Folk
and
BLUES
THE ENCYCLOPEDIA

Also by Irwin and Lyndon Stambler

Country Music: The Encyclopedia

The Encyclopedia of Pop, Rock and Soul

Also by Irwin Stambler

The Encyclopedia of Pop Music

The Encyclopedia of Folk, Country, and Western Music

Folk
and
BLUES

THE ENCYCLOPEDIA

IRWIN STAMBLER
& LYNDON STAMBLER

THOMAS
DUNNE
BOOKS

ST. MARTIN'S PRESS

NEW YORK

We would like to dedicate this book to our wives, Constance Stambler and Terry Ann Silberman, for their support and encouragement, and also to the parents and children who keep folk and blues music alive from generation to generation.

Thomas Dunne Books.
An imprint of St. Martin's Press.

www.stmartins.com

ISBN 0-312-20057-9

First Edition: May 2001

10 9 8 7 6 5 4 3 2 1

CONTENTS

BANJO IN THE WORST WAY

BY JOHN GORKA

*I*T HAD TO DO with the banjo and the letter J. I began an inappropriate liaison with the five-string banjo at an early age that was never technically consummated and actually continues till this day. I was captivated by the syncopated fingerpicking of Earl Scruggs in "The Ballad of Jed Clampett," the theme song of the *Beverly Hillbillies* TV show. Flatt and Scruggs were also occasional guests on the program. I also loved hearing Roy Clark play the banjo on *Hee Haw.* Bluegrass banjo was often featured in the chase scenes of movies in rural settings. The use of "Foggy Mountain Breakdown" in *Bonnie and Clyde* is a prime example. The playing of Eric Weissberg in "Dueling Banjos" from *Deliverance* was the final straw. I *had* to learn how to play the banjo in the worst way . . . and that is just what I went on to do.

Wanting to play the banjo would permanently lead me into the world of music as a participant rather than as a listener alone. I had abandoned the viola a year or so before because the school lessons had switched from the Suzuki method, which had a tablature approach, to standard notation, and nobody had taught me how to get from one to the other. I started picking up my brother's guitar about six months after starting on the banjo, and he showed me some easy chords and allowed me to borrow some of his song books. I started writing songs almost right away because (1) I wanted to see if I could, and (2) because it was easier to come up with my own tunes than it was to play other people's songs in a satisfactory way.

I performed in some high school shows and in the church folk group. I clearly remember the experience of being surrounded by people singing three-part harmony in the living room of Jennie Esposito's house, the group's leader in Colonia, New Jersey. The first concert I attended was the Earl Scruggs Revue in Asbury Park, New Jersey, and I also remember going to see Pete Seeger at a Blueberry Festival in Perth Amboy. I would go to the Woodbridge Public Library to read *Sing Out!* magazine when I first began to drive in the middle '70s. But it wasn't until I went away to college in Bethlehem, Pennsylvania, that my real musical education began. There I met some like-minded musicians and together we formed the Razzy Dazzy Spasm Band, a nontraditional bluegrass group that also played blues, country, and a few originals. Most of our repertoire came from Doug Anderson, who was a couple of years older than the rest of us and knew literally hundreds of songs. He also had a great record collection that he was very generous in lending out. The Bethlehem Public Library, across the street from my dormitory, had a great folk and blues collection, which I took advantage of extensively. I would sometimes put on Leadbelly records at parties where the usual party music was Bruce Springsteen, Boz Scaggs, and Thin Lizzy. I also borrowed a bunch of books on the history of the blues where I became enamored with the likes of Peetie Wheatstraw, "the Devil's Son-in-Law, and the High Sheriff of Hell," Son House, Robert Johnson, Sleepy John Estes, Furry Lewis, and many others. Their lives seemed so much more interesting than my own.

People I heard on the radio and saw on TV also led me inexorably to the world of folk music. Many had names that began with the letter *J.* I discovered them a song at a time or an album at a time. Their names in no particular order were: Joni, Joan, Judy, Janis(s), Jim, James, John(s), Jackson. There were also some non-*J* artists that I loved: Steve, Bonnie, Tim, Eric, and Emmylou, to name a few. The music they wrote and played and sang went deeper than most of the music that I had been exposed to. The more I found out about these artists the more it seemed they had common roots in American folk and blues music and to a lesser extent, jazz, rhythm and blues, and classical music. They also had a social conscience that indicated a bigger and more important world than I had known. They were writing songs in a way that was more about my own life than the songs I was writing. Their music was both an inspiration and a comfort to a nerdy young man who played the gregarious banjo and sang sad songs on the guitar. But all of those people seemed to come from a higher place, from another world that was very far removed from Bethlehem, Pennsylvania.

In late 1976 or early '77 Doug Anderson took me to a place on the south side of town called Godfrey Daniel's Coffeehouse. It was in the part of town school officials told us to avoid, so, being a contrary type, I was glad to go as often as I could. They were having an informal jam session in the front room, and I remember thinking this must have been what Greenwich Village was like in the '50s and early '60s. Later, when I found what Greenwich Village was like in the early '80s, I wished it were more like Godfrey's. Conveniently located near New York City and Philadelphia, Godfrey's was able to book a large number of high-quality performers from all around the United States, Canada, and Europe. The music included traditional folk, bluegrass, blues, Celtic, and singer-songwriters to a lesser degree. It was there I discovered the kind of performer I wanted to become. I didn't need to find a way into the unreachable world of my heroes on record. That music was no longer in vogue and the doors to that world were not only closed, they seemed to be nonexistent in the age of disco. There was this other world that I found to be incredibly inspiring, where you could do exactly the kind of music you wanted to do without compromising its best qualities for mass acceptance: the intimacy, the poetry, and the range of song possibilties. What I discovered in the music of Stan Rogers, Rosalie Sorrels, Claudia Schmidt, and Jack Hardy was to me living literature. You didn't have to be a great star with a larger-than-life image and an air of unapproachability to make great music. In fact, celebrity and artistry seemed to be opposing forces. In this alternate universe you could be an artist at any level of commercial success. You could do it yourself. You could make magic in whatever room you were in as long as you had the bare minimum of sound, lights, and a respectful audience. Godfrey's had all these things and more, and I loved being there.

I would go to shows as often as I could afford, sometimes going in at intermission, when they dropped the ticket price, so that I could experience new performers and new kinds of music. I was already playing at virtually every college coffeehouse in the Bethlehem vicinity and had started planning events with the program board at school. I started going to the open-mikes at Godfrey's as well. I didn't know exactly what kind of music I wanted to play but I had the feeling that this was the place I could discover it. I worked with Dave Fry (who booked Godfrey's) planning several events and festivals that featured some traveling professionals, local musicians, and college performers. Godfrey's was the most inspiring classroom I had ever been in, and so I stayed in Bethlehem after graduating from college with a degree in history and philosophy. I didn't know of any place like it anywhere, so I stayed put. The Razzy Dazzies disbanded upon graduation, and I started to pay more attention to the songwriting and less to the banjo music, especially after seeing Tony Trischka and Béla Fleck play at Godfrey's. Since they seemed to have banjo virtuosity more than covered, I felt I should point my energy into the songs. I also felt I could put more of my whole self into the songwriting than in banjo instrumentals.

I was able to get by, delivering flowers in the afternoon and playing in bars and restaurants at night. They were not listening rooms, but if you were able to reach an audience with a song that was not a well-known cover, you had really accomplished something. You had to learn to communicate on a more primitive level than what the lyrics alone were saying. I tended not to play the "hits," opting for more obscure covers and some of my own things as well. I was not the most popular performer in these settings because I tended not to give them what they wanted to hear. But by only doing songs I loved I never lost my emotional connection to music in general. I continued to go to Godfrey's when I wasn't playing, volunteering as open-mike host, sound man, MC, usher, counter worker, anything that needed to be done. I got to hang out after shows and bug the performers about how they wrote songs, who they were listening to, and hear their stories of the road and of the many worlds beyond my own. And I longed to be one of them. I wanted to be one of the performers whose signed pictures were on the wall that said "Thanks for having me, see you next time. Love, John Folksinger." I didn't care about being a star. I just wanted to play and discover the music that was inside me. If I could make a living playing my music, that was my ultimate dream, but if I could not I would still try to find a way to keep music as a special part of my life. It was always play for me. I worked at it but it has never been work itself.

I gradually became the house opening act at Godfrey's in the early to mid-'80s, and some of the people I opened shows for in Bethlehem opened doors for me in other parts of the country. Jack Hardy asked me to be a contributor to the *Fast Folk* musical magazine in 1983, and I started to perform in their live revues in 1985. And so I became an outpatient of the Greenwich Village folk scene of that time, which included the very inspiring company of Suzanne Vega, Shawn Colvin, Christine Lavin, Cliff Eberhardt, David Massengill, Frank Christian, and Lucy Kaplansky, to name a few. Dave Van Ronk and Tom Paxton, already well established, took an interest in the scene and provided inspiration and perspective. It was a great bunch of people, and living in Easton, Pennsylvania, I was free of the often contentious politics of the scene but close enough to observe these artists' growing talents firsthand. By the time we realized there was a scene the scene had disappeared.

Nanci Griffith encouraged me to enter the New Folk Concerts at the Kerrville Folk Festival in 1984. I won in the songwriting competition and I realized people who didn't know me personally might like my songs. I was encouraged that my songs might be real songs after all. Bill Morrissey gave Bob Donlin a tape to try to get me a booking at the venerable Passim, in Cambridge, Massachusetts. Christine Lavin was a champion, as she has been for countless other up-and-comers. Because these people and others were going out of their way to help me, I was getting the chance I had long hoped for.

In general I found the folk world to be a very supportive place, music being a common thread among performers and promoters. There are more places to play and more people doing it than there were in the 1960s before the Beatles came to America and Bob Dylan went electric. But folk music today as an expression of the "Folk World" is more an attitude or an approach than it is a discrete musical style. It is not just traditional music, ethnic music, protest music, or acoustic singer-songwriters. It is an increasingly organized, musically diverse network of performers and promoters, venues and festivals, dedicated to presenting quality music on a human scale from church basement coffeehouses and community halls to theaters and sheds. It is music over marketing. It is essence over appearance. Largely a grassroots, decentralized approach, it is slow growth versus the quick buck. As in other types of music on the popular margins, its basic noncommercial stance has made it possible to achieve a purity of vision that is so rare today. These forms of music will act like springs to feed and freshen popular music as it is needed. It is a place where premier artists can go to practice their craft and thrive even though they do not fit into an easily marketable package. Artists like Ani DiFranco and Dar Williams have proved Folk Music to be more than a baby boom generation phenomenon. Future artists will emerge from this world when they are talented and ambitious enough or when they are most needed. In the end the music's audience makes its stars. Folk music at its best offers music for all ages and for every important area of a person's life.

As songs are bigger than records so folk music is bigger than the folk world. Artists will create folk music whether they call themselves folk or not. Or whether they are part of the folk world or not. Not everything that comes out of the folk world is or will be folk music. Folk music is that which remains when everything else is discarded. It is a song like "The Water is Wide," where verses have been added, taken away, and adapted until what is left satisfies some deep human yearning. It is music that transcends its time and genre. It is, as in Jack Hardy's words, "where the song is more important than the singer." Whether it was composed purely to make money or for some higher purpose, if it has found a useful and essential place in peoples' lives it is folk music. In the end it is the sound of hope because it speaks to life.

INTRODUCTION AND ACKNOWLEDGMENTS

*W*HEN THE FIRST EDITION of this encyclopedia (then called *The Encyclopedia of Folk, Country & Western Music,* including roots blues entries) came out in 1969, interest in those fields was at a relatively low ebb. Not that there weren't many fans of those music forms, including the authors, but their numbers were a fraction of the audience for rock 'n' roll and soul. New young artists thronged the rolls of popular rock bands while a decade earlier many had been enamored of folk, blues, and down-home country.

Since then there has been a renaissance of interest in roots music, as reflected in the increased size of the second edition of *The Encyclopedia of Folk, Country & Western Music* in 1983. The pace picked up in the late '80s to the point where there were so many candidates that the decision had to be made to divide the third edition into two separate volumes: *Country Music: The Encyclopedia,* which came out in 1997, and this *Folk & Blues* encyclopedia. Even under those circumstances hard decisions had to be made about which performers to include in this twenty-first-century edition. (More information will be available on our Web site: www.folkandblues.com.)

We believe our efforts and love of the music are reflected in the pages of this volume. Over the past six years we have spent many hours collecting information, listening to live performances as well as recorded music, and interviewing many people in the field, from sidemen to solo artists like Charlie Musselwhite, Flaco Jimenez, Ry Cooder, members of the Seeger family, Dr. John, Patty Larkin, and Altan, to name just a few. We journeyed down Highway 61 in Mississippi to Clarksdale, home to Muddy Waters and many other Delta Blues artists. We attended Folk Alliance conferences in Albuquerque, Memphis, Vancouver, and Washington, D.C., to gain insight into the active performers, both veteran and newcomers.

The '90s spawned interest not only in fresh young artists like Sarah McLachlan, Keb' Mo', Ani DiFranco and John Gorka but also in pioneers in the field. This is demonstrated by the fact that the boxed set of 1930s blues legend Robert Johnson released by Columbia/ Legacy in 1990 went platinum, and the reissue of Harry Smith's 1952 *Anthology of American Folk Music* by Smithsonian/Folkways in 1997 has sold hundreds of thousands of copies.

Though the expanded field has become consider-

ably more complex from the standpoint of collecting information both from written sources and from interviews, we have tried to present a selection of artists and their experiences in order to give the reader a well-rounded picture of the field as it proceeds into the new century. But of course we could not have completed the volume without the valued contributions and assistance of many people and organizations. Among the organizations we wish to thank are: Phyllis Barney and Susan Martinez of the North American Folk Alliance of Music and Dance; Pat Mitchell of the Blues Foundation; Nancy Cardwell of the International Bluegrass Music Association; Mary Neumann of the Association for Independent Music; John Ruskey, curator of the Delta Blues Museum, Clarksdale, Mississippi; Lisa Carter, archivist of the University of Kentucky; Shirli Dixon Nelson of the Blues Heaven Foundation; Brenda Brown of Sing Out!; and Ann Willis of The House of Blues.

Among the record companies and industry personnel we wish to thank are: Glenn Dicker of Red Eye Distribution; Kerry Murphy and Steve Burton of Rounder Records; Bob Merlis of Warner Brothers Records; Randy Haecker of Columbia/Legacy; Cindy Byram of Shanachie; Judith Joiner of Green Linnet; Bob Feldman and Emilie Liepa of Red House Records; Bill Straw of Gift Horse Records; Watermelon Records; Dave Bartlett of Tone-Cool Records; Arista/Texas; Sharon Summers of Hollywood Records; Lilian Matulic of MCA; MCA/Nashville; Lellie Pittman-Capwell of Vanguard Records; Joel Amsterdam of Elektra Records; Glenn Fukushima of Atlantic Records; Epic Records; Mark Lipkin of Alligator Records; Jeff Place and Brenda Dunlap of Smithsonian/Folkways; Darcy Mayers of Rykodisc; Kurt Nishimura of Windham Hill; Jody Levy of Sugar Hill Records; David Dorn, Stephen Peeples, and John Hagelston of Rhino Records; Virgin Records; Chris Strachwitz and Annie Johnston of Arhoolie Records; Kelly Baird and Karen Shook of Quinlan Road; Holger Peterson of Stony Plains Records; Gary Cornelius of One Man Clapping Records; Tom Osborne of Mammoth Records; Tim/Kerr Records; High-Tone Records; Judy Kerr of Capitol Records; Dan Storper of Putumayo World Music; Steve Karas of Interscope Records; Melissa Dragich of Sony Music; Acoustic Disc Records; Rising Son Records; Dan Einstein of Oh Boy Records; Joshua Michaell of Appleseed Recordings; Jennifer and Dougie MacLean of Dunkeld Records.

Among the publicists and managers we'd wish to thank are: Tracy Mann, Lisa Shively, Les Eisner, Karen De Marco, Mark Pucci and Jill Kettles, Ellen Pryor, Michaela O'Brien of Young Hunter Management, Mike Kappus of Rosebud, Steve Macklam and S.L. Feldman, Carla Sacks, Mitch Greenhill of Folklore Productions, Cynthia Dunitz of Fleming Tamulevich, and Ralph Jaccodine.

Among the individuals we'd like to thank are: Michael Ochs and the Michael Ochs Archives, John Gorka (a gentleman who wrote the foreword about today's folk music), John Hannah (for his perceptive essay on Celtic music), jazz and blues writer Royale Johnson, Charlie Musselwhite, Roger Steffens, Lisa Pardini, Bart Bull, Jane Siberry, Jeff Warner, Gerret Warner, Jeff Davis, Megan Rubiner Zinn, Max Wolf, Terry Fowler, Wayne Mackenzie of Wolfstone, Martin Hadden, Peggy Seeger, Si Kahn, John McCutcheon, John Cohen of the New Lost City Ramblers, Robert Meitus, Carrie Newcomer, Ariel Rogers, Meg MacDonald, Pete Urbaitus, Ken Fabrick, Gary Glade, Richard Waldow, Frank Markowitz, Mitch Waldow, Richard Silverstein, Alice Seidman, Adam Seidman, Nancy Schimmel (daughter of Malvina Reynolds), Mary McCaslin, Roz and Howard Larman of Folk Scene, Liz R. McNeil, Nancy Felixson and Michael Hoover of McCabe's Guitar Shop, Johnny Dodd, Lorenzo Benet, Karen Brailsford, Lloyd Jassin, Mike Stroud, Neal Koch, Mary Katherine Aldin, Peter Figen, Roz and Ike Silberman, Susan Thau, Florence Nishida, Vicki Sheff-Cahan, Paula Yoo, David Craig, Craig Tomashoff, Tom Cunneff, Jim Oberman, Ron Arias, and Pete Lumsden and Bob Burk for listening on the bike rides.

We appreciate the opportunity to interview many people covered in this volume, and the archivists who provided information on some of these major artists. We would like to thank the many writers and reviewers whom we quote from *Sing Out!, Folk Roots,* and *Dirty Linen.*

We'd like to thank representatives of performers from other parts of the world who provided information about performers from Ireland, the United Kingdom, Scotland, Africa, Canada, Mexico, and the Caribbean. We also wanted to thank the production staff and our editors at St. Martin's Press: Cal Morgan, now with Judith Regan Publishing, for his yeoman work and support; and his capable successor Carin Siegfried, who shepherded the book from original manuscript to printed pages.

Culver City, California

LIVIN' WITH THE BLUES

BY ROYALE JOHNSON

I GREW UP in the heartland of the American blues tradition—Memphis and the nearby Mississippi Delta. Blues innovators were everywhere in the region and its practitioners were beginning to expand its horizons throughout the United States and, in time, the world. But religious families tried to shield their children from what some called the Devil's music and, in any event, if you were a child and not into performing, you didn't give too much thought to what was going on around you in terms of local musical culture.

Looking back on my youthful days in the Mississippi Delta, my imagination strains to make a connection between the notorious "old days" and the reputation the area enjoys today for its rich blues music legacy. The matter of the Delta's importance as the birthplace of the blues meant nothing to me then, though I'd heard my elders speak of it when they wanted to "hand down some learnin'." What I already knew from living there was the stuff I would read about years later as journalists and fiction writers spoke of "Mississippi hell" and neither needed room to exaggerate.

(But, as kids from upstream Memphis on summer visits to grandma's sharecropping farm, we never referred to that flat and rugged expanse of territory as the *Delta*. We knew it, with its endless rows of cotton, as the *country*. My grandparents' home in Hushpukena could easily have been poster material for the war on poverty folks, or the focal point of an essay on the cover of an old Gordon Parks novel).

Later I came to understand that this part of the U.S. is the "Mississippi Mud" which W.C. Handy referred to as the "best thing" that could have happened to him. This is where he of "St. Louis Blues" fame and other performers grew up and, in time, spread word of the blues far and wide. Handy settled in an area of the Delta only a mule's ride from my grandparents' home, an area that led him, as he put it, "inevitably to the blues."

(Of course, the blues was here long before the "Father of the Blues" ever thought of codifying that material in his own inventive way. Southern black folks in the earlier days of the last century have left America a rich body of musical materials because, as Handy noted in his autobiography, they "sang about everything: trains, steamboats, steam whistles, sledge hammers, fast women, mean bosses, stubborn mules. . . .")

I overheard some of that music as a youngster when grownup men worked the family's sharecropping cotton fields. We pre-teens couldn't work with them, often because the distaff side knew some of those songs were "nasty." Our family had what we called "big hawg" songs. The men would gather to slaughter the bigger hogs granny raised for home-made pork delicacies like "souse" and smoked sausages. Reading later about Skip James and the words taken from his experience used in "Little Cow and Little Calf Is Going to Die Blues" never failed to remind me of my remote kinship with Delta bluesmen. Songs like those and other work numbers eventually formed the basis for the "roots blues" folk material made popular by artists like Leadbelly and Robert Johnson.

But the "Every Day Seems Like Murder Here" sentiment among the sharecropper families caused many a bluesman (and blues woman) to want to abandon the Mississippi mud. I myself can recall the indignity of being sprayed by crop-dusting planes in a field crowded with workers. I think that bluesman Tommy Johnson (by coincidence my own father's name) and others became standard-bearers and artistic spokesmen for my many uncles and aunts who chose to remain in the Delta. His "Big Road Blues," a redesign of Charley Patton's "Down the Dirt Road Blues," is one of a body of work that accurately presents the black experience in the Delta.

Still, when my own exit from the Delta and Memphis came in the mid 1950s, everything I knew about the blues could fit into my small kit, the one I packed as I headed off to California as a new U.S. Navy recruit. You see, Memphis, as part of the Bible Belt section of the South, looked at the blues with mixed feelings. To whites, the blues was the distinctive province of black music, giving secular music expression in the same way religious conviction and inspiration was channeled through gospel music. But many in the black community felt that "no man could sing the blues and serve God too," a view still held by many today.

However, as the years went by, things began to change. Perhaps no single artist worked as hard or contributed more to seeking common ground between blues and gospel music than the late Thomas A. Dorsey. "Since the blues elicits the same feeling as church music," a passage in his biography reads, the same "grasping of the heart," the blues, he suggests, should be looked at on the same terms as any music expressing human feelings through song. His marriage of blues and gospel styles predates the pervasive influence the blues had in the early development of rock music forms and styles. But Dorsey's mission in the 1930s to infuse large gospel choir music with subtle elements of blues materials to establish the category of "gospel blues" eventually helped give birth to the soul stylings that finally allowed black artists to compete for the mass audience market in the 1960s.

After working as a music journalist in southern California in the 1960s and '70s, a financial windfall (from a municipal bus accident) inspired me to return home and seek my fortune on Memphis's Beale Street. At one time Beale Street had been for the outside world a special venue, a haven maybe where blues and jazz heroes exercised their art in the proud graces of an approving public and surrounding business environment. After all, I recalled, the story was that Champion Jack Dupree had once seen my mother's former neighbor, Memphis Minnie, performing classic blues songs on Beale. And Beale in years past had been the place where scores of blues troubadours, coming up from the Delta and down from Chicago, over from Louisiana and Texas and elsewhere, had come to hone their skills, many working as street performers.

But when I returned there in the 1980s I hadn't read where Rufus Thomas, a surviving Memphis music legend, said in an interview that "there's not a lot of blues being played on Beale Street today." My own imaginings about Beale Street and the blues were about to get a stiff dose of reality. The avenue exhibited a collection of dilapidated buildings and rock-strewn lots without any venues where old-time blues or jazzmen or eager newcomers could bring the music to life. In fact, there was no way that even street musicians could earn enough for a meager lifestyle.

Looking back, the mass audience exposure to blues material in the 1960s and '70s mainly came through the work of young white performers like Stevie Ray Vaughan, Paul Butterfield, Mike Bloomfield, and Johnny Winter. Young black performers mostly sought the rewards of the soul movement. Once-thriving blues locales like Beale Street (whose storied past also had included the musical exploits of major jazz figures like Ellington, Basie, and Hines) had fallen on hard times.

By the early 1980s, however, there were hints of a revival of interest in the blues and a coalition of government, citizens, and private industry had decided to put Beale Street and the blues in Memphis back on the entertainment map. Soon there was construction everywhere and plans for expansion. I was able to open my own Club Royale, which featured both well-known and up and coming rhythm & blues and blues people. Meanwhile, other clubs opened in the area and as tourist levels increased, a new wave of street performers began to assemble. In a sense, this was in keeping with the history of the blues where many legendary figures were itinerant musicians who played for contributions from passersby.

But often those artists became larger draws than club shows. Club owners started complaining and gained support from the city authorities to have those officials make rules and draw boundaries, issue permits and impose fees to limit the impact of street competition. In my case, I offered the street artists refuge in inclement weather and also a haven in times of conflict with other business owners on the street. For a time, Club Royale was one of the favorite rooms on Beale where bluesmen, especially Albert King, would drop by to enjoy the music or just shoot the shit.

And it was a place where new performers had the chance to work. One of the success stories was bluesman Preston Shannon. He started with an R&B group called Amnesty, but I'd encourage him to do blues numbers because I, along with many an appreciative audience, knew he had the sound and feel of an authentic blues talent. In the late 1990s, Preston became a hit recording artist for Bullseye Records; some of his work was nominated for Grammys.

It was a period when, despite the success of rap and hip-hop (which can also trace their lineage to blues), suddenly a new generation of young black roots blues players came along as well: Keb' Mo', Corey Harris, Guy Davis, and Alvin Youngblood Hart.

But by then Club Royale was long gone. In harboring street performers who were shunned by other club owners, I was on the wrong side, from a tactical standpoint, and it was one of the factors that led to my ending the saga of Club Royale. In truth, during those years, only a handful of the music clubs in the area programmed blues music with consistency, except during tourist season. The situation changed, however, with the arrival of B. B. King's blues club, whose doors opened just about the time I was closing mine. King's club committed itself full-time to the blues and to date that approach has brought overwhelming success. The street blues performers now can be found, for the most part, in the outside terrain of W.C. Handy Park.

Today, reflecting what has been a renaissance in the blues fortunes, Beale Street has, in a surprisingly short time, gone from rubble to glitter. Today it has become a major city attraction.

As those who love the music say, the blues is in the blood and it will never die.

THE ROOTS OF CELTIC MUSIC

BY JOHN HANNAH

*I*N AUGUST 1879 Robert Louis Stevenson left Glasgow aboard the steamer *Devonia* to join his lover Fanny Osbourne in America. It was a miserable crossing: ten days of nausea, constipation, and mange, as the writer told a friend. After days of dismal and rough weather, Stevenson was drawn from his tilting cabin by a familiar sound.

"It had been rumored since Friday that there was a fiddler aboard, who lay sick and unmelodious in Steerage No. 1," he wrote "and on the Monday forenoon, as I came down the companion, I was saluted by something in Strathspey time. A white-faced Orpheus was cheerily playing to an audience of white-faced women. It was as much as he could do to play, and some of his hearers were scarce able to sit; they had crawled from their bunks at the first experimental flourish, and found better than medicine in the music. . . .

"Humanly speaking, it is a more important matter to play the fiddle, even badly, than to write huge works upon recondite subjects. What could Mr. Darwin have done for these sick women? But this fellow scraped away; and the world was positively a better place for all who heard him."

The below-decks fiddler's repertoire included "Auld Robin Gray" and "Merrily Danced the Quaker's Wife," tunes that would have been familiar to any convivial emigrant a century or more earlier. (Robert Burns adapted the tender "Robin Gray" from an old Scots folk song, and he borrowed the reel from "Quaker's Wife" to create the outrageous "Nine Inch Will Please a Lady," fine examples of the adaptability and resilience of folk melody.) Both tunes have their roots in antiquity and are still popular in pubs and living rooms wherever musical Celts and Celtophiles gather to this day.

Stevenson lived in an age when the term "Celtic music" could be used with confidence. In his time the poems of Ossian, the songs of Burns, and the harp music of Ireland were heard in respectable drawing rooms of the United Kingdom. "Celtic culture" was all the go, even when much of it bore little relation to how the average Gael lived his life. Today, things are not so simple. In the era since the diasporas of the eighteenth and nineteenth centuries and the revolutions in recording and broadcasting, Celtic music has spread world-wide and diversified into forms that would sound distinctly foreign to the Edinburgh-born Stevenson.

He would feel at home with the music of Altan, Ca-

percaillie, Cherish the Ladies, the Chieftains, the Battlefield Band, Boys of the Lough, the Tannahill Weavers, and Ossian, to name the first few Celtic groups that spring to mind. He would probably be able to sing along with the Dubliners and the Clancy Brothers, too. He would surely love *Riverdance*—while being pleasantly scandalized by Jean Butler's legs. But how would he react to the mystical obscurities of Enya and Loreena McKennitt? Or to the anarchic discords of rockers like Horslips, Moving Hearts, and the late lamented Pogues (described once as a cross between the Chieftains and the Sex Pistols)? And would he find "better than medicine" in "When Irish Eyes Are Smiling"?

Between "Nine Inch Will Please a Lady" (eighteenth century, Scots) and "When Irish Eyes Are Smiling" (1912, American) is a cultural gulf wider and deeper than the Atlantic. I stumbled into this gulf as a banjoist in a Celtic band some twenty years ago. Between belting out meticulously authentic tunes in the Irish bars of the San Fernando Valley, we fielded requests for standards of doubtful pedigree. Goaded into a display of Celtic hauteur, I once challenged an audience: "Would you ask the Chieftains to play 'When Irish Eyes Are Smiling'?" Yes they would, they replied without hesitation.

Irish singer Robbie O'Connell put the same lesson in his song "You're Not Irish," with its refrain of: *You can't be Irish—you don't know Danny Boy. Or Toora Loora Loora or even Irish Eyes. You've got a hell of a nerve to say you came from Ireland. So cut out all the nonsense and sing MacNamara's Band.*

I had a lot to learn about Celtic music back then, but one thing I was sure of: "When Irish Eyes Are Smiling" is *not* Celtic music—which begs a question that I still can't answer with complete confidence: How do we define Celtic music, in all its renewed diversity, in the twentieth century?

This is a trick question, because it has as many answers as answerers. I posed it to several Celtic musicians and none could answer with a simple sentence. "It's the music of the Celtic peoples and it's a genuine music that comes from the heart," said Martin Hadden, of the sadly defunct Silly Wizard. "It's the part of the fabric of the place that it comes from. It doesn't have to be an old tune or a traditional song; it's more a feeling. It's music that's being played for the love of it. Its purpose is social rather than commercial."

For Alan Reid, founder of the Battlefield Band,

Celtic music is "a sound and a feeling: It's about extremes exemplified in wild, uninhibited dance music contrasting with the gut-wrenching emotion of songs and laments that recount the all-too-often tragic story of the Celtic peoples. I think it is that emotion combined with great soulful melodies that touch other people even if they don't fully understand the form of the music or the language of it."

In striving for a more precise definition, we should begin at the beginning. Put as simply as possible, Celtic music is the *traditional* music of Ireland, Scotland, Wales, Brittany, and Galicia—all areas where Celtic languages are (or were) spoken. It is still very much alive in those places, and it also survives in unadulterated form in several parts of the world where Celts have settled.

Galicians, Bretons, and in particular the Welsh have powerful national musical traditions, but today's most widespread Celtic music is Irish and Scots. Aficionados hear distinct differences between Irish and Scots music. Yet they have much in common, the result of centuries of cross-pollination.

Only a handful of Welsh groups have found a wide audience. They include Cusan Tan, Ceredwen, and Kornog. Some Welsh groups, such as Madra Rua and Pluck and Squeeze, supplement their Welsh repertoire with Irish and Scots tunes.

Brittany can boast a healthy crop of musical Celts, such as rockers L'Ange Vert and Karma.

Welsh and Breton music, however, have been upstaged by Scots and Irish.

The Scots, Irish, Welsh, and Bretons are among the descendants of the ancient Celts, a lively and talented people who dominated Europe for at least half a millennium B.C. From their homeland in what is now southern France and Germany, they migrated to Spain, Greece, Italy, and Turkey. Around 700 B.C. they spread into the British Isles.

That Celtic world began to decline in the middle of the first century A.D. under pressure from the Romans and the Germanic tribes. Its traditions survived strongly in Britain and Ireland, where the music continues to thrive.

"The Celts were hospitable, fond of feasting, drinking, and quarreling and incapable of prolonged concerted action," says an Encyclopedia Britannica author, who should know better. (This is a scholastic version of the stereotype that greeted immigrant Irish in the New World: the feckless, drunken brawling Paddy who can't hold down a job.) What we do know from archaeology and history is that the Celts were farmers, fighters, and dancers with great reverence for art, poetry, and music. That reverence is still very much alive in their descendants. Live music, played informally in pubs and in homes, is still part of the fabric of Scots and Irish life.

Musicologists distinguish among three major types of music: *fine art music,* professionally performed and written with the upper classes in mind; *popular music,* which is essentially professional, urban, and oral; and *folk music,* described by the Encyclopedia Britannica as "the spontaneous creation of peoples unencumbered by artistic self-consciousness" and which has always tended to be rural, oral, and amateur.

Judged by that template, Celtic music is a survivor of an ancient folk tradition. According to some scholars the folk tradition is dead—killed off by the recording industry. The theory is that folk music flourishes only in isolation and loses its vigor when the wide world intrudes.

In its long history the music has incorporated elements of all three types. Examples of fine art are the delightful tunes of Turlough O'Carolan, many of which were written for aristocratic patrons in the seventeenth century and are commonly heard in pub sessions today. Many of the lovely popular songs of Thomas Moore (Irish, nineteenth century) and Robert Burns (eighteenth century) are found in the modern Celtic repertoire. (The flow between popular and folk music runs both ways; Moore and Burns borrowed ancient melodies, added new lyrics, and returned them, much enhanced, to the folk tradition.)

Few would disagree that Burns's "Ca' the Yowes" and Moore's "Meeting of the Waters" are popular songs that count as Celtic music. So why doesn't "Irish Eyes" qualify?

The best answer I can give is that Moore's and Burns's productions survive because they are *good* songs. The lyrics are polished, the sentiments are honest, and the tunes are often derived from folk melodies that endure on merit alone. "Irish Eyes" is seen as ersatz, written for profit and based on a caricature of what it means to be Irish.

Robbie O'Connell says he still hasn't learned "Irish Eyes" or "Danny Boy." It's true that "Danny Boy" has become as iconic as shamrock and shillelaghs. It's also true that its sentiments are a little cloying. Yet it is a good song with a respectable history. The original lament was composed in the 1600s by Rory Dall O'Cahan and was first published as "The Londonderry Aire" (to the continuing amusement of the French) in 1855. The lyrics were supplied by an English lawyer, Frederick Edward Weatherly, in 1912. "Danny Boy" is a sappy song, but the limpid beauty of the melody still has the power to move the soul. Robbie O'Connell won't sing it, but uilleann piper Davy Spillane's duet with Sinead O'Connor on his album *The Sea of Dreams* (1998) demonstrates that "Danny Boy" is indeed one of the great Celtic songs.

Alan Reid has a more open-minded attitude: "There are some songs that we would regard as music hall or burlesque songs. They may be excessively sentimental or they might simply have been done to death. I wouldn't sneer at them."

Martin Hadden recorded "Too-re-loo-ra-loo-ra (That's

an Irish Lullaby)" (1912) on his Benachally Ceilidh Band's album *Happy Feet* in 1998. "Why should we be embarrassed?" he asks. "It's a good tune. This is living tradition. It's not a museum. You'll hear people saying that it has to be old to be traditional. They're fooling themselves. That's not being a purist. It's just nostalgia."

When Martin Hadden remarks that the music's purpose is "social, not commercial," he is touching on a signal feature of traditional music: that it depends on acceptance by the community for its survival. The relationship, of course, is symbiotic. In return, the music contributes to the survival of the community in many ways: it entertains, it consoles, it accompanies work (waukin' songs, sea chanteys) and war; and it fuels social dancing, long a component of village mating rituals. Traditional music also has a less obvious and more profound role: by expressing ideas and emotions that the group holds in common, the music helps to define and reinforce a sense of cultural identity.

Ultimately the music has turned out to be more enduring than the physical communities themselves. When hunger, war, ambition, or politics forces Celts to move on, they take their music with them. In the Australian outback, the Alaskan tundra, or the suburbs of Los Angeles, the mere sound of the pipes reminds a Scot of who, at heart, he really is.

A twelfth-century monk described a typical Irish harp recital: "The sounds are rapid and articulate yet at the same time sweet and pleasing. It is wonderful how in such speed of the fingers the musical proportions are preserved. The vibrations of the short treble string sport with such brilliancy along with the deep notes of the bass. They delight with such delicacy and soothe so charmingly that the great excellence of their art appears to lie in their accomplishing all this with the least appearance of effort." He could have been describing a typical pub session of the twentieth century.

From the time of the Druids, the harp became the supreme instrument of Ireland, and its players were the admiration of Europe for hundreds of years. Harpers accompanied the bards, who kept the sacred flame of the culture alive in stories and geneaologies, and serenaded the Gaelic chiefs. At the end of the seventeenth century, when Gaelic high culture finally collapsed under the weight of English imperialism, the harpers found welcome in the homes of the Anglo-Irish aristocracy.

Ireland's greatest composer for the harp was the blind Turlough O'Carolan (1670–1738). His contemporaries sneered at his harp playing (he started learning at the ripe old age of eighteen) but were silent at the beauty of his compositions.

In her introduction to a collection of O'Carolan tunes, Greanne Yeats points out that O'Carolan represented a bridge between art music and folk music. Yeats also notes that Gaelic art music composed by previous harpers "was absorbed by the oral folk tradition and is still played and sung today." This is certainly true of

O'Carolan himself, whose very first composition—"Si Beag Agus Si Mor"—remains a standard.

In 1792, hundreds of Irish musicians attended the famous Belfast Harp Festival. Edward Bunting, organist of St Patrick's Cathedral in Dublin, was there to note down the music and published three tune collections that helped to define what we now call Celtic music.

Ironically, it was the instability of Ireland during the seventeenth century that helped preserve its musical tradition. According to conductor Michael Bowles, "Ireland remained on the outside while Europe was developing the art and practice of music." In the middle of the seventeenth century Europe was developing the "equal temperament" system, which divides the scale into twelve arithmetically equal half tones: an attempt to solve tuning problems of keyboard instruments. The new scale became the basis of all music theory and composition.

In their cultural backwater, Ireland's folk musicians persisted in using a simpler and more "natural" system of *modes,* with a more limited range of notes, for all musical needs, secular and religious. The shorter scale can have an uncanny effect. The lament "Fil O Run," for example, has the haunting quality of a Gregorian chant. Many of the old Irish tunes are pentatonic— melodies formed from only five different notes.

Writes Bowles: "The same style of melody associated with liturgy is used for lively and amusing dance tunes, for love songs of every shade and intensity, for uproarious and, as may be, bawdy drinking songs."

For Bowles, Irish melody is "the music that comes to us from the eighteenth century." But the tradition has been "muddied, especially in recent years, with the fashion of using banjos and guitars and melodeons, instruments with a pre-fixed tuning in Equal Temperament. If we wish to analyze and identify what really makes a melody 'Irish' perhaps we ought to refer to the modal system of scales on which they are based."

In Scotland, folk songs, formerly always an oral tradition, began to appear in print during the seventeenth century. The first collection was John Skene's 1627 book of tunes for the mandora (mandola). Forbes's *Songs and Fancies,* a collection of melodies for lute, lyre, harpsichord, and violin, appeared in 1662.

The instrumental lineup of the time might sound rather sedate to lovers of the accordion, fiddle, banjo, flute, and tinwhistle. In fact, most seventeenth-century Scottish folk music is hard to distinguish from English and European Renaissance music. A popular, though probably erroneous, explanation is that the tunes had been tamed by the Anglicized upper-crust types who patronized them. A better explanation, as offered by the *Encyclopedia of Scottish Culture,* is that today's most ubiquitous Scottish fiddle style is largely a creation of a later period: 1720 to 1750.

This change was a result of technology: the importation of the newly redesigned Italian baroque violin into Scotland during the late eighteenth century. It displaced the mandora, lute, border bagpipe, and oboe. It also filled the role of the great Highland bagpipes, pronounced illegal after the battle of Culloden. During the years of proscription—1746 to 1782—the violin became the instrument of choice in the Highlands. Highland chieftains, who had always had their own pipers, acquired their own fiddler, too.

Folk song and dance music became hugely fashionable in eighteenth-century Scotland, when collections began appearing in overwhelming numbers. Allan Ramsay, Robert Burns, Lady Nairn, and other talented Scots lyricists were among the beneficiaries. Burns in particular liked to slow down the melody of dance tunes and rework them into songs. The spritely Strathspey "Duncan Davidson" becomes the heart-breaking "Mary Morison."

The six volumes of *The Scots Musical Museum*, which began appearing in 1787, are perhaps the finest collection of Scottish song. Robert Burns was its virtual editor and principal contributor. Songs from the *Museum* still enjoy world-wide popularity. The late Serge Hovey took on the Herculean task of arranging and recording the entire collection, with Jean Redpath as soloist, producing eight volumes before his death in 1989 (Greentrax CTRAX 029).

During this period the Scots aristocracy revived folk dancing, long frowned on by the Kirk, and created a demand for new dance music. Among those to take up the challenge was the Gow family of Inver, in Perthshire. Neil Gow became famous playing for aristocratic dances around the country toward the end of the century. His *Collection of Strathspey Reels* was published in 1784. (Gow's fiddle is still on view at Blair Castle; the current Duke of Athole sometimes lends it to local fiddlers, including Dougie MacLean and Pete Clark.)

In making a living from music, the Gows were luckier than most. The clearances that began in 1790 and continued for nearly a hundred years gradually displaced the Highland populations and replaced them with sheep. The old clan system crumbled. Overpopulation, land hunger, and near starvation forced many to emigrate.

When the fiddler of the *Devonia* settled in New York, or Boston, or any of the major cities in the United States, or perhaps moved on to Canada, he would be sure of a welcome from his kinsmen. His music had arrived in the Americas long before him. Celts have ever been pioneers. Wherever they wandered, their music went with them.

The Scots-Irish, whose ancestors had bounced from southwest Scotland to Ulster, took their music and their melancholy into the Appalachians and the Ozarks. In the Canadian hinterland, other Scots and their friends the French beguiled the Athapaskan Indians with their sprightly reels. On Canada's eastern seaboard, Scots Highlanders held on to their Jacobite dreams and their stately Strathspeys. "The heart is Highland," an anonymous emigrant mourned, "and we in dreams behold the Hebrides." Yet few of these Scots ever went home; they had brought their home, in the form of language, songs, and traditions, with them.

Hordes of poor Irish brought to the great cities of America a musical tradition of unparalleled richness. The great emptying of Ireland began in the famine year of 1846; more than 6 million were to leave in the ensuing sixty years. Perhaps 3.5 million sailed west. When Irish Americans went to the dance halls in Boston or New York on a Saturday night, they danced the way they did, and still do, in the village halls of the old country. In 1867 Elias Howe of Boston published *Howe's One Thousand Jigs and Reels,* the very subtitle of which paints a riotous picture of Hibernian and Caledonian social life: *Clog Dances, Contra Dances, Fancy Dances, Hornpipes, Strathspeys, Breakdowns, Irish Dances, Scotch Dances, &c, &c., for the Violin, Flute, Clarionet, Cornet, Fife, Flageolet, or any treble instrument.* Ryan's mammoth collection, republished by Mel Bay, is still an indispensable resource for the Celtic fiddler.

The music crossed ethnic barriers, too. Many of the performers of the minstrel craze that began in the 1840s were Irishmen. (Daniel Decatur Emmett, who has been credited with putting on the first minstrel show and writing "Dixie," was an Irish American who also did a comic Irish "Paddy" act.) Minstrel troupes touring Ireland introduced the banjo into Irish music, where it continues to flourish. Joel Sweeney, another Irish American, had the nerve to file a patent for his five-string banjo, even though such instruments had long been used by plantation instrumentalists. Irish entertainers were also to pioneer vaudeville and Tin Pan Alley, at the same time helping to create the American idea of what it is to be Irish.

There can be no culture without language, tradition, and music. Irish immigrants were quick to abandon their language, because Gaelic had become associated with poverty and helplessness. Most were willing to tone down their traditions, to reduce conflict with new neighbors who were already prejudiced against them. For Celts, however, music is indispensable. A rich instrumental tradition, with its roots in Bronze Age Europe, has helped the Celts preserve their *emotional* identity.

Any new American faces a conundrum: how to become "American" without severing cultural roots that nourish the soul. Other immigrant groups relied on their music to preserve their identity, but the Irish went a step further. They played and sang to console, to amuse, to make money, and to remind themselves of who they were. And the music was also to serve as a cultural passport.

A good tune is unequivocal in its ability to evoke feelings. It appeals to a part of the brain that predates speech. Put words to a tune and you can convey ideas and values with the intensity of emotion. A tune can preserve a tradition, but a song can start a revolution. So the Irish immigrants borrowed old tunes, made up new ones, and added lyrics that helped them shape a new variety of Celt: the Irish American.

In his delightful study "'Twas Only an Irishman's Dream" Professor William Williams traces that change. The incomers faced two Anglo-American-inspired stereotypes: "A romantic stereotype of the exile in flight from a tragic land of beauty; and a comic stereotype of the wild, irresponsible Paddy." The Irish embraced both stereotypes, both to reform their image and to make money. Irish music and culture, in the form of sheet music and theater, were to become an industry.

In 1808 *Irish Melodies,* with lyrics by Thomas Moore, became a sensation on both sides of the Atlantic. Songs like "The Meeting of the Waters," "Believe Me If All Those Endearing Young Charms" and "Oft in the Stilly Night" set the tone of Irish music for a century. Erin was sad and beautiful. Nostalgia was the prevailing mood. The airs were authentic, derived from the famed harpers' convention of 1792, and many of them probably ancient. Transcriber Edward Bunting ignored the Gaelic lyrics; Moore wrote his own. Debate still rages over the "authenticity" of Moore's lyrical sentiments. ("A musical snuff box," sniffed one reviewer.) Still the songs survive, testament enough to their excellence.

A less sublime stereotype—comic songs depicting Paddy's drunken, bellicose exploits—also became hugely popular. A complete subgenre of McGinty songs, filled with internal rhyming (a characteristic of Gaelic verse), describes celebrations that end in drunken donnybrooks, usually with a pig or two in attendance.

As the century progressed Paddy became gradually domesticated. No longer an ignorant savage but an idiot savant whose loyalty and stoutheartedness more than compensated for his enduring weakness for "the cratur." As described by Professor Williams, the Irish "negotiated" their identity as Americans by writing their own stereotypes. Paddy's arrival as a bona-fide American is marked by the comic song "Who Threw the Overalls in Mrs. Murphy's Chowder?" (1898), in which the misunderstanding is explained and the riot avoided. The Irish Americans now felt secure enough to parody themselves, and to emphasize their domestication.

Professor Williams demonstrates the interdependence of a culture and its music. In the years between 1890 and 1930 the Irish entered the mainstream of American life. As they became more American, and as the Irish American climbed the social ladder, the old music, with its wildness and its deep emotion, was left behind or adapted to suit a new identity. It was replaced by a sentimental version of the ancestral homeland as the "Emerald Isle." After 1900 Tin Pan Alley did a roaring trade in such songs, some that can still be heard around closing time in bars on both sides of the Atlantic:

"A Little Bit of Heaven, Sure They Call It Ireland," (Brennan and Ball, 1914), "Mother Machree" (Chauncy Olcott, 1910), and "My Wild Irish Rose" (Olcott, 1897).

Writes Professor Williams: "Their nostalgia was a translation of the 'culture of exile' into the language of American popular culture, into a series of images about a nonexistent Ireland that enabled Irish Americans to portray themselves in ways that both they and the rest of America could appreciate."

These are the same songs that now so irritate Irish musicians from the Old Country.

The Americanization of Celtic music continued wherever emigrants settled. The tunes, as always, are the most resistant to change. Many Old World fiddle tunes—like "Moneymusk," "Soldier's Joy," and "Fisher's Hornpipe"—are still played by old-time musicians in America. Others merely acquired new titles. In America, "Miss MacLeod's Reel" is called "Did You Ever See the Devil, Uncle Joe?" and "Lord MacDonald's Reel" becomes "Leather Breeches."

The same sense of antic irreverence characterizes American square dancing. When native fiddlers wrote their own dance tunes they gave them titles like "Jay Bird Died with the Whooping Cough," "Tramp the Devil's Eyes Out," and "There Ain't No Bugs on Me."

The way old Celtic songs and English ballads became domesticated also says something about the American character. The thirty-five verses of the rambling old ballad "The Lass of Loch Royal" were reduced to three and became "Who's Gonna Shoe Your Pretty Little Foot?" "The Gosport Tragedy" is a murder ballad in which the killer is torn apart by the ghosts of the girl and the baby he has murdered. Americanized as "Pretty Polly," the song loses the supernatural and is shortened to a matter-of-fact description of the crime itself. In some cases only the tune survives because the song fails to resonate with American sensibilities. An Irish song of the rebellion of 1798, "Hurrah for the Men of the West," is changed to "Old Settler's Song," a familiar song of scratching a living on the frontier surrounded by acres of claims. An even older Irish song becomes "Johnny Has Gone for Soldier" with fake Gaelic lyrics: *Shool, shool, shool a-roo, Shool a-sac-a-rac-ca bib-ba-lib-ba-boo. If I should die for Sally Bobolink, come bib-ba-lib-ba-boo so rare-o.*

The transition from Old World to New World music was completed with the revolution in recording and broadcasting. Fueled by new technologies, popular song eclipsed the folk tradition. The British music of the South evolved into country and western. "Ballroom" dancing edged set dancing from the floors of the Irish dance halls.

On the other side of the Atlantic, ballroom dancing and Irish and Scots country dancing coexisted happily. Big band leaders like Duke Ellington and Harry James had their equivalents in Jimmy Shand and Adam Rennie. On a more domestic level, the old tunes and songs continued to be played and sung in homes and pubs. When the British Broadcasting Corporation discovered Celtic music, it naturally favored a more genteel approach, less challenging to English ears. "There was a more operatic approach to Scots song," says Martin Hadden with a hint of disdain. Singers like Kenneth McKellar and Andy Stewart were classically trained and specialized in "tartan treasures" like "Scotland the Brave" and "Skye Boat Song." The mass media—which for many years meant only the BBC—ignored the curious beauties of the old tradition until the folk boom of the 1960s.

In America, the folk boom was an opportunity for Celtic musicians to find an audience. When three jolly Irishmen immigrants in hairy sweaters sang ballads on the Ed Sullivan show 80 million people were delighted with a music that was new, yet strangely familiar. Paddy, Bobby, and Finbarr Clancy were an overnight sensation. With the later addition of Tommy Makem, they achieved international fame. They played for President John F. Kennedy in the White House, shared a stage with Barbra Streisand and Bob Dylan, and made fifty-five albums.

The American folk song revival of the 1960s was echoed in Britain. "It meant people looking within to find the music in their own backyards," says Reid. "It meant discovering source singers and musicians, by which I mean folk who had been playing and singing this music all their lives, unnoticed by the media or the 'big city' culture.

"These people provided sources for academics and enthusiasts that gave a bedrock of material to revivalists."

The British Celtic revival spread to the United States in the late 1970s. Bands such as Boys of the Lough, Battlefield Band, and Silly Wizard were among those who spearheaded the revival and also built a doting following during regular tours of the United States. Since 1981 Glasgow's Battlefield Band, in its many incarnations, has toured America on an average of twice a year. Sales of its twenty or so albums are still healthy.

When Martin Hadden joined Silly Wizard in 1976 he was much criticized for his electric bass. "The attitude was 'You cannae play folk music with an electric instrument,'" he recalls. "The revival hadn't quite kicked in and people had this attitude. We thought, well, if the only instruments you can play are traditional Scottish instruments, you can only play the *clarseach* (harp) and the pipes. We decided we'd play what we liked. Towards the end (of the band's lifetime) we were being seen as conservative in our electronics."

The revival was slower to spark in America. At first gigs for the Battlefield Band were small and sometimes eccentric, but in the mid-1980s there was a sudden surge of people who "discovered" Celtic music. "Nowadays," says Reid, "we have lots of folk who range from Batty/Celto heads to people who have a sympathy to, or an interest in, things Scottish. I have fond memories, however, of some of our earlier, bizarre performances."

Every few years throughout the century Old World Celtic musicians seem to take the New World by surprise. In 1994 the hard shoe turned out to be on the other foot, when Michael Flatley launched *Riverdance*, a stage show combining the oldest Irish music and dance with Busby Berkeley flair, and took Europe by surprise. Irish audiences were predisposed to sneer at Irish music and dance coming from America. *Riverdance* easily won them over by returning something that was lost. Michael Flatley and Jean Butler made Irish dancing sexy again, the way it was always supposed to be. Celtic culture grows well in any soil; it might lie dormant for a while, but has a way of blooming anew indefinitely.

Marvelous Scots and Irish music has been recorded in the twentieth century, and although many fine musicians (to their own amazement in many cases) are making a living at it, Celtic music is still essentially folk music. As such it is best appreciated not by passive listening but by participating in it.

For every professional who lives by making records and touring there are hundreds of amateurs who are happy to join an informal, ad hoc, "session" in a pub or a living room. Such sessions are judged not by the quality of the music but by what is referred to as the *craic* (pronounced "crack"). This is a Gaelic word that, significantly, has no English equivalent. It describes the convivial joy of being in the same room with the music, a drink or two, and good people. It is the essence of the Celtic experience.

"Nowadays there are many young people learning, playing, and teaching traditional music," says Alan Reid. "More than ever before—so although it might not be evident from the newspaper or commercial radio, the revival is real and vibrant, especially here in Scotland, where there is an upsurge in national expression, consciousness, and confidence."

My own love of the music might be connected to my hearing so much of it when I was a child. But I know that Celtic music has a way of tugging at the soul without regard to ethnicity or upbringing. Whatever our ethnicity, the music speaks to our deepest emotions and our original innocence—to how we were before we grew smart enough to make ourselves unhappy.

For conductor Michael Bowles, Irish music is not a narrow ethnic category. In *The Celtic Consciousness* he wrote: ". . . we might come to think of the quality described as Irish as not particularly Irish, but rather as universal, in the sense that the modal scale, with its 'natural' tuning, is valid throughout the world at large."

A

ALLISON, LUTHER: *Singer, guitarist, songwriter, band leader (Rolling Stones, Four Jivers, the Tornados, etc.). Born Widener, Arkansas, August 17 or 18, 1939; died University Hospital, Madison, Wisconsin, August 12, 1997.*

Cancer cut down blues superstar Luther Allison in 1997, when he was enjoying major comeback success in his native land after an interim period of fame in Europe. Recognition of his great impact on the modern blues spectrum came with a virtual sweep of the W. C. Handy Awards in 1995 and similar dominance in 1997.

The confusion about his birthdate comes from the problem of knowing whether he was born just before midnight on August 17, 1939, or just after on the eighteenth. After childhood experience as a gospel singer, he became engrossed in the blues after his family moved to Chicago in 1951. In the mid-1950s, working with brother Grant Allison in a band first named the Rolling Stones and later the Four Jivers, he began to build a reputation as a major blues and rock artist who gained wider recognition throughout the 1960s into the 1970s, punctuated by his first album release in 1969, *Love Me Mama,* on Delmark Records. His U.S. following tapered off by the late 1970s and he moved to Paris, France, where his career prospered over the next decade. In the early 1990s he returned home to begin turning out superb albums on the Alligator label starting with *Soul Fixin' Man* in 1993, followed by *Blue Streak* (1995) and *Reckless* (1997). Referring to the first of those, a *Guitar Player* critic wrote, "Fever and chills performances . . . ferocious solos combines the wisdom of a master storyteller with the elegance of B. B. King, the elasticity of Buddy Guy, and the big sting of Albert King."

In 1997 he was nominated in the nineteenth W. C. Handy Awards in eight categories: Blues Entertainer of the Year (an award he won the previous year); Blues Band of the Year (Luther Allison and the James Solberg Band); Contemporary Blues—Male Artist of the Year; Blues Instrumentalist—Guitar; Contemporary Blues Album of the Year; Blues Instrumentalist—Guitar; Contemporary Blues Album of the Year (*Reckless*); and Blues Song of the Year ("Living in the House of the Blues," from *Reckless*). In 1998, RUF issued the video *Live from Paradise,* and in 1999 Alligator released a new album, *Live in Chicago.*

ALMANAC SINGERS, THE: *Vocal group, active in the early 1940s.*

At the end of the 1930s many talented folk artists lived or entertained in New York. These performers, including Woody Guthrie, Lee Hays, and Burl Ives, had gravitated there from many parts of the United States. The climate was not too favorable for folk music at the time and most had to work at other trades to make ends meet.

From this trying situation grew a new group called the Almanac Singers. It was a loosely knit gathering of fellow artists to gain the enjoyment of singing with each other and, in time, present their songs before whatever audiences they could find to listen. The original members of the group included Pete Seeger (who called himself Pete Bowers at the time), Woody Guthrie, Lee Hays, and Millard Lampell. During its early stages in New York, Burl Ives regularly joined the sessions.

At the start of the '40s, the group decided to go across the United States, singing on street corners, college campuses, or anywhere support could be found for their material. At various times they were joined by such other performers as Cisco Houston, Josh White, Bess Lomax (Hawes), Butch Hawes, and Earl Robinson. Part of the time, the Almanacs consisted of only Pete Seeger and Woody Guthrie.

The group emphasized union songs, performing before many union organizations. They also sang anti-war songs until Hitler attacked Russia, at which time the emphasis switched to U.S. involvement. A good part of their material, though, was traditional folk music. The group recorded a number of albums during its brief period of existence. These included *Dear Mr. President, Talking Union, Sod Buster Ballads,* and *Deep Sea Shanties.* The albums are considered classics of the folk music genre of the mid-twentieth century.

U.S. entry into World War II resulted in the breakup of the Almanacs in 1942. Some of its members joined the armed forces, some enlisted in the Merchant Marine, and others returned home to help in the war effort. The group never regrouped after the war, but it did serve as the forerunner of that great postwar group, the Weavers.

In 1996, MCA Records released a CD titled *Complete General Recordings,* including songs like "Blow the Man Down," "House of the Rising Sun," "I Ride an Old Paint," "The Dodger Song," "The Golden Vanity," and "The Coast of High Barbary." The group was also represented on CD in the Smithsonian/Folkways collections *Folk Songs America, Volume I* (1993), and *That's Why We're Marching: WWII and the American Folk Song Movement* (1996).

ALTAN: *Traditional Irish band. Mairéad Ní Mhaonaigh, lead vocals and fiddle. Born Gaoth Dobhair (Gweedore), County Donegal, Ireland, July 26, 1959. Frankie Kennedy, flute and tin whistle. Born Belfast, Northern Ireland, Sep-*

tember 30, 1955; died Belfast, September 19, 1994. Ciaran Tourish, fiddle, tin whistle. Born Buncrana, County Donegal, Ireland, May 26, 1967. Ciaran Curran, bouzouki, cittern. Born Kinawley, County Fermanagh, Ireland, June 14, 1955. Dáithí Sproule, guitarist, vocals. Born Derry City, Ireland, May 23, 1950. Mark Kelly, guitarist. Born Dublin, Ireland, March 15, 1961. Dermot Byrne, accordion, melodeon. Born Buncrana, County Donegal, Ireland, January 18, 1969. Paul O'Shaughnessy, fiddle. Born Dublin, Ireland, June 9, 1961.

After singing a sensual love ballad in a concert at UCLA's Wadsworth Auditorium in March 1996, Mairéad Ní Mhaonaigh (pronounced Nee WEE-nee) flipped her blonde hair and attacked the fiddle. Her melodic interplay with fiddler Ciaran Tourish and accordionist Dermot Byrne drove "Johnny Boyle's Jig" and the reel "Dogs among the Bushes." Bouzouki player Ciaran Curran and guitarist Dáithí Sproule (pronounced DA-hee Sprole) laid the rhythmic foundation. The infectious music got the staid audience to dancing. Such vibrant layers mark the sound of this excellent Irish band.

Altan rivals the Chieftains as the best traditional band in Ireland. The band rarely wavers from the jigs, reels, airs, and soulful ballads of Donegal. With the melancholic soprano of Ní Mhaonagh, and the double-fiddle sound of Ní Mhaonagh and Tourish, the group captivates live audiences and CD listeners with equal ease. Until he died in September 1994, Frankie Kennedy's flute and tin whistle added a sweet texture to the sound. In 1994 the group hired Dermot Byrne, an excellent button accordion player, to realize the two-fiddles-and-a-box sound Kennedy originally conceived.

The music of Donegal is tinged with the rhythms of the Scottish strathspeys and Highlands, Polish mazurkas and "Germans," or barn dances. Passed on from generation to generation, Altan's repertoire comes from such Donegal musicians as James Byrne, Vincent Campbell, and Tommy Peoples.

"Donegal is sort of isolated," Ní Mhaonaigh explains. "The Northern Ireland situation has cut it off politically as well. You're talking of an island within an island. It's made the people there very proud. They've retained their own music very strongly. The tunes, the jigs, and the reels—you'll find them all over the country. But the verses in Donegal would be slightly different and more individual. People used to go to Scotland to work and bring back certain tunes and songs and really make them their own then."

Ní Mhaonaigh grew up speaking Gaelic in the Gaoth Dobhair section of County Donegal, and learned to play the fiddle from her father, Proinsias Ó Mhaonaigh, who was well known in the region for preserving the traditional fiddle tunes. (He also had a little ceilidh band by the name of Altan.) Kennedy traveled to Donegal in his late teens to study Gaelic and music, and met the then fifteen-year-old Ní Mhaonaigh, his wife-to-be.

He started to learn the whistle and flute. "It was part of life for me," Ní Mhaonaigh recalls. "He was a big fan of rock music. [But] he loved Irish music. He learned it very quickly."

He attended Queens University in Belfast and studied political science. She received a bachelor's degree in education at a Dublin university. They both wound up teaching primary school. In their spare time they traveled throughout Donegal learning tunes from the old-timers who were eager to pass on the instrumentals, but not the ballads. "Certain songs become associated with certain singers, and you wouldn't want to sing them," Ní Mhaonaigh told the Boston Globe (May 11, 1995). "You have to be sensitive toward other singers' repertoires: there's a little politics going on. So I'd go to the archives in Dublin and Belfast, then to collectors, asking for more unusual stuff."

Ní Mhaonaigh and Kennedy brought their northern sound to Dublin, where they were popular members of the music scene. In 1983, they recorded their first album, Ceol Aduaidh (Music from the North) for Gael Linn Records (rereleased by Green Linnet in 1994). The album also featured Ciaran Curran on the cittern and Eithne Ní Bhraonáin, who would later become known as Enya, on keyboards. (Ní Mhaonaigh grew up just three miles from Enya, and her sister Maire Brennan of Clannad.) The album sparked interest in the music of the northern counties throughout Ireland. In 1986, Ní Mhaonaigh and Kennedy took a leave from teaching to make the album Altan on the Danbury, Connecticut–based Green Linnet label. Their band soon inherited the name Altan, from a lake at the base of the quartz Erigal Mountain in the stark and beautiful northwest Donegal. "Altan" is an old Gaelic word meaning a slope into water or a gorge. ("We're on the slippery slopes," Ní Mhaonaigh jokes.) The original group included Ní Mhaonaigh, Kennedy, Ciaran Curran on the bouzouki, Mark Kelly on guitar, Donal Lunny (formerly with Planxty and the Bothy Band) on bodhran and keyboards, and Anna Ní Mhaonaigh, Mairéad's sister, on background vocals.

In Sing Out! (February/March/April 1995), writer Andy Nagy described seeing Kennedy and Ní Mhaonaigh perform in those early years: "I was immediately transfixed by the grace, energy and abandon of his flute as he matched, harmonized and rhythmically punctuated the equally extraordinary fiddling of his wife."

Ciaran Curran, from Kinawley in County Fermanagh, was also a founding member. He plays bouzouki, a Greek instrument that was brought to Ireland in the late 1960s. At twelve, Curran started playing mandolin. A couple of years later he took up the bouzouki and the bouzouki-guitar, an instrument custom-made for him by the Northumberland luthier Stefan Sobell. Curran says that when the band gets new material, the players usually jam until they get an arrangement that works. "Maybe some instruments won't work, others will," he says. "Everybody gets together on it."

Dáithí Sproule, a guitarist and vocalist, began playing with Altan when the band started touring in the United States. He is originally from Derry City, but now makes his home in Minneapolis, where he plays in another group, called Trian. Like many Irish musicians, he played sessions and festivals growing up and has known Ní Mhaonaigh since she was a teenager. Only one guitarist plays with the group at a time. Mark Kelly usually tours with the band in Europe and Sproule handles the American tours.

During their concerts, Ní Mhaonaigh greets the audience and sings in her native Gaelic. "That's my first language," she says. "I think in Irish. The songs that I sing, some of them I learned as a child at home. I learned others from older people and archives. We're not on a crusade about the language. It's just that it happens to be the language that I sing in. People seem to like it as well. It has a mysterious quality."

In 1989, the group released *Horse with a Heart,* followed by *The Red Crow* in 1990, *Harvest Storm* in 1992 (which stayed on the World Music Charts for twelve weeks), and *Island Angel* in 1993. Each album increased the band's reputation in Ireland and the United States. *Island Angel* reached number two on Billboard's World Music charts. Like *Harvest Storm* and *The Red Crow, Island Angel* won a NAIRD "Indie" award for Celtic Album of the Year. Britain's *Q Magazine* also selected *The Red Crow* and the band as "Roots Album and Band of the Year" in 1990.

Fiddle player Paul O'Shaughnessey had played with the band in its early years, but he had a full-time job which made it difficult to continue touring. Ciaran Tourish began subbing for O'Shaughnessey and eventually joined the band permanently in 1990, beginning with the *Harvest Storm* album. Tourish is a powerful fiddler from Buncrana, Donegal, who recalls accompanying his older sister to a local music teacher named Dinny McGlaughlin when he was six. Dinny handed him a tin whistle and suggested that he stick around as well. Tourish began playing fiddle in pubs at thirteen.

He and Ní Mhaonaigh incorporate triplets and other flourishes common in Donegal. "They're coming from the same source in Donegal," Tourish says of their styles. "Within the band, because there's melody going on, that allows me to do improvisations, to work around that. Everyone subconsciously has a role. Everyone knows what they have to do."

In 1992, when the group was just beginning to gain worldwide acclaim, Kennedy was diagnosed with throat cancer. He continued to perform with the group while undergoing chemotherapy. As his health declined, he insisted that the rest of the band keep touring. Ní Mhaonaigh went on tour even though it pained her.

"He insisted that the band keep going," Ní Mhaonaigh says. "His excuse was if he got better at least the band would be there. I used to just go to please him. I realize now he was preparing me for other things as well. That was a torturous time. We had great hopes. I didn't think of how final it was. But then when it did happen, the music was there to help us through again. . . . It was ironic, the lower that he was getting in health, the more recognition the band were getting. That was kind of funny in its own way. He was delighted."

Kennedy joined Altan for his last performance on June 21, 1994, in London at the Union Chapel. "That morning he was actually between two minds of going or not," Ní Mhaonaigh recalls. "It was just after having a chemotherapy course and he was feeling a bit sick. As we were leaving the house, he decided to bring his toothbrush and flute and join us. He had a brilliant night. It was really a happy evening."

Three months later Kennedy died in Belfast and was laid to rest in Donegal. In an obituary in *Dirty Linen* (December '94/January '95), Maureen Brennan wrote about Kennedy's desire to focus on traditional music. "We could have made a conscious decision to try and broaden our appeal by fitting in songs from other areas, like perhaps trying a country song or a Cajun song or a pop song, or something like that," Kennedy told her. "What we've tried to do is make our traditional music interesting to people who might not be interested in traditional music."

The band dedicated its sixth retrospective CD to Kennedy: *Altan: The First Ten Years 1986/1995,* released on Green Linnet. They asked Donal Lunny to select fifteen tracks from the band's first five albums. The collection includes three flute airs by Kennedy. (The annual Frankie Kennedy Winter School is dedicated to maintaining the music of Donegal.)

Because he had wanted them to go on, Altan began touring just four weeks later. "I had a great loss, but the band as a unit we all lost a great friend," Ní Mhaonaigh says. "I think none of us said we'll get another flute player. Nobody seemed to want that. We're going to leave that void there."

The addition of Dermot Byrne in 1994 brought in one of Ireland's top accordion players. Byrne, like Tourish, comes from Buncrana. He learned to play from his melodeon-playing father, Tomás Byrne. He has played with De Dannan fiddler Frankie Gavin and been in concert with accordionist Sharon Shannon and bouzouki player Lunny. He released his first solo album, *Dermot Byrne,* on Hummingbird in 1995 (released by Green Linnet in the United States a year later).

"Dermot, being from Donegal as well, it was a natural thing for him to join the band. He knew all the tunes," Tourish says.

One of the few diversions for Altan was the time the group recorded a duet of "Barbara Allen" sung by Dolly Parton and Ní Mhaonaigh on Parton's *Heart*

Songs CD. Says Sproule: "We thought it was a rather surreal thing to be doing, but we were excited to meet everybody. 'Barbara Allen' is well known in the Appalachians and all the traditional areas of America. We have versions in Ireland too. . . . We got a great kick out of blending our approach to the song to her approach."

The band also performed at the White House for Saint Patrick's Day 1994, an honor that confirmed the group's sterling reputation.

By 1995, the band's popularity had grown considerably beyond its rural Donegal roots. *Island Angel* and *The First Ten Years* sold a respectable 100,000 units each in the United States and the United Kingdom. When Altan tours, the group draws crowds far beyond the size of the local Irish American population. Their American audiences are generally sophisticated, though once in a while, someone will still request "Danny Boy" or "When Irish Eyes Are Smiling."

Says Ní Mhaonaigh: "One time in Cleveland, an old Irish American man asked me why I wasn't singing the old songs. Dáithí Sproule, who studies and lectures in Old Irish, turned around and said, 'The songs that Mairéad is singing are actually older than the ones you're asking her to sing.' He said, 'The old country's falling apart.' But he was right too."

In 1995, Altan signed with Virgin Records, releasing its first major label album in June 1996. Like previous albums, *Blackwater* is an excellent collection of jigs, reels, hornpipes, and soulful ballads sung by Ní Mhaonaigh. She plays lead fiddle on "A Tune for Frankie," a mournful but uplifting tribute to her husband. Kennedy's loss didn't dampen the group's inherent good spirits, and the collection strengthened the group's reputation as one of the finest traditional bands in Ireland. Altan followed with *Runaway Sunday* on Virgin in 1997.

In the meantime, Green Linnet released a double CD called *Best of Altan.* The package includes a limited-edition bonus CD, *Altan Live in Concert,* recorded live in Germany in 1989, with extensive liner notes by Earle Hitchner. K-Tel released an Altan compilation in 1996. The band released a new studio album, *Another Sky,* in February 2000.

"Obviously we're trying to break new ground," Ní Mhaonaigh says. "We want to bring the music to as many people as possible. We're not trying to make it precious. It's a live music, as vibrant as any type of music. It has all the emotions that you want to feel."

Based on an interview by Lyndon Stambler with members of Altan

ALVIN, DAVE: *Singer, songwriter, guitarist. Born Los Angeles, Nov. 11, 1955.*

With childhood musical influences ranging from roots blues to jazz, it's not surprising that Dave Alvin has performed everything from revivalist rock with the Blasters to acoustic folk music as a solo artist in the course of his career.

He and his older brother Phil (born March 6, 1953), lead singer of the Blasters, grew up in Downey, a "melting pot" LA suburb where they heard blues, R&B, country, Cajun, and Tex-Mex. An older cousin named Donna introduced them to West Coast R&B groups like the Medallions and the Penguins, and to singers like Big Joe Turner. Another cousin, Mike, introduced them to folk-based musicians such as Bob Dylan, Sonny Terry and Brownie McGhee, and Phil Ochs.

They listened to Carl Perkins, Chuck Berry, Woody Guthrie, Leadbelly, Robert Johnson, Hank Williams, Muddy Waters, Curtis Mayfield, and Smokey Robinson, learning from the old records. Phil liked to play harmonica and sing, and Dave sat in his bedroom and concentrated on matching chords and notes on his guitar with what came out of the phonograph or radio. There were also the neighborhood bars.

"Two blocks from where we lived a blues piano player named Lloyd Glenn was playing," Dave Alvin recalls. "If we weren't following the Johnny Otis band, we'd go sneak into there and sit on the bar and go, 'Play some blues, play some boogie-woogie.' . . . You could see a country singer in the bar down the street. If you wanted to go find it, all that music was there. We developed an appetite for it."

Marty Robbins's "El Paso" struck Alvin's fancy. He played the 45 over and over. "Songs that told a story or painted pictures always attracted me," says Alvin. "I always try to tell stories."

The Alvins' father, Casimir, was a union organizer for the Steel Workers of America. He took his family on organizing trips throughout the Southwest for the steelworkers and copper and coal miners. The sounds and images of the Southwest crept into many of Dave's songs.

"I tend to write songs about people that maybe have gotten the raw end of the deal," he says. "By the time I was ten or twelve, I'd seen things most average American kids didn't see unless they're involved in that kind of work. Most kids don't go to union meetings. They don't see their dad on top of a beat-up car in an Indian village giving a spiel about organizing into a union. They don't see their dad getting into fist fights out in the middle of the desert with guys over political issues."

Both brothers performed with local bands before deciding to assemble the Blasters in the late 1970s, initially to play at a friend's wedding. The group's roster later shook down to Phil on lead vocals and guitar, Dave on lead guitar, John Bazz on bass guitar, Gene Taylor on piano, and Bill Bateman on drums. Their debut, *American Music,* came out on the obscure Rollin' Rock label in the late 1970s. The band became a favorite in Los Angeles's New Wave movement, and gained a faithful local following. (The first milestone for Dave occurred in 1980, when the Blasters got enough gigs so that he could quit his job as a fry cook.)

Their diverse musical tastes contributed to the band's unique sound. "My style at that time leaned heavily toward Johnny Guitar Watson and Carl Perkins," Dave says. "Phil was pretty much and still is a Blind Blake, ragtime blues kind of guitar picker. The two styles really worked together. That's what created what somebody saw as rockabilly about us. We always considered ourselves to be a blues R&B band. We just had a different approach to it."

The group's material was good enough to induce Slash, a small but influential record company, to issue *The Blasters* in 1981. It deservedly won high praise from music writers around the United States, something that in the 1980s had little impact on those who put together programming for the nation's disc jockeys. Even then, the album, which featured Dave's well-crafted song "American Music" from the earlier collection, sold over 60,000 copies, mostly by word of mouth. Slash signed a promotional agreement with Warner Brothers Records, which provided a little more exposure, but not enough to do much more than double the album's overall sales.

While much of the material could be classed as rockabilly, in truth it did not sound dated or trite, reflecting an approach to the music by the Alvins that looked both backward and forward simultaneously. As Dave Alvin told a reporter from the *Chicago Tribune* in 1983: "Rock and roll grew out of blues, out of hillbilly music, out of ethnic fiddle songs—out of all the folk musics of the past. To a real rock and roll band, the sense of past is mandatory."

Their next two albums, *Non-Fiction* and *Over There,* issued in 1982, continued to feature a mix of blues, swing, roots rock, and Cajun boogie while Dave wrote new lyrics that dealt with the complexities of day-to-day living. "I'm basically a pessimist," Alvin told one reporter, "but whenever I can, I try to leave a way out for people."

The new album was ranked high on many reviewers' lists. But again, it got a minimum of airplay. Dave felt that it was getting near do-or-die time. He told *People* (December 24, 1984) that he was counting on the group's fifth album, *Hard Line,* to turn things around. "We brought our music up-to-date lyrically on the last album. This time we wanted to bring the sound up-to-date." John Cougar Mellencamp wrote and produced one song, and John Doe of X wrote another. The album, released by Warner Brothers in February 1985, didn't do much better than its predecessors, however. (In 1990, Slash/Warner Bros. released a retrospective album, *The Blasters Collection.* HighTone reissued the Blasters' debut *American Music* in 1997.)

Meanwhile, Dave became involved in projects with John Doe and other members of LA-based X, including

performing with an offshoot band called the Knitters that emphasized country and folk rather than rock. (The name is a playful tribute to the 1950s folk group the Weavers.) With the Knitters, Dave helped record the 1984 Slash LP *Poor Little Critters in the Road.* (The group reunited in the late '90s.)

"The Knitters was kind of a way for John (Doe) and Exene (Cervenka) to kind of get away from their X image," Alvin says. "It was kind of a way for me to get rid of some of the stylistic restrictions that were placed on me in the Blasters. It was also a reason to go get a bunch of beers with John and Exene."

While Dave was touring with the Blasters in support of *Hard Line,* X was in the throes of a reorganization caused by lead guitarist Billy Zoom's decision to leave. The remaining members of X asked Dave to take Zoom's place and, with the disappointment over the new album and some internal strains in the Blasters, he accepted the offer in early 1986.

"My brother and I were seeing things differently," Alvin explains. "It really came down to [the fact that] I wanted to progress as a songwriter. That meant abandoning some elements of the Blasters to do that. I didn't think I could grow as a songwriter unless I sang the songs. My brother's a great singer and I'm not. But when you're writing a song for someone else you have to write about a shared emotion or experience. You can only do that for so long."

Dsve recorded *See How We Care* in 1987 with X on Elektra/Asylum. He also embarked on his solo career with *Romeo's Escape* on CBS/Epic in August. Backing him was his new band, the All-Nighters, comprising Greg Leisz on pedal and lap steel, six- and twelve-string guitars; John "Juke" Logan on harmonica and keyboards; Gil T on bass; and Jerry Angel on bass.

(Phil, meanwhile, released his first solo album, *Un "Sung" Stories,* on Slash and revamped the Blasters to a foursome: himself, Bazz, Bateman, and, on lead guitar, 250-pound Hollywood Fats.).

Dave found freedom in his solo career, but the next four years after X were rough. He no longer had band mates to cushion the blows that sometimes come from bad reviews or poor record sales. He grew disillusioned with the music industry. He saw other bands and musicians whom the Blasters had supported succeed, like Dwight Yoakum and Los Lobos. After his first solo record he went heavily into debt to pay musicians. He also became disgusted by the use of blues or rockabilly to sell products. "You'd turn on the TV and there'd be a rockabilly thing which used to be something you never heard and there it is for a health spa, or used or new cars," he says.

Dave emerged from his funk in 1990 after he saw Curtis Mayfield (who was paralyzed later that year after a lighting scaffold fell on him during a concert in Brooklyn) performing to a crowd of 100 at the now-defunct LA country bar the Palomino. "He was incredible, musically and spiritually," Dave recalls. "It was like seeing Big Joe Turner or T-Bone Walker. Here was a cat who had all this talent perfectly intact. He wasn't up there drunk or on drugs. . . . I was thinking, 'People Get Ready' is as great a civil rights song or greater than 'Blowing in the Wind.' I left there thinking I wanted to write songs again."

Alvin does not write on a schedule, but rather waits for inspiration. "Sometimes you're just walking down the street and something will knock you over," he says. "You go, 'Hey, that's not bad.' You go home and write it and hopefully it's not. Other times you sweat bullets. . . . You're moved by some emotion inside of you that eventually has to come out. The pain in the ass is actually the writing. It gets so lonely. I have to remove myself from everything: playing live gigs, seeing friends, eating. I have to get enveloped in the songs and the characters inside of them."

Dave joined Oakland-based HighTone Records and released two more solo albums: *Blue Blvd* (1991) and *Museum of Heart* (1993). He began writing more personal songs, some edging toward folk. "The first time I went out of my way to write a folk song was a song called 'Andersonville' on *Blue Blvd,*" Alvin says. "I was trying to write a song that sounded like it was a first person narrative folk song from the Civil War era. I wrote 25 verses and pared it down to four. The great thing you can do with folk music is use the past to light the way to the future. Andersonville was about my great-great-great-uncle who died there in the POW camp. It was also very subtly, maybe too subtly, about where I think the country is at now and how polarized everything is."

In addition to solo albums, Alvin has developed a successful career writing songs for movie sound tracks: *Wall Street* (1988), *Cry Baby* (1990), *Thelma and Louise* (1991), and *Honeymoon in Las Vegas* (1991). He also recorded with such performers as Syd Straw, Tom Waits, and Sonny Burgess, and produced albums for Chris Gaffney, the Derailers, Tom Russell, and Big Sandy and His Fly-Rite Boys.

In 1994, he paid tribute to one of his all-time favorites, Merle Haggard, co-producing *Tulare Dust: A Songwriter's Tribute to Merle Haggard* with Tom Russell for HighTone Records. He performed "Kern River" on the album, which includes eleven tracks by singers ranging from Rosie Flores to Lucinda Williams and Katy Moffatt.

The project evolved when Tom Russell and Alvin were talking about California songwriters. They mentioned Tom Waits, Brian Wilson, Frank Zappa, Buck Owens, and paused when they came to Merle Haggard. But five minutes into the discussion someone mentioned that there was already a Nashville tribute record in the works. So they decided to focus on Haggard as a great California songwriter. "We came up with this idea of doing an acoustic album of all of Merle's California songs and setting it up so it was autobiographical. Everything from 'They're Tearing the Labor Camps Down' to 'Kern River' to 'Sing Me Back Home' and 'Mama Tried.' "

When they first tried to contact Haggard about the idea, he didn't respond. But after they made the album, "he kind of flipped for it," Alvin says. Haggard gave out copies to friends and played it on the bus for his band.

Alvin followed the Merle Haggard tribute album with an acoustic album of his own, *King of California,* released in 1994 on HighTone. The album included some songs he previously recorded with the Blasters and X, but in an acoustic setting: "Border Radio," "Every Night About This Time," "Fourth of July," "Barn Burning," "Bus Station," and "Little Honey." It showcased his songs about drifters, love gone sour, and convicts. He got used to playing acoustic sets on his solo tours "because it was the only way I could afford to tour," he told one reviewer, "but what I noticed was that I was learning to sing better because I wasn't having to project my vocals over drums and loud electric guitars."

The Woody Guthrie–esque title song, "King of California," was suggested by a girlfriend who was impressed with Alvin's knowledge of the back roads of California. It sounds traditional, an effect that was deliberate. "That goes back to my Blasters days of how do I write something that sounds like it's from the 1950s that still stands up to now," Alvin says. "I was kind of half consciously trying to write a song about the way California is now—this place where people come expecting the promised land and all that kind of malarkey. It's about someone who comes here and comes face to face with the reality of what the place is."

The album, which was well-received by the critics, was more folk-influenced than any of his previous work. "In a way, it took a little arm twisting to get High-Tone to let me do it that way," Alvin says. "My reputation was pretty much as a sweaty rock 'n' roller. Gradually more of my audience was becoming the singer-songwriter audience. But HighTone was still scared. To some extent I was too. . . . Half the people running around the East Village, what right do they have to be called folk music? Rockabilly is as much a folk music as blues or bluegrass or anything like that. It's just a little louder."

In 1996 Alvin released *Interstate City* with live versions of his old standards, like "Long White Cadillac" and "Jubilee Train" and newer songs, like the title track and a song he wrote with Tom Russell, "Out in California." The album is a "road album," with his characters in bars, on interstates, in motels, or the byways of the imagination. In "Dry River," the Downey, California, native knows of what he sings—*I was born by a river / But it was paved with cement*—but finds a way to dream of being "soaking wet." He captures the anguish of a man in a motel by the airport in "Thirty Dollar Room": *Sign on the door says check out's at 11 / A woman's earring laying on the table / She said she'll be right back / But I get the feeling she's gone.*

He and his band, the Guilty Men, produce a powerful live sound, with strong work by Rick Solem on piano, Greg Leisz, Alvin's longtime producer and bandmate, on steel guitar, and Ted Roddy on harmonica. But this won't necessarily be the sound he limits himself to. In the summer of 1998, HighTone issued Alvin's new album, *Blackjack David,* his sixth solo release. Writing in the *Los Angeles Times* (" 'Blackjack' Deals a Dark View of Love," July 4, 1998, p. F12), Richard Cromelin called Alvin an artist to reckon with. The track "Mary Brown," Cromelin stated, "illustrates his ability to spin a yarn, and over the course of the collection he creates a gallery of characters victimized by personal betrayal, by the system, or by their own inertia, giving them due sympathy without sentimentality."

In August 2000 Alvin released an album of what he considers folk covers, a wide range indeed, titled *Public Domain.*

Based on an interview by Lyndon Stambler with Dave Alvin

ANDERSEN, ERIC: *Singer, guitarist, harmonica player, pianist, songwriter. Born Pittsburgh, Pennsylvania, February 14, 1943.*

In the mid-1960s, when it was fashionable to compare every new folk artist to Bob Dylan, Eric Andersen was considered one of the foremost candidates for Dylan's folk mantle. Andersen, who in his writing and concert work steadfastly hewed to what might be called "old-school folk," was overshadowed by the resurgent rock movement of the period. However, he persevered and remained a favorite of the small but enthusiastic folk audiences of the late 1960s and early 1970s, symbolizing the weary-struggle-against-fate theme voiced in many of his compositions.

Born in Pittsburgh to a metallurgist father ("with the heart of a poet") and an Ohioan mother, Andersen grew up in Amherst, in upstate New York. Influenced by the strong folk music movement and the Beat poets of the mid-1950s, he taught himself piano and guitar, and by his mid-teens often accompanied himself when singing folk songs in school shows. By the time he enrolled in Hobart College in New York at the start of the 1960s, he was an excellent guitarist and harmonica player as well. Between his freshman and sophomore years, he and a friend went to Boston, guitar and banjo in hand, and formed their own group, the Cradlers. They made their mark on the folk circuit throughout New England. Performing in group concerts and folk festivals, they sometimes shared the bill with such early 1960s luminaries as Joan Baez, the Kingston Trio, Ramblin' Jack Elliott, and Peter, Paul, and Mary.

By his sophomore year he tired of college and

dropped out in the fall of 1963 to hitchhike to San Francisco, where he met Allen Ginsberg, Lawrence Ferlinghetti, and Neal Cassady. (He was at a poetry reading with them when John F. Kennedy was assassinated.) Tom Paxton heard him sing and invited him to New York, where he met Phil Ochs and Bob Dylan.

In the mid-1960s Andersen made Manhattan his base of operations, often appearing at major folk clubs in Greenwich Village. Besides his headline appearances, including several acclaimed concerts at New York's Town Hall, he was sought out by other artists to work as a sideman or as a session musician in recording studios. From the mid-1960s throughout the 1970s, he backed top artists in every segment of pop music from folk through rock.

In 1964, he signed with Vanguard Records, making his album debut with *Today Is the Highway* in May 1965, followed in April 1966 by *'Bout Changes and Things,* which included his classic songs "Thirsty Boots" and "Violets of Dawn." As a *Harper's* magazine writer noted, he was one of the most promising young performers in the Big Apple. "At the age of twenty-three, he is one of the mainsprings of the folk world. Tall thin . . . with high cheekbones like Rudolph Nureyev (the ballet dancer), he is what everyone who is eighteen in the Village wants to look like."

In the late 1960s, he continued to perform not only in New York but across the United States, with occasional forays into Canada. During these years, he continued to add about forty compositions a year. His Vanguard albums of those years included a remake of an earlier LP backed with electric instruments, *'Bout Changes and Things, Take 2* (1967), *More Hits from Tin Can Alley* (1968), *A Country Dream* (1969), and *Best of Eric Andersen* (1970). During the summer of 1967, Beatles manager Brian Epstein talked to Andersen about managing his career, but Epstein died in August of that year—the first in a string of misfortunes.

Warner Bros. released *Avalanche* in 1968 and *Eric Andersen* the following year. As he had in most of his previous recordings, Andersen arranged and produced his original works. He also turned out the *Eric Andersen Song Book* and established his own music publishing company, Wind and Sand.

The Warner Bros. alignment was short-lived, though, and he moved to Columbia in 1972. His initial LP on that label, called *Blue River* (released in August 1972, reissued by Columbia/Legacy in 1999), was clearly one of his best efforts and made the national album charts, a rare accomplishment for a folk artist during those years. Recorded in Nashville with such background vocalists as Joni Mitchell and the Jordanaires, *Blue River* received critical acclaim. But bad luck prevented Andersen from following up that success. He worked up material for a new album, but the master recordings were lost en route from Nashville to the Columbia headquarters in New York, and with them a wonderful opportunity to expand his following. It was around the time of the Watergate scandal, and Andersen had conspiracy theories of his own about his missing tapes. "I felt shock and horror. It was like a bad joke—worse than being stood up on New Year's Eve," he told *Musician* later (August 1991).

After that experience, he left Columbia and signed with Arista Records, which issued several of his albums in the second half of the 1970s, including *Be True to You* (1975), *Sweet Surprise* (1976), and *Eric Andersen / The Best Songs* (1977). His recording career was floundering, but he persisted with a rigorous touring schedule. Throughout the decade he continued to appear in small folk clubs across the United States and tour Europe and Japan. In 1976, he became the first solo U.S. singer-songwriter to tour Japan. In the mid-1970s, he acknowledged the changing times and included an electric bass guitar in his band arrangements. The emphasis remained, though, on acoustic instrumentation. Typically, he performed on an acoustic guitar with a harmonica brace around his neck and one or two acoustic backing musicians.

In the early 1980s, Andersen moved to Norway to live with Norwegian artist Unni Askeland and began shuttling between his Norway home and a New York apartment. (They had four children together; Andersen had previously had a daughter with guitarist Debby Green.) He recorded three albums in Europe: *Midnight Son* (1980), *Tight in the Night* (1985), and the original sound track for the little-known movie *Istanbul* (1985). But he didn't regain his footing in North America until the 1988 release of *Ghosts upon the Road* (rereleased in 1995 on Plump Records). His new manager, Ron Fierstein, who coproduced the movie *Torch Song Trilogy,* and Suzanne Vega producer Steve Addabbo helped bring Andersen back to the United States. But songs like "Trouble in Paris," "Irish Lace," "Spanish Steps," and "Belgian Bar" clearly reflected his European orientation. "Ghosts upon the Road," which received the most attention, is a 10½-minute autobiographical account of Andersen's life as a struggling folksinger in 1964, living in an abandoned building on Boston's Beacon Hill and on the Lower East Side of New York. (He also released a compilation album, *Best of Eric Andersen,* in 1988.)

In 1989, the missing tapes—forty boxes of tapes and artwork—from the early 1970s were discovered in unmarked boxes in a Columbia Records vault in Nashville. In 1991, Andersen released *Stages: The Lost Album*—eighteen years after it was supposed to come out. Although the album sounds more like the era in which it was originally recorded, it includes several wonderful originals. Songs like "Time Run Like a Freight Train" and "Woman, She Was Gentle" (which features Joan Baez) reestablished Andersen's standing with the critics. He won two New York Music Awards in 1991, for Best Folk Artist and Best Folk Album.

In 1991 he recorded a collaborative album, *Danko/ Fjeld/Andersen,* on Norway's Stageway Records, with Rick Danko, formerly of The Band, and Jonas Fjeld, a Norwegian singer-songwriter known for his work with poet Ole Paus. (The album was licensed to Rykodisc in 1993.) They followed up the album with *Ridin' on the Blinds,* recorded in the fall of 1994 and released on Grappa Records of Norway.

Despite the touring and his earlier rambling ways, Andersen has turned into something of a homebody. As he told *Musician*'s Jon Young (August 1991): "Records come and go; music business attention comes and goes, but it's all illusory. The only thing that matters, in the final analysis, is your family."

In 1997 Archive Records released a CD with fifteen tracks from Andersen's years with Arista. Columbia/ Legacy reissued his classic album *Blue River* in 1999.

In January 1999 Appleseed Records released *Memory of the Future,* Andersen's first solo album since *Stages: The Lost Album* in 1991. Among the participants in the project were Richard Thompson, Rick Danko, Garth Hudson, Jonas Fjeld, and Howie Epstein, noted producer of John Prine's latest albums. It includes the song "Hills of Tuscany," which Andersen wrote while he was living in Italy in 1985, and "The Rain Falls Down in Amsterdam," which he wrote after playing a tour with Townes Van Zandt in Holland a year after the Berlin Wall fell. The song reflected his "uneasy feeling" about what might crawl out of the rubble—the death and destruction of Bosnia, for example. He also includes the Phil Ochs song "When I'm Gone," which he had recorded for the Ochs tribute album *What's That I Hear.* In 2000 Appleseed released *You Can't Relive the Past.*

ARMATRADING, JOAN: *Singer, guitarist, keyboards player, band leader, songwriter. Born St. Kitts Island, December 9, 1950.*

A creative, multitalented artist, Joan Armatrading always had an exellent reputation with fellow performers, critics, and a loyal, if not overwhelmingly large, band of fans. In the mid-1990s, she could point to a fine body of recorded work and an established status as an entertainer who almost always presented an exciting, professional concert. Her artistic integrity—a refusal to water down her material for purely commercial reasons—did not prevent her from achieving a secure niche in the blues and folk rock music scene, but probably stood in the way of superstar status.

In albums such as *Joan Armatrading,* she demonstrated that she could do it all: sing with feeling and emotion, play excellent acoustic guitar, and, most of all, write well-matched words and music. Though she spent her early years in the West Indies, her material typically had the rhythmic intensity of Afro-American blues, jazz, and rock with a flavor of sophistication different from West Indies folk music. In her LPs, where nearly all the songs were written or cowritten by her, almost every track has contributed to the overall effect. An example of her lyrical ability from *Joan Armatrading* are these lines from "Somebody Who Loves You": "Mistaken shyness can be costly / Too hasty a goodbye / And then you've lost me." While most of her songs over the years have dealt with personal relationships, some probe the general human condition, as in "People": "I got no place to hide / Nowhere to go / People all around me / Singing out of tune."

Joan was born on the Caribbean island of St. Kitts in 1950. In 1958 the family moved to England, settling in the industrial city of Birmingham, where Joan completed her formal education. One of six children, she was left on her own a good part of the time. Shy by nature, she recalled hanging back and watching other children at play, something "that went into my writing."

After a while, she became a radio addict back in the days when there was no Walkman available. She spent hours listening to whatever pop music was being broadcast in a period where the transition from old-style pop to the new rock style was affecting a generation of young Britons. As her interest in music grew, she began to teach herself to play instruments, first a piano, later a guitar. She credited that with giving birth to her percussive style of guitar performance. She told Barbara Graustark of *Newsweek* (February 11, 1980): "I was trying to be all the musicians in a band and my weird tempo changes came from not knowing what I was doing."

At the age of fourteen, she wrote her first song, "When I Was Young." She had Marianne Faithfull in mind when she wrote it, but had no idea of how to present the material to her. As her playing and singing improved, her brother and friends urged her to think of becoming a performer. She had already had some experience in school concerts when she finally did decide to take that step at fifteen. She still was hesitant, she recalled, because "I've always thought of myself as a songwriter first. I write all the time. The last thing I think about is how to sing it."

For a while she got work at local clubs, singing songs by people such as Bob Dylan and Paul Simon as well as some of her own compositions. She gained a local following, but wasn't thinking of becoming a major artist at the time. Later she moved to Bristol and at the end of the decade successfully auditioned for a U.K. touring company of the musical *Hair.*

At the start of the 1970s, she took up residence in London and slowly began to build up contacts in the music field. She still wanted to make her way mainly as a writer, staying "famous but faceless."

In London, she became friends with poet/lyricist Pam Nestor and soon the two were collaborating on new material. With Armatrading's unique guitar style and powerful voice, it made sense for her to make the demonstration records needed to sell the songs; it was only a step from that to her being offered a recording contract.

Their debut LP, *Whatever's for Us,* came out on Hifly Records in 1972. It only sold about 12,000 copies, but more than a few observers could detect something very promising in the neophyte recording artist. A&M was interested in releasing another album, but Joan took a two-year hiatus, in part due to a restrictive management contract. Her next LP, *Back to the Night,* did much better than the debut collection. In the year-end poll of English music critics, it was voted one of the top 10 releases of the year. She also added to her luster with her opening act work on concert tours with Supertramp and Nils Lofgren.

Her next album, *Joan Armatrading,* issued by A&M in July 1976, brought even more accolades on both sides of the Atlantic. English reviewers considered it one of the best collections of the mid-1970s. Phil Sutcliffe of England's *Sounds* magazine called it the number one album of 1976, writing: "We need Joan Armatrading like we need Bob Dylan and the Beatles. You'll play this record once in a while forever." In the United States, *Rolling Stone* voted it runner-up Album of the Year.

Joan wasn't quite as consistent in follow-up albums of the late '70s, but all of them contained a sizable number of gems, for most of which Joan wrote both words and music. Her late '70s releases were *Show Some Emotion* (1977), *To the Limit* (1978), *How Cruel* (1979), and *Steppin' Out* (1979). As a whole, her output from 1973 to 1979 made her a major influence on pop and rock music almost everywhere but in the United States. By 1980, she had earned eighteen gold records in seven countries, but none in the United States. Some of her releases made U.S. charts, but none rose to top levels.

She asked American interviewers, smiling but with some frustration: "Why aren't I famous?" The question remained valid in the mid-1980s, when she still was a cult favorite in the United States, but an acknowledged star at home.

Some of the problem might have been the macho nature of rock music when she was getting started. She recalled that people enthused over the guitar licks on her albums, but were sure it was a male lead guitarist. "I'm used to people thinking it's a guy playing guitar on my albums when it's actually me. I suppose a lot of girls think they're expected to just strum along—to get by—but it annoys me that people should automatically think that's the extreme of my capabilities, too. I've always had a different approach, concentrating on writing songs and playing the guitar rather than thinking in terms of being a singer."

A&M continued to release new Armatrading LPs in the 1980s, starting with *Me Myself I* in 1980, followed by *Walk Under Ladders* in 1981. The latter was one of her more successful efforts during the winter of 1981–82. In support of the album, she made well-received tours of the United States, parts of Europe, and several countries in the Far East. A notable departure from previous shows, much to the dismay of some older faithful fans, was her use of electric guitars instead of the acoustic instruments she'd played in previous years.

In 1983, A&M issued two more albums, *The Key* and a best-of compilation called *Track Record,* which also contained two new songs by Joan. Following *The Key,* it was two more years before another LP of all new songs by her came out.

Commenting on whether that album, *Secret Secrets,* represented any change in musical outlook, she told an interviewer in early 1985: "It's always difficult to answer that. . . . I can only say that if you listen to [*The Key*] and then listen to this one, you'll hear what the changes are. It can be something as simple as using different chords. For example, you can pick a chord as simple as a D; you've always used one particular inversion of the chord and you suddenly decide to use a different shape for it. That can make a huge difference. I've change the shape of my chords quite a bit this time."

The album credits indicated she also had assumed new duties, naming her as coarranger for horns and strings backing tracks. She responded: "I did all the arrangement on *The Key* and *Me Myself I.* I just didn't put it down on the album."

In 1986 A&M issued another Armatrading LP, *Sleight of Hand.* Later the company issued one of her best collections, *Shouting Stage,* which like earlier releases received across-the-board critical acclaim but little airplay, particularly in the United States.

She remained with A&M into the 1990s, releasing *Hearts and Flowers* (1990) and *Square the Circle* (1992), but by mid-decade had decided it was time to try another alignment in hopes of finally expanding her following. Her RCA debut, *What's Inside,* came out in the fall of 1995 and proved a worthy addition to her catalog with such listenable, well-crafted tracks as "Back on the Road," "Songs," "Recommend My Love," and "Everyday Boy."

Her debut album, *Whatever's for Us,* was reissued on Castle Classics. A&M released a compilation of her work in 1987 called *Classics Volume 21.* In 1996, A&M released a two-CD collection called *Love and Affection* which includes thirty-nine songs. Her voice was also heard singing the song "Willow" on the sound track for the movie *Boys on the Side* on Arista Records.

AUSTIN LOUNGE LIZARDS: *Comedy vocal and instrumental quintet formed in 1980. Original Lizards include: Conrad Deisler (guitar, vocals), born Oakland, California, October 19, 1955; Tom Pittman (banjo, pedal steel, vocals), born Charleston, South Carolina, May 19, 1948; Hank Card (vocals, rhythm guitar), born Medford, Oklahoma, March 31, 1955. Bass players have included Tom Ellis, replaced by Michael Stevens in 1982, Kirk*

Williams in 1987, Matt Cartsonis in 1994, and in 1995 Boo Resnick, born Royal Oak, Michigan, June 11, 1950. Mandolin and fiddle players have included Tim Wilson (mandolin, fiddle, vocals), who joined in 1983, making the Lizards a quintet. He was replaced by Paul Sweeney (mandolin, vocals) in 1986, Todd Jagger (mandolin) in 1990, and in 1991 by Richard Bowden (mandolin, fiddle, vocals), born Durham, North Carolina, April 18, 1952. Lineup as of 1999: Deisler, Pittman, Card, Bowden, and Resnick.

The cover photo for the Austin Lounge Lizards' 1998 CD, *Employee of the Month* (Sugar Hill), depicts a mouse running a treadmill. You can say a lot of things about the Lizards, but they're not nine-to-fivers. All have given up their day jobs except administrative law judge Hank Card. In the tradition of Homer and Jethro, Tom Lehrer, and the Smothers Brothers, the Austin Lounge Lizards poke fun at everything from the state of Texas ("Stupid Texas Song") to Newt Gingrich ("Gingrich the Newt") to born-again Christians ("Jesus Loves Me But He Can't Stand You"). About the only thing they take seriously is their musicianship. They especially like to lampoon country music, as in the song about Hank Williams ("I Want to Ride in the Car Hank Died In") and another about the Oak Ridge Boys ("Put the Oak Ridge Boys in the Slammer"). Folk music isn't safe either. "Leonard Cohen's Day Job" features Tom Pittman intoning such somber Cohen-esque lines as *I come down to work where the common folk throng / In my famous blue shirt with its patch that says "Len."*

Hank Card and Conrad Deisler, who both studied history at Princeton, began writing songs together in 1976. They wound up at the University of Texas Law School. Along with banjoist and pedal steel player Tom Pittman (a philosophy major at the University of Georgia), they formed the band in 1980 to prove they really could do something useful with their degrees. Initially they called themselves the Lounge Lizards, but they added "Austin" when they found out their name was already in use by a New York band. They started out playing local bars around Austin for tips and beers. By 1983 the band was a quintet with Michael Stevens on bass and Tim Wilson on mandolin and fiddle. They began touring, winning the Best Band award in 1983 at the Kerrville Bluegrass Festival. They have gone through a succession of bass players and fiddler-mandolinists. The late 1990s lineup includes bassist Boo Resnick, who has a history degree from the University of Michigan, and fiddler Richard Bowden.

The Austin Lounge Lizards are proud they were named Best None of the Above Band by the *Austin Chronicle* readers' poll several times. Among their most notable spoofs, the Lizards have taken on National Public Radio in "Mourning Edition," the mentally challenged in "Shallow End of the Gene Pool," Pink Floyd in a bluegrass version of "Brain Damage," and the Teflon-coated president in "Ballad of Ronald Reagan."

Their first album, *Creatures from the Black Saloon,* came out on Watermelon Records in 1985. Since then they have released *Highway Café of the Damned* (1983, Watermelon), *Lizard Vision* (Flying Fish, 1991), *Paint Me on Velvet* (Flying Fish, 1993), *Small Minds* (Watermelon, 1995), *Live Bait* (a six-song live EP on Watermelon, 1996), and *Employee of the Month* (Sugar Hill, 1998). The Lizards, whose next two recordings will be on Sugar Hill, plan to record: "Waitin' on a Call from Don" (a song about car repair), "80 Hillbillies in a Haunted House," and "Grunge" (a deconstructed interpretation of grunge music).

Written with the assistance of Conrad Deisler

AXTON, HOYT: *Singer, guitarist, pianist, songwriter. Born Duncan, Oklahoma, March 25, 1938; died Victor, Montana, October 26, 1999.*

With his craggy features and strong, broad-shouldered build, Hoyt Axton looked the part of a lumberjack, man of the soil, or football player. As it happened, he was a talented athlete in his early years. Although he developed into one of the major folk song performers and writers of the 1960s and 1970s, he never learned traditional ballads at his parents' knees. His background was urban, though his mother segued from her initial profession of teacher to a songwriter who helped make Elvis Presley famous and, in passing, changed her son's ideas of what he wanted to do with his life.

Hoyt and Johnny Axton were the two sons of Mae Boren Axton, who was teaching English and drama when her boys were little. In 1950, when Hoyt was ten, she turned her attention to writing songs with friends and musicians from the Jacksonville, Florida, area the Axtons then called home. She wrote a variety of songs from country to pop, and for a number of years, not much happened. But in the mid-1950s, she cowrote a song called "Heartbreak Hotel" that came to the attention of a new young artist named Elvis Presley. The song, of course, became a smash, one of the best-selling singles of 1956 and one that was a major spark in bringing the rock revolution to fruition. The impact on Hoyt and Johnny Axton was as great as it was on millions of other teenagers of the era. In Hoyt's case it triggered the writing of his own original songs.

As Mrs. Axton wrote in the C&W magazine *Picking Up the Tempo* (February–March 1976), "Hoyt was in high school in Jacksonville, Florida, when Elvis knocked the props out from under the classy, but staid music industry—daring to be himself—and Hoyt and Johnny [who later went on to become an attorney] found themselves among the mushrooming number of Presley fans. Hoyt sang such Presley tunes as 'I've Got a Woman (Way Over Town)' in high school assembly and variety shows."

As a boy he had taken classical piano lessons, although, as his mother noted, he didn't necessarily follow the music put before him: "Sometimes, to the dismay of his piano teacher, he would start playing the boogie in the middle of a lesson." He learned to play piano after a fashion but the instrument he really took to in his teens was the guitar. He also liked sports and played on several high school varsity teams, and was good enough in football to get scholarship offers from a number of colleges.

"As a freshman football whiz at Oklahoma State University," Mrs. Axton wrote, "Hoyt entertained his friends by singing and picking his guitar. Hoyt left college for naval service, which was ironic, since he was trying to forego the demands of R.O.T.C.—and inadvertently chose a more demanding way of life in the Navy."

Meanwhile, Hoyt's musical tastes were changing. He found less and less interest in rock music and more in the growing folk music boom of the late 1950s. When he got out of the service, he began to travel around the coffeehouses and small folk club circuit of the West Coast, initially concentrating on venues in the San Francisco Bay Area, then extending his performances to the northwest and south to Los Angeles, where he often was featured in the late 1950s and early 1960s in the prestigious Troubadour Club. He built up a small but loyal following during those years, though he didn't become a top star for several reasons. One was the fact that the East Coast "folk establishment" classed him as too "conservative" in outlook, apparently more because of his independence of mind, which kept him from blindly joining causes for the sake of joining, than any lack of humanity. A second reason, though, was his admitted fondness for excess in drink, romance, and high-speed driving.

The lack of nationwide attention didn't seem to bother him much. He went his own way, often hitchhiking from one job to another, playing engagements in many out-of-the-way places, working with others who had the same outlook. He was continually writing new material. One of those songs, cowritten with the late Ken Ramsey, was the 1962 "Greenback Dollar." The song was picked up by the Kingston Trio and became one of their major hits of the early 1960s.

Hoyt was offered a recording contract with Harmony Records in the early 1960s and had a series of albums issued on the label, including *Balladeer, Thunder 'n' Lightnin'* (5/63), and *Saturday's Child* (2/64). He continued to appear regularly at the Troubadour in the mid-1960s, as well as other folk clubs around the country, and more than a few pop and rock artists came to hear him sing. At one of those shows in 1964, a young musician named John Kay caught his act and was impressed by Hoyt's song "The Pusher." Later, when Kay formed his group Steppenwolf, which became one of the top rock bands of the late 1960s and early 1970s, "The Pusher" was a staple in the band's repertoire. It was included in four best-selling LPs and made top levels of the singles charts in the early 1970s. In the mid-1970s, the song was used in the sound track of the movie *Easy Rider*. Several other Axton songs also were featured by Kay, including one called "Snowblind Friend."

Other rock groups became interested in Axton's material. One band, Three Dog Night, arranged for Axton to go around the United States with them as their opening act during the 1969–70 period. The association provided unanticipated bonuses for both Hoyt and the group. During one concert series he played a new song called "Joy to the World" for Three Dog Night. The band recorded it and the single rose to number one on U.S. pop charts in early 1971 and also rose high on country lists. It was awarded a gold record by R.I.A.A. on April 9, 1971. Later, Hoyt's "Never Been to Spain" also brought the group a top 10 singles hit. At the time, Axton was recording for Capitol Records, which released his version of "Joy to the World" in the LP of that title recorded with the *Hollywood Living Room Band*. Another Capitol LP of his that came out soon after was titled *Country Anthem*.

In the mid-1970s he signed with A&M Records; his albums of those years included *Less Than the Song* (1973), *Life Machine* (1974), *Southbound* (1975), *Fearless* (1976), *Road Songs, Snowblind Friend* (1977), and *Free Sailin'* (1978). New covers of "Joy to the World" and Axton's other originals continued to be released during the decade, and Ringo Starr had a hit single with a new Axton composition, the "No No Song." His duet with Linda Ronstadt, "When the Morning Comes," hit the top of the Canadian charts, while his novelty song, "Boney Fingers," received U.S. airplay.

Though he tended to keep a low profile as far as his contributions to charitable causes were concerned, his mother emphasized that "a concern for people has always been foremost in his mind. He was affiliated with UNICEF and prisoners' work [a charter member of the Bread and Roses organization, founded by Joan Baez's sister, Mimi Fariña]. He has been helping to care for orphan children . . . and he and Linda Ronstadt recently did a benefit in Santa Fe, New Mexico, for needy Indians."

In the late 1970s, Axton's recordings came out on his own label, Jeremiah Records, including *Rusty Old Halo* (1979). Results of that affiliation included "Della and the Dealer" in early summer 1979 and the late 1979 top 10 singles hit "A Rusty Old Halo." In 1980, he added more charted singles on Jeremiah, including "Wild Bull Rider," "Evangelina," and "Where Did the Money Go." The last named song was the title track of another Jeremiah album, released in 1980. This was followed in 1982 by the LP *Everybody's Going on the Road*.

One project of that period he particularly enjoyed, Axton said, was the chance to appear in the Francis Ford Coppola film *The Black Stallion*. "We started filming in 1979 and I played the father [of the boy whose

love for a horse was the focal point of the film]. It came out in 1982. Later I performed in the film *Buried Alive* for the USA cable network."

Hoyt continued to find outlets for his talents as a performer on concert circuits at home and in many other parts of the world through the 1980s into the 1990s. As for recordings, he noted from his home in Hamilton, Montana, in April 1996, "I kept making records until there didn't seem to be a market for them. The last one I put out was five years ago called *Spin of the Wheel*. A&M also put together a compilation of some of my work for them. My songs have done great. [The royalties] from 'Joy to the World' have been incredible—a lot better than Social Security."

By then, however, he was struggling with more severe problems than economic success. "I'm still kicking around, but last July 4 [1995] I had a major stroke and was paralyzed on my left side. I'm almost walking again, though. Not very gracefully and not very fast, but it's better than the alternative."

In the spring of 1997, his mother, Mae Boren Axton, passed away. Later that year, Axton recovered from his stroke and began writing songs, acting, and performing again. He also got married again in August 1997—to Deborah Hawkins. Two years later Axton died of a heart attack at his Victor, Montana ranch.

Axton quotes from phone interview with Irwin Stambler

BAEZ, JOAN: *Singer, guitarist, songwriter. Born Staten Island, New York, January 9, 1941.*

At the start of the 1980s, on the verge of her third decade as a major artist, Joan Baez sang, as she always had, to entertain and to inform, advocating nonviolence, whether her stand infuriated one side of the political spectrum or the other. In the 1960s, she was condemned by one extreme for her efforts against the Vietnam War; in the late 1970s, many on the left objected vehemently to her concerts on behalf of the Vietnamese "boat people" and the Cambodian refugees.

A decade later, Joan's sentiments hadn't changed, but the world had. With the end of the Cold War there no longer was any incentive for organized protests against her appearances or causes. As the 1990s drew to a close, she was widely acclaimed for her great talents and personal integrity.

Her lifelong fight for the underdog came partly from her childhood days. She was the middle daughter of Albert Vinicio and Joan Bridge Baez. She told Dan Wakefield (*Redbook* magazine, January 1967, p. 114), "My mother is Irish and my father, a physicist, is Mexican (born in Brooklyn, New York) and I grew up in Redlands, California, where there were a lot of Mexicans and Mexican kids were looked down upon. Though my father had professional status, I was still in a sort of no-man's land; the white kids looked down on me because I was part Mexican and the Mexican kids didn't like me because I couldn't speak Spanish. In the fifth grade, I started singing and playing the ukulele—it was a way of getting accepted. At first, my singing got me accepted on a kind of 'court jester' level—someone who was all right because she could entertain."

Actually, her parents, who liked classical music, had earlier tried to get her to take piano lessons, but young Joan was rebellious and refused. At twelve, she took up guitar, using an instrument bought from Sears, Roebuck. Her first fervor wasn't for folk music but for the first wave of rock 'n' roll represented by artists like Elvis Presley and Bill Haley.

The family moved to the East Coast just after Joan graduated high school in Palo Alto, California, settling in the Boston area, since Dr. Baez had a teaching appointment at MIT. He took his daughter to Tulla's Coffee Grinder one night and Joan was entranced. Although she enrolled in Boston University's Fine Arts School of Drama, she began spending more and more time hanging around Tulla's, adding to her folk song repertoire. After a while, she knew enough songs to start performing on the folk circuit and began taking the stage at such spots as the Golden Vanity, Ballad Room, and Club 47. She became a local favorite but didn't feel ready for bigger challenges, turning down a bid from Harry Belafonte to join his troupe.

A brief appearance at the Gate of Horn Club in Chicago resulted in folksinger Bob Gibson's suggesting she appear at the 1959 Newport, Rhode Island, Folk Festival. (She went there in a Cadillac hearse with her name painted on the side.) Her name was not on the program but she won wild applause from the Newport crowd and became close friends with Odetta, the Weavers, and the Seeger family. Record offers came, but Joan turned them down, preferring to go back to Boston and spend her time singing in coffeehouses. After another successful appearance at the 1960 Newport show, she felt more confident of her recording capability and signed with Vanguard.

Her debut LP, *Joan Baez,* came out in 1960 and, in a short time, Vanguard was surprised and pleased to find a steady stream of orders and reorders coming in from record dealers. By early 1961, Joan was becoming known all over the United States and she set off on what became a triumphal tour of college campuses and concert halls. From then on, even though Joan continually turned down lucrative offers for TV shows, movies, and nightclub engagements, she remained one of the favorite artists of millions of fans all over the world.

She also made many free appearances every year for charities, UNESCO, civil rights, and, in the 1960s and early 1970s, for anti-Vietnam war rallies. Sometimes she rejected offers that she felt conflicted with her principles. An example was her refusal to appear on the ABC-TV show *Hootenanny* in 1963 unless blacklisted artist Pete Seeger was invited. In April 1964, she informed the Internal Revenue Service she would not pay the portion of her 1963 taxes she felt would be used for the armed forces. (That November, the IRS responded by filing a lien against her for $50,000.)

Meanwhile, she had become known as the "Queen of the Folksingers." Her increasingly anti-establishment (or at least that's the way it seemed to her critics) activity antagonized some segments of society but had little obvious impact on the size of her own musical audience. As she added to her catalogue, she continued to be one of Vanguard's most important artists. Her second album, *Joan Baez, Volume 2,* a two-record set issued in December 1961, was well received, as were such succeeding albums as *Joan Baez in Concert* (1962), *Joan Baez in Concert, Part 2* (1963), and *Joan Baez 5* (12/64). (Squire Records also released a *Best of* LP in January 1964 featuring Joan with Bill Wood and Ted Alevizos with whom she performed in 1959.)

During the increasingly turbulent mid-1960s, Joan still managed to turn out new albums, though much of her time was devoted to rallies, marches, and protests. Her mid-1960s offerings on Vanguard included *Farewell Angelina* (1965), *Noel* (1966), and *Joan* (1967). Among her activities in 1967, for instance, was a performance at an anti-war rally in Tokyo, organization of a draft card turn-in day, and performance at a free concert before 30,000 people at the base of the Washington Monument (after being turned down in a concert request for DAR-owned Constitution Hall for her "unpatriotic activities"). In October 1967, she, her mother, and sister were jailed for demonstrating at the Armed Forces Induction Center in Oakland, California.

She worked closely during that period with a Stanford University activist named David Harris. In 1968, they married. Shortly thereafter, David was sent to jail for three years for refusing to register for the draft. While this turmoil continued, Joan's popularity with album buyers remained strong. The 1968 LP *Baptism,* poetry recited and sung, was on the hit charts for the last third of 1968, and her next release, *Any Day Now,* a collection of Dylan songs, reached gold-record levels. In late 1969, her album in honor of her spouse, *David's Album,* came out and was on the charts for months. The year 1969 had its joys. One was the rousing welcome given her at the now legendary Woodstock, New York, Festival, during the summer (with her material included in the Woodstock set issued on Cotillion); another was the birth of a son, Gabriel Earl Harris, on December 2.

In 1970, Vanguard celebrated her first decade on the label with the retrospective two-disc set *The First Ten Years,* on the charts from year end into early 1971. Early in 1970, she was represented by a new studio LP, *One Day at a Time,* on hit lists for most of the spring and summer. In 1971, the LP *Blessed Are* was in the top 20 late in the year, eventually earning a gold record, and her single release, "Let It Be," was a top 50 hit at the same time. In late 1971, her Vanguard LP *Carry It On,* the sound track to the film, featured a cover showing her welcoming David home from prison. But hardly had the LP been completed than the two decided to separate.

Separation, in fact, seemed to be a theme in Joan's life at that point. In early 1972, she announced the end of her long association with Vanguard, signing with A&M Records. Ironically, even as she was leaving, Vanguard readied a new single of her version of The Band's "The Night They Drove Ol' Dixie Down." The single proceeded to go to number five on the pop charts for Joan's biggest singles hit ever. It stayed on the list for fifteen weeks, and, soon after it slipped off, her debut LP on A&M, *Come from the Shadows,* made the album lists. The LP essentially represented Joan's songwriting debut, with most of the material written either by Joan or sister Mimi Fariña.

Her next LP was taped during a visit to Hanoi, capital of North Vietnam, in December 1972. She was there as a guest of that country's politically organized Committee for Solidarity with the American People. The massive bombardment at the time by U.S. planes played a role in the tone of what was to be her next A&M release, *Where Are You Now, My Son.* It was a plea against war of any kind. As Joan said, "If my pacifism was ever going to be put to a test, this must have been the time. At the end of eleven days of bombing, I was only reconfirmed in my belief that right-wing violence and left-wing violence are the same, and if the human race cannot find a life-supporting substitute for them, we will exterminate ourselves."

The LP was on the charts several months in 1973. Vanguard issued the LP *Hits/Greatest and Others* the same year. Joan spent much of the year working to advance the organization called Amnesty International, dedicated to freeing political prisoners and ending torture. Also a member was the conservative exponent William F. Buckley, Jr.

Though Joan didn't give up fighting for causes, she was able to relax somewhat and give more time to music after the Vietnam War ended. Her remaining LPs for A&M toned down the "message content" with more emphasis on the joys of life or the problems of daily living. Those LPs comprised *Gracias a la Vida* (1974), sung completely in Spanish, *Diamonds and Rust* (1975), whose title song was issued as a single and became Joan's first completely self-penned hit, *From Every Stage* (1976), and *Gulf Winds* (1976). *From Every Stage* was a live LP based on her tour in the summer of 1975.

In the fall of the year Bob Dylan asked her to join his tour and she accepted. She and Dylan had been friends since the early 1960s when Joan had helped bring the then-newcomer to national attention by adding him to a series of her concerts. For a time they were lovers, a relationship which had a much longer emotional effect on her than on Dylan. The first phase of the Dylan series, called the Rolling Thunder Revue, got under way in November 1975. A second series of concerts was presented by the Revue in the spring and early summer of 1976. Her experiences on the tour provided the basis for several songs included in *Gulf Winds.* That 1976 release was her first LP having only songs by her and it also was her last recorded for A&M. By 1977 she had moved to Portrait Records, a label owned by Columbia Records.

Her debut on Portrait, *Blowin' Away,* came out in 1977. Meanwhile, A&M issued a retrospective titled *The Best of Joan C. Baez.* Joan toured in support of *Blowin' Away* as she did in 1979 for her next Portrait LP, *Honest Lullaby.* Issued in May 1979, it included more original songs, plus her renditions of numbers ranging from Jackson Browne's "Before the Deluge" to Bob Marley's "No Woman, No Cry." Joan's association with Portrait ended at the start of the 1980s.

In preparation for her 1979 album, she took voice lessons and noted, "It's so strange. I used to be a soprano, then all of a sudden I find I sing everything in a lower register. It's easier and smoother. But the higher register is really hard to get, so I have a voice teacher helping me to exercise the upper ranges. That's one thing I've never done before in my musical life . . . exercise my voice."

The Portrait alignment did little to further her career, she later pointed out. She had left A&M for Portrait/CBS, mainly expecting the larger record company would reverse the progressive declines in her record sales as the 1970s went by. As she told Dennis Hunt of the *Los Angeles Times* ("Joan Baez Raising Her Voice Again," June 14, 1987), "Leaving A&M was a mistake. I thought the grass was greener, but it wasn't." In the summer of 1982 she was represented on film by the documentary *There but for Fortune,* which covered the struggles encountered during her 1981 concert tour of Latin America. She had not intended to antagonize anyone, she said at the time, but simply perform in Chile, Brazil, and Argentina as a gesture of goodwill to their people. The governments then in power saw her concerts as encouraging revolutionary activities and set about trying to prevent her shows.

She told U.S. reporters she had not intended to make any political statements concerning human rights violations, but simply sing her songs and let the audience decide what they meant. "It was absolutely foolish on their [the Latin American governments'] part. We would have been very limited and restricted in regular concerts. If they'd treated us better, we never would have gotten a film like this."

After her contract with Portrait ran out, Joan continued to tour steadily year after year, but could not find a place on the roster of any mid-size or large record company. Finally she signed with Gold Castle Records, which released her first new album in eight years, *Recently,* during the summer of 1987. (Several compilations had come out on Vanguard and A&M.)

The album almost came out simultaneously with her autobiography, *And a Voice to Sing With,* published by Summit. The book, a best-seller, frankly discussed her private life in some detail, ranging from her romance with Dylan and marriage to David Harris as well as the lesbian relationship she had disclosed to a Berkeley, California, newspaper in 1972. Her words about Dylan recalled the tender phase of their time together and the not-so-relaxed events during the Rolling Thunder tour.

As for the lesbian episode, she reported it occurred with someone named Kim when Joan was twenty-two. She had discussed it in some detail, she said, because "there would have been a big hunk missing if I hadn't put that in. Besides, since I revealed it years ago, people have come up to me and told me that coming out in the open with it inspired them to take a step in their lives that they might not have taken otherwise." She also emphasized the joys she had found raising her son.

In the 1990s, as in earlier decades, she found eager audiences awaiting her in all parts of the world including crowds at concerts in Czechoslovakia and the other nations of Eastern Europe.

Her album output continued in the early '90s, starting with the excellent 1992 release *Play Me Backwards* on Virgin, which was nominated for a Grammy. In 1993 she was represented in record stores by a new boxed set, *Rare, Live & Classic,* an excellent collection that won wide praise, including a five-star review in *Rolling Stone.* In April 1995, she was booked into New York's Bottom Line for four nights to work on a new live album for EMI's Guardian Records label. In her first small club date in decades, she treated concert-goers to not only solo renditions but also a series of duets over the four-night span with some of the brightest names in modern folk, including both veteran artists and relative newcomers. The songs covered a broad range from some of her own songs, going back to her first composition, "Sweet Sir Galahad," to a new a capella version of her greatest singles hit, "The Night They Drove Old Dixie Down." She also performed a song written about son Gabe, "Coconuts." Gabe played tambourine on his mother and aunt's singing of the song most associated with Richard Fariña, "Pack Up Your Sorrows."

Of course, when the album was released on Guardian Records on September 26, 1995, it didn't include every number from the Bottom Line shows, but the fifteen tracks in *Ring Them Bells* made it a recording to rank with the best albums in her career. The first single, performed with the Indigo Girls, was the Dylan classic "Don't Think Twice, It's All Right." Other duets included one with Mary Black on the Dylan-composed title song, Janis Ian on "Jesse," Dar Williams on "You're Aging Well," Tish Hinojosa on "Pajarillo

Barranquero," sister Mimi Fariña on the late Richard Fariña's "Swallow Song," Kate and Anna McGarrigle on "Willie Moore," and two songs with Mary-Chapin Carpenter, the latter's original "Stones in the Road" and Joan's nostalgic remembrance of her romance with Dylan, "Diamonds and Rust." Her vocal on the last named suggested that there were still feelings of regret the affair had ended as it did.

One thing conspicuously absent from her schedule in the late '80s and 1990s was participation in major benefit concerts. She told Mark E. Gallo for the *Eccentric,* Birmingham, Michigan, "You know that's in my blood, probably from before I started singing. However, six years ago, when I made the decision to pursue the career with some gusto, I really tabled all of the activism for this time period. I think I made the right decision because I always put it first. I wasn't that concerned about a career, and then I think that the realization that the vocal cords have a terminal point sort of snapped me into realizing that it was time to go full bore into a music career—vocal training, all of the stuff you have to do to keep it going."

Baez continued to tour regularly in the late 1990s. In 1997 Guardian released *Gone from Danger,* her first new studio album in five years. In the summer of 1998, Vanguard Records issued the album, *Baez Sings Dylan* based on recordings made by Joan in the late 1960s, as well as *Live at Newport.*

BAND, THE: *Vocal and instrumental group. Original members, mid-1960s to 1976, Robbie Robertson, born Toronto, Canada, July 5, 1944; Richard Manuel, born Stratford, Ontario, Canada, April 3, 1943, died Winter Park, Florida, March 4, 1986; Garth Hudson, born London, Ontario, Canada, August 2, c. 1943; Rick Danko, born Simcoe, Ontario, Canada, December 9, 1943, died Marbletown, New York, December 10, 1999. Levon Helm, born Marvell, Arkansas, May 26, 1940. Group disbanded in 1976, reunited in 1983 without Robertson until death of Manuel in 1986. A later version of the band had Stan Szelest (born 1943, died 1991) in place of Manuel. New alignment formed in early 1990s comprised Helm, Danko, Hudson, Jim Weider, Randy Ciarlante, and Richard Bell.*

When *Music from Big Pink* became a best-selling album months after its August 1968 release, it was truly the pot of gold at the end of the rainbow for the Band, a group that had almost literally wandered in the wilderness, unknown and often booed, for more than a decade. The event was an important milestone, for rock 'n' roll in general and folk and country rock in particular. The orientation of many of their songs, such as "The Weight," was toward country music with a leavening in others of blues, soul, and folk.

Outwardly it seems strange that a group composed mainly of Canadians should become known for southern soul music. As some critics noted, the lyrics of the Band's classic "The Night They Drove Old Dixie

Down" sounded as if the song were traditional from Civil War days: "Virgil Cane is the name / And I served on the Danville train / 'Til Stoneman's cavalry came / And tore up the tracks again / In the winter of '65, we were hungry, just barely alive."

Almost all the members had been fans of country music in their early years. They received additional exposure to country music when they were the backup group for country-rock artist Ronnie Hawkins in the early '60s.

Lead guitarist and songwriter Robbie Robertson recalls listening to country music when he was five years old. Not long after that, he started to learn guitar and almost simultaneously began writing music. His interests switched as he grew up, from country to big bands to rock. He left high school to play with rock groups, including one of his own, in his home area of Toronto. In the late '50s, he met Ronnie Hawkins and joined his band, the Hawks, for several years of touring through eastern and northern Canada.

Richard Manuel also grew up in a family that enjoyed country music. He started learning piano at nine, got into an argument about lessons and dropped it, and then picked it up again at twelve. He had a good voice and became popular at local parties in Stratford, Ontario. He formed a band, the Revols, during high school years. Ronnie Hawkins took a liking to his style when the Revols shared a bill with the Hawks and later asked him to join the group.

Garth Hudson, born and raised in London, Ontario, recalls that his father "used to find all the hoedown stations on the radio, and then I played accordion with a country group when I was 12." He also became an excellent organist and used the organ as the central instrument in a rock group he formed in Detroit in the early 1960s after graduating from high school in Canada. In 1962 there was an opening for a keyboards player with the Hawks and he moved back to Canada to take it.

Rick Danko, bass guitarist and vocalist with the Band, played guitar, mandolin, and violin before starting high school and performed with local groups before he was in his teens. Like the others, he had been a country music fan for a long time. He began listening to the Grand Ole Opry when he was five. Midway through high school, he dropped out to concentrate on music and, at seventeen, joined the Hawks.

The only member from the United States was drummer/vocalist Levon Helm. He listened to country stations as a boy in Arkansas, but he also liked to play blues records, particularly those of Sonny Boy Williamson #2. In high school, he formed a rock group called the Jungle Bush Beaters. Afterwards, he joined fellow Arkansan Ronnie Hawkins as a member of the backup group that worked with Hawkins at the end of the '50s. When Ronnie decided to make Canada home base, Helm agreed to remain with him.

As Robertson recalled about his days with the Hawks in Capitol bio notes, "There were only three kinds of rock then: rhythm & blues, corny white rock, and rockabilly. We played rockabilly." But the group members tired of the format. One by one, they left the Hawks and drifted south of the border to look for new directions in the United States. Their previous association caused Robertson and the others to get together to form a new group that played in small clubs along the U.S. eastern seaboard. In 1965, they got their first big break when Bob Dylan (see Dylan, Bob) chose them to tour with him as his backing band.

"I don't remember exactly how it happened," Robertson said. "I think we were in Atlantic City at the time. Dylan had heard of us, I guess. And we'd heard of him, but we weren't into that kind of music and I didn't really know who he was or that we could play with each other at all. Then we jammed together and a lot of things happened. We've had a great effect on each other. Dylan brought us into a whole new thing and I guess he got something from us."

The group toured all over the world with Dylan. Sometimes, though, it was a trying experience. Often, Dylan fans who hated the thought of his abandoning folk music for folk-rock took out their frustration, not by booing Dylan, but by booing and heckling his supporting musicians.

In 1966, those engagements ended abruptly when Dylan suffered serious injuries in a motorcycle accident. The Band moved to Woodstock in upstate New York to be near his home. Part of their efforts included working on some new songs with him and helping him to complete *Don't Look Back,* a documentary film started in England in 1965. The Band also went to work on some new material of its own, recording it in the Woodstock Playhouse during 1967–68. Those songs formed the basis for the 1968 debut LP on Capitol. (Group members wrote and recorded many other songs during their years in the "big pink" house in Woodstock. For example, between the Band's 1966 tour with Dylan and its initial live shows under its own name in 1969, tracks were made by the Band and Dylan of all the songs that eventually surfaced in *The Basement Tapes* double album issued by Columbia in 1975. Besides that, the Band is known to have recorded some 150 other numbers that had not been released on any label as of 1999.)

The success of the album in late 1968 gave them a chance to be featured performers in their own right. In 1969, they gave memorable concerts in such places as San Francisco's Winterland, New York's Fillmore East, and (with Dylan, who approved of their solo efforts) in a Tribute to Woody Guthrie at New York's Carnegie Hall. The Band also was featured in the English Isle of Wight pop festival.

The group's reputation grew with each new album. Its second LP, *The Band,* was issued by Capitol in November 1969 and its third, *Stage Fright,* in midsummer 1970.

The latter two included songs that became Band classics, such as "Up on Cripple Creek," "The Night They Drove Old Dixie Down," "The Rumor," "The Shape I'm In," "Strawberry Wine," "All the Glory," "Just Another Whistle Stop," and "W.S. Walcott Medicine Show."

Both LPs easily went over gold-record levels. During 1971, the group's fourth LP, *Cahoots,* was released and quickly shot up to the national top 20. Though it stayed on the charts many months it did not match the success of earlier LPs. In the fall of 1971, the Band was warmly greeted on one of its increasingly rare in-person tours. Its first California concert in a year and a half took place in San Francisco's Civic Auditorium in late November. It was one of a series of concerts that served as warm-ups for appearances at New York's Academy of Music around New Year, the source for their first live album, *Rock of Ages.* Issued in August 1972, the two-disc set earned a gold record by year-end.

During the summer of 1973, the Band was one of the featured groups at the rock concert held in Watkins Glen, New York, attended by an estimated 600,000 people, an even vaster audience than had gone to Woodstock four years earlier. On October 29, Capitol issued album number six, *Moondog Matinee,* which stayed on the charts well into 1974. The LP presented Band versions of songs made famous by such artists as the Platters, Fats Domino, Clarence "Frogman" Henry, and other "roots" performers.

At the beginning of 1974, Dylan and the Band teamed up once more for one of the landmark concert series of the '70s. The coast-to-coast tour took them to forty cities across the United States, where they played to standing-room-only crowds in every venue. Starting in Chicago on January 7 and ending in the Forum in Los Angeles on February 14, they played to 658,000 fans, but promoter Bill Graham announced that that only represented a tenth of the over 6 million ticket requests that came in by mail. *Before the Flood,* the live LP made during the tour, came out on Dylan's label at the time, Arista Records, in the summer and received a gold-record award on July 8, 1974.

There were reports at the time that group members were becoming increasingly weary of touring after the Dylan concerts, something most members denied in later years, asserting it was only Robertson who had become restless about the restrictions of group work. They turned out new LPs from time to time, such as *Northern Lights/Southern Cross,* issued by Capitol in late 1975, and *Islands,* also on Capitol, issued in 1977 after the group's breakup. Those albums, while certainly above average, did not have quite the creative urgency of the group's earlier releases.

In mid-1976, it was announced by group representatives that the Band would go out on the road once more for the last time and disband. The cross-country series began in the East in the fall and ended with a gala banquet and concert in San Francisco on Thanksgiving Day, 1976. The series was titled "The Last Waltz," also the title of the LP issued by Warner Brothers in spring 1978, drawn from the music of the final concert. Besides the Band, it featured a galaxy of guests, including Dylan, Van Morrison, Joni Mitchell, Dr. John, and Muddy Waters. During the summer of 1978, *The Last Waltz* movie, which Robbie Robertson helped assemble from films of the concert, came out. It still ranks as one of the most influential pop music documentaries.

In his 1993 memoir, *This Wheel's on Fire,* Levon Helm took issue with some aspects of *The Last Waltz,* arguing that some of the best material either hadn't been filmed or wasn't included. As he wrote, "Nine cameras on the floor, and there wasn't even a shot of Richard Manuel singing the finale, 'I Shall Be Released,' his trademark song. It turned out that of the nine cameras, only two were used in the movie. . . . I was in shock how bad the movie was."

He also stressed the fact that every group member but Robertson objected to the 1976 ending date. According to him, the others had sought to keep the Band going but were dissuaded by "hints" from Robertson he might take legal action if they took that path. Helm's anger at his old bandmate continued to smolder in the years after the final '76 concert. Looking back in 1993, Helm told Bob Canon, "I believed the Band was a lot stronger than any adversity and disappointment. But when *The Last Waltz* saw the light of day, I didn't hold any fantasies like that anymore. I knew the cows had come home."

After the group's breakup, Capitol continued to release LPs, mostly reissues of earlier material: the retrospective *The Best of the Band* (December 1976), *Anthology* (1978), and *Rock of Ages, Volumes 1 and 2* (both 1982), repackaged versions of the earlier releases of that work.

The members went on to new projects of their own after disbanding. Levon Helm initially toured with the RCO All-Stars and later with the Cate Brothers Band. He cut a number of solo LPs, including *Levon Helm and the RCO All-Stars* (ABC, 1977), *Levon Helm* (ABC, 1978), *American Son* (MCA, 1980), and *Levon Helm* (Capitol, 1982). He also showed impressive acting talent in such roles as Loretta Lynn's father in the hit film *Coal Miner's Daughter;* an unsuccessful country singer in *Seven Brides for Seven Brothers;* and a fighter pilot in *The Right Stuff.*

Danko did some solo work and also performed in shows with other well-known artists, in one case with Paul Butterfield and another with Band alumnus Richard Manuel and guitarist Blondie Chaplin. For a while after the Band's breakup, Manuel took treatment for alcoholism, but seemed to be coping with his problems well by the mid-1980s. Hudson's activities included composing (including the synthesizer piece "Our Lady Queen of the Angels"), session work, and production of recordings by other artists.

Robertson, acknowledged as the creative leader of the Band, became involved in writing new music and working on film projects. In the 1980 release, *Carny,* he not only acted, but also produced the movie, cowrote the script, and assembled most of the music. Later in the decade, he worked on the score for Martin Scorsese's *The King of Comedy* and supervised production of its sound track album, issued in early 1983.

At about the same time, most of the original Band members announced plans to reform the group and tour. Robertson, however, demurred. He told a reporter he felt that step was "probably a business decision, not an artistic one" and commented he'd "feel like a fool" to rejoin. The remaining foursome, backed by the four-member Cate Brothers Band, toured widely in the second half of 1983 and through much of 1984, playing all over the United States and Canada plus doing a series in Japan. On New Year's Eve 1983, the group appeared with the Grateful Dead in a radio concert from San Francisco.

The Band's numbers were certainly listenable but, perhaps due to Robertson's absence, the group couldn't recapture the magic of its earlier days. That realization may have contributed to the despondency that resulted in Richard Manuel's suicide by hanging in a motel room in Florida following a show in March 1986. Manuel's place was taken over for a time some years later by another Hawks alumnus, Stan Szelest, but in the late 1980s, the Band was once more out of action. Again some of the members went their own way as in the case of the concert series by Danko and Hudson in 1988-89. The original group's strong following was recognized by its old label, which issued such retrospective collections as the two-CD *To Kingdom Come* set in 1989 and the three-CD package (prepared with some supervision by Robbie Robertson) *Across the Great Divide* in 1994. Neither, however, seemed to capture the full essence of the group's prime years.

Robertson continued to add to his credits in the mid-1980s in both movies and recordings. He composed the score and cowrote (with Eric Clapton) the song "It's in the Way That You Use It" for the sound track LP of the 1986 hit movie *The Color of Money.* He acted as creative consultant for the 1987 film *Chuck Berry: Hail, Hail Rock & Roll.* In October 1987, Geffen Records issued his first album of new songs since the Band's breakup. The core band backing him on the LP *Robbie Robertson* comprised Bill Dillon on guitar, Tony Levin on bass, and Manu Katche and Terry Bozzio on drums. Also sitting in on some tracks were Peter Gabriel, U2, Maria McKee, the BoDeans, and former Band musicians Garth Hudson and Rick Danko.

In the early 1990s, the Band reformed again with Helm, Danko, Hudson, and Stan Szelest as core members. In the 1990s, with the eager approval of producer Rick Chertoff, the Band signed with Sony Records; they had completed a number of tracks when Chertoff left the label in 1991. This departure, according to Helm, together with the poor showing of a solo album by Robertson, induced Sony to buy out the group's contract without completing an album. Meanwhile, tragedy struck when Szelest, taking part in 1991 rehearsals for the Sony sessions at Helm's barn in Woodstock, suffered chest pains and died of a heart attack on the way to the hospital.

Helms and his cohorts refused to give up. The group's 1992 edition (which comprised those three plus guitarist Jim Weider, keyboard player Richard Bell—once a member of Janis Joplin's backing band—and percussionist/second drummer Randy Ciarlante) then got a recording contract with Pyramid Records, Chattanooga, Tennessee, which started it working on what became its first studio-recorded collection in eighteen years. While this was moving ahead in 1993, two books about the Band saga were published, *Across the Great Divide: The Band and America* by British music journalist Barney Hoskyns (Hyperion) and Helm's *This Wheel's on Fire* (William Morrow). In anticipation of the group's induction into the Rock and Roll Hall of Fame in January 1994, Capitol, besides issuing the aforementioned *Across the Great Divide* set, reissued four mid-'70s albums on CD: *Northern Lights/Southern Cross, Moondog Matinee, Islands,* and *Cahoots.*

The debut album of the '90s version of the Band, *Jericho,* was issued by Pyramid and Rhino Records (which handled distribution) in late 1993. Almost all the tracks were covers of songs written by others, including Dylan, but they were exuberantly performed in true Band style.

The dearth of new songs, of course, reflected the absence of Robertson, but Helm maintained that all the original Band members had always had strong involvement in all the material. He told critic Geoffrey Himes of the *Washington Post* in April 1994, "We used to grow the tunes together. We'd record the song once and listen to it and then fix the weak parts. Rick and I would try different lyric feels until we found one we liked, and then we'd try different lead singers. Many times the actual melody didn't fall into place until we had worked out the harmony vocals, and a lot of the chord changes would sound ordinary until Garth had put some different voicings on the chords. Yet you never saw Garth's name on the songwriting credits." He stressed, for instance, that without some of Garth's touches "Cripple Creek" wouldn't have been the same song that became one of the group's most popular numbers.

When it was announced the original group had been chosen for the Rock and Roll Hall of Fame, everyone wondered whether Robertson and Helm would patch up their differences, at least for the awards show in January '94. The bitterness had been less marked among other founding artists; Hudson and Danko, for instance, played on Robertson's first solo album. Levon remained adamant. He told reporter Scott Jordan, "I don't run in the same circles as he runs in. I wish him well, and I'm glad to see him get the success he wants—and I'm happy to see the Band have some success on our own. He has his own destiny to fulfill, but things are moving along for us, also."

Robertson for his part told Robert Hilburn of the *Los Angeles Times* ("Reflections on the Age of a 'Real' Rock Band," January 19, 1994), he would be happy to perform with Helm in the upcoming Hall of Fame ceremonies but doubted it would occur. "A couple of months ago, I called Levon and said maybe we should talk about this Rock and Roll Hall of Fame thing and the Band box set that is going to be coming out this year. But it didn't get any further than that, and I've heard from the Hall of Fame that Levon has said he might prefer not to play, just to enjoy the evening. To me, what everybody wants to do is fine."

He also responded to Helm's complaints that Robbie wanted to be the boss of the new group. "I never wanted to be the boss and, in fact, I never thought I was the boss. I was just trying to organize things so we could . . . make records and got out and play a show somewhere. . . . In a group, one guy is really good at that, and it kind of all settles. I just kind of found myself in the position of 'If I don't do this, nobody's going to do it. We'll just be sitting here in a year saying, "I don't know, what do you think?"' So you have to get things moving."

In the end, Helm stayed away, but the other founding musicians took the stage with Robertson at New York's Waldorf Astoria to accept the ovation from their peers in recognition of the Band's continuing tremendous impact on modern pop music.

During the summer of 1994, Capitol released a three-CD boxed retrospective of the group titled *Across the Great Divide.* The set included performances going back to the group's Hawks years. In 1995, Capitol released *Live at Watkins Glen* from the Band's 1973 concert.

In the fall of 1998, Helm, Danko, and Hudson were represented by a new Band release, *Jubilation,* on River North Records. Although it was a listenable collection, most critics felt it didn't have anything to match the songs of the group's golden era. Tracks that received some airplay attention included the Danko number "Book Faded Brown" and "Last Train to Memphis," where the group was augmented by guest Eric Clapton. On December 10, 1999, tragedy struck again when Rick Danko died in his sleep. He was fifty-six.

BATTLEFIELD BAND: *Vocal and instrumental group from Scotland. Original members, 1969: Brian McNeill, born Falkirk Scotland, 1950, fiddle, viola, mandolin, bouzouki guitar, concertina, bass, hurdy-gurdy, and vocals; Alan Reid, born Scotland, c. 1950, vocals, keyboard, guitar; Sandra Lang; Jimmy Thompson. 1979 roster: McNeill, Reid; Duncan MacGillivray, joined 1978, Highland*

bag pipes; Ged Foley, guitar, Northumbrian pipes. MacGillivray left 1983, replaced by Douglas Pincock. Foley left 1984, replaced by Alistair Russell, born Northumbria, England, vocals, guitars, cittern. McNeill replaced in 1990 by John McCusker, born Scotland, c. 1973, fiddle, accordion, keyboards, cittern, whistle. Pincock replaced in late 1980s by Iain MacDonald, born Glenuig, Scotland, Highland pipes, flute, whistle. MacDonald replaced in 1995 by Mike Katz. Russell replaced by Davy Steele, guitar, cittern, bodhran. Members in 1997: Reid, McCusker, Katz, Steele, still together in 1999. (Besides above, other musicians who were band members at various times included Jenny Clarke, Jim and Sylvia Barnes, John Gahagan, Pat Kilbride, Jamie McMenemy, Eddie Morgan, and Ricky Starr.)

In a sense, the Battlefield Band might be considered Scotland's premier contribution to the post-Beatles U.K. folk music revival. Certainly its repertoire included dozens of traditional ballads, jigs, reels, and strathspreys. But band members felt free to experiment with that material while also adding many excellent original compositions over the years. One critic described its musical approach as combining "the classical Celtic music of the Scottish Highlands with the contemporary rock-oriented folk music of modern Britain."

The band, which is named after a suburb of Glasgow, came into being in 1969 almost by accident. At the time, university students Brian McNeill, Sandra Lang, and Jimmy Thompson had formed a group that got a job as the weekend house band at the local Iron Horse pub. Needing someplace to store their instruments between classes, Thompson made arrangements with a friend who worked as a janitor to put them in a storage locker. This worked out for the first two weeks but then a hitch occurred.

Keyboards player Alan Reid, who was to become a central figure in the band's development, was a friend of Thompson's who was interested in the operation but not yet a band member. As he recounted to Rob Weir for a *Sing Out!* article ("Battlefield Band's Colorful Past & Future," vol. 41, no. 3, pp. 37–41), "They were on their third week at the Iron Horse. They were late one Friday and discovered that the janitor had gone home and no one else had the key to the storage closet. So they went down to the Iron Horse and said they couldn't do their gig because they had no instruments. So the pub said right then, 'You're fired!' That was it for that lineup and I joined the next day."

Over the next few years, various combinations of musicians, but always including Reid and McNeill, took a desultory approach to performing. They found work, but considered it more a fun thing than a possible full-time occupation. After a while, however, the outlook for better paying performances improved but, Reid noted, dissension also took place. "I caused a stir when I suggested we not split the money after each gig, but put it in the bank instead. Someone would yell 'No! I need my four pounds; I've got no money for drink.' So we started to have lineup changes because no group works unless everybody's got the same goal."

The group slowly became more cohesive and by the mid 1970s was beginning to build a following at home. But for almost its first decade the band had no album follow-up. It finally started work on its debut disc, recorded live on a four-track system in a dance studio near a French air force base. This album, *Battlefield Band,* became available at concerts in 1977; after being out of print for some time, it was re-issued on the Temple label in 1994. The group wound up the 1970s with two more albums, *At the Front* in 1978 and *Stand Easy* in 1979. During 1978, a solo album by Brian McNeill, *Monksgate,* was issued on the FMS label. In 1980, the group's output included the promotional EP, *Preview,* for Temple, which was still the group's U.K. label in the later 1990s. (Temple reissued all of those collections in 1994, combining *Stand Easy* and *Preview* on one CD.)

The group had established itself as an important influence on the U.K. music scene by the start of the 1980s, but dramatically expanded its critical acclaim and audience with its 1980 full album, *Home Is Where the Van Is.* The roster by then comprised McNeill, Reid, Duncan MacGillivray on bagpipes, and Ged Foley on guitar and Northumbrian pipes. In 1981, Flying Fish Records released *Home Is Where the Van Is* in the United States to coincide with the band's first North American tour. The band's repertoire included originals like McNeill's "The Lads o' the Fair" and unique arrangements of traditional numbers like "The Battle of Waterloo," "Braw Lads o' Galla Water," and "The Presbyterian Hornpipe." The band continued to demonstrate its spirited dynamics with the 1982 album *There's a Buzz,* released in Europe by Temple and in the United States by Flying Fish. Both labels also brought out another album in 1981, *The Story So Far.*

By 1984, half the roster had changed, with Dougie Pincock replacing McGillivray on Highland bagpipes in 1983 and Alistair Russell taking over from Foley. (Unlike the others, Russell was born in England, but he emphasized his parents were Scottish). The group's output in the mid 1980s included *Anthem for the Common Man* (1984), *On the Rise* (1986), *Music in Trust* (1986, by the foursome of McNeill, Reid, Pincock, and harpist Alison Kinnaird), *After Hours* (1987), and *Celtic Hotel* (1987). McNeill's projects included another solo disc, *Unstrung Hero* (1985). All of those were issued by Temple with Flying Fish records handling U.S. distribution. Besides his recording efforts, McNeill continued his songwriting activities, with his composition "The Devil's Only Daughter" winning the British National Songsearch competition in 1987. The group closed out the 1980s with volume 2 of its *Music in Trust* collaboration with Alison Kinnaird (1988) and *Home Ground* (1989). In 1990, McNeill,

whose first novel, *The Busker,* was published in 1989, left the group to focus more on writing and solo projects, with teenage fiddling whiz John McCusker taking his place. Brian's original contributions to the Battlefield's material in earlier years, besides "The Lads o' the Fair," included "The Yew Tree," "Montrose," and "The Snows of France and Holland." His "The Rovin' Dies Hard" won the 1990 Texas Celtic Music Award. His song output after departing the Batties included "Strong Women Rule Us with Their Tears," "Any Mick'll Do," and "No Gods and Precious Few Heroes." His solo album credits expanded rapidly in the 1990s to include *The Busker and the Devil's Own Daughter* (1990) on Temple, *The Back o' the North Wind* (1991) on Greentrax, and *No Gods* (1995) with Tom McDonagh on FMS and *Stage by Stage* (1995, with Iain MacKintosh) on Greentrax.

McNeill didn't give up performing, touring for a while in the 1990s with Clan Alba and later appearing in concert assisted by Iain MacKintosh and/or guitarist Tony McManus. In 1997 he toured the United States as part of the Celtic Fiddle Festival with Martin Hayes of Ireland and Natalie MacMaster of Nova Scotia. Another project he developed that was widely offered in North America was the audiovisual show *The Back of the North Wind,* dealing with Scottish emigration to America.

The Battlefield Band regrouped after McNeill's departure with no loss in creative momentum. Now comprising Reid, Iain MacDonald, Russell, and McCusker, the band continued to electrify audiences at home and abroad while completing the albums *New Spring* (1991), *Quiet Days* (1993), *Threads* (1995), and *Across the Borders* (1997), all on Temple with distribution in the United States by Rounder. (*Across the Borders* is a live album recorded at the Edinburgh International Festival, where the program included appearances by Kate Rusby, Seamus Tamsey, Alison Kinnaird, Eric Rigler and the Radio Sweethearts.) Temple also issued a number of videos in the 1990s such as *Highland Hi-Light* (1991) and *At His Majesty's Pleasure* (1994).

Besides touring regularly with the band, members worked on solo albums such as John McCusker's self-titled disc in 1995 and Alan Reid's first collection, *The Sunlit Eye,* on which he was backed by four past and present Battlefield pipers. Reid's album combined some of his own originals plus music based on the work of Scottish icons like Robert Burns.

In the fall of 1995, Duncan MacGillivray performed briefly with the band when Iain MacDonald suffered a broken finger. With only about forty-eight hours' notice, MacGillivray joined the group for a concert at the First Baptist Church in Philadelphia, Pennsylvania, on November 17 and, despite having to play largely unfamiliar material, acquitted himself famously. At the same concert, John McCusker sported two black eyes and other facial bruises he said came from colliding with a door, an incident he recalled in a new song performed in the show called "The Unfriendly Door."

The group's mid-1990s concerts included songs like McCusker's "Miss Kate Rusby" and Iain MacDonald's "The Top Tier" (referring to the top layer of a wedding cake). Both were included in the 1995 album *Threads,* which contained familiar numbers like "Tramps and Hawkers," "The Same Old Story," and "MacPherson's Lament." In a review of the disc in *Rock N' Reel,* Ian Arbuckle enthused, "I will go so far as to predict that *Threads* will ultimately be regarded as one of the best albums of contemporary folk ever to be released and would therefore unhesitatingly recommend its purchase."

In 1997 more changes took place, with Davy Steele and Mike Katz taking over from Russell and MacDonald. Katz, who had been playing bagpipes since he was ten, had been a featured artist in Ceolbeg and when he had time also performed with the top-ranked Scottish pipe band, Scottish Gas. Steele also had been a member of Ceolbeg, where he won critical praise for being one of Scotland's most talented traditional singer/guitarists and also had performed with such "supergroups" as Clan Alba and Caledon.

Asked by Peter Grant of *People* (the Australian magazine) why he joined Battlefield, Steele replied, "I've listened to the Batties since they started. They were guiding, shining lights. [And] they've always got top-level musicians coming through."

Grant noted that the band's latest album (1998's *Rain, Hail or Shine*) and live act "both show there's still room for Davy's own contribution. His poignant 'Beaches of St. Valery'—based on his uncle's World War Two experiences—is one of the features of both the show and the new album. And Davy's treatment of the traditional song 'Norlan Wind,' following on from a poignant John McCusker low whistle piece, proved a rousing show-starter at their Hobart [Australia] concert."

The concert series (whose highlights also included Alan Reid's composition "The Arran Convict"), he pointed out, was a key activity to indicate how well the new foursome had gelled. He stated, "If Hobart in June [1998] is anything to go by, they're well on the way to becoming one of the best Batties lineups ever. . . . By the time the current tour reaches Germany (September 1998), my bet is that Battlefield Band will be in frighteningly good form." Among the albums available for sale at the group's concerts in 1998 was a new solo effort by Steele, *Chasing Shadows.*

As the band approached its thirtieth anniversary in 1999, there still were occasional criticisms from Scottish folk purists who objected to the way the band melded traditional material with contemporary sounds. Though the band's expertise on some two dozen instruments with roots in the past should have satisfied traditionalists, the latter took umbrage at the inclusion of such newfangled items as synthesizer keyboards and drum machines. Reid and his fellow artists brushed aside such complaints in the late 1990s as they'd done in decades past.

As Reid commented to John Roos for a *Los Angeles Times* article ("Future Celtic Shock," March 4, 1995), "We've been answering [objections to their modernizing time-honored songs] for years, but what it really comes down to is style and people's own taste. I think it's healthy to have a variety of tastes, and as long as we're entertaining people, that's enough for us. Doubters that don't think using the synthesizer is a valid thing . . . well, they'll go off on their own way while we live our life quite happily. We're not hung up about it."

BEAUSOLEIL: *Traditional Cajun Band. Michael Doucet, fiddle, vocals, born Scott, Louisiana, February 14, 1951. David Doucet, guitar, vocals, born Scott, Louisiana, July 6, 1957. Jimmy Breaux, Acadian accordion, born Breaux Bridge, Louisiana, 1968. Al Tharp, bass, banjo, fiddle, vocals, born 1950. Billy Ware, percussionist, born Lafayette, Louisiana, 1954. Tommy Alesi, drums, born Lafayette, Louisiana, 1951. Bessyl Duhon, original accordionist, left in 1979. Errol Veret, accordionist from 1979 to 1988 replaced by Breaux. Tommy Comeaux, bass, mandolin, left in 1992.*

In the mid-1970s, Michael Doucet, the lead fiddler and founder of BeauSoleil, began a personal quest to discover the real Cajun music. He visited an old-time Cajun fiddler, Varise Connor, one day as he was out cutting timber. Connor walked out of the forest with a cypress log. Several hours later, after Doucet helped him, Connor, a burly man, took out the Jack Daniels and began playing "the most gentle and delicate Cajun music," Doucet told *New Orleans* magazine (May 1995).

"Why are you interested in me and this old music?" Connor wondered.

Doucet's response was to form BeauSoleil to preserve and "bring the music out," as he has said. BeauSoleil did much more than that. It become the "best Cajun band in the world," as Garrison Keillor of *Prairie Home Companion* said. Mary-Chapin Carpenter's 1991 Grammy award-winning song, "Down at the Twist and Shout," contains a line that serves as a jingle for the band: *There ain't no cure for my blues today, except when the paper says BeauSoleil is coming into town.* Since the mid-'70s, the band has released more than sixteen albums, been nominated for seven Grammys, and played with the likes of Richard Thompson, the Grateful Dead, and Keith Richards. (Doucet played on Richards's 1988 *Talk Is Cheap* album.)

Doucet originally formed the band in 1973 with Bessyl Duhon on the accordion and Kenneth Richard on mandolin. They came up with the name BeauSoleil in 1976. "The reason the name came about was we were asked to play in France in 1976 and the French needed a name," Doucet says. "It had been a name in our family for a long time. Literally it means good sun. But it's an Acadian name that's been carried out for centuries. It's a name that all Acadians recognize."

BeauSoleil refers to a fertile area of Nova Scotia and to one of the Acadian resistance leaders, Joseph Broussard dit Beausoleil. A group of French settlers from Brittany, Normandy, and Picardy colonized an area they called L'Acadie in 1604 in what is now Nova Scotia. (Doucet's relatives came from Poitou, France.) In 1713, Nova Scotia was granted to England in the Treaty of Utrecht that ended Queen Anne's War. Life for the settlers, who opposed the British in the French and Indian Wars, went downhill until 1755, when they were expelled. For thirty years, the Acadians—'Cadians, or Cajuns, as they became known—wandered in search of a new home. They finally settled in Louisiana because they were given land grants by the Spanish. They lived in isolation, passed on stories of their struggles, and preserved their culture through their language and music.

Cajun is infectious, foot-stomping music, driven by the fiddler, button accordionist, and washboard player. BeauSoleil's audiences usually take to the dance floor during concerts, spurred on by Doucet's fiddling, the dual vocals with his brother David, and the pulsing accordion work of Jimmy Breaux. Drummer Tommy Alesi and washboard player Billy Ware provide the rousing beat. "The parts click like the workings of a Swiss watch," John Swenson wrote in *Rolling Stone* after seeing them at Tramps in New York.

Doucet grew up near Scott, Louisiana, five miles from Lafayette, in the heart of Cajun country. "I used to go to play baseball on my horse," he recalls. "Can you imagine doing that now?"

His father was Louis Pierre Doucet, a retired lieutenant colonel in the air force. His mother was Mary Francis Le Blanc, a housewife. Both enjoyed music and dance. "My dad had five sisters who sang songs and ballads," Doucet says. "One of them was married to a fiddle, banjo, and guitar player. My mother had a lot of close relatives who were classically trained and who played swing music and jazz."

Doucet absorbed the Cajun sounds and stylings. "Asking when I first learned Cajun songs is like asking when you first learned Christmas carols," Doucet says. "They were just around as I was growing up."

His uncle, T-Will Knight, taught him a few fiddle tunes but refused to let him take the fiddle out of the house. "He lived a couple of pastures over. He did all kinds of crazy stuff. He had a race track. It was just a quarter of a mile straight lane. That race track was between our house and his. No one could take the fiddle out of the house because you would never see it again.

That was the rule. You're talking about a dozen kids. I learned how to handle it. I was six or something."

Another source of inspiration was Doc Guidry, who played fiddle on a local TV show. In the 1960s, Cajun culture was on the decline. Doucet played guitar in some New Orleans–style swamp bands and rock 'n' roll garage bands. He learned how to speak French as a child. "Everyone spoke it. You had to understand two languages."

His parents had card games on a Friday or Saturday night. "Kids would only be allowed to stay in there if they spoke French. If they asked you something you had to answer in French. And of course they'd say something that you didn't understand to get you out of the room."

It was a different story for David Doucet, who was six years younger than Michael. As he told Kenny Berkowitz of the *Ithaca Times* (March 23, 1995): "I grew up hearing [French] my entire life. But I didn't grow up speaking French. My folks would speak French when they didn't want us kids to know what they were talking about."

Michael Doucet gradually became interested in the music of his ancestors, but it wasn't popular when he graduated high school in 1969. His parents' generation was influenced by country, western, and rock 'n' roll. "They called Cajun old people's music," Doucet says. "Kenneth Richard and I were buddies from Scott. He played mandolin. His dad played accordion. We'd go around to people around Scott. We asked them to play the old songs. That's how we learned it."

Doucet attended Louisiana State University, graduating with an English major and a minor in French and music in 1973. He played guitar and gave his brother his first guitar lessons. British folk-rocker Richard Thompson inspired him to look into his own culture. Doucet heard "Cajun Woman" on a Fairport album called *Unhalfbrickling*. "I couldn't believe someone outside where we were from knew what a Cajun was, and here's this English guy, Richard Thompson, writing a song about a Cajun woman."

In the spring of 1973, Doucet traveled to France and England for six weeks with his cousin Ralph Richard, intending to return for graduate school at the University of Albuquerque to study the Romantic poets. But the trip sent him in another direction.

"We were playing French music," Doucet says. "A promoter came through Louisiana and was amazed to see two young Cajuns playing this music. He asked us to go to this festival [in France]. It was amazing. The French were having their folk revival. Here we were in France and we heard some of the old songs from Louisiana. That opened my eyes. Here I was representing the music and I didn't know it at all. That's when I formulated the idea to come back to Louisiana to learn where they came from by going out and meeting the actual musicians in Louisiana."

When Doucet returned to Louisiana, he recovered his uncle's fiddle, which he found in pieces underneath a cousin's bed. "I had to put it together. I got it enough so I could play it. I still have it but I don't play it. It's a nice old dark fiddle."

Doucet formed a Cajun/French group called Coteau, dubbed "the Cajun Grateful Dead" because of their free-flowing instrumentals. The group became popular with the younger generation in southern Louisiana. Doucet played fiddle, Bessyl Duhon played fiddle and accordion, Bruce MacDonald played guitar, Dana Breaux played guitar, Gary Newman played bass, and Kenneth Blevins played drums.

"It was the first group that started the Cajun renaissance here," Doucet says. "We played old music. It was also a very danceable group."

Around that time, Doucet formed an early incarnation of BeauSoleil that included saxophone, clarinet, trumpet, flute, and a female vocalist, Françoise Chauber.

In 1975, Michael Doucet received his first grant from the National Endowment for the Arts to track down the artists who made the first Cajun 78-rpm records. He met and learned from fiddler Dennis McGee (1893–1989), who recorded with Creole accordion player and singer Amédée Ardoin (1896–1941), the first black to record Cajun and zydeco music. Doucet also met accordionist Freeman Fontenot, who established the area's first school for African-Americans and lived in the back with his family. On the weekends he turned the school into a dance hall where Clifton Chenier; Amédée's nephew Bois-Sec Ardoin, and fiddler Canray Fontenot would play.

"The dance halls took place in the '30s, '40s, and '50s," Doucet says.

With another grant, Doucet worked with Dewey Balfa, trying to bring French music to the school systems. He also met the Balfa brothers who had played at the Newport Folk Festival in the late 1960s and wound up going to Carnegie Hall. (They received a Lifetime Achievement award from the Folk Alliance in 2000.)

"When I got in touch with some of those old musicians, they were shocked," Doucet says. "Some of them hadn't played in thirty years, and they wanted to know how I found them and why I wanted to learn about the music. But I found gems, songs that I had never heard that just made me cry. Mostly I'd go over there and hang out. They just played and you just watched. That's how you learned."

David Doucet had paid no mind to Cajun music until 1974, when Michael and David played a song at their sister's wedding. While he was still in high school, David got a gig playing country and bluegrass in a bar. Michael would sit in and play Cajun with them. "I really got hooked," David says.

Most of the time the guitar was just a rhythm instrument in Cajun music, but David loved Doc Watson and one day Michael said, "Why don't you play Cajun fiddle tunes on guitar?" David went out to learn the tunes. He visited Dennis McGee's house. "He'd look at you and say, 'See if you can follow me on this one, Sonny.' And if I kept up with him, he'd say, 'Hey, you pretty good, but I'm gonna play you one you don't know.' He'd always do these little games with you," David recalled.

Michael Doucet recorded the first BeauSoleil album in 1976, *BeauSoleil La Nuit,* released only in France on EMI. The same year Doucet was joined by David on guitar and Billy Ware on percussion (Ware started playing the washboard in 1981) to release the American debut, *The Spirit of Cajun Music,* on Swallow Records. The album set the trend for more to follow on Arhoolie, Rounder, Rhino's Forward, and Music of the World.

"We took things from ballads, blues, Tin Pan Alley, accordion and fiddle songs, the whole gamut. That was the idea of the group, and we're still doing it," Michael says.

The band signed with Arhoolie Records in 1981. Doucet wanted Arhoolie founder Chris Strachwitz to tape Octa Clark on accordion and Hector Duhon, Bessyl's father, on fiddle. Michael was playing guitar and Strachwitz asked if he would record some songs as well. He assembled the group in two hours. For a while, BeauSoleil was the best-selling group on Arhoolie. Some of their classic albums include *Parlez Nous à Boire* in 1985 (reissued on CD in 1991), *Allons à Lafayette* in 1986 (reissued in 1990), with Canray Fontenot on fiddle, *Bayou Boogie* in 1987 (Rounder), an attempt to recapture the rocking spirit of Coteau, *Hot Chili Mama* on Arhoolie in 1988 (whose title track was later used in a Maalox commercial); and *Live! from the Left Coast* (Rounder, 1989).

The group has received seven Grammy nominations since 1985: In 1985, the *Zydeco Gris-Gris* album, whose title track can be heard in the movie *The Big Easy,* was tapped for Best Traditional Folk Recording; the soundtrack for the 1987 film *Belizaire the Cajun* (Arhoolie) was nominated in the same category. BeauSoleil was nominated in Best Contemporary Folk for *Bayou Cadillac* (1989, Rounder), *Cajun Conja* on Rhino's RNA label in 1991, which hit number three on *Billboard's* World Music Chart, *La Danse de la Vie* on Rhino's Forward label in 1993. *L'Echo* was nominated in the Best Traditional Folk category in 1994.

Richard Thompson played on *Cajun Conja,* their Rhino debut, and *La Danse de la Vie.* Mary-Chapin Carpenter recorded two duets with Doucet on the latter and was listed as "Very Special Guest"—"Quelle Belle Vie" and "Chanson Pour Ezra." During Carpenter's Grammy Awards performance of "Down at the Twist and Shout," Doucet insisted that they perform the song live—right after Metallica left the stage. "We don't like to pantomime," Doucet says. "The whole thing is the feeling of the song."

Doucet, who received the 1988 Clifton Chenier

Award as the best musician in French-speaking Louisiana, has recorded solo albums: *Michael Doucet & Cajun Brew* in 1987 on Rounder and *Beau Solo* in 1990 on Arhoolie. Other Arhoolie releases include *Dit Beau-Soleil* (1982), *Cajun Jam Session* with Danny Poullard and Alan Senauke (1989), and *The Mad Reel* (1994). He's also recorded as part of the Savoy-Doucet Cajun band: *Home Music* (1984) and *With Spirits* (1986). A combination of the two LPs came out on a CD entitled *Home Music with Spirits.* Savoy-Doucet released two CDs on Arhoolie: *Live at the Dance* (1995) and *Two Step D'Amédée* (1989).

Doucet's wife, Sharon, a French teacher and Cajun scholar who does the translations on many of Beau-Soleil's albums, encouraged her husband to put out an album of children's music, *Le Hoogie Boogie: Louisiana French Music for Children* (Rounder, 1992). The album, which includes his daughter Melissa 'Doucet' Maher on fiddle and vocals won a Parent's Choice Award.

BeauSoleil's *L'Echo* came out in September 1994 on Rhino's Forward. As the title suggests, the album recognizes their debt to the Cajun musicians of bygone years. It includes ballads, waltzes, and two-steps taken from the 78s of the '20s and '30s by artists like fiddler Dennis McGee, Amédé Breaux (grandfather of Beau-Soleil's accordionist Jimmy Breaux), Freeman Fontenot, and Cleoma Falcon, who along with her husband, Joe Falcon were the first to record Cajun music.

"Back then, it was just fun to play," Michael says of BeauSoleil's roots. "It was a thing you had to do, a wonderful music to be able to share in with these people. It was really to bring out the old musicians, the unsung heroes, people who were popular in the '30s but who had ceased to perform, but would still play at their house. It was the artists and musicians I was looking for. People with enough passion and who had the ability to perfect our music and just left it at that. That's what I found. I learned to love the music from these guys. Most of them didn't have any 78s. Dennis McGee didn't have any. I'd find one and take a tape of it and he'd go, 'I remember that.' In those days they must have got fifty dollars a side, which was a lot of money."

The cover photos from *L'Echo* show band members sitting on the front porch of Doucet's 174-year-old Cajun cottage, which he restored himself in 1974. The cottage is at the end of a long dirt road near Lafayette, nestled at the edge of a forest. Doucet has always had a sense of the transitory nature of his music and life.

"It's just the music coming through us. It will go through someone else at some other time," he told *Rhythm Music Magazine* (Vol. III, No. 8, 1994).

The group finally won a Grammy for the 1997 Rhino release *L'Amour ou la Folie* (Love or Folly), which combines such diverse influences as Cajun, Creole, blues, jazz, and Caribbean music. The title track, a

two-step about the ups and downs of marriage, was written by Doucet. Special guests on the album include Richard Thompson, Herbie Hancock, Augie Meyers, saxophonist Harry Simoneaux, and Dobro player Josh Graves.

Other BeauSoleil albums include *Louisiana Cajun Music* (1984), *Christmas Bayou* (1986), *Cajun Experience* (1988), and *Déja Vu* (1990) on Swallow; *Cajun Brew* (1988) and David Doucet's *Quand J'ai Parti* (1989) on Rounder; *J'ai Eté Au Bal* (sound track, 1990) on Arhoolie; and *Bayou Deluxe: Best of Michael Doucet & BeauSoleil* (1993) on Rhino. A retrospective, *Vintage BeauSoleil*, was released in 1995 on Music of the World. In 1997, Arhoolie released *The Best of Beau-Soleil,* which covers material recorded between 1981 and 1989 for that label. EMI Hemisphere also re-released the long-lost first album (*BeauSoleil La Nuit*) that BeauSoleil had originally recorded in Paris in May 1976 on CD under the new title *Arc de Triomphe Two Step.* In 1999, Rhino released a new studio album, *Cajunization*, nominated for a Best Contemporary Folk Grammy.

Based on an interview by Lyndon Stambler with Michael Doucet

BECK: *Singer, guitarist, harmonica player, band leader (the Crew), songwriter. Born Los Angeles, California, July 8, 1970.*

Trying to categorize Beck is like trying to catch light in a bottle. In the mid-1990s, he certainly qualified as one of the more unique innovators in alternative rock 'n' roll, but his persona went well beyond that. He enjoyed experimenting with all sorts of sounds, acoustic and amplified, in varied combinations that could cross almost all pop music boundaries from patterns culled from noises of chainsaws and hammers, to high-energy metal rock components. Like rap artists, he enjoyed the idea of "sampling," but in his case instead of sampling R&B or soul artists the way conventional rappers do, his samples for some of his folk-rap numbers might include bits from Dylan albums or recordings by old-time bluesmen. In any case, the original force for his creative efforts was folk music, and folk remains one of his major musical loves.

Beck Hansen grew up in a multi-ethnic neighborhood near MacArthur Park in Los Angeles. His birth father, successful pop-classical music arranger/composer David Campbell, left when he was a child (though the two remained in touch), but his mother, Bibbe Hansen, remarried. The family then comprised him; his mother; his stepfather, Sean Carillo; and a younger brother, Channing Hansen. (For five years Bibbe and Sean operated a coffee shop, Troy Café, where Beck performed a few times.) He said that the music he heard at home by artists like Henry Mancini and Antonio Carlos Jobim didn't turn him on and it wasn't until he became exposed to folk and roots blues that he became interested in performing.

However, Beck also profited from the musical interests of his father, David Campbell. The latter, though classically trained on the violin, enjoyed playing songs by people like the Beatles and Rolling Stones on the instrument and at one time earned some money by playing bluegrass for crowds waiting in line for movies at Los Angeles's Westwood Village theaters. Campbell went on to become a highly regarded strings arranger who as of 1999 had applied his arranging skills to more than eighty gold and platinum albums of such superstars as the Rolling Stones, Bob Dylan, Willie Nelson, and Neil Diamond. He also worked on some of Beck's projects.

Speaking of the years he spent with Campbell, Beck told *Los Angeles Times* interviewer Neil Weiss, "There was definitely an environment where it was cool to sort of do your own thing and be interested in whatever." His father, he added, "always had an ear for the weirder harmonies. That's probably what he passed on to me."

He dropped out of school after junior high and worked a variety of menial jobs without any definite idea of what he'd do with his life. The turning point, he told Steve Hochman for a *Los Angeles Times* article ("Don't Get Bitter on Us, Beck," Calendar section, February 20, 1994, pp. 4, 60–61), came when he was seventeen and visiting a friend's house. (He told another interviewer this occurred when he was sixteen.) The two were just hanging out "and his dad had a bunch of records. He had this Mississippi John Hurt record and the cover was just a close-up shot of his sweating, old face and it looked pretty cool. So I stole it.

"It totally blew me away. I'd never heard music like that before. But it was exactly the kind of music I wanted to hear. I wasn't into that much music before. I was into some punk bands. I liked Pussy Galore when I was fourteen or fifteen. But this was so great."

Inspired by this, he sought out recordings by other folk artists like Woody Guthrie and Blind Willie Johnson as well as old-time country performers such as the Carter Family, and spent hours poring over songbooks at local libraries, with the collections of John and Alan Lomax being particular favorites. He also learned to play guitar, focusing on finger picking techniques, which he later expanded to include slide guitar talents. Still, as he told Edna Gundersen of *USA Today* ("*Odelay* finds perfect mix of imperfections," July 11, 1996), he initially saw his musical interests as only an enjoyable hobby. "It was inconceivable to me that I could make a living doing this. I played Leadbelly covers. How far can you get with that? I wrote folk songs for my own amusement." He did, though, get around to performing on street corners for spare change.

In early 1989, the then eighteen-year-old Beck was beginning to have the notion that there might actually be some kind of niche for him in the music field. With a girlfriend, he boarded a bus and traveled to New York to see if the Big Apple might have an active folk scene. He did find that other young folk aspirants were performing in small venues on the Lower East Side, and eventually worked up enough courage to seek some club exposure. He told Gundersen, "I had to get fairly intoxicated for my first gig."

His girlfriend departed the city soon after they got there, but Beck stayed on, slowly adding to his entertainment experience. Fellow folk artist Roger Manning recalled for David Browne of *Entertainment Weekly* ("Beck in the High Life," February 14, 1997, pp. 32, 34–36) that during that New York period, "He was into his Woody Guthrie mode and he was really good at it." But Beck hated the cold winters, and by the early 1990s had gone back home to L.A. He found work on the local folk club circuit, but he wasn't happy about the way audiences treated his sets. He told Browne, "I'd be banging away on a Son House tune and the whole audience would be talking. So maybe out of desperation or boredom, or the *audience's* boredom, I'd make up these ridiculous songs just to see if people were listening." His first hit, "Loser," he noted, "was an extension of that." Its lyrics include the lines "I'm a loser baby / So why don't you kill me."

The song was touted by some critics as "the ultimate slacker anthem," but Beck strenuously refuted that reference. He told Hochman, "It wasn't intended to be [an anthem]. It was just goofing around at a friend's house on an eight-track. There's a lot of ideas floating around in the song, but it wasn't meant to be some like triumphant message."

In a similar vein, he told Gundersen, "The world is so fractured. How can anyone write a song representing a whole age group? I don't know any of those body-pierced Internet surfers. I hated seeing my song used as an example of Generation X. It was insulting."

Local L.A. college radio stations picked up on the record, however, and began to play it regularly, and soon other stations in other parts of the United States added it to their playlists. The disc gained its initial attention after being released on the independent label Bongload. After that, success brought offers from a number of major record companies; he decided on Geffen, signing an unusual contract that allowed him to record discs for other firms as well. After "Loser" was reissued on Geffen's DGC Records on January 18, 1994, it soon reached number one on the *Billboard* modern rock list, going on to earn a gold record award from the R.I.A.A. on April 11, 1996.

On March 1, 1994, Beck's first album, *Mellow Gold,* with "Loser" as one of its tracks, was released on DGC Records. It was a strange, but oddly affecting, collection. Hochman commented, "If you put a thousand monkeys in a room with a tape recorder and locked them up for a thousand years, you might end up with an album like this one, a sputtering synapse stream of consciousness punctuated by cowboy chords on an untuned folk guitar." Still, he gave it an above-average three-star rating. Soon after its release, the album rose up the charts, passing R.I.A.A. gold record requirements on May 3, 1994.

Taking advantage of the leeway given him in his Geffen agreement, Beck kept turning out new material for other companies, such as *One Foot in the Grave,* issued by K Records of Olympia, Washington, in mid-1994. Richard Cromelin of the *Los Angeles Times* commented that the album positioned Beck "as a cross between Woody Guthrie and Syd Barrett (founding member of the rock group Pink Floyd)—cogent and stubbornly spacey, lethally alert behind the somnolent facade created by his sleepy murmurs." At the same time, the CD of a DGC single drawn from *Mellow Gold* titled "Beercan" actually comprised an EP since Beck had included no less than five "bonus" tracks of new material plus an instrumental version of "Loser." Bonus numbers included the excellent ballad "Totally Konfused" and a different treatment of the *Mellow Gold* track "Pay No Mind," here titled "Got No Mind." Another collection compiled for small label release was Beck's *Stereopathic Soulmanure,* issued on Flipside.

By the end of 1995, Beck was ready to begin work on a new album for Geffen. When that album came out, on June 18, 1996, it laid to rest worries about whether the artist's previous achievements had been an aberration. With tracks like the funk–hip-hop "Where It's At," "Devil's Haircut," the rap-style "High Five (Rock the Catskills)," and "The New Pollution" (with sounds of buzz saws and forklift trucks), *Odelay* proved one of the freshest additions to the pop music catalog. Among the samples used in various places were snippets of Dylan's "It's All Over Now, Baby Blue," Dick Hyman's "The Moog and Me," and James Brown's "Out of Sight."

During the summer, Beck began an intensive tour that brought him to many parts of the United States and the world the rest of 1996 and well into 1997. *Odelay,* which debuted at number sixteen in *Billboard* in June, received a gold record award from the R.I.A.A. on August 21, 1996. In January 1997, when the Grammy nominations were announced, Beck proved a finalist in three categories: Album of the Year, Best Alternative Recording, and Best Male Rock Vocal Performance (for "Where It's At"). He also was asked to perform that last-named number on the Grammy telecast on February 26. He commented to Browne, "It was a little surreal. But it feels good to be validated, to be acknowledged. For a while, I was one of the scapegoats for the whole slacker–Generation X thing. Somehow the perception changed, and I'm grateful."

By then, he was much in demand for the celebrity TV circuit. In January he was featured on *Saturday Night Live,* Howard Stern's *E!* program, and the Rosie O'Donnell show. Backed by his band, the Crew, his performance of "Where It's At" certainly was one of the high points of the Grammy ceremonies in February. The song earned Beck the trophy for Best Male Rock Vocal Performance, and *Odelay* also was named Best Alternative Recording.

Beck's standing with the nation's music critics was underscored by the results of the *Village Voice* poll of some 300 reviewers, announced in February, which showed *Odelay*'s selection as best album of 1996. The album received 1,134 points, the publication reported, almost twice the 612 for the runner-up Fugee's disc, *The Score.*

Despite his success with alternative rock, rap, and other genres, he emphasized in early 1997 that he remained a fan of blues and folk. In his stage appearances, he praised people like country bluesman Fred McDowell and, when he did some harmonica playing, paid tribute to Sonny Terry, "whose incredible harmonica style I'm about to give a bad name." He also said one project he hoped to complete during the year was a new album of folk and country-style material.

Called *Mutations,* this disc was issued by DGC in November 1998 along with the disclaimer that this was a side project, not the follow-up to *Odelay* and wouldn't get the full-scale tour and promotional support. Beck described the album tracks as "space-age folk."

The album, however, really didn't need excessive promotion, standing on its own as an excellent collection that showcased another side of Beck's musical tastes. It won warm critical endorsements across the board, including a rare four-star rating from the *Los Angeles Times* and strong praise from *New York Times* reviewers. It showed up on the *Billboard* best-sellers list as soon as it hit record stores. It earned a Grammy and was followed on the lists in 1999 with the disc *Midnight Vultures.*

Beck emphasized that he drew on both old and new influences in his work, telling Jon Pareles of the *New York Times* ("A Pop Post-Modernist Gives Up on Irony," Arts & Leisure section, November 8, 1998, pp. 33, 40). "People write that I dig through the pickle barrel of the past. But I think of the music of the last hundred years as contemporary. It's all part of a fluid continuous line. People have a general sense of superiority to the past, but I don't think we're any smarter or more enlightened. We're still the same people 80 years ago as we were 20 years ago. I also think that when you come to the end of something you really have to go back to the beginning."

BELAFONTE, HARRY: *Singer, actor, TV producer, Born New York, New York, March 1, 1928.*

With his great voice and matinee idol features, Harry Belafonte was a natural to succeed in the entertainment field. However, it took a number of years of struggle and experimentation before he discovered his true bearings. Once he did, he became a major artist and innovator in folk music, a fine actor in films and on TV, and a potent moral force in the civil rights movement.

Though strongly associated with West Indies–style folk music, Harry George Belafonte was born in New York and lived there his first eight years. He did have an authentic heritage of the Caribbean region, since his mother came from Jamaica and his father from the French-speaking island of Martinique. In 1935, his mother went back to Jamaica with Harry. He spent five years there, a period when he learned much about the island's music and culture.

By 1940, his mother took him to New York again, where he first attended parochial school, then George Washington High School in upper Manhattan. However, with World War II under way, he left in 1944 before graduating to enlist in the U.S. Navy. He spent several years in the service, then got a job as a janitor in a New York building in the late 1940s after receiving his discharge. A tenant gave him tickets to the play *Home Is the Hunter.* Impressed by the drama, Harry decided to use the G.I. bill to study acting.

He enrolled in Erwin Piscator's Dramatic Workshop. One of his roles called for him to sing, which led to his discovery by the owner of the Royal Roost, a Broadway nightclub, who offered Harry a two-week engagement. Harry's vocalizing brought such enthusiastic response that the engagement was extended to a twenty-week stay. More engagements followed, until Capitol Records finally gave him a recording contract.

Harry became dissatisfied with singing the pop songs of the day and, in 1950, decided to take a break. He decided that folk music, then enjoying the first stirrings of what was to turn into a boom in the late 1950s, suited him more. He joined some friends in opening a small folk spot in Greenwich Village, where he hung around, listening to various folk artists and sometimes singing himself. He also made many trips to Washington to study the material at the Archive of American Folk Music. In the early 1950s, he had a considerable repertoire of American as well as West Indian folk songs and began working in an act with two guitarist friends, Millard Thomas and Craig Work.

The three opened at the Village Vanguard in New York for the familiar two-week stand, and once more Harry had to be held over. The show played to packed houses for twelve weeks. Harry and his friends went on to other engagements, including a highly successful one in New York's Blue Angel.

Some of Harry's film contacts were also interested in him, and he was invited to come to Hollywood to do his first film part, in *Bright Road.* Another opportunity came along back on Broadway for him to be a cast member of John Murray Anderson's *Almanac.* When it opened in New York in December 1953, Harry's

singing of "Hold 'Em Joe" and "Acorn in the Meadow" stopped the show. Then in 1954 he won the lead role in Oscar Hammerstein II's musical version of the opera *Carmen* (with a black cast) titled *Carmen Jones.* Late in 1954, Harry added to his steadily growing reputation by touring the country in a revue called *Three for the Road.* Everywhere he went, critics and audiences were thrilled by his treatment of fourteen folk songs.

His talents weren't lost on record industry executives; during 1954, he signed with RCA, for whom he ultimately sold tens of millions of records. Along the way, he also became the first pop music performer to sell over a million copies of a long-playing album.

The event that catapulted him to a mass-audience celebrity took place on June 23, 1955. Harry's singing of calypso and other folk songs on a CBS national telecast was one of the high points of the TV year and the beginning of a close association between Belafonte and the medium. He went on to guest on almost every major network variety or talk show. During the late 1950s and through the 1960s, he was featured a number of times on *The Ed Sullivan Show* and made a number of dramatic appearances on TV over the years, including an acclaimed role in *General Electric Theater*'s "Winner by Decision." During the 1960s, Harry added producing to his other credits, producing not only some of his own TV specials but hour-long shows on the subjects of black music, folk music, and black humor.

His 1950s film work included a movie version of *Carmen Jones* (his second film part), with Dorothy Dandridge in the lead role; and the controversial 1957 *Island in the Sun,* with its interracial romantic theme. At one point he formed a company to produce films, appearing in two movies under that arrangement, *The World, The Flesh and the Devil* and *Odds Against Tomorrow.*

He began to come into his own as a folk music recording star during 1956–57. The initial impetus came from his unique renditions of calypso numbers such as "Jamaica Farewell," "Day-O (Banana Boat Song)," "Matilda," "Brown Skin Girl," and "Come Back, Liza." One of his first RCA albums, *Calypso,* earned a gold record and remained a best-seller for RCA for many years. Some of his well-received singles of the 1950s included the American-style folk song "Scarlet Ribbons," "Danny Boy," "Shenandoah," "Hava Nagela," and "When the Saints Go Marchin' In," all recorded during 1956; and "All My Trials," "John Henry," and "Mama Look a Boo Boo" (recorded during 1959).

From the late 1950s on, Harry was a giant in the personal appearance field. For decades, he set attendance records in major auditoriums the world over. After his initial debut at New York's Carnegie Hall in the late 1950s, he sold out the facility many times in later years. The same held true for Los Angeles's Greek Theater, where, during the 1960s, he became almost an institution, returning regularly at two-year intervals to post SRO signs for three-week periods. He cut back on his touring for much of the 1970s, but when he returned after a long absence to the Greek in mid-1979, he still attracted large audiences to his series of concerts.

During the 1960s, Harry was very active in the fight for civil rights. He took part in benefit concerts and freedom marches, and in 1966 performed in Paris and Stockholm for the first European-sponsored benefit concerts for Dr. Martin Luther King, Jr. He was a member of the board of directors of the Southern Christian Leadership Conference and, after the tragic killing of Dr. King, served as chairman of the Martin Luther King, Jr., Memorial Fund. As a producer, he presented the much-honored drama by the late Lorraine Hansberry, *To Be Young, Gifted, and Black,* to New York audiences in 1969.

Over the years his creative and humanitarian efforts won him honors from many organizations, including the NAACP, City of Hope, and the American Jewish Congress. He was awarded an honorary Doctorate of Humanities by Park College in Missouri in 1968, and later the New York New School of Social Research awarded him a Doctorate in the Arts.

From the late 1950s on, he also accumulated many credits in television, including such firsts as being the first of his race to win a TV Emmy award and the first black producer in TV. Among the specials he produced and starred in were "The Strollin' Twenties" on CBS and "A Time for Laughter" on ABC. He also starred in a number of annual TV specials on Canada's CBC.

Always a strong album artist, Belafonte mainly made hit lists with his LPs after the first surge of singles successes in the 1950s. During his close to two decades on RCA, he turned out dozens of albums, both studio and live. Among his releases were *Harry Belafonte* and *Mark Twain & Folk* (early 1950s), *Calypso* (1955), *An Evening with Belafonte* and *Songs of the Caribbean* (mid-1950s), *Love Is a Gentle Thing* (4/59), *At Carnegie Hall* (two records, 9/59), *Sings Blues* (3/60), *What a Mornin'* (2/60), *Swing Dat Hammer* (5/60), *Harry Belafonte Returns to Carnegie Hall* (two records, 12/60), *Jump Up Calypso* (9/61), *Midnight Special* (5/62), *Many Moods of Belafonte* (11/62), *Streets I Walked* (7/63), *Harry Belafonte at the Greek Theater* (two records, 4/64), *Ballads, Blues and Boasters* (11/64), *An Evening with Miriam Makeba* (7/65), *An Evening with Nina Mouskouri* (2/66), *In My Quiet Room* (7/66), *Calypso in Brass* (12/66), *Harry Belafonte on Campus* (7/67), *Homeward Bound* (1/70), *By Request* (5/70), *This Is Harry Belafonte* (two records, 9/70), *Warm Touch* (4/71), *Calypso Carnival* (12/71), and *Belafonte Live* (two records, 11/72).

As the 1970s went by, Belafonte's recording efforts became more of a sideline as he devoted more time and energy to other projects, including charitable work and films. His contract with RCA phased out, and until the late 1970s he had no arrangement for U.S. releases, though in 1979 RCA did put out a retrospective of some of his major hits called *Harry Belafonte—A Legendary Performer.*

In the early 1970s, he teamed up on a film project with longtime friend Sidney Poitier, with whom he once had acted in the American Negro Theater. In that unusual western titled *Buck and the Preacher,* Belafonte played an aging "jackleg" preacher, Reverend Willis Oaks Rutherford. Harry showed a flair for satiric humor in a later 1970s movie called *Uptown Saturday Night,* where his role was a takeoff on Marlon Brando's portrayal of Don Corleone in *The Godfather.*

Harry signed a recording contract with CBS Records International in the late 1970s for material to be released outside the United States. The first of several late-1970s LPs for that label came out in 1977, titled *Turn the World Around.*

In 1981, there were indications Belafonte would have a resurgence of his entertainment activities in the new decade. He was featured on TV in a dramatic program about integration in reverse—the story of the first white student athlete (played by Bruce Jenner) to enter formerly all-black Grambling College. Belafonte played the part of Grambling's noted football coach, Eddie Robinson. During the year, Harry also completed a grueling, seven-and-half-month concert tour that took him to major venues all across the United States. In August, his first album for Columbia for U.S. release, *Loving You Is Where I Belong,* was issued.

Through the 1980s into the '90s, Harry remained active on the concert stage and contributed his name or services to many good causes, including the recording of "We Are the World" in support of USA For Africa, though his recording career continued to languish. A high point from a personal standpoint was his choice to replace Danny Kaye in 1987 as goodwill ambassador for the United Nations' International Children's Fund (UNICEF), a position he filled for some seven years. In 1995, he completed his first movie in many years, *White Man's Burden,* planned for a 1996 release, in which he costarred with John Travolta. At the induction ceremonies for newly chosen members of the Rock and Roll Hall of Fame at the Waldorf Astoria in New York City in January 1996, Harry paid tribute to folksinger Pete Seeger, voted into the hall under a special music legends category.

During the summer of 1996, Belafonte received plaudits for his role in Robert Altman's film *Kansas City,* which Altman described as a "jazz memory" of his hometown. In the movie, Belafonte played Seldom Seen, the gambler-gangster proprietor of the Hey Hey Club, a combination jazz spot and gambling den, who muses on race, politics, and life. Writing in the *Los Angeles Times,* film critic Kevin Thomas observed, "As handsome and charismatic as ever, Belafonte sparks the film, he is its live wire and he's got a great part." (Belafonte won the New York Critics' Circle Award for his role.)

In early 1997, a documentary (*Robert Altman's Jazz '34*) of the many excellent jazz performers from the film, featuring some initial voice-overs by Belafonte, was featured on the Public Broadcasting System's *Great Performances* series. On March 1, 1997, Belafonte starred in a seventieth birthday concert at a State University of New York auditorium. The show was taped for presentation over PBS, the first TV concert program by Harry to be presented in over a decade. The concert offered old standbys ("Matilda," "Jamaica Farewell," "Banana Boat Song") and some new songs, including one titled "Now You See It, Now You Don't," which incorporated tributes to South African heroes Steve Biko and Nelson Mandela. Before giving his rendition of the standard musical comedy ballad "Try to Remember" (from *The Fantasticks*), Belafonte recalled that during the years he worked on UNICEF with the late Audrey Hepburn she had called it her favorite song. As he had done in the past, Belafonte introduced promising new talent on his show, including the excellent singer-guitarist from the Cameroon in Africa, Richard Bula.

In 1997, Island Records released *An Evening with Harry Belafonte and Friends,* the sound track to the PBS special, while DDC reissued a collection of recordings from 1961 titled *Jump Up Calypso.* Belafonte also formed his own label, Niger (named for the river in West Africa), which was underwritten by Island Records. His intent was to release the work of black artists from rural America, Africa, and the Caribbean. At the year 2000 Grammys, Harry was presented with a Lifetime Achievement Award.

BELL, VINCE: *Singer, guitarist, songwriter. Born Dallas, Texas, September 16, 1951.*

Almost always, when it's said that someone brought back his career from the dead, the reference is merely symbolic. In Vince Bell's case, though, it had a basis in fact. He was so badly injured in an auto accident in the early 1980s that one newspaper apparently ran an obituary. As it happened, he survived the accident, but it took more than a decade of dogged rehabilitation work before he could resume performing and recording, turning out a 1994 album that demonstrated how much the world of music would have lost if his life had ended prematurely.

Vince was born in Dallas, Texas, but grew up in Houston. He was interested in music and taught himself to play guitar, but he also had considerable athletic skills and became a starter on the football team at Memorial High in the late 1960s. He told Joe Mitchell of the *Austin Chronicle* ("Back from the Obit," March 31, 1995), "I was the high school quarterback my senior year there. Our record that year was not too terribly good. I think we were 4-5-1, but we beat some good

teams. I'm so glad I played high school ball. Playing sports kept me outa shit. I was a crazy and rambunctious kid. I would have done anything my body could've worn. Thank God it was on a damned football field and not in the street. The worst penalty there is 15 yards."

After graduating from Memorial, he began to get serious about music, particularly the kind of folk material played in Houston bars and coffeehouses by artists like Guy Clark and Townes Van Zandt, who often performed at the Old Quarter. For some time in the early '70s he simply drank in the atmosphere and tried to memorize some of the songs he heard, but he finally worked up enough nerve to introduce himself to a favorite professional performer.

He told Mitchell, "I just went down by the stage one night and said, 'Golly, Mr. Van Zandt, how do you play that A minor chord?'" The ploy worked, and for the next few years he got help in songwriting from Townes and pointers on guitar playing from Guy. "They would teach," he told Mitchell. "I would learn. They weren't really teachers. They were moody, arty types. Teachers were down at the schools. But they were good-natured about it."

Before long, Bell was starting to make his presence known on the concert circuit. At one point in the mid-'70s, he flew up to New York for an audition at the Bitter End in Greenwich Village for the chance to get on a roster of candidates for folk circuit engagements. His performance was well received, and for the next few years he gained a lot of gigs at coffeehouses across the United States. After a while, he signed with a Texas booking agency that set up engagements at almost every sizable city in the Lone Star State in the late '70s. Those included a number of appearances at Houston's Anderson Fair, where Clark and Van Zandt were sometimes featured, and where Vince's path crossed the paths of other talented newcomers like Nanci Griffith and Lyle Lovett.

His songwriting abilities impressed his new friends; Nanci recorded his 1977 composition, "Sun, Moon & Stars," (also the title of his 1989 recording on Analog) and later included his "Woman of the Phoenix" on her 1993 Grammy Award–winning album, *Other Voices/ Other Rooms.* For his part, in the 1990s, Lovett sometimes included Bell's 1989 song "I've Had Enough" in his live concerts.

Both Lovett and Griffith testified to the potential everyone saw in Bell in the late '70s and early '80s. Nanci told the *Houston Post* in 1992, "From all of us who were beating paths around Texas in the seventies, I always felt Vince was the best of us." Lovett recalled that he had been intrigued by Vince's originals from the first time he heard them. He told a reporter from *New Country* magazine (May 1995), "He writes songs about his life, and when I would listen to Vince's songs I would want to know about the person singing the songs. I think that's what great songs do."

One of Bell's songs, "Bermuda Triangle," caught the attention of choreographer James Clouser, who enlisted Vince to provide the music for a ballet performed by Houston's Space Dance Theatre. For the performance, Vince played and sang the entire fifteen-song score. One of the things missing from his résumé was an album, but in late 1982 he got the chance to work up some demo tapes he planned to submit to record companies. Backing him on the sessions in an Austin, Texas, studio were such excellent musicians as Stevie Ray Vaughan and Eric Johnson. Things seemed to be going well when he left for home the evening of December 21, 1982, and his life was turned upside-down.

He was waiting at a traffic signal for the light to turn green when a drunk driver "hit me in the driver's-side door going 65 miles an hour. I was in a coma through most of January 1983." He awoke at last in a hospital bed with broken ribs, liver damage, a very serious head injury, and a very badly mangled right arm. His friends told him they had read his obituary in the *Austin American Statesman,* apparently prompted by the fact that his heart had stopped beating for a short time.

As Vince told Mitchell in 1995, "I still haven't seen that. We went looking for it once and there was no record. What I think happened was that it was an early edition. Some poor kid was in the obit section and said, 'Okay, this cat's dead' and wrote an obit. Then 20 minutes later, my heart starts pumpin' again and he has to rip it out of the next edition. I don't care if it's true or not. It's an interesting story."

Not only was his body badly beaten up, his head injury also caused memory impairment. His treatment, besides reconstructive surgery, also included a stay in a mental hospital to deal with depression. Part of his therapy involved transcribing whatever lyrics he could remember from songs he had written before the accident. He told Kevin Avery from the New York publication *Gallery* ("The Bionic Songman," April 1995), "A head injury is a real double-edged sword. When you're an amputee, they take your arms and legs. When you're head-injured, they take your thoughts. One day you wake up, and some B-rate movie star is president. You can't walk or talk or see straight.

"But a head injury is the best of teachers, as well. It showed me that my gift was relentless. It let me know that if anybody was going to get up off that mat that I'd been laid on, it was me. And so I did. I got the fuck up. That's invaluable and actually kind of a thrill in this life to know about yourself."

Besides learning how to walk and talk properly again (helped greatly, he stressed, by his wife and publishing assistant, Sarah Wrightson), he also had to teach himself new ways to play the guitar. Surgeons rebuilt his right arm but couldn't restore normal motion to his thumb and forefinger. No longer able to hold a pick, he worked out a playing method combining picking and strumming he calls "the claw," derived from a combination of techniques used by Guy Clark and Merle Travis. For many years he also had trouble with walking stability. He recalled many times when he would be walking along when he would suddenly fall; when friends asked if he was all right, he'd simply joke that it was nothing compared to what happened the week before, when he "fell down a flight of stairs."

After finally being discharged from the hospital, Bell found new creative opportunities difficult to come by, and he moved to Berkeley, California, where he stayed for over five years. "I didn't want people to see me drool or stutter or limp, or any of the things I'd been doing," he told *New Country.* "I couldn't peel a potato in Texas, because my buddies started to own the places I wanted to peel the potatoes at, and they didn't want to see me hurt any worse than I was. Nobody would venture a $40-a-night gig on me. I was lost and had nowhere to go between the Red [River] and the Rio Grande."

In California, he focused on writing new material and, after a while gained the attention of producer Bob Neuwirth, whose credits included projects with Bob Dylan and T-Bone Burnett. Vince's manager sent Neuwirth cassettes containing fifty-nine songs, from which Bob selected enough for an album and gained approval for the project from Austin-based Watermelon Records. Except for "Sun, Moon & Stars," "The Beast," and one number by another writer, all the choices were of songs Vince had written since the accident.

The one nonoriginal was Texas writer Gary Burgess's "Frankenstein," which ended up as the opening track. The song begins with the lines "I've got stitches all over my body," certainly setting the tone for an album of travail and regeneration. Those contributing to the sessions included Geoff Muldaur (guitar, banjo, and mandolin), Stephen Bruton (guitar), Lyle Lovett (backing vocals), David Mansfield (violin), John Cale of Velvet Underground fame (piano), and Mickey Raphael (harmonica player in Willie Nelson's group). Tracks included "Woman of the Phoenix," "I've Had Enough" (with Lovett handling backing vocals), "Hard Road" (with harmonies from Victoria Williams), and "Girl Who Never Saw a Mountain." After the sessions were completed, Vince and his wife moved back to Texas, settling in the town of Fredericksburg.

It was odd in a way that the album, *Phoenix,* represented only the debut release for such a seasoned artist as Bell. But it was a triumphal collection, thought-provoking and inspirational, that surely merited the almost unanimous applause it received from critics at both large and small publications. The *Sing Out!* reviewer, for instance, commented, "This is one of those albums whose songs reveal new insights with each subsequent hearing." Steve Hochman of the *Los Angeles Times* wrote, "The opening 'Frankenstein' gets to the monster myth in three minutes with much more grace than Kenneth Branagh's overwrought movie. From there, the veteran Texas troubadour explores the poetry of the misfit with understated passion."

In the second half of 1994 and well into 1995, Bell was warmly welcomed at concerts in many places in the United States, sometimes being joined by others from the recording sessions like Victoria Williams. He hoped his newfound success, as he told Kevin Avery, would provide a valuable inspiration to others who suffered head injuries. "I hope they can see my thing and go, 'Look at that short little son of a bitch. He worked his butt off, and he sang at Carnegie Hall last year.' And I did, doggone it."

While on tour in the United States and Europe, Bell wrote an autobiographical account of his experiences after his accident titled *One Man's Music.* He also began writing songs for a new album, *Texas Plates* on Paladin Records (and Warner Distribution), which came out in 1999; he described it as a "rock 'n' western" album. In 1998, Lyle Lovett included Bell's song "I've Had Enough" on his CD that paid tribute to fellow Texas songwriters, *Step Inside This House.*

BLACK, FRANCES: *Singer. Born Dublin, Ireland, June 25, 1960.*

Irish singer Frances Black has much in common with her older and more famous sister, Mary—a clear and pleasing voice and an ear for good material. But she is not a clone. Beginning in 1993 with the success of the *A Woman's Heart* compilation and then in 1994 with her solo debut, *Talk to Me,* Frances focused on fusing contemporary and even country music into a pop format and gained a sizable following at home and abroad.

Frances grew up as one of the five children in the musical Black family, along with Mary, Martin, Michael, and Shay. Her mother, Patricia, sang as an amateur in Dublin's dance halls; her father, Kevin, who was born on Rathlin Island in County Antrim, was a plasterer but played fiddle and mandolin with the family. Frances joined the rest of her family in 1986 to tour and promote their debut on Dara, *The Black Family Album,* singing lead vocals on "Tomorrow Is a Long Time" and the traditional song "The Ploughboy Lads." After singing lead vocals on four of the tracks for *Time for Touching Home—The Black Family* in 1989, Frances joined the traditional/contemporary Irish group Arcady. (The group was formed by former De Dannan percussionist Johnny "Ringo" McDonagh and also included button accordionist Jackie Daly.)

Her first marriage broke up in 1985. (She is currently involved with Brian Allen, who is also her manager.) She had a bout with alcoholism in the 1980s, but with the aid of an alcoholism treatment center called Stanhope Street, she gave up drinking in 1988, according to an article in *Woman's Way* (April 29, 1994). After that, her life and career rebounded. "I was so unsure of myself that if I met anyone in the street I'd blush bright red!" she told Pat Costello of *Woman's Way.* "Drink gave me confidence. I thought I was the only one to have feelings of insecurity, but they taught me that everyone feels like that."

Black recorded one album with Arcady, *After the Ball,* in 1991, a combination of traditional jigs and reels and ballads. The title track and the album broke into the top 10 of the Irish charts, and the group gained a following in the United States. Black left in 1992 to spend more time with her two children, Eoghan and Aoife, who attended all-Irish schools in Dublin.

In 1992 she joined up with Irish singer-songwriter Kieran Goss and released the album *Frances Black and Kieran Goss* on CBM, Shanachie in the United States. Shortly thereafter Black's career received a boost when two of her songs were included on *A Woman's Heart,* the compilation of Irish women singers put together by Mary Black's husband, Joe O'Reilly, who owns Dara Records. The songs "Wall of Tears," from the Black/Goss album, and "After the Ball," from the Arcady album, gained worldwide attention as the album sold more than 500,000 copies. In 1994, Frances had two songs on the follow-up album, *A Woman's Heart 2:* "Talk to Me" and "Fear Is the Enemy of Love" by Fairground Attraction's Mark E. Nevin.

Following the success of *A Woman's Heart,* Black released her first solo album, *Talk to Me,* on Dara Records in 1994. The album, which was number one in Ireland for eight weeks, was later released on Atlantic's Celtic Heartbeat label in the United States and has sold more than 100,000 units. It included songs by Nashville country artist Vince Gill ("Colder Than Winter") and four by Nanci Griffith ("On Grafton Street," "Talk to Me While I'm Listening," "Always Will," and "Time of Inconvenience") before Griffith had a chance to record them herself. Frances took a similar path as her sister, Mary, who prides herself in selecting material from a stable of songwriters. (Mary and Frances talk nearly every day.) A single from the album, "All the Lies That You Told Me," written by Christy Hennessey, rose to the number three chart position.

A year later she released her second solo CD, *The Sky Road,* on Dara. She supported the album with a tour of Ireland, the United Kingdom, and the United States. The album hit the second position on the Irish charts. In April 1995 she won an award as Ireland's best female artist and National Entertainer of the Year.

In November 1996 she released her third solo album on Dara, *The Smile on Your Face,* which included her hit song, "When You Say Nothing at All." She recorded the song despite some severe bruising on her vocal cords. The album reached number four on the charts and went platinum (15,000 sales) in Ireland on the day of release. In 1997, she won her second Irish award for best female artist.

She went into the studio with Declan Sinnott, who had produced many of Mary Black's albums, and released a single on the Sony label, "Love Me," backed with "Two Strong Hearts."

Black has also been involved in supporting various charitable causes, such as the Aoibhneas Women's Refuge, a battered women and children facility, and an antidrug campaign in Dublin. At a rally for the campaign, Black talked about being the mother of two teenage children and sympathizing with the struggle against drugs.

BLACK, MARY: *Irish singer. Born Dublin, Ireland, May 22, 1955.*

With a clear soprano voice and an ear for good songs, folk-pop singer Mary Black has become one of the most popular singers from Ireland. Several of her solo albums have opened at the top of the Irish charts, seven of them going multiplatinum in Ireland (20,000 copies). But her popularity transcends the Emerald Isle. When NBC's *Today Show* visited Ireland in March 1996, the network showcased Black performing her pop song "Summer Sent You" at a castle overlooking verdant hills.

Black grew up in Dublin as one of five children in the musical Black family. Her father, Kevin (born on Rathlin Island off the north coast of Ireland), was a fiddler, and her mother, Patty, sang in Dublin's dance halls. The family performed together in Dublin clubs. Mary sang in the school choir, where she learned harmony from the nuns, and later in the Young Dublin Singers. While she grew up singing traditional folk— her brother Shay taught her folk songs—Black also listened to Sandy Denny, and American singers like Billie Holiday, Bonnie Raitt, and Aretha Franklin.

She learns songs by ear. "I hear a song once or twice and I've got it," she told Marybeth Phillips of *Irish Edition* (May 1991). "I don't want to listen more because I'll be influenced by the person singing it. I'd rather make it my own."

She joined her first group, Terrace, at fifteen, with brothers Shay and Michael, John White, and Paschal Bermingham. On the weekends, she'd visit Shay, who was working in Castle Bar for the phone company, and they'd sing with other musicians. She also busked along the East Coast of the United States for a couple of months with her brothers. In 1975 they started a traditional folk band called General Humbert (other members included Shay Kavenagh on guitar, Rory Sommors on Uileann pipes, John Donegan on mandolin and keyboards, and Steve Dunford on bodhran). The band toured Europe and released a couple of cassettes: *General Humbert* on Dolphin Records (1975) and *General Humbert II,* on Gael-Linn Records (1978).

Popular Irish singer Christy Moore and his guitarist Declan Sinnott first heard Black in a Dublin pub called "The Meeting Place" in 1981, where she was jamming with Triona Ní Dhomhnaill (of the Bothy Band and Nightnoise) and Linda Ronstadt. "After the women traded leads on 'Heart Like a Wheel' and Buddy Holly's 'I Guess It Doesn't Matter Anymore,' there was no doubt that Mary Black was a great singer," Sinnott said.

In 1982, Moore invited Black to perform at a concert at the National Concert Hall in Dublin. Black didn't have a guitarist, so Moore recommended Sinnott, who had played electric guitar in Moving Hearts and Horslips. Despite his rock and her folk background, the pairing worked—Sinnott would produce seven of her albums and edge Black toward pop. Sinnott produced Black's first solo album, *Mary Black,* in 1982. Her debut, which included the Billie Holiday song "God Bless the Child" among several Irish traditional songs, rose to number four on the Irish charts and earned an Irish gold album (10,000 copies). She won the Irish Independent Arts Award for Music in 1983.

Shortly thereafter, De Dannan's Alec Finn asked her to join the virtuoso group with a tradition of great female singers: Black, Dolores Keane, and Maura O'Connell. Black went into the studio with little time for rehearsal. De Dannan's *Song for Ireland* came out in 1983 on Dara Records (a record company owned by Black's husband, Joe O'Reilly) in Ireland and Sugar Hill in the United States. It was followed by *Anthem,* released on Dara in 1985, which won the Irish Album of the Year Award.

While performing with De Dannan, Black continued her solo career, releasing *Collected* in 1984 and *Without the Fanfare* on Dara in 1985. (Both albums went gold in Ireland.) *Collected* included several tracks from her days with De Dannan and General Humbert but adds four new songs, including Stephen Foster's "Hard Times" and Eric Bogle's "My Youngest Son Came Home Today." *Fanfare* shows her moving toward a pop-electric sound under Sinnott's guidance. Black, who receives hundreds of tapes from songwriters, mostly sticks to her proven stable of homegrown writers: Jimmy McCarthy, Noel Brazil, Johnny Duhan, and Mick Hanly. "My talent isn't in songwriting," she told Jim Bessman of *Billboard* (August 28, 1993). "It's an art in itself, not something you can contrive, or that you can train to do if you don't have the talent. I've never felt inspired to write a song."

In 1986, as her solo career was taking off, Black decided to leave De Dannan. "I had recorded my second solo album and there was more and more of a demand for me to go solo." she told Denise Sofranko of *Dirty Linen* (February/March 1991). "So it was really because of the workload that I had to end with De Dannan." Singing with De Dannan bolstered Black's confidence. "I used to get very very nervous before then."

She was named the Entertainer of the Year in 1986 and was voted Best Female Artist in 1987 and 1988 in the Irish Recorded Music Awards Poll. Her album *By the Time It Gets Dark,* the title track by Sandy Denny, came out in 1987 and became her first multiplatinum disc in Ireland. She sang with Van Morrison and the Chieftains on their 1987 album *Irish Heartbeat.*

But it was her aptly titled next album, *No Frontiers,* that broke down barriers. The album, was released in August 1989, shot to the top of the Irish charts, going triple platinum and remaining in the top 30 for more than a year. It includes Burt Bacharach's "I Say a Little Prayer," which Black performed at concert dates in the United States.

Bill Straw, the owner of Gift Horse Records in Los Angeles, first heard Black in 1989 while listening to KCRW's *Morning Becomes Eclectic.* He traveled to Ireland to secure the U.S. distribution rights. Released in the United States in June 1990, *No Frontiers* broke into the New Adult Contemporary top 20 in October. In Japan, the album rose to number three on the pop charts, and Black toured there at the end of 1990 with a band led by Sinnott. In January 1991, *Rolling Stone* called her voice "pure and haunting, it resonates with folk tradition" (January 24, 1991).

San Francisco Chronicle music critic Joel Selvin enthused about a performance: "For a vocalist to carry this much weight in a two-hour performance, the quality of her voice has to be close to spellbinding, her delivery flawless. Black qualified on both counts. She lit into the material with surgical precision, slicing off syllables with a scalpel of a voice, cutting her way to the emotional heart of the songs."

Black also began to perform with American artists Nanci Griffith and Emmylou Harris. She included songs on her albums by American songwriters such as Patrick Alger ("Going Gone" and "Once in a Very Blue Moon"), Mary-Chapin Carpenter ("The Moon & St. Christopher"), and John Gorka ("Treasure Island"). In 1990, Philip King produced the *Bringing It All Back Home* BBC TV series (about the worldwide influence of Irish music) in Dublin and Nashville, a production that included, among others, Emmylou Harris, Elvis Costello, Paul Brady, Dolores Keane, Richard Thompson, and the Everly Brothers. The BBC aired the series and released a two-CD collection in 1991 with Black performing "No Frontiers" and Richard Thompson's "The Dimming of the Day" with Emmylou Harris and Dolores Keane.

Returning from tours in the United States and Japan, Black released *Babes in the Wood* in 1991. (By this time she had distribution agreements with Grapevine in England, Gift Horse in the United States, and King in Japan.) *Babes* soared to the top of the Irish charts, where it remained for six weeks. The album hit number nine on the Gavin Adult Alternative charts in the U.S. and her song "The Thorn upon the Rose," by Julie Matthews, was even used in a TV ad in Japan for a railroad company and hit number eight on the Japanese charts. She was named Best Irish Solo Artist for 1991.

In contrast to many artists in the United States who find themselves pigeonholed, Black feels a sense of artistic freedom in Ireland. "If I had to confine myself to any one area of music, I'd crackle completely, 'cause I just feel the need to express myself in different ways at different times," she told Paul Robicheau of the *Boston Globe* (October 21, 1993).

Several collections came out in 1992 on labels around the world. Dara released *The Best of Mary Black,* in conjunction with RTE, the Irish TV company. Grapevine released *The Collection* and a video of Black's concerts in London at the Royal Albert Hall in January, 1992. King released a compilation album that year.

Joe O'Reilly had the idea of putting out a compilation of the increasingly popular Irish women performers. *A Woman's Heart,* released in 1992, included six of them—Mary Black, her sister Frances, Eleanor McEvoy, Máire Brennan, Dolores Keane, and accordionist Sharon Shannon. The album sold more than 500,000 units in Ireland, making it the biggest seller of all time in that country. Black performed a duet with Eleanor McEvoy, her former fiddle and synthesizer player, on "Only a Woman's Heart," which gave the album its title. In 1994, Black participated in the sequel, *A Woman's Heart 2.* The lineup included Frances Black, Mary Coughlan, Dolores Keane, Sincad Lohan, Maura O'Connell, Sinead O'Connor, Maighread Ní Dhomnaill, and Sharon Shannon.

Dara released Black's *The Holy Ground* in 1993, which entered at number one on the Irish charts. The album opens with "Summer Sent You," which gained some airplay on adult alternative stations in the United States, where Black toured in late 1993 to strong reviews. (Black and her husband have three children, the main reason she doesn't tour for more than three weeks at a time.) In Ireland, she played five sellout shows at Dublin's Point Theatre in April 1993. She also released a songbook through Dara compiled by Declan Sinnott.

In 1994 she won two more awards in Ireland: Best Irish Female Vocalist and Best Irish Album. But she had yet to become a household name in the United States. She continued to make inroads into the U.S. market, however, releasing the retrospective album *Looking Back* on Curb and Gift Horse records in 1995. The album contains twelve tracks, two of them new: "Soul Sister," which includes the words "Looking Back" on it, and a John Gorka tune to balance it out called "Looking Forward."

In 1995, Black also sang a duet of Bob Dylan's "Ring Them Bells" with Joan Baez at New York's Bottom Line for Baez's live album of the same name. She also appeared at the Newport Folk Festival.

Her release of *Circus* in August 1995 broke into the top 20 on the pop charts in England. The album included four songs by her favorite songwriter, Noel Brazil and two by John Gorka. Curb released the album in August 1996 in the United States. Black also performed with Mary-Chapin Carpenter at the White House in June 1996.

Black worked with bassist Larry Klein, Joni Mitchell's ex-husband, on her next album, *Shine,* which came out in 1997 on Curb Records. *Shine* took Black away from her Irish roots and did not do as well at home or abroad. During a 5½-week tour of North America in the fall of 1998, Black acknowledged that she wanted to return to her roots. "For the first time since I began recording I want to make a real folkie record," she told Geoff Chapman of the *Toronto Star* (November 7, 1998.) In 1998, Gift Horse released an eleven-track greatest hits album, *Song for Ireland,* with some of her earlier, folk-oriented recordings. She returned to folk with her 1999 studio release, *Speaking with the Angel,* on Dara (Curb in the U.S.), which received strong reviews.

Mary is not the only member of the Black family to record an album. Her sister Frances has released several albums; the Black family recorded *The Black Family* in 1986 and *Time for Touching Home* in 1989, and brothers, Shay, Martin, and Michael released *What a Time* in 1995.

With help from Bill Straw, the owner of Gift Horse Records in Los Angeles

BLAKE, NORMAN: *Singer, songwriter, guitarist, multi-instrumentalist, born Chattanooga, Tennessee, March 10, 1938.*

A major name in the bluegrass revival of the 1970s, adept at playing many other folk and country styles, Norman Blake might well have been a superstar had he so desired. But he preferred to shun the mass audience, rejecting the musical compromises they required. For many years he and his former wife Nancy traveled 50,000 miles a year, performing their southeastern-style, old-timey rural string music, to the delight of their small but devoted following.

Since the 1960s, Norman Blake has been one of the best flat-picking guitarists in the business. Despite his technical excellence he impresses the listener with a spare, lyrical style rather than a blizzard of notes. "Just because you can put a lot of notes in there doesn't mean you should," he told a writer for the *Atlanta Journal and Constitution* in 1989. "You don't want to play everything you know in one tune, because then you're letting your technique get in the way of the music. You're a technician, not a musician."

Norman doesn't like the way music sounds when it's plugged in. The electricity comes from his fingers flying over a multitude of different fret boards. When he and his wife performed together, the stage looked like a music shop. Besides Martin guitars, Norman plays fiddle, mandolin, mandola, viola, and Dobro. Nancy plays cello, rhythm guitar, bass, single-row accordion, and viola.

During the 1970s and 1980s, when many musicians experimented with jazz and world music, Norman Blake returned to his roots in Georgia and Tennessee. His inspiration comes from old sheet music, fiddle tunes, 78 rpm records dating back to the 1930s and 1940s, and songs he remembers from his youth. Even his original material sounds like it comes from a bygone era. "We're after a tone, a feel, a texture that's completely removed from today's world," Norman said.

Born in Chattanooga, Tennessee, and raised in nearby Sulphur Springs, Georgia, a whistle-stop along the Southern Railroad, Norman Blake could play several instruments by his teens. He listened to Bill Monroe, Roy Acuff, and the Grand Ole Opry on the radio. At eleven, he picked up the guitar, learning from friends and relatives. He also learned the mandolin and Dobro. At sixteen, he quit Trenton High to play mandolin and Dobro with the Dixieland Drifters. They made their radio debut on the Tennessee Barndance program on WNOX, Knoxville, and played on other southern stations during the next few years, including WROM-TV in Rome, Georgia. The band recorded some cuts with Jerry Lee Lewis for Sun Records in 1957, two of which resurfaced on *Sun Sessions—The Country Years.* Norman left the band to team with banjo player Bob Johnson as the Lonesome Travelers, recording *12 Shades of Bluegrass* for Parkway Records. In the late 1950s they added banjoist Walter Forbes, and the threesome made two records for RCA. In 1959, Blake joined another group, Hylo Brown and the Timberliners, though he still worked with Johnson, appearing as a duet at the Opry.

In 1960 he briefly joined June Carter's road band but military service cut that short. Norman was drafted into the U.S. Army in 1961, and stationed as a radio operator at the Panama Canal. He formed a bluegrass band, the Fort Kobbe Mountaineers, playing mandolin and fiddle. They were voted the best instrumental group in the Caribbean Command, with Norman winning as best instrumentalist. When he was discharged in 1963, Blake moved to Nashville and began work as a session musician. He found the main emphasis in pop music to be either rock 'n' roll or "Nashville-sound" country. He might well have become a top artist in either category, but his refusal to adapt his repertoire and performing technique in those directions drastically restricted his musical options. To earn a living he became a guitar teacher—with as many as 150 students a week—and played in a country-western dance band.

His musical abilities were not lost on others in the country field. In the mid-sixties Norman was part of June Carter's road group and played on Johnny Cash's record *Understand Your Man.* In 1968, Blake returned to Nashville, playing Dobro and guitar on Bob Dylan's *Nashville Skyline* album. In the summer of 1969, Blake joined the band for Johnny Cash's CBS TV show.

Once he had relocated to Nashville, Blake's performing career took on new dimensions. At the start of the 1970s, he played guitar and Dobro in Kris Kristofferson's first road band and toured with Joan Baez, backing her on her hit rendition of Robbie Robertson's "The Night They Drove Old Dixie Down." Blake became a member of John Hartford's Aereo-Plain band, and recorded the *Aereo-Plain* album. When that group disbanded, Norman remained with Hartford for a year and a half as an accompanist. Blake also recorded material for his first solo album, *Back Home in Sulphur Springs* (with Dobro player Tut Taylor), on Rounder Records in 1974. As the title suggests, it includes songs influenced by his childhood. He contributed to the Nitty Gritty Dirt Band's 1973 landmark *Will the Circle Be Unbroken,* and toured for nine months with the Red, White, and Blue(grass) Band, then plunged into a full-time solo career.

As it turns out, he never really considered himself a "session" musician. "I really have a lot of respect for the heavy session players that can play any bag, that can really blow anything," he told *Frets.* "I wasn't that; I did specialty things. I worked with people who knew me and who needed that certain thing I could do—like mandolins, fiddles, and guitars. Folkier things."

In 1972, he met Nancy Short, a cello player who was born in Independence, Missouri, on June 11, 1952. Nancy had a classical background, learning the cello in junior high. She moved to Nashville after high school and briefly played with the Nashville Youth Symphony, but left her classical roots when she discovered the other musical forms in Music City. She started with the group Everything in the Garden. In 1972 she was playing in an acoustic-folk group, Natchez Trace, which opened for Blake at Nashville's Exit/In. "This was the first time I'd ever heard him and I thought to myself, 'This guy must be totally nervous to play this fast!'" she told *Frets.*

Norman played by ear, while Nancy could read music. "I went through this thing where I thought it was a big handicap," she told *Frets.* "So, on purpose, I didn't read for about six years to develop my ear. That worked, so now I do both."

She played cello on *Fields of November,* (Flying Fish, 1974). The Blakes were married in 1975 and performed together for the next twenty years. In 1976, they moved from Nashville to Rising Fawn, Georgia, near Sulphur Springs. Norman also released *Whiskey Before Breakfast* on Rounder, featuring his acoustic guitar work.

Norman recorded such albums as *Old and New* (1975), *Norman Blake—Super Jam Session* (with Sam Bush, Clements and Jethro Burns, 1975), and *Blackberry Blossom* (1977), all on Flying Fish. He was represented on Takoma Records with *Live at McCabe's* (1979) and *Directions,* and on County Records with *Darlin' Honey.* Blake recorded with other major folk and country artists, including Bryan Bowers on *The View from Home* (1977, Flying Fish), Doc Watson on

The Essential Doc Watson (Vanguard), and Mason Williams on *Fresh Fish* (Flying Fish).

In 1978 the Blake group expanded to become a trio with the addition of fiddler James Bryan, an old friend of Norman's. He had first recorded with Blake on the *Old and New* album. During the 1970s, he had sometimes toured with bluegrass great Bill Monroe. They called the group the Rising Fawn String Ensemble. Blake told Art Coates of *Frets* that the trio combination gave increased depth to the music: the fiddle at the top of the range, the guitar in the middle, and Nancy's cello on the bottom.

In 1979, Blake and his group signed with Rounder. The first product of the new association was the 1979 release *The Rising Fawn String Ensemble,* followed by *Full Moon on the Farm* (1981), *Original Underground Music from the Mysterious South* (1982), *Nashville Blues* (1984), and *Lighthouse on the Shore* (1985). Norman teamed up with guitarist Tony Rice on two albums for Rounder, *Blake and Rice* (1987), followed by *Blake and Rice 2* (1989), and with Nancy on the *Norman and Nancy Blake Compact Disc* (1986), *Natasha's Waltz* (1987), and *Slow Train Through Georgia* (1989).

When Bryan left the group in 1985 due to family commitments, Norman and Nancy went back to touring as a duo. "We don't do this for the money," Nancy told the *Chattanooga Times* in 1990. "And if we don't want a particular commitment, or if we want to do a benefit concert, it's our decision. Probably not as financially rewarding as it could be, but we prefer loving what we do. Yet, we try to make a living."

The duo has received its share of accolades. Norman and Nancy received a Grammy nomination in the country music instrumental category for *Lighthouse on the Shore* (1985). Nancy's first solo recording, *Grand Junction,* was selected by a *New York Daily News* critic as one of the ten best of 1986. *Frets* selected Norman as the best multi-instrumentalist in 1986. In 1990 they received a Grammy nomination for best traditional folk recording for *Blind Dog* (1988). In 1993, they received a nomination in the Best Traditional Folk Album, Vocal or Instrumental category for *Just Gimme Somethin' I'm Used To,* a 1992 Shanachie release. The Blakes followed on Shanachie with *While Passing along This Way* (1994), *Hobo's Last Ride* (1996), and *Chattanooga Sugar Baby* (1998), all of which received Grammy nominations in Traditional Folk.

But living and working together took a toll on the relationship, which broke down in the late 1990s. Norman went his own way and was represented on Shanachie by two more CDs in 1999: *Be Ready Boys: Appalachia to Abilene* (with Rich O'Brien) and *Far Away, Down on a Georgia Farm.*

BLAND, BOBBY "BLUE": *Singer. Born Rosemark, Tennessee, January 27, 1930.*

Sometimes called the "Sinatra of R&B singers,"

Bobby "Blue" Bland remained a favorite of much of the black community into the mid-1980s. To that time he was still able, after more than forty years as a performer, to place singles and albums on black charts. Over the years, his recordings had appeared from time to time on the general pop charts in the United States, but he never achieved the status with nonblack audiences that his vocal abilities merited, though he did make unexpected inroads in that sector in the 1990s. However, he did have an influence on white rock musicians and the development of blues rock formats at home and abroad, a contribution recognized by his election to the Rock and Roll Hall of Fame in 1992. In the late 1980s and into the '90s, the rise of rap and the appearance of many successful young black pop and soul performers eroded Bobby's potential for chart hits. By then, though, he was focusing more on the gritty roots blues stylings of his younger days and attracting a different, if smaller, audience.

He was born in the small town of Rosemark, Tennessee, though for quite a few years, record company biographies attributed that honor to Memphis. In his early years, he was singing gospel music, but later, influenced by records by Blind Lemon Jefferson, he tended to country-style blues accompanying himself on the guitar. After his family moved to Memphis in 1944, he began to pay attention to the urban blues personified by artists such as Sonny Boy Williamson and B. B. King. (*See King, B. B.*) In high school in the mid-1940s, he formed his own R&B group and played for school dances and assemblies. During that period, he also was part of a gospel group, the Miniatures.

Seeking to improve his contacts in the music field, Bobby got a job as a valet for B. B. King and later worked as a chauffeur for bluesman Rosco Gordon. But he didn't give up performing during those years. Among his sideline projects was singing with a Memphis-based group called the Beale Streeters, whose members included the late Johnny Ace.

By the early 1950s, Bobby had met many other artists in the dynamic R&B field, which was then helping give birth to what was to become known as rock 'n' roll. One of the people impressed with his potential was Ike Turner, who produced some demos for presentation to Modern Records. However, it was local promoter Don Robey, head of Duke Records, who gave Bobby his first big opportunity. After hearing Bland perform in a Houston, Texas, talent show, Robey signed the artist to his label. After several mid-1950s singles had small impact on the record audience, Bobby and Duke scored a major hit in 1957 with the single "Farther up the Road." He placed some records on lower chart levels in 1958 and then came back strong with a top 10 single, "I'll Take Care of You," early in 1960. He topped this with three major hits: "Cry, Cry, Cry" (1960), "Turn on Your Love Light" (1962), and "Lead Me On." Some of these not only made the R&B charts but the pop lists as

well, resulting in Bobby's gaining notice as a top rock artist.

Bland steadily increased his list of singles successes in the 1960s, starting off in 1961 with "Don't Cry No More" and the number-one–ranked "I Pity The Fool." In 1962, he had three more top 10 R&B singles: "Yield Not to Temptation," "Stormy Monday," and "Ain't That Loving You." He was now one of the most important names in the R&B and rock fields and commanded top fees for in-person appearances in major cities across the United States. He was also gaining a considerable reputation in Europe, as was underlined by the success of "Call on Me" in 1963, which was in the English top 10 and sold over a million copies in the United States and abroad. He also had a number one R&B hit that year, "That's the Way Love Is."

In the mid-1960s, Bland continued his steady pace. He hit with "Ain't Nothin' You Can Do" in 1964, "These Hands" in 1964, and three successes in 1966: "Poverty," "Good Time Charlie," and "I'm Too Far Gone (to Turn Around)."

Bland's career quieted down for a time in 1967 and 1968. His record sales fell and there seemed to be slightly less interest in him on the club circuit. Some observers thought Bobby might be losing rapport with the younger fans. But he came back strong in 1969 with singles hits "Gotta Get to Know You" and "Chains of Love." He continued to demonstrate his popularity as the '70s began with top 20 singles "If Love Ruled the World"/"Lover with a Reputation" in 1970, "Keep on Loving Me" in the winter of 1970–71, and "I'm Sorry" in 1971.

Bobby was more successful as a singles artist than an album performer. He did account for a reasonable sales total with such LPs as *Soul of a Man, Call on Me, Two Stops from the Blues,* and *Here's the Man* on Duke, although his LPs rarely made the top chart levels. This situation began to change in the early 1970s after Duke Records was purchased by ABC Records. The additional promotion of a larger record firm gave more impetus to that side of his career. ABC and later MCA (which acquired ABC) reissued many of Bland's early LPs until, at the start of the 1980s, almost all of Bobby's albums were in print. (MCA noted that Bland was the only artist to have recorded for Duke, ABC, and MCA in succession.) His album credits from his early years with Duke to his MCA affiliation included: *Two Steps from the Blues* and *Call on Me* (1963), *Ain't Nothin' You Can Do* (1964), *The Soul of the Man, The Best of Bobby Bland, Volume 2,* and *Touch of the Blues* (1968), and *Spotlighting the Man* and *Introspective of the Early Years* (all on Duke); *His California Album* (1973), *Dreamer* (1974), *Get on Down with Bobby Bland* (1975), *Reflections in Blue* (1977), and *Come Fly with Me* (1978) (on ABC); and *I Feel Good, I Feel Fine* (1979) and *Sweet Vibrations* (1980) (both on MCA). Reuniting Bland with his long-ago boss from his days as a valet were *B. B. King and Bobby Bland Together for the First Time . . . Live* (gold, 1974) and *Bobby Bland and B. B. King Together Again . . . Live* (1976).

His name continued to show up on the black music charts with such albums as *You've Got Me Loving You* (MCA, 1981), *Here We Go Again* (MCA, mid-1982, on charts into 1983) and *Members Only* (Malaco, 1985).

It was during Bobby's association with Malaco Records that he began moving away from his more polished R&B vocals to the rough-edged country-blues he favored in his teens. He continued in this vein in the follow-up albums for Malaco: *After All, Midnight Run, Blues You Can Use, Years of Tears, Sad Street,* and *The Best of Bobby Bland*. Meanwhile, renewed interest in the folk and blues genres among new generations of music fans in the 1990s expanded his potential audience. This was reflected, for instance, in his reception at the Long Beach, California, Blues Festival, held at California State College in late summer 1996. As reviewer Cheo Hodari Coker wrote in the *Los Angeles Times* ("Singer Bland Turns It On at Long Beach Blues Fest," September 2, 1996), when Bobby walked onstage he "looked out over the sea of faces and smiled. Hooting and hollering, the crowd acted as if it was honored to be in his presence. After 44 years of recording, Bland is only starting to get the kind of accolades he deserves, and he basked in the attention before singing his heart out for 80 minutes."

The fact that Bland was able to complete such a demanding performance surprised some music industry people, considering that he had undergone triple bypass surgery during 1995. But once recovered, Bland resumed his intensive touring schedule that kept him on the road twenty-five to thirty weeks a year as of the end of 1998.

During the February 1997 Grammy Awards TV program, Bland was honored by the National Academy of Recording Arts and Sciences, which presented him with its prestigious Lifetime Achievement Award. The following year, on November 10, 1998, he was similarly honored by the Blues Foundation at its awards meeting in the Los Angeles House of Blues. He was nominated for a Traditional Blues Grammy for his 1999 album *Memphis Monday Morning*.

Several compilations of his work came out on CD in the 1990s, including *I Pity the Fool/The Duke Recordings Volume 1* (1992), *Turn on Your Love Light: The Duke Recordings Volume 2* (1994), *That Did It! The Duke Recordings Volume 3* (1994), *How Blue Can You Get: Classic Live Performances 1964–94* (1996), and *The Voice: Duke Recordings 1959–1969.*

BLEGVAD, PETER: *Singer, songwriter, guitarist, cartoonist. Born New York, New York, August 14, 1951.*

As Peter Blegvad sings in one of his better-known songs, "King Strut," *Imagination, like a muscle, will increase with exercise.*

Blegvad, an underground alternative musician based in London, is certainly one of the more offbeat singer-songwriters around. He incorporates nonsensical, dreamlike palindromes in some of his songs: witness the line *"Peel's foe, not a set animal, laminates a tone of sleep."* His wordplay has allowed this thin, professional-looking man, who is reminiscent of Lou Reed, to gain a cult following. His more recent albums are more folkie and less convoluted. Since 1991 his cartoon strip, *Leviathan,* has appeared weekly in London's *Independent on Sunday* magazine.

Blegvad was born in New York City to Lenore Hochman Blegvad, a children's book author and illustrator, and Danish-born Erik Blegvad, an illustrator of children's books. He grew up in Westport, Connecticut. Blegvad's first instrument was the clarinet, but he stopped playing because his braces interfered with his embrasure. He took up the guitar in 1964 after Beatlemania swept the United States. As he wrote recently: "[I took] a few lessons but basically [I was] an illiterate autodidact."

In 1966, his parents moved to England. He attended St. Christopher's in Letchworth, Hertfordshire. An English teacher, poet Peter Scupham, inspired him to study literature and, as Blegvad put it, "the life of the mind." He became interested in William Butler Yeats, and William Blake. (It was at boarding school that he met pianist Anthony Moore, a musical accomplice.) "I thought in order to be an artist I've got to have vision, like William Blake I thought I should go mad," he told Phil England of *The Wire,* tongue planted firmly in cheek (January 1996).

He attended Exeter University and Exeter College of Arts. He was working on a bachelor of arts with combined honors in English literature and fine art but dropped out in 1971, a few months before his finals. He moved to West Germany and began his career with a number of politically leftist-leaning bands: Slapp Happy, Faust, and Henry Cow. He spent several months in 1971 and 1972 in Germany, leading the avant-garde Slapp Happy with Anthony Moore on keyboards and Dagmar Krause, a German, on vocals. "I was corrupted by Anthony Moore, who lured me from university to Hamburg to make parodic pop music," he wrote.

Blegvad made three albums with Slapp Happy: *Sort Of, Acnalbasac Noom* (Casablanca Moon backwards) for ReR Megacorp of London, and *Slapp Happy* for Virgin. Blegvad also played with a German group called Faust, which was closely aligned with Slapp Happy. He performed with Faust in both England and West Germany and recorded *Faust IV* for ReR in 1973.

In 1975, Slapp Happy merged with Henry Cow, a British band formed in 1968 at Cambridge University. Henry Cow included John Greaves on bass; Fred Frith on guitar, keyboards, and violin; Tim Hodgkinson on keyboards and sax; and Chris Cutler on drums. Blegvad made two albums with them: *In Praise of Learning* and

BLIND BOYS OF ALABAMA; FIVE BLIND BOYS OF ALABAMA; CLARENCE FOUNTAIN & THE BLIND BOYS OF ALABAMA: *Vocal group (sometimes a cappella, sometimes with backing band). Original members, late 1930s, Clarence Fountain, born 1930; Velma Bozman Traylor, died 1947; Johnny Fields; J. T. Hutton; Ollice Thomas; George Scott. Members in 1994, Fountain, Scott, Fields, Jimmy Carter, reduced to Fountain, Scott, and Carter in 1995.*

One of the most acclaimed and longest lasting gospel groups—still going strong with two founding members fifty years after it began—the Blind Boys group finally moved from the relatively narrow confines of its chosen field to win attention for its artistry from secular fans in the late 1980s and the 1990s. While its repertoire didn't exclude secular songs—numbers like the Pete Seeger favorite "If I Had a Hammer" and the Isley Brothers' "Shout" were features of their performances in later years—the members never moved away from their gospel roots, shunning the material successes that could have come their way from making rock or R&B recordings.

The nominal leader for much of the group's career, Clarence Fountain, recalled that hearing gospel singers on radio in the mid-1930s had influenced the youngsters' decisions in life. The first group he heard was the Heavenly Gospel Singers, but the main impact came from the broadcasts of the Golden Gate Quartet on the NBC *Magic Key Hour* starting in 1937. Fountain, singing in the glee club of the Talledaga Institute for the Deaf and Blind, along with Velma Bozman Traylor, helped organize some of their friends—Johnny Fields, J. T. Hutton (the only one who wasn't blind), Ollice Thomas, and George Scott—into a group they named the Happy Land Jubilee Singers. He recalled, "We were just a bunch of happy guys" who enjoyed singing together.

Starting in 1939, the members sought performances that might be economically rewarding. The onset of World War II in the early '40s and establishment of training camps near the school helped their cause. As Fountain told Dave Peabody for *Folk Roots* magazine, "The school was not happy for us to go off campus, but we would sneak out. We would go out and make some money. There was a big soldier camp up there, had about ten or twelve thousand soldiers. We'd perform for that soldier camp and we'd do alright." One of the favorites with the troops was their version of the 1942 Golden Gate Quartet song, "Stalin Wasn't Stallin.'"

Fountain and his friends covered a lot more songs featured on recordings by the Golden Gate Quartet and, although they added many others from different sources over the years, including originals penned by Fountain and other members, their concerts still included songs derived from Fountain's favorites. In the group's 1995 House of Blues album, for instance, they had three inspiring versions of such Golden Gate numbers: "Didn't It Rain," "Hush, Somebody's Calling My Name," and "Listen to the Lambs." Fountain told Peabody, "Those were the people that we really patterned ourselves after. They made the current chords and we made 'em, too; they didn't sing hard, they just sang jubilee. They sang a lot of music."

In 1945, the six friends decided to drop out of school and seek engagements on the gospel circuit. They were beginning to make a name for themselves with churchgoers in 1947 when lead singer Velma Bozman Traylor accidentally shot and killed himself. For a while his place was taken by the Rev. Paul Exkano, who shared lead vocals with Fountain. Now known as the Happy Land Gospel Singers, the group made its record debut in 1948 on New Jersey–based Coleman Records with the song "I Can See Everybody's Mother But Mine."

That same year, down to five members, the group suddenly became the Five Blind Boys of Alabama. Fountain told Larry Katz of the *Boston Herald* ("The Gospel According to Clarence Fountain," July 28, 1995), the Happy Land Singers had been slowly extending their circuit of church appearances and had an engagement in Newark, New Jersey, with another group, the Jackson Harmonies from Mississippi. "They had a great promoter there named Ronnie Williams," he told Katz. "He billed it as a contest between the Blind Boys of Alabama and the Blind Boys of Mississippi. He made a big deal of it. He didn't ask us, just did it. When we realized it was drawing people, we kept the name. And so did the other group."

The high spot of each concert came toward the end when Fountain and Blind Boys of Mississippi lead singer Archie Brownlee tried to outsing each other. As Fountain told Seamus McGarvey in a *Blues & Rhythm* magazine interview, "Every night I had to battle it out with him. Who would the people like best—and may the best man win! At the end of the show, we would come down the aisle, shake hands and collaborate together. That was really exciting. Archie, he could sing you to death."

The competition soon drew large crowds, and for a time Fountain and his associates were in better financial condition than other groups performing on the gospel circuit. Fountain told interviewer Pepper Smith of *Rejoice!* "We racked up. I must have had $5,000 in my pocket by December. In 1955, that was mighty good."

The group also had more recording opportunities. After three 1950s releases on Palda Records, *Come Over Here on the Table Spread, Livin on Mothers Prayers,* and *Sweet Honey in the Rock,* the Blind Boys signed with Specialty Records. In 1952, they had their best-selling single of the '50s, "When I Lost My Mother (I Lost the Best Friend I Ever Had)." Their releases on the label included *When I Lost My Mother* in 1953, followed by *Stand by Me* and *Marching to Zion.* In the late '50s, the Blind Boys were represented on still more labels, with Vee Jay issuing *I'll Never Walk Alone* in 1957 and *My Mother's Train* in 1958, and Savoy Records releasing *The Original Blind Boys* and *God Is on the Throne,* both in 1959.

As Mark Humphrey reported in notes for a House of Blues Blind Boys release, "In the early '60s, the 'hard Gospel' drive pioneered by groups like the Five Blind Boys of Alabama was effectively co-opted by R&B; Bobby 'Blue' Bland's 'Yield Not to Temptation' and Marvin Gaye's 'Can I Get a Witness' were secularized church exhortations." Fountain and his friends still found work performing in churches in the 1960s and had more opportunities to record, particularly for Vee Jay in the early to mid years of the decade. Long out of print by the 1990s, many of the group's 1960s recordings were reissued in a series of House of Blues albums: *I Saw the Light*; *Best of the Blind Boys, Volumes 1 & 2*; *Can I Get a Witness*; *True Conviction*; and *It's Sweet to Be Saved.*

The group closed out the decade with the 1969 Keen Records release *Fix It Jesus Like You Said It Would.* The album featured one of Fountain's most striking lead vocal efforts, "Do Lord Remember Me," performed with blues singer Koko Taylor. By the start of the '70s, Fountain had left the group. He hoped to do better as a soloist than a group member. He told Katz, "We figured if we could work our way into the white market, it would be great. But we could never figure out how to make it happen. That was why I left. When I came back, things came together."

The reorganized Blind Boys kept on seeking performing dates, and some of their material from those years was included in the PIR Records 1978 release *The Soldier Album* and the 1981 Messiah Records collection *Faith Moves Mountains.*

With Fountain back in the fold, the fortunes of the group took a turn for the better in the second half of the 1980s. The key milestone was their selection to be the stars of the 1988 Pentecostal Gospel version of the ancient Greek story of Oedipus. Called *The Gospel at Colonus,* the show created a sensation when it debuted in New York in 1988, winning an Obie Award. The Blind Boys toured with the stage production, winning new fans and excellent reviews, opening new opportunities for the group in the 1990s when audiences cheered the Blind Boys sets at major blues and jazz festivals in the United States and elsewhere.

The group had two new albums on the Wajji Records label as the '80s ended and the '90s began, *I'm a Changed Way* in 1989 and *Brand New Way* in 1990. The Blind Boys were also guest artists on country singer k.d. lang's platinum-selling 1990 release on Sire/Warner Bros., *Absolute Torch and Twang.* The group followed in 1991 with the Atlanta Int'l Records album *I'm Not That Way Anymore* and its first album on a major label, the superb *Deep River,* released by Elektra/Nonesuch in 1992. In the mid-1990s Fountain

and company signed with the House of Blues organization, leading to the critically acclaimed 1995 HOB label debut, *I Brought Him With Me.* The album was recorded live by the group in January 1995, its first live collection and, when issued on August 29, became HOB's first release of new material.

That album was nominated for a Grammy, like *Deep River* before it. Prior to the HOB project, the group completed one track with Bonnie Raitt and one with David Hidalgo of Los Lobos for the 1994 Capitol Records album *Beat the Retreat,* a tribute to Richard Thompson. Among the Blind Boys honors in these years was their presentation by First Lady Hillary Clinton of a National Endowment for the Arts Heritage Fellowship for Lifetime Achievement.

In 1997, the group again was touring major venues, like the Cerritos, California, Center for the Performing Arts, with *Gospel at Colonus,* jointly performing the role of Oedipus. Other artists taking part included the Original Soul Stirrers and, at Cerritos, the L. A. Joy. Roscoe Lee Browne was cast in the role of the Messenger-Preacher, handled in the original version by film star Morgan Freeman.

Looking back at the origins of the show, Clarence Fountain noted it had been created by writer-director Lee Breuer and composer–music director Bob Telson as a short, thirty- to thirty-five minute set piece. When he first heard that version, Fountain told Don Heckman of the *Los Angeles Times* ("Spirit of 'Colonus' Still Moves This Group," March 3, 1997, pp. F1, F4), "I thought it sounded horrible, because they had no concept of gospel as I preferred it. So we had to tear it up and piece it back together—add more singing, more everything, to help give it a whole new outlook. And that was a big change, a lot more than a face lift." The result was a full-length show that, over the years, won Obie (Off-Broadway), Tony, and Grammy Awards as well as being nominated for a Pulitzer Prize.

BLOCK, RORY: *singer, songwriter, guitarist. Born Princeton, New Jersey, November 6, 1949.*

Rory Block takes to the stage at B.B. King's Blues Club in Los Angeles like a *Tornado,* the title of her 1996 record on Rounder. Dressed in black from her top to her spike-heeled boots, she stomps, twirls, and shakes her long brown hair. Despite her frenetic movements, she somehow focuses on her singing and guitar playing as she opens with "Mississippi Bottom Blues" backed by a five-man band, including her son Jordan Valdina on percussion. Later, alone on the stage with a guitar and a slide, she plays Robert Johnson's "Terraplane Blues." She has studied Johnson's eerie slide sounds from scratchy old records. But she really haunts the audience with her rendition of Andy Barnes's "The Last Leviathan," a song about environmental and nuclear holocaust. With red, purple, and green stage lights highlighting her face, and a groaning organ accompaniment, Block modulates her voice and aches with the pain of the earth.

They say you can't just play the blues, you have to feel it. Block learned from some of the best—Son House, the Rev. Gary Davis, and Mississippi John Hurt—who used to drop by her father's sandal shop in Greenwich Village. But Block, a white woman who grew up in New York City, has also had enough pain in her life to match the Delta blues kings. She ran away from home at age fifteen with guitarist Stefan Grossman to embark on a music career. Onstage, night after night, she would play her steel-stringed guitar until her fingers bled. The biggest blow came in 1986, when her son Thiele died in an auto accident at the age of nineteen. But she has had her share of success. Her 1995 album, *When a Woman Gets the Blues,* won a W. C. Handy Award (she had been nominated twice before), and she has received wider airplay and recognition since then with her 1996 album, *Tornado.*

"I was often asked, 'Why is a young white girl from New York City bonding with music from the rural South, music from the black culture of the '30s?'" she told Paul Freeman of the *West County Times* (Richmond, California, April 8, 1994). "You can't explain why your soul resonates with something. It's just that you've fallen in love with that music."

She was born Aurora Block but was nicknamed Rory at an early age. Her mother, Eleanor Jean Keller, was a singer and painter. Her father, who owned Allan Block's Sandal Shop on West Fourth Street, played old-timey banjo and fiddle. He introduced his daughter to the music of Roscoe Holcomb and Charlie Poole. In the 1960s his shop became a gathering place for folk and blues musicians, including Hurt, Doc Watson, John Sebastian, and Bob Dylan. At age eight, Block began studying classical guitar. But with all the blues greats around, and with her discovery of records by Son House and Robert Johnson (the first album she heard was *Really! the Country Blues*), she was drawn to country blues. Starting at age twelve, she learned riffs note-by-note from the records. She now believes that her classical training, combined with the influence of Delta blues records and players she met, helped her develop a distinctive sound. At age fourteen, she played Robert Johnson's "Walkin' Blues" for Son House, who was shocked by the talent of the adolescent girl before him.

"I don't have any conscious awareness that I do what I do because of watching [Son House]," Block told Elijah Wald of *Acoustic Guitar* (December 1995). "But sometimes I see the connection myself and I realize, wow, he rolled his head back and rolled his eyes and did some similar things. So maybe I picked it up from him without realizing it."

Despite their apparent liberalism, her parents weren't supportive of young Rory's aspirations to sing the blues. "The message I got was that it was unfeminine to have a career, and that I should get married and have

children, despite the fact that I came from a musical, bohemian family," she told *Guitar Extra* in 1991. "I believed that if I tried to have a career, there would be something very negative about me as a person. It took me years to get over it." She and blues guitarist Grossman, who had given her her first blues album, went to Berkeley, California. A year later they cut an instructional album for Elektra called *How to Play Blues Guitar* for Grossman's Kicking Mule. But she dropped out of the music scene from the mid-'60s through the mid-'70s, during which time she had two sons, Thiele and Jordan.

In 1975 she returned to music, recording her debut, *Rory Block (I'm in Love)* on the Blue Goose label. While she hoped to return to the blues-influenced sounds she had learned as a child, instead she made a few, overly produced pop albums for Chrysalis Records: *Intoxication So Bittersweet* (1977) and *You're The One* (1978). She soon became disillusioned with the major record labels, who wanted her to record a disco album to capitalize on the craze.

She told Jym Fahey of *Relix* (June 1983): "Everyone said that the blues isn't commercial, and that I'd never make a living at it. I think the implication was that women artists have no idea what they're doing, so they have to be controlled by producers, all of whom were, of course, men. I did the vocals and went home. Everyone else made the record around me. I didn't like it at all." Her song "Big Bad Agent Man" on *Angel of Mercy* (1994) lashes out against the pinky-ringed agents of her past. "You got a wig for your hair, rings on every finger, big-time connections . . . ," she sings.

In 1981, she signed with Rounder Records, which gave her the artistic freedom she desired. She has made a dozen albums on the Rounder label, beginning with *High Heeled Blues* (1981), which was produced by John Sebastian and featured traditional blues and a smattering of originals. The blues tunes she selected, however, included subject matter that pertained to women, a trend that she would continue throughout her career on later albums such as *Mama's Blues* (1991) and *When a Woman Gets the Blues* (1995). As she progressed she began to include more of her own songs, some of them influenced by folk and country sounds, but always with a bluesy timbre.

"It took years until I felt really comfortable, until I got unself-conscious about songwriting, until I dropped the feeling that it was something I had to do in a certain way and it better be good or else—and just wrote songs for myself," she told Whitley Setrakian of *Spotlight* (June 3–17, 1993).

Like Bonnie Raitt, who was born under the same sign, Block put her own signature on the blues. *Mama's Blues* includes interpretations of Robert Johnson's "Terraplane Blues," Tommy Johnson's "Big Road Blues," and Bessie Smith's "Do Your Duty" and "Weeping Willow Blues." In the 1992 release *Ain't I a*

Woman, she shows off her slide guitar playing in another Robert Johnson tune, "Come on in My Kitchen," Lottie Beamon's "Rolling Log," and Tommy Johnson's "Maggie Campbell" and "A Cool Drink of Water." She includes six original compositions as well.

She seemed to be moving toward folk, gospel, and pop. She softened some of her vocals and used Joni Mitchell–like octave jumps on some of her songs. But the blues influence remains.

"It's still a blend," she told the *News Tribune* (Tacoma, Washington, April 15, 1994). "I can't imagine a show without a bunch of blues in it. . . . It's just a part of me. Even if I have a total songwriter album, there's blues influences throughout."

Angel of Mercy is almost entirely composed of originals. The album was supposed to mark an end of ten years of touring around in her big motor home, "spent in one massive, seemingly endless tour." "I'll Be Gone," which includes harmonica work by John Sebastian, is a touring song.

As Block, who now lives in Chatham, New York, told the *News Tribune,* "I got to a point where I had to come to a grinding halt . . . I was so fried and so tired of going back and forth to Europe and going out on the road here and not being out in my flower garden and missing everything."

In "Somebody's Baby" she sings about meeting a pregnant homeless woman on the highway. Three of her songs are about love as a woman grows older: "Love without the Heart," "You Deserve the Best," and "Angel of Mercy."

Linda Gruno wrote in *Westword* (April 20, 1994): "Block is known as a woman who doesn't hide her feelings, a quality that has endeared her to fans even as it has won her a reputation as temperamental and occasionally abrasive."

She returned to her country blues roots with *When a Woman Gets the Blues* a year later, and back to original compositions with *Tornado.* (Mary-Chapin Carpenter and fiddler Stuart Duncan back her on "You Didn't Mind," and David Lindley backs her on a single from *Tornado,* "Pictures of You.") She also returned to the road in 1996. She told Wald that she had contemplated retirement after having a "bad health episode" but that she hasn't "saved any money. I've made myself a beautiful surroundings in upstate New York; I've fixed up my old house, put in gardens and landscaping and trees so that I don't see the road, and I have my beautiful bus and creature comforts that make me feel a lot of joy. But sometimes I wish I could take some time off."

The death of her son Thiele is never far from Block's memory. Her 1987 album, *House of Hearts,* was a tribute to Thiele. As she told Gruno, "I'll never put it away. That would dishonor my son totally if I just sort of went past it. I feel like it honors him when people talk about him or ask me about him. It may make me sad, but then I needed to get sad. If he was not

mentioned again, I would probably be sad about that. It's a part of our living experiences that people die, and to deny it would be unhealthy."

She has recorded at least two songs with her other son, Jordan: "Walk in Jerusalem" on her *Ain't I a Woman* album and "A Father and Two Sons" on *Angel of Mercy.* Block and her son blend well together as they sing the story of the prodigal son in the latter. The American Bible Society, in an effort to recapture the oral traditions of the Bible, used the song to film a video of the parable. Jordan sings the part of the younger son in a song dedicated to his older brother.

"Because of Thiele," Block told Paul Freeman of the *West County Times,* "Jordan and I feel deeply connected to the words 'Your brother was dead and now he's alive; he was lost and now he's found.'"

Jordan played a big role in Block's concert at B.B. King's in March 1996. He introduced his mother, sang backup, and did a rapping introduction of the band as his mom danced around the stage. *Tornado* provided much of the material for the concert. She performed her single from the album, "Pictures of You," which she said was about meeting her husband, who accompanied her on the tour. It was clear by the end of the concert that she had expended all of her energy.

"I go directly into this performing mode with a massive amount of energy," she told Ed Symkus of the *Tab* (April 9–15, 1996). "I may even be sick beforehand, and I go out there and have this huge rush of energy, I play hard and I go into another dimension. Then I come offstage and I get almost hypothermia. I cool off too fast and start shivering."

Some of her other Rounder releases include *Blue Horizon* (1983), *Rhinestones and Steel Strings* (1983), *I've Got a Rock in My Sock* (1986) (with Taj Mahal and David Bromberg), *Best Blues & Originals* (1987) (which went gold in Holland), and *House of Hearts* (1987). She recorded *Color Me Wild,* a children's album, for Alcazam! in 1990. In 1990, she also released *The Early Tapes: 1975–1976* on Alcazar (and Munich) records, which included traditional blues songs and some originals. Munich Records also released *Turning Point* (1989, 1995). She has also recorded two instructional videos for Homespun of Woodstock, New York: *The Guitar of Rory Block: Blues and Originals* and *The Power of Delta Blues Guitar.*

In 1997, Rounder released Rory's next album *Gone Woman Blues: The Country Blues Collection.* As the title suggests, the CD includes twenty-four tracks (most of them previously recorded) of her playing classics by people like Robert Johnson, Tommy Johnson, and Bessie Smith. The following year she released her thirteenth recording on Rounder, *Confessions of a Blues Singer.* Bonnie Raitt played slide guitar on Robert Johnson's "Ramblin' on My Mind" track. Jordan plays piano and sings on Bukka White's "Long Way Home." The collection also includes Block's renditions of

Robert Johnson's "If I Had Possession Over Judgment Day," Blind Willie McTell's "Statesboro Blues," and Charley Patton's "Bo Weavil Blues."

In 1996, *Tornado* won the National Association of Independent Record Distributors Best Adult Contemporary Album award. In 1997 and 1998 she won W. C. Handy Awards for Traditional Blues Female Artist of the Year. She also won the Trophées France Blues International Guitariste Acoustique award for 1998. In 1997 she posed with her guitar for print ads for Martin Guitar Strings. In late 1998 she toured Holland, Belgium, and England. She also began a tour of the United States in January 1999.

BLOOM, LUKA: *Singer, guitarist, songwriter. Born Kildare, Ireland, May 23, 1955.*

The youngest of six children raised in a rural section of Ireland not far from Dublin, Luka Bloom could look up to the musical exploits of his much older brother, Christy Moore, one of the founding members of Planxty and Moving Hearts, whose reputation extended to almost every corner of the world from the early 1970s into the 1990s. In time, Luka established himself as a creative talent on the modern music scene, not as a band member but as a unique, charismatic solo performer. His stage career blossomed not under his original name of Barry Moore but under the new name he chose for himself on a flight from Ireland to the United States in 1987.

Singing or playing instruments always was an interest of his immediate family and relatives, and young Barry was nine years old when someone loaned him a guitar to play. He told Beth C. Fishkind of *Acoustic Guitar* magazine in 1992, "When I first put the guitar on my leg, I felt a bond with the instrument, like I had played it before." When he got a guitar of his own a few years later, he set about conscientiously to become an adept player, paying particular attention to finger picking performers such as Bert Jansch, John Renbourn, Ralph McTell, and Doc Watson.

Apart from guitar techniques, he stressed, his primary musical influences came from outside Ireland. As he told Link Yaco of the *Ann Arbor News*, Ann Arbor, Michigan ("Bloom: Irish sensibility, American style," July 12, 1994), that didn't mean he was unaffected by the rhythms of his homeland. "They're so deeply ingrained in me that I don't have to think about it. It's not something I study, not something I analyze, not something I promote. My Irishness is an accident of birth which I'm very happy about. . . . But the music that has influenced me has always come from America. . . .

"I started out being influenced by Joni Mitchell and the very early James Taylor records. They had an effect on me as a young 14, 15 year old guy in rural Ireland who walked around and wanted to write songs. They were the people I focused on. And some of the English guitar players as well, like John Renbourn."

While continuing to write new songs and also perform when the chance arose locally, he entered college for a time, then dropped out in the mid-1970s in favor of increasing his musical experience on the folk club circuit at home and in other parts of Europe. In the late '70s and early '80s as Barry Moore, he recorded three albums using his self-taught finger-picking guitar style: *Treaty Stone* (1978) on Mulligan, *In Groningen* (1980) on Kolet, Holland, and *No Heroes* (1982) on Ruby/WEA. Then that phase of his career came to an end due to development of severe tendonitis of his right elbow, partly the result of his self-taught technique. Surgery was suggested, but he decided against it because of, among other reasons, his lack of medical insurance.

He told Fishkind, "I decided to rest completely, rather than go a round of surgery," and took two years off from performing. At the end of that period, he went to a different instrument style. "I threw away my fingers and picked up a plectrum." This strumming approach is easier on his arm, but he still must be careful not to abuse it, icing the elbow after each show or recording session and taking physiotherapy treatments when home in Dublin.

Before resuming his performing activities, he got even more involved in songwriting and also listened closely to material performed by such rock bands as Simple Minds, the Waterboys, and U2. When he started working again in the mid-1980s, he briefly fronted a rock band called Red Square before deciding he didn't want to give up his solo format. He had changed in a number of ways by then, broadening his musical tastes to include inputs not only from rock and folk but all manner of new stylings coming to the forefront around the world. He also had ended the alcohol abuse of his teens and early twenties. He told Michael Azerrad for an article in *Rolling Stone* ("Luka Bloom doesn't want to be just another boring folkie," March 19, 1992), "I was very fortunate. Drinking did not stimulate my songwriting, did not stimulate my imagination—it completely deadened and depressed everything I wanted to do, and thank God it did. I probably wouldn't be alive today if I had some success."

In 1987, he pondered his situation and decided he needed to take some dramatic actions to jump-start his creative options. He told Azerrad, "I said, 'Okay, I'm thirty-two years old. I'm going to change my name, and I'm going to America, and I'm going to stay there until something happens.'" In the process he left behind a longtime girlfriend and a son by a previous marriage. He booked a flight to Washington, D.C., and on the plane conjured up his new name taking Luka from a song by Suzanne Vega and Bloom from the central character in James Joyce's book *Ulysses.*

Arriving in Washington with a guitar and only $200, he set about finding work, making the rounds of clubs until he finally won a hearing from one that was willing to book him for weekend gigs. He chose instead to perform on week nights as a way to draw listeners to his kind of act. Soon after he also gained a steady date at the Red Lion in New York's Greenwich Village, and for four months commuted on Amtrak between the Big Apple and Washington before making New York his main base of U.S. operations. He was beginning to attract attention not only from music fans but also from many other rising young performers including the Indigo Girls and Sinéad O'Connor. With his powers of persuasion, he soon expanded his audience to many other parts of the United States by talking his way into opening spots on tours by the Pogues and Hothouse Flowers bands.

Helped by glowing reviews of his performances, his following expanded steadily. As *People* magazine reported in a late 1980s issue, "Luka Bloom hoots like a steam engine, laughs like a madman, spits out the lyrics and strums acoustic guitar with the ferocity of a speeding locomotive."

Actually, Bloom played a semi-acoustic guitar. As he told Fishkind, "The acousto-electric is just perfect for me. It's the tool to do what I want to do with my life, without feedback and distortion I can play loud with a beautiful semi-acoustic guitar on my own and fill a stadium." His goal was to try to have his guitar, in effect, substitute for a band. "I'll do *anything* to get any possible noise, because as a solo artist, it's difficult to sustain an audience's attention for over one hour unless dynamics are written in."

A record contract was a key element in his plans, of course, but he took a different approach than many aspiring newcomers. He refused to send a demo tape around, but instead asked executives to attend various showcases, which eventually brought a contract with Warner Brothers' Reprise label in the summer of 1989. He commented, "If I had ever given a tape to anyone they would only have said, 'Yes, we love it, but how about adding a fretless bass here or something else there.' Anyone who wanted to sign me had to see my performance so as to understand where I was coming from and just where I was going to. They had first to understand the whole picture."

He recorded *Luka Bloom* in 1988 for Mystery Records in Dublin. But the album was withdrawn almost as soon as it came out. By the fall of '89, Luka was well along in completing the tracks for his Reprise debut. While not opposing the use of backing musicians, he took the approach that he would do his material first, singing and playing guitar simultaneously, with any backing tracks laid down afterward. He told Azerrad, "Everything I do goes down first, so the source of the record is coming from here (pointing to his heart)." Released in early 1990, the new collection, *Riverside,* ranked as one of the more impressive debuts of the year, featuring such excellent songs as "An Irishman in Chinatown," "You Couldn't Have Come at a Better Time," "Delirious," and "Hudson Lady."

By the time his second album, *Acoustic Motorbike,* came out in 1992, Bloom had once more made Ireland his primary residence, settling his family in a house on Raglan Road in Dublin. To prepare new songs and consider possible covers, he retired to a small house in the west of Ireland, escaping mental fatigue from time to time by taking long motorbike rides. This inspired the title track, a "folk-rap" composition written by Luka. It was one of two such songs in the album, the other being an innovative cover of the U.S. rapper LL Cool J's "I Need Love." While Bloom does the rap lyrics on the cuts, the musical accompaniment is much more melodic than on ghetto rap recordings. Luka's brother Christy Moore and the Hothouse Flowers were among the backing musicians, marking the first time the two worked together. Moore played the traditional Irish drum, the bodhran, on both rap tracks as well as on "Bridge of Sorrow" and "Listen to the Hoofbeat." On Luka's "This Is Your Country," a folk-style plea for Irish emigrants to look homeward, Christy sang backing vocals as well as playing the drum.

Album tracks included Luka's version of an old Elvis Presley hit, "Can't Help Falling in Love," the high-energy rocker "Bones," and "Exploring the Blue." The last named was one of a number of originals by Luka using the word *blue*—a nod to his favorite color, but also a tribute to Joni Mitchell, whose album *Blue* was a strong early influence on Luka's music.

Acoustic Motorbike was warmly received by his adherents, though like his earlier album it did not win universal critical acclaim. One strong vote in his favor came from critics of *Stereo Review,* who named it the best recording of the month for March 1992. Parke Puterbaugh wrote, "Bloom harks back to the days when troubadours converged on the Big Apple with beat-up guitars and a headful of dreams and ideals."

After touring on behalf of the new album, Bloom once more hunkered down in Ireland, doing no major tours for some twelve months from 1992–93. As he told Mike Boehm of the *Los Angeles Times* ("Back on Home 'Turf,'" Calendar section, June 14, 1994), "I felt I had detached myself from Ireland to pursue my work. I felt I had to get reattached to my family and to Ireland. Being on the road, you lose touch after a couple of years with the progress of other people's lives and you become so completely self-absorbed you're transported into this unreality, or maybe a different reality."

When he decided he was ready to renew his musical pursuits, he told Reprise he was going to work on a solo album with essentially no backing support, a return to the sound of his stage shows. In December 1993, with his engineer and coproducers, he began preparing the new tracks in a roomy Dublin studio with concert lights, monitors, and all the attributes of a live show in place, but no audience. Except for vocal backing on one song, "Sunny Sailor Boy" (written by Mike Scott of the Waterboys) by Mairéad Ní Mhaonaigh, everything else on the thirteen numbers in *Turf* is performed only by him. Songs that became high points of later concerts included "Diamond Mountain," expressing the sorrow of Irish emigrants forced to leave their homeland; "Freedom Song," which focused on the actions of Rosa Parks in the United States and Nan Joyce in Ireland in support of minority rights (in Joyce's case, Irish gypsies); and a series of comments on travails of love; "Cold Comfort," "Black Is the Colour," and "Holding Back the River."

Turf was released in mid-1994, and Luka was on the road again to perform before enthusiastic crowds across the United States and in Europe. Most album reviews were laudatory, but as before, there were a few objectors such as Geoffrey Himes of the *Washington Post*, who, while liking the traditional folk song simplicity of "Cold Comfort" and "Black Is the Colour" and the "bouncy playfulness" of "Sunny Sailor Boy," objected to what he called the artist's "narcissistic musings." Another critic, who considered *Turf* an excellent example of the artist's "evocative lyrics, rich voice and impressive guitar-playing," acknowledged, "Luka Bloom isn't everybody's cup of tea, but then again, he doesn't try to be."

He switched to the Columbia label, which released a new critically acclaimed studio album called *Salty Heaven* in 1998. The album, as opposed to previous albums, heavy on drums, bodhran, and strings, is nevertheless clearly inspired by his homeland with songs such as "Holy Ground," "The Hungry Ghost," "Ciara," and "Blackberry Time." He also sings "Rainbow Warrior," an antinuclear song inspired by the activities of Greenpeace. His song "You Couldn't Have Come at a Better Time" was also featured on *Bringing It All Back Home* on BBC Records and a Rhino collection of Irish music, *Legends of Ireland*, that also includes a track by Christy Moore.

BOGGS, DOCK: *Singer, banjoist. Born Dooley, Virginia, February 7, 1898; died February 7, 1971.*

"I was born February 7th, 1898, place of birth, Dooley, Virginia. Long time done away with. I was named after the 1st phisician ever was in Norton, Va. My dad nicknamed me 'Dock' and it has stuck with me ever since."*

It took retirement to bring Moran L. "Dock" Boggs to the forefront of the folk music revival of the 1960s. Many folk song experts had been enthusiastic about rare recordings made by this traditional Virginia mountain singer and banjo player decades earlier and wondered what had happened to him. As he later related, his wife had thought working as a miner a more honorable way to earn a living and to please her he had abandoned his music until he completed forty-one years in the mines in 1954.

Letter to the author, August 21, 1968

Dock first heard folk music from his older brothers and sisters and other family members who played and sang the songs popular in the mountain areas. Dock joined in as soon as he was old enough. The banjo was the main instrument in the Boggs' home, and Dock began to play it in traditional "knockdown or claw hammer style" (that is, with one finger and thumb) when he was twelve. At the same time, he started his long career as a miner.

Dock had been playing the banjo only a short time when he became aware of other techniques employed by black artists. He recalled going to dances frequented by black audiences in places like Dorchester, where "I heard this fellow play the banjo. . . . And I said to myself—I didn't tell anybody else—if I ever, I want to learn how to play the banjo kinda like that fellow does. I don't want to play like my sister and brother. I am going to learn how to pick with my fingers."

And he did just that as he wrote in *Sing Out!* (July 1964, p. 32): "My younger brother Rosco brought a colored man home with him one evening that used to be around Norton. I heard him play 'Alabama Negro.' He played with his forefinger and next finger—two fingers and thumb." From that time on, Dock developed that style of playing to a fine art.

Dock's banjo playing slowed down after he married in 1918. Though devoted to her husband, Mrs. Boggs had a religious upbringing in which secular music was considered sinful. Dock continued to play for his own enjoyment for most of the 1920s, though, and his ability gained much notice among people of his home area. Thus when representatives of Brunswick Records came to Norton in 1927 to look for country music talent, Dock was urged by friends to apply. He finally agreed to go to the tryout in the ballroom of the Norton Hotel. He played his favorite type of "lonesome songs": "Country Blues," "Down South Blues," and "Mean Mistreatin' Mama." The record executive signed him to record twenty-four songs, which he did during 1927 and 1928.

Among songs he recorded, besides those three, were "Sugar Baby," "New Prisoner's Song," and "Sammie, Where Have You Been So Long." One of the first singles issued by Brunswick featured "Down South Blues." According to Charles K. Wolfe ("The White Man's Blues, 1922–40," *Journal of Country Music*, vol. 15, no. 3, 1993), the releases did well enough for the record company to try to get Dock to record more songs, but "Boggs was afraid of being cheated by the company, and demurred."

Boggs, in his writings and interviews in the 1960s, asserted that he had not kept up his performing because the Brunswick contract had increased his wife's unhappiness. He indicated he had essentially put the banjo aside for many years until he retired from the mines. Wolfe, however, pointed out that Boggs had tried several times to find another outlet for his music at the end of the 1920s and in the early 1930s: "On one occasion, Boggs had lined up a new recording session for Victor in June 1931, but couldn't scrape up the money to go there. Another time he went to Atlanta to record for Okeh, but froze at the mike on a radio-show audition and lost out there as well. He signed to record for an independent West Virginia label called Lonesome Ace, but was forced to record compositions by a local lawyer named W. E. Myers."

The latter records, produced in 1929, weren't issued until after the stock market crash triggered the Great Depression, and they found few buyers. By the time Franklin Roosevelt became president, Wolfe noted, Boggs had abandoned thoughts of an entertainment career and resumed a full-time coal mining job.

When Dock began to draw his miner's pension and Social Security in 1954, he later wrote, he was able to concentrate again on his banjo playing. (His Brunswick recording of "Sugar Baby" from 1928 was included on Harry Smith's landmark 1952 collection, the *Anthology of American Folk Music.*) Among other things his wife's attitude had mellowed and he could practice at home whenever he liked. He soon was playing not only for friends and neighbors, but also was attending folk festivals throughout the region. The rising interest in traditional music among young urban artists eventually provided the groundwork for his rediscovery in the 1960s. Mike Seeger sought Dock out at a festival and encouraged him to expand his performing horizons.

Seeger brought word of Boggs's talents to the eastern folk music establishment and set wheels in motion that led to Dock's participation in major folk music festivals. Seeger also helped line up a new recording contract for Dock with Folkways Records. Boggs's debut on that label, *Dock Boggs*, was issued in 1964. In March 1965, another LP of his recordings was issued on the Disc label. In December 1965, Folkways released *Dock Boggs, Volume 2* (with Mike Seeger). Earlier that year, Folkways also issued the album titled *Dock Boggs Interviews* (9/65), in which Boggs's responses to questions by Mike Seeger recalled the environment in which mountain music was performed before the rise of popular recording stars like the Carter Family and Jimmie Rodgers. Verve/Forecast released an album titled *Legendary Dock Boggs* in June 1966, and, in 1967, a third volume of Boggs's performances came out on the Folkways label.

During the mid-1960s, Dock covered much of the United States in concert appearances at folk clubs and on many college campuses. He also was featured at the Newport Folk Festival several times as well as at a number of other major folk festivals.

At the start of the 1980s, three of his LPs remained in Folkways Records' active catalog: *Dock Boggs Interviews*, *Dock Boggs, Volume 2*, and *Dock Boggs, Volume 3*.

In 1983, Folkways issued *Dock Boggs: His Twelve Original Recordings*, which were remastered from Brunswick and Lonesome Ace 78s recorded in the 1920s. In 1997, when Harry Smith's *Anthology of American Folk Music* was reissued on CD by Smithsonian/Folkways, a new generation became entranced by the sounds of performers like Dock Boggs, Buell Kazee, and Bascom Lunsford. In early 1998 Revenant Records issued *Country Blues: Complete Early Recordings*, featuring seventeen recordings that he had made in the 1920s. In the fall of 1998, Smithsonian/Folkways released a two-volume CD set, *Dock Boggs: His Folkways Years 1963–1968*. The reissue featured his last recordings before his death on his birthday in 1971.

BOGLE, ERIC: *Singer, songwriter, guitarist. Born Peebles, Scotland, September 23, 1944.*

Although he was born in Scotland, Eric Bogle jokingly refers to himself as a Scossie. He resides in two worlds: physically in his adopted land, Australia; mentally and emotionally in Scotland. In 1972, perhaps because of his outsider's perspective, he composed one of the best-known Australian folk songs of recent decades, "And the Band Played Waltzing Matilda," although he much prefers a later antiwar song, "No Man's Land." Bogle wrote the powerful antiwar song after viewing a parade of Aussie soldiers who had survived the World War I battle at Gallipoli. The story, told from the perspective of an Australian soldier who lost both legs, has been recorded by June Tabor, Joan Baez, the Pogues, and Tommy Makem and the Clancy Brothers.

Since then Bogle has developed a devoted following for his ability to compress emotion into tightly written stanzas, and his often brutal sense of humor. Bogle's average but not unpleasant baritone voice—a touch of Scotch inflection mixed with Aussie tang—keeps the listener focused on his lyrics.

Born in Peebles, Scotland, Bogle was the only son of Nancy, a domestic servant, and Laurence, a railway ganger, with whom he had a strained relationship. As Eric jokes in his own "Bogleography," "he showed no apparent early musical leanings, except perhaps a strong aversion to bagpipe music." He began jotting down poetry when he was only eight years old. "I don't know why," he told SCALA (Songwriters, Composers and Lyricist Association of Australia) president Robert Childs in 1989. "I just found a facility to rhyme things, which is an easy facility, it's not something that's a great gift. I've mainly gone in for rhyming poetry, although I've written a lot more prose in latter years. My life has been concerned with music and I come from a country and a generation and a society where music played quite an important part in our lives. It wasn't just the social lubricant that it is these days.

"When we were kids in school, the games we played were always accompanied by music. So the music was an integral part of the games we played in the school yard. The music reflected what has been a fairly dominated culture, the economic casualty that Scotland has been for the last two thousand years. In Scottish music it was quite important to retain a sense of national identity within the 'British Empire,' so there was always lots of Scottish music sung around the place. In my own personal household, my father was a bagpiper and all his drunken mates played mouth organs, accordions, and so on. There was always music."

Bogle was a normal teenager of the 1950s. He liked Elvis, Lonnie Donegan, and Brigitte Bardot. He began playing guitar at sixteen and formed a rock group, Eric and the Informers, in the early 1960s. "They were very popular in Peebles, but then so was eating live ferrets," Bogle jokes, "and after three years of relative obscurity the band broke up, and the various members returned to total obscurity."

Bogle became involved in the Campaign for Nuclear Disarmament and attended a Ban the Bomb rally, where he was inspired by the folk music he heard. He distinguished himself by being able to sing sixty verses of "We Shall Overcome" as he accompanied himself on the ukulele. Writes Bogle: "In 1969, bored, disillusioned, broke, etc., he gratefully accepted the Australian Government's offer of free passage to the colony of New South Wales."

He was twenty-six years old when he settled in Adelaide, where he did menial work in a builder's yard. Within six months he was working in an air-conditioned office. As he writes about himself: "Eric then succumbed to a rare Scottish disease called Greed, and studied to become an accountant, and he did become one, more or less. About this time he also acquired a wife [Carmel] and a pair of steel-rimmed spectacles, both indispensable aids for aspiring accountants. He has long since got rid of the specs, but has kept his wife, a tribute both to her patience and her sense of humor."

Bogle discovered the folk scene in Canberra, joining a local folk club. He wrote humorous poetry about Australia. He told Childs: "Like most migrants I was cast in the role of observer in a totally new society. So you see a lot of novel ways and funny little things, that possibly the people who live here can't see, because they can't see the wood for the trees. I'm like that after twenty years here. Less and less do I see the anomalies in Australian society because more and more I'm part of it."

He performed his humorous songs for the folk club, and wrote two more serious songs, including his two best-known songs, "And the Band Played Waltzing Matilda" and "Leaving Nancy," about waving good-bye to his mother and Scotland. " 'Nancy' wasn't written for public consumption originally," he told Childs. "A lot of my songs are written for my own benefit, my own penance, if you like, an emotional escape. But friends who heard me sing it, begged me to sing it to audiences,

because they said there were lots of people out there who could identify with every word. You tend to think of yourself as a unique human being. You think nobody has gone through such pain and trauma as you have, and of course, there's millions out there who've gone through worse than you have."

"And the Band Played Waltzing Matilda" was Bogle's fourth or fifth song. He still has reservations about it. He told Childs about how he pared it down from eight verses to five after he noticed people nodding off as he played it. "The first lesson I learned about songwriting was: say what you want to say and say it in the least number of verses possible," he told Childs. "I really wanted to try to get it down to four, which I felt was the right length, but I just couldn't."

The song won third place in a Brisbane competition, although many felt it should have won. The controversy helped launch it on the Australian charts. In 1976, Bogle gained recognition when his songs were covered by various performers. Tommy Makem and the Clancy Brothers recorded "And the Band Played Waltzing Matilda" and had a number-one hit in Ireland. "Leaving Nancy" and "No Man's Land" were also number-one hits in Ireland. Encouraged by the success, in 1980 Bogle "chucked" his job as an accountant and began his career as a professional musician—at the age of thirty-six. He came out with his first LP, *Now I'm Easy,* on Larrikin Records in 1980, which also included such notable songs as "I Hate Wogs" and "Front Row Cowboy," about sitting in the front row of Roy Rogers movies as a child. Those songs, as well as "The Aussie Bar-B-Q" from *Plain and Simple* (1983), "earned him a reputation as a deep social commentor, a reputation he has been trying to live down ever since," Bogle writes.

In 1984, *Now I'm Easy* went gold in Australia. He has released several other albums as well: *Scraps of Paper* (1981) on Flying Fish; *Eric Bogle Live in Person* (1982) on Autogram Records in Germany; *Eric Bogle Down Under; Eric Bogle Pure* (1982) on Autogram; *Plain and Simple* (1983) (with John Munro) on Grass Roots and Tempo Communication; *When the Wind Blows* (1984) on Larrikin and on Flying Fish in the United States; *Eric Bogle in Concert* (1986) on Larrikin; *Eric Bogle: A Collection, Singing the Spirit Home* (1987) on Larrikin; *Something of Value* (1988) on Larrikin and Philo in the United States; *Songbook* (1990) on Greentrax in Scotland; *Voices in the Wilderness* (1990) on Festival Records and Alcazar Records (1991) in the United States; *Not the Worst of Eric Bogle* (1990) on Larrikin; *It's Not Cricket* (1992) on Dino and Larrikin; *Mirrors* (1993) on Larrikin; *Songbook Vol. 2* (1994) on Greentrax; *I Wrote This Wee Song* (a live double-CD set) (1995) on Greentrax; *The Emigrant and the Exile* (1996) (with John Munro) on Greentrax; and *Small Miracles* (1997) on Larrikin. His songs have also appeared on compilation albums, including *Songs for*

Peace (1983) Rounder, *Music and Songs of Scotland* (1989) Greentrax, *The Music and the Song: Scotland Now; the Music and the Song of Greentrax: The Best of Scottish Music* (1997) Greentrax, and *If it Wasnae for the Union* (1996) Greentrax. He recorded Kate Wolf's "Cornflower Blue" for the 1998 tribute *Treasures Left Behind: Remembering Kate Wolf* on Red House.

Bogle's work stands out for its keen social and political commentary. He wrote the song "Something of Value" to criticize Australia's failure to acknowledge the Aborigines during the bicentennial celebration. *Mirrors* included songs about Chernobyl and the Holocaust. He has also written songs about apartheid, nuclear war, and the changing culture. He's also got an impish sense of humor, writing about a cat crushed by a truck in "Nobody's Moggy Now" or about a chihuahua trying to get cozy with a Saint Bernard in "Little Gomez."

As his reputation grew, so did Bogle's itinerary. Beginning in 1980, he was often accompanied by John Munro, a Glasgow-born guitarist, mandolinist, singer, and songwriter who works as a social worker. (Munro has appeared on at least eight of Bogle's albums.) In contrast to Bogle, who moved willingly from Scotland, Munro was "dragged kicking and screaming from Maryhill to Australia by his parents." Brent Miller, an Australian by birth, plays bass for Bogle and works as a podiatrist in his spare time.

Bogle has been recognized in his adopted country as well as in Scotland. Ironically, in 1985 he was voted "The Most Australian Australian of the Year" by the Newcastle and Hunter Valley Australia Day Society." In 1986 he won a Gold Award for Song of the Year ("The Band Played Waltzing Matilda"). He also received the Peace Medal in recognition of his efforts to promote peace and racial harmony with songs such as "No Man's Land," a.k.a. "The Greenfields of France," written after he visited a graveyard in Flanders in the 1970s. When a twelve-year-old schoolgirl from Belfast wrote British prime minister Tony Blair asking him to contribute a poem for her "peace wall," Blair sent her the lyrics from "No Man's Land." One paper even reported that the author had died in World War I.

"I'm not quite dead, just 53," Bogle told Chris Mosey of *Folk Roots* (January/February 1998), who said of his visit to the graveyard, "You couldn't fail to be moved."

In 1992 he was honored by the Peebles (Scotland) Callants Club with an honorary membership in honor of his achievements. In his album *The Emigrant & the Exile,* recorded with Munro, the two Aussies look back on their Scottish upbringing. As Bogle writes in the liner notes: "John Munro and I have both lived in Australia a fair time now, in fact 31 years and 27 years respectively. A question that we are both frequently asked by many people, is 'after all these years, do you now consider yourself to be an Australian or a Scot?' . . . We're lucky, we have the best of both worlds, two cultures we're at ease in, two emotional homes etc., etc., bulldust, bulldust, waffle, waffle . . .' "

He told *Folk Roots*'s Mosey his main goal: "Feeling is what I seek in music—I hate the bloody technocrats. I can't stand jazz and all these people trying to be cool. Sometimes I'm accused of sentimentality in my songs. Well, I've never been able to be a cool cynic. . . . I like to get involved. A lot of people find it a bit embarrassing to see a grown man displaying his emotions on stage. Well, that's their hard luck. I'm not about to change at my time of life.

"All I want to do is to keep writing songs, and to keep enjoying myself," he writes. "That's all really, though I'd like to be taller, and I wish my hair would grow back."

Entry written with assistance from Karen Rodgers, who maintains the Eric Bogle web site (http://www.windbourne.com/ebogle/)

BOTHY BAND: *Vocal and instrumental group, Donal Lunny, born Newbridge, County Kildare, Ireland (guitar, synthesizer, dulcimer, bouzouki, bodhran); Mícheál Ó Dhomhnaill, born Dublin, Ireland (vocals, guitar); Tríona Ní Dhomhnaill, born Donegal, Ireland (vocals, clavinet, harmonium); Paddy Glackin, born Ireland (fiddle); Matt Molloy, born Ballghadareen, County Roscommon, Ireland (flute, whistles). Tommy Peoples (fiddle) replaced Glackin in late 1975. Peoples replaced in 1976 by Kevin Burke. Paddy Keenan (Uillean pipes, whistles) joined in 1976.*

Comprising some of the finest young musicians from Ireland, the Bothy Band set many a fan to dancing with its high-powered versions of Celtic music evolved in part from the traditional jigs, reels, and ballads its members had loved since early childhood days. The group's members had all performed with various local or well-known groups before joining forces in the new project, and most went on to notable new projects after the band's short performing life came to a close.

The group, which featured the dramatic singing voice of Tríona Ní Dhomhnaill and the noteworthy lead guitar work of her brother Mícheál Ó Dhomhnaill, had no lack of talent in its other founding members. Tríona and Mícheál had performed in a group called Skara Bral, playing songs of their native Donegal. Donal Lunny already had tasted success as a member of another top-ranked Irish folk rock group, Planxty (which he was to help reorganize in 1979), and flutist Matt Molloy later became an important member of the long-lasting Irish traditional band the Chieftains. Several members had recorded together on Mick Hanly's 1974 album *Celtic Folkweave*, as well as in a group called Sixteen Ninety-one.

Recalling his earlier years in an interview with Paul Byrne of *Irish Music Magazine*, Lunny noted that his initial influence was the jazz music his father liked to play on his radio. "I'd had piano lessons when I was very young and I just ran away from them. But I became interested again in my early teens when I started trying to work out the chords of these jazz records that I thought were being beamed from another planet. And then, when someone started a teenybop Beatles and Shadows band at school, I volunteered to be the drummer. After that, I just found my curiosity, my appetite for music grew stronger by the day." He soon fell in love with stringed instruments. "I just thought the guitar was the greatest thing ever invented. So I went out and bought a left-handed one and, for better or worse, I've never looked back since."

Thus, Lunny already was an established artist by the time he became involved with the Bothies. He told Byrne, "By the time I joined the Bothy Band they already had an identity of their own, but I definitely think we grew over [his years with them], even if we didn't quite achieve our full potential though. Since [the band] split up in 1979, it's always seemed like unfinished business to me."

The group began as a loose coalition of musicians who had gathered together for the celebration of the twenty-first anniversary of Gael-Linn Records. The band took the name initially of Seachtar (which means "seven" in Gaelic) for local gigs with a roster that included accordionist Tony MacMahon, but without Donal Lunny. MacMahon left when the group decided to turn professional, a move that also induced Paddy Glackin to bow out. After Lunny and fiddler Tommy Peoples joined Tríona, Mícheál, Matt Molloy on flute, and Paddy Keenan on Uillean pipes, it was decided to record the band's debut album on Mulligan Records, a new label established by Lunny, Mícheál Ó Dhomhnaill, and Seamus O'Neill to record traditional Irish music as well as other material not covered by major labels in or out of Ireland. The Bothy Band's debut on the label was titled *Bothy Band 1975,* released in November of that year. Some of its tracks won airplay at home as well as in England (where the LP was released on the Polydor label in 1976) and Europe, and the group's live shows quickly won praise from critics and attracted steadily growing ranks of fans lured in by favorable word of mouth.

Colin Irwin of *Melody Maker* remembered his feelings on hearing their first British concert: "It took place at Hammersmith Town Hall and their impact was staggering—when they let rip the effect was like being in a jet when it suddenly whipped into full throttle along the runway. I just couldn't BELIEVE the ferocity with which Paddy Keenan attacked the uillean pipes.... Keenan was, for me, their most breathtaking component. Yet he was also flexible and continued to develop throughout the Bothies' career—listen to his solo on 'The Death of Queen Jane' on the band's last album. Tommy Peoples was equally startling. I've never heard a fiddle performance like he played that night in Hammersmith: unorthodox, unpredictable and utterly breathtaking." However, he added that Peoples's replacement, Kevin Burke, proved equally brilliant in his own way.

The group followed with two more very listenable collections in 1976, *Old Hag You Have Killed Me* and *The Bothy Band 1976.* Though there were some changes in personnel, the group continued to be wildly popular with audiences not only in Ireland but in many other parts of the world, including England, France, and the United States. In the latter part of the 1970s, the band played both regular venues and a number of major folk and rock festivals in the British Isles and elsewhere. In 1977, Mulligan issued their fourth album, *Out of the Wind into the Sun,* followed in 1978 by *After Hours—Live in Paris.* Though the group stayed together into 1979, the last-named LP provided its last recording project. After appearing at the August 1979 Ballysadare Festival in County Sligo, the group disbanded. In 1980, the retrospective *The Best of the Bothy Band* was issued.

In the 1980s, Lunny performed with Planxty while also pursuing solo projects. Mícheál Ó Dhomhnaill and Kevin Burke both ended up in the United States, as did Tríona Ní Dhomhnaill. Tríona worked with Linda Ronstadt and also organized her own group, Touchstone. Mícheál's and Kevin's duet work embraced the recording of a number of albums, including the LP *Promenade* (which won the Montreux Jazz Festival's Grand Prix Du Disque) and *Portland,* prepared at the studio they established in Portland, Oregon, in the early 1980s. Mícheál's other projects included organizing the band Nightnoise, whose roster in the mid-1990s included his sister, Tríona, Brian Dunning, and Scottish-born John Cunningham.

Though the Bothy Band's career came to a close at the end of the 1970s, all of its albums were kept in print in the 1990s in the United States by Green Linnet Records. In 1994, previously unreleased tracks came out on the Windsong label under the title *The Bothy Band—Live in Concert.* Drawn from the British Broadcasting Company archives, the album presented material from two concerts taped for BBC Radio One on July 15, 1976, and July 24, 1978. In the first of those, Peter Browne subbed for Paddy Keenan. In 1996, the album was released in the United States by Green Linnet. Arfolk Records released a CD titled *Irish Traditional Pub Music,* which features some of the members playing in the pre-Bothy group Sixteen Ninety-one. The CD includes tracks from *Irish Music* (Escalibur) and *Chants et Danses d'Irlande,* both released in the early 1970s.

BOWERS, BRYAN: *Singer, guitarist. Born Yorktown, Virginia, August 18, 1940.*

The autoharp certainly isn't considered a virtuoso instrument by most people—unless someone like

Bryan Bowers plays it. With his five-finger Bowers picking style, he draws amazing melodic combinations from his carefully tuned autoharp, covering a range of material from Mozart to songs like "You Are My Sunshine," "My Bonnie Lies Over the Ocean," and "Will the Circle Be Unbroken." Not without reason, some reviewers have called him the world's best autoharpist.

With his broad shoulders and imposing height (6 feet 4 inches), Bowers gives an appearance of a rugged individualist, but he is anything but immodest. As he told Art and Leota Coats for an article about him for *Frets* magazine (May 1979), "When people write [that he's the 'best'], I just want to ask them if they have ever listened to Mother Maybelle Carter, Pop Stoneman, Kilby Snow, or Mike Seeger. 'Best' is simply a matter of personal taste. My style of playing and technique are different and I can do a lot of things that other people can't or won't do, but there are people who can do things with the harp that I can't do. I think anyone who writes that I am the best should listen to some other good players, and then put that story back together with me in perspective."

Bowers grew up in Virginia and was exposed to some folk music (including local barn dances and early classical lessons on the violin) but didn't consider getting involved in it until he was in college. In high school his height earned him a place on the basketball team, and that, in turn, brought an athletic scholarship from Randolph-Macon College in Ashland, Virginia. Shortly after both of his parents died, he quit college—just three credits shy of earning his degree. "Almost by accident," he told the Coatses, "I picked up a guitar about that time. As I started picking around on it I began to feel better about myself and a lot of things." In fact, it banished suicidal thoughts from his mind: "Music saved my life!"

After fooling around with guitar, slide guitar, dulcimer, and mandocello, he was introduced to the autoharp in the late 1960s by a Virginia friend named Dr. Rollie Powell. He fell in love with it almost immediately. "The harp filled up the void that was in me. It felt spiritual, all-embracing." For the next few years, though he didn't give up the other instruments completely, he spent more and more time learning to play the autoharp, trying to master the art of tuning, the key to good autoharp performance.

In the early 1970s, he headed west and settled for a time in Seattle, Washington, singing with autoharp accompaniment in Seattle streets. After a year and a half, he loaded his instruments and other possessions into an old Chevy panel truck and drove back to the East Coast to try to work into the folk club/coffeehouse circuit. Unfortunately, while stopping to visit some friends in Pennsylvania, he unloaded his gear to repaint the truck. At that point, someone asked him to come down to jam with other friends in Washington, D.C., and while he was away a rainstorm ruined all his things.

Reduced to only the autoharp, he tried street singing in Washington, D.C., but citizens of the nation's capital proved to be closefisted with money. Things looked bleak, but he managed to get the owner of the Childe Harold Club in D.C. to let him play between sets of the scheduled artist for a little pay and some food. That kept him going for a while, and soon after he met the Dillards, who liked his work enough to take him along to a bluegrass concert where he got some additional exposure.

After that, more and more people became interested in his talents. The opportunities in the late 1970s to perform in folk clubs, on college campuses, and at major folk festivals increased. Among his festival credits were the Philadelphia Folk Festival, Culpeper (Virginia) Bluegrass/Folk Festival, and the Walnut Valley Festival in Winfield, Kansas. He also appeared as an opening act for both folk and rock artists, including a number of concerts with Merle and Doc Watson, in all parts of the United States. Whether appearing at the Bottom Line in New York or the Roxy in Los Angeles, before several hundred fans or in front of 15,000 people at a bluegrass festival, Bowers was able to create a rapport that had his entire audience singing along on songs like "Will the Circle Be Unbroken."

Despite his increasing number of adherents during the second half of the 1970s, it took almost to the end of the decade before he found his way onto records. One stumbling block was the lack of interest of large record companies in signing an autoharpist; the other was Bowers's perfectionist outlook. He preferred not to cut a record until he felt he could do one that met his personal standards. He finally signed with Chicago-based, folk music–oriented Flying Fish Records, which issued his debut LP, *The View from Home,* in 1977. His second album was released by Flying Fish in the spring of 1980, *Home, Home on the Road.*

A major part of his success with the autoharp was the development of his special picking style. He described it to Art and Leota Coats in this way, "With the five-finger approach, I catch one string with the thumb, which would be the rhythm part, and play the high and low melodies and harmonies with the fingers." This was considerably different from the method favored by Mike Seeger and Mother Maybelle Carter, which, the Coatses note, "features primarily a back-and-forth strum with a melody note here and there."

Bowers's career patterns changed little during the 1980s and '90s. He continued to perform on the folk circuit, playing coffeehouses, concert halls (including college campus venues), and folk festivals in the United States and throughout the world. He was still on the Flying Fish label when it was acquired by Rounder Records in 1995. His album catalog, most of which was available at his concert dates, included, besides his 1977 release, *By Heart* (1984); *Home, Home on the Road* (1980); and the 1990 Flying Fish disc, *For You.*

Among the tracks from the last that made a number of public radio playlists around the United States were "Maggie Brown's Favorite" and "Reflections in a Crystal Wind." Also available in the mid-1990s was his instructional video, *Autoharp Techniques,* issued on Homespun Tapes. His next project is an album to be called *Friend for Life,* which takes its title from a song he wrote with Bill Danoff, who co-wrote "Country Roads." He currently resides in the foothills of the Cascades in Washington State.

BOYS OF THE LOUGH: *Vocal and instrumental group. Original members in 1967: Robin Morton, born Portadown, Northern Ireland, December 24, 1939 (vocals, concertina, bodhran); Cathal McConnell, born Enniskillen, County Fermanagh, Northern Ireland, June 8, 1944 (vocals, flute, whistle); Tommy Gunn, born Derrylin, County Fermanagh, Northern Ireland, c. mid-1940s (vocals, fiddle, bones). Gunn left in '67. Aly Bain, born Lerwick, Shetland Isles, Scotland, May 1946 (fiddle) and Mike Whellans (vocals, guitar) added in 1968. Dick Gaughan, born Leith, Edinburgh, Scotland, May 17, 1948 (vocals, guitar) replaced Whellans in 1972. Gaughan replaced in 1973 by Dave Richardson, born Corbridge, Northumberland, England, August 20, 1948 (guitar, madolin, cittern, concertina, tenor banjo, hammered dulcimer). In 1979, Morton replaced by Tich Richardson (guitar), born England c. late 1940s; died September 1984. Two new members added in 1985: Christy O'Leary, born Rathcoole, County Dublin, Ireland, June 7, 1955 (vocals, uilleann pipes), and John Coakley, born Cork, Ireland, July 30, 1951 (guitar, piano). Chris Newman (guitar) joined in 1995, replacing Coakley. Newman left in 1997, replaced by Garry O'Briain on guitar, mandocello and piano. O'Leary left and was replaced by Brendan Begley on accordion.*

Sometimes compared to the Irish folk group the Chieftains, the Boys of the Lough tended to range somewhat further toward rock and pop in its musical choices. Its roster certainly changed often over a span that started in the 1960s and extended into the 1990s. The band's jigs, reels, and ballads drew on the traditions of Ireland, England, and Scotland, the lands of birth of most of its members over the years.

The founding members were Cathal McConnell (the only remaining original member in the '90s), Robin Morton, and Tommy Gunn, all born in Northern Ireland. After coming together in the mid-1960s, the trio got the chance to tour England and Scotland in 1967, though the result was less than a rousing success. When it was over Gunn left, and for a time McConnell and Morton found work as a duo, recording *An Irish Jubilee* in 1969. A major step forward occurred in 1969 when the band expanded to a foursome with the addition of Aly Bain and Mike Whellans. Bain in particular, an exquisite fiddle player, brought a new intensity and direction to the group's sets.

One of Bain's Edinburgh friends in the early 1970s

was Dick Gaughan, who was rapidly gaining a reputation as one of Scotland's most promising new singers and guitarists in the folk field. (See separate entry.) In 1972 Bain joined Gaughan to record the album *Dick Gaughan/No More Forever,* produced by Bill Leader and released on the small Trailer label. (One of the songs on the LP was "The Green Linnet," eventually taken as the name of a U.S. folk music label.) During 1972, Mike Whellans left the Boys of the Lough (a name the group acquired at a TV taping session) and Edinburgh-born Gaughan took his place.

Soon after Gaughan joined, the quartet of McConnell, Morton, Bain, and Gaughan started work on the Boys of the Lough's debut album, recorded and produced by Bill Leader in a studio in his home. The album, *The Boys of the Lough,* issued by Trailer in 1972, included such tracks as the title song, the jig sequence "Wedding March from Unst/The Bride's a Bonny Thing/The Granny in the Corner," "Caoidneadh Eoghain Rua," "Docherty's Reel/Flowing Tide," "Andrew Lammie," "Sheebeg and Sheemore/The Boy in the Gap/McMahon's Reel," and "The Shaalds of Foulla." In the 1990s, the album was available in the United States on the Shanachie label. The track "Docherty's Reel/The Flowing Tide" was included by Trailer in its 1975 compilation album, *Our Folk Music Heritage.* The group released a second album on Trailer in 1973.

The band's schedule included a hectic series of dates in the United Kingdom and in the United States. When Gaughan opted out of touring, his place was taken by multi-instrumentalist Dave Richardson. Gaughan's decision may have resulted from difficulties in gaining visas for U.S. visits relating to his association with Socialist causes. The new quartet of McConnell, Bain, Morton, and Richardson remained intact for most of the rest of the '70s, recording such albums as *Recorded Live* (at a venue in Cambridge, Massachusetts) and *Lochaber No More* (both issued in 1975), *The Piper's Broken Finger* in 1976, *Good Friends, Good Music* in 1977, and *Wish You Were Here* in 1978.

In 1979 Robin Morton left the group to form Temple Records in Scotland, leaving Cathal McConnell as the only founding member still with the band. Of course, Aly Bain, a member since '68, remained. David Richardson's brother Tich Richardson was brought in to take Morton's place. The first result of the new alignment was the 1980 release *Boys of the Lough Reorganized;* this was followed by *In the Tradition* in 1981 and *Open Road* in 1983.

In September 1983, the band had another setback when Tich Richardson was killed in an auto accident. But they bounced back the following year, adding Christy O'Leary and John Coakley to the group, and resumed touring and recording. Its albums in the mid- and late 1980s included *Far, Far from Home* and *To Welcome Paddy Home* in 1986, *Farewell & Remember Me* in 1987, and *Sweet Rural Shade* in 1988. In February 1988, the band celebrated its twenty-first anniversary in concert at New York's Carnegie Hall. The album drawn from that, *Live at Carnegie Hall* (1992) was issued in the United Kingdom on the Sage Arn label, which also released the *Fair Hills of Ireland* that year. Chris Newman replaced John Coakley on guitar in 1995. Newman left in 1997 and was replaced by Garry O'Briain on guitar, mandocello and piano. Christy O'Leary also left and was replaced by accordionist Brendan Begley. Newman set up a record company in Yorkshire called Old Bridge Music, releasing *Fretwork* in 1998, and the first solo recording by piper O'Leary.

Over the years, many Lough members did solo work or worked as session musicians. The most prolific from an album standpoint was Aly Bain, whose early '70s credits, besides his work with Dick Gaughan, included the 1971 release *Aly Bain—Mike Whellans*. Other Bain albums were *Aly Bain First Album* (1984) on his own Whirlie Records, *Down Home, Volumes 1 and 2* (both 1985), *Aly Bain Meets the Cajuns* in 1988, *Aly Bain & Friends* on Greentrax in 1994, and *Lonely Bird* on Green Linnet in 1996.

Bain is also known for his work with accordion player Phil Cunningham of Silly Wizard. They toured together extensively and recorded as well. Their first album, *The Pearl*, came out in 1994. Bain made a series of television specials of his music, including *Shetland Sessions* for the BBC Scotland. In 1993 he published an autobiography, *Fiddler on the Loose* (Mainstream). He and Cunningham also recorded *The Ruby* for Green Linnet in 1997.

In the mid-1990s, most of the group's albums were still in print on various labels. The Rounder catalog offered (on cassette only) four 1970s releases: *Live at Passim* (1975), *Lochaber No More, The Piper's Broken Finger,* and *Good Friends, Good Music.* Other albums were available in the United States on the Shanachie label. The group released a Christmas album, *A Midwinter Night's Dream*, in 1994 on Blix Street.

BRAGG, STEPHEN WILLIAM "BILLY": *Singer, guitarist, band leader (Red Wedge, The Red Stars), songwriter, born December 20, 1957, Barking, Essex, England.*
From the mid-1980s on, Billy Bragg was well known in England and Europe as a political activist and a performer and songwriter of folk rock and folk-themed material, but until the end of the 1990s, he had only a small cult following in the United States. This promised to change as the century drew to a close thanks to a project proposed by Wood Guthrie's daughter, Nora, in which Billy joined forces with the U.S. country and folk-rock band Wilco to provide music to go with some of Woody's previously unreleased lyrics.

Billy grew up in a working-class section of Barking, where his father earned a living as a warehouseman. Like other U.K. youngsters in the 1960s, he was influenced by the Beatles, the Rolling Stones, and other groups in the British rock movement like the Jam and the Clash. In time it led him to learn how to play guitar with teenage dreams of making a name for himself in pop music. As was the case with many English working-class children, opportunities seemed limited in the humdrum part of the economy that seemed reserved for that economic group. Billy's sense of rebellion against the way things were was reflected in his rejection of the education system he was exposed to. As Cole Moreton wrote in the *Sunday Independent* ("A Rebel with a Cause," May 26, 1996, pp. 18–20), a school report from Barking Abbey Comprehensive described him as a student who "uses his obvious intelligence as a disruptive influence."

Bragg formed a band called Riff Raff in 1977 with his next-door friend Wiggy, who had taught Bragg the basics of guitar playing. The band gained limited exposure playing mainly covers of material by artists like Bob Dylan and the Rolling Stones. For a time the group lived in a recording studio in Northamptonshire, but this didn't lead to any recording successes. The group recorded one single. The shift in emphasis by Bragg and Wiggy to the punk rock genre also fell flat, and Bragg picked up needed personal funds by working as a painter and decorator. Then he decided to enlist in the army in 1981. He told Moreton, "That seemed to be the only alternative to being a punk. At school the options were, 'Would you like to go and work for Ford Motors at Dagenham. No? Well, then will it be the Army, the Navy or the Air Force?' The Army was still the great sop of working class youth; if you had nowhere to go, you went there."

After the minimum three months in the service, Bragg realized that wasn't the life for him and bought his release. He returned home, determined to make his way as a solo singer–guitar player. He drew attention to himself by entering talent contests, auditioning for gigs, and began finding work as a sideman with local bands. He also prepared demos of some of his material that he began trying to submit to record companies. By the end of the 1970s, some of the owners of independent labels were starting to take an interest in his potential, and this finally resulted in the opportunity to work on an album for the independent U.K. Utility/Go! Discs that was issued in late 1983 under the title *Life's a Riot with Spy vs. Spy.* From the start, Bragg insisted that he be allowed to retain title to his recordings, including any new material he wrote.

His debut album, which sold 150,000 copies in the United Kingdom and another 100,000 worldwide, included seven tracks he had originally prepared in demo form. They included perhaps his best known composition, "A New England," as well as such other favorites with his fans in later years, "The Milkman of Human Kindness" and "The Busy Girl Buys Beauty." His next release, *Brewing Up,* was issued on Go! Discs in 1984 and contained harsh comments on U.K. journalism in

"It Says Here" as well as comments on romance in such tracks as "A Lover Sings," "Love Gets Dangerous," and "The Saturday Boy."

Growing up in a working-class environment, Bragg early on became a fan of England's Labor Party. The ruthless suppression of a coal miners' strike by the Thatcher government radicalized him still further, and some of those feelings surfaced in the contents of his 1985 extended-play disc, *Between the Wars*, on UK Go! Discs. The album included Bragg's versions of songs by American folksingers Pete Seeger and Leon Rosselson as well as some sharp-edged originals by Billy.

Growing interest among young English music fans in Bragg's political stance as well as his considerable entertainment talents brought him to the attention of Labor Party leaders like Neil Kinnock, who thought he and others like him could play an important role in the upcoming 1987 elections. In February 1985, Kinnock invited Billy and nineteen other artists to a meeting at the country's House of Commons. Billy responded by organizing a group called the Red Wedge that toured widely in support of Labor Party beliefs and candidates. Unfortunately for them, the Conservative party had no problem in continuing its winning ways in 1987, which sounded the death knell of Red Wedge, although it did not fade away completely until the 1992 voting period.

Billy began to seek entry into the American market starting with the CD Presents, American-only release *Life's a Riot Etc,* which combined his debut album with the tracks from *Between the Wars*. For his next project, the album *Talking with the Taxman About Poetry,* issued in England on Go! Discs in 1986, Elektra Records agreed to handle U.S. distribution and remained his North American label through the 1990s. The collection, whose tracks include such finely honed numbers as "Greetings to the New Brunette," "Levi Stubbs Tears," "Ideology," "Honey, I'm a Big Boy Now," and "Help Save the Youth of America," was ranked by some of the U.K. critics as one of the best releases of the year. In 1987, Go! Discs and Elektra issued the retrospective *Back to Basics* whose tracks incorporated all the material from *Life's a Riot, Between the Wars,* and *Brewing Up*. The record company promotional material in describing the release asserted "the first 21 songs form the roots of urbane folk music."

Billy was represented on album release lists at the end of the 1980s and start of the 1990s with the EP *Help Save the Youth of America* in 1988 on Elektra; *Worker's Playtime,* issued by Go! Discs in September 1988; *The Internationale* (Utility, May 1990); and *Don't Try This at Home* (Go! Discs, September 1991). His career seemed to take a large jump upward in 1991 as he collaborated with former Smith's guitarist Johnny Marr and U.S. rock stars REM on the hit singles "Sexuality" and "You Woke Up My Neighborhood." He also performed before admiring audiences in the United Kingdom with his band, the Red Stars.

Then puzzled fans and critics wondered why things quieted down with no new recordings and a paucity of new songs. One of the reasons, it turned out, was a case of appendicitis that sidelined him for a time and, he told interviewers, caused him to rest and think about career goals. Then his partner, Juliet, gave birth to their son, Jack, causing Billy to try to spend as much time with the child as he could. Bragg, however, was hardly inactive. He worked on material for the movies and TV and honed his skills as a record producer.

Cole Moreton of the *Sunday Independent* ("A Rebel with a Cause," May 26, 1996, pp. 18–20) wondered whether the replacement of Margaret Thatcher as prime minister by John Major might have taken something away from Bragg's creative urge. Billy replied, "No, I'd much rather there hadn't been a Margaret Thatcher and I could have just written love songs. The price in suffering and frustration that she caused isn't worth a dozen Billy Bragg albums, no."

In the early and mid-1990s, Billy's credits included work on a number of movies, TV, and radio shows. In late 1993, for instance, the sound track for the BBC drama *Safe* included two new unreleased songs, "Piccadilly Rambler" and "The Gulf Between Us." At the end of November, he narrated a show on BBC Radio 4 about his hometown of Barking titled "Looking for an Old England." During the next few years his movie projects included serving as sound coordinator and providing several songs, such as "14th of January," "She's Got a New Spell," and "Must I Paint You a Picture," for the New York film *Walking and Talking,* and writing "As Long As You Hold Me" for Kristy MacColl, which she performed on the sound track of *Mad Love.*

Billy began to expand his personal appearances in 1994 both as an artist and an activist. For instance, he took part in the Campaign against the Criminal Justice Bill in the United Kingdom and traveled to the United States several times for concert projects. The latter included opening for Natalie Merchant in Newport, Rhode Island, at her first solo show after leaving 10,000 Maniacs and taking part in opening ceremonies in Boston for the new Fort Apache recording studio.

He continued to expand his activities in 1995, eventually starting work on songs for a new album. He also offered a Mail Order Live disc of some of his last concert work with Red Stars called *No Pop, No Style, Strictly Roots*. But perhaps the most significant occurrence of the year was an invitation from Woody Guthrie's daughter, Nora, to add music to lyrics her father had written but never turned into songs. In 1992 he had performed two songs for the Woody Guthrie Memorial Concert in Central Park, New York, as well as his own songs. Nora was impressed by his style. As Billy wrote in the liner notes to the album, *Mermaid Avenue,* Nora Guthrie "approached me in the spring of 1995 with the idea of writing some new music to accompany these lost songs. She runs the Woody Guthrie archive in New York and offered me access to over a thousand complete lyrics of her father that are in her care. Handwritten or typed, often bearing the date and place where they were written and sometimes accompanied by an insight into the process at work, they offer us a broader picture of a man who over the past 60 years has been vilified by the American right whilst simultaneously being canonized by the American left."

While discussions went on about the project, Bragg began assembling material for his own new album, *William Bloke,* issued by Cooking Vinyl in September 1996. It turned out to be one of his best, with the songs covering a variety of subjects—from political "Upfield," in which he argues for "a socialism of the heart," to romance in "The Fourteenth of February." While appearing at New York venues with fellow artist Robyn Hitchcock, he discussed the album and some of his views with Jon Young for an article in *Newsday* ("Daddy, the Singing Socialist," November 15, 1996, p. B18).

He talked about the new insight into societal concerns being a parent had given him, including more focused awareness of the danger of environmental pollution and also emphasized he had not abandoned his socialist tenets. He told Young, "Now we have an opportunity to make a new left-wing agenda that isn't tainted by the totalitarianism of the Soviet Union. Socialism was born because capitalism couldn't bridge the gap between rich and poor, and it still hasn't. So how can socialism be dead? That's a ridiculous notion." In 1997 Cooking Vinyl released a seven-song EP along the same lines titled *Bloke on Bloke.*

Starting in 1996 and with more time applied in 1997, Bragg turned his attention to the Guthrie project. He suggested it would make sense to bring in American artists for a more authentic evaluation of Woody's material. This led to the addition of songwriter-bandleader Jeff Tweedy of the country–folk rock group Wilco. (Besides Bragg on acoustic guitar and lead vocals and Tweedy on electric guitar and vocals, Wilco participants included Jay Bennett on keyboards, Ken Coomer on drums, and John Stirratt on electric bass.) The collaborators' final selection for the album comprised fifteen songs, with Bragg composing the music for seven, Tweedy for two, and various combinations of the musicians on the others.

The album, titled *Mermaid Avenue* (named after the street in Brooklyn's Coney Island where Guthrie and his family lived after World War II), was issued by Elektra Records during the summer of 1998 and proved a worthy addition to the Guthrie oeuvre. Writing in the *New York Times* ("What If Woody Guthrie Had Led a Rock Band?" Arts & Leisure section, June 28, 1998, pp. 26, 36), Robert Christgau suggested that two songs for which Bragg provided the music, "Walt Whitman's Niece" and "Way Down Yonder in the Minor Key," had the potential to rank with Woody's most memorable numbers.

In general, he wrote, "without in any way dishonor-

ing Guthrie (although a few leftist sober sides may demur), Mr. Bragg and Jeff Tweedy of Wilco have reimagined him. Moreover, the Guthrie they create is present in his biography and, since he did write these lyrics, in his work." Christgau also commented, "Most important, [the words] express purely personal longing, pain and insecurity and forlorn hopes—with a vanity his friends knew well and fans of his shambling Everyman act rarely glimpsed—that 'this scribbling' would earn him a little immortality."

The goal of *Mermaid Avenue* was to broaden the image of who Woody Guthrie really was. While he was best known for such powerful songs as "This Land Is Your Land," "Bound for Glory," "Deportees," and "Do Re Mi," he was cut down in his prime by Huntington's Corea and the anti-Communist climate of the 1950s—before he could take the next step in his artistic career. Bragg told Matt Greenwald of *Sing Out!* ("Billy Bragg Carries on for Woody," Winter 1999, vol. 43, no. 3) that he believes Guthrie "is the first singer-songwriter. . . . Well, it's difficult, because other people were obviously writing songs . . . people that Woody was influenced by, like Jimmy Rodgers. But, a singer-songwriter as a genre, that inward, self-exploratory, social comment, it's difficult to find anyone else. I mean, in 1942, he's writing about gender politics on 'She Came Along to Me.' No one else was doing that. . . . It wasn't like he came to New York and wrote these songs about dust, he came to New York and had written all these songs that he's written while he was on the radio in California, and even in Texas and Oklahoma, those were the songs he had. But then he sat down and wrote, and this is what he wrote. And this is the next phase of his songwriting. It's in the big city . . . where does he go on, how does he improve, where does he step out of the shadow of folk music?"

The album was nominated for a Grammy in the Best Contemporary Folk category. Bragg and Wilco had recorded more than forty songs for the project, and Elektra released a second volume in 2000, *Mermaid Avenue Volume 2.*

BRAND, OSCAR: *Singer, guitarist, songwriter, actor, author, emcee. Born Winnipeg, Canada, February 7, 1920.*

Best known in the music field, perhaps, for his series of "bawdy songs" recordings (which seem rather tame now), Oscar Brand's credits amount to a spectrum of careers. Besides his folksinging activities, he wrote many scripts for films and TV, authored several stage shows, and hosted a long-running radio program that helped introduce many important artists of the 1950s and 1960s.

He was born on a wheat farm in Canada, but moved with his family to Minneapolis, then to Chicago, and then to New York. He completed elementary school in Brooklyn and went on to graduate from the borough's Erasmus Hall High School in 1937. Because of the Depression and an interest in seeing more of the world, he worked his way across country as a farm hand the next few years, picking up more and more folk songs to play on the banjo that he carried with him.

He returned home and enrolled in Brooklyn College to work toward a B.A. with a major in abnormal psychology. World War II interrupted, and he entered the army. After his discharge in 1945, he decided to try to earn a living in music and toured as a singer with the *Herb Shriner Show*. But in late 1945 he gave that up and got a job with New York City's radio station WNYC as coordinator of folk music.

He also started his own program on WNYC called *Folksong Festival*, which remained a mainstay of Sunday evening radio for several decades. It provided a showcase for all types of folk music recordings and for live performances by everyone from Woody Guthrie and Pete Seeger to Bob Dylan. In the 1950s and 1960s, the show was rebroadcast overseas by the United States Information Service (USIS). In the mid-1960s, his government-sponsored show, *The World of Folk Music,* was broadcast every week over 1,880 stations.

As a performer, Brand appeared throughout the United States in almost every folk club, on many college campuses, and in many folk festivals, and during the 1960s he served as a member of the board of directors of the Newport Folk Festival. Besides doing concert work, he was a guest on many TV shows, ranging from *The Tonight Show* and *Today* to a number of early 1960s hootenannies.

His TV efforts included scriptwriting and serving as musical director of a number of programs. In the early 1960s, he was musical director of NBC-TV's *Exploring Show,* which won the Peabody and Edison Awards for contributions to U.S. education. In 1966–67, he was both music director and head of the cast of NBC-TV's *The First Look.* In his original homeland, Canada, he also was active, performing as star and host on CBC-TV's weekly show *Let's Sing Out* from 1962 into the mid-1970s and, in the late 1960s, handling the same tasks on CTV-TV's weekly show *Brand New Scene.*

Among his TV output of scripts, narrations, and scores were contributions to "Invisible Journey," "The Farmer Comes to Town," Agnes de Mille's "The Gold Rush" on CBS-TV, Frederick Remington's "Bay at the Moon," and more than fifty scripts for the National Lutheran Council. He provided music, lyrics, and script material for several musicals, including the Off-Broadway show *In White America* and the 1966 Broadway presentation *A Joyful Noise,* which starred John Raitt. His writing credits include a number of books, such as *Singing Holidays,* published in 1957, and *The Ballad Mongers,* one of the basic histories of folk music in the United States. He also wrote forty-five movie scripts, some of which won him awards at the Venice and Edinburgh festivals, as well as winning him Golden Reel, Valley Forge, and Scholastic film awards.

He recorded hundreds of songs and dozens of albums in a career that extended from the late 1940s into the 1990s. Most of those were of traditional folk songs or songs by other writers, but he also performed his own material, and some of his originals were recorded by artists including Ella Fitzgerald and Harry Belafonte. His initial albums included *Noah's Ark* in 1947, *Songs Inane Only, American Drinking Songs,* and *Absolute Nonsense* (all 1948); and *Riddle Me This* with Jean Ritchie (originally issued in 1949, reissued in the 1960s). One of his earliest song hits was a toned-down version of a bawdy ballad titled "A Guy Is Just a Guy." In later years he specialized in singing such barrackroom ballads and other risqué numbers without any protective editing. Examples of some of the other songs of that type in his repertoire were "Charlotte the Harlot" and "Blinded by Turds."

His many albums were issued on a variety of labels, both major and minor. While most were recorded by him for the specific label, some were reissues on completely different labels. His first bawdy collection, *Bawdy Songs and Backroom Ballads, Volume 1,* came out in 1949, followed that same year by *Volume 2* and, in 1950, *Volume 3.* The Audio Fi catalog by the mid-1960s included such titles as *Bawdy Sea Chanties* (late 1950s), *Bawdy Songs and Backroom Ballads* (late 1950s), *Bawdy Western Songs* (2/60), *Bawdy Songs Go to College* (early 1960s), *Singa-Long Bawdy Songs* (10/62), and *Bawdy Hootenanny* (2/64), plus *Rollicking Sea Chanties* (5/62).

He released *All Time Hootenanny Folk Favorites* on Decca in 1960. *Folk Songs for Fun* (Decca, 1962) teamed Brand with the Tarriers on such song as "Big Rock Candy Mountain," "Sweet Betsy from Pike," and "Cotton-Eyed Joe." In 1965, a compilation *Best of Bawdy Songs* was released.

He was represented on Elektra by such albums as *Wild Blue Yonder* (late 1950s), *Every Inch a Sailor* (2/60), *Out of the Blue* (5/60), *Boating Songs* (7/60), *Tell It to the Marines* (4/60), *Sports Car Songs* (10/60), *Up in the Air* (5/61), *Snow Job for Skiers* (1/63), *Songs Fore Golfers* (9/63), *Cough!* (10/63), *For Doctors Only* (10/63), and *Courting's a Pleasure.* On Folkways, he had such titles as *Election Songs of the U.S.* (2/61) and *Town Hall Concert.* His Tradition releases included *Laughing America, Pie in the Sky,* and *The Best of Oscar Brand.* Riverside Records issued a number of his albums, including *Give 'Em the Hook, Riddle Me This, Drinking Sons, Children's Concerts,* and *G.I.* Other albums included *Songs for Adults* on ABC (9/61), *Morality* on Impulse, *Songs for Fun* (with the Tarriers) on Decca (7/62), *Singing Holidays* on Caedmon, and *Brand X* on Roulette (early 1970s). One of his best LPs was *Oscar Brand and Jean Ritchie,* issued by the Archives of Folk and Jazz Music (3/67).

From the end of the '60s into the '90s, recordings new and old continued to reach the market, many of them children's recordings. His 1970s credits included *The Best of Oscar Brand* in 1975, *Singing Holidays* in 1978, and *Billy the Kid* in 1979. In the 1980s, the list expanded to such titles as *First Thanksgiving* in 1980; *Trick or Treat* in 1981; *Singing Is Believing* in 1982; *My Christmas Is Best* in 1983; *Happy Birthday* and *American Dreamer* (1985); *100 Proof, Brand X,* and *We All Sing 1* (1987); *Songs for Tadpoles, We All Sing 2,* and *Hop, Jump and Sing with Oscar Brand* (1988); and *The Best of the Worst* in 1989.

He began the '90s with the albums *MacDougal & Bleecker* in 1990 and, in 1991, *Let's Have a Party* and *Welcome to America.* He continued to be involved in activities aimed at improving prospects for a folk-music revival in the '80s and '90s, and sometimes contributed backing vocals for new albums by other folk performers. In 1994 Alcazar released *I Love Cats,* a humorous collection that included Jean Ritchie on background vocals, as well as Steve Guglielmo on sax, John Pickow on banjo, and John Foley on guitar. The songs included "Cat Rap," "The Great Big Little Cat Show," and "Them Doggoned Cats." Naturally, he followed that up with *Get a Dog* on Alcazar in 1996. In 1999, Smithsonian folkways issued his album, *Presidential Campaign Songs 1789–1996.*

BREL, JACQUES: *Singer, guitarist, songwriter, actor. Born Brussels, Belgium, April 8, 1929; died October 10, 1978.*

He wasn't particularly handsome; descriptions of his buck-toothed, lanky appearance suggest a musical Jerry Lewis rather than a matinee idol. He sang his wonderfully insightful lyrics only in French, yet he enthralled English-speaking audiences, who rarely understood a word he was singing. He abruptly gave up a highly successful concert career in the late 1960s and restricted his music output to records alone, yet retained the affection of his fans up to and beyond his early passing. In short, from a creative standpoint, Jacques Brel really could do no wrong; his impact on those artists who came after him remains strong to this day.

He was born and raised in Brussels, Belgium, the son of a successful owner of a family cardboard merchandising company. The family background was Flemish, but Jacques preferred French, the language he used almost exclusively through most of his life. He reached his teens during World War II, when Belgium was occupied by Hitlers's legions. His family's fortunes weren't irreparably damaged by the war, and when peace finally returned the business began to prosper. It was assumed Jacques would help run the concern when he was old enough, and, despite a strain of rebelliousness that caused him to be expelled from Catholic school before graduating, it appeared as though he would indeed heed his father's wishes.

While he wasn't all that happy about school, at home he enjoyed listening to whatever music was available in the first part of the 1940s, which tended to be limited to classical and regional folk music. By the age of fifteen he had taught himself guitar and by his late teens he was ready to experiment with his own versions of some of the popular music that was beginning to be aired on European stations.

He remained with the business for several years at the end of the '40s and start of the '50s, but spent as much spare time as he could on writing original songs. When he was called up to perform his required military service, the move finally made him feel free to pursue his musical goals. Once out of the service he moved to Paris, which was to remain his home base for most of the rest of his life. He found whatever work he could performing solo at small Left Bank cafés, slowly building a following and reputation that eventually won him a regular spot in 1953 at the Théâtre des Trois Baudets in the Pigalle section. Audiences loved his original material, on which he backed himself on guitar along with support from a small instrumental group.

In 1954 he took another step up the success ladder when he was given second billing at Paris's famed Olympia Music Hall. Now an established performer, he began to make recordings that won attention from record buyers not only in France but in many other parts of Europe. His first major success was *Quand On A Que L'Amour.* In the following years he topped many charts with singles like "Le Valse De Mille Temps," "Les Bourgeois," "Les Dames Patronesses," and "Les Flamandes." During the mid-1950s he charmed audiences in England, and in 1957 he gave his first concerts in the United States.

He continued to be one of the most admired performers in France for the rest of the '50s and into the '60s. When American entertainment executive Eric Blau visited the City of Light in the early '60s, he was deeply impressed by hearing some of Brel's recordings. His voice, which Marlene Dietrich at one point said made Brel "the greatest singer in the world," was an amazing instrument, but the combination of lyrics and music Brel could create was even more significant to Blau. Returning to New York to develop a show called *O Oysters!* for the Village Gate cabaret, Blau included two of Jacques's compositions, "Carousel" and "Ne Me Quitte Pas."

Other artists in both English- and non-English-speaking countries were attracted to some of Brel's writings. In 1964, the Kingston Trio took his song "Le Moribond" and converted it to a hit U.S. single, "Seasons in the Sun." Another folk star, Dave Van Ronk, included some of Brel's songs in his repertoire. In 1965 Brel was hailed for his performances at two sold-out shows at New York's Carnegie Hall. When the live album derived from those appearances was released, the critic from the *Herald Tribune* compared the singer's performance style with "the drama and personal intensity that marked the style of Edith Piaf."

Getting to know Brel and hearing him in concert and on records caused songwriter Mort Shuman, who passed away in 1991, to have great respect for Brel's art. As he told an interviewer, "The first thing that impressed me was the virility in his voice. The only time I'd heard this virility was in black singers. Here was a man who combined raw force with the most meaningful lyrics I had heard in songs, a deep understanding of the human condition. I began to translate the songs."

This led to a collaboration with Eric Blau that formed the basis for a Village Gate show called *Jacques Brel Is Alive and Well . . . and Living in Paris* that debuted on January 22, 1968, and quickly became a critical and audience hit. The show, which included such Brel songs as "Mathilde," "Jackie," "Amsterdam," "Final Tango," "Marieke," "You're Not Alone," and "Carousel," soon moved to Broadway, where it remained a major attraction into the early 1970s. It later became a film.

As for Brel, during his '67 visit he took in the Broadway musical *Man of La Mancha* and fell in love with it. He arranged to have it translated into French so that he could play the lead role in European theaters. The show opened in Brussels in November 1968 and then moved on to Paris for a number of additional performances. It was a period when Brel was rethinking his entertainment goals, and after 1967 he announced he would no longer appear in the United States in protest against the nation's involvement in the Vietnam War. But by the early '70s he had extended his personal performance ban: he would no longer give concerts anywhere in the world, he announced, preferring to limit his efforts in music to the recording studio. Instead, he turned his attention to acting, appearing in several films, including *Les Risques du Matier* and *La Bonde à Bonnet.* When *Mare Mont-Dragon* premiered in Paris in December '71, he received accolades for his lead role of Georges, a career soldier who sought vengeance on the family of a colonel who improperly caused his dishonorable discharge.

By mid-1970s, Brel had moved his residence to the French Polynesian Islands where Gauguin painted, only returning to Paris from time to time to make new recordings. His albums, which continued to feature new gems of original songwriting, continued to sell well, and his catalog kept providing singles successes for other performers, examples being the number-one U.K. hit by Terry Jacks of Brel's "If You Go Away" (also covered by several U.S. artists) and use of his "Next" as title track for an album by England's Sensational Alex Harvey Band.

In his last years, Brel's trips to Paris involved treatment of the lung cancer that finally killed him in October 1978. In the years following his death many albums of reissued or previously unreleased material became available, including *La Chanson Français* in 1979, *Music for the Millions* in 1983, *Les Plus Grandes Chansons* in 1984, *Jacques Brel* in 1986; and *Le Plat Pays* in 1988.

BREWER & SHIPLEY: *Vocal and instrumental duo. Mike Brewer, born Oklahoma City, Oklahoma, 1944; Tom Shipley, born Mineral Ridge, Ohio, 1942.*

Mike Brewer and Tom Shipley, who individually cut their musical eyeteeth on the folk boom of the early 1960s, proved adept at surviving the collapse of that movement later in the decade. In fact, although they fled the big cities and retired to the "heartland" of the United States, they still managed to become major forces in pop music with their folk and soft rock efforts in the mid- and late 1960s. Their careers began to fade in the 1970s, and they went separate ways in the '80s, but reunited to find new success in the 1990s thanks to the folk music resurgence of that decade.

Brewer, born and raised in Oklahoma City, started playing guitar as a boy, with the full approval of his father, an artist who supported the family by working as a post office supervisor. After high school, Mike set off to wander around the country working the then-thriving coffeehouse circuit. On occasion, his path crossed that of Tom Shipley, beginning an acquaintance that was to blossom into friendship later.

With the folk boom dying out, Mike moved to Los Angeles in 1966 to join a group whose members included a musician named Tom Mastin. Eventually Mastin and Brewer worked as a duo and won a recording contract from Columbia. But the arrangement didn't work out and the two went separate ways. After a brief period working with one of his brothers, Mike gave up performing for a while and signed a songwriting contract with Good Sam Music, an affiliate of A&M Records, in 1968.

As for Tom Shipley, he noted that his musical appetite was whetted as a child by his family's interest in "cowboy music": "I always liked that and the whole family used to sing, riding in the car or sitting around the house. Dad sang in the choir, my sister played piano, and I toyed with a trumpet. None of us had any formal training, but we had a lot of informal fun."

Tom did some singing in high school. As a student at Baldwin Wallace College in Ohio, he became interested in folk music, learning acoustic guitar and polishing his singing. His early interest at school was ecology, but, he recalled, "I studied singing to help my head. Also I learned guitar and luckily at that time there were a lot of hootenannies where you could go and sing your song for people."

After graduating, he worked as a house musician at a local club, performing both folk standards and occasionally some original material he was writing. Then he married, bought a trailer, and wandered first to California, then to Toronto with his wife, picking up whatever singing work he could find. "We went up to Toronto because I thought 'Why not?' The folk scene was peaking everywhere and they were great. Of course it didn't stay like that because nothing ever does, and when the clubs started to close, I came back to California."

The time was 1968, and one of the people he ran into was Mike. They found a mutual interest in the kind of material they were writing and decided to join forces. Mike noted, "I already had my publishing arrangement with Good Sam, but Tom didn't, so he linked with me in my deal and, after writing together for a year, we decided to form a total duo and perform our own material."

But they began to tire of the L.A. scene. "It was really a drag," Mike said. "It was really foreign to us to have to face it like a job, you know, just cranking out songs. We started to feel like a jukebox. And there wasn't anything personal happening, with anyone. It wasn't fun. It wasn't making sense. It had to be fun. So . . . we split."

Eventually, the duo plus their families settled on a small farm in Missouri near Kansas City. Before they got there, though, Tom lived in a tent on a Hopi Indian reservation for a time, an experience that eventually led to such songs as "Too Soon Tomorrow" and "Song from Platte River."

From their Missouri retreat, the duo sallied forth at the end of 1969 and the start of the 1970s to perform in the clubs throughout the neighboring states. At the same time, A&M, without their knowing it, issued an album of their material called *Down in L.A.* When they found out that the LP was made of old demo tapes for Good Sam that didn't show them at their best, they were far from happy.

But it did help bring their skills to the attention of some fans and indicated there was an audience out there for their songs. Stan Plesser of Good Karma Productions offered to manage their career. The duo accepted and soon had a recording contract with Kama Sutra Records. In early 1969, they went to San Francisco to work on their first album for that label, with Nick Gravenites as producer. The session musicians for the resulting LP, titled *Weeds,* included fiddler Richard Greene, guitarist Mike Bloomfield, and Nicky Hopkins on keyboards. Among the original compositions in the collection were "Indian Summer," "Lady Like You," and "People Love Each Other."

Weeds wasn't a blockbuster, but it did moderately well for what Brewer & Shipley considered their first release. The group supported the LP with a series of engagements in major cities, including shows at the Bitter End in New York and the Troubadour in Los Angeles. Their next LP, *Tarkio Road,* came out in early 1971 and quickly won highly favorable reviews. Featuring notable backing guitar work by Jerry Garcia of the Grateful Dead, the single "One Toke Over the Line" quickly became one of the most-played new releases on radio. It moved into the top 10 and helped make *Tarkio* a

strong entry on the album charts. The team now was one of the major acts in pop music and headlined concerts and festivals all over the United States. Brewer & Shipley also performed on a number of major network TV shows. As Shipley recalled for Lahri Bond of *Dirty Linen* ("Brewer & Shipley—More Tokes for Old Folks," February/March 1996): "Almost overnight we went from making five thousand dollars to fifteen thousand dollars to fifty thousand dollars."

In late 1971, their third LP on Kama Sutra, *Shake Off the Demon,* coproduced by Brewer and Shipley, came out. It appeared on best-seller lists in early 1972 but did not approach the success of *Tarkio.* Their fourth and final album on Kama Sutra, also self-produced, was *Rural Space,* which came out in 1973 and appeared on hit lists for some weeks. However, its reception was even less strong than the previous one.

When Kama Sutra went out of business in 1973–74, they signed with Capitol Records. The debut on that label, an untitled LP just bearing the number *ST-11261,* came out soon after. Among its contents were such new songs as "Look Up, Look Out," "Eco-Catastrophic Blues," the country gospel "Fair Play," and the folk rockish "How Are You?" It ranked with their best efforts to that point, but perhaps due to changes in the taste of their audience or problems with promotion, it made little headway in the marketplace. The same held true for their second, and last, Capitol release, *Welcome to Riddle Bridge.*

In 1979 the duo decided to end their work together. Brewer opted to go it alone and recorded a solo album in the early 1980s, *Beauty Lies,* which included backup contributions from Linda Ronstadt, J. D. Souther, and Tom Scott. Shipley gave up performing in favor of producing documentary videos. As Shipley told Lahri Bond, "For years I had essentially taken advantage of all the fun that you can have on the road. I was having too much fun. I decided to get off the road. I also met a lady and realized this was for keeps, and decided it was time to look at my life, which was rapidly looking like a mess. Eventually a television station came along in the town I live in down in the Ozarks and I went to work there and started a television production company." That company, which he and wife Laura Powell still operated in the mid-1990s, produced commercials, industrial videos, and educational material for public TV as well as documentaries.

Still, many people remembered their recordings fondly, and favorable comments following a reunion set on a Kansas City "classic rock" station in the summer of 1986 induced them to line up future joint appearances. In September they won an ovation from a crowd of 10,000 fans who cheered their first live show in seven years. This inspired them to begin collaborating on new songs, while slowly increasing their personal appearances in the late 1980s and first part of the '90s. In 1993 they completed a new album, their first issued on compact disc, *Shanghai,* released on their own One Toke Productions label. In 1996 a second album, *Heartland,* came out on the same label. By then they had expanded their concert itinerary considerably, including a 1995 series called the "California Schemin' Tour" with Maria Muldaur, the New Riders, the Mamas and the Papas, and the '90s version of Canned Heat. Except for Muldaur, the other groups did not have the exact same rosters as in their glory years (in some cases because founding members had died), which prompted Shipley to comment to *Dirty Linen,* "We're still here and we're still performing. Oddly enough, in this day of '60s and '70s reunion bands, when you go to see us, you actually get the real Mike and Tom."

BROMBERG, DAVID: *Singer, guitarist, pianist, banjoist, mandolinist, fiddle player, flutist, songwriter, record producer. Born Philadelphia, Pennsylvania, September 19, 1945.*

Said David Bromberg in the mid-1970s, "I figure that I'll get exactly as successful as I'm supposed to, no more, no less. I'm not going to fight it and I'm not going to grovel for it. I'm not going to act surly in order to preserve my anonymity or folklike status, and I won't eat dirt so that somebody will bill me in some special concert. I don't believe in that. The only time that I do get surly is when someone tells me how to do my music. That's *all* I've got. It's the sum total. I'm not married; I've got no kids; I spend my life on the road and I've no hobbies beyond playing guitar, fiddle, and mandolin. There's nothing else in my life, so don't mess with it." The single-mindedness helped make Bromberg one of the most respected session musicians in the country. It also helped bring him the respect of a small but loyal following for his performing efforts.

Born in Philadelphia but raised mainly in New York, Bromberg did not take up the guitar until he was bedridden with a bout of the measles when he was thirteen. Once he began, he took to the instrument with a passion, teaching himself by listening to records by people like Pete Seeger, the Weavers, Josh White, Django Reinhardt, and Big Bill Broonzy. He particularly recalls the album *Josh White Comes Visiting,* on which Big Bill Broonzy took part, as a major inspiration.

He continued to add to his instrumental repertoire while attending high school. After graduating he entered Columbia University to take courses in harmony and music theory, intending to become a musicologist. However, he found the musical environment in Greenwich Village too attractive. He started performing occasionally in small clubs and coffeehouses and soon forsook college to work at his craft full-time.

His first engagement in the mid-1960s was with Jerry Jeff Walker, of "Mr. Bojangles" fame, with whom he appeared for several years. He backed many other artists during those years, including Rusty Evans, Fred Neil, Screamin' Tony McKay, Tad Tuesdale, and Richie Havens. He told Michael Brooks of *Guitar Player* (March 1973), "The first time I was in the studios was either with Screamin' Tony McKay or Rusty Evans. I didn't get paid for it as it was just going in for the thrill of being able to record. And that's where I found out that studio situations are tricky and that recording is not always the same thing as playing."

He picked up session technique rapidly, though, and became one of the most sought-after studio musicians in the city. In the late 1960s and the 1970s, he supported artists from all segments of the pop music field, including albums with Bob Dylan, Jerry Neff, Tom Paxton, Carly Simon, Patrick Sky, Mississippi John Hurt, the Reverend Gary Davis, Ringo Starr, Chubby Checker, John Prine, Paul Siebel, John Denver, and many others. Through the mid-1970s, he participated in over eighty albums. He also tried his hand at producing during those years, including John Hartford's Warner Bros. release, *Aereo-Plain.*

When Richard Skelly of *Relix* ("David Bromberg," February 1990) asked him to recall memorable session incidents, Bromberg cited meeting Dr. John (Mac Rebennack) at a recording studio, as well as his work with Bob Dylan (whom he backed on the albums *Self Portrait* and *New Morning*): "Working with Bob Dylan was very exciting to me. I never knew what was going to happen when I went into the studio. He was very spontaneous, and always got good performances out of people, I always thought. It's hard to work with someone like him and not be completely floored by what he can do.

"I remember one time I was playing Dobro for him on a date, and it just fell out of my hands, and I just sat there with my jaw hangin' open, listening to him."

One of his first road engagements in the late 1960s was as backing guitarist for a group called the Phoenix Singers. For a while after that, he played electric guitar with the Mojo Four during another concert swing.

At the start of the 1970s, Bromberg finally decided it was time to move to center stage. He had a chance to showcase his solo ability at the Isle of Wight pop festival in England and won resounding cheers from the massive audience. Columbia Records signed him soon after. His initial LP, *David Bromberg,* came out the following year, followed by *Demons in Disguise* (1972), *Wanted Dead or Alive,* (1974) and, in mid-1975, *Midnight on the Water.*

The albums contained some original compositions as well as his versions of a variety of music from traditional folk songs to jazz blues and rock-oriented material. His wide range of stylings was noted in the early 1970s by John S. Wilson, the *New York Times* jazz critic, who wrote, "David Bromberg fits no pigeonholes. He is part of everything contemporarily musical. He is a product of blues, country jazz, folk and classical music. . . . From his early success as a guitar virtuoso, Mr. Bromberg has developed into a brilliant entertainer."

After the mid-1970s, David parted company with Columbia and signed with San Francisco–based Fantasy Records. (Columbia issued the retrospective LP *Best of David Bromberg: Out of the Blues.*) In the late 1970s, Bromberg's releases on Fantasy included *How Late'll Ya Play 'Til* (1976) a two-disc live and studio album; *Reckless Abandon* (1977); *Bandit in a Bathing Suit; My Own House* (1978); and *You Should See the Rest of the Band* (1980). His affiliation with Fantasy prompted him to move to the San Francisco Bay region for several years.

During the 1970s, Bromberg formed his own regular backing group, which he dubbed "The World's First Folk Orchestra." He noted, "The band just crept up on me. I started out with just a bass player. Wherever we played, musicians I'd met on the road would come and sit in. Sometimes there would be ten musicians on the stage. It was very inspiring. I loved it! But then as we went along I began to miss certain guys. And by then I was making enough to afford to pay whoever I wanted to play with me." The band roster at the end of the 1970s comprised: Dick Fegy (fiddle, mandolin, guitars, banjo, string synthesizer), born Hartford, Connecticut, May 8, 1950; John Firmin (saxophone, clarinet, flute, percussion), born Anchorage, Alaska, April 20, 1947; George Kindler (fiddle, mandolin), born Washington, D.C., February 6, 1943; Curt Linberg (trombone), born St. Louis, Missouri, November 3, 1940; Lance Dickerson (drums), born Detroit, Michigan, October 15, 1948; and Dan Counts (bass), born Roanoke, Virginia.

In the fall of 1980 Bromberg dissolved his band and moved to Chicago in order to spend time with his family. At the same time he enrolled in the Kenneth Warren School of Violin Making, from which he graduated in 1984. He never completely abandoned his music field activities. But a prime reason for his early 1980s withdrawal from active music making was a wrenching dispute with the Fantasy organization.

The main elements in the situation were disagreements with the company's new artist and repertoire director. When Bromberg declined to complete delivery of the last album called for in his Fantasy contract, the label prevented him from releasing any new material until the matter was resolved. As he told Glenn Mitchell of the *Dallas Observer* ("A Former Sideman's Serenade," November 2, 1989), Fantasy officials demanded that he either record the final album due (and already paid for) on the contract or give up recording for any other label: "That's where we left it for quite a few years. They didn't believe me at first. You know, performers are supposed to be desperate to perform, and when it became clear to them that I wasn't, they sued me."

Finally, Bromberg compromised by going through the Fantasy vault to collect material he'd previously recorded, from which he assembled the album *Long Way from Here,* issued in 1986. "The kicker of the whole story," he told Mitchell, "is that I agreed to relinquish some royalties in return for my freedom, but there were some things they would be obligated to pay me. Afterward, they didn't live up to part of it, and we called them. They said, 'Sue us.' Obviously that was the point; they agreed to things they had no intention of fulfilling."

After finishing his education in violin making, Bromberg, who had learned to play the instrument proficiently, added to his income by buying and selling fiddles. Once free of Fantasy, he arranged to prepare a new album for Rounder Records; yet, fate intervened, as a series of setbacks kept him from completing that project for some three years. He told R. Bruce Dold of the *Chicago Tribune* ("Roads Less Traveled," October 12, 1989), "I had it all set up and was going to record the album in a month and I got pneumonia and couldn't do a thing. I had to rebook everyone's schedule and well over half a year had passed and then my father died. Everything was up in the air again. I canceled all of the sessions. And that took me a lot longer to recover from than the pneumonia. Then in the course of making it, my mother died. It seemed like there was no end to it."

While slowly getting things together for the new album, he continued his occasional work with what he called his MVP band. The group, which included a small nucleus of session musicians and a trio in which his wife, Nancy, sang, typically performed only in Chicago and St. Thomas, the latter venue where Bromberg annually played on New Year's Eve. When he finally got his Rounder sessions organized, the band was represented by one track on the final disc. Many long-time friends contributed to what was to become the 1989 release *Sideman Serenade,* David's first release of original recordings in a decade. They included Dr. John on piano, Jefferson Airplane alumnus Jorma Kaukonen on guitar, Jackson Browne on rhythm guitar and backing vocals, guitarist David Lindley, harmonica player John Sebastian, and another pianist well known to Chicagoans, Howard Levy, as well as some members of Willie Nelson's band.

Chris Daniels and the Kings, the Jesse Dixon singers, and Nancy Bromberg backed Bromberg on one of his three original compositions in the new collection, the gospel-flavored "Testify." Main support for the two others, "Top of the Slide" and "Watch Baby Fall," came from the Nelson sidemen. All in all, the album was certainly up to Bromberg's musical standards and won high praise from critics in late 1989 and early 1990. Accompanied in many concerts by one or more of the "name" artists from the sessions as well as his nine-piece Big Band (or, in some cases, performing solo), Bromberg toured widely in the early '90s, meeting a typically warm reception from new fans as well as old.

Still, he didn't resume the hectic pace of his earlier career, when he had sometimes done twenty-eight shows a month. In the '90s he did a fraction of that, returning between shows to be with Nancy and their two young children in the Hyde Park section of Chicago. In 1998 Columbia/Legacy released a compilation of his material from his years with that label on the CD *The Player: A Retrospective*.

BROONZY, BIG BILL: *Singer, guitarist, fiddler. Born Scott, Mississippi, June 26, 1898*; died Chicago, Illinois, August 15, 1958.*

Big Bill Broonzy was one of the greatest country blues performers of all time. As John Swenson of *Rolling Stone* noted, "Broonzy is the key transitional figure between the delta style of Robert Johnson and the electric Chicago blues of Muddy Waters." Sadly, he received little of that recognition during most of his lifetime. In fact, he was famous in Europe before more than a handful of Americans knew his name. Like so many folk-blues greats, Bill led a hand-to-mouth existence until his final years, though he managed to maintain his good nature and zest for living to the end of his days.

As one of a family of seventeen children, William Lee Conley Broonzy knew hard work from his earliest days. His family wandered between Mississippi and Arkansas during the first fifteen or sixteen years of his life. In 1915, he farmed on a sharecropping basis, but gave it up in 1916 when drought wiped out his crops. During those years he picked up many songs, from spirituals to blues numbers, and, at ten, was inspired to learn some instruments. He built himself a fiddle from a cigar box that his uncle taught him to play and a guitar out of a goods box and began to teach himself some accompaniments for his vocalizing. After a while he was accomplished enough to play with a friend at picnics. Those informal dates included "two-stages" —picnics where the whites danced on one side of the stage and the blacks on the other.

During World War I he enlisted in the army and went overseas in 1917. He returned home in 1919 and went to Chicago, where he got a job with the Pullman Company and perfected his guitar playing with veteran musician Papa Charlie Jackson.

The pattern of his life in the Windy City typified his life in general. He worked at various jobs to earn a living and gained his main enjoyment, and a little extra money, from part-time jobs in music. For much of the 1920s, he entertained at Saturday night "house rent" parties. One of his first original compositions of those years was a guitar solo called "Saturday Night Rub." He wrote fairly steadily afterward, completing more than 350 compositions before his death. Among the many musicians he performed with in Chicago during the early phases of his career were Sleepy John Estes,

Shorty Jackson, Blind Lemon Jefferson, Blind Blake, Lonnie Johnson, Shorty George, Jim Jackson, and Barbecue Bob.

In 1923, he made his first two records of his own material, "Big Bill Blues" and "House Rent Stomp." He was known as "Big Bill" for many years. A friend wangled away the $100 he made on the records. He managed to hold on to some of the money he got for later efforts of the 1920s, such as "Date with an Angel Blues," "The Walking Blues," "Big Bill Blues No. 2," "House Rent Stomp No. 2," "Bull Cow Blues," "Milk Cow Blues," "Serve It to Me Right Blues," and "Mama Let's Cuddle Some More."

In the 1930s he found increasing work in Chicago nightclubs and made a number of records with various other blues players on Champion Records. In 1932, he was in New York with one of several bands he organized and made a number of recordings on such labels as Vocalion, Oriole, and Melotone, including "Too Too Train Blues," "Worryin' You Off My Mind," "Shelby County Blues," and "Mistreatin' Mama Blues." Soon he was back in Chicago, where his old routine resumed. He made many more commercial recordings and worked as a performer fairly steadily, but got little money for those activities. To survive, he had to keep working at various menial jobs. His reputation was growing with folk fans, though, and in 1938 and 1939, he was one of the stars of the "Spirituals to Swing Concert" at New York's Carnegie Hall.

Although the enthusiasm of folk fans for his talents brought opportunities for engagements in nonsegregated clubs and college concerts across the United States in the 1940s, the folk audience still was too small to allow him the luxury of concentrating on music. During the 1940s, he supported himself mainly by working as a cook, porter, molder, piano mover, and a half dozen other "trades." As the 1950s began, he didn't seem to be getting anywhere and, in 1950, considered giving up performing. But he had become part of a group formed by Chicago folk artist Win Stracke called I Come for to Sing (whose other founders were Studs Terkel and William Lane) that began to get a growing number of engagements thanks to the beginnings of the postwar folk boom. As demonstrated in the group's debut performance, sponsored by the Renaissance Society of the University of Chicago, its goal was to present a panorama of all types of American folk music. The group was welcomed by enthusiastic crowds on major college campuses across the United States.

This exposure helped bring Bill an offer to tour Europe in 1951. It was a triumphal concert series, marked by standing ovations and critical praise. Europeans were amazed to find that Bill was virtually unknown in the United States, but when he got home that began to change. He was featured on dates with many established folk artists, from Pete Seeger to his old friends Brownie McGhee and Sonny Terry, and he started to re-

---

*Broonzy himself gave the year as 1893; after his death his twin sister produced a birth certificate giving it as 1898, the currently accepted year.

ceive invitations to guest on radio and TV shows. He extended his overseas tours to Africa, South America, and the Pacific region, and kept on making new recordings. The sales of his available catalog began picking up. From 1953 on, his financial position improved to where he could live quite well on his music earnings. Unfortunately, by 1958 he was dying of cancer, finally passing away on August 15.

Bill had told the story of his life to Belgian writer Yannick Bruynoghe back in 1954, and the material was published in a book, *Big Bill Blues: Big Bill Broonzy's Story, as told to Yannick Bruynoghe* (1955). An updated revision later came out in paperback (Oak Publications, New York, 1964).

Fortunately, his legacy remains in recorded form. By the late 1950s, his album catalog had begun to increase sharply with the release of such Folkways LPs as *Big Bill Broonzy Sings Country Blues, Big Bill Broonzy's Story,* and a 1959 blues album featuring Bill, Sonny Terry, and Brownie McGhee. Two massive collections came out posthumously on Verve in October 1961, a five-record set called *Big Bill Broonzy's Story* and a three-disc set, *Last Session.* More releases came out in the next few years. Folkways issued *Big Bill Broonzy Sings* in May 1962, and Mercury issued a *Memorial* album in October 1963 and another titled *Remember Big Bill* in August 1964. Releases on other labels in the mid-1960s included *Big Bill Broonzy* on Scepter, *Big Bill Broonzy with Washboard Sam* on Chess, and *Big Bill Broonzy* on the Archives of Folk Music.

Continued recognition of Bill's importance as a performer and songwriter was indicated by the availability of his albums for decades after his death. At the start of the 1980s, all of his Folkways LPs remained in print. Some of his 1930s and 1940s recordings also were available in current catalog albums of other companies, such as *Big Bill Broonzy* on Everest Records, *Do That Guitar Rag* and *Young Bill Broonzy* on Yazoo; *1932–42* on Biograph; and *Feelin' Low Down* and *Lonesome Road Blues* on Crescendo.

In the 1990s, Big Bill's name and legend continued to resonate with blues fans around the world as well as with new generations of rock musicians who turned to his recordings for pointers. Prospects for continued availability of his Folkways material far into the future were enhanced when the Smithsonian Institution purchased that label's catalog in the late 1980s. Some of the other albums listed above remained in print. In the early 1990s, he began to be represented on reissues in the Columbia/Legacy Roots 'n' Blues series; he had a few tracks on compilations like *Legends of the Blues* and the album *Big Bill Broonzy—Good Time Tonight.*

In 1990 Rykodisc/Tradition issued *Blues in the Mississippi Night,* which features Broonzy, Memphis Slim, and John Lee Sonny Boy Williamson from recordings Alan Lomax made with them in the mid-1940s. Lomax promised to keep their identities a secret because of the frankness of their words and songs about life in the South before Civil Rights. It was only released after their deaths. That year Columbia/Legacy also released *Good Time Tonight.* Document released *Complete Recorded Works in Chronological Order, Volumes 1–11* in 1991. In 1998 Columbia Legacy released the CD *Big Bill Broonzy: Warm, Witty & Wise* as part of its Mojo Workin'′ series. Smithsonian Folkways released *Trouble in Mind* in 2000. Among the other CDs available are *Treat Me Right; Baby Please Don't Go; Big Bill Boonzy: 1934—1947* on Story of Blues, *Historic Concert Recordings; Bill Bill Broonzy & Washboard Sam* on MCA/Chess; *The Young Big Bill Broonzy (1928–35)* and *Do that Guitar Rag (1928–1935)* on Yazoo; *Legendary Big Bill Broonzy* on Collector's Edition; *Feelin' Low Down* on GNP Crescendo; *Big Bill's Blues* on Portrait; *Legends of Country Blues Guitar* (Broonzy, Rev. Gary Davis, Son House, Mississippi John Hurt) on Rounder's Vestapol; *Muddy Waters Sings Big Bill Broonzy* on MCA/Chess; *Sings Folk Songs* on Smithsonian/Folkways; and Memphis Slim's *Tribute to Big Bill Broonzy* on Candid Records. His complete discography is covered by author Chris Smith in the book *Hit the Right Lick: The Recordings of Big Bill Broonzy* (Blues & Rhythm).

BROWN, ALISON: *banjoist, guitarist, songwriter. Born Hartford, Connecticut, August 7, 1962.*

Alison Brown didn't exactly learn how to play the five-string banjo while rocking in a chair in the Appalachians. Given the choice between punching a Quotron the rest of her life or plucking a banjo, she chose the banjo. In the late 1980s, the Harvard history and lit major and UCLA M.B.A. was working as an investment banker for Smith Barney, but her heart wasn't in it. So she left one male-dominated profession, investment banking, for another, bluegrass, becoming one of the most innovative and influential banjo players of the 1990s. In 1991 she became the first woman to be named Banjo Player of the Year by the International Bluegrass Music Association. When she returned to the world of spreadsheets, it was to form her own record company.

Brown showed that she had an aptitude for stringed instruments at an early age. She grew up in Stamford, Connecticut, the daughter of an attorney. Her parents, John and Barbara Brown, took guitar lessons. Her father was a decent trumpeter, but couldn't quite get the hang of the guitar. When she was eight, her parents took a two-week trip to Europe. Alison found an old guitar gathering dust in a corner. When her parents returned, they found Alison strumming the guitar. Her parents passed on a few tips, and she started taking lessons from a teacher who also played banjo. When the teacher played Flatt and Scruggs's *Foggy Mountain Banjo* record for her, she flipped. Her father made a cassette tape of the album, labeled it "hillbilly music," and Brown played it so much she wore it out.

At ten, Brown started learning basic tunes like "Cripple Creek" and "Worried Man Blues" on a cheap Mayfair banjo. The next year, her family moved to La Jolla, near San Diego, California. She took some lessons and joined a local bluegrass club. She also picked up some licks playing at pizza parlors and in parking lots. "There's a Southern California tradition of pizza and bluegrass," she told Earle Hitchner of the *Wall Street Journal* (1996). She played in a band called Gold Rush with fiddler Stuart Duncan, who went on to play in the Nashville Bluegrass Band. They recorded a twelve-track demo called *Pre-Sequel.*

In the late 1970s Brown attended La Jolla High School, where surfing was in and bluegrass was out. Besides banjo, she took piano lessons. During her teens, she played at the bluegrass festivals and won some competitions, including the Canadian National 5-String Banjo championship in 1978 and the Topanga Banjo and Fiddle Contest in 1979 and 1985.

"To tell you the truth, we thought that after all that traveling, she wouldn't want to pursue (music) as a career," her mother, Barbara, told the *La Jolla Light* in 1996. In 1971, Brown had told the newspaper that she didn't see much of a future for herself in bluegrass— "just gigs in pizza palaces."

Instead, in 1980 she headed east to Harvard, where she studied history and English literature. In between classes, she hosted a Saturday afternoon bluegrass radio show for the Harvard radio station, WHRB. She also cut an album with the New England bluegrass group Northern Lights. After graduating with a bachelor's degree, she decided to attend UCLA to get an M.B.A. She earned the M.B.A. in two years and landed a job as an investment banker with Smith Barney in San Francisco.

"I grew up in a very career-minded family," she explains. "In fact, everyone in my immediate family is a lawyer. Even though I always loved to play the banjo, I never expected that it would be more than a hobby for me."

The investment-banking job, in which she crunched numbers on tax-exempt bond underwriting, consumed her, but it wasn't satisfying. "There were people there who you just knew woke up in the morning, got in the shower, and thought how they could refund a particular bond issue. I got up, took a shower, and thought about music," she told Hitchner.

She quit, wrote some tunes, and started to think about what she was going to do with her life. Then bluegrass fiddler and singer Alison Krauss had an opening in her band for a banjo player and offered it to Brown. She toured with Krauss's band, Union Station, from 1989 to 1991. "It was a great education in bluegrass music, right down to the cross-country van trips, and a real eye-opener to play in the Southern Appalachian states where the music comes from," she

says. She recorded one album with Krauss, *I've Got That Old Feeling,* on Rounder, which won a Grammy.

She spent six months writing songs to see what she could come up with, and also studied jazz guitar. (She's best known for her banjo playing but is an excellent guitarist as well.) The result was her first solo album, *Simple Pleasures,* which David Grisman produced in 1990 on Vanguard and was nominated for a Best Bluegrass Grammy. Banjo innovator Béla Fleck wrote in the liner notes: "Her technique is formidable and her playing is filled with twists and turns." The influences of Grisman and Fleck are there, but the album showed that Brown had a style and vision of her own. Her playing is melodic, crisp, and clear, with help from Grisman, Krauss, Mike Marshall on guitar, and Jim Kerwin on percussion.

While she was with Union Station, Brown went into the studio with Michelle Shocked to record a song for her *Arkansas Traveler* album. That was 1992, and Brown released her second solo album, *Twilight Motel,* for Vanguard; it had a couple of bluegrass tracks but edged Brown toward the progressive side. It was produced by Mike Marshall and included Jerry Douglas on Dobro, John R. Burr (one of the members of her quartet) on keyboards, Tony Rice on guitar, and Roy Husky Jr. on bass.

Brown left Union Station, but she soon got a call from Shocked, who asked Brown to become the musical director for her world tour. Brown traveled through Europe, Australia, Canada, and the United States with Shocked, playing acoustic and electric guitar, Dobro, and banjo. She told *Banjo Newsletter* (January 1995): "For me, it was a big change from being in a bluegrass band—which isn't necessarily entertainment-oriented. The whole point was to put on a great show. Michelle is a great showperson, an incredible entertainer. We had parts of the show where everybody was in costume. We did the *Arkansas Traveler* routine. She had a little outhouse on stage and a white picket fence. She even had a stuffed chicken that she put on wheels! She got it from a taxidermist in Los Angeles and smuggled it into Europe."

When she was in Australia, she became acquainted with Shocked's bassist, Garry West. They soon became business (and personal) partners in search of good didgeridoo players. One particularly good player, Alan Dargin, led them to two brothers who had started a company called Natural Symphonies. West and Brown arranged a deal to distribute the company's titles in the United States (she now lives in Nashville). The result was their company, Small World Music. In 1995 Brown and West formed Compass Records, which has issued works by singer-songwriters Clive Gregson, Kate Campbell, and Leslie Tucker, the instrumental group Kaila Flexer and Third Ear, and Béla Fleck's bass player Victor Wooten.

Until 1998 Brown hadn't put out any of her own albums on Compass, since she had a four-record deal with Vanguard. In 1994, she solidified her quartet with Rick Reed on drums, John R. Burr on keyboards, and West on bass. The quartet has traveled to Latin America for the State Department, performed at the Shetland Islands Folk Festival in Scotland and at the Antigua Jazz Festival.

They recorded *Look Left,* which moved even further away from bluegrass although Mike Marshall and fiddler Vassar Clements play on the album. Some of her innovation comes from the mix of players she enlists: Bill Miller, a Native American musician, plays wood flute, Seamus Egan plays uilleann (elbow) pipes, and Alan Dargin plays didgeridoo.

She followed that up in 1996 with her fourth release on Vanguard, *Quartet.* The album was an attempt to capture her quartet's sound without any guest contributions. "In spite of all the wonderful musicians who have guested on my past records, I often feel that the most unique setting for my tunes is the Quartet—just John R., Garry, Rick and me putting our own stripped down spin on the music," she wrote in the liner notes. The album opens with the jazzy "g bop" and takes off from there.

As a banjoist running her own label, Brown has not let her M.B.A. go to waste. "I feel fortunate in that I've created my own job: making my own albums, having a touring band, and running a distribution and record company," she told Hitchner. "Thank heavens I learned how to do spreadsheets when I was a banker."

In 1998 she released *Out of the Blue,* her fifth solo album and her first on her own label, Compass. Produced by Garry West, the new album is an even jazzier collection than *Quartet* and features Alison playing an electric nylon-string banjo to achieve the cool jazz tones that she desired. The album also continues her interest in Latin and Caribbean sounds on songs like "Out of the Blue," "Coast Walk" "Samba del Sol," and "Rebel's Bolero." "It was really important for us at the beginning not to be perceived as a vanity label," she said. "But after twenty-two releases, I think we're past that. So, it's great to finally be on the label." She released *Fair Weather* in 2000.

BROWN, CHARLES: *Singer, songwriter, pianist. Born Texas City, Texas, September 13, 1922. Died Oakland, California, January 21, 1999.*
Many people heard Charles Brown for the first time when he appeared in a PBS documentary with Bonnie Raitt who called Brown "the most extraordinary piano player I've ever heard." The broadcast and his tours with Raitt in the late 1980s and early '90s made people aware of Brown's piano playing and suave voice, not to mention his colorful stage persona and Navy-style caps. The appearances rekindled Brown's career in the

1990s, although he first hit the top of the R&B charts fifty years earlier.

Brown was born in Texas City, Texas, and was raised by his grandmother following the death of his mother. He started taking classical piano lessons when he was ten, but also listened to jazz and blues artists Art Tatum, Fats Waller, the Ink Spots, and Leroy Carr. He attended Prairie View A&M College, earned his bachelor's degree in chemistry, and taught high school science at Carver High School in Baytown, Texas. During World War II, he moved to Pine Bluff, Arkansas, where he made mustard gas for the military arsenal located there. In 1943, he was transferred to Berkeley, California.

He briefly played piano in a club in Berkeley, but began to focus on music in 1944, when he moved to Los Angeles. He liked the thriving club scene on Central Avenue and won a talent show at the Lincoln Theater for his performance of "Boogie with the St. Louis Blues," which he melded with the "Warsaw Concerto." He soon had gigs playing at clubs like the Chicken Shack and Lincoln Theater. He caught the attention of guitarist Johnny Moore who asked him to join a group called the Three Blazers, with Eddie Williams on bass. The group was modeled after the Nat King Cole Trio. The Three Blazers first recorded for Atlas, accompanying Frankie Laine. In 1946, after switching to the Philo/Aladdin label, the Blazers scored with Brown's original "Drifting Blues," which rose to number two on the R&B charts and won R&B Record of the Year honors from *Cash Box.* The Three Blazers also recorded for the Exclusive and Modern labels, and hit again the following year with "Merry Christmas, Baby."

In 1949, Brown formed the Charles Brown Trio and signed with Aladdin. He followed with such chart-topping hits as "Trouble Blues" and "Black Night," and other successful records like "Get Yourself Another Fool," "In the Evening When the Sun Goes Down," "Hard Times," "My Heart Is Mended," and "Seven Long Days." By 1950 Brown was the top R&B star on the West Coast. He influenced players like Ruth Brown (no relation), Ray Charles, and the Dominos.

His career faltered in 1952 with the onset of rock. Brown's ballads and piano playing were no longer in favor. He also had difficulties with the musicians union and ran afoul of the tax man. For the next twenty-five years he recorded albums but he never recaptured the popularity of the late 1940s early '50s. To make ends meet he took odd jobs like washing windows for a janitorial service.

During the 1950s, he continued to tour, traveling the South with Johnny Ace in 1954 and performing at clubs in Los Angeles. He recorded with the Ray Charles Singers in 1956 and Amos Milburn in 1959. He also performed with Jimmy Witherspoon. He reunited with Johnny Moore in 1961 and recorded for Mainstream in

1963. He released Legend (BluesWay) in 1969, and recorded with T-Bone Walker in 1973 and Johnny Otis in 1975. His fortunes began to turn around when he performed at Tramps in New York in 1983. Three years later he recorded *One More for the Road* for Blueside Records. Alligator reissued the album at the end of the decade.

Bonnie Raitt pulled Brown out of the doldrums for good in 1987 when she took him on tour. He would often appear on stage with Ruth Brown who belted out blues songs while he played the piano. The exposure enable Charles Brown to record a new album in 1990 entitled *All My Life* for the Bullseye Blues label. Dr. John and Ruth Brown appeared on the album, and Bonnie Raitt wrote the liner notes. That and his 1992 Bullseye follow-up album, *Someone to Love,* which featured Raitt on slide guitar, received strong critical acclaim and sold well. Brown formed his own band and went on tour again with guitarist Danny Caron.

In 1996, however, Brown's health began to fail. At the end of 1998 he was confined to a nursing home in Oakland. Friends such as Raitt, Maria Muldaur, Charlie Musselwhite, Dr. John, and John Lee Hooker held a benefit concert in January 1999 to help pay his medical bills. He died of congestive heart failure on January 21, 1999. In a statement, Raitt said that Brown "introduced the nuances of great pop and jazz singing into the world of R&B, and you'll hear it in everyone from Ray Charles to Sam Cooke to Marvin Gaye."

Brown is represented by numerous albums and CDs: *Sunny Road* and *Race Track Blues* (Route 66), *The Boss of the Blues* (Mainstream, 1963–64), *Driftin' Blues: The Best of Charles Brown* (EMI, 1990), *Just a Lucky So and So* (Bullseye Blues, 1994), *The Complete Aladdin Recordings of Charles Brown* (1994), *These Blues* (Verve, 1995) *Snuff Dippin' Mama* (1995), *Honeydripper* (Verve, 1996), *Please Come Home for Christmas* (King, 1998), *1946* (1998), *Cool Christmas Blues* (Bullseye Blues, 1998), *So Goes Love* (Verve, 1998), and *1944–1945* (Jazz Chronological Classics, 1999).

BROWN, CLARENCE "GATEMOUTH": *Singer, guitarist, fiddler, viola player, harmonica player, drummer, band leader, songwriter. Born Louisiana, 1924.*

His reputation as a blues artist was an important factor in bringing Clarence "Gatemouth" Brown's work to the attention of many fans and music industry peers, but he never thought of himself as purely a blues performer. In fact, a typical Gatemouth concert in the mid-1990s, like one performed before a packed house at B.B. King's Blues Club on the City Walk in Universal City, ran the gamut from a few blues to a fiddle tune cowritten by him ("Stop Time"), a version of Duke Ellington's jazz number "Take the A Train," country, honky-tonk, and Caribbean-based songs to his treatment of the old Righteous Brothers hit "Unchained Melody," which he

and his four-piece band began slowly and soulfully and then revved up to a breakneck pace as the crowd on the dance floor cavorted feverishly.

Brown himself sometimes took the lead on guitar or fiddle; other times, garbed in his black cowboy outfit topped by a black cowboy hat, he sat back on his high stool, lighted his pipe, and directed the band occasionally with a single finger. He liked having good bandsmen, he always said, and if you had them there wasn't much sense in not letting them display their skills.

Brown recalled learning to play his first instruments from his father, who performed with amateur groups in the Sabine River section of East Texas, not far from the Louisiana border. (Gates was born in Louisiana in 1924, but the same year his family moved to Range, Texas.) He emphasized that his father wasn't a blues musician but rather someone who likes country and bluegrass music, with some Cajun influence from nearby Louisiana. That was the kind of music Brown cut his musical eyeteeth on, he pointed out. He wasn't unaware of blues, but that was just one of a number of types of material he heard and played in his formative years. In his teens he enjoyed playing jazz, and at sixteen Brown started playing drums and singing in a group called Howard Spencer and his Gay Swingsters. Before joining the army he toured Texas with the group W.M. Bimbo & His Brownskin Models.

In his twenties, as Gatemouth found the musical options limited in his hometown, he went to Houston looking for better career opportunities. There, as he recalls, he was the benefactor of a lucky break and his own willingness to take chances. At the town's Bronze Peacock club, blues star T-Bone Walker took sick one night and had to leave the stage—whereupon Brown rushed onstage, grabbed Walker's guitar, and improvised a new blues song of his own on the spot. His performance won crowd approval and $600 in tips while also making Walker's promoter and club owner, Don Robey, take notice. Robey, Brown stated, quickly arranged for him to record on the Aladdin label, and also set up appearances at his club and other locales in the region. Robey liked Gatemouth's work so well he soon signed him for his own label, Peacock.

The recording collaboration between Gatemouth Brown and Don Robey led to many excellent blues-based singles and albums released on Peacock between 1949 and 1960. Many, like the early '50s self-penned "Sad Hour," became regional favorites, and one, "Okie Dokie Stomp," made the national charts. Other singles written by Brown in those years included "She Winked Her Eye" and "Gate's Salty Blues." In Texas and nearby states, Brown developed a considerable following. In 1960, however, Gatemouth and Robey went their separate ways. The reason, Gatemouth told Pat Collier for a *Sing Out!* article ("Clarence 'Gatemouth' Brown— American Music, Texas Style," vol. 40, no. 4, 1995): "They wanted me to keep playin' that blues, and I was gettin' interested in other stuff. I wanted to play country, work some country in. People weren't interested in this."

For much of the 1960s, people in the industry and fans of his blues artistry lost track of him. As he told Collier, "People think I was out of music during that time, but that's not right. That's when I was making my crossover, lettin' the different styles come into my music. I played all over the place. I moved up to Colorado and played at all kinds of joints. I played strip joints—I quit a couple of those jobs 'cause I didn't like it. I moved down to New Mexico and played in little clubs in mining towns. I was my same self but I was turning myself around, playing my country."

European audiences' love of the blues helped revitalize Brown's career in the '70s. French promoters sought him out in New Mexico and arranged for him to play several overseas gigs in 1971. In 1973 he was a featured performer at the Montreux Jazz Festival in Switzerland. He also eventually found time to make contact with Nashville writers and performers like John Loudermilk and Roy Clark. From the mid-1970s into the 1990s Gatemouth included several of Loudermilk's compositions on his albums, and in the 1996 release *A Long Way Home* Loudermilk backed Brown on a number of tracks and also sang his classic song "Tobacco Road."

In the 1970s interest in Brown's performances increased again, and albums of both his older material and new work began to appear. In 1975, Red Lightnin' Records released an anthology of his best Peacock tracks called *San Antonio Ballbuster.* That same year, MCA Records issued his collaboration with Roy Clark, *Makin' Music.* In a review of the album in his syndicated column, Irwin Stambler noted Roy Clark's recent accomplishments—which included cohosting TV's *Hee Haw,* touring the Soviet Union under U.S. State Department sponsorship, and taking the stage with the Boston Pops—and pointed out that Brown "is a veteran blues and jazz artist who deserves more attention than he's received over the years.

"The album might seem more on Gatemouth's home turf than Roy's, presenting as it does such blues and boogie numbers as 'The Drifter' (written by Brown) and 'Caldonia' and such jazz tracks as Gatemouth's 'Short Stuff' and the old Ellington standard (written by Billy Strayhorn) 'Take the A Train.' . . . Vocally, Roy's smooth, countrified style forms an effective foil to Brown's rough-hewn country-blues singing. Both as performers and as a writing team, the duo provides the best track in the LP, the slow, impactful 'Justice Blues.' "

Other Gatemouth albums issued in the mid- and late '70s included *Gate's on the Heat* on Blue Street in 1975, *Bogalusa Boogie Man* on Barclay in 1976, and, in 1978, *Blackjack/Music Is Medicine.* In the early 1980s he completed his first album on Rounder

Records, the 1981 release *Alright Again!* The disc won the Grammy Award for Best Traditional Blues Recording (announced on the TV Awards show on February 23, 1983). This was followed by a 1983 Rounder compilation, *The Original Peacock Recordings.* That same year Rounder issued *One More Mile,* reissued on CD in 1991. Continuing his busy recording work of that decade, Gatemouth completed *Pressure Cooker* on Alligator, his 1985 debut on that label. Two years later Rounder issued his collections *Texas Swing* and *Real Life.* In 1989, he had another release on Alligator, *Standing My Ground.*

Throughout the 1980s into the 1990s, Gatemouth continued to take part in festivals of various kinds in many parts of the United States as well as in other countries. In one concert series in England and on the Continent, he opened for English rock guitar superstar Eric Clapton. In one period in the mid-'90s, after touring U.S. venues, he spent five weeks in Europe, went for a year-end series in Japan, returned to do a boat cruise gig, and arranged for tour dates with Billy Gibbons and ZZ Top.

In 1992 Alligator issued his new album *No Looking Back,* whose contents included another special Gatemouth treatment of an Ellington number, in this case "C-Jam Blues." In 1993 Evidence Records issued his album *Just Got Lucky,* and in 1994 Verve reissued his 1975 *Gate's on the Heat* disc on CD. That collection originally was issued on the French Black and Blue and Barclay labels, as were *Blues in Montreux* and *Professor Longhair's Rock & Roll Gumbo,* also reissued by Verve. This was followed by a new collection, *The Man,* issued by Verve in 1995, and *A Long Way Home* from 1996.

Though Gatemouth never stopped writing new songs—besides those noted above, his credits include "Boogie Uproar" and "Blues Power" (the latter made famous by Clapton, who joined Brown in a duet of the song on *A Long Way Home)*—he took a great deal of pleasure in adding his own touches to music originated by others. In the case of Ellington's "Take the A Train," for instance, he noted he didn't want the song to remind a listener of Ellington's style. He emphasized to Collier, "I want it to sound like me." He did the same thing with Muddy Waters's trademark "Got My Mojo Working," to the point where during Clapton's "From the Cradle Tour" he was asked to omit it one night because it was being done in Clapton's set. Instead of improvising, he recalled, Clapton just played it the way Muddy did.

He philosophized to Collier, "If you're a young person, and you're up on stage playing like Muddy Waters or Howlin' Wolf, all these hardcore blues artists, I just don't see a point in that. The music's just a big joke. They're up there using the same thing over and over. It's not saying anything. . . .

"Everybody's trying to be somebody else, it seems to me. And in this world, it's hard enough just to be yourself. I've been noticin' in country music these days, it seems like nobody's got their own direction. Country music today is just people jumpin' on what's already been done."

Writing in *Option,* Bart Groomes commented, "Brown is best known for his uncomplicated Texas blues playing. But then he pulls out his violin or viola and his seasoned band launches into a Cajun or straight country number, and you realize that this man is U.S. roots music personified."

BROWN, GREG: *Singer, songwriter, guitarist. Born Ottumwa, Iowa, July 2, 1949.*

Performing at the Neighborhood Church in Pasadena in November 1996, Greg Brown came onstage wearing a hat, multicolored scarf, and dark glasses. He never took off the glasses. Instead, he took the audience on an imaginary musical and poetic trip stretching from Ottumwa, Iowa, to China. Backed by Nina Gerber on guitar and Bill Griffin on mandolin (longtime Kate Wolf accompanists), Brown regaled the audience with stories about growing up in the Midwest with his onetime preacher father. He sang "Where Is Maria?", longing for the diversity represented by the mythical Maria.

It doesn't matter that Brown's voice has been called a "gruff, seafaring baritone, trolling at the bottom of its register in search of a tune." In the tradition of Tom Waits and Leonard Cohen, Brown's voice is well suited to his poetic-story songs, which have been recorded by the likes of Mary-Chapin Carpenter, Shawn Colvin, and Carlos Santana. His songs are lessons in songwriting. The first couple of lines for "Brand New '64 Dodge" rattled in his head for two years. The rest didn't come to him until he was running for a plane at Chicago's O'Hare airport. He missed the plane but got the song, which tells the story of a family buying a Dodge in 1963, just before the Kennedy assassination.

He described the process of writing "Brand New '64 Dodge" in *Sing Out!* (November–December '95/January '96): "What is a song? It could start with the beat, walking down a street, the rhythm of your life that day, sitting in a bar mishearing a snatch of conversation—but you like the beat of it, you hear a melody inherent in the riff of words, and you find yourself humming under your breath, and there it is: a song. Children make them up without thinking, and so do I—good days. It's all there for whoever hears it. You don't need a guitar or a Casio or an orchestra. A stick will do, an old pan, tears on your face. Or a laugh from deep inside."

Brown didn't go too far for his musical influences. His kinfolk in the Hacklebarney region of southern Iowa always got together to play music. Their roots were in the Appalachians and Ozarks. As banjoist Art Rosenbaum told Brown after visiting his relatives: "Greg, there's a lot of folksingers who would give their left nut for your roots." His maternal grandfather played the banjo and fiddle, his grandmother played the pump

organ and sang Irish ballads. He started playing his grandma's pump organ at six. At twelve, he took up his mother's Gibson guitar and began writing songs. By seventeen, he knew he wanted to be a musician, but struggled with a more practical side.

"I always loved music, but I was interested in so many other things. I was interested in biology, anything to do with the outdoors, literature. I wanted to study and maybe keep music on the side. The urge [to do music] was just a little too strong. . . . I'm not that fond of the life that goes with it. In some ways I'm more of a homebody."

His father, William Brown, worked building telephone and radio broadcasting towers after he got out of the army. He opened a radio and TV repair shop and was doing well when he answered a calling to become a preacher with the Old Bible Church (later as a Methodist). Every few years, he moved the family, which included Greg's older sister, Sharon, around to small towns in Iowa, Kansas, and Missouri. They stayed the longest—five years—in the northeastern Iowa town of Earlville.

Greg heard gospel music, and learned how to spin a yarn while listening to his dad's preaching. His mother, Mary, played the "church lick" on a arch-top Gibson electric guitar. Greg would get up and sing at church.

Greg loved sports and made friends easily; it wasn't a problem that his family moved so much. But at fifteen, he suddenly didn't want to move. "The moving date came and I was playing the piano," Brown recalls. "My dad came in and said, 'It's time to move the piano.' I said, 'As soon as I finish this song.' He said, 'We've got to move it now.' We had that classic father-son moment. We just looked at each other for a while. He said, 'Go ahead and finish your piece, son, and then we'll move the piano.'"

Despite his religious leanings, Bill Brown, who once incurred the wrath of a small town for approaching the Bible as myth rather than fact, placed no restrictions on his son's musical listening habits. Brown was "knocked out" at ten when he found a Big Bill Broonzy album at a garage sale in Kansas. He loved Jerry Lee Lewis.

Fed up with the "narrowness of small towns and the role of the pastor," Bill Brown dropped out of the church when Greg was sixteen. He worked with juvenile delinquents for a while and later started a continuation high school in Des Moines.

Mary Brown, an English teacher, read poems to Greg at bedtime—Robert Frost, William Blake. There were always books at home. She was also a classical music fan. Greg took classical piano lessons. "But I cheated," Brown says. "I could always play so easily by ear. My sister would play my lesson and I'd learn it by ear. So I didn't learn to sight-read as well as I should have."

During his senior year of high school, he took voice lessons from an Italian woman who taught him how to breathe and sing, which he says kept him from having voice problems later on. He sang bass in the school choir.

Brown's piano playing ended at eighteen. He was working in a meat-packing plant when another worker sliced off part of his left thumb by accident. He wasn't devastated, although he only got $800 in compensation. "I could probably be an independently wealthy man if I had known anything then."

The day after the accident, he picked up his guitar and tried to play it, even though his thumb was bound and oozing blood. "My father, up until then, had really been wanting me to get my college degree," Brown says. "He saw me sitting there with that bloody thumb trying to play. He put his arm on my shoulder and said, 'I can tell you're going to go for this, so good luck to you.' He gave me his blessing."

Greg stopped playing the twelve-string guitar and concentrated on the six-string. He couldn't bring his thumb over the top anymore, or play bar chords up and down the neck, but he could still play and that's what was important to him. "If you know Django Reinhardt's story, you can't feel too sorry for yourself for missing part of one digit."

He was still writing songs when he entered the University of Iowa. Folksinger Eric Andersen was going to perform, and the university held a contest to find an opening act. Brown won and played three original songs at the concert. Afterwards Andersen invited Brown to New York. "I'll show you around," he told him. Brown went to New York as soon as his freshman year ended. But he couldn't find Andersen

Brown had a stash of $300 to $400, but, as he puts it, "I'd never seen people in such bad shape, so I just gave my money away. In two weeks my money was gone and I was out on the streets. It was hippie days and you had a lot of company. I would sleep in Washington Square Park until they chased me out, and then I'd go up to Penn Station. . . . The way I ate really was once in a while I'd get a little job singing at somewhere in the Village for $15 to $20. That would feed me for a week."

Brown played open mikes at Gerde's Folk City. The regular emcee was leaving and asked Brown if he wanted the job. He became the new emcee for $50 a week. He was set—for about eight months, until he fell in love with a woman from Oregon. "One day I just woke up, sold my guitar and flew to Oregon. That's what you do when you're nineteen."

A bit later on, Brown met up with guitarist Paul Bjerke and pianist Marcia Seeberger. They formed a trio for three or four years. Seeberger knew Buck Ram, founder of the Platters, who eventually named the trio the Comstock Load. Ram invited them to come to Las Vegas and ghost-write songs. "Buck was always looking for the next Platters," Brown says. "He liked our vocal harmonies, took us under his wing, and we worked for him for about a year and a half."

Brown wrote a number of "awful" songs for the bands Ram had in development. "It was like going to school. Buck would say I've got this guy, he's kind of a smooth pop singer, he needs a few tunes. Or I've got this quartet, they're playing rhythm and blues. I was writing in different styles. I'd listen to their tapes and then try to write some stuff."

The trio grew tired of waiting for Ram to record them, and disbanded in the early 1970s. "Paul and Marcia wanted to do other things. I wanted to quit the music business. I felt like I'd done it all and seen it all. I'd lived in New York. I'd lived in L.A. I traveled around the country, played all kinds of joints. I thought, that's enough of that."

Brown moved outside of Iowa City with his first wife, a pre-med student, and their baby. He didn't play professionally for two and a half years and found odd jobs: driving a truck, hospital and library work. He considered going to school to study forestry.

But in 1976 a musician friend, Dick Pinney, whom he had met in Wisconsin, settled on a farm nearby. They began playing gigs, cut a record "and things kind of kicked in again almost without me noticing it."

At the time, Brown was not a great performer. "I would sit up there with my head down kind of hunched over my guitar. I just played my tunes. I never said boo to the audience. I was playing in bars where nobody cared if you said boo or not anyway."

One night he was performing and didn't even notice that the cops had busted the bar and arrested ten to fifteen underage kids in the balcony. In 1978, he auditioned and got a job with the Iowa Arts Council's Touring Arts Team, visiting towns around the state in the summertime. The job paid $50/day. He compiled a twenty-five-song demo tape and sent it out to record companies. Nobody was interested. So he started his own label, which he named after his red barn. He called it Red House Records. In the early 1980s, he got a bank loan and produced his debut, *44 & 66,* during a four-hour session in Des Moines. He printed up a thousand copies and sold them at gigs and did the same thing for his next album, *The Iowa Waltz.*

He got bored and was ready to quit again in his early thirties. "I always had this pull to do something besides being a musician." As soon as he decided to quit, his luck turned around. Willie Nelson recorded one of his songs, called "They All Went to Mexico." "A terrible little song," Brown says.

Then Garrison Keillor's *Prairie Home Companion* offered him a job in the early '80s. Robin and Linda Williams and Bryan Bowers had performed some of his songs and they asked him to come in. He hit it off with Keillor. He moved to Saint Paul, Minnesota, as a regular in 1983 and worked through the fall of 1985. He wrote opening and closing numbers with Keillor, and enjoyed the spontaneous collaboration. One time Brown came in whistling "Bolero." Keillor started writing lyrics to the tune and before long they had a song about a bowling alley called "Don's Bowlero."

"Musically it felt like a feast," he recalls. "One week I'd be playing with the Preservation Hall Jazz Band and the next week I'd be playing with BeauSoleil. The next week I'd get to jam with some great gospel piano player."

While living in the Twin Cities, he met Bob Feldman who was teaching a business course. Both of Brown's albums were out of print. Feldman suggested that they print up more and he would handle the business end. They reissued *44 & 66* and *Iowa Waltz* and put out a new album, *In the Dark with You,* in 1985. He took two or three days to make *In the Dark with You.* (His engineer is Tom Tucker, who also worked for Prince.) The album got airplay on public radio, and eventually sold 25,000 copies, more than the first two. "It all kind of went hand in hand with being on the *Prairie Home* show, too," he says.

When Brown left *Prairie Home Companion,* he simply gave the label to Bob Feldman. "There was nothing to sell at that point," Brown says. "It was just my little records. I said, 'You just take it over. I don't have any financial interest in it at all.'" (Feldman turned it into a successful independent label.)

Brown lived in Chicago for a year and a half. In 1986, he put his own lyrical gifts aside and recorded an album setting William Blake's poetry to music, called *Songs of Innocence and Experience.* Fiddler Michael Doucet, founder of BeauSoleil, is said to have wept during the sessions because he was so moved. "I don't remember it as being at all difficult to record," Brown says. "It was simply a matter of loving those poems."

During the 1980s he found himself returning to his musical roots, moving to Iowa City in 1987. "One thing I like about Bruce Springsteen is it's like listening to New Jersey or, if you listen to Muddy Waters, that's the Delta and later the sound of Chicago. I think being from the Midwest is a big part of who I am. It's not like I do all my writing about small towns. It's more it just affects who you are and your outlook."

Each of Brown's albums built on the previous one, critically and artistically, most selling in the 20,000 and 30,000 range. In 1988 he released *One More Goodnight Kiss,* and in 1989 he released *One Big Town.* It won a NAIRD award for Adult Contemporary Album of the Year and three and a half stars from *Rolling Stone.* He released *Down in There* in 1990 and *Dream Cafe* in 1992, which received high marks from critics and drew comparisons to Bob Dylan's *Blood on the Tracks* from *Z Magazine.*

Brown acknowledges that *Dream Cafe* could be referred to as his divorce album. "I suppose 'You Drive Me Crazy' and 'Dream Cafe' itself, that song, they have that feeling to them of a relationship kind of coming apart, I guess."

Brown received a Grammy nomination for *Friend of Mine,* his 1993 release with his friend and fly-fishing comrade Bill Morrissey on Rounder/Philo. The album includes a song Brown wrote for Morrissey called "Fishing with Bill."

"*Friend of Mine* came about as a fluke," Brown said. "Bill was doing an album called *Inside* a few years back. We did 'Hang Me,' an old folk song. Bill said, 'We should do a whole record of old folk tunes.' I said 'Yeah, that'd be fun.' I thought that would be the end of it. Next thing I knew we were in the studio doing it."

While Brown had usually just made his albums in live sessions, Morrissey was more methodical, laying songs down track by track. Morrissey's "well-crafted" songs impressed Brown. "Every word's in place. Almost the opposite of my songs, where there is stuff hanging out all over the place."

In 1993, Brown released *Bath Tub Blues,* his first record of children's music, on Red House. His experiences touring the state for the Arts Council affected his songs. His daughters from his second marriage, Constance and Zöe, accompany him.

Brown returned to adult themes with *The Poet Game* in 1994, his most successful album to date, selling more than 50,000 copies. Alanna Nash wrote of the album in *Stereo Review* (February 1995): "*The Poet Game* is full of unforgettable images and well-lit snapshots of the human condition. . . . On its own terms it's a powerful statement about trying to make sense out of missed opportunity and discarded treasures—large and civic, small and private. Think of it as an elegant examination of scar tissue."

The album debuted on Gavin's Americana chart at number four and won a NAIRD Indie Award for Singer-Songwriter Album of the Year. It opens with "Brand New '64 Dodge," with images of innocence and doom with the assassination of Kennedy:

> *And Jesus loves our president,*
> *Even though he is a Catholic,*
> *There's a lot for a boy to think about*
> *As he walks along the railroad tracks.*

With the loss of innocence, the songs that follow are dark and skeptical: "Ballingall Hotel," "One Wrong Turn," and "Sadness." In "Boomtown," Brown sings about people from California and New York ruining once-idyllic places; "The Poet Game" is full of images of the troubled life of the poet. In the end, the narrator wonders, *If I had it all to do again/I am not sure I would/ play the poet game.* Brown balances the dark songs with some humor. In "Jesus & Elvis," for example, he compares the two 'kings': *Jesus sang down through the ages: 'Do like you'd have 'em do to you.'/Elvis rocked the universe with be-bop-a-lu-la.*

Brown says he can only write dark and cynical songs when he's feeling good, drawing a comparison with Richard Thompson, who is happy-go-lucky himself but writes gloom-and-doom songs. "One thing that happens when you write the dark stuff is you kind of get rid of all the darkness within you and you let it out," he says.

His songs for the most part aren't autobiographical. "There's little bits in there," he says. "But a lot of my songs are about other people. Any time you say 'I' it seems people make that mistake. . . . We all face heartache and trouble of all kinds in our lives. A lot of people also have some real pleasure and some stuff that fills them up good. That's what I really write about."

In 1995, Brown released his first live album, *The Live One,* recorded in summer 1994 during a concert at JR's Warehouse in Traverse City, Michigan. Brown didn't know that a friend was taping it on his DAT machine. When he heard the tape it was exactly what he was looking for: "A good night in a good club with a good crowd. To me that's what it's really about." (In 1999, Red House released *One Magical Night,* originally recorded in 1982.)

Following his successful *Poet Game,* Brown returned to the studio in 1996 with his longtime producer Bo Ramsey and the superb lap slide guitarist Kelly Jo Phelps. The result was *Further In,* an acoustic album that is much lighter than *Poet Game.* "I think of it as being quite romantic and kind of a sexy record. There are a lot more love songs on it. I've been threatening for the last couple of years to do my Barry White album. This one's not it. But it's a step on the road to the *Late Night Lovers album."*

One of Brown's songs, "Sadness," was used in the sound track for the movie *Dream with the Fishes.* In 1997 Red House released *Slant 6 Mind.* Brown used the "Slant 6"—"the dependable old engine that would keep going after the body rusted away"—as a metaphor for songs such as "Mose Allison Played Here," "Dusty Woods" about Robert Johnson, "Billy from the Hills" about his father, and "Vivid," a thank-you note to Ani DiFranco for a song she wrote about him called "The Bouquet." He hadn't expected to make the record. He was trying to put together a songbook of his old songs and found himself writing new ones instead. The contemporary album ironically was nominated for a Grammy in the Traditional Folk category. Regardless of categories, it was recognition of Brown's growing importance in music.

Among other projects, Brown is working on a songbook with snatches of prose pieces. He is considering another album of Blake poems, and an album that would tie together two or three short stories. In his spare time, he paints and hopes to build a big pond and a cabin on the forty-acre farm in southern Iowa he inherited from his grandparents. In 1999 he completed *Solid Heart,* to benefit In Harmony, a nonprofit organization based in Oregon. In 2000 he completed work on a new album, *Covenant,* on Red House.

For now, Brown continues to write songs, but he doesn't force it. "I think my subconscious does the real bulk of the work. A lot of it is a mystery to me as to where the songs come from or how they develop. I get in these periods where I feel very receptive. It generally will go for three to six months. Then it seems like I have to rest from that. Then I learn other people's songs or I'll work on some of these other projects. After maybe three months or so go by I'll feel receptive to songs again."

Based on a Lyndon Stambler interview with Greg Brown

BROWNE, JACKSON: *Songwriter, singer, pianist, guitarist. Born Heidelberg, Germany, October 9, 1948.*

It might be said that Jackson Browne was to the '70s as Bob Dylan was to the '60s. Not that they are alike in styles or songwriting approach; but if Dylan was the premier solo folk-rock artist of the '60s, Browne certainly could lay claim to that status for the following decade. His career seemed to stall creatively, with some exceptions, in the 1980s, as his concert audiences seemed far more interested in his landmark earlier work than in his new material. In the first part of the '90s there were some indications he was beginning to reverse that trend.

Browne was born in Germany, but moved to Los Angeles with his family when he was three. He studied several instruments at an early age and was a proficient pianist and guitarist by his late teens. By then, he had also demonstrated a budding talent for songwriting. In 1967 he went to New York City, where he worked at a number of local clubs through 1968. He picked up experience, but didn't make much headway in furthering his position in the music field.

In the late '60s, he headed back to the West Coast, which became his home base from then on. He picked up some jobs as a sideman and session pianist in Los Angeles, but his reputation began to rise with his peers mainly because of his songwriting skills. He became friends with Linda Ronstadt, J.D. Souther, future Eagles mainstay Glenn Frey, and other struggling young performers with a bent for blending folk and country elements with rock.

In fact, for a while, Frey and Souther joined Jackson in his frugal $60-a-month apartment in L.A.'s Echo Park district as all of them waited for the big break. Frey and Brown worked on song material together; one creation—"Take It Easy"—was to prove highly important later on for the Eagles. Browne's version of the song was included in his *For Everyman* album. But Browne began to make progress as a songwriter in the late '60s and early '70s as more and more artists recorded his material, including Tom Rush, Linda Ronstadt, Johnny Rivers, the Byrds, and Brewer & Shipley. During that period, he made several attempts to make his way as a solo artist, without notable success. However, in 1971 he finally struck pay dirt when David Geffen signed him for his new label, Asylum Records. His debut LP, *Jackson Browne,* came out in October 1971 and gradually garnered considerable airplay across the country, particularly on FM stations. It made the charts in early 1972 and stayed on them for months, helping to spawn two hit singles, "Doctor My Eyes" and "Rock Me on the Water." Browne backed it up with a steady round of concerts that included tours with J.D. Souther and the Eagles, in the fall.

After 1972, Jackson never looked back. Though his album output was relatively sparse in the '70s, every one contained a number of folk-rock gems, most completely written by him. Those songs plus other originals were often covered or introduced by other artists, among them Bonnie Raitt, Ronstadt, Joan Baez, Ian Matthews, Gregg Allman, and Warren Zevon. In his concert tours, Browne surrounded himself with excellent musicians, including noteworthy talents such as fiddler/pedal-steel player/guitarist David Lindley, and lead guitarist Waddy Wachtel. Unlike other stars, Browne never disdained playing smaller venues. Much of his concert work was on the college circuit, with ticket prices set within a typical student's budget.

His second LP, *For Everyman,* came out on Asylum in the fall of 1973; the single "Red Neck Friend" from it made regional charts. The album itself was on bestseller lists well into 1974. In the fall of 1974, he was represented by his third album, still one of his finest, *Late for the Sky,* which remained in upper chart levels into 1975.

Though Browne continued an intensive concert schedule, it was close to two years before he completed another LP. By the time that collection came out in late 1976, considerable anticipation had been built up among his now sizable following. Called *The Pretender,* the LP rose to the top 5 on the charts in December, having earned a gold record award from the RIAA on November 14, 1976. His next release, *Running on Empty,* found even more favor with the public. It turned up on the charts almost as soon as it was issued in late 1977, staying there into 1979, bringing a platinum record award along the way.

During the 1970s, Browne remained a strong advocate of protecting the environment and saving endangered species, often giving fund-raising concerts for causes he believed in. At the end of the '70s, he joined forces with Graham Nash in urging a stop to the proliferation of nuclear power. They helped assemble a number of concerts in 1979 both to express that opposition and to collect money to fight nuclear energy. They were joined in 1979 by many rock and folk-rock artists in a series of concerts in New York's Madison Square Garden that provided material for a two-record *No Nukes* live album.

Browne's strong interest in antinuclear and other social causes may have caused him to reduce his emphasis on writing new singles candidates or touring. His album releases and concert tours were considerably more sporadic in the 1980s than in the previous decade. He began the decade with the 1980 Asylum album *Hold Out,* a reasonably good collection, though not up to his earlier standards. But it was certainly far better than his 1983 LP, *Lawyers in Love.* The latter was on the charts the last nineteen weeks of 1983 and into 1984, earning gold record certification, but it was one of the major disappointments of 1983. His 1986 collection on Elektra, *Live in the Balance,* however, restored some of the luster in his writing credits and suggested he might have a brighter future in store for his still sizable following.

By the 1990s, Browne had joined a new crusade, at one point joining people like John Denver and Kris Kristofferson in concerts against drug abuse. Though he had stopped using drugs long before the end of the '80s, he said his own decision was nevertheless a delayed reaction to the 1979 drug-affected death of his friend Lowell George of Little Feat band fame. He stressed that he wished he had not waited the extra years. "The reason a person finally stops doing drugs is obvious. My children and my work were greatly affected."

He was also influenced, he told a reporter, by seeing many musicians who didn't take drugs, "to see how much longer they could last, how much harder they could work. Over the time that you take drugs, you begin to get a tally of the mistakes you made, the decisions you can't undo."

He emphasized that alcohol abuse can be as terribly harmful as any mainstream drug. As he told a *Los Angeles Times* interviewer, "Four kids in my neighborhood were killed in a flaming car crash not long ago. They were just burned alive in the car, and alcohol was the reason. The effects alcohol has on people's lives are just devastating."

His father, he noted, who died some years earlier from Alzheimer's disease, suffered from alcoholism. "It was hard to calculate the effects that his drinking had on us growing up. But in later years it was evident that the effect was considerable. Dad died of Alzheimer's, but it was vastly complicated by drinking. A neurosurgeon who was a friend of my father's took me aside and said, 'You should know your dad drank and drank and drank.' I guess Dad prided himself on his ability to hold his liquor."

Jackson completed one more album before the end of the 1980s, and for a time he was more prominent in the pages of gossip publications for his romance and tumultuous breakup (in 1992) with actress Daryl Hannah than in mainstream media for his musical activities. When his first album in four years, *I'm Alive,* came out in the fall of 1993, listeners associated many of the songs with the final stages of that relationship. Browne told Chris Willman of the *Los Angeles Times* ("Browne Getting on with Life after Daryl," November 27, 1993), "People imagine they know exactly what circumstances the song was being written in. But these songs were written over a period of four years in a lot of different states of the relationship, and if you imagine they were all written at one particular point after the dissolution of the relationship, that misses . . . Well, it's a drag to even imagine that people are thinking about that relationship instead of their own lives. I think if a song is any good, eventually it'll turn out to be about the life of the listener and not about the life of the writer. Anyway, that's my hope."

His concerts in support of the new album (from which the track "All Good Things" was the most notable) were vintage Browne, and won applause from both audiences and critics, including what he termed a "rave review" from the *New York Times*. While happy to get it, he commented, "I hate to have it be at the expense of trashing my last 10 years of work. Two nights ago I appeared at an Oxfam America hunger banquet in Boston, and there are a lot of places where the songs from the last two albums still really mean a lot to people." As that indicated, he continued to devote a good part of his entertainment schedule to what he felt were good causes, from fighting poverty and hunger to arguing in favor of Native American rights.

During 1995, he started working on a new album for Elektra Records, his debut on that label. Released in early 1996, *Looking East* won favorable comments from many (but not all) reviewers, including Stephen Holden of the *New York Times* ("Jackson Browne vs. Madison Avenue," February 18, 1996). Holden observed that in the track "Information Wars," Browne "mounts an attack on America's television culture that includes an ingenious collage of variations on familiar advertising slogans." The remaining contents, he added, represent "a mixture of lofty social commentary and love songs that recall the contemplative folk-rock style of Mr. Browne's 1970's albums." He concluded, "Having made detours through rock bombast and outspoken political protests, Mr. Browne seems to have recovered the reflective songwriting voice that began deserting him 20 years ago when arena stardom beckoned."

In truth, while the album is a listenable and well-prepared collection, it was hardly a resounding advance beyond his repertoire of the early career days. Certainly concertgoers still anticipated his performance of songs like "Stay," "For Everyman," and "Late for the Sky" rather than newer numbers. As Browne had said ruefully to Willman, "The longer you're around, the more certainly a part of your audience has memories tied in to certain songs and favorite times. I don't think there's any returning to an earlier time in your life—although some things are kind of cyclical, and it's possible to be in the same position later in life."

In the fall of 1998, Elektra issued the first retrospective collection of Jackson's material, *The Next Voice You Hear: The Best of Jackson Browne*. The set included two new songs by Browne, the title song and "The Rebel Jesus."

BRYNDLE: *Group originally formed 1969, disbanded in 1971, reunited in early 1990s. Karla Bonoff, (singer, songwriter, pianist, guitarist), born Santa Monica, California, December 27, 1951; Kenny Edwards, (singer, songwriter, mandolinist, bassist, guitarist, producer), born Santa Monica, California, February 10, 1946; Andrew Gold, (singer, songwriter, guitarist, keyboards, producer, engineer), born Burbank, California, August 2, 1951 (left band in July 1996); Wendy Waldman, (singer, songwriter, guitarist, pianist), born Burbank, California, November 26, 1951; Scott Babcock, (drums, percussion), born Pasadena, California, August 22, 1960; Matt Cartsonis, (bassist, vocalist, guitarist, fiddle, accordionist), born Philadelphia, Pennsylvania, June 19, 1959 (joined band in May 1996). Other members include Bill Bonk, bass, left band in 1996; Peter Bernstein, bass in original band; Dennis Wood, drums in original band.*

When Bryndle performed at McCabe's Guitar Shop in Santa Monica in 1996, the group's melodies and four-part harmonies recaptured the 1970s singer-songwriter sound. Karla Bonoff, Kenny Edwards, Andrew Gold, and Wendy Waldman had briefly joined together in 1969. After disbanding in 1971, Gold and Bonoff went on to have top 10 hits. Edwards and Waldman also had their own successes as performers, producers, and writers. Twenty-five years later, the four decided to get back together.

Kenny Edwards, who started playing upright bass (and later cello) in school, was influenced early on by 1950s R&B and rockabilly artists like Little Richard, Jerry Lee Lewis, Chuck Berry, and Eddie Cochran. In high school he began listening to traditional folk and blues and began learning banjo, mandolin, and guitar. He worked at the Ash Grove, where he met Roger McGuinn and David Crosby before they formed the Byrds. Bobby Kimmel introduced him to a singer he knew from Tucson—Linda Ronstadt. In 1965 they formed the Stone Poneys (named after a Charley Patton song), releasing three albums on Capitol before breaking up in 1968. The group recorded the rock classic, "Different Drum." Edwards met Waldman and Gold when he was playing at a local high school with the Stone Poneys.

Andrew Gold wrote his first songs at thirteen. His father, Ernest Gold, was a sound track composer who won an Oscar in 1961 for his score of *Exodus*. His mother, Marni Nixon, was the singing voice for Audrey Hepburn in *My Fair Lady*, Deborah Kerr in *The King and I,* and Natalie Wood in *West Side Story.* Gold was an extra in *Inherit the Wind,* which his father had scored. He released his first single, "Of All the Little Girls in the World," in 1967 on Polydor U.K. as part of a group called Villiers and Gold.

Waldman is a third-generation songwriter. Her grandfather, George Steiner, was a composer in Hungary who settled in New York. Her father, Fred Steiner, was a composer for radio in New York. Shirley, her mother, was a violinist and concert mistress for the New Haven Symphony. They moved to L.A. to find work in television. Fred wrote music for *Gunsmoke* and the theme to *Perry Mason.* Wendy describes her eclectic influences in the liner notes to the Warner Brothers retrospective album *Love Is the Only Goal: The Best of Wendy Waldman* (1996): "Any night in L.A. you could see great jazz artists, hear Latin music, ethnic bands and dance companies from all over the world, psychedelic acts from San Francisco, legendary bluegrass artists from the Southeast, political songwriters and folk revivalists from New York and Boston, the great Chicago bluesmen, bluesmen from the Delta and from Texas, English folk-rock bands, young white musicians experimenting with rock and blues, with songwriting, with the blend of several cultures at once, and so many others. . . ." At sixteen, Waldman began performing as a soloist and later worked with a jug band.

Bonoff also came from a musical family. Her mother, Shirley, a classical pianist, started Karla and her sister Lisa on the piano when they were in grade school. (Her father Chester P. Bonoff was a radiologist.) Karla enjoyed the piano, but was even more excited when someone gave her a toy guitar. By fifteen she was taking lessons with Frank Hamilton, who had played with the Weavers. For a while she and her sister formed a duo (The Daughters of Chester P.), and sang at a number of "Hoot Nights" at the Troubadour in the late 1960s and early '70s. "In those days Jackson Browne was doing Hoots, and so was James Taylor," she said. "It was an exciting place. You knew when you played there someone would hear you. It was really scary, though."

They auditioned for Elektra/Asylum and cut a demo. But Lisa decided to focus on college work. Karla pursued music. A chance meeting with Edwards (who had begun exploring Eastern Spiritual practices and music) at a Transcendental Meditation seminar in Lake Tahoe gave her musical career a boost.

Waldman, Gold, Edwards, and Bonoff formed Bryndle in 1969, naming the band after a multicolored animal, the brindle. (Gold, who liked the Byrds, encouraged them to change the *i* to a *y.*) They cut a debut album with producer Chuck Plotkin for A&M in 1970. But it never came out. "There was so much confusion and lack of experience, both in the band and in our producers, that our music wandered around hopelessly in search of a real direction," Edwards explained in a

Q&A on Bryndle's Web site. "We were new songwriters and were wary of cowriting and diluting our adolescent visions."

One single from the sessions, "Woke Up This Morning," written by Bonoff and produced by Lou Adler, became a hit in Northern California but soon disappeared. The group played locally for a short while, then disbanded in early 1971. Gold and Edwards briefly formed a group called the Rangers before joining Linda Ronstadt's band.

The early 1970s marked a transition from the traditional folk and folk-rock of the 1960s to a singer-songwriter tradition. The Eagles, Jackson Browne, and Linda Ronstadt were gaining prominence.

Edwards played bass and contributed background vocals for Ronstadt's 1974 album *Heart Like a Wheel,* which hit number one on the pop charts and achieved platinum status. Andrew Gold contributed the smooth guitar licks on such Ronstadt hits as "You're No Good" and "When Will I Be Loved?" Edwards and Gold toured with Ronstadt and contributed to Ronstadt's next album, *Prisoner in Disguise* (1975). Edwards cowrote "Lo Siento Mi Vida" and Gold cowrote "Try Me Again" for *Hasten Down the Wind* (1976) with Ronstadt.

During this period, Gold also released four solo albums: *Andrew Gold* (1975), produced by Plotkin, *What's Wrong with This Picture* (1976), produced by Peter Asher; *All This and Heaven Too* (1978), and *Whirlwind* (1979), his last album for Elektra/Asylum. "Lonely Boy," from his second album reached number five on the *Billboard* charts; he broke the top 10 with two songs from his third album: "Never Let Her Slip Away" and "Thank You for Being a Friend." The latter became the theme song for the TV series *The Golden Girls.* He also had a hit with "How Can This Be Love."

Waldman carved out a solo career. Maria Muldaur recorded two of her songs, "Vaudeville Man" and "Mad Mad Me" on her debut album for Warner Brothers. (She later recorded "Gringo en Mexico" for her *Waitress in a Donut Shop* album.) In 1973, at the age of twenty-two, Waldman released her first album on Warner Brothers, *Love Has Got Me.* Produced by Plotkin, it included her Bryndle cohorts on backup. The album didn't make Wendy an overnight star, but it did increase her stature. She contributed backing vocals on Ronstadt's *Don't Cry Now,* and *Heart Like a Wheel.* Earlier that year Waldman's second LP, *Gypsy Symphony,* recorded at the Muscle Shoals studios, came out on Warner Brothers. She followed with *Wendy Waldman* (1975), produced by Nick Venet. She went from the Muscle Shoals sound to a folk roots sound on her self-titled album. Commenting on the wide range of subjects covered in her songs at the time, Wendy said, "As many pictures and emotions as there are in the world, that's how many potential songs are out there." She followed with *The Main Refrain* in 1976, produced by her friend

Peter Bernstein. Other friends—Ronstadt, Muldaur, Taj Mahal, Bonoff, Gold, and Edwards—also participated.

The gap between albums four and five was somewhat longer than for her previous efforts. In between Wendy moved to Seattle, where she organized a new band with a stronger rock direction. She also enlisted the services of Mike Flicker, who had produced the first hit albums of the rock group Heart. *Strange Company,* released in May 1978, marked her strongest departure yet from the folk arena, and yet one of the songs, "Love Is the Only Goal," was written in honor of Steve Goodman and John Prine. The tradeoff probably brought her talents to a somewhat wider spectrum of fans. It still wasn't enough to make her album work commercially. She left Warner Brothers in 1978. After struggling for four years, she released another rock-influenced album, *Which Way to Main Street,* (1982, Epic), produced by Eddie Kramer, who had worked with Bad Company and Jimi Hendrix. Waldman moved to Nashville and became involved in writing and producing for the country market. She released *Letters Home* on Cypress Records in 1987. Her songs were recorded by Vanessa Williams and the Nitty Gritty Dirt Band. She produced Suzy Bogguss's debut album as well as albums for the Forester Sisters and Jonathan Edwards. Warner Brothers released a retrospective in 1996, *Love Is the Only Goal: The Best of Wendy Waldman.*

For Karla Bonoff, the road to a solo career went through Ronstadt. Edwards introduced Bonoff's material to Ronstadt, which helped both women's careers. As Karla told *Fullerton Hornet* editor Chip O'Neal (December 3, 1976), Ronstadt almost included "Lose Again" on her *Prisoner in Disguise* album. Karla's spirits soon rose when Linda selected "Lose Again" for *Hasten Down the Wind.* Linda also included two others, "Someone to Lay Down Beside Me" and "If He's Ever Near." "Someone to Lay Down Beside Me" was issued as a single and made top-chart levels. Soon more of Karla's songs were being discovered by a wide range of artists. During 1976, she signed with Columbia and began work on her debut disc. That self-titled collection, produced by Kenny Edwards and issued in March 1977, verified her skills as vocalist and song interpreter even if it didn't threaten to outstrip any of Ronstadt's late 1970s releases. She had a hit with her song "I Can't Hold On," and Bonnie Raitt would later record her song "Home." One of her problems, she agreed, was her relatively low volume of new songs. She told O'Neal, "When I write [lyrics] it comes out in a burst. Like I wrote 'Someone to Lay Down Beside Me' in about twenty minutes. I had the music and I just went and sat down and the words just sort of came out and I went 'Oh, far out!' and it was there. . . . But that kind of mood doesn't hit me too often."

With a good reception for her first album, she put together material for the next LP somewhat faster. *Restless Nights,* produced by Edwards even though they had ended their nine-year relationship, was issued by Columbia in September 1979. It included such new songs by Karla, besides the title track, as "The Letter," "Only a Fool," and "Never Stop Her Heart" plus two cowritten with Edwards, "Trouble Again" and "Baby Don't Go." Also included was the adaptation of the traditional "The Water Is Wide," on which Karla collaborated with Frank Hamilton and Pete Seeger. The album remained on the charts well into 1980.

As the disco craze edged into the 1980s, all four Bryndle members continued their careers, though at a slower pace. Gold, who once did the voice for Alvin of the Chipmunks, produced albums and tracks for Rita Coolidge, Art Garfunkel, Vince Gill, Nicolette Larson, and 10cc, which hired him to work on *Ten out of Ten* in 1982. He soon joined forces with Graham Gouldman of 10cc to form the group Wax. They released three LPs—*Magnetic Heaven* (1986), *American English* (1987), and *A Hundred Thousand in Fresh Notes* (1989)—and had two hits, "Right Between the Eyes" and "Bridge to Your Heart." He also cowrote songs for many others: "Show Some Emotion" with Celine Dion and "I Saw the Light" with Wynonna Judd. He sang the theme song "Final Frontier" for the TV show *Mad About You* (and once played a bodyguard on the show). Rhino released *Best of Andrew Gold* in 1996. Another project during these years was a collection of Halloween songs for children.

Edwards, who wrote teleplays for *Miami Vice, Crime Story,* and *The Street,* continued to work as a sideman with Ronstadt, Don Henley, Warren Zevon, Stevie Nicks, and J.D. Souther in the early 1980s. He produced Bonoff's third LP, *Wild Heart of the Young,* released in 1982. Bonoff had a hit in the early 1980s with the song "Personally" from the album. She became popular in Japan and toured there often. It took six more years before she released her next album, *New World,* in 1988 on Gold Castle, which was rereleased by JVC and Music Masters. She and J.D. Souther wrote songs for the movie *About Last Night.* She also teamed up with Wendy Waldman to write "Standing Right Next to You," a country hit that was also used in the movie *Eight Seconds.* (Edwards and Gold produced Vince Gill's version of "When Will I Be Loved?" for the same movie.) Bonoff's songs have been recorded by Wynonna Judd ("Tell Me Why") and Lynn Anderson ("Isn't It Always Love"). Ronstadt recorded three more of her songs for her album *Cry Like a Rainstorm, Howl Like the Wind,* including a duet with Aaron Neville ("All My Life"), which won a Grammy. Columbia/Legacy released *All My Life: The Best of Karla Bonoff* in September 1999.

More than twenty years after their initial foray into the music business, Edwards, Bonoff, Waldman, and Gold met at Gold's house one night and began to joke about getting back together. "I think everybody was at a point in their individual careers and life where it made sense," Edwards told Jim Lee of *Dirty Linen* (June/July '96).

They began recording a new album in the winter of 1994, releasing *Bryndle* in August 1995 on Music Masters/BMG. The album, produced by Bryndle and Josh Leo, includes fourteen tracks, most of them cowritten. "I cowrite for my daily bread, but to write for Bryndle is to cowrite a mural, to do a painting," Waldman told Lee. (Scott Babcock, who has played with Victoria Williams, Lyle Lovett, and Peter Himmelman, played drums.) The album sold reasonably well, thanks to a strong base of followers and a Web site that helped to promote the band (www.bryndle.com). They also released a promotional one-song Christmas CD in 1995, *Corn, Water, and Wood.*

The group toured extensively in the United States, but in June 1996 Gold announced that he was leaving to relocate to the East Coast with his wife Vanessa and their three daughters. The rest of the band members, including Waldman, Edwards, Bonoff, Babcock, and Matt Cartsonis on bass, continued to play. They were working on a second CD, *Bryndle 2,* due out in 2000.

The four members of Bryndle harbor few illusions of grandeur. As Andrew Gold told *People* in 1996: "Sometimes I'll pull out my credit card and the clerk will say, 'Hey, you're Andrew Gold from the '70s,' and I'll think, 'You're right. What am I doing here?' I was eating some granola, and suddenly here I am."

As Waldman told Robyn Flans of *Mix Magazine* (March 1996): "This is a world filled with angry alternative 22-year-olds and record companies that only want that kind of music. Will there be a place for us? Let's face it, we're not 20-year-old artists, which I personally think makes us unbelievably bitchin'. We kick ass; we're a very good band, and we can rock in the ways that 22-year-olds can't. . . . When you're older, you know how to lay it down. You know how to pull it out of yourself and control it, which gives it that much more impact."

BUCKLEY, TIM: *Singer, guitarist, banjoist, songwriter. Born Washington, D.C., February 14, 1947; died Santa Monica, California, June 29, 1975.*

Tim Buckley lived a scant twenty-eight years and never achieved the commercial heights that many expected of him. Yet he bequeathed much to posterity— fond memories of some great concert moments to many of his followers, and nine albums, including many gems and innovations likely to influence music lovers and musical innovators in years to come.

Born Timothy Charles Buckley III in Washington, D.C., he spent his first ten years in Amsterdam, New York, then moved with his family to Anaheim, California. Buckley's reminiscences of his early influences were given to interviewer Frankie Nemko (*Down Beat,* June 10, 1977): "I was only about twelve years old and I had probably five or six notes to my voice. I heard a recording of a trumpet playing things way up there. So I tried to reach those notes. Little Richard got them. It was like a falsetto scream. I'd ride my bicycle around the neighborhood screaming at the buses until I couldn't go any higher.

"Then one day I heard the opposite end, the baritone sax, waaaay . . . doooown . . . there. I said, 'There's gotta be a way to do that.'

"So I practiced, and I screamed, and I practiced some more, until I finally ended up with my five-to-five-and-a-half-octave voice."

As he moved into his teens, he was attracted to various musical styles, from Hank Williams to Miles Davis. He taught himself to play banjo from listening to country and folk records, and then played local dates with a country band.

During his brief stay in college, his interests were beginning to shift toward poetry and folk-flavored rock. He started to collaborate with a close friend, poet Larry Beckett, on original songs. At first Tim supplied music, but before long he was creating songs of his own. Buckley formed an act with bass player Jim Fiedler, later a member of the rock group Blood, Sweat and Tears, which played many of his songs at small clubs in the L.A. area. One of those shows was heard by drummer Jim Black of the Mothers of Invention, who told Mothers manager Herb Cohen of Buckley's striking voice. Cohen followed up, and selected six of Tim and Larry's songs for a demonstration record.

He booked Buckley into New York's Night Owl Cafe during the summer of 1966 and sent the demo material along to Jac Holzman, president of Elektra Records. Even before Buckley appeared in New York, Holzman had been so impressed by the advance recordings that he was ready to sign Tim: "I asked Herb to arrange a meeting, but I had made my mind up already. We spent a late afternoon together and my belief in Tim was more than confirmed." In a short time, Tim was in the studios back in Los Angeles working on his debut LP, *Tim Buckley,* released in October 1966. The album had a strong folk flavor that, as it happened, forced Buckley into a straightjacket he didn't want.

As Lee Underwood, who was a sideman in Buckley's first band and had worked with him in the years to come, wrote in *Down Beat,* "Tim liked the melodic and harmonic flow of 'Valentine Melody,' 'Song of the Magician,' and 'Song Slowly Sung,' but for the most part, he later regarded this first effort as just that, a first effort, naive, stiff, quaky, and innocent. It was, however, a ticket into the marketplace. There, because he played an acoustic guitar and strummed, they called him a 'folk' singer, a misnomer from which he never freed himself."

The album didn't make any waves, although it did help bring increasing opportunities to perform on the college campus and rock festival circuit. His abilities attracted attention from many musical peers. George Harrison, for instance, urged the Beatles' manager Brian Epstein to hear a Buckley concert at New York's Cafe Au Go Go in April 1967.

In 1967, his follow-up album did much better—the title song, "Goodbye and Hello" showed up on national charts, as did the antiwar song "No Man Can Find the War." By then, Buckley was moving away from the cerebral world of Larry Beckett to concentrate on themes closer to his heart. Almost all the material on his third Elektra release, *Happy/Sad* (1969) was by him. The album had much greater emphasis on jazz-related themes, including the song "Strange Feeling," which was patterned after Miles Davis's "All Blues." In 1969 Tim also composed the sound track for the film *Changes*.

However, Tim's creative restlessness alarmed Elektra officials, who felt he was abandoning the approach that promised to make him a major star. Rather than listen to the commercial pleadings, Tim went still further afield in the album *Lorca* (1970), where he was interested in developing music based on unusual sound and lyric patterns. Wrote Underwood, "The album, which was composed in 5/4 time, proved too experimental. It failed dismally with the public and also caused Elektra to drop him. When he essayed some of his new musical gymnastics in concert, he drew negative responses from unprepared critics and audiences."

Under pressure from management, he finally agreed to assemble some of his previously unrecorded songs in his earlier styles and turn out a new LP. The result was *Blue Afternoon,* issued on Straight Records in 1971. "The performances were perfunctory," Underwood wrote. "Tim's heart was not in them, and it showed." The album was a failure. Undaunted, Tim went back to playing music his way. The result was *Star-Sailor* (1971), in which most of the pieces return to the odd time signatures—particularly 5/4—Buckley was exploring. The album, issued on Straight Records, didn't set the charts on fire, but it won praise from a number of critics, particularly in the jazz field. *Down Beat,* for instance, gave it a five-star rating. Warner Brothers released *Greetings from L.A.* in 1972.

However, the impact on his career was even more catastrophic than *Lorca.* Buckley found himself without a recording contract and, for legal reasons, unable to perform except on the q.t. "After two years," stated Underwood, "he was strapped in every way. He needed money. He desperately needed the idolatry recognition of his long-vanished public. He needed to record. He needed to feel like a man again. He needed to come back!" Buckley also needed to come back from the drug and alcohol dependency he had developed.

He seemed to be achieving his goal in 1973–74, when he signed with DiscReet Records. They released his LPs *Sefronia* (1973) and *Look at the Fool* (1974). He cut back sharply on drugs and alcohol and got the chance to hit the concert trail again. He found audi-

ences interested in his modified mid-1970s folk-rock style. But in 1975, he once more was without a recording agreement. Watching him at the Starwood in May 1975, a *Los Angeles Times* critic praised his supple, roaming voice and wrote, "Tim Buckley is a bona fide legend and no record company should be allowed to sign another country-rock act or heavy-metal group until he is back in the studios."

Time, though, was running out. Late the next month, returning home from an engagement in Dallas, he hit the bottle in the afternoon and then, visiting a friend, accepted some heroin. Said Underwood, "Buckley's system had been clean. The combined dosage of alcohol and heroin proved to be too much for him." Tim was pronounced dead at 9:42 P.M. the evening of June 29, 1975, in Santa Monica.

In his farewell in *Down Beat,* Underwood wrote, "Tim Buckley held hands with the world for a while. He gave in fire and fury and perverse humor the totality of his life's experience, which was vast beyond his mere 28 years. . . . He had a beauty of spirit, a beauty of song and a beauty of personage that re-etched the face of the lives of all who knew him and of all who ever truly heard him. He burned with a very special flame, one of a kind. Bye, bye, baby. . . ."

In the years that followed, only a few die-hard fans kept his memory alive. Warner Brothers released *The Late Great Tim Buckley* in 1978, and Rhino released *Best of Tim Buckley* in 1983. He had never accumulated a backlog of unreleased material, another result of the general neglect of his talents by the recording industry. There was a glimmer of hope for his rediscovery when some live tapes from a 1968 concert in London, England, formed the basis for the 1989 release, *Dream Letter* on Demon Records. As his ever faithful friend Lee Underwood commented in the album's liner notes, "His first loyalty was . . . to the music itself, to the creative process, and to the unfathomable mystery and complexity of the human heart."

The early '90s saw a renewed interest in the man and his music by other artists. Some recorded cover versions of his songs, such as the Cocteau Twins' track of "Song to the Siren," and in 1991 a tribute concert was organized in St. Anne's Church in Brooklyn, New York. That year Strange Fruit Records also released *The Peel Sessions* from his radio interviews with British host John Peel. (Another collection, *Honeymoon,* was issued by Edsel Records in 1995, taken from a 1973 radio show in New York.) Then, in the mid-1990s, the discovery of a batch of unreleased tapes of still another concert, and the appearance on the pop scene of his very talented son, Jeff Buckley, seemed to confirm the revival of Tim Buckley's reputation. *Tim Buckley Live at the Troubadour 1969,* issued in 1994 by Rhino Records, captured the full flavor of Tim at his most passionate. Providing lead vocals that on occasion exhibited a range of five and a half octaves, and playing his beloved twelve-string acoustic guitar, he obviously was enjoying himself while delighting enthusiastic fans.

Reviewer Phil Gallo, writing in the *L.A. Weekly* (June 10, 1994), wrote: "*Dream Letter* was a whisper of a date, an evening alone with a tripper among the stars. *Troubadour* is a scream, a psychedelic frenzy that showcases all his directions and impulses: the folk roots, the rock leanings, his jazz influences and soul tendencies with an operatic bent. His voice goes from Lou Reed drone to Aaron Neville sweet—it was his greatest attraction then and it remains so now. The textures, the sentiments, the love songs—they all reek of incense and hashish." Most of the *Troubadour* numbers had been released on his old albums except for two previously unissued songs, "My Venice Mating Call" and "I Don't Need It to Rain." Also made available in the mid-'90s was a boxed set of Buckley's output offered by Enigma Records.

In a number of reviews, Tim's *Troubadour* was bracketed with son Jeff's 1994 release *Grace*. Jeff, whose father had left Jeff's mother soon after he was born, was not happy about that, rejecting Tim as a positive influence and maintaining that he himself was definitely not a folksinger. This certainly seems true from the contents of his debut album on Sony Records, the 1993 EP *Live at Sin-é*, where his high-pitched, almost falsettolike, vocal stylings would be hard to categorize. His homage to Edith Piaf, "Je N' en Commais Pas La Fin," might be construed as pop-folk in the vein of performers like Leonard Cohen, but elements of jazz, pop, rock, and even more traditional folk could be discerned in *Sin-é* (a nightspot in New York's East Village) and the follow-on, the highly acclaimed *Grace*.

Jeff, born in Anaheim, California, on November 17, 1966, was raised by his mother after his parents' marriage dissolved. Growing up in Orange and Riverside Counties, he was interested in a wide range of music formats as a child even without Tim's presence, and played guitar in teenage rock bands in the early 1980s. As his interest in music extended to writing original songs, he settled for a time in Los Angeles, then moved to New York at the start of the 1990s. Ironically, despite his avowed disinterest in being associated with his natural father, it was a tribute to the latter that proved a key career milestone.

Record producer Hal Willner had arranged for a 1991 tribute concert for Tim Buckley to be held at St. Anne's Church in Brooklyn, New York, a location well known in New York for hosting some notable music events. He called Jeff to ask him to take part—and Jeff at first said no.

As Jeff told Robert Hilburn of the *Los Angeles Times* ("Wading Beyond the Gene Pool," Calendar section, February 19, 1995), "I declined at first because his life had nothing to do with mine. If he wasn't involved then, I didn't know why I should be involved now. To me, [stepfather] Ron Moorhead was my father."

In fact, for much of his youth, Jeff was known to friends and family as Scott Moorhead. His decision to change his name, he stated, had nothing to do with his eventual career in music. After his mother and Moorhead parted, he told Hilburn, "I just wanted my own identity, so I asked my mother what was the name on my birth certificate."

Jeff finally agreed to perform at St. Anne's and that led to involvement in groups with some other musicians he met there. Building on that experience, in early 1992 he opted to work as a solo artist and began to build a following in Greenwich Village clubs performing his own songs and covers of material influenced by people like Van Morrison, Bob Dylan, Leonard Cohen, and Edith Piaf. Piaf, he told Hilburn, was a particular favorite. "I saw her on a PBS special when I was around 16 and fell in love with her. I said, 'That's for me'—the way she seemed to be giving you everything on stage. There was something about her I resonated with. She put what I was feeling into a certain clarity."

With the release of *Grace* by Columbia in 1994, Jeff became hailed as a potential new superstar. Stephen Holden of the *New York Times*, for instance, rated the album as "exceptional," stating: "Jeff Buckley reveals a world of astonishing emotional fire. Mr. Buckley's songs . . . express the same burning mysticism, and his voice, which shades from an ethereal soprano of heart-rending delicacy into a transported yowl worthy of Robert Plant, makes them indelible. The settings, which feature Mr. Buckley on guitar, harmonium, organ and dulcimer, strikingly underscore the songs' intense spiritual aura." Jeff's 1994–95 fall and winter tour in support of the album began appropriately with a gig at St. Anne's.

Though Jeff and Tim Buckley had never known each other, the younger artist's achievements did help restore interest and luster to the important creative achievements of Buckley Senior—milestones that were otherwise in danger of slipping into obscurity.

Tragically, Jeff's life also was cut short, though not from drug abuse. While in Memphis in the spring of 1997 to work on a follow-up album to *Grace,* he went swimming in the Mississippi River and drowned. His body was recovered on June 4, 1997.

After Jeff's passing, his mother, Mary Guibert, played a major role in making sure the second album became a reality. In her residence in Santa Ana, California, she listened to hours of Jeff's unreleased tapes before deciding which ones she favored for release. When the two-disc collection, *Sketches for My Sweetheart the Drunk,* came out on Columbia in the summer of 1998, it certainly seemed evident she had chosen well. Songs such as "The Sky Is a Landfill," "Everybody Here Wants You," and "Nightmares by the Sea" emphasized his continued progress as a writer and performer. Robert Hilburn of the *Los Angeles*

Times wrote that the album's contents "might have made Buckley a superstar if he had lived to promote them with a tour."

In an interview with Hilburn, (" 'Sketches' for Her Son," May 25, 1998), Guibert emphasized that Jeff was not a "tortured artist." "If artists are drugging themselves to death at an early age, then something is wrong with the psyche of those artists. But that wasn't Jeff. [He] was a very positive person . . . very much a seeker of truth. He was into a Sufi way of thinking, that we do not need a [go-between] between us and God, and that love is the highest power."

After his death, she said, "I knew I wanted to be the one to sort of monitor what was going to happen to his music. . . . At the moment that Jeff walked into the water . . . he was ready to finally go in and make the second album. He knew exactly what he wanted. He and I had a long conversation just previous to that. We talked about everything about his life. We even covered some stuff that we needed to clean house on as a mother and son."

She told Hilburn she didn't feel right about comparing the personal factors of Tim and Jeff, stating she really had known Tim very briefly and they had been separated for months before Jeff was born. "My biggest regret in life was that Tim couldn't have lived and they could have had a relationship. I'm sure Tim would have been so proud of him."

BUCKWHEAT ZYDECO: *Group led by zydeco accordionist, singer, songwriter Stanley "Buckwheat" Dural Jr. Born Lafayette, Louisiana, November 14, 1947.*

Although he had rejected zydeco as a child, Stanley "Buckwheat" Dural Jr. apprenticed with Clifton Chenier, the King of Zydeco, who encouraged him to return to the fold. Since Chenier's death in 1987, Buckwheat has done much to bring the driving music known as zydeco into the mainstream.

He was born and raised in Lafayette, Louisiana, with five brothers and seven sisters. There was always music around the house, which was once equipped with three pianos. His father, Stanley Dural Sr., who played accordion every day, urged his son to take up the instrument, but Stanley Jr. shunned the squeezebox as "unhip." Instead he started playing piano at four, and the organ when he was nine. Before long he was playing in clubs around Lafayette. He got his nickname from a schoolmate who compared him to Buckwheat from *The Little Rascals.* "I couldn't stand it but it stuck on me," he said.

He started out in junior high playing rock and soul covers in a band called Sammy and the Untouchables. For a time he played in bands backing Joe Tex, Barbara Lynn, and Clarence "Gatemouth" Brown. In 1971 he formed a fifteen-piece R&B band called Buckwheat and the Hitchhikers. His father never came to see him play. "It's no good music, what you're playing. You need to play music like Clifton Chenier," Stanley Sr. told his son (related in an interview with Michael Tisserand). The Hitchhikers folded in 1975, and the following year he was invited to play organ with Clifton Chenier. "From the very first night I went on the stage, I couldn't believe the energy, the roots and the people having so much fun. It just took me away," he told Steve Appleford of the *Los Angeles Times* (September 3, 1993).

Chenier inspired him to pick up the piano accordion in 1978. He formed his own band the following year, Buckwheat Zydeco and the Ils Sont Partis Band (meaning "they're off"). The band released *One for the Road: Buckwheat Zydeco Ils Sont Partis* in 1979, followed by *People's Choice* and *Take it Easy, Baby.* After he started playing the accordion, Dural's old man began showing up at his concerts. "My father turned out to be my best friend," he told Appleford.

The band released four albums on the Blues Unlimited label and then moved on to the Black Top and Rounder labels, releasing *100% Fortified Zydeco* (1985). In 1986 music writer Ted Fox became Dural's manager. When he signed with Chris Blackwell's Island Records in 1987, Dural became the first zydeco artist to sign with a major label. He has toured throughout the world and provided zydeco music for films such as *The Big Easy* and *Casual Sex.* He also played accordion on a Keith Richards album, while Eric Clapton played guitar on the group's cover of "Why Does Love Got to Be So Sad?" If you hear zydeco in commercials for Budweiser, Toyota, Cheerios, and Coca-Cola, it's probably Buckwheat.

Dural earned four Grammy nominations in the 1980s. He also combined zydeco songs with songs from rock, country, blues, and funk. For example, the group's Island debut, *On a Night Like This* (1987), which broke into *Billboard's* top 200, includes a cover of Dylan's song as well as the zydeco classic "Ma 'Tit Fille." It was named one of the year's ten best by the *New York Times.*

Dural is now one of zydeco's biggest cheerleaders. As he told Appleford, "This zydeco music was Creole black traditional music. This is what my father played, and my grandfather, and great-grandfather played. It took me back."

Buckwheat Zydeco has released a steady string of albums, including *Buckwheat's Party* (Rounder, 1987), *Turning Point* (Rounder, 1988), *Taking It Home* (PolyGram, 1988), *Ils Sont Partis* (Blues Unlimited, 1988), the compilation *Buckwheat's Zydeco Party* (Rounder, 1988), *Waitin' for My Ya-Ya* (Rounder, 1988), *Where There's Smoke There's Fire* (Island, 1990), *Menagerie: Essential Zydeco* (Mango, 1993), *Five Card Stud* (Island, 1994), *Choo Choo Boogaloo* (Music for Little People/Warner Brothers, 1994), *Best of Louisiana Zydeco* (AVI, 1996), *On Track* (Alliance, 1997), and *Trouble* (Mesa/Atlantic, 1997).

BUTTERFIELD, PAUL, PAUL BUTTERFIELD BLUES BAND; PAUL BUTTERFIELD AND BETTER DAYS: *Harmonica player, flutist, songwriter, band leader. Blues Band personnel as of 1971: Paul Butterfield, born Chicago, Illinois, December 17, 1942, died North Hollywood, California, May 4, 1987; Charles Dinwiddie, born Louisville, Kentucky, September 19, 1936; Roderick Hicks, born Detroit, Michigan, January 7, 1941; David Sanborn, born Tampa, Florida, July 30, 1945; Ralph Wash, born San Francisco, California, August 19, 1949; Steve Madaio, born Brooklyn, New York, July 18, 1948; Dennis Whitted, born Chicago, Illinois, July 1, 1942; Trevor Lawrence. Band broke up 1972. Better Days formed in 1973; original members: Billy Rich, Christopher Parker, Ronnie Barron, Amos Garrett, Geoff Muldaur.*

Paul Butterfield's series of blues bands never achieved many chart hits. Nonetheless, measured by the loyalty of his fans, Butterfield was an important influence on modern music. Some of his bands' alumni have gone on to fame in other groups or as soloists, while the amplified, rock-tinged arrangements of his blues numbers helped bring the blues new favor with American audiences.

Butterfield grew up in Chicago and studied classical flute in his youth. By the time he was high school age, he had concentrated on the harmonica. He began sitting in with blues artists of Chicago's South Side clubs when he was sixteen. Among the famous bluesmen who welcomed the young artist to their stages were Howlin' Wolf, Otis Rush, Magic Sam, and Little Walter. *(See Howlin' Wolf.)* Like Little Walter, Butterfield developed a style of playing a harmonica with a microphone cupped in his hands to provide amplification and, by varying the position of harmonica and mike, different tonal effects.

Paul went on to the University of Chicago, where he became friends with a versatile musician named Elvin Bishop. Butterfield, who by then had experience with local show bands (bands that play in nightclub lounges or as pit orchestras), joined Bishop in his spare time for harmonica duets. Bishop took up the guitar in 1960, becoming one of the most noted lead guitarists in the field as a member of the Butterfield Blues Band until mid-1968.

In the early 1960s, Bishop and Butterfield were the nucleus for Paul's first band. Its six members included a drummer, a pianist, and two more guitarists. The group aroused considerable controversy among blues purists because it used amplification and its material combined blues with elements of folk, rock, and jazz. Some critics referred to the group's music as "sound and soul."

The group became one of the best-known in Chicago. It found favor with young fans despite the fact that, by the mid-1960s, the once-flourishing blues field had declined sharply in popularity there. The group played to enthusiastic audiences for over a year at the Blue Flame and 1015 Club on Chicago's South Side,

and then achieved similar success at a nightclub called Big John's on Wells Street. The reputation of the band reached record company executives even though Butterfield remained basically a Chicago artist at the time.

His first album, *Butterfield Blues Band* on Elektra, won warm praise from many critics. Syndicated columnist Ralph Gleason wrote: "What is interesting about [the LP] is that a young white Chicagoan can play the blues this well. It is as if a Negro sharecropper from Mississippi were suddenly to be expert in Gaelic song. What is of further interest is that this is the blues band which attracts all the attention when the originals on which it is patterned (Howlin' Wolf, Muddy Waters) go unrecognized by this audience."

In 1965 the band was invited to appear at the Newport Folk Festival in Newport, Rhode Island. To that point festival organizers had ruled out amplified instruments. However, they decided that Butterfield's music was so important that they would relax the rules in his case. The group, which then consisted of Butterfield, Bishop on second guitar, Jerome Arnold on electric bass, Billy Davenport on drums, Mark Naftalin on electric organ, and Mike Bloomfield on lead guitar, won one of the most resounding receptions of any of the acts and wound up backing Bob Dylan's controversial debut with electric guitar at the festival. Bloomfield, considered one of the best technicians on guitar in the country, was singled out for an ovation after some of his solo runs.

Butterfield rearranged his band to include a brass section in 1967. The group then consisted of Butterfield, Bishop, Naftalin, Charles "Bugsy" Maugh on bass, Philip Wilson on drums, Charles Dinwiddie on tenor saxophone, Keith Johnson on trumpet, and Dave Sanborn (who won several jazz awards while studying classical music in college) on alto saxophone. The group earned generally favorable, though sometimes doubting, reviews for the new arrangements worked up by Butterfield for such LPs as *The Resurrection of Pigboy Crabshaw* (1968) and *In My Own Dream* (fall 1968).

Typical of comments on *In My Own Dream* was the review by Jerrold Greenberg in *Rolling Stone* (September 14, 1968): "Butterfield has had a dream of a new music, rooted equally in the blues . . . in the technical virtuosity of jazz and in the amplified immediacy of rock: with this record that dream starts elbowing its way into reality. . . . I say starts because, while most of the cuts are excellent in varying degrees, some of them almost extraordinary in their musical togetherness, there are several that are impaired by hangovers from the band's (or individual musician's) previous incarnations."

Subsequent Butterfield LPs included *Keep on Moving* (September 1969), *Butterfield Live* (December 1970), and *East-West* (July 1971).

Continuing in pursuit of his dream, Butterfield presided over a group that changed considerably in personnel during the late 1960s. In 1968, Bishop left to form his own band and was replaced for a while by Buzzy Fieton (born New York City, 1949) who, in turn, was replaced by the time the 1970s started. In 1971, with an eight-man group that retained only Dinwiddie and Sanborn from the 1967 band, Butterfield maintained his reputation as one of the best but most underrated band leaders in American pop music.

In 1972, in search of more creative and economic progress, Butterfield broke up his old group and formed a new one, Better Days. Original members of that band included Geoff Muldaur on vocals, Ronnie Barron on keyboards, Billy Rich on bass, Christopher Parker on drums, and Amos Garrett on guitar. While Butterfield was assembling his new group, Elektra released the 1972 retrospective album *Golden Butter/The Best of the Paul Butterfield Blues Band.*

By 1973, Paul had signed a recording contract for Better Days with Bearsville Records (distributed by Warner/Reprise Records), where his band remained into the early 1980s with mixed results. His Bearsville releases included *It All Comes Back* and *Paul Butterfield/Better Days* in 1973, *Put It in Your Ear* in 1976, and *North/South* in 1981. The band's personnel changed from time to time during those years. They could draw respectable audiences to smaller halls throughout the 1970s, but never built up enough of a following for regular appearances in large venues.

At the start of the 1980s, though, Butterfield ran into difficulties that made his entertainment business disappointments seem insignificant. As he told Don Snowden (*Los Angeles Times,* June 26, 1986), he was felled by an attack of diverticulitis while working on new album material in Memphis, Tennessee. "To make a long story short, my intestines burst. . . . I ended up having four operations and you don't realize what it takes out of you energy-wise. You think you can come right back to work so I went back and herniated the scar tissue in my stomach. I had three hernias from playing the harmonica, so it was a vicious circle.

"Sure it occurred to me that I might not be able to play anymore, but I got that Irish ornery thing going and said, 'I'm going to make it through this,' and I did with a lot of help from God. I came through the wars."

The illness sidelined Paul for some four years. When he finally recovered, he ran into disagreements with his record company that resulted in his arranging his own financing for his next album. That collection remained on his hands for some eighteen months while he tried to find a label to put it out. Butterfield's search finally won over executives of Amherst Records in Buffalo, New York, who issued *The Legendary Paul Butterfield Rides Again* in mid-1986.

To complete that and other projects, Paul moved from New York to the Los Angeles area in 1986. In May 1987, he was found dead in his apartment in North Hollywood.

BYRDS, THE: *Vocal and instrumental group. Original personnel, 1964: Jim McGuinn (McGuinn changed his first name to Roger in 1968), born Chicago, Illinois, July 13, 1942; Chris Hillman, born Los Angeles, California, December 4, 1942; Gene Clark, born Tipton, Missouri, November 17, 1941, died 1991; Michael Clarke, born New York, New York, June 3, 1944, died Treasure Island, Florida, December 19, 1993; David Crosby, born Los Angeles, California, August 14, 1941. Gene Clark left in 1966, returned briefly in 1967. Crosby and Michael Clarke left in 1968. Crosby was replaced by Gram Parsons, born Winter Haven, Florida, 1946, died Joshua Tree, California, September 19, 1973. Clarke was replaced by Kevin Kelly, born California, 1945. By the end of 1968, the group was reorganized to include McGuinn, Clarence White (died 1973), Gene Parsons, and John York. York replaced in 1969 by Skip Battin, born Galipolis, Ohio. Gene Parsons left in 1972, replaced by John Guerin. Group disbanded after February 24, 1973, show in Passaic, New Jersey. Reformed in 1973 to record album material for Asylum: members were same as original 1964 roster. Group reformed briefly in early 1990 comprising McGuinn, Hillman, Crosby, John Jorgenson, and Steve Duncan for Orbison Tribute show with McGuinn, Hillman, and Crosby, who later recorded new album tracks, August 1990.*

The two primal forces in the birth of folk-rock are considered to be the Byrds and Bob Dylan. Dylan may have been transitioning from pure folk to the new blend before the Byrds came into existence, but it was the treatment the newly formed Byrds gave a Dylan song, "Mr. Tambourine Man," that opened the door to a series of folk-rock superhits by both parties.

The catalyst in the birth of the Byrds was Californian Jim Dickson, a man in his early thirties who had been an artists and repertoire man with record companies for some years in the folk and jazz fields. He liked the Beatles but thought there was room for a new kind of U.S. band that combined the melodic approach of the English group with elements of American folk and rock. During the summer of 1964 in Los Angeles, he helped bring together the original group: Jim McGuinn (lead guitar and vocals), Chris Hillman (bass guitar and vocals), Gene Clark (harmonica, tambourine, and vocals), David Crosby (rhythm guitar and vocals), and Michael Clarke (drums). The group took the name Byrds because of McGuinn's belief that all music was related to the sounds and stresses of the age. In this case, he thought of the whining, persistent sound of jet engines, of his desire to write music that could soar and fly. This pointed to birds, modified for greater audience impact to Byrds.

The members were in their early twenties, but all had some years' musical experience. McGuinn had traveled to many parts of the country in his boyhood, accompanying his parents on publicity tours for their best-selling book, *Parents Can't Win.* In his teens, he became hooked on music, learned guitar, and began working as a folksinger. This led him to Greenwich Village in New York in the late '50s, where he worked in coffeehouses and made contact with many of the young stars of the folk boom. In the early '60s he wrote arrangements for many folk artists, including Judy Collins, was lead guitarist for Bobby Darin, and toured for two years with the Chad Mitchell Trio.

By mid-1964, David Crosby had some five years' experience under his belt as a singer-guitarist in folk clubs all over the United States. Gene Clark, also a product of the folk field, had been a member of Randy Sparks's New Christy Minstrels. Chris Hillman brought along a background that included both folk and country roots, He had spent much of his youth in the cattle-raising country in Northern California, where he worked for a while in his teens as a cowboy. He also organized his own country group, the Hillmen, with whom he sang and played bluegrass mandolin. (Their 1964 LP, *The Hillmen* on Together Records, was reissued in 1981 on Sugar Hill Records.) The only original member who varied from the folk pattern was jazz-based drummer Mike Clarke.

The group rehearsed for weeks in the World Pacific Studios in Hollywood before Dickson had them play for Columbia A&R man Terry Melcher (Doris Day's son). Also having a hand in the acceptance of the group was West Coast public relations director Billy James, who later took part in their management. The label signed the Byrds in September 1964.

The band was preparing its first album when Bob Dylan flew into Los Angeles in early 1965. A close friend of Dickson's, he was interested in hearing the new group. He had supplied Dickson with "Mr. Tambourine Man," a song he had written and recorded on Columbia but which had not yet been released. He listened to the band and expressed his approval. In March, the Byrds' single of the song came out, and by June 26, 1965, it was number one in the United States. It was featured in the group's debut LP, *The Byrds* (released in August 1965), which quickly won a second gold record and today is considered one of the all-time great rock releases.

The group made its public debut in March 1965 at Ciro's on the Sunset Strip for $30 a night per musician. The first night was a disaster. The equipment didn't work, the Byrds were nervous, and the audience wasn't very appreciative. The two-week engagement was a flop. However, with the success of "Mr. Tambourine Man" soon after, the group's confidence was restored. When the quintet played Ciro's again in April 1965, they were one of the sensations of the year. Every night, long lines of fans stretched around the block waiting to get in. Still another boost came in May, when the Rolling Stones came to town for seven concerts and the Byrds played on each bill. As the year went by, the group steadily expanded its performing schedule and added to its following. Late in the year, the band toured throughout the United States and also had a successful concert series in England.

During the mid-1960s, the band's reputation soared, though more for its recording work than its concerts. Their stage appearances tended to be somewhat wooden compared to other top groups'. In the studio, though, they came into their own. The result was a string of best-selling releases, including such other singles hits from Dylan's pen as "All I Really Want to Do," "Spanish Harlem Incident," and "Chimes of Freedom." They also had hits by other writers (such as "Turn! Turn! Turn!," a biblical passage set to music by Pete Seeger) and boasted an increasing repertoire of originals by McGuinn and other band members.

Almost all the band's albums of the mid-1960s did well, including *Turn! Turn! Turn!* (February 1966), *Fifth Dimension* (September 1966), *Younger Than Yesterday* (April 1967), and *Greatest Hits* (October 1967). Its top 40 singles successes after "Turn! Turn! Turn!" (which rose to number one in the United States in late 1965) were: "Eight Miles High," "Mr. Spaceman" (1966), and "So You Want to Be a Rock 'n' Roll Star" and "My Back Pages" (1967).

By 1967, though, internal problems were negatively affecting their performance. McQuinn, who by 1967 was acknowledged band leader, told *Los Angeles Times* reporter Pete Johnson in April 1968 that the difficulties began in England.

"I got sick. I had like 103 something fever. And we were in the BBC studios doing some show and the doctor came in and said 'This guy shouldn't work; send him home to bed.' So I'm lying on a couch or something and everybody's going crazy. Nobody has any organization any more. Michael [Clarke] left; he just walked out. . . . Then the other three guys started fighting about whether Michael should be fired or not.

"And everybody quit right there and said, 'I quit. I'm going home,' you know. . . . Everybody was out for himself and running scared. The Africans have an expression 'Living with someone is like asking for a fight,' or something like that. A group is even worse. You're boxed in when you're traveling. It's hard pressure.

"Gene developed a tremendous fear of airplanes, this was maybe a year later. One day we were going in New York [from L.A.] to do a Murray the K special and Gene was on the airplane. I got there late, just as the thing was closing up. I always do. Gene was already freaked out and they were holding his arms. He got off and decided to quit the group."

The group went on as a foursome but ran into more problems in late 1967 and early 1968 while making the LP *The Notorious Byrd Brothers*. In the middle of the project, Crosby and the others disagreed about the approach of the album. David left, later to become a founding member of Crosby, Stills, Nash & Young. Gene Clark came back to take Crosby's place for a while, but then left once more. *(See Crosby, Stills, Nash & Young.)*

Roger McGuinn (he changed his first name in 1968 as a result of membership in a religious group known as Subud) reorganized the band in early 1968, briefly adding Chris Hillman's cousin Kevin Kelly on drums. The fourth member was Gram Parsons, a guitarist with country roots who previously had been lead singer for the International Submarine Band.

The Byrds had previously shown great latitude in their approach to rock, starting with an emphasis on amplified folk-rock, proceeding to experimental combinations of Indian music and rock (some critics credited McGuinn with coining the descriptive phrase *raga-rock*), and then to arrangements using the Moog synthesizer. The addition of Gram Parsons signaled a new phase in the group's development: country-rock.

The Byrds went to Nashville to record their next LP, *Sweetheart of the Rodeo,* with fiddle, banjo, and pedal steel guitar accompaniment. The group was a little in advance of the times, however. The response to *Sweetheart* by record buyers was much weaker than for earlier releases. Still, the album had an impact on a number of young musicians who were to become factors in the country-rock surge of the 1970s.

Yet that foursome—McGuinn, Hillman, Gram Parsons, and Kelly—had advanced tremendously in stage presence over earlier versions. They seemed more relaxed, they conveyed a feeling of greater enjoyment of what they were doing, and they were tighter musically. However, the decline in record sales had its impact. Hillman and Gram Parsons left and soon started a new country-rock band, the Flying Burrito Brothers, which Michael Clarke later joined. McGuinn defied advisers who told him to forget the Byrds. He refused to give up, formed a new quartet with bluegrass picker Clarence White on lead guitar, Gene Parsons on drums, and John York on bass. The new aggregation seemed very promising, as indicated by its work on the March 1969 Columbia LP, *Dr. Byrds and Mr. Hyde.* During 1969, there was another change when York was replaced on bass by Clyde "Skip" Battin (formerly of Skip and Flip, who sang "It Was I" in 1959 and "Cherry Pie" in 1960). The feeling of a Byrds rejuvenation was further heightened by the group's music in the hit film *Easy Rider.* Also above average was the two-LP set *The Byrds (Untitled),* one live disc and one from studio sessions, issued by Columbia in September 1970. The album had advance sales orders for 100,000 copies and moved onto the best-seller lists for several months. Also making the charts was their next album, *Byrdmania* (released in August 1971).

The LP *Farther Along,* issued by Columbia in December 1971, was on the charts into 1972, but unfortunately didn't live up to its title. Also appearing on the album lists in late 1972 was the *Best of the Byrds, Greatest Hits Volume II.* During 1972, McGuinn broke up the current group, but during the winter of 1972–73 the five original members agreed to collaborate on a reunion album, *The Byrds,* on Asylum Records (distributed by Atlantic Records). Though it was on the charts for a time in 1973, it was an inferior effort. After the session, the members went their separate ways. (By then, the Byrds no longer were on the Columbia label, though the company did issue the LP *Preflyte,* essentially the original demo tape the group had made in its beginning phase.) In the mid-1970s and early 1980s, Columbia issued a few albums of previously recorded material, including *Mr. Tambourine Man/Turn! Turn! Turn!* in 1975, *The Byrds Play Dylan* in 1980, and *The Original Singles, 1965–1967 (Volume 1)* in 1981.

During the Byrds' active period, onetime members like Chris Hillman and David Crosby had gone on to other projects, and the same held true for many alumni after the group broke up. McGuinn initiated a solo career with support from Columbia Records, which issued the mid-'70s albums *Roger McGuinn* (1973); *Peace on You* (1974); *Roger McGuinn and Band* (1975); *Cardiff Rose* (1976); and *Thunderbyrd* (1977). Clarence White returned to his bluegrass roots with a new version of the Kentucky Colonels, a group he had performed with before joining the Byrds. That affiliation ended tragically with his death in a parking lot accident in mid-1973, following a 1973 Swedish reunion tour that formed the basis for the 1977 Rounder Records release *The White Brothers (The New Kentucky Colonels).* (The group's early sound was offered on other mid-1970s releases—*Livin' in the Past* on Takoma in 1975 and *The Kentucky Colonels* on Rounder in 1976.) Another album by a band alumnus during those years was Gene Parson's *Kindling* on Warner Brothers.

In the late 1970s, McGuinn got together with two other original Byrds members, Gene Clark and Chris Hillman, to form the McGuinn, Clark and Hillman group. Among Hillman's endeavors before that minireunion had been the Souther-Hillman-Furay Band, which had completed two disappointing LPs on Asylum, *The Souther-Hillman-Furay Band* (1974) and *Trouble in Paradise* (1975). Record output of McGuinn, Clark and Hillman comprised two Capitol LPs, *McGuinn, Clark and Hillman* (1979) and *City* (1980). Clark had decided to leave by the time the *City* recordings got under way and the remaining duo later recorded the 1980 Capitol LP *McGuinn and Hillman.*

Hillman, who had recorded two solo LPs before reuniting with McGuinn, the Asylum LPs *Slippin' Away* (1976) and *Clear Sailin'* (1977), returned to solo work in the early 1980s with the albums (on Sugar Hill) *Morning Sky* (1982) and *Desert Rose* (1984). In 1987 he was part of a new group whose debut LP, *Desert Rose Band,* came out on MCA. After parting from Hillman, McGuinn returned to solo work and was featured mainly in college or smaller venue concerts for the rest of the decade.

At the start of the 1990s, Byrds members were asked to take part in a tribute concert to the late Roy Orbison held on February 24, 1990. The band makeup for the concert comprised McGuinn, Hillman, and Crosby, plus John Jorgenson on guitar and Steve Duncan on drums. Live recordings of two songs, "Turn! Turn! Turn!" and "Mr. Tambourine Man," were included on the tribute album. For the latter song, Bob Dylan joined the group onstage. During the summer, Sony arranged for a series of new recordings by McGuinn, Hillman, and Crosby on August 6–8, 1990, in Nashville, Tennessee, for inclusion in a new boxed set under preparation at the company. The four songs, "He Was a Friend of Mine," "Paths of Victory," "From a Distance," and "Love That Never Dies" brought the total in the set (*The Byrds,* issued in October 1990), to ninety assembled on four CDs.

During the 1990s, the saga of the Byrds and other landmark bands with which Byrds alumni were associated was recounted in several "History of Rock" programs for TV and home video presentation. Roger McGuinn, Hillman, and Crosby were among the performers who provided commentary on some segments of those shows.

In December 1993, Michael Clarke died in his condominium in Treasure Island, Florida, from liver failure, ending one of the more controversial chapters in Byrds' history. In 1985, Clarke had organized his own band using the Byrds name. In 1989 Crosby, McGuinn, and Hillman filed a lawsuit charging that Michael was using the name illegally, and performed several concerts together as the Byrds with the apparent intent of bolstering their legal allegations. However, the five original members patched up their differences in time to appear together in early 1991, when the Byrds were inducted into the Rock and Roll Hall of Fame. From then until his death, Clarke called his group Michael Clarke's Byrds.

BYRNE, DAVID: *Singer, guitarist, band leader (Talking Heads), songwriter, actor, author, record producer, filmmaker, record company founder (Luaka Bop), born Dunbarton, Scotland, May 14, 1952.*

If anyone in the entertainment field from the 1970s on qualified for the title "Renaissance Man," it had to be David Byrne. Through the closing decades of the twentieth century, he applied his talents in a dizzying array of ways, from forming the "literate rock" band Talking Heads to writing and directing films, composing music for a Twyla Tharp ballet, and performing and promoting music based on diverse ethnic strains from around the globe.

He was born in Scotland, but long before his teens he was living in Baltimore, Maryland, where his interest in pop music led to his performing in rock groups during his high school years. After graduating from high school, he enrolled in the Rhode Island School of Design in the early '70s. He found a musical soul mate in drummer-percussionist Chris Frantz (born United States, May 9, c. 1951), and the two formed a group called the Artistics (also known as the Autistics) in 1974. Later, fellow student Martina "Tina" Weymouth (born United States, November 22, c. 1951) joined as bass guitarist.

Eventually the band evolved into the Talking Heads, becoming a quartet with the addition of Jerry Harrison (born United States, February 21, c. 1953). After achieving a growing following in the New York area in the mid-'70s, the band signed with Sire Records in January 1977. Sire issued its debut album, *Talking Heads '77,* in August. Over the next few years, the band attained star status with dynamic concert appearances throughout the United States and the world and such albums as *More Songs about Buildings and Food* in 1978 (a *People* magazine top 10 choice for the year), *Fear of Music* in 1979, and *Remain in Light* in 1980. The last-named, particularly in the track "Crosseyed and Painless," combined influences of new wave rock with funk and African style elements.

Byrne, by the start of the '80s, was becoming restless with his Talking Heads commitments and started looking for other creative challenges. One result was the 1981 collaboration with Brian Eno on the LP *My Life in the Bush of Ghosts.* The album, released on Sire / Warner, as Irwin Stambler noted in the *Encyclopedia of Pop, Rock, and Soul,* was "a striking, evocative album that highlighted a variety of percussion and trancelike vocal effects; it was a creative success if not a candidate for a gold or platinum record. Band members, besides Byrne and Eno, included several expert percussionists and bassist Basta Jones."

Another effort during that period was composing music for a ballet by the famous choreographer Twyla Tharp. His sound track album of the music, *The Catherine Wheel,* was a 1981 release.

Byrne returned to working with Talking Heads members for the 1983 release *Speaking in Tongues,* but he was looking ahead to other projects with and without the band. For one thing, he started writing songs and a script for a film to be called *True Stories,* discussed plans for a concert film of Talking Heads, and began considering song sketches for still another band LP. In late 1983 and into 1984, the band played major venues across the United States with a few appearances in Australia and New Zealand in early '84; when they reached Los Angeles, director Jonathan Demme filmed the show for the feature film *Stop Making Sense.*

Before the next Talking Heads album was issued by Sire / Warner in July 1985 (the platinum-selling *Little Creatures*), Byrne continued to toss off other work in a pinwheel fashion. As he reported, between the '83 LP *Speaking in Tongues* and *Little Creatures,* "I've been working on the *Knee Play* collaboration with [playwright] Robert Wilson, acting in *Survival Guide,* and co-writing a script [*True Stories*]. I also wrote the music for 'Alive From Off-Center' [a series of avant-garde TV shows for the Public Broadcasting System that emphasized dance and performance art] and did two short performance presentations at the Public Theater and the Kitchen in New York City."

Byrne's activities in 1986 included contributing to still another film sound track, this time for a major new feature film. When Bernardo Bertolucci's movie *The Last Emperor* came out in 1987, it featured a score cowritten by Byrne, Ryuichi Sakamoto, and Cong Su. That won the three composers Oscars for Best Original Score, one of nine Oscars the film was voted (including Best Picture) as it dominated the Academy Awards.

In 1988, Byrne and the Talking Heads once more were represented on the hit charts with the album *Naked*. The album's contents reflected Byrne's growing interest in music from other parts of the world, which often evidenced strong folk music influences. Recording was done in Paris with backing musicians from the United States, Africa, England, Ireland, and French Caribbean islands. Contributing to the Afro-French feeling of the project were the sounds of soukous from Zaire and Cameroon, mbalax from Senegal, and zouk from the French Antilles.

Byrne wound up the decade by touring not with the Talking Heads but with a fourteen-member Latin American ensemble. The group performed throughout the United States and Canada as well as in Europe and Japan, presenting songs from the 1989 album *Rei Momo*. Byrne began the '90s with projects that included development of a score for the German film *The Forest* (the sound track album came out in 1991) and an updating of the Babylonian myth of Gilgamesh. The goal in the last case was to apply the epic to the Industrial Revolution as the basis for both film and a theater version. Working with him on that were Robert Wilson, Chris Frantz, and Tina Weymouth. Byrne's album output in the early '90s included the 1992 release *Uh-Oh*.

In the mid-1990s, Byrne established his own label, Luaka Bop, with distribution by Sire / Warner Brothers, whose goal was to issue either Byrne originals with world music input or discs by world music performers, including some Brazilian groups. Albums prepared by Byrne for release on the label in early 1994 included a solo Byrne disc and another titled *Sabysylma* by the five-woman, Belgium-based group Zap Mama. Discussing *David Byrne* in the *CMJ New Music Report*, James Lien wrote: "[Byrne] is back from his musical travels and third world forays. . . . The Brazilian, Caribbean and soul influences on this album are like stickers on a suitcase or souvenirs for the mantelpiece, not an attempt to mimic the genuine article, just a whiff of spice, a hint of flavor, a pleasant, tingly memory of how good it felt to be there."

Still another improbable change in direction by Byrne occurred in the summer of 1996, when he installed an art show called *Desire* at the Massachusetts Museum of Contemporary Art in North Adams. The show incorporated billboardlike visual images and recordings of pitchmen-type comments against a background of Muzak-type music on an Acoustiglide headset. The headset commentaries, though, seemed to have little in common with the images surrounding the observer. Sarah Boxer of the *New York Times* ("Slogans and Images, with Talking Heads Bending Your Ears," Arts & Leisure section, August 18, 1996) pondered what it all meant: "If this is a brainwashing, it is just a post-modern one. Mr. Byrne washes the brain clean with paradox and pastiche, only to fill it with nothing. So what do we learn? We are all easy to brainwash. Money is connected to violence. Travel ads are like ads for hallucinatory drugs. Inspirational slogans are connected to corporate slogans. Television is numbing. Music is good manipulation. So are billboards. Who would question these platitudes? Probably no one. But, of course, there is always the possibility that Mr. Byrne meant more, or that he meant less."

C

CALE, J.J.: *Singer, songwriter, guitarist. Born Oklahoma City, Oklahoma, December 5, 1938.*

Few people know the name John W. Cale. Call him J.J. and his name recognition goes up significantly. (Jean Jacques was someone else's creation, and he chose J.J. Cale because John Cale was already taken.) But how many could describe what he looks like or tell you that he wrote two of the biggest hits in rock history, "Cocaine" and "After Midnight"? Not many. Cale avoids the limelight and quietly collects his royalties, occasionally going out on annual six-week tours. Nevertheless, his rootsy guitar style, offbeat lyrics, and smoky vocals have had a major impact on rock guitarists ranging from Eric Clapton to the Dire Straits' Mark Knopfler.

Cale grew up in Tulsa, Oklahoma; he picked up the guitar just before his teen years, soaking in the sounds of players as diverse as Chet Atkins, Les Paul, and Clarence "Gatemouth" Brown. He started playing in the Tulsa clubs in the 1950s, eventually becoming a bandleader. Oklahoma was a dry state, so Cale would play at the speakeasies till four or five in the morning. The bar owners would try to negotiate another hour or two at $5 to $7.50 for each player. Along with Leon Russell, he was one of the founders of the Tulsa sound, influenced by the end of the Big Band era and the dawn of rock.

"You had guys in their thirties—what we called old guys—who'd want to hear some big band stuff, like '[I] Can't Get Started' or Glenn Miller," Cale says. "Then the young people would want to hear Fats Domino or Little Richard or Chuck Berry. So you had to learn both kinds of music.

"I guess what we favored mainly was blues shuffles. . . . Something with four chords was really a pop piece to me. You'd play whatever was popular, and then as the evening wore on and people got drunker, we played more blues shuffles and rock and roll."

He took his band, Johnny Cale and the Valentines, to Nashville in the late 1950s, and toured with country stars Little Jimmy Dickens and Red Sovine. But his vain attempts to make it in country landed him back in Tulsa. As he put it, "There were only so many gigs." He had to work as a fry cook, hamburger flipper, elevator operator, steel grinder, and graveyard flower delivery man to make ends meet.

When Cale heard that Tulsa-ites Leon Russell, Chuck Blackwell, and Carl Radle had gone to California, he decided to follow them out in the early 1960s. Again, Cale had to be resourceful. "I'd put on a cowboy hat and do a country gig, if that's what they wanted," he said. "You want a blues gig? Here come the sunglasses."

He worked with Delaney & Bonnie, but mostly he struggled with the songwriting, releasing a number of singles, and learning how to be a recording engineer as a way to get by. "I never considered myself in the music business," he says. "I was just hanging out, having a good time, playing music. I had no idea the songs I was writing were going to do anything; that was just a deal on the side."

Cale had recorded a song called "After Midnight" on the Liberty label in 1965. They had given him a box of singles, and he tried in vain to get some radio airplay; before long it began to look like a worthless box of 45s. But British blues-rocker Eric Clapton had heard the 45, and liked the song and Cale's guitar style. When Clapton recorded "After Midnight" on his first solo album, it surprised Cale. "Bobby Keys, the sax player, told me, 'Hey, man, that Eric Clapton cut your tune,'" Cale recalls. "'Yeah, sure.' About six months later, I was going to a gig, and I heard it on the radio. Then I decided that I'd be a songwriter—although I really just wanted to play the guitar."

"After Midnight" climbed to number eighteen on the charts in 1970. It became a party anthem throughout the 1980s, and was even used in a commercial for Michelob beer. That didn't bother Cale. He told Jim Washburn of the *Los Angeles Times* (May 11, 1990): "I sold all my songs and have no control over them, but I do get paid when they use them. And I didn't think 'After Midnight' was one of those kind of special tunes, so it didn't bother me."

The Clapton hit helped Cale get his first record deal (although he had previously recorded *A Trip Down Sunset Strip* with a group called the Leather Coated Minds, a novelty act that poked fun at the psychedelic '60s). In 1971, Cale cut his first album, *Naturally,* on Leon Russell's Shelter Records. Clapton had "duped" the style of the Liberty 45, so Cale decided to make a slower version of "After Midnight." The album also included Cale's "Call Me the Breeze" and his hit single "Crazy Mama," which was recorded on a portable Panasonic tape recorder using an Acetone drum machine. (Says Cale: "That might have been the first song with electronic drums that was close to being a hit.") The song reached number twenty-two on the charts in 1972. He had a chance to play it on Dick Clark's *American Bandstand* but turned it down because he didn't want to lip-synch the song.

"I said, 'Oh, man, I'd feel stupid up there trying to lip-synch something,'" Cale recalls. "I'm not an actor, I'm a musician. I've either got to bring the band and we'll play this funky version of it, or we ain't comin'." The song fell to number fifty-nine on the charts the next week.

With the exception of "Crazy Mama," a rhythmic shuffle characteristic of Cale's laid-back style, most of Cale's hits have been recorded by other artists. Lynyrd Skynyrd recorded "Call Me the Breeze" in 1974. Then Eric Clapton recorded another Cale song, "Cocaine," in 1980.

Cale emphasizes that he wrote "Cocaine" before the '80s. "The song is not for cocaine, and it's not against cocaine," he told the *Los Angeles Times*. "It's something I observed and wrote a song about. That's what all writers do, in prose, poetry, whatever. I wasn't trying to turn anybody on to cocaine, or turn anybody off. When I wrote it I didn't realize that 10 years later it would be a big thing the government was going crazy over."

Several other Cale songs covered by others include "Same Old Blues" by Freddie King, Captain Beefheart, and Bryan Ferry; "Call Me the Breeze" by Johnny Cash and the Allman Brothers; "Cajun Moon" by Cissy Houston, Herbie Mann, and Maria Muldaur; and "Crazy Mama" by Larry Carlton, Leon Redbone, and Johnny Rivers.

In concerts in his early years he made little effort to "connect" with the audience, gaining an air of mystery and a reputation as a recluse. "I have a little more confidence now," he says. "Before, if you didn't get up and dance, if you sat and watched me play, I got real nervous. That's why you'd hear, 'I went to see J.J. last night. He was standin' over in the corner in the dark.' I wasn't trying to be mysterious; I was a sideman, and that's where sidemen stood. Even though it was my songs and my band, and I booked the deal and they were paying to see me, I still considered myself just a member of the band."

Cale became a self-described "gypsy," living in trailer parks and mobile homes. In 1971, he left Los Angeles and moved to Nashville, Tennessee. From 1971 to 1984, Cale released eight albums, including *Really* in 1972, *Okie* in 1974, *Troubadour* in 1976 (including a version of "Cocaine"), and *Five* in 1979. Unlike his smattering of earlier hits, his albums were not big commercial sellers.

He returned to Los Angeles in 1980 and began recording for Mercury. He released *Shades* in 1981, *Grasshopper* in 1982, *8* in 1983, and *Special Edition,* a compilation album, in 1984. Disillusioned with the music industry, Cale left Mercury and settled in Orange County, a good distance away from the music hub in Los Angeles. He didn't have a phone, he'd bike to most places, and he maintained a quiet life. He stopped recording for the latter half of the 1980s, only touring six weeks each year to stay sharp.

After this hiatus, he signed a deal with Silvertone Records in 1990 and released *Travel-Log,* his first album in six years. He had recorded the fourteen songs over five years as he moved from place to place—some in his trailer, others in fancy studios. The titles reflect the mood of the album: "Shanghaied," "Tijuana," and "New Orleans." As usual, he attracted some of the best musicians in the business: pianist Spooner Oldham, bassist Tim Drummond (who had worked with James Brown, Ry Cooder, and Bob Dylan), sax player Steve Douglas, and percussionist Jimmy Karstein. He followed that album with *Ten,* also on Silvertone.

Although he was a recording engineer, Cale was known for recording his songs on a cassette player or playing on an old beat-up Sears guitar.

"People would say, 'What did you do, cut the record on a cassette, man?' 'Yeah.' That was fun to me. And for a long time I figured people were not gonna buy my records, they're gonna buy somebody else doing my tune, so there's no use in me spending a lot of time and money trying to make my songs sound great."

In the early 1990s, Cale bought a house near San Diego and lived a more stationary life. "I thought I'd get me a little place and see what mowing the lawn was like," he told Washburn.

He also seemed more comfortable as a performer. Reviewing a concert, Washburn wrote that he was "a new man, talking and joking between songs and generally seeming comfortable with the idea that he was in a room full of people."

About a year later, Cale met blues guitarist John Hammond Sr. when they were performing on the same bill, and expressed an interest in producing his next album. That album, *Got Love If You Want It,* came out on Virgin's Pointblank / Charisma label in 1992 and included backup vocals by Cale and John Lee Hooker.

In 1994, Cale released his eleventh solo album, *Closer to You,* on Point Blank. In contrast to his *Travel-Log* album, Cale wrote eight of the twelve songs in a day on a new Martin guitar that he had custom-ordered (compared with the old beat-up models he was known to use before). He rented Capitol Studio in Hollywood and recorded the album in two days, with the vocals cut live. The album includes "Steve's Song," a tribute to

Steve Douglas, the sax player who died in an L.A. recording studio in 1993, and "Ain't Love Funny," which includes the Band's Garth Hudson on accordion. In typical Cale style, the album is a hodgepodge of racy, tongue-in-cheek, slick, and rough-edged songs. "It sounded real good, so I bought the stuff home and started muddying those tunes up and recorded three or four more, did some overdubs," he says.

Cale wrote some of the big hits of the 1970s and 1980s in spite of himself. He realizes that he has lived a charmed life.

"It's generally really hard to pay your rent playing music," he told Washburn. "Most people have to quit after a couple of years. I've been real lucky to be able to do it for 30 years. I didn't get rich. But I can pay my bills. . . . My days are all kind of like Saturday because I don't have a regular job to go to at 9 every day. I read a lot and have a lot of time on my hands."

In 1996 Point Blank / Virgin released Cale's twelfth album, *Guitar Man,* which includes eleven originals out of the twelve. He played nearly all of the instruments on the album and also produced and engineered the project. A retrospective of Cale's work was put out on the Mercury Chronicles label in the fall of 1997. *Anyway the Wind Blows—the Anthology,* comprised two CDs containing fifty songs, including his 1972 hit "Crazy Mama."

CALE, JOHN: *Singer, guitarist, bass guitarist, electric viola player, organist, songwriter, record producer, born Wales, United Kingdom, c. 1941.*

The multifaceted John Cale is best known for the wild rock performances he gave and, in some cases produced, for the Velvet Underground. But he pursued many other musical paths in his career, ranging from efforts to compose and play avant-garde classical material with strong rock elements to some forays into the folk-rock domain. In more than a few of the albums the tracks varied from urgent dissonant rock numbers to sensitive ballads, often with strong folk flavor.

Growing up in Wales after World War II, he was trained in classical music. After gaining a grounding in the accepted classical genres, he moved toward avant-garde styles, eventually studying in Europe in the 1950s under an exponent of those formats, La Monte Young. In the early 1960s, he moved to the United States, settling in New York (still his home in the late 1990s), where, while aware of the thriving folk scene in and around Greenwich Village, he soon found rock and roll more to his liking. As he played in various bands in small clubs in the New York area, his path crossed that of another performer on that rather seedy circuit, singer-guitarist Lou Reed. They decided to form their own band, bringing in Sterling Morrison on vocals, guitar, and bass guitar and Maureen Tucker on percussion. Lou Reed came up with a name for the band: Velvet Underground, taken from the title of a pornographic paperback.

A friend of artist and filmmaker Andy Warhol heard them play and, knowing a rock band fitted into a new project Warhol had in mind, brought Andy to hear them. Warhol was enthusiastic and set up a show featuring the German-born actress Nico, under the name Nico and the Velvet Underground. The band's wild visual effects and mostly original music, much of it provided by Cale and Reed, brought them a cult following and mixed responses from reviewers. The critic for *Los Angeles* magazine commented that the "screeching rock 'n' roll reminded viewers of nothing so much as Berlin in the decadent '30s."

Cale stayed with the group from the initial concerts set up by Warhol in 1966 to the end of the decade, leaving soon after the Velvets' 1968 album, *White Light / White Heat.* In 1970 Columbia issued his first solo LP, *Vintage Violence,* which contained a number of melodic, sometimes folk-flavored songs matched with often downbeat lyrics. He followed this with an album in the classical vein, *Church of Anthrax* on Columbia, recorded with avant-garde classical composer Terry Riley, who played keyboards and saxophone. In 1973, backed by folk rockers Richie Hayward and Lowell George of Little Feat, he recorded *Paris 1919* for a new label, Reprise.

In 1974 he gained still another record company alignment, this time with Island, which released the collection *Fear.* As Mikal Gilmore of the *L.A. Weekly* commented in the 1981 *New Rolling Stone Record Guide,* that album "sported a tougher, more deranged rock sound than anything since his work with the Velvets. 'Fear Is a Man's Best Friend' and 'Gun' are wild, frightening insights about brutality, far more cathartic than Lou Reed's similar recordings. Cale filled his quota of folk-based melodies as well."

John managed to demonstrate that kind of musical split personality in follow-up Island Records releases such as *Slow Dazzle* and *Helen of Troy* in 1975. Island didn't do much to promote those albums, but in 1977 they issued the retrospective collection *Guts.* By the start of the '80s, Cale had moved on to still another label alignment, turning out the LP *Honi Soit* on A&M, released in 1981.

In the 1970s and '80s, Cale's services as a record producer were as much in demand as his talents as a performer. Some of those projects were with friends from the Velvet days such as Lou Reed and Nico. He also supervised sessions by the Modern Lovers, Iggy Pop and the Stooges, Terry Riley, Eno, Phil Manzanera (like Eno, an alumnus of the U.K. group Roxy Music), Jonathan Richman, and Patti Smith, to name a few.

After Andy Warhol's death, Cale and Lou Reed joined forces for an album and concert series (one of which was telecast over the Public Broadcasting System) in Andy's honor titled *Songs for Drella.* The album was issued in 1991. Meanwhile, Cale kept his hand in with various unique projects, including work with songwriter–visual artist Bob Neuwirth on a theater piece commissioned for presentation at St. Anne's Church in Brooklyn, New York. After its debut (Neuwirth described the act's content as "an abstract Prairie Home Companion") at the church in 1993, it was taken to other locations, including a 1993 performance in Hamburg, Germany. After MCA executives, including public relations vice president Paula Batson, an old friend of the artists, heard tapes of the show's music, Cale and Neuwirth were asked to adapt the songs for an album. The result was the spring 1994 release *Last Day on Earth.*

Like many of Cale's projects, it was not easy to figure out what exactly *Last Day on Earth* was about. Cale told Steve Hochman of the *Los Angeles Times* ("The Meaning of 'Earth'? Duo Isn't Sure," April 29, 1994), "Well, it's certainly a Brechtian landscape that's got a lot of *Angst* and unresolved problems." Musically, they both told Hochman, it might be compared to *Songs for Drella,* though, as Hochman stated, "with everything from folk parodies to rock 'n' roll, it covers a wider range. Structurally it could be likened to a 'Canterbury Tales' in which all the pilgrims are different facets of one multiple-personality case."

In any case, the album was hardly a best-seller. Like many of Cale's projects, however, it seemed likely to be ahead of its time, perhaps eventually having unexpected influences on the work of future writers and performers.

During 1998 Cale began touring with a group called the Creatures, a drum-intensive band organized by U.K. vocalist Siouxsie Sioux (of Siouxsie and the Banshees) and her husband, Budgie, who played drums in the Banshees. Both Cale and Sioux at times took turns fronting the group while at others they performed together. The combination proved surprisingly effective, delighting audiences and critics alike. The encores highlighted different phases of Cale's career with Sioux handling lead vocals on a Velvet Underground song, "Venus in Furs," and Cale taking the lead on the Jonathan Richman composition "Pablo Picasso."

CAMP, HAMILTON: *Singer, guitarist, songwriter, actor, born England, c. mid-1930s.*

For most of his career, Hamilton Camp spent more time—and earned a lot more money—as an actor, but he made some important contributions to the folk music field, particularly as part of the duo Gibson and Camp. The team worked together sporadically over the years and recorded sparingly, but their early '60s LP, *Gibson and Camp Live at the Gate of Horn,* had a lasting impact on the development of U.S. folk music through its influence on many aspiring new artists.

Camp, originally called Bob or Bobby, was born in England but moved to the United States with his family at an early age and spent his formative years in Hollywood, California. Growing up in the movie capital of the world, he yearned for an acting career, and he took part in school plays while attending Hollywood High. In the mid-1950s he served for a time in the U.S. Army; after being mustered out late in the decade he gravitated to New York, seeking work in the theater while also taking part in the growing folk music movement centered in Greenwich Village. He hooked up with a rising star in the management sector, Albert Grossman, who at the time had a presence in both Chicago, where he roomed with another young musician, Bob Gibson, and the Big Apple.

As Gibson recalled for Jack Purdy ("Forty-Three Going on Fourteen," *City Paper,* March 22, 1991): "Albert and I shared this apartment in Chicago. He was back east looking for talent. So one day in 1959 I come home, walk in, and there's Bob [now Hamilton] in the living room. Albert had seen him singing in the Village and thought Camp would sound great with me. So we start fooling around, start getting a sound together and working at the Gate [the Gate of Horn folk club, owned by Grossman]. Then one day Albert calls.

"He says, 'Now that you're singing with Camp, I want you to try something else. I found this girl in New York. She's great. You and Camp are gonna hate her 'cause she's taller than both of you. But give it a try.' At this point, I say to Albert, 'No! This isn't what I want to do. It's working great with Camp. I don't want to see her.' So Albert dropped it."

Later, however, Grossman pursued his idea of a trio by helping shape the career of Peter, Paul and Mary. At the same time, he took over management of another promising newcomer, Bob Dylan.

Back in Chicago, besides working with Gibson, Camp found another outlet for his talents by joining the Second City comedy improv group, a move that soon led him to give up performing with Gibson. The latter appeared at the 1960 Newport Folk Festival as part of a trio with Dick Rosmini on guitar and Herb Brown on bass, with Gibson playing banjo. When the group performed the song "Well, Well, Well," cowritten by Gibson and Camp, Hamilton joined in on the vocal. This became one of the tracks on the LP released by Vanguard Records in January 1961, *The Newport Folk Festival, 1960—Volume 2.* Later, "Well, Well, Well" became a staple at Peter, Paul and Mary concerts.

Camp remained a member of Second City during the early 1960s, until he decided to move back to the West Coast, where he soon was working with the San Francisco–based comedy troupe called the Committee. Alan Myerson, who was that group's director, recalled in liner notes for a Rhino Records folk music set that Camp used his music skills to good advantage in the few weeks before he was scheduled to join the troupe.

"Hamilton was looking for something to do and one night went into a coffeehouse called the Coffee Gallery where they had a hootenanny night and anyone could get up and sing. The place was nearly empty and, like a bad 1940s musical, as soon as Hamilton began to sing, people started to drift into the place. In 15 minutes, it was packed."

In 1964, Camp, who had only recorded the single live album with Gibson, signed a solo contract with Elektra Records. His Elektra debut, *Paths of Glory,* had little effect on record buyers but it included Camp's version of the song "Let's Get Together," written by Chester Powers, Jr. (better known later as Dino Valenti of the Quicksilver Messenger Service). Another version of that song by We Five on A&M Records rose to number thirty-one on the *Billboard* pop charts in December '65 and several years after became a major hit for the Youngbloods on RCA, first hitting the charts in 1967 and resurfacing as a top 5 hit for the group in August '69.

Quicksilver included one of Camp's self-penned numbers, "Pride of Man," on its 1968 Capitol Records debut album. During that year, Camp had a new album out on Warner Brothers, *Here's to You,* which failed to make the charts.

Camp had somewhat better luck in the theatrical field, moving to New York for a time as a featured member of the cast of the Broadway production of *On a Clear Day You Can See Forever.* In the early '70s he joined a Virginia commune called Skymont, and in 1973 lived in Chicago for a while as the lead singer of the commune band the Skymonters. He kept up contact with Gibson, and the two performed together from time to time, appearing at folk venues like McCabe's in Santa Monica, California, in 1976.

By the late 1970s, Camp returned to Southern California as his acting career began to prosper. In 1978 he appeared in the movie *Heaven Can Wait,* and in 1983 was a cast member of the film *Under Fire.* He also began accumulating TV credits, appearing on such successful sitcoms as *Starsky and Hutch* and *The Mary Tyler Moore Show.* In the 1980s and '90s, he also gained many assignments doing commercials or voice-overs for cartoon animation projects. Shows he worked on in the mid- to late '80s included *The Smurfs* and *The New Flintstones.* His activities during those years included running the Heliotrope Theater in the Los Angeles area, staging concerts on Sunday afternoons and improvisational theater games on Friday and Saturday nights.

In the spring of '87, when Gibson and Camp got together for several shows at the Heliotrope, Camp talked about their musical relationship with Steve Pond ("Almost 20 Years of Reunion Music," *Los Angeles Times,* May 22, 1987): "Heck, I can't believe we played for more than a year together, all told. But now we do a few weeks every year, just to keep a hand in and to keep the people reminded that we're still here."

He noted that their first reunion had come in the early 1970s: "We hadn't seen each other for eight or nine years. We rehearsed for 15 minutes, then did an hour on stage. We barely knew what we were doing, but that thread was there, so we trusted it. And we raised the roof." In the late '70s, he pointed out, they had completed only their second album, *Homemade Music*. In 1986 they had gotten together to record an up-to-date version of their *Gate of Horn* disc.

In the early '90s, some of their music was included in the Rhino Records release *Troubadours of the Folk Era*. During the first half of the decade, Camp kept busy with his acting and commercial activities, but he came to his old partner's aid when Gibson was diagnosed with Parkinson's disease in the spring of 1994. Along with other friends of Gibson—including Roger McGuinn; Spanky McFarlane; Peter, Paul and Mary; and Josh White, Jr.—he helped organize a September '94 benefit concert in Chicago to defray Gibson's medical expenses. Earlier, in July '94, he joined other well-known folk artists as part of a backing chorus for the track "I Hear America Singing" on Gibson's new Arista *Makin' a Mess* album.

McFarlane, who starred in the '60s as head of the folk-rock group Spanky and Our Gang, fondly remembered how much she had valued being exposed to the Camp and Gibson music at the start of the '60s. As she told Lynn Van Matre of the *Chicago Tribune*, "Gibson & Camp were the coolest guys in town, sharp dressers who got all the chicks. We were underage, so we had to stand in the back of the [Gate of Horn] club and watch. After the show, we would go down to the Oak Street Beach and sing Gibson & Camp songs until dawn."

CAMPBELL BROTHERS/SACRED STEEL MUSIC:
African-American Sacred Steel group from Keith Dominion Pentecostal Church in Rochester, New York. Charles "Chuck" Campbell, (pedal steel), Darick Campbell, (eight-string lap steel), Phillip Campbell, (guitar), Carlton Campbell, (drums), and Katie Jackson, (vocals). Other Keith and Jewel Dominion steel guitarists include: Wille Eason, Sonny Treadway, Calvin Cooke, Glenn Lee, Henry Nelson, and Aubrey Ghent.

In most churches it's the organist that moves the congregation to singing. But in the Keith and Jewel Dominion churches, affiliated with the African-American Holiness Pentecostal Church, it's the steel guitar that brings the congregation closer to God. In the hands of an expert player, the fluid sounds of the steel guitar can mimic the human voice, touch the heart, and even move people to speak in tongues. The House of God-Holiness Pentecostal churches were founded by an African-American woman named Mary Magdelena Lewis Tate in 1908. After her death in 1930, there was a dispute over leadership and the church split into three dominions: Keith, Jewel, and Lewis. The steel guitar, usually played on the lap or flat on a table and fretted with a steel bar, took hold as the lead instrument in the Keith and Jewel dominions in the late 1930s.

"Before the steel guitar became the prominent instrument there were people who would play piano," pedal steel player Chuck Campbell told Dave Peabody of *Folk Roots* ("Holy Sliders!" October 1999). "They would have been beat-up pianos if the church was fortunate to have such a thing. If there was a piano someone would try to play on that, but it would be woefully out of tune 'cause it would be in a dilapidated condition. Mostly the music would be more percussive, hand-clapping, rub-board, tubs, and maybe a bass or hand drum, not a drum set or trap set as you see it today. And of course there were the voices with moans and the screams and the hollers, the back and forth, that was the music."

Willie Claude Eason is considered the father of the sacred steel guitar. His older brother Truman was taking lessons from a Hawaiian steel guitarist. Willie couldn't quite get the feel for the Hawaiian guitar but he incorporated some of the sounds into his own steel guitar playing. ". . . He would mimic the voices of the church and the way he sings," Campbell told Peabody. "And people thought this was the best thing since sliced bread because now, instead of coming to church and having to scream and yell yourself to death, you could go so far and then the steel guy would take it and do the rest. You could actually sit back and enjoy but still get the same kind of emotion from the steel."

Eason's playing caught on first in the Keith and then the Jewel Dominion churches, especially in Florida, as he toured with Bishop Lockley's "Gospel Feast Party" in the late 1930s. He also recorded with gospel groups in the 1940s and 1950s. Other steel guitar pioneers include Henry Nelson, Rev. Aubrey Valdis Ghent, Calvin Cooke, and Glenn R. Lee in the Keith Dominion, and Eston "Sonny" Treadway, and Bishop Lorenzo Harrison of the Jewel Dominion.

The Campbell Brothers, perhaps the best-known sacred steel group, are the sons of Bishop Charles E. Campbell and Deaconess Naomi Haygood Campbell, the ministers of the Keith Dominion Church of Rochester, New York. Chuck Campbell took up the lap steel when his father gave him one for Christmas when he was eleven. He started playing in church a year later, but it took him a few years to develop his own style. "I played all the time," he said. He later moved to pedal steel, changing the tunings with pedals and knee levers. "Steel is the instrument! Everybody wants to play steel," he told Peabody. Indeed, his younger brother Darick often takes the lead on his eight-string lap steel, and when he's not soloing, he gives the band a multi-textured steel guitar sound. Phil plays guitar, and Phil's son Carlton plays drums. They are often joined by Katie Jackson, a Baltimore-based gospel singer known as the "Mahalia Jackson of the Keith Dominion."

"In our church the steel is playing in some form or another for 90 percent of the service," Campbell told Peabody. "We start out with what we call testimonials service or praise service. What that's about is singing songs in a call and response manner where everyone is singing. The entire congregation is singing. . . . That means that anyone at anytime can sing any song we all know. . . .in any key."

The Campbell Brothers have taken their religious-based music to festivals in the United States and Europe. As Chuck told Peabody: "The music has bound us together, even as a family, even when we have arguments. We may not be on good terms at the time, but I grab my instrument, we'll start playing together and, after that, it's all right. . . . We're not in it for the money—we have day jobs. It's all about love. It's pure and simple because when we say 'Jesus' all we're thinking about is God's divine love personified."

Arhoolie Records has put out several Sacred Steel CDs, including: *Sacred Steel: Traditional Sacred African-American Steel Guitar Music in Florida* (1997), *Pass Me Not: The Campbell Brothers featuring Katie Jackson* (1997), *Sonny Treadway: Jesus Will Fix It, Aubrey Ghent & Friends: Can't Nobody Do Me Like Jesus,* and *Sacred Steel—Live at the House of God Church* (featuring the Campbell Brothers, Calvin Cooke, Ted Beard, Robert Randolph, and Willie Eason).

CAPERCAILLIE: *Celtic Band based in Scotland. Karen Matheson (lead vocals), born Oban, Argyll, Scotland; Donald Shaw (accordion, keyboards), born England; Marc Duff (recorder, whistles, bodhran), born Canada; Joan MacLachlan (fiddle, vocals); Shaun Craig (guitar, bouzouki); Martin MacLeod (bass, fiddle). All of the above except Matheson, Shaw, and Duff left the band by the late 1980s. Joining in 1985: Charlie MacKerron (fiddle), born England. Joining in 1988: Manus Lunny (bouzouki, guitars, vocals), born Donegal, Ireland. Joining late 1980s: John Saich (bass, guitar, vocals), born Irvine, Scotland. Other contributors include: James MacKintosh (drums); Fred Morrison (bagpipes, whistles); Wilf Taylor (percussion); and David Robertson (percussion).*

Although it has stretched the musical boundaries, Capercaillie is most definitely a traditional Celtic band. Sure, in concert they may use an electric bass, synthesizers, and drums, but at the heart of the band are the acoustic musicians: Manus Lunny on bouzouki, Charlie MacKerron on fiddle, Donald Shaw on accordion, and Marc Duff on whistles. The soul of the band is Scottish-born singer Karen Matheson. As one critic wrote, "Let's face it, vocalist Karen Matheson could transform any song into a masterpiece."

Although only Matheson and bass player John Saich were born in Scotland, the band certainly has Scottish roots, and several of the other members were raised there. The name comes from a large, endangered Scottish grouse. (One article estimated that there were only 2,000 capercaillies left in the entire country.) Like the bird it's named for, Capercaillie mostly stays close to home, playing material gathered from traditional Scottish sources. But while the band plays traditional reels and Matheson sings the ballads in Gaelic, as well as an ancient form known as mouth music, Capercaillie has also incorporated African, jazz, pop, and new age influences. Since it began in 1984, the band has sold more than a million albums and toured in twenty-five countries.

Donald Shaw, who won the All Britain Accordian Championship in 1984, formed the group, which was based in Oban, Scotland. He has been the band's leader and songwriter ever since. Other original members were Karen Matheson, whistle player Marc Duff, fiddler Joan MacLachlan, bouzouki player Shaun Craig, and bass player Martin MacLeod. Matheson learned to sing from her grandmother, a singer from the island of Barra, in the Outer Hebrides. She began performing in ceilidhs as a child and was recognized early on as a gifted vocalist. She was still attending Oban High School, on the west coast of Scotland, when she began singing with the group.

Capercaillie recorded its first album, *Cascade,* during a whirlwind three-day session. It was released by Greentrax Records in 1984 and immediately established Capercaillie as one of the best traditional bands in Scotland. In 1985 fiddler Charlie McKerron, considered one of Scotland's finest, joined the band. The group followed in 1987 with *Crosswinds* (Green Linnet). The next year they were asked to compose the music for a series called *The Blood Is Strong,* about the Gaelic Scots. The sound track album, released in 1988, went platinum in Scotland, and the band began its worldwide touring. Bouzouki player Manus Lunny joined in 1988. (His brother Donal Lunny has produced several of Capercaillie's albums.) He had grown up in Donegal, a Gaelic-speaking part of Ireland, and had previously toured with ex–Silly Wizard players Andy M. Stewart and Phil Cunningham.

In 1989 Capercaillie released the excellent album *Sidewaulk* (Green Linnet), a fine mix of instrumentals and songs featuring Matheson's powerful vocals, a voice that actor Sean Connery said "is surely touched by God."

A 400-year-old Scots Gaelic ballad, "Coisich A' Ruin" ("Walk My Beloved") from the band's 1991 album *Delirium* (Survival) made the British top 40. The following year, Survival Records released a compilation album titled *Get Out.* The band continued to put out new albums: *Secret People* (Survival Records, BMG, Green Linnet) in 1993; and *Capercaillie* (Survival) in 1994.

In 1995 the band contributed music to the movie *Rob Roy,* set in Scotland. Matheson appears in the movie singing a Gaelic lament, "Ailein Duinn," backed by piper Davy Spillane. The song is included on the band's 1996 album *To the Moon* (Survival, Green Linnet), in which the band began experimenting with African rhythms and Latin melodies. Later that year, Matheson released her solo debut, *The Dreaming Sea,* on Survival.

In 1998 the band continued its torrid pace, touring throughout the United States, Australia, and Brazil. Capercaillie released a second compilation album, *Dusk Till Dawn* (Survival), and a new studio album, *Beautiful Wasteland* (Survival), which received strong reviews. Besides Scottish material, *Beautiful Wasteland*, recorded in the Andalucia Mountains of southern Spain, incorporates the vocals of two singers from Equatorial Guinea. As Colin Irwin wrote in *Folk Roots* (October 1997): "We know Karen Matheson is an immaculate singer; we know Donald Shaw is a gifted song craftsman; and we know that few bands come within several light-years of matching Capercaillie's understanding and sensitivity when it comes to Scottish—and specifically Gaelic—material. What we didn't know was that their style and vision is flexible enough to incorporate the wonderful, wonderful vocals of Equatorial Guinea's Paloma Loribo and Piruchi Apo of Sibeba; or that they could sound so pure and so Celtic; while thoroughly modern and youthful at the same time."

CARTHY, MARTIN: *Singer, guitarist, songwriter, born Hatfield, Hertfordshire, England, May 21, 1940.*

An artist whose name appears as a thread connecting many facets of the British folk revival that came to life at the end of the 1950s, Martin Carthy certainly merited such descriptive terms as "living legend" and "the best-known urban revival singer in England." Besides playing a role in breathing new life into the traditional English ballads collected by nineteenth-century folklorist Prof. Francis J. Child (*see separate entry*), he added his own originals to the genre and also developed a unique guitar style that influenced instrumentalists such as Richard Thompson and Pierre Bensusan.

He was born in Hatfield, near London, where many London citizens were evacuated during the German air attacks of World War II. He was influenced to some extent by his mother, who had taken part in an earlier resurgence of interest in traditional music in the 1920s and 1930s, but his first performing experience was as a member of a church choir. His father was a politician at the TVC. Before reaching his teens he already was searching for an instrument he could play. As he told Steve Winick for liner notes on a 1993 retrospective album, "I took up the trumpet, at which I was unsuccessful; the euphonium, at which I was unsuccessful; the trombone, at which I was only marginally less [un]successful." Finally, inspired by the 1950s growth of skiffle, a music form derived from the roots blues of American black artists, he decided to try the guitar and this time eventually did succeed.

A chance encounter with a Norfolk fisherman named Sam Larner singing traditional songs had a life-long impact. As he told Charlotte Greig of the *Sunday Telegraph* ("Scarborough Unfair Bob Dylan and Paul Simon are in Martin Carthy's debt," September 7, 1997), "Here was this old bloke singing these outrageous tunes. His idea of music seemed to be all wrong, compared to all this perfect stuff I was used to, but he was obviously extremely musical. He made the whole song light up. I walked away thinking, this man is crazy, this music's crazy, but I'd experienced something that's never left me." At first, like many other English teens—including the Beatles—he emulated skiffle stars like Lonnie Donegan, playing somewhat garbled versions of blues songs. Before long, however, he heeded the arguments of Ewan MacColl and other English folk singers, who urged homegrown artists to promote neglected folk material rather than music imported from America. He began his career as an aspiring actor. But by the beginning of the 1960s he already was beginning to establish himself as a singer and guitarist with the growing cadre of U.K. folk entertainers.

His early gigs included a number of appearances at the Troubadour Cafe in London's Earl's Court. He joined various groups in the first part of the 1960s, including the Thameside Four and the Three City Four, before focusing on his solo work. The other members of the Thameside Four were Redd Sullivan, Pete Maynard, and Marian Gray. He also sang on a TV program called *Halleluja* with an ad hoc group comprised of Sidney Carter and Nadia Cattouse. His first recordings were on *Hootenanny in London* (1963), singing the novelty songs "Your Baby 'as Gone Down the Plug Hole" and "With the End of Me Old Cigar." He also recorded an LP with the Three City Four (Carthy, Leon Rosselson, Ralph Trayner, and Marion MacKenzie) on Decca called *Three City Four* in 1965, followed by *Smoke and Dust Where the Heart Should Have Been* in 1966.

He recorded his first solo album in 1965, backed by the Ian Campbell Folk Group, then one of the most popular in the folk field, whose members at the time included fiddler Dave Swarbrick. Martin and Dave became close friends, and in 1966 formed a partnership that became one of the most innovative and dynamic duos on the folk music circuit at home and abroad. Before they went their separate ways in 1969 (though they continued to work together from time to time in following decades), they also recorded several excellent albums. In addition to the debut *Martin Carthy* (1965), they recorded *Second Album* (1966), *Byker Hill* (1967), the EP *No Songs* (1967), *But Two Came By* (1968), *Prince Heathen* (1969), and the restrospective *Selections* (1971). Carthy also recorded the solo album *The Bonny Black Hare* (1967) during that period. (Swarbrick joined Fairport Convention around the same time that Carthy joined Steeleye Span.)

By then, more than a few artists had been influenced by both Carthy's vocal style and his guitar innovations. As was pointed out in the liner notes for the Rhino Records *Troubadours of British Folk, Volume 1,* many singers have taken note of the way "his clean-sounding, slightly nasal voice is augmented by a natural vibrato.

He will take liberties with a traditional song if he feels another tune or different words would better suit it. Many of his songs are such hybrids that they have come to be inextricably associated with him. He taught Paul Simon his version of 'Riddles Wisely Expounded,' which became 'Scarborough Fair.'"

As he told Greig, he was less than pleased with Simon: "I remember in 1964 he was living in the flat that I and my ex-wife had just moved out of, and he came round in this Sunbeam Alpine open-topped sports car. He'd heard me sing 'Scarborough Fair,' and he wanted it. I wrote down the words for him and he took the song away and made lots of money out of it, especially from *The Graduate*. When I saw a copy of the single saying 'Words and music by Paul Simon,' I was thunderstruck."

He had a better experience with Bob Dylan to whom he also taught "Scarborough Fair'" and "Lord Franklin": "He wrote 'Girl from the North Country' on the basis of 'Scarborough Fair' and 'Bob Dylan's Dream' from the tune of 'Lord Franklin,'" Carthy told Greig. "He gave me credit for both of them. With Bob everything was always done in a spirit of friendship."

The *Troubadours of British Folk* liner notes also stressed that Carthy's invention of a new guitar style was a key milestone in that it offered a change from the American-developed techniques previously used by British musicians: "He uses many open tunings, but most significant is the sound he produces: staccato, highly rhythmic and percussive, with a drone, and the melody line carried in the bass." Until the start of the 1970s Carthy stressed the acoustic guitar, but after joining the folk-rock group Steeleye Span he demonstrated equally impressive skill on the electric guitar.

He wasn't a founding member of the band, but he and fiddler Peter Knight replaced Gay and Terry Woods in 1969 for the group's second Chrysalis album, *Please to See the King* (1971). Carthy was still with the band for the third album, also issued in '71, *Ten Man Mop, or Mr. Reservoir Butler Rides Again.* The latter album included the notable track "Skewball" (about a race horse), one of Steeleye Span's concert favorites. As vocalist Maddy Prior recalled, "Skewball is sung and led on banjo by Tim Hart and has an early version of the guitar 'stabs,' played by Martin Carthy, that have become such a feature of the electric folk movement."

Carthy left the band soon after, and began work on new solo collections. His albums included *Landfall* (1971), *Shearwater* (1972), and *Kershaw Sessions* (1978). He also joined Steeleye Span for two more albums, *Storm Force Ten* (1977) and *Live at Last!* (1978) later in the decade. His superb 1970s releases on Rounder Records included *Sweet Wivelsfield* in 1974, *Crown of Horn* in 1976, and *Because It's There* in 1979. His offerings of a wide range of traditional or traditionally derived treatments of ballads from old English, Celtic, Scottish, or Welsh sources were presented in

those LPs as well as a number of albums available in the United States as imports in the '70s: *Second Album, Byker Hill, But Two Came By,* and *Prince Heathen.* In the early 1970s he married Nancy Waterson of the a cappella Watersons folk song group, and in 1976 his family expanded to include daughter Eliza Carthy, who was to carve out a folk music niche for herself in the 1990s.

Eliza became an accomplished fiddler. Recalling her childhood she told a *Folk Roots* interviewer in 1994, "People always assume that because my dad is such a great guitarist then I ought to be able to play the guitar, but in truth he just wasn't around so I've never learned. I've just started getting close in the last few years, since he's been playing with Swarb really and since I've been taking an interest in instruments. So yeah, I grew up as a singer and whenever I went with the Watersons I'd go on stage."

As to having an encyclopedic knowledge of British folk music history, she added, "No, I haven't a clue about the folk scene. Only in the last five or six years did I start taking notice. People mention all sorts of bands to me and I haven't a clue about them. I only really started going to festivals when I was thirteen and when I was little[,] folk clubs were places you'd go to sleep in."

After marrying Nancy, Martin in time toured many times with the Watersons, replacing her cousin John Harrison. But he continued with many diverse projects from the mid-'70s through the 1990s. He was on the roster of such other bands as the Albion Country Band and Brass Monkey. He participated in the *Albion Country Band* album, released in 1972. He also performed in *The Transports,* a folk opera created by Peter Bellamy. In the 1980s he formed a band called Brass Monkey with John Kirkpatrick (formerly of Steeleye Span) and Sue Harris. They toured and recorded, including *Brass Monkey* in 1983 and *See How It Runs* in 1986, both on Topic. (In 1993 Topic issued *The Complete Brass Monkey,* which was a combination of the two LPs.) He left off making new solo recordings during the mid-1980s, but in 1988 completed the first of a new series of solo releases. By the start of the '90s, he and Dave Swarbrick again were touring together. They released two new albums including *Life and Limb* in 1991 and *Skin and Bone* in 1992. The mid-1990s found him recording with Nancy and Eliza in a new family trio whose digital debut album, *Waterson: Carthy,* issued on the Topic label in 1994, included such tracks as "Bold Doherty," "Grey Cock," "Ye Mariners All," and "When First I Came to Caledonia."

In 1993, Green Linnet Records issued a retrospective of Martin's solo work titled *The Collection,* which drew on the contents of his three 1970s Rounder albums plus *Out of the Cut* (1982) and *Right of Passage* (1988). The tracks included one of his originals, "Company Policy," and "Palaces of Gold," written by former Three City Four associate Leon Rosselson, plus such traditionally based numbers as "Lord Randal," "Siege of Delhi," "Swaggering Boney," and "Lovely Joan." The 1995 Rhino Records *Troubadours* CD, besides including Steeleye Span's "Skewball," also included one of Carthy's favorite solo tracks, "Famous Flower of Serving Men." As he commented in the liner notes, "The Famous Flower is the Mayflower, which is traditionally the flower of bad luck and mischief (I bet the Pilgrim fathers knew that and named their ship in defiance!), and the story, drenched in secrecy, is one of betrayal and redemption in which this balladry is ankle deep."

In the late 1990s Carthy was not only touring all over the world (solo, with Nancy and Eliza, and Swarbrick) but he was also releasing new recordings. The retrospective *Rigs of the Time* came out on Music Club. In 1997 Waterson: Carthy released *Common Tongue* on Topic and released a third collection in 1999, *Broken Ground*. Martin joined with Chris Wood and Roger Wilson in the 1998 release *Wood. Wilson. Carthy* on RUF Records. He released an excellent solo CD, *Signs of Life*, in 1998 on Topic, including such songs as "New York Mine Disaster, 1941," "Heartbreak Hotel," "Barbary Ellen," "The Deserter," "The Wife of Usher's Well," and a cover of Dylan's "The Lonesome Death of Hattie Carroll." Somehow that year he also found time to participate in a new Brass Monkey CD, *Sound and Rumour*, on Topic. Among the group members are Carthy, Kirkpatrick on accordion, Howard Evans on trumpet, Richard Cheetham on trombone, and Martin Brinsford on percussion. He also was honored with the Member of the Order of the British Empire award by Queen Elizabeth for his contributions to English folk music.

CASE, PETER: *Singer, guitarist (six- and twelve-string), harmonica player, band leader (Plimsouls), songwriter. Born Hamburg, New York, c. 1952.*

More than a few performers and songwriters exhibit what amounts to split musical personalities, but not many have as strong a line of demarcation between their style preferences as Peter Case. On the one hand he has gained attention for wild, hard-driving punk or grunge rock in groups like the Nerves and the Plimsouls. At the same time, he has won cheers from folk audiences for his original folk and country compositions, as well as his passionate presentation of traditional folk and blues songs. Citing Neil Young as an artist who successfully straddles the rock and folk domains, he told interviewer Michael Kinsman that while some people might scratch their heads at his choices, "It makes sense to me. I'm going to do the rock thing and the folk thing. One of the things I've learned is that I've got to have both of those elements in my life."

His initial influences, he recalled, were the performers favored by his sister, ten years older than he, whose record collection included discs by Elvis, Link Wray, Chuck Berry, and the Everly Brothers. At school, she grew interested in Bob Dylan, and when she brought his albums home Peter turned his attention to folk and blues. In his early and mid-teens in the 1960s, while developing his instrumental skills, he kept up with new developments in rock while also finding time to listen to work by folk and blues artists like Mississippi John Hurt, Skip James, Lightnin' Hopkins, Mance Lipscomb, Leadbelly, and Woody Guthrie.

By the time he was sixteen, toward the end of the '60s, he had decided he wanted to try for a career in pop music, and managed to put together enough cash for a bus ride from Buffalo, New York, to San Francisco. Once there he began to earn whatever money he could by performing as a busker in the city streets. After a while he expanded his busking pursuits to other towns up and down the West Coast from Mexico to Portland, Oregon. When he was in San Francisco during that period of his life, he lived in an abandoned truck in a wrecking yard. "It was strange," he told Kinsman. "I found myself living in a car on blocks in a junkyard. It was just very weird. It taught me a lot about life."

After a while, though, he started to find gigs indoors at places like the Coffee Gallery folk club in the city's North Beach area, famous as the stamping grounds of the Beat poets and writers of the '50s. He formed friendships with other musicians from both the folk and rock sectors, which in the mid-'70s led to his joining with guitarist-songwriter Jack Lee and drummer Paul Collins in a high-powered rock trio called the Nerves. The group soon had a small following in San Francisco and growing respect from other rock artists. Among those it toured or played with locally were the Ramones, Mink DeVille, the Germs, and the Weirdos. The trio recorded a number of singles and a 1976 extended play album that for the most part made little inroads with record buyers. Later two Nerves numbers, including one written by Case, "When You Find Out," were included in a Rhino DIY compilation.

The three Nerves members went their separate ways in 1978, with Case moving south to Hollywood, where he kept writing new songs while earning most of his income as a house painter. In 1980, he founded another rock band, the Plimsouls, whose other members were Eddie Munoz, Lou Ramirez, and Dave Pahoa. The band played small clubs in the Southern California area while sending demo tapes around. After an EP disc was released on an independent label, the Plimsouls signed with Planet / Elektra Records, which issued a full album. The band received warm praise from Los Angeles writers, and began to gain a national reputation as it expanded its concerts to other parts of the United States. It seemed on the verge of stardom after moving to the Geffen label and completing the 1983 release *Everywhere at Once.*

Case, though, was becoming a little disenchanted with the rock routine, particularly since he often got more pleasure from playing folk music in his hotel room after a show than from his rock sets. In 1984 the

Plimsouls disbanded and Case focused on expanding his folk credentials, taking time at first to write some new folk- and blues-based numbers to expand his existing repertoire. During the mid- and late '80s he toured widely in the United States and Canada on the folk club and university circuits, typically working as a solo acoustic performer. He also appeared at some concerts as the opening act for Jackson Browne.

In 1986 he signed with Geffen Records, which released his solo label debut, *Peter Case,* during the year. Among the backing musicians were John Hiatt, Byrds founder Roger McGuinn, and Van Dyke Parks. The album showcased originals by Peter that presented the case for the down-and-out, as well as his version of Lightnin' Hopkins's song "Ice Water," for which he composed some new lyrics. The album ranked as one of the best releases of the year, folk or otherwise, and was included in the top 10 list of *New York Times* critic Robert Palmer. Case followed with an even more impressive collection on Geffen in 1989, *The Man with the Blue Postmodern Fragmented Neo-Traditional Guitar.* Among those contributing to his performances were such top-rank artists as T-Bone Burnett, David Lindley, Los Lobos's David Hidalgo, Ry Cooder, and Benmont Tench from Tom Petty's band, the Heartbreakers.

The original compositions on both those Geffen releases, Case said, reflected his feeling for the disenfranchised and disenchanted in the United States who ended up "losers in a society built exclusively for winners." Case told Kinsman, "I wrote the songs [for the albums] in the 1980s when we saw how the Reagan policies were affecting people. We saw homeless people and nobody seemed to care. I know the feeling of having to live in the rain and not having enough money to get out of it." Fortunately for him, those days were long past. By the 1990s, he had married writer Diane Sherry and lived in Los Angeles with her and their three children.

His third Geffen album, *Six-Pack of Love,* came out in 1992. It was a fine collection, though perhaps a little less powerful than his superb initial solo efforts. Songs of his that won critical approval included "Dream about You," "Never Comin' Home," and "Beyond the Blues." Among the people who collaborated with him on various tracks were Tonio K, John Prine, Billy Swan, Tom Russell, and Bob Neuwirth. In 1993 he left Geffen and was signed by Vanguard Records, which issued his label debut, *Peter Case Sings Like Hell.*

His second disc on Vanguard, the 1995 twelve-song collection *Torn Again,* certainly seemed on a par with his 1980s solo albums and was a candidate for top 10 honors by many reviewers. It got a thumbs-up signal, for instance, from the *Gavin Report,* which, after hailing Case's lyrics for "Baltimore," added that "the rest of the album is stunning, surely his best solo work ever. Over the years, Case has been living his original dream, bumming across the United States in the tradition of Woody [Guthrie] and Cisco [Houston] . . . 'Baltimore' will be the jump-start track, but 'Blind Luck' is another favorite." *USA Today*'s critic called it one of the year's most satisfying albums.

Even as Case continued a schedule of folk venue concerts, he also found time to return to his rock roots, appearing with a reorganized Plimsouls band comprising, besides Case, old friends Eddie Munoz and Dave Pahoa, plus former Blondie drummer Clem Burke. The group re-recorded its old concert favorite, "A Million Miles Away," for the sound track of the 1995 film *Speed,* and also developed material for a new album. As he told interviewers, he had found himself working with bands that sounded like the Plimsouls, which made him want to have the real thing.

But Case didn't abandon his solo efforts, completing work during 1996 on material for a new Vanguard album, *Full Service No Waiting,* issued in the spring of 1998. The contents again revealed his considerable abilities as a writer and performer. Critics enjoyed it even though, like most of Case's output, it wasn't fated to be a blockbuster, saleswise. Robert Hilburn of the *Los Angeles Times,* for instance, commented that, in the new collection, "Case reflects on the passing of time and the lessening of opportunities, about dreams and lost chances, 'We used to gather here to flirt and laugh,' he sings in one song, 'Now all my dreams are cut in half.' For those who loved Bob Dylan's *Time Out of Mind,* this is a good next purchase." In 2000 Vanguard issued *Flying Saucer Blues.*

CHAPIN, HARRY: *Singer, guitarist, songwriter. Born New York, New York, December 7, 1942; died Long Island, New York, July 1981.*

A singer-guitarist-songwriter whose original compositions incorporated musical elements stretching from folk to jazz to rock, Harry Chapin not only was a troubadour of modern times but also a social reformer. Besides entertaining audiences all across the United States, he often persuaded them to contribute to humanistic causes ranging from world hunger to support for the performing arts. Describing his code to one interviewer, he said: "Our lives are to be used and thus to be lived as fully as possible. And truly it seems that we are never so alive as when we concern ourselves with other people."

He was born in New York's Greenwich Village, the son of a big-band drummer whose credits included stints with the Tommy Dorsey and Woody Herman bands. It was a closely knit family. Harry and his three brothers all drew inspiration from their father's musical interests. One of Harry's early musical pursuits was singing in the Brooklyn Heights Boys Choir after the family moved to the Brooklyn Heights section of New York in the '50s. Among his acquaintances in the choir was Robert Lamm, later of Chicago rock group fame.

The first instrument Harry learned was trumpet; he later took up banjo and guitar. At fifteen, he organized a musical act with his brothers. The older one soon dropped music, but younger siblings Tom and Steve stayed with it and later were regulars in the band that accompanied Harry around the world. Their father, Jim, sometimes sat in with them when they were young; he too became a cast member of the Chapin troupe in the '70s, when he often opened one of Harry's programs with his own Dixieland jazz group.

Harry became enthused about the folk boom of the late '50s and '60s and played many of the folk hits of the day for his own pleasure or for friends while studying architecture at the Air Force Academy and then philosophy at Cornell University. In 1964, he decided he'd had enough of higher education and left school to join brothers Tom and Steve and his father in a group called the Chapin Brothers that worked in Greenwich Village spots. The group recorded an album, *Chapin Music,* on Rockland Records, but disbanded when Tom and Steve went back to school.

Meanwhile, Harry was also trying his hand in the film field, first working as a film packer, loading reels into crates, then moving into film editing. By the late '60s, he was making some of his own documentaries. Completed with associate Jim Jacobs, his documentary *Legendary Champions* won an Academy Award nomination for best documentary of 1969 and also received prizes at the New York and Atlanta film festivals. In the middle and late '60s, Harry also wrote original songs, mostly of the storytelling kind that was to become his trademark in the '70s.

In 1970, his family resurrected the Chapin Brothers and got a contract to cut an LP for Epic. Harry provided the songs but didn't play in the group. Among the tracks on the LP were "Dog Town," "Greyhound," and "Any Old Kind of Day," which later were re-recorded by Harry and became important parts of his repertoire. Not too much happened with the 1970 group, but the following year, Harry got back into action, assembling a new band including brother Steve. Instead of looking for paying engagements with others, Harry hit on the idea of renting the Village Gate in New York for a summer run. Critics praised their work. Soon, not only local fans were coming to hear them, but record company executives as well. In late 1971, this culminated in a contract with Elektra, which remained his label through the rest of the '70s.

In short order, he had a single and an album that made the national charts. The single, a story song called "Taxi," drew on Harry's short-lived efforts to get a taxi driver's license in the mid-1960s. (The song itself deals with a chance meeting between two onetime lovers— the man now driving a taxi—whose paths and dreams have diverged sharply.) It received considerable airplay despite its unconventional length of six minutes. *Heads and Tales,* his debut LP containing the song, was released in early 1972. Harry continued to build up a following across the world during 1973 and 1974 with the albums *Sniper and Other Love Stories* and *Short Stories.*

The most played track from *Short Stories* was the hit single "W*O*L*D," a bittersweet view of the AM radio world through the eyes of an aging disc jockey.

His fourth album, *Verities and Balderdash,* proved even more exciting. One of its tracks, "Cat's in the Cradle," was a telling indictment of a father who was more concerned about becoming a success in business than helping his son grow up. Both single and album soared past gold-record levels and verified that Chapin was a bona fide star even though his balladeering approach to music didn't fit neatly into any particular cubbyhole. He essentially was a folksinger, but in a completely modern idiom.

In the mid-1970s, without abandoning his steady recording pace (which included two LPs, *Portrait Gallery* and *Greatest Stories—Live*), Harry ventured into other entertainment areas. During 1974 he was working on a new musical, a multimedia concept show that opened on Broadway in 1975 under the title *The Night That Made America Famous.* The show was highly praised by reviewers and later was given two Tony nominations by New York theater critics. Two years later, this time across the country in Hollywood, a revue at the Improvisation Theatre based on his music and called *Chapin* achieved a seven-month run and later spawned similar productions elsewhere.

During the '70s, Chapin kept up a hectic touring schedule that averaged 200 concerts a year all over the United States and in many other nations, half of which typically were benefits.

Another continuing effort was his work to eradicate hunger throughout the globe. Chapin helped found the World Hunger Year, a campaign in which, besides giving many benefit concerts and enlisting other artists to do the same thing, he lobbied House and Senate members and the President of the United States to pass a resolution for a government commission on world hunger. At many of his concerts, he told the audience he would remain after the show as long as necessary to sign autographs and talk to people donating money to whatever charitable enterprise he was working on at the time.

Even with that hectic schedule, he still managed to write new songs and turn out new albums, though it must be said that sometimes the pace appeared to be reflected in some loss in creative results. After his 1976 LP, *On the Road to Kingdom Come,* he provided material for a two-album set released in August 1977, *Dance Band on the Titanic.* The theme running through its eleven songs was that the entertainment industry, to coin a phrase, was "on thin ice" and resembled the band on the sinking *Titanic.* However, the LP seemed far muddier and less interesting than his earlier releases. Harry was in better form for his next offering, *Living Room Suite,* issued in June 1978. Among the diverse groups providing backing vocals were the Persuasions, Dixie Hummingbirds, and Cowsills. Though he was still a favorite with concert audiences at the end of the

1970s, Chapin's recording efforts seemed to be bringing diminishing returns when he left Elektra to sign a new contract with Boardwalk Records. By the end of 1980, though, that part of his career was on the upswing with the success of his single "Sequel," in upper charts levels in December, and his Boardwalk LP of the same title, on the charts from late 1980 well into 1981.

"Sequel," as the title indicates, was a follow-up to his earlier hit "Taxi," in which the man and woman meet after ten years with their roles reversed—by then the one-time taxi driver is a success in the music field and the girl is divorced from her rich husband and working for a living. There turned out to be some irony in Chapin's comments to Paul Grein (*Los Angeles Times,* December 6, 1980): "My wife has been kidding me that in another ten years I've got to write a new song called 'Hearse' and finally haul 'em off."

Unfortunately, Chapin's own life was snuffed out in an automobile accident on New York's Long Island Expressway in July 1981.

Just before his passing, he had expressed his concern over political trends in the United States to Andrew Epstein of the *Los Angeles Times,* though at the same time indicating optimism that the younger generations would eventually improve things. (Chapin was somewhat apolitical himself; in the 1980 elections he had campaigned for five Republican and nineteen Democratic congressmen, basing his support on their stands in favor of action to alleviate world hunger.)

"Frankly," Chapin said, "there's more potential movement out of this generation than there was in the '60s. The real question is whether America is going to use Reagan as an excuse to forget about things it already knows it should stand up for. When David Stockman [Reagan's budget director] says to America that there's no such thing as entitlement, it's giving us all an excuse to not feel guilty about [the poor] and just be selfish. And we know that's nonsense. Because we know that Nelson Rockefeller, when he was born, was entitled to $400 million and somebody else was entitled to brain damage because of malnutrition.

"The scary thing about the current political situation is that it is allowing people to have a political excuse to go to sleep."

Soon after Chapin's passing, there were indications others would rally to his causes. Benefits were planned to collect funds for them as well as to salute his memory. His manager, Ken Kragen, announced establishment of a Harry Chapin Memorial Fund "to keep his work going and try to accomplish some of the goals he set." In 1999 Rhino/Elektra Traditions released the retrospective *Story of a Life.*

CHAPMAN, TRACY: *Singer, songwriter, guitarist. Born Cleveland, Ohio, March 30, 1964.*

Tracy Chapman is living proof that one should never take critics too seriously. In 1988, Tracy Chapman's year, she was just twenty-four and an unlikely star. She performed folk songs about serious issues at the end of the Reagan decade. But in August her self-titled debut album shot to number one on the charts, surpassing records by Def Leppard and Guns 'n' Roses. The shy young artist resonated with listeners around the world. The album eventually sold more than 10 million copies worldwide; she had a top 10 hit with "Fast Car," a song that provides a metaphor for a relationship going nowhere. Her success startled industry insiders. How could one woman with a guitar appeal to so many people? The answer: people were starved for something with meaning. They loved Chapman's husky voice and heartfelt, issue-oriented songs, a welcome refreshment to a public fed on a steady diet of heavy metal and dance music.

The problem with Chapman's meteoric rise was that it created unreasonable expectations. The albums that followed—*Crossroads* in 1989 and *Matters of the Heart* in 1992—were solid and commercially successful but could not match the intensity of her debut. The critics were too quick to write Chapman off, however. It took seven years, but Chapman's November 1995 release on Elektra, aptly titled *New Beginning,* would again break into the top 10 on the pop charts in 1996 and provide a hit single with "Give Me One Reason." By the time of her fourth album, she had sold more than 18 million albums worldwide and traveled around the globe. She sold millions more with *New Beginning.* Along with Suzanne Vega, Michelle Shocked, and k.d. lang, Chapman represented a new kind of female performer, a dressed-down, androgynous type with a less romanticized view of the world. In some ways she brought the singer-songwriter back to the pop mainstream. Her lineage harks back to the success of such artists as Jackson Browne, Joni Mitchell, and Bob Dylan, and paved the way for singers of the '90s—from Nanci Griffith and Mary-Chapin Carpenter to Sarah McLachlan and Paula Cole.

Chapman's early years in a working-class section of Cleveland shaped her musical themes. Her parents separated when she was four, and she was raised by her mother. She listened to gospel and Motown music. She told an interviewer that her father listened to John Coltrane, but she didn't have patience for jazz until she got older.

"I was very aware of all the struggles my mother was going through, being a single parent and a black woman trying to raise two kids," she told an interviewer. "[She noticed] all these forces in society making things more difficult than they ought to be."

As a teenager, she attended the private Wooster School in Danbury, Connecticut, on a scholarship sponsored by A Better Chance. At school she listened to Joni Mitchell and Bob Dylan, whose sounds blended with Chapman's earlier influences.

After Wooster she attended Tufts University, where

she graduated with a degree in anthropology in 1986. She began singing in clubs in the Boston area. The son of Charles Koppelman, president of the music publisher SBK, heard Chapman and brought her to his father's attention. Koppelman put her in touch with Elektra Records, which released *Tracy Chapman* in 1988. Elektra thought the album would sell 200,000 copies. No one could have predicted her overnight success. After all, as Elektra's vice president, Peter Philbin, told a reporter, Bruce Springsteen didn't start selling lots of albums until his third release, *Born to Run.* But Chapman's album followed Suzanne Vega's success in 1987—the road had been cleared.

Chapman was serious about her craft. "Music was never just a hobby for me," she told Robert Hilburn of the *Los Angeles Times* (April 17, 1988). "I'd pick up a guitar every day to work on whatever I was writing at the time. I would put my ideas in songs the way some people might put them in diaries or journals. One reason it didn't sound like most of the things you hear on the radio is I didn't listen to the radio. I tended to be more isolated."

She sang songs of racial injustice, domestic violence, economic exploitation, and love, set against the backdrop of the inner city. In "Talkin' 'Bout a Revolution" she almost anticipated the riots that would erupt in Los Angeles in 1992: *Poor people gonna rise up and take what's theirs!* In "For My Lover" she sings about a woman who is willing to do jail time for her lover: *Two weeks in a Virginia jail for my lover, for my lover. Twenty-thousand-dollar bail for my lover, for my lover.* In "Fast Car" the narrator is a woman tied to a lover who has little ambition and little to offer her except a fast car. "Behind the Wall" takes the listener into a chilling domestic violence scene: *Last night I heard the screaming—Loud voices behind the wall,* she sang; *The police always come late, If they come at all.*

Chapman was unprepared to be thrust suddenly into the spotlight. She made the cover of *Rolling Stone.* She went on the six-week, five-continent Amnesty International tour, along with Bruce Springsteen. She was nominated for six Grammys and won in three categories—Best New Artist; Best Pop Vocal Performance, Female; and Best Folk Recording—for her single "Fast Car."

When it came time to make a follow-up album, the pressure was tremendous. She was expected not only to meet the success of her debut album but to surpass it. Chapman told Robert Hilburn of the *Los Angeles Times* (June 10, 1990) how she retreated from the public view to cope with success, moving from Boston to San Francisco in 1990: "I think the biggest change I've found is how my time at this point has become very precious. Maybe in some ways I retreated a little more and hid from the success and attention of the first record. I tended to keep close to the people who I had known before."

Her second album, *Crossroads,* also on Elektra, received mixed reviews. Stephen Holden wrote in the *New York Times* (October 1, 1989): "On her compelling new album, her voice—judgmental but humane, embattled but nobly determined—infuses and elevates songs of freedom, justice and the struggle to maintain integrity that are so simple that were they sung by anyone else they might sound trite." Many other critics felt that the songs sounded too much like her first album.

Some of the songs on *Crossroads* reflected her ability to protest through music in much the same way Phil Ochs did in the 1960s. "Subcity" was critical of government cutbacks and their impact on the inner city. In "All That You Have Is Your Soul" she sings: *Thought I'd make history; making babies was the best I could do.* But there was a bitterness present in the second album that turned the media glare on her. In the title track, for example, derived from the Robert Johnson songs "Cross Road Blues" and "Hellhound on My Trail," she sings: *I look to the left, I look to the right; there're hands that grab me on every side.*

Although the song appeared to be railing against the travails of the recording industry, Chapman had written it in 1982, long before her stardom. "For me it just relates on a more general level to the challenges that individuals face in their lives," she told Hilburn. "There are lots more important things to write about than the record business."

Indeed, she participated in the Freedomfest in Britain honoring Nelson Mandela's release from prison. Two of her songs, "Freedom Now" and "Material World," had been banned by the South African Broadcasting Corporation in 1989.

Crossroads sold more than 5 million copies worldwide and reached number nine on the *Billboard* charts, respectable by any standards, but less impressive than her debut. She took a break before her next album; when she went on tour in 1990, instead of going solo, she added a five-piece backup band. She seemed to loosen up a bit in concert. She continued her contributions to protest movements, performing at the Farm Aid benefit in 1992 along with Willie Nelson, Neil Young, John Mellencamp, and Arlo Guthrie.

Then, in 1992, she released *Matters of the Heart* after several problematic delays. The album continued to show Chapman's superior songwriting talent, but she suffered vicious attacks from the critics. Karen Schoemer wrote in the *New York Times* (April 26, 1992): "Where the *Tracy Chapman* songs spoke volumes in whispers and minute details . . . *Crossroads* tried to deal with slavery, capitalism, urban decay, even the salvation of humankind's soul in one easy whack. 'Fast Car' worked because it balanced desperation with naive optimism; the sweeping statements of *Crossroads* harangued without offering hope. Overnight, Ms. Chapman seemed to have lost her innocence. The long-awaited and often-delayed *Matters of the Heart* regains little slipped ground. The first several songs come across like an issue-of-the-week tally sheet. . . . The songs are such downers they should be sold by prescription only."

The album topped out at fifty-three on the *Billboard* charts and quickly fell to 102. But in concert in September 1992, just five months after the Los Angeles riots, Chapman's songs, written in the early 1980s, seemed all too prophetic. She continued to sing about the poor and downtrodden. She wound up her set with "Talkin' 'Bout a Revolution." But as Steve Hochman wrote in the *Los Angeles Times* (September 21, 1992): "That's all well and good, but Chapman failed to offer any suggestions for how to achieve that utopia, save for a between-song plea for people to register and vote."

Her 1995 album, *New Beginning,* seemed to respond to Hochman's criticism. As the title suggests, she departed from her first three albums to show a softer side and more introspection with songs like "New Beginning": *There's too much fighting, too little understanding.*

During her concerts she gave away free packets of seeds to people who brought a coupon found in the compact discs. "I wanted people to think about the potential and possibilities that exist even in something as small as a seed," she told the Vanderbilt University newspaper (February 1996). She encouraged people to write messages on index cards and she read from the cards at her concerts.

She seemed genuinely happy with her lower profile. "I'm glad I'm not in that bright spotlight any longer," she told Steve Morse of the *Boston Globe* (November 10, 1995). "I'm just not comfortable with it. . . . I'm really happy with where I am musically now—and with the fact that I can walk around the streets of San Francisco without a problem. Some people may recognize me, but I can still live my life as I used to without feeling burdened. I met someone who said they'd love to be on the cover of *People* magazine and I said, 'Well, be careful what you wish for because it changes your life forever.'"

New Beginning moved steadily up the charts and remained in the top 10 for six months. Her bluesy single "Give Me One Reason," written before Chapman's 1988 breakthrough, was also a chart hit in 1996. In the album, Chapman reminded listeners of what made her so special in 1988: the ability to inspire people through deep, emotional songs. She is still "Talkin' 'Bout a Revolution," but these days it's a peaceful revolution. (Chapman received five Grammy nominations for *New Beginning* and "Give Me One Reason," and took home an award in the Best Rock Song category for "Give Me One Reason.")

"I don't think change has to be violent change," she told Sean Glennon of the *Springfield Advocate* (December 30, 1995). "If each individual who has the opportunity to vote and to work for change in the way the system works takes that opportunity we can make a change without any violence. . . . [The revolution] is not that far away; it's simply what you see as the rising up. I see the idea of poor people rising up in many different ways. It might be about voting, it might be about finding ways to look out for each other, it might be about making the system just a little better." In 2000 Elektra released Chapman's fifth solo CD *Telling Stories.*

CHAVIS, WILSON "BOOZOO": *Zydeco accordionist, harmonica player, singer, songwriter. Born Lake Charles, Louisiana, October 23, 1928.*

Although Clifton Chenier was the King of Zydeco, Boozoo Chavis had the first hit with "Paper in My Shoe" in 1954. But he became embittered with the music industry and in the early 1960s decided to hang up his accordion. He turned to training racehorses and didn't return to playing music professionally until 1984.

He was born Wilson Anthony Chavis, the son of a tenant farmer who played the accordion. Chavis learned the harmonica and accordion by observing his father. As a child growing up poor he'd walk miles to school each day. He'd stuff paper in his shoes because he'd wear out his socks. That's where the idea for his first hit came from.

He began playing in dance halls in the 1940s where he often ran into Clifton Chenier, who was playing the same clubs. (Unlike Chenier, Chavis developed his skills on the button accordion.) Eddie Shuler of Goldband Records heard about Chavis and asked him to come in to the studio to record. The result was "Paper in My Shoe," distributed by Imperial Records, which sold more than 100,000 copies. But Chavis feels Goldband never paid him what he deserved. "I'm mad now," he told Ben Sandmel for the book *Zydeco!* (University Press of Mississippi, 1999, with photographs by Rick Olivier). "If they came from Goldband today and asked me to make another record, I believe I'd have to shoot 'em." Among the last songs he recorded for Goldband was "Hamburgers and Popcorn" in the 1960s.

After a twenty-year hiatus, he recorded the single "Dog Hill" for Floyd Soileau's Maison de Soul Records of Ville Platte, Louisiana, in 1984. He followed that hit with another, "Zydeco Hee Haw," and his career suddenly took off again at the age of fifty-six. As he told Sandmel, "It spring up just like that, and sometimes I tell people, I say, 'I'm scared of myself.' Yessir. It's true. You get scared of yourself."

Boozoo, who wears a cowboy hat, draws large numbers to his concerts these days. "I wear a cowboy hat wherever I go," he told Sandmel. "You got to look clean. I don't like them damn hippies, with a scarf on their head, an earbob in their ear, their hair flyin' in their face."

Since he started making music again, several new and reissued Boozoo Chavis albums have come out, including several on Maison de Soul: *Louisiana Zydeco Music* (1986), *Boozoo Zydeco* (1987), *Paper in My Shoe* (1987), *Zydeco Homebrew* (1988), *Zydeco Trail Ride* (1989), and *Nathan and the Zydeco Cha Cha's* (1989). Elektra / Nonesuch released *Boozoo Chavis* (1990). Rounder released *Live at Richard's Zydeco Dance Hall* (1988); *The Lake Charles Atomic Bomb: Original Goldband Recordings* (1990), a fourteen-track compilation; *Boozoo, That's Who!* (1993); *Live at the Habibi Temple* (1994), and *Who Stole My Monkey?* (1999). Discovery Records released *Hey Do Right* in 1997.

CHENIER; CLIFTON, CLEVELAND, AND C.J.:
Clifton Chenier (accordionist, harmonica player, organist, pianist, band leader of the Red Hot Louisiana Band), born Opelousas, Louisiana, June 25, 1925; died Lafayette, Louisiana, December 12, 1987. Cleveland Chenier (washboard player), born Leonville, Louisiana, November 16, 1921; died May 7, 1991. C.J. Chenier (accordionist, saxophonist, band leader of the Red Hot Louisiana Band), born Port Arthur, Texas, September 28, 1957.

Wearing a regal crown and cape in concert, with his gold teeth shining, Clifton Chenier played his piano accordion (with its "Clifton Chenier" mother-of-pearl-inlay) as if it were an extension of his body. He not only looked like the king, he *was* the king—of zydeco. As Bob Marley had for reggae and Bill Monroe for bluegrass, Chenier put a rootsy spin on his music and brought it to the world beyond Louisiana. His sound, along with the rhythm provided by his older brother Cleveland, was irresistible. As Greg Drust wrote in the Rhino 1993 retrospective album *Zydeco Dynamite: The Clifton Chenier Anthology:* "If these scorchers don't make you move like an alligator in a pond of hot sauce, you'd better consult a physician." His son, C.J. Chenier, represents a new generation of zydeco players, mixing jazz in with the old tradition.

"What I did was to put a little rock 'n' roll into the zydeco to mix it up a bit," Chenier told *Rolling Stone.* "You see, people been playing zydeco for a long time, old style, like French music. But I was the first one to put the pep to it." Chenier described zydeco as "the traditional French two-step with new hinges so she can swing."

Zydeco takes its name from the French word for snap beans, *les haricot* (pronounced "lay-zahrico"), and also comes from the song "Zydeco sont pas sale" ("No salt in the snap beans"). The music evolved from Cajun, French, blues, and R&B influences. Before World War II, black and white music, like the food, was integrated in Cajun country, where descendants of French settlers of Nova Scotia relocated after the British expelled them in 1755. German and Czech settlers brought the accordion to the area in the 1870s. Creole accordionist and singer Amédée Ardoin was the first black man to cut a zydeco record, on Decca Records in New Orleans in 1928. After the war, the bayou became segregated and zydeco a black musical form.

Clifton and Cleveland heard both white and black musicians growing up, including Ardoin, who mixed the French dance tunes with Creole blues, and fiddler Freeman Fontenot. Their father, Joseph, was a sharecropper and weekend accordionist who taught Clifton how to play. Clifton and Cleveland played at weekend dance halls, including one that Fontenot held in the first black schoolhouse in the area.

Arhoolie Records founder Chris Strachwitz, who recorded many of the Cheniers' albums, thinks Clifton gravitated toward the accordion and Cleveland to the rubboard because Clifton "was obviously the more outgoing and he was going to be the main man. . . . The guy who wants to drink and have fun, that's the rubboard player."

Clifton designed the rubboard that Cleveland used, according to Strachwitz. He drew the design in the sand for a steel man. His rubboard had a collar so that it could be worn over ones shoulders. Cleveland wore it like a chest protector, playing it with bottle openers.

Cleveland was indispensible to Clifton's sound. "Whenever they played Creole music, it was basically Clifton and Cleveland," Strachwitz says. "The drummer just pounds a steady beat. But it was Cleveland's incredible syncopation that was going everywhere. He's so far beyond any other rubboard player. He had that bizarre old time syncopation that they don't have anymore that's really almost African."

The Cheniers cut sugar cane in New Iberia, Louisiana; worked in the Lake Charles oil fields; and drove oil refinery trucks in Port Arthur, Texas. "Clifton discovered that playing for the workers during the noonday break he could make more money than he was working for the goddam oil company," Strachwitz says.

In 1942, Clifton and Cleveland played at the Bon Ton Drive-In in Beaumont, Texas, owned by musician and entrepreneur Clarence Garlow (1911–1986) who had a local hit with "Bon Ton Roula." In the late 1940s and early '50s, the Cheniers played on the "crawfish circuit" from Port Arthur to Lake Charles with the Hot Sizzling Band.

They first recorded at KAOK radio station in Lake Charles. In the mid-1950s, J.R. Fulbright heard the Cheniers playing and was impressed. In 1954, the Elko label released the single "Louisiana Stomp" with "Cliston Blues" credited to "Cliston Chanier" (sic) on the B-side. Chenier had a regional hit with the record. Elko sold Chenier's contract to Imperial Records' Post division, which released four more sides.

His career took off when he recorded for Specialty in 1955 with sides like "Eh, Petite Fille" ("Ay-Te Te Fee"), a minor hit. (As Drust points out, "Eh, Petite Fille" sounds like Richard Lewis's 1954 song "Hey Little Girl," which in turn resembles a Paul Gayten song from September 1951 and a Professor Longhair cut from 1949). Chenier recorded a total of twelve sides for Specialty.

By 1956, the Cheniers quit their oil refinery jobs and begin spreading their zydeco sounds. As Drust writes, Chenier began touring with Etta James, who needed a legal guardian at the time. "Clifton Chenier used to lock me up in a room 'cause I used to like one of his little band boys," James said. "But that didn't help, really, 'cause I had a slick way of doing it. We could crawl out the bathroom window, along the pipes, crawl in somebody else's bathroom window, and get in another room. Anyway, Clifton taught me a lot about the road, and he tried to really keep me off the guys."

In the late 1950s and early '60s, Chenier's recording career slowed as rock 'n' roll took off. In 1964, that changed when Strachwitz was in Houston recording Lightnin' Hopkins. Hopkins's wife was Chenier's cousin, and they invited Strachwitz to see Chenier playing at a club in Houston's Frenchtown.

"It was unbelievably funky," Strachwitz recalls. "I had heard 'Eh 'Tite Fille' and some other R&B stuff. I wasn't all that excited. To me, it was R&B rather than low down blues. But hell, anyplace Lightning goes, shit, yeah, I went. It was this little tiny dive. All the people as far as I could tell spoke French, Creole patois. There he was all by himself with his accordion and a drummer, Madison Guidry. I was very impressed. He wasn't R&B at all. It was total French blues. I never heard anything like it in my life."

Chenier asked Strachwitz to cut a record with him the next day. Strachwitz somehow scraped together enough money for the session. "The next day he brought his whole goddam band—a bass player, guitar, and piano player. The piano player didn't play. The guitar, thank God, the goddam amplifier started burning. That was the end of that sonofabitch. The bass cone of the speaker was totally disconnected from the paper, so you didn't hear nothing." All that was left was Chenier and a drummer.

On February 8, 1964, Chenier recorded "Ay Ai Ai" (in English) for Arhoolie with "Why Did You Go Last Night?" on the flip side. Strachwitz encouraged him to play the old zydeco, but Clifton resisted. "He didn't seem to want to do any of those French numbers," Strachwitz recalls. "That's what knocked me out. So the next time we recorded I said 'We've got to have at least half the record in French.'" Chenier's first album, Louisiana Blues and Zydeco, came out in January 1966 on Arhoolie (reissued on CD in 1991), with one side devoted to zydeco and the other to R&B and blues. It produced the regional hits "Louisiana Blues," "Zydeco Sont Pas Sale," and "Hot Rod."

Strachwitz noted that Chenier would later change his act depending on his audience. "I saw him two nights running in the late 1960s," he told Daniel Wolff of The Nation (March 19, 1988). "The first night, for a white audience, he played a whole evening of two-steps

and waltzes. I didn't know he knew that much of the old stuff. And then the next night, in Lake Charles, he played the current soul hits and a little zydeco with some R&B riffs thrown in."

In April 1967 (reissued in 1991), Arhoolie released Bon Ton Roulet! and More (the title track is the French version of Louis Jordan's "Let the Good Times Roll"), which included Chenier's best-selling single "Black Gal." Black Snake Blues came out in March 1969. Other Arhoolie releases include King of the Bayous (February 1971; reissued June 1992), his most popular release, Bogalusa Boogie, (March 1976; reissued February 1991), Out West (May 1974; August 1991), Red Hot Louisiana Band (January 1978), 60 Minutes with the King of Zydeco (April 1987), Live at St. Mark's (September 1972; reissued January 1990), The King of Zydeco: Live at Montreux (March 1981; reissued February 1991); King of the Bayous (1970), and Sings the Blues (October 1987). (Half of the Red Hot Louisiana Band LP was also reissued on CD in February 1993.) None of his records were best-sellers, but he had a loyal following. Releases on other labels include Blues Festival (1966) with Lightnin' Hopkins and Mance Lipscomb, Live at a French Creole Dance (1972), Bad Luck and Trouble (1975), And His Red Hot Louisiana Band in New Orleans on GNP/Crescendo (1979), Boogie 'N' Zydeco (1980), and Boogie in Black and White later in the decade.

In 1966 he played at the Berkeley Blues Festival, which helped establish him with a wider audience. Chenier began to tour the world with the Red Hot Louisiana Band. The group included Chenier on accordion, his brother Cleveland on washboard, John Hart on tenor sax, and Paul Senegal on guitar. (Later members included C.J. Thomas on alto sax; Robert Peter, a.k.a. Robert St. Judy, on drums; and his son, C.J. Chenier, on sax and accordion.) In 1967, he played at the Ash Grove in Los Angeles, the Avalon Ballroom in San Francisco, and at the Royal Albert Hall in London as part of the American Folk Blues Festival tour, not to mention the Bon Ton Roulet in Lafayette, Louisiana. He appeared at the Newport Folk Festival in 1969 and toured Europe.

The Cheniers kept up their rapid pace in the early 1970s, including appearances at the New Orleans Jazz & Heritage Festival nearly every year from 1972 on. Documentary filmmaker Les Blank featured Chenier in the 1973 documentary Hot Pepper. He appeared on the PBS show Austin City Limits in 1976. He recorded Frenchin' the Boogie for a French blues label in 1976 (later released in 1995 on Verve). Classic Clifton, an LP compiled from other LPs and 45s, was released on LP in August 1980. But in the late 1970s, Clifton began suffering from diabetes.

As his health declined, Chenier prepared to pass on the zydeco crown to his son, Clayton Joseph "C.J." Chenier. C.J. grew up in Port Arthur, Texas, with his mother, Mildred Bell, and only saw his road-weary father twice a year. He had only one of his father's albums, and his friends ridiculed his father's music; he listened to James Brown, John Coltrane, and Miles Davis, and played the sax and keyboards in local bands.

One week before his twenty-first birthday, Clifton, whose sax player, John Hart, had left the band, asked his son to join him on the road. "It wasn't kind of scary," Chenier told David S. Rotenstein of the *Pittsburgh Tribune-Review* (August 24, 1995). "It was frightening. . . . I had been playing funk and didn't know a thing about zydeco."

But the band members helped him. "And then one day the music hit me, and I knew this is what I wanted to do," C.J. says.

Clifton's kidneys began to fail in the early 1980s, forcing him to receive dialysis three times a week. He continued to tour, recording *I'm Here* on the Alligator label in 1982 (with C.J. on sax), which won a Grammy. (Maison De Soul released *Country Boy Now Grammy Award Winner* in 1984.) His concerts lacked the drive of earlier performances. Reviewing a performance at the Club Lingerie in Los Angeles in 1983, *Los Angeles Times* writer Don Snowden wrote: "His normally effervescent stage personality wasn't in evidence and even his accordion solos lacked their customary fluency and authority" (August 6, 1983). Despite that, Snowden called Chenier and his band possibly "the most explosive band in American music right now." (His album *Live!*, released by Arhoolie in May 1985 (on CD in 1993), captured some of his best performances in the early 1980s at Long Beach and San Francisco Blues festivals.)

His condition worsened in the mid-1980s. He lost half of one foot and part of another leg due to diabetes, but insisted on traveling with the band. He encouraged C.J. to pick up the accordion. "He didn't push it," C.J. says. "But when he first called me to play with his band I think it was his idea all along that I would carry on his music."

C.J. became Clifton's bandleader. As he told Rotenstein. "His hands swirled around those keys and blended in with one another. He didn't have to work at playing the zydeco. I had to learn how to play that. All that came natural to him. . . . When I picked it up, I played blues. With zydeco, I had to work at it."

On December 12, 1987, Clifton died of kidney failure and complications from diabetes at the General Hospital in Lafayette. In Opelousas, where he was born, 4,000 people attended his wake. "It was a pretty good-sized crowd," Strachwitz recalls. "He was a well-known man." He was buried in sugar cane country in Loreauville, Louisiana, near New Iberia, apparently in an unmarked grave.

C.J. inherited his father's accordion and took over the Red Hot Louisiana Band. But wearing his crown was another story. At a concert in March 1988 at the Music Machine in Los Angeles, just three months after his father's death, C.J. made it clear that he wasn't trying to become the next king of zydeco. "The crown was his—it's not something to be handed down," he told Steve Hochman of the *Los Angeles Times* (March 14, 1988). "It won't fit any head but his."

Cleveland Chenier played in the band that night and told Hochman about the pressures C.J. faced: "If he plays like Clifton, people will say he's just a copy. And if he doesn't, people will be mad because he doesn't sound like Clifton."

Cleveland retired a couple of years later. He died in 1991 and was buried in a cemetery in Scott, Louisiana, at St. Martin De Porres.

A steady stream of albums have come out over the years. Maison De Soul released *Boogie & Zydeco* in 1987, and *Zydeco Legend!* in 1989. *Zodico Blues & Boogie* (1993) features his 1955 recordings for Specialty. Collectables put out *We're Gonna Party* in 1994, and Magnum America issued *I'm Coming Home* in 1996. Other albums include *Live at 1966 Berkeley Blues Festival, Bayou Bayou, Squeezebox Boogie,* and *Cajun Swamp Music.*

C.J. has forged his own sound, adding jazz and funk while keeping his father's legacy alive. He released five albums: *My Baby Don't Wear No Shoes* on Arhoolie (1988), *Let Me in Your Heart* (1989), *Hot Rod* (1990), and *I Ain't No Playboy* on Slash (1992), and *Too Much Fun,* recorded in Memphis for Alligator (March 1995). He described the latter release as a kind of "funky zydeco." C.J. does some traditional zydeco songs (including a cover of his father's "You Used to Call Me"), but on some tracks he mixes blues and jazz, adding Memphis-style horns. He sings most of his songs in English, with an occasional song in French, and his voice is deeper and smoother than his father's. *The Big Squeeze,* his second Alligator release, came out in 1996. On the album, he continues to blend his own sounds with his father's, juxtaposing a cover of Clifton's "The Moon Is Rising" with one of Elvis Presley's "Teddy Bear." C.J. has played at the New Orleans Jazz & Heritage Festival several years running, and also on Paul Simon's *Rhythm of the Saints* album.

When he returns to Lafayette, he finds himself in a time warp. "In Lafayette they've been having that music for years and years," he told me. "For me, since I'm not a traditionalist, nobody understands what I do there. For the traditionalists it's party every night. My style is very different. I mix a lot of different stuff—blues, boogie, funk. Not everybody in Lafayette goes for that kind of thing."

C.J., who plays at least 150 dates a year, no longer travels with his dad's accordion, however: 'I'm saving that one so I won't tear it up," he said. "The road is a tough place for an accordion." He recalls his playing days with his father fondly. "It was big fun," he says. "I play some of his music, but he always told me to play what I play so that's what I'm doing."

C.J. describes his style on the accordion as, "The kind of licks I hear. I don't know if they're sax or keyboard licks, they're just licks. I just play what I feel."

But his ultimate goal, like his father's, is to get everyone up dancing. During a 1990 concert at Bogart's in Long Beach, California, he led the audience in a dance line at 1:40 A.M. "It's happy feet music," he told me. "I hope to spread it all over the world. It needs to be heard by everyone so they can get a dose of that happy feet music."

Based on interviews by Lyndon Stambler with C.J. Chenier and Chris Strachwitz of Arhoolie Records.

CHERISH THE LADIES: *All female Irish American ensemble formed in 1983. Members have included: Joanie Madden (flute, whistles, vocals), born Bronx, New York, 1965; Maureen Doherty Macken (accordion, tin whistle, flute); Mary Coogan (guitar, tenor banjo, bouzouki, mandolin); Eileen Ivers (fiddle); Liz Carroll (fiddle); Siobhan Egan (fiddle, bodhran, flute); Winifred Horan (fiddle, dancing feet); Cathie Ryan (vocals, bodhran); Eileen Golden (dancing feet); Aoife Clancy (guitar, vocals); Mary Rafferty (accordion, flute, whistles); Donna Long (piano, fiddle).*

When American folklorist Mick Moloney first came up with the idea of putting on a series of concerts featuring Irish American women it was only supposed to last for ten days. But the group's leader, flute and whistle player Joanie Madden, held the excellent group together despite numerous personnel changes.

The group began in 1983, when Moloney approached the directors of New York's Ethnic Folk Arts Center about putting on the concert series. Madden, whose father, Joe Madden, was a champion accordion player in Ireland, was among the first Moloney contacted. Joanie, who studied the tin whistle and flute as a child, was inspired on the tin whistle when she heard Mary Bergin's album *Feadoga Stain*. In 1983 she became the first American to win the All-Ireland championships in the tin whistle. Later that year Moloney asked her to join the ensemble that would become Cherish the Ladies, the name of an Irish jig.

The group started out performing at high school auditoriums in the New York area. After a favorable review in the *New York Times*, their concerts began selling out. No one expected the group to last beyond those concerts. In 1985 Moloney went to the National Endowment for the Arts, which agreed to fund the group's debut album, *Cherish the Ladies*, released by Shanachie. There were more than a dozen participants in the debut effort, which was selected by the Library of Congress as one of the best folk albums of 1985.

Following the group's debut the NEA sponsored a Cherish the Ladies tour, which included Madden, accordionist Maureen Doherty Macken, guitarist-banjoist Mary Coogan, singer Cathie Ryan, and fiddlers Eileen

Ivers and Siobhan Egan (Seamus Egan's sister). This became the core of the group. Many of them were first-generation Irish Americans. Madden and accordionist Maureen Doherty Macken also participated in an album titled *Fathers & Daughters* (Shanachie, 1985), which brought together the two generations of musicians.

The group put out a second collection of instrumentals and ballads in 1992, *The Back Door,* released by Green Linnet. The title track, about the illegal Irish immigrants who came to New York, was written by Ryan, an Irish American who had studied with *sean-nos* singer Joe Heaney. The album was produced by Moloney. Their next, however, was produced by Johnny Cunningham, formerly of Silly Wizard. *Out and About* (Green Linnet, 1993) marks the departure of fiddler Eileen Ivers, who developed a solo career, and the arrival of classically trained fiddler and dancer Winifred Horan. The group had used step dancers such as Eileen Golden and Linnane Wick years before the *Riverdance* phenomenon. In 1994, Madden released a solo album, *A Whistle on the Wind,* on Green Linnet.

In 1996 the group released its final Green Linnet studio album, *New Day Dawning,* with Johnny Cunningham again producing. By this time Cathie Ryan had left the band and was replaced by Aoife Clancy, the daughter of Bobby Clancy, on vocals and guitar. Other new members included Mary Rafferty on accordion, flute, and whistles, replacing Maureen Doherty Macken. Donna Long took over on fiddle and piano, replacing Horan, who departed to join Solas.

In 1998 the group signed with RCA/BMG, which put out the group's major label debut, *Threads of Time.* That year, Green Linnet released the retrospective *Best of Cherish the Ladies.*

Although it started as an all-female group, Madden downplays the significance of gender. As she told Colin Irwin of *Folk Roots* ("Diasporadical," August-September 1998): "As far as I'm concerned that's the smallest thing about us. I don't see it as an issue at all—the issue is that when I look to my right or left I see a good accordion player or a good fiddle player and we've always been lucky to have good musicians in the band."

CHESAPEAKE: *Vocal and instrumental group, Mike Auldridge, born Washington, D.C., December 30, 1938 (Dobro, pedal steel guitarist, lap steel guitarist); T. Michael Coleman, born Leaksville, North Carolina (now Eden, NC) January 3, 1951 (fretless bass); Moondi Klein, born Port Jefferson, Long Island, March 13, 1963 (tenor vocals, guitarist, pianist); Jimmy Gaudreau, born Wakefield, Rhode Island, July 3, 1946 (mandolinist).*

When four veteran bluegrass musicians joined forces in 1994 to form the new band Chesapeake, one of their goals was to achieve creative freedom from a single musical format. Though they loved bluegrass and certainly had proven their expertise in it, as

T. Michael Coleman stressed to *Sing Out!* magazine, "One goal we have in common is a wider acceptance of what we do, of not being pigeonholed into 'This is a bluegrass band.'"

Multiinstrumentalist Mike Auldridge told article writer Rich Kerstetter ("Chesapeake," *Sing Out!*, vol. 41, no. 2), "Bluegrass sometimes has the attitude that 'We're here in the woods, if you want to join us, fine.'" Bass player T. Michael Coleman, looking back on his many years with Doc Watson, added, "With Doc, we were always embraced by the folk community and always felt like part of it. Bluegrass is kind of off by itself [usually considered a subset of country music]. Now, I feel part of it again." As the foursome demonstrated in concerts and their first albums in 1994–95, the band's repertoire blended elements of bluegrass, progressive country, traditional and modern folk, rock, and even jazz.

The prime mover in bringing the group together was mandolin expert Jimmy Gaudreau. Jimmy had been a professional musician since 1967, working with an early version of the Country Gentlemen, then moving on to J.D. Crowe & the New South before joining Tony Rice's backing band, the Unit, in 1985. His unique playing often drew attention from reviewers, as was the case at a concert in September 1992 when Steve Pick of the *St. Louis* [Missouri] *Post Dispatch* enthused over a Gaudreau solo in which Jimmy "picked the dickens out of his mandolin, pursuing melodic twists like he was gunning a canoe down the rapids." Jimmy was still part of the Unit in the early '90s, when he called Moondi Klein, then with the Seldom Scene band, for an informal jam session. Klein, in turn, lined up Seldom Scene band mates Mike Auldridge and T. Michael Coleman for the get-together, which was held in Auldridge's basement.

Auldridge, one of the original members of the Seldom Scene, had been with that band for some two decades as it rose to become for many years the foremost group in bluegrass. Coleman, besides his many years with Doc Watson before joining Seldom Scene in 1987, had also been active for many years as a sideman and record producer in Nashville. His session credits included work with such country stars as Johnny Cash and Don Williams.

Klein, the youngest member of Chesapeake, grew up in Long Island, New York, where his parental musical influence was mainly classical. When he was fourteen, though, his parents took him to a bluegrass concert in Virginia and he fell in love with the "high lonesome" sound. He had learned classical piano as a youngster and in his teens added bluegrass banjo to his abilities. In 1984, after finishing college as a voice and music theory major, he moved to Washington, D.C., where he was a member for a while of a bluegrass group called Rockcreek before joining Seldom Scene in the late '80s. Like many bluegrass artists, in between concerts by his main band he often played club dates or jam sessions with other musicians, including a few collaborations with Gaudreau.

For a year and a half, the four friends treated Chesapeake as a sideline while playing with what they considered their regular bands. Finally, in 1994, they decided to commit to Chesapeake full-time.

Once the musical Rubicon had been crossed, the group signed a recording contract with Sugar Hill Records, which issued their debut album *Rising Tide,* during 1994.

In 1995 the band released its second Sugar Hill collection, *Full Sail,* which matched its first release in well-honed arrangements. As in the debut disc, the contents covered the gamut from folk and bluegrass to rock and roll. Tracks included the old Carter Family number "Are You Tired of Me My Darling," Norman Blake's "Last Train from Poor Valley," Tom Paxton's longtime folk hit "The Last Thing on My Mind," and "Let It Roll," the last from the repertoire of the rock group Little Feat.

In 1998 Sugar Hill released Chesapeake's third CD, *Pier Pressure.* The album continues the band's eclectic mix of bluegrass, country, rock, and pop—even Caribbean stylings—on songs like Van Morrison's gospel-tinged "Full Force Gale" and the samba-flavored "Don't Lay Down," written by Klein. Linda Ronstadt joins Klein in a duet on the Steve Gillette–penned love ballad "Bed of Roses," and the album also includes four originals by Coleman, including the opener, "Once in a Day." The album, which includes electric instruments and drums, makes it clear that Chesapeake intends to remain in a category all its own.

CHESNUTT, VIC: *Singer, songwriter, guitarist, keyboardist. Born Jacksonville, Florida, November 12, 1964.*

Vic Chesnutt doesn't make a big deal about the accident that put him in a wheelchair for the rest of his life. "I was just drunk as hell and drove into a ditch and broke my neck. That was in 1983, on Easter morning," he says nonchalantly. "I wasn't in a coma much. In and out of consciousness for a few days. I couldn't talk. My mother was crying. She was getting the preacher to lay hands on me and try to heal me. It was freaking me out. I was mouthing the words, 'Get the fuck out. Leave me the fuck alone.' My mother was like, 'What?' She finally put her ear right up to my lips and heard what I was saying. She started crying. I was sad. I shouldn't have done that."

At first, Chesnutt, who had played in rock bands growing up, thought he would never be able to play music again. One hand was paralyzed and he had little movement in the other. He kept trying to rehabilitate himself until one day he took LSD, stayed up all night, and discovered that he could play guitar again. He superglued a pick to a glove so that he could strum the guitar, and now plays mostly open chords.

"People often ask me how come I don't write about my wheelchair and stuff," he told filmmaker Peter Sillen in his 1994 documentary about Chesnutt, *Speed Racer.* "I don't know, I guess every song is about the wheelchair. But what rhymes with wheelchair, anyway?"

One expects such answers from Chesnutt. After the accident, he began to write wry and quirky songs about all manner of things—suicide, odd childhood tales, whatever came to him in a burst of inspiration in the middle of the night. "I was a rural kid," he says. "I was out in the boonies. A lot of those kinds of images, they can't help but creep in. I write kind of nostalgic songs. Everybody does."

Chesnutt was born in Jacksonville, Florida. When he was four, his family moved to rural Zebulon, in Pike County, Georgia. His parents were born-again Christians; his father, James Thomas Chesnutt, worked as a baggage handler for Eastern Airlines in Atlanta. His mother, Miriam, worked for an insurance company and as a clerk for the Immigration and Naturalization Service.

"We said blessing before you ate," Chesnutt says. "I couldn't be too irreligious or I'd get a spanking. They weren't tyrants or anything. I had a great childhood." He loved church music. He remembers writing a song he called "God" when he was five. His father listened to country-western and loved Fats Domino and Conway Twitty.

Chesnutt hunted, fished, watched TV, and stayed away from books. He learned how to play the guitar by observing his maternal grandfather, Sleepy Carter, play his old Gibson L-7 (which Chesnutt still keeps). Sleepy played both kinds of music: country and western. "My granddaddy played the many-chorded, fancy country music and swing. . . . He'd show me how to play a song on guitar. Then I'd play the chords and he'd play lead," Chesnutt says.

As a teenager he remembers buying the Beatles' *Sgt. Pepper's Lonely Hearts Club Band.* He later discovered Styx, Bob Dylan, and Leonard Cohen. "I didn't want to be like my parents, [who] listened to country music. I wanted to be a rock 'n' roll kid."

He started playing trumpet in the school band at age ten. Randy Edgar, a band teacher who played saxophone like John Coltrane and "All Along the Watchtower" on guitar like Jimi Hendrix, became his mentor. Vic played trumpet with Edgar in a cover band called Sundance. "We did Bob Seger songs," Chesnutt recalls. "We played in a redneck bar in Griffin. I had a job doing that. I made good money. We played five or six sets a night on the weekends."

In the early 1980s, he formed a 'hick-punk' band with Todd McBride called The Screaming Ids when they were students at Gordon Junior College in Barnesville, Georgia. After the accident, Chesnutt moved to Athens to study English at the University of Georgia.

He thought he would become a high school English teacher but he got caught up in the nightclub scene and dropped out.

"I didn't go to Athens to play music," he says. "I was serious about getting my degree. But I enjoyed going to the clubs a lot. I'd see a band every night. A lot of bands came through Athens back then: the Replacements, News for Dues, the Minutemen, R.E.M."

McBride joined up with him in the La De Das, described by Chesnutt as "a bunch of rednecks, small town boys, basically the drunkest band in the world." He continued his self-destructive drinking even while he was holding down a regular Tuesday night gig. Vic's songwriting had become more sophisticated. "I was getting older and wiser," he says. "I had started reading books. I was writing teenage songs before. I wrote 'Isidore Duncan' when I was 19. That was kind of a watershed song for me. I wrote kind of hippy skippy songs before that, teenage, pseudomystical shit. They were kind of bad."

"[After the accident] he channeled all his guitar playing into songwriting," McBride, who now plays in the Dashboard Saviors, told the *Atlanta Journal & Constitution.* "That sounds like some sort of romantic notion, but it really seemed that way. But then he went to Nashville for a while, and when he came back I was amazed at what a great guitar player he'd become. . . . What impresses me is the poetry of his songs. Not just the words, but the way he puts the music together. It's sadly epiphanic. . . . if that's the word."

When REM's Michael Stipe came to hear the La De Das, the bandmates "were really freaked out," Chesnutt says. "They thought we were going to be the biggest shit in the world."

In October 1988 Stipe heard Chesnutt perform at the 40 Watt Club. Chesnutt "was reporting on everything that was going on in town in a very acerbic way." Stipe told Sillen. He wanted to record Chesnutt before it was "lost forever." He got him into a studio the next day. They ordered pizza and bottled water and recorded twenty-one songs. They culled ten songs from the batch to make Chesnutt's first album, *Little,* released on Texas Hotel Records in 1990. His nasal baritone, unusual, word-stretching phrasing, and eerie guitar playing produced a recognizable sound.

The band split in 1986 and he went solo. Stipe was the first one to get Vic to record. The session was stark, with Chesnutt accompanying himself on guitar. Songs like "Rabbit Box" and "Danny Carlisle" explore his conflict-laden childhood growing up "on the edge of redneckdom." The album also included personal protests such as "Speed Racer," in which he declares: *I'm not a victim/I am an atheist,* much to the chagrin of his religious parents. "Soft Picasso" is about a casual affair, so casual that neither one knew the other was there. Everyone in Athens thought it was about them.

"I didn't want to release [the album], that's for sure,

Chesnutt says. "But I'm not a perfectionist by any means. I thought, 'That's good enough, I don't care.' It wasn't a particularly great day for me." (It took Texas Hotel two years to release the album; Chesnutt had wanted it to come out before his father passed away.)

Although is debut sold only 4,000 copies, he and Stipe returned to the studio in 1992 to record his second album, *West of Rome,* on Texas Hotel. This time he brought a full band, including his nieces on violin and cello, and made a multitracked recording. The album included his song "Florida," about a friend who had moved to "the redneck Riviera" and committed suicide by shooting himself in the head with a nail gun. Chesnutt supports him in the song: *A man must take his life in his own hands, hit those nails on the head/And I respect a man who goes where he wants to be, even if he wants to be dead.*

"It had been a few years since any of my friends committed suicide," Chesnutt says. "For a while there everyone was popping themselves off. I was just sad that he did it. I was also kind of proud of him in a way because he finally made a big stand."

In another song, "Bug," he uses a line his grandmother gave him to express the elusive quality of creativity: *When the bug hits, that's the time to scratch it.* "I don't know how it all kind of squished together into a song, but it did."

Reviewer Mark Kemp of *Option* (January/February 1993) noted that Chesnutt is a "jumble of contradictions: pure at heart, perhaps, but broken by cynicism and hardly naive." While praising the album, Kemp asked, "How long can he remain so bitter and victimized in a world where people seem entirely willing to be there for him?"

There is a whimsical quality about Chesnutt that is only possible, it seems, for someone who has nearly lost his life. The extraordinary documentary about Chesnutt, *Speed Racer,* entered in the 1994 Sundance Film Festival, opens with Chesnutt in his bathtub, drawing a picture of himself in a wheelchair on the wall with grease pencils. That's the whimsy. But his anger and empathy show through when he talks about how investor Frank Lorenzo "murdered" his father when he took over Eastern Airlines. "It's just so wrong to do this," Chesnutt says of Lorenzo's actions, which led to his father's layoff. "It's like slavery all over again. It's not slavery—it's just disgusting, icky, it's terrible. It made me so mad at the time I couldn't function. Watching my father shrink as a human being because of what was going on 1,000 miles away in corporate boardrooms."

The documentary captures Vic singing about his father in the unreleased song "Flying," which he performed at the 1991 Black Mountain Festival in North Carolina. The film also has a hilarious account given by his wife, Tina, about how they got married at the Rip Rippon's World's Largest Truck Stop, outside of Dallas.

Vic formed a band called His Little Sharpie with Jeffrey Richards on drums and Tina on bass. He renamed it the Scared Skiffle Group, with Jimmy Davidson on drums, Alex McManus on guitars, and Tina on bass.

Chesnutt's third album, *Drunk,* released on Texas Hotel, was aptly titled. He recorded it during a lost, drunken weekend in 1993, precipitated by a fight with his wife. "It seemed like a title for the whole record," he told Steve Dollar of the *Atlanta Journal & Constitution* (May 8, 1994). "Because I was quite stinking drunk when I recorded it. I was trying to quit drinking, and was trying to quit using needles, and I was trying to be a better human at the time. So the whole record ended up being about a guy trying to reform himself."

The album was as dark and as personal as its title, with songs like "One of Many," "Sleeping Man," "Gluefoot," and "Naughty Fatalist." There was also the track "Supernatural," about a supposed out of body experience expressed in polysyllabic words: *Built a king on compliments, charisma and advertisements/Still they see him shimmer ephemeral.* "Chances are pretty damn good I was high when I was writing that song," Chesnutt says.

Rather than go to AA, he decided to quit drinking on his own. "I didn't need a new kind of obsession. Being married helped a lot because she could just yell at me. . . . Every now and then I slip up."

In 1995, he released his fourth and final album on Texas Hotel. *Is the Actor Happy?* is probably the most polished album, with songs like "Sad Peter Pan," a fictional account of a man whose lover leaves him. "Guilty by Association," which he wrote while he was driving up the motorway in England, shows an ability to compress images into haiku-like stanzas: *You've been sanctified (terrorized)/and I've been tried/Guilty by association.* Like any writer, Chesnutt says, his songs are part fiction and part satirical autobiography.

By 1996 some of the biggest performers in rock—REM, Smashing Pumpkins, Madonna, and Hootie and the Blowfish—clamored to record his songs for *Sweet Relief II* on Columbia Records to support a nonprofit fund to pay medical bills for musicians. Chesnutt, who knows most of the performers, had little to do with making the album, but was proud of the result.

Titled *Gravity of the Situation* for a song written after he shared a stage with songwriters Joe South, Allen Toussaint, and Guy Clark, the album increased his profile. "When I crashed, somehow I got on Medicaid," he says. "I got all my medical bills paid for. I didn't need it. That's what was so great about this record. I write my songs in a kind of selfish cave. It was great that I could help other people. Victoria Williams [who started Sweet Relief] is a great friend of mine. I was quite proud to be the second one."

In 1996 he also signed a major label contract with Capitol and released *About to Choke.* Recorded with the group Agitpop in three different studios, the album, as a Capitol press release puts it, "reflects his crazyquilt consciousness." Some of the songs on this album of Chesnutt satires have been in his repertoire for a while: "See You Around," "New Town," and "Giant Sands." He named a couple of new songs—"Tarragon" and "Myrtle"—after herbs. "It's weird how these little bulges kind of bulge out," he says. "It just kind of happened that out of my bag, I picked these herbal ones."

He also released a rock album with a band called Brute (Chesnutt and some members of Widespread Panic) called *Nine High a Pallet* on Capricorn in 1996.

At McCabe's Guitar Shop in Santa Monica in February 1996, four people lifted Chesnutt's wheelchair onto the stage. Wearing a black leather glove on his right hand with a pick attached to it, he began tentatively plucking the guitar. He squinted his dark, deep-set eyes over the crowd and asked for the house lights to be turned on. He burped, sneered, grimaced, and admitted, "I'm scared," as he worked his way through his set. He even gave his wife, Tina, a high-five because he was so pleased with one of the numbers. His disarming stage presence pleased the sellout crowd which seemed familiar with even his most obscure, unrecorded songs.

Chesnutt considers himself a songwriter first, but not like Phil Ochs or Bob Dylan—"Like my grand-daddy," he told the *Atlanta Journal & Constitution*. "I don't write pop songs that good. I write weird little songs. I don't know who would like 'em."

In November 1998, Vic's sixth solo album, *The Salesman and Bernadette*, was released, this time on Georgia-based Capricorn. In general, it could be said that the people "who would like 'em" included many major publication critics.

Based on an interview by Lyndon Stambler with Vic Chesnutt

CHIEFTAINS, THE: *Traditional Irish band. Paddy Moloney, (uileann [elbow] pipes, tin whistle), born Dublin, Ireland, August 1, 1938. Martin Fay, (fiddle and bones), born Dublin, Ireland, September 19, 1936. Seán Potts, (tin whistle, bones, and bodhran), born Dublin, Ireland, 1930. Left group in late 1970s. David Fallon, (bodhran), born in late nineteenth century; died in 1968. Left group after first album. Joining group for the second album, Peadar Mercier, (bodhran and bones), born circa 1914; died circa late 1970s. Replacing Mercier in 1976, Kevin Conneff, (bodhran, Chinese gong, lilting, vocals), born Dublin, Ireland, January 8, 1945. Michael Tubridy, (flute, concertina, tin whistle), born Kilrush, County Clare, Ireland, 1935. Tubridy and Potts left in 1979. Replacing Tubridy in 1979, Matt Molloy, (flute and tin whistle), born County Roscommon, Ireland, January 12, 1946. Joining the group in 1969, Sean Keane, (fiddle and tin whistle), born Dublin, Ireland, July 12, 1947. Since 1973, Derek Bell, (Celtic harp, dulcimer, harpsichord, medieval harp,* keyboards, synthesizer, and timpán [a form of hammer dulcimer]), born Belfast, Northern Ireland, October 21, 1935.

Each member of the Chieftains is a virtuoso: Paddy Moloney on pipes, Matt Molloy on flute, Sean Keane and Martin Fay on fiddles, Derek Bell on harp, and Kevin Conneff on bodhran and vocals. But when they play together, as they did at L.A.'s Universal Amphitheatre in July 1996, they sound like a finely tuned instrument.

More than any other band, the Chieftains have brought traditional Irish music to the world. The six-member group has released thirty-five albums, sold millions of copies, won six Grammys and an Oscar, and performed at thousands of concerts worldwide before powerful audiences: Pope John Paul II, Queen Elizabeth II, and the U.S. Congress. They have played at the Great Wall of China and the Berlin Wall, in Nashville and Japan.

"It was always a dream to me that maybe someday Irish music would be played in all the world's great auditoriums, that it would find its place in the world," Paddy Moloney, the group's leader, told Jim Washburn of the *Los Angeles Times* (December 13, 1991). "And now that's getting strong. We paved the way and have done a tremendous amount of letting people know what real Irish music is all about. It doesn't begin and end with 'Danny Boy' or 'Mother Machree.' When we go to other countries—Italy, China, Japan—I'm amazed at the reaction we get. They don't understand a word of the garbage I'm pouring out, but they respond to the music."

The Chieftains can play traditional jigs or accompany performers as diverse as Mick Jagger, Willie Nelson, and a group of 150 Buddhist monks. The 1995 release of *The Long Black Veil*, which included performances by Sting, Ry Cooder, Van Morrison, Jagger, and Marianne Faithfull, entered *Billboard*'s Top 200 charts at number twenty-four and became the group's first gold album in the United States. *Time* magazine selected it as one of the best albums of the year. It won a Grammy for Best Pop Collaborations for "Have I Told You Lately That I Love You" with Van Morrison, beating out Michael Jackson, his sister Janet, and Boyz 2 Men.

The album's success prompted some purists to question the band's allegiance to traditional music. But Moloney quickly points out that the album they recorded prior to that, *The Celtic Harp* (1993), featured traditional music from the eighteenth and nineteenth centuries. (The Chieftains' albums usually feature at least one song by Turlough O'Carolan, considered Ireland's greatest harpist. They released *O'Carolan's Favorite* with the New Ireland Chamber Orchestra in 1980, and Bell released *O'Carolan's Receipt*, a tribute to harpist Edward Bunting, both on Claddagh.)

On *The Long Black Veil*, Moloney brought the rock

stars into his tradition. He wrote the Gaelic phonetically and guided Sting in singing *"Mo Ghile Mear"* ("Our Hero"). "Coast of Malabar," sung by Ry Cooder, was inspired by a traditional song called "Little Maid from Malabar" that Moloney heard his grandmother sing.

The band dates back to 1961, when composer Seán Ó Riada, the musical director for the Abbey Theatre in Dublin, decided to add traditional instruments to an ensemble he called Ceoltóirí Cualann ("musicians of Cualann," named after a road outside his house). He formed the group to accompany a production called *The Golden Folk*. The group included the heart of what would later become the Chieftains: Paddy Moloney on uileann pipes, Martin Fay on fiddle, Seán Potts on tin whistle, Michael Tubridy on flute, and Peadar Mercier on the bodhran.

In the 1950s, traditional music was looked down upon in some quarters of Ireland. But Ceoltóirí Cualann and the folk revival of the 1960s brought it back. As Mick Moloney wrote in 1991 in the liner notes to *Best of the Chieftains*: "The sound that the ensemble produced was quite unlike anything ever heard in Irish music. The effect it had on widely diverse audiences, whether in live performance or on radio broadcasts, was nothing short of electric. They played the old dance music with a gay, lilting, infectious abandon and the old Gaelic airs with heart-wrenching pathos. Up to that time musicians in Irish ceilidh bands would simply play melodies in unison in strict rhythm."

Paddy Moloney, the driving force of the Chieftains, started playing a plastic tin whistle when he was eight. He had heard his grandfather playing the flute; his uncle belonged to the Ballyfin Pipe Band. He studied the uileann pipes from a master piper named Leo Rowsome. Before embarking on a career in music, Moloney worked as an accountant for a building firm called Baxendales. In the late 1950s he met Ó Riada while he was playing at a club and began pursuing a career in music. (Moloney has said he had the idea for a traditional band long before he met Ó Riada.)

After leaving Ceoltóirí Cualann, Moloney organized a band in 1963 with Potts on whistle, Fay on fiddle, Tubridy on flute, and Dave Fallon on bodhran. (The name was inspired by the book *Death of a Chieftain* by Claddagh Records director John Montague.) They recorded *The Chieftains*, released by Claddagh in 1963. As Sarah Adams described the debut, "It shows the young side of the Chieftains when they are still feeling their musical feet."

Over the next four decades, the Chieftains took their "musical feet" around the world. But the acclaim came gradually, and the band's personnel changed over the years. After the first album, bodhran player Peadar Mercier replaced Fallon, who was in his seventies. Mercier was in turn replaced by Kevin Conneff in 1976.

Fiddle player Sean Keane, who had played with Seán Ó Riada's ensemble, joined the Chieftains after the second album. The professorial-looking Derek Bell, who grew up in Northern Ireland, played harp in the Belfast Symphony, and continued to live in the civil war–torn area; he joined the group as Celtic harp player in 1973, when he played as a guest artist on *Chieftains 4*. He has done as much as anyone to popularize the ornate, slightly percussive folk instrument. He plays several other instruments well, including keyboards, oboe, timpán, and even synthesizers. Tubridy, the flutist, left the group in the late 1970s and was replaced by Matt Molloy, who had played with such landmark Irish bands as Planxty and the Bothy Band. Potts played with the group up until the late 1970s.

Claddagh released *Chieftains 2* (1969), recorded at Abbey Road Studio, *Chieftains 3* (1971) which featured lilting by Pat Kiduff, *Chieftains 4* (1974), *Chieftains 5* (1975), *Bonaparte's Retreat* (1976), the first to feature a singer, Dolores Keane, *Chieftains Live* and *Chieftains 7* (both in 1977), and *Chieftains 8* (1978).

Since 1978, the Chieftains' personnel has been fairly constant: Moloney on pipes and whistle, Fay and Keane on fiddles, Conneff on bodhran and vocals, Bell on harp, and Molloy on flute and whistle.

They continued with Claddagh releases *Boil the Breakfast Early/Chieftains 9* (1979), *Chieftains 10* (1981), the TV sound track *Year of the French* (1982), and a soundtrack for the documentary *Ballad of the Irish Horse* (1986). Claddagh released a number of solo albums by Tubridy, Moloney, Potts, Mercier, Keane, Molloy, and Bell. Among Bell's Claddagh releases are: *Carolan's Favourite, Derek Bell's Musical Ireland, Ancient Music for the Irish Harp*, and *Derek Bell Plays with Himself*. In 1996 Bell released *The Mystic Harp* on the Clarity Sound & Light label, in collaboration with J. Donald Walters, the founder of Ananda World Brotherhood Village in Nevada City, California.

The Chieftains had deals with Island and then CBS for the American market. Starting in 1991, Shanachie reissued many of their albums. In the mid-1980s the group signed with BMG and released: *Celtic Wedding* (1987), featuring the music of Brittany, *In Ireland* (1987, with flutist James Galway), *Irish Heartbeat* (1988, Mercury), *Chieftains Celebration* (1989), *Over the Sea to Skye* (1990, with Galway), *The Bells of Dublin* (1991) a gold record, *Reel Music* (1991), *An Irish Evening: Live at the Grand Opera House* (1992), *Another Country* (1992), *Celtic Harp* (1993), *Long Black Veil* (1994), *Film Cuts* (1995), *Santiago* (1996), and *The Celtic Minstrel* (1996, with Galway). Compilation albums include *Best of the Chieftains* (1992), and *The Magic of the Chieftains* (1992).

The group began to reach a worldwide audience with the Stanley Kubrick film *Barry Lyndon*, (Warner Brothers, 1976), the first of their many film scores. The sound track won an Oscar in 1976. "I get a gist of the story and I always find when I am reading the script, I get ideas on the spot and I write them down," Moloney told Kim Leddy of Columbus's *Alive Wired*. The group crafted several other sound tracks: *Tristan & Isolde, Three Wishes for Jamie, The Grey Fox, Circle of Friends, Treasure Island, Rob Roy,* and *Far and Away.* They compiled excerpts from the movies on two albums: *Reel Music* (1991) and *Film Cuts* (1996).

The group was also involved in some musical extravaganzas. When Pope John Paul II visited Dublin in 1979, the Chieftains performed for him at Phoenix Park. The audience of 1.35 million broke a record. Another big year for the group was 1983. They traveled to China and became the first Western group to perform with a Chinese orchestra on the Great Wall. Claddagh released *Chieftains in China* (1985). Former Speaker of the House Tip O'Neill invited the group to Washington, D.C., where they became the first group to give a concert in the Capitol Building. In 1994, the group traveled to Osaka, Japan, and played in *The Great Musical Experience* at the Todaji Buddhist Temple in Nara. They were joined by Bob Dylan, Ry Cooder, Joni Mitchell, Michael Kamen, the Tokyo Philharmonic, and 150 chanting Buddhist monks. The show was broadcast worldwide via satellite. In 1994, the group also played at Carnegie Hall for a Saint Patrick's Day concert.

Such "happenings" have led to criticism. Laura Evenson of the *San Francisco Chronicle* quoted one person who said, "If there is a dollar to be made anywhere in the world, Paddy Moloney will seek it out" (March 5, 1995). But Larry Kirwan of the Irish rock band Black 47 told Evenson: "They've always been at the forefront of taking Irish music into different areas, so they haven't gotten stuck in some kind of Celtic museum."

The first time they collaborated with a rock superstar was in 1972, when Paul McCartney asked Moloney to play on a project he was doing with his brother Michael. One of the best was *Irish Heartbeat* with Van Morrison on Mercury. Morrison sings traditional Irish folk songs on the collection, such as the tragic song "Carrickfergus." The band toured Europe with Morrison. Many fans would attend the U.S. concerts with the hope that Morrison might suddenly get on stage. They did eight songs with Van at a concert in Santa Rosa, California. "We were in the middle of the second half of our show and the boyo himself jumps up on stage," Moloney told Washburn.

In 1991, the group released *Bells of Dublin,* a compilation of traditional Christmas songs performed with Jackson Browne, Elvis Costello, Marianne Faithfull, Nanci Griffith, Rickie Lee Jones, Kate & Anna McGarrigle, and actor Burgess Meredith. Moloney came up with the idea of a Christmas album, but since he didn't know many Irish Christmas carols, he asked friends to

provide their own. Perhaps most impressive was Costello's rendition of "St. Stephen's Day Murders."

"Of course it has nothing to do with murder and more to do with an old Irish figure of speech," Moloney told the *Los Angeles Times*. "In fact, the Irish used to write songs with both Irish and English lyrics, and they'd sing them at parties when the opposition was there, if you know what I mean. One verse would be praising the British soldiers, and the next verse would be in Irish and would be making fools of them, and the British never understood why everyone would suddenly be laughing."

Irish Heartbeat and *Bells of Dublin* did not win Grammys, but several other Chieftains albums did. *Another Country* (1992), which matched them with a number of country artists, including Emmylou Harris, Ricky Skaggs, and Willie Nelson, won for Best Contemporary Folk Album. They also won a Best Traditional Folk Grammy for *An Irish Evening: Live at the Grand Opera House in Belfast.* Roger Daltrey, the lead singer of the Who, and singer-songwriter Nanci Griffith, were special guests. *The Celtic Harp* (1993), which grew out of a gathering of Ireland's best harpists, won for Best Traditional Folk. The fourth Grammy came for *The Long Black Veil.*

The album, originally titled *The Chieftains and Friends,* was designed to feature tracks recorded with famous guests. But they decided instead to record an album from scratch. As in *Another Country,* the Chieftains invited musicians to play with them, including Sting, Sinéad O'Connor, and Morrison. Mick Jagger wound up singing a country-western version of the title track, an American song. (Moloney could hear Irish roots in the ballad.) Performing with the Rolling Stones "turned out to be a great hoolie," Moloney told the *Los Angeles Times* (November 30, 1993).

Moloney composed a symphony to commemorate the Irish potato famine of the 1840s which killed and displaced millions. "It was our holocaust," Moloney said of the famine, and he hoped the project would encourage relief for other victims of famine. But the symphony has not been performed to date.

In late 1996 the group recorded *Santiago,* featuring Celtic music from Galicia in northwestern Spain. The premise was the pilgrimage from Ireland to Spain, to Cuba and Los Angeles. They went on tour with Carlos Núñez, a twenty-six-year-old from Vigo, Galicia. Núñez plays the gaita, a Galician version of the bagpipe that he plays alongside Moloney's uileann pipes on "Dueling Chanters." They also recorded "Guadalupe" with Los Lobos and Linda Ronstadt. In January 1996 they went to Cuba with Cooder and recorded with local musicians. *Santiago* garnered another Grammy for the Chieftains for Best World Album. Cooder, who performed at one of the Los Angeles concerts, told a reviewer about the forcefulness of Moloney: "You do what Paddy says. That's all there is to it." Cooder also recognized the important role that the Chieftains play, not only in Irish traditional but in all forms of music. "It's not just a band anymore, it's really become an institution," Cooder said.

The Chieftains worked on the soundtrack for a TV documentary about the immigration of the Irish to the United States entitled *The Irish in America: Long Journey Home*. The 1998 album by the same name, produced by Moloney and released on his Unisphere label, includes the Chieftains performing with Mary Black, Sinéad O'Connor, Liam O'Maonlai, and Elvis Costello. It won the Grammy for Best Traditional Folk Album. Moloney also produced an album released in the fall of 1998 entitled *Fire in the Kitchen*, featuring the music of Cape Breton Island and inspired by the fiery young fiddler Ashley MacIsaac. The new album includes contributions from other Canadian musicians: fiddler Natalie MacMaster, the group La Bottine Souriante, and Mary Jane Lamond. In 1999 Maloney released *Tears of Stone*, in which the Chieftains are joined by female singers Loreena McKennitt, Bonnie Raitt, Natalie Merchant, Joan Osborne, the Corrs, and Akiko Yano from Japan. Later that year Claddagh/Atlantic released *The Very Best of the Claddagh Years*, and planned to release the Chieftains' first eight albums beginning March 2000. BMG released *Water from the Well* in 2000, in which the Chieftains return to their Irish roots and are joined by guests like Altan and Ashley MacIsaac.

Entry written with assistance from John Glatt, author of The Chieftains: The Authorized Biography, *published by St. Martin's Press in 1997, and Charles Comer, longtime publicist for the Chieftains.*

CHILD, FRANCIS J.: *Folklorist, author, educator. Born Boston, Massachusetts, February 1, 1825; died Boston, Massachusetts, September 11, 1896.*

Harvard University isn't a strange place to be associated with folk music these days. To many, though, it does seem odd to connect the austere image of the Harvard of the 1800s with the field. However, not only is this so, but it was at Harvard that the groundwork was laid for the worldwide folk scholarship of the '50s and '60s.

The man responsible for this was a brilliant professor of English at Harvard, Francis James Child. Child's youthful goal was to go to the great university of his hometown, which he achieved despite his father's meager income as a sailmaker. His obvious gift for learning won him a series of scholarships that brought a degree from Harvard in 1846. A few years later, in 1851, he was appointed Boylston Professor of rhetoric, oratory, and elocution. By the time he gained this position, he was deeply immersed in literature studies in Berlin and Gottingen, from 1849 to 1853. It helped establish his reputation as a scholar in Europe and eventually led to a book contract that changed his life.

In 1855, he increased his stature by editing a five-volume edition of the works of British poet Edmund Spenser. He was then asked to prepare a study of Anglo-Scottish ballads as part of a series covering British poets. The result was an eight-volume set, *English and Scottish Ballads,* published in 1857–58. Child was not satisfied with the short period of time given him to prepare the material, particularly since he became intensely interested in the subject during his researches. From then on, his thoughts turned more and more to doing a proper study. Eventually, he was determined to spend years, if necessary, to compile a work covering all authentic old folk ballads.

He began to collect materials on ancient British folk music, increasing his efforts as time went on. He did not abandon his studies of English literature, however. In 1863 he wrote a famed treatise called "Observations on the Language of Chaucer." The university recognized his great contributions in 1876 by appointing him Professor of English. By this time, he had provided the university library with hundreds of manuscripts, song sheets, and other material on English and Scottish ballads. (He had secured a publisher for his projected new work in 1872.) This was to make Harvard one of the world's major repositories of information on folk music in later years.

From 1872 on, Child went at his task in earnest. He wrote to educators the world over for possible material and collected songs and verses from many states in the United States. His deep interest in the subject was from the standpoint of the poetry of the verses, for he was not deeply interested in music, nor is there any indication he ever tried his hand at singing.

In 1882, the first part of his work was completed. Between this time and the mid-1890s, Child continued to sift and judge hundreds of songs to turn out a work that included only authentic material. He had completed the last of ten parts of the work before his death in 1896 although the final volume did not appear until 1898.

Shortly after, the total collection of 305 ballads, covering such titles as "The Elfin Knight," "Sir Andrew Barton," "Sir Patrick Spens," and "The Marriage of Sir Gawain," was published in five quarto volumes. The work was called *The English and Scottish Popular Ballads.* A cryptic note of Child #10, 20 100, or whatever the case may be, after ballad references in the world's folk music literature testifies to the genius and effort of the great Harvard scholar.

CLANCY BROTHERS AND TOMMY MAKEM; CLANCY BROTHERS AND ROBBIE O'CONNELL: *Vocal and instrumental group from Ireland with all Clancy brothers born Carrick-on-Suir. Original members: Patrick (Paddy) Clancy, born 1923; died Carrick-on-Suir, November 11, 1998; Liam Clancy, born 1935; Tom Clancy, died Cork, November, 1990; Tommy Makem, born Keady,*

County Armagh, Ireland, 1932. Members in mid-1990s comprised Liam, Paddy, and Bobby Clancy and Robbie O'Connell.

The singing Clancy brothers and friend Tommy Makem formed one of Ireland's most likable and talented contributions to the American and international folk music scene from the 1950s into the 1970s. Their contributions went far beyond singing, embracing almost every area of entertainment from acting to management. The three Clancy brothers and Makem performed as a group from the mid-1950s to the early 1970s (though each had his own activities as well). In the late 1970s, the tradition was carried on by the twosome of Liam Clancy and Tommy Makem.

The first of the four to seek his fortune away from home was Patrick Clancy, oldest of the three brothers, but not of the nine children that made up the total clan in Tipperary. He enlisted in the RAF for two years and, from that activity as well as post-service civilian jobs, traveled to England, Canada, Wales, Venezuela, and India in the early 1950s. His occupations over three years included painter, insurance sales representative, welder, cab driver, diamond hunter, and actor. His acting hopes found fruition in the United States in the mid-1950s, where he found work with the Cleveland Playhouse and then on and off Broadway in plays by Yeats, O'Casey, and Synge.

His knowledge of Irish folk music was put to use editing and arranging songs for such New York–based firms as Folkways and Elektra Records. He became imbued with the idea of starting his own record company and finally saved enough to start Tradition Records. He soon signed people like Oscar Brand; Odetta; Josh White, Sr.; and Carolyn Hester.

Soon after this, a second Clancy arrived—Tom. After serving in the RAF, Tom won attention in Ireland as a pop band vocalist. Acting appealed to him as well, and he appeared with an English Shakespearean repertory company and in many Irish plays before going to the United States. Once in America, he emulated brother Patrick by finding work in summer stock and in New York productions. His acting career was hardly garden variety. Among his credits in several decades in the theater were appearances with Orson Welles in *King Lear,* with Siobhan McKenna in *St. Joan,* with Helen Hayes in *A Touch of the Poet,* and an award-winning portrayal of poet Dylan Thomas on CBS-TV's *Camera Three.*

Brother Liam also had an early love for the theater and took formal dramatic training at the National College of Arts in Dublin. After Pat started Tradition Records, he wrote Liam to be on the lookout for new material or artists. Liam then came across Tommy Makem.

He recalled, "It was . . . beyond that mystical border that separates the blessed subjects of the Queen from the Irish misfortunes that I first met Tommy Makem. I went to a ceilidhe in Newry town one night in a big dance hall there. I was very embarrassed when the band leader announced, in the midst of the fun and the dancing, that this one poor chap was going to sing and not a person in the hall stopped talking or looked up at the stage. Your man wasn't fazed the slightest. He just sat down and started silently to work on his boot.

"One person looked and then another, and in ten seconds you could hear a pin drop. Then when he had complete attention he began to sing 'O Me Name Is Dick Darby, I'm a Cobbler.' That was my introduction to Tommy. We both took the 'emigrant ship' to America the next year."

Makem's path to that dance hall began in County Armagh, where his family had a tradition of playing and singing Irish folk music. By the time he was five, he was on stage singing and acting with his parents. When he was in his teens, he had an excellent singing style and also could play a number of instruments. When Liam met him, he could handle banjo, guitar, pennywhistle, drums, piccolo, and bagpipes. In his teens, Tommy moved into the pop music field for a time before returning to the folk domain. At fifteen, he formed his own *ceili,* which translates as "Irish country dance band." At seventeen, he had become well known in Ireland as a pop vocalist in the American style.

After Liam and Tommy crossed the seas together, Liam went into acting while Tommy stuck to music. Liam starred at the Poet's Theatre in Cambridge, Massachusetts, and went on to New York to appear in Frank O'Connor's *Guests of the Nation* and to perform with Julie Harris in stage and TV versions of *The Little Moon of Alban.* He also won excellent notices for his work in Brendan Behan's *The Quare Fellow.*

Makem's first notable engagement was at the Circle in the Square, in New York's Greenwich Village. From there he went on to an acclaimed appearance at the Gate of Horn folk nightclub in Chicago. (Interestingly, perhaps influenced by the Clancys, he was also to establish himself as a talented actor in the late 1950s.) His reputation as a folksinger kept on growing and reached a high point with a show-stopping set at the 1960 Newport, Rhode Island, Folk Festival.

The Clancys and Tommy Makem had sometimes gotten together in informal songfests and by the late 1950s had begun to develop a joint repertoire. Their first public outing took place at the Circle in the Square. The response was so good they were booked into the prestigious uptown nightclub the Blue Angel. This led to engagements at major folk clubs across the United States, from the hungry i in San Francisco to the Village Gate in New York, and abroad until they announced at a 1969 concert in Sacramento, California, they were disbanding.

Looking back on the formative years of the group in October 1995, Liam Clancy reminisced in liner notes for a new album about hanging out with Bob Dylan in

Celtic Music in Germany, and *Clannad in Concert,* (from a Swiss tour), in 1979 by Oghm.

Enya made her presence felt on *Fuaim* (1981, Tara), singing lead on "An Tull" and "Buareadh An Phósta" and backing vocals and playing keyboards throughout. The album, cut in Dublin's Windmill Studios, includes "The Green Fields of Gaoth Dobhair," about the family's hometown. Frustrated with her role as the kid sister, Enya departed (along with Nicky Ryan) to go solo in 1982, the same year Clannad got its big break.

The band wrote the theme song for a drama about Northern Ireland written by Gerard Seymour. As Máire told Lahri Bond of *Dirty Linen* (August/September 1993): "When they approached us, they wanted to use a Scottish-Gaelic song from *Fuaim.* We thought it would be inappropriate to use it for something concerning Ireland. So we said we'll write something. My two brothers got together with me, and Ciarán had an old book of proverbs which belongs to my grandfather. In it was this proverb saying *Imtheochaidh sor is soir/A dtáinig ariamh An ghealach is an ghrian; Everything that is and was will cease to be.* He elaborated on it with the moon and the stars, the East and the West, a young man and his fame. It was a kind of lament. . . . We wrote it in a couple of hours and thought, great, it's a nice tune and everything, but we didn't realize the sound we created had developed over the six albums before with all the experimentations we did with words and voices and harmonies."

The exposure from the show on Granada Television sent "Harry's Game" to number five on the Irish charts. Besides the Ivor Novello Award, it was nominated for a British Academy Award. They included the song on *Magical Ring* (1983, Tara). For the first time, the band earned a gold record in the U.K. They were soon writing the soundtrack for another episodic TV drama, *Robin of Sherwood.* That led to their next album, *Legend,* released on RCA in 1984, which also went gold in Britain. The band received a British Academy Award for the soundtrack.

Clannad followed with an RCA release in 1986 titled *Macalla* ("echo" in Gaelic), produced by Steve Nye. They departed from tradition, composing most of the tracks and using electric guitar (Anton Drennan from Moving Hearts), sax (Mel Collins from King Crimson), synthesizers, and percussion. Máire sang a duet with U2's Bono on "In a Lifetime," a Top 20 hit in the United Kingdom. The next album, *Sirius* (1987, RCA), co-produced by drummer Russ Kunkel and Greg Landanyi and mixed in L.A., also includes guest musicians, among them Bruce Hornsby and J.D. Souther. The slick approach baffled critics but sold well, leading to the band's first world tour in 1988.

Atlantic Realm on BBC Records resulted from a project for a BBC documentary about the Atlantic Ocean. Clannad also produced the instrumental backing music for *The Angel and the Soldier Boy* (1990), a half-hour animated film.

Meanwhile, Pól, Ciarán, and Máire began pursuing their own goals. Máire released her solo debut, *Máire,* on RCA (distributed in America by Atlantic's Celtic Heartbeat label) in 1992. The album includes backing vocals by her sisters Dee, Olive, and Bridín, with bouzouki, and mandolin played by Lunny. (Máire includes another member of the clan, her daughter Aisling, who was born in 1992, on the album cover, the picture taken by her husband, photographer Tim Jarvis.) In 1993, Pól recorded an album with two Japanese musicians, Guo Yue and Joji Hirota, called *Trísan,* on Realworld. In 1994, Máire finished her second album, *The Misty Eyed Adventures.*

Clannad's next album, *Anam,* ("soul" in Gaelic), came out in 1992 on RCA in the United Kingdom minus Pól. Again, it was "Harry's Game" which provided a new break. The song had been used in the Harrison Ford movie *Patriot Games,* and then in a Volkswagen commercial, which led to its release in 1992 in the United States on Atlantic's Celtic Heartbeat label. The U.S. album broke onto the world charts and "Harry's Game" won *Billboard*'s "World Music Song of the Year."

They followed in 1993 with *Banba* on RCA (distributed by Atlantic in the United States). The more traditional album garnered Clannad's first Grammy nomination. "There's a song on it called 'Banba Oír,' " Máire told Bond. "Oír means gold and Banba is a very romantic mythical name for Ireland. . . . Ciarán wrote a song about the Golden Age of old Ireland, really talking about mythic Ireland. Each line is a visionary image of scenes you might see around Ireland." Another song, "I Will Find You," was used in the film *The Last of the Mohicans.* Máire actually sings it in Mohican and Cherokee. "[Michael Mann, the film's director] wanted us to sing in Gaelic," Máire told Bond, "but Ciarán said it wouldn't really be right because there were no Irish people around America in that time. So he said leave it with me and he researched it. Later, Michael said, 'Look, there're only 16 people in America who speak Mohican, but Ciarán somehow got the 17th at Yale or somewhere.' "

In 1996, RCA issued *Lore,* (distributed by Atlantic in the U.S.) which contained a mixture of the traditional Irish sounds and pop songs. The opening track, "Croi Croga," was written for the movie *Braveheart,* but didn't make the final cut. But with the increased interest in Celtic music worldwide, the album soared to the top of the world music charts. In 1998 Clannad released *Landmarks.* Like *Lore,* *Landmarks* mixed traditional and pop stylings on such tunes as "A Mhuirnin O," driven by the sound of the bodhran; and "Golden Ball," which includes a saxophone. Máire's voice stands out on such songs as "Let Me See" and "An Gleann." The album fared well with CD buyers. Clannad also won its first Grammy, in the New Age category.

The band also released several retrospectives: *Past Present* on RCA in 1989 (which went platinum and broke the top 10 in the U.K.), *The Collection* on K-Tel in 1992, *Themes* on Celtic Heartbeat in 1995, and *Rogha: The Best of Clannad* in 1997.

COCKBURN, BRUCE: *Singer, guitarist, pianist, dulcimer player, songwriter. Born Ottawa, Canada, May 27, 1945.*

Bruce Cockburn (pronounced "Coburn") has been hailed as one of Canada's foremost folk artists of current times, but he tends to back away from the description. He says, "I don't think of myself as a folksinger now and I never have. I do object to that kind of categorizing, though not strenuously. I don't feel my music fits any particular category. To me, folk music means music coming out of some identifiable tradition and Canada as a nation doesn't have any identifiable tradition except for the French one. I haven't tried to identify with that, so I don't consider myself a folksinger.

"I got the label because I showed up [during one career phase] playing acoustic guitar and playing solo. For the past few years I've been working with a band and, in fact, I played with a lot of bands early in my career. I felt confined by the folk music label, because people feel that kind of music has nothing to do with today and, for me, my music has to do with today because I'm living today and writing about today."

Bruce grew up in Ottawa, where his interest in music intensified when he entered his teens. He started learning to play guitar when he was thirteen and took up the piano at seventeen. Later he mastered such other instruments as the dulcimer and wind chimes. "Early on, when I first was developing a finger-picking style on guitar, I was playing ragtime and ethnic blues. I was listening to ethnic styles from all over the world. I still do. But my style covers everything—classics, rock, jazz. I played in rock bands for years, played in jug bands a while and jazz—sort of avant-garde jazz. In school I played jazz and country music, among other things."

After getting his high school diploma, Bruce felt his calling would be music. "It wasn't so much of a decision, but sort of a nondecision. When I got out of school it was the only thing I could do."

After high school, he took off for Europe, where he earned a living by singing in the streets in such cities as Stockholm, Copenhagen, and Paris during 1963. Deciding to pick up more formal music training, he recrossed the Atlantic and enrolled in the famed Berklee School of Music in Boston, Massachusetts, in 1964. He studied composition and theory there from 1964 to 1967 and also played in jazz and blues groups in his leisure time. During those years, he spent part of his time in Canada and, in fact, never did accrue enough credits for graduation.

One of the things that lured him back to Ottawa was the chance to join a promising rock group called Children. The project fell apart after a short time and he moved around to several other bands for similar brief periods, including such groups as the Esquires, Olivus, Flying Circus, and 3's a Crowd.

It was during that period he started to write in earnest. He says, "The first serious band I was in—this would be in 1965—was one in Ottawa that was into doing original material. Originally I wrote music for another guy's material and then got into writing words as well. During the next few years with a variety of bands I did more writing. None appeared on records that I know of. They weren't particularly good. It was a period of learning and growing."

In the late 1960s, he turned to the folk circuit, playing small folk clubs throughout Ontario. His performing ability and some of his original songs steadily added to his reputation with Canadian folk fans.

At the start of the 1970s, he signed his first solo recording contract with Canadian-based True North Records, distributed by Columbia Records of Canada. A decade later, it remained his "home" label, though his recordings were handled in other countries on other labels. His debut LP, *Bruce Cockburn,* was issued by True North in May 1970 and was hailed by Canadian critics as a major event. Pete Goddard of the *Toronto Telegram,* for instance, called it "the best Canadian folk-music record of the year."

Over the next few years, more and more honors came his way in Canada as additional albums came out on True North supported by extensive tours of Canadian colleges, folk clubs, theaters, and occasional festivals. By late 1972 he had received Canada's equivalent of the U.S. Grammy, the R.P.M. Juno Award, two years in a row as Folksinger of the Year (an achievement repeated in 1973, followed by such other Juno acknowledgments as Folk Artist of the Year in 1980 and both Male Vocalist of the Year and Folk Artist of the Year in '81 and '82) and two BMI songwriting awards. One of the latter was for the title song he penned for the movie *Going Down the Road.*

His second album, *Sunwheel Dance,* was completed in 1971 and issued only in Canada. The next year Epic Records contracted to provide some U.S. distribution for his follow-up release, but still his inroads into the United States remained very small through his next four LPs of the mid-1970s. This began to change in 1976, when an agreement was concluded with Island Records for U.S. marketing. The first offering was the True North/Island 1976 LP *In the Falling Dark.* He made a number of appearances in American cities in support of the collection, including a fine showing in November 1976 at New York's Lincoln Center.

Many of his best known compositions were included in the double live collection *Circles in the*

Stream, issued in 1977. This was followed in September 1978 by a new studio album, *Further Adventures of Bruce Cockburn,* a package that presented ten of his compositions, ranging from the semicomic "Outside a Broke Phone with Money in My Hand" to such other varied styles as "Rainfall," "Laughter," "Bright Sky," "Red Ships Take Off in the Distance," and "Ship of Fools."

At the end of the 1970s, Bruce switched to Millennium Records, distributed by RCA, for U.S. marketing. His first release on that label was the album *Dancing in the Dragon's Jaws,* which not only was a Canadian best-seller but made the U.S. top 50 and remained on U.S. album charts for most of 1980. His next album, *Humans,* was on U.S. charts the latter part of 1980, but didn't remain on them into 1981.

Bruce wasn't much worried about attaining ever higher sales. "I'm not really that concerned with the expansion or contraction of the audience. My main interest in terms of my career is that technically I want to do everything better—sing better, write better, play better, and do better shows. I'm not dissatisfied with the past, but there's always room for growth. As far as getting things across to people, I think there's been a sort of qualitative growth in recent years."*

In the early 1980s, his work was affected to some extent by his conversion to born-again Christianity, although, as Stephen Holden of the *New York Times* pointed out ("A Self-Effacing Ascetic in Folk-Rocker's Clothing," October 1, 1994), Cockburn "was a Christian mystic of a very undogmatic sort . . . continually finding intimations of divinity in the Canadian sky. But he also cries out against human cruelty, greed and thoughtlessness in a voice that even when raised in righteous anger, usually sounds more saddened than enraged."

Cockburn himself, soon after his conversion, told the *Atlanta Journal,* "Becoming a Christian was a factor [in his heightened involvement in social issues] . . . and having a child was a factor. But the single biggest crystallizing factor was travel, getting into situations where people don't have the luxury of sitting back and wondering if they should be involved in politics because someone who *is* involved may come along with a machete and remove a body part."

He continued to complete new album projects during those years, including *Mummy Dust* and *Inner City Front* in 1981, *The Trouble with Normal* in 1983, and *Stealing Fire* in 1984. *Stealing Fire* spent thirty-one straight weeks on the *Billboard* chart, and the single "If I Had a Rocket Launcher," a song influenced by his Central American visits, made the magazine's top 100 singles list. The album was certified gold by year-end in Canada and went platinum in 1986. During 1984, Cockburn's first home video, *Rumours of Glory: Bruce Cockburn Live,* was issued.

He began the second half of the '80s with the album *World of Wonders,* released by MCA/Gold Mountain in 1986, which was followed by the compilation *Waiting for a Miracle,* which contained all his singles issued in Canada from 1970 to 1987. (The title song was covered in a track in a Jerry Garcia Band 1991 album.) He closed out the decade with the album *Big Circumstance* in 1989. During that year, he was appointed honorary chairman of the environmental group Friends of the Earth: Canada. Besides that, he had been active in the fight for rights of Native Americans in both the United States and Canada for some time, a commitment he continued into the '90s.

After the album *Bruce Cockburn Live* was issued in 1990, he signed with a new label, Columbia Records, in the United States. His label debut, *Nothing But a Burning Light,* was released in 1991, followed by *Christmas* in 1993 and *Dart to the Heart* in 1994. *Nothing But a Burning Light* was named Best Album of the Year by the AP Wire Service and was certified gold by the R.I.A.A. in 1992.

As had much of his previous work, the focus of *Dart to the Heart* was on the power of love, which caused Joe Medwick of *HITS* magazine ("Love, Canadian Style," June 6, 1994, p. 60) to question how the artist could find the faith to write songs "given the state of the world these days." Bruce replied, "It's probably not so much faith and hope as it is recognition that nothing else is going to help you in the end. There are lots of different things we mean when we say love. I personally believe that at the core of all that, there is just one thing and, with the risk of sounding dumb about it, that's love with a capital L. It's a universal force. It's there whether we pay any attention to it or not. It's certainly part of our human nature and I suspect it's part of nature in a broader sense. . . ."

As part of its arrangement with Bruce, Columbia Records pledged to endeavor to make all of his album catalog available in the United States. As of 1994, it had reissued CDs of twelve albums: *High Winds White Sky, Sunwheel Dance, Night Vision, Joy Will Find a Way, In the Falling Dark, Dancing in the Dragon's Jaws, Humans, Inner City Front, The Trouble with Normal, Stealing Fire, World of Wonders,* and *Big Circumstance.* In 1997, another label, Rykodisc, issued *Charity of Night* followed in 1999 by *Breakfast in New Orleans, Dinner in Timbuktu.*

*Based partly on a phone interview with Irwin Stambler, early 1981

COHEN, LEONARD: *Singer, guitarist, songwriter, actor, author. Born Montreal, Quebec, Canada, September 21, 1934.*

Like a bird on a wire/Like a drunk in a midnight choir/I have tried in my way/To be free. Those lines from one of Leonard Cohen's most famous songs, "Bird on a Wire," exemplify both his poetic lyrics and the credo that made him one of the standard-bearers of folk and folk-rock in the 1960s and 1970s. Besides being included in his second solo album, the song was the title of a documentary of one of his European tours and a major pop singles hit for rock star Joe Cocker. Cohen has sold more than eleven million albums. The author of nine books of verse and two novels, Cohen continued "blackening pages" throughout the 1980s and 1990s, influencing a new generation of musicians. In his own quest for spiritual freedom, he began living in a California Zen Buddhist center in 1993, though he remained a practicing Jew.

His way with words preceded his foray into songwriting by many years. In fact, he already had a considerable reputation as a poet and novelist before he began adding music in the mid-1960s. Born and raised in Montreal, Canada, the son of Nathaniel Cohen, a successful clothing manufacturer, and his Russian-born wife, Masha, Leonard Norman Cohen began writing fiction and poetry at an early age and was considered a hugely promising writer when still in his teens. His father, who enjoyed singing World War I songs, died when Leonard was nine, and Masha, who sang Russian songs, raised Leonard and his older sister, Esther. Leonard studied piano, played clarinet in the high school band, and took guitar lessons.

He had just graduated with a bachelor's degree in English literature from McGill University in 1956 when his first book of poetry, *Let Us Compare Mythologies,* was published—rated one of the best volumes of the decade. It received McGill's MacNaughton Prize for creative writing. By the late 1960s, he had increased his total of poetry volumes to five: *Let Us Compare Mythologies* and *The Spice Box of Earth* (1961), *Flowers for Hitler* (1964), *Parasites of Heaven* (1966), and *Selected Poems (1956–1968)* (1968). He added *The Energy of Slaves* (1972), *Book of Mercy* (1984), and a complete anthology of his songs and poems, *Stranger Music* (1993).

Poetry readings first brought him before live audiences. In 1957 he toured the States, reading some of his poems against the backdrop of music played by jazz pianist Maury Kay. Though he hadn't turned to writing songs, he had been interested in folk music for a long time. He recalled that a friend's father, a union organizer, taught him to play folk and old union songs on the guitar. ("Only Socialists and Communists played the guitar in those days," he quipped.) He also was a member of a group called the Buckskin Boys in Montreal in 1954, a "strictly amateur band that played country music." Although he sometimes played the guitar to entertain himself or his friends, he didn't attempt to use it professionally until 1966.

Cohen increased his literary stature by writing two novels, *The Favorite Game* in 1963 and *Beautiful Losers* in 1966. The first won him a worldwide cult following; the second focused worldwide attention on his home

city of Montreal. The novels eventually qualified as best-sellers. (Both had eclipsed the 800,000-sold mark by the 1990s.) However, it took a 1967 documentary film about his life and works, prepared by the National Film Board of Canada, to really bring him large-scale attention at home. Called *Ladies and Gentlemen . . . Mr. Leonard Cohen,* the movie was released in 1967 as an Easter special by the Canadian Broadcasting Corporation. As a result of the film, he received several assignments to write themes or scores for NFB programs, including Derek May's *The Angel* and Don Owens's *The Ernie Game,* in which he also was a cast member. (He later had a cameo on NBC's *Miami Vice* playing the head of Interpol.)

Humanistic in outlook, Cohen is independent in thought and action. Much of his writing reflects his desire to find out for himself about events or situations that affect people's lives. After comparing many religious beliefs, he concluded, "Our natural vocabulary is Judeo-Christian. That is our blood myth." In 1961, he visited Cuba after the Bay of Pigs debacle and, unlike many intellectuals from Canada and Europe, didn't automatically take Castro's side. As he stated in his poem "The Only Tourist in Havana Turns His Thoughts Home," he left "not knowing which side to favor."

After studying at Columbia's General Studies Program in 1956 and 1957, Cohen won two Canada Arts Council awards and used his $3,000 in prize money to travel to Europe and to purchase a house (which he still owns) on the Greek island of Hydra, where he lived off and on for much of the 1960s with Marianne Jenson and her son, Axel. He wrote "Bird on a Wire" after looking out his window one day at some birds resting on a new electricity wire. Up to that point, the wires had enraged him. But when he heard the birds singing he was inspired. After Hydra, he took up residence on a 1,500-acre property in Franklin, Tennessee, near Nashville, before making Montreal home base once more in the 1970s.

The event that triggered his move into music occurred in 1966 when he was in New York for a poetry reading. CBS-TV approached him to do a program based on some of his readings that might also include some musical interludes. While in New York, Cohen attended a performance by Judy Collins, whose folk renderings inspired him to write songs. It was the beginning of a long association in which Judy tried to include Leonard's songs on her new LPs. The first instance was in her LP *In My Life* (Elektra, 1966), where she performed Cohen's classic song "Suzanne," about an exotic love interest who *feeds you tea and oranges/that come all the way from China* and includes the line *You've touched her perfect body with your mind.* (Later, Cohen explained that "Suzanne" was modeled not after a lover but rather a friend who was married to a sculptor in Montreal.) Collins also recorded "Dress Rehearsal Rag," depicting the rantings of a suicidal character. She recorded two more Cohen songs on her 1967 *Wildflowers* album, "Sisters of Mercy," and "Hey, That's No Way to Say Good-bye." Before long many other artists were discovering Cohen's songs.

Soon he started to perform his material himself. In 1967 his efforts were well received at the Newport Folk Festival, at Expo '67 in Montreal, and with Judy Collins at the summer Rheingold Music Festival in New York. From then on, he made many tours of the United States and Europe. He usually dressed in dark suits and ties, giving a somber impression while regaling audiences with his deadpan wit. "I grew up wearing suits," he told Robert Hilburn of the *Los Angeles Times* (September 24, 1995). "I wasn't trying to make a statement or set myself apart. I was never into blue jeans. I was older. I wasn't ashamed of my education. I didn't pretend that I came out of the country. I wasn't trying to be Paul Bunyan. My name was Leonard Cohen. My father was a clothing manufacturer. I wrote books. I went to college."

Meanwhile, he had been signed to Columbia Records by the label's vice president for talent acquisition, John Hammond Sr., after performing "Master Song" and "Hey, That's No Way to Say Good-bye" for him at the Chelsea Hotel in Manhattan. His debut album, *Songs of Leonard Cohen,* was released on December 26, 1967. Among its contents were "Suzanne," "Hey, That's No Way to Say Good-bye," and "Sisters of Mercy." The songs from that first album later provided a striking sound track for Robert Altman's western *McCabe and Mrs. Miller.*

His second album, *Songs from a Room,* was released on March 17, 1969, and included such tracks as "Bird on a Wire," "Story of Isaac," and "You Know Who I Am." He performed some of them before massive audiences in 1969 and 1970, including appearances before enthusiastic crowds at the Olympia Music Hall (Paris) in August and in front of over 100,000 people at England's Isle of Wight rock festival.

In 1969 Cohen also met a painter named Suzanne Elrod—not the Suzanne in the song written before they met. Although Elrod and Cohen never married, they stayed together for nearly a decade, living everywhere from New York to Greece, and had two children: Adam, who was born in September 1972, and Lorca (named after Spanish writer Frederico Garcia Lorca), born in September 1974.

Leonard's first album of the 1970s was *Songs of Love and Hate,* issued on March 17, 1971, whose tracks included "Joan of Arc," "Famous Blue Raincoat," and his version of "Dress Rehearsal Rag." This proved to be a commercial success, making the U.S. charts in May 1971 and staying on them for most of the summer. His fourth LP and his first live album, *Live Songs,* came out on April 27, 1973. The recordings were selected from several concerts between 1970 and 1972 and included "Bird on a Wire," "Story of Isaac," "You Know Who I Am," "Nancy," and "Tonight Will Be Fine." New songs

included "Queen Victoria," a fourteen-minute improvisation called "Please Don't Pass Me By," and "Passing Thru," which was issued as a single in 1973. *New Skin for the Old Ceremony* was issued on October 4, 1974. The album focuses on his trademark themes: loneliness, longing, the search for love, independence, depression, and lust. At one point Cohen let slip that "Chelsea Hotel No. 2" was about a brief fling with Janis Joplin, something he wishes he had kept private. He embarked on his first tour of the United States in five years, continuing into 1975. Columbia also released *Leonard Cohen: The Best of* that year. The LP was his last on Columbia for some time.

The next Cohen album didn't appear for two years, and when it did it was on a new label, Warner Brothers, and with a new collaborator. His wildly unlikely co-worker was Phil Spector, the boy wonder of rock in the early '60s. The two found a creative chemistry developing, and not long after their first meeting were getting together in Spector's Southern California mansion, combining Cohen's lyrics and Spector's melodies. Things went surprisingly well during that phase. Fifteen new songs were assembled in a short period of time. However, it became rougher when recording got under way. As Cohen told Janet Maslin of *The New York Times* (November 6, 1977), "I'd heard he was a genius who knew how to make records—I had no idea of the ordeal of a session with him. I never thought I would give up that much control. I didn't even know when [the record's various tracks] were being mixed—I never heard the mix and I don't approve of it. The mix is a catastrophe. No air. No breath. It's like what he has become himself. He doesn't know how to let a situation breathe. Let alone a song.

"But it's very hard to fight him—he just disappears. He was in possession of the tapes. His bodyguard took them back to his house every night. I knew he was mad, but I thought that his madness would be more adorable, on the ordinary daily level. I love the guy, but he's out of control. Finally, I just said let the thing go."

The LP, *Death of a Ladies' Man,* came out in late 1977 on Warner Brothers. As might be expected, it aroused a storm of praise and criticism from critics, some suggesting it was a disaster, others considering it one of the year's best. The collection, on first hearing, didn't seem in line with what one expected creatively from either individual. Though it found considerable interest in Europe, where Cohen has been compared to Jacques Brel, it sold poorly in the United States. Cohen described it best: "There's nothing I like about it—but it may be a classic."

In 1979, Cohen returned to Columbia with a new album, *Recent Songs.* Singer-songwriter Jennifer Warnes supervised the vocal arrangements and sang backup on several tracks. While Cohen's popularity soared in Europe—the British group Sisters of Mercy took its name from his song, and there is even an annual Leonard

Cohen festival in Krakow, Poland—the early 1980s were not a successful time for him in the States. He briefly turned to film. He scripted, directed, and scored *I Am a Hotel* in 1984, a half-hour short that won first prize at the Festival International de Télévision de Montreux. The following year he worked with songwriter Lewis Furey on a rock opera, *Night Magic,* which won a Juno Award for Best Movie Score.

Passport Records put out his next album, *Various Positions,* in 1984 (it was later licensed by Columbia), though distribution was limited. The album contained several songs whose titles revealed Cohen's penchant for religious exploration: "The Law," "If It Be Your Will," and "Heart with No Companion." Indeed, Bob Dylan remarked that Cohen's songs were sounding more like prayers. The most enduring song from the collection, "Hallelujah," later inspired such artists as the late Jeff Buckley and U2's Bono. The album again had backing vocals by Jennifer Warnes, who gave Cohen's career a boost with her renditions of his songs. In 1986 she recorded *Famous Blue Raincoat,* titled after Cohen's brilliant song from his third album. The album hit number seventy-two on *Billboard*'s charts and stirred a renaissance in Cohen's work.

When he released *I'm Your Man* on Columbia (with a picture of him eating a banana on the cover) the following year, he was met by wide critical acclaim, especially in Europe, where the album hit number one in several countries. As he explained to Stephen Saban of *Details* (September 1988), the Europeans "are not obliged, as they are here, to decide whether I have a voice or not, whether I *deserve* to be called a singer or not, whether I have the *right* to sing. Because they have a whole tradition of people who croak out their own versions of reality."

The album introduced his satire and wit to a new generation with songs like "First We Take Manhattan," set to pulsating beat, and "I'm Your Man." In "Tower of Song," he pokes fun at himself: *I was born like this, I had no choice. I was born with the gift of a golden voice.* The line drew laughs at his infrequent, but critically acclaimed, concerts in 1988. In 1990, one of Cohen's songs, "Everybody Knows," was featured in the movie *Pump Up the Volume.* The following year several younger admirers, such as R.E.M., Lloyd Cole, Ian McCulluch, the Pixies, and John Cale, complied a tribute album to Cohen, *I'm Your Fan,* on Atlantic.

Another fan in those years was actress Rebecca De Mornay, who had begun listening to Cohen's work when she was ten, as she told David Browne of *Entertainment Weekly* (January 8, 1993): "My mother was going out on a date, so she lit a candle and said, 'I'll put a record on that'll put you right to sleep.' And I remember it did put me to sleep. But it was comforting, too."

Despite their age difference, the two started out as friends, then became lovers in the early 1990s, and then friends again. De Mornay is credited with producing

"Anthem," on Cohen's next album, *Future* (Columbia, 1992). Cohen, notorious for taking years to chisel out his songs, had recorded several versions of the song until De Mornay helped perfect it. Cohen dedicated the album to her with a parody of the Book of *Genesis:* "And before I had done speaking in mine heart, behold, Rebecca came forth with her pitcher on her shoulder. . . . "

The title track for the album, which rated four stars from *Rolling Stone,* was featured in Oliver Stone's controversial movie *Natural Born Killers.* The song is an apocalyptic vision sung to "a hot little dance track." Cohen's bleak view came out just after the Gulf War, and in the year of the Los Angeles riots and Bill Clinton's presidential election. In "Democracy," Cohen sounds optimistic: *I'm sentimental, if you know what I mean:/I love the country but I can't stand the scene.* He also recorded "Always" by Irving Berlin, one of the few times he has recorded the work of another songwriter.

In 1993, Columbia Music Video released a one-hour documentary entitled *Songs from the Life of Leonard Cohen.* Originally produced in 1988 for BBC's *Omnibus* series, the video includes footage from Cohen's 1988 Carnegie Hall concert, encounters with Judy Collins, and home footage shot by his father. In the fall of 1993, Cohen published an anthology of his poems and lyrics from 1956 to 1992, *Stranger Music: Selected Poems and Songs.* Cohen described his writing process to Anthony DeCurtis of *Rolling Stone:* "Some people write great songs in taxicabs, and some people write great songs in offices in the Brill Building. I wish I could work that way. For me, I've got to surrender to it, struggle with it and get creamed by it in the process."

He added a second live set in 1994, *Cohen Live,* on Columbia, taken from concerts in 1988 and 1993. In 1995, another prominent group of singer-songwriters honored Cohen with *Tower of Song: The Songs of Leonard Cohen,* on A&M records. Kelley Lynch, Cohen's manager, produced the album along with David Anderle and Steve Lindsey, as a way of increasing Cohen's profile in the United States, where he had been largely ignored from 1975 to 1985. Don Henley, Sting, Tori Amos, Aaron Neville, Elton John, Willie Nelson, Peter Gabriel, Bono, Billy Joel, and Suzanne Vega perform their favorites. Joel and Vega do exceptional versions of "Light As the Breeze" and "Story of Isaac," respectively. In 1996, "Suzanne" was also included in the sound track for the haunting movie *Breaking the Waves.*

By 1997 there were three other tributes: a Norwegian album, a tribute to Leonard Cohen and Frederico Garcia Lorca by Spanish Flamenco performer Enrique Morente called *Omega,* and the third by Czech singer Juraj Kukura titled *Jsem tvuj muz.*

Despite his peripatetic ways, Cohen remained close to his children, Adam and Lorca. After his son had a bad car accident in 1990 when he was in the West Indies with a calypso band called Exile One, Cohen and

Suzanne Elrod transported him to Montreal and stayed by his side as he was treated for broken ribs, a collapsed lung, a broken pelvis, and a fractured spinal column. Following in his dad's footsteps, Adam became a singer-songwriter (his debut album *Adam Cohen* was released by Columbia in 1998). Lorca is a painter, sculptor, and pastry chef.

In the 1990s, Cohen divided his time between homes in Los Angeles and a cabin at the Zen Buddhist monastery on Mount Baldy, where Cohen moved in 1993, shortly after breaking up with De Mornay. ("She kind of got wise to me. Now it's just a friendship again," he told Robert Masello of *People* (March 25, 1996). At the center, Cohen wears traditional black robes and a shaved head and takes part in the daily routine of cooking, cleaning, and scrubbing. He typically wakes at 2:30 A.M. before preparing breakfast and meditates up to eighteen hours a day.

He found time in his regimen to come down from the mountaintop to Los Angeles frequently to meet with his manager and reporters from major publications. He was always thankful for his fans and his ability to make a living as a poet and songwriter. "I didn't want to write for pay, but I wanted to be paid for what I write," he told Masello.

He added words of love and hope to accompany 21 Henri Matisse paintings for the 1996 book *Dance Me to the End of Love*. He is currently at work on a new album and a collection of 130 poems, *The Book of Longing*. Looking back on his career, Cohen was pleased that people found his songs accessible. As he told Robert Hilburn: "People used to say my music was too difficult or too obscure, and I never set out to be difficult or obscure. I just set out to write what I felt as honestly as I could."

In 1997, Columbia, released a second greatest hits collection called *More Best Of*. The set includes thirteen tracks taken mostly from *I'm Your Man, The Future*, and *Various Positions*. It also includes two new songs ("Never Any Good" and "The Great Event") and a concert version of his best-known song, "Suzanne," from his 1994 album, *Cohen Live*. As he told Tim De Lisle of *The Sunday Independent* (October 12, 1997): "People know that song, and they want to hear it. It's sometimes hard for me to find the way into it, to locate the emotions that originally informed it. Anybody who's touring knows this problem, singing a song after 30 years. I was never so good that I could make a song sound real or authentic without it being that, and if it isn't, people know. I find that quite a lot of red wine will do it."

COLE, PAULA: *Singer, clarinetist, pianist, songwriter, record producer. Born Manchester, Connecticut, April 5, 1968.*

The impact that a new group of fascinating young folk-oriented female singers had on pop music was illustrated when the Grammy nominations for 1997's Best Female Vocalist were announced by the National Academy of Recording Arts and Sciences in January 1998. Four of the five nominees came from that group—Jewel, Shawn Colvin, Sarah McLachlan, and Paula Cole. All of them were nominated in other categories, with Paula Cole competing for Record of the Year for her single "Where Have All the Cowboys Gone?"; Album of the Year for *This Fire;* and vying with pop, R&B, and rap performers for Best New Artist.

It was a pinnacle she hardly dared dream of reaching while growing up in the small seaport town of Rockport, Massachusetts. One of two daughters of Jim Cole, who taught entomology at Salem State College (and later became a manufacturing quality-control executive) and artist Stephanie Cole, she recalled being influenced at a very young age by her parents' musical interests. In particular, she enjoyed listening to her father play several instruments (he helped pay his college tuition by playing bass in polka groups), and as she grew older she often sang along with him.

As a child she was very shy, she later told interviewers, and found her teen years particularly difficult. As she told Steve Dougherty of *People,* "I was the classic overachiever, getting straight A's, running for class president, trying so hard to be excellent and to please everybody." She was respected by other girls, but was paid little attention by boys; she later sang about these years on the track "Bethlehem" on *Harbinger,* her debut album: *Now I'm only 16 and I think I have an ulcer / I'm hiding my sex behind a dirty sweatshirt / I've lost five pounds these past few days / Trying to be class president and get straight A's.* She had few dates during those years and went alone to the junior prom; she was voted prom queen—but by other girls.

By her senior year in high school, though, she began gaining confidence in her abilities, and soon became interested in a wide range of pop music, from folk to jazz. By then she had also become reasonably proficient as a pianist, thanks in part to lessons her parents had arranged for in earlier years. To improve her vocal talent she started to commute to Berklee College of Music in Boston, where she worked with Bob Stoloff, a professor of vocal improvisation. Stoloff told Robin Rauzi of the *Los Angeles Times* ("Up-and-Coming Singer Knows the Score," Valley edition, Calendar, August 1, 1996, p. 18), "As a singer, she was all ready. She had a lot of focus and direction as a stylist. You could hear her just gliding through pop and rock with no problems. She had a beautiful sound and beautiful vibrato. She knew where she was going and what she needed to do."

After graduating from high school in 1986, she gained a scholarship to enroll full-time at Berklee. To earn much-needed additional income, she became a "wedding singer" and also got some work as backup vocalist for local bar bands. Now in a freer environment, she also started to kick over the traces—as she told

Dougherty: "I realized I was a repressed goody two-shoes." Her response to that was to begin "to have sexual experiences and make loads of mistakes."

Her rebellion also took the form of resisting some of the guidelines for her Berklee studies. She had continued to be a student of Stoloff's after enrolling full-time, but she became difficult to get along with, he later recalled. While she continued to demonstrate great skill as a vocalist, she persisted in showing up late for the choir rehearsals Stoloff directed. After he gave her a low grade for one class, she became angry and stopped speaking to him.

Such difficulties, however, may have been a reflection of inner turmoil that colored her view of life as her years at Berklee continued. She told interviewers she had felt frustrated and depressed after graduating from Berklee in 1990, though her school term also brought her in contact with musician and aspiring moviemaker Seyi Sonuga, who became her boyfriend. A Nigerian by birth, he had grown up in England before becoming a Berklee student. After finishing school Paula suffered a nervous breakdown, but six months of sessions with a Boston psychotherapist helped quiet her emotional demons.

Deciding that she wanted a career as a songwriter and vocalist, she worked up some material to present to people in the record industry. The GRP label offered to sign her, but she decided against it, moving instead to San Francisco, where she spent hours by herself writing more original songs. She made a demo tape, which eventually reached the president of Imago Records, Terry Ellis. He was impressed with the material but unsure of whether Paula could put them over in front of an audience. She seemed shy, he remembered, and hadn't done much performing after reaching California. Before committing his company, he arranged for Cole to appear in a showcase concert back east at Siné, a small venue in New York's Greenwich Village. He told Robin Rauzi, "Within 30 seconds, I knew what I wanted to know. She stood up and immediately she opened her mouth and started to sing—and there was a performer. . . . I immediately looked around the room to see if any other record companies were there."

Ellis quickly got Cole's name on a contract, and work began on her debut album, *Harbinger*. A prerelease copy of the album made its way to rock and world music artist Peter Gabriel, who was making plans for a 1993–94 concert tour in support of his album *Us*. He was impressed enough to hire her as a backup singer who also got to sing several duets with him. Her work also included performing on Peter's Grammy-winning video "Secret World Live." This opened other doors, including the chance to perform opening sets for such artists as Melissa Etheridge and Sarah McLachlan. Favorable critical response to *Harbinger* after it was released in 1994 began to expand her audience, as did personal appearances on the coffeehouse circuit in the

mid-1990s. By then she had left San Francisco to make New York her new home.

During 1995, Paula started preparing material for her next album. Her first had done well enough for Warner to arrange to distribute that collection, also due for release on Imago. She wrote new songs for the album, like "Feelin' Love" and "Throwin' Stones," and also looked at older material like "Where Have All the Cowboys Gone?" That song, originally considered for *Harbinger*, not only made the cut for the new disc but became her first single. The album, *This Fire*, which Paula also produced, was issued on October 15, 1996, and became a best-seller, aided by the success of the single. The album (which featured a revealing photo of Paula on the cover) was certified gold by the R.I.A.A. on May 8, 1997, and went platinum on October 22. The single moved up the national singles charts in early 1997, reaching number one in *Billboard* in mid-April 1997 and staying there for many more weeks.

The song's lyrics, which at first glance seem to encourage women to look for a beer-drinking, redneck kind of mate, shook up many feminists, but Cole said the meaning had been misinterpreted. It had been intended as sarcastic comment on the way women were treated by "John Wayne" types themselves. As she told *People*'s Dougherty, "I meant it totally sarcastically. [But now] people think I'm to the right of Tammy Wynette and 'Stand by Your Man.'" The confusion seemed merely to amuse rather than upset her, and it certainly didn't diminish her appeal to female music fans.

During the summer of 1997, she was one of the artists taking part in the all-female Lilith Fair tour series organized by Sarah McLachlan. Among others taking part in that highly successful event were Jewel, Shawn Colvin, Tracy Chapman, Cheryl Crow, and Fiona Apple. Starting in October 1997, Cole began her own tour as a headliner in major concert venues in the United States and abroad, which was still drawing enthusiastic crowds in the first half of 1998. In the midst of that tour she won another prize for her trophy case: the Grammy for Best New Artist, announced on the awards telecast in March 1998.

Cole was one of the artists represented on the Arista two CD set of the Lilith Fair project released in the spring of 1998 (*Lilith Fair: A Celebration of Women in Music*). Her track "Mississippi" was considered by many critics to be one of the highlights of the set.

COLLINS, JUDY: *Singer, guitarist, songwriter, pianist. Born Seattle, Washington, May 1, 1939.*

One of the brightest newcomers to the then thriving folk music field in the early 1960s was a slender, beautiful, blue-eyed young singer named Judy Collins. She burst on the Greenwich Village folk scene like a meteor, and in a short time her dazzling vocal treatment of traditional folk songs and the new folk compositions of Dylan, Paxton, Ochs, and others made her the talk of critics and folk audiences across the country. She proved to have flexibility and resilience as well, retaining an important place in both folk and pop in later years, despite the recurrence of personal problems and the periodic impact of new pop music forms—British 1960s rock, heavy metal, punk, etc.—on the record-buying concert-going public.

Although Judy became a celebrity at the start of the 1960s, she hardly was an overnight musical convert. Her interest and training in music went back to her early years. Show business, in fact, was part of the family heritage. Her father was a radio personality, and thus there was a lot of moving about. Soon after Judy's birth, the family relocated from Seattle, Washington, to Boulder, Colorado, then to Los Angeles. Judy showed an interest in music early on and, at five, in Los Angeles, she began classical piano. She picked up technique so rapidly she was considered a prodigy, and her teachers predicted she might have an important career in the classics. Her studies continued in Denver, Colorado, where her family finally found a permanent home base. It was in that city that, as a protégé of conductor Dr. Antonia Brico, she made her public debut at thirteen in a performance of Mozart's *Concerto for Two Pianos.*

But she was starting to pay attention to other, more popular forms of music. Folk music particularly enthralled her. It better suited her nature than the early wave of rock then being brought to the fore by Elvis Presley, Bill Haley, and their confreres. When she was sixteen, she took up the guitar, considering it a better instrument to accompany her new repertoire of folk songs. For several years, she mainly sang for her own pleasure or to entertain friends or school audiences. At nineteen, she decided to try for broader exposure. She auditioned for a job at a Boulder nightclub. As she told Donald Mullen of UPI in April 1967, "The manager said, 'I hate folk music. I'm sorry your audition was such a great success, because the demand is so popular I'm going to have to hire you for $100 a week. . . . ' "

For a while at the end of the 1950s, she played in her home region. As time went on, though, she gradually began to appear in coffeehouses and folk clubs in other parts of the country. The hub of folk music activity at the time was New York, so she headed east at the start of the 1960s. Once there, it didn't take long for her talents to become widely noted by other young artists and by talent hunters for record companies. By 1961 she was under contract to Elektra Records, then an independent, with whom she still remained at the start of the 1980s (by which time it was part of the Warner Communications conglomerate).

Her debut LP, *Maid of Constant Sorrow,* came out on Elektra in October 1961. An excellent initial effort, it found favor with a sizable number of folk adherents, though it came nowhere near gold-record levels. That was the way it was to be for many of Judy's releases in the 1960s, but considering the subsidence of the folk boom in the middle part of the decade, she did manage to do quite well.

Her concerts increasingly were eagerly awaited events in New York and elsewhere. Appearances at such major venues as New York's Town Hall and Carnegie Hall in the mid-1960s brought standing-room-only results. Similar receptions greeted her in medium- and even large-size auditoriums not only all across the United States but in Canada and throughout Europe. Meanwhile, Elektra continued to release new albums at the rate of about one a year in keeping with her desire to take her time and strive for maximum quality in each new group of recordings. Her second LP, *Golden Apples of the Sun,* came out in October 1962, and *Judy Collins No. 3* appeared in January 1964. In October of that year, her first live album, *Judy Collins in Concert,* was released.

Taken from her appearance at New York's Town Hall on March 21, 1964, it demonstrated her still-strong emphasis on folk material, something she was to change in coming years. Among her offerings were "Hey Nellie Nellie," "The Lonesome Death of Hattie Carroll," "Coal Tattoo," "Wild Rippling Water," "Tear Down the Walls," and "Winter Way."

During those years, like most young folk artists, Collins was actively involved in the civil rights movement. She often contributed her services to fund-raising events and also participated in marches in behalf of various civil rights causes. Though not quite as strident as Joan Baez or Bob Dylan, she still was proud of her efforts. As she noted in 1967, "I don't have the young rebel image. I'm trying to make statements as a woman. My message is in my music—what one woman is doing. One of my new songs is 'The Dove.' It says war is wrong. You have to answer 'yes.' There's no way to say 'yes . . . maybe.' "

As her albums continued to come forth, the content began to shift away from heavy folk orientation toward new, more sophisticated songs, both in the modern folk and pop vein. This was evident after *Judy Collins' 5th Album,* issued in November 1965; in such late 1960s releases as *In My Life* (11/66), *Wildflowers* (11/67), and *Who Knows Where the Time Goes* (11/68), the last two of which sold well over gold-record-award levels. On these albums she demonstrated a knack for selecting and interpreting material by such songwriters as Leonard Cohen ("Suzanne," "Sisters of Mercy," and "Hey, That's No Way to Say Good-bye"), Sandy Denny ("Who Knows Where the Time Goes"), Joni Mitchell ("Both Sides Now," "Chelsea Morning," and "Michael from Mountains"), Jacques Brel, and Randy Newman ("I Think It's Going to Rain Today"). By singing their songs, Collins brought them to the attention of the American public. With songs like "Marat/Sade" and Cohen's "Dress Rehearsal Rag" she also tackled complex and dramatic material. Another trend in the late 1960s was inclusion of a sprinkling of original compositions by Judy. Apparently she had taken to heart the criticism of her failure to do anything but interpret other writers' songs.

Judy also began to have chart-making singles during those years. One of them, "Hard Lovin' Loser" in 1967, was followed with her first blockbuster single, her 1967 rendition of Joni Mitchell's "Both Sides Now." The record won a Grammy Award for best single in 1968. In 1969, Collins had another vintage year with such singles as "Chelsea Morning," "Turn, Turn, Turn," and "Someday Soon." She continued her chart inroads in the early 1970s with such hits as "Amazing Grace" in 1971 and "Open the Door (Song for Judith)," an original composition, cowritten with actor Stacy Keach, in 1972.

Also on the album charts in the early 1970s were such releases as *Recollections,* issued in July 1969, *Whales and Nightingales,* released in November 1970, and *Living,* issued in November 1971 and on the charts well into 1972. By then, though, there already were signs of some difficulties in her private life, sometimes rumored, but previously not obvious in any change in her performing work. She announced she was taking a sabbatical for all of 1972 and planned to write a book. She was represented on the charts, though, by a May 1972 reissue of some of her early material, *Colors of the Day.* In January 1973 she released an album, *True Stories and Other Dreams,* which reflected her extensive feminist involvement of the time.

Collins began to try her hand at writing when she prepared some autobiographical material for the *Judy Collins Songbook,* published in the late 1960s. She was offered writing assignments by *Redbook* and *Ms.* magazines; for the latter, she decided to do an interview with her former teacher, Dr. Brico. A friend suggested filming the interview, and Judy enlisted the aid of Jill Godmilow for that. The resulting material caused them to pursue the matter further as a documentary dealing with Dr. Brico's life and particularly the frustrations of trying to gain acceptance as a female conductor in a male-dominated field. The film, *Antonia: A Portrait of the Woman,* was issued in 1974 to excellent reviews and has since won many honors. It was chosen to open the American Filmmakers Series at New York's Whitney Museum, was named by *Time* magazine as one of the ten best films of 1974, was nominated for an Oscar in the Best Documentary category, and won the Christopher Award and the Independent Film Critics Award.

Her relative inactivity extended for a few years, then she went back into the studios to work on a new LP that was released in March 1975, called *Judith.* One of the tracks on the album was her sensitive version of Stephen Sondheim's "Send in the Clowns." Released as a single, her recording was recognized as the classic handling of the ballad and since has been one of her best-known numbers. The album won a gold-record award in November. In the voting for the 1975 Gram-

mys, the single reached the final five nominees for best female vocal effort.

She finished another LP, *Bread and Roses,* which was released in August 1976, but then once more returned to the sidelines, although one single, "Special Delivery," received substantial airplay. (Elektra did, however, release an excellent double album retrospective, *So Early in the Spring: The First Fifteen Years,* in July 1977.) She remained there until early 1979, when she again was ready to tour in support of a new album, *Hard Times for Lovers* (which featured nude photos of Judy on the cover), released by Elektra in February. She told interviewers at the time that the mid-1970s had been particularly traumatic for her, with the onset of depression about her goals and personal relationships. As she said to Dennis Hunt (*Los Angeles Times,* February 16, 1979), she went into hiding at the end of 1976. "I didn't have an album out. . . . This is my first album since 1976. I've been taking it easy for a while. Last year [1978] was a quiet year, my first quiet year in many years and I desperately needed it."

She recalled when *Judith* came out, "I was having tremendous personal problems then. It was difficult to balance what was going on professionally with what was going on in my personal life. There was too much drama happening on the personal level for me to see anything clearly. It was a very painful time in my life and I can't really say that the pain has all disappeared."

However, she felt she had mastered her problems and was ready to go forward. "There has been a 180-degree shift in my perspective. . . . It's maturity. Maturity comes with age and I'm happier now than I've ever been, so aging does have its rewards."

Nonetheless, there were some anxious moments for her fans. Rumors persisted that she had lost most of her vocal effectiveness. This was given further credence by a near-disastrous vocal effort on NBC's *Saturday Night Live* in early 1979. She was better but still below par on a later appearance on Johnny Carson's *The Tonight Show.* However, she sounded in good voice on *Hard Times for Lovers,* and she held a concert series in which her voice, if somewhat more limited in range than in earlier years, returned to the purity of tone and clarity that always had been Judy's trademark.

During 1981, she worked on a new album, which she coproduced with Lewis Hahn, titled *Times of Our Lives,* released in January 1982.

During the 1980s, Judy continued to appear in concerts regularly, mostly in small or mid-size venues, and occasionally showed up on TV programs. Among her 1980s and 1990s releases were *Home Again* (Elektra, 1984), *Amazing Grace* (1985), *Trust Your Heart* (Gold Castle, 1987), *Sanity and Grace* (Delta, 1989), *Fires of Eden* (Columbia, 1990), *Wind Beneath My Wings* (Laserlight, 1992), *Judy Sings Dylan* (Geffen, 1994), *Judy Collins Christmas* (Rhino, 1994), *Live at Newport* (Vanguard, 1994), and *Christmas at the Biltmore Estate*

(Elektra, 1997). In the mid-1980s, she found a new interest in writing which led to preparation of an autobiography, *Trust Your Heart,* which was published in 1987. That effort, in turn, helped her to try her hand at fiction which eventually resulted in publication of a novel, *Shameless,* in 1995. Along with the release of the book, she was represented in record stores with a new CD, also titled *Shameless.*

Before that, however, her life was touched by great sadness when her thirty-three-year-old son, Clark Taylor (from her first marriage to Peter Taylor), committed suicide in 1992. (The fact that newly elected president Bill Clinton said that his and Hillary's decision to name their daughter Chelsea had been inspired by Collins's recording of the Joni Mitchell song "Chelsea Morning" was a positive note, but hardly made up for her loss.) In 1997, looking back on her son's death and other trying times in her life, she told Anthony DeCurtis, for an article in the *New York Times,* that music and the support of her second husband, Louis Nelson, had helped her to cope not only with her family tragedy but with previous problems with alcohol addiction and bulimia. As for her performing career, she told DeCurtis, "I do consider my work a calling, part of a journey of self-discovery. When you look at yourself, you discover something the rest of the world can relate to. Someone once reviewed me and said, 'When I walked out, it was as though I was scarred by the experience,' meaning 'I was changed.' If I go hear a singer and I haven't been down inside my own stuff while I'm listening, I might as well have been home channel surfing."

In 1996, she completed a new CD, the retrospective *Voices,* whose tracks included favorites of her own and her fans. The package included a booklet in which she wrote about some of the personal stories behind the songs. On March 20, 1996, the R.I.A.A. presented her with certification that her 1975 album *Judith* had reached platinum record level almost twenty years after its original release. In 1997, she and Roberta Flack joined to give a series of concerts to raise funds for the Nina Hyde Center for Breast Cancer Research at Georgetown University in Washington, D.C.

In January 1998, Elektra issued a two-CD package of her recordings for the label over the years, including a few of her own compositions such as "My Father." Other tracks in *Judy Collins, Forever: An Anthology* offered some of Judy's best-known vocals: her versions of Joni Mitchell's "Both Sides Now," Stephen Sondheim's "Send in the Clowns," Leonard Cohen's "Suzanne," and Sandy Denny's "Who Knows Where the Time Goes."

In 1998 she released a new CD, *Both Sides Now* (Interscope), featuring new versions of some of her best-known songs, and began work on a CD and TV special about Irish music. She also published her memoir *Singing Lessons* (Pocket Books). In it she chronicles her career, personal struggles with alcohol and depression, the pain of her first marriage, her relationship with her son, and how she dealt with his suicide, experiences that she hoped would help others. As she noted, the process of writing the book was therapeutic. "I couldn't have lived without writing this book. I wrote this so that I wouldn't have to die," she told Susan Cheever of *Newsday* ("One Verse at a Time," September 22, 1998).

COLVIN, SHAWN: *Singer, songwriter, guitarist. Born Vermillion, South Dakota, January 10, 1956.*

With a talent for interpreting other people's work as well as writing her own songs, Shawn Colvin was one of the select few folk performers in the early 1990s who showed an ability to cross over to a wider audience. Influenced by both Joni Mitchell and Suzanne Vega, Colvin somehow managed to develop a style of her own. That was evident at Los Angeles's Wiltern Theatre in December 1994, where Colvin headlined a concert shortly after releasing her album of covers called *Cover Girl.* She played Steve Earle's "Someday," Tom Waits's "(Looking for) The Heart of Saturday Night," and Sting's "Every Little Thing (He) Does Is Magic," backed effectively by Steuart Smith on guitar and bassist Larry Klein. But then she took a huge risk. Admitting to being awestruck, Colvin introduced her idol, Joni Mitchell.

Mitchell took the stage amid cries of "Joni." (It sounded like the 1970s again.) She played two songs, working the strings of her guitar as if it were two instruments. For most performers it would have been impossible to reclaim the stage. But Colvin gracefully regained her momentum, showing that she is not just a Joni Mitchell clone but a unique voice. Her musicianship and theatricality bring her recordings to life on stage.

Her first four albums have been critically acclaimed and have sold well. Her fifth album, *A Few Small Repairs* (with her hit single "Sunny Came Home") went platinum in the spring of 1998. Her debut, *Steady On* (1989) won a Grammy for Best Contemporary Folk Recording.

Colvin grew up in Vermillion, South Dakota, home of the University of South Dakota. Her father, Bob Colvin, owned a classified advertising newspaper, the *Broadcaster Press.* He introduced Shawn to the folk music of the early 1960s—the Kingston Trio, Josh White, Harry Belafonte, and Pete Seeger. He had a group of friends who would don Kingston Trio–inspired striped shirts and come over to sing folk songs. Bob played guitar and banjo, and Barbara, Shawn's mother, sang as well. When she was ten, Shawn picked up her brother's four-string guitar and a Mel Bay chord book and began to teach herself.

Both parents had other aspirations and moved the family around. Her father sold the newspaper and went back to school to be a psychologist; her mother went to law school. When she was eleven, the family moved to London, Ontario, for a year and a half (where Bob went to school to study psychology) and then to Carbondale,

Illinois, home of Southern Illinois University. They stayed in Carbondale because her father got a teaching position there. Shawn was already hooked on the radio— the Beatles, Simon and Garfunkel, Manfred Mann, the Association, and the Who. But Joni Mitchell had the biggest impact. When she first heard Mitchell, "all else changed," Colvin says.

The move to Carbondale unsettled Colvin. "Whatever instability I had, the move sent me into—I don't know—a dark part of myself," she told Helen Thorpe of *Texas Monthly* (April 1995). "It probably would have happened one way or another, but it took me the next fifteen years to recover—I needed to escape, and the notion of being cool and having an identity as a musician was a good escape."

She played in a folk duo and had the lead in several high school musicals. She enrolled at Southern Illinois University, taking the usual first-year requirements, but music called to her and she dropped out in the middle of her sophomore year. She got a job at a local club that paid $40 a night and began her career in music, eventually setting up the first of her two Shawn Colvin Bands, this one a hard rock group.

She broke up the band in 1976 and joined her boyfriend's country swing band, the Dixie Diesels. They moved to Austin, where songwriters such as Joe Ely, Butch Hancock, and Willis Ramsey caught her attention. After two years her relationship ended and she moved to San Francisco, where she became a local hit at LaVal's Subterranean, a small club in Berkeley, performing covers of Bruce Springsteen and other artists. In 1980, Buddy Miller, someone she had known in Austin, asked her to join his country-and-western band and move to New York.

Still fighting her own demons, she did. "In San Francisco I was just passing the time, getting drunker and drunker," she told *Texas Monthly*. "Sounded great to me—let somebody else do the bookings and figure out the gigs."

When Miller left the band, she took over as lead singer and renamed it the Shawn Colvin Band. Miller, who played guitar, was replaced by John Leventhal. He dazzled her with his playing, and they became entwined—he was producer, band mate, songwriting partner, and boyfriend in one. Her work with Leventhal gave her the confidence to write her own songs. But it was a stormy affair, "the all-time craziest f——ing thing I ever went through," she told *Texas Monthly*.

They played the clubs in a pop band modeled after Steely Dan, but in 1983 she decided to go solo. (She also quite drinking and began therapy.) She had been playing open-mikes at Folk City, but she landed her first extended gig at the Other End and began performing as many as five nights a week. The *Fast Folk Magazine* collective recorded an early version of one of her songs, "I Don't Know Why," the first song she had ever written in one sitting (in 1981). She began to perform in the

Boston area. A cassette of a live recording received some airplay on Boston's WERS-FM. Columbia Records took notice and signed her to a deal. She began recording her first album with Leventhal in December 1988.

Steady On, coproduced by Leventhal and Steve Addabbo, came out in October 1989. She released the title track and "Diamonds in the Rough" as singles. Colvin won the Grammy as well as a New York Music Award for Best Debut Female Vocalist. She appeared on *Late Night with David Letterman, The Tonight Show,* and at folk festivals in Kerrville, Telluride, and Winnipeg.

She had written most of the songs in 1986 and 1987, in part because she decided to take a break from performing. "I just stumbled onto it," she told Dennis Hunt of the *Los Angeles Times* (December 8, 1992). "I knew I could sing and play good rhythm guitar, but I didn't have anything special to offer. But in 1987 this inspiring event happened. I was working on this song called 'Diamonds in the Rough.' I decided to change it and write it in a way that was very personal and confessional. I stopped trying to be clever and just tried to be honest and put as much of me into the song as possible. Things changed after that."

Steady On included several other personal songs, including "Shotgun Down the Avalanche," written about her relationship with Leventhal, and "Cry Like an Angel," a song she had written with Leventhal in 1987.

Following *Steady On,* she began working on her second album with Leventhal, but their personal relationship was disintegrating. "It wasn't a disaster," she told *Rolling Stone* (February 4, 1993). "But we were like two wary, worn-out people." She started anew with a new producer, Joni Mitchell's then-husband and bassist, Larry Klein. Colvin originally planned to write a collection of songs about being single and independent. "I've been feeling my way through life and love, staggering here and there and going on—just like a lot of other women," she told Hunt.

But in 1991 she went on tour with Richard Thompson and fell in love again, this time with Simon Tassano, Thompson's sound man and touring manager. (The two married in 1993 and had their first child in spring 1998.) That changed the tone of her second album, *Fat City,* which was named after Tassano's world music band, Lights in the Fat City.

The introspective album, which came out in 1992, opens with the song "Polaroids" —*Please no more therapy—Mother take care of me/Piece me together with a needle and thread*—and ends with the first song she had ever written, "I Don't Know Why." Most of the critics liked the album, with an occasional complaint about the contents being too "self-involved." It included a long list of guest performers: Joni Mitchell, Richard Thompson, David Lindley, Booker T. Jones, and Bruce Hornsby. It was nominated for a Grammy in the Best

Contemporary Folk Album category, and "I Don't Know Why" was nominated in the Best Female Pop Vocal Performance category.

After releasing two albums featuring her own songs, she decided to release an album of covers. That album, called *Cover Girl,* came out in 1994 on Columbia. It was an impressive collection of twelve songs by such artists as Jimmy Webb, Bob Dylan, and Robbie Robertson. It has a different feel from Nanci Griffith's 1992 collection of folk covers, *Other Voices, Other Rooms.* While Griffith studiously reproduced the folkie flavor of the originals, Colvin puts more of a free-form pop stamp on her songs.

She toured extensively in support of the album, armed with a repertoire of covers and original material. At the Wiltern Theater concert, she even cleverly threw a cover medley into her own composition. When performing "Polaroids," she weaved in snippets of top 40 Motown songs such as "Just My Imagination" and "Put a Little Love in Your Heart."

Colvin released the collection of live songs that got her a contract with Columbia. *Live '88,* taken from concerts at the Iron Horse, in Northampton, Massachusetts, and the Somerville Theater, in Somerville, Massachusetts, came out in 1995 on Plump Records. It includes several of her best songs from *Steady On;* an unreleased track, "Knowing What I Know Now"; and an effective cover of Paul Simon's "Kathy's Song."

Along the way, Colvin developed some impressive alliances and friendships with other musicians. She met Mary-Chapin Carpenter in 1988 when she was opening for k.d. lang in Washington, D.C. Colvin performed on Carpenter's *Shooting Straight in the Dark* and *Come On, Come On* albums. They joined with Roseanne Cash to sing "You Ain't Going Nowhere" at Bob Dylan's 30th Anniversary Concert at Madison Square Garden. In 1990 she performed a duet called "Lost Soul" with Bruce Hornsby for his *A Night on the Town* album. Then, in 1994, she met Tony Bennett and recorded a duet of "Young at Heart" backed by a sixty-piece orchestra at Capitol Studios in Los Angeles. The song was featured in the movie *It Could Happen to You,* released by United Artists. She also had a cameo role as a singer in the Universal Pictures film *Grace of My Heart.*

In September 1996 she released her fifth album, *A Few Small Repairs,* on Columbia. It was her first album of original material since 1992 and received strong reviews. Andrew Abrahams of *People Weekly* (October 7, 1996) called *Repairs* brawnier and rootsier than her previous work: "Even amid the swelling ranks of female artists in pop, Colvin is a vibrant original."

When the Grammy Awards for 1997 were announced in the February 25, 1998, CBS telecast from New York's Radio City Music Hall, Shawn proved to be a double winner in the Record of the Year (single) and Song of the Year categories, both for "Sunny Came

Home," co-written by Colvin and John Leventhal. The single was number one on *Billboard*'s Hot 100 airplay charts and remained at the top of Gavin's Adult Contemporary Charts for a record eleven weeks, tying Celine Dion. *A Few Small Repairs* went platinum in the spring of 1998. Colvin's performance credits in the late 1990s included taking part in the Lilith Fair concert series in both 1997 and 1998. Columbia Records released a Christmas album titled *Holiday Songs and Lullabies* in the fall of 1998. She's currently working on her next record, slated for late summer 2000.

COODER, RY: *Singer, guitarist, banjoist, mandolinist, Mexican tiple, bajo sexto, saz, songwriter. Born Los Angeles, California, March 15, 1947.*

Restless, innovative, with almost unlimited musical curiosity, Ry Cooder left the musical mainstream in the mid-1970s and embarked on a journey to discover unadulterated forms of music. One moment he could be found playing avant-garde rock; the next, roots blues; then country and western and jazz. He combined such sounds with those of gospel, Hawaiian, Tex-Mex, Indian, Malian, Cuban, and Vietnamese musicians. For those who kept pace with him, he illuminated overlooked musical genres with striking results, even if his refusal to be typecast confused the musical establishment. Along the way he has played with the likes of Johnny Cash, John Haitt, Ali Farke Toure, and Buena Vista Social Club.

"When you make records, you're after something," Cooder said in an interview in November 1997. "You want an environmental experience to happen so that you can get that on tape. Because just another record of some other dark people who play guitars—forget it. The record stores are full of them. I'm not interested. I'm interested in the mood. . . . When you get in the habit of trying things out—wow, you can amuse yourself endlessly. That's all I've ever done is try things out."

Born and raised in Southern California, Cooder got his first guitar at age three—a Sears Silvertone tenor four-string given to him by his father. At that time he also started to wear a glass eye after he accidentally poked himself with a knife. After a while he began trying to play along with artists on his parents' folk records. "They bought me a Josh White album when I was eight. That was the first blues I ever heard. I learned all his runs, spent hours with him." He began listening to other folk and blues greats: Skip James, Leadbelly, Woody Guthrie, Blind Blake, Jesse Fuller, and Big Joe Williams. When Ry was ten, his father bought him a six-string Martin guitar and tried to set up a series of lessons, but Ry didn't like the teacher and dropped out.

Ry returned to self-teaching until, at thirteen, he became enthralled with some country-folk records that impelled him to find a teacher of Appalachian finger picking. This led him to what was the center of folk music in Los Angeles, the Ash Grove. As he noted in his biographical material for Warner Brothers Records, "Whenever there was a pretty good player [at the Ash Grove] I'd sit in the front row and watch. If someone like [Reverend] Gary Davis was in town, I'd talk to him, go where he was staying, give him five dollars and get him to play as much as he could while I watched. About a month later, I'd find that I'd start to remember how he did things.

"They used to have party nights at the Ash Grove, when people would get up out of the audience and play. And it seemed like when I was sixteen I was good enough and somebody said 'Get up! Get up!' and they pushed me on stage. I got up and was so scared I was petrified. I played and sweated and people laughed and clapped." This led to his forming a short-lived folk-blues act in 1963 with Jackie DeShannon.

Meanwhile Ry was expanding his musical skills, learning the banjo (he won the Advanced Bluegrass Banjo category in the Topanga Canyon Banjo and Fiddle Contest in 1962); he also perfected his bottleneck guitar playing, spending hours listening to records by Delta bluesmen until he had mastered every inflection.

"Sometime around 1964 or 1965, Taj Mahal showed up in Los Angeles. He was real raggedy and I was raggedy, so we got together and went to the Teenage Fair in Hollywood and sat in a booth for Martin Guitars and just played Delta blues. It was hard and it was good." The two started a rock group called the Rising Sons. The band won some attention from local appearances and they recorded some tracks for Columbia in 1964. The band broke up and Taj and Ry went their separate ways. (Columbia/Legacy put out some of the unreleased tracks as *Rising Sons Featuring Taj Mahal & Ry Cooder* in 1992.) Ry played on Taj Mahal's debut album in 1966.

Ry's next affiliation was with performer-songwriter Don Van Vliet, better known as Captain Beefheart. On the surface it seemed an unlikely alliance—the Zappa-ish Beefheart and the folk-oriented Cooder. But, Cooder proved an excellent session person for Beefheart and his Magic Band's first LP, *Safe As Milk*. Ry arranged two songs for the collection, "I've Grown So Ugly" and "Rolling and Tumbling." He did other session work in the late 1960s, including some with Paul Revere and the Raiders. He also got an assignment in England working with Jack Nitzsche on the score for the film *Candy*. (He worked with Nitzsche again two years later, playing guitar and dulcimer on the soundtrack for *Performance*, about Mick Jagger.) While there he did some backing work for the Rolling Stones's *Let It Bleed* album. He played the distinctive guitar lick on "Honky Tonk Women," though only his mandolin playing on "Love in Vain" remained in the credits. He did a number of other session jobs, including work on the Stones's *Sticky Fingers* album and Little Feat's first album.

With the help of friends Van Dyke Parks and Lenny Waronker, he finally gained a record contract from Warner/Reprise in 1969. The friends coproduced that LP, *Ry Cooder*, released in October 1970 to well-deserved critical acclaim. *Rolling Stone* called him "the finest, most precise bottleneck guitar player alive today, as well as the reviver of the lost art of blues mandolin." Ry demonstrated his finger-picking skills on "Police Dog Blues." Also presented were the songs "Alimony" and "How Can a Poor Man Stand Such Times and Live," a fiddle tune by country musician Blind Alfred Reed.

Cooder was paired with Captain Beefheart's Magic Band in a 1971 cross-country concert tour in support of both artists' new albums. The concerts produced a lot of publicity but not much buyer response to Cooder's LP. Things changed for the better with his second release, *Into the Purple Valley*, which made the pop charts in 1972. It was even more strongly received overseas, particularly in Holland, where it earned a gold record. Cooder played mandolin and bottleneck to good effect on "How Can You Keep on Moving" and "Billy the Kid." Other tracks included Leadbelly's "On a Monday" and a mid-1940s commentary, "F.D.R. in Trinidad."

Cooder continued to examine different aspects of American history in his 1972 album, *Boomer's Story*. The songs ranged from his version of "Rally 'Round the Flag" to one titled "President Kennedy." On "Maria Elena" he demonstrated his talent for classical guitar. On his next LP, *Paradise and Lunch*, released in 1974, Cooder turned his hat around to emphasize gospel music, employing backup singer Bobby King. Several tracks were in that vein, including "If Walls Could Talk" and "Jesus on the Mainline." Other kinds of music were included, ranging from an upbeat "Ditty Wa Ditty" (with jazz pianist Earl "Fatha" Hines) to such ballads as "Tattler" (cowritten by Cooder) and a folk-flavored version of Burt Bacharach's "Mexican Divorce."

In the mid-1970s, Cooder traveled widely to study and work with important but little-publicized musicians. In one direction, he sought out Hawaiian slack-key guitarist Gabby Pahinui to learn his techniques. Besides introducing slack-key stylings into his own work, Ry also arranged for Warner/Reprise to release an album by Pahinui in the United States. In a different vein, Ry went east to Austin, Texas, to study the accordion skills of Flaco Jimenez. As with Pahinui, Cooder not only spent time playing impromptu sessions with Flaco, he also took instructions on Jimenez's style on the accordion.

Both these influences were incorporated in Cooder's fifth album, *Chicken Skin Music* (Reprise, 1976). Slack-key was emphasized on such tracks as "Yellow Roses," "Chloe," and "Always Lift Him Up" (in some cases by

Pahinui, in others by Ry), and Jimenez provided accordion backing on such tracks as "Stand by Me" and "He'll Have to Go" (the latter an old Jim Reeves country hit).

"When Ry Cooder invited me to participate in his music, he checked me out because of my recordings," Jimenez recalled in an interview. "He searched for me and invited me to do that *Chicken Skin* album. That song that I participated in is a favorite of many, 'He'll Have to Go.' . . . I consider him a musical genius."

In 1977 Cooder put together a show featuring Tex-Mex and gospel sounds, with backing provided by Jimenez and four other Tex-Mex musicians, plus vocal support from three black gospel singers, Bobby King, Eldridge King, and Terry Evans. The entourage, called the Chicken Skin Revue, played clubs, campus halls, and theaters around the United States and in Europe. Again, he found greater attention overseas (especially in Germany and Holland) than at home. The tour spawned his sixth LP, the live *Show Time* (1977), recorded in San Francisco.

His next LP departed completely from his earlier offerings. Called *Jazz* (1978) it stressed some of the early jazz material from the 1920s and early 1930s with particular emphasis on the work of Bix Beiderbecke. Other material was inspired by guitarist Joseph Spence, whom Cooder visited in his native Bahamas. Spence's open-tuned guitar style had a great impact on Cooder. In 1978, Cooder again returned to film work with Jack Nitzsche as a special arranger for *Blue Collar;* he also performed the song "Available Space" for Jack Nicholson's movie *Goin' South.*

In 1979 Ry explored other aspects of jazz and pop in his LP *Bop 'Til You Drop,* which Warner Brothers said was the first commercial album to be digitally recorded. It proved his most popular LP up to that time, staying on the charts into 1980 and selling 850,000 copies.

In the 1980s, Cooder continued to demonstrate his multifaceted talents as recording artist, record producer, and composer of motion picture scores. His album credits include *Borderline* (1980) and *Slide Area* (1982). In 1980 he worked on his first soundtrack for director Walter Hill, writing music (along with David Lindley) for *The Long Riders.* Cooder later worked on several more for Hill, including *Southern Comfort* (1981), *Streets of Fire* (1984), *Crossroads* (1986), *Johnny Handsome* (1989), *Trespass* (1992), *Geronimo: An American Legend* (1993), and *Last Man Standing* (1996). For *The Long Riders,* he won the Los Angeles Film Critics Award for best score of 1980. He also performed on such notable soundtrack albums as *The Border* (1982), *Paris, Texas* (for Wim Wenders) (1984), *Alamo Bay* (1985), *Blue City* (1986), *Extreme Prejudice* (1987), *Cocktail* (1988), *Steel Magnolias* (1989), *Cadillac Man* (1990), and *The End of Violence* (1997), another Wim Wenders film.

In 1995, Cooder and his son Joachim produced an anthology of his motion picture work for Warner Brothers called *Music by Ry Cooder.* "About ninety percent of what I know about music, I learned on the job site," he writes in the liner notes, "so I'm grateful to have had the opportunity and encouragement to work out ideas and sounds in a totally intuitive and exploratory style, which is the only style I know.

Get Rhythm, Ry's first solo album since 1982, was released by Warner Brothers in October 1987. Besides scoring commercials (which had been a lucrative area for him), he found time in 1987 to produce a soul album by singers Bobby King and Terry Evans for Rounder Records. Turning his attention to a whole new genre—children's stories—Ry provided the music while comic Robin Williams narrated *Pecos Bill* (Windham Hill, 1988). The effort won a Grammy for Best Recording for Children.

In the '80s, he continued to emphasize the blues. Asked whether the blues might be passé for new fans, he replied: "It's so old that it's new. It has a picturesque energy that represents such an alien, mysterious environment that I think kids will be fascinated by it, no matter how much they actually know about the blues. It's like *Star Wars*—everyone wants to go somewhere they haven't been before."

In the 1990s, Ry continued exploring new frontiers. In September 1992, Kavichandran Alexander of Water Lily Acoustics brought Cooder together with Vishwa Mohan Bhatt, a classically trained musician from Jaipur in North India.

Bhatt, who had studied sitar with Ravi Shankar and his father Manmohan Bhatt, invented a slide guitar called a Mohan vina, which has the body of a guitar but a fret board that allows for twelve "sympathetic" strings in addition to eight others tuned at the head. Using analog equipment and custom-built vacuum-tube electronics, Alexander recorded Bhatt and Cooder after midnight at Christ the King Chapel in Santa Barbara, California. They sat cross-legged on a Persian rug. Cooder's son Joachim, then fourteen, provided rhythm on the dumbek, and Sukhvinder Singh Namdhari played the tabla. Bhatt, a classically trained musician, soon tired of the exercise. But the resulting album, *A Meeting by the River,* dedicated to Gabby Pahinui, won a Grammy.

Cooder's next collaboration, with Malian guitarist Ali Farke Toure, who had previously recorded the albums *The River* and *The Source,* put Ry in more familiar territory. The two first met in London in the summer of 1992. Toure cemented the relationship by giving Cooder a *n'jurkel,* a one-string instrument that was Toure's first instrument. "When I first heard Ali's record, I thought he was playing the blues backwards," Cooder told Philip Sweeney of the *Independent* (March 31, 1994), "but I don't think of him as a blues player now. I think of him as a rugged individual, but also one of the last of the real rural African bush musicians."

In September 1993, Toure, a farmer who grows

onions, carrots, and turnips at his farm on the outskirts of Timbuktu, came to California. He and Cooder rehearsed at Cooder's Santa Monica home and in three days cut *Talking Timbuktu,* which also included Clarence "Gatemouth" Brown on viola, Jim Keltner on drums, Hamma Sankare on calabash, and Oumar Toure on bongos. It was released in 1994 on World Circuit and distributed by Rykodisc. Cooder and Toure also performed some live dates together, including a memorable date at McCabe's Guitar Shop in Santa Monica.

On the album, Toure sings in several languages—Peul, Bambara, Songhai, Tamasheck—about love, spirits, war recruitment, happiness. "There is love, there is culture, there is cattle-rearing, there is criticism, bad government, injustice, racism, education," Toure told Thalia Griffiths of *Reuters* (April 26, 1995). "For us music isn't just a pleasure, it's an important participation in our society." Although Toure's sound has been compared to John Lee Hooker's, he emphasizes that it should be the other way around. "This system spread from Mali to the West African coast, and then by slavery to America." For the second year in a row, Cooder won the Best World Music Grammy. [Toure's album *Niafunke* (1999) on Rykodisc was nominated for a Grammy.]

In 1995, Cooder again found inspiration abroad. For *Dead Man Walking,* Cooder produced and played guitar on "The Long Road" and "The Face of Love," tracks recorded by Pearl Jam singer Eddie Vedder and the late, great Sufi singer Nusrat Fateh Ali Kahn. Cooder participated in the Chieftains' *Long Black Veil* album. He sings and plays slide guitar on "Coast of Malabar" and performs on the instrumental "Dunmore Lassies." In January 1996, Cooder went with the Chieftains to Cuba to make *Santiago,* an album showing the spread of Celtic music in the Latin world.

Just two months later, Cooder would return to Cuba for the most fortuitous two-week recording experience of his life. Nick Gold, the director of World Circuit who had produced *Talking Timbuktu,* invited Cooder to produce a collaboration of Malian and Cuban guitarists. But the Malians had visa problems, and Cooder, who arrived with his wife, Susan, and his percussionist son Joachim decided to make the most of the situation. "So we just said we'll make a record with whoever we can get our hands on," Cooder says. "Of course it was providential. It was the greatest good fortune. 'Cause it gave us a really valuable, rare opportunity."

Cooder met up with veteran Cuban musicians Francisco Repilado (a.k.a. Compay Segundo), then eighty-nine; guitarist Eliades Ochoa, fifty-one; pianist Rubén González, seventy-seven; and singers Ibrahim Ferrer, seventy, and Omara Portuondo ("the Edith Piaf of Cuba"), sixty-seven, for a series of recording sessions at the Egrem studio in Havana, built by RCA in the 1940s. Cooder produced three albums for World Circuit/Nonesuch: *Buena Vista Social Club,* the Afro-Cuban All Stars' *A Toda Cuba le Gusta* (Cooder plays on one track), and *Introducing Rubén González,* the pianist's solo debut. Cooder plays various stringed instruments on *Buena Vista Social Club,* which has sold more than one million copies worldwide.

Buena Vista Social Club, named after a Havana-area social club, sounds just like what it is, a group of veteran Cuban musicians playing their hearts out. Cooder reflected on the importance of the Havana sessions while sitting in his attorney's office, his gray hair pulled back in a ponytail. "Stuff comes through the air at you," he said. "You hear a lot in your life, especially as a musician. . . . Cuban music has for me something really special and compelling, which is kind of bittersweet. It's hard to say melancholy because the Cubans are not melancholy by nature. What they have is this kind of introspective, outgoing approach to music. So you get the energy that sends the music out but you also have this poetic wisdom that they have in their language and in their lyrics."

He compares the music to Japanese haiku. "*Son* is what they call it. A lot of people spent a lot of time refining this stuff. The songs tell a story about life, about people, about what's happening, about what your girlfriend did at the beach."

Folk Roots magazine chose *Buena Vista* as the best album of 1997; it was also awarded a Grammy for Best Traditional Tropical Performance.

In 1998, Cooder returned to Cuba. Although Compay Segundo was not part of the group, Ry gathered Ibrahim Ferrer, Omara Portuondo, Pio Leyva, guitarist Eliades Ochoa, pianist Rubén González, and bass player Orlando "Cacháito" Lopez. He added Gema Cuarto, an ensemble of four Cuban women. *Buena Vista Social Club Presents Ibrahim Ferrer* (a.k.a. "Buena Vista Two") released in May 1999, matched the first album in every respect and was nominated for a Grammy in Best Traditional Tropical Performance, as was Elias Ochoa's album *Sublime Illusion* (Virgin). "Buena Vista Two" incorporates styles ranging from American big band to Cuban-style *son* to songs inspired by Beny Moré. Ibrahim sings Arsenio Rodriguez's *son* "Mami Me Gustó," and duets with Portuondo on "Silencio" and Teresita Garcia Caturia on "Marieta." In 2000, World Circuit/Nonesuch issued *Buena Vista Social Club Presents Omara Portuondo.*

The documentary film by Wim Wenders, *Buena Vista Social Club,* (released in June 1999), won the hearts of people worldwide. Wenders captured the essence of the music, the personalities of people like Compay, Ibrahim, and Omara, and the spirit of the Cuban people. The film includes interviews, footage from the "Buena Vista Two" recording sessions, and from the landmark 1998 concert at Carnegie Hall.

In April 1999, Kavi Alexander's Water Lily Acoustics released a new Cooder project, *Fascinoma,* a jazzy collection featuring trumpeter Jon Hassell,

French-American jazz pianist Jacky Terrasson, and bansuri (flute) player Ronu Majumdar. Cooder produces and plays on the album, recorded using analog equipment at the stone church in Santa Barbara.

In essence Cooder wants to share his experiences with others. "When I was a kid, if somebody gave me a record that I loved, what it did for me I can never describe. It was like having something injected into my body. A world opened every time. If Woody Guthrie did this for me, then I want to do the same thing for other people.

"I play music so that I can feel it. Then you say, 'Let's take that feeling like this spherical ball, like this beach ball, and give it to the world and say, Here, boom, you try it.' And of course when you do that, you do two things. You create opportunites for the musicians to extend the life of their music. . . . The second thing you do is you open the ears and hearts of the rest of the world."

Based on interviews with Ry Cooder and Flaco Jimenez

COOLIDGE, RITA: *Singer, pianist, band leader (R.C. & the Moonpies), Born Nashville, Tennessee, May 1, 1944.*

With a background ranging from blues and R&B to folk and country music, Rita Coolidge was well adjusted. Her vocal talent brought her up through the ranks of backup singers at recording sessions to the threshold of superstar ranks by 1971, a pinnacle she never quite achieved.

Rita's heritage included a mixture of Cherokee Indian and southern white blood. Her father was a Baptist minister, and his children often sang in the church choir. All the children in the family were interested in music from their early years, following the country songs and, later, rhythm and blues in their home city of Nashville and, subsequently, in Memphis. By the time Rita was in her teens, Memphis had become a center of the rhythm and blues upsurge in the mass market paced by such artists of the Stax-Volt Record firm as Booker T. and the M.G.s and Otis Redding.

Rita and her sister Priscilla performed in shows in grade school and sang with small bands at high school dances. Rita continued to add to her musical experience while attending Florida State University where she organized her own band, R.C. & the Moonpies. Priscilla started gaining professional work that brought her in contact with Booker T.; they married and scored a number of chart albums. Rita learned much about R&B and rock from Booker T,. who introduced her to both established and up-and-coming stars.

In the late 1960s, this led to a friendship with Delaney and Bonnie Bramlett, who were then on the Stax label. The Bramletts liked Rita's singing style and added her to their act for several national tours. She began to gain a first-rank reputation with other artists. Leon Russell even wrote his hit song "Delta Lady" as a tribute to Rita.

In the famed Russell–Joe Cocker "Mad Dogs and Englishmen" act that toured the United States and Europe in 1970, Rita was a featured performer, receiving a standing ovation on many occasions for her delivery of the Delaney-Bramlett–Leon Russell composition "Superstar."

Before and after the "Mad Dogs" tour, she was in demand for major album work as a backup vocalist and, in some cases, as a pianist. Among the sessions she worked on were Eric Clapton's first solo album, Boz Scaggs's hit LP *Moments,* and Graham Nash's topselling *Songs for Beginners.*

Late in 1970, Rita was signed by A&M Records as a vocalist. Her debut album, *Rita Coolidge,* was released in 1971. Testifying to the music field's regard for Rita is the list of superstars who sat in: Leon Russell, Steven Stills, Graham Nash, Clarence White of the Byrds, and Booker T. *(See Byrds, The; and Crosby, Stills & Nash.)*

During 1971 and 1972, Rita made the charts with two more A&M albums: *Nice Feelin'* and *The Lady's Not for Sale.* Her marriage to Kris Kristofferson began a new phase in her career as the two toured together and recorded a number of duets in the middle and late 1970s before they separated at the end of the decade. Rita and Kris won two Grammy Awards for Best Vocal Performance by a Duo, one in 1973 for "From the Bottle to the Bottom" and the other in 1975 for a remake of Clyde McPhatter's "Lover Please."

Rita's A&M album credits included *Fall into Spring* (1974), *It's Only Love* (1975), *Anytime Anywhere* (1977), *Love Me Again* (1978), *Satisfied* (1979), *Heartbreak Radio* (1981), *Greatest Hits* (1981), and *Never Let You Go* (1983).

Her solo career gathered momentum in the late 1970s, even as her relationship with Kris Kristofferson unraveled. (They were divorced in 1980.) With Booker T. Jones handling production, she had several major singles hits during those years, starting with a remake of the Jackie Wilson hit "(Your Love Has Lifted Me) Higher and Higher," which rose to number two on U.S. charts the week of June 11, 1977, followed by her version of the Boz Scaggs composition "We're All Alone," which made number seven in *Billboard* the week of October 15, 1977. The next year she had a top 20 single of the Temptations' success "The Way You Do the Things You Do" in February followed by "You," which peaked at number twenty-five in *Billboard* the week of July 29. She began the 1980s with the top 40 single "I'd Rather Leave While I'm in Love," and in 1983 her contribution to the sound track for the James Bond film *Octopussy* resulted in the top 40 release (in August) "All Time High."

Her recording career tapered off in the mid- and late 1980s, though she did have a new album out in 1988, *Inside the Fire.* During those years and into the 1990s she remained active on the concert circuit, with occasional TV appearances, while also doing session vocals on albums by many other artists.

COPPER FAMILY: *Traditional English a cappella singing family from Rottingdean, East Sussex, England. Members as of 1999: Bob Copper, born January 6, 1915; John Copper (Bob's son), born 1949, Jill Copper Dudley (Bob's daughter), and Jon Dudley (Jill's husband), born 1949, and John Copper's children, Ben, Lucy, and Tom; and Jill's children, Mark, Andy, and Sean Barratt.*

For seven generations, the Copper Family has preserved the folk songs of Sussex, England. The quartet of Bob, John, Jill, and Jon represents the latest incarnatin of the singing Coppers who have been instrumental (despite singing unaccompanied) in preserving British folk music for more than a century.

Their songs are rooted in the countryside and farming life of Sussex. They sang about the conditions and the land, entertaining people to keep their spirits up, and preserving the community's heritage. As John Copper noted at a seminar at the Folk Alliance Conference in Memphis in Febuary 1998: "It is an unusual group of songs. There is not a note of complaint. James Brasser Copper [Bob's grandfather] realized the value of songs in bonding the community together."

The first record of the family residing in Rottingdean is 1593. "If it were left to people like the Copper family there wouldn't have been any English colonists at all," Bob Copper joked at the seminar. What the Copper family lacked in adventurousness was the world's gain, however. While most families knew two or three songs, the Copper Family collected more than 100 songs. For centuries the songs, collected from farm laborers and shepherds, were passed on orally. James Brasser Copper, who was born in 1845, the son of John Copper, changed that. When he was eight, Brasser was put to work as a shepherd, eventually learning all the jobs on the farm. But he also learned to read by attending evening classes. He collected songs from the farm gatherings. Migrant laborers would pass through and Brasser would learn their songs.

Brasser, a farm foreman, and his brother Thomas, an innkeeper, sang the family songs at local pubs and gatherings. In 1897, a folk music collector named Kate Lee heard about Brasser and his brother Thomas and traveled to Sussex to seek them out. "She put a bottle of whiskey on the table and said they couldn't leave until the bottle was finished," Bob Copper said. "She was impressed by the two Mr. Coppers of Rottingdean."

One of the songs Lee collected, "Claudy Banks," helped spark the creation of the English Folk Song Society in 1898, now known as the English Folk Dance and Song Society. In 1922 Brasser transcribed as many songs as he could remember, two years before he passed away. Brasser also passed the songs on to his sons James and John and grandsons Bob and Ron. The quartet continued to sing the family songs at taverns, folk clubs, and festivals. Fifteen million listeners heard a BBC broadcast in August 1951. A performance of the Copper family at the Royal Albert Hall in1952 played

a big role in the British music revival. The use of harmony and the singing style of the Coppers influenced such groups as the Watersons, the Voice Squad, and Young Tradition. The whole notion of singing English folk songs in harmony really comes from the Coppers.

In 1964, Folk Legacy released *Bob and Ron Copper: English Shepherd and Farming Songs* (recorded by Peter Kennedy). The album spread the family's music to the United States, which was then at the tail end of its own folk music revival. Other albums released by the Coppers include *Coppersongs* (1988), *Coppersongs 2* (1995), and *Coppersongs 3* (1999). A four-volume LP set of the Copper's music entitled *A Song for Every Season* was put out by Topic in 1971. Their landmark book, *The Copper Family Song Book—A Living Tradition* (published by Coppersongs) 1995, can still be obtained by writing to: 73 Telscombe Road/Peacehaven/East Sussex/England BN107UB.

In addition Bob Copper has written *A Song for Every Season* (William Heinemann Ltd., 1971); *Songs and Southern Breezes* (William Heinemann Ltd., 1973); *Early to Rise* (William Heinemann Ltd., 1976); *Across Sussex with Belloc* (Sutton Publishing Ltd., 1994); and *Bob Copper's Sussex* (S.B. Publications, 1997). Bob also wrote poems for a series of paintings about Sussex.

Written with assistance from folk song collector and musician Jeff Davis

CORDELIA'S DAD: *Rock band turned traditional. Tim Erikson (guitar, banjo, vocals), born 1966; Cath Oss (vocals, bass, dulcimer, accordion), born 1970; and Peter Irvine (drums, vocals), born 1965. Former members include: Tom King, (guitar), left band in 1993; Becky Miller (fiddler) on Comet; Laura Risk (fiddler) from 1995 to 1998; Bradford West (guitar); Steven Maggs (bass); and Jeff Davis (fiddle, mandocello).*

Like Bob Dylan before them, Cordelia's Dad proves the point that it really doesn't matter if you play acoustic or electric. What matters is the quality of the music. The members came from revved-up rock backgrounds but soon found inspiration in the dramatic ballads and traditional American music of the Appalachians. At times the band seemed a bit schizophrenic: singing a cappella at one date or blistering rock 'n' roll the next; opening for Nirvana here, playing an acoustic set at the Folk Alliance Conference, even playing electric and acoustic sets on the same night. Ian Anderson of *Folk Roots* described the band as "American hardcore meets the heart of the Appalachians, with the ghost of Martin Carthy in the wings."

Is there method in their madness? As Tim Erikson, guitarist and lead singer, told Elijah Wald of the *Boston Globe* in September 1994: "We support our research habit through doing rock. We had a tour this summer where we went to Appalachia State University to look at the I.G. Greer Collection, then we went to visit Ellis Wolfe, the best old-time banjo maker I ever heard of, and the climax of our tour was a shape-note sing in Winfield, Alabama. So it's not your average rock 'n' roll tour."

Tim Erikson, Tom King, and Peter Irvine, three college friends from Amherst, Massachusetts, formed the group in 1987. But they disbanded after graduation. Erikson traveled to India and other parts of the world. They reunited to record an album just three days after he returned to the Unites States. "It started out as kind of a joke, like a lot of bands do, so the big surprise to us at first was that it all sounded pretty good," Eriksen told Anderson ("Cordelia's Dad, the Best New Electric Folk Band Since . . . ," August 1993).

Irvine had played country music in Canadian strip clubs and listened to New Wave; King was inspired after seeing Martin Carthy in concert. Eriksen became familiar with traditional American music in college when he came across Frank and Anne Warner's *Traditional American Folk Music* and struck up a friendship with their son, Jeff Warner. When he was traveling in England, Eriksen also met Peter Kennedy, who made copies of the Warners' field recordings featuring Frank Proffitt, Lee Monroe Presnell, and Nathan Hicks available to Eriksen. "I love the tunes," Eriksen told Anderson. "They're just fantastic, and not the kind of thing that appears in other popular music. I get a little tired of the blues scale and the major mode after a while, and want to hear some minor stuff, or whatever."

They recorded their debut with Tim O'Heir in Boston. *Cordelia's Dad* was released on OKra Records (Normal in Europe) in 1990, and the album they describe as "folknoise" made top 10 college lists. The group followed its debut with *How Can I Sleep?* on OKra/Normal in 1992, produced by Dave Schramm. The second album reflected a blending of traditional and rock influences. The following year they released the acoustic-flavored nine-song EP *Joy Fun Garden* on Return to Sender (and Normal) in Europe. That year they were joined by Cath Oss on bass and vocals. King left, marking Cordelia's Dad's transition to a more acoustic sound. On October 31, 1994, they recorded *Comet* for Omnium (Normal in Europe). The album, which received a four-star review from *Rolling Stone*, reflects the group's change. The first eleven tracks are acoustic traditional, but then the band suddenly rocks out on the last track. Fiddler Becky Miller joined the group for *Comet*, while another fiddler, Laura Risk, joined the band from 1995 to 1998.

After the arrival of Oss, the band also became interested in shape-note singing, both a notation and an unaccompanied singing style that has religious roots. During a concert at the 1996 Folk Alliance Conference in Washington, D.C., the versatile band sang a couple of shape-note songs and also accompanied themselves on banjo (Eriksen), bass (Oss), and bodhran (Irvine) on

traditional American songs that they had discovered in the Warner Collection. (Eriksen and Oss also sing in a shape-note singing group called Northampton Harmony, which released an album called *The Hookes' Regular Sing* on Hazmat in 1996.)

By the mid-1990s Cordelia's Dad had developed a reputation for its iconoclastic ways. Their touring partners demonstrate their versatility: from Martin Carthy and Archie Fisher to Nirvana, Lemonheads, the Ass Ponys, and the Dead Milkmen. Despite their move to acoustic music, in 1996 Scenescof released a limited-edition live album called *Road Kill*, featuring the electrified Cordelia's Dad. (For a time they called themselves io for hard rock concerts.) In 1996 Omnium reissued the band's first two albums, which had been released on the now-defunct OKra. Along the way their songs have been included in compilations, such as "Narragansett Bay" on the 1995 Rhino Records *Global Gumbo* album, and "George Collins" on a *Folk Roots* "FROOTS" sampler the same year.

In 1998 the group signed with Appleseed Recordings, which released the highly acclaimed album *Spine*, produced by Steve Albini. The album, nominated for an Indie Award, is all acoustic and was recorded almost entirely without overdubs. It includes banjo and fiddle tunes, ballads, and a cappella songs. The group also has contributed to albums by banjoist Dwight Diller and Tony Trischka, as well as a cover of "How Can I Keep from Singing" for *Where Have All the Flowers Gone: The Songs of Pete Seeger,* released in 1998 by Appleseed.

COTTEN, ELIZABETH: *Singer, guitarist, banjoist, songwriter. Born Chapel Hill, North Carolina, January 5, 1895; died Syracuse, New York, June 29, 1987.*

It seems only natural that the folk music classic "Freight Train" would have its origin in the Seeger household. However, it wasn't the result of folk music jams among Pete Seeger, his friends and siblings, or something discovered by Pete's father, musicologist Charles Seeger, or his archivist friends the Lomaxes. Instead it came from an unusual source—Elizabeth Cotten, a lady who worked as the Saturday maid at Charles and Ruth Seeger's home in the Washington, D.C., area, ironing, baking bread, and performing other chores for the family that included Mike and Peggy Seeger and their two sisters.

Cotten, born and raised in North Carolina, had learned to play guitar in her youth, starting about age eight. She kept polishing her skills until she was about fifteen, when she was married and began working as a housekeeper. Her new responsibilities, plus the feeling among deeply religious people of her region that it was sacrilegious to play secular music, in time caused her to put guitar playing aside.

Some years later she moved to Washington, D.C., where she got a job in a downtown department store.

One day a young Peggy Seeger strayed from other family members and showed up alone and in tears in front of the store. Cotten came out and took the girl in hand, returning her to her family in Chevy Chase, Maryland. Very happy about this turn of events, Charles and Ruth asked if Elizabeth could work for them on weekends, which proved a fruitful arrangement for all parties.

A few years later, when the teenaged Mike and Peggy Seeger were carrying on family tradition by learning folk guitar and banjo, they belatedly discovered Libba's (a nickname coined by Peggy) musical talents. One day watching Mike practice in the kitchen while she was working there, Libba came over to tell him she knew the guitar herself. He gave her the instrument and was enthralled by her performance, which included original material. Before long the whole family was listening excitedly to their new discovery, finding her composition "Freight Train," which she had composed in 1903, particularly striking.

For the next few years, Libba often demonstrated her work for visitors to the Seeger home and as the folk boom took hold performed at folk festivals as a soloist or on many occasions with Mike Seeger's group, the New Lost City Ramblers. Musician, writer, and editor Ed Badeaux reminisced in Sing Out! ("Please Don't Tell What Train I'm On," September 1964) about his first meetings with Cotten. In the fall of 1953, he visited the Seegers, he wrote, "After we had been there a day or so, we met Libba and she proceeded to more than live up to her advance reputation. A small, slightly built woman with a great natural dignity, she calmly and deftly played a quite intricate two-finger picking style on guitar. Unlike many left-handed guitar pickers who decide to learn in reverse, Libba did not reverse the order of the strings. But she did fret with her right hand and pick the strings with the thumb and index finger of her left. Not reversing the strings meant that Libba's thumb picked the melody string while the nail of her first finger played a sharp pattern on the bass strings."

Though Cotten's repertoire included other originals besides "Freight Train" as well as her versions of traditional folk songs such as "Shake Sugaree" and folk music by other writers, her fame has consistently rested on that one song. (Badeaux, it might be noted, also contributed some verses to it.) But it took persistence by her friends to insure others didn't get credit for it. As Badeaux noted, during Peggy Seeger's tour of England and Europe in the late 1950s, while in London, two Englishmen came up after a concert with a tape recorder and asked if she would tape "Freight Train" for them. She obliged, and they soon proceeded to have singer Nancy Whisky make a disk, which became a major hit in the United Kingdom. The two credited themselves with writing it, however; incensed, Peggy helped set the wheels in motion for a lawsuit on Libba's behalf that eventually was settled out of court. In 1958, Libba's own version was included in her Folkways album, Folk-songs and Instrumentals With Guitar (a.k.a. Negro Folksongs and Tunes), which was recorded by Mike Seeger. In 1967, Folkways released another album, Elizabeth Cotten Volume 2: Shake Sugaree, also recorded by Seeger.

During the late 1950s and into the '60s Cotten performed at a growing number of concerts and festivals, including sets at the Newport Folk Festival. She also had some occasional TV exposure, including appearances on Pete Seeger's 1966 Rainbow Quest program. Problems of attribution for "Freight Train" continued into the early part of the '60s. Peter, Paul and Mary included it in their In the Wind album, with writing credit given to the trio plus someone called Mazzetti. It turned out a rights analyst at Warner Brothers concluded it was in the public domain and its arrangement open for claimants. When Peter, Paul and Mary became aware of the situation, they made sure the attribution was changed wherever possible.

Cotten continued to be active in the '70s and into the '80s, finding excellent response from audiences at major folk festivals. In 1979 Folkways released Elizabeth Cotten Volume 3: When I'm Gone. In 1984 she received the National Endowment for the Arts National Heritage Fellowship Award. In the Grammy voting for that year (announced on the TV awards show of February 26, 1985) her Arhoolie album, Elizabeth Cotten Live! was named Best Ethnic or Traditional Folk Recording. In the last years of her life, a video of her work, Elizabeth Cotten, was prepared by Stefan Grossman's Guitar Workshop and eventually released by Vestapol/Rounder in 1994. In the video, Mike Seeger sat with her and asked her about her career, while suggesting she play certain tunes. Besides her inimitable version of "Freight Train" she played some two dozen more, including "Wilson Rag," "Jesus Is Tenderly Calling Today," "Vestapol," "Old Georgia Buck," and "Rattler." For the last two songs, Cotten displayed considerable prowess on the banjo.

In her later years, Libba made her home in Syracuse, New York, (where she moved in 1978); she died there at ninety-two in the summer of 1987. The fact that she was still contributing to the folk-music tradition at her advanced age had been celebrated in Jon Pareles's New York Times article "Elizabeth Cotten at 90, Bigger than the Tradition" (January 7, 1983, section 3). After her death, her banjo and guitar were placed in the permanent collections of the Smithsonian Institution. In the 1989 photo documentary I Dream a World published by Stewart, Tabori, and Chang, she was one of seventy-five influential Afro-American women included in the coverage. Among the first releases following the Smithsonian's acquisition of Folkways in the late 1980s was the Cotten CD Freight Train and Other North Carolina Folk Songs, a reissue of her 1958 LP.

She influenced such performers as the Grateful Dead, who often performed "Shake Sugaree," and Taj Mahal, who toured with her. In the 1990s her other two Folkways LPs were reissued by Smithsonian/Folkways on CD. Over the years she was also included on various compilations: *Folk Music USA* and *Folk Song America Volume 2* on Folkways; the *Second Annual Farewell Reunion* on Mercury; *New Lost City Ramblers/20th Anniversary Concert* on Flying Fish; *Blues with a Feeling* on Vanguard; and *Mean Old World: The Blues from 1940 to 1994, A Fish That's a Song,* and *Smithsonian/Folkways American Roots Collection* on Smithsonian/Folkways. In 1998 Smithsonian also released material from Mike Seeger's field recordings of the 1950s and 1960s, *Close to Home: Old Time Music from Mike Seeger's Collection 1952–1967.* Among the thirty-eight tracks in the set is Cotten singing "In the Sweet Bye and Bye," which she recorded at home in 1952.

CRARY, DAN: *Singer guitarist, songwriter. Born Kansas, September 29, 1939.*

In modern folk music, it's never been too unusual for an artist to combine academic and musical backgrounds. Sometimes earning one's primary living as a college teacher was an economic necessity. In the case of flatpicking guitar exponent Dan Crary, he continued to hold a position as full-time associate professor of speech communication at California State University–Fullerton at a time when it seemed quite possible for him to support his family with his folk and bluegrass activities alone.

It wasn't that he didn't think about the matter from time to time. He told Mark Boehm of the *Los Angeles Times* ("Flatpicking Professor Enjoys a Double Life," Calendar section, June 4, 1989), "I bought into the 'music is for fun but it's frivolous' idea. It wasn't until I was in my 50s that I began to realize that what I had in my hand when I played the guitar was something important. Now I see what the traditional arts do for people, how it gentles them out and makes them nice to each other."

But he enjoyed teaching, and after a while learned to live with the suggestion that he could do more justice to either vocation if he chose one rather than continuously switching back and forth. "I used to worry about that issue," he told Boehm, "but music does not know these distinctions. It selects lots of unlikely people. I'm an ambitious person, but if I never achieve more than the way my life is today, I have no cause for complaint."

He grew up in a very religious, evangelical family in a small town in Kansas. As might be expected, he was exposed to church music in his early years, but when he was twelve, in 1952, his attention was captured by the sound of a guitar played by a local performer on a country music radio program. It was an odd choice; he hadn't seen anyone playing the instrument, and his peer group tended to favor accordion or piano.

He commented to Boehm, "It was a very esoteric instrument, and I'll be damned if I know why my parents agreed to buy me one. I was into nothing. I was kind of a nerdish kid who didn't have much going on. It may be that was the first thing I showed any initiative about."

As he told *Dirty Linen* in 1995, "When I started playing guitar, nobody was playing guitar. . . . For about two years of my playing the only other guitar player that I knew was the guy who sold me the guitar, an accordion teacher who was trying to teach me standard guitar lessons, which I resisted mightily but I still went to them. It wasn't until Elvis in the late 1950s that the guitar really took off, so it was a very lonely thing to do wanting to play traditional music on an acoustic guitar. The number of flatpicking instruction books was zero."

In the mid-1950s, Dan sought opportunities to play, entering local talent shows, and for a while joined a group that entertained at hospitals and orphanages around parts of the Midwest. In 1957 he entered the Moody Bible Institute in Chicago to study for the ministry. As it happened, the school was near the Gate of Horn, where many of the most talented musicians and singers in the burgeoning folk field were featured. Crary read the billboards but didn't attend any concerts. "When you're at Moody Bible College, you don't go to nightclubs. I was still sitting around working out traditional arrangements to play for people if I ever got the chance."

In 1960, deciding the ministry wasn't his forte, he entered Kansas University to study philosophy and speech communication. After graduation, he worked on graduate degrees in theology at institutes in Southern California and Louisville, Kentucky. Over the years he had developed his skills as a flatpicking guitarist from studying techniques of people like Don Reno, Doc Watson, and, in the early '60s, Clarence White.

Settled in Louisville, a hotbed of bluegrass music, he began to spend more of his spare time jamming with other young instrumentalists, which eventually resulted in the formation of the Bluegrass Alliance at the end of the '60s. He recorded an album with the band, *The Bluegrass Alliance,* and his solo debut (issued in 1970), *Dan Crary: Bluegrass Guitar,* both released on the American Heritage label. The Bluegrass Alliance project established the guitar for the first time as a lead instrument in bluegrass. On the solo LP, almost every track originated as a fiddle tune that was transposed to guitar by Dan, including such memorable tracks as "Blackberry Blossom," "Forked Deer," and "Salt Creek."

Now considered a rising star in the bluegrass field, Dan decided to forgo that opportunity while at the same time changing his academic goals. He told Boehm, "I'm very interested in ultimate questions, and I found my theological study to be fascinating and relevant. But I also knew damn well that in conservative circles a guy like me who likes to play guitar, drink a little wine, and read outrageous books didn't fit in. I was diskjockeying on a country radio station, and I was playing at the Red Dog Saloon. It was no moral problem for me—Jesus ate with publicans and sinners, and I played bluegrass for them. Nobody [at the seminary] gave me a hard time about it, but I knew that eyebrows were raised. Eventually I would have run into a conflict with it. So, at age 30, I started all over again, still resisting music."

He again moved back to Kansas, this time seeking a doctorate in speech communication. He focused on studying, only taking on occasional performing gigs until he earned his Ph.D. and got his teaching position at Cal State–Fullerton in 1974. The job suited him, and he was still teaching his course full-time in the 1990s with his family (his wife, a professor and consultant in business communications, brought two daughters from a previous marriage).

Once settled in at Cal State, Dan began to expand his musical activities, working closely with bluegrass fiddler Byron Berline and banjoist John Hickman, who formed the nucleus of Berline's mid-1970s band, Sundance. One product of that alignment was the MCA album *Byron Berline and Sundance.* While he went on his first solo performing tour of Europe during that period, classroom commitments prevented him from going on concert dates with Sundance in behalf of the MCA disk and another musician took his place. The same thing happened later for a State Department–sponsored series that took Berline, Hickman, and a stand-in for Crary to North Africa, Israel, and Katmandu.

In 1977, Crary's second solo album, *Lady's Fancy,* was issued by Rounder. Among the tracks was his guitar version of Byron Berline's composition "Huckleberry Hornpipe." As David McCarty of *Acoustic Guitar* pointed out, Crary's interpretation was so well crafted that, since then, the number had been far more popular with flatpickers than fiddlers.

As Crary told McCarty ("The Living Tradition," January/February 1991), adapting songs associated with other instruments to the guitar called for in-depth knowledge of the original melody and of the differences between instruments. "There's no formula I can point to. Just because 'Limerock' was thought up on a fiddle doesn't mean it must be my goal to play it exactly as it was played on a fiddle. I start with an appreciation of what the tune sounded like on the other instrument, and the way you get that is to bloody well listen to it played on the other instrument.

"If you want to play bluesy, go to some blues players and hear how they did it and remember that and reflect on it and get inside it and appreciate it and love it. Then when you go back to making the decisions of how you're going to play it on your own instrument, keep that in the back of your mind and let it influence you. You make music from your soul, but your soul needs a little education."

In the 1980s and '90s, Crary continued his collaboration with Berline and friends, for a time as the Berline, Crary, and Hickman trio, later as the group called California. In the mid-1990s, the latter group comprised, besides the three long-time friends, bassist-songwriter Steve Spurgin and singer-mandolinist John Moore. Albums resulting from those lineups came out on the Sugar Hill label, including *Berline, Crary, Hickman: Now We Are Four;* and a California collection released in 1996.

Dan's solo collections on the Sugar Hill label during the '80s and '90s included *Dan Crary: Guitar, Take a Step Over,* and the 1994 *Jammed If I Do.* In 1991 he took a slightly different creative turn, preparing an album (produced by Nightnoise's Billy Oskay) of what *Dirty Linen* described as Celtic-tinged contemporary instrumentals. As Crary told the magazine, his goal with music employing both six-string and twelve-string guitars "was simply to make a nice album, but in a different kind of studio environment. I just wanted to make a nice sounding album, and I wanted to do it with a recording strategy that would get it played on the radio more." The album, *Thunderation,* came out on Sugar Hill's Pamlico Sound Series, and won enough attention to support work on a second collection in that vein with Oskay as producer.

In 1990 he was asked to work with Michelle Shocked on her *Arkansas Traveler* recording project. His contributions included playing a guitar version of another old fiddle tune, "Worth the Wait."

By the late 1990s, Crary's credits included work on several movie and TV sound tracks, and also teaching at many flatpicking workshops at festivals and other gatherings across the United States and Canada and in many other parts of the world, from Japan and the South Pacific to many European nations. He also authored several instructional books on flatpicking techniques.

He expressed great confidence about continuation of the trend to greater worldwide interest in acoustic guitar playing. He told McCarty, "Traditional music is a rare and powerful and beautiful thing. . . . I'm actively optimistic that more people are listening to traditional music. They're standing around a campfire late at night, just as their ancestors did in barbaric times, with their shadows thrown on the side of a tree, and they're playing fiddles and banjos. And those slightly bacchanalian revelers give me a lot of hope for humanity."

CRAY, ROBERT: *Singer, guitarist, songwriter, band leader. Born Columbus, Georgia, August 1, 1953.*

Anyone who has been following the blues scene for the past two decades, even if only with a passing interest, will surely know of Robert Cray. With his soul-soaked singing and his clean, slick guitar playing, he has been one of the main forces behind the modern blues comeback of the '80s and '90s. Making his commercial debut in 1980, a time in which the pop scene was dominated by British new wave bands, Cray helped revitalize interest in a music genre that had been in hibernation since the mid-'60s.

Though he was born in Georgia, Cray called many places home during his childhood since his father was in the military. The Cray family lived in Virginia, California, and even Germany (where Robert began studying the piano) before settling down in Tacoma, Washington. His parents' fondness for Ray Charles, Otis Rush, Buddy Guy, and other Chicago blues artists helped steer Robert toward R&B and blues, yet the influence of such '60s rock bands as the Beatles and Jimi Hendrix can be heard in many of his tunes. Around the time of the British invasion Cray gave up piano to play guitar. "I was just 12, but being an Army brat had to do with why I stuck to it. I was pretty shy, not too outgoing. So when we'd move around I just had my friend in my hand, my guitar" (*People Weekly,* April 13, 1987). Shortly thereafter, Cray formed his first band, One Way Street. The rock-influenced One Way Street band died out after the "Master of the Telecaster," Albert Collins, performed at a graduation dance at Cray's high school. After meeting Collins at the dance, Cray decided to devote his life to more roots-based music playing.

In 1974 the first Robert Cray Band was formed (with Cray's childhood friend and bass player Richard Cousins); he immediately started touring the Northwest club and concert circuit and never looked back. Life on the road wasn't easy, but Robert showed that playing music was his life. He and Cousins would hitchhike seventy miles just to get to rehearsals, and when they weren't rehearsing, the Robert Cray Band would play three hundred nights a year, three to four sets a night, often backing visiting blues artists, including Collins himself. In 1977 Cray became friends with John Belushi during the filming of *Animal House* in Eugene, Oregon; in the film, Robert had a nonplaying part as a member of the fictional band Otis Day and the Knights. At the time, Cray was playing with a harmonica player and vocalist by the name of Curtis Salgado. Belushi actually adopted Salgado's goatee-and-shades look for the movie *The Blues Brothers.* Although Belushi was a good connection and a good friend (he would call Robert to ask him who he should have on *Saturday Night Live*), it was Cray's meeting with producer Bruce Bromberg at the 1977 San Francisco Blues Festival that was crucial for his musical career.

After being blown away with Robert's playing at the Blues Festival, Bromberg and co-producer Dennis Walker decided to produce the Robert Cray Band's first album. In 1978 *Who's Been Talkin'* was cut in just two sessions, and featured Cray on guitar and vocals, Cousins on bass, Salgado on harmonica and vocals on one track, some horns, and two different rhythm sections. The album was shelved for two years, when the short-lived Tomato label picked it up and released it in 1980. Unfortunately for Cray, Tomato went broke shortly after *Who's Been Talkin'* was released, and Cray's album died commercially.

Cray was gaining a loyal following, especially in the Northwest, but he needed another commercial break; enter HighTone Records. The HighTone label was created by Bromberg and Walker in order to record more Robert Cray Band albums, since the recording interest in blues at the time was minimal at best. The road was paved for Cray, and he didn't disappoint. His second album, *Bad Influence,* released in 1983, showed Cray's depth and creativity. Featuring Cray, Cousins, Dave Olson on drums, Mike Vannice on tenor sax and keyboards, and Warren Rand on alto sax, the new Robert Cray Band wrote all of the tunes for the album but two (with producers Bromberg, under the name of D. Amy, and Walker, writing and co-writing six of the ten songs). One of the cover tunes, "Got to Make a Comeback" by Eddie Floyd, announced Cray's desire to rise up out of the disappointment of his debut album. Indeed, he did make a comeback, garnering good record sales (helped in part by a spot on TV's "The Old Grey Whistle Test"), and catching the attention of two renowned blues artists: Albert King covered the powerful tune "Phone Booth," and Eric Clapton did his own version of the beautiful title track.

The Robert Cray Band was beginning to headline top venues, and two years later recorded their third LP, *False Accusations,* also on the HighTone label. Cray and company (now without Vannice and Rand, but with Peter Boe on keyboards) continued to sparkle on this album filled with ballads about adultery. *False Accusations,* a top 200 release, topped the U.S. and U.K. indie charts and prepared Cray for the success that was to come. Cray's breakthrough came later that year on *Showdown!,* an album that featured the playing of three guitar greats—Cray, Johnny Copeland, and Cray's longtime friend and inspiration Albert Collins. Released on Alligator Records, *Showdown!* introduced Cray to a much wider audience. The trio's album gave each artist his first Grammy and sold over a quarter of a million records.

Robert was on a roll. His guitar playing was getting increasingly better, he was establishing a spot in the international music scene, and he even had a Grammy under his belt. In 1986 Cray signed onto a major label, Mercury Records, and recorded what was to be his most successful release to date, *Strong Persuader.* Indeed, it was a strong persuader: the album handed Cray his second straight Grammy, reached double-platinum status, entered the top 20, and became the biggest blues hit since the mid-60s. Still with Cousins, Boe, and Olson, Cray exhibited his maturity on soul-based ballads such as "Right Next Door (Because of Me)" and showed that his blues/rock/funk/soul hybrid could work on the smash hit "Smoking Gun." As usual, the basis for the songbook is love, and all of the good and bad things that come from it. In an interview with Michael Segell,

Cray explained: "We're a bunch of guys who live on the road and try to keep relationships going. But it never works out, and that's what we write about" (*Cosmopolitan,* February 1987). A big difference between this album and the three previous ones was the addition of the Memphis Horns. Wayne Jackson (trumpet, trombone) and Andrew Love (tenor sax) rounded out the band's sound, hearkening back to the Stax soul recordings of the 60s.

Strong Persuader aside, 1986 was still a busy year for Cray. In October he was invited by Keith Richards to play at Chuck Berry's sixtieth birthday concert, which was later made into the film *Hail! Hail! Rock 'n' Roll.* In November he made his network TV debut with his appearance on NBC's *Late Night with David Letterman.* Later that month, he won a record six W.C. Handy awards at the seventh National Blues Awards. The following month, Robert taped a special for U.K. TV with Tina Turner, which appeared on HBO in 1987. Cray played the world over in 1987, including a one-month U.S. tour with Eric Clapton, appearances throughout Europe, and finally ending the year off in Japan, where he joined Clapton once again.

Cray and bandmates went to sunny Los Angeles, California, in 1988 to record their fifth album, *Don't Be Afraid of the Dark.* With the same Grammy-winning lineup of Cousins, Boe, Olson, the Memphis Horns, and the excellent producing skills of Bromberg and Walker, Cray added the raucous saxophone playing of David Sanborn and proved that his reputation as the best new blues artist in two decades was right on key. The album peaked on the British charts at number thirteen, reached number thirty-two on the U.S. charts, handed Robert his third straight Grammy, and sold more than half a million records.

In 1990 Cray once again found himself in Europe, this time opening at the Royal Albert Hall in London, playing with Clapton, Collins, Jimmie Vaughan, Buddy Guy, and pianist Johnnie Johnson. Later that year the Robert Cray Band released its sixth album, *Midnight Stroll.* Still with the Memphis Horns, but this time with a new rhythm section, this album and the 1992 release of *I Was Warned* showed Robert moving away from the blues and into soul and R&B. Utilizing his first chance to produce his own album, Cray showed his dark and somber side on the 1993 release *Shame + a Sin.* Relying less on the slick studio arrangements that characterized *Midnight Stroll* and *I Was Warned,* Cray returned to what made him the hit of the '80s: his sweet, soulful voice and his 1964 rosewood-necked Fender Stratocaster. On *Shame + a Sin,* Albert Collins became the first guest guitarist to lay down some licks on a Robert Cray Band project.

Touring consistently throughout the '90s, the Robert Cray Band (now featuring Jimmy Pugh on keyboards, Kevin Hayes on drums, and Karl Sevareid on bass) continued to pump out records. Focusing on Cray's voice,

the 1995 release *Some Rainy Morning* was the first Cray album without horns. Looking back to the past and into the future of the blues, the album is nostalgic yet modern. It was followed in 1997 by *Sweet Potato Pie,* recorded in Memphis, Tennessee. With the return of the Memphis Horns, the album attempts to recreate the Southern-style R&B of the '60s and early '70s while still remaining contemporary.

Although his mass market popularity seems to have diminished since the '80s, Cray continues to play on and impress. *Midnight Stroll, I Was Warned, Shame + a Sin,* and *Some Rainy Morning* each earned Cray a Grammy nomination. Robert (along with other greats such as B.B. King and Clapton) earned his fourth Grammy win for his work on "SRV Shuffle," from 1996's *A Tribute to Stevie Ray Vaughan.* Cray's music has been heard in half a dozen movies, including the 1996 Critic's Choice, *The Truth About Cats and Dogs.* Though many critics claim that his music isn't really blues, one need only look at the words and actions of top blues artists in order to see that Cray's reputation as one of the best modern blues artists is an accurate one. In the late '70s, Muddy Waters took him under his wing, calling Cray his "new adopted son." Clapton has toured, written songs, and shared albums with Robert, saying of him, "He's the only player I know who's absolutely, totally authentic." During the 1991 San Francisco Blues Festival, B.B. King unstrapped his beloved guitar, Lucille, and handed it to Cray to play; it was the first time that anyone besides B.B. had played Lucille in public. John Lee Hooker invited Cray to play on three of his hit albums: *The Healer* (1989), *Mr. Lucky* (1991), and *Boom Boom* (1992). In 1999 Rykodisc released *Take Your Shoes Off,* which earned Cray a Best Contemporary Blues Grammy. George Thorogood wrapped it up nicely: "He can sing like Sam Cooke, and he plays as well as he sings, and he looks like Sidney Poitier. The guy's got it all."

Entry by Adam Seidman

CROCE, A.J.: *Singer, pianist, songwriter. Born Bryn Mawr, Pennsylvania, September 28, 1971.*

A talented musician, A.J. Croce had little in the way of memories of his father, the late, great Jim Croce, who died in a plane crash only weeks before his son's second birthday. A.J.'s musical interests, at least through the mid-'90s, tended toward R&B and rock rather than the pop folk favored by his dad and folksinger mother, but he didn't completely ignore the family folk roots either.

Though he was born in Pennsylvania, by July '73 he had moved with his parents to a new home in San Diego, California. Hardly had the Croces settled in to their new environment when Jim Croce met his tragic end. As A.J. recalled, "Right after this, my mother decided we should leave the country for a while. We packed up the car and drove to Quapos, Costa Rica, where we lived for almost a year." Soon after he and his mother returned to the United States, he was enrolled in a boarding school in Arizona. Once more fate struck the family a harsh blow when, in November 1975, four-year-old A.J. was stricken with an illness that left him completely blind. Fortunately, after many operations and considerable medical expenses, in the end he did regain use of his left eye.

San Diego became home base for the Croces, and remained so into the 1990s. At six, A.J. began to play the piano, slowly picking up performing skills on his own. His mother backed his interest, though he got no formal piano lessons until he was twelve, a series that began almost at the same time he got the chance to make his public debut. He noted, "I was paid $20. And right then, I knew I would play music for the rest of my life."

By then he was listening to a wide range of music, starting initially with his father's collection of old 78-rpm discs that included material by Louis Jordan, Cecil Gant, and ragtime great Jelly Roll Morton. Later he added newer recordings by artists like Ray Charles, Randy Newman, Tom Waits, and a variety of blues and rhythm & blues performers. By his early high school years, in the mid-1980s, he was beginning to try his hand at original songs. Starting in 1984, he regularly played keyboards at a club founded by his mother, Croce's Top Hat Bar and Grille, a venue that also featured other promising local artists.

By 1988 he had joined his first band, the Hottentots, playing Vox Continental organ on a repertoire ranging from R&B and blues to high-powered rock. At seventeen, he decided to leave school and focus on solo piano gigs several nights a week at the family club and other San Diego bars while performing on weekends with the R&B group Romy Kaye and the Swinging Gates. By the early '90s he had a sizable following that insured good audiences for his Top Hat Bar and Grille appearances. In 1992 he was voted the Best Jazz Artist in the San Diego Music Awards. During one of A.J.'s sets that year, Ron Goldstein, then president and CEO of Beverly Hills–based Private Music Records, signed him to the label.

His debut album, A.J. Croce, came out in the spring of 1993 and won some critical attention. Meanwhile, Croce was beginning to widen his potential audience by playing small clubs as a headliner and larger venues as opening act for well-known artists. By the time his second disc, That's Me in the Bar, came out in early 1995, he had played in many parts of the United States and Canada and taken part in four different European tours. Noting that his debut album had been categorized as a jazz work, he argued that it certainly wasn't restricted to that genre: "As categories go, I would call my music rhythm and blues, with elements of New Orleans jazz, rock & roll, country, even folk." As proof, he pointed to the fact he had opened for such diverse performers as

country's Willie Nelson and Lyle Lovett, soul star Aretha Franklin, blues great B.B. King, bluegrass luminary Béla Fleck, and, among others, Morphine, Guru, and the Neville Brothers.

As was the case in his first album, That's Me in the Bar featured many new songs by Croce. Backing musicians included Ry Cooder on mandolins and guitar, Billy Payne of Little Feat on piano, David Hidalgo of Los Lobos on accordion, and producer Jim Keltner on drums. When the disc came out, Croce said, "I hope the release of my second album will clarify the broad influences in my music," influences that, to some extent, included those of his own father.

CROCE, JIM: *Singer, guitarist, accordionist, songwriter. Born Philadelphia, Pennsylvania, January 10, 1942; died Natchitoches, Louisiana, September 20, 1973.*

The countless times that Jim Croce's voice has beamed forth on rock and folk radio programs have brought acclaim far surpassing anything that accrued in his short lifetime. It is generally agreed that had he lived, this sensitive, highly creative folksinger turned rock artist might have become one of the brightest stars of the 1970s.

He grew up in south Philadelphia, where his initial musical training began with the accordion at age six. It was not until he was eighteen, working in a toy store and playing the blues in his spare time, that he bought his first guitar, a twelve-string. He became reasonably proficient on it while attending Villanova University, where he was emcee of a three-hour folk and blues show on the school radio station. While folk and blues were his primary interests, the various bands he formed during his Villanova years (he graduated in 1965) played everything from rock to folk and pop ballads. He was a warm, gregarious individual and made many lasting friendships during the college years, including one with Tommy West, later of the team of Cashman and West.

He loved music, but for a while after he left college it was mainly a sideline. One of his first jobs was selling ads for a black rhythm and blues station. After that, he began a series of jobs as a laborer. On one of these, he broke a finger with a sledgehammer, but he was able to regain the ability to play guitar by developing a picking style that didn't depend on the finger. In 1966, he got married and with his wife, Ingrid, worked at a summer camp in Pine Grove, Pennsylvania, teaching guitar and ceramics. In the fall he began a teaching job at a ghetto junior high school in south Philadelphia.

It wasn't easy, but Jim persevered until he and Ingrid decided to go to Mexico under a fellowship grant she received to study Mexican pottery. When they returned to the United States in 1967, they heeded the suggestions of Tommy West to put their folk music ability to work and soon were performing in coffeehouses and small clubs in the New York area. They also managed to get a recording contract with Capitol, which issued the LP *Jim and Ingrid Croce,* a disc that quickly sank without a trace.

At the end of the 1960s, the Croces moved onto an old farm in the Philadelphia area and lived a hand-to-mouth existence during 1969 and 1970. Jim eked out a meager living by working at a series of odd jobs, but at one point was forced to pawn his collection of guitars to make ends meet. He finally found a reasonably steady job as a truck driver, and composed new songs on his many long hauls to occupy his mind. When he had a half dozen completed that he liked, he recorded them on a tape cassette that he submitted to Cashman and West, who increasingly were more concerned with management than their performing activities.

Cashman and West liked the demo and arranged for Jim to record some of the songs at the Hit Factory studios in New York in the fall of 1971. ABC Records signed him, and Jim completed enough tracks for an album in early 1972. His debut LP, *You Don't Mess Around with Jim,* came out in the spring. Both title song and album made the charts after a while, and while they didn't zoom right to the top, the reception was promising. In the fall of 1972, another single from the album, "Operator," gained considerable airplay and also appeared on national pop lists. There was eager expectancy among many critics for his follow-up LP. When that collection, *Life and Times,* came out in early 1973, it confirmed that Croce was indeed a writer and performer with rare gifts. The album sold much more briskly than the first one, and a single from it, "Bad, Bad Leroy Brown," became one of the top hits of 1973, reaching number one on the *Billboard* list in June.

All seemed to be going well with Croce's career as he took off on a summer tour in support of his album. He had just completed a standing-room-only concert in Louisiana and was on his way in a private plane to the next one-night stand when fate stepped in. Something malfunctioned on takeoff and the plane hit the ground and burst into flames near Natchitoches. Even as his lifeless body lay in the wreckage, articles were appearing in three different music trade magazines hailing him as the next American superstar. As West told a reporter, "Jim became a star just three weeks before he died."

Instead of ending things, the shock of the accident caused millions of fans to realize what they had lost. Somewhat like what occurred with Jim Reeves, the country star who also died in a plane crash, years afterward reissues of old recordings or new releases of previously unreleased recordings resulted in a series of posthumous hits. The first impetus affected his already issued records. Elliott Abbott of BNB Associates, his management firm, told Jack Hurst of the *Los Angeles Times* (June 9, 1974), "His first album had sold about 10,000 or 50,000 and the second about 230,000 or so when he died." By mid-1974, both were over the half million mark.

Soon after Croce's death his single "I Got a Name" (a song presented in the movie *The Last American Hero*) moved into the top 10. In December, "Time in a Bottle" rose to number one. (The latter is a song whose hauntingly ironic lyrics include the prophetic words, "There never seems to be enough time to do the things you want to do . . .")

The Croce impact continued unabated into 1974. Early in the year, his seventh single on ABC, "I'll Have to Say I Love You in a Song," appeared on the charts, remaining for well over four months and rising to number one on some lists. In the summer, he made the top 40 with the single "Workin' at the Car Wash Blues." During the year, the *Don Kirshner Rock Concert* show devoted an entire ninety-minute concert to Croce. A seven-minute movie of Croce performing was used on the show and also presented on other TV programs, including several in Europe.

At intervals in the mid- and late-1970s, Croce's recordings were released in various album combinations. Unlike Reeves, who had been recording for quite a few years before he died, Croce's catalog was much more limited, so that by the late 1970s there was nothing available for new singles. Abbott told Hurst, "The last album was finished eight days before the crash and he hadn't recorded other things that are being held in the can. What he had done was it. That's all there is." Croce's memory remained green through the 1980s and '90s as his recordings remained in print for the most part and his recordings often were included on radio oldies programs. As of the mid-1990s he still retained a strong base of fans and was fortunate in having as part of his heritage a talented son, A.J. Croce.

CROSBY, STILLS, NASH & YOUNG: *Vocal and instrumental groups, David Crosby, born Los Angeles, California, August 14, 1941; Stephen Stills, born Dallas, Texas, January 3, 1945; Graham Nash, born Lancashire, England, February 2, 1942; Neil Young, born Toronto, Canada, November 12, 1945.*

The names of Crosby, Stills, Nash, and Young, in various combinations—solo, duos, trios, or quartet—bulked large on the pop music scene from the late 1960s into the 1990s. Their contributions included some of the finest folk rock material of the period, and some of their original compositions fit into all pop categories, from rock to folk and country.

By the time the members came together in Los Angeles at the end of the 1960s, all of them had impressive credits behind them. David Crosby, of course, had been a founding member of the Byrds, with whom he remained from 1964 to 1968, and, before that, had been a singer-guitarist on the folk music circuit for five years. Steve Stills and Neil Young, who helped form the landmark rock group Buffalo Springfield in the mid-1960s, first became acquainted when they were members of a folk song group called the Au Go Go Singers in 1964.

Young's earlier history *(see separate entry)* included his own rock band as a teenager in Winnipeg, Canada, followed by several years as a folksinger on the coffeehouse circuit. Stills, born in Texas but brought up in many different places by parents whose work kept them constantly on the move, already could play many instruments, from guitar to piano to drums, by his teens and was finding some work as a performer during his high school years. Later, after winning some local attention appearing in folk clubs while attending the University of Florida, he dropped out of college to concentrate on a show business career.

Graham Nash, raised in Lancashire, England, already had a stage act called the Two Teens with a friend named Allan Clarke while in grammar school. At fifteen, in 1957, they became the youngest artists to appear at a well-known English venue, the Manchester Cabaret Club. After several other group affiliations in the late 1950s and early 1960s, in 1963 the two founded a vocal and instrumental group called the Hollies, which became one of England's top rock groups (and was still active in the 1980s). With Nash as the main songwriter and lead singer, the group scored many major hits in the 1960s. When he announced he had decided to leave the group in 1968, fans flocked to his last shows with the band, including the standing-room-only farewell show at London's Palladium on December 8, 1968.

By then, Nash already was rehearsing new material with the first Crosby, Stills, Nash & Young alignment, Crosby, Stills & Nash. The origins of that threesome were described by Ellen Sander (*Hit Parade,* September 1969): "It all started one late summer afternoon in a picturesque house in Laurel Canyon [Los Angeles]. Crosby was preparing material for a solo album after having left the Byrds. Nash, still with the Hollies, was visiting, and Stills, after the breakup of Buffalo Springfield, had been sitting around and staring at the side of a mountain trying to decide what to do next between playing sessions. Goofing around in the California living room, they all began to play and sing together. And they loved it immediately and they talked about making an album and boy, it was going to be a hassle with each of them contracted to a different record company. Music biz wunderkind David Geffen, a twenty-six-year-old funky imp, was called in to move minds and signatures around to make it possible, no small feat, mind you, but he did it and then some."

The three went to England in the fall of 1968 to compose new songs and rehearse while Nash closed out his career with the Hollies. They then flew back to L.A. to record their debut LP, *Crosby, Stills & Nash,* which came out on Atlantic Records in the spring of 1969. The record, still one of the best in folk rock annals, included Stills's seven-minute-long "Suite Judy Blue Eyes," "Helplessly Hoping," "49 Reasons," and "Bye Bye Baby"; David Crosby's lament for Senator Robert Kennedy, "Long Time Coming"; Graham Nash's "Lady of the Island" and "Marrakesh Express"; and a song by Crosby, Stills, and Paul Kantner of Jefferson Airplane, "Wooden Ships."

The LP spawned several hit singles and earned a gold record before 1969 was over. The trio's concerts also were among the most welcomed appearances of the year. By the time the members were ready for a second album, Neil Young had agreed to join the loosely organized operation. The first offering of Crosby, Stills, Nash & Young, *Déjà Vu,* came out on Atlantic in the spring of 1970, matching the first one almost song for song in quality. It too was a success, rising to number one on U.S. charts in May and finding similar response all over Europe. The top 10 single "Woodstock," written by Joni Mitchell, was drawn from the LP. A year later the quartet had another number one hit, the LP *4 Way Street,* a live album. The band played before huge audiences all over the United States and abroad during 1971, including a memorable concert at New York's Carnegie Hall.

However, the individuality of the four superstars was beginning to cause strains. By 1972, Neil Young had dropped out of the alliance to concentrate on solo work and, though efforts were made from time to time during the 1970s to get him to take part in some reunion efforts, he kept on his own way. Stills, too, had his separate projects to work on during the mid-1970s, though he did return for trio work late in the decade. Besides *Déjà Vu* and *4 Way Street,* one other LP was issued of Crosby, Stills, Nash & Young recordings, a "best of" collection titled *So Far.*

In the mid-1970s, Crosby and Nash worked together steadily as a duo, making several extensive tours during that period. One of their albums, *Crosby and Nash,* came out on the old Crosby, Stills, Nash & Young label, Atlantic, but most of their releases were issued on a new label affiliation, ABC. Their first ABC release, *Wind on the Water,* was one of the best folk rock collections of 1975 and a top 10 hit in November 1975. They followed with two more ABC LPs, *Whistling Down the Wire* and *Crosby & Nash Live.*

Steve Stills returned to the fold briefly for the 1977 Atlantic Records LP, *CSN.* (Neil Young had been invited to take part but reportedly backed out at the last minute.) The trio toured in support of the album in 1977 and the sold-out signs in major auditoriums across the United States testified to the artists' standing with the mass audience. The album was in the top 5 on U.S. charts during the summer of 1977 and earned a gold record award from R.I.A.A.

However, following that flurry, the group broke up once more, with even Crosby and Nash giving up collaboration, at least for the last part of the 1970s. Nash turned most of his attention to solo work (with his solo LPs coming out on Warner Brothers during 1979–80) and cooperation with Jackson Browne on environmentalist issues. Those efforts included appearances by Nash and Browne in a concert series to raise funds to fight nuclear energy, One of those concerts formed the basis for a two-record album *No Nukes,* issued on Elektra at the end of 1979.

In November 1988, Atlantic issued a new Crosby, Stills & Nash album, *American Dream,* which quickly made the hit lists. It received a gold record award from the R.I.A.A. on January 10, 1989, and a platinum one the following January 27. On September 30, 1991, Atlantic issued a multi-CD box set of the group's hits, *Crosby, Stills & Nash,* which was certified gold by the R.I.A.A. on August 20, 1992. Meanwhile, earlier CSN and CSN&Y albums continued to sell steadily. On November 4, 1992, the 1977 *CSN* collection gained multiplatinum recognition from the R.I.A.A. for four million copies sold. Crosby, Stills, Nash & Young releases from the early 1970s also remained in Atlantic Records catalogs into the 1990s with R.I.A.A. awards including platinum and multiplatinum (4M) for *Déjà Vu* on November 4, 1992; platinum and multiplatinum (4 M) for *4 Way Street* on December 18, 1992; and platinum and multiplatinum (6 M) for *So Far,* on the same date.

The substance abuse pursued by David Crosby for so many years caught up with him in a near-death manner in the 1990s. He suffered liver failure, but fortunately was able to get a liver transplant that saved his life. The experience finally had a sobering effect on him, and his life took still another turn for the better when, soon after the surgery, he met his adult son, James Raymond, who had been given up for adoption as a baby. It turned out that Raymond also was in the entertainment field, trying to make his mark as a songwriter and keyboards player. In 2000 it was also revealed that Crosby was the father of the two children of Melissa Etheridge and Julie Cyper.

Crosby, Stills & Nash members commented on their careers and rock history in general on some of the rock and roll history series presented on both commercial and Public Broadcasting System TV stations during the 1990s. CSN also kept up its live appearance activities, though at a more leisurely pace than in earlier decades. In the fall of 1996 they made headlines for their objections to the use of some of their material in what they considered to be a violation of their pro–civil rights stance.

The bone of contention was use of an instrumental passage from the Stephen Stills composition "Carry On" (included in the *Déjà Vu* album) in a radio ad supporting passage of anti–affirmative action Proposition 209 on the November ballot in California. Crosby told Steve Hochman of the *Los Angeles Times* ("Crosby, Stills & Nash Object to Song's Use in Ad for Prop. 209," October 5, 1996), "In what lifetime am I going to support 209. I don't know where in hell they had the gall to use our song," adding he considered the measure "racist"; "To try to appropriate us to give them creden-

tials of the '60s as if they were out on the front lines of the civil rights movement . . . is the worst kind of lying."

Stills stated, "Until this country becomes color-blind and gender-blind and everything-else-blind, we have to have affirmative action or something."

By then Stills was aware that not only CSN, but his earlier band, the Buffalo Springfield, had both been chosen for induction into the Rock and Roll Hall of Fame the following May. This made him the first artist to be inducted twice on the same evening, May 6, 1997. Discussing the legacy of the short-lived Springfield band (original members Stills, Neil Young, Richie Furay, Bruce Palmer, and Dewey Martin) with Robert Hilburn of the *Los Angeles Times* ("For All It's Worth," May 6, 1997), he stressed its folk roots: "With the Springfield we took a brand of folk music and put electric guitars on top of it. Bruce Palmer was a Motown-styled bass player and we just burned with it. The truth is we never got on record what we sounded like live. Man, we were the Stones onstage . . . that intensity."

Asked about the ups and downs in popularity for CSN members over the years, Stills stressed it took a while to get over having swelled egos in the early phase when rock stars were treated like some sort of gods. "But it wasn't long before I got a grip on things and realized what really matters," he added. "But there is a hard part where you are too young to be a living legend and too old to be current, if you know what I mean. I remember Bruce Springsteen opening up for me. . . . There is a valley in everyone's career, but you just have to concentrate on the music and getting better at your craft. It's almost more rewarding getting up onstage at a time when you're supposed to be done . . . a has-been, and you just kill 'em with a show. That's a great feeling."

CSN received enthusiastic audience response during its 1997 concert tour, which wound up at the Universal Amphitheatre in late September. Attending the final tour event, reviewer Steve Hochman of the *Los Angeles Times* ("Crosby, Stills & Nash Display Special Chemistry," September 30, 1997, p. F2) pointed out that the threesome continued to be surprisingly formidable: "A decade ago the trio seemed ready for the scrap heap—or worse, given David Crosby's well-chronicled bouts with substance abuse and his consequent liver transplant. But from Sunday's opener, 'Love the One You're With,' to the closing 'Carry On' three hours later, Crosby, Stephen Stills and Graham Nash rocked harder and more joyously than ever."

Neil Young's association with the original supergroup was reflected in the encore presentation of his 1970 song "Ohio," written in protest of the killing of students by the National Guard at Kent State University. With Tom Petty standing in for Young, Hochman noted, the song "still raised goose bumps."

During 1997, Crosby joined with son James Raymond in a new band called CPR where the *P* stood for the group's third member, guitarist Jeff Pevar. The band's debut album, *CPR*, was released in the spring of 1998, and the band's supporting tour included a November appearance at the Wiltern Theatre in Los Angeles, the band's debut concert in that city. Joining the group onstage during the proceedings were many of Crosby's musical associates, including Graham Nash.

In early February 1999, during an interview on the CBS-TV's *Late Late Show with Tom Snyder,* Nash announced that Neil Young had agreed to a forty-date fall concert tour with himself, Crosby, and Stills. He also reported that the foursome was working on a CSN&Y reunion album, *Looking Forward* on Reprise.

CROWE, J.D.; J.D. CROWE AND THE NEW SOUTH: *Singer, banjoist, songwriter, band leader (Kentucky Mountain Boys, New South). Born near Lexington, Kentucky, 1936. Original members of Kentucky Mountain Boys, mid-1960s, Crowe, Doyle Lawson, Red Allen. Name changed to J.D. Crowe and the New South in 1975 with roster comprising Crowe, Ricky Skaggs, Tony Rice, Jerry Douglas, and Bobby Slone. New South roster changed many times over next twenty years with 1994–early 1995 group made up of Crowe, Richard Bennett (vocals, guitar), Phil Leadbetter (Dobro), Curt Chapman (bass), and Darrell Webb (tenor singer). Bennett replaced by Greg Luck during 1995.*

Bluegrass is a musical format that tends to defy categorization, particularly in its progressive evolution in the post–1960s period. Both folk and country adherents lay claim to bluegrass as their own with justification, but performers like J.D. Crowe and his many superb band combinations have never felt constrained to styles directly identified as traditional bluegrass. Over the years a typical Crowe-organized set included folk, country, and country-rock numbers as well as occasional R&B material. Crowe didn't hesitate to use electric as well as acoustic instruments, and eventually added drums to the arrangements.

Born and raised in Kentucky, he developed a love for country and the just-evolving rhythm and blues genre by the time he was thirteen, in 1949. His musical tastes were then shaped by exposure to the music of Flatt and Scruggs, who came to Lexington every Saturday night to perform on the *Kentucky Barn Dance* radio program. Managing to get a front-row seat in the audience almost every time, he was intrigued by Earl Scruggs's banjo picking and took mental note of Scruggs's fingering and chord progressions. After getting his own banjo for a Christmas present, he applied that knowledge to develop his playing ability.

As he told Jay Orr of the *Nashville Banner* (July 17, 1995), "There was something about that music that made you want to kick your foot up, drive or stomp or something. They had such power, they played with such

authority. Their 15- or 20-minute show was like five minutes. That's what I grew up listening to."

With constant practice, his instrumental skills continued to improve markedly, and he added to his experience by playing with friends and local groups. In 1956 he was given the opportunity to join Jimmy Martin's bluegrass band. In a Rounder profile based on material prepared by Herschel Freeman, it was noted that "his driving, bluesy style first came to national prominence with Jimmy Martin on classic mid-1950s recordings like 'You Don't Know My Mind' and 'Hold Whatcha Got.' At that time, Martin was one of the top three bluegrass names in the country." Crowe worked with Martin until 1961. After playing sporadically with other artists, in 1963 he lived in Nashville for a time, then decided to go home and give up full-time performing for a while.

In Lexington he worked a regular day job, picking up music gigs at local clubs nights and weekends. His goal, as he told Orr, was to play music that wasn't restricted by the "rules" of traditional bluegrass. His sets typically included blends of country, R&B, and traditional and avant-garde bluegrass.

Feeling more comfortable with his new musical approach, in the mid-1960s he formed his own group, the Kentucky Mountains Boys, whose original members were Doyle Lawson and Red Allen. Their sound featured trio harmonies, with Crowe singing baritone, in addition to powerhouse instrumentals. At the start of the '70s the band members included Larry Rice, whose brother Tony, a flatpicking guitar player par excellence, joined in 1971, the year Lawson left to join the Country Gentlemen. As the '70s went by, other changes took place both in sidemen and name. In 1975, now called J.D. Crowe and the New South, the group completed its first album for Rounder Records.

That album, *J.D. Crowe and the New South,* was recorded by what now is recognized as a superstar group: Tony Rice, Ricky Skaggs, Jerry Douglas, and Bobby Slone. It was a rousing clarion call to new directions for bluegrass and helped spur a broad revival of interest in the music.

The '75 album "was one of those things," Crowe told Orr. "It was meant to be and it clicked. It worked and it did become a classic recording."

By the time the band's next Rounder album, *You Can Share My Blanket,* came out in 1978, Ricky Skaggs and Jerry Douglas had left (in 1976) to form Boone Creek. By then the lineup included Glenn Lawson, Bobby Slone, and Jimmy Gaudreau. In 1979 the extremely talented but ill-fated Keith Whitley joined to add new creative dimensions for some four years. Keith's lead vocals are a prime feature of the *Live in Japan* album, which was recorded in 1979 but not released on Rounder until 1987. The band opened its 1980s efforts with the album *My Name Ain't in the Hall of Fame,* issued in 1980.

Increasingly, Crowe focused on finding a place for his band in the burgeoning commercial country market. To a rising chorus of complaints from old-line bluegrass fans, he added electric rhythm guitar, bass, pedal steel, drums, and piano to concerts and studio recordings. At the same time, he tended to downplay his banjo playing. Much of his creative time in the first half of the '80s was devoted to producing and arranging records for other performers. Still, he wasn't absent from the live performance scene, playing many club and festival dates with the New South through the mid-1980s. His New South output was limited, though; his only Rounder release from 1981 to 1989 was the 1986 album *Straight Ahead.*

He satisfied his interest in more traditional bluegrass by joining with Tony Rice, Doyle Lawson, Bobby Hicks, and Todd Philips to form the core of the Bluegrass Album Band (sometimes augmented by others such as Jerry Douglas, who played Dobro on their second collection). At of the start of the 1990s, that combination had provided five albums, all using a fully acoustic sound.

In 1990 Crowe disbanded the New South and let it be known he was going into semiretirement. During the early '90s he kept a low profile, though he performed at a few concerts and made an occasional guest appearance on Ricky Skaggs's TV program, *Pickin' Party.* After four years he admitted that he missed the camaraderie of band work, and recruited a new band to record his first New South album in eight years. The personnel comprised, besides himself on banjo and vocals, Richard Bennett (lead vocals, guitar), Don Rigsby (vocals, mandolin), Curt Chapman (bass), Phil Leadbetter (Dobro), and Randy Howard (fiddle).

The content of the new 1994 release, *Flashback,* ranged from dynamic instrumentals like renditions of Bob Dylan's "Nashville Skyline Rag" and the Osborne Brothers' "Sledd Ridin'" to sensitive treatments of traditional bluegrass numbers represented by Jimmy Martin's "Mr. Engineer" and Lester Flatt's "Bouquet in Heaven." Among other excellent tracks were "Ever Changing Woman," "If I Could Go Back Home Again," and "When the Angels Carry Me Home." Bennett, besides providing four original compositions, demonstrated vocal abilities no less impressive than such previous band lead singers as Skaggs, Rice, and Whitley. Steve Romanoski commented in *Bluegrass Music News,* "Bennett's style takes on elements of new country and folk music alongside its bluegrass base."

Bennett remained with the New South for extensive concert dates through 1994 and into early 1995, when he left to join the bluegrass group Carolina. His place was taken by Greg Luck. The other tour group members were Leadbetter, Chapman, and tenor vocalist Darrell Webb. In any case, nothing could detract from Crowe's unique banjo playing or the arrangements he provided for most of the group's material. Recognition for Crowe and his new material was quick to begin coming with

the International Bluegrass Music Association's naming him Banjo Player of the Year for 1994. *Flashback* was nominated for a Grammy Award for Bluegrass Album of 1994 and also was a finalist in the IBMA's 1995 Album of the Year category. The latter poll also selected "If I Could Go Back Home Again" as a candidate for Song of the Year and provided J.D. with a second straight Banjo Player of the Year nomination.

CURTIS, CATIE: *Singer, songwriter, guitarist. Born Biddeford, Maine, May 22, 1965.*

After hearing Catie Curtis sing at the Troubadour in Los Angeles in May 1996, it's no surprise to hear that a voice teacher once tried to smooth out her warble. But the subtle break in her voice gives Curtis the personality lacking in many singer-songwriters. Her background as a social worker also lends a unique sensitivity that comes through in songs such as "The Wolf," about child abuse, and "Hole in the Bucket," about the effect of social services cuts on the poor. Yet, she isn't preachy. In "Radical," a song about lesbian love, she sings that one can find love without having to label it.

"I don't want the risk of 90 percent of my audience not connecting to my songs," she told Daniel Gewertz of the *Boston Herald* (January 29, 1996). "When I hear she/he love songs in concert, even I can feel uncomfortable. There's internalized homophobia in all of us. I don't want to be onstage feeling my audience's discomfort. I don't even feel comfortable with labels for me. I've had a gay relationship, so I feel I can write 'Radical.' But I don't pigeonhole myself as a lesbian. I feel labels are appropriate for relationships, not people. People change."

Curtis grew up in southern Maine, where she juggled her interests in music and sports, especially basketball (she's a shooting guard). "I used to always love the way a basketball court would feel after the game was over and the lights were being turned off and it was really quiet. It's kind of like that when I go in to do a sound check," she told *Philadelphia Gay News* writer Harriet L. Schwartz (February 16–22, 1996).

Music eventually won out. Her parents loved show tunes. Her mother, Cathy, and three sisters would harmonize on the old standards: "Red Roses for a Blue Lady," "I Don't Know Why," and tunes from *Oklahoma!* and *The Sound of Music.*

"I used to listen to goofy Partridge Family songs and the soundtrack from *Oklahoma!* as a kid, and just really think, 'Man, I love music,'" she told Sheila Daughtry of *Dirty Linen* (June–July 1996). "I remember at a very early age wondering how people got to do music as a living. In my town, the only people who did were playing at the bars and clubs all their lives, not really ever being listened to. And I thought, 'Well, I guess that's what I'll be doing.'"

She sang in church and high school choirs. She also

took voice lessons from an 85-year-old man, As she told Chris Fisher of *The Worcester Phoenix* (February 2, 1996): "He was constantly trying to get me to smooth over the breaks in my voice by applying more technique, but I like the way I sing, so I've kept it." She started playing the drums in high school at Thornton Academy. She took up the guitar at fifteen because she wanted to play solo, though she still likes to play drums in concert. (As she took out a snare drum at the Troubadour, she said that as a girl she sold all her commemorative coins to buy her first cymbal.) In the late '70s she listened to artists like James Taylor, Karla Bonoff, Paul Simon, and Bonnie Raitt. She wrote songs, but mostly performed covers in local clubs before graduating high school in 1983.

At Brown University, she majored in history, and discovered Suzanne Vega, Greg Brown, Cheryl Wheeler, and Patty Larkin. She hung out with songwriters who encouraged her efforts. "They would say, 'Oh, play one of your own.' That's kind of unusual and that's partly because it's a neat school and people were really encouraging of the creative process instead of saying, 'Oh, play us another Bob Dylan song.'" she told *The Performing Songwriter* (September–October 1993).

After graduating, she moved to San Francisco and got a job as a waitress at Hopewell's. "It gave me a chance to go away from everybody I knew and just write for a while," she told the *Performing Songwriter.* "And I didn't have any friends out there. I didn't know anybody, so it was a good opportunity to spend a lot of time by myself writing." She compiled the material for her first tape and returned to Boston.

From 1988 to 1992 she worked as a case manager for the elderly by day, and performed in clubs by night. With money from family and friends, she produced her first recording, a cassette called *Dandelion* (now out of print) on her Mongoose Music label. She began to gain a following in 1991 with her second, independently released album, *From Years to Hours,* also on Mongoose.

Awards followed in the early '90s. She won the Telluride Festival Troubadour Contest. In 1993 she was nominated for the Boston Music Awards' Outstanding New Acoustic Act. In August 1995, she received a warm welcome at the Newport Folk Festival. Her songs were featured on two Putumayo compilations: "Mine Fields: From Years to Hours," on the *Best of Contemporary Folk Songs* and "Hole in the Bucket," on *Shelter: The Best of Contemporary Singer Songwriters.*

She released her third album, *Truth from Lies,* on Mongoose in 1994. By this time she had sold enough albums to return money to her investors.

Steve Murphy, the president of Guardian Records (the now-defunct singer-songwriter division of Angel), was in Washington, D.C., with his family, when his daughter Madeleine pulled him into a record store. They heard "Hole in the Bucket" from the Putumayo compilation. "I listen to dozens of tapes a week, but I was stopped in my tracks by that song," Murphy told *Billboard* (January 20, 1996).

The label signed her and reissued *Truth from Lies* in 1996. The title comes from her song "The Party's Over," a takeoff on the "Cinderella" myth: *The party's over, the clock's long struck twelve/Now you can be you and I can turn into myself.*

"I grew up with a lot of myths about what my life would be like, like what falling in love and getting involved in a relationship would be like, how you make those choices and how you structure your life," Curtis told Stephen Ide of *The Patriot Ledger.* "So many things that my life has turned into have not followed the expectations I have had. The title of the album reminds me of that process, separating myths from reality."

New England Performer magazine named it Best Folk/Acoustic Album. Standout tracks include the rocking "You Can Always Be Gone," "Radical," and "The Wolf," co-written with Jennifer Robohm, in which the wolf symbolizes the abusive stepfather, an allusion to Little Red Riding Hood. "I had a very specific kid in mind, and when I sing it, it's in the first person," Curtis told the *Patriot Ledger.* "I try to really imagine what it would be like to be the kid."

One of her more upbeat songs is "Dad's Yard," written to tease her pack rat father Phil when he retired from his job. In concert, Curtis talks about how her dad's motto was "never throw anything away . . . There would be sawdust and hammers as though someone were making things, but my dad wouldn't make anything. He would go to the dump and pick things up and start working on them. 90 percent of the things he brought in the house my mom would say, 'Take that back!'"

Curtis's lyrics are often semi-autobiographical. She sings in "Silhouette:" *I've always been an easy read/Just once I want to be a mystery.*

"I don't write anything down at all during the process," she told *Performing Songwriter.* "In fact, a lot of songs I've written I've never written lyrics down until I've recorded the song. The way I think about the lines is that if it doesn't stick in my head from line to line, I feel it's not worthy of keeping."

She also has an unaffected way about her in concert. At the 1996 Folk Alliance Conference in Washington, D.C., she performed at a showcase in torn jeans, a gray top, and boots. She introduced a song that takes an ironic look at social conventions called "Oops, I'm Sorry."

For a time she left New England to live in Michigan, but soon returned to Boston. "Every time I try to leave New England, I come back, because even if people are wonderful where I go, there's not a community of musicians who write and play and jam together. The scene here is so rich." (*Daily Hampshire Gazette,* February 5, 1996).

In October 1997 Guardian released her second album, *Catie Curtis.* For that CD, she had such top-notch players as Roy Bittan on keyboards, Kenny Aronoff on drums, Tony Levin on bass, and Jimmy Ryan on mandolin. When EMI closed down its Guardian division, Curtis was cast adrift. In 1999 she signed with Rykodisc, which issued *A Crash Course in Roses* in August 1999.

DANE, BARBARA: *Singer, guitarist. Born Detroit, Michigan, May 12, 1927.*

"Away with Rum" (the song of the Salvation Army) had the shabby walls of the Ash Grove shaking with a rhythmic beat while the audience laughed or clapped hands in time with the music. It was a rousing climax to an evening of folksinging that ran the gamut from low-down blues to classic folk ballads to comedy. The time was the late 1950s, and the singer was a good-looking, husky-voiced woman named Barbara Dane. The name has since become familiar to folk and folk-blues fans the world over.

Barbara (real name: Barbara Spillman) started with a folk music heritage. Her parents had moved from Arkansas to the motor city of Detroit, where Barbara was born. But they wanted to forget the struggles and slights of their humble origin and carefully avoided any mention of southern customs or music. They were interested in more sedate music, though, and saw that their daughter had piano and voice lessons. Young Barbara sang in the church choir and school glee club.

In her late teens, Barbara worked in a Detroit plant and joined the union. When the union went on strike, she began to learn her first folk songs, including some from a stirring performance by Pete Seeger. The Seeger union concert caused her to teach herself the guitar from a "'25 easy lessons' book and from records in the Detroit public library" (*Sing Out!* April–May 1964).

After getting nowhere trying to find radio work in Detroit, she went to Berkeley, California, in 1949. Folk songs still weren't in vogue, so she got a job as a popular singer on a program called *Sweet and Mellow*. She then tried out for the *Horace Heidt Amateur Hour* but didn't make it. Her first TV appearance was as the winner of a San Francisco bathing suit–talent contest. She kept up her folk efforts, though, and finally was given her own show, *Folksville, U.S.A.*, on KGO-TV. In 1952 she moved to KPFA radio. On one show she learned one of her most popular songs, "San Francisco Bay Blues," from blues singer Jesse Fuller. From Bessie Mercer she learned such songs as "Don't Sing Love Songs," also known as "Silver Dagger." Another song she learned during this period was "Spiritual Trilogy."

Soon after, she was asked to join the Dixieland band of Dick Oxtot. She sang many blues numbers and began to achieve notice for her blues work far beyond the bounds of San Francisco. By the early 1960s she had performed in concerts and at coffeehouses in many major cities. In October 1963 she returned to a scene of her earlier triumphs but now as a folk-blues artist. The result was a rousing ovation night after night from sell-out crowds.

By the mid-1960s she had been featured on many major TV shows and concert stages. These included a Timex TV special with Louis Armstrong, the Newport Jazz Festival, UCLA Jazz Festival, *Playboy*, *Penthouse*, and PM West. She also starred on a cross-country tour with comedian Bob Newhart. Over the years, Barbara turned out LP albums for a number of labels. The titles included *Trouble in Mind, Living with the Blues, Night at the Ash Grove,* and *When I Was A Young Girl.*

DAVIS, GUY: *Singer, songwriter, guitarist, harmonica player, actor, playwright. Born New York, New York, May 12, 1952.*

In a "Courting the Muse" essay in *Sing Out!* (November-December 1996–January 1997), bluesman Guy Davis rhetorically questions his own credentials for playing the blues. "I was born in Manhattan, raised in Westchester, I've lived in the Bronx, Queens and now Harlem, and I've never picked cotton a day in my life," he wrote. A talented actor and writer, Davis chose to focus on the blues. By the end of his essay, he makes the reasons clear: "I play this music because it resonates inside me."

It is his way of connecting with his ancestors. As Davis told Scott Alarik of the *Boston Globe* ("Guy Davis at the Crossroads," January 12, 1996), "If you think about the blues in its most raw roots, it is something that has been with us ever since slave times. . . . The blues moved along with the people, and as a people we've always been concerned with improvement, with getting that next leg up. . . . For a lot of people, what the blues was had to go by the wayside the same way minstrelsy did, with the black face and the big white lips. You didn't want to have to be singing about just surviving the hard times, you wanted to look at the good times ahead. . . . But this music is treasure, it's gold; part of the process of our people. It teaches us about ourselves, not just the hard times we had, but the things we did to survive and become who we are now."

Davis is the son of actors, directors, and storytellers Ossie Davis and Ruby Dee, who were born in Georgia and southern Ohio, respectively. His parents and grandmother Laura Davis raised Guy with a storytelling tradition, regaling him about life in the South. When he was thirteen, Guy went to see Buddy Guy and Junior Wells, which inspired him to look further into blues roots. As he told Alarik: "I love old things. I love old music, old stories, old people, old cups and saucers and tools. I love things that have some dust on them, the dust of time."

He spent five years studying acting. In the meantime, Davis taught himself guitar, listening to records by the blues masters like Skip James and Blind Blake as well as newer artists like Fats Waller and Taj Mahal. (He started with ragtime-style fingerpicking, later picking up the slide.) As a child, he appeared with his parents on a public television program in Dallas called *With Ossie and Ruby.* In his mid-twenties, he worked with Moses Asch of Folkways to cut his first album in 1978, *Dreams About Life.* Later he pursued his acting dreams with a part in the film *Beat Street* and in the TV soap *One Life to Live.*

He also demonstrated skills as a writer. In 1990 he wrote and starred in a one-act antidrug play called *The Trial,* which he later expanded into *The Trial: Judgment of the People.* Both were produced at the McGinn Cazale Theater. He made his Broadway debut in 1991 in *Mulebone,* written by Zora Neale Hurston and Langston Hughes and featuring Taj Mahal's music. His collection of three short stories, *Mudsurfing,* won a 1991 Brio Award from the Bronx Council for the Arts. Two years later he played the role of Robert Johnson in the play *Trick the Devil.* For his performance he won the W.C. Handy Keeping the Blues Alive Award in 1993. The following year he starred in a one-man show he wrote titled *In Bed with the Blues: The Adventures of Fishy Waters.* It was loosely modeled after the life of Muddy Waters, and Davis received a strong review in the *New York Times* for his performances of songs by Robert Johnson, Blind Willie McTell, Mississippi John Hurt, and Thomas A. Dorsey. He also performed in a play he had written with his parents titled *Two Hah Hahs and a Homeboy,* staged in New Brunswick, New Jersey, in 1995. (He also presented his father with a Lifetime Achievement Award from the Broadway Hall of Fame.) He arranged, performed, and composed music for the Emmy Award–winning film *To Be a Man;* his music was used in the 1995 PBS series *The American Promise.*

Davis self-released a live album from a concert at the Music Hall in Tarrytown, New York, in November 1993. Red House Records remixed and rereleased the album as *Stomp Down Rider* in 1995, which demonstrates his ability as a fingerpicking and slide guitarist, harp player, and interpreter of country blues. It was selected as one of the top 10 blues albums of 1995 by the *Boston Globe*'s Scott Alarik and by *Pulse!* Davis released a studio album, *Call Down the Thunder,* on Red House in 1996, followed by *You Don't Know My Mind* in 1998, and *Butt Naked Free* in 2000.

DAVIS, REVEREND GARY: *Singer, guitarist, banjoist, songwriter. Born Clinton, Laurens County, South Carolina, April 30, 1896; died New York, New York, May 5, 1972. (Some obits list place and date of death as Hammonton, New Jersey, May 3, 1972.)*
A towering figure in blues and gospel history, Gary

Davis during his many years of performing served as an inspiration and a musical model for countless younger artists. Generations of singers and instrumentalists, black and white, incorporated some of his techniques and some of his songs into their own acts. For much of his life, though, he was more intent on using his talents to save people's souls than to win acclaim.

Raised in rural South Carolina, he began singing gospel and blues songs while still a small child. Although he was sightless when he started to build a reputation as an artist with blues and folk music fans, he was not born blind, as was the case with many black troubadours of the early decades of this century. But he did have an almost inborn love of music, and before he was in his teens he could sing and play guitar and banjo so well that he often was asked to perform at cornshuckings, barn-raisings, and buck-and-wing dances.

He continued to improve his performing style and increase his musical repertoire. During his teens, in the early 1920s, he already was bent on making music a career. As the decade went by, he traveled all through North and South Carolina and into Tennessee picking up whatever work he could as a blues singer. His lifestyle paralleled that of most of the black artists of the period. Money was scarce and places to perform relatively few and far between. He sang and played on street corners at times, on other occasions in low-down bars and sometimes bawdy houses. It was a rough environment, and a person had to be handy with fists and sometimes more dangerous weapons to survive. Reportedly it was during one unfortunate incident that Davis lost his sight.

To cure the profound depression that swept over him after his loss, he turned to religion. He stopped singing blues and concentrated on hymns and gospels. He also began to develop a skill in preaching. He decided to study for the ministry in the early 1930s and was ordained in 1933. After that he sang and preached in churches throughout the Southeast, though not as a regular pastor of a particular congregation.

He returned to his musical wanderings, often teaming up with other famous names in blues and folk annals. Among the artists he worked with in the 1930s and 1940s were Blind Boy Fuller, Bull City Red, and Sonny Terry. In line with his new outlook on life, Davis mostly sang gospel and folk songs, though he occasionally was willing to do some blues as well.

Still essentially an itinerant performer, he settled in New York in the 1940s. His base of operations usually was Harlem, where he eked out a living in the usual way—performing or preaching on street corners, sometimes obtaining small amounts of money begging. After a while, though, things improved. For one thing, he got opportunities to preach in Harlem churches. At the same time, his skills as a folk artist gradually became known to an increasing circle of people in the thriving New York folk environment of the 1950s. As the decade went by, Davis was asked to perform on the growing number of small folk clubs in the city and in other parts of the Northeast. Soon he also was a familiar figure at the burgeoning circuit of folk festivals. He became an honored performer at the best-known folk festival of them all, Newport, where audiences loved his intricate five-string banjo and acoustic guitar accompaniment to his hoarse, gritty voice. In dark suit, white shirt, wearing a hat and dark, wire-rimmed spectacles, he seemed the living personification of the folk-blues and gospel genre.

Besides winning fans from the public at large, Davis was regarded with awe and affection by many young performers, including Bob Dylan, Taj Mahal, Donovan, and Ry Cooder. Cooder recalled learning some of his instrumental techniques from hearing artists like Davis perform at Ed Pearl's Ash Grove in Los Angeles: "Whenever there was a pretty good player, I'd sit in the front row and watch. If someone like Gary Davis was in town, I'd talk to him, go where he was staying, give him five dollars, and get him to play as much as he could while I watched. About a month later, I'd find that I'd start to remember how he did things." Some of Gary's performing skills also were recorded for posterity in two TV documentaries, one completed in 1967, another in 1970.

Helping to expand his reputation not only to other parts of the United States but to many other nations as well were the series of recordings issued by various small folk labels. Most of them, such as *Little More Faith,* issued on Bluesville in December 1961, and *Pure Religion,* released on the Command label in July 1964 (available on the Prestige label in the 1970s), contained gospel songs and hymns, though with strong blues intonations in the vocals and instrumental work. Among his other albums were *Blind Reverend Gary Davis* (Bluesville, October 1962); an album of the same title put out by Prestige Records in May 1964; *Singing Reverend,* issued by Stimson, in which he is joined by Sonny Terry; and *Guitar & Banjo,* available on Prestige in the 1970s.

In the 1970s, his new recordings, some issued posthumously, came out on Kicking Mule Records, Berkeley, California. Among his LPs on the label were *Ragtime Guitar; Lo I Be with You Always; Children of Zion;* and *Let Us Get Together.* Also in print in the early 1970s were the Biograph albums *Lord I Wish I Could See* and *Reverend Gary Davis.*

The days of begging or singing on street corners at least were past. During those decades he appeared in folk clubs, at festivals, and on college campuses across the United States. He also became a favorite in England. In the 1960s, he was part of the Blues and Gospel Caravan that attracted large audiences in many English cities. In the early 1970s he went there to give a number of performances on his own, including a show-stopping set at the Cambridge Folk Festival in 1971.

The renewed interest in the folk-blues and related music in the 1980s and 1990s led to many reissues of legendary artists like Davis. In 1991 he was represented by a compilation CD titled *Pure Religion and Bad Company.*

DE DANNAN: *Irish instrumental and vocal ensemble. Founding members: Frankie Gavin (fiddle, flute, tin whistle, viola, piano), born Corrandulla, Galway; Alec Finn (guitar, bouzouki); Johnny 'Ringo' McDonagh (bodhran, bones, percussion); and Charlie Piggott (banjo, whistles, and accordion), soon joined by Dolores Keane on vocals and Jackie Daly on accordion. Other accordion players: Aidan Coffey, born County Waterford; and Martin O'Connor. Vocalists have included Maura O'Connell, born County Clare, Ireland; Mary Black, born Dublin, May 22, 1955; Dolores Keane, born Caherlistrane, County Galway, Ireland; Eleanor Shanley, born County Leitrim; and Caroline Lavelle, who also played cello. Guitarist Andy Irvine, born London, June 14, 1942, was briefly with De Dannan after leaving Planxty in the mid-1980s and before joining Patrick Street. Guitarists Brendan O'Regan and Johnny Moynihan also played with the group briefly. Group ca. 1998: Gavin; Finn; Colm Murphy, bodhran; Derek Hickey, born County Limerick, accordion; and Tommy Flemming, born County Sligo, vocals.*

De Dannan, along with Planxty, the Bothy Band, and Clannad, has been one of the most influential Irish bands, despite the fact that it has been a revolving door for a series of top-notch accordion players and vocalists. The group has taken musical risks, covering songs by the Beatles and Queen and blending classical and klezmer with Irish instrumentation. The core of the group over the years has been provided by Frankie Gavin, the talented fiddle, flute, and tin whistle player; and Alec Finn on guitar and bouzouki. Over the years some of the best Irish female vocalists have performed with the band: Maura O'Connell, Mary Black, and Dolores Keane, all of whom went on to solo careers.

The band came together in 1972 in Connemara, an Irish-speaking area of County Galway. It was an informal pickup group at first—consisting of Johnny McDonagh, from Galway, on bodhran; Cork-born Charlie Piggott on melodeon and banjo; and Alec Finn on bouzouki and guitar—jamming at the local pubs.

Gavin, the son of fiddle-playing parents, grew up in Galway. By the time he was fifteen, he had won national championships for the fiddle and tin whistle. He was playing piano and fiddle at a local bar when he was joined by the other three. As Gavin put it: "At the time, there were these sessions on Sunday mornings in Hughes' Pub in Spideal [County Galway] and out of those sessions Alec Finn and I formed De Dannan. I was fourteen or fifteen when I first saw Alec playing the bouzouki in Connemara, and I immediately liked the sound of it."

Gavin supplied the fire with his fiddle playing ornamented with triplets and rolls, and tin whistle solos. Finn, one of the earliest proponents of the six-string Greek bouzouki, balanced out the sound with excellent backup. Finn was born in Yorkshire, but his parents were Irish and he lived mostly in the west of Ireland. Like many young musicians, he started out playing blues (influenced by Blind Lemon Jefferson) and rock and later took an interest in traditional music. He moved to Dublin and later settled in Galway.

The ensemble gained a reputation for musicianship and began getting gigs in Dublin. McDonagh met Dolores Keane, then an eighteen-year-old Galway native who came from a well-known musical family, in a pub and invited her to join the group. Keane performed on their first album, *De Dannan*, released in 1975 on Polydor Records. She left the group after a couple of years, moving to London to work on other projects. Shanachie released a duet album, *Frankie Gavin and Alec Finn*, in 1977, marked by their intricate interplay on fiddle and bouzouki.

The group followed in 1978 with *Selected Jigs, Reels & Songs* on Decca and then their best-known LP, *The Mist Covered Mountain*, on Gael Linn Records in 1980. The album includes traditional songs in the *seannos* tradition of Connemara. That same year, the group released a single covering the Beatles' "Hey Jude" that climbed the Irish charts.

In 1981 members of De Dannan heard Maura O'Connell singing at a party and offered her a job that was supposed to last for six weeks. She stayed with the band for two years. Her first album with De Dannan, *Star Spangled Molly*, features 1920s-era Irish American music. "Maggie" became a moderate hit in Ireland, and audiences came to identify one song with O'Connell, "My Irish Molly-O." She left the band in 1983 and settled in Nashville to pursue a solo career. The album won a National Association of Independent Record Distributors (NAIRD) award for best album.

By 1983 several of the original members had left the band, which once again needed a new singer. Alec Finn called Mary Black and asked her to join the group. They also added accordionist Martin O'Connor. Black had little time to rehearse before going into the studio to record *Song for Ireland*, released on Dara Records. The album also won a NAIRD award for best album.

Dolores Keane had since moved back to Galway, and De Dannan invited her to rejoin the group to sing a cover of the Beatles' "Let It Be." She sang it on the group's next album, *Anthem*, released on Dara in 1985, which won the Irish Album of the Year Award. In 1986, as her solo career was taking off, Black decided to leave De Dannan.

Keane stayed with the group for one more album, *Ballroom*, which was released in 1987. The album won a NAIRD best album award in the Celtic–British Isles category. The group then added Caroline Lavelle on cello and second vocals. Besides traditional Irish music, the band included two Jewish Reels, "A Shepherd's Dream" and "Onga Bucharesti." The band learned the klezmer-style reels from Andy Statman, a New York musician with whom they had played a series of concerts in New York and Philadelphia in 1986.

By 1987 the band released *The Best of De Dannan*. But by the late 1980s the band had lost several key members. Cellist Lavelle left. Bodhran player McDonagh, who had recorded nine albums with De Dannan, left and eventually created his own band, Arcady. Keane went solo and drafted accordionist Martin O'Connor for her first band.

Somehow Finn and Gavin managed to hold De Dannan together. They added Aidan Coffey, from County Waterford, who plays a German-style button accordion; Colm Murphy, from County Cork, on bodhran; and Eleanor Shanley, a native of County Leitrim, on vocals.

They followed with an original album, *A Jacket of Batteries*, on Harmac in 1988, featuring Shanley on vocals. They followed in 1991 with *½ Set in Harlem*, on Gavin's Bee's Knees label. The album again blends gospel, klezmer, and Irish influences. It includes a guest appearance by Bill Whelan before his *Riverdance* days.

Hibernian Rhapsody, released in 1996 on Bee's Knees and distributed by Gael-Linn (Shanachie in the United States), adds a male tenor vocalist, Tommy Flemming, to the mix of Gavin, Finn, Murphy, and Derek Hickey, a twenty-something musician from County Wicklow, on button accordion. Flemming, from Aclare, in County Sligo, switched from rock music to traditional music after hearing a former De Dannan alumnus, Mary Black.

The album's title track was inspired by the late Freddie Mercury (1946–1991), from the rock group Queen, and takes its melody from Mercury's "Bohemian Rhapsody," which was at the top of the British charts in 1976. "Freddie Mercury was one of our present-day Mozarts," Gavin said.

The group also performed with Nobel Prize–winning poet Séamus Heaney at the 1996 book fair in Frankfurt and appeared on the BBC-TV documentary *Bringing It All Back Home*.

Both Gavin and Finn have put together a number of solo projects over the years. Gavin has recorded three solo albums: *Croch Suas É* in 1983, *Frankie Goes to Town* in 1989, and *Shamrocks & Holly* on Shanachie in 1996. He has also recorded with jazz violinist Stephane Grapelli, classical violinist Yehudi Menuhin, and appeared on the Rolling Stones' *Voodoo Lounge* and Elvis Costello's *Spike*. Finn released a solo album in 1994 called *Blue Shamrock*, a collection of Irish airs on the guitar and bouzouki released in the United States on the Celtic Heartbeat/Atlantic label.

Commenting on the frustrations he experienced in two decades in the music business, Gavin told Anthony McCann of the *Living Tradition* in 1996: "We were skinned—by record companies, managers, you name it.

The record deals we've done in the past have been basically walking disasters. . . . It's twenty-one years since we started and the number of royalties we've received from any of the companies in that time you could pretty much count on two hands."

That is one reason Gavin decided to form his own label. He told McCann that the group has decided to take "on all the record labels in Ireland, England, and America, one by one, and we're taking them through the courts to get back the money that's owned."

Gavin also felt good about the latest De Dannan lineup: "I suppose it has a lot to do with experience and maturity. When you've been at it for so long you see things differently, and you approach things a lot differently, a lot more carefully."

DELAFOSE, JOHN & GENO: *John Delafose (singer, songwriter, accordionist, bandleader of the Eunice Playboys), born Duralde, Louisiana, April 16, 1939; died Lawtell, Louisiana, September 17, 1994. Geno Delafose (singer, songwriter, accordionist, rubboard, drums, bandleader of the French Rockin' Boogie), born February 6, 1971.*

While Clifton Chenier added blues and R&B to zydeco, accordionist John Delafose played a more traditional variant, harking back to before World War II when black and white musicians blended Cajun and zydeco. Creole accordionist Amadée Ardoin, the first to record zydeco, and Cajun fiddler Dennis McGee often played together. After the war, segregation crept into the bayou and black and white musicians played together less. John's son Geno, representing the next generation of zydeco, looks beyond race to include Cajun music in his blend. He often plays with musicians such as Steve Riley of the Mamou Playboys and Michael Doucet of BeauSoleil.

Zydeco, which has a driving dance rhythm, takes its name from the French word for snap beans *les haricot* (pronounced "lay-zahrico") as well as from the song "Zydeco sont pas sale" ("No salt in the snap beans"). The music evolved from descendants of French settlers of Nova Scotia and New Brunswick who relocated to Louisiana after the British expelled them in 1755, and "Creoles," who represent a mixture of French, Spanish, Caribbean, African-American, German, and Czech influences. One main difference between Cajun and zydeco is that Cajun music incorporates the fiddle while zydeco bands feature the rubboard, although the distinctions are blurring.

John Delafose, whose mother spoke only Creole, grew up near Eunice, Louisiana. He started playing violin, but soon began learning harmonica and the button accordion. He eventually formed a band called the Eunice Playboys, playing at Saturday night dances. In the late 1960s, John came out of a brief retirement to play again, infusing the zydeco and Cajun sounds with a touch of country. He wrote songs in Creole.

His best-known song was "Joe Pitre A Deux Femmes" ("Joe Pete Got Two Women"), a hit in the early 1980s. It was also the name of an album released by Arhoolie Records in 1990. Other albums include: *Zydeco Man* (Arhoolie, 1981), *Uncle Bud Zydeco* (Arhoolie, 1983), *Zydeco Excitement* (Maison de Soul, 1985), *Zydeco Live!* (Rounder, 1989), *Heartaches and Hotsteps* (Maison de Soul, 1990), *Pére et Garçon: Zydeco* (Rounder, 1992), and *Blues Stay Away From Me* (Rounder, 1993).

As the title *Pére et Garçon* ("Father and Son"), notes the group was a family affair. John's son Tony played the bass and Geno played the rubboard and the drums. From his younger days, Geno loved hearing his father sing and play the accordion. He picked up a rubboard at a young age, and it wasn't long before he joined the band. When his older brother went into the service, Geno stepped in at the age of eight. He began playing drums a few years later. "I just started playing a lot with my dad, you know, and it was kind of a full-time job. Every Friday, Saturday, and Sunday, I was out in the clubs playing," Geno told NPR's Jacki Lyden (September 17, 1994).

As a teenager, Geno came upon his dad's accordion. "The box was open, and I grabbed it, and the first day that I picked the accordion up, I played some songs on it, and I just kept on at it," he said. There was no father-son rivalry. John told Geno: "If you can't be better than me, there's no need for you to pick it up. Leave it alone."

Eventually, John began featuring his son's accordion playing. Geno would open the shows and John would tell the audience that his son was going to carry on the tradition after he was gone. Tony and Geno were featured in seven of John's albums.

Geno released his first solo LP, *French Rockin' Boogie* (1994), on Rounder, with Tony Delafose on bass and Paul Delafose on rubboard. His father, who was in poor health, had gone into semi-retirement. But he wasn't destined to provide an easy transition for his sons. On September 17, 1994, the band was playing at Richard's Club in Lawtell, Louisiana. Just after their set, John collapsed and died of a heart attack.

Tony Delafose produced *Tribute to John Delafose* to honor his father, a collection that came out in 1995 on Deep South Records.

At twenty-two, Geno, who played the traditional Cajun button style accordion, decided to carry on the tradition. But he asserted his own identity with his band, the French Rockin' Boogie. Geno, along with C.J. Chenier, represents the next generation of zydeco players. "What's happening is the older generation of zydeco is fading," Geno told Todd Mouton for the liner notes of *That's What I'm Talkin' About* (Rounder, 1996). "And (each member of) the younger generation is trying to be the top man."

The sound changed with the younger Delafose. "Anytime you are not with your family anymore, it is kind of different," Geno told Dan Willging of *ZydE-Zine* (December 27, 1997). "And the sound has changed quite a bit. We keep it on the traditional side, but it is not like it was with the family band. It's homegrown."

That's What I'm Talkin' About included such standout tracks as "Geno's Two Step" and "Teardrops," featuring Geno's soulful singing. He followed with *La Chanson Perdue* (Rounder, 1998). In contrast to other young zydeco musicians who jazzed up the sound, Geno retained the traditional sounds. He included songs by his father on all of his CDs, alongside traditional songs by Cajun and zydeco pioneers Irv LeJeune, Amedée Ardoin, and Canray Fontenot. On his third album, he included young Cajun accordian player Steve Riley and the Mamou Playboys, with whom he had attended Mamou High School.

"My music really doesn't have a color," Geno told Willging. "I play Cajun; I like Cajun. I like zydeco; I play zydeco. I play something for everybody. A little blues, a little bit of rock. It kind of depends on how the feeling is going, what's happening."

Geno toured incessantly but kept his residence at the Double D Ranch outside of Duralde, Louisiana, where he raised cows and kept horses. The ranch is also a gathering spot for musicians, nourished by Geno's mother JoAnn's fresh gumbo. In 1996, he began to hold an annual Barn Dance and Appreciation Party for his fans.

"I always like to stand out," he told Willging. "I like the traditional stuff. If nobody does it, we're going to lose it. I'm going to do my part, do my best. Otherwise, it'll be gone like yesterday. I like old things. Really, I am a young, old man."

Like his father, Geno also likes country music. Called "The Creole Cowboy," Geno is often seen sporting a black cowboy hat. "I would like to be the next Charlie Pride," he told Willging.

In 1999 Delafose and his band were featured on the PBS four-part documentary *River of Song* about the music found along the Mississippi River.

DENNY, SANDY: *Singer, songwriter, guitarist, pianist. Born London, England, January 6, 1947; died London, England, April 21, 1978.*

Sandy Denny, before her career was tragically cut short, established herself as one of England's foremost folk and folk-rock artists in the 1960s and 1970s. Interest in Denny only increased after her death, as several retrospective packages were released and extensive information about her life and work was posted on the Internet.

As a child growing up in Wimbledon, England, she bore the impressive full name of Alexandra Elene MacLean Denny, obviously too long for a theater marquee. The nickname Sandy proved a better choice as she made her way as a performer. She began playing piano and singing in the choir in high school and took up the guitar after graduation. Reaching her teens in the late 1950s, she was influenced by both the blues-based skiffle movement and the burgeoning folk scene at home and abroad.

She took classes at Kingston Art School, where she met John Renbourn, Eric Clapton, and Jimmy Page. She studied nursing for a year, but left to pursue a career in music. With a fine voice and the ability to relate emotionally to the content of her material, she first impressed friends and schoolmates and, in the 1960s, patrons at the small folk clubs that flourished throughout England. Among them were Paul Simon and Art Garfunkel, who encouraged her to pursue a career in music.

In the mid-1960s, inspired by the rise of folk-rock in the United States under the aegis of Bob Dylan and the Byrds, a parallel trend developed in England. Her earliest recordings were contained on two albums released in 1967, *Sandy and Johnny* (with Johnny Silvo) and *Alex Campbell & His Friends*. That same year, Saga Records compiled the tracks on which Denny appeared into *The Original Sandy Denny*, including traditional songs like "Pretty Polly" and two songs by Tom Paxton, "Last Thing on My Mind" and "My Ramblin' Boy."

Though considered one of the best young folksingers in her homeland, Sandy gave up the folk circuit to join the Strawbs. Dave Cousins, leader of the country-folk band, first heard Denny singing in 1967 at the Troubadour in Earls Court, according to his liner notes for the reissue *Sandy Denny & the Strawbs* (Rykodisc, 1991). "She was sitting on a stool playing an old Gibson guitar, about eighteen, wearing a white dress, a white straw hat, with long blond hair and singing like an angel. I don't know what came over me but I went up to her immediately afterwards, introduced myself and invited her to join the Strawbs."

The Strawbs recorded the album *All Our Own Work* on a cinema stage in Copenhagen in 1967. It included her first version of her most famous song, the wistful "Who Knows Where the Time Goes." (Judy Collins chose the song, only the second Denny had written, as the title track of an album that went gold.)

Before the album was released in England, Denny left the Strawbs to join Fairport Convention. The latter band was started in London's Muswell Hill section by five young folk musicians, including lead guitar-vocalist Richard Thompson, guitarist-vocalist Ian (now Iain) Matthews, bassist Ashley Hutchings, and guitarist Simon Nicol. Sandy was not a founding member—the original group had Judy Dyble as female lead singer—but the group reached its creative peak during her years with it.

Denny joined when the group was working on its second album, which included her original composition "Fotheringay." That LP, under the title *What We Did on Our Holidays,* came out on Island in 1968 and eventually became the band's U.S. debut release on A&M Records in 1969. She toured widely with the band in the late 1960s, and at the start of the 1970s received effusive praise from critics for concerts in Europe and venues across the United States, contributing as both a performer and a songwriter. Some of her songs ranked among Fairport's most successful numbers. Their next two albums, *Unhalfbricking* (which features a picture of Denny's parents with Fairport members in the background on the cover) and *Liege and Lief*, were among the best in the folk-rock genre.

In 1969 she left the group to form a new band with Australian musician Trevor Lucas, who had recorded a solo album in Australia *(See That My Grave Is Kept Clean)*. Lucas had moved to England in 1965. He played with Bert Lloyd and also played bass for a band called Eclection. In 1969 he had played on Fairport's *Unhalfbricking*. By that time he and Denny were an item. They were married on September 20, 1973.

The new group, called Fotheringay, turned out one LP called *Fotheringay*, produced by Fairport maven Joe Boyd (now with Hannibal Records in Salem, Massachusetts) and released in the United States by A&M. The group included Lucas on guitar, Gerry Conway on drums, Jerry Donahue on guitar, and Pat Donaldson on bass. The band disbanded as it started work on its second album. Trevor wanted to remake some of the '50s rocking tunes and got a group of musicians, called the Bunch, together for the endeavor. Denny participated in the ensemble that included former Fairport members Richard and Linda Peters Thompson, Ashley Hutchings, and Dave Mattacks. They recorded the album at a studio called the Manor and released *The Bunch: Rock On* in 1972 on Island.

Denny was voted best female singer by readers of *Melody Maker* in 1970 and 1971, which gave impetus to her decision to try for a solo career. (Led Zeppelin had her sing on "The Battle of Evermore" on their 1971 album, *Led Zeppelin IV.*) The first of four solo LPs, *The North Star Grassman and the Ravens*, came out in 1971 and included production work from Thompson and appearances by Conway and Lucas. The album includes the traditional song "Blackwaterside," and Denny's antiwar original, "John the Gun." She followed in 1972 with *Sandy* and in 1973 with *Like an Old-Fashioned Waltz*, which she recorded in London and Los Angeles. Those LPs, particularly the first two, were excellent offerings that won deserved acclaim from critics. Besides some ear-catching originals, she also did ample justice to Dylan with such fine tracks as "Down in the Flood" on the first LP and "Tomorrow Is a Long Time" on the second.

Though her solo work brought her star status at home, she still remained a cult figure among U.S. fans. During 1972, Trevor rejoined Fairport to help in the production of *Rosie*, released on Island in 1973. Denny rejoined Fairport Convention in 1974, working on the *Rising for the Moon* album, released in 1975, with the revamped group and taking part in a cross-country con-

cert series in the United States. The new albums did not match the quality of her earlier Fairport work, but she continued to demonstrate her ability as a show-stopper in concert appearances. Her concert work was featured on *Live Convention,* released as *A Moveable Feast* in the United States. Her earlier work also appears on *The History of Fairport Convention,* released by Island in 1972.

In 1975 she (and Trevor) again left Fairport and returned to solo work releasing *Rendezvous* on Island Records in 1977. In July 1977 she gave birth to her daughter, Georgia. (Shortly thereafter, she and Trevor were considering a move to the United States to revive her career.) In November 1977 she began performing again after a two-year hiatus. She played for the last time at the Royalty Theatre in London on November 27, 1977. By that time she had decided to stop performing traditional music. According to the liner notes for *Gold Dust,* a live recording of her last concert released on Island in 1998, she declared: "If I have to sing 'Matty Groves' one more time, I'll throw myself out of a window." She was nervous during that concert, and her voice had deteriorated somewhat from relentless smoking. But she brings her life experience to the seventeen songs, a set that ends with "Who Knows Where the Time Goes."

Her hopes to reestablish her solo career were dashed as a result of a fall down a flight of stairs on April 17, 1978, while staying at a friend's apartment in London. She collapsed in a coma and was taken to St. Mary's Hospital, but never recovered consciousness. Her death, on April 21, 1978, was found to have been the result of a cerebral hemorrhage. (Her husband was in Australia with Georgia at the time. He rushed back to London just before Denny died. He moved back to Australia, where he remarried and had a son, Clancy.)

But interest in Denny refused to die. In 1985, Trevor returned to the United Kingdom, where he appeared in Fairport's annual Cropredy festival and helped to put together a comprehensive retrospective Denny album, *Who Knows Where the Time Goes?* on Hannibal, which included several previously unreleased tracks. Hannibal also released a retrospective of her studio work, *The Best of Sandy Denny.* In 1994, Vicki Clayton recorded *It Suits Me Well,* a collection of covers of Denny's songs. Several compilations, the most famous of which is titled *The Attic Tracks 1972–1984,* have been released by friends and fans, including the Australian Friends of Folk. The *Attic* album came from the personal collection of her husband, who died of a heart attack in 1989, leaving his widow to raise his two children.

Denny's voice and spirit lived on. As Linda Thompson described her for an article in the *Independent* in 1996: "She was like a tornado. You didn't like Sandy, you loved her to death or you couldn't stand her, or often both. Extraordinary person, and such a wretch. She seemed robust. She was a girl. But she had such a breakable heart. I don't know why. She was a chubby teenager. . . . She'd say to me, 'Oh Linda you're so pretty and all the boys fancy you.' And I'd say, 'But Sandy, they fancy you too . . . and you're such a genius.' Maybe Sandy did secretly want to be a pretty thing."

DENVER, JOHN: *Singer, songwriter, guitar player, actor. Born Roswell, New Mexico, December 31, 1943; died Monterey Bay, California, October 12, 1997.*

Throughout the 1970s, John Denver was one of the most popular musicians in the country. He wholesomely epitomized the era's folk-rock and country-rock phase as well as the general feeling of "getting back to the basics" and "living in the country." At the height of his popularity, his music was played on country stations as well as on middle-of-the-road channels and his fans were said to range in age from three to ninety-nine. As could be expected, tastes change, and John Denver was not represented often on the hit lists in the 1980s; however, a star of his magnitude could still command attention from a great many fans.

Born Henry John Deutschendorf Jr., he was the son of an air force officer who was constantly being transferred to new locations. From Roswell, New Mexico, where he was born, the family moved to Tucson, to Oklahoma, to Japan, back to Oklahoma, and back to Tucson, where John's grandmother gave him an acoustic guitar and he started taking lessons. When the family moved again, to Montgomery, Alabama, ninth grader John found that his guitar-playing ability attracted attention, and soon people started seeking out his friendship.

A year later, John's family moved again, this time to Fort Worth, Texas, but he no longer had to be the lonely new kid in school, a role he had played so many times before. He immediately started meeting people by singing in a church choir and by bringing his guitar to school. For a time, John's family stayed in Forth Worth, and John found himself being asked to perform with local rock bands and to play at school proms and parties.

After running away from home to California for a short while, Denver, frightened and confused, returned to Texas. He graduated from high school and enrolled at Texas Tech in Lubbock as an architecture major. But soon he found himself spending more time making music than studying. Folk music was in vogue in the early 1960s and he became an avid fan of folksingers such as Joan Baez; Tom Paxton; Peter, Paul and Mary; and the Chad Mitchell Trio, singing their songs at local coffeehouses and college hootenannies.

Meanwhile, John's grades were slipping, which meant friction with his parents. At the semester break of his junior year, he dropped out of school and, for the second time in his life, headed for California. This time he reached Los Angeles with more confidence than before. He got a job as a draftsman and spent all his spare time trying to break into the music business.

After a year of floundering, John got his first big break when he sang at Leadbetter's nightclub, a folk music center in West Los Angeles near the University of California at Los Angeles. The club's owner, Randy Sparks, who was also the founder of the New Christy Minstrels, told John that he liked his voice and that he wanted him to work as a regular performer at Leadbetter's.

John became a member of the Back Porch Majority, a Sparks-supervised group that acted as a sort of "farm club" for the New Christy Minstrels. But soon the Back Porch Majority became a successful group in its own right, with Denver singing solos that were well received by the audience. However, he felt that the Back Porch Majority was a dead-end street, so he auditioned for and won a job at a club called the Lumbermill in Phoenix.

Before he moved to Phoenix, John heard that Chad Mitchell was leaving his trio and was looking for a replacement. He sent a tape and was called for an interview in New York with the trio's management. Around 300 other people were competing for the job, but Denver was selected. For nearly four years, he toured with the trio (renamed "the Mitchell Trio" due to Chad's departure). During this time, he also developed as a successful songwriter.

John had done some songwriting before joining the Mitchell Trio, but his efforts were sporadic and he often took eight or nine months to finish a song. One of those songs, "Leaving on a Jet Plane," he wrote in one evening in 1966, as he related in an interview in January 1971, "while holed up in a Washington, D.C., hotel room. You see, we [the Mitchell Trio] were always being invited to parties. I was never the type to play around on the road and time after time I'd be the only guy at these parties without a girl. This time I decided I'd had it with that. When the others left for the party, at eight, I got a pound of salami and a six-pack of beer and my guitar and locked myself in my room. When they came back about midnight, I had eaten the salami, drunk all the beer, and written 'Jet Plane.'"

The Mitchell Trio included "Leaving on a Jet Plane" in their stage act. Peter, Paul and Mary heard the song, liked it, and recorded it on their album *1700* in 1967. However, the song did not become a hit until 1969, when a girlfriend of a d.j. in Denver, Colorado, talked him into playing the song over and over again on the station. The song caught on and became one of the top hits of 1969.

Meanwhile, the trio was going through changes and suffering from tensions between the various members. Joe Frazier left to go more deeply into rock music. Mike Kobluk eventually left the trio in part because of personality clashes with Denver. John reorganized the group with new members David Boise and Mike Johnson. Chad Mitchell sued to remove his name from the group since none of the original members remained, but

Denver pointed out that he had assumed $40,000 worth of debts from the old group and that the suit would prevent him from continuing to pay it off. Mitchell dropped the suit, Denver paid off the debts and then changed the name of the group to Denver, Boise and Johnson.

In 1969 Mike Johnson decided to leave the group. At that point, John disbanded the aggregation to try his luck as a solo artist. He went to Aspen, Colorado, to perform at ski resorts. He was well received and was invited to perform at the Cellar Door in Washington, D.C.

During his run at the Cellar Door, he met Jerry Weintraub, a rising management expert then working out of New York. The two got along well, and Weintraub took over management of Denver's career. He placed Denver as a guest artist on several shows, such as Merv Griffin, and also got him a recording contract with RCA.

Denver's first album, *Rhymes and Reasons* (fall 1969), contained his version of "Leaving on a Jet Plane" as well as the title song, also an original Denver composition. (Most of the material, however, was written by other writers.) The album received good reviews but failed to hit the charts, as did his next two RCA albums: *Take Me to Tomorrow* and *Whose Garden Was This*. "Aspenglow," on the *Take Me to Tomorrow* LP, was one of Denver's few original compositions in these years.

John cowrote his first hit with Bill and Taffy Danoff, whom John ran into at the Cellar Door. The husband-and-wife songwriting team, also performing under the name Fat City, were having trouble completing a song. Denver's act already featured one song they had written for him, "I Guess He'd Rather Be in Colorado," which he later recorded on his *Poems, Prayers and Promises* LP. They got together and finished the song, "Country Roads," before the night was over.

John recorded "Country Roads" for his upcoming album, *Poems, Prayers and Promises*. The single was released in early 1971 and climbed to the number-fifty position on the charts, the highest a Denver single had ever reached. However, he and Weintraub were not satisfied with reaching number fifty. They pushed the song through performances on talk shows and by getting maximum radio coverage. The plan worked, and the song moved up to the number-two position. Before 1971 was over, Denver had his first two gold record awards, one for the single "Country Roads" and the other for the album *Poems, Prayers and Promises*.

Denver's next album, *Aerie* (released in November 1971), included "Eagle and the Hawk" (which he cowrote with Mick Taylor for a TV special) and the original composition "Starwood in Aspen," in which Denver sang the praises of his new home in Colorado, where he settled permanently with his then-wife, Anne, in the early 1970s. The album was certified gold by the R.I.A.A. in January 1972.

John took some time off from doing concerts in the United States to do a series of telecasts for BBC II in England. The idea was to improve his performing ability in front of TV cameras. His increased skills in this area were evident when Denver returned to the United States. In 1972 and 1973, he appeared on numerous talk and variety shows. He also hosted *The Midnight Special*, a late-night ninety-minute musical show on NBC, on which he not only sang some of his songs but also held discussions with other entertainers about the importance of getting young people to register to vote. Among Denver's other television endeavors was *Bighorn*, his first prime-time special, which emphasized ecology.

John's sixth album, *Rocky Mountain High* (late 1972), was soon certified gold by the R.I.A.A. The title song was released as a single and climbed to the top of the charts. His next album, *Farewell Andromeda*, contained the hit single "I'd Rather Be a Cowboy" and was certified gold in September 1973.

Denver continued to use television to boost the sales of his records. In 1973 he wrote the score for the TV drama *Sunshine*, one of the most highly acclaimed shows of that year. The score included his composition "Sunshine on My Shoulders," from the *Poems, Prayers and Promises* LP. The song was reissued on his next album, *John Denver's Greatest Hits*, which was certified gold within two weeks of its release in November 1973. "Sunshine on My Shoulders" received such enormous airplay that it was issued as a single in early 1974 and was certified gold by the R.I.A.A. not long afterward. It reached number one in *Billboard* the week of March 30.

In early 1974, Denver made some television appearances. He played a dramatic role on the TV series *McCloud* in February 1974. During that period, he served as guest host on *The Tonight Show*, standing in for Johnny Carson.

To coincide with a countrywide concert tour in the summer of 1974, RCA issued a new LP, *Back Home Again*. The album was certified gold within a week of its release. In addition, the governor of Colorado, John Vanderhoof, declared the week of June 24–30 as Welcome Back Home Again, John Denver, Week, and proclaimed Denver the poet laureate of the state.

Meanwhile, *Back Home Again* went gold, as did its single, "Annie's Song." Another of its songs, "Sweet Surrender," was featured in a Disney movie, *The Bears and I*. Denver won his fourth gold record award for a single for the song "Back Home Again" in January 1975.

(Before Denver's marriage to Annie Martell ended in divorce in the mid-1970s, they adopted two children, Zachary and Anna-Kate. Later he married Cassandra Delaney, with whom he had a daughter, Jesse-Belle, born in 1989. That marriage also ended in divorce. As mutual friend Suzanne Paris told Lyndon Stambler, the breakup was caused both by career competition—she wanted to succeed as a singer—and the show business demands on Denver's time: "It's difficult to be married to a big star because they're gone all the time. John was always working and he was always gone. He demanded a lot of attention. Cassandra needed to have a sense of herself, not just to be his shadow all the time. She needed to separate from him to do that. He didn't like it when other people would give her attention. He was possessive of her.")

In 1975 John Denver truly reached the heights of his profession and was generally agreed to be the number-one–selling record artist in the United States. Released in early 1975, *An Evening with John Denver* (a two-record set based on his 1974 concert tour) and the number-one single "Thank God I'm a Country Boy" were certified gold by the R.I.A.A. Denver's *Windsong* LP, released in October 1975, had gone gold before the year was out. So did both sides of the single release from the album, "I'm Sorry" and "Calypso" (a song celebrating undersea explorer Jacques Cousteau). The combined "I'm Sorry"/"Calypso" disc reached number one on *Billboard* charts the week of September 27, 1975. Another single from that album, "Fly Away," also became a chart hit. His 1975 Christmas album, *Rocky Mountain Christmas,* was certified gold almost as soon as it was released. His earlier albums, *Back Home Again* and *John Denver's Greatest Hits,* remained on the national hit lists through 1975, with the latter reaching a total volume of over five million units by December 1975, thereby becoming one of the biggest-selling albums in pop music history. Denver took the album title, *Windsong,* to be the name of his own record company, formed during 1975. Among the acts signed to the label was a group called the Starland Vocal Band, whose members included longtime friend Bill Danoff (born Springfield, Massachusetts, May 7, 1946) and Taffy Danoff (born Kathy Nivert, Washington, D.C., October 25, 1944). With Jon Carroll and Margot Chapman, they formed a quartet that earned a number-one single, "Afternoon Delight," on *Billboard* charts the weeks of July 10 and 17, 1976.

Among the many kudos received by Denver in 1975, one of the greatest was undoubtedly being named Entertainer of the Year by the Country Music Association. He accepted the award via closed-circuit satellite relay from Australia, where he was doing a concert tour.

After 1975, Denver's hit productivity declined somewhat. Still, the LP *Spirit* (1976) went platinum, while *John Denver* (1979) went gold. He continued to do TV specials, however, and he appeared in the box office smash movie *Oh, God!* with George Burns in 1977, receiving mostly positive reviews for his performance. As evidence of his continued popularity and respect as an all-around entertainer, he was asked by the record industry to serve as host of the annual televised Grammy Awards in 1979, and hosted the event several more

times. In the early summer of that year, his single "What's on Your Mind"/"Sweet Belinda" was on the country charts for two months. At year-end his LP *A Christmas Together* (with the Muppets) hit album lists, eventually going platinum. In 1980, his album *Autograph* was on both pop and country charts. His 1981 chart-makers included the country single "The Cowboy and the Lady" and the gold album *Some Days Are Diamonds.*

Though essentially absent from the hit lists during the rest of the 1980s, Denver was constantly popping up in television specials and commercials and on interview shows. He traveled to Russia, where he performed to enthusiastic audiences. In addition, part of his home in Colorado became a center for ecological research. Denver increasingly became a sort of goodwill American musical ambassador to Communist countries. In December 1983, for example, he was invited to sing at a banquet for Chinese Premier Zhao Ziyang in New York City hosted by Mayor Edward Koch, and that, in turn, led to an invitation to do a concert tour in China. In February 1984, he went to Sarajevo, Yugoslavia, to perform the theme song he wrote (at ABC-TV's behest) for the winter Olympics, "The Gold and Beyond." In March 1984, his twenty-second album on RCA, *It's About Time,* was released. But his album sales were dwindling and his increasingly diverse interests, which included hosting his own Annual Celebrity Pro/Am Ski tournament in Colorado, and such charitable activities as an African trip to focus attention on the continent's food crisis and serving as a spokesman for a UNICEF fundraising drive, tended to dilute any emphasis on restoring his songwriting and recording luster. He did not abandon the recording field, though, ending his long alliance with RCA in 1984 and signing a new contract soon after with Geffen Records.

His Geffen affiliation, however, failed to reverse his declining status with record buyers. While he was far from inactive in the late 1980s and first part of the '90s, he did not maintain a high profile in the entertainment field for close to a decade. His Windstar Foundation, founded in 1976, aided efforts in wildlife preservation, alleviating world hunger, and other environmental concerns. In the mid-'90s he agreed to work on a new concert project to help celebrate the hundredth anniversary of the Wildlife Conservation Society, headquartered in New York's Bronx Zoo. The plan called for taping by Columbia/Sony of a live concert as the basis for his first live album since 1975 followed later by a worldwide tour during 1995–96. The tour was launched with a sold-out show at the famed Radio City Music Hall in Manhattan the night of Saturday, June 17, 1995, which won positive comments from city reviewers.

On June 18, the A&E TV network presented a two-hour World Premiere Special Presentation of *THE WILDlife CONCERT,* which, A&E reported, drew an estimated one million viewers, making it the highest rated music special in the network's history. A few days later, Sony Music/Legacy Recordings issued a two-CD or -cassette package titled *JOHN DENVER—THE WILDlife CONCERT,* while Sony Music Video issued a two-hour expanded home video. (In 1997 a Sony-issued disc from the concert, *The Best of John Denver Live,* rose to the upper levels of the Country charts, his first charted album since '88). In support of the releases, Denver appeared on such programs as *The Today Show, Live at Five,* and *Late Show with David Letterman.* The album debuted briefly on the *Billboard* top 200 chart at number 104, but failed to become a blockbuster release in the United States.

Still, there was no lack of recognition of his creative talents. On June 12, 1996, for instance, he was inducted into the Songwriters Hall of Fame. The Baltimore Orioles baseball team used "Thank God I'm a Country Boy" as an alternative to "Take Me Out to the Ball Game" for the seventh inning stretch. Denver, who sang the song himself at an Orioles event, promised he would do it again if the team made the World Series. It appeared that might happen in October 1997, but the team fell one series short of achieving that, and Denver, in any event, was no longer alive.

His career came to an abrupt end in early October when he was killed in the crash of an "experimental" light plane that plunged into Monterey Bay, California, with Denver at the controls. Taking a cue from his air force pilot father, Denver had been an avid aerospace enthusiast for many years (going so far as to ask the Soviet Union in 1989 for the opportunity to travel to the orbiting *Mir* space station) and was an experienced pilot who had flown both piston-engine and jet-powered aircraft. It turned out that his medical certificate for piloting had been pulled some months earlier because of two incidents in which police had cited him for driving a motor vehicle under the influence of alcohol. However, an autopsy after the plane crash showed his system to be clear of alcohol or drugs.

Suzanne Paris and her husband, songwriter David James Holster (who wrote the song "Cowboy's Delight" on Denver's *Windsong* album), had gone to comfort Cassie and Jesse after news of the tragedy came out. Holster recalled that after Jesse was told in the morning she began screaming, "'Daddy, Daddy.' I couldn't stand it, it was really tough. Then she sort of, I guess it's a defense mechanism that kids have, she sort of took it in stride after a while. I don't think it's sunk in. The reality of it hasn't sunk in. I think it will come in waves."

Adding to the trauma, Paris said, was the fact Denver and Cassie had resolved their differences and talked of reuniting. "They were the love of each other's lives. She was his greatest love and he was her greatest love. They had recently become very good friends and healed a lot of the wounds that were difficult for them before. They've been talking. Cassie wanted to make

sure there weren't any bad feelings between them. They were feeling really good. They never really wanted to break up. But people go through different things and they grow. There was a peace between them, Cassie and John."

Denver's longtime manager, Jerry Weintraub, expressed shock and deep sadness over Denver's passing. He emphasized that Denver was never difficult and never had a problem with alcohol when he was managing him: "I never had one difficult day with him." Still, he noted that the relationship ended abruptly in 1980 when John fired him. "He wanted to go on to other things. He thought I was protecting him or something. I really don't know why. We never discussed the reason. It didn't matter. I was already making movies."

His recollection was that he first saw John at the Bitter End in New York, not the Cellar Door in Washington, D.C. He said John was playing solo in front of an audience of twenty-five people and Weintraub signed him right away: "He was a very different and a terrific performer, and a gifted writer. I thought he was tremendously talented. I think he was misunderstood as an artist, as successful as he was. He was probably the most successful artist in the '70s, record-wise.

"We made fortunes of money, tens and tens of millions of dollars. He was a huge concert artist, huge; he was a huge TV artist, his television shows got huge ratings; he was a huge movie star in *Oh, God.* His records all sold enormous amounts. Even though he was not critically acclaimed by a lot of critics in the '70s, he was the people's singer. He was true to the things that he believed in, the environment and all the things that he cared about. He worked for those causes and he never stopped working for them until the day he died. He gave of himself to a lot of people and a lot of causes. He did it without needing a pat on his back. I give him all the credit in the world for that.

"The most important thing I could say about John Denver was something he said to me many times when we were kids. He said, 'Jerry, I don't have to do an interview because my lyrics speak for themselves.'"

Weintraub regretted that the two had lost touch with each other: "All I can see is his face and I just miss him. I'd like to talk to him right now. I'd tell him I think he made a tremendous impact on the world, much bigger than he ever knew when he was alive. I think that his music will live forever. I think he'd like to know that. I told him that when he was alive, but I don't think he ever believed me."

Certainly many record buyers seemed to endorse that idea in the months after Denver's death. His albums once more made top chart levels and sold millions of copies during that period. At the end of 1997, River North Records issued the album *A Celebration of Life (1943–1997).* Described as "his last recordings," it contained studio tracks completed a little more than a year before his death.

His 1980s LPs also included *Seasons of the Heart* (1982), *Dreamland Express* (1985), and *One World* (1986) on RCA. He released several albums on his Windstar label, including *The Flower that Shattered the Stone* (1990), *Christmas Like a Lullaby* (1990), *Different Directions* (1991), and *Higher Ground* (1991). Among the mid-to-late 1990s CD releases of Denver's material were *Take Me Home* (1995) and *Annie's Song* (1997); *Sunshine on My Shoulder* (1997), *Take Me Home, Country Roads* (1997), and *Calypso* (1997) on Laserlight/ Delta; *Rocky Mountain Collection* (1996), a comprehensive two-disc retrospective distilled from his "greatest hits" albums of 1973, 1977, and 1984 on RCA; and *All Aboard* (1997, Sony). Other compilations and reissues include *Country Roads Collection* (RCA, 1997), *His Greatest Hits and Finest Performances* (1997) on Reader's Digest, and *Rocky Mountain Christmas* (1998) on RCA.

In October 1998, to mark the one-year anniversary of his death, the PBS show *Nature* aired a one-hour documentary titled "John Denver: Let This Be a Voice." The show features dramatic footage of Denver in wilderness settings, traveling along rivers and over mountains, with a sound track of songs that were inspired by the beauty of nature.

Quotes from Paris, Holster, and Weintraub from interviews with Lyndon Stambler

DeSHANNON, JACKIE: *Singer, songwriter, actress. Born Hazel, Kentucky, August 21, 1944.*

As befits one who early trumpeted the greatness of Bob Dylan and was a pillar of strength in the folk movement of the 1960s, Jackie DeShannon seemed to personify the words of "We Shall Overcome" by bouncing back from low points in her career with renewed vigor.

Born in Kentucky (named Sharon Myers), she spent most of her early years in Chicago, where she made her public debut in a nearby town at the age of six. Her talents matured rapidly, and at twelve she had her own radio show on a station in southern Illinois. Even at that stage, she was writing original songs, compositions good enough for Imperial Records' head, Lew Chudd, to seek her out and sign her to a recording contract for his Los Angeles–based firm.

By the start of the 1960s, this association prompted a relocation to Southern California, from where she sallied forth to become one of the better-known performers in the pop and folk field throughout the decade. She became a favorite of fellow artists from every segment of pop music. In her many concert engagements of those years she appeared with such stars as Glen Campbell, soul singer James Brown, Harry Belafonte, and many others from both folk and rock fields. At some of the folk festivals she appeared in, she shared the program with people like Bob Dylan and Joan Baez. In the mid-1960s, the Beatles sought her out to join on one of their tours. She also had close rapport with the Byrds, who included one of her compositions, "Don't Doubt Yourself Babe," on their landmark first album.

By the time the Byrds' first album came out, Jackie already had placed several singles on the charts, starting with "Faded Love" in 1963, followed the same year by "Needles and Pins" and, in 1964, with "When You Walk in the Room." In 1965, she gained her initial gold record singles award for her version of Burt Bacharach's "What the World Needs Now." Meanwhile, others besides the Byrds were profiting from her original compositions, including Brenda Lee, who made top chart levels with "Dum Dum," the Searchers, with the hit "When You Walk in the Room," and Marianne Faithfull, with a mid-1960s winner, "Come Stay with Me."

Her Liberty/Imperial album releases in the mid-1960s included *Jackie DeShannon* in November 1963; *This is Jackie DeShannon* (11/65); *In the Wind* (1/66); *Are You Ready for This* (12/66); *New Image* (7/67); and *For You* (12/67). Though she turned out many pop-oriented records in the early and mid-1960s, most of her offerings were in the folk vein. Particularly with college students, she was considered a major folk artist and played to capacity crowds on campuses around the United States.

She also was no stranger to TV, appearing on many programs, including *The Ed Sullivan Show*, the *Andy Williams Show*, and the *Johnny Cash* show. Her TV work expanded to include acting roles in the second half of the 1960s, including guest appearances on *My Three Sons*, *Wild, Wild West*, and *The Name of the Game*. In 1970 she had a cameo role on the Screen Gems TV movie *Hide and Seek*.

Her singing efforts seemed to flag a little as the 1960s drew to a close. A move to Atlantic Records helped lead to the success of her 1969 single of her composition "Put a Little Love in Your Heart." The song was one of the major pop hits of the year, earning DeShannon a gold record and bringing invitations to appear on the supper club circuit in such gilt-edged places as San Francisco's Fairmont Hotel and New York's Copacabana. The song's success helped push the LP *Put a Little Love in Your Heart* over gold record levels. She finished up 1969 with another single, "Love Will Find a Way," on the charts.

However, her image as a shallow club singer disenchanted many of her younger fans, reflected in a poor reception to her early 1970s college tours. She stressed to *Los Angeles Times* writer Richard Cromelin (December 4, 1977) that she never felt her songs lacked depth. She claimed they actually were similar in approach and content to the material that made Carole King a national favorite in the mid-1970s:

"I think if I had been more consistent in stringing things together, I might have made a little more sense. I just was not able to do that. I think I was ahead of a lot of what was to come. Sometimes when you're a pioneer in something you have to pay a little bit."

After things slowed for her in 1970, she moved to Capitol Records, which issued her debut single on the label, "Keep Me Warm," in June 1971. That recording also represented Jackie's debut as a producer. Her first Capitol LP, *Songs,* came out in mid-1971 and won some attention, but not as much as her next, *Jackie,* in 1972, which made upper-chart levels. A number of her singles showed up on national charts that year: "Only Love Can Break Your Heart," "Paradise," and "Vanilla Olay." Her total song catalog by then was over the 500 mark, including songs cowritten with such people as Randy Newman and the lead guitarist of Led Zeppelin, Jimmy Page.

In the mid-1970s, despite the 1975 release on Columbia of a first-rate album, *New Arrangement,* Jackie's career again hit some soft spots, and she gave up touring for a while to concentrate on writing. In late 1977 she reemerged with a new album on Amherst Records titled *You're the Only Dancer.* A single from the album, the composition "Don't Let the Flame Burn Out," made the hit lists, her first single to do that for several years.

Looking back over her career, she told Cromelin, "I've learned a lot from my low periods and I've been able to come out of them and make them work for me. You can sit here and say that this wasn't done right or that wasn't done right, but you can waste a lot of energy doing that. I really don't dwell on the negative aspects. Maybe I have too much Walt Disney in my eyes. Basically I think I'm a pretty positive kind of person. . . . Maybe I'm feeling how everybody else is feeling . . . that there's a lot of good in people, that you can make things better if you yourself get better, that you are the master of your own destiny. As I say, maybe it's a little too much Walt Disney, but I'm basically just a simple person."

In the early 1980s, DeShannon's recording career was in the doldrums, but some of her songs provided hits for others. One example was the single of her "When You Walk in the Room," recorded by Stephanie Winslow, which made the country top 30 in 1981.

Even more striking was "Bette Davis Eyes," cowritten by Jackie and Donna Weiss. A smash hit for singer Kim Carnes in 1981, it won Grammys for Record of the Year and Song of the Year.

DICKENS, HAZEL: *Singer, guitarist, songwriter. Born Mercer County, West Virginia, June 1, 1935.*

Small and wiry, at first glance Hazel Dickens gave an impression of fragility, but once she started singing her voice quickly captured her listener's attention for its robust sound. And her subject matter, often based on firsthand experiences, was uncompromising in its condemnation of the wrongs done to working people, particularly miners and women. Her original compositions included "Black Lung," inspired in part by the deaths of her older brothers and brothers-in-law from miner's black lung disease or related illnesses, and one objecting to sexism and the denial of women's rights, "Don't Put Her Down, You Helped Put Her There."

One of eleven children of a family headed by a hard-bitten Primitive Baptist minister who supported his brood by hauling timber to the mines, her early musical exposure was hindered somewhat by her father's refusal to allow musical instruments in the house in keeping with his religion's tenets. However, the many hours of the *Grand Ole Opry* still blared forth from the family radio on Saturday nights and, as a girl, Hazel sang in the church choir.

At sixteen, in 1950, she dropped out of high school to follow an older sister to Baltimore, Maryland, where she found a variety of jobs in ensuing years, including positions in plants that produced tin cans, paper cups, and electrical wires, as well as some waitressing and work as a salesclerk. She told Edward M. Silverman ("Working Heroine Folksinger Hazel Dickens," *Option Magazine,* September–October 1990), "Many of the mines had closed down and there wasn't a lot of work [back home]. Things were tough. There were different little patches all around Baltimore of people who'd come from Appalachia to find work in factories and construction."

During her early years in Baltimore, Hazel had no thoughts of trying her hand at entertaining. Later, when two of her brothers who played, respectively, banjo and guitar, settled in the city she joined them for some "pickin' parties" where they played traditional and bluegrass-style music at informal gatherings of friends and acquaintances. A major turning point came when one of her brothers was hospitalized with tuberculosis and met folksinger Mike Seeger, who, as a conscientious objector to military service, was working as hospital attendant. The brother, in turn, introduced Seeger to his sister.

As Seeger told Margie Sellinger for a *People* magazine article (November 16, 1987), "She was quiet, but I could tell she had a pretty sharp tongue and a sharp wit to go with it." Seeger soon was performing with Hazel and others at get-togethers and occasional bar gigs. During one of those shows, Dickens told *People,* she was pushed into becoming a guitar player. A group member, she recalled, worried that the bar owner would feel he wasn't getting his money's worth if one performer couldn't play an instrument, "handed me a guitar and said, 'Grab an A chord and hang on.'"

It was Seeger who introduced her to Alice Gerrard, a classically trained artist who had developed a love for old-timey music and bluegrass while attending Antioch College. Alice and Hazel formed a duo that was an important factor in the folk music scene for over a decade from the early '60s to the mid-'70s. Alice told Silverman, "There was an explosion of bluegrass around Baltimore and Washington, D.C., in the late '50s and early

'60s. I used to hang out at the Famous Restaurant in Washington. Hazel was a part of all that. For a lot of us not necessarily raised with this music, it was part of the folk revival. But it was real. We saw the connection to the original old-time music. Hazel and I met through a mutual friend. I was told that I'd like her. Hazel was described as a little, tiny girl with a great, big voice. She was streetwise and, in many ways, became a sort of mentor to me. She taught me a lot about singing."

The two decided to team up, adding to their song list by research at the Library of Congress and attendance at various folk festivals. At first they went to festivals mainly to pick up song ideas from others, but before long they were taking part in some of those as performers, with Alice providing solo and support vocals and instrumental work on fiddle, banjo, or autoharp. In 1965 their debut album was released on Folkways, *Who's That Knocking?*, the first of two releases on the label; the second, *Won't You Come and Sing for Me,* came out in 1973. When their first LP came out, the duo naively thought the door was open for them to earn handsome incomes in music. They soon realized folk recordings didn't provide openings for big bank accounts. Dickens could not support herself solely from music until 1979, by which time the duo had been dissolved for a few years.

In the early 1970s, the two artists signed with another label, Rounder, which issued *Hazel & Alice* in 1973. Besides covers of songs like the Carter Family's "Hello Stranger" and the Civil War number "Two Soldiers," the album included originals like Alice's "Custom Made Woman Blues" and Hazel's "Don't Put Her Down, You Helped Put Her There" was a gem. It was well-received by critics and the then-dwindling folk music audience. Hazel remembered their being cheered wildly by audiences at folk venues of the period by people who had bought the album. (The album was reissued by Rounder in 1995.)

A year or so after their next album, *Hazel Dickens & Alice Gerrard,* came out on Rounder in 1976, the two decided to go their separate ways. Hazel continued as a solo artist while Alice briefly worked with a group called the Harmony Sisters, which recorded two LPs before breaking up. Alice recorded a concert album with her husband, Mike Seeger, called *Mike and Alice Seeger in Concert* on King Records in Japan (1970). In 1975 Arhoolie released an album featuring the Strange Creek Singers (Hazel, Alice, Mike Seeger, and Tracy Schwarz from the New Lost City Ramblers) on an album called *Get Acquainted Waltz* (reissued in 1997). In 1980, Jean Ritchie's Greenhays label released *Mike Seeger and Alice Gerrard.* Alice recorded an album for Copper Creek, *Pieces of My Heart,* issued in 1994. Alice decided to devote more time to raising her children, and by the end of the 1980s published an old-time music magazine called the *Old-Time Herald.* Hazel had expanded her credits in the mid-1970s by singing four

songs on the documentary film of the coal miners' struggles, *Harlan County U.S.A.,* which was released in 1976. Her self-penned sound track song, "They'll Never Keep Us Down," later became the title song for a 1987 United Mine Workers video.

Discussing her 1979 move to work full-time in music with Stephen Holden of the *New York Times* ("Folk Tunes That Address Real Folks," May 29, 1992), she said, "I decided if I was going to starve, I was going to starve doing something I liked."

The move also gave her more opportunity to write songs about the continuing problems of working-class people. She told Holden, "I'm a home-made type personality who doesn't do anything on schedule. Right now I'm trying to write a song about the way the economy is and unemployment running so high among workers. What bothers me is the way that most people who have spent their entire lives working in factories, mills and mines are getting laid off without any benefits."

In 1981 Hazel made her solo debut on Rounder with *Hard Hitting Songs for Hard Hit People* (available on cassette in the 1990s). With music no longer a part-time activity, she was free to extend her performing activities as both a concert artist singing at festivals, folk clubs, and other venues and an activist taking part in benefits and rallies for working people and civil rights. As a board member of the Southern Grassroots Revival Project she continued that group's support of civil rights that had been under way since the late 1960s. In the 1987 John Sayles film *Matewan,* about a bloody coal mining strike in the 1920s, she had a brief on-camera appearance singing a funeral dirge at a miner's funeral. She told Silverman, "It was the first time I'd done anything like that and I really felt good about it. Here someone was paying attention, dug back and got those stories that aren't in the history books."

By the start of the 1990s her album output for Rounder included the 1984 *By the Sweat of My Brow,* the 1986 release *It's Hard to Tell the Singer from the Song,* and, in 1987, *A Few Old Memories.* The excellent and highly acclaimed *It's Hard to Tell the Singer* included such excellent originals as "You'll Get No More from Me" (about a failed relationship) and "Hills of Home," an antiwar gospel number; "Will Jesus Wash the Bloodstains from Your Hands"; a poignant number about the sad situation of nursing home patients in "Play Us a Waltz"; and an inspired rendering of Bob Dylan's "Only a Hobo."

In the 1990s Hazel continued to perform at benefits and in solo and festival concerts. In 1990 she was a featured artist at the hundredth anniversary of the United Mine Workers. Concert staples included such other originals as "Old Callused Hands," "Working Girl Blues," and "Your Greedy Heart." Her early '90s credits included feature sets at the International Bluegrass Music Festival in Kentucky. On some occasions in the '80s and

'90s she reunited in concert with Mike Seeger or Alice Gerrard.

In 1996 Smithsonian/Folkways released *Pioneering Women of Bluegrass,* a twenty-six-track collection from their 1965 and 1973 albums for the Folkways label. The CD demonstrates their roots: the soulful music of the Carter Family, Callahan Brothers, Bob Wills, Bill Monroe, and the Louvin Brothers. Among the tracks are the Carter Family's "Distant Land to Roam," a song Bill Monroe gave to them called "The One I Love Is Gone," "Walkin' in My Sleep," "Cowboy Jim," "Coalminer's Blues," and "Long Black Veil." In 1997 Hazel was one of the contributors, along with Phyllis Boyens, the Reel World String Band, and others, to the Rounder album *Coal Mining Women.* Back in 1984, Rounder had issued an album by the same artists called *They'll Never Keep Us Down: Women's Coal Mining Songs.* In 1998 she recorded a new album for Rounder, *Heart of a Singer,* along with Ginny Hawker and Carol Elizabeth Jones. Hazel's work can also be found on the 1994 Rounder collection *Old-Time Music on the Air, Volume 1,* and the *Matewan* sound track (1995, Daring Records). In 1996 she was honored as a featured performer at the Smithsonian Institution's Festival of American Folklife on the Mall in Washington, D.C. When asked by a reporter about her music, her response was direct: "I go for that feel, I go for the jugular. When I'm singing, I'm thinking about the real things."

DiFRANCO, ANI: *Singer, songwriter, guitarist. Born Buffalo, New York, September 23, 1970.*

Dressed in army fatigue shorts, a black vest, and combat boots, her purple braided hair flying behind her, Ani (pronounced "Ahnee") DiFranco looked more punk than folk as she whirled across the stage at the Mayan Theater in Los Angeles on June 2 1996. But despite appearances, DiFranco is a maverick who identifies with the spirit of folk music. She rejected lucrative major label offers to retain her integrity.

Early in her career, DiFranco shaved off her hair and donned a silver nose ring, a form of personal protest. "When I was about seventeen and guys were coming to hear me because I was cute, I thought, 'Maybe I don't want to be attractive at all. Maybe I want to shave my head and put on heavy black boots and see who'll listen to me then,'" she told *Interview* (July 1995). Later she grew her hair but dyed it greenish blond. In 1990 she started her wildly successful Righteous Babe Records. She created her own artwork, set up her own distribution deals, and filled 2,000-seat theaters. She sold more than two million copies of her first twelve albums by mail order and Internet, even though she received little airplay. In the process she stretched the limits of contemporary folk music.

Ani's songs are often laced with profanity on topics about abortion, rape, menstruation, exploitation, and bisexuality. Even when she doesn't use profanity, her

lyrics are brutally direct. "Blood in the Boardroom," from *Puddle Dive,* her fourth album, is the internal monologue of a woman who is menstruating while attending a board meeting: *I didn't really have much to say the whole time I was there/So I just left a big brown bloodstain on their white chair.*

"It was me, young artist going into a record company boardroom of a major label, and having this sort of poetic occurrence that I don't think this world is humanizing and affirming," DiFranco told Paul Robicheau of the *Boston Globe* (May 12, 1994).

Despite her frank lyrics, DiFranco is guarded about her upbringing. She grew up in Buffalo. At nine, she devoured a Beatles songbook, performing in local bars. Mike—a thirty-year-old "degenerate folk–singer barfly" concert booker whom she met at a guitar store—encouraged her. He booked artists John Gorka, Suzanne Vega, and Christine Lavin, and DiFranco's family put them up at their house.

A couple years later, however, her home life became unsettled. "My mother and I moved out of the house when I was about eleven," she told Robert Hilburn of the *Los Angeles Times* (May 5, 1996). "We were both kind of freaking out because my family was not a very happy one. The house when everyone lived together was like one scary scene after another. So it was a good thing we all kind of went our different ways."

DiFranco tried dancing and painting, but decided against those pursuits. She wrote poems first. But hanging out with the songwriters Mike booked, Ani began writing her own songs at fourteen. A year later her mother, an architect, took a job out of state. DiFranco started living on her own.

At sixteen, she graduated from the Visual and Performing Arts High School. By the time she was eighteen, DiFranco had played every bar in Buffalo, including a gig every Saturday night at Buffalo's Essex Street Pub. After a year of art classes at the State University of New York at Buffalo, she moved to New York City where she worked as a nude model, kitchen helper, and house painter. She took classes at the New School for Social Research. But, as she told Hilburn, "Music was just a way of life for me. I'm talking about people with guitars in bars—unknown people, if you will, open mike type scenes, lots of alcoholic, barfly types who wrote their own songs."

She cut a demo and approached some record companies but got nowhere. Instead she borrowed money from friends and looted her bank account to finance her first album, a cassette titled *Ani DiFranco* released in 1990. DiFranco produced 500 cassettes, which she sold at concerts, and Righteous Babe was born. He debut album revealed her ability to tackle personal subjects: "Lost Woman Song" is about an abortion she had. She was inspired by other female poets writing about the same topic. "Both Hands" is about the end of a love affair.

As word of her music spread, she began to tour extensively around the country in a VW Beetle. She told *Folk Roots* about some hairy moments: hitchhiking in Mexico without any money, spending a cold night on the streets of Cambridge, arriving in London without any money or gigs.

Tenacious Ani continued to release albums at an impressive rate: *Not So Soft* (1991), *Imperfectly* (1992), *Puddle Dive* and *Like I Said* (for which she re-recorded fifteen of her earlier songs) (1993), and *Out of Range* (1994), when she incorporated Righteous Babe. (Her Norma Ray-like logo is a sketch of a woman holding two fists above her head.) She continued apace with *Not a Pretty Girl* (1995) and *Dilate* (1996). In October 1996 she joined forces with folksinger Utah Phillips and released *The Past Didn't Go Anywhere,* which consists of Phillips telling stories and DiFranco laying down the music. Like Phillips, a longtime union man, Ani held on to her independence with religious fevor, spurning offers from the majors. "If you want to challenge the system, you don't go to bed with it," she explained to *Guitar Player* (December 1994).

An article in the *Los Angeles Times* business section (July 5, 1996), noted that DiFranco's royalty rate was double that of the biggest major label artists. She makes $4.25 per album, while Michael Jackson makes $2 an album. The article, by Chuck Philips, noted that the majors provide marketing, promotion, and distribution expertise and make up for lower royalties by selling many more units. Hootie and the Blowfish made only $1.25 an album but sold more than nine million copies of their debut.

"For me, it's not a question of why don't you sign with a label, it's why would you?" Ani told *Dirty Linen.* "If you can figure out how to do it for yourself and be your own boss, that seems to be much more gratifying and politically useful than supporting some guy with a fancy car and car phone and coke habit."

By 1995, DiFranco was called "the hottest young performer in folk" by *Guitar Player* and had write-ups in the *New York Times, Los Angeles Times, Ms. Magazine,* and *Rolling Stone. Puddle Dive* and *Out of Range* reached number fourteen and number twenty-two respectively on the Canadian charts. *Not a Pretty Girl* edged her into the mainstream, gaining critical as well as commercial success.

"DiFranco is a wonder to behold," Fred Goodman wrote in *Rolling Stone* (August 24, 1995). "A spiky-haired volcano who first glows smoky and warm and then explodes into a splendor of anger. Her songs, though mostly about independence and romance (with both men and women), often take unexpected, jarring turns—such as when she recites a poem about an abortion or sings about being felt up on the subway."

While praising her as one of the few artists "who can really paint the rainbows," Goodman noted a down side to her independence. "The torrential passion and volatility of both her lyrics and percussive guitar, so arresting in concert, aren't fully realized by production that consciously spurns the kind of full-fleshed arrangements associated with 'commercial' projects."

Ani acknowledged the growing pains in going solo. She had to tour incessantly to promote her albums and distribution was difficult. She eventually got an 800 number—(800) ON HER OWN—for people who wanted to order her CDs, tapes, and merchandise. She started selling T-shirts emblazoned with *Every tool is a weapon if you hold it right—a.d.* She maintains a large mailing list.

For four years, DiFranco and Scot Fisher, an old friend and longtime manager, ran Righteous Babe out of Fisher's apartment in Buffalo. In 1995 she signed a distribution deal with Koch International. She also hired a publicist, Tracy Mann, and Fleming Tamulevich & Associates to handle bookings.

Despite her punk appearance, DiFranco calls herself a folksinger in part because it's so out of fashion. "People think it's so uncool to be a folksinger," she told *Performing Songwriter* (May-June 1995). "And I think that anything that all the hipsters think is uncool must be cool. . . . I'm a real substance kind of gal. With folk music, it's subcorporate, it's political, it's grassroots and it's related to the community it comes out of, as opposed to being the creation of an industry that's making music that is marketed and passively consumed by big crowds of people in huge generic stadiums. So I've always been into folk music as sort of a weapon against the homogenization and the isolation of people."

Like *Pretty Girl, Dilate* received strong reviews. Robert Hilburn gave it four stars, the top rating. *Time's* Christopher John Farley called it "her best yet—her vocals and guitar work still seethe, but she's added atmoshperic touches, such as a trippy hip-hop beat on a cover of the song 'Amazing Grace'. . . . DiFranco makes folk relevant and fresh by incorporating other genres" (June 10, 1996).

DiFranco, who is openly bisexual, gave Hilburn a glimpse into what *Dilate* is about. "Well, I've made an album I never thought I'd make," she told him. "I've been sort of consumed with a relationship for a year now and the album is all about one subject. It's about a love affair from all these different angles. . . . The denial, the anger, the rapture, the insecurities."

Dilate hit number eighty-seven on *Billboard* and generated approximately $600,000 without a big ad push or radio airplay, according to Philips.

DiFranco developed a percussive style of guitar playing, using open tunings and Nailene press-on nails attached with super glue instead of picks. As she told Al Reiss of *Dirty Linen* (October/November '94): "My style comes out of survival techniques; years of playing in loud bars where you have to figure out some way of making people turn around and shut up and listen when they really just want to drink and pick somebody up."

She plays an Alvarez Weir guitar (the only hitch, she told *Guitar Player,* is the placement of the volume and tone controls: "Girls have tits"). For a long time she had just one backup musician—Andy Stochansky, a Canadian percussionist, who released an album called *While You Slept.* She added bassist Sara Lee during her 1996 tour. The sound is surprisingly potent. "We need tons of wattage and these rock sound company guys see acoustic guitar and drums [and say], 'Oh, that's some pansy ass folk show' and they very often show up with insufficient gear," DiFranco told *Pollstar* (December 4, 1995). "They just don't understand that this is a really heavy loud sound. I blow amps all over the place—the little fuckin' folk girl."

Her collaboration with Utah Phillips, *The Past Didn't Go Anywhere,* was decidedly noncommercial. The project grew out of their five-year friendship. She took his spoken word interludes about hobos, hustlers, and politicians, and set them to music. At first glance it would seem like an unlikely pairing: Phillips, a veteran of the Korean War and a member of the Industrial Workers of the World, and the much younger DiFranco. But Ani states: "I do appreciate the energy and dynamic of youth, but I think there's a lot we can learn if we are humble enough to pay attention to the people who have come before us." In February 1997, she presented the Lifetime Achievement Award to Phillips at the Folk Alliance convention in Toronto.

In April 1997, she released a two-disc live set (with a thirty-six-page photo booklet) from her spring and fall 1996 tour. The album, *Living In Clip,* a reference to overloading an amplifier, was recorded on ADAT, an eight-track videotape format. She included "Gravel," the first song she wrote after releasing *Dilate.* The set also includes poems and stories from her concerts.

In 1997 Bob Dylan invited DiFranco to open for him during an August tour of the East Coast. That year she also put out a four-song EP entitled *More Joy, Less Shame.* Maintaining her new-album-per-year pace in 1998, Ani issued *Little Plastic Castle.* While containing mostly new songs, the collection also included her studio version of "Gravel." Her defiant attitude is reflected in such tracks as "Swan Dive" and the title track (*People talk about my image/Like I come in two dimensions*).

In 1998 there were many other changes as well. Drummer Andy Stochansky left the band to pursue other goals. Daren Hahn, her new drummer, joined at the end of the year. And to the amazement of many, given her love songs for both women and men, she got married to Andrew Gilchrist, her longtime sound engineer, in May 1998 at a private ceremony in Canada. While Ani continued to wear combat boots (albeit with heels to boost her height) and army fatigues, she hasn't shaved her head for some time (although her hair color changes) which gives her a more feminine look. But her publicist Tracy Mann says Ani "would definitely define herself as queer." On April 12, 1999, she received a special OutMusic award at the third annual Gay and Lesbian American Music Awards.

In January 1999 she released her twelfth studio recording, *Up Up Up Up Up Up.* The album has a fuller band sound due to a band including Julie Wolf on keyboards, Jason Mercer on bass, and Hahn on drums.

DiFranco has received three Grammy nominations for Best Female Rock Vocal: in 1998 for "Shy," 1999 for "Glass House," and 2000 for "Gravel." She released another album with Utah Phillips entitled *Fellow Workers* in May 1999, which was nominated for a Best Contemporary Folk Grammy. In June 1999 she embarked on a nationwide tour with Maceo Parker, James Brown's longtime sax player. Later that year, she released *To the Teeth,* her thirteenth studio recording, which includes Parker on three tracks and The Artist Formerly Known as Prince on one. In 2000, Righteous Babe issued a Woody Guthrie tribute album, *'Til We Outnumber 'em.*

DiFranco's turquoise eyes, broad smile, and laugh belie the tough image she portrays in her songs. "I get these people who hear my album and come to interview me and say, 'So Ms. DiFranco, are you an angry woman?'" she told *Folk Roots* (March 1995). "It just seems such an odd thing to ask. Yes, if someone pisses me off I'm an angry woman. But how can anyone possibly be just one emotion? I'm an angry woman, but I'm also a happy woman and a hungry woman and a sleepy woman."

Some of her songs are like "a day in the life" and some are about "LIFE," she told *Performing Songwriter.* "Some are more like my little manifestos and some are more like small observations along the way. . . . I think it's important to tell our stories, just to add it to the soup. . . . That's all I intend to do in my songs, just tell my story and write about what I know."

Written with assistance from Tracy Mann

DILLARDS, THE: *Vocal and instrumental group. Personnel, early 1960s: Douglas Flint "Doug" Dillard, born East St. Louis, Illinois, March 6, 1937; Rodney Adean "Rod" Dillard, born East St. Louis, Illinois, May 18, 1942; Roy Dean Webb, born Independence, Missouri, March 28, 1937; Mitchell "Mitch" Jayne, born Hammond, Indiana, July 5, 1930. Doug Dillard left 1968, replaced by Herb Pedersen. Paul York added 1968. Pedersen replaced by Billy Ray Lathum, 1970. Jayne replaced by Jeff Gilkinson, mid-1970s. Lathum replaced by Doug Bounsall, 1977.*

Bluegrass has had several spurts of popularity since it was introduced on the national level by Bill and Charlie Monroe and the Bluegrass Boys in the 1930s. One of those "revivals" took place in the late 1950s and early 1960s as part of the folk boom and another in the 1970s as part of the "progressive" bluegrass period. Missouri's pride, the Dillards, participated in both revivals.

The founders of that band, Douglas and Rodney, were born across the river in Illinois, but their family home was in Salem, Missouri. Playing country and bluegrass music was a tradition in the Dillard clan, and both the father and grandfather of the boys played stringed instruments. While Doug and Rod still were in elementary school they began playing bluegrass on guitar and banjo. In their teens, first Doug and later Rod played at local events with friends and schoolmates. Doug, five years older than Rod, continued to perform whenever he could after graduating from school.

By then the brothers were writing original material and looking for ways to further their musical careers. In 1958 they went to St. Louis and found a backer for their first recording efforts. One of their first discs was a song cowritten by the brothers called "Banjo in the Hollow." Working with them at the time were such other young musicians as John Hartford (fiddle), Joe Noel (mandolin), and Buddie Van. The Dillards won support in the late 1950s from their friend, Mitch Jayne, then a disc jockey on Salem station KSMO. Mitch played their new record on the radio a number of times.

Jayne, who played banjo and bass, joined the boys in playing local school events, square dances, and other functions. Soon after, a fourth member, Dean Webb, mandolinist, was added. The group extended their efforts to playing folk clubs and coffeehouses in various parts of Missouri and nearby states in the early 1960s. In 1962, they decided to try to make the "big time" by journeying westward to Los Angeles.

Once in Los Angeles they followed the usual routine of working small clubs, making demo tapes, and looking for a recording opportunity. That came when Elektra Records officials gave them a contract. Their first album was released in July 1963 under the title *Backporch Bluegrass*. This was followed in November 1964 with the LP *The Dillards Live—Almost* and a year or so later by the album *Pickin' and Fiddlin'*.

During that period, a talent agent found them a job acting and playing music on the *Andy Griffith Show* on TV. For three years the band members played the roles of the slow-witted Darlin Family on the nationally televised program. Their skit showcased their excellent bluegrass playing for the national audience.

The group, meanwhile, had become somewhat controversial with bluegrass purists, who were upset that the band used electronically amplified instruments at one of the bluegrass festivals they appeared at in 1964. The Dillards, however, persisted in playing the music their own way. (In the 1970s, though, the band stressed acoustic rather than electronic offerings.) Later on, the band committed another heresy by adding a drummer to the roster.

In 1968 Doug left and was replaced by guitarist-banjoist Herb Pedersen. That same year, the group added Paul York on drums. The reorganized band continued to tour widely and record for Elektra, turning out *Wheatstraw Suite* in 1968 and *Copperfields* in 1969, the group's final offering on Elektra.

Pedersen departed in 1970 to do session work and to join Country Gazette, and his place was taken by Billy Ray "Hot Rod Banjo" Lathum, who took part in the band's first and only recording for Anthem/UA Records, *Roots and Branches,* issued in 1972. The Dillards then moved to Poppy Records, which released the LP *Tribute to the American Duck* in 1973. Soon after, Jayne departed and Jeff Gilkinson (bass, harmonica, cello) came aboard.

The Dillards kept active in the mid-1970s, performing in country and bluegrass festivals, folk clubs, and on college campuses across the United States and Canada, though their recording activities were at a standstill. The band made occasional TV appearances, as well, including a PBS *Live from Wolf Trap* (near Washington) concert.

By the late 1970s, interest in bluegrass, which had increased slowly but steadily throughout the decade, reached a new high, with many bluegrass nightclubs springing up in all parts of the United States and even overseas. All of this helped the Dillards' fortunes improve and brought a new contract with Flying Fish Records. Their debut on the label was the LP *The Dillards versus the Incredible L.A. Time Machine,* released in 1977. Soon after, the band had another change when Lathum left and was replaced by Doug Bounsall (electric guitar, banjo, fiddle). One of the first projects Bounsall took part in was the direct-to-disc album, *Mountain Rock,* issued on the Crystal Clear label.

In 1979, the band recorded its second LP on Flying Fish, *Decade Waltz.* Helping on this was Herb Pedersen, who, besides playing acoustic and electric guitar and banjo and contributing on vocals, mixed the final LP. Among the songs in the album were Pedersen's "Easy Ride," Bounsall's "10 Years Waltz," Jeff Gilkinson's "Gruelin' Banjos," and the Rod and Homer Dillard and Paul York collaboration on "Greenback Dollar." Besides performing at such festivals as the Telluride (Colorado) Country and Bluegrass Festival and the Jim and Jesse Third Annual Mid-America Bluegrass Convention, the band joined in the Dillards' reunion in Salem, Missouri, in August. For that event, the mayor of Salem proclaimed August 8 "Dillard Day." The reunion brought together not only former band members and close associates such as John Hartford and Byron Berline, but four generations of Dillards, ranging from seventy-eight-year-old Homer Earl Dillard Sr., on fiddle, to his grandson, eighteen-year-old Earl Dillard, on banjo. The proceedings provided the basis for the live album *Homecoming & Family Reunion,* issued by Flying Fish in 1979. The reunion also was taped for presentation on NBC-TVs *Real People* program in the 1979–80 season.

In the post-1970 years, Doug and Rod teamed from time to time with John Hartford for trio concerts under the group name Dillard-Hartford-Dillard. Dillards album credits in the '80s and '90s included the compilation *I'll Fly Away*, issued in 1988, the 1991 release *Let It Fly, There is a Time (1965–70)* in 1991, *Take Me Along for the Ride* in 1992, *Best of the Darlin' Boys* in 1997, and *First Time Live* in 1999.

In the mid-1990s, Rounder Records, which had acquired Flying Fish, kept a number of Dillard releases in its catalog. These included the Dillards' *Homecoming and Family Reunion;* Doug Dillard's *What's That* and *Heartbreak Hotel;* Rodney Dillard's *At Silver Dollar City* and *Let the Rough Side Drag;* and Dillard-Hartford-Dillard's *Glitter Grass/Permanent Wave*. All were available in CD or cassette, except for *What's That* and *Silver Dollar City* (cassette only).

DIXON, WILLIE: *Singer, songwriter, bass player, producer, arranger, band leader. Born Vicksburg, Mississippi, July 1, 1915; died Burbank, California, January 29, 1992.*

Willie Dixon, a huge man (six-four and over 250 pounds), might have made it as a professional boxer. Fortunately for blues fans, a dispute with his manager forced him to trade his gloves for an upright bass. He called the blues "the roots of all American music," and as producer, composer, and arranger for Chess Records, he became a chief architect of the postwar Chicago blues. His bass runs and studio production updated the rural Delta sound to an urban setting. Dixon made his most significant contributions as a songwriter and arranger. Titles such as "Little Red Rooster," "Hoochie Coochie Man," and "Wang Dang Doodle" have been recorded by blues legends Howlin' Wolf, Muddy Waters, and Koko Taylor. More than 450 of his songs are registered with BMI. Dixon also was an important link between the urban blues and rock 'n' roll, playing bass on Chuck Berry's early hits and giving inspiration for the Rolling Stones, Led Zeppelin, Cream, and the Doors.

He was born Willie James Dixon, but it's likely that his biological father was Anderson Bell. His mother, Daisy McKenzie Dixon, had divorced Charlie Dixon in 1913, two years before Willie's birth. He grew up as one of seven children in a poor, mixed-race section of Vicksburg, Mississippi. His mother managed a restaurant right next to a barrelhouse, where Willie heard Charley Patton and other ragtime and blues musicians. He heard Little Brother Montgomery playing piano on the back of a truck. His mother loved to recite religious verse, and Willie learned rhyming patterns. He began writing songs and poems in the second grade.

At eleven Willie ran away to Bovine, Mississippi, where he lived in a run-down shack and worked on a farm. Returning home a year later, Willie was arrested for stealing doorknobs worth $2 from an abandoned home and sentenced to a year on a prison farm. There he was exposed to the realities of American racism. "I really began to find out what the blues meant to black

people, how it gave them consolation to be able to think these things over and sing them to themselves or let other people know what they had in mind and how they resented various things in life," he wrote in his 1989 autobiography, *I Am the Blues: The Willie Dixon Story* (Da Copa Press), cowritten with music critic Don Snowden.

When he was thirteen, after his stepfather was killed in a sawmill accident, Willie rode the rails to visit a sister in Chicago, but was arrested for hoboing and sent to the Harvey Allen County Farm for thirty days, where he saw a man beaten to death. "They called him Preacher, and they beat him to death with a strap," he told Roger Wolmuth of *People* (September 11, 1989). "You never heard a man call on God like this old man called on God for his life."

Dixon received a blow to the head and lost his hearing for four years. He escaped from prison, wading through the Yazoo River to throw the bloodhounds off his path. He rode the rails up to Chicago and then New York, eventually returned to Vicksburg, where he worked on the docks for $1 a day. He added his bass voice to the Union Jubilee Singers, a gospel quartet, and learned harmony from Theo Phelps.

In 1936, Dixon again worked his way to Chicago. Within a year, he won the Illinois Golden Gloves (novice division) Heavyweight boxing title under the name James Dixon. He fought only four professional bouts, having been suspended for brawling with the boxing commission over prize money.

Instead, he went into music. "I was makin' more money passin' the hat than I was fightin'," he told Wolmuth. He and Leonard "Baby Doo" Caston, who had given him his first gut-bucket bass, formed a group called the Five Breezes, and cut an album in 1940 for Bluebird Records. His career was interrupted when he ignored draft notices as a conscientious objector. "Why should I go to fight to save somebody that's killing me and my people?" he told the draft board. He was arrested while performing one night and jailed for nearly a year. Dixon later emphasized the blues as a vehicle for spreading world peace in his song "(It Don't Make Sense) You Can't Make Peace:"

You have made great planes to scan the skies
You gave sight to the blind with other men's eyes
You even made submarines stay submerged for weeks
But it don't make sense you can't make peace

After his release in 1944, he joined a group called the Four Jumps of Jive, and recorded for Mercury. In 1946, Dixon joined the Big Three Trio, named after the "Big Three" of Franklin Roosevelt, Winston Churchill, and Joseph Stalin. He rejoined Caston and Bernardo Dennis, who was soon replaced by Ollie Crawford, to sing three-part harmony in the style of the Mills Brothers. The Big Three Trio recorded for Bullet in 1946, then signed with Columbia Records, scoring a moderate hit with the song "Wee Wee Baby (You Sure Look

Good to Me)." Their hit "Signifying Monkey," sold 40,000 records. They disbanded in 1952, after recording briefly for OKeh, even though they were making $375 a week performing.

In the late 1940s, Dixon met Elenora Franklin, the mother of his first seven children. The blues were attracting audiences to the South Side Chicago clubs, due to the large black migration from the South. Dixon would jam with Muddy Waters after his gigs with the Big Three Trio. One night while performing at the Macomba Lounge, Dixon met club owners Leonard and Phil Chess, who later formed Chess Records.

Dixon worked part-time for Chess in1948 as a session bass player, and started working full-time after 1951. After joining the label, he recorded some of his songs for Chess and wrote and produced for others, including Robert Nighthawk's "My Sweet Lovin' Woman" in 1948. Things took off in 1954, when he talked Muddy Waters into singing "Hoochie Coochie Man." Legend has it that Dixon taught Waters the distinctive five-note riff in a nightclub men's room. The song reached number three on the R&B charts. Waters had hits with Dixon's "I'm Ready" and "I Just Wanna Make Love to You." The following year Little Walter had a number one R&B hit with Dixon's "My Babe," later recorded by Elvis, Ricky Nelson, and John Lee Hooker. Sonny Boy Williamson (Rice Miller) had a hit with "Bring It On Home."

Howlin' Wolf also had hits with Dixon's "Evil," "Spoonful," "Little Red Rooster," "Goin' Down Slow," "300 pounds of Heavenly Joy," and "Back Door Man." He got Wolf to record some of his songs by suggesting that Muddy Waters was also interested. During recording sessions, Dixon would play the bass, arrange the tunes, and whisper the lyrics in Wolf's ear, as he belted out the song.

Dixon produced and did session work for Chess from 1954 to 1956. He played bass for Chuck Berry's first twenty songs, including the 1955 hit "Maybellene," "Johnny B. Goode," and "Sweet Little Sixteen." Bo Diddley recorded for Chess and had a hit with Dixon's "Can't Judge a Book (By Its Cover)" and "Pretty Thing."

In 1955, Dixon's relationship with Elenora Franklin ended. He later married Marie Booker, a waitress with whom he had five children. Although he wrote the majority of the label's blues hits, the Chess brothers only paid him $75 a week advance against royalties, having assigned the rights to their publishing company, ARC Music. Dixon, struggling to support his growing family, left Chess but continued his session work.

In 1957, he went to Cobra Records, where he created the "West Side Sound" with his recordings of Otis Rush (who had a hit with Willie's "I Can't Quit You, Baby"), Buddy Guy, and Magic Sam. He also formed Ghana Music Publishing in 1957. When Cobra began to fail, Dixon returned to Chess Records as chief song-writer and producer. One of his biggest discoveries was Koko Taylor, who was working as a domestic in the early 1960s. He was so anxious to record her that he called her in the middle of the night. "We've got to pick the chicken while the water's hot," he told her (*Gannett News Service,* January 24, 1994). In 1966, she hit with his party song "Wang Dang Doodle" and went on to win several W.C. Handy Awards and Grammy nominations.

In 1959, he released his first solo album, *Willie's Blues,* on Prestige/Bluesville. That year he reunited with Memphis Slim, with whom he had recorded in the 1940s, and played at the Newport Folk Festival. They toured the U.S. and Europe, releasing a series of albums: *Memphis Slim and Willie Dixon* on Folkways (1959); *The Blues Every Which Way* on Verve (1960); *At the Village Gate* on Folkways (1960); and *Live at the Trois Mailletz* on Polydor (1962). Dixon developed a strong following in Europe, paving the way for other blues artists. The American Folk Blues Festivals included artists such as Sonny Terry and Brownie McGhee, John Lee Hooker, and T-Bone Walker and exposed British rockers to the blues.In 1964, the Rolling Stones, in fact, recorded "Little Red Rooster" and "I Just Wanna Make Love to You." They cut their first American-made singles at Chess Studios. Later when the Stones stopped by Dixon's home in the 1980s, overzealous fans brought the visit to an abrupt end. "I was living on a one-way street at a little house, and here comes nine limousines full of folks," he told Wolmuth. "My doorbell was ringin', my telephone was ringin', kids was screamin'. The noise was too much to take." Willie's son Butch had returned home that afternoon from major surgery, so Willie invited them to catch a Muddy Waters show at a local club.

After Chess Records was sold in 1969, Dixon's commitment to bring the blues home to America was fulfilled when he produced the first Chicago Blues Festival in Grant Park. He released *I Am the Blues* on Columbia, recorded with his newly formed Chicago Blues All-Stars. His band was comprised of Big Walter Horton on harmonica, Clifton James on drums, Lafayette Leake (later Sunnyland Slim) on piano, and Johnny Shines on guitar. He released *Peace* (1971) on his own Yambo label and followed with *Maestro Willie Dixon and His Chicago Blues Band* on Spivey (1973). Two albums, *Catalyst* (1973) and *What's Happened to My Blues?* (1976), on Ovation, were both nominated for Grammys. His 1983 live recording with the All-Stars (released on Pausa Records, 1985) at the Montreux Jazz Festival also received a Grammy nomination.

Over the years, he battled diabetes. In 1977, his right leg was amputated and he had to have neck surgery due to vascular problems, but that didn't slow him much. He was nominated to the Blues Foundation's Hall of Fame in 1980.

Dixon battled to regain the rights to his songs, reaching a settlement with Led Zeppelin, whose song

"Whole Lotta Love" was virtually identical to his song "You Need Love." (His thirteen-year-old daughter Shirley pointed it out to Willie.)

Using some of the newly received royalties, in 1982 he started the nonprofit Blues Heaven Foundation, to help preserve the blues by giving scholarships to college students, distributing musical instruments to city schools, and providing support to needy blues musicians. In 1984, he moved to Glendale, California, and began doing TV commercials for Nabisco, Gain detergent, and Coca-Cola. He won a Grammy for best blues album in 1988 for *Hidden Charms* for Bug/Capitol, and worked on soundtracks for *La Bamba* (including his production of Bo Diddley's "Who Do You Love") and *The Color of Money,* on which he sang "Don't You Tell Me Nothin'." The following year he released his autobiography, and composed the soundtrack for *Ginger Ale Afternoon,* which also received a Grammy nomination. MCA/Chess issued a box set in 1989.

Dixon died on January 29, 1992, of heart failure in Burbank. He was 76. His family carried on Dixon's work by purchasing the Chess Studios building at 2120 S. Michigan that year. The remodeled building opened in 1997 as the home of the Blues Heaven Foundation. In 1994, a jury awarded his royalty rights to his wife, Marie. After his induction into the Rock Hall of Fame in 1994, Koko Taylor summed up Willie Dixon's legacy: "He put a fire under the blues. There'll never be another Willie Dixon."

Written with assistance from the Blues Heaven Foundation

DR. JOHN, THE NIGHT TRIPPER: *Singer, pianist, songwriter, guitarist, bassist, band leader, record producer. Born New Orleans, Louisiana, November 21, 1940.*

To say that Dr. John cut an unusual figure onstage when he appeared as the Night Tripper is an understatement. His spangled silver robes, ornate feathered headdress, and intricate necklaces brought to mind some of the characters in the jungle thrillers on TV's late, late show. His guise, though, did reflect the kind of music he often plays, which might be called voodoo rock. By the mid-1970s he had discarded his exotic garb, but continued to be a respected exponent of New Orleans R&B and rock stylings the rest of that decade and throughout the 1990s.

Dr. John grew up in New Orleans under the more prosaic name of Malcolm John Rebennack Jr., son of a professional model and an appliance store owner. His mother's contacts resulted in young Mac's being featured as an "Ivory Soap baby" in company ads. Mac Sr. first worked with Emblem Appliances on Gentilly Boulevard and later operated Rebennack Appliances.

As his son recalled: "That was near Dillard University. He sold a lot of records. Classical to the students with music classes and some jazz, blues, and hillbilly

records. He also had some sort of a deal with a jukebox distributor. I'd get the old 78s when they were returned from the machines. I was a fanatic for Gene Autry, Hank Williams, and Roy Rogers. I remember liking 'race' records by Big Bill Broonzy and Memphis Minnie, too."

At the age of eight, Mac already knew far more about hillbilly and black music than his playmates. His interest deepened when illness confined him to home for a long time. He had already learned a little boogie-woogie piano from an aunt and, while recuperating, he started guitar lessons.

Back in school, Mac eventually joined school pop bands and became guitarist with a group called Leonard James and the Nighttrainers. "I played guitar with them, even though I started out knowing only one chord." Barely into his teens, he hung around Cosimo Matessa's recording studio, where he met many professional musicians. "I was really taught to play guitar by Walter 'Papoose' Nelson and Roy Montrell. They were the guitarists in Fats Domino's band. Al Johnson, who had a record called 'Carnival Time' taught me some more piano, all kinds of boogie-woogie. I also learned piano by watching people like Huey Smith and Professor Longhair. James Booker showed me about the organ, how to use the stops and foot-pedals."

At fifteen Mac joined the musicians union and worked as head of his own group and as a sideman with others, such as the Paul Gayten group at the Brass Rail club. By 1956 Mac had performed on his first recordings. On one, he backed Professor Longhair, whom he had met while playing guitar behind singer Roy Brown at Lincoln Beach, a black amusement park. The Longhair record, "Mardi Gras in New Orleans," notes Mac, "is still a hit. Every year at Mardi Gras, it's pulled out and all the radio stations play it." His first album work was on *Boppin' and Strollin' with Leonard James* on Decca. In 1957 Mac recorded an instrumental album of his own, but it was never released.

In the late 1950s Mac worked as producer and/or session man with Ace Records of Baton Rouge and Minit of New Orleans. When several black artists formed AFO (All For One) Records, Mac was the first white act signed. With Ronnie Barron, he cut material issued under the names Drits and Dravy and also did an album of organ instrumentals. "I was the label's answer to Jimmy Smith. They also had a mystical act named Prince Lala. He was the original version of what would later become Dr. John the Night Tripper."

As to how he got his professional name, he told Lyndon Stambler, "First off they used to call me nicknames. One of them was Professor and one was Doc. One of them came because I read a lot of books. They used to call me Professor. It wasn't about like Professor Longhair, the piano professor from the 'ho' houses. It was because I read a lot of books. And Dr., it came from—there was a guy named Dr. John who was a famous hoodoo guy in the 1800s. I was making a one-off record that was about New Orleans gris-gris and give people a picture of that. And my middle name is John. So I figured it was mystically, politically, uncorrect and unfathomable.

"But I wasn't going [to use it]. I wanted Ronnie Barron to be Dr. John and then his manager thought Ronnie should be doing more like in the Staples Singers bag, or in the Curtis Mayfield and the Impressions bag. I just got mad and thought, 'I'm gonna do this record.' So I did and figured that will be the end of that and I'll go back to producing. It was at Santa Monica and Vine at Gold Star studios where we used to cut Sonny and Cher."

Mac decided to keep the new name, expanding it to Dr. John the Night Tripper. As he said in 1997, "I still use that. If I sign an autograph to this day it says Dr. John the Night Tripper."

Was the Night Tripper part related to voodoo or hoodoo? "Actually, I related it to something I always was. I've never been a day people. I always, just like my best Bela Lugosi, I always came to life at night. I worked all my life at night. That was just how I lived. Today I appreciate the day a whole lot different. But back then I never saw any. In fact, me and Harry Nilsson wrote a song about 'Damn the Daylight.' We'd see it, the sun would be glaring. We used to get off of gigs on Bourbon Street. We'd work from eight at night to eight in the morning, or midnight to noon, and walk out of a club. The last time you was going into a club it was pitch black and all of a sudden you'd walk out and it's broad daylight. It's something, you don't appreciate the sunlight in the same way. It's like a mole. Not a mole, some night critter that's caught in the day."

It was in those early years during his association with Ronnie Barron that he lost the use of part of his hand. He told Lyndon Stambler, "I got shot in this finger [raising his ring finger on his left hand]. I got shot in there and it came out there. Then he sewed it back on. It's the finger you bend strings with on the guitar. When I'd try to bend a string with that finger it goes 'bonk.'

"It [happened] in a motel room. Ronnie Barron was the vocalist with my band and he was very underage. Ronnie's mother told me, don't let anything happened to her son! So we're getting ready for the gig and the owner of the hotel was pistol-whipping [Barron]. My mind didn't really think about this guy's got a gun in his hand. It was Ronnie's mother's threat to me . . . when she said she was going to do me and my cojones with a butcher knife if anything happened to her son. I went harassing the guy for the gun and my hand was over the barrel and I was beating his hand against some bricks to get it loose and it went off on my finger.

"[Before then] I was a straight-up guitarist. I might have played piano a bit on a couple of recordings. 'Cause they knew I played, but I was hired as a guitarist all the time. After that my finger was in a big cast for a long time. I took a Dixieland gig playing bass at the Fa-

mous Door Lounge in New Orleans and I took some R&B gigs playing drums. Well, I hated carrying upright bass and I didn't know how to unpack and pack drums. I hated it. James Booker said, right when Jimmy Smith started getting popular, around 1961, he said if I could get him a gig, 'I'll teach you how to play Hammond B-3 organ.' He taught me and we went to work at three gigs, twelve hours a night, 365 days a year. That's what got my chops up on keyboard."

In the mid-1960s Mac moved to Los Angeles, where he slowly became a top session man working for many pop producers, including Phil Spector. In his spare time, he began developing an act based on voodoo ceremonies. "I'd been interested in the hoodoo ceremonies for quite a while in New Orleans. My sister worked in an antiques store and had some books on the subject. And I'd go down into the Ninth Ward to go to some of the church ceremonies. There's a place on Rampart Street called the Crackerjack Drug Store that deals in roots and incense. I'd go there to get some supplies. Though I hadn't done anything with them, I had written most of the songs on the first couple of [Los Angeles–recorded] albums before ever leaving New Orleans."

When the first Dr. John the Night Tripper album came out in 1968 its combination of soul and voodoo went over big with listeners to "underground" radio stations. On Atco, the album was called *Gris Gris,* after certain objects used in voodoo ceremonies. However, John noted, "I didn't really use much of the real [voodoo] church music. What I tried to get was the feel of what was going on there."

His reputation increased at the start of the '70s both from more Atco releases and from his garish rock concert appearances. Other performers, though, respected him for his musicianship rather than his showmanship. Thus, after his LP *Remedies* was released in 1970, his backing on the 1971 album *Sun, Moon & Herbs* included such famous English rock stars as Mick Jagger, Eric Clapton, and Ray Draper. The LP was on the bestseller lists during October and November 1971. In April 1972, Dr. John made the singles charts with the African-flavored "Iko, Iko." He continued with his voodoo-oriented material on the 1972 album, *Gumbo.* However, there was a change of pace in early 1973, when *In the Right Place* was issued. This album, one of the fastest-moving new releases on the hit charts in the spring, demonstrated Dr. John's background in blues and early rock. The title song provided Rebennack with a hit single.

During the same year, Dr. John was part of another project that had an album on the charts much of the year. The LP *Triumvirate* was recorded by a trio comprising Rebennack on keyboards, Mike Bloomfield on lead guitar, and John Hammond Jr. on vocals, guitar, and harmonica. The group made additional recordings for Columbia Records, but the promise of the embryo supergroup never was realized.

As it turned out, *In the Right Place* was the high point of Dr. John's record output as a solo performer for Atco. By the mid-1970s he had left the label. He continued to be active as a solo performer through the 1980s while also working as a session artist and record producer. One of his high points of the mid-1970s was taking part in the farewell concert for the Band in San Francisco, California, on Thanksgiving night, 1976. His contributions were included in the documentary film of the concert, *The Last Waltz,* and the sound track LP of the same title. *(See Band, The.)*

Asked about whether hits like "Such a Night" and "Right Place, Wrong Time," paid off financially, he recalled, "At the time, most of the money was spent on lawyers and stuff that had nothing to do with me keeping the money. I'm sure I got burned for a lot of money behind the fact that my lifestyle at the time [drugs and partying] wasn't conducive. I probably didn't figure I'd live past a certain point. I was trying to support my children and stuff but there was another part of me that really had a hopeless attitude toward making money. I didn't make much. From the days I worked for Ace Records, this [1997] is forty years later, I have not received one statement. I do not get paid royalties for any stuff no matter how many records they've sold. Only one label from the whole '50s into the '60s that were paying me any money, Specialty Records, out of California."

As to how he made ends meet, he replied, "Believe me, you have to figure something. I worked a lot of gigs. I worked as a studio musician. I produced records. I wrote songs. I just didn't get paid for the songs. As an artist that came later and I started getting stiffed in that area as an artist and a songwriter. But I just recently made a publishing deal and I'm starting to live like real people."

In 1979, Rebennack put two albums out on the Horizon label: *City Lights* and *Tango Palace.* His 1980s output included *Dr. John Plays Mac Rebennack* on Clean Cuts Records in 1981. Other labels that repackaged his material included Trip (*Dr. John* and *Sixteen Greatest Hits*), Springboard (*Dr. John*), and Alligator (*Gris Gris* and *Gumbo*). Throughout the 1980s, he kept busy as a performer and sometime record producer. His credits during those years included the Clean Cut LP *Brightest Smile in Town* and a role in the 1988 film *Candy Mountain.*

He completed his 1980s recording activities with the 1989 Warner Brothers album *In a Sentimental Mood,* whose tracks included a duet with Rickie Lee Jones on the old Eddie Cantor hit, "Makin' Whoopee." The album was a chart hit, and that single was awarded a Grammy for Best Jazz Performance by a Duo or Group. It was Dr. John's first Grammy and it was announced on the Grammy telecast of February 21, 1990.

Perhaps a more vital milestone of that period was the Night Tripper's decision to overcome his fondness

for heroin, which had begun some thirty-five years earlier. He told Tom Piazza for a *New York Times* article ("Night Tripping with the Good Doctor," Arts & Leisure section, May 22, 1994), "A lot of people were getting busted around me, for one thing, and I knew I was too old to do time. Then my daughter was really on me about it; she'd say things like, 'Every time you go into the bathroom I'm scared you're never going to come out alive.' Plus my interest in dope was getting way out of proportion to my interest in music. . . . So I had been thinking about cleaning up for a while, but not really doing anything about it. Finally, I wound up in a cardiac ward in Arizona, with all these wires sticking out of me. And the crazy thing was after I woke up, my first thought was to follow the nurse to the narcotics box. I was sitting in there, unplugging all these wires, and suddenly it was like something changed in me. I thought, 'I'm too old for this.' You know, if I had followed that nurse, the state of Arizona would have had me for the duration."

As for how he got into his habit, he told Stambler, "I think for thirty years I was chasing something that happened one day. I remember doing a bag of heroin and I felt, 'This is being high. I feel good.' I'd smoked weed and took pills, but I remember that one day. I think for all of the rest of them years that I did heroin I was looking to repeat that day. I know that now. Seven, I'm going on eight years away from it. It wasn't the most pleasant way to look. You know, looking over your shoulder, worrying about the police, being humiliated standing on a corner waiting for some guy to come with the dope is not my idea of fun and games."

For a time in the 1980s, he tried the methadone treatment. He hated it and decided to stop. "In 1985 I got off methadone. But I didn't understand that it's like a thing. If you don't watch yourself you'll be right back to where you was. I got off methadone and went back to shooting heroin again. It was during those four years that my daughter got hip to me. I was like losing my street smarts. I knew that eventually this was going to come to a bad end. I knew that in my heart, but I didn't want to stop because I felt like I couldn't do it. After I got off of methadone and I was back doing it I really felt like a lamebrain. Oh, man, I must be the biggest asshole in the world."

Then came the incident in the Arizona hospital that brought about the change. "That was in 1989. I'll tell you the exact date; December 17, 1989. I've been clean since."

In the early '90s, Rebennack, by then calling New York City home, though often going back to New Orleans for appearances at events like the New Orleans Jazz and Heritage Festival, worked on his next album in the Crescent City. Among the New Orleans notables backing him on tracks for *Goin' Back to New Orleans* (Warner Brothers, 1992) were Pete Fountain, Al Hirt, the Neville Brothers, Danny Barker, and Red Tyler. The tracks included a tribute to Mac's old friend and piano mentor, the late Professor Longhair ("Radiatin' the 88"), a track called "Scald Dog" that opened with the old Fats Domino tune "I Can't Go Rosalie" (featuring Fats's original tenor soloist, Herbert Hardesty), and new versions of such old classic New Orleans–style Dixieland numbers as "Milenburg Joys," "Didn't He Ramble," and "I'll Be Glad When You're Dead, You Rascal You."

It was a worthy effort that suggested that giving up his heroin habit had also rejuvenated Dr. John's creative abilities. After the album's release by Warner Brothers in 1992, it won some of the best reviews Rebennack had achieved in years. In the voting for the 1992 Grammys (announced on the February 23, 1993, telecast), the album won the award for Best Traditional Blues Album. In the fall of 1993, that disc was followed by a two-CD retrospective of Rebennack's career, *The Dr. John Anthology: Mos' Scoscious* (Rhino, 1993).

During those years, in between his recording projects and engagements at major venues in the United States and abroad, plus occasional TV appearances, he also worked on his autobiography. The book, published by St. Martin's Press of New York, *Under a Hoodoo Moon,* came out in the spring of 1994, around the same time his new album, *Television* (GNP), was released. Before starting his set at the '94 New Orleans Jazz and Heritage Festival, he spent lengthy amounts of time at book and record stores in town and the book tent at the festival signing copies for fans.

In the fall of 1997 Rebennack was engaged to marry a new love named Cat. Asked about how many times he'd been married, he replied, "It depends who you ask and it depends on what somebody considers the bonds of matrimony. Whether you considered common law and all the rest of it. So many considerations. I would say [I've been married] two or three times. Someone else might have some different numbers. [As for children] I have five that I'm sure of; I may have more. You know when you're out there living the lifestyle like I did, you're not sure of a lot of things."

He was queried about his favorite Professor Longhair story. "I used to love his vocabulary. Right before he passed away, he turned to me and he said—I was playing guitar for him, he always called me Max. He said, 'Max, you've got too much extortion on your amplifier.' He always had little stuff like that. I loved when he told the horn section, 'I want you all to make a spew.' The guy says, 'Fess, what is a spew?' Fess said, 'I want you all to spppeeeww.' He always called the key of E-flat E-minus. Always had his thing. Everything he said was his thing.

"He taught me something important. He taught me how to back up a soloist. He called that frolicking behind the soloist. But the whole band had to do that. It's like pushing, but don't pick the tempo up. Pushing so

that it's almost on the verge of picking it up, but just pushing it up so that it reaches a peak."

Besides Longhair, Rebennack over the years performed with many memorable artists, including Rickie Lee Jones and the Rolling Stones. To a question about who stood out in his memory, he said, "It's funny; if anybody stands out the most it was probably Joe Tex. I think 'cause Joe Tex used to walk in the studios—first off if it wouldn't have been for Joe Tex there wouldn't have been a James Brown, there wouldn't have been a Jackie Wilson show—he'd walk into a studio with a whole record, everybody's parts in his head. He'd sing everybody's parts to him. He really produced his own records. He was probably the first guy in the '50s that I met that really actually walked in, wrote the songs, produced, and did everything himself. Later other people did it, but he was the first guy and that stuck out to me.

"Later I had a lot of other people [who impressed him] from Ray Charles and other people. It was for different reasons. Charles Brown—I may have recorded with Charles Brown in the 1950s that later meant something different at different times. I got a big kick out of working with Dolly Parton. I got a kick out of working with Levon Helm. Just different people I liked. Not so much for their personalities; just for what they do with music. Johnny Clark Copeland recently passed away. Luther Allison. There's a lot of guys. Way back when I was young and I didn't know what I was doing Johnny Vincent let me produce some real gut bucket blues acts like Mercy Baby and Sonny Boy Williamson (#2). It's like over the years something sticks out for a certain thing.

"I thought [Sonny Boy Williamson] was something special. He scared me to death. He was tall and skinny. I was a kid. Johnny Vincent sent me over to do this record. They were with this old lady from Mississippi. All I remember was I walked into the studio and there were straight razors on the guitar amp and the harmonica amp. I thought, 'I'm not going in there.' Johnny Vincent told me to play piano. 'I'm gonna sit out here. This old lady's going in there. I ain't going. She's crazy enough to go in there. I'm not going in that room.' It was just fear. I was a kid."

During the summer of 1997, his first fully live album, *Trippin' Live,* was issued. As he told Lyndon Stambler, he had been waiting some forty years for this opportunity: "It was the first time someone would let me make a record with my band live. I've been wanting to do that for many, many years with a lot of labels. I believe that's what music is about—live music. Studio musicians playing for four walls—I did that most of my life and it's an industry to itself. But music was not made to be made records out of and all of that. It was made to be just played for people, live. The closest thing you can get on a record to that is a live record and that's what it is. It's a band that's been playing together that was tight. As a result we were able to go in [to a nightclub] and do some head music, play some songs we've never played before and probably will never play again, plus we did a lot of stuff we always do. There's a mixture of all that."

Looking back over his career, he commented, "I like to think that I was always square goods with people, as best as feasible and being a human being with all my shortcomings. I would like to be remembered as being fair. I would hate to be remembered as some shuckster. 'He was born to sing.' I can't sing. I can sing, but I ain't a singer. I don't think that I'm anything, but I think that I'm square goods. I treated musicians fair as possible. I'm trying to be that kind of guy."

His activities in 1998 included taking part in the B.B. King Blues Festival and touring in support of a new album, *Anutha Zone,* issued on Point Blank/Virgin. In this album, on which he was backed on some tracks by his own band and on others by British bands like Supergrass, Primal Scream, Portishead, and Ocean Colour, he re-created his image of New Orleans medicine man. As Steve Hochman of the *Los Angeles Times* enthused (August 9, 1998), "Perhaps his best album in 25 years, this is a full evocation of the Night Tripper, the gris-gris man persona he assumed early in his career. It's deep, spooky and trippy, a walk through the graveyards and bayous where Louisiana magic is real."

Other CDs by Dr. John include *The Ultimate Dr. John* (Warner Brothers, 1987), *Such a Night* (Makin' Waves, 1988/1992), *At His Best* (Special Music Company, 1989), *On a Mardi Gras Day* (1990), *Gumbo/In the Right Place* (Mobile Fidelity, 1994), *Afterglow* (Thumb, 1995), *The Very Best of Dr. John* (Rhino, 1995), *Cut Me While I'm Hot* (Magnum America, 1975/1995) from his 1960s session work, *Crawfish Soiree* (Aim, 1996), and *Duke Elegant* (BlueNote, 2000), his versions of songs by Duke Ellington.

Partly based on an interview with Lyndon Stambler on August 20, 1997

DOE, JOHN: *Singer, bass guitarist, songwriter, actor, poet. Born Decatur, Illinois, February 25, 1954.*

One of the most influential Southern California rock bands in the 1980s called itself simply X. The group excelled at throbbing, high-decibel, new wave or punk offerings, but its founding members, Exene Cervenka and John Doe, never restricted themselves to that artform, varying their spirited rock work with participation in poetry readings and sidebar efforts in softer musical genres like country and folk. In Doe's case, in the 1990s he embarked on a solo career starting with a debut album whose tracks covered a spectrum from folk-rock to a cover of country artist Hank Cochran's "It's Only Love."

Doe recalled, "I was born in Decatur, Illinois (both parents were librarians), but as a kid I moved all around America from Decatur to Knoxville (Tennessee) to Madison (Wisconsin) to Baltimore (Maryland). In Baltimore I started playing bass guitar in a bunch of bar bands. (He also wrote poetry and became friends with eccentric local artists such as film producer John Waters.) There was no place to go, musically speaking, in Baltimore and I wanted a big change, so I came to L.A. on Halloween in 1976."

In Los Angeles, Doe (whose real name is John Nommensen—he took his pseudonym from the Frank Capra film) soon met another former Illinois native, Exene Cervenka (born Chicago, February 1, 1956). He had heard her read some of her writings at a poetry workshop and had gone up afterward to make her acquaintance. He said, "She was wearing dark lipstick and read this poem about Lois Lane [*Lois Lane is a redhead/A neat slick chick/In a blue-eyed suit*]. We went out that night, got drunk, and became a couple." Later, in the fall of 1977, he found guitarist Billy Zoom through ads in a local throwaway paper and adding Exene as a lead singer, formed X.

During 1978 and '79, with a fourth member, Billy Bonebrake, playing drums, the group became increasingly popular with local fans through an extensive series of gigs in new wave clubs. As the band gained experience, it evolved its own special style that combined the high-speed instrumentals of new wave with all manner of influences from Applachian folk music to rockabilly to blues. The lyrics typically provided by John and Exene (by then man and wife) reflected their strong interest in avant-garde poetry. Exene told Irwin Stambler, "I think there's always been poetry in rock and the music styles it evolved from. I think if you look at an artist like Big Joe Turner, who's been around for years, his music is really poetic and that's the kind of stuff we love. 'Shake, Rattle and Roll' is really poetic. I think heavy metal bands play bad poetry and we think ours is like good poetry or word painting."

In 1978, X issued its first single, "Adult Books"/"We're Desperate," on the Dangerhouse label, and by the end of the decade had signed with Slash Records, which issued its first LP, *Los Angeles,* in 1980. The same year, some of the band's live performances of the songs "We're Desperate," "Beyond and Back," and "Johny Hit and Run Paulene" were on the Slash sound track LP of Penelope Spheeris's documentary about L.A. punk, *The Decline . . . of Western Civilization. Los Angeles* was a breath of fresh air for the rock movement and made more than a few reviewers' top 10 lists. It was followed by an even more striking collection, the 1981 *Wild Gift,* which *Rolling Stone*'s critic called "the finest American punk album ever."

The band's growing national (and international) reputation brought a contract from a major label, Elektra, which issued X's label debut, *Under the Big Black Sun* in 1982. The group (whose roster changed somewhat over the years) added to its Elektra catalog in the '80s with *More Fun in the New World* in 1983, *Ain't Love Grand* in 1985, *See How We Are* in 1987, and *X Live at the Whisky A G-Go on the Fabulous Sunset Strip* in 1988. The 1985 album, *Ain't Love Grand,* was one of the group's weaker collections, reflecting, perhaps, turmoil that included the breakup of John and Exene's marriage. However, the bitterness passed, and in 1986 they were reconciled—creatively, if not domestically.

In the mid-1980s, Doe and Cervenka, accompanied for a time by Dave Alvin of the Blasters, focused on folk and country material in a band called the Knitters (a takeoff on the name of the legendary folk group the Weavers). Increasingly, though, Doe was exploring other creative possibilities, including acting and a solo recording career. In 1989, for example, he took the role of bassist J.W. Brown in the film biography of Jerry Lee Lewis (released in 1990), *Great Balls of Fire.*

In late '89, Doe gained a contract from the David Geffen Company to do his first solo album. He worked on that from October 1989 to January 1990, writing or cowriting nine of the twelve songs on the disc, *Meet John Doe,* issued in April 1990. (The three covers were Hank Cochran's "It's Only Love," John Hiatt's "The Real One," and Bruce Hornsby's "Knockin' Around.")

Doe's supporting musicians didn't include any members of X present or past. He stressed, "It was both wonderful and scary! I didn't have the bandmembers who I've trusted and lived with for so long to provide that sounding board. But if I had used anyone from X on the album, people would think this was a rehash of X and it's not." Going it alone, he added, gave him a feeling of independence. "There's a do-it-yourself feeling. Like fixing the car yourself if it's busted. The way I look at it, no one carries my suit to the show, which I find important if I don't want to be jaded and removed."

Still, one number had Exene's mark on it. Talking about "Take #52," he noted. "Exene wrote most of the lyrics on a piece of paper and I've kept that paper in my guitar case for five years. I finally put the song together while I was in Memphis on *Great Balls of Fire.*"

In any event, by the early '90s, Doe had a new wife to consider. But, he said, "I haven't designed a new phase for myself; 1976 and now are the same thing. The only difference is that instead of living in Hollywood and getting loaded every day, I'm living out in the sticks and shoveling horseshit on my ranch every other day."

X continued to perform intermittently until it announced its disbandment in 1996. In 1997, the retrospective set *Beyond and Back: The X Anthology* was released. By the end of the year, however, plans were in the works for a series of reunion concerts in 1998 featuring the original lineup of Doe, Cervenkova (who in the 1980s used the shortened last name of Cervenka), D.J. Bonebrake, and Billy Zoom (real name Tyson Kindell), who hadn't played with the group since 1985.

DONOVAN: *Singer, guitarist, songwriter, arranger. Born Glasgow, Scotland, February 10, 1946.*

An artist who will always be remembered for his anti–Vietnam War songs during the heyday of the folk movement of the 1960s, Donovan P. Leitch was an idealist who finally became disillusioned with society's increasing apathy.

The son of working-class parents in Glasgow, Scotland, Donovan spent his first ten years in the Gorbals area of the city, one of the roughest in Scotland. In 1956 his family moved to the outskirts of London, where he developed an interest in art and learned to play the guitar. "At school, the teachers thought I was a little strange because I wrote a lot of fear and horror stories and drew sketches for them. One of them was about this man who got locked in a drain when it rained."

In college he continued his art studies until, after a year, his money ran out. With a friend, Gypsy Davy (who was later to figure in some of his songs), Donovan began to wander all over England, hitching rides on trucks and beachcombing. "We weren't working out the problems of the world," he writes, "we were letting our days fill us with strange encounters. We didn't talk much, but we moved fast a lot." During the months on the road, Donovan spent a good deal of time writing stories and folk-flavored songs.

Settled in London in 1964, he lived in a small basement flat and began to take his tapes around to music industry people. He was asked to perform on the top British Broadcasting Company pop music show, *Ready, Steady, Go;* audience response was so favorable he was signed for two more appearances.

Soon after, he turned out a single of his song "Catch the Wind," which rose to number two on the English charts and is still a favorite with folksingers. Two more hit songs, "Colors" and "Universal Soldier," followed, making the hit charts all over the world. His first two LPs, *Catch the Wind* and *Fairytale,* also created a stir.

In 1965 he appeared at the Newport Folk Festival, making his U.S. debut and creating a sensation. Similar encomiums and standing-room-only shows followed him throughout the 1960s and into the early 1970s, when he came to be considered a superstar and the perfect symbol of the flower children movement. When that movement phased out in the 1970s, Donovan's career seemed to wane with it.

His contract with Epic in 1966 marked his first U.S. label affiliation. "Sunshine Superman" was his debut on the label, a best-selling single and the title of a charted LP. Although some of the media tended to focus on his "message" songs, the compositions in the *Sunshine Superman* LP, and many of his later LPs, covered such topics as children, love, fairytales, beaches, and a girl who entangles her hair in a Ferris wheel.

For a large part of the late 1960s, it was rare if Donovan didn't have an album or single on the bestseller lists. His single "Mellow Yellow," issued the end of 1966, sold over a million copies and earned a gold record. His album of the same title, released in March 1967, was on the charts, as were several of his releases on the Hickory label. The latter, comprising material issued in Europe before Donovan signed with Epic, included *Catch the Wind, The Real Donovan,* and *Donovan* (all issued in January 1967). Also a chart hit was his third Epic release, a two-record set titled *Gift from a Flower to a Garden* (February 1968). His other Epic albums of the late 1960s and early 1970s included *Barabajagal* (10/69), *Open Road* (9/70), and *Wear Your Love Like Heaven* (1971). In a situation similar to Hickory's, Janus Records issued several LPs in the early 1970s, such as *Hear Me Now* and the two-record set *Donovan P. Leitch.*

Donovan's TV credits during the 1969–70 season included several segments of *The Smothers Brothers Comedy Hour* and an appearance on the Everly Brothers summer replacement show in 1970. Afterward his personal appearances began to taper off, as did most of his activity, though he did place a single or two on the charts, including "Celia of the Seals" in 1971. During 1970–71, he also had a contract with Warner Brothers to write the music and screenplay for a film combining live action and animation. Among the films he contributed to in the 1970s were: *If It's Tuesday, It Must Be Belgium; The Pied Piper;* and *Brother Sun, Sister Moon.*

Even at the start of the 1970s, Donovan's occasional live concerts showed he still had a strong following, but as the early 1970s went by he phased out concert work almost completely. Little was heard from him for several years until Epic came out with the first LP in a while of all original new songs, *Cosmic Wheels.* Another new collection followed, *Essence to Essence.* However, both LPs did much more poorly than earlier releases.

His next LP, *7-Tease,* which came out in late 1974, did not seem to reverse the trend, so he went on tour and finally ended his affiliation with Epic. The reason he had stayed away for the past three years, he told Dennis Hunt of the *Los Angeles Times* (December 1974), was: "I was disillusioned with the 1960s. I was also disgusted with the music business. I got so disgusted with all of the rotten aspects of it that I had to get out.

"Music and business just don't seem to mix. It's hard to be an idealist and just want to make good music and not get trampled on by all the ruthless people who just want to make money. That's why artists freak out, run away, get sick or do anything to escape.

"Recently I came to terms with this business and decided to work with it instead of against it. I've cooled down somewhat. It may be a mistake. I don't know yet."

By then he was happily married to Linda Lawrence, who was still his marital partner in 2001 and whom he sometimes called "my muse." With career opportunities becoming increasingly limited in the mid-1970s, he essentially gave up the entertainment field and lived quietly with his wife in the United Kingdom. At the time of their marriage, Linda had a son, Julian, by Rolling Stones founding member Brian Jones, and she and Donovan subsequently had two daughters, Astrelia and Oriole, respectively twenty-five and twenty-four in 1996. Donovan also had fathered two children with an American girlfriend, Enid Karl, and in the 1990s he surfaced in media articles as he sought to aid the careers of son Donovan Leitch and daughter Ione Skye. (Leitch Jr., twenty-seven in 1996, formed the band Nancy Boy, whose debut album came out in June 1996, while Ione pursued an acting career.)

This new exposure to the entertainment environment reawakened Donovan's creative interests and, encouraged by Linda, he began to develop new material based on Hindu and Buddhist themes. As he told Anthony DeCurtis, a *Rolling Stone* contributing editor, for an article in the *New York Times* ("An Apostle of Love Returns as a Pop Mystic," Arts & Leisure Section, October 13, 1996), "I was coming to the realization in about 1990 that the '90s may just well be the '60s turned upside down. So I was headed back into action. I was very excited."

But the record industry was less enthusiastic: "They all said no, very nicely, with little messages to me to say how much they loved my music. But they didn't know which box to put me in."

Finally he found a supporter in Rick Rubin, president and owner of American Recordings, who had revived the career of Johnny Cash in the mid-'90s. Rubin told DeCurtis, "I sought Donovan out, because I'm a fan. I've always felt a connection to the metaphysical aspect of his music." Supported by backing musicians from Tom Petty's band, the Red Hot Chili Peppers, and Spain, Donovan completed his first collection of new songs in some twenty years. They were released in the fall of 1996 under the title *Sutras,* containing such compositions as "The Way" and Nirvana."

It remained to be seen whether Donovan could find a substantial audience in an age dominated by rap music, grunge rock, and country, but his son, for one, pointed out that audiences at his father's new concerts spanned a considerable age range. Donovan felt there was room for his message of peace and harmony. He told DeCurtis he had asked Linda at one point what he really wanted to do with his new opportunities. "And Linda said, 'To offer as many as possible an alternative.' I said 'Sublime. Perfect.' It's really down to: 'I enjoy it. Here's an idea. It may open another door for you.' We need that kind of communication in this—dare I say it?—age of Aquarius."

DRAKE, NICK: *Singer, guitarist, pianist, clarinetist, saxophone player, songwriter. Born Rangoon, Burma, June 19, 1948; died Tanworth-in-Arden, England, November 25, 1974.*

In the years after his death in 1974, Nick Drake has

become recognized as an important contributor to the development of modern folk and folk-rock music. During his short lifetime, though, despite critical support in England, he remained essentially unknown—due partly to his retiring personality and partly the lack of FM radio outlets on the level available for recordings in the United States.

In the liner notes for the 1994 Hannibal/Rykodisc album release *Way to Blue,* record executive Joe Boyd, who produced Drake's first albums, reported, "The phone calls from people wanting to do a book or film on Nick Drake used to come in about twice a year. Now it's twice a month. Nick died 20 years ago, but his music seems more beautiful, more apt, more attuned now than it did when it was first recorded. I first met Nick Drake in 1968 when he arrived in my office carrying a reel-to-reel tape of songs he had demo'd at home. From the first few bars I knew he was an unusual and rare talent. Working with him on [his] first two records was rewarding and fun. He was shy and very quiet, but very firm about his musical opinions."

Nick's earliest years were spent in Burma (now Myanmar), where he was born in 1948 to English parents Rodney and Molly Drake (his father worked for an English lumber company). When he was two, his family returned to England, settling in the village of Tanworth-in-Arden. Nick showed proficiency on several musical instruments before reaching his teens, but attending boarding school at Marlborough he also was a top student and an above-average athlete. His musical influences were initially in the folk field but gradually also extended to folk-rock as one of his heroes, Bob Dylan, moved in that direction. Other artists he admired in the mid-1960s included Joni Mitchell, and guitar virtuosos Bert Jansch and John Renbourn.

By that time Drake had begun writing original songs, which he added to his repertoire of traditional folk music and material written by other folk artists. When he entered Fitzwilliams College at Cambridge University in 1968, he already was thinking about a career in pop music, finding gigs at coffeehouses and college benefits. After attending one of those shows, Ashley Hutchings, of the folk group Fairport Convention, was impressed enough by Nick's style and original compositions to suggest that Joe Boyd, who helped produce Fairport recordings, meet him. Boyd was rapidly establishing himself as a top independent producer of folk-rock acts, shepherding albums to completion not only for Fairport but also for the Incredible String Band and John Martyn. Martyn, a friend of Drake's, later wrote the song "Solid Air" in Nick's memory.

After hearing the 1968 demo tape, Boyd immediately made plans to work with his new find. This resulted in Nick's debut, *Five Leaves Left* (the title refers to the warning at the end of a roll of cigarette papers), released in July 1969 by Island Records. It included such notable tracks as "River Man," "Time Has Told Me," "Way to Blue," "Cello Song," and "Fruit Tree," which caught the attention of more than a few fellow artists and a number of U.K. reviewers but sold poorly. Among the 1969 milestones for Drake was his first major public appearance, at the Royal Festival Hall in London.

By then Nick was preparing the material for his second collaboration with Boyd, *Bryter Layter,* issued in 1970. Its contents included a number of excellent originals, some of which were covered by major performers in future years, such as "Northern Sky," "Poor Boy," "One of These Things First," "Hazey Jane I," and "Hazey Jane II." Like the first collection, the second album gained some critical praise but failed commercially. The same fate met the first U.S. release, which combined material from both albums into one LP. Boyd commented in 1994, "When they came out, [the first two albums] got good reviews, but his shyness about live performance meant it was hard to get his music known. In America, Leonard Cohen had achieved a poetic hit record without touring, but America had FM radio and Britain didn't."

Increasingly, Drake went into a shell. He found it even more difficult to perform in public. Though rapidly losing self-confidence, he still managed to complete tracks for a third album, *Pink Moon.* He recorded originals like the title track, "Which Will," "Things Behind the Sun," and "From the Morning," using only his guitar for accompaniment. The response to this collection, issued in 1972, paralleled that of its two predecessors. Further shaken, Nick retired to his parents' home known as FarLeys, and became almost a recluse. He spent hours looking up at the sky. He still had creative urges and set down the track "Black Dog" and three other songs before he died. In October 1974 he went to France and lived on a barge. He also contacted Francoise Hardy, a French folksinger interested in his music. When he returned to Tanworth-in-Arden he seemed optimistic. But on November 24, 1974, he had a hard time sleeping, as usual, and was found the next morning, dead from an overdose of the antidepressant Tryptizol. After his passing a fourth album of "rarities" was issued, *Time of No Reply* (1986).

Later, when Joe Boyd sold his production company to Island, he sought assurance that all of Nick's albums would remain in print. The agreement was honored and all remained available, initially in vinyl and later on CDs, first on Island and later on Joe Boyd's own Hannibal label. Meanwhile, Drake's star began to rise posthumously as many artists, including Elton John, Kate Bush, Lucinda Williams, Tom Verlaine (founder of the avant-garde rock group Television), and others included his songs in their shows or albums and the buying public became aware of his talent.

In the 1990s Hannibal additions to Drake's catalog (issued in the United States on the Rykodisc label) comprised the four-disc boxed set *Fruit Tree,* which included all of Nick's recorded material, and the 1994 *Way to Blue: An Introduction to Nick Drake.* The latter contained carefully culled choices from all of Drake's releases that showcased his thought-provoking lyrics and inspiring guitar playing. The reviewer at England's *New Musical Express* echoed the comments of many other critics by enthusing, *"Way to Blue* shows that we were robbed of a phenomenal talent. . . . Every single track on this collection is a work of genius. If Nick Drake means nothing to you go buy this album. It could be the best musical discovery you make this year."

Joe Boyd pondered, "It's hard to say exactly what makes his music timeless. He was a quietly powerful person. He would have loved the attention and the respect his music now commands, but listening to his lyrics, it begins to seem he may have planned it all this way."

According to an October-November 1992 article in *Dirty Linen* by T.J. McGrath, Nick had started composing songs on a tape recorder and recording them before he left to go to boarding school. His father salvaged the recordings, which are contained on *The Nick Drake Cassette.* Some of the early tracks were included in *Time of No Reply,* along with five unused tracks that were recorded during the *Five Leaves Left* sessions. Drake was buried in the Tanworth-in-Arden churchyard, and an annual recital of his music is held in the church. Author Patrick Humphries published *Nick Drake: The Biography* (Bloomsbury) in 1997.

DRIFTWOOD, JIMMY: *Singer, guitarist, fiddler, banjoist, songwriter. Born Mountain View, Arkansas, June 20, 1917, died Fayetteville, Arkansas, July 12, 1998.*

A true representative of the American folk heritage, Jimmy Driftwood grew up in the hill country of Arkansas, where he almost unconsciously fell into a pattern of listening for and preserving traditional songs from his early years. As a collector of rural music and a gifted songwriter who sometimes wrote brand-new songs in the folk tradition and other times expanded on earlier themes, he made important contributions to both folk and country movements in the United States over his many active decades.

As a boy named Jimmy Corbett Morris growing up in the Ozark Mountains, the major form of entertainment during his childhood was when his family and neighbors gathered 'round and played and sang songs whose roots went back to Elizabethan times. Before long Jimmy was taking part in the vocals and starting to learn how to play some of the instruments. His favorite instrument, one he remembered fondly all his life, was a homemade guitar given him by his uncle Morris. It was made, he once said, of "fence-rail, ox-yoke and bedstead." By the time Jimmy was nearing grade school age, he not only could handle the guitar quite well but had also mastered banjo and fiddle.

Jimmy's first educational lessons were in a one-room schoolhouse in Mountain View. Later he completed three years of high school at a Mountain View school, then finished his senior year at nearby Marshall. In those years, even a high school degree was quite an attainment, and, after receiving it, Jimmy embarked on a career as a teacher in rural Arkansas schools. Finally, after ten years, in the late 1940s he earned a B.A. with honors from Arkansas State Teachers College in Conway.

During the 1940s he took part in many folk festivals in his home area, including several appearances at the Ozark Folk Festival in Eureka Springs. During this period more and more musicologists and other academics were increasingly going through rural regions with notebooks and tape recorders to further their collections of traditional music. The contacts that Jimmy made helped bring his talents to the notice of folk fans outside the South and Southwest. In the 1950s, Jimmy began to take part in festivals and concerts in many other sections of the United States.

During the folk boom of the later 1950s, record executives at major labels sought out talented artists. As a result, Jimmy got the chance to sign with RCA Victor, which issued his debut LP, *Newly Discovered Early American Folk Songs,* in June 1958. Among the tunes in the collection were "Unfortunate Man," "Fair Rosamund's Bower," "Soldier's Joy," "Country Boy," "I'm Too Young to Marry," "Pretty Mary," "Sailor Man," "Zelma Lee," "Rattlesnake Song," "Old Joe Clark," and "Battle of New Orleans." The latter, an updated version of a folk tune Jimmy had discovered in his musical searches, caught the ear of country artist Johnny Horton. Horton turned out a cover record of it that became a major hit of 1959, rising to number one on country charts. The record also caught the fancy of the general public, reaching number one in *Billboard* in May to start a six-week run at that position. Horton's version only made the top 20 in England, but a version by Lonnie Donegan peaked at number two on U.K. charts.

Driftwood was represented by his own single of that song in the late 1950s, which also did reasonably well. Soon other country artists were recording some of Jimmy's material. In 1959, Eddy Arnold scored a top 10 hit with Driftwood's "Tennessee Stud."

During the 1960s Jimmy steadily expanded the range of his performances, but in between engagements he always returned home to his beloved Arkansas, where during the 1960s he had a career as a high school principal. There he continued to work with friends and folk adherents throughout the region to collect and preserve local folk material. One vehicle he helped found to further those aims was the Rackensack Folklore Society. He also helped start the Arkansas Folk Festival in 1963 and served as its director for many years. Besides taking part in that festival, he often was invited to other folk gatherings all over the world. He was a featured performer at many of the Newport Folk Festivals during the 1960s, and some of his work was included in Newport Folk Festival albums issued by Folkways and Vanguard. A prime goal for Jimmy in the '60s was gaining support to establish a cultural center in Mountain View devoted to preserving elements of the heritage of the Ozark Mountains region. He often solicited audience support for this project at Rackensack and other concerts. The dream finally became a reality in 1973.

Jimmy never concentrated his efforts on the commercial country music circuit, though he always was highly respected by many country fans and leading country artists. During the 1960s and 1970s, he was a guest many times on the *Grand Ole Opry*, and, indeed, some of his recordings were included in the RCA 1964 set *Stars of the Grand Ole Opry*. A highlight of many of his appearances was his playing of the unusual instrument called the "picking bow" or "mouth bow," one of many special instruments in a collection he assembled over the years.

Most of Jimmy's recorded output was released in the 1960s, including the RCA album, *Songs of Billy Yank & Johnny Reb*, issued in March 1961, the United Artists LP *Festival of Carnegie Hall*, and several albums on Monument Records, his label of the mid-1960s. Among the latter were *Jimmy Driftwood*, issued in March 1964, *Down in the Arkansas* (1965), and *Best of Jimmy Driftwood* (August 1966). In later years he had recordings on minor folk labels.

Jimmy didn't stray far from Arkansas much in the 1970s and '80s, but he still played occasional folk festivals in various locales. From time to time he also took part in country reunion shows in Nashville, Tennessee. Some of his recorded material was available in compilation albums like the 1970s release *Famous Country Music Makers* and the 1991 *Americana*. The last named, released by Germany's Bear Family Records, incorporated all of Driftwood's RCA recordings on three compact discs. He died of a heart attack at the age of ninety-one.

DROGE, PETE: *Singer, songwriter, guitarist, pianist. Born Eugene, Oregon, March 11, 1969.*

Like late-70s folk-rocker Elliott Murphy before him, when singer-songwriter Pete Droge (pronounced "drōj") entered the scene in the 1990s he was immediately compared to Bob Dylan, Tom Petty, Neil Young, and Gram Parsons, even though he had released only one album, *Necktie Second*, in 1993. Despite such lofty expectations, Droge's song "Fourth of July," about a friend who committed suicide on Independence Day, revealed a keen writing style and a slight touch of pain that exhibited flashes of Messrs. Dylan, Petty, Young, and Parsons: *On the Fourth of July it's a good day to die. They'll celebrate each year your independence from here.*

As Droge told *Los Angeles Times* rock critic Robert Hilburn: "The song was about a friend who climbed up a mountain on the Fourth of July and allowed himself to freeze to death. I was sitting around one afternoon thinking about him and wishing I had been around at the time he made that decision. So the song is partly about regret and guilt—feeling like I wasn't a good enough friend. But there's also part of the song that is a salute to him—and the fact that every year . . . I'll think about him and use all the fireworks to celebrate his independence from this world."

Not all of Droge's songs are so deep. In "If You Don't Love Me (I'll Kill Myself)," probably his best-known song, his tongue is firmly planted in cheek. He wrote it in the summer of '93 in his cramped Portland, Oregon, apartment. "There wasn't a whole lot going on in my mind at the time," he says of the song, which made the sound tracks of *Outbreak* and that great intellectual film of the '90s, *Dumb and Dumber.*

Droge was born in Eugene in 1969 and was adopted when he was less than a month old by a couple from Minneapolis. His mother, Janet, teaches elementary music to public school students from kindergarten to the fifth grade, and his father, Arnold, set up group homes for juvenile delinquents, then was a consultant for the state of Washington's Department of Social Health Services. He is now retired. The family moved to South Dakota and St. Louis before settling on Bainbridge Island, near Seattle. He started strumming a ukulele when he was four, singing: *Oh boy! You gotta get outta this town.*

He took piano lessons from the second grade until the sixth grade. (He still plays now and then, but seldom on record and never in public.) He got a guitar one Christmas and learned how to play it. As a teenager, attending Bainbridge Island High School, he played in a punk band called March of Crimes, modeled after the Fartz. Early on he was influenced by the rock bands KISS, AC/DC, and Black Sabbath. Then he discovered Dylan, Simon and Garfunkel, Muddy Waters, the Rolling Stones, and Kris Kristofferson. After high school, he studied music for one year at Cornish College. Then he went to Shoreline Community College and spent one quarter at Evergreen State College, but he never graduated.

In his early twenties, when grunge rockers Nirvana and Pearl Jam were taking off in the Seattle area, he formed Ramadillo, playing coffee shops and clubs, and making several demo tapes. "It was good-time, boot-stompin' boogie blues/country rock stuff," he told journalist Kim Ahearn. "But certainly the A&R people who were flocking up there all the time didn't pick up on it."

During the day he washed dishes, bused tables, and flipped pizzas at Piecora's Restaurant, near the University of Washington, with Mike McCready, who would go on to play guitar in Pearl Jam. They talked about music to break the monotony. McCready introduced him to Gram Parsons's music.

ALTAN (*Photo by Lyndon Stambler*)

JOAN BAEZ (*left*) and **DAR WILLIAMS** (*Photo by Lyndon Stambler*)

THE BATTLEFIELD BAND (*Photo by Gary Glade*)

HARRY BELAFONTE (*Courtesy of RCA Records*)

BRYNDLE (*l. to r.: Kenny Edwards, Karla Bonoff, Andrew Gold, Wendy Waldman*) (*Photo by Gary Glade*)

THE BYRDS 1964-65 (*Courtesy of Columbia Records*)

HAMILTON CAMP (*Photo by Gary Glade*)

PETER CASE (*Photo by Gary Glade*)

CLIFTON CHENIER (*Courtesy of Michael Ochs Archives*)

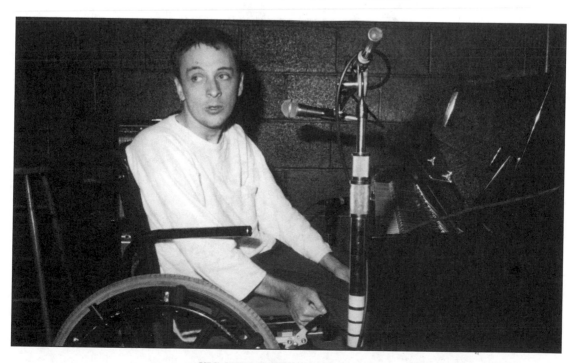

VIC CHESNUTT (*Photo by Gary Glade*)

THE CHIEFTANS (*Courtesy of Michael Ochs Archives*)

BRUCE COCKBURN (*Photo by Gary Glade*)

JUDY COLLINS (*Courtesy of Elektra*)

ROBERT CRAY (*Photo by Gary Glade*)

CROSBY, STILLS, NASH & YOUNG, late 1960's (*Courtesy of Atlantic Records*)

CATIE CURTIS (*Photo by Lyndon Stambler*)

In 1993 Droge mentioned that he wanted to make a new demo tape, and McCready gave him $5,000 and helped him with the demo. As a result Droge got a manager, Curtis Management, and a producer, Brendan "Bud" O'Brien, who had worked with Pearl Jam and the Stone Temple Pilots. After listening to the demo, O'Brien's initial thought was, "Why does this 40-year-old guy want to start making records now?" O'Brien told Hilburn. "There was such maturity in his voice and his songs. So I was amazed when I found out he was only 24."

In 1993 he moved away from the Seattle grunge scene, settling in Portland, Oregon. He played the South by Southwest conference in Austin. In June, he opened a couple of shows for Neil Young in San Francisco.

Droge signed with Burbank-based American Recordings and released *Necktie Second* ("necktie second" is a form of double-dealing in cards). Some of the strong cuts on the album besides "Fourth of July" and "If You Don't Love Me (I'll Kill Myself)" include "Straylin' Street," released as the first single from the album; "Sunspot Stopwatch"; and "Hampton Inn, Room 306." The latter, about missing a girlfriend, was recorded on a DAT player in a hotel room.

The critics liked Droge's album and concerts—for the most part. Richard Cromelin of the *Los Angeles Times* called Droge a singer-songwriter "with wit and bite, if not overwhelming originality . . . At 25 he's out to prove you're never too young to be world-weary and emotionally bruised" (October 20, 1994).

He went on two tours with Tom Petty, and played with Melissa Etheridge, LIVE, Freedy Johnston, and Sheryl Crow. In October 1994 Neil Young invited Droge to play at the annual fund-raiser at San Francisco's Shoreline Amphitheater for the Bridge School, cofounded by Young's wife, Pegi, to help children with speech and physical impediments. He also performed "If You Don't Love Me" on David Letterman's show in early 1995. He went back on the show in 1996 to play the song he wrote for the movie *Beautiful Girls,* by the same name.

In 1995 he began working on his second album, recording in Atlanta with Brendan O'Brien. That album, *Find a Door,* was released in June 1996 on American Recordings. It's a harder-rocking album than his debut. Droge describes it: "It's louder and more conducive to toe-tapping" than his first album. He calls his band Pete Droge and the Sinners to give some credit to his band mates: Robert Cooper on bass, Gregg Williams on drums, and Elaine Summers on background vocals.

Following the demise of American Recordings, Droge moved to producer Brendan O'Brien's 57 Records (distributed by Epic). O'Brien produced his third album, *Spacey and Shakin',* issued in 1998. Droge, who had been moving toward a mid-tempo rocking sound with *Find a Door,* moves even further into rock with *Spacey and Shakin'*. As he told John Roos of the *Los Angeles Times* ("His Climes They Are A-Changin'," July 1, 1998), "Most of the songs on [*Find a Door*] were rootsy, kind of mellower folk-rock stuff, but when we got out on the road, it just seemed natural to turn up the guitars and play a little faster. I wanted to give the songs more of an immediate punch, and that just carried over to my next record. Plus, I wanted to record some songs that were exciting, that would be more fun to play live every night."

The 1998 album reveals his varied influences (Tom Petty, Neil Young, Bob Dylan, the Kinks, Eric Clapton) on such songs as "Spacey and Shakin'," "I Want to Go Away," "Mile of Fence," "Blindly," "Motorkid," and the love song "Walking by My Side."

Based in part on written answers provided by Pete Droge

DYLAN, BOB: *Songwriter, singer, guitarist, pianist, harmonica player. Born Duluth, Minnesota, May 24, 1941.*

From songs of social consciousness such as "The Times They Are A-Changin'" and "Blowin' in the Wind" to songs about his faith in Christianity (which he embraced and then renounced), Bob Dylan's music has sparked controversy and set trends. Refusing to be classified in any specific political or artistic posture, he has written about whatever strikes his fancy, restlessly probing one area of popular music, then moving on to another. His frequent shifts in musical style and subject matter have often outraged and confused his fans, yet he always managed to maintain favor with a large segment of the record-buying public.

Born Robert Allen Zimmerman, the legendary Bob Dylan grew up in the mining town of Hibbing, Minnesota. Although at one time he professed to have been a rebellious teenager, often running away from home, he later disavowed these stories. Actually, according to his mid-1980s interviews, he had a fairly normal childhood that did not change direction until his freshman year at the University of Minnesota. (His father, Abraham, owned a hardware and appliance shop. His mother was named Beatty, and he had a younger brother, David.) During his six months of college, Dylan did some singing at the campus coffeehouse and changed his name from Zimmerman to Dylan, taken from one of his favorite poets, Dylan Thomas. He also was influenced by folk songwriter Woody Guthrie and, in fact, when he left school, traveled to visit the dying Guthrie at Greystone Park Hospital, New Jersey. He managed to get to see Woody, and the two became friends.

Dylan remained in New York, trying to make his living in folk music as either a performer or a songwriter. At one point he went to Hill & Range publishing to seek a $50-per-week job as a staff writer, according to then company VP Grelun Landon. Landon recalled recommending to the firm's top executives that Dylan be hired, but the advice was rejected. A short time later, he was discovered by Columbia Records executive John Hammond, who heard him by accident during a rehearsal session of folksinger Carolyn Hester, for whom Bob played harmonica. Hammond set up Dylan's first recording sessions. His first album, *Bob Dylan,* was released in 1962 and was followed by other folk-oriented LPs, *Freewheelin' Bob Dylan* (1963) and *The Times They Are A-Changin'* (1964). The second and third remained on the best-seller lists for many weeks. (Columbia came close to missing the boat on those successes and later Dylan classics. Hammond recalled that company executives talked about dropping the artist after his debut LP because they felt his style didn't fit the firm's roster.)

At the same time, Bob was appearing at various coffeehouses in New York City. The critics raved about his work, and he soon became a focal point of the short-lived folk music boom of the early 1960s. The dozens of folkish songs he composed during this time that became all-time standards included "Masters of War," "Don't Think Twice, It's All Right," "Spanish Harlem Incident," and "Chimes of Freedom." Some of his songs helped propel other artists to stardom, as "Blowin' in the Wind" did for Peter, Paul and Mary and "Mr. Tambourine Man" did for the Byrds. *(See Byrds, The.)*

With the folk boom on the wane, Dylan's songs began to veer more toward a blend of folk and rock elements. The symbolic transition point occurred on July 25, 1965, when Bob Dylan appeared at the Newport Folk Festival backed by the Paul Butterfield Blues Band. As Anthony Scaduto noted in the biography *Bob Dylan* (Abacus, 1972; Helter Skelter, 1996), Dylan bounded onto the stage dressed in "a wardrobe of the latest London mod fashions . . . carrying a solid body electric guitar. The audience sat transfixed as someone plugged his guitar into the amps and as a rock combo took its place behind him—the Paul Butterfield Blues Band. Dylan launched immediately into 'Maggie's Farm.' . . . The audience was bewildered, upset. This wasn't Bob Dylan." After playing "Like a Rolling Stone" Dylan left the stage in tears. He later returned to sing some acoustic numbers. There is still a great deal of controversy about the audience's reaction: some say they were upset because Dylan had changed, others because the sound was bad and you couldn't hear Dylan's voice. Nevertheless, the episode marks Dylan's move to folk-rock.

He now employed wildly upbeat arrangements and intricate but hard-to-understand lyrics that sometimes seemed written more for the sound and imagery of the words. These albums—*Another Side of Bob Dylan* (1964), *Highway 61 Revisited* and *Bringing It All Back Home* (1965), *Blonde on Blonde* (1966), and *Bob Dylan's Greatest Hits* (1967)—had considerable influence on that period's rock renaissance. His first single in his folk-rock vein to hit U.S. charts was "Subterranean Homesick Blues," which made the lists in April 1965. Later in the year he had a major hit, "Like a Rolling Stone," which reached number two. His other best-selling singles of the 1960s were "Positively 4th Street," "Rainy Day Women Nos. 12 & 35," "I Want You," "Just Like a Woman," and "Lay Lady Lay."

In 1966 Dylan suffered a near-fatal motorcycle accident and spent several years recuperating at his home in Woodstock, New York, away from the public eye. When he resurfaced musically at the end of the decade, he had once again switched his musical style to a blend of country and western and rock 'n' roll with lyrics emphasizing more basic, simple themes than his earlier songs. His best-selling Columbia albums *John Wesley Harding* (1968) and *Nashville Skyline* (1969) helped spark the growing trend toward the merging of country, folk, and rock.

In the 1970s Bob Dylan embraced many different themes and causes in his songs and tried several different musical styles. Although many critics felt his recordings in the early 1970s were not up to his earlier quality, his fans made up their own minds, propelling such albums as *Self-Portrait* (1970), *New Morning* (1970) and *More Greatest Hits, Volume 2* (1971) onto the best-seller lists.

If many people were concerned that Dylan had lost his sense of political concern, he demonstrated over and over again that this was not so. He expressed outrage over the death of George Jackson in San Quentin in his 1971 song "George Jackson." He also performed at a concert in support of the new nation of Bangladesh at Madison Square Garden in New York in 1971. This concert was organized by George Harrison and resulted in a three-LP album, *The Concert for Bangladesh,* which featured a number of tracks by Dylan. In 1975 he performed at a concert dedicated to freeing Rubin (Hurricane) Carter, an ex-boxer serving a life sentence for murder. Dylan felt he was falsely accused of this crime and wrote "Hurricane" specifically for the concert to free him.

All in all, however, the Bob Dylan of the 1970s was much more concerned with personal feelings and relationships than the Dylan of the early 1960s. He expressed this himself in one song from his 1974 album *Planet Waves: It's never been my duty to remake the world at large. Nor is it my intention to sound a battle charge.*

The 1970s also witnessed Dylan's involvement in modes of communication other than music. His stream-of-consciousness-style book, *Tarantula,* appeared in print in 1970. In 1973 he published his own authorized text, *Writings and Drawings by Bob Dylan,* which contained lyrics to most of the songs he had written up through 1971 and also included album notes he had written and drawings he had made. In 1973 Dylan made his acting debut in the movie *Pat Garrett and Billy the Kid,* directed by Sam Peckinpah and also starring Kris Kristofferson. The sound track album, which included Dylan's "Knocking on Heaven's Door," was issued by Columbia. This actually marked Dylan's third movie effort. His first appearance had been in *Don't Look Back* (released in 1967), a documentary about a British tour with Joan Baez in 1965. A book of the dialogue from the film was a best-seller in the late 1960s. His second movie, *Eat the Document,* was actually intended as a TV special. Completed in the late 1960s, it was turned down by ABC (which sued for return of advances) as not professional enough.

For a brief period, his recordings appeared on the Asylum label. After his recording contract with Columbia expired in late 1973, he organized his own firm, Ashes and Sand, with distribution to be handled by Asylum Records. Plans for this new operation dovetailed with his decision to return to the concert stage after a long hiatus.

When Dylan announced that he would make a coast-to-coast tour in early 1974, a deluge of mail-order requests hit box offices across the nation. Bill Graham, producer of the concerts, estimated that six million orders came in, roughly ten times the 658,000 seats available. Dylan sang many of his old standards but also introduced new songs from his upcoming Asylum debut album, *Planet Waves.*

He was backed by the Band, a rock group he had discovered in Atlantic City, New Jersey, in the mid-1960s. *(See Band, The.)* The use of the Band, therefore, not only provided Dylan with fine backup musicianship but supplied further continuity with Dylan's past, for he had been backed by the Band on his last tour, eight years earlier. The live album resulting from the 1974 tour, *Before the Flood* (Asylum Records), went gold.

In 1975 Dylan continued to build on the momentum he had gained the year before. He had meanwhile returned to the Columbia fold, which remained his label into the 1980s. As Robert Hilburn described his gold *Blood on the Tracks* LP: "The 10 songs . . . represent a variety of styles (acoustic, electronic, folk, blues, rock) and themes (tenderness, anger, sarcasm, humor, affection) that we've associated with Dylan's music over the years. The album's most arresting song—one that reflects the stinging intensity of 'Like a Rolling Stone'—is 'Idiot Wind.' Like so many of Dylan's songs, it contains a variety of crosscurrents and can be interpreted on several levels, but its most persistent theme is a sense of being disappointed or betrayed. (It has been called Dylan's divorce album.)"

Dylan also had a surprising best-selling album on Columbia in 1975, *The Basement Tapes*—surprising because the two-LP set had actually been recorded eight years earlier. The set was the long-awaited legitimate, professionally prepared tracks made from bootleg magnetic tapes of Bob Dylan and the Band that had circulated many years before. Even though eight years had elapsed since the tapes were made, the songs stood the test of time so well that many fans and critics felt the LP was the most exciting rock release of the year. *The Basement Tapes* was ranked number one in the *Village Voice* 1975 Jazz & Pop Critics Poll, in which thirty-eight music critics were allowed to divide 100 points among ten 1975 American-released LPs.

In the fall of 1975, Dylan embarked on the Rolling Thunder Revue, an informal tour of some small New England cities, playing mostly in small (several hundred) to medium-size (2,000–3,000 seats) auditoriums. Although Dylan was always the focal point and main attraction, the concerts featured a number of other excellent musicians, who stepped forward at various times in the concerts to do solo performances. Among the supporting cast of the Rolling Thunder Revue were Joan Baez, Joni Mitchell, Bobby Neuwirth, Roger McGuinn, Ramblin' Jack Elliott, guitarist Mick Ronson, Ronee Blakley, T-Bone Burnett, Rob Stoner, and violinist Scarlet Rivera. During this tour, Dylan introduced a few songs from his next album, *Desire,* which was released in January 1976.

Desire was received favorably by most music critics, further evidence that Dylan had indeed returned to the top of the rock heap. The album's songs could be seen as an overview of the major themes of Dylan's previous work, from social protest ("Hurricane"), to affection for the underdog ("Joey" about slain underworld figure Joey Gallo), to many different views about romance and man-woman relationships ("One More Cup of Coffee," "Oh, Sister," "Sara"). Dylan wrote all the music, but the lyrics to seven of the album's nine songs were cowritten with Jacques Levy. *Hard Rain* also came out in 1976.

Dylan tried his hand at filmmaking once again in 1978 with *Renaldo and Clara,* which Dylan starred in, wrote, directed, and coedited. Robert Hilburn, pop music critic for the *Los Angeles Times,* typified most critics' reaction to the movie when he wrote: "Bob Dylan will hopefully make a better film some day than *Renaldo and Clara,* but it's doubtful that rock's most acclaimed songwriter will ever make a more fascinating one. At once mocking and reinforcing his own almost mythical pop status, Dylan has crammed enough provocative symbolism into his nearly four-hour production to keep Dylan-cologists aflutter for years."

The film featured Dylan as Renaldo, his ex-wife Sara as Clara, and Ronee Blakely and Ronnie Hawkins as Dylan's parents. Joan Baez appeared as a reminder of the rumors about Dylan's long-ago romance with her. One of the film's scenes showed Dylan and poet Allen Ginsberg visiting the tombstone of novelist Jack Kerouac, affirming that one's art is all that will survive. In addition, a great deal of concert footage (forty-seven songs) was included in the film.

His next record was *Street Legal* (1978), which sold

well but seemed lightweight for Bob Dylan. His new songs incorporated Latin rock, reggae, and soul styles, the result being a more top 40 pop-oriented sound than usual. He surprised his fans during concerts in 1978 by playing totally new, almost unrecognizable versions of his old hits, such as a reggae-flavored rendition of "Don't Think Twice" and a soul-flavored version of "Just Like a Woman."

The next year Dylan did another unexpected about-face. His new album, *Slow Train Coming,* reflected his conversion to Christianity. If anything could surprise Dylan's fans after all his previous changes in attitude and musical style, it was his new incarnation, for the Jewish-born rock poet had always seemed to be something of a cynic.

Whatever his fans thought of Dylan's conversion, many soon concurred that his newfound faith added power to his music. His voice seemed stretched by a new force. In addition, Dylan went beyond his own personal conversion and probed new aspects and applications of the morality implied in the embracing of Christianity. In "When You Gonna Wake Up," he expresses the idea that America is a great country, but warns that it must "strengthen the things that remain," "wake up" to the corruption around it, and focus on a new set of values. *Bob Dylan at Budokan* also came out in 1979.

Not everyone received Dylan's conversion and gospel songs with pleasure, however. His 1979 concert tour was met with empty seats and, on some occasions, even boos. His 1980 album, *Saved,* continued in the gospel vein. By 1983 Dylan had renounced his conversion to Christianity and apparently returned to the Jewish faith, although this aspect of Dylan's life, like much of his private life, remains a mystery.

Dylan's twenty-fourth album, *Shot of Love,* was released by Columbia in August 1981. Some of its songs were included in the summer tour of Europe, a series of concerts played to standing-room-only crowds. In connection with these activities, he recorded a special, limited-edition promotional piece, *The Bob Dylan London Interview,* intended mainly for radio station use. (The world premiere broadcast of the interview was on station WNEW-FM in New York on July 27, 1981.)

Dylan's next LP was *Infidels* (1983), produced by Mark Knopfler of Dire Straits. In this gold album, Dylan returned to the criticism of aspects of the state of the United States and the world that had marked his rise to fame in the 1960s, including "Neighborhood Bully" (saluting Israel's brave struggle for survival) and "Union Sundown" (lamenting the greed in American business). The summer of 1984 saw Dylan once again touring Europe before enthusiastic audiences. Then in 1985, at the invitation of Soviet poet Yevgeny Yevtushenko, Dylan traveled to the Soviet Union, where he performed in Moscow at a gathering of international

poets. Yevtushenko introduced him as a "famous . . . singing poet."

Earlier in 1985, Dylan had appeared with many of the most popular U.S. entertainers to sing "We Are the World" to raise money to aid those starving in Africa. He also appeared in the Live Aid concert in Philadelphia for the same cause, and in September 1985 in the Farm Aid concert to assist failing farmers. He also released two albums, *Empire Burlesque* and *Biograph,* a five-record set including twenty-one selections not previously available on an album and thirty-two digitally remastered versions of previously released tracks. As he had done with his singles for *Infidels,* Dylan also made some music videos of his singles from *Empire Burlesque.* Columbia also released *Real Live* in 1985.

In early 1986, in tribute to his lasting contribution to American music, ASCAP (American Society of Composers, Authors & Publishers) gave Dylan the Founders Award, an award to salute musicians whose songs changed the direction of American pop music.

Proving that he was still actively contributing to pop music, Dylan toured the United States in the summer of 1986 with Tom Petty and the Heartbreakers, singing old songs and new songs to delighted crowds. He released another album, *Knocked Out Loaded,* that same summer.

In an interview in 1984, Dylan told Robert Hilburn of the *Los Angeles Times:* "When I started, I combined other people's styles unconsciously. . . . I crossed Sonny Terry with the Stanley Brothers with Roscoe Holcomb with Big Bill Broonzy with Woody Guthrie . . . all the stuff that was dear to me. Everybody else tried to do an exact replica of what they heard. I was doing it my own way because I wasn't as good technically as, say, Erik Darling or Tom Paley. So I had to take the songs and make them mine in a different way. It was the early folk music done in a rock way, which was the first kind of music I played. On the first album, I did 'Highway 51' like an Everly Brothers tune because that was the only way I could relate to that stuff."

Stating that he was glad that he had started his remarkable career in the 1960s, he said: "Everything happened so quick in the '60s. There was just an electricity in the air. It's hard to explain—I mean, you didn't ever want to go to sleep because you didn't want to miss anything. It wasn't there in the '70s and it ain't there now.

"If you want to really be an artist and not just be successful, you'll go and find the electricity. It's somewhere."

In the second half of 1986, Dylan's schedule included work on a new film project called *Hearts of Fire,* in which he played the role of Billy Parker, a reclusive singer-songwriter who retires to a farm for a decade before a bittersweet return to the stage in an oldies concert. In the summer of 1987, Bob went back on tour, this time with the Grateful Dead band. In September he went to Israel for two concerts eagerly awaited by the nation's rock fans. He downplayed any symbolism, though, telling reporters it was just another part of his concert schedule. He jokingly told Hilburn (*Los Angeles Times,* Calendar, September 20, 1987), "I wish people here well, but it's not like this show is my biggest goal of the year or anything. My biggest goal of the year is getting back home alive."

In January 1988, after Bob was inducted into the Rock and Roll Hall of Fame in a ceremony at the Grand Ballroom of the New York Waldorf Astoria, he performed "Like a Rolling Stone" backed by a chorus of Mick Jagger, Bruce Springsteen, Supremes alumnus Mary Wilson, and a band whose guitar roster included John Fogerty, George Harrison, Neil Young, Jeff Beck, and Les Paul.

For the rest of 1988, Dylan continued his hectic activities as a soloist and as a member of an all-star group that called itself the Traveling Wilburys. The other artists were Jeff Lynne, Tom Petty, George Harrison, and Roy Orbison. The first Wilburys album, *Traveling Wilburys, Volume 1,* was released on the Warner Brothers label in October '88 (preceded by a Dylan solo album on Columbia, *Down in the Groove,* released in May '88). For the collection, Dylan and Harrison contributed three songs each, with two each from Petty and Lynne. Commenting on Dylan's numbers in the *New York Times,* John Rockwell concluded that all three were strong entries. "'Congratulations' is full of upbeat romantic scorn, 'Dirty World' can be heard as a good-humored Prince parody, and 'Tweeter and the Monkey Man,' with its references to New Jersey and driving down highways and other Springsteen signposts, may well be a gentle send-up of the Boss."

In November, the unauthorized biography *Dylan* by journalist and former rock manager Bob Spitz was published. While it didn't savage Dylan, the book took note of the performer's self-indulgences once he had become a global icon and his occasionally mean-spirited treatment of friends and family.

Spitz pointed out that Dylan, like many superstars, sometimes fretted about the problems of living in what amounted to a fishbowl. He called attention to a 1975 interview with Madeline Beckman where "Bob romanticized his brother's modest lifestyle in contrast to his own public spectacle. [He told Beckman] 'David's got it all, a good marriage, and a family and . . . anonymity. Wish I had some of what he had—especially privacy. In the music business, everybody wants a piece of you until there's nothing left to give.'"

Dylan and other members of the Wilburys were deeply shaken by Roy Orbison's untimely death in December '88. After Roy's passing, the group's album rose to number one on the hit charts. In the Grammy Awards voting for 1989 (announced on the global telecast of February 21, 1990) the album was given the trophy for Best Rock Performance by a Duo or Group with Vocal.

In February 1989 Columbia released a live album taken from Dylan's tour with the Grateful Dead titled *Dylan and the Dead.* Starting in the summer, Dylan was on tour supporting a new solo album on Columbia, *Oh Mercy,* released in September. Produced by Daniel Lanois, it was considerably more technically polished than some of his albums, but without losing the sharp-edged treatment Bob gave his work. One of his best collections, it included such introspective numbers as "What Good Am I," "Shooting Star," and several songs of social commentary. As Bob Hilburn of the *Los Angeles Times* observed, the opening track, "Political World," . . . "offers the biting social inventory that has long characterized Dylan's most compelling work, and the view again is a bleak one that describes a society adrift: 'We live in a political world/Where courage is a thing of the past/Where houses are haunted, children not wanted/The next day could be your last.'"

In January 1990, before opening a European tour with a concert in Paris, Dylan accepted one of the nation's highest honors, Commander of the Order of Arts and Letters, from culture minister Jack Lang. When his next album, *Under the Red Sky,* came out on Columbia in September, it was lighter in tone that the previous one and provided very listenable folk-rock tracks. The following month, Warner Brothers released another Wilburys album, *Traveling Wilburys, Volume 2,* which in essence ended the Wilburys' saga.

During the Grammy Awards telecast on February 20, 1991, Dylan was to receive the National Academy of Recording Arts & Science's Lifetime Achievement Award. Some thought he might not show up, given the many years in which the Grammy voters ignored some of his most legendary creative work, but he and his backing group did indeed appear at the New York event. In his introduction, Jack Nicholson said, "He's been called everything from the voice of his generation to the conscience of the world. He rejects both titles and others that categorize him or analyze him. . . . He opened the doors of pop music wider than anybody else, yet returned time and again to the simplicity of basic chords and emotions to express himself. He's been, and still is, a disturber of the peace." Dylan responded with a searing, overdrive version of his classic antiwar song, "Masters of War."

A month later, Columbia issued a boxed set titled *Bob Dylan: The Bootleg Series, Volumes 1–3 (Rare & Unreleased).* Meanwhile, he continued his demanding concert schedule that took him not only to many parts of the United States, but on a five-night series in Spain in October, when he was joined by such U.K. stars as Keith Richards of the Rolling Stones and onetime Cream bassist Jack Bruce. Other '91 shows were presented in London, Paris, and Toronto, as well as cities in Mexico and South America. Those appearances, in effect, formed a warmup for 1992 plans of 100–125 concerts to help celebrate the thirtieth anniversary of the release of his first Columbia LP. In the fall of '91 Rhino Records issued a single CD (*I Shall Be Unreleased*) containing eighteen covers of Dylan compositions by well-known artists like Rod Stewart, Manfred Mann, Roger McGuinn, and the Staple Singers and relatively obscure ones like reggae singer Jah Malla.

In between 1992 concerts, Dylan went into the studio to record an acoustic collection of mostly traditional folk songs, live with no overdubs, harkening back to his first recordings for the label. Among the thirteen tracks finally chosen for *Good As I Been to You* were "Frankie and Albert," "Blackjack Davey," "Sittin' on Top of the World," "Hard Times," "Arthur McBride," "You're Gonna Quit Me," "Diamond Joe," and "Froggie Went a-Courtin.'" Release date for the album was just after the Columbia thirtieth anniversary show, held the night of October 16, 1992, at New York's Madison Square Garden.

Those taking part in the festivities ranged from some of his earliest friends in the field like Liam and Paddy Clancy to such other stars as George Harrison, John Mellencamp, Willie Nelson, Johnny Cash, June Carter, Sinead O'Connor, Tom Petty and the Heartbreakers, Eric Clapton, Neil Young, Eddie Vedder and Mike McCready of Pearl Jam, and others. For people unable to attend in person, the concert was offered on a pay-for-view basis on cable TV.

In February 1993, a slightly re-edited version was used as the opening show for the Public Broadcasting System *In the Spotlight* TV series. On August 17, 1993, Columbia released both audio and video sets of the Madison Square Garden show called *Bob Dylan: The 30th Anniversary Concert Celebration.* The audio sequence, on two CDs or two cassettes, presented twenty-eight songs covering over 145 minutes. The video sequence was marketed in two volumes opening with a montage of Dylan's career. The thirty-one songs on the video included one not used in the concert, Dylan's rehearsal of "It Takes a Lot to Laugh, It Takes a Train to Cry." Another highlight for Dylan in '93 was release of the disc *World Gone Wrong* in October. His fortieth album release, like *Good As I Been to You,* was an acoustic folk-based collection. His fall concert work included a tour with Carlos Santana.

During 1994 and '95, Dylan continued to show unflagging energy as he toured widely and worked on new material for upcoming projects, including an appearance on *MTV Unplugged.* This was captured on a new Columbia album release in April '95. Tracks included acoustic treatments of "All along the Watchtower" (a hit for Jimi Hendrix), "Knockin' on Heaven's Door" (which had provided Guns 'N' Roses with a chart success), "Like a Rolling Stone," and "The Times They Are A-Changin'." He talked about the project in a rare interview, this time with Edna Gundersen of USA

Today. Asked about his approach to planning it, he replied, "I wasn't sure how to do it and what material to use. I would have liked to do old folk songs with acoustic instruments, but there was a lot of input from other sources as to what would be right for the MTV audience. The record company said, 'You can't do that, it's too obscure.' At one time, I would have argued, but there's no point. OK, so what's not obscure? They said 'Knockin' on Heaven's Door'."

Gundersen wondered about why Dylan kept up a steady live concert pace. He answered, "There's a certain part of you that becomes addicted to a live audience. I wouldn't keep doing it if I was tired of it. I do about 125 shows a year. It may sound like a lot to people who don't work that much, but it isn't. B.B. King is working 350 nights a year."

Music fans around the world were worried about Dylan's future when it as announced in May 1997 that he had checked into a hospital suffering from a respiratory infection. However, he made a complete recovery and within several months' time was back on the concert trail.

In October 1997 his concert schedule included a special appearance before Pope John Paul II during the twenty-third National Eucharistic Congress in Bologna, Italy. The Pope commented to the audience of 300,000 people, in part, "The answer to your questions about life is blowing in the wind." After accepting a gift of a mother-of-pearl rosary from the Pontiff, Dylan, outfitted in a black cowboy suit and wearing a gray Stetson hat, sang such numbers as "Knockin' on Heaven's Door," "A Hard Rain's A-Gonna Fall," and "Forever Young."

That fall, he also was represented on the charts by the Columbia album *Time Out of Mind,* his first set of recordings of original songs in seven years. It is an excellent, if more introspective than usual, collection, reflecting the singer's concerns about the aging process and the unpredictable nature of life. He sang, on one track: *When you think that you've lost everything, you find out that you could always lose a little more.* Peter Ames Carlin noted in *People* his opinion that the "standout track is 'Highlands,' an epic, 16 minute talking blues contrasting the everyday hassles of being Bob Dylan with his vision of an elusive, heavenly reward. 'I'm gonna get there someday,' he says. Here's hoping he's with us a lot longer."

Dylan's career contributions to the arts were recognized further on Sunday, December 12, 1997, when he was one of the recipients of the 1997 Kennedy Center Honors (along with Lauren Bacall, Charlton Heston, Jessye Norman, and Edward Villella). The presentation was made in New York by President Clinton.

When the Grammy Awards nominations were announced in January 1998, not only was *Time Out of Mind* a finalist for Album of the Year (later winning the

Grammy), but his son Jakob earned three nominations. The latter, born in 1970, lived with his mother, Sara Lowndes, after his parents divorced in 1977 and was the only one of four children of Lowndes and Dylan to go into show business. He told *People* magazine ("Highway 61 Revisited," November 11, 1996), "They're all civilians. When it got to me, that's why I'm onstage. I guess the family luck ran out."

After attending Windward School in Los Angeles and Parsons School of Design in New York, Jakob formed a band called the Wallflowers in the early 1990s. The group's debut album sold poorly and the label dropped the band, but Jakob refused to be discouraged, signing with another label, Interscope, and winning critical praise for the band's second album, *Bringing Down the Horse,* which spawned a hit single, "6th Avenue Heartache." Looking back, he indicated no bitterness about his formative years. He told *People,* "I feel like I had a normal upbringing—I considered it normal at least. People have a lot of worse things happen to them. . . . The truth is, yeah, it was weird. Relatively interesting, but weird. I could write a book. But I'm not going to."

Robert Hilburn queried Bob Dylan about his attitude toward his son ("Reborn Again," *Los Angeles Times,* Calendar, December 14, 1997, pp. 3, 72). Did Bob worry when he heard Jakob was starting a band and did he advise him at all? "It was inconsequential what I thought." Was Dylan worried after the Wallflowers' first label dropped them? "I was concerned after the label dropped him and they were still involved in trying to get another record deal, but he made it on his own. If anything, his name would have held him back. I think that held him back on his first record, to tell you the truth. I think that first record would have been accepted if he wasn't who he was."

After *Time Out of Mind* won the Album of the Year Grammy in February 1998 its sales almost quadrupled, moving it from number 122 on the *Billboard* chart to inside the top 30. Soon after, plans were announced for a spring concert series starring Rock and Roll Hall of Famers Dylan, Joni Mitchell, and Van Morrison. Dylan appeared much more relaxed than usual, making occasional comments between songs and bidding audiences at venues like the University of California at Los Angeles a cheerful farewell after performing the final encore number.

In October, Columbia Legacy finally released a non-bootleg version of the May 1966 Dylan concert in Manchester, England, erroneously listed as taking place at a London venue. The two-CD 1998 title was, however, the same as the original bootleg material, *The Royal Albert Hall Concert.* The first CD features Dylan singing and playing acoustic guitar, while the second features Dylan with an electric backup band, marking his transition from folk to folk-rock.

ℰ

EBERHARDT, CLIFF: *Singer, songwriter, guitarist. Born Bryn Mawr, Pennsylvania, January 7, 1954.*

With his husky voice, dark eyes, and serious face, Cliff Eberhardt does, at first glance, look like the "bad boy of folk," as Christine Lavin once called him. But standing on a stage at two A.M. at the 1996 Folk Alliance Conference in Washington, D.C., it's difficult to be too serious. He does crack a smile and joke about his shiny National steel guitar: "I spent a lot of money to get something that sounds this bad." There is a refreshing, brooding quality about Eberhardt. "I've been writing a lot about good and evil because I'm confused," he said, introducing his song "Thieves and Kings." "I don't know which category I belong in." He explored that theme in *12 Songs of Good and Evil,* issued on Red House Records in 1997.

Eberhardt's interest in good, evil, and music started in Berwyn, a suburb of Philadelphia. His father was an atheist and his mother was Jewish. "I was brought up Baptist, and I got swimmer's ear when I was baptized so it got me off on a strange foot," he told Scott Simon of National Public Radio (December 6, 1997). His father was a guitarist, and his mother played the piano. At seven, he began teaching himself guitar and discovered what he wanted to do with his life. His desire to become a professional musician only became stronger after he saw the Beatles on *The Ed Sullivan Show.* His goal was reinforced by several forays to the Main Point in Bryn Mawr, Pennsylvania, where he heard Joni Mitchell, James Taylor, Muddy Waters, and Dave Van Ronk.

Eberhardt started playing in groups with his brothers when he was fifteen. At twenty-one, he moved to Carbondale, Illinois, where he began playing the bar scene. He also worked in a masking tape factory. After a short stint in Colorado, in 1978 he moved to New York, where he struggled. He rented a $125-a-month apartment and drove a taxi to make ends meet. One night after playing at the Bitter End, he had to put on his other hat—he got into his cab and picked up a group of people who had just seen him perform.

But that was soon to change. He started playing the clubs in Greenwich Village and opened for Tracy Chapman, Suzanne Vega, Michelle Shocked, the Band, Melanie, and Richie Havens, who took him on tour as his opening act and guitarist. Eberhardt played in Europe and Canada, taping a TV special called *In Session.*

He did commercials for Diet Coke and Miller beer. His first big break came from General Motors. The advertising mavens chose Eberhardt to sing the Chevrolet "Heartbeat of America" jingle in the mid-1980s.

"Luckily that ad was so long ago that a lot of people don't remember it," he told interviewer Jay S. Jacobs. "At the time I was driving a cab in New York. It allowed me to quit my job and really concentrate on writing and making tapes. I find the whole business, and life itself, to be rather ironic. It doesn't bother me [that the jingle may be his most popular musical moment to date]. It seems almost predictable to me that something like that would be the case." Nevertheless, he learned a lot about recording, production, and engineering from his "Heartbeat" experience.

In the late 1980s, Windham Hill, known mostly for its new age recordings, began to sign some young, edgy singer-songwriters, such as John Gorka, Patty Larkin, and Eberhardt. In 1989, Eberhardt recorded a song, "My Father's Shoes," for the Windham Hill *Legacy: A Collection of New Folksingers* album. He went on tour with a group of singer-songwriters and appeared in a VH-1 concert special.

The following year, Windham Hill released Eberhardt's first solo album, *The Long Road*. It opens with "My Father's Shoes." An anthem about the need of a son to break away from the past, the song was featured on a Putumayo Records folk music compilation a few years later. The album ends with Eberhardt's fine song "Goodnight," which has been covered by Shawn Colvin and Buffy Sainte-Marie, among others. In between the two are romantic ballads and the title track, which Eberhardt sings with Richie Havens. It, too, is about his father.

Commenting on "My Father's Shoes," Eberhardt told Peter Nelson of *Performing Songwriter* (November-December 1995): "He was a fundraiser. He helped form CARE, the organization that sent care packages abroad. Ultimately alcoholism strongly knitted itself into a self-defeating and insecure personality, which tended to make his life take a series of downward turns. He hurt himself and hurt his family and lost everything in the end. . . . It's a reminder to myself, on a nightly basis, what not to do with my life."

Although the album sold respectably for a new artist, Eberhardt left Windham Hill in 1992 after making one album. He moved to Shanachie Records, releasing *Now You Are My Home* in 1993 and *Mona Lisa Cafe* in 1995. For the latter album, he recorded "Voodoo Morning," a bluesy song he wrote with David Wilcox. "Brave Little Grey" is an homage to the Band, and "Everything Is Almost Gone" was written for his father, who had passed away. "Why Do Lovers (Have to Say Goodbye)" is a song about narcissism and self-doubt. As Eberhardt said during his showcase at the Folk Alliance: "It was a one-sided relationship where we both liked her and neither one of us liked me very much."

In the early 1990s Eberhardt was part of the touring folk show started by Christine Lavin called On a Winter's Night. He joined Cheryl Wheeler, Patty Larkin, and John Gorka for the shows. In 1994 he relocated from New York to Northampton, Massachusetts. Cherry Lane also published a collection of his songs, *Cliff Eberhardt Songbook.*

Eberhardt was unhappy with the control the recording companies had exerted over his work, however. "I decided I wouldn't make any more crap until I could do exactly what I wanted," he told J. Mark Dudick of the *Anchorage Daily News* (October 3, 1997). "I thought my career was over."

In 1997 he signed with Red House Records and released his most coherent album, *12 Songs of Good and Evil*. He avoids singing typical love and relationship songs. "There were just so many relationship-gone-wrong songs that I had left in me," he told NPR. "The Devil in Me" was a song about his Jewish-Baptist-atheist upbringing: *You can blame yourselves/But you can't blame me/This isn't my fault/It's the devil in me*. He followed with *Borders* on Red House in 1999.

ELLIOTT, RAMBLIN' JACK: *Singer, guitarist. Born Brooklyn, New York, August 1, 1931.*

A cowboy from Brooklyn? This seems a little incongruous, but it is perhaps no more so than a matador or flamenco dancer from the same territory. Elliott is indeed from the big city, as are many others of the urban folk movement of the 1950s and 1960s. However, most critics agree that his music has the true flavor of the plains and the hills.

As Elliott told interviewer Bill Yaryan (*Sing Out!* November 1965, p. 16), "People [in the United States would] . . . just laugh their heads off at the idea of a kid from Brooklyn singing cowboy songs. So I invented this Oklahoma thing to keep 'em quiet. Said I was born on a ranch."

Elliott gained his initial interest in cowboys from watching countless movie westerns in his hometown. Though born Elliott Charles Adnopoz, son of a doctor, he began to think of himself as "Buck Elliott" by the time he was high school age. When he was sixteen, he ran away from home to join Col. Jim Eskew's rodeo. His family notified the authorities, and Buck was sent home two months later. He finished high school in Brooklyn and went on to college, first to the University of Connecticut and later to Adelphi College in New York. Along the way, he had learned to play guitar and sang cowboy songs whenever he had the opportunity.

Asked by Lyndon Stambler who taught him to play guitar, he said, "Many teachers. My first person that I watched play was a cowboy named Tiny Westly. Then I hung out with a cowboy named Todd Fletcher. He was a bullrider, and he rode rodeos and liked to play Martin guitars. He sang a lot of songs by Jimmie Rodgers and Ernest Tubb. That was in 1948 and 1949."

Stories that claimed he was playing banjo during these years were wrong, he added. "No, that's just a journalistic lie. It was an old rodeo clown who played banjo and guitar that was my first inspiration. Someone wrote it down wrong and said it was a rodeo clown who taught me to play the banjo. That's a total lie. He didn't teach me how to play the banjo at all. I used to watch him play the banjo. I loved it. I started playing guitar, but I was around a lot of banjo players also in the early times of my playing on guitar."

The urge to escape was too great for Jack to finish school. He left Adelphi and moved to Greenwich Village. Here he moved in coffeehouses and folk music circles. In 1951, this led to a meeting and start of a warm friendship with Woody Guthrie. Guthrie was impressed with Elliott's talent and invited the young man to stay with the Guthrie family in the Coney Island section of Brooklyn. The two played and sang for hours each day, and Elliott learned many of the fine points of combining guitar playing with other folk instruments.

He also established close ties with Woody's family, particularly with Arlo. He noted in 1998, "I've known him since he was four years old. When they ask if Woody taught him how to play guitar, he tells them he learned from me. I do not remember ever giving him a lesson. But he was watching the whole time when I was playing with his dad."

Arlo had some of his father's knack of telling stories, Jack said. "'Alice's Restaurant' is kind of a rambling tale. I once recorded that on a radio program with Arlo. I sang along on the chorus. It was played on WBAI for four years every day. I wasn't in New York and I never heard it. Four years later, I went right up to [the station] and I demanded for them to play the tape for me. By golly, it had been stolen or lost. About two years ago I went to New York and went to WBAI, and Bob Fass had relocated the tape and played it for me."

When the Guthries moved to the Topanga Canyon area of Los Angeles, Elliott went there too. Here he met many other major folk artists, including Bess and Butch Hawes, Guy Carawan, and Derroll Adams. Elliott gained his first professional experience in Southern California at Knott's Berry Farm, acting and playing guitar in the farm's covered-wagon-encircled amphitheater. He also worked as a "faith-cured cripple" for local revival meetings.

When Elliott met and married actress June Hammerstein, he decided to take her suggestion to go to Europe. His association with Woody Guthrie helped pave the way for acceptance by European audiences, but his first foray in 1955 took the form of busking shows with another American folksinger, Derroll Adams. In a relatively short time Elliott became a major favorite in England, and he and Adams soon were recording material for Topic Records. During 1956 and 1957, Jack and his wife traveled throughout Europe appearing in concerts and major clubs and starring on TV. They appeared on Alan Lomax's show *In the Big Rock Candy Mountain* and, joined by Derroll Adams, played to enthusiastic audiences at the Blue Angel in London and later at the Brussels World's Fair.

At one point during Jack's years in London, Mick Jagger saw him play guitar at a train station. Elliott commented, "That was when Mick was a kid and he was going to school. He was waiting for a train to take him to school. I was on the opposite platform. He was in a group of schoolchildren, so I never noticed him individually.... I got my guitar and played a few cowboy songs while we were waiting for the trains. Eventually their train came and so did mine. I was going back to London. Mick said it's the first time he ever saw me and he ran out to the guitar store and bought his first guitar the next day. He claims I was his first influence. I was amazed when I heard that story."

In 1958 the Elliotts returned to California but went back to England in 1959. Elliott was then featured on a European tour with the Weavers and Pete Seeger. After his triumphal reception overseas, Elliott once more tried his hand in his home country. This time his engagement at Gerde's Folk City won critical and popular acceptance throughout the United States. In the years that followed, Elliott became a favorite with U.S. audiences in concerts across the country. He also played at most major festivals in the 1960s, including several appearances at Newport.

One of the first things Jack did on returning to New York in 1961 was visit the hospital where old friend Woody Guthrie was fighting the debilitating disease Huntington's chorea. At Woody's bedside he met a young Minnesotan who called himself Bob Dylan. It was the beginning of a friendship in which Dylan in effect apprenticed himself to Elliott much as the young Elliott had done with Guthrie.

Reminiscing with John Wesley Harding in the mid-1990s ("Talkin' Bob Dylan Blues with Ramblin' Jack Elliott," *BAM* magazine, June 2, 1995), Elliott said, "I went to visit Woody in the hospital after I arrived back from Europe. I'd just gotten off the ship, and I hadn't yet got my land legs. I met Bob the very next day at Greystone Park Memorial Hospital, where Woody was, and I remember Bob was wearing a little black corduroy hat. I'd never heard of him, but he was a very memorable person. He was an unusual sort of lad and, very obviously, he was profoundly awed with respect and admiration for Woody."

At gatherings of Woody's friends, Dylan began learning some of Elliott's repertoire. Dylan also started to pick up some of Elliott's vocal mannerisms and guitar style. "Oh yeah, I know damn well he did that too!" he recalled. "Saw him do it! But that's OK. For his very first gig at Gerde's Folk City, there was a sign up outside the building that said: 'Now appearing: Son of Jack Elliott.' I suffered the same thing when I was hanging out and singing with Woody. The people who fancied themselves friends or fans of Woody were very irritated with me singing like Woody. People said to me and later I think [I] said to Dylan, 'You ought to learn how to be yourself,' but it can't be learned overnight."

By the mid-1960s, Elliott's name appeared on LPs on several labels. On Prestige, he turned out *Guthrie Songs* (1961); *Country Style Ramblin' Jack Elliott* (1962); and *Hootenanny* (1964). His output on Monitor included *Ramblin' Cowboy* and *Jack Elliott Sings Guthrie and Rodgers*. In 1964 he was featured on the Vanguard label with *Jack Elliott*. His other 1960s albums included *Talking Woody Guthrie* on Delmark Records (5/66); *Songs of Woody Guthrie* on Prestige (6/67); and *Jack Elliott* on the Archives of Folk Music. At the end of the decade he signed briefly with Reprise Records, resulting in such LPs as *Bull Durham Sacks.*

During the 1970s and into the 1980s, Elliott performed regularly on the folk music circuit, appearing mainly in small clubs and on college campuses around the United States and in other countries. An exception to that routine occurred in the mid-1970s, when, as a member of Bob Dylan's Rolling Thunder Revue, Jack performed across the United States before crowds ranging from several thousand to tens of thousands. With rock 'n' roll on the ascendant, recording opportunities for folksingers were very limited. The only "new" album of his to come out in that period, and that one was composed of previously unreleased recordings from the 1960s, was the 1976 Vanguard two-record set *The Essential Jack Elliott.* The LP contained one original by him, "Guabi Guabi," plus a number of traditional folk songs ("House of the Rising Sun," "Buffalo Skinners," "Sadie Brown") and songs by modern folk writers, such as Bob Dylan's "Don't Think Twice, It's Alright"; Woody Guthrie's "Ramblin' Round Your City"; Derroll Adams's "Portland Town"; and Jesse Fuller's "San Francisco Bay Blues."

Besides that LP, his albums still in print at the start of the 1980s included *Hard Travelin'* on Fantasy; *Jack Elliott* on Evergreen; *Jack Elliott* and *Ramblin' Jack Elliott* on Prestige; and *Songs to Grow On* (Woody Guthrie children's songs) on Folkways.

Although people not too familiar with Elliott's work tended to think of him as a singer of traditional material or the songs of others, particularly Woody Guthrie, he took pains to correct that image in answering questions posed by *Guitar Player* magazine (October 1974). He replied, "I have always created my own sources, but I still sing Woody's songs. While a lot of people don't think I'm imitating Woody, I still feel I am in a way, you know, like he's looking over my shoulder. [Onstage] I do a lot of Woody's songs, a lot of Dylan's songs, and once in a while I'll make up a song onstage."

As to how he uses the guitar in the latter instance, he told *Guitar Player,* "I don't plan it. I just get my fingers rollin' on the guitar, and the strings are rollin'. It usually happens when I'm not paying attention to it. Just when I think I'm gettin' lost."

Though interest in folk music in general declined in the 1970s, Elliott continued to ply his trade, performing at festivals and small venues. When the fortunes of the field began to improve in the mid-1980s, Jack was there to take advantage of better bookings and musical exposure. As had been the case with rising folk and folk-rock stars of the '60s and early '70s (including such names, besides Dylan, as Ian Tyson, Guy Clark, Jackson Browne, John Prine, Jerry Jeff Walker, Peter Rowan, Kris Kristofferson, and Joan Baez), newcomers of the mid-'70s and beyond, like John Wesley Harding, Bonnie Raitt, Rory Block, and Bruce Springsteen, also considered Elliott one of their key influences.

All of those artists remembered the impact on their careers of hearing Elliott on records or in person. Jackson Browne said in the mid-'90s, "I first heard Jack singing 'Muleskinner Blues' on a live album, probably over thirty years ago. Or was it a live album? All his records have seemed live to me. I used to see him play in the clubs I hung around in when I was sixteen and used to see him in the houses I hung around in Laurel Canyon [in Los Angeles] in my twenties. His singing springs from the roots of folk and country and the bohemian/rhapsodic/hobo narratives of the American West."

While Jack really had never been away, a new segment of the music audience began to become aware of him in the 1990s. Some heard his work on new album releases by Guy Clark and Peter, Paul and Mary. Rounder also released *Me and Bobby McGee* in 1995 with tracks from two late-60s LPs, *Bull Durham* and *Young Brigham*. The timing also was right for new album projects by the veteran troubadour, and Red House Records in Saint Paul, Minnesota, arranged for him to prepare his first new domestic studio album in twenty-five years.

The reason for the hiatus, he told Lyndon Stambler, was unhappiness over his treatment by the record industry. "I felt very divorced from the people in the recording companies who owe me millions and won't pay up. It's a dirty deal. They're not my favorite people. It was just a bad relationship. I thought, 'No point in doing any more recordings.'" But he had kind words for Red House. "They're a nice, small record company in the Midwest. . . . They're pretty nice folks."

The result of the Red House project was a collection for which the word *superb* seems too tame—the spring '95 release, *South Coast*. Almost all the songs had been recorded by him before, but his treatment was as fresh and varied as if he'd just discovered them a few days or months before. For instance, Elijah Wald of the *Boston Globe* commented that the title track, "a melodramatic pseudo-ballad that he somehow transforms into a masterpiece, has doubled in length to almost eight minutes since he first recorded it more than 30 years ago."

Naming the album one of the top picks in the June 9, 1995, issue of the trade magazine *Gavin Report*, Rob Bleetstein wrote, "Elliott rolls through a collection of folk classics with enthusiasm, capturing the wandering spirit that defines his influence on countless numbers of musicians, actors and playwrights. With new versions of 'Pastures of Plenty,' 'The Buffalo Skinners,' and 'San Francisco Bay Blues,' Ramblin' Jack is not only back, but sounds like he's at his artistic peak."

During 1995 and into 1996 Elliott toured widely in the United States, Canada, and Europe in support of the album. When the final five nominees for the '95 Grammy Awards in the Best Traditional Folk Album, Vocal or Instrumental, category were announced in early January '96, *South Coast* was one of the contenders, along with releases by other long-established folk performers Norman and Nancy Blake (*While Passing along This Way*) and Dave Van Ronk (*From . . . Another Time and Place*). The March weekend before the winner was to be announced on the global Grammy telecast, long-time friends Elliott and Van Ronk were onstage at McCabe's Guitar Shop in Santa Monica, California, charming the small (but capacity) audience with their vocal and instrumental expertise, telling stories of career events, and sometimes making joking references to the Grammy sweepstakes. In any case, the honor went to *South Coast,* belated recognition for a giant in American and world music annals.

Meanwhile, Jack started work on a new album based on duets with many of the artists he had known or appeared with over the years. It was an approach, he said, he'd never tried before. "I thought it would be fun to get some of the people I admired to sing duets with me. Actually, the idea was thought of by my producer, Roy Rogers, not the king of the cowboys [but] the lap steel blues guy who is a record producer and produced some Grammy-winning albums with John Lee Hooker and Bonnie Raitt."

Among the artists who took part in the new album sessions, which extended over some seventeen months, were Jerry Jeff Walker, Arlo Guthrie, Tom Waits (who wrote a new song for the album), John Prine, Nanci Griffith, and Emmylou Harris. Returning from an out-of-town concert, Emmylou came straight from the airport in Nashville and worked for two hours to get her part right on a song by Townes Van Zandt called "Rex's Blues." Elliott noted that Townes, who died on New Year's Day 1997, had been a good friend. "I traveled with him and played concerts with Townes. It's about a friend called Rex Bell. Townes wrote this little song about him. It's very poetic and it's not specific. It doesn't tell you much about the person. Townes had a way with words. He would produce images like watercolor, vague images that you could draw your own conclusions from. It puts you in a mood."

The album, *Friends of Mine,* was issued by High-Tone Records in early 1998, and the company arranged for a tour featuring Elliott and three other label artists, Dave Alvin, Tom Russell, and Chris Smither. Jack hoped that, for a change, the album would pay off. "I just want everyone to like it. I want to sell a lot of records, make a lot of money. I've got forty record albums out and never made a dime. [Actually] there's

more than forty albums. A lot of unknown companies have come out with bootleg albums. I hear about them every trip I make. I'll find out about another new album that came out that I didn't authorize." The album received a Grammy nomination for Best Traditional Folk.

Though he continued to tour in the mid-1990s, he maintained a much less hectic schedule than in his earlier years. Asked about whether that meant his nickname wasn't as appropriate, he replied, "Well, I still ramble. The ramblin' part is not just because I travel. It's because of my style of storytelling. My stories have a beginning and a middle, but they don't have any end. They just ramble on, like many people have said sarcastically much to my embarrassment, but I'm getting used to it: 'I know why they call him ramblin'. They don't call him ramblin' because he travels.' "

Among important milestones in the late 1990s was the first U.S. release of a CD of the album *Kerouac's Last Dreams,* originally recorded in Germany in 1980. The album, prepared by Appleseed Recordings and marketed and distributed by Red House Records, contained versions of two songs written and recorded by Elliott, "912 Greens" and "Cup of Coffee." In mid-1998, when the names of artists whose contributions to national culture were to be recognized at the Kennedy Center Honors in Washington, D.C., in December, Elliott was one of those selected. In 1999, Fantasy reissued his album *Country Style/Live,* while his new release on HighTone, *The Long Ride* won a Grammy nomination.

Partly based on an interview with Lyndon Stambler, February 8, 1998

ENYA: *Singer, keyboard player, composer. Born Gweedore, County Donegal, Ireland, May 17, 1961.*

A recording artist who avoided touring on behalf of her albums (which typically took two to three years to complete), whose vocals often were in Gaelic or Latin (languages understood by a minute fraction of the music audience), would seem to have an uphill fight ahead of her. Enya, however, defied the odds and with her collaborators, record producer Nicky Ryan and his wife, poet/lyricist Roma Ryan, drew admiring fans by the millions. Her albums were unique collections drawing on Celtic folklore and Enya's classical and religious experience to achieve soothing, ethereal sound structures very different from other folk or pop releases. The recordings struck a responsive chord with many critics and a worldwide audience, though some nay-sayers argued that her output represented a more sophisticated form of "elevator music."

Enya argued that her music offered people a respite from the noise pollution that surrounded them, from rush-hour traffic to radio and TV. She told David Gritten for a cover story in the *Los Angeles Times* ("Enya Dreams," Calendar section, January 7, 1996), most people don't have time for themselves. "You know, when you go for a walk and be alone with your thought? It's calming, I think, when people listen to [one of her albums] they experience a little bit of this. They sit down and they're more peaceful than they're used to, and they think about themselves and interpret their own emotions and feelings in the music."

She was born the fifth of nine children in Ireland's County Donegal in a Gaelic-speaking section and given the name Eithne Ní Bhraonáin (pronounced "Enya Brennan"). Her grandfather was a schoolteacher on the tiny island of Tory, whose myths included reference to a Celtic goddess whose name she was given. Music was a staple in the family; her father, Leo Bhraonáin, was a musician and dance band leader, and her mother, the former Maira Duggan, taught music at Gweedore Comprehensive School. Enya started taking classical piano at a young age and continued her musical studies from age eleven through seventeen while attending a convent college run by the Catholic Loretto order in the town of Milford.

Although most of her schoolwork in music dealt with the classics, she also was exposed to traditional Irish songs and dances performed by her father and others at Leo's Tavern, a pub her father ran in the small town of Meenaleck. Among those who congregated there were other members of her extended family, who formed the first version of the band called Clannad in 1970. Enya was too young to be involved, and she soon left for boarding school, but she was aware of what Clannad was doing since its founding members were close relatives.

As the 1970s went by, Enya continued to exhibit growing skills on keyboards and other instruments, as well as a lilting, pure voice. Meanwhile, Clannad, managed by Nicky Ryan in the later 1970s, had slowly emerged as a highly regarded Irish folk group. In 1979 Ryan met Enya and was immediately enthralled by her talent, suggesting to Clannad it bring her in on keyboards, though they were hardly typical components of a traditional Irish band.

As she told Timothy White of Billboard magazine ("Enya: 'Memory,' Myth & Melody," November 25, 1995), "It was Nicky who asked me to join Clannad, even though it was a true family group [Clannad is Gaelic for "family"], with two of my brothers, Pól and Ciarán, a sister, Máire, and two uncles, Noel and Pádraig. So I did keyboards and backing vocals." She toured with Clannad for two years and also played on two band albums, Crann Ull in 1980 and Fuaim in 1982.

"All the while," she added, "I loved Nicky's wonderful concepts of the layering of vocals, and Roma had wonderful stories from Irish mythology, so late in 1982 we decided to leave Clannad to see what we three could evolve together. Our first project was the music for David Puttnam's film The Frog Prince, and then we did

the sound track for a six-part BBC television history of the Irish called The Celts." The BBC took the sound track vocals and instrumentals performed by her and issued the album Enya in 1986, a collection that drew excited attention from influential listeners in the United Kingdom and overseas. (U.S. distribution was arranged through a licensing agreement with Atlantic Records.)

The music for the sound track, Enya pointed out, represented a blend of influences, ancient and modern. She told Gritten, "With me it was Irish traditional music. Because I was brought up speaking Gaelic. With [Nicky] it was the Beach Boys and Phil Spector. And I can hear that combination of all those influences in the music." In time, her compositions also reflected some of her mother's ancestral roots after Enya visited Spain. At the time of the Spanish Armada, she stated, some shipwrecked survivors from the Spanish fleet had come ashore on the island of Tory, whence her mother's family had derived.

After hearing The Celts, Rob Dickens, chairman of Warners U.K., became determined to sign Enya to the label. He recalled that some people in the company weren't convinced, but since he was the head of the office, he could call the tune. In particular, he urged Enya to add more vocals than in The Celts since she had such a beautiful, unusual voice.

She and the Ryans eventually complied, but at their own pace. Before completing the first album for Dickens, the Ryans and their two children moved from their home in Dublin to a larger, gated place in Dalkey, while Enya, who had been staying with them in Dublin, got a house some twenty minutes' walk away, in Killiney. The team installed their own studio, "Aigle" (Eagle), on the Dalkey grounds, and worked and reworked the music and lyrics, using more overdubs than usual in search of what they felt was their ideal sound.

In October 1988 the first results of that project, the single "Orinoco Flow," came out in England; to many observers' surprise it became a major hit, climbing to number one on British charts, where it stayed for three weeks, and later rising to number twenty-four in the United States. It was one of several chart hits from the album Watermark, which rapidly made inroads on World Music charts around the globe. The collection stayed on the charts for years from the late 1980s into the '90s, gaining multiplatinum certification in fifteen countries and sales by the mid-1990s of over eight million. Enya didn't perform a single concert to promote Watermark, but her career didn't suffer. In fact, the album's success added luster to her composing talents, which were called on for many films in the late '80s and the first half of the '90s, including L.A. Story, Green Card, Ron Howard's Far and Away, and Martin Scorsese's The Age of Innocence.

Back at the Aigle studio, Enya and the Ryans started work on the next album, again following their determinedly slow pattern. It was a triumvirate working together, Enya told Gritten. "I'm the main performer and I write the melodies and play all the instruments, so I feel it's very much me. But the melody only starts the ball rolling—the lyrics happen, then the arrangement. I always say 'we' because it's a unique setup, and it's only when I start talking about it that I realize how unique it is."

Many people thought *Watermark* was something of a freak success and were dubious that Enya *et al* could follow it up successfully. But *Shepherd's Moon,* issued by Warner/Reprise in 1991, was not a letdown. It continued to provide the team's trademark of textured instrumentals and vocals, and delighted growing numbers of fans. The album debuted at number one in England the day of its release and also became a best-seller in the United States, which accounted for four million of the nine million copies purchased worldwide through early 1996. The disk went multiplatinum in eighteen countries and spent 199 consecutive weeks on the charts. In the 1992 Grammy voting (announced on the TV awards show of February 4, 1993), it was named Best New Age Album.

Once again the three collaborators withdrew to their home studio to prepare the next set of tracks. This time it took almost four years before they were satisfied with the material.

The complete album, *The Memory of Trees,* came out on Warner/Reprise in December 1995 and was on many charts in early '96. The title, she stated, derived from the origins of the name of the Druids of ancient Celtic history. The name translates as oak knowledge, referring to the fact the practitioners of the religion believed woodlands were the source of all earthly wisdom. Enya told *Billboard*'s Timothy White, "I love the ambiguity of the idea, but it's got more to do with what the trees have been through and their awareness of us, instead of them. That's why the Druids placed great importance on trees and their spiritual power."

By the time her fifth album, *Paint the Sky with Stars: The Best of Enya,* came out in 1997, worldwide sales of her collections had exceeded twenty-five million copies, making her the second most successful recording artist in Ireland. Only the rock band U2 had higher totals. For the first time since she started her solo career, Enya backed the release with a promotional tour. As J.S. Considine wrote in the *Baltimore Sun,* unlike U2, up to 1997 "Enya never has toured. In fact, she was for a while the world's most anonymous superstar, a performer whose one-of-a kind-sound—drawing heavily on classical and Celtic traditions—was instantly recognizable to millions, but whose face was a mystery."

In 1997, besides giving many more print media interviews than in the past, she also appeared on such major United States TV shows as *The Late Show with David Lettermen* and *Late Night with Conan O'Brien.* She told Considine her approach to new material was to either sing it or play it on the piano. "I just let it happen.

I like to treat [songwriting] like it takes me on a journey." After working out the melody, she then performs it for the Ryans. "And I can see by their reaction that, yes, this is what I'm trying to say." Once all are satisfied, she noted, it's still Roma Ryan's task to work out the words to go with the music.

FAHEY, JOHN: *Guitarist, songwriter. Born Takoma Park, Maryland, February 28, 1939.*

John Fahey's guitar work and original compositions, an eclectic mixture of blues, jazz, rags, and classical, inspired generations of guitarists, from Leo Kottke to Sonic Youth's Thurston Moore. But he all but disappeared in the mid-1980s. In 1994, after battling chronic fatigue syndrome and diabetes for several years, Fahey suddenly reemerged with an industrial and atonal sound, to the dismay of his old adherents.

"I've always been part of the avant-garde," he says. "I've always been looking for new stuff, new ways of doing things."

John Fahey was born and raised in Takoma Park, Maryland, near Washington, D.C. His father was a United States Public Health Service employee. Fahey also worked for the post office and Library of Congress. Every day, his mother would listen to big band music by Woody Herman, Stan Kenton, and Glenn Miller. John absorbed these sounds and studied piano and clarinet. His first leanings were toward classical music, but that changed by the time he was a teenager. As he told Michael Brooks of *Guitar Player* (April 1972, p. 20), "I was frustrated. I had been playing clarinet in a school band and was interested in orchestra and symphonic music, but I couldn't maintain my interest playing clarinet. I've always wanted to improvise and write things, more than I wanted to play them."

His frustration eased when he turned to the guitar at thirteen. "I was in a park in the summer and I saw these older guys playing guitar and picking up girls. They were singing country and western songs. I made friends with them so I could pick up girls. I got a guitar [from Sears for $17]. They taught me some chords. Right away I started trying to compose things. . . . There's something about the guitar that's always driven me crazy. It's so personal, it's so direct with our emotions, it's so pretty."

He got a chord book and made up a few of his own. "A lot of the chords I play, I don't even know what they are. If I stopped to analyze what I play, though, it would take all the fun out of it," he told Brooks.

He plunged into country and western: Hank Snow, the Stanley Brothers, Wilma Lee and Stoney Cooper, Roy Acuff, the Delmore Brothers, Merle Travis, Hank

Thompson, and Sam McGee. "My main idol was Sam McGee, of the *Opry!* I always tried (and try) to play like him, but never can make it," Fahey wrote in 1980.

He also listened closely to country records by Eddy Arnold ("I Really Don't Want to Know"), Hank Williams, and Bill Monroe. Fahey perfected his technique. by listening to 78-rpm records and observing people like Elizabeth Cotten and Mike Paley. He traced his interest in blues to a visit to Baltimore in 1957, when he came across a record by Blind Willie Johnson called "Praise God I Am Satisfied" while looking for bluegrass records with collector Dick Spottswood. "It was an overwhelming experience," he said in 1997. "Not only did I cry, I got nauseated and almost threw up. I had to ask them to take that off and put on some Bill Monroe. The Bill Monroe made me feel better. This noise kept going through my head and I had to hear it again. Then they put it back on and I just cried out of some sort of emotional release. Prior to that I hated anything by black folk musicians. That was probably because of where I was brought up, where there's so much race prejudice."

That experience inspired him to make a number of trips through the South searching for rare recordings of blues and traditional country material. He began some of those swings in his teens and continued his searches in his twenties.

Through all those years, Fahey continued his schooling, studying philosophy at American University in Washington, D.C. He always spent time practicing guitar and playing occasional dates in small folk clubs as an amateur. When he was nineteen, he recorded some blues songs for Fonotone records. In 1959, he decided to produce his own record. He scraped together the money from a job pumping gas and selling his motorcycle to press a hundred copies (five were broken). His first solo album had *John Fahey* written on one side and *Blind Joe Death* on the other. He released it on his own Takoma Records (named after his home town). The master tapes were lost or destroyed and Fahey rerecorded the songs in 1964, and again in 1967.

His first major professional appearances came during the summer of 1964 in Boston, where he was paid $200 a week for a stay at the Odyssey club. After that, he told Brooks, "I stayed around Boston that summer of 1964 playing most of the places there, little dives like the [Club] 47 and all in all didn't get along with the people there that well. So I moved to Berkeley."

He entered the University of California at Berkeley as a philosophy student in an accelerated Ph.D. program, but didn't take to it. In 1964 he switched to UCLA to work on a master's degree in folklore and mythology. That effort was just getting under way when he was asked to perform at the Jabberwock in Berkeley. Fahey's main objective in entering UCLA was to demystify the old blues singers. "I mean, all these guys had big romantic legends built up around them, so I

went down to try and get the facts." His thesis on blues singer Charley Patton was published by Studio Vista Ltd. in London. He received his master's degree from UCLA in 1969.

Fahey was also instrumental in "rediscovering" two blues greats, Bukka White and Skip James. He had heard Bukka White's song "Aberdeen, Mississippi Blues" so he figured he lived there. He addressed a postcard to "Booker T. Washington White, Old Blues Singer," for general delivery. One night he got a collect call from Bukka,who was living in Memphis. Ed Denson and Fahey met him. "He was a really nice guy. A very sociable guy. I knew he had a criminal record and I know he killed somebody. With me and everybody I saw he was very gregarious and loved to talk, never any violence."

Skip James was more difficult to find. Few remembered who he was. "He was the best of the sad blues singers," recalls Fahey, who had heard all of his recordings. For years he searched for James but he couldn't find him. Then, in 1964, when he, Bill Barth, and Henry Vestine (of Canned Heat) were in Dubbs, Mississippi, they stumbled upon someone who knew James. They found him at the Tunica County Hospital and asked if he would like to resume his musical career. "He called himself Skippy," Fahey recalls. " 'That might be a good idea. I don't know. Skippy tired.' "

The next day they went to his house and James showed Fahey his special open D-minor tuning. "He played three songs and thrust the guitar at me and said, 'Show me!' He was really into competitiveness. 'Can you do this?' Well, I had it. So he showed me more. He showed me a lot of stuff he never recorded, too."

They took James, a tenant farmer, to Washington, D.C. "That's where [record collector] Dick Spottswood lived who had all the money and wanted him the most. I personally paid off his debts to the plantation owner, who, for those days, was a very nice plantation owner," Fahey recalls.

John performed in California and expanded his recording efforts. He released *The Great San Bernardino Birthday Party* (1966) and *Days Have Gone By* (1967). (In 1967, Fahey rereleased his debut set under the title *John Fahey.* The first volume was entitled *Blind Joe Death,* the second *Death Chants, Breakdowns and Military Waltzes,* and the third *The Dance of Death and Other Plantation Favorities.*) A local record store owner agreed to distribute the albums for Takoma, until then a mail-order operation.

Fahey's talents came to the attention of Vanguard Records, which released three albums: *John Fahey Guitar 'Requia'* (1967), *Yellow Princess* (1969), and *The Essential John Fahey* (1974), a thirteen-track retrospective. The association brought about an intensive series of concerts by John in clubs and college campuses across the United States. But soon he returned to doing his own record work. Among his late 1960s and 1970s releases on Takoma were *The Voice of the Turtle* (1968), *The New Possibility* (1968), *America* (1971), *Fare Forward Voyagers (Soldier's Choice)* (1973), *Old-Fashioned Love* (1975), *Christmas with John Fahey, Volume II* (1975), *The Best of John Fahey 1959–1977* (1977), and *Visits Washington, D.C.* (1979). His most popular albums, he reports, both on Takoma, were *The Best of John Fahey, 1959-1977* and *The New Possibility—John Fahey's Guitar Soli Christmas Album,* the first of which had sold 70,000 copies as of 1980, and the second over 200,000 copies.

Fahey, who recorded three albums with a Dixieland band, also issued albums by young artists he respected. One of those was Leo Kottke, whose debut LP on Takoma came out in 1970. (Fahey's path crossed that of Kottke when John performed at the Scholar Coffeehouse in Minneapolis.) When Kottke moved to Capitol Records, he included a number of Fahey compositions in his various releases. Fahey also handled production chores on many of Kottke's Capitol releases.

Some of Fahey's stylings came out on Reprise in the '70s, including *Of Rivers & Religions* (1972) and *After the Ball* (1973). He had sold Takoma to Chyrsalis in the late 1970s, but continued to release albums on the label: *Yes! Jesus Loves Me* (1980), *John Fahey Live in Tasmania* (1981) and *Railroads 1* (1983). His music was also featured in the film *Zabriskie Point.*

Expressing some of his methods and frustrations in 1980, he stated, "I write most of my songs and I play, don't write them down. (I can't read or write music. Do it all by ear.) There's one thing about the guitar drives me nuts. I can't get over this year. I'm rated number thirteen on the *Playboy* magazine of pickers. But I can play better than Atkins or any of them except Sam McGee. [Besides performing and recording] I am an A&R man with Chrysalis. I would love to make a record someday in Nashville."

John's pattern during the late '70s and early '80s remained much as it always was. He lived modestly in Santa Monica, California, and received warm welcomes from audiences in college auditoriums, small folk music concerts, and occasional festivals. In concert, Fahey would hide behind his dark glasses and remain aloof from his audience in a trancelike state. " I don't think about notes, I think about emotions," he says. "Am I playing the emotion I'm feeling? If I'm not I can't play very well. It may be down deep but I can get to it pretty quick because I was in psychoanalysis for ten years."

He embarked on a personal quest. He spent time at a Hindu monastery in India. But in the 1980s, Fahey's career—and his life—spiraled downward. In 1981, he and his third wife Melody moved from LA to Salem, Oregon. He went into psychoanalysis. In 1986, he came down with chronic fatigue syndrome and began chugging beers as a way to gain the energy he needed to get on stage. He went into AA to deal with his drinking, but

he lost his house when he divorced Melody and moved to a welfare motel in Salem and then the Union Gospel Mission for a couple of years. He made ends meet by pawning his guitar, living off record royalties, and scouring thrift stores for vintage classical records, which he resold at a profit. He gradually regained his health after he was diagnosed as a diabetic and stopped eating sugar.

He continued to record. Varrick, a subsidiary of Rounder Records, released *Christmas Guitar, Volume One* (1982), *Popular Songs of Christmas and New Year's* (1983), *Let Go* (1984), *Rain Forests, Oceans and Other Themes* (1986), *I Remember Blind Joe Death* (1988), and *Old Girlfriends and Other Horrible Memories* (1992). Chrysalis was sold to Allegiance and then to Shanachie, which released *God, Time and Casualty* (1989), *Old-Fashioned Love, Death Chants, Breakdowns and Military Waltzes* (1991), *Railroad* (1992), and *Fare Forward Voyagers* (1992).

After a decade of obscurity, in 1994 *Spin* magazine (and the *Spin Alternative Record Guide*) ran favorable profiles about Fahey. Rhino released a retrospective album, *Return of the Repressed: The John Fahey Anthology.* (with liner notes by Barry Hansen, a.k.a. Dr. Demento). In 1997, the *New York Times* and *All Things Considered* ran pieces on him. Fantasy Records of Berkeley bought his catalog from Shanachie and began reissuing his old albums. He began working on a "pseudo autobiography" for Drag City Press in Chicago.

Suddenly Fahey received bigger royalty checks from his old work. He recorded his first of several new albums, *City of Refuge,* on a DAT recorder in his $139/week welfare motel room. The album, an experimental mix of industrial sound effects, atonal collages, and distorted guitar noises, was released in 1998 on Tim/Kerr Records. It sold more than 40,000 copies. The emphasis is more on texture than tune. In the song "Fanfare" he expresses his ambivalence toward technology.

"I've been using sounds and noises since before I made my first record," he says. "In the 1960s, I'd take a portable tape recorder and go out to record trains and bridges with steel mesh so that when cars went over it, it went *wooosh*. What's new is now I can get away with it. The audience is younger and they're interested and more appreciative of experimentalism. All those guitar records I made I frankly don't like most of them. There were a few songs here and there that I wrote that were pretty good. But most of it I'm not really interested in anymore."

Alternative musicians took notice. He collaborated with the band Cul de Sac on an album for Thirsty Ear Records. Thurston Moore of Sonic Youth talked about Fahey as his "secret influence." In 1997 Fahey released an "industrial" EP called *Womblife* on Table of the Elements records. In late 1998, Tim/Kerr released an album of Fahey playing background music for William

S. Burroughs's readings. He also started his own label, Revenant, with a partner from Memphis, releasing such "raw music," as he put it, as the Sun City Girls, a pre-war gospel album, and a jazz pianist named Cecil Taylor. The name Revenant comes from Freud. "It means someone who dies and comes back to life, or that same idea psychologically."

Fahey, who seems to have returned from the dead, began to play in a three-guitar trio he called the John Fahey Trio. One concertgoer characterized the sound as "completely abrasive, sheer noise."

In the late 1990s, many of his albums were available on CD, including *Death Chants, Breakdowns and Military Waltzes, Voice of the Turtle, John Fahey/Leo Kottke/Peter Lang, The Transfiguration of Blind Joe Death, The Legend of Blind Joe Death, America, Breakdowns and Military Waltzes* on Fantasy/Takoma; *Popular Songs of Christmas and New Year's* on Varrick; *The John Fahey Christmas Album* on Burnside; *Requia and Other Compositions* on Vanguard; and *The New Possibility: John Fahey's Guitar Soli Christmas Album* on Rhino.

Revealing his traditional roots, Fahey contributed to the liner notes for the Smithsonian/Folkways 1997 reissue of Harry Smith's *Anthology of American Folk Music*. The album and the liner notes won two Grammys. But he stays away from many of his old songs. "I like the good black blues, especially if it's pre–Second World War. I still play a lot of that stuff on stage. Some white mountain stuff. But what I leave out is the stuff I wrote that's sentimental."

As to his fans who ask for the old tunes: "I tell them to leave me alone. I don't play that stuff anymore. New Age means mellow," he says. "It's all for sale. It's background music. I don't like it."

Based on an interviews with John Fahey in August 1997 and a letter to the authors in 1980

FAIRPORT CONVENTION: *Vocal and instrumental group. Original members, 1967: Simon Nicol (guitar, vocals), born Muswell Hill, London, October 13, 1950; Richard Thompson (guitar, vocals), born London, April 3, 1949; Judy Dyble (vocals, autoharp, piano, recorder), born London, February 13, 1949; Ashley Hutchings (vocals, bass), born Muswell Hill, London, January 26, 1945; Martin Lamble (drums), born St. Johns Wood, London, August 28, 1949; died May 12, 1969; Ian Matthews (vocals), born Ian Matthews MacDonald, Scunthorpe, Lincolnshire, June 16, 1946. In 1968, Dyble replaced by Sandy Denny (vocals, guitar), born London, January 6, 1947; died London, April 21, 1978. Matthews left in January 1969 to form Matthews Southern Comfort. Dave Swarbrick (violin, mandolin, vocals), joined in July 1969. August 1969, Lamble replaced by Dave Mattacks (drums), born Edgware, Middlesex, March 1948. Hutchings left in November 1969 to form Steeleye Span; replaced by Dave "Peggy" Pegg*

(bass), born 1948. Denny left December 1969 to form Fotheringay. Thompson left in January 1971. Group makeup in 1971: Nicol, Swarbrick, Mattacks, and Pegg. Nicol left to join Albion Band; replaced by Roger Hill (guitar, vocals). Mattacks left in 1972 to join Albion Band. Replaced by Tom Farnell (drums). Joining 1972: Trevor Lucas (guitar, vocals), born Melbourne, Australia, December 25, 1943; died February 4, 1989; Jerry Donahue (guitar, vocals), born September 24, 1946. Mattacks rejoined 1973. Group makeup in 1973: Swarbrick, Pegg, Lucas, Donahue, Mattacks. Mattacks left again and was replaced by Bruce Rowland on drums. Denny rejoined in 1974, left same year, along with Lucas and Donahue. Breton guitarist Dan Ar Braz joined for six months in mid-1970s. Nicol rejoined 1976. Band disbanded in 1979, but played together for projects. 1985 Swarbrick replaced by Ric Sanders (fiddle). Same year joined by Maartin Allcock (guitar, mandolin, bouzouki, keyboards), born Manchester, January 5, 1957. Group lineup 1986: Nicol, Pegg, Sanders, Mattacks and Allcock. Allcock left 1996. Replaced by Chris Leslie (violin, guitar, mandolin, bouzouki), born England, 1956. Mattacks left January 1998.

A group whose history encompasses an intricate web of shifts and changes, Fairport Convention ranks as one of the finest in folk-rock music. The band gave rise to the British folk-rock sound of the late 1960s. The two best-known members were Richard Thompson and Sandy Denny, not only for Thompson's superb guitar playing and Denny's stunning vocals, but also for their original songs. Although Fairport played a farewell concert tour in 1979, the group hardly disbanded. In 1980, it held a festival at Cropredy near Banbury, Oxfordshire, establishing an annual mid-August tradition attended by up to 30,000 fans. Like the Grateful Dead, Fairport gained a cult following that allowed it to tour and record into the twenty-first century.

In 1967, bassist Ashley Hutchings gathered a "convention" of North London musicians to play folk music, mostly from America. The original band, briefly called Tim Turner's Narration, was composed of a group of young English folk-oriented musicians: vocalist, auto-harpist, and pianist Judy Dyble; lead guitarist Richard Thompson; Hutchings (who provided the band's early original material); rhythm guitarist Simon Nicol; and drummer Shawn Frater, who left after the first gig that spring. Martin Lamble replaced Frater on drums, and Ian Matthews joined the band in the fall.

Thompson, whose musical interests ranged from folk to jazz and classical, was the son of a Scotland Yard detective. Before joining Fairport, he worked as an apprentice to a stained-glass maker. Nicol's childhood home in Muswell Hill, called Fairport, gave the band a practice area and its name.

During 1967, the quintet began playing covers in small clubs in London. At first they gained recognition by word of mouth, with rumors of their potential even reaching across the Atlantic to American fans. By 1968, though, their American-born manager and producer, Joe Boyd, who was impressed by Thompson's guitar work during performances at London's UFO Club, lined up a record deal with Polydor, which led to a single, "If I Had a Ribbon Bow," and their debut LP, *Fairport Convention,* a collection of covers. The album sold poorly but later became a cult favorite. Dyble soon left to form her own group. Her place was taken by a superbly talented vocalist and writer, Sandy Denny, whose contributions to the band included some of its most favored songs, such as "Fotheringay," on their next LP, *What We Did on Our Holidays* (1968, Island Records). The band began exploring traditional British folk music and dance, jigs and reels. By the end of the '60s, the group had an American label, A&M, which distributed *What We Did on Our Holidays* under the title *Fairport Convention* in August 1969.

That album, which included covers of Joni Mitchell and Bob Dylan songs, remains a classic of the folk-rock genre, as does the next Island LP, *Unhalfbricking,* released in 1969. *Unhalfbricking* included three covers of Dylan songs, including a Cajun version of "Si Tu Dois Partir," which became a chart hit. Those LPs showcase Denny's vocal skills and Thompson's work as singer and lead guitarist. It also features their original songs: Denny's "Who Knows Where the Time Goes," recorded earlier with the Strawbs, and Thompson's "Meet on the Ledge" (later the band's sign-off tune), and "Genesis Hall." The group supported those albums with critically praised concerts in England and the United States in the late 1960s. An important member of those tours was guitarist-vocalist Ian (or Iain) Matthews, who soon left to form Matthews Southern Comfort (whose output included the top-ten 1970 hit "Woodstock").

Meanwhile, other changes kept occurring, both through intention and accident. In June 1969, the band was driving home to London from a gig in Birmingham when the band's roadie, Harvey Branham, fell asleep at the wheel. The van flipped over, killing drummer Martin Lamble and Genie Franklin, Thompson's girlfriend. Branham was charged with "causing death by dangerous driving." The accident had a profound effect on the band. The surviving members had doubts about whether to continue but after hearing the Band's *Music from Big Pink* and the Byrds' early-'70s offerings, they decided to record another album.

The band replaced Lamble with drummer Dave Mattacks, who had previously played with several dance bands. Also joining in 1969 was vocalist-violinist Dave Swarbrick, who had been a major folk figure in England for years, much of it in partnership with guitarist Martin Carthy. Swarbrick was only scheduled to so some session work on *Unhalfbricking,* but his style fit so well that he joined full-time.

The next album they recorded, *Liege & Lief* (1969), is considered their best. Five out of the eight tracks on the album are traditional. The classic Thompson-penned

songs "Farewell, Farewell" and "Crazy Man Michael," (written with Swarbrick) both relate to coping with the tragedy. One of the best tracks featured Denny's vocal on "Matty Groves." The album rose to upper-chart levels in England. It showed that songs that were hundreds of years old could be played effectively using electric instruments.

During late 1969, Hutchings, who wanted to focus on traditional music, left to start Steeleye Span. He later formed the Albion Band, the Ethnic Shuffle Band, the Etchingham Steam Band, and contributed to a revival of British Morris Dancing, including an albums of dance music called *Morris On* (1973, Island). The remaining members chose bass guitarist Dave Pegg as a replacement. Pegg had played with Ian Campbell's band for a year and had previously played with pop bands in the English Midlands.

By December 1969, Sandy Denny departed to form a group called Fotheringay, with Trevor Lucas, her future husband, who had performed on *Unhalfbricking,* on guitar and vocals, Gerry Conway on drums, Pat Donaldson on bass; and Jerry Donahue on guitar. (The group broke up in 1971 after releasing one album, *Fotheringay.*) When Denny departed, Fairport, became an all-male group with Thompson, Nicol, Swarbrick, Mattacks, and Pegg. The group was warmly received during a United States tour in the summer that included a featured spot in the Philadelphia Folk Festival. In the fall of 1970, the band played to capacity audiences in Britain.

Fairport continued to turn out new albums that stressed the use of electric instruments. The next on Island was *Full House.* (A 1970 concert recorded at LA's Troubadour was released in 1977 as *Live at the L.A. Troubadour* and as *House Full* in 1986 on Hannibal.) Richard Thompson, who worked on that LP, departed in January 1971. The remaining four members toured the United States, England, and Europe.

Swarbrick took over as lead vocalist and Simon Nicol handled the lead guitar, but the new albums, such as *Angel Delight* (which refers to Swarbrick's brush with death when a truck crashed through his bedroom in the Angel pub) and *Babbacombe Lee* (both 1971) did not have the impact of earlier ones, even though *Angel Delight* reached the top-ten in England. Nicol, and later Mattacks, departed in December 1971 to join Hutchings in the Albion Band. The group replaced Nicol with Roger Hill on guitar and vocals, and Mattacks with Tom Farnell on drums. Trevor Lucas joined in 1972, after Fotheringay disbanded. He was joined by American-born Jerry Donahue on vocals and guitar. Meanwhile, Island released a compilation album called *History of Fairport Convention* (1972), an effort to recapture the group's earlier popularity. But 1973 releases *Rosie* and *Nine,* did little to reestablish the group's popularity.

In 1974, Denny rejoined, revitalizing the band. She

took part in two albums issued on Island in 1975, *Rising for the Moon* and *A Moveable Feast/Fairport Live Convention,* and offered impressive vocal during tours of Europe and the United States. Mattacks, who had contributed to *Rising for the Moon,* left once again and was replaced by Bruce Rowland from Joe Cocker's Grease Band, on drums. However, the results still were less than breathtaking, particularly since the new material didn't match earlier favorites. By the end of 1975, Denny, Lucas, and Donahue were gone. Fairport, comprised of Swarbrick, Rowland, and Pegg, was in disarray. In 1976, they managed to release *Gottle O'Geer,* (Island) and *Fairport Chronicles.*

Nicol rejoined later in 1976. Vertigo Records issued *Bonny Bunch of Roses* and *Tippler's Tales.* In 1978 too much talent was lost when Sandy Denny died of a brain hemorrhage after falling down a flight of stairs. A year later, Fairport was ready to call it a day, as the punk rock movement swept across the land. They released one more album, appropriately titled *Farewell, Farewell* (the first album released on the group's Woodworm label). They set a date for a blow-out final concert (August 4, 1979), much as the Band did with the Last Waltz.

But while The Band had meant it, Fairport couldn't get away with it. Just a year later, on August 4, 1980, they reunited for a concert at Cropredy, a tiny village of 724 where the Battle of Cropredy Bridge had been fought during the English Civil War. This turned into a popular annual event, often graced with appearances by illustrious alums such as Richard Thompson, Iain Matthews, and Judy Dyble. Pegg, who toured with Jethro Tull from 1979 to 1993, and his wife Christine organized the festival, and ran Woodworm, which released many of the group's albums through the 1990s. The festival (the band doesn't like the term "reunion") attracted a new generation of fans. As Pegg told *Dirty Linen:* "For a lot of the people that come to Cropredy now, especially the younger people, they're only aware of Fairport from the current lineup. They don't know about any of the history. They don't know who Sandy was—which is awfully sad, and why we always try to do something of hers." (*Dirty Linen,* incidentally, takes its name from a Fairport medley.)

Fairport retrospective albums continued to come out—*The Airing Cupboard Tapes 71–74* (1981, Woodworm) and *Moat on the Ledge* (1982), a live album on Stony Plain. The Cropedy reunions became so popular over the next five years that the band decided to record a new album in 1985, *Gladys' Leap,* on Woodworm. Swarbrick left the band due to problems with his hearing (but went on to form a band called Whippersnapper). Fairport recruited Ric Sanders, a lively fiddler who had played with the jazzy Soft Machine and the traditional Albions. Maartin Allcock, originally a bassist, joined and promptly took on other instruments: guitar, mandolin, bouzouki, and keyboards. Both added songwriting and synthesizer skills to the mix.

Gladys' Leap, with a guest spot from Thompson, did so well that Fairport made it official once again. From 1986 to the end of 1996, the group of Nicol, Pegg, Sanders, Mattacks, and Allcock was so stable that Nicol quipped to Tom Nelligan of *Dirty Linen* (December '95-January '96) that they had been together "longer than the Beatles."

The group released a series of albums: *Expletive Delighted!,* an instrumental album (1986, Varrick), *In Real Time: Live '87,* (Island), *Meet on the Ledge* (1987, Island), *The Other Boot* (Woodworm), *Heyday,* (1987, Hannibal), *The Best of Fairport Convention,* (1988, Island) *Red & Gold* (1989, Rough Trade/New Routes), *The Five Seasons* (1990, Rough Trade/New Routes) *The Woodworm Years* (1992), *25th Anniversary Concert* (1994, Wormwood), *Encore, Encore* (1979/1997, Folkprint), and *Fiddlestix 1970–1984: The Best of Fairport* (1998, Raven).

In 1995, Woodworm released *Jewel in the Crown,* the title taken from their favorite Indian Tandoori Takeaway. Most of the songs were written by other songwriters, including Julie Matthews, Steve Tilston, Ralph McTell, Jez Lowe, and Leonard Cohen. "They must take pity on us because we haven't any songwriters in the band, and I'm not about to start being a writer," Nicol explained to Nelligan.

The album, distributed by Green Linnet in the U.S., was moderately successful on both sides of the Atlantic, though not a standout. It features Nicol's adequate vocals throughout on the mix of traditional ballads and folk covers. The band toured Europe, Australia, and the U.S. In 1996, they followed with an all-acoustic album, *Old.New.Borrowed.Blue.* The band also unplugged for a tour of the United States in 1996 called Fairport Acoustic Convention (minus Mattacks).

Allcock left the band in 1996 to spend time with his family. In 1997 he was replaced by guitarist/mandolinist Chris Leslie, who had played with Swarbrick in Whippersnapper, and with Jethro Tull. In August the band celebrated its thirtieth anniversary at Cropredy before 30,000 fans. The live, three-CD album of the concert-party was titled *The Cropredy Box.* Guests included Thompson, Swarbrick, Jerry Donahue, Judy Dyble, Hutchings, Dan Ar Braz, Ralph McTell, and Vikki Clayton. That year also saw the republication of Patrick Humphrie's book about Fairport Convention, *Meet on the Ledge,* which first came out in 1982, and a book by Kingsley Abbott called *Fairportfolio,* a scrapbook about the band's early years.

In January 1998 the band released *Who Knows Where the Time Goes?* on Woodworm. The use of Denny's song drips with irony about the tyrannies of time in the rock business, and reflects the band's rich and tragic history. The album includes a live version of

Richard Thompson singing "Heard It Through the Grapevine."

The following year Dave Mattacks left for the fourth time and was replaced by Gerry Conway, who had played drums in Fotheringay. Dave Pegg turned fifty in 1998 and invited his friends to a bash. *The Birthday Party* (Woodworm) included performances by Fairport members past and present.

Reflecting on the Fairport years, Nicol told *Dirty Linen:* "I just know that Fairport has always been bigger than the sum of its parts. It's always had a momentum that transcends any particular lineup. I have a vision of it as being the equivalent of one of the older musical organizations in the U.K., things like choral societies or brass bands, or even sports teams, which have a recognizable identity and last for decade after decade after decade with people coming in and going out. I think Fairport could be the first rock band to have that attitude."

In that regard, Fairport recorded a new studio CD, *The Wood and the Wire,* released in November 1999 on Woodworm.

FARIÑA, MIMI: *Singer, guitarist songwriter. Born Palo Alto, California, April 30, 1945.*

There were more than a few emotional hurdles Mimi Fariña had to overcome in achieving a career in folk music. One of those involved trying to avoid the long shadow of her older sister, Joan Baez, who already was a superstar when Mimi was just developing momentum for her own vocal efforts. But even more traumatic was the tragic death of her young and creatively dynamic husband, Richard Fariña, in 1966, when she was only twenty-one. Somehow, Mimi found the inner capacity to cope and develop her own identity as a performer and writer.

She was born in California, but, like sister Joan, traveled to many different places. Her Mexican-born father, who held a doctorate in physics and worked for the United Nations, took his family with him on his many assignments. He and his British-born wife both liked music and encouraged their children's interest in it. In Mimi's case, she learned to play piano and violin. Later, when the family settled in the Boston area during the late 1950s, she was attracted by the folk music enthusiasms of the time to add guitar playing to her skills. Joan, of course, was old enough to start performing in some of the small folk clubs in Boston and environs, but Mimi, still in her early teens, sang and played for her own pleasure or for friends.

For a time in the early part of the 1960s, while her sister established herself as one of folk and pop music's brightest stars, Mimi went to Paris. There, she recalled, her approach to folk music and guitar stylings was influenced by the methods of local street musicians.

Among the other Americans she met there, she was particularly attracted to the Cuban-Irish musician and writer Richard Fariña, whom she married in 1963. Joan Baez gave a fond capsule portrait of him in her foreword to his posthumous book *A Long Time Coming and a Long Time Going:* "He was my sister Mimi's crazy husband, a mystical child of darkness—blatantly ambitious, lovable, impossible, charming, obnoxious, tirelessly active—a bright, talented, sheepish, tricky, curly-haired, man-child of darkness."

The two seemed eminently compatible, both as a married couple and as a striking performing and writing team. Among the songs they unveiled to delighted folk fans in their brief span of concerts, with Mimi handling guitar and Richard dulcimer, were such originals by Richard as "Pack Up Your Sorrows," "Children of Darkness," and "Birmingham Sunday." Besides appearing in major cities all over the United States and Canada in 1964 and 1965, they gave memorable performances at a number of folk festivals, including a sensational debut at the 1965 Newport, Rhode Island, Folk Festival.

The Fariñas signed with Vanguard Records in 1964, and their debut LP, *Celebration for a Grey Day,* came out in June 1965. This was followed in March 1966 by *Reflections in a Crystal Wind.* A third album, *Memories,* came out after Richard's death, and later Vanguard issued a retrospective, *Best of Mimi and Richard Fariña.*

The glowing promise of their association came to an abrupt end on April 30, 1966 when Richard was killed in a motorcycle accident on his way home from a book signing for his novel, *Been Down So Long It Looks Like Up to Me.* It was Mimi's twenty-first birthday. For many months Mimi was unable to decide about continuing in the music field. Gradually, however, she put the tragedy behind her and began to try to reestablish her career on a solo basis. In 1967 she won heartfelt applause from Newport Folk Festival attendees for her first appearance there since her 1965 event with Richard.

In the late 1960s, Mimi settled in California, where she joined a troupe of political/social satirists called the Committee. She found that acting with that improvisational group was excellent therapy for the depression she still was fighting. She started writing new songs and began thinking about doing more singing work again. However, she still felt the need for an artistic partner, a need met for a time in the early 1970s by Tom Jans.

Recalling those events for interviewer Robert Beers in 1971, Jans said, "I was singing by myself in California and Mimi was looking for someone to sing with. She was writing songs at that time, about a year ago. I was singing at a little club, and some people from the Institute of Nonviolence asked me to come up and have dinner. That's when I met Joan and through Joan I met Mimi."

The two found common ground as writers and performers and developed a new act that included some of their own song collaborations. Mimi told Beers, "In the beginning, writing was something to do. Something to do to keep from not doing anything. Then it became more creative, and then singing together started to kind of work. And it was listenable and fun. But to set out to be a songwriter. I don't know how someone could do that. To decide 'I'm gonna write songs that are gonna sell,' I don't know how that can be done. And yet it is, all the time."

Jans noted, "The reason why we write is to tell people that even if you are lonely there are ways of fighting your way out of it. Fighting your way out of depression and being able to relate to each other better."

The result of their efforts was a joint album, *Take Heart*, issued by A&M in 1971, and a cross-country concert tour. The album itself was not that impressive, though, and critical appraisal of their stage show was less than ecstatic. In 1972, Tom and Mimi decided to go their separate ways as performers. But the partnership did seem to give Mimi more confidence in her own ability, a way station that allowed her to become psychologically aware that she could make her own way in music without needing another person as a crutch. For the next few years she toured extensively as a solo artist with many major folk performers, including Hoyt Axton, Phil Ochs, Gordon Lightfoot, Arlo Guthrie, Kenny Rankin, Mose Allison, and Leo Kottke. When not working in larger venues with such artists, she often headlined her own set at small folk clubs and on college campuses.

In 1973 she began to work on a solo album for A&M. When the Arab oil crisis caused temporary panic in the record field, Mimi left A&M, feeling that they were using the crisis as an excuse to hold back on her recordings. Returning to the San Francisco area, for a time she channeled her efforts into beginning a new organization called Bread & Roses, a nonprofit operation to provide free entertainment to people in hospitals, prisons, and convalescent homes in Marin County.

By the late 1970s, she resumed a relatively heavy concert schedule. Some of her appearances were with the Gordon Lightfoot concert series. In her headline concerts at colleges, folk clubs, and folk festivals, she often was accompanied by Banana, a multitalented musician who earlier had been a charter member of the Youngbloods folk-rock group. She continued to write new songs, some of which were included in late 1970s albums by her sister and Judy Collins.

In the early 1980s she completed material for a new solo album, which eventually came out on a small label. For the rest of the 1980s and into the early '90s she kept a relatively low profile, continuing to perform in small folk-circuit venues and having some of her songs included on other artists' albums from time to time. In April 1995, she was among the musicians supporting a series of concerts by sister Joan Baez at the Bottom Line nightclub in New York that formed the basis for the album *Ring Them Bells,* released by Guardian Records in September 1995. The tracks included Joan and Mimi's duet on Richard Fariña's "Swallow Song" and a new version of "Sweet Sir Galahad," a song Joan had written back in the mid-1960s as a comment on Farina's death and the agonizing trauma it caused for Mimi.

Mimi joined Joan on tour in support of the new album during 1995 and '96. The stage set included some songs not included in the final makeup of *Ring Them Bells* such as "Pack Up Your Sorrows," the song with which Richard had been most closely associated. The sisters' guitar instrumental on Bob Dylan's "Don't Think Twice, It's All Right" typically opened their concert collaboration. In 1999 a retrospective CD of the Fariñas' '60s work came out: *Pack Up Your Sorrows: Best of the Vanguard Years.* Mimi had survived Hepatitis C and in December 1999, as she was planning the 25th anniversary Bread and Roses concert, she had a new foe to contend with: lung cancer.

FELICIANO, JOSÉ: *Singer, guitarist, banjoist, mandolinist, harmonica player, pianist, bongo and timbales player. Born Lares, Puerto Rico, September 10, 1945.*

The dark glasses José Feliciano wears symbolize his blindness, caused by irreversible glaucoma at birth, but his musical achievements demonstrate how much better he can "see" than many people blessed with perfect sight. (Actually, though legally blind, he can see slightly. As he told an interviewer in 1980, "Apart from when I go to bed, I never take [the dark glasses] off because I can see better with them on.") As an interpreter of Latin songs and of music in many languages, he established a reputation as one of the most talented folk and pop performers of the 1960s and 1970s.

Recalling his early years, he stated, "I derive a lot from my origins. I was born . . . in Lares, Puerto Rico. It's about three hours away from San Juan. When I was four years old, my family—my father [José], my mother [Hortencia] and the nine surviving boys out of the eleven my mother gave birth to—came to New York."

By the time the move to the Spanish Harlem section of New York took place, little José already had shown some musical promise. He recalls his earliest musical experience at three, when he accompanied an uncle by tapping on a tin soda-biscuit can. When he was six, in the mainland United States, he started teaching himself the accordion. He first performed for his classmates at P.S. 57 when he was eight.

Tired of the accordion, he switched to guitar. "I did not begin playing the guitar until I was nine," he told Mark Thornton of *West Australian Today* (March 8, 1994). "I wish I could have begun earlier because when I began playing it blew me away. Once I heard what it could do I knew it was the instrument for me and it became like an extension of my body."

He spent up to fourteen hours a day practicing and didn't take lessons until he began studying classical guitar at sixteen. His playing was influenced by Andres Segovia, Johnny Smith, Tal Farlow, and Django Reinhardt. As he grew up he added many other instruments to his repertoire. Some of those talents, he noted, surfaced while he attended various schools for the blind, where music teachers gave him pointers in classical and other musical genres.

His father, a shipping clerk, encouraged José's interest in music but tried to make his son concentrate on Spanish material. José made his first public appearance at El Teatro Puerto Rico in Spanish Harlem when he was nine. "My father had to pick me up because it was so crowded no one could see me, and the audience stood up and screamed with joy," he recalled. He performed at local events for no pay, often entering and winning talent shows, until he was thirteen, when he became a full-fledged professional.

At seventeen, Feliciano quit school. His father was then unemployed, and the family needed help financially. In the early 1960s, Feliciano gained a following among folk music fans in New York's Greenwich Village with his renditions of both Spanish and American folk songs. In 1963 he was appearing at Gerde's Folk City when an RCA executive came to watch the show and was greatly impressed by his poise and impact. José was signed by RCA and released the single "Everybody Do the Click," but for his first five years on the label, most of his recordings were in Spanish for release to the Latin American market. He played before large audiences in Latin America long before he was widely known in the United States. He had recorded some boleros, which drew a strong reaction in South America. "It was bedlam," he told Mike Boehm of the *Los Angeles Times* (July 18, 1998). "The girls were screaming. I became a teen idol. At the time, it embarrassed me." RCA wanted him to change his name to Joe Phillips, but he refused. "I was proud to carry my father's name," he told Boehm.

Meanwhile, José added to his laurels with a show-stopping performance at the Newport Folk Festival in Rhode Island in the summer of 1964. During the mid-1960s, he established himself as a favorite with the Latin nations, underlined by the tumultuous welcome given him at major events like the Mar Del Plata Festival in Buenos Aires, Argentina. He also was the star of his own syndicated Spanish language TV program during those years, which was top rated all over Latin America.

He was one of the most popular recording artists south of the border when he began to make inroads in the U.S. market. His first breakthrough in the United States came in 1968 with his fourth LP, the hit *Feliciano!* and his top-selling single of the Doors' rock hit, "Light My Fire" (which started out as the B-side to

"California Dreamin'"). The single hit number three on the charts, and the LP hit number two. At the time he also had two hit singles and three LPs on RCA's International label on the Latin American charts. The singles were "La Copa Rota" and "Amor Gitana" and the LPs were *Sombras . . . Una Voz, Una Guitarra* (recorded in Argentina); *Mas Exitos de José Feliciano* (recorded in Argentina and Mexico); and *La Voz y la Guitarra de José Feliciano* (recorded in Venezuela and Argentina).

By the end of 1968 he was recognized by almost every segment of the U.S. population. He won two Grammys for *Feliciano!*—Best New Artist and Best Performance by a Male Vocalist for "Light My Fire." He followed with several more hit records ("Ché Sara" was a hit in Europe, Asia, and South America) and personal appearances. He was featured on TV and radio talk shows and on such programs as ABC-TV's *Close-Up* and on the first Bing Crosby TV special of the 1968–69 season. He also performed the title song for Gregory Peck's film *MacKenna's Gold* and won a standing ovation from the audience that attended his Las Vegas debut shows in August 1968. The reception brought a return engagement there in October. (Just before the latter series, he was the center of controversy because of his "Spanish soul" rendition of "The Star-Spangled Banner" before the fifth game of the baseball World Series in Detroit. Feliciano is credited with opening the door for other artists to interpret the national anthem more freely.)

It was more of the same in 1969, and his popularity carried over strongly in the 1970s. He starred on major TV shows on American networks and was often featured on the most popular programs elsewhere in the world. During the late 1960s and early 1970s he was the star of several of his own TV specials on U.S. networks. He headlined concerts in prestigious places all over the world, including a number of appearances at venues like the Greek Theater in Los Angeles, the London Palladium, and Paris's Olympia. He also was a soloist on several occasions with major symphony orchestras.

He placed several more singles on upper-chart levels in the late 1960s, such as "Hitchcock Railway" and Tommy Tucker's "Hi-Heel Sneakers." However, in the 1970s, his main successes were as an album artist. Among his charted LPs were *Souled* and *Feliciano/10 to 23* in 1969 and *Alive Alive-O,* issued at the end of 1969 and a top 40 entrant in January 1970. During the summer of 1970 his album *Fireworks* appeared on the charts, featuring the medley "Susie Q" and "Destiny," on the singles charts for a few weeks in July. Late in 1970, his Christmas album came out, with the song "Feliz Navidad" receiving much airplay. From then on, it was a standard number for the Christmas season. In the summer of 1971 he had a chart hit LP, *Encore,* and at year's end he had a highly ranked single, "That the Spirit Needs." The LP of that title was on the charts from late 1971 to early 1972. In the spring of 1973 his album *Compartments* was on the hit lists for several weeks. In 1974 he had a hit with the theme song for the TV series *Chico and the Man.*

He had several more LPs on the charts in the mid-1970s, but his record sales slowed and his association with RCA came to an end. In the late 1970s he did not record for any major label. At the end of the 1970s his albums still in RCA's active catalog included *And the Feeling's Good, Compartments, For My Love . . . Mother Music, Encore! José Feliciano's Finest Performances, Feliciano!, Fireworks, José Feliciano, Just Wanna Rock 'n' Roll,* and *Feliciano/10 to 23.* In 1976 he also had an LP on Private Stock Records, *Sweet Soul Music.* In the 1990s Feliciano often complained that his old LPs were no longer accessible to record buyers. He planned to release a retrospective CD, *In My Life,* to remedy the problem.

However, his achievements were still noteworthy. He continued to receive steady airplay with "Light My Fire," "Feliz Navidad," "Rain," "Chico and the Man," "California Dreamin'" and "Affirmation."

As he started the 1980s, Feliciano signed with Motown's newly formed Latin music label, releasing *José Feliciano.* He later signed with EMI and recorded several albums, including *I'm Never Gonna Change* and *Tu Immenso Amor.*

He continued to release albums throughout the 1990s. He released a jazz-flavored album, *Steppin' Out,* on the Optimism label in 1990. In late 1992 he released *Latin Street '92* on Capitol/EMI-Latin, playing styles ranging from rumbas to mambos. The album was nominated for a Grammy. His 1997 album *Americano* on PolyGram was also nominated for a Grammy. A single from the album, "No Me Miras Asi," was a regional hit on Spanish radio in New York and Miami. He released *Señor Bolero,* an album of traditional and romantic ballads in Spanish, in the summer of 1998 on PolyGram. It was nominated for a Grammy. The first single from the album, "Me Has Echado Al Olvido," received strong airplay from New York Spanish radio stations.

In the early 1990s he wrote the music for Ray Bradbury's 1965 play *The Wonderful Ice Cream Suit,* about six young Latino men who share the use of a white suit. In 1994, a dance single called "Goin' Krazy," which he recorded under the moniker of JF, made the *Billboard* charts. He continued his TV and film work, making a cameo appearance in the movie *Fargo,* for which he performed his song "Let's Find Each Other Tonight."

Throughout the 1980s and 1990s, Feliciano continued to tour extensively, playing as many as 150 dates a year. Some critics commented about tired or listless performances. But none could criticize his ability to play the guitar.

Feliciano has been nominated for Grammys sixteen times and received six awards. In 1984 he won a Grammy for Best Latin Pop Performance for "Me En-

amore." In 1986 he won Best Latin Pop Performance for "Lelolai." In 1989 he won Best Latin Pop Performance for "Cielito Lindo," from his album *I'm Never Gonna Change.* In 1990 he won Best Latin Pop Performance for "Porue Te Tengo Que Olvidar?" from his 1990 album *Niña.*

He continued to be a popular attraction both as a concert artist and TV guest. In 1994 Feliciano was invited to perform on the annual TV gala *Christmas at the Vatican* and had a private audience with Pope John Paul II. Public School 155 in East Harlem was renamed the José Feliciano Performing Arts School. In 1996 *Billboard* gave him its Lifetime Achievement Award for contributions to the Latin music industry. He often performed to support organizations serving the blind.

As of the late 1990s, he had attained worldwide record sales of more than $68 million and earned forty gold and platinum records. He had recorded more than sixty albums in Spanish and English. But Feliciano had yet to recapture the notoriety of 1968. "I'd like to get back on the American chart," he told the *Los Angeles Times* (July 18, 1996). "But it's difficult now with all the crappy music today."

Nevertheless, Feliciano is recognized as one of the breakthrough artists for the Latin population. Speaking to Sheila Rule of the *New York Times* in 1994, Feliciano outlined his diverse influences: "My influences are not only in Latin music, but in rock-and-roll and, of course, black music. I didn't learn to sing from Frank Sinatra or Jack Jones, whom I consider great singers, but my influences were people like Sam Cooke, Ben E. King, Ray Charles. I think I related to those singers more because we all suffered. I was born in extreme poverty and, like them, I had my own minority things to deal with, one of which is being blind. I had to really develop my skills before I became famous because at every turn, there was a 'no.'"

Feliciano overcame his disability. Indeed, he enjoys baseball, horseback riding, and fishing, as well as music. In 1990 he moved from California to Connecticut with his wife, Susan (who had started a Feliciano fan club before they met), where they live in a converted eighteenth-century inn. She home-schools their three children. "I respond to people I meet in the same way a sighted person would to a stranger over the telephone," he told Mark Thornton. "You cannot see them but you make judgments from what you hear—the person's demeanor, voice, breathing. I can tell things about people by the way they walk—I can hear whether they are big or small, heavy or light."

FERRON: *Singer, guitarist, songwriter, record producer. Born Toronto, Canada, June 2, 1952.*

Acclaimed by fellow performers (including Shawn Colvin, Tori Amos, and the Indigo Girls) and critics as both an unparalleled interpreter of songs and a superb songwriter, Ferron (a name that means iron and rust) for much of her career was one of the best-kept secrets in pop-folk music of the last decades of the twentieth century. She had her first album in print when she was only fifteen, but it wasn't until she was in her forties that it appeared she finally might break through to reach something other than a cult-size audience.

Born Ferron Foisy she spent her Canadian childhood in Toronto and Vancouver, which she indicated was rough and painful, in a blue-collar household where her father was a truck driver and her mother a waitress. As she recounted in her song "Girl on a Road," she left home on one morning in an event "that was the closing of my youth when I said goodbye to no one and in that way faced my truth." She was thirteen when she ran away from home and in a short time started a new career for herself singing in coffeehouses in Vancouver, Canada. As she told Roger Dietz of *Billboard* ("Female Folk Artists Fight Pigeonholing," November 11, 1995), it was a time when politically based songs were popular with many folk music fans in western Canada. Her "training," she said, took the form of singing to "political folk-type people, mixed audiences of men and women. We were all mixed up together, trying to get co-ops happening, live communally, make a better world."

Her debut album, *Ferron,* was issued by Lucy Records in Canada in 1977, followed in 1978 by the Lucy release *Backed Up.* Her third Lucy release, the 1980 *Testimony,* whose title track became a favorite with women's rights groups, was the first to also find distribution in the United States. It also brought opportunities for engagements in the States. She told Dietz, probably reflecting her experience with gay and lesbian audiences, "I was kind of stunned when I got flown to the States and learned that there were places where women played to just women or where men played to just men. . . . I don't feel separated like that."

With her reputation as a "women's songwriter" growing steadily, Ferron built up a sizable but far from massive following on both sides of the border. Her 1983 release, *Shadows on a Dime,* presented an artist whose music and lyrics could justifiably be compared to the work of such icons as Bob Dylan, Joni Mitchell, and Van Morrison. The media generally reacted enthusiastically; the *Rolling Stone* reviewer, for example, rated it a four-star effort. As Ferron commented, some of her original compositions reflected feelings of self-doubt and pain. Her music not only reflected a desire to communicate with others, but also something vitally important "to save my sanity."

For all the supportive comments from the print media, the '83 album didn't receive intensive promotion and was far from a best-seller. It proved to be the last album of her material to be issued in the 1980s. Ferron kept on performing at festivals and small clubs and on the coffeehouse circuit, transferring home base from Canada to the United States. For a time she lived on Cape Cod before settling on Vashon Island in Washington, near Seattle, as part of a long-term relationship with a female partner. In 1994 the family expanded to include a baby. She told Roger Dietz in 1995, she was "fiercely and proudly a lesbian person, living here, trying to get it all done. I'm trying to keep a house together, and I have child, and I have morals, and I have problems, and I have passions, just like everyone else. I'm living it out, and I will not be stopped."

At the end of the '80s she got the chance to restart her recording career, signing for a new album with Chameleon Records. The result was *Phantom Center,* issued in 1990, with such fine new self-penned songs as "My My," "Harmless Love," "Indian Dreams," "Heart of Destruction," "Higher Wisdom," and "Stand Up." Backing her on the last track was the increasingly successful folk-rock duo the Indigo Girls. The origin of the title track, she noted, went back to a 1983 discussion she had with the sound engineer working on *Shadows on a Dime.* As she told Seth Rogovoy of the *Boston Phoenix* ("Ferron Rising," October 27, 1995), "I said I didn't want the viola over so far to one side. The engineer said, 'Don't worry, phantom center will take care of that.' I can remember my hair standing up when I heard that. I thought, well then, why doesn't it take care of a lot more."

She continued, "Sometimes something happens that just kind of jars me into a focus, a way of looking. For *Phantom Center,* it was, 'If I can cut the fat out of all my feelings, can I look at something that makes me sad or cold or angry or whatever and just leave it be, and also put something sweet alongside it, and will there be a middle? And are we everyday, in fact, our own phantom center?'"

When the album came out, however, the record company was having financial and organizational problems. (It went out of business in 1993.) Despite its quality, not much happened with it at the time. In 1992 Ferron's first live album, *Not a Still Life,* was released, followed by *Resting with the Question,* an instrumental album. Recorded at San Francisco's Great American Music Hall, it was something of a retrospective in which Ferron, accompanied only by her own acoustic guitar playing, sang original songs she had written over the previous sixteen-year period. Soon after, Ferron's career prospects took a turn for the better when she got the chance to sign with EarthBeat!, a record company that had a joint-venture arrangement with a major label, Warner Brothers. As Ferron began working on a new album, she also got the green light to rework *Phantom Center,* for which she fortunately had retained rights to the recording masters. Her EarthBeat!/Warner self-produced debut *Driver,* came out in 1994, followed by the new version of *Phantom Center* (coproduced by Ferron and Dan Marnien, the latter a producer of Joni Mitchell albums) in 1995. Both albums proved to be among the most praiseworthy projects of her career.

Her low, throaty vocal style proved well able to cope with formats ranging from pop-folk ballads to folk rock to Cajun-and-reggae-flavored numbers while effectively backed by top-rank session musicians and well-known artists like the Indigo Girls and Tori Amos. Typically, as Rogovoy noted, the songs were "densely textured, lyrical investigations" of many facets of the human condition and Ferron's diverse life experiences. Some of the tracks certainly were suggestive of artists with whom she had often been compared. "Girl on a Road" in *Driver* recalled Kris Kristofferson's "Me and Bobby McGee," while the fast-moving "Cactus," in the same collection, was Dylanesque in construction. Another distinctive *Driver* track was "Love Loves Me," a down-home tune with some Cajun fiddle flavor.

Stephen Holden, in choosing *Driver* as one of his top 10 albums of 1994 (*New York Times*, January 5, 1995), commented: "*Driver* is an expansive sigh of joy. . . .The songs, the best of which recall the dreamy mood of Van Morrison's most enraptured reveries, take stock of life and love in language and music that is startlingly intimate, honest and aspiring. These expansive confessional road songs by the husky-voiced Canadian singer and songwriter communicate a lifetime's wisdom with bone-deep honesty."

In 1995 several of Ferron's songs were included in collections made by other artists. The Indigo Girls' treatment of Ferron's "It Won't Take Long" was included in the fall compilation *Spirit of '73: Rock for Choice*. (During the summer of '95, she and the Indigo Girls performed the song at the Newport Folk Festival in what turned out to be one of the event's high points.) Earlier her "Sunshine" was included in a children's collection, *Hand in Hand*, featuring people like Joni Mitchell, Jackson Browne, the Pretenders, and John Lennon.

As the 1990s went by, Ferron's concert career embraced shows at larger or more prestigious venues in the United States and Canada. Critics commented on her more upbeat, relaxed demeanor in her live performances. Richard Cromelin of the *Los Angeles Times* ("Ferron Shines as 'Women's Music' Muse," November 11, 1995), discussing her appearance at an L.A. nightclub, observed, "Ferron's image over the years has been that of a reserved, even severe woman, but on stage [at the Troubadour] she tempered her innate dignity with playfulness and an unself-conscious physical looseness. She offered self-deprecating jabs at her persona as the wise matriarch, her wit blending with and reinforcing her seriousness of purpose."

Ferron told Donna Larcen of the *Hartford Courant* that she felt better about herself and her personal environment in the '90s. "After getting through my 20s, when I worried about everything, I am finally in my 40s and I realize you have to lighten up. It's going to be OK sometimes.

"If I had known at 20 that the songs about my life that were so painful to record would be so fun to sing later, I would have started at 6 months, although it's rough to rhyme with gaa."

The accolades *Driver* received helped bring Ferron a contract offer from Warner Brothers, which resulted in her self-produced album *Still Riot*, issued in the summer of 1996. Commenting on the project, Tom Manoff, who reviews classical releases for National Public Radio's *All Things Considered*, pointed out that while the project wasn't the first time Ferron had produced her own music, "It is the first time she has had full support from a major record company." The important thing, though, was the excellent content of music and lyrics of songs like "Dazzle the Beast" (*Well, where's Houdini when you need him to make a Joker an Ace. To make light of the moment by turning Time back into Space*) and "Venus as Appearances" (*Some mountains you can wander in the night, and some mountains you're not supposed to know*). In 1999, Ferron released *Inside Out: The Ima Sessions*.

FLECK, BÉLA: *Banjoist, songwriter, band leader (the Flecktones). Born New York, New York, July 10, 1958.*

If Earl Scruggs represents the first modern banjo revolution, then Béla Fleck represents the second. Scruggs took the music he heard as a boy in rural North Carolina and created his own style. Fleck, who grew up in Manhattan, took the banjo into the realm of progressive jazz. In the process, Fleck not only influenced a new generation of banjoists but also made the banjo palatable to jazz audiences who would otherwise have turned up their noses at the five-string. *Flight of the Cosmic Hippo*, his 1991 album with the Flecktones, was number one on the jazz charts for two weeks.

Record stores sometimes don't know where to put Fleck's albums. Do they belong with the other bluegrass artists or with the jazz artists? Béla, named after Bartók rather than Lugosi, likes to keep it that way.

His cartoonlike album covers often featured a banjo floating in space, and the music is out there for bluegrass purists. He often plays a souped-up electric Deering Crossfire banjo. At the urging of Bonnie Raitt, Fleck even plays some tunes with a slide. The other members of the Flecktones include Roy Wooten, called Future Man, who sometimes struts across the stage dressed like a pirate; he developed a percussion instrument called a drumitar that looks like an off-kilter guitar. His brother Victor Wooten plays bass, taking the lead on jazzy solos. Until 1992, Howard Levy was on keyboards and harmonica.

"I'm trying to make music that is thought-provoking, emotionally satisfying and technically interesting with a band that plays instruments that are unusual and plays them unusually," Fleck told Zan Stewart of the *Los Angeles Times* (August 26, 1992). "We're not trying to do pop or jazz or anything. We're trying to blend it all together, sort of a melting pot of all these elements so that we find our own little niche."

Fleck grew up in Manhattan, the son of Jere Fleck, a language teacher, and Barbara Fleck Paladino, a schoolteacher. His father liked classical music and his mother played campfire songs on the guitar. Béla's first taste of the banjo came, naturally, from "The Ballad of Jed Clampett" and "Dueling Banjos." When he was fifteen, his grandfather gave him a five-string banjo he found at a garage sale, and he was hooked. "Once I heard the banjo, it was as if neurons were firing off in my head. The notes were so clean and fast. . . . It was the sound of mercury," he says.

He won a spot at the Fiorello LaGuardia High School of Music and Art in Manhattan by performing "Here Comes the Sun" on the guitar. He told *Acoustic Musician* (August 1995): "I found that if I brought my banjo and played bluegrass in front of my high school, that wouldn't attract as much attention as if I played the blues or if I tried to play a Yes song or a Led Zeppelin song on the banjo or even a Beatles song—those kids up in New York would relate to that a lot more. Some people thought I was strange to be playing bluegrass. So all that affected the music that I started writing."

Fleck's first banjo teacher was Erik Darling, who played in the Weavers and the Rooftop Singers. His second teacher was Mark Horowitz. At sixteen, Fleck started taking lessons from another major force in banjo innovation, Tony Trischka, whom he met through Horowitz. At that time, Trischka was experimenting with jazz.

"I wish all my students were like that," Trischka says. "He could play a few Scruggs things and some fiddle tunes, some straight-ahead stuff. I had just put out my first record. I just showed him all the progressive stuff I was into. I'd only been teaching a few years. I didn't realize I should probably teach someone the roots of the music first. Anyway, we really hit it off. I don't remember how long he had lessons. Three or six months. He got a strong dose of what I was doing and moved up to Boston. . . . Later on a guy named Pat Enright taught him about Scruggs style and got him on that path. He was also taking jazz lessons from Billy Novick, who is a saxophonist who got Béla into doing jazz things, like Charlie Parker. He got all my stuff, the bluegrass thing and the jazz thing, all within a couple of years."

In 1975, Fleck heard Chick Corea play at the Beacon Theatre in New York. "I'd been playing banjo for just two years and it changed my whole approach to the instrument," he says. Charlie Parker also influenced him. "Even though I hadn't been playing very long, I started trying to figure out 'An Oscar for Treadwell,' " he told David Okamoto of *Jazziz* (April 1995).

He played in two bands, the Brownstone Hallow and Wicker's Creek, during his high school years. After graduating from high school in 1976, he moved to Boston and joined his first professional band, Tasty Licks. The mandolinist in Tasty Licks, Jack Tottle, urged him to write songs. Fleck told *Acoustic Musician:* "I was only interested in it if things were pretty weird, pretty complex. At that time, I wasn't interested in coming out with anything traditional. But as time went on, and I got more interested in bluegrass itself, I found I wanted to write tunes that could be traditional as well, that might sound like a Bill Monroe tune or a Norman Blake thing or different style of bluegrass or different styles of acoustic music."

He moved to Lexington, Kentucky, and cofounded Spectrum, which played progressive and traditional bluegrass. He sent an audition tape to Rounder Records and got his first record deal, releasing *Crossing the Tracks* in 1980, which included Jerry Douglas on Dobro and Sam Bush on fiddle and mandolin. He played the Chick Corea's song "Spain" on the album. The next year, Fleck joined banjo legends Bill Keith and Tony Trischka for *Fiddle Tunes for Banjo* for Rounder, though the three only play together on one song, "Bill Cheatham."

In 1981, Fleck settled in Nashville and joined a new incarnation of the New Grass Revival, with Sam Bush, John Cowan, and Pat Flynn. The group, formed in the 1970s, is credited with blending traditional and modern sounds to create "newgrass."

When he wasn't touring with the Revival, he played with a traditional group called Dreadful Snakes, with Douglas on Dobro, Blaine Sprouse on fiddle, and Enright on guitar. The group released *The Dreadful Snakes* on Rounder in 1984. Fleck also had his own group, Banjo-Jazz. If that wasn't enough, he was in demand as a producer. He worked on albums with Maura O'Connell (*Just in Time* and *Helpless Heart*), Stuart Duncan; the Nashville Bluegrass Band (a self-titled album, *Idle Time* and *To Be His Child*), Mark Schatz (*Brand New Old Timeway*), and Tony Trischka.

He was a prolific writer as well, trying more and more to incorporate feelings into his songwriting. "If I sit down to write, I can't," he told Alana J. White of *Banjo Newsletter* (September 1986). "But if I just pick up my banjo and start noodling around, sometimes I'll hit on something; I have to be prepared to do that at any time of the day while I'm between calls, doing laundry, or whatever, and allow the process to happen if it's going to. Often, it happens when I don't have time for it, and I feel like my subconscious is playing a practical joke on me."

He came out with several albums on Rounder: *Natural Bridge* (1982), a cross between stringband jazz and bluegrass; *Double Time* (1984) with Bush, Douglas, David Grisman, John Hartford, Tony Rice, and Mike Marshall; *Deviation* (1984), with the New Grass Revival, in which Fleck begins to deviate into jazz; *Inroads* (1986); and the traditional bluegrass album *Drive* (1988). He received Grammy nominations for *Double Time, Deviation,* and *Drive. Inroads* received a five-star review from *Billboard.* Rounder preferred Fleck's bluegrass albums to his jazzier offerings, but still encouraged his experimentation. After Fleck left Rounder, the label released two compilations: *Daybreak* and *Places,* both in 1987.

He also recorded several albums with the New Grass Revival: *On the Boulevard* and *Live in Toulouse* on Sugar Hill; *New Grass Revival* on EMI America; *Hold a Dream* on Capitol, which received a Grammy nomination for Fleck's composition "Seven by Seven"; *Friday Night in America,* also on Capitol, nominated for a Grammy for Fleck's song "Big Foot." He recorded an acoustic album, *Strength in Numbers* in 1989 on the MCA Master Series with Douglas, Bush, Mark O'Connor, and Edgar Meyer.

By the late 1980s, Fleck had solidified his reputation as one of the most innovative banjoists around. He was voted best banjoist in *Frets Magazine* five years in a row. After eight and a half years with New Grass, Fleck decided it was time to move on. He played his last concert with the group on December 31, 1989, opening for the Grateful Dead. "Eventually, there were a lot of things I wanted to do that just weren't appropriate for New Grass. I started to feel the need to do other things," he told *Acoustic Musician* (August 1995). "The Dreadful Snakes came together partly because I wanted to play bluegrass as well as newgrass. I was making records and trying to pull all these musicians like Sam [Bush] and Jerry [Douglas] with me and do what I wanted to do. I hadn't really found the thing."

That "other thing" came together in 1988 when Fleck assembled a group to play for PBS's *The Lonesome Pines Special.* He called it Béla Fleck and Friends: Victor Wooten on bass, Roy "Future Man" Wooten on percussion and Howard Levy on keyboards and harmonica. "Everything stands out about the show," Fleck said in answer to written questions. "It was a very special performance as proven by the fact that the people are still playing together ten years later."

In 1989 Fleck renamed the group the Flecktones. "I found these musicians who were just like me, into stretching and trying everything," he told *Acoustic Musician.* "Suddenly, instead of trying to simplify, I would pull out the most complicated things I had ever written and throw it to them. I was being challenged to write difficult music for the first time in my life not the reverse, not 'You gotta make it dumb.' In New Grass Revival, we were getting a lot of pressure to 'Keep it simple, stupid' for country radio. We resisted that quite a bit."

Fleck raised his own funds to record the first album in 1990 and signed with Warner Brothers. The album was titled *Béla Fleck and the Flecktones* and received a Grammy nomination for Best Contemporary Jazz album. Fleck was concerned that it might take a while to regain his audience after leaving the New Grass Revival. But his risk paid off. "It was boom time for us," he told *Acoustic Musician.* "We sold a lot of records. The thing just went. We were on TV; being booked on major jazz festivals. Our first concert in New York was with Stevie Wonder and Take Six. We were on the Take Six tour and Bonnie Raitt's European tour. It was just cookin'."

The Flecktones made a video of "Sinister Minister" from their debut, which ran on VH-1, BET, and TNN. Fleck kept bluegrass tracks off the first album to get the album out of the bluegrass bins. The video started playing on Country Music Television and Fleck told them to take it off. "And now I think, why did I do that?" he told banjoist Alison Brown, who interviewed him for *Banjo Newsletter* (May 1995). "I should have been glad I was getting played. But at the same time we were getting played on VH-1 and BET and I thought if they hear that this is getting played on Country Music TV, they're going to take it off. I was really afraid that there would be some reverse discrimination. But the fact is, we're building fans from all over the place. A few from country, a few from jazz and funk, and even a few from the Grateful Dead!"

The Flecktones' second release, *Flight of the Cosmic Hippo* (1991, Warner Brothers) was more melodic than the first, but still includes jazzed-up versions of "The Star-Spangled Banner," the Irish song "Star of the County Down," and the Beatle's "Michelle." The album hit the top of the jazz charts for two weeks. It received Grammy nominations for Best Contemporary Jazz Performance and Best Instrumental Composition for Fleck's "Blu-Blop." They toured Europe that year with Bonnie Raitt and once again, Fleck found himself opening for the Grateful Dead's New Year's Eve show in Oakland, an experience Fleck simply calls "Amazing!"

The final Flecktones' album with a cartoon album cover was called *UFO TOFU* (1992, Warner Brothers). The title was a palindrome, and the song itself includes phrases played backward and forward. It also includes a song, "Bonnie & Slyde," on which Fleck plays banjo slide, and Fleck's return to bluegrass, "The Yee-Haw Factor."

"As time went on and we became established in the jazz world I felt like it was dishonest to say we were open to all different kinds of music but to keep bluegrass out for marketing reasons," Fleck told Brown. "So we started doing things like 'The Yee-Haw Factor' and started bringing the roll back into the music, and then for me it was even more honest and more complete because I wasn't shutting a side of myself out."

Howard Levy, the harmonica player known for his soulful and melodic jazz leads, left at the end of 1992. "Howard is a guy who can walk in and play 50 instruments, play anything," Fleck told *Acoustic Musician.* "People said they weren't surprised when he left; they were surprised he had stayed so long. That was a frightening time: I was afraid everything would fall apart."

The Flecktones became a trio. Since Levy often played the melody lines on harmonica, Fleck was forced to play more of those lines himself. The trio released *Three Flew Over the Cuckoo's Nest* in 1993, which included guest musicians Bruce Hornsby on piano and Branford Marsalis on sax. It is also marked by novel uses of technology: Fleck began playing a Deering Crossfire banjo, which included a MIDI (Musical Instrument Digital Interface) pickup. They used floor pedals to "trigger sounds."

Fleck was voted the best miscellaneous instrumentalist by *Jazziz Magazine* in 1993 and 1994. In 1993, Fleck also wrote the theme song for the new *Beverly Hillbillies* movie. Every now and again, Fleck also tours with Tony Trischka. The two know each other so well that they can play duets on any standard bluegrass tune as well as improvise on jazz tunes. "I move a little more towards Béla and he moves a little more towards me," Trischka told Bill Evans of *Banjo Newsletter.* They were both featured on the *Rounder Banjo Extravaganza* (1988) and *Solo Banjo Works* (1992).

When Victor Wooten went off to make a solo bass album, Fleck began thinking about making another solo album like his acclaimed *Drive* album. He invited Douglas, Bush, and guitarist Tony Rice. But then he decided he wanted the rest of the Flecktones to play too. Others agreed to participate: Marsalis, Hornsby, and Corea on a banjo-piano duet called "Bicyclops." The result was Fleck's solo release *Tales from the Acoustic Planet,* (1995, Warner Brothers), which blends jazz and bluegrass. "To me, this record is about trying to bring all these different worlds together and find a place where they can exist," Fleck told *Jazziz.* "It was an attempt to make peace with these different sides of myself."

At the beginning of 1995, the Flecktones went on a USIA-sponsored tour through Mongolia, China, Korea, Indonesia, Thailand, and Singapore. They performed with indigenous musicians, which gave Fleck new ideas for compositions. In 1995, he got a call from Kavi Alexander of Water Lily Acoustics to record with Indian slide guitarist V. M. Bhatt, who had previously recorded the Grammy-winning album with Ry Cooder, *A Meeting by the River.* Bhatt plays the Mohan Vina, an Indian version of the guitar. Fleck also recorded with Chinese musician Jie-Bing Chen, who plays a two-string violin called an *erh'hu.* The album, *Tabula Rasa,* was nominated for a World Music Grammy.

In 1996 the Flecktones released a two-disc concert album, recorded on the road between 1992 and 1996, called *Live Art* on Warner Brothers. It captures the Flecktones' remarkable jazz chops on stage. Fleck won Best Pop Instrumental Performance Grammy for "Sin-

ister Minister." The Flecktones played 200 concerts, including a tour with Hootie and the Blowfish, and performed music for the feature film *Striptease.*

Where he would go from there was unclear. He doesn't want to repeat himself, writing songs on guitar or piano to vary his approach. "I'm trying to get to where it comes from the heart and I'm certainly thinking a lot less and just letting it flow more these days," he told Alison Brown. "I used to be a lot more concerned about the technical stuff, but now I'm more concerned with conveying a feeling. It's a different intent and I'm really not into soloing so much. I get just as much pleasure being in a group and playing a part that makes the whole thing sound good."

In 1997 Fleck continued his eclectic ways, from jazz to classical to bluegrass. He joined with upright bassist Edgar Meyer and mandolinist Mike Marshall to put out a semiclassical album titled *Uncommon Ritual* on Sony. Meanwhile, to fill the void left by Howard Levy, the Flecktones invited saxophonist Paul McCandless to tour with them in 1995 and 1996. (His work is on *Live Art.*) Sax player Jeff Coffin came along next and is featured on the Flecktones' *Left of Cool* (1998, Warner Brothers). The album represents a departure for the Flecktones because it includes vocals and instrumentals. Future Man (who goes by Royel when he's singing), Dave Matthews, and Amy Grant sing on four of the fifteen tunes. But the instrumentals still stand out. Two songs from the album were nominated for Grammys: "Big Country" for Best Pop Instrumental and "Almost 12," composed by Fleck, Future Man, and Victor Lemonte Wooten, which won a best instrumental composition Grammy. Fleck was nominated for another Grammy for Best Country Instrumental Performance with Jerry Douglas for the song "The Ride" from Douglas's *Restless on the Farm* (1998, Sugar Hill).

In 1999, Fleck continued to tour with Mike Marshall and Edgar Meyer as well as Tony Trischka. Warner Brothers released a Flecktones retrospective, *Greatest Hits of the 20th Century.* In the meantime, Fleck returned to his bluegrass roots with the musicians who had worked on *Drive. The Bluegrass Sessions: Tales from the Acoustic Planet, Volume 2* (Warner Brothers) was nominated for a Grammy for Best Bluegrass Album. As Fleck told Bill Kohlhaase of the *Los Angeles Times* ("Finding the Bluegrass was Greener," May 22, 1998), "I was trying hard to be a jazz contemporary when the Flecktones were first beginning. . . . I wanted nothing to do with bluegrass rhythms. . . . The Flecktones were playing all kinds of music other than bluegrass, and, as time went on, I began to feel like a hypocrite. Bluegrass is probably what I'm best at. So around the third album, we started utilizing it more."

Based partly on written answers by Béla Fleck and an interview with Tony Trischka

FOGELBERG, DAN: *Singer, pianist, guitarist, song-writer, record producer. Born Peoria, Illinois, August 18, 1951.*

Daniel Grayling Fogelberg sometimes sounded somewhat like the Eagles in his mid-1970s recordings. The comparison is apt since both he and they were part of the Southern California–based folk and country-rock movement of that decade and also were represented by the dynamic Irv Azoff. But the point is that Fogelberg alone could sound like the entire Eagles group because he was adept at so many instruments and modern recording methods could put separate tracks of his work together to form what amounted to a one-man band.

Music was a long suit in Dan's family, so it's not surprising he finally chose it for a career. His father was a band leader and his mother a singer in his hometown of Peoria. They saw to it that he took piano lessons as a child, and his grandfather, after whom Dan is named, gave him an acoustic slide guitar. He played in a variety of bands in elementary and high school and, at fourteen, started writing original material. At the same time, he also developed an interest in painting that eventually became his major when he enrolled in the University of Illinois in the late 1960s. He left school after two years, however, because "I saw it was going to be tough to make a living out of painting."

He worked in various groups until he became friends with an eager young entrepreneur named Irv Azoff. They headed to California, where Azoff got his charge a contract with Columbia Records. Dan's debut album, *Home Free,* was recorded in Nashville, where Dan had settled on a farm in an outlying area. While waiting for his recording career to take off, he earned a good living as a session musician in Nashville studios, backing such artists as Randy Newman, Eric Andersen, Buffy St. Marie, Roger McGuinn, Michael Stanley, Joe Walsh, and Jackson Browne.

Walsh returned the favor soon after by producing Dan's second album, recorded mainly in Los Angeles. Session musicians on the effort included Glenn Frey, Don Henley, and Randy Meisner of the Eagles; Graham Nash; Kenny Passarelli (later lead guitarist for Hall and Oates); and many others. Called *Souvenirs,* the album established Fogelberg as an important addition to the folk/country-rock scene after its release on Epic/Full Moon label in October 1974. The album spawned Dan's first singles hit, "Part of the Plan," which peaked at number thirty-one in *Billboard* the week of March 1, 1975. Singles hits, though, were not his forte. While he placed a number on the charts, few reached the top 10.

Fogelberg made a point of expressing his dissatisfaction with the industry's stress on singles. He told Dennis Hunt of the *Los Angeles Times* (March 7, 1978), "Record companies still tell you that you can't make it if you don't have a hit single, but me and a few others are proving them wrong. I have an FM-based audience and could care less about AM radio. I'll take an AM hit if it comes along, of course, but I'm certainly not going to go after one."

By the time that discussion took place, Fogelberg had two gold records (eventually gaining platinum awards as well), one for *Souvenirs* and the second one for *Captured Angel,* issued by Full Moon/Epic in September 1975. (*Captured Angel* was originally released as a quad rather than stereo disc). The latter album presented an even more relaxed tone and a more poetic interest in nature that reflected Dan's move from Tennessee to a house in the Rocky Mountains near Denver. Fogelberg not only played most of the instrumental tracks on *Captured Angel,* but provided backing vocals and handled the production chores himself.

In line with his attitude about setting his own goals and timetables, Dan took a while before finishing his fourth LP, *Nether Lands,* issued in May 1977. The album's songs tended to be more introspective than much of his earlier work and dealt in part with his view on the rites of passage from adolescence to adulthood. The album, eventually was certified platinum by the Recording Industry Association of America.

In 1978 Dan teamed up with flutist Tim Weisberg for a new series of recordings. The album proved a finely crafted, very listenable blend of elements of jazz, folk, and even hints of classical music. The general public expressed approval of the effort by pushing *Twin Sons of Different Mothers* into upper-chart levels a short time after its release in August 1978. By the end of the decade the LP won a platinum record award from the R.I.A.A. The album also provided another chart single, "The Power of Gold," which rose to number twenty-four in *Billboard* the week of November 4, 1978.

His next solo album, *Phoenix,* was released on Full Moon/Epic in November 1979 and by early 1980 was in the top five spot on national charts. (It too passed platinum levels in the early 1980s.) At the same time, the track "Longer" from the LP (written by Dan with Robert Putnam and Marty Lewis) became his best-selling single, spending two weeks at the number two position on the *Billboard* list in January 1980. The album also provided the chart single "Heart Hotels," which peaked at number twenty-one the week of April 19, 1980. This was followed by *The Innocent Age,* a two-LP set released in August 1981, which Dan later called his favorite album. The collection went platinum by the fall of that year and provided such singles successes as "Same Auld Lang Syne," which rose to number nine in December, and "Run for the Roses," which peaked at number eighteen the week of April 24, 1982. The year 1981 was a banner year in singles for Dan. Besides "Same Auld Lang Syne," he made the top ten with "Hard to Say" (number seven in September) and "Leader of the Band" (number nine in December).

During 1982, Dan moved from Boulder to a 600-acre ranch in the southern Colorado Rockies, where he also took his new bride, Maggie—a marriage, however, that ended in divorce in 1985.

In October 1982, Full Moon/Epic released the first Fogelberg retrospective, *Greatest Hits,* which also included two new songs, "Missing You" and "Make Love Stay." Both of those made it to the *Billboard* Top 30, "Missing You" rising to number twenty-three the week of November 13, 1982, and "Make Love Stay" peaking at number twenty-nine the week of March 5, 1983. By 1983, the album had been certified platinum by the R.I.A.A. Next out in January 1984 was *Windows and Walls,* produced by Fogelberg and Marty Lewis, which contained eight songs written by Dan, including the first single, "The Language of Love." The latter provided another chart hit single, reaching number thirteen in *Billboard* the week of February 11, 1984. By the end of '84, Dan had received a gold record award for the album.

Inspired by attendance at a 1983 bluegrass festival in Telluride, Colorado, this music style became the prime theme of *High Country Snows,* issued on Full Moon/Epic in April 1985. Contributing to the album tracks were such country and folk music stars as Doc Watson, David Grisman, Ricky Skaggs, and Chris Hillman and Herb Pedersen of the Desert Rose Band.

His 1987 release, *Exiles,* later dubbed by some the "divorce album," was a collection that took some two years to complete at locales in Hawaii and Los Angeles. The disc, produced by Fogelberg and Russ Kunkel, contained eight more originals by Dan, including the charted single "She Don't Look Back." During the year Fogelberg met Anastasia Savage, a nurse and painter from Louisiana who at one point was a private nurse for famous artist Georgia O'Keefe, whom Fogelberg considered his favorite painter. Anastasia became his second wife and settled in at the ranch while Dan began building his own full recording studio, which he named the Mountain Bird Studio.

Some of the material for his next album, the self-produced *The Wild Places* (released in August 1990) was prepared there, but most of the material was recorded elsewhere. The nine original songs on the disc included "Bones in the Sky," dedicated to the recently deceased Georgia O'Keefe. Nonoriginal renditions included his version of Bruce Cockburn's "Lovers in a Dangerous Time" and the Cascades' "Rhythm of the Rain." The album made the charts but fell far short of the sales Dan had achieved with his hit collections of previous decades. Soon after, a two-disc live concert set, *Greetings from the West,* drawn from concerts in Saint Louis, Missouri, was put out in 1991 by Full Moon/Epic Records.

A good part of his next album, *River of Souls,* which turned out to be the last in his longtime association with Epic, was produced and recorded by Dan in his Mountain Bird Studio. It included ten songs written by him, including, besides the first single, "Magic Every Moment," the title track, "Serengeti Moon," "Holy Road," and "Faces of America." Much of the material was based on African rhythms and South African soca music.

Following that project, Dan was reunited with old friend Irving Azoff in the latter's new Giant Records organization. His label debut in September 1995, *No Resemblance Whatsoever,* represented another reunion—this time with Tim Weisberg, their first joint effort since the *Twins* album collaboration. The same month, Sony issued another retrospective album, *Love Songs.*

The contents of the *River of Souls* CD included songs with sharp commentary on the problems of homelessness and international conflicts. The track "A Voice for Peace" had been penned in protest against the Desert Storm incident, while another song, "Faces of America," took the side of the nation's homeless. As Fogelberg commented on the latter, "That song came to me in a dream and I've only had that once or twice in my life. In this dream, I was hearing this song and seeing this video of homeless people—maybe somewhere in Arizona, the camera panning by them. When I woke up, I jumped out of bed and grabbed the guitar and wrote it down. It was just so fresh and so strong in my mind that all I had to do was figure out the verses and what I wanted to say.

"There's a sentiment in this country that the homeless don't want to work, but really there are a lot of people out there who would love to be back in the work force and get back on their feet again. There are plenty of artists who have addressed the issue—I'm certainly not unique in that—but this was my take on it."

He acknowledged, "A lot of people say you shouldn't mix art and politics, but I don't think you can avoid it. I think that's what art is there for. In many ways, we are the last bastion, we are the conscience, as artists always have been throughout history. They've been the ones who have brought up the problems and forced the changes."

During the summer of 1997, Epic/Legacy released a four-CD box set, *Portrait: The Music of Dan Fogelberg 1972–1997.*

FORBERT, STEVE: *Singer, guitarist, harmonica player, band leader (Rough Squirrels), songwriter. Born Meridian, Mississippi, December 15, 1954.*

The new wave of folksingers of the late 1970s tended to avoid the emphasis on traditionalism of previous generations in favor of a flexibility in both style and content. Steve Forbert was a typical exemplar of the trend, a balladeer who, like Bob Dylan, wrote his own folk songs and blended several elements of music, including rock, blues, and country.

Forbert was born and raised in Meridian, Mississippi: as he proudly told the authors, "I'm from Meridian, the home of *the* Jimmie Rodgers, the father of country music. When I was a kid I went to five or six of the memorial concerts for him in Meridian. I don't get home much now, but I do go when I have some time."

At the same time, he also knew he shared the

His well-crafted albums did win praise from the folk music press, and his original writings in particular developed a life of their own, being covered again and again by other, sometimes much better-known folk musicians. Many of Franke's compositions, like "The Great Storm Is Over," "Thanksgiving Eve," and "For Real," Tom Paxton told Scott Alarik of the *Boston Globe*, ranked as hits in the folk-music world: "In our terms, it's a hit song when it really enters the tradition, when you hear that it's being passed along from singer to singer, that people who may have no idea who you are have taken it into their lives. They can identify with the feelings in the song, the words and melody fit, and it tastes good to sing it. Bob writes like that, like an ordinary thoughtful man who has turned to song to express himself."

Franke was born and raised in Michigan in a family that suffered from the problems his father had with alcohol. As Franke later told an interviewer, "When I was growing up, my dad was an alcohol abuser. I understand now, as an adult, why he saw that as his only option and I love the man dearly now, in fact as adults we are much closer than we ever were when I was a child, when the alcohol really obscured the love." It was a theme Bob turned to in his song "Hard Love," with the lyrics, *but the hard times and the liquor drove the easy love away/there was love in Daddy's house, but it was hard love. . . .* The song, he commented, was a "very healing" one.

Franke began his career as a singer-songwriter in 1965 while attending the University of Michigan. He became one of the first people to perform at the Ark Coffeehouse in Ann Arbor, which later became a landmark spot on the coffeehouse circuit. He graduated from the university in 1969 with a B.A. in English literature and moved to Cambridge, Massachusetts, as a seminarian with the objective of entering the ministry. He gave up that idea after a while, but never abandoned his faith. He stressed, "I'm an artist first, but an artist who is biblically rooted. I'm a Christian songwriter who's appalled by right-wing Christianity. I've entertained the fantasy of going into contemporary Christian music, but each time I do," he said half-ironically, "something in me says 'No, that's the devil talking.'"

From the time he got to the Boston area, Franke continued to add to his repertoire of secular songs—some having biblical connections, though, such as the 1973 "Breakthrough Angels." He gained attention from people in the local community as well as some folk-music artists starting in the early 1970s by becoming one of the area's more popular street singers. He also started his own coffeehouse and sought opportunities to perform in other small folk venues. But then the decision to settle down and raise a family caused him to reassess his plans.

As he recalled in *Sing Out!* magazine ("Courting the Muse," vol. 37, 1992), "My own quest for fame had come to a screeching halt midway through the 1970s as I prepared to leave street-singing for what seemed a more 'responsible' full-time job maintaining candy-making and candy-wrapping machines (my training for which was being a folksinger who'd had to learn how to maintain old cars to get from one gig to the next).

"The advent of fatherhood demanded that I reexamine my life and make the appropriate adjustments. I prepared with some anguish and bitterness to turn my back on the idea of making music for a living, but in the process, some unexpected things happened. First of all, the process of reexamination revitalized my songwriting. Secondly, other artists, many of whom had played at the community coffeehouse I'd started in Marblehead, began to be attracted to my songs and started singing them. And because a lot of people my age were reexamining their own lives, the songs became popular in folksong-oriented communities."

Of course, while he worked at the candy plant, Franke never completely abandoned his music efforts; in 1976 he completed the album *Love Can't Be Bitter All the Time,* issued on the Fretless label. As interest in his abilities as songwriter and performer slowly expanded through word of mouth and covers of his songs by others, new opportunities began to come along, particularly as folk music began to gather interest on college campuses in the 1980s. In 1983, his album *One Evening in Chicago* was released on the Great Divide label, a collection later reissued by Chicago-based Flying Fish Records, with whom he signed in the mid-1980s.

In 1986 he scored a major breakthrough with his Flying Fish release *For Real.* The album gained approval at home and overseas, where the reviewer for England's *Folk Roots* commented, "There is greatness here, in an intense album of enduring quality through which you feel you have met the man and been changed somehow by his experience." He followed up with an equally engaging release on Flying Fish, the 1989 *Brief Histories.* The *Dirty Linen* critic enthused that the album was "an unusual, wonderful record [reflecting] painstaking, loving craftsmanship . . . in a class well above the norm. Franke is a provocative singer and an able instrumentalist. Above all, he is an unusually gifted songwriter. *Brief Histories* is a classic." The album was nominated in the Outstanding Folk Album category in the 1990 Boston Music Awards, and Franke was nominated for Outstanding Folk Act.

The 1980s provided Franke with the opportunities he needed to make music his full-time occupation. He performed at venues across the United States and Canada and was welcomed in England on several occasions. He also got the chance to lead songwriting workshops at many festivals, education centers, and music camps, a scenario that continued into the 1990s. Besides workshops at the 1987 Philadelphia Folk Festival in Schwenksville, Pennsylvania, and the 1992 Kerrville

Folk Festival in Kerrville, Texas, his credits included five years at the Puget Sound Guitar Workshop in Port Orchard, Washington, three years at CDSS Folk Music Week at Pinewoods Camp, Plymouth, Massachusetts, and two years at the Swannanoa Gathering in Swannanoa, North Carolina. Besides lecturing on the blues at Boston University's College of Basic Studies, he took part in blues workshops at the Philadelphia, Winnipeg, and SMU Eisteddfod festivals. He also guested on a number of live radio programs, including *A Prairie Home Companion, A Mountain Stage, Our Front Porch, Andy Bradley's Potluck, Folk Scene, West Coast Weekend,* and *Bound for Glory.*

In August 1990, Franke wrote a set of songs for a ballet of *The Velveteen Rabbit,* commissioned by the ODC Dance Company of San Francisco. His compositional output up to then also included three cantatas and a number of hymns for the Church of Saint Andrew in Marblehead, Massachusetts. His 1990s album credits began with the 1991 *In This Night* on Flying Fish, nominated for Outstanding Folk Album in the 1992 Boston Music Awards and named Number One Album of 1991 by Boston radio station WUMB-FM. Like some of his previous releases, it also was cited in award selections in other parts of the country. In December 1992, as part of the Folk Project of New Jersey, the songbook *The Songs of Bob Franke* was published.

After a gap of almost four years, Bob's next album came out in late 1995. By then Flying Fish had been acquired by Rounder, and he formed a new association with Daring Records, which was distributed by Rounder. The contents of *The Hearts of the Flower* included his treatment of "Hard Love," which, though covered by many others, had not been in print on any of Franke's discs for years. The eleven originals included such new songs as "Eye of the Serpent," "Waiting for Nineveh to Burn," "Helicopter Simulator," "Krystallnacht is Coming" (comparing some of the 1990s attacks on civil liberties, such as anti–affirmative action steps, with the infamous forerunner to the Nazi holocaust), "Trouble in the World (It'll Be All Right)," and a duet with Noel Paul Stookey on "Turn Back, O Man." Backing him on the tracks was a talented group comprising Nina Gerber on guitar, Duke Levine on guitar, Cary Black on bass, and Billy Novick on woodwinds.

By the time his thirtieth anniversary tribute took place in January 1996, Bob's concert appearances at coffeehouses, colleges, festivals, bars, streets, homes, and churches had covered twenty-nine U.S. states, four Canadian provinces, and a number of venues in England.

In 1997, another album on the Daring label was released by Rounder, *Long Roads, Short Visits.* The 1998 Rounder catalog, besides offering both Daring discs, also included earlier Flying Fish releases such as *One Evening in Chicago, For Real, Brief Histories,* and *In This Night.*

FULLER, BLIND BOY: *Singer, guitarist, songwriter. Born Wadesboro, North Carolina, July 10, 1907; died Durham, North Carolina, February 13, 1941.*

In his brief lifetime, Blind Boy Fuller was so successful a bluesman that he was credited with founding the Blind Boy Fuller Piedmont fingerpicking style, though others, like Buddy Moss and Rev. Gary Davis made equally important contributions. Moss, in fact, recorded this kind of music before Fuller's releases began to appear.

Fuller, born Fulton Allen in Wadesboro, North Carolina, wasn't blind at birth, but his eyesight began to fail in his late teens, by which time his family had moved to Rockingham, North Carolina. He was partially sighted when he married young Cora Mae Martin in 1927 and about a year and a half later became completely blind. He then had to expand his previously limited guitar playing ability to start to earn a living as a street musician. He did this in part by listening to recordings of people like Blind Blake and picking up techniques from other performers. Sometime at the end of the 1920s or in the early 1930s, he and Cora Mae ended up in Durham, North Carolina, where he eventually caught the attention of white entrepreneur J.B. Long, who got him a contract from the American Recording Corporation in 1935.

In July 1935 he sent Fuller, Bull City Red, and Gary Davis to New York for sessions in which the numbers included "Rag Mama Rag" and "Baby You Gotta Change Your Mind." The first of those, backed with "I'm a Rattlesnakin' Daddy," did well with blues fanciers, and ARC put out the welcome mat for more Fuller tracks, including a highly successful collaboration of Fuller and Sonny Terry that began in late 1937. Before his death from blood poisoning in early 1941, Fuller completed an estimated 135 sides, including such classics as "Truckin' My Blues Away" and "Mama Let Me Lay It On You" (both based to some extent on work by other artists), "Step It Up and Go," "I Crave My Pig Meat," and "I Want Some of Your Pie." Some of his recordings were made on Decca in a vain attempt to break away from Long's domination.

On his deathbed, Fuller gave Brownie McGhee his guitar, and the record company later promoted McGhee for a time as Blind Boy Fuller number two. In the 1990s all of Fuller's recordings were released on CDs, Volumes 1 through 6, by Document Records. Some of his best tracks were issued on the Yazzo disc *Truckin' My Blues Away.*

FULLER, JESSE: *Singer, guitarist, harmonica player, "fotdella" player, songwriter. Born Jonesboro, Georgia, March 12, 1896; died Oakland, California, January 29, 1976.*

Most of Jesse Fuller's life was a fight for survival. He never knew his father, and his mother gave him away to another family when he was only six or seven.

Yet, instead of becoming bitter or despairing, he eventually became a folk-blues artist with a message of hope and beauty for several generations of fans.

When he was seven or eight, staying with a family named Wilson near Macedonia, Georgia, he made himself a mouth bow, something akin to a Jew's harp. Soon after, he made a simple guitar. Though not yet ten, he went to Saturday night dances and learned to play by observing performances of various musicians.

He finished the third grade before running away from the Wilsons when he was ten. Later, in his 1964 composition "Drop Out Song," he urged other youngsters not to follow his example but rather to see that they got good educations. Still, he was street-wise and, as his nickname of later years, "Lone Cat," suggested, independent. In the years after leaving the Wilsons, he got by in various ways. He grazed cows, worked in a buggy factory, did housework, delivered groceries, worked in a chair factory in Brunswick, Georgia, laid track on the railroads, and made extra money by singing on street corners. He attended minstrel and other shows when he could, picking up songs he could play on guitar (he developed a Piedmont finger-picking style) or harmonica.

His roster of occupations continued as he reached his late teens. At eighteen he was a wood chopper, and a few years after he worked for a junkman in Griffin, Georgia. In his early twenties, he finally left the South, going to Cincinnati, where he worked on a streetcar for a while. Then he joined the Hagenback Wallace Circus as a canvas stretcher. World War I had just ended when the circus went through Michigan, and Jesse earned what for him was a sizable amount of money playing his guitar in the streets for the returning troops.

When he was twenty-four, he hopped a freight and went to California, which became home from then on. He worked shining shoes near the gate of the United Artists Studio in Los Angeles. Douglas Fairbanks Sr. liked him and got Jesse bit roles in several movies, including *East of Suez, Thief of Baghdad, End of the World,* and *Hearts of Dixie.* Director Raoul Walsh later financed a hot dog stand for Fuller, and he also sold toy wooden, cloth-covered snakes, but Jesse left that for a job on the Southern Pacific Railroad.

In the 1930s he relocated to Oakland and vicinity, working as a construction worker days and playing occasional pickup music dates at night. The railroad gave him an annual pass for "self and wife." He returned to Georgia and married for the second time, then returned to Oakland. He worked in the shipyards during World War II, eventually buying a house in West Oakland, where he raised three daughters. In the late 1930s he played "John Henry" on an Oakland radio station. His musical activity gradually increased until, by the late 1940s, both jazz and folk artists in the San Francisco area often sought him out.

In the early 1950s he began to play steadily at a small club in San Francisco called the Haight Street Barbecue. He also opened a small shoeshine stand on College Avenue in Berkeley that attracted many folk music fans. They enjoyed hearing him play both traditional folk music, mostly blues, and some of his own originals, which, after 1954, included the "San Francisco Bay Blues." The following year he recorded *Folk Blues: Working on the Railroad* for World Songs.

During those years Fuller devised a new kind of instrument he called a "fotdella." Essentially a one-man-band rig, it included a right foot pedal to operate a hammer against an arrangement of seven piano strings that served as a bass, a left foot pedal to run a high-hat cymbal or a washboard, and a harness to hold a harmonica and kazoo. While sitting amid all this, he also played a six- or twelve-string guitar with his hands.

Helped by close friend folksinger Barbara Dane, Jesse's career began to blossom in the late 1950s. He and Barbara were featured at the Ash Grove in Los Angeles in 1958 and also performed at other folk venues in the state. In the summer of 1959 he played at a folk festival at the University of California directed by Alan Lomax. Later that summer, he went to the Monterey Jazz Festival uninvited, was set up outside the stands by Festival director Jimmy Lyons, and vied with major jazz acts as a highlight of the program. As a result, he received an invitation to tour Europe.

Things got even better for him in the 1960s. He got the chance to perform at an increasing number of festivals, concerts, and coffeehouses. As the decade went by, he delighted audiences in all parts of the United States. He created a sensation in England in 1966, starring twice with legendary rock groups—the Rolling Stones and the Animals.

Some of his songs were played by rock 'n' roll bands as well as by folk performers. Ramblin' Jack Elliott recorded "San Francisco Bay Blues" in the late 1950s, which influenced Bob Dylan in the early 1960s. Peter, Paul and Mary sold many records of their single of the song, which was recorded by dozens of other folksingers over the years. Jesse himself was represented by several albums titled *San Francisco Bay Blues,* one on Prestige Records that came out in 1963 and another of that title on the Good Time Jazz label shortly afterwards. Good Time Jazz issued *Jesse Fuller: Jazz, Folk Songs, Spirituals & Blues,* which came out in August 1958, and followed that with the LP *The Lone Cat* in May 1961. His singing and playing also were offered on the Folk-Lyric Records' release *Greatest Negro Minstrels* (11/63). His mid-1960s releases included *Favorites* on Prestige (5/65) and *Frisco Bound,* originally on Cavalier and later released on Arhoolie Records (7/67). Arhoolie also included Fuller in the compilation album *The Roots of America's Music.* In the mid-1960s, Vanguard also included work by Fuller on a couple of compilations: *The Great Bluesmen* and *Evening Concerts at Newport, 1964, Vol. 2.*

Fuller was admitted to the Dowling Convalescent Hospital and died in 1976 of heart disease.

By the start of the 1980s, though folk artists still included some of his songs in their repertoire, little of Jesse's recorded work was still available. A few albums of his 1960s work continued to be offered by small record companies, an example being Fantasy Records' 1972 release *Brother Lowdown* (reissued in 1992), a repackaging of Fuller's Prestige recordings; Fontana Records' *Session with Jesse Fuller,* released in 1965; and *The Lone Cat* on Good Time Jazz.

Jesse Fuller had a great impact on many rock bands. The Grateful Dead often performed Fuller's songs "Beat It on Down the Line" and "The Monkey and the Engineer." In the 1990s, Eric Clapton included "San Francisco Bay Blues" on his best-selling MTV *Unplugged* album, drawing renewed interest.

Original Blues Classics Records reissued several of his albums in the 1990s, including *The Lone Cat, Jesse Fuller's Favorites, San Francisco Bay Blues,* and *Jazz, Folk Songs, Spirituals & Blues.* Arhoolie reissued *Frisco Bound* in 1993.

GABRIEL, PETER: *Singer, guitarist, keyboardist, harmonica player, songwriter, record company founder (Real World Records). Born London, England, May 13, 1950.*

The English progressive rock band Genesis lived up to its name by giving birth to some of the most influential solo performers of the late 1970s and early 1980s. Among its alumni were Peter Gabriel, Steve Hackett, and Phil Collins. First to go out on his own was Gabriel, whose persona originally had given Genesis its upward impetus. He achieved stardom by eschewing the role-playing that marked his Genesis phase, concentrating instead on increasingly sophisticated social commentary in his new performing repertoire.

Gabriel, who grew up in reasonably comfortable surroundings in the England of the 1950s and '60s, began learning various instruments, including piano, in his preteen years. His early inclination was toward folk music. In fact, at one point in the mid-1960s, he quit a job in a London travel agency to work as a street musician, or busker, performing songs such as "Where Have All the Flowers Gone" at the Tottenham Court Road subway station.

The genesis of Genesis took form at Charterhouse School in London in 1966, when Gabriel formed a songwriters collective with friends Tony Banks, Michael Rutherford, and Anthony Phillips. The writing activities gradually evolved into a rock group, which became the basis for Genesis in 1969. With Gabriel as lead singer and a prime contributor of original words

and music, the band began to win attention from London rock fans in 1970, when its debut LP, *Trespass,* came out on ABC Records. Over the next few years, buoyed by enthusiastically received concerts in the United Kingdom and the United States, the band's albums reflected steady creative growth, though much of its popularity could then be traced in part to Gabriel's flamboyant stage presence.

In his live performances, Gabriel seemed more actor than vocalist. He affected heavy makeup, odd masks, and all manner of special costumes. For the song "Watchers of the Skies," for example, he wore a batwinglike garment; for "Dancing with the Moonlit Knight," he typically donned a "Britannia" outfit (a "cheap" Britannia format, as Tony Banks indicated, to represent the "degradation of the nation"). On "Willow Farms" (which dealt with a man who turned into a flower), Peter had a flowerlike getup. Gabriel also used unusual hairdos, for example, having his head half shaven, leaving a Mohawk-like sheaf of hair down the middle.

Other band members were appreciative of the visual impact he had on audiences, though uncomfortable that it tended to obscure the songs themselves. Tony Banks told Richard Cromelin of the *Los Angeles Times* in October 1974: "Unfortunately the publicity is angled very much around it, so the audience gets the wrong impression sometimes. They're all really overstatements of what the song's about just to try to get across the mood."

Even as Banks made those statements, the situation was about to change. Gabriel had become increasingly restless with the restrictions of the Genesis format. After a 1974 tour, he decided to go it alone though he performed with the band into 1975.

As he told Robert Hilburn (*Los Angeles Times,* April 13, 1977): "The writing process with the band had become a little stale. We had fallen into habits. We weren't challenging or testing anything. As the band got more successful, it was increasingly difficult to encourage people to take a risk with something that might jeopardize their livelihood. I finally decided it was time for me to make a move. We were at a point where the real money was starting to come in for the first time. I was afraid that if I didn't leave, I might get used to the new way of living and would have found it hard to go because of the financial security."

He took all of 1975 off to expand his record business contacts and work on new material. For a time, he toyed with the idea of remaining behind the scenes as a songwriter rather than returning to performing. His mood was further unsettled when Genesis's first post-Gabriel album, *A Trick of the Tail,* became a massive worldwide hit. Some people suggested his contributions to the band weren't as important as once thought.

However, he was encouraged by U.S. musician friends to persevere and in 1976 got the go-ahead from Atco Records to start work on a solo LP. With Bob

Ezrin as producer, the new collection took shape, including such Gabriel songs as "Solsbury Hill" (a country-flavored treatment of his breakup with Genesis), a high-powered rocker called "Modern Love," and a Randy Newmanish track "Here Comes the Flood." Reflecting his loss of confidence after Genesis's recent success, he began his concert tour in support of the well-received 1977 solo debut album, *Peter Gabriel*, in the United States instead of the United Kingdom.

In keeping with his search for a new image, Gabriel played down the theatrics. Though he did make some minor adjustments for certain songs, he no longer sported a punk haircut, and he came onstage without outlandish garb. In many of his concerts of the late 1970s and early 1980s, his dress comprised a black boiler suit with asymmetric white stripes down the side of one arm and one pant leg.

In early 1978, he began work on his second album, this time with former King Crimson leader Robert Fripp as producer. This LP, also called *Peter Gabriel*, came out on Atlantic in late 1978 and featured such notable tracks as "D.I.Y.," "On the Air," and "Home Sweet Home." In 1979, while touring in support of that LP, he began work on material for his next album, songs with such somber content that Atlantic demurred at releasing the new collection, claiming it would be commercial suicide.

As a result, Gabriel switched to a new label, Mercury, for U.S. distribution. Produced by Steve Lillywhite, the 1980 album (again titled *Peter Gabriel*) proved to be one of his most striking offerings yet and certainly not a commercial failure. Among its contents were "Games without Frontiers" (a top 5 hit in England), "Family Snapshot" (dealing with the motivations of an assassin), and "Biko" (homage to the South African black poet-activist murdered by that government's pro-apartheid regime). "Milgrams 37," as he explained to English reporter Lynn Hanna, was based "on the famous American experiment in which volunteers were split into 'teachers' and 'learners.' The teachers were told to assist the pupils by administering shocks in the form of electric shocks. It was discovered that 63% of the volunteers were prepared to administer charges of 450 volts, which would have severely damaged or exterminated the learner (unbeknownst to the teachers, the learners were actors simulating pain.) . . . It shows just how far they'd go without questioning authority."

In the 1980s, Gabriel continued his approach of careful preparation of new material for each new album. Just as there was a two-year gap between his second and third studio LPs, there was a similar spread before his fourth release came out in 1982. This album, *Security (Peter Gabriel)* was on another label, this time Geffen Records. Among its tracks was "Shock the Monkey," which was a chart hit in both the United Kingdom and United States.

In 1986 Gabriel released *So,* which was certified platinum by year's end and reached double platinum levels by early 1988. It yielded two hit singles: "Sledgehammer," a number-one hit in the United States in July 1986, and "Big Time," a top-10 hit in 1987.

Though Gabriel had several nominations in the Grammy voting in 1986, he failed to win anything. However, he was a big winner in the 1987 American Video Awards, accepting the trophies for Best Pop Video and Best Male Performance ("Sledgehammer") at ceremonies in the Los Angeles Scottish Rite Auditorium. During the program he was also inducted into the National Academy of Video Arts and Sciences Hall of Fame.

Gabriel joined Sting, U2, and other rock stars in a summer 1986 fund-raising concert series for the humanitarian Amnesty International organization. In a December 1987 press conference in São Paulo, Brazil, Gabriel and Sting announced they would perform as well in a 1988 tour called Human Rights Now to coincide with Amnesty's drive to collect public endorsements for the Universal Declaration of Human Rights. The objective was to present the endorsements to the United Nations on December 10, 1988, the fortieth anniversary of that declaration.

In the 1990s Gabriel continued to command the respect of his music industry peer group for his charitable and creative work, and he remained a favorite with millions of fans the world over even though for a time in mid-decade he kept a low profile as both a concert act and recording artist. In December 1990, Geffen Records issued a "best of" collection, *Shaking the Tree—16 Golden Greats,* which was certified gold by the R.I.A.A. on August 3, 1992, moving on to platinum and multiplatinum (2 M) certification on June 24, 1996. His 1986 collection, *So,* served as a kind of annuity for the record label, reaching the 3 million mark in December 1991, the 4 million level in December 1994, and 5 million in October 1996.

In 1992 Gabriel completed a new studio album, *Us,* the first in six years and, as it turned out, the last such project for another long time period. The album, issued by Geffen in September 1992, went past gold and platinum sales levels by year-end. Gabriel went on an extended tour to support the release that wound up in 1994, and again, more years went by without new live concert appearances.

Gabriel, however, was not resting on his laurels but was focusing his attention on a variety of other projects, including supervising the choice of performers to appear on his world music label, Real World Records. He also was investigating other possibilities in the multimedia field. Headquarters for this work was the Real World Campus, located near Bath, England. Besides record offices, the complex included recording studios, personnel and equipment for interactive products, presentations on a world web site, and production of limited-edition magazines with enhanced CDs. Gabriel also created and often starred in the annual WOMAD tours featuring music and dance from around the world.

In the spring of 1997, a CD-ROM (compact disc–read only memory) titled *Eve* was issued by Real World Multimedia. The package provided a wild combination of art, puzzles, overdub, and video-manipulating capabilities, among other things. Musical features included vocal material by Gabriel, Sinéad O'Connor, or Youssou N'Dour and original artwork prepared by well-regarded modern artists designed to be seen against the musical background of four Gabriel songs, "Come Talk to Me," "Shaking the Tree," "In Your Eyes," and "Passion." Facts about the contents and preparation of *Eve* were made available in various places, including the Radio Real World Internet site, which described *Eve* as standing for "evolutionary virtual environment."

On-line information also outlined the format used for the fan publication, *Real World Notes,* and the available magazine-enhanced CD products. Among those, the directory disclosed, was a disc that provided world music tracks and a multimedia description of the making of *Eve.*

A Gabriel concert in late 1996 in Modena, Italy, provided the material for a two-CD set, *Secret World Live,* and a video released by Geffen in the fall of 1997. Writing in *People,* David Hiltbrand favored the video since it explained the reasons for unexpected ovations heard on the discs that were seemingly unrelated to the music. He noted, for instance, one such reaction came from the sudden eruption of water jets onstage during the song "Steam," "or when the entire band prances through some tricky choreography on 'Shaking the Tree.'"

GARCIA, JERRY: *Singer, guitarist, banjoist, band leader. Born San Francisco, California, August 1, 1942; died Marin County, California, August 9, 1995.*

Although best known as the lead guitarist and key figure in the high-powered rock band the Grateful Dead, Jerome John "Jerry" Garcia had strong roots in country and folk music. While he continued to play and tour with the Dead for almost three decades, he still found time for moonlighting projects covering a variety of nonrock formats from bluegrass to folk. He enjoyed the work of many folk-rock or folk artists and tried to widen their audience if he could. Folksinger Dave Van Ronk was asked to open for the Dead on several occasions, and he recalled feeling uptight when Deadhead audiences impatiently ignored him as they waited for Garcia and company to appear. He told stories about cutting his set short and stomping toward the wings, where he saw Jerry with a wide smile pointing back and saying, "Dave, I think what you need is to play a whole lot more songs."

As noted in the *Encyclopedia of Pop, Rock & Soul,* Jerry, born and raised in San Francisco, became interested in rock as a teenager, "but switched his interest to folk music after dropping out of school for a short stint in the Army, from which he was discharged as unfit for service. By the late 1950s, he was one of the most talented folk guitarists performing around San Francisco. Traditional country music attracted his attention for a while in the early 1960s. He did considerable research on the subject, along the way developing into one of the best bluegrass guitarists in the west."

In 1964 he formed a group called Mother McCree's Uptown Jug Champions with Bob Weir (vocals, rhythm guitar) and Ron "Pig Pen" McKernan (vocals, organ, harmonica), based in Palo Alto, California. There weren't too many opportunities for groups like theirs in their region at the time so they accepted a proposition from a Palo Alto music store owner, who played bass guitar, to switch to amplified rock as a condition for his supplying them with musical instruments. With later additions (not including the store owner) that group evolved into the Grateful Dead, whose participation in the Trips Festivals organized by novelist Ken Kesey became part of rock legend.

The Grateful Dead gained national and worldwide prominence in the 1970s and continued to attract massive crowds of "Deadhead" fans to concerts up to Garcia's death in 1995. During those years Jerry was active on many other fronts, turning out solo albums (beginning with the 1972 Warner Brothers release *Garcia*) and performing with a variety of other talented musicians. One of those combinations was called Old and in the Way, a group comprising Garcia on banjo, Vassar Clements on fiddle, David Grisman on mandolin, John Kahn on string bass, and Peter Rowan (vocals, guitar). Recordings of a live concert at the Boarding House in San Francisco formed the basis for the 1975 album on Round Records—the Dead's own label—called *Old and in the Way.* The excellent collection featured two Rowan originals, "Midnight Moonlight" and "Panama Red." The album was reissued on Rykodisc in 1984 and later on CD. Some of the musicians from Old and in the Way worked with Garcia in the Jerry Garcia Band in the early 1980s, and Jerry recorded some other albums with Clements.

Garcia's solo output in the '70s and '80s included *Garcia* on Round Records in 1974, *Reflections* on Round in 1976, *Cats under the Stars* on Arista in 1978, and *Run for the Roses* on Arista in 1982. The last named includes a fine Garcia interpretation of Bob Dylan's "Knockin' on Heaven's Door." Jerry was a longtime fan of Dylan's and covered some other songs by Bob in concerts and on records. During 1987–88, Dylan joined the Dead for a series of appearances, including one before 75,000 excited fans—many of whom hadn't been born when the Grateful Dead came into existence—at Philadelphia's JFK Stadium. After sets by the two principals and an intermission, Dylan joined Jerry and the band onstage in what *Los Angeles Times* critic

Robert Hilburn said was a surprisingly close-knit performance.

He commented ("Icons of the '60s Paired on Tour," July 13, 1987), "Though this was only the second stop on the tour, the band played the Dylan songs with an ease and grace that made them seem like part of their own repertoire. There is an extraordinary sense of communication between the band members that lets them move freely in a song without threatening the overall texture or rhythm. The Deadheads did get a chance to whoop it up when Garcia, on pedal steel guitar, supplied some country seasoning for Dylan's ballad, "I'll Be Your Baby Tonight,' and when Dylan went into his familiar 'All Along the Watchtower.'" Columbia released an album based on the tour, *Dylan and the Dead*, in February 1989. Among the Dead's songs played in the concerts were numbers from its 1987 Arista release, *In the Dark*.

During the 1990s the Grateful Dead continued to be one of the most successful touring bands in the world. Besides doing that, Jerry kept working with his sidebar group, the Jerry Garcia Band, and, in fact, was booked to play with it at MCA's Universal Amphitheatre in Los Angeles in November '95, the year of his death. Typically, the Dead brought in $50 million or $60 million or more in ticket sales per year, and, for the first half of 1995, its total for concerts of $29.3 million was second only to the reunited Eagles in income. Over the years the band also contributed to many charitable causes through its Rex Foundation, which, *Variety* noted, "dispersed millions to individuals, philanthropic organizations and environmental groups."

Jerry, however, suffered a continuing series of life-threatening health problems based in part on his long history of drug abuse. In early August 1995 he checked into Marin County, California's, Knolls Treatment Facility, reportedly to try to kick a recurring heroin habit. Two days later he was found dead in his bed in the early-morning hours of August 9. On that day and for some time afterward, some radio stations repeatedly played the Dead's signature hits such as "Truckin'" and "Casey Jones." Some stations played only Grateful Dead songs all day long.

After Jerry's passing, Arista Records began distributing both band and Garcia solo albums previously only available on the group's Grateful Dead label. (That agreement had been finalized shortly before Garcia died.) First release was a two-CD live set taped in Germany in 1972 titled *Hundred Year Hall*. Arista then started issuing nineteen catalog albums plus two archival *From the Vaults* live collections and three Garcia solo albums. Mandolinist David Grisman also released albums on his Acoustic Disc label of acoustic material recorded with Garcia, including *Garcia/Grisman* (1991), *Not for Kids Only* (1993), *Shady Grove* (1996), *So What* (1998), and the *Pizza Tapes* (2000).

GARFUNKEL, ART: *Singer, actor. Born Queens, New York, November 5, 1941.*

Certainly one of the great folk/folk-rock duos of all times, Simon and Garfunkel set new standards for their art form in the 1960s before going their separate ways at the start of the 1970s. Though they reunited for a few concerts in later years, they never resumed their old partnership. While Simon was more active following the split, Garfunkel also made his mark on the entertainment field as a solo recording artist and actor.

Young Art started to sing at the age of four after his father brought home one of the first wire recorders. He stated, "That got me into music more than anything else. Singing and being able to record it." His interest in music still remained strong when he became friends with Paul Simon when both were in sixth grade in Queens, New York. Before long, the two were singing in school events—mostly popular songs of the day.

Their early attention from elementary school into their high school years went to the '40ish pop songs still dominating the field in the early '50s. "Then rhythm and blues . . . rock'n'roll came along." The two began developing material in those genres. "We practiced in the basement so much that we got professional sounding. We made demos in Manhattan and knocked on all the doors of the record companies with our hearts in our throats. Just a couple of kids."

Under the pseudonyms of Tom (Art) and Jerry (Paul), they actually did make an impact on the pop field in the mid-1950s. Their single "Hey School Girl" made lower chart levels in 1956. The duo appeared on Dick Clark's *American Bandstand* and in some of the multiartist shows playing eastern theaters.

The outlook looked promising, but Art decided not to take a chance on the vagaries of show business. "I left and went to college. . . . I was the kid who was going to find some way to make a decent living." He enrolled at Columbia University with a major in art history and minors in architecture and education, getting his B.A. in 1965 and an M.A. in 1967.

But he didn't abandon singing. He turned out some solo singles and in 1962 rejoined Simon to sing at a fraternity house at Queens College, which Simon attended. That led to a decision to try to find more joint engagements. At the end of their sophomore year, they played Gerde's Folk City in Greenwich Village. A Columbia executive who heard the act offered them a contract. Those recording sessions provided the material for their debut LP, *Wednesday Morning, 3 A.M.* (1964).

The basic material for that was provided by Simon. As Garfunkel noted: "Up until then we sang and wrote rock and roll songs together . . . but suddenly one of us could write poetic folk songs. I really connected with that . . . so the rejoining, after several years, was on the basis of the two of us as singers and Paul as the songwriter. People always asked why I didn't write songs. It was because Paul was so good. It seemed foolish to go for equal time."

It took a while, and even another brief separation, but the debut album finally brought them national acclaim, primarily through the success of the song "Sounds of Silence" in late 1965. Simon and Garfunkel rapidly became one of the most esteemed singing teams in the United States and the world. They still were at the peak of their careers when they both decided they wanted to try new creative directions.

For Garfunkel, one of his initial goals was acting. His work with director Mike Nichols on the soundtrack of *The Graduate* led to the chance for featured roles in the major films *Catch 22* and *Carnal Knowledge*.

Meanwhile, Columbia was urging him to record solo material. He finally got back into the studio in 1972 for his 1973 debut solo LP *Angel Clare*. The gold album tended toward the sophisticated ballad side, but had folk elements as well. One of the tracks, "All I Know" (written for him by Jimmy Webb) became a top 10 hit.

He followed that with the 1975 platinum album *Breakaway*. The album rose to number nine on U.S. charts and number seven in the United Kingdom. Three of its songs made the hit charts: his update of the old pop ballad "I Only Have Eyes for You," the title track, and "My Little Town," a new song written by his old partner, Simon. The two recorded it together and it was included not only on *Breakaway* but also on a new Simon solo album. The two also made a rare joint appearance to sing the song on a *Saturday Night Live* telecast.

For his early-1978 third album, *Watermark*, most of the material was written by Jimmy Webb. Garfunkel handled production himself in the famous Muscle Shoals Studios in Muscle Shoals, Alabama. Discussing his approach, he stated: "In the past, I would have saved vocals for last. I would start with guitar and piano and build from there. This time I brought my voice down lower. I'm more a baritone tenor [as compared to the mainly high tenor stylings used on his previous two albums]. I wanted to stand there at the mike and sing the song."

To support the new album, Garfunkel agreed to do his first tour since the farewell concerts of Simon and Garfunkel in 1970. In 1979, he completed another album, *Fate for Breakfast*, issued by Columbia in April. The song "Bright Eyes" reached number one in England (it had been used in the animated film *Watership Down*). While Garfunkel's career seemed to be prospering in that period, he was shaken by personal tragedy. His girlfriend, Laurie Bird, who had appeared as Paul Simon's on-screen girlfriend in Woody Allen's film *Annie Hall*, committed suicide in Art's apartment from a sleeping pill overdose while he was on location shooting Nicolas Roeg's film *Bad Timing: A Sensual Obsession.* (In 1972, Garfunkel had married Linda Marie Grossman, but they divorced in 1975.)

In August 1981, Art put out the Columbia LP *Scissors Cut,* which included a cameo vocal by Paul Simon. In September, the two reunited for a free open-air concert in Central Park attended by several hundred thousand people amid reports this might be a harbinger of a full-scale reunion that would include a new Simon and Garfunkel LP. The concert was taped for telecasting on the HBO cable channel and also provided material for the 1982 double album, *Simon and Garfunkel: The Concert in Central Park.*

The concert response encouraged the duo to do an international tour that was completed in the fall of 1983. The album project, though, fell through. The two began to record some new material for the LP, but Simon changed his mind and completely revamped the tracks, replacing Garfunkel's work with his own so that the final LP was a Paul Simon solo vehicle.

Garfunkel then resumed his own solo activities, which included a three-year effort to complete the album *The Animals' Christmas,* based on the Jimmy Webb cantata. Joining him on the recording was gospel star Amy Grant. While completing work on that project, Art found time in 1984 to start his Walk Across America. As time permitted, he would walk a certain distance, note exactly where he finished each stage, then return later to that point to walk still more miles. In all, it took some twelve years for him to complete that coast-to-coast journey. *The Animals' Christmas* material finally was completed in 1986, and the disc was released by Columbia that October.

After that, Art moved on to record a new secular album, *Lefty,* issued by Columbia in March 1988. The tracks included his version of Percy Sledge's "When a Man Loves a Woman" and a duet with Kenny Rankin on "I Wonder Why." His concerts that year included singing before Prince Charles and Princess Diana at the Prince's Trust event along with Elton John, Phil Collins, and James Taylor. During the year, Columbia also released a "greatest hits" album, *Garfunkel*. On a personal level, Art married for the second time in 1988, to Kathryn (Kim) Cermak; their son, James, was born in 1990. He wound up the decade with completion of a collection of prose poems, *Still Water,* some of which dealt with his years with Simon and Laurie Bird's suicide.

The early 1990s included continued additions to his Walk Across America, which alternated with other events like a performance at an outdoor rally for democracy in 1990 in Sofia, Bulgaria, a concert witnessed by an estimated 1.4 million people, and his 1992 recording of Hoagy Carmicheal's song "Two Sleepy People" for the sound track of the hit film *A League of Their Own.* Art's next album, the 1993 *Up 'Til Now,* included a compilation of Simon and Garfunkel songs, live and studio work by Art providing such new material as a duet with James Taylor on "Crying in the Rain" and the Jimmy Webb composition "Skywriter."

Garfunkel still had some acting credits in the 1990s, appearing in the controversial film *Boxing Helena* in 1992 and in an episode of TV's *Frasier* in 1994. He also was the voice of the moose on the PBS *Arthur* TV series and sang "The Ballad of Buster Baxter" on the *Arthur* CD. In 1998 he made a cameo appearance in the film *54*.

Art completed his cross-country jaunt in August 1996, having traversed more than 4,000 miles in 100-mile installments. He applied his master's degree in mathematics to determine that he took 2,112 steps per mile. In December 1996, Columbia released the album *Across America*, a live album from a two-night concert at Registry Hall on Ellis Island. The Disney Channel aired a one-hour special based on that appearance. Art also sang the song "Always Look on the Bright Side of Life" for the 1997 movie (which starred Jack Nicholson) *As Good As It Gets*.

In 1997, his wife, Kim, joined him on *Songs from a Parent to a Child*, issued by Sony Wonder/Columbia, which also included son James's recording debut. The album was nominated for a Grammy in the Best Musical Album for Children category. He was accompanied on his 1998 concert tour by Eric Weissberg. Besides appearing at various venues in the United States and abroad, he also performed at the White House Easter Egg Roll in April 1998. He also was starting to add plans for still more "walks," announcing that he was following his Walk Across America with similar walks across Great Britain, Ireland, and Europe. In 1990, he was inducted into the Rock and Roll Hall of Fame.

GATEWAY SINGERS, THE: *Vocal and instrumental quartet, Jerome Walter, born Chicago, Illinois; Mrs. Elmerlee Thomas ("Mama Lee"), born Oakland, California; Ernie Sheldon, born Brooklyn, New York; Travis Edmondson, born Nogales, Arizona.*

It seems proper that the Gateway Singers played such an important part in the folk-music ferment that swept the United States in the 1950s. One of the best-known folk groups of the period, it included performers representing almost every region of the country. Before it disbanded, near the start of the next decade, it popularized many of the folk songs in the current repertoire of most performers.

The members of the group hailed from the four corners of the country, but came together in San Francisco. By the time he met the other three, the group's spokesman, bass singer and banjoist Jerry Walter, lived in Palo Alto. He had a long career in show business behind him, having started as a professional radio actor at nine, with such diverse radio credits as Santa Claus and Jack Armstrong, the All-American Boy.

The distaff side was represented by Mrs. Elmerlee Thomas, who was born and raised in Oakland. At the time the Singers formed, she was working as a laboratory technician at the University of California at Berke-

ley. Her early training included some success as a classical singer.

Lead guitar was provided by Brooklyn-born Ernie Sheldon. He too had many years of experience, having worked his way from New York to Los Angeles during a thirteen-year career as a singer and guitarist. Rounding out the quartet was the youngest member, Travis Edmondson, born in Arizona but a longtime resident of San Francisco when he met the others. His background included some military service, a job as a truck driver, and college training in anthropology.

The Gateway Singers began performing in San Francisco in 1956. They gained an engagement at the increasingly important San Francisco basement coffeehouse, the hungry i. Their efforts met wild acclaim from the audiences and their stay was extended for many weeks. Before long, they were written up in many major national publications and had bids for appearances on TV and in many clubs across the country. A recording contract with Decca added impetus to their careers as they turned out a number of hit singles and LPs.

One of their best-known songs was the title of the Decca LP "Puttin' on the Style." The album included such others as "Sally Don't You Grieve," "Monaco," "Bury Me in My Overalls," and "Rock Island Line."

The group provided two best-selling LPs in 1958, *Gateway Singers at the hungry i* and *Gateway Singers in Hi-Fi*. The former offered such numbers as "Hey Li-Lee," "Let Me Fly," "Big Rock Candy Mountain," "Rollin' Home," "All Over This World," "Kisses Sweeter Than Wine," "Malagueña Salderosa," "Hard, Ain't It Hard," "Rio Grand," "Fais Do-Do" ("Bon Soir Dame"), and "Rock About My Saro Jane." The other LP included "Ballad of Sigmund Freud," "The Fox," "Roving Gambler," "Erie Canal," "Roll Down the Line," and "Oleanna."

Soon after the Gateway Singers disbanded in 1961, Jerome Walter formed a new group called the Gateway Trio. The other Trio members were guitarist Betty Mann and bassist Milt Chapman. The Trio turned out several LPs for Capitol in the early 1960s, including *The Mad, Mad, Mad Gateway Trio* and *The Gateway Trio*.

GAUGHAN, DICK: *Singer, guitarist, banjoist, songwriter, record producer, actor. Born Glasgow, Scotland, May 17, 1948.*

A talented guitarist, considered by his musician peers as one of the best produced by the United Kingdom, and an excellent singer and songwriter, Dick Gaughan was a star in his home area, but as of the mid-1990s almost unknown in the United States because for many years he was denied entry. His American visa problems stemmed from the leftist sympathies he expressed in some, though not all, of his songs. With the lifting of some of those stumbling blocks in 1995–96, his first U.S. concert series since 1983 showed critics and fans what they had been missing all those years. As Steve Winick commented in a *Dirty Linen* review of Gaughan's set at the Bluett Theater, St. Joseph's University, Philadelphia, "In any style, on any stage, Gaughan is one of folk music's guitar geniuses as well as one of Scotland's finest singers, and this evening will be hard to forget for anyone lucky enough to be there."

Gaughan was born in Glasgow and raised in Leith, a part of Edinburgh, Scotland, in an environment where music was as accepted as the air people breathed. His Scottish-born mother, Frances MacDonald, had a fine voice and won a silver medal at the Gaelic Mods while still attending secondary school. As Gaughan said, "She joined the Army during World War II and she met my father who was in the Navy. She was a socialist and a passionate advocate of a Scottish Republic."

His father, whose name was also Dick Gaughan, was born in County Mayo, Ireland, and, his son pointed out, "was a Republican during the War of Independence like most Mayo people, but left after the Civil War as he regarded the Free State as a sell-out. Never set foot in Ireland again. [He] started playing fiddle like my grandfather, but took up playing guitar in the mid-50s during the great [UK] Skiffle boom and eventually ended up playing semi-pro in local dance bands. Growing up in a family where everyone played and sang made it a natural thing for me to play. From both sides of my family I grew up immersed in the traditional music and culture of the [Scots and Irish] Gaels."

Gaughan started learning guitar when he was seven and enjoyed playing and singing with friends and family as he progressed to his teens. At the time he didn't think of it as a full-time occupation, instead finding day work as a plumber while he began singing evenings and weekends in the mid-1960s at local folk clubs and pubs. His interest in the folk field, he said later, was spurred by hearing Pete Seeger's recording of "Waist Deep in the Big Muddy." An accident in his plumbing work caused him to take a closer look at music possibilities, and by the end of the '60s he was committed to finding outlets for his creative talents.

In January 1970 he gained his first gig as a professional musician and by July 1971 was working on his first solo album, which, he recalled, was recorded on a two-track Revox in the front room of producer Bill Leader's home. "We had to stop recording and go to the pub when the traffic noise was heavy," he noted. That LP, *No More Forever,* issued in the United Kingdom by Trailer Records in 1972, established him as a newcomer to be reckoned with. Most of the songs were traditional in origin, such as "MacCrimmon's Lament," which became a staple of many of his concerts in decades to come. Other tracks included such traditional numbers as "The Friar's Britches," "The Thatchers of Glenrae," "The Fair Flower of Northumberland," and "The Green Linnet" and "Rattlin' Roarin' Willie"—

based, respectively, on a Robert Burns poem and Hamish Henderson's "The John MacLean March."

Gaughan then became an early member of the Boys of the Lough folk group, handling vocals and guitar on their debut album on the 1973 group-titled release on Trailer. He then contributed two songs, "Bonnie Woodha'" and "The Auchengeich Disaster," to a double album by the High Level Ranters titled *The Bonnie Pit Laddie,* issued on Topic Records in 1975. This was followed in 1976 by another solo LP, *Kist of Gold,* whose tracks included "The Gipsy Laddies," "Lord Randal," "Banks of Green Willow," and another future concert favorite, "51st (Highland) Division's Farewell to Sicily."

His 1976 projects included contributing two songs to *The Second Folk Review Record* and the debut album of a new band he helped form, the folk-rock Five Hand Reel. The first of those releases was intended to help raise funds for the magazine *Folk Review,* for which Dick served as a reviewer and columnist in the mid- and late '70s. *Five Hand Reel,* issued on the Rubber label in '76 and reissued in 1987 on Black Crow Records, introduced U.K. fans to an important new pop band whose members, besides Gaughan on vocals, guitars, cittern, and tenor banjo, included Bobby Eaglesham (vocals, guitar, mandolin), Tom Hickland (vocals, fiddle, piano), Barry Lyons (bass), and Dave Tulloch (drums).

In 1977, the second Five Hand Reel LP, *For A' That,* came out on RCA and, like the earlier one, was reissued on Black Crow in '87. Also issued in 1977 on Topic was the solo LP *Coppers and Brass,* in which Dick, accompanied by Tom Hickland on piano, played a pulsating series of jigs (the title song, "The Gander in the Pratie Hole," "Strike the Gay Harp," etc.), reels ("O'Keefe's," "The Foxhunter," "The Connaught Heifers," and others), hornpipes, and 6/8 marches.

The juxtaposition of traditional and rock-based material represented by those two albums might have seemed strange to many U.S. reviewers. Gaughan told correspondent Elijah Wald of the *Boston Globe* ("Dick Gaughan's New Traditions," July 1995) that he thought fitting music into narrow cubbyholes was foolish: "I have this problem with the use of the word 'traditional.' I grew up in a family of traditional singers and musicians, and to me those are just songs. This idea of dividing things into 'This is traditional and this is not traditional,' I don't understand those concepts. There are songs I sing now that I've been singing since I was a kid, and I didn't make any real distinction between them and rock and roll. I mean, I was aware that I hadn't heard them on the radio, but they were just songs that nobody else sang; they were just our songs, you know?"

During a busy year in 1978, Gaughan was represented by a third album with the Five Hand Reel, the RCA release *Earl O'Moray,* and more solo performances. The latter included solo tracks shared with Dave Burland and Tony Capstick on *Songs of Ewan MacColl,* issued on Rubber, and *Gaughan,* issued on Topic. In the early 1980s, still working on new music material, Gaughan also moved in a somewhat different creative direction, working as an actor and theater music director with the Scotland Theatre Company. For the 1981 *Folk Friends 2* album, he provided three solo tracks, "The World Turned Upside Down," "The Father's Song," and "Lassie Lie Near Me." That same year, he took over production chores on his *Handful of Earth* album (issued by Topic), a role he shared with Andy Irvine and Carsten Linde on the 1982 album *Parallel Lines* (issued on the Folk Freak label) and with Linde on the 1983 *A Different Kind of Love Song.* The last named was the first to present a significant number of original compositions by Gaughan. Also in 1983, he performed the track "Your Daughters and Your Sons" on the compilation album *Songs for Peace.*

He had never been bashful about his political beliefs, and his mid-1980s albums had much more of that content than earlier collections, an example being the 1985 *Fanfare for Tomorrow,* which included "Sharpeville '85," "Liberation," and "Political Prisoners." This was followed by the '85 album *Live in Edinburgh,* whose tracks offered such songs as "Revolution," "Which Side Are You On?" "Companeros," and "Workers Song." The 1986 *True and Bold: Songs of the Scottish Miners* offered numbers like "Drunk Rent Collector," "Collier Laddie," and "One Miner's Life." In 1987, Dick paid tribute to another songwriter concerned with the travails of the working class in the Woody Guthrie tribute album *Woody Lives.* He wound up his '80s output with the self-produced 1988 Celtic Music release *Call It Freedom.*

He commented to Elijah Wald that he believed politics and music truly went together. "It doesn't make sense to me that any human being could be singing about what they see, what they experience and what affects their lives and ignore politics—to me that's ludicrous. Scottish and Irish traditional music always had a large part of itself which would now be regarded as political. Folk music . . . in its own way is dangerous. It's subversive to admit that ordinary working class people have actually got a culture and artistic merit. This flies against the vested interests of those who would have us believe that the poor are poor because they are stupid."

The 1988 album was the last solo or group collection bearing Dick's name until the mid-1990s. He continued to compose (at one point in his career he provided music for several BBC-TV programs) and do session work. In 1990, for instance, he played electric guitar on "Quietly Sing You to Sleep" and acoustic guitar on "The Rose of Summerlee" for the *Davy Steele/Summerlee* album and performed a duet with Billy Bragg on "The Red Flag" for the Elektra/Utility disk *Billy Bragg/The Internationale.* During the first half of the '90s a few of Gaughan's performances were included in compilations like the three-CD 1992 *Folk Heritage* set, the 1992 Green Linnet release *Heart of the Gaels,* the 1993 *The Folk Collection* on Topic, and the 1993 live CD of the annual folk festival at Rudolstadt, Germany.

In the mid-'90s, when not adding to his solo touring credits in the United Kingdom, Europe, and, finally, the United States, Gaughan helped found the octet called Clan Alba. Joining him in the band were Mary MacMaster, Brian McNeil, Fred Morrison, Patsy Seddon, Davy Steele, Mike Travis, and Dave Tulloch. He co-produced the group's debut album, *Clan Alba,* released on the Clan Alba Productions label in 1995.

He had lost none of his live performance charisma, Bob Flynn noted in a review of a show at Edinburgh's Pleasance Theatre on December 17, 1995. Writing in the *Guardian,* he commented, "While Irish traditional music expands on to the international stage, the Scots have been somewhat overlooked. But Gaughan is one of the most powerful voices in the field. He takes 'folk' and shakes it until it rattles, making songs from 1707 as relevant as today's rap rants. A hard-hitting vital force, Gaughan batters his guitar with the blurring speed of a thrash metal band. . . . Those who welcomed a return to social realism in pop with Bruce Springsteen's depressive *The Ghost of Tom Joad* should seek out Gaughan's blast-furnace performances to hear how music from the gut really sounds like."

In mid-1997, Red House Records/Appleseed Recordings issued two Gaughan CDs, *Parallel Lines* and *Sail On.* The latter was his first new album in eight years. *Parallel Lines* was an album originally recorded in the 1980s that hadn't been issued in the United States before; when it first appeared, the *Irish Times* called it "one of the best acoustic recordings ever released."

GEREMIA, PAUL: *Blues guitarist, harmonica player, pianist, singer, songwriter. Born Providence, Rhode Island, April 21, 1944.*

In the early 1960s, Paul Geremia (pronounced "Jeremia") became captivated by the old blues players, people like Skip James, Son House, Howlin' Wolf, Charley Patton, and Fred McDowell, who were "rediscovered" during the folk revival. He hunted for old 78-rpm albums in the Salvation Army stores and re-created the riffs from the scratchy old records. He later met many of the musicians and learned blues riffs from the masters themselves. Eventually, Geremia developed a reputation as a top-notch country blues six- and twelve-string guitarist. Though he never had a hit record, Geremia remained true to the idiom and continued to play roots blues on all of his albums. But beginning with his first album, Geremia also wrote his own songs, with clever and satirical lyrics. He sang them in a "husky-throated voice" and accompanied himself on guitar, piano, and harmonica.

A third-generation Italian-American, Geremia likes to joke that he was "born in the Providence River Delta." His father, Albert, was a salesman and ranch hand. His mother, Ann, was a secretary. His first instrument was the harmonica that his uncle, a bass player who worked in a music store, bought for him. As a teenager, he played a friend's electric guitar. His father had an old plywood Stella guitar that he never played, and Geremia took it with him when he left for college at the University of Rhode Island. (He went for a couple of years but didn't graduate.) In college he started playing guitar with some friends who were influenced by Chet Atkins, Pete Seeger, and Ramblin' Jack Elliott. In 1963, when he attended the Newport Folk Festival, he started hearing the great black blues and R&B players who had moved up to the Northeast. The first live blues act he heard was Mississippi John Hurt. He also heard some young white guys, like Tom Rush and Tim Hardin, playing the blues.

Geremia began his career in the mid-1960s, playing in coffeehouses, folk clubs, and the northeastern college campuses. In 1966 he gave up all other means of support and became a full-time musician. Izzy Young and Patrick Sky, who produced his first album, put him in touch with Folkways Records, and he released *Just Enough* on Moses Asch's label in 1968. The album included his interpretations of Robert Johnson, Blind Lemon Jefferson, and Blind Willie McTell songs. One reviewer, George Kimball, joked in *Rolling Stone* (July 22, 1971) that Geremia spent so much time on the road that "within the space of a month one Toronto newspaper headlined a feature on him with 'The Man from Philadelphia,' another paper referred to him as being Canadian, and a third implied that he was from the West Coast." His debut received strong reviews with limited sales and airplay.

He followed in 1971 with *Paul Geremia* on Sire Records. His second album again included his own compositions, such as "Elegant Hobo," described by Kimball as "a Mr. Bojangles with class." At the time he had moved to Cambridge, Massachusetts, and was performing two nights a week at a bar called Jack's while maintaining a rigorous touring schedule. Next up was an album called *Hard Life Rockin' Chair* on the Adelphi label in 1973.

He moved on to the Flying Fish label, based in Chicago, releasing *I Really Don't Mind Livin'* in 1983, an album of originals, and *My Kinda Place* in 1987. The latter album included eleven old-time blues tunes, including Leadbelly's "Silver City Bound" and Lonnie Johnson's "Nuts about the Gal." He also plays a harmonica tribute to Big Walter Horton. It was one of the first country blues albums put out by Flying Fish. The two albums were combined into one release on Flying Fish in 1991 (now available from Rounder Records).

It took him another six years to release his next album, *Gamblin' Woman Blues*, in 1993. Red House Records of Minnesota distributed the album in the United States, and Austrian-based Shamrock distributed it in Europe. The album, nominated for a W. C. Handy Award, includes eight covers of old blues tunes (Skip James, Blind Lemon Jefferson, and Peg Leg Howell among them) and four originals. *Los Angeles Times* critic Mike Boehm gave the album a strong recommendation: "You won't encounter a guitarist with a more engagingly idiosyncratic sense of rhythm than Geremia. . . . If the estimable [John] Hammond (who doesn't write original songs) embodies the blues at its darkest, most driven and crazily wired, Geremia's blues more often amble with a light, hopping gait and wear a grin" (March 18, 1993).

Boehm writes that "each song is a tragedy wrapped in a comedy." In the opening track, "Gamblin' Woman Blues," Geremia sings "love don't last forever, but time and trouble never end." In "Cocaine Princess" he has the line "Thank God you don't snort up the Mason-Dixon line." In another song, Geremia imagines the dismay of the Statue of Liberty at the goings-on in the United States: *If she saw what went on behind her back, she'd forsake you and me, Saying, 'Where's your guts and soul? Take care your own! Clean up your own back yard!'*

He equaled his strong release with his next album, *Self-Portrait in Blues,* also on Red House and Shamrock, in 1995. *Self-Portrait* was also nominated for a W. C. Handy Award for Best Acoustic Album. It includes a striking abstract portrait on the cover by 1960s folksinger and artist Eric Von Schmidt, of Club 47 fame, who taught Bob Dylan how to play "Baby, Let Me Follow You Down." He brought out Howard Armstrong to play fiddle and mandolin. Armstrong, who was born in 1909, had first recorded "Louie Bluie" in the early 1930s with Ted Bogan.

The album includes covers of songs by Skip James ("Devil Got My Woman"), Leroy Carr ("Midnight Hour Blues," originally recorded in 1932), Charley Patton ("Shake It and Break It," originally recorded in 1929), Blind Willie McTell ("Drive Away Blues"), and an excellent version of Leadbelly's "Leavin' Blues." It also includes several of Geremia's originals. He wrote one of these, "Henry David Thoreau," as he explains in the liner notes, "after a heavy dose of Walden Pond and Chuck Berry's music." Thoreau is *a cat who learned to read and write so well/He could transcendentalate just like ringin' a bell,* he sings.

Geremia's work is also included on three compilations: *Live at Café Lena* on Biograph, *The Hudson River Revival* on Flying Fish, and the Mountain Stage compilation put out by Blue Plate Records in 1995.

Geremia tours around the country incessantly, driving from gig to gig with a couple of guitars and a harmonica, keeping his overhead low. Occasionally he tours Europe, where he is quite popular.

In May 1997 Red House released his eighth solo

album, *Live from Uncle Sam's Backyard*. The live 1991 concert recording at a small club in the West Bank area of Minneapolis features Geremia playing originals, as well as covers of Willie McTell, Blind Boy Fuller, Robert Johnson, and Skip James. He also tells stories about his encounters with some of the old greats. Again the album features artwork by Eric Von Schmidt. *The Devil's Music* his ninth album, came out on Red House in July 1999.

Although he's only produced nine albums since 1968 (during the mid-1970s and 1980s the record companies weren't interested in country blues, and he had done a second album for Adelphi that was never released), Geremia seems to improve with age. "As a young revival musician, Geremia was pretty damn good," one reviewer wrote in *Sing Out!* (August-September-October 1995). "As a veteran of three decades of playing the music night after night, Geremia has become a master of the idiom, worthy of discussion alongside Blind Willie McTell, Pink Anderson, and the other traditional legends he started out emulating."

Based in part on answers to questions by Paul Geremia

GIBSON, BOB: *Singer, banjoist, twelve-string guitarist, songwriter, record producer, folk-music collector. Born New York, New York, November 16, 1931, died Portland, Oregon, September 28, 1996.*

As a solo performer and part of the Gibson and Camp folk-song team, Bob Gibson had considerable impact on the U.S. folk-music movement. As a collector of a number of previously obscure folk songs of Ohio and the Midwest, he also enhanced other artists' repertoires.

Gibson himself was not a native of the Midwest. He was born and raised in New York City, which, by the time he was in his teens, was the center of thriving folk-music activity spearheaded by people like Pete Seeger, Woody Guthrie, Leadbelly, Oscar Brand, and Burl Ives. Listening to folk-music broadcasts and recordings inspired Gibson to develop skills on guitar and five-string banjo and to learn a number of folk songs. By the late 1940s he was performing in folk clubs and in folk-music concerts.

Like many young folk enthusiasts of the period, he started to go off on collecting trips, ferreting out authentic folk ballads, especially in the Midwest. Thus one of his first albums, on Stinson Records, titled *Folk-songs of Ohio*, included such songs as "Katey Morey," "Ohio River," "There Was an Old Woman," "Workin' on a Pushboat," and "Father Grumble."

By the mid-1950s Bob was ranked as one of the best new folk artists. Following his initial TV appearance in 1954 on a Cleveland station, he performed on several network shows in succeeding years. He also gave a notable concert at New York's Carnegie Hall, which was the basis for a live LP issued by Riverside Records. His concert selections demonstrated a wide-ranging repertoire with material not restricted to Midwest origins. Among his offerings were "Sail Away Ladies," "Michael Row the Boat Ashore," "Marry a Texas Girl," "Day-O," "Go Down to Bimini," "Wheel-a-Matilda," "Good News," "When I Was Single," "You Must Come in at the Door," "Alberta," "The Erie Canal," and "John Riley."

Riverside Records issued two other albums by Gibson in the 1950s, *Offbeat Folk Songs* and *I Come for to Sing*. In 1959 he signed with Elektra; his debut album was *Ski Songs*, followed in June 1961 with the album *Yes I See*.

At the start of the 1960s, he and Bob Camp (later known as Hamilton Camp) became one of the most popular acts on the folk-music circuit. They played before sizable audiences in folk clubs, coffeehouses, and college auditoriums all over the United States. They were featured on the Elektra album *Bob Gibson and Bob Camp,* issued in December 1961.

By the early 1960s, Gibson already was demonstrating considerable skill as a songwriter either by himself or in collaboration with people like Shel Silverstein. In 1963 country artist George Hamilton IV had a number one hit with "Abilene," cowritten by Gibson, John D. Loudermilk, Lester Brown, and Albert Stanton. Many other performers included some of Bob's material on their albums, among them Peter, Paul and Mary, who scored one of their greatest hits of the decade with his "Well Well Well." His influence went well beyond writing and performing, though. He is credited with discovering or encouraging some of the brightest names in folk music, including Joan Baez. His work in the early to mid-'60s included recording albums for such artists as Brian Wilson (of the Beach Boys), Richie Havens, and David Crosby.

Judy Collins recalled, "Bob Gibson was one of the most important influences in my early career. He's a marvelous singer who has led us to extraordinary songs." Richie Havens stated, "When I first came to the [Greenwich] Village, Bob Gibson was the first inspiration for me to pick up a guitar and it was his song that did it for me."

As the resurgence of rock in the Beatles era pushed folk music into the background again, Gibson and Camp decided to go their separate ways. Camp was more interested in combining folk with rock while Gibson preferred the more traditional approach. Elektra released another Gibson LP at the start of 1964 titled *Where I'm Bound.*

Compared to his status in the days of the folk-music boom, Gibson had a relatively low profile from the mid-1960s on. He continued to perform on the folk club circuit and on the college concert scene and also appeared at a number of folk festivals over the years. At the start of the 1970s he was represented on Capitol Records with the LP *Bob Gibson.*

In 1976 Gibson and Camp reestablished their duo and began to appear at small folk clubs like McCabe's in Los Angeles. The songs they offered were in a more modern vein than in their previous association, examples being Camp's rendition of a song once in the repertoire of the group Quicksilver Messenger Service, "Pride of Man," and Gibson's offering of Shel Silverstein's "You Should Have Seen Me in 1961." The latter recounted the saga of many of the leading lights of the early 1960s folk boom who were idolized by fans back then but who never adapted to changing times.

For most of the '80s and the better part of the 1990s, Gibson worked as a solo artist, though occasionally working with Camp or other folk performers. His appearances mainly were in small folk venues, though from the mid-'80s on he was an important presence at the Kerrville Folk Festival in Texas, which by the '90s was the largest such festival in the United States and one of the major folk gatherings worldwide. His Kerrville activities included establishing and helping run the highly regarded songwriting school and competition aspect. He, of course, continued to add to his own backlog of songs, which by the mid-1990s comprised some 200 published compositions. Other credits in the 1980s included work on children's music with backing from the OshKosh B'Gosh company, which sponsored his Chicago children's TV program, *Flying Whales and Peacock Tails.*

His appearances at the start of the '90s included a role in the World Folk Music Association benefit concert in Washington, D.C. Later he got the chance to work on his first major label album in a number of years when Asylum Records added him to its roster, with a target date for completing the initial tracks by the fall of 1994. The previous year he had switched home base from the Midwest to Portland, Oregon, to be near an adult daughter. With a resurgence of interest in folk music among many younger fans, prospects seemed brighter for him than for many years. But in the spring of 1994, fate dealt him a body blow when he was diagnosed with a degenerative brain disease, a condition that soon brought about steadily rising medical expenses.

Meanwhile, he worked on his album project, which would offer songs written by longtime friend Shel Silverstein or cowritten by the two of them. The numbers, recorded in Nashville, included such tracks as "The Man Who Turns the Damn Thing On and Off," a satirical treatment of the impact of modern technology; a humorous song about everyone's future, "Still Gonna Die"; and the cowritten "Dying for Love," whose subject is a mutual friend who died of AIDS complications. When the final album track, "I Hear America Singing," was laid down in Music City on July 25, 1994, many friends and folk-music luminaries joined in the session, including Tom Paxton, Emmylou Harris, Peter Yarrow, John Hartford, John Brown, Cathryn Craig, coproducer (with Gibson and Silverstein) and Asylum Nashville president Kyle Lehning, Dennis Locorriere, Oscar Brand, Ed McCurdy, Glenn Yarbrough, Barbara Bailey Hutchinson, Spanky McFarlane, Josh White Jr., and, of course, Shel Silverstein.

The album, *Makin' a Mess—Bob Gibson Sings Shel Silverstein,* was released in late '94, representing Gibson's eighteenth album. It won almost unanimous critical praise and did well in the niche market at which it was aimed by the label. Before its release, in September '94, Peter, Paul and Mary and many other friends of Bob's organized a benefit concert in Chicago's Vic Theater to raise money to help pay his medical bills. Those taking part included, besides Peter, Paul and Mary, Roger McGuinn, Spanky McFarlane, Josh White Jr., and Hamilton Camp, who joined Gibson onstage to reprise some of their best-known duets. Two years later he died of complications from progressive supranuclear palsy.

GOLD, JULIE: *Songwriter, pianist, singer. Born Philadelphia, Pennsylvania, February 3, 1956.*

Julie Gold's story is inspiring for anyone whose dreams have been dashed by fate or recording executives. For years she wrote songs on the side, but that didn't pay the bills. She took a number of odd jobs to make ends meet. She had her share of publishing and recording contracts that fell through but she never gave up. Her mantra was "they're wrong, they're wrong." Just before her thirtieth birthday, while working as a secretary at HBO, she began scribbling the lyrics to "From a Distance" on a notepad. That song, recorded by Nanci Griffith, Bette Midler, and thirty-eight others, won the 1990 Grammy for Best Song and changed Gold's life.

The song takes an optimistic look at the world. Some have criticized the song as Pollyanna-ish, but it has touched millions. "It's a song about the difference between the way things look and the way things really are, and the way things could be," Gold says. As she sings, *And it echoes through the land. It's the voice of hope, It's the voice of peace, It's the voice of every man.*

Gold grew up in Havertown, a suburb of Philadelphia. Her father worked for the personnel department of the Philadelphia Police Department, and her mother worked as a secretary in the school system. For her fourth birthday present her parents took her to see *My Fair Lady.* Beforehand they ran into some cast members at a restaurant. During the performance, they waved at Julie from the stage. "That changed everything forever—that was the magic," she says. So did the Beatles. When she saw them on *Ed Sullivan* she vividly recalls John Lennon with the words flashed on the TV screen, "Sorry girls, he's married." She remembers going to the store to buy new Beatles records.

She knew she wanted to write songs early on. "As a little girl, I would sit in the backyard on the swings strumming a plastic guitar and making up songs to my cat, the trees, the birds and the sky," Gold says. "In junior high school you're conscious of what's happening socially. There was a kid with sideburns in my class named Michael. He would give me poetry and I would put it to music."

She began taking piano lessons in the first grade and later studied cello. She focused more on the piano and accompanied the chorus in junior high. At the Philadelphia High School for Girls, she began writing songs. She spent more and more time writing songs and less time practicing piano. She attended Temple University and majored in English. From her freshman year on, she was performing in bars, usually on Thursday nights at the Khyber Pass. She'd play tunes by Carole King, Dionne Warwick, Todd Rundgren, and others. "I actually turned 21 playing at the Khyber Pass," she says.

She graduated from Temple in 1978 and moved to New York with a dream of becoming a singer-songwriter. "I had a manager, a car, a beautiful apartment, the promise of a record deal. I had a gig in the neighborhood that I walked to. It was cocktail hour, from 5 to 7:30 P.M. on a little white baby grand. I got free dinner. I made my first set of friends and I got to play my own songs. I played the Bottom Line. But I didn't get the record deal, my manager dumped me, my gig closed. I never played the Bottom Line again until 1990."

Instead she took a series of odd jobs, demostrating toaster ovens, vacuum cleaners, and the like. She didn't have a steady paycheck until 1983, when she started as a receptionist for HBO, working her way up to secretary. "I tell any aspiring songwriter to get a day job," she says. "Don't become cynical or bitter. Go to the movies and the beach. You don't have to be impoverished to be a songwriter."

She had a small publishing deal with a company called Blending Well. She kept writing songs. But nothing took.

A combination of things inspired "From a Distance." Gold was too young to participate in the antiwar and civil rights marches of the 1960s, but was affected by them nonetheless. At the end of 1985, she was approaching thirty, "a turbulent time when you haven't achieved your life dreams." She had just served on a jury, finding the defendant guilty of attempted murder. Her brother was just about to get married. She had written about seventy songs by that point—"twenty good ones, fifty not so good." She lived in a one-room apartment and played Wurlitzer electric piano. She thought this might *be* her life. But then her parents decided to send the family's Knight upright piano to her. "I took the day off from work. It came off the truck and into my apartment. The guy told me I couldn't play it for 24 hours because it was so cold. It was like a block of ice. All I could do was polish it and hug it and put stuff on it."

She looked down on the piano from her loft as she tried to sleep. The next day at HBO she began scribbling "From a Distance." When she came home and sat at the piano, "the chords rang out at me."

Gold had been friends with fellow folksinger Christine Lavin since a songwriting workshop in the mid-1970s. They had been through the ups and downs of the business. As Lavin gained success, she never forgot her friends. "She was always dreaming up new ways to expose other people's talent," Gold says.

In 1986, Gold sent Lavin a copy of "From a Distance." It had been rejected by music publishers up and down the eastern seaboard. Lavin asked her to make ten copies of the song and she sent it out. It began getting some airplay in Boston and New York. Lavin also sent it to Nanci Griffith as a birthday present. Gold didn't know who Griffith was.

Gold came home from work one day and turned on the answering machine. "Hello, my name is Nanci Griffith and I just heard 'From a Distance,'" came the voice with a sweet Texas accent. "I think it's the most beautiful song I've ever heard. I'd like to put it on hold and put it on my next record."

"That was the flashing light that changed my life forever," Gold says.

Griffith, who co-published the song with Gold, recorded the song for her 1987 album *Lone Star State of Mind* on MCA. Although they share the royalties, Griffith played an important role in popularizing the song. "She's treated my child with the love that any parent would hope for," Gold says.

Griffith sent Gold a copy of the album at HBO. "It was the moment I had dreamed of, seeing my name on a record label. There it was. I played it on one of my bosses' turntables. I shed a few tears of joy. Then I went back to work."

Griffith's version was a hit in Ireland. One time Gold was sitting at her desk at HBO and she received a call from Nanci Griffith, who had just performed it in Belfast, Northern Ireland. "Protestants and Catholics embraced and wept. Julie you should see what your song is doing," Griffith said.

In 1987, when Griffith's piano player, James Hooker, took a leave from the band, Gold toured with Griffith and played piano on "From a Distance," by then a standard part of Griffith's show. On June 16, 1988, when Griffith and John Prine played Carnegie Hall, Gold accompanied her on that song. While her immigrant mother and other relatives watched, Gold backed Griffith on a Steinway grand.

On July 9, 1989, she finally quit HBO to work full-time as a songwriter. At the end of six months, although she hadn't sold any new songs, she received her first royalty check from BMI for foreign sales of "From a Distance." Gold could finally afford to take the next six months off.

Several others, including Kathy Mattea and Judy Collins, recorded the song. But the windfall came when Bette Midler recorded it. Stephen Holden, the *New York Times,* music critic, had mentioned "From a Distance" to Midler, and 'Miss M' recorded it for her *Some Peo-*

ple's Lives album. The album and single sold millions of copies, and the song was nominated for a Grammy. In 1991, Gold attended the Grammy Awards at Radio City with Christine Lavin. Midler opened the show with the song, which won the trophy. "Can you imagine?" Gold says, still incredulous.

Midler's version came out the same year that Iraq invaded Kuwait and it became the most requested song on Armed Forces Radio in Saudi Arabia. When the U.S. ground war began in 1991, Gold was performing at a Fast Folk show at New York's Bottom Line. She wasn't scheduled to do the song, but singer-songwriter David Massengill announced the ground war had begun and Gold sang it. "Performing it myself is always an honor, a privilege, a responsiblity. But almost every time I perform it I can't believe this is a song that I wrote and touches people and changed my life."

Griffith has recorded other songs by Gold: "Heaven" on her *Late Night Grande Hotel* album and her *Anthology* album and "Southbound Train" on *Flyer.* Gold wrote a song that became HBO's holiday greeting in 1991, "Try Love." The following year she wrote another song for HBO, "One Voice, One Heart," performed by the New York City Boys Choir. She co-wrote a song with Patti LaBelle called "When You've Been Blessed (Feels Like Heaven)" that rose to number four on the R&B charts. Broadway singer Patty LuPone sang "Heaven" as her grand finale for her one-woman show. Gold also wrote a song for the movie *Andre* called "Thanks to You," and a theme for the Channel Four News in New York that was nominated for an Emmy. She performed with Lavin in the Bitchin' Babes and participated in the 1993 album *Buy Me Bring Me Take Me Don't Mess My Hair.* In 1998 Gadfly Records released a solo album entitled *Dream Loud!* which was not a critical or commercial success.

Nothing has had the impact of "From a Distance." The song "is a gift that has kept on giving. The amount of money is really beyond my wildest dreams.... It has paid my bills and given me a safe future, thank God. I invested very conservatively."

She has a publishing deal with Cherry Lane to write eight songs a year. "Eight for me is a lot." She sits down at the piano every day and plays scales and arpeggios to "keep up her chops" and also to begin the process of writing new songs. But if she never has another song like "From a Distance" she will still be happy.

Based on an interview by Lyndon Stambler with Julie Gold

GOODMAN, STEVE: *Singer, guitarist, banjoist, songwriter, record producer. Born Chicago, Illinois, July 25, 1948; died Washington, D.C., September 20, 1984.*

During the 1970s, Chicago was the center of a mini folk boom. A number of very talented young artists and songwriters attracted growing attention not only from an enthusiastic (though relatively small) group of local folk adherents but also from many established performers who enjoyed visiting folk clubs like the Earl of Old Town to catch the work of promising newcomers like Bonnie Koloc, John Prine, and Steve Goodman. Their work didn't spark any folk revival along the lines of a decade and a half earlier, but they did have an impact on the national scene at times. Steve Goodman, in particular, won music industry respect in 1972, when Arlo Guthrie's single of Steve's now-classic "City of New Orleans" made top-chart levels.

Goodman was born and raised in Chicago, the son (as he fondly recalled in his 1977 tribute to his father after his father's death) of a warm-hearted used car salesman. In his early years, Steve enjoyed the first wave of rock stars, but by the time he picked up his first guitar at the age of thirteen it was 1961 and folksingers like Pete Seeger, Bob Gibson, and Bob Dylan were all the rage. As Steve moved through high school, his interests expanded to the work of earlier folk greats such as Woody Guthrie and the roots blues often played in Chicago black area clubs. Country music also was an influence, particularly the work of the great Hank Williams.

When Steve graduated from Maine Township East High School in the mid-1960s, his repertoire already was beginning to include some original compositions to go with the other folk and country songs he liked to sing. In the late 1960s, he had pretty much decided that he would try to earn his keep as a professional musician. Steve found the pickings meager, as might be expected in the folk-song environment of those years. However, he found it possible to survive until better days came along by earning a side income writing radio commercials.

As he told Rick Ansorge of the *Chicago Lakes Countryside* (March 16, 1978), it came about unexpectedly. "I was playing in the Earl [of Old Town] about ten years ago and was on the bill with a group called John Garbo's Banjo Rascals. One of the people in that group worked with an ad agency and talked me into coming down and singing one of those jingles for sixty bucks. It was for Dial Deodorant." He worked other such jobs for small amounts of money. "But then all of a sudden I did this Maybelline Blushing Eye Shadow spot and I got three hundred bucks for it. I didn't give it another thought, but a few months later it went on the air and they sent me a check for $1,500. This was in January of 1970." Steve's first recorded exposure came from his Earl of Old Town performances. The 1970 Dulwich Records album, *Gathering at the Earl of Old Town,* included three cuts by him.

Shortly afterward came the marriage to his wife, Nancy, and, as it happened, the birth of "City of New Orleans." After their marriage, they went to visit Nancy's grandmother in the South and the train ride inspired Goodman to begin writing a song mourning the decline of railroad transportation. Steve outlined the song's origins to WGN radio host Roy Leonard in 1972: "Nancy and I were going down to a small town in southern Illinois on the Illinois Central to visit her grandmother who was in an old folks' home down there. I just took out this sketch pad and wrote about what I saw out the windows of the train. Nancy was still asleep after an hour and I went down to the club car and ended up playing cards with a couple of old men. Everything in the song actually happened; I wish I had made it up. I'm not too good at fiction. I guess I can surround real events with some fiction every now and then to dress them up. But I don't come up with fictional situations too often. I have to see it first."

In 1971, Goodman's career took an upward swing. Steve was on a double bill in Chicago with Kris Kristofferson. Paul Anka, he recalled for Ansorge, "was singing one of Kristofferson's songs in his nightclub act so he came to see him play on his night off. In the process he heard me play and paid for some demo sessions in New York." The result was a contract from Buddah Records. Kristofferson lent a hand by producing that debut LP for Steve. The album, *Steve Goodman*, came out in 1971 and earned some fine reviews, but not much else. However, it helped bring more engagements for Steve, particularly on the college circuit. For years after that, Goodman's good-humored style and relaxed stage presence won him so many followers that, for most of the 1970s, his concert income rather than records sales kept him afloat. His broad smile and typically upbeat demeanor belied the fact that he was beginning to suffer from the ravages of leukemia, which eventually claimed his life. As Kris Kristofferson later pointed out, "A truly gifted artist, he took such obvious joy in his work and his life that he was a joy to be around. Unlike most of us, he knew he didn't have time to waste on anything but the good stuff. His spirit is a candle in the darkness."

More important, the debut album contained "City of New Orleans," which caught Arlo Guthrie's interest. Guthrie's version became a gold record in 1972. Goodman noted Guthrie "slowed it down a bit, changed one of the chords and read the words so good that I learned the song."

Goodman's second Buddah LP, *Somebody Else's Troubles*, was issued in 1972. Steve's peer group respect was indicated by the people who helped out on the album. Besides such friends as Jimmy Buffett and John Prine, the credits include the name of Bob Landy, an anagram for Bob Dylan. The release, though a good effort, didn't do much better than the first one. Problems between Goodman and the record company then kept him on the recording sidelines for two years afterward. When the situation finally was resolved, Steve moved to Elektra/Asylum, which issued his first effort for that label, *Jessie's Jig and Other Favorites.*

Still, though both critical and audience acceptance was better than before, Goodman was more successful as a songwriter than a performer. During the summer of 1975, country star David Allen Coe had a single of Steve's "You Never Even Call Me by My Name," which rose high on the country charts. In April 1976, Steve's second Elektra/Asylum LP, *Words We Can Dance To,* came out. Coproduced by Steve and sometime cowriter Steve Burgh, the album included such highly listenable tracks as "Unemployed," "Old Fashioned," "Can't Go Back," and "Death of a Salesman." The album did somewhat better with the buying public, indicating that Steve was slowly widening his following. (During 1976, Buddah released the retrospective collection, *The Essential Steve Goodman.*) In October 1977, his next LP, *Say It in Private,* was issued, providing probably his best collection to that point. The songs ranged from a tongue-in-cheek "tribute" to the late boss of Chicago, "Daley's Gone," a Goodman version of Hank Williams's "Weary Blues from Waiting," and one of soul star Smokey Robinson's "Two Lovers," plus a fast-moving folk-country commentary cowritten with John Prine, "The 20th Century Is Almost Over."

Backing Steve on that album as well as several tracks on the other two Elektra/Asylum albums was country great Jethro Burns. In a series of concerts in support of the 1977 LP, Goodman and Burns blended their talents in fine fashion. Burns (of the famous comedy team of Homer and Jethro) not only backed Steve on many songs but provided some of the major highlights with solo work on the mandolin.

Besides his performing and writing efforts, Goodman also did some record production work during the 1970s. A good example of his expertise was John Prine's 1978 release, *Bruised Orange,* the latter's debut on Elektra/Asylum and one of the best folk/folk-rock releases of 1978.

Steve's next solo LP on Elektra/Asylum was *High and Outside,* which came out in February 1979. On one track, "The One That Got Away," Steve was joined in duet by Nicolette Larson, a song recorded just before release of her first solo album. In October 1980, his LP *Hot Spot* was issued by Elektra/Asylum, a collection that turned out to be his swan song on that label.

In the early 1980s, Steve realized he was steadily losing ground to his disease. Unable to line up an agreement with another major record firm, he and his management team of Al Bunetta and Dan Einstein decided to start their own label, Red Pajama Records. This led to the release in 1983 of two albums, *Artistic Hair* and *Affordable Art,* mostly comprising material from live engagements. (The title *Artistic Hair* referred to the hair loss that resulted from chemotherapy treatments). An avid baseball fan, he wrote and recorded a theme song for his favorite team, the Chicago Cubs, titled "Go Cubs Go." His death (from complications following a bone marrow transplant) on September 20 of the following year came only four days before Chicago clinched its first National League pennant in decades.

His passing triggered widespread sorrow among top artists in many segments of the pop music field from rock and country to folk. Many of them, besides performing on the Red Pajamas *Tribute to Steve Goodman* album, issued in 1985, also commented on their great regard for him as an individual as well as a seminal artist. (In late 1984, the company issued an album of studio material Steve had been working on the previous year, *Santa Ana Winds,* following that in 1987 with tracks from his last sessions, *Unfinished Business.*)

The *Tribute* album comprised tracks from two tribute concerts arranged by Bunetta and Einstein. Among performers contributing were Arlo Guthrie, Bonnie Raitt, Jethro Burns, Jimmy Buffet, and John Prine. (Other concerts in his memory were to follow in later years.) At one of the benefits held in the Pacific Amphitheatre in Southern California, a crowd of 12,500 jammed the facility to hear several dozen musicians in a $5^{1}/_{2}$-hour celebration of Steve's career. Emcee Martin Mull kicked off the proceedings, which involved such stars as Willie Nelson, Emmylou Harris, Jackson Browne, and the aforementioned performers, by saying, "We could get maudlin and stand around extolling his virtues, his songwriting prowess, and start pulling out the Kleenex. But that's the last thing Steve would want. So instead we're going to have a party." The two initial benefit concerts raised almost $250,000, which was donated to several leukemia research organizations. The tribute album in 1985 was given the first Grammy handed out in the new Best Contemporary Folk category.

During 1984 Willie Nelson had come out with a new version of Steve's "City of New Orleans" that became a number one hit on country charts. In the 1984 National Academy of Recording Arts and Sciences voting Steve was posthumously awarded the Grammy (presented February 26, 1985) for Best Country Song. For 1987, Grammy voters selected *Unfinished Business* as Best Contemporary Folk Recording.

In the following years, Red Pajamas made some of Steve's earlier work available again on releases like the 1988 *The Best of the Asylum Years, Volume 1* and the 1989 *The Best of the Asylum Years, Volume 2.* In 1994, the company issued *No Big Surprise: The Steve Goodman Anthology,* a two-CD set comprising twenty-three studio and nineteen live tracks. Many reviewers considered it the definitive collection of Steve's artistic life, including some new finds in addition to previously released material. Dave Hoekstra, writing in *New Country* (December 1994), observed, "The anthology closes with a chilling, previously unreleased version of Goodman singing 'As Time Goes By.' It should come as no big surprise just how timely the Steve Goodman songbook is."

GORKA, JOHN: *Singer, songwriter, guitarist, pianist, banjoist. Born Newark, New Jersey, July 27, 1958.*

It's 2:00 A.M. in a packed hotel room at the Folk Alliance conference in Washington D.C., in February 1996. The soft-spoken, even shy, John Gorka is livid. There are too many people making too much noise in the hallway. Gorka wants everyone to hear the young performers at the showcase: Martin Sexton, Sloan Wainwright (Loudon's sister), and Greg Greenway. "Tell them to shut the (expletive) up," Gorka screams out the door. Shocked by the uncharacteristic timbre of Gorka's voice, people get *very* quiet, as Gorka introduces "Out of the Valley."

"I wanted to start out with a party song, the kind of songs I'm known for," Gorka jokes. The young folksingers listen intently as Gorka sings: *Until long after it matters/You don't know if you're good enough/You can bet your dreams will be battered/So just go after what you love.*

Earlier that day, in a concrete stairwell at the conference hotel, Gorka, a dark bearded man with sad eyes, talked about that song. "It's about chasing after your dreams before it's too late. Sometimes you need to leave home in order to realize your dreams. The price of that is high, but there's no other choice."

The valley in Gorka's song is the Lehigh Valley in Pennsylvania, where Gorka got his start in folk music, but it could be any valley. Gorka got his start at Godfrey Daniels, a coffeehouse in Bethlehem, Pennsylvania, where he met performers like Jack Hardy, Stan Rogers, Claudia Schmidt, and Nanci Griffith. "I always wanted to be one of those people whose picture was on the wall in Godfrey Daniels, one of those people who signed it 'Thanks for having me in.' "

Gorka has dedicated himself to maintaining a loyal audience just in case his recording contract suddenly evaporates. "I never wanted to rely on record companies or radio stations or press people exclusively," he told *Face Magazine* (February 15, 1995). "By touring heavily you can stay close to the people the music touches, and you can maintain an independence that way."

Gorka's songs are about characters, places, even snippets of conversation. "Vinnie Charles Is Free," from *Temporary Road* began in a bar in Portland, Oregon. "I thought I overheard somebody saying that they were having a party for their uncle who was getting out of prison," he says. "I don't know if it was true or not. See, that's one of the things about being a songwriter. It doesn't necessarily have to start out with a true story, or a real-life experience. It can be something that's perceived or an experience that you observed." Other songs were inspired by legends. "That's Why" about Elvis Presley, and "That's How Legends Are Made" was inspired by Canadian singer Stan Rogers.

Gorka grew up in Colonia, New Jersey. His father,

of Polish descent, worked in a factory and ran a printing press that made tags and labels. His mother, of Italian descent (which explains Gorka's song "Italian Girls"), went to work as a draftsman after his father died of a heart attack when John was thirteen. "The event has had a strong effect on his songwriting," notes Eliza Wing of *Rolling Stone* (1991). "He sings of wanting to see his father, show him a picture of his girl, tell him his son made out okay."

At fifteen, Gorka went to hear one of his heroes, Earl Scruggs, in Red Bank, New Jersey. He bought Scruggs's record *How to Play the Five-String Banjo.* "I wanted to be a banjo player first," he says. "I just always loved the sound of the banjo."

The Beatles influenced him as well; he took up guitar. "I had a split personality—the happy banjo music and the sad acoustic guitar songs. . . . I started writing songs pretty much right away because it was easier for me to write songs that sounded good by myself than it was for me to learn other people's songs the right way."

Gorka, an "intense white guy from New Jersey," is blessed with a beautiful baritone. Greg Brown described it as "a saxophone kind of a voice. I'd love to put a tuxedo on that voice, put a good horn section behind him and let him croon." Songwriting became a way to express himself. "I can organize my thoughts better and present what I really want to say. My best thoughts go into my songs," he told Wing.

He wrote his first song at sixteen, about sitting in his room trying to write a song. He listed his interests in the high school yearbook as guitar, banjo, and songwriting.

Gorka left New Jersey in 1976 to attend Moravian College in Bethlehem, Pennsylvania, fifty miles north of Philadelphia. He played banjo and guitar at a freshman orientation event. Another freshman, Russ Rentler, played guitar and mandolin. Doug Anderson, also in the audience, got Gorka and Rentler together to form the bluegrass Razzy Dazzy Spasm Band, with folksinger Richard Shindell.

Anderson introduced Gorka to new kinds of music through his extensive record collection. He also introduced Gorka to a neighborhood coffeehouse called Godfrey Daniels on the south side of Bethlehem, which was run by Dave Fry. Gorka began playing the open-mikes. He tended the snack bar and cleaned up after the shows. Eventually he started planning some of Fry's festivals and emceeing the open mikes. He graduated college in 1980 with majors in history and philosophy but he learned his most important lessons at Fry's venue. After graduation, Gorka remained in Bethlehem, delivering flowers to make ends meet and beginning his apprenticeship.

In June 1979, Gorka and Rentler opened for Jack Hardy at Godfrey Daniels, his first time as an opening act. "He was the first writer that I ever met who wrote songs on a schedule," Gorka told Adrienne Redd and Mark D. Moss of *Sing Out!* (November-December

'94–January '95). "That turned me around. I had been basically just writing from inspiration, whenever it would strike, and I was frustrated that I wasn't writing as many songs as I wanted. Jack was finishing a song a week at the time."

Gorka vowed to write a song a month. By the end of the first year, he had written sixteen songs. Meanwhile, he gained the support of such musicians as Nanci Griffith, Rogers, Schmidt, and Hardy, the founder of *Fast Folk Music Magazine.* Gorka recorded his first songs for *Fast Folk* while on a trip to New York City in 1983.

By 1984 Gorka was opening for Nanci Griffith at Godfrey Daniels. She persuaded him to enter the New Folk category at the Kerrville (Texas) Folk Festival. He sang "Branching Out" and took first prize. "That was the first time I thought that the songs could travel beyond people who knew me, that people weren't just being nice to me," he told *Performing Songwriter* (July-August 1993).

Gorka knew he wanted to make a solo album, but his earliest solo efforts didn't work out. He met producer Bill Kollar at one of Hardy's gatherings. Kollar had his own studio and asked Gorka if he wanted to remix his recordings. Instead, they started over. That resulted in Gorka's 1987 debut, *I Know,* on Red House Records. The album included the first song he felt was a keeper, "Like My Watch," and such standard Gorka songs as "I Saw a Stranger with Your Hair" and "Love Is Our Cross to Bear." The album was a moderate success but didn't lead to a second one with Red House. Some friends, including folksinger Christine Lavin, sent *I Know* to Will Ackerman of Windham Hill Records. The label, known for its New Age music, included one of Gorka's songs ("I Saw a Stranger with Your Hair") on the album of new singer-songwriters *Legacy, A Collection of New Folk Music.* (Fellow folksinger Bill Morrissey is seen holding up a placard on the record cover saying "I wrote all of Gorka's songs.") Gorka signed with Windham Hill's High Street subsidiary and made *Land of the Bottom Line* in 1990.

Ackerman wanted Gorka to re-record the songs from *I Know,* but Gorka agreed only to include two songs from the previous release. The album, produced by Kollar, includes such standout tracks as "Land of the Bottom Line," inspired by his two-year stint as an associate editor at *Sing Out!* One line in the title track—*You fill your clothes with keys and damned responsibilities*—had "rattled around in my head for a couple of years before I found a place in a song [for it]," Gorka says.

Gorka lets his songs percolate. "They all seem to have their own way of making their way into the world," he says. "Sometimes it's a phrase I hear. Other times it's something I learn on the guitar. Other times it's just a feeling I get that points in the direction of the song and everything else follows from that. Every song is different. That's one of the things that keeps me interested in the creative process. There's still a real mystery to it. . . . There are certain times of the day—when I'm waking up in the morning or going to sleep at night are the best times for the lines to the songs to come."

Also on the album are: "The One That Got Away," with harmonies sung by Shawn Colvin, and the offbeat "Promnight in Pigtown." Like most of the album, there is a dark side to this novelty song: *After desserts they bobbed for apples/All knowing soon they could be scrapple/Another packaged processed food.* Many of the songs have a melancholy feel to them: "Armed with a Broken Heart," "Love Is Our Cross to Bear."

He followed in 1991 with the more upbeat *Jack's Crows* (named for Hardy), in which he is backed by Colvin, Lucy Kaplansky, and David Wilcox. "Emotionally I feel like I'm on more stable ground," he told Wing. "I don't have to say, 'Oh, woe is me' so much. I guess it's love. I've got a girlfriend who's an emotional base. Hopefully *Bottom Line* will be the only brokenhearted record I'll ever write."

Wing called Gorka "the preeminent male singersongwriter of . . . the New Folk Movement." But Gorka joked with *Performing Songwriter* that she had used a "double oxymoron," New/Folk and Folk/Movement. "As far as I know folk music has always been here, never gone away," he said.

"Houses in the Fields," is about the rampant development he saw as a boy growing up in New Jersey. When he saw it happening on the road between Bethlehem and Easton, Pennsylvania, he turned the image into a song. The album also includes "I'm from New Jersey," which draws laughs in concert with lines like *There are girls from New Jersey who have that great big hair / They're found in shopping malls. I will take you there.* ("I used to have big hair too. I miss it now," Gorka jokes.) Other witty concert songs include a spoof on country, "The Pilot Light Is Out on Our Oven of Love," and his "Body Parts Medley," best left to the imagination.

His next album, *Temporary Road* (1992), was his most commercially successful. (A video from the album, "When She Kisses Me," was voted the Country Music Television Best Independent Video of the Year.) He also appeared on Austin City Limits and CNN. He described the album, which came out just after the Gulf War, as "songs of love and war, with a secondary theme of crime and punishment." Four of the songs are war related: "Temporary Road," about a young soldier skating on a frozen river; "The Gypsy Life," written during the Gulf War "when I felt I couldn't believe anything I was reading, hearing, or seeing in the news;" "Can You Understand My Joy?" about the effects of war; and "Brown Shirts," which criticizes President Bush's use of the term "New World Order." He balances those topical songs with ones that indicate his mood swings have improved. "Gravyland" is about his real life exceeding his dreams. "I Don't Feel Like a Train," with Nanci Griffith on backing vocals, shows Gorka's ability to

freshen up an overused metaphor: *I don't feel like a train anymore / I feel like a track/And if you want to change your luck/Put a penny on my back/Now my feet go everywhere.*

Gorka recorded his album, *Out of the Valley,* in 1994. Produced by John Jennings, the album contains more character-driven songs than his previous work, and an all-star cast: Mary-Chapin Carpenter, Kathy Mattea, and Jonnell Mosser on vocals, guitarist Leo Kottke, bassist Michael Mannring, and Dobro player Jerry Douglas. Standout tracks include "Up until Then," the whimsical "Flying Red Horse," about "what might happen if one of those horses escaped from the gas station sign," and "Good Noise," urging people to give back to society.

He recorded the album at Imagine Sound Studios in Nashville, using the mixing board often used by Roy Orbison and Elvis Presley at RCA's Studio B. One of the songs, "That's Why," was Gorka's attempt to humanize Elvis, as the nation was dehumanizing him in its debate over whether to put the fat or skinny Elvis on a postage stamp. "He was a real person but almost everything we know of Elvis was not of his own doing," Gorka says. "His image was partly Colonel Parker's creation, partly the media's creation, and partly our creation. That's why people say he never died. I tried to make him into a human being again."

At this point, Gorka hardly faces the problems of Elvis, although he is considered a leader in the folk movement. His albums sell a respectable 60,000 to 70,000 copies, and he performs up to 150 shows per year. He had to overcome his shyness and a slight stammer to be able to perform. "For me, music is a way out, my way of connecting if not with the whole rest of the world, at least part of the world outside myself," he told *Face Magazine.*

Windham Hill gave him artistic freedom but when BMG took over the label, they wanted more control. "It was a bad situation," Gorka said in Febraury 1996. "In general they were really good to me early on in the way they promoted me. I thought it was in line with the kind of music I was doing. Somewhere along the line they felt in order for me to sell more records they'd have to change my image and also change the sound of what I was doing. That didn't set well with me."

In August 1996, High Street released *Between Five and Seven.* The album included "Blue Chalk," which had been recorded by Maura O'Connell and received some airplay. The song refers to a friend with addiction problems: *Hold tight hang tough/Love's not enough/To keep you off that stuff.* The album, co-produced by John Jennings and Gorka at the Paisley Park Studios in Minnesota, showcases Michael Mannring on fretless bass, J. T. Brown on a Martin acoustic bass, and Peter Ostroushko on violin and mandolin. It is a jazzier sound than his previous work.

In a concert at Santa Monica's Ash Grove in October 1996, Gorka came out on stage wearing a purple T-shirt, black jeans, and his trademark red shoelaces in black shoes. Accompanied by Mannring, he played a mix of old and new songs, from "Stranger with Your Hair" to "Blue Chalk." He joked that he used to have his songlist prepared in advance, but now tries "to cut down on the slickness with the right balance of chaos and order. I've been trying to make the shows more chaotic."

In the fall of 1997, Gorka signed a three-record contract with his original label, Red House, which released *After Yesterday* in 1998. Gorka's new songs reflect a change in life. In 1996 he got married and moved from Pennsylvania to Minnesota; the baby boy came along in 1997. As he sings in the title track: *Make way for a new day, make room for a child.* In "Cypress Trees" he sings, *Maybe we will grow together like cypress trees in summer standing tall.* After years of traveling on his own, Gorka suddenly had new priorities. "It's definitely harder to leave home now, and it's a little bit harder to make the transition from dad to performing musician," Gorka told Noah Adams of National Public Radio (November 24, 1998) for a story about how he inadvertently forgot about a concert in Alabama. But being a parent is not all sweetness and light. There is also piss and vinegar. As he sings in "When He Cries," *He looks like an angel when he's sleeping but he looks like Charles Bronson when he cries.*

Not to be missed is Gorka's superb rendition of Stan Rogers' "The Lock Keeper" on *Folk Scene Collection* (Red House, 1998), recordings made for Roz and Howard Larman's L.A.-based "Folk Scene" radio show. He also does a fine version of "The Water is Wide" for the Pete Seeger tribute album *Where Have All the Flowers Gone* (Appleseed, 1998). In 2000 Gorka and his wife had a baby girl and he went on "paternity leave." In the meantime he was working on a new album.

Based on an interview by Lyndon Stambler with John Gorka

GREENBRIAR BOYS: *Bluegrass vocal and instrumental group, formed 1958.*

The enthusiasm for bluegrass-style music that flared up across the country in the 1950s started with the traditional groups, such as Bill Monroe and Flatt and Scruggs. Before long, as in other areas of folk music, city artists began to appear. One of the best of the latter groups was the Greenbriar Boys, formed in 1958 by Bob Yellin, Eric Weissberg, and John Herald. Yellin, brought up in New York, studied violin, voice, piano, and trumpet in his early years, then picked up the bluegrass style of five-string banjo playing in college.

The group gained closer knowledge of the style by touring the rural areas of the South soon after assembling. They appeared in many small clubs and coffee-houses and proved their ability by winning the old-time band competition at the Fiddler's Convention in Union Grove, North Carolina, in 1959. That year, the first change occurred in the Greenbriar makeup when Ralph Rinzler replaced Weissberg. Rinzler was no stranger to the group, having helped introduce guitarist Herald, a descendant of poet John Greenleaf Whittier, to folk music some years earlier.

As the 1960s began, the group received favorable critical comment for appearances at concerts and folk festivals and on radio. They added to their laurels by winning the banjo contest at Union Grove two years in a row, 1960 and '61. In the early 1960s, the group added a beauteous lead singer, Miss Dian Edmondson. She appeared with them during several shows on ABC-TV's *Hootenanny* in 1963–64. She also joined them on one of their first LPs, on the Elektra label, *Dian and the Greenbriar Boys.* One of the hit songs in the album was "Green Corn."

In 1964 Rinzler left after accepting a position as folk talent coordinator of the Newport Folk Foundation. His replacement on mandolin was Frank Wakefield, who had heard much bluegrass music during his youth in the southern hill country. Wakefield also plays rhythm guitar.

Most of the group's recording efforts were on the Vanguard label. In the early 1960s, they were one of the several folk groups featured on a Vanguard series of LPs, *New Folks.* Their contributions included "Stewball," "Katy Cline," and "Rawhide." Later they assisted Joan Baez on her *Volume 2* record for Vanguard, singing with her on "Banks of the Ohio" and "Little Darlin', Pal of Mine."

Their first full album for Vanguard, *The Greenbriar Boys* ('62), included such songs as "We Shall Not Be Moved," "Stay All Night," "Down the Road," "Florida Blues," "Other Side of Jordan," and "Coot from Tennessee." Their next LP was *Ragged but Right* (December '64). Some of the songs in the album are "Sleepy-Eyed John," "Take a Whiff on Me," "Methodist Pie," "A Minor Breakdown," "Roll on John," and "The Blues My Naughty Sweetie Gives Me." Their third Vanguard LP, issued in 1966, included such numbers as "Alligator Man," "Up to My Neck in High Muddy Water," "The Waggoner's Song," and "Honky Tonk Girl."

GREENE, RICHARD: *Singer, violinist, mandolinist, band leader (Richard Greene and the Zone, Greene String Quartet, Grass is Greener). Born Los Angeles, California, November 9, 1942.*

One of the finest folk and country fiddlers of the 1960s to the present, Richard Greene at one time or another proved his ability to excel in every form of violin playing from classical to rock. He easily could have earned his living in either field, and, in fact, had he concentrated on rock might have built up a mass following. However, always an individualist, he ended up performing the kind of music he enjoyed, even if that meant performing mainly before small but "tuned-in" audiences.

Born and raised in Beverly Hills, California, Greene demonstrated phenomenal musical talent as a young child. His classically inclined family saw to it that he started taking violin lessons when he was five, a regimen he began to chafe over as he grew older. As he said, "I quit as soon as I was tall enough." It was that early grind that influenced his decision to turn away from classics later on.

In high school, though, he kept up the classical routine, and was named concert master of the Beverly High orchestra in his sophomore year. He was beginning to turn his attention to folk music, however, listening to recordings of some of the folk artists of the late 1950s and early 1960s and doing some exploratory playing of that material in his spare time. His interest in folk music grew when he enrolled in the University of California at Berkeley, and when he was eighteen he was a member of a mountain music trio on campus.

Increasingly, he looked to folk and country music as his career direction. Helping him move that way was an association with fiddler Scott Stoneman of the Stoneman Family, who introduced him to bluegrass. In a short time, Greene mastered mandolin and bass guitar and was a member of a folk group called the Greenbriar Boys. He spent a while with them, then moved on to a prestigious association in Nashville in the mid-1960s with the Father of Bluegrass, Bill Monroe. Another young urbanite who was in Monroe's group during Greene's tenure was Massachusetts-born guitarist Peter Rowan. Greene won a Grammy in 1997 for his work on *True Life Blues,* a tribute to Monroe on Sugar Hill.

Greene stayed with Monroe for a year, then left to join one of Jim Kweskin's Jug Band alignments. Richard toured the country with the Jug Band and performed on several albums (he had previously made some records with Monroe and the Greenbriar Boys). He also did session work and, at one point in the late 1960s, wrote the score to a critically acclaimed movie titled *Riverrun.* He stayed with the Jug Band until it disbanded in the late 1960s. After that occurred, Greene settled in New York for a while, doing some solo work and writing new material.

His New York sojourn was interrupted by a call from Andy Kulberg to join the new band he was forming called SeaTrain. Greene, in turn, encouraged Kulberg to bring Peter Rowan in as a founding member.

Greene became a SeaTrain band member in late 1969. Signed by Capitol at the start of the 1970s, the band went to England to record its debut LP on the label, *SeaTrain,* issued in early 1971. A second album, *Marblehead Messenger,* came out later in the year. Both made the national charts for many months and demonstrated Greene's technique of deftly blending his violin work in with the ensemble playing of the entire band.

Still, while Greene won applause as one of the music field's finest rock violin players, he was becoming restless with the genre. In 1972 he left SeaTrain with the avowed goal of concentrating on solo performances in the folk-country vein. In a short time, though, he organized a new group called the Zone, which resulted in the 1973 LP *Richard Greene and the Zone.*

Soon after, he began participating in several band groupings in what might loosely be called experimental folk-bluegrass. One of those was the Great American Music Band, formed in 1974 by Greene and mandolin virtuoso David Grisman with Taj Mahal playing string bass and composer John Carlini also among the bandsmen. The blend of jazz, bluegrass, folk, and blues favored in the band's repertoire pointed the way for Grisman when he organized his David Grisman Quintet a few years later. Greene also joined Grisman in the band Muleskinner, which had evolved from the 1973 group Old and in the Way. Jerry Garcia of Grateful Dead fame, who had performed with the latter band, was replaced by the great bluegrass instrumentalist Clarence White. The album *Muleskinner,* first released in the mid-1970s, was reissued in 1987.

In the late 1970s and early and mid-1980s, Greene performed as a soloist while also doing many hours of session work. His album releases of those years included *Duets* in 1978, *Rambling* in 1980, and *Blue Rondo* in 1987. In the late 1980s he formed the Greene String Quintet, still active in the mid-1990s, whose concerts typically covered a range of genres from classical to bluegrass and rock. He formed the instrumental group the Grass is Greener, releasing the *Grass is Greener* (1994), *Wolves A' Howlin'* (1996), and *Sales Tax Toddle* (1998), which earned a Grammy nomination.

GREGSON, CLIVE: *Singer, guitarist, keyboards player, songwriter, band leader (Any Trouble), record producer, born Ashton-Under-Lyne, Manchester, England, January 4, 1955; partner with Christine Collister, born Douglas, Isle of Man, December 28, 1961. Vocals, guitar, percussion in vocal and instrumental duo.*

A major figure on the British folk-rock scene during the last decades of the twentieth century, Clive Gregson's influence extended well beyond the United Kingdom's shores. He was not as well known to the general public outside England and Europe, but critics and fellow musicians throughout North America were well aware of his talents as musician and writer. *Guitar Player* included him in its list of "1,000 Great Guitarists," and *Rolling Stone* characterized his partnership with Christine Collister in the late 1980s and early '90s as "the state of the art in British folk rock."

Gregson, born and raised in Manchester, was an above-average guitarist in his teens when he focused on acoustic folk music. As he grew older he became more rock-oriented and switched to electric guitar and synthesizers. Already starting to gain notice from U.K.

quest—to make a connection to other people. Hopefully my music will move them."

In 1997 A&M released a three-track promo CD titled *Let Him Fly*, primarily for radio airplay. In 1998 the label issued her second CD, *Flaming Red*. She had toured with Shawn Colvin and Lilith Fair and gained a reputation as a diminutive woman who could really belt out her songs. Her second CD adds rock drummer Kenny Aronoff and guitarist Jay Joyce to the mix, revving it up compared to her acoustic *Living with Ghosts* CD. The opening title track is about a girl's love for her flaming red pumps set to a rock beat. But by the end of the album, she shows her more sensitive side with her ballad "Peter Pan."

GRIFFITH, NANCI: *Singer, songwriter, guitarist. Born Seguin, Texas, July 6, 1954.*

New Year's Eve 1991–92 might one day go down as a touchstone for folk music. That night Nanci Griffith spoke with Emmylou Harris about the "beauty and clarity" of Kate Wolf's music. "We spoke of both the sadness in her passing and the lack of new voices singing Kate's songs," Griffith wrote. "Emmy said songs need new voices to sing them in places they've never been sung in order to stay alive."

As a result Griffith recorded *Other Voices, Other Rooms* (1993), which encouraged a mini-folk revival. (The album sold more than 375,000 copies and won a Best Contemporary Folk Grammy.) Griffith covers seventeen folksingers, starting with Wolf's "Across the Great Divide," and includes songs by Dylan, John Prine, Townes Van Zandt, and Woody Guthrie. The title comes from Truman Capote's first novel, published in 1948—"a time of new voices in literature and . . . a rebirth of interest in folk music with the added twist of focus on the singer-songwriter," Griffith explains.

Griffith, who has suffered her own battles in the music industry, embarked on a mission. "Somebody up high above said folk music doesn't sell," Griffith told Sean Mitchell of the *Los Angeles Times* magazine (May 7, 1995), "even though we all know that's not true. But that passed around [record company] offices until everyone believed it. My whole reason for making *Other Voices, Other Rooms* was to take the F out of folk music, for it to cease to be called the F-word in the music industry. And if it is the F-word, then Nancy Griffith is the F-word."

Griffith grew up with a mélange of sounds on the 1960s radio airwaves in Austin, Texas. She fell in love with the music of Carolyn Hester, the Everly Brothers, Odetta, and Nat King Cole. "Without that open ear of radio then I would never have found my first love in folk music," she wrote.

In concert, Griffith sprinkles the songs from *Other Voices, Other Rooms* in with songs like Julie Gold's "From a Distance" (which won a Grammy), and "Love at the Five & Dime." Griffith has an excellent band, the Blue Moon Orchestra led by keyboardist James Hooker, formerly with the Amazing Rhythm Aces. But Griffith is most affecting when she stands alone at the microphone, guitar in hand, and sings "The Wing and the Wheel," a song about her own longings. She always wears an LBJ badge when she performs. She is a fan of Johnson's pioneering civil rights efforts.

Griffith, the youngest of three children, grew up a shy, bookish girl in a middle class neighborhood near Austin. Her father, Marlin "Griff" Griffith, was a book publisher who sang in a barbershop quartet. Her mother, Ruelene Strawser, was a real estate agent who also acted in amateur theater. They divorced when Griffith was six.

"I think there was a certain sadness in my childhood," Griffith told Richard Cromelin of the *Los Angeles Times* (March 28, 1993). "It gave me a lot to think about, and I spent a lot of time by myself. I think that is essential for a writer. I was a little kid, I was skinny. I wasn't very popular. I didn't get tall till the 11th grade. So I spent a great deal of time playing guitar and reading. Literature was my great escape. I wouldn't really call that happy, 'cause I was so into morbid things. I was really into Carson McCullers and Eudora Welty. They're not *The Secret Garden*." (She later would pose for record jacket photos clutching books by Welty, Larry McMurtry, and Capote.)

Her mother was a bohemian woman, a beatnik in the '50s, who taught Griffith that there was more to life than motherhood. Nanci put off having children, something she regrets. She expressed some of her longings in a song about her relationship with her mother called "Goodnight to a Mother's Dream."

Griffith learned to play guitar by watching a PBS series. At twelve she wrote her first song, "A New Generation." At fourteen she played her first concert on Thanksgiving at the Red Lion Hotel in Austin. Her take was $11. "I was really awful and I knew it," she said. "But I also had the opportunity to be exposed to some very left-of-center music I wouldn't have otherwise heard."

She was writing story songs by the time she graduated high school, revealing the influence of Townes Van Zandt and Guy Clark (her father's favorites). She attended the University of Texas, graduating with an education degree. She taught kindergarten and first grade in Austin. At night she played at Austin's Hole in the Wall Bar. She told Ed Bumgardner of the *Winston-Salem Journal* (October 18, 1991) that the only time she stopped midsong at the rough-and-tumble bar was the time a cowboy tried to "deposit the head of a fellow patron in the coin slot of a Lucky Strike machine."

Her goal was become a songwriter, not a performer, like her friend Harlan Howard, who composed Patsy Cline's hit "I Fall to Pieces." Willie Nelson, Emmylou

Harris, Suzy Bogguss, Kathy Mattea, and Mary Black have all recorded her songs. But she soon gained a reputation for her sweet yet stirring vocals.

She was married to singer-songwriter Eric Taylor from 1976 to 1982. "It was a very exciting time, a spontaneous combustion of a music scene," Griffith told Anne Hamner of the *Record Exchange Music Monitor* (December 1991). "You'd get up in the morning and call Vince [Bell] or Lyle [Lovett] and they'd say, 'I've just written something,' and you all end up at somebody's house hearing the new song."

Griffith recorded her first three songs in 1977 on a sampler disc for the now-defunct B.F. Deal records: "Texas Boy," "If I Were a Child," and "Double-Standard Blues." She recorded her first album, *There's a Light beyond These Woods,* live in an Austin studio in 1978 for B.F. Deal. (reissued on Philo in 1986). The title track—about the world beyond childhood—revealed her literate songwriting skills. After a four-year break, she released *Poet in My Window* (1982) on Featherbed Records (reissued on Philo in 1986). The album includes her standard "Workin' in Corners" and her father's barbershop quartet on "Wheels." In 1984, she released her first big album, *Once in a Very Blue Moon,* on Philo. Jim Rooney, former manager of Club 47 on Harvard Square, produced the album, which was recorded at Jack Clement's Nashville studio. The title song, which gave her band its name, is by Pat Alger.

In 1986, she followed with *Last of the True Believers* on Philo. The album received a Grammy nomination. It contains such Griffith classics as "Love at the Five & Dime," a country hit for Kathy Mattea in 1986, "Banks of the Pontchartrain," "The Wing and the Wheel," and "Goin' Gone" by Pat Alger, Bill Dale, and Fred Koller. Lyle Lovett, who is shown on the cover dancing in front of a Woolworth's Luncheonette, sings backup, and Béla Fleck plays banjo on the album.

In 1986, Griffith made several changes. She left Philo and joined MCA Records in Nashville. She began describing herself as a "folkabilly" artist as she took on a country sound. She made two albums in Nashville for MCA—*Lone Star State of Mind* (1987) and *Little Love Affairs* (1988), both produced by Tony Brown (who had signed Steve Earle and Lovett to the label). *Lone Star State of Mind* included "From a Distance," which became a standard for Griffith and a hit for Bette Midler. The album also included a remake of "There's a Light beyond These Woods." *Little Love Affairs* included "Outbound Plane," a song she wrote with Tom Russell and that became a hit for Suzy Bogguss, and "Sweet Dreams Will Come," a John Stewart song. *One Fair Summer Evening* (1988, MCA), was recorded live at Houston's Anderson Fair club, where she played as a teenager. (The album includes a rendition of her ex-husband's song "Deadwood, South Dakota.")

While her albums sold respectably at home, Griffith found fame in Ireland. *Last of the True Believers* (licensed by Demon Records) became her first U.K. release. She had a number-one hit in the mid-1980s in Ireland with "From a Distance." Irish singers Maura O'Connell, Mary Black, and Frances Black have had hits with her songs. She has long been affiliated with the Chieftains. In 1991, she sang "The Wexford Carol" on *The Bells of Dublin.* In 1993, she performed on the Chieftains' Grammy-winning album *An Irish Evening.* That year MCA released a second retrospective, *The Best of Nanci Griffith.*

In 1985, she bought a century-old farmhouse on six acres of land in Franklin, outside of Nashville. She also owns a loft in downtown Dublin. But for many years, she lived on the road, driving from club to club to promote folk music. "For so many years, that was the only way to tell people about my new songs," she told *Time.* "I created an audience, as opposed to waiting for a record company to create it for me."

Those were lean years. But they provided her with plenty of material for songs such as "Spin on a Red Brick Floor." She recalls returning to Texas after being on the road and not knowing if she had enough gas in the car to reach Austin.

MCA didn't know how to categorize her music. She moved to MCA's Los Angeles division and made two albums that tended more toward pop: *Storms* (1989), produced by Glyn Johns (who had worked with the Rolling Stones and the Beatles), and *Late Night Grande Hotel* (1991), produced by Rod Argent and Peter Van Hook. MCA released *The MCA Years—A Retrospective* (1993).

A low point, reflected in her album *Storms,* came in 1989. She told Cromelin. "Where was my peace of mind? I was on the road 350 days a year and I had no life, no happiness, nothing of my own. It all came together for *Storms.* It was my way of working it out. All this rhythm and percussion getting this anxiety out. It helped. It made me just say, 'Stop this, take everything as it is and do what you do.' There's a reason for everything, and everything happens in its own time."

Late Night Grande Hotel included "It's Too Late" and "It's Just Another Morning Here," with Phil Everly backing her. But while sales of *Storms* and *Late Night* increased, she grew disenchanted. She was disappointed that MCA didn't submit her albums to the Grammys and wouldn't release "From a Distance" as a single at home, despite its success in Ireland. In 1991, she told Bumgardner, it was time to stop touring so much. "When you see dirty dishes in your kitchen and your first instinct is to leave them outside the door for room service, you know it is time to come off the road."

She left MCA, which retained the rights to her next two albums in Europe, and signed with Elektra in 1992. Using her own money, she decided to take a risk to show that "folk music and rap music are the only two

American forms of music that have any kind of social conscience whatsoever, so I think it deserves. . . . to be heard."

She reunited with Jim Rooney who had produced *Once in a Very Blue Moon,* and wanted to do justice to the songs. She arranged for guest appearances from a Who's Who in folk: John Prine, Arlo Guthrie, Emmylou Harris, Carolyn Hester, Guy Clark, Chet Atkins, Iris DeMent, and Bob Dylan. "The Dylan piece, 'Boots of Spanish Leather,' was probably the most intimidating piece," she told Cromelin. "After I'd sent it to Dylan, to tell him we had recorded it and let him know it was done, we heard back from him that he wanted to come in and play harmonica. That was the first time I knew that I had done OK." (Dylan later asked Griffith to perform the song for his *30th Anniversary Concert.*)

Other Voices reads like a novel about folk music, including a rendition of "Are You Tired of Me Darling" by the Carter Family; "Wimoweh," a South African song popularized in the '50s by the Weavers; "Across the Great Divide," recorded in the '70s by Kate Wolf. In March 1993 Griffith gathered the stars of her album—songwriters—for a concert at Carnegie Hall, including Carolyn Hester, Odetta, Julie Gold, John Gorka, Vince Bell, and her father, Marlin.

Griffith followed up the success of *Other Voices, Other Rooms* with *Flyer,* her second album on Elektra. Released in 1994, the album sold more than 300,000 copies. Griffith wrote most of the songs which reveal Griffith, at forty, focusing on her personal life. The album opens with "Flyer," a song about a chance meeting with an air force flyer while stranded in an airport and the romance that never was. "In the past, I wrote mostly fiction, or things I observed, without being part of them," she told *Time* (October 3, 1994), "*Flyer* has been totally different: it is a very personal—real experience, walking into life instead of walking around it,"

She dedicates the album to 'John,' a man who Griffith has said she was in love with when she was twenty. John pops up on several of her songs, including "There's a Light beyond These Woods," "Daddy Said," and, from *Flyer,* "These Days in an Open Book," "Always Will," and "On Grafton Street." "You know twenty years of mourning is a long time," she told Mary Wood Littleton (*National Forum,* Fall 1994). "I feel like it was good for me to wake up for a little while. But I feel at the same time in some people's lives there's only one person that's ever going to make an impact on you emotionally. And I just happen to be one of those people."

As with previous albums, she attracted talented performers: Sonny Curtis of Buddy Holly and the Crickets, who plays Stratocaster on "This Heart," a tribute to Holly; U2's Larry Mullen Jr. and Adam Clayton; Peter Buck of R.E.M.; Adam Duritz of Counting Crows; the Chieftains; Mark Knopfler; and the Indigo Girls.

In the spring of 1997, Elektra released *Blue Roses from the Moon.* The album includes ten originals and four covers. One of the covers, "I Fought the Law," showcases Sonny Curtis, J. I. Allison, and Joe Maulden, also members of the Crickets. The album also features backing from the Blue Moon Orchestra, and Hootie and the Blowfish lead singer Darius Rucker in a duet on a remake of Griffith's "Gulf Coast Highway." (Griffith appeared on three tracks on Hootie's second album.)

On previous albums Griffith's voice is her most effective and powerful tool; here it seemed lackluster and strained, sometimes even disappearing behind the lush arrangements. She shows flashes of brillance on her lovely composition "Saint Teresa of Avila" and her cover of Guy Clark's "She Ain't Goin' Nowhere." Both songs feature simple arrangements, allowing the clarity of Griffith's vocals to show through.

Nanci's activities during 1998 included releasing her follow-up to *Other Voices, Other Rooms* entitled *Other Voices, Too (A Trip Back To Bountiful)* on Elektra. While a worthwhile collection, it pales in comparison to her landmark 1993 album. It starts off with a weak version of Richard Thompson's "Wall of Death," in which Griffith's voice is lost in the mix. Other songs include Sandy Denny's "Who Knows Where the Time Goes," Sylvia Fricker's "You Were on My Mind," Woody Guthrie and Martin Hoffman's "Deportee (Plane Wreck at Los Gatos)," and a rousing gospel arrangement of "Wasn't That a Mighty Storm" featuring Tom Rush. The album is a testament to Griffith's organizational skills. She gathered sixty-seven folk and country artists to sing nineteen songs.

Later in 1998 Griffith's book about folk music, *Other Voices: A Personal History* (Random House), came out. In 1999 Random House published her first novel, *Two of a Kind Heart.* In addition, Paul Vasterling, who heads the Nashville Ballet, put together the ballet *This Heart* using seven of Griffith's songs. Griffith played guitar and sang during performances. Griffith also took part in a Newport Folk Festival tour along with many other top rank artists in folk and folk-rock. Her set at the Greek Theatre in Los Angeles included "Wall of Death" with Richard Thompson who also performed in the concert. Steve Hochman of the *Los Angeles Times* ("Folk Music Renews Its Political Message at Festival," September 22, 1998, p. F4) noted that "Wall of Death," is "a song about living life to its fullest [which] took on extra meaning given that Griffith is being treated for thyroid cancer." (She had also battled breast cancer.) Griffith showed a return to form with *Dust Bowl Symphony* (1999, Elektra), in which Griffith sings some of her best-known songs backed by the London Symphony.

One can only hope that Griffith will win her battles against cancer and find new inspiration for her songs, as well as strength to champion folk music. As she told Noah Adams of *National Public Radio* (September 7, 1998), she practices the creed expressed in "Wall of Death." "It's the carnival ride where the motorcyclist goes up on the sides of the wall. . . . For me, when we sing 'Wall of Death,' it's great happiness. It's just like I'm on that motorcycle. I'm riding it. I'm doing it. I've mastered the wall of death. And you know, for me, it's elation."

GRISMAN, DAVID: *Mandolinist, mandocellist, guitarist, saxophonist, composer, band leader (David Grisman Quintet). Born Hackensack, New Jersey, March 23, 1945.*

There are some musicians who can weave their way in and out of a series of bands of varied styles without appearing to be out of place in any of them. Such a one is David Grisman, whose career took him from classics to folk to rock to bluegrass to an amalgam of his own that combined elements of jazz with touches of several other genres.

Born in Hackensack, New Jersey, and later raised in Passaic, New Jersey, Grisman could play a number of stringed instruments in his teens as well as saxophone and piano. His piano teacher, he recalled, told him the mandolin "wasn't a real instrument." Nonetheless, after he finished high school in Passaic and enrolled at New York University, he took the mandolin along and played it in various folk ensembles, including a stint with the Even Dozen Jug Band, where he met such artists as Maria Muldaur and John Sebastian.

For a time he moved to the San Francisco Bay region in the mid-1960s, where his musical acquaintances included guitarist Jerry Garcia, who hadn't yet made his international reputation. In the late 1960s he heeded a call to go cross-country to Boston to join a new group formed by Peter Rowan called Earth Opera. In the mid-1960s, Rowan had been a guitarist and backing vocalist with Bill Monroe's Blue Grass Boys, but the goal in setting up Earth Opera was to play rock 'n' roll–type material. The band made its concert and record debut in early 1968 (the debut LP came out on Elektra) and won some attention as the year went by from tours of the United States and Canada. It had several regional hits and considerable critical praise. However, faced with dwindling reserves, at the end of 1968 it disbanded.

For a while Grisman and Rowan went in different ways, both doing session work and playing with other groups for several years. By 1973 they had joined forces once more in a bluegrass-oriented band called Old and in the Way, whose members included Jerry Garcia, by then the famed lead guitarist of the Grateful Dead (playing banjo in this case). Another member of the group was fiddle virtuoso Vassar Clements. The band played a number of concerts in various parts of the United States, including a 1973 set at the Boarding House in San Francisco that was taped for the live LP *Old and in the Way*, released by Rounder Records. During the 1970s, Grisman and Rowan also were the featured artists of another bluegrass band called

Muleskinner. Whereas Grisman had been featured on saxophone in the Earth Opera days, with the bluegrass groups he rarely played an instrument other than mandolin. His work was recognized by folk and bluegrass adherents as some of the finest mandolin playing of modern times.

Another mid-1970s project of Grisman's was the group called the Great American Music Band, formed in 1974 with violinist Richard Greene. (Greene also worked with Grisman and Rowan in Muleskinner.) Among the musicians who performed with that band were Taj Mahal (who played string bass) and composer John Carlini.

In addition to his band work in the mid-1970s, Grisman continued to do some session work and also wrote film scores. Among his movie credits were scores for *Big Bad Mama, Capone, Eat My Dust,* and *King of the Gypsies.*

In 1976, the first version of the David Grisman Quintet made its debut. He assembled a group that stressed instrumental music, featuring, besides his mandolin playing, Tony Rice on guitar plus a stand-up bassist and one or two fiddles. The music the band performed, much of it written by Grisman, was strongly jazz flavored, but not easily typified. Grisman later commented, "Words like jazz, rock-fusion or crossover bluegrass don't really mean anything. I'd just as soon call it 'Dawg Music,' after a nickname I've been stuck with, than refer to it as anything else." (During that year, A&M Records issued the album *Hot Dawg.*) The band's debut LP, released on Kaleidoscope Records in 1977, was called *The David Grisman Quintet* and sold over 80,000 copies, surprisingly good for a release on a small label. In the late 1970s the group switched to Horizon Records, distributed by the major Warner Brothers record firm.

Some of the band's numbers were by French jazz greats, an example being the Grisman Quintet's version of "Minor Swing," written by the late jazz guitarist Django Reinhardt and jazz violinist Stephane Grappelli. That number, along with new compositions, was presented in the group's debut LP on Horizon Records, *Hot Dawg,* issued in mid-1979. Grisman wrote or cowrote five songs on the album, including "16/16," "Dawgology," and "Janice."

At the end of the 1970s, the Grisman Quintet performed in jazz clubs, some folk venues, and, at times, as an opening act for rock bands at places like the Universal Amphitheater in Los Angeles. Among the band's credits in 1979 was an appearance on Johnny Carson's *The Tonight Show.* Another high point of 1979 was a number of concerts in which Stephane Grappelli, in one of his relatively rare visits from France, performed with Grisman's group. At the time, the band comprised Tony Rice on guitar; Darol Anger on violin, violectra, cello, and mandolin; Todd Philips on bass; and Mike Marshall on mandolin, guitar, and violin. (Anger, Philips, and

Grisman all contributed article material to Grisman's publication, *Mandolin World News.*)

By the time Grisman's new album, *David Grisman—Quintet 80,* came out on Warner Brothers in July 1980, the band's makeup had changed somewhat. Rice and Philips had left, with Mark O'Connor (guitar, violin) and Rob Wasserman (bass) taking their place. Two months after the new LP had come out, it was voted the best album of the year by readers of *Frets* magazine. In the same poll, Grisman was voted the top mandolin player, beating out thirty-three other nominees. Grisman's talents were also recognized in an article in *Newsweek* (November 10, 1980), in which he was dubbed the "Paganini of the Mandolin."

In 1980, *The David Grisman Rounder Album* came out on the Rounder label, which was his main label home for the 1980s. In 1981, Warner Brothers issued another Grisman collection, again an eminently well done album titled *Mondo Mando.* His second album on Rounder, recorded with Andy Statman and titled *Mandolin Abstractions,* came out in 1982. This was followed by the mid-'80s *Acoustic Christmas* and the 1988 two-CD set *Home Is Where the Heart Is.* The latter was his last release on Rounder until a 1996 disc. In the 1990s, all of the 1980s albums were still available from Rounder, as well as the multiartist album *Here Today,* which featured Grisman along with other performers, including Herb Pedersen and Jim Buchanan.

After being sidelined by a severe case of tendinitis at the end of the 1970s, Grisman resumed his performing chores throughout the 1980s as a session musician as well as a featured artist at a variety of concerts on the folk, jazz, and festival circuits. In 1989 he formed his own label, Acoustic Disc, whose studios were based in his own home in Mill Valley, Marin County, California. He made that move, he told Joel Segel of *Rhythmmusic* ("At Acoustic Disc, the Boss Works Like a Dawg," vol. V, no. 3, 1996, pp. 26–29), because "I never found a record company that felt like home. One company would be interested in bluegrass, but they wouldn't care about some old classical mandolin recordings or jazz. None really embraced what I was doing. Or was that effective in selling it. Or wanted me that long. So I figured, well, hey, I can do this myself."

His first release on his own label was the 1990 *Dawg '90,* which earned a Grammy nomination. This got his feet wet in self-marketing, but the album that really gained Acoustic Disc major recognition was the next one, the 1991 release *Garcia/Grisman.* The motivation came from longtime friend and sometime collaborator Jerry Garcia. (Grisman recalled he first met Garcia in a parking lot at a Bill Monroe concert in Pennsylvania, where the two did some bluegrass picking together.) He told Segel that Garcia told him, "Let's make a record, so it'll give us a reason to get together." "And I said, 'Well, gee, I just started my own record company.' He said, 'Great, we'll do it for you.' So not

being an idiot, business-wise, I saw that it might be better for the company to put out that second record."

After that album hit the stores (also going on to gain a Grammy nomination), Acoustic Disc became an established independent label for the rest of the decade, providing a series of notable releases not only by Grisman as soloist, band leader, or coperformer with other top-ranked artists, but CDs, and cassettes of other performers in jazz, folk, and bluegrass. The success of the company, Grisman stressed in the mid-1990s, was based on two key principles—limiting the number of releases, and requiring payment from distributors on delivery.

The third Acoustic Disc release was *Bluegrass Reunion,* with an all-star cast of musicians that, besides Grisman and Garcia, included Red Allen (whose band of the '60s, Red Allen and the Kentuckians, was Grisman's first gig as a bluegrass sideman) on vocals, Herb Pedersen on banjo, Jim Buchanan (from Jim and Jesse) on fiddle, and Jim Kerwin (a current member of the David Grisman Quintet) on bass. After that came out in 1992, the first album by someone other than Grisman, Enrique Coria's *Solos from South America* was issued. The 1993 releases comprised a new David Grisman Quintet collection, *Dawgwood,* and a new collaboration with Jerry Garcia, the award-winning *Not for Kids Only.*

The Acoustic Disc catalog continued to expand in the mid-1990s with Grisman maintaining a breakneck pace as record company executive, recording and concert artist, and contributor to recordings by other performers including backing work on Mike Seeger's 1994 Rounder album, *3rd Annual Farewell Reunion;* Linda Ronstadt's 1994 disc on Elektra-MTH, *Feels Like Home;* the Frank Vignola Trio Concord Jazz album, *Let It Happen;* and Chris Isaak's 1995 Reprise release, *Forever Blue.* Among non-Grisman-featured CDs on Acoustic Disc in that time frame were Red Allen and Frank Wakefield's *The Kitchen Tapes,* Radim Zenkl's *Czech It Out,* and Jacob Do Bandolim's *Jacob Do Bandolim Volume II,* all in 1994, and the 1995 collection of Jethro Burns tracks, *Swing Low, Sweet Mandolin.*

Grisman's personal projects during those years included *Tone Poems* with Tony Rice in 1994, and, in 1995, *Songs of Our Fathers* with Andy Statman, the David Grisman Guintet on *Dawganova,* and, with Martin Taylor, *Tone Poems 2.* The Quintet roster on *Dawganova* comprised Grisman, Jim Kerwin (bass), Matt Eakle (flute), Joe Craven (percussion and violin), and Argentine-born guitarist Enrique Coria. Before Jerry Garcia's untimely death, he and Grisman discussed the possibility of reissuing the original *Old and in the Way* album. But they found that the Grateful Dead sound recording expert at that time, Owsley Stanley, had tapes of a number of other live numbers that had never been released. This formed the basis for a new *Old and in the Way* album (issued after Garcia's death), the 1996 Acoustic Disc CD *That High Lone-*

some Sound. In 1999, Acoustic Disc released *Retrograss,* featuring Grisman, John Hartford, and Mike Seeger. It was nominated for a Grammy.

GUTHRIE, ARLO: *Singer, guitarist, pianist, songwriter. Born Coney Island, Brooklyn, New York, July 10, 1947.*

In concert, Arlo Guthrie can do what few performers can get away with. He'll begin a song, come to a screeching halt mid-verse, launch into a whacky monologue, and then pick up the melody again seamlessly, all the while keeping his audience transfixed. For many, Arlo's digressions are worth the price of admission.

At the Ash Grove on the Santa Monica Pier in February 1997, Arlo began singing "This Land Is Your Land," written by his father, Woody. Suddenly, he stopped and talked about how he was embarrassed as a child because he was the only kid in school who didn't know the words. He came home in tears. Woody, who by that time was suffering from Huntington's chorea, was lying on a wooden lounge chair in the backyard. Arlo brought him his Gibson guitar. He not only taught him the sanitized version of the song, but he also gave Arlo three unsanitized verses that never made the schoolbooks. In one, the singer comes across a No Trespassing sign in a beautiful field. But since there is nothing written on the back of the sign, he's home free. "That sign was made for you and me," Arlo sings.

Most biographies of Arlo Guthrie tend to emphasize his links to his illustrious father, Woody. The link is present in Arlo's sense of humor, storytelling abilities, and especially his irreverence, but he forged a distinct style, influenced by Leadbelly, Pete Seeger, Ramblin' Jack Elliott, Bob Dylan, and others who hung around his house when he was a child. While Arlo carries on the folk music tradition of the Oklahoma balladeer, to many he is the distinguished Guthrie and Woody a shadowy figure from past decades.

Arlo rose to prominence in the latter part of the 1960s and has generally stressed optimism and hope rather than the cynicism or despair that gripped many artists in that decade. He expressed those views in 1968, when he had just gained national attention from his 1967 success, the eighteen-minute-plus "Alice's Restaurant Massacree." (The song won acclaim at the 1967 Newport Folk Festival, where Arlo upstaged Joan Baez and Judy Collins.) He told a reporter, "I'm not really politically minded in my songs. The songs are sometimes about politics, have things about politics in them, but the songs aren't political at all. Because they don't say to choose one politic or another. No one ever can be a spokesman for someone other than himself . . . and I'm a spokesman for myself."

He noted that "the music has changed from being against a lot of things to being for a lot of things. They're just different things. So this is why the protest thing has died, because people happen to be for things instead of against things."

Reflecting on his career in 1990, Arlo told Kevin Sullivan of the *Providence Journal* (July 15), that "Alice's Restaurant" helped to distinguish him from his father: "When I first started out, people were probably wanting a Woody Guthrie clone. 'Alice's Restaurant' fixed that problem. It was so vastly different than anything my dad had ever done. Philosophically, it was along the same lines; but practically, it was a different thing altogether. I really thank God for that."

Arlo was the second of four children born to Woody and Marjorie Mazia Guthrie. An older sister, Cathy Ann, died in a fire before Arlo was born. Arlo and his younger siblings grew up in an apartment in Coney Island. His mother, a dancer with the Martha Graham company, taught dance. His father, whose songs didn't bring in much in the way of royalties until later, gave Arlo a Gibson guitar when he was six, though it was his mother who taught him his first chords. In 1953 his father went into the hospital for Huntington's chorea and only came home for weekend visits. Arlo taught himself how to play the guitar and hung out with other budding musicians in Greenwich Village. Because of his father he had an impressive folk music pedigree. He had played the harmonica for Leadbelly when he was three and first performed in public at thirteen. That year, Dylan also showed Arlo a few tricks on the harmonica.

During the summers, his mother taught dance at an arts camp in Stockbridge, Massachusetts, near where Arlo attended a boarding school. It was there that he became close to the shop teacher, Ray Brock, and his wife, Alice, who was an excellent cook. The Brocks lived in a deconsecrated Episcopal church they had converted into a home.

After graduating high school in 1965, Arlo busked around Europe, then enrolled at Rocky Mountain College, in Billings, Montana. He only stayed in college for six weeks before he got restless and headed east. He got his first gig at Club 47 in Boston. That Thanksgiving, he returned to the Brocks' church/home for dinner. He volunteered to take the garbage out to the local dump, which was closed for the holiday, and got arrested (by the late Stockbridge police chief William Obenhein) for littering on November 27, 1965. The ultimate conviction and $50 fine kept him out of the draft and provided the material for his million-dollar song, "Alice's Restaurant," which took up an entire side of his debut LP, released by Warner Brothers in June 1967. The song was first played on WBAI radio in New York in the spring of 1967.

Arlo played the album for Woody just before he passed away. The irony of his success wasn't lost on him. "I had made more money in one year probably than my dad made in his whole life. It was so absurd," he told Tom Cunneff of *People Weekly.*

The musical odds worked out well for Arlo as he closed out the 1960s and came into the 1970s commanding growing respect as both an interpreter of new and old songs (mostly folk, but with forays into country and rock on occasion) and a writer of new ones, usually with a strong strain of humor, as in "The Motorcycle Song" and "The Pause of Mr. Clause," both featured on his 1968 album, *Arlo*. In August 1969 he was featured at the legendary Woodstock concert in upstate New York, where he won an ovation for the song "Coming into Los Angeles," which was included in his third Warner/Reprise album, *Running Down the Road*.

He toured around the country with a small band comprised of Bob Arkin on bass, Paul Motian on drums, and John Pilla on guitar. About those early years of stardom, Arlo told Bill Locey of the *Los Angeles Times* (March 24, 1994): "Oh man, I was 18; I had a hit, and I wasn't married. It was great. I highly recommend it. It was an entirely different world then, very innocent, very fun."

In 1969 he met his wife, Jackie Hyde, a former Miss Malibu, while he was performing at the Troubadour in Los Angeles. His next concert date was in Philadelphia, and he asked Jackie to join him. She quit her job, and the two were married by October and living on the 260-acre farm he'd purchased in the Berkshire Mountains with the money he'd earned from "Alice's Restaurant."

Arlo's positive outlook spurred him to raise a family despite the specter of Huntington's chorea, the scourge that killed his father and grandmother. He later told a reporter that while he had a 50 percent chance of developing the disease, his children would run only half the risk. "That gives them a 75 percent chance for safety. No matter how you cut it, that's pretty good odds." Arlo refused to be tested, but his brother Joady, a writer, tested negative, and by 2001 Arlo showed no signs of coming down with the disease.

Arlo decided to give up drugs shortly after the birth of the oldest of his children, Abe. (He now has four children and two grandchildren, Krishna and Mo.) He was stoned at home one snowy night with some friends when he wondered aloud about who would be able to drive the car to the hospital through the snow in an emergency. The answer was nobody, so he quit, although giving up cigarettes and caffeine has proven more difficult for Arlo.

In the early 1970s he maintained his momentum, building up a following that cut across generation and stylistic lines with albums like *Washington County* (1970) and *Hobo's Lullaby* (1972). The last named contained Arlo's version of Steve Goodman's "City of New Orleans," which made the pop charts. (Another of Guthrie's concert digressions is the story about how Goodman came up to him after a concert at the Quiet Knight in Chicago and asked to play the song for him. Arlo was tired but agreed to listen only if Goodman bought him a beer. The song became Arlo's biggest hit to date and has become a folk classic.)

In the mid-1970s Arlo began raising a family and became more closely involved with a longtime friend of the Guthrie family, Pete Seeger. The two often appeared on the same bill and, after a while, collaborated on a series of concerts that presented, in effect, a history of folk music from Revolutionary times to the present.

Arlo's increased emphasis on traditional folk material was demonstrated on such mid-1970s albums as *Last of the Brooklyn Cowboys* (1973) and *Pete Seeger/Arlo Guthrie Together in Concert*. *Last of the Brooklyn Cowboys* included several tracks featuring Irish jigs and reels performed by Irish fiddler Kevin Burke and several country songs ("Lovesick Blues," "Miss the Mississippi and You") with backing provided by Buck Owens's Buckaroos. His 1974 album, *Arlo Guthrie*, was a more contemporary collection that contained such tracks as "Presidential Rag," written in the midst of the Watergate scandal, and "Won't Be Long!"

Arlo's eighth solo album, *Amigo*, was issued on Warner/Reprise in 1976. Its tracks included such originals as "Grocery Blues" and "Massachusetts," plus Arlo's version of an old Rolling Stones hit, "Connection." During 1977, while Arlo was touring with his group, called Shenandoah, his first retrospective disc was released. *The Best of Arlo Guthrie*, issued in the fall, included, besides "Alice's Restaurant" and "City of New Orleans," such tracks as "Cooper's Lament," "Darkest Moment," and a rerecording with additional comedic lines of "The Motorcycle Song" called "The New Motorcycle."

Arlo's tenth Warners LP, *One Night*, recorded with Shenandoah, was released in the fall of 1978. The album included traditionally oriented folk numbers such as "Tennessee Stud," "Buffalo Skinners," and "St. Louis Tickle," as well as a nineteen-minute version of a Guthrie saga called "The Story of Reuben Clamzo & His Strange Daughter in the Key of A." Shenandoah, which at the time comprised David Grover on guitar and banjo, Carol Ide on guitar and percussion, Steve Ide on guitar and trombone, Dan Velika on bass, and Terry Hall on drums (all five members also handled vocal support), provided adequate backup.

His album *Outlasting the Blues*, released in June 1979, also featured Shenandoah. It was a controversial album with religious and spiritual themes. Later that year, his early composition "The Motorcycle Song" was featured in an animated short film titled *No No Pickle*. Peter Starr, who produced the picture, also featured Guthrie material in a semidocumentary movie, *Take It to the Limit*, about professional motorcycle racing, that won a Silver Venus Medallion at the 1979 Houston International Film Festival.

In February 1981 Arlo and Pete Seeger again joined forces in a new two-record set issued on Warner Brothers titled *Arlo Guthrie and Pete Seeger—Precious Friend*. Later that year, Arlo released his last album for Warner Brothers, *Power of Love*.

In the early 1980s singer-songwriters like Guthrie

faced increased pressure from disco and punk rock. Their audiences were dwindling. Arlo put together a collection of songs but Warners didn't want it. In 1983, Warner/Reprise dropped several big-name acts, including Gordon Lightfoot, Bonnie Raitt, Van Morrison, and Guthrie. So Arlo decided to start his own label, Rising Son Records. Slowly, he reacquired the rights to his Warner Brothers albums, which he has since been selling by catalog. In 1986 he began producing his *Rolling Blunder Review* newsletter, which has a circulation of more than 6,000 who pay $2 a year for a subscription and is a vehicle to sell his wares.

In 1986 he released the album *Someday,* recorded with Shenandoah in 1983 at Longview Farm, in North Brookfield, Massachusetts. Besides reissuing his Warner/Reprise albums, he released a compilation, *All Over the World,* in 1991; a collection of cowboy songs, *Son of the Wind* (including "Buffalo Gals," "Shenandoah," and "Red River Valley"), in 1992; and a two-volume album, *More Together Again,* in 1994, featuring an August 1993 concert with Pete Seeger, Seeger's grandson Tao Rodriguez-Seeger, and Arlo's four children (Abe, Annie, Sarah Lee, and Cathy) on background vocals. In 1985 he recorded a collection of songs with Holly Near, Ronnie Gilbert, and Pete Seeger in an album whose title is taken from their first names, *HARP.* Arlo also lent his voice to Nanci Griffith's 1993 album, *Other Voices, Other Rooms,* backing her on the Townes Van Zandt song "Tecumseh Valley."

In 1988, Arlo accepted Woody Guthrie's induction into the Rock and Roll Hall of Fame, and returned to the ceremonies in 1996, when Pete Seeger was inducted.

During the 1990s Arlo continued to look toward the future with an eye to preserving the past. In 1992 he purchased the Old Trinity Church in Great Barrington, Massachusetts, made famous by the infamous Thanksgiving "massacree" that took place there. He moved Rising Son Records into the building, as well as the Guthrie Center, a nonprofit interfaith church foundation he formed in 1991 for children recovering from abuse, and to help people with HIV/AIDS, and the elderly.

The following year, Arlo, his sister Nora, and his brother Joady released a collection of Woody's children's songs that had been lost for forty years. The collection, *Woody's 20 Grow Big Songs,* received a Grammy nomination for Best Children's Record. He also wrote a children's book, *Mooses Come Walking,* based on a poem he often recited in concert. Alice M. Brock, of "Alice's Restaurant," illustrated the award-winning book, drawing the ambling moose.

Twenty-five years after he starred in *Alice's Restaurant,* the movie directed by Arthur Penn, Arlo again got a chance to act—by a fluke. He had appeared on a late-night cable access show that a Hollywood producer, Charles Eglee, happened to be watching. Producer Steven Bochco was creating a new TV show called

Byrds of Paradise and was looking for someone to play the role of an aging hippie, Alan Moon. With his long gray hair and his experience in the late 1960s, Arlo seemed like a perfect choice. At first Arlo, who had turned down all offers since the 1969 movie, turned it down. But when he found out it was filming in Hawaii, he jumped at the chance. The show lasted only one season, so before long he was back on the road nine months out of the year, traveling with his son, Abe, backing him on keyboards.

In July 1995, to celebrate the third decade of his fateful arrest for littering, Arlo recorded a new version of his original album, this one titled *Alice's Restaurant: The Massacree Revisited.* The album and title track were much the same with a couple of small production tweaks, as well as a brief epilogue about Richard Nixon and the White House tapes. A bare-chested Guthrie (save for a white napkin over his chest) posed for the cover at a mock Thanksgiving table in the same pose he had assumed in the '60s, except his hair is longer and grayer than it was back then.

In 1996 he released his first original album in ten years, *Mystic Journey,* a reference to the spiritual journey he had embarked on in the 1980s and 1990s, covering many of the religions known to humankind. In the mid-1980s he met a spiritual guru based in Florida, Ma Jaya Sati Bhagavati, or "Ma" for short. She was actually a Jewish woman from Brooklyn before she became a Hindu spiritual leader. She is involved in helping people with HIV, and Arlo has lent comfort at the hospices and hospitals she supports.

"I've spent a lot of time in lots of religions," he told Ellen J. Bartlett of the *Boston Globe* (December, 1988). "I've been everything. Almost everything. I was raised as a Jew. My dad was a Protestant. I spent a lot of time wandering around the halls of Catholicism. I spent time meditating on the Hindu version of life, on the Tibetan Buddhist approaches. I think they're all fabulous. The truth is that in the presence of God, my sneaking suspicion is that they all melt away, that all of the forms disappear."

With assistance from Tom Cunneff of People Weekly

GUTHRIE, WOODY: *Songwriter, singer, guitarist. Born Okemah, Okfuskee County, Oklahoma, July 14, 1912; died Queens, New York, October 3, 1967.*

In his songs and legend, Woody Guthrie has remained a living part of America's folk-music heritage more than three decades after Huntington's chorea claimed his life in 1967. Young folksingers still perform his Dust Bowl Ballads and other classic compositions, as earlier generations did in the 1970s and during Woody's lifetime. Reissues of his recordings continue to appear in record stores, and his story has been told in books, including his autobiography, *Bound for Glory,* and the 1977 film of the same name.

Such a legacy seems appropriate for a man whose family helped settle this land, and whose own love for his country was enshrined in his great composition, "This Land Is Your Land." Woodrow Wilson Guthrie was born of pioneer stock in Oklahoma when it was still referred to as Indian Territory. His father, Charles Edward Guthrie, came from Texas and brought to the family a background of pioneering, prize fighting, and guitar and banjo playing with several cowboy bands.

After marrying Nora Belle Tanner, Charlie Guthrie settled down to run a trading post and then a real estate office, which was prosperous for a while, since it coincided with the first oil boom in Oklahoma. Thus, in Woody's early years, he was surrounded by folk music from his parents, grandparents, neighbors, from African American singing, and even from the many Indian villages in the region. At four, Woody himself started singing and continued to follow this lodestone for nearly the rest of his life. As a child Woody was a class clown and town jester. A scruffy kid, he liked to joke around, play the harmonica, and dance on the streets.

As Woody reached high school age, things disintegrated at home when his father's real estate business failed, his sister, Clara, died in a coal oil stove explosion, and his mother had to be committed to the state asylum. At the time no one could diagnose Nora Guthrie's true illness. Now it's clear that she was suffering from the degenerative nerve disorder now known as Huntington's chorea or Huntington's disease. All of this contributed to Woody's dropping out of school. He learned to play harmonica and, when he left home at age thirteen or fourteen, he used it for entertainment and to pick up extra money during his traveling.

After his father moved back to Texas, Woody "hit the road down south to Houston, Galveston, the Gulf and back, doing all kinds of odd jobs, hoeing fig orchards, picking grapes, hauling wood, helping carpenters and cement men, working with water well drillers. . . . I carried my harmonica and played in barber shops, at shine stands, in front of shows, around the pool halls, and rattled the bones, done jig dances, sang and played with Negroes, Indians, whites, farmers, town folks, truck drivers and with every kind of a singer you can think of" (*American Folksong/Woody Guthrie,* Oak Publications, New York; 1961, p. 3).

Later he wandered north to Pampa, Texas, where his father's half-brother Jeff taught him to play guitar. The two played at many local events and later had their own magic show. Woody joined with his friends Matt Jennings and Cluster Baker to form a group called the Corncob Trio. They played together constantly wherever they could find gigs—at a local skating rink, a market, sometimes just for their own enjoyment. Woody also took a liking to Matt Jennings's sister Mary. He married her in 1933. But in 1935 the Dust Bowl devastated the countryside and the economy and Woody took off for California. He wrote "So Long, It's

Been Good to Know Ya" about leaving home, one of his most enduring songs. He worked as a painter during the day and a singer in saloons at night. By now he not only was collecting songs but writing them as well. For most of his life, he wrote one or two songs almost every day, resulting in an estimated total of more than a thousand published compositions winnowed from an even greater mass of material. (It should be noted that, like many folk artists, Guthrie often put new lyrics to folk melodies. A believer in the folk tradition that true folk songs evolved over many generations through the changes and additions of many individuals, he always expressed opposition, in later years, to the restrictions of copyright laws.)

In California, he joined with a woman named Maxine "Lefty Lou" Crissman in an act called Woody and Lefty Lou. They gained a regular spot on radio station KFVD in Los Angeles. After a few years, Woody's restless nature took him to Tijuana, Mexico, where he performed on station XELO. After that he returned to KFVD for a time as a solo performer.

During the trying years of the Depression and the drought and dust storms of his native Southwest in the 1930s, Woody vagabonded through the West and Southwest. Touched by the pressures and troubles of ordinary people, he became strongly supportive of unions and left-wing organizations, donating his talents performing before union groups, migratory workers, and other victims of hard times. Their problems showed up in a steady stream of new compositions. One of the songs he wrote was called "Do Re Mi," poking holes in the myth of California as the Garden of Eden: "But believe it or not, you won't find it so hot if you ain't got the do re mi," Guthrie advises. But he also made a point of writing uplifting songs for the people. As he remarked, "I am out to sing songs that will prove to you that this is your world and that if it has hit you pretty hard and knocked you for a dozen loops, no matter what color, what size you are, how you are built, I am out to sing the songs that make you take pride in yourself and in your work."

In the late 1930s, he moved to New York, where he met many other folk artists, including a youngster named Pete Seeger who soon was joining him in concerts. Among other things, he wrote for the Communist *Daily Worker* and performed on the folk circuit throughout New England and other eastern states. Despite his leanings, Woody never admitted to being a Communist, instead joking, "I ain't a Communist necessarily, but I been in the red all my life." An important contact was made with folk song collector Alan Lomax, who asked Woody to come to Washington, D.C., to record some of his music for the Library of Congress Archive of Folk Song. Woody recorded enough material, much of it original songs, for twelve records called *Dust Bowl Ballads*. Not only did Woody record songs, he also took part in taped conversations with Lomax about those years and his approach to writing and collecting. Those albums remain the most important focal point of Guthrie's life and art. During the 1940s Alan Lomax gave Seeger and Guthrie a collection of protest songs he had been collecting for five years. He suggested that Seeger and Guthrie finish the project, which they did. Pete transcribed the songs and Woody wrote introductions. Seeger named it *Hard Hitting Songs for Hard Hit People.* But the collection would not be published until 1967, the year of Woody's death. Returning to New York, he received many opportunities to perform on radio and sang on such major shows as *Pursuit of Happiness, Cavalcade of America, Back Where I Come From,* and *Pipe Smoking Time.* He also performed on the *Music Festival* series broadcast over New York City's station WNYC.

In 1941, after a sojourn in California, the Bonneville Power Association commissioned Woody, who was then twenty-eight, to write songs for a documentary film to promote the Grand Coulee Dam along the Columbia River. The film never came out, but in the time he spent there, Woody, who was a strong supporter of the works project, wrote a series of songs such as "Roll On Columbia," "Pastures of Plenty," and "Grand Coulee Dam." He returned to New York, where he joined with Lee Hays, Pete Seeger, and Millard Lampell in a group called the Almanac Singers. During the early 1940s, the group toured the country, sometimes appearing in commercial concerts, other times performing at union meetings, radical meetings, and occasional charitable affairs. Among the songs in their repertoire were "Union Maid," in support of women workers; "Talking Union"; and "Union Train a Comin'," as well as traditional folk songs and originals by various members.

With World War II under way, Woody entered the U.S. Merchant Marine with two other folk song friends, Cisco Houston and Jimmy Longhi, who wrote a book about his experiences in the 1990s titled *Woody, Cisco, and Me.* He was torpedoed twice during those years, sang and collected material from the British Isles to Russia, and composed still more songs. Just before the end of the war he was briefly drafted by the U.S. Army.

After the war ended, Woody returned to the New York area and resumed his singing activities. By then he had been divorced for a long time from Mary Jennings. They had had three children together. Two of them died from Huntington's chorea, and one died in a car accident. Woody had settled down with his second wife, Marjorie Mazia, a dancer who had worked with Martha Graham, in Brooklyn, New York. In 1943 Woody published his autobiography, *Bound for Glory,* which received strong reviews. His first child with Marjorie, Cathy, died in 1946 in an electrical fire that burned down their apartment. A year later they had a son who would carry on the family musical tradition, Arlo. They also had two other children, Joady and Nora, who now runs the Woody Guthrie Archives.

In the years after 1945 until illness disabled him, Woody performed as a soloist and in concerts with almost all the best-known folk singers of those years, from Leadbelly to Seeger and the Weavers. In 1948 he was inspired to write one of his most enduring songs, "Deportee (Plane Wreck at Los Gatos Canyon)" after reading a news account about a plane crash in Los Gatos, California, that took the lives of several Mexican migrant workers. Woody was incensed that their deaths were treated as less than important by some reporters. In the mid-1940s, he also agreed to record for Moses Asch's Folkways Records. Woody met Asch in 1944 and soon after recorded songs with Cisco Houston, Sonny Terry, and Bess Lomax. Over a two-month period 132 master records were laid down. Guthrie wrote, "We tried hilltop and mountain harmonies and wilder yells and whoops of the dead sea deserts and all of the swampy and buggy mud bottom sounds we could make." The songs included "Waiting by the Gate," "Hangman's Knot," "Git Along Little Doggies," "Lost John," "Dollar Down and a Dollar a Week," "Union Burying Ground," "Ludlow Massacre," "Pretty Boy Floyd," "The Dying Miner," and "Buffalo Skinner," to name a few. After its initial release, material from the sessions provided the basis for a 1976 Folkways reissue called *Struggle* containing notes by Asch. Later, Smithsonian Folkways in the fall of 1990 released a CD of that album.

Guthrie went on to provide more tracks for dozens of Folkways albums from the late 1940s through the 1950s. Besides the above, among the many songs he recorded for Asch were such titles as "Goin' Down the Road," "Boomtown Bill," "I Ain't Got No Home in This World Anymore," "Tom Joad," "Jackhammer John," "Billy the Kid," "When the Curfew Blows," "Electricity and All," "Sharecropper Song," and "Pastures of Plenty."

In the early 1950s, while he was visiting his old friend in California, actor Will Geer, Woody met and fell in love with a much younger woman named Anneke Van Kirk, who was married to a man named David Marshall. He ended up leaving Marjorie and marrying Anneke. They had a daughter, Lorina, whom they put up for adoption. But the marriage soon fell apart after they both went to live in New York with Marjorie and it became clear that Woody was suffering from Huntington's chorea.

In his lifetime, he was represented by a series of LPs, mostly on Folkways, but some on various other labels (some reissues of earlier material). Among the albums available in the early and mid-1960s were *Bound for Glory, Dust Bowl Ballads, Ballads of Sacco and Vanzetti* (2/61), *Woody Guthrie Sings,* with Leadbelly (and others) (5/62), all on Folkways; *Bed on the Floor* (8/65), *Bonneville Dam* (12/66), on Verve/Forecast Records; *Dust Bowl Ballads* (RCA Victor, 7/64); *Library of Congress Recordings,* on Elektra (three discs,

12/64); *Folk Songs by Woody Guthrie and Cisco Houston* and *Guthrie, Terry and Stewart* on Stinson Records; *Woody Guthrie*, Archive of Folk Music (1/66).

By the 1960s, Woody was seriously ill with Huntington's chorea, a hereditary, degenerative disease of the muscles for which no known cure exists. Even as legions of young folksingers hailed him as the symbol of the folk music boom of the late 1950s and early 1960s, Guthrie himself had to withdraw from the activities he loved so much. Among those who sought out the bedridden artist in the early 1960s was a young college dropout from Minnesota named Bob Dylan. Though Guthrie had never heard of Dylan, Guthrie accepted his presence in his room at Greystone Park Hospital and the two became friends. In the years following, Dylan joined other friends and former associates in keeping Guthrie's songs and name before the public.

The end came for Guthrie in October 1967 in a physical sense, but his career had been thwarted by his illness for almost the entire decade. In the years after his death, he was honored by many memorial concerts, from New York's Carnegie Hall to the concert halls of California. In the 1970s, his widow, Marjorie, helped organize a number of concerts to raise money to support medical research on Huntington's chorea.

Meanwhile, reissues of his material continued to appear, such as Tradition Records' *Early Years* and the Folkways LP *Poor Boy: 13 of His Folk Songs*. When the film biography of his life came out in the late 1970s, it also set off a flurry of releases. Among his albums still in current catalogs at the end of the 1970s were RCA's *A Legendary Performer* (retitled from the 1964 *Dust Bowl Ballads* release); *Cowboy Songs, Folk Songs by Woody Guthrie and Cisco Houston* on Stinson; *Early Years, Legendary Woody Guthrie* on Olympic Records (University of Washington); *Woody Guthrie* on Evergreen; *Woody Guthrie* on Warner Brothers; *Library of Congress Recordings* On Elektra; and, on Folkways, *Poor Boy, Dust Bowl Ballads, This Land Is Your Land, Woody Guthrie Sings Folk Songs, Volumes 1 and 2,* and three albums of songs for children—*Songs to Grow On Volumes 1, 2, and 3.*

Besides Woody's tremendous creative legacy for the people of the world, he also unfortunately left his offspring to cope with the terrible awareness that they eventually could inherit his fatal disease. They were aware Huntington's had caused the death of Woody's mother and half-sister as well as his two daughters from his first marriage. Joady Guthrie, a year younger than Arlo and also a songwriter-folksinger, told Richard Cromelin of the *Los Angeles Times* ("For Joady Guthrie, an Unhappy, Fearful Legacy," January 25, 1986), "That's a pretty big thing in my life. I have these memories of seeing my father get worse. I tell you, sometimes it's pretty rough now."

He emphasized to Cromelin that his mother, Mar-jorie, and Woody separated when he was 2½ years old and he didn't have much contact with his father until he was in his teens and Woody was hospitalized. "I really got folk music from my dad, got some of those values, and that's about it. Personal stuff? Just a couple of early memories."

During 1987–88 work got under way on an ambitious project to help raise funds to permit the Smithsonian Institution in Washington to purchase Folkways, including previously unreleased material by various artists in the label's vaults. It was decided to prepare a tribute album to Woody and Leadbelly featuring such modern stars as Bob Dylan, Bruce Springsteen, the Irish rock group U2, John Mellencamp, Willie Nelson, Little Richard, Fishbone, Brian Wilson (of the Beach Boys), Taj Mahal, and Sweet Honey in the Rock, plus Arlo Guthrie and Pete Seeger. Both studio recordings and live video material were prepared. The album, *Folkways: A Vision Shared,* came out on Columbia in the summer of 1988 with a video documentary connected to the album shown on HBO in September followed by release of an expanded home video version in October '88 by CBS Music Video Enterprises. The overall plan also called for Smithsonian/Folkways to put out a companion album featuring the original treatment of the songs by Woody and Leadbelly called *Folkways: The Original Vision.*

Once the Smithsonian's acquisition of Folkways was complete, it began releasing a series of reissues of Woody's recordings in the 1990s. Besides *Struggle,* those included the 1994 album *Woody Guthrie: Long Ways to Travel—The Unreleased Folkways Masters 1944–1949.* The latter's contents included "Budded Roses," first recorded by country star Charlie Poole; "Warden in the Sky"; "Rocky Mountain Slim and Desert Rat Shorty"; "Girls I Left Behind Me"; and the title track.

Guthrie was inducted into the Rock and Roll Hall of Fame in 1988 as an early influence on rock, though his inclusion might have surprised some. Hall of Fame officials continued to pay tribute to his achievements, giving a ten-day celebration at the end of September 1996 (including such varied events as an exhibit of Guthrie family photographs and a Guthrie film festival) that culminated in a concert featuring many folk stars, old and new, and members, as well, of the folk-rock community. Those taking part included veteran folk artists Pete Seeger, Ramblin' Jack Elliott, and Woody's son Arlo; new folksingers Ani DiFranco and Billy Bragg; as well as Bruce Springsteen, David Pirner (of the rock group Soul Asylum), and the Indigo Girls. Springsteen's contribution included his version of Woody's "Tom Joad," which Guthrie wrote in the 1930s after seeing *The Grapes of Wrath,* the movie adapted from the John Steinbeck novel.

The prime goal of the celebration was to raise funds

to benefit the Woody Guthrie Archives run by Woody's daughter, Nora. At the concert, held in Cleveland's Severance Hall, British folksinger Bragg sang two songs he wrote to go with Guthrie lyrics newly discovered among the archive's material: "The Unwelcomed Guest" and "Against the Law." The concert closed with all performers joining in Guthrie's "Hard Travelin'" followed by the artists and audience joining in on "This Land Is Your Land."

In early 1997 Smithsonian Folkways issued the CD *Woody Guthrie, This Land Is Your Land: The Asch Recordings, Volume 1,* which presented many of his best-known songs taken from the original masters. This represented the first of a series of four reissues of the folksinger's repertoire; the other three volumes were issued during 1997–1998. Those included *Muleskinner Blues, Volume 2, Hard Travelin', Volume 3,* and *Buffalo Skinners, Volume 4.* The title track of volume 1 included a verse, discovered by archivist Jeff Place, thought never to have been recorded. The words, which had been part of the original sheet music, went, *Was a big high wall there that tried to stop me/A sign was painted said: Private Property / But on the back side it didn't say nothing / This land was made for you and me.* Place noted that Guthrie had recorded 160 songs in the Asch sessions, of which 120 survived in the Smithsonian/Folkways collection.

During 1997 Rounder issued a CD of material by Arlo and Woody titled *This Land Is Your Land—an All-American Children's Folk Classic.* Meanwhile, British folk artists Billy Bragg and the American country/folk rock group Jeff Tweedy and Wilco were working on a project organized by Woody's daughter Nora Guthrie to add music to lyrics she had discovered in her father's files. That collection, *Mermaid Avenue* (named after the street in Brooklyn's Coney Island section where Woody and his family lived after World War II), was released by Elektra Records in the summer of 1998. Though it was a listenable album, some critics didn't know exactly what to make of it, suggesting the songs were good but not necessarily exceptional. Robert Christgau of the *New York Times,* for one, was enthusiastic, naming at least two songs, "Walt Whitman's Niece" and "Way Down Yonder in the Minor Key," as possible future classics. Bragg and Wilco had recorded forty songs from the archives, and Elektra released *Mermaid Avenue Volume 2* in 2000. Woody was also honored in 1998 when the U.S. Postal Service used his likeness for a postage stamp.

In the late 1990s, Smithsonian/Folkways also had the following CDs in its catalog: *Woody Guthrie Sings Folk Songs Volumes 1 and 2, Songs to Grow on for Mother and Child, Nursery Days, Ballads of Sacco and Vanzetti, Poor Boy, Bound for Glory: Songs and Stories of Woody Guthrie,* and the collections *That's Why We're Marching: World War II and the American Folk Song Movement, The Original Vision,* and *Cowboy Songs.* Rounder Records had *Woody Guthrie: Columbia River Collection, Dust Bowl Ballads,* and *Library of Congress Recordings,* a three-disc set.

GUY, GEORGE "BUDDY": *Singer, guitarist, songwriter. Born Lettsworth, Louisiana, July 30, 1936.*

Recognized as one of the all-time great blues guitarists—British rock superstar Eric Clapton, for one, called him the greatest blues guitarist ever, and cited Buddy and the "last generation of the true blues musicians as we know them"—Buddy Guy has had a strangely erratic career. Musicians from rock, folk, jazz, and blues raved about his uninhibited stage persona—compared by many to the techniques that made Jimi Hendrix world famous (and Hendrix, in turn, credited Guy with being one of his major influences)—yet his recorded output was strangely uneven, and more than a few critics had unkind things to say about his work. Yet such comments seem rather extreme. Some of his own singles and albums, particularly from the 1960s, are certainly above-average, and his collaboration with Junior Wells on discs like *Hoodoo Man Blues* and his versions of some of the work of legendary blues writer Willie Dixon are as strong as any of the great blues masters.

Buddy was born and spent his childhood in the small town of Lettsworth, fifty miles north of the capital of Louisiana, Baton Rouge. His parents were sharecroppers, though his father sometimes found other work than farming, including occasional railroad construction jobs. As a child he picked cotton, but his parents wanted their children to get an education and only let him do farm work after school and on Saturdays, with church on the schedule for Sundays. Buddy fell in love with the guitar at an early age, picking up musical cues from listening to gospel, country, and blues recordings on the family's battery-powered radio. After a while, he began trying to make his own instruments, until his father finally got him a cheap store-bought guitar.

His sister Annie Mae moved to Baton Rouge in the late 1940s because educational facilities were better there, and Guy joined her in 1950 to start high school. He still showed great interest in learning blues music and, as was noted in the semiautobiography written by Donald Wilcox and Guy (*Damn Right I've Got the Blues,* Woodford Press, San Francisco, 1992), an uncle on his father's side in Baton Rouge bought him his first real guitar for $52.50. His high school career was cut short after his freshman year when his mother suffered a stroke and Buddy had to drop out and take whatever jobs he could find to help family finances.

When he could, Guy continued to teach himself guitar, while learning words to blues songs he heard others in the black community sing. At seventeen, he got the chance to play his first professional gig at a bar called

Sitman's with a local group headed by "Big Poppa" John Tilley. He almost blew the opportunity because his shyness prevented him from facing the audience. However, he was allowed to try again another night at Sitman's, and this time things worked out well. For a time he played the roadhouse circuit in and around Baton Rouge with Tilley before joining another band organized by harmonica player Raful Neal. They worked up a small band act in which they did covers of songs like B.B. King's "Sweet Little Angel," Bobby Bland's "Buzz on up the Road," and Little Richard's "Lucille." Though Buddy sometimes played with other blues artists in the area like Lightnin' Slim and Slim Harpo, he and Neal remained a team until he decided to try for bigger things in the thriving blues market of Chicago.

On September 27, 1957, Buddy left for Chicago with $100 in his pocket and a demo tape recorded at Baton Rouge station WXOK of "Baby Don't You Wanna Come Home." Record companies weren't particularly interested in unknown artists; Buddy was able to leave his tape at Chess Records, but weeks and months went by and he didn't hear from them. Finding work was equally tough and, his funds almost exhausted and wearing tattered clothes, he was about ready to give up when a man saw him wandering by with his guitar and, after buying him a drink, finally took him to the 708 Club. When they entered, Otis Rush was performing; when Otis's set was over, he let the young Louisianan try out. While Guy was demonstrating his ability, bar owner Ben Gold came in and was impressed enough to tell someone to hire him. This led to a steady three-nights-a-week job that brought not only audience approval but attention from other musicians. Among those who soon became friends and admirers were Muddy Waters and Willie Dixon.

In the late '50s Guy expanded his activities to include solo or supporting roles in other Chicago area clubs, including appearances with the Rufus Foreman Band at the Squeeze Club and with B.B. King at the Trianon Ballroom. During 1958 he was initially featured at Theresa's Lounge, an association that continued until 1970. One of the notable events of 1958 was a "Battle of the Blues" at the Blue Flame Club that pitted Buddy against guitarists Otis Rush and "Magic Sam" Marghett and harp player Junior Wells, with Guy being acclaimed the winner. Buddy got the chance to record some material with Magic Sam for Cobra Records and also did two tracks with his own band on Cobra's companion label, Artistic. The single of "I Sit and Cry and Sing the Blues" was released by Artistic, but with little promotion, died quickly.

In 1960 he finally signed with Chess, and his first sessions for the label in March 1960 provided the singles "First Time I Met the Blues" and "When My Left Eye Jump." That year he became a house guitarist for Chess, and for the first half of the decade he spent more time in the studios backing other artists than recording

his own material. Among those he played behind were Willie Dixon, Little Walter, Sonny Boy Williamson (Rice Miller), and Koko Taylor. In December '61 he recorded his self-penned "Stone Crazy," which reached number twelve on the R&B charts in early 1962. During those years he continued to be active in various venues in the Midwest as a soloist or with other artists, including a stint with the Guitar Jr. Band at Curley's Bar in Chicago. Though basically known as an electric guitarist, Buddy demonstrated his skills on acoustic guitar in sessions for the early '60s Muddy Waters album *Folk Singer.*

Word of Guy's blues expertise began to filter back to England as young British rock musicians began to come to Chicago to get firsthand experience with the American blues scene. During one 1964 session, when Guy was recording "My Time after a While," members of the Rolling Stones came in to watch the proceedings.

The first part of the 1960s also saw the flourishing of a performing partnership with harmonica artist Junior Wells, a longtime friend of Buddy's. Besides working with Junior on the concert circuit, Buddy also teamed up with him for recordings for the Delmark label. One result was the excellent *Hoodoo Man Blues* album, which referred to Buddy as "Friendly Chap"—he couldn't use his real name since he was still under contract to Chess. Later Buddy and Otis Spann joined Wells on the Delmark album *South Side Blues Jam.*

In 1965 Buddy joined the American Folk Blues Festival group for the first of several tours of England and the European continent that extended through 1967. The exposure made him a favorite performer for many British rock stars, including Eric Clapton, who became a close friend and a strong proponent of Guy's reputation. In mid-February he played on the U.K. TV show *Ready, Steady, Go,* where the hostess first introduced him as Chuck Berry. (He performed a song that became one of his best-known solos, "Let Me Love You Baby," which he had recorded for Chess in 1960.) Soon after he headlined at the major London venue the Marquee Club, where Clapton saw him, recalling that it was the first time he'd seen a blues master in person using an electric guitar.

In the United States he and Junior Wells often headlined Pepper's Lounge in Chicago from 1966 through 1968, but in general Buddy was making little progress in expanding his U.S. audience. After he returned from his overseas tour in 1965, he had recorded five more songs for Chess, but the label still hadn't issued an album of his material. Then in 1967, he started to break out of his low-profile position with a series of dynamic concert appearances, first at a show at Canterbury House in Ann Arbor, Michigan, and then a wildly successful set at the Mariposa Folk Festival, held near Toronto, Canada. Among other artists on the bill were Joni Mitchell, Rev. Gary Davis, Tom Rush, and Richie Havens. That year, he also left Chess and signed with

Vanguard Records, which over the next few years issued such notable LPs as *A Man and the Blues, This Is Buddy Guy,* and *Hold That Plane!*

In the late '60s and early '70s he became a familiar figure on the folk and blues festival circuit. His 1968 dates included the Philadelphia Folk Festival, Newport Folk Festival, and Central Park (New York) Music Festival. He also appeared on an episode of the *Camera Three* series on CBS-TV in '68 called "Really! The Country Blues." In 1969, besides gigs at Bill Graham's Fillmore West in San Francisco, the Monterey Jazz Festival, and the Ann Arbor Blues Festival, he performed in concerts in central and east Africa funded by the U.S. State Department. Things continued to look up for him in the early 1970s when for a time he owned and also starred in the Chicago venues Buddie's Club and the Checkerboard Club (the latter open from 1972 to 1979). In 1970 his credits included a European tour with the Rolling Stones and an appearance in the movie *The Blues Is Alive and Well in Chicago.* Through the mid-1970s he was constantly on the go to concerts throughout the United States and overseas, including sets at the Montreux Jazz Festival in Switzerland and the Newport Jazz Festival in New York in 1974 and in Japan in 1975.

However, Buddy's career hit a plateau in the second half of the '70s, and he made relatively little progress on the recording side throughout those years and most of the 1980s. In 1989 he turned things around again by opening a new Chicago club, Legends, which attracted large, enthusiastic crowds from then into the 1990s. The timing was right, with fans in the United States and overseas helping support a blues renaissance. In 1991 Eric Clapton asked Guy to join him for a concert at the Royal Albert Hall in London that proved to be a pop music event, hailed by critics and blues music aficionados in England. The show served as the basis for a concert film that was shown on European stations and also was featured several times on the Public Broadcasting System in the United States.

Buddy also gained a new recording contract with Silvertone Records, which issued the album *Damn Right, I've Got the Blues* in 1991. The album, which included contributions from Clapton, Jeff Beck, and Mark Knopfler, sold well, although it received mixed reviews. Silvertone followed with the 1993 release *Feels Like Rain.* Through the mid-1990s, Buddy had as many performing dates as he wanted, including taking part in many of B.B. King's annual blues festival shows at major venues across the United States. Many of his earlier albums were in print in the mid-1990s, including reissues of Chess tracks on MCA, which had acquired the Chess catalog in the 1970s. (Chess had compiled a number of Buddy Guy albums after he started to gain attention in post-Chess years.)

MCA/Chess discs included *I Was Walking Through the Woods; Left My Blues in San Francisco; Buddy Guy;* and *Buddy Guy: Complete Chess Recordings.*

Also available were *Stone Crazy* and *Alone & Acoustic* (with Junior Wells) on the Alligator label; on Rhino, *The Very Best of Buddy Guy* and *Play the Blues* (with Junior Wells); *Drinkin' TNT & Smokin' Dynamite* on Blind Pig; and *Buddy & the Juniors* (Wells and Junior Mance) on MCA.

HAMMOND, JOHN: *Blues guitarist, harmonica player, singer. Born New York, New York, November 13, 1942.*

John Hammond has shown over the course of a nearly four-decade career that you don't necessarily have to be poor and black to sing the blues. He has been playing Robert Johnson's songs longer than the singer, who died at twenty-seven, was alive. The blues haven't made Hammond rich, but he's brought his act to all corners of the globe. Since 1962 he has toured 200 dates a year and released an astounding number of albums—more than thirty in all. Onstage with a National Steel guitar and a harmonica wrapped around his neck and his foot stomping to the rhythm, Hammond makes for quite an emissary.

The son of legendary Columbia A&R executive John Henry Hammond, John Paul Hammond grew up in luxury in New York City compared to most bluesmen. His father signed Bessie Smith, Billie Holiday, Big Joe Turner, Bob Dylan, Bruce Springsteen, and Stevie Ray Vaughan to the label in his extraordinary career. John Paul Hammond says that his father had very little to do with his decision to go into music. It was the scratchy 78s of Johnson that inspired Hammond to spend countless hours learning the technique.

"People assume I grew up in a musical bonanza, surrounded by it all the time, which was not the case," he says. "My parents divorced when I was five and I lived with my mother and my brother Jason. I wasn't aware of the significance of my father's position until I was a lot older, until I had gone on the road as a musician myself. Then I had to clarify that in fact I got into this on my own and my dad didn't nurture me. He wasn't thrilled when I began this career."

Hammond heard a lot of jazz and blues before his parents split up. He told Jim Washburn of the *Los Angeles Times* (May 25, 1995) that maybe his father had a "subliminal" effect on him. But just as significant were the sounds he heard on the radio in the 1950s.

"When I was becoming a music fanatic . . . I began to focus on the stuff I thought was great—Jimmy Reed, Howlin' Wolf, Muddy Waters, John Lee Hooker and many others. Listening to WLAC [based in Nashville] was an American phenomenon—the shows were sponsored by Randy's Record Shop. How many people sent away to Randy's for those records? I know I was one."

He was drawn to performers like Bo Diddley, Chuck Berry, and Eddie Cochran, but Robert Johnson got to his soul when he first heard him in 1957. "In hearing Robert's music, I was moved so deeply that I felt changed inside," he told Sheila Daughtry of *Players* (January 23, 1992). "Something emerged in me and built up 'til it just had to come out."

Hammond attended several high schools, including the Skowhegan Art School in Maine, where he studied painting and sculpture.

He also picked up a Folkways recording of country blues artists such as Blind Willie McTell and Blind Boy Fuller, which inspired him further. "I saw it as the roots to the rock 'n' roll I heard on the radio, the most direct and incredible stuff I'd ever heard. Not long after that, I got a guitar myself and started fooling around," he told Bill Kohlhaase of the *Los Angeles Times* (June 3, 1994).

Hammond learned to play by ear; he had no lessons. "I got a guitar when I was 18 and drove all my friends nuts for about a year-and-a-half," he told Daughtry. "I got a little better and a little better, and became a raging fanatic."

Hammond attended Antioch College in Yellow Springs, Ohio, where he began playing his music for other people. He hitchhiked out to L.A. when he was nineteen, got a job in a gas station, and auditioned for gigs in the local coffeehouses and clubs. When the club dates were sparse, he busked on street corners. Singer-songwriter Hoyt Axton got Hammond his first gig at the Satire Club. He was such a hit that he was held over for another week. He played at such L.A. clubs as the Insomniac, the Troubadour, the Cat's Pajamas, and the Ash Grove. He also played a TV show with the Chambers Brothers and Long Gone Miles, a blues artist from Texas.

He soon had enough money to buy a car and take a trek across the country. He stopped in Minneapolis, where he encountered Spider John Koerner and the trio of Koerner, Ray, and Glover. In Chicago he met Mike Bloomfield and Sonny Boy Williamson (#2). In November 1962 he wound up in New York City. He played Gerde's Folk City, sharing a bill with Phil Ochs. Both artists were soon signed by Vanguard Records.

He played an impressive set at the Newport Folk Festival in 1963 that received a rave review in the *New York Times*. He soon recorded his first album, *John Hammond*. Hammond, who doesn't write his own material, began developing a reputation as one of the hot young blues interpreters, along with Paul Butterfield, Mike Bloomfield, and Charlie Musselwhite.

He began hanging out in Greenwich Village, where John Sebastian, Bob Dylan, Richie Havens, and blues greats such as Mississippi John Hurt and the Reverend Gary Davis were performing. For a time a guitarist named Jimmy Jones, later known as Jimi Hendrix, played in his band. "He was playing at a place called the Cafe Wha [in Greenwich Village] and a friend of mine said 'You've got to hear this guy, he's great,'" Hammond told Kohlhaase. "I was playing at the Gaslight and Hendrix had just been fired from Curtis Knight's band and was stranded in New York. He and I met between gigs and he asked me if he could play. I was delighted."

Hammond was amazed by Hendrix's talent. For two weeks, Hendrix backed him at the Cafe Au Go Go, where Jimi was discovered. Hendrix went off to England to cut his first albums. Hammond went to England too and in 1965 taped a *Ready, Steady, Go* TV show on which he was backed by John Mayall and the Bluesbreakers with Eric Clapton on guitar.

Hammond continued to make albums for Vanguard, cutting three in 1964 alone: *Big City Blues*, a pioneering effort in electric blues, in *Country Blues*, and *Blues at Newport*, a compilation that included Sonny Terry and Brownie McGhee, Mississippi John Hurt, John Lee Hooker, Gary Davis, and Dave Van Ronk. In 1965, he recorded *So Many Roads*, on which he was backed by three core members from the group that would later become the Band—Robbie Robertson, Garth Hudson, and Levon Helm. Charlie Musselwhite and Mike Bloomfield also played on the album. His 1967 album *Mirrors*, on Vanguard, also included members from the Band. That year he left Vanguard for Atlantic. On his 1967 debut for that label, *I Can Tell* (reissued in 1992 by Atlantic), Bill Wyman of the Rolling Stones, Robbie Robertson, and Rick Danko also played on the sessions.

Hammond recorded two more albums for Atlantic: *Sooner or Later* in 1968 and *Southern Fried* (with Duane Allman on selected cuts) in 1969. He appeared on a couple of compilation albums on Spivey records, a small label based out of blueswoman Victoria Spivey's house in Brooklyn, including *Encore* in 1969, *Kings and the Queen* in 1970, which featured a duet with Roosevelt Sykes, and a compilation in 1971, *The All Star World of Spivey Records*. Vanguard also released *Best of John Hammond* in 1970. Columbia Records president Clive Davis signed Hammond, who released *Source Point* in 1970 and *I'm Satisfied* in 1972. (Delaney Bramlett produced the latter album.) *I'm Satisfied*, which included big-band work and strings on some tracks, represented a departure for the bluesman Hammond, as did his R&B-flavored 1973 album, *Triumvirate*, a group that featured Dr. John, Mike Bloomfield, Blue Mitchell on trumpet, and Chris Ethridge on bass.

Hammond first broke into the film business in 1971, when he composed and performed the sound track for the Dustin Hoffman film *Little Big Man*. He later contributed to the sound track for John Sayles's 1987 film *Matewan*, and made an appearance in *Cross Creek*.

The 1970s and 1980s were tough for many blues players. Disco and punk rock had taken over the club scene and the blues clubs weren't doing well. Somehow Hammond was able to continue his career throughout that period. "There were folk festivals in the summer, coffeehouses and colleges that weren't dependent on the radio or media, and blues has never gone out of style, it's always been there," he says.

He had played with bands on many of his albums, while playing solo when he went on the road. In 1975 he released an album on Capricorn Records called *Can't Beat the Kid*. One side featured Hammond playing solo, and the other featured him with the Capricorn house band. "It had been seven years since I recorded a solo album," he says. "I had stopped working with a band because I felt the lifestyle was at odds with my personal goals. I was anxious to make some records that reflected my stage shows. It brought me into the classic confrontation with a rock-oriented record company as to what material they would release."

Following that LP, Hammond returned to Vanguard and to the solo acoustic realm. He made three more albums for Vanguard: *John Hammond Solo* in 1976, *Footwork* in 1978, again with Roosevelt Sykes on piano, and *Hot Tracks* in 1979, backed by the Nighthawks. Vanguard released a retrospective album in 1993, *You Can't Judge a Book by the Cover.* In 1980 he moved to Rounder and made *Mileage,* followed by *Frogs for Snakes* in 1982 and *John Hammond Live* in 1983, recorded at McCabe's Guitar Shop in Santa Monica. (Rounder reissued *Mileage* and *Frogs for Snakes* on a 1987 CD called *John Hammond.*) He also recorded an album for Flying Fish in 1988, *Nobody but You.*

Showing worldwide interest in Hammond, a British label, Edsel, released a compilation LP in 1984 called *Spoonful,* drawing from his *I Can Tell* and *Southern Fried* albums. A Greek label, Lyra, released *John Hammond Live in Greece* in 1984. Hammond performed at the Montreux Jazz Festival in 1983 along with Stevie Ray Vaughan, Koko Taylor, J.B. Hutto, Sugar Blue, and Luther "Guitar Junior" Johnson. The 1984 album from the festival, *Blues Explosion,* released by Atlantic, won a Best Traditional Blues Grammy.

In 1989 John Lee Hooker asked Hammond to play on his album *The Healer,* and later for his 1991 album, *Mr. Lucky.* The albums on the Pointblank label, had surprisingly strong sales and helped spark new interest in the blues. "I've worked a lot of gigs with John Lee over the years, going back to '62 and '63," Hammond told Mike Boehm of the *Los Angeles Times* (September 24, 1992). "We're friends, and he asked me if I'd like to be on his album."

During that time, Hammond shared a concert bill with J.J. "After Midnight" Cale, who told Hammond he wanted to produce an album for him. Cale produced his 1992 album for Pointblank/Charisma, *Got Love If You Want It,* which was nominated for a Grammy. It was the first solo album Hammond had done since 1988, and it included Cale, John Lee Hooker, and Little Charlie and the Nightcats. Tom Waits wrote a song for the album called "No One Can Forgive Me but My Baby," and Hammond covered Chuck Berry's "Nadine," but

the bulk of the album featured blues standbys—by Son House, Howlin' Wolf, and Little Walter.

Hammond released two more albums on Pointblank/Virgin. *Trouble No More* came first, in 1993. The album, produced by J.J. Cale, was again nominated for a Grammy. It includes a performance by blues great Charles Brown and backing by Little Charlie and the Nighthawks. His next release, *Found True Love* in 1996, was coproduced with blues performer Duke Robillard and features Charlie Musselwhite on blues harp. The album received a Best Traditional Blues Grammy nomination.

Another indication that the blues were starting to take off again was the seventy-two-minute documentary Hammond narrated in 1991, *The Search for Robert Johnson,* later released on Sony Home Video.

"It won't die; they can't kill it," Hammond told Boehm. "They tried. God knows, in the '70s they x-ed blues off the airwaves, and big labels axed all their blues-oriented artists. But the Robert Johnson boxed set [released by Columbia in 1990] changed everything. That gave a new focus for the record industry in general. Its almost immediate worldwide success made everybody go: 'Geez, there's a lot of blues clubs all over the place that we didn't even notice.' All these years, I've never been out of work."

Hammond has been touring almost constantly since 1962. He occasionally opens for Neil Young, whom he met in 1970 at the Cellar Door in Washington, D.C. As he told Bill Locey of the *Los Angeles Times* (April 14, 1994): "You have to go on the road to make money unless you are the best studio musician in the world. Then you have to learn how to live on the road. Since I don't make rock star money, I have to play a lot. I play smaller theaters and clubs. With experience you learn how to maintain your energy and not blow it."

One thing that makes traveling more palatable is he's now accompanied by his wife, Maria.

"Blues is sort of a timeless music," he told Daughtry. "It's not ever really dated. . . . Maybe you don't hit the Top of the Pops, you know, with a really young crowd, but you last a long time if you take care."

In 1998 Hammond went on the House of Blues–sponsored Highway 61 tour, named after the legendary stretch of highway that runs from Memphis to New Orleans. He toured with Booker T. Jones, the Blind Boys of Alabama, and Chicago singer and harp player Billy Boy Arnold. That year he also released a new CD on Pointblank titled *Long As I Have You.* The CD includes three acoustic tracks produced by J.J. Cale. Hammond records songs by Sonny Boy Williamson, Willie Dixon ("As Long As I Have You"), Baby Boy Warren ("I Got Lucky"), Howlin' Wolf ("Crying at Daylight"), Little Walter, and Blind Boy Fuller, and received his fourth Grammy nomination in a row. He was also nominated for W.C. Handy Awards for Acoustic Blues Artist of the Year and Traditional Blues Album of the Year. In 2000

Vanguard issued *Best of the Vanguard Years* and he was working on a new album with Tom Waits.

Based in part on answers to questions submitted to John Hammond

HANDY, W.C.: *Songwriter, composer, band leader, cornetist, publisher, conductor. Born Florence, Alabama, November 16, 1873; died New York, New York, March 28, 1958.*

Unarguably, the blues has had a tremendous influence on modern music. The rhythmic and lyrical presence of the blues can be heard in music styles ranging from jazz and R&B to rock and pop music. To claim to be the "father of the blues" would therefore be a grand accomplishment. There is only one person who has justifiably proclaimed this title: W.C. Handy.

This is not to say that Handy invented the blues. Rather, he was the first one to transcribe and publish blues songs, which had previously existed only as an oral tradition in the American South. Handy standardized and popularized the twelve-bar blues as well as "blue notes" (flattened third and seventh notes in a scale that give the music a strange blend of uplifting yet sad tones).

William Christopher Handy was born in Alabama just eight years after the end of the Civil War. Lincoln's Emancipation Proclamation of 1863 had freed Handy's parents and grandparents from the bonds of slavery, allowing his father and grandfather to become well-respected Methodist ministers. It was assumed that young William would follow in these religious footsteps.

But Handy was more interested in the music of brass bands than in church, and when he saved up enough money he bought himself a guitar. However, Handy's father was outraged at this purchase of what he called the "devil's plaything," and young Handy was forced to trade in the stringed instrument for a new dictionary. According to Handy's autobiography, *Father of the Blues,* his father exclaimed "I'd rather see you in a hearse, son, than have you a musician."

Luckily this incident did not deter Handy from his love of music. At the Florence District School for Negroes, Handy received a rudimentary introduction to vocal music. Not content to just sing, he bought a trumpet from a circus musician and quickly taught himself to play. At the age of fifteen, Handy took his trumpet to the road as a member of a traveling minstrel show. However, the troupe went bankrupt after playing in only a few towns, and Handy was forced to hop a freight car in order to return home.

Interested in becoming a teacher, Handy enrolled in the all-black Agricultural and Mechanical College in Huntsville, Alabama, and received his teaching degree in 1892. However, after realizing that he could expect a very small salary as a teacher, Handy moved to Bessemer, Alabama, to work in a pipeworks company. At this time, Handy organized a vocal quartet, which took to the road after hearing of the Chicago World's Fair. Upon arriving in Chicago, the quartet learned that the fair had been postponed a year, and dejectedly traveled south to St. Louis, Missouri, where they soon disbanded.

The year was 1893, and the country's economy was in a depressed state. The hungry and homeless days that Handy experienced in St. Louis would have an enormous impact on his future music. In fact, the nights spent in vacant lots and on the cobblestones near the Mississippi River would eventually lead to the birth of Handy's most famous composition, the "St. Louis Blues."

After drifting around St. Louis, Handy traveled to Henderson, Kentucky, where he started to garner attention as a cornetist in several local brass bands. Handy later recalled in his autobiography, "I had my change that day in Henderson. My change was from a hobo and a member of a road gang to a professional musician." In Henderson, Handy sought out the director of a local German singing society, from whom he learned a great deal about music. It was also in Henderson that Handy met Elizabeth Virginia Price, who was to be his first wife.

In 1896 Handy was invited to play cornet in W.A. Mahara's Minstrels, and a year later became the troupe's band leader. For the next four years, Handy and the Minstrels traversed the American South and performed in Canada, Mexico, and Cuba. Wanting to try his hand at teaching, Handy taught music and was bandmaster at his alma mater in Huntsville from 1900 to 1902. In 1902 he rejoined Mahara's Minstrels and directed the all-black Knights of Pythias Band. With this band Handy toured the South, playing the popular music of the whites.

The frequent travels through the South enabled Handy to hear the "sorrow songs" of the poor black workers. Handy first came in contact with the blues while waiting in a railroad station in Tutwiler, Mississippi. It was in that deserted railroad station that Handy heard a black man playing the guitar, using a pocket knife as a slide, and singing in what is now the standard blues form. However, it was at a dance in Cleveland, Mississippi, that Handy first saw the mesmerizing effects that the blues could have on audiences. At that dance, Handy watched as three black men, playing on a battered guitar, a mandolin, and a worn-out bass, were showered with coins from the audience for playing their folk music. Handy later recalled in his autobiography that "their music wanted polishing, but it contained the essence. Folks would pay money for it. . . . That night a composer was born, an American composer."

Handy's first blues composition started as a campaign song for Edward H. "Boss" Crump, who was running for mayor of Memphis, Tennessee, in 1909. Handy composed "Mr. Crump," which represented the folk style that was indigenous to the black population of Memphis. Crump won the election, and many believe that Handy's catchy tune was responsible for the victory, even though the lyrics actually mocked Crump's campaign proposals. "Mr. Crump" appealed to both black and white people because of its new twelve-bar blues form, which brought the blues from the backwoods and the cotton fields into the spotlight in a big city.

Because of the song's popularity among voters, Handy decided to add new, nonpolitical lyrics and published the song as the "Memphis Blues" in 1912. Handy believed throughout his life that this was the first published blues song, but in actuality two blues songs (Artie Matthews's "Baby Seal Blues" and Hart Wand's "Dallas Blues") were published earlier that year. Regardless, "Memphis Blues" was the first blues song to achieve worldwide popularity among all types of audiences.

A New York publisher acquired the rights to "Memphis Blues" for a mere $50, and Handy therefore failed to realize any of the profits that the instant commercial hit earned. Frustrated with the growing popularity of a song that was no longer his, Handy decided to compose another blues tune that would earn him some money. While thinking of a subject for his new composition, memories of his down-and-out days in St. Louis danced before his eyes. Flashes of his nights spent homeless and hungry, as well as an image of a drunk woman that he had heard mutter, "My man's got a heart like a rock cast in the sea," compelled Handy to write his most famous piece: "St. Louis Blues."

Although "Memphis Blues" had become quite popular by the time he finished composing his new song, Handy could not find anyone to publish "St. Louis Blues." Handy decided to take matters into his own hands. With Harry Pace, a songwriter and businessman, Handy formed the Memphis-based Pace and Handy Music Company. This new company allowed Handy to publish his masterpiece, and "St. Louis Blues" was released in 1914.

As the world found itself in the midst of an international war, Handy continued to compose and publish blues songs, including "Yellow Dog Blues" (1914), "Hesitating Blues" (1915), "Joe Turner Blues" (1915), "Ole Miss" (1916), and "Beale Street Blues" (1917). "Joe Turner Blues" dealt with a man whose job was to escort convicts from Memphis to Nashville, while "Beale Street Blues" involved hard-luck days on Memphis's famous main street.

In 1917 the Pace and Handy Music Company moved from Memphis to Manhattan and soon after was renamed Handy Brothers Music Company after Pace withdrew from the partnership. Handy's company can still be found at its Broadway location. Along with the music company, Handy moved to New York his Memphis Orchestra, with whom he recorded until the mid-1920s.

Handy continued to compose blues songs, and in 1920 released "Aunt Hagar's Blues" followed by "Loveless Love" (1921), which is better known as "Careless Love." These compositions finally brought Handy the financial success he had always dreamed of. With high hopes, Handy tried his hand at the recording business and founded the Handy Record Company in 1922. However, the label folded quickly before ever issuing any recordings.

The 1920s brought both happiness and sorrow to Handy. "St. Louis Blues," which upon its release had failed to attract much attention, had emerged from obscurity to become one of the most recorded songs of all time. One of the most popular renditions of Handy's standard is the 1925 recording with Bessie Smith on vocals and young Louis Armstrong on the trumpet. Many of Handy's other songs, such as "Beale Street Blues," were quickly becoming classics, and Handy's name was known to most musicians. In 1926 Handy edited his first book, *Blues: An Anthology,* and two years later he conducted the first concert of black music at Carnegie Hall.

However, amid all this glory, Handy was slowly losing his sight. Afflicted by an eye disease, Handy suffered temporary moments of blindness. This condition slowed down his live appearances and recording sessions and forced him to focus on his music publishing company.

In addition to publishing, Handy continued to compose blues songs, such as "Joe Henry Blues" (1922), "Atlanta Blues" (1923), and "East of St. Louis" (1937). But Handy was not limited to the blues. He composed instrumentals such as "Hail to the Spirit of Freedom," spiritual hymns such as "Aframerica Hymn," and even a symphony, *Blue Destiny,* which was inspired by the Gettysburg Address. Handy was a very prolific composer, with over 100 different hymns, marches, and blues tunes under his name.

Handy soon become immortalized by the American public. In 1931 Memphis named a public park, square, school, and theater after him. Handy's sixtieth birthday in 1933 was celebrated with a dinner and concert at Carnegie Hall, and with fifteen different performances of "St. Louis Blues" in Hollywood.

Tragedy struck in 1937 when Handy's wife of almost forty years, Elizabeth, died of a cerebral hemorrhage. Handy, however, continued to be applauded by the American public. He was paid tribute to at Carnegie Hall in 1938, and was honored at the 1940 New York World's Fair. Handy told the public his life story in 1941 through his autobiography, *Father of the Blues.*

Handy came close to his own death in 1943 after falling from a New York City subway platform. He fractured his skull, became totally blind, and was confined to a wheelchair. However, Handy refused to give in to his debilitated condition, and continued to run his music publishing company, compose songs, and play the trumpet in front of audiences. In 1954 the composer married his longtime secretary, Irma Louise Logan.

Handy's long and successful life came to an end on March 28, 1958, in a New York City hospital. Less than two weeks later, Handy's life was portrayed, rather inaccurately, in *St. Louis Blues,* a film that starred Nat King Cole as Handy. Handy's son and daughter took over the management of the music publishing company, renaming it the W.C. Handy Music Company.

Posthumous awards and recognitions continued to enhance Handy's image. He was elected to the *Ebony* hall of fame in 1959, and was immortalized in a statue along Beale Street in Memphis. The U.S. Post Office commemorated Handy by placing his image on the six-cent stamp in 1969, and ten years later a street in New York City was named after him. The Blues Foundation has been handing out W.C. Handy Awards annually since 1980 to recognize achievement in the field of blues music.

Handy was also the editor of *Book of Negro Spirituals* (1938), *Negro Music and Musicians* (1944), and *A Treasury of the Blues* (1949). He was also the composer of many notable songs not mentioned, including "Hooking Cow Blues," "Long Gone," "Chantez Les Bas," "Friendless Blues," "Harlem Blues," "Basement Blues," "Annie Love," "Big Stick Blues March," and "Roosevelt Triumphal March."

W.C. Handy did not invent the blues, but he introduced them to the American public. As a guardian, promoter, publisher, and composer of the blues, Handy made sure that the world would hear and remember the folk music of his people.

Entry by Adam Seidman

HAPA: *Hawaiian duo. Keli'i Kaneali'i (slack-key guitarist, vocals), born Oahu, Hawaii. Barry Flanagan (slack-key guitarist, vocals, songwriter), born New York, New York.*

There is nothing like listening to the soothing and mystical sounds of Hapa while driving along the Hana Highway in Maui. This is not a travel story, but it is the tale of how a New Jersey boy met a native Hawaiian to create one of the most successful Hawaiian bands in history. Quite simply, they both followed their musical dreams. Their lush harmonies and rich slack-key sound have been called the "sound of Maui." Hapa, slang for "half" or "ethnically mixed," describes the blending of Barry Flanagan, of Irish Catholic descent, and Keli'i Kaneali'i, who grew up on the island of Oahu. Their music is a blend of the traditional Hawaiian sounds of Gabby Pahinui and the singer-songwriter traditions of Kenny Loggins and James Taylor.

Flanagan was born in New York but raised in New Jersey. His parents loved Frank Sinatra and he listened to the Beatles growing up. His mom played guitar in the

church while his sister played the six-string instrument in a rock band. Barry didn't start playing until eighteen. In 1979, he was in Boulder, Colorado, when he was awestruck by the slack-key guitarist Gabby Pahinui he heard on Ry Cooder's *Chicken Skin Music.* "I've never, even to this day, heard anyone play the acoustic guitar with such depth and feeling," Barry told Mark D. Moss of *Sing Out!* ("Hapa," Summer 1998). "I couldn't get a handle on the vocals at first, but the slack-key sound really floored me. I knew immediately that I wanted to experiment with that kind of open sound."

Flanagan bought more Pahinui LPs and used some insurance money he collected from a house fire to finance a trip to Hawaii to study his newfound musical love.

Kaneali'i, the youngest of fifteen children, grew up outside Honolulu in Papakolea. His uncle taught him how to play slack-key guitar. He participated in the church choir and sang traditional Hawaiian songs in the high school glee club. When Gerald Ford was president Keli'i danced the hula in a Hawaiian-style revue at the White House. "I'm Hawaiian Chinese and my dad's a pure Hawaiian and my mom's Hawaiian Chinese," Kaneali'i told National Public Radio ("Hawaiian Band Melds Traditional and Pop Music," February 1, 1996). "But my whole family sings. Grew up in church and in the choir, like that. And I guess when I was a baby I had been around music all the time."

In 1978 he moved to Maui and started playing in a band with Gabby Pahinui's son Martin. Keli'i loved the music of Loggins, Taylor, and Kenny Rankin. "I guess I've been playing Hawaiian music for so long that I wanted to play something else, you know, for a little change," he told NPR.

Flanagan settled in Maui and studied slack key guitar with Manu Kahaialli, who had played with Gabby Pahinui. He also played music with a next door neighbor named Jimmie Kaopuiki, who played bass and ukulele. In 1983, Flanagan played briefly in a local New Orleans-style group.

Flanagan and Kaneali'i were destined to meet at a party on Christmas Eve, 1983. Flanagan brought his guitar and when he went to stash it in a closet he discovered someone else had brought a guitar as well. "We ended up talking and began to play a little together," Flanagan told Moss. "It was like meeting my other half! I knew a lot of my older Hawaiian stuff from my time playing with Jimmie, and K had really been bitten by a lot of the mainland pop music that I was very familar with. We had just met when we began jamming a bit at the party, but the rest of the guests thought we were a practiced act. The moment I heard Keli'i's voice, I knew I had met my musical soul mate. I just had to travel 6,000 miles to find him."

Hapa features Flanagan's songwriting (with lyrics translated into Hawaiian), and Keli'i's tenor voice. "We have a new different sound," Kaneali'i told NPR. "It's like grabbing an old Hawaiian song and then giving it life."

They performed in Hawaii for nine years before recording their first album, *Hapa* (1992), on Coconut Grove. The album, which included a guest appearance by Stephen Stills, fared well with the buying public on the islands and the mainland, and earned the duo three Hawaiian music awards: best group, album, and song. They won all six titles for which they were nominated in the 1994 Na Hoku Hanohano awards. In 1995, they followed with *Hapa Holidays*, traditional and Hawaiian Christmas music, which did not match their debut. They remedied that with two albums in 1997: *In the Name of Love*, a collection in keeping with their debut, and *Surf Madness*, featuring surfing classics like "Walk Don't Run," "Hawaii-5-0," and "Wipe Out." In 1999, Hapa released its fifth album entitled *Namahana*. Flanagan and Kaneali'i perform in up to 100 concerts a year. Flanagan's songs have also been featured on the TV show *Northern Exposure* and the film *Race the Sun*.

HARDIN, TIM: *Singer, guitarist, songwriter. Born Eugene, Oregon, December 23, 1941; died Los Angeles, California, December 29, 1980.*

A singer with a unique vocal style that influenced many new artists in folk and pop music in the late 1960s and early 1970s, Tim Hardin suffered from the minority status of the folk field in terms of receiving widespread recognition for his performing ability. However, many people who wouldn't have known his name were quite familiar with many of his excellent compositions, which provided hits for artists ranging from Joan Baez to such rock stars as Bobby Darin and the Youngbloods. At one point, Bob Dylan paid him an oblique compliment by issuing an album in 1968 called *John Wesley Harding*, the name of a legendary outlaw who was an ancestor of Tim Hardin.

Music was part of Tim's more immediate heritage. Both his parents were musically inclined. His mother, in particular, developed a major national reputation in the classical field. Both of his parents studied music in school and both earned master's degrees in the field. His mother, Molly Small Hardin, ranked as one of the world's most accomplished female violinists, and, when young Tim was growing up in Oregon, she served as concertmaster of the Portland Symphony Orchestra. His father tended to favor more popularly oriented music, having played in jazz bands during his high school years and while serving in the navy. However, he turned to selling real estate rather than the arts as his main vocation.

Tim's musical inclinations didn't start to take shape until his high school years. "I started fooling around with the guitar in high school and I sang in the Eugene high school choir. I never thought of going to college, really, in my life. If you've got any kind of talent, man, it just restricts you."

After high school, in the late 1950s, Tim enlisted in the marines as the way to strike out on his own. The military occupied most of his next four years, first involving duty in Cambodia and Laos followed by two years in the reserves. When he was off-duty, Tim kept improving his guitar playing, and also added to his store of folk songs. After he completed his hitch, he headed across the United States to Cambridge, Massachusetts, where he soon became an important part of the still-burgeoning folk scene. He became a favorite of Boston fans from his appearances at local coffeehouses and small clubs. Increasingly he introduced some of his original songs into his act.

In 1966, Verve Records signed him and issued his debut LP on the Verve/Forecast label, *Tim Hardin*, in September 1966. Close to a year later, his second album, *Tim Hardin II*, came out in July 1967. Two months later another release, *This Is Tim Hardin*, came out on Atco Records, an album he had recorded in the early 1960s but reportedly, by the mid-1960s, did not want released. Meanwhile, other artists were beginning to turn out recordings of some of Tim's writings, including such well-known tunes as "If I Were a Carpenter," which provided a hit single in 1966 for Bobby Darin and later for Johnny Cash and his wife, June Carter, and "Reason to Believe," covered by dozens of well-known performers over the years, including Rod Stewart in 1972. During the late 1960s, many of Hardin's compositions were written in his new home, Woodstock, in upstate New York, where his paths crossed those of people like Dylan and the Band.

In the late 1960s, Verve/Forecast issued such other LPs as *Tim Hardin 3 Live in Concert* and *Tim Hardin 4*. In August 1969, Verve/Forecast turned out a retrospective of his earlier records, *Best of Tim Hardin*. He also was represented on MGM Records with an album called *Tim Hardin*. In 1968 he signed with a new label, Columbia, which issued his first LP, *Suite for Susan, Moore and Damian* in April 1969. Among his other releases on Columbia were *One, All in One*, and *Bird on a Wire*, released in August 1971.

His albums didn't make national charts, though Hardin maintained excellent rapport with folk adherents, including many critics. One of them wrote, "I wear out Tim Hardin's records as fast as Billie Holiday's. I suppose that's because Tim and Billie experienced pain so hurtingly and have so hauntingly made it a musical experience."

In the late 1960s and at the start of the 1970s, Hardin toured widely both in the United States and abroad. His concerts graced the stages of many colleges and clubs and concert halls in almost every major U.S. city. Indicating his standing with his musical peers, at many venues the audience included some of the best-known entertainers in the music field, past and present.

Hardin was frustrated by the rather limited attention he received in his homeland and at the fact that his songs tended to provide hits for other performers rather than himself. (Ironically, Tim's only hit single, "Simple Song of Freedom," wasn't self-penned but was written by Bobby Darin.) In 1971 he moved to England, where he remained for seven years. During that period he concertized in England and on the Continent, occasionally taking time out to record new material, such as the 1973 album *Nine* for Island Records, later issued in the United States in 1971 on Island's Antilles label.

In the late 1970s Tim returned to the United States with renewed optimism about finding his audience at home. In April 1980, his path crossed that of old friend Don Rubin, in the 1960s Tim's executive producer and music publisher during his association with Verve/Forecast Records. As Rubin told Len Epand, public relations director of Polygram Records (recalled by Epand in notes for Hardin's posthumous album on Polygram), the two planned a new project. "It was like a dream come true. . . . He had returned to make a comeback here in the U.S. We immediately set about the task of preparing a new album. He had written ten new songs for the project and we began recording the LP, a never to be completed LP due to his untimely death."

A poignant commentary on his career came from observations from Nancy Covey (then in charge of booking acts for McCabe's folk-music venue) soon after his passing. As she noted to Robert Hilburn of the *Los Angeles Times,* the last time she'd seen him perform was at a country music club in Malibu called the Lone Star. Tim had gone there to say hello to longtime friend Ramblin' Jack Elliott, who was headlining the show. "The sad thing was people didn't seem to know who he was. They just thought he was just another guy singing 'If I Were a Carpenter.' They didn't realize he wrote the song. They just kept on talking. In some ways, that was the story of Tim's life.

In the same month that the music world lost John Lennon, Hardin was found dead of a drug overdose in Los Angeles. In early 1981, Polygram issued the *Tim Hardin Memorial Album,* at the time the only album of Hardin recordings in print. The tracks, all of his own compositions, mostly were culled from his first two Verve/Forecast LPs, with two from *Tim Hardin 4.* They were "If I Were a Carpenter," "Black Sheep Boy," "Misty Roses," "Green Rocky Road," "How Long," "Don't Make Promises," "Smugglin' Man," "Hello Baby," "Reason to Believe," "How Can We Hang On to a Dream," "Lady Came from Baltimore," and "It'll Never Happen Again."

By the start of the '90s, essentially all of Tim's recordings were out of print in the United States. People still turned out new covers of many of his best-known songs. By the mid-1990s, well over 100 different covers of "If I Were a Carpenter" had been issued, and totals rose for others like "Misty Roses" and "Reason to Believe." Performers who included cuts of

Hardin originals in albums issued during the first half of the decade included Robert Plant, Wilson–Philips, and the reunited Emerson, Lake, and Palmer rock group. In the fall of 1993 Rod Stewart included a new track of "Reason to Believe" in his *Unplugged . . . and Seated* album.

Hardin's long absence from record store bins finally was corrected in early 1994, when Polydor issued the package *Hang On to a Dream: The Verve Recordings* (available on either two CDs or two cassettes). The set included all forty-seven of the songs released on the Verve label from 1964 to 1966 plus seventeen previously unreleased tracks of both Hardin compositions and his treatments of songs by other writers.

David Browne, in his review of the release for the *New York Times* ("Tim Hardin Defied Convention," February 20, 1994), saw the package as more than a hits sampler: "It also reminds listeners that no one ever sang those songs like the writer himself. An egotist and something of an exhibitionist, Mr. Hardin didn't hesitate to use his songs to chronicle his marriage, the birth of his son, divorce and the inner turmoil brought on by success and its temptations. In those songs, pain and uncertainty was a given; love was something easily lost or betrayed."

The package contents, as Browne also noted, reflected the fact that Hardin's interests never were focused solely on "pure" folk music. He had absorbed some of his father's interest in jazz and was an early devotee of rhythm and blues, for instance. Browne observed, "His arrangements were those of a jazz musician's, and his phrasing lies somewhere between folk and blues. Few performers have roamed down that road since. One of them, the jazz singer Cassandra Wilson, turns songs by Robert Johnson and Joni Mitchell into desert-dry cabaret on her latest release, *Blue Light 'Til Dawn.* Yet that album is an anomaly; in some ways, Mr. Hardin is still waiting for everyone to catch up."

A succinct epitaph on Hardin's much-too-short career was given in the album liner notes by Colin Escott: "If Tim Hardin's life had one recurrent theme, it was excess. He took everything to the limits—then stretched them. He ate in binges, drank to excess, smoked constantly, doped himself up excessively, loved suffocatingly."

HARDING, JOHN WESLEY: *Singer, guitarist, songwriter, author, band leader (the Good Liars). Born Hastings, England, October 22, 1965.*

A creative will-o'-the-wisp who dabbled in writing plays and short stories as well as songs, folk rocker John Wesley Harding covered a wide range of genres in his musical output. (As he said in 1995, "I always wanted to be an amalgam of all my favorite musicians. It was the music of a music fan. It still is, I think.") His 1991 Sire/Reprise album, *The Name above the Title,* for instance, had elements of soul in the track "Facts of

Life," hip-hop in "Bridegroom Blues," country-folk in "Anonymous 1916," and a number called "Movie of Your Life," which he described as "a dead ringer for a Carpenters song." The album's name referred to the autobiography of movie director Frank Capra, reflecting Harding's deep interest in cinema. (His doctoral dissertation at England's Cambridge University dealt with the roles portrayed by American actor Jimmy Stewart in various films.) His excellent initial albums struck a responsive chord with reviewers in England and the United States, but perhaps because it was so difficult to categorize the material they didn't win a great deal of attention from record buyers.

Born and raised in Hastings, East Sussex, England, in a family with considerable artistic talents—his mother was an opera singer, his father a jazz pianist—Wesley Harding Stace (he later changed his name to John Wesley Harding after the title of a Bob Dylan 1960s album that took its cue in turn from a western U.S. outlaw of that name) didn't seem inspired by entertainment pursuits in his formative years. In his early teens he told friends that he aspired to become a professional sportscaster. Though surrounded by the sounds of British and American rock and roll, in his mid-teens he gravitated toward blues and folk, influenced by the recordings of the late Robert Johnson and the work of a Hastings area slide guitarist. Other favorites at the time were Loudon Wainwright and John Hiatt, some of whose material the seventeen-year-old incorporated into an act he presented at a local pub, accompanying himself on acoustic guitar.

Among other American performers whose recordings became part of his collection while attending Cambridge were Jim Croce, Steve Goodman, Phil Ochs, and John Prine. (Among the stories and plays he wrote at the time was a play based on the life of Ochs. That play never was staged, however, because the late singer's brother, Michael Ochs, threatened legal action.) Inspired by their music, he started to write and perform his own folk-flavored songs in the Cambridge area. During the summer of 1988 he got the opportunity to take the stage in London, where the audience included a music publisher, a booking agent, and a prospective manager. His work impressed all of them and soon resulted in broader exposure as opening act for the band Hothouse Flowers in the United Kingdom and his idol John Hiatt in Europe. In late fall 1988 he returned to London to make his initial recordings, aided by musician friends. All the tracks were laid down in a single night, with no overdubs and no edits, for a total cost of only 800 pounds. Called *It Happened One Night,* the new album was released on Jake Riviera's independent Demon Records.

Harding and his advisers decided he needed an affiliation with a label with broader distribution capabilities, and to help make this move Harding prepared new demo tapes backed by Elvis Costello's band, the At-

tractions. Those tapes won a contract in early 1989 from Seymour Stein, head of Sire Records, who assigned the production team of Andy Paley and one-time punk music star Tom Robinson. For recording sessions in London and Los Angeles, Harding assembled a band called the Good Liars (Kenny Craddock on keyboards, Steve Donnelly on guitar, plus Attractions members) and completed work on his Sire/Reprise debut, *Here Comes the Groom,* for release in 1990. (Initial single and video was "Devil in Me.")

The album indeed was a gem and won often-lavish praise from the print media. The *St. Petersburg (Florida) Times* critic, for instance, called it a breathtaking debut "blending folkie integrity with rock 'n' roll intensity . . . Harding's youthful urgency is tempered by his engaging melodies, a deadpan sense of humor and playful arrangements. . . ." *Rolling Stone*'s assessment included such comments as: "His sometimes acidic political and social commentary is cushioned by pure pop production . . . [an] impressive major label debut."

Starting in January 1990, John Wesley was on the road most of the year working on a Sire-sponsored Laughter Tour that featured the label's groups the Mighty Lemon Drops and the Ocean Blue. Later in the year he opened for rising star Michelle Shocked. Airplay of his material was limited, however, and the album was far from a best-seller.

During the summer of 1990 Harding went back into the studios to work on his second Sire/Reprise album. Members of the Good Liars for the project, besides Donnelly and Craddock, were Pete Thomas on drums and Bruce Thomas on bass. Many others pitched in, including Victoria Williams, Ronee Blakley, the Morgans Creek String Ensemble, and the Big and Brassy Brass Band. Most, if not all, of the fifteen tracks on the new early '91 release, *The Name above the Title,* were drawn from forty new songs written by Harding.

While he was recording his next album in Los Angeles, the 1992 riots erupted in the black community. Reflecting the mood of the time, the final collection, the Sire 1992 release *Why We Fight,* had a considerably darker tone than earlier material. The tracks included a commentary on "modern day fascism" titled "Hitler's Tears," and such other notable originals as "The Truth" and "Ordinary Weekend." (Also issued on Sire in 1992 was the extended-play album *Pett Levels/The Summer EP*). Among those who applauded the effort was Bruce Springsteen, who joined Harding onstage during a concert at the 100-seat local folk venue, McCabe's. Later in the decade, Springsteen asked Harding to open two shows on Bruce's acoustic tour. Besides Springsteen, many other notables in the folk and rock field guested on some of Harding's concerts, including John Prine, Joan Baez, Iggy Pop, Lou Reed, and Ramblin' Jack Elliott.

It took several years for Harding's next album project, though he continued to tour steadily from 1992 through 1995, appearing solo—sometimes accompanied by multiinstrumentalist Robert Lloyd, and sometimes with a band—either as headliner or opening act for other artists, including Michelle Shocked. Things hadn't worked out well in his dealings with the record industry to that point, and he decided to finance his next sessions himself. The new tracks were assembled in the studio of friend and coproducer Chris von Sneidern, located in the latter's basement in San Francisco. (That city had become Harding's home base after he shifted his activities from England to the United States.) He commented, "Being on a big label was like a funfair merry-go-round; too quick too soon then it took ages to slow down—neither was my preferred speed." The new sessions, he said, were "very relaxed; just friends making music. No clock on the wall, no pool table, just patience and a blank canvas. I wouldn't even remember how to do it any other way. There's orchestration and arrangements on the record, but the lyrics and my acoustic guitar are the focal points—and that's a first for me, which is surprising given I'm a folk singer."

The resulting album, including such mind-bending compositions as "Paradise," "Heart without a Home," "The Speed of Normal," and "The Triumph of Trash," was titled *John Wesley Harding's New Deal*. Issued on the Forward/Rhino label in 1996, it ranked as one of the more engaging folk discs of the year. He followed with *Awake* (1998), *Trad Arr Jones* (1999), and a series of outtake albums, *Dynablob 1, 2, and 3*.

HARRIS, COREY: *Singer, songwriter, guitarist. Born Denver, Colorado, February 21, 1969.*

When his debut album, *Between Midnight and Day,* came out in 1995, many hailed Corey Harris as a latter-day "bluesman," a throwback to the days of Charley Patton and Blind Lemon Jefferson. While he was inspired by musicians like Son House and Lightnin' Hopkins and has covered blues songs on his albums, Harris takes pains to avoid such classifications. He told Pat Collier of *Sing Out!* ("Corey Harris: Manifesting the Blues," Fall 1998). "There's a difference between playing a lot of blues and being a bluesman. Really, the term is really thrown around so much it doesn't mean anything anymore. The only living people I would call blues men are surviving masters at what they do." Still, with his National Steel that he plays with a slide, Harris has distinguished himself by incorporating sounds of his African-American ancestors into his music.

Harris was born and raised in Denver, Colorado. His father died when he was one, and he was raised by his mother, a guidance counselor and home economics teacher, and a stepfather, who loved music. Although Corey grew up in Denver, his roots were in the South. "We ate southern food," he told Collier. "We didn't go to church all the time, but when we did it was a southern church, with gospel music. On vacation, we went to the South to see our relatives."

He was given a toy guitar when he was three and started playing trumpet, violin, and drums in grade school. He sang in church groups and was also influenced by the music on such shows as *Hee Haw* and *Soul Train*. His mother, a pianist, gave him a real guitar when he was twelve and introduced him to the music of Lightnin' Hopkins. "Once I started getting into Lightning, I realized, 'This is from the country, and my people, they're from the country,'" he told Chris Nickson of *Folk Roots* ("The Country Blues Is Alive and Well in the Hands of Corey Harris," June 1996). "So it became very personal. It was also part of my re-education in general about my own history, and what my family had been through."

He learned to play guitar by listening to his favorite albums over and over, developing fingerpicking and flatpicking skills. In the meantime he played trumpet in the junior high school marching band, and later guitar in a rock band in high school. He studied anthropology at Bates College in Maine, playing music in coffeehouses. He had become fascinated by Son House and ended up buying a National Steel guitar, which he struggled to learn to play with a slide. He spent a semester abroad in France which inspired him to travel to Cameroon, West Africa, where he studied pidgin. While there, he also became immersed in the musical sounds and philosophies of West Africa, discovering the roots of African-American music, including Makossa, Bikutsi, and juju.

Returning from Africa, he moved to Louisiana, where he taught French and English in a middle school near New Orleans. In his off hours he would play on the streets of the Crescent City, as well as performing on WWOZ-FM radio. He traveled to Clarksdale, Mississippi, where he had a brief encounter with Big Jack Johnson and saw Muddy Waters's cabin at the Stovall Plantation. He developed his strong voice from singing on the streets and began to get gigs in coffeehouses, colleges, and clubs.

While playing in Helena, Arkansas, in 1993, he met producer Larry Hoffman, who wanted to produce his debut album. The following year, Harris recorded his debut in a six-hour session. *Between Midnight and Day* was released by Alligator Records in 1995. The album includes three Harris originals and has him covering classic blues songs by Lonnie Johnson, Bukka White, Charley Patton, and Mississippi Fred McDowell. It garnered strong reviews. Natalie Merchant invited Harris to tour with her. He also opened for Buddy Guy, B.B. King, and the Dave Matthews Band. He toured throughout the United States, Europe, and Japan, and guested on Junior Wells's 1996 Telarc CD, *Come on in This House*.

In 1997, Alligator released his second CD, *Fish Ain't Bitin'*. Again, the album includes a combination of classic blues numbers and originals (this time nine of them), such as "5-0 Blues," about police brutality against people of color. "I've been arrested and I've been fucked with by the cops," Harris told Collier. "Any black male in America can relate to that. And any Latino male." *Fish Ain't Bitin'*, which included a New Orleans brass section on four songs, also received strong reviews. As Robert Christgau of the *Village Voice* wrote, "After a debut that established his mastery of the Delta idiom, Harris does something really hard—proves he's big enough to fool around with it. . . . His virtuosity springs to life." Harris won a W.C. Handy Award for Acoustic Blues Album of the Year.

When Billy Bragg was working on putting music to some old Woody Guthrie lyrics, he mentioned to Natalie Merchant that he wanted to include a blues singer in the project. She suggested Harris. Harris joined Bragg, Wilco, and Merchant on the *Mermaid Avenue* album that was released by Elektra in 1998 and received a Grammy nomination. Harris wrote music for a Guthrie lyric titled "Teabag Blues," which was included as a bonus track on his next CD, *Greens from the Garden*, released by Alligator in 1999. Harris chose the title to make a point: that his music, while rooted in blues, springs from a mélange of influences. "It's called *Greens from the Garden* because when you make greens, you take a little kale and some turnips and some mustard greens, some spinach, and you boil them all together." Alligator released *Vü-Dü Menz* in 2000, with Henry Butler.

HART, ALVIN YOUNGBLOOD: *Singer, songwriter, guitarist. Born Oakland, California, March 2, 1963.*

With just two albums to his credit, Alvin Youngblood Hart is already considered one of the best new blues artists among a promising group of young African Americans. In 1997 he was honored with a W.C. Handy Award for Best New Blues Artist of the Year. But while his bedrock is in the blues tradition of the Mississippi Delta, his music also reflects a wide variety of influences such as the cowboy music of Roy Rogers and Gene Autry, the folk blues of Leadbelly, and the blues-rock sounds of Frank Zappa and Jimi Hendrix.

He was born Gregory Edward Hart in Oakland, California. He took the name Alvin from Alvin and the Chipmunks, and "Youngblood" was the nickname the old blues guys in Chicago gave him when he was still a teenager. His parents had roots in Mississippi, his mother in Carroll County, near Greenwood, and his father in the northern part of the state. Both of them listened to blues records. His music also reflects his Native American roots. His great-grandmother was a Chickasaw Indian.

His father worked for General Electric and moved the family with him as he took jobs in different parts of the country. During vacations, the Hart family often returned to Mississippi to visit relatives. Since it took a while to make new friends, this left Hart with a lot of time to learn guitar, which he began in his teens. He grew up watching Roy Rogers and Gene Autry on TV,

soaking in their music as well. When he was in his late teens his family moved to Illinois, where he had a chance to see Muddy Waters perform. He also hung out on Maxwell Street with some of the old-timers who gave him his sobriquet. He put together a garage rock band with three friends.

In his early twenties Hart was getting bored with his job at a furniture factory in Southern California. By 1984 he had also tired of electric guitars and began exploring acoustic blues.

One day in 1986 he wandered into a Coast Guard recruiting office, signing up for a seven-year hitch. For three years he was stationed on a riverboat in Natchez, Mississippi, not far from his relatives. When he wasn't setting buoys to mark deep-water channels, Hart spent time practicing the guitar. He began sitting in with bands at a saloon on the Natchez waterfront. When he was transferred to a Coast Guard chart school in New York City, he continued his musical exploration. He would jam on Sunday nights at Dan Lynch's Club. The Coast Guard transferred him again, to Bolinas, in the San Francisco Bay Area. He started hanging out at a guitar store in Berkeley, where he learned how to restore vintage guitars. That's also where he met his wife, Heidi Loetscher, who excelled at restoring old guitars. He met Joe Louis Walker at the store; Walker asked him to perform with him at the San Francisco Blues Festival in 1991.

Four years later he was opening for Taj Mahal at Yoshi's in Oakland when Michael Nash and Carey Williams were impressed by his music. They offered to produce his debut album, *Big Mama's Door*, which came out on Sony's OKeh subsidiary in 1996. The CD includes Hart's stirring version of old blues standards such as Charley Patton's "Pony Blues," Blind Willie McTell's "Hillbilly Willie's Blues," and Leadbelly's "Gallow's Pole." Taj Mahal plays mandolin and guitar and sings on three tracks. It won several awards in the 1997 *Living Blues* critics poll: Best Debut Album, Best Traditional Album of the Year, and Best Blues Album. Despite the accolades, Sony did not push the album, and Hart signed a deal with Rykodisc, which released *Territory* in 1998. It was a much more eclectic album than the first, including ska, rock, and western swing sounds he had gleaned from the TV westerns.

Hart also contributed two tracks, "Sway" and "Moonlight Mile," to the Rolling Stones tribute album, *Paint It Blue*, and sat in on guitar for Junior Wells's 1996 Telarc album, *Come On in This House*.

HART, MICKEY: *percussionist, songwriter, producer. Born New York, New York, September 11, 1943.*

Mickey Hart followed his heart and heartbeat. As a child, he learned the rudimental, or military, style of drumming, later playing in marching bands in the air force. In 1967 he began drumming for the Grateful Dead. That would have been enough for most. But Hart felt compelled to explore the spiritual side of drumming. As he wrote in his 1990 autobiography *Drumming at the Edge of Magic* (Harper, San Francisco), "I had a burning desire to know why the tradition of drumming I inherited as a young American percussionist in the '60s had become devoid of the spirit or trance side of the drum, a side recognized by almost every culture on the planet." Hart embarked on an exploration of "endangered" music: from the Gyuto Tantric Choir to the percussionists he assembled for his Grammy-winning *Planet Drum* album.

As he recounts in his autobiography, Hart was born into a drumming family. Both of his parents, Lenny and Leah, played drums. Lenny, an award-winning rudimental drummer, taught Leah how to play drums at the Coney Island American Legion drum and bugle corps. They won the mixed doubles competition at the 1939 New York World's Fair. Mickey was born in 1943, but Lenny soon abandoned the family, leaving a wooden drum pad and a pair of snakewood sticks behind. "When I found the sticks, I began playing," Hart recalled. At first his mother tried to hide the pad, but eventually she gave him toy drum set at age eleven. They moved to Lawrence, Long Island, and Mickey played in the high school band.

During the 1950s, he idolized Gene Krupa and Buddy Rich, practicing to recordings of Krupa on "Sing, Sing, Sing," at times working himself into a trancelike state. He listened to early rock and the Latin and Cuban sounds popular in New York. A 1960 recording by Nigerian drummer Babatunde Olatunji made a lasting impression.

Hart quit high school and joined the air force hoping to become a military drummer. He was completing basic training at Lackland Air Force Base when he came across a pamphlet advertising Remo Weather-King drumheads. The quote in the ad was from none other than Lenny Hart, his father. While stationed at March Air Force Base, near Riverside, California, Mickey went to Los Angeles in search of the Remo factory. Remo Belli, the drum inventor, told Mickey that his father worked at a savings and loan in the San Fernando Valley. They became reacquainted, and Lenny demonstrated his ability to play in the rudimental style. But they lost touch when Mickey was transferred to the Strategic Air Command in Spain.

While in Spain, Mickey played in a marching band by day and a sixteen-piece dance band at night. But he took a hiatus from drumming when a friend encouraged him to get involved in competitive judo. (He won his weight class at the European championships.) He left the air force in 1965 and settled in New York.

Lenny soon reappeared and invited Mickey to the San Francisco area to help him open a music store. Mickey helped convert a guitar store into Drum City where they held drum clinics. At one of these, with Count Basie's drummer Sonny Payne, Mickey met Billy Kreutzmann, who played drums in the Grateful Dead. Kreutzmann took Hart to see Janis Joplin with Big Brother and the Holding Company at the Matrix Theater, an experience that changed Hart's life forever.

"Kreutzmann and I became drum brothers after that first night at the Matrix," Hart wrote. "We started hanging out, drumming together, cruising around Haight-Ashbury in Billy's Mustang. The Haight was as noisy as you got in America in the mid-sixties, probably because it was a psychoactive community, maybe the first in the history of the planet. You can't talk about the Haight without taking into account the mutating presence of LSD. People were high all the time."

He heard the Dead play for the first time on September 29, 1967, at the Straight Theater. He sat in on the song "Alligator/Caution" for two hours. "You practice for years so that you reach a point of technical proficiency where the instrument becomes part of your body," Hart wrote. "You no longer have to think about fingering or counting beats, so your mind is free for higher matters, most of which involve the pursuit of a personal style, a distinctive voice. This is a doubly difficult passage because your training has involved learning to mimic the powerful voices of the great musicians within your tradition, the Krupas, the Riches, the Paynes. You work to become like them, to wear their technical clothing, and yet one day a moment like the one I experienced at the Straight Theater comes along—so totally unexpected that I have often wondered what might have happened if I hadn't crossed paths with Kreutzmann."

After that night, Hart joined the Grateful Dead as the second drummer. "Kreutzmann and I worked hard at synchronizing our drumming," he wrote. "Sometimes we'd play for hours with our arms around each other, Billy handling one drumstick, me the other. . . . I taught Billy what I knew of the rudiments, and he taught me how to rock."

He played on the *Live/Dead* album in 1969 and *Anthem of the Sun* soon after. Bassist Phil Lesh introduced Hart to other rhythms when he gave him an album called *Drums of North and South India*, featuring Alla Rakha on the tabla. After a Ravi Shankar concert on Long Island, Rakha introduced Hart to the concept of polyrhythms.

The Dead turned to Lenny Hart, who became its business manager, but the relationship soon turned ugly. In 1970, after creditors tried to repossess Ron "Pigpen" McKernan's organ, the band discovered that Lenny had been skimming funds. Lenny went to jail, and Mickey voluntarily left the band in 1971. He went into his own confinement in a place he called the Barn in Novato, California. Even while he was in his self-imposed exile, Warner Brothers offered Hart a three-record deal, releasing his first solo album in 1972, *Rolling Thunder*. The album was inspired by John Pope, a brakeman who claimed shamanic powers.

Living in the country, Hart became attuned to the sounds of nature: crickets, the sound of water. He developed a close musical relationship with Alla Rakha's tabla-playing son, Zakir Hussain, who stayed with him at the Barn while he taught at Ali Akbar Khan's school in Berkeley. Hussain and Hart eventually formed the Diga Rhythm Band, made up of eleven percussionists, some of them students at Ali Akbar Khan's school. They released *Diga* in 1976, which featured Jerry Garcia.

Hart rejoined the Grateful Dead in October 1974 for what was supposed to be the band's last series of concerts at Winterland. Instead they returned to the studio and produced *Blues for Allah* (1975), an innovative album. (Hart worked on at least 45 albums with the Dead.) Hart also invented percussion instruments during the 1970s. "The Beast" included several bass drums suspended at the back of the stage which he played with mallets. "The Beam" included twelve piano strings hung from a ten-foot aluminum girder and tied into a 170,000-watt sound system.

Although he had started making field recordings as early as 1967 or 1968, and had recorded music from North India, Hart began probing even deeper in 1978. That year, the Grateful Dead performed at the Great Pyramids in Egypt. Hamza el Din, a Nubian drummer who had introduced Hart to the tar drum (a shallow drum covered with goatskin) at the Barn years before, was the opening act. Hart recorded Hamza for the 1978 album *Eclipse*. Armed with a Nagra analog field recorder, Hart accompanied Hamza to his village, Kumombo, 600 km southwest of Cairo in the Nubian Desert. (A Deadhead followed him to the village and disrupted one of the ceremonies.) Hart recorded a tar orchestra. He then took off for three weeks to record Bedouins and Sa'edians. The recordings were used for *The Music of Upper and Lower Egypt*, released in 1988.

As he told Steve Hochman of *Escape* (Spring 1994): "Great parties! You really had to get in with these people or they wouldn't play. They would smoke enormous amounts of hashish in hubbly bubblies, mixed with tobacco. When you smoke that much you lose the power of your extremities, but you can play your instruments. That's the purpose of this trance music. But they would smoke for an hour or two and just talk, and you had to get high with them. It was hard to get back to the machine after celebrating with them. There were pigs being barbecued, dogs running around, horsemen, guns, music going on all night. I recorded until I ran out of batteries."

Hart also worked closely with talking drum player Babatunde Olatunji. He had heard Olatunji's album *Drums of Passion*, at eighteen. But he became reacquainted with him a few years later when the Nigerian toured the Bay Area. Hart produced two albums for Olatunji: *Drums of Passion: The Beat* (1986), a remixed version of Olatunji's *Dance to the Beat of My Drum*, and *Drums of Passion: The Invocation* (1988).

Hart incorporated his eclectic interests into the sound track for Francis Ford Coppola's movie *Apocalypse Now*. He invited the Brazilian drummer Airto Moreira, whom he had seen perform with Miles Davis years earlier, to his home. Airto introduced him to many of the instruments brought to Brazil by African slaves, such as the *berimbau* (a bowed instrument used in a secretive martial arts dance called *capoeira*), *bata,* and the *atabaque.* (Kreutzmann and Airto joined in a group called the Rhythm Devils for *The Apocalypse Now Sessions,* (1990) and *The Rhythm Devils Play River Music.*) Hart also produced an album with Airto and Flora Purim called *Dáfos* (1989).

Hart became familiar with the vocal abilities of the exiled Tibetan monks around 1968, just after he joined the Grateful Dead. "I received an anonymous tape of the monks and would listen to it to come down from Grateful Dead shows," he told Frankie Wright of the *Los Angeles Times* (November 16, 1991). He later became aware of the persecution of the Tibetans and helped form the Society for Gyuto Sacred Arts. "Before the monks, no one had heard polyphonic singing before; that was truly wild for the West," he told Michael Parrish of *Sing Out!* (February-March-April 1995). "I remember playing it for a record company executive when I had first recorded it. It was amazing for them to consider it as music, as something they could even think of selling—it's so far from business. Now hundreds of thousands of units later, it is business. Serious monk business!"

In 1987 he recorded them for an album called *Freedom Chants from the Roof of the World,* and later produced *Tibetan Tantric Choir* "They aren't somber, hooded monks, but very much of this world—light, joyful," Hart told Wright. "They celebrate life and teach you the impermanence of it. . . . I can hear them for months in my ears after they've gone."

Hart had recorded music from various cultures for his own label, 360 Degree Productions. In 1987 Rykodisc asked Hart if he wanted to put his recordings "under one roof." They created a series called *The World* which has released more than twenty recordings, everything from *Music to Be Born By,* which includes the heartbeat of Hart's son Taro (born in 1983) in the womb and was meant to help Hart's ex-wife during the birthing process; to *Honor the Earth,* recordings of Great Lakes Indian dance ceremonies; to *Voices of the Rainforest,* music of the Kaluli of Papua New Guinea, recorded by Steven Feld.

Hart also began serving on the board of Smithsonian/ Folkways. He became a technical adviser for transferring the Folkways collection, including fragile cylinder and acetate recordings, to digital recordings. He returns the royalties from the project to the community, to instill pride and keep the music going into the next century.

He is also involved in the *The Endangered Music*

Project at the Library of Congress Archive of Folk Culture, which draws from the 40,000 hours of sound recordings housed there. The first release, in 1993, was *The Spirit Cries: Music from the Rainforests of South America and the Caribbean*, coproduced by Hart and Alan Jabbour, the former director. The album included music from rainforest people like the Garifuna of Belize and the Maroons of Jamaica. The second project, released in 1994, was *Music for the Gods—The Fahnestock South Sea Expedition: Indonesia*. The album, which includes gamelan and vocal music, was taken from material recorded by Bruce and Sheridan Fahnestock in the early 1940s, when they explored the music of the region. Hart has completed other albums for the *Endangered Music Project*, including *The Bali Sessions: Living Art, Sounding Spirit*, a three-CD set, released by Rykodisc.

"When society is interrupted in some way, and taken apart, that kind of insecurity affects the people, and affects the music," he told *Option* (November-December 1990). "A big pipeline running through the Amazon wipes things out. For every inch that we travel, we lose a lot of things. We take all of those musics that contain all of the dreams, all the stories, whole oral traditions. And you bet it's getting wiped out. Alan Lomax calls it cultural gray-out."

Hart recounted his experiences, from his days in the military to his experiences in the Nubian Desert, in his 1990 book, *Drumming at the Edge of Magic*, written with Jay Stevens. It is a lively book that takes the reader along on Hart's extraordinary odyssey. Hart released a companion album with the book called *At the Edge*. He followed in 1991 with *Planet Drum* (Harper), written with the help of ethnomusicologists Fredric Lieberman and D.A. Sonneborn, and an album by the same name.

"Book one was about the search," Hart explained to Banning Eyre of the *Boston Phoenix* (November 22-28, 1991). "*Planet Drum* is the lumber. This is what we brought back. It makes a convincing case for rhythm and noise, pre-written history. These are the fascinating ways that man has made rhythm over the years."

In 1991, Hart assembled seven percussionists from around the world to play in an ensemble that resulted in the *Planet Drum* album (Rykodisc). The drummers included Babatunde Olatunji and Sikiru Adepoju of Nigeria; Indian tabla player Zakir Hussain; percussionists Airto Moreira and Flora Purim of Brazil; Vikku Vinayakram of India, who plays the *ghatam*, or clay pot; and Puerto Rican conga player Giovanni Hidalgo. As Airto told the *Boston Globe*: "Music is supposed to be a universal language and I think rhythm is an even more basic element. In this case, all you have to find is a pulse. When you find a pulse, no matter what country you are from you're pulsing together and everything is fine." The album topped *Billboard*'s World Music charts for twenty-three weeks and won the 1991 Grammy for Best World Music album.

Besides exploring the spirit of drumming, Hart has worked with the therapeutic benefits of drumming. He testified before the Subcommittee on Aging in 1991 about such health benefits, recorded the San Quentin Mass Choir, and experienced with the benefits of drumming in nursing homes.

All of this was a sideline to his day job with the Grateful Dead. He continued to tour with the band, performing in up to eighty concerts a year. He did this until August 1995 when Jerry Garcia died suddenly of a heart attack. At first the surviving members considered carrying on. But in December 1995, they called it quits. Hart's way of coping with Garcia's death was to record music. He went into the studio to finish *Mystery Box*, (1996, Rykodisc).

"This record was part of the healing process. It saved me," he told Steve Morse of the *Boston Globe* (June 14, 1996). "Music mediates my whole world.... And with something as catastrophic as [Garcia's passing], my whole life changed drastically. The most important thing was to be around music, so I went right into this project. I went very deep and finished it with a lot of passion."

Staying true to his craft, Hart started *Mystery Box* by laying down the rhythms. He joined with Zakir Hussain and Giovanni Hidalgo to create the foundation and turned to Grateful Dead lyricist Robert Hunter to add the words. "I told him listen to the drums and they'll take you there," Hart says. In the studio, the most moving point in making the album was when Hunter recited the lyrics to "Down the Road," bringing tears to the eyes of all present: *I heard a sweet guitar lick/It sounded like Garcia, but I couldn't see the face/Just the beard and the glasses and a smile on empty space.*

Hart took his Mystery Box band on the road with his former bandmates for the Further Festival, which traveled to more than thirty cities from June 20 to August 4, 1996. Hart's band included the Mint Juleps (a British *a cappella* quartet), Zakir Hussain, Giovanni Hidalgo, and Sikiri Adepoju. Bob Weir performed with his band Ratdog, and Bruce Hornsby, Los Lobos, Hot Tuna, and John Wesley Harding. Although Garcia wasn't there in person, his spirit was there. "He is constantly with me," Hart told *People* (July 8, 1996). "His guitar is ringing in my ear. I can't get it out. It's harder for some people to cope. But I have my music, I have my memories and I had a great time. It was one hell of a ride."

In the summer of 1998 Hart joined with ex-Grateful Dead members Bob Weir and Phil Lesh for a Dead reunion band, the Other Ones (from the 1971 song by the same name). It all started when Paul and Linda McCartney sent him a twenty-minute video featuring the Dead's music and Linda's photos of the band. When Mickey played the video he started dancing around his house. He ended his mourning period and contacted other members to tour, which resulted in a live album.

In August 1998 Rykodisc released a new CD (with a

bonus disc) entitled *Supralingua.* The album title, which means "beyond words," grew from his interest in the chants of African Pygmies, who communicate without words. As he told National Public Radio's Frank Stasio (October 4, 1998), the album features "utterances before speech, before language." He uses his voice as a percussion instrument.

The album features the use of a computerized instrument, the Random Access Music Universe, (RAMU), a robot, sound droid, and digital workstation. "You could stick it, you could mallet it, you could rub it, you could hit it with the palm of your hands or your fingertips. It's a live performance instrument, computer, sampler, processor, MIDI'd instrument. Sort of an instrument of the future," he told Stasio, making no apologies for the use of digital technology. "You realize that we have one foot in the archaic world and one foot in the digital domain. And anyone who doesn't know that, you better blink twice." Ryko issued *Indoscrub,* a two-song/two-video DVD taken from the album.

In 1999 Hart (with Lieberman) finished his third book, *Spirit Into Sound: the Magic of Music* (Grateful Dead), and a new CD, *Spirit Into Sound* (2000, Grateful Dead Records). He also hopes to record recitations of both the Koran and the Torah.

Hart lives in a Sonoma County home with his wife, Caryl Ohrbach, and his two children. If his previous work is any indication, his days will begin and end with the sound of drumming. As he wrote at the end of *Drumming at the Edge of Magic:* "In the beginning was noise, and noise begat rhythm, and rhythm begat everything else. When the rhythm is right you feel it with all your senses. The head of the drum vibrates as the stick strikes it. The physical feedback is almost instantaneous, rushing along your arms, filling your ears. Your mind is turned off, your judgment wholly emotional. Your emotions seem to stream down your arms and legs and out the mouth of the drum; you feel light, gravityless, your arms feel like feathers. You fly like a bird."

HARTFORD, JOHN: *Singer, songwriter, banjoist, guitarist, fiddler, mandolinist. Born New York, New York, December 30, 1937.*

A strong-willed individual, John Hartford gave up what looked like a sure-fire route to stardom as a pop artist to return to the environment he loved best—performing folk-country music with a bluegrass flavor and spending a good part of each year as a Mississippi riverboat pilot. "I was always very careful to make sure I would do exactly what I wanted to do. If I achieved some success I always wanted to be ready to buy back the limits so I wouldn't work just for the money. Like CBS offered me a detective series in the late 1960s, but I didn't want to be known as a detective."

He was born in New York, where his father, who was studying to be a doctor, was completing his internship. When he was two weeks old, the family moved back to St. Louis, Missouri. "Missouri is home. My family on both sides was from Missouri. My mom and dad used to square dance. I always did like square dance music. I was listening to the *Grand Ole Opry* on the radio every Saturday from the time I was a little boy."

Although early on he wanted to work on the riverboats, John also fooled around with various instruments before concentrating on the banjo and fiddle in his early teens. "I started with a four-string banjo, then made it into a five-string. We drilled a hole and added the string. The thing that really turned me on was hearing Flatt and Scruggs when I was about fourteen. I loved Earl Scruggs playing bluegrass and I also was greatly influenced by Stringbean.

"I've always kinda known things on guitar. I always just played on other people's instruments. I never had one of my own until 1965. I liked to play fiddle almost as far back as I can remember. I kinda picked it up myself. A friend named Dr. James Gray, a state fiddle champ, showed me a lot of stuff and I also used to play with an old fiddler named Gofoth in St. Louis."

His interest in country music continued as he progressed through high school. "I started to play professionally during those years. The music I loved was bluegrass. I had a band that did all the Flatt and Scruggs hits, as well as Don Reno, Red Smiley, Bill Monroe material. Occasionally we'd do a Roy Acuff song, but rearranged. I went to Washington University in St. Louis for a while in 1959–60 [to study art], but I didn't finish. There didn't seem to be any need for it. I was either gonna be a boat pilot [his first work on a steamboat was in 1947] or a musician, and college wasn't much use in either case."

After leaving school, he worked at a number of jobs, including commercial artist (some of his drawings adorn the covers of his Flying Fish albums), steamboat deckhand, and radio announcer. He continued to play for small affairs or his own pleasure, but music seemed fated to be more a sideline than a primary occupation.

The years went by and, apart from marriage and the birth of a son, nothing dramatic took place. He had a few minor credits in the recording field in the first part of the 1960s: "I had a record out on the Marlo label and one on the Shannon label out of St. Louis." Then, in the mid-1960s, he decided to try his luck in Nashville. "I was working in southeast Missouri at the time and I wasn't doing too well, moneywise, and I thought, well, you only live once, and a guy can starve to death as easily in Nashville as anywhere else and have more fun doing it, so I just packed up my wife and my little boy and moved to Nashville."

Drawing on his announcing credits, he got a job on a Nashville station. He began trying to place his original songs with a publisher. That effort finally won the attention of the Glaser Brothers, who added his name to their talent agency list and began playing some of his demo tapes for record company executives. The result was a contract for John with RCA. (Up to then, his last name was Harford, but it was decided that adding a *t* made it a catchier-sounding appellation.)

Under the supervision of Chet Atkins, he recorded a number of his own songs. The first single release, in 1966, was of "Tall, Tall Grass" and "Jack's in the Sack." In July 1966 his debut LP on RCA came out, called *John Hartford Looks at Life*. It included such original compositions as "Eve of My Multiplication," "When the Sky Begins to Fall," "I Shoulda Wore My Birthday Suit," "Corn Cob Blues," "Today, Front Porch," and "Like Unto a Mockingbird."

His songs won attention from other artists. The Glaser Brothers cut their versions of some of his songs in the late 1960s, as did George Hamilton IV, Waylon Jennings, Patti Page, and many others.

In 1967 his second LP came out, titled *Earthwords and Music,* with a song John had written the previous year titled "Gentle on My Mind." As 1967 came to a close, artist after artist covered the song. It provided a multimillion-selling smash vocal version for Glen Campbell and an instrumental hit for Floyd Cramer. Years afterward, the income from the song helped Hartford maintain his musical independence. (Reportedly, he still was receiving about $170,000 a year in royalties in the late 1970s, and by the late 1990s the song had been recorded by more than 500 artists, including one of Hartford's main influences, Flatt and Scruggs, and played on the radio more than 5 million times.)

He wrote the song after he had seen actress Julie Christie in *Dr. Zhivago.* "I've always been mystified as to why that song was a hit," Hartford told Ellen Geisel of *Dirty Linen* (February-March 1997), "because it violates every rule of hit-making. First of all, it has no chorus. Second of all, it has too many words in it. Third of all, it has one verse that's irregular. And fourth, it's complex in its thought patterns. And fifth, which is the cardinal sin of all hit songwriting, it's a banjo tune. That's the kiss of death right there."

Hartford was on the way to becoming a national celebrity. His next LP, in early 1968, *The Love Album,* made the pop charts, and John was given a contract by CBS-TV to help prepare a summer replacement for *The Smothers Brothers Comedy Hour* (for which he had been hired the previous year as a writer and performer, along with Mason Williams, Steve Martin, Rob Reiner, and McLean Stevenson, among others). In 1969 he was a featured performer on the *Glen Campbell Goodtime Hour* TV show. The show opened with his song "Gentle on My Mind" and closed with "Natural to Be Gone." At the end of the 1960s he did session work, including work on the Byrds' country-flavored album, *Sweetheart of the Rodeo.*

He continued to do more recordings for RCA, including the LPs *The Housing Project* (1968), *Gentle on My Mind and Other Originals* (1968), *John Hartford* (1968), and *Iron Mountain Depot* (August 1970). They

didn't do too well, partly he felt, due to lack of label support. He switched to Warner Brothers, for whom he did two albums in the early 1970s, *Aereo-Plain* (1971) and *Morning Bugle* (1972).

He then seemed to fade from view as far as the general public was concerned. He was intent on going his own way, a route that included achieving more status as a professional Mississippi steamboat pilot. By the late 1970s he had earned a Coast Guard license for vessels up to 100 gross tons and had piloted the paddlewheeler *Julia Belle Swain* in the annual Louisville Derby Days Steamboat Race. His goal was to pass the examination for a first-class pilot's license.

"After I left Warner Brothers," he notes, "I didn't record for several years. Then I decided I was ready to start again and I was looking around for some big label to go with when I was approached by Flying Fish [an independent label that was taken over by Rounder in the mid-1990s]. That was a decision, but it was kind of in line with my success through smallness approach, so I went with it."

The first result of that was the 1976 album *Mark Twang*—as the title indicates, an album with a lot of the flavor of steamboating and the Mississippi in it. He included a song called "The Julia Belle Swain." The album was recorded live. "I wanted to make it loose and spontaneous, like the radio shows I used to do," he told J. Seymour Guenther later. In the Grammy Awards voting announced in early 1977, it was named Best Ethnic or Traditional Recording. (Hartford previously had won two Grammys in 1967 for "Gentle on My Mind": Best Folk Recording and Best C&W Recording.) It was the first of a series of unique recordings on Flying Fish that included such albums in the 1977–80 period as *Nobody Knows What You Do* (1976), *Dillard-Hartford-Dillard* (1977), *All in the Name of Love* (1977), *Headin' Down into the Mystery Below* (1978), *Slumberin' on the Cumberland* (1979), *You and Me at Home* and *Permanent Wave* (1980).

In the last half of the 1970s Hartford became one of the favorite artists of the traditional country and folk music audiences, and his solo concerts at folk venues across the country usually were sold out.

Whereas in earlier times Hartford would play his face or make other sound effects, a feature of his act in the late 1970s was the clog-dancing routine (on a three-fourths-inch plywood platform) that accompanied many of his songs. He said of that in 1979, "I added that clog routine about four years ago. It kind of evolved. I started jogging in place to music just to get some exercise. Before I knew it I was doing it while I was playing and singing onstage."

With his bowler and vest, his love of steamboats and the river, Hartford seemed like a modern day minstrel. "My dreams are all in the last century, I guess," he told Geisel. "I guess I'm a Victorian at heart . . . but also too I'm very much of a realist."

In the late 1970s and early 1980s he rarely used other musicians in his act, but sometimes combined with other artists. "I work with different groups like the Dillards and the New Grass Revival. We'll each do a set of our own, then do a set together. It's an exciting time because bluegrass is doing pretty well again with a lot of involvement in it. It's certainly the main kind of music I play, and it's good to see good young artists coming along to keep it going."

In the beginning of the 1980s Hartford continued to release albums on Flying Fish, including *Catalogue* (1981); *Gum Tree Canoe* (1984); the retrospective album from his Flying Fish years, *Me Oh My, How the Time Does Fly; A John Hartford Anthology* (1987); and *Down on the River* (1989). During the decade, he released one album on Rounder, *Clements, Hartford, Holland* (1984), and one on MCA, *Annual Waltz* (1987).

He returned to Nashville, living on the Cumberland River and keeping a collection of riverboat memorabilia. He even co-authored a book in 1986 called *Steamboat in a Cornfield* (Crown). The book is for a young audience and tells the story in rhyme of a boat called the *Virginia*. From time to time, he likes to pilot a boat called the *Twilight*.

Beginning in the early 1990s John Hartford released several albums on his own label, including *Goin' Back to Dixie* (1992), *The Walls we Bounce Off Of* (1994), *Live at College Station, Pennsylvania* (1994), *Old Sport* (1994), and *No End of Love* (1996). The latter was a collection of river and steamboat songs. In 1995, Rounder released *The Fun of Open Discussion* (with Bob Carlin).

He also recorded with his son, mandolinist, guitarist, singer, and songwriter Jamie Hartford. In 1991 they released *Hartford and Hartford* on Flying Fish, which John has called his favorite album. They followed up later in the year with *Cadillac Rag*, this one on Hartford's own Small Dog A-Barkin' label, named after a noisy Lhaso apso he once took on the road. Jamie Hartford released a solo album in 1998 on Paladin Records called *What About Yes*.

Hartford also developed a keen interest in Ed Haley, an old-time fiddler from the Ohio River valley. He found some acetate recordings in Haley's home, which he mastered for a four-CD set called *Forked Deer*, released on Rounder Records at the end of 1997. In 1996, Hartford released a collection of fiddle tunes that he suspects Ed Haley played, titled *Wild Hog in the Red Brush: And a Bunch of Others You Might Not Have Heard* on Rounder, including detailed liner notes about each song. The band for the album included Hartford on fiddle, Bob Carlin on banjo, Mike Compton on mandolin, Ronnie McCoury on guitar, and Jerry McCoury on bass. The album was nominated for a Grammy.

In 1998 he released *The Speed of the Old Long Bow: A Tribute to the Fiddle Music of Ed Haley* on Rounder. On that album, Hartford played fiddle and vocal, along with Carlin on banjo, Compton on mandolin, Robert Gately on string bass, and Darren Vincent on guitar and percussion. Hartford also co-authored a book about Haley, who had shied away from commercial recording companies during his life.

In 1998, Whippoorwill Records released *The Bullies Have All Gone to Rest* featuring Jim Wood, the Tennessee Champion Old-Time Fiddler, and John Hartford on banjo.

Beginning in the 1990s, Rounder Record began reissuing several of Hartford's classic albums on CD, including *Morning Bugle* and *Aereo-Plain*. In the liner notes for *Aereo-Plain*, Hartford and mandolinist Sam Bush explained how the musicians, including Norman Blake on guitar, Tut Taylor on Dobro, and Vassar Clements on fiddle, created a jam session in the studio. "A tune would start and I would stand there and then I would look down and discover my hands busy at the music and that I was just two eyeballs floating in it," Hartford wrote. David Bromberg was brought in as the producer. "[He] basically just turned on the recording machines and the band proceeded to play, without even listening to playbacks," Bush wrote. "All of us acoustic music freaks found an undeniable joyful noise."

Perhaps Hartford's only concession to the new world order is that he now has a web site (*www.JohnHartford.com*). Besides selling his CDs, the web site advertises T-shirts featuring lyrics to "Gentle on My Mind" and videotapes, including *Banjoes, Fiddles and Riverboats,* an Opryland USA home video, *The Banjo According to John Hartford* on Homespun, and *John Hartford in Concert,* on Shanachie. The site features Hartford's drawings of riverboats and banjos, as well as Hartford imploring his fans to write lots of letters.

In 1996, Hartford played a tribute concert at Ryman Auditorium for the family of Courtney Johnson, the original banjo player for the New Grass Revival, who had died of lung cancer. Hartford performed "Cross-Eyed Child" as a tribute to Bill Monroe, who had also died that year. Hartford contributed to the Grammy-winning 1996 Sugar Hill tribute album for bluegrass legend Monroe, *True Life Blues: The Songs of Bill Monroe*. In 1999 Rounder issued a new studio album, *Good Old Boys*. Acoustic Disc released *Retrograss,* featuring Hartford, David Grisman, and Mike Seeger, which earned a Grammy nomination.

"I do what's in my heart," Hartford told Geisel, summing up his career. "If it works, that's wonderful. If it doesn't work, at least I haven't wasted my time. . . . I think I could honesty say that one of my great role models in all of this was Bill Monroe, who certainly never compromised his music. I just had that confidence that it could be done 'cause I'd seen other people do it. . . . I don't know if I could live with myself any other way."

Based partly on an interview with Irwin Stambler in the fall of 1979

HAVENS, RICHIE: *Singer, guitarist, sitar player, songwriter, actor. Born Brooklyn, New York, January 21, 1941.*

Following in the activist tradition of many modern folk artists, Richie Havens carried his commitment to peace and love, so much a part of the message of the Woodstock generation of the late 1960s and early 1970s, through the '80s and into the '90s. He did this not only through his singing, but also through practical activities such as helping to set up the National Guard, an organization whose goals included teaching young people about ecological issues so they "could play a role in affecting the environment." Like many products of the '60s folk boom, Havens's career opportunities dwindled in the late '70s and much of the '80s, but with the revitalization of that music genre by the 1990s, Havens found his talents in greater demand than ever.

Havens grew up in the Bedford-Stuyvesant area of Brooklyn, which is now a black ghetto area but was then racially mixed and not as poverty-ridden. He was the eldest of nine children born to his piano-playing father, who worked as an electroplater in a factory, and to his churchgoing mother, who worked in a bookbinding plant. As a youth, Richie sang in church as well as on street corners with other neighborhood children. By the time he was fourteen, had had organized a group called the McCrea Gospel Singers.

Actually, at that time he was as much interested in doo-wop vocalizing, something he'd started doing with friends when he was twelve, as church music. He told Richard Skelly of *Goldmine* ("Richie Havens—Mixed Bag," June 10, 1994), that the McCrea Gospel Singers "was a deal we had made with our lead singer's mother. He sang in the church choir, and so the deal was we'd come and sing in the church in the family choir, if he could come out and sing rock 'n' roll with us! That was the deal, and it was a good deal, because we learned a lot of hymns and sang in a lot of different churches."

"One group I was with must have had at least 30 names, different configurations. I remember one was the Chances, one was the Cavaliers.... We actually won two Apollo amateur contest nights in a row, we didn't win the third one.... And we got the chance to almost make a record. One person in the band, his father wouldn't let him sign the contract, so we never got to do the record that we almost made. At that time, we were the Cavaliers. That was the last doo-wop group I was in, actually."

At that time, Havens regarded singing as mainly for fun. He had his hopes set on becoming a surgeon. He was a very good student at Franklin K. Lane High School; however, he dropped out just before graduation. As he told one interviewer, "I loved school. I mean, here was this one big building with a lot of people in it. But we used to laugh a lot, and they'd never let us laugh. I liked learning too, but I couldn't see any reason why I had to go over something I already knew. You know, we'd go over a lesson a week and then on

Friday, the teacher'd say, 'It's time for review.' I said, 'Why?' I already knew it. So I quit! It was just time to go I guess. I've always known when it was time."

When he was seventeen years old, Richie felt it was time to leave home. For a few years, he held a variety of jobs. Eventually, he made his way to Greenwich Village, where he supported himself by painting portraits of tourists during the daytime and spent most of his nights hanging around the coffeehouses that were springing up in the Village in those years. In the coffeehouses he heard such artists as Len Chandler, Dino Valenti, and Paul Stookey, who later became a member of Peter, Paul and Mary. Richie was inspired to try singing.

Around this time, Havens bought himself a guitar and taught himself how to play it. He developed an unorthodox open-E tuning that allowed him to play chord patterns that were not possible with more conventional tunings. This new style of tuning was later used by other folk and blues singers.

His first album, *Mixed Bag,* was released in the fall of 1966 and added to his growing reputation, although it did not make the hit charts at the time. Album tracks included "Handsome Jerry," cowritten by Richie and Lou Gossett, Jr., an excellent cover of Bob Dylan's "Just Like a Woman," and "Follow," written by Jerry Merrick. Richie's second Verve/Forecast album, *Somthin' Else Again,* which came out in 1968, did a lot better, making the *Billboard* list and also pulling *Mixed Bag* on as well. The exposure from his albums led to bookings at some of the more important clubs and concert halls across the country, including the Fillmore West, New York's Cafe Au Go Go, and Expo '67 in Montreal, Canada, as well as numerous college campuses.

In 1968 Havens was asked to be one of the performers at the Woody Guthrie Memorial Concert at New York's Carnegie Hall. His performance received a standing ovation. Word of this spectacular concert led to a booking on Johnny Carson's *The Tonight Show.* When he finished singing on that show, the audience response was so deafening that Carson, on the spot, asked Havens to return the next night. Taking advantage of Havens's newfound popularity, Douglas International added more instrumental backing to some demo tapes Richie had made in 1963 to provide two '68 album releases, *Richie Havens' Record* and *Electric Havens.*

For the rest of the 1960s, Havens performed at many folk and rock concerts in the United States and abroad. One of these was the legendary Woodstock music festival in 1969. There, Richie's energetic performance delighted the Woodstock crowd of half a million, and when the film of the concert was released a year later, he became a worldwide star.

Richie actually opened Woodstock, though he originally was scheduled to be the fifth act on the program. When the others didn't show up, and the start already had been delayed two hours, the promoters in desperation asked Havens to kick things off—and he balked. As he told Joseph D. Younger for an article in *Amtrak Express* ("Richie Havens, American Troubadour," March–April 1993), "I said backstage, 'There's no way I'm goin' out there!' I said, 'You want people to throw beer cans at me because your concert is two hours late?' But they begged me. So I said, 'OK, but if I get one beer can thrown at me, you're gonna owe me—big.'"

Coming onstage, he said, "I was in a state of shock. There were hundreds of thousands of people stretching up the hill, as far as I could see from the stage. That doesn't even count the hundreds of thousands who were behind the hill, who couldn't see the stage, and the thousands who were in the woods at the crafts fair. But they were all waiting for something to happen and they responded very openly."

So openly that they cheered him on for almost three hours. He told Richard Skelly that he performed that long because no other acts had been able to get by the massive traffic tie-up that extended for miles around the concert site. "I had to go back out about seven or eight times, and at the end I didn't know what the heck I was going to sing, and the first thing that went through my mind was that we already had the freedom that we were supposed to be looking for. What are we talking about, we already got it! So I started singing the words, 'freedom, freedom,' and then 'Motherless Child' came back to me, which I hadn't sung in, like, eight years. And then another song that I hadn't sung in, like, 12 years. [Those provided the melodies to which he put the new words.] I had gone through every song in my repertoire, and by that point, I really knew a lot of songs, but I couldn't think of many after almost three hours of performing. It's kind of interesting that the tune I'm most known for was totally improvised on the spot."

During 1969 Richie's two-LP album, *Richard P. Havens, 1983,* his first project as a coproducer and his last album under contract to Verve, came out. He signed with the Stormy Forest label, distributed by the MGM group. His initial label release in 1970 was *Stonehenge,* followed later in the year by *Alarm Clock.* The latter climbed onto the *Billboard* album chart in January 1971, staying in the top 100 for a number of months, during which it became his first LP to make the publication's Top 30. His cover of the song by George Harrison of the Beatles' "Here Comes the Sun" rose to number sixteen in *Billboard,* his only Top 20 single as of the mid-1990s.

Richie continued to place albums on the charts as the 1970s went by. His Stormy Forest album *The Great Blind Degree,* was on the best-seller lists from late 1971 through early 1972. His double album, *Richie Havens On Stage,* made the charts in September 1972 and stayed there through early 1973. In the summer of 1973 his last Stormy Forest release, *Portfolio,* appeared on the hit lists. He turned out albums on various labels during the rest of the '70s: *Mixed Bag II* on Polydor in

1974; two on A&M, *The End of the Beginning* in 1976 and *Mirage* in 1977; and *Connections* on Elektra/Asylum in 1979.

His activities during that decade included many concerts throughout the United States as well as tours of the Middle East and Europe. He also demonstrated considerable acting talent in a series of roles on stage and screen. In 1972, for instance, he had a major role in a stage presentation of the Who's rock opera, *Tommy,* and in 1974 played the lead role in the film of the rock musical based on Shakespeare's *Othello.* In 1977 he costarred with comedian Richard Pryor in *Greased Lightning.*

Havens's music hearkened back to the peace theme of the Woodstock years in 1978. After watching Anwar Sadat's televised visit to Jerusalem, he wrote a song, "Shalom, Salaam Aleichum." Both Egypt and Israel invited him to visit. He did so and performed his song at the embassies of both countries, which resulted in a number one hit in Israel as well as an ecstatic response from both sides of the Suez Canal.

By the early 1980s Richie's acting work had also included a part in the TV movie called *The Girl, the Gold Watch and Dynamite,* performing with boxing great Muhammad Ali in *The Man,* and appearing with Rita Moreno in the film *The Boss's Son.* He also devoted time to working on a proposed stage musical based on the life of Jimi Hendrix titled *Electric God.* To the surprise of many of his fans, Richie became one of the more sought-after artists for radio and TV commercials. During the first half of the '80s, he provided voice-overs for, among others, CBS-TV, Kodak film, L.A. light beer, and Dial Soap. He told Matt Damsker for a *Los Angeles Times* article ("Richie Havens Sells His Soulfulness," Calendar section, September 16, 1984), "The whole thing really started as far back as 1968 when I did an Eastern Airlines commercial. And the reason I did that was for the song, not the commercial—it was a song about people, and the whole thing seemed a challenge in another art form.

"But then as now, it had to be a product I could get behind, otherwise I wouldn't have done it. For CBS it was the 'We've Got the Touch' theme, for Kodak it's 'Because Time Goes By,' and the L.A. beer spot I did for a couple of reasons. One, it's the first time that an above-ground corporation has corroborated what the '60s youth did to this country. The song goes, 'You shaped the world and changed it, made it better, rearranged it,' and I consider myself part of that for sure. Also the idea of a light-alcohol beer I agree with, though no alcohol would be better, I guess."

At the time, Richie and his wife and four daughters still lived in the same apartment he'd found when he first moved to Greenwich Village. Later in the decade he settled for a while in Italy, where he worked with an Italian composer friend on the album *Common Ground,* issued on his own label, Connection, in 1987. When not working on the album he toured throughout Italy, where he was warmly greeted by sizable crowds. After completing the album project, he returned home to record still more albums, the 1988 release *Simple Things* on the RBI label and, in 1991, *Now* on Solar/Epic.

On October 16, 1992, at New York's Madison Square Garden, Richie took part in the Columbia Records concert commemorating Bob Dylan's thirty years on the label. His contribution was an inspired performance of Dylan's "Just Like a Woman," a song going back to Haven's debut album. In January 1993 Richie had a featured spot at the Earth Ball celebrating Bill Clinton's election as U.S. president. The concert was sponsored by Renew America, a lobbying group for renewable energy and other environmental advances. In April 1993, Rhino Records issued the multi-CD retrospective of the early years of Havens's career, *Resume: The Best of Richie Havens.* In June 1994 an excellent album of new recordings by Richie, *Cuts to the Chase,* came out on Rhino's Forward label. During '94, Richie took part in an alternative Woodstock concert in Bethel, New York, set up to protest what he and some other artists felt was the overcommercializing of the Woodstock show planned by the promoters of the '69 event.

In 1995, besides putting down new tracks for an album due out in 1996, he narrated the HBO special *Politics and Sports* for screening in late '95. He also handled narration on the new CD-ROM interactive GeoSafari educational game created by Educational Insights of Southern California. The games in the package covered topics in geography, history, and science to increase the players' knowledge base. Havens's role, the producers noted, was to provide "a highly responsive verbal interface, calling players by name as he rewards their gaming and learning efforts."

He told an interviewer from the *Portsmouth Herald,* of Portsmouth, New Hampshire ("Talking 'bout this generation," November 2, 1995), "I've found a whole new audience since the old days. One that I think actually knows what I'm talking about. Most of the folks coming to my shows are young people who were born in the '70s and '80s, and have an amazing ability to identify. They understand inherently the differences between good and bad—we don't have to tell them, because they're of us. It's evolutionary, in a sense."

HAWES, BESS LOMAX: *Singer, guitarist, mandolinist, songwriter, folklorist. Born Austin, Texas, January 21, 1921.*

In the 1960s, the effect of the Lomax clan on folk music spanned the country. On the East Coast, Alan Lomax continued ably to carry on the tradition of his father, John, by collecting folk songs from all over the world and lecturing on folk music at leading universities. Across the continent, in Santa Monica, California, his younger sister, Bess Hawes, ranked as one of the foremost unofficial authorities on folk music in the West.

Bess naturally grew up in an environment conducive to musical scholarship. Her father had established a reputation as one of the foremost collectors of folk material in the nation and, in general, enjoyed the arts. However, when she was old enough to participate in musical activities, he had left university work to become an official in a Texas bank. Thus she had more exposure to classical music than to folk material during elementary school.

Her family started her on piano lessons and she showed excellent potential as a pianist. By the time she was ten, she had received intensive training in the classics and in basic music theory. Then several hard blows changed the course of all the Lomaxes. Just as the Depression began to erupt, her mother's death sent Bess to a boarding school in Dallas. In 1932 the effects of the Depression caused cutbacks in the banking field and her father was laid off.

While Bess continued her studies in Dallas, her father and brother Alan embarked on new careers in folk music collecting, based on a book contract from the Macmillan Company. Bess proved a precocious student, walking off with honors at school. At fifteen, she was able to enter the University of Texas.

In 1937, she left Texas to join her family, now living in Washington, D.C. She worked on transcribing material from field recordings for her father and brother's second book, *Our Singing Country.* When her father remarried soon after the book was finished, he took her along to Europe on his honeymoon. To keep busy on the trip, Bess bought a secondhand guitar for fifteen dollars and taught herself to play it.

When the family settled down in the United States once more, Bess enrolled at Bryn Mawr College. She soon met many of the folk music artists then living in New York and was welcomed as a talented artist and kindred spirit. Among those with whom she sometimes performed in folk music gatherings were Pete Seeger, Butch Hawes, Earl Robinson, Woody Guthrie, and Burl Ives. Soon a new, somewhat amorphous singing group was formed, called the Almanac Singers. She became a part of it and later married one of the group members, Butch Hawes. During these years, she learned a second stringed instrument, the mandolin, with the great Woody Guthrie as her teacher.

When World War II caused the Almanacs to break up, Bess decided to help the war effort by joining the Office of War Information. She served with the Music Division, helping prepare material for broadcast to Europe and the Near East.

After the war, she and husband Butch Hawes moved to Boston. An informal songfest she gave at a nursery school attended by one of her children resulted in requests from parents for guitar instruction. She then set up her first class and was on the way to a reputation as one of the best folk-music teachers in the country.

While in Boston, Bess took an active part in political campaigns. For one of these she wrote "The M.T.A. Song" with Jacqueline Steiner. The song later was made into a national hit by the Kingston Trio.

In the 1950s, when the Hawes family moved to California, she found herself in as much demand as ever as a music instructor. She also was sought out by many major folk artists when they traveled in the West and received many invitations to perform at both West Coast and national festivals.

She continued to increase her stature as a teacher, joining the faculty of San Fernando Valley State College. As an instructor in anthropology, she advanced to the rank of associate professor by 1968. In the 1960s, she took on additional teaching responsibilities as a member of the summer faculty of the folk-music workshops at Idyllwild School of Music and the Arts, Idyllwild, California.

During the 1970s, she continued to take part in folk-music events and appeared in various venues on the folk circuit.

HAWKINS, TED: *Singer, songwriter, guitarist. Born Lakeshore, Mississippi, October 28, 1936; died Los Angeles, California, January 1, 1995.*

Singer-songwriter Ted Hawkins lived the life of the old Delta bluesmen. Each time he was discovered and it looked like things were going his way, hard times cut him down. He'd been in and out of prisons, suffered nervous breakdowns, left homeless and forgotten. When he finally signed a major label deal he died months later. But he left behind a powerful legacy, recording in a variety of genres: blues, folk, R&B, soul, pop, gospel, and country.

Those who saw him playing on the Venice boardwalk or on Santa Monica's Third Street promenade will not soon forget him. He sat on a milk crate, wearing a black glove on his fretting left hand; his fine white beard contrasted with his rugged black face, topped with a leather cap. He seemed shy, or at least caught up in his own world as he looked out at the crowds, tapping rhythm with his foot on a laminated wooden board.

He grew up in Mississippi, and never knew his father. His mother was an alcoholic and a prostitute. He was molested by a neighborhood man and no one could protect him. In school, he was so dirty and smelled so bad that his classmates called him Dirty Junior. At twelve he was sent to a reformatory school called the Oakley Training School in Biloxi. When one of his teachers asked him what he wanted to be when he grew up, he responded simply: "A singer." The school invited Professor Longhair to perform. Fess taught Hawkins his first song, "Somebody's Knocking at My Door." When Ted performed it at a school assembly, he never wanted to lose that feeling.

But at fifteen he was caught stealing a leather jacket from a motorcycle shop and sent to the infamous Parchman Farm, where he picked cotton on a work detail.

One day a guard beat him so badly Hawkins thought he was going to die. When he got out, he spent the next ten years riding trains up and down the East Coast. He had been married and divorced twice before he married a third time, to a woman named Elizabeth (who sometimes sang background vocals) in his late twenties. They moved to Los Angeles in the mid-1960s, and Hawkins began pursuing his dream of becoming a singer. He bought a Gibson guitar and began singing on the streets, growing his nails long on the index and thumb of his right hand and protecting his left hand with a black glove.

He cut his first record in 1966 as Ted "Soul" Hawkins for Money Records, a subsidiary run by John Dolphin. Money issued a 45 called "Baby" backed with "Whole Lot of Women." But Hawkins alleged he never got paid. In 1971 he recorded an album produced by Bruce Bromberg and Dennis Walker, the first in a series of people who were impressed by his street singing. His album was finally released by Rounder in 1982 as *Watch Your Step.* But by that time, Hawkins was again in trouble with the law. He spent eighteen months in the Vacaville (California) Medical Facility for allegedly molesting a thirteen-year-old girl, a charge he denied, although he admitted to being arrested for indecent exposure. After he was released in August 1982, he returned to singing on the Venice boardwalk.

Watch Your Step, which received a five-star review from *Rolling Stone,* included such enduring songs as "Who Got My Natural Comb?", "Sorry You're Sick," and "The Lost Ones," about an abandoned child that parallels Hawkins's own life. The album captures Hawkins's street style and isn't overproduced. That wasn't true of his second album, *Happy Hour,* also produced by Bromberg and Walker and released by Rounder in 1986.

In the mid-'80s, Hawkins was discovered again, this time by H. Thorp Minister III, who recorded Hawkins in Nashville in September 1985. Hawkins recorded two albums of covers with only one original in the set, "Ladder of Success," in which he sings about the importance of connections in the world. The albums were called *On the Boardwalk: The Venice Beach Tapes* (1986) and *Dock of the Bay: The Venice Beach Tapes* (1987), released on Munich Records.

A year later, BBC Radio disc jockey Andy Kershaw, who was mesmerized by Hawkins's earlier work, came to Los Angeles in search of him. He recorded Ted in 1986 in a hotel room and brought him to England, where Hawkins enjoyed a much wider following than in the United States. In 1989, Hawkins self-produced an album called *I Love You Too,* which enjoyed some success in England. But in 1990 he returned to Southern California, where he continued as a fixture on the Venice boardwalk.

Except for a couple minor recording efforts, Hawkins somehow made enough money from tips to eke out a living with his wife, Elizabeth. In 1993 recording artist Michael Penn heard Hawkins performing on the street and told his producer, Tony Berg, that he had heard "the greatest singer in the world" right outside his window. Berg, who had produced such acts as Squeeze and X, heard Hawkins singing "Amazing Grace" at a benefit for a homeless shelter and decided to sign him to Geffen Records, giving him a $10,000 advance. Geffen released the excellent album *The Next Hundred Years* in 1994. It included such Hawkins originals as "Strange Conversation," "Groovy Little Things," "Ladder of Success," "Afraid," and "The Good and the Bad," and covers of Jesse Winchester's "Biloxi," and John Fogerty's "Long As I Can See the Light."

With Geffen's support, Hawkins went on a nationwide tour and began putting together songs for his next release. But on December 29, 1994, he suffered a stroke, and he died on New Year's Day 1995.

Despite his death, interest in Hawkins remained strong. In 1995, Evidence released *Songs from Venice Beach,* taken from the recordings he made with H. Thorp Minister III. (Another collection titled *Love You Most of All: More Songs from Venice Beach* came out on Evidence in 1998.) Rounder has reissued *Watch Your Step* and *Happy Hour.* The recordings Hawkins made between 1986 and 1989 with BBC DJ Andy Kershaw came out as *The Kershaw Sessions* in 1995, months after his death. In 1998, Evidence released *The Final Tour,* a live recording made at McCabe's Guitar Shop just weeks before Hawkins's death. In 1998, Rhino also released a twenty-song compilation album, *Suffer No More: The Ted Hawkins Story.*

HESTER, CAROLYN: *Singer, guitarist. Born Waco, Texas, January 28, 1937.*

There were few lists of suggested basic albums of folk music of the mid-1960s that did not include one by Carolyn Hester. It was not just her material that was impressive but her vocal ability as well. As *New York Times* critic Robert Shelton stated in a rave review following her first New York concert in the early 1960s, "Miss Hester has a vocal range from rooftop soprano to stunning chest tones."

Besides talent, Hester showed a great amount of feeling for folk songs, reflecting her southwestern upbringing. A distant relative of President Lyndon Johnson, she was born and spent much of her youth in Texas, where she was exposed to many folk and country-music influences. She began to sing first for her own pleasure and then for small gatherings during her teens.

Her formative years were all spent in Texas, starting with her hometown of Waco and later in Austin and Dallas. Her roots were thus urban, but she didn't apologize for that, telling Billy James for album liner notes in the early '60s that the new breed of folksingers didn't live in the hills "and never did. We earn our living singing folk songs and we've been influenced by time."

She added that one of her first influences was Burl Ives: "His recordings were the first folk music I ever heard outside my own family. My grandparents were folksingers and they still sing a lot of old songs. They sing very tragic songs—about Charlotte going out and freezing to death—things like that. Then I heard a lot of country music in Dallas—we heard shows like *The Big D Jamboree, Saturday Night Shindig*—and my father adores *Grand Ole Opry.*"

In 1956 she moved to New York City to become a student at the American Theater Wing. In a short time, though, she became involved in the burgeoning New York folk scene, and in 1958 began performing at small clubs in Cleveland and Detroit, which led to engagements in other locales. During that period she completed her first album on a small label, *Scarlet Ribbons.* (She next recorded an album in New Mexico with Buddy Holly but it was never released.) At the end of the '50s and the start of the 1960s both critics and fans were increasingly impressed with her talents, and by 1962 she had appeared at most of the folk clubs on the national circuit. She also received bids to appear in college concerts, and by early 1962 she had been warmly welcomed at the University of Texas, University of Virginia, Yale, Harvard, and elsewhere.

For several years she was married to singer-songwriter Richard Fariña, but they separated and divorced due to what she described to one interviewer as "financial problems." Fariña later married Joan Baez's sister, Mimi.

In 1961 the album *Carolyn Hester* was issued on the Clancy Brothers' label, Tradition. Her first release to gain widespread attention, it helped bring a contract from Columbia Records. The backing musicians on her Columbia debut in June 1962 included the young Bob Dylan (harmonica), Bruce Langhorne (guitar and violin), and Bill Lee (bass). The disc created a national sensation. She was rewarded with ecstatic reviews in all the music trade magazines and in many national newsstand publications, including *Time* and *Hi-Fi Stereo Review,* which compared her favorably with Joan Baez.

During 1962 Hester was the only native American artist invited to perform at Scotland's Edinburgh Festival. While there, she was asked to appear several times on the British Broadcasting Corporation network. She also toured most of the important British folk clubs. She returned to the United States to continued accolades on campuses and in concerts in many major auditoriums. Her English tours resulted in an invitation from the British government to take part in a sponsored tour of Russian cities in 1963.

In the mid- and late 1960s, Carolyn's concert credits included appearances throughout the United States and Canada. She remained a favorite as well with folk fans in the United Kingdom and in Europe. Her engagements included a number of major folk festivals at home and abroad. Her album releases of those years comprised *This Is My Living* in 1963, *That's My Song* (on the Dot label in 1964), *Carolyn Hester at the Town Hall* (1965), and *The Carolyn Hester Coalition* (1969). The last-named release was a rock and roll collection representing her effort to cope with the inroads on folksinging careers by the dominance of rock. Yet this was ultimately an unsuccessful effort, and she soon returned to focusing on folk-flavored material with the 1971 Tradition album *Thursday's Child Has Far to Go,* produced by old friend Tom Clancy.

Her activities continued to taper off in the 1970s. Her album releases included *Carolyn Hester* in 1974 and a reissue of her 1962 Columbia debut album on Columbia/Legacy in 1977. That CD included previously unreleased alternative versions of two songs on the original LP, "I'll Fly Away" and "Come Back, Baby."

In 1969 she married jazz pianist-record producer David Blume. They lived in New York for a while, then moved in 1972 to California where she spent most of her time from the mid-1970s through the 1980s raising two daughters. The couple began to look for a venue where they might continue their musical careers. As she told Denise Sofranko for a *Dirty Linen* article ("Folk Trailblazer Carolyn Hester sings to a new generation," December-January 1993–94, pp. 26–28), they ended up taking over the Cafe Danssa folk dance club on Pico Boulevard in west Los Angeles. "We fell into it because we were looking for a venue to buy to present people. I knew all the folksingers and David knew all the jazz singers. There was a bar near the club that was known as a jazz club. I nixed that because we had little children and I didn't want to leave them out. I had my children late in life. I was 37 with the first and 41 for the second and I didn't want to go leave them. It's only recently now that they're older teenagers that I can go out on the road."

Soon after, Dani Danssa, an Israeli choreographer who had originally opened the club, offered to return and supervise Israeli dancing on Thursday nights. Later arrangements were made to offer other ethnic music/dance combinations, including Greek and Brazilian nights, activities still going on in the 1990s.

Though Hester kept a relatively low performance profile throughout the 1970s and '80s, she never stopped her folk music efforts. She regularly performed or judged songwriting or other contests at the Kerrville Folk Festival in Texas and aided the careers of promising new artists like Nanci Griffith, whom she brought in as an opening act for some of her concerts in the early 1980s. Later, after Griffith achieved star status, she asked Carolyn to perform on some of the tracks of her 1993 *Other Voices, Other Rooms* album and invited Hester to appear on several gigs at home and abroad during the tour in support of the album.

Starting in the mid-1960s, Hester also took part in folk music events organized by Washington, D.C., disk jockey Dick Cerri. For decades she made annual appearances in the World Folk Music Association's showcase of new and old folk music, hosted by Cerri. In 1993, besides performing on the Troubadours of Folk Show in Los Angeles, she also introduced folk-country superstar Mary-Chapin Carpenter, who said she had been greatly influenced by Carolyn's recordings.

She continued to add to her recording credits in the 1980s, starting with the 1982 LP *Music Medicine,* released on her own label, Outpost. Her next release was the 1986 *Warriors of the Rainbow.* In the 1990s, she collaborated with Germany's Bear Family label, which was working on a multi-CD package reissue of all her recordings, including *At Town Hall* in 1990 and the compilation *Dear Companion* in 1995. She recorded her first new album in a decade in 1996, *From These Hills,* on the Road Goes on Forever label.

A memorable moment for her was the chance to appear with longtime friend Bob Dylan on the thirtieth anniversary concert at New York's Madison Square Garden (which referred to his first recording releases on Columbia in the 1960s). She told Sofranko, "To be at the Bob Dylan tribute was a great honor, especially when you think that four hours of music was all one man and it started with a pen and a piece of paper. We had a lovely time, were treated very well and Dylan was downright jolly that night. He had just pulled off this huge rock summit—Bobstock or something."

For her part, she foresaw her career continuing pretty much as it always had. She stressed to Sofranko, "My agenda is to continue supporting folk music," including trying to encourage new writers to persevere. Her advice to them, she said, despite the fact that "there are only so many record labels and so many spots to go around," was not to let that stop them: "You're writing songs, you're thinking, you're living. Please make a tape anyway, even if it's not on A&M or Columbia. The creative process is such a tenuous thing and sometimes tentative and sometimes goes away. If it's come and made a home with you, keep on putting it out."

HIATT, JOHN: *Singer, guitarist, pianist, songwriter. Born Indianapolis, Indiana, August 20, 1952.*

The great respect his musical peers had for John Hiatt's creative abilities was demonstrated by the many performers who included his original compositions in their concerts or albums. Stars who recorded his material covered the spectrum from rock 'n' roll to country and folk, including such artists as Bonnie Raitt, Bob Dylan, Iggy Pop, the Searchers, Nick Lowe, and Ricky Nelson. The music world also respected his talents as a performer and recording artist, yet as of the mid-1990s, making his mark with the mass album-buying public still evaded him.

This was so despite the many accolades given his releases by major media reviewers from the *New York Times* to *People* magazine. In praising Hiatt's excellent 1995 album, *Walk On,* Craig Tomashoff of *People* commented, "Hiatt is sort of the Cal Ripken, Jr., of the rock world. Like the Baltimore Oriole, he may not be the flashiest player, but he is a workhorse who never fails to deliver quality work. . . . It is unfortunate that in his long career he has never really had anything resembling commercial success. Perhaps it's because he has refused to work with one musical persona, playing everything from the angry rocker to the sensitive folkie to the country troubadour."

Hiatt, born and raised in Indianapolis, by the 1990s devoted some of his nonmusic time to the racing car field. He told Andy Smith of the *Providence Journal Bulletin* ("John Hiatt Takes an Acoustic Turn," October 30, 1995), "It's a childhood dream. I grew up in Indianapolis and the sound of the [Indy] 500 was always music to my ears. It's just great fun. It's like performing in a way, because it requires great focus."

It was not a childhood free from trauma, however. His father died when he was twelve, and one of his brothers died at a young age. Before he reached his teens, two older brothers had left home as teenagers. This left young John as the only male child in a house he shared with his mother and three sisters. Tongue in cheek, he told Jeff Spevak of the Rochester, New York, *Democrat and Chronicle,* "I was left with no male guidance. That's why it's taking me so long to grow up."

When his high school years began during the second half of the '60s, he already was paying attention to blues and folk-rock performers. Dylan was a particular favorite. As he told Scott Mervis of the *Pittsburgh Post Gazette* ("Perfectly good musician," November 3, 1995), "My biggest thrill was getting a song ["The Usual"] cut by Bob Dylan, because he was my early, main influence. He's the guy that really personalized this whole music thing for me."

In his teens, he developed considerable skill as a guitarist and performed with a number of rock and rhythm and blues bands in his home area, including one in the late 1960s called the White Ducks, resulting in *White Duck In Season* (1972). In 1970 he moved to Nashville, Tennessee, seeking greater opportunities in the music publishing and performing areas. After a few years there, he signed with Epic, which released two of his albums, *Hangin' Around the Observatory* in 1974 and *Overcoats* in 1975. Neither caught on with record buyers, and after leaving the label he toured for a few years as a solo artist while sending demos of his new songs to other artists and seeking another recording contract. The latter finally materialized with MCA, which issued two more LPs, *Slug Line* in 1979 and *Two Bit Monsters* in 1980.

By 1980 he was working as a member of the Ry Cooder band. He had submitted a demo tape to Cooder of some of his songs; Cooder wasn't sure any of them fit his musical goals, but he liked Hiatt's vocal and instrumental work and asked John to join his group. John took part in a number of concerts with Cooder and also contributed to Ry's 1980 album, *Borderline.* Hiatt soon went out on his own again, signing with still another label, Geffen. His early '80s output included the 1982 release *All of a Sudden,* which again contained some wonderful tracks but was mainly ignored by pop radio and record buyers.

Still, by the mid-1980s John had built up a cult following and could draw respectable audiences to smaller venues around the United States and abroad. He continued to turn out new albums in the '80s almost at the rate of one a year, with production work handled for the most part by veteran industry experts Nick Lowe and Nick Visconti. His credits in the first part of the decade included *Riding with the King* in 1983, *Warming up to the Ice Age* in 1985, and *Riot with Hiatt* in 1985. There was a gap after the last one caused by a series of painful events that included the suicide of his first wife and a deepening problem with drug and alcohol abuse. He finally pulled himself together, shook off his addictions, and focused again on his writing and recording capabilities in a three-album sequence, sometimes referred to as his "recovery trilogy," on the A&M label. These albums—*Bring the Family* ('87), *Slow Turning* ('88), and *Stolen Moments* ('89)—rank among the best folk- and country-influenced rock collections of the decade. By then many of his songs had made the charts for other artists, including Three Dog Night's version of "Sure As I'm Sittin' Here"; the Neville Brothers' single of "Washable Ink"; and Rosanne Cash's release "Pink Bedroom."

In the early '90s he was represented on album catalogs with the 1991 compilation *Y'All Caught? The Ones That Got Away.* He also renewed ties with Ry Cooder, joining with him, Nick Lowe, and drummer Jim Keltner in what seemed on paper a potential supergroup, Little Village. However, the project never quite gelled and the group's self-titled album, issued in 1992, gained little attention.

Feeling more comfortable about himself and his abilities, by the '90s Hiatt had remarried and avoided the more raucous aspects of his earlier music career. By the mid-'90s, in between tours and recording sessions, he lived quietly on a farm in Franklin, Tennessee, with his second wife, three children, and a menagerie that included cats, dogs, and nine horses. In 1993 he completed the album *Perfectly Good Guitar* for A&M that for most print media critics had all the elements of a multimillion seller. In support of the collection, he embarked on an intensive concert series with his band. That wasn't enough to turn the disc into a chart blockbuster, but it provided the environment for John to write new material for his next album project.

One of the new songs, he wrote in *Musician* ("How I Wrote Those Songs," February 1995), was done on the piano, something he only did about every five years.

(Most of his songs, he stated, were written using an old 1947 Gibson guitar.) "'Friend of Mine' [included on his '95 album *Walk On*] is about a good buddy I'd lost. We were in Sacramento and my tour manager at that time had a remarkable ability to get perks out of hotels. Somehow, he got me the Presidential Suite at the Hyatt. I put my key in, opened the door—there's a grand fucking piano in my room. I sat down, and the next thing you know it's evening, and I'm kind of sad and blue, and my friend had been dead for six months, and it just came out."

In 1994, as he continued to compile new songs, A&M issued the live collections *Hiatt Comes Alive at Budokan* and *Live at the Hiatt*. He hadn't been satisfied with A&M's promotional work on *Perfectly Good Guitar*, though, and he decided to get out of his contract with that label and prepare his next album on his own. Among those who took part in the sessions were multi-instrumentalist David Immergluck (previously with Camper Van Beethoven), whose mandolin playing gave an excellent underpinning to many tracks; longtime friend Bonnie Raitt, who sang duet with John on "I Can't Wait" (Raitt's hit single of John's "Thing Called Love" helped jump-start her move to superstar status in the '90s); and members of the Minneapolis folk rock band the Jayhawks.

After hearing the session tapes, officials at Capitol Records eagerly moved to sign Hiatt, releasing the album, *Walk On*, in mid-'95. The album had elements of a classic collection, whether or not it moved to top spots on major charts, and received well-deserved support from reviewers. Joel Selvin of the *San Francisco Examiner-Chronicle* commented, "As good an album as the perennially underrated Hiatt has made since his splendid 1987 *Bring the Family*, his Capitol debut uses some folky instrumentation beneath his trademark passionate vocals." Jon Pareles of the *New York Times* (January 4, 1996) included the album in his top 10 list of '95, and the editors of *Stereo Review* listed it among their Record of the Year Awards for 1995. Chris Morris enthused in *Musician* about all the tracks, calling such numbers as "You Must Go," "Cry Love," "Walk On," "I Can't Wait," "The River Knows Your Name," and "Mile High" superlative.

In mid-1997 Capitol issued his fourteenth album, *Little Head*, a worthy addition to his output that, as was usually the case, won considerable critical praise but relatively little airplay. David Handelman, writing in *People* (July 7, 1997) after bemoaning the fact that Hiatt was better known for his songwriting than his performing, stated, in the new disc, "Hiatt . . . serves up a new batch of tuneful chronicles about liars, babes and other passions. Peppered with horn blasts and sitar strains, as well as lewd puns and goofy rhymes (. . . *red sweater . . . Eddie Vedder*), *Little Head* . . . brims with great pleasure."

Meanwhile, other artists continued to benefit from his original material, including Linda Ronstadt, who sang two of his songs, including the title track ("When We Ran") on her 1998 Elektra Records release, *We Ran*. (The other Hiatt track was Linda's version of his honky-tonk ballad "Icy Blue Heart.")

Hiatt's concert work in 1998 included taking part in the Newport Folk Festival tour along with such other artists as Joan Baez, Richard Thompson, Nanci Griffith, BeauSoleil, Wilco, and Bruce Cockburn. That year Capitol issued the compilation album, *Best of John Hiatt*, and A&M released *Greatest Hits.*

HICKMAN, SARA: *Singer, guitarist, percussionist, band leader (Domestic Science Club), songwriter. Born Jacksonville, North Carolina, March 1, 1963.*

The irrepressible Sara Hickman cast a strong shadow across the U.S. folk-music scene from the late 1980s on. With her effervescent personality and strong stage presence, she promised to become one of the major figures in the expanding folk-music genre of the closing years of the century. She projected an infectious sense of humor and deep interest in humanitarian causes, but within her sunny exterior was a strong creative will as shown by her successful refusal to bow down to the guidelines of the major record companies.

Her birthplace was in North Carolina, but she grew up in Houston, Texas. Her interest in music began early, and, encouraged by her mother, by her teens she had learned to play guitar and sing in school events. As a teenager, she began to devote some of her skills to helping others. As she told an interviewer, "There was a high school teacher who saw something inside me. She started booking me for weddings, psychiatric hospitals, wherever. She knew I had a desire to create in a way that helped people, and she helped me find a place to share it." It wasn't a path she ignored in later years when she started to make a name for herself in show business. Her activities in the 1990s, for instance, included taking part in benefits for Jimmy and Rosalynn Carter's Habitat for Humanity program and Romanian orphan relief.

After finishing high school in the mid-'80s, she entered college in Denton, Texas, where she continued to add to her performing experience with gigs at local folk venues. By then she also had started to write original songs. In 1986 her grandparents lent her $400 to prepare a 45-rpm single comprising the songs "How Can It Be" backed with "As Much As Me." She had a number of copies pressed for sale at her concerts. After graduating college in 1987, she moved to Dallas, where her career flourished in local folk clubs. The *Dallas Times-Herald* described her shows as "a cross between a stand-up comedy routine and group therapy, with great music thrown in as a bonus."

She was named the city's best solo performer and best folk act of 1988 by the *Dallas Observer*. That same year she was back in the studio, coproducing tracks for an album with Carl Finch of the local polka-rock band Brave Combo. (After seeing her perform on a local cable TV program, Finch had contacted her and offered to help assemble an album for his group's Four Dots label.) Called *Equal Scary People,* it first came out on Four Dots in 1988. In the *Dallas Observer*'s 1989 awards, her album was chosen as the best independent album release, while Hickman was called the best acoustic/folk act.

The album was picked up by Elektra Records, which reissued it in the fall of 1989. The Elektra version was somewhat changed from the Four Dots one, Hickman noted. The track "Take It Like a Man" was omitted and some of the other ones were remixed. In one case, the song "Last Night Was a Big Rain" was augmented with vocal support from Debbie Talasek and Doug Bryan.

Hickman was starting to attract attention from fans and music industry people beyond the confines of Texas. One indication was inclusion of her song "Salvador" on the Windham Hill Records 1989 compilation *Legacy.* Other songs on the disc were provided by such folk luminaries as John Gorka, Bill Morrissey, Pierce Pettis, and Cliff Eberhardt, people with whom Sara was to tour in years to come. In 1990 her vocals could be heard on several industry samplers and also on the Hollywood Records sound track album for the movie *Arachnaphobia.* Her cut of "Blue Eyes Are Sensitive to the Light" was the first track on the CD.

During 1990 Elektra released her second album, *Shortstop,* whose tracks included "Salvador" and such other Hickman compositions as "I Couldn't Help Myself" and "The Very Thing." Videos were prepared for the last two numbers. "I Couldn't Help Myself" rose to number three on adult contemporary charts. Though Sara never wavered in thinking of herself as a folk artist, the recordings were marketed by Elektra to the country market. Elektra's fortieth anniversary compilation, *Rubiyat,* included a cover version of Dennis Lynde's "Hello, This Is Your Heart," recorded by Sara in New Orleans with the Neville Brothers' Meters band.

The two Elektra albums weren't blockbusters, but they still sold around 50,000 copies each, a quite acceptable level for folk-oriented discs in a rock- and rap-dominated environment. Happy about the way her career was proceeding, Sara began taping material for a third release. When she took the tapes to Elektra in 1993, however, her contacts at the label weren't enthused. They wanted her to go back and prepare new songs that might be the basis for a radio hit. She refused, and Elektra put the album on the shelf, ultimately dropping her from the roster.

She then requested that Elektra return the masters so she could produce the album herself. She was turned down; the company said they were its property. Her mother suggested she buy them back, and after extended discussions Elektra gave in, initially setting the price at $100,000, then coming down, first to $50,000 and finally to $25,000. That still was more than the Hickmans had at their disposal, so Sara sent messages via the Internet and at concerts asking for help from fans. The response was surprisingly good, providing enough seed money so that Sara, by selling her house, some guitars, and a few keepsakes, could meet the needed payment. When the album finally came out it was called *Necessary Angels* in honor of the outside contributors whose names were listed on the album cover and who also received hand-numbered bracelets inscribed with the album title.

While Sara was negotiating to get the album on the market, she wasn't sitting at home in a rocking chair. Her 1993 milestones including releasing a single (at her own expense) called "Romania," based on her trip to that nation to work with orphans. Some ninety fellow musicians donated their time to work on it and all proceeds were earmarked for orphan relief. She also prepared *Joy,* a video about a homeless woman that won first place in the 1993 USA Film Festival. She formed the group called Domestic Science Club with Robin Macy (previously with Dixie Chicks) and bluegrass veteran Patty Mitchell Lege to prepare a three-part harmony album intended as a 1993 Christmas present. (The album was independently issued in 1993, then rereleased in 1994 on Discovery and in 1996 on Crystal Clear Sound.)

By 1994 Sara had gained the support of Jac Holzman, president of Warner Music Group's Discovery Records, for production of *Necessary Angels.* The new collection actually was quite different from what she'd originally delivered to Elektra, containing five songs from that set plus seven new tracks. When issued during 1994, the album's tracks included such songs as "Shadowboxing," "Best of Times," "The Place Where the Garage Used to Stand," "Oh Daddy" (a confrontation between a daughter and her divorced father), "Room of One's Own," and "Pursuit of One's Happiness," the last named one where the lyrics question whether a career is more important than a person's life. After that disc was issued, Discovery later issued the *Domestic Science Club* album as a regular catalog item.

Looking back over her efforts at the time, she commented, "I like to think of myself as someone who takes an experience and searches for common ground in which a song can form. . . . As my experiences have grown, I've begun to sense how deeply spiritual making music can be. My first album, *Equal Scary People,* contained vignettes and love songs mixed with political statements. The second . . . seemed closer to the mark I was trying to hit, but *Necessary Angels* is the closest yet. The idea is to present people with the other side of the coin, to draw them in and have them realize there can be good in even the darkest of situations."

By 1995, however, Sara began to feel she was beginning to encounter some of the same problems with Discovery she had with her first label. She told Joe Mitchell of the *Austin Chronicle* ("Deliveries Abound for Sara Hickman," May 1996), "What started my frustration with Discovery was that I'd take a song to them and I'd be really excited about it and I'd walk in dancing and singing and there'd never really seem to be a reaction. They'd say, 'Just keep writing.' The key words that kept coming up were 'radio hit,' 'radio hit,' 'radio hit.' I don't think about that when I write. To me it's just the miracle of writing anything at all.

"What do I love to do? I love to make music. What's stopping me from recording the music I love to make? Other people. And why are other people stopping me? Because they feel like I'm not doing something that's going to make them money."

So she decided to go to the label and say, "Thanks. You've put out *Necessary Angels* and the first *Domestic Science Club* CD, but I think I'm going to do [the next album] by myself. It's not about fame and fortune for me. It's about satisfying this hunger in my soul."

She also emphasized her happiness at having become pregnant, a fact she'd shared with audiences in early '96 during a concert tour designed to spotlight artists who typically were featured at the annual Kerrville, Texas, Folk Festival. (She and the expectant father, a man named Keith, married in February '96.) The baby was due in August '96 and, since they knew ahead of time it would be a girl, had been named Lily. She emphasized she planned to be a good mother but didn't expect to give up touring, making new records, or working on other projects. She told Mitchell, "Keith has always wanted to be a housewife. He has the freedom to work at home on his computer and take care of the baby. That's something I don't have." Sara said she expected to spend lots of time with Lily, who at first would stay with Keith in Dallas while Sara maintained home base in Austin.

Her '96 music efforts included completing and self-marketing a live album called *Misfits* (projected to be the first of a series to be followed by *Misfits II, Misfits III*, etc.) and an album of new material tentatively called *Two Kinds of Laughter.* The plan was to issue *Misfits* in the fall while she was nursing Lily, followed by the album of new recordings in early '97. She also had started collecting material for a children's album.

As if those projects weren't enough, she discussed new work with her associates of the Domestic Science Club, which already had issued a new album, *Three Women,* on the Dallas-based Crystal Clear label in the spring of '96. Still another possibility was to perform and record with a group that called itself Too Many Girls. The latter had started spontaneously at the Austin Music Awards show when Sara joined a group of other talented female artists on stage: Kris McKay, Kelly Willis, Abra Moore, and Barbara K. Their performance was so well received by the audience that they began considering expanding the association into a regular act. Sara, who also dabbled in art, started trying in '96 to use a character called Pillow Man she'd drawn for some of her concert T-shirts as the basis for a comic book series.

By 1997 Sara had a new record company alignment with Shanachie, which issued *Misfits* on its label in 1997, *Two Kinds of Laughter* in 1998, and *Spiritual Appliances* in 2000.

HICKS, DAN: *Singer, guitarist, drummer, band leader (Dan Hicks and His Hot Licks, Acoustic Warrior), songwriter. Born Little Rock, Arkansas, December 9, 1941.*

With his background as a folksinger coupled with an interest in swing and blues of the 1930s and '40s, Dan Hicks seemed well positioned to take advantage of the folk-rock formats taking shape in the San Francisco area in the mid-1960s. However, never one to follow the crowd, he came up with a musical blend at odds with what was coming to the fore in Haight-Ashbury that combined a wry sense of humor with hard-to-categorize folk, C&W swing, and jazz elements that for a time in the late '60s and early '70s drew a fairly sizable following.

He was born in Little Rock, Arkansas, to a military family that eventually moved to Santa Rosa, California, where Dan spent much of his youth. He was exposed to folk and country music as well as pop in his early years and also developed an interest in Benny Goodman and other swing band stars. While in high school he began to play drums with several teenage bands before enrolling in San Francisco State College in 1959. Influenced by the folk-music boom of that period, he learned guitar and performed as a folksinger in local coffeehouses and at college events.

In the mid-'60s he turned his attention to folk-rock, using his drum skills to replace Sam Linde in a group called the Charlatans in 1965. The group, considered a forerunner of the "San Francisco Sound" period that made international stars of people like the Jefferson Airplane, the Grateful Dead, and Janis Joplin, had potentially good prospects, but Hicks felt he didn't have enough room for creative growth; he left to set up his own band called Dan Hicks and his Hot Licks, which debuted in January 1968 as an opening act for the Charlatans.

The initial roster comprised Dan handling vocals, guitar, and primary songwriting; David LaFlamme on violin; and Bill Douglas on bass. In a short time, he completely reorganized the group, this time with Sid Page replacing LaFlamme on violin, Jaime Leopold taking over from Douglas on bass, and featuring John Webber on guitar and Tina Gancher and Sherri Snow on vocals (the girl duos featured with the band were called the Lickettes). Some of the late-'60s tracks made with some of those musicians were contained in the 1969 Epic release *Dan Hicks & His Hot Licks: Original Recordings,* which demonstrated how much better the group became with further changes in the early 1970s.

Those changes included the departure of Webber and a new Lickette team of Maryann Price and Naomi Ruth Eisenberg. The latter singers meshed exceedingly well with Hicks and the remaining musicians in the 1971 live album, *Where's the Money,* recorded at the Troubadour nightclub in Los Angeles.

Hicks and the band drew exuberant crowds to venues across the United States and Canada during the first half of the '70s. It also gained exposure on many major TV shows of those years, including *The Flip Wilson Show,* Johnny Carson's *The Tonight Show,* and *The Dick Cavett Show.* The group's output of that period included *Striking It Rich* (with new member guitarist John Girton taking part) in 1972, and *Last Train to Hicksville,* 1973, both on Blue Thumb Records. Recalling the group's style in the *Rolling Stone Record Guide*'s 1979 edition, critic Ariel Swartley wrote, "Is Dan Hicks Haight-Ashbury's answer to Jim Kweskin (of jug band fame)? No. Hicks and the Hot Licks have more up the sleeves of their seedy furs than hip-camp and caberet. The violin virtuosity of Sid Page, the spiffy harmonies of Maryann Price and Ruth Eisenberg and all those quotable sources, from Western Swing to Fifties cool, serve Hicks' curmudgeon's eye-view of life in the breakdown lane. Hicks gives nostalgia a mordent, modern voice. . . . [He] has cultivated a twang, a yodel and an air of gum-chewing innocence that fools no one—if he can help it. Probe his sentimentality and you find a sneer."

Hicks's career seemed in excellent shape in 1974, with *Last Train to Hicksville* doing well on the charts and many opportunities on the concert circuit, but Dan surprised many in the industry by breaking up his group and keeping a relatively low profile for the rest of the '70s and the first part of the '80s. During those years he earned a living doing commercials, some solo tours, and support work on other artists' albums. He did make an initial stab at a solo career in 1975, when he recorded *It Happened One Bite* for Warner Brothers, assisted by Maryann Price, Sid Page, and John Girton. Originally intended as the sound track for a Ralph Bakshi animated film, the album was released on its own in 1978, when the film failed to materialize.

In the mid-'80s he assembled a new, more jazz-oriented group called Acoustic Warrior. He was joined in the band by James "Fingers" Sheyse on fiddle and mandolin and Alex Baum on bass. His album credits in the '80s included the 1984 reissue album *Rich & Happy in Hicksville* and the retrospective *Very Best of Dan Hicks and His Hot Licks.*

In the 1990s Dan continued his pattern of the '80s, recording the track "Gone with the Wind" with Rob Wasserman on an MCA album, "Keeping My Eye on You" on Michael Franks's 1993 Warner Brothers release *Dragonfly Summer,* dueting with Maryann Price on her 1993 Watermelon album *Etched in Swing,* and doing two tracks with the Hot Club of San Francisco on a Clarity Records album that same year. In 1994 he recorded his first new album in sixteen years, *Shootin' Straight,* with the '90s version of Acoustic Warriors. The disc was recorded live at McCabe's Guitar Shop in Santa Monica, California, one of the major West Coast folk-music centers.

HINOJOSA, TISH: *Singer, guitarist, songwriter, record producer. Born San Antonio, Texas, December 6, 1955.*

With her clear, lilting voice and impressive songwriting skills, Leticia "Tish" Hinojosa became a major force in the burgeoning impact of Mexican-American elements on many segments of late-twentieth-century music. Her material ran the gamut from American/Spanish pop stylings to country and folk. But she rejected efforts to name her as heir to the Tejano mantle of another Texan with Mexican heritage, Selena. She told Larry Kelp of the *San Francisco Examiner-Chronicle* ("Q and A with Tish Hinojosa," October 29, 1995), "I could've been one of the pioneers of Tejana music. Since the Selena tragedy [Selena was gunned down by the head of her fan club in March '95] it has become a forefront issue, one that I face daily, of Tejano music representing the Mexican American culture. But it's not representative of an entire culture. Until Selena's death, most of the country had never heard of her or Tejano music. I never listened to it because to me Tejano music in the '90s is pop wannabes copying Madonna bustiers and Janet Jackson headgear, a caricature of our culture."

The difference between that and the type of music she offered, she told Kelp, was "the difference between doing make-believe and real roots music. I respect my roots and I love conjunto, the South Texas border music that brings together the Mexican rhythm played by the bajo sexto [twelve-string guitar] and the accordion and its polkas brought in by German immigrants."

The youngest of thirteen children (including stepbrothers and stepsisters), as a youngster Tish heard traditional songs from her father, a native of Tamaulipas, and her mother, originally from Coahuila. She also absorbed elements of various genres from San Antonio radio, which, besides rock and pop strains, also played recordings by traditionally oriented singer-songwriters like Austin Lara and Jose Alfredo Jiminez. Among non-Mexican influences, she recalled, were Linda Ronstadt and folksingers Buffy Sainte-Marie and Joan Baez. In school, she also was exposed to rock and roll, with British bands like the Beatles and the Hollies being particular favorites.

By her teens she had learned to play guitar and had the strong approval of her mother to pursue those talents. She told Ramiro Burr ("Rooted in Two Cultures—Tish Hinojosa," *Sing Out!* May–June 1995), while she was in high school her mother strove to get her daughter's career started: "When I was about 16 or 17, I would go to coffeehouses. She called (local radio station) KCOR-AM and talked to the main DJ there. She told him that her daughter could sing and asked what she should do with me. He said, 'Send her on down here and we will see if we can put her to work.' I took my guitar and auditioned for him and he immediately put me in touch with Rober Grever. This was about 1973."

Grever, a music publisher who was just starting a new record label, Cara (later to become the dominant independent Tejano label in the region), had her record four singles, which had minimal impact on the market. After finishing high school, Tish enrolled in San Antonio College, but focused more on earning a living from singing than on most of her courses. In 1979 she left Texas for Red River, New Mexico, partly because, as she told Burr, "I figured that playing cover songs in San Antonio bars was pretty dead-end," and partly because she had an uncle living there who was very involved in progressive country music. It didn't occur to her to move to Nashville because country to that point was foreign to her.

"I considered Los Angeles or New York, but at that time I knew nothing about country music. . . . I had begun to write a little bit and had just won the Kerrville Folk Festival New Folk Award. I'd only written two songs at the time." In Red River, her uncle Murphy gave her a strong grounding in modern country, including having her work as part of country duos and trios. In 1983 she used that experience to gain a writing contract with a Nashville publisher. Once settled in Nashville, she also prepared demo tapes for various industry people. While not much came of that, it proved a good learning experience in what was required for studio singing. She also met and married Craig Barker, who later became her manager-attorney. Her first child, a son, also was born in Nashville before the family decided to return to San Antonio in 1985, where her mother was succumbing to a fatal illness. After Craig was accepted into law school at the University of New Mexico, he and Tish returned to that state where she paid $2,000 to complete her first album, *Taos to Tennessee*, which was issued in cassette form in 1987. (Eventually it was reissued on the Watermelon label.)

Pregnant with her second child (a daughter, Nina), Tish didn't worry about handling children and career simultaneously. She told Burr, "I think the important thing for me was just to get something out. I didn't really aspire it to even go that far. We only made cassettes, and for me it was just going to be a demo to send to record companies and to sell at gigs. I figured I could make my money back that way. It had a practical side and an art side to it. I also felt it was important to get this record made before my baby was born."

By the late '80s the Barkers had moved again, this time to Austin, Texas, where Craig enrolled to finish his law degree. Meanwhile, Tish decided to set up a showcase at the Bluebird in Nashville in hopes of aligning with a major record firm. As it happened, none of the executives she invited showed up, but Patrick Clifford from A&M Records just happened to be at the bar and liked her performance. He gave her his card and asked her to send more demo material and a résumé. That, in turn, brought an OK for recording sessions that spawned her 1989 album, *Homeland*. Among its tracks was her composition "West Side of Town," which capsuled the trials of her late parents in bringing up a family of thirteen children. Backing her on the song was accordian and conjunto star Flaco Jimenez (famed as a soloist and, in the first part of the '90s, as a member of the Texas Tornados). The collection marked her with national critics as a potential future superstar, but before she could follow up on that, A&M was acquired by another company and Tish was dropped from its roster.

She continued to tour, playing college campuses, Southwest area clubs, and venues in other parts of the country, building up rapport with country and folk fans and drawing the attention of other artists who began to consider covering some of her compositions. In Austin, tapes were made of a concert in honor of Mexican Independence Day, Cinco de Mayo, which formed the basis for the 1991 album *Aquella Noche (That Certain Night)*, released on the independent Watermelon label. The album found favor with Hispanic fans, as did her second Watermelon release of 1991, *Memorabilia Navidena (Christmas Memories)*. She followed with her first album on Rounder Records, *Culture Swing*, issued in 1992, the first of a three-CD agreement. Among her activities in 1991 was performing at the inauguration events for newly elected Texas governor Ann Richards, something she also did in 1993 during President Bill Clinton's inaugural parties.

For her second collection, initially intended for Rounder, she began work on a group of self-penned songs reflecting her Mexican heritage. In the interim she had signed with the Madonna-owned publishing firm Maverick, which is affiliated with Warner Brothers. The Maverick representative liked the new material and took it to the head of Warner Brothers Nashville, feeling that they could offer bigger commercial possibilities. After receiving a call from top producer Jim Ed Norman on that, Tish decided to go with Warner. She emphasized to Norman that the new album really wasn't a country music disc. However, she recalled, he responded that he wasn't planning to sign her as a country artist. Her Warner Brothers debut, *Destiny's Gate*, came out in 1994 and proved an excellent addition to her recorded output.

While agreeing to sign with Warner, she declined to buy back her contract with Rounder. She wanted to keep the Rounder option open, she stressed, because she felt it gave her the chance to do more roots-oriented music.

The first product of that was the Hinojosa-produced Rounder album *Frontejas,* introduced in the spring of 1995. The album title combines the Spanish words for border, *frontera,* and Texas, *Tejas.* In the liner notes she pointed out an inspiration for the album's songs, which included both new compositions and versions of traditional material, was the discovery just before her mother's death in 1985 of the latter's singing aspirations. Seeking to find out more about the background of her mother's repertoire, she began working with University of Texas anthropologist Don Americo Paredes, who told of the meaning of those songs while also teaching her some other *corridos,* or story-ballads.

All of the songs were sung in Spanish except for the track "Polka Fronterrestrial," performed with Ray Benson, leader of the Asleep at the Wheel band. Benson also sang the duet "Con Su Pluma en Su Mano" with her on another track. Reflecting her diverse influences, backing on some tracks was provided by Brave Combo, Robert "Beto" Skiles (and his band, the Fairlanes), and Peter Rowan, players not identified with Mexican traditions, and on others by, besides Flaco Jimenez, who provided sole accompaniment on "Dejame Llorar (Let Me Weep)," such *conjunto* experts as Santiago Jimenez Jr. (a brother of Flaco's), Mingo Saldivar, and Eva Ybarra. Among the traditional numbers was "Pajarillo Barranqueno (Little Riverside Bird)," written in the 1800s and a favorite at her concerts. Ostensibly about bird-watching, in fact it refers to men sitting around the plaza in a Mexican town, watching the girls go by.

Some of the idols of her youth paid tribute to Tish by including some of her material in their projects. In the mid-'90s, for instance, Linda Ronstadt sang Tish's "Adonde Voy" on her *Winter Light* album, while Joan Baez and Tish sang a duet of another song on Baez's 1995 album release, *Ring Them Bells.* Hinojosa also was a guest artist on other releases by many of her peers, including among those work with Beto and the Fairlanes on the Dos release *Salsafied* and Peter Rowan on the Sugar Hill collection *Awake Me in the New World.*

During 1995–96, Tish was in the studios working on a Spanish children's album *Cada Niño (Every Child)* for Rounder and a new Warner Brothers project, *Dreaming from the Labyrinth* (1996), released the following year in a Spanish version, *Soñar Del Laberinto.* Watermelon also released *Best of the Sandia* in 1997. She told *New Country* magazine (May 1995), "I'm a two-record-label gal now. It's not a common thing. There was a time when I was struggling to get on one and now I'm on two." She liked the idea, she indicated, that the arrangement prevented her from being pigeonholed as a country singer or a Mexican folk revivalist or . . . anything: "The thing that makes me not their biggest selling country artist is the thing that gives me freedom. As much fun as it is, it's still very nerve-racking, too. It's been a very busy two or three years. I just wish I could make days be 48 hours instead of 24."

HINTON, SAM: *Singer, guitarist, dulcimer player, educator, marine biologist. Born Tulsa, Oklahoma, March 21, 1917.*

When Sam Hinton graduated from high school in Crockett, Texas, he received two books, *American Reptiles* and Carl Sandburg's *American Songbag.* The gifts were to symbolize his lifelong combination of careers as a distinguished scientist and part-time folksinger.

During his boyhood days in Oklahoma and Texas, Sam spent long hours exploring the wonders of nature in his rural surroundings. When he wasn't studying the wildlife and botanical features or going to school, he often sang for pleasure, by himself or with family and friends in local get-togethers. "During my youth," he recalls, "I always sang. It wasn't until I went to college that I found out it was folk music."

This discovery came in 1934, when Sam entered Texas A&M College as a zoology major. Sam remained at Texas A&M for two years, supporting himself with a variety of jobs, including singing, painting signs, and selling snake venom to an eastern manufacturer. The venom came from sixty water moccasins that he maintained as a zoological hobby. In 1936 Sam entered and won a *Major Bowes Amateur Contest* and left school to travel throughout the country with one of the Bowes troupes.

During the next two years, Sam sang his folk songs in forty-six states and throughout Canada. Finally tiring of traveling, he moved to Los Angeles and enrolled as a zoology student at UCLA in 1939. Again, singing came in handy to help pay tuition, as did another of Sam's skills, science illustrator. Not long after settling down in Los Angeles, Sam gained a part in the long-running musical comedy *Meet the People.* Joining Sam in the cast were such soon-to-be famous individuals as Nanette Fabray, Virginia O'Brien, Doodles Weaver, and Jack Gilford.

At UCLA, Sam met and married Leslie Forster, an excellent violinist and soloist with the university's a cappella choir. Leslie provided Sam with his first introduction to the more formal aspects of music.

After earning his B.S. in zoology from UCLA in 1940, Hinton accepted a position as director of the Desert Museum in Palm Springs, California. He left there in 1943 to accept a post as curator of the aquarium and museum at the University of California's Scripps Institution of Oceanography at La Jolla. This was the start of a long relationship between Sam and UC–San Diego. In 1964 he was appointed to the post of assistant director for the entire university system of the Office of School Relations.

In 1947 Sam made his first recording for the Library of Congress Archive of Folk Song, *Buffalo Boy and the*

Barnyard Song, an album of Anglo-Irish songs and ballads. In 1950 he made his first commercial recording, "Old Man Atom," for Columbia Records. Among his other singles in the early 1950s were "The Barnyard Song" (two songs, 1952); "Country Critters" (four songs, 1953); and "The Frog Song" and "The Greatest Sound Around" (1954), all of which were for Decca Records' Children's Series.

Sam turned out his first LPs in 1952, *Folk Songs of California and the Old West,* on Bowmar Records and nine songs for the two-record RCA album *How the West Was Won.* Besides singing in the RCA album, which also featured Bing Crosby, Rosemary Clooney, and Jimmy Driftwood, Sam worked with Alan Lomax and Si Rady in selecting and arranging the material. His other LP credits on Decca include *Singing Across the Land* (1955); *A Family Tree of Folk Songs* (1956); and *The Real McCoy* (1957). In the 1960s, Sam was featured on such LPs as *American Folk Songs and Balladeers* (Classics Record Library, 1964); *Newport Folk Festival, 1963* (Vanguard); and, on Folkways Records, *The Songs of Men, Whoever Shall Have Some Peanuts* (1961), and *The Wandering Folksong* (1967).

From 1958 into the 1960s, he provided a continuing newspaper feature, *The Ocean World,* for the *San Diego Union.* He also coauthored two books on oceanology with Joel Hedgpeth, *Exploring Under the Sea* (Doubleday) and *Common Seashore Animals of Southern California* (Naturegraph).

Sam was also featured as a lecturer in his chosen subjects in many parts of the country, as well as receiving many engagements for campus folk song concerts. From 1957 on, he was featured every year as performer and discussion leader at the Berkeley, California, Folk Festival. Throughout the 1970s and into the early 1980s, Hinton continued to perform in folk venues and to take part in major festivals.

He continued to believe in the enduring nature of folk material despite the breaking of the folk song boom in the mid-1960s. "The *Variety* headline 'Folk Music Is Dead' made no sense to me," he once said. "In the 1930s, songwriters used themes from Tchaikovsky, Chopin, and other classical composers. When that era disappeared, you could just as well have written the headline 'Classics Are Dead.' "

HOLCOMB, ROSCOE: *Singer, banjoist, guitarist, songwriter. Born Daisy, Kentucky, 1911. Died 1981.*

Were there a Folk Music Hall of Fame, Roscoe Holcomb undoubtedly would be in it. For those dedicated to preserving traditional southern mountain music, his name evokes memories of some of the finest performances of such material ever presented onstage or in records. Still, his national exposure was brief; for most of his life only people in local areas of Kentucky were aware of his talents.

He was born and spent almost his entire life in the mountain region near Hazard, Kentucky, a longtime hotbed of mountain music, but perhaps better known for certain family feuds and for contention between coal miners and their often oppressive employers. Roscoe was introduced to music almost as soon as he could talk. Almost every week friends and relations would get together and play banjo, guitar, fiddle, and dulcimer as a form of relaxation. One of his earliest memories was listening to someone play the mouth harp. As a child he would sometimes walk to outlying farms to hear an expert on the harmonica.

By the time he was ten he had already learned to play the banjo. He was given a homemade banjo by his brother-in-law that lasted him many years. Soon after, he began to accompany a local fiddler. In a year's time, he learned to play and sing some 400 songs. He continued to learn new ballads, work songs, and square dance numbers as he grew up, sometimes adding new verses to them. When he was in his teens, he could play the guitar and other stringed instruments as well as the banjo.

His schooling, as was not unusual in his region, was scanty. He began working on local farms as a boy. After a while, he became a coal miner, his main occupation most of his life. When work in the mines was slow, he often worked on the railroads setting timber.

He kept up his music in his spare time. Between World War I and World War II, he built up a major reputation locally as a square dance musician. He recalled those days for John Cohen (*Sing Out!* April–May 1966, pp. 3–7): "I've played for square dances 'til the sweat dripped off my elbow. I used to play for square dances a lot. Used a bunch of us get out, maybe we'd go to a party somewhere and after the party was over the moon'd be a-shinin' bright, you know, and we'd all go back home and going up the road, somebody'd start his old instrument, guitar or banjer or something or other, and just gang up in the middle of the road and have the awfulest square dance right in the middle of the highway."

Roscoe was religious, and he felt increasingly guilty about playing. The "regular" Baptists, to which he belonged, considered secular music sinful. During the late 1920s, spurred on by his wife, he laid his instruments aside and stopped playing for some ten years. However, by the time World War II began, he was playing again.

He kept mining coal until the mines shut down due to competition from petroleum and other fuels, a situation that began to be reversed in the 1970s. He subsisted in the 1950s mainly by working at odd jobs. In 1959, John Cohen, a folk-music collector and then a member of the New Lost City Ramblers folk group, heard about Roscoe and sought him out. One of the first results was Roscoe's debut album on Folkways Records, *Mountain Music of Kentucky.* One of the best tracks was a song

Holcomb had constructed from earlier ballads called "Across the Rocky Mountain."

Cohen and Holcomb became close friends. Cohen wrote a number of articles about Roscoe for various folk publications in the early and mid-1960s and was inspired to start work on a documentary about Holcomb and his environment. The project got under way in 1962, and the film, *The High Lonesome Sound,* was issued in 1964. Folkways released an album of the same title. Later, Holcomb completed a third LP in conjunction with another mountain singer, *The Music of Roscoe Holcomb and Wade Ward.*

Once Holcomb's skills became known, opportunities arose for personal appearances in folk concerts and festivals all over the United States. Among his credits during the mid-1960s were performances at the Newport Folk Festival, University of Chicago Festival, UCLA, University of California at Berkeley, Cornell, and Brandeis. In 1965–66, he toured Europe as a member of the Festival of American Folk and Country Music troupe.

Holcomb had considerable impact on many of the young folk artists of the 1960s. Bob Dylan was one of his strong backers, calling *The High Lonesome Sound* album one of his favorites. By the end of the 1970s, that LP, which presented some interview material collected by Cohen as well as some of Holcomb's musical work, was the only album still in Folkways' current catalog. In 1998 Smithsonian-Folkways issued a CD entitled *The High Lonesome Sound,* a compilation of his three albums of the '60s and '70s. He died of emphysema and asthma at age seventy.

HOOKER, JOHN LEE: *Guitarist, singer, songwriter. Born Clarksdale, Mississippi, August 22, 1917.*

An enduring artist, John Lee Hooker influenced many phases of popular music from the post-World War II years through the 1990s, when, in his seventies, his career suddenly gained momentum. His blues stylings covered just about every facet from traditional country blues to rhythm and blues with excursions into rock 'n' roll. He carved out a justified reputation as one of America's greatest blues and folk-blues artists.

He spent his early years in the Mississippi Delta, a region that produced many of the legendary names in country blues. The first wave to gain recognition included John Lee "Sonny Boy" Williamson, Mississippi John Hurt, and Big Bill Broonzy. Those artists were sometimes looked upon as old-fashioned by the next generation, which encompassed such artists as Muddy Waters and Hooker.

The blues were a living, everyday tradition in John Lee's home area. Few children had the chance for much schooling or to do much else but work in the fields or at odd jobs, so music was one of the few pleasures of life. Hooker's father, William Hooker, was a preacher in a Baptist church where Hooker sang spirituals as a little boy. After his parents divorced, John Lee lived with his mother, Minnie, and his stepfather, farmer Will Moore, a noted guitarist in the area who played at local functions. Hooker remembers Charley Patton coming to visit his stepdad one day.

From an early age he knew he wanted to be a musician, not a farmer. He stretched an inner tube across a barn door to make his first instrument. But he learned to play on a Stella guitar. Hooker noted he always used the style of guitar playing he aquired as a boy—"percussive, with stomping chords slashed out, often laced with walking bass lines." Though he knew many great slide guitarists, he never mastered the techique. He told Jim and Amy O'Neal (*Living Blues,* Autumn 1979): "My style comes from my stepfather, Will Moore. . . . And nobody else plays that style."

Recalling his early years, Hooker told the O'Neals, "Well, I never did have a hard time 'cause my dad had a big farm down there. But I know it was rough. I didn't experience it 'cause I left there when I was fourteen, 'cause I was playin' music when I was twelve or fourteen. . . . I run off from my dad and I went to Memphis. I stayed around two months. I was workin' at a motion picture show, the New Daisy. . . . And my dad followed me. He come and got me."

Within a few weeks (1931 or 1932), John was on the road again. First stop was Memphis, where he played at house parties. Hooker moved to Cincinnati in the mid-1930s. He worked at various day jobs and performed his music wherever he could, for house parties or small clubs, often for little or no money. He sang in gospel groups called the Fairfield Four, the Delta Big Four, and the Big Six. He enlisted in the army, where he stayed for about a year until they found out he was too young. He settled in Detroit sometime before 1938. The pattern was much the same. He worked as a hospital attendant, then in an auto plant, while singing and playing at parties.

Eventually, Detroit proved lucky for him, bringing him together with "Bernie Besman and Elmer Barbee, this Jewish guy and this black cat." Barbee owned a record store, and Besman was a record distributor. Barbee heard Hooker play at a house party and approached John about making records. He arranged a meeting between Hooker and Besman to which John brought a tape. As Hooker told the O'Neals after hearing the tape, one of them said: " 'Man, I tell you, you got somethin' different, ain't nobody else got. I never heard a voice like that. Do you want to record?' I said, 'Yeah, but I've been jived so much, I don't know if y'all just puttin' me on.' They said, 'No, no, kid. We're not puttin' you on. You're really good. You written them songs on there?' I said, 'Yeah. You know, "Boogie Chillen," ' " "Hobo Blues," "I'm in the Mood." ' "

In late 1948, Hooker recorded his first single: "Boogie Chillen' " backed with "Sally Mae." Originally made for the Sensation label, the disc was leased to Modern Records, for distribution. The record became a massive hit in 1949, rising to number one on the R&B charts. Soon Hooker quit his day job and went on the road, aided by Besman, who was still a close friend decades later. After his success with "Boogie Chillen'" Hooker got his first electric guitar in 1949 from T-Bone Walker (born 1911 in Linden, Texas; died 1975 in Los Angeles) who found it in a pawn shop. Walker, the composer of "Stormy Monday," was known for his acrobatics on stage. "T-Bone was the greatest on electric guitar," Hooker told Chuck Phillips of the *Los Angeles Times* (April 23, 1989). "I used to follow him around like a puppy." Hooker himself would later be known for his soft hands and his wickedly percussive guitar playing.

He demonstrated he wasn't a one-hit artist by recording more favorites with blues fans on Modern Records: "I'm In the Mood," a number one R&B hit in October '51, "Hobo Blues," and "Crawlin' King Snake" (later recorded by Jim Morrison).

With his driving rhythms, Hooker claims to have originated the boogie sound. He certainly had an impact on rock. During the 1950s, his name became increasingly well known both in the United States and abroad. Hooker ran into problems with Modern Records on matters of royalties, which triggered his working for many other labels under a variety of pseudonyms: Texas Slim and John Lee Cooker for King Records; Johnny Williams for Staff and Gotham, and John Lee for Gotham; Delta John for Regent; John Lee Booker for Chance, Gon, and Deluxe, plus Johnny Lee on some Deluxe releases; Birmingham Sam and His Magic Guitar for Savoy; and the Boogie Man for Acorn. Though most of his output was on singles, there were occasional albums, like *John Lee Hooker Sings the Blues* on King.

He recorded for Chess in the early 1950s, and toured with Muddy Waters. Then in 1955, he signed an exclusive contract with Chicago-based Vee-Jay and remained on the roster until that company ran into financial problems in 1964. He released "Dimples" (1956) and "Boom Boom" (1962) on Vee-Jay. Hooker wrote "Boom Boom" after a barmaid named Willow chastised him for being late to a show: *Boom, boom, you're late again. Boom, Boom, I'm gonna shoot you down.*

Among the albums issued by Vee-Jay were *Burnin'* (1962), *I'm John Lee Hooker* (1959), and *Travelin'* (1960), *The Folklore of John Lee Hooker* (1961), *The Big Soul of John Lee Hooker* (1963) and *Best of John Lee Hooker* (1963). After several years with Vee-Jay, though, his name began to turn up on other labels, though most were reissues. Two of his most successful LPs came out on Riverside in 1959, during the folk boom, *The Folk Blues of John Lee Hooker* and *Burning Hell*. In 1960, *House of the Blues* came out on Chess, followed by *Plays and Sings the Blues* (1961) and *Real Folk Blues* (1966). (In 1991 MCA/Chess released *More Real Folk Blues: The Missing Album*.) Fantasy issued *Boogie Chillen* in 1962.

The folk movement of the late '50s and early '60s embraced country and folk blues artists, so John Lee Hooker gained a new following that cut across racial lines. He frequently performed at the Newport Folk Festival, and became an important figure on the coffee-house/folk-club circuit. To fit the "folk image," he cut down on the amplification or simply used an acoustic instrument. "I wish those days was here again," he lamented to Greg Drust for the liner notes of his 1991 Rhino retrospective, *John Lee Hooker: The Ultimate Collection: 1948–1990.* "I really enjoyed just sitting down with my guitar, playing soft, slow blues, quiet, not loud, talking to the people, and they were just around me in those coffeehouses. . . . I know those days are gone, but I still weep and wish they was here again. I wasn't making the money I am now, but it wasn't the money. It was the scene and the people, and what I love to do."

Meanwhile, as a regular in the American Folk Blues Festival in Europe he had a dramatic influence on English rock musicians. The Animals, for instance, had a hit with his song "Boom Boom" in 1964, and other bands included some of his material in their repertoire. While in the U.K., he recorded with an English blues-rock group called the Groundhogs, *John Lee Hooker with John Mayall and the Groundhogs* (Cleve Records). (Mike Kappus, Hooker's manager, notes that Mayall didn't play on the album.) He later joined the Rolling Stones for a TV broadcast during the Steel Wheels tour.

English fans noted his ability as a harmonica player. At times he would put his guitar aside and play the mouth harp. However, by the '70s, he rarely played harmonica and almost no records are extant in which he plays that instrument.

From the 1960s on, Hooker became primarily an album artist. He almost always had a number of LPs in the active catalog, as usual on a bewildering list of labels. Many were repackages of earlier recordings, but there always were some new ones. His early 1960s LPs included *Don't Turn Me from Your Door* (Atco), *John Lee Hooker* (Galaxy), and *Great Blues Album* (Fortune). Later in the decade, his new material included an LP with the Muddy Waters Band with Otis Spann on piano. Album releases from the mid-1960s to the early 1970s included *Alone* (Specialty, reissued Tomato in 1991), *Big Band Blues* (Buddha), *Coast to Coast Blues Band* (United Artist), *Simply the Truth* (ABC/Bluesway), *Mad Man Blues* (Chess), and *That's Where It's At* (Stax).

In 1970, Hooker moved to the San Francisco area. In 1971, he toured with the blues-rock group Canned Heat in support of a double-disc LP set called *Hooker 'n' Heat*, on EMI, on the national charts for months. Hooker and Canned Heat collaborated on several other albums. He was represented in the '70s by *Endless Boogie* (1970), *Never Get out of these Blues Alive* (1972), and *Free Beer and Chicken* (1974).

In the 1970s, Bonnie Raitt, a longtime devotee,

asked him to join her in a number of concerts, and in 1977 he was a featured artist for the "Tribute to the Blues" program at New York's Palladium, a show that also included Foghat, Paul Butterfield, Muddy Waters, Johnny Waters, and Honeyboy Edwards. A 1977 concert at the Keystone in Palo Alto, California, was taped for *The Cream* (Tomato Records).

Through the 1970s and 1980s, Hooker remained active as a performer, although he became disenchanted with the recording industry. In the summer of 1980, he appeared in the *Blues Brothers* movie that starred *Saturday Night Live* alumni John Belushi and Dan Aykroyd. Hooker sang "Boom Boom," for the soundtrack. He was also inducted into the Blues Foundation's Hall of Fame.

He continued to reflect considerable fire and enthusiasm well into his sixties. Commenting on an engagement at the Music Machine in Los Angeles, Terry Atkinson of the *Los Angeles Times* (December 14, 1983), wrote: "In black suit, black hat, black tie, and red shirt, the legendary blues singer gazed at . . . the crowd with an assured glare that would have sent shivers down Darth Vader's spine. . . . With exact images and the gutsiest of gut feeling [in his singing], John Lee Hooker showed that the blues and absolute cool can overcome a mere thing like time."

After releasing *Jealous* (1986), which captured few record buyers, he survived mainly by playing club dates and from royalties from reissues of his old material. But 1989 would be a pivotal year for the seventy-two-year-old Hooker. In June, Pete Townshend featured Hooker as "The Iron Man" in his concept album of the same name. Then in August Hooker's career got a big boost when Chameleon released *The Healer,* Hooker's 110th album. Produced by Roy Rogers, it included appearances from Raitt, Robert Cray, Carlos Santana, George Thorogood (who had a hit with "One Bourbon, One Scotch, One Beer"), Charlie Musselwhite, and Los Lobos. With the release of the album, which sold more then 1.5 million copies, Hooker was suddenly in demand. He won his first Grammy for the duet with Bonnie Raitt, "I'm in the Mood." He also dominated the W.C. Handy Blues Awards, winning for best contemporary blues artist, male blues vocalist, and contemporary blues album.

"My songs are like poetry," he told Chuck Phillips. "Some are pretty heavy—so heavy I can hardly carry them. Sometimes on stage, when I'm singing them, it gets so sad and deep and beautiful, I have to wear dark glasses to keep the people from seeing me crying. I'm not kidding. The tears just start running. With the words that I'm saying and the way I sing it, sometimes I give my own self the blues."

In 1990, a stellar cast held a tribute concert for Hooker at Madison Square Garden, including Ry Cooder, Raitt, Joe Cocker, Huey Lewis, Mick Fleetwood, Gregg Allman, Al Kooper, Johnny Winter, Albert Collins, John Hammond, Charlie Musselwhite, and Willie Dixon. The following year, Hooker was inducted into the Rock and Roll Hall of Fame.

Several compilation albums have come out over the years, including *John Lee Hooker: The Ultimate Collection: 1948–1990* (Rhino), *Introducing John Lee Hooker* (MCA), *The Complete Chess Folk Blues Sessions* (MCA), *Alternative Boogie: Early Studio Recordings 1948–1952* (Capitol), *The Best of John Lee Hooker 1965–1974* (1992), and *The Vee-Jay Years 1956–1964* (1992), and reissues of earlier LPs, including *The Rising Sun Collection,* a live concert recorded in 1977.

In 1990, Hooker was part of the Grammy-nominated sound track for *Hot Spot,* a Dennis Hopper film, along with Miles Davis, Taj Mahal, and Roy Rogers. Hooker also contributed to recordings by B.B. King (*Blues Summit* on MCA), Branford Marsalis (*I Heard You Twice the First Time* on Columbia), Charlie Musselwhite (*Signature* on Alligator), Santana (*Dance of the Rainbow Serpent* on Columbia), and Van Morrison (a duet of "Gloria" for Morrison's *Too Long in Exile* (1993). He has participated in charitable events: Berkeley's Bread and Roses, Neil Young's Bridge School Benefit, Magic Johnson's AIDS Foundation, and Willie Dixon's Blues Heaven Foundation. His songs were used for ads for Lee Jeans ("Boom Boom") and Pepsi.

Remarkably, Hooker's career accelerated as the '90s progressed. His 1991 release on Pointblank/Charisma, *Mr. Lucky,* debuted at number three on the U.K. charts. Both *Mr. Lucky* and *Boom Boom* were nominated for Grammys. *Chill Out,* released in 1995 on Pointblank/ Virgin, again featured Santana, on the title track, and Van Morrison on a duet called "Medley: Serves Me Right to Suffer/Syndicator." (He and Morrison first recorded together for John Lee's ABC LP, *Never Get Out of these Blues Alive* in 1972.)

Throughout the 1990s, as Hooker's career suddenly took off, he began appearing on TV shows, including *The Tonight Show*, BBC TV's *The Late Show,* and *Late Night with David Letterman.* In 1993 British TV aired a *South Bank Show Documentary* covering his career, including a recording session for *Chill Out.*

In 1993, Hooker's daughter Zakiya Hooker also launched a professional career as a blues singer, performing in the clubs around the San Francisco Bay Area and releasing an album in 1997 on Virgin called *Flavor of the Blues.*

Hooker's blistering pace continued in 1997. Besides opening a San Francisco club called the Boom Boom Room, he released *Don't Look Back* on Pointblank/Virgin, produced by Morrison. John Lee and Van sang duets on four songs; Los Lobos backed him on "Dimples." The album won two Grammys: best pop collaboration with vocals for his duet with Morrison, "Don't Look Back," and best traditional blues album.

Disaster struck in July 1998 when a fire destroyed

Hooker's Los Altos home. But he saved his guitar and got out alive. As befits a seminal blues singer, he took it in stride: "It's a shame so many things got burned but you can buy things and you can't buy life—everybody came out safe and that's what's important."

In October 1998, Hooker released a new album, *The Best of Friends,* featuring duets from his previous five albums and three new tracks. A highlight of the album was John Lee's version of "Boogie Chillen" to celebrate the fiftieth anniversary of his first big hit. Ry Cooder backs him up on the new rendition of "Big Legs, Tight Skirt," and Ben Harper and Charlie Musselwhite back him on "Burning Hell." He also turns in a solo performance on his haunting "Tupelo," about the flood in Mississippi.

In November 1998 Hooker was honored by his hometown when Clarksdale renamed a street John Lee Hooker Lane. In February 1999 he received a Lifetime Achievement Award from the R&B Foundation. At the ceremony he and Raitt sang "I'm in the Mood." "Boogie Chillen" was also inducted into the Grammy Hall of Fame. In 2000 he received a Lifetime Achievement award at the Grammys.

Although he reduced his touring in 1995 (an avid Dodger fan, he spent a lot of time watching baseball), Hooker still performed twenty to thirty dates a year even after he turned eighty in 1997. In May 1998, he played at the Doheny Blues Festival in Dana Point, California, and stole the show. "I never, ever imagined I'd have a career last this long. . . . but here I am," Hooker told John Roos of the *Los Angeles Times* (May 15, 1998). "If I stopped playing the blues, I'd be miserable. I've been given a gift from the good Lord. . . . I think doing what I do is just in my blood."

With assistance from John Lee Hooker's manager, Mike Kappus

HOPKINS, SAM "LIGHTNIN' ": *Singer, songwriter, guitarist. Born Centerville, Leon County, Texas, March 15, 1912; died Houston, Texas, January 30, 1982.*

"Twenty-one years ago, I went to Louisiana to get me a mojo hand and I got me a wife with it. I'm going to try to go back again soon. I might just end up with two wives . . . "

"It's not worth singing [the song "My Babe"], but I'll guitar to it . . . "

These song introductions alternately intrigued and convulsed a packed house at Los Angeles's Ash Grove in March 1967. The man delivering them and singing such original comic lines as "I tiptoed to her window just to see how sweet she snored" and others that etched many of the grim facts of life of ghetto living was one of the legendary names in blues history: Sam "Lightnin' " Hopkins.

It had taken him decades to advance from days of poverty and singing for his supper on street corners or in nondescript bars, but when he delivered some of his country blues, the audience knew he hadn't forgotten the rough spots of his life. His ability to improvise his poetic lyrics spoke to his audiences about the daily traumas and indignities of life for African Americans that still persist in many parts of the country. For example, in "Penitentiary Blues" he sings about doing time for another man's crime and ends the song by stating, "You'd better watch it, all the time."

Though he had been a consummate artist for decades, he only began to gain recognition from a broad cross section of his native land at the start of the 1960s. When his unique vocal and guitar style were introduced to a larger audience he had a great impact on the early '60s folk boom and on rock stars from the Rolling Stones to the Grateful Dead.

He was one of six children, several of whom had strong musical abilities, born to Abe and Frances Sims Hopkins in Centerville, in a rural section of Texas not far from Houston. His grandfather had been a slave and hanged himself because of the horrible conditions, according to the liner notes by Greg Drust for Rhino's 1993 *Lightnin' Hopkins Anthology: Mojo Hand.* And his father was killed as the result of a card game fight when Lightnin' was three.

There wasn't much chance for schooling for a black child in those years, much less any formal musical education. "I didn't get no schoolin', man," he told Les Blank for the 1967 documentary *The Sun's Gonna Shine.* "Oh, I got my education by sitting around talkin', looking at what this one do, that one do, and how they do things. You can go to the field. That was our school—hoe that field, plow that mule, chop that cotton."

He made a crude guitar out of a cigar box and chicken wire when he was eight. When he wasn't doing farm chores, he spent his spare time learning guitar from an older half brother, Joel, a blues singer, guitarist, and songwriter. He taught himself licks and picked up song material from listening to farm workers or sneaking into local bars. He also sang in the church choir.

In 1920, Sam heard Blind Lemon Jefferson play at a church picnic in Buffalo, Texas, and got up the courage to accompany him on guitar. As Hopkins recounted to blues historian Sam Charters (*The Bluesmen*), Jefferson asked, "Who's that playing that guitar?"

"Oh, that's just a little boy here knocking on the guitar," others said. "No, he's playing that guitar," Jefferson responded. "Where he at? Come here, boy. . . . Boy, you keep that up you gonna be a good guitar player."

The interaction inspired Hopkins to work on his guitar techniques. In the late 1920s, Hopkins met his cousin Alger "Texas" Alexander at a picnic in Normangee, Texas. Alexander, a one-time successful blues singer who had recorded with OKeh in 1927, didn't play any instruments and needed accompaniment. When he was still a teenager, Hopkins began accompanying Alexander in several East Texas towns. In the late '30s, Hopkins served some time in prison, although there are conflicting reports about what the offense was and where he served. He continued with Alexander after he got out, although the two never recorded together. He had tried Houston in the late 1930s, but the trip proved a disaster. Music jobs were almost impossible to find, and Sam had to work on the Missouri-Pacific Railroad tamping ties. Whatever money he got from music came from singing in the streets. He hustled back to Centerville after a few months.

He was still earning most of his small income from farm labor in the mid-1940s, playing an old beat-up guitar on evenings or weekends mostly for family and friends, and still accompanying Alexander throughout the 1940s. In the early '40s he married Antoinette Charles and worked as a sharecropper for a mean landowner named Tom Moore, an experience that provided grist for his songwriting.

One relative, fortunately, realized Sam's talent deserved a wider audience. His uncle Lucien Hopkins got Sam a new guitar and urged him to move to Houston, where there was more opportunity for a performer. Hopkins at first resisted the idea.

But the next trip proved more rewarding. Sam and Texas Alexander were singing on Dowling Street, the main black thoroughfare in Houston, when Lola Anne Cullum, a scout for the Los Angeles label Aladdin, spotted them. Hopkins traveled to L.A. accompanied by barrelhouse pianist Wilson "Thunder" Smith. (According to liner notes written by Chris Strachwitz of Arhoolie for *The Gold Star Sessions Volume 1,* Cullum was intimidated by Alexander, who had just gotten out of prison, and didn't invite him along.) Aladdin executives liked the duo, who made twelve recordings in their first sessions, in November 1946. When the first discs were released, the twosome were given nicknames for more oomph, calling Hopkins "Lightnin' " to match Wilson's "Thunder" sobriquet. He had a minor hit in the Southwest with "Katie Mae Blues." The newly named "Lightnin' " was getting homesick, though. He made some more recordings for Aladdin, including his second hit, "Short-Haired Woman." He then recorded for Bill Quinn, owner of Gold Star, a Houston label that released many of his best sides. He had some success with a remake of "Short-Haired Woman" and "Big Mama Jump," released in 1947 by Gold Star, which sold 40,000 copies; the follow-up, "Baby Please Don't Go," sold 80,000. One of the songs he recorded for the label was "Tim Moore's Farm," recounting how he and his wife were once cheated by a white landowner. The song peaked at number thirteen on the *Billboard* R&B charts in 1949. "T-Model Blues" hit number eight in 1949, and "Shotgun Blues" moved up to number five on the R&B charts in 1950. Quinn later sold some of Lightnin's masters to Modern Records in Los Angeles.

Back home in Houston, he left for other locales as little as possible during the late 1940s and 1950s. He made plenty of recordings—by the end of the 1970s, various estimates were that he had recorded anywhere from 800 to over 1,000 songs—during his career, once traveling to New York to record for Bob Shad in 1951, singles that were released on the Jax and the Sittin' In With labels. He had R&B chart hits in 1952 with "Give Me Central 209" and "Coffee Blues," which rose to the number six position. But almost a0ll his live performances were in Texas. As the 1950s progressed Chicago-style urban blues grew in popularity and Hopkins's recordings tapered off. He held forth at the clubs in Houston. "Here in Houston I can be broke and hungry and walk out and someone will buy me a dinner. It ain't like that in a strange place where you don't know no one."

And it was true, in the 1950s, that few people in the mass audience knew who he was, though many blues experts were aware of both his prodigious recording output and the fine quality his material. He had a following in the black community around the nation, sometimes providing enough response for some of his singles to become moderate ethnic hits.

In 1959 a Houston folklorist named Mack McCormick and blues historian Sam Charters sought out Hopkins. Charters, who found Hopkins's guitar in a pawn shop, recorded Lightnin' on January 16, 1959, for Folkways, which released *Lightnin' Hopkins.* Charters brought a bottle of gin for Lightnin' and convinced him to make a recording. He held a microphone in his hand to record Hopkins's voice and guitar. The resulting recording reintroduced Lightnin's blues to a much wider audience. The next month, he recorded for the Tradition label.

Another project was a hootenanny held in Houston's Alley Theater that featured Hopkins. That appearance was so well received that two more concerts followed. Soon Hopkins was receiving ovations from integrated audiences at the University of California in Berkeley and at Carnegie Hall in New York. Hopkins's debut at Carnegie Hall, which occurred on October 14, 1960, was on a bill that included such promising newcomers as Bob Dylan and Joan Baez and the veteran performer Pete Seeger. From there, Hopkins soon got the opportunity to do an extended engagement at the Village Gate in New York that solidified his newfound recognition as one of the most compelling artists in the blues-R&B genre. From then on his reputation grew to worldwide proportions, and invitations to perform came from clubs, theaters, and auditoriums across the United States and other parts of the world. In 1961 he toured throughout Texas with zydeco great Clifton Chenier, who was related through marriage.

With the growing interest in folk blues in the early 1960s, Sam was occasionally enticed away from Texas to concerts in other sections. Meanwhile, his catalog of LPs kept growing (even if none came close to making the national charts). Among the dozens of albums that collected some of his singles made for jukeboxes in the '50s were the two-record set *Lightnin' Hopkins and the Blues,* on Imperial; the two-record *Lightnin' Hopkins,* on Time Records; *Lightnin' Strikes,* on Vee; *Lightnin' Hopkins,* on Folklore (1959); and *Goin' Away, Gotta Move Your Baby,* and *Greatest Hits,* on Bluesville.

His 1960 "discovery" period extended to TV. On November 13 he was brought into the New York studios of CBS to tape a workshop called *A Pattern of Words and Music.* During the 1960s and 1970s he appeared on a number of other TV programs, mostly made for the Public Broadcasting System. Filmmaker Les Blank made two films about Hopkins: a short titled *The Sun's Gonna Shine* in 1967, featuring Hopkin and Mance Lipscomb, and a documentary released in 1968 titled *The Blues Accordin' to Lightnin' Hopkins,* which won a Gold Hugo Award at the Chicago Film Festival in 1970. In 1972, Hopkins also contributed to the sound track for the movie *Sounder.*

One of his other efforts of that period was the album produced by critic Nat Hentoff for Candid Records called *Lightnin' Hopkins in New York,* which included a number of his original compositions. The LP later was reissued in the mid-1970s by Barnaby Records as part of its Great Performance series. By the time Hopkins started the project with Hentoff, two new LPs on the Tradition label had come out in 1960, *Country Blues* in March and *Autobiography in Blues* in April, and an album on Herald, *Lightnin' & the Blues,* a reissue of '50s singles released in June 1960. In July 1960, Hopkins was at a house party in Los Angeles with Sonny Terry, Brownie McGhee, and Big Joe Williams. On July 6 the four (with Jimmy Bond on bass) recorded *Down South Summit Meeting,* for Capitol (rereleased in 1995 on CD).

Throughout the 1960s, almost every year resulted in two or three LP releases (or more), sometimes representing reissues of earlier material. (Some of his collections were reissued a number of times.) His Bluesville releases of the 1960s included *Lightnin'* (6/61), *Blues in My Bottle* (2/62), *Walkin' This Road by Myself* (9/62), *Lightnin' & Co.* (2/63), and *Smokes Like Lightnin'* (8/63). His Verve (later Verve/Forecast) LPs included *Fast Life Woman* (3/62), *Roots* (8/65), *Lightnin' Strikes* (2/66), and *Something Blue* (6/67). Among the Arhoolie titles were *Lightnin' Sam Hopkins* (9/62), *Early Recordings* (2/64), and *Lightnin' Hopkins with Barbara Dane* (10/66). Prestige releases included *Hootin' the Blues* (6/64), *My Life in the Blues* (two discs, 8/65), and *Soul Blues* (4/66). Other 1960s credits included *First Meeting* (5/64), on World; *Best of Lightnin' Hopkins* (7/67), on Tradition; *Blue* (12/67), on Jewel, and an electric album, *The Great Show and Dance* (1968).

Among his available LPs in the early 1970s were such additional titles as *Gotta Move Your Baby,* recorded with Sonny Terry on Prestige; *Keeps on Rainin',* on Supreme; and *Lightnin' Hopkins,* on Trip.

During the 1960s and 1970s, Lightnin' took part in a number of major folk festivals, including the Newport Folk Festival and the American Folk Blues Festival, touring England and the Continent. His music influenced such rock bands as the Grateful Dead and Jefferson Airplane. He also kept up a round of concerts at folk clubs and on college campuses, though he always avoided leaving Houston as much as possible. In the 1970s his recording pace slowed due to an auto accident that put him in a neck brace, and declining health, and later as interest in the blues sagged. He was inducted into the Blues Foundation's Hall of Fame in 1980. In the summer of 1981 he came down with cancer of the esophagus. He died in Houston on January 30, 1982.

Interest in his work continued after his death, especially in the 1990s. In 1990, Smithsonian/Folkways reissued the 1959 session with Charters on CD. In 1991, Fantasy/Prestige released a seven-CD retrospective, *The Complete Prestige/Bluesville Recordings.* Wolf released *Lightnin' Hopkins 1947–1969* in 1992. Recapping his earliest recording years, in 1992, EMI released *The Complete Aladdin Recordings* (now out of print), while Arhoolie reissued *The Gold Star Sessions—Volumes 1 and 2.* Other Arhoolie releases included *Po' Lightnin',* recordings made in 1961 and 1969 (released on CD in 1995) and *Sometimes I Believe She Loves Me,* a live recording with Barbara Dane in the early 1960s (released on CD in 1996); *Texas Blues, Joel, Lightning, & John Henry* (which features Lightnin's oldest brother, John Henry, said to be the best musician and songwriter in the family, and Joel, who taught Lightnin' the guitar); *Lightnin'!* and in 2000 *Live at the Berkeley Blues Festival,* with Lightin', Clifton Chenier and Mance Lipscomb. Rykodisc, which purchased the Tradition label, rereleased *Country Blues* and *Autobiography in Blues* in 1996.

Entry written with assistance from Chris Strachwitz of Arhoolie Records

HORTON, BIG WALTER "SHAKEY": *Singer, harmonica player, band leader, songwriter. Born Horn Lake, Mississippi, April 6, 1917; died Chicago, Illinois, December 8, 1981. Inducted into Blues Foundation Hall of Fame, 1982.*

Big Walter Horton was the consummate sideman, able to blend his harmonica playing seamlessly into the performances of groups big and small. But he also was an inspired soloist whose recordings rank with the best of the blues genre. Assuming his claims to using amplification with his harp playing starting in 1940 are accurate, he also would rank as the first harmonica player to make use of that technology.

Born in a small Mississippi town in 1917, Horton soon was taken by his mother to live in Memphis, Tenncssee, where he spent his formative years. He taught himself to play harp at five and was an accomplished performer before his teens, joining the Memphis Jug Band, with whom he claimed to have first recorded as a ten-year-old, in 1927 for a time. For more than a decade he worked alone or with other bluesmen on the party and picnic circuit and also on Memphis street corners. In the early part of his career he called himself Little Walter, but said he gave it up to Little Walter Jacobs, calling himself Big Walter instead. His nickname "Shakey" came from the way he moved his head while playing.

After spending some time in Chicago in the late 1940s, he returned to Memphis, where he recorded material for Sam Phillips's Sun label and Chess in 1951. Phillips leased some of that to Modern/RPM and issued some on Sun, including the major harp milestone "Easy." Other 1951 tracks included "Hard Hearted Woman," "Need My Baby," and "I'm in Love with You Baby (Walter's Blues)." In 1953 he returned to Chicago to play with Eddie Taylor's band, but soon joined the Muddy Waters group as a replacement for Junior Wells, who had been drafted. From then on he was a major recording session player and band sideman with most of the best-known Chicago acts while also having his own band from time to time. In 1964 his first solo album, *The Soul of Blues Harmonica,* was released with the backing band comprising Buddy Guy on guitar, Jack Myers on bass, Willie Dixon on vocals, and Willie Smith on drums. Other notable releases followed, such as the 1967 *Chicago/The Blues/Today! Volume 3; Offer You Can't Refuse* (1972, one side with other side by Paul Butterfield); *With Hot Cottage* (1972); *Big Walter Horton with Carey Bell* (Alligator, 1972); and *Little Boy Blue* (1980).

During the 1960s and 1970s, Horton was featured at a number of major jazz and blues festivals at home and in Europe. In 1965 and again in 1968 he toured England and Europe as part of the American Folk Blues Festival group. Willie Dixon, who said, "Big Walter is the best harmonica player I ever heard," also recruited Horton for many of Dixon's Chicago Blues All-Stars concerts. Big Walter's credits included an appearance in the hit 1980 film *The Blues Brothers.* Horton died in 1981 and was buried in Restvale Cemetery, Worth, Illinois.

Various sources have given different causes of death, one stating he had been "killed," another attributing it to the ravages of alcohol abuse. Johnny Nicholas, formerly a guitarist with the band Asleep at the Wheel, who had worked with Horton on many projects, said Horton didn't die of a heart attack or alcoholism. Walter, he said, had just come back from a foreign tour with Jimmie Rogers with considerable cash and family members tried to get the money from him. He surmises that Horton was drunk, got into a big fight, and was severely beaten and thrown down a stair-

well: "Walter went across the street to an abandoned building and died from internal bleeding."

It was a great musical loss, Nicholas stated. "Nobody could do what that cat could do. Walter and I used to travel together. We'd sit around playing music when the light was just right. Sweet afternoons. We would just play those old tunes. It was the coolest stuff. He played old medicine songs from Memphis, jazz standards, hillbilly songs. I wish I could have recorded it. It would have been a great legacy. Walter was a sweet cat. Unfortunately, people used to get a kick out of getting him drunk."

Nicholas said he used to ration the booze when he played with Walter, give him a nip between sets. But he didn't want to see Walter drunk on the bandstand, screaming at people as he had done in Chicago. He and Walter had collaborated on recordings for the Blind Pig label that provided the Nicholas album *Too Many Bad Habits,* on which Horton played, and Horton's disc *Fine Cuts,* on which Johnny played. Nicholas also noted he, Walter, and Eddie Taylor had made an album together that had never been released.

Based partly on phone interview between Nicholas and Lyndon Stambler April 17, 1999; Nicholas then was running a café in Fredericksburg, Texas, called the Hilltop Cafe

HOUSE, SON: *Singer, guitarist, songwriter. Born near Riverton, Mississippi. March 21, 1902; died Detroit, Michigan, October 19, 1988.*

A seminal figure in the history of country blues, Eddie "Son" House had an enormous impact on many far better known musicians, both black and white. Even the relatively limited recordings available today, made for the most part when he was past his prime, affirm that his open-tuned, gutty, bottleneck guitar playing ranks at the top of that performing style. Though his live performances had become legendary by word of mouth among folk and blues artists, most of whom never had heard him play, for long periods of time nobody knew where he was or, indeed, if he was still alive. Fortunately, the folk boom of the 1960s resulted in his rediscovery and appreciation by new generations of fans.

Born in rural Mississippi but raised in Tallulah, Louisiana, his mother was a strict churchgoer and forbade Son to touch the guitar or sing blues. Son did sing with the church choir, however, wherever his family lived at the time. Son's father, Eddie House Sr., who had separated from his mother when Son was young, played bass horn, later becoming a church deacon and, like Son's mother, giving up secular music.

At the start of the 1920s, Son's mother died and he made Clarksdale home base. He worked at odd jobs there and in neighboring states, plowing, picking, and chopping cotton, and, for a time, tending cattle.

In 1927, while in Matson, Mississippi, he heard two musicians named Willie Wilson and Reuben Lacy and was inspired to take up the guitar. In 1928 he bought an old one for $1.50 and had Wilson fix it up and show him some chords. In a little while, Son could play his first song, one learned from Wilson, "Hold Up Sally, Take Your Legs Offa Mine." Wilson thought he showed much promise and asked Son to work with him that Saturday night.

Soon Son had developed a distinctive style of his own and was building a backlog of songs, both from listening to other musicians and writing new ones himself. He began to play regularly on the blues circuit, forming a partnership in the late 1920s with another performer, Willie Brown. He told Lawrence Cohn for liner notes on a Columbia release, "Willie was the best guitar player around, although his voice wasn't too strong. He used to play the 'comment' [background], while I did all of the lead singing. I used to like to sing my own songs mostly. Never did care too much about singing other people's songs. We used to play the 'jook joints' a lot. Boy, were they rough! Every Saturday night someone got cut up or killed. I'd leave when the rough stuff started, even though they never bothered the musicians. I wasn't taking any chances." (In 1928 he was sentenced to Parchman Farm prison for allegedly shooting a man in self defense, but released a year later.)

The duo, he told Cohn, played all over Mississippi and occasionally in neighboring states at picnics, birthday parties, dances, levee camps, and even some "white only" events. "The white people liked our music fine. Anything fast and jumpy went over. They didn't like to hear any church music, though." He also recalled backing Dr. McFadden's medicine show. "I used to get on a small stage and play just as loud as I could to attract attention of the people. Boy, we sure sold lots of medicine."

In 1930 the paths of House and Brown crossed that of bluesman Charley Patton. Patton had made several recordings for Paramount Records in Grafton, Wisconsin, and when the company asked him to do some more, took Brown and House along with him.

During those sessions, House recorded several solos, including "Preachin' Blues," "Black Mama," and "Mississippi County Farm," and two with Brown, one of them "Clarksdale Moan." He recalled meeting the legendary Blind Lemon Jefferson in Grafton, where the latter also was doing some recordings. Son was paid forty dollars for his efforts and went back to Mississippi. Paramount liked his work and asked him to travel to New York later on, but by then Son was married and settled down and didn't want to make the long trip. He did make more recordings, however, in 1932, for Spears Phonograph Company in Jackson, Mississippi, recording several originals, including "I Had a Dream Last Night Troubled Me."

Afterward, he concluded his commercial recorded work and gave up playing for local affairs for some time while he concentrated on earning a living at nonmusical jobs. The music industry lost sight of him, but in 1941–42 Alan Lomax sought him out in Robinsonville, Mississippi, twenty miles south of Memphis, Son's home from the late 1920s to the early 1940s. At the behest of Lomax, House recorded a number of songs for the U.S. Library of Congress Archive of Folk Song.

In 1943 Son moved to Rochester, New York, where he worked for a short time in a defense plant, then as a rivet-heater in a boxcar shop of the New York Central Railroad, and finally as a porter in the railroad's Buffalo operation. Later, Willie Brown moved to Buffalo, and the two friends occasionally played together. Son only performed when Brown was available in those years and, when Willie died in Mississippi in either 1956 or 1957, House put his guitar aside completely. He told Cohn, "I didn't much like to play without Willie. . . . After Willie went I just didn't have the heart to play anymore and just gave the whole thing up."

House remained with the New York Central for over a decade. He was living in upstate New York when the collecting team of Nick Perls, Dick Waterman, and Phil Spiro caught up with him. On Father's Day 1964, they found the "long-lost" artist and began to record some of his music. Afterward, they spread the word that House was alive and well, and opportunities started to come along for House to appear as a featured artist on the folk circuit. One of his first live performances was at the 1964 Newport Folk Festival in Rhode Island. Among the songs he played there and at other festivals in the mid-1960s were "Death Letter Blues," "Empire State Express," and "Pearline." He was sought out by folk authorities not only for his music but also for reminiscences of such important blues figures as Patton, Willie Brown, Robert Johnson (who was strongly influenced by House), Ma Rainey, and others.

House began to record again, completing such albums as *Mississippi Delta Blues* on Folkways and *Blues from the Mississippi Delta* on Verve/Forecast, the latter released in August 1966. In January 1966 Columbia Records released the LP *Father of the Folk Blues*, still in the catalog at the end of the 1970s. Also still in print at the start of the 1990s was the LP *Son House*, on Arhoolie Records, comprising the recordings made by Alan Lomax. The songs recorded by Nick Perls and his coworkers were available on the Blue Goose label, titled *Real Delta Blues*. During the 1970s House continued to perform sporadically, but as the folk fervor of the '60s faded, interest in many of the pioneer blues artists also started to wane. Blues aficionados, of course, continued to keep Son's contributions in mind, and his music was particularly honored in Europe. He was inducted into the Blues Hall of Fame in 1980. Many of his recordings were out of print when he died in 1988, but in 1992 his complete April '65 Columbia sessions were reissued in a two-CD package, *Son House—Father of the Delta Blues,* as part of the Columbia/Legacy Roots N' Blues Series for which Lawrence Cohn was producer. The tracks included classic compositions like "Preachin' Blues," "Death Letter," and "Downhearted Blues," plus newer songs like "President Kennedy." Sony/Legacy issued *Original Delta Blues* in 1998.

In the mid-1990s, some of Son's performances were included in a series of packages issued by Vestapol Videos (distributed by Rounder). These comprised *Legends of Bottleneck Blues Guitar* and *Legends of Country Blues Guitar* (both 1994), and *Legends of the Delta Blues* (1995). Document issued *Son House and the Great Delta Blues Singers* including sides he cut for Paramount from 1928–30.

HOUSTON, CISCO: *Singer, guitarist, songwriter. Born Wilmington, Delaware, August 18, 1918; died San Bernardino, California, April 29, 1961.*

Gilbert "Cisco" Houston was regarded by his fellow artists as one of the greatest American balladeers as well as one of the finest human beings. His great legacy to folk music has been understood clearly only in the years since his untimely passing.

His close friend and longtime traveling companion Woody Guthrie once wrote for Folkways Records, "In my own mind, I see Cisco Houston as one of our manliest and best of our living crop of ballad and folk-song singers. He is showman enough to make the grade and to hold any audience anywhere and at any time, I like Cisco as a man. I like him as a person, and as a fun-loving, warmhearted, and likeable human being."

Cisco, Gilbert Vandine Houston, was born in the Wilmington, Delaware, area, but spent only his first two years there before the family moved to California. His family came from the Carolinas and Virginia. As a small boy he heard his mother and grandmother sing traditional folk melodies. He enjoyed listening to them and took particular pride in their Virginia origins, which later made him claim he had been born there rather than in Delaware.

The Cisco Houston papers at the Center for Folklife Programs and Cultural Studies Archive of the Smithsonian Institution in Washington, D.C., include some memoirs by him titled "Autobiographical Notes by Cisco Houston." These include a condensed summation of his formative years. He wrote, "My schooling began at Rockdale Elementary [Eagle Rock Valley]. It was here that I first gained some prominence as singer, actor and artist. I was commissioned to draw the posters for school productions, managed to be cast in leading parts, and was encouraged to follow a career of singing by 'perceptive' teachers. I remember singing Brahms' 'Lullaby' in 'Hansel and Gretel' in the fourth grade. I was cast as the angel—a colossal bit of miscasting ac-

cording to my mother. Junior high and senior high years were spent at Eagle Rock High. (Guy Logsdon, who prepared notes for a Smithsonian/Folkways album, noted that Cisco didn't graduate from high school). By this time I knew clearly what I wanted to do; it was to be acting and singing folk songs and anything I had to be in between to make this possible was okay with me. My acting started with courses at Los Angeles City College and other night classes; experience came at little theater groups in Hollywood and Pasadena Playhouse. My career as a folksinger started when I met up with Woody Guthrie."

Actually, there were a lot of years between his attending Eagle Rock High and becoming friends with Guthrie, as Logsdon pointed out in his annotated album material. When he was twelve, with the rigors of the Great Depression taking hold, he and his family moved for a time to Bakersfield, where in 1932, his father deserted the family. In taped conversations with Lee Hays, also stored at the Smithsonian, he said, "We were on relief for a while; that was a miserable deal. A lot of us kids used to go out on trucks and work in the rhubarb fields and truck farms and in return for so many hours of work we would get some vegetables." He bitterly remembered that farmers would destroy large surplus piles of oranges, potatoes, and other crops to prevent hungry, impoverished people from eating them.

He recalled for Hays the times when, as a teenager, he and his older brother went on the road to try to help the family finances. "I went up to Washington once and worked in the hop fields around Yakima. I hitchhiked, and rode freight trains, and walked the highways between jobs. I left there with twelve dollars. I nursed that money all the way home. . . . I rode the trains through the Cascade Mountains. It was beautiful country, but cold as hell. I would lie up on a freight car, and when we'd go through a tunnel, I wondered if I was going to see the other end. Still, I wouldn't spend this money, I was so proud to be taking money home."

He adopted his nickname after his wanderings took him through the town of Cisco, California. Eventually he spent time in Southern California again, where his little theater activities in Hollywood brought him in contact with actor Will Geer. It was Geer, in turn, who introduced him in 1938 to Woody Guthrie, who at the time had a folk-music show on station KFVD. It was the beginning of a lifelong friendship that started off with the two singing and playing guitars together, first on Woody's program and then in concerts around the West.

Houston claimed that among his occupations in the late 1930s was working as a cowboy on western ranches, though that might have been a ploy to lend credence to the western ballads he added to his repertoire. It is certain that at the end of the decade, he traveled to New York (having previously visited the city in 1936), where, among others, he met Moses Asch, later the founder of Folkways Records. Some months before that,

Geer and Guthrie had gone there in what Geer hoped would open recording industry doors for his friend. Once Cisco arrived, he and Woody resumed performances at small clubs, informal gatherings, and the like.

Despite very poor eyesight, Cisco managed to enlist in the merchant marine in 1940, just before the United States entered World War II. Guthrie later enlisted as well, and the two were shipmates for a time. During the war years, Cisco survived three separate torpedoings of ships he was on. While New York was home port, he reached others throughout the world; in each new port he picked up additional material for his folk collection. Back in New York between trips, he sometimes performed with Woody or the Almanac Singers.

After the war, Cisco settled for a while in New York, then moved to Hollywood. He increased his performing pace, singing with many of the most gifted artists in the folk field. Besides working with Huddie Ledbetter in the late 1940s and again teaming with Guthrie, Cisco sang with such others as John Jacob Niles, Burl Ives, and Lee Hays. He performed on two of the first LPs issued by Moe Asch's new company in 1948.

Throughout the 1950s Houston continued to perform before audiences across the nation. He was featured in concerts on college campuses, in churches, in leading nightclubs, and in such places as New York's Town Hall and Madison Square Garden. During the 1950s he was seen or heard on radio and TV, including the American Inventory program and folk music programs broadcast by Mutual Broadcasting System.

In the mid-1950s, Cisco got the chance to host his own radio program in Denver, Colorado. Called *The Gil Houston Show,* it debuted on November 15, 1954, on the Intermountain Network. The program, broadcast three times a week, soon developed a sizable audience. It did so well that beginning in January 1955 its coverage was expanded to the national Mutual Broadcasting Network. He also could savor a recording of the song "Crazy Heart," cowritten by him and Lewis Allen, which made hit lists on a Coral Records release featuring singer Jackie Paris. Then suddenly, although there was no apparent dip in his program's popularity, it was canceled. While Houston never was personally added to the blacklists of the era of McCarthyism, the fact that he worked with many performers who were on it was considered by his friends to have led to the network's decision.

In 1959 Houston toured India under the sponsorship of the State Department and the American National Theatre and Academy. In June of the following year he served as emcee for the CBS program *Folk Music, U.S.A.* Besides Cisco, program performers included Flatt and Scruggs, Joan Baez, John Jacob Niles, and John Lee Hooker. Later that summer, Cisco received a warm welcome from the crowd attending the Newport, Rhode Island, Folk Festival.

During these years, Cisco turned out recordings for many labels, including Folkways, Stinson, Disc, Coral,

Decca, and Vanguard. Releases of his performances continued at a steady pace after his death. His Folkways LPs included *Lonesome Valley, Railroad Songs, Cowboy Songs, Hard Travelin', Cisco Houston Sings, Songs of the Open Road,* and *Songs to Grow On.* In 1960 Vanguard issued its first Houston LP, *Cisco Special.* In later years it issued *Songs of Woody Guthrie* (1961) and *I Ain't Got No Home* (1962). In 1964 Disc issued an LP, *Legacy of Cisco Houston.*

Over the years, Houston showed himself to be a talented songwriter and arranger as well as a performer. Some of his compositions, such as "A Dollar Down," "Bad Man Blunder," and "Ramblin' Gamblin' Man," were included in a commemorative song book, *900 Miles'; the Ballads, Blues and Folksongs of Cisco Houston,* issued by Oak Publications in 1965.

After the encouraging career achievements during the first part of 1960, Cisco was diagnosed with cancer, and in the spring of 1961 he died in a hospital in San Bernardino, California. His passing at age forty-two was mourned not just in obituary columns but with the more positive tribute of songs to his memory, such as "Fare Thee Well, Cisco" by Tom Paxton; "Cisco Houston Passed This Way" by his protégé, Peter La Farge; and "Blues for Cisco Houston," by Tom McGrath.

At the start of the 1980s, a number of his LPs were still in print, including (on Folkways) *Cisco Houston Sings American Folk Songs, Cowboy Ballads, Hard Travelin',* and *Railroad Ballads; Cisco Houston* on Evergreen; *Cowboy Songs* (with Woody Guthrie) on Stinson; and, on Vanguard, *I Ain't Got No Home* and *Cisco Houston Sings Songs of Woody Guthrie.*

After the Smithsonian Institution bought the Folkways Records catalog in the late 1980s, it made sure that all of Cisco's Folkways albums remained in print. During the mid-1990s, Smithsonian Institution research associate Dr. Guy Logsdon began compiling and preparing album notes for a new reissue set titled *Cisco Houston—the Folkways Years 1944–1961.* Issued in 1996, it contained twenty-nine songs, including a number of previously unreleased tracks. The latter comprised Houston's self-penned "Rambling, Gambling Man" and "What Did the Deep Blue Sea Say" (recorded by Houston with Woody Guthrie); plus "Hobo Bill," "There's a Better World A-Comin' " (with Woody Guthrie), "Dark as a Dungeon," "Ship in the Sky," "Born 100,000 Years Ago," and "Farmer's Lament."

HOWLIN' WOLF: *Singer, guitarist, harmonica player, band leader, songwriter, disc jockey. Born West Point, Mississippi, June 10, 1910; died Hines, Illinois, January 10, 1976.*

The surly, guttural tones of country bluesman Howlin' Wolf have had a substantial effect on the evolution of popular music. Countless young, white English musicians took to his R&B recordings in the early 1960s and eagerly used them as the basis for their own performances. In particular, a then-unknown singer named Mick Jagger sought all recordings he could find of Howlin' Wolf, as well as other black American blues artists, and distilled a style of his own from their phrasing and inflections. Other British rockers of the period also borrowed from Wolf's repertoire in varying degrees. Jagger's Rolling Stones and the others redirected the course of rock as the 1960s went by, eventually causing feedback that prompted American musicians to look back again to their homegrown blues roots.

In time, this led to belated fame for Howlin' Wolf, represented by a series of albums in the late 1960s and early 1970s that often made the best-seller lists. For most of his life, though, Howlin' Wolf was largely unknown in his own country except for brief moments of success with minority black R&B fans.

Like many roots blues artists, Howlin' Wolf (born Chester Arthur Burnett) grew up in southern farm country. His parents worked on a cotton plantation in Mississippi. At an early age, young Chester also was working in the fields rather than going to school. He learned some songs in his early years from the chants the field hands intoned to lighten their toil. Sometimes he hung around the small bars where blues musicians entertained black workmen on weekends.

Young Burnett was not that enthused about black blues material at the time, strange to say. Instead, his fancy was caught by the recordings of another Mississippian, white country blues singer Jimmie Rodgers (1897–1933), who now is revered as the father of modern country music. In a way, of course, Rodgers did not sound that foreign to a young black, since many of his songs were derived from Negro blues. (For more details on Jimmie Rodgers, see *Country Music: The Encyclopedia*.)

However, Burnett found that his voice wasn't suited to the blues yodeling that was a feature of Rodgers's style. As Arnold Shaw noted in *The World of Soul* (Cowles 1970), Chester turned to a blues shouting style, eventually settling on the pseudonym Howlin' Wolf, from a series of nicknames that included "Bull Cow" and "Foot." "I just stuck to the Wolf. I could do no yodelin' so I turned to Howlin'."

In the 1920s and '30s, Howlin' Wolf sought out pointers on performing from well-known Delta bluesmen. In particular, he hung around Charley Patton in Cleveland, Mississippi. Patton's wife, Bertha Lee, recalled one time when "Charley worked with him all day before Chester Burnett would leave him alone." He also spent time studying the techniques of the legendary Robert Johnson and Rice Miller. The second of two bluesmen to call themselves Sonny Boy Williamson, Rice taught him how to play the harmonica after marrying Wolf's half-sister, Mary.

Burnett served in the U.S. Army during World War II from 1941 to 1945. After his discharge, he returned to his home region, working briefly on a plantation in Twist, Arkansas, then relocating to Penton, Mississippi, where he resumed his approach of doing farm work during the day and performing in local juke joints or at parties nights and weekends. Seeking greater opportunities, in 1948 he moved to West Memphis, Arkansas, across the river from Memphis, Tennessee, where he formed his own band to play the jukes and club circuits in that part of the South. Among the various musicians who performed in the group were two young harmonica players who were to become major names in R&B: James Cotton (born Tunica, Mississippi, 1925) and Little Junior Parker (born West Memphis, Arkansas, 1927; died Chicago, Illinois, November 18, 1971). Other bandsmen included guitarists Pat Hare, Matt "Guitar" Murphy, and Willie Johnson.

During 1948 Howlin' Wolf also got the chance to work as a disc jockey and sometime ad salesman for West Memphis radio station KWEM, an affiliation that lasted into 1952. Eventually, all that exposure led to his first recording opportunities. The fact that his initial discs were released on the Chess Records label masked the fact his first sides were made in the Memphis studios of Sun Records owner Sam Phillips. Ike Turner, who later gained fame as a band leader and half of the Ike and Tina Turner team, brought Wolf to Phillips's attention in 1951, and this led to his first singles, "Moanin' at Midnight" and "How Many More Years," which Phillips leased to Chess, which issued them the following year. During 1951–52, Howlin' Wolf recorded more sides for Phillips, who leased them to Chess, RPM, and Crown Records.

When "Moanin' at Midnight," self-penned by Wolf, made the R&B charts, he pulled up stakes and relocated in 1953 to Chicago, where he signed a contract with Chess. Phillips later acknowledged he had made a mistake in not insuring that Wolf stayed with him to record for Sun. He told an interviewer, "I just thought he was the most different singer in the world. His voice was so 'extremely bad' that it fascinated me." He added that he believed Wolf's departure from the Sun fold proved a career loss both for Sun and Wolf. "If he hadn't gone to Chess," Phillips said, "there's no telling how many hit records I would have cut with this man. He should have been a pop smash." In any case, once Wolf moved to Chicago, he became a major attraction in South Side clubs like the Big Squeeze (the word *big* also could have applied to Wolf, who was well over six feet tall and weighed in the neighborhood of 300 pounds) and in the better-known West Side nightclub, Sylvio's Lounge.

The move north brought some changes in Howlin' Wolf's performances, though he insisted to Arnold Shaw that these were minor. The changes were "not much, really, but of course I did have to step up the tempo. I used to play very slow, but I had to come up with the tempo of today. I didn't know my positions when I was playing those slow blues. But over the last few years [late 1960s] I went to the Chicago Music School and they taught me my positions."

During the 1950s Howlin' Wolf recorded many more songs for Chess that found a good-sized market by blues standards. Some were provided by legendary writer Willie Dixon, including "Spoonful," "Little Red Rooster," "Back Door Man," "Evil," and "I Ain't Superstitious." Many of his releases made the charts without gaining the national top 10, including his "Sittin' on Top of the World" (1957) and his 1960s original composition, "Killing Ground." Both of these songs were among his many stylings that were later recorded by well-known rock groups such as the Grateful Dead, Rolling Stones, Cream, and Electric Flag.

Howlin' Wolf performed widely in clubs and at jazz and folk festivals of the 1960s (including the First International Jazz Festival in Washington, D.C., in 1962 and the Newport Folk Festival in 1966), though for much of the decade he was relatively inactive in the recording field (an exception being his 1967 LP *More Real Folk Blues*). In 1961 he started to gain attention from young British blues fans when he toured England and the European Continent with the American Blues Festival, something he did annually with that operation into 1964. Some of his work at the '64 Musikhalle concert in Hamburg, Germany, was included in a Fontana Records collection of Blues Festival performers. He became a favorite of many of the British rock performers who gained global prominence in the '60s. He toured with some of them, and appeared on the U.S. rock TV show *Shindig* in 1965 with the Rolling Stones.

By the end of the 1960s he had gained such a strong following among mostly white young U.S. rock fans that Chess urged him to work up new tracks. This resulted in the LP *Howlin' Wolf*, released on Chess's Cadet subsidiary in 1969. In the early 1970s Chess found a growing audience for such new albums as *Message to the Young* and *The London Howlin' Wolf Session*, featuring Eric Clapton, Steve Winwood, Bill Wyman, and Charlie Watts playing alongside their aging artistic forebear. He followed that with the 1972 live disc *Live and Cookin' at Alice's Revisited* (the Chicago club), *London Revisited* (on which he was joined by Muddy Waters), and what was to be his last album, the 1973 *Back Door Wolf*. He died before completing another one, though he continued to make personal appearances almost to the end of his life. His final show took place in Chicago in November 1975 with B.B. King sharing the bill. In early 1976, Burnett died after his heart gave out during an operation.

His final album proved an excellent one that won highly favorable comments from reviewers on both sides of the Atlantic. Typical of those critiques were the words of *Rolling Stone*'s David Marsh: "Wolf's final album . . . is some kind of triumph. . . . The songs range over Wolf's life span from ancient Delta blues to Watergate and the Apollo moonshot program, and his easy mastery of such a broad set of songs, coupled with the spare, sympathetic backings he's given, make the album a minor Wolf masterpiece, and perhaps his finest memorial. To the end, a great one."

Many of his recordings were available on various labels in the 1970s, particularly in England, where respect for the blues far overshadowed the interest in the place of its birth. Among titles packaged in Britain and available in the United States as '70s imports were *The Legendary Sun Performers: Howlin' Wolf* on Charly (which presented material recorded in Memphis by Sam Phillips), *The Real Folk Blues* (originally released by Chess in 1966), and *More Folk Blues* (originally issued by Chess in 1967). *Going Back Home* came out on Syndicate Chapter Records: some of his early material was packaged on two Blues Ball releases: *Heart Like Railroad Steel: Rare and Unreleased Recordings, Volumes 1 and 2*. In 1977 Chess issued the LP *Change My Way*.

In the mid-1980s, the Chess catalog was sold to Sugar Hill Records, which in turn sold it to MCA Records along with masters of recordings by Wolf and other classic names on the company's roster.

New releases of Howlin' Wolf recordings continued to be issued in the 1980s, such as *Ridin' in the Moonlight* (Ace, import, 1982), *Howlin' Wolf: His Greatest Sides, Volume 1* (Chess, 1983), and MCA reissues from the Chess catalog in the late 1980s.

In 1980, Wolf was inducted into the Blues Foundation Hall of Fame, and in 1991 he was made a member of the Rock and Roll Hall of Fame in Cleveland, Ohio. During the 1990s MCA reissued many of his Chess albums on compact disc. The MCA catalog included the late fall 1991 three-disc box set titled *Howlin' Wolf*. The set contained seventy-five songs, including nineteen rare or previously unreleased numbers. Germany's Bear Family group also issued two sets of his early recordings during those years: *Memphis Days: The Definitive Edition, Volume I* and *Memphis Days: Volume II*.

The 1998 Rounder catalog included both audio and video material of Howlin' Wolf's work. The audio product, issued by Rounder in 1989, was the album *Cadillac Daddy: Memphis Recording 1952*, while the video from Vestapol Videos was the 1996 release *Devil Got My Woman/Blues from Newport 1966*, featuring Skip James, Howlin' Wolf, Son House, Rev. Pearly Brown, and Bukka White.

HURT, MISSISSIPPI JOHN: *Singer, guitarist, harmonica player, songwriter. Born Teoc, Carroll County, Mississippi, March 8, 1893; died Grenada, Mississippi, November 2, 1966.*

In July 1963 the audience at the Newport Folk Festival in Rhode Island saw a "ghost:" a legendary seventy-one-year-old artist who had dropped from sight thirty-five years earlier and had been thought to have died many years before. As soon as the crowd heard his syncopated, three-finger guitar-picking style and vibrant baritone voice, they knew Mississippi John Hurt was very much alive. His performance was considered a highlight of the festival, and in appreciation, the event organizers gave him a new guitar.

Mississippi John grew up without a father. He had eight brothers and two sisters and didn't get past the fourth grade in school. His interest in music began early. His mother, Mary, gave him a $1.50 Black Annie guitar as a present when he was nine, and in a short time he taught himself to play some tunes. Avalon, Mississippi, where he remained almost his entire life, was a small town in the northwestern part of the state, and he had little contact with the blues musicians who wandered through other parts of Mississippi. As he told one interviewer, "I taught myself to play the guitar the way I thought a guitar should sound."

As he grew older, he learned as many songs as he could from field hands and other workers. He played for enjoyment, earning a meager living from odd jobs. At one time or another, he worked as a field hand picking cotton and corn, worked cattle, spent time on the Mississippi River, was a railroad hand, and, in the 1930s, was on the WPA payroll.

Though he received little money, he played at many local dances and celebrations from the early days of the century on and occasionally picked up new material from both white and black itinerant singers who passed through Avalon. In the 1920s he listened to some of the new crop of country records turned out by many eastern companies. He was greatly interested in the songs of fellow Mississippian Jimmie Rodgers (many of them "white blues") that began to gain attention throughout the South after 1927. He also liked a local musician named William Henry Carson. In addition to using songs from other sources, Hurt sometimes wrote his own, including the murder ballad "Louis Collins," "Coffee Blues," and "Chicken."

Until 1928, practically no one had heard of him outside of Carroll County. In that year, OKeh Records recording director Tommy Rockwell was touring Mississippi looking for country artists. Two white musicians, guitarist Shell Smith and fiddler Willie Naramore, suggested he see Hurt. Rockwell did (at one A.M.) and was impressed enough to bring him to Memphis for a recording session. Hurt was paid $240 plus expenses for making eight recordings. Two of these, "Frankie" and "Nobody's Dirty Business," were released. They sold so well that Rockwell arranged to bring Hurt to New York. On December 21 and 28, 1928, Hurt recorded such songs as "Louis Collins," "Candy Man Blues," "Spike Driver Blues," "Stagolee Blues," and "Avalon Blues," a total of twenty sides.

Hurt went home to Avalon, his career seemingly on the verge of taking off. However, the Great Depression caused sharp cutbacks in sales of blues and country records, and people forgot about him. He followed his established pattern of hard work and leisure-time performing for the next three decades. After World War II, growing ranks of folklorists heard his old recordings (which had become collectors' items) and wanted to find him, but no one could recall his whereabouts. Many folk song enthusiasts searched for him without success and finally concluded he had died.

Then blues collector Tom Hoskins of Washington, D.C., realized the significance of the lyrics from his song "Avalon Blues": *Avalon my hometown/ Always on my mind.* He went to the town in 1963 and, sure enough, found the lost balladeer, who was living in a bungalow with his wife, Jessie, and working for a farmer. He talked John into going to Washington with him. In a short time people were thronging to see him at the local Ontario Place Coffee House. Later that year, at Newport, he achieved a national reputation. In the twilight of his life, Mississippi John was a celebrity sought out for engagements in folk clubs, festivals, and college concerts across the United States. He even appeared at Carnegie Hall and on *The Tonight Show with Johnny Carson.* In the few years left to him, he crowded many such performances into his schedule (always returning home to Mississippi), singing and playing guitar with obvious relish. In the summers of 1964 and 1965, he repeated his success at the Newport Folk Festival. (His performances were included in the Vanguard album sets covering both the 1963 and 1964 festivals.)

Soon after Hurt's "rediscovery," he began to make new recordings. One of the first new LPs, produced by Dick Spottswood's Piedmont Records in 1963, was titled *Presenting Mississippi John Hurt: Folk Songs and Blues.* Another LP, *Worried Blues,* was issued by Piedmont in October 1964. He also recorded two albums for the Library of Congress Folk Archives. After that Vanguard recorded additional material, both live concert work and studio sessions. Unfortunately, John's health began to fail, as was evident in his final studio sessions for Vanguard in 1966. He passed away in Grenada, Mississippi, in November of that year.

The greater part of Hurt's modern LPs came out after his death, and, in fact, there were more of his albums still in record company catalogs at the start of the 1980s than were available during his lifetime. Among them, most originally issued in the late 1960s, were such Vanguard titles as *Mississippi John Hurt—Today* (1/67), *The Immortal Mississippi John Hurt, Last Sessions,* and *The Best of Mississippi John Hurt.* The last-named was recorded live during a 1965 college concert and included such songs as "Coffee Blues," "Chicken," "C.C. Rider," and "Candy Man." Among the tracks included in *Mississippi John Hurt—Today* are "Louis Collins" and "Beulah Land." Also available at the start of the 1980s was the Biograph Records release *Mississippi John Hurt—1928—His First Recordings.* The Canadian label Rebel also released *Mississippi John Hurt: Volume One of a Legacy.*

Several of Hurt's albums were still available in the 1990s, including *1928 Sessions* on Yazoo; *Avalon Blues 1963; Worried Blues, The Legacy Of,* and *Legend*

(1998) on Rounder; *Memorial Anthology* (1993) on Genes; *Today, The Immortal, Last Sessions,* and *The Best Of* on Vanguard; and *Library of Congress Sessions/Avalon Blues* and *Library of Congress Recordings 1963/Sacred and Secular* on Flyright/Heritage. Guitar aficionado Stefan Grossman issued a six-cassette series titled *The Guitar of Mississippi John Hurt.* In 1995 Collectables issued *Satisfying Blues,* and the following year Columbia/Legacy rereleased the excellent collection of thirteen songs that Hurt had recorded in 1928 for Okeh on a CD titled *Mississippi John Hurt: Avalon Blues: The Complete 1928 Okeh Recordings.* Vanguard released *Rediscovered* in 1998.

His work influenced many musicians of the 1960s, some of whom had heard the OKch recordings and some who were introduced to Hurt through Harry Smith's *Anthology of American Folk Music,* released in 1952, which included Hurt's 1928 recording of "Frankie." Jerry Garcia recorded an acoustic version of Hurt's "Louis Collins" that was close to the original on *Shady Grove,* an album of folk tunes he recorded with mandolinist David Grisman. Doc Watson used to listen to Hurt's records on an old wind-up Victrola in 1929 or 1930. Bob Dylan, Tom Paxton, John Fahey, and John Sebastian all were influenced by Hurt. About Hurt's significance Dave Van Ronk told *Sing Out!* (vol. 39, no. 4): "The most important thing about John as a musician was how playable most of his guitar work was. He was a brilliant arranger, but more important, most of his guitar arrangements were simple. That made his music accessible to beginning guitarists, giving several generations the kind of encouragement they needed to get started."

T

IAN AND SYLVIA: *Vocal and instrumental duo, songwriters (developed solo careers after 1974). Ian Tyson, born Victoria, British Columbia, Canada, September 25, 1933 (singer, guitarist); Sylvia Fricker, born Chatham, Ontario, Canada, September 19, 1940 (singer, guitarist, pianist).*

The gifted team of Ian and Sylvia spearheaded Canada's contribution to the folk movement of the 1960s and became one of the favorite acts of American folk audiences in the mid-1960s. For a time late in the decade their career floundered when folk fans objected to their newfound interest in country music. However, they went on to become important in the Canadian TV field during the 1970s while pursuing separate performing and recording careers after mid-decade.

Sylvia Fricker grew up in the small farming community of Chatham, Ontario. Her father worked in the appliance department of an Eaton's store, and her mother taught music. When Sylvia was old enough, she joined the choir at the Holy Trinity Anglican Church,

where her mother was organist and choir leader. Mrs. Fricker gave her daughter lessons on piano until, when Sylvia got older, her tastes in music tended away from the classical and waltz music her parents admired. She preferred trying to catch the far-off signals at night of an R&B program on a Detroit radio station.

During her high school years she made few friends, and from the ages of fifteen to eighteen worked summers at a local agricultural operation hoeing beans, picking tomatoes and berries, and the like. As she told interviewer Larry LeBlanc, "I wasn't too popular in high school. I very rarely went out. By the time I was starting to go out, I was working. I was always interested in music and English literature, the logical combination."

Her interest in music took the form of learning guitar (her first instrument sported a red-and-white image of a cowboy lassoing a cow) and picking out English and American folk songs from library books. She began to have the feeling that she had to go elsewhere. "You didn't stay there if you had any kind of feeling that there might be something better in life. I'm not putting down the town because it's a great place to grow up in until you're about thirteen . . . but it's a lousy place to be an adolescent in. I wanted to be a folksinger from about the time I was fifteen. I decided I'd finish high school, if that's what everybody wanted, and then I'd go and do my own things."

For a year after graduation, Fricker worked at a jeweler in Chatham and traveled to Toronto when she could to try to break into show business. The commute was too trying, so she found a job in a Toronto clothing store. In Toronto she met another aspiring artist, Ian Tyson, with whom she formed a part-time partnership in the fall of 1959, working with him at a place called the Village Corner while doing her own solo sets on Thursday nights at the Bohemian Embassy.

Tyson had come to Toronto via a route that began in far off British Columbia in Canada's western region. Born and raised on a farm in that province, Ian dropped out of school in his teens to work at various jobs while adding to his store of folk music. For a while he was a farmhand, then a rodeo performer. As he wandered across Canada, he sometimes picked up spare change playing his guitar and singing at small clubs and coffeehouses. His other jobs during those years included working as a commercial artist and lumberjack.

Ian told LeBlanc that when he first started singing with Sylvia, he was puzzled, "She was very standoffish. She was unique. I didn't know what to make of her. Nobody did. She was very different, a loner, original, very introspective, very shy, very small-town, very green. But you could see she wasn't going to be small town very long."

Sylvia recalled that the team's approach to music "wasn't intellectualized. Ian did the lead. I did the harmonies, and he played guitar. Ian would learn a song and sing it until I worked out a harmony. We got along well. We didn't make any demands on each other during the early period. We would rehearse together, which in those days was unheard of. Everybody just fooled around on their own. If they worked with somebody, maybe they got together for an hour or so before they went onstage. Ian and I would rehearse three or four times a week."

The two decided to work together full time in 1961 as they found a steadily growing following in Toronto. That year they also gave their first U.S. concert, in Columbia, South Carolina. "It was at a cotillion ball," Sylvia reminisced. "Girls in hoop skirts, their partners from a nearby army base, plus terribly lost young soldiers that none of the girls would associate with. They didn't dig us. They found us a little raw. They wanted the Kingston Trio. Our music had a mountain flavor to it. They said, 'I don't want to hear that stuff. My grandmother sings it. That's not folk music.' "

To try to reach a wider audience, the duo moved to New York in the early 1960s, where artist's manager Albert Grossman agreed to handle the act. (When they first went there, they lived in separate places, but in 1964 decided to marry.) Grossman brought them to the attention of the leading folk-music label of those years, Vanguard, which gave them their first major recording contract. Their debut LP, *Ian and Sylvia*, was issued in September 1962 and brought the first stirrings of interest. Soon after, inspired by the example of Bob Dylan (whom Grossman also managed for a long time), the partners decided to try to write original material. One of the first results was Ian's "Four Strong Winds," the title song of their second Vanguard LP (issued April 1964) and still often re-recorded. Sylvia's first composition, "You Were on My Mind," is another standard, which provided a best-selling single for the group We Five in the 1960s.

By the time the duo's album *Northern Journey* came out in September 1964, they were considered major folk stars all over the United States. Earlier that year, their popularity with New York fans had been demonstrated by a standing-room-only concert at Town Hall. During 1964 and 1965, Ian and Sylvia played before enthusiastic audiences in all parts of the United States and were featured in major folk festivals at home and abroad.

During those years, besides presenting more of their own compositions, they were instrumental in showcasing material of other talented writers from Canada. Their LP *Early Morning Rain*, for instance, issued in July 1965, had several Gordon Lightfoot numbers, including the title track. They also were among the first to promote the songs of Joni Mitchell. Their other Vanguard LPs of the mid-1960s included *Play One More* (5/66) and *So Much for Dreaming* (4/67). In the late 1960s and early '70s, Vanguard issued several retrospective collections: *The Best of Ian and Sylvia* (1968), *Greatest Hits, Volume 1* (1970), and *Greatest Hits, Volume 2* (1971). (In the early '70s the duo recorded some

material for Columbia that was not among their most effective work; Columbia did collect some of that in the 1973 release *The Best of Ian and Sylvia*.)

Problems arose for them during 1965–66. After giving birth to their first child, Clay, Sylvia developed severe vocal problems. At loose ends during her pregnancy and after, Ian tried working as a solo performer, including appearances at the Riverboat in Toronto and in Dayton, Ohio.

Sylvia eventually recovered and they returned to their duo activities, but with increasing emphasis on country-related material. They signed with a new record firm, MGM, which released *Lovin' Sound* in June 1967. The single of the title track failed to catch fire, however, though appearances at folk venues during the year didn't indicate any major loss of popularity with their folk following.

Meanwhile, Vanguard had complained that their contract requirements weren't fulfilled and that another album was due. For that the Tysons went to Nashville to record a series of tracks, many of which featured what LeBlanc refers to as "extended, instrumental, free-form country jazz." That album was appropriately titled *Nashville*. It was followed by one in a similar vein on MGM titled *Full Circle*.

Enthusiastic about their new musical directions, the Tysons assembled a new show called the Great Speckled Bird, which they took on the road at the end of the 1960s. Once more they were ahead of the times. Audience reaction, to say the least, was negative. The fans felt they were being forced to hear country music when they bought tickets for a folk concert. Sylvia recalled, "People even got up and walked out. They would have a violent reaction to the steel guitar. They'd walk out on the first bars that the steel player would hit."

Undaunted, they persevered, and in 1970 seemed to turn the corner. Their set was warmly received at the Atlanta Festival and at a series of concerts across Canada. One notable performance took place in Calgary, where a standing ovation was given a rousing version of "Will the Circle Be Unbroken" in which the Tysons were joined by Bonnie and Delaney Bramlett and Rick Danko of the Band.

Now they looked forward to release of the debut *Great Speckled Bird* album on Ampex, an LP produced by Todd Rundgren. The album flopped, however, and, after another series of poorly received concerts, the show was disbanded.

The Tysons were again dispirited and wondering what course to follow when the Canadian Broadcasting System asked Ian to host a show called *Nashville North*, which soon became the *Ian Tyson Show*. The program became a top-ranked show on Canadian TV for most of the 1970s. Sylvia was a regular cast member on the program, though she didn't perform on every weekly show.

She told LeBlanc, "Ian having had his TV show for

five years really gave me a breather. I had money coming in, but I really did not have to give myself full-time to the television show. The period gave me a lot of time to decide what I wanted to do. I started out in a lot of different directions. Not in any visible way, but with a lot of different possibilities."

In the mid-1970s, she got an offer she couldn't refuse—to host her own show on CBC radio called *Touch the Earth*. The program featured a blend of folk, country, and pop music. Later it was groomed for TV. Sylvia also was signed to a new solo recording contract by Capitol EMI of Canada; her debut on the label was *Woman's World,* issued in 1975. Ian produced the album, though by then their marriage was in its final stages (they divorced in 1975).

Tyson began focusing on his solo career, whose results included the 1974 album *Ol' Eon* and the 1978 *One Jump Ahead of the Devil.* However, as he told Patricia Ward Biederman of the *Los Angeles Times* ("At Home on the Range," Valley Edition Calendar, April 3, 1997), for a while after he and Sylvia divorced he cut back sharply on his music activities. "I'd play on weekends in honkey-tonks to make a little money. But, for four or five years there, I didn't write more than two or three songs."

During the decade he married his second wife, Trylla, and they settled on a 160-acre ranch he bought in Longview, Alberta, Canada, where they raised cutting horses. Ian's recordings from the late 1970s on emphasized his love for the cowboy's life. His releases included *Old Corrals and Sagebrush* in 1983, *Ian Tyson* in '84 (both on Columbia), *Cowboyography* in '87, and *I Outgrew the Wagon* in '89. The last two were on the Stony Plain label, founded in Edmonton, Canada, in 1976 by Holger Petersen. *Cowboyography* was particularly successful, selling over 50,000 albums in Canada alone—a best-seller by Canadian standards—and providing the hit single "Navajo Rug" (cowritten by him with Tom Russell). The album also earned Ian the Canadian Juno Award for Best Country Male Vocalist of 1987. Among covers of "Navajo Rug" was a version by Jerry Jeff Walker. As Tyson told one interviewer about his emphasis on western-style numbers, "As the song says, 'My heroes have always been cowboys.' "

In 1988 Columbia combined the tracks from *Old Corrals and Sagebrush* and *Ian Tyson* on the album *Old Corrals and Sagebrush and Other Cowboy Culture Classics.* Among the disc's contents were "Night Rider's Lament," "Old Alberta Moon," and "Oklahoma Hills." Tyson wound up the 1980s with the 1989 Stony Plain release *I Outgrew the Wagon,* whose contents included a new version of his standard "Four Strong Winds."

Ian started off the 1990s with the well-received 1991 Stony Plain album *And Stood There Amazed.* The following year, Ian was inducted into the Juno Hall of Fame. In 1994, the year in which his autobiography *I Never Sold My Saddle* was published, he completed

work on his next album, *Eighteen Inches of Rain,* in Nashville, joined on one track by country star Suzy Bogguss. The album was issued in Canada on Stony Plain and in the United States on Vanguard. One of Ian's songs, "Summer Wages," was included in Nanci Griffith's 1998 album, *Other Voices, Too,* with Tom Russell joining Nanci on the track. Also included on the disc is Sylvia Fricker's "You Were on My Mind," performed by Nanci and Richard Thompson.

Tyson's next release on Stony Plain and Vanguard was the 1996 *All the Good'Uns.* As Lyndon Stambler commented in *People* (September 29, 1996), "Like the cowboy he sings about in his song 'Someday Soon,' Ian Tyson was a rodeo rider before he met Sylvia Fricker . . . [The new album] contains 19 of Tyson's best cowboy songs (including two new ones, 'The Wonder of It All' and 'Barrel Racing Angel'), including five from his best-selling 1996 album *Cowboyography.* In 'The Old Double Diamond' and 'M.C. Horses,' his cowboy narrators lament the closing of a ranch and the disappearing cowboy way of life. . . . Nothing in here has the commercial appeal of 'Someday Soon,' but Tyson still has the knack for writing pared down and powerful songs about the West. Like a shooting star in the night sky, they remain etched in memory."

Sylvia also continued to add to her performing credits on the concert circuit and TV in the '80s and '90s. After a 1992 concert with Colleen Peterson, Cindy Church, and Caitlin Hanford, the four organized a group called Quartette with which she toured from time to time, though all the artists also kept doing solo work. Her recorded output included *Woman's World* (Capitol, 1975) the 1986 self-produced release *Big Spotlight,* the 1990 disc *You Were on My Mind,* and *Gypsy Cadillac* (Folk Era, 1992) (After 1978, her recordings came out on her own label, Salt Records, which she set up for her own releases as well as those of other folk artists.) Vanguard reissued Ian and Sylvia material on CD, including *Live at Newport* (1994) *Best of Ian & Sylvia* (1997), and *Best of the Vanguard Years,* (1998).

IAN, JANIS: *Singer, guitarist, pianist, songwriter. Born New York, New York (some bios give place of birth as a chicken farm in New Jersey), April 7, 1951.*

With her Orphan Annie–like mop of hair and slight figure, Janis Ian (born Janis Eddy Fink), gave an impression of being very young indeed even in the early 1980s. This was increased by her 4-foot-10-inch height which made someone of average stature feel like a giant. And it is true that Janis is unusually shy for a performer. But in her creative persistence and the body of her excellent work she turned out, she stands tall.

Her association with music went back to her earliest years. "I started with classical music at two," she recalled with a shadow of a smile. "I lived in New Jersey until I was 13 and then my family moved to Manhattan. I started writing songs at 12. (Her first song was titled

"Hair of Spun Gold.") My early influences included Billie Holiday, Edith Piaf, and Odetta."

For most of her childhood, her family was constantly on the move. During her first fifteen years, she lived in thirteen different places in New Jersey and New York, attending a variety of public schools before entering New York's High School of Music and Arts. Her musical efforts, she later noted, "were the only things that kept me going as long as I did without totally freaking out. School was always absurd . . . but then the whole fame thing was happening and I was going to a school where most of the teachers were frustrated musicians—they didn't like it."

Janis had started singing for school events, then performing in small New York folk clubs. By that time she was well versed in piano and acoustic guitar. In 1966, her efforts led to a recording contract from Verve/Forecast, which soon found itself with a major—and controversial—hit composition, "Society's Child." Objections to the song were prompted by its story of a doomed love affair between a young white girl and a black boy. Compared to many of the popular hits of the late '60s and '70s, it seems in retrospect as mild as its folksong melody.

The success of the song made the sixteen-year-old a national celebrity. During most of 1967, Janis maintained a hectic schedule of concerts across the country. She achieved a chart hit with her debut LP on Verve, *Janis Ian* (January 1967), followed in January 1968 by the album *For All Seasons*.

But Janis wasn't particularly happy with her newfound attention. She gave her earnings away to friends and charitable causes and, after meeting a boy named Peter during the October 1967 peace march in Washington, D.C., decided to settle down with him in Philadelphia. She also gave up entertaining efforts. "I retired for a while. I just got very bored with performing, so I stopped doing it. It was basically the same thing night after night. I did the same songs, the same show. It becomes very predictable."

But in the 1970s, the urge to create new material took hold again. The comeback began in 1970 and, after several ups and downs, brought her to new heights with the superb 1975 album *Between the Lines*. "I felt more mature, that I had more insight. I feel the songs are better now and I'm a better singer so the whole thing becomes more interesting. It isn't easy. It's hard work. The reasons I came back to the music field come down to this: I was writing songs that I liked and I wanted to record them."

She signed with Capitol and her debut on that label, *Present Company,* came out in March 1971, accompanied by her first tour in a number of years. The response was mixed. Critic Richard Cromelin echoed many reviewers when he wrote in the *Los Angeles Times* (July 16, 1971): "Her most glaring defect is her writing. Her tunes are pretty, if forgettable, but her lyrics . . . lack both facility and depth."

After several albums for Capitol, Janis signed a new contract in the mid-1970s with Columbia. Her first album on the label, *Stars,* had good spots, but nothing to bring her to creative prominence. Then came *Between the Lines,* a platinum album whose songs in some ways harked back to Janis's early glory years describing problems and relationships of young lovers, but the treatment showed a more reflective, less bitter approach. It included such gems as "When the Party's Over" (which recorded the singer's despair, tinged with hope, at the prospects of finding a loving companion) and the top-10 "At Seventeen," a song touching on the oft-felt feelings of inadequacy of a teenage girl. ("I learned the truth at 17/That love was meant for beauty queens . . . the pain of Valentines that never came.")

The album and its related singles won a rash of nominations in the 1975 Grammy Awards. Discussing the TV program on which she sang "At Seventeen" and won two awards, including Best Pop Vocal Performance, Female, she noted, "That whole thing was great. I don't know if I'd like to perform again under that much pressure; it's pretty nerve-wracking. I wouldn't mind winning again. It's always nice to win."

Janis continued to turn out new albums on Columbia for the rest of the '70s. Most made the charts for a number of months, but none repeated the blockbuster success of *Between the Lines.*

There were fine things in all of them, but they lacked the consistency of the 1975 release. Still, all probably deserved better exposure than they received, particularly since Janis did not stand pat, but continued to experiment in subject matter and approach. In the 1977 album, *Miracle Row,* she introduced touches of Latin-style rhythms. "The *Miracle Row* influences essentially come from New York's Columbus Avenue. They're Puerto Rican rather than Latin. I thought it deserved a better reception—oh well, win some, lose some." In 1978, her album *Janis Ian* presented some of her best writing since *Between the Lines* and won a share of critical praise, though only moderate public support.

However, Janis wasn't able to sustain the promise of her 1978 material. Her 1979 Columbia LP, *Night Rains,* and the 1981 *Restless Eyes* didn't catch fire with record buyers.

After her contract with Epic expired in the early 1980s, Janis had trouble affiliating with another major label. Part of the problem, aside from her declining fortunes with record buyers, was the nature of some of her new material. Harking back to the outspoken approach of the early years of her career, she again started writing on topics many record company executives shied away from such as childhood incest, covered in her mid-1980s composition "Uncle Wonderful." Those taboos seemed somewhat ironic, considering the range of topics the majors accepted from rock groups covering other forms of sexual license, drug taking, and the like.

But the 1980s overall ended up as a very trying time

for the artist. Perhaps in hopes of having a family, despite her lesbian orientation, she had married a Portuguese businessman, Tino Sargo, in 1978, a union she later said turned into an abusive relationship that ended in the mid-1980s, though she told a *People* magazine reporter in 1986 that the marriage was "as solid as any marriage can be when two people are constantly questioning it." She also encountered severe physical problems during the 1980s, and late in the decade she discovered a former business manager had failed to pay her income taxes, causing the IRS to confiscate her home, savings, and other collateral. Fortunately, things took a turn for the better after she moved to Nashville, Tennessee, in 1988 and wrote a series of songs recorded by people like John Mellencamp, Amy Grant, Bette Midler, and John Gorka.

In 1992, Janis recorded her first album in twelve years, *Breaking Silence,* produced by Mellencamp and released by Morgan Creek/Polygram Records. The title referred partly to the end of a long drought in new recorded material as well as the fact that she had become more open about her lesbianism. Her efforts included writing articles for the gay and lesbian publication *The Advocate,* though she pointed out to an interviewer that her song lyrics didn't address lesbian issues. "I don't know that I would want to be a role model," she said. The album was well received and was nominated for a Grammy in the Best Contemporary Folk Album category. The track "All Roads to the River" was used by Mellencamp in his film *Falling from Grace* and was also recorded by him.

In 1995, Ian completed another excellent disc, *Revenge,* issued on the Beacon label, which included the track "Ruby," used in the sound track for the film *Street Girls.* Another album song, "When Angels Cry," was featured on six episodes of the TV show *General Hospital,* with Janis singing the song in person in the last of those. In the fall of 1997 she signed with Windham Hill Records, which released her album debut, *Hunger.* The second single from the disc, "Getting Over You," reached the top 30 on the adult contemporary chart in *Radio & Records* magazine in May. Windham Hill issued *God & the FBI* in 2000.

Based partly on personal interview with Irwin Stambler

INCREDIBLE STRING BAND, THE: *Vocal and instrumental group. Original members, 1965, both born in Scotland, Robin Williamson, born Edinburgh, November 24, 1943, and Clive Palmer; Mike Heron, born Glasgow, 1942, added soon after. Reformed as a duo of Heron and Williamson in late 1966. Expanded to quartet, late 1960s, with addition of Rose Simpson and Christina "Licorice" McKechnie. Simpson replaced by Malcolm LeMaistre in 1971; McKechnie by Gerard Dott in 1972.*

One of the most innovative folk groups of the 1960s and early 1970s was Scotland's Incredible String Band, whose repertoire is often described as avant-garde folk music. Although its various members all had early experience as part of the folk movement in Britain, the music they typically played as a group bore little obvious resemblance to the normally accepted folk music of Scotland, England, or the United States. Their influences were as diverse as the thirty different instruments its members played, incorporating elements of medieval music, Scottish Highland music, American blues, and, in particular, oriental or Arabic music.

The original Incredible String Band was a duo of Robin Williamson and Clive Palmer, considered among Scotland's finest folk musicians in the early 1960s.

Playing as Clive and Robin, their instrumental version of "Jazz Bo's Holiday" was included on a Decca recording of the 1962 Edinburgh Folk Festival. Clive and Robin played at local clubs in Edinburgh frequented by such people as Ralph McTell, Bert Jansch, and Archie Fisher. They soon met a young accounting student named Mike Heron, who, like them, could sing well, play the guitar and a number of other instruments, and write unusual original songs. Heron, Williamson, and Palmer opened the first all-night folk club in Glasgow, called Clive's Incredible Folk Club (hence the band's name) on Sauciehall Street. The club survived for nine months until the police shut it down.

By mid-1966, the trio found a steadily growing audience in England and completed its first record release. Producer Joe Boyd spotted them at the Incredible Folk Club and helped get them a contract with Elektra Records. The first result was the LP *Incredible String Band,* issued in 1966. Their debut revealed the trio's strong folk influences on the original compositions of Williamson ("October Song" and "Womenkind") and Heron ("The Tree," "When the Music Starts to Play"). Clive Palmer took on a diminished role, playing banjo on a traditional tune and contributing one original song. The three friends decided to part company for a while and sought new musical insights through travel, with Clive going as far as Afghanistan and Robin spending several months in Morocco. When the artists reunited, their new material reflected their recent experience, incorporating instruments like the oud, finger cymbals, tamboura.

Although Palmer contributed material and ideas, he didn't want to return to the concert circuit, so the Incredible String Band became a duo of Heron and Williamson. In November 1966, they made their first concert appearance outside Scotland, sharing a bill with Judy Collins and Tom Paxton at London's Royal Albert Hall. The audience responded enthusiastically, and word of the duo's talents was brought back to the United States by Judy and Tom. That helped generate interest for the duo's initial concert work in the United States in 1967 at the Newport Folk Festival.

But it was only a preliminary to the excitement created by the duo's second LP, *The 5,000 Spirits or the Layers of the Onion.* After its release in 1967, the album made England's top 10; it didn't do nearly as well in the United States, but brought a strong cult following in the States.

The second collection included such notable songs as Williamson's "First Girl I Loved," his offbeat "Way Back in the 1960s," and "Madhatter's Song," and Heron's beautiful "Painting Box," "Little Cloud," and the childhood ditty "The Hedgehog's Song." During one trip to New York, they met Jac Holzman of Elektra, who gave them 100 albums of world music (including one by Bahamian guitarist Joseph Spence) from the Nonesuch catalog that influenced the duo.

Even more impressive was their next LP, *The Hangman's Beautiful Daughter,* issued in 1968. The influences in the various tracks ranged even further afield than usual, sometimes embracing themes with Arabic flavor and, at others, such inputs as spirituals and even Gilbert and Sullivan. The album, considered one of the group's best, rose to number five on the British charts and led to a tour of the United States. It included such songs as "Koeeoaddi There," a title that came to Williamson either in a dream, while rolling dice, or while playing Ouija. By this time the group had expanded to include Heron's and Williamson's girlfriends, Rose Simpson (guitars, vocals) and Christina "Licorice" McKechnie (vocals, acoustic guitar, organ, piano), who are simply referred to in album credits as Rose and Licorice. In 1968 the band released a double LP titled *Wee Tam and the Big Huge,* released as two LPs in the United States.

The following year, the quartet of Williamson, Heron, Rose, and Licorice was invited to perform at Woodstock. They arrived by helicopter but refused to perform during a driving rainstorm. Melanie went on instead, receiving a career boost. The Incredible String Band, on the other hand, waited for better weather but fell flat when they took the stage after Canned Heat. Their performance was not included in the concert film. At the end of the 1960s the group became involved in Scientology and released the LP *Changing Horses,* indicating the change in their personal outlook.

At the beginning of the 1970s Elektra released *I Looked Up* and *U,* another double LP. The latter concept album was made in conjunction with a dance-mime troupe called the Exploding Galaxy (later called Stone Monkey), which included future band members Malcolm LeMaistre and Janet Shankman, who would also wed Williamson. The mime show was produced in New York and London.

While the Incredible String Band maintained a small but devoted U.S. following their albums never became best-sellers. In 1970 the band signed with Island, which released another concept album in 1970, *Be Glad for the Song Has No Ending,* an instrumental sound track for a movie called *The Pirate and the Crystal Ball.* The film also includes footage of the band performing, miming, and presenting stories. The following

year the band released another collection, *Liquid Acrobat as Regards the Air.*

In January 1971, Rose Simpson left and was replaced by Malcolm LeMaistre (bass guitar, hand drums). In late 1972, Licorice left and was replaced by Gerard Dott (clarinet, saxophone, piano, organ, banjo, violin, percussion, xylophone). Dott was an old friend of the original members, having attended the same school as Heron as a boy in Scotland.

The focus of the music continued to be on Heron and Williamson, who composed most of the songs and demonstrated their instrumental dexterity. In 1971 Elektra released *Relics,* a two-disc set of some of the band's most notable songs, including tracks from the first three Heron-Williamson sets.

Elektra gave up distribution in early 1972, and Warner Brothers took over. The first LP on the Warner/Reprise label was *Earthspan* in 1972 followed in 1973 with *No Ruinous Feud* and *Hard Rope and Silken Twine,* in 1974.

By then there were signs that Heron and Williamson were becoming somewhat restless with group work. Heron, for instance, in 1970 completed his first solo LP, *Smiling Men with Bad Reputations,* (1971), issued by Elektra.

Heron's album included contributions from John Cale, Pete Townshend, and Keith Moon. In 1972, Island released Williamson's solo debut, *Myrrh,* for which Williamson played almost all of the instruments.

The group may not have threatened the U.S. top 10 album list with its albums, but it remained a concert favorite from the late 1960s to 1974, with enough drawing power to fill medium-size halls in many major U.S. cities rather than just small folk clubs. Its popularity was even greater at home. The response to its 1973 British tour included a standing-room-only concert at London's Royal Festival Hall.

Just before the band split up, roadies Stan Lee and Jack Ingram joined to take over on bass and drums. The band played at a tribute concert for Scientology founder L. Ron Hubbard at the Rainbow Theatre, along with Chick Corea, and can be heard on the album released by the organization. (For a time Williamson dedicated his albums to Hubbard, but both Heron and Williamson left Scientology in the 1980s.) After a tour of the United States ended in October 1974, Williamson decided to leave the band, which had increasingly focused more on rock and less on the traditional music he favored. Producer Joe Boyd told Nigel Williamson of *Folk Roots* ("It's Incredible!" October 1997) that their involvement in Scientology increased their efficiency but diminished their inventiveness. But Heron and Williamson maintained that changes in the music industry actually led to the band's demise. They agreed not to use the name Incredible String Band for future work.

Heron went on to form a rock band called Mike Heron's Reputation with LeMaistre, recording and touring widely for the next three years. The group released *Mike Heron's Reputation* (1974), followed by *Diamond of Dreams* (1976). He released a solo album, *Mike Heron,* in 1979. Later Heron released *The Glen Row Tapes,* three volumes of recordings made at the cottages he once shared with Williamson, Rose, and Licorice. In the late 1990s Heron released *Where the Mystics Swim* (1996) on Demon, and *Conflict of Emotions* (1998).

Williamson continued to tinker in a remarkable number of genres—music, fiction, storytelling, and theater. He wrote a novel and an autobiography, and contributed music for the film *Willow.* He formed Robin Williamson and His Merry Band with harpist Sylvia Woods, Chris Caswell, and Jerry McMillan, releasing *Journey's Edge* (1977), *American Stonehenge* (1978), *A Glint at the Kindling* (1979), and a compilation, *Songs and Music* (1986). The group's farewell concert at McCabe's Guitar Shop in December 1979 was released on CD in 1997.

Williamson put out a vast array of LPs and CDs during the 1980s and 1990s, many of them on his own Pig's Whisker label. He released *Legacy of the Scottish Harpers* (1984); *Volume 2* (1986); *Songs for Children of All Ages* (Flying Fish, 1987), including two songs, "Witches Hat" and "Watersong," from *The Hangman's Beautiful Daughter; Winter's Turning* (Flying Fish, 1987); *Ten of Songs* (Flying Fish, 1988); *Songs of Love and Parting* (1981), later released on CD with *Five Bardic Mysteries* (1994); *Wheel of Fortune* (Flying Fish, 1994), a live album recorded with John Renbourn that was nominated for a Grammy; *Island of the Strong Door* (1996); *Songs for the Calendarium* (1996); *Memories/Erinnerungern* (1997); *Dream Journals 1966–1976* (1997); *Celtic Harp Airs and Dance Tunes* (Greentrax, 1997); *Mirrormans Sequences* (1997); *A Job of Journey Work* (1998); *Gems of Celtic Story, Volumes One and Two* (1998); *Ring Dance* (1998); and *The Old Fangled Tone* (1999), a live recording featuring Williamson with a five-piece brass band.

Williamson spent much of the 1980s following in the bardic tradition, adapting ancient Celtic myths and legends. In the early 1980s he wrote music for *The Mabinogi,* a TV production of Welsh legends performed by a theater group called Moving Being. Flying Fish released the sound track in 1983. He also made several spoken word recordings of Celtic folk tales and legends that were available on cassette.

"Paradoxically, as the world gets more technically sophisticated, the simpler things take more value," he told Steve Hochman of the *Los Angeles Times* ("Folk Singer Promises Christmas Eve Surprise," December 23, 1987). "When the world can be destroyed at the touch of a button, anything that reminds us of the eternal verities is of value."

After reading a story that there were rifts between Heron and Williamson, the two decided to perform together at concerts in Glasgow and London. In the autumn of 1997, Heron and Williamson shared the stage for the first time in twenty-four years. In January 1998 Pig's Whisker released *Robin Williamson and Mike Heron—Live at Bloomsbury 1997.*

A number of retrospectives and reissues reflect ongoing interest in the Incredible String Band. These include *Seasons They Change* (Island, Elektra, 1977); *On Air* (1991); *BBC Radio One Live in Concert* (recorded in 1971-1972, released in 1992 by Windsong); *Incredible Acoustic Band: Official Bootleg* (1993); *Chelsea Sessions 1967* (1997), which includes unreleased material recorded prior to their second album; and *First Girl I Loved* (1998). In 1994, Joe Boyd's Hannibal Records, a subsidiary of Rykodisc, reissued the band's first three LPs on CD.

INDIGO GIRLS: *Vocal and instrumental duo, Amy Ray and Emily Saliers, both guitarists and songwriters. Saliers born New Haven, Connecticut, July 22, 1963. Ray born Atlanta, Georgia, April 12, 1964.*

Exponents of what some critics dubbed "Nu Folk," the Indigo Girls made their mark on the music scene starting at the end of the 1980s as folk-influenced artists who crossed over to pop stardom. Almost from the start of their joint career, their supporters ranged over a broad spectrum of music styles from country-folk (Luka Bloom and Mary-Chapin Carpenter) to rock (supergroup R.E.M.). With their devotion to acoustic guitars, they fitted right in with the new MTV-inspired "unplugged" concept.

Both were born into middle-class households (Saliers's father was a professor of theology) and became close friends by the time they were ten and musical collaborators in their teen years, growing up in Decatur, Georgia. They debuted as a duo at a high school Parent-Teachers Association show singing covers of songs recorded by people like James Taylor and Elton John. Later both enrolled in college as English literature majors while continuing to polish their act during appearances at local coffeehouses. By the time they finished high school they already were writing original material as "Saliers and Ray" and the "B-Band" and making plans to succeed in the entertainment field. An initial step, they decided in the summer of 1985, was to record some of their collaborations, which led to their preparing the single "Crazy Game" backed by "Someone to Come Home To" on their own label, Indigo. In November 1986 they went a step further by issuing an EP on Indigo, *Indigo Girls,* which included such songs as "Cold As Ice," "Finlandia," "History of Us," "Land of Canaan," "Lifeblood," and "Never Stop."

Meanwhile, appearing in venues like the Little Five Points Pub, the duo was building up a local following while also attracting the attention of other locally based artists like the members of R.E.M. The girls continued to work on new recording projects, which resulted in the fall 1987 Indigo Records full-length LP, *Strange*

Fire. Major labels had become interested in their potential, and in 1988 Epic Records signed them and brought them out to Los Angeles to work on their label debut. Among the backing musicians on the project were Peter Buck, Mike Mills, and Bill Berry of R.E.M., who contributed to "Tried to Be True"; Michael Stipe of R.E.M. ("Kid Fears"); Hothouse Flowers ("Closer to Fine," "Secure Yourself"); and Luka Bloom ("Closer to Fine").

Epic released the album, *Indigo Girls,* in February 1989, along with the initial single "Closer to Fine." The duo's prospects were aided by their friends from R.E.M., who arranged to have them open for a major arena concert tour. Besides that, the girls were featured in headline shows in small clubs across the United States. Aided as well by strong play on college radio stations, the recordings soon began to make inroads into pop charts. The single entered the *Billboard* Hot 100 list in July, rising to number fifty-two, and the album also reached well inside the album top 40, peaking at number twenty-two on the way to exceeding R.I.A.A. double platinum sales levels. Almost overnight, the girls had reached a level of fame most performers, particularly those in the folk-music sector, might take years to achieve.

Even more major milestones came their way before 1989 was over. In November, Epic reissued *Strange Fire* with a new bonus track titled "Get Together." A video was made of the bonus song to help benefit former President and Mrs. Carter's nonprofit Habitat for Humanity program. In the voting for the thirty-second annual Grammy Awards (winners announced on the TV awards show on February 21, 1990), the Indigos were nominated for Best New Artist and the *Indigo Girls* album for Best Contemporary Folk Recording, with the album gaining the trophy in its category.

The girls' live performances, showcasing harmonies combining Amy's husky, growling vocal style and Emily's high, angelic alto and their standout guitar work, typically satisfied growing numbers of enthusiastic fans. Their original material offered melodies that were catchy and stayed in the listener's mind. Their lyrics, though, sometimes seemed labored and much more complex than the straightforward lines associated with folk song classics. That didn't bother their fans, but it did draw fire from some critics. What did cause fan controversy was their ardent support of causes like prochoice on abortion, strong support for the rights of Native Americans, and belief in the Greenpeace agenda.

When petitions in support of abortion rights were circulated during a concert at Vanderbilt University in Tennessee, many people got up and walked out. Amy Ray told a reporter from the *Los Angeles Times,* "We have some very fundamental Christian people that like our music because of certain songs that we never intended to be strictly Christian. We just intended them to be spiritual. We were brought up Christians, but we don't consider our music Christian music."

The new decade saw the duo represented by the January '90 release of their first home video, *Live at the Uptown Lounge.* During the summer, they were back in the studios in Athens, Georgia, and Los Angeles to record a new collection, *Nomads*Indians*Saints,* issued by Epic in September. Among the backing performers were drummers Kenny Aronoff and Jim Keltner and Mary-Chapin Carpenter. A single from the album, the rousing "Hammer and a Nail," was nominated in the Best Contemporary Folk Recording Grammy category. The girls continued their support for what they felt were worthy causes, headlining in a May benefit for the Children's Health Fund at the personal invitation of fund founder Paul Simon. In October 1991 they had a busy benefit schedule, appearing in San Francisco with Joan Baez and Mary-Chapin Carpenter on behalf of Humanitas; in Phoenix, Arizona, with Jackson Browne, David Crosby, and Graham Nash on behalf of the Verde Valley School; and in New York with Jackson Browne and Bruce Cockburn for Native American land rights in James Bay.

Career-wise, the Indigos started off 1991 with their first appearance on *The Tonight Show* with Jay Leno, having already appeared on the competing David Letterman program. (The girls made their fourth appearance on the Letterman show in December '91.) Their only new recording release was the eight-song live EP *Back on the Bus, Y'All,* which won another Grammy nomination in the Best Contemporary Folk Recording category. The Indigos' next full-length album was *Rites of Passage* issued by Epic in May, which climbed the *Billboard* pop charts soon after, earning a gold record in September.

The duo made singles charts in the fall with "Joking," released in both audio and video versions, and by year-end had earned another platinum record from the R.I.A.A. for *Rites of Passage.*

The Indigos' 1993 concert schedule led off with their second annual appearance on January 19 at Constitution Hall in Washington, D.C., on a benefit concert for "Voices of Choice." They joined David Crosby and Graham Nash, Elayne Boosler, and Melissa Etheridge in an event whose proceeds went on to the National Reproductive Rights organization. On February 2, in Des Moines, Iowa, they played the first of three Midwest concerts in support of the Indigenous Women's Network and its Honor the Earth campaign. After a series of small-venue shows in the spring where all tickets and T-shirts had to be priced at $10 each, the girls took part in more conventional college and medium-to-large-venue appearances climaxed by two stadium shows with the Grateful Dead in Eugene, Oregon, on August 21–22, after which they took time off to relax and prepare for a new album, *Swamp Ophelia,* which came out on May 10, '94.

Before that release, the Indigos' version of the old Crazy Horse song "I Don't Want to Talk about It" was included in the sound track album for the AIDS-themed movie *Philadelphia*. In March, the girls went from sound track only to actual movie presence when they went to Los Angeles to film scenes in *Boys on the Side*, which featured Whoopi Goldberg, Drew Barrymore, and Marie Louise Parker. In those scenes, Whoopi, playing a lesbian folksinger, runs into the Indigos in Tucson, Arizona, where the three sing some Indigo originals ("Joking," "Southland in the Springtime") plus a cover of Lou Reed's "Walk on the Wild Side." They told Christopher John Farley of *Time* ("The Power of Two," May 23, 1994) that they enjoyed their part but were of mixed minds about doing more film work. Ray said, "I don't have the patience," and Saliers commented, "I plan on writing music for movies." In July '94, *Swamp Ophelia* (which a *Time* critic called the Girls' "most complex and satisfying album" to date) was certified gold. The Indigos' summer tour included capacity concerts at New York City's Radio City Music Hall, Atlanta's Chastain Park Amphitheater, and L.A.'s Universal Amphitheater.

On January 5, '95, the duo received still another Best Contemporary Folk Recording Grammy nomination, this time for *Swamp Ophelia*. In the spring and summer they embarked on a tour of twenty-one western U.S. states on behalf of Native American environmental groups working to protect their land base and culture. In October '95, Epic released the double live album *1200 Curfews*, accompanied by the Epic home video package *Watershed: 10 Years' Underground Videos*. The video offerings, Epic noted, included all the music videos done up to that time by the Girls, "along with interview and performance footage from both recent and vintage sources." Like all the preceding Epic releases, *1200 Curfews* quickly made the hit charts, though it didn't rise as far as previous ones, peaking at number forty and falling out of the *Billboard* top 200 in early '96. Still, that was much greater success than the majority of folksingers of the '90s could achieve.

On the girls' next Epic Records album release in the spring of 1997, *Shaming of the Sun*, guest artists included such people as Steve Earle, Ani DiFranco, and violinist Lisa Germano. The album was of much more uneven quality than earlier discs, with some well-crafted tracks like the debut single, "Shame on You," and "Get Out the Map" and other compositions that seemed run of the mill or overorchestrated. The album did well with record buyers, earning a gold record award from the R.I.A.A. on July 7, 1997. Earlier in the year, their debut album, *Indigo Girls*, was certified multiplatinum (2 million copies) by the R.I.A.A. on June 3.

The duo's activities in 1997 included taking part in Sarah McLachlan's highly successful Lilith Fair concert series, a role they repeated in the 1998 spring-summer Lilith Fair dates. On the negative side, a free concert planned by the girls in the spring of 1998 at Irmo High School in South Carolina was canceled when the principal acceded to the protests of some parents about the Indigos' lesbian sexual preference. (This was followed by similar rejections at two other schools.) This brought angry responses in defense of the girls from fellow musicians like Hootie and the Blowfish and civil rights groups. Epic released *Come On Now Social* in 1999.

IRVINE, ANDY: *Singer, instrumentalist (guitar, mandolin, bouzouki, mandola, harmonica, hurdy-gurdy), band leader (Mosaic, Patrick Street), songwriter. Born London, England, June 14, 1942.*

The many-faceted Andy Irvine became a significant figure in the burgeoning folk movement in Ireland and Britain in the years following the 1950s. It sometimes seemed as though he had a hand in the fortunes of almost every important phase of Irish folk-music development from the '60s through the '90s, but his skills as a writer and instrumentalist impacted more than a few artists outside Ireland, including some of the new U.S. artists coming to the fore in the folk field in the years following the 1970s.

He spent his childhood years not in Ireland but in London, where he was born in 1942. His father, Archie Kennedy, was Scottish, though his family had roots in Donegal, and his mother, a musical comedy performer who used the stage name of Felice LaSalles, came from County Antrim in Ireland. As Irvine recalled for Earle Hitchner ("Never Tire of the Road—Trad Legend Andy Irvine Keeps on Truckin'," *Irish Echo*, April 28–May 4, 1993), "I sort of followed in [my mother's] footsteps, and I became a child star, I suppose, if only briefly. I acted with the BBC Repertory on stage, and I also appeared in a few films." His biggest part was in a Gina Lollobrigida movie, *A Tale of Five Cities* (called *A Tale of Five Women* in the United States), filmed in 1950 and released in 1951.

His other main interest besides acting, he noted, was music. He enjoyed listening to his father's jazz records as well as some of his mother's 78-rpm records of musicals. Still, he felt something was lacking in that material. Then, when he was fifteen, skiffle and Lonnie Donegan's hit record of "Rock Island Line" caught his attention. He told Hitchner, "I got heavily into that. I was playing the guitar by this time, classical guitar in fact, which I didn't get on with too well. So I switched suddenly to playing skiffle, which was really easy because having even a slight classical background I found playing three chords was dead simple. From there I got into Woody Guthrie, and from Woody Guthrie I got generally into traditional music. Irish music didn't really play much of a part with me until about 1962, by which time I was living in Dublin."

There was a thriving folk scene in Dublin in the early 1960s, and Andy performed at many folk clubs, including one of the most frequented by young performers, O'Donoghue's Pub. He continued to expand his local reputation while also making contacts with others in the folk movement. Among other things, he got the chance to travel with American folk stars Derroll Adams and Ramblin' Jack Elliott in the mid-'60s for concerts in his homeland. In 1966 he became part of a trio with Johnny Moynihan and Joe Dolan that took the name of Sweeney's Men. The group managed to get the chance to prepare some material for Pye Records, which resulted in the single "Old Maid in the Garrett" that rose to number two on Irish charts in the spring of 1967. In the summer, Dolan left and Terry Woods, who later had a hand in organizing the successful Steeleye Span group, took his place.

Overall, though, Irvine pointed out, Sweeney's Men didn't have much of an impact on pop music. The interest was in ballads like those performed by Peter, Paul and Mary, and the trio didn't do that type of music. The trio recorded the 1968 album *Sweeney's Men* for Transatlantic Records (issued on Shanachie in the United States) before a discouraged Irvine left in May 1968. More than a few critics since then have argued the disc deserved a better response than it received, particularly citing the track "Willie O'Winsbury," which featured new lyrics by Irvine to an old ballad listed in a Francis Child compendium published in the United States in the 1800s.

After leaving Sweeney's Men, Irvine traveled to Eastern Europe, listening to the folk music played in Bulgaria, Romania, and Yugoslavia. To earn money for food and incidentals, he sometimes did some busking on the streets of Balkan cities, accompanying himself on mandolin or harmonica. In 1969 he decided he'd had enough of sleeping in orchards or by the roadside and returned home, initially finding work as a solo artist and then forming a duo with Donal Lunny. In 1971, after the two had helped singer-guitarist Christy Moore record an album called *Prosperous,* they agreed to form a new band with a fourth member, piper Liam O'Flynn.

The result was the seminal Irish folk group called Planxty (*see separate entry*). One of the best tracks on the band's debut album was Irvine's song "The West Coast of Clare," inspired by the setting of his last gig with Sweeney's Men in May '68. When Planxty broke up in 1975 after three excellent albums and many concert appearances, Irvine teamed with Paul Brady for new tour dates and the 1976 Mulligan Records album, *Andy Irvine/Paul Brady* (issued in the United States on Green Linnet). Andy told Hitchner, "Paul and I were together from early 1976 until the end of 1977. But he didn't like to travel very much, so even while I was playing with Paul in Ireland and England and indeed once in the States, I was doing tours with Mick Hanly. Paul eventually did a solo gig and got such a hit off of it that he wanted to pursue music on his own."

After working solo for a while in the first part of '78, Andy joined with the three other original members for a renewal of Planxty. This project encompassed three more albums and a time span from the late 1970s through 1983. During this period, though, Andy kept his hand in on other projects, including solo concerts and new solo recordings. In the early 1980s, the latter releases included *Rainy Sundays . . . Windy Dreams* and *High Kings of Tara* on the Tara label in 1980 (issued in the United States on Shanachie); *The Gathering* on Greenhays, and *Folk Friends II* on Folk Freak (both in 1981); and the excellent, underappreciated collaboration with Dick Gaughan, *Parallel Lines,* on Folk Freak in 1982 (released on Green Linnet in the United States).

After Planxty disbanded again at the end of 1983, Irvine shifted his attention to playing music that reflected the wide range of influences he'd heard or become aware of throughout Europe. He assembled a group called Mosaic whose members were drawn from Scotland (Dougie MacLean), Denmark (Lisa), Austria (Hans Thessink), and Hungary (Márta Sebestyén). MacLean left early on, and his place was taken by Donal Lunny and Declan Masterston. The group completed one very well received tour of Europe and Britain, but there were scheduling and other conflicts among the members and Irvine had to abandon the concept.

Irvine moved on to continue his solo work and, in 1986, to organize a new band called Patrick Street. The latter had evolved from a series of U.S. concerts given by Andy with Kevin Burke (fiddle), Jackie Daly (melodeon), and Gerry O'Beirne (guitar). O'Beirne backed out soon after Patrick Street was assembled and Arty McGlynn took over on guitar. The new band's debut album, *Patrick Street,* came out on Green Linnet in 1987, and the band's concert work in support of it included an extensive tour of the United States which was repeated annually through 1990. By then the group had two more albums out on Green Linnet, the 1988 *#2 Patrick Street* and the 1989 *Irish Times.*

Taking advantage of a temporary hiatus in Patrick Street projects in the early '90s, Irvine focused more strongly on his songwriting and solo concert work. In 1991 he completed tracks for two more albums, *East Wind* and *Rude Awakening.* The first of those, recorded with Davy Spillane (uilleann pipes and low whistle) and some of his Mosaic friends like Márta Sebestyén, and released on the Tara label, offered Bulgarian and Macedonian music. The second disc, available in the United Kingdom in '92 and in the United States on Green Linnett in 1993, consisted mainly of songs by Irvine on North American themes, including a tribute to Woody Guthrie called "Never Tire of the Road." Other self-penned numbers included "Viva Zapata," about the Mexican revolutionary; "The Whole Damn Thing," dealing with U.S. novelist Sinclair Lewis; and "James Connelly," about the Irish labor organizer.

In the mid-'90s Irvine split his performing time between gigs with Patrick Street and solo concerts in which backing musicians were drawn from many of the band associations he'd had during his career. Already almost legendary on his home grounds, he steadily built up a core following in the United States and Canada, where critics tended to be on his side. The *San Francisco Examiner*, for instance, enthused, "His forte, his genius is playing his mandolin, mandola and bouzouki. I have never heard such clarity of sound, such perfect and precise rhythmic variations or such brilliant melodic figures from this family of instruments."

In the spring of '93 the fourth Patrick Street album, *All in Good Time*, came out on Green Linnet. Besides Irvine and Kevin Burke, the group roster included Dáithí Sproule on guitar and Jackie Daly on accordion. *New Yorker* magazine called the album "lively" and commented that Burke "plays the fiddle so smoothly, with such buoyancy and with such relaxed showmanship that even a large concert hall becomes intimate." The fifth band album, *Corner Boys*, issued in January 1996 on Green Linnet, was even more striking, causing some reviewers to suggest the group had assumed "legendary" status (and the band promptly titled its U.S. concert series of '96 as the Legends of Irish Music tour). Particularly striking was the band's vocal work on the ballads "Moorlough Shore" and "Sweet Lishweemore." Green Linnet issued *Made in Cork* in 1997. Quartet members this time around comprised Irvine, Burke, and Daly, plus Ged Foley on guitar and small pipes. (All four musicians had other projects when away from Patrick Street, Irvine's in '96 being the East-Wind Trio, Burke leading the band Open House, Daly often appearing with Buttons and Bows, and Foley moonlighting with the House Band.)

IVES, BURL: *Singer, guitarist, actor. Born Huntington Township, Jasper County, Illinois, June 14, 1909; died April 14, 1995.*

In the world of music, Burl Ives is considered, first and foremost, one of the most talented folksingers of the twentieth century. And he is more than that. Not only had his recordings of country music done well enough to reach the uppermost levels of the country charts, his recordings also could be found on national pop charts at times. Additionally, he was a compiler of folk-song books and one of the more accomplished actors of his generation.

Burl liked to be regarded for his folk efforts, but he demurred at being described as a classical folk artist. As he told a reporter in 1978, "I've never defined what a folk song is exactly. But now I think I do know what a folksinger is. It has to do with the country, the soil. Now you take Leadbelly—he was a folksinger, born and raised in the country and he sang like it. I was born in the country, on the Illinois prairies, and moved to the big city at age twenty-four. I sing folk songs, but I'm not a complete folksinger. I have a foot in both camps, don't you know."

Still, there's no doubt his upbringing was in the folk tradition. His English-Irish ancestors came to the New World in the 1600s with farming in their blood, as it was for his parents, Frank and Dellie Ives, who were tenant farmers in Illinois. They sometimes sang old-time songs for their son, named Burl Icle Ivanhoe Ives, as did his grandmother, Katie White. His first public performance was before an old soldiers' reunion when he was four. A gifted banjoist, he performed in school shows when he attended Newton High School. But for much of his teens music took a backseat to sports as Burl starred as a fullback on the high school team. In fact, he decided to be a physical education major at Eastern Illinois Teachers College after graduating from high school in 1927, figuring on later becoming a football coach.

But wanderlust gripped him after two years in college, and he left to roam around the United States and Canada, picking up money to keep going from odd jobs or occasional musical efforts. As he drifted across the land, seeing new places and gaining all sorts of experience, he taught himself guitar and picked up new ballads as he went along. After several years he settled down for a time to attend Indiana State Teachers College in Terre Haute, earning some of his tuition singing folk songs on a local station. He dropped out once more to work at various tasks, including a spell as a pro football player, before settling in New York in 1937. Taking vocal lessons at New York University, he also attended Julliard and concentrated on entering the entertainment field full time.

His first entree was through the theater. After playing summer stock at Rockridge Theater, Carmel, New York, in 1938, he made contacts that brought a small role in Rodgers and Hart's *The Boys from Syracuse*. Roles in other Broadway plays followed, and, in the meantime, he got a foothold in music by appearances at the Village Vanguard. After several guest shots on New York stations, he got his own program on CBS in 1940, where he soon had millions of people singing along on numbers like "Bluetail Fly" and "Foggy Dew." The title song for the show also became something of a nickname for Burl: *The Wayfarin' Stranger*. The program prospered until he entered the army in 1942. Before he received his discharge in 1944, he performed in Irving Berlin's service musical, *This Is the Army*.

Back in civilian life, he resumed his acting and singing career with a vengeance. Among his credits in the period from 1944 to 1949 were the Donaldson Award for Best Supporting Actor in the 1944–45 Broadway season; a sold-out debut concert in New York's Town Hall in late 1945; his initial movie appearance in the western *Smoky* in 1946; and his initial record releases (1949) on the Decca label, which included three albums (Volumes 1–3) of *Ballads & Folk Songs*. Prior to his singing with Decca he recorded for Columbia, which reissued albums of his material at various times in the 1950s and 1960s.

He was so well known by the late 1940s that he got the opportunity to write his autobiography, titled *Way-*

farin' Stranger, which was published by McGraw-Hill in 1948. Most of his later efforts in the book field involved folk song collections. The first of those, containing 115 songs, came out in 1953. For much of the early 1950s, Ives was in California on acting assignments. In 1954, he returned to Broadway for one of his most acclaimed roles, that of Cap'n Andy in a revival of *Showboat*. The next year he played his most memorable role, that of Big Daddy in Tennessee Williams's *Cat on a Hot Tin Roof*. It was a role he recreated on film for the 1958 movie that also starred Elizabeth Taylor and Paul Newman.

As he told an interviewer in 1978, he didn't consider the role autobiographical. "There's littler of me in it than people might suppose. Fact is, I'm the opposite to the Big Daddy that Tennessee Williams wrote. I'm soft spoken. Don't talk overly much. Don't yell and holler at people."

He stressed the role wasn't written with him in mind. "How it happened, I got into a brawl one night in a saloon in Greenwich Village. Elia Kazan, a great director, saw me put out a couple of hecklers and figures there was some Big Daddy in me, just lyin' dormant. And out it came. People still do call me Big Daddy, but to me, inside, I'm no Big Daddy at all."

Throughout the 1950s he kept up his movie work and folk recordings. Among his movie efforts, a notable high was his 1958 work in *The Big Country*, for which he was awarded an Oscar for Best Supporting Role. His Decca albums of the 1950s included *Folk Songs Dramatic and Humorous, Songs of Ireland, Down to the Sea in Ships*, and *Old Time Varieties* as well as many others. Some of his 1950s Columbia releases included *Sings Songs for All Ages* and *More Folksongs*.

With the onset of the folk boom in the late 1950s and early 1960s, Burl was in more demand than ever for concerts and appearances on radio and TV folk-music shows. He also tried his hand at country-flavored material in the early 1960s, and in 1962 hit the top of the country charts with three top-10 singles on Decca; "A Little Bitty Tear," "Call Me Mr. In-Between," and "Funny Way of Laughin'." The last of those earned him a 1962 Grammy Award for Best Country & Western recording.

The song also was the title song for a chart hit LP in 1962, a year in which Decca also issued the LPs *Sunshine in My Soul* and *Songs of the West*. Later in the decade, some of his Decca LPs were *Burl*, issued April 1963; *Singin' Easy* (10/63); *True Love* (7/64); *Pearly Shells* (1/65). Columbia issued the LP *Return of the Wayfaring Stranger* in August 1960 and *Wayfaring Stranger* (1/65). At the end of the decade he returned to the label for the album *Softly and Tenderly*, issued in December 1969.

During the 1960s and 1970s, Ives did some film work, returned to Broadway in 1967 for the short-lived drama, *Dr. Cook's Garden*, and amassed a considerable number of credits for TV, including his own series, *O.K. Crackerby*, and the role of lawyer Walter Nichols on *The Bold Ones*. Although his career slowed down in the

1970s, he made occasional guest appearances to sing on network TV programs and was an award presenter on one of the Country Music Association Award telecasts. In the mid- and late 1970s, his familiar countenance also greeted TV viewers in a number of TV commercials.

During that decade, he spent much of his time at sea sailing, his favorite pastime. He also owned a 225-year-old stone house in Ireland. As he said in 1978, "Ireland is the only other country except the States that I feel comfortable in."

Several of his albums were issued on CD, including *Greatest Hits!* (MCA, 1996), *Little Bitty Tear* (Members Edition, 1997), and *Burl Ives Sings* (Columbia, 1997).

J

JACKSON, MAHALIA: *Singer, gospel arranger. Born New Orleans, Louisiana, October 26, 1911; died January 27, 1972.*

In her lifetime Mahalia Jackson ranked as the greatest of all gospel singers; thanks to the many recordings she made, she remains a major force in religious music. She was influenced not only by early gospel artists but also by female blues pioneers like Ma Rainey and Bessie Smith. Her body of work, in turn, influenced new generations of gospel performers as well as major artists in many secular areas from rock to blues, jazz, and soul. Undoubtedly, if she had wanted to, she could have become a superstar in any of those popular music genres. Many of her religious numbers also were included in the repertoires of folksingers and musicians, and she herself recorded a few nonreligious folk-style songs.

Growing up in New Orleans, she was introduced to church music at an early age and, like many black youngsters, gained major grounding in music from choir participation. Though not unaware of developments in pop music areas by black artists in the mid- and late 1920s, she kept her focus on church music even as she moved to the more urbane environment of Chicago when she was sixteen. In the late '20s and early '30s she continued to hone her gospel techniques as she began to attract interest among churchgoers from concerts in many Midwest places of worship.

During the 1930s, she became a favorite performer for gospel songs from the prolific pen of Reverend Thomas A. Dorsey, sometimes referred to as the father of gospel. (He died in Chicago on January 23, 1993, at the age of ninety-three.) Mahalia and Dorsey appeared together in gospel concerts in many parts of the United States. After she began her recording career in 1937 with an independent "race" label, she recorded many of his compositions, sometimes joined in the recording sessions by Dorsey. Dorsey was a skilled pianist, but for most of her career on stage or in the studio she was accompanied by pianist Mildred Falls.

From the first part of the 1940s to the early 1950s, Mahalia turned out many singles and albums for the Apollo label. These later were reissued on Kenwood Records. Among the LPs were *In the Upper Room, Just As I Am, Christmas with Mahalia Jackson, Best of Mahalia Jackson, Sing Out, Mahalia! Mahalia! Mahalia!,* and *World's Greatest Gospel Singer.* The Apollo releases, accompanied by increased exposure of Mahalia's artistry to radio audiences and concert stages outside the black community, helped bring her acclaim from all segments of the U.S. population and, after the end of World War II, from European music fans as well. (Her U.S. appearances included a concert presented at New York's Carnegie Hall in 1951.) In the early 1950s reviewers in France hailed one of her discs as a masterpiece, which led to a very successful initial tour of Europe by her in 1952.

Critic and editor John Mortland described Mahalia's approach to singing in the *New Rolling Stone Record Guide:* "With her pliable contralto, she preferred to sing slow hymns; they gave her plenty of room to stretch out, to repeat lines endlessly, with the emphasis slightly different each time, to show off her full range of vocal slurs and bent notes. Because she did rely almost exclusively on slow hymns, her albums may appear sluggish to the casual listener; the trick is to listen for how many different things she could do with a group of songs so much alike.

"What's most amazing is how effortless she makes it all sound. There's no sense of strain when Jackson reaches for a high note, as is often the case with gospel singers pushing their voices to the limit; she sounds relaxed even when she's shouting."

In 1954 she moved to a major label, Columbia, which had both positive and negative effects. On the plus side, Columbia gave her releases much broader distribution at home and abroad. On the other hand, there was more pressure on her by company producers to dress up her recordings with more sophisticated but not necessarily more powerful arrangements, and to include more secular-sounding material to broaden the potential market base. In any case, Columbia issued a steady stream of albums, including the following, recorded from the late '50s to 1964: *Great Gettin' Up Morning* (1959); *The Power and the Glory* (1960); *Bless This House;* and *Mahalia Jackson's Greatest Hits* (both 1963). *Bless This House* included a medley of George Gershwin's "Summertime" and the folksinger favorite, "Sometimes I Feel Like a Motherless Child". *I Believe,* another LP, was issued in 1964.

During those years Mahalia continued to dominate the gospel circuit, while also being featured on major radio and TV programs as well as at secular festivals

like the Newport Jazz 1958 event, when she was joined onstage by Duke Ellington. She worked on a number of projects with the Duke over the years, including performances and recordings of his sacred compositions. Others with whom she collaborated (in concerts, TV programs, etc.) included Louis Armstrong and Nat King Cole, in Cole's case contributing to the W. C. Handy bio, *St. Louis Blues,* in which he starred. Other film appearances included a role in *Imitation of Life,* which starred Lana Turner, and featured status in the documentary *Jazz on a Summer's Day.*

In the 1950s and '60s she was active in the civil rights movement and was a strong supporter of the Reverend Martin Luther King Jr. (She also proved a very capable businesswoman as well, supervising operation of her own chain of restaurants.) At the start of the '60s, when Jack Kennedy was elected president, she was one of the honored guests at his inauguration and later performed at the inaugural festivities.

Her Columbia album releases in the second half of the '60s included *Garden of Prayer* (1966); *My Faith* and *In Concert* (both 1967); *A Mighty Fortress, Mahalia Jackson Sings the Best Loved Hymns of Dr. Martin Luther King, Jr.,* and *Christmas with Mahalia* (all 1968); and *Right out of the Church* and *What the World Needs Now* in 1969. As the last title indicates, the disc contains a variety of pop or folk-style secular songs. One of the tracks in her late-'60s albums was the folk lament for the assassination of great liberal leaders, "Abraham, Martin and John." Mahalia was a friend and strong adherent of all three and poured some of her feelings of tremendous sadness into her rendition at Reverend King's funeral in 1968 of Thomas Dorsey's "Take My Hand, Precious Lord."

Mahalia completed one more album for Columbia, the 1971 *Mahalia Jackson Sings America's Favorite Hymns,* before her life came to an end in 1972. In her memory that year, Columbia issued the retrospective *The Great Mahalia Jackson,* while Kenwood released *Mahalia Jackson—1911–1972.* In 1973 Kenwood issued *God Answers Prayers,* while Columbia in 1976 released *How I Got Over.*

Various reissues of her work came out in the late '70s and during the 1980s, and Columbia put together a boxed multi-CD set called *Mahalia Jackson—Gospels, Spirituals & Hymns,* released in 1991. The set included a number of songs, mostly traditional, arranged by Mahalia, such as "Keep Your Hand on the Plow," "Roll, Jordan, Roll," "Joshua Fought the Battle of Jericho," "Search Me Lord," and "Great Gettin' Up Morning." Tracks of compositions by T. A. Dorsey included "If We Ever Needed the Lord Before (We Sure Do Need Him Now)" and "Take My Hand, Precious Lord." Also among the contents was her version of the classic country and western song "A Satisfied Mind," which had been a chart hit for Ray Charles.

Biographical books about her career included the 1966 memoir *Moving On Up* by Mahalia and Evan McLeod Wylie (Hawthorn Books, New York), and *Just Mahalia, Baby* by Lorraine Goreau (Texas Word Books, Waco, Texas, 1975).

JAMES, ELMORE: *Singer, guitarist, band leader (the Broomdusters), songwriter. Born Richland, Mississippi, January 27, 1918; died Chicago, Illinois, May 24, 1963.*

Elmore James's career provided a key link between roots blues and the R&B/blues-rock era. As a teenager he picked up pointers on the musical styles of people like the legendary bluesman Robert Johnson, later adding innovations of his own that took advantage of the capabilities of new electrified instruments—innovations that had a major impact on the career of blues performers of the post–World War II years as well as many future rock stars in the United States and United Kingdom.

He was born Elmore Brooks near one of the small towns in the Mississippi Delta region, already in the 1920s a hotbed of roots blues music by itinerant black performers. Some of those artists were relations or family friends, and even as a boy Elmore was trying to learn to play the guitar and sing some of the songs he heard at local parties or entertainment spots. One of his most important discoveries, though, didn't come from local musicians, but from exposure to Hawaiian guitarists who came through the area on tour and used metal tubes to get unusual sounds from their instruments. Elmore began to experiment with this slide guitar technique, eventually developing a unique sound that in time made him a major attraction with black audiences on the Mississippi and Arkansas blues circuit.

Among performers he toured with from the mid-1930s into the '50s were Sonny Boy Williamson (Rice Miller) and Robert Jr. Lockwood. He was something of a mentor for Williamson, eventually helping him get a recording contract in 1951 with Trumpet Records. (In the early '50s, Trumpet recorded material from a number of blues artists in Jackson, Mississippi.) From Lockwood, stepson of Robert Johnson, he gained insight into Johnson's performing style, which Lockwood had learned from his stepfather. Elmore's sets typically included numbers derived from Johnson (whom he met in 1937), including "Dust My Broom," "Ramblin' on My Mind," and "Crossroads."

The post–World War II proliferation of electric guitar technology had a profound effect on James's career. As Sam Charters noted in *The Bluesmen*, "Suddenly effects were possible that hadn't been before—like the slide technique of Elmore James. With an electric guitar he could sustain tones and emphasize the dramatic elements of what he was doing in a way he couldn't do with an acoustic instrument. The electric guitar also made it possible for a musician to play for a large audience without essentially changing the individualistic or personally expressive aspects of the blues."

In 1952 Trumpet issued Elmore's single of "Dust My Broom," which quickly became a hit with black record buyers all the way from New Orleans to Chicago. Elmore quickly made it his theme song and organized a backing band he called the Broomdusters. Health problems in the mid-1950s tended to restrict his touring activities. While he spent time in other places, particularly Chicago, he tended to stay close to his home region, where, besides giving shows in "chitlin' circuit" venues, for a time he also was a disc jockey on local radio. Meanwhile he continued to turn out new sides for various labels such as Flair and Meteor, including such self-penned numbers as "Dust My Blues," "Bleeding Heart," "Shake Your Moneymaker," "The Sky Is Crying," "Twelve Years Old Boy," and "Hand in Hand."

In the late '50s and early '60s the growing dominance of rock 'n' roll hurt the sales of his recordings. To make ends meet he moved to Chicago, where income from shows at major blues clubs helped compensate for reduced record payments. Still, he continued to add to his recording catalog thanks to strong support from producer Bobby Robinson. Some of his most impressive tracks, in fact, resulted from those sessions, recordings that had important future influence on many rock and soul stars. Though few pop music fans in the United States were even aware of him, by the early 1960s he was gaining a major reputation with overseas music lovers in Britain and throughout Europe.

While staying at the home of a cousin, Homesick James (James Williamson) in May 1963, he suffered a fatal heart attack. In the years that followed Homesick James carried on Elmore's tradition, while people like Jimi Hendrix and original Fleetwood Mac guitarist Jeremy Spencer gained major recording and concert success with covers of some of James's songs and their own versions of Elmore's bottleneck guitar styles. English blues rock great John Mayall recorded "Mister James" in tribute to him.

Though James recorded for only a little more than a decade, he left a huge reservoir of music that was issued and reissued over the following decades in the United States and United Kingdom, with much still in print in the late 1990s on such labels as Ace and Charly. His album credits from the '60s included *Blues after Hours* ('61); *Original Folk Blues* ('64); *Something inside of Me* ('68); *To Know a Man* ('69); *Whose Muddy Shoes* (Chess, '69); and *Blues in My Heart, Rhythm in My Soul* ('69). Seventies releases comprised *The Legend of Elmore James* ('70); *Cotton Patch Hotfoots* ('74); and *All Them Blues* ('76). During the '80s, reissues included *One Way Out* (Charly, '80); *The Best of Elmore James* ('81); *Got to Move* (Charly, '81); *King of the Slide Guitar* and *Red Hot Blues* ('83); *The Original Meteor* and *Flair Sides* (Ace, '84); *The Elmore James Collection* ('85); *Let's Cut It* (Ace, '86); *Shake Your Moneymaker* (Charly, '86); *King of the Bottleneck Blues* and *Pickin' the Blues* ('86); *Greatest Hits* ('87);

and *Chicago Golden Years* ('88). In 1990 his biggest hit was the title track for still another reissue album, *Dust My Broom,* on Tomato Records, followed by *The Sky is Crying: The History of Elmore James* on Rhino in 1993.

JAMES, ETTA *Singer. Born Los Angeles, California, January 25, 1938.*

A singer with great vitality and the ability to modify her style as musical trends changed, Etta James remained a favorite of rhythm & blues followers for decades. Among R&B female vocalists, only Dinah Washington and Ruth Brown had more top-10 hits than Etta over the period from the early 1950s to the early 1970s. But Etta was at home with many other kinds of songs. She could sing low-down blues, fast-paced rock 'n' roll, and was adept at jazz singing as well.

She was born Jamesetta Hawkins in Los Angeles, California, the daughter of a fourteen-year-old-girl and an absentee father. For much of her youth she was brought up by foster parents, but when her foster mother died when she was twelve, she found a new home with her real mother in San Francisco. She had sung gospel music in a choir in earlier years, but in San Francisco her associations were secular, not religious, and by the time she was in her early teens she was influenced by the blues sounds of performers like Guitar Slim, Roy Milton, and Charles Brown. During those years, she told interviewers, she also sang jazz with a group called the Peaches. "We sounded like the Hi-Los. We liked Gerry Mulligan and Chet Baker."

Like dozens of other soul stars, Etta was brought into the spotlight by Johnny Otis. As Johnny recounts the incident: "I was playing the Fillmore in San Francisco in the early 1950s. That was before it became a rock center; it was a ghetto theater then. We got there early and I went to my hotel room to rest. My manager called the room and said: 'There's a girl here who wants to sing for you.' I said: 'Tell her to see me at the theater.' She grabbed the phone and said: 'No! I want to sing for you now.' So I said come on up. She arrived with two little girls with her. After she sang a little, I was so impressed I called her mother and said I was taking Etta to Los Angeles with me. She stayed at my house and we wrote 'Roll with Me Henry' and it became a hit."

That song was an answer to Hank Ballard's 1954 hit, "Work with Me, Annie," which has such lines as "Annie please don't cheat/Give me all my meat." Etta's song was slightly less off-color than "Annie." The opening verse ended: "Roll with me, Henry/You better roll it while the rollin' is on." The record was released by Modern Records (owned by the Bihari Brothers of Los Angeles, who recorded much of Otis's material over the years) under the title "Wallflower" and became a top-10 R&B hit in 1955. A milder cover version ("Dance with Me Henry" by white singer Georgia Gibbs) eventually gained the lion's share of the record sales.

During the mid-1950s, Etta became one of the most popular members of Johnny Otis's show. Her subsequent hits on the Modern Label included "Good Rockin' Daddy" and "Most of All."

In the late 1950s, though Etta remained popular with R&B fans as a performer, her recording success toned down considerably. At the start of the 1960s, however, she signed a contract with Chicago-based Chess Records and began a new and even more rewarding phase of her career. As a solo artist in 1960, she had such best-sellers on the R&B charts as "All I Could Do Was Cry" and "My Dearest Darling" on Chess and its Argo subsidiary. She also teamed with Harvey Fuqua, formerly of Harvey and the Moonglows, for the top duo of the year in soul. Their Chess single "If I Can't Have You" reached the top 5 on the soul charts and made the general charts as well. With Argo, Etta demonstrated a style of singing somewhat different from her earlier efforts. It had considerably more gospel and blues content rather than the rough, strident inflections of old-time R&B.

During the first half of the '60s, Etta's name was rarely off the charts. In 1961, she had the top-10 hits "At Last" and "Trust in Me" and, in 1962, "Something's Got a Hold on Me" and "Stop the Wedding." In 1963, she had one of her greatest successes, "Pushover."

During the mid-1960s, Etta's career was plagued by drug addiction that sometimes sidelined her to her home in Los Angeles for long periods of time. She fought back and managed to keep going, despite occasional lapses, gaining such hits as "Tell Mamma" (1968) and "Loser's Weepers" (1970), both on another Chess subsidiary, Cadet.

Her drug of choice at the time, she later recalled, was heroin. As she told Richard Cromelin of the *Los Angeles Times* ("Rollin' with Etta," Calendar Section, November 1, 1992), "All of my role models at the time, the ones I looked up to most, were heroin addicts. Ray Charles, Billie Holiday . . . Chet Baker, all those people I admired were like that, and I think subconsciously I thought that was a cool thing.

"Sometimes I look back on it and remember being in a hotel or something and being very sick and saying to myself, 'Should I just kill myself now?' A few times I remembered that. I remember being so devastated. Like, 'Oh my God, am I gonna be like this all my life?' It was really sad."

Etta had many Cadet albums that made the charts. Her LPs included *At Last* and *Second Time Around* (1961); *Etta James' Top Ten,* and *Etta James Sings for Lovers* (1963); *Etta James Rocks the House* (1964); *Queen of Soul* (1965); *Call My Name* (1967); and *Funk* (1970). One of her best (though flawed) collections came out in 1971. Called *Peaches,* the Chess LP of some of her early recordings demonstrated why the emotion she could pack into her husky, powerful voice made her one of the truly awesome performers in R&B.

But while *Peaches* chronicled her beginnings, renewed problems with drugs in the early 1970s threatened to write an early end to her career. Fortunately, she entered a drug rehabilitation center in late 1972 for a year and a half.

She then completed a new album on Chess, *Come a Little Closer* (1974), which unfortunately showed arrangements straining for commercial rather than creative success. Her last album for Chess, *Etta Is Betta Than Evah,* (1977), saw her focusing on raw R&B stylings, but again best-seller status eluded her. Still she remained a shining star to her musical peers, including Van Morrison (with whom she toured in the mid-1970s) and the jazz/R&B fans who gave her thunderous ovations for her sets at the Montreux and Monterey Jazz Festivals of those years.

After completing her 1977 album for Chess, she was contractually free to seek a new alignment and she signed with Warner Brothers. With famed producer Jerry Wexler supervising, she completed one of her freshest post-'60s LPs, *Deep in the Night* (April 1978). Though critically applauded, the album wasn't a best-seller. Etta continued to play mostly small clubs in the late 1970s before being asked to open for the major 1979 Rolling Stones tour. It gave her greatly increased exposure to new fans, but she developed a new addiction, this time to cocaine and alcohol. Her concert opportunities dwindled, and in the early 1980s many music fans were hardly aware she was still alive. Once more she struggled back, urged on by her husband and two young sons, and finally gave up her second set of drug crutches.

Knowing the Olympic Games were scheduled for Los Angeles in 1984, she sent a card to Mayor Tom Bradley asking if she could take part. This resulted in her singing "When the Saints Come Marching In" at the opening ceremonies and sparked renewed career chances for her, initially for movie and TV projects.

She told reporter Don Waller in late 1985: "What's happening is that all the kids who grew up listening to me on their transistor radios in the '50s and '60s are now working for Steven Spielberg and network television and all that and they remember me from my records."

She said that with a smile, but it wasn't far from the truth. Among other things, the soundtrack for Spielberg's film hit *Back to the Future* included her vocal of "Wallflower." She also recorded "The Blues Don't Leave" for the film *Heartbreakers*. Another mid-1980s break was a bar scene in an episode of the TV series *Insiders* that focused on her singing.

Still, she wasn't the mass-audience favorite she should have been, and she agreed her long bout with heroin abuse was a factor. She told Waller she had been able to stay clean of heroin for over ten years as of the mid-1980s, though the problems with cocaine had intervened. Looking back on her mid-'70s heroin times, she said, "I used to count how long I'd been off the stuff and now I don't. How did I do it? The judge sent me to a shrink 'cause I kept writing bad checks and I told him what was wrong. So they sent me to detox and helped me see that it was gonna be a matter of life or death, and I decided I wasn't gonna kill myself.

"That's why I don't care to associate with a lot of other entertainers. It's not the drugs, it's just that I've heard all that jive talk and ego games for too long. When I first started out, touring was fun—ridin' those old buses, eatin' sardines out of a can, white folks runnin' you out of town, and everybody talkin' about it for six months afterward."

By the late 1980s, both her career and personal finances were steadily improving. After "Wallflower" showed up on the movie soundtrack, she sued for royalties and won a healthy settlement. When MCA bought the Chess catalog not long afterward many of her albums became available to the public again, and she turned out some new ones on Island Records, *Seven Year Itch* in 1988 and *Stickin' to My Guns* in '89. She also performed at the concert honoring Chuck Berry's sixtieth birthday, and her contributions wowed critics and audiences when the film of the event, *Hail! Hail! Rock 'n' Roll,* was released in October 1987.

Coming into the '90s, she was drug-free and exuberant as she continued to establish new career milestones. For one thing, she could place on her wall a career achievement plaque from the Rhythm and Blues Foundation. For another, she had more headline opportunities in major venues and pop music festivals than ever before and she often was featured in TV variety shows at home and abroad. MCA released the *Essential Etta James* in 1993, a double-disc retrospective, and *Her Best* in '97. In January 1993 she was inducted into the Rock and Roll Hall of Fame, and in early 1994 she made the R&B and jazz charts with a new album, *Mystery Lady (Songs of Billie Holiday)*, that won the Grammy for Best Jazz Vocal Performance of 1994 (presented on the globally televised awards program in March '95). Etta previously had been nominated for Grammys on four different occasions, but this was her first victory in the competition. In a celebratory set at the House of Blues venue in West Hollywood she won standing ovations for a set that included such numbers as "I Just Want to Make Love to You," "How Strong Is a Woman," and even her soul version of the Eagles' "Take It to the Limit." In 1995, she wrote about her life in her autobiography, *Rage to Survive*.

On June 23, 1996, she received another honor when the National Association for the Advancement of Colored People presented her with its Lifetime Achievement Award during ceremonies at the Queen Mansion in Los Angeles's Hancock Park neighborhood. During 1997 Etta was on the road again, playing venues like the House of Blues in West Hollywood, California, in support of a fine new collection on Windham Hill's Private Music Records, *Love's Been Rough on Me*, followed by *Life, Love & the Blues* in 1998, and *Heart of a Woman* in 1999.

JAMES, SKIP: *Singer, guitarist, pianist, songwriter. Born Bentonia, Mississippi, June 9, 1902; died Philadelphia, Pennsylvania, October 3, 1969.*

The mid-1960s saw a great revival of interest in the folk blues, leading to rediscovery of many very talented performers. One was Nehemiah "Skip" James of Mississippi, who had achieved a reputation with folk purists on the basis of a handful of recordings made in 1931.

Skip had the advantage of being born into a musical family, though along with this went the problems of living in the black ghettos of the South. His father, a Baptist minister, could play both organ and guitar. At seven or eight, when Skip became interested in playing the guitar from listening to Bentonia performers Henry Stucky and Rich Griffith, his father was able to help his son learn to play.

The guitar, as noted by Bruce Jackson in *Sing Out!* Magazine ("The Personal Blues of Skip James," January '66, p. 27), cost $2.50. James and the guitar became almost inseparable. Jackson quotes James, reminiscing: "It was just in me, I guess, and I was just graftin' after it. I would just sit still until . . . I didn't have sense enough to know how far to go and how hungry I'd get . . . 'cause my mind was on the music, what I was tryin' to learn."

At twelve, when he was starting high school in Yazoo City, Mississippi, he began taking piano lessons, but abandoned them because the $1.50 cost per lesson was too high. Money problems caused him to leave high school before graduation. He worked at odd jobs from Mississippi through Texas and back. He took his guitar along and learned many new songs on the way. In his late teens, he got a sawmill job fifty miles south of Memphis. There he met a dance hall pianist, Will Crabtree, and teamed up with him for a while. He left Crabtree to work in a barrelhouse in Memphis.

In the 1920s, he went back to Mississippi moving to the state capital, Jackson. For most of the decade he remained in Jackson, working at odd jobs and playing at various clubs around town. His musicianship, coupled with some of his original compositions, won him a degree of fame among blues fans in the region. In 1931, his then-roommate, Johnny Temple, and two other friends found that H. C. Speir Music Company of Jackson was looking for new blues talent for Paramount Records.

They talked Skip into auditioning for Speir. Speir and several others listened to Skip play a song called "Devil Blues" and signed him to a two-year contract. Skip was sent to the Paramount studios in Grafton, Wisconsin, two days later. There he spent two days recording twenty-six songs, including several of his own compositions, such as "Hard Times" and ".22-20." The last named was composed to order on the spot in about three minutes' time.

Not too much happened. Only a few of the songs were released by Paramount. Skip went home to Jackson and for a while completely gave up music. Later in the 1930s, he returned to music briefly by organizing his own gospel quartet, the Dallas Texas Jubilee Singers, and becoming a Baptist Minister in 1932 in his father's church. By 1946, when he was ordained a Methodist minister, music had again become a thing of the past for him.

During the 1940s and '50s, Skip worked at various jobs, including timber cutter, tractor operator, and plantation overseer. In 1964, John Fahey, the head of a small label, Takoma Records, and his associates Ed Denson, Bill Barth, and Henry Vestine, went to Mississippi to look for old folk recordings and for Skip. After a lengthy search, Fahey and Barth found him in a hospital in Mississippi.

They taped several songs, including "Devil Blues" and "All Night Long." The material was used to gain financial help from folk enthusiasts in other parts of the country to help pay Skip's medical bills. Soon Skip was given his first singing job in decades at the Bitter Lemon in Memphis. In July 1964, Skip was taken to Newport where he won a standing ovation from the audience.

From then on, he was in demand for concerts and club jobs in many parts of the east. He appeared in short order at Toronto's Mariposa Festival, Ontario Place in Washington, D.C., the Unicorn in Boston, and the Gaslight in New York. Interest in James was spurred by the release of several albums he recorded in the mid-1960s, such as the Melodisc LP *Skip James: Greatest of the Delta Blues Singers* and the Vanguard Records releases *Skip James Today!* in 1966 and *Devil Got My Woman* in 1968. Right up to the present the latter collections are considered among the finest roots blues discs of all time. As Greil Marcus commented in the 1983 edition of the *Rolling Stone Record Guide,* "These two modern recordings are among the most important blues albums ever made. The sound is full of presence, and the performance full of life—charged with bitterness, love, desire, and a sense of fun (most evident on *Today!* with 'I'm So Glad,' first recorded by James in the thirties and later made famous by [the English rock group] Cream). James' high, ghostly voice pierces the night air—it always seems like night when these albums are playing—and his guitar shadows the moon."

In agreement with other blues critics, Marcus placed James among the top ranks of singers, guitarists, and pianists to work with the framework of Mississippi Delta blues. He argued that "because he was also one of the more idiosyncratic, his formal influence has been much less than that of Robert Johnson, Charley Patton,

Son House, or even Tommy Johnson. His impact has been as an *inspiration*—on hearing him play, either on his original recordings or, after his rediscovery [in 1965] in live performances, any number of musicians were moved to deepen the passion and commitment of their own music."

Unfortunately, James had only a few years in the spotlight before passing away in the fall of 1969. In 1971 Biograph Records issued the album *Early Blues Recordings—1931,* which provided such Paramount recordings by James as "Devil Got My Woman" and "If You Haven't Got Any Hay."

In 1996 Rounder released the Vestapol Videos tape showing Skip and other blues greats in concert at the Newport Folk Festival. The video was titled *Devil Got My Woman/Blues from Newport 1966 featuring Skip James, Howlin' Wolf, Son House, Rev. Pearly Brown, Bukka White.* In 1994 Yazoo Records issued *Complete Early Recordings.*

JANSCH, BERT: *Singer, guitarist, songwriter. Born Glasgow, Scotland, November 3, 1943.*

Though hardly as well known as the Beatles, or the Rolling Stones, the introverted Bert Jansch arguably ranked with them as one of the foremost products of the English music scene in the 1960s. As a writer and performer, he influenced the development of folk-rock at home and abroad, through his solo career and with the Pentangle, starting in the mid-1960s and continuing into the early 1980s. (Neil Young and Jimmy Page have acknowledged his influence.) After some gaps in his career, Jansch returned to form in the 1990s.

He was born in Glasgow but grew up in Edinburgh; his father was Austrian and his mother Scottish. His maternal grandfather used to play banjo in blackface with the New Christy Minstrels.

Jansch was inspired to take up the guitar after hearing British skiffle player Lonnie Donegan. Recalling his early years to Mark Humphrey (*Frets,* March 1980, pp. 18–23), he said, "When I was a kid, the first things I heard were people like Elvis Presley and Little Richard. That was very early. My interest in guitar started then. I did have piano lessons when I was about seven; they went on for six months. My mother couldn't afford to keep them up, which is why I didn't continue them. I actually tried to make guitars when I was nine or ten; in fact, the second one I tried to make was even playable, and I learned to chord a D on it. . . . But it wasn't until after I left school that I started to earn enough money to buy a guitar." (Among other things, he worked as a gardener, hence the title of a 1992 compilation album.)

His departure from school occurred when he was fifteen, a period when he also began hanging around a local folk club called the Halwff (Scottish for "meeting place"). He was influenced by American bluesmen Brownie McGhee and Sonny Terry, and by Jesse Fuller,

who performed in Scotland. He also knew Scottish folksinger Hamish Imlach and the music of Big Bill Broonzy. Jansch owned one of his EPs and "played it to death," as he told *Guitar Player.* He studied guitar with two of the co-owners of the Halwff, traditional guitarist Archie Fisher and Jill Doyle, guitarist Davy Graham's sister. One day she showed Jansch a record that included Graham's song "Angi," informing him that Graham was her brother. Like many guitarists at the time, Jansch had toiled to learn the tune. "If you could play 'Angi,' then you'd made it," Jansch said in the 1992 documentary film *Acoustic Routes.* "You could actually stand up in a folk club and say, 'Here I am.'"

Six months later, Doyle and Fisher left the Halwff club; Jansch was forced to fill in. "There was no one to continue with the lessons," Jansch told Humphrey. "Being the most advanced player there, I ended up giving the guitar lessons myself. I never even contemplated singing. They were usually Woody Guthrie songs, with some Big Bill Broonzy, Brownie McGhee, and Leadbelly. It was some time after that that I plucked up enough courage to actually sing in front of an audience. I got into performing because there was a pub down the road that used to have folk music and—being very poor at the time, and not earning enough money from the guitar lessons—I found that if I got up and did two or three numbers, everybody would buy me a beer."

In his late teens, Jansch was influenced by folk-music friends (and roommates in Edinburgh) Clive Palmer, who introduced Jansch to traditional American folk songs, and Robin Williamson, co-founders of the Incredible String Band. Bert decided finally to branch out beyond Edinburgh. He traveled to Morocco where, as Colin Harper of *Folk Roots* reported, he married "a young lady solely to get her a visa for Morocco." He was deported back to England three months later.

For a while he went back and forth between London and Scotland, increasing his contacts in the folk world and adding to his performing credits at folk clubs in both places. It was in those clubs that he developed his aggressive guitar style. He told Humphrey: "Some nights in a folk club, if the audience was too noisy, I would get much more aggressive with the guitar. Instead of just playing it, I used to pull the strings—snap them really, so that it became a percussive thing. And I slowly started to use that as an effect. But it used to be just from sheer anger at the audience being so noisy."

By then he had begun to write original material. He wrote his first song, "Green Are Your Eyes," when he was seventeen. One of his most haunting songs from that period was "Needle of Death" (about the loss of a friend, Buck Polly, to a heroin overdose), which he wrote when he was nineteen. The song about drug addiction broke new ground on the British music scene.

In the 1960s he met Paul Simon and came in contact with the music of Bob Dylan in London. "I didn't use to take much notice of Paul Simon, and I still don't," he told

Humphrey. "But Bob Dylan's songs, the early songs, I liked a lot. They probably influenced me quite a lot."

By the mid-1960s he had a growing reputation as one of England's best young folk artists, an excellent guitarist with a gruff but soulful voice. In 1965 his first solo album, *Bert Jansch,* came out on Transatlantic Records of London. He recorded it in the front room of producer Bill Leader's home. "We had to invite down the neighbors from upstairs and give them a drink to keep 'em quiet," Jansch told Jas Obrecht of *Guitar Player* (May 1994). Considered one of his best, the album includes Jansch's instrumental version of "Angi" and several of his own compositions, including "Needle of Death" and "Do You Hear Me Now," later recorded by Donovan. He quickly followed his debut with two more solo albums: *It Don't Bother Me* (Transatlantic 1965) and *Jack Orion* (Vanguard 1966), with a nine-minute title track (revival folksinger Anne Briggs had taught him "Jack Orion" and his trademark "Blackwater Side") and the traditional song "Nottamun Town."

As British critic Karl Dallas described Jansch's style in the liner notes for the Shanachie compilation *The Best of Bert Jansch* (1980): "Often, Bert's instrumentals at that time were almost little more than exercises in arpeggios—but such arpeggios! . . . Upon these shimmering bases, Bert would construct the melodies of his songs, sometimes rudimentary things in themselves, like a ground-bass derived upwards instead of downwards. His voice did not arouse universal admiration—I remember one fellow-critic describing it as 'like the sound of dirty water disappearing down a plughole'—but for me it had a sort of gritty credibility. . . .'"

In 1966 Jansch had the chance to appear on the British variety show *Ready, Steady, Go!,* which would have given his career a boost. Instead the opportunity went to Donovan, whose career took off. Donovan went on to record some Jansch songs in tribute to his mentor on the *Sunshine Superman* LP: "Bert's Blues" and "House of Jansch."

During a three-year period, Jansch roomed in various flats with another promising young guitarist, John Renbourn. They made an album together, released by Transatlantic in 1966 under the title *Bert and John.* (They later collaborated on *After the Dance* on Shanachie in 1992.)

"In my view, he is the most outstanding songwriter and the most outstanding guitar player, barring Davy Graham, who was the seminal figure just before Bert," Renbourn told Obrecht. "What sets Bert apart, really, is his individuality. There's nobody quite like him."

For a time, the two ran their own folk club in London's Soho district called the Scot's Hoose. Among those who frequented or performed at the club were friends and associates like singer Jacqui McShee, bassist Danny Thompson, and drummer Terry Cox, who soon were to join Bert and John in the Pentangle, which synthesized folk, jazz, and blues—even Indian—influences. The Pentangle, founded in 1967, was the first of the big three

British folk-rock bands to invade the United States in the late 1960s, followed by Fairport Convention and Steeleye Span.

Over the next half-dozen years the group achieved considerable success on both sides of the Atlantic. The group's albums include *The Pentangle* (Reprise, 1968), *Sweet Child* (1968), *Basket of Light* (1969), and *Cruel Sister* (1971). Pentangle was still held in high regard around the world when it disbanded in 1973. Jansch told Humphrey, "We'd all had enough by then. We had gone around the world about five times; it was literally like three-month tours at a stretch; then a week off and another two-month tour somewhere else. Also, the manager at that time had a policy of sending us out by ourselves to do two-hour shows. We never met any other musicians, because there was nobody else on the bill. It became so insular and you do need to play with other people and meet other people." There was also, as Colin Harper reported in *Folk Roots* (March 1994), a dispute over royalties with their record company. (Jansch told *Guitar Player* he didn't play his guitar for two years after the split.)

Nevertheless, in the mid-1970s Bert turned out more solo recordings, such as *Rosemary Lane* in 1971, considered one of his best; *Box of Love* in 1972 and *Moonshine* in 1973 for Reprise Records. Tony Stratton Smith signed Jansch for his Charisma label, and he made *LA Turnaround,* produced by ex-Monkee Mike Nesmith, in 1974; *Santa Barbara Honeymoon* (1975) and *Rare Conundrum* (1977). In the late 1970s Transatlantic released two compilations, *Guitar of Bert Jansch* (1977) and *Anthology* (1978). In 1986 the label also issued *Strolling down the Highway.*

Jansch also toured England and the Continent with various backing musicians. Preparing for one tour of Scandinavia, he found himself in need of a new fiddler when Mike Piggott, who had played on *Rare Conundrum,* couldn't make it. On the advice of a member of the road crew, he contacted Martin Jenkins. The artistic rapport proved excellent, and the new duo of Jansch and Jenkins became a featured act on the concert circuit from the late 1970s into the early 1980s. Adding a third member, bassist Nigel Portman-Smith, they formed the group Conundrum.

(Jenkins, born in London in 1946, brought skills not only as fiddler but also on guitar, mandolin, and mandocello. For some years he was a central figure in a band called Dando-Shaft that finally broke up in 1972. In the mid-1970s, he was part of a folk-rock band from Newcastle, England, called Hedgehog Pie. It was just after that group broke up that he got the invitation from Jansch.)

Among the projects Conundrum worked on at the start of the 1980s was a joint effort with the amateur Cambridge Symphony Orchestra. Jenkins also supported Jansch and Danny Thompson on the instrumental album *Avocet* (1979).

Besides a number of Pentangle collections and the solo LPs noted earlier, Jansch was represented by such solo releases as *Nicola* (1967) and *Birthday Blues* (1969) on Demon and *Lucky Thirteen* (1969) on Vanguard. On U.S.-based labels, Vanguard offered some of his work with John Renbourn on a compilation album titled *Stepping Stones* (1969) rereleased in 1992, while Kicking Mule, besides *Rare Conundrum,* also had the LP *The Best of Bert Jansch.*

In 1981 Los Angeles–based producers John and Richard Chelew brought Jansch to L.A. for a recording session at Silverlake Recording Studio. The result was Jansch's solo album *Heartbreak* (1982), available on the Hannibal/Rykodisc label. The album includes a new version of the traditional song "Blackwater Side," which Jimmy Page had "borrowed" for his tune "Black Mountain Side" years earlier. He also covers Tim Hardin's "If I Were a Carpenter," "Heartbreak Hotel," and the traditional song "Wild Mountain Thyme." He's joined by vocalist Jennifer Warnes and guitarist and mandolinist Albert Lee on the album, not considered one of his best.

Jansch told *Guitar Player* that he tends not to listen to his old albums: "I always tend to think that they could have been or should have been a hundred times better than they actually are, therefore I don't really tend to listen. In fact, I don't really listen to my own albums at all. It's off-putting for future stuff I may do."

The 1970s and 1980s were not happy times for Jansch. After Pentangle disbanded he signed with manager Bruce May, who also managed folksinger Ralph McTell. "I can't skirt around this," McTell told Colin Harper of *Folk Roots* (March 1994). "It was a very bad part of his life. He's had a lot of tragedy in his life; he's made some very bad decisions; he's had women trouble all his life, I think. When I first met John Renbourn—well, I'd known John before I met Bert, and I said 'What's Bert like?' and John said—and this would still stand as a quote—'Well, you can go into a room where he is and you won't see him. He's invisible, he's almost inarticulate, but put a guitar into his hands and he becomes a bloody monster. He just fills the room up and it speaks volumes.'"

In 1990 he released two more solo albums: *Sketches* (Temple Music) and *The Ornament Tree* (Capitol), a traditional album. He became involved in a BBC Scotland and Scottish Film production called *Acoustic Routes,* a 1992 documentary about British guitar music that includes performances by Jansch with Brownie McGhee. The sound track includes guitar work with the two seminal musicians. Jansch also began touring extensively around the world again, and worked on a score for the BBC-TV series *You Can't See the Wood.*

Jansch and Jacqui McShee added Nigel Portman-Smith on bass, for a time fiddler and guitarist Mike Piggott, Peter Kirtley on lead guitar, and Gerry Conway on drums to form what is known as the Second Pentangle. The group toured sporadically and released albums in the 1980s and early 1990s: *Thirteen Down* (1980, Kicking Mule), *Open the Door* (1985) on Varrick Records (with all of the original members except Renbourn; fiddler/guitarist Mike Piggott is added), *In the Round* (1986 Varrick), *So Early in the Spring* on Green Linnet in 1990, *Think of Tomorrow* in 1991 on Green Linnet, and *One More Road* in 1993 on Permanent Records. Some of the original members weren't happy with the new ensemble. "It's no real secret that neither John [Renbourn] nor Danny [Thompson] are at all comfortable with even the existence of such a group with the name 'Pentangle,'" Harper wrote (March 1994).

Jansch also released *From the Outside* in 1985, and *Leather Launderette* in 1988. Compilations include *The Essential Collection Volume 1* (1987), *The Essential Collection Volume 2* (1987), and *The Gardener: Essential Bert Jansch 1965–71* (1992). Transatlantic rereleased the 1969 retrospective album called *The Bert Jansch Sampler.* In 1992, Jansch was featured on *The Art of Fingerstyle Guitar,* on Stefan Grossman's Guitar Artistry imprint, along with Renbourn, Graham, Martin Simpson, and others.

In the 1990s many of Jansch's excellent early CDs were reissued, often two LPs at a time, such as *Nicola/Birthday Blues,* released by Transatlantic; *Bert Jansch/It Don't Bother Me,* by Essential; and *Jack Orion/Nicola* and *Birthday Blues/Rosemary Lane* on Castle, which also released the compilation *Collection. Live at the 12 Bar,* which features his work during 1995 and 1996 at the club, came out as an "authorized bootleg." Another live collection on CD was *BBC Radio 1 In Concert.* Virgin Universal also released *Three Chord Trick* in 1993.

Jansch's 1995 album, *When the Circus Comes to Town,* on Cooking Vinyl, was his first solo release in six years. The album, whose cover is made up to look like a poster for the Big Top, includes Christine Collister on vocals and Mike Piggott on fiddle. It received some favorable reviews; people were happy to see him back in the business. And on the album he returns to his jazz and blues acoustic roots, as well as his traditional British guitar style.

These days Jansch writes songs with a computer, which transcribes his guitar sounds into written notation. He told *Guitar Player* that he likes to write late at night or early in the morning: "The periods when it's quietest. It took me a long while. . . . I had to stop drinking to find that out, that if you get up early in the morning, it's got a completely different atmosphere to any other time of the day, whereas late at night, the other end of it, is sleepy feeling."

In 1997 Jansch toured the United States with his old friend, guitarist Archie Fisher. The following year he released a new solo album, *Toy Balloon,* on Cooking

Vinyl. The tracks include a cover of Jackson C. Frank's "Carnival" and the traditional "She Moved Through the Fair." The rest are Jansch originals, such as the bluesy "Hey Doc," the delicate title track, and the instrumental "Bett's Dance." Another project included a collaboration CD with vocalist Loren Auerbach. At the end of the year Castle released *The Transatlantic Story,* a four-CD retrospective of the label that features early work by Jansch, McTell, and Renbourn. He was also represented in 1998 by a thirty-nine track "best of" album taken from his first seven albums, titled *Blackwater Side* on Recall/Snapper Records. In 1999, Big Beat/Acec released *Young Man's Blues: Live in Glasgow 1962–64.*

The guitar means even more to him now than when he was fifteen: "The more I get older, the more it becomes the central thing," he told *Guitar Player.*

There are those who complain that Jansch never realized his potential. But British guitarist Martin Carthy had another perspective. "He was never somebody who was going to be marketed," Carthy told Colin Harper. "He was just so outrageous and different and hard to get hold of. You might say that Bert missed the boat when Bob Dylan became famous. Did he? Honestly, do you think he did? I don't think he did. I just think it was out of the question. He was never anywhere near where the boat was going from, and if he was he never knew where the gangplank was!"

JEFFERSON, BLIND LEMON: *Singer, songwriter, guitarist. Born Couchman, Texas, September 1893 (previously listed as July 11, 1897); died Chicago, Illinois, December 1929.*

If Blind Lemon Jefferson had only recorded "See That My Grave Is Kept Clean," he would have earned his place in the annals of folk and blues. But he made 100 recordings between 1925 and 1929 and established himself as one of the best-selling blues artists of the 1920s. His influence on the blues is immeasurable. Although he was born in Texas, he traveled widely (often by boxcar) from Chicago to Mississippi. His singing and guitar playing (marked by strumming, the use of harmonics, and intricate fingerpicking flourishes) were difficult to imitate. But he left his mark on Leadbelly (who was his "lead man" for a brief period), T-Bone Walker (who led him around Central Avenue in Dallas), Lightnin' Hopkins (who saw him play as a child), and countless other performers in the folk revival of the late '50s who heard three of his songs on the *Anthology of American Folk Music.*

One of those was "See That My Grave Is Kept Clean." Jefferson opens the song with the lines "There's one kind favor I ask of you. . . . See that my grave is kept clean." His clear voice expresses the fear of the unknown—"My heart stopped beating and my hands got cold"—and a desire for a dignified funeral with "two white horses in a line." At one point he uses his guitar to imitate the sound of death chimes. And yet when Jefferson died of mysterious causes in December 1929, he was laid to rest in an unmarked grave.

Such performers as Hopkins, Mississippi Fred McDowell, Furry Lewis, Dave Van Ronk, Mike Bloomfield, Canned Heat, and Bob Dylan have also recorded "See That My Grave Is Kept Clean" under various titles. Among the other classic songs (he was among the first blues artists to write his own compositions) that Jefferson recorded were "That Black Snake Moan," "Corinna Blues" (a.k.a. "See See Rider"), "Rabbit Foot Blues," "Long Lonesome Blues," "Jack O' Diamonds," and "Prison Cell Blues." He also recorded religious tunes under a pseudonym, Deacon L. J. Bates. In his heyday he sold thousands of records.

Despite his prolific output in the 1920s, little is known about his life and death. There is just one publicity photo of him that shows a rather husky man dressed stiffly in coat and tie and wearing wire-rimmed glasses over dark squinty eyes. At the bottom of the photo, in large cursive (probably not his own) is written "Cordially Yours, Blind Lemon Jefferson."

Recent research indicates that he was born in September 1893 on a farm near Couchman, Texas, not far from the town of Wortham. According to Sam Charters's *The Bluesmen,* Jefferson was the youngest of seven children born to farmer Alec Jefferson and his wife Cassie Banks. He was born blind (although he wore wire-rimmed glasses, an indication that he had some residual sight) and was playing on the streets of Wortham by 1912. Five years later he moved to Dallas, where he played on street corners in the "Deep Ellum" section of town, as well as at all-night parties in the surrounding areas. He did well enough to support a wife, Roberta, whom he married in 1922, and a son named Miles. He also was successful enough to afford a car and a chauffeur. Remarkably, he worked as a wrestler for a time.

In Dallas, he sang in brothels with Leadbelly and later performed with T-Bone Walker. Both remembered him fondly and sang songs about him, such as Leadbelly's "Blind Lemon's Blues." In 1925 a Dallas record store owner and pianist named Sammy Price spotted Jefferson and made a test recording. He sent the demo to Mayo Williams at Paramount, who liked what he heard. Jefferson journeyed to Chicago by early 1926 for his first session. Paramount advertised his recordings, "Booster Blues" and "Dry Southern Blues," in the black newspaper the *Chicago Defender* in April of that year. His records sold so well that record companies sent scouts to sign other male blues artists, such as Blind Blake. As Charters notes: "The high, clear sound of his voice, despite the inadequate acoustical recording techniques, had a startling intensity, and he kept the freely structured rhythms of the field holler and the Texas chain gang in his guitar. The accompaniments, especially on 'Dry Southern Blues,' were very complex, and the relationship between the guitar and the voice was very loose. . . . The guitar had some of the elements of country white 'frailing,' but because of the tension of the vocal line the patterns were often wildly unpredictable. . . . It was a desolate, lost sound, the voice tinged with loneliness, the restless guitar moving below it as though it were looking for a phrase or a run to end its incessant movement."

He became well known in 1926 for his sexually-explicit "That Black Snake Moan," revised from Victoria Spivey's less explicit "Black Snake Blues." Jefferson sings, "Uum, better find my mama soon/I woke up this morning, black snake was makin' such a ruckus in my room." The record sold well, and he later followed up with "Black Snake Dream Blues" and "That Black Snake Moan No. 2." Although most of his recordings were on the Paramount label, OKeh lured him away for a session in Atlanta in March 1927, releasing a revised version of "Black Snake Moan" and "Match Box Blues," later a hit for Carl Perkins in 1955. But by June, Jefferson returned to Paramount, which released a total of forty-three records from several sessions. Paramount even released a birthday record for him with a gray-and-yellow label and a streamer saying "Happy Birthday, Lemon."

Although he was likely never in prison, Jefferson sang such songs as "Blind Lemon's Penitentiary Blues," and "'Lectric Chair Blues." He also covered songs by Bessie Smith ("High Water Blues"), Lonnie Johnson ("Mean Old Bed Bug"), and Leroy Carr ("How Long How Long"). He made his last recordings in September 1929 for Paramount in Richmond, Indiana, a session that included "Bakershop Blues," "Pneumonia Blues," and "That Crawling Baby Blues."

His death, most likely at the end of December 1929, is still shrouded in mystery since no death certificate was ever found. In some versions he suffered a heart attack and was abandoned by his chauffeur, in others he froze to death on the streets of Chicago in subzero temperatures and was found with snow covering his body. Paramount paid pianist Will Ezell to take Lemon's body back to Texas, where he was buried in an unmarked grave in the black section of the Wortham cemetery. In the months following his death several songs were recorded in tribute to Jefferson, including "Wasn't It Sad About Lemon?" by Walter Taylor and John Byrd and "Death of Blind Lemon" by Rev. Emmett Dickinson.

His grave remained unmarked until 1967, when the state of Texas placed a metal historical marker at the site. In 1996 a fan visiting the grave posted a note on the Blues List Internet discussion group that led to a campaign to raise funds for a headstone. Rykodisc/Tradition, which reissued his music on CD, made a donation, as did the Scandinavian Blues Association. As a result, in February 1997 a marble headstone was dedicated at his gravesite with a new birthdate (September 1893)

from recently discovered census data, and backed by enough funds to see that Lemon's "grave is kept clean." He was inducted into the Blues Hall of Fame in 1980.

Jefferson's music can be found on *King of the Country Blues* (1990, Yazoo); *Volume 1, 1926–1929* (Biograph); *Volume 2: Master of the Blues* (Biograph); *Blind Lemon Jefferson* (Milestone); *Immortal* (Milestone); *Volume 2* (Milestone); *Black Snake Moan* (Milestone); *Legends of the Blues, Volume 1* (Columbia); *The Blues Volume 1—A Smithsonian Collection of Classic Blues Singers*; *Blind Lemon Jefferson: Complete Recorded Works, Volume 1–4, 1926–1929* (Document, 1991, four discs); *Penitentiary Blues* (Golden Classics); *Moanin' All Over* (1996, Rykodisc/Tradition); *Blind Lemon Jefferson* (Fantasy); and *Squeeze My Lemon* (1997, Catfish).

JEWEL: *Singer, guitarist, songwriter. Born Homer, Alaska, May 23, 1974.*

She wasn't a rocker, she didn't sing pop ballads like Celine Dion or Mariah Carey, she certainly wasn't into rap, but still Jewel Kilcher managed to place her debut album in the top ranks of the hit charts of 1996. The unique thing about it was the fact that her album was essentially a work of folk music, and avoided the cynicism or despair of many chart hits of the time. Her original lyrics didn't ignore the problems of mean-spiritedness and greed besetting the world, but, as she told Sara Scribner for an article in the *Los Angeles Times* ("Jewel's Folk Gem Is the Real Thing," May 4, 1996), she felt "that people are ready to start feeling hope again. I don't think there are any true cynics alive. They all killed themselves. And I don't think cynicism's necessarily smarter, it's just safer."

Her home state was Alaska, where her immigrant Swiss grandfather had homesteaded near the town of Homer. She and her two brothers grew up in what amounted to pioneering conditions, on a farm with no shower, no TV, and an outhouse bathroom that was ice-cold much of the year. But she recalled there was considerable warmth in family life in her early years with her parents, a singer-songwriting duo, often leading the children in singing or encouraging them to listen to music by artists like Odetta, Nina Simone, and Ella Fitzgerald. Her parents performed on the Alaskan folk circuit, and when Jewel was six she joined the act, bringing considerable audience applause for her yodeling skills.

A few years later, however, Jewel's parents divorced; her mother eventually relocated to San Diego, California. Jewel's father continued performing, and for seven years Jewel toured with him, singing in bars and restaurants. One of the things that took her mind off her family's breakup, she said later, was an interest in writing poetry. Her mother had always exposed the three siblings to art and poetry as well as music. "Through these lessons I was given a tool. After my parents divorced, I started writing poetry a lot because I didn't always know how to express myself. That, to me, is the real beauty of writing; it makes you more intimate with yourself."

In her mid-teens, Jewel began to save money to further her education. At sixteen she had enough put aside to finance her final two high school years as a performing arts student at the Interlochen Fine Arts Academy in Michigan. She stated, "My two years there were a turning point. I saw a bigger world. I immersed myself in everything—drama, dance, sculpture, music." During her senior year she learned to play guitar and used the instrument to develop some of her original song ideas. One of the compositions was the folk-based "Who Will Save Your Soul."

After graduating at eighteen, she moved to San Diego to be with her mother. For a time, she worked at conventional jobs like waitressing. Sexual harassment by her boss made her quit that position and was one factor that caused her to take a closer look at what she wanted for her future. Despite the pleasant surroundings of California beach city life, she said, "This was a difficult time for me. I felt a lot of social pressure to figure out what I was gonna do with the rest of my life. I had no desire to go to college, but I also felt no peace in traveling or just bumming around. I got a number of dead end jobs . . . got fired a couple of times. I was frightened and a little depressed. The idea of spending my life in a 9-to-5 job made me feel trapped and hopeless."

Her mother suggested that they both just live in their cars, which, in Jewel's case, was a van. Between them they worked out a close-to-the-bone budget; Jewel's diet consisted mainly of carrots and peanut butter. Surfing helped relax her, and when not at the beach she spent much of her time writing poetry and songs and making friends with local musicians at San Diego–area coffeehouses. She performed in small venues solo or with other musicians until she was given her own weekly set at the Innerchange Coffeehouse in the Pacific Beach section of the city. Before long, word of her excellent voice and innovative songs began to get around and her shows began drawing capacity crowds. She reminded many listeners and local media people of artists like Joni Mitchell and Rickie Lee Jones, though she said she'd never heard their music until after her own album came out.

Word about her promise reached executives at Atlantic Records before she was out of her teens, and she signed with the label in 1994. Her debut disc, *Pieces of You,* was issued in February 1995. Both Jewel and Atlantic knew it was a challenge for a folksinger to succeed with a mainstream audience in the mid-'90s musical environment. In support of the album she accepted engagements anywhere they could be gained—in small folk venues, coffeehouses, and college campuses. She won the attention, fortunately, of many established performers and was given the chance in 1995 and early '96 to open for people like Bob Dylan,

Peter Murphy, the Ramones, and Liz Phair. An indication that her star was rising was her selection to sing the role of Dorothy in a concert version of *The Wizard of Oz* presented at the Lincoln Center in New York City in the fall of 1995. Others in the program were Jackson Browne, Roger Daltrey of the Who, and Natalie Cole.

These efforts started paying off in 1996. The album's first single, "Who Will Save Your Soul," started to get airplay on alternative rock stations, and sales of the album started to accelerate. By May '96 it was inside the *Billboard* Hot 200 chart's top 50 and was number twenty in California. When Jewel hosted MTV's *Alternative Nation* show, there was a video of her debut single available. Watching the proceedings, she told Scribner, "All the other videos were the most angry, dark, depressing—and then along came my little song. I thought it was hilarious, this dorky little thing after [the group] Marilyn Manson."

But she didn't underrate what the song was meant to convey: "We can make each other's lives worth living . . . even miraculous, . . . or we can make it just hellish and spread a lot of crap. That's what the song was kinda about for me."

Jewel continued to build a sizable following during 1996 and 1997. *Pieces of You* became a best-seller, still in the national top 20 in July 1997. By then it had reached multiplatinum totals of over 5 million sold, one of only seven albums to do that in that time period. (On September 24 the R.I.A.A. certified the album had sold 6 million copies, and on November 5 an award for 7 million was presented.) The single "You Were Meant for Me" from the album also did well, receiving R.I.A.A. gold record certification on February 28 and platinum on June 20. During the summer of 1997 she was one of the artists taking part in the Lilith Fair series of concerts organized by Sarah McLachlan. In December it was announced that she would make her film debut in Universal Pictures' *To Live On,* which was to be directed by the highly respected Ang Lee.

Jewel was asked to sing "The Star-Spangled Banner" at professional football's Super Bowl XXXII. To overcome problems of crowd noise, it was decided she would lip-synch the song, but this resulted in an embarrassing moment when she missed her opening cue and had to catch up with the recorded version. Late in the year her second album, *Spirit,* was released by Atlantic. Issue date was November 17, and the disc sold 368,000 the first week to reach number three on the album charts, rising to number two before falling back to slightly lower levels. In 1999 Atlantic issued her Christmas album, *Joy—A Holiday Collection.*

JIMENEZ, LEONARDO "FLACO": *accordionist, singer, songwriter. Born San Antonio, Texas, March 11, 1939.*

Sitting in a Japanese restaurant in Los Angeles, Leonardo "Flaco" Jimenez looks slightly out of place. A tall and skinny man in cowboy boots, he does nothing to disguise his Tex-Mex roots. The tattoos on both forearms—on the left, a rose and his wife's name, Adela; on the right, an eagle—give him a worldly air. In fact, Flaco added rock, blues, and country to the *conjunto* music he learned as a child, and influenced people at home and abroad. He helped revitalize Tex-Mex accordion music, inspiring people like Los Lobos's David Hidalgo. He played with Linda Ronstadt, John Hiatt, Dwight Yoakam, Bob Dylan, and, of course, Ry Cooder. By the mid-1990s, even the Rolling Stones had incorporated Flaco's accordion into their sound.

Many have the misconception that Flaco plays Mexican music. Actually, the *conjunto* evolved from European dance hall music. The music dates back to the turn of the century in Texas's Rio Grande Valley combining German and Czech polkas and waltzes with Mexican *norteño* style. *Conjunto,* also refers to an ensemble featuring accordion, *bajo-sexto* (an oversize twelve-string guitar), bass, drums, and vocals.

Leonardo Jimenez was one of seven children born to Santiago and Luisa Jimenez. The accordion was passed on from his grandfather and father to him. "Blood speaks by itself," says Flaco, who plays by ear. "Music is in the blood."

Grandfather Patricio learned by hanging out at the dances in the German settlement, New Branfels, where he heard bands playing polkas on Hohner diatonic accordions. Leonardo's father, Santiago, the original "Flaco" ("skinny one"), started playing professionally in 1936, when he recorded his first song, "Dieces Pescado." He put his own spin on *conjunto,* adding vocals to the instrumental form in the late '40s. Santiago had regional hits with his 78s, recorded on Decca, Globe, Mercury, and RCA. His band packed them in at the El Gaucho Garden. He never taught his son. Leonardo learned by observing him teach children in the neighborhood. "There was no sit down and I'll teach you how to do it," he says. "When the student left I knew the piece already."

Santiago Jimenez performed with a *bajo-sexto* player named Henry Zimmerle, Sr. The two fathers decided to get their sons, Leonardo Jimenez and Henry Zimmerle, Jr., to play accordion and *bajo-sexto.* "Like father, like son," Flaco says. "We were not old enough to play in nightclubs but we played in birthday parties. We got paid with plenty of ice cream and soda." They called their band Los Caporales.

Flaco heard the German music coming out of KGMB radio and at night, the country music from KONO's *Cowboy Jamboree.* At seven, he played in his father's band for a few numbers. At fourteen, he sat in with his father on *bajo-sexto* to record a polka, "Alma de Texas," released as a 78 on Corona Records. "When I did my first recording with my dad I broke a string," Flaco recalls. "I got scared. I had to stop and I felt so guilty because it was sounding really good. My dad just

pats me on the back and says, 'We've got more strings here so put another one on and we'll hit it again.' "

In 1955, Flaco, then sixteen, and his friend Henry Zimmerle, Jr., fifteen, were recruited by bassist Mike Garza and drummer Richard Herrera, who were desperate for an accordionist and *bajo-sexto* player for their band during Christmas. They became known as Los Caminantes, the most popular band in San Antonio for the next two years before Flaco left in 1958. He began recording under his real name, Leonardo, for the RIO label, cutting more than sixty sides during the two years he was with the band. In 1957 he cut a polka, "Hasta La Vista," and had a regional hit for Tipico Records. (In 1995 Arhoolie issued a CD of Flaco's RIO recordings called *Flaco's First.*)

He began going by "Flaco" after his father started working as Santiago again. "My father said, 'You take over and start recording under Flaco Jimenez,' " he recalls. "That was quite a present. He handed it to me and I took over."

His reputation grew during the late 1950s and early '60s as he had a string of local hits. In the mid-1950s, Flaco developed a much faster style than his father's. "At that time I was just playing the traditional *conjunto* that my dad played," he says. "Still, I had it in mind that I was going to change the traditional sound. I made some additions of country and rock 'n' roll. I started changing from the traditional to more progressive. People didn't realize that a simple accordion could play more than polkas. So I started learning progressive and jazzy runs."

Beginning in 1962, Flaco served in the army. He spent a year in Korea, but says he was lucky: "I got drafted when Korea ended and got out when Vietnam started. I think they knew I'd rather hear an accordion than a rifle shot."

He left the service in 1964; while his father worked as a custodian and refused to travel, Flaco took to the road. Another San Antonio musician, Doug Sahm, noticed Flaco and took him along with his Sir Douglas Quintet when he went to New York, where the band jammed with Dr. John and Bob Dylan. "It was just the sound of the accordion," Flaco recalls. "They gave me credit but they didn't turn me loose."

In 1972, Flaco broke new ground for a *conjunto* artist and recorded an album with Doug Sahm on Atlantic. Two years later, Arhoolie's Chris Strachwitz and Les Blank made a documentary on Tex-Mex border music called *Chulas Fronteras* (1976). His father and brother, Santiago, Jr., appear, along with Flaco's son David, then nine.

During the filming Flaco got to know Ry Cooder which proved to be a pivotal meeting. Cooder asked Flaco to play on his 1976 album *Chicken Skin Music.* He cut loose on the song "He'll Have to Go." Cooder also took him on the road as part of his "Chicken Skin

Revue," which resulted in the live *Show Time* album the following year. Cooder introduced Flaco to thousands of people in the United States and abroad. At first Jimenez might have looked out of place, but his riffs and runs sounded right and went a long way to introducing accordion into rock. "That was when the attention from more rockers came along, from me and Ry combining that sound."

In 1981, when Jack Nicholson asked Cooder to craft the soundtrack for his film *The Border*, Cooder turned to Flaco to add accordion textures. Flaco went on *Saturday Night Live* with Cooder and PBS's *Austin City Limits*. Flaco always gives credit to Cooder for opening the doors. Years later, Flaco was playing a gig on the Santa Monica Pier with his own band. He was setting up when suddenly saw Cooder with his guitar. "He wanted to sit in. He was not announced or nothing. He automatically knows if I'm in charge, he's welcome."

In the early 1980s, guitarist and mandolinist Peter Rowan met Jimenez, who toured with Rowan throughout the United States and Europe. Jimenez lends his rollicking accordion sound on Rowan's cult hit "Free Mexican Airforce" from *Peter Rowan* (1979, Flying Fish). They recorded *Flaco Jimenez y su Conjunto* with Peter Rowan in 1984 for Waterfront. (Arhoolie released *El Sonido de San Antonio* in 1979.)

Flaco toured Europe in 1985, and again in 1986, this time with his own band. (He headlined the Montreux Jazz Festival in 1990.) Arhoolie released *Ay Te Dejo en San Antonio y Más* in 1986, for which he won his first Grammy for Best Mexican-American Performance for the remake of his father's song "Ay Te Dejo en San Antonio." "It means I am leaving San Antonio because I don't want you anymore," Flaco says. "In other words, you're telling a girl, it's over."

He made another record on Arhoolie, *Flaco's Amigos* (1988), and followed that with three on Rounder: *Entre Humo y Botellas* (1988), *Arriba el Norte* (1989), and *San Antonio Soul* (1991).

In 1989, Flaco joined guitarist Doug Sahm, keyboard player Augie Meyers, and country balladeer Freddy Fender, all from San Antonio, to perform as the Tex-Mex Revue at Boz Scaggs's nightclub in San Francisco. Paige Levy, of Warner/Reprise, liked the sound, signed the band, and released their first album, *Texas Tornados*, which came out in Spanish as *Los Texas Tornados*. The album won a best Mexican-American performance Grammy for "Soy de San Luis," a *conjunto* classic written by Flaco's father. The group's follow-up album, *Zone of Our Own*, (Reprise, 1991), was nominated for a Grammy for best country vocal performance by a group. Their third release, *Hangin' on by a Thread*, came out in 1992, and *Best of Texas Tornados* in 1994. Their fifth album, *Four Aces*, followed in the summer of 1996. The album rose to the top ten on the Americana charts, and included a single, "A Little Bit Is Better than

Nada," featured in the film *Tin Cup*. In 1999 the group relesed *Texas Tornados Live in the Limo Volume 1*. But Doug Sahm died later that year.

In 1992, Jimenez called in some chits and recorded *Partners* on Warner/Reprise, including performances by Dwight Yoakam, Linda Ronstadt, John Hiatt, Steven Stills, Los Lobos, and Emmylou Harris. When the Rolling Stones were making *Voodoo Lounge*, they asked Jimenez to play on one track, "Sweethearts Together." Jimenez was on tour with his band in San Francisco when Don Was, the Stones' producer, tracked him down. "Who in the hell is Don Was?" was Jimenez's first response. But when he found out the Stones wanted him, he went straight to the studio with no time to practice. Even so, the Stones recorded Jimenez's track while he was doing a sound check. "They caught me when I was rehearsing, so they punched the button," he says. "I told Jagger I was ready to record and he said, 'Why do you want to record it? We caught you on the spot.' So there was no take one."

In 1995, Jimenez switched to Arista/Texas, which issued *Flaco Jimenez*. He brought in Raul Malo, lead singer from the Mavericks, Lee Roy Parnell on guitar, and country singer Radney Foster. He earned his third Grammy for Best Mexican-American Performance. As Eric Levin wrote in *People* (February 6, 1995), "Jimenez and his electrified band rollick, frolic and swing. About the only mistake in an album that otherwise cries crossover is a failure to translate the Spanish lyrics." The opening rowdy song, "Seguro Que Hell Yes," featuring Raul Malo, was released as the first single.

"The word 'seguro' means 'sure, why not,' with a lot of gusto," Jimenez told Timothy White of *Billboard*. "So the song is the 'live it up' combination of country and conjunto that I've dreamed of since I was a boy." (Flaco returned the favor by playing on the Mavericks' hit "All You Do Is Bring Me Down," in 1996.)

In 1994 Flaco was inducted into the Conjunto Music Hall of Fame and the Austin Music Hall of Fame.

He followed in 1996 with *Buena Suerte, Senorita* (Good Luck, Miss) on Arista. Compared to the *conjunto*/country sounds of his first Arista release, this album returns Jimenez to his roots with waltzes, polkas, and rancheras, a sentimental Mexican song with a driving beat. From the opening "Borracho #1" (#1 Drunk), to the stately "Swiss Waltz," which Jimenez picked up on one of his European tours, he explores his roots.

Arhoolie released *Un Mojado Sin Licencia* (A Wetback without a Green Card) in 1993, featuring tracks recorded in San Antonio from 1955 to 1967 for Norteño and Sombrero Records. Many of the songs were jukebox *conjunto* hits that helped establish his reputation. In 1997 Rounder issued *Tex-Mex Party*, with tracks by Flaco and his brother. The following year Flaco signed with Texas-based label Barb Wire (distributed by Virgin) and released *Said and Done,* which ranged from traditional conjunto to Tex-Mex. In 1998 he joined forces with six other Mexican-American performers—Freddy Fender, tejano singer Ruben Ramos, Rick Trevino, Joe Ely, Cesar Rosas, and David Hidalgo—in Los Super Seven. The band first came together during the 1997 South by Southwest conference in Austin when they realized they all loved traditional Mexican music. Their first album *Los Super Seven* came out on RCA/Nashville in September 1998 and included songs that focused on subjects important to Mexican Americans. Joe Ely sings Woody Guthrie's "Deportee (Plane Wreck at Los Gatos)" about a plane crash in 1948 that killed migrant workers. Fender sings the bolero "Piensa En Mi," written by Mexican composer Agustin Lara.

Jimenez won two Grammys for his activities in 1998: Best Tejano Performance for his song "Said and Done" from his solo album, and Best Mexican American Music Performance for the song "Los Super Seven." In 1999 Flaco released a new album, *One Night at Joey's* on Sony.

Although he enjoys the traditional sounds, Flaco likes to experiment with new directions as well. "I respect the old traditions, don't get me wrong," he says. "But still I like to progress. I like to deal in up-to-date music, not just the old traditional things."

He never expected to become as popular as he did. "I didn't rush in and I didn't really have a crazy desire to do it. I just hoped and prayed. You just play it day by day and watch the world turn, as they say. If it happens, it happens."

Based on an interview by Lyndon Stambler with Leonardo Flaco Jimenez

JOHNSON, BLIND WILLIE: *Singer, guitarist, pianist. Born near Temple, Texas, in 1902 or 1903; died Beaumont, Texas, 1949.*

One of a number of performers known as "guitar evangelists," Blind Willie Johnson sang only religious songs, but his unique performing style, based on the use of a pocket knife for slide guitar playing, influenced many important secular blues and blues-rock artists. (All of his slide playing was done in open D tuning.) It's generally agreed he was born near Temple, Texas, but he grew up in Marlin, a small city about eighty-five miles south of Dallas. His second wife, Angeline Johnson, told Sam Charters in 1959 that Willie was blinded when only seven when his mother threw lye in his eyes in a fit of anger at his father. In later years he worked as a street singer and played both guitar and piano for services and revival meetings at Marlin Church of God in Christ.

A Columbia field recording unit made his first recordings on December 3, 1927, in Dallas, and a year later more tracks were laid down with his first wife, Willie B. Harris, singing backing vocals. His first 78-rpm single, "I Know His Blood Can Make Me Whole"/"Jesus Make Up My Dying Bed," sold more copies than a Bessie Smith single release during the same time period. His last recording session took place in Atlanta, Georgia, on April 20, 1930. In the late 1940s, after his house in Beaumont burned, he slept on wet bedding in the remains and contracted a fatal case of pneumonia. In 1993, Columbia/Legacy issued a two-CD set, *The Complete Willie Johnson.* Also available at the end of the 1990s were the excellent CDs on Yazoo *Praise God I'm Satisfied* and *Sweeter As the Years Go By.* During 1998, Columbia issued the CD *Dark Was the Night.*

John Fahey credited coming upon "Praise God I'm Satisfied" in 1957 with inspiring him to seek out little-known blues and traditional country artists for his Takoma label.

JOHNSON, ROBERT: *Blues singer, guitarist, harmonica player, songwriter. Born Hazlehurst, Mississippi, May 8, 1911; died Greenwood, Mississippi, August 16, 1938.*

Robert Leroy Johnson lived his short and tormented life, as he sang, with a hellhound on his trail. Although it is a fictional portrayal in which the narrator sprinkles powder on his doorstep to keep the devil away, in real life Johnson was a restless soul, traveling from town to town, rarely settling down. His guitar playing improved so much in such a short period of time that the story grew that he had gone down to the crossroads and sold his soul to the devil. Johnson, like other bluesmen, did nothing to discourage the myth with songs such as "Cross Road Blues," "Me and the Devil Blues," and "Hellhound on My Trail." As he sings in "Hellhound" in his eerie tenor voice: *I' got to keep movin' . . . Blues fallin' down like hail.*

If there is truth to the myth, the world is the beneficiary. Johnson only recorded twenty-nine songs (twelve alternate takes brings that to forty-one tracks), but he was arguably the most influential blues singer ever. He combined the Delta blues sound of Charley Patton and Son House, both of whom he knew, with a walking bass pattern he derived from boogie-woogie piano music. He provides a transition from rural to the urbanized sounds of people like Muddy Waters and Elmore James in Chicago in the 1940s and 1950s, who listened to his 78s. (James recorded an electrified version of "I Believe I'll Dust My Broom" that became his own signature tune.)

From the songs about the devil to his songs about murder ("32-20 Blues"), rambling ("Traveling Riverside Blues," "Rambling on My Mind"), women ("Love in Vain," "Terraplane Blues," "I Believe I'll Dust My Broom"), and sex ("Come on in My Kitchen," "They're Red Hot," and "Malted Milk"), Johnson sang about what mattered to him and his listeners. Many of his songs offered a level of dark insight few have matched: *I'm gonna beat my woman/Until I get satisfied,* in "Me and the Devil Blues." Johnson never held back, as such brutal lines reflect. As Eric Clapton put it, "In some ways a song like 'Hellhound on My Trail' is hardly there, it's almost in the air—what he doesn't say, what he doesn't play, it's so light and menacing at the same time."

Young British rockers "rediscovered" Johnson after 1961, when Columbia issued the first of two LPs of his work, *Robert Johnson: King of the Delta Blues Singers* (reissued on CD in 1994). Columbia released *Volume II* in 1970. Clapton vividly recalls first hearing Johnson when he was fifteen or sixteen. "It came as something of a shock to me that there could be anything that powerful," he wrote in the liner notes to Columbia's definitive boxed set, *Robert Johnson: The Complete Recordings.* "What struck me about the Robert Johnson album was that it seemed like he wasn't playing for an audience at all; it didn't obey the rules of time or harmony or anything." Clapton recorded "Cross Road Blues" with Cream, which rose to twenty-eight on the charts. Despite Clapton's success there is nothing quite like hearing Johnson's tortured voice as he sings, *Standin' at the crossroad, baby risin' sun goin' down/I believe to my soul, now po' Bob is sinkin' down.* Cream also recorded a lesser-known Johnson song, "From Four Till Late." The Rolling Stones, of course, had a big hit with Johnson's haunting love song "Love in Vain," and covered "Stop Breakin' Down Blues."

In August 1990, Columbia issued *The Complete Recordings,* a two-CD set that included every known recording by Johnson. The album, produced by Lawrence Cohn, was expected to sell only 20,000 copies. Remarkably, the boxed set stayed on the *Billboard* pop charts for thirty-one weeks. In five months the album had gone gold, and by 1994 it had gone platinum. There were stories that concert promoters wanted to book this amazing new artist named Robert Johnson, only to find out that he had been dead for more than fifty years! (Proceeds were used to build a memorial in 1991 at the cemetery where he was buried.) A new generation had discovered that Johnson's sound was as compelling in the '90s as it had been in the '30s. *The Complete Recordings* won a Grammy for Best Historical Recording. He was inducted into the Blues Hall of Fame in 1980 and the Rock and Roll Hall of Fame in 1986.

Johnson had more than enough tragedy in his life to fuel his haunting blues. According to the liner notes written by Stephen C. LaVere for *The Complete Recordings,* Robert Johnson, born in 1911 in Hazlehurst, Mississippi (thirty miles south of Jackson), had a confusing family background. The grandson of slaves, he was the eleventh child of Julia Ann Majors Dodds. She had taken up with a field hand named Noah Johnson after her husband, Charlie Dodds Jr. (né Spencer), a farmer, carpenter, and wicker furniture maker, fled Mississippi in 1907 due to a disagreement with the Marchetti Brothers. Charlie moved to Memphis, calling himself Spencer or Dodds for many years.

After Julia worked for a couple of years picking cotton, she and Charlie were reunited in Memphis, where he lived with a mistress named Serena and thirteen children by both women. Julia and Serena coexisted under the same roof for a short time. But Julia left her family and settled in Robinsonville, Mississippi.

In 1918, Charlie Dodds sent the increasingly restless Robert south to live with his mother. By this time she had married a man named Willie "Dusty" Willis (a.k.a. Robert "Dusty" Saunders), a short, stocky field hand. Johnson attended the Indian Creek School in nearby Commerce ("a collection of shacks at the end of a dirt road" as Samuel Charters wrote) where his mother and stepfather worked on the Abbay & Leatherman plantation. Johnson didn't stay in school long because he was plagued by a cataract in one of his eyes. As a teenager, Johnson began the Jew's harp and the harmonica. But his real passion was for the guitar, which he learned from an older brother. He also had some fine tutors—Willie Brown, Charley Patton, and Son House played in the Delta.

House remembers Johnson at a Saturday night dance when he was still a little boy. "He blew a harmonica and he was pretty good with that, but he wanted to play a guitar," House told Samuel Charters for *The Bluesmen* (1967). "When we'd leave at night to go play for the balls, he'd slip off and come over to where we were. His mother and stepfather didn't like for him to go out to those Saturday night balls because the guys were so rough. But he'd slip away anyway. . . . He'd get where Willie [Brown] and I were and sit right down on the floor and watch from one to the other. And when we'd get a break and want to rest some, we'd set the guitars up in the corner and go out in the cool. Robert would watch and see which way we'd gone and he would pick one of them up. And such another racket you never heard! It'd make the people mad, you know. They'd come out and say, 'Why don't y'all go in there and get that guitar away from that boy! He's running people crazy with it.' "

In February 1929, Johnson, seventeen, married fifteen-year-old Virginia Travis. They lived together on the Klein plantation outside of Robinsonville with Johnson's half sister Bessie and her husband, Granville Hines. Virginia became pregnant. Johnson was hopeful. But Virginia and the baby died in childbirth in April 1930. His anguish shows up in such songs as his version of Son House's "Preaching Blues (Up Jumped the Devil)": *And the blues fell mama's child/Tore me all up-side down.*

Rather than do plantation work, Johnson traveled to Hazlehurst in search of his father, Noah Johnson. It's unclear whether he found him. But his music career took off. He found a tutor in the blues, Ike Zinnerman. Even though he secretly married again in May 1931, this time to Calletta Craft, more than ten years his elder, he pursued his music with single-minded passion. "She idolized Robert, fussed over him, cooked for him, worked for him, treated him like a king, even served him his breakfast in bed!" LaVere wrote. "She trusted him away from her, too, and had no qualms about him staying all night at Zinnerman's to learn what he could about music. . . . He attached himself to Ike for the next couple of years and kept the older man up late into the night learning what he could about the guitar and the blues Ike played on it."

His wife would sometimes accompany him to the juke joints, occasionally sitting on his lap as he played. But that only lasted for a couple of numbers because, as LaVere wrote, "usually his legs and feet were too busy keeping time. He'd flail his legs up and down and back and forth at the same time and his feet would get a terrific rhythm going in accompaniment to his music."

He left Calletta, who died a few years later. Johnson returned to Robinsonville to visit his mother and show Willie Brown and Son House his guitar skills. "Willie and I were playing again at a little place east of Robinsonville called Banks, Mississippi," House told Charters. "We were playing there one Saturday night and, all of a sudden, somebody came in through the door. Who but him! He had a guitar swinging on his back. I said, 'Bill!' He said, 'Huh?' I said, 'Look who's coming in the door.' He looked and said, 'Yeah. Little Robert.' I said, 'And he's got a guitar.' And Willie and I laughed about it. Robert finally wiggled through the crowd and got to where we were. He spoke, and I said, 'Well, boy, you still got a guitar, huh? What do you do with that thing? You can't do nothing with it.' He said, 'Well, I'll tell you what.' I said, 'What?' He said, 'Let me have your seat a minute.' So I said, 'All right, and you better do something with it, too,' and I winked my eye at Willie. So he sat down there and finally got started. And man! He was so good! When he finished all our mouths were standing open. I said, 'Well, ain't that fast! He's gone too!'"

House warned Johnson about being too sweet with the women at the juke joints. Johnson was a small man and House worried about him. According to LaVere, Johnson would single out the homeliest women, thinking that he was safer that way. He had a number of women who took care of him. Johnson drank, smoked, and gambled, and was often the life of the party.

Rather than move back to Robinsonville, Johnson settled in Helena, Arkansas, across the Mississippi River, where he stayed with another older woman named Estella Coleman—when he was home. (Charters theorizes that Coleman was the "Kindhearted Woman" in his song.) He met several of the emerging Delta bluesmen: harmonica player Rice Miller, a.k.a. Sonny Boy Williamson and Little Boy Blue, Johnny Shines, Elmore James and Howlin' Wolf, to name a few. He took Coleman's son, Robert Junior Lockwood, under his wing as his "stepson."

He continued to ramble throughout the Delta and beyond to Saint Louis, Memphis, Louisiana, Chicago, and Texas, developing a reputation as a great performer. "Robert Johnson became a stone traveler," LaVere wrote. "He developed a penchant for it. . . . Moving around the way he did and playing in so many different places to so many different people all the time, he had to, out of necessity, be able to play almost anything which was requested." Johnson played pop, hillbilly, polkas, and square dances, including "Yes, Sir, That's My Baby," "My Blue Heaven," and "Tumbling Tumbleweeds." "He could be deep in conversation with a group of people and hear something—never stop talking—and later be able to play it and sing it perfectly," LaVere wrote.

Like many bluesmen, Johnson wanted to make records. He contacted H.C. Speir, a record store owner in Jackson who had contacts with the American Record Company (ARC). Speir, who had spotted Son House and Charley Patton, introduced Johnson to Ernie Oertle, an ARC salesman and talent scout. Oertle was impressed and took him to San Antonio, Texas, in November 1936 for his first recording sessions with producer Don Law. According to Charters, Law put Johnson up in a boardinghouse, and went to dinner. Law soon got a call from the police to report that Johnson had been arrested on a vagrancy charge. Law bailed him out, brought him back to the boardinghouse, and gave him forty-five cents for breakfast. Law received another phone call. "I'm lonesome and there's a lady here," Johnson said. "She wants fifty cents and I lacks a nickel."

Johnson had three recording sessions with Law in a studio at the Gunter Hotel in 1936—on November 23, 26, and 27. (Johnson was followed in the studio by Hermanas Barraza con Guitarras and the Chuck Wagon Gang.) ARC's Vocalion label released "Terraplane Blues" backed with "Kindhearted Woman Blues" from the first session and had a decent hit, selling several thousand copies. He also cut "I Believe I'll Dust My Broom," "Come on in My Kitchen," and "Cross Road Blues." Johnson brought copies of "Terraplane Blues" to family members and even met his father, Noah Johnson, according to Charters.

Based on the success of "Terraplane Blues," Vocalion called Johnson back to record with Law on June 19 and 20, 1937, in a Dallas warehouse. Vocalion released eleven 78s during his lifetime and one posthumously. At the later sessions Johnson recorded some of his eeriest songs: "Stones in My Passway," "Hellhound on My Trail," and "Me and the Devil Blues." On the last day he recorded "Love in Vain."

The recordings brought Johnson newfound fame. While he mostly traveled and performed on his own, he embarked on an extensive trip with Johnny Shines, whom he had met in Arkansas in 1933, and Calvin Frazier. They traveled the Midwest, through St. Louis,

Chicago, and Decatur. They appeared on radio with a preacher in Detroit in 1937, and in Windsor, Ontario. They also traveled to New York and New Jersey.

Johnson was unpredictable, often disappearing in the middle of the night. It was his womanizing that would finally catch up to him. In August 1938, Johnson made a final trip to Robinsonville to visit his relatives and then traveled to Greenwood, Mississippi, where he had an engagement at the Three Forks roadhouse. He played there for about two weeks with David "Honeyboy" Edwards on Saturday nights. On Saturday, August 13, 1938, Johnson was appearing with Little Boy Blue (Sonny Boy II) and later with Honeyboy Edwards. It was to be Johnson's last performance.

His fatal mistake was to befriend the wife of the man who ran the juke joint. As LaVere pieced it together, Johnson began paying attention to his lady friend, not realizing it was the owner's wife. During a break, someone gave Johnson a half-pint of whiskey with a broken seal. Sonny Boy told Johnson not to drink from an opened half pint and knocked it from his hand. But when a second bottle was offered with a broken seal, Johnson drank from it. A bit later, in the middle of his set, Johnson fell ill and had to get up and go outside. Many believe that the woman's jealous husband had someone put strychnine in the whiskey.

Johnson contracted pneumonia, and died on Tuesday, August 16, 1938. Johnsons's death at such a young age was almost inevitable. One need only look at one of the two existing pictures of Robert Johnson to see the sad stare in his eyes, his right eye slightly off center, a cigarette dangling from his mouth. He was buried next to the highway in the Mount Zion Missionary Baptist Church graveyard outside Morgan City, Mississippi. His tombstone is inscribed with the words from "Me and the Devil Blues" *Early this mornin' when you knocked upon my door/And I said, Hello, Satan I believe it's time to go. . . . You may bury my body down by the highway side/So my old evil spirit can catch a Greyhound bus and ride.*

A tragic sidenote is that later that year the famous A&R man John Hammond had heard Johnson's 78s and wanted him to perform in his "Spirituals to Swing Concert" at Carnegie Hall. (An early poster listed Robert Johnson as one of the acts.) Hammond contacted Law, who told him that Johnson was too shy and would freeze in front of a big audience. He asked Oertle to search for Johnson anyway. Oertle found out that he had just died. Instead, Hammond invited Big Bill Broonzy to perform at Carnegie Hall on December 23, 1938. The concert gave Broonzy a career boost.

Besides Charters's books (which included a 1973 book of song transcriptions entitled *Robert Johnson*), Peter Guralnick wrote *Searching for Robert Johnson,* (1989), which served as the basis for a 1992 documentary by British filmmaker Chris Hunt about his life— narrated by John Hammond, Jr., the son of the man who

searched for Johnson. The film also includes interviews with Johnny Shines, Honeyboy Edwards and Willie Mae Powell, a girlfriend mentioned in "Love in Vain." Mack McCormick is the other person (along with LaVere) who has doggedly pursued the details of Johnson's life for a book tentatively titled *Biography of a Phantom.*

The postal service commemorated Johnson in the 1990s with a U.S. stamp as part of a series on country blues artists. *Can't You Hear the Wind Howl,* a docudrama directed by Peter Meyer, came out in 1997 (released on video in 1998) and features Keb' Mo', as Johnson. Danny Glover narrates. Meyer had a difficult time convincing people to talk to him. When he approached Willie Mae Powell, she was reticent at first. But when he showed her the photo of Johnson with a cigarette in his mouth, she clutched it to her chest and exclaimed, "That's my little Robert" (" 'Howl' Brings a Bluesman into Focus," *Dallas Morning News,* April 23, 1997).

In 1998 a long-lost recording of "Traveling Riverside Blues" turned up. It was the first version of the song recorded on June 20, 1937. When *The Complete Recordings* were released in 1990 it was counted among the nineteen recordings believed to have been lost or destroyed. The test pressing, a ten-inch, single-sided, laminated shellac disc, was found in the Alan Lomax Archives and purchased (with five other Johnson recordings) by the American Folklife Center of the Library of Congress for $10,000. It was released in 1998 on the second Columbia/Legacy CD reissue of the landmark 1961 LP *Robert Johnson: King of the Delta Blues Singers.* Johnson sounds nervous and hesitant on the track. "It is precious because it does give more insight into him and his art," Alan Jabbour, former director of the Folklife Center, told M. Dion Thompson of the *Minneapolis Star Tribune* ("Happy News: We've Got 'Riverside Blues'," May 17, 1998). Another CD entitled *Beg, Borrow or Steal,* came out on Catfish Records in 1998, with recordings by Johnson, House, Skip James, Charley Patton, and Elmore James.

Despite haggling over Johnson's estate, his influence could not be diminished. As Keith Richards put it: "He was like a comet or a meteor that came along and, BOOM, suddenly he raised the ante, suddenly you just had to aim that much higher."

And Eric Clapton said: "His music remains the most powerful cry that I think you can find in the human voice, really."

JOHNSTON, FREEDY: *Singer, guitarist, songwriter. Born Kinsley, Kansas, March 7, 1961.*

Rock 'n' roll rooted in folk simplicity is the term a number of critics have used to describe the songs written by Freedy Johnston. They reflected, in part, his roots growing up in a sparsely populated part of Kansas that, rather than inspiring joy in the surroundings of nature, appeared to induce in him as a boy a feeling of loneliness and a desire to escape to a more challenging social environment. Perhaps a comment on his feelings was the fact he literally sold the family farm to finance what became a breakthrough album project.

Though Freedy grew up on a farm, he wasn't cut off from the wider world, thanks to the modern entities of radio and TV. Like most youngsters in the '60s and early '70s, he was caught up in the rock revolution, and in his teens longed to become a rock star. At sixteen he ordered his first guitar from a mail-order catalog, since there was no music store in Kinsley—there were hardly many stores at all. He learned to play the instrument and could handle it tolerably well by the time he entered Kansas University in Lawrence.

He stayed only one semester, spending most of his time making contacts with local musicians and writing his own songs. For a long time, however, he avoided exposing his writing efforts. He recalled later, "Music looked like the most agreeable 'job' out there, but even though I was writing songs, I could never go so far as to play them for anyone, let alone in front of a crowd."

For the first part of the 1980s, he supported himself mainly by working in a restaurant while gaining musical experience with local bands on whatever opportunities were available—parties, club dates, campus events. After a while he did work up courage to let others in on his writing output and began to make demos of some of them. In 1985 he decided Lawrence was not the place to pursue a career in music and moved east to New York. Once there he made more demos and tried to get them to the attention of major labels. Not much happened until he was contacted by the independent Bar None label, based across the river from New York in Hoboken, New Jersey. Freedy hadn't sent them anything, but they had been given a tape by someone else and liked it.

After signing with Bar None at the end of the '80s, Johnston completed his debut album, *The Trouble Tree,* which was released in 1990. The album got little attention at home, but a copy reached Holland, and one of the tracks started to get considerable airplay and soon made top levels of Dutch charts and in Belgium. The situation seemed ripe for a follow-up album, but Bar None was strapped for cash to complete the project. To help finish the album and keep his band afloat, he sold the farm he inherited from his grandfather. He wrote about selling "the house where I learned to walk" in the song "Trying to Tell You I Don't Know," on the new album, *Can You Fly.*

The album, issued in 1992, proved as good or better than the previous one, but this time songs like "Down in Love" got airplay on a number of U.S. stations and the album got much more critical attention, acclaimed by some reviewers as heralding the arrival of a major new talent. Johnston also was starting to get opportunities to share bills with important new rock acts such as the Lemonheads, Soul Asylum, and Matthew Sweet. Major-

label executives also were beginning to evaluate him, and in 1993 Elektra Records succeeded in adding him to its roster. He soon was in the studio working on his third album, this time without having to worry about selling family heirlooms to pay for the sessions. To support him, he and his producer, Butch Vig, assembled no less than five guitarists, including top session players Marshall Crenshaw and Dave Schramm, plus a cellist, drummer, and several other musicians. In the spring of 1994 *This Perfect World* was released, to almost immediate approval from critics and more than a few radio programmers.

The songs typically matched deceptively cheerful rhythmic patterns with lyrics more in the tradition of Edgar Allan Poe. The title track, for instance, on the surface seems initially like a father apologizing for his shortcomings to his daughter, until it turns out that he murdered her mother and threw the body in the lake. The fast-paced, country-flavored "Gone Like the Water" describes the odyssey of a young man who leaves a small town with his mother's red suitcase and father's leather coat to make a name for himself in New York City—only to find he has become a very small fish in a big pond, someone who is "disappearing in the city."

That song and several others carried over characters and themes from *Can You Fly.* Johnston told Barbara Davies of *Billboard* ("Freedy Johnston's 'Perfect World,'" May 21, 1994), "I worried about that. When I wrote 'Gone Like the Water,' 'Disappointed Man,' and 'I Can Hear the Laughs,' I thought, 'Oh God, a theme record.' I really do relate to kind of disaffected youth from any rural areas who want to come to the city but they don't know yet that what they want isn't there. And at the same time, I didn't want to knock songs off the record because they had pretty much the same characters. Some people write the same damn songs, same chord changes, same melodies all their lives." The songs in the album also touch on unrequited love and, in "Evie's Tears," the disturbed feeling of a woman who has endured the physical horror of rape.

In any case, the collection was a worthy successor to both of Freedy's Bar None projects and whetted the listener's taste for the second Elektra album Freedy began working on for 1995–96 release. Before that it won accolades from just about all major media sources, including *Rolling Stone* where Barbara O'Dair gave it four stars. The magazine named him songwriter of the year in 1994. She commented, in part, that on *This Perfect World* the songs were "finely crafted and sung in a clear tenor voice that echoes the aching country voices he grew up listening to. Yet Johnston writes pop-folk songs—12 here about loss, loneliness and grief—that snap like small but potent firecrackers. When he wordplays like Elvis Costello or phrases like Neil Young or recalls Simon and Garfunkel in a verse and chorus, forget it. *Nobody* sounds like Freedy Johnston. He's an American original."

While Freedy's lyrics tended to deal with topics like thwarted love, feelings of despair, even death, he emphasized this didn't necessarily reflect his general state of mind: "I wouldn't say I'm a morbid person, but I have to admit that I usually don't write happy songs. To me, sad songs just seem to say so much more."

After completion of *This Perfect World,* he did feel he was making creative progress. "With each record, I've gotten closer to what it is I want. This record is the closest yet. I think it's more focused, and I'm very happy with how it turned out. I want to make something I can stand by. When I'm gone, I want to know that I got it right."

Johnston, who got his nickname when someone mispronounced his real name, Freddy, followed his successful *This Perfect World* with *Never Home,* released on Elektra in 1997 and produced by Danny Kortchmar, who had previously worked with Neil Young, Don Henley, and the Spin Doctors. There are even a few upbeat songs on the album, such as "I'm Not Hypnotized," while he maintains his Poe-like outlook on songs such as "Gone to See the Fire," about an arsonist. *Never Home* also received strong reviews, but none of the songs received the airplay of *This Perfect World.*

"I'm not trying to be self-effacing but I'm not the kind of guy who sells a lot of records. If it ever happens it's going to be accidental," he told Betsy Powell of the *Toronto Star* ("Every Song Tells a Story for Tunesmith," October 15, 1998). "I want to be liked. I would hate it if I put out a record that was slagged. So I work very hard to make sure that doesn't happen."

He next worked with producer T. Bone Burnett on his third Elektra release called *Blue Days Black Nights,* issued in July 1999.

JONES, RICKIE LEE: *Singer, guitarist, pianist, record producer, songwriter. Born Chicago, Illinois, November 8, 1954.*

A tough-talking, hard-drinking child of the streets, Rickie Lee Jones burst from obscurity in 1979 with her first album, which became one of the major successes of that year. That LP and her next one established her as potentially one of the more influential writers and performers in the rock/pop idiom. However, the very environment that nurtured her unique style proved a stumbling block to steady creative progress. Problems with alcohol as well as management difficulties sidelined her for a number of years in the early 1980s before she surfaced to try to resume her career in mid-decade.

Rickie Lee was born in Chicago in a neighborhood near the Chicago Cubs' ballpark, Wrigley Field. Some of her grandparents had been in vaudeville, but her parents earned a living, she jokingly said, "in the restaurant business," which meant that they had worked as a waiter and waitress. Her father did like to sing and, at one point, wrote a song called "The Moon Is Made of Gold," which Rickie Lee included in her stage performances of the late 1970s and '80s.

It was not a tranquil upbringing. Her parents were often at odds with each other. During her childhood, they separated for a while and then got back together. The family, which included several other children, was uprooted a number of times as her parents drifted from one state to another, working at a series of relatively unsatisfying jobs. The environment helped make Rickie Lee more unhappy and rebellious than the typical teenager. Her formal schooling ended when she was expelled from high school in Olympia, Washington.

She already had started drinking and after that incident she went out on her own as a drifter and member of the seamier underclass of modern society. She found occasional work to pay the rent, but much of the time she simply hung out with friends and drank. As she later said: "I've been as far down as I can go and I made it out. So there's nothing to be afraid of anymore."

Her wanderings took her to many cities on the U.S. West Coast as the 1970s went by. Eventually she made her way to the Los Angeles area in the mid-1970s, where she settled for a time in the Venice section. Her income came primarily from work as a waitress in small bars and restaurants, but she had always liked to sing and increasingly the idea of going into show business crossed her mind. By 1978, she was finding occasional gigs, most of which she did for no pay. Sometimes she sang with local bands, including one called Spanish Logo she later used as the theme for one of her songs. In general, during that period, she said: "I performed in dives and little bars that pay about $10 per four sets. If I could get one, I'd use a jazz trio. If not, I'd go solo." The audience, she recalled, typically was "full of bikers, degenerates, drunken men, and toothless women."

Her friends and acquaintances included a mixture of down-and-outers and some creative types, like Tom Waits, who drew inspiration from living in the rough milieu of the urban jungle. (*See Waits, Tom.*) Among that group was a close friend named Chuck E., also a member of the Waits circle, about whom she later wrote, he was "king of the sidewalk, the most popular guy on Santa Monica Boulevard."

By the fall of 1978, a demonstration tape found its way to the desk of Warner Brothers artists & repertoire executive Len Waronker. He and fellow executive Russ Titlemen checked her out and soon signed her to the label. In short order, they had Ms. Jones in the studio recording her first album. That collection was issued in February 1979 under the title *Rickie Lee Jones.*

The songs she provided had subjects somewhat akin to the offbeat themes proffered by Tom Waits, sometimes described as '70s Beat (though Waits always bristled at being compared to a movement of the '50s). There were elements of '50s pop, jazz, R&B, and rock in the melodies, as might be expected from a writer who listed among her favorite artists Van Morrison,

Sarah Vaughan, Marvin Gaye, Laura Nyro, and Peggy Lee. (The subject matter and treatment of some of her material also reflected folk leanings as recognized by Australian critic Ralph Douglas after attending a concert in Brisbane in 1994: "With a blend of R&B, jazz and folk, her acoustic set was simply astonishing.")

She acknowledged she wrote about things she knew about. She told Jeff Melvoin of *Time* magazine: "My writing is all from a particular neighborhood. I can pick any person on this street or the next and just be them."

"When people start comparing me to other singers and writers, I just ignore it. I've gotta laugh. My music is real personal. I think that's what—if anything—will make it noticed."

It certainly was noticed and in rapid order. The album soon became a favorite of reviewers and her cross-country tour that began in the spring of 1979 proved that she could win over a good share of the general public as well.

Describing one of her shows that won over New York City fans, Jay Cocks wrote in *Time* (May 21, 1979): "The titles [of her original compositions] fix the tone and set the stage ("Easy Money," "Coolsville," "The Last Chance Texaco") while the songs spin out little narratives of hard luck and high spirits in the big town: 'There was a Joe / Leanin' on the back door / A couple little kids with their eyes on a couple of bills / Their eyes was starin' / They was waitin' / To get their hands on some Easy Money.'

"Jones sings of such capers in a musky voice that slides across the lyrics, scatting between them and eliding words in vintage hipster style, as if English were a foreign language learned in a speed-speech course."

Rickie Lee Jones went past platinum levels. It was a hit in Europe and other countries as well. In Australia, it was number one on the album charts for five straight weeks. In the spring and summer, her single "Chuck E's in Love" made the top 5 in the United States. The track "Company," among others, also got considerable airplay on AM and FM radio.

Her eagerly awaited second album came out in 1981 on Warner Brothers. Called *Pirates,* it was more uneven than the first LP, but overall had enough high points to make it one of the more interesting releases of the year and won Rickie Lee a gold-record award from the RIAA.

She completed two more albums on Warner Brothers, *Girl at Her Volcano* (1983) and *The Magazine* (1984), before her career came to a temporary halt. She recalled that period for Jonatha Brooke of *The Performing Songwriter* (March–April 1996), a time when the events in her life drastically shook her self-confidence: "I still knew how to sing, but I didn't . . . you know I think that my life had a complete breakdown. My father died and somebody really close to me died, everybody died . . . and all this English music, and Madonna was the thing, and what I did was not the thing. I turned 30,

which is a really difficult birthday. And that all happened in the mid-80s and I had to stop and reform, and that took a while. I got married and tried to reform myself as that, and I knew I wanted to work, but I knew it wasn't the time. . . ."

For a while, some columnists conjectured her problems might be too great for her to overcome. But by the late 1980s she had resumed in-person appearances and signed a new recording contract with Geffen Records. Her terse description of her hiatus and return went as follows: "I left. I lived in France for a few years . . . I returned to America and gave birth to a big healthy baby girl. I met Walter Becker (of Steely Dan) and he spent nine months producing [the Geffen debut album] *Flying Cowboys* (released in 1989)." By the time her second Geffen album, *Pop Pop,* came out in 1991, though, she was beginning to feel uneasy about that label affiliation. Meanwhile her marriage ended in divorce.

She also was having problems in writing new material, but she said that upon hearing Leo Kottke's album *Great Big Boy* her creative instincts were reinvigorated and she came up with what she felt were some of her best originals for her next Geffen release, the 1993 *Traffic from Paradise.* The album won critical approval at home and abroad, but was not a best-seller, which had been the case with her previous Geffen discs. She attributed that to lack of understanding and support from label executives. She told Jonatha Brooke, "It's incredible . . . how we're treated. The thing is that new artists probably think they're the only ones treated that way and they're not. Everybody's treated really badly unless they're making a lot of money, and then they have power."

One aspect of Kottke's album that affected her, she told Australian journalist Stuart Coupe (*Sydney Melbourne & Brisbane Rhythms Magazine,* June 27, 1994), was the fact that "he had a little bit of that folk singer thing in him which, for good or bad, reminded me of the old days and what it's like to begin."

On hearing of her interest in his work, Kottke agreed to let Rickie Lee produce his next album. She had done some production of her own material in the past, but found taking that role for another artist's project was somewhat different. She told Coupe, "The hardest part for me about producing somebody else was that I found out that they have control because it's their record, and I'm not used to that."

She fought to get a release from the Geffen contract, she told interviewers, but for a long time was turned down. Finally her efforts paid off, and by 1995 she had signed with a new label, Reprise, part of the same corporation that owned her old record group, Warner Brothers. The first fruit of this alignment was the 1995 disc *Naked Songs,* whose tracks all came from live performances, mostly solo acoustic work with guitar or piano. Folk-based numbers included "Stewart's Coat," the only new song on the album; "The Horses"; "Magazine"; and "The Last Chance Texaco." Her concert appearances in support of her album included October '95 shows in London, Paris, Dublin, Amsterdam, and Berlin, the last two cities ones she hadn't performed in since 1979. By early 1996 she was writing new material and starting to record tracks for her first Reprise studio collection, *Ghostyhead*, released in 1997.

JOURNEYMEN, THE: *Vocal, instrumental group. John Phillips, born Parris Island, South Carolina, August 30, 1941; Scott McKenzie, born Arlington, Virginia; and Richard Weissman, born Philadelphia, Pennsylvania.*

The exact reasons for the rapid rise to national attention of folk music in the late 1950s and early '60s and its rapid decline in popularity among the mass audience in the mid-1960s is still being debated. The shifting winds of the mid-1960s did not eliminate folk music, of course, but there came a retrenching that shortened the careers of a number of well-regarded groups, including the Journeymen.

For several years, this group was considered one of the most promising of the new crop of the 1960s. Weissman, a noted folklorist and musicologist, studied at the Philadelphia Conservatory of Music, completed college at Goddard in Vermont, and attended Columbia's graduate school of sociology. By the beginning of the 1960s, his skill as a banjoist and guitarist—instruments in which he conducted seminars at New York's School of Folk Music—made him one of the most sought-after accompanists at folk recording sessions.

At one such session, he met Carolina-born John Phillips and his friend Scott McKenzie. They were part of a group known as the Smoothies. Phillips, an allstate basketball and track star in school, had attended the University of Virginia and George Washington University, and received a Presidential appointment to the U.S. Naval Academy. An intramural basketball injury ended his hopes of a navy career and turned him toward his long-time love of bluegrass music.

During his travels, he met McKenzie, who had attended a number of prep schools and colleges and had made many popular appearances as a vocalist, including several guest spots on Dick Clark's American Bandstand.

With Phillips as leader, the group made its debut at Gerde's Folk City in the spring of 1961. Frank Weber, who had managed the Kingston Trio, heard them and quickly notified Capitol A&R man Andy Wiswell. Wiswell signed them and set up a session at the firm's New York studios. The first LP was issued in October 1961. Called *The Journeymen*, it sold well enough to mark them as coming artists. In 1962, Capitol issued a second LP, *Comin' Attractions*, and in 1963, another titled *New Directions*.

After the Journeymen broke up, Phillips went on to national fame as Papa John of the top pop group the Mamas and the Papas.

KAHN, SI: *Political activist, singer, songwriter, guitarist. Born Boston, Massachusetts, April 23, 1944.*

Si Kahn never intended to become a folksinger; he was a grassroots organizer first. But Kahn began writing and performing for friends, who were so impressed by the poetry, stories, and emotion in his lyrics that they urged him to record his powerful first album, *New Wood*, in September 1974. At their best, Kahn's songs have a timeless quality, as in "Aragon Mill," a bluegrass standard that has been covered by such artists as Planxty, Dolores Keane, Rosalie Sorrels, Hazel Dickens, the Red Clay Ramblers, and the Dry Branch Fire Squad.

Kahn grew up in State College, Pennsylvania, in a middle-class Jewish household. His father, Benjamin, was a rabbi and executive director of Hillel, a Jewish organization serving college campuses. His mother, Rosalind, was an artist. They raised him to care about the less fortunate. Kahn told Steve Hochman of the *Los Angeles Times* (February 19, 1987) that they "had a very deep sense of justice . . . which is where I believe I got my politics from."

They used to sing at the dinner table and in synagogue, which gave Si a sense of the importance of song in all cultures. In first grade, Kahn wrote a song, and his teacher remarked on his report card that the whole class was learning to sing it. "We hope to encourage him in this activity," the teacher wrote, according to an article by Scott Alarik in *Performing Songwriter* (September-October 1995).

Later in life, his father once asked Si how he had become a country singer. Kahn learned it at home, he told his father. "If you think about the music we sang around the dinner table and you think about traditional Appalachian folk music, they have a great deal in common," he told Alarik. "They're both styles rooted in unaccompanied singing, and the vocal traditions are quite similar, based on solo artistry where there is a basic tune which is highly embellished. You also hear that in traditional Jewish music, and at the same time both of them are traditions where there is extensive harmony singing."

As a student at Harvard in the mid-1960s he did volunteer carpentry work in the South for the Student Non-Violent Coordinating Committee (SNCC) during the southern civil rights movement. Later he worked with black farmers in west Georgia, helping them form cooperatives. "The southern civil rights movement was my first experience of the public and strategic use of music," he told Alarik. "The lyrical improvisation of the civil rights movement, taking an old tune and putting new lyrics to it to suit the particular struggle or situation, taught me a lot about how music could be used to effect change." (Those songs included "We Shall Overcome," and "We Shall Not Be Moved.")

He graduated magna cum laude from Harvard in 1966 with a degree in medieval history and literature.

From 1965 to 1972 Kahn traveled and worked as an organizer throughout Georgia, working on civil rights, voter registration, and grassroots organizing. In the early 1970s he worked with the United Mine Workers of America (UMWA) during the Brookside strike in Harlan County, Kentucky. Later, as a strategist in the Carolinas for the Amalgamated Clothing and Textile Workers Union (ACTWU), he helped organize the campaign at the J. P. Stevens mills. He met other political activists and a number of folksingers, including John McCutcheon, Hazel Dickens, Roscoe Holcomb, and Guy Carawan. Up till then, he had been learning folk songs, but he soon began writing his own.

In September 1974 June Appal Records asked him to record an album. He and some close friends gathered in a little home in Wise, Virginia. John McCutcheon played Appalachian dulcimer, mandolin, fiddle, harmonica, guitar, and banjo on the album. The album included songs about a "Backroom Lady" who ministers to the leaders of society for $20 an hour; "Brookside Strike," written while he was working with the UMWA, about the coal miner who's *tired of working for nothing/And bad top that's ready to fall*; and about a ninety-pound "Truck Driving Woman." The most enduring song on the album was "Aragon Mill," a song whose last lines tell the story of the eerie silence after the mill is closed: *And the only tune I hear is the sound of the wind/As it blows through the town. Weave and spin, weave and spin.*

Kahn's songwriting, including his emotional and personal songs, is inseparable from his political work. "The essence of organizing is learning how to communicate simply and directly," he told Alarik. "That means both how to talk and how to listen, and that's what I've practiced for 30 years, in mining camps, mill towns, farming communities, little villages here and there. . . . If you're going to do organizing with folks, you have to pay attention not just to what is said, but to what is heard. And I carry that skill into my songwriting."

The album was first released in 1975, but was reissued in 1994 by Philo/Rounder after being remastered and remixed by Cathy Fink and Dave Glasser. "Somewhere during those three days," John McCutcheon recalled of the original recording session, "I remember realizing that the songs I was hearing were great not because my best pal had written them. They were great all on their own. They captured the simplicity, the honesty, the cut-to-the-heart qualities that Woody Guthrie penned."

Kahn continued primarily as an organizer. In 1980 he formed Grassroots Leadership, which does civil rights, labor and community organizing throughout the South. Proceeds from his concerts and lectures help fund the organization. He has lived in Charlotte, North Carolina, with his spouse, Elizabeth K. Minnich, a feminist philosopher and educator, since the early 1980s. In the mid-1980s he founded the Jewish Fund for Justice, which gives grants to Jewish and non-Jewish social activist groups. He served as the chair of the organization for several years and is still an active board member.

He has written several books on grassroots organizing, including *How People Get Power,* (McGraw-Hill, 1972; NASW Press, 1994) and *Organizing: A Guide for Grassroots Leaders,* (McGraw-Hill, 1981, NASW Press, 1991) In 1990, Hal Leonard Publishers released the *Si Kahn Songbook.*

"The great majority of my time is spent doing organizing work," he told Hochman. "The music is a sideline. But there aren't lines on my calendar where the organizing work stops and the singing begins. I see myself by profession an organizer and by avocation a musician."

New Wood was critically acclaimed, but the distribution was limited. His next five solo albums came out on the Chicago-based Flying Fish label, including *Home* (1979), *Doing My Job* (1982), *Unfinished Portraits* (1984), *I'll Be There* (1989), and *I Have Seen Freedom* (1991). The Red Clay Ramblers, as well as singer Claudia Schmidt, backed his earlier albums on Flying Fish. Kahn never developed a large following, but his albums sold in the 5,000 to 7,000 range, respectable for a folk artist during those years.

He didn't start performing until 1979, when he appeared at the Chicago Folk Festival. Since then he has toured in the United States, Canada, England, Scotland, Wales, Northern Ireland, the Netherlands, Belgium, and Portugal. He also gives workshops on organizing and music to local groups.

In 1985, during the Reagan years, Kahn and McCutcheon collaborated on an album called *Signs of the Times,* released the following year on the Rounder label. The album includes such Kahn songs as "Government on Horseback," "Signs of the Times," and "The Senator," about a Jesse Helmsian right-to-life senator who finds out he is pregnant. McCutcheon also first recorded his song "No Mas!" on the album. The album was reissued on Rounder in later 1994, with two additional tracks from each artist, including "Let's Keep It Straight," a McCutcheon song about the ban on gays in the military, and "By the Side of the Road," a multiracial murder ballad by Kahn.

The most powerful element in Kahn's songwriting is his ability to tell stories that instruct without hitting you over the head. "A guitar is not a sledgehammer," he told Hochman. "Part of my philosophy is slip it by them if you can."

In 1986 Kahn recorded with fellow activists Pete Seeger and Jane Sapp. The album, *Carry It On: Songs of America's Working People,* was issued by Flying

Fish. Kahn stayed with the label until his friend, producer and Flying Fish owner Bruce Kaplan, died in the early 1990s and then, at the urging of John McCutcheon and Cathy Fink, Kahn went to Rounder.

In 1989 Kahn recorded song and narration cassettes (along with Cathy Fink and Marcy Marxer) for two children's books, *Goodnight Moon* and *Runaway Bunny,* for HarperCollins. In 1993 he released an album for children, *Good Times and Bedtimes,* on the Rounder label. The album, seven years in the making, centers on the "universal ritual of bedtime" and begins with two Kahn protest numbers for children: "No More Bedtimes" and "I'm Not Going to Go to Sleep." The album was delayed for so long because Flying Fish wasn't interested in children's albums, and because the album could be considered hostile to parents, "of which I am one," Kahn admits. It also includes humorous songs, such as "Brush to the North" and "Stay in the Bathtub Till the Soap Disappears," and lullabies such as "Will You Remember?"

In 1994 Kahn released a retrospective live album called *In My Heart* on Rounder. (The album was recorded in the Netherlands in April 1993, and was released there first on the Strictly Country label.) It includes many of his standards: "Gone Gonna Rise Again," "Aragon Mill," "Mississippi Summer," and "Brookside Strike."

In addition to albums and books, Kahn has written lyrics and music for three musicals: *200 RPM,* first produced by the Playgroup in Knoxville in 1976; *Some Sweet Day,* about white and black sharecroppers organizing together, performed by the Tennessee Repertory Theater in Nashville in 1991; and *Mother Jones,* which premiered at the Milwaukee Repertory Theater in 1992. In addition he has recorded songs for several videos.

In 1997 Appleseed Records released *Companion,* a collection of songs about "the people who've been living, loving, and working companions over the years," Kahn says. He includes three songs for his spouse, Elizabeth; one song for his youngest son, Gabe; a song for Cathy Fink's fortieth birthday; and one for Pete and Toshi Seeger, among others.

In 1998 Kahn recorded a bluegrass album produced by former Hot Rize banjoist Pete Wernick that also features Laurie Lewis, Tom Rozum, Todd Phillips, Charles Sawtelle, and Sally Van Meter. The album, *Been a Long Time,* was released on Sliced Bread Records in 2000. In December 1999 Kahn recorded his thirteenth album, *Threads,* in Wolfenschiessen, Switzerland, produced by and featuring the instrumental work of Jens Krüger, of the Swiss-based band the Krüger Brothers. The album begins in 1846 when a young woman leaves her family farm in New Hampshire to work in the cotton mills in Lowell, Massachusetts, the town where Kahn's Russian Jewish grandparents settled when they came to this country. The "threads" of the title connect South to North, cottonfield and cotton mill, field hand and mill

hand, black and white. The CD will be released on the Swiss "double time music" label on 2001.

Kahn still spends most of his time organizing throughout the South with Grassroots Leadership. Songwriting remains a sideline. "My music is a hobby that got out of hand," Kahn says. "I still see myself as a passionate, amateur musician who would like nothing better than to play rhythm guitar and sing harmony with Ralph Stanley's band. What I'm trying to do is draw on the roots music of southern African American and white communities where I've spent my organizing life and to give back a music that is about the everyday lives, hopes, fears, and dreams of the people I've lived with and learned from. I'm trying to create a music that's for everybody, a music that people can sing and make their own."

Based on an interview by Lyndon Stambler with Si Kahn

KAISER, HENRY: *Guitarist, songwriter, record producer, folk-music collector. Born Oakland, California, September 19, 1952.*

After establishing a reputation with other musicians in the jazz and rock fields for his talents as an innovative and improvisational electric guitarist over almost two decades, Henry Kaiser suddenly switched gears in the 1990s and joined fellow Californian David Lindley in a program of unusual folk performances in countries across the globe. In a supporting role to captivating folk performers in Madagascar and Norway, he showed he was as much a master of acoustic guitar playing as he was on a highly amplified instrument.

He was born and raised in the San Francisco Bay Area under comfortable circumstances and with little initial thought of making his career in entertainment. Like many people in their teens in the mid- and late 1960s, he enjoyed the folk-rock sounds of artists like the Jefferson Airplane, Janis Joplin, and, in particular, the Grateful Dead, but was a listener rather than a participant. He recalled, "Before I played guitar, I used to go see the Grateful Dead and sit at the edge of the stage. The band was an early model for me in terms of improvising and thinking about music as a positive social force. Oddly enough, though, I didn't play rock and roll when I first picked up the guitar. Now I not only have fun playing rock, but I get to play on stage with some of those guys."

Nor was his interest in the Grateful Dead the spur for him to learn guitar, something he didn't pursue until he was twenty in the early 1970s and attending college. The inspiration, in fact, was listening to a jazz recording by British guitarist Derek Bailey with saxophonist Evan Parker and percussionist Han Bennink. After hearing the disc, he went out and bought a guitar and began experimenting with it. By the mid-1970s he had mastered the electric instrument and was starting to win attention as a unique free improviser who added all manner of unusual touches to his playing style. One of his approaches that fueled this development was his curiosity about all manner of music, from twentieth-century classical compositions to hard-driving rock. Over the years, he drew on such other sources as shamanistic Korean music, Hawaiian guitar, country blues, and North Indian classical styles.

As a supporting artist or musical collaborator, he found opportunities to play with dozens of artists, including Grateful Dead stars Jerry Garcia and Bob Weir. Among those he worked with from the '70s into the 1990s were, besides Garcia, Weir, and their group, Herbie Hancock, Diamanda Galas, Raymond Kane, Terry Riley, Bill Frisell, John Oswald, Freddie Roulette, Sang-Won Park, Evan Parker, Cecil Taylor, the Golden Palominos, Sonny Sharrock, Miya Masaoka, Negativland, and his most important early influence, Derek Bailey. In all, through the early 1990s, his album appearances encompassed some 100 discs. Some of the releases that featured his rock 'n' roll abilities were *Those Who Know History Are Doomed to Repeat It* on the SST label, *Heart's Desire* and *Hope You Like Our New Direction,* both on Reckless Records, and, as part of FFKT (John French, Fred Frith, Kaiser, and Richard Thompson), *Invisible Means* and *Live, Love Larf & Loaf* on Windham Hill. The latter went out of print and was reissued by Shanachie in June 1996.

Among the contacts he made in the music field was one with David Lindley, the multiinstrumentalist and longtime associate of folk-rocker Jackson Browne. At the start of the '90s, the two decided they would like to track down music in other parts of the world that might open completely new vistas for composers and performers everywhere. They discussed going off the beaten path to places in Africa or Asia, but with support from Shanachie Records ended up traveling to the island of Madagascar, in the Indian Ocean, off Africa's east coast. Not knowing exactly what to expect, they arrived there with their recording equipment in the spring of 1991.

They originally expected to collect material for a single CD in which they laid down tracks with the major Malagasy artists from the popular, folk, and traditional sectors. Instead, they were amazed at the range and quality of material their newfound friends could offer. During their stay they typically recorded performances for sixteen to eighteen hours a day, usually finding the Malagasy rhythms and interactions so compelling that they themselves didn't take part. Kaiser commented, "We had so much great stuff that after we'd been recording for a week we called Shanachie and said 'There's going to be a lot more.' " When the first release, *A World out of Time (Volume 1),* came out in 1992 (with Kaiser handling production chores) it proved one of the most satisfying CDs in the world music sector for the year. Similar accolades greeted *A World out of Time (Volume 2)* issued by Shanachie in 1993. That album earned a 1994 Grammy nomination.

By 1995 Kaiser was working on production of *Volume 3,* released in August 1996.

In his contributions to some of the tracks on those albums, Kaiser mainly used acoustic rather than electric instruments. This also held true when he and Lindley went to Norway in 1994 to record some of the little-heard (on records) folk music of that country (issued on the '95 Shanachie CD *Sweet Sunny North*). *Sweet Sunny North (Volume 2)* was released in October 1996. Discussing that with Michael Parrish for an article in *Dirty Linen* ("Musical Ambassadors to Norway," April–May 1995), he said, "The last couple of years I've been playing acoustic guitar a lot more. It's because I've played a lot in the last few years with Richard Thompson, Lindley, Bob Weir of the Grateful Dead, people who are real masters among folk musicians. They've been really, really kind to me in allowing me to understand that kind of music a lot more than before."

Of course, Kaiser didn't abandon his electric guitar probings and continued to turn out a dizzying number of new or reissued albums in the mid-1990s. Some of his projects drew on his exposure to the Grateful Dead. For instance, for Shanachie he completed the collection *The Music Never Stopped: The Roots of the Grateful Dead,* coproduced with David Gans, which presented an anthology of original and influential source music that affected the group's development. In late '95 the label issued the disc *Eternity Blue,* which included four Dead-related tracks from Kaiser's personal archives and three new 1995 recordings in honor of the band's late leader, Jerry Garcia. Among those who collaborated on the project were former Dead members Tom Constanten and Bob Bralove; guitarists David Gans, Danny Carnahan, and Bruce Anderson; vocalists Cary Sheldon, Diana Morgano, and Robin Petrie; pianist Marilyn Crispell; bassist Gary Lambert, and a number of other musicians.

In addition, there were several other mid-'90s projects involving Kaiser's instrumental talent and production skills. One of those, on the Immune label, was a rock collection recorded with former Frank Zappa guitarist Mike Kenneally, former Dixie Dregs bass guitarist Andy West, and Tubes/Todd Rundgren/Jefferson Starship drummer Prairie Prince titled *The Mistakes.* During 1995 Shanachie issued the album *Wireforks,* on which he performed guitar duets with Derek Bailey. The disc *Second Sight,* released by Shanachie in '96, was a fusion effort that featured contributions by Bralove, Weir, and Jerry Garcia. On Cuneiform Records, Kaiser joined with Bruce Anderson, Dale Sopheia, Tom Constanten, and Lukas Ligeri in *The Siamese Step Brothers* album. In February 1996 some of Kaiser's early improvised recordings became available on the Dexter's Cigar label, titled *Outside Aloha Pleasure.* Besides all that, he occasionally joined Bob Weir as coleader of the Valentines, described as a "psychedelic good-time dance party band."

In August 1998 Kaiser and Wadada Leo Smith co-produced *Yo Miles!*, a two-disc high-definition CD dedicated to an exploration of Miles Davis's electronic era, from the mid-1970s to the mid-1980s. The set includes Smith on trumpet and musicians Nels Klein and John Modeski.

KAPLANSKY, LUCY: *Singer, guitarist, songwriter. Born Chicago, Illinois, February 16, 1960.*

By the time Lucy Kaplansky's impressive debut album, *The Tide,* was released by Red House Records in late 1994, she had accumulated many hours of performing experience going back to her early teens. But it was not a matter of an artist having an extended period of dues-paying before gaining attention; in fact, a *New York Times* critic had tapped her for potential stardom as early as 1981. Nor was it a lack of opportunities to bring her talents to a large sector of the music audience. Each time those arose, she backed away, insisting that music was a hobby for her rather than a profession. Fortunately, she finally realized in the 1990s that it was fear of failure rather than creative desires that had hindered her career as long as it had.

Looking back to her formative years, she recalled, "My father was a professor of mathematics at the University of Chicago and a semiprofessional piano player, and from when I was a kid I did a lot of singing leaning over the piano while he played. Mostly he played stuff from the '30s and '40s like George Gershwin and Irving Berlin and he also loved Gilbert and Sullivan. So really from the time I was little I was singing. I took lessons on guitar when I was thirteen and started performing in high school, and people said you should try doing it professionally. I met a guy named Elliot Simon who'd just graduated from the University of Chicago, and we began working together and got a bass player and another singer to become a folk-rock group. I used to play in Chicago bars when I was too young to be in clubs legally.

"There was a big article in the *New York Times* in December 1977 saying there was a new folk music revival in Greenwich Village. It had a picture of the Roches, Steve Forbert, and some others. So when I graduated from high school Elliot and I packed up and went back east and began performing in New York. We broke up after a couple of years, and I started doing a solo thing in 1980, first in a few clubs in the Village and later extended that to New England. Things really were going very well and in April 1981 I got a great review in the *New York Times* after opening for Jesse Winchester in Folk City."

Both her many friends in the folk and folk-rock communities and music critics believed it was only a matter of time before she gained a record deal with a major label. But, Lucy said, "All of a sudden in 1983 I kind of freaked out and decided I wasn't happy, wasn't using my real talents, and I decided to quit and go back to college. [She enrolled in New York University and earned her bachelor's degree there late in the decade.] In reality, looking back I was very scared that I wasn't good enough and couldn't be successful partly because of the extraordinarily talented people I was hanging around with—Suzanne Vega, Bill Morrissey, Shawn Colvin, the Roches. I was scared but didn't know it, so I quit.

"Actually, I never quit completely. I kept singing and doing backing vocals for people like Nanci Griffith, Suzanne Vega, Shawn Colvin, and John Gorka. Also in the mid-1980s I formed a duo with Colvin for a couple of years. It was sort of informal at first, but it became more and more formal as people heard us. We were nominated as Best Folk Act in the New York Music Awards. One night at Folk City a record company executive said, 'I'd like to record you.' I was back in college and thought I was performing as a hobby and I said, 'Oh no! I don't want to make a record,' and that was the end of our duo. Shawn said she hoped I didn't mind but she did want to make a record."

During those mid-'80s years and onward, though, Lucy was not unfamiliar with recording studios. She sang harmony on tracks on albums by Griffith, Vega, Gorka, and Colvin, and backed some of them on sound track music. That included a song with Suzanne Vega for the 1986 film *Pretty in Pink* and one with Griffith for the 1987 movie *The Firm* (the last-named a cut from Nanci's *Little Love Affairs* album). Besides that, she pointed out, "I sang the jingle 'The Heartbeat of America' in 1986 for a Chevy commercial. It was written by Robin Batteau, who also wrote a song I used on *The Tide.*" Later Lucy harmonized with Shawn Colvin on songs for the latter's *Steady On* album on Columbia Records, which earned the 1990 Grammy for Best Contemporary Folk Recording.

Through it all, Lucy continued to pursue her academic goals, earning her doctorate in clinical psychology from Yeshiva University in 1992. After graduation she took a position at St. Luke's Hospital in Manhattan, where many of her clients were substance abusers or people with chronic mental illness. Her friendship with Shawn Colvin remained close, and Colvin, who wanted to gain experience in record production, urged Lucy to let her work on a solo album. "So we made the record," Lucy said, "and only when we were in the process of shopping it around the music industry did I realize I had been lying to myself about my career goals, and since then I've been pursuing a music career seriously."

When Colvin brought Lucy's material to the attention of Bob Feldman of Red House Records, she recalled, he was very enthusiastic, saying "he thought it was the best album he'd heard in years." Most of the songs were written by others—Batteau, Richard Thompson, Bill Morrissey, Tom Russell, David Massengill, Cliff Eberhardt, and Sting—but Lucy provided three songs, including the title track. Released in late 1994, *The Tide* qualified as one of the more intriguing releases of 1994–95. Critical response was overwhelmingly favorable. The United Press reviewer enthused, "In the 1960s a composer and vocalist of her brilliance would have been accorded superstar status. . . . *The Tide* showcases Kaplansky's talents perfectly, introducing the audience to her sensitive, imaginative writing . . . and demonstrating her interpretive skills." Stewart Francke, in *CD Review* (February 1995), commented, "Her singing style is worth noting. She has something of a pinched delivery, clarified by Ciceronian diction and an adroit use of dynamics. . . . A marvelous interpretive singer, Kaplansky stands no less tall than Nanci Griffith, Lucinda Williams, or even her old friend Colvin."

In early January '96 she was preparing material for a second Red House album: "This will have a lot of original songs because I've been writing a lot of original stuff myself or with my husband, Rick Litvin. I cowrote 'The Tide' with him. I hope the new album will come out this fall. As for my writing approach, what seems to work for me is to allow my subconscious to speak. I sit down with my guitar and a tape recorder and sing whatever comes out. A couple of my songs came from suggestions by my husband, but usually I don't start with a specific idea. I can't say I'm going to sit down and write a song about subject X or subject Y. It doesn't work that way for me."

She expressed her optimism about the future of neofolk music. "For the last few years there have been more and more places to play and more and more talented people to perform in them. The Internet has fueled this trend to a considerable extent, because there are a lot of discussions about artists on smaller labels, which has been good for albums like mine."

During 1995 Lucy continued to back her new collection with concerts in many parts of the United States, though still doing work as a clinical psychologist. She hoped to tour overseas during 1996, she said, particularly since *The Tide* was doing quite well with record buyers in England.

In 1996 Kaplansky followed her fine debut with her second CD release on Red House, *Flesh and Bone*, which like *Tide*, sold 20,000 copies and was nominated for an Indie Award. This time eight of the twelve tracks were originals, written by Kaplansky and her husband. Kaplansky expanded her following with her second release. She continued to succeed with strong covers of songs by excellent writers, including "(What's So Funny 'Bout) Peace, Love and Understanding" by Nick Lowe, "Don't Renege on Our Love" by Richard Thompson, and "The Return of the Grievous Angel" by Gram Parsons.

Kaplansky teamed up with Dar Williams and Richard Shindell to produce an album called *Cry Cry Cry*, released in 1998 on X. The album includes covers of the trio's favorite songs, including R.E.M.'s "Fall on Me," Ron Sexsmith's "Speaking with the Angel," and Robert Earl Keen's "Shades of Gray." The three toured widely around the United States in late 1998 in support of the collaborative project.

Kaplansky released her third Red House CD, *Ten Year Night,* in March 1999.

Based on phone interview with Irwin Stambler in January 1996

KAZEE, BUELL: *Singer, banjoist, minister, composer, author. Born Burton's Fork, Magoffin County, Kentucky, August 29, 1900; died August 31, 1976, Winchester, Kentucky.*

There is an obvious close connection between folk music and religion. Many of the folk standards sung by all manner of artists and groups in the 1950s and 1960s are gospel songs or spirituals or are derived from this genre. Thus, some of the best-known names in folksinging, particularly prior to the mid-twentieth century, have religious or ministerial backgrounds.

A case in point is Bible scholar, minister, and folksinger Buell Hilton Kazee. During his youth in Kentucky, he heard many old ballads and religious songs from his parents and the neighbors. His father, who was in charge of music at their church, made his son a banjo when the boy was five. By the time Buell was old enough to attend the log schoolhouse in the area, he could play and sing many old-time songs.

Buell completed high school in 1920 at the Baptist Magoffin Institute in Salyersville, Kentucky, and went on to nearby Georgetown College. By this time, he was already an ordained minister, having taken up religious studies in 1917. Though some people looked on singing and dancing as sinful, Buell was not troubled by such thoughts. From his teens on, he often performed for local gatherings. By the time he was in college, he had learned to play the piano, guitar, and banjo.

When Buell gained his degree from Georgetown, he had considerable local repute as a folksinger. In 1925, he was featured in a concert at the University of Kentucky, the first of hundreds of such recitals he was to give.

His college years helped whet his interest in American folk music and he became an avid collector. This was his major hobby throughout his ministerial career. He worked at various places in Kentucky for the Baptist Church before settling down to a twenty-two year tenure as pastor of the First Baptist Church in Morehead, Kentucky. His church duties included directing the choirs, for some of which he composed original music.

Kazee was one of the pioneer recording artists in the folk-music field. During the 1926–30 period, he turned out more than fifty recordings for Brunswick and Vocalion labels. These included many of the best-known folk songs, such as "Rock Island Line," "Hobo's Last Ride," "Darling Cora," "East Virginia," "The Little Mohee," and "The Roving Cowboy." These activities came to a close in the early 1930s, due to the Great Depression.

He continued to perform at many folk concerts, however, including recitals at colleges and universities, throughout the Appalachian region. In the 1930s, he also recorded some material for the Archive of American Folk Songs of the Library of Congress.

Kazee found time to write many articles on religious subjects. He also turned out a book in 1941 titled *Faith Is the Victory*. He never went far afield from his beloved Kentucky, though, and in 1950 moved over to Lexington Baptist College as professor of Old Testament studies. In 1952 Harry Smith included two of Kazee's songs in the *Anthology of American Folk Music:* "The Butcher Boy" and "The Wagoner's Lad." Both were recorded in New York in January 1928. (The anthology was rereleased on CD in 1998.) In 1959, Folkways Records once more made Kazee's music available to the general public with the LP *Buell H. Kazee, His Songs and Music*. This included some of the songs mentioned above and such others as "Yellow Pups," "John Henry," "The Moonshiner," "Cumberland Gap," "Old Grey Mare," "Amazing Grace," "Bread of Heaven," "Eternity," and "The White Pilgrim."

After retiring from preaching, Kazee performed frequently at colleges and folk festivals around the country. In the 1960s he performed at the University of Chicago and at the Newport Folk Festival with Joan Baez and Pete Seeger. "They were a little radical for him but he performed there anyhow," says Loyal Jones, a retired professor who first met Kazee in 1965. Kazee served on a committee with Jones at Berea College in Kentucky and performed at a celebration of traditional music.

Kazee retired to Winchester, Kentucky, and died there just two days after his seventy-sixth birthday. He was buried in Burton's Fork, Magoffin County.

Two years after Kazee's death, Loyal Jones, John McCutcheon, and Jonathan Greene produced an album for June Appal Records titled *Buell Kazee*, which includes extensive notes by Jones and William Tallmadge. The album, based on field recordings of Kazee, includes "Roll on, John," "Jay Gould's Daughter," "The Lady Gay," "Steel A-Going Down," "The Roving Cowboy," "Sporting Bachelors," "The Orphan Girl," "Black Jack Davie," "The Blind Man," and "Amazing Grace."

Kazee's son, Phillip Kazee, a Baptist preacher, has carried on Buell's tradition. "He sings remarkably like Buell and plays the banjo in the same way," Loyal Jones says.

Entry written with the assistance of Loyal Jones, a scholar living in Berea, Kentucky

KEANE, DOLORES: *Singer, songwriter, band leader (the Reel Union, Kinvara), actress. Born Caherlistrane, County Galway, Ireland, ca. mid-1950s.*

A favorite of almost all music fans in Ireland as well as of such U.S. artists as Emmylou Harris and Nanci Griffith, Dolores Keane's pure, crystal-clear voice set

new standards of excellence in traditional and modern folk music of the closing decades of the twentieth century. As Colin Irwin enthused in *Folk Roots,* "She could sing the small print on a Guinness bottle and make it heartstopping. Fortunate indeed is that songwriter who gets a song covered by the blessed Dolores. And when she gets a genuinely good song . . . then the sheer depth of her artistry is mesmerizing."

Nanci Griffith, who treasured Keane's recordings, told the *Irish Independent* newspaper, "As long as Dolores Keane is walking around the Earth, I won't call myself a singer. I think she's the voice of Ireland. I'm a huge fan of Maura O'Connell and we're dear friends with Mary Black as well and I love their voices. But there's something about the soul of Dolores Keane to me and it's just that I want the world to hear her voice."

People of Ireland began hearing her voice on radio and TV long before she reached her teens. The first radio recordings were made when she was five by Kieran MacMohan, who used to visit her home with a mobile recording unit to collect material by her aunts, Rita and Sarah Keane, adepts at *sean-nos* (unaccompanied) vocals. Over the years of her youth she appeared on many TV programs, usually with Rita and Sarah. As she recalled for Lahri Bond of *Dirty Linen* ("The Voice of Ireland, Dolores Keane," June–July 1993), "I was actually brought up in my grandmother's house, the house of Rita and Sarah. They're maiden aunts, never married. I lived there from when I was about four years old, with my aunts and uncles and my grandparents, in what would be in West Ireland 'a big farm.' It wouldn't be over here [in the United States]; just over ten acres, it was quite a large farm for that part of Ireland."

As she grew older she extended her musical boundaries as a performer to a point where she began gaining attention for her solo artistry. Her first breakthrough to a broader audience came in the mid-1970s, when she became a key member of the De Dannan band. She told Bond, "Johnny Moynihan asked me one night in a pub in Galway if I would like to join a group that they were forming. Would I like to sing? It was the first time I ever sang accompanied. I took them up on it and decided to go for it. We used to rehearse out in Spidell in Alec's [band member Alec Finn] house at the time and we'd do a lot of rehearsing at the pub. Just sessions for the locals."

Dolores remained a member of the group, whose vocal roster at times also included Mary Black, for four years, touring with them throughout Ireland and other parts of the world, and contributed to the band's first album, *De Dannan,* issued on Boot Records in 1976 and available only in the United Kingdom. Two tracks on which she sang lead vocals, "The Rambling Irishman" and "The Mountain Streams," later were included in the Shanachie Records retrospective, *The Best of De Dannan*. When "The Rambling Irishman" was first issued as a single in 1976, it rose to number one on the Irish

see his jazz band on Monday nights, and I'd bring my guitar and sit in, start playing the blues. He'd look over the drums and holler, 'Keb' Mo'!' It's like if I was playing jazz, I could be Kevin Moore—but if I was gonna play the blues, I had to be Keb' Mo'!" Denard later played drums behind Keb' Mo' on the latter's debut album.

It was a meeting with Kevin's idol Taj Mahal that opened the door to the artist's solo career. A mutual friend took Keb' Mo' to meet Mahal, and producer John Porter was also present. As Mo' told Dave Peabody, "I gave [Porter] one of my tapes and we hit it off . . . kind of cool and everything. He just started calling me up . . . 'You got anything else on tape you can give me?' I said, 'Well, I've got a few tunes here.' And I gave him some more stuff and he went on his way with it."

Learning that Epic Records was reviving the illustrious OKeh label, Porter gained label approval for a Keb' Mo' project, which resulted in the June 1994 release *Keb' Mo'*. The disc contained thirteen songs, eleven written or cowritten by Keb' Mo' and two by Robert Johnson, "Come On in My Kitchen" and "Kind Hearted Woman Blues." Supported by extensive touring by the artist, including opening for artists like Buddy Guy, Joe Cocker, and Jeff Beck, and featured spots at major festivals, the album became one of the most talked-about blues stylings of the mid-1990s. Keb' Mo' originals from the disc like "Don't Try to Explain" and "Victims of Comfort" also received considerable attention from blues critics and fans. The album was voted Country Acoustic Blues Album of the Year in the sixteenth annual W. C. Handy Blues Awards and placed second in the "Beyond" category of *Down Beat*'s forty-third annual Critics Poll.

Keb' Mo''s 1995 performing credits included a well-received set at the Newport Folk Festival, where he used his slide guitar talents and powerful vocal delivery to good effect on songs like "Angelina," "Every Morning," and "She Just Wants to Dance." Late in the year he was featured on his first European concert series.

Among the artists who reacted enthusiastically to the new collection were Bonnie Raitt and Jackson Browne. In Bonnie's case, she was given a tape of the album by bassist James "Butch" Hutchinson. Keb' Mo' said, "She was listening to it in the car one day, then she switched to the radio. I was doing a radio interview at that moment, and she called me at the station from her car phone! Then she came to a gig and hung out, and then I opened for her on a couple of dates. She said, 'I'd like to do something with you—and I'm not just jerking your chain.' And when Bonnie says she's gonna do something, she always shows up. A good friend of mine, Kevin McCormick, is in Jackson Browne's band. He introduced me to Jackson when we were both playing the Bumbershoot Festival in Seattle." Both Raitt and Browne provided backing vocals for the title track of Keb' Mo''s second OKeh album, *Just Like You*.

The latter, again produced by John Porter, contained twelve new originals plus one Robert Johnson number, "Last Fair Deal Gone Down." The album, released during 1996, again gained good critical response, and when the Grammy winners were announced on the February 1997 awards TV program, the album was named Best Contemporary Blues Album of 1996. The growing public association of Keb' Mo' with the late Robert Johnson brought him the opportunity to play the Johnson role in the 1997 docudrama *Can't You Hear the Wind Howl?* narrated by Danny Glover. (The film was released on video in 1998.) The U.S. Post Office launched its Robert Johnson stamp release by having Keb' Mo' perform at a Boulder, Colorado, post office.

By the end of 1998, Keb' Mo''s credits at major festivals included, besides Newport, the Chicago Blues Festival, Montreux Jazz Festival, and North Sea Jazz Festival. During the year, his third Keb' Mo' album was released on Sony 550, *Slow Down*. That album rose to number one on the *Billboard* blues chart and won the artist a second Grammy for Best Contemporary Blues Album of 1998. In early 1999 he was a featured artist, along with such other notables as McKinley Morganfield Jr., Buddy Guy, and Charlie Musselwhite, in a tribute to Muddy Waters at the Kennedy Center in Washington, D.C., telecast over the PBS network. In 2000 he released an album on the Sony 550 label, *The Door*.

KEITH, BILL: *Singer, banjoist, pedal steel guitarist, songwriter. Born Massachusetts, December 20, 1939.*

In terms of banjo innovations, the two artists who contributed most in the post–World War II decades were Earl Scruggs and Bill Keith. If Scruggs's advances helped bring about a surge in bluegrass banjo interest in the late 1940s and during the 1960s, Keith's efforts laid the groundwork for the evolution of such new forms as "newgrass" and "jazzgrass" in the 1970s.

Bill, who grew up in Brockton, Massachusetts, near Boston, was interested in the banjo during his high school years in the mid-1950s. Initially he played tenor banjo in local dixieland groups, but the thriving folk music atmosphere of those years soon caught his attention. He was particularly impressed with the banjo styles of Earl Scruggs and Pete Seeger, though he didn't really set about to master those methods until he was attending Amherst College in Amherst, Massachusetts, in the late 1950s. He purchased a used five-string banjo for fifteen dollars as well as Pete Seeger's book, "How to Play the Five-String Banjo," in the fall of 1957 and learned the basics of both Seeger's and Scruggs' techniques before he started to experiment with variations of his own.

Meanwhile, he had found a kindred spirit in guitarist Jim Rooney, also attending Amherst, who liked folk and bluegrass music. The two began to jam together and soon formed a duo to play in local coffee houses and in campus shows. They also made other contacts in the music field, including a promoter named

Manny Greenhill who helped them form a folk music organization called the Connecticut Valley Folklore Society. Those activities led to a series of concerts in many college areas of New England in which Keith, Rooney, and other college folk groups took part. During one of those late 1950s concerts, Keith unveiled the first version of his own picking style (the tune was called "Noah's Breakdown"), which later became known as melodic (chromatic) banjo style. In years to come, that invention had as great an impact on the banjo field as the earlier Scruggs style.

Comparing the two approaches, Keith told Roger H. Simonoff (*Frets* magazine, March 1980, pp. 32–37), "I would say that the basic difference between [his approach] and the regular Scruggs style is that [in chromatic banjo style] the hands are working together in a much higher degree of cooperation. . . . When you play chromatically, you're playing pretty much note for note, whereas in the regular Scruggs style, it's more apt to be lick for lick. One of the big differences in the way the left hand is used is that you're using different kinds of chord positions than are used in the regular Scruggs style. And, of course, you use open strings, so very often you're fretting on the second string and the first string is open, or you're fretting on the third string and the second string is open. . . ."

In addition to developing a new playing technique, Keith also developed new banjo components, such as a special tuner. In that case, he worked with a fraternity brother of Rooney's named Dan Bump. Bump suggested forming a banjo company in 1963, and Keith suggested they needed some kind of innovation to set such an operation apart. Between them, they decided an improved tuning peg would make sense, and the result of their work was a system incorporating the pitch-changer function into the peg. He told Simonoff, "Earl Scruggs had come up with his own cam-type pitch changers, . . . but those involved drilling holes in the peghead for installation. We felt the advantage of ours was that you could just substitute one for an existing peg." Later they showed the design to Scruggs, who was so impressed he joined them in producing Keith-Scruggs tuners in the mid-1960s. Dan Bump eventually set up his own firm in Putney, Vermont, to turn out Keith tuners.

Keith and Rooney continued to perform whenever the chance arose, including an appearance at the Newport Folk Festival. They also managed to get a recording agreement with Prestige that resulted in 1963 distribution of their 1962 album, *Livin' on the Mountain,* which included debut renditions of two of Keith's best-known instrumentals, his version of "Salty Dog Blues" and "Devil's Dream." After completing his studies at Amherst, and a stint in the Air Force Reserves Keith moved to Washington, D.C., for a while to study banjo-making methods from an expert named Tom Morgan. Rooney also migrated there and, through Mor-

gan, the duo met bluegrass musicians Red Allen (guitar) and Frank Wakefield (mandolin), who asked Keith to become banjoist of their group, the Kentuckians. During that period, Manny Greenhill was promoting some of the Flatt & Scruggs concerts. While that famed team played Baltimore, Greenhill introduced Scruggs and Keith. Earl needed someone to do banjo tablature for a new book on the five-string banjo he was working on and asked Bill Keith to come to Nashville to help out.

Keith agreed, his work eventually appearing in the book, *Earl Scruggs and the 5-String Banjo,* when it was published in 1968 by Peer International. His stay in Nashville had other ramifications. Backstage at the *Grand Ole Opry* one night, he was overheard playing "Devil's Dream" by the Father of Bluegrass, Bill Monroe. In 1963 Monroe brought Keith (whom he called Brad) into his Bluegrass Boys, an association that lasted less than a year. Said Monroe, "There's not a banjo picker in the country that can beat Brad!"

Keith had too many interests to remain in the group and left to become the banjoist for Jim Kweskin's Jug Band in 1964. He stayed with the group for the next four years and then played banjo with a group called the Blue Velvet Band with Rooney and Eric Weissberg. Over the years, he did session work, spent some time as banjo player for the Woodstock Mountain Review, did solo sets, such as the one at the 1967 Newport Folk Festival, wrote new material and continued to refine both his melodic style and banjo innovations. He also found time to perfect his performance on another instrument, pedal steel guitar, at one point dropping the banjo for a while.

He never dropped his friendship with Rooney. Throughout the 1970s and into the 1980s, they often toured together, playing the folk music circuit in the United States and Canada. Together or separately, they also made a number of trips to Europe; France, in particular, held Keith's work in high esteem. Besides his concert work, Keith also devoted considerable amounts of time to banjo workshops in many parts of the United States. When the magazine *Frets* began publication in the late 1970s, he was one of the charter columnists on banjo techniques.

Although Keith took part in many recording sessions during the 1960s and 1970s, only a limited number were albums featuring his work. In 1976, Rounder Records released *Something Auld, Something Newgrass, Something Borrowed, Something Bluegrass,* which featured Keith, Rooney, David Grisman on mandolin, Tony Rice on guitar, Vassar Clements on fiddle, and Ken Kosek on fiddle. In 1981 he joined Béla Fleck on the Rounder album *Fiddle Tunes for Banjo.* Keith followed in 1984 with his second solo album, *Banjoistics,* released by Rounder. Other album releases on which he was represented were, on Rounder, *Banjoland* and *Mud Acres—Music Among Friends*; on Musigrass-Diffusion, *Banjo Paris Sessions*; on Ridgerunner, *Muleskinner* and *Jazzgrass*; on MCA, *Bluegrass Time.*

In the 1970s, though he could play many styles of bluegrass, Keith made considerable contributions to the general classification of progressive bluegrass. He told Simonoff, "I think people generally will admit that there's a difference between newgrass and traditional bluegrass and I think the difference is the material that's dealt with. These days, there is a higher percentage of material that has more complicated harmonies in it. Also newgrass, jazzgrass, and what I call fusion music are taking bluegrass instrumental styles and playing other kinds of music, including jazz and old standards. . . . There's more of a variety of chords. In fact, you get into this kind of variety when you include more notes in the chord that you're playing (than in 'traditional' chording)."

In 1989, Keith, Rooney, and Eric Weissberg reestablished the New Blue Velvet Band, adding Kenny Kosek on fiddle. In the 1990s Keith also played with other ensembles, including the John Herald Band. In 1992, Green Linnet released his third solo album, *Beating Around the Bush,* on which he is joined by Mark O'Connor, Kenny Kosek, Sam Bush, Roy Huskey Jr., and Gordon Titcomb.

KELLY, PAUL: *Singer, guitarist, songwriter, band leader (the Messengers). Born Adelaide, Australia, January 12, 1955.*

Australia has spawned more than a few artists who gained sizable followings in the United States—straight-ahead rock performers Men at Work and AC/DC come to mind—yet has not contributed much to advancing the musical state of the art. But one of its most talented people, singer-songwriter Paul Kelly, a superstar at home, turned out a series of superb albums released in the United States in the late 1980s and early 1990s without causing more than a ripple in the consciousness of the American music public. Critical comments, though, remained very positive, and there was hope that the tables might be turning in his favor in the mid-1990s.

Paul showed an interest in a broad spectrum of popular music from his preteen years, ranging from rock and folk-rock to country. By his teens in the 1970s he had learned to play guitar and already was demonstrating promise as a songwriter. He surfaced as a professional musician in 1980, first as a soloist and then as front man for the talented group the Messengers. By the mid-1980s Kelly and the band had established themselves as one of the dominant groups in Australia and New Zealand. They turned out five albums released locally during that period, which became top sellers on the Australian market and drew enthusiastic capacity crowds to many major venues in their homeland.

By the late 1980s Paul and his associates felt they were ready to seek approval from American fans. The impetus for that was outlined by Paul to Dan Kening of the *Chicago Daily Herald,* in a 1995 interview. (Even at that late date, Kenning commented, "Paul Kelly is one of the best songwriters you've probably never heard of.") "Every artist in Australia wants to be successful in the States. It's as simple as that. I've got a pretty good following in Australia, but to make my living I need to sell records in Europe and the U.S. as well. I'm not that big of a star back home that I can sit back and let Australia alone support me."

Kelly and the Messengers began their campaign for U.S. recognition under their 1987 album debut on the A&M label, *Gossip,* followed by *Under the Sun* in 1988 and *So Much Water, So Close to Home* in 1989. Critics across the United States hailed him as a creative artist whose writings were on a par with people like John Hiatt, Bruce Springsteen, and country-folk innovators Butch Hancock and Jimmie Dale Gilmore. (Hancock and Gilmore, in fact, recorded cover versions of Kelly's song "Special Treatment".) A *Rolling Stone* writer commented that Kelly "is one of the finest songwriters I have ever heard, Australian or otherwise." More than a few reviewers ranked *Gossip* and *Under the Sun,* the latter including such notable tracks as "Untouchable" and "To Her Door," both featured in his mid-'90s concerts, as among top releases of the decade.

While Kelly's music was typically well above average, his lyrics, as was the case with writers like Bob Dylan, often verged on the poetic. In the 1980s a book of his lyrics was published in Australia to good response. Geoffrey Himes of the *Washington Post* wrote, "He has a rare instinct for the kind of quirky details that separate everyday life from bad fiction, and he has sewn his narratives about bitter ex-lovers and bewildered children into catchy folk-rock guitar figures." Kelly's literary bent was indicated by the 1989 album, *So Much Water, So Close to Home,* which, he pointed out, was inspired by a short story by Raymond Carver that he admired. The track "Everything's Turning to White" reflected the mood of the Carver piece.

Live performances in many parts of the United States and Europe in the late 1980s, those who attended believed, were among the most exciting and emotionally charged events they'd experienced. Unfortunately, his U.S. appearances were in small venues that helped build a cult following but did little to expand his fan base to a national level. In 1991 his last studio album with the Messengers, *Comedy,* was released, another fine effort that included such songs as "Sydney from a 727" (a tip of the writer's hat to Jimmie Dale Gilmore's "Dallas") and "Buffalo Ballet," which had been written years before by John Cale, an alumnus of the Velvet Underground. In 1992 Mushroom Records released *Hidden Things,* a collection of eighteen songs Paul Kelly had recorded with the Messengers between 1986 and 1991. All except Woody Guthrie's "Pasture of Plenty" and Kelly's "Bradman" had appeared on previous albums. In the same year, Mushroom released a double-CD collection of concert recordings, *Live.*

After completing *Comedy,* Paul went his own way

and signed with Vanguard Records as a solo performer. This resulted in his 1993 label debut, *Wanted Man,* another well-honed collection that suffered much the same fate in the United States as previous releases— glowing critical backing but little or no radio or large-scale concert coverage. In 1995 he lined up a new band to back him in studio sessions in Melbourne for his next Vanguard project. The bandsmen included Shane O'Mara on the guitar, Stephen Hadley on bass, Bruce Haymes on keyboards, and Peter Luscombe on drums, and provided an excellent, well-rounded sound to the new disc, *Deeper Water,* issued in late '95.

Without a doubt this brilliant folk-rock album ranked among his best releases. It won glowing comments from the media from large circulation publications to small newspapers. The *Rolling Stone* reviewer, for instance, punned that Kelly "has always worked in deep waters. Even something as apparently matter-of-fact as the insistent affection in 'Give in to My Love' . . . has a wicked undertow of gray guitar jangle and unhealthy obsession (*My love is like a drunkard/Holding up the bar/And he'll say the same thing over/And he'll fix you with his stare*)." The *USA Today* critic, noting that *Wanted Man* made many '94 top 10 lists, called *Deeper Water* "the sleeper album of the year . . . The fuller-sounding *Water* . . . is prime grown-up rock: a dozen uncommonly resonant songs, played tight and written deep." Just about all of the album's songs, which included "Blush," "Anastasia Changes Her Mind," "Madeline's Song," and "I'll Forgive But I Won't Forget," seemed prime candidates for possible cover hits by other performers, even if the album itself failed to achieve the best-seller status it deserved.

Kelly discussed his approach to writing with reporter Sean Glennon in late 1995, saying among other things, "I do resist being put in a category with Graham Parker or Richard Thompson—although I have a lot of respect for Richard Thompson—or Elvis Costello. I want to range a little wider than that . . . I'm not trying to trick people or mystify them. My taste in music is pretty wide and I want to be just as wide in the kind of music I play."

Despite the tributes to his lyric writing, he emphasized that he considered music his main concern. "I think lyrics are important, but I don't write the lyrics first and then try to find music to go with them. Great lyrics aren't going to get over unless you've got great music first. Music's first. I'm a songwriter, not a poet."

In 1996 Kelly released *Live at the Continental and the Esplanade* on the White Records label, followed by a greatest hits album for the Australian market, *Songs from the South,* released in 1997. In May 1998 Vanguard Records released Kelly's album *Words and Music.*

THE KENNEDYS/KENNEDY, PETE AND MAURA:

Husband and wife duo. Pete Kennedy (guitar, banjo, mandolin, bass, keyboards, percussion, vocals), born Arlington, Virginia, February 9, 1952. Maura Kennedy (guitar, keyboards, lead vocals), born Syracuse, New York, October 25, 1963.

As they performed during a showcase in the 1996 Folk Alliance in Washington, D.C., Pete and Maura Kennedy made no secret of their love for one another. Full of energy, they smiled, mugged, and laughed. They even leaned back-to-back strumming their guitars. Theirs is a textured sound, heavily influenced by the Byrds, the Everly Brothers, and Buddy Holly. Pete Kennedy has been known for years as a premier East Coast session guitarist. He has played with Kate Wolf, Danny Gatton, Mary-Chapin Carpenter, and Nanci Griffith. Maura, who formerly played with an Austin-based group called the Delta Rays, sings lead and balances Pete's guitar playing on rhythm.

Pete grew up in Northern Virginia, where he gained a reputation playing at local clubs. He played guitar in Kate Wolf's band when she toured the East Coast. During the mid-1980s, he began recording a string of solo albums, including *Live at the Birchmere* and *Distant Thunder* on Potomac Disc; *Bound for Glory* on Rosewood Records; *Rhythm Ranch* and *Sunburst* on Rooster Records; *Channel 3* and *Highway 10* on Third Floor Records; and *Shearwater: The Art of the Unplugged Guitar* on Guitar Acoustics. He accompanied such artists as John McCutcheon, Fred Small, Sally Rogers, Carpenter, and Nanci Griffith, who invited him to play on *Other Voices, Other Rooms.*

Maura (nee Boudreau) grew up in Syracuse and began playing with the Delta Rays, which relocated to Austin, Texas. The country-rock group cut four songs for Warner publishing and cut one single, "Fancy Dreams."

Fate brought them together. Pete was touring through Austin in 1992 and Maura went to see him at the Continental Club. "My jaw dropped the minute he went into a guitar solo," she told Tom Nelligan of *Dirty Linen* ("Pete & Maura Kennedy," December '94/January '95). They met at a picking party and Maura suggested that Pete stay in town another day to write a song with her. To her surprise, he agreed. They wrote "Day In and Day Out."

Pete headed out of town to play at the Telluride Festival with Nanci Griffith. But the bond with Maura had been established. Both are Buddy Holly fans, so they decided to meet in Lubbock, Texas at Buddy Holly's grave site. They left their guitar picks in the dirt surrounding his tombstone, like many other musicians. For the next year they continued to write together, and established a long distance relationship.

Pete went on tour in 1993 to support *Other Voices, Other Rooms.* Iris DeMent was the opening act for the show but by the end of the American tour, DeMent left to pursue her own path. Griffith, who had heard Maura sing, invited her to sing backup in the Blue Moon Orchestra. She also asked Pete and Maura to open for her in England. They played their first perfomance in Liverpool, home of the Beatles. During that tour, they visited Abbey Road, the Beatles' recording studio. They also had harrowing experiences in Northern Ireland. While huddled in a Belfast hotel room, afraid to go outside, they wrote the material for their debut album, *River of Fallen Stars* (Green Linnet, 1995). "That was because the theater we were supposed to play in had gotten blown up and that was right next door to the hotel," Maura says.

Pete and Muara were married in the fall of 1994. They told Nelligan about how compatible they are on stage and off. "We think the same way," Maura said. "Someone commented that we even breathe at the same time. It's just the perfect match, musically and personally." They followed up with their second album, *Life is Large* (1996), their last album for Green Linnet before they decided to leave the label. The album featured an all-star cast of backup musicians: Roger McGuinn, Nils Lofgrin, Kelly Willis, and Steve Earle.

Despite their short-lived relationship with Green Linnet, don't expect the Kennedys to get down. At the Folk Alliance showcase, Maura introduced the uplifting "Life is Large" by saying, "We're generally happy people, we're not angst-ridden. We like to leave a positive message."

As singer-songwriters they found a better fit with Rounder in 1997 and came out with *Angel Fire* in 1997 and *Evolver* in January 2000. Like many young performers, they have a web site: www.kennedysmusic. com.

KING, ALBERT: *Singer, guitarist, songwriter. Born Indianola, Mississippi, April 25, 1923; died Memphis, Tennessee, December 21, 1992.*

Big Albert King, six feet four inches and 250 pounds, became the darling of the young audiences at the Fillmore East and West in the late 1960s. His raucous, infectious renditions of songs based on the Mississippi Delta blues tradition had the fans marking time with hands and feet and shouting for more when each number ended. It had taken a while for Albert, but he had persevered through the lean years to become recognized as perhaps the greatest living country blues artist of them all. Though the passionate '60s interest in blues and blues rock tapered off in the 1970s, King still was able to sustain his performing career throughout that decade and the 1980s.

Albert's story was the usual one of black rural bluesmen. He grew up in poverty, his father dead and his mother hard-pressed to pay the bills. He had a smattering of schooling, but had to work as a field hand, chopping cotton and doing other chores, when he was only nine. He was aware of the blues before that, however. His birthplace was Indianola, Mississippi, a town replete with dozens of barnlike clubs where blacks sought respite from their cares on weekends. Indianola is also the home region of B.B. King. There is still controversy about whether B.B. and Albert are half brothers; they decline to settle the matter. (*See King, B.B.*)

There also were many clubs with blues performers in Forest City, Arkansas (a town seventy-five miles from Memphis, Tennessee), where Albert's mother took the family when he was a child. As he told Phyl Gardner (*Sound of Soul,* Henry Regnery Co., 1969): "Like I was a little bitty boy when I used to listen to a blues singer called Dorothy Dailey (a man). Back in those days, now, Lonnie Johnson used to play the guitar and Mercer D. was a piano player then. He kept time with his feet; he played the bass with one hand, played the lead with the other, and sang and they would record him. If you listen to him, he really gets your attention because he's a man who really played from the heart, you know what I mean?"

King waited some years before he started playing music himself. In his early teens, he bought a guitar from another boy in Forest City for $1.25. He spent every spare hour he could for months on end learning to play the instrument which he played left-handed and upside down. Once he had mastered it reasonably well, he played it for friends or for his own pleasure and occasionally for parties and in small clubs. For many years, though, it remained a sideline as he earned his living in other ways. When he was full grown, he found work in the construction field, eventually specializing as a bulldozer operator.

At the end of the 1940s, he settled in Little Rock, Arkansas, working on levee construction days and, in time, assembling his own band to perform in local clubs nights and weekends. He bought his first amplified guitar then and used it as he handled lead vocals for his band. The group, called the In the Groove Boys, came into existence in the Arkansas city of Osceola. Slowly it built up a following. While King's group was overshadowed by better-known bands from nearby Memphis, it was considered the best homegrown organization. In the mid-1950s, King noted that things had improved to the point that he would get $14–$15 for each weekend night he worked.

Things went along at this pace for the rest of the decade. In 1962, King moved north to try to improve his lot. He spent half a year as a service station attendant in South Bend, Indiana, and then moved to Gary, Indiana, just below Chicago. Soon after he got to Gary, he became acquainted with people at a small record firm called Parrot. He recorded a single, "Lonesome in the Night." The record didn't bring any money to King, but it received enough airplay to bring him recognition from Muddy Waters and other Chicago bluesmen.

In Gary, King became friends with singer–disc jockey Jimmy Reed. The two worked together in small Chicago clubs and also cut some discs for Vee Jay Records. These included a joint effort, "Baby You Don't Have to Go," and one King did with a group he led called the Dutones, "Shake a Tail Feather." They were local hits in the R&B market and received some attention in other parts of the country too. Reed later went on to fame as a solo artist.

By the mid-1960s, King had returned to Osceola briefly, then decided to make home base in Love Joy, Illinois, a St. Louis suburb across the river from the city. He assembled a new band from St. Louis–area musicians and won his greatest reception yet from audiences throughout the Southwest. His work in Memphis was well appreciated by Al Bell, an executive with the rising recording firm of Stax/Volt, the company responsible for the Memphis Sound of the 1960s. Bell signed King and the result was a steady string of top hits, including such singles as "Blues at Sunrise," "Let's Have a Natural Ball," "Ooh-ee, Baby" and "Travelin' to California." The recordings showed up initially on the soul charts, but by the late 1960s, King's releases were just as likely to gain the top 20 or top 50 on the pop charts.

Critics were hard-pressed to find enough praise for his ability. *New York Times* reviewer Albert Goldman called King's style "a fusion of the ancient Mississippi 'bottleneck' style (the fret finger sheathed with glass or metal tubing) and the sighing, swooning, 'psychedelic' sound of the Hawaiian steel guitar. King's blue note is so 'nasty,' so cruelly inciting, that after a quarter of an hour under its spell, one itches for a bottle to break and a face to cut."

Like B. B. King, Albert became a major album artist in the late 1960s and early 1970s. A major boost in that direction was his creative collaboration with Booker T and the M.G.s at Stax Records in the mid-1960s. An early product of that was the fine album *Born under a Bad Sign* (1967) containing two cuts that became particularly associated with King, the title song (cowritten by Booker T Jones and William Bell) and "Cross Cut Saw." Both became staple items in his concerts from the late '60s on. Additions to his album credits in 1969 were the Chess release *Door to Door* and Stax Record's *Years Gone By*. For about half a decade, into the early '70s, Albert placed a series of albums on the charts, such as *Live Wire: Blues Power, Albert King Does the King's Thing, Jammed Together, Lovejoy,* and *Years Gone By.*

A new generation of rock fans in the mid-1970s lost interest in some of rock's blues roots and King's career went into a decline for a while. He continued to perform, but mainly in small clubs. By then he had left Stax, though the label continued to reissue some of his material, such as the 1976 LP *The Pinch.* Meanwhile, he signed with a new label, Utopia, which issued *Albert* and *Truckload of Lovin'* (1976) and *Albert Live* (1977). In 1977, some of his Stax recordings were reissued on Atlantic Records' Atco subsidiary under the title *King of the Blues Guitar.* In the late 1970s, Berkeley-based Fantasy Records controlled his Stax catalog and reissued most of his albums from those years.

In the early 1980s, King's star began to rise again, powered by successes scored by new blues-rock performers such as Stevie Ray Vaughan who credited much of their guitar style to Albert's influence. Vaughan was cited by a writer in England's *New Musical Express* as "a young Texan who apparently believes that Albert King is God and the Lord should be praised regularly."

Asked about that by reporter Don Snowden of the *Los Angeles Times* in September 1983, King responded: "He's a good player. He's trying to play too much like me, but he'll never get it all. How's he gonna do it when I don't know how I'm doin' it?" Some of his guitar work was essentially intuitive and some of the things he did at one time had slipped from his memory later on.

The new publicity helped bring new concert opportunities for King in the mid-1980s, both at home and abroad. Besides more chances to play rock clubs, he was featured in some of the blues festivals beginning to be organized in the United States, such as the annual event in Long Beach, California. In 1983, he signed a new recording contract with Fantasy Records, which in midyear issued *San Francisco '83,* his first new LP in five years. A featured track on the album was titled "Floodin' in California." Fantasy later released *I'm in a Phone Booth, Baby* (1984) and (on compact disc only) *The Best of Albert King.* Using the Stax logo, in 1988 Fantasy reissued the triple-guitar *Jammed Together* teaming Albert with Steve Cropper and Pop Staples of the Staple Singers.

His career plans as of the mid-1980s, were modest, he told Snowden. "I never had the desire to be a millionaire. I never had the desire to be a big star. If I feel like playing a gig, I will. If I don't, I won't. Everybody needs money to live, but as long as I can make a decent living, I'll be all right."

With good engagement opportunities at home and abroad in the late 1980s and the early 1990s, King indeed was able to make enough money to meet his needs. In late 1992, alas, he suffered a fatal heart attack. But through the medium of records and videos his creative presence has lived on, and will continue to for years to come.

Several collections of Albert King's work have been reissued on CD, including *King of the Blues Guitar,* a collection of his Stax sides, released in 1989 by Atlantic records; *The Ultimate Collection,* released in 1993 by Rhino Records; and *The Tomato Years,* released in 1994 by Tomato Records.

KING, B.B.: *Guitarist, singer, songwriter. Born Itta Bena (near Indianola), Mississippi, September 16, 1925.*

It's lucky that B.B. King never worried all that much about personal schedules or he might not have attained his eventual eminence in blues and rock. Though considered one of the major interpreters of country blues, he really didn't focus full attention on that genre until he left his native "Delta blues" region. And he didn't

teen," and "Every Day I Have the Blues," as well as his treatment of the old Billie Holiday number "Ain't Nobody's Business," Louis Jordan's "Let the Good Times Roll," and Fats Domino's "Whole Lotta Lovin'." He followed with *There Is Always One More Time* in 1991.

King earned two more of his eight Grammy Awards in the first half of the '90s, both for Best Traditional Blues Recording. In the 1991 voting by the members of the National Academy of the Recording Arts and Sciences, he won for the MCA release *Live at the Apollo* and in 1993 for his MCA album *Blues Summit.*

Though in his late sixties and early seventies in the 1990s, King kept up his demanding touring schedule for an average of close to 300 dates a year at home and abroad. He received a Kennedy Center Honor in 1995, along with Neil Simon, Marilyn Horne, and Sidney Portier. By 1996 he had added to his lengthy list of honors with the Songwriters Hall of Fame Lifetime Achievement Award, a presidential Medal of the Arts, and a Lifetime Achievement award from N.A.R.A.S.

During those years he headlined many solo concerts and was a major figure in a variety of blues festivals, including an annual show at the Greek Theater in Los Angeles's Griffith Park, inaugurated in 1992. Joining him for the August '95 concert were Etta James, guitarist Jimmie Vaughan (brother of the late Stevie Ray Vaughan, with whom King had performed a number of times), and Elvin Bishop. For the August 1996 event, the bill included the Neville Brothers, Delbert McClinton, and Taj Mahal. Typically, after performing part of his set with his twelve-man B.B. King Orchestra, he waved all but a small core group off and drew up a chair at center stage. He told the crowd with a smile, "Just because we're sitting doesn't mean we're tired," then demonstrated some dazzling runs on his trusty guitar and a voice as emotion-filled as ever.

His recorded credits in the summer of 1996 included taking part in a tribute album to Stevie Ray Vaughan with such other top artists as Dr. John and, naturally, Jimmie Vaughan.

In 1991 his namesake B.B. King's Blues Club opened on Beale Street in Memphis. A second club was later opened at Universal City Walk in Los Angeles. In 1992, MCA records released a four-CD box set, *King of the Blues.*

A biography of King, *The Arrival of B.B. King* by Charles Sawyer, was published in 1980 by Doubleday. In 1996 King decided to put out his own words on the subject. Avon published King's autobiography, *Blues All Around Me,* written with David Ritz. In the book, King described his fifty years of constant touring, during which he sired fifteen children by fifteen different women. "I'm a simple man, but I've had a complicated love life," he explained to Liz McNeil of *People Weekly* ("Talking with . . . B.B. King," December 2, 1996.) Earlier in 1996, King came out with an interactive autobiography, *On the Road with B.B. King,* released on CD-ROM. King's permanent residence is Las Vegas, if he gets a chance to go home with his busy schedule.

In 1997 MCA released *Deuces Wild,* a collection of thirteen duets teaming King with several top musicians, including Eric Clapton ("Rock Me Baby"), Tracy Chapman ("The Thrill Is Gone"), Bonnie Raitt ("Baby I Love You"), Willie Nelson ("Night Life"), Van Morrison ("If You Love Me"), Heavy D. ("Keep It Comin' "), Joe Cocker ("Dangerous Mood"), and Marty Stuart ("Confessin' the Blues"). B.B. King earned a gold album for *Deuces Wild.*

King visited with Pope John Paul II in December 1997 and gave him a special gift: Lucille, one of his signature Gibson guitars. The origin of the name Lucille went back many years to an occasion when King was playing at a dance in Twist, Arkansas. A fight broke out and a fire was started when a kerosene stove was knocked over. King raced outdoors to safety with everyone else but went back to save his $30 acoustic guitar. He later found out that the fight had been over a woman named Lucille and decided to give that name to his guitar.

Perhaps due to the Pope's blessing, MCA and King continued a fast pace of new releases and reissues in 1998. In April 1998, MCA reissued four classic albums on CD, including *The Electric B.B. King—His Best* (eleven recordings from 1965 through 1968), *Live in Cook County Jail, Completely Well* (his first top 40 chart LP, including "The Thrill is Gone"), and *Take It Home* (originally released in 1979). In August, MCA released *B.B. King—Greatest Hits,* a compilation of his hits from 1965 through 1993. In October, King produced and performed on a new album, *Blues on the Bayou,* recorded primarily at Dockside Recording Studios in Maurice, Louisiana. The album earned a Best Traditional Blues Grammy.

KING, CAROLE: *Singer, songwriter, pianist. Born Brooklyn, New York, February 9, 1942.*

Carole King had what amounted to two phenomenal careers in pop music embracing two different decades. In the '60s, her songwriting partnership with Gerry Goffin provided dozens of superhits in the R&B/soul/rock vein. In the '70s, as a writer and performer, she played a pivotal role in development of a softer, more reflective sound in pop music, a sound closer to folk music than the more strident compositions of her earlier years.

Carole Klein was born and raised in Brooklyn, New York, where jazz, swing bands, and the last stages of romantic ballads dominated pop music in her childhood. In her teens, she veered away from most of that, influenced by the rock revolution represented by Bill Haley, Elvis Presley, and Fats Domino. As she progressed through high school, she delved a little deeper than her classmates into the roots of rock, finding a strong interest in the still submerged rhythm and blues stylings that were mainly restricted to the black population.

By the time she finished high school, though, R&B groups were beginning to show up regularly on the pop charts. She had started writing songs by then, some in the R&B format. (Neil Sedaka, in turn, wrote his 1959 hit "Oh! Carol" to her.) Gerry Goffin and Carole King met in the lounge at Queens College, New York. She was studying to be a teacher and he was studying to be a chemist. They wrote their first song on a piano at King's house, Goffin focusing on the lyrics and King the music. That song, "Kid Brother," was recorded by Mickey and Sylvia as a B-side, and the two made about $150 apiece. After marrying Goffin (born Queens, New York, February 11, 1939), she became part of a writing team that soon won the attention of New York publishers. Using the pen name Carole King, by the time she was twenty she and Gerry already had a reputation as songwriting greats of the future.

Their first massive success came with the Shirelles' "Will You Love Me Tomorrow" in 1961. Soon they had another top-10 hit with the Drifters' "Up on the Roof." Goffin and King compositions proved winners for an ever widening group of artists. "Locomotion" provided a number-one hit for Little Eva (Eva Boyd, Carole and Gerry's babysitter) in 1962 and for Grand Funk Railroad in 1974. "Ili-De-Ilo" became a major hit in 1970 for Blood, Sweat & Tears. Other successes included the Chiffons' "One Fine Day" (1963), the Drifters' "Some Kind of Wonderful" (1961), Bobby Vinton's and Tony Orlando's releases of "Half Way to Paradise" (1961 and 1968, respectively), Maxine Brown's "Oh No, Not My Baby" (1965), the Righteous Brothers' "Just Once in My Life" (1965), Gene Pitney's "Every Breath I Take," (1961), and Aretha Franklin's "A Natural Woman" (1967).

In the early '60s, Carole tried her hand at singing some of the Goffin-King songs. Several discs made the charts, the most successful being the 1962 "It Might as Well Rain until September" on Dimension records. However, Carole preferred to take time out to raise a family rather than pursue the pressure-laden route to pop stardom.

The Goffin-King writing partnership continued to be highly productive until they ran into problems with their marriage. The two finally divorced, after which Carole went into semiretirement to concentrate on looking after her two young daughters. In the second half of the '60s, that goal led her to move to the Los Angeles area. She kept on writing songs, though she didn't do much else in the music field for the first part of her stay in California. While she collaborated with various writers in the late '60s (including Toni Stern and musician Charles Larkey, who became her second husband), much of her new material was written alone.

In 1968, she formed a group called City with Larkey and Danny Kortchmar. Carole had known record-company owner Lou Adler since 1963 and he agreed to sign the group. His firm, Ode Records, issued City's LP, *Now That Everything's Been Said,* but it was a failure. However, Kortchmar introduced her to his friend James Taylor, who urged her to go on as a solo artist.

She finally agreed with that idea and was buoyed by a good reception to several West Coast concerts and the faith expressed in her by Adler. Her first album, *Writer: Carole King,* was issued at the start of the '70s and had a reasonably good if not sensational reception. But the next one provided the turning point. Titled *Tapestry,* it was released in early 1971 to coincide with a national tour in March and April on the same bill as James Taylor. So well were both album and tour received that by midyear, people were clamoring for her to headline rather than be a supporting act. The gold album provided a number-one single in *Billboard,* "It's Too Late," plus her classics "I Feel the Earth Move," and "You've Got a Friend." In 1971, the last named also became a number-one hit for Taylor and a top-30 hit for the team of Roberta Flack and Donny Hathaway.

Tapestry was a sensation, making its way to number one on *Billboard* charts during 1971. It was still on the charts in late 1976, having sold over $13^1/_2$ million copies, the most ever sold by an LP up to then. In the Grammy Awards for 1971, Carole won no less than four trophies: Album of the Year, Best Pop Female Vocalist, Song of the Year (songwriter's award) for "You've Got a Friend," and Record of the Year for the single "It's Too Late." Before 1971 was over, Carole had added another gold-record award to her collection for her third Ode solo LP, *Carole King Music.*

As the '70s went along, while her sales were far less than the blockbuster levels of *Tapestry,* all her Ode collections reached gold-record status except the 1975 TV soundtrack LP, *Really Rosie.* Her LP *Rhymes & Reasons* gained the award on November 1, 1972, followed by *Fantasy* on June 26, 1973, *Wrap around Joy* on October 16, 1974, and *Thoroughbred* on March 25, 1976.

Always jealous of her privacy, Carole cut back on her live appearances sharply after the banner year of 1971. She did give concerts, but only at widely spaced intervals. In between, she stayed behind the scenes, spending as much time as she could with her family, which, by the early '70s, included another daughter born to her and second husband Larkey. That approach probably tended to cut down on the potential sales of her new albums, but she never felt that was the overriding concern of her life. It was a theme she was to emphasize in her gold 1977 album *Simple Things,* whose title song (written by Carole and musician Rick Evers), said: "Simple things mean a lot to me."

The album represented a change in affiliation. In late 1976, she announced she had severed relations with Ode, though Ode stated it still had several LPs of her work to release. In December 1976, she signed with Capitol Records, which set up a new label, Avatar/Capitol, for *Simple Things.* Carole finished out the decade with two more LPs for Capitol, *Welcome Home* (1978) and *Touch the Sky* (1979). She began the '80s with the Capitol LP *Pearls,* which comprised her versions of Goffin-King songs that had been major hits for other artists.

By then she was living on her Robinson Bar Ranch near Stanley, Idaho, where she had moved in the late 1970s after her marriage to Larkey fell apart, followed by another brief marriage to Rick Evers. She liked being away from the hype and the pressures of Los Angeles, she stressed, and enjoyed trying to fit in as just another citizen. An example of that was her acceptance of a role as featured speaker at a convocation at Hemingway Elementary School in Ketchum, Idaho, in December 1982, where she told the gathering she was "a singer and a songwriter—also a notary public." A main theme of her speech was the need to carry on the fight for peace symbolized by artists such as the late John Lennon.

For the most part, Carole continued to maintain a low profile in the 1980s, spending much of her time on her ranch and restricting much of her live concert work to shows for special causes. Among those were a series of appearances to raise money for Senator Gary Hart's 1984 presidential bid. She also appeared at Willie Nelson's Farm Aid concert in September 1985. During some of them, she acknowledged that she hadn't made much impact with record buyers after *Tapestry.* She opened a show at Los Angeles's Dorothy Chandler Pavilion with the comment: "So many people thought I died after *Tapestry.*" As it happened, though much of her performance focused on new songs she had written in the '80s, the ones that brought the most intensive audience response were from *Tapestry.* Some of the new material had been included on her 1983 LP, *Speeding Time,* on Atlantic Records, which had also released her album *One to One* the previous year.

In the mid-1980s, her career as a recording artist had, in effect, come full cycle as she got back together with her old associate, Lou Adler, who produced some of her new sessions. Despite the production assistance from Adler, however, *Speeding Time* did not do well with record buyers.

At the end of the 1980s King began to change her focus a bit. She composed the score for *Murphy's Romance,* with James Garner and Sally Field, and began to try her hand at acting with some success. She appeared in the movie *Russkies* and Off-Broadway in some plays. Later she appeared on the TV show *The Trials of Rosie O'Neill* and an ABC after-school special. In 1994 she appeared in the Broadway production of *Blood Brothers,* an engagement that ran for six months.

She returned to Capitol in 1989 and released the moderately successful *City Streets.* She continued to write songs, including "If It's Over," written with Mariah Carey, and "Now and Forever," the theme from the movie *A League of Their Own,* a star-studded female baseball film. In 1993 she released *Color of Your Dreams. In Concert,* released in 1994, was taken from her concert tour in support of her *Color of Your Dreams* CD. She followed those with *A Natural Woman, Time Gone By,* and reissues, including *Carole King—Hits and Rarities from the Sixties* and *The Carnegie Hall Concert, June 18, 1971.*

But she continued to receive accolades for her songwriting. In January 1987 she and Gerry Goffin were inducted into the Songwriters Hall of Fame. Two months later they received a Lifetime Achievement Award from the National Academy of Songwriters. In 1990 Goffin and King were inducted into the Rock and Roll Hall of Fame. She performed at Bill Clinton's Arkansas Inauguration Ball on January 20, 1993. In 1996 a group of '90s acts paid tribute to King by recording their versions of her songs in *Tapestry Revisited: A Tribute to Carole King* on Lava/Atlantic. Included in the collection are Eternal singing "I Feel the Earth Move," Curtis Stiger singing "Home Again," All-4-One singing "Tapestry," and Amy Grant singing "It's Too Late." That year, Goffin released an album of politically oriented songs called *Back Room Blood* on Adelphi Records.

In the meantime, after twenty-five years, *Tapestry* continued to sell steadily. A 1996 *Entertainment Weekly* report on the twenty-five best-selling albums in May 1996 indicated that her album was still number twenty-five on the list, with 10 million in U.S. sales. It was on the charts for 302 consecutive weeks, a record for a female artist. The *Entertainment Weekly* piece also indicated that 5,800 copies of *Tapestry* were sold in the week of April 14, 1996.

Certainly, King's music had the ability to transport many people back to the early 1970s. In October 1998 she performed at a dinner in honor of California Senator Barbara Boxer and President Clinton remarked: "You were saying I was singing those songs with you. Every time Carole King opens her mouth you can make thirty years of my life vanish."

KINGSTON TRIO: *Vocal and instrumental group. Original members, 1957–1961, Bob Shane, born Hawaii, February 1, 1934; Nick Reynolds, born Coronado, California, July 27, 1933; Dave Guard, born near San Francisco, California, October 19, 1934, died Rollinsford, New Hampshire, March 22, 1991. Guard left May 1961, replaced by John Stewart, born San Diego, California, September 5, 1939. The Shane-Reynolds-Stewart group disbanded in 1967 and Shane later assembled the New Kingston Trio with Roger Gamble and George Grove. In the 1970s, separate versions of the trio were active, one led by Shane and another headed by Reynolds. The founding members reassembled briefly in late 1981. A "Kingston Trio" act was still performing in the late 1990s.*

The Kingston Trio often was disparaged by the "serious" members of the folk boom of the late 1950s and early 1960s as being, in effect, opportunistic. The Trio, they said, was essentially a pop group that happened to sing folk or folk-flavored material rather than an authentic folk group. But the fact remained that the Trio had a hand in making the American mass audience aware of the pleasures of folk music, and its enormous success provided an environment that allowed all types of folk artists to prosper for a time.

Two of the original threesome grew up in Hawaii; Dave Guard and Bob Shane learned to play ukuleles and sometimes sang Hawaiian songs together while attending Punahou School in Honolulu. Their paths didn't cross that of Nick Reynolds until they came to the San Francisco Bay area to attend college, Bob enrolling at Menlo College to major in business administration and Dave working his way through nearby Stanford University as an economics major. (Both earned B.A. degrees in their specialties in the mid-1950s.) Nick, the son of a navy man, was born in Coronado, but lived in many different places during his youth. By the time he enrolled in Menlo College in the early 1950s, he could play guitar well, having been tutored at the start by his father, who also played the instrument.

Reynolds and Shane, both business administration students, became friends and started casually singing pop and folk songs for the fun of it. Soon they brought in Bob's friend Dave Guard to form a group that picked up spare income performing for college events. Still, they didn't think of making music a career at first. In fact, after graduation, Shane went home to Hawaii and worked in business for a time. But inspired by the growing public interest in folk material, they decided to re-form their act and try for a professional career. They performed at a college hangout near Stanford called the Cracked Pot, being paid essentially in free beer and meals. A San Francisco publicist named Frank Werber heard them and was so impressed he used a table napkin as paper for a contract they all signed one night. The group decided a distinctive name was needed and they chose "Kingston Trio" because calypso was in vogue then and "Kingston" sounded both collegiate and calypso.

They spent months polishing their act before debuting at the well-known cellar club of San Francisco, the hungry i. That 1957 engagement lasted a week. They won polite applause, but nothing to suggest their future superstar status. Then they moved across the street to another famous cellar spot, the Purple Onion, and things started to jell. By the end of the first week, audience response had picked up to the point that their engagement was extended a week, then another, until finally their stay extended to seven months. Other well-received dates followed in such San Francisco spots as Facks II and the hungry i. With their reputation starting to build, the boys took off across country to star in places like Mr. Kelly's in Chicago and the Blue Angel and Village Vanguard in New York.

In January 1958, the Trio signed a long-term contract with Capitol Records and also began considering overtures from major concert venues and from TV. One of their first major milestones was an appearance in both acting and singing roles in a *Playhouse 90* TV program, "Rumors of the Evening." In June 1958, their debut album, *The Kingston Trio,* appeared. The record did fairly well, but its main impact proved to be one track titled "Tom Dooley." Released as a single late in 1958, it began to receive widening airplay until it finally rose to the top of the charts. In January 1959, it passed the million-copy mark, bringing the group its first gold-record award. The Kingston Trio by then was nationally known and on the way to becoming one of the most popular acts in the world in 1959 and the early 1960s.

("Tom Dooley" was thought at first to be a traditional ballad. One of the approaches the Trio favored was to sing updated versions of public-domain songs, often with new lyrics that could permit copyrighting of the song. As it happened, a long, drawn-out lawsuit eventually demonstrated the song was the contemporary creation of a hill-country artist named Frank Proffitt.)

The group quickly showed that "Tom Dooly" wasn't a one-shot success by turning out a series of singles and albums that rose high on the hit charts. In 1960, they earned gold records for their first album, *The Kingston Trio,* and the follow-up *Kingston Trio at Large* in April and added two more awards in October for the LPs *Here We Go Again* and *From the hungry i.* In June 1961, their album *Sold Out* won another gold record. Also doing well on the charts those years were such songs as "Tijuana Jail," "M.T.A.," "Molly Dee," and "Green Grasses." The last two songs were written by a close friend, John Stewart, who had become a primary arranger for the group. When Stewart decided to switch from rock to folk performances at the start of the 1960s, the Trio members helped him form his folk trio, called the Cumberland Three.

In the spring of 1961, the Trio went on a highly successful tour of Australia, New Zealand, and Japan. Things were going well outwardly, but Dave Guard was becoming restless. He wanted to go his own way and finally decided to leave after the tour. His first move was to form a new folk group, the Whiskeyhill Singers, and he later made his headquarters in Australia in the mid-1960s, where he was host of a TV show for a time before moving back to the United States in 1968. His activities in succeeding years included writing books on fairy tales and a manual on guitar technique.

After his departure, the other two members asked John Stewart to be Guard's replacement.

The changeover went smoothly and, if anything, the Trio's shows seemed to achieve a new vitality. The band took cognizance of new trends in the folk field by including songs from Bob Dylan in its repertoire, making the charts with its version of "Blowin' in the Wind." Stewart continued to add new compositions of his own like "Song for a Friend." By the mid-1960s, typical concerts included such other songs with which the group had become identified as "Lemon Tree," "Raspberries, Strawberries," "A Worried Man," Pete Seeger's "Where Have All the Flowers Gone," the Hoyt Axton-Ken Ramsey composition "Greenback Dollar," Ed McCurdy's "Last Night I Had the Strangest Dream," the Woody Guthrie opus "Reuben James," Rod McKuen's "Two-Ten, Six-Eighteen," and Billy Edd Wheeler's "Ann." Sometimes included were folk-flavored songs from the musical theater such as "They Call the Wind Maria" and "The Merry Minuet."

Still, the inroads of the "British Invasion," and the rock resurgence it spawned, affected the group's status by the mid-1960s. Trio records made the charts, including gold-record attainment for the LP *String Along* in June 1962 and *The Best of the Kingston Trio* in September 1963, but more and more the releases tended to only go as high as mid- or lower-levels. (Other album releases of the mid-1960s included *New Frontier, Time to Think,* and *The Kingston Trio No. 16* in 1963; *Back in Town* and *The Folk Era* in 1964; *Nick-Bob-John, Stay Awhile, Somethin' Else,* and *The Best of the Kingston Trio, Volume 2* in 1965; *Children of the Morning* and *The Best of the Kingston Trio, Volume 3* in 1996.)

The group continued to be a top-rated act and could bring out sizable audiences on cross-country tours of the United States and on swings through Canada, Europe, and the Far East, but it seemed obvious that the Trio's main glory days were behind them. As the latter 1960s came into view, both Shane and Reynolds were getting a little tired of the grind and Stewart was becoming increasingly eager to try to succeed as a solo artist. (The road proved to be much longer than he imagined. Solo stardom escaped him until the end of the 1970s.) In 1967, the group decided to disband and its *Farewell Album* was released by Capitol that year. In 1969 the label added another disc to the Trio catalog, *Once upon a Time.*

In the 1970s, Bob Shane decided to organize a new version of the Kingston Trio but without any of the other charter members taking part. The group toured widely the second half of the 1970s, mostly playing vintage Trio material, though with occasional new songs like "Aspen Gold." Besides playing small to medium-size clubs, the group also made some TV appearances, including a mid-1979 set by Shane's group on the nationally televised Mike Douglas show. Most of the Kingston Trio album releases in the '70s were retrospectives of the 1957–67 musicians, though the titles included some by the newer alignment. The discs included *The Kingston Trio* and *Where Have All the Flowers Gone* in 1972, *American Gold* and *The World Needs a Melody* in 1973, *The Historic Recordings of the Kingston Trio* in 1975, and *Aspen Gold* in 1979.

In late 1981, the original members of the Trio, Reynolds, Dave Guard, and Shane, reunited for their first performance together since 1961. The performance was given at Six Flags Magic Mountain amusement park near Los Angeles and was taped for presentation later on PBS. There was some talk of making it a continuing association, but nothing came of it. (Also taking part were John Stewart and Shane's associates of the 1970s-early 1980s group.)

The first new album of Kingston Trio recordings in some years—essentially remakes of early Trio hits—was issued on a new label, Xeres Records, in early 1982, titled *The Kingston Trio—25 Years Non-Stop.* The group making that LP contained Shane, George Grove, and Roger Gambill, the latter two having performed with Shane for over six years. In 1987 another retrospective album was issued on CD, *The Very Best of the Kingston Trio.*

During the 1980s, Guard had made his home in New England, and in the closing years of the decade was diagnosed with cancer. On March 22, 1991, he died at his home in Rollinsford, New Hampshire. Nick Reynolds told reporters, "I'm very upset. I visited him two months ago and he was in remission. We were talking about a reunion. We were going to have John Stewart and George Grove and the rest of us sing in different combinations. . . ."

Reynolds recalled that Guard was the tallest of the original trio and the others considered him the most intellectual. "Bobby was considered the sex symbol and I was the short, little guy."

KOERNER, "SPIDER" JOHN: *Singer, guitarist, songwriter. Born Rochester, New York, August 31, 1938.*

He played concerts in Minneapolis with a then-unknown performer named Bob Dylan and was thought by many observers of the late '50s folk scene to be the superior artist. His performances and recordings influenced such "name" artists at home and abroad as John Lennon, Ray Davies of the Kinks, Jim Morrison and the Doors, and Bonnie Raitt. Yet he never became a superstar, and for many years was almost invisible to the public, even to the relatively knowledgeable fans of modern folk who knew the name vaguely but never connected the legend with an actual individual. Then, in the mid-1980s, new interest in his music brought the release of a new album, followed in the '90s by reissues of his superb 1960s LPs and a rebirth of his career as a concert and festival performer and recording artist.

He was born and raised in Rochester, New York, but in his late teens enrolled as an engineering major in the University of Minnesota. He enjoyed blues and traditional folk music and liked to pick out tunes on a guitar, but he didn't think of a career in entertaining when he entered college. He left the Midwest for a time to serve in the U.S. Marine Corps, but when he got out and returned to Minnesota he began to dig out blues and folk songs from library sources or albums by Sam Charters, Leadbelly, Woody Guthrie, etc., and in 1959 began appearing in local Minneapolis clubs, sometimes working solo, sometimes with other young musicians, including Bob Dylan.

While Dylan moved on to New York to take the first steps to national acclaim, Spider, so called because of his thin, gangly, somewhat sprawling frame, continued to hone his skills in the Twin Cities. He had a particular love for the blues, not as performed by young urban artists, but as originated by veteran Delta and Chicago bluesmen. In 1962 he formed a trio to focus on that kind of music, though not ignoring traditional white folk roots, with twenty-four-year-old singer-guitarist Dave "Snaker" Ray and nineteen-year-old harmonica player–singer Tommy "Little Sun" Glover.

During early 1963 they got the chance to record their debut album, *Blues, Rags and Hollers,* in a local studio. It was originally released in June '63 on the Audiophile label, and was reissued on Elektra that November. The album, which featured Koerner playing an unusual seven-string guitar (with Glover performing on a twelve-string) included excellent versions of songs like Leadbelly's "Hangman" and Robert Johnson/Elmore James's "Dust My Broom," plus some similar originals. It was then, and remains, one of the best folk blues albums ever made.

That album and a series of others in the mid-'60s expanded their following not only to most parts of the United States, but also to England and the rest of Europe and opened opportunities to tour widely and be featured at major festivals including the Newport Folk Festival. Koerner, Ray and Glover Elektra releases of that period included *The Blues Project* (issued 3/'64); *Lots More Blues, Rags and Hollers* (6/64); *The Folk Box* (various artists including Koerner, Ray and Glover, '64); *The Return of Koerner, Ray and Glover* (11/65); and *Folksong '65* (sampler of various Elektra folk artists including Koerner, Ray and Glover). Koerner also recorded solo albums for the label such as *Spider Blues* (5/'65) and *Running, Jumping, Standing Still* (Koerner and Willie Murphy, 12/'67). The trio's offerings also were among the contents of the Vanguard releases *Newport Folk Festival 1964* (issued 5/'65) and *Newport Folk Festival 1965* (issued 1966). In January 1972, some of the trio's live concert material from 1963–64 was released on the Mill City album *Good Old Koerner, Ray and Glover.*

Though the '60s were the years of the hippie and flower children culture, Koerner wasn't a serious participant in those movements. As he told Brett Anderson of the *Twin Cities Reader* for a 1990s interview, "You could hardly avoid the hippie culture, especially when you were into music like we were. I personally never became anything that I would consider a hippie, but I was interested in hippies and I knew a million of them. But I never thought of myself as one.

"I mean, as far as drugs go, I wound up being one of those people who likes to drink and smoke pot and that's it. On the other hand, I was surrounded by people who were taking every damn thing you could imagine, and I was watching them do it so I was definitely in the middle of it. Plus the ideas that were floating around at the time came from all kinds of different corners, anywhere from the hippie movement to the civil rights movement to the Black Power movement, whatever. A lot of that stuff was interesting, so we wound up assimilating a lot of it."

Despite the praise from critics and folk musicians for *Standing Still,* (which became a cult favorite, though never a chart hit), by the early 1970s Koerner's interest in performing was waning. Willie Murphy recalled that their Elektra arrangement called for a follow-up album. Koerner later on wasn't sure about that, but he hadn't been keen on pursuing the project further at the time, he told interviewers in the '90s. He told Anderson, "Music once filled my life, now it doesn't . . . if I had enough money to live without playing, I probably wouldn't play."

However, he did issue some albums in the early 1970s on his own label, Sweet Jane: *Music Is Just a Bunch of Notes* (with Willie & the Bees), issued in May '72, and *Some American Folk Songs Like They Used To,* released in October 1974. In the mid-'70s Koerner cut back on his concert work, perhaps influenced by the decline in the folk-music audience in that decade, and focused on other pursuits, including experimental filmmaking. During the second half of the '70s he moved to Denmark for a few years before returning to Minnesota. While overseas he had been inspired by finding books of traditional American folk material, and back home in 1980 he assembled a team of other musicians, including Peter Ostroushko (mandolin), Butch Thompson, Willie Murphy (piano), Tony Glover (harmonica), Dakota Dave Hull (guitar) and a bones-player who called himself Mr. Bones, to record some of those songs.

In the mid-1980s, it became obvious to many in the music field that folk music was coming back into vogue on college campuses and among members of the baby-boom generation. Elektra, for one, decided to take advantage of it with some retrospective multiartist releases such as the January '84 albums *Bleecker & MacDougal: Folk Scene of the 1960s* and *Crossroads—White Blues in the 1960s,* both of which included Koerner, Ray and Glover tracks. In 1985, executives at Red House Records in Minnesota became aware of Koerner's unreleased 1980 sessions and acquired the rights to them. This resulted in the album *Nobody Knows the Trouble I've Been,* released in January 1986.

The album won enthusiastic support from reviewers across the media spectrum (*Spin* magazine called it "One of the Top 10 Folk Albums of the Decade" and *Frets's* critic hailed it as "Comeback of the Year") and won new attention from the folk-music audience. This brought new chances for Koerner to return to the concert and festival circuit, which in the late 1980s and into the 1990s kept him busier than he had been in the '60s. Red House fueled the process with new releases and reissues such as the January 1990 album *Legends of Folk,* which teamed him with Ramblin' Jack Elliott and Utah Phillips; the new Koerner album *Raised by Humans* (issued March '92); and CD versions of the '60s classics, *Running, Jumping, Standing Still* (2/'94), *Blues, Rags and Hollers* (2/'95), *Lots More Blues, Rags and Hollers* and *The Return of Koerner, Ray and Glover,* both in 1999. The trio reunited for the live album *One Foot in the Groove* released by Tim/Kerr in 1996.

Other collections came out in the '90s capturing some of Koerner's work. In the August 1992 package from Rhino, *Troubadours of the Folk Era,* some numbers by Koerner, Ray and Glover were presented as was also the case in the Vanguard '93 CD, *Blues with a Feeling—Newport 1963–66.* Tony Glover also wrote and produced the documentary *Blues, Rags and Hollers— the Koerner, Ray and Glover Story* (Latch Lake Music Productions). Meanwhile Red House made arrangements for a Koerner–Willie Murphy reunion album recorded in New Orleans and released under the title *StarGeezer* on May 21, 1996. The album name reflected Spider John's love for returning to a cabin in the Minnesota woods to focus his telescope on the heavens.

Koerner in the mid-'90s continued to separate his musical activities from the rest of his life. As he had told Richard Cromonic of the *Boston Phoenix* ("The Spider's Web," July 20, 1990), "I put out 100 percent when I'm playing and everybody has a good time [but then] I put my guitar in the corner and forget about it."

Once he's done that, he added, "I do some bartending and some construction work now and then . . . simpleminded stuff. Also I'm an amateur astronomer, and I'm a lot hotter on that than I am the whole music thing."

KOTTKE, LEO: *Singer, guitarist, harmonica player, songwriter. Born Athens, Georgia, September 11, 1945.*

Readers of *Guitar Player* magazine voted Leo Kottke "best folk guitarist" five consecutive years in the 1970s. He is still renowned as a masterful guitar player and composer, comfortable in styles ranging from folk and country to classical. Among his fans, he is nearly as well known for his wry tales and unusual lyrics.

Throughout his three-decade career, Kottke has evolved from an early emphasis on flashy, lightning-fast guitar work to a more balanced, often quieter approach. He winces today when he recalls early, laudatory reviews that said he "sounded like he was playing with three hands." However, he still impresses fans and musicians with his speed, along with his technical mastery and his relish for communicating with his audience.

Kottke grew up in twelve states, the result of his father's career moves, first as a golf pro, then as an administrator for the Veterans Administration. Listening to Burl Ives, the Kingston Trio, and Jimmie Rodgers as a youngster sparked his interest in folk music. Although he also learned the harmonica along the way, as well as trombone and violin, the guitar early on proved to be his favorite, and it's turned into a lifetime romance. As he stated during a recent telephone interview, "I'm still hooked on the guitar. I literally can't get enough of it."

He learned to play guitar just by fooling around with the instrument. "I just sort of picked it up. I'm definitely self-taught. Which has some disadvantages." Banjo playing also made important contributions. "Most of the technical inroads that I made came from trying to learn how to play the banjo," Kottke told Gil Podolinsky in a *Guitar Player* interview (August 1977).

In the mid-1960s, after stints in the navy (where he almost sank a submarine) and the University of Missouri (where his college career was sinking), Kottke went north to St. Cloud State College, Minnesota. Since a relative was a dean there, he figured, he would likely have a smoother time preparing to be a high school teacher. However, his involvement with music made it difficult for him to keep up with his regular classwork. By 1968 he had given up college and was working bars and coffeehouses to pay for his room and board. After a while, he settled down to a regular weekend job at the Scholar Coffeehouse in Minneapolis. Slowly, word of his skills on six- and twelve-string guitar began to circulate among folk and pop fans in the area.

While having equipment problems during one club date and embarrassed by the delay, Kottke tried telling humorous stories to the audience. "Has anybody ever tried to kill a chicken?" he asked, starting off an offbeat tale about another musician. The immediate rapport he established convinced Kottke that his stories could enhance communication with the audience. (Today he is so well known for his stories that concertgoers occasionally yell out requests for favorite yarns, which makes Kottke uncomfortable.)

His debut album came out on the small, local Oblivion label in 1969. Called *12-String Blues,* it was initially produced in an edition of only 1,000 copies. Feeling that his ability deserved a wider audience, Leo began looking around for another possible outlet. He heard of the Takoma Records label headed by another fine guitarist named John Fahey, whose travels occasionally took him to the Scholar Coffeehouse for an engagement. "John sounded like the right guy, so I sent him some tapes."

Fahey concurred that Leo had considerable potential as a guitarist, but he wasn't impressed with Leo's baritone voice. Thus Leo's 1970 debut on Takoma contained thirteen instrumentals.

After a disastrous trip to Portland to play with Fahey (where his guitars were stolen and his wife got sick), he visited Los Angeles to try to jump start his career. For a while, though, not too much happened. Takoma was a mail-order company, so Leo spent a lot of time mailing his own debut album. (Despite its slow start, the album, titled *Six- and Twelve-String Guitar,* has sold about a half-million copies over the years. It included fourteen instrumentals, primarily Kottke's own compositions, ranging from the blistering "Vaseline Machine Gun" to Bach's "Jesu, Joy of Man's Desiring.")

His debut album on the Capitol label came out in 1971. Called *Mudlark,* it included such tracks as an instrumental version of "Eight Miles High" and a collaboration with Kim Fowley called "Monkey Lust." In a series of club dates in support of the LP, he thrilled critics and fans alike with his lightning skill on the twelve-string and his powerful bottleneck slide work. Despite his friend Fahey's doubts about his voice, he demonstrated an excellent ability to win audience attention with his occasional vocal efforts.

His 1973 album, *Greenhouse,* did nothing to lower his reputation. It included two tracks that remain among the most popular he has recorded, one his version of a Paul Siebel folk song, "Louise," the other a Ron Nagle composition, "From the Cradle to the Grave." These songs and his performance of country star Tom T. Hall's "Pamela Brown" were key elements of the vocal part of his act in the mid-1970s. Also included in the LP was his composition "The Spanish Entymologist," in which he interwove parts of such songs as "Jambalaya," "Pretty Redwing," and "Tumbling Tumbleweeds."

As his name became more widely known among folk and pop fans throughout the United States and overseas (in 1973 he won rousing ovations from concertgoers in Europe—particularly in Germany), Kottke decided he could keep a career going outside the Los Angeles region. So he packed up and moved back to Minnesota from Pasadena. He got the chance to put together his own program to be presented at the Tyrone Guthrie Theater in Minneapolis, which became an annual event in that city in the 1970s. His 1973 appearance there was the basis for his third Capitol release and his first live album. In 1975, his fourth release, *Ice Water,* sold in the neighborhood of 200,000 copies.

By the time the all-instrumental *Dreams and Other Stuff* came out in 1975, his talents had received attention from a broad cross section of the mass media, including several pieces in *Rolling Stone* and a feature story in *People.*

He made several more albums for Capitol in the mid-1970s before parting company with the label, "run down" by the company's expectation of an album every six months. (In November 1978, Capitol put out a "best of" retrospective.) His debut on Chrysalis, *Leo Kottke,* was issued in 1977. Kottke continued to perform in smaller venues throughout the United States and in other countries, either holding the stage himself or with only a small backing group. He also appeared on the soundtrack of Terence Malick's 1978 film *Days of Heaven.*

After moving to Chrysalis, production values and musical variety improved. *Guitar Music* (1982) was his first all-instrumental LP since his *Six- and Twelve-String Guitar. Time Step* (1983) was produced by T. Bone Burnett with guest vocals by Emmylou Harris and Albert Lee. Other Chyrsalis albums included *Burnt Lips* (1978) and *Balance* (1979).

Tired of making albums, Kottke concentrated for several years on touring. In 1986, he switched labels to Private Music and in the next decade released seven albums through that small company: *A Shout Toward Noon, Regards from Chuck Pink, My Father's Face, That's What, Great Big Boy, Peculiaroso,* and *Live. Regards from Chuck Pink* (1988), whose title refers to life's nagging regrets, was an all-instrumental album marked by a softer sound and controlled, often delicate strings arrangements by Buell Neidlinger, a bassist Kottke has long admired. On songs such as "Dan's Tune" and "Pink Christmas," guitar and string lines weave around each other in the kind of gentle counterpoint usually associated with chamber music.

His 1989 album *My Father's Face,* produced by T. Bone Burnett, mixed vocal and instrumental numbers. It is notable for the tender lyrics of "Everybody Lies," the novelty song "Why Can't You Fix My Car," and a traditional, blazing fast, take on "William Powell."

Great Big Boy (1991), which Kottke considers one of his personal favorites, featured an arrestingly broad range of catchy vocals and lush sound, from jokey novelty songs to a somber number about the death of illegal aliens ("Driver"). The marimba-flavored "Running up the Stairs" matches melancholy lyrics to vibraphone. "The Other Day (near Santa Cruz)" discusses the merits of "hippie chicks" according to a beer-bellied barfly. "Pepe Hush," a duet with Margo Timmins, from the band Cowboy Junkies, recounts a sleepless night in a motel. Lyle Lovett also provided backup vocals on a couple of songs.

In 1991, he premiered a symphonic suite, composed along with Stephen Paulus, playing with the Fort Worth and Kansas City symphony orchestras. He found the challenges of coordinating timing with a large orchestra difficult, and the experience convinced him that guitar is far from an ideal concerto instrument.

Kottke played on Rickie Lee Jones's *Traffic from Paradise* and so enjoyed the relaxed collaboration that he invited her to produce his 1994 album, *Peculiaroso.* She also sang backup vocals on the largely instrumental album. Van Dyke Parks arranged the string quartet for a cover of the Bert Kaempfert tune "Wonderland at Night" and also played accordion on "Porky and Pale."

Peculiaroso included two songs with unusual lyrics. "Parade" referred to a troubled period as a boy in Cheyenne, Wyoming. Here a youthful Kottke saw "Roy Rogers or Gene Autry in a parade and tried to disturb his horse." "Turning into Randolph Scott (Humid Child)" refers to "the sense that there's no forward motion, just multi-motion," that the child and the grizzled cowboy actor he turns into actually exist simultaneously.

A very favorable review in *Acoustic Guitar* by Jeffrey Pepper Rodgers compared the "compelling vocals" to Tom Waits and commented on its further evidence that Kottke is "one of the acoustic guitar's most evocative and enduring voices."

Leo Live (1995) presented a Colorado concert, including a couple of humorous monologues. One describes his father's army manual on hand-to-hand combat.

In the summer of 1996 Kottke went to Nashville to record an album with the assistance of country guitarist Chet Atkins. The album, *Standing in My Shoes*, came out in early 1997 to mixed reviews. Producer-engineer (and longtime friend) David Z, a Prince alumnus, laid down funky drum machine and live percussion tracks over old Kottke tunes to add rhythmic bite. The experimental approach even included sitar accompaniment to a high-energy cover of the old Fleetwood Mac song "World Turning." But Kottke balanced mostly uptempo numbers with his somber, poignant singing of the traditional folk song "Corrina, Corrina."

Two Kottke compilations also were issued in 1997: *The Leo Kottke Anthology* on Rhino Records (which featured selections originally recorded before 1984) and the Dutch album *Hear the Wind Howl*.

He continues "to spend 80 percent" of his time touring. Kottke considers the demands of live performances and the audience interaction a great aid to staying fresh and improving, even after nearly thirty years of touring. "The longer you play, the better you get at filling the pocket," Kottke explains, referring to the elusive tempo and dynamics that perfectly match the character of each piece.

Although he prefers live dates, Kottke is satisfied with his recording career and the different recording companies he's worked with: "It's been a fairy tale. They have all treated me like a grand poobah."

Kottke lives in Wayzata, Minnesota, a suburb of Minneapolis, with his wife, Mary. He has two older children.

Entry written by Frank Markowitz based on an interview with Leo Kottke

KWESKIN, JIM: *Singer, band leader (the Jug Band). Born Stamford, Connecticut, July 18, 1940. Band members on original album, 1963, included Geoff Muldaur (vocals, guitar, kazoo, washboard), Bob Siggins, Bruno Wolf, Fritz Richmond (jug, washboard bass).*

The history of jug bands in rural parts of the United States goes back many decades, probably to times before the twentieth century, but by the 1940s and early '50s such groups had essentially faded from the musical pantheon even in remote backwoods areas. With the onset of the folk boom of the late 1950s, folk music collectors started to pay attention to such old-time material, and in the early and mid-1960s, a number of young urban musicians brought on a brief jug band revival through groups like Dave Van Ronk's Jug Stompers, the Even Dozen Jug Band, and, most notably, Jim Kweskin's aggregation.

All of those bands became seedbeds for artists who went on to become major players in modern folk music. The Jug Stompers leader, Dave Van Ronk, became one of the most influential solo artists for the last three decades of the twentieth century, and his group included jug player Sam Charters, a folk music collector, writer, and eminent folk and blues historian. Some of the Even Dozen roster later became members of important folk or rock bands or successful soloists. But probably the most impressive total of successful alumni came from the Kweskin group, including Geoff Muldaur; his wife for a time, Maria Muldaur; banjoist Bill Keith; and fiddle virtuoso Richard Greene.

Kweskin was born and raised in New England. As a teenager he was drawn to folk and blues music and began performing those styles in local clubs before heading west to San Francisco. In the Bay Area, he was exposed to ragtime jug band styles and gained experience during 1961–62 before heading back to his home area to organize his first band that began finding gigs in folk clubs in and around Boston.

(Sam Charters, who did considerable research on rural music, told Paul Nelson for an article in *Sing Out!* magazine ["Jug Band! Jug Band!" December-January 1963–1964], "The jug had all the necessary qualifications for a rural instrument. It was cheap, easy to carry around, it was durable, and it wasn't hard to play. Its tone, dark and heavy, made a strong contrast with the high-pitched harmonicas, or the shouting voices. . . . [To play it] the jug player tightened his lips, then blowed between them, letting them buzz. The small opening of the jug was held close enough to the mouth so that the jug acted as a resonant chamber.")

By mid-1963, jug bands had become one of the popular favorites in the northeast, and turnaway crowds greeted appearances of the best-known ones in major nightclubs and concert halls. One concert in the fall of the year brought together many jug groups at New York's famed Carnegie Hall. Major record labels soon came calling, with Elektra signing the Even Dozen band, Mercury the Jug Stompers, and Vanguard Records the Kweskin group. All three bands recorded debut LPs in 1963, with the Kweskin album, *Jim Kweskin and the Jug Band*, coming out in December of that year. Joining him on the disc were Geoff Muldaur, Bob Siggins, Bruno Wolf, and Fritz Richmond (jug, bass, washboard).

Soon after that, Siggins left and banjo player and pedal steel guitarist Bill Keith joined. During 1964 the band's first female member, vocalist Maria D'Amato was added. She later married Geoff Muldaur and, though they eventually divorced, maintained Muldaur as her professional last name. Over the next few years, Kweskin's group continued to find an audience for its live appearances and new recordings. The band expanded its performing locales to many other parts of the United States, including the West Coast, where, in February 1964, it was the first of its genre to play the then-prestigious Troubadour nightclub. In a typical program, he noted, his group performed "some jug band tunes, a lot of ragtime . . . some Leadbelly numbers." Besides those, Paul Nelson added, their shows typically included "a number of things that delightfully defy classification."

From 1965 through 1967, a steady output of both solo and jug band albums by Kweskin came from Vanguard Records. These included the 1965 *Jug Band Music,* the 1966 releases *Relax Your Mind* (whose contents included a fine rendition of "Woman" by Maria Muldaur) and the *Jim Kweskin* solo album (on which Mel Lyman played harmonica), and three 1967 collections, *See Reverse Side for Title, Jump for Joy,* and *Garden of Joy. See Reverse Side* had some of the band's best renditions, including "Blues in the Bottle" and "Fishing Blues," which became staples in the repertoire of John Sebastian's band, the Lovin' Spoonful, and a Geoff and Maria Muldaur's duet, "Chevrolet." *Garden of Joy,* which turned out to be the band's last album, contained some excellent contributions on fiddle from Richard Greene.

Mel Lyman, who worked closely with Kweskin on both solo and jug band efforts (the two recorded an album issued by Reprise in 1971 titled *Jim Kweskin's America with Mel Lyman*), turned away from music in favor of organizing a rather strange commune in the Boston area. (Some journalists described him as the psychedelic dictator of Boston.) Kweskin for a time became an acolyte and disbanded his group. Vanguard issued albums of previously unreleased or retrospective material, including the 1968 releases *Whatever Happened to the Good Old Days in Club 47* and *The Best of Jim Kweskin.* In 1969 Vanguard released the LP *American Aviator,* followed in 1970 by the two-LP *Greatest Hits.*

By the early 1970s Kweskin had resumed his entertainment career, primarily as a soloist. Though he never came close to the levels reached in his jug band period of the mid-1960s, he kept active in the 1990s while more albums were added to his discography of new or retrospective material. These included *Jim Kweskin* and *Jim Kweskin Lives Again* in 1978, *Side by Side* and *Swinging on a Star* in 1980, and the 1990 rerelease of *Greatest Hits.*

LADYSMITH BLACK MAMBAZO: *South African a cappella group. Joseph Shabalala, singer, songwriter, producer, leader. Born Ladysmith, Natal Province, South Africa, August 28, 1940. Other members: Headman Shabalala (killed in 1991); Ben Shabalala (left group in 1991); Jockey Shabalala, born November 4, 1944; Albert Mazibuko, born April 16, 1948; Abednego Mazibuko, born March 12, 1954; Russel Mthembu, born March 12, 1947; Inos Phungula, born March 31, 1945; and Jabulani Dubazana, born April 24, 1954. After Headman Shabalala's death, his son, Thulani Shabalala, born February 2, 1968, joined the group. After Ben Shabalala left, his sons, Sibongiseni Shabalala, born May 20, 1972, and Thamsanqa Shabalala, born July 7, 1974, joined. (All members born in Ladysmith except the sons.)*

In the mid 1980s, when the white minority in South Africa still imposed apartheid on the black majority, Ladysmith Black Mambazo represented a ray of hope and protest. The ten-member a cappella group captivated audiences by performing the song "Homeless" on Paul Simon's *Graceland* album, which sold more than 11.5 million copies. Although some antiapartheid activists criticized Simon for violating the cultural boycott of South Africa, his album brought the traditional sounds and dancing of Ladysmith Black Mambazo to the world. The group became a symbol for peace. In December 1993 they accompanied Nelson Mandela and then South African President F. W. de Klerk to the Nobel Peace Prize ceremony in Oslo, Norway. In May 1994 the group performed at President Mandela's inauguration. In June, as the group performed for 10,000 people in front of New York's Museum of Natural History, Joseph Shabalala declared: "Hey! Look at me! I'm free! I have a black president in Pretoria. I'm not a slave anymore. Look at me! I am free!"

But it was a long struggle. "Homeless," cowritten by Simon and founder Joseph Shabalala, spoke of a people who had been systematically uprooted and displaced.

"Music creates order out of chaos," Shabalala told Lynne Heffley of the *Los Angeles Times* (March 8, 1994). "When the people came, the white people in South Africa, the [indigenous] music was there a long time, but they don't understand. They built many schools and many universities, but the music of the regional people has no home."

In the 1920s and 1930s, as South Africa became industrialized, black workers were forced to work in mines and factories far from their homes. They lived in all-male hostels under oppressive, overcrowded conditions. The men developed a cappella singing groups to break up the drudgery of their lives. The 1939 song "Mbube," one of the first recordings to have an impact outside South Africa, came out of that milieu. The song, by Solomon Linda, sold 100,000 copies and inspired the Weavers' hit "Wimoweh" in 1950 and "The Lion Sleeps Tonight" by the Tokens in 1961.

Black Mambazo's music has its roots in Zulu traditional songs for marriages and special occasions, but the harsh conditions brought a more urbanized feel to the sounds. "When our fathers came to Johannesburg to work there, they stay in the hostels and start to sing alone," Shabalala told Don Snowden of the *Los Angeles Times* (June 10, 1987). "They try to imitate the girls, to sing the high parts, because at home there used to be only girls who will sing those parts."

The men would work for six days straight and then in the wee hours every Saturday night, they would mix Zulu songs with a touch of R&B and gospel. They danced quietly and gently so as not to draw the attention of the guards. They came to be known as *cothoza mfana,* or "the tiptoe guys." The music became known as *isicathamiya,* the Zulu word meaning "to stalk or step softly."

"When you stand up and dance, it means that you are powerful," Shabalala told Jon Pareles of the *New York Times* (March 21, 1993). "You stomp the floor until, if it was wooden, it would be broken. But in the cities the neighbors were complaining. So they started to tiptoe."

Joseph was born Bhekizizwe ("leader of men") Shabalala. The eldest of eight children, Shabalala grew up on a farm near Ladysmith Township, a rural grassland area roughly 200 miles north of Durban, South Africa. He came from spiritual stock. His father worked on a farm but was also an herbalist. His mother was a diviner. When his father died, it was his responsibility to look after the family.

In the late 1950s he left the family farm and migrated to Durban in search of work. It was there that he began singing with a group called the Highlanders, led by veteran vocalist Galiyane Hlatshwayo. When he returned home in 1958, he formed his first group, the Durban Choir, with his brothers and cousins. The group usually performed during the Christmas holidays, when workers returned home. In the mid-1960s the group changed its name to Ezimnyama ("The Black Ones"), after Shabalala's favorite black oxen. In the late 1960s they changed their name to Ladysmith Black Mambazo—Ladysmith for their township, Black for Shabalala's black ox, and Mambazo, which means "ax" in Zulu, because they cut down their competition. They usually took home the winning prize—a goat—in the township contests. They became so good that they were forbidden to enter the competitions.

Despite their dominance, Shabalala was never satisfied with the results. In 1964 he had a fateful dream that inspired him to go after a certain sound. "There is a stage but the children are not on the stage," he described the dream to Snowden. "They were in between the stage and sky, just floating there and always singing. They are like my teachers who teach me exactly this sound."

He recruited members of his immediate family, including his brothers Headman, Jockey, and Ben, and cousins Albert and Abednego and taught them the sounds he had heard in his dreams. It wasn't until 1969 that the group perfected the sound with a choir of ten: seven basses and three singing in the upper registers. Joseph sang lead above the rumbling bass voices.

Shabalala told Snowden: "The first time we sing in the big halls, we have no instruments. We did the tours without microphones for a long time. It's easy to hear this high voice but those basses are singing in deep voices and there must be many people to be strong."

During the 1960s the South African Broadcasting Corporation asked various a cappella groups to perform on Radio Zulu's popular *Cothoza Mfana* program. Ladysmith Black Mambazo performed the first of several live broadcasts for Radio Zulu in 1970, resulting in a flood of requests for records. West Nkosi, a producer for Gallo Records, brought the group to Johannesburg to cut a record. (The group has remained with Gallo ever since.) They released *Amabutho* in 1972, and followed quickly with a second album, *Isitimela,* in 1974, and a third, *Amaqhawe,* in 1976. Before Black Mambazo, groups would release a series of singles and compile them into a "greatest hits" album. But Black Mambazo broke new ground by putting out LPs from the beginning. (The group sings mainly in Zulu, and also in Sotho, Xhosa, Shangaan, and Venda.)

The early albums contained traditional folk songs with cryptic antiapartheid references. After Joseph Shabalala became a minister in 1970, the albums also contained religious themes. The group released *Ukukhanya Kwelanga,* an album of religious songs. Since then the group has released more than thirty albums, many of which have gone gold (25,000 units) in South Africa, and become one of the most popular groups in Africa. *Ukusindiswa* was the group's biggest-selling album, more than 300,000 units. Other albums on Gallo include *Ezinkulu, Ezulwini, Ibhayibheli Liyi, Imbongoni, Indlela Yasezulwini, Inkazimulo, Intokozo, Ngongotha Mfana, Phansi Emgodini, Phesulu Emafini, Shinisha Sithothobala,* and *Thandani.*

Black Mambazo took its first overseas trip in 1980 to perform at an outdoor festival called African Fest held in Frankfurt, West Germany. The group was so popular that they returned in 1981 and 1983. Paul Simon first got interested in the group after seeing the film *Rhythm of Resistance,* produced for the BBC by Jeremy Marre of Harcourt Films in 1979 and distributed by Shanachie Records. He called Shabalala in 1985 about performing on the *Graceland* album. Black Mambazo recorded two tracks for the album, "Homeless" and "Diamonds on the Soles of Her Shoes." Rather than try to change the group to fit his style, Simon wisely allowed the band to perform its music in its original form, except that they sang in English, not Zulu. Black Mambazo went on a worldwide tour with Simon after the release of *Graceland.* Simon introduced audiences around the world to the sights and sounds of South Africa, not just Ladysmith Black Mambazo, but also the *mbaqanga,* or township, style of Ray Phiri.

Many antiapartheid activists criticized Paul Simon

for traveling to South Africa in the middle of the cultural boycott. Many American and British performers had refused to play in South Africa's Sun City, a huge entertainment complex. But Simon had gotten approval from the black musicians' union in South Africa. The United Nations Anti-Apartheid Committee dropped its objections. Shabalala, who was not ostensibly political in nature, always defended Simon. He gave him a Zulu name, Vulindela, which means "he who has opened the gate."

"Paul Simon used our music, yes," Shabalala told Tamela Hultman of *Africa News Service* in 1993. "This kind of music is meant to be used by many people. . . . but he helped us in so many ways, he became our friend. Because of him our music is known all over the world."

The world fell in love with Black Mambazo's rhythms, synchronized dancing, and uplifting sounds. Following *Graceland,* the group signed with Warner Brothers and released *Shaka Zulu* in 1987, produced by Simon. The album won a Grammy for Best Traditional Folk Recording. The next album, *Journey of Dreams,* came out in 1988, coproduced by Paul Simon and Russ Titelman. "For the first time I have made the music on record exactly as my dreams would tell me and for this sound I am grateful," Shabalala wrote in the liner notes. "Because the world listens now and that means the Journey of Dreams goes on and on."

They followed with *Two Worlds, One Heart* on Warner Brothers in 1990. The album included a gospel collaboration with the Winans and a "Zulu-funk/rap" number with George Clinton. That year they also backed Simon on his *Rhythm of the Saints* album.

One of the group's most memorable performances was on *Sesame Street.* They were one of many celebrities to sing "Put Down That Ducky" in 1987 which became one of the top three requested segments in *Sesame Street*'s history.

They appeared in award-winning commercials. They sang "Rain Rain" for a 7-Up commercial, and appeared in ads for Lifesavers and Reebok. They did a successful ad for Heinz Ketchup in which they sang "Inkanyezi Nezazi" ("The Star and the Wiseman"), from the album by the same name. They performed in Michael Jackson's *Moonwalker* video; Spike Lee's *Do It A Cappella;* on the soundtrack of *Coming to America,* the Eddie Murphy film; *A Dry White Season,* starring Marlon Brando; and *Cry the Beloved Country,* starring James Earl Jones.

In December 1991, a time of tumultuous change in South Africa, tragedy struck. Headman, a founding member, was shot dead by an off-duty private security guard during a traffic dispute. The guard was sentenced to three months' house arrest and was later freed on appeal.

At first, Shabalala was angry about the lack of justice for his brother's death. "In South Africa, a black man is worth nothing," he told Pareles (March 21, 1993). "It is very easy for the judge to say five years of home arrest, not to put him in jail, because he is white."

But by 1994 he had taken a more spiritual look at the situation. "I was thinking this is the way of God telling me to not continue," Shabalala told Heffley. "From that day, I was telling myself I'm not going to sing anymore. But as the time goes, the dream came to me at night, it was like somebody telling me that this is your gift. You must carry on."

And so the group continued. After Headman's death, Joseph's son Thulani Shabalala joined the group. When Ben Shabalala also left, his sons, Sibongiseni Shabalala and Thamsanqa Shabalala, joined.

The group worked with the Steppenwolf Theater Company of Chicago to create a play called *The Song of Jacob Zulu.* Written by Tug Yourgrau, a white playwright who was born in South Africa, the play is based on the true story of Andrew Zondo, who was hanged for planting a bomb in a shopping mall.

When first approached about participating in the play, Shabalala was hesitant. "At first I thought, 'Oh, no, forget about it, Black Mambazo are Christian; they are not talking about politics,'" he told Pareles (March 21, 1993). "But when I read the script, I discovered this was my cousin! I thought, 'This is wonderful for me, this is the truth, this is exactly right.'"

The play premiered in Chicago in the spring of 1992 and on Broadway in the spring of 1993. It was nominated for six Tony awards. Shabalala and won the Drama Desk Award for Best Original Score.

In 1995 Black Mambazo returned to the stage again to perform in the play *Nomathemba,* based on a song by Shabalala by the same name. Nomathemba is the name of a woman as well as a word that means "hope" in Zulu. The play, about two lovers separated as they moved from rural Ladysmith to the urban areas, won a Chicago Theater Jeff Award for Original Musical Score.

The group reunited with Paul Simon in the fall of 1993 for twenty-one sold-out concerts at the Paramount Theater on Broadway. In 1994 Black Mambazo released *Liph' Iqiniso* on Shanachie. The album hit number thirteen on *Billboard*'s world music charts. It was nominated for a Grammy, the group's fifth nomination in eight years. Other Ladysmith Black Mambazo recordings available on Shanachie include *Ulwandle Oluncgwele* (1985), *Induku Zethu* (1987), *Inala* (1987), *Umthombo Wamanzi* (1988), *Classic Tracks* (1990), *The Best of Ladysmith Black Mambazo* (1990), and *Thuthukani Ngoxolo* ("Let's Develop in Peace"), nominated for a Grammy in 1996. On the back of the album, Shabalala thanks the group's international supporters: "During all the turbulent times in our society, you were there for us. . . . We gladly present this album to you. The trick to succeed all evils is the ability to use our inborn consciousness, a gift that was bestowed on us by our mighty lord."

In 1997 Ladysmith released *Heavenly,* a gospel recording that included Phoebe Snow and Bonnie Raitt. They followed with *The Best of Ladysmith Black Mambazo Volume 2,* released by Shanachie in October 1998 and *In Harmony: Live at the Royal Albert Hall* in 1999.

Increasingly, Shabalala, a father of nine and grandfather of four, became concerned that the youth were not carrying on the traditions in South Africa. He began to see his mission as preserving indigenous music. Black Mambazo released a children's album in 1994, *Gift of the Tortoise,* on Music for Little People/Warner Brothers. *How the Leopard Got His Spots* came out in 1997 on Rabbit Ears Records. He donated the proceeds to the Ladysmith Black Mambazo Academy of Music, the country's first academy for the teaching and preservation of indigenous South African music and culture. "It's time to follow the footsteps of our ancestors," Shabalala told Heffley. "That's the only way to know ourselves."

The academy has begun to conduct classes at Natal University (where Shabalala was appointed an associate professor of ethnomusicology) and has been raising funds for the construction of an independent facility.

Shabalala told the *Africa News Service* in 1993 that he was on a mission: "The nature of this group Ladysmith Black Mambazo is to spread our culture and its tradition, to encourage our musicians and composers that their music should remain as close as possible to their roots. Ladysmith Black Mambazo are like teachers, to share this culture that is our gift all over the world."

Written with help from Cindy Byram, Shanachie Records; C. Vaughn Hazell and Ivor Haarburger of Gallo Records; and Mitch Goldstein, Right Side Management

LA FARGE, PETER: *Singer, guitarist, songwriter. Born Fountain, Colorado, 1931; died New York, New York, October 27, 1965.*

Sensitive and poetic, Peter LaFarge was one of the first of the American "angry young men" who sparked the folk boom of the 1950s and '60s. He functioned on many creative levels, providing some of the best of the "composed" new folk music as well as turning out articles, plays, and poetry in his short lifetime.

As Julius Lester wrote in *Sing Out!* (January 1966, p. 11), "It is too easy to feel sorrow for a poet who dies young. 'If he had only lived . . .' is the pathetic plaint of those who stand at the grave. But he did live and our sorrow and our tears are wasted on him now. He is beyond us—the audiences that never quite understood him, and the friends who pitied him. . . ."

Of American Indian ancestry, LaFarge grew up in the Rocky Mountain area, where he learned the ways of the rodeo cowboy. He became interested in folk music early in life, and at fourteen had his own radio program on a Colorado Springs station. He played many of Woody Guthrie's recordings, which led to a meeting with Guthrie's close friend Cisco Houston. Houston helped LaFarge learn many of the fine points of singing, guitar playing, and, most important, songwriting. Another part of Peter's training came from the man who adopted him, Pulitzer Prize–winning novelist and Indian champion Oliver LaFarge. He was later adopted by the Tewa Tribe of the Hopi nation.

LaFarge continued to develop his talents as performer and songwriter during the late 1940s. His career was interrupted by the Korean War. He won five battle stars and suffered a serious head injury before leaving the service. Returning home, he indicated his disdain for physical hurt by working as a rodeo bull-dogger and bronco rider. He also put in some time as a boxer.

Finally, he returned to writing and singing. He performed in local coffeehouses, then moved on to star at major folk concerts, including the Newport Folk Festival. His byline also began to appear on articles on folk music and folk performers in *Sing Out!* By the early 1960s, many major folk artists including Bob Dylan, and Johnny Cash, were singing and recording his songs, including "Black Stallion," "The Ballad of Ira Hayes," "Coyote," and "As Long as the Grass Shall Grow."

In the early 1960s, LaFarge recorded the first LP of his own material for Columbia Records, *Ira Hayes and other Ballads,* produced by John Hammond. He followed up with several more LPs on Folkways, the first of which was the 1963 *As Long as the Grass Shall Grow.* His talents were beginning to win him a reputation as a budding dramatist and author when his life ended in New York in the fall of 1965.

The cause of death was officially listed as a stroke, although there were persistent rumors that he had committed suicide. Investigators found several empty medical bottles and syringes near his body when he died in his New York City apartment. He was involved in organizing for the rights of Native Americans, activities that apparently attracted the attention of the F.B.I.

LaFarge was part of the group hanging around with Bob Dylan in the early 1960s. According to Anthony Scaduto's biography, *Bob Dylan,* some women asked LaFarge to keep an eye on Dylan, in particular to keep him away from pot smoking. As Mrs. Sid Gleason told Scaduto: "Pete would walk into a party where Bob was and stand with his arms crossed, not saying a word, just watching. And Bobby called me one day and said, 'Mom, please get that Indian off my back. I promise I won't do anything like that again.' Every place he was, Pete would come and show up."

In 1998 LaFarge's LPs were available on CD through Smithsonian/Folkways, including *As Long as the Grass Shall Grow, Iron Mountain and Other Songs, On the Warpath, Sings of the Cowboys, Sings Women*

Blues–Sings Love Songs. Bear Family Records released *As Long as the Grass Shall Grow/On the Warpath.*

LANOIS, DANIEL: *Singer, guitarist, songwriter, record producer, sound engineer. Born September 19, 1951, Hull, Quebec, Canada.*

One of the most successful behind-the-scenes experts of the late twentieth century, Daniel Lanois played an important role in the careers of artists across a broad range of musical genres from straightforward rock to folk-rock and world music as a sound engineer and record producer. But he was also a talented performer in his own right, sometimes working as a backing musician for others, other times showing talent on his own as a singer and instrumentalist.

He was born and spent his early years in Quebec, Canada, in a family where there was considerable love for music. His mother enjoyed singing and his father played the fiddle. In 1963 his parents separated and Daniel moved with his mother to Hamilton, Ontario. Daniel was influenced by the rock formats of the early and mid-'60s, but also had been exposed to more traditional styles. By his mid-teens he showed considerable skill as a guitarist and, with his brother Robert, set up a small recording studio in the basement of their mother's home. There the two experimented with some of their own work while also earning income by making discs for local artists. In 1978 Daniel served as producer for an album by Raffi, who went on to become a major concert and TV star in children's music. The folk LP, *Singable Songs for the Very Young,* was issued on an independent label.

Over the next few years, others in the music industry became aware of Lanois's abilities, including avant-garde artist and fellow producer Brian Eno. In 1982 Lanois was coproducer with Eno on the latter's EG release, *On Land.* The next year, Lanois collaborated with Brian and his brother Roger as coproducer, coengineer, and cowriter of the EG album *Apollo, Atmosphere & Soundtracks.* In 1984 Lanois worked with Brian Eno and Harold Budd as coproducer and cowriter of Budd's album *The Pearl.* That same year, Lanois gained a worldwide reputation for his assistance in launching the breakthrough album of an Irish band that was to reach superstar rank in the mid-1980s, U2. With Eno he coproduced the group's *The Unforgettable Fire,* which soon became a best-seller on the Island Records label. Lanois went on to produce Peter Gabriel's sound track album *Birdy.* (He later worked with Billy Bob Thornton on the score for 1986's *Sling Blade.*) He wound up the first half of the decade with two more projects, coproduction of the Michael Brook EG Records disc *Hybrid* and a similar task (with Roger Eno) on Eno's *Voices* collection for the same label.

Daniel's interaction with major creative forces continued unabated during the rest of the 1980s. In 1986 he coproduced Jon Hassell's album *Power Spot* (issued on ECM) and went on to collaborate with Brian Eno in co-producing what was to become another global hit for U2, *The Joshua Tree.* The album was named Album of the Year for 1987 in the Grammy Awards voting, and the band, Eno, and Lanois all received trophies. In 1988 he handled all the production chores for the Geffen Records self-titled debut of the famed alumnus of the Band, Robbie Robertson. Also in '88, he coproduced the Jon Hassell/Farafina Intut'n Records album, *Flash of Spirit.* Daniel also was enlisted to produce a new album by the legendary Bob Dylan, *Oh Mercy,* released by CBS Records during 1989. Lanois closed out the '80s with his first solo album, which he also produced, *Acadie,* issued on Opal/Warner Brothers. Lanois's impact on the musical spectrum was recognized by *Rolling Stone* in its retrospective look at the 1980s, when he was named the most important record producer to emerge in the decade.

The early 1990s found him once again engaged in a U2 project, this time as coproducer of the 1991 Island release *Achtung Baby.* Like earlier U2 releases, this was a multimillion-copy seller. Also that year, Daniel produced and performed the Opal/Warner Brothers track "Sleeping in the Devil's Bed," which was included in the sound track for the film *Until the End of the World.* His 1992 efforts included production of the Peter Gabriel Geffen release *Us.* (He had produced Gabriel's *So* in 1986.) In the 1992 Grammy voting, Lanois earned his second award, this time for Producer of the Year, an honor shared with Brian Eno.

In early 1993 his second solo album came out on Opal/Warner Brothers. Called *For the Beauty of Wynona,* it took its cue from a small Canadian town near where Lanois grew up. Also produced by him, the thirteen songs included such originals as "Death of a Train," "Rocky World," "Brother L.A.," and "Still Learning to Crawl." A live set, *Cool Water,* came out in 1994.

During the '80s and '90s, other artists Lanois worked with as producer, coproducer, engineer, or cowriter included the Parachute Club *(The Parachute Club);* Martha and the Muffins *(Danseparc, This Is the Ice Age, Mystery Walk);* M + M *(M + M);* and the Neville Brothers *(Yellow Moon).* In the mid-1990s he extended his production work into the country and folk field, holding the reins on Emmylou Harris's notable album *Wrecking Ball.*

Wrecking Ball won the Grammy for Best Contemporary Folk album, beating out albums by Bob Dylan and John Prine. In 1997 Lanois produced Dylan's *Time out of Mind* CD, which broke into *Billboard*'s top 10, won the Grammy for Album of the Year, and reestablished Dylan as a force in the 1990s. The following year, he produced Willie Nelson's album *Teatro,* recorded in an old Mexican movie theater in Oxnard, California. He also worked that year on the score for Thornton's film of Cormac McCarthy's book *All the Pretty Horses,* and produced Scott Weiland's solo album, *12 Bar Blues,* released on Atlantic Records.

LARKIN, PATTY: *Singer, songwriter, guitarist, mandolinist, accordionist. Born Des Moines, Iowa, June 19, 1951.*

If Patty Larkin were just an excellent guitarist, singer, and songwriter, that would be enough. But she's also a performer who possesses a wicked wit and a knack for theatrics. Take, for example, her song "At the Mall," a vaudeville-like schtick in which she puts on lipstick, holds her nose, and sings off-key to assume the persona of screen legend Marlene Dietrich, followed by Carmen Miranda and Ethel Merman. The laughter spills out of the audience at McCabe's Guitar Shop in Santa Monica like the fruit out of Miranda's hat—the song is a satire about their own behavior.

Larkin mesmerizes them again with "Me and That Train," a harrowing ride in a snowstorm that is a metaphor for life's vicissitudes. One verse is based on a true story about how Larkin was held up while working in a health food store. As the robber pointed a gun at her, she laughed out of fear and the absurdity of it all. "I want the listener to experience the songs and make them their own, use their imagination and come along for the ride," she says.

She's best known in Boston, which declared July 18, 1995, Patty Larkin Day, marking the release of her album *Strangers World.* She has won eleven Boston Music Awards. She even sang "The Star-Spangled Banner" at a Boston Red Sox game. But Larkin has also developed a national following. With eight albums to date and appearances on NBC's *Today Show,* CBS's *This Morning,* and ABC's *Good Morning America,* Larkin seemed on the verge of breaking into the mainstream. *Angels Running* (1993) and *Strangers World* both topped the Adult Album Alternative charts.

Larkin was born in Des Moines, Iowa, and raised in Whitefish Bay, Wisconsin, outside Milwaukee. Music was an integral part of her family. Her mother, a painter and artist, played the piano, and her father, a businessman, sang in the church choir. Her sisters were musicians also. "I remember listening to music when I was a little kid," she recalls. "Both grandmothers were avid piano players. One was a party girl, the other was a church choir leader. Whenever we visited them, we would sit around and sing. I got a lot of encouragement from my folks to play piano, sing, and be in college."

She studied classical piano for eight years, but didn't take to it. On her *Tango* CD, Larkin jokingly credits a strict piano teacher, Sister Guadilla, "for making me want to quit piano lessons and play the guitar. . . . She was incredibly strict and she'd hit you with a ruler. She didn't impart the love of the music, just the discipline," Larkin says.

Larkin found a better match when she took up guitar in seventh grade. She began composing songs a year later—"the teenage, pre-teen sort but they were meaningful to me," she says. "I liked singing and playing at the same time rather than reading music and being very strict about it. There was a social thing—hanging out with your friends, exchanging information about the D chord and trying to figure out a new, cool song. I was able to go up and hide in my room and make up chords and learn new songs and start making up my own songs. It was something that was private rather than in full public view in the living room."

She started out on Simon and Garfunkel, and then Joni Mitchell. "I remember when Joni Mitchell first came out, that was pretty amazing stuff for me," she told Scott Alarik of *Performing Songwriter* (September-October 1993). "It seemed personal, seemed to really cut through. There was a sense that she had a view that wasn't as distant as other writers. She had a sense of humor, and that came through. . . . For me, it was the first woman singer-songwriter I had heard that really moved me."

After high school, she planned to go out west with a boyfriend. When the relationship broke up, she went anyway—to the University of Oregon. There she got a taste for the outdoors, hiking, backpacking, and rock climbing. She graduated in 1973 with a bachelor's degree in English lit. But it was a course in the folklore department—Jug Band 101—that influenced her the most. She began playing in a jug band called Willie and the Egyptians. Around that time, Bonnie Raitt came out with her *Give It Up* album. "Here was a woman for the first time that not only played guitar and sang great, but she also took the solos," Larkin says. "I found her very inspiring."

Larkin moved to Boston in 1974 and soon found out how hard it was to be a musician. "Early on, when I made the decision to go into music, I was extremely hard on myself," she says. "I think at that time I had what would probably be termed a nervous breakdown. Who knows what was going on for me? It might have just been being twenty-two, which is a tough time. I didn't think I deserved to do what I wanted to do, just for the joy of it. I think probably if I had any advice it would be to just go ahead. Give yourself permission to do what you're going to do. I just at some point said, 'I don't care, I'm going to be a musician.' Good or bad. If I have to wear white boots, if I have to play lounges the rest of my life, that's what I'm going to do."

The rough period lasted for about a year and a half, and she returned to music. She attended the Berklee College of Music for a summer. She studied jazz guitar there and later with various teachers, especially Chet Krule, a big-band jazz stylist. "We had these combos, four guitarists playing horn parts and one guitarist playing rhythm parts," she recalls. "They were like bebop charts. I learned a lot from Chet. I wouldn't call myself a jazz player. I was still writing folk music and light jazz and some Brazilian-influenced stuff. I was interested in Flora Purim, Airto, Milton Nascimento, and Jobim."

She played Brazilian-flavored music in a trio that included flute, conga, and acoustic guitar. She also played mandolin and rhythm guitar on the Cambridge streets in the Celtic-style Brattle Street Band. "I was just starting to get into mandolin when the band broke up," she says. "Mostly I learned how to use a pick."

She wrote original music and played guitar in the rock Patty Larkin Band from 1979 to 1981. They played covers of the Pretenders and R&B classics. But she found rock limiting. "The whole time also I was performing solo or duo gigs, all acoustic," she says. "I realized I didn't like the writing I was doing for the rock format. I was opening for Leon Redbone, the Persuasions, Jesse Colin Young. I was getting these gigs because I was doing this pop acoustic thing. . . . It was a musical choice and a personal choice to let go of the rock and concentrate on acoustic guitar."

Over the years she became skilled in many guitar styles, exploring Paul Simon, and Joni Mitchell, Brazilian players, John Renbourn, John Martyn, Ry Cooder, Richard Thompson, and Delta blues. She incorporated the influences into a rolling, percussive guitar style, dazzling her audiences on a 1946 Martin D-18.

In 1982, she made the transition to a solo act. She began developing a reputation in New England. The owners of Rounder Records took note and signed her. In 1985, she released the first of three albums on Philo/Rounder, *Step into the Light*. She followed her debut with *I'm Fine* (1988) and *In the Square* (1990). *In the Square,* recorded at the Sanders Theater in Cambridge, won three Boston Music Awards: Outstanding Folk Act, Outstanding Folk Album, and Outstanding Song/Songwriter.

The latter album (as well as her first album on Windham Hill/High Street) included a song she wrote in 1989 called "Metal Drums," about a toxic waste disaster in Holbrook, Massachusetts. "After I wrote it I went to a folk festival and someone was playing a Woody Guthrie song about a fire in a union hall. It was like, well, that's the form I use. A song about a disaster that just grabs you when you're writing."

Her first three Philo/Rounder releases sold under 15,000 copies, not bad for an emerging acoustic artist. In those years, she says, "My goal was to write songs that were influenced by traditional and pop music. To try to use the mandolin and the slide, but still have some chord changes that were probably more modern in some ways. And to get the kind of drive out of the guitar I was getting with the band."

By the late 1980s, aided by Rounder's national distribution and promotion network, she began touring nationally. She played the Newport Folk Festival in 1988 and was featured on the album on Alcazar. She was one of the original Four Bitchin' Babes (with Christine Lavin, Megan McDonough, and Sally Fingerette) playing on the 1990 Rounder/Philo "Babes" live album: *Buy Me, Bring Me, Take Me, Don't Mess My Hair.* "The thing that was fun was the camaraderie and just how funny these people really were," Larkin says. "It was very much a cabaret show. Megan has so much background in theater. Her music is so varied. Sally also plays piano and guitar. Then, of course you have the genius known as Christine Lavin." She also played with John Gorka, Cheryl Wheeler, and Cliff Eberhardt in the On A Winter's Night tours.

Soon after, she left Rounder and joined High Street/Windham Hill, founded by Will Ackerman. At the time Windham Hill had a larger distribution network and bigger recording budgets than Philo/ Rounder in the pre-Alison Krauss days. Larkin's first album on that label, *Tango* (1991), blended various rhythms and themes. On one song, "Dave's Holiday," she is accompanied only by bass and drums. "Not a lot of overdubs on that album," Larkin says. "Will [Ackerman] is very much a strong believer in live takes. Not a lot of repairs, if any. What I learned from Will was don't overdo it."

The album included such backup musicians as electric guitarist Lyle Workman, John Gorka, and bassists Richard Gates and Michael Mannring. As the title suggests, the album is about the intricate dance of romance: love gained and lost as depicted in "Tango," "Time Was," and "Chained to These Lovin' Arms." Larkin spells it out in the liner notes: "It takes two to tango. . . ."

The album reflects Larkin's conscious effort to combine her background in jazz with her maturing songwriting ability. As she told Kevin Ransom of *Guitar Player:* "I felt like I needed to put more tension in my chords, move around the neck more, and add more colors." One source of inspiration, she told the magazine, was a Richard Thompson Homespun guitar instructional tape of Irish fiddle tunes. Homespun later released *The Guitar Techniques of Patty Larkin*.

While *Tango* represented an artistic breakthrough, *Angels Running,* produced by John Leventhal and Ben Wisch, broke new commercial ground, selling around 60,000 copies. Her songwriting was inspired by Greg Brown, Lou Reed, and especially Bob Dylan. "The lyric wasn't necessarily hemmed in by a particular melodic phrase," she says. "I really went back and started listening to Dylan on his old albums and I was blown away by what he did with lyrics and his imagination—how he stuck with a particular idea and kept turning it around and looking at it from different angles."

"A song starts with the guitar for me," Larkin told Nalini Jones, of the *Newport Folk Festival 1995* program. "It's interesting to hear people talk about their process of writing. Greg Brown said that he generally waits to be inspired, listening, staying open, which is, of course, the essence of it. But I'm more of the hands-on school. . . . I go in to work as a songwriter and do it every day I'm home. To me the process is about crafting. It takes a couple of weeks of bad songwriting before I can weed out the bad ideas and find something that might work."

More heavily produced than her previous efforts, *Angels Running* has Larkin playing a Stratocaster, mandolin, and accordion. She is joined on backup vocals by Mary-Chapin Carpenter, Jonatha Brooke, and Jennifer Kimball. She makes her social commentary on songs like "Do Not Disturb," a "song poem of urban angst and feminism," as she describes it. In "Video" she parodies a Dire Straits song about MTV. She acknowledges there is a bite to songs like "Video" and "At the Mall." She told Alarik: "There is anger in those songs. It's the kind of thing that I feel so intensely that sometimes I'm afraid I would come on way too strong, so it comes out as satire. I think people are able to laugh and still get it. I include myself in that consumer group; that group; that has to fight to turn the television set off, that's fascinated by the mall."

Larkin created a stir when she appeared on the *Today Show* on Thanksgiving, 1994 and identified herself as an acoustic singer-songwriter rather than a folksinger. One folk fan started a letter-writing campaign criticizing her position. The debate raged in the folk magazines and on the Internet. Larkin, who draws on folk, jazz, and rock influences, didn't feel right categorizing herself as a folksinger. Pete Seeger, who does not call himself a folksinger anymore, defended her. "I think it was unfortunate because it was divisive," Larkin says. "But it spawned great discussion and debate in the folk community, which I think needs to take place, about what to call this music and how strict do we want to be about the definitions of who is and who isn't. I owe the folk community a lot, I owe them my career. There's no way I forget that. But when I think of my music, of the influences and what I do, I think of myself as a songwriter."

Angels Running made the top ten on the AAA charts and set up her sixth album, *Strangers World* (1995), which was projected to sell 80,000 copies. The album received consistently strong reviews and moved to the top of the Adult Album Alternative charts. As *Music Review Quarterly* wrote (Fall 1995), "Although possessed of a fine voice and excellent guitar skills, Larkin has always seemed to work just a little too hard to get all the songwriting pieces to fit together. . . . Here she blows those obstacles away completely. She's tight lyrically, loose musically, and completely in control."

Her mother wanted her to be more upbeat in her songs. "I understand that," Larkin says. "For one thing I'm her daughter. She doesn't want to think I'm unhappy. I'm not unhappy. But I think I just wasn't editing the darker end of things."

The album does contain some optimism in "Open Arms," "Me and That Train," and "Carolina." But a thread of alienation runs throughout. Three or four close friends had died within a year and she was trying to deal with the loss. "I'm trying to resolve feeling alienated and angry and frustrated and not being able to

vent it. That's where some of the other songs come from," she says. "But I got to a place of hope."

The album was produced by John Leventhal (who worked with Rosanne Cash and Shawn Colvin), with backup singing by Bruce Cockburn, Colvin, Jonatha Brooke, and Jennifer Kimball. "I wanted to create a mood, this atmosphere that you walk into and hang out in, instead of just being song, song, song. I wanted a whole piece, not a sampler," she told Alarik.

"Johnny Was a Pyro" is a scathing account of a failed marriage: *Johnny was a pyro and he acted like a baby/Wanted all of this attention I couldn't give.* It was about her marriage to the percussionist in the Brazilian band, which ended in 1980, she says. She is "happily relationshipped," and now has no plans to remarry. "That was enough."

For many years, Larkin, who lives on Cape Cod, had been performing 150 concerts a year. She told Martin Zyla in 1995 that she was happy with her career but wanted stability. "The only thing that I would say that's hard for me right now is to not be home as much as I'd like to, because that has an impact on my personal life and it also has an impact on my writing, which, to me, is the most important facet of what I do."

Her sly, sarcastic song, "Don't," balances the sadness of some of the others: *Don't believe I want a Happy Meal/Don't believe blondes have more fun/ Don't believe those pills will make me feel/Loved by everyone.* In concert, she joked that the song is about a "young girl growing up Irish Catholic in the Midwest and wanting to question authority and still wanting to be liked." Her beautiful song "Mary Magdalene" is a feminist commentary on the past and the present. As Larkin writes in the liner notes: "I think I saw her coming out of the subway at rush hour."

With such wry observations, Larkin has been recognized as a leading songwriter. She has participated in a number of compilations and tributes, from *Legacy II* in 1992 to *Live at the Iron Horse* in 1997. She recorded "Poverty Train" for *Time and Love,* a tribute to Laura Nyro, who died in 1997. She performed "You Can't Always Get What You Want" (along with Bruce Cockburn) for the *Slide Summit* album. She also covered Fred Neil's "Everybody's Talking" for *Bleecker Street: Greenwich Village in the '60s* (Astor Place, 1999). For a Windham Hill compilation she performed "Bachianas Brasileiras No. 5" by Brazilian musician Heitor Villa-Lobos.

BMG purchased Windham Hill in 1996 and Will Ackerman was no longer affiliated. Nevertheless in October 1997 Larkin released her final album, *Perishable Fruit,* on Windham Hill's High Street label. In the album, Larkin uses everyday symbols—a road, an unread book, and a rearview mirror—as metaphors to depict the tenuous nature of life. In "The Road" she sings about the fears and rewards of breaking away: *Then the road rose up to meet me/and gathered me in its arms/ whispered to me sweetly/I'll keep you safe from harm.* Larkin also asked percussionist Ben Wittman to keep time on stringed instruments: he drums on a mandolin, brushes on a guitar, and pounds the strings of a detuned lap steel guitar.

In 1999 Vanguard released *À Gogo,* a live CD from her 1997 Perishable Fruit tour. Although Larkin is not a household name yet, a concert at McCabe's Guitar Shop indicated just how loyal her audience is. She sang "These Boots Were Made for Walking" and asked the women to sing the line, *One of these days these boots are going to walk all over you.* They did, with gusto.

Based on interview by Lyndon Stamble with Patty Larkin

LAVIN, CHRISTINE: *Singer, songwriter, guitarist. Born Peekskill, New York, January 2, 1952.*

Christine Lavin, the effervescent singer-songwriter known for her unselfish support of other songwriters, had her first brush with fame when she performed her song "Prince Charles" on NBC's *Today Show* in 1981. The song urges Prince Charles not to go through with his marriage to Lady Di: *Oh Charles, Prince Charles / Can you hear my heart break? / Can you hear me telling you / Marrying her is a big mistake?*

Like most comics, Lavin strikes a sensitive nerve. Whether it's about the grandmother on the subway observing a young couple making out in "Ain't Love Grand?" or the delusional woman encouraging people to jump onto the subway rails to save what she thinks is a puppy in "Waiting for the B Train," potential tragedy often lurks behind her comedy.

"See, I try my best to write songs about life as it is truly lived; I try to observe and record my observations as honestly as I can," Lavin wrote in a hilarious article about her semifamous life as a folksinger in the *Washington Post* (December 15, 1996). "It's important that I stay anonymous for this work so that my presence doesn't change the situation."

She's an especially keen observer of sensitive men with growing foreheads. One of Lavin's best-known satirical songs, "Sensitive New Age Guys" (written with the sensitive John Gorka), takes loving aim at the kind of man who *likes to cry at weddings / Who thinks Rambo is upsetting.* She often calls on sensitive new age guys (SNAGs) in the audience to help her sing it, as she does with her homage to bald men, "Bald Headed Men."

While she is at her best when writing humorous songs, Lavin is one of the few comic folksingers who can also write serious tunes, much like Loudon Wainwright III. She sings one about a friend going through a divorce, "Compass," and another, "Until," about a friend with a drinking problem. "The Dakota" is her response to coming upon the apartment where John Lennon was gunned down.

Never mind that she likes to bring people onstage when she plays "Jeopardy" or that she twirls a baton during her concerts and calls herself the Paula Abdul of folk music: Lavin is a serious force in the folk world.

She was a cheerleader when folk music was in the pits. While her own career was building slowly, in the early 1980s she helped Suzanne Vega (whom she later kidded in one of her songs), and later Julie Gold, whose song "From a Distance" won a Grammy. In 1989 she put together a tape of love songs by fifteen singer-songwriters, *On a Winter's Night—Ballads to Warm the Heart,* which evolved into the On a Winter's Night tours (with Cliff Eberhardt, John Gorka, Cheryl Wheeler, and Patty Larkin). (In 1991 Lavin produced a second Winter's Night collection called *When October Goes—Autumn Love Songs.*)

In the summer of 1990 she organized an all-woman ensemble called Four Bitchin' Babes, including Megon McDonough, Sally Fingerett, and Patty Larkin. The tours gave a boost to all of the performers. Then, in September 1992, she invited dozens of folksingers to the Wintertide Coffeehouse on Martha's Vineyard for the First Annual Martha's Vineyard Singer-Songwriter's Retreat. The gathering lasted three weeks, and resulted in an album of seventeen folksingers performing their compositions live, *Big Times in a Small Town: The Vineyard Tapes* (Rounder Records 1993). The retreat was so popular it was held the following year and produced a two-disc set on Rounder with thirty songs: *Follow That Road: Highlights of the Second Annual Martha's Vineyard Singer-Songwriter's Retreat.* The elegant title song was by Anne Hills; its simple lyrics contain directions to a house in the country.

Lavin was born and raised along with eight brothers and sisters on the campus of a military academy in Peekskill, New York. Her father was an administrator at the academy. Her mother bought her a cheap Silvertone guitar and she learned to play it by watching the New York City public television guitar lesson shows when she was twelve. As a child she listened to Bob Dylan, Judy Collins, Joni Mitchell, Pete Seeger, and Peter, Paul and Mary. She began writing songs when she was thirteen. She made her first public appearance, at fourteen, at a hootenanny for the Peekskill Boy Scout and Girl Scout troops.

Then she heard Phil Ochs. "'The Power and the Glory' was one of the first songs that I remember hitting me, and I really loved it," she told *Sing Out!* "'Changes' was the first full song that I ever learned."

Her family moved to Geneva, in the Finger Lakes region of upstate New York. She attended the State University of New York at Brockport, graduating in 1974 with a bachelor's degree in English, although she changed her major seven times, according to her personal bio. She moved to Florida and then to Saratoga Springs, New York, in 1975, where she worked as a waitress and bread maker at Caffe Lena. In the next six months, Utah Phillips, Kate Wolf, Jay Unger, and Arlo Guthrie performed at the café. Don McLean's manager heard her playing and encouraged her to take guitar lessons. That same night Dave Van Ronk was playing at the café. Lavin played "The Rambling Waltz" (written about Ramblin' Jack Elliott), and Van Ronk suggested she move to New York, which she did. She began taking weekly guitar lessons from Van Ronk in 1976. She soon landed a $50-a-night-plus-tips job as a singer at a Mexican restaurant.

One day, as she told Daniel Zwerdling of National Public Radio, things turned ugly in front of the restaurant: "This big mean guy started to insult this little guy's dogs. He said, 'Your dogs are ugly. They are ugly, ugly dogs.' And so, they happened to have on the counter a huge knife—to cut pecan pies. Anyway, the little guy with the dogs got so mad at his dogs being insulted he picked up the knife and he started chasing the big, ugly mean guy up the street, and then the manager ran after them and tackled the guy who had the knife. And then the assistant manager came out to me and said, 'Sing. Sing. Sing.' So I'm going, 'Michael, row the boat ashore.' . . ."

In 1981 she released her first album (on tape only), *Christine Lavin: Absolutely Live*, on Lifesong Records. The album showed her talent for humorous songs, including some that would become concert standards: "The Air Conditioner Song," about the necessity for a boy to own an air conditioner in New York during the summer, and "Prince Charles."

In 1982 she became involved in a folk-music cooperative called Speakeasy, which put out a magazine, *The Fast Folk Musical Magazine*. She recorded some songs as part of the co-op, but her musical ventures didn't pay the bills. So she worked full-time from 1982 to 1984 at Bellevue Hospital as a secretary, taking a break from her folk singing pursuits. "Those were my giving-up years," she told *Sing Out!*

She found time to release an extended-play album, *Another Woman's Man* (also on tape only), in 1983. In 1984 she released her first breakthrough album, *Future Fossils*, on her own label, Palindrome. Philo/Rounder picked it up and released it in 1986. It soon became one of the fastest-selling folk albums put out by Rounder. With songs like "Sweet Irene the Disco Queen" and "Don't Ever Call Your Sweetheart by His Name," Lavin continued to build her reputation as a witty and offbeat songwriter. She stirred up some controversy by singing "Don't Ever Call Your Sweetheart by His Name" at a dinner party for then-mayor Ed Koch. Her second performance was canceled and Koch told her that she was "promoting promiscuity and an immoral lifestyle," according to an interview with *Sing Out!*

Her next several albums included a blend of humorous and serious songs. *Beau Woes (and Other Problems of Modern Life)*, in 1986, was her second release on

Philo/Rounder. The album included "Ballad of a Ballgame," about the tribulations of a child playing in a softball game, and "Biological Time Bomb," an offbeat look at the biological clock. Another wry song is "Summer Weddings," about marriage among thirty- and fortysomethings.

She followed that album with *Good Thing He Can't Read My Mind* in 1988. The title track is about a woman suffering in silence as she skis, eats sushi, and goes to the opera, all to please her man. The album won the Folk Album of the Year award from the National Association of Independent Record Distributors.

But she still considered herself a struggling folksinger. As she joked in her tongue-in-cheek article in the *Washington Post*, she once saw a man in a record store walking to the counter with the album and impulsively went up to him and said, "Wow! Thanks for buying my record!" The man "looked at the album cover, then looked at me, then at the cover, and said, 'That's not you! Get away from me!' I was so shocked that I backed away, with the fleeting thought that maybe it wasn't me, and maybe I was nuts."

More objective critics have been kinder to Lavin. "Christine Lavin has been a driving force and enthusiastic cheerleader of the eighties urban accoustic Folk Revival," Vin Scelsa wrote in *Penthouse* (June 1988). "But don't let the F-word scare you. This is no wimpy-dip, time-warp hippie I'm talking about. This is one of the country's best songwriters. Period."

In 1989 she won the first of two New York Music Award's Folk Artist of the Year. (She received the second in 1992.) She also received the annual World Folk Music Association's Kate Wolf Memorial Award.

In 1990 she came out with *Attainable Love*, which included "Sensitive New Age Guys" and another concert standard, "Shopping Cart of Love: The Play," about a woman who finds love after she brings thirteen items to a ten-only checkout stand. She followed with *Compass* in 1991. She was finally beginning to receive mainstream attention. *People* wrote, "If we could get [Christine] and Loudon Wainwright III named our national folk music laureates, we'd have most of the country's problems accurately described, if not solved, in no time."

She recorded *Live at the Cactus Cafe: What Was I Thinking?* in 1993 at the University of Texas at Austin. The album included "Bald Headed Men," inspired by the TV commercials for spray-on hair. She believes it took a woman to write this homage to bald men. "I want to tell men: Don't fall for it, it's this giant black hole that will suck your money for the rest of your life the same way cosmetic companies make us [women] feel we cannot live without the stuff," she told Kristen A. Conover of the *Christian Science Monitor* (March 6, 1992). "I want bald guys to feel good. . . . I imagine these guys at the show ripping their toupees off and [shouting] 'I'm really bald!'"

After a two-year hiatus, she switched from Rounder

to Shanachie in May 1994 and released *Please Don't Make Me Too Happy* in 1995. As she said in a press release about the title, "Like many songwriters, I'm afraid that if I'm too happy my songwriting will turn to sappy mush—so I've told everybody at the Shanachie/ Cachet to stop being so gosh darn nice to me, but do they listen? No!" The album, recorded at the Magic Shop in New York, includes "Star 69," a Big Brother-ish song exposing male infidelity through a traced telephone call; "The Sixth Floor," about stumbling upon the Kennedy Museum in Dallas; and "Oh No," about aging and forgetfulness but with a Lavinian touch. The protagonist in the song loses her glasses, car keys, the remote control, and purse just as the pizza man arrives.

At the end of 1996 she completed work on her ninth solo album, *Shining My Flashlight at the Moon*, released in early 1997. Each song was inspired by a person or event in Lavin's life. The title track came about after she got horribly lost one night after a concert in Vermont and stood in awe as the moon nearly sucked the light out of her flashlight. The album has its share of Lavin humor: her song "Two Americans in Paris," about gazing at the Mona Lisa in the Louvre for twenty-five seconds while the cab waited outside; and "Music to Operate By," intended as a sort of cautionary pep talk for surgeons.

Besides her solo albums, Lavin has produced several compilations. She recorded three albums with the Four Bitchin' Babes. The first group of "Babes" to go on tour included Lavin, Patty Larkin, Megon McDonough, and Sally Fingerett (who dubbed them the Traveling Pillsburys). A live album taped at the Birchmere in Alexandria, Virginia, produced *Buy Me Bring Me Take Me: Don't Mess My Hair . . . Life According to Four Bitchin' Babes,* released on Rounder in 1991. Larkin moved on, and Julie Gold joined them to make their first studio album, *Buy Me Bring Me Take Me Volume 2,* issued on Rounder in 1993. In 1995 the group released its third album, *Fax It! Charge It! Don't Ask Me What's for Dinner! More Life According to Four Bitchin' Babes,* with McDonough, Fingerett, and Debi Smith of the Smith Sisters. Mary Travers of Peter, Paul and Mary makes a cameo appearance on the album, released on Shanachie. Other "Babes" have included Cheryl Wheeler, Kristina Olsen, and Janis Ian. Camille West replaced Lavin on the fourth Bitchin' Babes CD, *Gabby Road: Out of the Mouths of Babes,* released on Shanachie in October 1997.

Christine continued her support of other artists in the late 1990s. In the summer of 1996 she invited many of her more humorous colleagues to a two-night concert at the Bottom Line. In October, Shanachie released a two-volume set, *Christine Lavin Presents Laugh Tracks: Live at the Bottom Line, Volumes 1 and 2.* The collection features Vance Gilbert singing "Country Western Rap," the Foremen singing "Every Man for Himself," and Megon McDonough singing "Microwave Life."

After three years with Shanachie, Lavin left to create her own label, ChristineLavin.Com Records, and began marketing her CDs and other assorted wares on her web site (www.christinelavin.com). In May 1998 she self-released her tenth CD, *Christine Lavin: One Wild Night in Concert,* recorded at the Blue Moon Coffeehouse in Bloomington, Illinois.

She also spread the gospel of reading to concertgoers by creating the Lavin Lending Library, sans overdue notices. At each of her concerts she would read a couple of lines from a book and then give the book to an audience member. The only condition is that the recipient needs to write a one-line review on the inside cover and then pass it on to somebody else. Lavin's philosophy is that books are meant to be shared. Besides, she doesn't have enough space in her home for the books.

After all those years of supporting other artists, the artists got together and created a tribute album to her. Called *Big League Babe: The Christine Lavin Tribute Albums, Parts 1 and 2,* the two CDs were produced in 1997 and 1998 by David Seitz of PrimeCD. Each artist performs a different Lavin song, from Dave Van Ronk to Jane Kelly Williams. "It is so good that I feel that I could retire after this is released—in fact, I almost feel that I should retire!" Lavin wrote about the CDs.

Throughout the '90s, Lavin's following grew, as she continued to promote other folk musicians. As she told *Sing Out!,* "I was reading *Billboard* the other day and I looked at this pie chart which was carved into big slices for pop, rock, and country, and there's not even a sliver for folk music. Not a sliver! I shouted, 'How unfair!' A woman I was with said, 'Look, you're not trying to get a slice of that pie, you're baking your own pie.' That's really true, we're all baking our own pies!'"

LEADBELLY: *Singer, guitarist, songwriter. Original name Huddie Ledbetter. Born near Mooringsport, Louisiana, January 21, 1885;* died New York, New York, December 6, 1949.

He was, simply, larger than life. Somehow escaping the ravages and impact of oppression and prejudice, he had a monumental impact on pop music the world over. Sure of his ability and proud of his bull-like strength, calling himself the "King of the Twelve-String Guitar," he was a legend in his lifetime. His saga went on afterward, in performance of his songs by countless other artists, in reissues of his recordings, in the creation of myths of his life and times, and in plays and movies about his life.

His early years are shrouded in some degree of mystery. He himself said he was born on a farm in the Caddo Lake district near Mooringsport, Louisiana, and it's pretty certain he grew up there, but one east Texas historical society claims his true birthplace was in the

Date open to question.

Lone Star State. Wherever he was born, Louisiana was home and a rugged one, where he was out working the fields with other blacks as soon as he was able. Similarly his date of birth is also uncertain. Leadbelly gave January 21 as his birthday in talks with John and Alan Lomax in the mid-1930s, but it isn't certain that's the true date. His year of birth is variously given as 1885 and 1888.

While he was growing up he was exposed to Negro work songs, hymns, and the thrum of voodoo drums. His Uncle Terrill gave him a concertina when he was barely past toddling stage, and before long Huddie (pronounced Hew'-dee) could pick out many melodies on the instrument. A few years later his father gave him a guitar, which became his pride and joy. In his teens, when he left home to wander through the countryside playing at local affairs or on street corners, he almost always had a guitar in his hands or slung over his shoulder.

In the years near the turn of the century, Huddie spent much time playing for coins in the street for his daily bread. He sang songs he had picked up in his travels and others that he had made up on the spot. By the early years of the century he had grown into a tall, muscled strongman, and he was able to find work during the day in construction or cotton picking. He picked up his nickname during those years, but there are various stories of its origin. It's said by some that he was given it by field hands because he was so powerful, and by others that he got it from knife-wielding opponents who said his stomach muscles could fend off knife blades. Another version is that he received it from whorehouse occupants for his sexual prowess. (The latter is the one used in the 1970s movie of his early years.)

Leadbelly had what amounted to a Jekyll-Hyde nature. He could be a pleasant companion, full of humor and good nature, but if antagonized or whipped up by liquor, he could be extremely violent. The latter facet of his personality kept him in trouble—and prison—much of his life. His towering talent, however, saved him from obscurity.

His wanderings took him across Louisiana and into Texas. In 1917 in Dallas, he met another since-famed folk musician, Blind Lemon Jefferson. They teamed up to play for coins on street corners or for better pay in the brothels of East Dallas. One story has it that Huddie took a bus driver's holiday one night at a traveling carnival. While moving along the midway, he is said to have come upon a man playing a twelve-string guitar. Falling in love with the sound, the story goes, he spent the night listening to the man play, then went out and bought himself one the next day. However, Frederic Ramsey, Jr., writing in *Sing Out!* (March 1965), states that Leadbelly actually had learned to play the instrument some years earlier.

The pattern from the World War I years through the early 1930s was the same; Leadbelly was constantly getting into scrapes that landed him in prison more often than not. In between he wandered around playing his guitar and singing songs like "Pick a Bale of Cotton" or "Good Night Irene" for whoever would listen. He was working in Shreveport, Louisiana, whorehouses during World War I and sometimes making his way to towns in Texas. During that period he got caught for killing a man in one of his numerous fights and was tried for murder. He was committed to a Texas prison called Harlem on May 24, 1918, and remained there until early 1925.

At Harlem, an all-black unit no longer in existence but then located near Sugar Land, just outside Houston, Leadbelly composed one of his most famous songs, "Midnight Special." The words *Let the Midnight Special / shine its everlovin' light on me* referred to the prison myth that if the light from that train from Houston shone on an inmate he would be freed.

A major—and true—part of his legend springs from Harlem. As Alan Lomax said, "He'd perform his way into more compassionate treatment." His wonderful singing and playing got him better assignments on work gangs and finally gained his release, which resulted from a visit to the penitentiary by Texas governor Pat Neff. After hearing Leadbelly sing, including a song where he interpolated the words, *If I had you, governor, like you have me / I'd open the doors and set you free,* Neff did indeed grant a pardon. Leadbelly left the prison on January 15, 1925.

He resumed his former life, scrapes and all. The inevitable denouement caught up with him in 1930 in Louisiana. He almost killed another man and was sent up to the rugged Angola prison in the Bayou State. Again he survived, easing his burdens with songs, sometimes picking up new material from the other prisoners. While he was in Angola, he was fortunate in being befriended by the folk-song collector Dr. John Lomax. Lomax came to the penitentiary in 1932 to collect songs for the Library of Congress Archive in Washington and was amazed at Leadbelly's repertoire and musical ability. Huddie not only recorded a number of his trademark numbers for Lomax, together they also prepared a plea for freedom to be given to the state governor. This time, Huddie's music failed to move the state executive; Governor O. K. Allen turned down the appeal.

However, Lomax went back east to enlist support from friends and other folk-song collectors, a campaign that finally won Leadbelly a good-conduct release in 1934. Huddie arrived in New York later that year, carrying a beat-up green guitar held together with a piece of string. His first performances in the city in January 1935 brought strong praise from both critics and fans. He followed that with an equally acclaimed concert at Harvard University. There was no doubt in anybody's mind that a talent of immense proportions had been brought forward.

The Leadbelly legend was beginning to blossom, but the man himself still was flawed. As John Lomax's son, Alan Lomax, told Jeff Millar, "He had a terrible violent nature. He drove my father's car for him and my father handled his bookings and when he didn't have whiskey in him, Leadbelly could be a good companion. But when he was drunk or suffering the effects of a hangover, he was unapproachable. He finally pulled a knife on my father in the late 1930s and my father got shuck of Leadbelly after that. I'm positive Leadbelly was guilty of everything he went to prison for and other things he got away with. There's no telling how many people he killed."

On stage, however, he could do no wrong. From the mid-1930s to the end of his life, audiences eagerly awaited his appearances all over the world. He went to those concerts in relative style, staying in comfortable motels rather than sleeping in the streets as he once did. And he was on the same bill or sang with many of the greatest names in folk music, people like Sonny Terry, Brownie McGhee, Josh White, Cisco Houston, Big Bill Broonzy, Woody Guthrie, and Pete Seeger. He was featured on network radio shows as well, and his music became available on records that captured permanently, if not necessarily perfectly, his renditions of songs like "Goodnight, Irene," "Gray Goose," "Midnight Special," "Whoa Back Buck," "Easy Rider," "Keep Your Hands Off Her," "Fannin Street," "Rock Island Line," and a great many others. Still, for all his activities in the last fourteen years of his life, he never gained much financial return.

Though he mellowed considerably under less stringent circumstances, he never reformed. In fact, in 1949, the year in which he died, he was jailed briefly in New York on assault charges. His growing overseas reputation brought the offer of many engagements in Europe. He went there to give a series of concerts in the fall of 1949. While in the midst of the tour, he came down with a disease that caused his muscles to atrophy. The symptoms became intense in Paris, and he went back to New York for treatment at Bellevue Hospital. There was nothing doctors could do to save him; he died in the hospital on December 6.

His great legacy has been reflected in the popularity of his songs ever since then. His own recordings have been reissued on various labels over the years. Among those available in the 1960s were *Leadbelly Sings* (with Guthrie, Josh White, and others), issued on Folkways Records in May 1962; *Ledbetter's Best* (Capitol, 1/63); *Midnight Special* (RCA Victrola, 9/64); *Goodnight Irene* (Allego, 11/64); *Play-Party Songs* (Stinson); *Memorial* (four discs, Stinson); *Leadbelly Legacy* (Folkways, four 10-inch discs); *Last Session* (four discs, Folkways); *Library of Congress Recordings* (two discs, Elektra); *Take This Hammer* (Verve/Folkways, 9/65); *Leadbelly* (Archive of Folk Song, 1/66); *Hands Off Her* (Verve/Folkways, 2/66); and *From the Last Sessions* (Verve/Folkways, 3/67). Coming into the 1970s, the pattern continued with additional reissues, such as

Legend on Tradition Records, *Leadbelly* (11/70) on Columbia Records, and *Shout On* on Folkways.

In 1974, a film crew under director Gordon Parks went on location in central Texas to start work on a film dealing with part of the Leadbelly saga. The movie, called *Leadbelly,* dealt only with the artist's life from 1908 through 1934 and, as its writers admitted, wasn't necessarily historically accurate. The completed movie, which was affected by executive changes in Paramount Pictures, initially was shown mainly in black areas and was not released to wider distribution until early summer of 1976. The script for the film was written by Marc Merson, who noted that the emphasis on Leadbelly's early days dealt with the fact that "his struggle [then] was not to make music, but simply to stay alive."

Summing up Leadbelly's troubled life, Alan Lomax said, "Women and liquor, that was his problem. My father got him to marry his girl, Martha Promise, and that settled him for a while, a week or two, but that was all. He called himself 'the twelve-string champion guitar player of the world,' and I guess he was. I never heard anybody who could play it better. He loved being the best. He wanted to stay the best as long as he was alive."

Leadbelly's legacy remained intact throughout the 1980s and the 1990s. The number of covers of his songs by artists from many segments of the pop and folk fields continued to grow, and many of his own recordings became available on compact disc.

In late summer 1988 a tribute album and video to Leadbelly and his friend and sometime concert-mate, Woody Guthrie, *Folkways: A Vision Shared—A Tribute to Woody Guthrie and Leadbelly,* was released by Columbia Records. Contributors ran the gamut from folk and country artists to pop and rock practitioners. Little Richard joined with Fishbone, for instance, on a gospel-funk version of Ledbetter's "Rock Island Line." Others performing on the fourteen album tracks were Bob Dylan, Bruce Springsteen, U2, Willie Nelson, Brian Wilson, Emmylou Harris, John Mellencamp, Pete Seeger, Doc Watson, and Sweet Honey in the Rock. *Los Angeles Times* reviewer Randy Lewis commented that the above roster offered "sterling testimony to the fundamental roles [of Leadbelly and Guthrie] in shaping the conscience of postwar popular music [and] how strongly those two voices are still felt in the music of today's socially conscious singers."

Proceeds from sales of the album and video were earmarked for the Smithsonian Institution's fund for the purchase of Folkways Records, the company founded by Moses Asch that for decades had been one of the world's key sources of folk-music albums and songbooks. The Smithsonian project was successful and insured preservation of an important American musical legacy. The Folkways catalog, of course, included some of the best recorded work of both Ledbetter and Guthrie.

Rounder Records, which had worked out an agreement with the Library of Congress Recordings section to release Leadbelly's recorded material in that archive on CD and cassette, in 1994 listed three available albums in its catalog, *Midnight Special, Gwine Dig a Hole to Put the Devil In,* and *Let It Shine on Me.* Three more were added for 1995–96: *The Titanic, Nobody Knows the Trouble I've Seen,* and *Go Down Old Hannah.*

In 1996 Tradition/Rykodisc released *In the Shadow of the Gallows Pole.* Smithsonian Folkways has released *The Leadbelly Legacy,* a three-volume set of the performances recorded by Moses Asch during the 1940s. Volume 1, *Where Did You Sleep Last Night,* came out in 1996; volume 2, *Bourgeois Blues,* came out in 1997; and volume 3, *Shout On,* which includes accompaniment from Woody Guthrie and Cisco Houston, came out in 1998. Many of the recordings were previously available only on 78-rpm recordings. In 1999 Smithsonian-Folkways issued *Songs for Children.*

TRO Folkways Music Publishers, Inc. of New York published the 128-page songbook *Leadbelly, No Stranger to the Blues* in 1998. The songbook includes thirty-two songs in standard notation and guitar tablature transcribed by Harry Lewman. Among the songs are "Where Did You Sleep Last Night," "Goodnight, Irene," "Fannin Street," "Midnight Special," "Rock Island Line," and "Good Mornin' Blues" (web site: www. hlmusic.com).

Leadbelly has also been covered by mainstream artists. Eric Clapton covered Leadbelly's song "Alberta" on his *Unplugged* CD, released in 1992 on Reprise. Kurt Cobain covered "Where Did You Sleep Last Night" on Nirvana's *Unplugged in New York,* released in 1994 on Geffen Records. Some of Leadbelly's descendants used the royalties to erect a new statue at his grave site at the Shiloh Baptist Church in Mooringsport, Louisiana.

The Leadbelly Society, a clearinghouse for information about Leadbelly, was formed in 1985. It published a quarterly newsletter until 1998. The address for the society is P.O. Box 6679, Ithaca, NY 14851.

LIGHTFOOT, GORDON: *Singer, songwriter, guitarist, pianist. Born Orillia, Ontario, Canada, November 17, 1938.*

Starting as a folksinger-songwriter, Gordon Lightfoot never really abandoned his first love, though he often combined folk elements with rock to good effect during a long and eventful career. Even in the late 1980s, when the folk boom of the late '50s and '60s was only a fleeting memory for most music observers, he commanded respect from a large segment of the music public embracing almost all age brackets.

Lightfoot was born in the small town of Orillia, eighty miles north of Toronto. During his late teens, he spent summers playing in bands and driving trucks in northern Ontario. In 1958, after finishing high school, he went to Los Angeles to study piano and orchestration at a since-departed music school, Westlake College. For a time, he earned money at such behind-

the-scenes jobs as arranging, copying music, and writing and producing commercial jingles.

"Then in 1960, I started to listen to some people like Pete Seeger and Bob Gibson. That's when I got interested in folk music and that's when I started to play guitar. Ian and Sylvia [a Canadian folksong team] were friends of mine from before and we used to hang out at the folk clubs and coffeehouses. I just started singing folk stuff. I used to get up on stage and play and sing like everybody else. Ian turned me on to the guitar because he was so adept with flat pick. The style of Bob Gibson also affected me a great deal.

"Actually, I'd written some songs before then, but they didn't have any kind of identity. I wrote 30 or 40 songs up until the time I started to write stuff that I could do on stage. Then the writing explosion started with Bob Dylan and Phil Ochs and Tom Paxton and everybody else who followed them and I started to get a point of view and that's when I started to improve." Gordon went back to eastern Canada in the early '60s and "sang in a lot of bars in and around Toronto."

In the early '60s, he began recording for a Canadian label, Chateau, and had a number of hits in his homeland. The first, "Remember Me," was followed by others on various local labels, including "I'm Not Saying," "Spin, Spin," "Go Go Round," "The Way I Feel," and "Black Day in July." But it was performances of his songs by others that focused attention on him south of the border.

His career moved faster after Ian Tyson of Ian and Sylvia brought his manager, Albert Grossman (then partners with John Court), to hear Lightfoot at Steele's Tavern in Toronto. Grossman became Lightfoot's manager and Court his record producer. Just as Grossman had previously boosted his then unknown protégé Bob Dylan by having another of his acts, Peter, Paul and Mary, record Dylan's compositions, he publicized Lightfoot by having the trio popularize his "For Lovin' Me" and "Early Morning Rain" (both of which Ian and Sylvia had already recorded for U.S. listeners). Grossman also landed him a contract with United Artists, which issued *Lightfoot* in 1966.

Over the next three years, UA followed with *The Way I Feel, Did She Mention My Name, Back Here on Earth,* and *Sunday Concert.* In 1969, he changed record companies, moving to Warner Brothers.

The move seemed to bring new vitality to his work. The debut album on Reprise, *Sit Down Young Stranger* (1970) went gold eventually. It was retitled *If You Could Read My Mind* when its song of that title became a top-10 hit. *Summer Side of Life* (1971) also gained the hit lists. A little later, UA repackaged his earlier work on *Classic Lightfoot.* In 1975, Warner Brothers released the platinum two-LP retrospective, *Gord's Gold,* featuring many of the memorable songs from his first decade as a U.S. recording artist. These included "Cotton Jenny," "If You Could Read My Mind," "Carefree

Highway," "Canadian Railroad Trilogy," and "The Last Time I Saw Her."

His career was then in excellent shape, but it must be said that it had slowed a bit not long before. For a time in the early 1970s, he appeared to lose some momentum. For instance, his two albums of 1972, *Don Quixote* and *Old Dan's Records,* while certainly above average in many ways, still seemed weaker than most of his previous work. Gordon returned to top form with the platinum 1974 album *Sundown,* which also provided him with a gold record for the title song (a number-one hit in *Billboard*). In 1975, he was represented by the commendable album *Cold on the Shoulder.* The well-crafted *Summertime Dreams* (1976) went platinum. In 1978, the gold *Endless Wire* was released.

He began the next decade with his tenth release on Warner Brothers, *Dream Street Rose* (March 1980)—a good album, but not a major hit. The same held true for his 1983 *Salute.* Though he continued to tour steadily in the mid-1980s, Gordon sought different directions both in his musical efforts and career-wise. One step in a new direction was a debut acting role in the film *Harry Tracy* (starring Bruce Dern) for which he also wrote the theme song. In early 1984, he began studio work on a new album, starting with over fifty song "concepts" that finally were winnowed down to ten tracks for the album. That LP, *East of Midnight* (Warner Brothers, June 1986) had for its first single release "Anything for Love," cowritten by Lightfoot and David Foster. The LP represented his twenty-third album.

After that album came out, there was a long pause in his career before his next album project. It was a time, he said later, during which he went through a period of reflection and reassessment of his music and life. Among other things, he wanted to insure that he had put his problems with alcoholism behind him. In the early 1990s he resumed work on a new album, *Waiting for You,* issued by Reprise in 1993.

After touring on behalf of that release, there again was a long period before his next release came out, *A Painter Passing Through,* issued on Reprise in April 1998. Not long before that, in November 1997, he was presented with the Governor General's Award, the highest official Canadian honor for contributions to the culture and prestige of the nation.

By this time in his career, he pointed out, he tried to take more time in honing the final album product. "I start by assembling material, which can take a year and a half. Then I go into the studio—and it can take that long again! So the ten songs on the [new album] are the best that I could put together in a five-year period." Eight of the ten songs on the album, coproduced by Lightfoot and engineer Bob Doidge, including the title track, were written by Gordon. An exception was his version of longtime friend Ian Tyson's "Red Velvet," about "a guy living alone on a ranch after his girl leaves him."

Backing him on his 1998 concert dates in support of *A Painter Passing Through* was his core band comprised of Terry Clements on guitar, Rick Haynes on Bass, Mike Heffernan on keyboards, and Barry Keane on drums. In 1999 Rhino released a four-CD, 88-song anthology, *The Gordon Lightfoot Songbook.*

LIMELITERS, THE: *Vocal and instrumental trio. Louis Gottlieb, born Los Angeles, California, October 10, 1923; died Sebastopol, California, July 11, 1996; Alex Hassilev, born Paris, France, July 11, 1932; Glenn Yarbrough, born Milwaukee, Wisconsin, January 12, 1930.*

Witty bassist Lou Gottlieb, who earned a Ph.D. in musicology from the University of California, was, in effect, the glue that held the literate folk group the Limeliters together. His humorous comments and unique arrangements made the trio one of the most popular folk acts in the early '60s, but his abrupt departure at the end of 1962 quickly ended the trio's place in the limelight.

The group was formed in 1959 in the Cosmo Alley coffeehouse in Hollywood. Each artist had been working as a single supper club and coffeehouse act, though Yarbrough and Hassilev had been associated in running a club in Aspen, Colorado, called the Limelite. A few years earlier, Yarbrough had been engaged by the club and became a regular performer there. In time, he and Hassilev joined to buy the lease and run the club themselves.

Hassilev, born in France of Russian parents, had been brought to the United States as a boy. By the time he met Yarbrough, he was trying for a career as an actor, having spent some years working in off-Broadway productions. In 1959, Alex got a part in a horror movie in Hollywood and took a singing job at the Cosmo Alley to help pay expenses. Later that year, Glenn came to town and sang with Alex. Gottlieb heard them perform one night and suggested they make it a trio, but left after three years to complete work on his Ph.D. at the University of California at Berkeley, awarded in 1958. His dissertation was titled "Liturgical Polyphon of the Fifteenth Century."

When he became a Limeliters member, he had already had considerable professional experience. He had been one of the original Gateway Singers, a top folk group of the 1950s, but left after three years to complete work on his Ph.D. He had already gained a major reputation as an arranger. During the early 1960s he sometimes provided song arrangements for other acts, including "Miss Bailey" and "Good News" for the Kingston Trio.

The three men agreed to start work after Glenn and Alex finished their Cosmo Alley run in late July 1959. They based their name on the title of Glenn and Alex's Aspen club. Combining Gottlieb's arrangements and droll comic interludes with Yarbrough's lyric tenor and Hassilev's command of several languages, they moved to San Francisco to become a smash hit at the hungry i basement nightclub. Their repertoire included such songs as "Gari Gari," "When I First Came to This Land," "The Monks of St. Bernard," "Ya Se Murio el Burro," "The Cumberland Mountain Bear Chase," "Rumeynia, Rumeynia," "The Hammer Song," "Have Some Madeira, M'Dear," "Molly Malone," and the show-stopping comic renditions of "The Ballad of Sigmund Fraud," "Charlie, the Midnight Marauder," and "Mama Don't 'Low."

From that time until the group disbanded in the mid-1960s, they were featured on radio and TV and in concerts throughout the United States and the world. These included extended engagements at the Blue Angel, Roundtable, and Village Vanguard in New York and Mister Kelly's in Chicago, and a concert with Eartha Kitt at the Hollywood Bowl. The group also toured the country with Shelley Berman, Chris Connor, and George Shearing; joined Johnny Mathis in a show at the Greek Theater in Los Angeles; and formed an act for a time with comedian Mort Sahl.

The group signed with RCA Victor Records soon after its formation. Limeliter LPs were still finding a wide audience after the group had ceased performing. The list of titles included *The Limeliters* (1960); *Tonight in Person, Slightly Fabulous* (1961); *Sing Out, Children's Eyes, Folk Matinee* (1962); *Our Men in San Francisco, Makin' a Joyful Noise, 14 14K Folk Songs* (1963); *More of Everything, Best of the Limeliters, Leave It to the Limeliters* (1964); and *London Concert* (1965).

The breakup of the trio in 1963 came after Gottlieb survived a plane crash in Colorado in December 1962. He decided he no longer wanted to endure the concert grind and for a while took a job as a classical music critic for the *San Francisco Chronicle*. This affiliation lasted only a short time, after which he eventually set up an alternative-lifestyle community on Morningstar Ranch in Sonoma County in 1966. Some of the alleged events at the ranch made juicy tidbits in gossip columns over the next few years. Yarbrough, meanwhile, had a hit in 1965 with "Baby the Rain Must Fall." In 1973, Gottlieb, Hassilev, and Yarbrough agreed to revive the original group and made appearances from time to time on the folk club and festival circuit. Lou, Alex, and tenor Red Grammer reformed the group in 1981.

Gottlieb died in 1996 at Palm Drive Hospital in Sebastapol, California. According to a friend, Ramon Sender, who spoke to William Grimes of the *New York Times*, the entertainer had been taken to the hospital suffering from internal bleeding "and had refused heroic measures to save his life." His survivors included his wife, Lee Hartz Gottlieb, three children, and four grandchildren.

LINDISFARNE: *Vocal and instrumental group. Original members, 1965, Rod Clements, born North Shields, Tyne and Wear, United Kingdom, November 17, 1947 (vocals, bass, organ, piano, violin, guitar, songwriter); Ray Laidlaw, born North Shields, Tyne and Wear, United Kingdom, May 20, 1948 (drums). Over next few years added Simon Cowe, born Jesmond Dene, Tyne and Wear, United Kingdom, April 1, 1948 (vocals, lead acoustic and twelve-string guitars, mandolin, banjo); Ray Jackson, born Wallsend, Tyne and Wear, United Kingdom, December 12, 1948 (vocals, mandolin, harmonica); Jeff Sadler (lead guitar). In 1969, Sadler left and group reformed with addition of Alan Hull, born Newcastle-upon-Tyne, Tyne and Wear, United Kingdom, February 20, 1945 (vocals, acoustic and twelve-string guitar, keyboards, songwriter). Laidlaw, Cowe, and Clements left in 1973, replaced by Kenny Craddock (keyboards), Charlie Harcourt (guitar), Tommy Duffy (bass), Paul Nichols (drums). Group disbanded in 1975, later in '70s reformed with original members Clements, Hull, Laidlaw, Jackson, and Cowe.*

With a repertoire ranging from Beatlesque pop songs to blues, folk, and folk-rock numbers reflected in several excellent LPs released in 1969 and the early '70s, Lindisfarne seemed to have all the elements for mainstream success. Though achieving considerable popularity in their homeland, the group never gained a foothold in the vital U.S. market, which tended to discourage large-scale promotion by the recording industry. Still, after breaking up in the mid-'70s, the band came back to maintain an ardent following in the British Midlands well into the 1990s.

The founding members all grew up in the Newcastle area, where Clements and Laidlaw cut their musical eye-teeth starting in 1965 as part of a blues band, which Clements claimed was the first such band in Newcastle. Over the next few years with the addition of various new members their group evolved into what eventually became Lindisfarne. Clements told *Music Maker* magazine in 1970, "We used to be called Brethren, and were the local folk band, blues band and progressive band." Paced by guitarist Jeff Sadler, whom Clements called "the most futuristic guitarist in the world," by the late '60s the group was focusing on hard-driving rock. (Before becoming known as Brethren, the band had assumed and discarded a series of names, including the Aristocrats, Downtown Faction, Impact, and the Druids.)

When Sadler left, Clements told Michael Watts of *Melody Maker* ("A breath of early Beatles from Lindisfarne," December 19, 1970), the group faced a crisis. "We could not play on without him. Before, we had been into heavy rock and when he left we decided to quieten down a bit. We changed the style and started to play quieter, and then we got to know Alan, who was playing at the time in folk clubs and had a single released the previous year on Transatlantic. Eventually he joined us in May ['69]."

Alan recalled for *Melody Maker* at the time he was thinking of starting a band with Graham Bell and John Turnbull when he met some of the Brethren members. "Ray Jackson is a brilliant harp player [for one]. I had my own folk club in Whitley Bay at the beginning of the year and Brethren came along and did three numbers acoustically, and it was fantastic. Then they wanted to back me on some tapes I was making and this led to a booking together which was really terrible, but we gave it another try and it was fantastic, so I joined. Then when we got to know each other it turned out that we had exactly the same ideas in mind, and singing exactly the same sort of things."

With the addition of Hull, the group now had two skilled songwriters to diversify the band's concert flavor. After Hull joined up, the group decided to switch home base to London, and they prepared some tapes that their manager presented to Tony Stratton-Smith, director of Charisma Records. The latter was impressed and arranged for a session that summer at the Trident Studios. He also suggested in August that the band rename itself Lindisfarne, after an island off the Northumberland coast that had been one of the first centers of British Christianity.

By mid-1970 the debut album, *Nicely Out of Tune*, was ready for release on Charisma. Elektra Records was assigned U.S. distribution rights. The titles, Hull said, reflected the band members' belief "it's out of tune with what other people are doing, metaphorically speaking. Seven of the songs are mine, two are by Rod Clements, and there's also [Woody] Guthrie's 'Jack Hammer Blues' and a Rob Noakes song, 'Turn a Deaf Ear.' At times they are very reminiscent of the old Sonny Terry/Woody Guthrie/Cisco Houston sound—happy, but nicely out of tune." The debut single was the excellent "Clear White Light, Part 2." Later the group made the singles charts with "Lady Eleanor."

The critical reaction was uniformly supportive. The *New Musical Express* reviewer said of the album, "I personally rate this as the best debut album that I've heard this year by a hitherto unknown British band." The original songwriting by Clements and Hull, it was noted, was "outstanding." Charisma signed the group to record three more albums, which resulted in *Fog on the Tyne* in 1971 and, in 1972, *Meet Me on the Corner*, which peaked at number five on U.K. lists, and *Dingly Dell*. To try to start making inroads in the U.S. market, an intensive tour schedule was arranged for 1972. Unfortunately, this turned out so badly that in 1973, the band, in essence, fell apart, with Laidlaw, Cowe, and Clements trying to change their luck by forming the group Jack the Lad.

Lindisfarne reorganized with Hull and Jackson being joined by Kenny Craddock on keyboards, Charlie Harcourt on guitar, Tommy Duffy on bass, and Paul Nichols on drums. In 1974 the band was represented by the LP *Happy Daze*. (The retrospective LP *Take Off Your Head* also came out that year.) This didn't improve the band's fortunes, though, and in 1975 it disbanded.

A few years later, the original quintet from 1970 reunited and won a new recording contract with Mer-cury/England. The group's Mercury debut, *Back and Firth*, in 1978, provided the top-10 U.K. single "Run for Home." The band wound up the decade with the 1979 album *The News*. While not becoming mass audience favorites in the 1980s, Lindisfarne did well enough to add to its recording credits. Its '80s output included the 1981 compilation *Singles Album; Sleepless Night* in 1982; *Lindisfarne Tastic Live, Volumes 1 and 2,* and *Dance Your Life Away* in 1984; *C'mon Everybody* in 1987; and *Amigos* in 1989. In the fall of 1990 the group was joined by an internationally known soccer player, Paul Gascoigne, in a ploy that resulted in a number two U.K. single with a revised version of "Fog on the Tyne."

Into the mid-1990s the group maintained a fervent, basically cult following at home, as indicated by the large audiences that attended its annual North of England Christmas concert.

LINDLEY, DAVID: *Singer, multiinstrumentalist (fiddle, guitar, banjo, Turkish banjo, sodina, kabosy, bouzouki, oud, saz), band leader (Kaleidoscope, El Rayo-X), songwriter. Born Los Angeles, California, March 21, 1944.*

Though many people know about David Lindley mainly from his longtime work on fiddle and guitar in support of close friend Jackson Browne, his overall career might be better compared to the name of the 1960s band he founded: Kaleidoscope. With his longtime interest in world music, his projects through the years covered a kaleidoscopic spectrum in melodic content and rhythmic structure, involving everything from blues, country, and folk to international folk and pop. In the course of seeking out diverse music forms he learned to play a dizzying array of instruments, many completely unfamiliar to American musicians. During one concert in the 1990s, Jackson Browne joined him onstage and scratched his head at the instrument selection, noting there wasn't anything there he knew how to play.

Lindley, who grew up in Southern California, had his interest in music initially whetted by the family music collection, which included recordings by various country, folk, and pop artists as well as classical albums. In his mid-teens he developed skills on banjo and fiddle, focusing on bluegrass stylings. He won a first-place award at the annual Los Angeles Topanga Canyon Banjo Competition at age eighteen in the early '60s and repeated that victory for the next four years in a row. Like many young folk performers, he followed the coffeehouse circuit and also hung out at L.A.'s Ash Grove, where, besides becoming friends with other promising artists including Ry Cooder, he also gave guitar lessons.

During the first part of the '60s, Lindley was a familiar figure on the bluegrass circuit, playing with bands like the Mad Mountain Ramblers and the Dry City Scat Band. He appeared on *String Band Project*, issued on Elektra in 1965. He kept his eyes open for developments in global music and, when he founded the band

Kaleidoscope in 1965, incorporated elements of some of that into the band's repertoire. The group signed with Epic Records, and in its more than five years of existence completed four albums on the label, starting with *Side Trips* and *A Beacon from Mars,* both issued in 1967. (Those were followed by the LP *Incredible Kaleidoscope.*) The band never attracted a mass audience, partly due to reviewers' and radio programmers' never coming to terms with the group's unorthodox music mix, but it still won attention from more than a few discerning fans.

The roster in March 1970, when Epic issued its fourth album on the label, *Bernice,* consisted of Lindley (five-string banjo, guitar, harp guitar, fiddle); Paul Lagos, born New York City, ca. 1940 (drums); Chester Grill, born Oklahoma City (piano, organ, violin, harmonica); Jeff Kaplan, born California (vocals, guitar, piano); Richard Aplan (saxophone, flute, oboe, *petie,* hosephone, piano); and Ronald Johnson from Detroit, Michigan (bass guitar, piano, violin, drums). On some of the group's recordings, members played such unfamiliar (to U.S. record buyers) instruments as the oud and vina. By the end of the '70s all the band's albums were out of print, but in 1991 Epic/Legacy issued a CD of fifteen representative tracks from the earlier albums plus three previously unreleased numbers. Lindley pointed out that his banjo instrumental "Sefan" had been omitted before as being "too strange," though it didn't seem that way to 1990s listeners.

In 1971, with Kaleidoscope disbanded, Lindley began his long association with Jackson Browne, touring and recording with Browne until 1981. *Dirty Linen* magazine pointed out, "On Browne's first five albums, it was Lindley creating musical sparks with his lap slide guitar licks, his Persian-based fiddle accompaniments, and that crazed falsetto vocal turn on 'Stay,'" the last named a staple of just about every Browne concert of that decade. When not working with Jackson, Lindley performed session work or toured with people like Linda Ronstadt (his cousin) and Crosby, Stills and Nash. In 1980, he and Ry Cooder collaborated on the sound track for the film *The Long Riders* and participated in recording the Ry Cooder Band's seminal digital album, *Bop Till You Drop.*

After deciding to go his own way again in 1981, Lindley founded a new band called El Rayo-X whose members at various times comprised Ras Baboo on percussion, Jorge Calderon on bass, William "Smitty" Smith on keyboards (sidelined for a time in the '80s from a stroke), Ian Wallace on drums, later replaced by Wayfredo Reyes, and Ray Woodbury on rhythm guitar. The group recorded three albums and a live extended-play record for Elektra/Asylum. Looking back, Lindley told an interviewer from *Dirty Linen* (February–March 1994), "El Rayo-X was kind of Kaleidoscope again, but with a heavy reggae reference. I loved reggae from that period. Our 'Bye Bye Love' was a nod to the Pioneers,

the Melodians, and the Greyhounds. I was a big fan of all of them: Toots [of Toots and the Maytals], Desmond Dekker. I felt it was too good not to participate in."

The Elektra/Asylum debut, *El Rayo-X,* was issued in 1981, followed in 1982 by *Win This Record.* The first of those continues to cast a warm glow among Lindley fans to this day. Those two albums were joined in the Elektra/ Asylum catalog by the 1983 EP *El Rayo-X Live* and the 1988 album *Very Greasy.* In 1985, Lindley's solo album, *Mr. Dave,* was issued only in Europe by WEA International (WEA stands for Warner/Elektra/ Asylum).

Major career problems arose from the label's contract requirements, which forbade him from doing session work or performing with other individuals or groups. For much of the second half of the 1980s, this interfered with Lindley's creative efforts. At the end of the decade, for instance, he and Ry Cooder formed an acoustic duo that appeared at clubs and major festivals at home and abroad but were prevented from recording new material by the Elektra/Asylum legal department.

Exasperated at the start of the 1990s, Lindley swore he would never sign with a major record label again. He formed several partnerships with highly talented artists such as Jordanian percussionist Hani Naser and guitarist–world folk-music enthusiast Henry Kaiser. Among other things, Naser coached David on the finer points of the *saz,* a long-necked Turkish lute. In October 1991 Kaiser and Lindley took a recording team to the island of Madagascar, in the Indian Ocean, to record and interact with local musicians. It originally had been planned as a short stay to record one CD's worth of material, but so much unique material was available that the recording work took up to sixteen to eighteen hours a day without coming close to compiling all the compelling songs and instrumentals at hand.

Kaiser recalled calling Shanachie Entertainment, the organization backing the project, to say they needed extra time. "We had so much great stuff that after we'd been recording for a week we called Shanachie and said 'There's going to be a lot more.'" Over a two-week period, the duo collaborated with over seventy Malagasy artists to record more than 150 songs. When the recordings were brought back to the United States, it was decided to issue two CDs of songs on which the duo had participated and four solo CDs by individual Malagasy performers.

The songs were drawn not only from Malagasy originals, but in true world-music fashion, from other lands and genres, including the U.S. country field. An example presented on the 1992 Shanachie release *A World out of Time, Volume 1,* was the treatment by the Tarika Sammy Band with vocalist Claudia Ramasimanana of the song "Hana," written by Shoukichi Kina of Okinawa. When that first CD came out, it created a sensation among world music fans across the globe, doing so well the producers were able to return significant amounts of money to the Malagasy performers.

1. to *r.*: **MIKE SEEGER, HAZEL DICKENS, ALICE GERRARD** (*Photo by Lyndon Stambler*)

ANI DiFRANCO (*Photo by Gary Glade*)

JESSE FULLER (*Courtesy of Michael Ochs Archives*)   **WOODY GUTHRIE** (*Courtesy of Michael Ochs Archives*)

W. C. HANDY (*Courtesy of Michael Ochs Archives*)

JOHN WESLEY HARDING, BRUCE SPRINGSTEEN and **ROBERT LLOYD** (*Photo by Gary Glade*)

JOHN HARTFORD (*Irwin Stambler Collection*)　　　　**BESS LOMAX HAWES** (*Courtesy of Bess Lomax Hawes*)

JOHN LEE HOOKER (*Courtesy of Michael Ochs Archives*)

INDIGO GIRLS (*Courtesy of Urbaitis*)

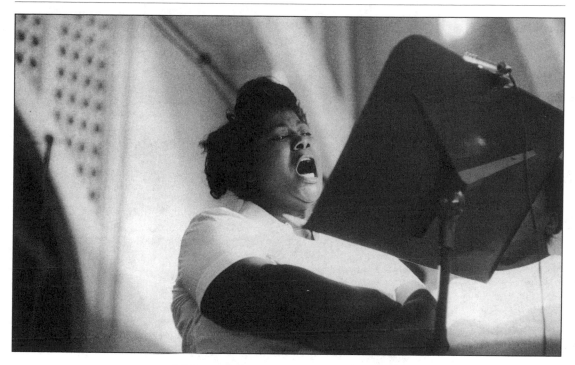

MAHALIA JACKSON (*Courtesy of Columbia Records*)

LITTLE WALTER (*Courtesy of Michael Ochs Archives*)

BERT JANSCH (*Photo by Gary Glade*)

FREEDY JOHNSTON (*Photo by Gary Glade*)

In August 1993 Shanachie released *A World out of Time, Volume 2,* another amazing collection of truly unique music. The leadoff track, "Lemur Rap," resulted from the recording engineer's accidentally laying down rhythm tracks on a tape of the sounds of indri lemurs, one of the exotic species native to the island. This is followed by "O Isa," in which Rossy, leader of the most popular band on Madagascar, joins forces with seventy-two-year-old flutist Rakota Frah to demonstrate close-knit harmony vocals against sounds by Rossy on the *valiha,* a bamboo harp, while Frah plays his *sodina,* a flute made from an aluminum tent pole. On another track, Frah's flute meshed impeccably with Lindley's slide guitar on what is, to say the least, an unusual format for country star Ray Price's "You Done Me Wrong." Kaiser's guitar contributions included backing on such tracks as "Tsaiky Mboly Hely" and "Tsihai Akory Atao," the latter a wild number intended to back salegy dance audiences. The tracks also included the quadrille "Afrindrafindrao," a number that became one of the highlights of the mid-1990s concerts by Lindley and Hani Naser. As was the case with *Volume 1,* the second CD also won ecstatic reviews in the United States and elsewhere and rose to top levels of world music charts.

Besides touring with Naser in the '90s, Lindley also arranged to release material under his own imprint, Pleemhead. The first to come out was the 1993 *David Lindley and Hani Naser Live in Japan, Playing Real Good, You'll Really Like It,* followed by a second collection in 1996. David also found time for new sound track work, collaborating with Ry Cooder on material for *Geronimo,* issued on CD by Columbia in 1993. He also played banjo on tracks for the *Beverly Hillbillies* movie and did session work with a singer from Borneo, Tanina Takoum. In 1994 he and Kaiser went to Norway on an expedition similar in style to the Madagascar project. This led to the release of the 1995 album *Sweet Sunny North,* issued on Shanachie, followed by *Volume 2* in October 1996. In 1998 Lindley released a solo CD, *Twango Banjo,* on the Ulftone label.

In 1995 Lindley and Kaiser looked back fondly on their accomplishments. However, as Lindley emphasized to Michael Parrish for *Dirty Linen* ("Musical Ambassadors to Norway," April–May 1995), as creatively successful as the Madagascar journey had been, it didn't seem likely as an approach they would continue to take. He commented, "With the Madagascar stuff, I produced all these things and we ended up with nine (they haven't all come out yet) CDs of Malagasy stuff, but it's too much work . . . I'm kind of backing out of that position."

LITTLE WALTER: *Blues harmonica player, singer, songwriter, bandleader (the Aces, the Jukes). Born Marksville, Louisiana, May 1, 1930; died Chicago, Illinois, February 15, 1968.*

A fiery man offstage, Little Walter Jacobs channeled his considerable energies onstage into the mouth harp and became a giant of postwar blues harmonica players. Throughout the Chicago clubs in the late 1940s and early 1950s, Little Walter distinguished himself with his powerful amplified sound, taking on a role similar to a sax player in a jazz band with his soulful and precise solos. His playing influenced younger harp players, from Charlie Musselwhite and Paul Butterfield to George "Harmonica" Smith. He was also a dynamic singer (with a husky voice) and songwriter and enjoyed a string of fourteen hits on *Billboard*'s top 10 R&B charts from 1952 to 1958, including "My Babe," "Blues with a Feeling," "Mean Old World," and "Juke."

He was born Marion Walter Jacobs and raised on a farm in Marksville, Louisiana. He taught himself how to play the harp when he was eight and left home four years later. At twelve, he began playing on New Orleans street corners. After stints as a teenager in Helena, Arkansas (where he played on Sonny Boy Williamson's radio show in 1944), Memphis, and St. Louis, he arrived in Chicago in 1946. There, Little Walter started out playing on Maxwell Street in Chicago, where established Chicago players Tampa Red, Big Bill Broonzy, and Memphis Slim recognized his talent. He cut his first records for Ora-Nelle ("I Just Keep Loving Her") with Jimmy Rogers, and later with Tempo-Tone and Parkway. In 1948, just two years after arriving in Chicago, Muddy Waters invited him to play harp in his legendary band, with such notable players as drummer Fred Below, pianist Otis Spann, guitarist Jimmy Rogers, and bassist Willie Dixon.

Walter's harp work meshed perfectly in the ensemble and can be heard on many of Muddy Waters's hits of the 1950s, and on recordings he made with the Jimmy Rogers Band. During recording sessions with Muddy Waters, the Chess Brothers heard his harmonica solo on a song called "Your Cat Will Play" and decided to release it as "Juke" in 1952 under the name of Little Walter and His Night Cats. "Juke" went to the top of the R&B charts that year.

Following his success, Walter left the Muddy Waters Band (although he continued to record with Waters) and joined a group called Louis Myers' Four Aces with guitarists Louis and David Myers and Fred Below. Harp player Junior Wells was a member of the Aces and soon took Little Walter's place in Muddy's band.

Walter was a temperamental man, and Louis and David Myers soon left the group. The void was filled by guitarist Robert Jr. Lockwood, Robert Johnson's adopted "stepson," and Luther Tucker. Walter and his Jukes went on a cross-country tour in 1954. The following year his version of Willie Dixon's "My Babe" soared to the top of the R&B charts. Among his other hits were "Mean Old World," "Sad Hours," "Off the Wall," "You're So Fine," "Blues with a Feeling," "Last Night," "Mellow Down Easy," "I Hate to See You Go,"

"Boom Boom Out Go the Lights," and "Everything Gonna Be Alright."

His popularity spread to Europe in the late 1950s. He was part of the Rhythm & Blues USA package that toured Great Britain and the Continent in 1962. The Rolling Stones took him on a tour in England two years later. But by that time Walter, although he was just thirty-four years old, was on the decline due to a drinking problem and his tendency to get into fights. In 1967 he played in the Super Blues Band with Muddy Waters and Bo Diddley, but his harp skills had declined. He took part in the American Folk Blues Festival in England and Europe, where he got into a knife fight with Sonny Boy Williamson. In 1968 he got into a brawl in Chicago in which he was hit over the head with a lead pipe. He developed a blood clot and died of coronary thrombosis.

Walter recorded ninety-five sides for Chess. *The Best of Little Walter,* first released in 1958, includes many of his hits, followed by *Best of Little Walter Volume Two,* both reissued in the 1980s. In 1969 Chess released *Hate to See You Go,* a fifteen-track compilation of his work between 1952 and 1960. In the 1990s, MCA/Chess reissued his earlier work. *Essential Little Walter* (MCA/Chess 1993) contains forty-six tracks on two discs spanning his career. *Little Walter: His Best* (MCA/Chess, 1997) is a fine twenty-track retrospective. *Blues with a Feeling* (1995) includes alternate takes among its forty tracks. *The Chess Years 1952–1963* (1992) is a comprehensive four-disc set. Other recordings include *The Blues World of Little Walter* (Delmark, 1988), *Confessin' the Blues* (1974/1996), *Chess Masters Volume 1* (1981), and *Volume 2* (1983).

LOGGINS, KENNY: *Singer, guitarist, songwriter. Born Everett, Washington, January 7, 1948.*

When you've been part of as successful a team as Loggins and Messina you aren't surprised when people shake their heads in doubt about the wisdom of sallying forth to try a solo career. Kenny Loggins, however, was certain he could do as well as a soloist as part of a team, emphasizing in the summer of 1977: "I love being on my own. It's been very exciting. It's very difficult to put the whole thing into words. Just the feeling of being responsible for your own fate and having the direction of your life in your own hands is the ultimate goal for an artist and I'm enjoying the hell out of it.

"I don't expect to do more work with Jim [Messina] at this time. But we keep in touch and we may help each other out now and then if it seems of value to do it. For instance, there may be a song he might be the right guitarist for or he may want me to help on one of his songs. But otherwise I don't see us reforming as a team."

At the time Kenny said that, his solo career was still on a touch-and-go basis. His debut album was finding a reasonable reception with record buyers, but it didn't seem quite as strong as some of the Loggins and Messina

efforts. But Kenny persevered, turning out successively more impressive albums until, by the end of the '70s, the folk-music and soft-rock alumnus had retained most of the old Loggins and Messina following and added a sizable number of new enthusiasts as well.

He was born in Everett, Washington, but moved first to Seattle and then to Alhambra, California, with his family. In the seventh grade in Alhambra, he started to learn the guitar and was a proficient guitarist by the time he finished high school and entered college. His main musical preference then was folk music. As a sophomore in college, he joined a folk group. However, as time went by, he became more and more rock-oriented, although usually retaining elements of folk in both his performing style and songwriting approach.

As he said in the late '70s, though he hadn't considered himself a folk artist for many years, it still affected his approach to music. "I can't escape from my folk roots because it's a part of me. I remember when I showed [arranger] Bob James the material for my solo debut album and I'd sing and he'd write down notes and chords that totally were blowing my mind, he kept laughing as he did it. The reason, he said, was that he couldn't write the musical phrases down the same way I did it because I used folk phrasing 'and that's unwritable.' His jazz roots interpreted what I was doing as folk while folkies would interpret it as rock."

In the late '60s, Kenny's main goal was to succeed in the rock field. He joined two rock groups during those years. One, Second Helping, recorded on Viva Records; the other, Gator Creek, did some tracks for Mercury. Neither band made any waves with the public at large. Kenny left Second Helping in 1969 to concentrate on writing and, hopefully, a solo effort.

Soon after, he got a writing contract with ABC Wingate Publishing. One of his compositions for that firm was the delightful "House at Pooh Corner," a hit for the Nitty Gritty Dirt Band. The song later became a staple of Loggins and Messina shows and still is often included in a Loggins concert.

In September 1971, Columbia Records executives were impressed sufficiently with his writings and performing potential to give him a contract. Jim Messina was assigned to produce Kenny's first solo effort, but as the sessions proceeded, Messina became involved in the performing as well as producing end. By the time the album was issued in early 1972, it bore the title *Kenny Loggins with Jim Messina Sittin' In.* The album became a major hit and also was the launching pad for one of the duo's most famous singles, "Danny's Song," which also was a top-10 hit for Anne Murray.

The tremendous acceptance of the Loggins and Messina team caused Kenny's solo career to recede into the background for a while as the group turned out a series of best-selling albums and singles in the mid-1970s and also became a headline concert act. However, by 1976, the group's popularity began to fade. Part of the reason was the lack of striking new songs for the duo's repertoire, perhaps reflecting a loss of enthusiasm on Kenny's part at being a team member rather than soloist. The slowdown in audience interest, whatever its cause, helped make Kenny and Jim decide to try new directions.

This time, Loggins was determined to go all out to make his solo ambitions pay off. Besides spending as much time as possible in writing and recording new material, he stressed performing before as many people as he could reach. "This is my shot and I'm taking it seriously. Part of my philosophy is giving 100% of your effort in the things that mean something to you creatively and that means going out and working in front of the public."

Part of his approach in the early phases of this campaign was to open for Fleetwood Mac shows. He was aware he could fill medium-size or small venues on his own as a headliner, but he took the approach that, in the long run, it would pay off more handsomely if he took second billing in order to showcase his talents to Fleetwood Mac's massive audiences. He noted in 1977: "I had to make a decision whether to be the headliner in 3,000- to 5,000-seat halls or opening for Fleetwood in 15,000- to 17,000-capacity auditoriums. I know I only have so much time to show people who I am and what I do. It made sense to do the Fleetwood thing and hopefully turn a lot more people onto my music."

The strategy worked. His solo debut, *Celebrate Me Home* (1977), didn't shoot up to the top of the charts. But it did stay in the middle levels for a long time, selling steadily all the time, eventually going platinum. His rising prestige was reinforced with his second LP, the platinum *Nightwatch* (summer 1978). Something of a change in tone and content, it indicated that Kenny was not afraid to experiment with new musical and lyrical material. Though he was basically a solo act, he was hardly working totally alone. He coauthored *Nightwatch*'s top-10 single "Whenever I Call You Friend" with Melissa Manchester and recorded it as a duet with Stevie Nicks of Fleetwood Mac.

Discussing his approach to songwriting, he stated: "Essentially, it requires self-discipline. I find that creativity, inspiration will come into the room if I open the door. If I don't, if I don't work at it, it rarely arrives on its own. I wrote some things with the Bergmans [Alan and Marilyn Bergman, winners of several Academy Awards for movie songs] and Alan says songwriting is more perspiration than inspiration. I rather think at this point in my life it's more inspiration for me, but I feel there's always at least a small degree of perspiration.

"That's particularly true of my lyrics much of the time. Every once in a while I'll write a song and lyrics and music will be born almost simultaneously, but usually the music comes first and I wait until that moment comes when the lyrics fall into place. An example is my song 'Why Do People Lie?' from my 1977 solo album. I sat down four times after I wrote the music before the

words came. I had a feeling about it; I felt I knew subconsciously what the theme would be, but it took several tries before it came. Then the fourth time I knew somehow the timing was right and the lines just came to me. I feel you're only a vehicle; the song writes itself. You have to wait for it to come out. It's wonderful, but it's scary too."

The 1980s for Loggins were marked by a steady broadening and deepening of his creative accomplishments before an audience covering an age spectrum from teens to middle years. He began with a banner year in 1980 with gold albums *Keep the Fire* and *Alive*. He had three singles high on the charts during the year: "This is It," "Keep the Fire," and "I'm Alright." On the Grammy Awards telecast, he and cowriter Michael McDonald (of Doobie Brothers acclaim) won for Song of the Year for the 1979 hit "What a Fool Believes." In the 1980 voting, he won a Grammy for Best Pop Vocal Performance, Male, for his single "This is It."

During 1982, he had another solid Columbia LP, *High Adventure*. Its single, "Heart to Heart," made *Billboard*'s Top 20. In 1984, he hit number one with his single of the theme from the movie *Footloose* soundtrack album. Kenny followed this with the 1985 hit album *Vox Humana*. In 1986, he again contributed soundtrack material to one of the movie blockbusters of the year, *Top Gun*. He had a top-10 single from the soundtrack with "Danger Zone" (cowritten by Giorgio Moroder and Tom Whitlock) and also contributed the song "Playing with the Boys," which he wrote with Peter and Ina Wolf.

Loggins continued his successful foray into the movies with "I'm Alright," the theme from *Caddyshack;* "Nobody's Fool," the theme from *Caddyshack II;* "Meet Me Half Way," from *Over the Top;* and "For the First Time," a song from the movie *One Fine Day,* which was a hit and also earned an Oscar nomination.

In 1988 Loggins released his seventh solo album, *Back to Avalon,* on Columbia Records. It was not one of his more successful efforts. "It certainly is impressive sounding pap," wrote David Hiltbrand in *People Weekly* (September 26, 1988). His concert notices weren't much better in those years. "His approach is pleasant, but nothing you'd want to get unruly over," wrote Connie Johnson in the *Los Angeles Times* (October 3, 1988).

His next album, *Leap of Faith,* released in 1991 on Columbia, focused on the personal issues he was going through in the late '80s: divorce, single parenthood, finding new love. The confessional album eventually was certified gold and included the song "Conviction of the Heart," sung on behalf of a suffering planet, which has been designated as an unofficial anthem for the environmental movement. His next album, *Outside: From the Redwoods,* released in 1993, was recorded live in a natural amphitheater in Santa Cruz. He invited 1,000 people from EarthSave to serve as his audience. A year before, his TV Special, *This Island Earth,* was aired on the Disney Channel. It won Emmys for Outstanding Achievement in Writing (Special Class) and Outstanding Original Song for Loggins's "This Island Earth." In 1998 Loggins sang in support of Green Mountain Energy Resources, a leading provider of electricity from renewable sources.

Loggins performed some of his favorite children's songs in *Return to Pooh Corner,* released in 1994 by Sony's Wonder Family Artist Series label. The title track is a revised version of Loggins's "House at Pooh Corner."

In 1997 Loggins and his second wife, Julia, collaborated in a book/CD project. The book, *The Unimaginable Life: Lessons Learned on the Path of Love,* a chronicle of the couple's love affair, was published by Avon Books. They compiled the book from seventy-five handwritten journals they both kept. The CD *The Unimaginable Life* includes the song "I Am Not Hiding," which could sum up their relationship. The two met in 1984, when he hired her to give him a high colonic, and espouse 100 percent honesty. When they got married in Big Sur, California, in 1992, they asked everyone in the wedding party to shed their clothes. But it started raining so they all put their clothes back on.

In October 1998 Loggins released an album of Christmas standards called *December.* In 2000 Sony Wonder issued the CD *More Songs from Pooh Corner.*

Based in part on interviews with Irwin Stambler

LOMAX, ALAN: *Singer, author, folk music collector. Born Austin, Texas, January 15, 1915.*

The name Lomax is almost synonymous with folk-music scholarship in the United States. First the late John A. Lomax and then his son Alan provided the dynamic force that helped make the Archive of Folk Song of the Library of Congress one of the most comprehensive in the world. The archive itself has been of major importance for many scholars and folk artists who built up their repertoire from browsing through the collection. In addition, the discovery or rediscovery of many greatly talented artists is directly traceable to the survey tours of John and Alan Lomax.

In 1997 Rounder Records joined together with the Library of Congress to release the first six of a projected 100 CDs in the Alan Lomax Collection. Comprised from five decades of field recordings made by Lomax in the United States, the Caribbean, the United Kingdom, Spain, and Italy, it will surely be one of the most definitive collections of folk material ever made available to the general public. In 1998 Rounder released CDs from his Deep River of Song series, and in 1999 another three from his Caribbean voyages.

Alan spent most of his boyhood in Texas, where he was exposed to many folk songs in his home environment. He went to grade school in Austin and later attended a college preparatory school in Dallas. In 1933, he went on his first collecting tour as an observer and sometime helper to his father. The trip made him a confirmed folk-music collector in his father's image. Soon after the trip was over, the Lomaxes moved to Washington, D.C., where John Lomax began his monumental work of collecting folk-music material for the Library of Congress.

Now that the family was based in the East, young Alan enrolled at Harvard. After one year, though, he went back to Texas, entering the University of Texas, from which he was graduated in 1936. Returning to Washington, he settled down as assistant curator of the Archive in 1937. That year he spent three months in Haiti recording Haitian songs and dances.

In the next half-dozen years (he left the Archive in 1942), Alan recorded new and established artists both in Washington and on field trips. Among those with whom he worked were Vera Hall, Muddy Waters, Son House, Fred McDowell, Horton Barker, and, in 1939, the great Leadbelly. During 1939, he also recorded famous jazz pianist Jelly Roll Morton (writing the book, "Mr. Jelly Roll" in 1950) and began a new folk-music series for Columbia Broadcasting's School of the Air, called *Wellsprings of America.* Alan played recordings of old and new artists, discussed folk-music aspects, and sang some songs himself. He recorded Woody Guthrie and Leadbelly for the Library of Congress in 1940.

During World War II, Alan was active in government-sponsored morale programs. In 1943 and 1944, he worked for the Office of War Information, and in 1944 and 1945 with the Army's Special Services section. When the war ended, he accepted an invitation from Decca Records to serve as its director of folk music. His selections helped make the Decca catalog one of the strongest in the field in the late 1940s and early 1950s.

Lomax continued to collect and classify folk material in the post–World War II era, augmented with a 1947 Guggenheim grant. He continued his broadcast work with a 1950 program for Mutual Broadcasting, *Your Ballad Man Alan Lomax.*

During most of the 1950s Lomax lived and worked in Europe, as the McCarthy hearings heated up in Washington. In those years, he traveled extensively in Italy, Spain, England, Scotland, and Ireland, making field recordings. His extensive work is reflected in the *Columbia Encyclopedia of Folk and Primitive Music,* an eighteen-volume collection, and *Folk Songs of Great Britain,* a ten-volume set compiled with Peter Kennedy.

In 1958, Tradition Records issued an LP featuring Lomax's voice called *Texas Folk Songs.* Among the album numbers were "Billy Barlow," "Ain't No More Cane on This Brazos," "The Dying Cowboy," "My Little John Henry," "All the Pretty Little Horses," "The Wild Rippling Water," "Black Betty," "Rattlesnake," "Sam Bass," "Lord Lovell," and "Godamighty Drag."

Lomax remained active in the 1960s as an artist and scholar. He performed at a number of festivals, including Newport. He also helped in the direction of some of these, an example being his service as a member of the board of advisors of the American Folk Festival at Asheville, North Carolina. He was one of the founding members of the Newport Folk Foundation and served on the Board of Directors of the Folk Festival for several years starting in 1963. In the 1960s, Kapp Records produced another album of Lomax singing, *Folk Song Saturday Night.*

Over the years Lomax also wrote many books and articles, both scholarly and of popular interest. He worked on a number of books with his father, including *American Ballads and Folk Songs* (1934); *Cowboy Songs and Other Frontier Ballads* (revised edition, 1938); *Negro Folk Songs as Sung by Leadbelly* (1936); *Our Singing Country* (1941); and *Folk Song, U.S.A.* (1947). With Sidney Robertson Cowell he compiled the *American Folk Song and Folk Lore* regional bibliography in 1942. In 1960, Alan was represented by *The Folk Songs of North America in the English Language.* In 1967 Oak Publications published *Hard Hitting Songs for Hard Hit People,* a compilation by Lomax, Woody Guthrie, and Pete Seeger that included protest songs that Alan and John Lomax had collected in the 1930s but could not release due to political pressures.

His activities in the 1950s and 1960s included lecturing on folklore at such schools as New York University, Columbia University, University of Chicago, and the University of Texas. From 1951 to 1957, he served as editor for the Columbia Records World Library of Folk and Primitive Music. Beginning in 1963, he started a comprehensive study in comparative musicology, including field recordings in the Caribbean Islands. His activities continued along similar scholarly lines in the 1970s.

Lomax returned to the United States in the late 1950s and traveled extensively throughout the South in 1959 and 1960. His field recordings were released by Atlantic and Prestige on twenty LPs, reissued in 1993 by Atlantic on a four-CD set called *Sounds of the South.*

In 1989 Hunter College agreed to house Lomax's extensive archives. As the 1990s began, Lomax, well into his seventies, continued an active schedule. He wrote and hosted a five-part video series about traditional music called *American Patchwork,* which aired on PBS in 1990. In 1993 he recounted his experiences from his travels throughout the Deep South in his National Book Critics Circle Award–winning book, *The Land Where the Blues Began* (Pantheon). He began an ambitious multimedia project, *Global Jukebox,* an effort to use his archives (thousands of tapes and records) to show the interconnections of folk music and dance around the world. Lomax also began working with Rounder Records to make his field recordings available on compact discs.

He was in the middle of the *Global Jukebox* and Rounder projects when he suffered two strokes in 1995, his eightieth year. His daughter, Anna Lomax Chaire-

takis, became coproducer of the latter project along with Jeffery Greenberg. (She also continued work on *Global Jukebox.*) Anna, who accompanied her father on his collecting trips, was an informal apprentice. "He was meticulous in his efforts," she told Logan Neill of the *St. Petersburg Times* ("Fields of Opportunity," July 10, 1997). "Everything from microphone placement to song selection—he was totally consumed by the need for the recordings to paint a portrait of the singer. It just had to be right."

The first six CDs were released in 1997. Titled *Southern Journey,* they chronicle Lomax's journeys to prisons, churches, and farms in 1959 and 1960 through his recordings of blues, hymns, reels, spirituals, and shanties.

As Pete Seeger once said, "Alan Lomax is the man who is more responsible than any other person for the twentieth-century folk-song revival." Indeed, Lomax's contributions have been recognized with a Lifetime Achievement Award from the North American Folk Music and Dance Alliance, a Presidential Medal of the Arts, and a Media Achievement Award from the American Anthropological Association.

LOMAX, JOHN AVERY: *Folklorist, folk-music collector, educator. Born Goodman, Mississippi, September 23, 1875; died Greenville, Mississippi, January 26, 1948.*

The name Lomax is a pioneer name in many ways. Lomax ancestors were among the first settlers of the nation and of the Southwest. One of the descendants of this hardy family, John Avery Lomax, helped preserve the musical heritage of pioneer days while pioneering the new areas of American folklore scholarship of the twentieth century.

Born in Mississippi and raised in the Southwest, John Lomax had an ear for folk ballads of the hills and plains from his very early years. When he reached his teens, he began to collect some of this material, listening to farmers, itinerant musicians, and cowboys near his home. He scrawled their lyrics down on an assortment of papers, including the backs of envelopes and pieces of cardboard and wrapping paper. By the time he was in his late teens, he had a considerable pile of those odd-looking manuscripts.

In the mid-1890s, he gathered his belongings, making ready to enter the University of Texas at Austin. In among his clothes and some tattered textbooks was his collection of song material. He had no way of knowing that collecting this kind of material was almost unheard of in academic ranks in those years. At the university, he had occasion to show the notes to one of his English professors, Dr. Morgan Callaway, Jr. Dr. Callaway glanced through them and suggested they were of little value.

The disappointed Lomax filed them away and went on to gain his B.A. in 1897. Moving toward a career as an English instructor, he attended a number of schools over the next decade. He took some courses at the University of Chicago in 1903 and 1906 and also continued to attend the University of Texas, receiving his M.A. in 1906. He then moved north to Harvard, having received an Austin Teaching Scholarship to work toward another master's in American literature (1907). In one course given by Barrett Wendell, he received an assignment to bring in examples of native literature. Lomax dug out his old files and this time won the wholehearted attention of his teacher.

Wendell introduced young Lomax to the nation's first-ranked folklorist, George Lyman Kittredge. Kittredge shared Wendell's enthusiasm and both supported further collecting by Lomax. From then on, collecting was an important part of Lomax's life and, in time, the lives of his children. Helped by a Shelden Traveling Fellowship, he went back to the Southwest. There he spent three years on its backroads with an Ediphone recording machine to make on-the-spot cylinders of folk melodies.

He returned to the East and, after several rejections, got a publisher. The firm of Sturgis and Walton agreed to produce a book with 122 song texts, eighteen with the music. Included in the book was a letter in praise of Lomax's work from Theodore Roosevelt, who had been shown the manuscript by Lomax during a Frontier Day Celebration in Cheyenne, Wyoming. Published in 1910, Lomax's *Cowboy Songs and Other Frontier Ballads* was a landmark that compared with the publication in the previous century of Francis James Child's ballad books.

Lomax continued to follow the usual pattern of collectors, earning a living in other ways and pursuing new material in his spare time. From 1903 to 1910, for instance, he held the title of Associate Professor of English at Texas A&M College. From 1910 to 1917, he was Secretary of the University of Texas in Austin.

For a while, from 1925 to 1932, he varied his pattern by entering the banking business. Although still interested in folk music, his bank work kept him from spending much time on it.

In 1933, he finally embarked on another major collecting tour, this time with his seventeen-year-old son, Alan. The Depression, which resulted in the failure of his bank, was the reason for the tour. To make ends meet, John signed a contract with a publisher for a folksong book. He and Alan built a 350-pound recorder into the back of their car and garnered hundreds of new songs.

These were published by the Macmillan Company in 1934 under the title *American Ballads and Folk Songs*. The raw material collected on the trip was sent to the Library of Congress in Washington. It so impressed Library officials that John Lomax was asked to come to Washington in 1934 as Honorary Consultant and Archivist, Curator of the new Archive of Folk Song.

During the 1930s and 1940s, John and Alan built this collection up into the most impressive in the world. Thousands of songs were added either through field trips or folk artists brought to Washington. In time, Alan succeeded his father as curator.

In the years between 1934 and his death, John gained a worldwide reputation. He continued to write books on folk-music subjects, many with Alan, and lectured before learned and lay groups. The final fruits of his labors were a new public awareness of the importance of folk material and the use of the collection as a basis for growth by new folk artists who came to the library to help increase their knowledge of the field.

LOS LOBOS: *Vocal and instrumental group. Original members, born Los Angeles, California, David Hidalgo, born LA, October 6, 1954 (vocals, multiinstrumentalist, songwriter); Conrad Lozano, born LA, March 21, 1951 (vocals, bassist); Cesar Rosas, born Hermosillo, Mexico, September 26, 1954 (vocals, guitarist, songwriter); Louie Perez, born LA, January 29, 1953 (drummer, songwriter). Steve Berlin added early 1980s, born Philadelphia, Pennsylvania, September 4, 1955 (vocals, saxophone).*

East Los Angeles, for many decades the center of Mexican-American life in the City of the Angels, appeared ready to exert a strong impact on the still young rock field in the late 1950s with the emergence of a prospective superstar in teenage Ritchie Valens. But after his tragic death in a plane crash in 1959, years passed without an artist or group from the area gaining widespread notice. Then, almost thirty years later, a film about his brief career, *La Bamba*, catapulted the band Los Lobos to national and international prominence, the first East L.A. rock act to achieve that since his passing.

The four founding members—Conrad Lozano (vocals, bass, *guitarron*), Cesar Rosas (lead vocals, guitars, *bajo-sexto*, mandolin), David Hidalgo (lead vocals, guitars, accordion, lap steel, percussion), and Louie Perez (drums, guitar, quinto)—all grew up in East L.A. and still lived there in the late 1980s after Los Lobos had achieved star status. The four became close friends while attending Garfield High School in their home barrio and in the late 1960s became involved in the backyard party band activity that was the milieu of many Chicano teenage musicians. Their interest then was in Beatles-influenced rock, but in the early '70s Hidalgo, Perez, and another friend switched to an emphasis on learning Mexican folk material, particularly Norteños music from northern Mexico. That became the basis for Los Lobos when it was formed in 1973. The Band became a quartet of Hidalgo, Perez, Lozano, and Rosas.

The band played Mexican folk material using acoustic instruments. Rosas told Don Snowden (*Los Angeles Times*, December 18, 1982), "We got satisfaction from being able to play something that was real traditional, our own kind of roots. We were just doing it for the love of the music and would learn songs because they were really tough. They were a challenge to the max because all the cross-rhythms and different things are so difficult to play."

The group gained a sizable following in its own

community, but the members were stymied in attempts to get gigs in other parts of the city. They tried to expand their audience by recording some of their folk songs on a self-distributed label, starting with the 1978 LP *Just Another Band from East L.A.* By the end of the '70s, however, the band had started to go to electric guitars along with formats that blended their Mexican roots music with everything from rock and blues to country music. The new repertoire brought increased exposure, including club appearances outside the barrio area. In 1981, band members had a chance meeting with Dave and Phil Alvin of the Blasters, who remembered the group from a program on which it played on Los Angeles Public Broadcasting Station KCET-TV. The Alvins asked the group to open for them at a Whisky-A-Go-Go show on L.A.'s Sunset Strip.

The Los Lobos set won audience approval and attracted attention from local pop music reviewers. One result was an opportunity to provide a Spanish version of the song "Devil with a Blue Dress On" for the soundtrack of the cult comedy film *Eating Raoul.* The performance also helped open doors to more engagements at L.A. area rock clubs that built up a growing fan following that crossed ethnic boundaries. The Whisky set also brought them in contact with saxophonist/percussionist Steve Berlin, who then was with the Blasters. Berlin was attracted to the group's music and eventually became the fifth member in 1983.

Things soon began to move briskly for the group. They signed with Slash Records and Steve Berlin and T-Bone Burnett produced the Los Lobos label debut, an Extended Play album called *. . . And a Time to Dance.* The track "Anselma" won the Grammy Award for Best Mexican-American Performance of 1983. In the fall of 1984, the band's LP *How Will the Wolf Survive?,* also produced by Berlin and T-Bone Burnett, won raves from many critics, including those from *Time* and the *Los Angeles Times.* The album's quality also helped earn the group a tie for Best Band of the Year in the *Rolling Stone* critics poll. Sharing the honor with them was Bruce Springsteen and the E Street Band.

The group followed with another excellent album, *By the Light of the Moon,* issued by Slash/Warner Brothers (Warner Brothers handles U.S. distribution for Slash), in early 1987. By then, the group had another noteworthy credit, its work on the "All Around the World Track" on Paul Simon's 1986 smash LP *Graceland.*

But the real breakthrough was just over the horizon. After the film biography of Valens came out and became a hit with moviegoers, the soundtrack music by Los Lobos created a sensation. The album, *La Bamba,* became a best-seller soon after its release in mid-1987 and Los Lobos's single of the title track reached number one in *Billboard* in August and stayed there for several weeks more. Soon after, a second Los Lobos single from the soundtrack, "Come on, Let's Go" (a staple of the band's act for a number of years) charted. Late in the year, the group had another single out, "One Time, One Night" (from *By the Light of the Moon*) which provided it with three discs on *Billboard*'s Hot 100 at the same time.

Instead of coming out with a follow-up album directed at the pop-rock audience, Los Lobos recorded an all-Spanish LP of traditional Mexican songs, the 1988 release *La Pistola y la Corazon.* As Perez told Jerry Crowe of the *Los Angeles Times* ("Wolves out of the Den," Calendar Section, March 17, 1996), "We didn't want to go for the obvious. We didn't want to put on the funny hats. When 'La Bamba' hit, the stage was set for us to sell Doritos for the next 25 years.

"[Selling out] would have perpetuated that legacy, those same stereotypes that have gone on forever about Mexican people. We said, 'We're not going to take it,' and we probably turned down a whole pile of dough. But we still had to look at ourselves every day—and at each other."

The group continued to tour extensively in the late '80s and early '90s before completing work on the 1992 album release *Kiko.* The album certainly was as good a collection as the group had completed to that time and was widely praised by critics. The *Los Angeles Times* reviewers voted it 1992 Album of the Year, and it was ranked high by critics at places like *Rolling Stone* and the *Village Voice.* Despite that, by 1996 it had only achieved total sales of around 250,000. In 1993 the two-disc retrospective *Just Another Band from East L.A.* was issued by Slash, a package that amply demonstrated the band's superior work over twenty years in the folk and folk-rock veins, but one that again did not win massive support from record buyers.

In the mid-'90s, the band members kept up a hectic pace with diverse projects that included recording tracks for tribute albums of other performers and handling of soundtrack assignments. The album contributions included those honoring Buddy Holly, Johnny Thunders, Doc Pomus, Jimi Hendrix, and Richard Thompson. Soundtrack projects included work on music for such films as *Mi Vida Loca, Desperado,* and *Feeling Minnesota.* One of the attractions of such activities, Perez told Crowe, was: "It keeps us off the road. It's nice to sleep in your own bed every night and still be able to make a living. We're not 20. We have obligations that go along with being [in our 40s] and having families. This allows us to satisfy the creative urges and also to make a living."

However, a prime reason the band members did such side projects, including helping Chicano folksinger Lalo Guerrero record a children's album, *Papa's Dream,* was unhappiness with their record company's limited success in marketing their band releases, particularly outside the United States. This was a factor in the long delay between *Kiko* and the next Los Lobos studio album. While waiting for the smoke to clear on that matter, Perez and Hidalgo worked as the Latin Playboys on a separate album issued in 1994. (*Papa's Dream* earned a Grammy nomination in the voting for 1995 recordings.)

In the spring of '95 the group finally obtained an agreement with Slash that allowed it to find another label home. The band didn't go very far afield, signing a new contract soon after with its longtime U.S. distributor, Warner Brothers. The first product of the new alignment was the very listenable album *Colossal Head*, released in early 1996. With its release Los Lobos put aside its other activities to support the new disc with an extensive tour schedule extending into 1997. However, band members still weren't satisfied with label support and decided to leave Warners even without having another contract lined up. This spawned a lot of sidebar projects by the artists.

Steve Berlin told Alisa Valdes Rodriguez of the *Los Angeles Times* ("Prowling, Howling," Calendar Section, February 24, 1999), "I think all of us just got involved in other projects partly because we didn't know what would happen to us as a band." He also noted one reason the group was unhappy with Warners was that the company rarely promoted them in the Latino community, just assuming they automatically would have a big audience there "and that was a mistake."

Berlin moved into production, working on projects with the groups Tragically Hip, Los Super Seven, and Great Big Sea. Joining the Los Super Seven aggregation were David Hidalgo and Cesar Rosas of Los Lobos along with five other veteran musicians: Rick Trevino, Freddy Fender, Ruben Ramos, Joe Ely, and accordionist Flaco Jimenez. The album won the Grammy for Best Mexican American musical performance for 1998. Besides that association, both Hidalgo and Rosas lined up separate tours for later in 1999, David to support his album *Houndog,* recorded with multiinstrumentalist Mike Halby, who once performed with Canned Heat (issued in March on Columbia Legacy); and Cesar to back his solo release *Soul Disguise,* issued in February by Rykodisc. Before that, Hidalgo and Louie Perez had worked together in the Latin Playboys band, whose second disc, *Dose,* was issued the week of the Grammys. Conrad Lozano's outside projects included working in a band with his twenty-five-year-old drummer son and writing a play titled *Song of Orfeo*.

However, Los Lobos didn't disappear. The five members signed a new contract in the fall of 1998 with the Disney Company's Hollywood Records, with the first release on the label, *This Time,* in June 1999. In October 1999 a pall was cast over the group with the kidnapping and murder of Sandra Ann Rosas, the wife of Cesar Rosas.

LOVE, LAURA: *Singer, songwriter, bassist. Born Omaha, Nebraska, January 5, 1960.*

You might call Seattle-based Laura Love folkadelic. She certainly offers up an eclectic brew, calling on influences as diverse as Broadway musicals, the Weavers, the Jackson Five, and Ladysmith Black Mambazo. She delights audiences with her powerful and expressive voice, her funky licks on her Fender bass, and her infectious stage presence. At first you listen to her lilting voice and you could swear she is Celtic, but then she plays a running bass riff and the Afro part of it comes in. (She actually is part black, part white, part Native American.) She calls her style "Afro-Celtic"—mournful northern sounds, African rhythms, and a touch of Native American chanting thrown in.

Love was born in Omaha, Nebraska, the daughter of alto sax player Preston Love, who played with Count Basie, Johnny Otis, and Lucky Millinder, and Winnie Winston, who sang in Preston's band. Preston was married to another woman, and Winnie decided to leave the band when Laura was an infant. Laura, who grew up in Omaha and Lincoln, would not see her father again until she was sixteen.

She had a very difficult childhood. Her mother suffered from depression and psychosis. Laura and her sister Lisa were shuttled from orphanages to foster homes, to homeless shelters, as her mother went in and out of state hospitals. As she wrote in the liner notes of the *Laura Love Collection* released by Putumayo in 1994: "Sometimes it seemed like I couldn't win, but now I am grateful for the experience, however painful it was then. I learned what it feels like when people are unkind. I learned that I never want to feel like that again, and I sure don't want to make someone else feel like that."

As an African American with light skin she experienced what it was like to be the only black child in an all-white school and also, when she moved to the ghetto in Omaha, the only white child in an all-black school. As she told Scott Simon of National Public Radio (June 28, 1997), "I was almost accepted into white culture, but not quite, and almost accepted into black culture, but not quite."

Her experiences politicized Love and gave her much to write about. In the Putumayo liner notes, she explains: "I write about relationships, i.e., the relationship of people to each other, people to animals, people to the Earth, men to women, black to white, gay to straight, rich to poor."

She first performed at the Nebraska State Penitentiary at sixteen. She was singing in the glee club in high school when a couple of guitar players who were looking for a singer approached her teacher. They had a grant to perform in the prisons. The teacher suggested Laura, and that's how she ended up singing Chaka Khan covers at the penitentiary. "It was so funny becasue they were so sweet," she said of the prisoners. "Even then I realized they were thinking tenderly towards me. And they were saying things like, you know, 'I got a daughter looks like you.'"

She earned $50 for the gig, which made her consider becoming a performer. She moved to Portland, Oregon, and then on to Seattle, Washington. She longed to pound out rhythms on the bass. She began playing in grunge bands. While she was playing with a band called Boom Boom GI, a *Rolling Stone* contributor named Gillian Garr complained that she was singing racist and misogynist lyrics, and wasting her talent. Love did some soul searching, began taking classes in race and gender issues at the University of Washington, and ultimately completed the requirements for a psychology degree. (During that time she also played in an all-female group called Venus Envy, releasing *I'll Be a Homo for Christmas* on De Milo in 1988.)

She continued to pursue music, composing, performing, and playing bass. She tried to get a major label deal but instead formed her own Octoroon Biography label, financing the venture with her credit cards. (Octoroon is a slave auctioneering term for a person of one-eighth black ancestry.) "The slave auctioneers didn't research it," Love told Gene Stout of the *Seattle Post-Intelligencer* ("Love Will Find a Way," July 31, 1997). "They just looked at you and decided how light you were. The lighter the skin, the lighter the duty—and the higher the price." She released four albums: *Menstrual Hut* (1989); *Z Therapy* (1990); *Pangea* (1992); and *Helvetica Bold* (1994).

It was Dan Storper of Putumayo World Music who brought Love to a wider audience, releasing one of her songs, "I'm a Givin' Way," on *Shelter: The Best of Contemporary Singer-Songwriters.* Storper invited her to perform at Carnegie Hall with some of the other singer-songwriters including Shawn Colvin, Nanci Griffith, and Mary-Chapin Carpenter. She took the stage backed only by her bass. "Laura Love stole the show," a *New York Times* critic enthused. In 1994, Putumayo put out a compilation of her recordings on *The Laura Love Collection.* Along with her originals, she has recorded such folk standards as "Wayfaring Stranger," "Swing Low, Sweet Chariot," and "Amazing Grace."

Following that, Love played in a bluegrass band with Jo Miller and recorded a traditional album, *Jo Miller and Laura Love Sing Bluegrass and Old-Time Music.*

As a result of the national interest in Love and the difficulties in maintaining an independent label, she signed with Mercury Records. Her first album for Mercury, *Octoroon,* came out in 1997. The album includes a cover of a Kurt Cobain song, "Come as You Are," which she decided to record after Cobain committed suicide. She followed with *Shum Ticky* on Mercury in 1998. But after putting out two of her albums, Mercury dropped Love. It didn't faze her. "I'd rather pour hot lead into my eyeballs than continue with someone who doesn't want me," she told Fish Griwkowsky of the *Edmonton Sun* ("Crazy Little Thing Called Love," April 23, 1999).

LUNSFORD, BASCOM LAMAR: *Singer, fiddler, banjoist, folk festival organizer, and director. Born Mars Hill, North Carolina, March 21, 1882; died September 4, 1973.*

The folk festival has played a major role both in preserving much of America's folk heritage and in rekindling widespread interest among new generations. Not all of the festivals have maintained a relatively catholic outlook on the kind of material played, but high standards were always a hallmark of the many festivals organized and/or directed by longtime folklorist Bascom Lunsford.

Lunsford was taught to love folk music when he was a child by his schoolteacher father and musically inclined mother. While he was in grade school, he often sang folksongs at local affairs and school parties. By the time he was high school age, he had a considerable repertoire of traditional music and was accomplished at playing both fiddle and banjo.

Folk music seemed an unlikely way to earn a living, so he pointed toward a profession. After finishing high school at Camp Academy, Leicester, North Carolina, he went on to Rutherford and Trinity Colleges. In 1913, he received his law degree. Law was not completely to his taste, however, and he sought other ways of earning rent money. For a time he was a teacher. He also worked as an auctioneer and newspaper editor.

He continued to perform whenever he could and, in 1920, began to collect folk music in earnest after meeting the avid collector Robert W. Gordon. In the 1920s, he and Gordon went on tours throughout the southern hill country collecting songs, meeting performers, and taking part in local dances and other celebrations. Lunsford made his first commercial recording in 1924, when he cut "I Wish I Was a Mole in the Ground" for the OKeh label. The song, which he later recorded for other labels, was included on Harry Smith's *Anthology of American Folk Music,* released in 1952 and reissued on CD in 1997.

As Lunsford's interest deepened, he began to think of organizing some kind of annual event that would provide a meeting place for folk artists and enthusiasts to exchange information, and also to be a showcase for folk artistry. In 1928, this resulted in his starting the Mountain Dance and Folk Festival at Asheville, North Carolina. Over the years, the festival matured under his direction until it became one of the most important in the country.

By the early 1930s, Lunsford had a national reputation among folklorists. He was asked to record some of his songs for the Columbia University Library in 1935 and he complied by singing 315 of them. Later, John and Alan Lomax asked him to provide material for the Archive of America Folk Song of the Library of Congress. So great was his backlog of material that he sang an additional 400 numbers for the Washington collection, and still had several thousand more in his files.

During the late 1930s, he was director of a group of Appalachian folk dancers and singers who appeared in major cities throughout the United States. President Franklin D. Roosevelt admired Lunsford's work and asked him to bring a troupe to perform for the king and queen of England at the White House in 1939.

Lunsford helped the war effort in the mid-1940s and entertained for charitable events. He organized the Annual Folk Festival at Renfro, Kentucky, in 1946, and two years later helped set up the North Carolina State Fair Folk Festival at Raleigh. In 1949, he delighted audiences in London and at the First International Folk Music Festival in Venice.

He continued to expand the folk-festival spectrum in the 1950s. In 1952, he directed the first East Carolina Folk Festival at Kenansville, North Carolina.

Despite his many folksong laurels, Lunsford was not represented on many commercially available records. There were a few such LPs available, however, in the 1960s, on Riverside and Folkways. The Riverside LP was called *Minstrel of the Applachians.* It included such songs as "Go to Italy," "I Shall Not Be Moved," "Sundown," "Poor Jesse James," "The Miller's Will," "The Old Man from the North Country," "Black Jack Davy," "Weeping Willow Tree," "Swing Low, Sweet Chariot," and "The Sailor on the Deep Blue Sea." For Folkways, Lunsford recorded an LP called *Smoky Mountain Ballads,* which included "Mr. Garfield," " "Jennie Jenkins," "Little Margaret," "On the Banks of the Ohio," "Springfield Mountain," and "The Death of Queen Jane."

Lunsford is credited with composing the song "Old Mountain Dew," which he wrote in 1921 and which became a bluegrass standard and was even used in a Mountain Dew soft drink commercial. In 1996, Smithsonian/Folkways released a collection of Lunsford's work that was recorded for Brunswick Records in the 1920s and the Library of Congress in 1949, *Bascom Lamar Lunsford: Ballads, Banjo Tunes, and Sacred Songs of Western North Carolina.*

Pete Seeger often credits Lunsford with inspiring him to pick up the five-string banjo. His father took him to Lunsford's Mountain Dance and Folk Festival in 1935. Seeger, who up to that time had been playing the ukulele and the tenor banjo, heard old-timey banjo played by people like Samantha Baumgarner. Lunsford gave him a ten-minute lesson on how to pick the banjo as well, teaching Pete the "basic strum."

M

MACCOLL, EWAN: *Singer, songwriter, folk music collector, record producer, playwright, actor. Born Salford, Lancashire, England, January 25, 1915; died London, October 22, 1989.*

Ewan MacColl, best known to U.S. audiences as the author of "The First Time Ever I Saw Your Face," played a vital role in initiating and extending what is now called the "folk song revival" in Britain. For sixty years, Ewan was at the cultural forefront of numerous political struggles, producing plays, songs, and scripts on the subjects of apartheid, fascism, industrial strife, and human rights. He had a large impact on the North American folk music scene as well, not only through his songs but through the numerous articles he wrote on the subject for U.S. publications.

He was born Jimmie Miller in Salford (Lancashire), the child of William Miller, a Scots ironmolder and militant trade unionist who was also a "sweet singer," and Betsy Hendry, his fit and fiery mate. Both were active left-wing socialists. William had left his native Stirlingshire in his mid-twenties. He met Betsy, one of fourteen children from Perthshire, at a pawnshop in Falkirk, falling in love with the young red-haired manageress. William stumped around the country with Scots revolutionary John MacLean. As a result he was blacklisted in almost every foundry in Scotland. In 1910 the Millers moved to Salford in search of work. They had four children, but Jimmie is the only one who survived.

He grew up amongst a community of émigré Scots. From his earliest days he was as familiar with the cut-and-thrust of political discussion as he was with the songs and stories his parents had brought from Scotland. His parents often entertained themselves and friends with their large repertoire of songs. In 1930, after an elementary education, Jimmie left school. It was the middle of the Great Depression, and he went directly into the ranks of the unemployed. Seeking warmth at the Manchester Public Library, he began a life-long program of self-education. He found intermittent work as, among other things, a mechanic, factory worker, builders' laborer, and street singer. He joined the Workers' Theatre but found it too pedestrian and conservative and departed to form his own agit-prop street performing group, the Red Megaphones. His next two decades were devoted to theatrical and political activities.

In the early 1930s he wrote for and edited nine factory newspapers, writing satirical songs and political squibs. He also wrote advertising jingles for local restaurants. After taking part in the hunger marches and unemployed demonstrations of 1932–33, he joined forces in 1934 with Joan Littlewood, a young theater student who had attended the Royal Academy of Dramatic Arts. They married and set up an experimental theater in Manchester called the Theatre of Action. Jimmie played the lead role in *Draw the Fires,* produced by radical German dramatist Ernst Toller. In 1935 Joan and Jimmie moved to London, where they formed a workers' dramatic school called the Theatre Workshop. The next year they returned to the north of England and founded the Theatre Union, which they modeled as a "theater of the people." Jimmie and Joan produced Lope de Vega's *Fuente Ovejuna,* Jaroslav Hacek's *The Good Soldier Schweik,* and Jimmie's original script *Last Edition.* Called a "living newspaper," *Last Edition* dealt with the events leading up to the Munich Pact. In 1939 the police raided a performance of *Last Edition.* Miller and Littlewood were arrested, charged with disturbing the peace, fined, and bound over (barred from taking part in theatrical activity) for the next two years.

World War II temporarily disrupted the work of Theatre Union. Within weeks the members were scattered and serving in the war effort. They continued to correspond about theater art and techniques, however, and when the war ended a number of them pooled their armed forces gratuities and launched the Theatre Workshop, inspired by the work and thoughts of Miller and Littlewood. It was around this time that Jimmie Miller changed his name. Like many of Scottish descent, he was inspired by the Lallans poets of the nineteenth century who attempted to create a standard Scots language and literature to preserve their identity in the face of English dominance. These contemporary writers took the names of earlier writers, and Jimmie took the name Ewan MacColl, a pseudonym that eventually usurped his given name.

In an attempt to create a popular theater for the masses, the Theatre Workshop traveled extensively from 1945–1952. Littlewood directed and produced while MacColl rehearsed the actors and wrote eleven new plays. In his plays, Ewan experimented with language in an effort to close the gap between literary and oral traditions, stressing speech rhythms and cadences, constantly challenging his audiences. He used many of the same ideas and techniques in his songwriting and radio work. In the 1970s he would coauthor (with Howard Goorney, one of the TW actors) a book of political plays and reminiscences about the Theatre Workshop titled *Agit-prop to Theatre Workshop*.

In the late 1940s Ewan and Joan Littlewood divorced. In 1949 he fell in love with and married the dancer Jean Newlove. They had two children, Hamish and Kirsty, both of whom became singers and musicians. Kirsty later established herself as a pop vocalist and songwriter. She placed a number of songs on U.K. charts over the years and was a backup singer on recordings by such top acts as Simple Minds, the Rolling Stones, Talking Heads, Robert Plant, Van Morrison, and Morrissey.

When the Theatre Workshop moved to London and became "fashionable," Ewan turned his attention to traditional music and song. In 1956 he met and fell in love with Peggy Seeger of the North American Folksinging Seeger family. It was for her that he wrote "The First Time Ever I Saw Your Face," which many singers recorded during the 1960s until Roberta Flack's cover version took it to the top of the charts. It reached number one in *Billboard* magazine the week of March 25, 1972, and stayed there for five more weeks. In the Grammy voting for 1972, Flack received the award for Record of the Year while MacColl accepted the trophy for Song of the Year. In England, the song also won an Ivor Novello Award in 1973.

Ewan MacColl wrote an estimated 300 songs, many of them created for theatrical or media-oriented programs. Among his best-known songs are "Dirty Old Town," about his childhood town of Salford; "The Shoals of Herring"; "Freeborn Man"; "My Old Man"; "The Thirty-Foot Trailer"; and "The Manchester Rambler." Many of these songs were born out of MacColl's work in folk clubs. In 1953 Ewan and such notable folk stalwarts as Alan Lomax, Bert Lloyd, and uilleann piper Seamus Ennis founded the Ballads and Blues Club, later known as the Singers Club. The latter club launched the careers of many young singers and groups until it closed in 1991. Ewan sang there regularly until just a week before his death.

Ewan MacColl's involvement with the media was a constant thread throughout his life. Beginning in the early 1930s, he worked in radio as a narrator, actor, writer, and producer, collaborating with experimental producers such as D.G. Bridson, Dennis Mitchell, and John Pudney. When he was only nineteen, the BBC commissioned him to prepare a program called *Music in the Streets*. In 1957 he collaborated with Peggy and BBC producer Charles Parker on a series of musical documentaries for BBC radio that came to be known as *Radio Ballads*. These represented a major breakthrough in radio techniques, featuring a combination of recorded speech, sound effects, new songs, and folk instrumentation. As noted in *Sing Out!* magazine in November 1964, the series "provided new dimensions in folk music broadcasts. . . .We have nothing comparable here. They are usually hour-long programs combining documentary recording and interviews with contemporary ballads created in traditional forms . . . [on subjects including] 'Boxing' . . . 'Gypsies and Tinkers' and 'Teen Agers.'" The eight *Radio Ballads* in the series were issued by Topic Records in 1999.

By the late 1950s Peggy and Ewan were joined in both personal and public life, becoming well known as a singing duo. They toured in Britain and abroad as singers of traditional and contemporary songs from 1957 to 1989. Between 1959 and 1972, they had three children: Neill and Calum (both musicians), and Kitty (who works in desk-top publishing and public relations). They gave concerts, conducted workshops, and toured widely, singing traditional and contemporary songs. They wrote scripts and music for films and commercial television shows. Their involvement in and influence upon both theory and practice in the British folk revival was legendary.

From the late 1950s through the 1980s, MacColl was a prolific recording artist, completing dozens of albums of traditional and contemporary songs both as a soloist or with other artists, mainly Peggy. His (and their) LPs came out on such labels as Decca, Topic, Argo, EMI, Riverside, Rounder, Tradition, Stinson, Folk Lyric, and Folkways. Seeger and MacColl also formed their own recording company (Blackthorne Records). Among their recorded works were *The Long Harvest* (a ten-volume series of traditional ballads), *The Paper Stage* (a two-volume set of Shakespearean sung narratives), and *Blood and Roses* (a five-volume set of rare British and North American ballads). A complete discography may be found on Peggy Seeger's web site (www.pegseeger.com).

In 1965 they founded the Critics Group, a cooperative company of revival singers interested in studying and combining folksinging and theater techniques. From 1965 to 1971 Ewan wrote an annual musical stage documentary called *The Festival of Fools,* a dramatic musical review of the year's news performed by the Critics Group. Seeger and MacColl were avid folk song collectors, chiefly among Gypsies and travelers in Britain. They produced two anthologies: *Travellers' Songs of England and Scotland* and *Doomsday in the Afternoon,* a profile of the Stewarts of Blairgowrie, a singing family of Scots travelers.

In 1979 Ewan suffered the first of many heart attacks. Nevertheless, he continued to work, tour, lecture, and write songs. In 1980 he wrote his last play, *The Shipmaster,* a story of a sailing ship captain who cannot adopt to the coming of steam. It was in many ways analogous to his personal and professional life as his health was deteriorating. In 1987 he began writing his autobiography, *The Journeyman,* which he completed a year later. On October 22, 1989, he died of complications following a heart operation. The following year *Journeyman* was published by Sidgwick and Jackson, but it went out of print when MacMillan bought the company. It may be republished in the near future.

In the summer of 1989 he recorded his last album with Peggy, *Naming of Names* (Cooking Vinyl, 1990). His sons Calum and Neill assembled a compilation of their father's music, *Black & White—The Definitive Collection* (also Cooking Vinyl, 1990). In 1993 another compilation came out, *The Real MacColl* (Topic). He was also represented by his rendition of "Dirty Old Town" on Rhino's *Troubadours of British Folk Era, Volume 1.* As of 1999 the Rounder catalog included two albums by Ewan and Peggy: *At the Present Moment,* originally issued in 1973, and *Freeborn Man,* first issued in 1983. Ewan and Peggy were also represented on CD by *Scottish Drinking and Pipe Songs* on Legacy, and *Scottish Voices* and *English and Scottish Folk Ballads* on Topic. Ossian has reissued a number of his early collections of Scottish songs—it is becoming quite difficult to keep up with releases and re-releases of his material. The best way to keep track is to keep an eye on Peggy's web site.

Peggy Seeger compiled a collection of 200 of his songs in *The Essential Ewan MacColl Songbook,* published by Music Sales in 1999. Their children put together a three-CD set, much of it previously unissued recordings, to go with the book.

Written with the assistance of Peggy Seeger

MACISAAC, ASHLEY: *Fiddler, dancer, composer. Born Antigonish, Nova Scotia, February 24, 1975.*

Jumping and prancing around the stage like a dervish in army boots, flashing a Canadian maple leaf T-shirt and who knows what else from beneath his tartan kilt, "bad boy fiddler" Ashley MacIsaac seems more grunge rocker than Cape Breton fiddler. In fact, his Celtic rock style has ruffled some feathers among the purists. He inadvertently exposed his privates when he performed on *The Conan O'Brian Show,* and Nanci Griffith, who was performing with him and the Chieftains in 1996, left the tour because she couldn't take his wild antics. But his formula has worked. His debut album *Hi How Are You Today?* (A&M, 1995), a blend of traditional Scottish fiddle tunes set to rock, disco, and hip-hop beats, sold more than 500,000 copies worldwide (130,000 in the U.S.).

MacIsaac was actually a straightlaced shirt and tie boy who studied traditional fiddling until he was seventeen. He was born in Antigonish and raised in Cape Breton, the son of a homemaker and an electrician. His father played fiddle and his mother was interested in music and dance. He began studying step dancing at five and fiddle at eight, not unusual in Cape Breton, which was experiencing a renaissance in traditional Scottish music in those years. He studied Scottish fiddle tunes with Stan Chapman. For the next decade Ashley played fiddle at square dances and weddings and practiced four hours a day. By the age of thirteen, he was performing as far away as Boston and Detroit. He even step danced in front of the Pope when he visited Nova Scotia in 1984.

But at seventeen MacIsaac discovered *The Village Voice* and became entranced with New York. Philip Glass and his wife Joanne Akalaitis heard MacIsaac play and invited him to perform in an ensemble group for the 1992 Off-Broadway production of *Woyzeck.* Glass put MacIsaac up at his home in the Hell's Kitchen section of New York during the performances. He came in contact with other kinds of music, from rock to punk, and began experimenting with his own music. As he told Paula Yoo of *People:* "That was the first time I had listened to anything other than my own music that I really got into and liked. Which made me come up with the rock 'n' roll gig. I figured I'd put my music in context of a dance record. Then I started doing more freaky things, like showing up to gigs with sunglasses on or with dyed hair, which was considered crazy because it's such a traditional-laced gig."

He recorded two albums—*Close to the Floor* in 1992 and *A Cape Breton Christmas* in 1993. A&M signed him in 1993 and released his debut album, *Hi How Are You Today?* in 1995. He won an East Coast Music Award (Best Live Act) and the Canadian Country Music Association Award in 1995, and two Juno Awards the following year (Best New Solo Artist and Best Roots and Traditional Album—Solo). He also won the hearts of fans with his daring, high energy performances, not to mention his costumes. He often wears heavy army boots, a tartan kilt, and a white maple leaf T-shirt. Sometimes he dons a feather boa which was a gift from RuPaul. (MacIsaac is openly gay.) He once busted his fiddle on stage a la The Who's Pete Townshend. And then there was the *Conan O'Brian Show*, which required the show to blur the camera a bit during one of MacIsaac's high kicks. As he explained to Yoo (*People*, "The Cat with the Fiddle," May 5, 1997): "I never wear underwear with my kilt. They blurred it so you can't see anything."

Despite his flamboyant style, MacIsaac stays rooted in traditional music. A&M released a single from his debut album called "Sleepy Maggie" in 1997. He followed with a more traditional album, balancing out *Hi How Are You Today?* with *Fine, Thank You Very Much*, released in Canada in 1998.

But beginning in 1999 MacIsaac's boisterous style got the better of him. He was working on his next album for A&M Canada when A&M merged with Universal. He split with Universal and signed a three-CD deal with Loggerhead Records in July. In October MacIsaac stunned many by buying a 1975 sky blue Cadillac Seville that Elvis had bought for his manager Colonel Tom Parker. The price tag: $75,000. Later that month, MacIsaac admitted he had kicked a 2½-year addiction to crack cocaine, revealing that at one point he had tried to sell his fiddle for $25 to support his habit.

In November 1999 he finally put out his new album, *Helter's Celtic*, on Loggerhead, in which he again takes bold risks, combining disco, electronic, and blues-pop with traditional sounds. But his antics continued. In December 1999 he told *New Yorker* writer Rebecca Mead that he fantasized about staging his death, undergoing a sex change and coming back as a Cape Breton girl fiddler. "I think I am going to become weirder than Michael Jackson," he told Mead.

He lived up to the latter prediction at an appearance on New Year's Eve in Halifax, Nova Scotia. MacIsaac unleashed profanities and racial epithets at his audience during a scheduled seventy-minute performance that lasted only twenty minutes. "He was an idiot," one seventeen-year-old said. "It was eff this and eff that and you're a bunch of effin' idiots. He also made crude comments about genitalia. He just completely made an ass of himself. All around, people were saying, 'What a jerk.'"

Loggerhead denounced his behavior and his career seemed to be unraveling amid reports that he had made threatening comments to young girls at the New Year's Eve concert and had originally planned to slaughter rabbits on stage. He tried to claim that he had intended his rave as a performance art stunt to warn kids against drugs.

At the end of January 2000 he told a newspaper that he was filing for bankruptcy and owed the Canadian government and Loggerhead $750,000. There were questions about whether MacIsaac really was in debt or if that was just another publicity stunt. By February, however, he toned down his act, giving a subdued performance at New York's Carnegie Hall to benefit a charity in support of a free Tibet. At least for a few concerts after that the "bad boy fiddler" seemed to be on his best behavior.

MACLEAN, DOUGIE: *Singer, songwriter, guitarist, fiddler, mandolinist, didgeridooist, record producer. Born Perthshire, Scotland, September 27, 1954.*

In 1996, far from his native Scotland, in concert at McCabe's Guitar Shop in Santa Monica, California, Dougie MacLean, with his shoulder-length hair, jeans, and white T-shirt, sings about universal themes: the environment, love, indigenous people. But he gets angriest when he introduces a song even closer to his heart, "Rank and Roses," about persisting inequities in his native land. MacLean saw the remnants of feudalism as his father worked for forty years as a gardener for a wealthy lord. He grew up in a tiny house on the lord's property, and watched his parents act deferentially, saying "Yes, m'lord" or "Yes, m'lady," so concerned were they about losing their jobs. A successful singer and independent record producer, MacLean declares, "We won't take that shit anymore!" and sings, *We are our father's dreams, we are our mother's pride and joy/And we will be the ones to tell you now that it's over.*

MacLean breaks with tradition in this song, yet at the same time he is rooted in the music of his ancestors. It's a common theme throughout his music, in which old images, ancient ruins, and the land combine with contemporary themes. He is one of the premiere soloists and writers of contemporary material in Scotland, and one of the best interpreters of the songs of Robert Burns. His has extended his influence by writing music for Hollywood movies, appearing on the BBC, touring constantly and forming his record company, Dunkeld, with a roster of Scottish musicians.

MacLean is one of the Scottish musicians who helped save their music from the British overlords and update it through the 1970s, groups like the Tannahill Weavers and Silly Wizard. "It was quite difficult sometimes," he told Scottish journalist Neil Trotter, "because Scottish music wasn't fashionable at all. People steered away from it because they were almost embarrassed about being Scottish." In the late '70s he recorded his "wee homesick" song "Caledonia," written while sitting on a beach in France and pining for his homeland. It became an unofficial Scottish anthem in 1993 when it was used in a Tennents Lager ad and Frankie Miller had a hit with it.

"He sings of the dignity of the individual, the need to keep the beauties of the land sacred, the devastation that selfish interests can cause, past and present," wrote Dawn Arnold in the *Scottish Fiddling Revival Newslet-*

ter (October–December 1995). "Of course, he refers to Scotland. It is both his reality and his metaphor. Yet, his thoughts hit home to me, for they are universal concerns, my concerns."

MacLean was born in Perthshire, Scotland. Like Robert Burns, he was the son of a gardener. He was surrounded by music and the love of the land in the verdant pastures of Scotland. His mother played the mandolin and his father the fiddle. They imparted their skills on both instruments to Dougie. His grandfather, a shepherd who grew up in the west coast islands, would sit in the corner of the house and sing in Gaelic as tears rolled down his face.

MacLean began performing at an early age. "I remember we used to run a little folk club at home and I used to get up there and sing one of my own songs, and it was just terrifying," he told Lydia Hutchinson of the *Performing Songwriter* (May–June 1995). "You would always choose to sing somebody else's songs rather than to sing one of your own, and then slip yours in and don't say anything about it."

MacLean—who has worked as a gardener, pipeline worker, and who majored in engineering in college—gained a reputation as an excellent fiddler and played with several semiprofessional groups. One was Puddock's Well, formed with fellow Perthshire residents Andy M. Stewart (vocals and tenor banjo) and Martin Hadden (bass). The band disbanded circa 1973. (All three of the members would play for Silly Wizard at one time or another.)

Shortly thereafter, the Tannahill Weavers recruited MacLean while he busked the streets of Kinross. He played fiddle and mandolin and toured throughout Europe. In 1974 they recorded *Are Ye Sleeping Maggie?* on PlantLife Records.

He left the Tannahill Weavers in 1977 and formed a duo with Alan Roberts, a fellow Scot. They toured Europe, playing the European folk festivals, and recorded the album *Caledonia* on PlantLife (1979), which sold respectably. He also recorded an album with Roberts and Alex Campbell called *C.R.M.* In 1980, when fiddler Johnny Cunningham left Silly Wizard to settle in the United States, MacLean took his place for six months, playing on the album *Wild and Beautiful*.

MacLean formed a duo with Edinburgh guitarist Donald MacDougall. They toured in England, Europe, and Canada. MacLean recorded his first solo album, *Snaigow* (1980) on PlantLife, followed by *On a Wing and a Prayer* (1981).

After briefly rejoining the Tannahill Weavers, MacLean returned to Perthshire. Along with his wife, artist Jennifer MacLean, who has illustrated many of his album covers, Dougie formed Dunkeld Records. The MacLeans converted the Old Schoolhouse (which Dougie and his father had attended) into a home where they live with their two children. It also houses a recording studio, and serves as headquarters for the record company near the town of Butterstone. (He released an album titled *Butterstone* on Dambuster Records in 1983.) The first album he released on his own label in 1982 was called *Craigie Dhu* ("black mountain") which includes traditional fiddle tunes, songs by Robert Burns, and "Caledonia." The song is an anthem signifying his return home from travels in far-flung lands like Australia and New Zealand. *Let me tell you that I love you and I think about you all the time,* the chorus goes; *Caledonia, you're calling me and now I'm going home.*

They borrowed money from Jennifer's sister to form Dunkeld; within three months they had sold enough copies of *Craigie Dhu* to repay her. With more than a dozen albums, MacLean has become known for his spare songwriting style and versatility. He's facile on fiddle, mandolin, and guitar. He's been described as Scotland's James Taylor because of his understated vocal style and sweet guitar picking. Nevertheless, like Taylor, his songs pack an ironic and mystical punch.

"I like dealing with songwriting as a kind of magical art," he told Hutchinson. "Nobody can put their finger on what is or is not an infectious melody. You can give the same eight notes to people and they'll all come up with different things, but one of them might just be something that will break your heart."

Another song from *Craigie Dhu,* "Ready for the Storm," was later recorded by Kathy Mattea on her 1991 album *Time Passes By.* (MacLean received a gold record for his co-production work.) In concert, MacLean introduces the song with a hilarious story about how he decided to buy a boat while living in Australia. He went to the docks to view the vessel, which had a confusing array of bells and whistles. The Aussie selling the boat let him take it for a joy ride, handing him little more than an old map. MacLean, who'd never taken control of a boat, still isn't sure how he survived. "I'd like to dedicate this to myself," MacLean joked.

MacLean followed with his albums *Fiddle* (1984), *Singing Land* (1986), and *Real Estate* (1988). As its name implies, *Fiddle* is comprised of original fiddle tunes, with backing by guitar, didgeridoo, bass mandola, and keyboards. On *Singing Land*, MacLean dedicates the title track to the Aborigines. The song contains images of the Australian outback: the dingo, burning skies, red brush plains. In songs like "Singing Land" and "Solid Ground" (from *Real Estate*) he sings about the connections of people with the land.

"I feel privileged being able to live in the place where my father grew up and my grandfather spent his time as a young man," he told T.J. McGrath of *Dirty Linen* (October–November 1990). "I know all the hills and woods around the area intimately and feel very much a part of it. I think it's an important part of human contentment, this 'sense of belonging' to the actual soil on which you stand. Native peoples, like the North

American Indians and the Australian Aborigines, put a large emphasis on this connection—there is a respect, love, and deep caring for the land that they depend on. One of the problems with the modern Western way of things is a general lack of this 'connection,' and as a result the ability to do terrible things to the land without any feelings of guilt."

The MacLeans began producing albums by a number of Scottish artists: piper Hamish Moore, singer Sheena Wellington, guitarist David Allison, Gordon Duncan, Frieda Morrison, and the Celtic group Black-eyed Biddy. Dunkeld handled the recording, promotion, and distribution. The artists retained the rights to their material.

In 1989 and 1990, MacLean led this group on two United States tours in connection with Fiona Ritchie's American Public Radio program *Thistle & Shamrock*. MacLean continued to release his own albums: *Whitewash* (1990), a collection of protest songs, *The Search* (1990), an instrumental album based on the search for the Loch Ness Monster, and *Indigenous* (1991). That year, *Real Estate* and *Whitewash* received Gold Discs from the Scottish Music Industry Association. The following year Frankie Miller recorded "Caledonia;" the song reached the top of the Scottish charts in February 1992. Irish songstress Delores Keane also recorded it for *A Woman's Heart* and "Solid Ground" for *A Woman's Heart 2,* two compilations featuring Irish women.

Indigenous includes two more Robert Burns songs ("Slave's Lament" and "Ae Fond Kiss") and the song "Turning Away." In concert, MacLean introduces "Turning Away" by pointing out that in Scotland there are reminders of people who had lived there before: old forts and ruins. "This is a song about things ancient," he says.

MacLean began to gain recognition at home and abroad. In 1992, two of MacLean's songs were featured in *The Last of the Mohicans,* starring Irish actor Daniel Day Lewis. He received a gold record (sales of over 500,000) for the songs on the soundtrack. In January 1993 the BBC Scotland produced a forty-minute film on his life titled *The Land: Songs of Dougie MacLean.* The film also features his wife, Jenny, their children, Julie and Jamie, and his father. He shot nine takes of his father coming out of the cottage where his grandfather was born. "It wasn't until we got into the editing suite that we noticed that every time he came out from the door to light his pipe, he'd look at the sky to check the weather," MacLean told Lahri Bond of *Dirty Linen* (October–November 1995). "He did it completely instinctively, because he grew up in the country. So many people don't even bother about the weather, now. These old people were wonderfully in touch with it."

MacLean became the composer and musical director for the TAG Theatre Company's production of a play entitled *A Scot's Quair,* inspired by Lewis Grassic Gibbon's Scottish trilogy. (Gibbon's real name was James Leslie Mitchell.) MacLean's 1993 album, *Sunset Song,* is a recording of the instrumental music he created for the play. He intended the music to evoke the mood of the story. MacLean worked on farms as a lad, not unlike the farms Gibbon wrote about.

In *Marching Mystery* (1994), he returns to the same themes of land and spirit in the title track, "The Land," and "Broken Wings." "Marching Mystery" refers to a discovery of seventy-eight haunted chess pieces in Scotland in 1831. "He has never been one to come at the listener with claymore and battering ram," Alastair Clark wrote in the *Scotsman* (July 2, 1994). "His is more the protest and rebellion of stealth. . . . Now you see him, now you don't, now he's got you thinking."

In October 1994, he played at Carnegie Hall as one of several performers at a singer-songwriter festival presented by Putumayo as a benefit for the National Coalition for the Homeless. The next year Dan Storper of Putumayo paid tribute to MacLean with an anthology called *The Dougie MacLean Collection.*

Back in Scotland, MacLean filmed a seven-part series for the BBC called *Transatlantic Connections* in November 1994, bringing artists from both sides of the Atlantic together: Kathy Mattea, Iris DeMent, Dónal Lunny, Phil Cunningham, Aly Bain, Jerry Douglas, Emmylou Harris, Davy Spillane, and Richard Thompson. The show aired at the end of 1995. He also wrote and recorded the music for a BBC series called *A Mug's Game* (December 1995).

In 1995, MacLean released *Tribute,* an album of traditional songs by Robert Burns, Robert Tannahill, and Neil Gow, some from previous albums: "Are Ye Sleepin' Maggie," "Slave's Lament," and "Banks & Braes" among others. He contributed a song for an album commemorating the stones of Calanais, which have stood on the island of Lewis for 5,000 years. The album, *Calanais,* came out on An Lanntair Records in 1995.

In January 1996, MacLean played at the Glasgow Royal Concert Hall during the Celtic Connections Festival as part of "The Song Field," a concert that brought five singer-songwriters from Scotland and Ireland together. That year he was involved in a BBC production which traces the musical friendship between MacLean and Kathy Mattea. BBC2 first aired the 50-minute documentary, *SongRoads: A Musical Friendship from Nashville to Dunkeld,* in January 1997.

In the summer of 1997, MacLean released a new album on Dunkeld, *Riof* (after the Gaelic word for reef, or to use a knot to lessen a sail in a storm). All of the tracks except one traditional tune are originals. He also continued to expand his Scottish enterprises, converting an old bank in Dunkeld into MacLean's Real Music Bar. "Time was, here in my village, when someone in a pub would just sing a song or pick up a fiddle—to raise his spirits, to make others laugh or make them think," he told Steve McGrail of *Folk Roots* ("Holding Up the

Bar," December 1998). "But over the years, all that died. Now, I want to bring it back." He issued *Perthshire Amber* in 1999, a tribute to classically-trained Celtic ensembles.

MacLean is so bent on preserving the Scottish heritage that he told the story to Bond about how he was bothered by the auctioning of old farming implements as farmers retired. He was at an auction with a friend when a big butter churn came up for auction. He and his friend pooled their resources to outbid the dealers. The farmers, who knew MacLean as a boy, cheered as the bids went higher and higher, thirty-five pounds, forty-five pounds. "Come on Dougie, you can get it!" they yelled. A cheer went up when he bought it for eighty-five quid. "I would have spent anything on that churn. Even if I didn't have the money, I would have still bought it because it became a matter of principle, rather than the value of the butter churn," he said.

MACMASTER, NATALIE AND BUDDY: *Buddy MacMaster (fiddler). Born Timmins, Ontario, Canada, October 18, 1924. Natalie MacMaster (fiddler, composer, singer). Born Cape Breton, Nova Scotia, Canada, June 13, 1972.*

Natalie and her uncle Buddy MacMaster represent two generations in the vibrant Cape Breton fiddling tradition. Wearing shiny leather pants, a lace top over her black bra, and shaking her blond locks as she step dances around the stage at UCLA's Royce Hall in 1997, Natalie MacMaster does not look like she comes from a traditional folk background. She powers her fiddle with a miniamplifier attached to her hip. It's hard to take your eyes off her. But her sound comes straight from out of the music her Scottish ancestors brought to Cape Breton Island, Nova Scotia, in the early 1800s. Her uncle Hugh Alan "Buddy" MacMaster, one of the great fiddlers from Cape Breton, helped keep the music going, reviving it after the 1960s when there were fears that the younger generation might turn their backs on the music.

Buddy's parents settled for a short time in Ontario, but returned to Cape Breton in the early 1930s. Influenced by local fiddlers and pipers who played at the local dances and ceilidhs held at his home, Buddy found an old fiddle in the attic and began playing at the age of eleven. His parents loved music and often invited musicians into the home. Buddy taught himself how to play the fiddle and began playing in public at the Christmas concerts held at his school. Before long he was playing at local square dancing and step dancing parties.

He worked for forty-five years with the Canadian National Railways as an operator, telegrapher, and station agent. In 1949 he began working at the Mabou railway station and playing fiddle in earnest at the local dance hall. During the 1950s, he began playing gigs in Boston, Detroit, Toronto, and Halifax. But in the 1960s, people lost interest in fiddlers. "Fiddling seemed to be

on the way out," he told Ken Perlman of *Sing Out!* ("An interview with Buddy and Natalie MacMaster," March/April 1996). "About 30 years ago, or maybe a little less, there was a video documentary made called *The Vanishing Fiddler.*"

Buddy has released the following albums: *Judique on the Floor* (SeaCape, 1983) and *Glencoe Hall* (self-released, 1991) and a video entitled *The Master of the Cape Breton Fiddle* (1995).

Out of concern for the "vanishing fiddler," locals formed the Cape Breton Fiddlers Association which sponsored annual concerts, ceilidhs, and workshops. The association helped revive the tradition. One of the youngsters who took up the fiddle was Buddy's niece, Natalie. Because her mother loved to dance and listen to Celtic music, Natalie took up step dancing at age five. She studied Gaelic as well. When she was nine, her great-uncle, Charlie MacMaster, gave her a fiddle. She began playing it that night. Her father, Alec MacMaster, encouraged her and she took lessons from Stan Chapman (who also taught Ashley MacIssac). She was influenced by the music of her uncle and other local fiddlers.

Natalie played at her first dance when she was twelve, and then at local festivals. At thirteen, she traveled to Boston to play the fiddle, and the following year she played at the Expo '86 in Vancouver. She put together a cassette tape of her music called *Four on the Floor* at 16. It was clear from the start that she would break from tradition. In addition to the Cape Breton/Scottish tunes, she included a few Irish tunes on her first album. She also included Irish tunes on her second collection, *Road to the Isle,* which she released on cassette. Each of the first two albums sold more than 12,000 copies.

She took some flak for breaking with tradition. "I'm the type of person—even with my dancing, too—if I like a certain style or something about it, or a new step or a new tune, well, I want to learn it," she told Perlman. "I don't care if it's Irish or Spanish or Greek. . . . But the Cape Breton style will always be my favorite." (She has recently been performing with Mark O'Connor and teaching at his fiddle camp in Nashville.)

Word spread about this young, blond fiddler and her dancing ability. She is a charismatic performer, often backed by pianist Tracey Dares and guitarist Dave MacIssac. In 1992, she won the East Coast Music Association's Roots/Traditional Artist Award.

Her third album, *Fit as a Fiddle* (1993), which included percussion on three tracks, sold more than 30,000 copies on CD and cassette. It won the East Coast Music Association's Instrumental Album of the Year. In 1996 she signed with Warner Music Canada, which put out her fourth album, *No Boundaries.* She went on tour with the Chieftains (later with Solas and Carlos Santana). She also signed with Rounder, which in 1997 released *Fit as a Fiddle* and *No Boundaries* for the U.S. market. The following year, Rounder released

Compilation (released in Canada in 1996), which included tracks from her first two albums.

She followed with a return to her Cape Breton roots in the appropriately titled *My Roots are Showing.* But she veered away from tradition again with her 1999 Greentrax album, *In My Hands,* featuring Mark O'Connor, Sharon Shannon, and the singing of Alison Krauss. She sings on the title track and switches genres on the album from jigs to flamenco to jazz or rock 'n' roll.

MAKEBA, MIRIAM: *Singer, actress, author. Born March 4, 1932, Johannesburg, South Africa.*

Anyone who heard Zensi Miriam Makeba sing the "Click" song of her native Xhosa tribe during her first exposure to American audiences in the 1950s had to agree she was one of the unique folk artists of the post–World War II years. In her U.S. concerts of 1959 and the '60s, initially as part of Harry Belafonte's concert series, she also demonstrated she could be as much at home with songs from U.S. musicals or the folklore of other lands as she was with those of her native Africa. In an interview with *Newsweek* (January 25, 1960), Belafonte enthused, "[She is] easily the most revolutionary talent to appear in any medium in the past decade."

Her career might have prospered even more if she did not have the burden of coming from a country that actively suppressed its black African and Indian citizens. Increasingly in the 1960s and '70s she did all in her power to overcome the forces of apartheid and achieve a democratic form of government at home, something she had to do in other places since she was barred from performing in her native land. Fortunately, she was able to continue her career to a time when Nelson Mandela was released from prison to become the president of South Africa in the 1990s and she could travel freely and perform where she wished in the nation.

Though of noble lineage, Miriam was born in Prospect Township, an African shantytown outside Johannesburg, when South Africa was a colony of Great Britain. Her parents were from the Xhosa tribe, closely related to the Zulus. Her father was a schoolteacher and her mother worked as a domestic and traditional healer, or *Sangoma.* Music was an important part of her family atmosphere and Miriam loved to sing. When she was grade-school age, she was a member of the choir at the Methodist-operated Kilmerton Training School in Pretoria. During a visit of King George VI, she appeared as a soloist in one number.

She remained at Kilmerton for eight years. After this, she went to work as an assistant to her mother. The life of a domestic didn't interest her, and she sang as much as she could at dances, weddings, and other local affairs. A male singing group heard of her talent and asked her to accompany them on a tour through South Africa, Rhodesia, and the Belgian Congo in 1954. She continued to perform with the eleven-man group, called the Manhattan Brothers, for several years. By the late 1950s she had achieved a rising reputation in South Africa, recording with a harmony-based group called the Skylarks.

Her first starring role was in the jazz opera *King Kong,* which opened in Johannesburg on February 2, 1959. She took the part of Joyce, owner of an illegal drinking place called a *shebeen,* and her singing of "Back of the Moon" became a show-stopper. The previous year she had taken part in a semidocumentary film, *Come Back Africa,* which received wide acclaim at the 1959 Venice Film Festival. This plus her eight-month run in *King Kong* helped bring her to the attention of Harry Belafonte, who brought her to the United States in 1959 to appear with his troupe. She became the first South African to win a Grammy Award for the album *An Evening with Harry Belafonte & Miriam Makeba.*

Her first TV appearance on the Steve Allen network program on November 30, 1959, won rave notices. This was followed by highly successful appearances in 1960 at the Village Vanguard in New York and clubs in Boston and Los Angeles. From 1960 through the mid-'60s, she was often featured on TV and radio; she also turned out a series of well-received LPs on RCA Victor during the first part of the decade, including *Miriam Makeba* (1960), *Many Voices of Miriam Makeba* (1962), *The World of Miriam Makeba* (1963), *The Voice of Africa* (1964), and *Makeba Sings.*

As she reached star status, Miriam's efforts turned more and more to the cause of African freedom. In 1960 she was banned from returning to South Africa and spent the next thirty years in exile. In early 1963 she was an honored guest at the Addis Ababa, Ethiopia, meeting of African leaders. On July 16, 1963, she spoke before the United Nations against apartheid. She addressed that body again on behalf of jailed South African leaders on March 4, 1964, a year in which she also performed in the Independence Day ceremonies in Kenya.

In 1964 she also married band leader trumpeter Hugh Masekela (born Wilbank, South Africa, April 4, 1939), another strong voice in favor of African liberation. The marriage to Masekela, one of five husbands for her as of the late 1990s, ended in divorce in 1966. The following year, Miriam had her biggest singles hit in the United States with "Pata Pata" on the Reprise label, which peaked at number twelve in *Billboard* the week of October 28. Meanwhile, Miriam had become a supporter of U.S. black power organizations, including the Black Panthers. Her 1968 marriage to Panther leader Stokely Carmichael brought major media condemnation, and her performing opportunities rapidly dried up.

However, she had no trouble finding concert opportunities in other parts of the world, including newly independent African nations, and at venues in Europe and Latin America. Among other things, she appeared regularly in the '70s and '80s at the Montreux Jazz Festival in Switzerland and such other events as the Berlin Jazz Festival and Northsea Jazz Festival. She continued to record new albums issued overseas, including *Live at Conakry* in 1975, and sets presented at the Pan-African Festival of Arts and Culture (FESTAC) in Lagos, Nigeria, where she was an unofficial representative of South Africa. The latter performances were available in the *FESTAC 1977–78* releases.

In 1982 she teamed up once more with Hugh Masekela for a memorable concert in Botswana, one of the countries neighboring their homeland. In the mid-1980s she was made a member of the Guinean U.N. delegation, and in 1986 that body awarded her the Dag Hammarskjold Peace Prize. In 1987 she agreed to join Ladysmith Black Mambazo and Paul Simon on the latter's *Graceland* tour, which included a historic concert in the capital of Zimbabwe whose audience included not only many black fans but large numbers of whites who had come across the border from South Africa. The concert was taped for a documentary telecast in the later 1980s over the U.S. Public Broadcasting System and reflected hope that apartheid would soon be ended in South Africa.

Other career milestones for Makeba in the second half of the '80s included the 1985 retrospective album *Greatest Hits from Africa,* and the 1989 disc *Sangoma.* In 1989 Miriam's autobiography, *Makeba, My Story,* was published. In 1992 she joined the cast of the film *Sarafina,* playing the role of Sarafina's mother. In 1991, Makeba released the Polydor CD *Eyes on Tomorrow,* featuring Dizzy Gillespie, Nina Simone, and Hugh Masekela. In 1994 Makeba went on an extensive Hope tour with Hugh Masekela throughout North and South America and Europe. That year, Sonodisc released *Sing Me a Song.* In 1997 two of her songs were featured on the Mango-released sound track for a documentary about Nelson Mandela. In the meantime, several of Makeba's earlier LPs were reissued on compact disc, including the compilation disc *Miriam Makeba & the Skylarks,* featuring her work with the group in the late 1950s.

The '90s saw the realization of Miriam's dreams for her homeland with the rise to power of Nelson Mandela and the African National Congress. Makeba, who returned to South Africa in December 1990, took part in the celebration of Mandela's election to the presidency, and he and other ANC officials recognized her decades-long devotion to their cause. Putumayo released her album *Homeland* in honor of South African Freedom Day in April 2000.

MALLETT, DAVE: *Singer, guitarist, pianist, songwriter, producer. Born April 21, 1951, Dover-Foxcroft, Maine.*

If you examine a list of performers who have recorded songs written or cowritten by Dave Mallett, you might be tempted to label him either a country or a folk-music talent. The roster includes country stars like Hal Ketchum, Kathy Mattea, Marty Stuart, and Emmylou Harris, and folksingers like Pete Seeger, Arlo Guthrie, and Peter, Paul and Mary. Mallett, like most artists, prefers to avoid categorization. Still, as he told J.

Doug Gill for an article in the *Baltimore Sun* ("Songwriter for the stars sees himself as just a guy with his guitar," February 17, 1995), "I will admit that I'm partial toward the folk audience. The folk audience tends to compare their songwriters to poets. Well, I love Robert Frost, and not a songwriter alive, me included, can even approach the power of that material."

A New Englander by birth, Mallett grew up in Maine. When he was only eight he teamed with his brother to perform at local country fairs, Grange halls, and school auditoriums throughout the region. Most of the material he sang in those preteen years, he said, was "Webb Pierce country style music." He was just entering his teens when John F. Kennedy was assassinated, and the shock of the event, he recalled, caused him to write his first "serious" song. He kept on writing new ones while also perfecting his guitar technique through his high school years and adding to his concert experience up to the time he entered the University of Maine in Orono in the late 1960s.

While there he became more aware of singer-songwriters like Gordon Lightfoot, Bob Dylan, Paul Simon, and John Prine, and his own songwriting began to reflect their influence. He stressed, "They combined elements of country music with the lyrical quality of folk and that served as a beacon for me."

After leaving college in the early 1970s, he focused on performing at the coffeehouses and small venues on the New England folk circuit. Audiences and other folk artists enjoyed hearing some of his new song efforts, such as the 1975 "Garden Song," which he told *Performing Songwriter* (May–June 1995), "was a gift from as pure a place as there can be. I was working with my father, who was an avid gardener, and I remember I was on my knees, my hands were in the dirt and we were planting peas. The song just came to me." In time his work caught the attention of Noel Paul Stookey of Peter, Paul and Mary, who was active in record production. Under Stookey's guidance, Mallett recorded his first album in 1978.

Over the next seven to eight years, Dave's career progressed slowly. The routine remained essentially the same. He recorded more albums for small-label release that achieved a cult following and extended his appearances to folk venues and fairs beyond the New England area. Friends in the country field suggested he might have greater success by moving to Nashville to collaborate with some of the writers or singer-songwriters based there. He finally did shift home base to Music City in 1987, and his work with people like Danny O'Keefe (writer of "Good Time Charlie's Got the Blues") and Hal Ketchum began paying off when recordings by Ketchum and others brought his songs high up on the country charts at the end of the '80s and first part of the '90s. His performances during those years included sets at such major events as the Newport Folk Festival, the Philadelphia Folk Festival, and the Seattle Bumbershoot Festival, plus concerts ranging from the Barns at Wolf Trap and New York's Bottom Line to the Great American Music Hall in San Francisco.

Mallett had seven album releases on Neworld and Flying Fish to his credit when he signed with Vanguard Records in 1992. In 1993 his label debut, *This Town*, came out and earned positive reviews from many critics and opportunities to tour more widely in the United States and Canada, as well as some European nations.

For his next project, he acted as producer as well as performer. Called *...In the Falling Dark*, it had a more somber tone, with lyrics that focused on loss—loss of love, loss of innocence, loss of loved ones. Mallett agreed it was the darkest album he had created, one that gave some indication of what was going on in his personal life. He commented, "It reflects where I've been in the last year." Not that the songs directly outlined events he was involved in, or that elements of optimism didn't come in on a number of tracks. Examples of "downer"-type material included "Daddy's Cadillac," cowritten with Ketchum, which told of the decline in a family's fortunes to the point where they lived in their car (recorded by Hal in his *Star Love* album); and "Closer to the Truth," cowritten with Lance Cowan, which includes the lines *We are dying for love/In dangerous times*. The closing song on the album, though, the sprightly "Hope for One and All," suggests that people enjoy the small things in life like the rebirth of grass in April after a long winter and the rocking of a child's cradle.

The album, while not a hit chart maker, was one of the better releases of the year and suggested much more important contributions to the folk and country domains could lie ahead for him. Another positive milestone of 1995 was the publication of a children's book called *Inch by Inch* (HarperCollins), based on "The Garden Song." In 1996 Hal Leonard published a songbook, *Songs of David Mallett*. In the fall of 1997 Rounder/ Flying Fish released a live album, *Parallel Lives*.

When *Performing Songwriter* asked him if he had any advice for aspiring singer-songwriters from his career experience, he replied, "Do your pushups, because it's a tough life. It doesn't matter what kind of music you do. If you get real famous, people are taking potshots at you, and if you don't get real famous, the bank is taking potshots at you. So I'd say, do your pushups and question your motives."

MARLEY, BOB: *Singer, guitarist, songwriter, band leader (the Wailers). Born Nine Miles, St. Ann's Parish, Jamaica, February 6, 1945; died Miami, Florida, May 11, 1981. The Wailers (1973): Carlton ("Carlie") Barrett, born Kingston, Jamaica, December 17, 1950; died Kingston, Jamaica, April 17, 1987; Aston ("Family Man") Barrett, born Kingston, Jamaica, November 22, 1946; Neville ("Bunny Wailer") Livingston, born Kingston, Jamaica, April 10, 1947; Peter Tosh, born Winston Hubert McIntosh in Church Lincoln, Westmorland, Jamaica, October 19, 1944; died Kingston, Jamaica, September 11, 1987; Earl Wilber Force ("Wya") Lindo, born Kingston, Jamaica, January 7, 1953. The Wailers later comprised Aston Barrett, Carlton Barrett, Tyrone Downie, Alvin Patterson, Earl Smith, Donald Kinsey, Al Anderson, Junior Marvin (lead guitarist) and Stevie Golding.*

"Greeting in the name of His Imperial Majesty, Emperor Hail-e-eye Selass-e-eye . . . Rastafar-I! Ever livin', ever faithful, ever sure Selass-e-ey the First. . . . Yeh! . . . Yeh! . . . Rastafar-I ever lovin'.'"

Intoned from a concert stage by a slight yet striking Jamaican with long, black corkscrew curls falling past his shoulders, these words signaled the typical beginning of a show by the king of reggae, Bob Marley, and his group, the Wailers. Anyone fortunate enough to attend a live performance by Marley and his cohorts could not fail to experience the excitement generated by his style of reggae, that intriguing blend of rock, R&B, soul, and Jamaican folk rhythms. The difference between his roots reggae and the watered-down versions by non-Jamaican artists such as Eric Clapton (who had a 1973 hit with a cover of Marley's "I Shot the Sheriff") was like day and night. Though it took close to a decade before Bob was able to reach out successfully to the general U.S. and British audience, by the mid-1970s he was an acknowledged superstar whose legacy only strengthened after his untimely death from cancer in 1981.

As Marley indicated in opening his shows, he was a devout adherent of the Rastafari way of life, which was influenced by Jamaican black nationalist leader Marcus Garvey (1887–1940), who advocated repatriation to Africa. The pivotal figure of that belief was the late ruler of Ethiopia, Haile Selassie (whose noble name was Ras Tafari, meaning "head creator"), who was seen as the personification of Jah (God). Part of the teachings of Rastafari is that Selassie, who visited Jamaica in 1966, was God returned to lead his followers back to Africa (a theme touched on in Marley's 1977 hit "Exodus"). Rastas and Marley also advocate the use of ganja, or marijuana, as a means of inducing a spiritual state. Bob's "sighting of the faith" as a young man in 1966 shocked his devoutly Christian mother, Cedella Marley Booker (who later espoused the Rastafari way), and influenced both his songwriting and his attitudes toward life.

The development of reggae, of course, is strongly (though not exclusively) related to Rastafari. But unlike some gospel singers in other religions, the writers of reggae never saw anything strange in adapting all topics to the pulsating rhythms of the music (rhythms, as one American drummer described them, based on "inside-out rock 'n' roll with accents on the second two beats and you break your back just trying to keep it going"). Reggae has roots in *mento*, a Jamaican rhythmic form popular in the 1930s and 1940s, the raucous double-time ska of the early 1960s, and rock steady, a harmony-rich, languidly paced style popular among the "rudeboys" in the ghettos in the 1960s.

Bob Marley was deeply affected by folk and blues music. "Marley's music has always been informed by the folklore of Jamaica, both in terms of the metaphors he used and the language as well as the subject matter," says Roger Steffens, Marley archivist and founding editor of *The Beat,* an international reggae magazine. "He was listening to the blues from the New Orleans and Miami stations in Jamaica. Many of the major [R&B artists] came through Jamaica in the '50s and '60s and he would often be in the front row."

If reggae sometimes sings praises of the Rastafarian religious beliefs, more often it reviews the ills, joys, and dreams of humanity, particularly from the vantage point of the downtrodden people trying to escape from the slums of Jamaica's ghetto life.

It was an environment all too familiar to Marley— the son of a middle-aged white Jamaican plantation overseer, who took no part in the boy's upbringing, and a teenage Jamaican mother, Cedella. Born in the northern part of the island, Robert Nesta Marley grew up in restricted circumstances. In 1957 his mother moved to Trench Town, a housing project in Kingston, where she worked for "t'irty shillings a week," barely enough to keep the family going. Because of his light complexion, Marley was often taunted and challenged by his peers. He developed the nickname "Tuff Gong" because of his ability to defend himself in fistfights, as well as his skill as a soccer player. It was in Trench Town that Marley learned to play a crude sardine can guitar. In 1959 he began to be tutored privately by a Rasta named Joe Higgs, who taught Marley, and later his friends Bunny Livingston and Peter McIntosh, the art of three-part harmonies.

Marley dropped out of school at fourteen. In 1961, while the sixteen-year-old Marley was learning the welding trade (along with Desmond Dekker, who sang the hit "The Israelites"), a piece of metal hit him in the eye and he decided to focus on music instead. Marley cut two singles in 1963 with producer Leslie Kong: "Judge Not" and "One Cup of Coffee." He formed his first harmony group with Bunny and Peter, which they initially dubbed the Wailers, because, as Marley said, "We start out cryin'."

In January 1964 the Wailers scored their first local hit with a ska song about gang violence called "Simmer Down," featuring Bunny Wailer on lead vocal, backed by Marley, Peter Tosh, Junior Braithwaite, and Beverley Kelso. They recorded the single for Clement "Coxson" Dodd's Studio One label, for whom they would record more than 100 songs in the mid-1960s. They followed with "It Hurts to Be Alone," with Braithwaite singing lead, and "Lonesome Feeling," with Bunny on the lead. Kelso, Braithwaite, and another girl (Cherry Green) all left by 1966.

In February 1966, Marley married Soulettes singer Rita Anderson, who had had some hits in Jamaica as a Studio One recording artist. "I had sympathy for Bob," Rita recalled in *Essence Magazine* (February 1, 1995). "He didn't know his father, his mother had moved to America, and he was living in a recording studio, sleeping on the floor. Life was rough for him."

The day after the wedding, however, Marley left Jamaica for Wilmington, Delaware, where his mother had relocated. "I wrote him every day," Rita, who had a daughter, Sharon, from a previous relationship, remembers. "He was very sad. He would not eat. He had a job in housekeeping at a Delaware hotel. One day when he was vacuuming the machine exploded and dust went everywhere. That was it. So after about eight months, he decided to come back to Jamaica. . . . Deep down he always knew he was a singer and that he would not spend his life in America doing odd jobs."

He and his cohorts were trying to raise enough money to start their own record label. When Marley returned to Jamaica in October 1966, the Wailers reunited and recorded "Bend Down Low," a song they produced on their Wail'N Soul'M label. It was their last disc recorded at Studio One. By that time, rock steady was on the verge of becoming the dominant form, replacing ska.

Bob and Rita, meanwhile, settled into a domestic life. For a time they moved back to Marley's hometown, Nine Miles. They had their first daughter, Cedella, in August 1967. Ziggy was born in October 1968, and Stephen in April 1972. Marley had other children by other mothers. "At first I said to him, 'Are you crazy? Is this something I'm going to have to live with?'" Rita wrote. "But I asked God to give me the understanding, 'cause our love was more than for flesh or looks, it was something so deep. I found tolerance. I grew to love what he loved."

In 1970, Bob, Peter, and Bunny began working with Lee "Scratch" Perry, the legendary and controversial Jamaican producer. Perry matched the Wailers up with his own group, the Upsetters which included Carlton and Aston Barrett, who provided the strong drum and bass component for the group.

Marley, who formed Tuff Gong Records with Bunny and Peter, was recognized as a rising talent in the competitive reggae world of Jamaica's capital, Kingston, but the financial rewards were meager. His group cut five albums in the '60s and early '70s (including *Wailing Wailers* in 1965 on Studio One and *Soul Rebels* with Perry on the Trojan/Upsetter label in 1970) that did well in Jamaica but nowhere else.

Other artists began to record his work, such as American singer Johnny Nash, who had hits with Marley's "Guava Jelly" and "Stir It Up." From 1968 to 1972, Nash and his partners Arthur Jenkins and Danny Sims (whose first names provided the label's acronym, JAD) signed Bob, Peter and Rita to a contract that lasted four years. Although Nash enjoyed several hits with Bob Marley's material, he could never get a hit for the Wailers.

The Wailers briefly returned to producer Leslie Kong, who released a "Best of" album in 1970. In 1972 the Wailers were signed by British/Jamaican producer Chris Blackwell, who founded Island Records in 1957. The label had had hits with Millie Small's "My Boy Lollipop," reggae's first million-seller, in 1964; Desmond Dekker's "The Israelites"; and Jimmy Cliff's "Wonderful World." But it was the Wailers who put Island on the world map. Island released the Wailers' superb *Catch a Fire* in 1972. Marley's first U.S.-released LP, it received little attention from record buyers. They added Earl "Wya" Lindo and followed up in 1973 with the brilliant *Burnin'* album (containing Marley's version of "I Shot the Sheriff"). The album, which won critical acclaim then, has withstood the test of time. When asked in 1996 to choose an album that would be around in 100 years, *New York Times* music critic Jon Pareles selected *Burnin'*. "In 2096 when the former third world has overrun and colonized the former superpowers, Bob Marley will be commemorated as a saint," Pareles wrote.

In 1974 two albums of pre-Island material, *African Herbsman* (the title track written by Richie Havens) and *Rasta Revolution,* on the Trojan label, became available in the United States as imports. After a tour of Britain, Peter Tosh, Bunny Wailer, and Earl Lindo decided to go their own ways. The original Wailers performed together for the last time in 1975.

Marley added the I-Threes (wife Rita Marley, Marcia Griffiths, and Judy Mowatt) to sing backup, and began touring as Bob Marley and the Wailers. *Natty Dread* (which contained Marley's breakthrough U.K. hit "No Woman, No Cry") came out in 1974, and the group began gaining popularity on the U.K. and world scene, playing before sellout crowds. They followed in 1975 with *Live,* recorded at the London Lyceum.

With the release of *Rastaman Vibration* in 1976, Marley, already acclaimed in the United Kingdom and Europe, finally became a recognized star with U.S. fans. The album hit number eight on the *Billboard* charts. But even as Bob gained acceptance outside Jamaica, he found himself almost a man without a country. He had to spend much of the late 1970s away from his homeland after political turmoil resulted in an attack on his life. On December 3, 1976, just two days before his group was to give a free government-sponsored, "Smile Jamaica" concert in Kingston, five men forced their way into Marley's home, injuring Bob and three others. (It was conjectured that the raiders were partisans of the opposition political party.) Marley was wounded in the arm but escaped with his life. Despite the attack, Marley performed in the concert in front of 80,000 people. After the incident, though, he spent much of his time in other parts of the world, even when he wasn't touring.

Though disenchanted with politics, Marley returned to Jamaica for the April 1978 One Love Peace Concert following a cease-fire declared by rival gunmen. During his performance he brought Jamaica's main political rivals, Michael Manley and Edward Seaga, onstage and had them join hands in a symbolic effort to spread peace in the divided country. (Marley received the United Nations Medal for Peace for his efforts.) In 1979, Marley released his *Survival* album, which included a song, "Zimbabwe," about the African struggle for independence from the white Rhodesians. The following year, Marley was invited to celebrate Zimbabwe's independence.

But all along he had been fighting his own battle for life. In July 1977, Marley had cancerous cells removed from a toe in Miami, the first sign of the disease. Meanwhile, he continued to record spine-tingling new reggae on *Exodus* (1977), the two-disc live set *Babylon by Bus, Kaya* (which hit number four on the U.K. charts in 1978), and *Uprising* (1980). Worldwide his audience was growing, as indicated by the 100,000 people who attended a concert in Milan in 1980. Dubious reissues of his earlier work came out on other labels in the late 1970s and early 1980s.

Though other reggae artists gained followings in the United States, none could match the successes achieved by Marley and his band. One of the reasons for his rapport with fans in the United States, where few had even heard of most other reggae stars, is indicated on *Babylon by Bus.* Other major reggae exponents such as Tosh and Bunny Wailer tended to turn out more somber, almost atonal material. Marley, on the other hand, always maintained a lighter touch. In fact, in mid-1970s concerts he changed the arrangements of songs such as "Rat Race" and "Rebel Music" to make them more accessible. But this didn't mean he sugar-coated his message. In "Rat Race," the music was compellingly danceable but the words retained their sting ("Oh, it's a disgrace to see the human race / In a rat race / You got the horse race / You got the dog race / You got the human race.")

Marley's subjects covered a range of sociological topics from lighthearted love songs ("Is This Love," "Stir It Up") to the optimistic overview ("Positive Vibration") to the political warnings of "War." ("Until the philosophy / Which holds one race superior and another inferior / Is finally and permanently discredited and abandoned / Well everywhere is war.") It seems likely the words struck home even more effectively due to the light mood. Certainly this is the case in "Concrete Jungle" (one of the best musical indictments of recent times about the terrible plight of many inner cities), in which the singer cries out "A light must somehow be found / Instead of a concrete jungle" while making the point: "No chains on my feet / But I am not free / I am down here in captivity."

Although he was still advancing creatively and at the height of his writing and performing powers, as indicated by his excellent Island release *Uprising* in the summer of 1980, the cancer had spread to other parts of his body. He collapsed after performing at Madison Square Garden. After an eight-month battle, on May 11, 1981, Marley was struck down by cancer. Hundreds of thousands of people attended his state funeral in Jamaica, including Seaga and Manley. Marley's body rests in a mausoleum in his birthplace, Nine Miles.

"I miss Bob," his widow wrote in 1995. "When I feel things are too much to bear—particularly with the legal battles [over the Marley estate]—I especially wish he were here. It was cancer that took him. As a Rasta, though, you'd never hear him saying 'If I did . . .' or 'When I die . . .' To Rastafarians life is an everlasting gift. But one day in the hospital Bob was ready to go. I heard him say, 'God, take me, please.' I held him in my arms and started singing to him. Then I started to cry. Bob looked up at me. 'Don't cry,' he said softly, 'keep singing.'"

Marley, who was awarded Jamaica's Order of Merit and had his birthday declared as Bob Marley Day, left the magnificent legacies of his record catalog and his family survivors, his highly gifted children, who include seven professional singers. David "Ziggy" Marley and the Melody Makers especially keep his traditions alive. Rita had released *Who Feels It Knows It* on Shanachie while Bob was still alive, and *Harambe* on Teldec in 1984. Cedella Marley Booker released *Awake Zion*, a tribute to her son, in 1990.

In the years after Bob's passing, there was a profusion of Marley/Wailer relations and/or alumni on the concert circuit or in recording studios. At the same time, albums of earlier Bob Marley material, some previously unreleased, came out. In 1982 a controversial, pop-inflected posthumous collection, *Chances Are,* was released on Atlantic/Cotillion. In 1983, though, Island issued the well-prepared LP *Confrontation,* offering only songs never before released or previously unreleased in the United States. That was followed by a militant anthology called *Rebel Music.* Island released a ten-album boxed set, *Bob Marley—The Boxed Set,* in 1982. Other releases included *Soul Revolution I and II* on Trojan in 1988 and *Interviews* on Tuff Gong in 1988.

In 1997 a revived JAD Records, in conjunction with the estates of Bob Marley and Peter Tosh, and with Bunny Wailer, began releasing a projected twelve-CD project called *The Complete Bob Marley and the Wailers 1967–1972,* containing over 200 tracks from that period, about a quarter of them collected or released for the first time. (In 1996, JAD released *Soul Almighty: The Formative Years,* both a regular CD and also a CD-ROM with ten hours of interactive material from Roger Steffens's Marley archives. It is the only CD-ROM that has been made about Marley.)

In 1984, Bunny Wailer began coordinating a new album, *Never Ending Wailers,* which mixed tracks made by the Wailers in the 1960s and new recordings by Bunny, Peter Tosh, Junior Braithwaite, and Constantine Walker. Braithwaite, who had moved to Chicago in 1965, had been lead singer of the first Wailers band in 1963. Walker had replaced Marley as lead singer for most of 1966 and later toured with Tosh.

Bunny, who had gone into seclusion on a rural Jamaican farm in 1975, returned to action as a solo performer in 1982 and had such U.S. releases on Shanachie Records in the 1980s as *Roots Radics Rockers Reggae* (1983) and *Marketplace* (1986). In 1990, Bunny released *Time Will Tell* on Shanachie, another tribute to Marley. In 1994 came *Crucial,* a collection of mostly Jamaican releases, and *Hall of Fame: A Tribute to Bob Marley's 50th Anniversary,* each of which won a Grammy.

When Marley died, according to Rastafarian custom, he did not leave a will, which led to more than a decade of legal wrangling among record companies, Marley's family, his widow, his unwed wives, and even the Jamaican government. The disputes kept large amounts of unreleased material locked up in the vaults. The Jamaican government seized control of the estate after Rita Marley was charged with forging Bob's signature (she was later cleared), and then sold the rights to Chris Blackwell for $8 million, a move that was challenged legally by the Marley family. Finally, in December 1991, the Jamaican Supreme Court awarded control of the estate to Rita, his eleven children, and Chris Blackwell for $11.5 million. Since that time the family has regained 75 percent of the estate, with Blackwell retaining 25 percent.

The group that bore the Wailers title during the last years of Bob's life also had major problems for years thereafter because, they stated, six months after Bob's death they had signed an exclusive recording contract with Rita Marley in which they agreed to relinquish control of the Wailers name. The legal and financial problems involved kept that group, which included the Barrett brothers, Al Anderson, and Junior Marvin (who had joined as guitarist in 1977), from doing any extensive touring until early 1987, after they had filed an $8 million lawsuit against the Marley estate. The suit demanded an audit of royalty payments made to the estate after Marley's death. The group now calls itself the Wailers Band.

Hardly had the group gotten its new career under way when drummer Carlton Barrett was shot to death in April 1987 by a gunman hired by his wife and her lover. (Peter Tosh was murdered in the same year.) By summer bassist Aston Barrett revamped the band by adding Cornell Marshall on drums, former Third World member Irvin Jarrett on percussion, and Martin Batista on keyboards, backing lead singer Junior Marvin.

Still, it appeared that the true torchbearers of the Marley legacy would be his own family. The 1984 European success of the Island greatest hits LP, *Legend,* encouraged Rita to organize a European tour featuring members of the old Wailers, the I-Threes, and son David "Ziggy" Marley, who bears a physical and vocal resemblance to his father.

Before Bob's death he had been able to hear the promise of his youngsters in 1980 when they recorded a song he'd written for them, "Children Playing on the Street." The children took the group name the Melody Makers, which they used in 1985 for their debut album on EMI-America, *Play the Game Right,* including the song written by their father. Nine of the LP's ten songs were written by Ziggy and were of high enough quality to warrant a Grammy nomination in 1985. They followed up with *Hey World* on EMI in 1986. The group was made up of Ziggy, his brother Stephen, and sisters Sharon, and Cedella. The Melody Makers' first U.S. tour occurred in 1986. Ziggy told Don Snowden (*Los Angeles Times,* July 19, 1986), "We're just trying to make our own style and to also make new trends. We can't be keeping the same thing. We have to keep adding on."

In 1988, after the group switched to Virgin, EMI released a compilation album, *Time Has Come: The Best of Ziggy Marley and the Melody Makers.* The group was represented on Virgin by the strong release *Conscious Party,* which won a Grammy for 1988 and sold nearly a million copies, *One Bright Day* in 1989, *Jahmekya* in 1991, and *Joy & Blues—Ghetto Youths United* in 1993. They have since won two more Grammys.

By the 1987 sixth annual Bob Marley Day concert in Santa Monica, California, Ziggy had progressed to being one of the stars of the show. His charismatic performance suggested that he had the ability to lead reggae to new creative heights. He didn't feel any pressure from that, he told Steve Hochman (*Los Angeles Times,* February 10, 1987). "It feel good and so that why I do it." But he also hoped reggae would find new leaders. "Even my father say reggae can't die. It's not only one man to carry on. It's many people."

After sagging interest in reggae during the second half of the 1980s, the form experienced a resurgence in the '90s. Ziggy's success in the late '80s rekindled interest from the public. His single, "Tumbling Down," was number one on the black singles charts. In the late 1980s dance hall, a faster form of reggae, began to make inroads with African Americans through combinations with rap and hip-hop. The Reggae Sunsplash, begun in 1978, continued to tour year after year. And Bob Marley tribute concerts were too numerous to list. In the mid-1990s there was a renewed interest in ska, one of the roots of reggae, as Ernest Ranglin, who had been Marley's guitar teacher, traveled to Senegal to record with Baaba Maal. His album, *In Search of the Lost Riddim,* came out in 1998 on Palm Pictures Records.

In the mid-1990s Ziggy continued an active touring schedule, but his record sales sagged. There were no Bob Marley replacements on the horizon, although his influence was evident in artists such as Burning Spear, Luciano, and African reggae artists Lucky Dube, Alpha Blondy, and Majek Fashek. "There's a handful of people still out there trying to maintain the rootical perspective," says Steffens. "But there's no major figure that's emerged since Bob. Ziggy tours all the time, he does great live shows but his album sales don't reflect his popularity. All of the kids have a piece of Bob but nobody has the whole combination."

It is that unique combination of talent that has kept Bob Marley's legacy alive. As the millennium approached, record labels continued to reissue old material and mine unreleased material. The most successful of all was the 1984 Island release *Legend,* which dominated the *Billboard* top pop catalog charts throughout the late 1980s and 1990s with more than 12 million in unit sales. It was at the top of the catalog chart for more than seventy-six weeks, longer than any artist in history, beating out releases by Pink Floyd, Michael Jackson, and the Beatles.

Says Steffens: "Marley in death has become a bigger and more important figure in the music than in life. In 1997, he sold more records than any year in his lifetime and he'd been dead for seventeen years. I think it's a combination of a beguiling and melodic musical sensibility, coupled with some of the most deceptively profound lyrics of the twentieth century, inspired by his God."

In 1991, *Talkin' Blues,* an album of previously unreleased live performances recorded from a '73 concert, came out on Tuff Gong/Island. In 1992, *Songs of Freedom,* a four-CD boxed set that includes seventy-eight songs spanning his career from the earlier Wailers to the late incarnations, sold out its limited million-copy release and was rereleased in the jewel box format in 1999. Heartbeat released *One Love at Studio One,* a two-CD set that includes some of the Wailin' Wailers' earliest recordings, including their first hit, "Simmer Down." In 1993, Real Authentic Sounds released *Never Ending Wailers,* originally titled *Together Again.* In 1995, Island and Tuff Gong released *Natural Mystic: The Legend Lives On,* a compilation of Marley's spiritual and political songs, followed by *Chant Down Babylon* in 1999.

The best of the dozen or so books that have come out on Marley included *Bob Marley: The Biography,* by Stephen Davis; *Bob Marley: Spirit Dancer,* by Bruce W. Talamon and Roger Steffens; *Catch a Fire: The Life of Bob Marley,* by *Billboard* music editor Timothy White; *Soul Rebel—Natural Mystic,* by Adrian Boot and Vivien Goldman; *Bob Marley: Reggae King of the World,* by Malika Lee Whitney and Dermot Hussey; and *Songs of Freedom,* by Chris Salewicz and Adrian Boot.

Naturally, the commercialization of Marley has continued unabated. In 1995, to commemorate the fiftieth anniversary of Bob's birth, there were all kinds of celebrations. The Jamaican government issued six stamps, put his image on two coins, and adopted Marley's song "One Love" for a tourist board advertising campaign. There have also been trading cards, posters, T-shirts, calendars, two Marvel comic books, and countless bootleg recordings. "Next to the Beatles, he's probably the most bootlegged artist in the world," says Steffens.

But Marley, who was inducted into the Rock and Roll Hall of Fame in 1994, has an impact that goes way beyond music. His lyrics and image are known throughout the world, even in remote regions. In Sierra Leone, rebels of the Revolutionary United Front who were fighting against the military government wore Bob Marley shirts as part of their uniform, which meant that ordinary citizens wearing the T-shirts were putting themselves in grave danger. Both sides in the Nicaraguan civil war marched off to battle to his music.

"It's astonishing to me just how ubiquitous a figure he is," says Steffens. "I've traveled all over the planet lecturing on Bob. There's not a corner of this world where I haven't found Bob in evidence. As Jack Healey, the president of Amnesty International, said, 'Everywhere I go in the world today, Bob Marley is the symbol of freedom.'"

Entry written with assistance from Marley archivist Roger Steffens

MARTYN, JOHN: *Singer, songwriter, guitarist. Born Glasgow, Scotland, June 28, 1948.*

During the 1960s and 1970s, Scottish-born singer-songwriter John Martyn composed romantic folk ballads of ineffable grace and delicacy. The Island Records two-CD anthology *Sweet Little Mysteries* captures the quintessential Martyn songs: "Bless the Weather," "Head and Heart" (covered by the rock group America), "Solid Air," "Don't Want to Know" (covered by Eric Clapton), "May You Never," "Lay It All Down," "Spencer the Rover," "Sweet Little Mystery," and "You Can Discover." Martyn, in these works, created an unsurpassed romantic style: his melodies are alternately lilting and playful or achingly heartbreaking; his singing style is alternately soft, warm, and earthy or gruff and slurred; and his delicate guitar styling is influenced by performers like Richard Thompson and John Renbourn.

A sampling of three Martyn songs highlights his lyrical gift. "Solid Air" both expresses Martyn's devoted friendship with Nick Drake (it was written one year before Drake's death) and captures the paradoxical, wraithlike nature of a man living in the world but not of it . . . and who would shortly leave it: *You've been painting the blues and you've been looking through solid air, . . . Don't know what is going on inside your mind, I can tell you don't like what you find when you're moving through solid air.*

In Martyn's love songs, the exquisite interplay be-tween his guitar and Danny Thompson's bass mirrors the playful relationship of two lovers. One of his best is "May You Never," a plea for lasting love. And in "You Can Discover," the alternating joy and pain of love seems to make the lovers and their relationship stronger: *One day our laughter comes floating with the rain, On the very next day our sorrow sees us crying again, But darling you can discover the lover in me, And I can discover the lover in thee . . .*

It is startling that such a gifted songwriter has never won more than a cult following in the United States. Several reasons account for this: Martyn can be ornery, irascible; he is far too demanding and uncompromising to remain satisfied in a single genre like the romantic ballad. No sooner did he write these gorgeous ballads than he restlessly turned his hand to the technowizardry of a song like "Root Love." While Martyn's journeys across the musical landscape earn him credit as a continually experimenting and expanding performer (ever the contrarian, Martyn says his "sense of adventure came from the need to avoid boredom rather than a need to constantly experiment and evolve"), his audience, radio stations, and record companies didn't know what to make of him. Also, a broken marriage and alcohol dependency sidetracked his career for three years beginning in 1976.

Colin Escott's masterful liner notes for *Sweet Little Mysteries* capture Martyn's grit and iconoclasm. Life has been "a hard bloody slog, John Martyn would be the first to tell you," Escott writes. He was brought up in Glasgow, Scotland, a city of working-class neighborhoods whose inhabitants work the textile mills and seaside docks. It is gray, bleak, and brooding. The street life is replete with petty crime and drug dealing as described in the film *Trainspotting*.

Martyn was an only child whose parents divorced when he was five. His mother returned to England, and he shuttled back and forth from Glasgow to southern England. During the mid-1960s, he worked the London folk club circuit, eventually securing a record contract from Island Records. His first album, *London Conversation* (1967), was heavily influenced by British guitarist Davy Graham, who was also a musical hero to Paul Simon when he lived in London during this period. His second album, *The Tumbler*, was produced by Al Stewart.

He had a hardscrabble youth and, as with Van Morrison (who grew up in Belfast), you can hear it in his voice: at times gruff and scuffling; at other times warm, smooth, and whiskey-drenched. His diction, like Morrison's, makes no concessions to intelligibility. The growling and slurring lend an emotional authenticity to the songs. His highly autobiographical, introspective songwriting calls to mind Tim Buckley and Nick Drake.

Martyn met his first wife, Beverly Kutner, in 1969 at art college. At the time, she was involved with Joe Boyd, the legendary producer of Fairport Convention.

When she earned her first record contract, Martyn played guitar and wrote many of the songs with her. Their first album released in America is the delightful *Stormbringer* (1969), produced by John Simon (who did the early Leonard Cohen recordings) and featuring accompaniment by many members of the Band from the Big Pink era. They followed with *The Road to Ruin* and *Bless the Weather* before John recorded *Solid Air.*

In 1973, his musical explorations caused him to turn away from simple folk songs in favor of electronic experimentation. He introduced the fuzz box, phase-shifter, and Echoplex on the recordings *Inside Out* and *Sunday's Child,* using them to add a darker, more threatening edge to his music. In particular, Martyn's work on the Echoplex influenced U2's lead guitarist, the Edge, and helped give that group its distinctive sound.

His romance with musical technology can become oppressive. Martyn's album, *No Little Boy* (1992), is an uneven attempt to update his old folk-oriented material in a jazz groove. This work is an uncomfortable musical amalgam in which Martyn attempts to get his folk material to swing and groove in the jazz idiom.

Escott characterizes Martyn's music at its best when he says: "All kinds of sound and furies meet here, brought together by a keen, intuitive musical intelligence. . . . The albums are the work of a true eccentric. 'Every record,' John once said, 'is totally autobiographical. That's the only way I can write. Some people keep diaries. I make records.'"

Martyn's *The Church with One Bell* (Independiente, 1998), is an album of covers of disparate originals ranging from Billie Holiday's "Strange Fruit" to Randy Newman's "God's Song" to Portishead's "Glory Box." A rather audacious concept the result of which, by most critics' accounts, is rather spotty. Writing in the *Jerusalem Post,* David Brinn calls it "a good concept gone awry in execution. . . . Amazingly enough, Martyn manages to make all this seemingly incompatible music sound exactly the same—a droll, lazy shuffle that's perpetually stuck in first gear."

Almost simultaneously released were a limited-edition "official bootleg" *Live at Bristol* (Voiceprint, 1998) and *Serendipity* (Island, 1998), a compilation album of previously released material issued by Martyn's former record company.

Entry written by Richard Silverstein

MATTHEWS, IAIN: *Singer, guitarist, band leader (Matthews Southern Comfort, Plainsong), songwriter. Born Scunthorpe, Lincolnshire, England, June 16, 1946.*

The haunting strains of Joni Mitchell's song "Woodstock" remain to this day one of the striking reminders of that legendary concert, and the version that has by far sold the most records and received the most radio coverage over the decades was the one prepared by the English band Matthews Southern Comfort. The leader of that group, singer-songwriter Iain Matthews, established a presence in the folk/folk-rock scene in the United Kingdom and the United States that had many high points but never quite brought him the star status that he initially seemed destined for.

As a teenager, Matthews (born Ian Matthews McDonald, a name later changed to Iain Matthews to avoid confusion with King Crimson bandsman Ian MacDonald) performed with a number of groups in his home area of Lincolnshire including the Classics, Rebels, and Imps. In 1966 he moved to London, where he earned money to live on by working in a shoe store while performing with a "surf group" called Pyramid. In 1967 he became a member of Fairport Convention, the folk-rock band formed by a group of highly talented folk-based musicians, including lead guitarist Richard Thompson, bassist Ashley Hutchings, and vocalist Judy Dyble. His stint with them was relatively short, but he was there long enough to perform on the group's first single, "If I Had a Ribbon Bow"; the group's debut, *Fairport Convention,* released by Polydor in 1968; and the follow-up *What We Did on Our Holidays,* issued by Island Records.

Matthews left Fairport Convention in 1969 and got the go-ahead to prepare a solo album for the MCA label. That disc, called *Matthews Southern Comfort,* came out in 1970. Whereas his backing for it comprised studio musicians and former Fairport band mates Thompson, Nicol, and Hutchings, he proceeded to form a tour band for gigs in the United Kingdom and the Continent and for a series of recordings released on Decca in both England and the United States. (Band members included Gordon Huntley, Mark Griffiths, and Andy Leigh from England, Ray Duffy from Scotland, and Carl Barnwell from California.) Decca LPs included *Second Spring,* and *Later That Same Year,* the first including the single "Woodstock." The song peaked at number twenty-three in *Billboard* the week of April 24, 1971, but did even better in the United Kingdom, rising all the way to number one. The single became a classic, being played often in the decades since then on rock oldies programs and included on several collections of British all-time favorites.

He left Southern Comfort even as "Woodstock" was rising on the charts. Matthews soon arranged a solo deal with Vertigo Records that resulted in the albums *If You Saw Thro' My Eyes* in 1971 and *Tigers Will Survive* in '72. His Vertigo output included the chart single "Da Doo Ron Ron" (originally a 1963 hit for the Crystals). In 1972 he organized a new group, Plainsong, in collaboration with Andy Roberts, Dave Richards, and Bob Ronga. The band signed with Elektra Records, which issued *In Search of Amelia Earhart* in 1972, in part a concept album revolving around the career and disappearance of that aviatrix. Before the group could complete more LPs, disagreements between members caused its breakup.

Matthews picked up the pieces by doing some work

with Michael Nesmith of Monkees fame and getting the green light from Elektra for solo efforts that produced *Valley Hi* in '73 and *Some Days You Eat the Bear . . . and Some Days the Bear Eats You* in 1974. Neither of those were best-sellers, and Iain moved to Columbia in hopes of reigniting his career. His CBS output comprised *Go for Broke* in '75 and *Hit and Run* in '76. In 1978 he signed with a U.K. label, Rockburgh, which issued the album *Stealin' Home* in England and licensed Canadian-based Mushroom to handle North American distribution. The album provided a U.S. singles hit, "Shake It," which made the *Billboard* top 20 in December '78. With support from that label, which had prospered with the rock group Heart, it seemed as if Matthews might score a U.S. breakthrough, but the label's owner and founder died and the operation disintegrated. His 1979 album *Siamese Friends,* on the Rockburgh label, found few buyers.

At the start of the '80s Rockburgh issued the LP *A Spot of Interference,* which was followed by a "best of" compilation, *Discreet Repeat.* Still hoping for U.S. stardom, Matthews signed with a Seattle label and formed the band Hi Fi, which released the 1981 live extended-play disc *Demonstration Record* and full album *Moods for the Mallards,* both issued in the United States on First American Records and in the United Kingdom on Butt Records. Next came an agreement with Polydor in Germany, which resulted in the '83 album *Shook,* which was only released in Europe.

Discouraged by the sluggish momentum of his performing career, in 1984 he took a behind-the-scenes position as artists and repertoire man for Los Angeles–based Island Music and later for Windham Hill Records. (His main accomplishment was bringing Canadian art song singer-writer Jane Siberry to U.S. audience attention via Windham Hill's subsidiary Open Air.) In 1986, when he took part in the Fairport Convention Cropredy Festival in Oxfordshire, United Kingdom, to excellent audience response, he was inspired to try to revive his entertainment credentials. Back in the United States, he completed a record that was issued by Windham Hill in '88 called *Walking a Changing Line,* an entire album of his versions of songs by Jules Shear with New Age instrumentation.

Once more on the concert circuit, in 1989 he moved from California to Austin, Texas, where he formed a partnership with guitarist–record producer Mark Hallman. Hallman supervised recording and production of a cassette-only product, *Iain Matthews Live,* sold at early-'90s Matthews appearances. In 1990 Iain found still another record company alliance, this time with Goldcastle, whose roster also included Joan Baez and Karla Bonoff. His label debut was the 1990 album *Pure & Crooked.* Also encouraging was an enthusiastic welcome given by the crowd at the Cambridge Folk Festival for a reunion set with former Plainsong associate Andy Roberts. Matthews added two more albums to his credits in 1991, *Nights in Manhattan—Live* and *Or-*

phans & Outcasts, Volume 1 followed by *Orphans & Outcasts, Volume 2,* a collection of demos and live recordings, before suffering another career setback with the collapse of Goldcastle in 1992. *Orphans & Outcasts, Volume 3* came out in 1999.

Despite the setback, Matthews forged on with his career, releasing the solo album *Skeleton Keys* in 1992 on the German Line Records. He signed with Texas-based Watermelon Records, releasing *The Dark Ride* in 1994. A reunited Plainsong had recorded *The Dark Side of the Room* in 1992, released the following year on Mesa Records. In 1994 the group released *Voices Electric* on Line Records. The following year he joined with Mark Hallman and singer-songwriter Michael Fracasso in a group called Hamilton Pool and released a country-rock album, *Return to Zero* on Watermelon. He released another solo album, *God Looked Down,* on Watermelon in 1996, followed by *Sister Flute* with Plainsong on Line in 1996. The group released a live mini-CD in 1997, *Live in Austria,* following a European tour. Matthews signed with the German label Blue Rose and released the solo CD *Excerpts from Swine Lake* in 1998, followed by *A Tiniest Wham* solo CD in 2000.

Plainsong recorded a new album, *New Place Now,* released in 1999. Matthews formed a band called the Swinelakers (taken from the name of the town where he resides in Texas) for his European touring, featuring Bradley Kopp on guitar, Mark Andes on bass, and Larry Thompson on drums.

MAYALL, JOHN: *Singer, guitarist, organist, harmonica player, record producer, songwriter, band leader (the Blues-breakers). Born Manchester, England, November 29, 1933. (See footnote* for partial listing of band personnel 1963–75.) Roster in 1982, Mayall, Mick Taylor, Steve Thompson (bass), Colin Allen (drums). Band members in 1997–1999, Mayall, Buddy Whittington (guitar), John Paulus (bass), Joe Yuele (drums).*

Tall, gangling John Mayall could always be counted on to defy existing musical tradition. He formed his first major band at thirty at a time when a pop musician over twenty was considered ancient. He played blues-rock and jazz-rock in his own relatively subdued way when hyperamplification was the rage. He continually experimented, varying groups and musical content no matter how commercially successful a particular pattern seemed to be. Despite a lack of best-sellers for most of his career, he persevered and outlasted many of the big-name stars of the moment.

He told Douglas MacPherson of *Keyboard Review* ("John Mayall—Just Call Me Mr. Blues") that his father played guitar, but John's first favorite was the piano. "When I was 13, there was a girl at school who one day sat down at a piano and played the boogie-woogie thing. From that point on I was gone. I can't read or write music, and I can't think of many of my musical partners who can. I sometimes wish I had learned music, that I had a little more technique and that I had learned to play a scale, which I still can't do. But at the same time, my keyboard style, through having been self taught, doesn't sound like anybody else."

After graduating from art school, where he majored in graphic design, in the early 1950s, he spent many years in the advertising field and won a reputation as one of Manchester, England's, best typography and graphic design experts. (He later put this experience to work in preparing the artwork for several of his album covers.) He also worked as a window dresser.

During the 1950s, Mayall was caught up in the skiffle craze then sweeping England, a movement that helped solidify his interest in traditional blues. He performed with small groups in Manchester for a while, moving to London at the start of the 1960s to work as a sideman with some of the blues-rock groups flourishing as an aftermath of skiffle. He started his own band in 1964 and soon won approval from most of the English

---

* Partial Listing of Mayall Bands Personnel

1963—guitar: Bernie Watson; bass guitar: John McVie; drums: Peter Ward. 1964—guitar: Roger Dean; bass guitar: John McVie; drums: Hughie Flint. 1965—guitar: Eric Clapton; bass guitar: John McVie and Jack Bruce; drums: Hughie Flint. 1966—guitar: Eric Clapton (six months), Peter Green; bass guitar: John McVie; drums: Hughie Flint (six months), Aynsley Dunbar. 1967—guitar: Peter Green (six months), Mick Taylor; bass guitar: John McVie (nine months), Paul Williams; drums: Mick Fleetwood (six months), Keef Hartley; saxophones: Dick Heckstall-Smith, Chris Mercer. 1968—guitar: Mick Taylor; bass guitar: Andy Fraser (three months), Tony Reeves (three months), Steve Thompson; drums: Keef Hartley (three months), John Hiseman (three months), Colin Allen; saxophones: Dick Heckstall-Smith, Chris Mercer; trumpet: Henry Lowther. 1969—guitar: Mick Taylor (six months), Jon Mark; bass guitar: Steve Thompson; drums: Colin Allen; saxophones: Johnny Almond. 1970—guitar: Jon Mark (six months), Harvey Mandel; bass guitar: Steve Thompson (three months), Larry Taylor; drums: none; saxophone: Johnny Almond (six months); violin: Sugarcane Harris. 1971—guitar: Harvey Mandel to Jimmy McCulloch to Freddy Robinson; bass guitar: Larry Taylor; drums: Paul Labos to Keef Hartley to Ron Selico; violin: Sugarcane Harris; saxophones: Clifford Solomon; trumpet: Blue Mitchell. 1972—guitar: Freddy Robinson; string bass: Victor Gaskin; drums: Keef Hartley; horns: Blue Mitchell (trumpet), Clifford Solomon (saxophone), Fred Clark (saxophone). 1973—guitar: Freddy Robinson; string bass: Victor Gaskin; drums: Keef Hartley; horns: Blue Mitchell (trumpet), Red Holloway (saxophone and flute). 1974–75—Larry Taylor (bass); Sugarcane Harris (violin); Dee McKinnie (vocals).

---

rock stars as one of the most innovative band leaders around. In particular, Mayall from the start was a superb judge of young performers. Because so many Bluesbreakers alumni went on to international fame, John was given the nickname "grandfather of British rock."

His 1965–66 band featured two of the most impressive talents in rock history: lead guitarist Eric Clapton and bassist Jack Bruce. The recordings made by the group, which strangely never became hits, are now considered classics of rock. Clapton and Bruce later influenced an entire generation of young guitarists when they left Mayall to join Ginger Baker in Cream. Mayall's album releases during those years included his debut LP (on Decca), *John Mayall Plays John Mayall*, and *Bulldogs for Sale* in 1965 and *Bluesbreakers with Eric Clapton* in 1967.

Personnel changes never seemed to worry Mayall. In fact, on at least one occasion, he dissolved a group to give a musician a chance to join another internationally successful band. One reason probably was Mayall's faith in his judgment. If one skilled sideman left, he always seemed able to find another expert to take his place. Thus his band rosters through the early 1970s look like a who's who of rock: besides Clapton and Bruce, there were such artists as Aynsley Dunbar, Peter Greene, Mick Taylor, lead guitarist during mid-1967–mid-1969, who took Brian Jones's place with the Rolling Stones, and many others.

Despite the great competence of Mayall's bands, it took most of the 1960s before his hard core of avid followers were complemented by the mass audience. He gained some success in England in the mid-1960s, after signing with London Records, with such 1967 albums as *A Hard Road* and *The Blues Alone*, but he was hardly a threat to top 10 groups. But he persisted with intensive touring and a steady output of new albums in the late 1960s, including *Crusade* in 1967; *Diary of a Band (Volumes 1 and 2)*, *Bare Wires*, *Blues from Laurel Canyon* (all in 1968), and *Empty Rooms* (1969). Slowly, however, rock fans became aware of his musical contributions and, by the end of the '60s, Mayall was receiving the attention he deserved.

His tours of the United States, which started in the late 1960s, made him decide to buy a house in the Los Angeles area, where he spent half of each year from then on. Fans were impressed with his 1969–70 group that included John Thompson on bass and versatile Johnny Almond (born 1946), who could play a dozen instruments, including saxophone, flute, vibraharp, organ, and guitar. This group, as was to be expected, was unorthodox. It was a jazz-blues band, but it had no drummer. The introduction of jazz elements into a pop format was daring, considering the tastes of most rock fans.

By this time, Mayall was recognized for his new and old work. In 1969, he played the Newport Jazz Festival and his final LP for London Records, *Looking Back* (reviewing his material and group makeup during 1964–67) was a top-20 U.K. hit, while his new label, Polydor, released the gold LP *Turning Point,* recorded live at the Fillmore East.

In the early 1970s, some of Mayall's albums seemed to be assembled more for quantity than quality. London Records reached into its vaults to release *Diary of a Band* (1970) and *John Mayall in Europe, with the Bluesbreakers* and *John Mayall through the Years* (1971). Ampex Records reissued an album of his early work with Eric Clapton, while Polydor issued *Empty Rooms, Memories, USA Union,* the two-disc *Back to the Roots, Jazz-Blues Fusion, Moving On,* and *10 Years Are Gone.* London kept on repackaging his older material on *Down the Line* (1973), *A Banquet in Blues* (1976), and *Primal Solos* (1978).

Through it all, Mayall continued to go his own way, playing what Leonard Feather called his "blues without bedlam." John showed his independence in the lyrics he wrote for many of his songs, which avoided the stereotyped response of many rock artists to police brutality, drugs, and other problems. Thus in "The Laws Must Change" on his first Polydor LP, he wrote: "You're screaming at policemen, but they are only doing a gig." He expanded on his intent at one point to Feather. "I meant that it's not the law enforcers we should worry about—after all, they're only the hirelings—but rather the laws themselves. In the same songs, I hinted at [late comedian] Lenny Bruce's much more extended discussions and theories along these lines, about not throwing rocks at cops, but getting the knots of laws untied."

In 1975, he switched to a new label, ABC, which released *New Year, New Band, New Company* and, later in 1975, *Notice to Appear.* He followed with such ABC albums as *A Hard Core Package* (1977) and *Last of the British Blues* (1979). By the end of the decade, Mayall had left ABC and his new material, such as the albums *The Bottom Line* and *No More Interviews,* came out on DJM Records.

Mayall took some time off at the start of the 1980s, but was soon back in musical harness with the 1982–1983 reunion concert tour. Band members comprised Mayall on vocals, keyboards, guitar, and harmonica; Mick Taylor on guitar; Steve Thompson on bass; and Colin Allen on drums. An appearance at the Wax Museum in Washington, D.C., provided the basis for the live CD *The 1982 Reunion Concert.*

For the rest of the 1980s and throughout the 1990s Mayall continued to tour and work on new recording and video material with the United States as his main base. In the summer of 1997 he released what many reviewers enthused was one of his best-ever collections, *Blues for the Lost Days.* For instance, Buddy Siegal commented in the *Los Angeles Times's* Orange County Edition, "The sonic crunch and energy level of the opening 'Dead City' (which Mayall said he wrote about urban decay, violence and the benefits of moving to the country) are every bit as potent as anything from his landmark 'Bluesbreaker' album from 1966 and 'Lost Days' sustains its excellence from start to finish. He may be one grizzled old geezer, but Mayall delivers his blues with all the punch and enthusiasm of his glory days." Band members for the album were John Paulus on bass, Buddy Whittington on guitar, and Joe Yuele on drums.

As of 1999, Mayall typically booked some 120 concerts a year, including many dates at venues in nations across the globe. He often was one of the featured acts at a blues or blues rock show such as the Long Beach Blues Festival at the California State University Long Beach Athletic Field in September 1998, where he led off the final session with the comment "We've got the limey brigade onstage tonight." Besides the Bluesbreakers band, the performers included Bluesbreakers alumnus Peter Green, finally recovered from years of mental illness, who headed his Splinter Group band.

Reviewing the show, Natalie Nichols, writing in the *Los Angeles Times* ("British Brand of Blues Is Celebrated at Long Beach Fest," September 8, 1998), gave high marks to the Green set as well as to numbers by such other veterans as drummer Jim McCarty and guitarist Chris Dreja of seminal U.K. 1960s rock group the Yardbirds, but saved her highest praise for Mayall, noting that he and his current Bluesbreakers "offered the most dynamic and varied set, a blend of standard blues, newer material and early classics, such as 'Room to Move.'"

She also noted that Mayall proved an "adept ringleader" for a closing jam session "casually assembling some incredible firepower, including Green, Dreja, McCarty, organist Keith Emerson and American guitarist Ronnie Earl, as well as former Bluesbreaker and Rolling Stones guitarist Mick Taylor and Savoy Brown leader Kim Simmonds."

McCASLIN, MARY: *Singer, guitarist, banjoist, songwriter. Born Indianapolis, Indiana, December 22, 1946.*

As a solo performer or teamed with Jim Ringer, Mary McCaslin kept the flame of folk music burning bright for a small but devoted audience in the mid- and late 1970s and 1980s while formats like heavy metal and rap dominated the charts and major concert circuits. In the 1980s, when she couldn't gain new record projects even with small independent labels, fans of her gentle vocal renditions and sophisticated finger picking guitar style in many parts of the world had no idea she was still active on the western folk scene and were pleasantly surprised when she began to surface on a broader stage with the renewed public interest in the folk domain of the 1990s.

She was born in Indiana, but from her formative years was basically a California native. "I don't remember much about the Midwest. Our family moved out when I was six. My parents just wanted to come to California. So I grew up in the Los Angeles area. We moved to Redondo Beach and then to Norwalk, which was just the pits. In my teens I went to high school in Whittier, which was close to Norwalk."

Among her earliest pop-music influences, she recalled, were the Marty Robbins singles "El Paso" and "Big Iron," which gained extensive radio coverage in 1959 and 1960. "Besides Marty, those early influences included Joan Baez, Hedy West, and, in the early '60s, the British Invasion groups like the Beatles and the Animals. I started playing guitar at fifteen and banjo at twenty-one. In my teens I sang at church functions, but I didn't take part in school plays. The music I really liked listening to in my early times in high school was country, but later I switched to folk and to some extent rock."

By the mid-1960s, she had begun to pattern her guitar technique on the approach of artists like Baez and Joni Mitchell. In time, she evolved an open-tuning method of playing, and her finger picking style eventually influenced a new generation of acoustic guitarists. When she added the banjo to her instrumental abilities she employed the clawhammer method that had been a favorite of many country, old-timey, and folk performers over the years.

She recalled, "I started performing professionally when I was eighteen. There were a lot of coffeehouses in California at the time, and my first gig was at one called the Paradox in the city of Orange or Tustin. It all happened a long time ago and it's hard to remember some of the details. My first record release was my cover single of the Beatles' 'Rain' on Capitol in 1966. I got that chance through a friend named Larry Murray, and when Capitol didn't happen he connected with Barnaby Records and that opened the door for my first album. It was the only one I recorded in Los Angeles. I recorded *Good Night Everybody* in early 1969 and it didn't come out until I was living in Hollywood."

In the early '70s she met folk-music soul mate Jim Ringer at a folk-music camp in the Sierras, and the two began a musical (and personal) collaboration that lasted for two decades. "Jim had already connected with Folk Legacy Records in Connecticut, and he wanted to go back and record some of his material. Meanwhile we began working together, and in the fall of 1972 we went back east and while there went to Vermont and met the people who started the Philo label. We came back to California and gave more concerts before returning to the East Coast in the spring of '73, where I recorded my first Philo album, *Way Out West*. Later that year Jim recorded his album *Good to Get Home*, which came out in 1974."

Now they had a foot in the entertainment door, but the duo had a lot more dues to pay before gaining a wider audience. "We went touring as much as we could. We were kinda starting out, trying to establish ourselves. It took a couple of years to do that. We recorded several more albums before we started getting some recognition." Those mid-'70s albums included Mary's

Prairie in the Sky and *Old Friends* and a duet album with Jim, *The Bramble and the Rose*. Tracks of the various Philo releases included some striking originals by Mary, as well as compositions written together or by Ringer alone. Besides her other activities, Mary also got the chance to work on some movie sound track projects. She contributed to the sound track of the late-'70s cult western film *Cattle Annie and Little Britches*. She added, "I also sang a song for the documentary about the Flint, Michigan, auto strike in the early 1930s." The latter film, *Of Babies and Banners,* which focused on women in the labor movement, was nominated for an Academy Award.

In the late 1970s Philo had financial problems. Mary and Jim had to find other recording connections. Mary completed an album for Mercury called *Sunny California* and one in 1980 on Flying Fish, *A Life and Time*. After the latter came out, a recording drought of over a decade followed. Not that Mary left the field. In the early '80s she was active on the folk circuit from a home base in the Santa Cruz area. However, because of Ringer's increasing health problems, the duo's performances in the 1985–89 period were restricted to limited appearances in California and the Northwest. "Because of Jim's health," she recalled, "we moved to Humboldt County, in the Arcata area, and lived there until we separated in the summer of 1989. He went down to Fresno and I went to Santa Cruz." Jim's difficulties with alcohol remained, however, and were a factor in his death in 1992. He was fifty-six years old.

In the early 1990s the folk-music revival offered opportunities for many veteran artists like Mary to renew their careers. "Starting in 1992 and '93, I worked with Philo/Rounder on an compilation album of early Philo tracks. (The result was the fine CD release, *Things We Said Today*.) I hadn't been in the studio since 1980, and in the fall of 1993 I went back in and recorded a new album (issued in 1994), *Broken Promises*. The record company also started reissuing some of my vinyl albums on CDs." First of the latter to be released was *Prairie in the Sky* in '95, with reissue of *Old Friends* in October '96, and *Way Out West* in 1998.

With the reactions to *Broken Promises,* it seemed Mary had come full circle to the glory days of her early career. Reviewers in publications large and small reacted enthusiastically. The *Boston Globe* critic, for instance, commented, "That this is ultimately such a lovely recording is testament to McCaslin's rare talent, spirit and grace." *Dirty Linen* suggested the album might be her best recording. And the *New England Folk Almanac* chimed in, contending that "*Broken Promises,* her first recording in over 10 years, should assure her fans she is indeed back; her sweet melodic gifts intact; her lyrics informed with a tough and ennobling wisdom."

With the new music environment of the '90s, McCaslin began to find more places to showcase her talents. Through mid-decade, her concerts took place at such venues as New York's Bottom Line; the Great American Music Hall in San Francisco; McCabe's Guitar Shop in Santa Monica, California; and Caffe Lena, in Saratoga Springs, New York. Her festival credits included two or three appearances at the Philadelphia Folk Festival, including a 1995 gig in which, in addition to performing a solo set, she co-emceed a Sunday-night concert with folk radio personality Gene Shay.

At writing songs, she noted, she tended to be painfully slow. But while her output was not as extensive as that of other songwriters, more than a few were covered by other artists, among them "Young Westley" by David Bromberg, "Ballad of Weaverville" (cowritten with Jim Ringer) by Kate Wolf, and "Circle of Friends" by Chris Williamson.

Based partly on personal interview with Irwin Stambler in July 1996

McCUTCHEON, JOHN: *Singer, songwriter, hammered dulcimer player, fiddler, guitarist, banjoist, jaw harp player, autoharpist, record producer. Born Wausau, Wisconsin, August 14, 1952.*

One of the most versatile musicians in any segment of popular music, John McCutcheon seemed capable of playing almost any instrument there was. Though considered one of the world's foremost exponents of hammered dulcimer playing, his work in concerts or on record demonstrated his far-from-average abilities with guitar, banjo, and other unique instruments. Those skills and his insight into the roots of folk music were honed in an approach similar to the way an earlier generation of folk artists had prepared themselves—hitchhiking and walking to remote areas where the old ways of playing and singing still held sway.

McCutcheon was born and raised in Wausau, Wisconsin. He moved to Tennessee when he was twenty, and three years later he settled in Virginia (which later led some observers to name him "the Virginia rural renaissance man"). Recalling his early influences for Keturah Truesdell Austin of the *Newton Kansan* ("McCutcheon 'coming home' for concert," November 10, 1995), he said, "I listened to everybody—from Beethoven to Trini Lopez to the Ink Spots—those were the things my parents had." Later he began a collection of his own with albums by the Beatles and country performers before shifting his focus to people like Pete Seeger, Woody Guthrie, and Bob Dylan. When he got his first guitar from a mail-order catalog he began to emulate some of his favorite performances. Then the folk-music boom of the early sixties inspired him to concentrate on learning and perfecting his skills on the banjo.

Though the folk-music wave of those years began to fade in the mid-1960s, John's love for the music remained strong as he went through high school and enrolled in St. John's University in Minnesota, where he majored in American folk studies. After a while at the school, he often hitchhiked on weekends or holidays to hear folk concerts in venues as much as 500 miles away. He sometimes went to folk festivals where besides listening to other artists he could sit in with them in impromptu jam sessions. Before completing work on his degree he left to travel extensively through Appalachia, his banjo by his side.

He told *Bluegrass Unlimited*, "A banjo case is the best passport in the world. It's a sign that says 'Pick me up.' People would stop and give me a ride and right away they'd ask me if I played. I'd get the banjo out. 'Oh you play that old style,' they'd say, 'so-and-so plays that old style.' 'Well, where does so-and-so live?' I'd ask." Improving his playing ability, he said, was only part of what resulted. "I thought I was coming to learn to play the banjo, but I found that was only a small part of what excited me when I went into the homes, the churches, the union halls and the schools. I learned the athletics of how to become a good musician, but those people also taught me where the music comes from. That's universal. Whether you're Rachmaninoff or [country artist] Wilma Lee Cooper you go through the same process of getting the music from inside to outside."

His travels brought him in contact not only with skilled banjo players but with superlative exponents of other instruments, including the mountain dulcimer. After learning the instrument himself, McCutcheon remained on the lookout for artists from whom he could learn. At one folk festival he met a man named I.D. Stamper who, he told Donald E. Wilcock of the *Troy (New York) Record* was "one of the most remarkable musicians I ever spent any time with . . . He was an incredible musician, incredibly influenced by the blues, and built these huge, low-toned mountain dulcimers and played them in a way that was totally unique, very bluesy, with a sound and a style that would change anybody's ideas about what a mountain dulcimer player was."

After McCutcheon introduced himself to Stamper, the latter invited him to visit. "He was a really sweet guy, and our personalities hit it right off. So I went and I visited him the next week. He played some for me, and I said, 'Would you mind if I taped you?' Then he heard me play and he asked if he could tape me. So it was an interesting kind of exchange."

By the mid-1970s McCutcheon was beginning to make a name for himself with folk fans by performing at small clubs and major festivals. A number of times he shared the bill with Johnny Cash, who was so impressed with McCutcheon's artistry that when his daughter Rosanne married Rodney Crowell in 1979 he asked John to perform. Introducing him to a wedding group that included people like Ricky Skaggs and Chet Atkins, McCutcheon recalled for Wilcock, "he said, 'This is just the most impressive instrumentalist I've ever heard.' I was sitting next to Tommy Thompson of the Red Clay Ramblers, and he wrote the comment down on a napkin and shoved it over to me. He said, 'If you don't use that quote, you're crazy.'"

After his travel odysseys of the early 1970s, John taught for a year at Clinch Valley College in Wise, Virginia, where he combined his academic pursuits with as many live performances as he could squeeze into his spare time. In the years that followed, his concert work took him to many parts of the United States and Canada as well as to such other places as Europe, Nicaragua, and Australia. He organized the U.S.–U.S.S.R. Friendship Tour, which included Gregory Gladkov. They played twenty-five concerts in each of the two countries. In the 1990s, still a familiar figure on the folk circuit, including serving as the headliner for many years at the Walnut Valley Festival in Winfield, Kansas, he was dubbed by one newspaper reporter as "the hardest working man in folk music."

In the late 1970s and early 1980s McCutcheon was beginning to accumulate recording credits, starting with the June Appal albums *How Can I Keep from Singing?* (1975) and *The Wind That Shakes the Barley* (1977), the latter being the first release to showcase his unique dulcimer skills. Those were followed by *Barefoot Boy with Boots On* (1980) on Front Hall Records and *Fine Times at Our House* (1982) on the Green Hays label. A *Washington Post* critic called the latter album a gem. By the mid-1980s he had signed with Rounder Records and turned out albums like *Howjadoo!* in 1983 and *Signs of the Times* (1986) and *Step by Step* (1986). The first of those was a children's album, reflecting in part the insights he gained from his two young children, born in the early 1980s. *Howjadoo!* won the National Association of Independent Record Distributors Indie Award for Best Children's Album, while *Step by Step* won the 1986 Indie for Best String Album. *Signs of the Times,* a live album which won the Parent's Choice Award for 1986, was reissued by Rounder in 1994 with additional cuts.

In the second half of the 1980s McCutcheon continued to record albums for both adult and children's audiences that sparkled with ingenuity and sensitive singing and playing. Rounder releases comprised *Winter Solstice* (1984) (called one of the ten best albums of the year by the *Kansas City Star*); *Gonna Rise Again* (1987) (named one of the year's ten best by the *Boston Globe* critic); *Mail Myself to You* (1988) (a Parent's Choice Gold Medal winner, also named a Recording of Notable Merit by the American Library Association); and *Water from Another Time* (1989). In the '90s there was no letup in McCutcheon's prodigious recording efforts, nor in the quality of his new releases. His children's albums included *Rainbow Sign* (1992) and *Family Garden* (1993), both widely praised, as were his other albums of the first half of the decade, *What It's Like* (1990); *Live at Wolf Trap* (1991); *Between the Eclipse* (1995); and

the early '95 *Summersongs,* the first of his *Four Seasons* series of seasonally themed family albums. The album won the 1995 National Association of Parenting Publications gold medal. The second in the series, *Wintersongs,* was issued by Rounder in the fall along with John's nineteenth collection, *Nothing to Lose.* Besides his recordings, by the mid-1990s he had two songbooks, both published by the Hal Leonard Corp., *John McCutcheon—Stone by Stone* and *Water from Another Time—Songs from John McCutcheon.*

Over the years McCutcheon remained active in many activities he believed were socially important. An example in the '90s was his chairmanship of the "Libros para Niños" books-for-kids project, which was founded by an American woman living in Nicaragua. It was supported by the University of Wisconsin Platteville Center for the Arts in 1992 as part of a sister-city project. (The Platteville City Council in 1992 passed a resolution officially recognizing Mateare, Nicaragua, as its sister community.) McCutcheon, who first went to Nicaragua in 1986, oversaw the transfer of the program to Nicaraguans. It is currently in use in nearly every school in the country. In 1994 and 1999 McCutcheon went to Mateare to sing and play for the children of the town. McCutcheon also served on the board of Grassroots Leadership, a regional community organizing group in the south, for ten years.

In the spring of 1997, Rounder released *Sprout Wings and Fly,* John's first all-acoustic (mostly traditional) album in fifteen years, followed by *Bigger than Yourself* in the summer of 1997. The latter includes songs (written with Si Kahn) about organizing for kids. "The idea was to write all the songs about these ideas—playing fair, pooling resources," McCutcheon says. It won the Parent's Choice Gold Medal Award and received a Grammy nomination for Best Children's Album. He has also received Grammy nominations for *Summersongs* (1995), *Wintersongs* (1995), *Autumnsongs* (1998) and *Springsongs* (1999).

In the fall of 1997 Rounder released a live album with Tom Chapin called *Doing Our Job.* McCutcheon also had a children's book published by Little, Brown called *Happy Adoption Day,* based on his song by the same title from his 1992 album *Family Garden,* with illustrations by Julie Paschkis. Rounder Records is currently reissuing McCutcheon's earlier recordings on CD, including 1980's *Barefoot Boy with Boots On,* rereleased in October 1998.

In 1997 McCutcheon began his term as the first president of the American Federation of Musicians Local 1000, formed for the traveling folk musicians whose issues differ from symphony and studio musicians who mostly stay in one place (www.local1000.com). "It's an Un-local, it's nongeographical," says McCutcheon. Members in the local range from Pete Seeger and Bernice Reagon to Dan Bern, Ani DiFranco, and Christine Lavin.

Holding regular meetings is difficult, but the local has set up a web site and a permanent chat room. They also hold informal get-togethers ("showcase free zones") at the annual meeting of the North American Folk Alliance of Music and Dance. The meetings are unique, to say the least. "It's amazing to say, 'Brother Pete Seeger, why don't you open it up with a song, and then Brother Utah Phillips, please tell us a story,' " says McCutcheon.

More information about John McCutcheon can be obtained at his web site: www.folkmusic.com.

Based in part on a phone interview with John Mc-Cutcheon on December 24, 1998

McDONALD, COUNTRY JOE: *Singer, guitarist, harmonica player, songwriter, band leader (the Fish). Born Washington, D.C., January 1, 1942.*

Country Joe McDonald didn't grow up in the country nor did he specialize in country music. He was essentially a member of the urban folk movement of the 1960s and, as such, identified with the many protest songs of the period. This identification tended to mask the fact that he was first and foremost an entertainer, and a good one, whose repertoire included songs of all kinds covering a wide range of topics.

He was born in Washington, D.C., and raised in the Los Angeles suburb of El Monte, which at the time had a strong following for country music, providing a sizable audience for the Los Angeles–area country radio and TV programs. During Joe's preteen years he did listen to a lot of those programs, but by the time he entered high school in the mid-1950s, rock 'n' roll was all the rage. Like most of his peer groups, Joe was a fan of early rockabilly stars like Elvis, Jerry Lee Lewis, and Bill Haley.

In high school, Joe became involved in teenage bands and, to a limited extent, school politics. He formed a rock group called the Nomads that performed at local parties and school events, with Joe handling lead vocals plus some still tentative instrumental work on guitar and harmonica. When a friend of his ran for student body president at El Monte High School, Joe wrote his campaign song, aided in the effort by other band members. The song, called "I Seen a Rocket," was composed "while we all were high on cigarettes and black coffee." It was, he noted wryly, "my first political act."

Ironically, considering his future course as a major antiwar activist, McDonald's first step after leaving high school was to sign up for a four-year hitch in the U.S. Navy. During those navy years, though, his musical tastes gradually shifted from rock to the folk music that swept the United States for a time in the late 1950s and early 1960s. Before he received his discharge, he had added a number of traditional folk songs to his repertoire.

From the navy, McDonald went back to the L.A. area and spent a year at Los Angeles City College. Af-fected by the growing restlessness among people of his generation, caused in part by the civil rights movement and growing opposition to involvement in the Vietnam War, he became discouraged about the LACC environment. His views about political conditions at home had started to alter and, while still at LACC, he had written a number of protest songs. He always stressed that he believed in basing one's views on the conditions that existed at the time. "The most revolutionary thing you can do in this country is change your mind."

Changing his mind about where he wanted to live, McDonald left Los Angeles and moved north to Berkeley, where he soon was performing in some of the small folk clubs and coffeehouses in the Bay Area. He made his first recordings in 1964 with Blair Hardman, released in the 1970s as *The Goodbye Blues*. He soon met and formed a strong friendship with guitarist Barry Melton, who, in 1965, joined him in forming Country Joe and the Fish with such other performers as David Cohen and "Chicken" Hirsh. In a short time, the group was a familiar presence at various festivals and political gatherings and also often was featured at a coffeehouse called the Jabberwock. The group soon developed a trademark routine, which began with the "Fish cheer," where the audience was asked to spell out either the band name or another four-letter word, followed by the band's rendition of the Country Joe composition "I Feel Like I'm Fixin' to Die Rag." The song, which became an anthem of the antiwar movement, first appeared in recorded form on an extended-play version of a music magazine called *Rag Baby* in 1965. The magazine, one of the first notable underground publications, was published by Joe and Ed Denson, a onetime editor of *Sing Out!* magazine who became Joe's manager.

In late 1966, Denson got the band its first record contract with New York–based Vanguard Records, and their debut LP, *Electric Music for the Mind and Body,* came out in April 1967. The album contained some songs that appealed to some of the radical adherents of the political movements of those times, but many that were more general in tone. In fact, though McDonald was against the Vietnam War, in many ways he was a moderate in philosophy. He often performed at the love-ins of the "flower children" of those years, sometimes passing up radical political gatherings to do so. In an effort at "cross-pollenization," he usually appeared at love-in concerts with all kinds of political buttons pinned to an old army shirt and at mass demonstrations with the band's amplifiers covered with daisies.

His debut LP did reasonably well, thanks to word of mouth promotions, and the song "Not So Sweet Martha Lorraine" became a favorite with fans both in the United States and in Europe. The band's first European tour in December 1967 demonstrated they were a hit with overseas rock fans. In the summer of 1968, McDonald demonstrated anew his nonviolent stand. Though he was supposed to lead the Fish at the Yippie Festival of

Life in Chicago during the Democratic convention, he withdrew the Fish at the last moment. As he said at the Chicago conspiracy trial, "The vibrations were so incredibly vicious that I thought it was impossible to avoid violence on the part of the police. . . . there was a possibility that people would follow us to the Festival and be clubbed and maced and tear gassed. . . . I had no choice."

His second LP, which contained "I Feel Like I'm Fixin' to Die Rag," came out in early 1968 and his third, *Together,* in October 1968. Album number two included one of his best-known compositions, "Janis," a moving song about the great Joplin that, as Norma Whittaker pointed out, "turned out to be a tragically prophetic song."

Joe's interest in experimentation was emphasized in his fourth LP, *Here We Are Again,* released in May 1969. Joining him and original Fish members Cohen, Melton, and Hirsh were such varied contributors as members of the Count Basie Band, musicians from the Oakland Symphony, David Getz and Peter Albin of Big Brother and the Holding Company, and Jack Casady from Jefferson Airplane. Some rock critics complained he had retreated from his hard rock posture of previous years to more restrained stylings. His reply was "There is absolutely no reason why electronic music cannot draw on every musical tradition."

The year 1969 was a busy one for McDonald and the Fish. In the summer they were cheered by the half million attendees at the now legendary Woodstock concert. In midyear, Vanguard released *The Greatest Hits of Country Joe & the Fish* and, after a highly successful European tour in the fall, it issued *C. J. Fish,* a live compilation from that tour. In Europe, Joe completed an assignment to write and perform the music for a Danish film based on the Henry Miller novel *Quiet Days in Clichy.*

Joe was beginning to find his band association restrictive. In November 1969, he began to work on his debut solo LP on Vanguard, *Thinking of Woody Guthrie.* The collection suggested he was becoming more interested in his early folk and country roots. After the *Woody* LP, issued in January 1970, he stated thinking about a new collection of country-flavored material. During 1970, he went to Nashville to record that material, released under the title *Tonight I'm Singing Just for You.* He continued to add to his solo catalog throughout the early 1970s with a series of albums that caused one reviewer to write, "To an ever greater extent, he is the closest thing to the Woody Guthrie of the 1970s." His third solo LP was *Hold on—It's Coming;* his fourth, released in 1971, was based on the Robert W. Service World War I book of poems, *Rhymes of a Red Cross Man;* and his fifth, issued in early 1972, was *Incredible Live.* Also released in late 1971 was a retrospective album of his band years, *Life and Times of Country Joe and the Fish.*

By then, Joe had essentially turned his back on rock in favor of being a folk-music troubadour. The road was a tough one to travel in a period long past folk music's halcyon days. McDonald found himself playing to small audiences in minor halls with a sprinkling of college dates as well. One of his political causes at the time was women's equality. During 1973, for example, he toured with a band called the All Stars whose four members included three women, his song sets typically including several numbers condemning sexism.

In early 1975, he ended his long association with Vanguard, which often had been marked by stormy arguments about musical directions between Joe and that label's executives. His credits on the label comprised sixteen albums, both solo and with the Fish. Later that year he signed with Oakland, California–based Fantasy Records, which issued his first LP on the label, *Paradise with an Ocean View,* and first single, "Breakfast for Two," in late 1975. In 1976 Fantasy issued his second album on the label, *Love Is a Fire.* The same year, Vanguard released a retrospective set, *The Essential Country Joe McDonald,* and Warner Brothers issued *A Tribute to Woody.* In early 1978 Fantasy issued a new LP of his titled *Rock and Roll Music from the Planet Earth,* which featured, significantly, the track "Bring Back the Sixties, Man." He closed out the decade with two more Fantasy LPs, *Goodbye Blues* and *Leisure Suite.*

Joe admitted that one of the things hampering his career in the 1970s was his image problem as a "protest music" artist. Since such songs had become somewhat passé with new generations of fans in that decade, that label tended to keep people away from his concerts. As he told an interviewer in the mid 1970s, he felt that it was a bum rap. "People who know my music know that not much of it is protest stuff. Out of a catalog of about two hundred and fifty songs, I have about ten songs that you could call protest songs. The rest are all kinds of songs."

Of course, if Joe avoided politics as such, that didn't mean he wasn't involved in causes. During the 1970s, for instance, he worked for conservationist causes such as the Greenpeace Foundation. In connection with those activities, he wrote the song "Save the Whales" in the mid-1970s. He also spoke out for veterans' rights and performed at a Washington, D.C., rally in the spring of 1982 against federal cutbacks in veterans' health care programs.

During the 1980s, Joe became more outspoken about the need for a change of attitude toward Vietnam servicemen and women. While he still felt the war was wrong, he stressed he had always been proud of his own navy years, even when he was singing "I Feel Like I'm Fixin' to Die Rag." He told Steve Hochman of the *Los Angeles Times* ("Country Joe Singing a Pro-Veteran Tune Now," February 24, 1986), "At Woodstock there was such a negative feeling toward the military that I subconsciously blocked it [his service] from my mind."

As a step toward making what he believed were deserved amends to Vietnam servicepeople, he was one of the organizers of the February '86 Welcome Home Inc. concert, intended to raise funds for various Vietnam veteran outreach and counseling programs and public consciousness-raising projects. He told Hochman at the time, "I don't think that being a veteran is acceptable today in any mainstream sense, and I find that a very strange contradiction in the American mind-set. The fantasy Rambo is in, but the reality of what it means to be soldiering is not in.

"People can correct me if I'm wrong, but I thought that military service to your country was an honorable thing to do and recognition of those who served is also an honorable thing." Besides McDonald, others performing in the show included Kris Kristofferson, Brian Wilson, Herbie Hancock, Charlie Daniels, Neil Young, and Richie Havens.

McDonald continued to pursue this theme in his solo concerts through the 1980s and into the '90s, sometimes including songs on the subject in the albums he released on his own Rag Baby label, like the '86 LP *The Vietnam Experience.* On November 11, 1996, he unveiled a memorial in Berkeley, California's Veterans Memorial Building honoring the city's twenty-two Vietnam War dead. He told *People* magazine ("Making Amends, Country Joe McDonald Honors the Veterans of a War He Scorned," November 27, 1995), "Blaming soldiers for war is like blaming firefighters for fire." At the dedication ceremonies for the memorial, which he designed and funded, he said, "The healing is still going on. It may take the rest of our lives."

In addition to his work with Vietnam veteran groups, McDonald became interested in the life of military nurse Florence Nightingale, even traveling to Turkey to conduct research on her activities during the Crimean War. He wrote a song about her activities in the Crimea called "The Lady with the Lamp," which he included on his 1995 CD, *Carry On,* licensed to Shanachie.

In 1990 Vanguard released the retrospective CD *The Best of Country Joe McDonald.* The following year he released a collection of originals on his CD *Superstitious Blues,* released on Rag Baby and licensed to Rykodisc. The CD included two songs that he recorded with Jerry Garcia. He followed that with *Carry On* and *Something Borrowed, Something New* in 1998, licensed to Big Beat Records. In 1998–99 McDonald began working on a project with Stephen Barsottie, who plays bass with his band. The goal was to create moods similar to his 1966 Country Joe & the Fish release, *Electric Music for the Mind and Body.*

McDOWELL, "MISSISSIPPI" FRED: *Singer, songwriter, guitarist. Born Rossville, Tennessee, January 12, 1904; died Memphis, Tennessee, July 3, 1972.*

Though he was born and died in Tennessee, "Mississippi" Fred McDowell earned his nickname because he spent much of his life in Como, Mississippi. More important, his gritty slide guitar sound emanates from such Delta greats as Son House. Unlike Son House, however, McDowell never got a chance to record until he was fifty-five. He was a purist, of sorts, who didn't care much for rock music and even titled his 1969 Grammy-winning album for Capitol *I Don't Play No Rock and Roll,* a tongue-in-cheek title since he played electric guitar throughout the album. He influenced such blues-rock artists as Bonnie Raitt and the Rolling Stones, who recorded his song "You Gotta Move" on *Sticky Fingers.*

McDowell, whose parents were farmers, spent his youth in Rossville, Tennessee. His parents passed away when he was young. As a child he taught himself how to play guitar, using a slide made from a steer bone. He began performing at local dances, though he couldn't afford his own guitar. He later moved to Memphis and began traveling throughout the Delta in search of work, playing at dances, picnics, and fish fries in the 1920s and '30s. (In 1928 he heard Charley Patton play at a work site, which influenced his playing.) He settled in Como in 1940 with his wife Annie Mae Collins, a singer with whom he recorded. He worked as a farmer in Como and played for neighbors at local dances or for tips at a candy store in town. He could finally buy his own guitar.

But he wasn't "discovered" by an audience beyond the Delta until 1959. That year folklorist Alan Lomax recorded McDowell for his *Southern Folk Heritage* twenty LP series released by Atlantic and Prestige. In his book *The Land Where the Blues Began,* Lomax called McDowell "a bluesman quite the equal of Son House and Muddy Waters but, musically speaking, their granddaddy."

During the early 1960s McDowell played at the Newport and Chicago folk festivals, among others in the United States. (Portions of his live performances at Newport were released by Vanguard.) In 1964, Chris Strachwitz of Arhoolie Records came to Como and made the first of several recordings that broadened McDowell's following: *Fred McDowell (Volumes 1 and 2).* In 1965, McDowell toured with the American Folk Blues Festival in England and Europe, and at folk clubs throughout the States. During the 1960s he also recorded for the Testament, Biograph, Everest, Polydor, and Revival labels. He was featured in several documentary films: *The Blues Maker* (1968), *Fred McDowell* (1969), and *Roots of American Music: Country Urban Music, Part 3* (1971).

Before he passed away, McDowell managed to buy a gas station on Highway 61, near Como. But in 1971, he was stricken by cancer. He died the following year in Memphis, but was buried at the Hammond Hill Church cemetery in Como, Mississippi. In 1991, he was named to the Blues Foundation Hall of Fame.

Many of his albums are still available on CD or on vinyl, including: *Mississippi Fred McDowell* (Flyright), *Shake 'Em on Down* (Tomato), *Somebody Keeps Calling Me* (Antilles), *I Do Not Play No Rock 'n' Roll* (Capitol), *I Do Not Play No Rock 'n' Roll: Complete Sessions* (an expanded reissue of his 1969 album), *Fred McDowell and His Blues Boys* (Arhoolie), *You Gotta Move* (Arhoolie), *Good Morning Little School Girl* (Arhoolie), *This Ain't No Rock 'n' Roll* (Arhoolie), *Fred McDowell* (Testament), *Amazing Grace* (Testament), *My Home is in the Delta* (Testament), *Levee Camp Blues* (Testament), *Standing at the Burying Ground* (Sequel, a live recording from a 1969 London concert), *Steakbone Slide Guitar* (Rykodisc/Tradition), *Long Way From Home* (Fantasy), *Ain't Gonna Worry* (Drive Archive), *Mississippi Blues* (Black Lion), *This Train I Ride* (New Rose), *Live at the Mayfair Hotel* (Warner Brothers), *What's the Matter with Papa's Little Girl* (Iris), *Mississippi Fred McDowell* (Rounder), *Fred McDowell and Johnny Woods* (Rounder), and *First Recordings* (Rounder).

McEUEN, JOHN: *Singer, guitarist, five-string banjo player, mandolinist, accordionist, steel guitarist, fiddler, record producer. Born Oakland, California, December 19, 1945.*

For some twenty years multitalented instrumentalist and singer John McEuen was a central figure in the saga of the band variously known as the Nitty Gritty Dirt Band or the Dirt Band. He played a major role in shaping the band's blend of folk, country, and rock, which helped it maintain its position as a landmark group despite many changes in membership and in the public's musical tastes. Through it all, though, McEuen retained an independent spirit, finding time for his own solo projects as a recording artist and live stage act. His live sets showcased his diverse performing skills and puckish sense of humor.

Early on, McEuen was inspired to learn banjo by Doug Dillard of the Dillards. By his mid-teens in Long Beach, California, he could already play banjo and guitars well enough to earn entry into groups with high school friends, including comedian-banjoist Steve Martin. He was particularly influenced by the folk-music boom of those years, and spent time at some of the favored hangouts for local folk artists, like the Los Angeles Ash Grove and McCabe's Guitar Shop in Santa Monica. It was two other Long Beach High students, Bruce Kunkel and Jeff Hanna, who founded the first version of the Nitty Gritty Dirt Band, drawing on the talents of other young performers they met at McCabe's—Les Thompson, Jimmie Fadden, Ralph Barr, and Jackson Browne—for the first roster in May 1966. Browne, however, only stayed with the group a few months; when he left, John McEuen took his place.

McEuen helped record the group's first two LPs, issued during 1966–67: *Nitty Gritty Dirt Band* and *Ricochet,* from which came the group's first hit single, the

top 20 "Buy for Me the Rain." By 1968 Bruce Kunkel had left and Chris Darrow was added, but McEuen remained on board to contribute to the albums *Rare Junk* and *Alive* and take part in concert work that included jamming with jazz great Dizzy Gillespie and opening for Bill Cosby at Carnegie Hall in New York. After the group disbanded in 1969, deciding to shift home base to Colorado, McEuen made that move and joined Hanna, Fadden, Les Thompson, and Jimmy Ibbotson in a new quintet that recruited many country-music greats for the August 1970 Nashville sessions that resulted in the three-record *Will the Circle Be Unbroken* set, which earned a platinum record from the R.I.A.A. and earned two Grammy nominations. The band also earned a top 10 single for its version of Jerry Jeff Walker's "Mr. Bojangles" in January '71.

(Reflecting on buyer response to *Will the Circle Be Unbroken* in 1996, McEuen said, "We've been told the *Circle* album did over a million units as a three-record set. I think it brought to the attention of the Dirt Band's audience and a lot of other people . . . where that inspiration came from. It showed that the bridge [between different genres] was possible.")

For the rest of the 1970s and into the 1980s, McEuen was a pillar of strength in a group that became famous in many other parts of the world while turning out a string of albums and singles that often made top chart positions in markets like Japan, England, and Europe. Besides conventional tour venues, the band's credits included being featured at a wide range of festivals at home and abroad, including—at various times—folk, country, bluegrass, blues, and rock gatherings, an example of the last-named being an appearance in the mid-'70s before a crowd of 190,000 people in 103° heat in Sedalia, Missouri.

McEuen's and the group's highlight memories of the mid-'70s included a 1977 concert tour of the Soviet Union, the first such series permitted for an American pop group by Russian authorities. The visit included a concert presented on Soviet TV that was watched by an estimated 145,000,000 people. As John enthused, "Russia was very exciting. Being part of America's first band to go to Russia in 1977 was an extremely exhilarating experience. Russia wanted to bring over an American group and they ended up picking us. We had nothing to do with it." That was one of his favorite experiences, he said. "Other than that I'd say playing on the Grand Ole Opry stage, the couple of times that I've done it, was a favorite. Pretending I was Uncle Dave Macon and doing an old-time traditional thing."

Among his fond memories of the 1970s, he also noted, was performing on a radio show with Lester Flatt. To do that, he had to get up at the ungodly hour (for an entertainer) of 5:00 A.M. "It was Marty Stuart who picked me up and said, 'Be in the lobby in fifteen minutes.' Marty and I had been friends a long time and he knew that I'd grumble, but I'd be there. He said, 'Bring your banjo.' 'Where are we going?' 'You'll find out when we get there.' We get there and it's WSM [in Nashville], the morning show where he was playing with Lester Flatt.

"There I am watching the Martha White morning show and it actually happened. It was like going back in history. The thing that surprised me was just before the commercial break Flatt said, 'We've got a young man in the studio who's going to sit in on the banjo right after this commercial.' So here I am looking around and I'm the only guy with a banjo that was visiting. So here I am frantically tuning up and Flatt says, 'John, what song have you got picked out to play for us today?' The only one I could think of was 'Earl's Breakdown' [written by Earl Scruggs, Flatt's former partner]. He said, 'That sounds mighty fine.'

"This was," McEuen noted, "way after they broke up. This was when Marty Stuart was playing with him and hadn't started his own career yet. I'd hire Marty to back me up and usually pay him $50 or $60 a night—on good nights, maybe even $65. And all the food, of course."

From the late '70s into the first half of the 1980s, McEuen remained in the Dirt Band fold, but increasingly performed on his own between band engagements. Besides concert work, he was also featured from time to time on major TV programs like *The Tonight Show* and *Saturday Night Live*. He was still performing with the Dirt Band during the 1983–86 time period when his band mates comprised Hanna, Fadden, Ibbotson, and Bob Carpenter. The group's record output during those years included the albums *Let's Go* (Universal, 1983), *Plain Dirt Fashion* ('84), and *Partners, Brothers and Friends* ('85), and the hit singles (on country charts) "Dance Little Jean," "Long Hard Road (Sharecropper's Dream)," and "Modern Day Romance," the last two providing the NGDB with its first number one singles.

Among other things in the mid-'80s, John performed with the group at the 1984 Olympic Games and at Willie Nelson's Farm Aid. His contributions also were key elements of the *Twenty Years of Dirt* album issued to coincide with the standing-room-only twentieth anniversary concert at the McNichols Arena in Denver. The show, in which stars like Ricky Skaggs, Emmylou Harris, Michael Martin Murphy, Doc Watson, John Prine, Rodney Crowell, and others appeared in support of the group, commemorated the NGDB's first performance at the Paradox in Orange, California, on May 13, 1966. McEuen had not yet become a member at that time, but he could celebrate his own twentieth anniversary with the group during the summer.

In 1987, after having released twenty-two albums and earning four Grammy nominations, John left the band to focus on a solo career. Though some observers thought the separation might only be temporary, as of the late-'90s the band continued on its way without McEuen. He commented in 1996 about rejoining the group, "That's not my call. I've played with them a couple of times since I left. I don't control that. I love that music. I love playing behind the guys when they're singing. I hope that happens."

The 1987–88 time period, McEuen told Lyndon Stambler, was one of the most difficult ones of his life. "There was a month in 1988 when I had separated from my wife. We had been married eighteen years and I had six kids. I left the Dirt Band and I moved out to live on my own for the first time in my life. That was a tough month. In a nutshell, that was a significant down. I didn't have a record label, agent, or manager." While he and his wife never got back together, John stated in 1996, "It's one of those things where people are inclined to say, 'Yeah, now we're really good friends.' And not understanding why we couldn't have been good friends then. It was tough. Six kids, grew apart, whatever it was, but things are OK. About two years ago, I feel like I got my career started. It's under way at a better level than it's ever been."

His breakup with his wife and the Dirt Band situation caused a lot of soul-searching, he recalled. "It took me a couple years before I felt worthy of going into a studio after leaving the Dirt Band, which was also a separation. The difference with the Dirt Band was I was president of the corporation. I was responsible for handling things, signing the contracts. I did about 95 percent of the interviews. That was over. No more interviews, no more agents to talk to. I was going out on the road and working, but it was not progressive. Sometimes it was the best therapy a person could get through. It was very difficult to go on and come off and have people say, 'Oh, man, I loved the show. That was great, your music's great.' Here you are in the middle of your life being shattered, right? 'Well, thank you very much.' Now I've got to go back to a hotel room by myself, call no one because the kids are asleep, then go home and wait."

By the early '90s McEuen had begun to put his life and career back in some kind of order as he continued to maintain a schedule of concerts at folk and country venues or festivals each year. He formed a group called the String Wizards, which included Tom Corbett on mandolin, Randy Tico on bass, Phil Salazar on fiddle, Jesse Siebenberg on percussion, and McEuen's son Jonathan on guitar (Jonathan released his debut CD, *Sampolin 14,* in 1998.) Vanguard released the group's *String Wizards* in 1991, followed by the Grammy-nominated *String Wizards II* in 1993. In 1997 the label released *String Wizards' Picks,* a "best of" collection from McEuen's Vanguard years, which was put out in the "enhanced" CD-ROM format.

He was a familiar presence at the annual get-together of the Folk Alliance organization formed by artists and entrepreneurs from that field in the late 1980s, typically performing at some of the workshop sessions. At the

1996 Alliance meeting, he was looking forward to release of a new album on Vanguard, *Acoustic Traveller.* "With *Acoustic Traveller* I'm trying to bridge all the experiences I've had on the road, which is playing over four thousand different places. And that goes from bluegrass to folk music to pop music to sometimes being in a foreign country in Europe and hearing those sounds that people are making that somehow the notes seem to be related to what you might hear out of Kentucky. Even if you're in Armenia. Trying to put that together in a sound picture. It's like musical photographs of places I've been over the years."

The album production, he also pointed out, drew on his many years with his old band. "One thing I think that's important in recording is to try to create depth instead of just a right-left stereo picture, where you have a guitar on the right, the bass in the middle, and another instrument between right and left and then something on the hard left. What you need to do is give things a sense of space, like there's one guy right in front of you and there's someone beside him playing. Maybe somewhere between the two of them there's a percussion guy. Or there's somebody hitting a certain chord that washes across the entire sweep that goes from back left to front right. By treating your EQ and your echo sends during your mix you can create a depth in the mix with acoustic instruments that you quite often hear on pop records or rock 'n' roll type of recordings. I've mainly come to that through working with the Dirt Band for twenty years and the recording process and doing film scores and different kinds of recording and working with great engineers."

McEuen has also done work for movies and television. He composed the score for the National Geographic Society's *Braving Alaska,* which received an Emmy nomination for best score. He also produced the music for a PBS miniseries called *The Wild West,* composed the score for the Tommy Lee Jones–directed movie *The Good Old Boys,* and produced a ninety-minute video documentary on the Dillards, *A Night in the Ozarks.* In 1997 he made a cameo appearance on the Nitty Gritty Dirt Band's *Christmas Album* on Rising Tide Records. The following year, he produced an album by Seminole chief Jim Billie called *Alligator Tales,* released on Sound of America Records. In 1999, McEuen released *Round Trip* on Chrome Records, a live album.

McEuen quotes from interview with Lyndon Stambler at 1996 Folk Alliance Convention in Washington, D.C.

McGARRIGLE, KATE AND ANNA: *Vocal duo, songwriters, guitarists, pianists, accordionists, banjoists. Anna, born Montreal, Quebec, Canada, December 4, 1944. Kate, born Montreal, Quebec, Canada, February 6, 1946.*

Kate and Anna McGarrigle have not yet achieved the level of popularity and record sales of contemporary performers such as Linda Ronstadt, Emmylou Harris, the Roches, Leonard Cohen, or Maria Muldaur, but they comprise one of the most musically and lyrically gifted sister folk duos originating in the early 1970s' second-generation folk-pop movement. They went their own musical way, never slavishly imitating anyone for the sake of tagging onto a popular style. Because of their iconoclasm they are all the more adored by their devoted musical followers.

Kate and Anna were born in Montreal in 1946 and 1944, respectively. An older sister, Jane, also sang professionally with them for a short period. They grew up in St. Saveur-des-Mont, in the Laurentian Mountains of Quebec, about forty-five miles north of Montreal. Their interest in music came from their father, Frank, and his side of the family. Frank's father became the first movie theater exhibitor in New Brunswick around 1906, according to an article by Mike Regenstreif, "Kate & Anna McGarrigle: On Their Own Terms" (in the February–March 1997 issue of *Sing Out!*). Between screenings, the young Frank and his sister, Anna, would sing Stephen Foster tunes and turn-of-the-century parlor songs.

"Music was always there at home," Kate told Regenstreif. "My father would sit at the piano at night and play those songs. At parties, somebody would get up and sing, and my father would accompany them and sing the harmony. There were lots of friends and uncles and each would get up and give their big song."

Kate continued, in an interview with Richard Silverstein: "We were children of the middle class. My dad played funny ditties and drinking songs from the 1930s. We didn't really have an Irish folk tradition even though we were half Irish. . . . There was no Irish folk tradition because they were subsumed under the prevailing English Canadian culture. The French, on the other hand, were quite the opposite. As an oppressed people, it was quite important for them to remember their language, history, and music. No conqueror would take that away from them."

The McGarrigle sisters' mom, Gaby, was also musical. She once played violin in the Bell Telephone Orchestra. Gaby loved the old music hall songs that were popular in the era after she was born (1904). The daughters told Regenstreif the story of their mother accompanying her father to the burlesque shows at Montreal's legendary Gayety Theatre during World War I: "Gaby's dad was French Canadian and didn't understand English that well and she used to go to translate for him." One morning during that period, she came to school quite late. "Gabrielle, why are you late?" demanded a nun. "I had to go to the Gayety with my father," she replied, to the consternation of her classmates.

The young McGarrigle sisters took piano lessons from the nuns of St. Saveur. At the age of ten, Kate remembers her dad showing her guitar chords. There were also a ukulele, a banuke (a banjo with a ukulele neck), and a zither around the house.

In the 1950s Kate and Anna listened to popular

music of the era: Carl Perkins and the Everly Brothers. "Janie had gone away to boarding school in Ontario when she was fourteen, and she really got into country music. . . . She introduced us to a lot of songs that otherwise we might not have heard," Anna told Regenstreif. On Saturday nights "on a good night, the clear signal [of WWVA] from Wheeling, West Virginia, crossed hundreds of miles and international borders" to be heard by two sisters hungry for this music from another world.

In the 1960s the McGarrigles were Montreal high school students. They once sneaked out of the house to see a Pete Seeger concert with an older friend of whom their parents disapproved. They discovered folk music, and from that moment Kate wanted her own banjo. Then they saw the Weavers and quickly formed a folksinging trio with a high school friend. They sang songs like "Swing Low, Sweet Chariot" and appeared at the Finjan, an early-'60s Montreal coffeehouse owned by Simon Asch.

In 1962 they met Peter Weldon and Jack Nissenson, members of a Montreal traditional folk group called the Pharisees. Weldon and Nissenson knew folk legends like Ewan MacColl and Peggy Seeger. They even owned Montreal's first Joseph Spence albums. The McGarrigles joined Nissenson and Weldon as the Mountain City Four.

Kate told Silverstein: "We entered into the folk scene through the records of Joan Baez and Bob Dylan. But when we met Nissenson and Weldon, they introduced us to music at the sources and said, 'Forget about Joan Baez! Go to the sources at all times. Don't copy styles, just learn the original music.' I think that's why we have an original sound. We didn't try to imitate anyone, with the possible exception of Dylan, who everyone tried to imitate at one time or another."

While performing with the Mountain City Four, Kate and Anna began singing traditional standards like "Willie Moore"; Carter Family songs like "Lonesome Valley"; French Canadian songs like "V'La L'Bon Vent"; contemporary folksongs like "Land of the Muskeg"; and Arthur Crudup's "Mean Old 'Frisco." In the Montreal folk scene, the McGarrigles met Galt McDermott, who later composed the music for *Hair*, Broadway's first rock musical. McDermott songs "No Biscuit Blues" and "Cover Up My Head" made it onto the McGarrigles' second and third Warner Brothers albums, *Dancer with Bruised Knees* and *Pronto Monto*.

Eventually, Chaim Tannenbaum, Dane Lanken (who later married Anna), and others joined the Mountain City Four. Meanwhile, Kate studied engineering at McGill and Anna took painting courses at L'Ecole Beaux Arts. It was during this period they met the French lyricist Philippe Tatartcheff, who studied at McGill and eventually completed his Ph.D. at the Sorbonne in Paris.

Kate decided to pursue a musical career in New York after college. She and Roma Baran formed a duo: with Kate on piano and Roma on guitar, performing old blues and folksongs as well as McGarrigle originals. They played the Gaslight and Gerde's Folk City in New York. They received a record offer but turned it down.

In this period, both Kate and Anna began to write their own songs. Anna's first song was "Heart Like a Wheel." Incredibly (when one thinks of the song's subsequent popularity after it was recorded by Linda Ronstadt), Anna had no performing ambitions. The way Anna tells it, her lack of interest in performing helped her hone her writing skills.

Kate's musical maturity came slower, until, inspired by the burgeoning folk songwriting scene, she wrote "The Work Song" and one of their most haunting ballads, "Talk to Me of Mendocino."

Kate and Roma's musical breakthrough came at the 1970 Philadelphia Folk Festival, where their Saturday night performance drew a rave *New York Times* review. They opened for Jerry Jeff Walker at the Gaslight. When Jerry Jeff heard their closing tune, "Heart Like a Wheel," he asked for a demo tape to send to Linda Ronstadt, who was putting together songs for a solo album.

In 1971, Roma and Kate split up. Roma returned to school and Kate married Loudon Wainwright III, who covered "We've Come a Long Way." Maria Muldaur covered "The Work Song." The group McKendree Spring recorded "Heart Like a Wheel" in 1972. Kate and Anna's big break came in 1974, when Ronstadt put "Heart Like a Wheel" on her album by the same name.

Maria Muldaur invited Kate to sing harmony on a gospel song for one of her records. Muldaur also chose to sing Anna's "Cool River," for which producer Joe Boyd asked Kate to play piano. As Regenstreif recounts, when Kate told him she didn't know the piano track, he said, "What do you mean you don't know it? You wrote it!" She explained that Anna, her sister, wrote the song. Soon Anna said good-bye to her coworkers in Montreal and boarded a plane to L.A. When they entered the studio to make a demo tape for Warner Brothers, they didn't know each other's tunes very well because they hadn't performed together in years. "It was that afternoon [in 1974] that we became Kate and Anna McGarrigle," Kate told Regenstreif.

In May 1974, Warners offered them their first record contract. During 1975, they recorded their first album, *Kate and Anna McGarrigle*. The McGarrigles and their two producers, Greg Prestopino and Joe Boyd, had conflicting musical visions during the recording process. "Warner, at first, thought we could become the next Laura Nyro," Kate told Silverstein. "They saw us as soulful piano player chicks. When we first got into the studio, there were fights between Greg, who wanted us to have a pop sound with no folk instrumentation, [and] Joe (who claimed to have created the English folk-rock sound), who wanted an eclectic folk-pop sound. When they recorded Anna's 'Complainte Pour Ste. Catherine,' for example, we heard it Cajun," Kate recalls. "Greg heard it pop and Joe heard it reggae."

Remarkably, they completed the album, which has gone down in history as a classic. It made an auspicious debut in February 1976. *Stereo Review* named it Record of the Year, and *Melody Maker* called it Top Rock Album.

The McGarrigles had a surprise in store for record executives who saw them as the "next Nyro." It was their "quaint" idea to put childraising before their career. They never toured to support their first album—certain death for a new release—because Kate was pregnant with her second child when it came out. They went so far as to hire a band of studio musicians and book a series of dates at a Boston venue, but when they were dissatisfied with the band, they decided to bag the tour. Similarly, as they completed their second and third albums, Anna's two pregnancies complicated plans for extensive touring—enough to drive record executives to an early grave.

The debut album contains the gorgeous "Talk to Me of Mendocino," a description of a cross-country car trip in which the songwriter takes leave of the mountains of Quebec and other natural markers of her youth, only to come face-to-face with the majestic power of the Mendocino redwoods: *Talk to me of Mendocino / Closing my eyes I hear the sea: / Must I wait? Must I follow? / Won't you say: Come with me?* Rarely have poetic image, natural sound, and musical setting wedded so touchingly.

In 1976, Kate's marriage to Loudon Wainwright III ended. Returning home to Montreal with her young children, Rufus (who now has a successful recording career) and Martha, she began to collaborate more closely with Anna. They made *Dancer with Bruised Knees* (1977), which contains the gothic, alternately charming and horrifying "Perrine Etait Servante," in whose lyrics you have the diabolical charm of the McGarrigles' star-crossed lovers mixed with the nononsense "make something funny and useful out of a hard life" attitude, which represents traditional French Canadian life.

Pronto Monto (1978) contained the wonderfully quirky "NaCl," a song dedicated to the romantic possibilities inherent in physical chemistry: *Just a little atom of chlorine, valence minus one / Swimming through the sea, digging the scene, just having fun . . .*

They toured sporadically, joining Bonnie Raitt, playing New York's Bottom Line, and doing foreign gigs in England and Holland. In 1980 they played Carnegie Hall and were featured in a National Film Board of Canada documentary.

Also in the 1980s, they released *The French Record* (1981) and *Love Over and Over* (1983) (rereleased on CD in 1997 by Rykodisc). The former was originally commissioned at the height of the Quebeçois separatist movement. Says Kate: "There was a French-Canadian record company which wanted to extend a hand of friendship to us and asked us as English Canadians to produce a record for a French audience. It was a political gesture in a sense. The odd thing is that it never came out in France and we've never played in France!"

When asked why, Kate suggests, "I think their music can be insular. Also, with few exceptions, music doesn't play that large a role in French culture. You just don't hear in French music the kind of cross-fertilization that you hear in American music, for example. If you listen to Chuck Berry, the influence of New Orleans blues is unmistakable."

The French Record contains one of their finest efforts, a rocking Cajun rendition of "Complainte pour Ste. Catherine," and their first collaboration with Philippe Tatartcheff.

Much of their recording during the 1980s came about through happenstance. The mid-1980s were a fallow time for the McGarrigles and their relationship with the industry. After a National Public Radio interview, a Private Music executive called and offered them a contract to make *Heartbeats Accelerating,* which came out in 1990. "Musically, Anna and I like all different styles of music. *Heartbeats Accelerating* was written completely on synthesizers. But the record company wanted more of a folk sound, so we toned it down for them."

Kate bemoans the stresses and strains of a large touring band. "For a while that was fun," she told Regenstreif. "But then it got to be less fun. We couldn't say to so-and-so on the drums, 'Why don't you sit this one out.'"

The McGarrigles are sometimes compared to another folk-pop sister group, the Roches; in a strange coincidence, Loudon Wainwright later married Suzzy Roche. While the Roches are a trio of New Jersey native Irish-Americans whose first musical encouragement came from Paul Simon, the McGarrigles are usually a duo, except when sister Janie sings with them. The lyrics of both are lushly, even tragically, romantic. The Roches have slicker production values, and their sisterly harmonies are breathtakingly beautiful. Many listeners who enjoy the McGarrigles will also find themselves taking to the Roches.

Matapedia was the first new McGarrigle recording in six years. Bob Franke, the great songwriter, wrote an homage to the album: "Anna's 'Goin' Back to Harlan' celebrates the role that traditional music took in the lives of those of us who first discovered it in the mid-1960s. The myths it offered were not the ones that our parents, damaged by the traumas of World War and Great Depression, sought to create. Ozzie and Harriet had little to offer us compared to the likes of 'Lord Thomas' and 'Fair Ellender.' The original singers of these songs had a different relationship to history and culture than our parents did."

The McGarrigles' songwriting is drenched in musical and lyrical references to traditional songs and heroes, from 'Shady Grove' to 'Barbara Allen.' "Anna and I make references in our own songs to traditional folk songs because these people lived lives of great drama," Kate told Silverstein. "In modern life, you cannot find the same pure passion and romance. Yes, people love and die today, but where is the grand passion that unites the hearts of 'Barbara Allen' and her lover?"

Kate's brilliant "Jacques et Gilles" speaks to us in two ironic contexts. Again, to quote Franke: "She creates a myth—to a wonderful variation on the tune of the old nursery rhyme 'Jack and Jill'—that turns a loving but not flattering eye on her mill worker forebears. In doing so she crosses a line, becoming a social historian, coming to terms with her history, [and becoming in turn] something of a tradition-bearer herself."

Kate described how she came to be interested in the New England mill towns that she writes about in "Jacques et Gilles": "I came to write it because of my interest in Jack Kerouac and *On the Road*. Ten years ago, I realized the similarities in Kerouac's and my own backgrounds. Though he was born in Lowell, Massachusetts, his family came from the same Quebec region as mine. Like him, I learned French in school and spoke English at home. Both of our upbringings were terribly insular. Our contact with the outside world was minimal. Perhaps that's why he wrote a book about traveling. But you'll recall that all his traveling, searching for a better life, ended up back in his mother's home, where he died a terrible death.

"I didn't come to understand any of this until I took a trip to Lowell. I brought along a video camera and asked a local woman for permission to film the local cemetery, where Kerouac is buried, from her balcony. When we got to talking, I realized how similar her background was to Kerouac's and my own. She was born in the States, yet she knew almost no English and spoke only French. I found it amazing that you could live in this country for so long, yet still be apart from it. This woman lives through French Canada. Those are the only photographs on her wall.

"It wasn't until I began doing research on this subject that I discovered that fully half the population of French Canada left for the factory mills of New England! That's an astounding fact, yet very few people are aware of it. Despite these huge numbers, French Canadians have had nowhere near the impact on the greater American culture that Italian, Irish, and Jewish Americans have. There are no traces of their cuisine, language, customs, etc. I think Kerouac responded to this insularity by writing *On the Road*. Yet his search for freedom and liberation ended with death."

In the McGarrigles' 1998 Rykodisc release, *The McGarrigle Hour*, they have created yet another under-stated musical masterpiece. They hit upon the brilliant idea of integrating all of the values in life that they hold dear, most notably family and music, in a single musical recording. As Jane McGarrigle states in her liner notes: "*The McGarrigle Hour* reunited many of the same people who worked on the first Kate & Anna record in 1975." It also brings together the sisters with their respective spouses, an ex-spouse (Loudon Wainwright III); their children, including Rufus and Martha Wainwright; several distinguished musical interpreters (Linda Ronstadt and Emmylou Harris); and current and former musical collaborators (including Joe Boyd, producer of their first two recordings).

The song selection, too, epitomizes the celebrated McGarrigle eclecticism: new versions of previously recorded material ("Talk to Me of Mendocino" and "NaCl"), plus the old pop standards like "Gentle Annie" (Stephen Foster) and "What'll I Do" (Irving Berlin). Unlike *Matapedia*, there is no newly written material here; but neither is there anything stale or nostalgic about this record. It gives us a fresh new perspective on individuals we felt we knew all along.

In a contemporary music business increasingly dominated by a frenzy for the next sensation or the smash hit, Rykodisc deserves enormous credit for its commitment to the McGarrigles' musical canon. In addition to releasing their previous *Matapedia*, it rereleased on CD such long-out-of-print titles as *Kate & Anna McGarrigle, Dancer with Bruised Knees, The French Record* and *Love Over and Over.*

Entry written by Richard Silverstein based on an interview with Kate McGarrigle

McGHEE, BROWNIE: *Singer, guitarist, songwriter. Born Knoxville, Tennessee, November 23, 1915; died Oakland, California, February 16, 1996.*

One of the great folk and blues artists, Brownie McGhee is inextricably linked with his longtime partner, Sonny Terry. But Brownie and Sonny both had long careers in music before joining forces, and, even over the decades of their close collaboration, they stressed the importance of each having his identity.

Brownie's early years were spent on the family farm near Kingsport, Tennessee, in a musical environment. His father, George, was an excellent singer-guitarist who often teamed with Brownie's uncle, John Evans, a fiddler, to play for local parties and dances. Even when George gave up the farm for a time to earn a living in various mill towns in eastern Tennessee, he often found time to join Evans for performing dates.

When young Walter (Brownie's given name) was four, he was stricken with polio, from which he recovered though he walked with a limp ever since. His illness ruled out working long hours on farm chores in his youth (something his younger brother, Granville "Sticks" McGhee, later a professional guitarist who had a hit in

1949 with "Drinkin' Wine Spo-dee-o-dee," couldn't escape). That left more time for Brownie to indulge his interest in music.

Even as a small child, he loved to listen to his father, uncle, and friends play blues and gospel music. When he accompanied them occasionally to performances, he got the chance to learn some of the basics of playing stringed instruments. His father taught him some of the skills involved in playing guitar and, before he was eight, he also had his own banjo to practice on, a homemade gift from Uncle John. He started picking out music on the piano as well.

The family (his parents split up when he was five) settled in Lenoir City, Tennessee, for several years, where Brownie completed elementary school. His musical endeavors included playing the organ in Solomon Temple Baptist Church and singing in the choir at Sanctified Baptist Church.

Next stop for the McGhees was Marysville, Tennessee, where Brownie started high school. After finishing his freshman year, he spent the summer performing at resorts in the Smoky Mountains. In 1928, when he was thirteen, he decided to drop out of school and earn whatever he could as a singer and guitarist. (He went back to school, earning his high school diploma in 1936.) For the rest of his teens, he drifted across Tennessee, working in medicine and minstrel shows and, for a while, with the Hagg Carnival.

In the early 1930s, his family needed his help back on the Kingsport farm. For several years he stayed home, pitching in on farmwork, though he still found time to sing with a gospel quartet, the Golden Voices. He grew restless of rural life and, when he got the chance to head to Knoxville in the mid-1930s, he did so and formed a number of small bands that worked local events. But things got tight in the city in the late 1930s and Brownie went back to playing for coins on street corners. He started in Asheville, North Carolina, then made his way to Winston-Salem, where he formed a team with harmonica player Jordan Webb. Word reached them that things were good for itinerant musicians in Burlington and Durham. While playing in those towns, Brownie became friends with such skilled performers as Blind Boy Fuller, Sonny Terry (then playing harp with Fuller) and Bull City Red. More important, they impressed OKeh Records talent scout J. B. Long with their ability, and Long offered to pay the duo's way to Chicago to make some recordings.

McGhee's first single was "Me and My Dog," which was pressed as the reverse side to Blind Boy Fuller's "Bus Rider Blues." He and Webb also made a number of other recordings in those initial sessions.

The OKeh schedule for June 1940 called for Blind Boy Fuller to make a number of recordings. Fuller went to Chicago, but a kidney infection, which eventually caused his death, kept him from going into the studios. Long then turned to Brownie and suggested he write a song in praise of Fuller. McGhee complied and cut the song, "The Death of Blind Boy Fuller," using Fuller's own steel-bodied guitar. The artist's name on the record, instead of McGhee, was listed as Blind Boy Fuller No. 2. That was one of many pseudonyms under which Brownie was to record during his career. Some of the others were Spider Sam, Big Tom Collins, Henry Johnson, Tennessee Gable, and Blind Boy Williams.

After Blind Boy Fuller died, Long decided Sonny Terry and Brownie would be a good combination. They debuted in the early 1940s at a blues concert at the Riverside Stadium in Washington, D.C., where they shared the bill with Leadbelly. They didn't decide to make it a permanent team right away. However, after they recorded "Workingman's Blues" together in 1942, they agreed to make it a regular alignment.

The two moved to the New York area in the mid-1940s and soon became one of the most popular acts on the folk and blues circuit. Besides working with Leadbelly (with whom Sonny and Brownie lived for a few years) and other famous blues musicians, they often appeared with Pete Seeger, Woody Guthrie, and the Weavers. From that time throughout the 1950s, 1960s, and 1970s, the twosome appeared in countless coffeehouses, clubs, and folk festivals across the United States and the world. In the 1960s and 1970s, they performed on dozens of major network TV shows and were practically institutions at the annual Newport Folk Festival. During the 1960s, they also made several national tours working with Harry Belafonte.

Not that they were anywhere near inseparable. Although they cut dozens of albums together, each sometimes made solo recordings under various noms de plume. Terry joined the cast of *Finian's Rainbow* in 1947 and McGhee formed a six-piece band (washboard, guitar, piano, drums, bass, and saxophone) called Brownie McGhee and His Mighty House Rockers. In 1948, McGhee started a blues school in Harlem called Home of the Blues. They also appeared in several Broadway shows, including Tennessee Williams's *Cat on a Hot Tin Roof* and Langston Hughes's *Simply Heavenly,* and the movie *Face in the Crowd.*

McGhee and Terry, together and separately, recorded for a dizzying array of labels over the years. Their work appeared, among others, on such labels as Folkways, Savoy, Alert, Decca, Jade, King, Verve, Bluesville, Main, and Prestige. Among their releases were *Blues, Traditional Blues, Blues and Folksongs* (1958); *On the Road with Burris* (1959); *Brownie's Blues, Blues and Folk* (1960); *Blues around My Head* (1960); *At the Second Fret* (1963); *Blues Is My Companion* (1961); *Back Country Blues, Terry and McGhee, Just a Closer Walk with Thee, Blues and Shouts, At Sugar Hill* (1962); *Down Home Blues* (1963); *Work, Play, Faith, Fun* (1960); *At the Bunkhouse, Home Town Blues* (1965); and *Guitar Highway* (1966). In the 1970s, the duo recorded for Fantasy Records. Their LPs available on the label at the start of the 1980s included *Back in New Orleans* and *Midnight Special*. Other LPs still in print at the start of the 1980s were *Brownie McGhee and Sonny Terry Sing, Brownie McGhee Sings the Blues, Preachin' the Blues;* on Folkways Records, *Live At the 2nd Fret,* and *The Best of Brownie McGhee and Sonny Terry* on Prestige.

Terry and McGhee toured for thirty-five years before they went their separate ways in the mid-1970s. Terry died in New York in March 1986. Some have said that the two only tolerated each other in a business sense. "They had a rancorous, bitter relationship," guitarist Happy Traum told *People Weekly* ("Last Licks," March 4, 1996). But in an interview with *Sing Out!* ("Yesterday Is Today & Today Is Tomorrow," by Cathy Signorelli, November–December 1995–January 1996), McGhee said, ". . . me and Sonny never did have no fallin' out. If we hated each other we couldn't have lasted 35 years. People get these ideas because we didn't eat in each other's lap. We had separate contracts. We didn't need to stay together in motels. The only time we lived together was at Leadbelly's. We pooled our resources. There never was anyone as good as Sonny Terry. We were partners. Our deal was he'd carry my weight and I'd see for him."

Brownie discussed his philosophy of music and the blues with Michael Brooks for *Guitar Player* magazine (October 1973). He told Brooks, "My definition of the blues is 'truth.' Man being true to himself and being true to his listeners when he's performing or singing any song that the people consider the blues. Blues is words which have been hooked onto black people so long—but you don't have to be lonely to sing the blues. Just be honest with yourself as you tell your stories of the past and present, with a smile on your face. I'm not ashamed of my past, and that's why I say blues is truth, because I tell it like it is. I don't mess it up at all. Blues is my life, my living, my joy, my everything. And I can live with it."

He argued against arbitrary typecasting of blues artists. "A man could come from Mississippi and hang out around Texas for a while and he'd get marked 'Texas blues.' I'm from Tennessee so automatically I can't play slide guitar, according to those people, because I've got to come from Mississippi to play slide. They mark people. I'm marked as a blues singer, a folk singer.

"Personally I mark myself as an entertainer and I don't care whether it's blues, folk, gospel, spiritual, jazz or what. I tell stories, and I'm an entertainer. I don't go out and tell people I'm a blues singer, because I could be wrong to them."

Though he slowed down his pace a bit, McGhee, who claimed to have composed 600 songs and made 500 recordings, continued to perform and record until his death in February 1996 from stomach cancer. He had bit roles in two movies, Steve Martin's *The Jerk* in 1979 and *Angel Heart,* with Lisa Bonet, Robert DeNiro,

and Mickey Rourke, in 1986. He was inducted into the Blues Hall of Fame in 1989. He was invited to perform at the 1995 Chicago Blues Fest and that year also recorded his last album, *Brownie's Blues,* with the Elmer Lee Thomas Blues Revue. Much of his earlier work was reissued on CD, including *The Complete Brownie McGhee* on Columbia/Legacy, *Brownie McGhee and Sonny Terry Sing* (a remastered version of their 1958 recording), *Brownie McGhee: The Folkway Years, Brownie McGhee Sings the Blues* (a remake of a 1959 LP), *Traditional Blues Volumes 1 and 2, Sonny Terry and Brownie McGhee, Get on Board* on Smithsonian Folkways, and *Whoopin' the Blues: The Capitol Recordings, 1947–1950,* a Sonny Terry compilation featuring McGhee on eight tracks.

McGUINN, ROGER: *Singer, guitarist, songwriter, band leader (the Byrds). Born Chicago, Illinois, July 13, 1942.*

When folk music began to pale as a commercial force in the face of the British-spearheaded rock resurgence, artists like Bob Dylan and the Byrds held onto the attention of at least part of the pop audience by blending elements of folk with rock. The man who was the driving force behind the Byrds and kept that group as an important contributor to the music scene for almost a decade was Roger McGuinn. At the end of the 1970s, he was part of a new alignment of onetime Byrds stars called McGuinn, Clark and Hillman.

McGuinn was born to parents with an active interest in writing and public relations, who gave him the name James. He changed his name to Roger in 1967 as part of his conversion to a religious movement. During his early years, he was constantly on the move because his parents' activities required them to travel widely. For instance, at one point he accompanied them around the country during a publicity tour for their best-selling book, *Parents Can Win.*

Like many of high-school age, Roger was enormously impressed with the rise of Elvis Presley in the mid-1950s. He hadn't really thought much about playing an instrument before that, but Elvis's music caused him to ask his parents to give him a guitar for his fourteenth birthday. However, though his first inclination was toward rock, he soon switched allegiance to folk music. As he recalled, "One of my high school teachers knew Bob Gibson [the folk-music performer] and had him play for the class. I'd heard folksingers before, the Weavers and such, but I was really impressed by Gibson. I began to listen to folk music and some of the traditional blues people."

Roger not only taught himself guitar, but started to learn five-string banjo at the Old Town Music School in Chicago, in the late 1950s. "I had to quit because the lessons cost ten bucks apiece—I was still in school. I finally tried playing in a small club and one of the Limeliters heard me. He offered me a job backing them which I turned down until I graduated from high school. There was about a ten-minute lag between my graduating from high school and becoming a professional musician. I got a telegram from the Limeliters and they hired me to work at the Ash Grove [in Los Angeles] as an accompanist."

After two months with them, McGuinn moved to San Francisco, where he did some solo work in local folk clubs. The Chad Mitchell Trio was looking for a replacement and Roger got the chance to audition for them in New York, which led to an association that lasted for two and a half years.

He left the Trio in the early 1960s and served as lead guitarist for a folk segment of Bobby Darin's cabaret act for a time. In 1963, he settled in as a session musician-arranger and occasional songwriter in New York, often taking part in programs in Greenwich Village folk clubs. Among the artists he either worked or became friends with were Bob Dylan, Judy Collins, and a duo known as Tom and Jerry. He helped prepare some material and also accompanied the latter twosome, who are better known as Simon and Garfunkel. "I worked with Judy Collins on her third album. It was my first chance to really stretch out and try to do something. . . . She chose the material and we worked together to arrange things. I never toured with her though."

In mid-1964, McGuinn got the call to come to Los Angeles to take part in a new group being assembled there, the band soon to take shape as the Byrds. Although McGuinn wasn't the original catalyst for the group, he soon became its central figure. He chose the name, for example, and his lead guitar work helped provide the ringing sound that was to be the group's trademark. *(For more details, see the Byrds entry.)* The group included three other folk-music alumni, Gene Clark, David Crosby, and Chris Hillman, plus rock drummer Michael Clarke.

The Byrds signed with Columbia Records in September 1964 and started working on their initial recordings. One of the first results was the group's version of Dylan's "Mr. Tambourine Man," released in March 1965 and a top-10 hit around the world a few months later. The group solidified its rapidly rising status in the rock field with its debut LP, *The Byrds,* which came out in August 1965 and in a short period of time earned the group a gold-record award. Although only an indifferent in-person act for much of its early phase, the group kept turning out inspired new recordings that kept it in the forefront of the folk-rock movement from 1965 through 1967.

Ironically, even though McGuinn held the band together through numerous personnel changes from the mid-1960s and early 1970s and inspired steady improvement in its stage presence during the latter part of Byrds history, the band's recording success waned. The group continued to have an impact on developments in pop music even if its prestige with the mass audience slipped. For instance, in some tracks of *The Notorious Byrd Brothers* and particularly the 1968 LP *Sweetheart*

of the Rodeo, the Byrds pioneered the country-rock field and were a forerunner of such late-1960s–early-1970s bands as the Flying Burritos, Poco, and the Eagles. During the last four years of the Byrds' existence, McGuinn had honed their musicianship to where they could play rings around the organization of the early years and expanded their repertoire to all manner of rock stylings, but they never did regain their onetime prominence. Roger sang the "ballad" to the 1969 hit film *Easy Rider.*

During 1972, McGuinn finally closed down the Byrds as a continuing organization. He had become increasingly interested in solo work in the early 1970s, and for a number of years in the middle of the decade he concentrated on that aspect of his career. He turned out a number of LPs that are among some of his best work, though they never achieved mass audience acceptance. These releases include *Roger McGuinn, Peace on You, Roger McGuinn and Band, Cardiff Rose,* and *Thunderbyrd.*

Toward the end of that phase in 1976–77, Roger became part of the Bob Dylan Rolling Thunder Revue, which was one of the major concert attractions of the time. Among those who shared the stage with him and Dylan were such major artists as Joan Baez, Joni Mitchell, and Mick Ronson. Interest in the series ran high and McGuinn's guitar work often won rousing ovations from tens of thousands of people who crowded into large stadiums to catch the show.

In 1978, McGuinn and two other original Byrds, Gene Clark and Chris Hillman, decided to form a new band called McGuinn, Clark and Hillman. By year end they were in the Criteria Studios in Miami working on their debut LP on Capitol Records. This time, Roger told a reporter, the personality clashes that brought major problems in the mid-1960s were past.

"We have a lot of the old rapport and memories. We've taken what we've learned and applied it. But we've all grown up and it's easier to work together. We're more accommodating. Patience is the key word."

The trio also hoped to develop a sound different from the Byrds. "The track on one of Gene's songs that might have come out 1960ish and Byrdsish sounds more like Steely Dan or the Average White Band. That gets me off."

The debut LP, *McGuinn, Clark and Hillman,* when it came out in February 1979, reflected the change in emphasis to some extent, though the group would not be mistaken for a heavy metal rock group. In early 1979 concerts, however, audiences tended to cheer loudest for the old Byrds replays, which indicated that McGuinn and company had an uphill fight to make a new way for themselves. On the other hand, the LP remained on pop hit charts for months, proving there still was an audience interested in what they might offer. By 1980, though, Clark had decided to stop touring, and the second LP was attributed to McGuinn and Hillman *with* Gene Clark (who provided only two songs for the collection).

By the early 1980s, Roger and Chris had decided to go their separate ways again. For most of the 1980s and 1990s, McGuinn pursued a solo career despite urging from former Byrds members that he try to reform the group. He did agree to appear at a tribute concert to the late Roy Orbison in February 1990, joined by Hillman, Crosby, John Jorgenson on guitar, and Steve Duncan on drums. Two of their numbers, "Turn! Turn! Turn!" and "Mr. Tambourine Man," were included in the tribute album. During the summer, he joined McGuinn, Hillman, and Crosby to record a few songs for inclusion in a new four-CD retrospective boxed set, *The Byrds,* issued by Sony in October 1990.

In 1991 he was appearing in support of his new solo album, his first in almost a decade, *Back from Rio* (issued by Arista), on which he was backed by many well-known artists, including old friends Crosby and Hillman, Elvis Costello, and Eagles alumnus Timothy Schmidt, as well as Tom Petty and the Heartbreakers. One of the best tracks was a song he cowrote with Petty, "King of the Hill." The disc also had material Roger wrote with his wife, Camilla, such as "The Trees Are All Gone" and "Without Your Love." Some of those songs later were featured onstage when Petty, his band, and Bob Dylan joined with McGuinn on the Temple in Flames tour. During the year, Roger also joined with other original Byrds members to accept inductance into the Rock and Roll Hall of Fame. (Gene Clark passed away a few months after that event.) In a separate project, McGuinn, Hillman, and Crosby provided commentary for a series of *History of Rock* programs for TV release that also were offered in commercial video form. Hollywood Records issued *Live From Mars* in November 1996.

McGuinn continued to hold sway as an elder statesman in folk rock throughout the 1990s. He told John Tobler late in the decade ("The Man Who Made Folk Rock," *Folk Roots,* October 1997) that he hoped never to retire and emphasized he also didn't want to take part in any Byrds reunion. To Tobler's query about his decision never to appear with the Byrds again, he responded, "That's right, because I'm not interested in doing it, that's all. I'm happy doing what I do." (As of 1997–1998, this included an acoustic folk-flavored tour.)

Tobler wondered whether Roger was surprised at continuing interest in his old band. "Yeah, especially in the light of the fact that during the '70s, the Byrds were completely erased from the map. I mean, we were gone. And then in the '80s, with the advent of Tom Petty and R.E.M. and various others, the Byrds became cool again."

McKENNITT, LOREENA: *Singer, songwriter, harpist, guitarist, pianist, accordionist. Born Morden, Manitoba, Canada, February 17, 1957.*

Many assume Loreena McKennitt is from Ireland. After all, she plays the concert harp and sets W. B. Yeats's poetry to music. She has a great mop of reddish blond hair and the fair skin of a Celt. But McKennitt comes from the Canadian prairies. She once thought of becoming a veterinarian; she is a good businesswoman, exhibiting the traits of her livestock-dealing father. But she trades in music, not beef.

"Growing up on the farm, you learn to persevere, and create things for yourself. If there are problems, you have to be creative in how you solve them if there are not the resources to buy the solution," she told the *Courtyard Group* (Winter–Spring 1994).

In concert she accompanies herself on harp, piano, and accordion, while singing her ethereal music. She calls her music "eclectic Celtic" and bridles when her ethereal sound is called New Age. As she told John Schafer, host of *New Sounds* of KUOW Seattle in late 1995: "There's a fusion of many, many things going on. At the heart of it, there's definitely a Celtic sound, but I've woven in these East Indian, Spanish, Moroccan kinds of elements and on top of that the musicians that I'm working with. . . . They each have their own individual careers that come from rock and jazz and world music, very experimental music, kinds of backgrounds, and then my own. I come from a classical and folk background."

Some have claimed that she is a devotee of Pagan beliefs, citing her songs entitled "Samain Night," "All Soul's Night," and "The Old Ways." She is not affiliated with any religion or political group, but is fascinated with spirituality and the meaning of God. As she told one interviewer: "I derived my own spiritual sustenance from the natural world. . . . When I reflect upon our contemporary society where people seem to be more and more restricted in their jobs that do not allow an opportunity for them to tap into their own creativity, they become, I feel, in some way, spiritually deprived. But for my own part, I find that that is why the music, for me, is a very spiritual experience."

McKennitt, the daughter of Irene and Jack McKennitt, grew up in Morden, about eighty miles outside of Winnipeg. Her mother is a nurse and her father came from a long line of livestock dealers, or drovers and auctioneers. In the 1830s her father's family emigrated from County Donegal in northwestern Ireland. Her mother's family came from Belfast. But there wasn't much music or Irish evident around their house, except for her father's red hair. As a child, Loreena took to Highland dancing, but a car accident in which she broke both her legs ended that. She began taking voice lessons, and classical piano lessons at five on her grandmother's piano. She sang in youth choirs and played the organ in the United Church.

As a child, Loreena didn't see much of her father, since he worked from 6 A.M. till 10 P.M. They spent time together when they could. "Often we'd just talk," she told Peter Feniak of *Saturday Night* ("Irish Soul," February 1994). "They could be very ethical kinds of conversations. My father would talk about 'the little guy,' explain that you gave him just as much attention as the big guy. Not for better business, but because it was a *good thing to do*."

Growing up in a small town was difficult for a young girl with red hair interested in sports and music. "I was playing sports and I was playing music in my own kind of creative and willful way," she told Feniak. "But I was *different*, you know? I wasn't kind of a real social creature like a lot of other girls my age. And because I felt older and different from many of my school chums, I spent time with my phys-ed teachers."

In the eleventh grade, after she was placed on a list for delinquent kids because she was often playing sports or music away from school, her parents enrolled her in the Balmoral Hall School for Girls in Winnipeg. The move came a year after the Winnipeg Folk Festival began, fortuitous timing for McKennitt: she started performing in the burgeoning local folk scene. She enrolled in the Agriculture Department at the University of Manitoba to pursue a career as a veterinarian, but music drew her in.

By day, she worked in her father's Winnipeg livestock office. Occasionally, she would have to round up cattle. At night she played dinner theater, performing Broadway show tunes at the Hollow Mug. (She also sang in a television commercial.) In 1977–78, she was one of 1,500 performers to enter the du Maurier Search for Talent Competition. She was one of six finalists, winning $5,000 for performing a scene from *My Fair Lady*. From 1979 to 1980, she helped run a folk club located above a woodworking shop. She heard recordings by Steeleye Span, Pentangle, Planxty, the Bothy Band, and Breton harpist Alain Stivell, whose album *Renaissance de la Harpe Celtique* inspired her to take up the harp a few years later. As usual, she taught herself. She was instinctively drawn to Celtic music. She took a correspondence course in Irish history. She took a trip to Ireland in 1982, visiting County Donegal and County Clare, where she now owns a cottage.

In 1981, she returned to Stratford, in southern Ontario, to be with an actor boyfriend. (She still lives in Stratford, in a stone farmhouse with her dogs and cats.) She worked as a composer, actor, and singer at the Shakespeare Festival. Appropriately, she played Ceres, the goddess of agriculture, in *The Tempest*, and composed music and performed in *Two Gentlemen of Verona*, in 1984. (Act IV, scene ii, has lines that have been used by fans as a tribute: *Who is Loreena? What is she/That all our swains commend her?/Holy, fair, and wise is she;/The heavens such grace did lend her,/That she might admired be.*)

Throughout the 1980s and early '90s, McKennitt composed music for plays and films. She wrote music for a play called *Blake* at the Stratford Festival in 1983, and scores for two Canadian feature films: *Bayo* (1985) and *Heaven on Earth* (1986). She briefly composed music for the Royal Shakespeare Company in England

in 1985. She was the musical director and performed in *Lilly* at the Blyth (Ontario) Summer Festival in 1986, and was a composer and performer in *St. Stephen's Green* at Dublin's Abbey Theatre in 1988. (That year she also appeared in a half-hour Canadian Broadcast Corporation TV broadcast called *Breaking the Silence* on *Adrienne Clarkson's Summer Festival*.) She was musical director and performer for *Kidnapped*, based on Robert Louis Stevenson's book, at the Young People's Theatre in Toronto in 1989. She composed music for several Canadian National Film Board films: *To a Safer Place* (1987), *A Wake for Milton* (1988), *Adam's World* (1989), and *Bridging The River of Silence* (1991), as well as for the three-part NFB Studio D series "Women and Spirituality": *Goddess Remembered* (1989), *The Burning Times* (1990), and *Full Circle* (1992).

In 1985, armed with $10,000 from her parents and a book called *How to Make and Sell Your Own Recordings* by Diane Sward Rapaport, she self-produced *Elemental,* a nine-song cassette on her Quinlan Road label. (The label was named for the street she lived on.) She sold the albums as she busked on Saturday mornings at the St. Lawrence Market in Toronto, lugging her forty-five-pound Lyon & Healy troubadour harp in her 1978 Honda Civic. She had a brief bout with depression at the time, having just broken up with actor Cedric Smith, who performed and arranged some of the songs on the album. "It lasted about three months," she told Feniak. "I didn't have any money, I didn't want to eat. I couldn't sleep. Tuesdays, just to force myself out of the house, I'd go down and quilt with the ladies at the Red Cross. . . . [I was in] a very dark place. It scared the hell out of me."

But she sold a remarkable 30,000 copies of *Elemental* in the first two years of its release. *Elemental* included "Stolen Child," a poem by Yeats that she set to music, and traditional Celtic songs such as "Carrighfergus," "She Moved Through the Fair," and "Blacksmith." The album has gone on to sell over 250,000 copies worldwide.

McKennitt has set to music the words of Shakespeare, Blake, Tennyson, and Yeats, which means that her listeners need to keep their *Norton Anthology* handy. "I suppose it's not surprising in that I live in Stratford, Ontario, worked at the Stratford festival there for a number of years, and the point was very much driven home of how substantial Shakespeare's work is in reflecting a variation and depth of humanity," she told KUOW FM in Seattle. "Part of the reason I've been drawn to Yeats is that his work seems to embody a lot of that mythology of the Celts and folklore and spin it out in a mystical, earthy kind of way. So, I've found a sympathetic soul. Some have accused me of working with the Dead Poets Society, who can't defend themselves."

In 1987, she released *To Drive The Cold Winter Away,* a collection of lesser-known winter songs and Christmas carols with spare arrangements. She recorded the songs at some unique settings, including Glenstal Abbey, a Benedictine monastery outside Limerick, Ireland, an artist's retreat near County Monaghan, and at the Church of Our Lady in Guelph, Ontario. She produced her own first concert in 1987, renting out the Trinity St. Paul's Church in Toronto.

Her next album, *Parallel Dreams* (1989), was her first to include original compositions along with traditional songs. It was also her first album to go gold in Canada, (more than 50,000 copies) and has since sold half a million copies. The album reveals McKennitt's interest in the supernatural. Her composition "Samain Night" incorporates images of the moon, the sun, the eagle's wing, and the owl's cry. She also mixes Native American and Celtic influences in "Huron 'Beltane' Fire Dance."

She toured throughout Canada and abroad to sold-out audiences, drawing the interest of major labels, including Warner Music Canada. The administrative duties had begun to overwhelm her creative side. She opened an office in Stratford in 1991 and hired staff to help her with promotion and distribution. Because she was in such a strong position, she garnered a favorable distribution contract with the Warner Music Group, retaining creative control and the right to sell her albums at concerts and by mail. She encourages other artists to do the same. She told the *Courtyard Group,* "I can hardly think of any people in other lines of work saying, 'Well, I'm just this sensitive, creative creature and I don't want to contaminate my head with business.' It's horribly naive, and furthermore, if you don't look after your best interests, other people will come along and look after it for their best interests, or they won't come along at all."

Her first album distributed by Warner Music Group was *The Visit,* released in Canada, Europe, and Australia in 1991 and, in 1992, in the U.S. via Warner Brothers. During a trip to Venice, Italy, she saw an exhibition of Celtic artifacts (*I Celti* at the Palazzo Grassi), including items gathered from Hungary, Spain, and Asia Minor. "Until I went to that exhibition, I thought that Celts were people who came from Ireland, Scotland, Wales, and Brittany," she says. She realized that the Celts emigrated to Ireland and Scotland from tribes in Central and Eastern Europe dating to 500 B.C.

The album incorporates Eastern European influences. There are also Latin sounds in "Tango to Evora," originally recorded for *The Burning Times* and later used on the TV show *Northern Exposure.* She includes "Cymbeline," derived from Shakespeare's play, an eleven-minute version of Tennyson's "The Lady of Shalott," and a self-described Tom Waits–ish version of "Greensleeves." She reveals her deep interest in Celtic rituals in "All Soul's Night" and "The Old Ways."

The album sold two million copies worldwide (in more than forty countries) and has since certified quadruple platinum in Canada (400,000 copies). She won a Juno award for Best Roots and Traditional Album, and gained worldwide acclaim, making a number of critics' year-end best album lists. But as her popularity grew, she suffered a tremendous personal loss: her father died of cancer in 1992.

Her next album, *The Mask and Mirror,* continued her musical quest, mixing Spanish, Eastern European, Moroccan, and Celtic music. She looked into Spanish history and found that it was a crossroads for literature, music, art, science, and religion. The album did even better commercially than *The Visit,* selling 2.25 million copies worldwide. She uses diary entries in the liner notes to give history on the songs. "The Dark Night of the Soul," for example, is taken from the work of St. John of the Cross, a fifteenth-century Spanish mystic and visionary. McKennitt's "Marrakesh Night Market" was inspired by the sounds of the market during Ramadan and includes *balalaika* and *dumbek.* "The Mystic's Dream," also used in the film *Jade,* was inspired by her interest in Sufi mysticism, which she theorizes "may be an association with the Druidic order of the Celts." The last two songs are by her favorite poets: "The Two Trees" by Yeats and "Prospero's Speech" from *The Tempest.*

She won a second Juno Award for Best Roots/Traditional Album and embarked on a worldwide tour. Jim Washburn of the *Los Angeles Times* wrote (November 29, 1994): "She plays Celtic harp and sings in a Celtic manner, in echoey, ethereal, atmospheric settings. Her songs list such heady and significantly dead co-writers as St. John of the Cross and Alfred Lord Tennyson. This is Loreena McKennitt and, despite one's worst apprehensions given the above information, she's not the least bit pretentious."

McKennitt is known for the excellent musicians who accompany her. Brian Hughes coproduced *Parallel Dreams, The Visit,* and *The Mask and Mirror.* Rick Lazar plays percussion, including the *dumbek,* or Arabic jar drum. Patrick Hutchinson played uileann pipes on *Parallel Dreams, The Visit,* and *The Mask and Mirror.* Hugh Marsh, an Ottawan who started as a classical violinist, plays electric fiddle.

Among McKennitt's various other projects: she wrote a song for Disney's Tim Allen vehicle *The Santa Clause* and recorded a five-track Christmas EP, *A Winter Garden: Five Songs for the Season,* at Peter Gabriel's RealWorld Studios in Wilshire, England, in July 1995. She also released a six-track recording via mail-order from Quinlan Road only from a May 1994 concert in San Francisco called *Live in San Francisco at the Palace of Fine Arts* and made a video called *No Journey's End* that aired on PBS. The half-hour documentary includes McKennitt talking about her musical influences, performing some of her better-known songs, and walking through fields. She also toured Japan with the Chieftains in the latter part of 1995. She expanded her Quinlan Road label by opening a second office in London.

In 1996 the CBS drama *EZ Streets* used three of her

songs on its pilot: "Old Ways" and "Bonny Portmore" from *The Visit* and "The Mystic's Dream" from *The Mask and Mirror.* The show also used songs by Carolyn Lavelle and Maire Brennan.

By the end of the 1990s, McKennitt had sold more than eight million records in more than forty countries, earning *Billboard's* International Achievement Award. *The Visit* and *The Mask and Mirror* both went gold in the United States (more than 500,000 each).

Over an eighteen-month period, she recorded her seventh CD, *The Book of Secrets,* at RealWorld. Quinlan Road released the CD via Warner Music in 1997. Rather than promote the album, McKennitt went on a two-week bike trip in China. Despite her initial absence, the CD hit the top of the *Billboard* World Music chart and broke the Top Twenty on the *Billboard* album chart. A remix of her song "The Mummers' Dance" also reached the Top Twenty of the *Billboard* Hot 100 Singles Chart, gaining airplay on rock stations. Within four months the album had topped 800,000 in sales (gold status) in the States alone. It sold 3.2 million copies worldwide.

McKennitt has been inspired by such experiences as taking a trip on the Trans-Siberian railroad and reading Dante's *Divine Comedy,* which shaped her songs "Night Ride Across the Caucasus" and "Dante's Prayer." "The Mummers' Dance" was about the traditional folk custom of mumming often performed as part of Spring and May Day celebrations. She also sings about fictional and historical figures such as a seventh century Irish monk in "Skellig," and thirteenth century explorer Marco Polo. The album marked the end of her three-CD distribution deal with the Warner Music Group.

She went on a spring '98 tour of 33 cities. In July 1998, when she went to RealWorld to mix a live album, she learned the tragic news that her fiancé Ronald Rees had died in a boating accident in Georgian Bay with his brother Richard Rees and friend Gregory Cook. To help prevent other tragedies, McKennitt co-founded the Cook-Rees Memorial Fund for Water Search and Safety. In 1999 Quilan Road released *Live in Paris and Toronto,* a two-disc set distributed in the U.S. by Valley Entertainment, and donated proceeds to the Cook-Rees fund.

She has often composed music for important causes. *Parallel Dreams'* "Dickens' Dublin (The Palace)," in which a Dublin street girl expresses her desire for a home, expresses the plight of homeless children. The ballad "Bonny Portmore" mourns the loss of ancient Irish oak stands and parallels the destruction of old-growth forests. She wrote "Breaking the Silence" from *Parallel Dreams* for Amnesty International.

Although her music takes on mythical proportions, she takes pains to reveal the sources of inspiration, as Shakespeare does by unmasking Prospero at the end of *The Tempest.* As she explains in the liner notes, the speech is "delivered with the sense of the actor removing his mask as an artist . . . . The illusion has ended, and reality and God are left for us to determine for ourselves."

McLACHLAN, SARAH: *Singer, guitarist, pianist, songwriter. Born Bedford, Halifax, Nova Scotia, Canada, January 28, 1968.*

A major trend in the final decades of the twentieth century was the appearance on the music scene of a group of young, inspired female singer-songwriters in the pop and folk domains, including some notable artists from north of the U.S. border. Among the latter was Sarah McLachlan, whose ethereal soprano voice and finely crafted self-penned songs resulted in recordings that successfully competed for places on the hit charts with gangsta rap as well as with grunge and conventional rock releases.

Though brought up in Bedford, a suburb of Halifax, Nova Scotia, she was the daughter (an adopted daughter, she found out later) of parents from the United States. Her father had migrated to Canada to pursue his work as a marine biologist, and her mother also had academic roots. Neither of them were particularly fond of pop music and tried to instill in their youngest child (Sarah has two older brothers) a love for the classics. Her lengthy classical training, she told an interviewer, embraced twelve years of guitar, six years of piano lessons, and even five years of voice training.

Still, Sarah was well aware of what was going on in pop and rock, and in her teens she often used her instrumental skills to play some of the hit songs of the day. Her impressive vocal skills brought the opportunity to sing with a local new wave group at a Halifax venue when she was seventeen. Her career might have started right then, but her parents didn't like the idea of her signing a record contract before she had even finished high school.

(Her teen years, though, as she told Michael Small for a *Mademoiselle* article, were not without their downside. She felt self-conscious, she noted: "I had braces and greasy hair. I was called Medusa. Boys would fall down on the ground and writhe and scream and say they were going to turn to stone.")

She told rock star Stevie Nicks in a phone discussion for *Interview* magazine (March 1995), "I started singing professionally when I was nineteen. I got a record contract offered to me on a silver platter. A couple years previous, I was in a band, and the first gig we ever did, a guy from a record company (Vancouver-based Nettwerk Records) saw me and wanted to sign me. . . . But my mom kind of freaked out. And in retrospect, it was a really good thing. Because I forgot about it and I went to college (Nova Scotia College of Art and Design) for a year and was really feeling like I fit in someplace for the first time in my life. Then they came back to me and offered me a contract. I had never written a song up until that point."

hiking from one town to the next, he found renewed interest in rock caused by the emergence of the Beatles. "I became a Stones freak for a time and I also dig [soul man] James Brown—his band is fine."

In 1966, he began performing summers at the Caffe Lena in Saratoga Springs, New York, a folk art center run by Lena Spencer. The association proved particularly valuable two years later when the New York State Council on the Arts asked Lena to recommend someone to give free concerts in a special program. He recalled: "It was the summer of 1968 and I was broke. Lena got me a job with the state, figuring I'd make a good bureaucrat. I had to play in 50 river communities (billed as the Hudson River Troubadour), three a day a month or more while the state paid me $200 a week. Man, they got their money's worth. I sang about 40 songs a day, sometimes 60. That's cheaper than the juke box."

Those efforts, plus Don's activities on behalf of restoring the Hudson's ecology, brought him in contact with Pete Seeger. Seeger contacted him to join in the 1969 cruise of the sloop *Clearwater,* a voyage from South Bristol, Maine, to New York City, undertaken by a group of folksingers to enlist public support against industrial pollution of the rivers. The project resulted in a National Educational TV special, "The Sloop at Nyack." Besides performing on that show, Don also edited a book about the voyage, *Songs and Sketches of the First Clearwater Crew.* Seeger, meanwhile, had become one of McLean's major enthusiasts, calling Don "the finest singer and songwriter I have met since Bob Dylan." Following the *Clearwater* activity, Don became a familiar figure at many folk concerts, appearing with people such as Arlo Guthrie, Janis Ian, Josh White, Lee Hayes, and Seeger.

But he was finding favor with the broad spectrum of pop artists as well. At the start of the '70s, he shared bills with Blood, Sweat & Tears, Laura Nyro, Dionne Warwick, and the Nitty Gritty Dirt Band. He had built up a repertoire of original songs besides continuing to try his hand at prose and poetry. He also was interested in films, working in 1971 with Bob Elfstrum, who helped prepare the Academy Award–nominated *Other Voices,* a movie in which twenty-five of Don's original songs were used.

But while many well-known entertainers thought highly of Don's growing body of songs, he was consistently frustrated in his efforts to land a record company. He approached twenty-seven different firms with tapes of what was to be his debut LP, *Tapestry,* and was turned down by all of them. Finally, the small Mediarts put it out in 1970 with very little fanfare and very little notice from the public.

McLean toured the country's coffeehouses in support of *Tapestry.* The tour didn't help sales much, but during his travels, he began slowly assembling "American Pie," finishing it in early 1971. By then, United Artists was interested in him and gave him the go-ahead

to work on a new album. The song debuted long before the LP came out, being presented on station WPLJ-FM in New York the day Bill Graham closed his Fillmore East rock theater. It reached number one in *Billboard* the week of December 4, 1971, and stayed there for four weeks. It remained high on that list into 1972 and also rose to number one on other industry charts.

The album reached number one in early 1972, and in some cases both single and album were at number one at the same time. McLean was the rage of pop music all over the world. Soon the attention given his work caused a second song from the album, "Vincent" (an ode to painter Vincent Van Gogh), to become an international hit. It peaked at number twelve in *Billboard* the week of April 1, 1972, and rose even higher on charts in other countries. (Later, when the Vincent Van Gogh Museum opened in Amsterdam, the Netherlands, the song was played at the inaugural ceremonies and still is played at the entrance area.) Also a chartmaker at the time was the single "Castles in the Air" from his first album.

McLean soon became unhappy about the whirlwind success of "American Pie." It had, he believed, caused people to overlook the messages in such other compositions as "Three Flights Up," "And I Love You So," and "Tapestry." He also felt most people had missed what he considered the song's main theme "which isn't nostalgia, but that commercialism is the death of inspiration. If only one person can relate to it on that level, I'll be satisfied."

Much of his bitterness colored his next album, *Don McLean* (1972), as reflected in the strident tone of songs such as "The Pride Parade" and "Narcissisma." The LP did provide him with another hit single, though, the fast-moving "Dreidel." That song's words in places were far from optimistic: *My world is a constant confusion/My mind is prepared to attack/My past a persuasive illusion/I'm watchin' the future—it's black.*

For close to a year, McLean's state of mind prevented him from writing any new material. He also sharply curtailed his concert work. However, a friend from Caffe Lena days, bluegrass mandolinist Frank Wakefield, helped restore McLean's interest in music. The result was the album *Playin' Favorites* (1973), which contained no originals but various folk, country, and bluegrass songs that appealed to Wakefield and McLean. Well-received tours of Europe and Australia added to Don's rebound and he finally set to work on his next LP, the 1974 *Homeless Brother,* whose title track sang the praises of the American hobo.

But though Don was writing again, he had lost the attention of much of the audience. His record sales declined and his association with UA came to an end. For two years, little was heard from him, but in 1976, he signed with Clive Davis's new label, Arista. Late in the year he appeared in clubs across the United States in his first concerts since 1974. Among his material were

"Echo" and "Color TV Blues," new songs included in his first Arista release, *Prime Time* (1977), a collection not up to his earlier standards.

At the end of the 1970s, Don signed with a new label, Millennium (distributed by RCA), which issued *Chain Lightning* in 1979. That album received some attention from record buyers and his next collection on the label, *Believers*, did even better, spending several months on the charts in late 1981 and early 1982. During 1981, McLean had his first singles hit since the mid-1970s when his version of Roy Orbison's "Crying" made *Billboard*'s top 5. "Crying" did even better in the United Kingdom, peaking at number one. Also in record stores in 1980 was the retrospective release *The Very Best of Don McLean*. Before 1981 was over, Don had two more chart singles, "Since I Don't Have You," which peaked in *Billboard* at number twenty-three the week of May 2, and a remake of "Castles in the Air," which was a top 40 entry in December.

McLean's recording fortunes declined again after "Crying," but he retained a core of fans who assured him the opportunity to remain active as a solo concert artist in small clubs or on college campuses for the rest of the decade. Though in most cases he appeared on stage as a one-man act, he sometimes worked with other groups ranging from bluegrass bands to the Israel Philharmonic Orchestra. For some appearances in the late 1980s he handled lead vocals for Buddy Holly's old band, the Crickets. He and the Crickets played some of Holly's songs on a segment of the 1988 Grammy Awards Telecast from Radio City Music Hall in New York.

McLean's album releases in the late 1980s and early 1990s included the country-tinged *Love Tracks* in 1987, *Don McLean's Greatest Hits—Then and Now* in 1987, *Headroom* in 1990, and *The Best of Don McLean* in 1991. The retrospective collections drew new attention to his music, particularly in the United Kingdom, where "American Pie" rose into the top 20 in 1991.

For himself, McLean was happy people still enjoyed the hit that made him a star, if only briefly, but his memories of that "stardom" weren't particularly satisfying. He told a *Los Angeles Times* reporter, "When you're really hot, it's dangerous. Back then, I recall it was quite unpleasant. I didn't commit suicide and I didn't go into bankruptcy but it was quite a swim upstream until I got my bearings." However, he added, "American Pie" was "not just another song I wrote. It belongs to the people. If children keep singing it, it will be around forever, long after I'm dead."

McLean had moderate success in 1987 with singles from the *Love Tracks* album, including "Can't Blame the Wreck on the Train," which peaked at number forty-nine on the U.S. country charts, and "Love in My Heart," a top 10 hit in Australia. Much of the material was released in the United Kingdom in a 1989 album titled *And I Love You So*. In 1995 McLean put out a new album of originals titled *The River of Love*, a mixture of pop, country, and blues that revealed a man satisfied with his station in life.

McLean signed a record deal with Hip-O Records (a division of MCA) which planned to reissue several of his earlier albums, including *Chain Lightning* and *Believers* in 1997. In early 1997, Hip-O Records issued a two-CD set titled *Don McLean—Greatest Hits Live!* (previously released as *Dominion* in 1983). The twenty tracks in the collection were taped at the final concert of a lengthy English tour performed in 1980. In the liner notes for the release, McLean, who produced it, stated, "We traveled in two buses around the English and Scottish countryside in the fall of 1980 as my version of my friend Roy Orbison's song 'Crying' was reaching number one on the British charts. Instead of a solo tour, as I had done in the past, a rock orchestra was put together with a full string section and musicians like the Kinks' drummer Bob Henritt, and his friends Bob Metzger on guitar and Dave Wintour on bass."

In October 1997, Hip-O released *Christmas Dreams*, a collection of Christmas songs. The following month Hip-O announced plans to release a six-CD boxed set containing material from McLean's years with United Artists, scheduled for late 1999. By late 1998 McLean was working on an autobiography, recordings of children's songs, and a collection of songs from the Wild West. Martin Guitars also issued a special edition Don McLean guitar for $5,750, which was selling briskly by year's end.

McTELL, BLIND WILLIE: *Singer, songwriter, six- and twelve-string guitarist. Born near Thomson, Georgia, 1898 (also reported as May 5, 1901); died Milledgeville, Georgia, August 19, 1959.*

Best known for his blues classic "Statesboro Blues," which has been covered by Taj Mahal, the Allman Brothers, and Rory Block, Blind Willie McTell spent most of his life singing and playing guitar for tips on the streets of Atlanta and in small Georgia towns. He was never a commercial hit, largely because many of his records came out during the Great Depression, but his vast recorded material from 1927 to 1956 established him as one of the great blues guitarists, playing his Stella twelve-string with an innovative fingerpicking and slide style. He could play blues, folk, ragtime, boogie woogie, religious, and pop standards of the day.

According to liner notes for *The Definitive Blind Willie McTell* (Columbia, 1994) written by folklorist David Evans, he was born Willie Samuel McTell in a cotton-growing area thirty miles west of Augusta, the son of Minnie Watkins and Ed McTear (or McTier). It's not known how he became known as McTell. Blind from birth or shortly thereafter, McTell nevertheless compensated with an extraordinary sense of hearing and touch. He is said to have been able to make his own way from town to town by train or bus or to negotiate the New York subway, as well as thread a needle. He gravitated to music from an early age, starting with harmonica or accordion and graduating to the guitar. Both of his parents were excellent guitarists, and he was related to such artists as Georgia Tom Dorsey, Buddy Moss, and Barbecue Bob and his brother Charlie Lincoln.

In 1907 he and his mother moved to Statesboro, Georgia (between Savannah and Augusta) in search of work. His mother, who died in 1920, became a cook for a local family. Before her passing, McTell found work performing with traveling medicine shows, including the John Roberts Plantation Show in 1916 and 1917. Over the years, he would often play for relatives in Thomson and Statesboro, at school assemblies, and in church, for white and black audiences. He played with other blind musicians, including guitarists Lord Randolph Byrd, a.k.a. Blind Log, in towns throughout Georgia.

In 1922 he enrolled in Georgia's school for the blind, where he learned to read Braille and developed skills in clay modeling, broom making, and leather working. He later attended schools in New York City and Michigan. He returned to Atlanta by 1927, where he often played at the 81 Theatre during matinees, or at the Pig 'n' Whistle barbecue, which served whites only. Like Blind Lemon Jefferson, only one publicity photo of McTell remains. In it he looks dapper in a suit and vest with a watch on a chain and a cap, sporting a small mustache.

On October 18, 1927, he had his first session, set up by Ralph Peer of Victor Records. McTell cut four songs using the six-string: "Writin' Paper Blues," "Stole Rider Blues," "Mama, 'Taint Long fo' Day," and "Mr. McTell Got the Blues." A year later he switched to a twelve-string and recorded four more songs for Victor, including "Three Women Blues," "Dark Night Blues," "Love Talking Blues," and the classic "Statesboro Blues." As Sam Charters noted in his 1977 book, *Sweet as the Showers of Rain,* Willie's first eight recordings were his best. "For the earliest sessions it was the plaintive quality of his singing voice that was immediately identifiable. His voice was high and rather light, sounding much younger than someone in his late twenties, and there was almost a pleading quality to it, a helplessness to his phrasing."

On October 30 and 31, 1929, he began recording for Frank Walker of Columbia Records, using the pseudonym Blind Sammie. While he recorded blues songs for Victor, he also recorded ragtime songs for Columbia, which released four of his six cuts: "Atlanta Strut," "Travelin' Blues," "Come on Around to My House Mama," and "Kind Mama." (His first 78, released in 1930, sold 4,205 copies. When the next one was released, in 1932, only 400 were pressed.) In November 1929, he recorded eight more sides for Victor, which released two songs. He recorded again for Columbia in April 1930. On October 23 and 31, 1931, he recorded again, this time for Columbia's OKeh subsidiary using

a new pseudonym, "Georgia Bill." Among the songs he recorded were his classic "Broke Down Engine Blues" backed with "Southern Can Is Mine," which sold a scant 500 copies in 1931.

For the OKeh and Columbia sessions, McTell brought his longtime friend Curley Weaver (who had recorded with Barbecue Bob and Buddy Moss in the Georgia Cotton Pickers in 1930) on second guitar and Ruth Day/Mary Willis on background vocals.

He recorded as "Hot Shot Willie" in 1932 for Victor Records and in 1933 as "Blind Willie" for the American Recording Company, recording twenty-three songs, twelve of which were released by Vocalion. Curley Weaver played guitar and vocals for the 1933 sessions. Among the songs were "Death Cell Blues," "It's Your Time to Worry," and "East St. Louis Blues." But again they did not sell well. By 1934 he had married a woman named Ruthy Kate Williams, whom he put through nursing school and who would occasionally sing and dance while he performed.

By 1935 McTell was still in demand. This time he was spotted by J. Mayo Williams of Decca Records. Ruthy Kate Williams, Curley Weaver, and McTell traveled to Chicago, where he recorded sixteen sides, including gospel, blues, and Appalachian-style music in April. He recorded again for Vocalion in 1936 at an Augusta, Georgia, radio station with a musician known as Piano Red (Willie Perryman), but the masters were either destroyed or disappeared and nothing was ever released.

McTell's recording career was put on hiatus for the next four years. In 1940 folklorist John Lomax's wife spotted him performing in front of a barbecue stand in Atlanta. After guiding Lomax and his wife in their car, McTell went up to Lomax's hotel and received one dollar plus cab fare to record some of his folk songs ("Delia"), spirituals ("I Got to Cross the River Jordan"), and blues ("Dying Crapshooter's Blues") for the Library of Congress Archive of American Folk Song. During this session, McTell also gave Lomax an account of his life and of race relations; he told Lomax that he had been friends with Blind Willie Johnson. Following Pearl Harbor, McTell and his wife drifted apart when she found a job as a military nurse. McTell began living with another woman, Helen Edwards.

He also began to play more in front of the Pig 'n' Whistle stand. According to Evans, who interviewed Ruthy Kate, McTell obtained a preacher's license and often played in church, but never became a minister. Still, his interest in religious songs became more evident in his recorded work and performances. In May 1949 he recorded several sides (backed by Curley Weaver) for Fred Mendelson of Regal Records, which listed McTell as "Pig 'n' Whistle Red" after the barbecue stand where he played. Later that year he was "discovered" once more, this time by Ahmet Ertegun of the newly formed Atlantic Records. McTell recorded fifteen sides for Atlantic, which released his songs as "Barrelhouse Sammy (the Country Boy)."

In the 1950s McTell made an annual trip to a school for the blind in North Carolina. But his health began to deteriorate. He suffered from diabetes and high blood pressure, and began drinking heavily. He continued to play on the streets and at the Pig 'n' Whistle; by then he was a grizzled man who drank whatever was offered. But he continued to wear a suit and tie. In the fall of 1956 an Atlanta record store owner named Ed Rhodes gave McTell some whiskey and got him to record for an hour in his shop. The whiskey slurred his voice some, but his guitar playing was still fine during his "last session."

McTell's girlfriend, Helen Edwards, died of a heart attack on November 1, 1958, and Willie's health continued to decline. He suffered a stroke in the spring of 1959 and moved in with relatives in Thomson. In August 1959 he suffered a second stroke. Unable to pay for treatment at the local hospital, the McTears had to take Willie to a state hospital fifty miles away in Milledgeville, where he died on August 19 of a cerebral hemorrhage. He was laid to rest at the Jones Baptist Church, near Thomson. That was the year Charters's book *The Country Blues* came out. It mentioned McTell. Rhodes, realizing that he had the tapes he had made of McTell in 1956, contacted Charters in 1961 and went to New York, where they listened to the tapes. Prestige released the *Last Session* LP on its Bluesville label.

McTell's music is readily found on CD, including *The Definitive Blind Willie McTell* (Columbia Legacy, 1994), from his Columbia, OKeh, and Vocalion sessions; *Blind Willie McTell: Complete Recorded Works 1927–35, Volumes 1 through 3* (Document, 1990); *Complete Library of Congress Recordings* (Document, 1990), from the John Lomax session; *Last Session* (Original Blues Classics/Fantasy, 1991), from his session with Rhodes; *The Early Years (1927–1933)* (1989, Yazoo); *Blind Willie McTell 1927–35* (Yazoo, 1990); *Doing that Atlanta 1927–1935* (Yazoo, 1991); *Pig 'n' Whistle Red* (Biograph, 1993), from his 1949 session with Regal; *Atlanta 12 String* (Atlantic, 1991), fifteen tracks from his session with Ahmet Ertegun; and *Victor Recordings 1927–1934* (1996).

McTELL, RALPH: *Singer, guitarist, songwriter. Born Farnborough, Kent, England, December 3, 1944.*

A phenomenally talented writer and musician, Ralph McTell remained what amounted to one of England's best-kept creative secrets, at least from an American vantage point, for decades. Britain's *The Guardian* noted, "McTell is a technically brilliant guitarist . . . some of his songs, delicate tunes, are as powerful as early Dylan." Indeed, some of his songs, like "Streets of London" and "From Clare to Here," were covered by so many established performers in the United Kingdom and the United States that members of the public thought they were traditional folk tunes rather than original compositions by one person.

His original name, when he was born in Farnborough in the waning months of World War II, was Ralph May. His father abandoned the family when he was two, leaving his mother to raise him and a younger brother. He told Tom Nelligan for a *Dirty Linen* article ("Ralph McTell Still Weathering the Storm," April–May 1996), "I came from a broken home like a lot of kids after the war. And although I was brought up by a very firm mum who kept us straight, pretty much, there was a time when I was alienated and alone, and disturbed."

Music interested him at an early age, though, and when he was seven he started teaching himself the harmonica. "I actually wrote a tune when I was about eight or nine that I can still remember, only because someone said they liked it—probably the lady upstairs in the tenements where we lived." Another factor that helped his outlook on life as a child, he added, was attention from a neighbor named Connaughton. He told Nelligan, "Not everybody had a dad, so they were sort of shared around." Later he paid tribute to that person in his song "Mr. Connaughton."

In the mid-1950s, as the skiffle craze took hold in the United Kingdom, Ralph took up the ukulele and formed a band. By the late 1950s he'd dropped ukulele playing in flavor of using a guitar. Fifteen at the start of the '60s, the restless teenager quit school and enlisted in England's boy soldier program. He was assigned to the Queen's Surrey Regiment Junior Leaders Battalion, but after five months he found army life didn't agree with him and he borrowed money to buy his way out. Once a civilian again, he returned to school but also sought to improve his musical skills. A turning point in his career, he said later, was hearing U.S. folk performer Ramblin' Jack Elliott play "San Francisco Blues" at the College Jazz Club. After that, McTell spent as much time as he could listening to folk and blues records and catching concerts in folk clubs in London and Brighton.

He listened closely and picked up pointers about guitar playing from albums by Elliott, Woody Guthrie, Blind Boy Fuller, Blind Blake, Blind Willie McTell, Mississippi John Hurt, Robert Johnson, and Bahamian musician Joseph Spence. He also was intrigued by books by American writers like Jack Kerouac and John Steinbeck. Before long he felt confident enough to try to establish himself as a performer, supporting himself with odd jobs while he gained experience playing gigs or doing street corner busking along England's south coast. Sometimes he played solo and sometimes he teamed up with other folk musicians like Wizz Jones or some of the founding members of Fairport Convention.

It was a time when bands like the Beatles and the

Rolling Stones were revolutionizing world rock 'n' roll, but McTell was so engrossed in blues and folk and "learning to play like Blind Willie McTell" that he hardly noticed the other developments.

Of course, American blues music had an impact on U.K. rock artists as well as folkies. The rapport with an art form that took shape somewhere else, McTell suggested to Nelligan, was that "white working-class kids in England just identified with blues so completely. The music had this authenticity and a purity; it was regarded by some as a music of protest. It's easily available if you can play three chords. It understates things to such a huge amount. There's sexual innuendo, there's power of manhood in it. And it's your own, you make it your own."

During the mid-1960s, Ralph extended his itinerant musician activities to Europe and Scandinavia, hitchhiking, busking, and finding occasional club or bar opportunities. While in Norway he met an attractive girl named Nanna whom he married and with whom he soon had a son. Back in England, he decided the time had come to settle down and start earning a living to support his family. He pursued teaching credentials at Training College while also seeking work at folk clubs, calling himself Ralph McTell. He soon had the chance to appear regularly at a leading London folk club, Les Cousins, in Soho. His treatment of traditional music and the quality of his original writings won approval of audiences and other folk artists, which opened up opportunities for engagements in other venues in the United Kingdom. The contacts he made were translated into a recording deal with the major folk label Transatlantic Records.

His debut album, *Eight Frames a Second,* came out in 1968 and won excellent reviews from the media in general. As record buyers became acquainted with McTell's abilities, openings began to arise for appearances at colleges and universities and, as the 1970s began, as a supporting act or headliner in concert halls and theaters. His 1969 credits included his debut set at the Cambridge Folk Festival in July, and in December his first London headline show at Hornsey Town Hall. By then his reputation soared with the release of his second Transatlantic album, *Spiral Staircase.* Though he had written "Streets of London," a song dealing with homelessness and despair, in 1965 or '66 when he was living in Paris, he first recorded it for that album. He had hesitated to do it, but his record producer persuaded him to include it. Before '69 was over, he had a third collection in print, *My Side of Your Window,* followed in 1970 by his last Transatlantic contributions for some time, the compilation *Revisited.*

As the 1970s went by, McTell began to attain star status in the United Kingdom and Europe. In May 1970, he was able to attract a capacity audience to a concert at London's Royal Festival Hall. A TV documentary was made of some of his concert work, and he also was signed to take part in the Isle of Wight Festival. Over the next few years he continued to expand his following at home and in Europe through concerts, festival appearances, and new recordings. His album output included *You Well Meaning Brought Me Here* in 1971 on Famous Records (reissued as *71/72* on the Mays label in 1981 and again on Mays in 1986 as *The Ferryman*); *Not Till Tomorrow* on Reprise/Warner Brothers in 1972; and *Easy* on Reprise/Warner Brothers in 1974. His '72 LP release coincided with his first U.S. appearances, in which he played with Patti LaBelle in New York, opened for Randy Newman in Philadelphia, and also performed in Los Angeles.

He returned home to a series of concert dates in England and Europe, culminating in a sold-out show at London's Royal Albert Hall. The audience was as entranced by his guitar technique as by the sound of his baritone voice. He had developed an approach in which he could, if he desired, play melody, countermelody, bass lines, riffs, and fill-ins all at the same time, a style a *London Daily Express* writer described as "an orchestra in six strings."

In 1974 he rerecorded "Streets of London" for Reprise/Warner Brothers and ended up with his first major hit. The single rose to number two on U.K. charts and also made German lists in four different versions, three by him and one by a German artist. It was the start of a floodtide of covers by artists around the world that by 1996 had gone past the 200 mark. Overwhelmed by the sudden attention given him by the media and music fans in his home area, in March '75 he announced he would take a leave of absence from the entertainment field for a while. He spent most of the year in the United States, keeping a low profile and doing some writing before surfacing for a Christmas concert in Belfast.

During 1975 Warner Brothers issued the disc *Streets,* which was reissued on Leola Music in 1995. McTell added several more albums to his Warner Brothers catalog in the mid-'70s, including *Right Side Up* in 1976 (reissued as *Weather the Storm* on Mays in 1982); *Ralph, Albert & Sydney* in 1977 (a live album based on concerts at the Royal Albert Hall and Australia's Sydney Opera House—reissued on Mays in 1982); and *Slide Away the Screen* in 1977 (reissued on Mays as *Love Grows* with new tracks in 1982 and with the original title and new tracks on the Road Goes on Forever label in 1994). Backing him on the latter album were longtime friends from Fairport Convention—Richard Thompson, Simon Nicol, and Dave Pegg. Members past and present from that band backed him on many of his recorded material before and after that release.

Over the years, Fairport included a number of McTell's compositions in its concerts and albums. Among them was "The Girl from the Hiring Fair," "Wat Tyler" (cowritten with Simon Nicol), and "Bird from the Mountain." The "Wat Tyler" song, dealing with a failed

English rebellion of several centuries earlier, underscored McTell's interest in historical events. His compositions also included "Red and Gold," based on a 1644 battle in the English civil war, and "Maginot Waltz," about blithely happy picnickers just before the start of World War II. In the 1990s he commented on the horrors of the war in Bosnia in "Peppers and Tomatoes," with lyrics reflecting how easily hatreds could spring up among people who had been neighbors and friends. While Fairport members performed McTell's songs and backed his recordings, he, in turn, took part in a number of the group's annual Cropredy Festivals, including an appearance at the 1992 twenty-fifth anniversary show.

In much of the 1980s Ralph shifted career gears a little to focus some of his attention to children's TV, where he surfaced as a composer and performer on the *Alphabet Zoo*. This was so successful that the network developed a program for him called *Tickle on the Tum*. After his 1982 Mays LP *Water of Dreams,* which featured his song "Bentley and Craig," *Songs from Alphabet Zoo* was issued in 1983. (It was reissued on Music for Pleasure in '84 and as *The Complete Alphabet Zoo* on Road Goes on Forever in 1993.) In 1986, the collection *Best of Tickle on the Tum* came out on Mays. His other 1980s albums comprised a contribution to the CBS album *Just Guitars* ('83); *At the End of a Perfect Day* (Telstar '85); *Bridge of Sighs* (Mays, '86); *Blue Skies Black Heroes* (Leola Music, '88); and the compilation *Affairs of the Heart* (Castle Communications, '89).

He led off the new decade with the 1990 Castle Communications album *Stealin' Back* while starting to work on an ambitious project to capsule the life of poet Dylan Thomas through a combination of words and music. He prepared two versions, one for presentation on BBC Radio and one for the 1992 album on Leola Music, *The Boy with a Note*. Both of those were hailed by British critics, with the *Folk Roots* reviewer calling the album "the most adventurous of his 25 year career . . . and arguably the greatest." The twenty-fifth anniversary of his first album release also was celebrated through release of two retrospective albums by Castle Communications in '92, *The Best of Ralph McTell* and *Silver Celebration*. The tracks on the last-named included "From Clare to Here," about an Irish worker in England who longs for home. Included in Nanci Griffith's Grammy-winning album, *Other Voices, Other Rooms,* it proved one of the most noted tracks in the acclaimed collection.

The attention given that song and the familiarity by many American music fans with "Streets of London" inspired new attention to the U.S. market by McTell and his advisers. After his 1995 album, *Sand in Your Shoes,* was issued by Transatlantic, he headlined a series of standing-room-only appearances at venues along the U.S. East Coast, his first live performances in this country in fourteen years. Also helping to expand his North American audience was the May '96 release of *Silver Celebration* by Red House Records, retitled *From Clare to Here*.

In 1997 McTell began hosting a folk music show for BBC Radio Two called *Folk on Two*. The following year, Leola Music began rereleasing his back catalog on CD, including *You Well Meaning Brought Me Here, Not Till Tomorrow, Easy, Right Side Up,* and *Water of Dreams*.

MELANIE: *Singer, guitarist, songwriter. Born Astoria, Queens, New York, February 3, 1947.*

Though she often appeared with rock groups or in rock venues, there was never any doubt that most of the music Melanie sang, much of it original material, was in the folk tradition. She often gave it a modern twist that allowed her to vie for the attention of the mass audience even in the late 1960s and early 1970s, when folk music had retreated to a minority status.

Melanie, who was born in New York's borough of Queens, was the daughter of Fred and Polly Safka, her father of Ukrainian extraction, her mother of Italian. As she recalled, "My mother sang. She used to sing in clubs and she always sang interesting music, the kind of songs Billie Holiday sang. She always taught me as a little girl to sing songs she sang. Although I was too young to always understand the words, I knew the words meant something to mother and that inspired me."

While attending a variety of schools in New York, including William H. Carr Jr. High School in Bayside, Safka taught herself to play guitar and, by the time the family had settled in Long Branch, New Jersey, already was interested in pursuing a music career. During her early teens, the folk music boom was in full swing and Melanie was attracted to the work of Pete Seeger, Woody Guthrie and, later, Bob Dylan. At sixteen, while she was attending high school in Long Branch, she began singing in local clubs on Monday nights and going into New York on weekends to sing in folk clubs and coffee houses.

She also became interested in acting and attended the American Academy of Dramatic Arts in New York City after graduating from Red Bank High School in the mid-1960s. For a while during that period, Safka studied ceramics at Penland School of Crafts in Penland, North Carolina.

Although she was doing some work as a performer and had been writing original songs for some time, Melanie's move into the recording field came as an accident. While at the Academy, she went to audition for an acting role in an office building on Broadway and the doorman accidentally sent her to a music company. Noting her guitar, people at the company auditioned her and were impressed enough to sign her to a contract. It was a double find for her—while there she met Peter

Schekeryk (born June 23, 1942), who later became her husband.

The alignment helped bring her a recording contract with Columbia Records in 1967 and release of her first single in the fall of the year, "Beautiful People," backed with "God's Only Daughter." However, though she stayed with Columbia into 1967, not too much happened until she left to go with Buddah Records the following year. Her composition "What Have They Done to My Song, Ma," issued late in 1969, became a major hit. Melanie performed at the Woodstock concert in the summer of 1969, although her set was not included on the original album or movie of that landmark event. A song "Birthday of the Sun" was released on the *Woodstock 2* album, and she was included on the video released twenty years after the event, *Woodstock: The Lost Performances*. In 1970 she made the singles charts with "Lay Down/Candles in the Rain" and "Peace Will Come" as well as the album charts with her Buddah LP, *Candles in the Rain*. (*Candles* was her third album, having been preceded by *Affectionately Melanie* and *Born to Be*.) Her next albums on Buddah came out in rapid-fire fashion—*Leftover Wine*, a live album recorded at Carnegie Hall, in mid summer 1970 and *The Good Book* in early 1971. The latter, though on the pop charts, didn't sell quite as well as *Candles in the Rain*. In 1970, she released one of her best-known performances, a single of the Rolling Stones' "Ruby Tuesday" sung in a slow, mournful voice.

Melanie was beginning to feel restless with her association and in 1971 decided to change direction in several ways. She and her husband set up their own label, Neighborhood Records, just about the same time that Melanie chose to cut back on touring in favor of raising a family. Earlier in the year she had been honored with an invitation to play at the opening of the United Nations General Assembly. This led to her being named the official spokeswoman for UNICEF.

One of her first efforts for Neighborhood was her song "Brand New Key," a frothy pop song that was released in the fall of 1971 and rose to number one in the United States in January. Also doing well was her first Neighborhood LP, *Gather Me*, which rose to top-chart levels and earned a gold record, as had "Brand New Key." Her newfound popularity wasn't lost on Buddah, which struck paydirt with material Melanie had recorded while still under contract to them. The single of the "Nickel Song" was a hit the first half of 1972, and so were the albums *Garden in the City* and *Four Sides of Melanie* in 1973. On Neighborhood, Melanie had such other chartmakers in 1972 as the album *Stoneground Words* and the singles "Ring the Living Bell" and "Together Alone."

The phenomenal public appetite for songs like "Brand New Key" and "Nickel Song" wasn't matched by critical approval. She was scolded in print, as she put it, for being "an ingenue, a sickly sweet person singing sickly sweet songs." The fact that she had written songs with considerably more depth over the years was forgotten. Melanie was thin-skinned about the subject and that, coupled with her desire to raise a family, caused her to drop out of the limelight for several years while two daughters were born and a son in 1981. A live album from a 1972 concert at Carnegie Hall, *Melanie at Carnegie Hall*, and the retrospective *Very Best of Melanie* were issued in 1973, followed by another Buddah release, *Please Love Me*. She still found time to release a few albums—*Madrugada* and *As I See It Now* in 1974; *Sunset and Other Beginnings* the following year. But none sold well, and she and her husband shut down Neighborhood Records.

In 1976, she came out of that temporary retirement to record a new album for Atlantic Records that was released with the title *Photograph*. The original material she provided was more complex in lyric structure than her previous work. It won accolades from the critical establishment, including a paean from John Rockwell of the *New York Times*, who wrote that Melanie was "singing adult songs for adult people." He called the album one of the top-10 LPs of the year. However, the album fell far short of her earlier efforts in the market place.

Not too much was heard from her for a while after that, though some of her recordings continued to sell years after their original release. As of early 1978, she had recorded nineteen albums and sold over 22 million records worldwide.

She returned to the recording wars in 1978 with a new release on Midsong International Records called *Phonogenic: Not Just Another Pretty Face*. The album contained four new original compositions, including "Runnin' After Love," "Spunky," and "Bon Appetit." The remaining ten songs were by other writers, including perhaps the most effective tracks of the album, her version of Jesse Winchester's "Yankee Man" and of Carole Bayer Sager's "I'd Rather Leave While I'm In Love." She released *Ballroom Streets* in 1979 on Tomato Records, her last original album until 1982, when she released *Arabesque* for Blanche Records. The latter was released in the United Kingdom by RCA and gained enough interest to support a series of concerts there. She followed up with her Neighborhood release, *Seventh Wave*, for the British market in 1983. At the end of the 1980s, she received an Emmy for writing the lyrics to "The First Time I Loved Forever," from the television series *Beauty and the Beast*. For the most part, she was content to raise her children. However, she continued to appear at folk festivals and clubs in the United States and in Europe. She also appeared at the twentieth and twenty-fifth anniversaries of the Woodstock concert.

Melanie was represented in the late 1980s and 1990s by *Am I Real or What* (Amherst, 1985) in the United Kingdom, *Melanie* (CNR, 1987) in the Netherlands, *Cowabonga* (Food for Thought, 1989) in the United

Kingdom, *The Best of Melanie* (Rhino, 1990), *Precious Cargo* (Precious Cargo, 1991), *Freedom Knows My Name* (Lonestar Records, 1993), *Silence Is King* (Hypertension, 1993), *Silver Anniversary* (Dino, 1993) in the Netherlands, *Old Bitch Warrior* (Creators BMG/Ariola, 1995) in the Netherlands, *Golden Hits Collection* (Intercontinental, 1995), *Her Greatest Hits Live & New* (Laserlight Digital, 1996), *Unchained Melanie* (VTM Entertainment Company, 1996), *Low Country* (Special Edition, 1997), *Melanie—On Air* (Strange Fruit, 1997) taken from BBC recordings, a Christmas album *Antlers* (Blue Moon, 1997), *The Very Best of Melanie* (Camden, 1998), and *BBC Radio I Live in Concert* (Imprint, 1998).

In 1998 Melanie and her husband, Peter Schekeryk, briefly opened a restaurant/coffeehouse called Melanie's in Tarpon Springs, Florida, near their home in Clearwater. "For a while there, it wasn't cool to be Melanie," she told Michelle Miller of the *St. Petersburg Times* ("Look What Melanie's Done to the House, Ma," April 20, 1998). "Now it's cool to be Melanie again."

MELLENCAMP, JOHN: *Singer, guitarist, band leader (the Zone), songwriter. Born Seymour, Indiana, October 7, 1951.*

An exponent of the straightforward, mainstream rock favored by most midwestern U.S. fans in the 1970s and '80s, John (Cougar) Mellencamp, as his career progressed, increasingly took note of the problems besetting society from the plight of the small farmer facing foreclosure to the blue-collar workers suffering the pains of recession. His lyrics and his musical treatment of his songs, which in some cases employed arrangements based on instruments like the fiddle and accordion, certainly were in the folk tradition. He sometimes was called the midwestern Bruce Springsteen, but in his self-penned songs of the '80s and early '90s, Mellencamp demonstrated a far less romantic outlook in his lyrics than Bruce, and his often bitterly cynical comments turned off some critics, though not his many admirers in the Midwest and all over the world.

John grew up in the working-class town of Seymour, Indiana, not far from the industrial city of Bloomington. Though his father had brought the family into a middle-class environment, John noted their roots were rural. He told a reporter from *Billboard:* "We were farmers, basically, of Dutch stock. My grandfather was a carpenter, never got past the third grade, could barely speak English. My dad became a vice president of an electrical company—one of those self-made guys. I'm the runt of the litter [referring to his short, stocky shape]; everybody else has big muscles."

Like many a rock musician, Mellencamp was a rebellious, outspoken teenager. He had some athletic ability and made his high school football team but was thrown out for violating smoking rules. He also didn't take to any of his peers trying to order him around. He had a quick temper that, he recalled, often led to fights with other teens. "You had to fight," he claimed. "Your dignity depended on it."

Rock 'n 'roll became a strong influence during those years. He listened to records and radio programs and also ventured into playing guitar with school friends and some early attempts at songwriting. His carefree phase came to an abrupt stop when his girlfriend, a relatively mature twenty-three to his eighteen, informed him she was pregnant; the two eloped and moved in with her parents in Louisville, Kentucky.

She got a job with the local phone company, but John demurred at 9-to-5 work since he was determined to carve out a career in music. To his in-laws' dismay, he was underfoot all the time, often just drinking, smoking, or listening to records with occasional time out for songwriting. After eighteen months, they gave him an ultimatum: work or leave. He took off and sought work with local bar bands in the Midwest, living from hand to mouth for the next few years.

After a while, he felt ready to try for bigger things. He recorded a demo tape of some of his songs and headed to New York to seek recording contracts. In 1975, he finally caught the ear of David Bowie's manager, Tony DeVries, who liked the tape enough to actively pursue a recording contract for his new client. He won approval from MCA executives and Mellencamp's debut came out under the title *Chestnut Street Incident* (1976). When Mellencamp saw his first copy, he was upset to find that someone had given him the pseudonym of Johnny Cougar.

He told writer Martin Torgoff: "So I get the record finally—my first record—and it says Johnny Cougar on it! Nobody ever called me 'Johnny' in my whole life, ever—and that's the name people in the Midwest know me by now because of that record. It's a ridiculous name, but I'm stuck with it. It doesn't bother me that much anymore. I just laugh about it now."

From 1976 to 1978, Mellencamp's subsequent album output included *Kid Inside* (issued by MCA in the United States) and *Biography* (released only in Europe in 1978). Little happened with his MCA material and he was dropped from the label, which later licensed his two U.S. LPs to Rhino Records for reissue. He, in turn, left DeVries's organization and moved under the wing of Billy Gaff, at the time the manager of Rod Stewart. Gaff soon arranged for Mellencamp to record an album for Gaff's label, Riva. John worked on that for the first part of 1979 and rehearsed his band, the Zone, for live performances in support of the LP the latter part of the year. The band comprised Larry Crane and Mike Wanchic on dual lead guitars, a bass guitar player called Ferd, and a pianist only known as "Doc."

The band began to play small clubs and work as an opening act before the first Riva LP, titled *John* (rather than Johnny) *Cougar,* came out in the fall of 1979. With Cougar in top singing form and the band giving compelling backing, the group won praise in newspaper columns around the country. Some of their musical associates thought the group sounded too good. Thus, during October 1979, Cougar and company were dismissed as opening act for a Kiss tour because they tended to upstage the better-known band.

Though disco and new wave were the musical buzzwords in 1979, Mellencamp had no apologies for his somewhat "conservative" approach to rock. He told Jo-Ann Wong of the *Deseret News* that with punk or new wave, "You can't tell by listening who's who. With disco there's nothing personal. I'm not into fads. They cost too much money. I can't afford to go out and buy a disco shirt, shoes, and pants or go to discos every night. Same for new wave. I can't go out and buy a leather jacket."

Enough fans agreed with him to allow his Riva debut to do reasonably well, even if it fell far short of gold record sales. Songs such as "A Little Night Dancin',", "Small Paradise," "Sugar Marie," "Great Mid-west," and "I Need a Lover," suggested that an important new force had appeared in pop music for the 1980s. With "I Need a Lover," John had his first singles hit, peaking at number twenty-eight in *Billboard* in December 1979.

The second Riva release, *Nothing Matters and What If It Did* (1980), met with about the same response as his debut on the label. It did produce two moderate hit singles: "This Time" (which reached twenty-seven in *Billboard* that December) and "Ain't Even Done with the Night" (number seventeen the next May).

In late 1981 and early 1982, Mellencamp put the finishing touches on his third album on Riva (which was by then part of the Mercury Records organization). It was to provide the breakthrough he had been seeking for almost a decade. Called *American Fool,* the album remained number one in *Billboard* for nine straight weeks in summer 1982, earning John his first platinum record certification. Its success pulled the previous LP, *Nothin' Matters and What If It Did,* onto the hit lists in late 1982.

Helping propel *American Fool* to the heights were several hit singles, the first being "Hurts So Good." He recalled a friend had been with him at his home in Bloomington and suggested that "a great idea for a song" was based on the phrase "It hurts so good!" Right after that, John went to take a shower and "the song came to me so fast that I grabbed a piece of soap and wrote it on the glass of the shower door. That's what I call a good, clean song." The single made a clean break to the top, faltering just shy of number one at the second position in *Billboard* the week of August 7, 1982. It stayed at number two for four weeks while another single, "Jack and Diane," entered the top 10, giving Mellencamp the rare accomplishment of having two discs in the top 10 simultaneously. "Jack and Diane" did even better than "Hurts So Good" ranking number one for four weeks starting October 2. In the Grammy Awards for 1982, "Hurts So Good" won the trophy for Best Rock Vocal Performance, Male.

During 1982, Mellencamp demonstrated he was not without compassion for others by giving a free concert in Fort Wayne, Indiana, for 20,000 high schoolers who had worked for eight days in March to pile up sandbags and save the city from flooding. He said: "These kids don't have money to go to concerts or have much of a good time. The point of this free show was to help them have a little fun." Later in the 1980s, he contributed his services to benefits intended to help impoverished Midwestern farmers.

As Mellencamp began working on his next LP, he was determined to restore his full original name to his album listing. Though the label argued it might confuse his audience, he persevered and the platinum fall 1983 release, *Uh-Huh,* bore his full name on the cover. Its top 10 *Billboard* singles included "Pink Houses" and "Crumblin' Down."

His 1985 album proved his biggest success to date. Called *Scarecrow,* by year-end, it was number three in the United States. Easily exceeding triple-platinum levels, it provided two top 10 1985 singles, "Small Town" and "Lonely Ol' Night" (like most Mellencamp singles, written by him). In the 1985 Grammy competition, *Scarecrow* was one of the finalists in the Best Rock Vocal Performance, Male, category. In 1986, *Scarecrow's* track "R.O.C.K. in the U.S.A." hit number one in *Billboard.*

During the summer of 1987, PolyGram released a new LP by John, *The Lonesome Jubilee,* which by early 1988 had sold over 2 million copies. The material obviously wasn't aimed at teenagers, though Mellencamp still drew sizable numbers from that age bracket to his concerts. The song "The Real Life," for example, had for its hero a forty-year-old who still had no sense of purpose about his life.

Mellencamp told Robert Hilburn (*Los Angeles Times,* February 26, 1988), "Every song on the album came out of table talking. Anybody who knows me knows you can come over just about any night of the week and there will be four or five people sitting around the kitchen table, drinking coffee, smoking cigarettes and talking about all sorts of things.

"Take 'The Real Life.' It was just another night at the table. Jackson Jackson is a real person, though that's not his name. He said to me one night, 'I'm 40-something years old and divorced and, hell, I haven't done one thing with my life that I really wanted to do when I was young and strong and a worldshaker.' But when I asked him what it was he wanted to do now, he looked at me and said, 'I don't know.'

"I think that is a very common thing among people who aren't very directed and I don't think 98 percent of the world is very directed."

In the fall of 1988, Mellencamp recorded his version of "Do Re Mi" for *A Vision Shared,* a Folkways tribute to Woody Guthrie and Leadbelly. John ended the decade with the 1989 album *Big Daddy,* then announced he was going to take some time off to do some painting. His move in that creative direction was relatively short-lived, as he soon became involved in filmmaking and recording new material in the early 1990s. This resulted in the 1992 album release *Whenever We Wanted* and the movie, which he helped script and also directed and starred in, *Falling from Grace*. In 1993 his album *Human Wheels* was released, followed in 1994 by *Dance Naked*. The album spent a number of months on the charts, though it never reached top positions.

The first part of the '90s, though, brought some unsettling personal problems, including a heart attack in 1994. The decade began with the breakup of his second marriage, which ended in divorce in 1990. The demise of his marriage, coupled with his continued hectic professional activities, likely played a role in his health problems. Recalling what happened for Robert Hilburn of the *Los Angeles Times* ("Oh Yeah, Life Goes on . . . and Thrill of Living Is Back," September 10, 1996), he said, "I woke up after a show in New York and I was sick as a dog. I thought I was getting the flu or something. My hands were trembling and I couldn't walk. I never imagined I was having a heart attack. I did like 15 more shows before I went to the doctor in Bloomington [Indiana] for my annual physical and learned it was a heart attack. So, I went straight to the hospital where they found the end of an artery had closed out. . . . It was definitely due to my lifestyle. You can't lay your face in cholesterol day after day, smoke 80 cigarettes a day, stay out all night, stay up all day and not expect repercussions."

He noted that for six months after he couldn't escape a form of panic and depression that made it difficult to relax. "You keep thinking that you've had a heart attack and you may have another one. But once you get out of the depression, things kind of get into focus for me. I never thought I'd ever say this, but the heart attack was probably the best thing that could have happened to me." It brought about a change in outlook about what was most important in life, he indicated, and also made him realize how fortunate he had been in many ways. Also helping to make him feel better about himself was starting a new family with a supportive third wife, Elaine. He decided to cut back on touring in favor of spending more time at home getting to know his infant children, Hud and Speck. (He also had three children from his first two marriages.)

Though he limited his appearances in the mid-1990s, he always found time for some of his favorite benefits, such as the annual Farm Aid concerts. Meanwhile, his album catalog continued to sell steadily. In early 1996 the R.I.A.A. presented him with a multiplatinum (3 million copies) award for the 1981 release *Uh-Huh;* one for 4 million copies for the '82 LP *American Fool;* gold and platinum for *Nothin' Matters & What If It Did* (1984); 4 million copy award for the 1985 *Scarecrow;* gold record for the 1987 *John Cougar Mellencamp;* and a 3-million-copy award for the '87 *The Lonesome Jubilee.* In September 1996 Mercury released a new, post–heart attack

disc, *Mr. Happy Go Lucky,* which took a more optimistic look at life than typical in his earlier releases.

He released his first retrospective album, *The Best That I Could Do: 1978–1988,* in late 1997. The album was certified platinum in 1998. He switched from Polygram-Mercury to the Columbia label and released *John Mellencamp* in October 1998, his fifteenth album. He received strong reviews in *Time* and *People Weekly*. He culled the twelve tracks, including "Your Life Is Now," "Eden Is Burning" (in which Jack and Diane make a cameo appearance), and "Fruit Trader" from more than fifty songs he had written. Later in the year he also released a book showcasing seventy-five of his paintings titled *Mellencamp: Painting and Reflections* (HarperCollins).

MEMPHIS MINNIE: *Singer, songwriter, guitarist. Born Algiers, Louisiana, June 3, 1897; died Memphis, Tennessee, August 6, 1973.*

A fine guitarist, singer, and composer best known for her song "Bumble Bee Blues" and her performance of "Me and My Chauffeur," Memphis Minnie McCoy picked up where Bessie Smith and Ma Rainey left off. She was a self-sufficient and appealing woman who carved out a successful career through sheer force of will, personality, and talent. She outlasted three husbands who were often her accompanists, and projected a sense of independence and playful sexuality that continues to inspire female performers into the 1990s. She made more than 200 recordings, and legend has it that she was such a good guitarist that she even beat Big Bill Broonzy in a cutting concert in Chicago in the early 1930s. She was also tough—willing to use a pocketknife or pistol if need be.

She was born Lizzie Douglas, the first of Abe and Gertrude Douglas's thirteen children. When she was seven, the family moved to Walls, Mississippi, thirteen miles southwest of Memphis, and then into Memphis. She started on the banjo and soon taught herself guitar. By her fifteenth year she was playing on Beale Street for tips. Between 1916 and 1920 she performed with the Ringling Brothers Circus. Known as Kid Douglas, she often played with the Memphis Jug Band and was romantically involved with original member Casey Bill Weldon.

By 1929 she had married guitarist and singer Joe McCoy (born Raymond, Mississippi, May 11, 1905; died Chicago, January 28, 1950). They recorded for Columbia Records in June 1929 under the names Kansas Joe and Memphis Minnie. Initially, Columbia released "That Will Be Alright" backed with "When the Levee Breaks" and "Goin' Back to Texas" backed with "Frisco Town," all four featuring Kansas Joe on vocals. It was Mayo Williams of Vocalion Records who recognized Memphis Minnie's talent, recording her with Kansas Joe in February 1930. Vocalion released the seductive "Bumble Bee Blues" featuring her vocals, which became a hit in 1930. She followed with "Bumble Bee No. 2" and "New Bumble Bee" for Vocalion. Among Kansas Joe and Memphis Minnie's early recordings was "Hoodoo Lady," which demonstrated their excellent guitar picking. Before the end of 1930 they moved to Chicago.

She continued to make recordings for Vocalion, seventeen of them in the first five months of 1931. As Samuel Charters notes in *Sweet as the Showers of Rain,* "She was a handsome, talented woman, with a successful career and an open enjoyment of the things of life she found around her. She made a comfortable living for the Depression years and she lived well in Chicago. Her marriage did end with Joe McCoy, but she didn't have the series of drab affairs that she described in her songs. The image which she projected of herself, however, was poor, often alone, often resentful—sometimes even pathetic in her need for affection." (Kansas Joe and his brother Charlie McCoy later got together with trumpeter Herb Morand to form the Harlem Hamfats, a popular band in Chicago in the 1930s.)

According to Charters, between 1934 and 1942 record buyers could find a new Memphis Minnie record in the stores each month. She received $12.50 a side. She began to record without Kansas Joe in 1935, performing two songs about boxer Joe Louis: "He's in the Ring" and "Joe Louis Strut," the latter with pianist Black Bob. That year she cut four songs with her first partner, Casey Bill Weldon, for the Bluebird label.

In 1939 she married Ernest Lawlars, a.k.a. Little Son Joe, with whom she would record for the next decade. She had a hit in 1941 with the memorable song "Me and My Chauffeur Blues" backed with "Can't Afford to Lose My Man" for the OKeh label. It became a trademark song for Memphis Minnie through the end of the decade. She also recorded Lawlars's "Digging My Potatoes" and "I'm So Glad," and the semiautobiographical "In My Girlish Days" and "Hustlin' Woman Blues."

Among other pursuits, she owned a blues club in Indianapolis and lived in Detroit during the 1940s. In 1952 she recorded for the JOB label, and for Checker two years later. She cut records with Sunnyland Slim and Little Walter. During the 1940s Minnie also began playing an electric guitar; she was always a step ahead of most other female performers.

In 1957 Lawlars had a heart attack, and they returned home to Memphis, where he died in 1961. She suffered a stroke in 1960 that spelled the end of her singing career. Over the last thirteen years of her life, Minnie lived in various nursing homes and with her sisters. She suffered a fatal stroke and died in Memphis at her sister Daisy Johnson's home on August 7, 1973. Charters notes that she had outlived her fellow musicians; only Furry Lewis attended her funeral. She was buried at the New Hope Cemetery in Walls, Mississippi.

She left behind voluminous recorded material, much of which can now be found on CD. These include *Complete Recorded Works (1935–1941), Volumes 1–5* (Document/RST, 1991); *Complete Recorded Works: Memphis Minnie & Kansas Joe (1929–1934), Volumes 1–4* (Document, 1991); *Hoodoo Lady (1933–1937)* (Columbia/Roots 'n' Blues, 1991), which includes her work with Lawlars; *I Ain't No Bad Gal* (CBS/Portrait Masters, 1988); *Hot Stuff (1930–1941)* (Collector's Edition, 1996); *Me & My Chauffeur 1935–1946* (E.P.M. Blues Collection, 1997); *Memphis Minnie: The Complete Post-War Recordings in Chronological Order 1944–53, Volumes 1–3* (Wolf, 1991); *Early Rhythm & Blues 1949* (Biograph, 1992); and *Memphis Minnie: Queen of the Blues* (Columbia Legacy, 1997). In 1992, Da Capo published a book about Memphis Minnie titled *Woman with Guitar: Memphis Minnie's Blues,* by Paul and Beth Garon.

MITCHELL, JONI: *Singer, songwriter, guitarist, pianist, artist. Born Fort Macleod, Alberta, Canada, November 7, 1943.*

In February 2000, Joni Mitchell sat in the middle of her home art studio like a lady at court, surrounded by paintings, easels, a Fender Strat, dulcimers, and drums. She picked up a Collings acoustic guitar and began strumming in her unorthodox, self-taught style. It's an image—the girl with the acoustic guitar—that she'd been trying to live down for thirty years, since she helped create the confessional singer-songwriter genre with her classic folk composition "Both Sides Now."

During her 1974 concert tour, Joni Mitchell changed one of the verses to "Both Sides Now" to *But now old friends are acting strange / They shake their heads, they say I've changed. . . . And I have!* Indeed, at the time, Ms. Mitchell was shedding her image of a shy, soft-spoken folk artist. She continued to change, moving toward jazz until, by the end of the '70s, her music ranked among the more dynamic experiments in avant-garde jazz. Whatever genre she worked in, she made lasting contributions. Even as some jazz enthusiasts welcomed her sounds, folk performers still covered her earlier writings and aspiring rock performers drew musical insight from her up-tempo recordings. What most of her fans didn't realize (although it infused a great deal of her art) was that during all of those years in the spotlight, Joni was struggling with the longings of having given her only child up for adoption when she was twenty-one.

Born Roberta Joan Anderson in Fort Macleod, Canada, she was the only daughter of Myrtle and Bill Anderson, a schoolteacher and a former Royal Canadian Air Force officer turned grocery store manager. When Joni was six, her family settled in Saskatoon, Saskatchewan. From an early age she demonstrated a creative (and rebellious) bent. She started classical piano lessons when she was seven, and began smoking at age nine, though she kept it a secret.

Joni contracted polio in the fall of 1952 and was

hospitalized for several months. She feared she might never walk again, but through sheer willpower she found the strength to walk and was able to go home by Christmas. Her mother helped nurse her back to health and home-schooled her for the next year. Her bout with polio "made an artist out of me," she says. "Staring into the eyes of death as a young person deepens you a lot." She found an early interest in art and, with encouragement from her teachers, became a capable painter. By age eleven, her paintings, which she signed "Joni," were exhibited at her school. "I grew up with an identity as an artist, and although I was encouraged to write and my writing was praised, I didn't develop a sense of myself as a writer," she says. Nevertheless, a seventh grade English teacher, Arthur Kratzman, singled her out as one of the best writers in class. "Someday I think you'll love to paint with words," he told her.

As a child, Joni was something of a tomboy, playing cowboys and Indians with the boys. But then the hormones kicked in. She had a rebellious adolescence. She loved to dance all night at clubs. She listened to country, jazz, rockabilly, and rock 'n' roll. At thirteen she even entered a contest to become the "Girl From Saskatoon," a pageant inspired by a Johnny Cash song. A friend of hers won and got to go to Cash's concert. She began to listen to folk musicians such as Pete Seeger, Leadbelly, Woody Guthrie, Bob Dylan, Joan Baez, and Canadians Ian & Sylvia and Gordon Lightfoot. In her senior year she bought a baritone ukulele for $36 and learned a few chords.

After high school, she enrolled in the Alberta College of Art in Calgary with the thought of making a career in commercial art. She took along her baritone ukulele just for the fun of it and started singing folk songs during leisure moments. When friends urged her to go further with her musical talent, she found work at a local coffeehouse called the Depression. Eventually she bought a guitar and taught herself. Music became more engrossing and her interest in commercial art faded. The same wasn't true for her painting, which remained a major love. (Later on, she did many original pieces of art for use on her album covers and had major exhibits of her work.)

She started to go farther afield to perform. On a train trip to the Mariposa Folk Festival in Toronto, where she traveled to see singer Buffy Sainte-Marie, she wrote her first song, "Day by Day." Once in eastern Canada, she became enthused about the folk scene. She moved to Toronto and began to pursue a career in folk music. She wrote contemporary folk-style songs and built a reputation with folk fans and other young performers in the city. But shortly after she settled in Toronto, she discovered that she had become pregnant by "fellow painter" Brad MacMath. On February 19, 1965, she gave birth to a baby girl, Kelly. She was too embarrassed to tell her parents that she had had a child out of wedlock.

She wanted to keep her daughter but she was penniless and couldn't afford diapers or housing. At the Penny Farthing coffee house, she met a young American folksinger named Chuck Mitchell who initially agreed to take on Joni and her daughter. Joni and Chuck were married in June 1965 at his parents' home in Rochester, Michigan. She soon adopted her stage name, Joni Mitchell. But a couple of months into the marriage, she was forced to give Kelly up for adoption. "It says in the notes, on the adoptive papers, 'Mother had very difficult time signing this,'" she says. (Kelly was adopted by David and Ida Gibb, two teachers who lived in the Toronto area.) "A piece of me was missing," Joni says. "Right after that of course I began to write. And right after that I was reeled up into celebrity land. The combination play was kind of disastrous. . . . It left a hole in me that I didn't fill until the day I saw her again."

It was as Joni Mitchell that she began to perform in coffeehouses in Detroit, where she and her husband billed themselves as Joan and Chuck Mitchell. Joni drew the attention of folk artists like Eric Andersen, Tom Rush, and Ramblin' Jack Elliott. She and Chuck divorced soon after, but Joni Mitchell she remained. Meanwhile, the impact of her performance and the quality of her original material continued to improve.

She performed at the Newport Folk Festival in 1966. In 1967 Joni moved to New York, encouraged by Tom Rush, who recorded her song "Urge for Going." There she quickly met David Geffen, Elliot Roberts, who became her manager in late 1967, and David Crosby. Word of her talents spread among her musical peers. Soon Judy Collins, Buffy Sainte-Marie, and Dave Van Ronk were also performing her songs.

As a Detroit critic enthused in 1967: "She is a beautiful woman. Her voice and her acoustic guitar are free, pure instruments in themselves; there is additional beauty in the way she uses them to convey such a full range of emotions. But if she knew only three chords, her performance would be justified by her songs alone. As a songwriter, she plays Yang to Bob Dylan's Yin, equaling him in richness and profusion of imagery and surpassing him in conciseness and direction."

With the help of Crosby, she landed a recording contract with Reprise Records and moved to Los Angeles. Crosby also produced her debut LP, *Joni Mitchell: Song to a Seagull* (March 1968). The allegorical album, with one side called "I came to the city" and the other "Out of the city and down to the seaside," received rave reviews. But her first national success came when Judy Collins' version of Joni's song "Clouds" (retitled "Both Sides Now") peaked at number eight on *Billboard* in November 1968.

By 1968, Joni had moved to a home in Laurel Canyon above Los Angeles, where she spent much of her time when not on the road throughout the '70s. During the years she recorded for Reprise, she continued to be identified with contemporary folk music. Her second record on Reprise, *Clouds* (which featured Joni's self-portrait on the cover), came out in October 1969 and was a chart hit. She won her first Grammy for Best Folk Performer. The album included her versions of "Both Sides Now," "Tin Angel," and "Chelsea Morning," with lines that inspired Bill and Hillary Clinton to name their daughter Chelsea. By the end of the year, Joni had gotten involved with Crosby's bandmate, Graham Nash. They settled into a late '60s lifestyle in Los Angeles commemorated by Nash in his song "Our House." (Joni knew Stephen Stills and had first met Neil Young at the 4-D coffeehouse in Winnipeg in 1964.) In August 1969, she was supposed to join her friends at the Woodstock festival in upstate New York but the massive traffic jams kept her away. Nevertheless, her song "Woodstock" captured the euphoria and idealism of the festival. Crosby, Stills, Nash and Young's single of the song hit number eleven on the *Billboard* charts in April 1970. Matthews Southern Comfort topped the U.K. charts with the song that year. The song was an early intimation of some of the directions Joni's writing would take in the '70s.

Her third album, *Ladies of the Canyon* (May 1970), which included "Big Yellow Taxi," "For Free," and "Woodstock," went gold. But by June 1970, her romantic relationship with Graham Nash had ended. She retreated to Crete where she was visited by James Taylor—she had sung backup on "You've Got a Friend"—and where she was inspired to write songs for her romantic confessional masterpiece, *Blue.*

Blue, Mitchell's best-selling album, was certainly one of the best of 1971 and arguably one of the best of the century. It hit number fifteen on the *Billboard* charts. Many of its songs underscored her ability to work several themes into a single song. An example is "All I Want": *Alive, alive, I want to get up and jive / I want to wreck my stockings in some juke box dive,*" but it ends suggesting those are daydreams to supplement the more restrained yearnings for love. The quality remained high in every song, whether slow or fast, and such tracks as "My Old Man," "This Flight Tonight," "Carey," and "The Last Time I Saw Richard" remain favorites. There still was a contemporary folk feeling to *Blue.* She had written some songs on the piano, which she had played during preparation for *Ladies of the Canyon.* On *Blue,* Joni was struggling with her own demons and crises: "To ask what I was going through when I wrote *Blue* is a really strange question because everything I was going through when I wrote *Blue* is on *Blue,* in incredible detail."

One of the songs, "Little Green," relates to her daughter. The song "was like sending her a message in a bottle," says Mitchell, who had named her daughter after the color, Kelly Green. "It was a song of goodwill addressed to her out in the world, wishing her happiness and joy." Over the years she consulted gypsies in an effort to find out what had happened to her. After completing *Blue,* she realized she was feeling increasingly uptight about the inroads of her career on her private life. She decided to take time out to reevaluate things and for the next year and a half stayed away from concerts—traveling, visiting with friends, and concentrating on painting and songwriting. In 1972, she toured with another rising star, Jackson Browne.

She sold her house in Laurel Canyon and built a retreat near Vancouver, British Columbia. However, she didn't give up writing and recording. She moved from Reprise to Asylum Records (newly founded by David Geffen), and released *For The Roses* (November 1972). Its country-flavored "You Turn Me On, I'm a Radio" became a hit single, peaking at number twenty-five on *Billboard*'s charts; she earned a gold record.

Though Joni stressed about rock and jazz, by the time *Court & Spark* came out in January 1974, it didn't diminish her appeal. Backing her was rock-jazz artist Tom Scott, who helped put together the "band sound." "It took me six projects to find a band that could play my music," she recalls. "And when I did it came in a hybrid, with one foot in the jazz camp and one foot in a very original kind of pop music." She held on to most of her earlier fans and added a host of new ones. Proof was the success, both critical and commercial, of the gold LP, which also spawned three hit singles: "Raised on Robbery," "Help Me," and "Free Man in Paris" (a song about Geffen). One song, "Same Situation," reflected one of her enduring themes: *My search for love it don't seem to cease. Court & Spark* was nominated for four Grammys and won for Best Arrangements.

In 1974, she went on her first major tour in a long while, accompanied by Tom Scott and the L.A. Express, which included drummer John Guerin, her boyfriend at the time. Her rock image was met by shrieks of joy, thunderous applause, and dancing in the aisles. Unlike earlier tours, when mellow acts such as Jackson Browne opened for her, the L.A. Express began with a hard-driving electric set. The results of that combination were captured in the gold double disc *Miles of Aisles* (January 1975). Her updated treatment of an earlier favorite, "Big Yellow Taxi," brought another hit single.

She diverged from rock to avant-garde jazz the next time out with the November 1975 LP *The Hissing of Summer Lawns.* The lyrics, as often held true in the '70s, were richly poetic, accompanied by complex, usually minor key melodies. In addition, a complex rhythmic background, influenced by drummer John Guerin (with whom she shared a sixteen-room, Spanish-style villa in the canyons of Bel Air, California) and an ensemble from Burundi, pulsated throughout the album. Discussing the material in the liner notes, she cryptically wrote: "The whole unfolded like a mystery. It is not my intention to unravel that mystery for anyone, but rather to offer some additional clues."

In 1975–1976 she appeared in a number of shows with Bob Dylan's Rolling Thunder Revue and toured with Tom Scott's group. Jazz continued to preoccupy her to a greater extent. She continued to experiment with her styles on her next few albums, much to the dismay of her older fans who wanted her to return to the folk stylings of *Blue*. In November 1976, bassist Jaco Pastorius of Weather Report was one of those who contributed to her LP *Hejira*. An Arabic word for flight, *Hejira* again reflected Joni's mood at the time, during which she went on a road trip across the country following another romantic breakup. Although the album received many negative reviews, it is truly one of Mitchell's most complete works.

Pastorius contributed to Joni's next effort, the double album *Don Juan's Reckless Daughter* (Asylum/ Elektra, January 1978). He was joined by such artists as Wayne Shorter, Guerin, Chaka Khan, and Brazilian Airto Moreira. The Afro-Latin percussionists and jazz artists combined to produce an intricate sound of near symphonic complexity. Her song "Paprika Plains" captivated jazz great Charles Mingus, who asked Mitchell to help set T.S. Eliot's *Four Quartets* to music as well as add lyrics to his song, "Goodbye Pork Pie Hat."

But Mingus died of Lou Gehrig's Disease in Mexico on January 5, 1979, before the project was finished. Issued that summer, *Mingus,* which included Wayne Shorter on sax, Herbie Hancock on keyboards, Don Alias on percussion, Peter Erskine on drums, and Pastorius on bass, was dedicated to Mingus and included some impressive paintings of him by Joni on the cover. *Mingus* spent months on the charts during 1979.

The following year, Joni had a hit with another jazz-based Asylum album, *Shadows and Light*, a live set recorded at L.A.'s Greek Theatre, with backing from such jazz fusion performers as Pastorius and Pat Metheny, and vocals from the Persuasions. The tracks included a revision of Frankie Lymon and the Teenagers' 1956 hit "Why Do Fools Fall In Love." Many observers were surprised that Joni could bring a large segment of her folk-pop fans along with her into the jazz domain as shown by the continued chart status of her new releases.

During the 1980s, Joni edged away from jazz, blending elements of other types of music into her albums. She spent some time in the Caribbean painting and writing. Reggae influenced her album on the Geffen label, *Wild Things Run Fast* (November 1982). She lyrically explored the problems of aging in the album. Bassist Larry Klein worked with her and the two became involved romantically. They were married on November 21, 1982. She embarked on an extensive tour of Europe and Asia in 1983, which was exhausting and financially unsuccessful. As a result she vowed not to tour anymore, a decision she honored into the late 1990s. In early 1985, she dismissed Elliot Roberts and signed on with Peter Asher Management. (In the '90s, she signed with S.L. Feldman & Associates of Vancouver.)

Joni and Klein narrowly escaped major injury when a drunk driver smashed into their car on Pacific Coast Highway, but they were still able to attend the record release party for *Dog Eat Dog* issued on Geffen in November 1985. The bleak and controversial album received lukewarm reviews, and her popularity with fans and critics seemed to drop off in the mid-1980s. In 1987, she received a personal blow when Pastorius died after he was beaten outside a nightclub.

But in 1988, she turned her career around with an excellent album co-produced by Klein, *Chalk Mark in a Rainstorm*. Recorded in nine different studios in England and Los Angeles, it included Joni's version of the traditional "Corinna, Corinna" which she titled "A Bird That Whistles." The album spent months on the charts. Joni was nominated for a Best Pop Female Vocalist Grammy, losing out to Tracy Chapman.

At the beginning of the 1990s, singer-songwriters were again in favor. Many female singers cited Joni Mitchell as a primary influence, including Tori Amos, Shawn Colvin, the Indigo Girls, and Alanis Morissette. Some of them joined the Lilith Fair concerts started by Sarah McLachlan. In Los Angeles, a cast of performers put on *The Joni Mitchell Project,* performing their favorite songs. Joni again found time to focus on her art work. Her paintings were part of a traveling exhibit in Europe in 1991.

In March 1991, she released her next album, *Night Ride Home*, on Geffen, which Joni recorded at her home studio. The album included her song "Come in from the Cold," which was cast as a video on VH-1. This was her most critically acclaimed album in many years, a fusion of jazz, acoustic, synthesizers, and a collection of strong songs such as "Cherokee Louise," about a friend who had been sexually abused.

In the meantime, her search for her long lost daughter came out in the *Globe* tabloid published on July 12, 1994, entitled "Songbird Joni Searches for Love Child." Joni decided to tell her version of the story in an interview with *Vogue*. At the same time she was having difficulties in her marriage. That summer, she and Larry Klein announced they were divorcing, but they remained friends.

In August 1994, she signed a five-album deal with Reprise. Her first release, *Turbulent Indigo*, included the song "Not to Blame," whose lyrics Jackson Browne later asserted represented a veiled assault on his relationship with Darryl Hannah. The album was critically acclaimed and spent some time on the *Billboard* charts, although sales were lower than hoped. The song "Sex Kills" (*Sex sells everything / Sex kills*) and her Vincent Van Gogh-like self portrait on the cover indicated her ever keen eye toward the ills of society in both music and art. She also recorded "Yvette in English," a song she and David Crosby had co-written years earlier. She won two Grammys. But still, as she told KCRW-DJ Chris Douridas in March 1998, "The record didn't sell enough units to recoup the cost of making it."

Billboard announced in early 1995 that she was chosen to receive its fifth annual Century Award. *Billboard*'s Timothy White interviewed her at her Bel Air home. At that point she was involved with Canadian songwriter Donald Freed, a Saskatoon native who had been introduced to Mitchell by her mother. Freed travels from reservation to reservation teaching Native American children to write songs. "In a cathartic way, he's writing the nursery rhymes of the north," Mitchell says.

She intensified her search for her lost daughter, telling Canadian television in 1996: "I just want to tell her I didn't give her up for lack of love." Stephen Holden of *The New York Times* also wrote about her search, as Canadian journalists chased the story.

In late 1996, Reprise also released two single disc retrospectives, ironically titled *Hits* and *Misses*. Who could argue with the list of hits: "Urge for Going," "Chelsea Morning," "Big Yellow Taxi," "Carey," to name a few. But the *Misses* album, which was Joni's selection of tracks that should have been released as singles, perplexed reviewers who argued that it left out some of Mitchell's most compelling songs. Her fans were still waiting for a true retrospective of her considerable oeuvre.

In March 1997, she was finally reunited with her daughter, who was now named Kilauren Gibb and who once worked as a model, like Joni. Gibb had been told by her parents that she had been adopted and was searching for her birth parents. To Mitchell's surprise, Kilauren also had a four-year-old boy with her, Marlin. Joni was a grandmother. She told Bill Higgins of the *Los Angeles Times* (April 8, 1997) about the "joy and celebration" of seeing her daughter. She reflected about the scandal of having a child out of wedlock. "The main thing at the time was to conceal it," she said. "The scandal was so intense. A daughter could do nothing more disgraceful. It ruined you in a social sense. You have no idea what the stigma was. It was like you murdered somebody." But Mitchell sought greater privacy for herself and her reunited family, which in 1999 expanded to include a granddaughter, Daisy.

In early 1997, she was selected to the Rock 'n' Roll Hall of Fame after Holden of *The New York Times* berated the institution for ignoring her. That year, she also gave approval to Janet Jackson to sample "Big Yellow Taxi" for a single entitled "Got 'Til It's Gone." As Q-Tip raps, you hear Mitchell's high pitched voice singing "Don't it always seem to go." Like countless other young female singers, Janet had been influenced by Mitchell. "I called her and told her I wanted her to hear it before she made a decision," Jackson said. "Everyone was surprised when a couple of days later she said yes."

Mitchell, for her part, loved the single, but after hearing the refrain, "Joni Mitchell never lies," joked to Douridas: "It makes you want to cut down a cherry tree."

For the first time in twelve years, Mitchell agreed to go on tour, playing a few dates in Seattle, the San Francisco area, and Los Angeles. The extraordinary tour harked back to the early '60s, with Bob Dylan, Joni Mitchell, and Van Morrison all sharing the bill. In a set at UCLA's Pauley Pavilion, Mitchell seemed to relish her role as a mature artist, gently swaying as she played her electric guitar backed by ex-husband Larry Klein on bass and a small combo. About her only concession to her early years was a souped-up version of "Big Yellow Taxi." Most of the songs she played were from her post-*Blue* era: "Slouching Toward Bethlehem" from *Night Ride Home,* "Amelia" from *Hejira*. Mitchell, who wore a red dress and performed in front of a backdrop of a river scene she had designed, was elegant and subdued compared to Morrison and Dylan's rollicking sets. In August 1998, Mitchell finally made it to Woodstock to perform along with people like Lou Reed, Stevie Nicks, and Pete Townshend.

She might never have made another album had it not been for a New Orleans merchant who introduced her to two new instruments, a Roland "computer guitar," which held her unusual tunings in memory, and a Roland keyboard. The instruments give her a "palette" of sounds and greater flexibility. She released *Taming the Tiger* in September 1998, the "tiger" reflecting disdain for the music business. "You can't tame the tiger," she sings.

"I'd gotten to the point where the process of making records is still enjoyable to me," she told radio DJ Chris Douridas (March 1998). "I still have growth potential, but the business and the marketing have become unbearable. And I've painted myself into a corner where the tunings wreak havoc on the neck of an acoustic instrument. I spend tremendous amounts of time in concert tuning, tuning, tuning. I just felt I didn't want to do it any more, and I wanted out of the business. I'm a painter first anyway. I got seduced into (music) in art school. I felt at this particular time that the energy had gone back into the painting. I waited for the music, I was uninspired."

She was disenchanted with the music she heard. "What you hear on the radio is not music, it's ick. The muse has gone out of it," she says.

But she still loves making music. "The music has always been free in spite of the industry. I've insisted on making the music the way I wanted without producers or without the influence of the company. As a result I've been difficult to market because I don't fit a demographic or a genre. . . . The marketplace is very limited to me."

Taming the Tiger features sax player Wayne Shorter and percussionist Brian Blade. She sings in a huskier voice (due to years of smoking), about more mature themes, in songs like "Love Puts on a New Face" or in the refrain "Happiness is the Best Facelift" about her relationship with Donald Freed, who cowrote "The

Crazy Cries of Love" with Mitchell. She also looks back to her youth in Saskatoon in "Harlem in Havana" about two girls who sneak into an Afro-Cuban burlesque. Donald and Joni had grown up on opposite sides of the river in Saskatoon. She was an eastside girl, and he was a westside boy, but he was six years younger. "The places that interested me were on the wrong side of town," Mitchell says. "I wanted to go where the jukeboxes were."

She made the album during the time that she was reunited with her daughter and grandson, and took off a few weeks to get to know them. "I'd work a bit more and then we would rendez-vous again and take off some more time. That time was all so joyous and so experiential. Writing takes withdrawal and introspection and I just haven't had time. Between the commitments that I had prior to their arrival and the time actively spent with them when they're with me, I haven't had much contemplative time."

She is a doting grandmother. "I saw Daisy when she was born," she says. "And I love my grandson. I just adore him." But she is also protective of them and her privacy. "I don't like being a public person, especially at this time," she says. "It's the most unpleasant time in the history of the world to be famous."

Mitchell's next project, *Both Sides Now* (March 2000), was an album of jazz covers popularized by the likes of Ella Fitzgerald, Nina Simone, Frank Sinatra, and Billie Holiday. (Holiday and Edith Piaf are Joni's favorite singers.) Joni, who recorded the songs with 70 members of the London Symphony Orchestra, updates two of her classic songs, "Both Sides Now" and "Case of You." She conceived the album as a play representing "the rise and fall of a romantic relationship." It begins with "You're My Thrill." "That's when you're smitten: seeing someone across the room and going all woofy," Mitchell says. It ends with "Both Sides Now," which Joni has reclaimed after all these years. But now she sings it with the maturity of a 56-year-old woman, in somber tones. "I was kind of dismissive of the song. But every time I played it, it was everybody's favorite. It wasn't my favorite of my songs at that time so I kind of let it go. I think it's beautiful on this record. It works very well as a closing statement because of the first verse full of clouds and because of where it takes you. I like it as the ending to the play."

In May 2000 Mitchell went on a nationwide tour performing the songs from *Both Sides Now* backed by a seventy-piece orchestra. For the time being Mitchell says she has little desire to write new songs. "I don't want to be a doomsday prophet. If I was to scrape my soul at this time as I think about the future of the planet and the human species, with what I know, it's not a pretty picture."

She graces her home with some of her work, like her portrait of Miles Davis which she began painting the day after he died, and a cubist-abstract landscape of a storm in Saskatchewan, "The Road to Uncle Lyall's." In the future she hopes to be able to paint her dreams and "develop a kind of surrealistic sophisticated naivete in my art." She also wants to restore balance in her life. "Spiritual, ritualistic, taoistic, tai chi, yoga under a tree. I want to develop some good habits of saying grace in nature."

Based in part on an interview with Joni Mitchell for People *in February 2000*

MORRISSEY, BILL: *Singer, songwriter, guitarist, harmonica player, novelist. Born Hartford, Connecticut, November 25, 1951.*

Bill Morrissey, who looks as lean and sparc as a character etched out in one of his songs, hardly looks tough enough to sing the blues. Morrissey is a New England version of the blues, a "Swamp Yankee." He has a talky "cracked husk of a voice," as one reviewer described it. His songs are about the drifters and down-and-outers, the missed opportunities of a cabbie (in "Handsome Molly") he came across during his years struggling to eke out a living. By the late 1980s Morrissey had gained a reputation as one of the most literate songwriters around, frequently compared to John Prine and writer Raymond Carver.

As novelist Robert Olmsted wrote about Morrissey: "They call Morrissey a folksinger, but to me, he is New England's own bluesman—not hot and humid Delta blues, but deep snow and sharp pine blues. In his weathered voice there are dreams gone awry, there is old Hank Williams, there is Tom Waits, there is a wedding at the Legion Hall where maybe the bride did not wear white and the cars in the parking lot are all secondhand. This is the cabin fever blues of dead-end jobs and busted relationships, the place where life and consequence meet."

Morrissey grew up in Hartford, Connecticut, and Acton, Massachusetts. In grammar school he wrote lyrics to pop songs. In high school he bought a Silvertone guitar with the names of the Beatles carved in front. He didn't last much more than freshman orientation at Plymouth State College in New Hampshire. He left in the late '60s to become a singer-songwriter. But it wasn't until 1984 that he recorded his first album, *Bill Morrissey*.

In the intervening years, he performed in smokey bars and gin joints, sometimes sleeping in his '65 Beetle, and survived by doing odd jobs, working in factories, gas stations, on an Alaskan fishing boat, and in fast-food joints. His audiences didn't always appreciate his songs. "Life would have been better had I learned all the words [to] 'American Pie,'" he told the *New York Times* (January 16, 1994).

Sometimes they were downright hostile. One time at a tavern in Haverhill, New Hampshire, a drunk came up to him and asked, "Can I play your guitar?"

"Sorry, but it's my tool," Morrissey responded.

The drunk pulled a .38-caliber gun on him and said, "Can I play it?"

"You need a flat pick?" Morrissey responded.

Over the years he learned how to come back at his hecklers and entertain his audiences with humor. "I realized that, even if you weren't the greatest musician, if you could entertain people, they'd hire you back," he told *Performing Songwriter* (March–April 1994).

He began to focus on his experiences discovering they were also those of his audiences. "I'd play these mill town songs, and people would start to listen," he told the *New York Times*. "That's when I thought I was really onto something. Guys would come up and say, 'We really like that "Small Town on the River" song you were singing—what are you drinking?'"

Over the years, he honed his songwriting skills, acknowledging his debt to such contemporary writers as Raymond Carver and Richard Ford. He heeded the advice of Thomas Williams, a writing teacher at the University of New Hampshire: "Say what you mean, say it in the most economical way possible and get out." When he's on the road he makes note of fragments and song ideas on a microcassette recorder and often develops the songs when he returns home.

He edits as much as he writes. "What I really strive for is no excess," he told *Performing Songwriter* (March–April 1994). "I worry a lot about . . . overloading, gilding the lily. You can actually become rococo; you know, too much information, overstating. I guess that probably started with listening to Mississippi John Hurt, how he would sometimes not sing a line, just play it. You realize certain things can be said with just the music, and my whole approach is to keep everything as spare as possible."

Morrissey's first album, *Bill Morrissey,* a solo acoustic release, came out on Rounder's Philo label without much notice in 1984. (He rerecorded all of the songs and added three new tracks in 1991.) In 1985, however, Morrissey performed at the Newport Folk Festival, which established his name in the folk world. His second album, *North,* recorded in 1986, was rather severe and was not a commercial success. But he began touring around the country.

His big breakthrough came with the 1989 Philo release *Standing Eight,* which he calls his "divorce" album, recorded right after his first marriage broke up. "It caught me totally unprepared," he told the *Boston Phoenix* (January 24, 1992). "I'd come back off the road, and it was, 'Well, when are you moving out?' So I just stopped the tour and made enough to pay the rent and write songs for *Standing Eight*—and put my life back together."

Suzanne Vega, Patty Larkin, and Shawn Colvin also perform on the album, Morrissey's favorite. "I was in a pretty weird place for a while," he told the *Boston Phoenix.* "I would do things like drive down to Pennsylvania to take a woman out to dinner and drive home the same night. A lot of the songs from *Standing Eight* came out of that. 'These Cold Fingers' I wrote over the course of a couple of months, one verse at a time." (He now lives in the suburbs north of Boston with his second wife, Ellen Karas, who is his producer and manager.)

His next album was *Inside,* recorded in 1991 at Massachusetts's Long View Farm. *Rolling Stone* gave the album a four-star rating. The title track started in a dressing room with the lines: *This ain't Hollywood / It never really gets that good / Call it love if you think you should / There's no need to explain.* It took a month to finish this portrait of a humdrum love affair.

Morrissey enlisted the support of fiddler Johnny Cunningham and John Jennings, who played guitar and coproduced. One of the tracks, "Robert Johnson," is a tribute to the famed Delta bluesman. "Man from out of Town" reveals Morrissey's Raymond Carver–like wry storytelling abilities: *The house burned down on a rainy night / And they never did find out why / I just stood alone beneath the silver maple / Trying to keep my cigarettes dry.*

During a fly-fishing trip in 1991, Morrissey convinced folksinger (and fellow fly-fishing fanatic) Greg Brown to perform on *Inside.* They recorded an old folk song called "Hang Me." In the spring of 1993 they decided to collaborate on an album of covers called *Friend of Mine.* Although both of them are storytellers with river-bottom voices, they found they have very different styles. "Bill records very meticulously," Brown told *Dirty Linen* (August 1993). "I just go into the studio and turn on the machines. But with Bill, you go in, lay down the guitar tracks and, then, you lay down the vocals and the harmonies. You try to get everything just right." The album includes covers of songs by Willie Dixon, Hank Williams, Chuck Berry, Ferron, and Mick Jagger and Keith Richards. Brown's "Fishing with Bill" is a tongue-in-cheek tribute to his buddy. The album was nominated for a Traditional Folk Grammy.

Morrissey's 1993 release, *Night Train,* is his most commercially and critically successful album. Ellen Karas produced it. The song "Birches," about a woman's longing for excitement versus security in a relationship, came to Morrissey's mind, appropriately, when he was at a friend's house in Maine hauling four white birch logs (*as white as a wedding dress*) from a friend's cellar. He built the song around the images of birch and oak. Rather than go for the fast-burning birch logs, the man urges his wife to go for the more practical option, long-burning oak wood. After he goes to bed, she throws the birch logs on the fire to enjoy a fleeting, but life-affirming moment: *And she knew the fire would start to fade / She thought of heat, she thought of time / And she called it an even trade.*

Morrissey's star was never bright, and consequently it's unlikely to fade. As he told *Performing Songwriter* (March–April 1994): "I'm in it for the long haul, and I

429 • MULDAUR, MARIA

think if I hadn't had that attitude in the very beginning, I might have gotten out. I mean, I have nothing against making some money, and I don't mind the attention when I get it, but that's not the goal. . . . My goal has always been to write well, to have the next song be better than the last one."

In April 1996 he released his seventh album, *You'll Never Get to Heaven,* to positive reviews. Recorded in New Orleans and coproduced by Karas and Scott Billington, the album includes a wide variety of rock, jazz, and electric sounds, including Michael Toles on electric guitar and Hammond organ, Jamil Sharif on trumpet, and Bill Samuel on saxophone. The release coincided with the publication of his first novel, *Edson* (Alfred A. Knopf). His editor was Gary Fisketjon, who had championed his songwriting to novelist Richard Ford.

His novel actually started out as a song. "Songwriting is sprinting the 440, and a novel is a marathon," he told Seth Rogovoy of the *Berkshire Eagle.* It contains a familiar character: Henry Corvine, a recently divorced folksinger struggling along in a fictional New Hampshire mill town. "The thing with Henry is that he and I have gone through a lot of the same experiences, but we reacted differently," Morrissey told Rogovoy. "At least I as the author have first-hand knowledge of what he's gone through, and that was very important to me—that allows me to go into a little more detail than if I were just making it up."

Morrissey, who released a second novel, *Slow Blues,* enjoyed the experience. "I would wake up thinking about my characters," he told Leslie Boyd of Gannett News Service. "I couldn't wait to get to work to see what would happen to them. It's kind of like watching a Polaroid picture develop. . . . It was more work to do a novel. With a song or a short story you can see the horizon. But with a novel it's long."

In 1998 Morrissey returned to New Orleans to record an album of Mississippi John Hurt's songs. The 1999 album on Rounder was nominated for a Grammy.

MULDAUR, MARIA: *Singer, fiddler, guitarist. Born New York, New York, September 12, 1943.*

Over a lengthy and noteworthy career, Maria Muldaur has proved herself one of the most versatile and talented vocalists in popular music. She originally made her mark as a folk artist and played an important part in the folk movement of the 1960s but, as she also demonstrated, she could handle almost any style of music with skill and freshness, ranging from ballads to jazz, blues/R&B, and rock 'n' roll.

Born and raised in New York's Greenwich Village, Maria (born Maria Grazia Rosa Domenico D'Amato) didn't have far to go to hear the music she enjoyed. The Village was a hotbed of jazz activity during her childhood years and the core of the burgeoning folk boom in her teens. She described her early years as a "non-stop hootenanny" replete with "bluegrass, folk, blues, gui-

tar, and Italian accordion players. It was like a miniature folk festival every Sunday afternoon."

Although she enjoyed listening to blues and R&B artists and joined her peer group in admiring the early wave of rock 'n' rollers, folk music remained her main love as she moved into her late teens. Many of the leading folk artists of the time, such as the Seegers and the New Lost City Ramblers, made a practice of seeking out little-known but highly talented rural artists. One group founded to arrange for city appearances of such musicians was the Friends of Old Time Music. Maria, then a recent high-school graduate, attended the first such concert, which featured the legendary Doc Watson and his North Carolina associates. She was inspired by Doc's vocals and striking guitar work, and by the fiddle playing of Doc's father-in-law, Gaither Carlton.

By that time Muldaur had already decided to try her lot as a performer and had started collecting folk songs for her repertoire. Like many urban folk aficionados, she decided the best way to become attuned to the authentic folk sound was to spend time with people who, in essence, lived it. So not long after the concert she made her way to Watson's hometown, where she spent some time with the Watson family. Besides learning many of the songs Doc and his friends and neighbors knew, she took pointers from Gaither Carlton on country fiddling.

She returned to the Village, where she was a familiar figure at many of the informal get-togethers of young folk artists who had flocked to New York from all over the United States. She got the chance to sing and play the fiddle at some of the small clubs and coffeehouses and also picked up change from working the party circuit. Muldaur arrived at her first major performing milestone in late 1963 when she was twenty-one. Blues luminary Victoria Spivey assembled a group to make a jug band record for her label; called the Even Dozen Jug Band, its members included, besides Maria, such people as John Sebastian and Steve Katz. Sebastian, soon after, was to go on to national fame with his folk-rock group Lovin' Spoonful while Katz later was a key figure in such major rock bands as the Blues Project and Blood, Sweat & Tears. The only LP of the Even Dozen Jug Band was released under the Elektra Records banner in January 1964.

Jug bands were a big thing in the folk field at the time. Among others vying for attention were Dave Van Ronk's Ragtime Jug Stompers and the Jim Kweskin Jug Band. The groups often crossed paths, sometimes sharing the same bill. This resulted in the meeting of Maria and a member of Kweskin's group named Geoff Muldaur, then living in Cambridge, Massachusetts. After the Even Dozen group broke up, Maria went to join Geoff, and, soon after, the two were married. Their relationship became an artistic partnership as well; when an opening came up in Kweskin's band, Maria was added to the roster.

For the rest of the decade, the Muldaurs remained members of that assemblage, helping Kweskin record a series of albums, mostly on Vanguard, but some on Reprise, including *Jug Band Music* (4/65), *Relax Your Mind* (3/66), *See Reverse Side* (2/67)—all on Vanguard—and *Garden of Joy* (11/67) on Reprise. The group toured throughout the United States and to a number of foreign countries and also played many major festivals, including a number of appearances at the Newport Folk Festival.

At the start of the 1970s, after Kweskin disbanded his group, the Muldaurs moved from Cambridge to Woodstock, New York. There they worked on a new act featuring just the two of them. This effort won them a new contract from Reprise and resulted in two LPs, *Pottery Pie* and *Sweet Potatoes.*

Unfortunately, personal problems were beginning to crop up which finally resulted in their separating and, in 1972, divorcing; however, Maria kept Muldaur as her professional name. (Geoff's career stalled after that. He made some solo albums that didn't gain much attention and also performed for a while with Paul Butterfield's band, after which little was heard from him until he resurfaced in 1998 with his first new solo disc in over twenty years, *The Secret Handshake* on the HighTone label. Writing in the *New York Times* ("Danceable, Eclectic Folk-Pop," December 13, 1998), Tony Scherman stated "I haven't heard a better album this year. . . . Mr. Muldaur has always had an encyclopedic knowledge of American roots music styles. What's new is his power to fuse them, to grasp the essence of an idiom and, blending it with another come up with something new. This is pop music for grownups. Existing beyond trends, it shows how much further from obsolescence folk music is than the latest top 40's styles.")

After spending some time considering her next direction, Maria decided the time had come to try for a solo career. In 1973, she signed a solo agreement with Warner Brothers, the parent company for the Reprise label. Her debut solo LP, *Maria Muldaur,* was issued in the early summer of 1974 and Maria set out on a cross-country tour in support of it. The initial single release, a novelty number by David Nichtern called "Midnight at the Oasis," caught fire and moved high on the charts. By the time Muldaur finished her tour in June 1974, she had a gold record award for the single (which peaked at number six in *Billboard* that April) plus a second one for the album (the album later went platinum). In January 1975 she had the hit single "I'm a Woman," which rose to number twelve in *Billboard.*

Although her emphasis was moving away from folk toward R&B, rock, and jazz influences, a folk flavor remained on *Maria Muldaur* as on the succeeding Reprise releases, *Waitress in a Donut Shop,* issued in 1975, and the 1976 release *Sweet Harmony. Waitress,* for instance, included her performance of songs by the Canadian folksinging sisters, Kate and Anna McGarrigle. (Her debut album also had contained material from the McGarrigles as well as songs by Dolly Parton and Wendy Waldman.)

After the last of those albums came out, Maria decided a change of scenery was in order and relocated in Marin County above San Francisco. Once there she assembled a new band and made regular swings up and down the coast, besides playing extended engagements in clubs in the Bay Area. She also appeared with such diverse groups as the rock-oriented Jerry Garcia Band and the jazz-based Benny Carter Orchestra. On several occasions she was a featured performer at jazz festivals in various parts of the country.

In 1978, after a two-year hiatus, Muldaur was represented by a new LP, *Southern Winds,* with stylings ranging from soft folk ballad to driving R&B. She continued to explore different vocal shadings in her June 1979 release, her fifth solo LP, *Open Your Eyes.* Describing the evolution of her vocal approach in the 1970s, she told a biographer from Warner Brothers Records, "My depth of expression is growing; my voice is more relaxed and it's getting heavier as I get older. It's like I've had a flute all these years, a little delicate flute. But I started wanting to express other things. I thought somehow I'm gonna find a corner in my voice to convey more than just a crooning lullaby. Now I find there's a saxophone in there."

Maria started off the 1980s with the album *Gospel Nights.* Two years later her collection *There Is a Love* came out on the Christian music label, Myrrh. She continued to complete albums on various labels for the rest of the 1980s and into the '90s, mostly on small ones like Takoma and Spindrift. Those releases included *Sweet and Slow* in 1984, *Transblucency* in 1985, *Live in London* (on the Making Waves label) in 1987, and in 1991, the children's album *On the Sunny Side,* for the Music for Little People series, followed by *Swingin' In the Rain.* In 1992 she released *Louisiana Love Call* on the Black Top label, followed by *Jazzabelle* in 1993, and *Meet Me at Midnite* in 1994. Telarc released *Fanning the Flames* in 1996, *Southland of the Heart* in 1998, and *Meet Me Where they Play the Blues* in 1999. She remained active as a concert artist in the '80s and '90s, often performing at venues or festivals in other parts of the world besides North America. In addition to her solo recordings, she provided support vocals on a number of albums by other artists during those years.

MUSSELWHITE, CHARLIE: *Harmonica player, guitarist, singer, songwriter. Born Kosciusko, Mississippi, January 31, 1944.*

As Charlie Musselwhite puts it, "A lot of people think of the harmonica as a toy." But a harmonica is a weapon in Musselwhite's hands. He has one of the purest sounds of any blues harpist, having learned his trade from blues legends Little Walter, Big Walter, Will Shade (a.k.a. Son Brimmer), and Muddy Waters. Musselwhite, along with Paul Butterfield, became one of the first white roots blues players in America.

Musselwhite's bio is the stuff of legend. Journalists have written that his father was a mandolin maker and traveling musician and that Charlie was part of the act; that he was raised by a mean aunt; that he was introduced to Will Shade by some black women when he worked in an all-black factory; and that he didn't switch from guitar to harmonica until he met Little Walter in Chicago. None of it is true. He may have some Choctaw Indian blood, but even that's not certain. "I'll say something to someone and years later I'll hear it and it's just so different from what I said," Musselwhite says.

Musselwhite was born in Mississippi, the son of Charles Douglas Musselwhite, Jr., and Ruth Maxine Miller. His father was a cab driver and machinist who served in the navy (including a dangerous stint in mainland China). He played guitar, harmonica, and mandolin (and once built one); Charlie's mother played the piano. He was also influenced by an uncle, Archie Stevens, who had a one-man band act called the Sunshine Band. He said he could play seventeen instruments at once, and claimed he invented a gut bucket-like instrument. "He was a character," Musselwhite says.

His parents moved to Memphis in 1947. "They borrowed a dumptruck, put everything in there, and drove up," Charlie says. "Just looking for a better life I guess. My daddy came home from the navy. My mother had been in Philadelphia working for the navy too during the war. I remember being left with a lady named Velma, a black lady. When my mother came home I wouldn't eat nothing unless Velma had fixed it." He also had an Aunt Urville who would help out when his mother was working. "But she wasn't mean," Musselwhite says. "She was pretty nice to me."

In Memphis, Musselwhite heard all kinds of music: street musicians, buskers on Beale Street, Main, and Poplar. Rockabilly stars Johnny Burnette and Slim Rhodes were neighbors; he went to parties hosted by Elvis Presley. Elvis used to rent out the Memphian Theater and show Road Runner cartoons, or he'd rent out the skating rink in town from midnight till 8:00 A.M. Charlie listened to the radio and bought records from junk stores. He started playing harmonica before his teens. "They were given to me as a toy when I was a kid," he says. "That's when they were cheap. The way they cost today you don't be givin' them away as toys too much. Then my father gave me his guitar when I was about twelve or thirteen, he had an old Supertone. The only time I saw another one was on the cover of a Bill Broonzy album, I think on Columbia."

At thirteen, Charlie decided to focus on the blues. "I loved the way it sounded," he says. "I thought, 'Well, I have a harmonica, why don't I try to play it?' It felt good to make those sounds. I didn't have any idea about playing professional or nothing like that. I just loved the music, I loved listening to it, I loved the way it made me feel. It felt great to be able to play your own blues. It's the best feeling in the world."

He had read *Country Blues* by Sam Charters and knew the names of Memphis blues players like Will Shade and Furry Lewis. He could also track them down in a local directory called the *Blue Book*. "One way or another everybody kind of knew each other," he says. "The funny thing is, you'd be at one guy's house hanging out and you'd say, 'I think I'm going to visit so and so.' They'd say don't go over there. If any money was going to be spent for alcohol they didn't want to miss out on the party."

He got caught up in the rivalry between Will Shade and Furry Lewis. "If I was at Will's house, he wouldn't want me to go visit Furry," Musselwhite says. "The two courted Jenny Mae Clayton. Will Shade wound up with her. They'd never been friends since then. I even saw them in a regular fist fight."

Musselwhite absorbed the music around him, teaching himself the harp. "It's a blind man's instrument, you can't see how to play it," Will Shade told him. Charlie was always welcome to sit in with the local blues bands on guitar or harmonica, but he never expected to become a professional. As a teenager, he worked for the Southern Paper Company, cutting stacks of paper for writing tablets, and in a cardboard box factory as a printer-sorter. "It was so hot, I remember sweating," he recalls. "On this concrete floor there'd just be a big puddle all around me. My shoes just rotted off my feet 'cause of the sweat." At one factory, he moved loads on a dolly; when the women wanted his services they'd sing, *Dolly Boy, dolly boy, bring your dolly 'round / If you don't like your dolly, put your dolly down.* They'd also trade lines on blues tunes and standards.

He got construction jobs laying concrete for cotton warehouses at a dollar an hour. He took odd jobs, fixing up washing machines or mowing lawns. He ran moonshine from rural stills to Memphis for $50 a trip. "I would drive out in the country to this community where these people lived who were making it," he says. "I'd go to this fellow's house and give him the keys to my car. He'd drive out and he'd come back a little later and my trunk would be full. I'd drive to Memphis, go to another guy's house, give him the keys and he'd drive off and come back and my trunk would be empty." But when the state police followed him home one day, he decided to give up that profession. It was a good time to move to Chicago, since Memphis was so depressed.

"It seemed like a dead end," he says. "I had friends who would leave Memphis and they'd go up to Chicago and get a job in a factory that paid $3 an hour with benefits. That sounded like a helluva lot of money. I'd see them leave town in an old jalopy and they'd come back for Christmas in a brand new car. I didn't connect Chicago in any way to music. I just thought it was a big town up north that had a lot of jobs."

So in 1962, as soon as he got out of Memphis Tech high, he moved to Chicago in search of factory work. He only had enough money to rent a room for a week. He looked all week and couldn't find a job. Then, on his last day, Sunday, he was taking a last look around town and walked by a store with a Help Wanted sign. An exterminator told Charlie to return the next morning to work as his driver.

"I drove all over Chicago," Musselwhite says. "I would see posters and pass by clubs advertising blues singers: Muddy Waters, Howlin' Wolf, Elmore James. What a thrill! Whenever I'd see one of these I'd write down the address for where the club was and I'd go. Here were all these people I'd been listening to on records and the radio. You could see Muddy Waters for 25 cents and with your ticket get a free beer, Tuesday nights only, at Peppers Lounge. I was never disappointed. Seeing Howlin' Wolf for the first time, he was even more than I thought he would be."

Chicago had a laid-back blues scene in the early '60s in which non-professionals, even doormen and housewives, could get up on stage to jam with established blues players. Musselwhite played slide guitar and harmonica on Maxwell Street on the North Side with Robert Nighthawk and Johnny Young, from 8:00 A.M. to 2:00 P.M. He went to the clubs every night on the South Side and wound up playing with Big Walter, John Lee Granderson, Little Walter, Sonny Boy II (Rice Miller), and Muddy Waters. He lived around the corner from Junior Wells.

Even though Musselwhite was eighteen, he could get into the bars without a problem. He had the look— the slicked back hair, shades, and black suit—which inspired Dan Aykroyd to mimic him in the Blues Brothers. "He used to see me when I toured up in Canada where he was going to school." He hung out with Little Walter. "He'd always buy me a set up [a bowl of ice, a couple of glasses, a fifth of whiskey and a mixer]," Musselwhite says. "He'd always have me sit in. He'd play and sometimes just hand me his harp and his microphone and just say, 'Play something, Charlie.'"

Although Musselwhite was white, he never experienced much prejudice. "My mother she always taught me not to be prejudiced," he says, adding that her family had taken in and raised a black child. "The idea of being racist was foreign to me. I couldn't tolerate that in any way. Every person was another single person. It had nothing to do with what color they were or where they were from or what church they went to."

One night a waitress Musselwhite was dating told Muddy Waters that he "ought to hear the boy play." Waters got him up on the stage, and the word got out. "For me to be invited to sit in wasn't a big deal except that I was so young, and I was white, and I played blues," he says. "Those three things were all unusual in one person, which made me kind of a hit." Through Waters, he met other white blues artists: Mike Bloomfield and Paul

Butterfield. "For a long time people would address me as Paul," Musselwhite says. "I'd say my name's not Paul. We kind of looked alike and we both played harmonica. Paul used to joke that we had harmonica player's eyebrows because our eyebrows go up. It didn't take me long to realize there was some guy about my age who kind of looked like me playing harmonica. We eventually became friends."

Butterfield, who grew up in Chicago and had a working band, was already serious about the profession. But Musselwhite still worked in factories and played music on the side. "There was no plan at all," Musselwhite recalls. "Things just fell into place. I was having a good time."

Butterfield released *East West: Butterfield Blues Band* on Elektra in 1965. The success of that album and his friendship with Sam Charters led to Charlie's first deal with Vanguard. He played a duet with Big Walter Horton on the 1965 Vanguard release, *Chicago/ The Blues Today, Volume 3* (1966), and recorded *Stand Back! Here Comes Charlie Musselwhite's Southside Blues Band*. The album was produced by Charters and included backup work from drummer Fred Below, bassist Bob "Little Bob" Anderson, guitarist Harvey Mendel, and keyboardist Barry Goldberg.

Musselwhite still had a factory job when his album came out. "I remember thinking it was interesting making an album and not having a band or working anywhere," he says. "One day Mike Bloomfield came over and he's got the record. Vanguard never even sent me a record. They sent me a check for 36 cents. That's no lie. I was really counting on getting the session fee. I thought I should buy myself an amp, maybe start taking this a little more seriously. The union called up and said come down we've got a check for you from Vanguard. I said great and I went down there. They said you have to give us $4 dollars in union work dues to get the check. I said let me see the check. It was for 36 cents. I couldn't believe it. They deducted everything they could think of. . . . According to Vanguard that album has never earned a penny. They still send me statements showing that that album is in the red."

He followed with *Stone Blues* (1968) (produced by Barry Goldberg) and *Tennessee Woman* (1969), both on Vanguard. The label continued to press him to match Butterfield's sales. *Tennessee Woman* included "Christo Redemptor," a twelve-minute instrumental that helped build Musselwhite's reputation. He was one of the few who could keep up with blues great Big Joe Williams, accompanying him on an Arhoolie release, *Thinkin' of What They Did to Me* (1969).

"Joe was typical of the early country style players," says Musselwhite. "He's one of the last of that style from Charley Patton and all those guys. His playing could be erratic. You had to anticipate which way he was going to go, which really was valuable for me to learn. Being able to apply that anticipation allowed me to play with just about anybody, even in foreign countries. For instance, I was in Norway and I met Knut Buen, he's a folk master fiddle player. There's a classical harmonica player in Oslo. They tried to have a jam session but they couldn't find the groove because the classical guy was not an improviser. But me and Knut could play together with no problem because I could anticipate what he was going to play."

Musselwhite, who once roomed with Big Joe, remembers how he held his old guitar together—a shoehorn under the bridge to raise the strings, a bit of tape. "He took pride in making it like that instead of having it be all squeaky clean. He liked to have that down home country look to it."

In the late 1960s, Musselwhite got an offer to play for a month in San Francisco. He was married at the time with a baby boy and stuck in a factory job. But the money was good so he took a leave of absence. He liked California. "They didn't seem to know you didn't have to pay blues musicians," he recalls. "Suddenly I was in this whole scene where I had a band and I was playing in nightclubs, just overnight. I didn't see any reason to go back to the factory. So my family moved out and that was that."

He left Vanguard and recorded for many labels. In 1970, he released *Memphis, Tennessee* on Paramount and *Louisiana Fog* on Cherry Red Records. He recorded two excellent albums for Arhoolie: *Takin' My Time* (1971) and *Goin' Back Down South* (1974), playing guitar on the latter. The records were reissued as *Memphis Charlie* by Arhoolie. His strong 1975 release on Capitol, *Leave the Blues to Us*, reunited him with Mike Bloomfield, followed by *Times Gettin' Tougher Than Tough* on Crystal Clear Records in the late '70s, produced by guitar player Johnny Heartsman.

Musselwhite released the album and instructional book, *Harmonica According to Musselwhite* in the mid-1970s on Kicking Mule (later on Blind Pig) and wrote an instructional book called *Power Harp* for Mel Bay with Phil Duncan. He also cut three more albums—*Tell Me Where Have All the Good Times Gone* on Blue Rock'it (1980), *Mellow-Dee* in West Germany on Cross Cut (1982), and *Cambridge Blues,* recorded at the Cambridge Folk Festival in England, on Blue Horizon in the mid-1980s.

Things were hardly smooth sailing for Musselwhite. In the 1970s he got into a devastating car crash in Utah. It was snowing and his bass player from Wisconsin suggested that he do the driving. As soon as he took over the van went out of control and started rolling. Musselwhite was thrown from the van. His pelvis was broken in three places, and he had numerous lacerations. His first thought was the van was rolling, coming his way. "I started just swimming through the snow down this embankment. I got down to the bottom and laid there and didn't hear nothing. I started walking up the embankment and my leg was going funny. I got up to the top and there was the van upside down. Everyone was OK so I just laid down on the highway. I remember feeling very peaceful, thinking 'Thank God, I don't have to go to work.'"

In the mid-1970s, when interest in the blues hit rock bottom, Musselwhite hit rock bottom too: he was in San Jose working in a plastics factory. "I was disgusted with the whole thing. I was doing a lot of drinking. I got up to two quarts of gin a day."

In 1987, Musselwhite realized his drinking had plagued his career. He'd repeat songs, forget tunes, and sometimes get rough. "It was an old Southern tradition," he says. "Growing up I was around a lot of alcohol, especially the home brew I had going there. It was part of life. I was good at it. I could drink a lot and not have a hangover, which is a bad sign. Then I would drink so I wouldn't give the hangover a chance."

Most of the old Chicago bluesmen were heavy drinkers too. In the mid-1980s he tried to reduce the amount he drank and thought it was a big victory if he could refrain from drinking before noon. But he still had to drink to get on stage. "I'd never been on a bandstand sober. . . . It got to the point where no matter how much I drank I didn't feel good. That old glow that used to come with alcohol was no longer there."

He had to figure out a way to get on stage sober. That came in October 1987, when he was driving to work and heard on the radio that Jessica McClure had fallen into a well in Texas. "She was being really brave," he says. "She was singing nursery rhymes to herself. Here I was on my way to this gig to do something I had done a 1,000 times and knew perfectly well how to do it. Why couldn't I be as brave as this little girl? As a prayer to her I decided I was not going to drink until she got out of the well. That meant getting on stage that night sober. It was the scariest thing in the world. My knees felt like jelly. Saying that it was scary would be like saying falling out of an airplane is scary. But I did it, and it felt really great." He hasn't had a drink since.

After he quit drinking, his career improved, as did his personal life—he's happily married for the third time. He signed with Alligator in 1990 and released *Ace of Harps,* followed by *Signature* in 1992, both receiving critical acclaim. He won a W.C. Handy award for Blues Instrumentalist of the Year in 1994, and his band won for Blues Band of the Year. His 1994 release, *In My Time,* an album that combines original compositions with blues favorites by Sonny Boy II and Big Walter, also showed he had returned to form. The album features backing by the Blind Boys, and Musselwhite plays guitar. He resumed a feverish touring pace, as many as 300 appearances a year. He usually takes 15 to 30 of the hundreds of his Lee Oskar models on the road.

Musselwhite has won seven W.C. Handy Awards and been nominated for several Grammys. In 1997, he released *Rough News* on Virgin/Point Blank. Dick

Sherman produced tunes in Chicago, Cesar Rosas of Los Lobos produced a session in Los Angeles, and Keith Keller produced one in New Orleans. "There are a lot of different flavors and they're all connected to blues. They come from the heart," he says.

In 1998, Musselwhite recorded *Continental Drifter,* released by Virgin/Point Blank in April 1999. He recorded four of the tunes with a Cuban band called Eliades Ochoa y Cuarteto Patria. Musselwhite had hoped to travel to Havana to record with the band in January 1998. But the Cuban government barred most U.S. passport holders at the time due to the visit by Pope John Paul II. Luckily, Musselwhite played at the Bergen Blues and Roots Festival later that year and recorded with the Cuban band in a Norwegian studio. As a result of the sessions, as well as Ochoa's performances on the *Buena Vista Social Club* CD with Ry Cooder, Virgin signed Cuarteto Patria to a recording contract. *Continental Drifter* received a Grammy nomination. In 2000 Vanguard released *Best of the Vanguard Years.*

In December 1999 Musselwhite was in yet another accident when a tractor-trailer broadsided his car in Mexico. But that couldn't dampen his spirits. "Ain't no broken bones going to keep me down," he told the *Clarksdale Press Register.* "The people here at the hospital said I came as close to death as you can get."

Based on an interview by Lyndon Stambler with Charlie Musselwhite

NEAR, HOLLY: *Singer, songwriter, actress. Born Ukiah, California, June 6, 1949.*

Possessing an excellent voice and fine songwriting skills, Holly Near might well have become a fixture on U.S. hit charts had she opted to sing rock or been born a little earlier. In the tradition of the folk-song protest movement of the 1960s, she reached maturity in the 1970s when the folk genre had been relegated to a minority position in music. Nonetheless, Near had the courage of her convictions and refused to change her folk style or writing approach for the sake of financial success.

Born in Ukiah in northern California, she spent her early years on a ranch in Potter Valley just outside town. When she was ten, her family moved back into Ukiah. Her family enjoyed music and exposed Holly to folk music, country and western, Broadway musicals, and some of the popular music of the 1950s.

Holly enjoyed singing at a very early age and made her public debut in her home area at seven. From then on, she took part in many entertainment activities in the Ukiah region, including plays and musical events at school and in local playhouses. By the time she was in

her teens, Holly sought and won assignments in a number of films and TV programs. She appeared in *Slaughterhouse Five, The Partridge Family, Room 222,* and *Sesame Street.* At the end of the decade, she headed east to audition for the cast of the rock musical *Hair* and won one of the leads in the Broadway production.

She had already become politically active, having taken part in protests against the Vietnam War. In the early 1970s, she was the featured performer in Jane Fonda's controversial "Free the Army" show that toured Vietnam.

Near was making a name for herself on the folk-music circuit (folk clubs and college campus concerts) in the early 1970s. Throughout the 1970s she was a featured performer in folk festivals all over the United States, including most of the major ones, and recordings of some of her sets often could be heard on stations that featured folk material.

She might have signed with a major record company, but Near decided she would have to give up too much control over her material if she went that route. Instead, she set up her own label in Ukiah, Redwood Records. Her debut LP, *Hang in There,* was recorded in 1973, and in 1974 she completed work on a live album. Working with her on both of these, providing local and instrumental backup, was Jeff Langley, a friend from Ukiah. He also helped record her third Redwood LP, *You Can Know All I Am,* issued in 1976. Her fourth LP *Imagine My Surprise,* came out in 1978 and in 1980 she began work on her fifth album. Most of the songs in these, lyrics and music, were written by Holly.

Although her exposure to the music public was limited, she still managed to have considerable impact. As of the end of 1979, sales of her four albums totaled 155,000, a very respectable figure for a label that depended essentially on word-of-mouth advertising. In 1979, the National Association of Independent Record Distributors named *Imagine My Surprise* best album of the year. *BAM Magazine* also named the LP the best album of the year by an independent label.

Holly toured steadily during the 1970s, albeit restricted mainly to small venues. Often the concerts were intended to tie in with some of the causes Near believed in. Thus her March 1979 set at the Fox Venice Theater in the Los Angeles area followed the benefit premiere of the labor-struggle film *With Babies and Banners.* She told the audience she wanted to put her energies into "community organizing, not Bahama vacations." Similarly, a year later she returned to Los Angeles (soon after having completed a forty-city national tour) to perform in a benefit concert for WAVAW (Women Against Violence Against Women). One of WAVAW's successful campaigns was to stop Warner Communications from using violent images of men and women on the record jackets of its various labels.

At the beginning of the 1980s Near released two more LPs, *Fire in the Rain* (1981) and *Speed of Light*

(1982). She also went on tour in 1982 with her sisters, Timothy, an award-winning actress, and Laurel, a dancer and choreographer. She released a retrospective album, *Journeys,* in 1983, covering the years 1972 to 1983. She made the first of her three recordings with Ronnie Gilbert of the Weavers in 1984, *Lifeline.* (Gilbert and Near went on tour several times in the 1980s and 1990s.) She followed that year with *Watch Out!* and a collaboration with a Chilean ensemble, Inti Illimani, titled *Sing to Me the Dream.* In 1985 Near's label released a live recording, *H.A.R.P.,* with Holly, Arlo Guthrie, Ronnie Gilbert, and Pete Seeger. That was followed by another recording with Gilbert in 1987, *Singing with You.*

As the 1980s drew to a close, Near made an attempt to move to the mainstream. She released her thirteenth album in 1987, *Don't Hold Back,* which focused more on emotional than political topics. Bonnie Raitt and Kenny Loggins were guest performers on the album. Despite her conscious attempt to move toward a pop sound, she continued to focus on her political agenda in concert, supporting feminism, labor issues, and opposing U.S. involvement in the wars in El Salvador and Nicaragua. "Instead of worrying about whether one is preaching to the converted, we need to figure out how to spiritually energize the converted," she told Chris Willman of the *Los Angeles Times* ("Holly Near Edges Closer to a Mainstream Sound," November 4, 1987).

In 1989 she released *Sky Dances,* a concept album that focused on different approaches to life and death. "I wanted to make a record which was a hand for people to hold in these times, that allows the raging, grieving, mourning, and at the same time allows the celebration of that person," she told Joe Brown of the *Washington Post* ("Songs Support Near and Dear," October 20, 1989). She also toured with the exquisite Argentinian singer Mercedes Sosa. In 1990 she released her first recording on another label, *Singer in the Storm,* on Chameleon.

At the beginning of the 1990s Near published her autobiography at the age of forty-one. Called *Fire in the Rain . . . Singer in the Storm* (William Morrow), the book covers her film and TV career, her political activism, her friendships and affairs with men and women, her support of lesbianism. As the *New York Times* critic wrote, "It shows how a talented performer can be marginalized because of her sexuality and politics. And it documents a rare case in which an artist who was determined to fight the power actually succeeded." Beginning in 1992, she appeared in a one-woman show based on her autobiography. *Fire in the Rain . . . Singer in the Storm* was directed by her sister Timothy, and was staged in Los Angeles, San Francisco, and New York to mixed reviews. As the *Newsday* critic, Ira Robbins, wrote in 1993: ". . . 'Fire in the Rain' is as palatable as an auto-canonization can be. . . . She can't quite get around the contradictory impulses that began driving her as a child in northern California: to save the world and to become a Broadway actress."

The play indicates that Near went through a breakdown of sorts in the mid-1980s but that she was able to work her way through the difficult times to find peace and serenity. It also dropped a bombshell for her lesbian fans: Near, who had long been a vocal supporter of the lesbian community, was in a relationship with a man. As Near wrote on her web site, that didn't mean a lack of commitment to gay rights: "Although Near now is in a relationship with a man, she is still a powerful voice for love and continues to include lesbian material in her work."

She released some of the songs she had performed in the play in *Musical Highlights,* issued by Redwood in 1993, the last solo album she would release on the label. In the middle of the 1990s she dissolved Redwood Music. In 1996 she released another live collection with Ronnie Gilbert. Called *This Train Still Runs,* the CD was issued on Abbe Alice Music in 1996. The following year she released *With a Song in My Heart* on Calico Tracks Music, with John Bucchino, her longtime pianist, backing her up.

She continued to act, appearing over the years in *All in the Family, L.A. Law,* and the films *Dog Fight* and *Heartwood.* She authored a second book, called *The Great Peace March* (Henry Holt), with lyrics based on a song she originally wrote for the 1986 Great Peace March for Nuclear Disarmament (from Los Angeles to Washington, D.C.). A collection of her songs was also available in the songbook *Singing for our Lives.*

After twenty-five years of touring throughout the United States and the world, Near decided to take a "semi-sabbatical" beginning in May 1998, touring only one week a month. She spent most of her time at her home in Ukiah. She continues to make occasional concert appearances and to perform as a guest for gay men's choirs while cowriting songs and choral works with her songwriting partner, Jeff Langley.

NELSON, TRACY: *Singer, songwriter. Born French Camp, California, December 27, 1944.*

At times during her career it seemed as though Tracy Nelson was better known for having the same last name as Willie Nelson or for a supposed performing resemblance to Janis Joplin than for her vocal work. Her peers in the pop and country field valued her abilities highly, as indicated by the artists who wanted her to contribute to some of their recordings. At the start of the 1980s, however, her recording opportunities faded. Tracy moved to Nashville and went into retirement for a decade, only to reemerge in the 1990s.

Born in California and raised in Madison, Wisconsin, her early interests had little to do with the country-music mainstream. As she told Jay Milner of the *Rocky Mountain Musical News,* "I started out as a folkie—spent a good deal of my time singing 'Silver Dagger'—and then I became a blues fanatic."

Helping to kindle her interest in blues and blues

rock when she was in her teens were rock performers like Boz Scaggs and Steve Miller, both of whom attended the University of Wisconsin in the 1960s. She told Milner, "Steve and Boz played the Chi Psi house when I was in high school in Madison. I used to go hear them a lot. They'd left by the time I got to college, but they came back occasionally. . . . Anyhow, by the time I got out of high school the activist stuff had died out and there wasn't much going on, musically, there."

Tracy entered the University of Wisconsin as a social work major in the early 1960s. She sang in the Madison coffeehouses and at frat parties with an R&B band called the Fabulous Imitators. She would travel to Chicago, where she became familiar with the blues scene. She recorded her debut album, *Deep Are the Roots*, for the Chicago-based Prestige label in 1965. Charlie Musselwhite played harmonica, Peter Wolfe played guitar, and Sam Charters produced the blues-flavored tribute to Bessie Smith and Ma Rainey.

After a while, Tracy, who had become convinced she had the vocal ability to make a career out of music, left the Midwest for the San Francisco area. She found the going rough for a female artist, despite the prominence of Janis Joplin and Grace Slick in the West Coast rock sound. Most rock groups she contacted didn't even want to give a woman an audition because they feared possible problems that might result from adding a woman to an all-male band.

Nelson got some jobs, then decided to put together her own band. "There were so many people out there making so much money playing what I thought was substandard music and I said to myself, 'If they can do it, I can do it.'" She assembled her first band partly by recruiting the rhythm section from Doug Sahm, of Texas folk and blues-rock fame. "Doug's band was breaking up and I got his drummer, piano player, and bass player. Of course, they were all Texans. . . ." Thus the band, called Mother Earth, had a strong Texas flavor and resulted in the misconception that Tracy herself came from the Texas music scene.

The band made some demo tapes showcasing Nelson's impressive vocal skills and, in short order, had a recording contract. They made a number of albums in the late 1960s and early 1970s that brought them a cult following and predictions that Tracy and the group would reach superstar status. Many critics tended to bracket Nelson with Janis Joplin in the sense that she was seen as an heir to Joplin's rock eminence. However, it was an inaccurate comparison and one that never sat well with Tracy.

Nelson and her band signed with Mercury, which issued the debut album, *Living with the Animals*, in 1968. The band set out on a cross-country tour of the United States that had the unexpected outcome of starting Tracy on the path toward country-music involvement.

The tour, as it happened, ended up in Nashville. A friend, guitarist Harvey Mandell, suggested she consider doing some recordings at the local Bradley's Barn studios. "We just did it for the hell of it," she recalled. As she got into the project, she began working with backing musicians like Pete Drake and fiddler Johnny Gimble. The product of that union was the album titled *Mother Earth Presents Tracy Nelson Country*, issued by Mercury in November 1969.

Tracy enjoyed that experience as well as the musical friends she made so much that she moved from California to Nashville in 1970. She made a number of additional albums with Mother Earth in the early 1970s that stressed rock elements, such as *Make a Joyful Noise* and *Satisfied* on Mercury and *Bring Me Home* on Reprise.

By the mid-1970s, Nelson had lost most of her interest in rock and was spending more time singing country material. When Atlantic Records started a country-music department during those years, they signed Tracy and released several albums that started to win her some attention from country fans. Helping to solidify her reputation as a rising young artist was the success of a duet single with Willie Nelson, "After the Fire Is Gone," which received a Grammy nomination.

"The record did well everywhere," she told Milner. "It astounded me that country people accepted it. It really established me in my neighborhood in Tennessee. I live out in the sticks, outside of Nashville, and there are really old country people who just didn't have any use for me until I'd made a record with Willie. Then I was OK."

In the late 1970s, Tracy recorded a number of country albums for MCA Records and also toured many country venues all over the United States with her band. She sometimes worked on projects with other country stars, including a contribution to the 1979 Amazing Rhythm Aces album, singing the role of Elaine in Amazing Rhythm Aces' Russel Smith's story song, "Rodrigo, Rita and Elaine."

Her albums included *Poor Man's Paradise* (1973) on Columbia, her last with Mother Earth; then solo albums *Tracy Nelson* (1974), *Sweet Soul Music* (1975), and *Time Is on My Side* (1976) on MCA/One Way Records, and *Homemade Songs* (1978) and *Come See About Me* (1980) on Flying Fish.

Throughout most of the 1980s she stayed at home on the farm she bought outside of Nashville in 1973. She wrote commercial jingles to survive. "Busch beer supported me for five years," she told Miriam Longino of the *Atlanta Journal and Constitution* ("Late Success Surprises Blueswoman," April 17, 1998). "But you know, for 10 or 12 years, touring was all I did, and it got to the point it wasn't worth it to me. Most people work a lot because they're driven or have a lot of bills. But I got over it, and I have no mortgage, no car payments, tiny utility bills—I just cut way back. I was very lucky to just have a life."

She did some touring in 1990 and then signed a new

recording contract with Rounder Records, recording two bluesy albums. She released *In the Here and Now* in 1993 to excellent reviews. She followed with *I Feel So Good* in 1995, which included a strong version of Bessie Smith's "Send Me to the 'Lectric Chair." She won a Nashville Music Award for Best Blues Album that year. Next was the more gospel, R&B-flavored *Move On* in 1997, which won a Nashville Music Award for Best R&B album. She released *Sing It!,* a recording she made with Marcia Ball and Irma Thomas, in 1998. She was nominated for a W.C. Handy Award for female artist of the year in 1996, and received a nomination in 1998 for Best Female Vocalist for a Nashville Music Award.

Suddenly Nelson was back, and some of her back catalog became available on CD. Reprise Archives released *Best of Tracy Nelson/Mother Earth,* including selections from the first five Mother Earth Records, in 1996, as well as *Mother Earth Presents Tracy Nelson Country;* Flying Fish reissued *Homemade Songs/Come See About Me* in 1992. MCA/One Way reissued *Sweet Soul Music* and *Time Is On My Side.* Another collection released was *New City Blues—the Prestige/Folklore Years Volume 2,* which includes two songs from Tracy's first record in '65. In 2000 she released her twentieth album, *Ebony and Irony.*

NESMITH, MIKE: *Singer, guitarist, songwriter, band leader (First National Band, Second National Band), film and video producer, novelist. Born Houston, Texas, December 30, 1942.*

As a writer and musician, Mike Nesmith made a number of contributions to the folk and country fields. Some of his songs became hits for other artists over the years and several of his country-flavored solo rock albums are still among some of the underrated gems in pop music of the 1970s. For all that, he remained best known for his part in *The Monkees* TV show of the mid-1960s, a part of his career about which he always had decidedly mixed feelings.

His first musical love was the blues, a by-product of his early environment. He was born in Houston but spent most of his youth in Farmers Branch, just outside Dallas, where his family had inherited some property that turned out to be in the black ghetto. (His mother, Betty Graham, invented Liquid Paper.) Recalling those years to Todd Everett (*Phonograph Record,* December 1970), he said, "Most of my friends were black, my first girl friend was black. I'm surprised that I didn't marry a black girl. I was married by a black preacher."

"Music didn't really mean anything to me until I was twenty. It was just something I'd hear in the back of a bar while I was shooting illegal pool. The kind of music I was exposed to? Well I remember when B.B. King had something like six hits in a row. They were hits to me because they were what got played a lot on the juke boxes. People like Ray Sharpe, Jimmy Reed. . . . Hell, they lived right there."

During high school, Mike did play a little saxophone, but he didn't begin to take a serious interest in music until he finished a two-year air force hitch in 1962. Inspired by the early 1960s folk boom, he took up guitar and, after about a year he was proficient enough to start playing rhythm guitar with local groups. He soon became an itinerant musician, working with bands around the country and doing some session work, including some backing assignments at Stax-Volt Records in Memphis. His travels eventually took him to Los Angeles in search of musical advancement, where he continued to perform in small folk clubs. In the fall of 1965 he heard about auditions for a new TV show and tried out in October. Considering that his competition included people like Steve Stills, he didn't expect much to happen, but to his surprise he was offered the job. His career with the Monkees was under way.

Selected to join him were David Jones, Peter Tork, and Mickey Dolenz, chosen mainly for their appearance and potential acting ability rather than their musical talent. Nesmith was upset when Monkees recordings initially were made by session musicians and falsely presented as being done by the TV foursome. Angered, Mike finally organized a revolt that changed the situation. However, the damage had been done—even after the Monkees did their own recordings, many people still were sure they were faked. The TV show debuted in September 1966 and remained on the air for three years. The group made fifty-six episodes in all of the half-hour show.

The group also gained a series of gold records for such albums as *Monkees Headquarters, Pisces, Aquarius, Capricorn and Jones Ltd.,* and *The Birds, the Bees and the Monkees.* The quartet also had many chart hit singles, including such Nesmith compositions as "Circle Sky" and "Tapioca Tundra." Linda Ronstadt and the Stone Poneys had a top 20 hit with Nesmith's "Different Drum" in 1967. Tork left in 1967, but the other three continued to do the program and also extended concert tours. Program ratings began to dwindle in 1969, and the Monkees disbanded by midyear.

Nesmith wasn't particularly sad about the breakup. Although the situation had been lucrative he hadn't held on to much of the money and, in addition, felt it had been creatively stifling. He wanted to concentrate on improving his image as a writer and musician and to do that assembled a new group in November 1969 and got a recording contract from RCA. Called the First National Band, its members were Red Rhodes, pedal steel guitar and slide Dobro; John Ware, drums and keyboards; and John London (legal name, John Carl Kuehne), bass guitar. Symbolizing the strong country roots of the group was Rhodes (born East Alton, Illinois, December 30, 1930), who had headed the house band at the famed Los Angeles Palomino Club for nine years and who was voted best steel guitarist for 1967 and 1968 in the Academy of Country and Western Music poll.

Things started off well. The debut LP, *Magnetic South,* issued in May 1970, made the charts, as did a single from the LP, Nesmith's song "Joanne." A second album, *Loose Salute,* came out in late 1970 and also won considerable critical praise. That album spawned a charted single, the top 40 "Silver Moon."

Before Mike's third solo effort came along, the band was reorganized. Now called the Second National Band, its members included Rhodes, Johnny Meeks on bass guitar, and Jack Panelli on drums. That group worked on the next LP, *Nevada Fighter,* issued in May 1971. The change in lineup, according to Nesmith, related to the ambitious plan he had for a series of concept albums that emphasized elements of folk and country and western music along with rock.

As he described the plan in the early 1970s, "The idea is to do a trilogy based on one of this country's original musical art forms, the music of the West and Southwest. My goal is to have three groups of three albums each—nine albums in all—providing insight into different consciousness at different periods of time. The first three albums were intended to present music from the consciousnesses of the old West, the second three on present day themes, and the third more futuristic.

"Musically, then, the First National Band arrangements were very simple and less complicated than later work. It was not only less sophisticated, but more sparse within the boundaries of music. The first three albums have some unusual effects on them, but these were achieved on the instruments themselves without special electronic manipulation. The second series is planned to use techniques used by today's groups, but not going overboard. The third series may just be an extension of the second or it may be much more advanced. For the Third National Band, almost anything may go, but there is one limitation. I don't intend to do anything in the studio that we can't reproduce on stage. If it can't be performed, there's no need to record it. There's very little truth in just being a recording act, from my standpoint."*

The first LP in the second grouping came out in late 1971, *Tantamount to Treason, Volume 1,* which included a recipe for home-brewed beer in the liner notes. The notes listed José Feliciano on congas. This was followed by a second album in early 1972, and the tongue-in-cheek titled *And the Hits Just Keep on Comin'* in August 1972. In 1973, RCA released *Pretty Much Your Standard Ranch Stash.* However, the response to the series was less enthusiastic than RCA hoped for, with the result that Nesmith never was able to complete the overall project.

In the middle and late 1970s Nesmith concentrated on songwriting, providing hit singles for various pop and country performers, including "I've Never Loved

Quotes from early 1970s interview with Irwin Stambler

Anyone More," which was recorded by Lynn Anderson. After leaving RCA, Nesmith recorded many albums on his own Pacific Arts label: *The Prison* (1974), a concept LP (reissued on CD in 1990) in which listeners were encouraged to read a story while the music served as a "sound track"; *From a Radio Engine to the Photon Wing* (1976), which included his song "Rio"; *Compilation* (1973); *The Best of Michael Nesmith* (1976, released by RCA in the United Kingdom); *Wichita Train Whistle Sings* (1978, first issued by Dot Records in 1968); *Live at the Palais* (1978, recorded in Australia); and *Infinite Rider on the Big Dogma* (1979), his last album for a decade.

By the end of the 1970s he was increasingly engrossed in the production of video films. In fact, Nesmith is credited with developing the idea that became MTV for Warner Brothers. He set his song "Rio" in a video format in 1977. A longer version of the "Rio" video, *Elephant Parts,* won the first Grammy Award for Video of the Year in 1981. He also was involved in producing several critically praised films, including *Timerider* in 1983, *Repo Man* in 1984, *Square Dance* in 1987, and *Tapeheads* in 1988. In 1985 he produced a television series for NBC called *Television Parts.* In 1989 he released a collection of his music videos in *Nezmusic.*

That year he also released a collection of the music he had recorded but not released commercially over the past decade in Rhino's *The Newer Stuff.* (Beginning that year, Awareness Records in London, now defunct, reissued all of Nesmith's solo albums on CD.) Two years later, he released a collection of his earlier music in Rhino's *The Older Stuff.* In 1992 he released *Tropical Campfires,* and in 1993 he released *Complete,* which included all of the songs he had recorded with the First National Band. *The Garden,* released in 1994, was a follow-up to his book-music LP *The Prison,* released two decades earlier. Again, he included a story booklet meant to be read while listening to the music. Two more compilations came out in the late 1990s: *Michael Nesmith—Listen to the Band* on Camden/BMG in 1997 and *Michael Nesmith—The Masters* on Eagle Records in 1998, both for the U.K. market, and a collection for the Japanese market in 1998.

In the mid-1980s there was renewed interest in the Monkees when old episodes were placed in TV syndication. Nesmith, however, still had no desire to relive those days and declined to tour with the other members of the group. Rhino Records reissued several of the group's albums and TV programs, and the other Monkees toured again in 1989. But in the mid-1990s, the four got together to make some music and decided to cut a new album in celebration of the group's thirtieth anniversary. Rhino released *Justus* in 1996, the first album of new material released by all four Monkees since 1969, to decidedly negative reviews. "Let's hope that, if they decide to record another album, the Monkees evolve a little," Al Brumley wrote in the *Dallas Morning News* (October 20, 1996). Despite the bad reviews, the following year Nesmith scripted and directed a one-hour ABC Monkees special called *Hey, Hey, It's the Monkees*. In 1997 the four also embarked on a ten-date tour in the British Isles and Ireland. But Nesmith backed out of the planned tour of the United States in the summer.

At the end of 1998 Nesmith released his first novel, *The Long, Sandy Hair of Neftoon Zamora* (St. Martin's Press), in which the main character is named Nez, and began working on a second novel. When asked to compare the young generation in the 1960s to the '90s Nesmith said, "In the sixties, kids were focused on television and rock 'n' roll. There were also some political and lifestyle issues that were important if you were under age thirty. Today the emphasis from kids is much more on computers and the Internet, on reinventing institutions, and economics. Television has changed dramatically in its influence, becoming a small part of a huge information landscape. Music is also less important as a cultural imperative than it was thirty years ago. However, the energy and drive of today's youth seem the same, as do the spiritual issues involved with growing up."

NEW CHRISTY MINSTRELS: *Vocal and instrumental group.*

What's in a name? Several million dollars, if the name happens to be New Christy Minstrels. This was the evaluation of the marketplace on the title associated with one of the most exciting folk sounds of the 1960s. As is often the case with groups, the personnel of the Minstrels changed many times during its existence, but the general style remained what was expected by the group's fans throughout the world.

The founder of the group was a young San Francisco–based folk artist named Randy Sparks (born Leavenworth, Kansas, July 29, 1933). Sparks had lined up a number of other singers and instrumentalists in 1961 to supply an up-to-date version of the famed Christy Minstrels of the 1800s. Started by Edwin "Pops" Christy in 1842, the original group had become legendary. In the years before the Civil War, Christy had led one of the most imitated minstrel troupes in the United States, credited with introducing many of Stephen Foster's greatest songs. The Christy Minstrel Show was the longest-running show on Broadway, and gave such performers as Eddie Cantor and Al Jolson their start. The group disbanded in 1921.

The New Christy Minstrels differed widely from the older organization. They performed old-time folk songs, but with up-to-date arrangements. They did not perform in blackface, and from the start included several female performers. In addition, many of their hit songs were original compositions by Sparks or other members of the troupe. Among the national hits turned out by the

group in the early 1960s were "Green, Green" (written by Barry McGuire and Sparks), "Today," "Saturday Night," and "Liza Lee."

In 1962 and 1963, the group was featured in personal appearance tours across the United States and on many major network TV shows, and was represented on national hit charts with singles and LPs on the Columbia label. By 1964, the New Christy Minstrels was one of the best-known folk groups in the nation. During the summer, the group was featured on its own summer replacement TV show. That same year, the Minstrels performed on the White House steps at the invitation of President Lyndon Johnson.

During 1963 and 1964, Randy Sparks had withdrawn as an active performer to concentrate on managing the business affairs of the Minstrels. In 1964, he sold his interest in the group to the management firm of George Greif and Sid Garris for the not insignificant sum of $2,500,000. Sparks went on to form a group called the Back Porch Majority.

Under the new management team, the group continued as a major attraction for several years. In early 1965, the New Christy Minstrels were the toast of Europe during their first overseas tour. The tour took them to England, Holland, and Scandinavia, and they capped the climax with a performance at the San Remo Festival in Italy. They gained top honors at the Festival with their renditions of "Si Piangi, Se Ridi (If You Cry, You Laugh)" and "Le Colline Sono in Flore (The Hills Are Full of Flowers)." Both songs were released on records shortly thereafter and made the top rungs of the Italian hit charts.

The sales count of New Christy Minstrels LPs through 1969 exceeded 11 million. Among the album titles were *Cowboys and Indians, Lands of Giants, Today, Presenting the New Christy Minstrels, New Christy Minstrels in Person, Tall Tales, Ramblin', Merry Christmas, Wandering Minstrels, Chim Chim Cheree, All Star Hootenanny, Greatest Hits, In Italy . . . In Italian,* and *New Kick.*

At the start of 1967, the personnel of the Minstrels were as follows: Dave Ellingson, born Ladysmith, Wisconsin; Peter Moore, born Chicago, Illinois, July 27, 1944; Michael McGinnis, born near Peoria, Illinois; Mark Holly, born St. Petersburg, Florida; Terry Benson (Williams), born Hollywood, California, June 6, 1947; Kenny Rogers, who later formed the First Edition, born Texas; Monica Kirby, born Detroit, Michigan, 1946; Sue Pack, born Hollywood, California, 1946; and Mike Settle, born Tulsa, Oklahoma, March 20, 1941. Other musicians who got their start with the New Christy Minstrels include Barry McGuire, who wrote the song "Eve of Destruction," Kim Carnes, Gene Clark, John Denver, and Karen Black.

Settle, who previously sang with the Cumberland Three on tour with Shelley Berman (including a Carnegie

Hall concert), was musical director of the group in the mid-1960s. After performing in coffee-houses in Oklahoma, he had returned to a feature spot at New York's Bitter End. Before he joined the Minstrels, several of his original compositions were recorded by major folk groups, including the Limeliters, Peter, Paul and Mary, and the Brothers Four.

By the 1970s, none of the original members were still with the group. The name stayed the same, but the roster was usually in flux. After the mid-1960s, the group did little new work, though it was still in existence in the early 1990s.

In May 1988 they performed for the queen of England. They have also performed around the world and at major events such as the World Series and the Super Bowl. The New Christy Minstrels continued to perform until 1995, when Sid Garris and George Greif decided to take a breather for a couple of years. In 1997 they considered starting the group up again. They even began advertising on the Internet for talented musicians and singers between the ages of eighteen and twenty-five with a "vision of future folk music for the year 2000 and beyond" to make up the group of six or seven minstrels.

One of those who answered the Internet ad was none other than Randy Sparks. Garris and Greif signed a two-year contract with Sparks on May 1, 1998, to see if he could get the ensemble going again. As of January 1999, not much had happened, according to Garris, the owner and vice president of the New Christy Minstrels. Despite the recent setbacks, Garris has no regrets about paying $2.5 million for the group in the 1960s. "Not only was it worth what we paid for it, but I think Randy deserved to get some money from it," Garris says. "We were running red hot at the time."

Several compilations were released in the 1990s: *Greatest Hits* (1990, Columbia), *The Best of the New Christy Minstrels* (1996, Vanguard), *Golden Classic Edition* (1997, Collectables), and *Definitive New Christy Minstrels* (1998, Collector's Choice). They also were featured on Rhino's *Troubadours of the Folk Era, Volume 3* (1992).

Based in part on a phone interview with Sid Garris in January 1999

NEW LOST CITY RAMBLERS: *Vocal and instrumental group, Mike Seeger, born New York, New York, August 15, 1933; Tracy Schwarz, born New York, New York, November 13, 1938; John Cohen, born New York, New York, August 2, 1932.*

A major feature of the folk-music renaissance in the decades after World War II was renewed interest in the traditional hill country music. A landmark group in transmitting some of the feeling of old-time country music to the urban audiences of the 1960s was the famed New Lost City Ramblers.

The Ramblers came into being in the summer of 1958, sparked by the interest of young Mike Seeger, half brother of the renowned Pete Seeger, in collecting old-time country songs. In his late teens, Mike had become engrossed in the playing techniques employed by rural artists. He first studied their methods of playing such instruments as fiddle, banjo, guitar, mandolin, and autoharp by listening to records in the Library of Congress. During the mid-1950s, he went into the back country with recording equipment to gain firsthand experience with the music.

At the time, many other city-bred folk enthusiasts followed similar paths. Among them was mathematician Tom Paley (born New York, NY, March 19, 1928) and freelance photographer John Cohen. Cohen, Paley, and Seeger were acquainted through common folk-music activity in the New York area. They compared notes and finally decided to form their own group to concentrate on preserving and extending the traditions of rural folk music.

Their first efforts before audiences in New York and other eastern cities were encouraging. Their first Folkways album, released later in the year, helped extend their reputation throughout the United States. The songs in the LP, which was titled simply *The New Lost City Ramblers,* pretty much set the future style of the group. Basically, as Mike Seeger stated in the album notes, "The songs . . . were recorded by commercial companies and the Library of Congress in the southeastern mountains between 1925 and 1935, and show the first attempts of the hill musicians to 'make a hit' with old traditional songs that had been in the mountains since pioneer days."

The Ramblers' selections had originally been featured by such groups as Gid Tanner and his Skillet Lickers, the Fruit Jar Drinkers, the North Carolina Ramblers, Dr. Smith's Champion Horse Hair Pullers, and the Piedmont Log Rollers. Examples of the LP's contents are: "Tom Cat Blues," "Don't Let Your Deal Go Down," "East Virginia Blues," "Battleship of Maine," "Roving Gambler," "Take a Drink on Me," "It's a Shame to Whip Your Wife on Sunday," "The Old Fish Song," and "Brown's Ferry Blues."

Demands for more recordings and requests for in-person appearances multiplied rapidly as the 1950s gave way to the 1960s. The Ramblers sang in coffee-houses and on college campuses across the nation. They were invited to the first Newport Folk Festival in 1959 and returned for most of the succeeding ones in the 1960s. They also performed at other major festivals in the United States and abroad. The group also found a steady market for their series of LPs for Folkways. *Volume II* was issued in 1960, *Volume III* in 1961, *Volume IV* in 1962, and *Volume V* in 1963.

By the time *Volume V* appeared, Tom Paley had left the group (in August 1962) to concentrate on teaching mathematics. His place was taken by Tracy Schwarz. Schwarz's interest in country music came from listening to country radio programs in New York in the 1940s. At ten he started playing guitar and, in his teens, also mastered fiddle and banjo. When he went to college in Washington, D.C., in the late 1950s, he played in bluegrass and country-style bands. When he joined the Ramblers, he proved to be as talented and versatile as his predecessor and the ovations for the group were as loud as ever. Oak Publications published the *New Lost City Ramblers Songbook* in 1964, edited by Seeger and Cohen.

New Lost City Ramblers records continued to appear with regularity after Schwarz's arrival. They include, on Folkways, *American Moonshine and Prohibition Songs* ('62), *Gone to the Country* ('63), *Instrumentals* ('64); on Verve/Folkways, *Rural Delivery No. 1* ('65) and *Remembrances* ('67). Their Newport performances are included on several Vanguard LPs, such as *Newport Folk Festival, 1959, Newport Folk Festival, 1960,* and *Country Music at Newport, 1963.*

By the late 1960s the Ramblers had moved on to other projects, although the members occasionally got together to record or perform into the late 1990s. Seeger and Schwarz formed the Strange Creek Singers along with Alice Gerrard, Hazel Dickens, and Lamar Grier. Seeger continued to make solo and field recordings, as well as to perform with Peggy Seeger. Cohen went on to teach at the State University of New York at Purchase. He photographed traditional musicians over the years and also produced several documentary films, including *That High Lonesome Sound, Sara and Maybelle, Musical Holdouts, Post-Industrial Fiddle,* and the *End of an Old Song.* He played with the Putnam String County Band, a group that included Jay Ungar, Abby Newton, and Lyn Hardy, and released the *Putnam String County Band* on Rounder. Paley continued to perform and record into the 1990s. In 1978 the Ramblers reunited for a twentieth anniversary concert, which included Elizabeth Cotten, the Highwoods String Band, Pete Seeger, and the Green Grass Cloggers. The 1978 Flying Fish LP received a Grammy nomination.

Smithsonian/Folkways makes many of the Ramblers' earlier Folkways recordings available by copying the masters onto cassettes or CDs. Smithsonian has also reissued their work through compilations in the 1990s, including *The Early Years, 1958–1962* (1991), *Out Standing in their Field: Volume 2, 1963–1973* (1993), and *There Ain't No Way Out* (1997), the group's first new recording in more than twenty years. The latter contained twenty-six newly recorded tracks and received a Grammy nomination for Best Traditional Recording. In 1994, Vanguard released *New Lost City Ramblers & Friends, 1963–65.* The friends included Cousin Emmy, Maybelle Carter, Eck Robertson, Roscoe Holcomb, Dock Boggs, and Sam and Kirk McGee. In 2000 Rounder released *Forty Years of Concert Performances.*

NEWCOMER, CARRIE: *Singer, songwriter, guitarist. Born Dowagiac, Michigan, May 25, 1958.*
Like most good songwriters, Carrie Newcomer looks

to her own life for songs that will connect with her audience. "There are things that are happy and sad and bittersweet and embarrassing," she says. "I have stories to tell and I've learned to trust those stories and experiences and appreciate them for what they are."

She often sings about spirituality and feminism, giving listeners an introspective look at love and relationships. But she is not afraid to take on a controversial political issue, as in "Wisdom Is Watching," from *The Bird or the Wing,* about the senseless killing of Dr. David Gunn at a Florida abortion clinic in 1993. She pulled the car over when she heard the news of Gunn's death.

"The song is my way of dealing with the anger," she says. "The argument has gotten to the place where people are killing people in the name of life. This song says, 'Come on now, this is ridiculous.' I consider myself a feminist and I consider myself a strong woman and a very deeply spiritual person. There's a very loud and vocal group of the religious right that equates religion and spirituality with being pro-life or anti-choice. That's not the case." Some have walked out of her concerts after hearing the song, but most have supported her call for "sanity in an insane situation."

Her style, both in singing and writing, is reminiscent of Bonnie Raitt and Mary-Chapin Carpenter, but with a midwestern sound. Newcomer sings in a powerful alto, backed by a six-person (including herself) folk-rock band.

The daughter of Donna Baldoni Newcomer and James Newcomer, a high school principal, Carrie grew up in Ekhart, Indiana, close enough to Chicago to hear Motown and Stax artists on the radio. "One of my first ambitions was to be one of Aretha Franklin's backup ladies," she jokes. She remembers dancing in the junior high gym to Franklin and other soul acts during lunchtime. Newcomer had a little record player and remembers buying her first Beatles 45. But Elkhart was once home to wind instrument makers Selmer, Armstrong, and Conn, and everyone started playing a band instrument by the time they were eight. Carrie played flute in her school orchestra. "As a kid you try different things and have different experiences," she says. "But sometimes you stop and go, 'Wow, I like this.' That's what happened when I started playing music."

Later she fell in love with the "singing poets": Bruce Cockburn, Joni Mitchell, Janis Ian, and Leonard Cohen. She was captivated by their lyrics and melodies. "You can't really sing and play flute at the same time, so I picked up the guitar." Her sister got a Sears guitar when Carrie was in junior high. "I really wanted to learn how to play so I would kind of swipe her guitar when she wasn't around," she says. "I remember playing 'Red River Valley' until my fingers bled."

Her father, a teacher and counselor before becoming a principal, bought her an Alvarez classical guitar with nylon strings. She paid him back eventually by mowing the lawn and baby-sitting. (Those would be among her more conventional jobs.) She taught herself the guitar by getting songbooks and listening to records. Her friends taught her some licks. She took classical guitar in college. "My first vocal teacher was probably a book of Joni Mitchell songs," she says. "I just remember singing 'Blue' over and over again so I could get those high notes and low notes and do it like she did."

Her mother was from an Italian Catholic immigrant family, and her dad had a Mennonite, Amish, and Methodist background. "They didn't know what to do with us," she says. "I wound up going to a Methodist church with my dad and mom. I was one of those people who thirsts for spirituality, even as a kid. I was interested in the peace churches and peace movements. I discovered Gandhi when I was in high school." Newcomer attended Ball State College and transferred to Goshen College, a Mennonite school in Indiana. "It was nice, small and peace oriented, a socially conscious kind of place."

To fulfill her missionary requirement at Goshen she spent six months in Costa Rica in 1979. She was moved by the poverty and the richness of the culture. She learned to value the cultural and religious differences. She visited a Quaker commune in the mountains. "I was impressed with the silent meeting there," she says. "The idea of silence and unstructured meetings. Women are so valued. The piece of light that women have is equal to the piece of light that men have. . . . When I came back to the States I started looking for Quaker meetings. People think that I'll have a bonnet or be very conservative. But they're like Zen Christians, very much on the mystical side."

She graduated from Purdue in 1981 with an art education degree. To put herself through school she painted refrigerator magnets in Lafayette, Indiana, and later took jobs she wouldn't dare tell her art professors about. "I could do fine detail work with a brush," she says. "I was painting pigs and doing John Deere caps on cows. I'd paint those racy pinstripes on vans, and that really awful stuff, like 'woman with sunset' or 'sailing boat into the sunset.'"

But rather than pursue the visual arts, she opted for music. "My heart was leading me to music," she says. "I was ready to risk it. I think at first when I went to school for visual art, I was ready to deal with tough critiques but I wasn't with my music yet. It was too close to my heart. Afterwards, I decided this is what I wanted to do."

Performing didn't come easy for the "insufferably shy" Newcomer. "Performing was a way for me to learn how not to be so shy and to be easy on stage and laugh at myself. It really did push me. It's been a long process from singing my songs for friends in the living room to getting my first job in a bar in Michigan."

Along the way she taught guitar and worked as a truck stop waitress outside Indianapolis. She sings of her experiences in "Under Your Skin" on *The Bird or the Wing: I was wearing my hair long, I was loving an angry man / I wore too much eyeliner,* she sings. "Pour a good cup of coffee," she recalls. "I learned how to carry four glasses in one hand and put the plates up the arm. . . . I worked with a couple of women who had real thick accents. I found myself sliding into it, 'Pass the sugar honey.' I'd find myself getting a little more southern each night."

All the while she performed in bars and clubs. In 1982, she was playing at a club when guitarist Larry Smeyak asked if he could sit in. A percussionist named Dennis Leas began sitting in as well, adding an ethnic beat. They formed a folk trio called Stone Soup. She was the lead singer and songwriter. (Newcomer and Leas, a computer programmer, became husband and wife.) She stayed with the group for six years. They released *Long Fields* (1984) and *October Nights* (1987) on her Windchime Records. It was mainly a weekend band because the two men had full-time jobs. Newcomer worked as office and business manager. She sent the first album to public stations and followed up with phone calls. "We were amazed at how much it was getting played," she says. "I'd get calls from all over the country from people who wanted to know where they could get the album. There was no distribution. I'd say, 'You can't find the albums, because they're all in my basement.' I'd send them out."

From 1984 through 1986, Newcomer also sang with a three-woman group called the Aluminum Singers. Other members were Susan Denton Staley, who sings backup on all of Newcomer's albums, and Fran Berman, who taught Carrie how to laugh on stage.

Stone Soup broke up at the end of 1988 when Newcomer's marriage to Leas ended, a difficult breakup. "I had a little girl," she says. "I'd worked so hard in Stone Soup. It was doing so well. When the marriage split that also meant the band would split. It was a tough time. It was a real time of transition where I was trying to make a living as an artist and support myself and my daughter. Just going through the whole grieving process of a marriage that didn't work."

Newcomer embarked on a solo career in 1989. She scraped together money from friends and gigs to release her first solo album in 1991, *Visions and Dreams,* on Windchime. She had recorded a first version of the album, intended as a Stone Soup release, but she wasn't happy with it. So she tossed out half of the album and rerecorded the second half. Several of the songs were written when she was breaking up with her husband and becoming a single mom. Remarkably, she sold 10,000 copies out of the back of her Toyota station wagon. (Following the success of her two Rounder/Philo albums, the label licensed and rereleased *Visions and Dreams* in October 1995.)

With daughter Amelia (she wrote "Amelia Almost 13" for her *My Father's Only Son* album), she currently lives on seven acres of land near Bloomington, Indiana, with her second husband and manager, Robert Meitus. She met Meitus in 1991; he was living in New York and had come to Indiana to record an album of his own with an engineer named Michael Graham, who wound up recording the second half of *Visions and Dreams*. Meitus hired Newcomer to perform at a small festival and returned to New York. They got to know each other through letters. "Sometimes you'll write things that you're not quite ready to say," she says. "That was fine with me at that point in my life. I was really just happy to be on my own."

Meanwhile, she had been corresponding with Ken Irwin of Rounder Records, who encouraged her but also felt she needed to develop a grassroots following. After she sold 10,000 copies on her own, he signed her to Rounder/Philo in the fall of 1993, which licensed her solo second album, *An Angel at My Shoulder* (February 1994), selling more than 20,000 copies. The title track was inspired by spirituality and nostalgia. "Right before I left Lafayette, it was like there were ghosts everywhere. It's always a little nostalgic whenever you leave a place where you've lived for a while."

Her spiritual life has always been important in her music. "I'm a real no-holds-barred kind of writer," she says. "It's my personal life, my relationship with my daughter, my political views sometimes, and my spiritual life. It's all up for grabs."

She doesn't wait for inspiration. When she's on the road she jots down her ideas in a notebook. "I'm a real plugger and chugger when it comes to writing," she says. "I try to write every day. Starting out in visual art, I would draw better or paint better if I kept my skills sharp. I write a lot of essays and short stories. I'm always mulling over experiences and what I'm thinking and dreaming."

Another song, "Only One Shoe," is about falling in love with Meitus. "I kept waiting for the other shoe to drop," she says. "I guess I'm chiding myself and saying sometimes there's only one shoe. The other one hasn't dropped."

Angel sold 20,000 copies and received favorable critiques. *Rolling Stone* called it "an album that impresses with the bite of her intelligence, the bluesy warmth of her voice and the support of musicians who give these confessions an edgy propulsion."

Her February 1995 album, *The Bird or the Wing*, received even more attention, selling slightly more copies than *Angel at My Shoulder*. Newcomer had opened for Bonnie Raitt, Bruce Hornsby, and Richard Thompson and was beginning to receive more airplay. The title track was inspired by a poem by Rainer Maria Rilke which asks, "Are we the source of creativity and art, or does the art merely pass through us?" Newcomer doesn't claim to know: *I don't know if I'm the bird or if I am the wing / But that's all right.* Chris Wagoner provides a nice fiddle solo in the song.

"The Yes of Yes," with Jennifer Kimball of the Story

singing backup, and "Holy Ground" are just two of the songs with spiritual overtones. The latter was inspired by a dream about a young woman. "She offered me a bowl with the spirit of God in it. It was liquid and shimmering. I realized that it moved like water. If she poured it into a different kind of bowl it would fit. . . . The second part of the dream is a man offering me an old book. He said, 'This is the spirit of God and take it.' I kind of turned and looked at it. It looked old and like a good-sized wind would blow it away. So I went back to the woman with the spirit of God in a bowl. I woke up from it feeling really wonderful. It was a wonderful gift, that dream. So I wrote a song about it."

While spirituality is a primary force for Newcomer, she doesn't proselytize. "There's a thread of spirituality running through my work," she told the *West County Times* in Richmond, California (June 23, 1995). "But I want it to remain inclusive, not exclusive. Quakerism is very inclusive, that whole idea that everybody has a little piece of light inside themselves that connects to God."

She released her fourth solo album, the richly produced *My Father's Only Son,* in the fall of 1996. She had been touring with a band to support *The Bird or the Wing.* She recorded the album with the band and singers Jennifer Kimball and Susan Denton Staley. The album is much more upbeat and pop than previous releases. The opening track, "Crazy in Love," was written with Meitus, who coproduced it with Mark Williams.

The title track, cowritten with John Prine's guitarist, Jason Wilber, was originally called "Throwing Back the Little Ones." "When there's only girls in the family one of the girls usually gets to be the son," she says. "I got to be the tomboy. It's kind of that experience of getting to hang out with my dad in a boat." Another song, "The Rooms My Mother Made," is about her relationship with her mother, who died of cancer in the early '90s. "This song is about being able to look back and say these are the wonderful things I learned from my mother," Newcomer says. "These are the things that are carried on woman to woman, and I'm going to take those with me."

One of the songs, "Up in the Attic," comes from rediscovering her childhood through a box in her attic. "My dad was moving, and he was clearing out his attic," she told Frank Rabey of *Mountain Express.* "He gave me a box of stuff I had from when I was a kid. . . . I opened up the box and there's my marbles. And I was running around for about a week going, 'I've found my marbles! I'd lost them!' "

Newcomer describes each album as a book. *Visions and Dreams* is about getting through a tough time intact. *An Angel at My Shoulder* is about trying to decide on a new direction. *The Bird or the Wing* is about spirituality. *My Father's Only Son* is about appreciating her well of experiences. In March 1998, she added the next volume in her canon, *My True Name.* Barbara Kingsolver, who inspired the song "Moon over Tucson," was one of her avid fans. "To my mind—a writer's mind—Carrie Newcomer is much more than a musician," Kingsolver wrote. "She's a poet, storyteller, snake-charmer, good neighbor, friend and lover, minister of the wide-eyed gospel of hope and grace." Again, Newcomer explores themes of spirituality, feminism, and hope in such songs as "When One Door Closes (Another One Opens Wide)" and "Something Worth Fighting For." While touring in support of *My True Name*, she donated 10 percent of her concert CD sales to local organizations for hunger, health, and the homeless. In March 1999 Rounder released a limited edition concert CD, *Bare to the Bone*, with all profits going to Planned Parenthood. She came under fire from anti-abortion groups, most notably Rock for Life, a group that targets musicians, which called for a boycott.

Based on an interview by Lyndon Stambler with Carrie Newcomer

NIGHTNOISE: *Vocal and instrumental group, original personnel, 1983 Mícheál Ó Domhnaill, born Dublin, Ireland (vocals, guitar, whistles, synthesizer); Billy Oskay, born Ireland (fiddler). Reorganized group, 1987, comprised Ó Domhnaill; Oskay; Tríona Ní Dhomhnaill, born Donegal, Ireland (lead vocals, piano, synthesizer, accordion, whistles); Brian Dunning, born Ireland (vocals, flutes, accordion, whistles, songwriter). Oskay was replaced in early 1990s by Johnny Cunningham, born Edinburgh, Scotland.*

In the constantly changing spectrum of Celtic music in the late decades of the twentieth century, it might be said that you can't tell the players without a scorecard. Over the years, gifted performers got together, separated, and surfaced as soloists or members of new bands, often taking on a new alignment while still occupied with other career activities. Such was the case, for instance, with Nightnoise, whose members had honed their skills with other notable assemblages including the Bothy Band and Silly Wizard.

The founding musician was Mícheál Ó Domhnaill (pronounced "Meehall O Donnell") who had settled in Portland, Oregon, after a U.S. tour with fiddler Kevin Burke. Before then he had been among the best-regarded young performers in his native Ireland, as was his sister Tríona Ní Dhomhnaill ("Trina Ne Donnell"). The two had sung and played together from childhood, and had both been involved in a band called Skara Brae, which also included Altan guitarist Dáithí Sproule and their sister, Maighread Ní Dhomhnaill, before becoming original members of the Bothy Band in 1975, a band which in its short lifetime established itself as one of the favored folk and folk-rock groups in the Emerald Isle. After the group disbanded in 1979, Tríona as well as Mícheál pursued projects in the United States, Tríona settling in North Carolina in the early 1980s, where she formed the group Touchstone.

After Mícheál and Kevin Burke decided to call Portland home, they set up a recording studio where they made several duet albums of their own work and also backed recordings by other artists. In 1983, Mícheál began the Nightnoise project with another friend and fiddle player, Billy Oskay, whose father was a violin maker. The debut collection, titled *Nightnoise*, came out on Windham Hill in 1984. Before moving on to develop a second Nightnoise album, Mícheál recruited his sister for lead vocals and her multiinstrumental skills and vocalist and fiddler Brian Dunning (who also played several other instruments as well as having a background in composing that promised to mesh well with the other members' writing abilities).

Tríona brought to the group a striking singing voice, which a *New York Times* critic described as "one of the glories of current Irish folk music." She recalled as influences in her vocal style such diverse artists as Ella Fitzgerald, the Beatles, Bob Dylan, and the folk-rock group the Pentangle.

Dunning had played classical and jazz flute in Ireland before coming to the United States in 1977 to expand his musical background at the Berklee College of Music. Among the things that had inspired his interest in the flute were hearing a song by Van Morrison's rock band Them featuring a flute solo and listening to the recordings of classical flutist James Galway (who, of course, also played flute versions of pop songs by people like John Denver and the Beatles). He recalled attending a music festival in Birmingham, Alabama, as a turning point in his career. Mícheál Ó Domhnaill and Kevin Burke joined in duets that combined elements of jazz and Irish folk music that embodied the kind of material Dunning envisioned performing. He later sought out Mícheál, and the two worked so well together that they formed a group called Puck Fair in which they were joined by bodhran artist Tommy Hayes. In between Nightnoise or solo efforts, that band came together for sidebar work in the late 1980s and into the '90s, including a recording, *Fair Play,* for Windham Hill in 1987.

In 1987 the foursome of Mícheál and Tríona, Oskay, and Dunning completed work on the second Nightnoise album, for Windham Hill, *Something of Time.* The band appeared at many venues and festivals in the late 1980s in support of their album releases, which received many accolades in the general media and in folk magazines. By the start of the '90s, Nightnoise had added two more albums to its Windham Hill catalog, *At the End of the Evening* and *The Parting Tide.* As Dunning commented, "The best way to describe playing in Nightnoise is that it's like playing in a chamber music group—but you get to have a bit of a blow. The music is quite delicate and takes place in a very disciplined setting, but at the same time there is that chance for self-expression and freedom."

Soon after *The Parting Tide* came out, Oskay's place was taken by Edinburgh, Scotland–born Johnny Cunningham. The latter had been a key member of the Silly Wizard group that had featured vocal star Andy M. Stewart. He was also in a Boston-based band called the Raindogs. Cunningham's, Mícheál's, and Tríona's paths had crossed before, when the three of them plus John's brother Phil had been in a band called Relativity. In 1992, Windham Hill released *Nightnoise: A Windham Hill Retrospective*. In 1993 Windham Hill issued the first album of the revamped quartet, *Shadow of Time*, followed two years later by Nightnoise's sixth Windham Hill disc, *A Different Shore*.

After the latter's release, Mícheál stated, "I think we've managed to distill the Celtic elements that are in each one of us individually. When I say Celtic, I don't mean it in the 'diddley-diddley' sense, but rather that deep Celtic emotion that you can feel when you hear the music. That is coming more and more to the forefront as we journey along in this present incarnation, although it's not something we're consciously doing; it's just something that seems to be coming out of us."

All four musicians kept on pursuing personal projects in between concertizing and recording for Nightnoise. Tríona worked on a solo album effort while Dunning played with jazz groups in the Portland area and Cunningham performed solo or with other musicians at many East Coast venues or in recording projects. Dunning collaborated on a series of albums with synthesizer player Jeff Johnson (the fourth of which was released in 1995). Mícheál's sidebar work included providing music for four projects by film painter Rose Bond.

By the late 1990s most of the members had moved back to Ireland. At the beginning of 1997 they released the *White Horse Session,* a live recording made in Oregon and Spain for Windham Hill that included Cunningham, who left the group in 1996. Johnny composed the music and lyrics to accompany *Peter and Wendy,* a puppet show adapted from J.M. Barrie's *Peter Pan.* The band recorded an album with Japanese vocalist Mimori Yusa for an Epic Records release. In 1998, Windham Hill remastered and reissued *Something of Time.*

NILE, WILLIE: *Singer, guitarist, keyboards, songwriter. Born Buffalo, New York, June 7, 1948.*

Though by the early 1990s Willie Nile had completed three fine albums for major labels, mostly of original material, his name didn't ring many bells with music fans in either the folk or rock domains. But he continued to be held in high regard by other musicians not only for his live concert work but also for his many excellent compositions. This was underscored by the roster of stars who helped out on his '91 album on Columbia, which included Roger McGuinn, Loudon Wainwright III, Eric Bazilian and Rob Hyman of the Hooters, Mark Johnson, and Terry and Suzzy Roche.

Born Robert Noonan, music was something of a family tradition in his hometown of Buffalo, New York.

His grandfather Dick Noonan was a vaudeville house pianist who accompanied many visiting stars of the time, from Bill "Bojangles" Robinson to Eddie Cantor. Two of Dick's six children—Willie's uncles—he recalled as being "incredible" boogie-woogie and ragtime pianists. As a child of the 1950s, his early exposure to pop-music trends came through in the albums his older brothers brought home of Buddy Holly, Fats Domino, the Everly Brothers, and Elvis Presley.

With the piano-playing influences all around him, Willie's first efforts at learning the instrument came when he was eight. For the next four to five years, he took classical lessons, but he was inspired by British Invasion groups like the Beatles and the Rolling Stones to focus instead on rock numbers. By then in his early teens, he kept up with pop music by listening to local stations and, on clear nights, to Boston station WBZ. One of those shows changed his early musical directions, he remembered. "One night I was up in one of the garrets on the top floor of the house, listening to 'BZ and they're saying, 'This is a brand-new song we think you're gonna like from a band called the Byrds.' And they played 'Mr. Tambourine Man' and I couldn't believe it, it was electrifying."

The song whetted his interest in folk and folk-rock genres, but not in his wildest dreams did young Willie think about someday meeting McGuinn and other famous artists. However, in time he became friends with many of them, including the Byrds' founding member. Over a decade and a half later, Willie commented, while he was working on tracks for his Columbia debut, "I got a call from Roger McGuinn. He wanted to do one of my songs on his new album; instead he wound up playing on my new album. I have a song called 'Rite of Spring' which is very Byrdsy, so I came into the studio late one day and I could hear his guitar playing the tune. And I had chills because I'm just a fan. I'm a kid, still am. I just stood there watching him and remembering the first time I heard 'Mr. Tambourine Man' on the radio."

By his mid-teens, Willie had begun teaching himself guitar, though he wasn't sure what career path he'd follow. One of his high school teachers introduced Willie's class to many of the great English writers and poets, including Shakespeare, Shelley, Keats, and Blake, which inspired Nile to begin writing poems of his own. Before he enrolled in the University of Buffalo as a philosophy major in the late 1960s, he was able to see some of them in print in small poetry magazines. After a while, he switched to writing song lyrics instead, and during summer vacation from college, he hitchhiked to New York to enjoy the city environment—often sleeping in the park—and earn occasional change from busking. After he graduated in the early '70s, he decided to live full-time in Gotham, moving into an $80-a-month apartment in Greenwich Village at the corner of Bleecker and MacDougal Streets.

It took him a little while to work up the courage, but

one night he got up and performed at a Village hoot night, the first of a number of times he used that outlet to gain stage experience. He told an interviewer, "It's kind of funny, actually, but there I was in blissful innocence and ignorance, just moving forward with the confidence of a poet who had already done a long journey of self-discovery, I suppose you'd call it, or self-exploration." One trick of self-defense at those events was to use a variety of funny pseudonyms: He performed as Umberto Snortz, Osgood Pequod, Huey Rosinbag, and Moe Downs.

To pay the rent, though, he picked up whatever work was available. His jobs included working in the mail room of a publishing firm, at a health food store, clerking in a bookstore, and so on. Meanwhile he kept writing new songs while finding occasional gigs at small folk clubs. To keep up his piano skills, he went into music stores saying he was looking to buy one and spent time practicing on the instruments. The hectic pace caught up with him that winter, however, at one time bringing him down with pneumonia and later resulting in a case of mononucleosis he fought by returning home to Buffalo to recuperate.

In the mid-1970s he focused less on folk and more on folk-rock, caught up in the avant-garde rock scene at venues like CBGBs. Of the latter, he stated, "I caught the whole scene. Patti Smith, Television, the Ramones, Talking Heads. It was a wonderful time, very spiritual, very mystical, one of my favorite times in New York."

He kept on adding to his credits with engagements at various rock clubs in the New York area before lining up what became a fairly steady gig at Kenny's Castaways. He built up a strong following there, and word of his shows reached many in the rock scene, including English star Robert Palmer. Palmer enthused about Nile to a *New York Times* reporter, calling him "the most gifted songwriter to emerge from the New York folk scene in some while . . . He writes rock 'n' roll songs that combine the innocence and lyricism of Buddy Holly with the rogue intensity of Gene Vincent . . . He is an exceptional talent."

By this time, Willie had a wife and two children to support back in Buffalo (later to expand to four children), and the chance to improve his career circumstances was more than welcome. Things like the *Times* article opened doors for him, and by 1979 brought a pact with Arista Records. The first album project was a strange experience for Nile. "The thing is, I'd never played with a band until one week before I made my first record, and then we just rehearsed for four days." His backing group comprised two members from the Cryers, Patti Smith Group drummer Jay Dee Daugherty, and Boston guitarist Peter Hoffman. The album, issued in March 1980, contained eleven originals by Nile, including "Vagabond Moon," "Dear Lord," "It's All Over," "Across the River," and "She's So Cold." Reviews of *Willie Nile* were almost all positive.

Rolling Stone's critic gave it a four-star rating. And Arista helped set up a cross-country tour that introduced him to many new fans. During a stop at the Roxy on Los Angeles's Sunset Strip, his act was caught by the manager of the Who, who gave Willie the opportunity, quickly accepted, to open for that legendary band on a three-week U.S. concert series.

In December 1980, Willie was starting work on his second Arista disc at the Record Plant in New York. He soon became aware that John Lennon was recording material in an upstairs studio. "We got a call saying he was out of guitar strings, and do we have any? And we all went diving into our bags. I was going to send up a note with the strings, thanking him for all his great music, but then I thought I'd tell him, when I saw him. The engineers told us he played the whole night using those strings, 'Walking on Thin Ice,' the Yoko songs, the last thing he recorded. The next night, December 8th, ten o'clock, ten fifteen, his friend Tom Pannunzio came in and told us the news [about his death]. It didn't make sense."

By early 1981 Nile had completed his second album for Arista, *Golden Down,* issued a little later in the year. The collection was above average, though perhaps not quite as effective as its predecessor. Reviewer Jean Costa commented in the *New Rolling Stone Record Guide* that while the 1980 release did "a wonderful job of capturing the interplay between Nile's folkie roots and rock and roll instincts, *Golden Down* gets dragged down by its overambitious production, some of which comes dangerously close to Springsteenism." Most critics, however, tended to rank the album as favorably as *Willie Nile.*

Unfortunately, some legal problems arose in connection with *Golden Down* that took some two and a half years to clear up and interfered with Nile's performance activities even longer. In fact, it took five years for his next concert, for which he flew to Oslo, Norway, during 1987 for a show that also featured folksinger Eric Andersen. Before that, while commuting between Greenwich Village and his family in Buffalo, Nile's income came from work on screenplays and royalties from songs covered by other artists such as the Hooters' version of "Washington's Day" and Patty Smyth and Scandal's recording of "Sue Lee."

Willie had kept on writing new songs in the mid-'80s, and a videotape of his Oslo set combined with demos of some of his new material helped bring a recording contract with Columbia in 1988. Willie took his time in selecting the contents of his Columbia debut, which wasn't completed until the start of the '90s. Besides the aforementioned "Rite of Spring," on which Roger McGuinn sang backing vocals and played twelve-string guitar, the disc included such other effective numbers as the title track, "Heaven Help the Lonely" (cowritten with Dean Chamberlain of the group Code Blue), "Cafe Memphis," "Children of Paradise," and "Renegades." In all, *Places I Have Never Been,* issued in March 1991, included eleven tracks, all written or cowritten by Willie. It was an album that ranked with his previous efforts and won deserved praise from most media reviewers. But while his musical peers respected the work, it made relatively little headway with the general public.

Razor & Tie Records reissued *Willie Nile* and *Golden Down* in the 1990s. Nile released his fourth solo album, *Hard Times in America,* on Polaris in 1992, and *Archive Alive* on Archive in 1997. In 1999 River House Records issued a studio album, *Beautiful Wreck of the World.* He has also appeared on several albums for other artists. He played guitar on Eric Andersen's *Stages: The Lost Album* and provided background vocals on David Massengill's *Coming Up for Air,* Curtis Stigers's *Time Was,* Andrew Dorff's *Hint of Mess,* and on *Largo,* an album put together by Rick Chertoff, Eric Bazilian, and Rob Hyman and inspired by Antonin Dvorak's "New World Symphony." In 1998 he joined Marshall Crenshaw, Jill Sobule, and Amy Rigby in the cast of *The Beat Goes On: The British Invasion Revisited.*

NILES, JOHN JACOB: *Singer, instrumentalist (dulcimer, lute, piano), songwriter, folklorist, folk-music collector. Born Louisville, Kentucky, April 28, 1892; died near Lexington, Kentucky, May 1, 1980.*

The multitalented John Jacob Niles was a major force in preserving traditional folk music for close to six decades. In concert, his high-pitched, falsetto voice took a little getting used to, but once that barrier was crossed, folk purists could delight in renditions of many of the finest folk songs to evolve during the long history of the genre. Niles, however, probably contributed more in other ways to preserving the folk-song heritage than as a performer. Besides keeping alive the tradition of homebuilt musical instruments, he was an avid collector of songs and related material, compiling one of the largest folk-music collections in the world.

John was born into a family with deep roots in the tradition of folk and classical music. His father, a farmer and skilled carpenter, was one of the best-known folksingers in the region and one of the best square dance callers. His mother played the organ in church and also was an excellent classical pianist. From his father John learned to play several stringed instruments, and he was given a basic grounding in piano by his mother.

When still in public school, he was given a store-bought three-stringed dulcimer by his father, who told the boy he expected him to make his own instruments in the future. John learned to play that dulcimer, but when he was about twelve replaced it with one he made himself. From then on, he always made his own stringed instruments, including many interesting variations of three- to eight-stringed dulcimers and a number of lutes.

Niles began his folk-music collection in high school, devising his own system of musical notation. At fifteen, he started a notebook of songs from his home region. According to Ray Lawless (*Folksingers and Folksongs in America,* p. 176), Niles's first paid performance took place about this time "when he accompanied a group of Chatauqua performers in a Saturday afternoon show." In 1907 Niles wrote his first song, "Go 'Way from My Window," which he had collected from an African American farm worker. The song would influence Bob Dylan fifty years later.

John graduated from DuPont Manuall High School in 1909 and took a job as a surveyor. His work took him through the mountains of the Kentucky region and gave him the chance to continue his folk-music collecting. By 1910 he had an impressive collection of songs and began to perform for local churches and other groups.

His budding career as a folk artist was interrupted by World War I. He enlisted in the U.S. Army Air Corps and went to France in 1918, where he almost lost his life in a plane crash. He was partly paralyzed; it took some seven years before he could walk completely normally once more. Instead of returning home, he took his discharge and attended the University of Lyon and the Schola Cantorum in Paris, improving his background in classical music. In 1919, Niles returned to the United States and continued his studies at the Cincinnati Conservatory of Music. He also soon resumed his spare-time activity of giving folk-song concerts.

After two years at the Conservatory, he moved to New York. He supported his folk-music work with a variety of jobs, including that of emcee at the Silver Slipper Club, grooming horses for *Ziegfield Follies* extravaganzas, and working as a rose gardener. During the early 1920s, he gave folk concerts at major universities. At Princeton, John met Marion Kerby. The two developed a folk-song program and toured widely in the United States and in most of the countries of Europe.

For several years during this period, Niles also worked as a chauffeur for photographer Doris Ulmann. He drove her throughout the Southwest, collecting folk material while she photographed various localities. He moved to New York in 1925 and published collections of music, *Impressions of a Negro Camp Meeting* in 1925 and *Seven Kentucky Mountain Songs* in 1928. In the late 1920s, he had books published, based on his World War I experience: *Singing Soldiers* (1927) and *Songs My Mother Never Taught Me* (1929). During the 1929–30 period, he also wrote a number of short stories for *Scribner's* magazine.

In the 1930s, his reputation continued to grow as he turned out more books, arranged and composed new folk material, and gave upward of fifty concerts a year. His published song collections included *Songs of the Hill Folk* (1936) and *Ballads, Carols and Tragic Legends from the Southern Appalachian Mountains* (1937). In 1939, he made one of his first major albums for RCA Victor, *Early American Ballads.*

In 1940, troubled by Hitler's excesses, he began an oratorio called "Lamentations." The piece was finally completed ten years later and given its initial performance March 14, 1951, at Indiana State Teachers College, Terre Haute. The work in its final form expressed opposition to all forms of authoritarian rule, including, as it did, what John called "a prayer to deliver the world from the curse of communism." Other long works by Niles are "Rhapsody for the Merry Month of May" and "Mary the Rose."

His recordings of the 1940s included *Early American Carols and Folk Songs* (1940) and *American Folk Lore* (1941). The latter was reissued on RCA's Camden label, with minor changes, in 1954. His concerts, which won critical acclaim for the choice of songs and Niles's sensitive dulcimer playing, continued to draw capacity audiences in the 1940s and 1950s. Particularly noteworthy was the 1946 midnight concert at New York's Town Hall in which an appreciative gathering heard him sing such favorites as "Black Is the Color of My True Love's Hair" (sung to a melody written by him), "The Seven Joys of Mary," "The Rovin' Gambler," and "I Wonder as I Wander" (for which he wrote the music).

His output of recordings and collections continued through the 1950s and 1960s. In 1957, RCA Camden issued the LP *John Jacob Niles: 50th Anniversary Album.* Niles also issued several albums on his own label, Boone-Tolliver, including *American Folk Songs* and *Ballads.* He was featured on a number of Tradition LPs, including *I Wonder as I Wander* (1957); *Ballads* (two LPs); and *An Evening with John Jacob Niles* (1960).

Other collections of Niles's material issued after World War II included *The Anglo-American Study Book* (1945); *Shape-Note Study Book* (1950); and the massive *Ballad Book of John Jacob Niles.* Among other well-known original Niles compositions and arrangements presented in these books are such songs as "Sweet Little Jesus Boy," "The Cherry Tree," "Froggy Went a-Courtin'," "Down in Yon Forest," and "You Got to Cross That Lonesome Valley."

In the 1960s, despite his advanced years, Niles remained active as a performer, appearing on many a concert hall and college stage in the eastern United States. In 1965, RCA issued the LP *John Jacob Niles: Folk Balladeer,* and in 1967 Tradition Records presented *The Best of John Jacob Niles.*

In the 1970s, Niles, who always kept close to his roots in Kentucky, spent most of his time at his Boot Hill Farm near Lexington. One of his last major projects was the *Niles-Merton Song Cycles,* published in 1972. In this work, he provided music accompaniment to poems of the Trappist monk Thomas Merton. At the start of the 1980s, his albums still in print included *The Best of John Jacob Niles* on Tradition and, on Folkways Records (including another of his best-known renditions, "I'm So Glad Trouble Don't Last Forever"), *John Jacob Niles Sings Folk Songs.*

His long career came to a close in May 1980 when he died at Boot Hill Farm.

In the 1990s Rykodisc purchased the Tradition Records master discs, which included albums recorded by Niles in its catalog. His family made a donation to the University of Kentucky to create the John Jacob Niles Center for American Music, which included his manuscripts, recordings, photographs, and personal papers, as well as those of his wife, Rena Lipetz Niles, a Russian-born writer. In 1992, Gift Horse Recordings released *The Collection,* a cassette that includes several of Niles's best-known songs.

NILSSON, HARRY: *Singer, pianist, guitarist, songwriter. Born Brooklyn, New York, June 15, 1941; died Los Angeles, California, January 15, 1994.*

The saga of Harry Nilsson, born Harry Edward Nelson III, combined elements of triumph and tragedy. He made many lasting contributions, including original songs and excellent recordings. He was essentially a pop stylist, but many of his self-penned numbers contained folk elements—some were recorded by artists in the folk field—and his greatest singles hit, "Everybody's Talkin'," was written by folksinger Fred Neil. Still, he seemed to lose his creative touch in his mid-thirties and died much too young, a victim in part of excesses that included wild partying with rock stars like John Lennon and the Who's Keith Moon.

In 1967, Nilsson often could be found having a sandwich or coffee at Revell's Coffee Shop near the RCA Victor building in Hollywood, California. During working hours, he could sometimes be discovered hanging around RCA's fourth-floor public relations office, where he went mainly to escape from his closet-like office elsewhere on the floor. Tall (six feet two inches), clean-shaven, blond, and blue-eyed, usually wearing sports clothes and a sweater, he gave the impression of an all-American boy of Scandinavian ancestry.

In conversation, he handled himself well on a range of subjects from computer theory to philosophy to music. The picture one gained was of someone quite intelligent with strong self-control, a quick sense of satire, and, particularly, an underlying toughness of the kind needed to succeed in show business. While RCA hadn't provided this young unknown with lavish office space, it had signed him to an exclusive $75,000 contract (nonrecoupable advance against royalties). The reason became obvious, within a year, with the release of his first RCA album, *Pandemonium Shadow Show.*

The LP focused critical attention on Nilsson, almost all of it highly favorable. Typical was Pete Johnson of the *Los Angeles Times,* who enthused: "His voice has a three-octave range, his imagination a somewhat wider one. He is a vocal chameleon, but, unlike some singers whose lack of limitations robs them of identity, each voice shares a personality common to every [Nilsson] voice. Nilsson is easily identifiable whether he is shouting the dramatic lyrics of '10 Little Indians' or musing tenderly in 'Sleep Late My Lady Friend,' or screaming in 'River Deep, Mountain High.' . . .

"His phrasing is perfect, but there is more. He embellishes many of his songs with bits of scat singing, sometimes noodling through an octave or two, sometimes imitating an instrument, sometimes doing things for which there is no adequate description. His voice doubles and triples and quadruples in harmony and counterpoint. All the singing voices on the album are his, even on the Beatles' 'She's Leaving Home,' with its latticework of complex harmony. He can be a one-man group."

The Beatles' reaction to Nilsson matched Johnson's. Derek Taylor, just moved from Los Angeles to London to join the Beatles' Apple Records, gave them copies of the LP. He called Nilsson long-distance and then put John Lennon on the phone. Lennon, who had spent thirty-six hours listening to the album, said to Nilsson: "It's John . . . John Lennon. Just wanted to tell you that your album is great! You're great!" Later, Beatles manager Brian Epstein tried unsuccessfully to lure Nilsson onto Apple.

Despite all this, the LP sold poorly. However, cuts from the album provided songs for other artists: "Ten Little Indians" for the Yardbirds, "Without You" for Herb Alpert. ("Cuddly Toy" had been recorded by the Monkees before the album came out.) But the exposure paid off later. *Aerial Ballet,* released in late 1968, had a good run on the charts the next year. Its track "One" became a top 10 hit for Three Dog Night. Harry finally was on his way.

Much of Nilsson's songwriting is autobiographical. "1941" on his first album refers to his year of birth in the Bushwick section of Brooklyn; other material obliquely mentions his father's separation from the family in Nilsson's early years. His mother took him (then called Harry Nelson) and his sister to Southern California in 1958. There, Nilsson attended St. John Vianney's Parochial School in Los Angeles, where he won letters in baseball and basketball.

After graduating, he spent half a decade trying to find his niche. He worked at several odd jobs, including theater usher, before settling down to work in a San Fernando Valley bank. By the mid-1960s he was a supervisor in the computer-processing department with thirty-two people working for him. However, he had slowly grown fonder of music, expanding his ability to play piano and guitar and beginning to compose. Working the night shift at the computer center, he had his days free to make the rounds of music publishing and recording firms.

For a while, nothing encouraging resulted. But his persistence paid off when dynamic producer Phil Spector selected three of his songs: two for the Ronettes and one for the Modern Folk Quartet. Harry made several singles and the 1967 LP *Spotlight on Nilsson* for Tower Records. Meanwhile, he was earning side income from singing radio commercials. In 1967, RCA simplified

things by signing him to a long-term writing-performing contract. By 1968, Harry had resigned from the bank and was devoting full time to creative work, including fitful efforts at novel writing.

Nilsson's second RCA album brought him success with the mass audience. In particular, his version of "Everybody's Talkin'" became a top 10 hit. Ironically it was the only one of the LP's thirteen cuts not written by him (rather, by Fred Neil), except for "Little Cowboy," a song his mother made up and sang to him when he was a child. Adding to the irony was the fact that the song, which earned him his first Grammy, became the theme of the hit movie *Midnight Cowboy,* edging out Nilsson's own candidate, "I Guess the Lord Must Be in New York City"—a hit for Nilsson in 1970, a year in which he also made singles charts with "Waiting."

"Waiting" was one of thirteen he performed on his third RCA LP, *Harry* (1969). The selections demonstrated his interest in lyric inventiveness, as reflected in such diverse titles as "Nobody Cares about the Railroads Anymore," "The Puppy Song," and Randy Newman's "Simon Smith and the Amazing Dancing Bear."

Nilsson's talent and versatility resulted in many offers from various segments of show business. He was retained to do the score for Otto Preminger's comedy *Skidoo* in 1968. Preminger even gave him a cameo role in the movie, which starred Jackie Gleason. The film, as it turned out, received far less praise than the score. In 1969, Nilsson also provided the background score for the TV series *The Courtship of Eddie's Father.*

Nilsson's record sales might have been higher if he had been more interested in performing. He was featured on a number of TV shows in the late 1960s; however, except for the special programs that interested him, he preferred to spend his time writing and composing.

Early 1970s included *Nilsson Sings Newman* (a 1970 tribute LP to fellow songwriter Randy Newman), plans for Broadway musicals, and the script and music for a ninety-minute animated TV special, *The Point.* Shown in early 1971, the program generally was considered by TV critics to have been an excellent achievement. Nilsson's own album of the score for the program (RCA, April 1971) made the charts.

Other Nilsson chart successes in 1971 included the single "Me and My Arrow" and the LPs *Aerial Pandemonium Ballet* and gold *Nilsson Schmilsson.* One of *Schmilsson*'s singles, "Without You" (written by Pete Ham and Tom Evans of Badfinger), proved his biggest singles hit ever, staying at number one in *Billboard* for four weeks starting February 19, 1972. He earned his second Grammy for the song. In August 1972, Nilsson had another top 10 single, "Coconut." Other chartmakers that year were the singles "Jump into the Fire" and "Space Man" and the gold album *Son of Schmilsson.* Nilsson's next album, *A Little Touch of Schmilsson in the Night* (1973), also made the charts.

Nilsson's relationship with Beatles alumni had become quite close, particularly with Lennon and Ringo Starr. Lennon, who called Nilsson his favorite American singer, produced Harry's 1974 RCA LP *Pussy Cats.* Ringo also worked with him on the score and sound track album for the 1974 movie *Son of Dracula.*

After 1974, Nilsson's recorded output seemed to enter a decline. Such LPs as *Duit on Mon Dei* (1975), *. . . That's the Way It Is* (1976) and *Knnillssonn* (1977) were pale shadows of his earlier collections. For some reason, Nilsson had run out of emotional energy for his music and increasingly seemed to seek excuses to get out of doing new work. In the late 1970s RCA ended its association with him with release of such albums as *Nilsson's Greatest Hits* (1978), *The World's Greatest Lover,* and *Harry and . . .* (1979).

The 1980 Robert Altman film *Popeye,* included Nilsson contributions on its sound track, but the film was not a success. Hampered by health problems like diabetes and a tendency to drink and eat too much, after that Nilsson essentially retired from creative work to pursue business interests, particularly in the movie field. In the late 1980s he owned a film distribution company in Studio City, California. Sensing continued interest among a segment of the buying public in Nilsson's work, in 1988 RCA issued *A Touch More Schmilsson in the Night.* Also available that year was the retrospective *Diamond Series: Nilsson.*

The Nilsson of the late 1980s and early 1990s was a far cry from the slim, athletic-looking individual of his prime. He was badly overweight and often in need of a shave. He was felled by a major heart attack in 1993, but recovered and began to reconsider his career objectives. In the early '90s he started to work on an autobiography and also started seeking a new recording contract. However, before any of that came to fruition he suffered a second, fatal heart attack in January '94.

In February 1995, RCA released *Personal Best: The Harry Nilsson Anthology,* a two-disc, forty-eight-track boxed set covering the years 1967 to 1977. Four months before his death, several artists began to put together an album of Nilsson's songs as a "get well" project. After mourning his passing, the artists made plans for a tribute album in his memory. The album, *For the Love of Harry: Everybody Sings Nilsson,* was released in 1995 by Music-Masters Rock and included performances by twenty-three artists, including Aimee Mann, Randy Newman, Joe Ely, Ringo Starr, Stevie Nicks, LaVern Baker, Steve Forbert, Al Kooper, Victoria Williams, Marshall Crenshaw, Brian Wilson, Ron Sexsmith, the Roches, and Jimmy Webb. The first annual Harryfest was held in 1998, as was a tribute concert at the Roxy in Los Angeles.

NYRO, LAURA: *Singer, songwriter, pianist. Born Bronx, New York, October 18, 1947; died Danbury, Connecticut, April 8, 1997.*

A shy, soft-spoken, highly capable artist, Laura Nyro had an almost across-the-board impact on pop music of the late '60s and early 1970s with original songs that combined often poetic lyrics with musical elements ranging from urban folk (somewhat in the Dylan tradition) to jazz and soul. The appeal her songs had to artists of all genres could be seen from the names of those who recorded them: Peter, Paul and Mary, Three Dog Night, 5th Dimension, Blood, Sweat and Tears, Mongo Santamaria, Frank Sinatra, Linda Ronstadt, and Aretha Franklin.

Music was a part of her life from her earliest years on College Avenue in the Bronx. Her father, a jazz trumpeter, spent many hours practicing at home. Young Laura Nyro was intrigued by his playing and by other music she heard on the radio and on records. When she was eight, she wrote her first songs. She attended Manhattan's prestigious High School of Music and Art, depicted in the film *Fame.* Always independent, though not always articulating herself well, she was often trying to her teachers, but they had to admit her considerable creative potential.

In her teens, she experimented with both songwriting and drugs. On a harrowing LSD trip, for nine hours she imagined a stream of half-men, half-rat monsters were coming into her room to destroy her. She later referred to that incident as a turning point in her life when she gained confidence in her ability to succeed. Later she stopped using LSD.

Her interests musically at the time ranged from Bob Dylan to jazz great John Coltrane. She began singing in local clubs in her late teens and impressed more than a few people in the music field with her promise. When she was eighteen, she went cross-country to San Francisco, where for two months she performed at the hungry i nightclub (long a proving ground for new folk stars).

Back in New York, Verve/Folkways Records released her first album, *More Than a New Discovery,* in 1966. Rights to the LP later were purchased by her next record label, Columbia, which reissued it in January 1973 under the title *The First Songs.* By 1967, so many people in the pop and folk audience were interested in her that she was asked to take part in the Monterey Pop Festival. It proved to be a disaster. Her low-key, introspective music seemed out of place against the high-powered acid rock of Jimi Hendrix and Janis Joplin. She was hooted off the stage.

However, it proved only a temporary setback. People in other segments of music began to appreciate the subtleties of her work and the expert craftsmanship that made her songs adaptable to different musical arrangements. Six months after Monterey, Nyro-penned songs started to show up on the hit lists. The 5th Dimension's versions of her "Stoned Soul Picnic" rose to number three in *Billboard* and number one on other industry charts and "Sweet Blindness," to the top 20 in 1968. By the time "Stoned Soul Picnic" moved to the top of the charts, Laura had completed her first album for Columbia, *Eli and the Thirteenth Confession* (March 1968).

Its songs revolved around the central theme of a young girl's path from childhood to maturity. An example was the song "Emmie": *Emily / You're the natural snow / the unstudied sea . . . and I swear you were born a weaver's love / Born for the loom's desire.* In "The Confessions," she wrote, *Love is surely gospel.*

That album wasn't an immediate smash, but by word of mouth its excellence was relayed among fans. Though some termed Laura's frequent jumps in volume and tempo mere gimmickry, eventually the LP was on the charts for many months. Her next album, one of her best, *New York Tendaberry* (August 1969), almost immediately was on the charts. It included such fine tracks as "Save the Country" and "Time and Love." This was followed by *Christmas and Beads of Sweat* (November 1970). Her only album of nonoriginal material, *Gonna Take a Miracle* (R&B oldies recorded with the soul/R&B group LaBelle), came out in November 1971.

During the late '60s and early '70s, other artists continued to do well with covers of her songs. In late 1969, Three Dog Night won a gold record for their recording of "Eli's Coming." In 1970, the 5th Dimension had a million-seller in "Wedding Bell Blues" as did Blood, Sweat and Tears with "And When I Die." In 1971, Barbra Streisand scored a major success with Laura's "Stoney End."

But after *Gonna Take a Miracle,* though Laura made some concert appearances, nothing new took shape in the recording studios. Finally in 1972, she retired completely from the music field and for a long time nothing much was heard from her. She got married, severed all ties with industry people, and moved to a small town in New England. Later, discussing the reasons for that sudden and complete break, she told Michael Watts of England's *Melody Maker:* "It just got to the point where people who met you had preconceived notions. And your phone rings 20 times a day. It's really nice to get away to a place where you can say 'Now wait a minute' and throw the phone out the window. I think it's good to get away from this horrible business when you begin to feel like a commodity. There are many other things in life."

For some three years, she remained in artistic seclusion, but eventually she got the incentive to take up writing and performing again. For one thing, she felt a new maturity in her approach to the art; for another, her marriage ended in divorce after three years. In late 1975, she made Columbia executives happy by agreeing to go into the studios and work on a new LP. That collection, *Smile* (February 1976), proved to be a coherent, well-written, and well-sung group of songs that matched many of her finest efforts of the past. Though most were new songs, including "Midnight Blue" (which provided a hit for Melissa Manchester), a major track was "I Am the Blues," a song she had performed in 1971 on a British TV special. In support of the album, Laura made a coast-to-coast tour of the United States in early summer that showed her to be at the peak of her form as an entertainer.

That four-month tour with a full band provided the material for the live album *Seasons of Light,* stressing versions of older songs. In June 1978, over two years after *Smile,* she was represented on Columbia by *Nested,* an album of new songs. During that year she gave birth to a son and stopped touring for a decade to focus attention on her offspring. While continuing to avoid personal appearances, she returned to the recording scene in 1984 with *Mother's Spiritual,* inspired by her own motherhood.

Many adherents began to wonder whether she'd given up her career altogether, as she issued nothing from 1985 through 1987. Then in 1988 she resurfaced to begin an extensive concert tour that extended into 1989, whose aim was to build up interest in a new album collection due out in '89. Backed by a four-piece band, she performed both older numbers and some of her new work.

Commenting on the song contents, Robert Hilburn of the *Los Angeles Times* noted ("Nyro Returns to Public Eye with Artistry Intact," August 15, 1988), "While the new songs share many stylistic similarities to her early material, there was a slight shift in attitude. Instead of the questioning, introspective edge of those days, Nyro now tends to deal lyrically with finding comfort and harmony in a world overloaded by indifference."

Queried by Richard Cromelin of the same paper about the reasoning for her long sabbatical ("Laura Nyro Returns for a Soulful Connection," August 11, 1988), she replied, "Sometimes you trade one success to find another. At any time that I have not been very active in the music business, it means that I'm busy doing something else.

"I really think music is my strongest calling, but at times in my life I did what felt natural for me to do. Over the years I've taken time to live life, have different experiences, sort it out, catch up with myself. I feel that I've always been involved in music, whether I was coming on like the goddess of creativity or whether I was just writing music on the sidelines. I just feel there's a difference in how you handle the world at 40 than how you do when you're 20."

In the '80s and '90s, Nyro continued her strong support of feminist issues and, starting in the late 1980s, added advocacy for animal rights to her concerns. In her 1993 Columbia Records album, *walk the dog & light the light,* the tracks included "Lite a flame," called "the animal rights song." Nyro wrote eight of the ten songs on the album and also served as coproducer with Gary Katz. The album had little commercial success, but that wasn't important. Nyro had already left an indelible musical mark. In January 1997, Columbia Legacy released *Stoned Soul Picnic: The Best of Laura Nyro,* a two-disc retrospective that was very well received. Just three months later, Nyro died at her home in Connecticut of ovarian cancer, leading some to wonder about the line she had written in her song "And When I Die": *I swear there is no heaven and I pray there is no hell.*

At the time of her death, several prominent artists were already at work on a tribute album, *Time and Love: The Music of Laura Nyro,* which came out in May 1997 on Astor Place Records. The album included covers by Phoebe Snow, Rosanne Cash, Jill Sobule, the Roches, and Suzanne Vega, among others.

O

OCHS, PHIL: *Singer, guitarist, songwriter. Born El Paso, Texas, December 19, 1940; died Far Rockaway, New York, April 9, 1976.*

Tremendously talented and passionately devoted to human rights, Phil Ochs gained a national reputation in the 1960s as one of the foremost exponents of politically related folk music. An activist for civil rights and against U.S. involvement in the Vietnam War, he often sang his sharply effective original songs on those subjects while taking part in marches or rallies favoring the causes he espoused. (He could and did write less controversial material, though he tends to be remembered mainly for his protest writings.) Perhaps, however, he cared too much. After considerable achievements during the 1960s, he seemed creatively exhausted in the 1970s when he took his own life at the age of thirty-five.

From a middle-class family, he was born in Texas, but for most of his youth his family lived in either New York or Ohio. His initial introduction to music emphasized the classics. He learned to play the clarinet and saxophone during his high-school years and was good enough to make the college orchestra later on. His brother, Michael Ochs, recalls that though the first wave of rock 'n' roll came along while Phil was in his teens, it didn't have much impact on him, though it did on Mike. Nor was Phil into folk music at that time. Mike notes, "After classics, he was into country for a while, then into black music—rhythm & blues. The first time we agreed was on [Elvis] Presley. When the Kingston Trio surfaced in San Francisco, that had an effect on him and later [in college] Jim Glover turned him onto the Weavers and [Woody] Guthrie."

Before Phil went to college, he attended Staunton Military Academy in Virginia, where his classmates included notables like Barry Goldwater, Jr. The choice, Mike Ochs states, was Phil's. "Basically our parents gave him the choice of a private or public [preparatory] school. He probably decided to go there because of the way the movies portrayed military schools and an identification with John Wayne."

From Staunton, Phil enrolled in Ohio State University in the late 1950s. His roommate, Jim Glover, was a folk-music aficionado who played guitar and banjo. Besides impressing the pleasures of the genre on Phil, Glover also taught him to play guitar. Phil later won his first guitar from Jim as the result of a bet on the Kennedy-Nixon election. While still at Ohio State, he wrote his first song, "Ballad of the Cuban Invasion," which took a pro-Castro stance.

Phil had matriculated at Ohio State as a journalism major. He was in line to become editor of the school publication *The Lantern* when school authorities rejected him because they felt his views were too "left wing," Mike states. "He quit because of that with only one quarter to go to graduate. He decided to become a full-time singer and in the summer of 1961 played in Farragher's Bar in Cleveland as an opening act for a number of performers, including the Smothers Brothers, Judy Henske, and Bob Gibson. He learned basically from all the artists who came through and in the fall headed for New York's Greenwich Village."

It was a golden time for folk music in that locale. There were many small folk clubs in and around the Village with a now legendary group of young artists on hand, people like Bob Dylan, Joan Baez, and Judy Collins. Like them, Phil got his start by singing in the many basket-type clubs in the area, where whatever pay performers got resulted from passing a basket around the audience. "His first major gig," recalls Mike, "was in a place called the Third Side."

The contacts he was making began to pay off in opportunities for new exposure to the public. "His biggest break back then," Mike says, "came from appearing at the Newport Folk Festival in 1963 and 1964. [He was invited back again in 1966 and 1967]."

Those appearances helped focus attention on him from both fans and record executives. Actually, he already had been given the chance to audition for Vanguard for an album planned to present a number of promising new folksingers, called *New Folks.* He was signed by Elektra soon after. While his tracks for *New Folks* were recorded before his Elektra debut LP came out in early 1964 (titled *All the News That's Fit to Sing*), the two albums were released at about the same time. On the Elektra disc, Phil wrote all but one song. It was a promising first effort, but not as good as his next release on Elektra, *I Ain't a-Marchin' Anymore.* Issued in 1965, it included such songs as the title number and "Draft Dodger Rag," major expressions of antiwar sentiment, the pro–civil rights composition "Here's to the State of Mississippi," and another of his best-known numbers, "Heat of the Summer."

His third Elektra LP, *Phil Ochs in Concert,* was on the pop charts in 1966. Among its contents was "There but for Fortune," a song that provided Joan Baez with a hit single and that was covered by many other artists, including Peter, Paul and Mary, who called it one of the strongest songs they'd recorded. Also on the album was the love song "Changes," a song recorded by many artists over the years.

During the mid-1960s, Ochs kept up a busy performing schedule, including many free appearances at civil rights and anti-war events. He was a regular on the folk festival circuit, appearing at such concerts as the 1965 New York Festival, 1965 Canadian Mariposa Festival, 1966 Berkeley, California, Folk Festival, and 1966 Beaulieu Folk Festival in England. One of his concerts included a 1966 appearance at New York's Carnegie Hall, where the material for his *Live in Concert* LP was taped.

In the summer of 1967, Phil switched from Elektra to A&M Records. His label debut, *Pleasures of the Harbor,* came out in late 1967. Besides songs like "Crucifixion," which philosophizes on assassination (reflecting great sadness over President Kennedy's death), the album included a number of more light-hearted numbers, such as "The Party," "Miranda," and "Small Circle of Friends," which provided Ochs with one of his rare singles successes. Over the years, the album sold over 200,000 copies, the best sales total of any of Phil's LPs.

His next effort was the 1968 album *Tape from California,* whose title track is a rare rock-style type rendition by Phil. An excellent collection including such protest tracks as "The War Is Over" and "When in Rome," it also has a more bitter, less optimistic tone than in Ochs's previous collections. In his next A&M LP, *Rehearsals for Retirement,* issued in 1969, that tone is struck to an even greater degree. Both in title and content it suggested the end of an era, which, for Ochs, was indeed the case. It was reflected in his next album, the early 1970s LP *Greatest Hits,* which proved to be Phil's weakest effort yet. It was to be the next to last album recorded in his lifetime. The last album, *Gunfight in Carnegie Hall,* came out in Canada in 1974 and wasn't released in the United States. The only other album of his recordings to come out in the 1970s was the 1976 posthumous two-record set *Chords of Fame,* issued shortly after his suicide and containing material from both his Elektra and A&M catalog.

As to what caused Phil to take his life, outwardly it could be considered an outgrowth of his increasingly heavy drinking. Mike Ochs believes that the drinking was a symptom of underlying problems. "He was never a drug user. In the 1960s he drank on and off, but he was more a social drinker than anything else. As things began to go wrong for him he drank a lot more. But he was never an alcoholic as much as he drank.

"The problem was that he found he had writer's block and couldn't complete his songs anymore. He stopped writing them in the early 1970s. Then he decided he wanted to see the world and so he did. He visited Africa, South America, and Australia. In Australia he recorded one single and one in Africa. Basically, since he couldn't write songs he began looking for

other things to justify his existence. He felt he had been a shaper of society and couldn't figure out how to keep doing that. He dabbled in other kinds of writing, doing some articles for the *Los Angeles Free Press.*"

He spent a lot of his time in New York in the mid-1970s, where his activities included organizing two major benefit concerts. One of those was a celebration of the end of the Vietnam War, held in Central Park and featuring such artists as Paul Simon, George Harrison, Joan Baez, and Harry Belafonte. The second was a concert to raise money for Chilean refugees, a concert, Mike Ochs remarks, "which brought Dylan out of political retirement."

After spending some time in California, in 1975 Phil went back to New York to live. He already had been subject to increasing fits of depression marked by manic drinking binges. He had refused to seek psychiatric help and, in early 1976, his feelings of hopelessness overwhelmed him and he killed himself.

Several months after his death, a memorial concert in his honor was held in New York, featuring many luminaries of folk music's golden era, including Pete Seeger, Odetta, Tim Hardin, Ramblin' Jack Elliot, Melanie, Bob Gibson, Dave Van Ronk, and Eric Andersen. The show was taped for TV by the Public Broadcasting System and is still shown at times on various PBS stations.

By 1996 most of Phil's work was available on CDs or cassettes. The first two Elektra collections, *All the News That's Fit to Sing* and *I Ain't a-Marchin' Anymore,* had been reissued on the Hannibal/Rykodisc label. The third one, *Phil Ochs In Concert,* came out in '96 on Elektra Tradition/Rhino. Previously, in 1986, a two-disc compilation composed mainly of acetates in Michael Ochs's possession called *Phil Ochs—A Toast to Those Who Are Gone* came out on Rhino. In 1988, A&M issued the CD *Best of Phil Ochs—The War Is Over.* The next year, Elektra released the "best of" collection, *Phil Ochs—There But for Fortune.* The 1990 Rhino release *Phil Ochs There and Now—Live in Vancouver* was based on previously unreleased material from the A&M vaults. As of 1996, the first four A&M albums were available on CD, but only through Japan (manufactured by Pony Canyon, Inc.).

In 1996 an official biography of Phil, *There But for Fortune,* by Michael Schumacher, was published by Hyperion. Besides that, Michael Ochs reported, a long-awaited feature film on Phil was in development.

In 1998, Sliced Bread Records released a Phil Ochs tribute album, *What's That I Hear? The Songs of Phil Ochs.* The two-disc collection, compiled and produced by folk DJ Gene Shay, included covers of Ochs's songs by Eric Andersen ("When I'm Gone"), Peter Yarrow ("There But for Fortune"), Magpie ("Power and the Glory"), Arlo Guthrie ("I Ain't Marching Anymore"), Iain Matthews ("Flower Lady"), Tom Paxton ("Draft Dodger Rag"), Sid Griffin and Billy Bragg ("Sailors and Soldiers"), Katy

Moffatt ("Here's to the State of Mississippi"), and Karen Savoca ("No More Songs"), among others. Phil's sister Sonny Ochs also helped keep the tradition alive by organizing the annual Phil Ochs Song Night.

Based partly on 1981 and 1996 interviews with Michael Ochs by Irwin Stambler

ODETTA: *Singer, guitarist. Born Birmingham, Alabama, December 31, 1930.*

Until she was almost twenty, Odetta knew practically nothing about folk music. When she finally did become interested, classical music lost an average performer and folk music gained a star.

Though known as simply Odetta, she has had a series of last names. She was born Odetta Holmes, but soon after her birth her father, a steel worker, died and her mother remarried. Odetta took the surname of her stepfather, Zadock Felious. When she was six, the family took what was to be an important step in her career by moving to Los Angeles.

Odetta's first interest in music came from picking out notes on a piano in her grandmother's home. By the time she reached junior high school, she had a deep desire to gain more musical background. She joined the glee club and took vocal lessons for a while. She continued her musical activities, with emphasis on classical studies, in Belmont High School. Her work level was high in all subjects, and she won the Bank of America's achievement award on graduation.

Odetta helped finance her night courses at Los Angeles City College by working as a housekeeper during the day. Her major was in classical music. In 1949, she was accepted for the chorus in a Los Angeles production of "Finian's Rainbow." During this period, several of her friends were deeply interested in folk music. After hearing some, she decided she preferred it to other musical forms. "I knew I was home," she told one interviewer.

Now she taught herself to play the guitar and began to perform in small folk-music establishments. She tried out for a job at San Francisco's hungry i, and was accepted, but she never got the chance to go on the bill because of objections from the featured artist. Soon she won a year's engagement at the Tin Angel, and her reputation increased so rapidly that she followed the San Francisco stint with a month's run at the Blue Angel in New York. Here such artists as Pete Seeger and Harry Belafonte were greatly impressed with her talent.

She was asked to return to California to sing the chantey "Santy Anno" in the movie *Cinerama Holiday.* She followed this with a hit appearance at the Gate of Horn in Chicago. Her first LP was turned out by Tradition Records in 1956, including such songs as "Joshua," "Deep Blue Sea," and "I'm on My Way." The LP title is *Odetta Sings Ballads and Blues.* In 1957, her Gate of Horn engagement was the basis for a second LP, which

included "He's Got the Whole World in His Hands," "Take This Hammer," and "Greensleeves."

Now an established performer, Odetta toured the United States and Canada in 1958 and '59. Her Town Hall debut in April 1959 won rave notices. In December 1959 she starred on a Belafonte television special, "TV Tonight." In 1960, she signed with Vanguard Records. Her first LP for the new company *My Eyes Have Seen,* featured "Water Boy" and "I've Been Driving on Bald Mountain." On May 8, 1960, she again took New York by storm with a recital at Carnegie Hall. In the 1960s, she was a regular performer at the Newport Folk Festival.

Throughout the 1960s and early 1970s she continued to produce excellent collections of live and studio albums: *Christmas Spirituals* (1960) on Alcazar Records; *Ballads for Americans* (1960), *At Town Hall* (1962), *At Carnegie Hall,* and *One Grain of Sand* (1963) for Vanguard; *Sometimes I Feel Like Cryin'* (1962), *Odetta Sings Folk Songs* (1963), *It's a Mighty World* (1964), *Odetta Sings of Many Things* (1964), and *Odetta in Japan* (1965), *Odetta Sings Dylan* (1965) for RCA; and *Odetta and the Blues* (1962) for Riverside. Several "best of" collections were released: *The Best of Odetta* (1967, Tradition), *Odetta Sings* (1971, Polydor), and *The Essential Odetta* (1973, Vanguard).

She also appeared in several movies, including the film adaptation of William Faulkner's *Sanctuary, The Effect of Gamma Rays on Man-in-the-Moon Marigolds,* the TV version of *The Autobiography of Miss Jane Pittman,* and the TV special *Dinner with the President* in 1963. She performed in the Gian-Carlo Menotti opera *The Medium* and in Arthur Miller's *The Crucible.*

By the mid-1970s she had released some nineteen LPs and traveled all over the world. Her music had influenced a generation of folksingers like Bob Dylan, Joan Baez, and Janis Joplin, and a generation to come, such as Tracy Chapman and Joan Armatrading. But in the mid-1970s she became disenchanted with the recording industry and stopped making LPs for more than a decade. In 1986 she released *Movin' It On,* which was recorded in Madison, Wisconsin, and represented her first new album in twelve years. She also rerecorded her *Christmas Spirituals* album. As she told Craig Harris for his book *The New Folk Music* (White Cliffs Media Company, 1991): "The songs are the same but I'm a different person now. I know so much more about how to approach a recording studio. I used to think that you sang in the studio like you sang on the stage. But that doesn't really work. It's a completely different medium."

The 1990s have represented a renaissance for Odetta. She continued to tour and perform in the United States and around the world, often going solo or with symphony orchestras. She was included in Rhino's compilation *Troubadours of the Folk Era, Volume 1,* released in 1992. Nanci Griffith invited Odetta to sing on "Wimoweh" for *Other Voices, Other Rooms* (1993).

Odetta also performed on Griffith's 1998 CD, *Other Voices Too: a Trip to Bountiful*. Then Rykodisc purchased the Tradition catalog and reissued Odetta's early classics, *Sings Ballads and Blues* and *At the Gate of Horn*. In 1998 Odetta sang "One Grain of Sand" for the Pete Seeger tribute, *Where Have All the Flowers Gone* (Appleseed Recordings), as well as issuing her own tribute to Ella Fitzgerald, *To Ella*, released on the Silverwolf label. She received the first Lifetime Achievement Award of the World Folk Music Association in 1994.

As a solo artist she backs herself with a guitar she calls "Baby," which she plays with her characteristic "Odetta strum." During her concerts, she continued to use music as a weapon in the continuing struggle for peace, justice, and freedom. At a concert at the First A.M.E. Church in Los Angeles a few months after the 1992 riots, she sang standards such as "Kumbayah" and "Amazing Grace." After the concert, she told Steve Hochman of the *Los Angeles Times* ("A Homecoming for Odetta," November 24, 1992): "Los Angeles is where I discovered folk music. I think of where I started and the stuff we've gone through and I come back another person. It's a reminder and encouragement that maybe I'm still on the right path. . . . Music alone doesn't solve anything but it can be healing. And it can give you the motivation and strength to carry on . . . to fight city hall . . . or whatever we need to fight." Odetta's 1999 album *Blues Everywhere I Go* on MC Records received a Grammy nomination. Vanguard also released *Best of the Vanguard Years,* and *Livin' with the Blues* in 2000.

OLSEN, KRISTINA: *Singer, songwriter, guitarist, slide guitarist, concertina, sax, hammer dulcimer, pianist, multi-instrumentalist. Born San Francisco, California, May 26, 1957.*

A versatile singer-songwriter Kristina Olsen might never have found her true calling if she had listened to her elders. Her father, a classical pianist, discouraged her from playing the guitar. A junior high teacher told Kristina that she had a bad voice and advised her not to sing in public. But rather than discourage her, these negative comments actually helped Kristina find her own voice. During the time that she was afraid to sing in public, she mastered several different instruments, which became her ersatz voice. Later in life, she took lessons to develop her husky, expressive alto, which she uses to great effect in her bluesy songs and ballads.

Kristina grew up in San Francisco's Haight-Ashbury District during the 1960s and early 1970s. Her parents didn't have a television, something Kristina sings about in her song "Better Than TV." At an early age, her mother took her to see John Prine, Steve Goodman, and Joan Baez. Since her father was a classical pianist, she started piano lessons at a very early age. She hated it. Her fingers were too small and her teacher demanded perfection.

At eleven, when she was at summer camp, she fell in love with the guitar. "Nothing sparked my interest more than my father telling me not to play," she told Chris Flisher of *Performing Songwriter* (March–April 1994). After he died, she wrote a song for him called "My Father's Piano."

The teacher who told her she couldn't sing also had an impact on her. "I was crushed because I loved to sing," she told Flisher. "This teacher told me that I shouldn't play guitar because it made me sing! . . . I became a multi-instrumentalist out of complete frustration over my voice. . . . I was trying to force my voice through my instruments. When I wanted to say something in a different way I would go out and learn a new instrument. They are like languages, once you learn one of them the rest come pretty easy."

She took up more than fifteen instruments, including the accordion, banjo, saxophone, concertina, bass, and guitar. Songwriting also became a natural form of expression for Olsen during adolescence. "I wrote my songs to escape but I would go to the roof of my house and sing them over the sound of the traffic," she told Flisher. "I was so completely convinced that I couldn't sing and that way no one could hear me."

Listening to her own muse, she started voice lessons, which helped broaden her range and tone. She is best suited to her shouting anthems or blues songs, which she accompanies with a steel-body slide guitar, but she can also hold her own singing a delicate folk song.

After graduating high school she began writing and performing songs and supporting herself with odd jobs. She had lived in many cities but settled in Venice, California. She continued to support herself by working in music stores, teaching music, and working as a computer consultant. She still likes to teach every summer at guitar camps. "Total heaven," she told Todd Ellison of *Acoustic Guitar* (April 1996). "Guitar camp is just like regular camp when you're a kid, only better, because you can have sex at night."

She self-released her first cassette, *It Don't Take Too Much,* in 1983, on her Take A Break label. Two years later she released her second cassette, *Cupid Is Stupid,* on Take A Break, recorded live at McCabe's Guitar Shop in Santa Monica. In 1985 she won the New Folk Songwriting Contest at the Kerrville (Texas) Folk Festival. The song, "Keeping This Life of Mine (Song for Battered Women)," was written for a friend of hers who wound up in the hospital with broken bones after her husband beat her. Michelle Shocked, whom she met at the festival, invited Kristina to play hammer dulcimer on her 1988 debut for Mercury, *Short Sharp Shocked.*

After she opened for singer-songwriter Christine Lavin at the Chocolate Church in Bath, Maine, Lavin encouraged Philo Records to sign her. Kristina released her debut album, *Kristina Olsen,* in 1992, followed by *Love, Kristina* in 1993, *Hurry On Home* in 1995 (produced by former Kate Wolf guitarist Nina Gerber, who often tours with Olsen), and *Live from Around the World* in 1997, recorded during performances in Scotland, New Zealand, Australia, and the United States.

Olsen has also played in ensembles. In the fall of 1993 she went on a national tour with other Philo artists, including Bill Morrissey, Cheryl Wheeler, and Vance Gilbert, to celebrate the twentieth anniversary of the label. She was included on the album *Philo So Far . . . the 20th Anniversary Folk Sampler,* released in 1994. She has also toured as a member of the Lavin-inspired group Four Bitchin' Babes, and participated in Lavin's songwriter retreats held on Martha's Vineyard.

She formed a songwriting group in Los Angeles in the late 1970s that provides constructive criticism for its members. "I love writing songs," she told Flisher. "But my favorite songs don't seem to come from me, they seem to come through me, like maybe I am the channel for that song. It is an absolutely euphoric feeling when it happens, it is such a jolt, like the high that runners get."

One of her best songs is "The Man with the Bright Red Car," about a man she met in England who learned to drive at forty-five so that he could take care of his mentally handicapped siblings. As she sings: *I said I don't know how you cope / You've so much weight to bear / A full-time job, some overtime, and your brothers' full-time care / He looked at me like I was slow, he shook his head and told me, 'No, / Don't you see they take care of me. That's how it is with family.' / And I saw a man who was a king / The man with the bright red car.*

Olsen's songs are replete with sexual and political allusions. "I like to write about human experience," she told Ellison. "I have a lot of strong convictions, but I really don't like songs that stand on a soapbox and tell someone else what to think, because I hate it when people tell me what to think. I like thinking for myself."

Other artists have picked up on her songs. Fairport Convention, whom she met at the National Folk Festival in Canberra, heard her song "Dangerous" and recorded it for their CD *Who Knows Where the Time Goes.* Lucky Bags from England recorded "Cry You a Waterfall," and New Hampshire singer-songwriter Doug Clegg recorded "My Father's Piano."

In 1998 she put out a CD with Australian cellist Peter Grayling called *Duet* for the Australian and U.K. markets.

OYSTERBAND, OYSTER BAND: *Vocal and instrumental group from England. Founding members included John Jones, born Aberystwyth, Wales, October 19, 1949 (lead vocals, accordion, melodeon, piano); Alan Prosser, born Woverhampton, England, April 17, 1951 (vocals, guitars, banjo, mandolin, violin); Ian Telfer, born Falkirk, Scotland, May 28, 1948 (violin, viola, tenor concertina); Ian Kearey, born London, England, October 14, 1954 (twelve-string guitar, bass guitar, epinette, autoharp). Ros-*

ter of Oyster Ceilidh Band, late 1970s, comprised Jones, Prosser, and Telfer, plus Chris Taylor (mandola, banjo, bouzouki, dulcimer, mouth harp, melodeon); Cathy LeSurf (lead vocals, bodhran, bells); Chris Wood (vocals, bass, percussion); Will Ward (bassoon). Wood left 1980, replaced by Kearey to form initial Oyster Band group, LeSurf, Jones, Prosser, Telfer, Taylor, Kearey. LeSurf left 1982 with Jones taking over lead vocals. Taylor left '84, Russell Lax added in mid-'80s on drums. Roy "Chopper" Cooper, born Romford, Essex, England, September 22, 1954 (vocals, bass, cello) added late '80s. Lax replaced by Lee (drums, percussion, bodhran) early '90s.

One of England's best-kept secrets in the 1980s and early '90s, the Oysterband ranked among the best U.K. folk-rock groups of the period. With a repertoire ranging from politically oriented originals (examples being a song deploring the conditions of Turkish immigrants in Germany—"This Year, Next Year, Somewhere"—and protests against U.K. class divisions) to high-energy versions of traditional numbers like "Hal-an-Tow," the band could provide insights into global problems while generating feverish audience participation among sizable audiences in England and Europe.

Their U.S. appearances were equally exciting, although these were typically restricted to smaller folk venues through the early '90s. After attending a concert at McCabe's in Santa Monica, California, Steve Hochman of the *Los Angeles Times* ("The Oyster Band: In One Era and Out Another," April 4, 1989), commented approvingly, "The veteran band finds as much folk value (i.e., topicality) in such rock material as New Order's "Love Vigilantes" as it finds rock value (i.e., explosiveness) in the traditional words and music it sometimes employs. . . . Solid rock drums and bass pushed along melodeon and fiddle lines for a blend that—though building on the folk-rock of Fairport Convention and Richard Thompson—was strikingly original."

The group's origins went back to the 1970s, when several of the founding members were part of a band organized by fiddler David Arbus called Fiddler's Dram. The musicians assembled for it in 1973 comprised Cathy LeSurf on lead vocals; Ian Telfer on fiddle, viola, and concertina; Alan Prosser on guitar and mandolin; and Chris Taylor on mandola, banjo, harmonica, and other instruments. In November 1975 the foursome joined with such others as John Jones and Ian Kearey to play a benefit dance, calling themselves the Whitstable Oyster Co. Ceilidh Band. The concert worked so well it was decided to continue the collaboration as a sidegroup to Fiddler's Dram, playing dances under the name the Oyster Ceilidh Band.

Fiddler's Dram naturally was seeking recording exposure, which led to the 1979 release on the Dingles label, *To See The Play.* This found little favor with record buyers but in late '79 spawned an unexpected hit with the single "Day Trip to Bangor." The high hopes this inspired soon evaporated as a follow-up LP, *Fid-*

dler's Dram, brought another failure. The Oyster Ceilidh Band had a little better luck with an LP on Dingles called Jack's Alive, recorded by LeSurf, Jones, Prosser, Telfer, Taylor, Chris Wood, and Will Ward. After Fiddler's Dram essentially ceased to exist by the end of 1980, Oyster Ceilidh musicians reorganized under the banner of the Oyster Band (with Ward no longer taking part and Wood replaced by Ian Kearey) and had their debut LP, English Rock 'n Roll: The Early Years (1800–1850), out on Pukka Records in 1982. Soon after that came out, Cathy LeSurf departed to take over as lead singer in another group, Ashley Hutching's the Albion Band. Undaunted, Jones became lead vocalist and the Oyster Band came out with an excellent second collection on Pukka, Lie Back and Think of England. Their live concerts in support of those albums, which increasingly included some new compositions by band members, won good critical response at home and growing interest from first U.K. and then European audiences.

While the band's styling had the raw energy of rock, the music never abandoned folk elements; indeed, several band members in the late '70s and '80s did session work on albums by more traditional folk artists. Telfer and Prosser, for instance, played on the 1977 release by Ewan MacColl and Peggy Seeger, Cold Snap, and Telfer contributed fiddle support in 1983 to some tracks on their Freeborn Man album.

The band had two more albums released on the Pukka label in the mid-1980s, 20 Golden Tie-Slackeners in '84 and Liberty Hall in '85. It continued to expand its followers during that period with tours throughout the United Kingdom and Europe as well as Japan and other parts of the Far East. In 1986 the Oyster Band moved to a new label, Cooking Vinyl, which remained its U.K. outlet into the mid-1990s. Its label debut, Step Outside, produced by U.K. folk-rock notable Clive Gregson, included its first track of "Hal-an-Tow," which became one of its best-known concert numbers. Other songs on the album included "Another Quiet Night in England," "Ashes to Ashes," "Bully in the Alley," "Gaol Song," and "The Old Dance." The album was issued on CD in the United States by Rounder. By this time, Chris Taylor had left and drummer Russell Lax had been added. The same group (Jones, Kearey, Lax, Prosser, and Telfer) recorded the next album, Wide Blue Yonder, also produced by Gregson, issued in the United Kingdom in 1987 by Cooking Vinyl and in North America by Polygram. (Kearey left soon after the album was completed.) That year the track of "Liberty Hall" was included in Folk Roots Record's anthology titled Square Roots.

The band closed out the 1980s with such releases as the EP Love Vigilantes, the twelve-inch EP The Lost and Found, the twelve-inch EP New York Girls (which included live tracks recorded at a London concert), and the full album Ride, all issued during 1989. For Ride, the group no longer included Kearey, but welcomed another new member, Chopper (who used only that single

pseudonym), previously bassist for the group 3 Mustaphas 3. During 1988 more of the group's material was included in U.K. folk-music anthologies such as "Kentish Cricketers/Galopede" (from the album 20 Golden Tie-Slackeners), included in the Folk Roots Tap Roots release, and a remix version of "Hal-an-Tow" and "The Oxford Girl" (the latter from Wide Blue Yonder), incorporated in Cooking Vinyl's Hot Cookies.

The band began the '90s with the 1990 album Freedom and Rain, issued on Cooking Vinyl in the United Kingdom and Rykodisc in the United States. The collection, whose songs included "Mississippi," "Lullaby of London," "Dives and Lazarus," "Susie Clelland," and "Finisterre," was recorded with the exquisitely talented U.K. folksinger June Tabor as co-lead vocalist. She then joined the band for a critically well received U.S. tour. The Oysters also had the live album Little Rock to Leipzig on the Cooking Vinyl label in U.K. stores in 1990. It came out on Rykodisc in the United States in '91. Not long after completing that project, the Oyster Band had a new drummer and percussionist, also a single-name artist, Lee, who played on their next CD, Deserters.

For this collection, issued by Cooking Vinyl in the United Kingdom and Rykodisc in the United States in 1992, the band sported a new name arrangement: Oysterband. Asked about the contrast between the somber lyrics of many of the tracks ("Elena's Shoes," for instance, focused on the decadence of dictator's wives like Imelda Marcos of the Philippines and Elena Ceaucescu of Romania) and the joyous driving energy of the musical treatment, Jones observed, "I love the juxtaposition of dark lyrics delivered uptempo with an edge. I find the clash of things very, very intriguing."

In 1993 the group was represented by an overseas "best of" compilation, Celtic Junkies, released on the Continent by P&C/Cooking Vinyl. It completed a new collection, Holy Bandits (the roster was Jones, Chopper, Lee, Prosser, and Telfer), issued by Cooking Vinyl in the United Kingdom in '93 and by Rykodisc in the United States in '94. In '94, Cooking Vinyl released Trawler, a CD set of favorite band songs remixed for this package. By 1995 the band's U.K. record firm had set up a North American outlet, Cooking Vinyl America. The first Oysterband album released under this arrangement was the very listenable The Shouting End of Life. Except for Leon Rosselson's "The World Turned Upside Down," all of the tracks were originals, mostly cowritten by Telfer, Jones, and Prosser. Topics ranged from the romantic ("Put Out the Lights") to the romantic put-down ("Don't Slit Your Wrists for Me") to the anticonservative polemic in the rap-rock "Jam Tomorrow." The group was represented on the Rhino Records compilation Troubadours of British Rock, Volume 3 with the track "Moving On" from the Holy Bandits album.

In 1996 a limited-edition CD, Alive and Shouting, was offered by mail order or purchase at the band's concerts. It was described by them as an "Official Bootleg Live Oysterband CD," issued to raise funds to keep the band's free newsletter *F-Word* operating. In addition to helping that cause, band members noted, it also offered much better quality than the various unauthorized bootleg tapes of their shows. The CD contents were intended to provide the flavor of typical concert sets played by the band in the mid-'90s.

In 1997 the Oysterband released *Deep Dark Ocean* on Cooking Vinyl, an uncharacteristically apolitical collection released shortly after the Labour Party and Tony Blair had taken over the British Parliament. "Yes, we voted Labour, but we didn't inhale," the band jokes in the liner notes. It was a much tamer album than *The Shouting End of Life.* That year the Oysterband performed on Chumbawamba's *Tubthumping* album on the song "Farewell to the Crown," while Chopper played cello on "Tea Room England" for *Tubthumping.* In 1998 they released *Alive and Acoustic,* an album recorded during an acoustic tour of England. Another compilation album, *Pearls from the Oysters,* was taken from the band's first four albums. In 1999 Omnium Records issued *Here I Stand.*

PATTON, CHARLEY: *Singer, songwriter, guitarist. Born Edwards, Mississippi, ca. 1887 (also listed as 1891); died Holly Ridge, Mississippi, April 28, 1934.*

Although there was no single inventor of the blues, Charley Patton can be considered one of its "fathers": during the '20s, when the blues was still in its "infant" years, Patton had already developed his own mature style. One of the first blues artists to ever be recorded, his harsh, mumbling voice, sharp yet melodic guitar lines, and personal lyrics reflect the heavy life of traveling that this bluesman led. A popular entertainer with both white and black crowds, known in most every city in Mississippi, Patton became an idol to young aspiring musicians such as Howlin' Wolf and Bukka White, while preserving and spreading the blues throughout the Delta.

Patton's early years are somewhat unclear, but according to Patton's sister, Viola Cannon, he was born on a farm outside Edwards, Mississippi, in 1887. His father, Bill Patton, was a preacher, but it is possible that his real father was his mother's secret lover, Henderson Chatmon, the father of the Chatmon brothers, the most famous of whom were Sam and Armentier, a.k.a. Bo Carter, who were later to record their own blues records in the '20s and '30s. Either way, it is clear that both the Chatmon clan and his father influenced the blues and gospel songs that Patton was soon to write. When he was a young boy, Charley, his parents, and his four siblings moved from Edwards to Dockery's, a fairly large

plantation, where his father became the elder of the church. According to his sister Viola, it was at Dockery's that Charley started playing guitar. Also at Dockery's, Charley met Henry Sloan, one of the earliest Delta bluesmen, who also became a large influence on Patton's playing.

The thin, rather short Patton soon began playing at the plantation during Saturday night festivities. It appears that he married a girl named Gertrude in the early 1900s, and another by the name of Minnie Toy in 1908, but not much is known about them. Charley decided to take to the road, working in timber and levee camps, hauling logs, and of course, playing guitar and singing to the other laborers. According to J.D. Short, a Delta singer, Patton "mostly followed timber camps and levee camps and stuff like that . . . he always kept a guitar, but he didn't usually carry it with him. He would come along driving a wagon or something back in them days and somebody had a guitar around playing and he wasn't in a hurry he'd just stop by and play the guitar some and let the people hear him" (*The Bluesmen,* Sam Charters).

Right after leaving Dockery's in 1921 Charley met Minnie Franklin, and they were soon married. With Franklin, Patton traveled around the Delta region, playing wherever he could make a few dollars. In addition to the logging camp shows, he would play on the streets, in picnics, at dances for white audiences, and at Saturday night parties for the sharecroppers, either in the backcountry or in lively "juke" joints.

With all of this traveling and playing, Patton soon became well known all throughout the Delta region to both white and black audiences. He was regarded as a "clowning" entertainer onstage, which earned him applause and money as well as disapproval from other artists such as Son House, who felt that Charley was sacrificing his music just to make a buck. According to Sam Chatmon, his probable half brother, Patton would offer crowd-pleasing tricks such as playing "his guitar all between his legs, behind his head, [laying] down on the floor" ("The Devil's Music"). While these tricks turned heads and made the performance a show, critics such as Son House noted that his lyrics would often be slurred, and he often would throw in vocal lines that had nothing to do with the rest of the song. These criticisms didn't stop Patton, however, who knew that he had to put on these types of shows to make a living.

Traveling regularly, drinking heavily, changing women constantly, getting into and out of fights. These were the stereotypical years of a bluesman's life that Patton actually lived, but he lacked one thing that he sorely needed and would soon receive: a recording contract. The 1920s saw the beginning of blues recordings, but few artists were lucky enough to land a paying recording gig. Enter H.C. Speir, a music store owner in Jackson, Mississippi, who had an arrangement with Paramount Records to do tests on anyone he thought might sell some records. In 1929 Charley found himself drifting around Jackson, and this is when Speir "discovered" him. Speir sent him on to the recording directors of Paramount, and Patton was soon doing his first recordings at Richmond, Indiana, in the old Gennett Record Studios, on June 14, 1929. Patton recorded, quickly returned to Jackson, and within six weeks his first release, "Pony Blues," was out. Charley had been playing this song around the Delta for years, but this was the first time that audiences outside of Mississippi were able to hear his gruff voice and screaming guitar.

At about the same time Paramount released two of Patton's religious songs, "Prayer of Death" and an alternate take of "I'm Going Home," under the pseudonym Elder J.J. Hadley. Using other names was one of Paramount's marketing ploys, and Patton had releases under the names Charley Peters and "The Masked Marvel." Overall, his first issued recording sold well, packing bars where customers danced to tunes such as "Pony Blues," as well as other songs such as "Screamin' and Hollerin' the Blues" and Charley's popular rendition of a Delta classic, "Mississippi Bo Weevil Blues."

The fourteen sides that Patton recorded that June day in 1929 did so well that Paramount invited him back to record just a few months later. Late in 1929, Charley and Delta fiddler Henry "Son" Sims traveled up to Paramount's home studio in Grafton, Wisconsin, to record what would be released the following year as thirteen Patton records. In addition to Patton and Sims, there is another guitarist and "commentator" on these songs from the second recording session, most likely Patton's longtime friend and fellow Delta bluesman Willie Brown. The success of the sales of these records most likely convinced Paramount to record Sims and Brown individually in the following years.

After these recording sessions Charley found himself living in Lula, Mississippi, a small town off of Highway 61, north of Clarksdale. It was in Lula that Patton met both Son House, a fellow Delta blues singer and guitarist who would play with Patton for the next four year until Patton's death, and Bertha Lee, who would be Charley's last wife. Paramount invited Patton back to Grafton, Wisconsin, in July 1930, and Charley brought with him his new friend Son House, Willie Brown, and Louise Johnson, a female pianist from Brown's hometown of Robinsonville. This recording session, a very significant group of Delta blues songs to ever be recorded, was Patton's last session with Paramount.

Patton's songs from these three sessions reveal his harsh, personal style, as well as his breadth of topics, ranging from an account of the 1927 flooding of the Mississippi River in the two-part "High Water Everywhere," to his real-life account of jail life for blacks in the Delta in "High Sheriff Blues." Patton recorded religious songs ("Prayer of Death") as well as anticlerical tunes ("Elder Greene Blues"), and of course songs about women ("Shake It and Break It But Don't Let It

Fall Mama") and death ("Oh Death"). The majority of Charley's songs used the now-standard twelve-bar blues, with lyrics consisting of three lines, the first two usually identical, and the last line different but end-rhymed. Sometimes he would finger-pick the guitar, and sometimes he would use a bottleneck or a knife to produce a slide effect. His guitar lines often mimicked his vocal lines, as in "Banty Rooster Blues" and "Tom Rushen Blues."

Upon returning to Lula after the 1930 recording session, Patton began living with Bertha Lee. He was in his forties and she was only sixteen. After about a year, they moved to Holly Ridge, in west-central Mississippi. Lee also sang the blues, learning the majority of her songs from Patton. Charley was suffering from a heart leakage at this point, so he wasn't able to work in the fields; this meant that he had to keep playing and singing every night to make money. During this time Patton began teaching his blues style to a young singer named Chester Burnett, who would later be known as "Howlin' Wolf." In the fall of 1933 the recording director of Vocalion Records got in touch with Patton, and he and Bertha Lee went to New York in January 1934 to record Patton's last songs. The equipment at this studio was better than the instruments used at Paramount three years earlier, and they revealed Patton's hoarse, strained voice. The three years had not done much to change Patton's style, which remained basically the same as it had sounded on Paramount's recordings, although he tended to use less finger-picking.

After the three days of recording Patton and Lee went back to their small, run-down cabin in Longswitch, Mississippi. Four months later, on April 28, 1934, Patton died of a bad heart. Although it was clearly heart disease that had killed Patton, rumors started to spread that Charley had been murdered, a not-uncommon event in the Delta. Patton's influence did not die with him; his style was carried on by his student Howlin' Wolf; his contemporary musicians Son House, Tommy Johnson, and Bukka White; as well as by his friends and fellow bluesmen Willie Brown, Henry Sims, and Bertha Lee. His influence on later artists such as Robert Johnson and Muddy Waters is immeasurable, but his biggest contribution to the music world was his intense, personal style, which spread to the group of Delta musicians that were associated with him. This original Delta "showman" can best be heard on Yazoo's *Founder of the Delta Blues 1929–1934* (1989), which highlights twenty-four of Patton's more than sixty released songs, as well as another Yazoo release, *King of the Delta Blues: The Music of Charley Patton* (1991). In 1970 guitarist John Fahey wrote a biography, *Charley Patton* (Studio Vista Ltd., 1970), and in 1980 Patton received long overdue recognition by being inducted into the Blues Foundation's Hall of Fame.

Entry written by Adam Seidman

PAUL, ELLIS: *Singer, songwriter, guitarist, harmonica player. Born Fort Kent, Maine, January 14, 1965.*

With his flyaway, shoulder-length hair and torn blue jeans, Ellis Paul looked more grunge than folk as he played in a hotel room at the 1996 Folk Alliance Conference in Washington, D.C. But once he began his traveling song "3,000 Miles" it became clear that Paul owes more to the folk-troubadour tradition than to grunge rock. Blessed with a strong sense of lyric and melody and a pleasing tenor voice, Paul has established himself as one of the most promising singer-songwriters in the nation.

"There are a lot of rock elements in my music," Paul said in an interview at the conference. "It tends to be a roots rock, folk kind of approach. Major chords, open tunings. I write from sort of a fictional approach. I try to do some sort of character sketch and development in the songs. I made a vow to always write about the things I know very well."

His repertorial approach is similar to that of his idol, Woody Guthrie. Indeed, Paul once made a pilgrimage to Woody's hometown, Okemah, Oklahoma. It was a stormy day, with ominous clouds threatening to spawn tornadoes. Ellis asked around at the fire department and the police station to see if anyone knew where Woody's boyhood home was located. No luck. He was about to give up when he saw a man sitting on a porch strumming a guitar. Sure enough, this man knew the way to Woody's home. All that was left was a foundation and a pile of orange-colored rocks, one of which Ellis took with him for posterity. He thought he was the only folksinger who possessed one of the rocks. But as he traveled on to the Key Door in Oklahoma City and to the Kerrville Folk Festival, he met other singers who had the distinctive orange rocks.

"Folksingers are taking the stones and then they're going their various ways and this foundation is completely covering the entire country. It's disappearing at its source but it's spreading," says Paul, who tattooed Guthrie's likeness on his right shoulder.

He was born Paul Plissey in Fort Kent, Maine, but began using the name Ellis Paul when he started his performing career in the mid-'80s. His family moved to North Dakota and Minnesota before returning to the northern Maine town Presque Isle, which he still considers to be his hometown. His paternal grandfather was a potato farmer, and his father, Ed Plissey, worked as the potato specialist for the state of Maine. "I grew up with potatoes all my life in the fields up there," he says. His mother, Marilyn, was a nutritionist.

Ellis considered becoming an artist and was interested in creative writing. He also played the trumpet in high school. "If I'd known what I was going to become when I was fifteen, I probably would have shot myself on the spot," he says.

Most of the music he heard was on top 40 radio in the late 1970s and early 1980s: Billy Joel, Elton John.

"I didn't discover folk music until Dylan released *Biograph* when I was about twenty years old and somebody played it for me in college," he says, adding that he was particularly moved by Dylan's voice on "The House of the Rising Sun." "Most of my youth when I heard folk music I was making fun of it like every other youth in my generation."

Ellis was a state cross-country champion in Maine, running a 9:07 two mile when he was eighteen. He went to Boston College on a track scholarship. He ran cross-country and indoor track in college and was even named All Big East once. But when he was a junior his overtraining caught up with him. He injured the tendons in his right knee. He had to have surgery and take a year off. A friend named Allison Higgins lent him a guitar and he spent his free time playing it. "I think I just needed a creative outlet. Before college so much of my life was around being an athlete I had to let the creative part go for about two and a half years."

A few years later Allison died, and he wrote the song "Conversation with a Ghost" for her. "It's actually a song about what she would, sort of, be telling me from the grave because I . . . never really got to say goodbye to her," Paul told Katie Davis of *All Things Considered* (August 8, 1993).

Many of Paul's songs seem like dialogues with friends, acquaintances, even inanimate objects, such as "Autobiography of a Pistol," written from the perspective of a .45. "It was a chance for me to make fun of the NRA and take a risk by giving the gun a voice," he told *Everybody's News Issue* (September 16, 1995). As he sings: *Some things they never tell you, when you're riding the assembly line. / Like who'll be the hands to hold you, and what's their state of mind.*

Paul graduated from Boston College with a B.A. in English. For three years he was a case worker at an inner-city school in Jamaica Plain, working with children suffering from behavioral problems: transvestites, murderers, drug dealers, and children with attention deficit disorder. Says Paul: "What it mainly did was open my eyes up to seeing the world in a broader, more open-minded way."

In his early twenties, Ellis began playing the open-mikes at the coffeehouses around Boston. He found himself hanging out with up-and-coming artists like Dar Williams, Vance Gilbert, and Jonatha Brooke. Paul formed a songwriter's collective with Jim Infantino, Jon Svetky, and Brian Doser called End Construction. "Suddenly we went from being unknown to being popular as a group." Like Crosby, Stills, Nash, and Young, they backed up one another's original compositions. But, as usual, egos got in the way and they broke up. Around that time, Paul began getting airplay on some of the college radio stations.

He made some recordings and sold the cassette tapes at concerts. His first cassette was called *Urban Folk Songs* in 1989, followed by *Am I Home* in 1991. He sold up to twenty cassettes per show, for a total of 5,000 copies of the two cassettes. "It made me know I could do it as a living," he says. (The master tapes exist but Paul has stopped taking orders for the cassettes. "They're green enough," he says now. "They have some value to anyone who loves what I do, probably.") By the time he was twenty-seven, Paul was playing music full-time.

In 1992 he won the Boston Acoustic Underground Competition, and the following year he won a Boston Music Award for Best New Folk Acoustic Act, the first of seven Boston Music Awards.

Paul's manager, Ralph Jaccodine, formed Black Wolf Records. New England signer-songwriter Bill Morrissey agreed to produce Paul's first album, *Say Something,* issued by Black Wolf in 1993. "It was great because I got to hang out with him and I tend to get very nervous talking to him because he's one of my heroes," Ellis says.

Known for his taut writing style, Morrissey helped Paul pare down his songs. "When we were recording the album, Bill kept looking over at me and saying, these are four-minute songs," he told Scott Alarik of *Performing Songwriter* (January-February 1994). "We were shaving and editing and cutting things out that were unnecessary. His writing is so right to the point, he helped me a lot."

Say Something received strong reviews in the *Washington Post* and *College Music Journal.* In the meantime, he was playing up to 200 concerts a year. One of those performances was at the Kerrville Folk Festival in 1994, where he won the prestigious New Folk Award. That year he also won the Boston Music Award for Best Song ("Conversation with a Ghost") and Best Songwriter.

His second album for Black Wolf, appropriately called *Stories,* came out in 1994 and continued to receive critical acclaim. The album, produced by guitarist Duke Levine (who had played with Mary-Chapin Carpenter), exhibited Paul's ability to write catchy and yet poignant songs: "All Things Being the Same," "3,000 Miles," "Autobiography of a Pistol," "Last Call."

Paul usually writes his songs between ten P.M. and three A.M., a time when he can find some peace and quiet. He usually starts with the chord changes and then he'll sing free verse until he finds a phrase around which he can build the song. Then he'll pare it down. "I do character sketches and talk about a moment in a person's life," Paul says. "But I think you get a sense of where they've been up to that point and where they're going after the song is over."

Both *Say Something* and *Stories* sold more than 20,000 copies, a respectable amount for an independent. It was enough to attract the interest of Rounder/Philo Records which signed Paul in 1995 and agreed to rerelease *Stories* in the fall of 1995. Paul was also included early on in several compilations: High Street Records' *Legacy II* and Putumayo's *Best of Singer Songwriters.* He also contributed "Last Call" to a nineteen-track CD for Joyce Maynard's novel, *Where Love Goes,* which

also featured Nanci Griffith, Emmylou Harris, and Townes Van Zandt.

He soon returned to the studio to record his third album, *A Carnival of Voices,* for Rounder, released in 1996. This album, with a more economical sound than his previous ones, was produced by Jerry Marotta, a drummer who had worked with Peter Gabriel, and included backup from bassist Tony Levin and guitarists Bill Dillon and Duke Levine. One of his songs, "All My Heroes Were Junkies," is about a friend who is a recovering drug addict and once ran the sound system for a major rock club in Boston. Besides sound, he also supplied drugs to the big rock bands who played there, but he eventually paid the price. The folk world helped to turn his friend's life around, Paul says. "He's got a really great sense of humor about it, so I kind of took a humorous stance in the song," he says.

The album includes another traveling song, "Paris in a Day," a spoof about a tourist trying to accomplish the impossible. *Carnival* helped to build Paul's reputation as a songwriter. The album hit number three on CMJ's AAA chart and number four on Gavin's AAA chart. By the end of 1997 his three CDs had sold close to 60,000 copies.

In 1996 Woody's daughter Nora, the director of the Woody Guthrie Archives, invited Paul to perform at the Rock and Roll Hall of Fame induction for Guthrie, along with Billy Bragg, Ani DiFranco, Jimmie Dale Gilmore, Arlo Guthrie, Bruce Springsteen, and the Indigo Girls. He met Nora at the February 1996 Folk Alliance Conference. "She chased me down at the bar and demanded I take my clothes off and show her my tattoo," Paul told Paul Robicheau of the *Boston Globe* ("Ellis Paul's got Woody Guthrie under His Skin," 1996). "We developed a good friendship and she's the one that has sort of been in charge of his [archive] library and getting the show going."

He won his seventh Boston Music Award in January 1998 for Outstanding Contemporary Folk Act. In July 1998 Paul was invited to participate in the First Annual Woody Guthrie Free Folk Festival in Okemah, Oklahoma, along with Billy Bragg. Ellis played "Hard Travelin'" and "Lonesome Valley" for the concert, which was filmed by the BBC and PBS.

In September 1998 Paul released his fourth CD, *Translucent Soul,* which he recorded in Woodstock, New York, and which was again produced by Jerry Marotta. The title track, about interracial friendship, was inspired by his good friend Vance Gilbert, a noted African American folk artist. "It was half-way done at one point and he had me in tears," Gilbert told Charlene J. Arsenault of *Worcester Magazine* ("Ellis Paul Catches a Buzz," July 17, 1996). "He basically defines how the lines get broken down. Not that he said anything new, but he has an inimitable way of saying things. Through his eyes it's like another field of colors."

Paul infused the album with the pain and introspection resulting from his divorce from a woman he had been involved with since he was fourteen. He included such personal songs as "Did I Ever Know You?" and "Take Me Down." "I was in this reflective mode and we put all those songs on the record to give them a home, side by side. There is something about talking in the first person that makes people feel like they're being talked about, like it's their story."

In a phone interview in late 1998, Paul said he was hoping to record a live album for Rounder and then he plans to write a new batch of songs for his next album. Regardless of whether he records for Rounder or a larger label, Paul remains committed to folk music. "I might have an electric guitar on my albums but I still consider it folk."

At the Folk Alliance Conference in 1996, Paul said he wasn't trying to become an overnight success. "I want to be like Ray Charles and be seventy and still be improving," he said. "I'm a good songwriter now, if I do improve, I'm going to be as good a songwriter as can be. I'm after the art, I'm not really after the fame. If I could write a couple of masterpieces before I die, I'd be happy."

Based on an interview by Lyndon Stambler with Ellis Paul in February 1996 and a phone interview in 1998

PAXTON, TOM: *Singer, guitarist, songwriter. Born Chicago, Illinois, October 31, 1937.*

In some ways Tom Paxton might have seemed an anachronism in the 1970s and 1980s, a throwback to the folk scene of the 1960s. But what goes around comes around; Paxton was still performing and winning new fans in the late 1990s, when another folk-music renaissance seemed to be gathering momentum. He still wrote material in the spirit of the earlier period, and was not interested in trying to make it in the rock field by slanting his material or performing style that way. Asked by Jeff Bradley of the *Denver Post* (" 'My Best Shot,' Folksinger Tom Paxton Says of New Album," January 22, 1995) whether he regretted missing the chance to reap the huge monetary rewards rock stars obtained, he responded, "Maybe for a few minutes watching 'A Hard Day's Night' I thought, 'God, that looks like great fun.' I've got nothing against rock, it's just that to me the sound of acoustic instruments is what really moves my soul. I've never heard an electric instrument that can touch me in the way a beautifully played acoustic instrument can."

Financial bonanzas aside, in his quiet way, Paxton continued to have an impact on at least some members of the post-late-'50s-early-'60s folk boom generation. Besides that, many of his compositions had become classics in their own right and, over the years, artists of many different musical persuasions turned out their own versions of songs like "Bottle of Wine," "Morning Again," "Mr. Blue," and "The Last Thing on My Mind."

Tom spent many of his formative years in Oklahoma, a state laying claim to folk-song legend Woody Guthrie, so it might be said he came by his love for that kind of music naturally. However, Paxton spent his first decade on the South Side of Chicago and was far more interested in athletics than music. His family moved to the small town of Bristol, Oklahoma, in 1948, but soon after they arrived his father died. It was young Tom's first harsh exposure to the realities of life, though his mother managed to keep the family going in reasonable shape despite the loss.

In high school he spent more time in the drama department than music, though he started to learn guitar after an aunt gave him one when he was sixteen. He could play the instrument well by the time he entered the University of Oklahoma as a drama major, though he never was to come close to being a superior guitarist. After hearing a folk album by Ed McCurdy at a campus party, he began to work up his own repertoire of folk songs and later debuted as a folk performer in a campus variety show.

Still, he kept his eye on the stage, moving into summer stock after graduating from college in 1959. He wasn't bad in that field, as indicated by the starring role he gained in *The Spoilers*. But his interest in music was increasing. He spent six months in the army stationed off the coast of New York. On the weekends he would take the ferry and train to New York City, where he "haunted the coffeehouses of Greenwich Village."

He found the Greenwich Village folk scene as active and interesting as he'd heard it would be. It was a heady time to be on hand, with such brash newcomers as Bob Dylan, Joan Baez, Phil Ochs, and dozens of others performing whenever and wherever they could and getting together at other times to compare material and talk about the music field. He recalls seeing Dylan perform for the first time in New York: "Gerde's Folk City had Monday night hootenannies where you signed up and did three songs (no encores, no exceptions). Dave Van Ronk and I had done ours and were drinking beer when this skinny kid with a corduroy cap and a harmonica rack got up and did three Woody Guthrie songs. We instantly agreed that he had something special. Turns out, he did." Looking back in 1977, he noted "The Village coffeehouses were the dearest of blessings to a beginning performer, a place to be terrible and to learn from being terrible."

Paxton took advantage of it, working the small venues, often for no pay, with any money coming from passing the hat. His efforts impressed many of his peers and in a short time he felt confident enough of his abilities to audition for a replacement spot in the Chad Mitchell Trio. Milt Okun, the group's director, at first gave Tom the nod, then changed his mind. It was a bitter blow, but Okun kept in touch with Paxton, whose original songs—particularly one called "The Marvelous Toy"—had impressed him. He suggested to Tom that his forte was writing more than performing.

For a while, Paxton stressed entertaining alone, working the U.S. coffeehouse circuit during 1961–62, usually accompanied by folksinger Gil Robbins. Starting in 1962, however, he turned out a growing list of new, often topical compositions. The quality of his work impressed many fellow artists, some of whom began incorporating Paxton songs in their repertoire. One such was the Weavers, who gave their version of his "Rambling Boy" in their 1963 Carnegie Hall concert.

Many of his songs of the first half of the 1960s were of the protest variety. He never gave up commenting on the shortcomings of society—his 1977 LP on Vanguard, *New Songs from the Briarpatch* examined such topics as capital punishment ("Bring Back the Chair"), the Nixon era ("Talking Watergate"), and the death of Chile's President Salvador Allende ("White Bones of Allende"). However, his approach to writing such material changed with time.

As he told Lorraine Alterman of *GO* (August 9, 1968), he thought the typical protest song missed the mark. "The main problem with the so-called protest song is that the writers—and I include myself of a few years back—believed that it was enough to say what they felt was the truth. It was not important to say it well. That changed, at least for me. You must say what you think with the same skill that you would write a hit song with.

"There is a technique to the way I write, and that's relaxation. I'm learning how to sit down with a blank piece of paper and relax. For example, with the song 'Morning Again' I sat down with a blank piece of paper and nothing in my head but the phrase 'morning again.' The best hitters in baseball have all their concentration on hitting; they are relaxed."

As his catalog of new material expanded, Tom was ready for an assault on the recording side of things. In 1964, Elektra signed him. (He had recorded some material earlier and an album, *I'm the Man Who Built the Bridges,* of his stylings had come out on the small Gaslight Club label.) His debut LP on Elektra, *Ramblin' Boy,* was issued in December 1964, and, if it wasn't a top 10 hit, it served to introduce him to a growing number of adherents around the country. Although the folk movement was beginning to wane under the onslaught of the British rock invasion, it still was strong, particularly on college campuses, and Paxton was regarded as one of the finest artists in the field.

His stature already was on the rise in Europe when he visited England with his wife, Midge, in 1965 for a series of concerts. The English audiences took him to their hearts, and he was still attracting relatively large crowds for shows over there when only a minute segment of the U.S. music audience was aware of him in the late 1960s and throughout the 1970s. In the mid-1960s, though, he was active on the U.S. college and small-club scene and, before that period was over, he had appeared in those venues in all the states.

He continued to turn out a series of finely honed albums on Elektra as the 1960s went by, many now collector's items. Among them were *Ain't That News,* issued

in December 1965; *Outward Bound* (11/66); *Morning Again* (1967); *The Things I Notice Now* (1968); *Tom Paxton 6* (1969); and a live two-record set recorded at the Bitter End, *The Compleat Tom Paxton,* issued in 1970. Among the songs that appeared in those releases were "The Man Who Built the Bridges," "What Did You Learn in School Today," "Brand New Baby," "The Willing Conscript," "Victoria Dines Alone," "Talking Vietnam," "Potluck Blues" (one of the most famous antiwar songs of the 1960s), "A Thousand Years" (a strong condemnation of neonazism), "What a Friend We Have in Hoover," and "Georgia on the Freeways."

In 1968 the Fireballs (led by Jimmy Gilmer) had a top 10 hit with his song "Bottle of Wine." Later he penned "Wasn't That a Time" after appearing on a TV show with the Irish Rovers, who had a million-selling single with the song. Paxton also has written one of the best-known baseball songs around, "My Favorite Spring." Showing his respect to another great songwriter, Paxton performed two songs, "Pastures of Plenty" and "Biggest Thing Man Has Ever Done," for the 1972 collection *A Tribute to Woody Guthrie.*

In the early 1970s he moved from Elektra to the Warner/Reprise label, which released four albums in the first half of the decade. These were *How Come the Sun* (1971), *Peace Will Come* (1972), *New Songs for Old Friends* (1973), and *Something in My Life* (1975), released on Private Stock.

As the folk audience seemed to dwindle at home, Paxton spent more and more time abroad, where he remained a highly regarded troubadour. In the mid-1970s, he and his family settled down in England for a number of years. He enjoyed living there, but the lure of home eventually proved too strong and in early 1977 he and his family came back and settled in East Hampton on New York's Long Island.

As he said, "I've seen a good deal of the planet in the last seven or eight years and spent the better part of three or four of them living in England. I loved it, but it feels good to be back home again. In the last year," he noted in mid-1977, "I have been seriously rediscovering my own country. Everywhere I go, I meet people who remember the old songs and welcome the new ones." The first of the latter were presented on his debut LP on the Vanguard label, *New Songs from the Briarpatch,* issued in July 1977. The following year Vanguard issued another Paxton album, *Heroes.* He closed out the decade with the 1979 album *Up & Up* on Mountain Railroad/Flying Fish, which also released the 1980 disc *The Paxton Report.*

Throughout the 1980s and into the 1990s Tom continued to tour widely, performing on the college campus and folk club circuit, though sometimes appearing in larger venues, particularly overseas. By 1995, when he celebrated thirty-one years of marriage to Midge, he had turned out some thirty-two albums, including a number of children's albums. The latter included *The Mar-*

velous Toy & Other Gallimaufry, issued on the Cherry Lane/Alcazar label in 1984 (this originally had been *Tom Paxton's Children's Songbook*), and a series on Pax Records/Sony Kids: *Balloon-alloon-alloon,* originally issued in 1987, reissued in 1992; *A Child's Christmas,* 1988–92; *A Car Full of Songs,* 1990–92; *It Ain't Easy,* 1991; and, on Sony Kids, *Peanut Butter Pie,* 1991–92 and *Suzy Is a Rocker,* 1992. His output also included a series of songbooks and children's books, the last available from Morrow Junior Books.

Tom's album credits in the '80s and '90s, besides his children's works, included *Bulletin* on the Hogeye label (1983); *Even a Gray Day* ('84), *A Paxton Primer* ('86), *Politics* ('88), and *The Very Best of Tom Paxton* ('89), all on Flying Fish; *One Million Lawyers and Other Disasters* ('86) on Bradley, United Kingdom; *A Folk Song Festival* ('86), and *And Loving You* ('87) on his own Pax records; and *Wearing the Time* on Sugar Hill in 1995. The '95 release produced by Jim Rooney indicated that Paxton remained at the peak of his powers as a writer and performer. His originals included the title track, cowritten with Susan Graham White, "Getting Up Early" (which premiered on radio's *A Prairie Home Companion*), "Johnny Got a Gun" and "Verdigris," the last a duet with Iris DeMent. The album was nominated in 1995 as Best Folk Album by the National Association of Independent Record Distributors.

The increasingly important younger folk artists held Paxton in the highest esteem. John Gorka, for instance, commented, "I would give every hair on my head to be able to write songs like Tom Paxton." Nanci Griffith, who recorded "I Can't Help But Wonder Where I'm Bound" for her 1993 *Other Voices, Other Rooms* album, told an interviewer, "He has such an amazing ability to write these classic songs like nobody wrote 'em. No folk tribute album would be complete without a Tom Paxton song. I think he really defined that era of folk songwriting."

Asked by Lydia Hutchinson how he defined a folk song ("Tom Paxton—A Songwriter for All Seasons," *The Performing Songwriter,* January–February 1994), Tom replied, "You wouldn't believe the near fistfights that used to break out in coffeehouses over these questions of what a folk song was. Oh God, there [were] bitter, angry fights over this nonsense. A folk song, to me, is a song over 50% of which I can reproduce after one hearing, because it's simple and it addresses something beautifully, simply, urgently, tells a story, or expresses an emotion that we've all experienced."

He also expressed his pleasure at the talents of up-and-coming new writers. "I think this is the golden age right now. People talk about the 60s, and they were fun, and they were important; it was a wonderful time to be young and starving and all that. But I think the level of talent now is higher and the artistry is just wonderful. There's just so many really good musicians out there. . . .

Because of all this talent, there is becoming such a growing consciousness on the part of the public of the value of this kind of music. So as the old restaurant business adage goes, it's better to have two restaurants on the block than one. It creates an atmosphere of excitement. So the fact that you can go out just about any night of the week in cities around the country and hear really good acoustic music makes it good for every acoustic musician."

By 1996 Tom and Midge were taking their winters in Virginia to be near their oldest daughter, Jennifer, and their grandson, Christopher. They continued to spend their summers in East Hampton.

In February 1996 Paxton recorded a performance at the Birchmere in Alexandria, Virginia. Sugar Hill released the album, *Live! For the Record,* later in the year. Produced by Jim Rooney, it includes twenty-nine tracks, among them "Rambling Boy," "The Last Thing on My Mind," "I Can't Help But Wonder Where I'm Bound," and his baseball song, "My Favorite Spring" (a duet with John Gorka). In 1997 he released two more children's albums, *Goin' to the Zoo* and *I've Got a Yo-Yo,* for Rounder Records. In January 1999, Rhino Records released the retrospective *I Can't Help But Wonder Where I'm Bound: The Elektra Years.* He continued to record and perform in 1999. The BBC gave him a radio show called *Paxton's Picks,* which included invited guests like Guy Clark, Pete Seeger, Iris DeMent, John Prine, and Hal Ketchum.

Although Paxton has not been nominated for a Grammy (yet), he is considered one of the masters of the topical song. As he wrote in *Sing Out!* ("Courting the Muse," August-September-October 1996), the first topical song he learned was Ewan MacColl's "Springhill Mine Disaster" in 1960, when he was in the army. He wrote his first topical song, "Mister Woolworth," on an army typewriter. He wrote such effective anti-Vietnam songs as "Lyndon Johnson Told the Nation" and "Jimmy Newman." In the 1990s he wrote "On the Road from Srebrinca," about the massacres of Muslim men in Bosnia. He urged others to write topical songs: "I simply try to draw an honest picture with words and music that is true to these people who have, it almost seems to me, chosen me to tell their story. . . . There is far more ambiguity to handle in 1996 than there was in 1966, but it's the stuff of our lives and deserves to be sung."

He has won two Wammys (Washington Area Music Association Awards), one for Best Children's Artist (Male) and the other for Best Traditional Folk Artist (Male). In addition, he was inducted into the Kerrville Folk Festival Hall of Fame and received the Lifetime Achievement Award from the Swannanoa Gathering at Warren Wilson College in Asheville, North Carolina.

Based in part on answers to written questions submitted to Tom Paxton in January 1999

PEDERSEN, HERB/LAUREL CANYON RAMBLERS: *Singer, banjoist, guitarist, Dobro player, songwriter, band leader (Laurel Canyon Ramblers). Born Berkeley, California, April 27, 1944. Original band members: Kenny Blackwell (mandolin, vocals), Bill Bryson (bass, vocals), Gabe Witcher (fiddle), and Billy Ray Lathum (guitar, vocals). Lathum left in 1996, replaced by Roger Reed (guitar, vocals). Bruce Johnson (lead guitar, second fiddle) substituted occasionally after Reed injured his hand.*

Herb Pedersen's Laurel Canyon Ramblers takes its name from a famous street in Los Angeles that traverses the Hollywood Hills, and from the Redwood Canyon Ramblers, a bluegrass band that influenced him. Pedersen, in a white T-shirt, blue jeans, wire-rimmed glasses, and shaggy haircut, looks more Berkeley than Hollywood when we met at a coffeehouse on the corner of Laurel Canyon and Ventura Boulevards one sunny Saturday in April 1997. Yet during his thirty-year musical odyssey he has straddled the line between Tinseltown and bluegrass, playing Earl Scruggs, the Dillards, and on TV and movie soundtracks.

Born in 1944 to a policeman who liked the Mills Brothers and a housewife who played piano and guitar, Pedersen discovered bluegrass despite his urban upbringing. In 1959 the Kingston Trio sparked his interest in folk music and the banjo. In 1960, he found a Stella guitar at home and began playing it with high school friend Butch Waller. They were drawn to the Everly and Louvin Brothers' harmonies.

Pedersen was impressed by Billy Faire's album, *New Adventures for Five-String Banjo.* But like many banjoists, Flatt and Scruggs' *Foggy Mountain Banjo* changed his life. "To paraphrase Keith Richards, the world was black and white. And as soon as I heard them it became Technicolor," Pedersen says. His style came primarily from Scruggs, but he acquired "tone, taste, and timing" from Alan Shelton, Sonny Osborne, and J.D. Crowe. He observed two banjoists in the Redwood Canyon Ramblers: Neil Rosenberg (influenced by Scruggs) and Pete Berg (influenced by Ralph Stanley).

Pedersen bought his first banjo, a four-string with a hook on the side of the neck for a fifth string, at Louis Prince Rare Violins in Berkeley. His first "real" banjo was an open-backed S.S. Stewart. He acquired a Gibson Mastertone RB-250 and learned by slowing down records to half-speed. He later bought a 1930 RB-4 Mastertone.

While a senior in high school, he and Waller formed the Pine Valley Boys in 1961, with Waller on mandolin, Pedersen on banjo, Rich Conley on guitar, and Dale Hollis on bass. In 1964, the group added David Nelson (later of New Riders of the Purple Sage) on guitar. Richard Greene sat in occasionally on fiddle. Pedersen considered becoming an architect. He worked by day, attended Oakland City College at night, and played in the Pine Valley Boys on weekends. "For some reason bluegrass just got me," he says. In 1964, he joined Vern & Ray, the California Louvin Brothers.

He met Jerry Garcia during those years. "He was in Palo Alto. I was at Berkeley, so we'd see each other from time to time," Pedersen says. "We listened to new stuff like the Beatles. He had a really good attitude about life and music. He was always trying new stuff, literally. Right around the time the Dead got started I moved to Nashville."

Anxious to develop his bluegrass chops, Pedersen followed Vern & Ray to Music City in 1967. One gig led to another. At age twenty-three, Pedersen began playing with former Blue Grass Boy Joe Stuart with Carl Tipton and the Midstate Playboys, featured on Channel 8 in Murfreesboro Saturday afternoons. Little did Herb know that Earl Scruggs would be watching. "He got my name through the union and called me up," Herb recalls. "I thought it was a big joke, 'Hi, this is Earl Scruggs.' I went, 'Who is this?' I thought it was one of my buddies from back home. Well it wasn't that at all. It was him. He said, 'I saw you on Carl's show.' At that point he invited me to his house. He said, 'Bring your banjo with you.' I said, 'OK.' So I went over there. I was scared to death, of course. He was living in Madison which is where I was living too, a suburb of Nashville.

"I parked out in front of his house and waited fifteen minutes before going and knocking on the door. It was a ranch style house in the suburbs, very nice, with a big lawn all the way around the property and a big white picket fence. That's where they raised the three boys—Randy, Gary, and Steve. So Louise [Scruggs] answered the door and I walked in. We just sat down and talked for a while. I told him I was from San Francisco. He had just played out there. It was interesting to him for some kid to come all the way to Tennessee from California to do this.

"Anyway, we went in the back room and he said, 'Yeah, take out your banjo, let's play some.' He picked up the guitar and I picked up the banjo. He said, 'Do you know "Reuben"?' So we played some of that. We played 'Lonesome Road Blues.' He said, 'Do you know the Martha White theme?' I said, 'Yeah.' We played that. Then he said, 'How about the "Flint Hill Special"?' 'Yeah,' so we played that. Afterwards, he said, 'Well, I kinda got you over here under false pretenses.' I remember him saying those words. I said, 'What do you mean?' He said, 'I have to go to the hospital next week to have a hip replacement put in and I was wondering if you'd be interested in filling in for banjo.'"

Pedersen was flabbergasted. The next Friday night Scruggs took him to the Opry to meet Lester Flatt and the rest of the band: Josh Graves on Dobro, Paul Warren on fiddle, Jake Tullock on bass, Johnny Johnson on sock rhythm guitar. Flatt said, "Get out yer banjo, let's pick one;" they played "Salty Dog Blues." "That band was so incredible that as a moderately good banjo player you just felt yourself being pushed to that next level. It was an amazing feeling that I've never felt before or since. They'd been together thirty years. They breathed in harmony."

It was 1967 and Flatt and Scruggs and Bill Monroe were not on speaking terms. "At the time Monroe was the only bluegrass on the Opry. Flatt and Scruggs got a sponsor, Martha White, and they just went on the show. Bill felt it was kind of a snub to him that they didn't come to him and ask permission to bring their band on and play the same kind of music that Bill was playing. I think that's what prompted that whole thing."

Within a year Doug Dillard had left the Dillards and they were looking for a new banjoist. Mandolinist Dean Webb called Pedersen. "We remembered each other from the Troubadour in the early '60s," he recalls. "They were looking for a good tenor at the time. Nobody could really replace Douglas on banjo and vocally it would be different because Douglas sang baritone. With my voice we stacked it differently harmonically."

Herb returned to California to audition. "We went over to Rodney Dillard's house and played for half a day. Our first gig was at Santa Monica City College in the outdoor amphitheater there. After our show I remember Rodney running in with a big grin on his face saying, 'Boys we're back in business.'" They recorded *Wheatstraw Suite* (1968) for Elektra, and *Copperfields* a year later.

"That was a big thrill for me," he recalls. "It was so experimental. We were one of the first bluegrass bands to use strings or steel or drums. I know the Osborne Brothers did that prior to us. But we did multitrack vocals. I think it was before Crosby Stills and Nash did it. We had a whopping budget. It was incredible because we had enough money to have a string arranger come in by the name of Al Kapps. Nowadays when you record a bluegrass album people are into the tradition of it and keep it really straight, real simple. Back then we were just kind of free."

In 1970 Pedersen left the Dillards and began playing with the biggest performers on the Southern California scene: Jackson Browne, Emmylou Harris, Linda Ronstadt. "The first major session other than the Dillards stuff was Linda Ronstadt. She had heard me sing with them. I started singing on her records. One thing led to another. And it was just word of mouth. The people who did that kind of music all knew each other. So I'd get calls from various people to sing and play acoustic guitar. I play rhythm guitar. So if there wasn't a lot of banjo work, which there wasn't in this town, ever, then I would do rhythm guitar and vocal."

His most recognizable riff was the opening banjo solo on "Love Is a Rose." "David Lindley was playing fiddle," Pedersen recalls. "We got into this slow groove. I just started using the tuner on it. It was a bluesy approach as opposed to some fast frantic picking." He backed Emmylou Harris on the Louvin Brothers tune "If I Could Only

Win Your Love," J.D. Souther on "Faithless Love," and toured with Jackson Browne, playing the banjo solo on "Take It Easy." In the mid-'70s he joined Country Gazette and recorded *Trader in Our Midst* and *Don't Give Up Your Day Job,* both on United Artists. He cut two solo albums for Epic: *Southwest* (1976) and *Sandman* (1977).

He played on *The Rockford Files* starring James Garner for eight years. Songwriters Mike Post and Pete Carpenter, who knew Pedersen from the Troubadour, got him onto the show. Herb learned how to read chord charts. Since then he has done a great deal of work for TV and movie soundtracks (*City Slickers, Maverick,* and *Fire Down Below*). "It keeps you disciplined. You don't know what you're going to be recording, you don't know who you're going to be recording with. . . . Sometimes the music's right for the banjo and sometimes it isn't. You do the best you can."

Besides his banjo playing, Pedersen has done session work as a backup vocalist. "I am completely blessed with the ability to hear harmonies very quickly. It's not something that I work on constantly. It's just something that I do. I know where they should go. That's kind of what sustained me over the last twenty-five years."

He has modeled his singing after such tenor singers as Jim McReynolds, Bob Osborne, Curly Seckler, and Ira Louvin. Two of his songs, "Wait a Minute" and "Old Train," became part of the Seldom Scene's repertoire for another famous bluegrass tenor, the late John Duffey. "He was a great guy," Pedersen says of Duffey. "I loved his sense of humor. I'd always invite him to come to the Birchmere [in Alexandria, Virginia] when we played back there. But he'd never come because it was bowling night or something. I really respected him for that. He wasn't one who said, 'Oh yeah, I'll be there.' He'd say, 'No, I can't. It's bowling night.' At least he was honest with us. He broke the mold as far as that east coast bluegrass scene goes."

"Wait a Minute" came out of a spat Pedersen had with his first wife, who didn't approve of his constant touring. "I came home. I had a tour with Johnny Rivers coming up. I said to my wife, 'We're going to go to Europe and do this tour.' 'Wait a minute,' she responded. She didn't want me to go." The phrase led to the song. (Pedersen's current wife, Libby, a music editor who has worked on such TV shows as *Law & Order* and *LA Law,* is more accepting of his touring.) Sometimes Herb will only write one song a year, three in a good year. "I don't really consider myself a songwriter's songwriter. . . . I have to have something I really want to say that just kind of comes out."

In the mid-1980s, Pedersen was ready for new challenges, this time in the country-rock realm. He had first met Chris Hillman in 1963. Pedersen was playing in the Pine Valley Boys and Hillman in the Scottsville Squirrel Barkers from San Diego. "There was an immediate kinship. . . . We liked the same kind of music. We lived in the same neighborhood in Hollywood. When he joined The Byrds I didn't see him for a long time because he was really busy with that. Then he joined the Flying Burrito Brothers."

The two stayed in touch. Herb worked on Chris's solo albums. When Herb recorded *Lonesome Feeling* for Sugar Hill in 1984, he invited Hillman to play mandolin. "From that point on we really sort of struck up another relationship." They played on Dan Fogelberg's album *High Country Snows*. He hired Pedersen and Hillman to open for him on tour. The first configuration of the "California-country" tinged Desert Rose Band was Bill Bryson, John Jorgensen, Hillman, and Pedersen (on rhythm guitar) in an acoustic format. After that tour, Jorgensen suggested an electric sound. They added Jay Dee Maness on pedal steel and Steve Duncan on drums. "Working with Chris was a challenge, it was fun, it was never boring," Pedersen says. "We played in places that normal country music couldn't get into because of his past being more rock 'n' roll oriented or country rock, . . . like the Bottom Line or Carnegie Hall."

The group recorded six albums and had five number one hits on country radio. But after eight years together, they disbanded. "Nashville always had that thing about us being from California and not being part of that clique. There were the generic hat acts coming out. We felt, as Chris puts it, our shelf life was just about up." Pedersen and Hillman teamed up for the 1996 Sugar Hill release *Bakersfield Bound*. He and Hillman also joined Tony and Larry Rice to release *Out of the Woodwork* (1997) on Rounder, followed by *Larry Rice, Tony Rice, Chris Hillman and Herb Pedersen* (1999).

Pedersen was practicing one day in 1994, when his wife came in. "Honey, why don't you put something together and have some fun with it?" she suggested. Pedersen called Bill Bryson, Kenny Blackwell, and Billy Ray Lathum, all of whom liked the idea of playing traditional bluegrass. Byron Berline joined. "We played some old standards to see what it would sound like," Pedersen says. "It sounded pretty damn good."

Sugar Hill president Barry Poss liked the demo. "The name came from this street right here, Laurel Canyon," Pedersen said, pointing to the busy road. "The Laurel Canyon Ramblers is basically a tip of the hat to the Redwood Canyon Ramblers as far as I'm concerned. . . . It's straight bluegrass and original tunes done in the Rambler style. We don't do much that's really left of field or right of field."

Berline departed after the first album on Sugar Hill (*Rambler's Blues*, 1995). They invited fiddler Gabe Witcher to join. When Lathum left after the band released its second Sugar Hill CD (*Blue Rambler #2, 1996*), Roger Reed joined on guitar and tenor vocals. He lost his index finger on his left hand in a Skil-saw accident. "The middle finger actually came off too but they reattached it," Herb says. Bruce Johnson filled in until Reed rejoined the band in 1997. "He's a good enough guitar player where he can get around on it OK. He went through some intense hand therapy," Herb says.

In the '90s, Herb also played banjo in the Bluegrass Reunion Band, the recent version of Old & In The Way (whose roster originally included Jerry Garcia on banjo) with David Grisman, Peter Rowan, Vassar Clements, and James Kerwin. Pedersen, who plays a Deering Golden Era banjo these days, practices every day for an hour and says his playing has gotten stronger over the years. "I'm not as interested in playing fast as I am in making the notes really sound fat and true."

In 1997 Sugar Hill issued the Ramblers' third CD, *Back on the Street Again*. In 2000 the group was mulling over an offer to record for Grisman's Acoustic Disc label. Despite the group's straight-ahead bluegrass approach, the band still has Hollywood roots. They played a party for producer Douglas Kramer in the Santa Clarita Valley attended by Dennis Hopper, Tony Bill, and other Hollywood types. "About halfway through our fourth or fifth tune I feel this tug on my pant leg and I look down and it's Steve Martin," Pedersen says. "He said, 'Do you guys know . . . ?' I just cracked up because I hadn't seen him in so long. I said, 'Why don't you get up and play one?' 'Oh no, I couldn't do that,' he said. 'I don't have my picks with me.' I said, 'I've got picks in my banjo case. So that's really not an excuse.' He said, 'Let me practice a little bit.' So we took a break. He came back and tried my banjo on. I gave him some picks. We actually got him up to play 'Foggy Mountain Breakdown.' The people dug it."

Adapted from an interview with Herb Pedersen in April 1997 for Banjo Newsletter

PENTANGLE: *British folk-rock-jazz group. Original members from 1967 to 1973: Bert Jansch (guitarist, songwriter, vocals), born Glasgow, Scotland, November 3, 1943; John Renbourn (guitarist, songwriter, vocals), born Marylebone, London, England, August 8, 1944; Jacqui McShee (vocals), born London, England; Danny Thompson (bass), born England, April 1939; Terry Cox (drums and percussion). Group disbanded in 1973, reformed in 1983 with Jansch, McShee, Thompson, Cox, and Mike Piggott (fiddler, guitarist). Thompson left in 1985, replaced by Nigel Portman Smith (bass) born in Sheffield, Yorkshire, England. Piggott and Cox left in 1989, replaced by Gerry Conway (drums), born King's Lynn, Norfolk, England, 1947. Also joining was Peter Kirtley (vocals, guitarist). Jansch left in 1994. McShee reformed band in 1995 as Jacqui McShee's Pentangle with McShee; Gerry Conway (drums); Spencer Cozens (keyboards); Alan Thomson (bass and guitar); and Jerry Underwood (tenor and soprano sax).*

The mid-1960s were a heady time on the London club scene. Many of the musicians had been influenced by the skiffle movement of the 1950s. American blues artists such as Big Joe Williams and Muddy Waters began touring England in the 1960s. Folk revivalists sparked an interest in traditional British music. The Pentangle, considered one of the most influential British groups of the late 1960s, came out of that milieu. The group is usually called folk-rock but it also fused blues, jazz, and Indian influences, and played everything from traditional folk to Charles Mingus.

Guitarists Bert Jansch and John Renbourn had their own folk club in London's SoHo district called the Scot's Hoose. They had recorded an album called *Bert and John* for Transatlantic in 1966, and put Pentangle together the following year. Renbourn knew Jacqui McShee, who began singing professionally with her sister Pam when she was seventeen. He introduced McShee to Jansch, bassist Danny Thompson, and drummer Terry Cox, who were playing nearby in a group called Alexis Korner's Blues Incorporated. Thompson came from an eclectic background, having played with Sonny Terry, Brownie McGhee, Josh White, Nick Drake, and Roy Orbison. The others were exploring musical forms as well. As Jansch told Mike Joyce of the *Washington Post* ("Pentangle's 'New Colors,'" July 22,1986), "I remember I was very much into Charlie Mingus, among other people, at the time. And if someone was listening to Indian music—for instance, I've listened to a lot of Ravi Shankar—the Indian flavor would just show up in our music sooner or later. It was all very natural."

Pentangle's first performance was in late 1967 at the Horseshoe Pub on Tottenham Court Road in London. The group was noted for the interplay between Jansch and Renbourn on guitar, the jazz stylings of Thompson and Cox, and McShee's wonderful singing. At first glance it would not seem an easy fit. As Shel Talmy, who produced their early albums, told Karl Dallas (liner notes for Rhino's *Troubadours of British Folk*), "On the face of it, it shouldn't have worked. Throw together three of the most individual folk artists, Bert Jansch, John Renbourn and Jacqui McShee, with two of the better jazz musicians, Danny Thompson and Terry Cox, and it should have been chaos. Instead some sort of amazing synergy resulted."

In 1968 Transatlantic released the group's debut, *The Pentangle*. The eight-track LP includes some of their most enduring songs, "Let No Man Steal Your Thyme," the instrumental "Pentangling," and "Bruton Town." They followed later in the year with an excellent double LP titled *Sweet Child* (Transatlantic). One album was recorded in the studio, the other in concert. It included two Mingus compositions, "Goodbye Pork Pie Hat" and "Haitian Fight Song." In 1969 Transatlantic released *Basket of Light,* which hit number five on the British charts. The group had a moderate hit with the single "Light Flight" and embarked on a tour of the United States in February 1969. While playing at the Newport Folk Festival in the summer of 1969 their set was inter-

rupted by the announcement that Neil Armstrong had walked on the moon. Despite the general excitement, some people booed because they just wanted to hear Pentangle play.

Transatlantic issued *Cruel Sister* in 1970, which was also an excellent album. The group was at the height of its popularity when it performed at New York's Carnegie Hall in April 1970. As Don Heckman wrote in the *New York Times* ("The Shadowy Territory Between Jazz and Folk," May 10, 1970): "One was constantly aware of a precise, but almost intuitive improvisational interaction between the musicians. Singer Jacqui McShee's bell-toned, vibratoless vocals acted as a kind of sustained *cantus firmus* against which John Renbourn's electric and Bert Jansch's acoustic guitars wove intricate, jazz-colored threadings.

"As if in compensation for the absence of physical, body moving rhythms, the Pentangle used a selective array of unusual meters. In songs like 'Bruton Town,' 'Light Flight' and 'Pentangling,' strange stop-and-go, suddenly changing rhythms in 5/8, 7/8, 6/4 and the like appeared and disappeared with an effect as tartly surprising as the tongue-curling flavor of English sour candy balls."

Two compilation albums followed, *Reflection* on Transatlantic in 1971, and *Solomon's Seal* on Reprise in 1972. But by 1973 the group had played itself out creatively. The group broke up mostly because they were seeking new creative opportunities and had tired of the constant touring. They also ran into contractual difficulties.

After they disbanded, Jansch and Renbourn went back to recording solo albums. Thompson and Cox went on to play at London's jazz club Ronnie Scott's. In his distinguished career, Thompson would accompany everyone from Richard Thompson and John Martyn to African kora player Toumani Diabate.

McShee joined the John Renbourn Group (along with Sue Draheim on fiddle, Tony Roberts on flutes and pipes, and Keshav Sathe on tabla), releasing *A Maid in Bedlam* (Transatlantic, 1977), *The Enchanted Garden* (1980), and *Live in America* (Flying Fish, 1981), recorded at San Francisco's Great American Music Hall and McCabe's Guitar Shop in Santa Monica. The last-named album was nominated for a Grammy. Shanachie also released a video, *John Renbourn Group in Concert.*

McShee spearheaded the reunion of the band in 1982, when Jansch, Thompson, and Cox joined her for a brief European tour. In 1985 the four original members plus Mike Piggott on violin and guitars released a new studio album titled *Open the Door* on Spindrist in the United Kingdom, Varrick in the United States. Renbourn, who went back to study music in college, was never impressed with the newly formed group and declined. Other albums by the "New Pentangle" include *In the Round* (Plane, Varrick, 1986), *So Early in the Spring* (Plane, Green Linnet, 1989), *Think of Tomorrow*

(Green Linnet, 1991), and *One More Road* (Permanent, 1993).

While competent, the group never re-created the energy and inventiveness of the original Pentangle. Thompson left after *Open the Door* and has continued his multifaceted career. He was replaced by bass and keyboard player Nigel Portman Smith, who studied at the Guildhall School of Music. Cox departed after recording some tracks for *So Early in the Spring*. Gerry Conway, who had played with Alexis Korner, Steeleye Span, Francoise Hardy, and the Incredible String Band, replaced him on drums. Piggott, who had replaced Renbourn for the 1985 reunion album, left shortly after the band recorded *In the Round* (1986). The band recruited Peter Kirtley, the house guitarist at the famed Star Club in Hamburg, where the Beatles once played, to play guitar, vocals, and mandolin. He also added "handclapping" for the band's 1991 release, *Think of Tomorrow*.

By 1994 Jansch had also decided to leave Pentangle. That left Jacqui McShee as the only original member. In August 1994 she got together with Conway and keyboardist Spencer Cozens to record a new album. Other performers joined them, including Ralph McTell on vocals, Albert Lee on guitar, Mike Mainieri on vibes, John Giblin on bass, and John Martyn on guitar. The result was the album *About Thyme*, released in 1995. Following the success of that album, she put together a new incarnation of the group that she called Jacqui McShee's Pentangle. Conway, Cozens, and McShee were joined by Alan Thomson on bass and guitar, and Jerry Underwood on sax to round out the quintet. The new ensemble recorded *Passe Avant* ("Go Forward") in 1998, released by Park Records.

Renbourn and McShee continued to tour together, including a Spirit of the Tradition tour with Kathryn Tickell and Maddy Prior, and performances in England in June 1999. In the meantime, besides his duties with Pentangle, Conway took Dave Mattacks's place in Fairport Convention.

A large number of Pentangle retrospectives and compilations have been released, including *History Book* (Transatlantic, 1972); *This is Pentangle* (1973); *Pentangling* (Transatlantic, 1973); *Pentangle Collection* (Transatlantic, 1975); *Anthology* (Transatlantic, 1978); *At Their Best* (Cambra, 1983); *Essential, Volumes One and Two* (Transatlantic, 1987); *A Maid that's Deep in Love* (Shanachie, 1987); *Collection* (Castle, 1988); *25 Year Anniversary* (Permanent, 1992); *Early Classics* (Shanachie, 1992); *People on the Highway 1968–1971* (Transatlantic, 1992); *Live at the BBC* (Bank of Joy, 1995); and *Light Flight* (1997).

PETER, PAUL AND MARY: *Vocal and instrumental group, songwriters. Peter Yarrow, born New York, New York, May 31, 1938; Noel Paul Stookey, born Baltimore, Maryland, November 30, 1937; Mary Ellin Travers, born Louisville, Kentucky, November 7, 1937.*

In the mid-1960s, when revived rock 'n' roll ended the short-lived dominance of folk music, only a handful of the most talented performers managed to retain a hold on a large following. Peter, Paul and Mary, who came together in Greenwich Village at the start of the 1960s during the folk music ferment, remained headliners when folk music was no longer the vogue without moving markedly from their folk roots. Even more unusual, after the trio had been apart for a decade, they demonstrated that they still had major drawing power with their reunion concert tour of seventeen major U.S. cities in 1978.

Paul Stookey's early history seemed to make him an unlikely candidate for the Village scene. He was an early fan of rock 'n' roll as a teenager growing up in Baltimore. Later, he used his skills with electric guitar to work in a rock band, which helped pay his tuition at Michigan State University. He added to his earning by working as an emcee in local clubs.

After receiving his degree, he moved to Pennsylvania with his family and worked at a number of odd jobs before deciding he wanted to try his hand as an entertainer again. After moving to New York, he went through months of near starvation trying to find show business jobs. It got to the point that he took a position in a chemical company to keep going while he sought work as a stand-up comic in his spare time. His persistence paid off, though, and he began to make a name for himself as a comic in Greenwich Village clubs by the end of 1960.

Mary Travers's family originally came from Louisville, Kentucky, but moved to New York when she was still a small child. She became interested in folk music, and while still in elementary school, took lessons in the genre from teachers like Charity Bailey. In high school, in the early 1950s, she followed that interest still further, singing with various teenage folk groups. During those years, as a member of a group called the Songswappers, she made two appearances at Carnegie Hall.

Still, for a time it looked as though she too might have to find other routes to a professional entertaining career. One of her first efforts after finishing high school was to get a job in the chorus of a Broadway show. Unfortunately, it flopped, and she worked at various literary and advertising jobs during the day while trying to increase contacts in the music field nights and weekends. Among the people she became acquainted with were Stookey and a one-time music teacher and folksinger named Milt Okun. In the early 1960s, Okun was turning his attention away from working as an entertainer himself in favor of handling management and production of the new flood of young talent he could see around him in New York.

Okun took an interest in Mary and Paul and encouraged them to form a team, which they started doing in 1961. He felt the act would work better if it expanded to a trio, which helped open the door for Peter Yarrow.

Yarrow, born and raised in New York, learned to play violin and guitar in his youth and was adept at both instruments by the time he enrolled at Cornell University, in upstate New York. His major was psychology, but he enjoyed music and played in school functions and in local clubs. After getting his degree, he considered making psychology his career, but when he returned to New York, he couldn't avoid the lure of the folk music boom. He began working with various folk groups and attracted the attention of local folk fans. In May 1960, he was chosen as a cast member for a CBS special, "Folk Sound, U.S.A." That exposure, in turn, gained him a spot in the 1960 Newport Folk Festival, which reaffirmed his decision to make folk music his main occupation.

His reputation had increased still more by the time he joined forces with Paul and Mary in 1961. With Okun providing advice and assistance, things moved forward rapidly. The trio made their performing debut in New York in 1962 and in a matter of months were ranked among the most promising newcomers on the Manhattan folk scene. They also signed a recording contract with Warner Brothers, which was still their recording firm in the 21st century. By May 1962, their debut LP was out; titled *Peter, Paul & Mary*, it proved one of the top debut releases of the year. Before 1962 was over the trio had its first hit singles, "Lemon Tree" and "If I Had a Hammer."

If 1962 was successful, 1963 proved better. Their second LP, *Peter, Paul & Mary–Moving*, issued in March 1963, was a chart hit as was their next album, *Peter, Paul & Mary–In the Wind*, released in December 1963. The group had four major single hits that year: "Puff (the Magic Dragon)," written by Yarrow; "Stew Ball"; and two Dylan songs, "Blowin' in the Wind" and "Don't Think Twice It's Alright." Their version of "Blowin' in the Wind" won the Grammy Award for the Best Folk Music Record of the year. By the end of 1963, Peter, Paul and Mary were one of the most sought-after acts in music and were featured on major TV shows and in concerts all over the United States and Canada. The group also headlined many major folk festivals (and even some rock festivals) through most of the 1960s, including a number of appearances at the Newport Folk Festival. During those years, some of the songs in their repertoire were written by one or more of them (sometimes all three, sometimes in collaboration with Okun), including such tunes as "On a Desert Island," "A-Soulin'," "Talking Candy Bar Blues," "Early in the Morning," and "It's Raining."

As the 1960s went by, the group kept adding to its credits both as stage attractions and recording artists. In 1964 they had the hit single "Go Tell It on the Mountain." In 1965 their album releases included *Peter, Paul and Mary in Concert*, issued in March, *A Song Will Rise*, released in May, and, in December, *See What Tomorrow Brings*. That year, they helped bring a very talented Canadian songwriter to the United States' attention with their single of Gordon Lightfoot's "Early Morning Rain." Later in the decade they were to do a similar favor for another then unknown troubadour with their gold-record version of John Denver's "Leavin' on a Jet Plane."

Their seventh LP release on Warners was *Peter, Paul and Mary Album*, issued in October 1966. That year they were represented on singles charts with "The Cruel War." One of their best collections came out the following year with *Album 1700*, released in September 1967. They also had two singles that made national charts in 1967, "I Dig Rock 'n' Roll Music" and "Great Mandella." They followed with an album a year the next three years: *Late Again*, issued August 1968; *Peter, Paul and Mommy*, issued May 1969; and *The Best of Peter, Paul and Mary, Ten Years Together*, issued May 1970. They placed two more singles on hit lists in 1969, "Too Much of Nothing" and "Day is Done."

By then the group was on the way to closing out that phase of its history. Part of the reason for the breakup was the natural desire of artists to strike out in new creative directions. But perhaps having the greater impact was a court case involving Yarrow in which he was charged with having illicit relations with a fourteen-year-old girl. He served three months and was pardoned in 1980 by President Jimmy Carter.

Stardom's pressures were partly to blame. Other members also could feel that impact. Paul Stookey, for instance, had become aware of a loss of contact with his family and decided that a return to a closer involvement with Christianity might help. That experience in 1968, he said, opened his eyes. "After the discovery that I needed God in my life, it became obvious that I had allowed a great distance to develop between me and my family, but since my body moves about two years after my mind, it wasn't until 1970 that I spoke about retiring."

Paul moved his family to several rural areas, eventually settling in Maine in 1973. As of 1982, his family included a seventeen-year-old daughter, Elizabeth, and twin daughters, Anna and Kate, ten. His activities after leaving the trio included writing three albums on biblical parables and work on recording/animation projects in his own studio in Maine.

He also wrote a song in honor of Peter's marriage to Marybeth McCarthy, a niece of Senator Eugene McCarthy, titled "Wedding Song (There Is Love)." Yarrow eventually settled in Malibu, California, where as of 1982, his children were an eleven-year-old daughter, Elizabeth, and a son, Christopher, nine. Throughout the 1970s, he remained active in the folk movement, appearing on folk shows on local California stations and taking part in various concerts and festivals.

Mary also continued to be active in various ways as the 1970s went by. At times she had her own music and interview program on Radio Pacifica in Los Angeles (KPFK). She also performed in many college concerts, did some nightclub work and was featured on occasion with symphony orchestras, including those of Denver and Baltimore. Besides that, she lectured in colleges on the subject of "Society and Its Effect on Music." She also devoted much of her time to raising her two daughters, Erika (twenty-two in 1982) and Alicia (sixteen in 1982).

Reflecting on the way their lives had developed for a biographical article in connection with their 1978 recombination, Mary said, "We are the children of Pete Seeger. We came from the folk tradition in a contemporary form where there was a concern that idealism be a part of your music and the music a part of your life. If Paul explores it vis-à-vis a political activist position, it is all the same. It's a concern, wanting your music not to be schizophrenic. So the music becomes an extension of your caring and your soul—there's no schism between what you can do on stage and who you are. What we're trying for is a kind of health—and that's what we were always trying for."

The trio's decision to get together once more resulted in the September 1978 album *Reunion.* The songs included Dylan's "Forever Young," Margie Adams's "The Unicorn Song," Billy Joel's "Summer Highland Falls," and two new numbers co-written by Yarrow with Barry Mann and Cynthia Weil, "Sweet Survivor" and "Like the First Time."

In the mid-1980s, the trio's visit to Central America made them aware of the terrible suffering of the local population and inspired Stookey's song "El Salvador." This was coupled with another song by Peter Yarrow, "Light One Candle," in favor of the peace process in Israel in an independent 1985 single whose profits were used to support the Sanctuary Movement and efforts for free elections in Central America.

The title track of the trio's 1986 album, *No Easy Walk to Freedom,* expressed dismay over the apartheid system of South Africa. At a special benefit held at the Kennedy Center in Washington, D.C., the group was honored by the Free South Africa Movement. Later in the year during a concert series at a venue on New York's Broadway, the trio hosted a fund-raiser for the New York Coalition for the Homeless. Since 1986 represented the twenty-fifth year since they first got together, they taped a PBS special *25th Anniversary Concert,* that has been replayed many times on the network.

Two years later the trio taped another show for PBS, *A Holiday Concert,* performed before a live audience in New York. Backing them on their songs were the 160-member New York Choral Society and a 40-piece orchestra. Some of the material formed the basis for a new album, *A Holiday Celebration.* Gold Castle issued *Flowers and Stones* in 1990.

In 1992, Peter, Paul and Mary went back to their original record affiliation, signing with Warner Brothers Records. Their first label release was their second children's album, *Peter, Paul & Mommy, Too.* (The original of that title, coined by Mary's daughter Erika, was the 1969 *Peter, Paul & Mommy.*) Album tracks included live versions of "Puff (the Magic Dragon)," "The Fox," "The Garden Song," "Blowin' in the Wind," "Inside," and "If I Had a Hammer."

The trio enlisted the aid of many friends from the folk music field for their 1996 TV show and associated album, *Lifelines.* Those taking part included Weavers alumni Ronnie Gilbert and Fred Hellerman, Richie Havens, Tom Paxton, Odetta, Dave Van Ronk, John Sebastian, Boddy Mundlock, and Susan Werner. They continued their humanitarian efforts in 1997 by helping make two Public Service announcements, one focusing on gun violence against children, the other in support of steps to eradicate hunger in the United States. The gun violence spot, developed by the trio with the National Crime Prevention Council, the Ad Council, and ad agency Saatchi & Saatchi, featured Pete Seeger's song "Where Have All the Children Gone" in a moving appeal to stop the loss of young lives.

During 1998 the trio turned their attention to the travails of the farm workers, organizing a benefit on behalf of the United Farm Workers union in Santa Cruz, California, on March 19, 1998. The event, they noted, represented the thirtieth anniversary of the trio's first benefit for Cesar Chavez and the UFW, presented at Carnegie Hall in New York in 1968.

In April 1998, Warner Brothers issued the double-CD album *Around the Campfire,* which included previously recorded versions of some of the group's best-known songs plus four new tracks of longtime folk music standbys, "Down by the Riverside," "Kumbaya," "Michael Row Your Boat Ashore," and "Goodnight Irene." Reader's Digest released a four disc set, *The Collection,* in 1998, followed by *Songs of Conscience and Concern* on Warner Brothers in 1999.

PHILLIPS, U. UTAH: *Singer, guitarist, harmonica player, songwriter. Born Cleveland, Ohio, May 15, 1935.*

During a concert in the early 1990s, Bruce "U. Utah" Phillips, self-professed left-of-center activist and anarchist, told some college students in the crowd, "You are about to be told one more time that you are America's most valuable natural resource. Have you seen what they do to valuable natural resources? They're going to strip-mine your soul, they're going to clear-cut your thoughts for the sake of profit, unless you learn to resist, because the profit system follows the path of least resistance, and following the path of least resistance is what makes the river crooked! Make a break for it, kids! Flee to the wilderness. There's one inside you if you can find it."

Those acid-tinged words from a white-bearded man who looked like Santa Claus were part of Phillips's stock-in-trade. In concert after concert he raised the voice of the gadfly, typically interrupting his versions of folk songs, old and new—most his own—with witty, often sarcastic comments such as: "If you're set on having heroes, make sure they're dead so they can't blow it" (which he said was coined by his friend Amnon Hennessey of the Catholic Workers Movement), or "A melting pot is when the people at the bottom get burned and the scum rise to the top."

The content of his stories and songs reflected an outlook shaped from the start by his impulse to question accepted attitudes in his native land. Born in Cleveland at the height of the Great Depression, he was the son of parents who were ardent union supporters. His stepfather became a Depression-era Communist, and his mother worked for John L. Lewis's labor organization, the C.I.O. (Congress of Industrial Organizations). They moved to Dayton and then Utah in 1947. In his mid-teens, longing to see more of the world, he left home to ride the rails, sharing the world of large numbers of hobos, tramps, and bums. (More definitions: a tramp is "someone who dreams and wanders; a hobo is someone who works and wanders; and a bum is someone who drinks and wanders.") He first developed skill on the ukulele to help entertain his new friends, from whom he learned many tales of the wandering life; later he taught himself guitar as he started writing songs about life on the road. Those songs, he later noted, reflected the influence on him of material by the original Jimmie Rodgers and Gene Autry's films and recordings.

In the 1950s he was inducted into the U.S. Army. Sent to Korea during his two-year hitch, he became disillusioned with the American presence over there and with war in general. He told Bill Ainsworth of the *Sacramento News & Review* ("Anarchy in Song—Utah Phillips Keeps the Wobbly Flame Alive," July 25, 1991), "I saw the arrogance of this white army treating the people they were supposed to be helping as if they were subhuman. That's where I learned about sexism, racism and imperialism."

After his discharge, he returned to Utah, where he found a position as a social worker at the Joe Hill House, named after the slain leader of a once-powerful labor union called the International Workers of the World, or "Wobblies." (He joined the surviving IWW, a shadow of its former self, at the time and was still a member in the 1990s.) From the mid-1950s on, he helped union causes in a variety of ways, such as walking picket lines and aiding migrant farm workers and, in the '60s, as an ardent pacifist was one of the early opponents of the U.S. involvement in Vietnam. He continued to add to his repertoire of songs, which included, besides union numbers like "Solidarity Forever," "There Is Power in a Union," and "Joe Hill," and traditional ballads, an increasing number of originals such as "Railroading on the Great Divide." Sometimes he appeared with other regional folksingers, in particular working with Rosalie Sorrels. Where possible he performed at local folk venues or at union rallies, but his main income came from teaching guitar to children and, for a

time, as a Utah state archivist. He released his first album, *Nobody Knows Me,* on the Prestige label in the early 1960s, produced by Ken Goldstein. Phillips did not see it as his best effort. Later, Rosalie Sorrels recorded six of his songs on an album called *If I Could Be the Rain,* released on the Folk Legacy label. (The album later inspired Kate Wolf to become a songwriter. Utah and Kate became close friends and nurtured each other's development over the years.)

In the mid-1960s Phillips got the idea of organizing his own political organization to run for president. He called it the Sloth and Indolence Party. Later that merged into the Peace and Freedom Party, which named him its presidential candidate in 1968. Utah took a leave of absence from his state job to run a tongue-in-cheek campaign, earning a total of 6,000 votes. While he was away, the state managed to phase out his archival position. In later years, Phillips continued to run under the Sloth and Indolence banner. He told a reporter in 1991, "I've won every election so far. I'm not in the White House, and I consider that a stunning victory."

He remained a part-time troubadour, supporting his family with a variety of day jobs, until the end of the 1970s. In 1979, at the urging of Rosalie Sorrels and other folk-music friends, he agreed to try making his living solely from music. As he described it, he left Utah in a pouring rain in the dead of night with $75 in his pocket in a VW van he called "Hitler's revenge" and drove back to join a folk music "family" loosely grouped around Caffe Lena in Saratoga Springs, New York. Phillips recorded a collection for Biograph Records called *Welcome to Caffe Lena.* The alignment worked out and from then on he was a full-time performer, working with other important folk artists or as a soloist. He later said, "Singing together and sharing food is a holy activity. Not consuming, but creating. The folk family is the healthiest thing to happen in the United States. They helped raise my family and helped me to buy a home. I'm deeply indebted to the family. I want to do everything I can to nurture it."

True to his pacifist beliefs, he strongly opposed the Gulf War of 1991. He was attacked by others in the audience when he attended a pro-war meeting wearing an anti–Gulf War button.

Through the 1980s and into the '90s, he became a familiar figure on the folk circuit, drawing typical SRO crowds (to small folk venues or on college campuses) in the United States, Canada, and elsewhere. Other artists covered some of his songs like "I Remember Loving You," "Touch Me," and "Starlight on the Rails," which also appeared on his own albums. Through the mid-'90s, he typically performed in some 100 cities from September to May, after which he returned to his home, which then was located in the rural locale of Nevada City, California. His activities then focused on his family and his garden with occasional work on new songs. His recorded output as of 1995 included five records on

Rounder/Philo (*Good Though!, El Capitan, All Used Up: A Scrapbook,* and *We Have Fed You All for a Thousand Years*), one on Alcazar (*I've Got to Know*) and a live one with Ramblin' Jack Elliott and Spider John Koerner on the Red House label called *Legends of Folk.* In 1994 he was given a grant from the Rex Foundation to prepare a songbook of his material, which was released in 1995.

Still a strong union proponent, he recalled for the *New England Folk Almanac* (January 15, 1992), "Although my mother couldn't sing, she could quack and honk and bleat and make other feral utterances she characterized as American folk song. You know, labor songs like Joe Hill's 'Power in the Union' or 'Solidarity Forever' are as much a part of our folk music as 'On Top of Old Smokey.' I think you don't hear them as much because what they say is very often more threatening. Those songs tell stories about common ordinary people, often with the cards really stacked against them—immigrants with no education, no ability to go to school—taking control of their lives and the condition of their employment.

"That's how we got mine safety laws and child labor laws and the eight-hour day. Because working stiffs, ordinary men and women, were willing to commit a whole lot to make sure those things happened. They were not benevolent gifts from an enlightened management."

In 1996 Red House released *The Long Memory,* recorded with Rosalie Sorrels. They won the Best Traditional Folk award from the National Association of Record Distributors.

Another collaborative effort, with Ani DiFranco, was *the past didn't go anywhere,* released in 1996 by her Righteous Babe Records. DiFranco contacted Phillips and asked him to "send every live recording of yourself that you have lying around and give me your blessing to mess with um," as she says in the liner notes. He complied. She transferred them to DAT and drove to Austin, listening to Phillips's words for three days "at 75 mph, alternately laughing, weeping, and jotting cryptic notes on napkins while swerving lane to lane." She took his stories, poems, rants, and raves only (not his songs) and set them to music—strains of hip-hop, blues, and percussion. Songs included "Bridges," which begins *Time is an enormous river;* "Korea," a story about his stint in Korea; "Bum on the Rod;" "Anarchy;" and "Nevada City, California," where Phillips now operates No Guff Records.

In the late 1990s Phillips came down with a heart condition that limited the amount of traveling he could do. He did fewer concerts. He also hosted a weekly radio show for the Pacifica Radio Network called *Loafer's Glory: Hobo Jungle of the Mind. Loafer's Glory* was also the title of his next CD, released on Red House Records in 1997.

Jody Stecher and Kate Brislin recorded *Heart Songs: The Old Time Country Songs of Utah Phillips,* which was nominated for a Best Traditional Folk Grammy for 1997. That year, Rounder/Philo released *The Telling Takes Me Home,* a compilation of Utah's albums *El Capitan* and *All Used Up.* At the Folk Alliance Conference in Toronto, Phillips was awarded a Lifetime Achievement Award, which was presented by Ani DiFranco. She invited Phillips to her studio in Buffalo to work on a second album in 1998. Phillips also performed "See Here, She Said" for *Treasures Left Behind: Remembering Kate Wolf,* on Red House Records. Utah and Ani collaborated on a second album in 1999, *Fellow Workers,* on Righteous Babe, which was nominated for a Grammy. Utah followed with *Moscow Hold* on Red House in 1999.

Phillips discussed his health problems at a concert at McCabe's Guitar Shop in Santa Monica, California, on January 9, 1999, his first appearance in some time. His physicians had sharply restricted his activities during his rehab from congestive heart failure, but he began to feel restless. Then he said, " 'If you want to continue to do this you'll no longer be extant,' my cardiologist said. As my condition improved I told him that I could do one thing a month away from home and this is it." His reasoning in choosing McCabe's was that when his heart problems caused him to cancel an extensive tour "the last engagement I had was here."

PHRANC: *Singer, guitarist, songwriter. Born Santa Monica, California, August 28, 1957.*

With her flat-top hairstyle, male attire, and cowboy boots, Phranc's appearance on the L.A. pop scene in the late 1970s in some ways seemed a predecessor of country star k.d. lang's couture. She didn't seem out of place as part of the Southern California hardcore punk scene, whose participants, male and female, obeyed no rules as far as their appearance was concerned. When she turned to folk music, though, she did look somewhat odd to many fans, though they couldn't gainsay her obvious skills as writer and performer.

She was born Susan Gottlieb in Los Angeles, the daughter of an insurance salesman and a dental hygienist, and spent most of her formative years in the middle-class environment of the Mar Vista area. Allen Sherman's "My Son the Folksinger" inspired her to pick up the guitar at age nine. Early on she realized she had different feelings and emotions than most of the people in her classes at school. As she told an interviewer, "When I was growing up, I really hated being a girl. I couldn't do the things I wanted to do. I couldn't look the way I wanted to look. When I was going to school I had to wear a dress. I definitely couldn't have had my brother's haircut then."

By her teens she had realized that she was a lesbian, and at seventeen she dropped out of Venice High and became actively involved in the local lesbian-feminist community. She was interested in pop music, both folk and rock, though for a time as a student at Santa Monica College she was more into sports, becoming a member of the school's swim team. (She later worked as a swim teacher.) Then in the late '70s she turned her attention to the burgeoning punk rock scene in L.A., though as she told a reporter from the *Los Angeles Times* in 1981 she felt a little ambivalent: "It was new, refreshing, exciting. People were getting mad and saying something. For the first time in my adult life I was involved with people my own age. I never thought I would be performing for anybody but women. It freaked me out. Was I a traitor to the women's movement? I still feel guilty sometimes. But I had to move along and find these things out for myself."

During that period, she moved to Pasadena, where she became friends with a neighbor who enjoyed listening to music by a variety of artists. The neighbor got Phranc enthused about performers of the folk–folk-rock genre such as Bob Dylan, Lou Reed, and Patti Smith.

Meanwhile, Phranc sang solo, accompanying herself on electric guitar at small punk venues. One night, she recalled, she met "a guy wrapped in black plastic named Edward." A month later he called to ask her to become lead vocalist for his group, Nervous Gender. She decided to join what the *Times* critic referred to as "one of the most extreme groups to ever come out of Los Angeles. [One that] produced a grating sort of electro-shock music played by three arhythmic synthesizers blaring out chunks of white noise." Besides that group, she went on to appear with other hardcore bands such as Catholic Discipline and Castration Squad.

One of her punk period associations was with an all-girl group. She wasn't too happy with that experience. "All-girl bands turned out to be worse than Nervous Gender. All these girls would act tough and then would fix their hair and see their boyfriends. I was the only lesbian in the all-girl group, which was worse than being the dyke in the all-male group."

In 1980 she decided to go back to seeking gigs for her earliest musical love, folk music, using an acoustic rather than electric instrument. Rather than perform at "accepted" folk venues like McCabe's, she decided to play for the audiences and musicians she knew best, the avant-garde rock types. She debuted at Club 88 and went on to do solo sets at other rock venues, including the Whisky A-Go-Go on the Sunset Strip in West Hollywood. Her Whisky shows proved so popular they became regular events in which many punk fans, instead of throwing things or spitting, listened attentively to her numbers. Many other artists came by to join her on occasion, including groups like X, the Blasters, and Tito Larriva of the Plugz punk aggregation.

Resisting the lure of rock stardom, which offered larger crowds and potentially more lucrative recording opportunities, Phranc, who called herself "an all-American Jewish lesbian folksinger," persevered with her folk material, ranging from songs by other folk writers to some of her own originals. In 1985 she made her album debut with *Folksinger* on Rhino Records (rereleased on Island in 1990), whose contents included the tracks "Female Mudwrestling," "Amazons," and "One O' the Girls." Jon Pareles of the *New York Times,* who particularly liked her treatment of Bob Dylan's "The Lonesome Death of Hattie Carroll" on the disc, noted she contrasted "an angular image—a flattop haircut, cowboy boots and a stance that makes her look more like a 1950's teen idol than a folksinger—with songs that are sweet and basic, praising women with muscles and decrying female mudwrestling and people who park in spaces for the handicapped."

After *Folksinger* came out, however, she hit a writer's block and was unable to write for several years. In the late '80s, though, she overcame that problem and recorded a new album at her own expense whose title track was a folk version of Rodgers and Hammerstein's "I Enjoy Being a Girl." To some the choice might have seemed strange, but she stressed it reflected a feeling of freedom to wear and say what she wanted to. She often sang another standout track, "Take Off Your Swastika," during her punk rock days to protest neonazi slam dancers. Most of the tracks were self-penned, with topics ranging from the whimsical to the serious, including some reflecting her anger at current political conditions. After she sent the album tapes to several record companies, Island Records decided to acquire it for a 1989 release.

By then the outlook for the folk field was decidedly brighter than when Phranc had first opted for that kind of music. She told Richard Cromelin of the *Los Angeles Times* ("Folk Singer Enjoys Being Phranc at Last," July 22, 1989), "I think it's pretty amusing that 10 years ago I wanted this folk thing to happen so bad. I was singlehandedly trying to do this thing at the Whisky and get everyone together to do these acoustic nights. I kept saying, 'This folk thing is coming, it's coming.' My friends are like, 'I don't know, Phranc, I don't know,' and then 10 years later—boom—it's here."

By then Phranc was finding opportunities to perform at folk venues well beyond California borders. Island also helped bring the new album to the attention of record buyers in the United Kingdom and the European Continent. In 1991, with a new album *Positively Phranc,* in record racks, she was cheered by overseas audiences in a concert series in which she opened for the British singer Morrissey.

Phranc moved to New York and became involved in performance art projects such as her send-up on Neil Diamond, "Hot August Phranc," in 1993 at the Dance Theater Workshop, and her homage to the Automats, called "Phranc-o-mat," set up in a New York storefront in July 1994. Three years earlier, her brother was murdered, and she began working on a project to cope with her grief.

In 1995, Phranc released an EP-CD called *Goofyfoot,* released on the Kill Rock Stars label, which featured a photo of Phranc on a surfboard (she's an avid surfer) strumming a guitar on the cover. In 1998 she released *Milkman*, a thirty-minute CD on Phancy Records. Besides covers of "The Handsome Cabin Boy" and "Tzena, Tzena," Phranc also includes songs that delve into the pain she suffered from her brother's murder.

PLANXTY: *Vocal and instrumental group. Original members, 1972, Christy Moore, born Dublin, Ireland, May 7, 1946 (vocals, guitar); Andy Irvine, born London, England, June 14, 1942 (vocals, guitar, harmonica, mandolin, mandola, bouzouki, songwriter); Dónal Lunny, born Ireland (mandolin, bouzouki); Liam O'Flynn, born Ireland (uileann pipes). Lunny left in July 1973 replaced by Johnny Moynihan (bouzouki, tin whistle); Moore left in 1974, replaced by Paul Brady, born County Tyrone, Northern Ireland, May 19, 1947. Group disbanded in 1975, re-formed in 1978 with four original members plus Matt Molloy, born County Roscommon, Ireland, January 12, 1946 (flutist). Christy Moore and Lunny left at the end of 1982. For 1983 tour, group comprised Irvine, O'Flynn, Bill Whelan, James Kelly, Dolores Keane, and Arty McGlynn, broke up again after conclusion of tour.*

One of the most innovative Irish bands of the 1970s and early '80s, Planxty set new standards for folk and folk-rock performances in the United Kingdom and Europe. Its style extended well beyond those bounds, influencing musicians in many North American groups. As critic Dan Doyle wrote in the *New Rolling Stone Record Guide*, "Planxty was the most ambitious band of its type and displayed an awareness of other ethnic music from Bulgarian to blues. [An album like] *The Well Below the Valley* is a must for anyone interested in contemporary Celtic music."

The band evolved from recording sessions organized by singer-guitarist Christy Moore for a new album issued by Trailer Records in the early '70s titled *Prosperous*. Various articles have credited either Andy Irvine or Dónal Lunny with founding Planxty, but Irvine told *Irish Echo* the idea came from Moore. During 1971, he noted, "Christy Moore, whom I only recently met when he was living in London, said he was going to do an album in Ireland. So we got together and went to Prosperous in Kildare, Christy's home county, and went down in the basement of this marvelous Georgian house and did the album. It was a good feeling, that album and I was playing with Dónal Lunny at the time in a duo."

Lunny worked on the album, as did Liam O'Flynn and bodhran player Kevin Conneff, who would later join the Chieftains. Later on, discussions among some of the musicians gave birth to Planxty. Irvine stated, "It was Christy, the great decision maker, who suggested a band of the four of us. At the time, Dónal and I were playing a local Dublin residency at Slattery's on Cabel Street and Christy was there one time. Afterward, he asked what I thought of forming a band. I was taken

aback because I had never thought of it at all. I said, 'Well, who?' And he said, 'You, Dónal, Liam, and me.' My very first thought was my duo days with Dónal would be done. But Christy said Dónal and Liam were into it, and that made up my mind on the spot. From there it started."

The first order of business was choosing a name, and the four musicians closeted themselves in a room to figure it out. They decided to start with the word *Planxty*, which is Gaelic for "in honor of," a term Irish troubadours had used for centuries when a song was performed to pay tribute to a friend or sponsor. The bandsmen kept thinking Planxty this or Planxty that, before as Irvine recalled, one of them said, "Well, what about just Planxty?" And that stuck.

The group had a hit single in Ireland with "The Cliffs of Doneen" and soon laid down the tracks for its debut album, *Planxty*, issued on Polydor in the United Kingdom in 1972. The "Black Album," as it was called for its black cover, received enthusiastic critical acclaim, as did the 1973 Polydor release *The Well Below the Valley*. The band's concerts in support of those releases were also crowd-pleasers. However, in July 1973, Lunny left to play in another group called Bugle. The remaining members kept things going and, with some session musicians, including bouzouki and whistle player Johnny Moynihan, completed a third album, *Cold Blow and the Rainy Night*, that came out on Polydor in 1974. The album was named *Melody Maker's* folk album of 1974. Not long afterward, Moore stepped down and his place was taken by Paul Brady, a friend of Irvine and some of the others, who had been trying his luck in the United States. The new alignment kept things going into 1975, when the remaining members decided they'd rather try other musical combinations and Planxty disbanded.

In 1976, Polydor in Europe and Shanachie Records in the United States issued the retrospective LP *Planxty Collection*. In 1979, Shanachie reissued all three initial band discs for U.S. record buyers. Meanwhile in 1978, the original quartet had come back together for the second phase of Planxty's odyssey. For a while, they had a fifth member, flute player Matt Molloy, who stayed until 1979, when he accepted a bid to join the Chieftains. During 1979 and into the early 1980s the band continued to tour, the schedules bringing them to venues in Ireland, England, Scotland, Europe, and other parts of the world, including some U.S. concerts. Planxty's output during 1979–80 included *After the Break* in '79 and *The Woman I Loved So Well* in '80. Both were released on the Tara label at home and Shanachie in the United States.

In December 1982 the group completed tracks for the album *Words & Music*, on which the original foursome was supported in the sessions by James Kelly, Bill Whelan (later of *Riverdance* fame), Eoghan O'Neill, and Nollaig Casey. The album was issued on

WEA Ireland in Europe and Shanachie in the United States. During 1982, Moore and Lunny, besides their Planxty activities, had become key members of another band, Moving Hearts, whose repertoire combined Irish folk music with jazz and rock. Starting in 1983, they decided to opt for the new group full-time.

Irvine and O'Flynn put together a new version of Planxty including Whelan, James Kelly, Dolores Keane, and Arty McGlynn. This was the roster for what proved to be a farewell concert series during '83. A compilation album, *Aris*, came out on Polydor in 1984. In the years since then, Planxty has been gone, but not forgotten, as its key albums remain in print and some of the songs are often included on radio programs at home and overseas.

PRINE, JOHN: *Songwriter, singer, guitarist. Born Maywood, Illinois, October 10, 1946.*

To paraphrase Dylan, with whom John Prine was often compared, "The times they have a-changed." Had Prine come along at the start of the '60s and Dylan in the '70s, it might well be Prine who would now be hailed as a giant of the times. But despite the "new Dylan" tag, Prine soon developed his own quirky style. His songs have become standards for performers like Bette Midler ("Hello in There"), Bonnie Raitt ("Angel from Montgomery"), and Nanci Griffith ("Speed of the Sound of Loneliness").

Prine stands squarely in the folk and country-rock art form; his music is tinged with the high lonesome sound of western Kentucky. One of his songs, "Paradise," about the Kentucky coal mining town where his ancestors worked, even gained notice from bluegrass father Bill Monroe, who initially thought it had been written in the 1920s.

Prine kept in touch with his working class roots, even after gaining a measure of acclaim. John grew up in Maywood, a blue-collar suburb of Chicago, where he was born the third of four children in 1946. John's songwriting about grassroots America relates directly to his background. His parents, William and Verna, and grandparents came from Kentucky. His father moved to Chicago to escape the coal mines and found work as a tool and die maker, later becoming president of the Maywood United Steelworkers Union local. John's brother, Dave, taught him guitar when he was fourteen and introduced him to Carter Family songs.

He wrote two songs at the time, "Sour Grapes," and "The Frying Pan," which he cut for his second album *Diamonds in the Rough*. "I guess I started writing as soon as I learned a couple of chords," Prine writes. He credits his ability to a strong imagination. "I was a real daydreamer in school and that kind of got me into trouble sometimes," he told Scott Simon of *National Public Radio* (June 10, 1995). "As soon as the teacher would start talking that was kind of my signal to go off into a daydream."

John also had an interest in rock and country in his teens, listening to Hank Williams, Hank Snow, and Roger Miller. He saw other aspects of working-class life after he graduated high school in 1964 and worked as a mailman. "I took it because it's about the best job that you need no training for, and you get health insurance," Prine writes. "You get sick pay from day one. . . . I'm sure some mailmen, that's what they want to be. But it's a good place for somebody that doesn't know what they want to do."

He spent two years in the army in 1966 and 1967, serving as the head of a motor pool in Germany. He brought his guitar and occasionally entertained his barrack mates. When he was discharged, he went back to the post office and began writing down songs he composed in his head while doing his rounds as a mail carrier.

At the start of the 1970s, urged on by a desire to get away from the vicissitudes of tramping city streets in the wind, cold, and rain, he began performing in Chicago clubs. His performing debut came in 1970 at the Fifth Peg. "There were all these amateurs that were getting up and they were terrible," Prine recalls. "So I started making some comments about it and the next thing I knew, somebody said, 'Well, if you think you can do it better. . . .' I said, 'I could.'"

In his raspy voice, he got up and sang "Sam Stone," about a drug-addicted Vietnam vet, "Paradise," and "Hello in There," a bittersweet portrait of an elderly couple. He soon began appearing regularly at Chicago's Earl of Old Town. Before long, he was making enough money to quit the post office. He became friends with folk singer Steve Goodman. In the summer of 1971, Goodman brought Kris Kristofferson to the Earl of Old Town to hear Prine. It was closing time so Prine gave Kristofferson a private concert. "No way somebody this young can be writing this heavy," Kristofferson remarked. Prine flew to New York and within 24 hours had signed a $25,000 contract with Atlantic Records. "It was rough to take," he recalled. "I felt like Lana Turner for the first couple of years, everything happened to me so fast. Sitting in a folk bar in Chicago just because I don't want to walk in the snow and deliver mail. And that was it; no sights or goals. Then in walk Paul Anka, Kris Kristofferson, and Samantha Eggar and it might as well have been Donald Duck and Mickey Mouse, it made as much sense. Next thing I know I'm on a plane to New York City. I'm in the Village and Kristofferson asked me to get up on stage [at the Bitter End] and I sing three songs and the house comes down and Jerry Wexler [from Atlantic Records] asks me to sign his shoe and all this [excitement] happens and my father dies and I get a record out and I'm in Los Angeles, running around the country and people are calling me the next Bob Dylan and it was really just fuckin' goofy."

In 1971, he went to Memphis to cut his debut album, *John Prine*, with some of the musicians who had worked with Elvis Presley. The album received glowing reviews and introduced audiences to his wonderfully quirky characters in songs like "Sam Stone," "Hello in There," "Illegal Smile," "Angel from Montgomery" (about the quiet desperation of a middle-aged woman), "Paradise," and "Spanish Pipedream." Prine found humor in his subjects, adding a dash of satire. "Illegal Smile" gained a reputation as a doper song, but Prine told *Performing Songwriter* (May–June 1995) that "it was more about how, ever since I was a child, I've had this view of the world where I would find myself smiling at stuff nobody else was smiling at."

He didn't know "Sam Stone" would be about a Vietnam veteran when he began writing it. "I just knew I liked the chorus and the image of a hole in daddy's arm," he told *Performing Songwriter.* He wrote "Paradise" for his father: "Paradise was a real place in Kentucky, and while I was away in the army in Germany, my father sent me a newspaper article telling how the coal company had bought the place out. It was a real Disney-looking town. It sat on a river, had two general stores, and there was one black man in town, Bubby Short, who looked like Uncle Remus and hung out with my Granddaddy Ham, my mom's dad, all day, fishing for catfish. Then the bulldozers came in and wiped it all off the map. When I recorded the song, I brought a tape of the record home to my dad, I had to borrow a reel-to-reel machine to play it for him. When the song came on, he went into the next room and sat in the dark while it was on. I asked him why and he said he wanted to pretend it was on the jukebox."

Prine became known as a songwriter's songwriter. Bob Dylan got an advance copy of *John Prine* and liked it. He later played harmonica and sang harmony with Prine at a 1972 concert at the Bitter End.

The predictions of overnight stardom proved a trifle optimistic. There was nothing wrong with his output— the four albums he recorded on Atlantic from 1971 through 1975 [*John Prine, Diamonds in the Rough* (1972), *Sweet Revenge* (1973), and *Common Sense* (1975)] were among the high points of folk music in the 1970s. They included such compositions as "Far from Me," "Six O'Clock News," "Grandpa Was a Carpenter," and "Christmas in Prison." But folk music in those years was a minority art form, and while the albums sold reasonably well they didn't storm top-chart levels. Prine became accustomed to a slow, steady upward struggle. As he noted, "I'm surprised I'm in one piece; there's a thin line between *Billboard* and Bellevue."

He recorded "Dear Abby" live for his third album, *Sweet Revenge.* Prine got the idea when he was in Rome with his first wife. He bought a copy of the *International Herald Tribune* and found that Dear Abby's column provided the only relief in the newspaper. His first three albums were produced by Arif Mardin. For his fourth LP, he switched to producer Steve Cropper of Booker T. and the MG's for *Common Sense,* a modestly

successful album that was too daring at the time for his fans.

Reflecting on those early years, Prine says he was not at all disappointed. "I've read things where, like, 'He must have been really discouraged and really pissed off not being a star' and that couldn't have been further from it," he states. "I think I was just feeling pretty cocky by that time in my career. A lot had happened in three years' time. At that time, I was rolling and the press that those records were getting was usually so great. I was just starting to realize that not everybody is afforded that."

After the retrospective *Prime Prine* came out in 1976 (gold by the '90s), it looked as though Prine was backing off a bit. He did some shows, but for a long period no new records appeared. Meanwhile, he had, in effect, moved sideways, switching from Atlantic to another part of the Warner conglomerate, Elektra/Asylum. The move made practical sense since Atlantic's product, for the most part, leaned toward up-tempo rock and soul while Elektra's roster had Linda Ronstadt, Jackson Browne, and Judy Collins.

In the summer of 1977, Prine had a false start, recording a rockabilly style album with songwriter-producer Jack Clements which was never released. He brought Steve Goodman in to salvage the project. In midsummer 1978, John's first Elektra album, *Bruised Orange,* proved to be a gem. The title song is reminiscent of Kristofferson in his salad days but with lyrics that are more cerebral. *(For a heart wrapped in anger grows weak and grows bitter / You become your own prisoner as you watch yourself sit there / Wrapped up in a trap of your very own chain of sorrow).* There were some hints of rock in the ballad cowritten with Phil Spector, "If You Don't Want My Love," but the other tracks, such as "Fish and Whistle," "That's the Way That the World Goes 'Round," the offbeat "Sabu Visits the Twin Cities Alone" and "Crooked Piece of Time," remained in the folk-country domain. While hardly setting any sales records, the LP did gain the national charts for a number of months, a step forward compared to earlier releases. Prine's following was small but growing, as indicated by the capacity crowds at the clubs he played during his concert tour. *Bruised Orange* won plaudits from critics, and *Time* cited it as one of the ten best albums of 1978.

John's next LP, *Pink Cadillac* (1979), was recorded at Sam Phillips Studios in Memphis and had a stronger rock flavor than previous collections. *New York Times* reviewer Robert Palmer was one of the few who liked the album, exclaiming that it "embodied the most authentic honky-tonk ambiance in a new record in at least twenty years." Prine toned things down again on his third Elektra LP, *Storm Windows* (1980), which covered a spectrum from rock ("Shop Talk," "Just Wanna Be With You") to ballads ("Storm Windows," "One Red Rose") to country ("It's Happening to You"). Despite the excellent content of those albums and continued critical praise, Prine, whose style never suited the pop or country radio stations in the late '70s, still could not find a mass following, with the result that his contract with Elektra/Asylum expired in 1981.

Prine had reached the point where he couldn't stand being in the same elevator with the record executives. "I was wondering where the fun was with the music, this thing that I took on as a hobby years earlier that I used to get so much out of long before I ever sang a song for anybody else except myself. . . . If it meant the only way I could enjoy taking the guitar down off the wall and sitting around playing it was to not be a recording artist, then I was wanting to do that."

He moved to Nashville in 1980 and began cowriting songs with Roger Cook, one of which, "Love Is on a Roll," hit number one on the country charts for Don Williams. (In 1998, Prine and Cook had another number one country hit with "I Just Want to Dance with You," performed by George Strait.) The song received a Country Music Award nomination. Prine also authored songs with John Mellencamp, including "Jackie O," recorded by Mellancamp on his 1983 LP, *Uh Huh*.

Rather than sign with a major, Prine formed his own label, Oh Boy Records, in 1981 with manager Al Bunetta and associate Dan Einstein. Prine credits the move with saving his career. He recaptured the creative freedom he sorely missed. The break-even point for a small label meant that he could make a profit by selling his albums at concerts or through the mail. "If an artist is dropped from a label, it doesn't mean the audience disappears," Einstein told *Investor's Daily* in 1986. "It's a matter of alerting the public there are Prine albums available." His first release came out in late '83: a red vinyl Christmas single "I Saw Mommy Kissing Santa Claus" backed with "Silver Bells."

Prine's 1984 release, *Aimless Love,* produced with Jim Rooney, took two and a half years to complete and had a strong acoustic folk-country flavor. One indication of his emotional state at the time is the album title and the picture on the back of the LP of Prine reading *True Love* magazine. One standout track, "Unwed Fathers," was written with Bobby Braddock and later recorded by Tammy Wynette. The song is about a pregnant and abandoned Appalachian woman: *From a teenage lover to an unwed mother / Kept undercover like some bad dream.*

On September 20, 1984, Prine's pal Steve Goodman succumbed to his sixteen-year battle with leukemia. "You'd think you'd be halfway prepared for it when it came. But he might as well have gotten hit by a train. . . . I miss him now just as much as I did back then," Prine told David Fricke for the liner notes of his 1993 Rhino retrospective *Great Days: The John Prine Anthology.* Prine led a strong cast at a tribute for Goodman on January 26, 1985, including Arlo Guthrie, John Hartford, Michael Smith, and Bonnie Koloc. The tribute album came out on Goodman's Red Pajamas Records in 1985. Prine sang "Souvenirs," a song he had often performed with Goodman; "Angel from Montgomery" with Bonnie Raitt and David Bromberg; "My Old Man," a heart-wrenching Goodman song; and "Please Don't Bury Me."

His next release, *German Afternoons,* recorded in two weeks on a budget of $30,000, came out in 1986. The album, nominated for a Best Contemporary Folk Grammy, opens with a Carter Family song, "Lulu Walls," and ends with an old-timey rendition of "Paradise." But the enduring track is "Speed of the Sound of Loneliness," a poignant song of alienation following a failed romance. Despite the Grammy nomination, it would be the last original release for several years except for the 1987 green vinyl novelty single, "Let's Talk Dirty in Hawaiian" backed with "Kokomo."

Prine toured extensively, releasing a double LP *John Prine Live* in 1988, taped mostly during three concerts at the Coach House in San Juan Capistrano, California. The album sold more than 75,000 copies. After nearly two decades in the business he still hadn't had a best-selling album (although his independent releases routinely sold more than 50,000 copies). That would soon change. He had hoped to scale back a bit, but fate wouldn't let that happen. "I wanted to make one really good record, then not make one for a while," Prine told Michael McCall of *Nashville Scene* (June 29, 1995). Bassist Howie Epstein of Tom Petty and the Heartbreakers had just produced a successful album for Carlene Carter in 1990, *I Fell in Love.* Prine invited Epstein into the recording studio for two or three days. It turned into a nine-month, $100,000 project that resulted in *The Missing Years,* issued in September 1991. "Howie and me, we'd argue about the most minute things, until we got what we wanted," Prine says.

The album title was taken from Prine's "Jesus the Missing Years," a tongue-in-cheek song in which he imagines what happened during the lost, unrecorded years of Christ. It also includes "All the Best" and "The Sins of Memphisto," a song that juxtaposes Memphis and Mephistopheles. The album featured Bonnie Raitt, Tom Petty, David Lindley, and Bruce Springsteen. For the first time in his career, Prine had a hit, not to mention strong airplay for his video of "Picture Show." The album sold over 400,000 copies and this time won the Grammy for Best Contemporary Folk album. Prine attributes the album's success to the sound, production, "and a good bit of luck."

By the early '90s Prine had finally shaken the "new Dylan" comparison, although he still cited Dylan as an influence. In 1993, Rhino released an excellent retrospective collection, *Great Days: The John Prine Anthology,* which spans Prine's career from 1971 to *The Missing Years.* The album compiles Prine's most enduring songs, from "Sam Stone" and "Hello in There" to "The Sins of Memphisto."

Prine's songs were featured by other artists as well. Nanci Griffith recorded "Speed of the Sound of Loneliness" for *Other Voices, Other Rooms,* which came out in 1993. Prine also sang as part of the ensemble for the version of "Wimoweh" (which means "the lion is sleeping") along with Odetta, Leo Kottke, John Gorka, and John Hartford. He sang backup on a Harlan Howard/ Tompall Glaser song, "The Streets of Baltimore," for Griffith's 1998 follow-up, *Other Voices, Too.* A version of the song "If You Were the Woman and I Was the Man," which Prine recorded with Margo Timmins of the Cowboy Junkies, appeared on the *Dead Man Walking* soundtrack in 1995.

Prine returned to the studio with Epstein in November 1992 to produce his next solo album, *Lost Dogs + Mixed Blessings,* but the new work didn't come out until 1995. Prine is notorious for taking a long time between albums. "If you asked me to go across the street and get a hot dog, I'd leave the most important song I was ever writing, I'd just leave it floating," he told *Performing Songwriter.*

The album, with more of a rock edge, sold more than 300,000 copies, received some radio and video airplay ("Ain't Hurtin' Nobody" was number one on Country Music Television in the U.K.) and was nominated for a Best Contemporary Folk Grammy. It's another quirky Prine album with songs like "Humidity Built the Snowman," "Quit Hollerin' at Me," and "Big Fat Love." The title came from a newspaper story calling a camp where Cuban refugees were held "a mixture of lost dogs and mixed blessings."

Marianne Faithfull, who listened to Prine's "All the Best" as she was writing her autobiography (especially the sections about Mick Jagger), provides backup on "This Love Is Real." A strong cut is "Lake Marie," which starts out with memories of first love on the shores of the small lake on the Wisconsin-Illinois border and somehow segues into news of a double homicide. Prine sings: *Saw it on the news / The TV news / In a black and white video / Do you know what blood looks like / In a black and white video?*

In June 1995, he embarked on an extensive tour in support of *Lost Dogs.* He followed with his second live album, *Live on Tour,* in 1997. A collection of some of his old and new concert standards, the album garnered another Grammy nomination but the award went to Bob Dylan's *Time out of Mind.*

In his late forties, Prine settled into being a dad for the first time. He and third wife Fiona Whelan had two children, Jack and Tommy, which turned his life around. "I certainly had enough time to do whatever I wanted to do," Prine told McCall. "I was married twice before, and I guess we were just young and selfish. . . . I always knew I wanted a kid. But I had no idea I'd enjoy having a kid this much." (Around that time Prine also underwent radiation for squamous-cell carcinoma.)

Fatherhood provided a break from the slow process of songwriting. As Prine said: "Writing is about a blank piece of paper and leaving out what's not supposed to be there." In 1992, he appeared in a feature film, *Falling from Grace,* written and directed by John Mellencamp. He played Billy Bob Thornton's brother in a movie called *Daddy and Them,* which includes an original song by Prine called "In Spite of Ourselves." That provided the name for an album of country covers in 1999, featuring duets with Emmylou Harris, Dolores Keane, Patty Loveless, Lucinda Williams, Iris DeMent, and country stars Melba Montgomery and Connie Smith. The album, produced by Jim Rooney, was nominated for a Contemporary Folk Grammy.

Written with the assistance of Dan Einstein of Oh Boy Records

PROFESSOR LONGHAIR: *Pianist, singer, whistler, songwriter, guitarist, dancer. Born Bogalusa, Louisiana, December 19, 1918; died New Orleans, January 30, 1980.*

Some have called pianist Professor Longhair, born Henry Roeland Byrd, the first rock 'n' roller. Although that is debatable, Fess, as many called him, was certainly an innovator. His rhumba, calypso, and country-blues-influenced "rhumba-boogie" sound blended in New Orleans rhythm & blues, which led to rock. His songs "Tipitina" and "Go to the Mardi Gras" are classics, the latter the Mardi Gras theme song in the Crescent City. He influenced a long line of pianists, each of whom has had his own impact on R&B and rock—Dr. John, Art Neville, James Booker, Huey "Piano" Smith, Fats Domino, and Allen Toussaint, who called him the "Bach of Rock." But his contribution wasn't fully recognized until after his death. He was inducted into the Blues Hall of Fame on November 16, 1981, and the Rock and Roll Hall of Fame on January 15, 1992.

Both of his parents were musicians. He was born in Bogalusa to James Lucius and Ella Mae Byrd. (His paternal grandfather, Americus Byrd, was a slave in Alabama.) But when he was just a couple of months old his parents split and he moved with his mother to New Orleans. He learned music and other lessons on the streets. He worked briefly as a stuntman for the CJK Medicine Show in the mid-1920s. In the tradition of Bill "Bojangles" Robinson, young Henry sang and danced on the streets of New Orleans for tips, learning acrobatic moves from childhood friends Streamline Isaac and Harrison Hike. "The very first instrument I played was the bottom of my feet, workin' out rhythms, tap dancing," Professor Longhair told Tad Jones and Mindy Giles, who wrote liner notes for his *Crawfish Fiesta* album. "We used to dance all up and down Bourbon Street."

He danced in front of such taverns as the Caldonia Inn and the Dew Drop Inn and heard the barrelhouse pianists: Kid Stormy Weather, Sullivan Rock, Robert Bertram, and his mentor, Isidore "Tuts" Washington. He is said to have started playing on an abandoned upright piano that was missing some keys which might have contributed to his unique style. Essentially, he played Caribbean-tinged boogie-woogie in his left hand and intricate, embellished sounds with his right hand, along with the kind of African polyrhythms commonly heard in the "second-line" at New Orleans funerals. "This isn't on sheet music," he told Peter Brown shortly before his death, "You have to remember it." (The interview was published in *Welcoma* on December 8, 1993).

He created a gumbo out of the jumble of rhythms that he heard. "I used to take all these things and put 'em in one big bag and shake 'em up and make a gumbo out of 'em," he said.

Fess sang whimsical, seemingly nonsensical lyrics in a crooning, playful voice. In his offbeat song about a bald woman, he shouted, *Looka here, she ain't got no hair,* while the rest of the band responded in unison: *Bald head.* In later songs, he threw in a nursery rhyme. Sometimes he opted for a reedy whistle instead of his voice.

Longhair lived an often-harsh existence. As he told Timothy White of *Rolling Stone,* he took up prizefighting in his mid-teens to get by. He lost his two front teeth in a bout with an older man. Afterward, Longhair told White, he beat up the man with a metal pipe in an alleyway. "I was just a boy and he took advantage," Longhair explained (*Rolling Stone,* March 20, 1980).

He played guitar and piano at parties and danced at the local clubs in the early 1930s. For a time in 1937 he formed a dance team with Redd Foxx and Champion Jack Dupree, performing at the Cotton Club in New Orleans, until Foxx and Dupree moved on. In 1937, he joined the WPA's Civilian Conservation Corps, repairing roads, sewers, and bridges. He took to the piano when he realized he could get out of the hard labor and drills by entertaining workers at the recreation hall.

When he returned home, he found more profitable pursuits than music: as a cook and boxer, but mostly as a gambler from 1937 to 1942. He was in the army from 1942 to 1943. In the next few years he began his musical career, forming a combo that played club dates in New Orleans. In 1947 he got his famous sobriquet, Professor Longhair. He sat in for Dave Bartholomew's keyboardist, Salvadore Doucette, at the Caldonia Inn. Mike Tessitore, the club manager, wound up firing Bartholomew and hiring Byrd.

He told John Broven, according to the liner notes for Rhino Records' *Rum and Coke:* "We had Big Slick on drums, Apeman Black on sax, and Walter Nelson on guitar. We had long hair in those days and it was almost against the law. Mike said, 'I'm going to keep this band—we'll call you Professor Longhair and the Four Hairs Combo.'" Professor was a nickname given to pianists who played in the bordellos. He became one of the most popular acts in New Orleans.

In 1949 Fess cut his first records with the Star Talent label, based in Dallas. Star Talent released his first two 78s in November 1949, "Mardi Gras in New Orleans" and "She Ain't Go No Hair." He recorded for Mercury in August and September of that year. His song "Bald Head," a rerecording of "She Ain't Got No Hair" cut as Roy Byrd and the Blues Jumpers, climbed to number five on the *Billboard* R&B charts in 1950. Using the name Professor Longhair, he moved on to Atlantic and recorded "Tipitina," one of his standards, "In the Night," "Hey Now Baby," and "Walk Your Blues Away." He cut records on Federal from 1950 to 1954 and six sides for Ebb in 1957. (During this time, for some unexplained reason, Professor Longhair was barred from performing in the New Orleans clubs and returned to his second profession as a card sharp.) Despite that, in 1959 he made "Go to the Mardi Gras" for Ron Records, that became the standard played each year in New Orleans. Besides his piano playing he was known for his flamboyant costumes—such as tuxedos, red gloves and feathers—and "his habit of kicking the beat on the front of the piano until the instrument splintered," according to the *Crawfish Fiesta* liner notes.

He recorded under such names as Roy "Bald Head" Byrd, Professor Longhair and His Blues Scholars, and Professor Longhair and His Shuffling Hungarians. As he joked to Jones and Giles: "I had one Hindu in the band, but there weren't no Hungarians." He recorded for Rip Records in the early 1960s. Rip folded in 1964 and Longhair, in poor health, was ready to quit the music business. Before he went into retirement he recorded three singles for Watch Records, including "Big Chief," and returned to making a living as a card hustler and pushing a broom at a record store called the One-Stop.

He was sweeping floors when Quint Davis and Allison Minor, who had spent a year looking for him, tracked him down. He reunited the original Four Hairs Combo for the New Orleans Jazz and Heritage Festival in 1971 and created a sensation, reestablishing his reputation as one of the pioneers of R&B piano. He became one of the biggest draws at the festival every year until his death.

Davis spearheaded Longhair's return to the studio. In September 1971, Longhair recorded in Baton Rouge for the first time since the early 1960s. He played with blind guitarist Snooks Eaglin, drummer Shiba, and bassist Will Harvey. He returned to the studio in June 1972, this time in Memphis's Ardent Studios. The backup musicians included Eaglin, drummer Joseph "Zigaboo" Modeliste, George Davis on bass, and a horn section. The sessions, produced by Davis, were released years after his death. Rounder Records issued *Houseparty, New Orleans Style* in 1987 which garnered a Grammy for Best Traditional Blues Album. Rhino released *Mardi Gras in Baton Rouge* in 1992.

After resurfacing at the New Orleans Jazz and Heritage Festival, Longhair was suddenly in demand again.

He resumed playing in the New Orleans clubs. In 1971 he appeared on a show with Dr. John that aired on PBS and again in 1974 as part of *Dr. John's New Orleans Swamp Show,* which also featured Earl King and the Meters. He played the Festival of American Folklife in Washington, D.C. In 1973 he toured throughout Europe as part of the Night in New Orleans group, including a performance as a headliner at the Montreux Jazz Festival in Switzerland. He performed at the Newport Jazz Festival in 1973, Philadelphia Folk Festival in 1975, Monterey Jazz Festival in 1977, and in London in 1978, which led to the release of *The London Concert,* on the JSP label.

In 1974 Professor Longhair returned to the studio once again. This time he recorded in his birthplace, Bogalusa, with Clarence "Gatemouth" Brown on guitar for the Blue Star label. The album, *Rock 'N' Roll Gumbo,* was remixed and reissued on the Dancing Cat label and is considered one of his best, with Brown's guitar work complementing Longhair's driving piano stylings.

The following year, Paul and Linda McCartney flew Professor Longhair to Los Angeles to play at a private party on the *Queen Mary.* They produced a live album that was released a year later.

On February 3 and 4, 1978, Longhair performed at Tipitina's in New Orleans, the club named after his song. He played with Alfred "Uganda" Roberts on congas, George Davis on bass, David Lee on drums, "Big Will" Harvey on guitar, Tony Dagradi on soprano and tenor sax, and Andy Kaslow on trumpet. The sessions were released in 1982 by Atlantic on a double album called *The Last Mardi Gras,* and in 1993 Rhino released *Big Chief* and *Rum and Coke.* That year, Rhino also released *Fess: The Professor Longhair Anthology,* a two-disc retrospective of his music from 1949 to 1980.

In November 1979 he recorded for Alligator at the Sea-Saint Studios in New Orleans. The album, called *Crawfish Fiesta,* included Dr. John on guitar, Alfred "Uganda" Roberts on congas, David Lee Watson on bass, John Vidacovich on drums, Tony Dagradi, Andy Kaslow, and Jim Moore on saxophones. "He reigned supreme from the piano bench, pounding out funky licks, rocking in his seat, crooning like a seductive lounge singer, then breaking into his trademark yodel like an adolescent boy whose voice is changing," wrote Jones and Giles in the liner notes. "And every song was propelled by the second line beat." Unfortunately, that album was not released until after his death.

As 1980 approached, the Professor was getting ready to play a documentary with pianists "Tuts" Washington and Allen Toussaint. In one of the rehearsals just a few weeks before his death, he played "Boogie Woogie" with the other two, a session that was caught on video; it was released on PBS in 1984 and called *Piano Players Rarely Ever Play Together.* The rehearsal number, later released on Rhino's *Fess: The Professor Longhair Anthology,* was one of his last recorded sessions.

In November 1979, Professor Longhair agreed to an interview-performance session with Canadian radio producer Keef Whiting at Ultrasonic Studios in New Orleans. The resulting tape was never broadcast due to union regulations and sat on a shelf until Holger Petersen of Canada's Stony Plains Records released it as a CD in July 1996. *Fess' Gumbo* includes piano solos of some of his most famous numbers interspersed with interviews. In 1996, Rounder also released *Collector's Choice,* a reissue of some of his 45s from the late 1950s and early 1960s.

The Professor died in his sleep of a massive coronary at 3:00 A.M in early 1980. "Trembling in his sleep, he gagged, spat out a gold front tooth and then lay still," Timothy White wrote. "Alice, his wife of forty years, was at his side, begging him to wake up."

A thousand mourners, mostly friends and neighbors, turned up for the slow traditional funeral procession to the Mount Olivet Cemetery on a cold and gray morning. An American flag was draped over his coffin, a nod to his status as an army veteran and a member of the local Civil Defense Special Force. Trumpeters from a brass band played him into his powder-blue hearse. Afterwards, his family served a dinner of corn bread, fried chicken, ham hocks, red beans, and rice at their home.

In life, he never made much from his music. He made $32,000 in 1978—and that was one of his most profitable years. Even though 15,000 copies of *Mardi Gras in New Orleans* are sold each year, he never received any royalties, according to an article in the *Toledo Blade* (March 2, 1994).

For years after his death, record companies continued to earn money from the Professor's records. In 1993 six of his heirs formed a corporation called Song-Byrd to recapture Professor Longhair's legacy and royalties. In just five years, according to an article in the *Minneapolis Star Tribune* ("Longhair's Heirs Lead Effort to Win Musicians Their Dues," November 26, 1998), his publishing and artist royalties brought in nearly $1 million. SongByrd was involved in the production of *Fess: The Professor Longhair Anthology*; the Stony Plains project; and *Byrd Lives!,* a double CD taken from several concerts in 1978 and released by Nighttrain/Tuff City Records in 1998.

His legacy lives on in New Orleans, along with those of Louis Armstrong, Jelly Roll Morton, and Fats Domino. At Tipitina's, behind the stage is a painting of Fess looking down on all the performers, encouraging and daring them to play well as he did.

PROFFITT, FRANK: *Singer, guitarist, banjoist, songwriter, instrument maker. Born Laurel Bloomery, Tennessee, 1913; died Vilas, North Carolina, November 24, 1965.*

Except to folk-music experts, the name Frank Proffitt doesn't mean much these days. However, the song he belatedly received credit for writing, "Tom Dooley," is an acknowledged folk classic. In addition to that, Proffitt was an important link in the chain that has preserved many traditional hill-country songs for today's and future generations.

The Proffitt family moved to the Cracker Neck sections of the eastern Tennessee mountains from Wilkes County, North Carolina, just after the Civil War. When Frank was a boy, his family moved to Reese, North Carolina, a few miles below the Tennessee border. There his father, Wiley Proffitt, earned a living as a farmer, cooper and tinker.

Young Frank grew up in an atmosphere of what is now called folk music, where songs that were the forerunners of modern country music and today's "traditional" folk music provided one of the few forms of relaxation. His father, his Aunt Nancy Prather, and his Uncle Noah often sang old songs of the hills. Frank's father also made banjos and passed some of his skills along to his son. As Proffitt told the collecting team of Anne and Frank Warner (Sing Out! October-November 1963, p. 7):

"As a boy I recall going along with Dad to the woods to get the lumber for banjo-making. He selected a tree by its appearance and sounding . . . hitting a tree with a hammer or ax broadsided to tell by the sound if it's straight grained. . . . When the strings were put on and the pegs turned and musical notes began to fill the cabin, I looked on my father as the greatest man on earth for creating such a wonderful thing out of a piece of wood, a greasy skin, and some strings."

Young Frank managed to finish sixth grade in the rural school before he had to devote all his hours to the farm. He continued his deep interest in music and spent most of his few free hours singing or listening to songs. As he grew older, he took more and more part in local gatherings, trading songs with others from the region and playing the banjo. In 1922, still a young boy, he had gotten his first store-bought instrument when he gathered enough premiums from selling goods of the Lee Manufacturing Company to trade them for a guitar.

He also was learning how to make his own instruments from his father and later in life became an expert at the craft. In fact, as time went by, he became as noted in the region for his instrument making as for his performing skills. He was particularly admired by the folklorists, who eventually sought him out for his ability in playing the fretless banjo he built for himself.

In 1932, he married Bessie Hicks, daughter of another musical family in the area, and moved to his own farm in Pork Britches Valley. The years passed much as they had before. The Proffitts raised a family of their own and farmed, and Frank played and sang whenever he could. A turning point occurred in 1938 when the Warners met Frank's in-laws while passing through the hill country seeking folk material. Nathan Hicks, in turn, introduced them to Frank. In the next few years, the Warners returned to record 120 of Frank's folk

songs. One of those was a ballad about a tragedy involving the local people, Tom Dula and Laurie Foster. Other songs bore such titles as "Dan Doo" and "Moonshine."

The Warners, who performed as well, included "Tom Dooley" in their repertoire for decades, always mentioning its origins in Proffitt's home in the Tennessee-North Carolina hills. They maintained contact with Frank in the years after World War II, sometimes visiting him to compare notes or collect new material. In 1952 they recorded "Tom Dooley" for Elektra. Then in 1958 the Kingston Trio came out with a single of "Tom Dooley," a song they learned from an Alan Lomax book. They believed it was traditional and thus in the public domain. At first nobody connected it with Proffitt, but that changed after a story about him came out in the Carolina Farmer in 1960. The revelation inspired a groundswell of support for Frank among folk-music people that eventually led to a lawsuit that established Proffitt's rights to authorship.

One result of the furor was an invitation for him to appear at the University of Chicago's First Folk Festival. His work proved one of the Festival highlights and other invitations poured in. Although Frank was uncomfortable being away from home for extended periods of time, he did travel to New York for some concerts and also appeared at the Country Dance Society's Folk Music Camp near Cape Cod, Massachusetts, in the early 1960s. He continued to do some live performances in the mid-1960s, including taking part in the traditional music portions of the Newport Folk Festival in Rhode Island in 1964 and 1965. His material was included in some of the Vanguard Records LPs of the festival.

Interest naturally arose in making new recordings for commercial release, and Sandy Paton took recording equipment to Proffitt's home to make tapes for Folkways Records. His first album, Frank Proffitt Sings Folk Songs came out at the start of the 1960s. His second LP, on Folk Legacy, titled Frank Proffitt, Trifling Woman, came out in 1962.

Although his name had become famous in many parts of the world besides the United States, Frank spent most of his time on his beloved tobacco farm in North Carolina. In late 1965, after driving his wife 115 miles to a hospital in Charlotte for a needed foot operation, he returned home in seeming good health. He finished his dinner, lay down on his bed, and died in his sleep on November 24. In 1966, folk artists dedicated a number of concerts to his memory. In 1969, Folk Legacy released A Memorial Album, from recordings he had made shortly before he died. He accompanies himself on guitar, dulcimer, and fretless banjo during his "final session."

By the start of the 1980s, he still had two albums in print, the original Folkways release and a Folk Legacy LP titled Reese, North Carolina, which contained Proffitt's version of "Tom Dooley." In 1974, Rounder Records released High Atmosphere: Ballads and Banjo Tunes from Virginia and North Carolina Collected by John Cohen in November of 1965, which included recordings by Proffitt, Wade Ward, E. C. Ball, and Gaither Carlton. His son, Frank Proffitt Jr., a singer, dulcimer and fretless banjo player, also recorded a collection of folk songs, including "Tom Dooley," on an album titled *Kickin' Up Dust*.

R

RAINEY, GERTRUDE "MA": *Singer, dancer, songwriter. Born Columbus, Georgia, April 26, 1886; died Columbus, Georgia, December 22, 1939.*

When most members of the public read about or attended the stage show of the late 1980s called *Ma Rainey's Black Bottom,* they probably thought the woman of the title was a mythical character. Blues aficionados, however, knew it was a real person who certainly deserved the reputation of being "Mother of the Blues." While forms of the blues certainly were sung before her time, it's generally agreed she was the first female singer to perform blues stylings as part of stage show events. The exact year she did that is open to question, but undoubtedly isn't too far off the 1902 date she herself claimed.

She was born Gertrude Pridgett in Columbus, Georgia, in 1886, daughter of parents who were active in minstrel shows for some period before the turn of the century. She was only fourteen when she made her stage debut as a singer-dancer in the talent show *A Bunch of Blackberries,* staged in her hometown during 1900. For years after that she was almost always involved in show business with various minstrel and vaudeville troupes that played the black theater and tent show circuit. At times she also performed alone at various saloons in the southern U.S. region.

For part of her early career, she teamed with dancer-singer William "Pa" Rainey, whom she married on February 2, 1904. The two toured under the professional names of Rainey and Rainey or "Ma and Pa Rainey, Assassinators of the Blues." Gertrude adopted the "Ma" designation even though she was still a teenager. Through the World War I years, together or separately, they were cast members of groups like the Moses Stokes Show, Fat Chappelle's Rabbit Foot Minstrels, Florida Cotton Blossom Show, Donald MacGregor's Carnival Show, and Tolliver's Circus and Musical Extravaganza Show. Bessie Smith worked with the Stokes troupe briefly in 1912 and also sang with the Rabbit Foot Minstrels in 1915, engagements where she reportedly received encouragement from Ma Rainey. Whether they were actually close friends or whether Smith simply took courage from Rainey's rapport with the blues audiences, there's no doubt that it had an influence on the younger artist's career.

Ma Rainey's portly figure, of course, contrasted sharply with Bessie Smith's more svelte appearance in her starring years. Her vocals had a rougher edge and more closely reflected the work chants of plantation crews. She certainly had the ability to get listeners heatedly involved in her music, as she demonstrated as the star of her own show in 1917–18: Madam Gertrude Rainey and Her Georgia Smart Sets. Though she became a favorite of black music fans throughout the South, she also built a reputation as a tough, hard-drinking individual who had a multitude of affairs with various men during her stage years. Piano player Jack Dupree is quoted as saying about her, "She was really a dreadful woman. But when she opened her mouth, she was fascinating, and she made you forget everything. What a character. She was such a great singer."

For a time in the early 1920s she retired from U.S. show business and lived in Mexico. After a few years away, she returned to her home area and inaugurated a new phase of her career that helped earn her place in the blues pantheon. The key to this newfound success was the brash new technology of recording. She signed with Paramount Records in 1923, and between then and 1928 she recorded over 100 songs in various studio sessions. When Paramount first signed her, it enthused in print: "Discovered at last—Mother of the Blues." The first numbers were recorded in Chicago and Illinois, with backing from the Lovie Austin Blues Serenaders. Later sessions were held in either Chicago or New York. On her last recordings, made in 1928, she was accompanied by barrelhouse pianist Georgia Tom Dorsey and guitarist Tampa Red.

Among her songs that were favorites with record buyers or concert audiences were "Ma Rainey's Black Bottom," "Jelly Bean Blues," "Lawd Send Me a Man Blues," "Bo' Weevil Blues," "Broken Hearted Blues," and "C.C. Rider." Those songs and others in her repertoire were covered by blues performers black and white in later years; "C.C. Rider" (slang for a good sexual partner) was a particular favorite that brought chart hits for both rock and R&B performers.

In the mid-1920s she was a headliner on the Theater Owners Booking Association (TOBA) circuit in the Midwest and South, backed on many dates by her own group, the Georgia Wild Cats Jazz Band. During 1927 she performed with her Louisiana Blackbirds Revue and the following year starred with Boisy De Legge and His Bandanna Girls. Through the end of the 1920s and into the early '30s, she continued intensive touring with her own show or with others, but the opportunities faded away as the depths of the Depression took hold. Looking back, she could recall not only many dazzling performances of her own, but also appearances with other legendary names in blues and jazz, including singer-cornetist Louis Armstrong, saxophonist Coleman Hawkins, pianists Fletcher Henderson and Lovie Austin, cornetist Tommy Ladnier, Papa Charlie Jackson, Jimmy O'Bryant, clarinetist Buster Bailey, and others.

In 1935 the Mother of the Blues (she was also known, at one time or another, as the Paramount Wild Cat and the Golden Necklace of the Blues) retired to her home-town of Columbus, Georgia. Despite her high living in her halcyon years, she had saved enough money to be comfortable and invested some of it in two theaters, one in Rome, Georgia, the other in Columbus. She lived quietly with her brother, a church deacon, Thomas Prid-gett, until she was felled by a fatal heart attack just be-fore Christmas 1939. She died in the local hospital.

Though her records were out of print for a time, the situation was reversed after World War II, when her out-put was reissued several times. Almost all of her catalog came out in the 1970s on either the Biograph or Mile-stone label. Those included, on Biograph, *Ma Rainey, Oh My Babe Blues* (1970), and *Queen of the Blues* (1972); and, on Milestone, *Blame It on the Blues, Down in the Basement,* and *The Immortal Ma Rainey* (1975). In later years, VJM Records reissued all of her work in *Ma Rainey: Complete Recordings in Chronological Order,* and in the late 1980s Yazoo Records came out with *Ma Rainey's Black Bottom.*

In 1981 a biography written by Sandra Lieb, *Mother of the Blues: A Study of Ma Rainey,* was published by the University of Massachusetts Press. The extensive influence of Rainey on much of the pop music of the century was recognized by her induction into the Blues Foundation Hall of Fame in 1983, followed by election to the Rock and Roll Hall of Fame in 1990.

RAITT, BONNIE: *Singer, guitarist, keyboard player, songwriter, band leader (Padlock), record producer. Born Burbank, California, November 8, 1949.*

When Bonnie Raitt's first albums came out in the early 1970s, it seemed evident that here was an artist destined for stardom. And, in fact, those discs' blend of folk, blues, and rock later made them cult classics. While they had little impact on the record-buying pub-lic, Bonnie told interviewers that it didn't bother her, her goal was to do quality work and perform the music she believed in and she really didn't like the idea of becom-ing a household name. As the years passed, she seemed to make some concessions to try to gain hit albums, but by the end of the '80s, without a recording contract, it seemed as though she would remain a low-profile artist. Then, at a time she really wasn't expecting anything dra-matic to occur, she started putting out albums on a dif-ferent label—records that soon made her one of the dominant figures in pop music of the 1990s.

The daughter of John Raitt, a very successful star of stage and screen musicals such as *Carousel* and *Pajama Game,* she was born in California and raised in New York and the Los Angeles area. As she told Robert Hilburn of the *Los Angeles Times* ("Not Fade Away," Calendar Sec-tion, March 20, 1994), her father's career bred in her an insecurity reflected in a number of her original songs, like the mid-'90s "Circle Dance." She commented,

"Childhood was where I got that first lesson about being afraid of people leaving . . . the fear of loving someone so much and that person always leaving. [My father] was a traveling musician. In fact, he is still out on the road. . . . As a child, I just remember how he wasn't home enough, and I didn't understand why at the time."

Her earliest attempts at performing, she recalled, in-volved singing some of the songs from her father's mu-sicals in school plays, but by her teens she found folk and blues more to her taste. She told Hilburn, "My brothers and I would go to this sort of progressive Quaker camp in the early '60s that had a lot of counselors from the East Coast colleges where a lot of interest in folk music and civil rights and the peace movement was all mushrooming.

"So that kind of tied music and politics together for me . . . Pete Seeger, Joan Baez, Odetta, Bob Dylan. Then I heard my first acoustic blues record and there was a whole new world . . . Mississippi John Hurt, Mis-sissippi Fred McDowell, John Lee Hooker, Muddy Wa-ters, Howlin' Wolf."

She received her first guitar at eight, took some piano, and by the time she was twelve she was becom-ing proficient on the guitar. As time went by, her inter-est in blues encouraged her to work on a slide guitar style that became a feature of her concerts and record-ings. Besides guitar, she also developed skills on key-boards, and a number of tracks on her future albums showcased her work on acoustic and electric piano and the organ. The year 1967 found Bonnie enrolled in Radcliffe college, in the Cambridge, Massachusetts, area, where she reveled in the folk and blues music per-formed at venues like Club 47. After a while she gained access to the folk club circuit, first in Boston, then in Philadelphia. By the start of the '70s she had gained a manager, Dick Waterman, who also handled blues artists like Mississippi Fred McDowell. Waterman arranged her professional New York debut as an open-ing act for McDowell at the Gaslight Club in Green-wich Village. From the latter she learned the basics of bottleneck slide guitar playing that, as one reviewer in the '90s commented, made her one of the most power-ful and expressive exponents of that style.

Engagements at Philadelphia's Main Point, the Philadelphia Folk Festival, and many concerts on the college circuit began to build a following among young music fans. Record company interest was whetted, and in 1971 she signed with Warner Brothers. Her debut album, *Bonnie Raitt,* recorded at Dave Ray's studio in Minnesota, was issued that year and proved a gem. The contents included covers of country, blues, and R&B numbers, and some original compositions by Bonnie, who was backed by people like Chicago bluesmen A. C. Reed and Junior Wells. The album won consider-able critical praise but was far from a best-seller. She followed with an equally excellent collection in 1972, *Give It Up,* featuring such notable blues or folk-flavored tracks as "Too Long at the Fair," Chris Smither's "Love Me Like a Man," and the Eric Kaz–Libby Titus composition "Love Has No Pride." Next came *Takin' My Time* in 1973; backing artists included Lowell George and Bill Payne of Little Feat, Van Dyke Parks, and John Hall. Favorite tracks with many fans were her treatment of Jackson Browne's "I Thought I Was a Child" and Randy Newman's "Guilty."

Her first three albums were all well received in the print media, and several writers included one or the other of them in their year's top 10, but despite that, they were not major successes. The rest of her releases on Warner Brothers in the '70s seemed watered-down compared to her initial collections, reflecting a record company push to get hit singles, and perhaps Bonnie's growing problems with alcohol abuse. The albums comprised *Streetlights* in 1974 (which included John Prine's "Angel from Montgomery"); *Home Plate* in '75, *Sweet Forgiveness* in '77, and *The Glow* in 1979. All of those had standout tracks but many employed slick, more commercially oriented arrangements than typically associated with Raitt's talents. For the last named, she worked with Peter Asher, whose production credits included preparation of hit albums for Linda Ronstadt and James Taylor. The association was not well received by many of her supporters.

She told Dennis Hunt of the *Los Angeles Times* ("Faces: In Charge of Her Career," Calendar Section, December 9, 1979), "I knew I'd catch hell for working with Peter. I know some of my fans are saying that I sold out. I don't feel I have to defend myself. I don't feel I made any artistic compromises. I can't stay at the same level like these fans want me to."

She added that her thinking about career goals had changed: "I want to be famous. I want a hit record. I want to make accessible records. I figured Peter could help me with that."

The Glow did a little better than some of her earlier releases, but the big economic breakthrough escaped her. This held true for her next Warner Brothers release, *Green Light,* in 1982. This was her last solo studio album to be completed for half a decade. In the interim she was actively involved in lending her support for a variety of causes, starting with the 1982 series of MUSE concerts protesting the arms race. For those performances she joined an array of stars that included Jackson Browne, Graham Nash, John Hall, Bruce Springsteen and the Doobie Brothers, which later formed the basis for a film and an album. This was followed by other benefit appearances by Bonnie, including more No Nukes concerts and fund-raisers for environmental causes.

She began work on some new recordings in late 1983, but after completing six tracks the project was put aside as Bonnie began a new series of dates with her band, Padlock, that extended over the next two years. In early 1986 she finally got the green light to finish the album, supported again by members of Little Feat. Is-

sued in June 1986, *Nine Lives* showcased some fine work by Bonnie that gave rise to hopes this might be an important career boost. She commented, "I have the funny feeling that popular music has caught up with me. I've been doing the same thing, singing the same kind of music, my whole career. It's what I love . . . that mix of R&B, rock and blues, whatever. It seems now that the barriers between black and white music are finally coming down. I knew that if I just kept at it long enough, it would be my time."

It turned out it wasn't quite her time yet. The album made no chart inroads, and soon after its release Warner Brothers dropped her from the label. But meanwhile Bonnie had decided to take some steps to regain control of her life, particularly by curbing her alcohol dependency. She entered a substance abuse program, joining Alcoholics Anonymous, and by the late 1980s was completely sober for the first time in years. Then she got the chance to sign with a new record company, Capitol. The first fruit of that alignment was the 1989 album *Nick of Time,* which suddenly caught fire with critics, radio programmers, and record buyers. With excellent tracks like the title song, "Cry on My Shoulder," and "Too Soon to Tell," it was a collection that ranked in feeling and style with her first classic releases. The album, produced by Don Was, quickly made the album charts on its way to multiplatinum status by 1990 and, as of the mid-'90s, achieved sales of over 4 million. Also gratifying for her was the considerable praise given by critics and fans to her two original songs on the album.

Recognition of her dramatic career comeback came in the voting for the 1989 Grammy Awards (presented on the globally televised TV awards show on February 21, 1990), which resulted in her winning four of the trophies: Album of the Year for *Nick of Time;* Best Pop Vocal Performance, Female, for the track "Nick of Time"; Best Rock Vocal Performance, Female, for the album; and Best Traditional Blues Recording for "I'm in the Mood," a duet with John Lee Hooker on his album *The Healer.* Though she continued to reward her longtime fans with shows at the small venues that had kept her career going during the period of struggle, she now was asked to play much larger rooms before crowds in the thousands to tens of thousands. This also gave her more opportunity to showcase the skills of many friends from the blues community, something she had done regularly in years past. With a new wave of interest in Raitt, Warner Brothers released *The Bonnie Raitt Collection* in 1990, a compilation of twenty songs from earlier albums such as "Love Me Like a Man," "Love Has No Pride," "Guilty," "Angel from Montgomery," and "Louise."

By the time her next studio album, *Luck of the Draw,* came out in 1991, Bonnie had posted another milestone in her life—her first marriage, to actor Michael O'-Keefe. She told Chris Willman for a *Los Angeles Times* article, "I'd lived with people since I was 18—really, the first time I was ever single was at 37—and suddenly I found I kind of liked being in my house by myself. I was newly sober and really wanted to establish a relationship with me.

"I wasn't looking to get involved—it was the last thing I wanted—but as they always say, 'When these things happen . . .'" She emphasized it hadn't been done on impulse. Michael's courtship lasted a year before they decided to wed. After that, they settled down in the house she'd owned in the Hollywood Hills since 1975.

The couple found they also were compatible creatively, cowriting the song "One Part Be My Lover" for the new album, one of four songs Bonnie wrote or cowrote on *Luck of the Draw*. The collection, which featured such other cuts as "Something to Talk About," "Tangled and Dark," and "I Can't Make You Love Me," proved her Capitol debut was not a one-shot event. If anything, the new album, which she coproduced with Don Was, was even more engaging than the previous one, and it quickly moved into the top 10 in *Billboard* on the way to sales of over 5 million by the mid-'90s. As Bonnie exulted during a second encore at the Universal Amphitheater, where she was joined onstage by John Prine and Jackson Browne, "Here's to middle age!" She and Prine sang a duet of his composition "Angel from Montgomery," which had been a feature of many of her shows from the mid-1970s on. In the Grammy Awards poll for 1991 (announced on the TV show of February 25, 1992), she scored three more victories: Best Pop Vocal Performance, Female, for the single "Something to Talk About"; Best Rock Vocal Performance, Solo, for the *Luck of the Draw* album; and Best Rock Performance by a Duo or Group with Vocal for the album track "Good Man, Good Woman," performed by Bonnie with Delbert McClinton.

While happy with the 1990s' turn of events, Bonnie told Chris Willman she still had some darker memories. For instance, she felt bitter at making what she felt was fine music that was being ignored. "I don't expect to be No. 1, but when record companies sank below the level of even being able to get records into the towns I was playing and making sure that the 100,000 or 200,000 people that wanted to buy my records got a chance to find them in the stores, I got pissed.

"But I was more bitter and angry about a lot of other things and personally just brokenhearted. What does *bitter* mean? I'm bitter every time Jackson Browne can't get airplay because his music is too political. I wish the Democratic Party had a decent candidate, I wish Ry Cooder was president of the airwaves.

"I wish blues people got appreciated while they were still alive. I mean, dream on; I've been like this since I was a kid. You'd have to be pretty naïve not to be realistic, having grown up with counterculture values in a culture that is mainstream."

In the mid-1990s Bonnie performed for appreciative audiences across the United States and around the world, including several more shows at which John Prine appeared, such as the Troubadours of Folk festival at UCLA's Drake Stadium in June 1993, which also featured such other stars as Arlo Guthrie and Joni Mitchell. She also made many TV appearances, including some spots with father John Raitt, with whom she also recorded duet material during those years. One of her mid-'90s concerts in San Francisco was taped for presentation on the Public Broadcasting System.

In early 1994 her third Capitol album came out, *Longing in Their Hearts,* whose title track was another collaboration between Bonnie and Michael O'Keefe. Reviewing the album in the *New York Times* ("Bonnie Raitt Takes a Journey into a Heart of Darkness," March 29, 1994), Ken Tucker commented that those who became acquainted with her work only through her first two Capitol albums "may not be prepared for the depth of emotion the new album draws upon. In some ways, this collection might be called 'Raitt's Revenge': After establishing a new peak of popularity, Ms. Raitt, 44, has returned with the sort of soulful, brooding album that used to consign her to mere cult status." Tracks that appealed to him, besides the title number, included "Storm Warning," Richard Thompson's "Dimming of the Day," and the reggae-flavored "Cool, Clear Water."

The album peaked at number one on the *Billboard* top 200 soon after release, and had gone past platinum sales levels by year's end. In the fall of 1995, Capitol issued a two-CD live set, *Road Tested,* drawn from six West Coast concerts during the summer of 1994. Among the cuts, besides solos, were duets with Jackson Browne, Bruce Hornsby, Kim Wilson from the Fabulous Thunderbirds, Bryan Adams, and R&B artists Charles and Ruth Brown. *Road Tested* received a Grammy nomination for Best Album. In 1996, Capitol released an enhanced CD, *Burning Down the House,* taking five songs from a live home video that included twenty-one songs. Raitt received a Grammy nomination for Best Female Vocal for the title track.

After taking a year off, in the spring of 1998 she released *Fundamental,* her first full album since 1994's *Longing in Their Hearts.* With new producers Mitchell Froom and Tchad Blake she attempts to strip away all pretension and falseness in sound and relationships with songs such as "The Fundamental Things," "Meet Me Halfway," and "Round & Round." Although the album received strong critical acclaim and sold well, it was nowhere near the levels of *Nick of Time* or *Luck of the Draw.* In mid-1998, Raitt joined the Lilith Fair tour, and later in the year her version of John Hiatt's "Lover's Will" was included in the sound track release from the movie *Playing by Heart.*

Raitt became active as a board member of the Rhythm and Blues Foundation in setting up a program to assist performers who were exploited by the record companies. (Atlantic's Ahmet Ertegun donated $1.5 million to the cause.) She also became the first woman to have her name on a Fender guitar. Raitt suggested that Fender create a program to donate guitars and provide lessons to inner-city children, primarily girls. By January 1999, 2,000 children had benefited from the program. "Hopefully . . . I'll get the word back from one of the programs that there'll be a new female Stevie Ray Vaughan ready to come on and cut heads with me," she told Bill Ritter and Kevin Newman of ABC's *Good Morning America* (May 19, 1998). "I'll bring her out, and she'll knock me off the lead guitar perch, which is my aim." In 1999 her marriage with O'Keefe ended in divorce. She was inducted into the Rock and Roll Hall of Fame in 2000.

RANKIN FAMILY, THE: *Vocal and instrumental group from Canada, all born Mabou, Cape Breton Island, Nova Scotia: Jimmy Rankin, born May 28, 1964 (vocals, guitar, percussion, songwriting); John Morris Rankin, born April 28, 1959 (vocals, fiddle, keyboards, songwriting), died January 16, 2000; Raylene Rankin, born September 15, 1960 (lead and backing vocals, percussion, step dancing); Cookie Rankin, born May 4, 1965 (lead and backing vocals, percussion, step dancing, songwriting); Heather Rankin, born October 24, 1967 (lead and backing vocals, percussion, step dancing).*

A Canadian entertainment phenomenon of the 1990s, the Rankin Family emerged from a remote section of Nova Scotia to become one of the brightest stars in that nation's musical firmament in half a decade's time. To the surprise of many in the music industry, the group's album blend of pop-folk, country, and traditional Celtic songs outperformed releases by the top-ranked Canadian, U.S., and U.K. artists in rock, rap, and Nashville-style country from 1989 to 1999. It was a matter of being in the right place at the right time, the band's primary songwriter, Jimmy Rankin, suggested. He told Brant Zwicker of the magazine *Acoustic Musician* ("The Rankin Family," December 1995), "There's so much music available out there now that people . . . just don't have rock 'n' roll to listen to, or blues. . . . So, I think that's probably part of it, and maybe people are—a lot of people wanna get back to things that are more acoustic, more simplistically based."

In the family's home area on the rugged west coast of Cape Breton Island in Nova Scotia's Inverness County, music was almost an everyday activity among local residents, most of whom had originally emigrated to Canada from Ireland or Scotland. Jimmy told Jack Hurst of the *Chicago Tribune* ("The Rankins Bring Canadian Stardom across the Border," April 30, 1995), there are similarities between their kind of music and traditional U.S. country music. "A lot of the music that the Scots and Irish brought over to Canada was [also] brought over to the Appalachians. Basically they're the same kind of cultures, only it developed into an even more distinct thing in the States. Certainly [American country music] is and always has been a heavy influ-

ence on [our country's] country scene. Where we're from, luckily, we're isolated enough that we've kept a lot of elements of our traditions that have influenced our music and style—although we do tend to meld other styles into our music making. There are elements in our music that may sound country, but I think the best title I've heard for our style is 'contemporary folk.'"

Enough children—twelve in all—were born to the Rankin parents (their father was a heavy machinery mechanic who played the fiddle, while their mother, who has a good voice, worked in a home for the "adult mentally challenged") to have started a full-scale marching band. Neither parent played professionally although both had a strong musical appreciation. While not all twelve children were part of an organized group at one time, over the years they interacted in various ways in different-sized musical formats.

Jimmy recalled, "People ask me why we do so many different [musical] styles. My answer is that growing up we always had a band together. We used to play on the weekends at dance halls and taverns, and we used to play traditional fiddle music for square dancing. We also played what we called 'round dance' music, which ranged from waltzes to rock 'n' roll—anything people would dance to."

All five members of the '90s band returned home from college in the late 1980s to carry on the Rankin musical tradition. Some of the progeny had included music courses in their studies, while one, Raylene, earned a law degree. At first, playing music was thought of as a part-time activity while everyone pursued other job opportunities. The quintet was following the typical family approach, performing at local pubs and special events like weddings, when a music production company based in Cape Breton asked them to join it for a tour series. Jimmy told Victor, "We were fairly well known in our home area of Nova Scotia. This company got us together to do a series of concerts across Nova Scotia and we got a lot of good responses. We decided to make a record that fall, and it snowballed from there."

Their debut album, *The Rankin Family*, which combined three originals with a group of traditional Scottish songs, came out on an independent label in 1989 and was followed two years later by another independent disc, *Fare Thee Well Love*. Some of the tracks from the albums gained Canadian airplay while the quintet began to extend its reputation outside Nova Scotia with appearances in small Canadian venues and some folk festivals in the United States. In those early days, the Rankins' technique of gaining radio coverage was to go to local stations and demand their recordings be played. Surprisingly, it worked in many cases, mainly on smaller local outlets, and people in many parts of Canada began to pay attention to some of the newcomers' work.

By the end of 1992 the two albums had amassed the very respectable sales totals of some 80,000 copies, which caused executives at the major label EMI Canada to offer the group a contract. The initial albums were reissued on the EMI Canada label and preparations started for the band's third album. (*Fare Thee Well Love* was issued in the United States by Liberty Records in 1992, but gained little support from the label and soon went out of print on Liberty.) Meanwhile, a single issued by EMI (Jimmy Rankin's "Orangedale Whistle," written to support restoration of an old Canadian Pacific Railroad station house in Cape Breton) made the Canadian top 10 and *Fare Thee Well Love* also became a Canadian best-seller, rising to number one on the pop charts and staying there a total of three weeks.

In 1993 the band's debut on EMI Canada, *North Country,* came out and quickly found rapport with not only Canadian audiences but record buyers in the United Kingdom, particularly in Ireland and Scotland. In a short period of time sales of the disc reached the multi-platinum level, a remarkable achievement in the relatively small Canadian market. (In Canada, the total required for platinum is 100,000.) Besides concert, radio, and TV appearances throughout Canada, the Rankins also conducted intensive engagements in England and Scotland during 1993–94. Their 1995 credits included headlining concerts at major cities throughout Australia and New Zealand as part of the prestigious Guinness Festival series.

During 1994 the group's acceptance by fans and musical peers alike was reflected in its dominance of the Juno Awards, the Canadian equivalent of the U.S. Grammys. They won the trophies for Group of the Year, Single of the Year (for Jimmy's composition "Fare Thee Well Love"), Country Group of the Year, and the People's Choice Award for Canadian Entertainer of the Year. They won the Entertainer award over such non-folk favorites as Celine Dion, Barenaked Ladies, and the Tragically Hip. The band extended its success streak into 1995 with release of the special limited-edition extended-play album *Grey Dusk of Eve,* featuring a striking title track arranged by Jimmy. EMI Canada had projected likely sales for that of around 25,000, but instead it rocketed past that to a total of 70,000 bought by Canadian and United Kingdom fans.

Coming into 1995, the Rankin Family hadn't focused much effort on the U.S. market. It did appear from time to time at U.S. venues, but didn't attempt extended tours. Cookie stressed that the Rankins wanted to have a U.S.-released collection available before taking the risks of incurring heavy expenses for a series that involved nine musicians—the five Rankins and a four-man backing group that included Howie MacDonald on fiddle, mandolin, and synthesizer; Ray Montford on guitars; John Chiasson on bass guitar; and Scott Ferguson on drums and percussion.

They decided that the right choice was Guardian Records, a firm connected with EMI with offices in New York and Nashville. The '95 release was titled *North Country,* but actually comprised a selection of songs from the band's second and third albums plus the EP title number. Geoffrey Hines of the *Washington Post* was one of many U.S. critics who loved the album: "Cookie Rankin sings the melancholy alto lead on the separation ballad, 'Border and Time'; Raylene lends her high soprano to the pastoral paean, 'Gillis Mountain'; and Heather belts out 'Fisherman's Son,' a sing-along tribute to Cape Breton's chief industry. All three sisters are standout lead singers and when they blend voices on the old Irish folk songs, 'My Nut Brown Maiden' and 'Tell My Ma,' they're overpowering. Fiddler-pianist John Morris Rankin is the family's instrumental whiz who leads the way on a medley of reels. The group's most crucial talent, though, is Jimmy Rankin, who has written some of the finest folk-pop songs of the '90s."

In support of the album, Guardian helped arrange a U.S. tour that included an appearance with bluegrass luminary Alison Krauss at Columbus, Ohio's, Capital Theater and several shows with Mary Black, one of which was held at New York's Town Hall in May. In keeping with the idea of making haste slowly, the concerts headlined by the Rankins typically were held in 500-seat halls.

Before working on their next album, intended for release in both Canada and the United States, family members decided they should seek out a new producer with strong credits. Raylene noted, "After *North Country,* we decided we really wanted to go for a change. We put out the feelers for different producers, looking for someone who had an affinity for what we do." The choice fell to John Jennings, who had produced some of Mary-Chapin Carpenter's best work. "Mary-Chapin also came from a folk background. So, we thought it might work for us."

The project culminated in the late 1995 Canadian release of the disc *Endless Seasons.* The backing musicians recruited by Jennings included Carpenter, who played rhythm guitar on the title track, and longtime bluegrass band and session musician Sam Bush, who played mandolin and mandocello. The final collection included traditional Irish folk songs like "As I Roved Out" and a Gaelic medley called "Oganaich An Or-Fhuilt Bhuidhe/Am Braighe," the latter arranged by the Rankins from tunes they heard in their home area. It also included some new songs by other members besides Jimmy. Raylene commented, "The nucleus of our material is always Jimmy and traditional tunes, although this time the album features a song from Cookie, 'The River,' and a pair from John Morris, 'Blue-Eyed Suzie' and 'Eyes of Margaret.'" Jimmy provided four new compositions, including the poignant "Your Boat's Lost at Sea," drawn from the press reports of the death of two Cape Breton brothers in a fishing boat tragedy.

By the time *Endless Season* was issued in the United States by Guardian on March 4, 1996, it already had passed platinum sales in Canada. The U.S. release was followed by a U.S. concert series that got under way in April.

In 1996, EMI released the retrospective *Rankin Family Collection.* The following year, the three female members of the group recorded a Christmas album, *Do You Hear . . . Christmas with Heather, Cookie, & Raylene Rankin,* issued by EMI. They picked up another Juno Award for Country Group of the Year in 1997. In 1998 the family released *Uprooted,* a collection of songs that had been recorded between October 1997 and March 1998. Now calling themselves the Rankins, the group dedicated the new album to the memory of their late parents, Kathleen and Alexander (Buddy) Rankin. The group disbanded in the summer of 1999 and was further shaken by the death of John Morris Rankin, whose car slid off the road in January 2000.

READER, EDDI: *Singer, songwriter, actress. Born Glasgow, Scotland, August 28, 1959.*

Many a headliner in pop music got his or her basic experience by doing session work or providing backing vocal or instrumental support for touring groups. Eddi Reader took that route, contributing to the success of a number of U.K. artists for over a half decade before moving to center stage herself in the mid-'80s.

Born in Scotland, Reader demonstrated considerable vocal ability at an early age before deciding to enter art school in her teens. While taking art courses, she performed at local folk and rock clubs and made contact with a number of young musicians coming to the fore in the U.K. pop-music scene of the 1970s. A particular hotbed for new performers was Leeds University, where a band called the Gang of Four began to be one of the standouts. Eddi got the chance to sing backing vocals for the group, which released a number of striking LPs at the end of the '70s and in the early '80s. Their U.S. credits in the '80s, issued by Warner Brothers, included such excellent albums as *Gang of Four* in 1980 and *Solid Gold* and *Another Day, Another Dollar* in 1981.

In 1983, Eddi moved to London, where she found session and tour work with still more up-and-coming performers, including the synth-pop duo the Eurythmics and Alison Moyet. Among the musicians she met in London was bass guitarist-songwriter Mark Nevin, with whom she began working on demos. One result was the chance to perform on two songs included in the Compact Organization's sampler album, *The Compact Composers.* Among their mid-1980s activities was to perform as part of the group Jane Aire and the Belvederes in 1985.

After that, the two organized their own folk-rock band, Fairground Attraction, which included Simm Edwards on guitarron and Roy Dodds on drums. The group began to attract notice as an opening act for some name

performers and as headliners in small venues in and around London. This led to a recording contract with RCA Records/UK whose initial fruits included the number one U.K. single "Perfect" in 1988. The title track for the 1988 album *First of a Million Kisses* and the album itself won U.K. awards for Best Single and Best Album of the Year. In 1989 the group completed work on a video for the single "Clare" in Nashville, Tennessee. The disc made English charts, and Nevin hoped the '90s would bring success with U.S. as well as U.K. audiences. However, plans had to be put on hold when Reader became pregnant. After giving birth, she rejoined the band for a series of concerts in 1991–92 in which the group added Graham Henderson on accordion and Roger Beaujolais on vibraphone.

Unfortunately, internal strains, coupled with the group's failure to grow a substantial following, resulted in its breakup in 1992. Reader accepted acting offers and also completed the solo album *Mirmama,* issued in 1992 on Compass Records. In the spring of 1993 she joined Clive Gregson (whose duo work with Christine Collister had ended the previous year) and Boo Hewerdine for a series of concerts throughout the United Kingdom during spring and summer months.

In 1994, Blanco y Negro and Reprise in the United States released *Eddi Reader,* which included songs she cowrote with Boo Hewerdine, Kirsty MacColl, Teddy Borowecki, and Mark Nevin. As she noted, the album came at a crossroads: "My relationship ended, my previous deal ended and there were two years of single parenthood in which I felt totally divorced from the world. The songs are sympathetic to how I was feeling, and hopefully will be sympathetic to others too."

She followed in 1996 with *Candyfloss and Medicine,* which came out on Blanco y Negro and Reprise in the United States in 1997. That year, she toured Britain and Europe with the Levellers, a group from Brighton, and Boo Hewerdine.

REAGON, BERNICE JOHNSON/REAGON, TOSHI/ SWEET HONEY IN THE ROCK: *All-female African American a cappella ensemble formed in November 1973. Since its inception, twenty-two women have been part of Sweet Honey in the Rock. Original members were: Bernice Johnson Reagon (vocalist, songwriter, activist, historian, artistic director), born Albany, Georgia, October 4, 1942; Carol Maillard, born Philadelphia, Pennsylvania, 1952; Louise Robinson; and Mie. Joining in 1979, Ysaye Maria Barnwell (vocalist, songwriter, assistant artistic director), born 1946. Joining in 1980, Shirley Childress Johnson, American Sign Language interpreter. Joining in 1981, Aisha Kahlil, born 1954. Joining in 1985, Nitanju Bolade Casel, born 1953. Members in 1999: Bernice Johnson Reagon, Maillard, Barnwell, Kahlil, Casel, Shirley Childress Johnson. Also producing and playing with Sweet Honey, Toshi Reagon (Bernice's daughter, solo artist,* *singer, producer, songwriter, guitarist, bassist, drummer, leader of Big Lovely, and member of Casslebery-Dupree group), born Atlanta, Georgia, January 27, 1964. Other members have included: Evelyn Maria Harris, Rosie Lee Hooks, Ayodele Harrington, Patricia Johnson, Ingrid Ellis, Dianaruthe Wharton, Tia Juana Starks, Yasmeen Williams, Laura Sharp, Tulani Jordan, Geraldine Hardin.*

The name Sweet Honey in the Rock comes from a spiritual Bernice Johnson Reagon heard as a child about a land so rich that honey flows from the rocks. Formed in November 1973, the group combines strength and sweetness. As Reagon wrote in the biography *We Who Believe in Freedom* (Anchor/ Doubleday, 1993): "From the beginning, the phrase—with sweetness and strength in it—resonated in a deeply personal way with me. As African Americans and as women, we have had to have the standing power of the rocks and the mountains. . . . If our world is warm, honey flows, and so do we; if it is cold, honey gets stiff and stays put, and so do we."

The women of Sweet Honey sing about racism, sexual and economic oppression, people with HIV, and freedom in a multitude of genres from spirituals and gospel to blues, rap, African, and jazz. Although they have recorded more than a dozen albums it is their live shows that move audiences. During the shows the six women, who accompany themselves only with shekeres or tambourines, connect with the audience. They do not have set lists but actually decide what they will sing from moment to moment. During a concert in Harare, Zimbabwe, in 1989, the women of Sweet Honey whispered together before each song; they were checking in and taking the audience's pulse before deciding what to do next.

Bernice Johnson was the third of eight children born to Beatrice, a housekeeper, and the Rev. Jessie Johnson, a carpenter who also was a pastor at four different Baptist churches, including Mt. Early Baptist Church. The church didn't have a piano until Bernice was eleven, which is one reason she was drawn to a cappella music. The first music she heard was in church and the harmonies of southwest Georgia. "I didn't even think of them as songs," she told Bill Moyers for his PBS show *Bill Moyers' Journal.* "I didn't think of them as things I needed to learn. They just came with the territory."

After graduating high school, she enrolled at Albany State College in 1959. She planned to study music but became an active participant in the civil rights movement, joining the youth chapter of the NAACP. She was suspended from college in 1962 for marching with the Student Non-Violent Coordinating Committee (SNCC). At meetings disrupted by local sheriffs she learned the power of song. "The only way to take the space back was by starting to sing," she said. "People would join in."

She was later jailed for two weeks. While in jail she and the other women sang together to lift their spirits. It was there that she met her husband-to-be, Cordell Hull

Reagon, a field secretary with SNCC. Cordell formed the Freedom Singers in late 1962 with Bernice, Rutha Mae Harris, and Charles Neblett; they drove around the country in a beat-up Buick station wagon to raise money for SNCC. The group performed at the Newport Folk Festival in 1963, singing "We Shall Overcome" with Bob Dylan, Joan Baez, and Pete Seeger. They performed at the March on Washington. "The civil rights movement is where I found song as a language," Reagon told Rochelle Jones of *People Weekly* ("Raising Her Voice," 1994). It's also where she learned the power of song to fight for social justice.

In January 1964 she had her first child, Toshi, and decided to leave the Freedom Singers. The following year she also had a son, Kwan Tauna. (During this period she managed to travel around with Guy Carawan putting together civil rights song leader conferences.) She self-produced her first solo album, *The Sound of Thunder,* in 1965, followed by other solo releases, including *River of Life.* In 1967 she and Cordell were divorced.

The following year, Bernice founded an all-black female group called the Harambee Singers (with Mattie Casey and Mary Ethel Jones) that performed songs about the black political struggle. In 1968 she enrolled at Spelman College to finish her undergraduate degree. Following her graduation, Bernice moved to Washington, D.C., in 1971 with her children and enrolled in a doctoral program in history at Howard University. She soon began working as a curator at the Smithsonian. She worked in the Division of Performing Arts/African Diaspora Project and published an article titled "African Diaspora Women: The Making of Cultural Workers."

During those years Bernice also began working as the vocal director at the Black Repertory Company in Washington, D.C. Sweet Honey in the Rock sprang from a workshop Reagon offered in the spring of 1973. She put up an announcement for a rehearsal for a new singing group and three women showed up: Carol Maillard, Mie, and Louise Robinson. "For some reason, we were the only three people who saw the sign," Carol Maillard told Audreen Buffalo of *Ms.* magazine ("Sweet Honey: A Cappella Activists," March–April 1993).

The first song Reagon taught them was "Sweet Honey in the Rock." It was a fortuitous and spiritual beginning. "So I started a song, they joined in and the chord was . . . tight!" Reagon told James Attlee of the *Weekly Journal* ("Sweet Spirits on the Rocks," October 28, 1993).

Over the next two years they performed at colleges and folk festivals across the country. In the spring of 1975 they were performing at a folk festival in Chicago when Bruce Kaplan of Flying Fish Records asked if they wanted to record an album. That resulted in the group's debut, *Sweet Honey in the Rock,* on Flying Fish the following year.

By May 1975 Reagon had completed her doctorate

in oral history at Howard. She continued to perform with Sweet Honey while pursuing her academic interests as a professor of history at American University and curator at the Smithsonian's National Museum of American History.

Sweet Honey has enjoyed the voices and *signing* of twenty-two women over the years. The only remaining original members as of 2000 were Reagon and Carol Maillard. Maillard grew up in Philadelphia in a home that was broken up by drugs. She started out at Catholic University on a violin scholarship but soon transferred to the drama department. It was while attending Catholic University that she saw the flyer for the tryout that resulted in Sweet Honey. "At the end of that rehearsal Bernice said, 'Well, I've got a gig coming up. Do you guys want to do it?'" she told *Ms.* magazine.

Maillard stayed with the group but left for a time to perform in plays on and off Broadway. She also recorded with Horace Silver on his Blue Note recording *Music of the Sphere.*

Ysaye Maria Barnwell joined in 1979. Her father played violin in a string quartet, and Barnwell studied classical violin as a child. When she was ten she met a Haitian girl who was deaf and decided to learn how to sign. She later pursued a doctorate in speech pathology, and a masters in public health administration. While "signing" at a local church she met Reagon who invited her to join the group. For a year, Barnwell sang and interpreted the concerts for the deaf. But then she realized there was no way one person could do both. She decided to sing.

In 1980 the group added Shirley Childress Johnson, who is fluent in American Sign Language. Shirley was born to deaf parents and learned sign language to communicate with them and others. She earned a bachelor's degree in deaf education and is considered a full member of Sweet Honey. "When I see deaf people touched, really enthralled at a Sweet Honey concert, I know we've connected," she told *Ms.* "That energizes me. . . . My first goal is to convey Sweet Honey's message in a way that reflects its tempo, passion, and melodious intent."

Aisha Kahlil joined the group in 1981, followed by her sister Nitanju Bolade Casel in 1985. Besides Sweet Honey they codirect First World Productions, which teaches music and dance in the Washington area. Both have studied African dance and bring that to their work with Sweet Honey. Kahlil brought a knowledge of jazz and an improvisational flair to the group and is considered the strongest blues singer. She released a CD, *In This Land* (Earthbeat!/ Warner Brothers), and the Contemporary A Cappella Society named her Best Soloist in 1994 for her performances of her songs "Fulani Chant" and "Wodaabe Nights." Casel studied dance in Dakar, Senegal, for four years and was awarded a grant from the D.C. Commission of Arts and Humanities to teach dance in the school system when she returned.

Although she has not been a regular member of Sweet Honey, Toshi is certainly an honorary member. As an infant her mother took her with her as she rehearsed and performed. Toshi often performs and produces for her mother and vice versa. She put together a collection called *Demonstrations* in 1985. Her debut, *Justice,* on Flying Fish in 1990, includes Bernice singing backup on a cover of Sting's "Walking in Your Footsteps." Toshi followed up in 1994 with *The Rejected Stone,* in 1997 with *Kindness* (Smithsonian/Folkways), and *The Righteous Ones* (Razor & Tie) in 1999.

Sweet Honey has received several honors, including Parent's Choice Awards for their children's albums and several Indie Awards: *We All . . . Every One of Us* (1983) and *Feel Something Drawing Me On* (1985) for best gospel albums, *The Other Side* (1985) and *Live At Carnegie Hall* (1988) for best women's music, and *All for Freedom* (1989) for best children's album. In 1989, Sweet Honey received a Grammy nomination for its song "State of Emergency," written by former member Evelyn Maria Harris, who was in the group for eighteen years; it was recorded on the 1988 album *Live at Carnegie Hall.* The group won a Grammy in 1991 for its participation in *A Vision Shared: A Tribute to Woody Guthrie and Leadbelly* (1989, Smithsonian/Folkways); they covered Leadbelly's "Grey Goose" and "Sylvie." That year Bernice Reagon also received a $285,000 MacArthur Award. She was honored a few years later with a presidential medal. Ken Burns set Sweet Honey's version of Sojourner Truth's tribute to the Colored Michigan Regiment to the tune of "John Brown's Body" for his documentary *The Civil War.*

While Sweet Honey maintained a full concert schedule, traveling throughout the United States and abroad, Reagon continued her academic pursuits. In 1992, Smithsonian Press published a book she edited about black gospel music titled *We'll Understand It Better By and By: Pioneering African American Gospel Composers.* Reagon interviewed many of the early gospel singers for the book. The following year, Anchor/Doubleday published a biography about Sweet Honey titled *We Who Believe in Freedom: Sweet Honey in the Rock, Still on the Journey* to celebrate its twentieth anniversary. In 1994 National Public Radio and Smithsonian cosponsored her twenty-six part radio documentary on the history of African American song titled *Wade in the Water: African American Sacred Music Traditions.* The latter was released as a four-CD set by Smithsonian/Folkways. She served as a consultant on a number of PBS documentaries about African American history, including *Eyes on the Prize, We Shall Overcome,* and *Roots of Resistance: A Story of the Underground Railroad.* In 1997, Smithsonian/Folkways released *Voices of the Civil Rights Movement: Black American Freedom Songs 1960–1966* (Smithsonian/ Folkways), a two-CD set of historical recordings from the civil rights movement. The following year, Rykodisc released the Reagon-produced sound track to the PBS series *Africans in America.*

In addition to their self-titled debut in 1976, Sweet Honey in the Rock has released the following CDs and LPs: *B'lieve I'll Run On* (Redwood, 1978); the live *Good News* (Flying Fish, 1981); *We All . . . Everyone of Us* (Flying Fish, 1983); *Feeling Something Drawing Me On* (Flying Fish, 1985); *The Other Side* (Flying Fish, 1986); *Live at Carnegie Hall* (Flying Fish 1988); *Breathes* (Flying Fish, 1988); combining *Good News* and *We All . . . Everyone of Us;* Sweet Honey's first children's album, *All for Freedom* (Music for Little People, 1989); *In this Land* (Earthbeat!/Warner Brothers, 1992); *We Who Believe in Freedom* (Earthbeat!, 1993), *Still on the Journey* (Earthbeat!/Warner Brothers, 1993); *I Got Shoes* (Music for Little People, 1994); *Sacred Ground* (Earthbeat!/Warner Brothers, 1996); and *Selections 1976–1988* (Rounder, 1997), and *Freedom Songs* (Sony Classics, 2000).

In 1998, to celebrate Sweet Honey's twenty-fifth anniversary, Rykodisc released the CD *Twenty-five* (1998), with covers of Bob Marley's "Redemption" and "Motherless Chil'." The group also released a songbook, *Continuum: The First Song Book of Sweet Honey in the Rock* (Third World Press). That year Ysaye Barnwell released a children's book, *No Mirrors in Nana's House* (Harcourt Brace).

In 1999 the North American Folk Alliance honored Bernice Johnson Reagon with a Lifetime Achievement Award. As she told *Ms.,* she is glad that she took the risks in her life: "The civil rights movement was the most wonderful thing I experienced in my life. Day by day, I found courage to be who I was. This was different from who people wanted me to be. Finding courage. Taking the risk. There was something about doing things that I had always been warned would kill or ruin you. Well, I did get suspended and I did go to jail—things I had been told to avoid at all costs. I saw people die so I knew that some risks could kill. But I found that if you avoided everything that was a risk, there would be many things you'd never know about yourself. Septima Clark [activist-educator] told me black people survived because we understood that to be alive meant you had to struggle. She also explained struggle as a way of knowing your life. If you stay in the safety zone all the time, you'll never know about your strength, you'll never know yourself at your most brilliant."

REDPATH, JEAN: *Singer, guitarist. Born Edinburgh, Scotland, April 28, 1937.*

Scottish folksinger Jean Redpath became known by millions of Americans with her performances on Garrison Keillor's *Prairie Home Companion* in the 1980s. But folk devotees recognized her long before as one of the foremost interpreters of Scottish traditional music, especially the extraordinary songs of eighteenth-century poet Robert Burns.

Although she left Scotland and settled in the United States in 1961, in a spiritual sense she never really left home. She spent the next three decades singing and interpreting traditional Scottish tunes. She has recorded seven albums devoted to Burns's songs, and hopes to record all of his songs. But her repertoire is not limited to Scottish music. She knows a thousand songs, from bluegrass and country ("Sonny's Dream") to fifty-verse Scottish ballads.

Redpath, who was raised in East Fife, Scotland, inherited rich musical traditions from both parents. Her father played the hammer dulcimer and his brothers played bagpipes and drums. Her mother came from a family of self-taught musicians. "In my family, it was assumed that one could turn one's hand to something musical," she told the New Bedford, Massachusetts, *Standard-Times.* "I had the piping and drumming on one side of the family and my mother's siblings all played or sang something, all self-taught, usually keyboards because that was what was around."

She describes her career as the result of "dumb luck and happy accidents."

She attended the University of Edinburgh, studying medieval history and English. She also took classes at the School of Scottish Studies. Afterward, she worked for ten years as a teacher, driving instructor, and super at a boardinghouse. In March, 1961, at age twenty-three, she came to the United States with just $11 in her wallet to see the world and get away from the home and academia. A friend had agreed to sponsor her trek if she sang at her wedding. She sang at a hootenanny in San Francisco and impressed a Philadelphia club owner. But by the time she traveled cross-country, the gig fell through. She moved to New York City and "walked straight into the folk scene," as she told the *Standard-Times.* She performed at a Greenwich Village apartment with Bob Dylan, Ramblin' Jack Elliott, and the Greenbriar Boys. Soon afterward, she performed at Gerde's Folk City in New York, which was reviewed favorably in the *New York Times.*

Audiences then and now respond to her rich, mezzo-soprano voice. She prefers to sing a cappella, but learned early that audiences in the 1960s expected performers to play at least some guitar. "When I first stood up at Folk City in 1961, an unaccompanied singer in folk clubs or coffeehouses was almost unheard of," she told the *Standard-Times.* "What I did was take a guitar on stage with me, lean it against the back and that made all the difference in the world. Oh, guitar, a badge—now we know what she's doing—and they'd listen with slightly different ears."

She released her first album, *Scottish Ballad Book,* on Elektra in 1964, followed by *Skipping Barefoot through the Heather* on Prestige International in 1965. *Songs of Love, Lilt and Laughter* came in 1966, *Laddie Lie Near Me* in 1967 (both on Elektra), *Frae My Ain Country* in 1973 on Folk Legacy, *Jean Redpath* on Philo in 1975, and *There Were Minstrels* in 1976.

She built her recording (three dozen albums) and

touring career on her voice. As North Cairn of the *Cape Cod Times* described it: "Much of the reason for her success lies, no doubt, in the sheer power of her talent: the clarity of her voice, the poignancy and depth of its emotional character, the breadth and substance of the material which flows so effortlessly from her. Her voice has an almost flutelike texture to it, and her music reaches deep into the heart, creating an attitude of acceptance of the scope of human life as sad and hard, but also serene."

She never expected to become a premier interpreter of Scottish traditional music. "I don't think I ultimately realized it until I'd been doing it for 10 or 15 years," she told Parry Gettelman of the *Middlesex News*, Framingham, Massachusetts (January 22, 1988). "It was one of these happy accidents. If I were to look back at the music we did around the piano at school, it probably would have been light opera I was singing—mostly because that was what was in the piano stool. I think I managed to survive school with my interest in traditional music intact because it was never taught as a formal subject."

She never learned to read music and says she can pick up songs she likes just by listening two or three times. "If it's a song that's within the tradition that's very familiar to me, I only have to hear it two or three times and I've got it—tune and text both," she told the *Standard-Times*. "I still find that songs I have force-fed to myself don't ever sit quite as well as the ones that I've fallen for, one at a time."

Poet Robert Burns has become a lifelong fascination for Redpath. She collaborated with the late American composer Serge Hovey (1920–1989) to produce seven volumes of the poet's songs, all for Rounder's Philo division. She released the first in the series, *The Songs of Robert Burns Volume 1* in 1976 and *Vol. 7* in 1990. (All have been reissued on CD.) "You wouldn't have to look further than Burns if you wanted to spend a lifetime on Scottish music," Redpath told Daniel Gewertz of the *Boston Herald* (January 23, 1988). "Musically, he was very consciously preserving a whole vocal and pipe and fiddle tradition. His work ranged from very formal songs full of classical allusions, written in standard English, to the simple, Scottish dance melodies that everybody knows. He was a universal kind of bard, the voice of the common man. And it's remarkable how much his lyrics still have relevance today."

Hovey put together *The Robert Burns Song Book,* matching 323 of Burns's lyrics with their original tunes. Although Hovey was born in New York City and raised in Los Angeles, he developed a keen appreciation for the Scottish poet. "The Burns and Scottish tunes worked their way into the bloodstream of American music," he wrote. "The hopes and dreams of early America found many forms of cultural expression and, together with the writings of Paine and the spirit of the Enlightenment, we also find the songs of Burns."

Redpath told one writer that she doubts if she'll ever live to see the Robert Burns project finished, "but that's no reason not to start chugging along with it right now" (*Middlesex News,* January 22, 1988). She told the *Standard-Times:* "In the 18th century, Burns was already concerned about when we were ever going to manage to live in harmony before we either finished ourselves or the planet off."

She doesn't limit herself to Scottish music. In her 1990 Philo album, *Leaving the Land,* whose title track was composed by Scottish and Australian singer-songwriter Eric Bogle, she performs country and western songs as well. She performs contemporary folk music as well. She does not plan her concerts beforehand. "One of the things I obviously fear most in life is a repetition factor," she told Kyle MacMillan of the *Omaha World-Herald* (October 9, 1988).

During her concerts, Redpath will explain the significance and history of tunes that were composed hundreds of years ago. As one reviewer, North Cairn of the *Cape Cod Times* (May 2, 1988), put it: "She seems to sing to an ear in another place, at another time, in a different life and circumstance. The effect is as eerie and moving as many of the lyrics are melancholy."

During the 1970s she lectured on folk music at Wesleyan University. She is also a faculty member at Stirling University in Scotland.

After years of touring small clubs—Redpath, who returned to live in Edinburgh after residing for a time in Long Island, New York, but jokes that she really lives mostly out of a suitcase—the Scottish singer gained the ultimate recognition back home. In 1977, Queen Elizabeth II awarded the MBE (Member of the British Empire) to Redpath at the royal family banquet at Edinburgh Castle.

Besides her seven volumes of *The Songs of Robert Burns,* Redpath has released the following albums: Christmas songs with Lisa Neustadt, *Angels Hovering Round* (1978) and *Anywhere Is Home* (1981) on Fretless, and the following albums on Philo: *Song of the Seals* in 1978, *Father Adam* in 1979, *Lowlands* in 1980, *Shout for Joy!*, a collection of Christmas songs with Lisa Neustadt and the Angel Band in 1980, *Haydn's Scottish Songs* in 1983, *Lady Nairne* in 1986, and *A Fine Song for Singing* in 1987. In 1990, Rounder released *First Flight,* a compilation of her first three Elektra albums. She has also issued several collections on her own Jean Redpath Records: *Love is Teasin'* in 1994 (a reissue of songs originally produced for *A Prairie Home Companion*); *Summer of My Dreams* in 1995; *The Moon's Silver Cradle,* a collection of Celtic lullabies, in 1996; *A Woman of Her Time* in 1997; and *Think on Me* in 1998. She also issued three volumes of Robert Burns's songs on Jean Redpath Records.

R.E.M.: *Vocal and instrumental group from Athens, Georgia. Michael Stipe (lead vocals, main songwriter), born Decatur, Georgia, January 4, 1960; Peter Buck (guitar),*

was shaping up to be another major success, and Warner Brothers had hastened to sign the band to a new contract covering five more albums. Industry observers suggested the pact marked the biggest record deal in history to that point estimated to guarantee the band some $80 million. Before '96 was over, the band had another product in stores (in October) to fatten its royalty statement, a ninety-minute film, *R.E.M.'s Road Tour,* shot in Atlanta in 1995 during the final three nights of the *Monster* Tour.

In October 1997, EMI, which had acquired the right to IRS's catalog, released a retrospective CD called *Essential—R.E.M. in the Attic.* The fifteen-track CD includes songs that had previously appeared on *Dead Letter Office* and *Eponymous,* as well as songs dating back to 1981 ("Gardening at Night"). There are also acoustic versions of "The One I Love," "Disturbance at the Heron House," and "Maps and Legends," which were recorded in 1987 during a live concert at McCabe's Guitar Shop in Santa Monica. At the end of October 1997, drummer Bill Berry, citing "personal reasons," decided to retire, throwing the band into some turmoil.

While band members discussed their next step, Stipe, a longtime Patti Smith fan, published a book of photos he had taken during a 1995 tour with Smith and Dylan titled *On the Road with Patti Smith,* which came out in the spring of 1998. R.E.M.'s first recording effort after Berry's retirement came out in an unconventional way. They recorded and released the song "Why Not Smile" for a music sampler published in a mid-1998 issue of John Grisham's bimonthly magazine, the *Oxford American.* The trio was featured on the cover of the magazine, which carried a seven-page spread titled "Visions of R.E.M."

In October 1998 the band released its first studio album after Berry's retirement, *Up,* on Warner Brothers. The band did not try to replace Berry, instead bringing in Barrett Martin to play drums and relying on synthesizers and drum machines to lay down the rhythm. "This album forced the three of us to become essentially a new band," Stipe told Miriam Longino of the *Atlanta Journal and Constitution* ("*Up* unbuttons three-piece R.E.M. from its past," September 3, 1998). "All the things we used to be doing, and the way we worked in the studio, were thrown out the window. We didn't want to bring in a drummer to be the new Bill Berry. That wasn't going to work. . . . This is about the saddest and most romantic record I've ever made. It's like, 'Here's an alternative universe. Please come in. Expect anything.'"

The album, which revealed the band's upbeat mood despite the loss of Berry, received strong reviews for songs like "The Apologist," "Sad Professor," "Walk Unafraid," "Diminished," and "Falls to Climb." Stipe, Buck, and Mills did not tour in support of the album, preferring to make TV appearances. In December 1998 they were featured in VH-1's *Storytellers Featuring R.E.M.,* in which Stipe expounded on the meaning of several tunes, including songs from *Up.* Three of their songs were featured in the soundtrack to *Man On the Moon* (1999) about comic Andy Kaufman.

RENBOURN, JOHN: *Guitarist, singer, songwriter. Born Marylebone, London, England, August 8, 1944.*

When John Renbourn joined the London folk club scene in the 1960s, he forged a new sound by combining a distinctly British finger picking style with the sounds brought to England by country blues and jazz artists from America. Classically trained, with an even, fluid style, Renbourn's sound contrasted effectively with the powerful guitar of Bert Jansch in the Pentangle, the group they cofounded in 1967. After the group disbanded, Renbourn began to focus on medieval and Renaissance music as a solo act; in his own ensemble, the John Renbourn Group; and with other folk stars such as Robin Williamson.

Renbourn grew up in Torquay in southwest England. His father, Edward Tobias Renbourn, was a country doctor. His mother, Dorothy Louise (Jopling) Renbourn, played piano at church functions. At thirteen, he got his first guitar. He wanted to be like the singing cowboys he had seen in movie westerns early on, like Roy Rogers in *Son of Paleface.* As a teenager he played guitar in various skiffle groups such as the Black Cats. In the early 1960s he studied harmony and counterpoint as well as classical guitar with Frank Winslade for two years at the George Abbot School in Guildford. He moved to London in 1964, when he was twenty. He had no intention of making a career of music.

Instead, like John Lennon before him, he took art classes at the Kingston Art School, which at the time had such musicians in attendance as Eric Clapton, members of the Yardbirds, and later Sandy Denny. "And a year later I came out of art school without any real hope of making a living as a painter and found myself playing in the pubs just to survive," he told Jim Washburn of the *Los Angeles Times* (April 29, 1995).

He played with a couple of bands, including the blues-influenced Hogsnort Rupert and His Famous Porkestra, an R&B band (at Farnham Art School) that performed Muddy Waters, Jimmy Reed, Bill Doggett, and Ray Charles covers. "It was the same era as the young Rolling Stones. All the bands were influenced by Alexis Korner's 'Blues Incorporated,' " Renbourn recalls.

He then hit the folk club scene, which was split into two camps at the time. As he told Washburn: "The main clubs then were under the auspices of the English Folk Dance and Song Society and also very heavily under the sway of Ewan MacColl [writer of "The First Time Ever I Saw Your Face" and father of rock singer Kirsty MacColl], and the general feeling was that they were preserving the tradition, and it was a very serious proposition. As a result guys like Bert, Robin [Williamson], and Davy Graham and other people who were playing guitar were considered to be total heresy, because the steel-string guitar wasn't a British instrument to start with, and the music they were playing initially was American folk blues stuff. So the camps were really split but very much in favor of the traditionalists for a while."

Davy Graham, who had released a 1960 album called *The Guitar Player* that influenced many young guitarists, teamed up with a traditional singer named Shirley Collins, known as "the rose of English folk music," creating a dilemma for the traditionalists. "Davy was arranging these tunes in exciting ways that had never been done before and they couldn't ignore it," Renbourn said.

The American blues and jazz artists were beginning to make the English circuit, performers like Little Walter Jacobs and Big Bill Broonzy. They had a huge impact on the younger set in London. As Renbourn told Dave Helland of *Down Beat* (December 1986), "They'd never seen a black American before and wondered how he had escaped from the plantation. Broonzy would tell them he had a real good master who took off the shackles once in a while and let him go play guitar. People actually believed that. Broonzy, Jesse Fuller, Jack Elliott, and Josh White got us skiffle players into playing American fingerstyle guitar."

After being dismissed from art college—"for playing more than painting," Renbourn writes*—he met Dorris Henderson, a singer from Watts in Los Angeles. She sang blues and gospel and they recorded together in the early 1960s. Dorris was the resident singer on the BBC-TV show *Gadzooks It's All Happening.* Renbourn describes the show as "a sort of '60s musical mishmash. They first had Alexis Korner as the house band. I accompanied Dorris on guitar. There I met Danny Thompson (bass) and Terry Cox (who played drums with Alexis) and later persuaded them to join Pentangle." (Renbourn backed Henderson on two albums: *There You Go,* released on EMI in 1964, and *Watch the Stars,* on Fontana in 1966.)

He soon struck up a friendship with Bert Jansch. Renbourn first heard Jansch when he backed up legendary blues harpist Little Walter at a London club run by producer Bill Leader. (The guitarist Leader had slated to back up Little Walter didn't show up.) Jansch and Renbourn became close friends, rooming together in several flats for three years. They started a folk club on Tuesday nights called the Scot's Hoose. Shortly after Jansch released his eponymous album, Renbourn did the same, releasing *John Renbourn* on Transatlantic Records in 1965 (with Jansch playing backup). The two teamed up a year later on *Bert and John* in 1966. (Compilation albums were released in the United States called *Stepping Stones* on Vanguard in 1969, and *After the Dance* on Shanachie in 1992.) Renbourn's third album, *Another Monday,* released in 1967 on Transatlantic, revealed his keen abilities as a solo guitarist.

After playing a club called Les Cousins for a while, Renbourn and Jansch decided to form their own band. The two guitarists brought singer Jacqui McShee, bassist Danny Thompson, and drummer Terry Cox together to form the Pentangle, which fused folk and jazz.

The Pentangle was the first of the big three British folk-rock groups. Fairport Convention and Steeleye Span soon followed. The group toured around the world and gained a strong following. Jansch and Renbourn complemented each other well on guitar, though it took some doing. "John Renbourn is the quietest player in the world—his touch is so light, the opposite of me," Jansch told Mark Humphrey of *Frets* magazine (March 1980). "To get the balance right was difficult."

The Pentangle was a whirlwind experience. As Renbourn told Washburn: "It was strange but all very exciting. The first tours we did in America, somehow we were billed as an underground band, which was this sort of buzzword with a lot of groups in the old days. Our label, Warner Bros., classed us in there as well. So we shared bills with the Grateful Dead, Jethro Tull, Canned Heat, Spirit, Alice Cooper. They were pretty odd pairings."

The group released four new albums on Transatlantic—*The Pentangle* and *Sweet Child* in 1968, *Basket of Light* in 1969, and *Reflection* in 1971—and one compilation on the Reprise label—*Solomons Seal*—and then disbanded in 1973. "Pentangle drifted apart after intensive touring, largely due to contractual difficulties with management and the recording company," Renbourn writes. There were the usual disputes over royalties; as Jansch told David Cavanagh of *Q Magazine* (1995), the band had gotten used to the fast life: "Pentangle were rather spoiled. We'd stay at the Algonquin Hotel in New York. . . . You know you get used to standards, which are rock 'n' roll standards. When we finished and came back to what I would call reality, we were a bit lost."

Like Jansch, Renbourn had continued to release solo LPs while the Pentangle were together: *Sir Johnalot of Merrie England* on Transatlantic in 1968 (on Reprise in the United States and later on Shanachie) showed Renbourn's increasing interest in medieval and Renaissance music. He also released *The Lady and the Unicorn* in 1970 (later released on Shanachie), and *Faro Annie* in 1972, both on Transatlantic. Renbourn took a brief respite from the music industry during which he released two more Transatlantic albums, *The Hermit* in 1976 (later on Shanachie) and *The Black Balloon* in 1979 (later on Stefan Grossman's Kicking Mule label). In 1979 he released *So Early in the Spring,* a solo album on Nippon Columbia.

Renbourn was "living quietly in South Devon and touring less," he writes of the mid-1970s period.

He formed a group on an informal basis called the John Renbourn Group, which included Jacqui McShee, Sue Draheim on fiddle, Tony Roberts on flutes and pipes, and Keshav Sathe on tabla. The group debuted with *A Maid in Bedlam,* released on Transatlantic in 1977. The album had a "much stronger medieval/Renaissance flavor than Pentangle's work," Ken Roseman wrote in the liner notes for a later album. "This reflected

Sesame Street, and she recorded three children's albums, *Artichokes, Griddlecakes* (1970), and *Funnybugs* (1972) on the Pacific Cascade label, followed by *Magical Songs* (1978) on her own Cassandra label. She also reissued *Malvina Reynolds* on Cassandra and recorded two new albums for adults, *Malvina* (1972) and *Malvina—Held Over* (1975), both on Cassandra. She published three songbooks for children and one, *The Malvina Reynolds Songbook,* for adults. The publishing company she founded, Schroder Music Company in Berkeley, is now run by Malvina's daughter, Nancy Schimmel (also a songwriter, with two Parents Press Award–winning albums on her Sisters' Choice label) and Malvina's business associate, Ruth Pohlman. A Malvina Reynolds web page appears on the Sisters' Choice website, designed by Nancy Schimmel's daughter, Nancy Beth Ibsen.

Malvina's last recorded album, *Mama Lion,* was issued in 1980, two years after her death. In the years since then, some of her songs continue to be included in concerts by veteran folk artists as well as by some members of the new generations of folksingers, as represented by Nanci Griffith's inclusion of "Turn Around" on her 1993 *Other Voices, Other Rooms* album.

Entry revised by Nancy Schimmel, Malvina Reynolds's daughter

RICE, TONY: *Singer, guitarist, songwriter, band leader (the Tony Rice Unit). Born Danville, Virginia, June 8, 1951.*

A spur to the bluegrass revival of the 1970s was the arrival on center stage of many young, extremely talented exponents of the style. An important member of that group was Tony Rice, one of the finest flatpicking bluegrass guitarists. He was involved in many of the major changes in bluegrass playing, including the use of electrified instruments (which outraged purists then and still does today) and the format known as "Dawg" music, which he pioneered in collaboration with David Grisman.

Rice spent his formative years in Southern California, and biographical material in the '70s suggested his birthplace was Los Angeles, but he actually was born in Danville, Virginia, and moved to California with his family at an early age. His father, whom he described as "a serious amateur on mandolin and guitar," loved bluegrass music and was friends with a number of important artists, including Doc Watson. Rice recalled that he could hardly remember a time in his childhood when he wasn't able to pick out bluegrass and folk melodies on a guitar. But his interests weren't restricted to those formats. He pointed out that, besides hearing recordings by Bill Monroe, Flatt and Scruggs, and new performers of the 1960s, he also enjoyed work by jazz musicians like Dave Brubeck, John Coltrane, and Lester Young.

In the early 1960s rising newcomers such as the Dillards and the White brothers, Clarence and Roland, had particular impact on his own development. He told Bill Eichenberger of the *Ohio Columbus Dispatch* ("Rice Has His Own, Perfect Style of Bluegrass," July 28, 1994), "My style kind of came out of my own limitation, to tell you the truth. Seeing Clarence White when I was 9, seeing this big kid who was 16 years old playing bluegrass like that—well, you go through a period when you think, 'I'd do anything to play guitar like Clarence White.'"

For a time he did try to imitate his idol, but as he accumulated performing experience with various local groups during his high school years he started to develop his own approach. Joining him in some of the bands was his brother Larry Rice, and both picked up tips on musical trends from the Whites, Ry Cooder, Herb Pedersen, and other artists on the California scene. In 1970, at the request of Sam Bush, Tony moved to Louisville, Kentucky, to work with the Bluegrass Alliance, leaving soon after to become a member of the innovative J.D. Crowe's New South group. While working with Crowe, his path eventually crossed that of mandolinist David Grisman, who was experimenting with new material that blended jazz, bluegrass, and classical styles.

The New South members enjoyed trying out concepts that could expand the horizons of bluegrass, including addition of electric instruments and drums. Rice told Eichenberger, "At the time, I didn't particularly like the electric instruments and drums, to tell you the truth. It was just one of those things that was happening at the time. During the early 1970s, bluegrass music was undergoing big changes; we're talking about a music that had remained unchanged for the previous 25 years.

"Myself and J.D. Crowe and a few others sort of jumped on that bandwagon. Then Ricky Skaggs came [in 1974] and Jerry Douglas. You know, things came in from the periphery to change your way of thinking." Rice worked with Crowe on a number of '70s recordings, including the seminal Rounder debut, *J.D. Crowe & the New South.*

In the mid-1970s, David Grisman recruited Tony for his new, California-based, all-instrumental David Grisman Quintet. As part of that group, Rice said, he expanded his horizons past three-chord bluegrass, studying chord theory, learning to read charts, and incorporating elements from other musical genres such as jazz. Working with Grisman, he helped develop a new kind of acoustic style that became known as "Dawg" music, taken from Grisman's initials. Discussing that with *Country Guitar* ("Tony Rice: Him and His Guitar," April 1994), he described Dawg as, essentially, music "played on stringed instruments—an extension of bluegrass and old-timey, with the same timbre but more structured." Tony took part in recording the quintet's independently produced debut album and also performed on the group's first LP on the Horizon label, the 1979 release *Hot Dawg.*

At the end of the 1970s Rice began polishing his solo credentials, beginning with the excellent 1979 Kaleidoscope Records album *Acoustics* (reissued by Rounder on CD in the mid-'90s), which was followed in 1980 by *Manzanita*. The latter, which focused as much on Rice's vocal abilities as his guitar work, was praised by *Frets* magazine as the starting point for "acoustic music's brilliant future." In 1981 he became part of a new all-star coalition called the Bluegrass Album Band, whose other members were Crowe, Bobby Hicks, Doyle Lawson, and Todd Phillips. As of 1995, the group's catalog covered five album releases. Rice's '80s output included the experimental jazz "spacegrass" album *Backwaters, Native American, Cold on the Shoulder,* and *Me and My Guitar,* which combined elements of jazz, bluegrass, and folk. In 1987, he collaborated with Norman Blake on *Blake and Rice* and a follow-up album, *Blake And Rice 2*.

As of the early 1990s, critics noted that it had been fifteen years since Rice had recorded a straight-ahead solo bluegrass album. He remedied this with the late 1993 Rounder album, *Tony Rice Sings and Plays Bluegrass*. Tracks in the collection included his versions of songs made popular by such artists as Bill Monroe, Flatt and Scruggs, the Stanley Brothers, Hylo Brown, and the Country Gentlemen, as well as a bluegrass rendition of Bob Dylan's "Girl from the North Country." The album was nominated for Best Bluegrass Album in the 1993 Grammy Awards voting. In support of the album, Rice toured widely with his band, the Tony Rice Unit, whose roster, besides Tony, comprised Jimmy Gaudreau on mandolin, Rickie Simpkins on violin, Ronnie Simpkins on bass, and Wyatt Rice on guitar.

Country Guitar wondered if Tony had considered trying for major-label success like that attained by bluegrass graduates Skaggs, Vince Gill, and Marty Stuart. He commented, "In order to become a contemporary country music artist, I always felt that I'd have to give up a big part of myself. I thought about going mainstream country, but whenever I did, it was in terms of Nashville coming to me."

In 1996, Rounder released *Tony Rice Sings Gordon Lightfoot,* which includes such standards by the Canadian folksinger as "Early Morning Rain," "Cold on the Shoulder," "Wreck of the *Edmund Fitzgerald,*" and "Bitter Green." Later in the year, Rounder also released *Out of the Woodwork,* an excellent album in which Tony Rice joined with his brother Larry, Herb Pedersen, and Chris Hillman. Among other songs, they perform Richard Thompson's "Dimming of the Day" and Aretha Franklin's "Do Right Woman." He followed on Rounder with *Rice, Rice, Hillman and Pedersen* in 1999. In 2000, Rice released a solo album on Rounder called *Unit of Measure*.

Other Tony Rice albums include *Church Street Blues* (1987) and *River Suite for Two Guitars* (with John Carlini, 1995) on Sugar Hill; the Tony Rice Unit's *Mar-*

West (1980), *Devlin* (1988), *The Rice Brothers* (1989, with Tony, Larry, Ron, and Wyatt), and *Rice Brothers 2* (1994) on Rounder; and *Guitar* and *California Autumn,* both on Rebel in 1991. Grisman also showcased Tony's work on CDs issued by his Acoustic Disc label.

RIDDLE, ALMEDA: *Singer, fiddler, pianist. Born West Pangburn, Arkansas, November 21, 1898; died Heber Springs, Arkansas, June 30, 1986.*

One of the artists who became legendary with folk purists as a result of the research into the American folk heritage by the father-and-son team of Professor John Lomax and his son Alan Lomax was Almeda Riddle. It was Alan Lomax in particular who preserved some of her finest traditional renditions in several extensive folk-music collections he prepared after World War II. Apart from that, the Arkansas balladeer's album work was relatively sparse, but always provided important contributions to folklore annals. By the time of her death, she was renowned for her repertoire of more than 600 songs and her a cappella "feather singing" style.

Almeda grew up in rural Arkansas and still resided there at the end of the 1970s, known to folk adherents as Granny Riddle. In her youth, the old folk ballads derived from the music of Elizabethan times—and earlier—in the United Kingdom and Ireland still were sung at family gatherings in many parts of the South, Southwest, and border states. From her father, J.L. James, and other relations and friends, Riddle learned many folk songs that she preserved and sang throughout her life. Her father, who was a fine musician, also helped her learn to play both fiddle and piano.

In her home area her ability was well known, but hardly anyone outside the region took much notice. However, in the years after World War I, there was increasing interest in searching out and preserving the old songs, secular and religious, that were in danger of dying out with the advent of advanced methods of communication and the rising tide of popular music. After Almeda got married to Price Riddle and had children, she continued to sing. But in 1926, Price and one of her sons were killed in a tornado. She was left to raise her children and tend the farm. She was an avid quilter and a member of the Bee Branch Bethlehem Primitive Baptist Church.

Throughout the 1930s and 1940s, Alan Lomax worked steadily with his father to find previously unknown folk balladeers and bring their talents to wider notice. One of John Lomax's most famous discoveries, of course, was the art of Leadbelly. Equally important was Alan Lomax's work in preserving Almeda Riddle's trove of songs (and her performing style), which he pursued in the years after the elder Lomax's death in 1948. In 1952 folklorist John Wolf of Southwestern University at Memphis took out a newspaper ad looking for people who knew the "old songs." One of Almeda's neighbors wrote to Wolf about her singing skills. Wolf arranged for her first concert and introduced her to Alan Lomax.

During the 1950s, Alan went to Arkansas to tape some of Riddle's material for the Library of Congress archives. Later, in wide-ranging efforts for commercial folk companies, he included more of her material. In some cases, folk scholars excitedly discovered that her renditions were rare modern-day equivalents of ballads collected in the nineteenth century by the first great American folklorist, Professor Francis J. Child of Harvard. Some of these tracks were included in the twelve-volume set on Prestige/International Records called *Southern Journey* and others in Lomax's seven-record set for Atlantic called the *Southern Folk Heritage Series.*

With the broad interest in folk music in the United States in the late 1950s and early 1960s, eager young folk enthusiasts sought Riddle out either to listen to her sing at home or to try to include her in various festivals. She took part in some of them during the '60s. She also agreed to make her first solo album for Vanguard, *Almeda Riddle,* issued in February 1965. On the album, she sings without instrumental backing.

After that, though she continued to be alert and active, there was a long hiatus before another album appeared. Finally, in the early 1970s, Rounder Records made a new collection titled *Songs and Ballads from the Ozarks.* Some years later, in early 1979, Almeda's third solo album was issued by Rounder, *More Songs and Ballads from the Ozarks.* In 1983, Riddle received a National Heritage Award for her music and balladry. The following year she made a film in which she talks with Starr Mitchell about her desire to preserve her music. When she died in 1986, she had traveled widely, bringing her unique brand of singing to the rest of the country. She was survived by a daughter and a son, eight grandchildren, and twelve great-grandchildren. In 1997, when Rounder issued the first six CDs from the Alan Lomax Collection, Almeda Riddle was represented with her versions of "Jesse James" and "Hangman Tree" (Child No. 95), recorded in Arkansas in October 1959.

RINGER, JIM: *Singer, guitarist, songwriter. Born Yell County, Arkansas, February 29, 1936; died Fresno, California, March 17, 1992.*

It is difficult to think of folksinger Jim Ringer without also bringing to mind his collaboration with Mary McCaslin, his musical partner and for some years also his wife. But he had been performing in the folk field for many years before their paths crossed, and even while the two shared billing on recordings and on the concert circuit, he continued to amass credits as a solo artist and an excellent songwriter.

He was born in the Ozark Mountain region of Arkansas in 1936 to a family steeped in the tradition of hill country ballads and string music, some of which could be traced back to the folk songs of medieval England.

McCaslin wrote in the liner notes for the 1996 Philo/Rounder retrospective of Jim's recordings, "Most of the old ballads came from his mother's side; his dad knew Jimmie Rodgers songs and played a bluesy style of piano." As was the case with Doc Watson, she added, "Jim grew up with an appreciation for whatever music he heard and enjoyed. Rock and roll licks and jazz chords were as much a part of Jim's early music [in the late 1950s] as any country song or 200-year-old ballad. His recall of song lyrics was remarkable. He could remember the words to old ballads, country songs, pop standards, and rock and roll songs. When I wanted to learn 'Ghost Riders,' 'Wayward Wind' and 'Don't Fence Me In,' Jim sat down and wrote out the words."

In the mid-1940s, Ringer's father decided to give up farming and move west in search of a better-paying occupation. The family stayed for a time in Oklahoma, then left for California, finally settling in Clovis, a small town near Fresno where Ringer Sr. got a job in the construction field. As time went by, the children helped the family budget by picking crops for area farms at harvest time. Coming into his teens at the end of the 1940s, Jim became bitter and rebellious. He was interested in music, but life for him seemed a dead-end street. Like another young person in a similar position, Merle Haggard, Ringer was wild and undisciplined, and finally ended up in prison in the late 1950s on a two-year burglary conviction.

But after serving that sentence and returning to society, he found a wife and started a family. While he still sometimes drank too much, essentially he focused on staying out of trouble and finding ways to meet his responsibilities. He found whatever work he could, including jobs in construction and logging, and supplemented that income with whatever he could earn at gigs in bars and honky-tonks in the Fresno area.

His skills as a singer and guitarist improved with experience in the mid- and late 1960s, and his various appearances also led to more contacts in the entertainment field. By the early '70s, besides solo efforts, he had become a member of a Fresno-based string band, with whom he performed at various festivals, including summer appearances at the Sweet's Mill folk-music camp/retreat in the Sierra Mountains east of Fresno. His early recording credits included singing and playing guitar on string band LPs such as *Kenny Hall and the Sweet's Mill String Band* and *Kenny Hall and the Sweet's Mill String Band, Volume 2,* both on Bay Records.

It was at the Sweet's Mill camp that he met Mary McCaslin in the summer of 1972. As she said in the liner notes, "Jim was 36 years old. . . . He was separated from his wife and children in Fresno and had been living in Berkeley. After years of performing music part time, he was restless to travel and make music his life.

"When we met, Jim was just beginning to find his way as a songwriter. The first time I heard him sing 'Waitin' for the Hard Times to Go,' I was moved by the incredible power of this song's unadorned lyrics. . . . Over the years, Jim's writing flourished. He painted stunning portraits and his love of words was obvious, but he retained his lean style of writing. There were no 'filler' lines in his songs. Jim could come upon an idea for a song and would have it written within a couple of hours. I don't remember him ever struggling over lyrics—he would complete the song, including the melody, in one sitting."

The two became friends, then musical collaborators. Word of Ringer's abilities had started to filter back to record executives at small labels in the eastern United States, and during the 1972–73 period both Jim and Mary returned east for possible recording projects. His solo debut was the Folk Legacy release *Waitin' for the Hard Times to Go,* which was followed by his first Philo Records collection, *Good to Get Home.* The title song was a rare semiautobiographical composition by him; its lyrics reflected the failure of his marriage and sadness at being apart from his children. Another original, "Open Door at Home," was written in a similar vein.

From 1973 into 1976, either as a solo performer or partnered with Mary McCaslin, Ringer gradually began to gain more attention from folk adherents. Mary wrote: "The 'Glory Days' of our career together started in late 1976. We began to work steadily and were finally getting the recognition we had been striving for since the early 1970s. We married in 1978 and bought a home on the outskirts of San Bernardino (east of Los Angeles) that fall." During the late 1970s and early 1980s, the duo was featured in folk-music venues across the United States and Canada and continued to add to their festival credits. By the early '80s Philo had issued several more Ringer solo albums, such as *Any Old Wind That Blows* and *Tramps and Hawkers,* plus the highly successful duet LP *The Bramble and the Rose.*

The situation deteriorated for Jim and Mary after 1982, however. The original Philo Record label (it later was acquired by Rounder Records) ran into financial problems and stopped releasing new albums. Finding another record outlet was a challenging task; Flying Fish did issue one album apiece for the twosome (Ringer's was titled *Endangered Species*), but there were no follow-ups. At the same time, the growing depression in the folk field caught up with them and concert jobs decreased sharply. Though Ringer continued writing new songs, he seemed to suffer an increasing feeling of helplessness, which contributed to his tendency to drink too much.

In the fall of 1985, Jim and Mary moved from San Bernardino to the Eureka/Arcata area in northern California just south of the Oregon border, hoping the change of scenery might produce a change in their sagging fortunes. The duo essentially stopped touring after 1988 except for a few shows on the West Coast, and separated in 1989. Ringer, still unable to overcome his drinking problem, moved back to Fresno, where he died in early 1992.

In the spring of 1996, Philo/Rounder released the retrospective CD *The Best of Jim Ringer: The Band of Jesse James.* The album's seventeen tracks included seven songs for which Ringer wrote both words and music, one cowritten by him and Larry Murray ("Linda's on Her Own"), and a traditional number with new words by him, "Tramps and Hawkers." The seven others noted above, many of which had been covered over the years by other performers, were "Open Door at Home," "Good to Get Home," "Tulsa," "Rachel," "The Band of Jesse James," "Dusty Desert Wind," and "Still Got That Look."

Steve Netsky, who compiled the album, stated, "When Jim Ringer sang, it was hard to believe he hadn't lived every line. . . . Known for his solo albums and his recordings and performances with Mary McCaslin, Jim helped define folk music in the 1970s. Jim Ringer lived hard, but he sang gently. . . ."

Based partly on a Mary McCaslin interview with Irwin Stambler

RITCHIE, JEAN: *Singer, dulcimer player, autoharpist, guitarist, songwriter, author, folk-music collector. Born Slabtown Hollow, Viper, Kentucky, December 8, 1922.*

At the Folk Alliance conference in Memphis in 1998, Tom Paxton had the honor of introducing Jean Ritchie, who was receiving a Lifetime Achievement award. He talked about how Ritchie's songs and dulcimer playing influenced him and other folksingers in the late 1950s. "Tradition is what Jean has been about," he said. "In my opinion she is a true national treasure."

Indeed, in a video presentation about her life, Ritchie talked about her memories of a childhood home overrun with people (she was the youngest of fourteen children) and of the songs she learned as a child. When she met Alan Lomax in the mid-1940s, he wanted to record everything she knew. "That would be difficult because my family knows three hundred songs," she told him.

When she was finally introduced to the Folk Alliance crowd, which included many prominent folksingers from the early 1960s through the 1990s, the audience erupted in riotous applause. Ritchie slowly made her way up to the podium to receive her award; a reverent hush settled over the audience. "I'm kind of a shy person, so it's hard to think of what to say," she said quietly. "I'm not sure I've done anything to deserve this. I want to thank you for giving me the roses while I was still alive."

Music has been such an integral part of Jean Ritchie's life that it is no surprise that she would downplay such an award. Music is her lifeblood.

In her 1955 book, *Singing Family of the Cumberlands,* she described how the folk-music heritage had been handed down from parents to children in her family in an unbroken line going back to colonial times. In telling the story of her roots and upbringing, she also described a way of life common to many other families in the hill-country culture whose original members were in the first wave of emigration from England, Scotland, Wales, and Ireland. The book, in effect, constituted a sort of road map to the development of the traditional folk music that was the core both of the folk revival of post–World War II years and the parallel rise in the popularity of country music.

Ritchie was born near the tiny hamlet of Viper, deep in the Cumberland Mountains of Kentucky. Jean's ancestors had been among the first settlers of the region in the 1700s. Jean's father, Balis Ritchie, had taught school in the nearby town of Dwarf before marrying her mother, Abigail Hall, of Viper, when she was fifteen.

Although their house looked more like a dormitory, Ritchie recalled it as a lively and happy place to be. All the children lent a hand, tending the cornfield in summer as soon as they were old enough. When work was done, all looked forward to evenings of fun with friends and relations, singing and playing the banjo, guitar, dulcimer, and fiddle. As a child, Jean would take her father's dulcimer off the mantel and sneak behind the couch to strum it. She taught herself to play "Go Tell Aunt Rhody." When her father finally got around to teaching her the instrument, he was so amazed at her progress that he called her a "natural born musician."

Singing was an integral part of life in the Cumberlands. The people sang as they worked in the fields, joined with their neighbors in sings at socials and other events, and sang hymns and gospel songs lustily in church on Sundays. Many of the songs were traditional tunes handed down and modified by generations of settlers from the British Isles. In the case of the Ritchies, some of the songs the family sang had been brought from England by James Ritchie, Jean's great-great-great-grandfather, in 1768. Among those traced back to James and his son, Crockett Ritchie, were "Nottamun Town" (Nottingham, England), "Lord Bateman," "Old Sally Buck," and "Killy Kranky."

Other songs that Jean and her brothers and sisters sang included "Fair Ellender," "Hush Little Baby," "Twilight A-Stealing," "Shady Grove," "Somebody," "I'm Goin' to Boston," "I've Been a Foreign Lander," "Maria," and "Old Tyler." Their repertoire made the Ritchie family one of the best-known singing clans in the region. During Jean's childhood, folk-music collectors used to come to the Ritchie house to note down some of those numbers.

Jean's singing and collecting continued steadily as she went through elementary school, the new high school of Viper, and, after that, college. Despite the family's limited resources, quite a few of the children managed to get to college. She attended Cumberland Junior College in Williamsburg, Kentucky. World War II interrupted her studies, and she taught school in Little Leatherwood, during which time she realized she didn't want to be a teacher. She graduated from Cumberland and then she entered the University of Kentucky in Lexington. She completed work for her B.A. in social work in 1946, graduating Phi Beta Kappa. She won the Founder's Day Award, impressing both classmates and instructors with her knowledge of folklore and traditional music, as well as her skill as an instrumentalist. Ritchie's work on the dulcimer was particularly striking and, later on, she awakened considerable interest in the instrument from her concerts and festival appearances in the 1950s and 1960s.

In 1947, armed with a degree in social work, she moved to New York City and found a position at the Henry Street School, where she worked as a music counselor and social worker at an inner-city school whose students were primarily Italian and Jewish. "We sang and danced a lot, and I learned so much from them," Ritchie told Mary DesRosiers of Sing Out! ("Jean Ritchie: An Unbroken Circle," November-December 1996–January 1997).

In the years immediately after graduation, she began to make a name for herself in the folk field with a series of concerts in eastern and southeastern states. By 1948 she had met Alan Lomax, who recorded her songs for the Library of Congress. A year later, she was a guest on Oscar Brand's radio show. In 1950 she married New York photographer George Pickow, with whom she had two sons. And in 1952 she made her first solo recording Jean Ritchie Sings Traditional Songs of Her Kentucky Mountain Family, released by Elektra. She applied for and won a Fulbright Scholarship to do folk-song research in Great Britain.

In 1952 she traveled throughout Scotland, Ireland, and England, recording music to discern the roots of her own music. Her husband, meanwhile, took photographs. Among those she recorded were uileann piper Seamus Ennis and singer Tommy Makem. As she told DesRosiers, while traveling in Aberdeen, Scotland, she played the song "Loving Hannah," which she had heard her father and uncle sing, for singer Jeannie Robertson. The song got passed around from person to person, and in 1983, when Mary Black recorded the song, it was listed as a "traditional Irish song." "I guess I should take it as a compliment," Ritchie said.

Back home in the 1950s, Ritchie quickly became an integral part of the folk-music boom. She performed in folk clubs and concert halls, festivals, and college campuses all over the United States. Besides singing traditional material, she also wrote original songs or variations of older ones, including "A Tree in the Valley-O," "The Cuckoo She's a Pretty Bird," "Let the Sun Shine Down on Me," and "What'll I Do with the Baby-O." She also compiled several books of folk songs—The Swapping Song Book, From Fair to Fair, and Folk Songs of the Southern Appalachians.

Her Singing Family of the Cumberlands was first

published by Oxford University Press in 1955; it was released in paperback in 1963 by Oak Publications, and later reprinted by the University Press of Kentucky in 1988. She also wrote *Apple Seeds and Soda Straws: Love Charms and Legends Written Down for Young and Old,* published by Henry Walck in 1965. She wrote some of the earliest dulcimer instruction books, such as *The Dulcimer Book,* published by Oak in 1963 (accompanied by *The Appalachian Dulcimer,* an instructional LP on Folkways), *The Dulcimer People,* published by Oak in 1974, and *Traditional Mountain Dulcimer,* published by Homespun Tapes in 1984.

Among her recordings released in the mid-to-late-'50s were *Appalachian Mountain Songs* (1953) on HMV, *Songs from Kentucky* (1953) on Argo, and *Kentucky Mountain Songs* and *Courting Songs,* both on Elektra in 1954. She recorded *American Folk Tales and Songs* (1956) for Tradition, and for Folkways *Children's Songs and Games from the Southern Mountains* (1957), *Singing Family of the Cumberlands* (1957) for Riverside and *The Ritchie Family of Kentucky* (1957).

During the 1960s, Jean was a familiar figure at the major folk festivals in the United States and abroad. She appeared several times at the events at the University of Chicago, University of California at Berkeley, and at traditional gatherings in the South and Southeast. She was very active in the Newport Folk Festival, both on stage and off, and performed there in 1963, 1964, 1965, 1966, and 1967. Some of her performances were included in the Vanguard Records festival coverage. When the Newport event was reorganized in 1963, she became one of the original seven board members, and later became a member of the Newport Folk Festival Foundation when her term as director terminated. The National Endowment for the Arts also asked her to serve on its first folklore panel in the early 1960s.

Ritchie was represented by a number of albums from the late 1950s to the late 1970s. One of her earlier efforts, originally released in 1959 but still in the Folkways Records active catalog in the early 1980s, was called *Jean Ritchie and Oscar Brand at Town Hall.* Her album *Carols of All Seasons* came out on Tradition in 1959 (reissued by Rykodisc/Tradition in 1997), followed by *Riddle Me This* on Riverside. Her 1960s output included several on Folkways: *British Traditional Ballads in the Southern Mountains* (1961), *Precious Memories* (1962), and *Jean Ritchie and Doc Watson at Folk City* (1963, reissued Smithsonian/Folkways). *The Best of Jean Ritchie* came out on Prestige in 1961. Warner Brothers released *A Time for Singing* in 1965.

Although the mass audience interest in folk music had subsided by the 1970s, there still was a sizable number of devotees. She recorded several albums for Sire Records, including the January 1970 release *Clear Waters Remembered* and the 1977 LP *None but One,* which surprised many folk fans with its underlying

rock format in several numbers. *Rolling Stone* named *None But One,* which also featured Janis Ian, Mary Travers, Eric Weissberg, and Oscar Brand, Best Folk Album of 1977.

Several of her songs have been recorded by others, including "Black Waters," about the pollution of rivers by coal mining in Kentucky: "Dear Companion" by Dolly Parton, Linda Ronstadt, and Emmylou Harris in 1987; and "The L&N Don't Stop Here Anymore," by Michelle Shocked and Johnny Cash. Nanci Griffith invited her to perform on *Other Voices, Too (A Trip Back to Bountiful),* released by Elektra in 1998.

She and her husband had settled in Port Washington, New York, in 1955, but built a house out of recycled logs in Viper that they visited two or three months a year, especially in June, when the Ritchie family reunion takes place. In the 1970s she and her husband created their own company, the Folklife Family Store, to market the "Jean Ritchie Dulcimer" her husband had learned to make (others had begun to pirate his design), and also to sell her CDs and books. They released several recordings on their Greenhays label, including *None But One, High Hills and Mountains* (1979) (they reissued *None But One* and *High Hills* on a double CD in the 1990s), *The Most Dulcimer* (1984), *Kentucky Christmas Old and New* (with her sons Jon and Peter Pickow), and *Mountain Born: Jean Ritchie & Sons Sing Cabin Country.* She had first written the title track for a Broadway show directed by Arthur Penn called *Hillbilly Women,* which was performed at the Actor's Studio in New York. Ritchie notes that like most of her forty albums, her latest takes the "slice-of-life" approach: "Some love songs, a child's song, a hymn, a play-party, honor songs for home, for family. A collection of songs to celebrate, again, a way of life, a loved place in the world, and pass on the memories gathered by all the people there."

Released in 1995, *Mountain Born* was also the title of a documentary about her life produced by H. Russell Farmer and Guy Mendes for Kentucky Educational Television which ran on PBS stations in 1996. Looking back on her career, she wrote in the Folk Alliance conference book for 1998: "I believe that old songs have things to say to the modern generation, and that's why they've stayed around. That's also why I am still singing. I'm not afraid to be myself. Agents say you have to change and grow, but I believe you can sing the same songs and sing them better and grow new songs out of the old. If I had to categorize myself or pin down what I do, I'd have to say I'm a carrier of tradition."

ROBERTSON, ROBBIE: *Singer, guitarist, songwriter, film composer, record producer. Born Toronto, Ontario, Canada, July 5, 1943.*

A pivotal figure in the saga of the Band, one of the greatest groups in rock 'n' roll history, Jaime Robbie

Robertson went on to create a solo career for himself in the years following the breakup of the original aggregation in 1976. His early influences included the country music that was popular in his home area at the time as well as the folk music of the Mohawk Indian tribe. Both types of music affected his future work as a musician and songwriter, his Indian heritage providing the inspiration for his 1994 album *Music for "The Native Americans,"* written for the sound track of the six-part TBS-TV program on that subject. As he said on its release, "I've been wanting to make this record all my life."

Robertson was born in Toronto, Canada, and grew up in the Cabbagetown section of that city. His father, of Jewish descent, died in an automobile accident while Robbie was a baby, but he formed a close bond with his mother, of Mohawk descent, who had been raised on the Six Nations reservation. Robbie spent summers at the reservation, where he enjoyed listening to his Mohawk relations play Native and country music. As he grew older he asked his mother to get him guitar lessons, but she sent him to a teacher of Hawaiian guitar, which he quickly rejected. Instead he began teaching himself, partly by listening to guitarists on recordings and radio and, in the mid-1950s, taking tips from relations during his reservation visits.

In the later 1950s he became active on the local band scene, playing in such teenage groups as Little Caesar and the Consoles, Robbie and the Robots, and Thumper and the Trambones. He was already writing original material during those years, and managed to bring some of this to the attention of rockabilly artist Ronnie Hawkins. After recording two of Robbie's songs, "Hey Boba Lu" and "Someone Like You," on his *Mr. Dynamo* album, Hawkins asked Robbie to become lead guitarist in his backup group, the Hawks. From 1961 through 1964, the Hawks, which included future Band members Levon Helm, Rick Danko, Richard Manuel, and Garth Hudson, toured with Hawkins to many parts of the United States and Canada. Some of those gigs were part of package tours with such rock and roll performers as Jackie Wilson, Chuck Berry, and Carl Perkins. Critics and other artists began to take note of Robertson's guitar talent, exemplified by tracks on other Hawkins albums like "Who Do You Love" and "Come Love."

Members of the Hawks already were starting to think about making separate career moves for themselves. As the Canadian Squires, they had the singles "Leave Me Alone" and "The Stones That I Throw" come out on the Atco label. Robertson also did some session work, including backing folksinger John Hammond Jr. on the latter's *So Many Roads* and *I Can Tell* LPs.

In 1965 the pivotal event in the history of the group's career came when a meeting between Robertson and Bob Dylan in New York City led to their becoming his backing band for several years. Robertson contributed to Dylan's *Blonde on Blonde* album in '66. The next year a bootleg of recordings they made in the basement of a pink house in West Saugerties, New York came out as *Great White Wonder* (released in '75 as *The Basement Tapes*). In 1968, calling itself the Band, the five-man group had its debut album, *Music from Big Pink,* come out on the Capitol label followed in 1969 with their self-titled LP. In short order the Band became one of the premier rock 'n' roll acts in the world, turning out one classic album after another and becoming one of the most popular groups on the global concert scene, as detailed in the separate entry. In 1970, Robertson produced Jesse Winchester's self-titled debut album.

In 1976 the sixteen-year association of Band members came to an end with the Thanksgiving night Last Waltz concert, although *Islands,* their last studio album with Robbie Robertson, came out in '77. Other members later emphasized they hadn't wanted to split, but had to accede to Robertson's desires. Levon Helm was particularly bitter about the breakup, and played an active role in later versions of the group that Robertson pointedly refused to have anything to do with. Robertson told Robert Hilburn of the *Los Angeles Times* ("Reflections on the Age of a 'Real' Rock Band," January 19, 1994) he never regretted his actions. After Hilburn asked if he did, he responded, "No, because I really felt that the circumstances dictated it. It wasn't me saying, 'OK, 16 years, I've had enough.' Things had run their course. It became so difficult to do things that used to be so easy. . . . To get everybody together to come to the studio."

Robertson didn't have any trouble keeping busy afterward. First he worked with director Martin Scorsese on the concert film *The Last Waltz,* released in 1978. The three-record sound track on Warner Brothers included new material called "The Last Waltz Suite," whose contents included the song "Out of the Blue," written and sung by Robbie. The previous year he also had produced Neil Diamond's live album *Love at the Greek.*

Over the next few years, Robbie continued to add to his movie credits. In 1979, for instance, he cowrote, produced, and composed music for the 1980-released film *Carny,* starring Gary Busey and Jodie Foster, while also acting in the film. The next year he worked on background and source music for Scorsese's *Raging Bull.* In 1982 Scorsese again enlisted his help to assemble the score for the *King of Comedy,* released in 1983. His contributions included a solo recording of "Between Trains," his first new song in five years. In 1986 he produced the score for Scorsese's *The Color of Money,* which included songs cowritten with Eric Clapton ("It's in the Way That You Use It") and blues legend Willie Dixon.

Robbie's solo debut album on Geffen Records, *Robbie Robertson,* came out in 1987 with the first single release being "Showdown at Big Sky." The single "Somewhere Down the Crazy River," for which Scorsese directed a video, later became a European hit. The album, which included performances by Danko, Hudson, Peter Gabriel, Daniel Lanois, and members of U2, made the *Billboard* Top 40 and went on to earn a gold record. Robertson also received a Grammy nomination in the Best Rock Vocal category. In 1988 the album and its contents won major trophies at the Canadian Juno Awards. He also was joined onstage by other members of the Band for the group's induction into the Juno Hall of Fame.

In 1991 his second Geffen album, *Storyville,* which takes its name and sounds from a nightclub area of New Orleans, was released with "What About Now" as first single. The album, coproduced by Robbie and Stephen Hague, fell short of the sales results of the earlier collection but won considerable respect from reviewers and other musicians. The disc won Grammy nominations for Best Rock Vocal Performance (Solo) and Best Engineered Album.

Robbie moved back to his old label, Capitol, in 1993 and began considering a variety of projects, including solo work and preparation of new Band anthologies. In January 1994 the Band was inducted into the Rock and Roll Hall of Fame at ceremonies in the New York Waldorf Astoria. The other founding members agreed to perform with him except for Levon Helm, whose unhappiness with Robertson caused him to boycott the affair.

During 1994, Robbie provided additional material with Scorsese for the laserdisc reissue of *The Last Waltz.* He also had a role in the movie *The Crossing Guard,* which starred Jack Nicholson and was directed by Sean Penn, and provided the score for the Barry Levinson film *Jimmy Hollywood.* The most important event from his standpoint, though, was release of the album of the music prepared by him for the TBS documentary that chronicled the history of Native Americans. As he told Don Heckman of the *Los Angeles Times* just before the album's release by Capitol in October '94, "If I had called the record company five years ago and told them I was going to do what I've just done, they would've said, 'I'm sorry, we've got a bad connection here. Did you just say something weird.'"

The album featured some songs written or cowritten by Robertson, but much of its contents comprised material from traditional sources or composed by others of Indian descent. The contributing performers were described as Robbie Robertson and the Red Road Ensemble, where the latter term included artists such as Rita and Priscilla Coolidge and Priscilla's daughter Laura Satterfield, Kashtin, the Silver Cloud Singers, Douglas Spotted Eagle, Ulali, Bonnie Jo Hunt, and Jim Wilson. Also singing backing vocals were Robertson's son Sebastian and daughter Delphine. One of the most striking tracks was the song "Mahk Jchi" ("The Heart of the People"), recorded by the female trio Ulali. Other tracks ranged from traditionally based numbers like "Ancestor Song," "Cherokee Morning Song," and "Coyote Dance" to the rock-flavored "Skinwalker."

As Robertson told Don Heckman, "Most of my younger Native American friends are not in any way looking for sympathy, and they're not looking to lay guilt on anybody. They have their dignity, and they do what they do. . . . Look, half of this record is not even in English. And I don't think it matters. I just want to send out this heartbeat and this mood to the world and say, 'Here's a taste of it'. . . ."

Robertson continued his sound track work by scoring Scorsese's *Casino* in 1995, incorporating music ranging from J.S. Bach to B.B. King. The following year, he suggested that Eric Clapton include a song called "Change the World" in the sound track for *Phenomenon,* starring John Travolta. Kenneth "Babyface" Edmonds produced the track, performed by Clapton, and it won 1997 Grammys for Song, Record, and Producer of the Year.

In 1997, Robertson received a Lifetime Achievement Award from the National Academy of Songwriters. But perhaps his most gratifying award was one he received in May 1998, a Lifetime Achievement Award given during the first annual Native American Music Awards held at the Mashantucket Pequot reservation in Connecticut.

Just two months earlier, Robertson had released his fourth solo album, *Contact from the Underworld of Red Boy,* in March 1998 on Capitol. He recorded the album at various locations: at the Six Nations reservation, in Los Angeles, in New Mexico, and in London. The use of "Red Boy" in the title, Robertson explains, reflects his personal odyssey in coming to terms with his heritage. "'Red Boy' is the 'N' word I was once called when I was a kid," Robertson says. "For Native people, it's okay to use it—it's derogatory when others do. The album is really the music accompanying this journey of Red Boy."

Again he included an eclectic variety of contributors, from producer Howie B., who had worked with Bjork and Tricky, to a Native American throat singing duo called Tudjaat. Robertson uses a phone conversation with imprisoned activist Leonard Peltier on a song called "Sacrifice."

The album received strong critical praise, including a four-star review in *Rolling Stone.* Despite the Native American theme, it was nominated for a Grammy in the Best World Music Album category. The irony was not lost on Robertson, who said when the album was released, "This is not from Borneo; this is from down the road. We're talking about something that's right here but people don't hear it. This is truly underground music."

In August 1998, PBS aired a documentary based on Robertson's 1996 visit to the Six Nations reservation called *Robbie Robertson: Making a Noise—A Native American Musical Journey.* The one-hour film explores Robertson's musical background and Native American heritage and includes comments by Peltier and American Indian Movement leader John Trudell.

By November 1998 Robertson was back in Hollywood. He joined DreamWorks Records as a "label muse" who would work on recording projects, including sound tracks, animation, and with new artists. Robertson's guitar work during the heyday of the Band can be heard on the Columbia/Legacy release, *Bob Dylan Live 1966,* the Royal Albert Hall bootleg that was actually recorded at the Free Trade Hall in Manchester, England, on May 17, 1966.

ROBESON, PAUL: *Singer, actor. Born Princeton, New Jersey, April 9, 1898; died Philadelphia, Pennsylvania, January 23, 1976.*

Despite his important contributions to American arts, Paul Robeson for many years almost became a nonperson. Condemned in his homeland for his political beliefs during the McCarthy era, he was blacklisted as a performer and his recordings were withdrawn from record stores. It was not until his waning years that his reputation was restored and he again received acclaim for his many achievements. Typical of the witchhunts of the 1950s, he was condemned for being a "left-wing activist" although he stated publicly he had never been a communist. There were many who tried to quell his influence, but there is no doubt of his artistic abilities and of his impact on many aspects of twentieth-century culture, including folk music.

Born and raised in relatively comfortable circumstances in New Jersey, Paul was the son of a highly regarded Presbyterian minister, William Drew Robeson, who had escaped slavery. The father-son relationship was always supportive and loving. As Robeson said in later years, "When people talk about my voice, I wish they could have heard my father preach." His mother, Maria Louisa Bustill, a schoolteacher who came from one of the oldest black families in the United States, died when he was six.

After graduating with distinction from Somerville, New Jersey, High School in 1915, Paul (full name Paul Leroy Bustill Robeson) passed the scholarship examinations for Rutgers University and became the third black man to be accepted. At Rutgers, he continued to achieve good grades while also starring on the football team, where he was an All-American end in 1917 and 1918. After gaining his bachelor's degree in 1919 and receiving his Phi Beta Kappa key, he went on to enroll in Columbia Law School the following year.

In 1921 he married Eslanda Cardozo Goode, a biology and chemistry major who went on to have a distinguished career as a pathologist, anthropologist, and writer. While at Columbia, he began to show a flair for acting. His wife encouraged him to take the title role in Ridgely Torrence's play *Simon the Cyrenian.* He appeared in a major role as an amateur in the production at the YMCA in Harlem in 1921. When the play moved to the Lafayette Theater, Robeson made his professional debut in the same role.

He received his law degree from Columbia in 1923,

one of the first African Americans to do so, but law no longer seemed as appealing as the theater, especially after a white secretary in the firm he worked at for a short time refused to take dictation from a black man. In 1922, Robeson appeared in *Taboo* (later retitled *The Voodoo*) and then *Shuffle Along.* When the opportunity came to join the Provincetown Playhouse in Greenwich Village for the summer of 1923, he took it. His performances in the lead roles in Eugene O'Neill's *The Emperor Jones* and in *All God's Chillun Got Wings* made a strong impression on critics. In 1924, he starred in the New York production of the O'Neill play.

Although Paul had an excellent voice, for which he took some classical training, he didn't sing professionally until 1925. Early that year, he and close friend Larry Brown, a talented pianist-composer, organized a concert act that featured Negro spirituals and folk songs. In April 1925, the act won standing ovations from a packed house in a New York concert hall. For the rest of the year and into 1926, the concert was presented to enthusiastic audiences across the United States and in England and Europe. In 1926, Robeson signed a recording contract with a major company and was to prove a top-selling artist on records. From 1926 through the early 1940s, he recorded more than 300 numbers, ranging from operatic arias to folk and pop songs.

In October 1926, he was on Broadway playing the lead role in *Black Boy.* The play was short-lived, but his acting was as fine as ever. During that period, the musical *Show Boat* was drawing capacity crowds in its initial run, but while Robeson is almost always identified with it, he did not perform the role of Joe in the original cast. He first made his mark, particularly for his show-stopping treatment of "Old Man River," in the London version of 1928. It was not until 1930 that he performed in *Show Boat,* in New York at the Casino. That year he also first appeared in his most acclaimed acting role, as Othello in Shakespeare's classic. It was a part he took up again to great effect from 1943 to 1945.

During the 1930s, he continued as one of the major concert artists in the world, performing a wide variety of songs on stages throughout the United States and in many other countries. His repertoire included lyrics in most of the world's major tongues; a talented linguist, he mastered some twenty languages in his lifetime.

He also made an impact on the burgeoning film industry in the early 1930s with the recreation of his lead role in *Emperor Jones* for United Artists. In 1936, he sang "Old Man River" for the cameras as Joe in the Universal film of *Show Boat.* In all he made eleven films, his last efforts being *Tales of Manhattan* and *Native Land* in 1942.

Robeson's singles and albums sold reasonably well in the 1930s and early 1940s, some occasionally becoming best-sellers. His greatest success as a recording artist came in 1939, when he premiered in the radio broadcast of Earl Robinson's *Ballad for Americans,* a collection of songs celebrating multiethnic and multiracial America. The broadcast received a tremendous response from listeners. When his disc *Ballad for Americans* came out that year, it was one of the year's most popular releases.

By then, he had become increasingly active in fighting for black rights. He credited his first trip to Russia in 1934 with his growing awareness of racial problems. Because he found no apparent racial bias in the Soviet Union, he became an open admirer of their system and, in fact, sent his son, Paul, then nine, to school there in 1936 to avoid racial prejudice. In the late 1930s, during the Spanish Civil War, he entertained the Loyalist International Brigade at the front. With the onset of World War II, his friendship with the Russian system actually stood him in good stead, but all that changed when the Cold War erupted in the second half of the 1940s.

The first tremors of the coming political storm occurred in 1946, when Robeson was called before a commission of the California state legislature. Questioned about his political affiliations, he stated he was not a Communist Party member. When the same questions were put to him a few years later by the House Un-American Activities Committee, he refused to answer on grounds of principle, and his long ordeal began. In 1949 he gave a controversial speech in front of the World Peace Conference in Paris that complicated matters for him at home. "It is unthinkable that American Negroes will go to war in behalf of those who have oppressed us for generations . . . against a country [the Soviet Union] which in one generation has raised our people to the full dignity of mankind." The statement was taken out of context and made it seem as if Robeson was telling blacks not to go to war against the Soviet Union. As a result Robeson was condemned by prominent African Americans.

Pressure began to build on concert agencies and record companies to no longer feature his work. When he tried to appear at the Peekskill Music Festival in New York in 1949, riots broke out against his performing. A week later he performed in Peekskill while black and white trade unionists and veterans formed a human wall to protect the area. Although he would have been welcomed by European fans, from 1950 through 1958 the U.S. State Department revoked his passport and refused to issue him a new one. Still the object of inquiries by the U.S. Congress, when he was asked by a committee member in 1956 why he didn't move to Russia, Robeson replied, "Because my father was a slave and my people died to build this country, and I am going to stay here until I have a part of it just like you."

Despite that statement, when the climate changed in the late 1950s and the U.S. Supreme Court restored his passport, Robeson went into a sort of voluntary exile for some years. Before moving to England, though, he gave a farewell concert at New York's Carnegie Hall in 1958, his first performance there in eleven years. The concert was recorded and released in several volumes.

Later, a repackage of Volume 1 was available in the late 1970s on Vanguard Records under the title *The Essential Paul Robeson*. In 1958, Robeson published his autobiography, *Here I Stand*. It was republished in 1988 by Beacon Press. After a short tour of the U.S. West Coast, Robeson left for Europe. In April 1958, he was in Russia, where there was a massive birthday celebration in his honor.

He returned to the United States in 1963, which remained his home for the rest of his life. He made his last appearance in April 1965. His wife, Eslanda, died of cancer at the end of the year, and Robeson, whose health began to fail due to problems with his circulatory system, went to live with his sister in Philadelphia. By the early 1970s, he lived in complete retirement. He remained a hero of the black civil rights movement, his stature increasing with each passing year. On April 15, 1973, a seventy-fifth birthday salute was given him at Carnegie Hall, attended by celebrities from stage, screen, and the civil rights movement. Among those paying tribute was the widow of Dr. Martin Luther King, Jr., Coretta King.

Meanwhile, releases continued of some of his earlier recordings. In 1972, RCA Victor issued *Songs of My People*. Vanguard included three of his LPs in its catalog, *Paul Robeson at Carnegie Hall*, *Paul Robeson Recital*, and *Ballad for Americans/Carnegie Hall Concert, Volume 2*. Also available in the 1970s were *Spirituals and Popular Favorites* on Columbia Records and *Songs for Free Men* on Odyssey Records.

Robeson suffered a stroke in late 1975 and died in Philadelphia in early 1976, but honors continued to come his way posthumously, including the belated placement of his name on the Walk of Stars on Hollywood Boulevard.

For many years, Robeson's legacy was all but lost. Few of his recordings were available, and his name was not regularly mentioned in the schools. However, as the centennial of his birth approached in 1998, people around the world took steps to remember him. Some wrote plays about his life and committees put together celebrations in his honor. In 1995 he was finally inducted into the College Football Hall of Fame. He also won letters in baseball, basketball, and track.

In the latter half of the 1990s a growing number of Robeson's recordings were reissued on CD, an indication of a renaissance of interest. In late 1997, Folk Era released *The Peace Arch Concerts*, originally recorded in 1952 and 1953. At the time, his passport had been revoked and he was stopped on his way to attend a conference in Canada. The Mine, Mill & Smelter Workers union sponsored a concert on his behalf. He stood on a flatbed truck at the U.S.-Canadian border and sang songs such as "Joe Hill," "Ol' Man River," "Go Down Moses," and other folk songs and spirituals. The concerts became an annual event. In 1998, Sony's Masterworks-Heritage released *Songs of Free Men,* which originally came out in 1942 and had eight numbers—two American songs, a Spanish Civil War song, a song from the German concentration camps, and four Russian songs.

Other CDs available include *Paul Robeson: The Legendary Moscow Concert,* originally recorded in 1949 on Fenix Entertainment and reissued by Revelation; *Paul Robeson and Elisabeth Welch: Songs from Their Films with Hattie McDaniel* on Conifer; *Green Pastures, Ol' Man River, Freedom Train,* and *A Lonesome Road* on Living Era; *The Glorious Voice of Paul Robeson* on EMI; *Collector's Paul Robeson, Favorite Songs Volumes 1* and *2,* on Monitor; *Essential Paul Robeson, Live at Carnegie Hall,* and *Ballad for Americans* on Vanguard; *Paul Robeson Sings Ol' Man River and Other Favorites* on Angel; *The Odyssey of Paul Robeson* on Vanguard Classics; *A Man and His Beliefs* on Legacy; *21 Songs & Spirituals* and *Songs & Spirituals Volume 2* on Memoir Classics; *Paul Robeson* on Pearl; *The Power & the Glory* on Columbia Legacy; and *Political Years* on MCC.

In 1998, in honor of his centennial, the National Academy of Recording Arts and Sciences also awarded him a posthumous Lifetime Achievement Grammy. But a longstanding campaign to honor Robeson with a U.S. postage stamp has been unsuccessful.

ROCHES, THE: *Folk-pop trio. Maggie Roche (keyboardist, guitarist, singer, songwriter, born Detroit, Michigan, October 26, 1951; Terre Roche (singer, songwriter, guitarist, pianist), born New York, New York, April 10, 1953; Suzzy Roche (singer, songwriter, guitarist, keyboardist), born Bronxville, New York, September 29, 1956; David Roche (guitarist, pianist), born Bronxville, New York, March 19, 1958.*

In the 1970s, when there was plenty of testosterone to go around in the music business, the Roche sisters brought a badly needed feminine perspective to the stage. They sang crisp three-part harmonies with Maggie at the bottom of the register, Terre at the top, and Suzzy in the middle, and wrote wry songs about riding the train to New York, washing panties at the Laundromat, or in "ing," using gerunds to depict a relationship stuck in a rut. Although they never had a hit record, the Roches were praised by critics and managed to stay together for more than fifteen years. Along with Bonnie Raitt and Joni Mitchell, the Roches helped break down barriers for the female singers with guitars who would follow in the 1980s and 1990s.

Their father, John A. Roche, was an actor who met their mom, Jude Jewell Roche, while both were performing in a play. "He was a star and I was a walk-on," Jude says. The Roche siblings grew up in suburban Park Ridge, New Jersey. "We weren't like the Osmonds or something, where our parents formed us into a singing group when we were seven years old," Maggie told Mike Boehm of the *Los Angeles Times* (July 11,

1991). "But we're a close family, and we all did the same things. We all made up songs, we all played the piano that was in the house, we all wrote stories, we were all cut from the same cloth."

They sang in church and school choirs, at talent shows, and in local coffeehouses. They sang Christmas carols on the streets of New York. Their father, who used to cry while reciting Gerard Manley Hopkins poems, encouraged his children to go into the arts. "That was the thing that was most revered when we were growing up—art and artistic expression," Terre told Colin Irwin of *Folk Roots* (January-February 1996).

John, a teacher, training consultant, director, and writer, wrote songs in support of political candidates, which Maggie and Terre would perform from the backs of flatbed trucks. Once the political scheme backfired: Maggie told Lahri Bond of *Dirty Linen* (October-November 1995): "We had worked up this victory song and we wanted to get a chance to sing it. So we sang it anyway—at the losers party. I don't remember that going over well."

When they were eleven and twelve, their parents gave Maggie a guitar, which she shared with Terre. "Terre learned to play Maggie's guitar from Laura Weber's instruction on television," says Jude, a writer and artist who runs the Roches' fan club. "Soon the house was full of guitars."

Maggie and Terre learned some Phil Ochs songs from the public television program. When they were still in high school, their father would take his eldest daughters to New York, where he encouraged them to sing at the hootenannies in Greenwich Village. Maggie began writing songs influenced by Bob Dylan and Paul Simon. She found out that Paul Simon was giving a songwriting course at New York University, and Maggie and Terre, still teenagers, auditioned some songs for him.

"We thought he was going to listen to these songs and say, 'This is the greatest thing I've ever heard,'" Terre told Boehm. "Instead, he just said, 'If you like, you can join this songwriting class.' For us, that was the beginning of the reality of the music business, as opposed to your fantasies of it."

They took the class for a semester. Simon liked their voices enough to have them sing backup for his 1973 album *There Goes Rhymin' Simon* on Columbia. A talent agent booked the duo at college coffeehouses in places like North Dakota, Idaho, Wisconsin, and Louisiana. In 1975, Simon produced Maggie and Terre's first album, *Seductive Reasoning* for CBS Records. Besides Simon, the album was produced by Paul Samwell-Smith, David Hood, and Jimmy Johnson; they were backed by top-notch studio musicians such as the Muscle Shoals Rhythm Section, and their songs featured offbeat stories.

But it was not a great experience. "By the end of the thing we were feeling intimidated about our own musicianship," Terre told Boehm. "We were working with the top people in the business, and we'd never even played with other musicians in New Jersey. We had never taken any instruction, and didn't know the names of half the chords. We were in over our heads. We felt we had absolutely no talent, that we had nothing to say. We did about four shows, and they were disasters."

Maggie and Terre also felt intimidated because they were women in a male-dominated profession. They decided to drop out. They traveled to Hammond, Louisiana, where a friend ran a Kung Fu school. They studied Tai Chi and Kung Fu and waitressed. In retrospect they felt it was "absolutely necessary" to stop out. "Hammond Song," written by Maggie, was inspired by their decision. *If you go down to Hammond, you'll never come back,* the song begins.

"We did come back, or at least part of us did anyway," Terre told Bond.

A year later, they returned to New York. In 1976, Suzzy Roche, a senior studying drama at the State University of New York at Purchase, left college and joined her older sisters. She encouraged them to sing Christmas carols on the streets of New York and under the arch in Washington Square. (Suzzy was actually born as Susannah and went by Suzy until her grandfather added another *z* on a Christmas stocking.)

"I totally idolized them," Suzzy, the most outgoing of the sisters onstage, told Boehm. "They were older, and I never saw myself as part of it. But after they quit, I felt I could get them back singing again."

The trio returned to singing in the folk clubs in Greenwich Village—Kenny's Castaways and Gerde's Folk City, where Terre and Maggie tended bar. They gained a strong reputation and soon started drawing an audience. One person who took notice was British rocker Robert Fripp. He had disbanded his group, King Crimson, and settled in New York, and he began accompanying them in concerts. "You wouldn't have really thought of the match at first, but I think we shared certain sensibilities together," Maggie told Bond.

"He would play with us whenever we were together at a gig. He was a riot; we were a strange combination," Suzzy added.

By 1979 the Roches had signed a record deal with Warner Brothers. Fripp produced their critically acclaimed debut, *The Roches.* He played guitar and added Larry Fast on keyboards, Jim Maelen on percussion, and Tony Levin on bass. Fripp took a very different approach from Paul Simon.

"I don't know what Paul is like now, but at the time he'd have everybody overdub things and you'd have to play something 50 times and you'd have to punch in notes," Terre told *Folk Roots.* "But Robert had this phrase 'No pussyfooting!' What he meant was you get into the studio, you sit down, you play the songs and that's it. . . . So we basically sat around in a circle and we sang the songs and that was basically it."

The album included "Hammond Song" and their anthem "We," "The Train" and "The Married Men." The

trio began headlining concerts. At a concert in Washington, D.C., in 1980, it was clear that Maggie Roche was the most subdued of the three, hiding behind the keyboards or guitar. Suzzy was the ham, and Terre threw herself into her performances. The album made the *New York Times* top 10 list, among others, and was one of their top two best-selling albums. (*We Three Kings,* their 1990 Christmas album, was the other one.)

They followed with *Nurds* on Warner Brothers in 1980, an album that did not match the quality of their debut. They continued to write from a feminine and offbeat perspective, in songs such as "The Death of Suzzy Roche," a farce about being done in by a Laundromat attendant. Fripp returned to produce their third album, *Keep On Doing,* for Warner Brothers in 1982. The album is noted for the a cappella song "Hallelujah Chorus," which became a concert standard, and its title track about perseverence. The next album, *Another World,* released in 1985, featured the use of drum machines and synthesizers but didn't generate much airplay. It was their last for Warner Brothers, even though it included some excellent material, such as "Face Down at Folk City," a tale of debauchery taken from their years at the famous folk club.

In 1986 they cut a four-song demo called *No Trespassing,* which they sold at concerts. It was rereleased by Rhino Records in 1990. Suzzy played a supporting character, Marilyn Cohen, in the 1988 film *Crossing Delancey,* and the group performed on the sound track. In 1990 the youngest Roche, brother David, joined the tour as opening act and tour manager. Sometimes he'd join his sisters in a song or two. The group developed a faithful "cult" audience.

At the end of the 1980s they signed with MCA/ Paradox, releasing *Speak* in 1989. "Big Nuthin'," written by Suzzy, received some play on VH-1. They performed the song, about how a talk show appearance does nothing for their career, on *The Tonight Show.* Their album in 1990 for MCA, *We Three Kings,* hearkens back to their days as Christmas carolers. The album went out of print and was rereleased by Rykodisc in 1994. *A Dove,* which includes the song "ing," released by MCA in 1992, was their last for MCA.

Suzzy Roche was inspired to make a children's album by her child, Lucy, whose father is Loudon Wainwright III. She produced the group's first children's album in 1994 on Baby Boom Records, *Will You Be My Friend?* with Stewart Lerman, who had also produced *A Dove* and their 1995 album on Rykodisc, *Can We Go Home Now.* The children's album received a Parent's Choice Gold Award. About the children's album, Suzzy told Bond in 1995, "I have a 13-year-old daughter and I have been thinking about it for a while. That was a real personal and joyful album. My daughter sings on it and co-wrote one song."

In 1997 Suzzy completed her first solo effort, *Holy Smokes,* released by Red House in August. Suzzy played a number of solo engagements in support of the CD, which required some adjustment after years of performing with her sisters. "It's terrifying," Suzzy told Kristin Tillotson of the *Minneapolis Star Tribune* ("Suzzy Roche, Singular Sister," September 19, 1997). "I'm trying to connect—in a very visceral way—my voice, my guitar and my words with the people listening." In November 1998, Terre released a solo CD on Earth Rock Wreckerds called *The Sound of a Tree Falling,* which was "produced by Nobody." All songs were written and performed by Terre. In 2000 Red House issued Suzzy's second solo CD, *Songs from an Unmarried Housewife and Mother.*

In a role only Hollywood could have dreamed up, the Roches guest-starred as singing roaches for Steven Spielberg's animated film *Tiny Toons.* "They came to one of our shows and drew us and based our characters around our personalities," Suzzy told Bond. "Then we had to go in and play the characters, too."

The Roches also performed a track for the tribute to Harry Nilsson that came out on Music Masters in 1995, *For the Love of Harry.*

The first album they recorded for Rykodisc, *Can We Go Home Now,* was the most intensely personal for the group. It was conceived and produced when their father was suffering from Alzheimer's disease and released just a few weeks before he died in June 1995 of emphysema. The experience caused the sisters take stock.

"It was very hard to go through his illness with him," Terre told *Folk Roots.* "It was almost as if the heart of the group grew very tender as a result of that experience. But I think we also drew something very positive from it. Like Suzzy's song, 'Home Away from Home,' which goes back to early childhood. She was put in touch with her early self in a way which I think is quite profound."

The title track, written by Maggie, shows a mature woman confronting her place in life. Terre's song, "Christlike," was inspired by a conversation with her boyfriend, who said, "I don't want to be jealous, I want to be Christlike" (*Dirty Linen*).

"It is definitely an album by 40-year-old women," Suzzy told *Dirty Linen.* "The record industry interests, especially towards women, are really geared towards people who are younger. Just because you're 40 doesn't mean you're dead."

After the release of *Can We Go Home Now* the Roches took a break from recording together. Maggie went into teaching, and the three only occasionally appeared together, as they did on Tracey Ullman's HBO program. Terre performed with her band, the Moodswings, and Suzzy appeared with an ensemble called the Wooster Group. Despite the potential for sibling rivalry—and according to one article, there have been some fights over the years—the Roches have somehow been able to keep singing together and even improve their relationships.

"We've had so many years of working out our differences," Terre told Boehm. "Many times we would come to the point where we would think we would have to stop, 'This is not going to work.' Then it would break through to a different place. I can't remember one argument about (musical differences). It's more the kind of stuff that happens in families: 'Since you were a kid, you're always saying this to me and I can't stand it anymore.' We're constantly checking the working relationship, asking, 'How is everybody doing?'"

With assistance from Jude Jewell Roche

ROGERS, GARNET: *Singer, songwriter, guitarist, violinist, flute player. Born Stony Creek, Ontario, Canada, May 3, 1955.*

When Canadian folksinger Stan Rogers died in a tragic plane fire in June 1983, he cast a long shadow over his younger brother, Garnet. But Garnet simply picked up where Stan left off. He continued to write and perform songs that depict the extraordinary lives of everyday people. Throughout the 1980s and 1990s, Garnet has performed up to 250 nights a year, putting hundreds of thousands of miles on his car. Just one year after Stan's death, Garnet released his debut, *Garnet Rogers,* on Snow Goose Songs and released seven other albums through 1999.

Garnet grew up near Hamilton, Ontario, the son of Al, a bricklayer, and Valerie, a housewife. His parents loved music of all types, especially folk, country, swing, and the blues. During the summers he and Stan would visit their relatives in Nova Scotia, getting in touch with the music and the stories in that maritime province. One of Garnet's biggest influences was his older brother. When he was six and Stan was twelve, they would lay in their beds and listen to radio broadcasts of the Grand Ole Opry. He started playing the ukulele when he was eight, but soon began to teach himself flute, violin, and guitar.

By the time Garnet was eighteen, he began traveling full-time as part of Stan's band, accompanying him on flute, violin, guitar, and vocals. Like Stan, Garnet is a big man, standing six feet, four inches tall with a smooth baritone voice that complemented Stan's vocals well. For the last ten years of Stan's life, they traveled extensively throughout Canada and the United States.

Garnet has chosen to maintain his independence, releasing all of his albums on his own label, Snow Goose Songs, despite several offers from major labels. He has shunned the established music industry and all that it represents. His loyal but small following (which includes Mary-Chapin Carpenter) has come to respect him as a man of integrity who makes excellent music. He is known for his storytelling and offbeat humor in concert. He has shared the stage with such performers as Carpenter, Billy Bragg, Bill Monroe, Ferron, and Guy Clark.

Following his debut, he released *The Outside Track*

(1986); *Speaking Softly in the Dark* (1988); *Small Victories* (1990); *At a High Window* (1992), which was nominated for a Juno Award; *Summer Lightning—Live* (1994); and *Night Drive* (1996). The last album, which favors an electric rather than acoustic sound, includes backing from Mary-Chapin Carpenter's guitarist Duke Levine, Junkhouse guitarist Dan Achen, Mike Bonnell on organ, and singer David Sereda. In 1999, Rogers released his eighth solo album, *Sparrow's Wing.*

On the album, Garnet finally includes two songs that deal with his brother's death, "Night Drive" and "Golden Fields," about their travels through western Canada. "Of all the songs I've written, 'Golden Fields' and 'Night Drive' are the hardest ones I ever wrote, and the most honest," he told Nick Krewen of the *Toronto Star* ("Garnet Rogers Finding His Voice," December 26, 1996). "There's no line I would change. I'm going to, at least in some sense, journey back there every time I perform those songs."

ROGERS, STAN: *Singer, songwriter, guitarist. Born Hamilton, Ontario, Canada, November 29, 1949; died Hebron, Kentucky, June 2, 1983.*

The songs Stan Rogers left behind after his tragic death at age thirty-three captured Canada's history in much the same way Woody Guthrie spoke of the United States. They encompassed the vast geography of his nation—from the East Coast in his first album, *Fogarty's Cove,* to the West Coast in *Northwest Passage,* to his native Great Lakes in his last studio record, *From Fresh Water.*

A bald man with a Paul Bunyanlike, 6'4" physique and beard, Rogers cut an imposing figure. "They aren't just songs, they're literature," songwriter John Gorka told Stephen A. Ide of the *Patriot Ledger.* (July 1991). "They're rich with detail and full of life. You felt like you could learn something from them." Toronto songwriter Nancy White said Stan's baritone was "a voice you could take a bath in."

Stan was born in Hamilton, Ontario, the son of Al, a shy bricklayer with a good singing voice, and Valerie, a housewife. Uncle Lee Bushell, who lived in Nova Scotia, built Stan his first guitar when he was five out of birch plywood with metal welding rods and an old toothbrush. (The family still has it.)

Rogers summered with relatives in Nova Scotia, learning the music from his ancestral home. His parents loved folk, country, swing, and blues. There were records by Leadbelly, Cisco Houston, Guthrie, and Bob Dylan around the house. His later influences included Steeleye Span (he was dubbed Steeleye Stan; the band's influence comes through in his song "The Nancy"), Gordon Lightfoot, Eric Bogle, Joni Mitchell, and Friends of Fiddlers Green, the house band at Toronto's Fiddlers Green Club.

He first appeared in a high school variety show at thirteen. "I was pretty scared," he told *Artsbeat,* published by the Hamilton Regional Arts Council in 1973. "I wasn't a very popular kid, and to get up in front of a thousand kids and play and sing was pretty scary, but they all seemed to like it; they were still clapping a couple of minutes after the curtains had closed. I've never really considered any other career but music since that night."

He played bass in the rock band Stanley and the Livingstones while attending the Saltsleet Secondary School in Stoney Creek, Ontario. His mother wanted him to be a dentist, but it wasn't to be. He started at McMaster and then Trent University. He met up with his first touring partner, guitarist Nigel Russell (now living near Austin, Texas) and dropped out to become a folksinger—not an easy road. "Most of the songs I wrote the first year were pretty bad," he told *Artsbeat.* "I was an amateur trying to become a professional and I made a lot of mistakes. And I damned near starved to death. I remember one month after I paid my rent I had exactly eight dollars to live on for the rest of the month. I bought some guitar strings and ate a lot of macaroni."

He cut two 45s on RCA Canada, but the label considered him a novelty act. "Here's to You, Santa Claus," with "Coventry Carol" on the B-side, came out in 1970; "Fat Girl Rag" backed by "Seven Years Along" followed in 1971. "Seven Years Along," about painter Bill Powell, was a regional hit in Nova Scotia for six weeks, but the other sides bombed. Rogers parted with RCA Canada. He also had a bad experience with Vanguard. "They wanted him to be Burl Ives II," says Rogers's wife, Ariel.

In the early '70s, Stan began working on documentaries about Canada for the Canadian Broadcasting Corporation. He performed his songs on *Entertainers* and *Showcase 73.* The CBC made limited-edition 45s of three songs: "Three Pennies," "Past Fifty," and "Guysborough Train." He recorded for several CBC producers, including Paul Mills (a.k.a. "Curly Boy Stubbs"), producer of most of Rogers's albums, and Bill Howell, on shows like *Touch the Earth, CBC Playhouse,* and *Nightfall.*

Rogers eventually found a home in clubs like Smale's Pace in London, Ontario, sharing an apartment with two brothers from Nova Scotia, Mike and Tim Curry. "The first time I played Smale's Pace in London, it felt like coming home," he told *Artsbeat.* "There were people who could really listen to what a song had to say, and everytime I went there, I had such a high time that I went on a two week songwriting spree. My best songs were written in London."

Traveling with a small band, his reputation as a performer increased in the early 1970s. For the first couple of years, he toured with Nigel Russell, who wrote Rogers's concert standard "White Collar Holler." For the last ten years of his life, his younger brother Garnet accompanied him on fiddle, flute, and guitar. "Curly

Boy Stubbs" occasionally sat in on guitar. Stan had several bass players over the years: Jim Ogilvie, David Woodhead, David Alan Eadie, Craig Jones, and Jim Morison. The band became more versatile with time, ranging from folk to a hint of country-rock.

An aunt, June Jarvis from Canso, Nova Scotia, persuaded him to write songs about the people of Nova Scotia and relatives gave him stories. He included the songs on his first album, *Fogarty's Cove*, released in 1976 on Barnswallow Records. Mitch Podalik, the former director of the Winnipeg Folk Festival, created the company to get Rogers going. Rogers, gunshy from his experiences with RCA and Vanguard, bought back the tracks and founded the Fogarty's Cove label as a sole proprietorship. His mother filled the orders from her house, while Ariel worked as a full-time nurse until 1982 to make ends meet. "Otherwise we would have starved to death," she says. Rogers married the former Ariel McEwen on September 30, 1977.

Fogarty's Cove included songs that were used in various CBC programs and some of his best-known songs: "Barrett's Privateers," a sea chanty; "Forty-five Years," a touching love song for Ariel; and other Nova Scotia tales. What was striking was Rogers's ability to take the stories of common Canadians—fishermen, miners, sailors—and chisel them to life. Roger's most popular tunes remain "Barrett's Privateers," "Northwest Passage," "The Mary Ellen Carter," and "Forty-five Years."

"This is my first album, and I hope you enjoy it," Rogers wrote in the liner notes. "It's really where I'm from and I think that's appropriate for a first album." This has caused some confusion, with some people thinking that he was actually born in Nova Scotia. "His roots were from there," Ariel explains. "I think he really felt like a maritimer spiritually, trapped in upper Canada."

He followed with *Turnaround* (1978) on Fogarty's Cove. Standards on the album include "The Bluenose" and "The Jennie C," an allegory about a fisherman who loses his boat; "Song of the Candle," written in 1972 when he was in London, Ontario; and Scottish folksinger Archie Fisher's "Dark Eyed Molly." "So Blue" shows Joni Mitchell's influence with the line, *I want to listen to Joni Mitchell on the radio and make love.*

Between the Breaks . . . Live! came out in 1979. "It was done in the Groaning Board in Toronto in front of a live audience," Ariel says. "They had to cut a hole in the back wall of the building and feed the cables out to a truck outside in the alley." It included some previously unrecorded concert standards, including Fisher's "The Witch of Westmoreland," "The Flowers of Bermuda," inspired by his trip to Bermuda in 1978, and the hopeful "The Mary Ellen Carter," about a group of men who raise a sunken ship. "I really like the guy in this song," Rogers wrote. "He's every person who ever had experts tell him what he wanted to do was impossible, then did it anyway." In fact, Ariel tells the story about a man whose boat capsized in the Atlantic Ocean. To keep himself awake until help arrived, he sang "The Mary Ellen Carter."

Northwest Passage, issued in 1981, is a tribute to Roger's perserverance and skills as a songwriter. He wrote: "As the result of much traveling in the West and North of Canada, I had amassed a number of songs that dealt specifically with that area and some bright soul suggested that this album become yet another 'theme' album, and incorporate the Western tunes." Songs like "Free in the Harbour" and "Field Behind the Plow," dedicated to Saskatchewan grain farmers he had seen plowing the fields at 4:00 A.M., depict the hard lives of the Northwesterners.

In 1982, Folk Tradition approached Rogers to record an album of quintessential Canadian folk music. The result was *For the Family,* a collection of songs he, Garnet, and Ariel researched. Three of the songs—"Lookout Hill," "Strings and Dory Plug," and "Up in Fox Island"—were written by uncle Lee Bushell. The album also includes a heart stopping rendition of "Cape St. Mary's." "Three Fishers" is modeled on a Charles Kingsley poem. Garnet and Stan considered doing it a cappella, but, as Ariel put it, "Garnet took the fragment of the melody and added the Jimi Hendrix violin."

After having written about Nova Scotia in *Fogarty's Cove* and the west in *Northwest Passage,* Rogers began work on the final album in the trilogy, *From Fresh Water,* in 1981. He wanted to do an album about the Great Lakes and Ontario, but as Ariel explains, he had a growing family (four children) and couldn't drop his rigorous touring schedule. The Canada Council, and later the CBC, gave him funds to reduce his touring. He rented a small office and began research, which included an unsettling day on a Lake Erie fishing boat with a friend. ("The man was green when he got home," Ariel recalls. "Everyone thought of him as this strapping sailor but he wasn't good in a boat at all.") Rogers found, Ariel says, "an Ontario he had not known or suspected, more unsung heroes of Canadian history and enough information, useful and otherwise, to enliven supper table conversation wherever he was."

After eighteen months, Rogers began recording in Hamilton with Mills producing and playing guitar, Garnet on fiddle, guitar, and flute, and Jim Morison on bass. The album depicts several historical incidents like "The Nancy," about a battle from the War of 1812 to 1814, and "MacDonnell on the Heights," about a major from the "right" kind of family whom nobody liked. Photographer Bruce Kemp told Rogers about a man who was restoring the "Blue Dolphin," a pleasure craft, a research ship, and a World War II sub tracker. Other classics include "White Squall," "The Last Watch," and the "Lock-Keeper." "Tiny Fish for Japan" was a topical song about the many unemployed fishermen in the Great Lakes area. His last number, "The House of Orange," written at the last minute, was highly critical of the civil war in Northern Ireland.

Rogers went on a three-week tour shortly after he finished the album. He started in Western Canada, traveled down to Seattle, then to San Francisco, L.A., and Texas. A week before he died he appeared at McCabe's Guitar Shop in Santa Monica. Writing in the *Los Angeles Times* shortly after his death, Marc Shulgold described how Rogers "bounded center stage, dressed in ever-present long-sleeved shirt and tie and looking more like a computer engineer from IBM than a folk singer (and much older than his 33 years), Stan exuded tremendous energy. . . . Many leaned forward in their chairs, greeted each familiar tune with ripples of applause, and joined right in on the chorus of every song." (June 12, 1983).

He played at the Kerrville Folk Festival in Texas. Then he boarded Air Canada flight 797, a DC-9, from Dallas to Toronto, en route to his home in Dundas, Ontario. A fire broke out in one of the rest rooms and the plane was forced to make an emergency landing at the Cincinnati Airport located across the river in Hebron, Kentucky. Half of the forty-six passengers died of smoke inhalation. Rogers was one of them.

He had achieved immortality in his short life. He was awarded the Diplome d'Honneur of the Canadian Conference of the Arts. Several of his songs have been covered by such artists as Peter, Paul and Mary, Eric Bogle, and the Tannahill Weavers. John Gorka turns in a brilliant rendition of "Lock-Keeper" on *Folk Scene Collection* (1998), recorded live by L.A. radio personalities Roz and Howard Larman and issued by Red House. Others, including Eric Bogle, Gorka ("That's How Legends Are Made"), and Kate Wolf, have written songs about him. Garnet wrote two: "In These Golden Fields" and "Night Drive." There have been tribute concerts, the largest being *Remembering Stan Rogers: An East Coast Music Tribute* on April 23–24, 1995.

Since his death, a documentary video by Kensington Productions, *One Warm Line: The Legacy of Stan Rogers,* has been issued, including forty-five minutes of his music. In 1993, Fogarty's Cove released an album from a 1982 concert at the Rebecca Cohn Theatre in Halifax called *Home in Halifax,* including one previously unrecorded song, "Sailor's Rest." The label also released a songbook from his first four albums called *Songs from Fogarty's Cove,* and is working on a full anthology. In 1993, Chris Gudgeon wrote a book for Penguin called *An Unfinished Conversation: The Life and Music of Stan Rogers.* (The title was taken from an unreleased song.)

In 1996, Fogarty's Cove released an album called *Poetic Justice,* two CBC radio plays for which he wrote the music. The label also released another concert collection called *From Coffee House to Concert Hall* (1999), twenty unreleased songs recorded between 1968 and 1983. The label plans two more albums, one culled from CBC archival tapes, and the other of Stan doing other people's songs.

Perhaps the greatest tribute to Rogers came during a call-in program to the CBC. Peter Gzowski of the CBC asked people to submit nominations for an alternate Canadian anthem. The top two pieces were both songs by Rogers: "Northwest Passage" and "The Mary Ellen Carter."

"At the time of his death, he was beginning to attract attention beyond the traditional folk audience in Canada," Ariel says. "He had in fact begun to redefine Canadian folk music and was being sought after internationally. . . . I think that Stan, in addressing some basic issues about being human, said things that became part of the Canadian cultural matrix. . . . The nature of his death [has] made him a legend. He now has, I would say, cult status. People have enormous arguments about what he meant in his music. He'd probably have a good chuckle and say, 'Shit, put a sock in it.'"

Based in part on an interview by Lyndon Stambler with Ariel Rogers

RONSTADT, LINDA: *Singer, songwriter. Born Tucson, Arizona, July 15, 1946.*

One of the most popular female singers since the early 1970s has been Linda Ronstadt. She has kept her star shining brightly by following her heart in what she sings and by not being afraid to try new material while still remaining true to her roots. In the 1970s she did a lot to popularize country-rock, but in the 1980s she daringly ventured away from this sound and performed in an opera and operetta and also did three albums of nostalgic, 1950s-type ballads, managing to maintain old fans while gaining new ones.

Linda grew up in Tucson, Arizona, where her preteen idols were Hank Williams and Elvis Presley. She liked rock music but also listened to country and Mexican music. After a year at the University of Arizona, Linda left for California to pursue a career as a singer.

With two friends, Bob Kimmel and Ken Edwards, Linda formed the Stone Poneys. They made three albums for Capitol and had a top 20 rock hit in 1967 with "Different Drum." (Written by Michael Nesmith of the Monkees, it was one of numerous songs in her early repertoire she got from records by the folk-bluegrass Greenbriar Boys.) However, the group broke up about that time and Ronstadt started off in her own direction.

Her first solo album, *Hand Sown, Home Grown* (1969), evidenced a shift from the soft-rock sound of the Stone Poneys to a stronger country emphasis. The album was a good one, featuring such songs as "Silver Threads and Golden Needles," a favorite with audiences through the late 1970s, and country standards like John D. Loudermilk's "Break My Mind" and Ivy J. Bryant's "The Only Mama That'll Walk the Line." However, she had no chart hits from the album. Her second solo LP, *Silk*

Purse (1970), continued in the country vein. The album was on the pop charts for a few months, while its top 30 single, "Long, Long Time," won Ronstadt her first Grammy nomination.

For her third album, *Linda Ronstadt* (1972), she assembled a new band, which included Glenn Frey and Don Henley. They went on to form their own influential country-rock group band, the Eagles. In 1973, Ronstadt left Capitol for Asylum Records and released the shallow but successful album *Don't Cry Now* (1973).

The turning point in Linda's career came in 1974, when she signed Peter Asher (formerly of Peter and Gordon) as her manager and producer. From that time on, all of Linda's albums were gold or better. She still owed Capitol an album under her previous contract so she and Asher decided to get it out of the way. Ronstadt and Asher's first collaboration, the platinum *Heart Like a Wheel* (Capitol, 1973), reached number one on the LP charts. Its remakes of "You're No Good" (a 1963 R&B hit for Betty Everett) and the Everly Brothers' "When Will I Be Loved" also made number one and top 10 respectively. Its tearful version of Hank Williams's "I Can't Help It" won her the Grammy Award for Best Female Country Vocal. In addition, *Don't Cry Now* returned to the charts to become Linda's second gold record.

Ronstadt's second album produced by Asher (the platinum *Prisoner in Disguise,* Asylum, 1975) was more rock-oriented than some of her previous albums. The big hit single was "Heat Wave" (a remake of Martha and the Vandellas' 1963 soul hit). There were also country-influenced cuts such as Dolly Parton's "I Will Always Love You" plus Neil Young's "Love Is a Rose" (a hit on the country charts).

The year 1976 witnessed a continuation of Linda's previous successes. *Hasten Down the Wind* included, for the first time, two songs that she had written herself: "Lo Siento Mi Vida" (cowritten with former Stone Poney Kenny Edwards as well as Linda's father) and "Try Me Again" (cowritten with sideman Andrew Gold). Other cuts were "That'll Be the Day" (a Buddy Holly classic, which added fuel to the growing Buddy Holly revival craze) and Willie Nelson's composition "Crazy" (a 1961 hit for the late Patsy Cline). Both became pop as well as country hits. The album achieved platinum status and won a Grammy for Best Female Pop Vocal Performance. That year, the *Playboy* poll named her the Top Female Singer in both pop and country categories.

Ronstadt's next album, *Simple Dreams* (August 1977), contained five major hits. Two were smash rock hits, "Tumbling Dice" from the Rolling Stones and "It's So Easy" from Buddy Holly. Its three country hits were Roy Orbison's "Blue Bayou" (which won a Grammy Award for Best Single), "Poor, Poor Pitiful Me," and the traditional folk ballad "I Never Will Marry"

(recorded with Dolly Parton). Linda was once again named Top Female Singer in both pop and country in the *Playboy* poll. *Simple Dreams* sold 3.5 millions copies in less than a year in the United States alone. Ronstadt appeared on the covers of *Time, Rolling Stone,* and *People* magazines.

September 1978 saw the release of Linda's platinum *Living in the U.S.A.* Its opening cut, "Back in the USA," written by Chuck Berry, made the upper echelons of the country and rock charts. In 1980, she reflected the growing punk and new wave movements on the platinum *Mad Love* with its top-10 single "Hurt So Bad."

After this, Ronstadt took a hiatus from rock and appeared in a Joseph Papp production of Gilbert & Sullivan's operetta *The Pirates of Penzance,* in New York City. The production was a big hit and Ronstadt's voice adapted itself well to the operetta.

In the meantime, her *Greatest Hits, Volume 2* (Asylum, late 1980) was certified gold by year-end. The next album with new material, *Get Closer* (fall 1982), also went gold.

Ronstadt's next move was a surprise—an entire album of ballads from the 1920s through 1950s, backed with rich orchestrations by arranger-conductor Nelson Riddle. The resulting album, *What's New* (1983), surprised everyone by going platinum, attracting young audiences as well as older ones. *What's New* was followed by a similar Riddle-backed LP, *Lush Life* (1984), featuring a few up-tempo numbers along with the ballads. A third LP in the genre, *For Sentimental Reasons,* appeared in 1986. Asylum released a three-record set of the Ronstadt–Nelson Riddle LPs titled *Round Midnight.*

Ronstadt returned to the New York opera scene in 1984 as Mimi in Puccini's *La Boheme.* Her performance was given mixed reviews. She had done operatic training prior to taking on the role, but some critics felt that her voice, though certainly beautiful, had not been trained early enough to adapt to the rigors of opera.

Linda continued to do concerts of her pop-rock-country material. She even performed at a mariachi festival at Los Angeles's Universal Studios in September 1986, which was natural for her as her father, a Mexican-German, often listened to and sang *rancheras,* the songs sung to mariachi music. Her *Canciones de mi Padre* (1987) preserved these songs on disc. The album won a Grammy for Best Mexican American Performance.

In 1987 came the album *Trio* (Warner Brothers)—the long-awaited and second attempt at a collaboration between Linda Ronstadt, Dolly Parton, and Emmylou Harris on an idea they had been germinating for ten years. The album was mostly country and folk songs, and the blend of the three voices, a lovely experience. *Trio* won a Grammy for Best Country Performance by a Duo or Group with Vocal. At the same ceremony, "Somewhere

Out There" (written by James Horner, Barry Mann, and Cynthia Weil and recorded in a duet by Ronstadt and James Ingram) was named 1987 Song of the Year.

Ronstadt returned to the studio with Peter Asher to make *Cry Like a Rainstorm-Howl Like a Wind,* released in September 1989 by Elektra. The album represented a return to her 1970s pop style and would become her last mainstream hit record for a decade, selling more than 5 million albums worldwide. At the heart of the album are four duets with Aaron Neville. "Don't Know Much" won a Grammy for Best Pop Performance by a Duo or Group with Vocal. The following year "All My Life" won for Best Pop Performance by a Duo or Group with Vocal. Asher won a Grammy for producer of the year. She also recorded "I Need You" and "When Something Is Wrong with My Baby" with Neville, a combination that was widely praised by critics and fans.

At the start of the 1990s, Ronstadt continued to experiment with her range and style of music, a move that whipsawed her fans as well as company executives. She had gone from folk-rock, country, and pop to big band, jazz, opera, Broadway, and mariachi music. As she told one reporter: "I sing songs that I really want to sing and that I admire, regardless of what they are. And if I don't get to sing them, they keep me awake at night."

Although most of her albums went gold, she no longer achieved the kind of multiplatinum success of earlier years. The big question among record executives when Ronstadt announced a new project was often "What language is it in?" Her next two albums were made in Spanish. *Mas Canciones,* released in 1991 by Elektra, was a follow-up to the album she made of her father's songs. She won a Grammy for Best Mexican American Album. In August 1992 she released another Latin-flavored album, but this time she focused on the music of Cuba. *Frenesi,* released by Elektra, included eleven Afro-Cuban songs from the 1930s through the 1950s. Her timing was slightly off, although she was on the right track. The album missed the intense renaissance in Cuban music in the late 1990s but still won a Grammy for Best Tropical/Latin Album.

With her 1993 album, *Winter Light,* she returned to the English language. It was praised for such songs as "Anyone Who Had a Heart" and "I Just Don't Know What to Do with Myself" by Burt Bacharach and Hal David, "Heartbeats Accelerating" by Anna McGarrigle, and "A River for Him" by Emmylou Harris. But the album, which Ronstadt coproduced with George Massenburg, seemed uneven and overproduced. She returned to her 1970s country-pop sound with *Feels Like Home,* released in April 1995. The album includes a Nashville-tinged cover of Tom Petty's "The Waiting" and pared down versions of Neil Young's "After the Gold Rush" and A.P. Carter's "Lover's Return." The songs were originally intended to be used in a sequel of

1987's *Trio.* But Linda and Emmylou couldn't get together with Dolly, so Ronstadt made it a solo project, with Emmylou providing background vocals. She went on tour for the first time since 1990. (She's known to suffer from stage fright.)

In 1996, Ronstadt took another turn, making an album for children called *Dedicated to the One I Love.* It was a collection of lullabies fashioned from rock and pop hits such as "Be My Baby," "In My Room," "We Will Rock You," and (not a pop hit but popular nevertheless) "Brahm's Lullaby," the strongest track, a duet with Aaron Neville. The album was inspired by her adopted children, Carlos and Mary Clementine. "I didn't think I could love anything so much," Ronstadt told Letta Tayler of *Newsday* ("Ronstadt Reveling in a Lullaby Style and Motherhood," July 19, 1996). "It's such ferocious love that you just don't think you can bear it sometimes."

The album sold surprisingly well—more than 600,000 copies—for an album of lullaby covers of pop songs and received a Grammy for Best Musical Album for children.

She followed in 1998 with *We Ran,* which received strong critical acclaim. Backed by guitarists Bernie Leadon and Waddy Wachtel, Ronstadt returned to her country-rock versions of folk-rock artists such as Bob Dylan ("Tom Thumb's Blues"), Bruce Springsteen ("If I Should Fall Behind"), and John Hiatt ("When We Ran"). It was certainly one of her best albums in a long time, but it didn't sell well, in part because Ronstadt refused to tour to support it.

But for Ronstadt, who turned fifty in 1996, selling is not as important as it once was. She is one of the top female artists of all time, having sold more than 50 million records worldwide. Her earlier albums still sell briskly. She is viewed as one of the godmothers of Lilith Fair. And in 1999 she was involved in several projects likely to reestablish her credentials as one of the top vocalists around. She made an album of duets, *The Western Wall: The Tucson Sessions,* with Emmylou Harris that includes Neil Young on a couple of tracks. The album was nominated for a Grammy. She also recorded *Trio II,* a reprise of the winning combination of Harris, Parton, and Ronstadt. They won a Grammy for their rendition of "After the Gold Rush." Elektra also released a box set, covering Ronstadt's career from the early 1960s, when she recorded with Frank Zappa and the Stone Poneys, to the late 1990s.

Linda Ronstadt had her first hit at the age of twenty-one, and more than thirty years later, she was still going strong. She seems to be a person without pretenses, which, along with her lovely voice, has endeared her to her fans. This charm has always helped her career. Girls and women could identify with her giggling stage manner and her songs about failed romance. Men found her pretty and sexy in addition to enjoying her voice.

Ronstadt carried her honesty into the songs she chose to record. As she told Robert Hilburn of the *Los Angeles Times* in December 1974: "Though the melody has to match up with what I can do, the lyrics are the main thing. I look for something that feels like it is about me. Just like a songwriter will write a song that is about some feeling he just went through, I can't really sing a song that doesn't express my feelings in some way."

Entry by Alice Seidman, revised by Lyndon Stambler

ROOFTOP SINGERS: *Vocal and instrumental group. Erik Darling (vocals, guitar, banjo), born Baltimore, Maryland, September 25, 1933; Bill Svanoe (vocals, guitar); Lynne Taylor (vocals). Taylor replaced by vocalist Mindy Stuart. Stuart replaced by Patricia Street.*

Most anyone living in the United States in 1963 who listened to the radio will remember a song called "Walk Right In," which rose to the top of the pop charts in January. The song so defined an era that it was used as part of the sound track for the movie *Forrest Gump* in 1995. The group that performed the song, the Rooftop Singers, got together mainly to record it.

The song was written by Gus Cannon (born Red Banks, Mississippi, September 12, 1883; died October 15, 1979), a Memphis banjoist, who formed a band called the Jug Stompers in 1928. Cannon, who had previously recorded with Blind Blake, decided to form a jug band after hearing Will Shade's Memphis Jug Band. He was an innovator on the banjo. He'd sometimes set the banjo on his lap and play it with a knife. He'd also suspend a jug around his neck so that he could play it and strum the banjo. He recorded several sides for Victor Records, among them "Walk Right In" in 1929.

The song had legs. Johnny Cash recalled that after he got out of the air force in 1956, he was selling appliances door to door in Memphis. He wasn't a very good salesman. Whenever he heard music inside a house he would offer to sing along. Cash remembers knocking on Gus Cannon's door and then singing songs on his porch day after day, including "Walk Right In."

Erik Darling, who played with the Weavers for several years as a replacement for Pete Seeger before leaving to pursue a solo career, came across a recording of "Walk Right In" by Cannon and His Jug Stompers. Seeing the commercial potential for the song, he decided to form a group to record it. He was no stranger to forming groups, having put together the Tarriers in 1956. The Tarriers helped start the ball rolling for "The Banana Boat Song," which later became a nationwide hit for Harry Belafonte. The Rooftop Singers' genesis came some years after that, however, in 1962. To his own aptitude on guitar and five-string banjo, Darling added the skills of guitarist Bill Svanoe and vocalist Lynne Taylor.

Svanoe, who attended Oberlin and the University of Minnesota, spent seven years playing his guitar throughout the United States and Europe before joining the Rooftop Singers. Taylor provided a cosmopolitan touch, having impressive jazz and popular credits. These included working with the Benny Goodman band for a year, with Buddy Rich, feature spots on such TV shows as Steve Allen, Ernie Kovacs, Robert Q. Lewis, and Dick Van Dyke, and appearances at the Blue Angel, Birdland, and the "Jazz on a Sunday" series at the Little Theater. In the early 1960s she also showed her folk music abilities in a twenty-eight-week engagement at the Village Vanguard.

Darling came up with the notion of using two twelve-string guitars to bring out the acoustic backing for "Walk Right In." Although Leadbelly had popularized the twelve-string, in the early 1960s there were not many around. Darling special-ordered a twelve-string from Gibson Guitars, but before they could record they had to wait until the company made a second guitar for Svanoe.

The group won favorable notice in appearances at concerts and festivals in the eastern states in 1962. Then, at the start of 1963, they scored a nationwide hit with "Walk Right In," which hit the number one spot in January. The song was featured in their first Vanguard LP, *Rooftop Singers,* released in April 1963, which also included "Tom Cat" and "Stagolee." The album was nominated for a Grammy for Best Folk Recording of 1963, but lost out to Peter, Paul and Mary, who had released *Blowin' in the Wind.* Other nominees included the New Christy Minstrels (*Green Green*), Judy Collins (*Judy Collins No. 3*), Odetta (*Odetta Sings Folk Songs*), Pete Seeger (*We Shall Overcome*), and Miriam Makeba (*The World of Miriam Makeba*). The Rooftop Singers also performed the song at the Newport Folk Festival in 1963, and it was included in Vanguard recordings of that event.

In 1964, Vanguard turned out a second Rooftop Singers album, *Good Time,* followed by *Rainy River* in 1965, and the compilation *The Best of the Rooftop Singers.* The latter, produced by Mary Katherine Aldin, is available on CD and cassette from Vanguard.

The group continued to play concerts, including a tour of Australia and New Zealand. But they never had another hit. Taylor was replaced by Mindy Stuart, who in turn was replaced by Patricia Street. The group recorded some songs for Atlantic Records before disbanding in 1967. Darling has continued to record and perform since then. (Folk Era Productions released his *Border Town at Midnight* in 1994.) He had the distinction of being Béla Fleck's first banjo teacher.

Besides the *Forrest Gump* sound track, "Walk Right In" has also been included on *One Hit Wonders of the '60s* on Rhino (1990), *Havin' a 60's Hootenanny* on K-Tel (1991), *Folk Song America* on Smithsonian/Folkways (1991), and *Troubadours of the Folk Era, Volume 3, the Groups* on Rhino (1992).

ROSE, TIM: *Singer, guitarist, songwriter. Born Washington, D.C., September 23, 1940.*

Tim Rose never quite made it to stardom, though he came agonizingly close a number of times. A gifted songwriter and effective if low-key performer, he seemed destined for great success when he first appeared on the New York pop scene in the early 1960s, but somehow there always seemed to be a piece of the puzzle missing. Nonetheless, he turned out an excellent body of work over the years and had an influence on both folk and rock.

Born and raised in the Washington, D.C., area, Rose came from a musical family. His maternal grandmother played piano in silent movie houses; his mother played piano as well. She started Tim out on the accordion, an instrument that didn't inspire him. He was much more motivated when she bought him a guitar. Rose played in a number of bands in his teens, winning his high school's highest musical award. He went on to a seminary to train for the priesthood, but he was thrown out after six months. At the University of Virginia he majored in history and psychology, earning money for college by working in one of Lester Lanin's society dance orchestras. After a year and a half of college he decided that neither school nor old-style pop music was exciting enough and enlisted in the air force, where he was trained as a navigator for the Strategic Air Command. While stationed in the Midwest, Tim formed a rock group with other fliers called the Abstracts, considered one of the best in the air force in 1962.

After receiving his discharge, Tim moved to New York. He briefly joined Michael Boran to form a group called Michael and Timothy. Then he joined John Phillips and Scott McKenzie of the Journeymen, although he did not record with the group. In the fall of 1962 he met Cass Elliott, later to become famous with the Mamas and the Papas, and formed a group called the Triumvirate with her and John Brown. While performing in Omaha, Nebraska, Rose fired Brown and added James Hendricks (who went on to write a number of songs that became hits for Johnny Rivers). They called themselves the Big 3 and worked together from May 1963 to May 1964. They recorded two albums for FM Records, *The Big Three* (1963) and *The Big Three Live at the Recording Studio* (1964). The group had great potential, but was ahead of its time. It featured folk material, but with the then unusual approach of employing some electric guitar plus drums.

Rose said later, "I remember the big names in the business throwing hands to heads at the thought of mixing folk with rock. But a couple of months later, folk-rock became an accepted musical form. That proved one thing to me. In this business you've got to go ahead and do what you want to do."

But the Big 3 had other problems. Rose told a reporter, "I was 'fired' from the group when Cass and Jimmy decided they didn't want to work with me anymore. They had gotten married—and had been married for months—and they didn't even tell me. That's how close we were."

After performing briefly with an obscure group called the Feldmans and another called the Thorns, Tim decided to make his way as a solo act only, come what may. He worked when he could, wrote new material, and made the rounds of recording companies in the mid-1960s, for the most part meeting only frustration. It was an outlook he expressed incisively in the lyrics to his song "Goin' Down Hollywood": *Soon I met reality / It hit me in the face / No one cared to hear my songs / Was dreamin' all a waste? / First I had to sell my car / Just to buy a meal / My lady found another man / This whole thing sounds unreal / But it's all goin' down in Hollywood.*

He didn't lack for near misses, though, as he told Richard Trubo (*Los Angeles Times* Calendar, July 16, 1972): "I had a chance to join the Rolling Stones, but I was extremely anti-group at the time and turned it down. I also refused an opportunity to join the Christy Minstrels. I was considering an offer George Harrison made to produce an album of mine and put a group around me, but the label I was with then [Columbia] nixed the idea before it got off the ground."

However, Tim's signing with Columbia in 1967 was a promising step forward. The debut disc, *Tim Rose,* contained such songs as "Hey Joe (You Shot Your Woman Down)," "Morning Dew," "Come Away, Melinda," "Where Was I?," and "I Got a Loneliness." Rose's arrangement of "Hey Joe" was adopted by Jimi Hendrix for a chart hit single. Rose never got any royalties from Hendrix's version because it was a traditional Appalachian song arranged by Rose. "Morning Dew" has been covered by many artists over the years. The album and Rose's debut single on CBS Records in England, "I Guess It's Over," found a wider audience in that country than either the LP or the U.S. initial single, "Long-Haired Boy," achieved. During 1968, Rose was well received in such places as London's Royal Albert Hall, Yugoslavia, and the international pop music festival, Musica '68, held on Majorca.

A second album by Rose came out on Columbia in 1969, *Through Rose-Colored Glasses,* but it fared relatively poorly with the U.S. public. In 1970, Tim moved to Capitol, which released the album *Love, A Kind of Hate Story.* It had some good cuts but, as Rose himself agreed later, suffered from a lack of consistency and from overproduction. He remedied many of those defects in his fourth solo LP, *Tim Rose,* which came out on Playboy Records in 1972. The release provided an excellent showcase for Rose's composing and performing skills and received considerable critical praise and more airplay than previous efforts. Overall, though, perhaps because he was the first artist on the new Playboy label, it never received enough sustained promotional support to expand Rose's cult following to a broader audience.

Rose, whose album *The Musician* was issued in 1975 by Atlantic, moved to London in the mid-1970s, occasionally performing with Tim Hardin, whose drug and alcohol addiction made him unpredictable. As the decade wore on, his music career was going nowhere. He moved back to New York in the late 1970s and did a wide variety of non-music-related jobs. He worked in construction and laying Sheetrock. For a number of years he lent his voice to commercial jingles, such as ads for Wrangler blue jeans, Pepsi, and Wheaties. Later he did voice-overs. In the late 1980s he went back to college to finish his degree. He worked as a Wall Street stockbroker, but left that field after the 1987 stock market plunge. That same year a retrospective, *I Got to Get a Message to You,* was completed by See for Miles Records but never released. Rose had been married and divorced before returning to the music business.

At the beginning of the 1990s his long-forgotten albums were suddenly available again. His first album, *Tim Rose,* was reissued by Edsel in 1988 under the new title *Morning Dew. The Gambler,* which had been made in 1977 for Phonogram but never released, was finally released in 1991 on President Records. Demon/Edsel rereleased *The Musician* in 1995. With a sudden groundswell of interest in Rose, in the fall of 1996, when he was in London making demo tapes, a friend called and asked him if he wanted to perform at the Half Moon Club. To his surprise 200 people came out to see him. Nick Cave asked him to perform with him at the Royal Albert Hall. In 1997, Rose recorded his first new album since the 1970s, *Haunted,* on Best Dressed Records. Some of the tracks were recorded in the studio, some live at the Garage and Royal Albert Hall. BGO Records also rereleased his first four albums in 1997 and 1998.

ROWAN, PETER: *Singer, songwriter, guitarist, mandolinist, band leader (Earth Opera, Rowan Brothers, Panama Red Riders). Born Wayland, Massachusetts, July 4, 1942.*

In a 1996 concert at West Hollywood's Troubadour, alongside singer-songwriter Steve Earle, guitarist Norman Blake, and bassist Roy Huskey, Jr., Peter Rowan lifted his guitar to the microphone and began singing "Land of the Navajo." At the end of the song, he chanted in a falsetto that echoed eerily throughout the club. Storytelling, whether it be about the Navajos or the Texas Rangers, is second nature to Rowan, who first read *Huckleberry Finn* as a child. He has taken his own picaresque journey from sock hops in the '50s, bluegrass in the '60s, psychedelic rock at the decade's end, and back to bluegrass, country, and folk in the '70s, '80s, and '90s.

The son of a textile salesman, Rowan grew up on a small farm in Wayland, Massachusetts, twenty-five miles outside of Boston and ten miles from Walden Pond. He read Thoreau and learned about Paul Revere as a child, but also recalls hearing country music. World War II had ended, and the radio stations were playing "hillbilly music" for the sailors returning to the Boston Naval Yard. His parents, Paul and Elizabeth Rowan, played piano. His father was an amateur musician who performed in musicals and plays at the Volk Theater. But it was his Uncle Jimmy, back from the South Pacific, who impressed him as he stood in the living room in a grass skirt and sailor's cap, playing ukulele. "Oh, I want to do that," Rowan recalls. "He was the fun guy."

Rowan would ride his bike to a grocery store a mile from home, where he bought his first 45-rpm record, Homer and Jethro's spoof "The Ballad of Davy Crew Cut." Before long, rock 'n' roll had taken over and he bought 45s by Little Richard ("Tutti Frutti") and Elvis ("I'm Left, You're Right, She's Gone"). Peter learned to square dance at the annual Strawberry Festival, which featured a bluegrass band. He remembers when rock entered his consciousness. He had been listening to a gospel station on his parents' Zenith radio. Then one day he heard Buddy Holly singing "That'll Be the Day" on every radio station. The gospel station had been replaced by a rock station.

His dad gave him a ukulele at age twelve, with an Arthur Godfrey chord finder. Rowan learned to play "Down by the Old Mill Stream." A great-uncle, who played the guitar and accordion, threw a family party each year. "The guitar, an old Monterey, would be sitting in his basement on a table. It marked my growth as a child: first looking at it, then being allowed to touch it. Finally, I would have it in my arms the whole time."

Rowan's first guitar was a Fender Telecaster. In high school, he formed a rock 'n' roll quintet called the Cupids (including Bill Emery, at one time of Northern Lights) which played at sock hops—"the girls had their beautiful white socks on." The band recorded a 45, and received airplay in Boston. It was after one of the sock hops that he got his first taste of the folk movement. The band went to Harvard Square and discovered a girl singing in front of Club 47. It was Joan Baez, who came outside to sing some doo wop songs with them. He hung out at the coffeehouses and heard jazz, conga, and folk. He sold his Telecaster, something he now regrets, and bought a Martin. "The sound of an acoustic guitar being projected the way Joan Baez did it was cool."

He had heard about another kind of music at a bar called Hillbilly Ranch near the Combat Zone, a rough part of town. Rowan wasn't twenty-one yet, but one night he sneaked in. A band called the Lilly Brothers from Clear Creek, West Virginia, was on stage. Don Stover was playing banjo and Tex Logan was on the fiddle. "There was a difference between the folk and the bluegrass scene," he says. "I liked the bluegrass scene. Somebody in the folk scene turned me on to a record of Lightnin' Hopkins. I began to see that rock 'n' roll had roots. I could hear where Chuck Berry was coming from. I got interested in the blues. The more I heard of bluegrass, the more I liked the fact that it had a bluesy feeling. But it also had the ballads, the old story songs, the legends. When I finally heard Bill Monroe it all came together, the blues and the Celtic tradition, in this powerful, rocking sound called bluegrass."

In 1961 he enrolled at Colgate, but only lasted two years. He took philosophy, English lit, and history courses, but neglected his studies. He played mandolin in a bluegrass band with banjoist Bill Keith and Jim Rooney. He also joined the Charles River Valley Boys, which evolved into the Mother Bay State Entertainers. The group recorded three tracks for *The String Band Project* released in 1964 on Elektra, which was produced by Paul Rothchild, who later worked with the Doors.

Rowan hitchhiked to Washington, D.C., to hear the Country Gentlemen. He met Ralph Rinzler, Monroe's road manager, who had discovered Doc Watson playing in North Carolina, and later became director of the Smithsonian Folk Life Center and the Newport Folk Festival. When Monroe came to Boston, Rowan was primed to meet him. Bill Keith, who played banjo in the Blue Grass Boys, called Rowan: "Of course Bill plays mandolin. How would you feel about playing guitar?"

"Is there any other answer but yes?" Rowan says. "When you get into bluegrass and you're flatpicking with Bill Monroe, you're locked in. It's hard to think of much else. His mind was a genius mind. It's like going into Einstein's lab or Picasso's studio." Rinzler saw the chemistry between Monroe and Rowan and assured Rowan, "You can do this." "I didn't know what he meant," Rowan says. "Actually what he meant was I could drive the bus, book the dates, and take over managing Bill Monroe."

So Rowan began playing guitar and singing in the Blue Grass Boys in 1964. "In those days there was only one microphone on stage," he recalls. "You had to learn how to project an acoustic instrument into one mike, which is something I love about bluegrass, the dynamics that were created by necessity. Bill would lift his mandolin up and play into the vocal mike. When you played guitar, you had to physically approach the person next to you. He had to make room for you." (Rowan still lifts his guitar to the mike to signal a change in dynamics.)

In concert, the Blue Grass Boys were expected to keep their hair trimmed short. One time, Rowan was on stage and Monroe came up behind him, lifted his hat and said, "Now, look at that hair right there folks, he's a longhaired boy." As the youngest band member, Rowan wanted to bring people his own age into the group. He enlisted fiddler Richard Greene, who was playing with the Green Briar Boys. The band also included Bill Keith (later Lamar Grier) on banjo. "Finally we were all of the same generation," he says. "We added a focused intensity to Bill's sound."

Monroe was a father figure. Once, while they were shoveling hay at his "Bean Blossom" farm in Indiana, Monroe left them some sandwiches and a note: "I've gone to Charlie's [his brother]. Here's some food for you boys. Be back later. Love, Bill."

Late at night, when everyone else had gone to bed, Rowan would ask questions of the man, something the others thought was rude. "He'd sit there in silence for four minutes, as if he was deciding if he even wanted to tell you this. Bill would take out his mandolin and he'd moan the blues or play these things that sounded like American Indian songs. I would listen and never say anything. He'd always talk about this other music he would play. He didn't want to let his fans down and change his style."

Monroe played a song called "Cheyenne," in which he would chant at the end, something Rowan applied to "Land of the Navajo." He's also carried on Monroe's mandolin teachings. By 1966, Rowan had fallen in love and wanted to move on. "I tried to follow his way," Rowan says. "I was just wanting to, as Bill said, be a beatnik. I wanted more of that *On the Road* style."

Monroe was hurt by his departure and advised: "Pete, don't go too far out on that limb and flowery it up too much. There's enough flowers out there already." Rowan cowrote "Walls of Time" with Monroe and had performed at the Grand Ole Opry. He recorded one studio album, *Bluegrass Time* (Decca, 1966) with Monroe; tracks can also be heard on *Bill Monroe Bluegrass, 1959–1969*, released in 1993.

In 1967 Rowan joined with mandolinist Dave Grisman, whom he had met in Union Grove, North Carolina, when he was playing with the New York Ramblers. They moved to Cambridge and formed Earth Opera, playing "somnambulistic trance music." They recorded two albums for Elektra: *Earth Opera* (1968) and *The Great American Eagle Tragedy* (1969), including the minor hit, "Home to You." "American Eagle Tragedy" was a Vietnam protest song full of "grandiose bombast and explosive sounds. It was my chance to be a real rock lead singer and stalk the stage." Rowan and three others played a saxophone intro, which was cut from the final mix. They started out with Rowan on guitar and Grisman on mandocello. They were experimenting, adding drums performing the introspective songs Rowan had written while traveling with Monroe.

The band had some regional hits: "The Red Sox Are Winning," "Time and Again," "Dreamless," and "When You Were Full of Wonder." They opened for the Doors. "Jim Morrison could magnetize a crowd," Rowan recalls. "He could crawl on the ground and entertain them. He was acting out something in the psyche of the time."

So were Rowan, Grisman, and Janis Joplin, with whom they also toured. Earth Opera fell apart in 1968. "When Earth Opera broke up on the West Coast with all the drugs and all the various personalities and hysteria, it was very depressing," Rowan says. "What was such a supportive unit to begin with suddenly dissipated." (Since the '70s, Rowan has studied the Vajrayana Buddhist path, a practice that precludes drugs.)

Rowan returned to Nashville. He got a call from Richard Greene in California who had formed a rock band called Seatrain. "Earth Opera was a mood-altering sound with strange lyrics," Rowan says. "Seatrain was punchy, hard driving, up-tempo rockin' stuff with strong classical music influence."

The group put out two albums on Capitol: *Seatrain* (1970) (produced by George Martin) and *Marblehead Messenger* (1971). When the band reorganized, Rowan departed. He moved to Stinson Beach in Marin County, California, and returned to his first love, bluegrass, joining Greene, Grisman, Keith, and flatpicker Clarence White in a short-lived but potent group called Muleskinner, which recorded one album in 1974 on Warners. The band gave a number of notable concerts in clubs and at festivals around the United States. White died too young, cut down by a drunk driver. In 1991, Sierra Records issued a CD and video of an original television soundtrack of Muleskinner. "Clarence White, of course, was so refined at a young age and had distilled so many musical ideas that, really, they just linger on as little jewels, little seeds," Rowan told Stephanie P. Ledgin of *Bluegrass Unlimited* (April 1986).

At the time Grisman was producing an album with Rowan's younger brothers, Chris and Lorin, who were living in Stinson Beach. (Columbia released *The Rowan Brothers* in 1972.) Another person in the area was Jerry Garcia. "Garcia was always up for a pickin' session," says Rowan, who jokes that he would look for knobs on his banjo. David [Grisman] is a precise and infectious mandolin player who can just start playing and make everybody want to play. He lit the fire in Garcia to want to really get good on the banjo again. Jerry would take the banjo on the road. He'd call us from the hotels. We'd go up to his house and Mountain Girl [Carolyn Adams, Garcia's second wife] would say, 'Jerry is going to call in fifteen minutes.' We'd sit there and Jerry would call and we'd all talk to him. 'How's it going, man?' 'Oh great, man, I'm pickin' the banjo, man.'"

Garcia coined the name for the band: Old and in the Way. The group, which began playing in the San Francisco area, included Rowan on guitar, Grisman on mandolin, Greene on fiddle, occasionally John Hartford on several instruments, and John Kahn on bass. Greene left the group, so Rowan tracked down country fiddle virtuoso Vassar Clements. The group began playing on alternate nights from the Grateful Dead during an East Coast run. Clements returned with the group to the West Coast for a series of shows. They were scheduled to play at San Francisco's Boarding House on two successive weekends in 1973. Owsley Stanley, who had taped most of the group's performances, set up microphones in the dressing room and in the club.

Garcia would show up at the Boarding House before anyone else to practice. "He'd be sitting on the stage with his carton of Camels on the table playing the banjo. . . . We'd show up and we'd start picking, take a break for a bite, then we'd pick in the dressing room. Then we'd walk on stage. Basically what they got on stage was a culmination of a full day of picking. In other kinds of music it's called rehearsal. In bluegrass you don't rehearse. Playing with the group was a burst of energy."

Rowan wrote and sang several of the songs performed by the group: "Midnight Moonlight," "Land of the Navajo," and "Panama Red," a song later recorded by The New Riders of the Purple Sage. (*The Adventures of Panama Red*, Columbia, 1973).

The resulting album, *Old and in the Way*, released on the Dead's Round Records label in 1975 and reissued on Sugar Hill and Rykodisc, was the best-selling bluegrass album until Alison Krauss's 1995 Rounder album, *Now That I've Found You*, surpassed it. It was like a "busman's holiday" for Garcia. All he had to do was show up. But egos got in the way and the band broke up, according to Rowan, who fell out of touch with Grisman until after Garcia died in 1995.

Rowan reunited with his brothers in 1975 and they recorded three albums on Asylum: *The Rowans, Sibling Rivalry*, and *Jubilation*.

At the end of the decade, Rowan shifted from bluegrass to write songs with a Southwest flavor, compositions about cowboys, Indians, and Mexican Americans. Native Americans have become an important influence for Rowan (who wears a turquoise ring). He doesn't have any Indian blood, but feels a spiritual connection. "All my childhood was an awareness of a certain presence of these people," he said. "I just followed that. I sat in the sweat lodges out in Colorado with northern Ute elders and sun dancers. I've sat with Sioux people. Basically you talk it over and you pray. 'Land of the Navajo' is a sort of prayer song. It takes people into a nonverbal realm. It sparks their intuition, imagination, and their spiritual essence."

Native Americans provided the main input for his self-titled LP released in 1978, which included "The Free Mexican Air Force" (recorded with accordionist Flaco Jimenez) and "Land of the Navajo," and also for *Medicine Trail* (Flying Fish Records, 1980). Members of the Free Mexican Air Force band included Richard Greene, fiddler Tex Logan, and Jimenez, whom he had met in San Antonio while traveling with Seatrain. Rowan followed with *Texican Badman*, (Apaloosa Records, 1981).

He and Jimenez recorded a live album in 1982 when they toured in London: *Flaco Jimenez and Peter Rowan: Live Rockin' Tex-Mex* (Waterfront Records). Other Waterfront releases included *Revelry,* and *Rowan, Keith, and Rooney: Hot Blue Grass.* He also played on *Flaco's Friends,* released on Arhoolie Records, nominated for Best Mexican American album Grammy.

Traveling has often inspired Rowan. In 1978, he toured Japan with an ensemble known as the Red Hot Pickers—Tony Trischka, Andy Statman, Greene, and Roger Mason. They released two albums in Japan, later issued by Sugar Hill as *The Red Hot Pickers.* He sought out his roots when he went to Ireland, releasing a Celtic-influenced album, *The Walls of Time* (Sugar Hill, 1981). It was the first time he had recorded with Dobro player Jerry Douglas and mandolinist Sam Bush.

In the mid-1980s, he returned to Nashville, formed the Wild Stallions, and wrote songs recorded by Ricky Skaggs ("You Make Me Feel Like a Man"), George Strait ("Dance Time in Texas"), Janie Fricke ("Where Does Love Go When It's Gone").

In 1984, he began recording for Sugar Hill and again returned to bluegrass. The following year he toured Ecuador on a State Department–sponsored tour. He returned and released *The First Whippoorwill* (1985, Sugar Hill), an album of Bill Monroe's songs selected as Album of the Year by WAMU, a PBS station in Washington, D.C. *New Moon Rising* (1988) with the Nashville Bluegrass Band was a Grammy nominee for best bluegrass album. (His song "Meadow Green" was used in the film *Steel Magnolias.*)

Rowan again showed a capacity to grow with two more Sugar Hill albums: *Dust Bowl Children* (1989) and *Awake Me in the New World* (1993). *Dust Bowl Children,* selected as the best folk album of the year by NAIRD, is a Woody Guthrie–esque look at the Great Depression and environmental issues. Rowan sings about people who live off the land, from Tennessee farmers to Hopi Indians. *Awake Me in the New World* was another thematic album about Columbus's voyage to North America as seen through the eyes of a cabin boy named Pulcinella. Rowan was reunited with his brothers and included Caribbean and Latin stylings.

He recorded two more bluegrass albums for Sugar Hill: *All on a Rising Day* (1991), selected as NAIRD's Best Bluegrass Album and a Grammy nominee; and *Tree on a Hill* (1994) with his brothers, which includes traditional songs of the Stanley Brothers, the Carter Family, and Doc Watson. He joined with Jerry Douglas to record *Yonder* (1996) on Sugar Hill. The album, which received a Best Contemporary Folk Grammy nomination, was recorded using old tube equipment to give it an old-timey feel. Rowan had been hanging out with Norman Blake, listening to 78 rpm records. "I wanted to make a recording that gave Jerry and I the chance to play the roots of what later became country and bluegrass."

Douglas and Rowan began recording the album in October 1995 in Béla Fleck's living room, setting up microphones in different parts of the house to get the ambient sounds. Rowan included some of his own songs, like "Wayside Tavern" and "You Taught Me How to Lose," that fit in with the old tradition. He also recorded a stunning ballad about the Indian Wars called "Texas Rangers." In a concert at McCabe's with Douglas, Rowan performed "Texas Rangers," occasionally strumming on the mandolin as he sang. Douglas's Dobro accompaniment was simple and mournful. *Yonder* was another step in Rowan's quest for roots: "It's a metaphor of where we have been, where we are and where we're going in terms of this imaginary road." It received a Best Contemporary Folk Grammy nomination.

In 1995, after Jerry Garcia died suddenly, Rowan renewed contact with Grisman. They got to talking about the Old and in the Way days. "I've got these Old and in the Way tapes," Grisman said. "Jerry really wanted to put them out."

They decided to get the old band together, with one major component missing: Garcia. In March 1996 they played together for a reunion. They played the Telluride Folk Festival in 1996 with Herb Pedersen on banjo, Grisman on mandolin, Vassar Clements on fiddle, Rowan on guitar, and Roy Huskey, Jr., on bass. (Rowan is also playing in a bluegrass group called the Panama Red Riders, with Greene on fiddle, Michael Munford on banjo, Viktor Krauss on bass, and Charles Sawtelle on guitar.)

In 1996, Sugar Hill released *Bluegrass Boy,* his tribute to Bill Monroe, who died that year. It was nominated for a Best Bluegrass Grammy. "It's a way of me saying I was a Blue Grass boy—and still am a bluegrass boy," he told Jim Bessman. "And that I inherited from Bill Monroe certain things that have allowed me to continue his style of bluegrass. I'm the same age as Bill was when I came to work with him." The album also includes former Blue Grass Boys Del McCoury and Richard Greene. Rowan was also featured on a Monroe tribute, *True Life Blues: The Songs of Bill Monroe,* a Sugar Hill release that won a Best Bluegrass Grammy.

In the last part of the 1990s, Rowan was constantly in demand as a singer and musician. He participated in *Rig Rock Deluxe,* a collection of truck driving songs released in 1996 by Upstart/Diesel Only Records. His singing and picking can be heard on sequel recordings of Old and in the Way released by Grisman's Acoustic Disc label. He provided backup for Ramblin' Jack Elliott's 1998 HighTone album, *Friends of Mine.* In May 1998, he sang four of the fourteen cuts on Daniel Gore's CD *Ways That Are Dark,* on Elephant Rock Records. He sang two tracks for Czech banjo virtuoso Lubos Malina's 1998 CD, *Piece of Cake,* and performed with Malina's group Druha Trava on *New Freedom Bell* (1999). The group also released *Czech Mate* on Compass in 2000.

After his multifaceted journey, it would seem impossible to pin Rowan down to a definition of his music. But that's not true, as he says simply: "The only style I play is bluegrass. The rest of the time everyone's groping in the dark."

Based on an interview by Lyndon Stambler with Peter Rowan

RUSH, TOM: *Singer, guitarist, pianist, songwriter. Born Portsmouth, New Hampshire, February 8, 1941.*

For a while in the first half of the 1960s the name Tom Rush brought the image of a major force in current music trends to the minds of a sizable segment of the American music audience. However, with the resurgence of rock 'n' roll and the British invasion of the mid-1960s, Rush, like most other folk luminaries, moved into the wings. Tom has continued to turn out finely crafted, sensitive records since then, but their delights have been sampled by a select few of the general public still faithful to the folk idiom. Still, to those individuals, Rush remained a major name, and his concerts at various folk centers always were eagerly awaited. And, as a look at the albums of contemporary artists like Jackson Browne and others in the California folk-rock movement indicate, Rush's abilities as a songwriter continued to be recognized by artists with mass followings.

When he was growing up in Concord, New Hampshire, where his father taught mathematics at St. Paul's School, Tom's initial exposure to music took the form of classical piano lessons. Ivy League education was very much a family tradition; Rush was sent to Groton School, in Groton, Massachusetts, in the eighth grade.

He recalled, "It was straight out of Dickens. They had a black mark system and depending on the nature of the offense, you could be given up to six black marks. Each was worth an hour's time doing something. Sometimes it was copying out of the Bible, sometimes it was walking in circles. Every now and then they would have you do something constructive, like sweep up the woodworking shop or model for an art class."

In retrospect the most important event during his high school years was when he received his first guitar during his junior year at Groton. "I never did take lessons on the guitar, which is probably why I enjoyed it so much. I got a little band together and we played before the Saturday night movies and for parties and things. We were doing Gene Vincent imitations and Carl Perkins imitations, you know, old time rock 'n' roll. Subsequently, I became interested in folkier type of music. When I went to Harvard, I found that Cambridge was the hotbed of folk."

At the time he was accepted there, in the late 1950s, the folk boom was in full swing, inspiring such then-unknowns as Joan Baez to sing in local coffeehouses. Rush also followed that path, working one or two nights a week for small amounts of money, sometimes passing the hat.

His popularity encouraged him to begin his recording career. "I made a record on a little fly-by-night label. It wasn't quite a vanity record. Somebody was paying me to make it. It was really a small scale operation. The guy was distributing it to stores out of the trunk of his car. Then a friend of mine, Paul Rothschild, got a job as A&R man for Prestige Records and signed up most of the Cambridge folk scene, except for a few artists who went with Vanguard Records."

Tom made some albums for Prestige in the early 1960s, such as *Got a Mind to Ramble* (1963) and *Blues, Songs, Ballads* (1965), then dropped out of school. "Most of the time I was staying around Boston working two nights a week. I was only taking home $10 a night, but somehow I managed. I ate a lot of liver."

Having proved he could support himself, albeit marginally, he went back to Harvard and got his degree. "I didn't really intend to be a professional singer, but I graduated with a degree in English Lit, which doesn't really prepare you for anything." He continued to work as a Boston folksinger for a while, his reputation slowly growing not only locally but in other folk centers. After Rothschild moved to Elektra and worked out a new contract with Rush, Tom became a fixture on the New York folk scene and took up residence for a while in a Manhattan apartment. His concertizing took him far afield in the mid-1960s, including appearances on campuses and in concert halls and clubs throughout the United States, as well as three tours of England.

His Elektra albums rank among the more notable folk releases of the mid- and late-1960s. His debut on Elektra, *Tom Rush*, was released in March 1965 and was followed by such other Elektra releases as *Tom Rush—Take a Little Walk with Me* (1966), *The Circle Game* (1968), and *Classic Rush* (1971). Commenting on *The Circle Game*, whose title track was written by the soon-to-be-discovered Joni Mitchell, the *New York Free Press* (March 28, 1968) critic echoed many reviewers in writing, "[the album] screams for recognition. . . . Tom Rush is a musician who projects sensibility. He can handle the dangerous emotions of love and tears as few have ever been able to bare themselves with their voice and eloquence." The LP included another Joni Mitchell song, "Urge for Going," his versions of songs by Jackson Browne ("Shadow Dream Song") and James Taylor, and the self-penned "No Regrets." The cover art was contributed by Linda Eastman, who later married Paul McCartney. Elektra also released the retrospective *Classic Rush*, which included "Urge for Going" and "The Circle Game."

Although Rush retained a faithful following, the sales of his recordings by the end of the 1960s paled compared to the reigning rock and soul royalty. There was still enough demand for his output, though, for Columbia to welcome the chance to add him to its roster in late 1969. His debut release on the label, *Tom Rush*, was on record racks in 1970. The album contained one of Tom's best-known originals, "Lost My Drivin' Wheel." In 1971, his second Columbia LP, *Wrong End of the Rainbow,* was issued, following in May 1972 by *Merrimack County* and, during the summer of 1974, by *Ladies Love Outlaws.* In 1975, Columbia issued the retrospective album *The Best of Tom Rush.* His early '70s album credits also included the 1972 Fantasy release *Tom Rush.*

In the 1970s, Tom moved back to New Hampshire, where he took up residence on a 400-acre farm. An environmentalist, he spent some of his time at home in the mid-1970s building a windmill electrical generation system. He also indulged in such other hobbies as sculpting and hang gliding.

Into the 1980s, he continued to turn out new songs while sometimes reworking arrangements for earlier ones. Although he could hardly sell out large rock venues, as might have been possible during the early 1960s, he commanded respectable attendance in college auditoriums and folk clubs whenever he chose to tour. His show usually included such favorite original compositions as "No Regrets," "Rockport Sunday," and "Wrong End of the Rainbow" and a sprinkling of songs by other writers, often promising newcomers whose careers Rush enjoyed aiding.

IIis 1980s albums, released on his own label, Night Light, included the live *New Year* in 1982 and *Late Night Radio* in 1984. Much of the work on those and other 1980s projects was accomplished in his own recording studio on his New Hampshire farm. In 1990 he lost studio and home completely to a fire. Rather than try to rebuild, he established his new residence on the other side of the country in Wyoming. It was in Jackson, Wyoming, that Rush met his wife, Renee Askins, an environmentalist who works to protect wolves through the Wolf Fund. Rush helps with the fund when he's not touring around the country. In 1986, Night Light reissued *Tom Rush at the Unicorn,* which was taped live in 1962 at the Unicorn in Boston. In 1994 he released *Work in Progress,* a six-song cassette collection on Night Light. In 1998, Nanci Griffith included "Wasn't That a Mighty Storm" on her album *Other Voices, Too (A Trip Back to Bountiful),* a traditional song arranged and popularized in the 1960s by Rush and Eric Von Schmidt. Rush sings background vocals and plays acoustic guitar on the track. Rush also recorded "River Song" for a Sony/Legacy Tom Rush anthology *The Very Best of Tom Rush: No Regrets 1962–1999,* issued in 1999.

RUSSELL, TOM: *Singer, guitarist, band leader (Tom Russell Band) songwriter, record producer, author. Born Los Angeles, California, March 5, 1951.*

Most creative individuals have an intense aversion to being assigned to a particular category, but in most instances the artist's body of work can be attributed to a general music sector, at least from the standpoint of a reporter or critic. Someone like Tom Russell, though, clearly could qualify as an important contributor to a variety of genres from country to blues and folk. His

songs brought successful record releases for many others, including country stars like Emmylou Harris and Suzy Bogguss and folk notables like Ian Tyson and Nanci Griffith, but his own excellent recordings typically were overlooked by mainstream pop and country radio programmers, which tended to restrict his own audience to a cult following, at least in the United States. In England and Europe, on the other hand, he was justly honored as a major factor in the modern folk and country fields.

While much of Russell's writings and recordings tended to be classified as "country," the folk-music shadings of some of his output was commented on by a *Rolling Stone* reviewer who wrote, "Russell's songs, mainly about American heroes and anti-heroes, offer insight and wryly observed detail reminiscent of John Prine and Steve Goodman."

Russell spent his formative years in a then largely undeveloped section on the outskirts of Los Angeles. As a youngster in the early to mid-1950s, he enjoyed listening to recordings or watching some of the stars of the local country TV shows (like Cliffie Stone's *Hometown Jamboree*) such as Merle Travis, Joe Maphis, Tex Williams, Spade Cooley, the Collins Kids, and the Maddox Brothers and Rose. He recalled, "We had a small ranch in Topanga Canyon in the late 1950s. Real drugstore cowboy scene up there with movie stuntmen and amateur bullriders. I stole my brother's Tijuana gutstring guitar during the folk boom in the '60s and began to learn cowboy songs like 'Sam Bass' and 'Jesse James.'"

"Later on I heard Buck Owens, Wynn Stewart, and Merle Haggard out of Bakersfield. Then folk artists like Dylan and Ian and Sylvia came along and I realized people actually wrote their own songs. Later on, it was a thrill writing songs and recording with both Ian and his ex-wife Sylvia."

After playing at school events during his high school years, he eventually decided to try to make his living as a musician. He ended up performing in house bands at skid-row country bars in Vancouver, Canada, for a time in 1971. He commented, "We were backing topless dancers, strippers, female impersonators, dog acts, and sword swallowers. Then, in 1973, I heard about a progressive country scene down in Austin, Texas." Picking up stakes, he traveled to Texas and after a while became part of the alternative country movement that numbered people like Joe Ely, Butch Hancock, and Jerry Jeff Walker among its prime innovators. (Both Walker and Ely in later years recorded some of Russell's compositions.) In Austin he teamed up with pianist Patricia Hardin to form a band that started to draw attention from reviewers and club goers in the region. They got the chance to record for the Dark Angel label in the mid-1970s, turning out the fine albums *Ring of Bone* in 1976 and *Wax Museum* in 1978.

Russell was not only writing songs during those years, he was also experimenting with fiction. The Russell-

Hardin band never became a mass audience favorite, and after it disbanded in San Francisco in 1979, Tom moved to New York to seek publishers for the novels he was working on. In 1981, Grateful Dead lyricist Robert Hunter looked him up and urged him to return to the music field. With mutual friend guitarist Andrew Hardin, he formed a new partnership that found fertile ground for their collaborations in Europe. This resulted in preparation of three albums by Russell, on two of which he was backed by his own band. These comprised *Heart on a Sleeve* in 1984 (available in the 1990s on Germany's Bear Family label), *Road to Bayamon* in 1987, and *Poor Man's Dream*, released in 1989. These were issued in the United States on, respectively, Philo Records and Philo in the United States and Round Tower Records in Europe.

Based in the United States again from the late 1980s on, Russell found an increasing number of artists interested in recording his songs or cowriting new material with him. One of those was Canadian folk artist Ian Tyson, with whom he wrote "Navajo Rug," a major singles hit for Tyson in both Canada and the United States. It was named the Country Music Association Single of the Year for 1987. Later, Tyson sang a duet of the song on Tom's 1991 Philo disc *Cowboy Real*, which also included a Russell/Tyson duet on the track "Gallo del Cielo," a song first recorded on *Poor Man's Dream* about a fighting rooster from heaven. During 1991 the Tom Russell Band also had the Philo/ Round Tower album *Hurricane Season* on record store shelves. In 1992, Round Tower compiled a retrospective of Tom's recordings, *Beyond St. Olav's Gate 1979–1992.*

Besides writing and performing, Russell developed skills in record production. The dozen or so albums he coproduced from 1988 through 1995 included two for Sylvia Tyson, two for Katy Moffatt, and two for soul singer Barrence Whitfield: *Hillbilly Voodoo*, issued in 1993; and *Cowboy Mambo*, released in 1994, both on East Side Digital/Round Tower. Both albums, as well as Russell's own 1993 solo collection on Philo/Round Tower, *Box of Visions*, showed up on a number of best-of-the-year lists in publications like *Billboard, CD Review, CMJ,* and the *Austin Chronicle. Cowboy Mambo* was nominated for an Indie of the Year Award by voters from the National Association of Independent Record Dealers and Manufacturers.

The 1990s proved rewarding career-wise for Russell. More and more of his songs appeared on albums by people like Johnny Cash, Katy Moffatt, Nanci Griffith, Dave Alvin, and Peter Case. While not receiving the massive attention his skills seemed to deserve, he still had accumulated a sizable following, and his recordings won acclaim from folk and country musicians at home and in many other countries. After Suzy Bogguss scored a top 10 hit with his "Outbound Plane" in 1993, the song was given an ASCAP Country Award as one of the most played radio songs of the year.

Russell joined forces with Dave Alvin in the mid-1990s on an ambitious project in honor of Merle Haggard, *Tulare Dust—A Songwriters' Tribute to Merle Haggard.* Among those taking part in the recording sessions, besides Russell and Alvin, were Peter Case, Marshall Crenshaw, Iris DeMent, John Doe, Joe Ely, Rosie Flores, Robert Earl Keen, Billy Joe Shaver, Barrence Whitfield, Lucinda Williams, Dwight Yoakam, and Steve Young. The disc, issued on Russell's new label home, HighTone, in November 1994, won glowing accolades. England's *Mojo* magazine called it "the country album of 1994," and the *CMJ (College Music Journal)* critic enthused, "Of all the country music compilations that were released in 1994, *Tulare Dust* is without a doubt the best . . . in fact, this is one of the finest country records released in the '90s."

The album quickly showed up on the Americana chart in the industry trade press publication, the *Gavin Report,* remaining at the number one position for eight weeks. In *USA Today*'s review of top releases, the album was ranked the number five country album of the year. In 1995 the *Gavin Report* named *Tulare Dust* the Americana Album of the Year.

In 1995 Tom's solo debut album on HighTone, *The Rose of the San Joaquin,* was released. Most of the material was written by Russell, but also contributing to the disc were Alvin (who coproduced the album with Greg Leisz), Chris Gaffney, and highly regarded songwriter Peter Case. The tracks also included Russell's version of the late Jim Ringer's song "Tramps and Hawkers." As was the case for *Tulare,* the new collection became a top 10 success in the *Gavin Report*'s Americana chart and was among albums listed in a number of best-of-the-year selections by newspaper and magazine critics. The title track also was issued as a video and received airplay on both U.S. and European TV outlets.

Russell's 1995 credits included publication of a new book, coedited with Sylvia Tyson, *And Then I Wrote: The Songwriter Speaks,* published by Canada's Arsenal-Pulp Press.

In 1997, HighTone issued a captivating retrospective album, *The Long Way Around,* which included seventeen songs, nine of them recorded live. He sings duets with Nanci Griffith ("St. Olav's Gate"), Iris DeMent ("Big River," about the midwestern floods; and "Box of Visions"), and Katy Moffatt ("Gallo del Cielo"). The album received strong critical praise, as did his other 1997 release, *Song of the West: The Cowboy Collection,* released by HMG, a HighTone subsidiary. In 1998, after HighTone released the promotional *Monsters of Folk* CD, which also included Chris Smither, Dave Alvin, and Ramblin' Jack Elliott, the four troubadours embarked on a nationwide tour.

That year, Russell traveled to Europe to put together an ambitious and creative new album, *The Man from God Knows Where,* recorded at a barony farmhouse in Norway. The folk opera, as Russell calls it, tells the story of his family's migration from Ireland and Norway to the United States in the 1800s and everything they went through along the way. Released in March 1999 by KKV in Norway and HighTone in the United States, the album features Andrew Hardin and such guests as Iris DeMent, Dolores Keane, Dave Van Ronk, and even a guest appearance by poet Walt Whitman, from an old recording.

$\int$

SAHM, DOUG: *Singer, guitarist, band leader (Sir Douglas Quintet), songwriter. Born San Antonio, Texas, November 6, 1941; died Taos, New Mexico, November 18, 1999.*

Many artists are hard to classify, and that certainly holds true for Doug Sahm, whose body of work extends across a spectrum from rock to country and folk. As was noted in Dave Marsh's and John Swenson's *Rolling Stone Record Guide,* Sahm "is a walking encyclopedia of Texas music—blues, country, Western swing, vintage rock 'n' roll, Cajun, R&B, even Mexican border music—all of which is melted into a bright, pulsating sound [in his Sir Douglas Quintet days] nobody else has ever matched."

Born and raised in San Antonio, Texas, his early influences came from the country and western genre. He became skilled as a steel guitar player while in elementary school, and by eight, known as "Little Doug," he was amazing audiences in Texas and surrounding states with his instrumental talent. He soon became a featured player on the *Louisiana Hayride* radio program. At twelve he was featured on *Grand Ole Opry* programs and other country shows, and in December 1952 he was brought onstage by country legend Hank Williams shortly before the latter's death in January 1953.

By Doug's late teens he was influenced by the first wave of rock artists, such as Texan Buddy Holly and Elvis Presley, and started to assemble bands (the Pharaohs, the Dell-Kings, the Markays) with friends and acquaintances performing that type of music. One fellow teen whose path crossed Doug's at that time was Augie Meyers, who was polishing his skills as a keyboards player. Meyers, who fronted a band called the Goldens, remembered meeting Doug in 1960 when Sahm came with his parents to shop at a grocery store run by Augie's mother. Typically, Augie said, "Doug would say, 'Yeah, I got a band,' and I'd say, 'I got a band I'm working with.' He was always on one side of town and I was on the other."

After a while, though, they found common musical ground that led in the mid-1960s to formation of the Sir Douglas Quintet, which began to draw interested audiences on the Texas bar circuit. The group signed with Tribe Records and, after placing some releases on regional charts, gained a singles hit called "She's About a Mover" that rose to number thirteen on the *Billboard* national chart the week of April 17, 1965. Critics took note not only of Sahm's vocals and guitar playing, but also of the excellent support of Augie Meyers on his Farfisa organ. In early 1966 the band placed another single on the hit lists, "The Rains Came," which peaked at number thirty-one in *Billboard* the week of March 5.

The band's album releases in the mid to late 1960s included *Best of the Sir Douglas Quintet* (1965) on Tribe (reissued on Crazy Cajun Records in 1975), and, on the band's new label, Mercury's Smash subsidiary, *Honkey Blues* in 1968 and *Mendocino* in 1969 (issued by Oval in the United Kingdom in 1975 and by Mercury in Holland in 1980). As the last album suggests, the group had shifted its base from Texas to California, for a time calling Big Sur home. The title track of *Mendocino* provided the band's last top 40 hit, peaking at number twenty-seven in *Billboard* the week of March 15, 1969.

During the 1970s and early 1980s, Sahm kept the band together with various personnel changes and kept turning out new albums with the group or solo on a succession of labels. Taken as a whole, the album contents included country-rock, folk-rock, Tex-Mex blends, and what might be called Texas soul. The series included *Together After Five* (1970) on Smash; *1 + 1 + 1 = 4* (1970) and *The Return of Doug Saldaña* (1971) on Philips Records; *Rough Edges* (1973) on Mercury; *Doug Sahm and Band* (featuring Bob Dylan, Dr. John, David Bromberg, and Flaco Jimenez) and *Texas Tornado* (both in 1973) on Atlantic; *Groover's Paradise* (1974) on Warner Brothers; *Texas Rock for Country Rollers* (1976) on Dot; and, on John Fahey's Takoma label, *Hell of a Spell* (1980), *Best of the Sir Douglas Quintet* (1980), *Border Wave* (1981), and *Live Texas Tornado* (1983). In 1972 Sahm and the Quintet appeared in the film *Cisco Pike* with Kris Kristofferson; in 1979 Sahm had a bit part in *More American Graffiti*. His song "Michoacan" was featured in the former film, while his cover of Bo Diddley's "I'm a Man" was in the latter.

Through the mid-1980s, Doug kept busy with various projects, working as a record producer at times and trying out new band alignments. In 1983 Sahm and Meyers signed with Sweden's Sonet label and toured Europe. "Meet Me in Stockholm," from their *Midnight Sun* LP, went platinum in Sweden. In 1985, however, following a traffic accident, Sahm moved to Canada, and three years later returned to Texas. In 1988 he released *Juke Box Music* on Antone's.

Late in the decade he helped found a new group, which took its name from one of his albums, the Texas Tornados. Originally intended as a Tex-Mex rival to the Traveling Wilburys, the Tornados stayed together much longer. Joining Sahm were longtime collaborator Augie Meyers plus country Tex-Mex star Freddy Fender and Tex-Mex accordion superstar Flaco Jimenez. The group signed with Reprise Records, which issued its debut album, *Texas Tornados,* in the summer of 1990. It was released as *Los Texas Tornados* for the Latino market. The album became a hit, reaching upper levels on the *Billboard* top 200 and helping to set the stage for a well-received tour of major venues throughout the United States. A track from the album, "Soy de San Luis," won the 1990 Grammy for Best Mexican American performance. The group completed several more albums for Reprise, including *Love of Our Own* (1991), nominated for a Grammy for Best Country Vocal Performances by a Group; and the excellent 1992 release *Hangin' On by a Thread.* The first three albums sold more than 800,000 copies, but in 1994, their impact on the music-buying public had tapered off and the members went their separate ways. Reprise released *Best of Texas Tornados* that year. In 1996 Sahm returned to make *Four Aces* with the Texas Tornados. The album rose to the top 10 of the Americana charts, and included a single, "A Little Bit Is Better than Nada," that was featured in the film *Tin Cup,* starring Kevin Costner.

By 1994 Sahm had put together a new "Quintet," but with seven members instead of five. The group released *Day Dreaming at Midnight* on Elektra, followed by *The Last Great Texas Blues Band* on Antone's. In 1998 Sahm released *Get a Life* on Munich Records.

SAINTE-MARIE, BUFFY: *Singer, songwriter, guitarist, actress. Born on Piapot reserve, Qu'Appelle Valley, Saskatchewan, Canada, February 20, 1941.*

For most of her career, Buffy Sainte-Marie was classified as a fighter for Indian rights and a charter member of the antiwar protest movement of the 1960s. In fact, her composition "Universal Soldier" was almost an anthem for the protestors of the Vietnam War. But, as she often pointed out, that was only one side of her musicianship, albeit one for which she never apologized. She told a reporter from *Life* (December 10, 1965, pp. 53–54), "I have written hundreds of songs and only a half dozen are of protest. I believe in leaving politics to the experts, only sometimes the experts don't know what's going on."

And, in fact, Sainte-Marie's writings contained many sensitive songs about love and life in general, including her late 1960s offering "Until It's Time for You to Go," and her 1980s Oscar-winning "Up Where We Belong," both of which gained record successes for a number of artists and provided steady royalty checks for Sainte-Marie. Still, her protest image worked against her for a long time, pushing her into the background on the U.S. music scene while she kept her performing career alive by finding work outside the United States.

Although she seemed a bit uncertain of her heritage in the 1960s, later on Buffy ascertained that she was born in Canada of Cree Indian extraction. When she was a few months old, she was adopted by a couple from Maine who were part Micmac Indian. Most of her growing up years, however, were spent in Wakefield, Massa-chusetts, where she attended high school and also taught herself to play guitar. With a view toward a teaching career, she entered the University of Massachusetts, from which she received a degree with honors in Oriental Philosophy and Education in the early 1960s. She later returned to school to earn a teaching credential and a Ph.D. in fine arts from the University of Massachusetts.

However, folk music proved too strong an attraction, particularly after a guest appearance at a hootenanny at the Gaslight Cafe in Greenwich Village brought a management offer from Herb Gart. Under his aegis she soon was working the East Coast coffeehouse circuit, often appearing with many of the stars of the folk boom.

A bout with bronchial pneumonia in 1963 incapacitated Buffy for six months, having an adverse impact on her voice and almost ending her performing career. She also had to fight off an addiction to codeine that resulted from the illness, which she described in her song "Cod'ine."

In 1963 Buffy was waiting for a flight in the San Francisco airport when she saw some injured soldiers coming home from Vietnam. At the time the U.S. government was denying any involvement in Vietnam. As soon as she arrived in Toronto, Sainte-Marie wrote the song "Universal Soldier" in the basement of the Purple Onion coffeehouse. It appeared the following year on her debut album for Vanguard Records, *It's My Way.* The album also included "Now That the Buffalo's Gone," a protest song in support of Native American rights. Several artists recorded "Universal Soldier," but it was Donovan's recording in 1965 that established it as an anti–Vietnam War anthem.

Her career by then was on a strong upswing, with concert offers from across the United States and Canada and opportunities to appear on major radio and TV shows. She continued to turn out new albums on Vanguard, including *Many a Mile* (April 1965), *Little Wheel Spin and Spin* (8/66), *Fire and Fleet and Candlelight* (8/67), which included her version of the "Circle Game" by Joni Mitchell, whom she had met in Canada in the early 1960s, *Illuminations* (9/69), and *She Used to Wanna Be a Ballerina,* (1971). Other Vanguard releases of the 1960s and 1970s were *I'm Gonna Be a Country Girl Again* (1968), *Moonshot* (1972), *Quiet Places* (1973), *Native North American Child (An Odyssey)* (1974), and *Best of Buffy Sainte-Marie, Volumes 1 and 2.*

A number of Sainte-Marie's songs continued to deal with the Indians' plight. Among those were "Native North American Child," "My Country 'Tis of Thy People You're Dying," and "Now That the Buffalo's Gone." Sometimes she punctuated her performances with a demonstration of the native Indian mouth-bow, an instrument she learned to play from another Cree Indian folk artist of the period, Patrick Sky. Besides folk and protest music, Buffy recorded *I'm Gonna Be a Country*

Girl Again in Nashville, and her song "Piney Wood Hills" made the country charts in 1967 for Bobby Bare.

"I've had hits in country songs, in pop songs, in protest music, as well as in indigenous music, and the only way that I can explain it is that I write about whatever is out there, whatever is happening in my life," she told Martin Dunphy of the *Georgia Straight* ("Sainte-Marie Seeks Heaven Here," April 25–May 2, 1996). "I travel so much and in such a variety of intense communities that I think there's a variety in my music which has been consistent from the very beginning."

By the late 1960s, her career was in decline in the United States. A steady series of tours throughout Europe and countries of the Far East (Japan, Australia, New Zealand) made her a favorite of those audiences. In the United States Buffy's appearances became increasingly rare in the late 1960s and much of the 1970s, a situation intensified by her decision to take up residence on a hilltop in Hawaii in 1967, her home into 2001. Her hopes of returning to the top in the United States were never completely abandoned. She switched record labels from Vanguard to MCA in the early 1970s. For her new label, she recorded *Buffy* (1974) and *Changing Woman* (1975). When that didn't bring any rewards, she signed with ABC Records in September 1975. That affiliation also proved disappointing, leading to one of her weakest LPs, *Sweet America* (1976).

In 1975 Sainte-Marie had a son, Dakota Wolfchild Starblanket, and following *Sweet America,* she decided to step out of the recording industry to raise her child, although she continued to be featured in Canadian concerts (often on tiny reserves) and TV specials. In 1976 she became a regular member of the cast of Public Television's *Sesame Street* program, in which she contributed not only as a performer but as a writer of special material, including children's songs. (In the children's field, she already had written and illustrated a book.) In early 1978 she introduced viewers to her son, Dakota, born of her marriage to Dakota Sioux artist and TV producer Sheldon Peters Wolfchild.

In 1978 Buffy decided to take her recording activities back into her own hands. She bought back rights to the last four LPs she'd made on Vanguard, MCA, and ABC, noting that they had received little exposure when they first were released. Her plans were to reissue those on her own record label.

Looking back on the ups and downs of her career in early 1978, she told Jennifer Sedor of the *Los Angeles Times* (March 31), "It only takes a feather to tip the scale in this business, but it took me a while to realize my fall was also a matter of politics rather than mass listener turn-off. But I've accepted myself as an alternative performer in America. My time will come again. Meanwhile I'm doing other things. I travel, I write, I'm rich, I buy the clothes I want, and if I'm not a tremendous success here, at least I have the respect of the industry and success abroad." That success, among other things, included a command performance for Queen Elizabeth in the mid-1970s.

While she no longer recorded albums or toured much in the 1970s and 1980s, Sainte-Marie became involved in composing sound tracks. She scored such movies as *Soldier Blue, Starman, 9½ Weeks,* and *Jewel of the Nile.* She cowrote the music with her husband, Jack Nitzsche, for "Up Where We Belong," from the movie *An Officer and a Gentleman,* which earned them, and lyricist Will Jennings, Oscar and Golden Globe Awards. The recording by Joe Cocker and Jennifer Warnes was a number one hit and garnered a Grammy. She also worked worldwide on behalf of UNICEF's Committee for Refugees.

During those years, she became interested in "digital art." She had drawn with crayons as a child and with paints as an adult. After buying a Macintosh computer in 1984, she began making computerized digital paintings, which were exhibited in museums and galleries. "Sixteen million colors in your palette are hard for any artist to turn down," she says.

After a fifteen-year hiatus, she began recording a new album using her Macintosh. When she had finished recording the songs, she sent the music via modem from her home in Hawaii to her English record company, Ensign. One of the more computer-literate folksingers, Buffy had made the first ever electronic quadraphonic vocal album in the '60s for *Illuminations.* She became familiar with synthesizers in the 1970s and 1980s as she began composing sound tracks. When she appeared in concert, she played a Roland MIDI guitar. Later on she used computers made for composing music, first a Fairlight, then a Synclavier, graduating to the Macintosh. *Coincidence (and Likely Stories),* issued on Ensign (EMI) in 1992, was viewed as her comeback album. It fared well in Canada but received little exposure in the United States.

Sainte-Marie sees no irony in being a computer-literate Native American folksinger. "It's natural for any indigenous community to be online, because of our desire to remain in the local community, yet be part of the global community," she told Nick Coleman of the *Independent* ("Cult Folk Heroines on the Loose," March 8, 1996). "It's so nice, if you're studying, to have a friend online who's living on another reserve."

After *Coincidence* came out, she was named Best International Artist in France. She was inducted into the Canadian Music Award Hall of Fame. She established a special category at the Juno Awards for the Music of Canadian Aboriginals, an award that Sainte-Marie won in 1997.

In 1995 she became involved in the HBO animated musical series *Happily Ever After: Fairy Tales for Every Child,* singing Native American rock 'n' roll for the "Snow White" episode.

In 1996 she put together her follow-up album, *Up*

Where We Belong, released by EMI in Canada and Angel in the United States. It was a best-of album for which Buffy rewrote and rerecorded many of her best-known songs: "Up Where We Belong," "Piney Wood Hills," "Until It's Time for You to Go," "Universal Soldier," "Now That the Buffalo's Gone," and "Bury My Heart at Wounded Knee." She recorded "God Is Alive," with lyrics taken from Leonard Cohen's book *Beautiful Losers,* and "Goodnight" by Cliff Eberhardt. The album also includes a sampling of powwow singing, and drums from the Red Bull singers and from a Stoney Park song.

Since then, she has cut back on her touring to work on the Cradleboard Teaching Project, an education project to improve the curriculum about Native Americans in both mainstream and Native schools. She received funding for her efforts from the Kellogg Foundation. As of 1997, there were pilot sites among the Lakota, Mohawk, Cree, Northwest coast and Ojibway tribes. Sainte-Marie also has adjunct professorships at York University in Toronto, the Indian Federated College in Saskatchewan, and Evergreen State College in Washington. She teaches digital art at the Institute for American Indian Arts in Santa Fe, New Mexico. Her son, Dakota, went on to attend Boston's Berklee School of Music.

SEBASTIAN, JOHN B.: *Singer, harmonica player, guitarist, pianist, arranger, band leader (Lovin' Spoonful). Born New York, New York, March 17, 1944.*

John Sebastian gave the audience at McCabe's Guitar Shop in Santa Monica, California, a musical history lesson during his performance in January 1996. After more than thirty-five years in the music business, during which time he and his rock band the Lovin' Spoonful scored seven consecutive top 10 hits, Sebastian showed that he never really left his roots. With Fritz Richmond, an alumnus of the Jim Kweskin Jug Band, backing him on jug and washtub bass, Sebastian demonstrated where his inspiration came from: the jug band and blues masters.

Much of his music over the years contained folk, blues, and, to some extent, country elements. Reflecting that influence, in fact, was the name of his extremely successful rock group of the mid-1960s, the Lovin' Spoonful, derived from one of the songs of Mississippi John Hurt.

Sebastian, the son of classical harmonica virtuoso John Sebastian Sr., and a mother who wrote for the radio, was born and raised in New York City's Greenwich Village. His parents saw to it that he took classical piano lessons as a child; in addition, he played the harmonica in emulation of his father, who had introduced his son to blues harp player Sonny Terry. As his interest in the growing folk-music movement of the late 1950s and early 1960s grew, he added guitar playing skills as well.

In his mid-teens, John began to frequent some of the folk clubs and coffeehouses in the Village, where he often got the chance to join other aspiring young performers or, on occasion, to do some solo turns. His particular focus at the time was on blues, and all he had to do was walk down the street to the Night Owl Café or the Village Vanguard to meet some of the masters of the genre. One of his first contacts was Lightnin' Hopkins. Sebastian spent a great deal of time studying Hopkins's musical style. Another of those artists was Mississippi John Hurt, who taught Sebastian many of his favorite songs, including one that contained the line "I love my baby by the lovin' spoonful."

After graduating from high school, for a time Sebastian went to Marblehead, Massachusetts, where he worked as a sailmaker. He wasn't quite sure what he wanted to do, but finally decided to return home and enter New York University. He spent a short time in college, then dropped out to follow music full-time. One of his first formal associations in the early 1960s was with the Even Dozen Jug Band, formed by blues guitarist Stefan Grossman and guitarist Peter Siegel and also included Dave Grisman on mandolin, Steve Katz (who later joined Blood, Sweat and Tears), Maria Muldaur, and Josh Rifkin. The band made one album in 1964 on Elektra Records—on which John performed—before breaking up. In 1962, he teamed up with three others— Zalman Yanovsky, Cass Elliot, and Denny Doherty—in a group called the Mugwumps. That folk quartet stayed together only a short time, but the individual members were all heard from again. Elliot and Doherty later became half of the Mamas and Papas, and recalled some of the history of both their group and the Mugwumps in the song "Creeque Alley." Yanovsky eventually became a charter member of the Lovin' Spoonful.

At the end of 1963, back in New York, John organized a band whose members included Yanovsky on lead guitar, Steve Boone on piano and bass guitar, and Joe Butler on drums. The band practiced for six months before landing a job playing at the Night Owl Café. One night Phil Spector came to see them, which, Sebastian told KPFK radio hosts Roz and Howard Larman, was "pivotal because the next night everybody was down there. They'd heard that Phil was there yesterday and, by golly, they weren't going to miss out on another thing that Phil found out about first." The band became a favorite of New York pop fans, and, after Kama Sutra Records signed them, soon extended their sway coast to coast. The band's repertoire covered just about all musical bases: jug band, folk, country, gospel, ragtime, blues, and pop ballads, all with an underlay of rock 'n' roll. Sebastian sang lead on a succession of hits, most of which were original compositions, including "Do You Believe in Magic" (a massive hit in late summer of 1965), "Younger Girl," "Nashville Cats," "Summer in the City" (number one in the summer of 1966), "Daydream," "You Didn't Have to Be So Nice," and "Did You Ever Have to Make Up Your Mind." Sebastian demonstrated his arranging skills in many innovative numbers, such as "Groovin'," "Big Noise from Speonk,"

"Jugband Music," "Lovin' You," "Your Eyes," "Lonely," and "Bes' Friends."

Sebastian managed to sandwich in work on two film scores during those years, Francis Ford Coppola's *You're a Big Boy Now* (which included Sebastian's beautiful "Amy's Theme") and, for Woody Allen, *What's Up, Tiger Lily?* The Lovin' Spoonful provided sound track music in both cases. Besides those activities, the band toured widely, headlining rock shows across the country and also guesting on many network TV programs.

They released several LPs on Kama Sutra, including *Do You Believe in Magic* (1965), *Daydream* (1966), *What's Up, Tiger Lily?* (1966), *Hums of the Lovin' Spoonful* (1966), *The Best of the Lovin' Spoonful* (1967), *You're a Big Boy Now* (1967), *Everything Playing* (1968), *The Best of the Lovin' Spoonful Volume Two* (1968), and *24 Karat Hits* (1968).

Their productivity came to a sudden halt in 1967, when members of the band were picked up on drug possession charges. However, there were other pressures causing members to lose interest in the operation. The band might have kept going, but the enforced layoff caused by the legal entanglement led to some soul-searching that precluded such a step. Zal Yanovsky left the group in 1967, and Sebastian left shortly thereafter.

John stated later, "It wasn't fun anymore. The band for about two years was really groovy. I guess what made it groovy was the chemistry of the people in the group. But after about two years, it began to get really muddied.

"We could have gone on cranking it along for a few more years and started to collect the enormous sums we were just beginning to get. Of course, breaking up wouldn't have been the best thing from a businessman's point of view. Lots of people were really brought down, but they were concerned with money rather than the music."

Having made up his mind, Sebastian moved on to new projects, beginning with work on music for a Broadway play, *Jimmy Shine,* starring a then relatively unknown actor named Dustin Hoffman. The show didn't do much, but it helped give John confidence he could do well on his own.

The Lovin' Spoonful briefly went on without Sebastian, recording *Revelation: Revolution '69* in 1969 before disbanding. (They reunited briefly in the late 1970s to record "Do You Believe in Magic" for Paul Simon's movie *One Trick Pony*.) Kama Sutra released *John Sebastian Songbook Volume I* and *The Very Best of the Lovin' Spoonful* in 1970, and *Once Upon a Time* in 1971. Buddah reissued *The Best of the Lovin' Spoonful* in 1976, Aristides released *Best of the Lovin' Spoonful Volume One* in 1983, and Rhino released *Best of the Lovin' Spoonful Volume Two* in 1984. Rhino also released *The Best of John Sebastian* in 1989 and *Anthology* the following year. In 1996, King Biscuit Flower Hour released a live John Sebastian concert CD that was taped in 1979.

At the end of the 1960s Sebastian settled in Los An-

geles and started a relatively low-key approach to life in which he did a lot of composing and arranging with personal solo appearances mixed in. His music continued to stress folk content combined with a pop-rock flavor. He began to make his mark as a festival artist, first with a set at Big Sur, California, then with a gripping performance at the now legendary Woodstock, New York, event. His contributions to that show were featured both on the live album and the successful film.

Although his Woodstock effort is considered a highlight of his career, he wasn't even an original invitee. A close associate recalled, "Ironically, he wasn't even supposed to be in the festival. He happened to be there and they needed another act so he filled in. As a result, he was featured on the record and in the movie and made a small fortune." (The reports were that he ended up with something like $150,000 in royalties.)

That incident helped get things going for him as a solo artist in the early 1970s. He gave several hundred concerts during those years and appeared at more festivals, including a show-stopping appearance at Britain's Isle of Wight Festival in mid-1971, where a crowd of some 200,000 urged him on for two hours with several standing ovations.

His recording work the first half of the 1970s was for Warner Brothers, which released his debut solo LP, *John B. Sebastian,* on Reprise in 1970. The LP provided a charted single, "She's a Lady." MFG released *John Sebastian Live,* taken from an audience tape, in 1970. The following year, Reprise released *Cheapo-Cheapo Productions Presents Real Live John Sebastian.* This was followed by such other albums as *The Four of Us* and *Tarzana Kid.* Sebastian also wrote the theme song for the TV show *Welcome Back, Kotter* and both the single of "Welcome Back" and the Reprise album of that title made the pop charts in 1976, though the LP was well below the creative levels of other Sebastian recordings.

In the mid- and late-1970s, Sebastian was less active as an in-person artist and concentrated more on writing material for films and TV. An example was his score for a 1979 animated TV feature called *Romie O and Julie 8.*

Sebastian moved to upstate New York with his wife and two children. He took a seventeen-year hiatus from solo recording, sometimes doing session work for top artists like Bonnie Raitt, Tom Petty, and NRBQ, sometimes writing jingles or hosting TV shows. He made a cameo appearance on the TV show *Married with Children* and appeared on Garrison Keillor's radio show, *A Prairie Home Companion.* He composed the score for the *Care Bears Movie.* He hosted the weekly "Golden Age of Rock 'n' Roll" for Arts and Entertainment; completed his first children's book, *J.B.'s Harmonica,* for Harcourt Brace; and wrote instructional books on harmonica and autoharp for Homespun Records. Later on, he also played guitar for Jewel's debut album, *Pieces of You.*

In 1992 former Even Dozen Jug Band leader Stefan

Grossman, an executive with Shanachie, invited Sebastian to return to the studio. Shanachie released Sebastian's *Tar Beach* in 1993, his first solo album since 1976. The album included a collaboration with the Band's Levon Helm (a neighbor in Woodstock, New York) on "Someone Standing in Your Door," as well as songs that take a look back in time, such as "Night Owl Café," about the café where the Lovin' Spoonful got its start. There were also bleak songs such as "Freezin' from the Inside Out," and "Bless 'Em All," and more upbeat numbers such as "You and Me Go Way Back" and "Smokey Don't Go," a tribute to Smokey Robinson.

At the same time, Sebastian wanted to return to his jug band roots. He had been gigging with guitarist Jimmy Vivino and drummer James Wormworth. Sebastian wanted them to try the jug band sound. But for that they needed someone who could play the jug. So Sebastian called on jug virtuoso Fritz Richmond. (They called themselves the J-Band rather than Jug Band in deference to the Jim Kweskin Jug Band.) In 1994, Sebastian and the J-Band played at the twenty-five year Woodstock reunion concert held in Bethel, New York, at Max Yasgur's farm.

When Vivino took a job as the guitarist on the *Late Night with Conan O'Brien* show, Sebastian brought in singer-guitarist Paul Rishell and his singer–blues harp partner, Annie Raines. Blues guitarist Rory Block also joined, and they drafted mandolinist James "Yank" Rachell, an eighty-six-year-old jug band veteran who was then living in Indianapolis. (He passed away in 1997.) With various personnel and in different recording studios, they finally recorded fourteen tracks for the album, *I Want My Roots,* released by Music Masters/BMG in 1996. A follow-up album called *Chasin' Gus's Ghost,* with contributions from Yank Rachell and Geoff Muldaur, came out in 1999.

Although there have been offers for a Lovin' Spoonful reunion, and two of the members (Joe Butler and Steve Boone) reformed the group in the early 1990s, Sebastian has always resisted, saying he is only interested in playing a few gigs with Zal Yanovsky. "I'm proud of those songs, they're some of the best I've written," he told Parry Gettelman of the *Orlando Sentinel* in 1993. "On the other hand, I'm also really glad I don't have to do *only* those songs. . . . It's very easy to find a slot on an oldies show. It's a little harder to run around and push a new record."

SEEGER, MIKE: *Singer, guitarist, banjoist, pianist, Jew's harp, viola, autoharpist, mandolinist, fiddler, harmonica, ukulele, songwriter, record producer, writer, folkmusic collector. Born New York, New York, August 15, 1933.*

The name Seeger almost has become a synonym for the folk-music movement in the United States since the 1930s. What seems to be a dynasty was founded by musicologist and folklorist Dr. Charles Seeger Sr. His interest in folk music was passed along to his seven children by two wives. His first family of three included the great Pete Seeger. Of the four children by his second wife, Mike, Peggy, and Penny Seeger all had an impact, in varying degrees, on the folk-music field.

Michael, called Mike, the eldest of the four offspring of Charles Seeger's marriage to Ruth Crawford (who was a noted female composer of the early twentieth century and a folk song collector), spent many of his early years in Bethesda, Maryland, near Washington, D.C., where his parents were assisting the Lomaxes in compiling the Archive of Folk Song at the Library of Congress. Thus young Mike was exposed to a wide range of folk information and met the many accomplished folk artists who visited the Seeger household. His half brother was another good source of information.

By the time Mike began high school he was pretty well indoctrinated. For a while, he learned the Spanish guitar, but when he was eighteen he switched to the banjo and the guitar, more conventionally used in folk music. One of his deep interests was the traditional hill-country music that laid the foundation for the more urban folk-song genre of the post–World War II years. In the early 1950s, he began to travel through the rural parts of the United States, seeking out old-time performers and collecting traditional folk songs. He was a conscientious objector during the Korean War, and a lack of funds kept him from traveling too far afield. Although only in his twenties, he contributed greatly to folk research, making tapes of many important songs and bringing many "lost" artists, such as Dock Boggs, to the attention of current audiences.

Mike's first recording subject was actually the great singer and guitarist Elizabeth Cotten, who had worked for the Seeger family for many years before revealing that she could play the guitar. He recorded Cotten for Folkways in 1957, reissued in 1989 by Smithsonian/Folkways. Seeger is also credited with recording the first bluegrass LP, *American Banjo, Three Finger & Scruggs Style,* for Folkways in 1956 (reissued in 1990), *Mountain Music* in 1958 (reissued in 1990), and *The Country Gentlemen* in 1959 (reissued in 1990). He also recorded the Stoneman Family, the McGee Brothers, Fiddlin' Arthur Smith, the Lilly Brothers, and Don Stover.

By the mid-1950s, Seeger was performing at many coffeehouses and festivals in the United States. In 1958 he joined forces with two other artists, John Cohen and Tom Paley (later replaced by Tracy Schwarz), to form the New Lost City Ramblers, which became the premier old-timey group of the late 1950s-early 1960s folk boom.

Among the many songs that won sustained applause from audiences throughout the United States and abroad were "Oh Babe It Ain't No Lie," "The Girl I Left Behind," "Lady of Carlisle," "Red Rocking Chair," "Battleship of Maine," "Hopalong Peter," "The Cannonball," "Old Bell Cow," "East Virginia Blues," "Freight Train," "Fly Around My Pretty Little Miss," "The Girl on the Greenbriar Shore," "Tom Dooley," "Whoop 'Em Up Cindy," and "Arkansas Traveler." These and many other songs were included in their book, *The New Lost City Ramblers,* issued by Oak Publications in 1964.

While his association with the group continued on a limited level into the 1990s, Mike Seeger continued to make solo recordings or recordings with various other bands and also found time for other music-related activities. He provided liner notes for folk-song albums, went off on collecting tours, and provided articles on folk music for various folk music magazines and journals. His solo LPs of the 1960s included, on Folkways, *Oldtime Country Music* (issued 1962) and *Tipple, Loom and Rail* (1965), and on Vanguard, *Mike Seeger* (7/64).

In 1966 he made *Mike and Peggy Seeger* for Argo, followed by *Mike and Alice Seeger in Concert* in 1970 (with his ex-wife, Alice Gerrard) for Japan's King label. Jean Ritchie's Greenhays label also released *Alice and Mike* in 1980. He recorded two albums on the Mercury label, *Music from True Vine* (1971) and *The Second Annual Farewell Reunion* (1973). In 1986 he made an album for Flying Fish called *Old Time Music Dance Party.*

At the end of the 1970s, several of his albums were in the current Folkways catalog—his 1965 release, *Tipple, Loom and Rail,* plus *American Folk Songs* and *Old-time Country Music.*

His efforts through the 1970s and '80s continued pretty much as they had been in the 1960s, though with much less public attention in that rock-dominated period. He was a familiar face on the folk-music concert circuit and also performed regularly at many of the major folk festivals, sometimes with other Seegers or in conjunction with other well-known soloists, and sometimes with other bands such as the Strange Creek Singers whose members in the late '70s included Mike, Tracy Schwarz, Lamar Grier, and former wife Alice Gerrard. Arhoolie reissued a Strange Creek Singers CD in 1997 from recordings made in the 1970s. Over the years, Mike mastered an amazing variety of instruments, his capabilities embracing a dozen or more by the 1990s. In the '90s, with folk music experiencing a strong resurgence, he remained one of the artists respected by new young performers as well as veterans for his devotion and innovation to the folk domain.

The New Lost City Ramblers, whose demise was reported or announced several times from the mid-1960s on, never completely disappeared from concerts or recordings. The group did go on hiatus for a while after 1979, but by the start of the '90s were coming together for some festivals and concerts. Mike told Mark Greenberg for *Sing Out!* magazine ("The State of Old-Time Music from New Lost City to Siberia," 1993), rumors of its passing were incorrect: "That's right. We'll continue until we can't, I reckon. I look forward to playing another fifteen, twenty, twenty-five years myself."

He added the trio had just recorded a blues song on which Mike provided vocals, for the CD *Third Annual Farewell Reunion,* issued by Rounder in 1994. (The album, nominated for a Grammy in the Traditional Folk category, also included contributions from Etta Baker, Hazel Dickens, Michael Doucet, Bob Dylan, Carol Elizabeth Jones, Maria Muldaur, Tim O'Brien, Pete Seeger, Ralph Stanley, and Jody Stecher and Kate Brislin.) "So the music goes on. John hurt his hand about two years ago, and it's given him a hard time. Tracy's [Tracy Schwarz, who replaced original trio member Tom Paley] working full-time, mostly at Cajun dances. . . . He and Ginny Hawker, his new spouse, are singing and playing together, and they make a wonderful pair because they're both such strong singers. John's not making a great deal of music these days because he's working on his films." In 1997, following an appearance at the Merle Fest in 1996, the New Lost City Ramblers reunited to record their first new recording in twenty-three years, *There Ain't No Way Out,* which was nominated for a Traditional Folk Grammy.

Among Seeger's 1980s projects was a documentary about southern step dancing. With support from the National Endowment for the Humanities and a Smithsonian Institution Fellowship, he, associate Ruth Pershing, and a film crew went to a variety of locales in the mid-1980s and videotaped veteran artists perform styles like flatfoot, buck, hoedown, and mountain tap, backed by music ranging from fiddle and banjo to country and western for the video *Talking Feet.* His video work in the early '90s included several instructional compilations for Happy Traum's Homespun label, including one on old-time banjo featuring artists like Greg Hoven, Kirk Sutphin, Etta Baker, Doc Watson, Joe and Odell Thompson, and Pete Seeger. This was followed by another on traditional southern guitar mainly performed by Mike, though with some segments by Doc Watson.

From a creative standpoint, Seeger took some new approaches in the 1980s. He told Stephanie Shapiro of the *Baltimore Evening Sun* ("Mike Seeger: Preserver of Mountain Music," May 24, 1990), "In the early to mid-'80s, I began changing what I was doing. I'm not exactly sure how. Before that time, I reached much more . . . for sounding like the people I was learning from. . . . Now I'm feeling like I've designed it a little bit more. I've also made up a couple little tunes, which sound more archaic than a lot of the things I've learned from."

Actually, that change in concept first began to occur to him before the '80s, he indicated to *Bluegrass Unlimited* in July 1989: "In the late 1970s, I began thinking of more alternative ways that the music might have been played or ways that it still might be developed without losing its country feel or sense of spontaneity. I applied for a Guggenheim Fellowship to develop and record some of these musical ideas and in 1984 was successful."

Not that he meant to revolutionize the genre or seek to make it more commercial. Rather it was to take a close look back, as he told Greenberg, "at the depth and the wonderful variety of the old-time styles and sounds . . . [with the idea] of being able to create within the genre . . ." But commercialization, including going to electric instruments, was to be avoided. "I believe that the kind of music I like should remain noncommercial, but still should have a great number of people who will play it. I think that merely by playing traditional music, I'm making an anti-commercial statement. There's thousands of people playing this music who have nothing to do with the commercial scene whatever."

One of the first fruits of those studies was the 1988 Rounder release *Mike Seeger: Fresh Oldtime String Band Music.* The album contained a variety of Seeger's alternative treatments of traditional numbers such as his mandolin quartet version of "Black Jack Davey" recorded with Norman and Nancy Blake and James Bryan and a version of "Mabel" on which Seeger plays viola and support comes from his band of that period, the Stokes County String Quartet. On some tracks, like "East Tennessee Blues—Goin' Crazy," "Pork Fat Makes My Chicken Tan," and "Wagnerd," he provided arrangements without performing, and in "Cotton-Eyed Joe," played by the Agents of Terra, he only sang harmony vocals.

In his next album, though, he displayed his diversity as an instrumentalist, vocalist, and, on a few cuts, songwriter. The 1991 Rounder release *Solo: Oldtime Country Music,* besides his originals, contained sixteen traditional ballads, including, as one reviewer wrote, "an eerie holler sung in a diatonic progression and a number of proto-blues (such as 'Roustabout') that reveal the deep influence of African styles on early American music." The album was nominated for a Grammy in the Best Traditional Folk Album category.

In the early '90s Mike also got together with the three other children of Ruth Crawford Seeger—Peggy, Penny, and Barbara—and their children to record the songs their mother (and grandmother) had collected long ago for her songbook, *Animal Folksongs for Children.* The result was a fifty-eight song collection, *Animal Folksongs for Children and Other People!* issued by Rounder on two CDs or two cassettes in 1993, a release hailed widely by childrens' librarians and music teachers. A companion book containing forty-three of the songs was published by Linnet Books/The Shoe String Press in January 1993. As might be expected, accompaniments to the Seeger vocals were all performed on traditional instruments. Interestingly, the children included Neill and Calum MacColl, sons of Peggy and the late U.K. folksinger Ewan MacColl, who had a rock 'n' roll band in England called Liberty Horses. Mike had previously recorded two other collections based on Ruth Crawford Seeger's songbooks: *American Folksongs for Children* in 1977, with Peggy, and *American Folksongs for Christmas* in 1989, with Penny and Peggy.

In the '90s, Mike called Rockbridge County, Virginia, home. He told Mark Greenberg in 1993, "This is my 60th year and I'm still finding this music something that I love to do. I play it for my own pleasure a great deal more than I play in public."

At the Folk Alliance Conference in Washington, D.C., in February 1996, Seeger performed a set with longtime friends Tracy Schwarz, Hazel Dickens, and Alice Gerrard. Afterward, Lyndon Stambler asked Mike when they had first been together as a group. Seeger replied, "Back in the '60s. We were all friends in the '60s. We found common musical ground and loved the area of southern music that existed between the very oldest sounds and early bluegrass, plus some of the songs that Alice and Hazel were beginning to write at that time. This was the Strange Creek Singers."

The fifth member back then, he said, was Lamar Grier. "He's the banjo picker who used to work with Bill Monroe. I work mostly as a soloist now, almost entirely. Tracy works with his wife, Ginny, or with a Cajun band. Sometimes Tracy and I work with John Cohen of the New Lost City Ramblers. Alice works mostly as a soloist and is an editor. Hazel works on her own largely." Getting back together again "was wonderful. Those songs that we sing together, I can't sing them with anybody else. There are just certain things that we can do that are entirely unique to this group. Certain harmonies, feelings, and ways of singing."

The Folk Alliance reunion with Hazel, Alice, and Tracy, he noted, was the first time all four had been onstage together in some two decades. "In the mid-1970s, Alice and Hazel stopped singing together. Tracy and Alice and I sometimes sang together after that. The last time the four of us sang together was in 1975 or 1976. Tonight was all because BMI asked us to do a round robin. We asked Tracy if he would join us."

But, he emphasized, "I've been a solo musician for thirty-five years. From about 1960 through 1970, I worked with the New Lost City Ramblers. Actually, we've played all the way down through the years. But those were the main years that we had a significant amount of time playing together. Much of old-time traditional music is solo. A mountain banjo player, a fiddle player, a Jew's harp player on their own. I like to present and represent that tradition to a wide variety of people. I think it has a significance that is similar in its way to the other great musics."

Stambler asked Seeger's views on the difference between the music of the 1960s and folk music of today. "There's quite a number of differences. There's not as much consciousness of continuity of traditions now. People in the '60s usually knew some of the older songs and had some grounding in traditional music as well, especially people like Bob Dylan, Tom Rush, Arlo Guthrie. Those people cherished old-time or traditional music. They brought it into their music. Now times have changed so much that people don't have much of a mind for history. Perhaps five or ten years is a generation now. I would like to see younger singer-songwriters be conscious of some of the other kinds of music, the older kinds of music.

"Why do I think that? Because their music would be richer for it, for one thing. Also, I think it's very important for people to have an idea of roots, of someplace to come from and go to. The old songs have a great, great value. They've been going on for hundreds of years and there's hundreds of years of people's lives that went into those songs. The ones that have come down to us now are the survivors. They have a great deal of value. It's as if we would be without a Shakespeare or a Bach."

Asked whether he practices a lot, Seeger said, "Never as much as I want to. If I'm lucky I play half a day. These days I'm recording a CD of different banjo styles. I've been managing to play for an hour or two nearly every day, which is very unusual for me."

Seeger recorded his next CD with Paul Brown, *Way Down in North Carolina,* released by Rounder in 1996. It's a collection of southern mountain songs on banjo, gourd banjo, guitar, fiddle, dulcimer, autoharp, harmonica, and trump (Jew's harp). Mike followed in 1998 with a survey of traditional southern banjo songs and styles for Smithsonian/Folkways. The CD, *Southern Banjo Sounds,* includes instrumentals and songs played on twenty-three different kinds of banjos, ranging from nineteenth century African American Mississippi style to 1940s-era Earl Scruggs bluegrass picking. "One track of bluegrass, but most of them are old-time styles," Mike explained. "There's a world of older banjo styles, some of them different, some of them pretty well brotherly." *Southern Banjo Sounds* was nominated for a Grammy in the Best Traditional Folk category.

In 1998, Smithsonian/Folkways also released two albums of material from Mike Seeger's field recordings of the 1950s and 1960s, *Close to Home: Old-Time Music from Mike Seeger's Collection 1952–1967* (which includes thirty-eight tracks featuring people like Maybelle Carter, Dock Boggs, and Eck Robertson) and *Dock Boggs: His Folkways Years 1963–1968.* In 1999 Acoustic Disc issued *Retrograss* featuring the playing of Seeger, David Grisman, and John Hartford.

For the future: "I would like to take traditional American music to more people than are listening to that now. It has a lot of value and it's not being considered very much. I feel that along with all the new [folk-music] approaches, the approach of presenting the music of the past 100–150 years just to keep these songs and ideas alive I think is important. It's not a matter of economic need quite so much. I do have to make a living and this is my living."

(See also New Lost City Ramblers: Seeger, Peggy: Seeger, Pete)

SEEGER, PEGGY: *Singer, songmaker, instrumentalist (guitar, piano, five-string banjo, English concertina, Appalachian dulcimer, autoharp). Born New York, New York, June 17, 1935.*

Another member of America's first family of folk music, Margaret ("Peggy") Seeger was the second of four children of musicologist Charles Seeger's second marriage (to Ruth Crawford). She is the half sister of Pete Seeger and full sister of Mike Seeger, and her contributions to the folk-music revival in all parts of the world surprised no one. She made her mark as a feminist and activist, writing such songs as "Gonna Be an Engineer," which has become an anthem for the women's movement; "Woman on Wheels," about a woman in a wheelchair protesting the presence of cruise missiles on British soil; and "The Ballad of Springhill," about the 1958 Nova Scotia mining disaster.

Peggy heard a great deal of North American folk songs from her earliest years, since her parents were continuously collecting and listening to records and visiting singers. As the children grew up, they became more interested in performing the music than in the analytical pursuits of their academically oriented parents. Peggy recalled that the family was not a singing family in the sense of the Ritchie Family, but "we always heard songs and we chose our own favorites." They did, however, have singing evenings every week, and thus the children became acquainted with vocal, instrumental, and performing skills.

The many talented folk artists who paid house calls inspired her to learn a number of instruments, including piano and guitar. Her half brother Pete, of course, was making a name for himself as a stellar folk artist, and he and folk-music friends often visited the Seeger house in Washington, D.C. She had taken piano lessons from the age of seven, and began learning guitar at twelve years old. Her interest in folk music continued to grow while she attended Radcliffe College as a music major in the early 1950s. Leaving Radcliffe after two years, she went to Europe in 1955, traveling to Holland to study Russian (in the language of Dutch!) at the University of Leiden. Afterward she traveled to Belgium, France, Italy, Russia, China, and Poland.

In 1956 the opportunity to perform a role in the English production of *Dark of the Moon* played a major role in the course of her life. Alan Lomax, son and coworker of Dr. John Lomax, curator of the Archive of Folk Songs of the Library of Congress, helped her get the part. (The Lomaxes were longtime friends of the Seeger family.) Once in England, Seeger soon joined a folk song quartet, the Ramblers, that included Scottish folk expert and songwriter Ewan MacColl. Two years later she married MacColl and settled in England, which remained home into the 1980s. They had three children: Neill, born in 1959; Calum, born in 1963; and Kitty, born in 1972.

Before they married, Peggy returned to the United States early in 1957 to perform at concerts, festivals, and clubs in many parts of the country. She was particularly well received at the Gate of Horn in Chicago, where she remained for a six-week engagement. That summer she took part in the World Youth Festival in Moscow. She journeyed from the Soviet Union to the People's Republic of China, then back through Russia to England to meet Ewan MacColl. After their marriage, they continued to be familiar figures on the folk scene, separately or together, in Europe and the United States. They became one of the leading duos in Britain, traveling up and down the island for over three decades.

With BBC producer Charles Parker, Peggy and Ewan created the Radio Ballad form, which combined field recordings, speech, and sound effects with new folk songs. One of the Radio Ballads, *Singing the Fishing,* won the 1960 Italia Prize for best radio documentary. The eight Radio Ballads were issued on CD by Topic Records (England) in April 1999. They also formed Blackthorne Records, which produced a yearly political theater show (the Festival of Fools) with the London Critics Group. In 1971, Granada Television put together an hour-long documentary on Peggy for its series *The Exiles.* Over the years, she also compiled the *New City Songster,* which included more than 500 contemporary songs collected from singers around the world (1965 to 1985).

By the late 1950s Seeger had made a number of recordings, including *We Sing America* (with Guy Carawan) for Pye Nixa in the late 1950s, *America at Play* in 1958 (with Guy Carawan) for EMI, and for Folkways *Folksongs of Courting and Complaint* in 1955, *American Folksongs Sung by the Seegers* (with Mike, Barbara, and Penny) in 1957, *American Folksongs for Christmas* in 1955, *Animal Folksongs for Children* in 1957, and *Songs of Robert Burns* (with Ewan MacColl) in 1959. She recorded *Folksong Saturday Night* (with Guy Carawan and Alan Lomax) in 1958 for Kapp; *Matching Songs of Britain and America* (with Ewan) in 1957, and *Folksongs and Ballads* in 1958 for Riverside; and for Topic *Peggy Seeger* in 1956, *Early in the Spring* in 1957, *Pretty Little Baby* in the late 1950s, and *Troubled Love* in 1958. She made *Three Sisters* (with her two younger sisters, Penny and Barbara) for Prestige International in 1957.

She continued to turn out LPs on various labels (including their own Blackthorne) during the 1960s and 1970s as a solo performer or with other artists, including her husband. Her 1960s albums included *Who's Going to Shoe My Pretty Little Foot?* (with Tom Paley) on Topic, and with Ewan, *Classic Scots Ballads* on Tradition (available in the 1990s through Rykodisc/Tradition), *Lover's Garland* for Prestige, and *Bothy Ballads of Scotland* on Folkways. She recorded *Peggy 'n' Mike* for Argo in 1967. Her solo albums in the 1960s included *Peggy Alone* in 1967 on Argo; *American Folksongs for Banjo* and *Popular Ballads* for Folk-Lyric; and *Best of Peggy Seeger* in 1961, and *A Song for You and Me* on Prestige. In the 1970s, nearly all of her releases were performed with Ewan, except for a number of recordings she made with a women's chorus. A box set about Peggy and Ewan called *Parsley, Sage & Politics* came out in 1986. She recorded *Familiar Faces* (with a women's chorus) for Blackthorne in 1988.

Throughout the 1970s, Peggy and Ewan remained active on the folk-music concert circuit, mainly in England and on the Continent, though they occasionally performed in folk clubs and colleges across the United States. Many of the songs in their repertoire were originals by MacColl, plus some written or adapted by Seeger. One of Ewan's compositions (inspired by Peggy) that had been part of their repertoire as well as other folk artists' for much of the 1960s suddenly gained mass audience attention in 1972, when Roberta Flack's version of "The First Time Ever I Saw Your Face" became a million-seller and later won MacColl a Grammy.

By the start of the 1980s, Peggy and Ewan were represented by two albums recorded during the 1970s, *Folkways Record of Contemporary Song* and, on Rounder Records, *American Folksongs for Children* (1977), ninety songs from Ruth Crawford Seeger's book, and *At the Present Moment.* The latter two were still in the Rounder catalog in the 1990s along with another joint album, *Freeborn Man,* recorded in 1983.

During the 1980s the pattern for Peggy and Ewan was much the same as in previous years. They continued to perform on the folk circuit in Europe and occasionally in the United States while each worked on new song material separately or together. Ewan died in October 1989, but earlier that year he and their son Calum and daughter Kitty backed Mike, Peggy, and Penny Seeger on preparation of a new album for Rounder Records, *American Folk Songs for Christmas.* The collection, recorded mostly in London, England, in February and March 1989, was based on a book of the same title assembled by Ruth Crawford Seeger (1901–53). Among the fifty-three songs in the multi-disc release were numbers like "Bright Morning Stars Are Rising" and "Go Tell It on the Mountain."

Following the death of MacColl, Peggy began performing with Irene Scott, an Irish singer whom she had first met in Belfast in 1964 and with whom she had been friends ever since. They formed a duo called No Spring Chickens as well as a record company called Golden Egg Productions. In 1992 they released *Almost Commercially Viable,* characterizing their music as "free-range and organic." The album of political and love songs (reissued in 2000 by Sliced Bread) included Peggy's song "Give 'Em an Inch (and He'll Take a Mile)," a feminist perspective on the birth of a baby boy, and many love songs for Irene and Ewan. In 1992, Smithsonian/Folkways also put out a CD that compiles her years of recording for Mo Asch's label titled *The Folkways Years: 1955–1992, Songs of Love and Politics.*

Around the same time, all of Ruth Crawford Seeger's children—Peggy, Mike, Penny, and Barbara—and their children recorded another of Crawford's books, *American Folk Songs for Children.* This time Peggy's two sons, Calum and Neill, took part. On their own, Neill and Calum fronted a rock band in England called Liberty Horses that had an album come out almost simultaneously with Rounder Record's release of *Animal Folk Songs* in 1992. As had been the case with the 1989 album, the new release, containing fifty-eight songs on two CDs or two cassettes, was warmly welcomed by educators, including elementary school music teachers across the United States. A sampling of the tracks included "The Mole in the Ground," "The Grey Goose," "The Old Bell Cow," "Crocodile Songs," and "Wolves a Howling." Peggy and Mike (and their grandchildren!) regard this CD set as the best of the three audio versions of Ruth Crawford Seeger's books.

After that project, Peggy produced her first solo album in many years. The album, *An Odd Collection,* was issued in early 1996. Only four tracks contained previously recorded material. The remainer were new songs written by Peggy (or cowritten with her partner, Irene Scott) over a period from 1989 through 1995. The album contents included a union song ("If You Want a Better Life"), a feminist-oriented spoken-word piece ("You Men Out There") that capsuled a plea for a better world, and an antismoking composition ("It's a Free World").

In 1996, Fellside released *Classic Peggy Seeger,* a compilation of recordings she had made for Topic Records. Cooking Vinyl has also reissued several studio and live collections in the 1990s. In 1997, Oxford University Press published a biography of Ruth Crawford Seeger titled *Ruth Crawford Seeger: A Composer's Search for American Music,* by Judith Tick. The following year, Rykodisc/Tradition released *Period Pieces,* a compilation of women's songs written by Peggy between 1963 and 1994. Music Sales also published a new songbook, *The Peggy Seeger Songbook, Warts and All,* which included 149 songs. Peggy has also compiled *The Essential Ewan MacColl Songbook* (Music Sales). Her next project was a book of love poetry accompanied by a CD of love songs, *Love Will Linger On,* issued by Appleseed in 2000.

Since moving back to the United States in 1994, Seeger has been touring again, traveling the country in her nineteen-foot camper that she calls "Maggie."

"These last seven years have been traumatic—years of change, insecurity and adventure," Peggy wrote in an article posted on her web page (http://www.pegseeger.com). "I am rediscovering the pleasure of singing with Mike and Pete . . . I have ploughed up my back garden in Beckenham and converted it into a wildlife sanctu-

ary . . . I am renewing contacts with old friends, finding new spirits and seeing new sunrises."

With assistance from Peggy Seeger

SEEGER, PETE: *Singer, banjoist, guitarist, songwriter, musicologist, author. Born New York, New York, May 3, 1919.*

By the mid-'90s, Pete Seeger had attained such heights in the music field that he became both a Rock and Roll Hall of Fame inductee and a Kennedy Center honoree. At an awards ceremony from the Kennedy Center stage, Arlo Guthrie looked at the balcony where Seeger was clad in his father's tuxedo and couldn't resist the irony. "I'm wondering what we're going to do now that you've become official," Arlo said.

He was referring to Woody's words about "This Land is Your Land": "The worst thing you can do is make a song official." But in some ways, Pete Seeger has become an institution, a giant of twentieth-century music. In 1996, just before he turned seventy-seven, he released *Pete* on Living Music Records, his first studio recording in fourteen years. His voice sounds tentative, but his banjo, guitar, and words are fiery as ever. "The artist in ancient times inspired, entertained, educated his fellow citizens," he wrote. "Modern artists have an additional responsibility—to encourage others to be artists. Why? Because technology is going to destroy the human soul unless we realize that each of us must in some way be a creator as well as a spectator or consumer. . . . Make your own music, write your own books, if you would keep your soul."

Pete sold more than 35,000 copies in the first three months and won the Grammy for Best Traditional Folk album. Such good fortune had not always followed his career. During the 1950s, anti-Communist factions accused Seeger of subversion. More than a few U.S. officials called him unpatriotic. He was not without defenders, including the American people who valued his contributions as an artist.

In none of their rhetoric could anti-Seeger people damn him as a recent immigrant to American shores. The Seeger lineage could be traced back to colonial times. Several members of the family made important contributions to many facets of American life. His mother, Constance de Clyver Edson, was a violinist and teacher. His father, Dr. Charles Seeger, was recognized as one of the world's foremost musicologists and classical conductors before Pete was born. Charles became interested in American folk music when he met Alan Lomax in 1935. "They hit it off immediately," Pete told Craig Harris of *Dirty Linen* (December '94–January '95). "They tried to decide what had gone wrong with the attempts to revive folk music in Europe, where they tried to arrange everything for chorus and piano. . . . They took the sex out of it and the protest out of it. No wonder some of the young people said, 'This is boring.'

When people in England and Europe heard American folk music, they said, 'This is exciting, this is fun.' What my father and Alan did was to lay the basis for the revival. It let young people hear the music as it was recorded out in the fields."

Charles Seeger, who later married composer and folk music collector Ruth Crawford, continued his research in ethnomusicology into the 1970s.

Young Peter R. Seeger went to private schools in Nyack, New York, and in Connecticut before entering Harvard. He had little interest in folk music until he was sixteen (although he began singing at five and was aware of pop hits by his eighth year.) But a trip with his father to a festival organized by banjoist Bascom Lunsford in Asheville, North Carolina, changed his life. "In 1935 I was sixteen years old, playing tenor banjo in the school jazz band," he later recalled. "I was uninterested in studying the classical music which my parents taught at Juilliard. That summer I visited a square dance festival in Asheville, North Carolina, and fell in love with the old-fashioned five-string banjo, rippling out a rhythm to one fascinating song after another. I liked the melodies, time tested by generations of singers. Above all I liked the words. Compared to the trivialities of most popular songs, the words of those songs had all the meat of human life in them. They sang of heroes, outlaws, murderers, fools. They weren't afraid of being tragic instead of just sentimental. . . . Above all, they seemed frank, straightforward, honest. By comparison, it seemed to me that too many art songs were concerned with being elegant and too many pop songs were concerned with being clever. So in 1935 I tried learning some of this music."

He entered Harvard in 1936 as a sociology student and hoped to become a journalist. But in 1938, he became disillusioned and left. He cycled around New England exchanging watercolors of barns for room and board. He formed a traveling puppet show with three friends, performing at summer camps and resorts. He drew closer to Alan Lomax, curator of the Archive of Folk Song at the Library of Congress in Washington. "There were stacks of thousands of old 78 rpms," Seeger told Harris. "He [Lomax] said, 'Listen to each one of these and give me an idea. Weed out the worst ones and make notes on what you think are the more interesting ones.' That's where I first heard Uncle Dave Macon."

By 1939–40, Pete was an archive assistant and went on field trips with the Lomaxes. In the fall of 1940, he hitchhiked through Kentucky, Tennessee, Alabama, Florida, and Georgia, picking up tips from old-time banjo players like Rufus Crisp in Kentucky. He met Woody Guthrie at a midnight benefit in New York for California agricultural workers. "He stood on the stage and was so relaxed, spinning out story after story," he told Harris. "It was a remarkable evening. Burl Ives was

there, Leadbelly, the Golden Gate Quartet, Josh White, and my wife, Toshi, was there, dancing with Margo Meyer's American Square Dancing Group. We weren't married then. We weren't even going together."

After failing to get a reporting job, he found a Stewart banjo for $5 at a pawn shop and toured the United States with Woody Guthrie, riding the rails, performing, and collecting songs. (He broke the banjo jumping off a train and bought a Vega Whyte Laydie for $10.)

Seeger helped form the Almanac Singers in association with Lee Hays and Guthrie. It was a loosely knit framework that also included Millard Lampell, Josh White, Bess Lomax, Peter Hawes, and other folksingers of the time; "anybody who happened by," as Arlo put it. Seeger, Guthrie, and the others sang at labor and migrant meetings and composed pro-union and antifascist songs, including an album of peace songs in April 1940. Much of their repertoire came from traditional music. Although the Almanacs were only in existence a few years, they made several albums: *Songs for John Doe* (Keynote, 1941), *Talking Union and Other Union Songs* (Keynote, 1941, Folkways, 1955), *Sod Buster Ballads* and *Deep Sea Shanties* (General Records, 1941), and *Dear Mr. President* (Keynote, 1942). Along with the Lomaxes and Cis Cunningham, Seeger formed the Almanac People's Music Library, the first collection of union songs. The event that broke up the Almanacs was America's entry into World War II. In 1942, Seeger was drafted and spent more than three years in the army, mainly entertaining troops throughout the Pacific. He sent two collections of soldiers' songs to the People's Music Library.

After his discharge in December 1945, Seeger helped create the songwriters' union People's Songs, Inc. He ran the group's magazine out of the Greenwich Village flat he shared with his Japanese American wife, Toshi Ohta Seeger. At its pinnacle, the union had 3,000 members, including folk and blues luminaries like Sonny Terry, Tom Glazer, Alan Lomax, and Guthrie. They held "hootenannies," a term Seeger and Guthrie first heard in Seattle when they were in the Almanacs. These were forerunners of the more ambitious hoots of the late '50s and early '60s. People's Songs also provided songs for labor and civil rights movements. But a lack of funding forced them to declare bankruptcy at the end of the 1940s.

Seeger's projects included a movie short, *To Hear Your Banjo Play,* in 1946, and a Los Angeles revival of the folk musical *Dark of the Moon*. In the 1940s, Seeger also recorded or participated in the following: *Songs of the Civil War—Vol. 1* (Folkways, 1943, 1960); *Lonesome Train* (Decca ten-inch, 1943); *America's Favorite Songs* (1943, rereleased by Asch); *Lonesome Valley* (Folkways, 1943–1946, ten-inch); *Songs for Victory* (Stinson/Asch, 1943–44); *Folksay I–VI* (Folkways, 1943); *Songs for Political Action* (CIO Political Action

Committee, 1946); *Bawdy Ballads and Real Sad Songs* with Betty Sanders (Charter, 1946–47); *Roll the Union On* (Asch, 1947).

In 1948, Seeger rejoined Lee Hays (with whom he cowrote "If I Had a Hammer"), to create the Weavers. The initial foursome, which debuted in November 1948 after the defeat of Progressive Party candidate Henry Wallace, included Seeger, Hays, Fred Hellerman, and Ronnie Gilbert. (Hays and Hellerman sang baritone, Gilbert alto, and Seeger tenor.) Their first efforts were hardly financially rewarding. "We couldn't earn a dollar," Seeger said. "The Weavers was about to break up when we were offered a job at a shoddy nightclub [The Village Vanguard in Greenwich village]. In six months, we found ourselves with a recording contract, a best-selling record, managers, agents, publicity men, and the whole thing."

After a six-month run at the Village Vanguard in late 1949, the Weavers began performing in major concert venues (including appearances at Carnegie Hall) and on TV shows. Gordon Jenkins, Frank Sinatra's arranger, got them a contract with Decca, and they released their first single, "Goodnight, Irene." The song, which sold more records than any other pop song since World War II, came out a year after its author, Huddie Ledbetter, had died penniless.

From 1949 to 1952, the Weavers produced hit after hit, including "On Top of Old Smoky," "Kisses Sweeter Than Wine," "So Long (It's Been Good to Know You)," "Wimoweh (The Lion Sleeps Tonight)," "Tzena, Tzena," (in Hebrew and English), "Guantanamera," and Zhonkoye." They were on the verge of signing a network TV show in 1950 when a blacklisting organization attacked them and the network nixed the contract. Through 1952, when the onslaughts of the McCarthy era forced the group to disband, the Weavers' record sales totaled many millions.

Seeger, who quit the Communist party in 1951, according to an article in the *Los Angeles Times,* felt the effects of the blacklist. "They started chopping us down," he said. "First they kept us off TV. Then, they kept us out of the big nightclubs. Finally, after two years, we were working in Daffy's Bar and Grill and we looked at each other and said that this was a waste of time. We took a sabbatical."

The Weavers made several records: *The Weavers* (Charter, 1949); *Folk Songs of America and Other Lands* (Decca ten-inch, 1951); *Best of the Weavers* (Decca, 1959); *We Wish You a Merry Christmas* (Decca, 1952); *The Weavers on Tour* (Vanguard, 1958); *The Weavers at Home* (Vanguard, 1958); *The Weavers Songbag* (Vanguard, 1967); *Traveling on with the Weavers* (Vanguard, 1959); *Reunion at Carnegie Hall* (Vanguard, 1963); and *Reunion at Carnegie Hall, Part 2* (Vanguard, 1965). At the insistence of manager Harold Leventhal, the Weavers broke the blacklist in 1955 for a

sold-out Christmas concert at Carnegie Hall (released 1957 as *The Weavers at Carnegie Hall*).

Before rejoining the Weavers in 1955, Seeger forged a solo career. His efforts included a series of six concerts at Columbia University in 1954–55 on "American Folk Music and Its Origins." For a long time Seeger kept his career going in the face of widespread blacklisting on U.S. TV and concert circuits. He expressed his perseverance through "How Can I Keep from Singing," the nineteenth-century hymn, with a verse written by Doris Plenn during the McCarthy era: *When tyrants tremble sick with fear / And hear their death knell ringing—When friends rejoice both far and near / How can I keep from singing?*

His legal woes with the U.S. began in 1955, when he refused to answer questions put to him by the House Committee on Un-American Activities. ("I took the First Amendment and not the Fifth," he told Harris. "Arthur Miller and I and a couple of others decided to challenge the Committee of Un-American Activities. The Fifth, in a sense, is 'You have no right to ask me this question.' The First is 'Nobody has the right to ask anybody these questions.'") He was indicted on ten counts of contempt of Congress, and awaited trial for five years. He was found guilty on some charges and sentenced to a year in prison. (His lawyer bailed him out after he spent four hours in jail). The charges were dismissed by the U.S. Court of Appeals on May 18, 1962. "Ironically, it was the same judge who sentenced the Rosenbergs to the electric chair, Irving Kaufman," Seeger told Harris. "The decision was most obtuse. He said, 'We are not inclined or likely to dismiss charges of unconstitutionality even though they may be made by those unworthy of our respect.' However, after three pages of talking around the subject, I was acquitted." Seeger could finally get a passport. In 1963–64, he traveled the world with Toshi and his three children.

The blacklist kept him off network TV until 1967. He was hardly inactive, however. He worked with the Weavers from 1955 to 1957 and then helped revive the Newport Folk Festival. He contributed to *Sing Out!*, which he raised from the ashes of People's Songs. Besides writing his regular "Appleseeds" column in *Sing Out!*, he wrote several books. *How to Play the Five String Banjo*, first issued in 1948, had sold over 250,000 copies by the mid-'80s. Seeger transcribed in tablature, a musical notation used by lutists during the Middle Ages, and coined terminology such as "hammer-ons" and "pull-offs." Other books included *American Favorite Ballads, Henscratches and Flyspecks: Or How to Read Melodies from Songbooks in 12 Confusing Lessons,* and *The Incompleat Folksinger.* David King Dunaway wrote a biography, *How Can I Keep from Singing?* (McGraw-Hill, 1981). In 1993, *Sing Out!* published Seeger's autobiography, *Where Have All the Flowers Gone,* filled, naturally, with 200 songs.

From the 1950s on, his recordings continued to pour

out on a variety of labels, including Columbia, Vanguard, Folkways, Decca, and Warner Brothers. Among his 1950s and 1960s LPs were a five-volume set on Folkways titled *American Favorite Ballads,* issued between 1957 and 1962; *Hootenanny at Carnegie Hall* (Folkways, 1960); *Champlain Valley Songs* (Folkways, 1960); *The Unfortunate Rake* (Folkways, 1960); *Gazette with Pete Seeger, Vol. 1* (Folkways, 1958); *Gazette, Vol. 2* (Folkways, 1961); *The Rainbow Quest* (Folkways, 1960); *Sing Out with Pete!* (Folkways, 1956–1961); *Story Songs* (Columbia, 1961); *Highlights of Pete Seeger at the Village Gate Vol. 1* (with Memphis Slim and Willie Dixon) (Folkways, 1960); *Pete Seeger at the Village Gate Vol. 2* (Folkways, 1962); *Songs of the Civil War* (Folkways, 1960); *Indian Summer* (soundtrack, Folkways, 1961); *The Bitter and the Sweet* (Columbia, 1963); *Broadside Ballads Vol. 1* (Folkways, 1963); *Broadside Ballads Vol. 2* (Broadside Records, 1965); *Ballads of Sacco and Vanzetti* (Folkways, 1963); *Little Boxes and Other Broadsides* (Verve/Folkways, 1963); *We Shall Overcome* (Columbia, 1963, expanded live album reissued on CD in 1989); *Hootenanny* (Prestige/Folklore, 1963); *Strangers and Cousins* (Columbia, 1963–1964); *Folk Songs* (Capitol, 1964); *Broadsides* (Folkways, 1964); *Freight Train* (Capitol, 1964); *I Can See a New Day* (Columbia, 1965); *Songs of Struggle and Protest* (Folkways, 1965); *On Campus* (Verve/Folkways, 1965); *Pete Seeger* (Arc Folkways, 1966); *God Bless the Grass* (Columbia, 1966); *Dangerous Songs!?* (Columbia, 1966); *Pete Seeger Sings Woody Guthrie* (Folkways, 1967); *Waist Deep in the Big Muddy* (Columbia, 1967); *Greatest Hits* (Columbia, 1967); *Pete Seeger Sings Leadbelly* (Folkways, 1968); *Pete Seeger Sings and Answers Questions* (two records, Broadside, 1968); *John Henry and Other Folk Favorites* (Harmony, 1969); *Tell Me That You Love Me, Junie Moon* (soundtrack, Columbia, 1969); and *Pete Seeger Young vs. Old* (Columbia, 1971).

Among his other recordings were the following (Folkways unless noted): *Darling Corey* (1950); *South African Freedom Songs* (1950); *Frontier Ballads Vol. 1 and 2* (1954); *Goofing Off Suite* (1954); *Pete Seeger Sampler* (1954, ten inch); *A Pete Seeger Concert* (Stinson, 1953–54); *Birds, Beasts, Bugs and Little Fishes* (1954); *How to Play the Five String Banjo* (1954); *The Folksinger's Guitar Guide* (1955); *Bantu Choral Folk Songs* (1955); *Love Songs for Friends and Foes* (1956); *American Industrial Ballads* (1956); *With Voices Together We Sing* (1956); *Nonesuch* (with Frank Hamilton) (1959); *Pete! Folk Songs and Ballads* (Stinson, 1963, rerelease of 1944 *American Banjo* on Asch); *The Seegers* (with Peggy and Mike) (Prestige, 1965); and *Big Bill Broonzy and Pete Seeger in Concert* (Verve Folkways, 1965).

Seeger has also issued a number of albums for children on Folkways, including *Songs to Grow On* (1951); *American Folksongs for Children* (1953); *Camp Songs* (Folkways/Scholastic, 1959); *Sleep Time* (1958); *Song and Play Time with Pete Seeger* (1958); *Folk Songs for Young People* (1959); *Pete Seeger and Brother Kirk Visit Sesame Street* (Children's Records of America, 1974); and *Abiyoyo, Other Stories and Songs for Children* (Smithsonian/Folkways).

During the 1960s, many of Pete's songs were played by other musicians in fields ranging from folk and country to rock. The Kingston Trio and Peter, Paul and Mary had hits with his "Where Have All the Flowers Gone." "A good song can stand various treatments," Seeger told Harris. "The way they sang it was very different from the way that I would sing it. But who knows?" His song "Turn! Turn! Turn!" (with lyrics derived from the Bible) was a hit for the Byrds. "I love those twanging guitars, they're like bronze bells," he told Harris. "What a voice [Roger McGuinn] has. . . . I hope that he keeps on singing until he's a hundred years old."

Seeger was the master of ceremonies at Newport when Bob Dylan went electric, and regrets that he didn't stick up for him. "I was furious at the distortion of the sound," he told Harris. "I couldn't understand the words. I went [to the sound booth] and said, 'Get rid of that distortion. Turn it down a little bit.' They said, 'No, this is the way that they want it.' I said, 'I wish that I had an axe, I'd cut the cable.' But he was singing a great song—one of my favorites ('Maggie's Farm'). . . . I should have come out and said, 'Folks, don't boo Bob Dylan's guitar. You didn't boo Muddy Waters or Howlin' Wolf. They have electric guitars. Why can't Bob have an electric guitar?' "

Along with folksingers like Phil Ochs and Joan Baez, Pete, a favored performer for decades on college campuses, took part in concerts opposing U.S. involvement in Vietnam. In late 1967, he made his first appearance on TV since the blacklisting when the Smothers Brothers invited him on their show. They had to fight an effort by CBS executives to continue the ban. Pete later appeared on two more Smothers Brothers shows. On one, he sang "Waist-Deep in the Big Muddy," whose rejection by network censors from his first appearance created a national furor. "Once or twice in my life I've wished I could have a million seller," he told Ken Hunt of *Folk Roots* (March '94). "When I made up the song 'Waist Deep in the Big Muddy' I really wished that it could have gotten around. It might have saved lives. But the distributor of the record thought it was too dangerous to promote the record so my record didn't leave the shelves."

Seeger told Hunt that little has changed. "Songs get blacklisted now. People get blacklisted. The people who own the media call it 'editing.' They don't call it 'censoring.' In my own opinion I'd like to see everybody in the world be an editor and a censor, in a sense. I don't think the world will survive if we don't learn to limit ourselves in one way or another. Scientists have given all sorts of goodies to us and it's only a matter of time before somebody discovers how to make a very powerful plastic explosive out of some very common products that you can get in any drug store or hardware store and they'll be able to blow up planes, tunnels, boats, houses, bridges and be thousands of miles away before anybody tries to chase them. The *only* solution—and it is the *only* solution—is a world where people realize that our lives depend on each other and we're going to have to be a lot more careful with each other than we ever were before."

At the end of the 1960s, Seeger helped organize a campaign to restore the ecology of the Hudson River. He and other folksingers cruised the river in the sloop *Clearwater,* giving concerts to publicize their concerns. Among those he enlisted was a young folksinger named Don McLean, who went on to write *American Pie.* The National Educational Television special, *The Sloop at Nyack,* telecast at the start of the 1970s, resulted from the concert series. Prior to that, in 1965 and 1966, Seeger had his own show on public TV, called *Rainbow Quest.* He also hosted a number of programs on folk-music topics in the 1970s. One of his appearances on public TV in the late '70s was a concert from Wolf Trap (in Vienna, Virginia) with Arlo Guthrie.

Pete's albums were issued on various labels during the 1970s. They included *Rainbow Race* (Columbia, 1973) and *The World of Pete Seeger* (Columbia, 1974). No longer a pariah, he played venues, large and small, across the U.S., including New York's Lincoln Center. His albums in the late 1970s were on Warner Brothers and included *Pete Seeger and Arlo Guthrie in Concert* (1975). By 1981 he had left Warners, but the preceding LP and *Circles and Seasons* (July 1979) remained in the company's catalog. Vanguard released *The Essential Pete Seeger* in 1978.

At the decade's end, Seeger reunited with Hays, Gilbert, and Hellerman at Hays's Pennsylvania farm. "Our voices just started singing the old arrangements," Seeger said. "We hadn't sung them in 15 or 20 years. But once our tongues started going. . . . It's like once you learn to ride a bicycle or ice skate, you never completely forget. Lee's voice slipped into the bass part, mine slipped into the high part."

The Weavers again returned to Carnegie Hall. Hays's godson, director Jim Brown, captured it all for the award-winning documentary *Wasn't That a Time.* Hays had lost both legs to diabetes and died before the film aired on public television in 1982. Vanguard also released a box-set, *The Weavers: Wasn't That a Time,* in 1993.

On August 8, 1993, Arlo, Pete, and family members, including Seeger's grandson Tao Rodriguez-Seeger, who has released his own recording, and Arlo's son Abe, performed at Wolf Trap. Arlo released a two-volume set from the concert on his Rising Son Records called *More Together Again: In Concert* (1994). Rodriguez-Seeger began singing with Pete in concert.

"My voice is 75 percent gone," Pete explained to Harris. "I can get away with some songs. But I can't hold a note or sing way out there anymore. It wobbles uncontrollably. On the other hand, when I sing with my grandson, he can hold the note. People think they're hearing me when they're really hearing him. It's a new way of doing a Milli Vanilli."

On December 4, 1994, Seeger received Kennedy Center Honors and the National Medal of Art. Joan Baez sang "Where Have All the Flowers Gone," Arlo "If I Had a Hammer," and Roger McGuinn "Turn! Turn! Turn!" President Bill Clinton called Pete "an inconvenient artist who dared to sing things as he saw them. . . . He was attacked for his beliefs, and banned from television. . . . Now that's a badge of honor."

In January 1996, he was inducted into the Rock and Roll Hall of Fame in a ceremony at the Waldorf Astoria. Harry Belafonte emphasized Pete's role in the civil rights movement. Seeger, who popularized "We Shall Overcome" and took part in the 1965 march in Selma, Alabama, was dedicated to "the great task of overthrowing injustice." Arlo led the audience in "Goodnight, Irene," saying, "When we sing together, nothing can bring us down."

For many decades he and Toshi, his wife of more than fifty years, lived in a log-cabin home overlooking the Hudson near Beacon, New York, that Seeger built using instructions from books he checked out of the New York Public Library. "We've been swimming in the Hudson for the past ten years or so, largely thanks to Clearwater and other organizations that kept pushing," Seeger told the *Los Angeles Times* (1992). "Of course, it took the whole nation to push through various water-pollution amendments, and as a result there are rivers, lakes and bays all over America that are cleaner than they were in 1972 when the laws were passed—over Richard Nixon's veto, I believe."

Seeger has appeared on more than eighty albums and made more than thirty solo recordings. In 1982 he made *Precious Friend* with Arlo on Warner Brothers. He recorded *H.A.R.P.* (with Holly Near, Arlo Guthrie, and Ronnie Gilbert) on Redwood Records (1985). The next year, Seeger recorded *Carry It On: Songs of America's Working People* with activists Si Kahn and Jane Sapp, a two-CD set on Flying Fish.

As they were driving home from a festival in June 1982, jazz saxophonist Paul Winters (who had formed Living Music Records in 1980) asked Seeger if he would be interested in making an album of his "Earth" songs. "Oh, I've done over eighty albums and I think that's enough," Seeger responded. "I'm through recording."

Five years later, Seeger took one look at Winters's barn in Litchfield, Connecticut, and said, "Wouldn't this be a great place to get a group of people together and do some singing!" They held the first "sing-in" in July 1988, but Seeger didn't like the recording. They tried again in April 1995. This time Pete sang with three choirs—Gaudeamus, of Norfolk, Connecticut, the Union Baptist Church Singers of Bloomfield, New Jersey, and the Cathedral Singers of New York, New York. "I'll be 80 in three years—and I sound it! So having a chorus take over from time to time makes sense," he told Jim Bessman of *Billboard* (April 13, 1996).

Jam-packed with Seeger's liner notes about the origins of various songs, *Pete* was released on April 16, 1996, a month before his seventy-seventh birthday. The album includes: "My Rainbow Race," "Kisses Sweeter Than Wine," "Well May the World Go," and three new songs: "Huddie Ledbetter Was a Helluva Man," "Natural History (The Spider's Song)" based on an E.B. White poem, and Beethoven's "Russian Song Ode to Joy" with lyrics by Seeger and Don West.

In the liner notes, Pete wrote about getting a call from Otto Preminger, who was directing the movie *Tell Me That You Love Me, Junie Moon.* He wanted "a song about the will to live." A month later Seeger had written several versions when he met Preminger in Los Angeles, but none was quite right. On the flight to the set in Fresno, Seeger wrote "Old Devil Time." "Why didn't you sing that one to me first?" the director asked. Seeger told him he had just written it. "Oh, don't tell me that. You had it all along," Preminger retorted. Seeger played it at the beginning and end of the film.

After decades of collecting and singing folk songs, Seeger no longer calls himself a folksinger. When approached for an interview at the Folk Alliance Conference in Washington, D.C., in February 1996, he balked. "Do you include Chinese music? Do you include Afghanistan music?" he asked. "If you don't, don't call it folk. Call it Appalachian Music." Without another word, he walked away. Instead, Seeger took to calling himself "Pete Seeger, River Singer."

"Course, I will say that I have a disagreement with both old John and Alan [Lomax]," he told *Folk Roots* (March '94). "I think they should have kept the word 'folksong' as an academic term and have called a song whatever it is: a farmer's song, a miner's song. . . . People think I'm a 'folksong singer' because they've heard it [said]. But I'm not so much of a folksong singer as some grandmother sitting in a rocking chair singing some old song to her grandchild. The average person would say, 'Oh, they're not folksingers. They're not on the stage. They don't make a living at it.' Ah! Bunch of crap! Commerce distorts things and changes things and not always for the good."

Seeger's impact transcends commerce. In March 1998, Appleseed Recordings released the first and only (to date) Pete Seeger tribute album, *Where Have All the Flowers Gone: The Songs of Pete Seeger.* The collection demonstrates the remarkable breadth of Seeger's music and features a who's who of contemporary recordings artists: Bruce Springsteen singing "We Shall Overcome," Bonnie Raitt and Jackson Browne singing

"Kisses Sweeter Than Wine," John Gorka singing "The Water Is Wide," Cordelia's Dad singing "How Can I Keep from Singing," Roger McGuinn singing "Bells of Rhymney," and Richie Havens singing "Of Time and Rivers Flowing." The two-disc CD, produced by Jim Musselman, features Pete Seeger with the Weavers singing "Wimoweh." Pete also recorded a new song for the finale, "And Still I Am Searching." In 1998, Sony Legacy reissued two of Seeger's albums from 1966 on CD, *Dangerous Songs!?* and *God Bless the Grass,* the latter including songs by Malvina Reynolds and liner notes by former Supreme Court Justice William O. Douglas.

In the '90s, Pete seemed melancholy about the way society was going. "I have to confess that the main thing I wanted to do with my life I've not done—namely, getting the country singing again," Seeger told John D'Agostino of the *Los Angeles Times* (January 31, 1992). "And, by and large, I haven't succeeded. Of course, community singing remains an important part of church services across the country, and many ethnic groups have choruses. And I believe that a number of families still get together and sing songs, and that countless individuals sing along with the radio or a recording. So I haven't given up hope."

Indeed, after winning the Grammy in 1997, Seeger summed up his devotion to the cause: "The important question is not 'Is the music good?' but 'What is the music good for?' If we do our jobs well we'll all be able to enjoy music in one hundred years."

SEXSMITH, RON: *Singer, guitarist, songwriter. Born St. Catharines, Ontario, Canada, January 8, 1964.*

Though as of 2000 Ron Sexsmith's total album output was three, the original material in those collections marked him as a potential star of the future. His compositions, somewhat in the vein of folk songsmiths like Tim Hardin and John Prine, still had a freshness and special quality that reflected the skills of their writer.

He was the product of a broken home. His parents divorced when he was young, and he and his two brothers moved to a government housing project with his mother. When he was ten, his mother remarried and the family expanded to seven children with the arrival of Ron's new stepfather and his family. Those conditions, he indicated later, did not make for a relaxed atmosphere as he grew into his teens. It was a struggle to complete high school, he told interviewers, but one saving grace was his interest in music, where his favorites included rockabilly artists like Buddy Holly and English performers like the Beatles, the Kinks, and Elton John. Ray Davies of the Kinks was a particular icon. He told Robert Hilburn of the *Los Angeles Times* ("Exile in Sensitive Guyville," Calendar section, July 20, 1997, pp. 9, 67), "To me, Ray had the melodic gift of McCartney, the wit and bite of Lennon. Plus, his music had all these sad overtones that somehow gave you strength."

"SPIDER" JOHN KOERNER (*Photo by Gary Glade*)

ALBERT KING (*Courtesy of Stax Records*)

PATTY LARKIN (*Photo by Gary Glade*)

HOWARD AND **ROZ LARMAN**, whose Folk Scene program has aired on KPFK for 30 years, interview Wendy Waldman of Bryndle. Their albums, *FolkScene Collection Volumes 1 and 2*, came out on Red House Records in 1998 and 1999.

(*Courtesy of Howard and Roz Larman*)

THE LIMELITERS, *l.* to *r.*: **GLENN YARBROUGH,
ALEX HASSILEV,** and the late **DR. LOU GOTTLIEB**
(*Courtesy of RCA Records*)

DOUGIE MACLEAN (*Courtesy of Dunkeld Records*)

BOB MARLEY (*Courtesy of Island Records*)

JOHN McCUTCHEON (*Courtesy of Urbaitis*)

LOREENA McKENNITT *(Photo by Ann Elliott Cutting;*
Courtesy of Loreena McKennitt)

JONI MITCHELL *(Courtesy of Reprise Records)*

KEB' MO' *(Courtesy of Urbaitis)*

BILL MORRISSEY *(Photo by Gary Glade)*

CHARLIE MUSSELWHITE (*Photo by Norman Buller of Woldwide Images; Courtesy of Charley Musselwhite*)

ANDY WILLIAMS and two members of the 1960's version of the **NEW CHRISTY MINSTRELS** (*Courtesy of Columbia Records*)

NEW LOST CITY RAMBLERS (*Courtesy of Michael Ochs Archives*)

CARRIE NEWCOMER (*Courtesy of Jim McGuire*)

JOHN JACOB NILES (*Courtesy of University of Kentucky Collection*)

PHIL OCHS *(Courtesy of Michael Ochs Archives)*

ODETTA *(Courtesy of RCA Records)*

ELLIS PAUL (*Photo by Lyndon Stambler*)

TOM PAXTON (*Courtesy of Elektra*)

After graduating high school, he worked at various day jobs while performing in a local tavern on weekends, singing folk/folk-rock songs by well-known artists. He found an admiring if limited audience, but after a while became frustrated because he wanted to focus on his own material. In the mid-1980s he moved to Toronto where he fought for attention from the local music industry while being strongly encouraged by his wife, Jocelyn. (The couple still call Toronto home, it's where they live with their two children, a thirteen-year-old son and an eight-year-old daughter, as of 1998.)

Sexsmith made tapes and sought interviews with record company executives, but for years little happened. He told Hilburn, "Well, it was hard all around. There was a lot of pressure on us financially and I couldn't get any gigs so I worked as a courier. I was getting near 30 and wondering whether anyone would ever want to hear the songs. But you keep going because it's the only thing you are good at. You keep thinking, let's just try a little longer."

One might think that Canada, which generally has seemed more attuned to folk-flavored material than the United States for some years, might have been a logical starting point. However, the first breakthrough for Ron came when he gained a songwriting agreement with U.S.-based Interscope Records in 1994. In time, he got to demonstrate his performing talents for company co-owner Jimmy Iovine, who signed him to a recording contract and arranged for Sexsmith to start work on his first album. The result was the finely crafted 1995 release, *Ron Sexsmith*. The album sold a modest but satisfactory 100,000 copies worldwide, with the largest share being bought outside the United States. More than a few established performers spoke highly of the disc, and Elvis Costello even displayed it for a cover picture on the prestigious United Kingdom magazine *Mojo*.

In mid-1997, Interscope released Sexsmith's second album, *Other Songs,* which proved a worthy successor to his debut disc. While his concert performances at venues like the Los Angeles Troubadour emphasized his original material, he also showed the ability to effectively handle songs by other artists. For instance, he gave a rousing version of John Lennon's "Nowhere Man" in his encore period, then won equally enthusiastic audience response for his own "April After All" (whose lyrics included the lines *But there'll be other days/And things will turn our way/The rain has got to fall/It's April after all*). The last named, along with tracks like "Average Joe" and "Thinking Out Loud," were among the highlights on *Other Songs*. In 1999 Interscope issued his third CD, *Whereabouts.*

SEXTON, MARTIN "MARTY": *Singer, guitarist, songwriter. Born Syracuse, New York, March 2, 1966.*

An intriguing example of the new breed of folk artists coming to the fore in the 1990s, Marty Sexton energized audiences with an amazing vocal range—from deep bass to very high notes culminating in a throbbing falsetto—and with his impressive songwriting abilities. The content of his concerts went well beyond traditional or modern folk, embracing elements of soul, jazz, blues, and anything else that struck his fancy. Onstage, his repertoire included effective imitations of a trumpet and pan flutes and vocal inflections reminiscent of singers like Al Green and Ray Charles. As Neil Fagan wrote in *The Performing Songwriter,* "While other singer/songwriters play their guitars and sing their songs, Sexton plays his guitar, plays his voice, plays his song and plays his audience, creating a one man symphony."

Growing up in Syracuse, New York, as part of a family of twelve, he developed an outgoing persona as a way to keep from getting lost in the crowd. He told Frank Rabey of the North Carolina publication *Mountain Xpress* ("You Ain't Heard Nothin' Till Hearing Marty Sexton Sing," March 6, 1996), as a youngster he was "a trouble-maker and a rabble-rouser. I was practiced in the art of getting attention, which led to my career in entertainment."

His initial foray into music came when he was in the eighth grade and began playing in a rock band with school friends. In high school in the early 1980s he was a member of various "garage bands in church basements" who copied pop hits by Jimi Hendrix, Janis Joplin, and Led Zeppelin at school dances and beer blasts. After graduating high school, he told Rabey, "I got a haircut and into a Top-40 band, singing Huey Lewis and hits of the '80s." Though he continued to focus on mainstream rock, over the years he also had gained an interest in black soul and blues from listening to radio programs in his home area.

In 1989 he decided he needed to widen his musical horizons and left home for Boston, Massachusetts. He had honed his guitar technique by then and also had begun writing his own material. After losing his job as a waiter, he soon started to perform on street corners in Cambridge and in subway stations, while also demonstrating his vocal skills when possible at open-mike nights in local clubs and gigs at coffeehouses. He also listened eagerly to music played by other young street buskers, which gave him his first insight into the folk genre. As he told Seth Rogovoy of the *Boston Phoenix,* until that time he "didn't even know what folk music was." After that, some of his songwriting incorporated folk influences.

He expressed amazement to Rabey about the high caliber of Boston subway performers. "At every subway stop there were these incredibly talented artists playing original stuff or really obscure covers. I said, 'I gotta do that.'" Taking up the challenge, he soon was earning enough from his underground efforts to pay his rent and other living expenses.

Some episodes of busking were particularly rewarding, he said. "People could hear me as they were coming down the escalator, but they couldn't see me. One morning, I was singing—probably 'Hard Times' by Ray Charles—and this old African American woman came around the corner and did a double-take. Her jaw sort of hit the pavement. The train was on its way so she pulled this crumpled one-dollar bill out of her bag and hunched over to drop it in my case. And as she was walking away, she looked over at me and said, 'You black. There's some black in you some way.'

"That was a nice day."

This pattern continued into the early '90s. In 1992, Sexton self-produced a cassette tape of some of his songs called *In the Journey* on his Kitchen Table label. Word of his ability had begun to spread by word of mouth to newfound fans in Boston and Cambridge, and he began to find more opportunities to play on local stages and hawk the cassette to audiences. Over the next few years, sales of the tape continued steadily until it went past the 16,000 mark, an amazing achievement for a self-produced product. After listening to the cassette, a critic from the *CMJ New Music Report* commented, "Sexton's wide vocal range allows him to take a variety of styles with uncommon ease, while his writing talent is equally impressive. . . . His tape left me wanting more."

Meanwhile, more than a few members of the press and radio began to extol his performing skills and the quality of his original songs. After seeing him take part in a multiartist concert, a reviewer from the *Boston Herald* enthused, "Every act was worthy, but Martin Sexton was the only one of brilliance. He simply has to be seen to be believed! At first he comes across as a supple singer drenched by the mannerisms of '70s black pop. Yet his style is not just blue-eyed soul, it dips back to early jazz, blues, ragtime. He has a vaudevillian way of selling a lyric. He yodeled, displayed a keening wild falsetto, purred like a slinky sex symbol, and made it all seem easy."

Growing recognition of his gifts led to his winning a Boston Music Award two times (New Acoustic Act of 1995 and Best Song/Songwriter of 1996 for "Glory Bound") and being named the 1994 National Academy of Songwriters Artist of the Year. Such laurels paved the way for a copublishing deal with Sony Music Publishing and a recording contract with the independent Eastern Front Records. By then he already was extending his activities to other parts of the United States, headlining small clubs or college shows and also getting the chance to appear on bills with established artists like Art Garfunkel, Jackson Browne, Stephen Stills, and John Hiatt.

His debut album on Eastern Front, *Black Sheep* (originally on Kitchen Table), was issued on May 21, 1996. The title song referred in part to his feelings of inadequacy when he first compared himself to the excellent artists he heard around him on the streets and in the subway. Though somewhat uneven in content, the album still showcased an individual with almost unlimited potential.

Reviews in publications big and small were unfailingly positive. Carole and Josie Connare commented in the *New England Folk Almanac*, "Sexton is a soul poet who is unafraid to tackle diverse styles, conquering them all with his vocal prowess. 'Diner,' a snappy '50s ditty that could have been part of the *Grease* sound track, couches the only scat singing on the album. 'Freedom on the Road' soars with a gospel sound. 'Can't Stop Thinking about You' borrows from Billie Holiday and Stevie Wonder, while 'Candy' wails and plummets like an alternative rock anthem." Much of the material, as might be expected, was autobiographical. For instance, the "hard traveling" aspect of a rising pop musician was captured in lyrics to "Glory Bound," which talked of his "living out of a VW bus" accompanied only by "a pipe dream and my guitar."

In 1996 he could consider his "pipe dream" of musical success an emerging reality as he was cheered by audiences in small to medium venues across the United States. He also was a main stage featured performer at such prestigious festivals as Telluride, Kerrville (Texas), High Sierra, and Newport. While tracks from the new album didn't crack the top 40 programming barrier, they still gained airtime on many smaller stations, particularly college and public radio outlets.

He left Eastern Front Records and signed with Atlantic Records, releasing his label debut, *The American,* in November 1998. Produced by Danny Kortchmar, who has previously worked with Freedy Johnston and Don Henley, the twelve songs on the album range from folk, country, and boogie-woogie to jazz. Two songs, "Glory Bound" and "Candy," appeared on the *Black Sheep* album. Some of the new tracks include "My Maria," "The Way I Am," "Beast in Me," and "The American." He followed with a second Atlantic release in late 2000, *Wonder Bar.*

SHANNON, SHARON: *Accordionist, fiddler, songwriter. Born Corofin, County Clare, Ireland, June 8, 1967.*

For a folk-music artist to outsell rock groups is remarkable, even in a place where traditional music has a great following such as Sharon Shannon's native Ireland. It's even more remarkable when you consider that Shannon is an instrumentalist, not a singer, and that her primary instrument is the somewhat unique button accordion. Yet that was what Sharon did in the early 1990s, extending her influence, though not on as grand a scale, to many other parts of the world including the United Kingdom and the United States.

As is the case in more than a few Irish families, traditional folk music was beloved by her parents and easily adopted by Sharon and her siblings. She told Oliver P. Sweeney ("That Was the River," *Hot Press*), "My parents got us all started. They're really interested in music—they're set dancers themselves. There's four of us in the family—my brother Gary, my older sister Majella, myself and my younger sister Mary. We all had tin whistles and we learned them.

"Gary was brilliant, a great encouragement. When I was about eleven, he must have been fourteen or fifteen, and he decided to take up the concert flute—so he suggested that instead of us staying on tin whistles, we should all take up different instruments. Majella took up the fiddle, I got an accordion and Mary got a banjo. The parents bought them all one day, the whole lot of them, and we all just played in the house like mad."

Their musical skills impressed neighbors and friends, including a man named Frank Custy, a fiddle teacher and an organizer of ceilidhs in Toonagh, a village near where Sharon's parents grew up. The affairs were held every Friday night, and Sharon and her family went there to play music and dance. Sharon's abilities as an accordionist continued to improve, and by her mid-teens many other musicians were becoming aware of her unusual talents. Soon she got the chance to appear at dances and folk venues in other parts of Ireland, including the capital city, Dublin. When she was seventeen she began teaching herself the fiddle and soon was a good, if not great, fiddler. As a teenager she began playing with the group Disirt Tola, which included her brother Gary and sister Mary, concertina player Gearoid O'hAllmhurain, and piper Ronan Browne. The band released one album, *Disirt Tola.* She also toured with Comhaltas Ceoltoiri Eireann (where she came into contact with piano accordionist Karen Tweed). She appeared on the album *Ceol Tigh Neachtain,* released by Gael Linn in 1989.

In the mid-1980s well-known (in Ireland) theater director Jim Sheridan of the Druid Theatre asked Sharon, then in her teens, to provide music for a touring production of the Brendan Behan play *The Hostage.* Following that well-regarded project, she joined a traditional Irish music group called Arcady. Late in the decade she had just begun recording some of her material when she was asked by Mike Scott to join the Waterboys. She put her recording efforts aside and toured with the band for eighteen months, performing on the Waterboys' album *Room to Roam* (Ensign, 1990). Her stay with the group, as she told Sweeney, was a fun time that also helped her learn a lot more about performing in general. "It was fantastic, brilliant, great altogether. They were great people to be around. There were sessions all the time, on buses and at airports—we used to do an awful lot of hanging around airports and we ended up doing great crack (Irish slang for jam sessions—not the drug) even doing sessions on airplanes." After the band broke up in 1991 she decided to go back and complete her solo album.

Critics and concert goers newly introduced to Sharon's accordion work were amazed at what she could do with the instrument. Don Meade, writing a concert review in the *Irish Voice* ("Super Show from a Young Legend," June 15, 1993), noted, "Still in her early 20s, she has become a celebrated musician by finding her own distinctive and highly influential sound. All over Ireland, young accordionists are busily copying her patented single-note triplets and retuning their instruments to approximate the clean, concertina-like tone she gets from her pint-sized Castagnari 'box.'"

By then Shannon already had taken a first step toward stardom with her debut album, *Sharon Shannon,* issued in Ireland in 1991 on Solid Records. In the studio sessions of 1991, she was backed by such top-rank musicians as Mike Scott and Steve Wickham from the Waterboys, Liam Ó'Maonlaí from Hothouse Flowers, bass guitarist Adam Clayton from U2, and traditional instrumental artist Dónal Lunny on bouzouki and Phillip King. Tracks included a tribute to fiddler Tommy Peoples in "Glentown," a medley combining the traditional "O'Keefes" with the American Cajun song "The Happy One Step," and originals such as "The Munster Hop," a rock-flavored number Shannon wrote while on tour with the Waterboys. The album rose high on Irish charts and sold more than 50,000 copies, a substantial volume for the Irish market.

In support of the album, Sharon organized her own band, which toured the United Kingdom and the European continent in 1992–93 and then backed her at U.S. venues after Philo/Rounder released the disc to the American market in the summer of 1993. Primary band members were guitarist Gerry O'Beirne (whose credits included backing Mary Black and Maura O'Connell and performing with Andy Irvine and the Patrick Street Band), fiddler-mandolinist Mary Custy (daughter of Frank Custy), and former Waterboys stand-up electric bass player Trevor Hutchinson. (During 1992, Sharon also contributed two instrumentals to *A Woman's Heart,* a compilation album that also had tracks by Frances Black, Maura O'Connell, Dolores Keane, Eleanor McEvoy, and Mary Black. The disc became the best-selling Irish folk collection of the year.)

Her repertoire of traditional and traditional-style music charmed many American concert goers in 1994 and 1995. She told Paul Robicheau of the *Boston Globe* ("Irish Voices . . . Sharon Shannon's Road to Success Follows the Traditional Route," Calendar section, March 17, 1994), "Traditional music isn't all boring and serious. You can have a great crack with it." To his comments about how well she blended songs from other cultures, like Cajun or Portuguese, with Celtic tunes, she responded, "It's a lot of the same instruments and the tunes are very similar to Irish tunes. It doesn't matter really where the tune comes from. If we like the melody, we just play it."

Shannon's second solo effort, *Out the Gap,* was issued in 1994 on Solid Records and the following year on Green Linnet. Although there were a few holdover tunes from the 1990 recording sessions for her first CD, the new album in general had a less traditional feel. She deliberately hired reggae producer Denis Bovell to add a Caribbean and calypso beat to some of the songs with overlaid drums and horns on her accordion sound. The reggae-flavored tracks include "The Mighty Sparrow" and "Sparky." She also plays a traditional American tune, "Sandy River Belle," and a polka-meets-calypso-meets-Norwegian-style song, "Bjorn Again Polka." Backup artists on the album include Trevor Hutchinson on bass, Donogh Hennessy on guitars, Mary Custy on fiddle, and Gerry O'Beirne on guitars.

In her tours to support the CD, she was backed by her own Sharon Shannon band: Hutchinson on bass, Hennessy on Guitar, and on fiddle Winnie Horan, who has also played with Cherish the Ladies and Solas.

Dónal Lunny produced her excellent CD *Each Little Thing,* issued on Grapevine in Ireland and Green Linnet in the United States in 1997. She included the traditional French Canadian song "Mouth of the Tobique" and also features the vocals of Kirsty MacColl, daughter of Ewan MacColl, on "Libertango."

In an acknowledgment of Shannon's growing influence on both sides of the Atlantic, Nanci Griffith invited her to play the accordion on three tracks for *Other Voices, Too (A Trip Back to Bountiful),* released by Elektra in 1998. That year Grapevine Records also came out with *Spellbound: The Best of Sharon Shannon,* a compilation of her first three albums that includes five new songs. The CD came out on Green Linnet in January 1999.

SHOCKED, MICHELLE: *Singer, songwriter, guitarist, mandolinist. Born Dallas, Texas, February 24, 1962.*

It's no surprise that Michelle Shocked took on her *nom de plume.* She has always revealed a strong dose of skepticism in her music. She is constantly remaking herself, to the delight of her fans and the dismay of record company executives, altering her musical style from the rural, countrified folk of her Texas roots to the R&B and funk style of her current home, New Orleans. She adopted her punkish name in the '80s when she was traveling around the United States with a group of peace activists. Since then, Michelle has used her creative powers to sing for peace, feminism, and against racism.

She has maintained integrity in the face of the muscle of the record industry. After a four-year battle with Mercury Records over artistic rights, she emancipated herself, filing a $1 million lawsuit in 1995 invoking the Thirteenth Amendment abolishing slavery and the Indentured Servitude Act of California. The parties reached an out-of-court settlement in 1996. But the struggle kept Shocked from releasing a new album on a commercial label for several years.

"The system that you use to get your music out there has to be dealt with, but it's a tough fight," she told P.J. Huffstutter of the *San Diego Union-Tribune* (April 18, 1996). "It took me three years to get free from Mercury

Records. All that time, I felt like I was back . . . out there as a protester with a picket sign on the sidewalks."

Despite her maverick outlook, she has done some conventional things, like getting married to journalist Bart Bull on July 4, 1992. In concert at McCabe's in March 1996, she talked about coming down with "nestosterone" in her thirties: "We have to nest." (She struck a more feminine pose, wearing her hair in a shag. She also wore a Jimi Hendrix T-shirt, red tennis shoes, and played a white Fender Stratocaster.)

While her personal story initially was obscured in marketing put-on and inaccurate articles, there is one consistent truth about Shocked: she has written some of the best songs of any contemporary singer-songwriter. From "Come a Long Way," about the strange and twisted life in L.A., to "Quality of Mercy" for the *Dead Man Walking* soundtrack, Shocked challenges her audiences. She has criticized the music industry for its failure to acknowledge the contributions of black artists. But she has sometimes vented her anger on well-meaning fans. She reportedly walked off the stage at one concert in May 1996 in Portsmouth, New Hampshire, complaining that her mostly white audience lacked diversity.

She was born Karen Michelle Johnston, the daughter of Bill Johnston and a mother whose name she doesn't reveal. Her parents divorced a year after she was born. She grew up poor and entertained herself by making music. She stayed with her mother who married an army man, providing young Michelle with an army brat upbringing. They moved around to Maryland, Massachusetts, and West Germany, and eventually settled in Gilmer, Texas, the East Texas setting for many of her songs. In "Memories of East Texas," she sings about the perils of childhood: *You had to watch out for all the curves / down by Kelsey Creek / And detour thru the Lindsay's Pasture / When the waters ran too deep.*

"I knew I wasn't talking about roads," she told the audience at McCabe's.

Michelle's mother was a converted Mormon whom she has described as a Tammy Bakker type. High school was no better. "I had to teach my government teacher how to pronounce bourgeoisie," she told *People Weekly* (November 7, 1988). At sixteen, she ran away for the summer to stay in Dallas with her father, a "hippie atheist type." While her Mormon mother "wouldn't let her listen to anything but the Osmonds," her father was an avid country and blues fan who liked Guy Clark, Doc Watson, and Big Bill Broonzy. He played the mandolin and took her and her brother Max around to bluegrass and folk festivals. She bought a $75 Yamaha guitar from a pawnshop at his urging and "flew with it," Bill Johnston told *People.*

She put herself through the University of Texas and graduated in May 1983 with a bachelor's degree in speech with an emphasis in interpretive literature. After graduating, she left Texas and lived the hobo's life, squatting in abandoned buildings in San Francisco, New York, and Europe. She toured with a group of peace activists called the War Chest Tour, staging protests at both the Republican and Democratic conventions in 1984. At the Democratic Convention in San Francisco she was arrested while sitting peacefully with her cohorts. A picture, taken by *San Francisco Examiner* photographer Chris Hardy, shows her being choked by the police. She would later use the photo for the cover of her 1988 album *Short Sharp Shocked.* (In the late 1980s, she testified in a successful civil suit filed by some of those who were arrested.)

She was twice committed to mental hospitals against her will. While living on the streets in Northern California, she was arrested by police and thrown into a mental institution. Her father helped her get out and brought her back to Dallas. When Michelle resumed her vagabond lifestyle, her mother had Michelle committed to a psychiatric hospital in Dallas, where she stayed until the insurance ran out. She later legally changed her name to Michelle Shocked, or 'Chel-Shocked, which had been her punk name (not because she received electric shock therapy as has been widely reported).

She left for Europe in 1985, squatting in Amsterdam and London. While traveling through Italy, she was raped and was taken by friends to a woman's crisis center. "I didn't fit in there, either," she told *People.* "I didn't fit in anywhere."

"I was an angry and resentful person, and I was milking my past hurts, and past injuries for all they were worth," Shocked told Kevin Ransom of the *Detroit News* (May 16, 1996). "I blamed God for my pain. My mother was a strict Mormon, and I found a lot of her ideology to be so reprehensible that it literally drove me away from God."

She returned to Texas via New York. She began living the life of a troubadour. In 1986, Shocked was trading tunes with other singers by a campfire at the Kerrville Folk Festival. British producer Pete Lawrence heard her and asked if he could tape her. He turned on his weak-batteried Sony Walkman, which picked up the sounds of the crickets and rumbling trucks along with her songs. Without her permission, Lawrence released the recording as *The Texas Campfire Tapes* (1986, Cooking Vinyl) in England. Remarkably, it hit the top of the British independent charts. The album showed her raw skills on "Chain Smoker," "5 AM in Amsterdam," about her days as a vagabond in Europe, and "Necktie," a wry look at injustice in which she sings, *And they said it was suicide / Now you can blame the social system / But I still say it was his necktie.*

Michelle's experience is a cautionary tale. After her unplanned debut, she signed with PolyGram and moved to London, where she lived on a houseboat on the Thames. PolyGram offered a $130,000 advance; she took $50,000, suggesting the balance be used to help other artists. To regain the rights to her songs, she had to sue Lawrence, the first in a line of difficult legal battles. They eventually settled out of court. "It was a lawsuit that caused this very bitter attitude on my part, which is where I picked up the term 'Texas Campfire Thefts,'" she told Robert Wilonsky of the *Dallas Observer* (April 25, 1996). "That was settled out of court eventually, but I went through a real seven-year English, powdered-wig, m'lord-m'lady kind of legal battle, and it was hard." Now that she owns the rights, she'd prefer they remain out of print, she told Wilonsky.

She eventually signed with managers, and booking agents, and her alliance with one manager in the United Kingdom, Martin Goldschmidt of Cooking Vinyl, in 1987, was another business relationship that went sour. The English courts eventually ruled in Goldschmidt's favor after a protracted battle.

She signed a major label contract with PolyGram's Mercury label. For her debut she was matched up with Pete Anderson, who had produced Dwight Yoakam. "I came into the whole studio thing very much alienated," she told Jim Washburn of the *Los Angeles Times* (May 29, 1990). "I'm not much in the record-buying tradition, and a good reason for that was, having sampled the radio, I had a real strong distaste. And I thought that was a lot to do with the technology and the producers. I didn't really even know what a producer was. I just figured that whatever they were, they were going to try to make me sound like all the other crap on the radio."

Anderson wanted to use synthesizers for the song "Anchorage." Shocked didn't want computers on her record. "If your intuition tells you that it's not right for this song, we won't use it," Anderson told her, gaining her respect.

"He obviously has an agenda that is very similar to mine, which is to shake up the status quo and question formula production," she told Washburn. "He's a strong ally, and what we have is a collaboration in the best sense of the word."

Short Sharp Shocked, released in 1988, included some of Shocked's best songs, including "Memories of East Texas," "When I Grow Up . . . I Want to Be an Old Woman," "Hello Hopeville," Jean Ritchie's "The L&N Don't Stop Here Anymore," "Graffiti Limbo" (about graffiti artist Michael Stewart, who died while in police custody), and "Anchorage." The latter was in the form of a letter from a friend who settled into a domestic life: *Kevin lost a tooth, he's starting school / I got a brand new eight month old baby girl / I sound like a housewife / I think I'm a housewife.* The single hit number sixty-six on the charts, and the album rose to number seventy-three.

Her image as a runaway, iconoclastic, waiflike folksinger was cemented in feature stories across the country. Here's how the 1988 *People Weekly* story began: "Skinny and pale, she wears the uniform of the defiant: close-cropped hair, black T-shirt and sweats, a British

Tell Wizard" and "Hard Core Hornography." Her most moving song was called "Little Billy," powered by the funeral tradition of the "second line." It tells the story of a mother whose son was killed on the streets. They brought his coffin into the house. The mother changed from her black funeral dress to her powder blue dress. They lifted her up and she danced, scuffing "the coffin with her shoes."

The song reveals her resiliency and vulnerability. "Life deals out certain frustrations no matter how charmed a life you think you lead," Shocked told Rayburn. "But . . . I had to get real honest [and] . . . realize that I was doing this for no one but myself. In the past, I felt like I had to please the record company or please my manager or the audience. When I realized that I was doing this for me, I found the courage to fight. Then God set about to work on my heart, and love took the place of bitterness."

Based in part on a phone interview with Bart Bull

SIBERRY, JANE: *Singer, guitarist, keyboard player, record producer, filmmaker, author. Born Toronto, Ontario, Canada, October 12, 1955.*

With an excellent soprano voice, a probing mind, and skills on both acoustic and electronic instruments, Jane Siberry represented one of Canada's important contributions to the folk movement in the late decades of the twentieth century. Not that she considered herself purely a folk artist. She told Jonathan Taylor of the Los Angeles *Daily News* (August 29, 1985), "I don't use 'folk music' as words in my language. I'm part of the populace, so I guess that's part of folk, and I'm expressing what I feel I need to express. You can say it's part of folk, but you could say the same thing about heavy metal."

She grew up in a suburb of Toronto, Canada, under comfortable conditions but not surrounded by a musical environment. She told David Furnish of *Interview* magazine ("Music View Woman," March 1996), "My parents weren't musicians. Basically, our record collection was created by what they won at bridge parties." She did study piano in her preteen years and went on to play by ear and later as a teenager taught herself to play the guitar. As she went through high school, she became increasingly engrossed in music, trying to write original songs in her midteens. During those years she took music classes and also joined the school band.

When she began to attract attention for her creative achievements in the 1980s, some critics compared her to artists like Joni Mitchell and Laurie Anderson. This attempt at pigeonholing her talents seemed somewhat strained, but she acknowledged that Mitchell had been a major influence. She told Stephen Holden of the *New York Times* ("Jane Siberry," May 30, 1986), "Joni . . . has been a real inspiration to me for her lyrics. I also

used to listen a great deal to Neil Young and Leonard Cohen. And because I was interested in their intricate rhythms, I also liked rock groups like Yes, Emerson, Lake and Palmer, and Steely Dan."

In 1974, at nineteen, she enrolled at the University of Guelph in Guelph, Ontario (about 100 miles from Toronto). She began as a music major but found the courses didn't add to anything she already knew intuitively so she switched to science. She completed courses for a degree in science, with a major in microbiology. "I was sort of the oddball in the science class, but it was a good experience. Before I took microbiology, if someone asked me what time it was, I'd round it off to the nearest hour. Now I round it off to the nearest fifteen minutes." Seriously, though, she felt the new insight into the physical world and the discipline involved proved valuable in shaping her songwriting approach.

Jane continued to work on her writing as she proceeded through college, and after graduating she decided to seek a career in music, taking whatever gigs were available in local coffeehouse and other venues. To help meet her room and board requirements she took various jobs as a waitress, typist, and file clerk. In liner notes for one of her albums, guitarist John Switzer recalled the first time he heard her perform in 1977 at the Carden Street Cafe folk club in Guelph: "She seemed shy and a bit nervous, even on that tiny stage; but at the same time there was a strange confidence and a sense of humor that rewarded your attention, that promised a mind and a spirit that you would benefit from knowing. And her songs confirmed these impressions: melodies that seemed truly inspired by the words they conveyed, and words that seemed like true poetry, in that they made you feel things you had never felt; or had felt but never articulated; or had articulated, but never so exactly, never with that ring of the pure tone of truth."

Gradually the two became friends, and in 1979 Siberry, who had formed a duo with singer Wendy Davis called Java Jive, asked Switzer to join as bass guitarist. For the rest of that year into 1980 the trio played whenever the opportunity arose at clubs and folk festivals. At one festival they met an artist named David Bradstreet, who asked them to help back him and partner Carl Keesee on the album *Black and White,* recorded in their basement studio in Toronto. In lieu of salary, Siberry and her associates were given studio time, which she gradually used to tape tracks for her first album. She helped finance production of the album with tips gained from waitressing. Titled *Jane Siberry,* it came out on an independent label in 1981 and was sold almost exclusively at her concerts.

She kept touring and writing new material in the next few years, gradually building up a following among folk and pop fans in Canada. In 1984 her second album, *No Borders Here,* was released on Duke Street Records in Canada and won applause from critics and a place on many radio playlists in her home country. It made the Canadian charts and helped earn her a Juno nomination for Most Promising Artist of the Year. (The Juno is the Canadian equivalent of the U.S. Grammy.) The record was called to the attention of Jeff Heiman, then handling A&R for Windham Hill Records in the United States, who helped arrange for its U.S. release on Windham Hill's new subsidiary, Open Air Records. With tracks like "I Muse Aloud" (with an unusual 5/4 time signature), "Extra Executives," "Dancing Class," "Symmetry (The Way Things Have to Be)," "Mimi on the Beach" (which provided a hit single in Canada), and "Waitressing," it was one of the most exciting U.S. debut albums of the year. Just about every reviewer cited the lyrics of the last song, which included the lines *I'd probably be famous now / If I wasn't such a good waitress.*

The album was a commercial success in Canada and didn't do badly in the United States. It certainly won the attention of a far greater number of listeners than her first LP, she said, "when I was doing traditional acoustic folk music." A major difference was her use of a Fairlight computer synthesizer, which, as Stephen Holden observed, enabled her "to program and sample different sounds and create fluid, constantly changing musical atmospheres."

In 1985 her album *The Speckless Sky* came out on Windham Hill and was warmly received by reviewers in both the United States and Canada. It quickly made Canadian charts and earned a gold record for that market. It earned her two People's Choice Awards (CASBY) in Canada, one for Album of the Year, the other for Producer of the Year. Before work began on her next collection, she left Windham Hill and was signed by Reprise/Warner Brothers Records. The first result of the new alignment was the LP *The Walking,* issued in 1987. Support for that album included her first tours outside North America, covering engagements in Europe, Japan, and Australia. Her concerts won many ecstatic reviews from foreign critics including columns that employed terms like "heart stopping" and "spellbinding."

For her next Reprise project she backed away from her technopop electronic layerings to move back toward acoustic folk-oriented stylings. The new album, the 1989 *Bound by the Beauty,* was recorded in the middle of an apple orchard. Coming into the '90s, she continued to demonstrate a winning stage presence in sets at a variety of venues and at major festivals. She began work on tracks for her new album in June 1991, but didn't complete the material until January 1993. Called *When I Was a Boy,* the disc was issued by Reprise/Warner later in '93, and among its cuts was "Calling All Angels," which formed part of the sound track for Wim Wenders's film *Until the End of the World.* Wenders also used her composition "Slow Tango" on the sound track for his movie *Faraway So Close.*

From mid-'93 through 1994 Jane was involved in an array of projects, including accepting an invitation from Peter Gabriel to take part in his Real World Recording Week in Bath, England. She commented, "It was like a huge gift to me from Peter Gabriel. I was reminded in one week of the power of music generated by the musicians who pray when they play. The glamour of high-tech manipulation (i.e., fix it till it's perfect) was returned to its appropriate place." On the four compilation albums made from the gathering Jane was featured on several tracks, including "Arcane" and "Harmonix."

During this period, she also cowrote and recorded "It Won't Rain All the Time" for the sound track of *The Crow,* issued by Atlantic Records in 1994. For Hector Zazou's 1994 Sony album *Songs from the Cold Seas* she contributed the track "She's Like the Swallow," a traditional song from Newfoundland. Jane also was invited to sing on the 1994 Indigo Girls album on Epic, *Swamp Ophelia,* handling backing vocals on "Language of the Kiss" and "Mercury."

In 1995, Siberry's seventh album was released, the Reprise/Warner collection *Maria.* The jazz-flavored offering included a twenty-minute suite, "Oh My My"; a ballad titled "Goodbye Sweet Pumpkinhead"; "Begat Begat," in which Jane exhibited her scat singing skills; and the track "See the Child," which *Rolling Stone* approvingly described as "a nursery rhyme with bebop cadence."

The contents of *Maria* confirmed that Siberry was not afraid to experiment with new musical directions—although, as she said when similar comments by critics were made before, she thought some were going overboard "when they talk about how 'different' I am. I'm drawing from a lot of things around me. I don't see my music as groundbreaking or unique. It's just my way of doing what others do, and it's different simply because I'm a different person. On the other hand, I don't like being called 'quirky' and so on. I think some people like my music on first hearing, but for others it definitely takes some getting used to. The chords don't always move the way you'd expect; there is some reorientation involved. I like the fact that the album grows on you."

After the marketing of *Maria* had run its course, Reprise wanted to renegotiate her contract (which still had called for two more albums). This gave her an opportunity to leave, and so in 1996 she set up her own Toronto-based independent label, Sheeba Records. She told Jim Bessman of *Billboard* ("Siberry's Sheeba Takes Indie Route," June 1, 1996), "I'm very grateful to Reprise, because if it weren't for them, I wouldn't have such well-established media and marketing channels."

But she welcomed the prospects of being her own boss. The first project undertaken was to record pieces from her early writing days. The album, recorded and mixed one week in March 1996 and released in June '96, was titled *Teenager.* In album liner notes, she pointed out, "I wrote my first song when I was 16 for an English class. It got a low grade for being too sweet. Whatever. And the original recording you hear was done in the first blush of my excitement at being able to create my own harmonies." She also recalled these songs were ones she first recorded "in my bedroom with two ghetto blasters" and the new album gave her the chance "to go way back before going way forward."

Though Sheeba was based in Canada, by the 1995–96 period Jane had made her home in New York. The plan was to have Sheeba not only be the source of new Siberry albums but also to offer such other items by her as songbooks, a short story trilogy, and a novelette she was working on. *Teenager,* at least initially, was not available in stores but was sold via phone and web site links. During the summer of '96 Jane scheduled a series of shows with full band backup to help, in part, with start-up costs of her new label. These included appearances at the Vancouver Folk Festival, the Ottawa Rideau Falls Festival, the Harbourfront Vocals Series, the Hillside Music Festival in Guelph, the Bottom Line in New York, and the Michigan Women's Festival.

Meanwhile, she still found time for other activities, including singing and writing lyrics for violinist Nigel Kennedy's song "Innig" on his summer '96 album *Kafka.*

She contributed the song "When I Think of Laura Nyro" to *Time and Love: The Music of Laura Nyro,* a tribute album released by Aston Place Recordings in May 1997. Other collaborative projects included backup vocals for Patty Larkin's "Coming Up for Air" on *Perishable Fruit;* "Haint It Funny," a song she wrote for k.d. lang's *Drag* album; and "The Bridge," recorded on Joe Jackson's album *Heaven and Hell,* a modern-day look at the "Seven Deadly Sins."

In the spring of 1997 Jane moved back to Toronto to focus on developing Sheeba. Through her web site she communicated more directly with her fans. Her second project on the label was *A Day in the Life,* released in June 1997. A twenty-nine-minute soundscape-audio collage, the recording follows Jane through a frantic day in New York, complete with hair appointments, cab rides, message machine missives, and songs.

She came out with her next recording, *Child,* in October 1997. A Christmas-flavored album that was recorded live at New York's Bottom Line in December 1996, it includes some traditional French and German songs as well as Siberry originals. She embarked on an international tour in support of *Child.* At the end of 1997 Siberry returned from touring, found her business affairs in a state of disarray, and proceeded to lay off her entire Sheeba staff and begin running the office single-handedly. She studied bookkeeping and revamped the entire office. "I had to take responsibility for a few mistakes I made," Siberry says. By 1999 things were back on track. Despite the rebuilding period, in 1998 Siberry self-released her first book of poetry titled *Swan,* something she hopes to do more of. She also completed her *New York Trilogy* with two other collections from the

Bottom Line concerts in 1999: *Tree,* music used in film sound tracks and those that should have been, and *Lips,* a say-what-you-mean collection of songs.

With assistance from Jane Siberry and Rebecca Campbell, a singer who also works with Sheeba and as Siberry's tour manager

SIEBEL, PAUL: *Singer, guitarist, songwriter. Born Attica, New York, September 19, 1937.*

A sensitive songwriter, a fine balladeer in the folk-country-blues tradition of Dylan, Kristofferson, and even the early king of country music, Jimmie Rodgers, Paul Siebel had a lot going for him, except timing. He came along just after the folk boom of the late 1950s and early 1960s had peaked and never got the attention his talents seemed to deserve.

Though he loved the work of country greats like Rodgers, Hank Williams, and Hank Snow and wrote a number of songs on country and western topics ("Pinto Pony," "Nashville Again"), his roots were in the North. He was born and raised on a farm in Attica, a town in upstate New York not far from Buffalo. His first exposure to music took the form of classical violin lessons when he was still a small child. As a teenager, he became interested in folk and country music and learned to play the guitar, singing traditional folk songs, tunes of Woody Guthrie, and songs made famous by Jimmie Rodgers and Hank Williams.

Siebel started to perform in small clubs and coffeehouses in Buffalo when he was drafted; he spent two years in the armed forces. After his discharge, he headed for New York in 1963, where he worked in a baby carriage factory in Brooklyn and became a part of the Greenwich Village folk scene nights and weekends. Part of the time, he added to his income by singing in Village "basket houses," so called because the basket was passed around for contributions from the audience.

In 1966, Paul began to supplement his country and folk repertoire with original compositions. Among the songs that he penned in the mid-1960s were "Louise," the sympathetic story of a truck-stop prostitute, "The Ballad of Honest Sam," a satirical look at politicians, "Then Came the Children," and perhaps his best-known piece, "Any Day Woman." The lyrics of the latter demonstrate his understanding of the human condition (*If you don't love her / Better let her go / You'll never feel her / You're bound to let it show / Love's so hard to take / When you have to fake / Everything in return*).

Songs like that helped make him a favorite with Boston folk fanciers in the mid- and late 1960s. Though he achieved a considerable reputation locally, his name remained unfamiliar outside the East. As the 1960s drew to a close, he became part of the movement among many folk-country and rock artists to Woodstock, New York, joining such well-established artists as Dylan and the Band in residence there.

Still, as the 1970s began Siebel remained obscure, partly because he had never been given a contract by a major record firm. It looked as though this would at least be remedied when Elektra signed him. His debut LP on the label, *Woodsmoke and Oranges,* won strong approval from all sides in 1970. *Rolling Stone* magazine called it a milestone event in country/rock/pop. The effort illustrated the force and flexibility of his vocal style and his storytelling talents in tracks such as "Nashville Again" and "She Made Me Lose My Blues," in which he displayed yodeling skills that would have made Jimmie Rodgers proud. Siebel had an amazing number of stellar musicians backing him on his albums, including guitarist David Bromberg, fiddler Richard Greene, mandolinist David Grisman, pedal steel guitar player Buddy Emmons, and guitarist Clarence White.

He followed up with another highly satisfying collection in his second album, *Jack-Knife Gypsy.* The title song showed that Siebel could handle the folk-rock idiom well when he wanted to, while other tracks extended over a range of folk and country stylings, such as the western-oriented "Pinto Pony" and "Legend of the Captain's Daughter," which included fiddle backing by Doug Kershaw in the Cajun-flavored number. The album included such other excellent originals as "Prayer Song," "Jasper and the Miner," and "Hillbilly Child."

More encomiums resulted, such as this glowing tribute by Ellen Sander in *Saturday Review* (January 30, 1971): "His writing is precise, tight and full of images that appear in a phrase, develop into flesh and feeling and flash through changes that live throughout the song. . . . After Siebel finishes his musical novelette, one is left with a dramatic impression of a brief lifetime having passed, its every aspect explored, the net result established, played and gone."

Despite many deserved tributes of that nature, Siebel did not break through to the mass audience, partly because of his own reluctance to endure the grind of continuous concertizing. He noted in 1971, "If I go on tour and make $40,000 a year and live in motels, what will I have after it's over?" That he could do well touring was indicated when he opened one show for the Band in California and won a standing ovation from the crowd. However, Siebel drew back from heavy touring in the mid- and late-1970s. He continued to make appearances at folk clubs in various parts of the country, but this low profile kept his name from wider prominence despite his high standing with other artists.

During the 1970s, many of his songs were performed by singers from diverse parts of the pop spectrum. Bonnie Raitt, for instance, recorded a number of Siebel's compositions (as did Linda Ronstadt) and often spotlighted "Any Day Woman" in her concerts.

During his years in Woodstock, Paul took part in many informal sessions with other talented performers who lived in the area. Eventually folk-music performer and enthusiast Artie Traum organized a group called the Woodstock Mountain Revue, whose members included Paul Butterfield, Eric Kaz, Rory Block, Jim Rooney, and others. The group cut some material issued on Rounder, and Siebel performed on the second of those, the 1977 LP release, *Woodstock Mountains (More Music from Mud Acres).* Artie Traum's brother Happy noted that Siebel didn't perform any of his own songs on the album. He told Ellen Geisel of *Dirty Linen* ("Timeless Treasures: The Music of Paul Siebel," June–July 1996), "It didn't mean much to us that he didn't choose any original song, but it became kind of clear around that time that his muse had sort of left him. We had spoken a bit around that time that he didn't feel he had any more songs left in him."

Siebel continued to appear on the concert circuit from time to time until the early 1980s, when he seemed to fade from view. In fact, little was heard from him for well over a decade after that. (There is a live album recorded at McCabe's Guitar Shop in Santa Monica that came out on the Rag Baby label in 1981.) He told Geisel, "I wasn't getting anywhere, so I stopped. Folk lost its popularity possibly a little in the early '80s. It picked up again since. In fact, it's quite popular nowadays, the number of people in it supporting one another and the Irish influence is very strong. I'm impressed at how big it is now, [even if it's] not with the same intensity there was in the late '60s, the Dylan era, Joan Baez and those magic concerts at Newport."

The growing new following for folk helped induce Philo Records to obtain rights to Paul's Elektra output. In late 1995 the reissue titled *Paul Siebel* came out on the Philo/Rounder label. It incorporated all the tracks from *Woodsmoke and Oranges* and five from *Jack-Knife Gypsy.* The album disclosed to new generations how effective a performer and writer Siebel had been in his prime.

Siebel by then was in Maryland, where he worked as a bread-baker in a café and in his spare time satisfied an interest in wooden sailing ships by doing some model building and sailing when the occasion arose. What would he like people to think about him? Geisel asked. His reply: "Well, 'He was a guy who wrote a couple of pretty good songs. What ever happened to him?' I guess it's gonna go down something like that."

SILLY WIZARD: *Vocal and instrumental group from Edinburgh, Scotland. Andy M. Stewart, born Blairgowrie, Perthshire, Scotland, September 8, 1952; Phil Cunningham, born Portobello, Scotland, January 27, 1960; John Cunningham, born Portobello, Scotland, August 27, 1957; Gordon Jones, born Birkenhead (Merseyside), England, November 21, 1947; Martin "Mame" Hadden, born Aberdeen, Scotland, May 23, 1957; Bob Thomas, born Glasgow, Scotland, July 28, 1950; Madeline Taylor, born in Perth; Neil Adam, born in England; Freeland Barbour, born in Aberdeen; Alistair Donaldson, born in Edinburgh. Group disbanded in 1988.*

One of the growing number of very talented bands from the United Kingdom and Ireland that combined traditional music with hard-driving rock, Silly Wizard built up a sizable following in its native Scotland in the 1970s and early '80s before winning notice from many North American critics in the mid-'80s. Among those echoing the praises of U.K. commentators were Leslie Berman of the *Village Voice,* who said the band's offerings represented "the best marriage of traditional and modern music," and Ken Roseman of *Folk Roots,* who wrote that Silly Wizard's sound was "not only brilliant instrumentally and vocally, but [had] a special magic which sets them apart." The group broke up in the late 1980s, but many of its albums were still popular with record buyers in the 1990s.

All the band members were influenced by the rock sounds of the '60s, from Elvis Presley to the Beatles and Rolling Stones, as well as by the folk scene, which remained more dynamic in Europe even after it faded from view in the United States. The pop music center of Scotland for many years has been Edinburgh, where there were opportunities for teenage musicians to meet and perform at a variety of local clubs and pubs. Among them in the early 1970s was Martin Hadden, born in Aberdeen but brought up in Blairgowrie, whose first folk band, Puddock's Well, included vocalist Andy Stewart from Blairgowrie and fiddler Dougie MacLean. In the fall of 1972, Silly Wizard formed as a trio that included Gordon Jones, Bob Thomas, and fiddler Johnny Cunningham, who had left home at the age of fourteen and lived in run-down flats in Edinburgh before hooking up with the other two. They ran the Triangle Folk Club on Saturday nights. In 1973 the group began performing with a singer named Maddy Taylor and recording an album for Transatlantic, but it was never released. They asked bassist Neil Adam and later Andy M. Stewart to join and take over lead vocals in 1974, following the breakup of Puddock's Well. In March 1975 they started recording their debut, *Silly Wizard,* for Transatlantic (later released by Highway), with Alistair Donaldson on bass and Freeland Barbour (occasionally Phil Cunningham) on accordion. Donaldson and Barbour soon left and were replaced by accordionist Phil Cunningham and bassist Martin Hadden. The resulting group recorded Silly Wizard's second album, *Caledonia's Hardy Sons* (1978), released by Highway in the United Kingdom and Shanachie in the United States. Guitarist Bob Thomas got married and left soon after that album. The group then recorded *So Many Partings* (1979) as a five-piece band, embarking on their first trip to America to play the Philadelphia Folk Festival in the summer of 1979.

The Silly Wizard roster that evolved in 1978 was still playing together a decade later, except for a four-year hiatus by one bandsman in the first half of the '80s. Besides performing with the band, all of them from time to time became involved in projects of their own from solo albums to record production. The '78 group

comprised Stewart (lead vocals, tenor banjo, and pennywhistle); Hadden (bass guitar, keyboards, guitar, vocals); the Cunningham brothers, Phil (vocals, accordion, piano, synthesizers, pennywhistle, cittern) and John (vocals, fiddle); and Gordon Jones (vocals, guitar, bodhran).

The members typically began gaining experience as musicians in their preteen years. Phil Cunningham, for example, started to learn accordion as a boy and won six Scottish Accordion Championships before he was sixteen. His brother John started playing the fiddle in his native Edinburgh when he was seven and was considered one of Scotland's best young fiddlers when he reached his teens. Andy Stewart gained attention for his renditions of traditional folk music of Scotland and Ireland before teaming with Hadden and MacLean.

Silly Wizard started accruing fans in Scotland from the mid-1970s on, and by the 1980s was playing in concerts and festivals in other parts of the United Kingdom and in Europe. Their releases in the 1980s included, on Highway in the United Kingdom and Shanachie in the United States: *Wild and Beautiful* (1981), *Kiss the Tears Away* (1983), and *Best of Silly Wizard* (Shanachie, 1985). Green Linnet in the United States and REL in the United Kingdom released *Golden Golden* (1985), *Live in America* (1985), and *Live Wizardry* (Green Linnet, 1989). The group's album output also included the 1986 release *A Glint of Silver,* which won the Indie award in the British Isles category. While continuing to tour and record under the Silly Wizard banner, all the members kept finding other outlets for their talents, a situation that in time contributed to the decision to disband. For instance, John Cunningham left the band completely in 1980 to focus on a solo career (he was replaced briefly by Dougie MacLean), then rejoined in 1985 though continuing solo work into the mid-1990s. His solo albums included *Thoughts from Another World* (Shanachie, Highway, '81) and *Fair Warning* (Green Linnet, '84). He also tried his hand at record producing; during one period he produced the debut album for the rock band Rain Dogs, whose home base was Boston, Massachusetts, releasing *Lost Souls* (Atlantic, 1990) and *Border Drive-In Theatre* (Atlantic, 1991).

Not to be outdone, his brother Phil started doing solo discs of his own. He released *Against the Storm* on Highway in 1980. His solo effort, *Airs and Graces* (1984), gained the Indie from the National Association of Independent Record Distributors as British Isles Album of the Year. The following year he teamed with John Cunningham and Tríona and Mícheál Ó'Domhnaill in a band called Relativity, whose album *Relativity* (1985) won the British Isles Album of the Year Indie. They followed with *Gathering Pace* (1987). He later joined Nightnoise (*see related entry*). Hadden's sideline activities included recording the album *When These Shoes Were New* with Jane Rothfield and Alan Carr, with whom he also toured, and working on production for

Dougie MacLean's Dunkeld Records. Gordon Jones's credits included producing albums for Pete Coe and Pete Morton, one of which won them the Best New Artist Award from *Folk Roots* magazine.

Lead vocalist and primary songwriter Andy Stewart was particularly successful in establishing an identity for himself as a soloist. As a writer, Stewart not only made some of his traditionally styled compositions like "The Ramblin' Rover" and "The Valley of Strathmere" part of the Silly Wizard repertoire, but also saw them recorded by many other artists. His solo album debut, *By the Hush* (1982), was named Folk Album of the Year by the British music trade magazine *Melody Maker.* He also placed second in the tenor banjo category in the *Frets* magazine readers' poll.

Stewart and Manus Lunny (guitar, bouzouki, bodhran) got together with Phil Cunningham, who had recently recovered from a bad traffic accident, to record the album *Fire in the Glen,* released by Shanachie in 1986. As a duo, Stewart and Lunny recorded *Dublin Lady* in 1987 and *At It Again* in 1990, both on Green Linnet. Stewart followed with *Songs of Robert Burns* on Green Linnet in 1991. His touring experience after Silly Wizard's breakup included concerts with Lunny and Irish musician (twelve-string guitar, guitar, keyboards, ukulele) and record producer Gerry O'Beirne. The latter produced Andy's 1994 solo album, *Man in the Moon,* issued in the United States by Green Linnet, and backed Stewart's tenor vocals in a series of American concerts in 1996. Album contents included Stewart originals like "Kathy-Anne's Waltz" and traditional numbers such as "Sweet King Williams Town" and "The Echo Mocks the Corncrake." In 1997, Green Linnet issued Stewart's *Donegal Rain,* with backing from Phil Cunningham and Gerry O'Beirne. An *Andy M. Stewart* songbook was also released in 1997.

Silly Wizard albums still in the Green Linnet catalog as of 1996 included *Live in America* and *Golden, Golden* (on cassette only) and a single CD, *Live Wizardry,* incorporating both of those albums. Their last studio album, *A Glint of Silver,* also remained in print. Green Linnet offered band videos *Live Wizardry—The Video* and *Silly Wizard Live at Center Stage.* Video material showcased the group's farewell concert, performed in the United States in the spring of 1988. The record company's catalog also included two Phil Cunningham albums, the 1984 *Airs and Graces* and the 1989 *Palomino Waltz.*

In 1995 Phil Cunningham joined touring partner fiddler Aly Bain and recorded the Green Linnet CD, *The Pearl.* He also released a songbook titled *The Phil Cunningham Collection Volume 1.* He has produced albums by such groups as Altan and Wolfstone.

John Cunningham composed the music and lyrics for the puppet play *Peter and Wendy,* adapted from J.M. Barrie's *Peter Pan.* An album, *Peter and Wendy,* came out on Alula Records in 1997, featuring Cunningham

with backing from Solas's multiinstrumentalist Seamus Egan, harpist Jay Ansill, accordionist Mick McAuley, and singer Susan McKeown. Cunningham is also featured among other excellent fiddlers on *Celtic Fiddle Festival,* released by Green Linnet in 1993.

SIMON AND GARFUNKEL: *Vocal and instrumental duo. Paul Simon, born Newark, New Jersey, October 13, 1941; Art Garfunkel, born Queens, New York, November 5, 1941.*

Simon and Garfunkel were sometimes described as urban folksingers, folk-rock artists, or soft-rock musicians. Their music, of course, was closer to folk than rock, but whatever its style, it reflected one main color—gold—the color of an almost unbroken series of phenomenally successful recordings.

Considering their relatively meager output compared to other pop stars', their total sales of singles and records by the time they broke up in the early '70s came to a surprising 20 million plus. Painstaking craftsmen, both often polished and repolished their material for months before presenting a new song, usually an original composition by Simon. (Garfunkel contributed to some songs, but almost all the duo's material, both words and music, was written by Simon.) Thus, they rarely recorded more than one album in a single year. Their only singles release in 1969, for example, was "The Boxer," a song included in their sole LP of 1970, *Bridge over Troubled Water.*

During their 1960s heyday, the duo could have reaped considerably higher income from even a small increase in concert dates. However, they kept their in-person appearances to a relative minimum while Garfunkel pursued graduate school studies. When they did give a concert, it was certain to be a sellout within hours after tickets went on sale.

The two were friends from childhood, having first met as cast members of a sixth grade presentation of *Alice in Wonderland* at Public School 164 in Forest Hills, Queens. Art appeared as the Cheshire Cat while Paul acted the part of White Rabbit. As their friendship flourished, a mutual interest in pop music led to their collaboration on their first song, "The Girl for Me," in 1955. Two years later, they had a song on the hit charts, "Hey Schoolgirl," on the Big Records label. Then calling themselves Tom and Jerry, the duo appeared in 1957 on Dick Clark's "American Bandstand." However, after the next two singles went nowhere, the boys went to college, doing some music-business efforts on their own during the early '60s while spending most of their time hitting the books.

Both boys favored pseudonyms. Under the name Art Garr, Garfunkel recorded some material for Warwick Records. Paul's efforts included recording the 1962 single "Motorcycle" as leader of Tico and the Triumphs and, in 1963, the single "The Lone Teen Ranger" as Jerry Landis. He also used the name Landis for the

As Simon had noted earlier to Robert Hilburn, he sometimes was plagued with self-doubts about his ability to create viable new material. "I'm neurotically driven. It has always been that way. What happens is I finish one thing and start to take a vacation. I lay off for a while and then I get panicky. . . . I say to myself: 'Oh my God, I'm not doing anything. I can't write anymore. It's over.' All that kind of thing. . . . Then I laugh and tell myself: 'Don't be silly. This is exactly what happens every time you finish an album. So, of course, you write again.'"

In the late '70s, disputes arose between Simon and Columbia Records that caused a long delay in the next phase of his career. After a long legal wrangle, Simon ended his association with Columbia and, in 1979, signed with Warner Brothers. In the interim, Columbia had issued a retrospective album of his '70s solo work, *Greatest Hits, Etc.*

His Warner Brothers album debut in 1980 was the sound track from *One-Trick Pony,* a film Simon scored as well as starred in. The record was far more successful than the film. A single from the gold LP, "Late in the Evening," provided Paul with a top 10 hit.

In 1981, Paul reunited with Art Garfunkel for a free summer concert in New York's Central Park that drew an estimated 500,000 fans. This inspired them to schedule a series of shows overseas (not for free) that also were dramatic successes. The concerts drew some 130,000 people in Paris, and 75,000 each in London, Tokyo, and Sydney, Australia. In early 1982 a concert film of the Central Park engagement was telecast on the Home Box Office cable TV channel.

All of that made the team agree to a wide-ranging U.S. tour in 1983 in places such as Dodgers Stadium in Los Angeles and Jack Murphy Stadium in San Diego that could accommodate crowds of tens of thousands. They also announced they would work together on a new album, tentatively titled *Think Too Much,* which Paul originally had started as a solo project. Later, however, Paul decided to eliminate new Garfunkel material and return to the solo concept. A spokesperson for Warner Brothers said: "Paul simply felt the material he wrote is so close to his own life that it had to be his own. Art was hoping to be on the album, but I'm sure there will be other projects that they will work on together. They are still friends."

When the revised LP, now called *Hearts and Bones,* came out in October 1983, the duo was completing concert commitments in Europe that followed the U.S. appearances. The album was in the top 40 by year end but didn't go gold. Among Simon's other high points of 1983 was his much-publicized marriage to actress Carrie Fisher of *Star Wars* fame.

Paul's next major project was the album *Graceland,* recorded with many black music stars of apartheid-torn South Africa. The blend of his songwriting skills with strains of such South African musicians as the a cappella Zulu male choir Ladysmith Black Mambazo had both a creative and social impact on listeners. When the platinum LP first came out in 1986, Simon was criticized widely for violating the antiapartheid boycott of South Africa by recording there, but he claimed he was helping blacks and "coloreds" there through the attention *Graceland* brought them. It also demonstrated the tremendous talent to be tapped among the oppressed black majority in South Africa while providing spine-tingling African rhythms. It was named Album of the Year in the 1986 Grammy voting. During 1986, Simon and many black performers struck a symbolic blow against apartheid with a concert in Zimbabwe that drew a massive, integrated audience of black and white fans, including many whites who crossed into Zimbabwe from South Africa to attend the show.

The title track from *Graceland* (which referred to Elvis Presley's Memphis mansion) was voted the Record of the Year in the 1987 Grammy poll. (The album also provided other hit singles, such as "You Can Call Me Al" and "The Boy in the Bubble.") One of the high points of the Grammy Awards telecast in March 1988 was an appearance by the Ladysmith Black Mambazo group, which won the Best Traditional Folk Recording Grammy for *Shaka Zulu.*

Warner Brothers released the retrospective album *Negotiations and Love Songs 1971–1986* on October 18, 1988. This was followed two years later (October 16, 1990) by a new album by Paul, *The Rhythm of the Saints,* that featured many Brazilian artists, some of whom joined him on his Born at the Right Time tour. That series ended in a massively attended free concert in New York's Central Park in 1991 that was taped for video release, as had been the case with the *Graceland* tour and also came out in audio form on the two-disc set *Paul Simon Concert in Central Park. The Rhythm of the Saints* received both gold and platinum awards from the R.I.A.A. on January 8, 1991. On March 3, 1991, *Negotiations and Love Songs* was certified gold, later receiving a platinum award on August 17, 1994. Before 1991 was over *The Rhythm of the Saints* disc surpassed multiplatinum levels, earning an award for 2 million copies sold, on September 12. During 1991 a Japanese box set, *Paul Simon: The Collection,* was released.

Graceland kept right on selling throughout the 1990s, earning awards from the R.I.A.A. for 4 million copies on February 5, 1992, and for 5 million on January 31, 1995. On March 28, 1993, Warner Brothers released the career-spanning box set *Paul Simon 1964–1993.* That collection received R.I.A.A. gold record certification on December 17, 1993. A two-disc set, *The Paul Simon Anthology,* (not available in the United States) was issued in 1993.

At the start of the 1990s Simon began work on one of his most ambitious projects, his first musical. Besides conceiving and writing more than three dozen songs for the production, he also coauthored the book and lyrics with author Derek Walcott. The show was titled *The Capeman,* after the nickname of a Puerto Rican gang member named Salvador Agron, who was known for wearing a black silk cape. Agron, who grew up in New York, became a member of the Vampires gang as a teenager and made headlines in Manhattan in 1959 when he was sentenced to death at age sixteen for murdering two teenage boys.

In advance of the show's opening in Broadway's Marquis Theater on January 8, 1998, Warner Brothers released the *Songs from the Capeman* disc on November 18, 1997, representing Simon's first new studio album in over six years. Joining him on those numbers were cast stars from the Broadway production: Ruben Blades, Marc Anthony, and Ednita Nazario. Simon blended elements of Caribbean, salsa, doo-wop, gospel, and rock in his score, which included such numbers on *Songs from The Capeman* as "Trailways," "I Was Born in Puerto Rico," "Bernadette," "Satin Summer Nights," and "Adios Hermanos." Beyond that, the plan, which wasn't carried through, was to issue a separate, original cast album during 1998.

The show opened to generally unfavorable reviews and closed in March after only sixty-eight performances. Most critics, while finding fault with the script, were impressed with Simon's score. On a more positive note, during the year Simon was inducted into the Songwriters Hall of Fame.

As of 1999, Simon and his third wife, singer-songwriter Edie Brickell, and their son, Adrian, reportedly shared living quarters in a duplex on Central Park West in New York and a house in Montauk. He also had an older son by his first marriage to Peggy Harper. (*See Garfunkel, Art; Simon and Garfunkel; Ladysmith Black Mambazo.*)

SIMPSON, MARTIN AND JESSICA RUBY: *Martin (guitarist, banjoist, singer, songwriter). Born Scunthorpe, Lincolnshire, England, May 5, 1953. Jessica (songwriter, singer, percussionist). Born Los Angeles, California, February 18, 1952.*

For two and a half hours one night in June 1996 Martin Simpson played with heart and soul at McCabe's Guitar Shop in Santa Monica. He took the audience from the British Isles with the traditional song "Gypsy Davy," to the Mississippi Delta with his slide playing, to the depths of his soul in his moving a cappella song about alcoholism, "Fool Me Once." Simpson tapped his reserve to soar in his last song of the night, "Icarus," based on the Greek myth of Icarus and Daedalus. With his expressive voice and guitar work, Simpson sang of the pain of the father as he sees his son fall to the sea:

Then I saw your white wings fail
I saw your feathers falter . . .

Simpson, a member of the British scene that produced Martin Carthy and the Watersons, has the life experience that allows him to pull off a song like "Icarus." From a young age, he was known as one of the best acoustic guitarists in England, playing traditional fingerpicking, country blues, and slide with equal skill. But a series of career mishaps kept him from achieving commercial success. It is remarkable that a person with so much talent has never achieved the notice of a Richard Thompson or John Renbourn. Simpson has made his musical mark in other ways. He toured with U.K. folksinger June Tabor for ten years. For decades he has imparted his mastery of the guitar through teaching others. Since 1984, he has been performing with his wife, Jessica Ruby Simpson. He has tried to break down musical barriers, playing, for example, with a Chinese pi-pa player named Wu Man. "It's all the same stuff, the music itself," he says. "It's a tapestry woven of threads that start in Ireland and West Africa and extend into North Carolina and Mississippi."

Simpson grew up in Scunthorpe, Lincolnshire, in northeastern England. His parents were Henry and Mary Simpson, members of the "fallen middle class" who sold insurance. His father, who was born in 1899 and served in both World Wars, introduced Martin to Gilbert and Sullivan and Victorian parlor ballads. His two older brothers favored jazz, R&B, blues, and rock. In the '50s, Martin began listening to 78-rpm recordings of Little Richard, and in the early 60s, he began listening to country blues and old-timey banjoists. He got his first guitar at twelve and bought his first banjo a year later in a second hand shop for fifteen pounds. "I fell head over heels in love with musical instruments," he says. "The moment I picked up the guitar I knew I was going to be a professional musician."

When he was twelve, Martin started going to the Scunthorpe Folk Club every Tuesday night. The British folk revival was in full swing. For the next five years he heard an incredible assortment of performers: Maddy Prior before she joined Steeleye Span, Martin Carthy, Nic Jones, Christy Moore, John Renbourn, Bert Jansch, Davy Graham, Pentangle. He would join in the local hootenannies.

"It was a training ground," Simpson says. "They had what they called floor singers. So you could go along and you could sing a few songs. In a sense it didn't matter how bad you were. There were singers' nights where you were encouraged to get up and sing. If you were really fuckin' awful people just hoped that you got better."

He saw great blues acts at the Lippman and Rau festivals in Manchester and Sheffield. At fifteen, Simpson saw Jimmy Reed, John Lee Hooker, T-Bone Walker, Big Walter, and Big Joe Williams. He got up the nerve to talk to Big Joe. "He was a heavy-duty guy," Simpson recalls. "He was incredibly kind and polite to me. In a sense we were from another planet. In another sense we weren't at all."

Simpson picked up Williams's guitar but didn't play

it. He knew Joe didn't like that. The guitar was jury-rigged. "He had this old Harmony Sovereign at the time," Simpson says. "It was covered in mud. It was the dirtiest thing you've ever seen in your life. . . . He had a nine-string guitar, the funkiest thing you have ever seen."

When they were finished talking, Williams took out a big Swedish pine plank with a round hole sawed in one end that he used as a walking stick. The stick was covered with autographs. "It was like a who's who of American folk and blues music. I signed as close as I could get to Bob Dylan and Joan Baez."

Simpson had started to play at the Scunthorpe Folk Club, "well before I was good enough." He started getting paid by the time he was fourteen. At seventeen, he started performing on radio shows with groups like the Watersons, who lived close by. By his early twenties, singer Barbara Dickson, later a mainstream British star, recommended Simpson to producer Bill Leader, who had made the first recordings with the Watersons, Bert Jansch, and Dick Gaughan. At twenty-two, Simpson recorded his first album for Leader/Trailer Records, *Golden Vanity* (1976). The album included songs by Randy Newman and Bob Dylan, traditional British material, and old-timey banjo and guitar tunes. It was critically acclaimed, but didn't sell well. When Leader sold his company to Transatlantic, Simpson's record was deleted from the catalog. "It will begin to sound like the story of my life," he says.

In 1976 Simpson opened for Steeleye Span at places like the Hammersmith Odeon and rock 'n' roll venues. "Being on the road with Steeleye Span was not a barrel of laughs," he says. "Some major personal problems and drinking going on, some major bad tempers. It was great in career terms. In personal terms it was really hard."

His manager had plans that didn't match his own. "I was going to be a rock 'n' roll star," Simpson says. "That's what they told me. Needless to say, it actually was an uncomfortable situation for a lot of reasons. Nothing to do with Steeleye themselves."

It took several years before he wanted to make another record. "I felt damaged by it," he says. He made four records with Andrew Cronshaw: *Earthed in Cloud Valley* (Leader, 1977), *Wade in the Flood* (Trailer Highway, 1978), *The Great Dark Water* (Waterfront, 1983), and *Till the Beast's Returning* (Topic, 1988).

In 1977, Simpson got a call from June Tabor, the stately queen of British folk who had only begun touring the year before with guitarist Nic Jones. She asked Simpson to tour with her. "There are a very limited number of people who can play the British guitar style in a way that is convincing," says Simpson, who includes Jones and Martin Carthy in the group. "I was the youngest of those players. I was lucky that I had these guys' examples before me. I was the man for the job."

The alliance lasted ten years. "I loved working with

June," he says. "I love to accompany, I love songs. June Tabor has the best natural instrument in the universe. She'd come to me with these great traditional or contemporary songs. I would take her a song. We'd build stuff from the ground up. It was always exciting."

Simpson met the luminaries of the British scene, including Richard Thompson, Mike Oldfield, and Steve Winwood. In 1979, Ashley Hutchings (of Fairport Convention and Steeleye Span) invited Simpson to play in the Albion Band at the National Theatre. He recorded *Lark Rise to Candleford* (Charisma, 1980) with the Albion Band.

Tabor and Simpson recorded their first album, *A Cut Above*, on Topic in 1980 (rereleased by Green Linnet in 1992). The album includes backup work by Ric Saunders on violin, Dave Bristow on piano and synthesizer, and Jon Davie on bass. Simpson made a solo album using the same musicians on Waterfront Records called *Special Agent* (1981), and followed with two solo albums: *Grinning in Your Face* (1983) and *Sad or High Kicking* (1985), both eclectic albums that included songs by singers like Buddy Holly and Hank Williams. He recorded two other albums with Tabor: *Abyssinians* (1983) and *Aqaba* (1988), both on Topic.

Sad or High Kicking included material from Jessica Radcliffe, an American woman whom he met in 1984, who changed Martin's life, after two failed marriages. With an unusual, soaring soprano voice, Jessica was on her way to Ireland to sing at an annual Fleadh when they were introduced in London. "It was pretty much love at first sight," Simpson says. "I asked Jessica if she would marry me after sixteen days of our being together. She said, 'I'm really glad you asked because I have to go back to the States soon and I was going to have to ask you.'" They put together Flash Company, a five-member band that included British singer-songwriter John B. Spencer, Irish singer Mary McLaughlin, and fiddler-mandolinist Laurie Harper.

Jessica's life is like something out of a Theodore Dreiser novel. Her mother was of Irish descent and her father of Spanish heritage. She inherited an interest in music from both sides. Her maternal grandfather was imprisoned for fraud and met Leadbelly in a segregated jail. "I have a mixture of gypsies and landowners that makes for a confusing family history," she says. She ran away from home at thirteen, lived in tents, slept on people's floors, wound up in juvenile hall and in mental hospitals. "I lived on the lam until I was eighteen," she says. "I sort of hid out."

She didn't realize how much folk music she knew until she was sixteen or seventeen and folklorist Dillon Bustin took an interest in her. She began singing at folk festivals and with bands and became interested in Irish music (in addition to guitar, mandolin, and dulcimer) which is why she was heading to the Fleadh.

Martin and Jessica were married in 1985 in Bloomington, Indiana. They returned to England and Simpson made two more albums: *Nobody's Fault but Mine* (Dambuster, 1986), a solo instrumental album, and *True Dare or Promise* (Topic, 1987), a duo album with Jessica including two of her compositions. They moved to the United States at the end of 1987 and settled in Ithaca, New York. Jessica had three children whom Martin adopted; the couple wanted them to attend an alternative high school. They formed the Martin Simpson Band with Doug Robinson on bass, Hank Roberts on cello, Eric Aceto on violin, the Burns Sisters on vocals, and Tommy Beers on harmonica.

It was when he moved to the United States that Simpson realized he had a drinking problem. He had played in bars for years. "I didn't have a drink problem—I could always get it," he says wryly. "Alcohol is really so subversive because it takes over so gently, so slowly, and takes away so much time and energy. I watched friends go into treatment and become religious members of AA. I didn't think I had any problem really. Then I realized I drink all the time."

One night in 1989 he was ready to hit someone and he realized he needed to give up drinking. He's been sober ever since.

Moving to the States was good for the children but a career risk for Martin. He had just finished his stint with Tabor and had a strong following in the United Kingdom. Simpson made a series of albums for Stefan Grossman's Guitar Artistry label, a subsidiary of Shanachie. The first was called *The Music of Ireland,* a compilation that also included Davy Graham. Jessica suggested that he make an album of the Irish, English, and Scottish airs his audiences loved. The result was the instrumental album *Leaves of Life* (Shanachie, 1989). He followed with another instrumental album, *When I Was on Horseback* (Shanachie, 1991). Jessica says that people often tell Martin that they played his instrumental albums when their babies were born or to ease the pain when a parent was dying. Topic released a compilation of Simpson's Topic albums in 1992 called *The Collection,* which included tracks from *Sad or High Kicking, Grinning in Your Face,* and *True Dare or Promise.* While he was in England he cut three tracks for a 1992 video compilation for Grossman—*The Art of Fingerstyle Guitar.*

Martin began working on another album with his wife—*Red Roses* (Rhiannon, 1994, in England, Thunderbird in the U.S.). The album reveals Jessica's lyrical skills on "We Are All Heroes," "The Company You Keep," "Red Roses," and her translation of the traditional "Gardener's Child" from Scots English into American English. She developed the Band of Angels with Lisa Ekstrom on whistle, accordion, and vocals; Alisa Fineman on guitar, harmonium, and vocals; Kimball Hurd on vocals, mandolin, and guitar; Barry Phillips on cello and bowed psaltery; and Doug Robinson on bass.

Her songs have fairy-tale elements. She uses traditional tunes and nursery rhymes and incorporates them into her songs. "I have a lot of respect for inspiration which is the same as being filled with spirit," she says. "It's the same as breathing. The best folk rock is like a meeting of the supernatural and the natural worlds."

Others are based on her hard life. "We Are All Heroes," for example, is an autobiographical song about a group of teens living in a vacant building. A father once told her that the song helped give him patience with his own children. "I'm keeping some guy who grew up on the streets from beating up his kids," Jessica says. "It's just such an honor to be allowed into people's lives in that way."

Martin wrote a couple of songs on the *Red Roses* album: "Dreamtime" and the delightful fairy tale, "The Turtle and the Asp" (he enunciates the *p*). He also takes special pleasure in interpreting other people's works. In concert he performed Richard Thompson's "Down Where the Drunkards Roar" and Bob Dylan's "Boots of Spanish Leather," which he had wanted to make his own since he first heard it as a teen. He is also known for versions of "The First Cut Is the Deepest" by Cat Stevens, P.P. Arnold, and Rod Stewart, and Anne Lister's "Icarus," included on *Red Roses* and Rhino Record's 1996 compilation *Troubadours of British Folk.*

He heard "Icarus" in the early 1980s and fell in love with it. "It's a song that works on so many levels," he says. "Mostly I sing songs and write songs because of a need to express the deepest emotions. In some cases, that's anger. . . . 'Icarus' is so tragic and yet so triumphant. It knocked me sideways. I had no choice."

In 1994, Simpson released an instrumental album called *A Closer Walk with Thee,* a collection of hymns released by Gourd Records in the United States, and released by Fledg'ling Records in the United Kingdom. (Fledg'ling also reissued Simpson's '81 album, *Special Agent.*) As Simpson said at the concert at McCabe's, the album upset fundamentalist Christians and New Agers alike. The fundamentalists didn't like it because he didn't sing the lyrics to the hymns, and the New Agers didn't like it because he was singing Christian songs. In concert he played a slide guitar solo on "Wayfaring Stranger" and went right into a fingerpicking version of "Go Down Moses," subsequently moving effortlessly into "The Turtle and the Asp."

Martin and Jessica moved to Santa Cruz in 1992, which was like coming home for the California-born Jessica. Simpson continued to make records, teach guitar, work on soundtracks, books, and videos. He had started teaching at seventeen to make money but soon realized he learned from his students. "I learn about music, I learn to expand my playing." He has produced three instructional videos for Homespun and a book called *The Acoustic Guitar of Martin Simpson.*

In 1993 Simpson developed an alliance with a record company, Thunderbird Records, but it faltered badly. "Thunderbird was a record company put together by some well meaning people who wanted to be involved in the music business for many of the best possible reasons," Simpson says. "Unfortunately they really didn't do it, they actually mismanaged it." The company licensed *Red Roses.* In 1995, Thunderbird released Martin's *Smoke and Mirrors,* a collection of blues tunes such as "See That My Grave Is Kept Clean." But the album had mistakes in the credits that made it look like Simpson had written some of the traditional songs. "There were 15,000 copies," Simpson says. "They said they could not afford to reprint. They overprinted stickers that said, 'Contains the following traditional songs.' But the damage was already done."

Simpson also recorded folksinger Bob Franke's masterpiece "Hard Love." He wrote new lyrics for Skip James's "Rather Be the Devil" after the L.A. riots, which he calls "Road Kill." He dedicated the album to Big Joe Williams, who inspired his frailing guitar style on "Broke Down Engine" and "I Want My Crown."

In 1996, he and Jessica left Thunderbird and joined Minnesota-based Red House Records. The company released *Band of Angels,* with five of her songs.

Simpson also recorded an experimental album with Chinese performer Wu Man, who plays a lute-like instrument called the pi-pa. The collaboration was arranged by Kav Alexander, who introduces musicians from disparate backgrounds and encourages them to play together. Simpson's album with Wu Man, *Music for the Motherless Child* (1997), was released by Alexander's Water Lily Acoustics, and nominated for a Grammy. Simpson has also collaborated with an Indian vina player, N. Ravikiran, and a Chinese fiddle player, Jie-Bing Chen. He worked with Los Lobos guitarist David Hidalgo on a project with violinist Viji Krishnan and *mridangam* player Puvalur Srinivisan. The album, *Kambara Music in Native Tongues,* was released by Water Lily in 1998. "It received incredible reviews and sank without a trace," Simpson says.

"We tried to find areas where we could readily communicate and that mostly worked around Western scales," Simpson told *Sing Out!* (August-September-October, 1996). "A lot of that stuff is incorporated into Eastern music, but there's so much more. The pentatonic scale is sort of a sawn-off scale. We mostly used traditional themes as a jumping off point for improvisation. Every one of those situations is a different challenge. You sit down with somebody you really don't know much about and go, 'OK, let's open up, let's see what happens.'"

Simpson also worked on the soundtrack for a PBS documentary called *Breaking Ties,* about children escaping poverty.

Jessica Simpson has self-published two books of poetry: *Delicate Strange* and *Ruby Slippers.* Her middle name is Radcliffe, after her mother's family name, but she disavowed her surname, changing it to Ruby. "It's

all part of running away," she says. "All I need to do is click my heels together and I can go home now."

In October 1994, Simpson performed at Oxford's Holywell Music Room, the oldest music venue in Western Europe. A seventy-minute live solo album, *Martin Simpson Live* (1996), was released by Beautiful Jo and issued the following year in the United States by Red House. In the fall of 1995, Martin toured with blues rocker Steve Miller, a fan of Simpson's. The following year, he toured with Bob Brozman and Debashish Bhattacharya on the World of Slide Guitar Tour. *Guitar Player* named him one of the best acoustic guitarists. In 1997 Red House released *Cool and Unusual,* which won the Best Instrumental Album award from the Association for Independent Music. The CD includes Kelly Jo Phelps on lap slide guitar.

In 1998, Martin and Jessica moved from Santa Cruz to New Orleans so there is no telling what wondrous sounds they will produce. In 1999 they formed their own label, High Bohemia Records, and released Martin's live album *Bootleg U.S.A.,* including his version of "Boots of Spanish Leather." In August 2000 they released a winter solstice album by Jessica called *Beautiful Darkness.* Still in the pipeline are an album of Jessica's songs, an experimental guitar record by Martin called *Righteousness and Humidity,* and a CD of Jessica's poetry called *Ruby Slippers.* Martin is also working on a solo record of English songs and an album of traditional English music, both for Topic. He's been performing with Jackson Browne, and produced his first multi-media show in Santa Cruz with Dutch wildlife photographer Frans Lanting.

At the concert in McCabe's, Simpson spoke about how he likes to go home to see Jessica, and how sometimes he arrives to find the added bonus that she has written a new song. "I feel extraordinarily lucky," Martin says. "To have a life partner who is a working partner and a musical partner is an extra blessing. I feel blessed because at a very young age I discovered the world of traditional music. That world is full of melody and full of the absolute essential elements of humanity. I'm extremely fortunate to be involved in such a vital tradition. The tradition is not something you attempt at any point to keep in one place. If you've done that, you've killed it."

Based on an interview by Lyndon Stambler with Martin and Jessica Ruby Simpson

SKY, PATRICK: *Singer, guitarist, banjoist, harmonica player, mouth-bow player, songwriter, author. Born Live Oak Gardens, Georgia, October 2, 1940.*

Though not too well known by the end of the 1970s, and represented by only a handful of recordings from the mid-1960s to the start of the 1980s, Patrick Sky had an important influence on folk music. Many of his songs became staple items in the folk-music repertoire of other artists and his knowledge of folk music and willingness to impart it to others played a role in the success of artists like Buffy Sainte-Marie.

Patrick "Pat" Sky was born in Georgia but spent most of his youth in the LaFouche Swamp region of Louisiana, where some of his ancestry, Cree Indian, originated. He was exposed to folk and country and western influences from his earliest years, playing the banjo, guitar, and harmonica before he was in his teens. Many of the songs in his concerts of the 1960s and 1970s were traditional songs his grandmother had taught him as a child.

After performing in his home area for a few years, Pat went on to college, spent some years in the army, and then, after leaving the service, decided to concentrate on music. In the early 1960s he began to sing in small clubs and coffeehouses in various parts of the country. In time, he moved on to New York, the center of folk-music activity in the 1960s.

There he soon won over the Greenwich Village folk fans and also became friends with many of the promising folk artists thronging the Village and other parts of the city. As his popularity increased, so did the interest of recording firms, resulting in a contract from Vanguard in late 1964. His Vanguard debut, *Patrick Sky,* came out in the summer of 1965 and won immediate critical acclaim. *HiFi/Stereo Review* called the LP "very good" and the performance "infectious." Among the songs included were "Everytime," "Hangin' Round," "Come with Me," "Love," and "Many a Mile."

The last of these was one of a number of original Sky songs on the album. It also was a song on the way to becoming a classic in the modern folk idiom. His friend Buffy Sainte-Marie used it as the title song for her second album. She also included it and other Sky compositions in her concerts, appearances that also featured her use of the mouth-bow. Sky had begun using that primitive Indian instrument in his act, having recreated its design and use from his knowledge of his Cree Indian heritage. He, in turn, coached Buffy in mouth-bow technique. Among his other original songs that have been used by other folk artists are "Separation Blues," "Hangin' Round," "Nectar of God," and "Love Will Endure."

Sky's second album on Vanguard, *Harvest of Gentle Clang,* came out in 1966. Though an interesting album, it didn't have much of an impact on the increasingly rock-oriented audience. Pat left Vanguard and made two albums on the MGM label in the late 1960s. His last two 1960s releases came out on Verve/Forecast Records, *Reality is Bad Enough* and *Photographs.*

As the 1970s progressed, Sky became involved in Celtic music and less concerned with the American music scene. He gave occasional folk concerts, made a few recordings, and spent part of his time building Irish

uileann pipes (which he played expertly). Sky was also involved in forming Innisfree Records, one of the first U.S. record companies specializing in Irish music. The name was later changed to Green Linnet. For the better part of a decade Sky spent much of his time trying to get the label off the ground. He recorded and produced many of the best Irish musicians during that period. He brought Irish piper Liam O'Flynn (of the band Planxty) to America, and hired him to perform as his opening act. "It was the first time people had heard the uileann pipes on the American stage in seventy years," Sky says. In 1975 Sky wrote *A Manual for the Uileann Pipes,* the first book of its kind published for the pipes.

He continued to make recordings during the decade although none of them were commercially successful. In 1972 the small Adelphi label released his album *Songs that Made America Famous* (reissued in 1997). With songs like "Vatican Caskets" and "Bake Dat Chicken Pie" it was quickly relegated to cult status. The album came out on a small label because the lyrics (which satirized many aspects of American life) were too outspoken and vulgar for a major label to accept them. Later in the 1970s he completed an album of traditional folk music issued on the Leviathan label titled *Two Steps Forward—One Step Back.*

In the 1980s and 1990s Patrick Sky continued to pursue his varied interests. His last album was *Through a Window* on Shanachie in 1985. He retired from the recording business since then. He received a master's in folklore from the University of North Carolina at Chapel Hill. He wrote the introduction to *Ryan's Mammoth Collection: 1,050 reels and jigs, hornpipes, clogs, walk-arounds, essences, strathspeys, highland flings, and contra dances with figures, and how to play them.* The collection was first published in 1883 and republished by Mel Bay in 1995.

Over the years he produced twenty-four albums for other artists, including Mississippi John Hurt, Mick Moloney, and piper Seamus Ennis. He wrote film scores, including the sound track for *Down the Road,* a documentary film about pollution. He cowrote *The Dixie Dewdrop,* the first musical about Uncle Dave Macon. His first album, *Patrick Sky,* was still available, as was *Songs that Made America Famous.*

In the late 1990s he was working in North Carolina as a certified local area network engineer for IBM. In his spare time he makes and plays the uileann pipes and plays music with his wife, Cathy, a fiddler. "I've become apolitical in my old age," he acknowledges.

He never made much money for his recordings, including *Songs that Made America Famous,* which he estimates probably sold more than 40,000 copies. "I've never made any money on records," he says. "It's really kind of a joke. The contracts weren't very good."

However, when George Thorogood recorded "My Friend Robert," a song Sky wrote about Robert John-

continued to attract adoring crowds to her late 1920s theater performances while her record sales held up quite well in an environment where other blues artists were beginning to lose fans.

A major reason for the downward slide in the blues field was the growing impact of movies with sound—the "talkies"—which promised greater profits to theater owners than live shows. This soon was compounded by the stock market crash in the fall of 1929 that hit the black population even more ferociously than the jobless white citizens. Earlier in 1929, Bessie recorded a song that captured the feeling of most of the nation in the Depression years, her version of the Jimmie Cox mid-1920s song "Nobody Knows You When You're Down and Out." Ironically, the song, which became her last big hit, was recorded on May 15, the day after she opened in one of the biggest Broadway musical failures she was associated with, *Pansy*.

Bessie continued to tour in the early 1930s, though now she often was faced with many empty seats. But she had a new lover, old friend Richard Morgan, and the two apparently were well matched. The two started a small "bootlegging" business in Philadelphia that provided a stable income while Bessie sought to keep her career afloat. On November 20, 1931, her association with Columbia ended when she recorded two songs, "Safety Mama" and "Need a Little Sugar in My Bowl," accompanied only by pianist Fred Longshaw.

In 1932 Bessie had her worst year ever as a major artist with minimum bookings and no record contract. But she refused to give up, performing wherever she could get a date and working to update her repertoire to meet the new demands of the swing era. In late 1933 she got the call from John Hammond to cut some new sides for the OKeh label (which eventually was acquired by Columbia). The four numbers recorded on November 24 included "Gimme a Pigfoot," on which her backing musicians included Buck Washington on piano, Benny Goodman on clarinet, and Jack Teagarden on trombone. The other three sides were "Do Your Duty," "Take Me for a Buggy Ride," and "I'm Down in the Dumps."

During 1934 and 1935, Bessie's career began to revive. A new owner of the Apollo who had booked her in years past into the Lafayette Theater in New York asked her to appear there, and she soon was building a new fan base as she sang with bands headed by musicians like Don Redman and Benny Carter. In 1936, when young singing star Billie Holiday took ill and needed a replacement for an appearance at Connie's Inn in downtown New York, Bessie was called upon to substitute and showed again the poise and dramatic vocal style that had made her a star. Her one-week date was turned into a two-month engagement. Word of her successful comeback began to circulate among people in the entertainment industry, and it seemed likely important new opportunities would soon begin to open up. By the end of 1936 there already was talk of her being added to the RCA Victor roster.

Her appearance credits in major eastern cities continued to increase in 1936 and 1937. They included dates at the Famous Door, the Savoy Ballroom, and the League of Rhythm Revue at the Apollo in New York and Art's Cafe in Philadelphia during 1936 and at Philadelphia's Wander Inn in 1937. When she was asked to be a featured artist with the Broadway Rastus troupe for a fall 1937 southern tour, she readily accepted. Rather than travel with the other cast members, she and Richard Morgan decided to use his big Packard automobile. The cast finished a show in Memphis the night of September 25 and was due to go on to a matinee the next day in Mississippi. Bessie talked Morgan into driving to Clarksdale, Mississippi, rather than staying over in Memphis with the other performers. After midnight, Morgan failed to see a large truck in the road around a curve, plowed into it, and Bessie was badly injured.

There were conflicting reports of exactly what happened in the next few hours, when Bessie died from her injuries. For many years the consensus was that she might have survived if she hadn't been refused treatment at a whites-only hospital. But an intensive study by Chris Albertson indicated that the incident developed differently. He found that Dr. Hugh Smith, an intern at Campbell Clinic in Memphis, and his friend Henry Broughton had come upon the scene of the accident, where they saw Bessie's body lying on the road and a truck driving off in the distance. (Morgan, he recalled, appeared stunned but unharmed.) The doctor said he attended to Bessie as best he could, and Broughton went to a nearby house to call for an ambulance. The situation was further complicated when another car driven by a white couple hit the other vehicles. It turned out the truck driver had gone on into Clarksdale and said an ambulance was needed so that eventually two ambulances showed up, Dr. Smith told Albertson, one of which took Bessie to an African American hospital while the other ferried the white couple to a whites-only facility. By the time Bessie reached the hospital, however, it was too late to save her.

She was buried in Mount Lawn Cemetery, Sharon Hill, Pennsylvania, after a funeral in Philadelphia reportedly attended by some 10,000 people. Amid reports that there hadn't been enough money available to pay for a proper headstone, a benefit and tribute performance, From Spirituals to Swing, was held in her honor at Carnegie Hall on December 23, 1938.

A number of books were published in the decades following World War II recalling her career, including *Bessie Smith*, by Paul Oliver (Cassel Ltd., 1959); *Somebody's Angel Child*, by Carman Moore (Thomas Y. Crowell Co., 1969); *Bessie* (Stein & Day, 1972) and *Bessie Smith, Empress of the Blues* (Walter Kane &

Son, 1975), both by Chris Albertson; and *Bessie Smith,* by Elaine Feinstein (1985). In 1971 the Columbia album *The World's Greatest Blues Singer* won the Grand Prix du Disque Award at the Montreux Jazz Festival in Switzerland. Starting in 1991, as part of its Roots 'n' Blues Series, Columbia Legacy released the first of five box sets that, when completed in 1996, covered all of Bessie's Columbia/OKeh recordings.

In 1980 Bessie was inducted into the Blues Foundation's Hall of Fame, and in 1989 she was chosen for the Rock and Roll Hall of Fame.

SMITH, DARDEN: *Singer, songwriter, guitarist, pianist. Born Brenham, Texas, March 11, 1962.*

Singer-songwriter Darden Smith, like Mary-Chapin Carpenter and Nanci Griffith, is difficult to place in one genre. Like the others, Smith has forged a storytelling style marked by a hybrid of country, folk, and rock. His first two labels, Epic and Columbia, didn't know whether to market Smith as a country-folk or a folk-pop artist. Eventually they dropped him, even though he had built a solid following. He continued his career with releases on small labels such as Plump and Valley Entertainment records.

Smith was born and grew up on a farm in Brenham, Texas, seventy-five miles northwest of Houston, where his family raised cows and chickens. When he was nine, Darden sang in the church choir. "I remember the pipe organ rattling my wooden chair during practice one day and I was hooked," he says. He had a brother who also played guitar, although his parents weren't musical. His first taste for popular music came from listening to pop and country radio.

Darden bought his brother's guitar for $26. "I was writing poetry, and [then I] realized that Neil Young actually wrote all the songs on *Harvest* and *After the Gold Rush,*" Smith recalls. "Somehow I just started doing it myself."

When he was fourteen, his parents picked up and moved to Houston when his father got a new job. The move shocked Darden and encouraged him to turn to songwriting. "I went from wandering across hundreds of empty acres to living in a condo," he recalls.

He attended the University of Texas in the early 1980s, majoring in American Studies. He played the club circuit in Texas in his early twenties and recorded his first country-folk album, *Native Soil,* in 1986 (re-released by Watermelon in 1992), which he put out himself. His debut effort caught the attention of several major labels and he soon had a contract with Sony's Epic division in Nashville. In 1988 Epic released *Darden Smith.* As Melinda Newman wrote in *Billboard* (April 24, 1993), the album was "an underappreciated little gem that got stuck between country and rock."

"The reason I was signed in Nashville is because I was a guy from Texas with an acoustic guitar," Smith told Tom Nuccio of the *Illinois Entertainer* (November

1993). "At the time, there were a lot of hip people being signed, Texans and former Texans like Dwight Yoakam, Steve Earle, Lyle Lovett, Nanci Griffith. I put out one record and it was obvious because of the songs I was writing that I was going to be unhappy in Nashville. I never got much support from country radio and realized I wasn't going to be able to do the music that was coming out in Nashville. Since I believe that what comes naturally is what one does best, I walked away from the record deal—which is hard to do as an artist. Nashville was pretty much happy to see me go."

From Epic, Smith went to another Sony division, Columbia Records. In January 1989, before releasing an album on Columbia, Smith met British-born singer-songwriter Boo Hewerdine, who fronts a folk-rock group called the Bible. The two quickly became friends and songwriting partners. "In about twenty minutes we completed 'Reminds Me (a Little of You),'" Smith told *Rolling Stone* (November 2, 1989). "Then we went out to lunch, came back and wrote 'Under the Darkest Moon.'" They wrote six more songs in three days, made a demo, and decided to cut an album. *Evidence,* written and recorded in two weeks, came out in 1989 on Chrysalis and received four stars in *Rolling Stone*'s *Album Guide.* (It was reissued in 1997 by Compass.)

The experience freed Smith. "It showed me that there was a lot of music inside my head that I had to let come out," he told Nuccio.

He released a solo album on Columbia called *Trouble No More* in 1990. The album included excellent pop-country songs such as "Midnight Train" and "2000 Years." Columbia featured those two songs on its *Hitchhiker Exampler* albums, which also included Mary-Chapin Carpenter, Shawn Colvin, the Indigo Girls, and Rosanne Cash. In March 1991, *Trouble No More* received three and a half stars from *Rolling Stone*'s David Handelman, who compared Smith to John Cougar Mellancamp and Tom Petty. "Smith may indeed prove a savior for thinking persons' roots rock," Handelman wrote. But he also pointed out "clichéd but catchy" writing in such songs as "Ashes to Ashes" and "All the King's Horses."

Smith did not have an easy time of it on that album. "It was a very difficult record to make because I was experimenting, and you can experiment only so much within a major label context before they say, 'What are you doing?'" he told Nuccio. "There were two different producers on the record, which led to difficulties, especially when combined with the fact that I was unsure of myself."

He embarked on fifteen months of touring in 1991 and 1992. At one point he was part of the In Their Own Words tour of singer-songwriters. Along with Don Henry, Rosie Flores, Chip Taylor, and Midge Ure, Smith would discuss his songs and then perform them. When the marathon touring session ended, he settled in Austin, Texas, where he composed music for a dance theater piece called *9 Chains to the Moon*. The production was based on the writings of the architect and visionary thinker R. Buckminster Fuller.

Smith wrote enough new songs to put together his next release for Chaos/Columbia, *Little Victories*. The album, released in April 1993, again received critical acclaim, including a four-star review from *Q* magazine. Rosanne Cash joined him on "Precious Time"; he cowrote "Love Left Town" with Boo Hewerdine. He finally generated some minor airplay on alternative radio with the single "Loving Arms." He toured with Peter Himmelman and Brenda Kahn and then opened for rising star Shawn Colvin and Fleetwood Mac's Stevie Nicks. He appeared on *The Tonight Show, Austin City Limits,* and NBC's *Today Show.* In 1995 he toured Europe with Joan Baez. The album was accessible and moved toward the pop vein. But all of that wasn't enough. Columbia Records dropped him. "It was a mutual decision; it was time for a change," Darden says.

Despite the setback, Smith has persevered. As the title track for the album goes, he was looking for "Little Victories." He told Judy Black of *Cleveland Scene:* "Green lights, good cups of coffee, a telephone call from a friend or a really great kiss—it's those kind of things that make up the whole of our life. It's not necessarily the big winning-the-lottery kind of thing. That's a fluke. Most of us live this sort of life where we win these little battles every day. Put them together at the end of our life, and that's what has led to the whole of our life."

In 1994 he moved on to AGF Entertainment and Plump Records. Smith released his sixth album, *Deep Fantastic Blue,* on Plump Records in 1997. The songs reflect the self-examination that comes from becoming a father and going through a divorce. He parted company with Plump, releasing his seventh album, *Extra Extra,* on Valley Entertainment in 2000.

Based on written answers to questions submitted to Darden Smith

SMITH, HOBART: *Singer, banjoist, guitarist, fiddler. Born Smyth County, Virginia, May 10, 1897; died Saltville, Virginia, January 11, 1965.*

The 1960s was a time of rediscovery in folk music. Many of the great traditional country music artists existed for most people in the form of recordings made by such collectors as the Lomaxes and the Warners. As folk music interest expanded in the post–World War II era, many of the older artists were brought before audiences throughout the country. The charm and ability of such performers as Hobart Smith was as infectious to college students and big city groups as it had been for years in rural areas of the country.

Smith's music ability showed up at a very early age. As stated in his *Sing Out!* autobiography (January 1964, pp. 10–13, based on taped interviews with George Armstrong), "I started playing banjo when I

was seven years old. When I was three, I commenced playing on an old fire shovel . . ."

Both of Smith's parents played banjo and he learned to play from them. When he was seven he could pick out a tune on the banjo, and his father bought him a small, short-necked banjo from the Sears, Roebuck catalog. As he notes, he originally used the "old-timey rapping style" of banjo playing rather than the three-finger picking style of Flatt and Scruggs. Later he concentrated on the double-noting (double-thumbing) style. His father ". . . kept his thumb on the thumb string and that thumb string was just a-going all the time. Now, John Greer came along and went from thumb string to the bottom—double noting—and he was the best man I ever heard on the banjo. And I patterned after him. . . ."

When he was in his early teens, Smith learned to play the guitar from listening to traveling blues musicians, including Blind Lemon Jefferson. He also learned fiddle playing as a boy from an old black man.

Smith was raised in an environment of music. He and his father and many of the neighbors played twice a week at the local square dance, and often gathered for an evening at home of singing and playing. In his youth, Smith helped his father run the farm and also ran the family wagon in a local hauling and moving business. He also worked as a painter and, for twelve years, as a butcher with the Olin-Mathieson Company.

During the 1920s Smith continued to be active in music. For two years he played and danced in a local minstrel show that played engagements in nearby towns. For a time he had his own band and also played with Clarence Ashley in the late 1920s. As interest in old-style music died down in those years, Smith gave up the banjo. In the early 1930s he played fiddle at local dance halls, providing such music as "Golden Slippers" and "Comin' Around the Mountain."

With his sister, Mrs. Texas Gladden, he played more traditional songs, such as "Coo Coo Bird," "Claude Allen," "Banging Breakdown," "Last Chance," and "Cumberland Gap" at local folk-music festivals. During most of the '30s, they were regular performers at the Whitetop, Virginia, event. In 1936 they were heard by Mrs. Eleanor Roosevelt, who invited them to the White House to play for President Roosevelt. In 1941–42 and in 1959–60, much of their material was recorded for the Library of Congress Archives by Alan Lomax.

For most of the '40s and '50s, Hobart Smith received little notice beyond his Virginia home country. When folk enthusiasts began to search out the old-time musicians, Hobart was one of those contacted. He and his sister won a standing ovation at the 1963 Third University of Chicago Folk Festival in February. That fall, they were asked to give a concert at Chicago's Old Town School of Folk Music. While there, Smith recorded his first LP album for Folk-Legacy Records at WFMT Radio. Other folk collectors taped interviews with Smith. From then on, he was in demand for appearances at nationwide concerts and at major folk festivals. Just after his performance at the Newport Folk Festival in the summer of 1964, he suffered a stroke that claimed his life in January 1965. Smith was represented on Vanguard recordings of the 1964 Newport Folk Festival. His music was also recorded by the Tradition, Folkways, and Prestige International labels.

With the 1990s came a renewed interest in American roots music, including that of Hobart Smith. Alan Lomax's extensive travels throughout the South in 1959 and 1960 resulted in a series of LPs released by Atlantic and Prestige. Among these were several field recordings made of Hobart Smith. The series was reissued in 1993 on a four-CD set called *Sounds of the South*. Hobart Smith was also well represented on the first six (of a projected one hundred) CDs from the Alan Lomax Collection released by Rounder in 1997. Among the songs included are "O Day" and "It Just Suits Me" (with African American singer Bessie Jones, from the Georgia Sea Island Singers), "Katy Went Fishing with Her Hook and Line," "Peg and Awl," "See that My Grave Is Kept Clean," and "Lonely Tombs," sung with his sister Texas Gladden and brother Preston Smith.

SMITHER, CHRIS: *Singer, songwriter, guitarist. Born New Orleans, Louisiana, November 11, 1944.*

Carrying his weathered blue guitar, Chris Smither sits down on a folding chair on a piece of plywood at Santa Monica's McCabe's Guitar Shop in February 1997. It's hard to take your eyes off Smither. He shakes his shaggy-haired head as he pulls and coaxes the strings on his Alvarez-Yairi acoustic/electric. He mesmerizes the audience with his fluid right hand, his rhythmic toe tapping, and his offhand raspy baritone. He plays a seamless set of originals and covers: Jesse Winchester, Bob Dylan, even Elizabeth Cotten's rendition of "Shake Sugaree." When Smither sings "Everything's I've got's in pawn," you can believe him. His sad eyes show his hard years.

Like the character in his song "I Am the Ride," Smither has taken control of his life, surviving a ten-to-twelve-year period (beginning in the mid-1970s) when alcoholism nearly destroyed him. But he recovered from alcohol and his career has flourished as a result.

Just after singing his best-known song, "Love You Like a Man," popularized by Bonnie Raitt as "Love Me Like a Man," Smither confesses that he has been in a trancelike state. "Sometimes I float out of myself and watch myself play," he tells the audience, just glad to be along for the ride.

Smither grew up in New Orleans, where his father was a language professor at Tulane University. (Chris, who has lived in France a couple of times, speaks fluent French.) As a child he took piano lessons, but without much enjoyment. He credits his uncle Howard with showing him some chords on the ukulele. He told Kerry Dexter of *Acoustic Musician* (November 1995), "He

showed me that if you know three chords, you can play almost everything you come across. So I started learning songs. I played that ukulele all the time!"

While working as a director of the junior year abroad program in Spain, Smither's father bought Chris his first guitar. "I didn't know how to play it," he told Dexter, "but I figured out a few three-chord variations." He began to learn songs by the Kingston Trio and the Everly Brothers. Smither acknowledges learning a lot by sitting in the front row at concerts. He was good enough to win a battle of the bands at the Saenger Theatre on Canal Street in New Orleans. "Remarkably enough, New Orleans has never really been a guitar player's town," Smither says. "A piano town, a horn town, but not a guitar town."

When he was seventeen, Smither heard Lightnin' Hopkins's *Blues in a Bottle* album, which inspired him to learn every song on the record. "He sounded like a one-man rock 'n' roll band," Smither told Bryan Powell of *Acoustic Guitar* (May–June 1995). Smither listened to Hopkins and other favorites, like Mississippi John Hurt, Skip James, Robert Johnson, and Willie McTell, but he didn't try to copy them note for note. "If you can't do it the way they do it, just fake it!" he advises budding guitarists. "In faking it and trying to come up with something that's acceptable, you come up with something that's valid in its own right."

Intending to become an anthropologist, Smither enrolled at Tulane. But on a trip to Florida he met 1960s folkie Eric von Schmidt, famous for teaching Dylan "Baby, Let Me Follow You Down," who was impressed by his guitar playing and encouraged Smither to move to Cambridge, Massachusetts.

Smither heeded von Schmidt's advice and moved to Cambridge when he was twenty-one. "I was playing a lot of Lightnin', some Robert Johnson, and some Mississippi John Hurt and just starting to write my own songs too," he told Dexter. "There wasn't really anybody in New Orleans I could learn from. And there's really no place to play in New Orleans. . . . Rightly or wrongly, there's a certain amount of music hipness associated with New Orleans, and when people would hear I'm from New Orleans, they'd say, 'Oh God, he must be good!'"

On his first day in town, von Schmidt gave Smither a guest slot at the famed Club 47. He began to make a living touring and playing clubs and festivals. *Broadside* magazine voted him best new performer (*Playboy* later nominated him as best instrumentalist of the year). Smither lived around the block from and became friends with Bonnie Raitt, who has called Smither "my Eric Clapton." Raitt's producer, Michael Cuscuna, brought his demo tape to Poppy Records (which was also home at the time to Texas folksinger Townes Van Zandt). Cuscuna coproduced Smither's first LP, *I'm a Stranger Too*, with Ronald Frangipane. Smither's debut included a mix of originals and covers, including songs by Neil Young, Randy Newman, and Skip James. It also included "Love You Like a Man," which Bonnie Raitt first recorded in the early 1970s. ("When I wrote that song I was twenty-one," Smither joked at McCabe's. "I never thought there would be a day when it would tire me out just to sing it.")

Smither followed with his second LP, *Don't It Drag On,* released in 1971 on Poppy and produced by Cuscuna. The album includes covers of Bob Dylan ("Down in the Flood") and Willie McTell's "Statesboro Blues" and the Jerry Garcia/Robert Hunter/John Dawson classic "Friend of the Devil." It also included "I Feel the Same," the second Smither song recorded by Bonnie Raitt, as well as his cult favorite, "Mail Order Mystics." (John Mayall recorded "Mail Order Mystics" and Smither's songs have also been recorded by Christine Collister and Rosalie Sorrels.)

In December 1972 and the spring of 1973, Smither went into the studio with Lowell George, Dr. John, Bill Payne, and Bonnie Raitt. He recorded his third album, *Honeysuckle Dog,* produced by Cuscuna. But the album was never released. United Artists absorbed Poppy Records and dropped Smither. (Smither's first LPs went out of print; Capitol Records owned the masters. In 1997 Collectables Records reissued his two Poppy LPs on a single CD. But *Honeysuckle Dog* was never released.) On his Internet web site, Smither recalled playing with Lowell George, who died in 1979: "He could have done anything and I'd have thought it was great, but in fact everything that he did *was* great. I drank so much myself at the time that I doubt I would have noticed anything like that on his part. As for his songwriting, he's a genius when it comes to contemporary lyrics with a roots feel, and since that's what I try to do myself, I use him as a benchmark."

The album included a song called "Tribute to Mississippi John Hurt." In another Internet note, Smither wrote that he first saw Hurt at the Gaslight in New York in September 1964. Tom Paxton was the opening act, and John Sebastian was backing Hurt on harmonica, which annoyed Smither because "I just wanted to hear (Hurt) play guitar."

In the mid-1970s, after he was dropped by United Artists, Smither went into a tailspin. "There's not much to say. . . . I was a drunk," he told Dexter. "Addictive drugs will tend to mess up people's lives and render them completely ineffective for long periods of time. I wasn't out hustling, working at [music] in an artistic sense or a business sense. I would play once in a while, if somebody would call up and say, 'Hey, come play,' but I didn't have any representation. I didn't have a record company, I wasn't writing . . . it was pretty sad. I mean, I was just very sick, and it lasted a long time."

Even when he had a gig in those years, it was demoralizing. In a July 1993 interview with NPR's *All Things Considered* he remembered once getting onstage but not being able to play. "I just sat there and

tried to get started on the first song, and it wouldn't happen. I mean, it just literally wouldn't happen—sitting there, looking at a whole crowd of people. I'd play a few notes. And stop and think, and, finally, I just said, 'You know, I don't think I can do this,' and I got up and walked off. That was an awful feeling."

Smither worked mostly as a carpenter in those years. In 1984, Gene Rosenthal of Adelphi Records called Smither and asked him to record again. The result was *It Ain't Easy,* first released on LP in 1984 and rereleased on CD in 1989 with two additional tracks. "I recorded a bunch of tunes, solo, that I thought I'd never have the opportunity to record," he told interviewer Richard Skelly. "I was extremely disappointed when I finished it but now the more I listen to it, the more I realize I did a good job with that record."

He recovered shortly thereafter. "Why did I get better? I don't know. I do know that it's not because I'm smart or stupid . . . strong or weak, or any personal virtue on my part. Some people look at themselves and say, 'I can't do this anymore. There's got to be some way out of this hole.' You keep looking and you keep trying and you get out."

As he became sober he began touring again and eventually writing new songs. On December 28 and 29, 1989, he recorded his next album before a live audience at Soundtrack Studios in Boston. The album, *Another Way to Find You,* came out on Flying Fish Records in 1991. The eighteen tracks include several that he had recorded on previous albums, and it rekindled interest in Smither. He eventually began a touring schedule of 130 dates a year. "Every time I'm tempted to feel sorry for myself," Smither wrote on his web site, "I remember all the years that I would have given anything to have this much work."

In 1993 he married a woman named Carol Young, who now manages him, and is a partner in Young/Hunter Management, which also manages Don Williams and Richard Shindell. "She tends to favor the trips to Ireland and France over the ones to the Midwest, but sometimes she comes on those too," he wrote on the Internet. (She must have gotten used to the Midwest since they bought sixty acres of land in Missouri in 1996.)

More audiences became familiar with Smither's unique style and his trademark blue guitar. He played an Epiphone Texan for twenty-five years and when it finally began falling apart his repairman suggested that he find another guitar. As he told Dexter, the blue guitar "spoke to me immediately, because it was blue. Now that's strictly because, when I was in high school, I was crazy about a Wallace Stevens poem called *The Man with the Blue Guitar,* and I thought, 'Mm, I could be the man with the blue guitar.'" (The Wallace Stevens poem includes the line: "Why do you play a blue guitar? Things as they are are changed upon the blue guitar.")

He released *Happier Blue,* produced by John Nagy, in 1993 on Flying Fish Records. The album, named

Best Folk Recording by NAIRD, reestablished Smither as an insightful writer with songs like "Happier Blue" and "The Devil's Real." As he told *Acoustic Guitar,* he writes most of his songs while singing the melody lines over the chord progression. He told Powell: "I don't sit down and say, 'I'm going to write a song about bank robbers,' or 'I'm going to write a heartbreak song.' . . . There's a point when the song declares itself."

He has also been great at covering other artists. His versions of Roland Sally's "Killing the Blues," Lowell George's "Rock 'n' Roll Doctor," and J.J. Cale's "Magnolia" demonstate his remarkable ability to make them his own. As he told NPR's *All Things Considered* about "Killing the Blues": "I sort of listened to the song and . . . put it in the back of my mind and then, months later, sat down to work out an arrangement of it and had a difficult time working it out. And eventually, I realized that one of the difficulties in this song is that there isn't a single rhyme in it." But there is no mistaking Smither's song for anyone else's version. He plays it slowly, deliberately without a hint of sentimentality, as he sings: *Now I am guilty of something I hope you never do/Because there is nothing sadder than losing yourself in love. Happier Blue* was the first of Smither's albums to hit the Triple-A charts.

In 1995 he signed with HighTone Records and released *Up on the Lowdown,* produced by Bonnie Raitt's lead guitarist, Stephen Bruton. The album again broke onto the alternative charts. It opens with "Link of Chain," an upbeat blues number Smither often uses to start his concerts. It also includes his "existential" song, "I Am the Ride," which, he jokes in concert, he didn't know was existential until he read his reviews. Santa Monica director John Flanders made a thirty-minute film called *The Ride* based on the song. "The central character is a musician much like myself, but played by the director John Flanders," Smither told Jim Bessman of *Billboard* (December 21, 1996). "(The song) is kind of a mystical/philosophical piece about trying to analyze one's position in the universe and to remember that you're not along for the ride—but are the ride."

His career began to pick up. "The last two records, each of them has just about doubled [in unit sales]," he told Chris Morris of *Billboard* (November 11, 1995). "But we're still talkin' small numbers. We're not even talkin' to the point where major labels are pickin' up your options yet."

In September 1996 Smither assembled the same band that he used on his *Up on the Lowdown* album to produce his next album, *Small Revelations,* also produced by Bruton. The performers include Chris Maresh on bass, Brannen Temple on drums, Riley Osbourne on keyboards, and Mickey Raphael on harmonica. The album came out in January 1997. Again he opens the album with an uptempo song, this one "Thanks to You" by Jesse Winchester, whose "Talk Memphis" Smither had recorded for *Up on the Lowdown.* In concert he

jokes that Winchester lives in a cabin and won't come out—"that's nice for people like me who want to sing his songs without competition." He jokes that his off-beat song "Cave Man" (*When I was a cave man, paintin' on the wall/I never had a dollar, man, I had it all*) stems from his days as an anthropology/paleontology student. His song "Help Me Now" suggests his solitary life as a journeyman performer: *Where do I go to close this show/This one-man band to the bone.* He even strikes a humorous note with his song "Winsome Smile," a wry tune with the line *Your winsome smile will lose some of its innocence.* "Winsome," Smither deadpans in concert, means "charming with a hint of naiveté."

In 1998 Smither embarked on the Monsters of Folk tour with three other HighTone artists, Tom Russell, Dave Alvin, and Ramblin' Jack Elliot. A couple of his songs were included on the accompanying *Monsters of Folk* promotional CD. HighTone also began distributing Smither's two albums from his years with Flying Fish: *Another Way to Find You* and *Happier Blue.* In a further sign that Chris's songwriting talent was gaining notice, Emmylou Harris recorded his song "Slow Surprise" from *Small Revelations* for Robert Redford's *The Horse Whisperer,* which also includes songs by Iris DeMent, Gillian Welch, Steve Earle, and Lucinda Williams. His song "Hold On" was featured in an independent film titled *Love from Ground Zero,* directed by Stephen Grynberg.

In December 1998 Smither returned to the Hit Shack studio in Austin to record a new CD, *Drive You Home Again,* produced again by Bruton and issued by HighTone in March 1999. HighTone released *Live as I'll Ever Be* in 2000.

In concert, Smither no longer performs "Wine Spodee-Odee," from Lightnin' Hopkins's *Blues in a Bottle,* because he doesn't drink anymore. He attributes a great deal of his success to his sobriety. "I hate to sound like the antithesis of the carousing musician," he wrote on his web site, "but any stamina that I have is a result of clean living and lots of exercise. Doing it the other way almost killed me, and this is actually a lot more fun."

SOLAS: *Irish American ensemble formed in 1995. Members include: Karan Casey (vocals), born Ballyduff Lower, County Waterford, Ireland, 1969; Seamus Egan (flute, banjo, whistles, mandolin, nylon string guitar, bodhran, uilleann pipes), born Hatboro, Pennsylvania, 1971; John Doyle (acoustic guitar, vocals); Winifred Horan (fiddle, vocals); John Williams (accordion, concertina, vocals); Joining in 1998: Mick McAuley (accordion, concertina, low whistles, vocals), replacing Williams. Casey left in 1999.*

True to its name, Solas has brought light to the music world, playing some of the best Celtic jigs, reels, and ballads around, especially considering that several members of the talented quintet were born in the United

States. Philadelphia-born Seamus Egan, who won the All-Ireland championships on an unprecedented four instruments (tin whistle, tenor banjo, mandolin, and flute) by the time he was fifteen, serves as the group's musical linchpin. Karan Casey, of County Waterford, Ireland, cuts to the heart of her carefully selected songs. The rest of the band—fiddler Winifred Horan, formerly with Cherish the Ladies; guitarist John Doyle; and accordionist John Williams, who was replaced in 1998 by Mick McAuley—are all virtuosos who know how to accompany as well as to solo.

Although Seamus Egan was born in Pennsylvania, his parents moved to County Mayo, Ireland, when he was three, settling in the town of Foxford. He began studying tin whistle with Martin Donaghue, who was wheelchair bound and inspired young Seamus. But it was when he saw flautists James Galway and Matt Molloy on TV that he was inspired to take up the flute as well. He dedicated himself to the flute and other instruments. His parents supported his habit. When he heard American folklorist Mick Moloney playing banjo on the radio, his parents went out and bought him a tenor banjo. Then when his family moved back to the United States when he was twelve, he began studying banjo with Moloney. Initially he played in a trio with his sisters, recording his first album, *Traditional Music of Ireland* (Shanachie, 1985), when he was sixteen. He released his second solo album, *A Week in January* (Shanachie, 1990), three years later. Soon he began playing in a group called Green Fields of America with Moloney and Eugene O'Donnell, releasing the album *Three Way Street* on Green Linnet in 1993.

It was by chance that Egan's music began to reach a wider audience. In February 1993 he was traveling in Rhode Island with Tony Furtado and Dirk Powell as part of the Young Turks of the Banjo tour. Their van broke down in the middle of a cold winter storm. A kind couple took the three of them in for the night, and Egan left a copy of *A Week in January* to repay them. Their son, Andy Yarmes, who was working as a technician on the film *The Brothers McMullen,* took the CD back to the set and director Edward Burns liked what he heard. When the film came out at the end of 1994 it included much of Egan's music, as well as a Sarah McLachlan/Seamus Egan song that went on to become a pop hit: "I Will Remember You," based on Egan's instrumental "Weep Not for the Memories." *The Brothers McMullen Soundtrack* (Arista, 1995) broke into *Billboard*'s top 10. The following year, Shanachie released Egan's *When Juniper Sleeps,* which included contributions from Winifred Horan on fiddle, John Doyle on guitar, and John Williams on accordion.

This would become the core of Solas. Horan had studied Irish dance in Brooklyn with Danny Golden and was quite successful, winning nine North American dance titles at the Oireachtas competitions. She joined the all-female group Cherish the Ladies as a dancer but focused on the fiddle after Eileen Ivers left. She studied classical violin at the New England Conservatory of Music but switched back to fiddle after a bout of tendinitis. Egan met her at a Celtic jam session in New York and encouraged her to play more traditional music. She often sat in with other members of the group Chanting House along with guitarist John Doyle, fiddler Eileen Ivers, and singer Susan McKeown. Egan, Doyle, Horan, and Chicago-born accordionist John Williams played together at the Lowell Folk Festival in 1994 and began thinking about forming a group.

They first encountered vocalist Karan Casey at the end of 1994. She grew up in a family that encouraged singing at home, church, and school. As a child she was inspired by Seamus Brady, and later by Dublin's Frank Harte, Dolores Keane, and Belfast-born Aine Ui Cheallaigh. Later she studied classical music at the University College in Dublin and at the Royal Irish Academy of Music. But she also began gravitating toward jazz singers like Ella Fitzgerald. She moved to New York in 1993, taking jazz courses at the Brooklyn campus of Long Island University. She was singing in a group called Atlantic Bridge when Horan and Egan took notice. "She has the quality of voice I've always enjoyed listening to; sort of high, but strong," Egan told Scott Alarik of *Sing Out!* ("Solas: Innovative Tradition," Fall 1997). "And she knows how to sing. She doesn't gesture with her voice. She's certainly placing emotion into the song with her interpretation, but she's not in any way bludgeoning the point. If it's a good song, people are going to know what it's about."

Solas debuted at Georgetown University in the spring of 1996. Silly Wizard's Johnny Cunningham produced the group's debut, *Solas,* released in May 1996. As soon as the album was released by Shanachie, it became clear just how well they worked together. As Horan told Alarik: "We're never coming to show off, never coming just to show we can be different. It's always the music first, definitely the music first. That's the motto."

The debut album features Casey's vocals on five of the thirteen songs. She makes a point of choosing feminist and politically charged songs like "My Johnny's Gone for a Soldier." The other tunes are made up of excellent instrumentals performed by Egan, Horan, Williams, and Doyle. The album received rave reviews and won an Indie for Best Celtic/British Isles Album.

The band's second album, *Sunny Spells and Scattered Showers,* also produced by Cunningham, came out the following year on Shanachie. Casey sings six songs on this album, including "The Wind That Shakes the Barley," about the United Irishmen's uprising of 1798; "Vanished Like the Snow," about the disappearance of women from the history books; and the finale, "Adieu Lovely Nancy," a tragic love song. The other seven tracks include fiery reels, jigs, a barn dance, and a slow air.

Casey recorded a solo album, *Songlines,* released in 1997 by Shanachie, which was produced by Egan, who plays flute, whistles, mandolin, and bodhran. Horan, Doyle, and cellist Michael Aharon also accompany Casey. Among the eleven tracks, which include traditional songs, are her versions of Ewan MacColl's "Ballad of Accounting," Leon Rosselson's "The World Turned Upside Down," and Jean Ritchie's "One, I Love."

In 1998, continuing the CD-a-year pace, Solas released its third album, *The Words that Remain,* on Shanachie, which features a new box player, Mick McAuley. Produced by Egan, the album, which includes more songs than instrumentals, also features guest performances by Iris DeMent, banjoist Béla Fleck, and Michael Aharon on bass, keyboards, and cello. Among the songs on this album are Woody Guthrie's "Pastures of Plenty," which Casey discovered on an Odetta album, and "Song of Choice," a Child ballad that adds Iris DeMent's vocals to the mix of Doyle and Casey. Later that year, the group also recorded the song "Reel Friends" for the Walt Disney Winnie-the-Pooh album *Friends Forever.*

Among other musical adventures, Egan played at Bonnie Raitt's wedding along with Mick Moloney and Eugene O'Donnell, performed on a hip-hop track with Living Color's Vernon Reid, on the *Dead Man Walking* sound track, and was featured on *Out of Ireland,* a PBS documentary about Irish emigration. Horan joined with accordionist Sharon Shannon on a couple of projects. In 1999 Casey left the group to pursue a solo career. She was replaced by Irish singer Deirdre Scanlon.

SON VOLT: *Vocal and instrumental group. Jay Farrar, born Belleville, Illinois, December 26, 1966 (singer, guitarist, songwriter, band leader); Jim Boquist, born Rosemont, Minnesota, May 30, 1961 (singer, bassist); Dave Boquist, born Rosemont, Minnesota, October 21, 1957 (guitarist, banjoist, lap steel guitar, Dobro, fiddler); Mike Heidorn, born Belleville, Illinois, May 28, 1967 (drummer).*

WILCO: *Jeff Tweedy, born Belleville, Illinois, August 25, 1967 (vocals, guitar); Jay Bennett, born Chicago, Illinois, November 15, 1963 (keyboards, vocals, harmonica, lap steel guitar, accordion, banjo, guitar); John Stirratt, born New Orleans, Louisiana, November 26, 1967 (bass); Ken Coomer, born Nashville, Tennessee, November 5, 1960 (drums); Max Johnston, born Dallas, Texas (mandolin, banjo, fiddle).*

Many critics and a small but devoted following bemoaned the breakup of the roots-rock midwestern U.S. band Uncle Tupelo in 1994. Powered by the writing skills of coleaders Jeff Tweedy and Jay Farrar, the band had turned out four excellent country-rock or folk-rock

(depending on your vantage point) albums that, while far from chart busters, seemed harbingers of greater things to come. Surprisingly, though, in place of one band, two new ones with perhaps even more promise emerged in its place; Tweedy's Wilco and Farrar's Son Volt. Wilco took shape first, releasing its debut, *A.M.,* in 1995 on Reprise, but by the fall of that year Son Volt's debut on Warner Brothers Records, *Trace,* containing ten originals by Farrar, demonstrated that his creative vision was as distinctive as ever.

Farrar grew up in the small conservative town of Belleville, across the Mississippi River from St. Louis, Missouri. He could listen to guitar playing in the living room from his earliest years, since both his parents played the instrument and encouraged their four sons to learn to play as well. His father was a fan of old-time country artists like Jimmie Rodgers, whereas his mother preferred modern performers like Bob Dylan and the bluegrass group the Dillards. In Jay's formative years, for a while he opted for the popular rock bands of the day, but eventually he changed his mind. He told Bob Gulla of the Peterborough, New Hampshire, *New Country,* "It takes a while to be able to reconcile that you like the kind of music your parents like."

His influences soon included artists like Hank Williams Sr. and folk legend Woody Guthrie, performers who he told Gulla, "were passionate men who wrote simple, passionate songs. It all just stuck with me." Also among his favorites were Neil Young and Young's band, Crazy Horse, whose folk-rock approach was reflected in some of Farrar's writing and performing efforts.

He recalled first being in a band at the age of eleven, "a garage and rockabilly combo I played in with my brothers." In high school, he performed with many more groups of that kind, sometimes with his brothers, other times with friends from town. By his late teens he had become part of a group that included Tweedy on bass and Mike Heidorn on drums.

This evolved into the three-member Uncle Tupelo group in the closing years of the decade. The band soon became one of the favorites on the St. Louis rock scene. In 1990 the band made its record debut on the Chicago-based independent label Bloodshot Records with *No Depression.* (The title track, which was used as the title of a magazine about the alternative country music spawned by Uncle Tupelo, was a rock version of an old Carter Family song.) This was followed in 1991 by *Still Feel Gone,* whose tracks included originals by both Tweedy and Farrar, the latter's input including the fine composition "Still Be Around." The band's third collection was titled *March 16–20, 1992,* an album that brought a contract offer from the major Reprise/Warner Brothers label. The group, now expanded to five members, worked on tracks in 1993 for its Reprise/Warner debut, and the result was the critically well received *An-*

odyne. The title track by Farrar ranked among the best he'd written and, along with such other Tupelo Farrar originals as "Slate," "Fifteen Keys," "Postcard," and "Chickamauga," remained in his repertoire for later Son Volt concerts.

Great things were foreseen for Uncle Tupelo when it suddenly broke up in 1994. From all reports it was due to Farrar's decision that he and Tweedy really were trying to go in different creative directions. Tweedy, though acknowledging some disagreements over band directions, expressed surprise when Farrar suddenly stepped down. He told Alan Scully of the *St. Louis Post-Dispatch* in April '95, "I think it was a personal decision for Jay, but he wasn't very communicative about anything to us, which was fairly normal for Jay." Farrar told Derk Richardson of the *San Francisco Bay Guardian* ("All Americana," November 29, 1995) that the differences between him and Tweedy "would have gotten to the point where we would have had to put out double albums, which would have been kind of strange."

In mid-'94 Farrar's first step in forming a new group was to recruit bassist and backing vocalist Jim Boquist, formerly with a band called Joe Henry that had appeared on some bills with Uncle Tupelo. Jim, in turn, suggested adding his brother, Dave, who could play a wide range of instruments. Finally, Farrar recruited onetime Tupelo drummer Mike Heidorn, who'd left that band after the sessions for its third album were completed in favor of new family obligations. Heidorn told Peter Blackstock of *No Depression* magazine ("Son Volt—Jay Farrar Traces a Path Away from Uncle Tupelo," Fall 1995), "I had just gotten married, and we have a couple of kids, and I didn't really want to hold the band back in getting their music out and all that stuff. We had some offers from bigger labels, and Jeff and Jay were writing some really good songs, and I figured maybe they could use somebody at that juncture who could just go, go, go."

After Farrar inquired about Heidorn's availability to work on the new Son Volt album, it was Mike's wife who urged him to think about it. He recalled her saying "something like, 'Give him a call, see what he's doing.' So I just called to see if he needed any help to record . . . and he said, 'Sure.'"

When the project got under way, Farrar, by then living in New Orleans, drove from there to Minneapolis, Minnesota, where the Boquists lived, and to Heidorn's home in St. Louis, Missouri, and then back again in setting up the operation. It was during the long hours alone in his Honda Civic, listening to National Public Radio and various AM stations and watching scenery along the way—including billboards, small town main streets, and occasional glimpses of the Mississippi River where his father had once worked on a dredge—that his thoughts for new songs for the band's debut album on Warner Brothers took shape.

The new songs the band began recording in a North-field, Minnesota, studio had lyrics that probed more deeply into the joys and sorrows of day-to-day life than typical pop compositions. The country-flavored "Tear-Stained Eye" paid tribute to the courage of residents of Ste. Genevieve, Missouri, during the disastrous floods of 1993. "Drown" received airplay on alternative rock stations. In "Windfall," which clearly falls into the folk domain, he capsuled the atmosphere of "searching for a truer sound" in his car journeys while also urging the listener to "Let the wind take your troubles away." Rural blues are tapped for "Ten Second News," which describes the abandonment of another Mississippi River town (Times Beach, Missouri) whose soil was found contaminated with dioxin.

When the album, *Trace,* came out in the summer of '95, it won almost universal approval from the print media, though it was up against problems of category restrictions among radio programmers. The band overcame that to some extent by intensive concert work that took it to places like New York's Tramps, San Francisco's Great American Music Hall, and venues in other major cities in between. Writing in the *New York Times* (October 30, 1995), Jon Pareles took note of the Neil Young vein: "Like Mr. Young, [Son Volt sings] about disorientation and displacement, a feeling that they can never return to what they might have had. The music craves durability, turning resolutely away from anything that might seem trendy and sinking its roots into country and folk-rock." With *Trace,* the band won honors from many quarters, including selection by *Entertainment Weekly* as one of the Most Promising Newcomers. Son Volt made the top 10 lists of many publications, including being among the Ten Best Albums of 1995 in the *Rolling Stone* Critics' Poll presented in the January 25, 1996, issue.

Son Volt followed up with its second CD, *Straightaways,* released by Reprise in 1997. Like *Trace,* the new album had been inspired by the road. It includes such songs as "Been Set Free," sung from the perspective of a woman who had been murdered by her lover. Farrar's wife was unhappy with an earlier Tupelo version of a traditional murder ballad called "Lilli Schull." She didn't feel the Tupelo song adequately represented a woman's perspective, and so she wrote the first verse of "Been Set Free." "Caryatid Easy" is a title Farrar came up with after browsing through the dictionary. The word *caryatid* is an architectural term for a support column that has the form of a draped female figure. Edifices also play a role in his song "Way Down Watson," similar in theme to Joni Mitchell's "Big Yellow Taxi." Farrar's song was inspired by the destruction of the old Coral Courts Motel on Route 66. "It represents what I've seen all over the country," Farrar lamented to Paul Hampel of the *St. Louis Post-Dispatch* ("Don't Call Him Prodigal," August 7, 1997). "The prevailing mentality seems to be to tear down historic buildings and put up parking lots or pre-fabbed condos."

In 1997 Son Volt converted a lingerie warehouse in Millstadt, Illinois (not far from Belleville), into a rehearsal space and recording studio. It was there that they developed the songs for their third CD, *Wide Swing Tremolo,* issued by Warner Brothers in 1998. Farrar took the title from a phrase he came across while reading a Gibson catalog advertisement for an amplifier. The album takes a different approach from the first two. It seems less self-conscious and more relaxed. The harder-driving "garage-style" sound is evident in the opener, "Straightface," which includes distorted guitars and harmonicas à la Neil Young. Other tracks include "Hanging Blue Side," "Carry You Down," and the closer, "Blind Hope."

By 1997 Farrar had apparently mended fences with his old band mate Tweedy. "I just think that Jeff and I needed to step away, reflect, let the air settle a little bit," he told Hampel. "It was difficult for both of us, doing interviews and being asked to answer the same questions about each other over and over again. I don't want to get into specifics, but a lot of things got taken out of context. But we get on all right now."

There is a symmetry in the post–Uncle Tupelo existence. Wilco will come out with an album and then Son Volt will follow, or vice versa. During a concert in New York, Son Volt was joined onstage by one of Farrar's early influences, Roger McGuinn, who played "Fifth Dimension" with them. Wilco performed at a New York show with Johnny Cash. Brian Paulson, who had produced Uncle Tupelo's last album, produced the debut albums for both bands.

Wilco comprised many of the folks from Uncle Tupelo: Tweedy, Ken Coomer on drums; Max Johnston (Michelle Shocked's brother) on Dobro, fiddle, mandolin, and banjo; and John Stirratt on bass, violin, and piano. For the band's debut, *A.M.,* Tweedy wrote all but one of the tracks, including "Box Full of Letters," "Casino Queen," "Pick Up the Change," and "Too Far Apart."

After *A.M.* they added Jay Bennett on guitar, keyboards, harmonica, accordion, lap steel guitar, and songwriting. Tweedy wrote the nineteen songs for *Being There,* the 1996 double-disc release on Reprise. The CD received almost unanimous praise for its brooding, country-rock sound, as well as the fine songs penned by Tweedy. In the meantime, Tweedy relocated to Chicago, where his wife, Susan Miller, co-owns a rock club, and the couple had a son, Spencer. He also found the time to work with a side band called Golden Smog, which put out a couple of CDs. Johnston left the band and played with the Austin-based band The Gourds, as well as with Freakwater.

In 1998 Wilco collaborated with Billy Bragg on the album *Mermaid Avenue,* setting music to lyrics the legendary Woody Guthrie had written following World War II. The album title came from the street in Coney Island where Guthrie lived. In 1995 Guthrie's daughter Nora gave Bragg access to more than 1,000 of Woody's song lyrics and asked him to bring them to life musically. Bragg invited Wilco to help with the project. The result is a unique CD, released by Elektra, which reveals a much different side of the Dust Bowl balladeer. Bragg recalled coming across one song about flying saucers during his research. The phrase "supersonic boogie" was scrawled in the margin, an indication of Guthrie's eclectic and offbeat approach. Tweedy, Bragg, and Jay Bennett brought Woody's songs into the 1990s with their melodies and arrangements. "I think the last thing Nora wanted to do was sound like an archaeology dig," Tweedy told Kevin McKeough of the *St. Louis Post-Dispatch* ("Woody Guthrie Cuts a New Album," June 28, 1998).

The subject matter ranges from "Ingrid Bergman," in which the narrator dreams of making love to the film actress; to the romantic "California Stars"; to "Christ for President" and "Eisler on the Go," about Hans Eisler, who was called before the House Un-American Activities Committee. The album was nominated for a Best Contemporary Folk Album Grammy. Elektra released *Mermaid Avenue Volume 2* in 2000, since they had recorded more than forty songs for the project. In March 1999 Wilco released a new studio album on Reprise, *Summer Teeth.*

SORRELS, ROSALIE: *Singer, guitarist, songwriter, author. Born Boise, Idaho, June 24, 1933.*

With a powerful alto voice and a way of bringing the gut feelings of joy, pain, and sorrow home to listeners through her repertoire of songs—both original and covers—and stories, Rosalie Sorrels remained a pillar of strength in the folk movement in a career that began in the 1960s and was still thriving as the century drew to a close. Her presentations in concert or on records reflected lifetime experiences ranging from teenage abortion, marriage, motherhood, divorce, and the struggles of the "travelin' lady" to support her family of five children through income from music. And always, like her close friends, the late Malvina Reynolds and U. Utah Phillips, she lent her voice to support the underdog, the single parent, or the average working person.

Her childhood memories for the most part were idyllic. She had a loving relationship with her parents, a father who was a state highway engineer, and a mother, Nancy Stringfellow, who ran the Book Shop in downtown Boise, Idaho, for twenty years and wrote poetry in her spare time. She recalled enjoying her father's singing while she was growing up, and fondly remembered a scrapbook of songs a grandmother had assembled. More than a few songs included in future concerts came from those times, such as "Jerusalem," learned from a grandfather, and "Then You'll Remember Me," which her father liked to sing. She also liked listening to records by artists like Edith Piaf, Hank Williams Sr., and jazz greats Charlie Parker and Miles Davis.

But despite the understanding of her parents, in her teen years she started having curiosity about the opposite sex, and, with some girl friends from high school, started hanging out evenings on the corner of Eighth and Bannock Streets outfitted in white shirts, jeans, penny loafers and sporting ponytails. As she said at one concert, they were "desperately looking for someone. I don't know who. To this day I don't know who."

Eventually experimentation led to a short-lived romance, and when she found herself pregnant at sixteen in 1949, she opted for an abortion. It turned out to be a bloody, botched affair, as she wrote in the liner notes of the album *Be Careful, There's a Baby in the House,* at the hands of "the midwife from hell in a dirty motel." She became pregnant again afterward, by which time she was an honors student in high school, and this time had the baby, a daughter, whom she immediately gave up for adoption. Those experiences made her a strong "pro-choice" advocate the rest of her life.

Sorrels loved her home area, though she realized its shortcomings. As she told John Ross of the *Bay Guardian* ("The Travelin' Lady Alights," April 2, 1986), "Boise's always been weird. Louis Armstrong and his All-Stars with, can you imagine, Jack Teagarden on trombone, played my high school graduation. But then years later, in 1968, when I invited Pete Seeger to town, the locals pulled out the old McCarthy-hearing bullshit and near ran poor Pete out of town. I guess you could say there weren't any '60s here in Boise."

She married soon after completing high school at the age of nineteen. She joked that her husband, Jim Sorrels, married her to get her Miles Davis records. They moved to Salt Lake City, Utah, where Rosalie had five children in the course of their fourteen-year stay together. They shared an interest in collecting and singing folk material as a hobby, activities that brought them into contact with many offbeat creative individuals—beat generation writers and poets, folk musicians, painters, and others, some of whom used their house as a way station in their travels. From the local folk-music community, Rosalie became friends with the wife of U. Utah Phillips before meeting that musician-songwriter, who became a strong supporter of her career steps and often joined her in future years in concerts and festivals.

Her marriage began disintegrating in the early 1960s, and she finally decided to leave in 1966. As she told Roger Dietz of *Billboard* magazine ("Sorrels Remains True to Her Green Linnet 'Heart,'" November 11, 1995), "I never really thought about becoming a performer. My marriage broke up, and I had to do something. I tried to get a job, and I just couldn't find one. Then, somebody offered me a concert that made me more money than anybody would pay me for working a whole month. I thought I'd try it. It's all I've ever done since."

Contributing to her decision, as she told Lynn Van Matre of the *Chicago Tribune* ("Liberation? She's Too Busy Being Free," September 7, 1973), was her limited work experience. "All I knew how to do was cook and sing. And I sure didn't want to make a living slinging hash in some truck stop. I told my parents what I was going to do. I figured they'd be upset—there I was, 33 years old, with five kids. They just said, 'Great.' "

She piled her kids into a Ford truck and took to the road, playing concerts at various locations until she arrived at the Newport Folk Festival in Rhode Island, where she made a strong impression on audience members as well as more seasoned folk artists. (The saga was recounted decades later in Nanci Griffith's tribute song, "Ford Econoline.") It was the first phase of a lifestyle she was to pursue for decades, which she capsuled in part in what was to become her signature composition, "Travelin' Lady." Her mother was proud of her daughter's efforts, saying Rosalie had a voice that combined "wine, honey, and cayenne"; Sorrels, in turn, often quoted from her mother's poetry and pithy sayings in concert or festival appearances.

In short order, Rosalie had the chance to make her first album, a 1961 Folkways release titled *Folksongs of Utah and Idaho.* This was followed by such others as *Rosalie's Songbag* (1962), *If I Could Be the Rain* (1967, whose title track was one of Utah Phillips's classic compositions), *Somewhere Between* (1963), and *Songs of the Mormon Pioneers* (1964). During those years she also met and became close friends with singer-songwriter Malvina Reynolds, making Malvina's Berkeley area her own home base for a while as she picked up pointers on writing and performing. Sometimes the two performed together, and over the years Rosalie added many of Malvina's songs to her concerts and albums.

In 1971 Rosalie could point to an album rated one of the year's best by many critics, *Travelin' Lady.* Original songs in her early '70s concerts, besides "Travelin' Lady," included a comment on her lifestyle, "All I Ever Do Is Say Goodbye." She continued to maintain a full touring schedule, including sets at many major folk festivals the world over. And she kept on adding to her album catalog with such '70s releases as *What Ever Happened to the Girl that Was* (1972), *Always a Lady* in 1976, *Moments of Happiness* in 1976, and *Travelin' Lady Rides Again* (1978), on the Philo label and reissued on CD by Green Linnet. The 1975–76 time period was one of her psychological low points because of the suicide of a son, which she sometimes referred to obliquely in future compositions. That was not the only negative occurrence with her family—another son, for example, spent time in prison. It was part of the price, she indicated, a single parent had to pay. As she wrote, "I really know I did the best I could. . . . Goddamn, it was a hard row to hoe . . . no one can take care of five children by themselves." But the good times still outweighed the bad. Most of her children carved out satisfying lives for themselves, and by the mid-'90s they had added six grandchildren to the family roster. One daughter eventually took over as Rosalie's manager.

In 1979 she formed a touring triumvirate with Terry Garthwaite (a member in the early '70s of the all-female rock group Joy of Cooking and later a jazz and blues devotee) and writer Bobbie Louise Hawkins. The threesome combined music with poetry and prose readings and was well received at folk clubs, coffeehouses, and major festivals like the annual Vancouver (Canada) Folk Festival. The artists worked together off and on for three years, going their separate ways after 1982. The high points of their show were covered in the 1982 Flying Fish album *Live at the Great American Music Hall*. Rosalie's solo album output included *The Lonesome Roving Wolves (Songs and Ballads of the West)*, issued in 1979; *Then Came the Children* (recorded live at the 1984 Vancouver Folk Festival and initially issued only in Canada in 1986); and *Miscellaneous Abstract Record No. 1*, issued in 1982 on Green Linnet.

In the late 1980s Rosalie made her primary residence the cabin her late father had built, where she had spent most of her childhood. It was partly because she longed for the colorful woodland surroundings and partly to be near her mother, whose health was declining. Suddenly, though, it was her life which was at risk as she was hospitalized with a brain aneurysm in August 1988. Fortunately, corrective surgery was successful, and by the start of the '90s Rosalie was pursuing her entertainment career with new energy. In January '89 she gave her first concert since the surgery, an almost-two-hour program for the Twelfth Night Celebration at St. Michael's Cathedral in Boise. The only evidence of the crisis was her close-cropped haircut, which she called her "Gertrude Stein look." The program included an Italian carol, a Basque Christmas song sung a cappella, her own "Waltzing with Bears" and "I'm Going to Tell on You" and Malvina Reynolds's love song "If You Love Me," which, Sorrels noted, Malvina had written when she was sixty-five.

Tongue in cheek, she told Mark Freeman of the *San Francisco Weekly* (February 21, 1990) that the brain surgery had been another liberating experience: "Now when someone tells me I have to do this or that, I figure I should have been dead by now. I don't have to do anything."

That same year she shepherded a book of her mother's writing through publication. She provided the introduction to the tome, *Report from Grimes Creek After a Hard Winter*, issued by Limberlost Press in Boise. In 1991 she completed a concept album derived from the book project, the Green Linnet release *Report from Grimes Creek*, which combined some of Rosalie's memories of childhood years, some of her mother's poetry, and some songs. Coming out almost simultaneously was the album *Be Careful, There's a Baby in the House*, with songs and spoken passages about raising

children and growing up in general. During 1990 she toured the United States during which she read some of the material from the *Grimes Creek* book, including appearances at the National Storytelling convention and the Cowboy Poetry Gathering in Elko, Nevada.

Her 1991 achievements included still another book project, *Way Out in Idaho—A Celebration of Songs and Stories Compiled by Rosalie Sorrels*, published by Confluence Press in association with the Idaho Commission on the Arts.

During 1992 and '93, Sorrels worked on tracks for a new album, *What Does It Mean to Love?* which Green Linnet issued in late '93. Besides originals like the title track, it included an a cappella traditional song, "There Was an Old Woman," Rosalie's rendering of Emily Dickinson's poem "When Much in the Woods As a Child," and Malvina Reynolds's compositions "A Place to Be" and "Turn Around."

Another gem of a collection was released by Green Linnet in 1995, *Borderline Heart*. This included such excellent self-penned tracks as the title track, "Come and Be My Driver," and a moving remembrance of her dead son, "Hitchhiker in the Rain"; a new version of Utah Phillips's "If I Could Be the Rain"; Mayne Smith's "Tucson, One More Time" and Townes Van Zandt's "Snowing on Raton." For her next project, she joined with longtime friend Utah Phillips to record an album containing a collection of songs that capsuled the history of the American labor movement. This album, *The Long Memory*, was issued by Red House Records in March 1996.

Generally speaking, Sorrels was more upbeat about the music she loved in the mid-1990s than in earlier years. She told Eric Snider of the *Sarasota Herald Tribune* ("Singer Rosalie Sorrels Has Laughed All Her Life," February 1, 1994), "I must tell you that I think it's a very hopeful time for folk now. I don't necessarily think folk being a viable *commodity* is a good thing for it. But people do, in fact, want personal contact. They love a story that's more than a soundbite. I think the attention span is making a comeback. That would be nice."

Nanci Griffith invited Rosalie to sing on two songs for her 1998 CD, *Other Voices, Too (A Trip Back to Bountiful)*. Sorrels also had an impact on Kate Wolf, who was inspired to study folk music after hearing her LP *If I Could Be the Rain*. Sorrels has been a regular performer at the Kate Wolf Memorial Music Festival, held in Sebastopol, California, each June. In May 1998, just weeks before her sixty-fifth birthday would have qualified her for Medicare, Rosalie underwent breast cancer surgery. Folksingers around the country quickly put together benefit concerts for the Rosalie Sorrels Recovery Fund. The surgery was successful, and Sorrels soon resumed a steady touring schedule, including performing at the Kate Wolf Festival in June 1998. In 1999 Limberlost Press released *An Imaginary Christmas in Idaho: Rosalie Sorrels and Friends*, and in July 2000

Red House released *No Closing Chords: The Songs of Malvina Reynolds.*

SOUTHER, J. D.: *Singer, guitarist, saxophonist, pianist, songwriter. Born Detroit, Michigan, November 2, 1945.*

Although he was a part of the Southern California folk and country-rock explosion of the late 1960s to early 1970s that made stars of Jackson Browne, Linda Ronstadt, and the Eagles, J. D. Souther took somewhat longer than his friends and associates to reach that status. He made important contributions as songwriter, session musician, and sometime musical adviser to the success of the others. Finally, after several starts as soloist and band member, he achieved a growing number of hits under his own name in the late 1970s and early '80s, but wasn't able to sustain his solo career momentum beyond that although his songs old and new remained popular with other artists.

Born in Detroit, John David Souther moved to Texas with his family at an early age and grew up in the city of Amarillo. He showed musical talent as a boy and, in his teens, learned to play a wide variety of instruments, from guitars and piano to drums. His early musical interests were diverse, ranging from the classics through jazz and bebop to country and rockabilly. Among his early favorites were Buddy Holly, Ray Charles, and Hank Williams. His schooling covered many aspects of music, from musical history to theory, harmony, and composition. While in high school, he played with a group called John David and the Senders.

During the mid-1960s, Souther made the Los Angeles area his home, where he sought to further his career as a songwriter and musician. He had worked with a number of local pop bands when his path crossed that of a recent arrival from the Midwest, Glenn Frey, in the late 1960s. Frey began dating a woman whose sister was Souther's girlfriend, bringing Frey and Souther in contact. Finding common musical ties, they soon formed a duo called Longbranch Pennywhistle. At first things seemed to look promising for them. They gained a record contract from Amos Records, which issued a debut album of their work in 1969. The duo made some progress in the pop club scene. Still far from flush economically, Frey and Souther shared a sixty-dollar-a-month apartment in Los Angeles's Echo Park district with another struggling artist, Jackson Browne.

In 1970, the duo sought to get out of their contract with Amos and the resultant legal entanglements sidelined them. Unable to work, they finally decided to go separate ways. Frey moved on to become part of Linda Ronstadt's backing band, and later formed the Eagles in 1971, while Souther began to perform as a soloist. In 1971, he signed with Asylum Records, which brought out his debut LP, *John David Souther,* in the summer of 1972, the same year Asylum released the first Eagles' album.

Unlike the Eagles' debut, Souther's album was not a chart hit, but he collaborated with Eagles' members on several songs in the band's second LP, *Desperado.* Both Linda Ronstadt and Jackson Browne generally included one or more Souther songs in their albums. When the Eagles began work in early 1974 on what was to become their first massive hit album, *On the Border,* the first two songs they recorded were collaborations with Souther, "The Best of My Love" and "You Never Cry like a Lover." The title song of Linda Ronstadt's *Prisoner in Disguise* LP was a song by Souther. He produced Ronstadt's 1973 album *Don't Cry Now.* She also covered his songs "Silver Blue" and "Simple Man, Simple Dream." Among the songs he wrote with Frey and Don Henley were such standards as "The Heart of the Matter," "New Kid in Town," and "Heartache Tonight."

In late 1973, rather than continue on as a solo performer, Souther joined with two veteran artists, former Byrds and Flying Burritos member Chris Hillman and Buffalo Springfield/Poco alumnus Richie Furay, in a new band. The debut LP of that band, the *Souther Hillman Furay Band,* came out on Elektra/ Asylum in the summer of 1974. Initially, it seemed that the threesome was on the threshold of impressive new success. The group was warmly received in an extensive tour of the United States in the summer and fall of 1974 and the LP stayed on upper pop chart levels during that time, earning the band a gold record award from the R.I.A.A on September 23, 1974. (The Eagles' "Desperado" was awarded a gold record the same day.)

Encouraged, the band went back to the studios to work on the next LP in late 1974 and early 1975. That album, *Trouble in Paradise,* came out in the spring of 1975. Unfortunately, the title proved quite appropriate. There already was discontent among SHF members about musical directions, and, when Furay was injured and incapacitated, the group broke up, with Souther once more seeking a solo role.

With Elektra/Asylum supporting his plans, he started work on his second solo LP, with Peter Asher as producer, in the fall of 1975. That LP, *Black Rose,* came out during 1976, showcasing a new group of Souther songs, which, however, seemed more pretentious than his previous work. In his concert tour in support of the album, in fact, there was great audience response to his performance of songs such as the Grammy-nominated "Faithless Love" (a hit for Linda Ronstadt), "Don't Cry Now," "Run like a Thief" and "Silver Blue." Despite the response the new album did not do particularly well.

For the next few years, though Souther's material continued to show up on new releases by many artists and Souther himself did considerable session work and some concerts with major folk-rock artists, his own entertainment career essentially was in limbo.

Then he signed with a new label, CBS Records. His first LP on that label, *You're Only Lonely,* came out in mid-1979, and this time all the elements for success seemed in place. Backed by a tight-sounding band, he offered an interesting array of numbers, ranging in style from fast-paced folk-rockers to country-tinged ballads. The concerts he gave in places like New York's Bottom Line to the Los Angeles Roxy, with stops at important venues in between, were among the most effective of his career. The new album remained on the pop charts from soon after its release to the first part of 1980. The title song, aided by excellent live shows in New York and Los Angeles, became a singles hit on both the pop and singles chart, peaking at number seven in the former the week of October 20.

His next Columbia sessions provided the singles hit "Her Town Too," recorded with James Taylor. The disc rose to number eleven in *Billboard* the week of March 14, 1981. In 1984 he added the album *Home by Dawn* to his credits. For the rest of the 1980s into the '90s, aside from benefit appearances, most of his focus was on doing session work with other artists and adding to his songwriting catalog.

Souther had bit roles in films and TV shows. He made his acting debut in the 1989 film *Always,* in which he briefly appears as a lead singer in a band performing "Smoke Gets in Your Eyes." He also had cameos in *Postcards from the Edge, My Girl 2,* and in several episodes of the 1980s TV show *thirty-something.* Two of his songs were included in the *About Last Night* sound track, "Step by Step," written with Karla Bonoff and performed by Souther, and "If Anybody Had a Heart," written with Danny Kortchmar. He and Ronstadt also performed "Hearts Against the Wind" on the *Urban Cowboy* sound track. He and Jackson Browne sang the Everly Brothers' "'Til I Kissed You" at Don Henley's 1995 wedding to Sharon Sumerall in Malibu.

In the '90s Souther continued to write and perform songs. He performed "Rock & Roll Doctor" on the Lowell George tribute album. The Dixie Chicks included his "I'll Take Care of You" on their hit album *Wide Open Spaces* in 1998. He cowrote the song "Where Love Has Been" with Brian Wilson for his album *Imagination,* released in June 1998.

SPANN, OTIS: *Singer, keyboards player (piano, organ), harmonica player, songwriter. Born Jackson, Mississippi, March 21, 1930; died Chicago, Illinois, April 24, 1970.*

Otis Spann was a prime contributor to the sound of the Muddy Waters blues band from 1953 to 1969, and his keyboard mastery can be heard on dozens of albums of Chess Records artists as well as his own solo releases. Spann, Waters told *Jazz Journal* writer Sheldon Harris in the late 1960s, "is the best blues piano player we have today. There is no one left like him who plays the real, solid, bottom blues." Samuel Charters, in the liner notes for the Vanguard 1966 release *Chicago/The Blues/Today! Volume 1,* commented that Spann, "with-

out argument or qualification, is one of the greatest blues piano men who ever lived."

The son of a minister, Spann grew up in his hometown of Jackson, Mississippi, starting to teach himself piano at age five and making his first public appearances in his father's church. By his teens he was playing in local bars, at house parties, and at other events in the Jackson area while also demonstrating athletic skills that eventually led to experience as a semipro football player and a boxer. After his mother died, he was sent to stay with relatives in Chicago, but he joined the U.S. Army in 1946 (presumably faking his birth date, if the given year is correct). After his discharge in 1951, he returned to the Windy City, where he joined the Muddy Waters group in 1953, taking the spot once held by his idol and mentor, Big Maceo Merriweather. He made his recording debut with the Waters group on September 24, 1953, and performed regularly with the band in concerts and on records until 1969. His work with Waters included the 1960 Newport Jazz Festival set captured in the live album *Muddy Waters at Newport* whose tracks included Spann's vocal performance of "Goodbye Newport Blues" and a rousing version of Muddy's trademark number, "Got My Mojo Working " (Spann's boogie-woogie piano style also can be heard on such Waters classics as "I'm Ready," "Hoochie Coochie Man," and "Just Make Love to Me.")

In 1960 Spann recorded his first solo album, *Otis Spann Is the Blues,* on the Candid label accompanied by guitarist Robert Lockwood Jr. Over the next eight years, while continuing to tour and record with Waters, he turned out a series of memorable solo collections, often backed by all or part of Waters's group (including Muddy under the pseudonym "Dirty Rivers"). His solo albums included *The Blues of Otis Spann* (1962); *The Blues Is Where It's At* (ABC Bluesway, 1965); *The Bottom of the Blues* (featuring vocalist Lucille Jenkins, whom he married in 1967, and the Waters Band; issued by ABC Bluesway in 1967).

In 1969, after turning over his piano chores with Waters to Pinetop Perkins, he signed with Vanguard Records and embarked on what many foresaw as a path to stardom as a solo artist. On his label debut, *Cryin' Time,* lead guitar work was done by Barry Melton of Country Joe and the Fish. Other late 1960s releases included *Cracked Spanner Head* and a set with the British rock band Fleetwood Mac for Blue Horizon that included his fine rendition of "Hungry Country Girl." In Spann's final recording work, he collaborated with Buddy Guy and Junior Wells on the latter's 1970 Delmark LP, *Southside Blues Jam.* Spann by then already was suffering from the cancer that took his life at Cook County Hospital, Chicago, in April. Most of his albums were reissued in the late 1980s and in the 1990s, though not all remained in print.

Spann was inducted into the Blues Foundation's Hall of Fame in 1980.

SPENCE, JOSEPH: *Singer, guitarist, songwriter. Born August 3, 1910, Small Hope, Andros, Bahamas; died Nassau, New Providence, Bahamas, March 18, 1984.*

Though his recorded output was relatively small, Joseph Spence had an enormous influence on many guitar players in the folk field and other genres as well because of his unique two-finger picking style. His playing was so distinctive, in fact, that musician–folk-music collector–author Sam Charters, who first recorded him on the small Bahamian island of Andros on July 23, 1958, noted that it was almost impossible for artists in the forefront of the U.S. folk boom of the late 1950s to copy his style accurately.

Actually, it was through a streak of luck that Charters discovered Spence at all. Along with Ann Danberg (later Ann Danberg Charters), he had gone to Andros in the summer of 1958 to try to tape folk musicians who had not been influenced by pop music trends, including calypso performers. He had heard some unique Bahamian material in recordings made by Alan Lomax in the 1930s and hoped to find artists who had not been tainted by modern entertainment developments. As he recalled in notes for a Spence album, he and Danberg had been walking from their rented house in the Fresh Creek Settlement area on the island when they heard what sounded like multiple guitars being played somewhere near. They soon discovered that the source of the music was one man sitting on a pile of bricks "in a faded shirt and rumpled khaki trousers" and picking out melodies on a large acoustic guitar.

As Charters wrote in 1958, "I had never heard anything like Spence. His playing was stunning. He was playing simple popular melodies, and using them as the basis for extended rhythmic and melodic variations. He often seemed to be improvising in the bass, the middle strings and the treble at the same time. Sometimes a variation would strike [a group of workmen, who were building a new house nearby] and Spence himself as so exciting that he would simply stop playing and join them in the shouts of excitement. One of the men sent for a bottle of rum, and the others drifted back to work."

Finding and recording Spence turned out to be the highlight of the visit, but it could have easily been a missed opportunity. Spence at the time lived in Nassau, where he worked as a stone mason, and had only come to Andros to visit his sister and some friends.

Back in New York City, Charters placed an initial six of Spence's numbers with Moses Asch of Folkways for an inexpensive ten-inch album. Later Asch used more of the material for a full-size disc, *Music of the Bahamas, Volume One.* Some of the tracks also were included in compilations of Bahamian music. When Charters played his original tapes for other guitar players, the typical reaction was tremendous interest. Performers and folk fans alike eagerly sought out Folkways releases of Spence's initial output for some years. Contents of the original 1959 Spence album, which was reissued by the label in 1964, included one track of his version of a U.S. World War II pop song, Harold Adamson and Jimmie McHugh's "Coming in on a Wing and a Prayer," and eight Spence adaptations of traditional material. The latter comprised "There Will Be a Happy Meeting in Glory," "Brownskin Gal," "I'm Going to Live That Life," "Face to Face That I Shall Know Him," "Jump in the Line," "Bimini Gal," "The Lord Is My Shepherd," and "(Glory, Glory) When I Lay My Burden Down."

Spence had actually worked in the U.S. construction field from 1944 to 1946 under a program that allowed non–U.S. citizens to come to the country for employment during World War II. In 1946 he returned to the islands, settling in the Bahamian capital of Nassau with his wife, Louise, whom he had married in 1937.

Among others, Pete Seeger was enthusiastic about Spence's work and sought his address from Charters for a possible invitation to the Newport Folk Festival. Also intrigued with Spence's Folkways material were collectors Paul Rothchild and Fritz Richmond, of the Jim Kweskin Jug Band, who went to the Bahamas specifically to seek out Spence. This resulted in the Elektra album *Happy All the Time* (reissued by Hannibal/Rykodisc in 1985). As Rothchild wrote in the LP's liner notes, "In January 1964, Fritz left for the Bahamas on the first leg of his search and, during his second day, met [the Bahamian artist] Blind Blake, who introduced him to Spence, now living in Nassau."

Also in 1964, the Newport Foundation asked Charters to help shepherd Spence and two female family members on a tour of New York and Boston. The women were deeply religious and most of the concerts focused on gospel music. Charters recalled that Spence was much more restrained as a person and a musician and the numbers lacked the exuberance Charters remembered from the Andros meeting. Although Charters made a few new recordings, he was disappointed in the results. For a variety of reasons, he found Spence's work weaker than in 1958; his job as a stone mason had apparently robbed him of practice time and made his hands less supple for guitar playing.

Spence, though, was asked to make new tracks for other organizations. For Arhoolie, for instance, he was featured on the LPs *Bahamian Guitarist* and *Good Morning Mr. Walker.* Several of his collections became part of the Rounder Records catalog and were still available from the label as of 2000. Those included *Living on the Hallelujah Side, Glory, Kneelin' Down Inside the Gate: The Great Rhyming Singers of the Bahamas,* and *The Spring of Sixty-Five.* The last contained tracks obtained by Peter Siegel and Jody Stecher, who flew to the islands in early June of that year and, among other things, recorded one of the most notable Bahamian numbers, Spencer with the Pinder Family's version of "I Bid You Goodnight." (The song originally was part of the Siegel/Stecher-produced mid-'60s

Nonesuch album *The Real Bahamas,* which was reissued in 1998.) During 1968 it made an impression on many folk fans through a cover version by the Incredible String Band on its Elektra LP *The Hangman's Beautiful Daughter.* The song, which was included in the 1995 Shanachie release *The Music Never Stopped: The Roots of the Grateful Dead,* also made an impact on Jerry Garcia and company.

Musicians continued to be impressed by Spence's work in the 1970s and early '80s, and some enthusiasts went to the Bahamas in hopes of listening to him play. Most notably, Spence influenced Ry Cooder, who traveled to the Bahamas to study with him. Cooder included a version of Spence's "We Shall Be Happy" on his 1978 album, *Jazz.* Still, Spence himself maintained a low profile up to his death in 1984.

In the mid-'90s, Smithsonian/Folkways reissued the album *Joseph Spence—The Complete Folkways Recordings 1958.* The reissue, which included pictures taken by Ann Danberg Charters, was prepared for reissue and annotated by Sam Charters.

In 1994, ten years after his death, several artists made the album *Out on the Rolling Sea,* released by Green Linnet as a tribute to Spence. Performers include David Lindley, David Grisman, the Watersons, Taj Mahal, Van Dyke Parks, Henry Kaiser, Michael Chapman, and the Malagasy groups Tarika Sammy and Rossy. Spence's version of "Santa Claus Is Comin' to Town" was also included in the 1997 Rykodisc compilation *Xmas Marks the Spot.*

SPRINGSTEEN, BRUCE: *Singer, songwriter, guitarist, band leader (The E Street Band). Born Freehold, New Jersey, September 23, 1949.*

Unlike many artists who become popular and stick to a set format, Bruce Springsteen hasn't been afraid to change. He built his popularity as a skillful exponent of mainstream rock, but there always were elements of folk and blues in his material, such as his 1982 album *Nebraska.* His folk orientation was becoming more pronounced in the 1990s, when his album *The Ghost of Tom Joad* won the Grammy for Best Contemporary Folk Album of 1996.

The blue-collar rocker burst on the national scene in 1975 with the album *Born to Run.* Its tracks featured his original "street-drama" compositions, laden with images and characters from his native New Jersey shore. As he matured as an artist Springsteen began gradually to shift his attention to America. His songs in the 1984 album *Born in the U.S.A.* are stark; his characters struggle against a landscape of decaying cities and shuttered factories. His fans have stayed faithful throughout. To them, Springsteen remains "the Boss."

Even in such venues as the Los Angeles Coliseum, in front of 80,000 people most of whom could only see him via gigantic video screens, he has the ability to touch each individual with his energy. He runs from one end of the stage to the other, jumping atop speakers while wielding his guitar. Or he clowns around on stage with longtime friend and saxophonist Clarence "Nick" Clemons.

In short, his concerts are a celebration. Because of Springsteen's power on stage, it's fitting that in 1986 he released *Bruce Springsteen & the E Street Band Live/1975–1985,* a five-disc retrospective capturing the essence of his live performances plus the evolution of an artist—from his performances in clubs such as Los Angeles's Roxy to progressively larger arenas, from his early introspective and heavily textured anthems to his stark dramatic monologues about despair and futility. No artist during that period had a larger impact on the American rock scene.

Indeed, in 1984 his influence had become so great that President Reagan and Walter Mondale each claimed that Springsteen shared their views of an America filled with hope and prosperity. Springsteen was forced to disassociate himself from both presidential candidates, becoming openly critical of "blind faith" in anything, according to *Los Angeles Times* columnist Robert Hilburn. "Here's a song about blind faith," Springsteen said, introducing "Reason to Believe." "That is always a dangerous thing, whether it's in your girlfriend . . . or if it's in your government."

Since 1980, Springsteen has become a powerful spokesman for America's dispossessed. In that year, he turned to Woody Guthrie's "This Land Is Your Land," sung in minor tones to reflect his view that something is amiss in the land. He reminds his audiences of the importance of commitment to their local communities as a way of bettering the world.

"Life is a struggle," Springsteen explained to Hilburn in 1980. "That's basically what the songs are about. It's the fight every one goes through every day. . . . I'm a romantic. To me, the idea of a romantic is someone who sees the reality, lives the reality every day, but knows about the possibilities too. You can't lose sight of the dreams."

Indeed, Springsteen's career began with dreams set against the backdrop of a working-class family. His father, Douglas, held jobs as a bus driver and factory worker. Bruce attended elementary and high school in his hometown, Freehold, New Jersey, a place offering few role models. "It's like I come from an area where there was not a lot of success," he told Hilburn in 1978. "I didn't know anyone who made a record before me. I didn't know anybody who had done anything. It was like climbing the mountain or something."

In the late 1950s, he was attracted to rock by Elvis Presley. As he later told a reporter: "Anybody who sees Elvis Presley and doesn't want to be like Elvis Presley has got to have something wrong with him." (And indeed, one night in 1976 when he was performing in Memphis, Springsteen hopped the gate of Elvis's Graceland mansion in an attempt to see the rock legend, only to be turned away by a guard.) When he was nine, Bruce got a guitar, but his fingers couldn't handle it and he gave up. At fourteen, he tried once again; this time he stuck with the instrument. Once he could play reasonably well, he organized the first of a series of bands that worked high-school parties and small Jersey clubs in Asbury Park. It was there that he met such musicians as Southside Johnny Lyons of the Asbury Jukes. He formed a hard-rock group called Steel Mill. Later he started a soul group under his own name that had ten members and incorporated the brass section sound that Springsteen continued to stress in his smaller bands of the '70s.

Two members of that band—keyboard artist David Sancious and saxophonist Clarence Clemons—remained with Bruce when he formed the E Street Band. Other early members of the E Street Band, most of whom he met in his Asbury Park days, were: Danny Federici, organ; Roy Bittan, piano; Garry Tallent, bass; Max Weinberg, drums; and Steve Van Zandt, guitar. Sancious left the band in 1974, signing a recording contract with Epic, and Van Zandt left the band in 1983 to begin a solo career. Van Zandt was replaced by Nils Lofgren in 1984. Patty Scialfa joined the band in 1988 as a background vocalist-guitarist on the "Tunnel of Love Express" tour.

Bruce briefly attended Ocean County Community College, but left when he got the chance to play at Bill Graham's Fillmore West. That experience didn't open any doors, so he returned to New York and worked whenever he could at clubs around the city. A meeting with two management executives, Mike Appel and Jim Cretecos, finally led to an audition with John Hammond, Sr. of Columbia Records. Hammond was impressed with Springsteen's original street dramas such as "It's Hard to Be a Saint in the City," which evoked insistent images (*The sages of the subway sit just like the living dead/As the tracks clack out the rhythm/Their eyes fixed straight ahead.*)

Appel became Bruce's first manager, a relationship that eventually ended in a legal dispute. According to Dave Marsh, who wrote *Born to Run: The Bruce Springsteen Story* (Dell, 1979), the arrangements with Appel were not favorable to Bruce: "Prolific Bruce may have been. Shrewd he was not. He signed a long-term management contract only a few days later, on an automobile hood in the unlighted parking lot of a bar."

That contract with Columbia was signed in 1972, and Bruce's debut album, *Greetings from Asbury Park, N.J.,* was released in January 1973. Many reviewers didn't even give the disc passing notice, but a few found it extremely powerful. It was not a commercial success, selling about 25,000 copies initially. Hammond and his associates urged him to complete a second LP: *The Wild, the Innocent, and the E Street Shuffle* (September 1973).

At first, the record-buying public also stayed away from this record, in part because the songs did not lend themselves to widespread radio airplay. But this time, almost all the critics paid attention. *Rolling Stone* selected the album as one of the best of 1973. Jon Landau, who became Springsteen's manager–record producer in 1977, wrote the most often-quoted Springsteen review after seeing Springsteen in a 1974 concert: "I saw my rock and roll past flash before my eyes. . . . I saw rock and roll's future and its name is Bruce Springsteen."

The critical acclaim paid off in the short term. By August 1974, sales of *E Street Shuffle* were approaching 100,000, according to Marsh.

But it was another year before Landau's prophecy came true. Part of the problem seemed to be Springsteen's low profile; he liked playing the small East Coast clubs where he had become a celebrity but shied away from coast-to-coast touring. Springsteen also suffered from inertia in creating new material, accounting for a long gap between albums. It took much prodding from admirers such as Landau before Bruce capitulated and wrote enough songs for album three. When *Born to Run,* which was coproduced by Landau, was released in August 1975, it was hailed in most quarters as a landmark in rock. The LP was aided by Springsteen's first national tour and, on October 8, 1975, brought him his first gold-record award. Accompanying it on its chart journey were the two earlier albums, which also went gold.

Springsteen became a national celebrity. His face graced the covers of both *Time* and *Newsweek* in the same week. In the pictures, he seemed a throwback to an earlier rock era with his black leather motorcycle jacket, T-shirt, and jeans. But his music, almost all agreed, had not been heard before. It was a blend of many things in pop from R&B and swing to hard-driving rock, but, as often happens, the sum of the parts added up to something considerably removed from any individual element.

In his first three albums, Springsteen focused on New Jersey plus his youth, independence, and coming of age. Many were dazzled by such songs as "Blinded by the Light," and "Growin' Up" on *Greetings.* "Rosalita" and "4th of July, Asbury Park (Sandy)" continued his focus on specific involvements in his second album, which had an adventurous and heavily textured sound.

But despite the critical and popular acclaim of *Born to Run,* Springsteen did not release another album until 1978's *Darkness on the Edge of Town.* The three-year hiatus was in part caused by legal entanglements. In 1976, Springsteen and Appel had a series of disagreements over the management deal, royalties, and the rights to his songs, according to Marsh. The two sued one another in July of that year, and one ruling restrained Landau from producing any of Springsteen's albums. A settlement was not reached until May 1977. But Springsteen was also attempting to deal with his newfound stardom. Early in his career, Springsteen had said: "There's no way we'd ever play in one of those barns." But in 1978, he switched from playing clubs such as New York's Bottom Line (where he kicked off the '75 tour in support of *Born to Run*) to such "barns" as the Nassau Coliseum and the 18,000-seat Los Angeles Forum. It took him a while, though, to learn how to project his personality to all parts of huge arenas, for the timing and musicianship needed to be a bit different from the techniques used on the club circuit.

In *Darkness,* Springsteen also began to change his focus. He had fulfilled his dream of becoming a rock star and now had to deal with its realities. As Irwin Stambler wrote in his "Pop, Rock & Soul" column: "It is a work that diverges sharply from what has gone before. For the most part, it talks of the problems and frustrations of a real, recognizable world rather than the special surroundings of Bruce's youth in New Jersey."

Though *Darkness* reached the top 5, it did not receive the acclaim of *Born to Run.* Nevertheless, such songs as the title track, "The Promised Land," and "Badlands" all became Springsteen concert standards.

It was clearly a time of transition for Bruce. "I felt like I had lost a certain control of myself," he told Hilburn in 1980. "There was all the publicity and all the backlash. I felt the thing I wanted most in life—my music—being swept away and didn't know if I could do anything about it."

In 1980, Springsteen released *The River,* a two-album set recapturing the artistic energy of his first three albums. His reputation as a performer also improved sharply in 1980, when he showed he not only could sell out arenas night after night, but also could electrify the largest crowds. He displayed tremendous endurance, with shows often lasting more than four hours. He told Hilburn: "I don't count on my tomorrows. . . . If you do that, you begin to plan too much and begin rationing yourself. . . . If you start rationing, you're living bit by bit when you can live it all at once."

The River was more accessible and commercially successful than *Darkness.* "The Boss" received more widespread radio airplay with such spirited songs as "Hungry Heart" and "Out on the Street." But his work also included dramatic songs such as the title track, written from the perspective of a young man whose dreams and aspirations are cut down when his girlfriend becomes pregnant and they are forced to get married. "Independence Day" paints a bittersweet image of a decaying hometown seen through the eyes of a man who is leaving his family. *(Now the rooms are all empty down at Frankie's joint/And the highway she's deserted clear down to Breaker's Point.)*

Such concerns about recession and decay could in retrospect be seen as leading directly into Springsteen's next album, *Nebraska* (1982). The album seemed like such a departure from his earlier work that it caught many by surprise. It received critical acclaim, but did not do as well with record buyers as previous releases.

The album is a collection of stories about drifters and criminals. Springsteen recorded it at home on a four-track cassette recorder, accompanying himself on guitar and harmonica. The acoustic, rough-cut quality reminds one of Woody Guthrie singing "Pretty Boy Floyd."

The title track was based on the true story of Charles Starkweather, who went on a killing spree in Nebraska in 1958 and was executed the next year. Springsteen ended speaking in the matter-of-fact voice of the murderer: *They wanted to know why I did what I did/Well sir I guess there's just a meanness in this world.*

But he changed gears again in his next, and most successful album. In *Born in the U.S.A.* (1984), Springsteen returned to the E Street Band but retained the themes of *Nebraska.* He reportedly culled the twelve songs from more than sixty tracks recorded during an eighteen-month period.

Many critics hailed *Born in the U.S.A.* as another landmark. As Stephen Holden of the *New York Times* wrote: [Springsteen] forged a dense metallic sound that embraces more mechanical rhythms and textures, but without severing Mr. Springsteen's ties with Chuck Berry, Motown, rockabilly, and other traditional rock and roll idioms. . . . [It] is a sad and serious album about the end of the American dream—of economic hope and security, and of community—for a dwindling segment of our society."

On the album cover, Springsteen posed in blue jeans and T-shirt in front of what looked like an American flag. The image was taken by many, including Reagan, as emblematic of Springsteen's patriotism. But for his fans, the album's upbeat sound could not mask the disillusionment in his lyrics. The album began with the title track, a song about a downtrodden Vietnam vet: *Born down in a dead man's town/The first kick I took was when I hit the ground/You end up like a dog that's been beat too much/Till you spend half your life just covering up.*

Songs such as "My Hometown" and "Reason to Believe" depicted the decay of the towns and the determination of many to escape, as well as the blind faith some seem to need to survive. Even the catchy single "Dancing in the Dark" portrayed the loneliness of a man who "could use just a little help."

The album sold more than 11 million copies worldwide. The posters of Springsteen in front of the American flag could be seen in stores worldwide as he embarked on an international tour in 1984. At many stops, Springsteen urged fans to contribute to local food banks. For example, in an Oakland concert, Springsteen introduced "My Hometown" by asking people to "help the Berkeley Emergency Food Project . . . to feed people—people who have been cut down by the injustices in our social system and by the economic policies of the current administration."

Springsteen continued to show his commitment to

combating hunger by playing a key role in the 1985 "We Are the World" album and video. His distinctive voice was easily recognizable on the song, which raised millions of dollars for relief of the famine in Ethiopia.

"The Boss" was now being called things like "rock's popular populist" as critics compared him to Guthrie, Dylan, and Presley. Many fans, including rock critic Robert Hilburn, began to make pilgrimages to New Jersey to discover Springsteen's roots. But others also began wondering if Bruce's immense popularity would lead to a backlash. Most critics discounted the notion. But in the *Los Angeles Times* article "Tellin' Off the Boss," Kristine McKenna criticized Springsteen's "pedestrian thematic vocabulary. There's some serious Stone Age thinking going on in Bruce's songs, which basically begin and end with girls."

Amid the hoopla, Springsteen found time to break many hearts in May 1985 by marrying actress and model Julianne Phillips. That too was well covered by the media. In fact, according to Dave Marsh, who wrote *Glory Days: Bruce Springsteen in the 1980s* (Pantheon, 1987), the media even intruded upon the ceremony. "The guy looked at me at the end of that wedding scene (which included photographers shooting from helicopters) and said: 'I do not believe or comprehend the world that I live in. Put that at the top of the chapter,'" Marsh told *USA Today*.

In 1986, the publicity died down a bit until the release of the five-LP live set in November. Despite the $25 price tag, record buyers besieged the stores, which received advance orders of more than 1.5 million copies.

The *Live* set was the end of an era. He told Edna Gundersen (*USA Today,* March 15, 1988): "We played it in my room. We all sat there and listened to it. And I said, 'Well, 10 years, there it is. When you have those little babies and they want to know what you did these past 10 years, you play them this record.' I think it's something to be proud of. After that, I said, 'Well, time for a new adventure.'"

That adventure was *Tunnel of Love* (September 1987), which represented a change in direction. Songs such as the title track, "One Step Up," and "Brilliant Disguise" focused on the dashed hopes and desires in modern romance. The album was perhaps more autobiographical than most had thought at first, since in 1988 rumors began circulating that Springsteen and Julianne Phillips had separated.

The album was certified double-platinum and earned Springsteen the distinction of being the only artist in the past ten years to chart four number one LPs in *Billboard*.

In February 1988, Springsteen embarked on the "Tunnel of Love Express" tour, a carefully crafted show that represented a shift from his previous, more spontaneous concerts. "It felt like the time to break with the past a little bit," he said.

On March 30, 1992, Columbia released two albums on the same day, *Human Touch* and *Lucky Town*. They were the first studio collections "the Boss" had released in nearly five years. It was something most artists couldn't get away with, and Springsteen was no exception. Certainly much had happened in the interim. He had divorced Julianne Phillips and the E Street Band and married his Jersey backup singer, Patti Scialfa, in 1991. He had become a father twice over. He had purchased a $14 million mansion in Bel Air. Critics and record store owners questioned whether a domestic Springsteen could still captivate his audience. He recorded most of the fourteen-song *Human Touch* in 1990 with a full band, including keyboards player Roy Bittan from the E Street Band, Jeff Porcaro on drums, Randy Jackson on bass, and backup singers Bobby King and Sam Moore. Springsteen took eight weeks to record the ten songs of *Lucky Town* at his Beverly Hills studio, playing most of the instruments himself. Some of the tracks on the latter reflected his new life: "Book of Dreams," about his wedding to Scialfa, and "Living Proof," about the birth of his son. He seemed to have lost his edge, or perhaps it was just that he had passed forty. As he sings in "Better Days": *Now a life of leisure and a pirate's treasure don't make much for tragedy/But it's a sad man, my friend, who's livin' in his own skin and can't stand the company.*

The albums certainly didn't capture the power and bite of his earlier work. David Browne of *Entertainment Weekly* commented, "Strained and verbose, both *Lucky Town* and *Human Touch* are his most confused albums since his 1973 debut. In trying to follow up the emotional and musical resonance of 1987's bravely folkish *Tunnel of Love,* on which he stripped the veneer from his first marriage, Springsteen takes one step up. But his burning desire to still rock the stadiums takes him two frustrating steps back." The record buying public, the ultimate critics, stayed away. *Human Touch* and *Lucky Town* debuted at number two and number three, respectively. But within weeks the former had dropped off to number thirty-three and the latter to number forty-four, although international sales remained strong.

But as in the late 1980s, he retained his principles and his dignity in the 1990s. He remained committed to fighting against living in a world of mirrors and illusions, he told Bill Barol (*Newsweek,* November 2, 1987). "People deserve better. They deserve the truth. They deserve honesty. The best music, you can seek some shelter in it momentarily, but it's essentially there to provide you something to face the world with."

Bruce followed those principles in the 1990s when his songs dealt with such issues as AIDS and homelessness. His composition, "Streets of Philadelphia," written for Jonathan Demme's 1993 film *Philadelphia,* which dealt with the AIDS plague, was a touching, insightful ballad that won the music industry's Oscar for

Best Song, presented to him on the March 1994 awards telecast. "Streets of Philadelphia," issued by Columbia, received a gold record certification from the R.I.A.A. on April 26, 1994.

When the Grammy Award winners were announced on March 1, 1995, "Streets of Philadelphia" was named Song of the Year for 1994. At the 1995 Grammy show, Springsteen also took home awards for Best Male Rock Vocal, Best Rock Song, and Best Song Written for a Motion Picture or Television. After receiving the first trophy, he took time to thank "the folks who have come up to me in restaurants and on the street who have lost their lovers or their friends and said that the song meant something to them." With his Grammy victory, Springsteen became the first rock writer ever to win best-song honors in both the Oscar and Grammy voting.

During 1994 his 1975 *Born to Run* album received a certificate from the R.I.A.A. for 4 million copies sold on November 17 and his 1984 disc, *Born in the USA,* was certificated for going past the 14 million mark. Meanwhile his 1980 LP, *The River,* passed the 3 million sales level. In February 1995 Columbia released his *Greatest Hits* collection, which rose to number one on the charts soon after. On November 14, 1995, his folk-style collection *The Ghost of Tom Joad* came out and, after peaking at number eleven in *Billboard* late in the year, went on to earn a R.I.A.A. gold record award on August 1, 1996.

In the Grammy nominations for 1996, announced in January 1997, *The Ghost of Tom Joad* was named a finalist in the Best Contemporary Folk Album category. On the awards telecast in February, folk legend Pete Seeger made the introduction to Springsteen's performance of the title track, calling him "my good friend." After singing the number, backing himself on acoustic guitar, Springsteen went offstage to hear soon after he had won the trophy. In his comments to the audience, he thanked Elaine Steinbeck for giving him the rights to write about the central character in her father's book (and the film based on it) about the Depression years, *The Grapes of Wrath.*

Showing his debt to folksingers like Woody Guthrie and Pete Seeger, Springsteen performed "We Shall Overcome" for the Seeger tribute *Where Have All the Flowers Gone,* released in March 1998 by Appleseed Recordings. He was also heard performing the title track for the film *Dead Man Walking* and on the sound track, released by Sony in 1995.

In the late 1990s Bruce and Patti relocated their family (children Evan, Jessica, and Sam) to a farm in New Jersey, which Springsteen had fled to as a fledgling rock star. In the meantime, he took another look back on his multifaceted career. In November 1998 Columbia released *Tracks,* a four-CD collection of sixty-six songs, fifty-six of which were never officially released. The set begins with four songs that were recorded for his 1972 demo for John Hammond Sr., and

follows his career from *Greetings from Asbury Park, N.J.* to *The Ghost of Tom Joad.* He writes in the liner notes, "This collection contains everything from the first note I sang in the Columbia recording studio, my early and later work with the E Street Band, through my music in the '90s. It's the alternate route to some of the destinations I traveled to on my records, an invitation into the studio on the many nights we spent making music in search of the records we presented to you. Here are some of the ones that got away." (In fact, in 1998 Springsteen went to court in England to attempt to squash the unauthorized distribution of his earliest recordings, which popped up as imports in the United States.)

As tribute to Springsteen's place in the pantheon of rock stars, he was inducted into both the Rock and Roll Hall of Fame and the Songwriters' Hall of Fame in 1999. In the summer of that year he also reunited for a tour with the E Street Band for the first time in a decade, selling out shows at home and abroad.

STAINES, BILL: *Singer, guitarist, banjoist, autoharpist, songwriter. Born Medford, Massachusetts, February 6, 1947.*

A writer and performer of sensitive, "instantly memorable" songs, Bill Staines remained tough-minded about the need to focus on the traditions of folk music rather than give in to the popular music trends of the moment. In a career that straddled the folk booms of the early '60s and the folk revival that began in the late 1980s, Staines continued to find an audience for his appearances in the United States and Canada through good times and bad and managed to maintain consistent quality in his album and songwriting output.

Growing up in the Boston area, he tuned in on the extensive folk movement spawned in part by the many colleges in and around the city. By his late teens he was taking an active role in music, performing informally with friends and, as time went by, appearing on bills in small clubs with people like Bonnie Raitt and Tom Rush. For a while in the mid-1960s he became the master of ceremonies at the Sunday hootenanny at the Club 47 in Cambridge, Massachusetts. Before the end of that decade he had built up a solid following among fans in the Boston area as well as other parts of New England and had begun to impress critics and fellow performers with his warm baritone voice and writing abilities. In 1966 he made his album debut with *Bag of Rainbows,* followed by *Somebody Blue* on Champlain Records in 1967. This was followed by the 1971 Evolution Records release *Bill Staines.*

Coming into the '70s, his standing with a sizable number of folk-music adherents and magazine and newspaper critics remained high. After a 1971 concert, a reviewer for the *Boston Phoenix* called him "simply Boston's best performer." By then his original songs were finding their way into the repertoires of other artists like Tom Makem and Liam Clancy, Mason

Williams, and country music's Grandpa Jones. Meanwhile, in what was a down decade for folk music in the main, Staines continued to find an outlet for his stylings either on independent labels or on his own Mineral River Records. His releases through the '70s included *Third Time Around,* on Catfish Records in 1973; *Miles,* in 1976, and *Old Wood and Winter Wine,* in 1977, both on Mineral River; *Just Play One More Tune,* in 1977, and *Whistle of the Jay,* in 1979, both on the Folk-Legacy label; and *Rodeo Rose,* on Philo in 1981.

Throughout the '70s Staines kept expanding his potential audiences with appearances at major folk festivals and literally hitting the road in a van to travel all over the United States and Canada. He had taken a great interest in yodeling, listening closely to the techniques on records of performers like Jimmie Rodgers and Montana Slim. In 1975 he demonstrated his yodeling skill at the Kerrville Folk Festival, Kerrville, Texas, where he won the National Yodeling Championship. Afterward, he was instructor at a series of yodeling workshops on the folk festival circuit.

In 1978 he had a streak of writing inspiration that led to what are probably his three best-known songs, "A Place in the Choir," "Roseville Fair," and "River." "Roseville Fair," which later became a favorite of Nanci Griffith, who included an inspired version of it on her *One Fair Summer Evening* album, took its cue, in part, from the Rose Bowl Parade in Pasadena on New Year's Day. For some reason, Staines recalled, while he was slowly developing the lyrics about an old couple remembering how they fell in love at a fair, the Pasadena event stuck in his mind, so he named the song's locale Roseville.

In almost all his songwriting efforts, he told interviewers, he worked out the patterns with his old Martin guitar, which he plays left-handed, like Elizabeth Cotten. A lot of his ideas came to him while driving his van between concerts. For the most part, he wanted to save the thoughts until he got home, though some originals were composed on the road, as was the case with "Roseville Fair." Wherever he did them, he told Steve Givens of the *Performing Songwriter* ("Bill Staines—Passing It on with Clarity," September–October 1994), he needed to be alone. "The thing that I'm sort of limited by is that I really have to be secluded to write. So if I'm staying with people while I'm on the road and they're off at work and I have their house to myself, then I'll write. When I'm home and I'm by myself, that's when I do my writing. I can't write in hotels and I don't use a tape recorder to sort of spit images into while I'm driving along. I really need to have my guitar."

In the 1980s Staines's career proceeded predictably: more hard traveling, more new songs, and another string of new albums. After completing *Sandstone Cathedrals* on his Mineral River label in 1983, he added to his catalog in 1984 with the excellent *Bridges,*

issued on Coffeehouse Extempore Records. (The album was reissued in 1989 by Red House Records.) In 1985 he began a series of discs on Philo-Rounder with *Wild, Wild Heart.* This was followed by *Redbird's Wing* in 1988, *The First Million Miles* (referring to the road miles he'd chalked up in his series of minivans) in 1989, and *Tracks and Trails* in 1991. During those years, besides completing some 200 concert dates a year, he was also active on radio and TV, appearing on *A Prairie Home Companion, Mountain Stage,* and the *Good Evening Show,* as well as hosting some local programs in the new England area on PBS and network TV. His home base was near Dover, New Hampshire, where he lived with his wife and young son, born in the late 1980s.

By the start of the '90s some eighty of Staines's songs were available in published form in three books. The first to enter print was the 1977 *Movin' It Down the Line,* followed by the 1980 *If I Were a Word, Then I'd Be a Song,* and *All God's Critters Got a Place in the Choir* in 1989, *River,* and *Music to Me,* in 1993 and 1994.

In 1991 he was one of several contributors to the Alacazam Records release *A Child's Holiday.* Two years later he had his own new children's collection, *The Happy Wanderer,* in record stores, an album that also served as his debut on Red House Records. Besides "A Place in the Choir," it included such fine originals as "Four Little Sailors" and "This Song Is for the Birds." Though aimed at children, the collection was just as attractive to adults. The columnists and editors of *Pulse* magazine named the album both number one children's album and best folk release for 1993. In the children's list, the album was described as "Homey as a cross-stitch sampler, with classics and Staines originals for all ages."

In 1993 Bill's first Red House disc for adults was issued: *Going to the West.* Two years later the record company released his eighteenth album, *Looking for the Wind.* Aiding in expanding his audience in the mid-1990s was the growth of the Internet, through which entertainers can reach whole new audiences. Staines tried to adapt to the new situation, though he had strong reservations, as he told reporter David W. Johnson, who was preparing an article on the growth of folk music as a business ("Move Over, Woody, Make Room for My Manager," *Boston Globe,* May 7, 1996). "I really have mixed feelings about it," Staines said. "Aesthetically, it's almost like walking around without your clothes on. You can say something on stage and everybody in the world knows it. So as an artist, I feel very vulnerable." Besides that, he added, "I would hate to see folk music become nothing but marketing, because there is so much drivel out there. When it's marketed real well, it becomes mega-drivel."

Earlier, in talking to Steve Givens, he had emphasized that he had a very strict vision of what qualified as true folk music: "This is not to put anybody down, but I think there are two [acoustic] genres today. The people who are writing acoustic pop may be very talented writers, but I think that's what it is—acoustic pop. I consider myself a folkie because I think I know the roots of the music I write. Once again it goes back to that human spirit and being accessible to people. The 'pretty melodies' are the melodies that are memorable. They are the melodies that somebody will go away singing. That's why I consider myself a folkie."

As the 1990s progressed, Staines added to his diverse catalog. In 1994 he released *Alaska Suite,* a string and brass exploration of the largest state, on his Mineral River label. Rounder released his second retrospective album, *The First Million Miles Volume II,* including nineteen songs recorded between 1979 and 1990, in 1998. He also compiled another children's album, *One More River,* for Red House in 1998. The latter includes such traditional songs as "The Riddle Song," "Ash Grove," "Mr. Rabbit, Mr. Rabbit," and the classic children's song by Henry Clay Work, "My Grandfather's Clock." In 2000 Red House issued *October's Hill,* an adult collection.

STEELEYE SPAN: *Vocal and instrumental group from England. Original members (1969): Tim Hart, Maddy Prior, Ashley Hutchings, Gay Woods, Terry Woods. Gay and Terry Woods replaced in 1971 by Martin Carthy and Peter Knight. Hutchings and Carthy replaced in 1972 by Bob Johnson and Rick Kemp. Nigel Pegrum added in 1974. Group disbanded in late 1970s. Regrouped in 1980s with Prior, Knight, Johnson, Kemp, and Pegrum. John Kirkpatrick joined in 1977, left in 1978. Tim Harries and Liam Genockey joined in 1989. Gay Woods rejoined in 1995. Maddy Prior left in 1997.*

Over the lifetime of many rock bands, so many personnel changes take place you might quip you can't tell the players without a scorecard. This certainly was true for the excellent folk-rock group Steeleye Span during its first decade. Though the group's style changed with its shift in members and record producers, there was continuity provided by founding members Tim Hart and Maddy Prior—the only original performers to remain with the band throughout its first incarnation.

Like the other original members, Hart and Prior emerged from the British folk scene of the 1960s. As a duo, they were major draws on the folk-club circuit late in the decade before helping form Steeleye Span.

Guitarist–dulcimer player Hart actually started out as a rock adherent in the Beatles–Rolling Stones era. His first group experience came during his teens when he and some school friends started a rock band called the Ratfinks. But when he met a promising folk singer named Donovan at a St. Albans pub, he changed his musical goal.

He told a reporter from England's *Melody Maker* magazine in 1973: "I started singing folk at the Cock. I'd already started getting fed up with the group and

Don [Donovan] was a big influence on me. Together with records by people like Dylan, of course, and Jesse Fuller and Peter, Paul and Mary, which were flying about that time.

"We used to have great times at the Cock, although it wasn't a proper pub, just a bar where all the folk freaks used to gather, most of them underage. It's remarkable how many well-known singers got started there."

Among the talented performers who showed up there was clarion-voiced Maddy Prior, who soon found common musical ground with Hart. Prior had made her stage debut at eight with the Blackpool Opera. Her career didn't burgeon then or in her teens, though she continued to sing various kinds of pop music when she got the chance. She had some interest in early rock and the kinds of folk songs Joan Baez and July Collins recorded in the early 1960s, but didn't develop a particularly individual style at the time.

For some years, she was better known among folk artists as a rare female roadie rather than as a singer. For a while she chauffeured American folk duo Sandy and Jeanie Darlington around the United Kingdom, and later helped do concert setup chores for blind American blues singer Reverend Gary Davis.

But she desired to be onstage rather than behind it. Her chance finally came in the late 1960s through her association with then-boyfriend Tim Hart. Initially they performed songs drawn from American pop folk of the 1960s, but gradually they incorporated more and more upgraded versions of traditional British tunes such as "Maid That's Deep in Love" and "Prince Charlie Stuart." They recorded two albums of traditional material, *Folk Songs of Old England, Volumes I and II,* released in 1968 on Teepee Records.

While appearing at a folk festival at Loughborough University in 1969, Tim and Maddy got into conversation with another highly regarded musician, Ashley Hutchings. The son of a north London dance band leader who got the nickname "Tyger" from his aggressive play on the football field, Hutchings had just left Fairport Convention (after recording *Liege and Lief*) because he wanted to continue to focus on traditional music. He began searching for musicians who shared his outlook. He had started rehearsing a new band whose other members were drawn from the disbanded Irish folk act Sweeney's Men. The latter were Terry Woods (later of the Pogues) and his then-wife Gay, Johnny Moynihan, and Andy Irvine. Shortly before the festival, Moynihan and Irvine quit to form Planxty and Hutchings was looking for replacements. He asked Tim and Maddy to join and they agreed, provided that they still could continue fitting in their duo gigs.

The new quintet took its name from a Lincolnshire folk song, "Horkstow Grange," about an argument between two characters named John Bowlin and Steeleye Span. It was collected by Percy Grainger from George Gouldthorpe of Goxhill, North Lincolnshire, in 1905.

Martin Carthy suggested the name to Tim Hart. After rehearsing for some months, the band got a go-ahead to record a debut album. That collection, *Hark! The Village Wait* (RCA, 1970), came out in England only. The group had hardly finished the project when Gay and Terry Woods left. In fact, the first version of Steeleye Span never did make any public appearances.

The band regrouped by adding harsh-voiced veteran English folksinger and instrumentalist Martin Carthy and fiddler Peter Knight. Knight, whose eventual tenure with the band was second only to Maddy's, came from a musical family. His father, a dance band member who played guitar and mandolin, taught the latter instrument to Peter when the boy was eight. Initially grounded in the classics, he was accepted in the Royal Academy of Music in his teens, but left because he saw little chance for a rewarding career.

Instead, he got a job selling musical instruments, which inspired him to make his own collection. He spent some of his spare time listening to folk artists at local clubs, but didn't consider a folk career until a friend played him a record by Irish fiddler Michael Coleman. "I thought that if I could achieve anything like that sort of lilt and could understand the feel of the music, then that was what I wanted. [I began] listening to people like Coleman and Bobby Casey and Jimmy Power as well as a lot of flute players. That was my first introduction to any form of folk music, but at that time it wasn't specifically English folk music that I liked."

He and guitarist Bob Johnson began to appear in folk clubs. The money from music was minimal, but Knight loved performing. He quit his job and gained living expenses by selling instruments from his collection. In 1971 he told *Melody Maker:* "I'd been going a year without work when 'Tyger' Hutchings phoned me up one day and asked me to join Steeleye. Apparently Martin Carthy had been to see some gigs that Bob and I had done, but whether that had anything to do with it or not I don't know. I'd also done a BBC gig with Maddy. I was shocked to find out how many professional musicians knew me just on the strength of those gigs I'd done with Bob."

In 1971 the new band put out two albums: *Please to See the King* (on Big Tree in the United States) and *Ten Man Mop or Mr. Reservoir Butler Rides Again* (issued in England only on Pegasus). Tracks by Steeleye also were included in a Charisma sampler titled *Individually and Collectively.* Those releases and audience reaction to a number of concerts by the new group brought attention not only in Europe, but also in the United States. The band, which had no drummer for several years, used bass guitar or percussion instruments to provide a strong rhythm base.

Though the future looked promising, there were disagreements about direction and Hutchings left, complaining that the band focused too much on Irish rather than British folk tradition. Carthy also decided the format was too constraining and took leave. (He and Hutchings then played in the Albion Country Band. Carthy later put out such fascinating solo traditional folk LPs as *Crown of Horn* and *Because It's There,* released in the United States on Rounder.) Their places were taken by Knight's former partner, Bob Johnson, and bass guitarist Rick Kemp (who eventually married Prior). Both had extensive experience as session musicians and rock bandsmen.

Johnson originally liked the trumpet, but when he asked for one at thirteen, his father said it was too noisy an instrument, so Bob began learning harmonica. He told *Melody Maker:* "I passed a second-hand shop and I saw a battered guitar in the window. It was totally unplayable, of course, but it was my fourteenth birthday, so I got it. I just loved the feel of it round my neck, standing in front of the TV when '65 Special' was on and miming. I really had delusions of grandeur. I really wanted to be a pop star."

In the next few years he got a decent guitar and learned to play well enough to join a band in the town of Tooting named Earl Sheridan and the Houseshakers. After Earl left, the band continued on as the Pack. Afterward, Johnson said: "We got picked up by this singer called Paul Raven, who is now known as Gary Glitter, and we backed him as Paul Raven and the Pack for about two years, but we never made any money."

Discouraged, Johnson took a regular job for a while, but Raven's brother helped him get session work as part of the house band at Immediate Records. He was asked to join a folk-oriented band, Thane Russell, which piqued his interest in traditional music. He liked the songs' content, but felt they could use more of a current feel. "Then I started working with Peter and what was nice about that was he had this classical feel and I had all these pop influences. Then [Fairport Convention] and Steeleye happened and I was really jealous because this was what I'd thought of many years before."

Naturally, he jumped at the chance to join Steeleye. Once aboard, he imparted more electric instrumentation to the band's arrangements.

Kemp's introduction to pop music went back to the skiffle period in England. At 12 his group won the all-England skiffle contest at a club called the Cafe de Paris. He told *Melody Maker:* "Larry Parnes offered me a contract, but I was only 13 and my old man wouldn't hear of it. He thought I was going to be an airline pilot or a brain surgeon or something."

He continued to play guitar in his later teens when his family moved to Hull. There, he got his first professional job with a group called the Aces as bass guitarist. "After a while I really fell in love with the bass because I was at the bottom of it all instead of being out in front and that appealed to me."

After that band broke up, he got a job in a music store, where he was befriended by songwriter–band organizer Mike Chapman. He did some backup on two of

Chapman's albums and then toured the United States with him. Back in England, Kemp did more session work, where he met the producer of early Steeleye recordings, Sandy Roberton. When Hutchings left, Roberton brought Kemp into the band.

The first two albums with the new roster, *Below the Salt* (1972) and *Parcel of Rogues* (1973) on Chrysalis Records, were thought by some to have added too much electric influence. The albums, however, still were impressive for unusual material (such as the a cappella Latin hymn "Gaudete" and numerous tales of bewitchings, human transfigurations, and struggles for eighteenth-century pretender to the British throne Bonnie Prince Charlie Stuart) and Maddy Prior's bell-like soprano on tracks such as "One Misty Moisty Morning" on *Parcel of Rogues*. The band by then had a healthy, if not massive, following in the United States, which enthusiastically performed an in place dance called jigging to Steeleye Span music in rock clubs across the country. Also unique to Steeleye's live shows was a recreation of a medieval mummers play.

For the 1974 Chrysalis release, *Now We Are Six,* the group finally added a drummer—Nigel Pegrum, who also played the flute. With this sixth member, Steeleye also had shaken down to a stable grouping (and had a new manager, Jo Lustig). *Now We Are Six,* whose title came from an A.A. Milne book, was the group's sixth studio recording. It was produced by Ian Anderson of Jethro Tull. This sextet turned out what some consider the band's best trio of albums: *Now We Are Six* and, in 1975, *Commoners Crown* and *All Around My Hat,* the latter, produced by Mike Batt, the group's most commercially successful album. Some novel additions were a saxophone solo by David Bowie on the hardly folk Phil Spector composition "To Know Him Is to Love Him" on *Now We Are Six* and Peter Sellers's ukulele playing on *Commoners Crown's* "New York Girls."

Though the group continued to concertize and record new material after the mid-1970s, the quality didn't match the previous releases. After the Chrysalis album *Rocket Cottage* (1976), Peter Knight and Bob Johnson left to make an album called *The King of Elfland's Daughter,* released on Chrysalis in 1977. Without those two key players, the group was cast adrift. They enlisted Martin Carthy, who returned to the group accompanied by his friend John Kirkpatrick on accordion. The group of Carthy, Hart, Pegrum, Kirkpatrick, Prior, and Kemp released two albums, *Storm Force Ten* (1977) and *Live at Last* (1978), recorded during the band's farewell tour. In 1977, Chrysalis issued a two-disc retrospective, *The Steeleye Span Story—Original Masters.*

In 1978 Steeleye disbanded. Prior tried for a solo career, releasing her contemporary LPs *Woman in the Wings* and *Changing Winds* (both in 1978), as well as the Maddy Prior Band's *Hooked on Winning* (1981). Tim Hart recorded a solo album in 1979 for Chrysalis.

Carthy and Kirkpatrick returned to traditional folk music in Brass Monkey and the Albion Country Band. Shanachie licensed most of Steeleye's albums for reissue in the United States, along with Prior and Hart's sterling 1971 *Summer Solstice* and Prior and June Tabor's rich (and hardly silly) 1976 *Silly Sisters* duets. (Tabor and Prior reunited in 1988 for a second Silly Sisters album, *No More to the Dance,* on Topic.)

After a two-year hiatus, in 1980 the group of Kemp, Johnson, Knight, Hart, Prior, and Pegrum reunited for their last studio album for Chrysalis, *Sails of Silver.* Produced by Gus Dudgeon, who had worked with Elton John, the album includes only one traditional song. It would be the last featuring the six core members of Steeleye Span. In 1981 the act reassembled informally for a few dates. At the end of a tour in 1982, Hart decided to leave the group to spend more time with his family. He recorded two children's albums for Music for Pleasure, *My Very Favourite Nursery Rhyme Record* in 1981, and *Drunken Sailor and Other Kid's Songs* in 1983. Prior, Knight, Kemp, Johnson, and Pegrum regrouped in 1983. (Hart by then had gone into music management and eventually headed off to the Canary Islands.)

The group (minus Hart) reunited in 1986 to record the LP *Back in Line,* released on the group's Flutterby label in 1986 and licensed to Shanachie in the United States. It was not one of their better albums, and mostly featured their own compositions rather than traditional fare. Shortly after that album, Kemp left the band due in part to a repetitive stress injury he suffered in his shoulder from years of playing the bass. After several attempts to replace Kemp, the band brought in bassist Tim Harries. In 1989 the group of Prior, Harries, Pegrum, Knight, Johnson, and Martin Ditchum put together a new studio album, *Tempted and Tried,* for Dover.

Nigel Pegrum then left the band and moved to Australia. He was replaced by Irish drummer Liam Genockey, who played on the band's Twentieth Anniversary Celebration tour in September 1989. The new ensemble went on a tour in 1991 from which *Tonight's the Night—Live,* released by Shanachie in 1992, is taken. The following year, Prior had trouble with her voice, and the band called on Gay Woods, one of the founding members, to help out. (In the meantime, Park Records released *Steeleye Span in Concert,* a retrospective live album taken from a tour in 1986 and one in 1994.)

The band continued to retain a place in the affections of many English folk and folk-rock fans, new and old, as shown by the enthusiastic reception given Steeleye's twenty-fifth anniversary concert at the Forum in London in September 1995. Almost all the musicians who had performed under the Steeleye banner over those years took part, including second-generation performers like Martin Carthy's daughter, Eliza, who played several numbers with the Kings of Calicutt ensemble she had formed with Nancy Kerr. Some alumni, like John Kirkpatrick and Ashley Hutchings, gave samples of the material used in their groups like Home Service and Albion.

The main part of the four-hour show included sets by all of the main band combinations over its history, starting with original members Prior, Hart, Hutchings, and Gay Woods. Only Terry Woods from the founding makeup was absent, and his part was taken by Kirkpatrick. Also contributing on banjo was Martin Carthy, and Michael Gregory added drum support. This was followed by the second version of the band from the early '70s, including a stunning performance of "Lark in the Morning" featuring Knight, Carthy, and Hutchings. Later Carthy, Kirkpatrick, Rick Kemp, and Nigel Pegrum combined on late-'70s material like "The Maid and the Palmer." The program closed with the 1990s band alignment, whose roster once more included founding member Gay Woods. Its renditions included a rousing version of "Thomas the Rhymer."

To celebrate the band Chrysalis released *Spanning the Years* in 1995, a comprehensive retrospective. The compilation includes extensive liner notes by Maddy Prior about the history of the band. Numerous Steeleye compilations and reissues have been released. In 1996 the group released its first studio album in seven years, *Time*. Gay Woods joined Prior, Bob Johnson on guitar, Peter Knight on fiddle, Liam Genockey on drums, and Tim Harries on bass.

In 1997 Maddy Prior left the band, as did Genockey. Gay Woods took over the lead vocals and Dave Mattacks on the drums on *Horkstow Grange,* a new studio album released in 1998 by Park Records. The title track is the traditional Lincolnshire folk song that gave rise to the band's name in 1969.

Prior has continued to put out solo albums, including *Going for Glory* (1983) on Spindrift, and on Park Records *Happy Families* (with Rick Kemp in 1990), *Year* (1993), *Memento: The Best of Maddy Prior* (1995), *Flesh and Blood* (1997) and *Ravenchild* (2000). She has also recorded several albums with the Carnival Band (which focuses on medieval and Renaissance music): *A Tapestry of Carols* (1986) and *Sing Lustily and with Good Courage* (1990) on Saydisc; and *Carols and Capers* (1991), *Hang Up Sorrow and Care* (1995), and *Carols at Christmas* (1998) on Park. Her husband, Rick Kemp, has released *Escape* (1996) and *Spies* (1998), both on Fellside. In 1998 Prior went on an extensive tour of North America with Kathryn Tickell, who plays the Northumbrian pipes and fiddle.

STEWART, JOHN: *Singer, songwriter, guitarist. Born San Diego, California, September 5, 1939.*

One of the outstanding singer-songwriters to emerge from the folk boom of the early '60s, John

Stewart has long earned critical praise for his distinctive songwriting style. While his recordings have variously been found in the folk, country, pop, and rock racks, his roots are set firmly in the folk tradition. At certain points in his career, Stewart has seen heights of commercial success unattained by nearly any other folk artist—as a member of the Kingston Trio, then as a solo act, and also as the writer of hits for other artists. Yet, ironically, just before his greatest chart success as a solo artist, it took a letter-writing campaign by his fans to help win him a record deal. Today, having established his own label, Stewart continues to record and perform throughout the United States and Europe and to add to his reputation as a fine songwriter with an original artistic vision.

Stewart, whose father was a racehorse trainer, was born in San Diego, California, and grew up in that state. As a teenager in the mid-1950s, he was influenced by Elvis and the other rock pioneers. After learning to play guitar, he formed his own rock band in high school. The band, called John Stewart and the Furies, played small clubs in the Southern California area and recorded a single called "Rocking Anna" that came out on Vita Records. After finishing high school, John entered Mount San Antonio Junior College in Walnut, California, leaning toward music, but not sure whether he could make a living at it.

By then the folk-music explosion was under way, and John found his calling. As he noted, "The lyrics were adventurous, you could play the songs with a guitar, and they were easy to sing." John not only worked up versions of traditional folk songs but also began writing new ones. In 1959, after attending a Kingston Trio concert, he managed to get backstage to talk to the group that was becoming one of the favorites of the mass audience of the late 1950s. The meeting led to the group's adopting some of Stewart's material for their repertoire. "They said, 'Sign right here.' It was that easy. They recorded 'Molly Dee' and 'Green Grasses.' Then their manager told me that Roulette Records wanted a folk group, so I formed one. We rehearsed on the airplane to New York."

The group named itself the Cumberland Three. During its two-year span, the trio recorded three albums, none of which made much impact on the market. Besides that, it found a respectable amount of concert work on the folk-club coffeehouse circuit. Meanwhile, Stewart kept in close contact with the Kingston Trio, helping with arrangements and supplying new songs from time to time. When charter member Dave Guard tired of the grind and decided to leave in 1961, Stewart was the natural choice to replace him.

The Trio was still riding high with concert goers and record buyers, and the momentum continued after Stewart joined. During his years with the group, John was able to place a sizable number of awards in his collection, including gold records for the LPs *String Along* (1962) and *The Best of the Kingston Trio* (1964). He also contributed to a number of top 10 singles, such as "Greenback Dollar," "Where Have All the Flowers Gone," and "The Reverend Mr. Black."

By 1966, though, the glory years of the group were behind it. The resurgent rock movement of the mid-1960s drastically cut into the following for folk groups, and it was finally decided to disband (though new incarnations sprang up in later years). John's last work with the Trio appeared in the 1967 Capitol release *Farewell Album*. After that, he set his cap for a solo career. He told an interviewer he was happy for that development: "I was bored. It was a very formal group, so we were limited in what we could do."

When the spotlight dimmed for folk music in the mid-1960s, many artists accepted the fact and adjusted to playing before small audiences and recording for specialty labels. Stewart rebelled against taking such a role. He was determined to develop broad interest in his material. Yet the road to individual stardom proved a rougher one than he expected. For a decade, though he had a following on the folk circuit and turned out many excellent albums, it seemed a lost cause.

In the mid- and late 1960s, he achieved better results as a songwriter than as a performer. A number of his compositions were chartmakers for other artists, including the Monkees with "Daydream Believer," the Lovin' Spoonful with "Never Going Back to Nashville," and several artists with "July, You're a Woman." Stewart signed with the Trio's old label, Capitol, and completed such superb LPs as *California Bloodlines* and *Willard* in the early 1970s.

Those albums included splendid songs of romance and wanderlust, but the selections on *California Bloodlines* and *Willard* that cemented Stewart's reputation as a songwriter were thoughtful, challenging explorations of America's political and social direction, often set against a wistful recollection of the America of yesteryear. A number of those songs grew from Stewart's personal involvement with Bobby Kennedy's presidential campaign. But while the LPs received near-unanimous critical acclaim (*Rolling Stone* once listed *California Bloodlines* among the 200 best albums of all time), they were all but ignored by the public at large.

Stewart switched to Warner Brothers Records in the early 1970s, and such LPs as *Lonesome Picker Rides Again* and *Sunstorm* were issued, again with disappointing sales results despite the excellence of Stewart's songwriting and performing. John still received a warm welcome from folk diehards on college campuses and in small folk clubs around the country, but without commercial record breakthroughs. Still searching for the right combination, he signed with RCA, which issued several albums in the mid-1970s: *Cannons in the Rain*, a rousing 1974 live album titled *The Phoenix*

Concerts, and *Wingless Angels*. Each of those albums showcased Stewart's incisive songwriting talent and distinctive vocal abilities. Yet, once more, the commercial reaction was less than monumental.

As the late 1970s came into view, the outlook appeared increasingly dismal for Stewart. He had no recording contract and his income from concert work was marginal. As he played for small, admiring crowds on the folk circuit, he asked his listeners to help him by writing record companies he was approaching to give him another opportunity. Whether that resulted in a flood of letters is hard to say, but he finally did complete an agreement with RSO Records, then riding high on the disco hits of the Bee Gees.

His first album for RSO, *Fire in the Wind*, came out in 1978. Receiving more promotion than most of his previous solo albums, it didn't threaten any of the best-selling LPs of the year, but made a respectable showing with record buyers. But then, finally, Stewart's perseverance paid off with major commercial success. In 1979, RSO released *Bombs Away Dream Babies* (a title that came from Stewart's close friend, Dave Guard). Helping out were two backing artists who felt Stewart was a major talent too long ignored, Lindsey Buckingham and Stevie Nicks of Fleetwood Mac. There was more of a rock tone to the tracks than in Stewart's previous work, something that didn't escape the notice of folk-music critics. However, the mixture proved to be what was needed to attract attention both from John's staunch folk supporters and new groups of fans.

The single "Gold" from the collection received airplay across the United States in the summer of 1979. The song gave voice to John's longstanding frustration with his lot in pop music (*There's people out there turning music into gold*). The single lived up to its name, reaching the top 5 nationally and helping make the album a chart success. The other songs issued as singles from the LP, "Midnight Wind" and "Lost Her in the Sun," also did very well.

In early 1980 Stewart's third LP on RSO, *Dream Babies Go Hollywood*, came out. Among those supporting him this time were Phil Everly, Linda Ronstadt, and Nicolette Larson. *Dream Babies Go Hollywood* failed to match the huge commercial success of *Bombs Away Dream Babies*, and Stewart eventually parted company with the RSO label. But rather than mount the same kind of effort that resulted in his RSO signing, Stewart elected to start his own label, Homecoming Records, to release his recordings as well as those of other artists.

Although Stewart has not since matched his commercial success of the late '70s, he maintains a devoted following that appreciates his well-crafted work, and has continued touring widely and releasing well-received solo recordings (by now totaling over thirty). His Homecoming releases include *Centennial* (1984) (an instrumental album, re-released as *American Sketches* in 1991 on Laserlight, which was played for a year at the National Archives in Washington, D.C., during a photo exhibit on the American West), *Neon Beach* (1990), *Deep in the Neon* (1991), and *Escape to Arizona* (1993).

In addition to his Homecoming releases, Stewart has also recorded albums for other labels in recent years, including *Punch the Big Guy* (1987) on A&M, *Blondes* (1983) on Allegiance, *Trancas* (1984) on Affordable Dreams, and *Bullets in the Hourglass* (1992) on Shanachie. In 1992, Capitol Records released *John Stewart/ American Originals,* a CD compilation of tracks from *California Bloodlines* and *Willard,* along with a number of songs from Stewart's solo and Kingston Trio years. His 1995 Shanachie collection, *Airdream Believer,* featured reworked versions of some of his best-known songs in addition to new material. He was joined on the CD by such notable artists and admirers as Nanci Griffith, Johnny Cash, Rosanne Cash, and the current version of the Kingston Trio. He followed with *Teresa & the Lost Songs* (Homecoming, '98), and *Darwin's Army* (Appleseed, '99).

Stewart has also continued to find success through covers of his work by other artists. The Monkees' version of "Daydream Believer" remains a staple on radio airwaves (having received over 2 million airplays), and Anne Murray's version sold 2 million copies in 1980. The song was also covered in 1993 by an Irish band, Boyzone. In 1989, Rosanne Cash charted a number-one country hit with Stewart's composition "Runaway Train." Other artists continue to cover his catalog, including Nanci Griffith, Joan Baez (who recorded Stewart's "Strange Rivers" in 1993), and the Beat Farmers.

Stewart has expanded his creative interests in other directions as well. He has been an artist in residence at Pennsylvania State University, which has initiated the John Stewart Library of American Folk Music. He has also written four books, including one on songwriting. Additionally, his paintings and photographs have been featured in gallery shows across the country.

Contributed by Richard Waldow

STRACKE, WIN: *Singer, guitarist. Born Lorraine, Kansas, February 20, 1908. Died Evanston, Illinois, June 29, 1991.*

One of the most popular folk acts on college campuses and in folk concerts of the late 1940s and early '50s was "I Come for to Sing." The group featured the almost legendary name of Big Bill Broonzy. However, even Broonzy's great talents failed to overshadow the bass renditions of midwestern singer Win Stracke.

Win was born in a small town in Kansas. Within a short time, however, his German-born father, Robert Stracke, a minister, was called to a new pulpit in Chicago, the second German Baptist Church. Win thus grew up amid the sights and sounds of the bustling Second City. His parents sang many songs, of both classical and folk origin, from their native Germany. Win learned some of the folk songs but was even more impressed with the heritage of Bach, Beethoven, Handel, and Brahms. In high school he was a member of a well-known Chicago a cappella choir. Before attending college, Win held a series of jobs. He worked as a suit salesman, police officer, gas station attendant, coal miner, oilfield worker, ship's engine room attendant, and fruit picker. As a result he gained sympathy for the labor unions. He kept up his interest in music during his years at Lake Forest College, near Chicago, from 1929 to 1931.

When he left college he sang with a number of symphony orchestras in the Midwest as a soloist and as part of oratorios. With the advent of radio, he sang on a number of classical programs on various stations. In the early 1930s, he was signed as a soloist for the program *Hymns of All Churches,* which was broadcast over a good many stations across the United States and featured Win for eight years. During the decade he was a regular on such Chicago radio shows as *National Barn Dance, Alec Templeton Time,* and *The Chicago Theater of the Air.* He also sang with the University of Chicago opera and in 1937 joined the Chicago Repertory Group.

In his spare time, he still enjoyed singing folk songs, both the old German songs of his youth and American ballads. He numbered many folk artists among his friends in the 1930s, including Burl Ives and Carl Sandburg. They suggested that he had a flair for folk music and should consider giving folk concerts.

His career as a classical singer was interrupted by World War II. He joined the army and spent four years in an antiaircraft battery in many of the battle areas of North Africa and Europe. During these years, he often entertained his fellow soldiers with folk songs. He also learned much about folk music from them, including more about how to play the guitar. After his discharge he entered the American Conservatory of Music for three years. At the same time, he began to focus more on folk music, adding to his repertoire by studying folk-music books, listening to records, and collecting from other artists.

By 1947 he had a growing reputation as a folk artist. The following year, with Broonzy, Lawrence Lane, and Studs Terkel, he helped form "I Come for to Sing." The first performances of this panorama of American folk music were sponsored by the Renaissance Society of the University of Chicago.

The group continued to tour nationally until the early '50s. In mid-1952, Stracke was featured on an NBC program, *America's Music.* The show struck pay dirt with audiences and developed into a series called the *Meaning of America.* Besides appearing on this show for several years, Stracke sang on many TV shows throughout the 1950s, including *Studs' Place* with his friend Studs Terkel, the daytime serial *Hawkins Falls,* and *The Garroway Show.* He eventually had his own children's shows including *Animal Playtime* and *Time for Uncle Win.* He also worked up a program called "A Minstrel's History of the U.S.A." for concerts in many parts of the country. But Stracke was blacklisted during the McCarthy era and his TV career was cut short.

Many of his favorite songs were included in his 1957 LP *Americana.* Some of these were "Venezuela," "Acres of Clams," "Single Girl," "Big Rock Candy Mountain," "Wanderin'," "Paul Bunyan's Manistee," and "Cold Water vs. Rye Whisky." Later in 1957, Stracke started a school for folk-song study called the Old Town School of Folk Music. It became a folk music and cultural center in Chicago and a place where people like Steve Goodman, Roger McGuinn, Bonnie Koloc, and John Prine got their start. In 1963 Stracke founded the Old Town Folklore Center.

Another Stracke LP was issued by Golden Records in 1958. Called *Golden Treasury of Songs America Sings,* it included such numbers as "Shenandoah," "Black-Eyed Susie," "Old Dan Tucker," "John Henry," "The Erie Canal," "Buffalo Gals," "Aunt Rhody," "Elanoy," "Rio Grande," "Hush Little Baby," "Boll Weevil," "Poor Lonesome Cowboy," "Leather Winged Bat," "Cindy," and "One More Day." Stracke became involved with an informal folk-music group called the Golden Ring, which got together for the joy of making music. The group, which included George and Gerry Armstrong, Ed Trickett, and Howie Mitchell, recorded several albums released on the Folk-Legacy label, including *Golden Ring, New Golden Ring: Five Days of Singing, Volumes 1 and 2,* and *For All the Good People: A Golden Ring Reunion.*

In the 1960s Stracke devoted much of his time to his Old Town School. The school celebrated its first decade with a well-established curriculum and faculty and with a growing number of respected alumni. Many major artists visited the school and gave concerts under Stracke's aegis, including Jimmy Driftwood, Pete Seeger, and Doc Watson.

In 1965 Stracke coauthored *Songs of Man* with Norman Luboff. They also composed a musical cantata called "Freedom Country" in 1967. The following year, Stracke was Illinois's unofficial Voice of the Sesquicentennial, traveling and performing throughout the state to celebrate the state's 150th birthday.

In 1991 he died of natural causes in his apartment in the North Shore Hotel in Evanston. He was eighty-three. He remained friends with Studs Terkel throughout his life. "Win, to me, is my oldest friend," Terkel told Laurie Goering of the *Chicago Tribune* ("Folk Music Dean Win Stracke," June 30, 1991). "He was a big man in more ways than one. When his bass voice was heard at a peace rally or a labor rally during a strike, you knew it was going to be OK."

TABOR, JUNE: *Singer. Born Warwick, England, December 31, 1947.*

When June Tabor takes the stage, as she did at McCabe's Guitar Shop in Santa Monica in February 1996, she does so with a solemn grace. Whether singing a cappella or backed by her accompanists, Huw Warren on piano and Mark Emerson on violin, it's hard to separate the singer from the song. When she sings a "love gone wrong" song, it's as if she herself had been wronged. When she sings a traditional murder ballad, it's as if she had observed the crime. Tabor, who is content to interpret songs rather than write them, takes her job seriously. "One of the main functions of music for me is it requires the entire mind," she said in a phone interview. "You have to concentrate, you have to listen, it's not wallpaper. If music, and song particularly, moves you, you don't have to feel embarrassed by it. You should let the music take you where it wants you to go. If that means you cry, that's fine; if it means you laugh, that's good too. If it makes you think, that's probably the most important thing of all. But it is a total experience, and not for the fainthearted or the feeble-minded."

Tabor has one of the best instruments in the business: a deep and expressive alto voice that could have served her well in the cabarets of pre–World War II Berlin. She is a favorite of Elvis Costello. "If you can't appreciate June Tabor, you should just stop listening to music," he has said. *Folk Roots* magazine readers voted Tabor Vocalist of the Year so many times that they retired the category. Her 1992 album, *Angel Tiger,* was named Celtic Album of the Year by *Pulse!* magazine. *Rolling Stone* has called her "one of the classiest, boldest and most respected singers in Great Britain."

She chooses her material from such diverse songwriters as Eric Bogle ("No Man's Land"), Si Kahn ("Aragon Mill"), Ralph McTell ("Bentley and Craig"), Bob Franke ("Hard Love"), poet Les Barker, and Richard Thompson. The remarkable thing about Tabor is that she never had any voice training. She didn't sing in a glee club or high school choir. She was completely self-taught: "Listen, copy, imitate, try it out, and then leave most of it out," she says.

Her father worked as a manager for a clutch manufacturer; her mother was a housewife. "Singing really was a natural form of expression," she says. "My parents would sing around the house. Anything: songs of the day, standards, anything they felt like. So I did as well. That was just purely for fun. No formal musical training ever."

June listened to the radio as a child. When she was

sixteen, she went to a local folk club and was "volunteered" one day to sing "Michael Row Your Boat Ashore" and "Kumbaya." "Those were the only folk songs I knew," she recalls.

She soon heard recordings of folksingers Anne Briggs and Gypsy singer Belle Stewart and began to emulate their styles. As a student at Oxford in the mid-1960s, she came in touch with several members of the British folk-music revival and began to develop her own distinctive smoky, evocative, and controlled singing style. "June Tabor has the best natural instrument in the universe," says British guitarist Martin Simpson, who toured with her for a decade.

She got a degree from Oxford in modern and medieval languages, specializing in French and Latin. After that she went to school to become a librarian, working in the English public library system for a number of years. It was this experience, she says, that helped develop her love of words.

"The singing thing just came very gradually," she says. "I went to folk clubs. Then I went to a number of festivals. That way you get to know people from other parts of the country and they get to know you. I was just doing the open mike spots. Eventually in December 1968 I was asked to actually perform for money for the first time."

She got paid eight pounds plus expenses to perform in Kingston-on-Thames. "It was a lot of money then. All a cappella," she recalls.

Indeed, she is one of the few singers who can get away with singing unaccompanied. She met Steeleye Span's Maddy Prior through the folk club circuit, and they began singing together for fun. They did a few gigs a cappella. Chrysalis Records asked Prior if she wanted to make a separate project and she suggested a duet album with Tabor. June didn't start singing with other musicians until she recorded *Silly Sisters* with Maddy Prior in 1975 (Chrysalis, 1976). They sing beautiful harmony on some tracks and are accompanied by some of Britain and Ireland's best musicians—Martin Carthy, Nic Jones, Andy Irvine, Johnny Moynihan. "That was the first time I'd sung with any form of accompaniment," Tabor says. "It was doing that album led me to ask Nic Jones to be the guitarist to be on my first solo album."

Tabor released *Airs and Graces* on Topic in 1976 and began touring with Nic Jones. The following year, Tabor released her second solo album, *Ashes and Diamonds*, on Topic.

Jones couldn't tour to support *Ashes and Diamonds,* and so in 1977 Tabor asked Simpson if he would tour with her. "My producer and best friend said, 'I've seen this cracking new young guitarist called Martin Simpson. He's really good. Why don't you ask him?' That's how Martin and I got together."

"I loved working with June," Simpson recalls. "It's always been totally expansive to me. I love to accompany; I love songs. That's what I do. She'd come to me with these great traditional songs, or sometimes contemporary songs. We'd build stuff from the ground up. It was always exciting."

Tabor and Simpson collaborated on a classic album of traditional and contemporary songs, *A Cut Above,* on Topic in 1980. The cover shows Tabor (wearing thigh-high suede boots) and Simpson standing on a bridge over the Thames with the London skyline in the background. It includes backup work by Ric Saunders on violin, Dave Bristow on piano and synthesizer, and Jon Davie on bass.

She followed in 1983 with *Abyssinians* on Topic and *The Peel Sessions* in 1986 on Strange Fruit (a live a cappella session recorded in 1977 for the English radio presenter John Peel), and *Aqaba* on Topic in 1988. She again teamed up with Silly Sister Maddy Prior in 1988 to record *No More to the Dance* on Topic. And then she released another solo album, *Some Other Time,* in 1989 on U.S.-based Rykodisc/Hannibal. That album was a collection of jazz standards, including "Round Midnight."

Music was still just a sideline for Tabor. After her library work, she started a restaurant with her then-husband in the Lake District called Passepartout, named after the man servant in Jules Verne's *Around the World in 80 Days.* Her husband was the chef, and she "did starters and puddings, front of house, did the books, ordered the wine, served the wine, walked the dogs. You name it. I did pretty much everything else."

When she and her husband got divorced, she was forty years old and she turned to music full-time. "I'd done a few things and it seemed like the right decision. I'd gotten old and awkward enough to think perhaps I can do it on my own terms," she says. "I thought, 'What shall I do now? Maybe I'll just start singing full-time.' "

The divorce was a watershed for Tabor. "Previously, however committed I felt to music, a lot of the energy had always gone into my other career," she says. "Particularly running a restaurant, as anyone will tell you, takes all your energy and then some. When I did decide to turn to music all that energy that had been doing something else went, 'Hey, okay, let's try all these things.' Hence the various project albums and collaborations with different people. I've been doing it ever since."

In 1990 she broke away from her traditional and contemporary act to record with the British folk-rock group the Oyster Band. Cooking Vinyl released *Freedom and Rain,* and she toured extensively with the band in support of the album. (They also released a promotional tour sampler, which came from a live radio show.) The album received a strong review in *People Weekly*—"She gives the Oysters an emotional depth that they lacked on three previous albums," wrote reviewer Michael Small (November 26, 1990). Steve

Pond wrote in *Rolling Stone* (May 2, 1991) about a concert at McCabe's: "Tabor's solo records are austere, decorous works that set the warmth of her voice against sparse, chilly and minimalist arrangements, and the fiery backing of the Oysters pushed her to become more aggressive and spirited."

Tabor was recognized as one of the most talented singers in the United Kingdom. Conifer Request released a compilation of her work titled *Aspects,* which scored high marks with critics. In 1993 Music Club released *Anthology,* another retrospective.

She has participated in several collections, including *Hard Cash,* released in 1990 by Special Delivery, and *Beat the Retreat,* the 1994 Richard Thompson tribute album, released on Capitol Records. For the latter, she sings two songs, the title track and an a cappella version of "Genesis Hall." Rounder Records included Tabor on its 1997 release *Divine Divas: A World of Women's Voices,* for which she sings "Sudden Waves," a Ronald Jamieson–Les Barker song. Other "divas" include Cassandra Wilson, Ani DiFranco, and Alison Krauss.

She continued to gain acclaim with her solo releases. In 1992 she released *Angel Tiger* on Cooking Vinyl (Green Linnet in the United States) to strong reviews. The album includes the songs "Hard Love" by Bob Franke and the above-mentioned "Sudden Waves," and songs by Billy Bragg and Richard Thompson. Elvis Costello wrote the song "All This Useless Beauty" for Tabor, the title track for a 1996 album by Costello. He also wrote a song, "I Want to Vanish," that Tabor recorded for her 1994 Cooking Vinyl CD, *Against the Streams.* On the latter album, producer John Ravenhall notes that Tabor decided to forgo studio technology and chose to record each song as a "live performance. . . . All the vocals on this album are therefore *true* performances, underlining her unique talent as a presenter and interpreter of songs. A rare gift, indeed."

She sang on an album by harpist Savourna Stevenson called *Singing the Storm,* with backing by bassist Danny Thompson. The album was released in 1996 by Cooking Vinyl. *Aleyn,* a solo album in the true sense of the word (the title means "alone" in Yiddish), came out in 1997. The album follows the theme of isolation, whether she's singing Richard Thompson's "The Great Valerio"; Ralph McTell's murder ballad "Bentley and Craig"; "Shallow Brown," a West Indian shanty about a slave sold away from his loved one; or "Di Nakht," a Yiddish song about a lonely emigrant. The album was recorded live at four different venues in England and later remixed, and was released in 1997 by Topic (Green Linnet for the United States market). It was produced by John Ravenhall and features Huw Warren on piano, Mark Emerson on violin and viola, and Andy Cutting on accordion.

In October 1998 Strange Fruit released another collection from her radio show appearances called *On Air.*

In March 1999 she returned to the studio to record *A Quiet Eye* for Topic, with accompanists Warren, Emerson, and sax player Mark Lockheart, and the brass and woodwinds ensemble the Creative Jazz Orchestra.

Tabor now lives in the border country between England and Wales, where she keeps three dogs and two cats. She has no hesitation when asked about her musical goals: "Words first. What I do is to sing songs that tell good stories. It doesn't matter where they come from. It doesn't matter what musical background they come from. It can be traditional, it can be modern. It can be from the jazz repertoire, it can be a standard, anything if it tells a good story. That's usually done with the kind of accompaniment that underscores the strength of the words rather than obscuring them. A minimalist approach."

Based on a phone interview with June Tabor by Lyndon Stambler in January 1999

TAJ MAHAL: *Singer, guitarist, pianist, harmonica player, bassist, vibraphonist, mandolinist, dulcimer player, songwriter. Born New York, New York, May 17, 1942.*

From the mid-1960s to the early 1970s, if you wanted to find Taj Mahal, most of the time all you had to do was go down to the Ash Grove folk club on Melrose Avenue in Los Angeles. He was almost always there, teaching classes in mouth harp or folk blues during the day, watching folk and blues artists or taking part in occasional jams at night. He had a growing reputation among his peers for his musicianship and writing ability, but it took a while until he had more than a folk following. In time, though, he gained his due as an interpreter of American folk, rock, and blues material and as one of the first U.S. artists to focus attention on African roots. In the 1980s he moved to Hawaii, but he remained a familiar figure on the pop and blues scene, taking part in varied projects throughout the '80s and '90s, including touring the United States with folk and rock stars, and, in the early '90s, writing the music to lyrics by Langston Hughes and Zora Neal Hurston for the Broadway show *Mule Bone.*

Taj was born in New York City. His father, Henry St. Claire Fredericks, grew up in Brooklyn and was a respected jazz arranger and pianist. Benny Goodman played from his charts, and Ella Fitzgerald was familiar with his work. He spoke seven languages and was a devoted Marcus Garvey follower. Taj's schoolteacher mother, Mildred Shields, grew up in Cheraw, South Carolina, and loved gospel music. His family moved to Springfield, Massachusetts, when he was young. His father worked as a molder for Fisk Tires and was starting to develop his own business when he died in a tragic accident. Taj was eleven. As he writes in the liner notes of *Taj Mahal in Progress & in Motion 1965–1998* (Columbia Legacy, 1998): "I saw a tractor crush him in our backyard. I was so traumatized I couldn't do full-on grieving, so I never spoke to anyone about it."

His mother went back to school and earned a master's degree in early childhood education. She married a Jamaican man named Hughan Williams when Taj was thirteen. By then Taj had started trombone and clarinet lessons. But he had his musical epiphany when he found Williams's guitar in a coat closet. He took it to the basement to learn it, strumming and plucking with teeth from a broken comb. He briefly took guitar lessons from a neighbor named Lynwood Perry, but he mostly taught himself. When Taj was young, a music instructor gave up after a week of trying to get him started on piano. "He'll never be a musician," that worthy said. It turned out that Taj was just a late bloomer. During high school years he began to learn a whole range of instruments on his own, including piano, guitar, and harmonica. Still, he didn't play any of them exceptionally well. So when he went to the University of Massachusetts in Amherst, he took his degree in animal husbandry, with a minor in veterinarian science and agronomy.

Before he finished college, however, his skill as a singer and musician began to show marked improvement. In the early 1960s, he started winning some attention as a blues artist in local Boston-area coffee houses. By then he had changed his original name of Henry St. Claire Fredericks to Taj Mahal, a nom de plume he derived from dreams he had in the late 1950s. From 1961 to 1963 he had an R&B band called Taj Mahal and the Elektras. He and a guitarist named Jesse Lee Kincaid played some shows in Detroit and Canada, and then, in 1964, they drove Jesse's uncle's Cadillac to Los Angeles. Taj settled in Santa Monica and frequented the Ash Grove, where he made friends with many aspiring young folk artists over the years.

He worked as a soloist whenever he could find gigs and sometimes teamed with other musicians in blues or rock bands. In the mid-1960s, one of the initially promising efforts was a group he formed with Ry Cooder called the Rising Sons, with Gary Marker and Ed Cassidy on bass and drums. The band won a Columbia Records recording contract and started work on an album that was never completed. Cooder later said the reason was that too many other good blues-rock bands had come to the fore in the meantime. In 1992 Columbia Legacy finally released their recordings in *Rising Sons Featuring Taj Mahal and Ry Cooder.*

Columbia executives, though, felt there might yet be a future for Taj on their label. Renewed public interest in blues and blues-rock late in the decade opened the door for him to do some solo work for the label. The first fruits of his labor, *Taj Mahal,* in early 1968, won mixed reviews but brought increased interest in him in places other than Southern California. This trend received a little more impetus with his next LP, *The Natch'l Blues,* which he supported with a series of concerts in clubs around the United States backed by a band that featured guitarist Jesse Ed Davis. Both album and show won praise from *Rolling Stone* magazine, which stated, in part, that Mahal "is one of the most enjoyable and entertaining performers around."

One result was a rising level of sales for his next album, issued in November 1969, *Giant Step/De Ole Folks at Home.* Along with his increased exposure Mahal was also becoming more active with black organizations fighting for increased civil rights. He gave benefit performances for a number of these groups and that also heightened a new interest in exploring roots music on an international level. He won attention for his versions of country-blues songs like "Stealin'," "Statesboro Blues," and "Divin' Duck Blues." As the 1970s went by, he constantly probed other black-related music forms—African music, mainly West African, Caribbean forms from calypso to reggae, and various forms of jazz.

To further explore his international background he moved from California to Spain in the early 1970s, from there making some trips to Africa and also embarking on several tours of Europe that won him an enthusiastic following in many nations. He had several LPs on U.S. charts during those years, including the two-disc set *Real Thing* (recorded live at the Fillmore East) released in August 1971. During 1971, he returned to the United States for several activities, including appearances at folk festivals in Big Sur, California, and Washington, D.C., and to work on material for the movies. In particular, his score for the movie *Sounder* was credited with achieving much of that film's overall effect on the audience. Besides providing the scoring, he also played the role of Ike. In another movie project, he provided the "Whistlin' Dixie" segment of the sound track for *Clay Pigeon.*

In 1972, his next two LPs on Columbia, *Happy Just to Be like I Am* and *Recyclin' the Blues and Other Related Stuff* (featuring a photo of Taj standing next to blues great Mississippi John Hurt on the album cover) were on U.S. album charts part of the year. Over the next few years, he was represented on Columbia by several more albums: *Oooh So Good 'n' Blues, Mo' Roots,* and *Music Keeps Me Together.*

In the mid-1970s, Mahal's association with Columbia ended and he began a new alignment with Warner Brothers. An early project there was to write the score for a film about prison injustices, *Brothers.* After that, Warner's issued his debut solo album on the label, *Music Fuh Ya' (Musica Para Tu).* The tracks, which presented material ranging in styles from blues to reggae/ calypso, included such songs as "Sailin' into Walker's Cay," "Freight Train," "The Four Mills Brothers," "Baby You're My Destiny," "Curry," and "Truck Driver's Two Step."

His second Warner's album, *Evolution (The Most Recent)* was issued in 1977. Typical of Taj's sometimes tongue-in-cheek approach to his craft was the name of the instrumental title track, "The Most Recent (Evolution) of Muthafusticus Modernusticus." Other songs ranged from salsa to country blues, as in Mahal's original composition "Queen Bee." Though not a commercial success, the LP was, like most of Mahal's albums, interesting and often challenging. In late 1977 one of his new credits was a feature spot on NBC-TV's late-night satirical show *Saturday Night Live*. In 1979 Taj had a new album on the Crystal Clear label titled *Live and Direct*. In 1981 Columbia issued the retrospective album *The Best of Taj Mahal*.

Taj had no major record label project in the early 1980s, though he was far from inactive even while establishing a new home base in Hawaii in the early years of the decade. His recorded output during those years included *Conjure: The Text of Ishmael Reed* on American Clave in 1984 and an impressive collection of songs for youngsters in 1987 called *Shake Sugaree*, released on the Music for Little People label. In 1988 he joined with other notable artists, including Pete Seeger and Bob Dylan, to record songs by Woody Guthrie and Leadbelly as part of a project to help the Smithsonian Institution in Washington, D.C., raise funds to purchase the Folkways records catalog. The album, *Folkways; A Vision Shared*, was issued by Columbia. In addition, in 1986 Gramavision released *Taj*, followed by a live set in 1988, *Big Blues, Live at Ronnie Scott's*, and the sound track from *Hotspot* in 1990. His sound track from *Mulebone* came out on Gramavision in 1991.

In 1990, Windham Hill Records issued a collaboration between Taj and film star Danny Glover on the story of *Brer Rabbit and the Wonderful Tar Baby*. Later Taj was teamed with Morgan Freeman to relate the saga of the underground railway that brought blacks to freedom during slavery years, a very well received release on the Rabbit Ears label called *Follow the Drinking Gourd* (a reference to the Big Dipper). In 1992 he worked with Bob Marley's mother, Cedella Marley Booker, on another collection for Music for Little People, the 1992 release *Smilin' Island of Song*.

In an interview for *Dirty Linen* magazine by Ellen Geisel ("Taj Mahal—The Root of the Matter," February–March 1996), she asked whether this reflected the influences of some of his own children. He replied that while "some of them are musical," his motivation was more broadly based. "I was aware that there was a tremendous generational gap . . . and that the kids would like music at a particular point in their life, and if you start it early enough with them, they don't have any of the prejudices or head hang-ups. It sounds good, it's clear, it moves. They'll move with it." Columbia Legacy released a couple of albums from Taj Mahal's archives, including *Taj's Blues* (1992), which contains most of his 1974 album *Mo' Roots*, and *World Music* (1993), with songs influenced by Caribbean, West Indian, and African sounds and rhythms.

In 1991, Taj had a new label debut, *Like Never Before*, on Private Music. This was followed in 1993 by the CD-cassette release *Dancing the Blues*. The album included some excellent new songs by him such as "Blues Ain't Nothin'" and "Strut," featuring some fine instrumental work by Taj on harmonica and electric guitar, new versions of Fats Domino's "Going to the River" and "I'm Ready," as well as a duet with Etta James on "Mockingbird." The collection earned a Grammy nomination in the Blues Best Contemporary Album category.

Audiences around the United States and abroad had many chances to see Taj perform in the '90s. In 1995 his schedule included taking part in a tour by Tom Petty and the Heartbreakers, with the Black Crowes on the H.O.R.D.E. Festival series, concerts with the Neville Brothers and Robert Cray. The shows helped bring Taj to the attention of many members of younger generations. In 1995 Water Lily Acoustics released *Mumtaz Mahal*, a collaboration including Taj Mahal and Indian master musicians Vishwa Mohan Bhatt and Narasimhan Ravikiran. Water Lily is the brainchild of Kavi Alexander, who likes to match musicians from different cultures. *An Evening of Acoustic Music* (1996), recorded live during a 1993 tour of Europe, was also released.

Coming into 1996, Taj didn't lack for things to keep him busy. For one, he was collaborating with Bob Weir of the Grateful Dead on a musical based on the life of baseball pitching star Satchel Paige. He also was putting the finishing touches on a new album due out on Private Music called *Phantom Blues* (1996). Working with him on many of the tracks were first-rank artists such as Bonnie Raitt, who backed him on "I Need Your Lovin' Every Day," and such other musicians as guitar wizard Eric Clapton, Mike Campbell from Tom Petty's group, and David Hidalgo of Los Lobos. Other songs included his composition, "Lovin' in My Baby's Eyes," and Taj's treatment of Fats Domino's "Let the Four Winds Blow." *Phantom Blues* received a Grammy nomination for Best Contemporary Blues Album.

In 1997, Private Music released Taj Mahal's thirty-sixth album, *Señor Blues*, which featured him on guitar, harmonica, kazoo, and Dobro. Taj scats and smokes through the thirteen tracks on the album, including two originals. The title track is a remake of Horace Silver's jazz classic; he also covers songs by James Brown ("Think"), Otis Redding ("Mr. Pitiful"), and Delbert McClinton ("Having a Real Bad Day"). The album earned Taj Mahal his first Grammy, for Best Contemporary Blues Album.

The following year, Private Music issued *Sacred Island*, which again demonstrates Taj's eclectic tastes. Recorded with what he called the Hula Blues Band, the album fuses the blues with the Hawaiian music he heard while living on the island of Kauai for twelve years (before moving back to the Los Angeles area in the mid-1990s to be closer to the film and TV industry). He includes two veterans from his International

Rhythm and Intergalactic Soul Messengers bands: Rudy Costa and Kester Smith. In 1999 Taj teamed with Malian *Kora* player Toumani Diabate on the unique album *Kulanjan* (Hannibal), followed by the retrospective *Best of the Private Years* on Private Music and *Shoutin' in Key* on Ryko in 2000.

In 1998, Columbia Legacy released the most comprehensive retrospective album to date, *Taj Mahal: In Progress and in Motion 1965–1998.* The extraordinary three-CD set includes fifty-four tracks, fifteen of them previously unreleased. It starts from Taj's years with the Rising Sons with such songs as Blind Willie McTell's "Statesboro Blues" and Charley Patton's "Bye & Bye." The collection takes Taj from blues to reggae, gospel, soul, jazz, African, Latin, even his tuba ensembles. Taj's liner notes, revealed his dedication to the music of his ancestors. "I got to stay on that path. Because the truth is that I come from a people disenfranchised from their roots. In the music of my people, I have found a power and energy and purposefulness that makes the struggle worthwhile. You see, the music is the property of humankind. It emanates from African-American humankind, but it extends all the way to embrace the planet. To be a part of that embrace is enough for me."

TALLEY, JAMES: *Singer, guitarist, songwriter. Born Tulsa, Oklahoma, November 9, 1943.*

If laudatory press clippings were gold, James Talley would have been a millionaire by the end of the 1970s. One of the finest writer-performers in the American folk-balladeer tradition, his down-to-earth offerings ranged from folk and country to blues and western swing. He was compared to people like Woody Guthrie and Hank Williams. He even numbered among his fans President Jimmy Carter and wife Rosalynn, who invited him to appear at the Inaugural Ball and greeted him after his performance. Unfortunately, his newfound prestige was not convertible into mass public acceptance.

Born in Oklahoma to blue-collar parents, his family moved to Washington state when he was three so his father could find construction work. His father, a proud Okie, helped build the Hanford plutonium factory and worked as a chemical operator handling radioactive material used to make the atomic bomb dropped on Nagasaki. Talley, who believes his father's work with plutonium contributed to his death, wrote a song about the factory called "Richland, Washington." His mother was raised on a two-mule farm in north-central Oklahoma. She graduated from high school at sixteen and worked her way through Oklahoma State to become an elementary school teacher.

Talley senior gave his son some of his original musical delights, singing songs by Jimmie Rodgers, Woody Guthrie, and others of country and folk fame. He also admired western swing, an influence James Talley later paid tribute to in his song "W. Lee O'Daniel and the Light Crust Doughboys" on his debut album.

The family moved southward again when James was eight, this time to Albuquerque, New Mexico. He played trumpet in his junior high school band, then switched to guitar when he was fifteen. The first song he worked out on the guitar was a Leadbelly song about prison life called "I Got Stripes." His musical interests included not only Anglo folk and country material, but the influences of Albuquerque's Mexican American population. Still, he wasn't thinking of making a career of music. Instead, he got his bachelor's of fine arts and went on to graduate school at the University of New Mexico and, briefly, at the University of California at Los Angeles for a Ph.D. in American Studies, with emphasis on art in the 1930s. It wasn't long before he became discouraged with the art scene. He never completed his doctorate. He enjoyed painting, but later noted, "Art at graduate school was just like [commercial] music. It's what's hip, what's in."

While in Los Angeles, Talley read *Born to Win,* a collection of Guthrie's work edited by Robert Shelton. "I got the idea from that that I needed to experience life and study it from a different viewpoint," Talley recalls. "That's when I abandoned the Ph.D. program and went to work as a welfare case worker in Albuquerque. It changed my perspective on life."

He was making some early attempts at writing when he met Pete Seeger, who stressed that the best songs are "in your own backyard." Taking that to heart, Talley wrote a song called "Ramón Esteban" about a highway worker he met during summer employment. That was the first of a collection of songs about the New Mexico Chicano experience called "The Road to Torreón." He finished the collection in Nashville, where he relocated in 1968 after driving up from Albuquerque in a 1949 Willys panel truck. He had hopes of making his way as a songwriter and artist, but Music City doors didn't swing open readily. To make ends meet, he found work as a case worker, which introduced him to the hopes and difficulties of the poverty ridden. He met his wife of more than thirty years, Jan, who also worked as a case worker.

His insight into the blues was reflected in the song "Bluesman" on his third LP. (The song was a tribute to B.B. King, who made his first trip to the Nashville studios to play guitar on the track.) When Talley asked King why he had never recorded in Nashville before, B.B. responded, "No one ever invited me."

In the early '70s, he made slow progress in his musical pursuits. He met talented sidemen, like Texas fiddler Johnny Gimble and Dobro player "Uncle Josh" Graves, who contributed fine backing work on his albums. He also began to find occasional engagements in small clubs and on college campuses. In 1974 he was invited to take part in the Smithsonian Festival of American Folklife.

By then Talley, who had married and started to raise a family, earned his living with construction and carpentry jobs. He kept trying for a recording contract and was finally signed by Atlantic, which was trying to start a country division, but with little result. Then James met a Nashville businessman who wanted to build a recording studio, and bartered his carpentry work for studio time. This allowed him to make his first album, *Got No Bread, No Milk, No Money, But We Sure Got a Lot of Love.* He borrowed $3,000 to press 1,000 copies, some of which he offered for sale at concerts and others of which he mailed to country stations and record executives. In time, this led to Capitol buying the original master for the bargain price of $5,000.

The almost unanimous critical acclaim for the work raised hope that the next LP, *Tryin' Like the Devil* (February 1976), would start Talley on the road to stardom. Again the critical response was glowing. But the brutal honesty of the songs made it difficult for commercial outlets to back the album. As an example, one song, "Give My Love to Marie," told of a coal miner ill with black lung disease. (*There's millions in the ground/But not a penny for me.*) There were indications of an audience out there. The track "Are They Gonna Make Us Outlaws Again" was issued as a single and made lower country chart levels.

Talley found strong critical support for his concert appearances. Indeed, audiences at the small clubs he worked across the United States generally shared that enthusiasm. However, without much support from radio stations, most people were unaware of his talents. Refusing to water down his material in favor of "commercial" success, James still felt he could find a large following if he could just get a fair hearing. He told *People* magazine (July 11, 1977), "I don't want those mothers of mine on the radio, but it seems next to impossible for a James Talley song to break into an AM playlist. In this industry, executives just want to sell plastic—they may as well melt down records into ashtrays—and radio guys just want to sell ad time. So they program the Conways and Lorettas, the Tammys and Georges to keep listeners on until the next station break."

Talley's third LP, *Blackjack Choir* (January 1977), came out on Capitol. The content was as strong and diverse as the other two, but again the response was disappointing. The critics cheered and the buyers stayed away in droves. Talley followed with a fourth LP on Capitol, *Ain't It Something* (August 1977). He had left his manager in the spring of 1977, not long after playing at Carter's inaugural. For a time, Talley tried to handle the bookings himself, but he soon realized he needed a new manager. After his fourth LP received little promotion, Talley's new manager suggested that he leave Capitol, even though the label wanted him to make a fifth album. Talley left Capitol in 1978 at a time when the music business was entering a recession. "There was a sea of red ink. It was impossible to get re-signed by a label at that point," Talley says. "It was the worst mistake and the worst timing that I could have made in my life."

He continued to play clubs like the Lone Star Café in New York and the Great Southeast Music Hall in Atlanta. But he had to lay off his band. "A career just goes down like a set of stairs with a long landing and another step down," Talley says. "I had a wife and two children. I came from humble beginnings. I had no resources behind me. So I had to figure out what I was going to do."

In 1983, he returned to school and became a real estate broker in the Nashville area. "I've made enough of a living to make these damn records, which is my passion. I don't think I'll be remembered for my great real estate deals."

His first love was still music. In 1985, he met Richard Weize of Bear Family Records in Germany who asked him to perform at the label's tenth anniversary party. After the concert, Weize asked Talley, who had eight or nine new songs recorded, if Bear could release his next album. Talley recorded three more songs, and Bear released his fifth recording, *American Originals,* in 1985.

In 1989, Bear released his sixth album, *Lovesongs and the Blues.* Finally, in 1992, Bear released Talley's late 1960s effort, *The Road to Torreón,* a box set with a book and photographic essay by Cavalliere Ketchum, along with other writings by Talley. "The songs were written between 1967 and 1971, the photographs were taken between 1967 and 1970. I took it around in Nashville, but I came to the wrong city. No one gave a shit about Chicanos."

At the time, he had even presented the material to John Hammond, Sr. who wanted CBS Records to sign him. But Talley's timing was off. With Bear, Talley paid for production and retained ownership of the masters. The label reissued his first four Capitol LPs on two CDs in the 1990s, and a new CD, *Live* (1994), recordings of 1978 concerts at the Lone Star and the Great Southeast Music Hall. By 1994, Talley, who says he never received royalties, ended his relationship with the label. Despite this, Talley says, "everyone in Europe knows my work. I've been inundated with letters from England, Germany, Italy, Holland, Scotland. I had no idea there was so much good will out there."

Talley began negotiating with Capitol to reissue his early recordings and to release two new collections dear to his heart: *Woody Guthrie and Songs of My Oklahoma Home* and *Nashville City Blues,* both recorded at the Stepbridge Studio in Santa Fe, New Mexico. While still negotiating with Capitol, in 1999 Talley formed his own Cimarron Records and released his *Woody Guthrie* collection. He was also working on an album with Native American themes. Talley is more interested in music than in the music business. "I'm just a guy out here who writes songs and wants to share them with people," he says.

Based on a February 1999 interview with James Talley by Lyndon Stambler

TANNAHILL WEAVERS: *Vocal and instrumental group from Scotland. Original personnel in 1968, all born in Scotland, included John Cassidy (vocals, flute, guitar, whistles); Davie Shaw (guitar, bass); Stuart McKay (vocals, guitar); Roy Gullane, born Maryhill, Glasgow, Scotland, March 19, 1949 (lead vocals, guitar, songwriter), joined 1969, still with band in 1999. Roster for first album sessions, 1975, comprised Gullane; Hudson Swan (bouzouki, fiddle, guitar), joined 1972, born Paisley, Renfrewshire, August 31, 1954; Phil Smillie, born Kelvin Hall, Glasgow, Scotland, December 22, 1955 (harmony vocals, flute, whistles, bodhran, composer, arrangements), joined 1971; Dougie MacLean, born Dunblane, Scotland, September 27, 1954 (fiddle). Numerous band changes took place in late 1970s and 1980s. Personnel in early 1990s comprised Gullane; Smillie; John Martin (harmony vocals, fiddle, cello, viola, arrangements), born Bellshill, Scotland, April 1, 1953, joined 1990; Leslie Wilson (lead and harmony vocals, guitar, bouzouki, keyboards, bass pedals, harmonica, vocal arrangements), born Johnstone, Scotland, January 7, 1955, joined 1981, left 1982, rejoined 1989; Kenny Forsyth (highland bagpipes, Scottish small pipes, whistles), joined 1990. In 1995, Forsyth replaced by Duncan J. Nicholson (highland bagpipes, Scottish small pipes, whistles, keyboards, arrangements), born Inverness, Scotland, January 5, 1973. Other band members have included Wullie Beaton (fiddle), Willie Begg (fiddle), Mike Ward (fiddle, guitar, lead and harmony vocals), Dave Carmichael (bouzouki), Bill Bourne (lead and harmony vocals, guitar, bouzouki, fiddle), Alan MacLeod (highland bagpipes, mandolin, keyboards, bodhran), Ross Kennedy (lead and harmony vocals, bouzouki, bass pedals), Stuart Morison (fiddle, guitar), Iain MacInnes (highland bagpipes, Scottish small pipes, whistles), and Gordon Duncan (highland bagpipes).*

It would take a book to describe the comings and goings of the musicians that made the Tannahill Weavers one of the best-known groups in the United Kingdom folk–folk-rock pantheon in the last three decades of the twentieth century. The band, which was formed in the weaving center of Paisley in 1968, started out as a regional assemblage playing small bars and dance hall venues in its home area of Scotland. The group takes its name from Robert Tannahill (1774–1810), who was a weaver and poet from Paisley. He modeled his poems and songs after his contemporary, Robert Burns. But ultimately Tannahill burned many of his manuscripts and died in despair in May 1810.

By the time the group began to branch out to find a wider following in the mid-1970s, all of the founding members from 1968 were gone, with only Roy Gullane, who joined the Weavers in 1969, being considered an original bandsman. Over the following years, Gullane stayed as the main connecting line to the group's origins, though Phil Smillie, who joined at age sixteen, also could claim veteran status in the 1990s, having joined in the early 1970s. Meanwhile, the Weavers' creative efforts had a strong impact on many other groups, with some of its alumni winning new laurels as solo performers or as important members of other Celtic bands.

As the band's music evolved in the early 1970s with original members leaving and new artists taking their place, opportunities began to arise to enhance the group's reputation. The trade press and some print media critics started to take note of them during 1974, when they gave some concerts in Germany followed by an extended tour of England. The following year resulted in a recording agreement with Plant Life Records in England, which released the band's first album, *Are Ye Sleeping Maggie*, in 1976. Performers on that disc were Gullane, Smillie, Hudson Swan and Dougie MacLean. By the time their second Plant Life LP, *The Old Woman's Dance*, came out in 1978, MacLean had left and Gullane, Smillie, and Swan were joined by Mike Ward (fiddle, mandolin) and Alan MacLeod (bagpipes, whistles). For the second album, the Tannahill Weavers broke new ground by recording and performing onstage with a Highland bagpipe player. The blend of the bagpipes with Gullane's guitar playing and Smillie's flute runs gives the group its distinctively Scottish sound.

During 1978, besides headlining at some venues in the United Kingdom and abroad, the Tannahills also opened for a Steeleye Span tour of England and for the rock group Dire Straits' appearances in the Netherlands. In an unusual event in the band's saga, the same five musicians recorded the next LP, *The Tannahill Weavers*, released in 1979. In 1980 the album won the group the Scotstar Award for Best Folk Group of the Year. When *Tannahill Weavers IV* was released in 1981, Swan and Ward had left and multiinstrumentalist Les Wilson had joined for what was only a short stay.

There were more changes both in personnel and band activities in 1982–83. The remaining trio of Gullane, Smillie, and MacLeod were joined by the first non-U.K. artist: Canadian Bill Bourne (vocals, bouzouki), born in Red Deer, Alberta. The quartet severed relations with Plant Life Records and recorded a new album, *Passage*, on a Dutch label, Munich Music. Band members didn't like the album's quality and, after aligning themselves with an American label, Green Linnet (still their primary record company in 1999), rerecorded it for U.S. release in 1983. A change from previous albums in supporting musicians was the use of electric guitar and a drum kit, steps that helped attract new fans while offending some traditional-style music loyalists. In 1982 the Tannahills made their first tour of U.S. venues, winning good reviews from many critics and establishing an annual concert series still going strong in the mid-1990s.

The second Green Linnet disc, *Land of Light*, issued in 1986, featured still another revised lineup. Gullane and Smillie remained, but the other spots were taken by

Ross Kennedy (vocals, bouzouki) and Iain MacInnes (bagpipes). The album contents included some striking originals by Gullane composed in traditional Scottish folk style. Those four members were joined by fiddler Stuart Morison for the 1987 Green Linnet collection, *Dancing Feet.* By then the band was well established in both Europe and North America as one of the most intriguing exponents of dynamic Celtic-style rhythms. The Tannahills closed out the decade represented on the retrospective Green Linnet album *The Best of the Tannahill Weavers 1979–1989.*

The Tannahills ended the 1980s and began the 1990s by welcoming back Les Wilson and adding John Martin on fiddle, viola, and bass vocals. (Martin's credits included membership in the highly regarded Contraband, Ossian, and Easy Club groups. He also had done solo work on a fiddle album and a duo LP with Billy Ross, *The Braes of Lochiel.*) At the same time, Ross Kennedy and Stuart Morison took their leave. The new quintet started off the decade with the 1990 album *Cullen Bay.* In 1991 the Tannahills celebrated their tenth annual U.S. concert series. They were joined on the tour by bagpiper Kenny Forsyth, who worked with Gullane, Smillie, Wilson, and Martin on the 1992 album *The Mermaid's Song.* The same five artists prepared the 1994 Green Linnet collection *Capernaum.* That disc proved to be one of the band's most notable achievements. It was well received by both critics and band adherents in the United States and Europe. In May 1995, at the National Association of (U.S.) Independent Record Distributors and Manufacturers' annual meeting, the Tannahills were presented with the Indie Award for Celtic Album of the Year 1994. In 1993 the band bought back the rights to the Plant Life LPs and brought them out as CDs on their own Hedera label.

In 1995, Forsyth was replaced by highland piper Duncan J. Nicholson, whose skills also included composing pipe tunes. Nicholson joined Gullane, Smillie, Martin, and Wilson in recording the band's twelfth album, *Leaving St. Kilda,* released on Green Linnet in 1996. Green Linnet issued a second compilation in 1997, *Choice Cuts 1987–1996,* which included fourteen tracks. The band appeared in a live album called *Live from Mountain Stage,* along with Dougie MacLean, Altan, and the Battlefield Band. In September 1998 Green Linnet released the band's fifteenth album, *Epona.* The lineup remained unchanged for the band's next album, released in August 2000.

TAYLOR, ERIC: *Singer, guitarist, songwriter. Born Atlanta, Georgia, September 25, 1949.*

Highly regarded by Texas-based artists and songwriters for decades, before the release of his self-titled album in 1995—only the second album of his to come out in a career going back to the late 1960s—Eric Taylor had been better known in Europe than at home. This promised to change in the second half of the 1990s, as U.S. audiences and record buyers became familiar with his considerable talents.

Though closely associated with the many young performers who gave new direction for the folk and country genres in the 1970s and 1980s, he spent his formative years in Atlanta, Georgia. One of his first influences, he recalled, was a recording by blues great Lightnin' Hopkins that he heard on a jukebox in a black section of town. He learned to play guitar by his teens in the 1960s and focused on soul music, which he first played with a garage band. He told Michael Miller of the Columbia, South Carolina, newspaper *The State* ("Texas' Influence Is Apparent in Eric Taylor's New Album," October 6, 1995), "Soul music was real big. That's still the stuff I have the most affinity for, and it's really what got me into writing. Since I wasn't black, it came out my own way."

In his late teens he expanded his interests to include among his favorites folk icons like Tim Hardin, Richard Fariña, and Bob Dylan. He began to find opportunities to perform in local folk clubs; then, looking for greater exposure, he moved to Washington, D.C., for a while. In 1970 he decided he could find more creative chances in California, but in working his way west he decided Houston, Texas, was more to his liking. He'd first come to Houston, he noted, "because I got a ride with someone who was going that way." He told Rick Wittenberg of the *Houston Chronicle* ("Eric Taylor Not a Secret Anymore," September 21, 1995), "It was great. I saw Townes Van Zandt the first night I got to Houston and Lightnin' Hopkins the next. For a writer, it seemed like the place to be."

To pay for living expenses, he found a job as a bill collector on rental TVs and also worked as a dishwasher at the Family Hand restaurant and club. He kept meeting other artists, and soon was opening for people like Townes Van Zandt and Guy Clark at the Old Quarter Bar folk venue. "Back in those days," he told Mitchell, "the way the Montrose was, you could play around and find a place to stay and make a living. Vince Bell was around in those days, and Steve Earle played some. I fell in with Mike Condray, who had the Family Hand and later started Liberty Hall."

In the early 1970s Taylor worked for a booking agent (the Blue Squirrels Agency) who put out a sampler record of his clients called *Through the Dark Nightly.* Taylor had a few cuts on the album, which was supposed to be for promotional use only. But the late Bob Claypool, a journalist with the *Houston Post,* gave it such a strong review that it became a cult favorite.

As the 1970s went by, Taylor's reputation with musical acquaintances and folk fans continued to grow as he moved from opening act status to headliner in Houston, Austin, and other Texas cities. He formed friendships with established artists like Jerry Jeff Walker and a steady influx of promising newcomers such as Rodney Crowell, Lucinda Williams, and Nanci Griffith—

Nanci for a time becoming Mrs. Taylor. It was a time, he remembered, that was particularly inspiring for songwriters. "The music was presented for writers. It was a time when club owners really loved the music, and it really bred a feeling in the writers that we were doing something that was important."

By the end of the 1970s Taylor himself had become an important influence on the younger generation. One of them was a journalism major at Texas A&M University named Lyle Lovett, who sought Taylor out for an article for the school's paper. As Lovett began to focus more on music than journalism, the interviews with Taylor became the starting point for a friendship that evolved into a working relationship in which Lyle served an apprenticeship as opening act for Taylor at places like Anderson Fair and various folk festivals. Lovett told Rick Mitchell, "I'm always the opening act when I'm around Eric. I love his voice, and he has a great narrative quality and sense of detail. He sort of takes you out of your own reality and into the reality of his songs."

Lovett and Taylor also collaborated on some songs, an example being the comical "Fat Babies Have No Pride," written while the two were driving to appearances at the Kerrville, Texas, Folk Festival in 1980. (Lovett included the song in his 1994 album, *I Love Everybody*.) In the early 1980s friends and fans set up a record label to issue the first album featuring Taylor and some of his compositions. Released in 1981 on a label called Featherbed, *Shameless Love* also contained contributions from Nanci Griffith, Gurf Morfix (later a guitarist and producer for Lucinda Williams), James Gilmer (a future percussionist with Lovett's Large Band), and John Hagen (also a future Large Band member). The LP was praised both locally (four stars from the *Houston Chronicle*) and nationally (three stars from *Rolling Stone*), but won record buyer support only in Europe.

There seemed to be enough music industry enthusiasm for Taylor's songs and new album effort to open the door to wider success. But Eric was falling prey to drug abuse. He said, "I got pretty strung out on methamphetamine and alcohol, but I got clean and sober in 1983, and went ten solid years without anything. I became a licensed drug counselor and worked with addicts and alcoholics, and I liked what I was doing." For over a decade he spent most of his working time as a counselor, only keeping his hand in the music field by occasional appearances at venues like Houston's Anderson Fair and the Cactus Cafe in Austin, though he continued to write new songs. "It wasn't that I didn't want to be in the music business," he said in 1995. "There were record offers five and six years ago." But he felt a sense of achievement from his work in rehabilitating others and hated to give that up.

Also delaying his decision to return to music full-time was meeting a lady named Martha Seymour, who became his new wife. "And that changed my life again," he enthused. "And then we had this little miracle baby [a girl they named Alex]—we weren't supposed to be able to have kids, and then wham!" The Taylors settled in Columbus, Texas, between Austin and Houston. For a while he wanted to spend more time with his little girl as well as his teenage son, Nathan, from an earlier relationship. By 1993, with his daughter now three and his son in college, he believed the time was right for a new move into music. "I decided I wanted my daughter to grow up knowing artists and writers, so she was a big influence on my coming back to give this thing another shot."

Providing encouragement was the fact that other artists still used his songs in concert or included them in new albums. Among those doing that were Lovett, Nanci Griffith, and English folk star June Tabor, who has covered "Shameless Love" and "Joseph Cross," both from the *Shameless Love* album. (Taylor's songs recorded by Griffith in the 1990s included "Deadwood," on her live album *One Fair Summer Evening*, and the title track on *Storms*.) TV viewers also applauded his guest appearance with Griffith on *The Texas Connection*. Taylor soon had a new songwriting contract with Songs of Polygram International, and a record contract with Watermelon Records of Austin, Texas. During the first part of 1995 he was in the studios working on tracks for an album with coproduction handled by well-known performer and sometime record company executive Iain Matthews and guitarist Mark Hallman. Vocal harmonies were provided by Matthews, Lovett, Betty Elders, and Denice Frank. Instrumentalists included Hallman, Gene Elders (from George Strait's Ace in the Hole Band), Hagen, and former BoDeans members Michael Ramos and Rafael Gayol.

The album, *Eric Taylor*, was released in August 1995, and from then through much of 1996 Eric was on the road supporting it, including a six-week European tour at the end of 1995 that took him to Germany, Austria, and the Netherlands. The album, which included such excellent originals as "Whooping Cranes," "Dean Moriarty," and "Prison Movie," proved one of the better releases of the year, and most concert critics gave him high marks for his stage presence. Michael Miller, for instance, commented, "With a voice that falls somewhere between Tom Waits' growl and Waylon Jennings' mournful howl, Taylor sings about hard men having a hard time understanding love and about the colorful thrills and chills of the American West. He takes the listener on road trips to happiness or heartbreak, depending on which fork in the road the song takes."

Though by 1996 Taylor had many songs to his credit, he emphasized that he was not really a prolific writer; lyrics in particular are something he prefers to take time to craft very carefully. As he told Tex Rogers of the Columbus, Texas, *Colorado County Citizen*, "My songs are story songs that make a point. I work hard on my songs. Sometimes things just happen and I can write one in a setting, but most take a lot of work."

In 1998 Koch Records released Taylor's third album, *Resurrect*. The album received strong reviews from outlets ranging from *No Depression* magazine to the *Oxford American*. He toured in support of the release and issued *Scuffletown* on Eminent in 2001.

TAYLOR, JAMES: *Singer, songwriter, guitarist, cellist. Born Boston, Massachusetts, March 12, 1948.*

A child of his times, James Taylor initially expressed the alienation and restlessness that beset those who came of age during the years of the Vietnam War. Later, his music conveyed the more relaxed atmosphere combined with the desire to come to terms with life that ensued in the United States and Western society in general once the agony of Vietnam was over. However, while finding favor with his peer group, because of the strong country-folk elements in his writings, he also bridged the generation gap to appeal to all age groups.

When he became a superstar in the early 1970s, he was only in his early twenties, but in his brief lifetime to that point, he had packed experiences ranging from exultation to despair. In this sense, his background was similar in part to some of the black blues artists. Unlike most of them, his scars were self-inflicted. He was born into a loving and affluent family, his early years were sheltered and—in what was probably a major element in the problems he and his three brothers and sister encountered—few of his wishes were denied.

He was born in Boston's Massachusetts General Hospital, where his father, Isaac, from an old, affluent southern family, was completing work on his medical degree. His mother, Gertrude, daughter of a Massachusetts fisherman and boat builder, was trained as a lyric soprano, but gave up the idea of a career to raise a family. She allowed her children to start lessons on various instruments, but did not pressure them to continue when they resisted formal instruction.

As James grew up, he moved between two beautiful locales. During most of the year, the family lived in a twenty-eight-room house near the campus of the University of North Carolina in Chapel Hill, where his father was a member of the medical faculty and eventually dean of the medical school. Summers were spent in another large house near the white beaches of Martha's Vineyard off the coast of Massachusetts.

The family enjoyed music, and James heard both his father and mother singing at family get-togethers as he went through public school and then the expensive Milton Academy near Boston. One of his close friends on Martha's Vineyard was musically oriented Danny Kortchmar (born Kootch). When Taylor was fifteen, he and Danny won a local hootenanny contest with Danny

playing harmonica and Taylor guitar and both alternating on vocals. But each soon turned his attention from folk to rock.

James found his time at private school trying. He was not sure of his goals and missed his family and friends. At sixteen, he felt he had to get away and left school for a term to return to North Carolina and join his older brother Alex in a rock band, the Fabulous Corsairs. He then returned to Milton, but at seventeen found himself increasingly despondent. When he began to have suicidal urges, he signed himself into a mental institution, McLean Hospital in Belmont, Massachusetts.

During a nine-month stay there during 1965, he managed to improve his emotional outlook, though he still had stretches of sadness. He completed work for a high school degree before leaving for New York, where he reestablished contact with Danny Kortchmar, who was forming a new band, the Flying Machine, which enjoyed a number of low-paying engagements in the New York area. Taylor, who played guitar and sang, also wrote original compositions for the band, some of which—"Knocking 'Round the Zoo," "Night Owl," and "Rainy Day Man"—appeared on his debut LP a year later.

Living in a small apartment, mostly on money from his parents, eighteen-year-old Taylor provided a haven for many alienated people. After a while, he began to join some of them in experimenting with drugs. He tried increasingly stronger stuff and soon became hooked on heroin, something he commented on in his song "Fire and Rain": *Won't you look down upon me, Jesus/You've got to help me make a stand/You've just got to see me through another day.*

Realizing he had escaped one trap just to fall into another, he decided to leave New York and try to kick the drug habit. He went to London in 1968 and rented studio time to make tapes of his material. He took them to the Beatles' Apple Records and managed to get them auditioned by producer Peter Asher (originally of the Peter and Gordon vocal duet and later producer of Linda Ronstadt's big hits of the '70s). Asher liked them, as did Beatle Paul McCartney, and the debut LP *James Taylor* came out in November. The promising LP didn't sell well, though one of the tracks, the folk-flavored "Carolina In My Mind," later became a hit.

Taylor returned to the United States in December 1968 and spent another brief period in a mental hospital, Austin Riggs, in Stockbridge, Massachusetts. By mid-1969, he felt well enough to go back to work. Peter Asher had become his manager and, with Apple in legal difficulties, he gained Taylor a new contract with Warner Brothers and produced Taylor's label debut, *Sweet Baby James* (spring 1970). With strong promotion help from Warners, this LP slowly sold more than 2 million copies. It also brought the Apple album new attention, so the debut too went gold. In late 1970, Tay-

cessful composers of blues numbers, who worked with her on her December 1965 single of his "Wang Dang Doodle," a staple in Howlin' Wolf's repertoire that went on to sell over a million copies for Taylor. Dixon helped arrange a contract for her with Chess Records, which led to such superb albums as *Koko Taylor* in 1968 and *Basic Soul* in 1970, and such excellent singles as "What Kind of Man Is This," written while she was pregnant with her first child, and "I Got What It Takes." In 1970 she made her film debut in the documentary *The Blues Is Alive and Well in Chicago*. She also recorded a live album for the Black & Blue label while in Europe, *Southside Lady*.

She continued to expand her audience beyond Chicago in the early 1970s with concert appearances in many parts of the United States and well-received sets at the Montreux Jazz Festival in Switzerland and the Ann Arbor Blues and Jazz Festival in Michigan. By the mid-1970s she had left Chess and signed with a new label, Bruce Iglauer's Alligator. Label releases included *Chicago Baby* in 1974, *I Got What It Takes* in 1975, which received a Grammy nomination, and *Earthshaker* in 1978. She backed her album releases with high-powered engagements supported by her band, the Blues Machine.

She led off her 1980s recording work with another fine collection, *From the Heart of a Woman*. In 1984 she and her band were represented on the Atlantic album *Blues Explosion*, which also included tracks by John Hammond, Stevie Ray Vaughan and Double Trouble, Luther "Guitar Junior" Johnson, and J.B. Hutto and the New Hawks. The album was a chart maker, and in the Grammy voting for the year, announced on the awards telecast on February 26, 1985, was named Best Traditional Blues Recording. By then Koko had the unofficial title of Queen of the Blues, and her rights to the title were buoyed by data indicating she was the top-selling female blues artist in the world. That status was claimed in the title of her new Alligator 1985 release, *Queen of the Blues*.

New releases of Koko's work came out regularly in the late 1980s, including *An Audience with the Queen—Live from Chicago* in 1987, *Blues in Heaven* in 1988, and *Jump for Joy* in 1990. By the end of the 1990s, Koko's honors included winning the W.C. Handy Award eighteen different times, more than any other blues vocalist. In 1988 a van carrying Taylor and her band plunged forty feet off a mountain on a rural Tennessee road. She was seriously injured, and some feared she might not survive; she did pull through. In January 1989, she was featured in one of the shows during the inauguration of George Bush as president of the United States. But 1989 was a bittersweet year. In March, her longtime soul mate and manager, husband Pops Taylor, died in a car accident. By 1990 she was ready for new challenges. That year she released her sixth album on Alligator, *Jump for Joy*.

She remained one of the best-loved performers with blues and jazz fans the world over and kept up a full schedule of appearances. Her credits also included a part in David Lynch's movie, *Wild at Heart*.

Some of her early recordings began to become available in the early 1990s, due to MCA Records' acquisition of the Chess catalog. Her mid-1990s output of new material included the 1993 Alligator album *Force of Nature*. The renewed interest in blues and R&B that began to develop in the United States in the 1980s brought an awareness of her talents by new young fans, as well as members of the "Baby Boomer" generation. In June 2000 Alligator released Koko's *Royal Blue*. She has also received eighteen W.C. Handy awards as of 1999.

TAYLOR, LIVINGSTON: *Singer, guitarist, songwriter. Born Boston, Massachusetts, November 21, 1950.*

Although all the members of the famous Taylor clan, whose musical scion was Livingston's older brother, James, had elements of folk and country music in their styles, Livingston perhaps stressed those aspects the most. In fact, much of his original body of work was essentially in the folk vein, and he was considered a part of the Northeast folk fraternity when he started to make his mark as a performer in his late teens.

All the Taylor children, of course, found themselves straddling different cultures with their father, Dr. Isaac Taylor, a member of an old southern family, and their mother, Trudy (a lyric soprano by training), from long-established New England roots. As the family shuttled between New England and Chapel Hill, North Carolina, where Dr. Taylor became dean of the medical school, Livingston and his brothers and sister were exposed to diverse musical influences, from country to blues and pop.

Emotional illness was a dark thread in their early years, perhaps triggered in part by drug experiences. In succession, James, then Livingston, and later Kate all entered McLean Hospital, a private sanitorium in the Boston area. Livingston began to experience acute depression while attending a private Quaker-run high school in Westtown, Pennsylvania, in the mid-1960s and, aware that James was completing treatment at McLean, followed him there in 1967. He was, he recalls, suicidal, but somehow kept pulling back from the brink, telling himself, "Liv, you're really on the deep end this time."

Music therapy was a part of the treatment, and he soon became engrossed in singing and playing guitar. After he left the hospital at the end of the 1960s, he settled in a secluded house in Weston and sallied forth to perform in small clubs and coffeehouses.

He might have been happier if brother James hadn't hit it so big just about then. The national spotlight that glared on James's activities tended to make Livingston's efforts seem like an attempt to ride on his brother's coattails. Liv, on the other hand, already was embarked on his own musical odyssey when James became famous and probably would have made an impact on the music field under any circumstances.

As he told an interviewer in 1970, soon after he had signed his first record contract with Capricorn, "I don't want 'superstardom' or anything like that word implies. I want to develop and become known gradually, so that I can build something that will last for a lot of years. Something that gets better and better with every album. I don't write a whole lot of songs, because every one I write has to be as good as it can possibly be."

His music was different from other Taylor family members'. It was softer, with much less emphasis on rock rhythms. That difference perhaps worked against him at a time when rock was the overwhelming arbiter of pop music. He turned out a series of albums on Capricorn in the early 1970s that won him a following. His debut LP on Capricorn, produced by Jon Landau (later to become Bruce Springsteen's manager), came out in the summer of 1970. Called *Livingston Taylor,* it made lower chart levels and provided two songs, "Carolina Day" and "Sit on Back," that made national pop singles charts in 1971. Landau produced his next album, *Liv,* released in late 1971, which had much greater impact, remaining on the charts well into 1972, though never achieving gold-record levels. The single "Get Out of Bed" also received good response in early 1972. In 1973, his third LP on Capricorn, *Over the Rainbow,* also showed up on pop charts for some months. The LP included backing from James Taylor and Carly Simon on some tracks.

During those years, Taylor toured through much of the country, where his quiet, ingratiating manner made the slender, tall, blond artist many friends among folk and soft-rock fans. He enjoyed performing, though he felt somewhat dissatisfied with the way his career was going. Those feelings and other personal and record business considerations caused him to essentially retire from the recording field for almost all of the mid-1970s. But while he kept a low profile in that sense, he stayed on the concert circuit, working mostly small clubs and college venues, and kept experimenting with new approaches to songwriting.

He felt he was growing creatively even without the exposure of nationally promoted albums and singles. As he noted when he finally returned to those endeavors in 1978, "I know what my audience wants and they're going to get it. Playing live is how you make a career. I've been playing to audiences for the last five years and the only way they can be exploited is with quality and good taste. There's no 'new and improved Livingston Taylor'—I've always been good. And, above all else, I'm an entertainer."

During the summer of 1978, Epic Records released Liv Taylor's first new album in five years. Called *3-Way Mirror,* it indicated that he had moved more strongly into folk-rock than basic folk stylings, though many of the compositions could have been performed in the latter vein. Among his new songs were the relatively fast-paced "L.A. Serenade" and such others as "How Much Your Sweet Love Means to Me," "Train off the Track," and "No Thank You Skycap," the latter featuring Maria Muldaur as a guest vocalist. During his touring efforts, he got the chance to play before a number of very large audiences, since many of his late 1978 appearances were as opening act for Linda Ronstadt.

The song "I Will Be in Love with You" from *Three-Way Mirror* made the *Billboard* charts, peaking at number thirty in mid-December 1978. The following year, his old label, Capricorn, issued the retrospective album *Echoes,* containing material from his first three LPs. His 1980 Epic disc, *Man's Best Friend* (which had him posing on the cover with his dog), provided the top 40 hit in the track "First Time Love," which rose to number thirty-eight in September. But it would be eight more years before his next studio release, *Life Is Good,* on Critique Records. The single of "Loving Arms," a duet with Leah Kunkel, also made lower chart levels in 1981. Through the 1980s into the 1990s, Taylor continued to perform on college and folk club circuits throughout the United States, with occasional sallies to venues in other countries.

He picked up the pace of album releases in the early 1990s, releasing *Good Friends* on Chesky Records and *Our Turn to Dance* (featuring Garth Hudson on accordion) on Vanguard, both in 1993; *Unsolicited Material,* a live album, on Whistling Dog in 1994; and *Bicycle* on Coconut Bay in 1996. The latter includes a song inspired by Ken Burns's documentary on the Civil War. The lyrics for "Last Letter" come from the letter Lt. Sullivan Ballou wrote to his wife, Sarah, on the night before he died at the first battle of Bull Run. His next CD was *Ink,* released on Chesky in 1997. It includes covers of Don Henley's "The End of Innocence," and the Jackson 5's "Never Can Say Goodbye." In 1998, Razor & Tie Records issued the retrospective *Carolina Day: The Livingston Taylor Collection.* He issued a live album, *Snapshot,* in 1999 on Whistling Dog Records.

In addition to his albums, Taylor composed and performed themes for TV shows and commercial jingles (Ringling Brothers, Folgers Coffee, and Little Debby Snack Cakes). He has written two children's books: the first, *Pajamas* (Harcourt Brace), was adapted from a song he cowrote with Maggie, his wife of twenty-plus years, called "I've Got My Pajamas On." His second book, *Can I Be Good Now?* (Harcourt Brace), was illustrated by Ted Rand of Seattle. For Homespun Tapes, Taylor made an instructional video, *Livingston Taylor's Excellent Guitar Lesson,* and recorded an audiotape lesson, *Hit Guitar Styles.* Livingston is also a competent pilot who often travels to his concerts in his 1964 Cessna 205/A.

both taken from 1963 recording sessions including Lightnin' Hopkins. Collector's Edition had *Not Guilty Blues*. Rounder's Vestapol label had *Sonny Terry: Whoopin' the Blues—1958-1974*, *Sonny Terry & Brownie McGhee: Red River Blues 1948-1974*, and *Brownie McGhee: Born with the Blues—1966-1992*.

In 1998 Sonny was honored by the U.S. Postal Service when he was featured on a thirty-two-cent stamp playing his harp alongside stamps honoring Woody Guthrie, Leadbelly and Josh White Sr.

THOMPSON, RICHARD: *Singer, songwriter, guitarist, mandolinist, banjoist. Born London, England, April 3, 1949.*

Standing alone with his acoustic guitar, Richard Thompson squints into the stage lights at the Universal Amphitheatre in July 1996. Being on stage is nothing new for Thompson, who writes songs about love gone terribly awry. But the 6,000-seat venue is big for him. "I can't see a thing," he says, shielding his eyes. "It's a Gestapo interrogation."

Unfazed, he begins a crisp guitar intro for "1952 Vincent Black Lightning," a modern tale in traditional ballad form inspired by American rock songs about cars and motorcycles. *Nothing in this world beats a '52 Vincent and a red headed girl*, he sings. "A Vincent motorcycle is a rare and beautiful beast. It is romantic. It is a thing of myth, and it's used that way in the song," he told Karl Dallas (liner notes, Rhino's 1996 *Troubadours of British Folk*).

It is difficult to define Thompson's impact on British and American music. He has cut an impressive figure on the British folk-rock scene, starting as a member of Fairport Convention in the late 1960s, through his tempestuous period with ex-wife Linda Thompson from 1972 to 1982, and then as a soloist. He hasn't had the commercial success of a Bruce Springsteen or a Bob Dylan, but many aficionados consider him their songwriting equal. His songs can make you laugh but just as often make you drip sweat. In "Cold Kisses" from *you? me? us?* (1996) the protagonist looks through a girlfriend's dresser for signs of past lovers. "Keep Your Distance," from his Grammy-nominated *Rumor and Sigh* (1991), is about temptations that can destroy a relationship.

British folksinger June Tabor, who performed two Thompson songs on the *Beat the Retreat* (1994) tribute album, said, "I see the hallmarks of a truly great songwriter as being a simple but powerful use of language, a strong sense of visual image, the power of suggestion, an economy of expression and a range of melodies that runs from the direct to the elusive. Add a wicked sense of humor and you have the blessed Richard Thompson. He plays the guitar quite nicely, too."

Thompson is such a hit among fellow songwriters that three tribute albums have been made: *The World Is a Wonderful Place* (Green Linnet, 1993); *Beat the Retreat* (Capitol, 1994), in which artists as diverse as June

Tabor and Dinosaur Jr. recorded his songs; and Dave Burland's *His Master's Choice* (Road Goes On Forever, 1992).

Thompson grew up in the "leafy and bohemian" north London section of Highgate listening to classical, jazz, Scottish traditional, rock, and blues. His father, John Thompson, was born in Dumfriesshire, Scotland, and worked as a Scotland Yard detective. His mother, Joan Rawlins Thompson, was a secretary and homemaker. "My father didn't talk much about his work," Thompson told *Grooves* (August 1994). "But it was interesting to be walking down the street with him, and he'd greet someone like an old friend. They'd chat and then as we walked away he'd say, 'I put that guy inside for seven years.'"

His father played guitar in Scottish country dance bands and introduced Richard to guitarists Django Reinhardt and Les Paul through his eclectic record collection. His older sister Perri also influenced him. "When I was six," he told *Grooves*, "she bought 'Rock around the Clock.' She had all of Buddy Holly, all of Jerry Lee Lewis. She even had Lightnin' Hopkins when I was twelve. Not bad for a white kid from the suburbs."

Thompson began playing acoustic guitar at eleven. (He also worked in a snack bar at the London Zoo.) He took classical guitar lessons for a year, and listened to classical guitarists, as well as '50s rockers Gene Vincent and Eddie Cochran. His sister's boyfriends also had an impact on him. "They'd come 'round to pick her up, and she was always two hours late. We'd listen to the latest Buddy Holly songs and such, and I learned a lot," he told *Mix* magazine (June 1994).

As a teenager, he attended the William Ellis School. He played a Hofner V3 electric guitar in a band called Emil and the Detectives, covering songs by the Shadows, the Ventures, Duane Eddy, and Chuck Berry. When he was fourteen, Thompson frequented the London clubs, where he saw the Who, Yardbirds, and guitarists Davy Graham and Bert Jansch. He studied the lyrics of Phil Ochs, Bob Dylan, Joni Mitchell, and Richard Fariña and wrote his first song at sixteen. After secondary school, Thompson, unsure if music could pay the bills, served as an apprentice to a stained glass maker for a year. He began playing blues, folk, and pop with guitarist Simon Nicol and bassist Ashley Hutchings in the London pubs and clubs. They named themselves Fairport Convention after Nicol's house in Muswell Hill, called Fairport, where they rehearsed.

By the end of 1967, the group included vocalist Judy Dyble, Hutchings, Nicol on autoharp and guitar, drummer Martin Lamble, and guitarist-vocalist Iain Matthews. In June 1968 the group released its first album for Polydor, *Fairport Convention*. Thompson shared writing credit on five tracks on the album, which also included Dylan and Mitchell covers. In the spring of 1968 Dyble left, and Sandy Denny took her place. In January 1969, the band released its second album, *What*

We Did on Our Holidays on Island in the United Kingdom and A&M in the States. The liner notes described Thompson's eclectic tastes: "His unkempt individualism and affection for Coltrane and Debussy led the others to look to him for wisdom and new material which, after some hesitations, he now supplies in ample doses."

The album included traditional songs with updated electric arrangements—"Nottamun Town" and "She Moves through the Fair." "What we were doing was a conscious revival of traditional music to make it something that would sound contemporary and appealing to British people, so that they could reclaim it for their own," Thompson told *Grooves*. But folk purists thought the band's approach to traditional songs was heretical. Thompson mined his traditional roots throughout his career, although he rarely played traditional songs on albums or in concert.

"To come from tradition gives you solidity and a confidence to experiment and explore," he told *Mix*. "As they say, 'Those who don't know their history are doomed to repeat it.' If you don't know what the past is, you can't invent the future. . . . There is such strength in traditional music. Compare a typical pop song with a Scottish ballad—no question which is the greater song, by several hundredfold."

Denny and Thompson were soon writing songs that felt like ballads but with a late-'60s psychedelic spin. Fairport released *Unhalfbrickling* in July 1969, which included Denny's "Who Knows Where the Time Goes" and Thompson's "Genesis Hall" and "Cajun Woman" (which influenced fiddler Michael Doucet of Beau-Soleil to investigate his Cajun roots). The songs became hallmarks for Fairport for decades.

Fairport was developing a reputation on both sides of the Atlantic when disaster struck. In the spring of 1969, the band was driving to London from a gig in Birmingham when the band's roadie, Harvey Branham, fell asleep at the wheel. The van flipped over, killing drummer Martin Lamble and Thompson's girlfriend Genie Franklin. Branham was charged with "causing death by dangerous driving." The accident had a profound effect on Thompson. On their *Liege & Lief* album (December 1969) the classic Thompson-penned songs, "Farewell, Farewell" and (with fiddler Dave Swarbrick) "Crazy Man Michael," relate to the tragedy.

Liege & Lief silenced many of the purists. But Hutchings and Denny soon departed, leaving an all-male group behind: Thompson, Nicol, Swarbrick, Mattacks on drums, and Dave Pegg on bass. None had Sandy Denny's expressive power. As Thompson told *Mix*, "We looked at each other, looking for the next vocalist and there wasn't an apparent one, so we just shared it. Three of us sang, and we weren't born singers, so we had to learn, and I'm still learning."

The band toured the States in the summer of 1970 and was featured at the Philadelphia Folk Festival in August, followed in the fall by an extensive tour of En-

gland. Thompson made one more album with Fairport, *Full House,* released in July 1970 (audiences enjoyed hearing Thompson's guitar solo on a song called "Sloth"), and embarked on his solo career in 1971. Despite the band's success, Thompson hadn't made a killing during his Fairport years. He started off making twelve pounds a week and was only making twenty pounds by the time he left. "It was great because we wouldn't have cared if there was no money," he told *Mix*. "It was total enthusiasm, and you can do that for a while when you're young."

Thompson played guitar on several of Denny's solo albums for Island. Denny introduced him to one of her backup singers, Linda Peters, who was born Linda Pettifer in East London and raised in Glasgow. Her father, Charles, ran electronics shops. Her mother, Jessie, was a vaudevillian who called herself "Vera Love, Specialty Dancer." As Linda told *Time* (August 30, 1982): "I'd be scared to ask her what 'specialty dancer' meant; it may have been something risqué." Linda sang in folk clubs in the late '60s.

Richard and Linda both performed on the 1972 album *Rock On,* with a group called the Bunch that included Denny, Hutchings, and Mattacks. That year Thompson also played guitar and sang on the Island release *Morris On,* a collection of traditional songs. Richard and Linda soon established a romantic and musical partnership, and were married in 1972. Thompson released his first solo album, *Henry the Human Fly!,* in June of that year on Island (Warner Brothers in the States). The cover featured a picture of Richard wearing a fly mask complete with buggy red eyes; record buyers didn't quite get the joke, and the album sold poorly. "It's supposed to be the smallest-selling record," Thompson joked to *Hits* (September 16, 1991).

The album showed Thompson's amalgam of traditional and modern stylings, as well as the influence of Scottish accordion player Jimmy Shand, whose name and tunes crop up in a number of his songs. His nonsense lyrics on "Nobody's Wedding" resemble the Beatles of the late 1960s: *Everybody came to nobody's wedding/Everybody knew it was bound to be a hoot/What can you do when nothing else is cooking/Make your own amusement, bring a pile of loot.*

In 1973, he recorded his first album with Linda, *I Want to See the Bright Lights Tonight,* while she was pregnant with their first child. The album includes some of Thompson's best songs: the allegorical "Cavalry Cross," "The Great Valerio," the bitter "Withered and Died," and the vivid "Down Where the Drunkards Roll." Leslie Berman, who wrote liner notes for the retrospective album *Watching the Dark,* describes how Linda augmented his style: "Linda's voice is strong and supple, and warmer in its spareness than Thompson's, which propels the relentless beat of his 'dirge und drang,' poised to rake open wounds and probe tender places with romantic and cynical lyrics."

They recorded five more albums together: *Hokey Pokey* (1975), *Pour Down Like Silver* (1975), *Almost Live (More or Less)* (1976), *First Light* (Chrysalis, 1978), *Sunnyvista* (Chrysalis, 1979), and *Shoot Out the Lights* (Hannibal, 1982). In the mid-1970s Linda and Richard became Sufi Muslims after hanging out with a group of Muslim musicians called Mighty Baby. Thompson, who was born Christian, didn't consider it a "conversion." "I don't *practice* religion, it's just a way of life," he told Berman. Their belief in Sufism waxed and waned throughout the '70s. For a time, they retreated from music, living at a Sufi community in the English countryside.

Thompson kept bringing more and more emotion into his songwriting, in pieces like "A Heart Needs a Home" on *Hokey Pokey* and "For Shame of Doing Wrong," "Beat the Retreat," and "Dimming of the Day" (later recorded by Shawn Colvin and Bonnie Raitt) on *Pour Down Like Silver.* In the late 1970s, tensions between Richard and Linda emerged in songs such as "Strange Affair" on *First Light.* In 1980, the Thompsons recorded an album produced by Gerry Rafferty and Hugh Murphy, but the album was never released because Thompson thought the tracks were "oversweet and overdone," according to Berman. (*Watching the Dark* features three tracks from the sessions.) In 1981, Thompson took a vacation from lyrics with his instrumental album, *Strict Tempo!,* recorded on his Elixir label with Mattacks on percussion. (He had previously released *Guitar/Vocal* (1976, Island) which has two short instrumental cuts, while the remainder are live guitar and vocal tracks.)

Despite marital strains, the Thompsons recorded what many feel was their masterpiece, *Shoot out the Lights,* released on Joe Boyd's Hannibal label in 1982. The song titles reveal a relationship on the brink of collapse: "Walking on a Wire," "A Man in Need," "Wall of Death," and "Did She Jump or Was She Pushed?"

The album was on many critics' top 10 lists, and was considered a masterpiece for years afterward. Thompson had met another woman, former McCabe's concert booker Nancy Covey, while on a solo tour in the States in 1981. But Richard and Linda still went on an extensive tour in 1982, attracting media attention. Many said at the time that the tensions actually heightened their performances.

"The marriage has run aground," Jay Cocks wrote in *Time* (August 30, 1982). "Further collaborations are uncertain. *Shoot out the Lights* may have to stand as the summing up of one of the most extraordinary creative partnerships in rock." Linda told Cocks about her husband's intensity: "He was a vegetarian for years and years and wouldn't wear leather. Then he became a Muslim, and we had to go to this Islamic commune in London and give all our money away, give all our clothing away. And now he loves this woman. With a vengeance."

Following their divorce, in the mid-1970s, Linda began suffering from a rare condition called hysterical dysphonia, a stress-related disorder that affects the vocal cords. As she told *People* ("Sound of Silence," October 14, 1996): "I would open my mouth to sing, and nothing would come out." She made a guest appearance on Simon Nicol's *Before Your Time* (1987), and on the 1990 album *Circle Dance.* A song she cowrote with Kentucky musician Betsy Cook, "Telling Me Lies," received a Grammy nomination after Linda Rondstadt, Emmylou Harris, and Dolly Parton recorded it on their *Trio* album. But generally she developed a life outside of music. She married Steve Kenis, the managing director of the William Morris Agency in the United Kingdom in 1986 and sold antique jewelry in London. She performed at the British National Theatre in 1984 and released a solo album, *One Clear Moment* (Warner Brothers, 1985). She recorded a follow-up album, but never released it, and sang on the *World is a Wonderful Place* tribute album. She didn't release another album until her retrospective *Dreams Fly Away: A History of Linda Thompson* (Rykodisc, 1996).

Richard, meanwhile, continued on with a vengeance. In *Hand of Kindness* (Hannibal, June 1983), Richard reflects on the difficulties of his breakup with Linda in "Tear Stained Letter" (a top-10 country hit for Cajun accordionist Jo-El Sonnier in 1987) and "How I Wanted To," while "The Wrong Heartbeat," recorded twice before their breakup but never released, resonates even more strongly afterward. In 1984, Hannibal issued Thompson's *Small Town Romance,* recorded live at the Bottom Line in New York in 1982. According to Berman, Thompson, painfully aware of the imperfections on his recordings, can't bear to listen to them. In this case he actually asked that the album be withdrawn. Hannibal reissued it in 1997. Indeed, Thompson rarely listens to contemporary pop music for inspiration, preferring jazz and classical. "I don't mind inflicting popular music; it's just having it inflicted on me that I don't like."

Thompson returned to Polydor in 1985 and recorded *Across a Crowded Room,* his last album with Joe Boyd, which again featured his songwriting prowess on "When the Spell is Broken," "I Ain't Going to Drag My Feet No More," "Walking Through a Wasted Land," and "Love in a Faithless Country." That year, a fan bootleg tape aptly called *Doom and Gloom from the Tomb I* became available (*Doom and Gloom II—Over My Dead Body* came out in 1991).

Thompson followed with *Daring Adventures* (1986), the first of several produced by Mitchell Froom, who has worked with Elvis Costello, Los Lobos, and Suzanne Vega. Enduring tracks include "Al Bowlly's in Heaven," a song in which the narrator, a World War II veteran, reminisces about the good old days reflected by a banjo and guitar player who died in the bombing of London in 1941. Another heart-wrenching song, "Jennie," relates to dashed dreams of love.

In 1988, Thompson joined Capitol Records and released his first album on the label, *Amnesia*. His stunning but anguished lyrics continued on songs like "I Still Dream," "Can't Win," and "Waltzing's for Dreamers." It's no surprise that he is constantly searching for material. "It starts with anything: words, music, riffs, hooks, lines—ideas, concepts, television, telephone directories, it doesn't matter," he told Jim Washburn of the *Los Angeles Times* (September 5, 1990). "If you're going to write, you have to keep your ears and eyes open. . . . You're walking down the street and suddenly lightbulbs go off and you take out your little notebook. It's a full-time job, but the tax man doesn't believe that."

He made four more solo albums for Capitol: *Rumor and Sigh* (1991), *Mirror Blue* (1994) (including another ode to British machinery, "MGB-GT"), *you? me? us?* (1996), and *Mock Tudor* (1999), continuing to write edgy songs, perhaps too much for the general public. For the acclaimed *Rumor and Sigh,* whose title comes from an Archibald MacLeish poem (*Rumor and sigh of unimagined seas*), Thompson includes bittersweet songs like "I Feel So Good (I'm going to break somebody's heart tonight)," and "I Misunderstood." The album features "1952 Vincent Black Lightning" and a picture of Thompson sitting next to a Vincent in a mock desert with a howling wolf and a star and moon backdrop. Fairport guitarist Simon Nicol and drummer Jim Keltner played on the record, as well as Clive Gregson and Christine Collistor (regulars in Thompson's touring band) on backing vocals.

Many artists were amazed by Thompson's ability to straddle folk and rock without losing either audience. In 1996, he experimented with *you? me? us?,* a nineteen-song, two-disc set. One disc, called "Voltage Enhanced," was all electric. The other, entitled "Nude," was all acoustic. "I suppose some of the reasoning behind this was that the electric side could be more wholly electric and the acoustic stuff could be more indulgently acoustic," he told the on-line 'zine' *Salon* (1996). "Without having to compromise, without having to say, this Jimi Hendrix freakout doesn't exactly fit on the same record as this 14-verse acoustic murder ballad. . . . When you stand up acoustic in front of an audience, you really are a man without any clothes on. And that can be fun—it depends how much of an exhibitionist you are, I suppose. I quite enjoy it."

In 1981, Thompson recorded with a group called The GP's (the Grazed Pontiffs), with Mattacks, Pegg, and Ralph McTell at Broughton Castle, Oxfordshire, England. The album was called *Saturday Rolling Around* (1991). He has also played on albums for Bonnie Raitt, BeauSoleil, T-Bone Burnett, Loudon Wainwright III, J. J. Cale, Shawn Colvin, Everything But the Girl, Nick Drake, and the Golden Palominos, to name a few. He's recorded two albums with the avant-garde lineup of John French (the former Captain Beefheart drummer), Fred Frith, and Henry Kaiser: *Live, Love, Larf and Loaf*

(Rhino, 1987), and *Invisible Means* (Windham Hill, 1990). He also collaborated with Peter Filleul on soundtracks: *The Lives and Loves of a She Devil,* released by the BBC in 1986, *The Marksman* in 1987, and *Sweet Talker* (Capitol, 1991).

Several compilation and retrospective Thompson and Fairport albums have been released, including Fairport's *House Full* (Hannibal, 1986) from a 1970 recording, and *Heyday* (Hannibal) recorded in 1968–69. Island released Fairport's *Live at the L.A. Troubadour* (1976) and Woodworm and Stony Plain released *Moat on the Ledge* (1982). In 1990, he worked on a soundtrack for a film by Taylor Hackford and put together the soundtrack for a BBC series about exploitation in the workplace, *Hard Cash* (Special Delivery Records and Green Linnet, 1990), which includes three Thompson songs. For those interested in guitar instruction, Homespun released *The Guitar of Richard Thompson* in 1986.

The best introduction to Thompson is the three-disc retrospective CD *Watching the Dark: The History of Richard Thompson* (Hannibal/Rykodisc, 1993). The set includes a comprehensive bio by Leslie Berman, and several previously unreleased tracks, such as Thompson's excellent "From Galway to Graceland." He's also represented on all three volumes of Rhino's 1996 *Troubadours of British Folk.*

In 1997, Thompson teamed up with former Pentangle bassist Danny Thompson on the album *Industry* (Hannibal/Rykodisc), about the rise and decline of the industrial complex in Britain. It includes five instrumental tracks written by Danny and seven songs written by Richard. In 1998, Nanci Griffith included "Wall of Death" on her *Other Voices, Too* tribute to songwriters. Thompson plays guitar on other tracks, but strangely not on Griffith's tepid version of his song.

In his solo performances, Thompson affects a self-deprecating attitude (performing such ghoulish songs as the John French number "Now That I Am Dead" and his own "Psycho Street") and appears to be mocking the audience, which might lead some to believe that he's inaccessible. In truth, many interviewers have remarked on how direct and nice he is in person, though he's a master of droll British humor.

"I'm not sure the English understand irony either," he told *Salon.* "But they are more used to it. I just think the British are more cynical. Americans are much nicer people and tend to take you at face value. That's why American humor sometimes strikes me as too safe, or too conservative. Anyway, irony's there and you either get it or you don't. If you explain it, then you've lost it somehow."

Richard and Linda had had three children together and kept in touch. For years, Richard Tompson has maintained residences in Santa Monica, California, and Hampstead, outside London. He is a homebody who likes to garden. "It's the English disease," he told *Grooves.* "It strikes you at midlife. None of the things I enjoy doing look good on a rock 'n' roll résumé: hiking, bird watching, botany, architecture."

While many have scrutinized Thompson's lyrics for signs of his autobiography, he has repeated constantly that the characters depicted are fictional, an expression of subconscious moods rather than the reality of behavior. "A song can be a mood that passes very quickly," he told *Mix*. "Sometimes you feel sad, but it doesn't last forever. Sometimes you feel crazy. It's good to have these things that change all the time, and it's good to have a song for those things. It's good to reflect those things. 'Easy there, Steady Now' is about someone pulling themself back from the brink, and in the end, perhaps, he doesn't succeed. It's open ended."

THORNTON, BIG MAMA: *Singer, drummer, harmonica player, songwriter. Born Montgomery, Alabama, December 11, 1926; died Los Angeles, California, July 25, 1984.*

Literally and figuratively, Willie Mae "Big Mama" Thornton cut a huge figure in the history of rhythm and blues and its later pop offshoots. Her booming voice, sometimes 200-pound frame, and exuberant stage manner had audiences stomping their feet and shouting encouragement in R&B theaters from coast to coast from the early 1950s on. In later years, she won attention from white audiences the world over as well. Her early recording career, though she didn't plan it that way, helped assure the future popularity of Elvis Presley, who sold millions of records of his 1956 version of "Hound Dog," a song first released by her four years earlier for the R&B market.

One of minister George Thornton's seven children, she began singing at an early age in Montgomery, Alabama. Her gospel-singing mother, Mattie Hughes, died in 1940, and the following year, when Willie Mae was only fourteen, she joined Sammy Green's Hot Harlem Revue, traveling throughout the South until she settled in Houston in 1948.

She was playing in small clubs in the West years later when she came to the attention of band leader Johnny Otis. Otis, a supreme judge of talent, added her to his touring show, which included such famous names as Little Esther and Mel Walker. By the time the show reached the Apollo Theater in New York on her first circuit with the band, she already had people in other cities discussing her talent, and she knew a success at the Apollo would really give her career momentum.

She told columnist Ralph Gleason that she got her nickname after her initial Apollo performance. "They put me on first. I wasn't out there to put no one off stage. I was out there to get known and I did! I didn't have no record and I was singing the Dominoes' hit, 'Have Mercy Baby.' They had to put the curtain down. Little Esther never got on that first show. That's when they put my name in lights and Mr. Schiffman, the manager, came backstage to Johnny Otis, who packaged the

show. Poking me in the arms with his finger—it was sore for a week. 'You got to put her on to close the show!'" It was decided, indeed, that "Big Mama" would have that coveted spot.

"I traveled with Johnny Otis," she continued. "But I went even further on my own after I recorded 'Hound Dog.'" Her chance to do the song came after she signed a contract with Peacock-Duke Records of Houston, Texas. One of her first numbers for Peacock, it was written by two young New Yorkers, Jerry Lieber and Mike Stoller (with some contributions by Johnny Otis) and recorded in Los Angeles in August 1952.

As she told Gleason: "They were just a couple of kids then and they had this song written on a paper bag. So I started to sing the words and join in some of my own. All that talkin' and hollerin'—that's my own. That song sold over 2 million copies. I never got what I should have. I got one check for $500 and I never seen another." Another side she recorded in that session was "They Call Me Big Mama."

During the mid-1950s, Big Mama was a featured attraction in the R&B field, placing several discs on the charts. She toured with Clarence "Gatemouth" Brown, Junior Parker, and Johnny Ace. She was in the dressing room with Johnny Ace on Christmas Eve 1954 at the Houston City Auditorium when he put a bullet through his head while playing Russian Roulette. By 1957, though, interest in her had waned, and Peacock-Duke did not renew her contract. For several years, she kept active in the music field by playing drums and harmonica with small bands in the San Francisco Bay Area. Among the songs she sometimes sang was her composition "Ball and Chain," which Janis Joplin later featured in her act.

As the folk boom, with its emphasis on blues, developed in the late 1950s, Big Mama became better known to white fans. Her career picked up again after a well-received appearance at the 1964 Monterey Jazz Festival in California. She performed in leading folk clubs and was invited to major folk and blues festivals throughout the world.

In late 1964, she made a new recording of "Hound Dog" for Fontana Records in Europe during a tour of the Continent. Her European appearances during 1964–65 were made as a member of the American Folk Blues Festival troupe. In October 1966, Chris Strachwitz's California-based Arhoolie Records put out *Big Mama Thornton in Europe* followed by *Big Mama Thornton with the Chicago Blues Band* (Arhoolie, July 1967), with backing from blues greats Muddy Waters, James Cotton, and Otis Spann. *Ball and Chain* (Arhoolie, 1968) featured separate tracks by Big Mama, Larry Williams, and Lightnin' Hopkins. In the early 1970s, still touring theaters and clubs across the country, Big Mama could point to several more album releases: *The Way It Is, Maybe* and the Backbeat LP *She's Back*, all in 1970; and in 1973, *Saved* on Pentagram Records. In 1975, Vanguard Records released the LPs *Sassy Mama!* and *Jail*. Recorded live in two penitentiaries, *Jail* included such Thornton classics as "Hound Dog," "Ball and Chain," and Willie Dixon's "Little Red Rooster." She wound up the '70s with two more albums among her credits, *Mama's Pride* in 1978 and *Live Together* in 1979.

She continued to play the big jazz festivals into the 1980s. As time went on, an increasing number of festivals were devoted solely to the blues. At the 1983 Newport Jazz Festival, which actually was held in New York, she joined such blues greats as Muddy Waters, B.B. King, and Eddie "Cleanhead" Vinson in one session that provided material for the Buddah album *The Blues—A Real Summit Meeting*. Toward the end of her life, alcohol abuse had taken a toll on Thornton. She appeared gaunt, having lost a tremendous amount of weight, and lost her stamina.

Though Big Mama died of a heart attack in a Los Angeles boardinghouse in 1984, her Arhoolie albums, *Jail* and *Quit Stompin' 'Round My Door* (a British import on Ace), remained in print years later so listeners could still discover a classic blues shouter. She was inducted into the Blues Hall of Fame in 1984. In 1993, MCA released *Hound Dog: The Peacock Recordings*, a retrospective. Her original version of "Hound Dog" was included in several compilations, including Rhino's *Blues Masters Volume 3: Texas Blues*, the *Rolling Stone Women in Rock Collection*, a three-CD set on Razor & Tie, and *The King's Record Collection*, a collection of originals that Elvis remade, released on Hip-O. In 2000 Vanguard issued *Complete Vanguard Recordings*, a three-disc set.

TICKELL, KATHRYN: *Northumbrian small piper, fiddler, composer, band leader (Kathryn Tickell Band). Born June 8, 1967, Wark, North Tyne Valley, Northumberland, England.*

Her music is grounded in the traditions of Northumberland, the northeastern region of England, but Kathryn Tickell has taken the lesser known Northumbrian small pipes to a world audience, in part due to her session work with Sting, the Chieftains, and the Oyster Band. She distinguished herself on the small pipes with her emotional and versatile play, but she is also quite accomplished on the fiddle, which she features on her albums on which she mixes traditional tunes with her own originals.

Like many traditional players, Tickell grew up in a musical family. Her father sang ballads, her mother played the concertina, her paternal grandfather played accordion, fiddle, and church organ, and her maternal grandfather, Matt Robson, introduced her to many other musicians. Kathryn started on piano at six, and began playing the Northumberland pipes and fiddle at nine.

"There's always been women players," she told Tom Nelligan of *Dirty Linen* (December '97/January '98) of her decision to take up the small pipes. "In the village I come from there's a bagpipe museum, and I was looking through some of the old photos and archive stuff, and I found quite a few female pipers. They're all from the valley I come from."

She started competing on the pipes at thirteen. Before long, she was appearing at festivals and gaining a reputation as an up-and-coming musician. She made her first recording at fifteen while performing on a local radio show. She began selling the tape in record shops. Not long afterwards she recorded her first album, *On Kielder Side*, in her parents' home. The album, released by Saydisc Records in 1984, expanded the audience of the seventeen-year-old Tickell. It even included one of her original compositions. She was appointed the Official Piper to the Lord Mayor of Newcastle in 1984. It was the first time someone had held the post for 150 years.

In 1987, Black Crow Records released *Borderlands*. She followed in 1988 with *Common Ground*, with backing by bassist Danny Thompson and guitarist Chris Newman. She then combined traditional and rock sounds in the Kathryn Tickell Band, which included Karen Tweed on accordion, bass, and guitar backing up her piping and fiddling. The band released its debut album, *The Kathryn Tickell Band*, in 1991, followed by *Signs* in 1993, both on Black Crow. She then signed with Park Records, which released *The Gathering* in 1997, the name taken from the annual "Gathering" festival in Cork. Tickell recorded the latter with a trio including Ian Carr on guitar and Neil Harland on bass. *The Gathering* included a fiddle tune she wrote for her mother entitled "Kathleen" and another for her grandfather, "Tune for Matt Robson." "I don't feel that I can really take credit for it; it felt like it was there waiting for me," she told Nelligan.

She has lent her piping skills to several albums by fellow Newcastle denizen Sting. (She played with him at Carnegie Hall for a concert to aid the Rainforest Foundation.) She's also played with jazz saxophonist John Surman, the Oyster Band, and the Chieftains. In 1998, she toured the United States with singer Maddy Prior. While only in her thirties, Tickell has taken it upon herself to assist and encourage young traditional musicians and singers. "I remember that when I was younger there were two extremes of people, people that helped and people that were not very encouraging," she told Nelligan. "The people that weren't very encouraging didn't put me off in the slightest. It just made me determined that if I ever got anywhere I wouldn't behave in that manner. So I always try and encourage wherever possible."

She organized BBC radio performances featuring promising artists. She set up the Young Musicians Fund (supported by the Tyne & Wear Foundation) to subsidize music lessons for underprivileged children in northeast England. "I started playing fiddle at school but now, unless your parents pay, you can't learn an instrument," she told Colin Irwin of *Folk Roots* (July 1997).

"It doesn't seem fair, so the charity is just trying to counter that a little bit."

In 1998, Tickell also put together an album of friends called *The Northumberland Collection* on Park Records, featuring music and players from her home region. The following year, she released an instrumental album entitled *The Debateable Lands* on Park, the title referring to the border land separating England and Scotland which was long disputed by the two peoples. She is backed by Kit Haigh on guitar, Julian Sutton on melodeon, and Gregor Borland on fiddle and bass.

TOSH, PETER: *Singer, guitarist, keyboardist, band leader, songwriter. Born Winston Hubert McIntosh, Church Lincoln, Westmoreland, Jamaica, October 19, 1944; died Kingston, Jamaica, September 11, 1987.*

One of reggae's founding giants, Peter Tosh was overshadowed for many years by Bob Marley outside the bastions of the art form in Jamaica and the West Indian ghettos of England. In those locales, however, he was always considered on an equal footing with Marley and even a more important influence. Some of Marley's best-known recordings, after all, were of songs written by Tosh. On many of those, of course, Tosh himself could be heard, since for a decade, those two Jamaicans and a third artist, Bunny Livingston (also known as Bunny Wailer), were the heart of reggae's landmark group, the Wailers.

During Peter's childhood in the western part of Jamaica, he was interested in the pop music he heard on broken-down record players or echoing from radios. Reggae had not been born yet, but those who would give it life were picking up influences from such varied sources as West Indian folk music, gospel, and American rhythm & blues and rock. Even before his teens, Tosh was experimenting with instruments. His first love was the Hawaiian guitar, after which he began to try his hand at the organ and, at twelve, the piano. At fifteen, he learned to play guitar and determined that a career in music might be the only route from the poverty-stricken environment that afflicted most black islanders.

The center of an essentially youth-based music movement was in the Jamaican capital of Kingston, where Tosh gravitated in his midteens. In the ghetto area called Trench Town, where teens were as likely to become petty crooks as musicians, Tosh made his new home and became acquainted with other aspiring artists such as Marley and Livingston, who had moved to Trench Town from other parts of the country. In the mid-1960s, they started the band that gained fame as the Wailers. Because Peter was from the west, Bob from the middle, and Bunny from eastern Jamaica, they were referred to as "the three wise men" of music by Jamaican reporters.

Although he was raised as a Christian, Tosh was inspired to follow the Rastafarian way of life, whose pivotal figure is the late ruler of Ethiopia, Haile Selassie (also known as Ras Tafari). Drawing on a combination of West Indian and mainly American black styles and Rasta themes, Jamaican performers experimented with exciting new musical forms. After passing through variations of ska, bluebeat, and rock steady, the genre known as reggae evolved. Among the major innovators of this home-grown musical revolution—a format that sprang not from a large culture like the United States or United Kingdom, but from a small, economically depressed island—were the Wailers.

Although there were hundreds of groups and solo artists coming to the fore in reggae in the late 1960s and early 1970s, until the original Wailers broke up in 1974, it was regarded as "the" reggae band. In its glory years, Marley, Livingston, and Tosh were considered equal partners in writing, arranging, and performing their material. The group made a number of recordings on small local labels before getting wider exposure on Island Records in the 1970s. Some of its most notable discs employed songs written by Tosh, including "Get Up, Stand Up," "One Foundation," "Stop That Train," and "400 Years."

For a number of reasons, including conflicting career goals of the three main artists and hopes by each to gain more attention outside the relatively small West Indian community, the original Wailers association ended in 1974. For a while, Tosh kept his activities close to home, writing and producing new records for release in Jamaica. His songs continued to protest the inequalities and indignities faced by the black population of Jamaica and by blacks everywhere. Tosh's anger reached out to many of the oppressed after an unprovoked beating by Jamaican police in 1972 caused him to record "Mark of the Beast," a song quickly banned from airplay on the island.

A similar initial fate befell his 1975 single, "Legalize It," which argued for free use of marijuana. For Rastafarians, this was considered a religious matter, since marijuana (also called, among other things, ganja) was thought to be part of the way to commune with God. Rastafarians, however, opposed the use of alcohol and other drugs as well as meat consumption.

Meanwhile, interest in Tosh's music was growing outside the country. This gave incentive for him to record his first solo LP, *Legalize It* (Columbia, 1976). In London, he told a reporter from *Melody Maker:* "Reggae is only what you hear and think is reggae. Most people don't know what the word means. The word *reggae* means king's music, and that means it is highly sophisticated and should be highly appreciated. But it is black kings and that is why they keep a good man down, because it is getting to the people; it is relating to the people and the voice of the people is the voice of the almighty. It is dangerous to keep back anything that is relating to the voice of the people, very dangerous, man."

In 1977, Tosh completed his second solo album for Columbia, *Equal Rights*. As the title song put it: "I don't want no peace. I want equal rights and justice." Other tracks continued the theme of struggle against oppression and the need for all blacks to look to Africa as a common homeland. Peter's other compositions for the collection included "Apartheid," "Jah Guide," "African," "Downpressor Man," and his cover of the Wailers' teacher Joe Higg's song "Stepping Razor."

Despite the message of the lyrics, the album spoke to all people through its joyful, infectious melodies and complex, but highly listenable rhythms. The *Village Voice* reviewer commented: "In this mix, melody merges with rhythm, harmony with polyrhythm, each instrument fulfilling both functions." The album was undoubtedly Tosh's most impressive to that time and one of the classic reggae collections ever released. But while critics enthused over it in the United States and Europe, it had minimal chart impact. Tosh did have a small, dedicated following of several million outside his homeland, but not enough for him to rival Bob Marley as a popular favorite. In 1978 he joined Marley to play in the successful One Love Peace Concert in Jamaica. Whereas Marley sought to join the hands of political rivals Michael Manley and Edward Seaga, Tosh represented a more militant approach toward solving the problems in the divided country.

In the late 1970s, Tosh moved to Rolling Stones Records, becoming the first artist on the label other than the Stones. The Rolling Stones, like many English rock stars, were passionate reggae fans and welcomed the chance to sign Tosh to their label (distributed by Atco Records in the United States). Peter's label debut (*Bush Doctor,* 1978) included a Tosh–Mick Jagger duet on a Temptations song, "Don't Look Back." Though it indicated an effort to water down his roots-reggae approach for more commecial impact, overall, it was still a fine collection, only a shade less powerful than earlier albums. The second and last Rolling Stones LP (*Mystic Man,* 1979) was weaker in content and style.

However, the worldwide tour Tosh undertook to help promote *Mystic Man* proved a sensation. Backed by his excellent band, Words, Sound and Power, he proved he could excite crowds of all sizes and ethnic makeup. As one reviewer described Tosh's stage work: "He is an explosive performer. His voice, honey-toned, soulful, and exquisitely restrained, is a beguiling and accomplished instrument. . . . [He] roams the stage with the grace and agility of a panther, often stopping in midstage for a martial arts routine that looks like his own blend of T'ai Chi and Kung Fu."

The band also epitomized the finest in reggae. Besides Tosh on rhythm guitar, its members included Sly Dunbar on drums and Robbie Shakespeare on bass, a still legendary reggae rhythm section, Mikey "Mao" Chung on guitar, Robbie Lyn on keyboards, Sterling on guitars and percussion, and Donald Kinsey (the only American member) on lead guitar. As an onlooker commented, when Tosh and the band went into his new song "Jah Seh No," in which he demanded that the walls in Babylon be torn down, corruption rooted out, and "the captives set free": "There is not a person on the site that doesn't buy his ideas, at least speculatively, at least for the moment."

It was a tour with other rewards as well. On August 23, for instance, Brooklyn's Deputy Borough President Ed Townsend presented Tosh with a proclamation of freedom of the borough. It also was declared "Peter Tosh Day" in Brooklyn.

That and other shows across the world made it seem like Peter Tosh year in reggae. Indeed, his *Mystic Man* album did outsell *Bush Doctor* (his most successful commercially up to then). But it still fell far short of top-10 status in the major U.S. and U.K. markets.

Tosh continued to tour and record excellent new material over the next half dozen years, including *Mama Africa* in 1983, *Captured Live* in 1984 (nominated for a Grammy for Best Reggae Album), and his fine 1987 collection *No Nuclear War.* The latter won the Grammy for Best Reggae Album of 1987, but the award had to be presented posthumously to his twenty-year-old son Andrew Tosh in the spring of 1988, because Peter's life had been snuffed out the previous September by an apparent robbery at his home in Kingston in which two others were killed and four seriously wounded.

Many Jamaicans wondered whether robbery had been the prime motive, since Tosh had gained many enemies for his outspoken criticism of social ills in his country and corruption in government and business. However, the authorities, after arresting one person who was charged with murder (with two suspects still reported at large), stated the evidence did not support any cloak and dagger theories.

In 1988, Andrew took his father's place as lead singer for Peter's Word, Sound and Power band. The tour included a "Tribute to Peter Tosh" performance at the Starlight Amphitheater in Burbank, California, with proceeds earmarked for a proposed museum near Peter Tosh's grave, the Freedom College in Tanzania, and the magazine *Music Times,* a Los Angeles reggae-oriented publication.

Andrew told Don Snowden (*Los Angeles Times,* April 7, 1988), "There are people watching me towards what I got out of it [his father's death]. They see I'm serious and strong, so they may want to keep a bullet behind my head. I got to keep watching.

"It feels good that Peter will receive a Grammy for his good works. It's nice to know they're still respecting him. I'm sorry he's not here to come forward and receive it, so I'll receive it and do my work."

Later in 1988, the twelve-track retrospective album *The Toughest* was released by Capitol. In the late 1980s and the 1990s, Peter Tosh's memory remained fresh with reggae fans, who continued to seek out his albums. Nicholas Campbell and Wayne Jobson made a documentary film about Tosh titled *Stepping Razor-Red X,* released in 1992. The song "Stepping Razor" became something of an anthem and a nickname for Tosh. The "Red X" referred to his experience of seeing a red *X* marked against his name in an official Jamaican document. Long before he was murdered, he felt that he was a marked man.

Heartbeat Records released *The Toughest,* a nineteen-track CD, in 1996. The first thirteen tracks include recordings he made for Clement Dodd at Studio One. He cut the last six tracks with Lee Perry. In 1997, Columbia Legacy released *Honorary Citizen,* a three-CD, forty-four-track box set. Although it sold briskly in the United States and in Europe, family squabbles kept it from being released in Jamaica through mid-1998. The album sold so well outside of Jamaica, in fact, that Columbia decided to rerelease his first two LPs, *Legalize It* and *Equal Rights,* in 1999 with liner notes by Marley/Tosh archivist Roger Steffens. In 2000 Intel-Diplo also released recordings made of the One Love Peace Concert.

Tosh continued to inspire reggae stars such as Lucky Dube in South Africa. Other artists covered some of his songs during those years, while reggae stations in Jamaica and throughout the world often played his recordings. "Peter was the person who drank the deepest from the draught of Jamaican folk music and country aphorisms, filtered through the church, then spit out in a bombastic hellfire-and-brimstone baritone that made Babylon shake in its boots," says Steffens. "He was Malcolm X to Bob Marley's Dr. King. He was a fearless fighter against inequity, who put his life on the line more than once in the face of overwhelming Babylonian forces. His music is especially beloved in Africa, where he is still viewed today as the most militant of musical freedom fighters, an icon of resistance." (*See Marley, Bob.*)

Entry written with assistance from Roger Steffens

TOUSSAINT, ALLEN: *Singer, pianist, songwriter, arranger, record producer, record industry entrepreneur. Born New Orleans, Louisiana, January 14, 1938.*

Equally at home with rock, R&B, country, folk, and regional ethnic styles, Allen Toussaint was a prominent force in the post-1950s decades as a record producer and songwriter. While he turned out a number of solo albums, his contributions to the hit charts primarily came from covers of his songs by others or the production treatment he gave to material from other writers. Headliners benefiting from his talent ranged from artists like Dr. John, Paul Simon, and Bonnie Raitt to country stars like Glen Campbell and rock legends like Ringo Starr and Paul McCartney and Wings.

Toussaint, whose father played trumpet, was born and raised in New Orleans and already was a skilled keyboard player in the Professor Longhair style in his mid-teens. In the early '50s he found work touring with a duo called Shirley and Lee, and the Flamingos. After David Bartholomew, longtime partner and collaborator with R&B great Fats Domino, heard him, he decided to take Allen on as a protégé. One thing that impressed Bartholomew was young Toussaint's ability to mimic the playing of other pianists, including Domino. In the process of finishing a Fats Domino session when Fats was away on tour, he called on Allen to lay down finishing piano tracks in the Domino style. This worked out so well that Bartholomew helped get Toussaint more session assignments, which included backing Smiley Lewis and other performers—and led to his own recording contract in 1955.

Toussaint's debut album, *Wild Sounds of New Orleans,* released under the pseudonym "Tousan" a few years later, included his song "Java," which later became a major hit for jazz trumpeter Al Hirt. Unfortunately, the record company agreement involved Allen's signing away his royalty rights to the song. Another original of that period, "Whipped Cream," later became a favorite with Herb Alpert audiences.

At the end of the 1950s Toussaint joined Minit Records as a producer. His first work was with Jessie Hill, resulting in the chart hit "Ooh Poo Pah Doo," which reached the *Billboard* Top 30 in May 1960. This was followed by well-received recordings by such Minit artists as Irma Thomas, Ernie K-Doe, Joe Jones, and Aaron Neville. He also continued to be active as an independent producer, one of his clients being Lee Dorsey, then on the New York–based Fury label, who made *Billboard* charts with the singles "Ya Ya" in 1961 and "Do-Re-Mi" in early '62. Among the songs recorded by the various artists who worked with Toussaint during those years and later in the decade were several that he wrote under the pseudonym Naomi Neville (his mother's name). The titles included "I Like It Like That," "Out of My Life Woman," "Pain in My Heart," "Workin' in a Coal Mine," "Ride Your Pony," "Mother-in-Law," "Holy Cow," and "Everything I Do Gonna Be Funky."

The U.S. Army claimed his services from 1963 to 1965, though he kept his hand in by playing with an army-base band called the Stokes. After returning to civilian life, he resumed his activities, helping Lee Dorsey make the singles charts during 1965–66 with three "Naomi Neville" compositions, "Ride Your Pony" reaching the top 30 in July '65, "Workin' in a Coal Mine" the top 10 in August '66, and "Holy Cow" reaching number twenty-three in November '66. (Dorsey, born in New Orleans on December 24, 1924, also died there, of emphysema, on December 1, 1986.)

Allen also formed a new label called Sansu with fellow producer Marshall Sehorn on which performers like the Meters (Toussaint produced the group's eponymous debut in 1969) and Betty Harris were recorded. Other artists whom they worked with for their own or other labels included Lou Johnson, Wilbert Harrison, Diamond Joe, Clarence "Frogman" Henry, Chris Kenner, and Willie West. Some of those performers and many others were able to take advantage of the twenty-four-track Sea-Saint Studios that Toussaint and Sehorn set up in 1972. The facility was built to answer the need for a state-of-the art operation in New Orleans, and it soon became a gathering place for local band members and visiting musicians.

Toussaint started off the '70s by completing his first solo album in years, the 1971 release *Allen Toussaint*. A particularly exciting track was his "From a Whisper to a Scream," which became the title for a reissue of the album in 1991. During 1972 he laid down the tracks for his first album on the Reprise label at the new studio. That album, *Life, Love and Faith,* was followed by the 1975 Reprise release *Southern Nights.* By then Toussaint and Sehorn could point to major new chartmakers by other artists beginning with a top 10 hit (in May '73) by Dr. John (Mac Rebennack). Toussaint was a producer, arranger, and background vocalist on Mac's *Right Place, Wrong Time.* In 1973 the Pointer Sisters achieved their first big hit on the Blue Thumb label, "Yes We Can Can," from Toussaint and associates' production work. The song peaked at number eleven in *Billboard* the week of September 8. In 1975, Patti LaBelle could thank Toussaint for a number one hit, "Lady Marmalade," which reached that pinnacle at the beginning of February. Another highlight of 1975 for Toussaint and company was the use of Sea-Saint Studios by Paul McCartney and Wings to record the album *Venus and Mars.*

In 1976 he and Sehorn completed preparation of the double album *New Orleans Jazz and Heritage Festival 1976,* whose contents included Toussaint's lively rendition of his "Play Something Sweet." The following year, Allen's name again was on the credits of a hit single, this time Glen Campbell's version of "Southern Nights," which topped the *Billboard* mainstream list the week of March 5 and reached top levels of the country charts. The song was nominated for a Best Song of the Year Grammy in the 1978 voting. During 1978 Toussaint's new solo album, *Motion,* came out on the Warner Brothers label. It included what many considered his best original song to that point, "Night People." Coming out almost simultaneously on ABC Records was a new Lee Dorsey album written and produced by Toussaint using that song as its title track.

As the '70s drew to a close Toussaint could look back on a decade in which he continued to influence almost every segment of the pop music field at home and abroad. Besides Dorsey and the Meters, artists who recorded his music included Van Dyke Parks, Ringo Starr, Little Feat, Johnny Winter, Joe Cocker, Robert Palmer, Boz Scaggs, Bonnie Raitt, and Maria Muldaur.

The picture remained essentially the same for Toussaint in the 1980s and into the '90s. The list of artists who recorded some of his songs continued to grow, as did the albums he produced or helped to produce. Among the latter were new projects by Dr. John and Paul Simon. In 1994 he had two new releases for his solo catalog, a reissue of *Life, Love and Faith,* and the appropriately titled *Mr. New Orleans.*

In 1996 Toussaint joined forces with Joshua Feigenbaum, president of MJI Broadcasting, to create New York/New Orleans Records. The label debut was Toussaint's *Connected,* his first new album since the late 1970s. It featured Toussaint on piano playing a wide range of his songs from "Java" and "Whirlaway," first recorded in the 1950s, to "Computer Lady," a song for the '90s about cyber-romance (although Toussaint remarked that he would rather play the piano than surf the Internet). Following the debut, Toussaint made plans to produce albums by more than a dozen Crescent City artists. In 1998, NYNO released *A New Orleans Christmas,* a funky blend of holiday songs, including performances by Toussaint.

Among the CDs looking back on Toussaint's career were *The Complete 'Tousan' Sessions,* a Bear Family reissue of Toussaint's initial recording sessions, and the *Allen Toussaint Collection,* which includes songs from his four solo albums on Warner-Reprise. In recognition of Toussaint's contributions to rock 'n' roll, he was inducted into the Rock and Roll Hall of Fame as a nonperformer in January 1998. As ever, prominently displayed on his office wall in Crescent City was the motto "Life is like a piano. What you get out of it all depends on how you play it."

TRAUM, HAPPY AND ARTIE: *Singers, musicians, songwriters, composers, producers, vocal and instrumental duo, authors, teachers. Happy (Harry), born New York City, May 9, 1938. Artie, born New York City, April 3, 1943.*

Reading the bios of Happy and Artie Traum, one might be reminded of the character, Forrest Gump, in the movie of the same name, who happens to be present at numerous important world events. Happy and Artie could be considered the Forrest Gumps of the music world, a combination of talent and being in the right place at the right time.

New York City in the 1950s was the right place to be growing up in terms of folk and blues music. The first concert Happy went to was to see Pete Seeger in 1954, and he was enormously inspired by that performance. As he said in one interview, he realized that "you could make music that's socially meaningful, that has historical and cultural value, and that can involve other people in some meaningful way. Not just some icon standing onstage, but music that includes everybody for some common good." Seeger, as well as such other folk music greats as Woody Guthrie, were sowing the seeds for a folk music renaissance. Happy and his younger brother,

Artie, were both inspired to learn to play folk guitar. They were also moved by traditional blues, and Happy sought out blues great Brownie McGhee, who helped teach him blues guitar. He started making a name for himself as a talented folk and blues instrumentalist.

By the early 1960s Happy was a member of a folk group called the New World Singers. In 1963 the New World Singers, including Happy Traum, joined other folk musicians, such as Bob Dylan, Phil Ochs, Pete Seeger, and Peter LaFarge, to record an album called *Broadsides.* On that record (Happy's first), Happy and the New World Singers sang the first recording of Dylan's "Blowin' in the Wind," and Happy sang a duet with Dylan on his song "I Will Not Go Down Under the Ground." Happy toured the United States with the New World Singers and participated in their 1964 release on Atlantic Records, *New World Singers,* with liner notes by Bob Dylan.

Meanwhile, Happy taught much of what he learned to his younger brother, Artie, and Artie began to make a name for himself as a sessions musician, later joining the True Endeavor Jug Band, a folk-blues group. Next came a stint with the Danny Kalb Quartet, a blues-rock group, which later metamorphosed into the Blues Project. Artie's first recording for a major record label was with a group called the Children of Paradise. Artie also was composing music for the groups he played with. In the late 1960s he composed and performed the score for Brian DePalma's first feature film, *Greetings!,* starring Robert DeNiro.

Continuing with their knack for being where things were happening musically, the Traum brothers moved to Woodstock, New York, in the late 1960s. Around this time they started performing together as a vocal and instrumental duet. They toured the United States and Europe, appearing in various folk festivals and in small clubs. In 1970 they signed a contract with Capitol Records. Their first album, *Happy and Artie Traum,* was hailed by the *New York Times* as "one of the best records in any field of pop music." Their next album, *Double Back,* was equally well received. But, as Artie later told one reporter, they had hoped to become household name performers; what they ended up doing was making a few highly regarded albums that became collectors' items. Nevertheless, the brothers continued to perform together, at least until the late 1990s, if not constantly, at least now and then.

In 1971 Happy played guitar, banjo, and bass and sang harmony on *Bob Dylan's Greatest Hits, Volume 2.* Happy and Artie both contributed as producers and musicians to *Mud Acres, Music Among Friends,* the first of five albums of the Woodstock Mountains Revue for Rounder Records, featuring the Traums and other folk and rock musicians. The Traums recorded a solo album for Rounder, *Hard Times in the Country,* for which poet Allen Ginsberg wrote the liner notes.

Concomitant with their recording career, Happy also had a career writing about music. Two of his books, *Fingerpicking Styles for Blues Guitar* and *The Blues Bag,* were published in the mid-1960s. He has written fifteen books in the instructional music genre. He had been a contributor to the folk music magazine *Sing Out!* and took over as editor for that publication for three years in the late '60s and early '70s. Artie and Happy also wrote a book together, *Rock Guitar.*

Happy always enjoyed teaching music and felt that the written format was inadequate for teaching instruments. In 1967, Happy, along with his wife, Jane, founded Homespun Tapes, a company that is still going strong. Homespun Tapes is a mail-order business that carries instructional audio and video cassettes and CDs taught by first-rate professional musicians. Customers can choose from such titles as *Swingin' Jazz Violin taught by Matt Glaser, The Joy of Uke: A Hands-on Guide to Playing Ukulele, taught by Jumpin' Jim Beloff, How to Play the 5-String Banjo, taught by Pete Seeger, New Orleans Piano and the Roots of Rock, taught by Dr. John,* and *The Guitar of Chet Atkins, taught by Chet Atkins,* to name just a few of the hundreds of tapes available for musicians of all instruments, all levels, and all different musical tastes. In a telephone interview with Happy Traum, he stated that he felt that his most important contribution to the music field was through his Homespun Tapes because the tapes are sent all over the world and provide the closest thing to a private lesson with a world-class musician most people will be able to get.

While Happy was concentrating on his tape company, Artie was spending more time as a solo jazz musician. In the 1980s he put out two solo albums, *Life on Earth* and *Cayenne,* and a duet album with Nashville songwriter Pat Alger (who, among other songs, cowrote "And the Thunder Rolls" with Garth Brooks) titled *From the Heart.* His 1993 instrumental CD, *Letters from Joubeé,* on Shanachie Records, was ranked number one for six weeks on the Gavin Report in the Adult Alternative category and received nearly unanimous rave reviews. A few years later, Artie recorded another instrumental CD for Shanachie, *The View from Here,* and *Meetings with Remarkable Friends* on Narada. Artie also produced albums for other artists, including two with Livingston Taylor.

Happy also had a solo career going on. He toured Europe as a solo artist in the 1970s and 1980s. His recorded output during that time period included *Relax Your Mind* (Kicking Mule) in 1975, followed by *Bright Morning Stars* and *Friends and Neighbors.* A sampler of his recordings, titled *Buckets of Songs,* was released by Shanachie in 1988.

Though working solo for the most part, Happy and Artie still performed together at clubs, concerts, and festivals. Together they hosted a radio show called *Bring It on Home,* recorded "live" and broadcast monthly from the performance studio at National Public Radio affiliate WAMC in Albany, New York. Sony Records recently (in the late 1990s) released a two-CD set with highlights from the radio show. Another "brotherly" effort was the recent *Test of Time*, the first album the Traums had recorded together for years.

Whether together or apart, the Traum brothers enriched the music scene for over thirty years. Through their contacts over the years, they were always able to call on an enormous wealth of talent from fellow musicians. As an article in the *New York Times* summed up, "Between them they've been studio musicians, composers, comedians, writers, editors, folklorists, and a host of other things. . . . A brilliant and unique entity in the world of country-folk music."

Based in part on phone interview with Alice Seidman

TRAVELERS 3: *Vocal and instrumental group; Pete Apo, born Hawaii; Michael Gene Botta, born Sacramento, California; Charles Oyama, born Honolulu, Hawaii; Joseph Ronald "Joe" Lamanno, born Sacramento, California.*

One of the better known folk "trios" of the mid-1960s, the Travelers 3 billed themselves as the "world's first and finest four member trio." The group actually began as a trio in 1959 when Apo, Oyama, and bassist Dick Shirley met at the University of Oregon in Eugene. The group became a foursome in 1964 with the addition of Botta. In 1965, Lamanno joined the group as a replacement for Shirley.

The foundation of the Travelers 3 was provided by Apo and Oyama, who were both students at the university. Oyama at first was more interested in athletics than music. He was an excellent swimmer as a child, and in his teens was a top boxing prospect. His boxing prowess led to an athletic scholarship at the University of Oregon. While working for his master's degree in educational psychology, he served as swimming and tennis coach and psychologist at a local high school. Apo, who came to Oregon from Lahaina, Maui, also was interested in psychology.

Both Apo and Oyama had found some time for music in their growing-up years. By the time they met, Apo had done some composing and singing and Oyama was a skilled twelve-string guitarist. They decided that they had the potential for musical careers and added Shirley to form a trio. They started playing at dances and in clubs in the Eugene area. The reception was good enough for them to decide to devote full time to music, at which point Apo left college with a year to go for his B.A. and Oyama abandoned plans for a Ph.D.

During the early 1960s, the group began to branch out, playing engagements in many other parts of the country. Their style initially was basically folk-oriented. Later they also incorporated some of the rhythms of rock 'n' roll. The growing interest in folk-rock in the '60s, spurred by success of such performers as Bob Dylan, also helped increase the Travelers 3 popularity. When the ABC-TV *Hootenanny* show got under way, the group was featured on four different occasions. Through 1967, they also appeared on such other TV shows as *Roy Rogers, Hullabaloo, Mike Douglas, Al Hirt, Regis Philbin,* and *Let's Sing Out.*

In 1962 they were featured on their first major album release, the Elektra LP *Travelers 3*. Later that year, Elektra issued a second LP, *Open House*. In 1963 they were represented on Elektra with the LP *Live at Last*. After adding Botta on drums in '64, they moved to Capitol Records and recorded the LP *New Sounds* in '65.

During the mid-'60s, they played before audiences at many college campuses, including appearances at UCLA, Whittier College, Oregon Technical Institute, Santa Monica City College, and Adams State. They also starred at such folk clubs as the Gate of Horn in Chicago, Shadows in Washington, D.C., Troubadour in Los Angeles, Exodus in Denver, and Buddhi in Oklahoma City. Their nightclub engagements included such places as the Blue Angel in New York, Sherman House in Chicago, Harrah's in Lake Tahoe, Embers in Indianapolis, and a six-month stay in the Shell Bar in Honolulu.

TRISCHKA, TONY: *Banjoist, pedal steel player, songwriter. Born Syracuse, New York, January 16, 1949.*

Many bluegrass banjoists believe life begins and ends with Earl Scruggs. But banjo innovator Tony Trischka never saw it that way. He explored "newgrass" and even jazzier strains in the 1970s and suffered criticism from purists for his renegade style. After passing the experimentation baton to his former student, Béla Fleck, Trischka began looking backward; in his 1993 album *World Turning,* he explored the rich history of the banjo, from the gourd banjos brought to America by African slaves to the electric banjos made by Deering.

Trischka told Tim Farrell of *Bluegrass Canada* magazine (September–October 1993) that he has left the way-out innovation to Fleck: "I'm not into that right now. I'm more into the old stuff. I think that what I laid out in the '70s is my statement on progressive music, and now I say, 'Well, I did that.' Now I want to go back and research the history of the banjo and the music."

In the 1990s Trischka alternated between his love for the past, and his exploration of the future, with his jazzier ensemble, the Tony Trischka Band, formed in 1997. He occasionally toured with Béla Fleck; in *Banjo Newsletter* (August 1993), Bill Evans described Fleck and Trischka jamming at a 1984 bluegrass festival in Louisville: "The two musicians trade chorus after dizzying chorus on familiar pieces such as 'Salt Creek,' 'John Hardy,' and 'Foggy Mountain Special.' The tunes are turned inside out, deconstructed and then reassembled in improvisations which delve deeply into an encyclopedic knowledge of both three-finger banjo techniques and modern musical styles. Tony and Béla have enjoyed this jamming ritual for many years, since the earliest days of their teacher-student relationship."

Trischka grew up in Syracuse, New York, listening to his father, John Wilson Trischka, a physicist, play Duke Ellington and Fats Waller tunes on the piano. His mother, Coryl Cattel Trischka, sang folk songs at night to the children. Tony played the flute, piano, and guitar before the banjo. His parents had Pete Seeger, Weavers, and Almanac records. In 1962 Trischka discovered the Kingston Trio and the banjo break in "Charlie and the MTA."

"The banjo player, Dave Guard, took his break. I just fell in love with it and it made me want to play the banjo," he told Farrell.

His first instructor, Jon Gaines, taught Tony clawhammer style. "It was a different style than I really wanted, but he was a banjo teacher," Tony says. It was Gaines, who had been friends with Bob Dylan in New York's Greenwich Village, who took Trischka backstage to meet Dylan in 1963. Dylan came to Syracuse to play at the Regent Theater for a Conference on Racial Equality concert. Tony was fourteen. After the show, Trischka and Gaines went to the Hotel Syracuse to visit Dylan. He bought Trischka a Coke. "That's my great claim to fame," Trischka jokes.

In 1965 he went to his first bluegrass festival, where he heard Bill Monroe, Red Smiley, Don Reno, and the Stanley Brothers. "Bill Monroe had a very profound effect on my music," he told Lee Kessler of *Banjo Newsletter* (October 1986). "Seeing his band with Peter Rowan, Richard Greene, and Lamar Grier in the mid-'60s was . . . literally a transcendant experience."

While attending Nottingham High School he got together with a couple of friends and played at the University Club in Syracuse. He earned $10 for playing ten minutes and decided it wasn't half bad. He formed his first band, the Southern Planters, when he was a senior in high school. "We wanted to be sponsored by the Simmons School of Embalming of Syracuse, New York, and get its T-shirts . . . but it didn't come to pass," he joked to Farrell.

After high school, they changed their name to the Down City Ramblers and stayed together for a few years. "That was where I started getting into it seriously," he told Farrell. "Then I went to college [at Syracuse University] and I was taking art and music history and I was never planning on doing anything in the art. . . . It was like I never had to make a decision what I was going to do when I grew up, I just kept playing the banjo. It's like it chose me. I didn't really have a say in the matter."

He followed with a succession of bands with similar names: Country Granola, Country Cooking, and Breakfast Special. "Just strictly coincidence," Trischka says. "I didn't have anything to do with naming those bands."

Country Granola, which performed songs like "I Am a Lineman for the Giants," was a "sports rock band." He also played pedal steel for the country-rock group Cross Creek. In 1971 David Bromberg performed at a club in Syracuse, and brought another young banjoist onstage to play banjo duets. This was Peter Wernick of Country Cooking, and Trischka wound up playing in that band for a few years.

He made his first recording with Country Cooking, *Fifteen Bluegrass Instrumentals,* released on Rounder in 1971. The band backed mandolinist Frank Wakefield on his *Frank Wakefield* album for Rounder in 1972. Country Cooking followed that with its own *Barrel of Fun* in 1974 on Rounder, which included Kenny Kosek on fiddle and Andy Statman on mandolin. (A compilation album, *Country Cooking,* came out in 1989.)

Trischka recalls experimenting after a session with Kosek and Statman. "We all had such a good time we decided to put a band together," Trischka says. "We were all thinking the same way, trying to stretch the boundaries of bluegrass and add in jazz, Hasidic, Hawaiian, and rock 'n' roll, whatever."

Trischka moved to New York City in 1973 and formed Breakfast Special with Kosek, Statman, and Stacey Phillips on Dobro. Trischka played banjo and pedal steel. In the meantime, Trischka recorded *Bluegrass Light,* his first solo album, on the Rounder label in 1974. In it Trischka showcased his progressive banjo style. He followed with *Heartlands* on Rounder in 1975, which is even jazzier. (Rounder released his first two records on CD.) His third solo album, *Banjoland,* released on Rounder in 1976, was more traditional, with his versions of old standards such as Bill Monroe's and Bill Keith's "Salt Creek" and Scruggs's "Foggy Mountain Breakdown."

At the end of 1975 Trischka left Breakfast Special and moved to Syracuse. Then he went to California for a couple of months in the spring of 1976. He got a job playing banjo in *The Robber Bridegroom,* a bluegrass musical set in Mississippi in the 1800s, and returned to New York in the summer to do the show on Broadway. "It was just sort of fun not to have to worry about where the next gig is coming from," he told Farrell. "They paid you really well, you did eight shows a week, and you knew it was going to be going on for a while. . . . They had two lofts on either side of the stage, and you would come down and play, and go up on the other side. Once in a while, one of us would walk out onstage and be in with the townspeople in the show."

He performed *The Robber Bridegroom* until 1977, and later performed it at Ford's Theater in Washington, D.C., as well as on a bus-and-truck tour in 1978. That year he also took a tour of Japan and Hawaii with guitarist-mandolinist Peter Rowan and fiddler Richard Greene. They were called the Red Hot Pickers and recorded two albums in Japan that were rereleased on a Sugar Hill compilation called *The Red Hot Pickers.*

In 1980 he formed his longest-lasting group, Skyline, with Danny Weiss on lead guitar, Larry Cohen on

years, which I think has a lot to do with my sometime multifrantic behavior." (His "behavior" problems went deeper than that, however. Singing his song "Two Girls" at a New York nightclub performance in 1995, he stopped after the opening chorus line "I've got two girls" to add "because I'm a schizophrenic." The interpolation harked back to his teens, when he was diagnosed as a manic-depressive with suicidal tendencies.)

"Then I went to the University of Colorado for a while, then finally dropped out of school and became a folk singer," he added. "College was, well, I sorta went off the deep end at the University of Colorado. I was apparently not stable enough to go there. I hit that place like a saddle bronc hits the arena—coming right out of military school and all. No way it could last, and it didn't." His escapades at college, he told writer Ben Hedgepeth, included times when he would lock himself up in his apartment for a week, "taking my phone off the hook, being drunk all the time, drinking Bali Hai wine, playing the guitar, listening to Lightnin' Hopkins and Hank Williams and early Bob Dylan. . . . Then I'd come out at the end of a week of this and throw a giant party.

"I lived on the fourth story of this apartment building, and at one point during one of those parties, I went out and sat on the edge of the balcony and started leaning backwards. I decided I was gonna lean over and just see what it felt like all the way up to when you lost control and you were falling. I realized that to do it I'd have to fall. But I said I'm going to do it anyway.

"So I started leaning back really slow and really paying attention. I fell. Fell over backwards and landed four stories down flat on my back. I remember the impact and exactly what it felt like and all the people screaming. I had a bottle of wine and I stood up. Hadn't spilled any wine. Felt no ill effect whatsoever. Meanwhile all the people jammed into the elevator, and when the doors opened they knocked me over comin' out. And it hurt more being knocked over than falling four stories."

After leaving school, he told Claypool, he came to Houston "and started singing. Got into town about a year after the folk boom had died down, in like 1966, and the first place I played was a club on the Westheimer called the Jester. That was the first place I ever got real money for singing. This guy, who turned out to be Don Sanders, came up to me in there and said I also oughta try this place called Sand Mountain. So I went over there with him and we did a little short set. . . . There was this song I used to do called 'The Blues,' and I sang it that night. It was a talking blues about, you know, dropping out of the second grade to join the KKK and the guy said 'You got too much education.' Then I did another one called 'The Vietnamese Blues,' which had a chorus about 'leaving Vietnam to the Vietnamese.' "

Although Sand Mountain's operators were a little dubious at first, they finally asked Townes back, and he became a regular attraction there and at such other places as the Old Quarter and local coffeehouses. Not only did local folk and country fans sing his praises, so did fellow musicians and writers. One of those impressed with his talents was Mickey Newbury, who suggested that Townes try for a recording contract. His first album, produced by Jack Clement, was placed with the small regional label Poppy, which issued the disc *For the Sake of the Song* in 1968. The album included a number of impressive originals, including "Tecumseh Valley," which later was recorded by country star Bobby Bare and, in the 1990s, by Nanci Griffith on her *Other Voices, Other Rooms* album.

Van Zandt completed a series of additional albums issued by Poppy in the late 1960s and early 1970s, including *Our Mother the Mountain, Townes Van Zandt* (issued 12/69), *Delta Momma Blues* (11/70); *High, Low and in Between,* and *The Late Great Townes Van Zandt.* More than a few artists mined those collections for cover songs in the years to come. Among the notable tracks were "To Live Is to Fly" on *Delta Momma Blues* and, on the last LP, "If I Needed You" and "Poncho and Lefty." "Poncho and Lefty" was covered by Emmylou Harris and Hoyt Axton in 1977 and, in the early 1980s, provided a number one country hit for Willie Nelson and Merle Haggard. In the 1983 Country Music Association voting, their version was nominated for Single of the Year. Don Williams and Emmylou Harris also recorded "If I Needed You," a number three hit on the country charts in 1982.

In the mid-1970s Townes added the albums *Live at the Old Quarter, Houston* (a double LP) and *Flying Shoes* to his list of credits. *Flying Shoes* (issued in 1978) contained such excellent originals as "Loretta" and "No Place to Fall." The latter was covered in an excellent recording by country artist Steve Earle. Earle later commented, "Townes Van Zandt is the best songwriter in the whole world, and I'll stand on Bob Dylan's coffee table in my cowboy boots and say that."

Discussing his approach to songwriting with John T. Davis of the *Austin American-Statesman* ("Sinking 'no deeper'—Van Zandt Hangs in the Real Balance between Melancholy and Redemption," January 19, 1995), he remembered that "If I Needed You" literally was a dream song: "I just woke up and wrote it down. I had the guitar part and everything. I was staying with Guy and Susanna (Clark), and we all had the flu. So we were taking cough syrup and antibiotics, so the dreams were like, Technicolor! I dreamt I was a folksinger, and I played 'If I Needed You.' In the morning, I played it for Guy and Susanna when we were having coffee. And they said, 'That's a beautiful song; where did that come from?' I told them I wrote it in my sleep."

He said that he started more songs than he finished: "If I think a song is not going to be good, I just stop writing it. Get it away from inside my brain, so another good one can come along. Some take 30 minutes, and some take a year. You have to be in the right chair at the right time. There is a certain craftsmanship involved. But I've heard kids dancing around in a circle making up a song which is just as pretty as any song can be."

Part of the reason for Van Zandt's slow progress in the music business was his individualism and the desire to keep a low profile. In the early 1970s, for instance, he spent the entire summer in an isolated spot in the Colorado mountains. He told Claypool, "I stay in the mountains until the weather runs me out and then I come back into the world in September." Finally, in 1976, his manager, John Lomax, convinced Van Zandt that he should put more emphasis on his career. In October 1976, Townes finally moved to Nashville (even there, he managed to find a place for himself and his then-wife, Cindi, in a mountain area fifteen miles from town) and signed a new recording contract with Tomato Records. His initial effort was to help prepare the double live *Houston Old Quarter* album from tapes of appearances during 1973–74, followed by *Flying Shoes.*

Of course, Van Zandt continued to be plagued by his many demons, particularly alcohol abuse and fits of depression. He told Hedgepeth that random attacks of "total loss of meaning and motivation" sometimes culminated in severe, prolonged bouts of misery. "Boy, there's been a lotta times when depression with me just became physical, it hurt so bad it was wrenching me apart, wrenching my brain apart, my whole body to the point where I was holding my head and screaming. There's been times when my hands—I took them—and I have the feeling, a very strange feeling that if I had a machete and could just chop my hands off then everything would be fine."

His personal problems plus the unfortunately limited market for folk recordings played a role in his long absence from new album catalogs—an absence that extended from 1978 to 1987, when an alignment with Sugar Hill resulted in the release of *At My Window,* which once more demonstrated his extraordinary writing skills. Not that Townes was inactive during his recording hiatus. He still could get performing gigs, and his outlook took a turn for the better after a new marriage in the early 1980s and the birth of two children helped him to cut back on some of his self-destructive actions. He told Terry Atkinson of the *Los Angeles Times* in 1985 ("Life Isn't Quite So Blue for Van Zandt," July 26, 1985) that he was restricting his drinking to apple juice, had settled a dispute over royalties, and was making enough money from concerts to support his household in Austin, Texas. "I can't go out and buy a Cadillac right now, but I can support my family. [The marriage] keeps me anchored. It's nice to have someone else to consider. When I'm alone, I can come up with some strange ideas. If I didn't have a family at home right now and a gig to do—man, I'd do *anything.*"

The stirring contents of *At My Window* plus a new awareness of folk music by new generations of fans helped enhance Van Zandt's prospects on the college and coffeehouse circuit. He already had an overseas following whose ranks increased with each new album on Sugar Hill, which included *Live and Obscure* in 1989, *Roadsongs* in 1994, and *No Deeper Blue* in 1994, the latter released in Europe on the German Veracity label.

No Deeper Blue, his first studio album in seven years, actually was assembled in Ireland. He told a *New York Times* reporter in a phone interview from Germany, where he was on tour (November 24, 1994), that his dreams again played a role: "I was asleep in Nashville, and I had this real vivid dream that just said, 'You have to go to Ireland, get ahold of [Irish guitarist] Philip Donnelly and produce your next record.' So I got up in the middle of the night, and miraculously got ahold of him. From the time I had that dream until somebody handed me the finished cassette was about a year. I can't believe I pulled that together." The album contents included songs like "Marie," dealing with the searing pain of homelessness; the darkly humorous "Billy, Boney and Ma"; and a touching tribute to his daughter, "Katie Belle Blue."

During 1993–94, Townes also spent considerable time in U.S. studios producing new versions of some sixty of his songs in duets with other artists. Backing him on various tracks were people like Willie Nelson, Freddy Fender, and Doug Sahm. He told the *New York Times,* "It's either going to be a giant tax write-off, or some company with a lot of money is going to release it. It's out there." The album was delayed for several years and finally came out in 1999 on Arista titled *A Far Cry from Dead.*

On New Year's Day 1997, Van Zandt, only fifty-two, died unexpectedly of a heart attack. Townes had fallen and broken his hip on Christmas Eve 1996. He went in for surgery on New Year's Eve and was at home with third wife Jeanene and children William and Katie Belle when he died. The songwriting community mourned his passing. His memorial service on January 5, 1997, was attended by Steve Earle, Nanci Griffith, Rodney Crowell, and Guy Clark. Several songwriters held a tribute concert in February at the Bottom Line in New York, including Nashville singer Jonell Mosser (who covered Van Zandt's songs on her 1996 album *Around Townes*), Jimmie Dale Gilmore, Joe Ely, Gillian Welch, Tom Russell, Rosie Flores, and Margo and Michael Timmins of the Cowboy Junkies. On Sunday, March 2, 1997, his oldest son, John Townes Van Zandt, and a host of musician friends gave an emotionally charged six hour concert in his memory at Ed Pearl's Ash Grove on the Santa Monica, California, pier. The performers included Peter Case, Mare Winningham, Butch Hancock, Bob Neuwirth, David Olney, and Kimmie Rhodes. The twenty-seven-year-old John Townes Van Zandt hadn't followed in his father's footsteps, becoming instead a fly-fishing guide, but his comments indicated there had been a close relationship between the two. He told the audience, "Thank you for coming. I know that tributes to people who have died . . . tend to get a little heavy, but Townes had a sense of humor that was unmatched." His father, he indicated, would not have wanted everyone to feel sorry for him but rather to enjoy themselves and remember the good times. Several friends recounted some amusing incidents involving Townes senior, and the evening ended with all joining in on a rousing rendition of "Pancho and Lefty."

Sugar Hill released two albums shortly after his death: *Rear View Mirror,* recorded live in 1979, was reissued in February; and *The Highway Kind,* including eleven songs recorded in concert and three studio tracks, came out in March. Rhino has rereleased several of Van Zandt's early albums on CD, including *For the Sake of the Song* under the title *First Album, Our Mother the Mountain, Townes Van Zandt, High, Low and in Between, Flying Shoes,* and *The Nashville Sessions* (from recently discovered tapes). *Rain on a Conga Drum,* a 1991 live CD available as an import on Exile Records, is now available through the Townes Van Zandt web site. Several retrospectives have also come out, including *Best of Townes Van Zandt,* released in Germany by Charly Records in 1996; and *Zandt Anthology: 1968–1979,* released in Germany by Charly in 1998.

Van Zandt's legacy will clearly live on with the Texas singers and songwriters who revered his work. One of those, Lyle Lovett, included two of his songs on his 1998 album on MCA/Curb Records, *Step Inside This House:* "Flying Shoes" and "If I Needed You."

VAUGHAN, STEVIE RAY: *Singer, guitarist, songwriter, record producer, band leader (TRIPLE THREAT, DOUBLE TROUBLE). Born Dallas, Texas, October 3, 1954; died Alpine Valley, Wisconsin, August 27, 1990.* Although his life was cut short tragically at the age of 35, Stevie Ray Vaughan was undoubtedly one of the main players responsible for the blues revival of the 1980s. Not only did Stevie rise from relative obscurity to international fame, he also battled with and eventually overcame addictions to drugs and alcohol. Top-rated musicians and fans worldwide continue to garnish his memory with posthumous awards and recognitions.

For Stevie, the die was cast from his childhood in Dallas. Like many traditional blues guitarists, Stevie grew up dirt poor. Born in Dallas to an asbestos worker who drank to kill the pain of poverty, Stevie watched the first record he ever bought, Lonnie Mack's *Wham!,* get smashed in one of his father's drunken rages. Luck-

ily for Stevie, he had an older brother Jimmie Vaughan, who went on to gain a measure of success with the Fabulous Thunderbirds, was a blues-rock fanatic and active in amateur bands with his friends while Stevie was in elementary school. Before Stevie was eight, he already was being taught guitar chords by Jimmie and had his music appetite whetted by listening to his brother's collection of blues discs. At age eight, Stevie had mastered guitar playing well enough to be accepted as a member of bands organized by older boys. He had more performing credits when he approached teen years than most musicians could point to by their middle or late teens. Jimmie Vaughan told John Swenson of *Rolling Stone* (October 4, 1990) about his younger brother's fast start: "I ran off when I was about fifteen. Left him my guitar." When he saw his brother two years later, Jimmie was astonished. "He worked twice as hard as I did because he was trying to beat me. He just whooshed past, and I'm still over here."

From adolescence through high school, Stevie paid little attention to class work, focusing his energies on performing professionally with Dallas-area bands. Among the groups that welcomed his phenomenal guitar licks from the late 1960s through the early 1970s were the Chantones, Blackbird, and Night Crawlers. When the chance came for somewhat more interesting band work outside the Dallas region at the start of the '70s, Stevie dropped out of high school in his senior year and moved to Austin, Texas, which was still the place he called home in the late-1980s.

In 1975, he joined Austin-based blues/R&B group the Cobras, whose reputation as one of the most exciting local blues bands grew steadily, sparked to considerable degree by the intricate string work of its young lead guitarist. Feeling more confident about his audience rapport, Stevie left the Cobras in 1977 to form his own R&B revue, Triple Threat. Though there were rough periods when engagements and performance money was hard to come by, Stevie kept things going until 1981, when he disbanded the group with a view toward incorporating blues and R & B themes into a more hard-driving rock format.

The vehicle he chose for that was a "power-trio" concept somewhat in the tradition of that "little ol' band from Texas," ZZ Top. For his new act, Stevie Ray brought in bass guitarist Tommy Shannon and drummer Chris Layton. The backing twosome was given the name Double Trouble after a song in blues singer Otis Rush's repertoire. (Rush had made some of his best recordings on a label called Cobra, incidentally.) In the trio's early period, it wasn't easy finding work or financial support, but slowly the group began to pick up a following in Texas among blues-rock fans, to a considerable extent by word of mouth.

As the band's musical peers sang their praises, chances arose for Stevie and Double Trouble to perform in small clubs and as opening act in places outside Texas. This exposure finally brought an opportunity for the trio to go overseas to Switzerland in mid-1982 for the annual Montreux Festival. They proceeded to take full advantage of what festival organizers had seen as a relatively minor role in the event. It truely was a rags to riches story. As James McBride wrote in *People,* Vaughan came "roaring into the 1982 Montreux festival with a '59 Stratocaster at his hip and two flame-throwing sidekicks he called Double Trouble. He had no record contract, no name, but he reduced the stage to a pile of smoking cinders and, afterward, everyone wanted to know who he was."

Montreux typically lures famous musical personalities and a good share of record-industry excutives, which augured well for the trio's future. One of the first to respond was David Bowie, who, after seeing the group's virtuoso performance, asked Stevie Ray to handle lead guitar on his next album, *Let's Dance* (spring 1983), Bowie's debut on a new label (EMI-America) and one of the biggest hits in his career. Meanwhile, the Montreux showcase had brought other offers for Stevie and his cohorts, including a suggestion by Jackson Browne that the trio record an album at his studio in Los Angeles. Negotiations also got underway with Columbia for a contract, an agreement urged on the company by Columbia record producer and fabled discoverer of new talent, John Hammond.

Ranging from undated versions of roots blues to high-powered blues-rock, the debut, *Texas Flood* (early 1983), was produced by Hammond and released on Columbia's subsidiary Epic. It broke *Billboard's* top 40 and eventually went double platinum. At the end of 1983, Stevie Ray made himself felt via a number of awards and readers' polls. Grammy voters provided two nominations: Best Rock Instrumental (for the song "Rude Mood") and Best Traditional Blues Recording. While Stevie didn't win the Grammy, he and Double Trouble did take number one honors in three categories of *Guitar Player* magazine's readers poll. *Texas Flood* was named Best Blues Album and Stevie headed the lists for Best New Talent and Best Electric Blues Guitarist.

For the second album, *Couldn't Stand the Weather* (summer 1984), Stevie and his associates brought to bear other influences, including jazz and mainstream rock on a new version of Jimi Hendrix's "Voodoo Chile" and jazz-flavored "Stang's Swang." It broke the top 20, went double platinum, and brought the group a third Grammy nomination. *People* magazine noted in 1984, "For a kid who failed music theory in high school, the past two years have been a wild ride from local legend to stardom, from sleeping on club floors to playing Carnegie Hall. If Stevie's dizzy from this sudden height, it ain't showin'."

Stevie and Double Trouble won their first Grammy trophies in early 1985. This wasn't for their Epic album, but for a track on Atlantic Records' *Blues Explosion,* voted Best Traditional Blues Recording of 1984. Besides Stevie's group, that album featured John Hammond, Jr. (son of the CBS executive), Sugar Blue, Koko Taylor & the Blues Machine, Luther "Guitar Junior" Johnson, and J.B. Hutto and the Hawks.

Increasingly, Vaughan was providing original songs to complement his group's versions of blues and R&B numbers written by others. The October 1985 LP, *Soul to Soul* (platinum), included his "Empty Arms," "Life Without You," and "Ain't Gone 'n' Give Up on Love." By this time, he had revamped Double Trouble to include new member Reese Wynands on keyboards. In voting for the 1985 Grammy Awards, Stevie and Double Trouble were Best Rock Instrumental Performance finalists for the track "Say What!" from *Soul to Soul.*

Vaughan in the mid-1980s established credentials as a record producer as well as a performer. Besides producing all the tracks for his second and third albums, he supervised all work by other artists, including a comeback collection by blues-rocker Lonnie Mack, *Strike Like Lightning* (Alligator, 1985). When not working with his own band, Stevie liked to sit in with many legendary blues artists. Among those he played with in the mid-1980s were Big Mama Thornton, Albert Collins, B.B. King, Bobby "Blue" Bland, Johnny Copeland, and Albert King. 1986 saw the release of *Live Alive,* a two-LP live set that eventually went platinum. A live version of "Say What!" handed Stevie and bandmates their second Grammy award for Best Rock Instrumental.

Life as a musician finally caught up to Stevie Ray. For years he had been playing and recording fervently, as well as abusing cocaine and alcohol. However, it was the grief of his father's death that finally put Stevie into a rehab clinic. Although his marriage came apart and his relationship with his manager deteriorated, Vaughan cleaned up his act and stuck to the one thing that he truly loved: playing the blues. Stevie teamed up once again with Double Trouble to record, but it wasn't until 1989's *In Step* that their hard studio work was released. Not only did *In Step* showcase a reinvigorated Stevie Ray, it also was the band's first commercial breakthrough. The album, which reached double platinum sales, earned a Grammy award for Best Traditional Blues Recording and contained the band's first number one radio hit, "Crossfire."

Unfortunately, Stevie Ray did not get to enjoy his success for very long. On August 26, 1990, Vaughan flew into Alpine Valley, Wisconsin, to play an outdoor concert with friends Eric Clapton, Buddy Guy, Robert Cray, and brother Jimmie; as usual, Stevie stole the show. After the show ended, Stevie opted to take the last remaining seat on a Chicago-bound helicopter. Battling early morning fog, the helicopter crashed into a man-made ski slope, killing Vaughan and four others, including Clapton's agent, tour manager, and bodyguard. Stevie just missed his 36th birthday (October 3) and his fourth anniversary of being drug and alcohol free (October 13).

A month later, an album that Stevie and brother Jimmie had recorded, *Family Style,* was released and quickly reached number seven on the *Billboard* charts. The record went platinum a mere two months following its release, and garnered two Grammys: the album won as Best Contemporary Blues Recording, and a track, "D/FW," took the honor as Best Rock Instrumental. The recording was the first time that Stevie and Jimmie had laid down some tracks together. Stevie Ray, in an interview with Jesse Nash and George Flowers less than a week before his premature death, related his feelings about recording with his older brother. "We had a great time making this record. We spent more time together than we have since we were kids, so it's been more than just making a record together for us. We've been getting to know each other again." (*Billboard,* September 8, 1990.)

Stevie, who had been placed in *Guitar Player's* "Gallery of the Greats," was named Musician of the Decade at the 1990 Austin Music Awards. The following year Governor Ann Richards proclaimed October 3 "Stevie Ray Vaughan Day" in the state of Texas. Also in 1991, Jimmie Vaughan compiled, mixed, and released ten studio performances by Stevie Ray and Double Trouble recorded during the five years between *Couldn't Stand the Weather* (1984) and *In Step* (1989). The compilation, entitled *The Sky Is Crying,* is a tribute to many of Stevie's heroes and includes songs written by Elmore James ("The Sky Is Crying"), Jimi Hendrix ("Little Wing"), Lonnie Mack ("Wham"), Howlin' Wolf ("May I Have a Talk with You"), and Kenny Burrell ("Chitlins Con Carne"). The album eventually went double platinum, reached number ten on the *Billboard* charts, and was voted album of the year at the 1992 Austin Music Awards. The success of *The Sky Is Crying* led to the 1991 Sony Music Video release of *Live at the El Mocambo* (platinum) and 1992's *In the Beginning.*

On May 11, 1995, Stevie Ray's friends paid tribute to Stevie himself at the Austin City Limits Sound Stage, a show that would later be made into the Epic album and home video, *A Tribute to Stevie Ray Vaughan* (1996). The all-star cast included Jimmie Vaughan, Eric Clapton, Bonnie Raitt, Buddy Guy, B.B. King, Robert Cray, Art Neville, and Dr. John as well as the Double Trouble crew of Tommy Shannon, Chris Layton, and Reese Wynans. Later that year Epic Records released *Stevie Ray Vaughan & Double Trouble's Greatest Hits,* which was accompanied by the Epic Home Video *Live from Austin, Texas.*

In 1997 Epic pleased Stevie Ray's fans by releasing his great October 4, 1984 concert from New York's Carnegie Hall. *Live at Carnegie Hall* captures Stevie at his prime, playing crowd favorites such as "Scuttle Buttin'" and "Cold Shot," as well as songs not available on any other albums, such as Vaughan's great renditions of Guitar Slim's "Letter to My Girlfriend" and Albert King's "C.O.D." In 1999 Sony/Legacy reissued *Texas Flood, Couldn't Stand the Weather, Soul to Soul,* and *In Step,* along with *The Real Deal: Greatest Hits 2.* In 2000, the label released *Blues at Sunrise,* featuring ten of Vaughan's performances.

Although Stevie Ray Vaughan is no longer here with us, his memory is carried on by his family, friends, and albums. Dr. John (Mac Rebbenack), a long-time friend and keyboardist of Stevie Ray, told Don McLeese: "His spirit is with us here. You can take all the meat, the bones, the dust—whatever's left—and it don't mean a whole lot. But the music is what he loved and where the spirit came, and we've got that. That way he's always with us." (Rolling Stone, June 29, 1995)

Entry by Adam Seidman

VEGA, SUZANNE: *Singer, guitarist, keyboards, songwriter, producer. Born Santa Monica, California, July 11, 1959.*

With her breakthrough chart hits of the mid-1980s, Suzanne Vega showed there was a market—and a sizable one—for female urban folksingers. Her achievements are credited with opening the door to major-label support for many talented artists, including Tracy Chapman, Michelle Shocked, and Shawn Colvin. Though there certainly are elements of rock and pop in her material, she continued to be a major contributor to the modern folk movement of the last decades of the twentieth century and was often featured at folk festivals in the United States and Canada (including, for instance, the Calgary Folk Festival in 1995), as well as in England and on the Continent, where she retained a very strong following.

She was born in California but grew up in the East Harlem section of New York populated mostly by people of Puerto Rican Hispanic descent. She had a close relationship with her Puerto Rican–American stepfather, a novelist by profession, and for years thought she herself was half Puerto Rican. She didn't meet her real father until she was almost out of her teens; when she did, he informed her, among other things, that her grandmother, Helen Ward, had been a drummer with a group called the Merry Makers' Ladies Orchestra. The band, which played boogie-woogie, was billed as "the hottest band this side of Hades."

She experienced an urge to perform from an early age, she told Karen O'Brien for the book *Hymn to Her: Women Musicians Talk* (Virago, United Kingdom, 1995), so that even at five or six she "was always dancing up and down the hallway or making costumes for myself, or getting the other kids to do stuff with me, or

hit of the magnitude of "Dead Skunk." At the end of the 1990s Wainwright seemed to be making another major contribution to the arts in the form of two of his children, Rufus and Martha, both of whom have chosen to carry on the family tradition of their father and their mother, Kate McGarrigle, to become singer-songwriters.

Wainwright was born in North Carolina in 1946. His father, Loudon Wainwright Jr., was a well-known editor and writer for *Life* magazine. The family was well-to-do, and Wainwright grew up, for the most part, in Westchester County, New York, though for a short period the family lived in Beverly Hills, California, where one of Loudon's playmates was Liza Minnelli; he wrote the song "Liza" about his boyhood crush on her. He was sent to the same boarding school in Delaware his father had attended. Along the way, he heard Bob Dylan play at the Newport Folk Festival. He was later often compared to Dylan ("Talkin' New Bob Dylan"). He started playing guitar.

After attending about a year of Carnegie-Mellon College, where he studied drama, Loudon dropped out and headed west for the Haight-Ashbury district of San Francisco and the Summer of Love. He ended up being arrested in Oklahoma for possession of marijuana and spent a few days in prison there. After his father bailed him out, Loudon returned to New York City, where he started working odd jobs. Around this time he began writing his own songs and performing in some folk music clubs, including the Village Gaslight, where Milton Kramer heard him perform and became his manager. Loudon got his first record contract with Atlanta and put out his first album, *Loudon Wainwright III*, in 1970, followed soon after with *Album II*. His third album, *Album III*, contained the number one hit "Dead Skunk," which Loudon allegedly wrote in just fifteen minutes.

The huge success of "Dead Skunk" brought Wainwright the reputation of a singer of novelty songs, though previously much of his material had been more serious in nature. His live performances were notoriously lively and full of his wry humor. His albums, on the other hand, have been criticized for failing to convey that sense of fun and humor. Of course, the record management wanted Loudon to come up with another "Dead Skunk." As he told Sam Sutherland of *Music Central On Line* in 1996, "When you start off, everybody needs a shtick, and when I started being that angst-ridden 21-year-old, the songs in the beginning were very bleak and serious for a while, but when I got up and performed them, I started to squirm around and physicalize them, and I noticed that people started to laugh. And then I went with that, and then I would write silly songs, like 'Nice Jewish Girls' or 'Plane, Too.' Or 'Dead Skunk,' for that matter—songs that were designed to make audiences laugh because I enjoyed that. But I also enjoyed getting an audience to gasp, or to just think, or to even get upset or pissed off. So over the

years, in a 90-minute show what I try to do is do all of that. And people would say to me, particularly early on, 'Oh, those silly songs that you write. I hate that. I hate "Dead Skunk," and I hate all that funny stuff. Why don't you just sing the serious stuff?' The answer is that I enjoy making people laugh, and the other thing, too, so why not do it all?"

However, his next few albums—*Attempted Mustache* (1974, CBS), *Unrequited* (1975, CBS), *T Shirt* (1976, Arista), and *Final Exam* (1978, Arista)—featured songs more reflective of his personal life. He had married folksinger-songwriter Kate McGarrigle, half of the sister duo of Kate and Anna McGarrigle. Loudon chronicled the events of his life in song, including childbirth ("Dilated to Meet You"), his son's breastfeeding ("Rufus Is a Tit Man"), and also the difficulties with the relationship ("Your Mother and I"), which ultimately ended in divorce after the birth of their second child, Martha. Around this time he also parted ways with his longtime manager, Milton Kramer.

Nevertheless, performing remained a constant for Wainwright. In 1975 he had a brief but recurring role on the hit TV show *M*A*S*H* as singing surgeon Captain Calvin Spaulding. He later appeared in a few films—Neil Simon's *The Slugger's Wife* and David Jones's *Jacknife,* starring Robert DeNiro—several other television shows, and some plays, including *Pump Boys and Dinettes* on Broadway.

Wainwright also spent time in England and acquired a devoted following over there. He first went to London in 1971 and recorded a show for BBC Radio One and developed an immediate fan base. When his career in the United States was stagnant in the late 1970s and early 1980s, he continued to enjoy success in England, playing concert halls, whereas in the States he was appearing in small clubs. He also appeared on BBC 1 TV on the *Jasper Carrott Show* as a resident American, wiseguy singer-songwriter, and on another show, on BBC 2 TV, *Loudon and Co.*

Back in America, Wainwright kept recording albums, *A Live One* (Radar, 1979) and *Fame and Wealth* (Demon/Rounder, 1982), followed by *I'm Alright* (Demon/Rounder, 1985) and *More Love Songs* (Demon/Rounder, 1986), the latter two of which were nominated for Grammy Awards. More albums included *Therapy* (Silvertone, 1988), *History* (Virgin, 1992), *Career Moves* (Virgin, 1993), *Grown Man* (Virgin, 1996), and *Little Ship* (Virgin, 1997), the latter featuring duets with Shawn Colvin. He was married briefly to singer-songwriter Suzzy Roche, and their union produced one child, but that marriage also ended in divorce.

Among Wainwright's other achievements, he has written and performed some topical songs for National Public Radio and has been featured on ABC-TV's *Nightline* with Ted Koppel, singing songs he wrote: "Brand New Braver World," about the declining birth rate; "Tonya's Twirls," about Olympic skater Tonya

Harding; and "Talkin' Woodstock '94," about Woodstock's twenty-fifth anniversary. Among other career highlights was when Johnny Cash recorded one of his songs, "The Man Who Couldn't Cry," on his 1994 album *American Recordings.* Throughout the years, Wainwright has provided backup vocals and guitar for Earl Scruggs and various other performers and groups.

The late 1990s were busy for Wainwright. He appeared on *Austin City Limits* on PBS. He was a performer-emcee on the Newport Folk Festival tour in June and July 1998. He performed on the CD *The McGarrigle Hour,* featuring ex-wife Kate and her sister, Anna, and children Rufus and Martha Wainwright, as well as some other McGarrigle family members, along with Emmylou Harris and Linda Rondstadt. Later that same year, his old albums *Attempted Mustache* and *Unrequited* were rereleased as CDs. In 1999 Rykodisc issued *Social Studies.* His son, Rufus, considered one of the brightest new talents of the late 1990s (and quite openly gay), released his first CD on the DreamWorks label.

Taken as a whole, Wainwright's body of work can be said to document not only his own private journey through life but that of much of the so-called Baby Boomer generation, with all its seriousness, fears, anxiety, and humor. For example, on his 1996 album, *Grown Man,* the first cut on the CD, "The Birthday Present," was recorded in the shower and tells about turning forty-eight and soon facing turning fifty. Next is "Grown Man," in which he tells his girlfriend that she has a grown man for a boyfriend so she better treat him just like a kid, and that as long as she continues to look and act like a sixteen-year-old he'll adore her. Then comes "That Hospital," about the various life events that took place at the nearby hospital, from birth to death. Another song, "A Year," is about how he avoided his baby daughter for a year because he knew he wouldn't be able to stay with her—he didn't want to pick her up because then he'd have to put her down. Perhaps most interesting is "Father/Daughter Dialogue," recorded with daughter Martha, in which she sings: *Daddy, daddy with your songs, do you hope to right your wrongs? You can't undo what has been done to all your daughters and your son. The facts are in and we have found that basically you're not around.* . . . He replies: *Darling daughter, can't you see, the guy singing the songs ain't me. He's someone people wish I was. What I can't do this dude does. And if the songs seem slightly pat, I know life's messier than that.* . . . The album also contains the funny, "Dead Skunk"-like, "IWIWAL" ("I wish I Was a Lesbian and Not a Hetero"). Loudon Wainwright remains, over thirty years into his career, someone worth listening to, and has undoubtedly been a major influence on many of today's singer-songwriters as well.

Entry by Alice Seidman

WAITS, TOM: *Singer, songwriter, pianist, actor. Born Pomona, California, December 7, 1949.*

A wondrously gifted lyricist and music writer, Tom Waits had considerable influence in the entertainment field beyond his recording and concert work. His music contributed to the careers of singers as diverse as Bette Midler and Crystal Gayle and enhanced several striking films of the 1980s. From a record-industry viewpoint, he was considered a cult favorite since he probably numbered his audience in the millions worldwide instead of the tens or hundreds of millions. One element of his work that perhaps limited his following was its diversity—jazz, blues, R&B, and rock. Besides that, more than a few folk-music fans claimed him as one of their own because his blend of music and multilayered lyrics provided vignettes of many odd corners of modern life in the folk tradition.

Waits himself seemed to be living the kind of Damon Runyonesque existence on the seamy underside of American culture he described in many of his songs. In the late 1970s, when Waits's star was strongly on the rise, he still resided in a run-down motel in a seedy section of Santa Monica Boulevard in Los Angeles and greeted callers in a room littered with empty beer cans and wine bottles and butt-filled ashtrays scattered over such oddities as an old stove, an ancient-looking upright piano, and a slightly askew, aged card table.

As he talked to this writer in 1978, he flicked ashes from his cigarette on a pile of books near one elbow, appearing to reflect more kindly on the recent past than the apparently bright future ahead. (That year his activities included releasing his hit album, *Foreign Affairs;* writing special songs for Diane Keaton; and providing three songs for the score of Sylvester Stallone's movie *Paradise Alley* in which Waits acted as well.) Said Tom: "I've got a lot of miles under my belt. Played a lot of dives and a lot of small clubs. I'm still playing beer joints—just played one called the Choo Choo Room. I still keep a low profile. I still keep one foot in the streets."

He indicated with a wave of his hand that it was the back alleys, the flophouses he'd slept in (and where he still holed up at times on the road) that enriched his creativity and provided the themes for many of his songs.

He compared most of his songs to mini-short stories. "I don't think I'd write stories for books or magazines. If I'd write a short story, I'd put it in an album. 'Potter's Field' [a song on *Foreign Affairs*] is like a short story for me. Anything I write isn't valid for me unless I can perform it on stage or use it in an album."

California was always home. "I grew up in East Whittier. My father, Jesse Frank Waits, was named after the James Brothers and he grew up in LaVerne, California."

He noted that, while he liked to show off a bit as a teenager, he never thought of going into show business at the time. "I used to take regular jobs. I never really looked at the world of entertainment as a thing I could parlay into money. You don't really find it; it finds you. I had a lot of different jobs before moving over. It takes a great deal of courage to get up on stage. It's really an unnatural act."

After dropping out of school and working at everything from driving delivery trucks to selling vacuum cleaners, Tom got a job as a doorman at a club in San Diego in the late '60s. "I started working at the door taking tickets. I saw a variety of acts—string bands, country & western, comedians, miscellaneous performers. I liked it. I made eight bucks a night and lived next door." Almost without his knowing it, he became interested in music. One time while visiting his parents, he came across an old piano of his mother's in the garage and started to teach himself to play. Soon he had a small repertoire. "I played a couple of Ray Charles songs. I used to do an Elvis Presley impersonation. I did some folk songs and I was also sort of toying with writing."

After a while, he felt confident enough to drive up to Los Angeles and try out on the amateur shows called Hoot Nights at the Troubadour nightclub. One of those visits in 1969 resulted in his acquiring long-time manager Herb Cohen. The two met at the bar and Cohen suggested they work together. With Waits's typical tongue-in-cheek recall, he noted: "We met and he asked to borrow a dollar. Actually, he told me he just needed it until his brother straightened out. . . . His brother is a hunchback."

The alliance worked out, but it took a lot of persistence and hard work on both sides. Once Cohen started getting engagements for Waits, he toured constantly, which he still did at the start of the '80s. "I usually hit about 50 cities per tour. At one time I might have stayed in a joint for a while, but these days generally I do all one nighters so I can play in more cities."

As Tom's following slowly began to build in the early '70s, he gained a recording contract from Asylum. His 1973 debut album, *Closing Time,* was followed by *The Heart of Saturday Night* (1974) and *Nighthawks at the Diner* (1975). Though Waits had started playing low-down bars, by the mid-1970s he was a major attraction on college campuses. However, Waits stressed he felt good about the fact that his audience wasn't restricted to academia. "I'm not limited to the college scene. It's not just young people that listen to me. I get letters from waitresses, truck drivers, fry cooks, people from all different walks of life."

The offbeat nature of much of his material caused some critics to refer to him as a musical evocation of the beat generation of the 1950s. In truth, his music, while having some of the flavor of the beat movement, went off in many other directions. He disliked being so typecast. "I didn't even have a driver's license back in the '50s. I think some of the books written by beat writers represent an important event in the content of American literature. But I'm not nostalgic. I wouldn't want to live in the '50s. I mean I've read a lot of those cats. But, y'know, I'm not a throwback. I don't live in a vault. I try to stay abreast of current affairs."

Certainly, by the latter half of the 1970s, Waits had proven his ability to stay abreast of the musical tastes of his growing audience. His 1976 LP *Small Change* and 1977 *Foreign Affairs* and *Blue Valentine* (1978) were among the more interesting releases of those years and did well on the charts. Even before *Foreign Affairs* came out, its song "I Never Talk to Strangers" had appeared on Bette Midler's LP *Broken Blossom.*

His parents, he stressed, were well satisfied. "My dad teaches a language course in downtown L.A. now. He supports what I do. Thinks I'm a chip off the old block. He's proud of me." He indicated his mother was a little dubious about his career direction in the past, but things such as the mid-1970s Public Broadcasting TV special on him had brought her around. "I was in *Vogue* magazine a while back. A little shot of me in a club in New York. It said I was 'up and coming.' My mother liked that."

Tom began the 1980s with another excellent and unusual album on Elektra/Asylum, *Heartattack and Vine.* Soon after he was working on the Oscar-nominated score for a Francis Ford Coppola movie, *One from the Heart.* The sound track album, issued on Columbia Records, featured both Waits and country singer Crystal Gayle. More than a few critics commented that Gayle's versions of Waits's songs added new dimensions to her singing. Tom's work on *One from the Heart* had another, more important consequence. He met Kathy Brennan, who was working as a script editor for Coppola's Zoetrope Studios, and she later became Mrs. Waits as well as a collaborator on some of Tom's projects.

In 1983 he signed with a new label, Island Records, and his first album after his marriage to Kathy was *Swordfishtrombones* in September '83. It was the first album he produced himself, and he credited Kathy with giving him the self-confidence to do it. (Asylum released the retrospective *Asylum Years* in 1984.)

Meanwhile, Waits had worked on material for another Coppola film, *Rumble Fish* (1983). He once more demonstrated his acting skills with a role in the movie. In 1985 he had another record on store shelves, *Rain Dogs,* followed by the 1987 *Frank's Wild Years.* Perhaps his biggest triumph of 1987 was the role of a Depression Era derelict in director Hector Babenco's film version of William Kennedy's novel *Ironweed.* In 1988 he completed a concert film, *Big Time,* from which a live album of that title was drawn.

At the end of the '80s Tom began an ambitious project in which he worked with novelist William Burroughs *(Naked Lunch)* and director Robert Wilson on a pop opera based on the story from which Carl Maria von Weber derived his 1821 opera *Der Freischutz.* Waits and Burroughs began their collaboration at the latter's home in Lawrence, Kansas, and Wilson took score and script to direct a German cast to premiere the opera, called *The Black Rider,* at the Thalia Theater in Hamburg, Germany, in March 1990. (The show had its American premiere on November 20, 1993, as part of the Next Wave Festival at the Brooklyn Academy of Music.) Where the von Weber version had a happy ending, the Wilson-Waits-Burroughs one kept the downbeat conclusion of the original story. Waits's album *The Black Rider* was released in 1993 by Island.

His 1991 activity included acting and providing the score for Jim Jarmusch's *Down by Law,* which many considered some of the most impressive acting work of the year. In the early 1990s he added to his acting credits with roles in Francis Ford Coppola's *Bram Stoker's Dracula* and Robert Altman's late-'93 release *Short Cuts.* He told Robert Palmer for an article in the *New York Times* ("Tom Waits, All-Purpose Troubadour," Arts & Leisure Section, November 14, 1993), "I don't really consider myself an actor. I do some acting. I've chosen to just identify myself as a creative person. I don't have the confidence I'd like to have as an actor at this point. But I've learned that the acting and the music and the other projects all serve each other. There's things you learn in one that you can bring with you to the other."

During 1991 he helped longtime friend jazz saxophonist Teddy Edwards by contributing some guest material to Edwards's album *Mississippi Lad,* the latter's first release on a major label. Waits recalled that Edwards had been part of his band in the early '80s and the two also had worked together on *One from the Heart,* after which they had toured together in Europe and the South Pacific. Edwards had suggested Waits sing two of his own compositions, but Tom preferred doing Edwards originals. Waits told Zan Stewart of the *Los Angeles Times* ("Waits Does a Guest Turn with Saxophonist Edwards," November 22, 1991) that he particularly wished to do "Little Man," in which a father talked to his son: "I've loved that song since I first heard it, and now that I've got a couple of kids, it took on new meaning." (As of the early '90s, he and Kathy, who then lived in Northern California, had three children.) In the early 1990s Waits's early manager, Herb Cohen, released two collections of recordings made in late 1971 before his deal with Asylum, *The Early Years* and *The Early Years, Volume 2* on Bizarre Records.

During 1992 Tom worked to complete a new album, whose songs mostly were cowritten with his wife. Released in the fall by Island Records, *Bone Machine* proved one of his truly classic releases. Critical praise generally was lavish. For instance, James Lien, writing in *CMJ New Music Report,* commented, "It's about time the claim was made for Tom Waits as not just a multitalented songwriter and musician, but as one of the great all-around talents of this century. Indeed, there are those who keenly realize that Waits and his art just may have more to do in the long run with the monu-

mental contributions of modern composers like Harry Partch, novelists like Henry Miller, boundary-pushers like Charlie Parker, or immortal songsmiths like Kurt Weill than with most of his current pop brethren alongside him in the CD bins. . . . As usual the songs (such as "Earth Died Screaming," "The Ocean Doesn't Want Me," "I Don't Want to Grow Up," "Who Are You" and "Black Wings") . . . carry small, beautiful images and turns of lyric in virtually every line."

The album won a Grammy for Best Alternative Album. As if that effort wasn't enough, Waits also found time for a new collaboration with Burroughs and Wilson, which led to their second joint pop opera, *Alice,* based on the story of Alice in Wonderland and its creator, Lewis Carroll. This again premiered in Hamburg's Thalia Theater, in December 1992.

His name also appeared in legal stories in the early 1990s as, like friend Bette Midler in a similar case against the Ford Motor Company, he filed suit against Frito-Lay and its ad firm for unauthorized mimicking of his voice in a Doritos commercial. Pointing out that Waits for years has refused to perform in commercials, his attorneys presented testimony from people who thought the voice on the commercial was his. The defendants argued that while they consciously imitated Waits's style they did not deliberately imitate his voice. After lower courts granted Waits a $2.5 million award, the case was taken to the U.S. Supreme Court, which in January 1993 let the earlier decision stand.

In the mid-1990s Tom continued to pursue diverse projects, including contributing two songs, "Walk Away" and "Fall of Troy," to the sound track of the Tim Robbins–Susan Sarandon film *Dead Man Walking.* (The sound track album was issued in late 1995.)

In 1998, Island released *Beautiful Maladies: The Island Years.* Waits selected the twenty-three tracks for the retrospective, including "Frank's Wild Years," "Straight to the Top (Rhumba)," "Singapore," "Downtown Train," "Black Rider," "Johnsburg, Illinois," "16 Shells from a Thirty-Ought Six," "Time," and "Jesus Gonna Be Here." Waits left Island and signed a one-record contract with Epitaph Records in 1998. In the meantime, Waits coproduced *Extremely Cool* (Slow River/Rykodisc), the second album in eighteen years by L.A. artist Chuck E. Weiss, the subject of Rickie Lee Jones's "Chuck E's in Love." His 1999 Epitaph album, *Mule Variations,* won the Grammy for Best Contemporary Folk Album.

Based partly on an interview with Irwin Stambler

WARNER, FRANK AND ANNE: *Husband-and-wife folk music collectors, producers, performers. Anne Warner, born St. Louis, Missouri, October 18, 1905; died Grafton, Massachusetts, April 26, 1991. Frank Warner, born Selma, Alabama, April 5, 1903; died Glen Cove, New York, February 28, 1978.*

In 1938 Frank and Anne Warner were living in Greenwich Village when a professor named Maurice Matteson showed them a dulcimer made by Nathan Hicks of Beech Mountain, North Carolina. The Warners were so intrigued by the instrument that they wrote to Nathan asking him to make them a dulcimer. But times were tough and Hicks didn't have enough money for glue and other materials. So he wrote back dejectedly explaining why he couldn't make them a dulcimer. In June 1938 the Warners packed up their car with food and clothes and headed to Beech Mountain to meet the Hicks family. It was there that they encountered Nathan; his wife, Rena Hicks; a large number of Hicks children; and Nathan's son-in-law Frank Proffitt, who had walked eight miles from his home in Pick Britches Valley, Watauga County, to be there. Among the first songs Proffitt played for them was "Tom Dooley."

So began a lifelong friendship and an extraordinary musical relationship. Frank Warner, who often performed songs by people he had met during his travels, taught "Tom Dooley" to Alan Lomax, who included it in his book *Folk Song U.S.A.* in 1947. Although Frank recorded it for Elektra in 1952, the Kingston Trio got their 1958 version from Lomax's book. "Tom Dooley" sold millions of copies and helped spark the folk music revival of the late 1950s. When Proffitt first heard the Trio's song he was offended. He thought they were making fun of his family. Eventually, after an out-of-court settlement, Proffitt and his family began to receive royalties from the song in 1962.

Before meeting the Hicks family and Proffitt, Frank and Anne were interested in learning and performing folk songs. But it was really that experience in 1938 that made them passionate about collecting traditional American folk music. Over the next three decades they made numerous trips to Beech Mountain and Watauga County to record members of the Hicks family and Frank Proffitt. Although Frank Warner worked as an executive for the YMCA in New York, he and Anne took their month-long vacations each year to travel to several key locales to collect folk music along the eastern seaboard: to the Appalachians, the Adirondacks of New York, the White Mountains of New Hampshire, the Outer Banks of North Carolina, Tidewater, Virginia, and Long Island.

By 1941 David Grimes, a vice president of Philco, had developed the first battery-powered recording machine (the Wilcox Gay Recordio), which allowed the Warners to make field recordings. The music they collected was kept in the vaults at the Library of Congress; their notes and photos were housed at Duke University.

In 1984 Syracuse University Press published the most comprehensive book of material from their travels: *Traditional American Folk Songs from the Anne and Frank Warner Collection.* The 501-page book, compiled by Anne Warner and edited by her son Jeff Warner, includes songs, archival material, and an engaging narrative about the people they met along the way. Wayland D. Hand, a musicologist at the University of California at Los Angeles, called it "the richest single volume of folk songs and ballads to come from the hands of any American folk song scholar."

But the vast recorded material remained in the vaults. That changed in the late 1990s, when Tim Erikson, of the band Cordelia's Dad, and Joshua Michaell, of Appleseed Recordings, approached Frank and Anne's sons Jeff and Gerret about getting some of the material out before the public. As a result, in 2000 Appleseed released a CD titled *Her Bright Smile Haunts Me Still: Music from the Anne and Frank Warner Collection.* The title comes from a song collected in 1951 from the Gallop sisters (Eleazar Tillett and Martha Etheridge), who lived on the Outer Banks. Appleseed released a second CD from the collection focusing on the music of Frank Proffitt, *Nothing Seems Better to Me: Frank Proffitt and the Music of North Carolina.*

Among the other artists the Warners met were Yankee John Galusha in the Adirondack Mountains of New York. He sang "The Days of Forty-Nine," a minstrel song about the Gold Rush. In New Hampshire Lena Bourne Fish sang 100 songs for them. Among those were "Whiskey in the Jar" and "Gypsy Davy." On their trips to North Carolina's Outer Banks they collected songs from an African American woman, Sue Thomas, who worked as a cook. In 1933 Thomas first taught Frank the song "He's Got the Whole World in His Hands," later popularized by Mahalia Jackson and Odetta. At Crab Tree Creek, in Piedmont, North Carolina, they recorded Rebecca King Jones, who lived in a cabin in the woods. Jones was born in 1866, and her father had fought at Gettysburg. Among the songs she performed were "Barbara Allen" and "Chimbley Sweeper."

Besides the many songs they collected by Frank Proffitt and Roby, Nathan, Rena, and Buna Hicks, they also recorded songs by Lee Monroe Presnell, a man with a bushy mustache and an extraordinary singing style they first met in Beech Mountain in 1951. He sang "George Collins," "Red Rosy Bush," and "Farewell to Old Bedford."

Frank Warner, whose father also worked for the YMCA, spent his first six years in Selma. The first song he remembered was sung by a black woman who was washing clothes in her backyard. When he was twelve, his family moved to Durham, North Carolina. He attended Duke University, where he sang in several groups and became interested in traditional music after meeting Dr. Frank C. Brown, a music collector specializing in the folk music of North Carolina. In 1932 he moved to New York to work for the YMCA, where he met his wife-to-be, Anne Locher. Anne was born in St. Louis and raised in the Midwest. She attended Northwestern University and then moved to New York. They were married in 1935.

Anne kept meticulous notes and coauthored several articles for publications like the *Christian Science Monitor* and *Sing Out!* She wrote liner notes for her husband's albums. As Alan Lomax noted in a forward to *Traditional American Folk Songs:* "When Frank was preparing to sing, you would note the delight rising in him. You could see his eyes glowing with fun, the corners of his mouth twitching. He was remembering the person whole, getting ready to relive the strange fantasy of the ballad story, to play the part for you in the multilevel way he had, so that the original singer was there, presented through Frank."

In 1963 Frank Warner authored *Folk Songs of the Eastern Seaboard: From a Collector's Notebook,* published by Southern Press, a series of lectures he often gave about the singers that also includes lyrics from the most famous songs. Warner recorded *Songs of the Hudson Valley* (Disc Records) in 1946. He recorded folk songs he learned from his trips to North Carolina for the Elektra LP *Frank Warner Sings American Folk Songs and Ballads* (1952), followed by *Songs and Ballads of America's Wars* (1954), *Our Singing Heritage* (1958), *Songs of the Civil War* (Prestige, 1961), *The Civil War* (Heirloom, 1962), and *Come All You Good People* (Minstrel, 1976).

Word of their trips to North Carolina spread to Folk-Legacy co-owners Sandy and Caroline Paton, who made their own trips to Beech Mountain. As a result, Folk-Legacy issued *Beech Mountain Ballads Volumes I and II* (1964), *Frank Proffitt, Reese, North Carolina* (1962), and *Frank Proffitt, Memorial Album* (1968).

Jeff and Gerret Warner grew up listening to their father perform the songs, and accompanied their parents on field trips. Although Frank and Anne have passed on, Jeff and Gerret are carrying on the tradition. Jeff has been a traditional performer for most of his life. Gerret is a filmmaker. They were at the Folk Alliance Conference in Albuquerque, New Mexico, in 1999, when Frank and Anne were awarded a Lifetime Achievement Award. After singing the cowboy song "The Chisholm Trail," which their father had them sing at his concerts, Jeff and Gerret explained why their parents were so good at what they did: "The Warners collected not just songs but singers of songs. . . . The people were first, the music was second."

Written with the assistance of Jeff Warner and Joshua Michaell

WATERS, MUDDY: *Singer, guitarist, harmonica player, band leader, songwriter. Born Rolling Fork, Mississippi, April 4, 1915; died Chicago, Illinois, April 30, 1983.*

As a performer, writer, preserver of traditional black music, and pioneer electric guitarist, Muddy Waters contributed to developments in blues, R&B, folk, and rock. One of his most famous songs, "Rollin' Stone," inspired the names of the English rock group, a song by Bob Dylan, and a rock magazine. He was a father figure to such rockers as Johnny Winter, Chuck Berry, and the Rolling Stones, and next-generation bluesmen like Buddy Guy and Robert Cray. As Muddy put it; "The blues had a baby, and they called it rock 'n' roll"—and the blues he had in mind was his own.

Born McKinley Morganfield on the Kroger Plantation in Sharkey County, Mississippi, the second son of Berta Jones and Ollie Morganfield, a farmer and musician, Muddy was heir to the Delta Blues tradition. In rural Mississippi poverty was the normal state of affairs, and music a way of coping. After Muddy's mother died when he was three, his father remarried, sending his son north to his grandmother's house in Clarksdale, Mississippi. He taught himself harmonica at nine and sang in the church choir. He even considered becoming a preacher. By ten, McKinley was working as a field hand for fifty to seventy-five cents a day.

Muddy heard many blues renditions by local performers, both while they worked and at get-togethers. (According to Alan Lomax, he owned records by Arthur Crudup, Peetie Wheatstraw, Tony Hollins, and Sonny Boy Williamson.) He earned his nickname in those years. "[My grandmother] used to say I'd sneak out and play in the mud when I was little so she started calling me Muddy. The kids added Waters; it was a 'sling' [slang] name and it just stuck."

He sang at local events in his youth and said he was playing harmonica at thirteen, earning fifty cents a night plus food, which later escalated to $18 a night working with several sidemen in the 1930s. He started learning guitar at seventeen, basing his bottleneck style on bluesmen Robert Johnson and Eddie "Son" House, who showed him how to tune his guitar "three ways—nachul, Spanish, and cross note" (*The Land Where the Blues Began,* Lomax, pg. 411). "He'd always call Son 'the ol' man,'" Johnny Winter told Mark A. Humphrey (liner notes for MCA's *Blue Sky* CD, 1992). He first began performing at local parties with a couple of friends, Scott Bohannon and Henry "Son" Simms and their string band, the Son Simms Four.

Word of Muddy's ability circulated among folk-music collectors. In the summers of 1941 and 1942 folklorist Alan Lomax went to Mississippi and recorded Son House and Muddy for the Library of Congress Archive of American Folk Song. Muddy was working as a tractor driver on a cotton plantation at the time, living in a small sharecropper's cabin with his wife, uncle, and grandmother on eight acres with four hogs and seven chickens. "I remember thinking how low-key Morganfield was, grave even to the point of shyness," Lomax wrote. "But I was bowled over by his artistry. There was nothing uncertain about his performances. He sang and played with such finesse, with such a mercurial and sensitive bond between voice and guitar, and he expressed so much tenderness in the way he handled his lyrics, that he went right beyond all his predecessors—Blind Lemon, Charley Patton, Robert Johnson, Son House, and Willie Brown."

Initially, with associate John Work, Lomax recorded "I Be's Troubled" and "Country Blues." Later, they recorded several more sides. Those 1941–42 tracks are available on *Down on Stovall's Plantation* on Testament, reissued by MCA as *Complete Plantation Recordings* (1993).

In 1943, eager to break away from the drudgery of farm labor, Muddy briefly joined the Silas Green tent show playing harmonica. That work inspired Muddy to look for new opportunities. The turning point came in 1943, when he asked the Stovall Plantation overseer to raise his pay from $22^1/_2$ cents to 25 cents an hour. The overseer refused, and so Muddy took the Illinois Central from Memphis to Chicago (like 250,000 other blacks migrating north during the war years), where he soon got a job on the loading docks of a paper mill. For the next few years he held several other jobs, while performing in the evenings. He met other artists, including Big Bill Broonzy and John Lee "Sonny Boy" Williamson, and his name came up when recording executives were in the market for new blues artists. In 1946 he recorded three sides for independent producer Lester Melrose, who sold them to Columbia. But the sides were never issued (until 1971). In 1947 things finally fell into place when he signed with Chicago-based Aristocrat Records, recording "Johnson Machine Gun" and "Fly Right Little Girl." His debut single paired "Gypsy Woman" with "Little Anna Mae," which went nowhere. Soon after, however, he provided the label with two big hits: "I Can't Be Satisfied" backed with "I Feel Like Going Home," briefly on the R&B charts in 1948. He slowly increased his stature with his own recordings and as a sideman for other artists.

In the meantime, he was playing the nightclubs where Muddy came to exemplify the Chicago Sound, a plugged-in "city" version of the earthy Delta blues. "Mine was a rustier sound, a grittier sound," Muddy told Tom Wheeler of *Guitar Player* when asked to compare his sound to Big Bill Broonzy and Tampa Red. As Studs Terkel quoted Big Bill Broonzy for the liner notes of *The Best of Muddy Waters* (Chess, 1958; reissued on CD by MCA): "It's real. Muddy's real. See the way he plays guitar? Mississippi style, not the city way. He don't play chords, he don't follow what's written down in the book. He plays notes, all blue notes. Making what he's thinking."

The Muddy Waters Blues Band included such legendary performers as Little Walter on harmonica, Otis Spann on piano, Willie Dixon on bass, Jimmy Rogers on second guitar, and Elgin Evans and Fred Below on drums. Alan Lomax theorizes that Muddy kept such a talented ensemble together because of his "deep-rooted sociability."

"When one of my band members goes over big, I really like it," Muddy told James Rooney for his book *Bossmen.* "A lot of people ain't like that. They don't want to give their band members a break. . . . I let them all try. They feel good behind that, you know. Everybody wants to be a star. So I give 'em a chance."

When aspiring bluesmen arrived in Chicago, they headed to the bars where Muddy was playing. Harmonica player Charlie Musselwhite recalls seeing him for twenty-five cents and getting a free beer at the Peppers Lounge. At the behest of a waitress, Muddy invited Charlie to sit in, giving him his first big break. "Muddy would always talk to me, invite me over to his table, buy me drinks, have me sit in," Musselwhite says. "Any time I came he would have me sit in, which was just about a lot, not every night. Muddy would go on the road. He didn't just stay there."

After another fling with Columbia in the late '40s, he returned to Aristocrat, which had been absorbed by Chess Records. Muddy soon became one of the label's bread-and-butter artists. In 1951, he had top ten R&B hits with "Louisiana Blues" and "Long Distance Call," following those with "She Moves Me" (1952) and "Mad Love" (1953). In 1954 he had a vintage year as he presented "Rollin' Stone" (also known as "Catfish Blues") and such R&B top 10 singles as "I'm Ready," "I'm Your Hoochie Coochie Man," and "Just Make Love to Me." In 1955 he made R&B hit lists with "Mannish Boy," adding "Close to You" and "Got My Mojo Workin' " later in the decade.

His career hit a new high in 1958 when he made a triumphal tour of England, where his concerts influenced many young musicians. (The Beatles listed Muddy as a primary influence during their American tour; when a journalist asked where Muddy Waters and Bo Diddley were located, one of the Beatles shot back, "You Americans don't seem to know your most famous citizens.") His universal appeal was apparent in the way artists and audiences from folk, jazz, and rock all loved his music. From the late '50s into the '80s, he and his band were favorites at festivals worldwide. Among the major events to which he returned again and again were the Monterey Jazz Festival, Newport Folk Festival, and Newport Jazz Festival in the '60s and '70s.

Over the decades, Muddy made dozens of albums on a variety of labels. In the latter 1970s, his albums were marketed by Columbia, finally bringing him success with the alignment. Among his Chess LPs were *Best of Muddy Waters* (1958) (with hits from the early 1950s recorded with Little Walter, Jimmy Rogers, Otis Spann, and Willie Dixon), *Muddy Waters Sings Big Bill Broonzy* (1959), *Muddy Waters at Newport 1960* (1961), *Folk Singer* (1964), *Real Folk Blues* (1966), *Brass and the Blues* and *More Real Folk Blues* (1967), and (on Chess's Cadet subsidiary) *After the Rain* (1969). *They Call Me Muddy Waters* (1971) and *The London Muddy Waters Sessions* (1972) won Grammys for Best Ethnic or Traditional Recording two years in a row. Accompanying him on the 1972 tracks and *London Revisited with Howlin' Wolf* (1974) were British stars Stevie Winwood and Rick Grech and Ireland's Rory Gallagher. Other Chess albums in his catalog as of the mid-1970s included *Live at Mr. Kelly's, Can't Get No Grindin', Electric Mud,* the excellent *Fathers and Sons* (with Otis Spann, Mike Bloomfield, Paul Butterfield, and Buddy Miles), *Sail On, Unk in Funk,* and *McKinley Morganfield a.k.a. Muddy Waters.* He contributed several songs to *The Blues: A Real Summit Meeting,* Buddah's 1975 LP of the New York Newport Jazz Festival, *Mud in Your Ear* (1973) and, with Luther Johnson, *Chicken Shack* (1974) on Muse Records. He won another Grammy for Best Ethnic and Traditional Recording in 1975 for *Muddy Waters' Woodstock,* released on Chess, which also issued *Rolling Stone* in 1982.

Though Muddy was in his sixties in the second half of the '70s, his career seemed to generate new momentum. Throughout those years, he maintained a breakneck schedule that might have sent much younger artists to the sidelines, touring worldwide thirty-five to forty weeks a year.

Nor did his recording work suffer. He signed with Blues Sky in the mid-1970s for a series of new albums (produced by Johnny Winter) that explored new facets of the man and his music. He earned three consecutive Grammys for Best Ethnic or Traditional Recordings. The first LP, *Hard Again* (1971), showed Muddy at the top of his form backed by a band comprised of Winter, James Cotton, Charles Calmese, longtime Waters sidemen "Pinetop" Perkins, Bob Margolin, and Willie "Big Eyes" Smith. The equally impressive follow-up, *I'm Ready* (1978), reunited him with '50s sidemen harmonica player Big Walter and guitarist Jimmy Rogers. In 1979 material recorded during his 1977 and 1978 national tours was issued on *Muddy "Mississippi" Waters Live,* which also won a Grammy. *King Bee,* the last Winter-produced Waters album, was recorded in 1980. It was Muddy's last session.

There were many other highlights of Muddy's illustrious career that took place in the '70s. In 1971, he and his group were the subject of an award-winning one-hour documentary presented by the National Educational network. It gave insight into Muddy's skills and philosophy by showing a typical live program (at a Chicago blues club) beginning with rehearsals and continuing through the set.

In November 1977, Muddy was a guest of honor at "The Last Waltz," the farewell concert for the Band in San Francisco, where he shared the stage with Bob Dylan and Van Morrison. His performance of "Mannish Boy" was an important part of the concert album *The Last Waltz* (Warner Brothers, 1978) and director Martin Scorsese's film of the event. Muddy's audience had shifted. "I think it surprised him that the first part of his life he played completely for black people, and towards the latter part of his life he was playing mostly for young white teenagers," Johnny Winter said.

On August 9, 1978, he performed at the annual White House staff picnic in Washington, D.C. His forty-minute set included "Hoochie Coochie Man," "Got My Mojo Working," and "The Blues Had a Baby and They Called It Rock and Roll" to several ovations from more than 700 guests. Commenting on Muddy's musical stature, President Jimmy Carter told the gathering: "Muddy Waters is one of the great performers of all time. He's won more awards than I could name. His music. . . . represents accurately the background and history of the American people."

In the 1980s, dozens of Muddy's albums were reissued, including *Trouble No More/Singles 1955–1959,* (1989), *The Chess Box: Muddy Waters, One More Mile,* the 1992 *Blues Sky* compilation, and a two-disc compilation of outtakes and alternate takes called *Rare and Unissued* (1994). In 1997, MCA/Chess issued an excellent compilation, *His Best 1947–55.* In 1999, two albums from concerts were issued: *Honey Bee* on Wolf, and *Hoochie Coochie Man* on Just a Memory Records.

He remained active on the concert circuit during the 1980s despite failing health, continuing to entertain audiences almost up to his death of a heart attack in April 1983.

In a tribute to Waters's work, in 1988, blues-rockers Z. Z. Top gave Clarksdale Delta Blues Museum a white electric guitar fashioned from a cypress log taken from Muddy's childhood cabin. (The museum also displays a life-size wax statue of Muddy playing guitar.) Until 1995, Muddy's cabin—a roofless shack reduced from four rooms to one by a tornado—stood off the side of the road at Stovall's Plantation outside of Clarksdale. In 1995, the House of Blues leased the shack, refurbished it, and took it on a world tour. It is scheduled to return to Clarksdale in 2000. In 1980 Waters was inducted into the Blues Hall of Fame, and in 1987 the Rock and Roll Hall of Fame.

In January 1999, PBS broadcast a one-hour documentary, *A Tribute to Muddy Waters, King of the Blues.* The bulk of the show (which included clips of Muddy Waters in his early years and interviews with Bob Dylan and Keith Richards) featured a tribute concert at the Kennedy Center with performances by his son, McKinley Morganfield, Keb' Mo', Buddy Guy, Bo Diddley, Charlie Musselwhite, and Phoebe Snow.

With help from John Ruskey, curator, Delta Blues Museum, Clarksdale, Mississippi

WATERSONS, THE: *Vocal group from Hull, England. Original members, mid-1960s, all born England, Norma Christine Waterson, born August 15, 1939; Mike Waterson, born January 16, 1941; Elaine Lal Waterson, born February 15, 1943, died September 4, 1998; John Harrison. Harrison left 1966, group disbanded 1968. Reformed 1972 with Bernie Vickers taking Harrison's place, in turn replaced by Martin Carthy, born May 21, 1940, Hatfield,*

Hertfordshire, England. Rachel Waterson, born April 3, 1966, joined 1985 as temporary replacement for Lal. Norma Waterson, Martin Carthy, and Eliza Carthy (born 1975) performed as Waterson:Carthy in 1990s.

The singing Waterson family, whose extended membership over three decades from the mid-'60s to the mid-'90s included cousins, husbands, and children, gave new life to English traditional music with its a cappella harmonies. Not that group members couldn't play instruments: family elder Norma Waterson, whom *Folk Roots* magazine called the very heartbeat not only of the Watersons but of English folk music itself, learned guitar and concertina and taught her siblings Mike and Lal to play, and her husband, Martin Carthy, ranks as one of the all-time U.K. guitar greats. But they enjoyed unaccompanied harmony singing and felt it gave better expression to traditional compositions than band-based music. Their live performances and recordings influenced many other artists at home and abroad not only in the folk domain but in pop and rock as well. (Their version of "John Barleycorn," for instance, spurred Steve Winwood to adapt it for a hit single by the rock group Traffic in the mid-'60s.)

Singing and playing music for the sheer enjoyment of it was ingrained in the Waterson children—Norma, Lal, and brother Michael—from their early years. They were raised in the Yorkshire city of Hull by a grandmother, their parents having died when they were very young, in such an environment singing seemed as natural as breathing. Norma told *Folk Roots,* "We used to have these great big parties where we all got together and sang and my uncle would play 'cos he played cornet in the pit bands in the silent cinema at Hull. All our relations either played or sang and we'd have these huge gatherings of the tribes playing music hall songs and all sorts."

The family ran a small club in Hull in the '50s and '60s where several of the Waterson children began to perform in public. Norma, Mike, and Lal had fallen in love with traditional songs, but she stressed that the music at the venue wasn't restricted to that. Other forms of music from pop-folk to American roots blues were welcome. And, she stressed, her first husband was a jazz drummer. The group that was to become the Watersons evolved during the early 1960s from earlier combinations like the Mariners and the Folksons. Finally the family name was adopted by a quartet consisting of Norma, Mike, Lal, and their cousin, John Harrison, who soon built a following among U.K. folk fans. In 1964 the tracks they provided on the *New Voices* anthology album brought critical praise and national attention.

They followed that with a series of mid-'60s albums on Topic that ranked among the best U.K. folk releases of those years: *Frost and Fire* in 1965, and *The Watersons* and *A Yorkshire Garland,* both in 1966. The lead-ing British trade magazine, *Melody Maker,* selected *Frost and Fire* U.K. Folk Album of the Year for 1965. By 1967, however, John Harrison had left, and in 1968, when Norma decided to move to Montserrat in the West Indies, the group's breakup was signaled.

In the early 1970s, when Norma returned to Yorkshire, she helped Mike and Lal complete the 1972 LP *Bright Phoebus* on Trailer Records. (The album, intended not as a traditional collection but rather a folk-rock disc, included such originals as Mike's "Rubber Band" and Lal's "Fine Horseman," and backing by Richard Thompson and Ashley Hutchings.) Norma's marriage to Martin Carthy provided a Watersons roster in which he took the place of John Harrison. The new alignment continued to thrill folk-music record buyers in the United Kingdom and United States with releases like *For Pence and Spicy Ale* (1975), *Sound, Sound Your Instruments of Joy* (1977), and *Green Fields* (1981). The group was featured on the concert circuit in the United Kingdom and Europe with occasional tours of other parts of the world. Some of the members worked on side projects, examples being Lal's and Norma's 1977 album *A True Hearted Girl* and Mike Waterson's solo LP of the same year. Lal's daughter Maria Knight made her recording debut on *A True Hearted Girl.* (Martin Carthy, of course, maintained a separate career from his Watersons work.)

In the mid-1980s Lal fell ill for a long time, and the future of the singing group was endangered. She decided to stop live concert or festival gigs, and that in turn resulted in Mike's retreat from the group. Norma told *Folk Roots,* "When Lal made the decision it did unsettle everybody because we'd done it so long and it unsettled the whole balance. Michael didn't want to perform if Lal wasn't there and I didn't want to perform if they weren't there. When you've sung with your family for so long you get a sound in your head, and then all of a sudden it's not there." In 1985 Mike's daughter Rachel took over for her aunt.

By the early '90s still more Waterson offspring were making their mark, including Eliza Carthy, who exhibited excellent fiddling skills and a fine voice, and Lal's son Oliver Knight. Eliza's debut album on Topic, *Heat, Light & Sound* (1996), marked her as a likely coming star. The combination of Eliza and her parents (with accompaniment at times by her brother Martin Carthy Jr.) in the Waterson:Carthy group also became a feature on the folk venue and festival circuits. Topic issued *Waterson:Carthy* in 1994. Meanwhile, Lal and son Oliver Knight recorded an album of originals by her, *Once in a Blue Moon,* that was a contender for Best Folk Album of 1996. Another memorable event in '96 was the release of Norma's first solo album, recorded in Los Angeles for release by Hannibal/Rykodisc, which contained, besides such tunes as "Rags and Old Iron" and Lal's "Anna Dixie," a rare original by her, "Hard Times

Heart," and versions of songs by writers like Elvis Costello, Billy Bragg, and Jerry Garcia. In addition to Eliza and Martin Carthy, Norma had backing on the album from Richard Thompson on guitar, Danny Thompson on bass, and Roger Swallow on percussion. The album was nominated for England's prestigious Mercury Music Prize.

While less active as a group in the '90s, the Watersons still did some a cappella singing performances, typically involving the longtime core members Norma, Lal, Mike, and Martin Carthy, joined by Eliza Carthy.

Several of the Watersons' earlier works were reissued on CD in the 1990s, including *Frost and Fire* (1990, which included half of *Sound, Sound Your Instruments of Joy*), *For Pence and Spicy Ale* (1993), *Early Days* (1994, including most of *The Watersons: A Yorkshire Garland*, and five tracks from the *New Voices* anthology), *Green Fields* (1998). *A True Hearted Girl* (1999), and *Mike Waterson* (1999). Waterson:Carthy released a second collection, *Common Tongue*, on Topic in 1997. Eliza, Norma, and Martin followed with a third album, *Broken Ground* on Topic in 1999.

In the early 1990s Eliza Carthy joined with Nancy Kerr to record *Eliza Carthy & Nancy Kerr* in 1993 on Mrs. Casey Records. They followed two years later with *Shape of Scrape.* In the mid-1990s Eliza and Nancy formed the Kings of Calicutt with guitarist Dan Plews. Plews and Kerr left the band in 1997. Remaining members included Saul Rose on melodeon and vocals, Andi Wells on drums, Barnaby Stradling on bass, and MacLaine Colston on hammered dulcimer and vocals. They released *Eliza Carthy & the Kings of Calicutt* on Topic in 1997. The album includes traditional songs like "Whirly Whorl" and "Bonaparte's Retreat" played in a folk-rock vein. In the meantime, Eliza formed the Eliza Carthy Band, a more electric-sounding ensemble with her cousin Oliver Knight on guitar, Barnaby Stradling on bass, and Sam Thomas on drums.

In 1998 Topic released Eliza Carthy's second solo album, *Red Rice*, a two-disc, limited-edition set. The first disc included contemporary songs while the second one comprised traditional music. Indeed, in a symbolic gesture of the contemporary-traditional mixture that she represents, Eliza poses on the album cover holding her violin while also sporting a pierced lower lip and red hair. The album was nominated for a Mercury Music Prize and chosen as one of the top ten albums of the year by *Entertainment Weekly* critic David Browne. Eliza signed a deal with Warner Brothers and released a new solo album in 2000. She also embarked on a U.S. tour with Joan Baez.

On a sad note, on September 4, 1998, Lal Waterson died suddenly after she had been diagnosed with cancer only ten days earlier. Her obituaries noted the impact that Lal had as a songwriter with the Watersons and later while performing with her son. Among her most popular songs, recorded by the likes of June Tabor and Anne Briggs, were "Red Wine Promises," "Fine Horseman," and "Scarecrow." In addition to her musical gifts, she was a painter, stained-glass designer, and sculptor.

WATSON, DOC; DOC AND MERLE WATSON: *Doc, singer, guitarist, banjoist, harmonica player, born Deep Gap, North Carolina, March 2, 1923; Doc and Merle, father-and-son vocal and instrumental team. Merle born North Carolina, February 8, 1949; died North Carolina, October 23, 1985.*

Fads came and went—folk music was in, then it was out, then it seemed to find favor again; the British invasion and acid rock prospered, then waned; progressive country came to the fore; but through it all Doc Watson blithely went his own way, playing his vast repertoire of songs traditional and new, folk, country, blues, and even rock, with skill and feeling. And for almost two decades, accompanied by his son, Merle, he continued to be a favorite of a sizable number of fans, drawing capacity crowds to as many shows (at small venues) as he had done when first introduced outside his home state as a solo artist at the start of the '60s. That phase came to a close with Merle's fatal farm accident in 1985, but Doc regrouped from the tragedy and still was performing and recording new material in 2001.

At one point many audiences cheered Doc as much for his magnificent spirit in overcoming blindness (the result of an illness in his first year of life) as for his performing work. Like Riley Puckett, one of Doc's boyhood heroes, he had the ability to charm and entertain people despite the great handicap of sightlessness. But he also brought to the music field in general his unique talents, becoming perhaps the finest exponent of guitar flatpicking in the world. Smithsonian folklorist Ralph Rinzler, who first brought Doc's abilities to general attention, commented, "He is single-handedly responsible for the extraordinary increase in acoustic flatpicking and fingerpicking guitar performance. His flatpicking style has no precedent in earlier country music history."

Besides that, Doc was a virtual walking encyclopedia of folk and country songs, from classic ballads to modern country; his interests even extended to rockabilly, which resulted, for instance, in his making such unlikely additions to his songbook as Carl Perkins's "Blue Suede Shoes." For many years, contributing to the warmth of a Watson concert was the fine second guitar work of Merle Watson, who exhibited, among other things, excellent bottleneck slide guitar work.

For both Watsons and particularly for Doc in his childhood, music was a way of life. His father, a farmer, led the singing at the local Baptist church. In addition, General Dixon and Doc's mother, Annie, gathered the family around each evening for Bible reading and hymn singing. But young Arthel (his real name) didn't hear gospel music only. As he told Ralph Rinzler, (*Sing*

Out!, February–March 1964), his mother sang the children to sleep with such songs as "Omie Wise," "House Carpenter," and "The FFV." From his grandparents he learned such folk songs as "Waggoner's Lad," "Uncloudy Day," "Talk about Suffering," and "Tom Dula."

The first instrument Doc learned to play was the harmonica. His father gave him one one Christmas and then handed the boy another new one each succeeding holiday. When he was six he heard a cousin play "Goodbye Little Bonnie Goodbye" on a five-string banjo and fell in love with the banjo sound. He didn't get his own until a few years later when his brother Arnold married and Arnold's new brother-in-law gave Doc a homemade instrument. Doc's father helped him learn to play it, then made him a better banjo out of hickory, maple, and catskin.

A few years later, when Doc was attending the Raleigh School for the Blind, he added the guitar to his attainments. His father provided the difference between Doc's savings and the amount needed to buy a guitar. Before long, Doc could play guitar well too and organized a duo with his older brother Linny, with Doc holding forth on lead guitar and lead vocals and Linny playing supporting guitar and singing tenor. The music they played came from a variety of sources—material friends and neighbors played, phonograph records, and the country-music programs that Doc loved to listen to. Among the artists whose material they sang were the Carter Family, Skillet Lickers, Monroe Brothers, and Delmore Brothers.

When Doc was seventeen, he earned enough money cutting wood to buy a new guitar from Sears, Roebuck. He used this to play "The Mule Skinner Blues" in his first stage appearance, at a fiddlers' convention in Boone, North Carolina. From then on, he played at other local functions when the chance arose. When he was eighteen, he joined a group that was sometimes heard over local radio stations. It was during one of those shows, when he was nineteen, that he got his nickname. The announcer liked the name of Doc's friend Paul Greer, who played with Doc, but felt that Arthel seemed too stuffy. While this was being discussed on the program, a woman standing outside listening to it on a loudspeaker shouted "call him Doc," and from then on Doc it was.

Those activities remained a low- or nonpaying sideline for many years until, he told writer Chet Flippo, "In 1954 I met a man from Johnson City, Tennessee, whose name was Jack Williams. He came to my house that summer and when he heard me play the guitar, he said, 'Doc, let's start a little band. We'll get you an electric guitar and I'll teach you a few of the pop standards.' Jack and I worked together for eight years, sometimes with a five-piece band and sometimes four. We played in V.F.W. clubs and for lots of other organizations in eastern Tennessee and western North Carolina. The music we played was a combination of rock and roll, country and western, old pop standards and a few of the old square dance tunes."

As it turned out, it was old-time music that paved the way for Doc's step into the national spotlight. He kept on playing traditional music at home with friends, family, and particularly a banjoist named Clarence Ashley. Ashley taught Doc such songs as "The Cuckoo" and "Rising Sun Blues," better known as "House of the Rising Sun."

Ashley's reputation as a traditional artist lured some of the folk-music collectors from New York and vicinity to North Carolina. As Doc recalled, "Ralph [Rinzler] came to record Clarence Ashley [in 1960] and Clarence introduced him to me. After hearing me, Ralph persuaded me that I had something to offer in the way of entertainment. Ralph showed me the ropes and got me started on the road. If it hadn't been for his encouragement, I wouldn't have done it—no way." Some of the playing that kindled Rinzler's enthusiasm can be heard in the LP that resulted from his visit, the Folkways release *Old Time Music at Clarence Ashley's*.

The session led to an invitation for Ashley's group to come to New York for a Friends of Old Time Music concert at Town Hall in early 1961. Doc's solo spots in the concert attracted attention that finally brought the chance for him to appear at Gerde's Folk City in December 1962. He won well-deserved rounds of applause for such renditions as "The Storms Are on the Ocean" and "Willie Moore." In 1963, Doc really broke through with a thunderous ovation from 13,000 fans who listened to his set at the Newport, Rhode Island, Folk Festival and with a concert at Town Hall with Bill Monroe and the Blue Grass Boys.

Doc was beginning to make a name for himself with folk-music fans, but he found it difficult to cope with the changes in lifestyle it required. In particular he missed spending time with his wife, Rosa Lee, and two children, though he welcomed the chance to earn a living from music instead of depending on piano-tuning work and state aid. As he recalled for Dana Andrews Jennings of the *New York Times* ("Doc Watson, Down-Home Virtuoso," Arts & Leisure Section, November 12, 1995), "Being on the road is tough on a man. And there was a time in 1963 when I came close to quitting. I almost said, the hell with it. But music was the only trade I knew.

"My father instilled in me the fact that if a man can work, he should. That's why Daddy put me on one end of a crosscut saw when I was 14. So, the road was lonely, but it was a way to provide for my family. I'll never forget how proud my daughter, Nancy, was when we were able to cancel our aid from the state."

In the mid-1960s, with folk followers across the United States eager to hear more of this newly discovered troubadour, Doc not only toured more and more widely, but also was represented by a growing catalog of recordings. Folkways issued a series of albums, including one with Jean Ritchie called *Jean and Doc at Folk City,* as well as *Progressive Bluegrass* and *The Watson Family, Volumes I and II.* Joining Doc in the family albums were his mother, his brother Arnold, and Arnold's talented father-in-law, Gaither Carlton on the fiddle. Those discs included "The House Carpenter," "Bonaparte's Retreat," "Ground Hog," "Darling Corey," "The Train That Carried My Girl from Town," and "Every Day Dirt."

In 1964 Doc signed a contract with Vanguard Records, and that remained his main label throughout the 1960s. His debut on the label, *Doc Watson,* was issued in September 1964. The following year, he introduced a new individual to Watson fans when he added his then fifteen-year-old boy Merle on second guitar. The first collection featuring the father and son team was *Doc Watson & Son,* issued on Vanguard in June 1965. From then on Merle was almost always part of his father's concerts and record releases, with his playing gaining in purity and dexterity with the passing years. Though better known for his slide guitar work, when Merle wanted to he could handle the flat pick almost as adeptly as Doc.

As the 1960s went by, each year brought new LPs from Vanguard, including *Doc Watson and Family: Treasures Untold* (1964), *Home Again* (1966), *Southbound* (1966), *Ballads from Deep Gap* (1967) (which featured a number of solos by Merle), *Good Deal* (1968), and *Doc Watson on Stage* (1971). At the end of the 1960s and start of the 1970s, Doc had a number of releases on Poppy Records: *Then and Now,* and *Two Days in November.* Columbia also could point to his work on two albums, one titled *Strictly Instrumental* (with Flatt & Scruggs) in 1967 and the other *Earl Scruggs, Family and Friends.*

For a time in the late 1960s and at the start of the 1970s, Doc and Merle were relatively submerged as a result of the fadeout of the folk-music movement in favor of revitalized rock. However, they always were welcomed in concerts on college campuses and in small folk venues. However, with the new surge of interest in mainstream and progressive country, they bounced back easily to featured status. Helping to highlight their importance were two Grammy Awards voted them in successive years, both for Best Ethnic or Traditional Recording. In 1973 they won for the Poppy album *Then and Now* and in 1974 for *Two Days in November.*

In the 1970s they signed a new recording contract with United Artists, which turned out one or more albums of their work into the 1980s. Among those releases were *Elementary Doc Watson* (1972), *Doc Watson/ Memories, Lonesome Road, Look Away!* and *Live and Pickin'.* Doc and Merle also won a Grammy for Best Country Instrumental Performance (Song) for a medley of "Big Sandy/Leather Britches" from *Live and Pickin'.* Doc Watson played on the landmark 1972 Nitty Gritty Dirt Band album *Will the Circle Be Unbroken.* Other United Artists albums included *Bottle of Wine* and *Doc and the Boys.* (During the 1970s, Vanguard also issued the retrospective *The Essential Doc Watson (Live at Newport '63–'64),* and the reissue of a 1967 LP, *Old Timey Concert.*) In 1980, RCA released *Reflections,* on which Doc joined guitarist Chet Atkins.

Throughout the 1970s, Doc and Merle had more concert offers than they could handle. Among the songs they played in the mid- and late-1970s were such original Jimmie Rodgers tunes as "Mean Woman Blues," "T For Texas," "The Mississippi and You," and "I Recall a Gypsy Woman"; such old-time songs as "Little Maggie" and "The Cuckoo Bird"; a bluegrass number like "Salt Creek," Carl Perkins's "Blue Suede Shoes"; the old country standard "Rollin' in My Sweet Baby's Arms"; Mississippi John Hurt's "Spikedriver Blues"; Woody Guthrie's "Goin' Down the Road Feelin' Bad," "Tennessee Stud," and many others.

Merle spoke for both himself and his father when he told an interviewer in the late 1970s, "There are a lot of good musicians coming up, but they aren't going into the old-time music, or at least playing it really well. I think one problem is they just don't feel the music. The old traditional folk-type tunes are really a music of the people, and if you didn't grow up with it and don't know the feeling of what you're playing, it's hard to play it."

In the '80s Doc and Merle recorded for Flying Fish: *Red Rocking Chair* (1981), *Guitar Album* (1983), *Pickin' the Blues* (1985) and the retrospective *Watson Country* (1997). In October 1985 Merle died in a freak accident when a tractor overturned on him. "I don't know if we'll ever get through it," Doc said. After that grievous loss, Doc formed a partnership with guitarist Jack Lawrence, while retaining the talents of bass player T. Michael Coleman, who had backed Doc and Merle starting in 1980. He continued to tour regularly during the second half of the '80s and into the late 1990s while recording new material from time to time for his record label of those years, Sugar Hill. By 1995 he claimed to be essentially retired, but that didn't preclude a concert swing in the fall that included shows in Washington, D.C.; Valley Forge, Pennsylvania; and New York City's Bottom Line.

His output on Sugar Hill included the 1984 release *Riding the Midnight Train,* which won a Best Traditional Folk Grammy award. The label issued two albums in 1990, *On Praying Ground,* which won a Traditional Folk Grammy award, and the children's collection *Doc Watson Sings Songs for Little Pickers* (on Sugar Hill/Alacazam!). He dedicated the latter to his great-granddaughter "and to all the other little children who love fun songs." Sugar Hill also released *Down South* (1984); *Portrait* (1988); *My Dear Old Southern Home* (1991); *Remembering Merle* (1992), including recordings he had made with his son; *Memories* (1993); and *The Doc Watson Family: Songs from* the Southern Mountains (1994). Doc did not work on new studio tracks until 1995, when he prepared songs for Doc-a-billy, which focused on Doc's electric guitar period as a member of Jack Williams's rockabilly group. The year before, Sugar Hill reissued Then and Now/Two Days in November, comprising the compilations that earned Doc and Merle their 1973 and '74 Grammys. In 1997 Sugar Hill issued Mac Doc Del, followed by Home Sweet Home in '98, nominated for two Grammys.

In early 1996 Vanguard Records issued the four-CD set Doc Watson—The Vanguard Years, whose tracks mainly were drawn from his albums on the label in the late '60s and early '70s. Besides those, the package included some fifty minutes of previously unreleased live concert material. On six songs he performed duets with the late Country Hall of Famer Merle Travis, his son's namesake. The label issued Best of Doc Watson in 1999. Warners released Groovegrass in 1998.

In 1997 David Grisman's Acoustic Disc released Doc & Dawg, featuring recordings of the guitar and mandolin virtuosos. Smithsonian/Folkways reissued The Watson Family, originally recorded for Folkways in 1963. Also available in 1996 were two Smithsonian/Folkways retrospectives, the forty-eight-song collection Doc Watson and Clarence Ashley: 1960–1962 and Bill Monroe and Doc Watson: Live Duet Recordings 1963–1980. Among the tracks on the latter was a performance of "Paddy on the Turnpike" played at a White House barbecue in 1980 hosted by President Jimmy Carter.

In 1997 President Bill Clinton awarded Watson the National Medal of Arts at a ceremony at the White House. The following year, the town of Boone, North Carolina, proclaimed the third Saturday in July Doc Watson Appreciation Day. In 1999 Doc and Merle were nominated for a Grammy for Best Country Instrumental Performance for a living room recording of "Reuben's Train," with overdubs by Sam Bush, Marty Stuart, Michael Coleman, and Alan O'Bryant. At the end of the 1990s Watson was still living with his wife, Rosa Lee, on land that was homesteaded by his great-great-grandfather. In 1999 Sugar Hill issued the album by Doc and Richard Watson, Third Generation Blues. The Folk Alliance presented a Lifetime Achievement Award to Doc Watson in 2000.

WEAVERS, THE: Vocal and instrumental group. Original personnel (1948): Pete Seeger (vocals, banjo, guitar), born New York, New York, May 3, 1919; Lee Hays (vocals), born Little Rock, Arkansas, March 14, 1914; died Tarrytown, New York, August 26, 1981; Ronnie Gilbert (vocals), born Brooklyn, New York, September 7, 1926; Fred Hellerman (vocals, guitar), born Brooklyn, New York, May 13, 1927. In 1957, Seeger replaced by Erik Darling, born Baltimore, Maryland, September 25, 1933. In 1962, Darling replaced by Frank Hamilton, born New York, New York, August 3, 1934. In 1963, Hamilton replaced by Bernie Krause.

One of the most successful groups in folk-music history, the Weavers might have accomplished far more than they did if not for the congressional investigations into "un-American activities" of the 1950s. The group proved that folk music could enthrall mass audiences years before the folk boom of the late '50s. The Weavers inspired other ensembles like the Kingston Trio and Peter, Paul and Mary. The group reunited several times, including legendary concerts at Carnegie Hall in 1955, 1963, and 1980. The latter led to a 1982 documentary film called Wasn't That a Time. Vanguard also released a retrospective four-CD box set in 1993, The Weavers: Wasn't That a Time.

The group began in 1948 under the aegis of veteran folksingers Lee Hays and Pete Seeger. Seeger, the son of a musicologist and a violin teacher, grew up in Manhattan but dropped out of Harvard and hitchhiked around the country, with his banjo in hand. Hays, the son of a Methodist preacher, grew up in Arkansas and became involved in the labor movement. In December 1940 Hays and Seeger met in New York and they tried to publish a collection of labor songs. They performed together in the Almanac Singers, another landmark folk group. (Seeger actually kicked Hays out of the Almanacs, but the two later patched up their differences.) The onset of World War II broke up the group, with Seeger entering the service for several years.

Seeger and Hays corresponded during the war and in 1946 started People's Songs Inc., a mimeographed newsletter that had a circulation of 2,000. People's Songs went bankrupt at the end of the decade. In November 1948 Hays suggested to Seeger that they assemble a singing group but make it more organized than the Almanacs, according to liner notes by Mary Katherine Aldin for Wasn't That a Time. The group evolved from hootenannies in the basement of Seeger's Greenwich Village home in 1949. Hays and Seeger met Fred Hellerman and Ronnie Gilbert through People's Songs when the four of them were asked to sing accompaniment for some folk dancers. Initially, they were called the No-Name Quartet. Hellerman was reading a play called The Weavers, by Gerhart Hauptmann, hence the group's name.

The son of a Latvian immigrant in the rag business, Hellerman taught himself the guitar when he was in the Coast Guard during World War II. Gilbert, whose father came from the Ukraine and mother from Warsaw, took piano lessons as a child and inherited her political identity from her mother, a member of the Garment Workers' Union. She sang with the Priority Ramblers in D.C. before joining the Weavers.

The group made its New York debut at the Village Vanguard during Christmas 1949, an engagement that lasted for six months. Seeger and Hays did most of the songwriting at first, but as the demand for material increased Hellerman wrote as well. All four cowrote "Kisses Sweeter Than Wine." Seeger's wife Toshi managed the group at first, but in 1950 Pete Kameron and then Harold Leventhal, a music publisher whom Seeger had known through his political work, took over the managerial duties. Band leader Gordon Jenkins (best known as one of Frank Sinatra's arrangers) attended a Village Vanguard show and insisted that Decca Records sign them.

Looking back on those times for a *Sing Out!* interview in 1979, Lee Hays stated, "When we first went to audition for Decca Records, one of the Kapp brothers [Dave Kapp, then a Decca executive, later a founder of Kapp Records] came out and said, 'You have to decide whether you want to be good or commercial.'

"I told him when he came back that we decided we wanted to be good *and* commercial."

Decca signed the group after hearing that Mitch Miller of Columbia Records was ready to offer the Weavers a contract. Says Hays: "What orchestra leader Gordon Jenkins did was to take our songs and package them with big orchestras and choruses, and immediately we had two enormous hits."

In June 1950 the Weavers recorded Leadbelly's "Goodnight Irene" backed with "Tzena Tzena." As Ronnie Gilbert told Aldin: "The day after we closed at the Village Vanguard, I got married, and we had the wedding party at the Vanguard. And then my husband and I went off on our honeymoon, which was a camping trip across the country. And while we were traveling west, every time we stopped in a place to have coffee, the jukebox was playing 'Tzena Tzena.' And then we got out to the west coast . . . when a telegram came which said something like, 'Can you cut your trip short and be back by such and such a time? We have an engagement at the Strand Theater and the Café Society uptown.' . . . All the way back, people were playing 'Goodnight Irene,' which was the other side of the record. And from then on we were a marketable, commercial commodity."

"Goodnight Irene" topped the charts for months, selling 2 million copies. But as Gilbert told Aldin, "It's important to recognize that we weren't making huge amounts of money. . . . For us it was a large amount; I bought an automobile with the proceeds from 'Goodnight Irene.' But . . . a car wasn't that expensive in those days."

With a hit record and radio and TV exposure, the Weavers gained a national reputation. The group followed up with several songs on the charts, including the traditional folk ballad "On Top of Old Smoky" and Woody Guthrie's "So Long, It's Been Good to Know You." Their success carried into 1951. They sold over four million 78-rpm records. Their recording of Solomon Linda's "Wimoweh (The Lion Sleeps Tonight)" later inspired the Tokens (who had a number one hit in 1961), R.E.M. (on *Automatic for the People*), and Nanci

Griffith (on *Other Voices, Other Rooms*) to record the song. Also in their repertoire was the Hays-Seeger classic "The Hammer Song," "Wreck of the 'John B.,'" "Hush Little Baby," "Darling Corey," "Hard Ain't It Hard," and other songs that have become American standards.

Why were they so popular? "Before we came on the scene, popular music was all big band stuff," Hellerman told the *Los Angeles Times* (June 24, 1982). "Then along comes a kind of music that has a homemade quality. There was an identification with the music. [The] music wasn't reserved for the elite anymore."

McCarthyism halted the group's progress. In 1952 an informant told the House Committee on Un-American Activities that three group members were members of the Communist Party. (The informant later recanted his testimony.) A TV appearance sponsored by Van Camp Beans was canceled, and it became increasingly difficult to get club dates. Decca bought out their contract and refused to record them again.

The Weavers disbanded in 1952 partly due to the political climate, and partly because of career and personal goals. Gilbert moved to California and had a baby, Seeger began playing solo dates, Hellerman wrote songs and did session work, and Hays wrote short stories and commercial jingles. In an effort to break the blacklist, Harold Leventhal reassembled the Weavers in 1955 for a Christmas Eve concert at Carnegie Hall. Based on the success of that performance, they began performing again but only on weekends. Vanguard's 1957 release *The Weavers at Carnegie Hall* was number three on Sam Goody's "Album Bestsellers" list in October 1957.

In 1957 Seeger left the group. "There was an argument over a commercial, as I recall, Pete not wanting to do it and the rest of us wanting to do it; but that was just the spark," Gilbert told Aldin. "My personal opinion is that Pete was never really happy as a Weaver. There were too many conflicts for him."

Three different people took Seeger's spot: Erik Darling, Frank Hamilton, and Bernie Krause. Darling, a singer, guitarist, and banjoist, born in Maryland but raised in New York, was in the Tarriers with Bob Carey and Alan Arkin who had a hit in 1956 with "The Banana Boat Song" on Glory Records. He worked with the Weavers from 1958 to 1961. He later joined the Rooftop Singers, which had a number one hit in 1963 with "Walk Right In," originally recorded in 1929 by Gus Cannon's Jug Stompers.

Frank Hamilton replaced Darling in 1962. He had been in the Sierra Folk Singers in the late '40s and played with Bess Hawes, Odetta, Guy Carawan, and Bob Gibson in the early '50s. He recorded a couple of sides with the Weavers and toured with them for a year and a half. He grew tired of trying to raise his family in New York and returned to California. Bernie Krause joined the group shortly before it disbanded.

The Weavers' album releases included *The Weavers* (Charter, 1949); *Folk Songs of America and Other Lands* (Decca ten-inch, 1951); *We Wish You a Merry Christmas* (Decca, 1952); *Greatest Hits* (Decca, 1957); *Best of the Weavers* (Decca, 1959); *Folk Songs around the World* (Decca, 1959); and *Weavers' Gold* (Decca, 1962). Most of the later releases were on Vanguard, including *The Weavers on Tour* (1958); *The Weavers at Home* (1958); *Traveling on with the Weavers* (1959); *At Carnegie Hall* (1960); *At Carnegie Hall, Volume 2* (1960); *The Weavers Almanac* (1962); *Reunion at Carnegie Hall–1963* (1963); *Reunion at Carnegie Hall, Part 2* (1965); *The Weavers Songbag* (1967); and *Wasn't That a Time?* (1993). The Weavers disbanded after a 1964 farewell concert at Chicago's Orchestra Hall.

On November 28 and 29, 1980, the four original Weavers—Seeger, Hellerman, Gilbert, and Hays—reunited to celebrate the twenty-fifth anniversary of their blacklist-busting concert at Carnegie Hall. Both concerts were sold out. Lee Hays's health had been failing for some time, though; in August 1981 he suffered a fatal heart attack in his upstate New York home. *Wasn't That a Time,* a documentary about the concert directed by Jim Brown and dedicated to Hays, aired in 1982 and is available on video.

Hays could be difficult and drank at times. He suffered from diabetes and tuberculosis in his later years. He had both legs amputated before he died and, in the documentary, introduced himself from his wheelchair as "Lee Hays, more or less." About the blacklisting, he said: "If it wasn't for the honor of it I'd just as soon not have been blacklisted." Journalist Charles Kuralt recalled living in an apartment building with Hays in the early '50s. When Seeger left the group they thought he was irreplaceable, but he wasn't. Hays was another story. As Hellerman told Aldin: "Aside from whatever musical qualities he brought to the group, I think that Lee gave more to define the character of the group than anyone else." Doris Willens Kaplan wrote a biography called *Lonesome Traveler: The Life of Lee Hays* (University of Nebraska Press).

As far as the other members: Ronnie Gilbert lives in Berkeley, California, with her partner Donna Korones. She has written a one-woman play about Mother Jones, *The Most Dangerous Woman in America,* and has continued to record over the years, including *H.A.R.P.* with Holly Near, Arlo Guthrie, and Seeger for Redwood Records. In 1996, she released an album with Holly Near called *This Train Still Runs* on her own Abbe Alice label. Seeger released *Pete* in 1996 on Living Music, his first studio album for many years, and has also written an autobiography, *Where Have All the Flowers Gone* (Sing Out!). Hellerman continues to work in the music field, producing records, scoring films, and composing songs. Darling performed with the Rooftop Singers, and then with Patricia Street; he was on the short-lived *The Lorenzo and Henrietta Music Show,* and

later studied to become a therapist. He lives in Santa Fe, writing music, painting, counseling, and studying flamenco guitar. Hamilton, finally, now lives in Decatur, Georgia, and continues to perform with two groups, Meridian and the Uptown Strollers.

WELLS, JUNIOR: *Singer, harmonica player, band leader (the Three Deuces, the Aces, Three Aces, Four Aces), songwriter. Born Memphis, Tennessee, December 9, 1934; died Chicago, Illinois, January 15, 1998.*

The period from the late 1930s to the years following World War II in Chicago might be called a golden age of blues harmonica, with artists like the two Sonny Boy Williamsons, Little Milton, Little Walter, and others enthralling audiences in local clubs. Among the younger exponents of the blues harp was Junior Wells, who outlasted most of the stars of the '40s and '50s to hold almost legendary status in the 1990s.

Wells, whose original name was Amos Blakemore, was born in Memphis, Tennessee, but grew up across the Mississippi River in the West Memphis section of Arkansas. As a child, he listened to the original Sonny Boy Williamson on the radio, which inspired him to take up the harmonica. Wells has indicated that he started to teach himself to play when he was eight years old. Soon after, he began to play on West Memphis–area streets to earn tips from passersby. In his early teens, he moved to Chicago, finding various nonmusical jobs while seeking jobs in music at night and on weekends.

His obvious talent with the mouth harp soon gained work with various bar bands, including those of Tampa Red, Little Johnny Jones, and Memphis Slim. In 1948 he formed his own band with the Myers brothers, Dave and Louis; originally called the Little Boys, the band changed its name to the Three Aces in 1949. During '49 Wells also played briefly with Muddy Waters's group. His own group became the Four Aces in '49 with the addition of drummer Fred Below, an alignment that lasted into 1952. During that year he was recruited by Muddy to replace Little Walter in his band; Walter, in turn, took Wells's place in the Aces.

Though he remained part of the Waters group into 1955, like many musicians, he found time for other projects, including occasional dates with Memphis Slim and his first recording sessions for the small States label in '53. (His States output in the mid-'50s included "Hoodoo Man Blues," "Bout the Break of Day," and "Lawdy! Lawdy!") He had to take a temporary hiatus from the music field when he was drafted into the U.S. Army in 1953. He was only in the service a short time when he went AWOL and returned to Chicago to rejoin Waters (cutting some sides with that band on the Chess label) and record some more of his own material on States. Deciding it was better to finish his military requirements than end up in federal prison, he went back to the army and stayed until getting his discharge in

1955; then, after a short stay once more with Muddy, he re-formed the Three Aces and alternated gigs in Chicago clubs with appearances in black blues clubs in many other parts of the United States.

A major milestone in his career occurred in the late 1950s, when he and singer-guitarist Buddy Guy developed a close friendship. In 1958 the two gave a sensational concert at Pepper's Lounge in Chicago, where they often were joint headliners for more than a decade until 1972. Wells backed Guy on a series of sessions for the Chess label during 1960–61. Besides that, he continued his own recording efforts, making the charts in 1962 for the first time with the single "Messin' with the Kid." In the 1960s Wells toured many times with Guy but also performed at folk and jazz festivals and at clubs in Chicago and elsewhere as a soloist or with his own band. Two years after recording some sides for the USA label in 1963 he backed Buddy Guy on new sessions for the Vanguard label. In 1965 Guy played backing guitar and collaborated with Wells on a series of tracks for a Delmark Records album. Called *Hoodoo Man Blues,* it provided a turning point in Wells's saga, marking him as one of the most innovative instrumentalists and singers to emerge from the Chicago blues scene. (Wells also gained a reputation as a flamboyant dresser, wearing sharkskin and black satin suits, fancy cowboy outfits, gold jewelry, and porkpie and fedora hats.)

Of course, he had been considered a first-rank artist for years by Windy City audiences, but the new album expanded his reputation not only throughout the United States but globally as well. This was indicated by the excellent reception given his sets as part of the American Folk Blues Festival tour of the United Kingdom and the European Continent in 1966. Besides the concerts, the tour included TV coverage and recordings of some of his festival numbers by Fontana/Amiga Records during a Berlin show. The year 1966 also saw release of another excellent LP by Wells, *It's My Life, Baby* (partly recorded live at Pepper's Lounge) on the Vanguard label, which two years later issued the disc *Coming at You.*

In the late 1960s, Blue Rock released *You're Tuff Enough* and *Junior Wells Sings Live at the Golden Bear.* In 1970, Blue Thumb released *Buddy and the Juniors* (Wells and Junior Mance). Wells continued to be a familiar presence in Chicago, often appearing solo or with Buddy Guy at Theresa's Lounge, a venue he enjoyed playing well into the 1970s. Other 1960s highlights included performances at the Philadelphia Folk Festival in 1966 and '67, a U.S. State Department tour of Africa in 1967–68, a set at the Newport Folk Festival in Rhode Island in 1968, and concerts in many parts of Canada and on the U.S. West Coast.

In the early '70s, Wells added to his following in Europe. In 1970 he worked with the U.S. blues rock band Canned Heat at the Bath Festival in England and also joined Buddy Guy on a European concert tour with the Rolling Stones. His overseas efforts included recording sides with Memphis Slim on the Barclay label in Paris and headlining a concert at the Palais des Sports in that city. Junior's album credits in the early '70s included the 1970 disc for Delmark *Southside Blues Jam* and the 1971 British import on the Red Lightnin' label *In My Younger Days.* In 1972, Wells and Buddy Guy collaborated on an album for Atco Records (*Play the Blues*) where supporting musicians included Eric Clapton, Dr. John, and the J. Geils Band; they also worked together on the live LP (on the Blind Pig label) *Drinkin' TNT 'n' Smokin' Dynamite.* Delmark issued the albums *On Tap* (1974) and *Blues Hit Big Town* (1977).

Wells was as busy throughout the 1970s as he had been during the previous decade, performing at clubs and festivals the world over, though he always returned to star at major venues in his beloved Chicago. In 1972 European film audiences could see some of his work in the movies *Blues under the Skin* and *Out of the Blacks Into the Blues.* That year he made his performing debut on the other side of the world as a member of an American Blues Festival concert series in Australia. His festival appearances in the mid-'70s included sets at the Montreux Blues Festival in Switzerland in 1974 and '75; the Newport Jazz Festival in New York City in 1974; the Toronto Blues Festival in 1974; the New England Blues Festival in Providence, Rhode Island, in 1976; the Jazz Life Festival in Dortmund, Germany, in 1976; and the Nancy Jazz Festival in Nancy, France, in 1977.

In the early 1980s, Wells was represented in record stores by the import albums *Pleading the Blues* and *Going Back* on the Isabel label. Other 1980s albums included *Buddy Guy & Junior Wells Live in Montreux* on the Black & Blue label, *Buddy Guy & Junior Wells* (live in Japan) on the Bourbon label, *Universal Rock* and *Chiefly Wells* on Flyright, *Messin' with the Kid* on Charly (a collection of tracks Wells had recorded for the Chief and Profile labels), *Win or Lose—Brian Kramer with Junior Wells* for Monsoon, and *Blow by Blow* for Sundown.

Into the 1990s, Wells continued to showcase his unique performing skills at major festivals and at clubs, college auditoriums, and overseas venues, including some stops in Japan. In 1990, Alligator Records issued his album *Harp Attack!* in which he was joined by such exponents of harmonica blues playing as James Cotton, Carey Bell, and Billy Branch. In 1991 Wells and Buddy Guy were featured on the Alligator album *Alone & Acoustic.* In the late '90s all of his Delmark albums were still in print, as was a good part of his Vanguard catalog. Also available was the MCA collection *Buddy and the Juniors* and the Paula CD *Messin' with the Kid, 1957–1963.*

Other CD releases were *Drinkin' TNT 'n' Smokin' Dynamite* on Blind Pig and *Buddy Guy & Junior Wells Play the Blues* on Rhino. Wells continued to tour and record during his last years. He cut several albums for the Telarc label: *Better Off with the Blues* (1993); *Everybody's Gettin' Some* (1995), including guest appearances by Bonnie Raitt and Carlos Santana; *Come On in this House* (1996), which was nominated for a Grammy and won a W.C. Handy Award for best traditional blues album; and *Live at Buddy Guy's Legends* (1997). Shortly before his death Wells also completed scenes for the film *Blues Brother 2000.* In September 1997 Wells suffered a serious heart attack. Soon after that he came down with lymphoma, and he died in a Chicago hospital in January 1998. Later in the year, several retrospectives were released; *Best of the Vanguard Years, Keep on Steppin': The Best of Junior Wells* on Telarc, and *You're Tuff Enough: The Blue Rock Studio Recordings.*

WEST, HEDY: *Singer, banjoist. Born Cartersville, Georgia, April 6, 1938.*

A singer of many of the most traditional folk songs, Hedy West heard her first folk music in her mother's arms in the hill country of western Georgia. Her grandmother played the banjo and sang classic ballads or nonsense songs to the children, and her father, Don West, besides being a union organizer, was one of the best-known poets of the South. Other friends and relatives also came to the West home to sing and play, including her Uncle Gus, one of the most popular fiddlers of the region.

Hedy's parents wanted her to learn music and started her on piano lessons when she was only four. Her interest in music continued to increase as she got older, veering more and more toward the folk idiom. In high school, she taught herself to play the banjo, following her grandmother Lillie Mulkey West's example. Soon she was singing some of the old songs at local gatherings. Word of her ability spread beyond Cartersville and she was asked to appear at other folk-music events. In 1956, seventeen-year-old Hedy won hearty applause for her singing in a festival at Boone, North Carolina. Two years later, her reputation was further increased when she won first prize in a folk-song contest in Nashville, Tennessee.

After this, her career began to move into high gear. She traveled north to play in coffeehouses in Chicago and New York, making the latter city her home in 1959, when she began studying music at Mannes College and drama at Columbia. This led to an invitation to appear in a hootenanny run by *Sing Out!* magazine at Carnegie Hall. Pete Seeger was impressed with her ability and asked her to join him in a two-week engagement at the Village Gate in New York.

In 1961 Vanguard talent executive Manny Solomon heard her perform at the Indian Neck Festival and made arrangements for some of her renditions to be included in the LP *New Folks.* Soon after she was featured on her own LP, *Hedy West Accompanying Herself on the Five-String Banjo,* followed later by *Hedy West, Volume 2.*

By the mid-1960s West had sung at most major festivals in the United States and given recitals across the country. Audiences were enthralled with her performances of such songs as "Mister Froggie," "Single Girl," "The Wife of Usher's Well," "Lord Thomas and Fair Elender," "Little Old Man," "Cotton Mill Girl," "Pan of Biscuits" and "The Brown Girl."

In addition to singing, Hedy wrote words and music to classical material and composed her own songs. Her output included music to go with her father's poems, "Anger to the Land." The 1963 country hit by Bobby Bare, "500 Miles Away from Home," is credited to West, Bare, and Charlie Williams.

During the mid-1960s she moved to Los Angeles for a time, where she got married and, at the end of the decade, she took up residence in London. Her albums of that period included the 1967 *Ballads,* recorded with Bill Clifton, and *Pretty Saro and Other Songs from My Family* recorded on the U.K. label Topic. She recorded *Serves 'em Fine* for Fontana-Philips Records. In the early 1970s she moved again, this time to Germany, where she and Clifton recorded *Getting the Folk out of the Country,* issued on Folk Variety Records in 1974.

Though she occasionally returned to perform at folk events in the United States in the '70s and '80s, most of her concert work was on the European folk club and folk festival circuit. At the end of the '70s only one album of hers was generally available in the United States, the excellent *Old Times and Hard Times* LP on Folk-Legacy. The album, originally released in 1967, was out of print until it was reissued in 1981. Other additions to her catalog in the early '80s included *Love, Hell and Biscuits* on Bear Family Records, and the 1981 reissue of *Pretty Saro and Other Songs from My Family.*

WHEELER, CHERYL: *Singer, guitarist, songwriter. Born Baltimore, Maryland, July 10, 1951.*

A talented songwriter whose compositions were covered by well-known artists from pop, country, bluegrass, and folk music, Cheryl Wheeler also possessed an intriguing voice bracketed between the styles of friend and sometime musical collaborator Mary-Chapin Carpenter and Emmylou Harris. Long a well-kept secret on the folk circuit, at the start of the '90s she seemed poised to make a commercial mark in country music, but Nashville's mechanisms didn't mesh with her own creative goals, and by the mid-1990s she was turning out some of the best albums in the folk domain.

Her interest in folk music went back to her early childhood years, in the Baltimore area, when she spent many hours listening to folk programs on the radio and to discs in the family record collection. She told Steven Libowitz ("Capturing Details of Life's Poignant Moments," *Santa Barbara News-Press,* September 22, 1995), "I remember being a little tiny kid and just loving to listen to that Stephen Foster song, 'Swanee

651 · WHEELER, CHERYL

River.' It's still one of my favorites. I remember thinking how beautiful it was and how sad a man had to be to write it."

She started to write songs when she was only ten, an occupation that was to keep her busy for decades to come. After performing for friends and in high school events she began to branch out. In 1976 she moved to New England, where she was starting to gain a local reputation by performing on the coffeehouse and bar circuit, initially in Rhode Island. Among artists with whom she shared bills in the late 1970s were Tom Rush, Jesse Winchester, Gordon Lightfoot, and Jonathan Edwards. In time her friendship with Edwards ripened into romance, and when he indicated the need for a bass player for a 1978 tour, Cheryl bought a bass guitar and in a short time could play well enough to join the group.

She got her first chance to record an album in the early 1980s, *Newport Songs* (1983). In her folk circuit activities her path had crossed that of Mary-Chapin Carpenter, who provided backing vocals and instrumental support for the disc, which came out in 1983. Not much notice was attracted by the release, but this changed when North Star Records issued the album *Cheryl Wheeler,* produced by Jonathan Edwards, in 1986. Tracks from the album were played on folk-music programs in many parts of the United States and other artists took note of the quality of some of the originals it contained, such as the song "Addicted." Country performer Dan Seals covered it, obtaining a number one country hit as well as a Grammy nomination. (There was a promotional cassette, *Live and Otherwise* in 1987, and then her second album, *Half a Book,* came out in 1987 on Cypress just before that label went out of business. North Star Records rereleased it in 1991. The album also included Jonathan Edwards on background vocals and John Jennings on guitar.) Others began to examine her writing catalog, and by the end of the '80s among those who had recorded Wheeler material were Bette Midler, Irish singer Maura O'Connell, Juice Newton, and Suzy Bogguss. Bogguss had a top 10 hit with Cheryl's "Aces," an achievement that played a big part in getting her career off the ground.

Cheryl's name on credits for such country block-busters sparked interest in her from Nashville-based record labels, and in 1990 she moved to Nashville to work on an album for Capitol (which dropped the release soon after it came out). The result was the 1990 disc *Circles and Arrows,* a high-quality collection that failed to win over the country radio programmers. She told Steven Libowitz, "My songs are much more Nashville than I am. I never belonged there. I don't fit into the scene. I don't want to get a band. I don't want to get an outfit. I don't want a light show. And I don't want to get all high-falutin' about it. I just want to go around in jeans and a T-shirt and stand there and sing the songs and that seems more suited to folk venues."

She recalled for Ed Condran of the *Bucks County*

Courier Times, Levittown, Pennsylvania ("The Wheel Deal in Newtown," October 5, 1995), "The DJs down in Nashville didn't know what to make of me." Of course, other radio programmers were similarly insensitive to the tracks from her next albums on the Philo folk-oriented label. She told him she had learned to take it philosophically. "If they're going to play my records that's fine. But it has to be on my terms. Right now I am going on the road and whatever happens will happen."

By 1993 Cheryl had signed a new recording contract with Philo, distributed by Rounder, which issued her label debut *Driving Home* that year. Again she was helped by Mary-Chapin Carpenter, who sang harmony on one track, as well as Mike Auldridge on Dobro and Allison Krauss on background vocals. Pop programmers may have ignored the many excellent tracks, but the folk community considered it one of the best releases of the year. Much of her original material was autobiographical and the track "Seventy-five Septembers," written for her father's seventy-fifth birthday, took a somber look at how an aging parent might deal with a world so different from his earlier life, asking, in part, "Are you more amazed at how things change/or how they stay the same?"

She followed up with an equally acclaimed fall 1995 release on Philo/Rounder, *Mrs. Pinocci's Guitar.* The radio music trade press publication *FMQB* noted it deserved good airplay, calling it "a marvelous fourteen song collection [that] highlights the enthralling, robust voice of Cheryl Wheeler and is a praiseworthy successor to her *Driving Home* and *Circles* albums. The title track, 'Does the Future Look Black,' 'The Rivers' and 'The Storm' caught our ears first." (During '95, Philo/Rounder reissued the *Circles and Arrows* album.)

The track "So Far to Fall" mourned a relationship that had failed though it once had seemed "almost perfect." As she told Libowitz, "It was a situation where everything seemed to be great, but the romance died along the way. I cried a lot when I wrote that song. But then almost all the songs are autobiographical or about a situation with someone really close to me."

Kathy Mattea recorded "Further and Further Away" for her 1997 album *Love Travels* on Mercury.

In January 1999 Rounder/Philo released *Sylvia Hotel* which includes some live and some studio tracks. The album was originally intended for release in 1998, but most of the songs she had recorded reflected the melancholy following a divorce, so she wrote some more upbeat numbers. One of the tracks, "Potato," is a novelty song about the spud sung to the melody of the "Mexican Hat Dance." *Sylvia Hotel* also includes "Right Way to Do a Wrong Thing," about going through the divorce.

Wheeler has been part of the On a Winter's Night tours with John Gorka, Patty Larkin, and Cliff Eberhardt. She is represented on numerous collections, including performances at the Ben & Jerry's Newport Folk Festival, *Big League Babe* (a tribute album for

White, Jr. Album, came out on United Artists in 1967, followed by *One Step Further* in 1968.

During the years after his father's death, Josh paid homage by presenting his concerts in the same fashion made famous by the elder artist. He almost always appeared alone, sitting on a straight-back chair and accompanying himself on acoustic guitar. His program included a range of material, from traditional folk songs to musical theater numbers and some original compositions. In the mid-1970s concerts, for instance, his program included songs by such diverse writers as Mickey Newbury, Cole Porter ("Miss Otis Regrets"), Bobby Darin ("I've Been Down So Long"), and Gordon Lightfoot. Among the original songs he presented were numbers like "Think About Me, Think About You," a lighthearted song with a little rock 'n' roll flavoring.

During the 1960s and 1970s White performed in clubs all over the United States. His New York appearances included programs at Madison Square Garden, Lincoln Center, and Town Hall. He also made several trips to Europe and, in addition to his live concerts, was a guest many times on Swedish TV and the BBC and Granada networks in England. He gave many of his concerts in those years on college campuses, averaging about 150 college appearances a year.

In the mid-1970s he cut back on touring because he wanted to spend more time with his growing children in his upstate New York home, where he had moved following the death of his father and his first wife, Jackie. In 1978 Josh decided it was time to increase his activities once more. One move was a new recording contract with Vanguard that resulted in the mid-1978 release *Josh White, Jr.* A single from the LP, "Marco Polo," received considerable airplay on FM stations that summer. In support of the album, he also went on a five-week, eleven-country tour of Europe later in the year.

During 1978 and 1979 White appeared at major folk festivals in Philadelphia, Vancouver, Canada, and at the Bread and Roses Festival in San Francisco. His TV work included guesting on an Irish Rovers TV special in Canada that won a Canadian Emmy Award. He also was onstage once again at venues on the East and West Coasts.

In 1970 White provided narration for *Dream Awake* (with James Earl Jones and Josephine Premice), a recording of an Owen Dodson poem released on Spoken Arts. At the end of the 1970s Mountain Railroad Records released a live album called *Sing a Rainbow.* The pattern remained much the same during the 1980s, as Josh continued to perform at folk clubs, on college campuses, and on TV and radio at home and abroad. In the mid-1980s he developed a production called *Josh: The Man and His Music,* a tribute to his father that he performed on a number of Midwest stages. In the 1980s he moved to Detroit, Michigan, with his second wife and six children. National Archives issued *Sings Traditional Folk*

Songs (1980) and in 1984 Eagle Records issued *Almost Alone.* Rykodisc released his fine collaboration with violinist Robin Batteau titled *Jazz, Ballads & Blues* in 1986. The disc included ten songs recorded and popularized by Josh White Sr. In the 1990s his career took a slightly different turn as he began to work on projects aimed at children.

As he told Rick Richards for *Dirty Linen* ("Josh White, Jr.—Singing for Single Digit People," December '94–January '95), this phase of his work went back to 1976, when he responded to a request from a teacher friend to sing for elementary school classes. In time he also started to write songs he felt would appeal to young people. Some of them, which he described as "common denominator songs," he found worked as well with older audiences as with younger ones. He told Richards, "I had never really geared my music for a younger audience, so I wasn't sure. The more I got exposed, and listened to different kinds of music, singers and story tellers, the appeal got stronger and stronger. I realized that I didn't have to do anything different. I didn't have to be other than what I was when I sang for their parents. My material may change. My demeanor may be a little more of being a leader for young kids, but basically I am no different and that's the thing that is important. I don't have to alter what I do when I sing for single digit people."

In late 1990 he collaborated with playwright Randi Douglas on a theme song for a toy exhibit at the Detroit Historical Museum. The song later became the title track for an album of children's songs called *My Favorite Toy.* After first performing it at a children's set at the 1991 Kerrville, Texas, Folk Festival, Josh regularly included "My Favorite Toy" in presentations at schools, libraries, and other venues in many parts of the United States. He also performed some of his children's songs repertoire on a number of TV programs, including Nickelodeon's *Eureka's Castle* and a special for a Detroit PBS channel, *Josh and Ron's Family Adventure.*

Josh also tried his hand at playwriting in the mid-'90s, collaborating with Randi Douglas on *Buster, the Bodacious Bear.* He and Douglas provided six new songs for the show. While developing projects for children was his main interest in the '90s, he didn't retire from the adult field. He continued to make appearances on the folk circuit around the United States and in '94 one of those concerts was the basis for a new album on Oceansong Records, *Live at the Soft Rock Cafe.* In 1999 Silverwolf Records released Josh's tribute to his father, *House of the Rising Sun,* including "One Meatball," recorded by father and son on Duke Ellington's radio show in 1945 when Junior was four years old.

WHITE, JOSH, SR.: *Singer, guitarist, songwriter. Born Greenville, South Carolina, February 11, 1914 (also listed as 1908); died Manhasset, New York, September 5, 1969.*

A lighted cigarette placed behind one ear, one foot

resting on a chair while he sang and played, Josh White personified the magic of folk music for decades. He had become such a trademark of the idiom by the 1930s that future audiences all over the world could visualize his stance while listening to that vibrant voice pour forth blues, ballads, gospel, and work songs from his long career. Even today, long after his death, those often matchless performances still remind millions of people of his importance to folk music in particular and every phase of popular music as well.

Like many black artists over the years, Joshua Daniel White's roots were in religious music. His father was a Baptist minister in South Carolina, his mother sang in church choirs, and the gospels and hymns he often heard at the church meetings were a regular part of his life. Later he was to break from his religious background, and from his home, where his parents had separated.

He moved into the "entertaining" field as an assistant to one of the blind Negro minstrels who made a precarious living singing on street corners and in small clubs, mostly in the South and Midwest. As Mark Humphrey noted in the liner notes for Columbia Legacy's *Josh White: Blues Singer 1932–1936,* he was badly treated by a succession of blind musicians. He started at eight as the lead boy for John Henry "Man" Arnold in 1922 and for the next seven years traveled throughout the country playing the tambourine and collecting tips for the "guitar evangelists." White claimed to have been the "eyes" for the legendary Blind Lemon Jefferson during his travels through North Carolina, although some blues historians have questioned this. It was a legendary circle, whose teachings helped lay the groundwork for Josh's equally brilliant contributions to folk-music history. Besides committing the many different songs each sang to his memory, Josh also blended elements of their different guitar styles to form his own unique instrumental technique. As a teenager, he already was gaining a reputation among his music peers, if not in the broad population.

He made his first recordings in 1928 in Chicago with Blind Joe Taggart (whom White recalled as "nasty mean") for the Paramount label. In 1932 he moved to New York and recorded for the American Recording Corporation, cutting twenty tunes for $100. When he recorded religious songs he called himself "Joshua White, the Singing Christian," but for his blues numbers he sang as "Pinewood Tom" (to spare the feelings of his religious mother). His first solo recording was under the Pinewood Tom sobriquet, "Black and Evil Blues"; he recorded "Milk Cow Blues" in a 1934 session.

In the 1930s, his career was abruptly threatened when an accident caused paralysis in one hand. His voice was still as good as ever, though, and he managed to find enough work to survive. In New York he was to become almost a fixture on the folk scene for the rest of his life. His initial breakthrough was gaining the role of Blind Lemon Jefferson in the play *John Henry,* starring Paul Robeson.

Between the mid-1930s and the end of the 1960s, he recorded material released on dozens of albums for a wide range of companies, including Decca, Mercury, London, Columbia, Folkways, Stinson, Period, and ABC Paramount. He also recorded many songs for the Archive of American Folk Song of the Library of Congress. Most of the songs were traditional folk music, including a wide variety of blues, spirituals, and work songs. Besides providing his own arrangements and interpretations of these folk songs, he occasionally wrote new songs. Examples of material he wrote in whole or part are "The Gray Goose," "I Had a Woman," and "Ball and Chain Blues."

White's strength of character and determination to surmount adversity enabled him to overcome the injury to his hand. Over a five-year period through the mid-1930s he continued to exercise his arm and fingers day after day and year after year until he finally regained the ability to play guitar. Not only did he restore mobility to his hand, he toiled over his playing skills until he was once more a first-rate guitarist. By the mid-1930s, he was accompanying himself successfully on concert tours of college campuses and clubs around the country. As his fame grew, he expanded it still further with appearances on network radio, including sessions with a group called the Southernaires on NBC, on the *Harlem Fantasy* radio show, as well as fronting the Josh White Singers and playing with the Carolinians (White, Carrington Lewis, Bayard Rustin, and William White).

At the start of the 1940s, White's name was well-known throughout the United States and in many other countries around the world. During 1941 and 1942 he gave many programs with singer Libby Holman. He had a solo show at the Cafe Society Uptown club in New York that ran for three years in the 1940s, and was asked by President Franklin Delano Roosevelt to give a special concert at the White House. In 1941 he was asked to make a goodwill tour of Mexico for the United States with the Golden Gate Quartet. At other times in the 1940s he was featured at such New York clubs as the Village Vanguard and Cafe Society Downtown. When he wasn't booked into New York venues, he was welcomed on the club and concert circuit in major cities all over the land. A guest on many radio shows, in 1944 he had his own fifteen-minute program on station WNEW in New York. In the mid-1940s, he also made a number of broadcasts for the Office of War Information. In 1947 he appeared with Sonny Terry and Brownie McGhee in the film short *To Hear Your Banjo Play.*

In the 1950s White's career was severely hampered after he testified before the House Committee on Un-American Activities. He was asked to identify communists within the folk community and wound up being blacklisted himself for much of the decade, as well as shunned by his old friends. At the end of the 1950s, as the McCarthy era subsided and the folk boom began to pick up, White reestablished his career. He had a hit with the novelty song "One Meat Ball" and became known for such diverse songs as "Foggy, Foggy Dew" and "House of the Rising Sun." In fact, Lonnie Donegan, who launched the British skiffle craze in the 1950s, said White's version of "House of the Rising Sun" inspired him to go into music. "This was the first American folk song I heard and the experience kicked off my career, starting me singing American blues and folk," Donegan told Jennifer Rodger of the *Independent* ("The First and Last Records Bought by Lonnie Donegan," January 15, 1999). "I believe that Josh White started the British rock scene."

President John F. Kennedy invited him to sing at the White House, also citing him as an inspiration. In the 1960s Josh was featured in clubs and folk festivals in the United States and overseas, where his repertoire often included such favorites as "Ballad of John Henry," "Jim Crow Train," and "Strange Fruit." He performed a number of times at the annual Newport Folk Festival over those decades. TV also showcased his talents at times: a guest on many network programs, he was particularly in demand for the folk-oriented shows of the late 1950s and early 1960s. Among his credits were several spots on the 1963–64 ABC-TV *Hootenanny* presentation.

Although Josh White recorded for many record labels, his longest association was with Elektra. Among his albums on that label were such late-1950s releases as *Josh at Midnight, Josh,* and *Chain Gang Songs* (issued in April 1959). His 1960s LPs on Elektra included *Spiritual and Blues* (2/61), *House I Live In* (7/61), *Empty Bed Blues* (2/62), *Live* (4/62), a two-record *Best of Josh White* set, and the *25th Anniversary Album.* The entire first side of the last named constituted a musical narrative prepared by Josh. Besides that, he presented many of his familiar renditions, including "Black Girl," "Free and Equal Blues," "Live the Life," "Sam Hill," "Where Were You Baby," "Delia's Gone," "Run, Momma, Run," and "You Don't Know My Mind."

His other releases included albums on Mercury, such as *Josh White with Josh, Jr.,* and *Beverly* (3/62), *Beginnings, Volume 1* (5/63) and *Volume 2* (1/64). His Stinson LPs included *Josh White Sings* and *Josh White Sings the Blues.* A Period release teamed him with another famous blues musician—*Josh White and Bill Broonzy* and Decca released the LP *Josh White* in April 1958. Other albums were *The Josh White Story, Volumes 1 and 2* and *Josh White Live* (4/62) on ABC Paramount; *Josh White Program* on London; and *Josh White* on Archive of Folk Music (issued 3/67). The songs presented on *The Josh White Story* included "Boll Weevil," "Frankie and Johnny," "House of the Rising Sun,"

"Hard Time Blues," "Good Morning Blues," "The Gray Goose," "Trouble in Mind," "Sometimes I Feel like a Motherless Child," "Red River," "I Has a Woman," "Strange Fruit," and "Two Little Fishes and Five Loaves of Bread." The London album included such numbers as "Call Me Darling," "Like a Natural Man," "Foggy, Foggy Dew," "Waltzing Matilda," and "He Never Said a Mumbling Word."

Josh continued his hectic appearance schedule throughout the mid-1960s, headlining concerts across the United States and Canada, including the Village Gate and the Bitter End in New York, Mother Blues in Chicago, the Troubadour in Los Angeles, and the Bunkhouse in Vancouver, Canada. His 1965 credits included a tour of the United Kingdom and the Continent and a set at the Newport, Rhode Island, Folk Festival. In 1966 he performed in major cities in Australia, and in '67 returned to England for a series of concerts. He returned to the Bitter End several times during those years and some of his renditions there were included in the syndicated TV program taped by WOR-TV New York called *From the Bitter End.* Among his work in Canada in the mid-'60s was a featured spot on the CBC show *The World of Music* in '66. As the '60s drew to a close, he still was filling engagements including concerts in Canada and at the 1969 Berkeley Blues Festival in Berkeley, California.

White was in ill health the last few years of his life and died in a Manhasset hospital the afternoon of September 5, 1969, while undergoing heart surgery. After his death, the commemorative album *In Memoriam* was released on Tradition Records.

His passing was mourned by young and old pop and folk artists as well as countless fans the world over. Commenting on White's legacy for *Sing Out!* magazine, singer-songwriter Don McLean said Josh "was one of the finest artists America has ever produced." Thanks to recording technology, White's artistry remained available to new generations long after his death. Among the albums available in the mid-1990s were *Joshua White (1929–1941),* a very complete four CD-set on Document; *Joshua White, Volume 1* and *Joshua White, Volume 2,* on Earl Archives; and *The Legendary Josh White,* on MCA. His blues work is represented on the Columbia Legacy CD *Blues Singer 1932–36,* released in 1996; *Plays the Blues and Sings,* on Collectables; and *Free and Equal Blues,* a twenty-six-song collection originally recorded in the 1940s and reissued by Smithsonian/Folkways in 1998. That year the U.S. Postal Service put out a stamp in Josh White's honor. Also helping to keep memories of his career alive was his son, Josh Junior, who often included some of his father's songs in his concerts. In the mid-1980s he mounted a stage show tribute to White Senior called *Josh: The Man and His Music,* which he was considering reviving in the late 1990s.

WILCOX, DAVID: *Singer, songwriter, guitarist. Born Dayton, Ohio, March 9, 1958.*

In the early 1990s David Wilcox was a rising star among the new singer-songwriters. His smooth baritone voice, often compared to James Taylor's, and clean-cut look were deceptive. The subject matter of his songs, at least in his first three albums, often dealt with serious themes: fear, addiction, intimacy.

Wilcox usually lets his guitar tunings suggest melodies and lyrics. But his brilliant song "Chet Baker's Unsung Swan Song" from his 1991 A&M release, *Home Again: For the First Time,* came to him in a flood of inspiration and without the use of his guitar. "The pen was moving as fast as I could write, and I did not rewrite it, it's just the way it was, start to finish," he told Lydia Hutchinson of the *Performing Songwriter* (September–October 1993).

The result is a song that reveals Wilcox's use of imagery and metaphor: *My old addiction is a flood upon the land/This tiny lifeboat can keep me dry/but my weight is all that it can stand.*

Wilcox grew up in Mentor, Ohio, the son of George and Anne Wilcox. His father was a psychologist and his mother a teacher. He had no early musical influences or music lessons, although he was interested in the guitar. He attended Mentor High School and went on to Antioch College in Yellow Springs, Ohio, where he studied humanities and religion. In 1977 he had his first encounter with a guitarist. He heard a woman playing Bob Dylan's "Buckets of Rain" in a stairwell. He asked the woman to write the chords down, but she was playing in an open tuning. Instead, she showed him how to position his hands on the guitar.

Wilcox fell in love with the guitar and open tunings. The woman taught him songs by Joni Mitchell, his first influence. He also learned songs by John Martyn and the late Nick Drake. Six months later he started writing his own songs. "I learned other people's songs," he told Hutchinson. "I learned a lot of Joni Mitchell's songs. And it was only when it was harder for me to find songs that really moved me that I started to make up a few of my own. Then little by little I was telling my own story because that's what was the most powerful emotionally."

By 1979 he had begun modifying his own capos so that some strings would be left free while others were pressed, an idea he got from watching Richie Havens. "Songwriting for me is based mostly upon my belief that the guitar knows the song," he told James Jensen of *Acoustic Guitar* (November–December 1994). "If I listen to the guitar, put it into some weird tuning and begin to experiment, it plays me a melody. I say to the guitar, 'Wow, that's beautiful, what's it about?' and the guitar replies, 'How does it make you feel?' And I might say that it makes me think about this or that, and the guitar says, 'Well, that's probably what it's about then.'"

Wilcox has modified that of late: "My guitar does still suggest the songs, only now my Matchless Amp does too."

He graduated from Warren Wilson College in Asheville, North Carolina, where he settled largely because of McDibb's, a club where he developed his performing skills. In 1987 he released his first record, *The Nightshift Watchman,* on an independent label owned by Jerry Read Smith of Black Mountain, North Carolina, called Song of the Wood Music. The title track was about a worker in a nuclear missile silo who takes pride in his work but admits ominously: *If I do my job/my job is over.* It's the type of dark twist, reminiscent of Martyn or Drake, that is evident in Wilcox's earlier work. His song "Come Away to Sea" was inspired by the Nick Drake song "Place to Be."

After a stint repairing motorcycles, Wilcox began performing at the Bluebird Cafe in Nashville. One night an A&M executive came in and signed him to the Americana division. His 1989 label debut, *How Did You Find Me Here,* sold 100,000 copies, a healthy amount for a folk performer. Early on, critics compared Wilcox to James Taylor. Robert K. Oermann, writing in the *Tennessean,* described Wilcox as "a rainy-day man, a troubadour with a soft, flannel voice. . . . Wilcox touches you in the same place that 'Sweet Baby James' did so long ago. He's a serious fellow who sings in a dark, intimate baritone with sparse acoustic backing."

The song "Leave It Like It Is" was inspired by an artist he hung out with in college: *Leave it like it is, never mind the turpentine/Just leave it like it is, it's fine.* "Language of the Heart" is one of the strongest tracks on the album. Two of his songs were inspired by his experiences with motor vehicles, "Rusty Old American Dream" and "Eye of the Hurricane," although he says he "was more into motorcycles and motocross racing than cars."

Wilcox began playing the folk festival circuit—Kerrville, Newport, Telluride. He played on the first On a Winter's Night tour with John Gorka, Patty Larkin, and Christine Lavin. Despite his fresh-faced appearance, Wilcox was dealing with his own inner demons. In his 1991 A&M disc, *Home Again: For the First Time,* Wilcox confronts some of his issues. "While the first album had a lot of escapist songs about wanting to disappear and find my life somewhere else, *Home Again* was me realizing that I could run, but I couldn't hide," he says. "It had to do with the work that got done once I went back and tried to fix the things that needed to get fixed."

The album, jazzier and fuller than the one before, includes "Covert War," about why he stopped visiting his family and breaking down barriers with his parents; "Last Chance Waltz," inspired by Sue Wintersein, about his decision to avoid his reunion and thus miss an opportunity to see an old flame; and "Advertising Man," which takes aim at the cigarette industry: *Crack will kill you quickly/that's why it's got to go/they'll get more of your money if they kill you nice and slow.*

Wilcox says Chet Baker's "Swan Song" could also be about himself. "I think that addiction defines the visible end of the spectrum of something that is so pervasive you might as well call it human nature," he told Bill Demain of *Song Talk* (Winter 1991). "Although I haven't had a substance addiction myself, I feel like the tendencies are definitely there in wanting to get some fix to make my life happy."

In 1992 Wilcox married Nance Pettit, and a year later they had a son, Nathan. His next album, *Big Horizon,* released in 1994 on A&M, suggests his newfound contentment. "Dog Block" reflects on what an old hound dog he was, and songs like "Strong Chemistry" and "Please Don't Call" also show an effort to put past behaviors behind and move forward.

Wilcox talked about his transformation with Gil Asakawa of the *Colorado Springs Gazette-Telegraph:* "When I started playing, I'd play nothing but the saddest of the sad . . . I wanted the emotion in my music to be like wasabe in sushi—just Blam! It brings tears to your eyes. . . . The older songs, they were like, 'Gee, do you really want to hear this stuff?' . . . What I'm singing about is good for people. It offers solutions. . . . The album is a testimony, a credo. I've come to conclusions about how I live my life, and what brings me joy."

Wilcox says his life is not devoid of conflict but that it's okay even for a brooding singer-songwriter to be happy. Wilcox told Robert Levine of the *Los Angeles Times* (April 29, 1994): "I had my records of delving into the depths of this and that. I think it's great to offer up solutions as well as questions."

About his religious beliefs, he told Robyn Schwartz of the *Metropolitan* (April 1, 1994): "It depends on who's asking. I go to friends' churches sometimes and people are saying things like . . . 'AIDS is God's punishment.' They're not asking me if I love who they love, they're asking me if I hate who they hate. I feel very scared about that. . . . I don't want to send people away from my music because I feel like my music can lead people to something."

Big Horizon was, as John McAlley of *Rolling Stone* (September 8, 1994) put it, the "fourth in a string of unjustly neglected albums." Over the years, A&M had put out a number of promotional CDs, including *Eye of the Hurricane* in 1989, *(Mostly) Live—Authorized Bootleg* in 1991, *She's Just Dancing* in 1991, *Make It Look Easy* in 1994, *New World* in 1994, and *It's the Same Old Song* in 1994. But just as Wilcox was feeling contented, A&M dropped him.

To some critics, *Big Horizon* made the songwriter just a bit too earnest and sentimental. "When Wilcox slips as a writer, it's usually because he gets carried away with metaphors and grand concepts," wrote Mike

Boehm of the *Los Angeles Times* (July 11, 1994). "That tendency toward the big statement crops up more often on *Big Horizon* than on its two precursors, giving songs like 'That's What the Lonely Is For,' 'Farthest Shore' and 'Make It Look Easy,' all of them life-lessons rather than capsules of lived life."

In 1996 he released *East Asheville Hardware* on Fresh Baked Records (distributed by Koch) a live album containing twenty tracks of previously unreleased material. The album includes covers of such concert standards as "Blow 'Em Away," a take-back-the-road song by Chuck Brodsky; "Barbie," written by Nance Pettit; and "For Real," by Bob Franke; as well as his own compositions: "Johnny's Camaro," "Roadside Art," and the title track. Wilcox released a new disc in May 1997 called *Turning Point* on Koch. With *Turning Point,* Wilcox, known for his fine acoustic work, employed electric guitars, a sign that he was again ready for a change. He even recorded a song, "Human Cannonball," about his experience of being dropped by A&M: *I was a fool to fall/I'm going to leave your three-ring circus/a human cannonball.*

Rather than perform solo, he toured with a four-piece band in support of the album in the summer of 1997. The Wilcox-Pettit family briefly relocated to Columbia, Maryland, while his wife finished acupuncture school, but they planned to return to North Carolina.

In 1998 Wilcox signed with Vanguard Records, which released *Underneath* in February 1999, his seventh album. Recorded in Nashville, it features such fine musicians as Steuart Smith on electric guitar, Victor Wooten (of Béla Fleck's band) on bass, Alison Krauss on viola, and Sonny Landreth on slide guitar. His new songs are filled with irony and introspection as in "Sex and Music," which criticizes measuring music by rankings, and "Hometown," about his parents' compromises. In "Underneath," Wilcox urges people to make real changes in their lives, not superficial ones. As he puts it: "A lot of what my music stands for is the strength to follow your heart. If your heart is pulling you in a direction that has mystery and wonder, trust it and follow it." He released his eighth album on Vanguard in 2000, *What You Whispered.*

Entry written with help from David Wilcox

WILLIAMS, DAR: *Singer, songwriter, guitarist. Born Mount Kisco, New York, April 19, 1967.*

The contrast between the two supple-voiced folksingers performing at Los Angeles's Wiltern Theater in early 1996 could not have been more apparent. Joan Baez, the seasoned veteran of more than thirty years, filled the house with her mature voice even while singing a cappella. Dar Williams, the petite, auburn-haired folksinger who was born after Baez was already established, sang delicately as she squinted apprehensively into the bright lights. But despite their different styles, the two share a common bond: a commitment to the folk song as a powerful means of expression.

In 1996, at that time twenty-eight years old, Williams was young enough to recall her youth yet sophisticated enough to tell her stories with humor and wit. On her first album, *The Honesty Room,* she included a song called "The Babysitter's Here," about a young girl who idolizes her hippie baby-sitter. On the same album she included "You're Aging Well," which she also sings as a duet on Joan Baez's live album *Ring Them Bells.* Williams came out of nowhere in 1995 to be considered one of the most promising folksingers in the business. *The Honesty Room* sold 40,000 copies, and she followed a year later with *Mortal City,* further establishing herself as a self-reliant new voice.

She was born Dorothy Snowden "Dar" Williams, the daughter of Gray Williams, a medical writer-editor who went to Yale, and Vassar-educated Marian Ferry, who worked as a fund-raiser for Planned Parenthood. As Williams describes her upbringing in her Internet autobiography, she grew up in the "deep suburbs" of New York, the youngest of three girls. As a child she was "exposed to folk music in the suburban way: my sisters went to camp and taught me all the songs on the way home from Vermont." She listened to Baez, Judy Collins, Simon and Garfunkel, and the Byrds, and had lots of teachers who played guitar in class. She began to learn guitar at age nine. She wrote her first song at eleven, called "I Should Be Happy Where I Am," but gave up songwriting for six years because of some "indelicate critiques," according to a column by *Billboard*'s Timothy White (January 28, 1995). "All in all it was a colorful childhood, filled with hippie housepainters, *Life* magazines, folk-rock, and, as the seventies progressed, fluorescent gum," she writes.

She auditioned for *Godspell* in high school and, after surviving an "existential crisis" at the age of sixteen, began writing music and plays. She attended Wesleyan College in Connecticut, where she became a theater and environmental religion major. After her sophomore year, she spent a summer in Berkeley, California, where she played her first open-mike at the Plough and Stars. She finished college, produced a play for her senior thesis, and graduated as a theater major.

In 1990 she moved to Boston and worked as a stage manager for the opera company. In the meantime she began taking voice lessons from Jeannie Deva, who encouraged her to play open-mikes at the coffeehouses in Boston. She struggled with depression over the end of a relationship and professional woes at the end of 1992 and into the next year, and debated going for a graduate degree in theater, speech therapy, or psychology. Instead she moved to Northampton, Massachusetts, and began her life anew.

"There's a rhythm to where I live that helps my music," she told White. "And it includes the mountains, high snows to constantly dig yourself out of, and geese clucking along the shoulder of the main road into town."

After releasing a couple of cassette tapes (*I Have No History* and *All My Heroes Are Dead*), Williams recorded her first album, *The Honesty Room,* in the fall of 1993 in a basement studio in Belchertown, Massachusetts. She used her own savings to fund the project. By January 1994 singers Christine Lavin and Chris Smither were touting the album. In February Williams played three unofficial showcases at the Folk Alliance Conference held in Boston. By August, Williams received a standing ovation for a four-song segment at the Newport Folk Festival, opening for the Indigo Girls. She began getting radio airplay in Boston, Philadelphia, and New York. In December she was voted Artist of the Week on WXPN in Philadelphia.

In February 1995, Razor and Tie Records rereleased *The Honesty Room,* which sold more than 40,000 copies based on limited airplay, word of mouth, and the power of the Internet. (Williams was one of the earliest folksingers to have her own web site.) In January 1995 White called Williams "the hottest young performer on the New England folk horizon."

The album opens with "When I Was a Boy," a clever ditty about the socialization of little girls (and boys) that incorporates literary allusions to *Peter Pan.* As she told White, "It's not surprising that the original Peter Pan character had some menace in him. In the story, Wendy wanted to be just like Peter and also in love with him—but somebody like Peter, who won't grow up, would be terrible in any real-life relationship."

Dar wrote the songs "You're Aging Well" and "I Love, I Love (Travelling II)" while she was coping with depression. "The point of those songs," she told White, "is that I'm looking forward to aging, affirming the ancient but currently unpopular idea that getting older can make you wiser and physically and emotionally stronger." Nevertheless, when Baez sang a duet with Williams during the 1996 concert, she couldn't help but mark the irony of a twenty-eight-year-old woman singing about aging.

One of Williams's best songs, "Alleluia," begins with the line *Ron and Nancy got the house, but Sid and Nancy rule,* comparing the Reagans to Sid and Nancy Vicious. The offbeat and humorous song tells of a young punk who wrapped a Chevy around a tree and went to heaven. Williams portrays a punk perspective of Heaven: *The cafeteria's got everything, it's gonna drive me mad/ 'Cause it looks just like this big Hawaiian party that my mother had.*

Her lilting and sometimes quavery three-octave voice invites comparison to early Joni Mitchell, especially with her soaring soprano. As Scott Alarik wrote in the *Boston Globe* (February 3, 1995), "Williams' songs are deceptively sophisticated, with complex yet

began using a larger instrumental group, and on many of his later Bluebird recordings between 1937 and 1941, the sound was closer to the small bands working in the Jackson [Mississippi] area than it was to the spare Delta accompaniments."

From 1935 on Big Joe turned out new recordings year after year, including such successes as his own composition "Highway 49" and the 1941 Bluebird chartmaker "Crawlin' King Snake." Besides solo appearances, his live credits in the late '30s and the 1940s included shows with pianist Peetie Wheatstraw, guitarist Robert Nighthawk, and harmonica player John Lee "Sonny Boy" Williamson. In addition to his own recordings, he sometimes backed some of those artists on their releases. For some tours he organized his own band or trio, on one occasion in the early '40s fronting a group that included Muddy Waters.

After his contract with Bluebird expired in 1945, Big Joe turned out new recordings on a dizzying array of labels, including Chicago Records; St. Louis–based Bullet Records; Trumpet Records in Jackson, Mississippi; Delmark; and VeeJay in Chicago; Arhoolie in California; and such others as Testament, Milestone, World Pacific, Bluesville, Adelphi, Storyville, Cobra, and Blues on Blues. Starting in the 1950s, with the growing interest in roots blues outside the black community, Williams began to attract a wider, more diverse audience not only at home but also in England and on the European Continent. The rise of TV also helped, with one of his first exposures being the early '50s set on Studs Terkel's *I Come for to Sing* show on a Chicago station.

He kept on churning out new singles and albums as the 1950s went by and the 1960s began. Among his LPs were *Piney Woods Blues* in 1958 on Delmark; the Arhoolie releases *Tough Times* (1960, reissued in 1981) and *Thinkin' of What They Did to Me* (early '60s with Charlie Musselwhite, reissued in 1981); and Delmark's *Nine String Guitar Blues* (1971, reissued in 1990), *Blues on Highway 49* ('62), and *Blues for Nine Strings* ('63). His *Blues on the Highway* album won the Grand Prix de Jazz of the Hot Club of France for 1962. Folkways released *Mississippi's Big Joe Williams and His Nine-String Guitar* in 1962 (reissued on CD in 1995 by Smithsonian/Folkways). His mid-1960s albums included *Big Joe Williams at Folk City* ('63); *Studio Blues* ('64); *Starvin' and Heaven Sent* and *Classic Delta Blues* (both '66); and *Big Joe Williams* ('69).

By the late '50s and early 1960s he was in demand for concerts on the coffeehouse and folk festival circuits. Among the places he headlined in the 1960–63 period were the Gate of Horn in Chicago, Ash Grove in Los Angeles, and Gerde's Folk City in New York. In 1963 he made his first visit to England and the European Continent as a member of the American Folk-Blues Festival. He recorded tracks for several overseas labels during the tour (as he was to do on later overseas trips) and also was included in the *I Hear the Blues* TV program on Granada TV in London, England. That was the first of many tours that won him a considerable audience overseas, including concerts in 1968, 1971, 1972, 1973, 1976, and 1977.

In the liner notes for Delmark's *Nine String Guitar Blues,* former manager John Simmons took a stab at describing Big Joe's guitar: "It is a big flat-top Sovereign acoustic, amplified as an afterthought. Masking tape holds the body together and keeps the pick-up from falling out. An extra set of pegs is attached to the top of the head, and the holes are drilled in the bridge to accommodate the three extra strings. These double the first, second and fourth strings. The guitar is tuned in G (open tuning): d-g-d-d-g-b-b-d-d. Joe plays with the first, sometimes the second fret capoed. The extra three strings are there not without reason. Joe aims at power; his voice needs complimenting by accompaniment of equal force. The nine-string guitar fills that purpose quite well. When his voice rings, his guitar doesn't just follow—it rings too."

He was invariably courteous to aspiring young artists who attended some of those shows. Martin Simpson, who became one of the top U.K. musicians, recalled approaching Big Joe after a concert and being treated with great kindness. Williams let the fifteen-year-old Simpson examine his odd-looking self-built nine-string guitar and asked Martin to sign his wooden walking stick. Simpson remembered how impressed he was to see the signatures of many of the most famous blues and folk performers, including Bob Dylan and Joan Baez.

Though Williams had the nickname "Grouch" with some U.S. musicians, harmonica great Charlie Musselwhite, who roomed with Big Joe in Chicago for a while in the early 1960s, said that while Williams sometimes packed a knife, he was not hard to get along with and was, indeed, a good guy. Musselwhite, who sometimes backed Big Joe, noted that, as was typical of country blues musicians, Williams could be very erratic in his musical patterns and an accompanist had to anticipate sudden changes that could be difficult for someone who didn't grow up in that musical environment.

Big Joe's schedule continued at a hectic pace from the mid-'60s into the 1970s. Just a few of the mid- to late-'60s high points included 1965 participation in the Downbeat Jazz Festival in Chicago, the Folksong '65 concert at New York's Carnegie Hall, a 1968 role in the U.K. film *American Folk Blues Festival,* and a 1969 set at the Ann Arbor, Michigan, Blues Festival. Among his 1970s credits were appearances at the New Orleans Jazz & Heritage Fair in 1972 and '79, concert dates in Japan in 1974 as part of the Blues Festival group, participation in the Festival of American Folklife in Washington, D.C., portions of which were included on the NBC-TV *Glorious Fourth* telecast, and appearances at the annual Delta Blues Festival in Greenville, Mississippi, from 1978 through 1980. His '70s album credits included the 1974 release *Legacy of the Blues Volume 6.* Among documentaries in which he was featured in the last half of the 1970s were *The Devil's Music—A History of the Blues,* shown on BBC-1 TV in the United Kingdom in 1976, the 1978 PBS-TV program *Good Mornin' Blues,* and the PBS-TV film of the 1980 Delta Blues Festival, initially telecast in 1981. In 1980 a book by rock guitarist Michael Bloomfield called *Me and Big Joe* was published. Besides the Arhoolie reissues mentioned above, he also was represented by the 1982 one titled *Big Joe Williams 1974.*

Williams was still active in the music field in the early 1980s even though in his late seventies. He finally was felled by a heart attack in December 1982. After his death, a variety of albums were issued, including the 1988 *Melvina My Sweet Woman,* his *Complete Recorded Works in Chronological Order Volumes 1 and 2* in 1991, and *Delta Blues—1951* (with Luther Love and Willie Love, reissued in 1991). Many of the songs he recorded during the 1935–1947 years were available on the Mamlish Records release *Big Joe Williams* and, on RCA, *Big Joe Williams and Sonny Boy Williamson.* Among the reissues of his work available in the late 1990s on CD were *Down South Summit Meeting* and *Rediscovered Blues* on Capitol, both featuring tracks recorded by Sonny Terry and Brownie McGhee, Lightnin' Hopkins, and Big Joe; *Have Mercy!* on Tradition; *Shake Your Boogie* on Arhoolie; *Stavin' Chain Blues* on Delmark (with J.D. Short); *The Final Years* on Verve; *Watergate Blues* on CMA; *Nine String Guitar Wizard* on Collectables; *Walking Blues* on Fantasy; *Giant of the Nine-String Guitar* on Jazz Archives; *Hand Me Down My Old Walking Stick* on Sequel; *Back to the Country* on Testament; *Blues Masters Volume 2* on Storyville; and *No More Whiskey* on Evidence, sixteen tracks originally recorded between 1978 and 1980. In 1992 he was inducted into the Blues Foundation's Hall of Fame.

Based in part on interviews with Lyndon Stambler

WILLIAMS, LUCINDA: *Singer, songwriter, guitarist. Born Lake Charles, Louisiana, January 26, 1953.*

Lucinda Williams is in the top rank of American songwriters. Her reputation has soared as some of the best performers in country, pop, and folk have made powerful covers of her finest songs like "Passionate Kisses" (Mary-Chapin Carpenter), and "The Night's Too Long" (Patti Loveless). Loveless had a top-10 country hit, and Carpenter her breakout hit, with "Passionate Kisses." Tom Petty has recorded "Changed the Locks." These songwriting successes raised Lucinda's stock in the music industry and transformed her from a cult act to a performer with broader appeal. And thanks to Daniel Lanois's haunting production, Emmylou Harris has made a memorable cover of "Sweet Old World," one of the best songs written in recent years.

Williams's musical influences are broad and diverse. As she notes, "I've had tremendously eclectic musical influences. My mother was a music major at Louisiana State University. There was always sheet music lying around the house. Mom's favorite was Judy Garland, and all those great musicals from the '50s, like *South Pacific.* But I also loved the Beatles . . . Go figure it! Dad was a big country blues fan. He also loved jazz. So I heard a lot of Coltrane, Dinah Washington, and of course, Ray Charles. I would hear Hank Williams one day and Wilson Pickett the next."

As for musical influences that determined her own subsequent development, she says, "1965 was a big year for me. I took my first guitar lesson and discovered Bob Dylan and Joan Baez. My dad taught college literature. One day, one of his students brought over *Highway 61 [Revisited]* and he was raving about it. I was lucky because I was surrounded by college students, who turned me on to musicians like Leonard Cohen and Joni Mitchell."

When she talks of the music that gripped her the most personally and deeply, she gravitates to the blues: "Some of my earliest memories are of the Delta blues. I don't know what it was about it, but it got right to me and cut me to the bone. A friend introduced me to Robert Johnson and I ate it up."

Williams didn't study music or theory. "I just started playing what I loved," she says. "I'd find a song that spoke to me and listen to it over and over. It's kind of addictive . . . until I master it."

She broke into the music business in the 1970s. "Then the music world seemed bigger and broader," she says. "You could work a few days a week, play a few clubs, share a house with a few friends, and get by on $125 a week. Now you have to work forty hours a week and squeeze the music into what's left over. It's really hard for young kids starting out today."

She made her first recordings for Folkways, recording her first album, *Ramblin' on My Mind* (1978) in a single day. She followed with *Happy Woman Blues* on Folkways in 1980. "I had a few songs I'd written but I didn't use them," she recalls. "Boy, I was so naive! I was a real purist. I thought Folkways wouldn't want anything contemporary. I thought they'd want nothing but the blues."

During the 1980s she was heavily influenced by the Pretenders, Talking Heads, Bruce Cockburn, Nick Drake, and Pentangle. "I have an eclectic perspective on music," she says. "I never thought in terms of having an image or limiting myself in terms of what I could or couldn't do."

Of all her albums, the 1992 *Sweet Old World* is her most masterful. Its title song—a gentle rebuke to a lover or friend who chose suicide over "this sweet old world"—is filled with pathos and a clear-eyed look at the suffering and joy of human life.

Lucinda has a spare singing style that tends to focus attention on the lyrics of her songs. At first her earlier recordings, including *Lucinda Williams* (1988) and *Passionate Kisses* (1989) on Rough Trade, can seem nasal and whiny, but later recordings, like *Sweet Old World,* have fuller arrangements and higher sound quality, which gives her singing style sharpness and bite.

On recordings like *Sweet Old World,* Gurf Morlix's guitar style provides the perfect instrumental accompaniment to Lucinda's singing and lyrics. On "Something about What Happens When We Talk" it takes on a slow, lingering, lonely quality that reinforces the lyrics, in which a woman describes the tingling excitement she feels when she speaks to a male friend, and a sense of lost erotic opportunity: *All I regret now is I never kissed your mouth.*

Though Lucinda's upbringing and background are in the South, the melodies and lyrics of her songs seem to have more in common with the big, lonely, open spaces of Texas or California. The characters in her songs are reminiscent of the characters in Edward Hopper's canvases or in Bruce Springsteen's contemplative albums like *Nebraska* or *The Ghost of Tom Joad.*

Early in her career, she was heavily influenced by rhythm and blues. Currently her music alternates between uptempo anthems like "Passionate Kisses" and slow, meditative ballads like "Little Angel, Little Brother." Her ballads seem more authoritative, as if they come from a "deeper well" within her psyche.

Much has been made of the literary quality of Lucinda Williams's songwriting. In her best songs, she finds a convergence between her inner life and the external reality of a fictional character. "Side of the Road" is a ringing feminist defense of the need for a woman to retain her independence and self-awareness while in a relationship with a man: *I just stood and looked at the open space and a farmhouse out a ways. I wondered about the people who live in it; and are they happy and content? Were there children and a man and a wife? Did she love him and take her hair down at night?* Notice the simple prose and accumulation of prosaic detail, (the field, the grass, the farmhouse) leading to the climactic last line, with its juxtaposition of a profound question with a loving observation of domestic life. The scene harkens back to Edward Hopper's domestic portraits of himself and his wife sitting on a bed in their sun-filled bedroom. In a published interview, Williams has said that she had Andrew Wyeth's portrait of a lone woman looking up at a house high on a hill in mind when she wrote the song.

The imaginary happy family in "Side of the Road" is a mirror image of the first-person narrator, who wonders whether she can find sustenance and support in the midst of her own relationship. She concludes her revelry by alternately warning and reassuring her lover: *If I stray away too far from you, don't go try to find me. It doesn't mean I don't love you.* In "Sidewalks of the City" each verse begins with a scene peopled by homeless men and women haunting the city streets and ends with the songwriter pondering her own life, the transitory nature of human love, and the innate frailty of human relationships. The song asks a profound question: Can any human being promise another permanence and security? It also ponders the narrow gap separating those who are homeless and those who lead comfortable middle-class existences.

Williams's close relationship with her younger brother is chronicled in two songs over the course of several years. In the honky-tonk ode "Crescent City" she brags: *My brother knows where the best bars are.* In the later "Little Angel, Little Brother" she views him through a lens of love and regret: *I see you now at the piano, your back a slow curve/Playing Ray Charles and Fats Domino, while I sang all the words . . . I see you sleeping in the car . . . an empty bottle at your feet.* The poignancy of the song turns it into a beautiful but mournful requiem.

Williams and her band were at work on a new record by the late '90s. Emmylou Harris and Daniel Lanois have had an important influence on the new album because they brought her together with Steve Earle. "In May 1995 Lanois invited me over to the studio where he was recording *Wrecking Ball* with Emmylou. He wanted me to play the song for her so that she could get a feel for the way I do it. Steve Earle was also there because Emmylou was recording 'Goodbye,' one of Steve's great songs. He and I got to talking and playing a bit and I got excited. I heard Steve's new album and liked it a lot. I talked with him about going back into the studio with him and his producer. We decided to go back into the studio to recut some tracks for the new album. I'm going to work out of Ray Kennedy's studio, where Steve recorded his new album. I'm also going to use his producer on a few tracks." (Later, Williams departed from Earle and Kennedy and produced the final version of her next recording, *Car Wheels on a Gravel Road,* with Ray Bittan, Bruce Springsteen's producer.)

Williams has had some less-than-satisfying business and professional relationships with several record companies over the years. She described their uneasiness with her unclassifiable sound: "Record labels always had trouble knowing how to market me. I was too rock for country and too country for rock. It's always a constant uphill struggle.

"When you're signed to a deal, you sign with people who are committed to you and your musical vision. But then they are fired and then you've got new people to deal with who have different ideas. The label is only as good as the people running it. In the past, you had the John Hammonds at Columbia who had tenure and stature. These guys had great vision and passion. You don't find that anymore. Record executives come out of business school. They have no history in the [music] business. They fly around from label to label."

Williams is a fierce champion of the artist's right to pursue his or her vision without consideration of commercial appeal: "Hasn't that always been the case with really great artists trying to make it commercially? The music business is Big Business. It's hard to be an artist in this business with all the slickness and marketing. You look at all those music videos with Joe Blow singing about something or other that someone told him would sell records. It's pretty pathetic . . .

"Buffalo Springfield couldn't be marketed nowadays. Back then, if you had an interesting sound and a musical vision you stood for something. You'd get airplay and people would pay attention. It's not true anymore. Partly, this is due to the economy. There's no room for experimentation and no room for mistakes. That's got to be tough for kids starting out today.

"At American Recordings, my new label, communications are good between the band and the record company. [After a record company reorganization, she left American Recordings for Mercury.] Our bass player is managing the band. Everything must be open. Everyone must be straight with each other . . . try to be human. You must demand respect . . . none of this nonsense about the artist being told what to wear or what to sing. It comes down to an artist taking a stand and saying, 'I'm not going to do this.' . . . like when union organizers got workers together who said, 'I'm not going to work for these wages anymore. . . . Which side are you on?' You have to know you have something that no one else can take away. You can make it by yourself.

"Neil Young and others didn't let the music industry push them around. I've had this rebel streak in me. You can't be a good artist without vision. When I was recording 'Six Blocks Away,' Rough Trade wanted to boost the rhythm track to make it more playable for radio. I wouldn't let them. You've got to look at the big picture. I'm not willing to make those compromises. The only thing that lasts is your art and principles and staying true to them. Finding the musical mainstream shouldn't be the be all and end all of your existence. Taste changes quickly. Some want to go for it and get it quickly. Do you want a long, slow ride or a short, quick one?"

Returning to her audience with the first new material in six years, Williams made *Car Wheels on a Gravel Road* (Mercury, 1998), a recording that was worth the wait—it won a Grammy for Best Contemporary Folk album of 1998. Her fans often wondered during this period what was causing the silence. A September 1997 *New York Times Magazine* article noted that she went through three different record labels during this period, and as many producers. Gurf Morlix, a longtime collaborator and fixture in her musical universe, quit in frustration. Hers was the record industry's most notorious nonexistent album. But Lucinda has turned everyone around who wondered whether she had "lost the touch." *Rolling Stone* bestowed a near-perfect rating, calling it "a country-soul masterpiece." *Spin* declared it an album of the year contender.

Songs like "Drunken Angel" and "Lake Charles" take us back over familiar Williams lyric territory: the sad folly of a sensitive soul's self-destruction at the hand of alcohol, rage, or violence. Yet she manages to add a new inflection to make something new: in the latter song the character has such passion for the Delta blues that he creates an accent and a personal history rooted in Lake Charles, but conceals his former alien identity.

This recording raised Williams's visibility among those who had not heard her music (she toured the high-profile Lilith Fair). Mercury (which bought the rights to the album from American Recordings for $450,000) hoped for a "breakthrough hit." Danny Goldberg, the company chairman, said hopefully, "Bonnie Raitt, Tracy Chapman, [and] Shawn Colvin . . . have had major success with unorthodox records, just by sheer emotion and talent. But this is not where Williams's interests lie. She wants to make music that is art and that will live for the ages. Fame and celebrity are not in her vocabulary." What seems clear is that Williams has chosen a long, slow ride to musical greatness.

Entry written by Richard Silverstein; based on an interview with Lucinda Williams

WILLIAMS, MASON: *guitarist, singer, songwriter, artist. Born Abilene, Texas, August 24, 1938,*

Mason Williams does not consider himself a Renaissance man. But the Grammy- and Emmy-winning composer, writer, artist, author, and environmentalist has had a career that belies his modesty. Williams spent his childhood with his mother in Oregon and his father in Oklahoma. He might have spent his professional life as an actuary for an insurance company; that was the future he was considering when he enrolled as a math major at Los Angeles City College in the fall of 1956. He had arrived in L.A. with his lifelong friend, artist Edward Ruscha, fresh out of high school in Oklahoma City. But the allure of the jazz houses and other music venues in Southern California had a profound influence on Williams. He decided to seek a career in music. He moved back to Oklahoma, enrolled as a music major at Oklahoma State University, and studied piano, flute, and double bass.

Williams considers 1958 to be a key year in the formation of his career. For $13 he bought a used Stella guitar and began studying folk and ethnic music with musician and musicologist Bill Cheatwood. In 1959 Williams and schoolmate Baxter Taylor joined Cheatwood in forming the folk group Wayfarers Trio. They recorded a single for Mercury in 1960 featuring the songs "Little Billy Blue Shoes" and "Run, Come See."

Williams also performed at the Gourd, an influential Oklahoma City coffeehouse, and in August 1960 he recorded his first album, *Folk Music As Heard at the Gourd.* He wrote his first song that year and, with the Wayfarers Trio, released an album on Mercury called *Songs of the Blue and the Grey.*

In 1961, after touring as the opening act for the Kai Winding Jazz Septet, the Wayfarers broke up, re-formed, and toured the West Coast. From 1962 to 1963, while on active duty with the navy out of San Diego, Williams formed the Hootenaires. They performed at folk clubs throughout Los Angeles and recorded an album on the discount Crown label called *More Hootenanny.* Williams, who by 1961 had taken up the five-string banjo, made his first instrumental recordings with that instrument and the twelve-string guitar. These pieces appeared on anthologies for the Horizon label: *The 12-String Story* (two volumes) and *The Banjo Story.*

After leaving the navy in 1963, Williams returned to Oklahoma, planning to finish college. But a club offer in Denver proved to be the detour that ended his college career. In 1964 Williams moved to Los Angeles, which became his home base for two decades.

Williams signed a publishing agreement with Davon Music for a $200-a-month retainer. Several of his songs were recorded by the Kingston Trio and Glenn Yarbrough. Williams's clever "Them Poems," short, limericklike verses, were such a big hit for the Kingston Trio that Williams made his own record of all of them for Vee-Jay.

The year 1964 also saw the publication of Williams's first book, *Bicyclists Dismount,* a whimsical collection of lyrics, poems, and photographs, published in limited editions by Davon Music. In 1969 *The Mason Williams Reading Matter,* published by Doubleday, used roughly the same formula and sold more than 167,000 copies.

Williams's association with Tom and Dick Smothers began in 1964. The Smothers Brothers were enjoying tremendous success as a comedic folk duo, and they used his songs to good effect; Williams backed them up on their 1965 album *Tour de Farce.* He toured with them and signed with their managers, Ken Kragen and Ken Fritz.

In 1966, Williams began a steady five years of television writing, starting with the *Roger Miller Show,* a variety series for NBC. Williams worked on fifteen of those shows that year, produced the record *The Smothers Brothers Play It Straight,* and recorded the single "Love Are Wine" for Mercury. He also conceived his best-known artwork, a life-size reproduction of a Greyhound bus, titled simply *Bus.* The work measures eleven feet high by thirty-seven feet long and was printed with the process used in producing billboards. *Bus* was featured in the Museum of Modern Art's Word and Image exhibition, and was published in a limited edition in 1967. The work remains in the museum's permanent collection. Williams's art, like his books, though overshadowed commercially by his recording and television output, offers valuable insight into the creative development of a conceptual artist who took the playfulness inherent in that art form and brought it to television.

In 1967 Williams began writing for the *Smothers Brothers Comedy Hour* on CBS. He received an Emmy nomination for Outstanding Achievement in Comedy, Variety and Music, and published three more books, including *Royal Road Test,* written with his friend Ruscha, who was by then a well-known Los Angeles painter. This book, really a work of art, is a spiral-bound still photograph documentary marking the fate of an old Royal office typewriter as it is tossed out of a speeding Buick onto a desert road. Much as a homicide crime scene is documented by police photographers, so too is the demise of this typewriter—from point of impact to the exact distance traveled by every recovered piece of the ill-fated machine. Another conceptual piece, *Sunflower,* took place in the high desert north of Los Angeles, where a skywriter sprayed the outline of a giant flower into the sky, with the sun as the heart of the blossom.

Later that year Williams began work on his first Warner Brothers album, *The Mason Williams Phonograph Record,* which was to feature photographs of both his *Bus* and *Sunflower* on the cover. The album was released in February 1968, concurrent with Williams's continued work on the Smothers Brothers television show. "Classical Gas," a single pulled from the album, became a number-one hit that summer. "I originally called it 'Classical Gasoline,'" Williams said. "I was trying to connote the idea of *cool,* like, *it's a gas,* but the copyist shortened it to 'Classical Gas.' I think it kind of defines the idea of pop music meeting classical music."

Another successful merger, one that blended Williams's sense of whimsy with his sharp satirical talents, resulted in the presidential political campaign of comedian Pat Paulsen. What began as a sketch on the Smothers Brothers show soon became a fledgling campaign, complete with personal appearances by the candidate, a televised campaign special, folksy and intentionally trite campaign literature, a book, and enough public response that Paulsen's television appearances eventually led to cries for equal time from the other candidates. The satire was so successful that Paulsen reprised his campaign in subsequent presidential elections.

The success Williams saw in 1968 was recognized early the next year when "Classical Gas" received three Grammy awards. Williams won for Best Instrumental Composition and for Best Instrumental Performance. Mike Post received a Grammy for Best Instrumental/Orchestra Arrangement of the song. For his work on the Smothers Brothers show, Williams received an Emmy for Outstanding Writing Achievement in Comedy, Variety and Music.

Throughout 1969 and 1970 Williams maintained a heavy concert schedule, released two more albums, and published five books, including a scathing review of the state of American commercial television, *The Mason Williams F.C.C. Rapport.* He continued his work on the Smothers Brothers shows and also for the *Glen Campbell Goodtime Hour* on CBS.

PENTANGLE (*Courtesy of Reprise Records*)   **U. UTAH PHILLIPS** (*Photo by Gary Glade*)

JOHN PRINE (*Courtesy of Urbaitis*)

BONNIE RAITT (*Photo by Gary Glade*)

JOHN RENBOURN (*Photo by Gary Glade*)

STAN ROGERS (*Photo by Finn Larsen; Courtesy of Ariel Rogers*)

JOHN SEBASTIAN (*Photo by Gary Glade*)

TRACY SCHWARZ and **MIKE SEEGER** (*Courtesy of Michael Ochs Archives*)

EWAN MACCOLL and **PEGGY SEEGER** in 1981 (*Courtesy of Peggy Seeger*)

PETE SEEGER (*Courtesy of Michael Ochs Archives*)

MARTIN SEXTON with **JOHN GORKA** in *l. rear* (*Photo by Lyndon Stambler*)

MICHELLE SHOCKED (*Photo by Lyndon Stambler*)　　　　**PAUL SIEBEL** (*Courtesy of Elektra*)

MARTIN SIMPSON (*Photo by Lyndon Stambler*)　　　　**DARDEN SMITH** (*Photo by Gary Glade*)

DAR WILLIAMS (*Photo by Lyndon Stambler*)

KATE WOLF (*Photo by Peter Novak; Courtesy of Owl Productions*)   **WILLIE DIXON** (*Photo by Peter Figen Photography*)

In 1971 Williams's fifth and final Warner Brothers album, *Sharepickers,* offered a review of some of his earlier compositions along with two featured songs written and performed by Rick Cunha. The album's liner notes, written by Williams, provide a glimpse of his own assessment of the state of his career and life. He writes, "I had used music, God bless it, just to get to the top. . . . I had become rich and famous, a star, just so everything would come to me, even more than I could use, and I could take my pick from it without risking rejection." Hinting that he was searching for a new direction, in 1972 Williams left Hollywood and spent six months traveling the West in a camper.

Settling in Santa Fe, New Mexico, Williams bought a Martin D-28, learned to play with a flat pick, and began playing rhythm guitar with a country, folk, and bluegrass group he formed called the Santa Fe Recital. It was about this time that Williams began experimenting with the concept of melding bluegrass and classical music forms. Williams had earlier appeared with symphony orchestras, but more as a soloist and not with a bluegrass program. In the summer of 1974 Williams premiered his *Concert for Bluegrass Band and Orchestra* in Denver, Colorado. He also wrote twenty-six *Tommy Banks* shows, a Canadian television variety program, and in December of that year returned to Hollywood to write for the Smothers Brothers NBC show. His efforts on that program won him a Writers Guild nomination in 1975.

Throughout 1976 Williams performed his *Symphonic Bluegrass* concert with orchestras in California, Colorado, Oklahoma, and Oregon. He spent three years playing bluegrass festivals and symphony concerts. In 1979 he stopped off in Hollywood to write for the *Dinah Shore Show.*

Williams reunited with the Smothers Brothers in 1980 for two NBC specials and then went to New York as head writer for *Saturday Night Live.* A Steve Martin special, *All Commercials,* which Williams wrote in June of that year, won him a Writers Guild Award for Outstanding Script in Television Variety.

In the early 1980s, after a ten-year hiatus, Williams began writing music for guitar. He also took part in a Vail, Colorado, symposium on water resources. Although there to perform, Williams discovered that a utility was planning to construct a string of dams along his favorite trout stream on a fork of the Willamette River in Oregon. This led to an activism that produced a concert dedicated to protecting the nation's rivers and waterways, named after a Pete Seeger song, "Of Time and Rivers Flowing." Williams's efforts led the state of Oregon to declare the North Fork of the Willamette River a protected waterway. In 1984 Williams released an album of river-themed songs from his concerts, and for the next three years he toured with a special "river" show band that included author Ken Kesey. In 1987 Williams released his *Classical Gas* album recorded with Mannheim Steamroller. The album is still in stores and went gold in 1991.

Williams returned to television, and CBS, in 1988 for another stint as writer for the *Smothers Brothers 20th Anniversary Reunion Special.* The show received an Emmy nomination for Outstanding Writing in a Variety or Music Program. Williams also received a Grammy nomination that year for Best Instrumental Performance for the song "Country Idyll," which appeared on the new *Classical Gas* album.

In 1990 Williams received the Governor's Award from the state of Oregon for his contribution to the arts. In 1992 Williams added a holiday concert program to his repertoire, featuring Christmas music that was included in his 1992 CD *A Gift of Song.* In 1993 Belwin published *Classical Gas—The Music of Mason Williams.* By 1998 Williams's original recording of "Classical Gas" had surpassed 3 million radio airplays, according to BMI.

Williams continues to tour with a band that includes such musical heavyweights as pianist Art Maddox, drummer Hal Blaine, championship fiddler Byron Berline, guitarist Rick Cunha, and author Kesey, and through 1999 he performed numerous concerts with the Oregon Children's Choir. He also was a featured performer at the 1999 Oregon Gubernatorial Inauguration.

When Williams was asked how it felt to know that despite all of his accomplishments he might best be remembered for "Classical Gas," he said, "I'm fortunate in that the song has had a lot of radio airplay. If you have a tune that people make use of for other things, like in school marching bands, it gets a bigger life. But what you do and what you are are two different things. I think one wants a creative life more than anything else, and having a hit song has nothing to do with the totality of everything you've done."

Entry written by Mitch Waldow; based on an interview with Mason Williams in December 1997 and published biographical material provided by Williams

WILLIAMS, ROBERT PETE: *Singer, guitarist, songwriter. Born Zachary, Louisiana, March 14, 1914; died Rosedale, Louisiana, December 31, 1980.*

The great black folk artists of the pre–civil rights era had every reason to sing the blues. They grew up in a segregated, often violent society where white man's "law and order" had only a negative meaning. And many of them, like Robert Pete Williams, never had the chance for formal education, much less the opportunity to learn the rudiments of reading and writing. Yet many of them, like Williams, proved that in spite of everything talent will out against insurmountable odds.

He was born and raised on a farm in Zachary, Louisiana, not far from the state capital of Baton Rouge. His family earned a meager living from sharecropping, and Robert Pete toiled long hours in the fields from his early years through his teens. Though he heard friends and an occasional touring performer sing the blues, he didn't think of it as something he could do until he was twenty, when, he later told interviewers, he fashioned a guitar for himself out of a sugar box. Over the next two decades he slowly expanded his repertoire from material picked up from other bluesmen and some songs he made up himself. With a wife and family of his own to support, he couldn't make entertaining a full-time career, but he loved to sing and play, and whenever possible picked up additional income from playing at dances, parties, and bars.

It was a rough environment; in many cases, it was every man for himself. Williams had his share of arguments and fights, often the result of one party or the other having had too much to drink. In 1956 he was picked up by police after he shot and killed a man, something he always claimed was done only in self-defense. That version didn't convince the authorities, and he was convicted and sent to the notorious Angola Prison Farm on a life sentence. Though it didn't seem so at the time, it turned out to be a lucky break. Two years later folklorists Dr. Harry Oster and Richard Allen came to Angola in search of blues artists and were impressed with the raw emotion and inspired guitar skills of the forty-four-year-old Williams. They set up their recording equipment and taped such songs as "Angola Penitentiary Blues," "Prisoner's Talking Blues," and "Pardon Denied Again," which were included in an album released on Arhoolie in 1958, *Angola Prisoners' Blues* (reissued by Arhoolie in 1996).

As the Lomaxes had done for Leadbelly, Oster and Allen began taking steps to persuade Louisiana officials to pardon Williams. With such outside help he had much better chances than the meager legal resources usually available to the typical black citizen, superior artist or not. In 1959 this finally won him his release. At a time when folk music was on the upswing, there was a sizable audience for roots-blues performers, and a great deal of interest in this previously unheard voice was inspired by the '58 album and several follow-ups. Many people outside the South wanted to hear him in live performances, but under Louisiana law a parolee was forbidden to leave the state for five years. That time limit expired in 1964, and he was asked to appear at the Newport, Rhode Island, Folk Festival where his set proved to be one of the highlights of the event.

From then on his career blossomed. He was featured in many other festivals in the United States and other countries and headlined many concerts on the folk and folk-rock circuits. His credits included performing in the United Kingdom and on the Continent in the 1966 American Folk Blues Festival, an association repeated in 1972. Closer to home, he often appeared at the annual New Orleans Jazz and Heritage Festival in the '60s and '70s. During those years he sometimes performed with such other blues greats as Mississippi Fred Mc-

Dowell (who died in July 1972) and Roosevelt Sykes. Meanwhile he continued to turn out new albums on a variety of labels including, besides Arhoolie, Takoma, Fontana, and Storyville. His catalog by the start of the '80s included *Those Prison Blues* on Arhoolie, *When I Lay My Burden Down* on Southland; *Free Again* on Prestige (also included in the two-LP Fantasy package *Robert Pete Williams and Snooks Eaglin); Sugar Farm Blues,* recorded 1972 on the United Kingdom label Blues Beacon; and *Louisiana Blues* on Takoma in 1980. In 1973 he also was represented in the compilation *Legacy of the Blues, Volume 9.*

Williams died in 1980, but new releases of some of the many tracks he laid down during his career continued to appear. Those included the 1988 albums *Robert Pete Williams Live with Big Joe Williams* and *Robert Pete Williams and Roosevelt Sykes;* the two-volume release of 1994 on the Arhoolie label, *I'm As Blue As a Man Can Be* and *When A Man Takes the Blues;* and *It's a Long Old Road* in 1999.

WILLIAMS, ROBIN AND LINDA: *Husband-and-wife vocal, instrumental, and songwriting team, band leaders (Their Fine Group). Robin, (vocals, guitar), born Charlotte, North Carolina, March 16, 1947. Linda (vocals, guitar, banjo), born Anniston, Alabama, July 7, 1947. Their Fine Group members in mid-1990s comprised Robin, Linda, Jim Watson (vocals, bass), and Kevin Maul (vocals, Dobro, Hawaiian, and slide guitars).*

A performing team familiar to many regular listeners of Garrison Keillor's *Prairie Home Companion* and *American Radio Company of the Air* programs, Robin and Linda Williams ranked among the top exponents of folk and traditional country-style music in the closing decades of the twentieth century. Their many albums are gems of the folk and country genres, which appeal to many listeners without becoming mass-market bestsellers. Their skills have been well recognized by performers beloved by mainstream audiences—such as Mary-Chapin Carpenter, for whom they provided harmony vocals on her platinum 1993 *Stones in the Road,* and Iris DeMent, whom they backed on her acclaimed 1994 disc *My Life.*

Both spent their early years in the South. Robin lived first in Virginia's Shenandoah Valley, then in North and South Carolina, as his father, a Presbyterian minister, moved to different parishes; Linda moved slowly north as her father changed jobs. By their teens, each of them had learned to play the guitar and enjoyed playing folk and country music for their own pleasure or with friends. Until she met Robin, Linda had never considered becoming a professional musician, while Robin already was earning money as a performer in his college years. For a time Linda's family lived in Michigan, where she attended high school and went on to get a degree from the University of Michigan. Meanwhile, her parents' odyssey took them back to their original home in South Carolina. It was while Linda was visiting them in 1971 that her path crossed Robin's.

Robin was in the same South Carolina town for a brief stay when he met Linda at an open stage event. He liked her musical abilities, but more than that, he felt attracted to her as a person. As he told Mike Parrish for *Dirty Linen* ("Robin & Linda Williams—From the Exit Inn to the Circle," December 1993–January 1994) "We stayed in touch, and then things started getting real tight between us during the two years between when we first met and when we got married. During that period of time, Linda moved to Nashville. I was on the road and single, and Nashville seemed like a great place to go for that, especially as Linda was there. She was working for the state government then."

As their relationship deepened they began writing songs together, some of which they presented at Tuesday writers' nights at the Nashville Exit Inn. Then they started working up some duo numbers that they began performing at pass-the-hat shows at a bar called the Bishop's Pub in 1972. Some country artists who later moved on to stardom caught their show and urged them to develop it into a full-scale professional act. The question was whether Linda could get accustomed to the demands of touring, They collaborated on expanding their repertoire and lined up some out-of-town appearances to see if Linda would feel comfortable on the road. They made their debut on that schedule in May of 1973, and with Linda warming to the idea of giving concerts, got married in June.

Robin recalled for Parrish, "When we first started out playing, we were playing a lot of colleges. They had a coffeehouse circuit and we worked for them for a couple of years and that brought me out to the Midwest. I made some musical contacts in Minneapolis and started getting a recording contract through those folks. One of them was Peter Ostroushko, and he came and played on our first record [*Robin and Linda Williams*]. After we'd made the record, Peter and Linda and I decided to team up as a trio. Peter came down to Virginia (to which Robin and Linda had relocated from Nashville), and we went out on the road as a trio. That was 1975."

Ostroushko was friends with Garrison Keillor; he knew that the latter was planning a new radio program on a Minnesota Public Broadcasting System station and suggested they try to get on it. Keillor agreed to drive over and hear them in Menominee Falls, Wisconsin, where they were appearing five nights a week at a college coffeehouse. As he wrote in liner notes for a 1990 album, "It was impressive . . . to meet them and to see their motel room, which was one of the neater rooms ever lived in by a musician. Their clothes were hung up, and their stuff wasn't spread out on the floor, nor were they. I could tell they had grown up in the right kind of homes. Despite this advantage, they turned out to be a lot of fun, more fun than the earnestly messed up musicians I know, and that night at the coffeehouse, which

deserved a niche in the Bad Gigs Hall of Fame, they were even more fun. [The Williamses], then as now, have a sort of kryptonite bond with an audience so that nothing can come between them and us. They were magnificent. All the distractions were somehow incorporated into their show, as comedy, and of course it helps to have talent. Individually, their voices can melt cheese and, in duet, they can do all-purpose welding. They sang for three hours, and nobody left, and other people kept arriving."

Keillor indicated he would be happy to have them on his new program, and from then on they came in one or two times a year to guest on the *Prairie Home Companion;* they also made other occasional appearances while traveling through the area. Later, when Keillor began his New York–based program, Robin and Linda's appearances increased to ten to twelve times a year from 1980 until the program closed down in 1987. When Keillor reinstituted *The Prairie Home Companion,* the Williams duo continued as welcome guests. The three also became close personal friends.

Robin and Linda's decision to leave Nashville and make Middlebrook in the Shenandoah Valley of Virginia home reflected their desire to retreat from the pressures and problems of a metropolis like Music City. They continued a busy schedule touring the college and folk club circuit, and turned out a steady stream of new material while not ignoring traditional folk and country strains, including gospel renditions. Through the 1970s into the early 1980s, they released several new albums for small record companies. These comprised *Shenandoah Moon, The Welcome Table, Dixie Highway Sign,* and *Harmony.* In the 1980s they signed with Chicago-based Flying Fish Records, which released the LPs *Close As We Can Get* and *Nine Till Midnight.*

In the 1980s the Williamses often were featured at major folk and country festivals—not only in the United States and Canada but also in other parts of the world. They accumulated many radio and TV credits, including occasional sets on *Grand Ole Opry.* By the late 1980s they had decided to expand their regular roster to a band format, a move that took shape in 1988. First added was highly regarded founding member of the Red Clay Ramblers, vocalist and bassist Jim Watson, followed soon after by Dobro expert Kevin Maul.

As Robin told Chris Nickson of *Folk Roots* magazine ("Companions," June 1995), "We were real careful when we started putting it together. There are a lot of other things to think about besides music when you put a band together. We wanted to make sure everyone got along. And it's worked out real well." Linda commented to Parrish, "Not only are they great musicians, and bring a great knowledge of the tradition of the music with them, they're great guys too. . . . We've known Kevin almost as long as we've been together." They had known Watson since his Red Clay Rambler days in the 1970s.

After the quartet was assembled and began performing together, Robin and Linda began searching for a group name. It was a greater challenge than they thought it would be. As they stated on liner notes for an early 1990s album, "There is an unwritten rule somewhere that says when an ensemble becomes four, the band needs a name. We don't make the rules, we just live by them. The addition of Kevin made us realize the time had come. In our search for the perfect band name the four of us kept returning in our minds to one of our first gigs [as a group]. We were playing the Grand Ole Opry and one of the Four Guys introduced us as 'Robin and Linda Williams and their fine group.' Since then we have spent an inordinate amount of time looking for a band name, but nothing we can think of says it better than 'Robin and Linda Williams and Their Fine Group.' It just sounds right."

The first two albums completed by Robin and Linda for a new label, Sugar Hill, with which they signed in 1989, employed session musicians, not the new band. In the first of those, 1989's *All Broken Hearts Are the Same,* except for their versions of Tom Paxton's "Panhandle Wind," M. McKee's "After the Flood," Merle Kilgore's "Baby Rocked Her Dolly," and the traditional "Across the Blue Mountains," all of the tracks were written by one or both of the Williamses, usually in collaboration with Jerome Clark. Besides the title track, the originals included "Rollin' and Ramblin' (The Death of Hank Williams)," "Leaving This Land," "Annie," "Pine County," "Riding on the Sante Fe," and "Stone Wall Country." This was followed by the 1990 release *The Rhythm of Love* that contained eight originals by Robin, Linda, and in some cases Jerome Clark, like the title song, "Gone to the West," "Hired Gun," "The Six O'Clock News," and "The Devil Is a Mighty Wind." Also among the tracks was the traditional "Poor Wayfaring Stranger," Hank Williams's "House of Gold," and "You Done Me Wrong," the last by Ray Price and George Jones.

Their next album marked the debut of Their Fine Group. Called *Live in Holland,* it incorporated May 1992 recordings at three Netherlands venues: De Muzeval in Emmen, the home of Strictly Country Records in Harpel, and the Colonial Country Club in Valthermond. The album contained four originals, including "Don't Let Me Come Home a Stranger," to accompany, among others, the Delmore Brothers' "Pan American Boogie," Jack Logon's "Herding Cattle in a Cadillac Coup de Ville," and the traditional numbers "Wild Hog in the Woods" and "Across the Blue Mountains."

In the mid-1990s the duo, usually with their band, provided Sugar Hill with new collections that won praise from critics and increased audience attention in the United States, Canada, and overseas. These included *Turn Toward Tomorrow* in 1994, for which Robin and Linda, Robin alone or with Clark, or all three wrote nine of the eleven songs; the 1995 country gospel

disc *Good News,* by the Williamses and Their Fine Group (dedicated to Robin's father, Reverend R. Murphy Williams); and the 1996 *Sugar for Sugar.* For the latter, Robin, Linda, and Clark accounted for all but one of the eleven tracks of another excellent compilation. Among the notable tracks were the title song, "Together All Alone," "Honky Tonk Nation," "Traffic Light," and the bluegrass gospel track "Streets of Gold."

Sugar for Sugar was nominated for Gospel Album of the Year by the International Bluegrass Music Association. Their next album, *Devil of a Dream,* came out in January 1998 on Sugar Hill and soon broke into the top 10 of *Gavin Report's* Americana charts. In contrast to the gospel-flavored *Sugar for Sugar, Devil of a Dream* incorporates styles ranging from country and bluegrass to Cajun and folk. In addition to Watson and Maul, the album includes backup work by Stuart Duncan, Tim O'Brien, and Rose Sinclair. They released their next album in January 2000, *In the Company of Strangers* on Sugar Hill. The other members of Their Fine Group have also released solo efforts. Jim Watson released *Don't Tell Me, I Don't Know,* and Kevin Maul released *Toolshed.*

In addition to their concert efforts, starting in the early 1980s Robin and Linda also became involved in working up material for musicals, initially developing two projects for the open-air Lime Kiln Repertory Group in Lexington, Virginia, near their home in Middlebrook. This led to other opportunities like a project with New York's Circle Repertory Theater. In some ways, the latter work proved more demanding, as Linda told Parrish. Working with the New York organization was an entirely different undertaking from the Lime Kiln association. "The Lime Kiln is a local group; they use some repertory people, some professional actors, but they also use a lot of kids who acted in college and so on, so it's in a way sort of semi-professional. The Circle Repertory Theater is definitely professional."

In the 1990s they were obliged to decide which aspect of their career would win their primary attention. Their new albums for Sugar Hill—and heralded appearances at major festivals, *Grand Ole Opry* and *Austin City Limits* TV programs, plus their backing of stars like Mary-Chapin Carpenter and Iris DeMent—greatly increased demand for their live shows. In fact, major record companies sought to sign them, but as of 2001 they had not been willing to move in that direction. They told Nickson, "We've got a long-term career going. It's been slow and steady moving, but that's what we wanted. Our goal has always been to spend our lives making music. We've never had a huge hit to propel us into the forefront of the scene. On the other hand, we've always been there."

In fact, they liked the idea that, unlike Nashville-based performers, they didn't have to worry about having hits. "Our decisions are creative ones. It's a tough row to hoe when your bottom line is you have to have hits and sell records that get played on the radio. That really puts a wrench in things." As for musicals, while not stating they planned to abandon that entirely, Robin and Linda emphasized they would be stretched thin to work intensively in both areas, so they decided performing and recording would be their main pursuit.

They weren't averse to trying out new things in the music field. Thus in 1993 they inaugurated a tour with Kate MacKenzie and Garrison Keillor as the Hopeful Gospel Quartet. The show blended gospel offerings with some secular songs with Kate and Garrison joining to sing some of the numbers. But they continued extensive touring with their regular act and found time to write still more songs. Linda told Parrish, "Our audiences are growing, people seem to be responding to what we're doing. There are all these little pies for us to dip into. Our songwriting is getting noticed—Emmylou Harris recorded one of our songs and we're getting nibbles from people in Nashville all the time, but still, it's just a matter of time. The more you become visible . . . the more people turn to you as a source. That makes us want to write more, and it all comes back to the goal of keeping the band together so we can go out and play for people."

WILLIAMS, VICTORIA: *Singer, songwriter, guitarist, pianist. Born Shreveport, Louisiana, December 23, 1958.*

In the spring of 1995, Victoria Williams opened for Hootie and the Blowfish at the House of Blues in Los Angeles. The crowd, anxious to hear Hootie, talked through Williams's set, missing out on her delightful songs. She tried to ask them to quiet down, to no avail. But when Williams called Soul Asylum lead singer Dave Pirner to the stage, the crowd suddenly grew quiet as they began "Summer of Drugs," Williams's song about adolescence: *Sister got bit by a copperhead snake in the woods behind the house/Nobody was home so I grabbed her foot and I sucked the poison out/Sister got better in a month or two when the swelling it went down/But I'd started off my teenage years with her poison in my mouth.*

"My sister gets so mad at me," Victoria muses. "She did get bit by a snake, and she says, 'You didn't suck the poison out of my foot.' 'Yeah,' I told her, 'but that's my poetic license.' . . . It seems like the songs just beg to be told."

Another song "Crazy Mary," is based on a woman with that nickname. "People called her Crazy Mary because she would never get in an automobile," Williams says. "She had this fear. One night an auto went out of control and hit her house. Fifteen years later I had this dream that she was in a better place."

Williams's songwriting skills, a quirky brew of truth and fiction, were evident beginning with her 1987 debut, *Happy Come Home,* on Geffen Records, and her 1990 Rough Trade release, *Swing the Statue!* But bad luck initially stymied her career. In 1989, she and L.A.

folksinger Peter Case divorced after six years of marriage. Rough Trade went bankrupt shortly after her release on that label. But the biggest blow came just when people were beginning to take notice. In the spring of 1992, while opening for Neil Young in Detroit, she found that her fingers "were just flopping and wouldn't do what my brain told them to," she told *People* (May 1, 1995). She returned to Los Angeles where a doctor diagnosed her with multiple sclerosis. "When I asked, 'What now?' they shook their heads," Williams said. "They don't know either."

She was confined to a wheelchair and went temporarily blind in 1993. Williams, who had no health insurance, soon had amassed more than $20,000 in doctors' bills. Luckily, she had friends. Shortly after the diagnosis, Lou Reed's ex-wife Sylvia Reed and Sony Music's Kelley Walker came up with the idea for *Sweet Relief: A Benefit for Victoria Williams.* They produced the album, which came out on Columbia in 1993. It included a superstar lineup: Soul Asylum, Lucinda Williams, Pearl Jam, Lou Reed, Evan Dando of the Lemonheads, Giant Sand, the Waterboys, and Michelle Shocked, all performing Williams's songs. The album sold more than 250,000 copies and the publishing royalties went to help pay Williams's medical expenses. (She regained her strength, in part through swimming, digging in the garden, and her strong belief in God.) Her follow-up album, *Loose,* which came out in 1994 on Mammoth/Atlantic, received glowing reviews. Steve Hochman of the *Los Angeles Times* gave the album the top rating—four stars—and called Williams a "national treasure." "Her third and best album is filled with distinctive revelries in the many small joys and large awes she finds in life, feelings that apparently were only intensified by her battle with multiple sclerosis," he wrote (October 23, 1994). "They are given finer detail in Williams's own miniatures, filled with the kind of eccentric characters and peculiar insights that would be at home in a Eudora Welty story."

One of those stories, "Century Plant," is about finding new life and spirit in old age. "Happy to Have Known Pappy" was inspired by a saloon owner she met in the California desert. She wrote "Harry Went to Heaven" after attending the funeral for a jazz player from Shreveport, Louisiana.

Williams, the youngest of three children, was born in Shreveport and lived in a house once occupied by pianist Van Cliburn. "My grandmother and grandfather, my mother and father too are natural storytellers. That must be where I got it from."

Patricia, her mother, was a schoolteacher and painter. She would take Victoria out to the country where she painted wildflowers and plantations for descendants. "She couldn't let anyone know," Victoria recalls. "She'd be hiding out in her car with her paints working on painting these people's old houses." Victoria, meanwhile, would be down by the Cane River Cutoff float-

from her song titles: "Grandpa in a Cornpatch," "Train Song (Demise of the Caboose)," "Allergic Boy," "Kashmir's Corn," and "Periwinkle Sky." Whether she's singing about her childhood in "Train Song," or a boy who is so allergic that he can't eat milk and pie, Williams expresses desires in a whimsical, subconscious manner. "My favorite song is always the next one bubbling underneath the surface."

She followed with *Water to Drink,* released on Atlantic in July 2000.

Based on an interview by Lyndon Stambler with Victoria Williams

WILLIAMSON, JOHN LEE "SONNY BOY" (SONNY BOY #1): *Singer, harmonica player, songwriter. Born Jackson, Tennessee, March 30, 1914; died Chicago, Illinois, June 1, 1948.*

Harmonica innovator Sonny Boy Williamson's life was brutally ended when he was only thirty-four years of age. And for much of his career he labored in relative obscurity, performing in juke joints and other small venues on the southern blues circuit. But he still left an indelible stamp as musician and songwriter in the folk-blues and R&B genres, and, long after his death, influenced the birth of blues-rock formats. His legacy was strangely affected by the confusion caused when another great harp player, Aleck Rice Miller, assumed his professional name. This resulted in blues observers denoting John Lee as Sonny Boy #1 and Miller as Sonny Boy #2.

Williamson was born in Jackson, Tennessee, and in his preteen years taught himself to play the harmonica. By his midteens in the early 1930s he had become an accomplished player and often performed with bluesmen like Sleepy John Estes, Big Joe Williams, and Robert Nighthawk. He developed a peculiar style of singing, a slurring approach he adapted to get around his problem of stammering. Essentially it was his original method of harmonica playing and his creation of blues songs that since have been covered by artists in many fields from blues to rock that set him apart. His harp technique, as was pointed out in the *Guinness Encyclopedia of Popular Music,* was almost always based on "cross-note" tuning "in which the key of the harmonica is a fourth above that of the music. This technique encourages drawn rather than blown notes, thus facilitating the vocalization, slurring and bent notes that are basic, in conjunction with intermittent hand muting, and various tonguing and breath control effects, to most blues harmonica playing."

In 1934 Williamson moved to Chicago, where his path crossed those of such blues greats as Big Bill Broonzy, Tampa Red, and Big Maceo. He had already performed with some of the most talented people in the Chicago blues scene and had done some initial session work with some of them when he signed a solo contract with Bluebird Records. He soon began providing the label with singles that were best-sellers in the black community in the late '30s and the 1940s, such as "Good Morning Little School Girl," "Sugar Mama Blues," "Bluebird Blues," "Early in the Morning," and "Check Up on My Baby." In his lifetime, the record firm released a series of albums, starting with *Sonny Boy Williamson, Volume 1* in 1938 and ending with *Sonny Boy Williamson, Volume 5* in 1947, plus many other collections such as *Big Bill [Broonzy] and Sonny Boy.* By the start of the 1940s Sonny Boy had become one of the top stars in Chicago blues clubs, a position he enjoyed for the rest of his life. He continued to record new material of his own while backing dozens of other performers in recording sessions. He still retained a devoted following and probably would have benefited greatly from the soon-to-arrive popularity of R&B and rock if he had lived. However, on the night of June 1, 1948, while walking home from a gig at a local South Side Chicago club, he was assaulted and killed.

In the decades following his death, reissues of his recordings continued to appear in record company catalogs. In 1964, *Big Bill and Sonny Boy* became available. Blues Classics reissued *Sonny Boy Williamson, Volume 1* in 1965, *Volume 2* around 1968, and *Volume 3* in the early 1970s. RCA Records in the pre-1980s period also released the collections *Sonny Boy Williamson* and *Sonny Boy Williamson Volume 2.* The RCA Heritage series also included the album *Throw a Boogie Woogie (with Big Joe Williams).* In the 1980s more reissues were released: *Bluebird 1* around 1982, *Bluebird II* in mid-decade, *Sonny Boy Williamson* around 1986, and *Rare Sonny Boy, Volume 1* in 1988. The latter was issued on CD in 1991. That year Document Records released *Sonny Boy Williamson Complete Recorded Works 1937–47,* a five-CD set, from his Bluebird catalog. BMG reissued his recordings later in the 1990s. In 1991 Rykodisc released *Blues in the Mississippi Night,* a documentary recording made in the mid-1940s by Alan Lomax of Sonny Boy, Big Bill Broonzy, and Memphis Slim speaking about racism in the South and the roots of the blues. Lomax agreed to keep their identities sealed and only revealed their names after they were all dead.

WILLIAMSON, SONNY BOY "RICE MILLER" (SONNY BOY #2): *Singer, harmonica player, guitarist, drummer, songwriter. Born Glendora, Mississippi, December 5, 1899 (year of birth also has been variously given as anywhere from 1894 to 1909 or 1910); died Helena, Arkansas, May 25, 1965.*

Facts about the life and career of the harmonica great, who gained fame by appropriating someone else's professional name, are, to say the least, somewhat elusive. He performed in his lifetime under a variety of pseudonyms and even his original name is open to question. But there is no question about his skills: he was one of the finest harmonica players to ever come out of the roots-blues tradition as well as an above-average singer. His influence extended well beyond basic blues to such genres as R&B, rock, and jazz.

The illegitimate son of a woman named Millie Ford, his given name at birth was either Aleck or Alex Ford. As he grew older, though, he began using the last name, Miller, of his stepfather, and chose to be called "Rice." Sometimes he called himself Aleck Rice Miller. There wasn't much in the way of education available for a young black man in the early years of this century, but fortunately for him he had the inherent musical talent that allowed him to teach himself the harmonica in his preteen years, also picking up skills on the guitar and drums. It's not certain exactly when he left home to work as an itinerant musician, but he was already working on the blues circuit in his early teens.

In the 1920s he performed at local juke joints and parties before moving farther afield at the end of the '20s or the start of the '30s. He played wherever he could find an opportunity, sometimes in clubs or dance halls, sometimes in parks or on street corners. His path crossed those of many other bluesmen of the period, including Robert Johnson, Robert Jr. Lockwood, Elmore James (who played an important role in the evolution of his career), Howlin' Wolf, and others. Howlin' Wolf's half sister Mary became his first wife during that period of his life. Before appropriating the name of Sonny Boy Williamson in the late 1930s he performed under many other pseudonyms, including Little Boy Blue, Willie Williams, Willie Williamson, and Willie Miller. He also acquired the nickname "Foots."

Tall (six feet) and strong, he also was known for his less savory habits—drinking too much and never avoiding a fight. In the rough-and-tumble environment of the blues world, however, he was a survivor and managed to avoid the fate of so many blues performers who were killed or maimed. On the other hand, he could be charming and persuasive to other artists or members of the opposite sex. He was respected as a musician and songwriter by other artists, but his career was only moving ahead slowly in the late '30s, when he started to call himself Sonny Boy Williamson after the better-known Chicago-based Sonny Boy #1. It was as Sonny Boy Williamson that he scored his first breakthrough when he joined guitarist Robert Jr. Lockwood for a noon-hour show on Helena, Arkansas, station KFFA in 1941 called the *King Biscuit Flour Time.*

KFFA reached many states in the region, and Williamson and Lockwood used the exposure to good advantage. The publicity brought work in many clubs in the region, while they also were featured, as the King Biscuit Entertainers (eventually with several backing musicians), in shows sponsored by KFFA. B.B. King made his radio debut on same the show. After 1944, Williamson resumed his roving ways, often performing with people like Elmore James, Willie Love, and Joe

Willie Wilkins. When he returned to Helena from time to time, he still was welcomed at the microphone.

Considering the fact that he had become a name artist for great numbers of black music fans in the Mississippi Delta area, it's surprising that it took him so long to start recording his own material. Thanks to help from Elmore James (whom he backed on his hit "Dust My Broom"), he laid down his first tracks in 1951 for the Jackson, Mississippi, label Trumpet Records. Over the next few years, while he called Memphis, Tennessee, home, he recorded many songs for the label, among which was his classic rendition of "Mighty Long Time."

In 1954 he pulled up stakes again, heading to Detroit, where he and Baby Boy Warren had a featured act in local night spots. After spending some time in Cleveland, in 1955 he moved to Chicago, a city he had avoided during the years when Sonny Boy #1 was active there. By 1955, of course, the latter had been dead for seven years and Rice Miller felt the coast was clear for him. Trumpet closed its doors that year, and Williamson signed with a larger label, Checker, part of the Chess Records organization. He soon had a hit single of his self-penned "Don't Start Me to Talkin'," the first of many releases that made the blues and R&B charts. Over his years with Checker/Chess, which lasted into the early 1960s, he turned out dozens of albums, some in which he was accompanied by such other top-rank performers (many who worked with the Muddy Waters Band) as guitarist Luther Tucker; piano players Otis Spann, Willie Love, and Lafayette Leake; drummer Fred Below; and bass player Willie Dixon.

Through based in Chicago during the second half of the '50s and the first half of the '60s, he never lost touch with his roots. He regularly included stops in the Delta, Helena, and Memphis on his tours before returning to his Chicago home, shared with his second wife, Mattie Lee Gordon. In 1963 he joined the American Folk Blues Festival group for a tour of Europe in which he became one of the concert showstoppers. After the '63 AFBF series, he stayed overseas for a while to take advantage of the growing enthusiasm for blues music on both sides of the Iron Curtain. His well-received appearances took him to many parts of Europe, including Poland. He went back to the United States afterward, then joined another AFBF European tour in '64, savoring the fact that he had become a major star in the eyes of fans in Britain and on the European Continent. During both his 1963 and '64 visits he added to his recording credits with sessions for the Storyville label in Denmark, with other American blues artists in France, and collaborations with young blues-rock notables in the United Kingdom.

By 1965, though he had become an established favorite of large numbers of blues fans at home and abroad, his health was deteriorating. His association with station KFFA in Helena had never been completely severed, and in '65 he became a regular again as host and main artist on the *King Biscuit Time* show. In late May '65, he died quietly in his sleep.

His legacy was immense, including songs covered by many other performers and an array of recorded material that continued to be recombined and reissued over the decades from the mid-'60s through the 1990s. His classic songs, besides the ones noted above, included "One Way Out," "Cross My Heart," "Nine Below Zero," "Fattening Frogs for Snakes," "Eyesight in the Blind," and "Help Me." Album releases during the latter part of his career included the 1959 *Down and Out Blues*, *A Portrait in Blues* (Storyville 1964), and *The Real Folk Blues* (also known as *In Memoriam* 1965). Posthumous releases during the second half of the '60s included *Final Sessions 1963–64* (a French import on the Blue Night label); *Don't Send Me No Flowers* and *Sonny Boy Williamson and the Yardbirds* (both 1966); *More Real Folk Blues* ('67); *One Way Out* ('68); and *Bummer Road* ('69). The last three Chess LPs were available as reissues by overseas companies in the mid-'70s. In 1972, Chess issued the collection *This Is My Story,* one of the best compilations of Williamson's work that often served as a reference point for blues and rock performers. Other LPs available in the '70s included *King Biscuit Time* on Arhoolie (1976); *Sonny Boy Williamson* (Chess, French import 1977; *The Real Folk Blues* and *More Real Folk Blues* (Chess, French import); and *Sonny Boy Williamson and Memphis Slim in Paris* on Crescendo.

In the 1980s reissues became available on the MCA/Chess label after MCA acquired the Chess catalog. MCA releases as of the '90s included *One Way Out Blues, The Real Folk Blues,* the excellent 1992 *Sonny Boy Williamson: His Best, More Real Folk Blues,* and *Bummer Road.* His recordings at the end of the '80s and in the '90s began to be issued on CDs, such as the albums *King Biscuit Time, The Animals with Sonny Boy Williamson,* and *Clowning with the World,* recorded with Willie Love, all issued in 1989; Charly Records' 1991 box set *The Chess Years; Boppin' with Sonny* (1992); and the Optimism album *Sonny Boy Williamson and the Yardbirds Live in London.* Other albums in print in the mid-'90s included the Alligator Records discs *Keep It to Ourselves* and *Going in Your Direction.*

WINCHESTER, JESSE: *Singer, pianist, drummer, songwriter. Born Bossier City (near Shreveport), Louisiana, May 17, 1944.*

It's generally conceded that Jesse Winchester would have been a star, perhaps even a superstar, by the mid-1970s if he hadn't fled to Canada to express opposition to the Vietnam War. As it is, the series of finely crafted albums he turned out from 1969 through 1977 did reasonably well considering he wasn't able to tour in support of them in the United States until 1976, when President Carter pardoned war protesters. In the late

1970s Jesse started touring U.S. cities, and his new album sales rose perceptibly. Equally important were the number of folk, country, and pop artists who gained chart successes with some of Jesse's songs in the '70's, '80s, and '90s, including Wynonna Judd and Emmylou Harris.

Jesse was born in Louisiana into a proud family tradition. (He originally was named James R. Winchester after his father, an air force captain.) One of his forebears invented the famous Winchester firearm, Robert E. Lee was a blood relation, and other family members were prominent in Memphis affairs from the city's earliest times. He was in direct line of descent from a co-founder of the city, and his grandfather gave the funeral oration at the burial of blues great W. C. Handy.

When Jesse's father returned from the war in the South Pacific, he came back a pacifist and took up farming. Jesse noted that his father was "one of the original hippies in the late forties; he decided against joining the family law firm to take up farming instead and get closer to the land." Jesse grew up on the farm until he was twelve, when his father decided to move back to Memphis, where he finally gained a law degree and practiced until he died in 1962. Jesse already had become immersed in pop music by then, finding particular empathy with the early R&B and rockabilly artists such as Elvis Presley, Carl Perkins, Chuck Berry, Bo Diddley, and Jerry Lee Lewis. In high school in Memphis, he played with various bands, first as a drummer, later as a piano player, in groups called the Midnighters and Church Keys.

He continued his interest in music as a sideline when he entered Williams College in Massachusetts, from which he received his B.A. in 1966. His major was German, and he spent some time traveling in Europe before he returned to Memphis to work as a pianist in local clubs. When his draft notice came in 1967, he had a hard choice to make. "It was a very hard decision and my mother didn't tell me what she thought at the time—she said I had to do what I felt was right. She later said she thought it was the right decision. The hardest part was hurting my grandfather, who was the patriot of the family. He was my father's father and I was very close to him spiritually. He had a strong sense of honor and duty and his attitude could be summed up by the phrase, 'my country, may she always be right, but right or wrong, still my country.'"

Deciding he had to leave, Winchester moved to Montreal, where he answered a newspaper ad to become a member of a band called Les Astronauts. By the end of the 1960s he had gone out on his own, playing piano in small clubs like the Back Door Cafe, across from McGill University. In 1969 he opened a concert for the Band at Montreal's Place des Arts, and his performance, plus the original songs he was writing by then, so impressed the Band's Robbie Robertson that he became one of Jesse's most ardent proponents.

Robertson helped Jesse get a recording contract from Ampex and produced the first album, *Jesse Winchester,* issued in 1970. The album contained such striking numbers as "Yankee Lady," "Biloxi," and "Brand New Tennessee Waltz," the latter a bittersweet song about the travail of exile ("I've a sadness too sad to be true/So have all your passionate violins/Play a tune for the Tennessee Kid"). The album won critical praise in the United States, including praise from *Rolling Stone,* which called him the most promising new artist of 1970, but the album failed commercially without adequate promotion.

Some of the songs have done well for others, however. "Yankee Lady" was recorded by Tim Hardin and Melanie, and "Brand New Tennessee Waltz" has appeared on many albums, including those of Joan Baez. The well-known manager Albert Grossman shared Robertson's continued faith in Jesse and signed him for his Bearsville label in 1972. *Third Down, 110 to Go* (the title refers to Canadian football, where the field is 110 yards long rather than 100 as in the United States), fared almost exactly the same as the Ampex effort. It too provided songs for others: "Isn't That So" was recorded by Peter Yarrow and became an English chart hit for a British group. Undaunted, Winchester and Grossman kept on with new releases, such as *Learn to Love It* (1974) and *Let the Rough Side Drag* (1976). Important tracks from the former include "Defying Gravity" and "Mississippi on My Mind," the latter giving country artist Stoney Edwards a top-level hit. The 1976 album had many delights, including the title track and "Blow on Chilly Wind."

Although Jesse could travel freely to and from the United States after 1976, he had decided Canada was his true home. He received Canadian citizenship in 1973, though he became increasingly active on the U.S. concert circuit. His debut tour of the States in early 1977, backed by a Canadian band he'd assembled the previous year called Midnight Bus (Martin Harris on bass, Bobby Cohen on lead guitar, Ron Dann on pedal steel, and Dave Lewis on drums), proved to stateside audiences that Winchester provided a highly entertaining, professionally polished show. The tour, which coincided with release of his new Bearsville LP, *Nothing but a Breeze,* received coverage from *Newsweek, Time, People, Rolling Stone,* and an extended segment on the NBC network show *Weekend.* In 1978, however, the initial frenzy had died down, and his sixth album (fifth on Bearsville), *A Touch on the Rainy Side,* though as consistently rewarding, failed to make the U.S. charts as its immediate predecessor had done.

Jesse, who lives in the Eastern Townships of Quebec, continued to tour in Canada, the United States, and abroad in the 1980s and into the '90s, though he didn't match his recording achievements of the '70s. His album credits in the 1980s included *Talk Memphis* in 1981 (which included the hit song "Say What") and, in

1988, the retrospective *The Best of Jesse Winchester* and *Humour Me.* In the mid-1990s Stony Plain Records of Canada reissued Winchester's albums on CD.

In January 1999 Winchester returned to Nashville and recorded his first new album in a decade, *Gentleman of Leisure,* released by Sugar Hill in June of that year. Dobro wizard Jerry Douglas produced it. Also appearing on the album were Steve Cropper on electric guitar and Vince Gill and the Fairfield Four singing background vocals. "I enjoyed making this latest record so much, I've started preparing for another one," Winchester wrote in response to an E-mail. "Otherwise, I still write for other artists."

WITHERSPOON, JIMMY: *Singer, bassist, songwriter, Born Gurdon, Arkansas, August 8, 1923; died Los Angeles, California, September 18, 1997.*

Jimmy Witherspoon had one of the smoothest, smokiest voices around, which enabled him to shift from blues to R&B to jazz during a prolific career (more that 200 recordings) that spanned five decades. He was influenced by the gospel sounds of his youth, and by such veteran blues stars as Muddy Waters, Big Joe Turner, T-Bone Walker, Big Bill Broonzy, and Jay McShann.

'Spoon, as he was called, later developed a strong following in Britain and around the world. He was a charismatic performer. "I've had people crying when I come on stage," he told National Public Radio (September 21, 1997). "I've had people laughing laughing and crying. Oh, it turns me on, makes me feel good. Sometimes I get carried away on stage. I'm only human. But I'm blessed to be able to sing and get carried away. It's a marvelous tool. And I'm smart enough to realize it."

He grew up in Gurdon, Arkansas, soloing in the Baptist Church choir when he was five. He took first prize at the Clark County singing contest while still young. At sixteen, he left home, using a forged rail pass (his father had worked on the railroad) to travel to Los Angeles. He was washing dishes at an Owl Drugstore when T-Bone Walker invited 'Spoon to sing at a show in Watts. He later sang for Art Tatum's band. A couple of years later, he joined the merchant marine. During a stop in Calcutta, India, he sang in pianist Teddy Weatherford's band at the Grand Hotel Winter Garden. He performed with the band on Armed Forces Radio.

In 1944, he went home to visit his mother and heard Jay McShann perform. His timing was perfect, since blues singer Walter Brown had just left the band. Witherspoon took his place and brought the house down with his version of "Kansas City Blues." He remained in McShann's band for the next four years, recording for several labels, including the hit song "Confessin' the Blues."

At the end of the 1940s, Witherspoon decided to try his hand at a solo career and formed his own touring band while continuing to record extensively. In 1949, with McShann's band backing him, he scored with his rendition of "Ain't Nobody's Business" on Supreme Records, which hit the top of the R&B charts. Later in the year, his version of "In the Evening When the Sun Goes Down" hit number five on the charts. He continued strong for the next few years, but when rock 'n' roll edged out R&B, Witherspoon had to file for bankruptcy in 1953. He continued to perform and record throughout the 1950s, however.

He struggled along until 1958 when he switched to jazz, recording with such greats as Earl Hines, Coleman Hawkins, Buddy Tate, Gerry Mulligan, and Ben Webster. His appearance at the 1959 Monterey Jazz Festival helped rebuild his career. The live album from his perfomance and a follow-up recorded at the Renaissance Club helped him gain even wider attention. He toured Europe with Buck Clayton's band in 1961. He performed at Carnegie Hall that year, and at the Newport Jazz Festival. In 1963, he toured Japan with the Count Basie Orchestra and appeared on the *Steve Allen Show*.

Throughout the 1960s, 'Spoon put out a steady stream of albums crossing blues, jazz, R&B, and rock genres. He had another minor hit with "You're Next" in 1965, and later with "Blues Around the Clock," "Some of My Best Friends are the Blues," and "Blue Spoon." In 1971, he toured with Eric Burdon and the Animals, appearing at festivals throughout the States.

Beginning in 1972, he had his own radio show on KMET-FM in Los Angeles. He even made an appearance as an actor: in *Black Godfather* in 1974, for which he won a Billie Holiday Phoenix Award from the Black American Cinema Society. That year he also appeared on *The Tonight Show Starring Johnny Carson*. His recording of "Love is a Five Letter Word" rose to number 31 on the R&B charts in 1975.

In 1984, Witherspoon was diagnosed with throat cancer. He went through radiation therapy and returned to singing a year later. His voice was never the same, but he continued to tour and record albums. In 1996, he played an itinerant blues shouter in a film called *Georgia*. "I play Trucker, a dirty old man," he explained to Paul A. Harris of the *St. Louis Post-Dispatch* ("Ain't Nobody's Business If He Does," January 18, 1996). "I had to do a lot of research for the part, of course. Practice, practice, practice." The following year in September 1997, police found him dead of natural causes at his home in the Baldwin Hills section of Los Angeles. Earlier that year his *Live at the Mint* album was nominated for a Grammy in the Best Traditional Blues category.

A profuse number of his LPs and CDs can be found, including: *Jimmy Witherspoon & Jay McShann* (DA, 1949), *New Orleans Blues* (1956), *Goin' to Kansas City Blues* (RCA, 1958), *Jimmy Witherspoon at the Monterey Jazz Festival* (HiFi, 1959), *The Spoon Concerts* (Fantasy, 1959), *Singin' the Blues* (1959), *Jimmy With-erspoon at the Renaissance* (HiFi, 1959), *Feelin' the Spirit* (1959), *There's Good Rockin' Tonight* (1961), *Spoon* (1961), *Sings the Blues* (1961), *Jimmy Witherspoon* (1961), *A Spoonful of Blues* (1962), *Roots* (1962), *Hey Mrs. Jones* (1962), *Baby, Baby, Baby* (Original Blues Classics, 1963, Fantasy, 1993), *Evenin' Blues* (Original Blues Classics, 1963, Fantasy/Prestige, 1993), *Blues Around the Clock* (Original Blues Classics, 1963, Fantasy), *As Blue as They Can Be* (1963), *Some of My Best Friends are the Blues* (Original Blues Classics, 1964/Fantasy, 1994), *Blue Spoon* (1964), *Blues for Easy Livers* (Original Blues Classics, 1966/Fantasy, 1996), *Spoon in London* (1965), *Goin' to Chicago* (1965), *Blues for Spoon and Groove* (1965), *Hey Mr. Landlord* (Route 66, 1965), *Bluesbox* (1966), *Blue Point of View* (1966), *In Person* (1966), *The Blues Is Now* (1967), *Spoonful of Soul* (1968), *The Best of Jimmy Witherspoon* (1969), *Handbags and Gladrags* (1970), *Blues Singer* (1970), *Guilty* (1971), *The Spoon Concerts* (Fantasy, 1972), *Huhh* (1973), *Groovin' & Spoonin'* (1973), *Jimmy Witherspoon & Ben Webster* (1974), *Love Is a Five Letter Word* (1975), *Spoonful* (Avenue Jazz, 1975/Rhino, 1994), *Live* (1979), *Spoon's Life* (1980), *Big Blues* (1981), *Patcha, Patcha, All Night Long* (1985), *Midnight Lady Called the Blues* (Muse, 1986), *Rockin' L.A.* (Fantasy, 1988), *Live at Condon's* (Chess, 1990), *Spoon Go East* (1990), *Spoon So Easy: The Chess Years* (Chess, 1990), *Blowin' in from Kansas City* (Ace, 1991), *Call Me Baby* (Night Train, 1991), *The Blues, the Whole Blues and Nothing But the Blues* (Indigo, 1992), *Witherspoon/McShann* (1992), *Jimmy Witherspoon Sings the Blues* (Aim, 1993), *Hot Licks: Ain't Nobody's Business* (Polydor, 1967, Drive, 1994), *Amazing Grace* (1994), *Ain't Nothin' New About the Blues* (Aim, 1994), *Spoon's Life* (Evidence, 1994), *Rockin' with the Spoon* (1995), *American Blues* (1995), *Taste of Swing Time* (1995), *Cold Blooded Boogie* (1995), *Spoon's Blues* (Stony Plain, 1995), *Spoon and Groove* (Tradition/Rykodisc, 1996), *Jay's Blues* (Charly, 1996), *Live at the Mint* (1996), *Ain't Nobody's Business* (Polydor, 1996), *Tougher than Tough* (1997), *Jimmy Witherspoon with the Junior Mance Trio* (Stony Plain, 1997), *Kansas City* (1998), *Jimmy Witherspoon Meets the Jazz Giants* (1998), *Jazz Me Blues: The Best of Jimmy Witherspoon* (1998).

WOLF, KATE: *Singer, songwriter, guitarist, bandleader (the Wildwood Flower). Born San Francisco, California, January 27, 1942; died December 10, 1986.*

For one who departed so early, Kate Wolf left behind an enduring legacy: from 1971 to 1986, she wrote 200 songs and recorded fifty-six of them. Her significance exceeds her modest commercial success. Nanci Griffith was so moved by her work that she opened her 1992 tribute album to songwriters, *Other Voices, Other Rooms*, with Wolf's song "Across the Great Divide."

The words from the last verse, about life's mysteries, resound in light of Wolf's death of leukemia at the age of forty-four: *The finest hour that I have seen is the one that comes between/The edge of night and the break of day when the darkness rolls away.*

By focusing on the world around her, Wolf wrote timeless songs: "Give Yourself to Love," written for a friend's wedding; "Emma Rose," inspired by a woman's name on a mailbox; and "Eyes of a Painter," inspired in part by former husband Ché Greenwood's father in Oklahoma. "She would take certain influences from people, add things to it and through that process have a more universal impact," says Terry Fowler, Wolf's last husband, who comanages her music with her son Max Wolf and Jamie Keller, and works with people who want to use Kate's copyrighted songs.

"Kate's songs often hold a sadness that's like clear water in cupped hands," wrote Marja Eloheimo in the *Fax* (October 1984). "Indeed she says that's one reason she started singing as a child was to touch that sadness."

She was born Kathryn Louise Allen, the daughter of Fred and Ruth Allen. Ruth was a high school teacher, Fred was in the merchant marines. The family moved around in her early years to Oregon and Michigan, to accommodate Fred's career or to live with relatives when Fred and Ruth were separated. They returned to Berkeley where Wolf attended junior high and high school. They called her Katie Lou as a child. People didn't call her Kate until the mid-1960s. She started taking piano lessons from her grandmother at four until she was sixteen. She stopped because she felt shy and self-conscious, according to a biography found on the official Kate Wolf Web site written by Max Wolf and Jamie Keller in 1987. "I think it was just a little awkward for her to go from learning how to play piano and then going in front of her classmates," Fowler says.

Wolf listened to the folksingers of the late '50s and early '60s—Bob Dylan, the Weavers, the Kingston Trio. She also liked the rootsy country music of the Carter Family, Merle Haggard, and Lefty Frizell. Among other favorites were Peggy Lee, Frank Sinatra, Hank Williams, Jo Stafford, Joan Baez, Jean Ritchie, Malvina Reynolds, Johnny Cash, Buffy Sainte-Marie, and Stevie Winwood. "It's been kind of a progression through honest songs and honest singers; that kind of clarity. I guess it's that heart that's out there," she told Tim Van Schmidt in August 1985.

Kate began playing in coffeehouses in the early '60s while she was attending San Francisco State. Max Wolf has a 1965 flyer announcing a performance at the Cedar Alley Coffeehouse in San Francisco. "She wasn't a full-time singer songwriter at that point," Max says. "In the 1960s it was an exploration." She met Berkeley architecture student Saul Wolf in 1961; she was nineteen. They married when she was twenty-one, and she dropped out of college to have a family. Max was born

in 1964, and Hannah in 1967. (Both work as computer consultants and manage Wolf's web page.)

When Hannah was one, her babysitter gave Kate an album of Rosalie Sorrels singing Utah Phillips songs, which inspired her to play folk music. In 1969 she met some musicians in Big Sur, who encouraged her to write songs. "Anyone can write a song. Just sit down and sing your conversations," George Schroder, who wrote "The Redtail Hawk," told her. She also met Gil Turner, an early influence. "It was a hippie hangout commune kind of thing, very down-to-earth," Max says. "She didn't think she could write and they encouraged her to write down whatever she was feeling. They helped her hone her skills."

She left her family in San Francisco to follow her muse. In 1971, after an amicable separation from Saul, she moved to Sonoma County, north of San Francisco, and lived in her '50s Plymouth station wagon for a few months. "She was homeless," Max says. "We lived with my father. He did all the child care. Then we started alternating years between my dad and her. She must have felt strongly about wanting to go into music. I think she developed a pretty strong, supportive network of friends."

While raising her children, she continued to perform her music. "She met Don Coffin at the Stage Coach establishment at a shared gig. He began backing her and later that year they began living together," Fowler says. In January 1974 she married Coffin, a rural mailman. Kate found a job doing layout for the *Sebastopol Times* and began performing in local bars, notably the Painted House in Santa Rosa, where she performed Tuesday and Saturday nights after dinner. On her album *An Evening in Austin,* recorded at *Austin City Limits,* as she introduced "One More Song," she talked about how it got so bad that the bartender stopped taking the chairs off the tables. "There's nothing wrong with your music, you're just in the wrong place," he told her.

"She was out to play music," Fowler says. "She would go wherever she could. She got to know restaurant owners, radio people, and volunteer organizations." In a newspaper article of the time, she described her calling: "It meant singing for all kinds of situations for their own sake and getting other people involved in presenting music where there had been none. It meant having a commitment to the community in return for their support and spending time and energy being accessible to everyone, not just other musicians." She and a group of musicians got together on the weekends at O'Connell's Grove to play concerts, using a flatbed truck as a stage.

In 1973–74, she formed her first band, the Wildwood Flower, with Don Coffin, who sang backup and played mandolin, harmonica, and lead guitar; Rod Dickinson on guitar; and Bill Rodgers on bass. Other musicians would become part of the Wildwood Flower for periods of time up to and including Kate's first two albums, *Back Roads* and *Lines on the Paper.* They included Paul Ellis on fiddle, Will Siegel on Dobro and banjo, Pete Wiseman on bass, and David West of the Cache Valley Drifters on guitar.

She hosted a live radio show called *Uncommon Country* on KVRE radio and played country artists not usually heard on commercial radio. She later hosted a show called the *Sonoma County Singers Circle* on KSRO. She also put together the first Santa Rosa Folk Festival in 1974 and invited Utah Phillips to perform. "Kate was a go-getter; taught herself to play guitar," Phillips told Michael Parrish of *Dirty Linen* (June–July '94). "She wanted to meet me. I couldn't figure out why; I was pretty new at the game myself. She had left the home she was living in and loaded everything she owned into a station wagon to work in the roadhouses and learn her skills. She had heard an album called *If I Could Be the Rain* that Rosalie Sorrels had made for Folk Legacy right after leaving Utah that had six of my songs on it. Kate listened to the album, said 'I can do that,' and started doing it."

A fan who lived in Sonoma, Alice Hall, gave her $4,000 to record her first album, *Back Roads,* with many songs inspired by the sights and sounds of the county. Rather than try to sign with a major label, she formed her own Owl Records (after her love of owls, which show up in her lyrics), becoming one of the first female artists to do so. She formed Another Sundown Publishing Company in 1973 and retained the rights to her songs. "The only way an artist can get a fair shake from the industry is to do it yourself," she told Jim Rigby of the *Hartford Advocate* (September 28, 1977). "You set a track record and then you can deal with the music industry."

Wolf recorded the album over five days in July 1975, in the living room of a house on the Sonoma coast near Goat Rock. It included eight original songs and four by other artists, including "Red Tail Hawk" by George Schroder. She wrote the title track one day after she took back roads to get home rather than the highway. The album helped Wolf gain a grassroots following. It sold 7,000 copies in a year and a half. She gained a wider recognition, performing at San Francisco's Boarding House with Phillips and Sorrels in April 1976, and at the San Diego Folk Festival.

Says Fowler: "She basically struggled through a lot of her life, carrying her albums around in a '71 Dodge camper van which she acquired in 1976 as she began to perform out of the area. That's the way she made her living."

In 1977 Wolf released her second album, *Lines on the Paper,* again with the Wildwood Flower (Coffin on harmonica, mandolin, and backup vocals, Ellis on fiddle, Blair Hardman on bass, and Eddie B. Barlow on Dobro and backup vocals). The album was recorded in November 1976 in a living room at a Chanslor Ranch bunkhouse, a five-minute drive from Bodega Bay, and in October and December in Roger Gans's studio in San Francisco. She also invited members of the Cache Valley Drifters—Bill Griffin and Wally Barnick on bass, David West and Cyrus Clarke on lead guitars—to sit in. Griffin had filled in as a band member on a gig in 1974 and wound up producing many of her albums. *Lines on the Paper*'s first pressing of 2,800 copies sold out in the first month.

"I heard a side of Kate I hadn't seen before," Griffin told *Dirty Linen.* "All of her songs up to that point had been about life in rural Santa Rosa, friends, riding in the country, and so on. 'The Heart' got into a new area that was almost a dark side, and I don't mean that in a bad way. All of a sudden, I started to see a lot of depth that told of things to come. 'She Rises Like a Dolphin' comes from the same place, 'The Medicine Wheel,' and all these things that were to come later."

Wolf began touring nationally in 1977 in her Dodge van with Coffin. In 1978, Utah Phillips invited her to tour back east. He tells the story of driving with her to Washington, D.C. for a rally for Karen Silkwood sponsored by the Oil, Chemical, and Atomic Workers Union. Kate wrote a song on the way called "Links in the Chain," which she never recorded, and performed it at the rally. She also performed at the Philadelphia Folk Festival (singing Paul Siebel's "Then Came the Children," which was included in a Flying Fish compilation), at Telluride in Colorado, and at Canadian festivals in Calgary, Winnipeg, and Vancouver.

In January 1978, Wolf split with her husband, Don Coffin, and the Wildwood Flower. She was too busy to put out her own albums and formed an alliance with Tom Diamant and Jeff Alexson who owned Kaleidoscope Records. They began distributing her first two albums. She co-produced her 1979 album, *Safe at Anchor,* with Griffin, who played mandocaster and piano. The album marked the arrival of mandolinist and guitarist Nina Gerber, who was inspired to become a musician after seeing Wolf play at a Sebastopol pizza parlor. Nina took mandolin lessons from Coffin and filled in for him in 1977. Gerber accompanied Wolf for the remainder of her career (although guitarist Pete Kennedy, who would later play "Across the Great Divide" with Nanci Griffith, performed with her during some East Coast trips, as did renowned Dobro player Mike Auldridge).

Safe at Anchor reveals the delicate interplay of Griffin and Wolf. As Philip Elwood, music columnist for the *San Francisco Examiner,* wrote in the liner notes: "Griffin, as you will note from the very first stanzas, has a feeling for Kate's voice—he treats it with affection, supporting it (indeed fondling it) with original and enhancing instrumental mixes."

Griffin told Parrish that his musical relationship with Wolf evolved. "About every two years Kate would call me and say "It's time to make another record,' so I would end up living in San Francisco for six months while we were doing it. For the last several records she would just send me a tape of herself playing these songs she had written on a boom box in the living room and my job was to turn it into what you hear on the record. She and I had an understanding that my job was to crawl inside her songs and flesh them out. It was always a labor of love first, because Kate and I had a connection that made it work easily."

By the time of *Close to You,* released in 1981 and produced by Griffin and Diamant, Wolf had arrived musically. The album includes some of her most enduring songs: "Unfinished Life," "Like a River," "Across the Great Divide," "Stone in the Water," and "Eyes of a Painter." Guitar virtuoso Tony Rice sang background vocals on the album, which also features harmonica player Norton Buffalo.

In the spring of 1982, after she participated at a week-long Vision Quest in the Joshua Tree National Monument with Terry Fowler and others, she started living with Fowler, who sells natural foods domestically and overseas through his Fowler Brothers Company. Fowler became her third husband. (Wolf was married for a few months in 1979 to Ché Greenwood, but the marriage was annulled.) She moved to West Marin County and became deeply involved in environmental causes in groups such as No Nukes, Big Mountain, and SEVA, a nonprofit organization to bring together surgeons and healers in developing countries. Wolf performed at several benefits supported by social activist Hugh Romney, commonly known as Wavy Gravy. "She was always the first person I would call to do stuff, she was solid like a rock that way, and trusted my feel for what good causes were," Wavy Gravy told *Dirty Linen.*

In the spring of 1983 she toured the Southwest with the Academy Award-winning documentary film, *The Four Corners: A National Sacrifice Area?,* about the cultural and ecological impact of energy development in the Southwest. Kate performed "Medicine Wheel" on the tour. "She was definitely influenced by Native American symbolism, although she wasn't a Native American," Fowler says. The tour was set up at the Hopi, Navajo, and Taos reservations. "Thomas Banyacya from the Hopi reservation would speak. Then Kate would perform, then they'd show the film and people would ask questions." Other musicians joined her on the tour including Tom Rigney (later of the Sundogs) and Eddie B. Barlow (Wildflower). Billy Roberts showed up in Taos, New Mexico, to play his harmonicas.

Wolf was nominated for a Bay Area Music Award in the singer-songwriter category in the early '80s. Her live, two-disc album *Give Yourself to Love* won a NAIRD award for Best Folk Album of 1983. Wolf attended the NAIRD convention in San Francisco. The album included covers of songs by her favorite songwriters. It was dedicated to Canadian songwriter Stan Rogers, who had died that year in a plane fire, and to Fowler. Besides her own compositions, it includes her

performances of Jack Tempchin's "Peaceful Easy Feeling," John Stewart's "Some Kind of Love," and Sandy Denny's "Who Knows Where the Time Goes." After that, Wolf decided in 1983 to take a year off. "The road is wearing me down," she said. "For twelve years I had been moving fast and furious with my career, so I thought it was time to take a sabbatical."

She sought out a different lifestyle, working for the *Point Reyes Light* of Marin as a part-time production artist. She practiced massage (she had gone to massage school in '82 after returning from Vision Quest) and planned activities at a community center in the San Geronimo Valley. By year's end she realized there was nothing she'd rather do than play music. "It's really nice to take a year off to discover that what you want to do is what you've been doing all along," she said in concert (The *Fax,* October 1984).

She appeared on *Prairie Home Companion* for the first time in 1984, and again in 1985. Then she began working on her last studio album, *Poet's Heart,* with Griffin. The album was released in January 1986 and received a NAIRD award as Best Folk Album. She dedicated it to "all the poets and friends whose words and thoughts appear in these songs: Eric Bogle, Utah Phillips, Luke Breit, Judy Mayhan, Dough Boyd, and the late Stan Rogers." The album shows her effort to seek spiritual guidance and connection with songwriters like Bogle (whom she met at the Winnipeg Folk Festival in 1982), Phillips, and Rogers, in songs such as "All He Ever Saw Was You," about Rogers, and "See Here She Said," for Judy Mayhan.

In the fall of 1985, she toured from Boston to Florida and through Michigan, Wisconsin, and Minnesota. She flew to Texas and appeared on PBS's *Austin City Limits.* (The concert was issued on video, which Max remastered in 1989. A soundtrack came out entitled *An Evening in Austin.*) She was on the verge of raising her career to a new level. On January 25, 1986, she performed on the East Coast one last time for the 25th anniversary of the popular Washington, D.C. folk radio program "Music Americana." Dick Cerri's long-running show benefited the World Folk Music Association. Kate led the entire cast in one of the evening's three finales, "Give Yourself to Love." Others performing were a surprise reunion of the Chad Mitchell Trio, Tom Rush, Bob Gibson, Carolyn Hester, Steve Gilette and Dave Guard of the original Kingston Trio, Schooner Fare, Dave Mallett, the Seldom Scene, Jonathan Edwards, Pete Kennedy, Christine Lavin, Buskin and Batteau, and Mary-Chapin Carpenter.

In late February Kate entered the hospital for a hysterectomy and during a post-surgery examination she was diagnosed with acute leukemia. After a course of chemotherapy at the U.C. San Francisco Medical Center, she went into full remission. When friends found out she was ill, they put together concerts and benefits for her, including one at the Cotati Cabaret. John Stewart, Reilly and Moloney, and Caswell and Carnahan performed. Wolf was feeling a bit better, so she showed up too.

Realizing that she would not be able to record again "for a long time, if ever," she returned home and compiled the songs for her retrospective album, *Gold in California,* released in January 1987, a month after she passed away. She selected the songs, the sequence, and the photographs. The album is an excellent compilation, with only one new song, a cover of Alice Stuart's "Full Time Woman."

She was scheduled to perform at Wavy Gravy's fiftieth birthday party benefit, but couldn't because of her illness. She managed to write "The Wind Blows Wild," her last song. Nina Gerber and Ford James came to the hospital to record the song, which became the title track for a posthumously released album. It was recorded on May 9, 1986, in Kate's hospital room and played at the beginning and end of Wavy Gravy's birthday party. In September 1986, Wolf re-entered the hospital for a bone marrow transplant but the treatment wiped out her immune system. She never recovered.

Besides *The Wind Blows Wild,* another retrospective, *Looking Back at You,* was released by Rhino Records in 1994. The album is a compilation of concert dates in 1978 and 1979 at McCabe's, an appearance on Howard and Roz Larman's Folk Scene (KPFK) radio show in 1977, and an appearance in 1977 at the San Diego Folk Festival. In 1996 Flat Rock Records released an album called *Carry It On,* a compilation of appearances Kate made on KPFA Radio in Berkeley in 1978, 1979, and 1981.

Wolf's friends hold an annual memorial concert for her. Among those performing at the June 1996 event were Rosalie Sorrels, Utah Phillips, Terry Garthwaite, Cache Valley Drifters, the remaining members of the Wildwood Flower, and Alice Stuart. A recording of the festival was released on Gargoyle Recordings. The 1998 Kate Wolf Memorial Music Festival included Nanci Griffith, Guy Clark, Nina Gerber, and Greg Brown, among others. Gerber produced a tribute album released by Red House in August 1998. *Treasures Left Behind: Remembering Kate Wolf* includes performances by Gerber, Kathy Mattea, Dave Alvin, Nanci Griffith, Lucinda Williams, Utah Phillips, Rosalie Sorrels, Greg Brown, Emmylou Harris, and John Gorka. "Love Still Remains," performed by Harris, was nominated for a Best Female Country Vocal Grammy.

While she was ill, she felt so obliged to her fans that she asked Utah Phillips to take over her concert dates, which he did. When he played Berkeley's Freight and Salvage, Kate managed to attend with a scarf around her head to cover the fact that she lost her hair from chemotherapy. Someone in the audience asked "How's Kate?" "Don't ask me, there she is," he said, pointing her out. At dinner afterwards she urged Phillips, who had retired, to go on performing, to carry on the struggle.

Her final resting spot is on Highway 49 on the way to Downieville in a small graveyard where other headstones date back to the Gold Rush Era. Her friends have planted golden poppies and wildflowers around her grave. "She had a turbulent and in many ways painful life and she was able to reach into her own heart of darkness and come out with songs of enormous forgiveness, which is as heroic as I can imagine," Utah Phillips told *Dirty Linen.* "I can't imagine anyone using their art more heroically and gently. That music deserves to continue and do its work, and it's the music's work now, of course, Kate's not here."

Wolf has sold 300,000 albums, two thirds of them since she passed away. She always found opportunity in times of darkness. "I remember once after a concert someone came up to Kate and said they had just lost their job," Fowler recalls. "She would always turn it around. She'd say that's great. Now it's open for you to do what's next in your life. The same thing with 'Across the Great Divide.' *The finest hour* is that change. It was always a part of her life, no matter what was happening, to always take those mysteries and make the most of them and to move on to change for the better."

Based in part on interviews with Max Wolf and Terry Fowler

WOLFSTONE: *Vocal and instrumental group from Scotland. Personnel mid-1990s, Duncan Chisholm, (fiddle) born October 31, 1969; Struan Eaglesham, (keyboards) born January 17, 1969; Stuart Eaglesham, (vocals, guitars) born September 11, 1965; Wayne MacKenzie (bass, vocals) born December 17, 1965; Ivan Drever, (vocals, bouzouki) born June 10, 1956; Graeme "Mop" Youngson, (drums) born August 18, 1960. Stevie Saint (pipes, whistles) added fall 1994. Struan Eaglesham, Youngson, and Drever left in 1996. Andy Simmers (piano, keyboards) born September 2, 1974; and Tony Soave (drums, percussion) born November 29, 1962, joined late '90s.*

Combining torrid rock and traditional Scottish folk music, Wolfstone became one of the most popular bands in the United Kingdom and Europe in the early 1990s, and by the mid-'90s had also begun to make inroads with American audiences. Their music, to a great extent, was derived from the jigs and reels of their homeland, but that did little to assuage the negative feelings of Scottish folk purists, who complained the group was selling out an important part of the country's heritage. Founding member fiddler Duncan Chisholm responded, "Plenty of traditionalists hate our guts, but if anything we're keeping the tradition alive. You just have to look at all the young kids (who, he noted, previously knew nothing about jigs, reels, or Scottish folk songs in general) queuing to get into our gigs. Hopefully, for every one person we upset, we'll please three others."

The saga of the band began in 1988, when Chisholm, who had been performing mainly as a soloist in local clubs for several years, got together with the brothers Stuart Eaglesham (vocals, acoustic and electric guitars) and Struan Eaglesham (keyboards) to form a group to play for ceilidhs (Scottish dances). (Before organizing the trio, Chisholm at one time had been in a local band with another Eaglesham brother.) The origins of the band's name, Chisholm told Lahri Bond for a *Dirty Linen* article ("A Thistle up the Kilt of Celtic Music," February–March 1994), came from "a Pictish stone which was found in a stone wall just 20 miles north of Inverness and along the road where we used to go to practice. When we were deciding on a name, we went through a lot of terrible, terrible names and decided on Wolfstone because it was a strong title and it was Pictish as well. . . . It was also two syllables and easy to chant."

Soon after the initial version of the band came into being in the late '80s it signed with Rowan Records, which issued the album *Wolfstone* in 1988 and *Wolfstone 2* in 1989. It was an arrangement the members of the 1990s roster wanted to forget. For one thing, they stress that the recordings didn't represent the music the larger group was playing; for another, they claim that the contract was completely one-sided in favor of the English producer. As Struan Eaglesham pointed out to Eric L. Reiner of the *Boulder [Colorado] Weekly,* Wolfstone was shut out from all the money earned on sales of those albums. "We were only about 18 or 19. The price of an education."

Starting in 1990, the founding threesome began adding new members and moved away from mainly folk-flavored rhythms to a greater emphasis on rock 'n' roll. In 1990 the roster included Andy Murray on lead guitar and an assortment of bass players, bagpipers, and drummers. In late 1990 Ivan Drever (vocals, acoustic guitar, bouzouki) joined, bringing to the group his excellent songwriting abilities. Drever, from the island of Sanday, in Orkney, had been playing traditional music in a group called the Knowe O'Deil with Ian Cooper. They had put out two albums, *Orkney Anthem* in 1986 and *The Viking's Bride* in 1987. He joined with Dick Clarke to release *October Bridge* in 1988. He had a solo album to his credit, *Homeland,* before joining Wolfstone. In July 1992 Wayne MacKenzie was brought in as regular bassist, accompanied by drummer Mop Youngson. The first album recorded by the expanded group was *Unleashed,* issued on the Scottish-based Iona/Lismor label in 1991. Chisholm, noting that the 1980s LPs were essentially dance records played by an "embryonic band," told Bond, "We as the band feel that the *Unleashed* album, which is the first album we worked on with Ivan, is really our first album, proper."

As Wolfstone's live concerts rapidly attracted a large following in Scotland and in other parts of the United Kingdom, their album became a hit at home, earning a Silver Disc Award from the Scottish Music Industry Association. With the release of the second Iona collection in 1992, *The Chase* (which also reached Silver Disc sales), the group extended its concert work to Europe and North America. (The band's first video, *Captured Alive,* from a concert in Aberdeen, also came out in 1992.) Employing what Jim Caligiuri of *CMJ* magazine referred to as an "intense mix of frenzied fiddle, spirited pipes, heavy bass, edgy electric guitar and ardent vocals," Wolfstone found many enthusiastic followers in many places beyond the Scottish Highlands. As headliners at the Avante Festival in Portugal, the group was cheered by over 70,000 people, and their appearance at the international Tonder Festival in Denmark in 1992 resulted in their being the first band to be invited back for four years in a row.

Variously described as "Celtic grunge" and "bagpipes with an attitude," Wolfstone's high-energy sound was infectious. As Drever put it, "There's nothing really sedate about us." Some of the songs, like Drever's "Song for Yesterday," besides traditional Scottish elements, had echoes of American country and blues. Drever pointed out that he had been brought up on country and western, which shared popularity in Scotland with home-grown compositions.

Though Drever remained the group's primary songwriter, by the time *The Chase* came out the other bandsmen were beginning to focus more on originals. In that album, "Jake's Tune" was penned by Struan Eaglesham and Andy Murray; Struan and Stuart were cowriters of "The 10 Pound Note"; and Chisholm and Drever collaborated on "The Prophet." The three-song extended-play album *Burning Horizons,* issued by Iona in 1993, featured the title track written by Struan.

By the end of 1993 the band had a solid base of fans on the European Continent. As Struan told Sheila Daughtry of *WMNF* (July–August 1994), "In Spain and parts of France they're very familiar with [Scottish music] because the Celtic music spreads right across the north of Europe, really, and they have their own form of bagpipes and stuff. Their own traditions are not that far removed from ours. And as far as Germany goes, they really have adopted Scots and Irish music as their own tradition. Because during the war their own traditional music was used as propaganda, which they're very embarrassed about—they don't consider it their own anymore. So Scots and Irish stuff is really popular."

Eager to extend their welcome in the United States and Canada, the band gained a U.S. distributor, Green Linnet Records, which reissued Wolfstone's first two Iona albums as well as a new studio album, *Year of the Dog,* in 1994. To support the releases the band scheduled a major tour of the United States that included opening for Los Lobos on several occasions and performing in the summer at the Strawberry Festival in California and the Telluride Festival in Colorado. The audiences literally danced in the aisles at some performances, and the band's sets at the above festivals brought invitations to return in 1995. For the mid-1990 concerts Andy Murray was not on the roster, and for the 1994 tour Martyn Bennett played bagpipes, being replaced in the fall for the '95 North American schedule by Stevie Saint.

During the first half of the '90s, Drever told Bond, "At the moment, we're using a pool of pipers, if you like. On the *Unleashed* album we used Allan Wilson, on the [early, '90s] American tour we used [the late] Roddy McCourt. For the Tonder Festival we had Duncan McGillivray, who used to play with the Battlefield Band. . . . We use Battlefield Band pipers a lot; we've had Dougie Pincock on *The Chase,* and we've played with Ian McDonald, who is the present Battlefield Band piper. We have also had Kenny Forsyth from the Tannahill Weavers and . . . Gordon Duncan on the next tour."

As is not uncommon for U.K. artists, all of the members had alternative projects besides their Wolfstone work. One example was the solo album by Drever (backed by Wolfstone), *Every Breaking Heart,* issued by Attic Records in 1992. In the mid-1990s the others performed as soloists in combinations of twos or threes or with other bands. As Struan told Sheila Daughtry, "Duncan's doing a solo album. Mop and Stuart and Wayne, they've got things they're going to do as well. Over the next few years I would expect you'd see a solo album from just about every member of the band."

Drever released *Isles Ne'er Forgotten* on Attic and *Four Walls* on Iona. He joined with Struan on the album *Back to Back* on Attic, and with Duncan Chisholm on the Iona album *The Lewis Blue.* Attic Records also released a compilation of Drever's work, *The Orkney Years 1986–1992 Volume 1.*

In 1996 Green Linnet released a new Wolfstone album, *The Half Tail,* produced by Chris Harley. Some of the excellent tracks include "Glenglass," "Gillies," and "Bonnie Ship the Diamond." *Pick of the Litter: The Best of Wolfstone 1991–1996* came out in 1997 on Green Linnet. The group disbanded at the end of 1997 due to management and record company disputes. Struan Eaglesham left to focus on being a dad and a recording engineer, Mop Youngson left to join Old Blind Dogs, and Ivan Drever concentrated on a solo career. Despite the changes, the core group of Chisholm, Stuart Eaglesham, MacKenzie, and Saint remained, adding Andy Simmers on keyboards and Tony Soave on drums. The group put out *This Strange Place* in 1998, followed by *7* in 1999, both on Green Linnet.

𝒴

YOUNG, JESSE COLIN: *Singer, guitarist, band leader (the Youngbloods), songwriter. Born New York, New York, November 22, 1941.*

Among the names that crop up in a rundown of the early 1960s folk ferment in New York are artists like Bob Dylan, Joan Baez, Pat Sky, Phil Ochs, John Sebastian—and Jesse Colin Young. Young, a fine singer and reasonably proficient guitarist, moved over to folk-rock just about the same time as Dylan. Although he never achieved the resounding success of the Minnesotan, his work had an impact on the genre that was still being felt at the beginning of the 1980s.

Jesse, born Perry Miller, came from an Ivy League, upper-middle-class family. He grew up in Queens, attending school with Paul Simon and Art Garfunkel. As he stated in biographical information for Elektra Records in 1978, "My father and his brother both went to Harvard, and both taught there and then my uncle went on to become the dean of the graduate school at Yale and my father became an executive comptroller in business, so it was a real heartbreaker for my family for me to be thrown out of school. [At fifteen, Young was discharged from the prestigious Phillips Andover Academy in Andover, Massachusetts, for playing his electric guitar during study hour]. But it probably saved me from going to Harvard and getting locked into the corporate challenge."

As a child, he recalled loving some of his family's opera records of Caruso. In the early 1950s he was attracted to Alan Freed's rock program on New York radio and the R&B show called *Jocko's Rocket Ship* on WWRL. At eight he sang at a reunion of his father's Harvard class (1925). "The old man had taught me all the Harvard fight songs and there I was singing in front of hundreds of people, accompanied by an accordion player."

Although he'd been sent down from Phillips Andover, Jesse completed public high school and went on to enter Ohio State University (a school that spawned other folk artists, such as Phil Ochs). There was strong interest in folk music on campus and Jesse was captivated by the bluegrass sounds of Bill Monroe as well as roots blues as performed by people like T-Bone Walker. The next year, his love for folk and blues caused him to leave school abruptly and head east to join the growing group of young musicians playing that kind of material in and around major East Coast cities.

"A couple of years later I was sitting in this apartment on the lower East Side, sitting at Lightning Hopkins' knee and being allowed to play music with him, and being patted on the shoulder! Later I took Lightning to a motorcycle race. He was in his blue serge suit, wearing a big ring; he was King of the Blues and perfectly at ease in a place where there were no black people."

Jesse sang in small clubs and coffee houses on the Greenwich Village circuit, often earning money by passing the hat. In the early 1960s a musician named Bobby Scott, a sideman for Bobby Darin, became enthusiastic about Young's talents and paid for and produced his first album, *Soul of a City Boy.* The album was released by Capitol in 1963 and, while not a howling success, helped bring Jesse an engagement at the major Boston folk center, Club 47. That , in turn, led to other dates in folk clubs. However, Young, like Dylan, was already leaning toward blending rock into his material, which sometimes didn't sit well with folk listeners. Scott continued to support Jesse, producing another LP, *Young Blood,* which was issued by Mercury and which included the John Sebastian band for backing. (Soon after, Sebastian was on the way to stardom with a band called the Lovin' Spoonful.)

The experience encouraged Young to start his own band. He got together with another folk-music artist, Jerry Corbitt, to form the Youngbloods. The idea took shape when Corbitt and Young crossed paths in Cambridge, Massachusetts. Soon after, they added Memphis-born (September 26, 1941) Joe Bauer on drums and hit the road. "The PA's weren't set up for the folk-rock sound and some people hated it, as it was not too quiet. We made a circuit of Toronto, Springfield, and Philadelphia and when we got to New York, Banana joined." The band had started in Cambridge, and that, oddly, was Banana's hometown (born circa 1946), though he joined in Manhattan. His real name was Lowell Leringer, and he brought considerable experience on electric guitar and keyboards to the new band. Young played bass.

The group rehearsed for much of 1966, occasionally playing club dates that helped bring notice from underground fans and publications. It also helped whet record company interest; several offered contracts before the year was out. The group finally settled on RCA and began recording initial material in late 1966. The debut album, titled *The Youngbloods,* was issued in February 1967. It attracted some attention mainly on the East Coast, and one song, "Grizzly Bear," became a regional hit in the East and Midwest. It was another track that eventually became the band's most famous, "Get Together" (written by Dino Valente), a plea for human cooperation that still is often played on rock stations and sometimes at folk festivals.

RCA released their second album, *Earth Music,* in November 1967. Before their next LP got under way, they had moved to San Francisco in 1968. In 1969 their last LP for RCA, *Elephant Mountain,* came out, just when they achieved their first gold record for "Get Together," recently issued as a single. The single peaked at number five in *Billboard* the week of August 2, 1969. That success prompted RCA to reissue the debut album under the name *Get Together.* RCA also issued a retrospective called *The Best of the Youngbloods.*

In 1970 the group's contract with RCA ended and, about the same time, Jerry Corbitt departed to try a solo career. The others went on for a time as a trio, setting up their own custom label, Raccoon, for their new work. They signed a distribution agreement with Warner Brothers, which issued four LPs of the band in the early 1970s: *Rock Festival, Ride the Wind, Good and Dusty,* and *High on a Ridge Top.* Raccoon also added other acts, producing and issuing several bluegrass and folk albums, including those of singer-songwriters Michael Hurley and Jeffrey Cain.

However, Young was becoming restless with the band alignment, as indicated by his debut solo album on Warner Brothers, *Together,* which reached upper-chart levels in late 1972. By 1973, when he had similar response to his second solo effort, *Song for Juli,* the Youngbloods were no more.

Since then, Young has stressed his solo work, which reached a peak in his Warner Brothers phase with the 1974 album *Light Shine* and 1975 *Songbird,* both works that effectively combined Young's diverse musical interest with tracks that varied from folk or blues-dominated rock to more hard-driving material. The songs for the latter LP were composed by Jesse during a cross-country tour in which he opened for Crosby, Stills, Nash, and Young. In 1976 Warner Brothers issued a live album titled *On the Road.* In 1977 his final Warner's collection came out, *Love on the Wing,* coproduced by him and Felix Pappalardi, an old friend who had produced the first two Youngbloods albums. (Charlie Daniels produced the third RCA disc.)

In 1978 a new stage in his career began with a move to Elektra/Asylum, which issued his debut on the label, *American Dreams,* in the fall. The album, which was somewhat uneven, included such unusual items as a disco-flavored song, "Slow and Easy," a remake of a Buddy Holly tune, "Rave On," and an ambitious "Suite," which Young states is autobiographical. "I really didn't start out to write a suite; it just started out as pieces and, as more of these pieces came together, it became a bigger picture. The suite, which has five sections, with other movements within them, encompasses elements of blues, rock 'n' roll, Jamaican music and all the American influences." The disc also included a fine duet with Carly Simon titled "Fight for It."

American Dreams was not a chart hit, which Jesse attributed to a great extent to lack of label promotional support. Later, in the 1980s, he bought the master of the album and had it reissued on an independent label. His '80s output included the 1982 collection *Perfect Stranger* and 1987's *The Highway Is for Heroes* on Cypress/A&M. Though he continued to tour, mainly playing smaller venues, in the '80s and in the '90s he became increasingly upset about the way major record firms operated, and what records he did make tended to come out on small, independent labels. Some of the old Youngbloods numbers, particularly "Get Together," continued to be played on oldies stations. "Get Together" in the '80s and '90s was given new exposure as the theme song for the National Council of Christians and Jews. It also was included on the sound track of the superhit movie of 1994, *Forrest Gump,* as well as on the multiplatinum-selling sound track album.

His songs were featured in movies such as *1969* and the TV series *90210.* Rhino Records released *The Best of Jesse Colin Young: The Solo Years* in 1991, a compilation of his post-Youngbloods work. Tracks include "Morning Sun," "Sunlight," "Four in the Morning," and "Sugar Babe."

In the 1980s Young went through a divorce and released only two albums. He remarried and relocated to Hawaii, where he now cultivates and markets Morning Sun Coffee, grown on a small farm in Kona located 2,000 feet up the slopes of the Jualalai volcano.

In 1993 Young formed his own record company, Ridgetop Music (named after his other home and studio, located on a ridgetop overlooking Point Reyes, California), to reissue his classic albums. His first new album on the label was called *Makin' It Real.* He also reissued *Song for Juli* and *Songbird.* He followed with *Swept Away,* a new acoustic album in which he chronicles meeting his second wife, Connie, in the title track. He also sings about being separated from his two grown children in "Cheyenne" for his son and "Street of Broken Dreams" for his daughter, Juli.

In 1998 Award Records released another retrospective, titled *Greatest Hits.* Among the tracks on that album are a remix of "Get Together," "Grey Day," "Sunlight," "Darkness," and "Song for Juli."

YOUNG, NEIL: *Singer, guitarist, songwriter. Born Toronto, Canada, November 12, 1945.*

A variety of influences shaped Neil Young's evolution into one of the foremost folk-rock writers and practitioners of the late 1960s and throughout the next three decades. His musical interests first were stirred by the initial wave of rock stars from south of the Canadian border. Later he briefly became a part of the folk movement before combining those forms into folk-rock and later country-rock.

Neil was born in Toronto, the son of Scott Young, a sportswriter, and Rassy, who would become his first manager. He grew up in Omenee, Ontario. At six he was hospitalized during a polio epidemic. He was later afflicted with epilepsy. He became interested in rock when Canadian radio began to broadcast the mid-1950s recordings of people such as Bill Haley and Elvis Presley. In his teens, he made his first serious efforts to become a musician, teaching himself to play on an Arthur Godfrey-style plastic ukulele. When he was thirteen,

his parents split up and he moved to Winnipeg with his mother. At this point he began playing banjo and a Harmony acoustic guitar. In the early 1960s he worked the coffeehouse circuit with various groups and then organized his own folk-rock band, Neil Young and the Squires, which became a local favorite in Winnipeg. In 1965, while performing with the Squires at the Fourth Dimension Club in Ontario, Young met Stephen Stills, who was playing on the same bill with a group called the Company. On a later trip to New York, he met singer-guitarist Richie Furay. While playing the folk circuit in Canada, he also met Joni Mitchell, who would play a key role in putting together the members of Crosby, Stills, Nash and Young (CSN&Y). Young briefly played guitar with a group called the Mynah Birds, which included a lead singer, Ricky James Matthews, who later gained fame as Motown chartmaker Rick James. But after James was arrested for going AWOL from the U.S. Navy, the Mynahs split up.

Looking for more career opportunities, he gave up band work and moved to Los Angeles in 1966, intending to focus on writing and solo vocalizing. There, he renewed acquaintances with Steve Stills and Richie Furay, who persuaded him to join their new group, Buffalo Springfield. It was an excellent match. Neil's fine guitar work and original songs played a key part in making the band one of the all-time great folk-rock combinations, even though it remained intact for less than two years. Among the classic Springfield songs Neil provided were "On the Way Home," "Broken Arrow," "Expecting to Fly," "Mr. Soul," and "I Am a Child."

After the band broke up in 1968, Young again wanted to strike out as a solo performer, but was sidetracked to some extent by the arguments of Crosby, Stills, and Nash in favor of his joining their superstar assemblage. He accepted only because they stressed it would be a loose alignment with each member free to pursue his individual music goals if he so desired. However, before he joined them in mid-1969, he had already released his debut solo LP *Neil Young* (Reprise, January 1969), and moved on to a second one, *Everybody Knows This Is Nowhere* (May 1969). For that collection he brought in a new backup band, Crazy Horse, a group he had first enjoyed at the Whisky A Go-Go on Los Angeles's Sunset Strip some years earlier. At that time the band, which called itself the Rockets, comprised Danny Whitten on guitar, Billy Talbot on bass guitar, and Ralph Molina on drums. Neil expanded it to a quartet for a time by adding producer-arranger-songwriter-instrumentalist Jack Nitzsche. The album went platinum, and Neil's solo reputation was assured. In decades to come Crazy Horse was to work on many albums and concert projects with Neil; Frank Sampedro (vocals, guitar, keyboards) joined Talbot and Molina to form the core trio.

As Talbot told Irwin Stambler, "We were friends

with Neil for some time before Crazy Horse. One of Danny Whitten's girlfriends brought Neil up to the house one time when he was making the Buffalo Springfield album. We'd get together and talk and play music at times. After the LP *The Rockets* [on White Whale Records] came out, we'd been seeing each other for two to three years while he'd been working with the Springfield and we got together and listened to our album and he liked it. We were playing at the Whisky, and he came to see us and jammed with our band.

"He was getting his solo career under way then. He showed up with 'Cinnamon Girl' and several other things and asked us to work with him. We got together at the studio and helped record *Everybody Knows This Is Nowhere,* and went on tour with him. Neil thought of the name Crazy Horse. We were discussing names, all of us together. It was between Crazy Horse and War Babies at the end, and you know who won."

Even as he began working in CSN&Y he was thinking about his next solo effort. He only remained a regular member of that now legendary band into the early 1970s, but helped turn out two classic albums for Atlantic: *Déjà Vu* (1969) and the live *Four Way Street* (1971), both gold and number one in *Billboard.* (Following the killing of four students at Kent State in May 1970 Young wrote "Ohio," which he recorded as a single with CSN&Y. It reached number fourteen on the charts.)

In between those two, Reprise released his third solo effort, *After the Goldrush* (1970, platinum), arguably one of the all-time great folk-rock LPs for such songs as "Southern Man," "Tell Me Why," "Only Love Can Break Your Heart," "Don't Let It Bring You Down," and "I Believe in You." The album was certainly rock 'n' roll, but with the subtle flavor of folk music and lyrics tinged with poetry. This was Neil's second album recorded with Crazy Horse, and included backing from Stephen Stills.

Young's next solo LP didn't come out until February 1972, but it too was a platinum blockbuster. Called *Harvest,* it contained such hits as "Old Man," "War Song," and, most notable of all, Neil's gold, number-one rock standard, "Heart of Gold." In addition to his other projects, in the early 1970s Neil wrote, directed, and took part in the unsuccessful film *Journey through the Past,* whose charted sound track album came out in November 1972. *Time Fades Away* (October 1973) won another gold record. However, as a whole it didn't measure up to the previous few albums and some critics wondered whether Neil might have written himself out. Backing him was a band he named the Stray Gators, whose members were Ben Keith on steel guitar, Tim Drummond on bass, and Kenny Buttrey on drums.

As the decade went by, though, Young proved those fears were groundless with a body of material that often matched his best work of the early 1970s. His LP *On the Beach* (1974, gold) was much better than *Time Fades Away* and his two 1975 releases, *Tonight's the Night* and *Zuma* (issued, respectively, in June and November) reflected considerably more despair and disillusionment than his earlier work. *Tonight's the Night,* for instance, was a concept album that explored his feelings about the drug-overdose deaths of Crazy Horse's Danny Whitten and another friend from the CSN&Y band, Bruce Berry. *Zuma* was the first album where the Crazy Horse roster comprised Talbot, Molina, and Sampedro.

In the mid-1970s Neil returned to recording and concert work with Steve Stills, which resulted in the 1976 LP *Long May You Run* (Reprise, 1976, gold). After that he went back to focusing on solo projects, starting with *American Stars 'n' Bars* (June 1977, gold). In October 1977 Reprise issued one of the period's best retrospective collections of a major pop artist, the three-record *Decade.* September '78 saw the release of another gold solo LP, *Comes a Time.*

Always interested in experimenting, during the summer of 1977 he joined a group based in Santa Cruz, California, called the Ducks, organized by a friend from the Buffalo Springfield days, vocalist Jeff Blackburn. The group played up-tempo "country rock" sets in small clubs in the area. In the spring of 1978 he played and recorded solo acoustic tracks in five nights at the small San Francisco club the Boarding House. Some of that material was used in his June 1979 platinum release *Rust Never Sleeps,* also the title of a concert film directed by Young, released in 1980. Neil and Crazy Horse embarked on a coast-to-coast U.S. concert tour, his first in several years. Those concerts were among the best of the late 1970s. The LP based on those shows, *Live Rust,* quickly went gold and later surpassed platinum levels. Now that the 1970s had come to a close, *Village Voice* and *Rolling Stone* editors alike named him the Artist of the Decade.

Some of Young's side projects in the 1980s were in movies. He developed the "nuclear comedy" *Human Highway* in the early '80s, a movie released in 1982 whose cast members included Dennis Hopper, Sally Kirkland, Dean Stockwell, Devo, and Neil himself. Later in the decade he also had parts in the films *'68, Made in Heaven,* and *Love at Large.* (The last named, filmed in the '80s, was released in 1990.)

In the 1980s Young demonstrated a considerably more conservative outlook than in previous decades. From *Hawks & Doves* (Reprise, late 1980), the track "Union Man" was called not just conservative but reactionary by many critics. Neither it nor its follow-up *Re-Ac-Tor* (1981), sold as well as earlier LPs.

Whereas his 1982 shows involved a great many musicians, for Neil's next project, he whittled the cast down to one—himself. The 1983 performances were an outgrowth of his first LP for Geffen Records, *Trans* (1982), based on the computer/electronics age. In his live concerts (perhaps an overstatement), the backing vocals and music came from various electronic devices: synthesizers, taped tracks of other instruments, and videos. He used the videos at times to sing duets with images of himself on the large stage screens.

But Neil also varied his approach during that period by bringing a 1950s rockabilly flavor to his sets with the Shocking Pinks, whose members were Drummond, Keith, and drummer Karl Himmel. This resulted in the 1983 album *Everybody's Rockin'*, which included updated versions of '50s numbers like "Mystery Train" and "Betty Lou's Got a New Pair of Shoes," plus new Young compositions. The next year he was back touring with a five-piece band and demonstrating his less strident political leanings, emphasizing patriotism via lyrics such as *I'm proud to be livin' in the U.S.A.*

He marked another change in direction the following year with his Nashville-recorded *Old Ways* (1985), featuring duets with country superstars Waylon Jennings and Willie Nelson. Absent from the album's songs were protest numbers such as the early '70s "Southern Man," a severe indictment of anti-black sentiments. In 1986, though, he reassumed his rock 'n' roll mantle with a hard-driving LP with Crazy Horse, *Landing on Water*. Following a demanding 1986 "In a Rusted-Out Garage" tour, he recorded the 1987 release *Life*, whose contents included the self-penned "Inca Queen" and "Prisoners of Rock and Roll."

Sampedro and Molina of Crazy Horse were among the musicians who performed on Neil's next album, *This Note's for You* (Reprise, 1988), along with another longtime Young associate, saxophonist Ben Keith. The album reflected increased emphasis on the blues in Neil's oeuvre, and that type of music was featured in live shows performed by Neil Young and the Bluenotes. (With his penchant for interesting band names, Neil later tabbed his blues backing artists as the Restless and the Lost Dogs.) The album title track, "This Note's for You," was issued as a video and, since it took aim at corporate sponsorship, was banned for a time by MTV. In a surprising turn of events, it later was named Video of the Year in the 1988 MTV Music Video Awards.

During 1988 Neil briefly returned to do a project with Crosby, Still and Nash, something he'd promised to do if David Crosby managed to overcome his drug addiction problems. The foursome completed *American Dream*, whose contents included three more Young originals, the title track, "Name of Love," and "This Old House."

Young closed out the 1980s with two more albums in 1989, *Eldorado* and *Freedom*. He was joined for the five tracks on the extended-play *Eldorado* by the Restless. The album was released only in Australia and Japan. Some of the same session musicians backed him on *Freedom*, on which he presented both acoustic and electric versions of his song "Rockin' in the Free World." For his 1989 tour he performed mostly solo with some support from Ben Keith and Frank Sampedro. That

year, a collection of up-and-coming rockers put together a benefit record for the Bridge School titled *The Bridge: A Tribute to Neil Young*. Among those performing Young's songs were Soul Asylum, Dinosaur Jr., Sonic Youth, and Victoria Williams.

As the 1990s began, Neil again called on Crazy Horse to join him for recording and touring, starting with the 1991 album *Ragged Glory*. Neil and his friends took off on an extended Don't Spook the Horse tour, whose best moments were captured on the 1991 double-CD release *Weld*. Opening acts for many of those shows were drawn from the ranks of "grunge rock" bands like Sonic Youth, Soundgarden, and Dinosaur Jr. Some of the grunge feeling was present in Neil's other 1991 release with Crazy Horse, *Arc*, an album featuring high-voltage electric guitar, and *Arc-Weld*. In 1992–93 Young reversed course from intense electric rock to less strident acoustic songs in the albums *Harvest Moon* in 1992, with the Stray Gators and Linda Ronstadt, James Taylor, and Nicollete Larson, and the '93 *Unplugged*, the latter drawn from his February 1993 performance with the Stray Gators, his half sister Astrid Young, Nils Lofgren, and Nicolette Larson on the *MTV Unplugged* program. Young's 1992 career events included performing Bob Dylan's "All along the Watchtower" in the October '92 Thirtieth Anniversary Concert for Dylan. That song, as well as Neil's version of Otis Redding's classic "Dock of the Bay," was featured in a series of 1993 concerts Young performed with Booker T & the M.G.s. That year Geffen released the retrospective *Lucky Thirteen*.

For the sound track of Jonathan Demme's 1993 film *Philadelphia*, which won an Oscar for Tom Hanks as a lawyer whose career was ruined by society's fear of AIDS, Neil and Bruce Springsteen were asked to contribute original songs. Neil got the assignment for the picture's title song, which was nominated for an Academy Award, and he performed it onstage during the global awards telecast.

The following year, another collaboration with Crazy Horse, *Sleeps with Angels*, was released on Reprise. The album, nominated for a Grammy, contained such new Neil songs as "Change Your Mind," "My Heart," "Western Hero," and "Piece of Crap." In January 1995 Neil was inducted into the Rock and Roll Hall of Fame. His performance at the ceremonies included previews of songs from his next project, a collaboration with Seattle-based grunge supergroup Pearl Jam. That album, *Mirror Ball*, was released by Reprise in May '95.

With *Broken Arrow*, released in July 1996 by Reprise, Young reunited with Crazy Horse, his group of nearly thirty years. Seven of the eight tracks are Young originals: "Baby What You Want Me to Do" is a cover of a Jimmy Reed tune recorded at a small bar called the Old Princeton Landing. Standout tracks include "Big Time," "Scattered (Let's Think About Livin')," "Changing Highways," and "Music Arcade."

In 1995 Young put together the sound track for Jim

Jarmusch's film *Dead Man,* an existential nineteenth-century western starring Johnny Depp as a character named William Blake. Like the score for *Paris, Texas,* put together by Ry Cooder, Young took a minimalist approach. He played a pump organ, piano, and acoustic and electric guitar to accompany the stark imagery in the film. While it worked in the theaters, the music was less successful on its own when Young released the sound track on his Vapor label in 1996.

When Neil was set to embark on tour with Crazy Horse in 1996 in support of the *Broken Arrow* album, he asked Jarmusch if he would make a long film featuring the "rawness" of the band. Jarmusch went on the road and filmed the concerts in Super-8 in an effort to capture the band's essence. Released in October 1997, the concert film, *Year of the Horse,* didn't gain much of an audience. But for Neil Young and Crazy Horse fans it includes wonderful live footage, interviews with Young and members of the band, and archival footage showing band members in their younger days. Earlier in 1997, Reprise released a live two-disc set from the same tour called *Year of the Horse.*

In May 1997 Young was scheduled to be inducted for the second time into the Rock and Roll Hall of Fame as a member of Buffalo Springfield. But he chose to stay away from the festivities in protest. He complained that televising the event cheapened it. He called the dinner a "VH1 TV show . . . that has nothing to do with the spirit of rock 'n' roll. It has everything to do with making money." In February 1999, however, Neil and his wife, Pegi, showed up at the House of Blues in Los Angeles to accept the Rock the Vote Patrick Lippert Award, honoring them for their community activism for their work with Farm Aid and the Bridge School Benefit. In 1999, Neil reunited with Crosby, Stills and Nash on the Reprise CD *Looking Forward,* followed by a successful tour. In 2000 Neil released a new acoustic-flavored album, *Silver & Gold,* on Reprise.

While Young's career in general was a rewarding experience, his private life was not free of the pains and sorrows of ordinary existence. Neil's youngest son with Pegi suffered from cerebral palsy, and in the mid-'80s attended the Bridge School, where children with that affliction are taught how to communicate with computers and other technology. In 1986 the Youngs inaugurated the Bridge School Benefit concerts at the Shoreline Amphitheater in Mountain View, California, to provide funds to aid the school in accomplishing its mission. Among performers who took part in the annual event over the years were Willie Nelson, Don Henley, Simon and Garfunkel, Bruce Springsteen, and, of course, Young himself. (*See Crosby, Stills, Nash and Young.*)

ZEVON, WARREN: *Singer, songwriter, guitarist, pianist, record producer. Born Chicago, Illinois, January 24, 1947.*

For a while in the 1970s, the Los Angeles area was a hotbed of a form of rock 'n' roll that might have been called the California folk-rock movement. It was a genre whose members included luminaries Jackson Browne, Linda Ronstadt, J. D. Souther, and the Eagles. Warren Zevon was associated with that scene but not really of it. His melodies had some of the flavor of the kinds of songs Browne or the Eagles wrote, yet it was more raucous in tone and featured lyrics that dealt more forcefully with the darker side of life—violence, deceit, and death—than those of his musical compatriots.

One reviewer called him the Sam Peckinpah (the movie director) of rock. Charlie McCollum of the *Washington Star* (March 9, 1978) commented: "Both [Zevon and Peckinpah] have a feeling of the internal workings of a violent society; both find beauty in the strangest of places, like death. Peckinpah lacks Zevon's intuitive humor, so what listeners get on [an album such as] *Excitable Boy* [where the subject of the title song is a 'boy' who rapes and murders his girlfriend, yet gets off with only a ten-year sentence] is a cross between Peckinpah and Randy Newman—a combination born of some other world."

It took considerably more time for Warren's career to blossom than for most successful rock artists'. He was nearing thirty before he began to take the steps that won him recognition from his fellow musicians, critics, and, to a lesser extent from the general public. Though he was almost totally immersed in music from an early age, it took a lot of soul searching and some breaks before he decided to try for a solo career rather than remain in a supporting role.

Zevon was born in Chicago, but the family moved to California when he was young and he spent most of his formative years there. His mother, Beverly, was from the Midwest. His father, William, was a Russian immigrant whose family name originally was Livotovsky before Warren's grandfather changed it to Zevon. Zevon Senior was a onetime boxer and professional gambler, a profession that tended to keep the family moving from one place to another. Talking about him to Judith Sims of the *Washington Post* (February 27, 1978), Warren said, "[he] looks like George Burns. Well, not exactly like George Burns."

As for those early years, he told her: "We always had enough to eat, but it was definitely . . . up and down. Friends tell me I should write a screenplay about it." Apparently his relationship to his parents was somewhat strained. He indicated he had not remained close to his father and, as of the mid-1970s, didn't stay in touch with his mother, who was divorced from his father when he was in his teens.

He learned to play piano as a child, concentrating on the classics, which remained his prime musical interest into his teens in the early 1960s. His desire to continue in that vein was strengthened briefly when a high school music teacher introduced him to the great composer Igor Stravinsky. But as family tensions intensified, he rebelled, turning his sights toward pop music and also becoming something of a delinquent, though "I never was a big-time hood."

Once his parents separated, the sixteen-year-old Warren headed for New York City in a Corvette (which his father had won in a card game) with a guitar in the backseat. He was inspired by reports of the folk ferment in New York and had dreams of emulating a rising young singer-writer named Bob Dylan. However, things didn't work out and he headed back west, this time to San Francisco.

In the Bay Area, he told Sue Reilly of *People* magazine (May 2, 1978), he formed a "preppy" band "that tried to sound like the Beatles and looked like Yale. We finally broke up because of dramatic lack of potential." For a while after that he remained in the region, picking up performing gigs and also becoming involved in the drug scene in Berkeley. But the psychedelic music and flower-power phase dominant in that locale in the mid-1960s faded and Zevon betook himself south once more to Los Angeles.

Back in Southern California, he teamed up with a vocalist named Tule Livingston to form a duo called Lyme and Cybelle. Their single "Follow Me" received airplay and something more than negligible sales. But it didn't do quite well enough to insure any major record-industry support. After that, Warren remained active in the music field in a variety of ways: performing as a record session pianist and guitarist ("I learned to play frustrated banjo-style guitar from listening to folk music. I still play that way"), writing original songs, and even doing some commercials.

While he paid those dues, he also made friends with many aspiring musicians and songwriters in the same boat he was in. Among them was Jackson Browne. The two first met in 1968 and remained close friends and occasional writing collaborators from then on.

Despite setbacks, Warren had no plans for seeking another work outlet. He told Robert Hilburn of the *Los Angeles Times* (August 8, 1976): "There were times when I was very frustrated, points at which I was writing bad songs and resenting the fact that they weren't regarded as good ones. But I never considered doing anything else. Besides, I felt I was making progress. It may have been slow, but each new song was a step closer to what I wanted to do."

Some of his songs were finding interested ears,

though. He got the chance to record an album for Imperial Records, *Wanted Dead or Alive* (1970). It was a flop—deservedly, Zevon said some years later. One of his songs from the album called "She Quit Me" was used in the *Midnight Cowboy* sound track—"He Quit Me Man," sung by Leslie Miller.

Then the Everly Brothers asked him to serve as musical director and instrumentalist for their backing band. He chose the band members, including guitarist Waddy Wachtel (an important contributor to many of Warren's solo recordings of the mid-1970s). He worked with the brothers for two years and then with each alternately after they broke up their partnership.

Warren told Hilburn: "There were some great nights. A lot of gooseflesh, a lot of pride. We may have played the songs 1,000 times before, but they're good songs and Phil and Don—no matter how they felt offstage—would always go out and perform with passion. If anything, I learned that when you go out on stage, you give your all even if you have been doing it for 15 years and are sick of giving your all."

He was inspired from what he called the emotional feeling he got from the Everlys to write a song called "Frank and Jesse James," later featured on his 1976 solo album. He found time to write other songs that found favor with his California folk-rock friends. Among them were "Hasten Down the Wind," "Poor Poor Pitiful Me," "Carmelita," and "Mohammed's Radio," which Linda Ronstadt eventually recorded and included in many concerts.

The Everly Brothers' breakup forced Warren to try to take stock of what he wanted from his career and his life. He was getting old for a rock performer and hadn't made any major impact on his chosen field. In 1974 he decided to drop his other projects and take a sabbatical in Spain, playing the piano and singing in a small club in the tourist town of Sitges while spending his spare time relaxing, writing, and pondering his future. In 1975 he was in the midst of negotiating a recording agreement with a European company when he got a message from Jackson Browne urging him to come back to L.A. Browne had suggested to Asylum executives that they assemble a solo LP of Zevon songs. Warren assented, though he took time off on the way back to stop in London, England, and arrange Phil Everly's solo album *Mystic Line* (Pye, 1975).

Back in the States, with Browne acting as producer, Zevon completed the new collection, *Warren Zevon* (May 1976), a stunning offering that his peers acknowledged as a potential classic. Despite that and Zevon's pulsating live performances, the LP was not a major commercial success. But it received enough buyer support and critical praise that the record company gave the green light for a follow-up.

Zevon, though, was not to be rushed. He took a lot of time writing and polishing the songs for the next album and, where he had written both words and music to all the tracks on his Asylum debut, he brought in Browne and others to help on the next candidates. As on its predecessor, he got heartwarming support from his musical friends. Among those helping to lay down the new tracks were Browne, Linda Ronstadt, Waddy Wachtel and other members of Ronstadt's band (the Section, which often backed Browne and James Taylor), and Fleetwood Mac. The gold *Excitable Boy* (early 1978), if not quite as consistently unique as the earlier LP, still had sterling moments, such as the comically eerie hit single "Werewolves of London."

That was a period when Zevon was as well known to his friends in the music industry for his carousing as for his creative work. His personal life was becoming a shambles by the late 1970s, and for a short time he finally sought help from his drinking and drug abuse problems in a rehab center during 1978. He also had to cope with divorce proceedings.

Though Zevon by the end of the 1970s was a concert headliner, he had trouble maintaining his creative momentum. *Bad Luck Streak in Dancing School* (1980, top 20) had some excellent tracks, but there were relatively uninspired ones as well. It was also far less successful commercially than its predecessor, though more popular than its follow-ups. Standout numbers on the album included "Jeannie Needs a Shooter," cowritten by Zevon and Bruce Springsteen; "Play It All Night Long"; and "Bill Lee."

Meanwhile, Asylum's gold sound track LP for the 1980 hit film Urban Cowboy included a song by Warren. His first live album, *Stand in the Fire*, was also issued by Asylum in 1980. A fine compilation, it caught much of the fervor and excellent musicianship that made Zevon shows among rock's best in the early 1980s. Besides presenting driving versions of Zevon's previous best writing, the album showcased some new songs that demonstrated his creative well had not yet run dry. Zevon followed with more studio albums as the 1980s moved along, such as *The Envoy* (1982).

In the mid-1980s Warren's career slowed down. Whether due to writer's block or a desire for a more low-key existence, Zevon had little new to match his classic work of the mid-1970s. He maintained a devoted but small following and performed mainly in smaller clubs and concert sites. By 1986 Zevon was no longer on the Elektra/Asylum roster. That year the label released the retrospective *A Quiet Normal Life: The Best of Warren Zevon*. The following year his long silence in terms of new recordings finally ended when he began his comeback on the Virgin label with *Sentimental Hygiene*. The supporting artists included Bob Dylan, Don Henley, Neil Young, Flea from the Red Hot Chili Peppers, and members of R.E.M.

He had told Hilburn in the mid-1970s that he always tried to keep things in perspective. "I think in songs that are supposed to have a wry or humorous twist, I'm trying to remind myself not to take myself seriously. I would not presume to tell my friends or colleagues what kind of attitudes they should take, but I find it very important to remind myself not to take myself seriously. So that may be the basis for humor in my songs."

He didn't want to be considered a cynic or one who had no sense of social responsibility, however. "But it has been stressed to the point where certain writers seem to see me as a comedian or something . . . a kind of extreme satirist, which I don't see at all. I'm very much not a cynic. I think, actually, that I'm quite idealistic. I think caring is perhaps the most positive force in life."

In 1989 Zevon's second album on Virgin, *Transverse City*, was issued. The album, whose tracks included a solo on the title track by the Grateful Dead's Jerry Garcia, was up to Zevon's standards, but had little support from record buyers. In 1990 he and three members of R.E.M. were represented as a band called the Hindu Love Gods on an album issued by Giant Records. The quartet comprised Bill Berry, Peter Buck, and Mike Mills from R.E.M. with Warren replacing Michael Stipe on guitar. The tracks had been recorded during studio sessions for *Sentimental Hygiene,* and his management had okayed their release despite opposition from the R.E.M. artists. For a time this resulted in strained relations between Warren and the latter. In any case, it did result in a charted album.

In 1991 Zevon had his first solo debut collection on Giant, the excellent disc *Mr. Bad Example*. His composition "Searching for a Heart" provided him with his first charted single since "A Certain Girl" in 1980 (from *Bad Luck Streak in Dancing School*). That song and the song "Lawyers, Guns and Money" (included in his next Giant album) were included in the sound track for the Lawrence Kasdan film *Grand Canyon*. The track "What to Do in Denver When You're Dead" was employed in the sound track for the film of the same name.

In 1993 Giant released the collection *Learning to Flinch*, a live album whose seventeen tracks included both new and old songs from Zevon's repertoire. Among the notable new songs were "The Indifference of Heaven" and "The Piano Fighter," both also included in his next album. In *Learning to Flinch,* Zevon demonstrated his skills on piano, synthesizers, guitar, and, for the first time on a recording, slide guitar. He demonstrated his slide talents on "Worrier King." For his next project Zevon decided to record all the songs digitally at his home studio. The result was the 1995 Giant release *Mutineer,* which, he told *People* correspondent Craig Tomashoff, was dedicated to his mentor and guru Hunter S. Thompson, "the original mutineer." It was a fine disc, but once more met limited sales response, bringing his affiliation with Giant to an end. Its contents included both up-tempo numbers and such moving ballads as the title track and "Similar to Rain."

In 1996 Rhino Records came out with a two-CD box set, *Warren Zevon: I'll Sleep When I'm Dead (An*

Anthology), containing forty-four songs covering Warren's work at Asylum, Virgin, and Giant. Besides offering essentially all of his best-known releases from all of those, it also contained several of his sound track compositions that hadn't been released before, including material he had written for TV projects like William Shatner's *TekWar* and the short-lived *Route 66* series.

He had recorded some of the songs at his home studio and tried out new material in his concerts, songs with such Zevonish titles as "For My Next Trick I'll Need a Volunteer" and "Hostage-O." Zevon counted David Letterman as one of his fans, and he sometimes filled in for band leader Paul Shaffer on *The Late Show with David Letterman*. In 1998 he also performed at benefits with author Stephen King and humor columnist Dave Barry in an ad-hoc rock band called the Rock Bottom Remainders. When former pro wrestler Jesse "The Body" Ventura won the governorship of Minnesota, he made it known that Zevon was his favorite rocker. He invited Warren to perform at his January inaugural ball. Zevon canceled some engagements and performed "Werewolves of London" and "Lawyers, Guns and Money" at the event.

While he certainly wasn't overjoyed that his recording career was at loose ends, his comments to interviewers didn't reflect the bitterness he might once have conveyed. He also was looking forward to trying something different—classical composing. He told Marc D. Allan of the *Indianapolis Star and News* ("Warren Zevon Hopes to Perform His Classical Music with Local Symphonies," March 14, 1996), "I think the prospects of getting such a thing played are probably fairly good. I'm optimistic about it. I may be deluding myself, but we know there's an orchestra in every town, much less city, in America." About his own outlook, he commented, "I'm in remarkably good health, the best shape I've ever been in. My kids are doing great and they like me. And what I explain to people about the misadventures of the recording industry is: Not winning the lottery is not a personal problem." Zevon's year 2000 album was titled *Life'll Kill Ya.*

AWARDS

NATIONAL ACADEMY OF RECORDING ARTS AND SCIENCES GRAMMY AWARDS BY CATEGORY IN FOLK, FOLK ROCK, AND BLUES

*T*he National Academy of Recording Arts and Sciences is a nonprofit organization composed of more than 4,500 members nationwide representing the entire spectrum of creative people in the phonograph recording field. It was formed, in 1957, to advance the arts and science of recording and to foster creative leadership for artistic, cultural, educational, and technical progress in the recording field. The organization is also known as the Recording Academy or by its initials, NARAS.

The Recording Academy is best known for its annual Grammy Awards, which are given for outstanding artist and/or technical achievements during each award's eligibility year to those deemed by their voting peers to be most worthy of the honor. The Grammy Awards are presented on nationwide television in late February or early March. The program reached over 55 million viewers throughout the world each year in the early 1980s, a number that increased severalfold by the mid-1990s.

BEST NEW ARTIST

1968   Jose Feliciano (RCA)
1969   Crosby, Stills and Nash (Atlantic)
1976   Starland Vocal Band (Windsong)
1979   Rickie Lee Jones (Warner Brothers)
1988   Tracy Chapman (Elektra)
1995   Hootie and the Blowfish (Atlantic)
1997   Paula Cole (Warner Brothers)

RECORD OF THE YEAR

1968   "Mrs. Robinson," Simon and Garfunkel (Columbia)
1970   "Bridge over Troubled Water," Simon and Garfunkel (Columbia)
1971   "It's Too Late," Carole King (Ode)
1977   "Hotel California," Eagles (Asylum)
1987   "Graceland," Paul Simon (Warner Brothers)
1997   "Sunny Come Home," (track from *A Few Small Repairs*) Shawn Colvin (Columbia)

ALBUM OF THE YEAR

1970   *Bridge over Troubled Water,* Simon and Garfunkel (Columbia)
1971   *Tapestry,* Carole King (Ode)
1975   *Still Crazy After All These Years,* Paul Simon (Columbia)
1986   *Graceland,* Paul Simon (Warner Brothers)
1989   *Nick of Time,* Bonnie Raitt (Capitol)
1997   *Time out of Mind,* Bob Dylan (Columbia)

BEST POP ALBUM

1994   *Longing in Their Hearts,* Bonnie Raitt (Capitol)
1995   *Turbulent Indigo,* Joni Mitchell (Warner Brothers)
1997   *Hourglass,* James Taylor (Columbia)

BEST NEW AGE ALBUM

1992   *Shepherd Moons,* Enya (Reprise)
1996   *The Memory of Trees,* Enya (Reprise)
1998   *Landmarks,* Clannad (Atlantic)

BEST ALTERNATIVE MUSIC ALBUM

1991   *Out of Time,* R.E.M. (Warner Brothers)
1996   *Odelay,* Beck (DGC)
1999   *Mutations,* Beck (DGC)

BEST POP VOCAL PERFORMANCE, FEMALE

1971   *Tapestry,* Carole King (Ode)
1975   "At Seventeen," Janis Ian (Columbia)
1976   *Hasten Down the Wind,* Linda Ronstadt (Asylum)
1989   "Nick of Time" (track from *Nick of Time*), Bonnie Raitt (Capitol)

BEST POP VOCAL PERFORMANCE, FEMALE (cont.)

1991 "Something to Talk About," Bonnie Raitt (Capitol)
1997 "Building a Mystery" (track from *Surfacing*) Sarah McLachlan (Arista)
1999 "I Will Remember You" Sarah McLachlan (Arista)

BEST POP VOCAL PERFORMANCE, MALE

1980 "This Is It" (album track), Kenny Loggins (Columbia)

BEST POP VOCAL PERFORMANCE BY A DUO OR GROUP WITH VOCAL

1990 "All my Life," Linda Ronstadt and Aaron Neville (Elektra Entertainment)
1991 "Losing My Religion," R.E.M. (Warner Brothers)
1995 "Let Her Cry," Hootie and the Blowfish (Atlantic)

BEST POP INSTRUMENTAL PERFORMANCE

1995 "Mariachi Suite" (track from *Desperado* sound track), Los Lobos (Epic Soundtrax)

BEST POP VOCAL COLLABORATION

1995 "Have I Told You Lately That I Love You," the Chieftans with Van Morrison (RCA Victor)
1997 "Don't Look Back," (track from *Don't Look Back*), John Lee Hooker and Van Morrison (Pointblank/Virgin America)

BEST COUNTRY VOCAL PERFORMANCE, FEMALE

1975 "I Can't Help It If I'm Still In Love with You," Linda Ronstadt (Capitol)

BEST COUNTRY COLLABORATION WITH VOCALS

1999 "After the Gold Rush," Linda Ronstadt, Emmylou Harris and Dolly Parton (Elektra)

BEST CONTEMPORARY POP VOCAL PERFORMANCE, MALE

1968 "Light My Fire," Jose Feliciano (RCA)
1969 "Everybody's Talkin'," Harry Nilsson (United Artists)
1971 "You've Got a Friend," James Taylor (Warner Brothers)
1972 "Without You," Harry Nilsson (RCA)
1975 "Still Crazy After All These Years," Paul Simon (Columbia)
1977 "Handy Man," James Taylor (Columbia)

BEST ROCK VOCAL PERFORMANCE, MALE

1979 "Gotta Serve Somebody," Bob Dylan (Columbia)
1982 "Hurts So Good," John Cougar (Mellencamp) (Riva/Polygram)
1984 "Dancing in the Dark," Bruce Springsteen (Columbia)
1989 "The End of Innocence," Don Henley (Geffen)
1994 "Streets of Philadelphia," Bruce Springsteen (Columbia)
1996 "Where It's At," Beck (DGC)
1997 "Cold Irons Bound," Bob Dylan (Columbia)

BEST ROCK VOCAL PERFORMANCE, FEMALE

1989 *Nick of Time,* Bonnie Raitt (Capitol)

BEST ROCK VOCAL PERFORMANCE BY A DUO OR GROUP WITH VOCAL

1979 "Heartache Tonight," Eagles (Asylum)
1989 *Traveling Wilburys, Volume One,* Traveling Wilburys (Wilbury/Warner Brothers)
1991 "Good Man, Good Woman," (track from *Luck of the Draw*), Bonnie Raitt and Delbert McClinton (Capitol)

BEST ROCK VOCAL PERFORMANCE, SOLO

1987 *Tunnel of Love,* Bruce Springsteen (Columbia/CBS)
1991 *Luck of the Draw,* Bonnie Raitt (Capitol)

BEST ROCK INSTRUMENTAL PERFORMANCE

1990 "D/FW" (track from *Family Style*), The Vaughan Brothers (Epic Associated)
1992 "Little Wing," (track from *The Sky is Crying,* Stevie Ray Vaughan & Double Trouble (Epic)
1995 "Jessica" (track from *2nd Set—an Evening with the Allman Brothers Band*), Allman Brothers Band (Epic)
1996 "SRV Shuffle" (track from *A Tribute to Stevie Ray Vaughan),* Jimmie Vaughan, Eric Clapton, Bonnie Raitt, Robert Cray, B.B. King, Buddy Guy, Dr. John, and Art Neville (Epic)

BEST ROCK SONG

1994 "Streets of Philadelphia," Bruce Springsteen; Bruce Springsteen, songwriter (Columbia/Epic)
1996 "Give Me One Reason," Tracy Chapman; Tracy Chapman, songwriter (Elektra)

BEST CONTEMPORARY POP PERFORMANCE, VOCAL, DUO OR GROUP

1968 "Mrs. Robinson," Simon and Garfunkel (Columbia)
1975 "Lyin' Eyes," Eagles (Asylum)

BEST POP VOCAL PERFORMANCE BY A DUO OR GROUP WITH VOCAL

1989 "Don't Know Much," Linda Ronstadt and Aaron Neville (Elektra)
1990 "All My Life," Linda Ronstadt and Aaron Neville (Elektra Entertainment)

BEST POP INSTRUMENTAL PERFORMANCE

1989 "Healing Chant" (track from *Yellow Moon*), Neville Brothers (A&M)
1996 "The Sinister Minister," Béla Fleck and the Flecktones (Warner Brothers)

BEST COUNTRY AND WESTERN PERFORMANCE

1958 "Tom Dooley," The Kingston Trio (Capitol Records)
1959 "The Battle of New Orleans," Jimmy Driftwood (Columbia)
1962 "Funny Way of Laughin'," Burl Ives (Decca)

SONG OF THE YEAR

1959 "The Battle of New Orleans," Jimmy Driftwood, composer (Columbia)
1970 "Bridge over Troubled Water," Paul Simon, songwriter (Columbia)
1971 "You've Got a Friend," Carole King, songwriter (Ode)
1972 "The First Time Ever I Saw Your Face," Ewan MacColl, songwriter (Atlantic)
1979 "What a Fool Believes," Kenny Loggins and Michael McDonald, songwriters (Warner Brothers)
1987 "Somewhere Out There," Linda Ronstadt and James Ingram; James Horner, Barry Mann, Cynthia Weil, songwriters (MCA)
1994 "Streets of Philadelphia," Bruce Springsteen; Bruce Springsteen, songwriter (Columbia/Epic)
1997 "Sunny Come Home," Shawn Colvin and John Leventhal, songwriters (Columbia)

BEST CONTEMPORARY SONG

1970 "Bridge over Troubled Water," Paul Simon (Columbia)

BEST COUNTRY AND WESTERN SONG

1967 "Gentle on My Mind," John Hartford, songwriter (RCA)

BEST PERFORMANCE, FOLK

1959 *The Kingston Trio at Large,* the Kingston Trio (Capitol)
1960 "Swing Dat Hammer," Harry Belafonte (RCA)
1967 "Gentle on My Mind," John Hartford (RCA)
1968 "Both Sides Now," Judy Collins (Elektra)
1969 "Clouds," Joni Mitchell (Warner Brothers)

BEST FOLK RECORDING

1961   *Belafonte Folk Singers at Home and Abroad,* Belafonte Folk Singers (RCA)

1962   "If I Had a Hammer," Peter, Paul and Mary (Warner Brothers)

1963   "Blowin' in the Wind," Peter, Paul and Mary (Warner Brothers)

1964   "We'll Sing in the Sunshine," Gale Garnett (RCA)

1965   *An Evening with Belafonte/Makeba,* Harry Belafonte and Miriam Makeba (RCA)

BEST PERFORMANCE BY A VOCAL GROUP

1962   "If I Had a Hammer," Peter, Paul and Mary (Warner Brothers)

1963   "Blowin' in the Wind," Peter, Paul and Mary (Warner Brothers)

BEST PERFORMANCE BY A CHORUS

1962   *Presenting the New Christy Minstrels,* the New Christy Minstrels (Columbia)

BEST TRADITIONAL FOLK RECORDING

1986   *Riding the Midnight Train,* Doc Watson (Sugar Hill)

1987   *Shaka Zulu,* Ladysmith Black Mambazo (Warner Brothers)

1988   *Folkways: A Vision Shared—a Tribute to Woody Guthrie and Leadbelly,* various artists (Columbia/CBS)

1989   *Le Mystere Des Voix Bulgares, Vol. II,* Bulgarian State Female Vocal Choir (Elektra/Nonesuch)

1990   *On Praying Ground,* Doc Watson (Sugar Hill)

1991   *The Civil War* (original sound track), various artists, producers Ken Burns and John Colby (Elektra/Nonesuch)

1992   *An Irish Evening Live at the Grand Opera House, Belfast,* the Chieftains (RCA Victor)

1993   *The Celtic Harp,* the Chieftains (RCA Victor)

1994   *World Gone Wrong,* Bob Dylan (Columbia)

1995   *South Coast,* Ramblin' Jack Elliott (Red House)

1996   *Pete,* Pete Seeger (Living Music)

1997   *L'Amour Ou La Folie,* BeauSoleil (Rhino)

1998   *Long Journey Home,* The Chieftains with Various Artists (Wicklow)

1999   *Press On,* June Carter Cash (RISK Records)

BEST CONTEMPORARY FOLK RECORDING

1986   *Tribute to Steve Goodman,* Arlo Guthrie, John Hartford, Richie Havens, Bonnie Koloc, Nitty Gritty Dirt Band, John Prine, and others (Red Pajamas)

1987   *Unfinished Business,* Steve Goodman (Red Pajamas)

1988   *Tracy Chapman,* Tracy Chapman (Elektra)

1989   *Indigo Girls,* Indigo Girls (Epic)

1990   *Steady On,* Shawn Colvin (Columbia/CBS)

1991   *The Missing Years,* John Prine (Oh Boy)

1992   *Another Country,* the Chieftains (RCA Victor)

1993   *Other Voices/Other Rooms,* Nanci Griffith (Elektra)

1994   *American Recordings,* Johnny Cash (American)

1995   *Wrecking Ball,* Emmylou Harris (Asylum/Elektra)

1996   *The Ghost of Tom Joad,* Bruce Springsteen (Columbia)

1997   *Time out of Mind,* Bob Dylan (Columbia)

1998   *Car Wheels on a Gravel Road,* Lucinda Williams (Mercury)

1999   *Mule Variations,* Tom Waits (Epitaph)

BEST BLUEGRASS RECORDING/ALBUM

1989   "The Valley Road" (track from *Will the Circle Be Unbroken, Volume Two*), Bruce Hornsby and the Nitty Gritty Dirt Band (Universal)

1990   *I've Got That Old Feeling,* Alison Krauss (Rounder)

1991   *Spring Training,* Carl Jackson and John Starling (and the Nash Ramblers) (Sugar Hill)

1992   *Every Time You Say Goodbye,* Alison Krauss and Union Station (Rounder)

1993   *Waitin' for the Hard Times to Go,* Nashville Bluegrass Band (Sugar Hill)

1994   *The Great Dobro Sessions,* Jerry Douglas and Tut Taylor (Sugar Hill)

1995   *Unleashed,* Nashville Bluegrass Band, (Sugar Hill)

1996   *True Life Blues: The Songs of Bill Monroe,* various artists, (Sugar Hill)

1997   *So Long, So Wrong,* Alison Krauss and Union Station, (Rounder)

1998   *Bluegrass Rules!* Ricky Skaggs and Kentucky Thunder, (Skaggs Family Records)

1999   *Ancient Tones,* Ricky Skaggs and Kentucky Thunder, (Skaggs Family Records)

BEST TRADITIONAL BLUES RECORDING

1982 *Alright Again,* Clarence Gatemouth Brown (Rounder)
1983 *Blues 'n Jazz,* B.B. King (MCA)
1984 *Blues Explosion,* John Hammond, Stevie Ray Vaughan and Double Trouble, Sugar Blue, Koko Taylor and the Blues Machine, Luther "Guitar Junior" Johnson, J.B. Hutto and the New Hawks (Atlantic)
1985 "My Guitar Sings the Blues" (track from *Six Silver Strings*), B.B. King (MCA)
1986 *Showdown!* Albert Collins, Robert Cray, and Johnny Copeland (Alligator)
1987 *Houseparty New Orleans Style,* Professor Longhair (Rounder)
1988 *Hidden Charms,* Willie Dixon (Bug/Capitol)
1989 "I'm in the Mood" (track from *The Healer*), John Lee Hooker and Bonnie Raitt (Chameleon Music Group)
1990 *Live at San Quentin,* B.B. King (MCA)
1991 *Live at the Apollo,* B.B. King (MCA)
1992 *Goin' Back to New Orleans,* Dr. John (Warner Brothers)
1993 *Blues Summit,* B.B. King (MCA)
1994 *From the Cradle,* Eric Clapton (Reprise)
1995 *Chill Out,* John Lee Hooker (Pointblank)
1996 *Deep in the Blues,* James Cotton (Verve)
1997 *Don't Look Back,* John Lee Hooker (Pointblank/Virgin America)
1998 *Any Place I'm Going,* Otis Rush (House of Blues)
1999 *Blues on the Bayou,* B.B.King (MCA)

BEST CONTEMPORARY BLUES RECORDING

1987 *Strong Persuader,* the Robert Cray Band (Mercury/HighTone)
1988 "Don't Be Afraid of the Dark," the Robert Cray Band (Mercury)
1989 *In Step,* Stevie Ray Vaughan and Double Trouble (Epic)
1990 *Family Style,* the Vaughan Brothers (Epic Associated)
1991 *Damn Right, I've Got the Blues,* Buddy Guy (Silvertone)
1992 *The Sky Is Crying,* Stevie Ray Vaughan and Double Trouble (Epic)
1993 *Feels Like Rain,* Buddy Guy (Silvertone)
1994 *Father Father,* Pops Staples (Pointblank)
1995 *Slippin' In,* Buddy Guy (Silvertone)
1996 *Just Like You,* Keb' Mo' (OKeh/Epic)
1997 *Señor Blues,* Taj Mahal (Private Music)
1998 *Slow Down,* Keb' Mo' (OKeh/550 Music)

1999 *Take Your Shoes Off,* Robert Cray Band (Rykodisc)

BEST ETHNIC OR TRADITIONAL RECORDING

1971 *They Call Me Muddy Waters,* Muddy Waters (Chess)
1972 *The London Muddy Waters Sessions,* Muddy Waters (Chess)
1973 *Then and Now,* Doc Watson (United Artists)
1974 *Two Days in November,* Doc and Merle Watson (United Artists)
1975 *The Muddy Waters Woodstock Album,* Muddy Waters (Chess)
1976 *Mark Twang,* John Hartford (Flying Fish)
1977 *Hard Again,* Muddy Waters (Blue Sky/CBS)
1978 *I'm Ready,* Muddy Waters (Blue Sky)
1979 *Muddy "Mississippi" Waters Live* (Blue Sky/CBS)
1980 *Rare Blues,* Dr. Isaiah Ross, Maxwell Street Jimmy, Big Joe Williams, Son House, Rev. Robin Wilkins, Little Brother Montgomery, Sunnyland Slim (Takoma)
1981 *There Must Be a Better World Somewhere,* B.B. King (MCA)

BEST ETHNIC OR TRADITIONAL FOLK RECORDING

1982 *Queen Ida and the Bon Temps Zydeco Band on Tour,* Queen Ida (GNP/Crescendo)
1983 *I'm Here,* Clifton Chenier and His Red Hot Louisiana Band (Alligator)
1984 *Elizabeth Cotten Live,* Elizabeth Cotten (Arhoolie)
1985 "My Toot Toot," Rockin' Sidney (Maison De Soul)

BEST WORLD MUSIC ALBUM

1993 *A Meeting by the River,* Ry Cooder and V.M. Bhatt (Water Lily Acoustics)
1994 *Talking Timbuktu,* Ali Farka Toure with Ry Cooder (Hannibal)
1996 *Santiago,* the Chieftains (RCA Victor)
1999 *Livro,* Caetano Veloso (Atlantic/Nonesuch)

BEST COUNTRY INSTRUMENTAL PERFORMANCE

1979 "Big Sandy/Leather Britches" (album track), Doc and Merle Watson (United Artists)

1995 "Hightower," Asleep at the Wheel with Béla Fleck and Johnny Gimble (Capitol/Nashville)

BEST ENGINEERING CONTRIBUTION— OTHER THAN CLASSICAL OR NOVELTY

1959 *Belafonte at Carnegie Hall,* Harry Belafonte; Robert Simpson, engineer (RCA)

BEST ENGINEERED RECORDING

1970 *Bridge over Troubled Water,* Simon and Garfunkel; Roy Halee, engineer (Columbia)

1989 *Cry Like a Rainstorm—Howl Like the Wind,* Linda Ronstadt; George Massenberg, engineer (Elektra)

BEST ARRANGEMENT ACCOMPANYING VOCALIST(S)

1970 "Bridge over Troubled Water," Simon and Garfunkel; Jimmie Haskell, Ernie Freeman, and Larry Knechtel, arrangers (Columbia)

1974 "Down to You," Joni Mitchell; Joni Mitchell and Tom Scott, arrangers (Asylum)

BEST INSTRUMENTAL ARRANGEMENT ACCOMPANYING VOCALS

1983 "What's New," Linda Ronstadt; Nelson Riddle, arranger (Asylum/E.A.)

1985 "Lush Life" (track from *Lush Life*), Linda Ronstadt; Nelson Riddle, arranger (Asylum)

BEST ARRANGEMENT FOR VOICES

1976 "Afternoon Delight," Starland Vocal Band, arranged by Starland Vocal Band (Windsong/ RCA)

BEST HISTORICAL ALBUM

1990 *Robert Johnson: The Complete Recordings,* Robert Johnson; Lawrence Cohn and Stephen LaVere, producers (Columbia/CBS)

1997 *Anthology of American Folk Music* (1997 Expanded Edition); Jeff Place, Pete Reiniger, and Harry Smith, producers; David Glasser and Charlie Pilzer, mastering engineers (various artists) (Smithsonian/Folkways)

BEST ALBUM COVER

1970 *Indianola Mississippi Seeds* (B.B. King); Robert Lockart, cover design; Ivan Nagy, photographer (ABC)

BEST ALBUM NOTES

1970 *The World's Greatest Blues Singer* (Bessie Smith); Chris Albertson, annotator (Columbia)

1997 *Anthology of American Folk Music* (1997 Expanded Edition); John Fahey, Luis Kemnitzer, Jon Pancake, Chuck Pirtle, Jeff Place, Neil V. Rosenberg, Luc Sante, Peter Stempfel, and Eric Von Schmidt (various artists) (Smithsonian/Folkways)

BEST RECORDING FOR CHILDREN

1969 *Peter, Paul and Mommy,* Peter, Paul and Mary (Warner Brothers)

1980 *In Harmony/A Sesame Street Record,* the Doobie Brothers, James Taylor, Carly Simon, Bette Midler, Muppets, Al Jarreau, Linda Ronstadt, Wendy Waldman, Libby Titus and Dr. John, Livingston Taylor, George Benson and Pauline Wilson, Lucy Simon, Kate Taylor and the Simon/Taylor Family (Sesame Street Records/ Warner Brothers)

1982 *In Harmony,* Billy Joel, Bruce Springsteen, James Taylor, Kenny Loggins, Carly and Lucy Simon, Teddy Pendergrass, Crystal Gayle, Lou Rawls, Deniece Williams, Janis Ian, and Dr. John (CBS)

1988 *Pecos Bill,* Ry Cooder, music; Robin Williams, narrator (Windham Hill)

1996 *Dedicated to the One I Love,* Linda Ronstadt (Elektra)

1997 *All Aboard,* John Denver (Sony Wonder)

BEST ORIGINAL SCORE WRITTEN FOR A MOTION PICTURE OR TV SPECIAL

1968   *The Graduate,* Paul Simon (Columbia)

BEST SONG WRITTEN SPECIFICALLY FOR A MOTION PICTURE OR TV

1987   "Somewhere out There," Linda Ronstadt and James Ingram; James Horner, Barry Mann, and Cynthia Weil, songwriters (MCA)
1994   "Streets of Philadelphia" (from *Philadelphia*), Bruce Springsteen; Bruce Springsteen, songwriter (Columbia/Epic)

BEST SOUL GOSPEL PERFORMANCE

1973   "Loves Me Like a Rock," Dixie Hummingbirds (ABC)
1974   *In the Ghetto,* James Cleveland and the Southern California Community Choir (Savoy)
1976   *How I Got Over,* Mahalia Jackson (Columbia)

BEST ALBUM PACKAGE

1977   *Simple Dreams,* Linda Ronstadt; Kosh, art director (Asylum)
1982   *Get Closer,* Linda Ronstadt; Kosh with Ron Larson, art directors (Elektra Asylum)
1985   *Lush Life,* Linda Ronstadt; Kosh and Ron Larson, art directors (Asylum)
1995   *Turbulent Indigo,* Joni Mitchell; Robbie Cavolina, art director (Reprise)

BEST LATIN POP PERFORMANCE

1986   "Lelolai" (track from *Te Amare*), Jose Feliciano (RCA)
1990   "Por Que Te Tengo Que Olvidar" (track from *Niño*), Jose Feliciano (Capitol/EMI Latin)

BEST TROPICAL LATIN ALBUM

1992   *Frenesi,* Linda Ronstadt (Elektra)
1997   *Buena Vista Social Club,* Ry Cooder (World Circuit/Nonesuch)

BEST MEXICAN AMERICAN PERFORMANCE

1989   *La Pistola El Corazon,* Los Lobos (Warner Brothers/Slash)
1992   *Mas Canciones,* Linda Ronstadt (Elektra Entertainment)
1995   *Flaco Jimenez,* Flaco Jimenez (Arista/Texas)
1998   *Los Super Seven,* Los Super Seven (RCA Nashville)

BEST TEJANO PERFORMANCE

1998   *Said and Done,* Flaco Jimenez (Barb Wire Productions/Virgin)

BEST REGGAE ALBUM

1994   *Crucial! Roots Classics,* Bunny Wailer (Shanachie)
1996   *Hall of Fame: A Tribute to Bob Marley's 50th Anniversary,* Bunny Wailer (RAS)
1997   *Fallen is Babylon*, Ziggy Marley and the Melody Makers (Elektra/EEG)
1998   *Friends,* Sly and Robbie (EastWest America/EEG)
1999   *Calling Rastafari,* Burning Spear

BEST MUSIC VIDEO, SHORT FORM

1991   "Losing My Religion," R.E.M.; Tarsem, video director; Dave Ramser, video line director (Warner Brothers)
1992   "Digging in the Dirt," Peter Gabriel; John Downer, video director and video line producer (Geffen)
1993   "Steam," Peter Gabriel; Stephen R. Johnson, video director; Prudence Fenton, video producer (Geffen)

MUSIC VIDEO, LONG FORM

1995   *Secret World Live,* Peter Gabriel; Francois Girard, video director; Robert Warr, producer (Geffen)

PRODUCER OF THE YEAR (NONCLASSICAL)

1992   Daniel Lanois and Brian Eno (tie with L.A. Reid and Babyface)

W.C. HANDY BLUES AWARDS

The Blues Foundation awards W.C. Handy Awards each May, based on votes sent out to more than 30,000 blues fans worldwide.

Twentieth Annual W.C. Handy Blues Awards (1999)

Blues Entertainer of the Year: B.B. King

Blues Band of the Year: Rod Piazza and the Mighty Flyers

Contemporary Blues—Male Artist of the Year: Keb' Mo'

Contemporary Blues—Female Artist of the Year: Susan Tedeschi

Soul/Blues—Male Artist of the Year: Bobby "Blue" Bland

Soul/Blues—Female Artist of the Year: Etta James

Traditional Blues—Male Artist of the Year: Robert Lockwood, Jr.

Tradtional Blues—Female Artist of the Year: Koko Taylor

Acoustic Blues—Artist of the Year: Keb' Mo'

Best New Blues Artist: Susan Tedeschi

Blues Artist Deserving Wider Recognition: W.C. Clark

Blues Instrumentalist—Guitar: Ronnie Earl

Blues Instrumentalist—Harmonica: Charlie Musselwhite

Blues Instrumentalist—Keyboards: Pinetop Perkins

Blues Instrumentalist—Bass: Willie Kent

Blues Instrumentalist—Drums: Willie "Big Eyes" Smith

Blues Instrumentalist—Other: Gatemouth Brown (violin)

Contemporary Blues Album of the Year: B.B. King, *Blues on the Bayou*

Soul/Blues Album of the Year: Etta James, *Life, Love & the Blues*

Traditional Blues Album of the Year: Robert Lockwood, Jr,. *I Got To Have Me A Woman*

Comeback Blues Album: Peter Green, *Robert Johnson Songbook*

Acoustic Blues Album of the Year: Rory Block, *Confessions of a Blues Singer*

Reissue Album of the Year: Ruf Records, *Hand Me Down Moonshine,* Luther Allison

Blues Song of the Year: "Soon As I Get Paid," by Kevin Moore and John Lewis Parker

Nineteenth Annual W.C. Handy Blues Awards (1998)

Blues Entertainer of the Year: Luther Allison

Blues Band of the Year: Luther Allison and the James Solberg Band

Contemporary Blues—Male Artist of the Year: Luther Allison

Contemporary Blues—Female Artist of the Year: Marcia Ball

Soul/Blues—Female Artist of the Year: Ruth Brown

Soul/Blues—Male Artist of the Year: Little Milton

Traditional Blues—Male Artist of the Year: Carey Bell

Traditional Blues—Female Artist of the Year: Rory Block

Acoustic Blues—Artist of the Year: Keb' Mo' (Kevin Moore)

Best New Blues Artist: Johnny "Yard Dog" Jones

Blues Instrumentalist—Guitar: Luther Allison

Blues Instrumentalist—Harmonica: Rod Piazza

Blues Instrumentalist—Keyboards: Pinetop Perkins

Blues Instrumentalist—Bass: Calvin "Fuzz" Jones

Blues Instrumentalist—Drums: Willie "Big Eyes" Smith

Blues Instrumentalist—Other: Roomful of Blues— Horn Section

Contemporary Blues Album of the Year: Luther Allison, *Reckless*

Soul/Blues Album of the Year: Ruth Brown, *R + B = Ruth Brown*

Traditional Blues Album of the Year: Carey Bell, *Good Luck Man*

Comeback Blues Album: Eddie King, *Another Cow Is Dead*

Acoustic Blues Album of the Year: Corey Harris, *Fish Ain't Bitin'*

Reissue Album of the Year: Jimmy Rogers, *The Complete Chess Recordings*

Blues Song of the Year: Jerry Lynn Williams, "Living in the House of the Blues"

Eighteenth Annual W.C. Handy Blues Awards (1997)

Blues Entertainer of the Year: Luther Allison

Blues Band of the Year: Luther Allison and the James Solberg Band

Contemporary Blues—Male Artist of the Year: Luther Allison

Contemporary Blues—Female Artist of the Year: Debbie Davies

Soul/Blues—Male Artist of the Year: Bobby "Blue" Bland

Soul/Blues—Female Artist of the Year: Irma Thomas

Traditional Blues—Male Artist of the Year: James Cotton

Traditional Blues—Female Artist of the Year: Rory Block

Acoustic Blues—Artist of the Year: Keb' Mo'

Best New Blues Artist: Alvin Youngblood Hart

Blues Instrumentalist—Drums: Willie "Big Eyes" Smith

Blues Instrumentalist—Guitar: Ronnie Earl

Blues Instrumentalist—Harmonica: William Clarke

Blues Instrumentalist—Keyboards: Pinetop Perkins

Blues Instrumentalist—Bass: Willie Kent

Blues Instrumentalist—Other: Clarence "Gatemouth" Brown

Contemporary Blues Album of the Year: William Clarke, *The Hard Way* (Alligator Records)

Soul/Blues Album of the Year: W.C. Clark, *Texas Soul* (Blacktop Records)

Traditional Blues Album of the Year: Junior Wells, *Come On in this House* (Tel Arc Records)

Acoustic Blues Album of the Year: James Cotton, *Deep in the Blues* (Verve Records)

Reissue Album of the Year: Freddie King, *Live at the Electric Ballroom* (Blacktop Records)

Comeback Album of the Year: Floyd Dixon, *Wake Up and Live* (Alligator Records)

Blues Song of the Year: William Clarke, "Fishing Blues" (Alligator Records)

Seventeenth Annual W.C. Handy Blues Awards (1996)

Blues Entertainer of the Year: Luther Allison

Blues Band of the Year: Joe Louis Walker and the Bosstalkers

Contemporary Blues—Male Artist of the Year: Luther Allison

Contemporary Blues—Female Artist of the Year: Koko Taylor

Soul/Blues—Male Artist of the Year: Little Milton

Soul/Blues—Female Artist of the Year: Etta James

Traditional Blues—Male Artist of the Year: Jimmy Rogers

Traditional Blues—Female Artist of the Year: Katie Webster

Acoustic Blues—Artist of the Year: John Hammond

Best New Blues Artist: Coco Montoya

Blues Instrumentalist—Guitar: Luther Allison

Blues Instrumentalist—Harmonica: Charlie Musselwhite

Blues Instrumentalist—Keyboards: Pinetop Perkins

Blues Instrumentalist—Bass: Willie Kent

Blues Instrumentalist—Drums: Willie "Big Eyes" Smith

Blues Instrumentalist—Other: Clarence "Gatemouth" Brown

Contemporary Blues Album of the Year: Luther Allison, *Blue Streak*

Soul/Blues Album of the Year: Percy Sledge, *Blue Night*

Traditional Blues Album of the Year: John Lee Hooker, *Chill Out*

Comeback Blues Album: Jimmy Johnson, *I'm a Jockey*

Acoustic Blues Album of the Year: Rory Block, *When a Woman Gets the Blues*

Reissue Album of the Year: Delmark Records for Otis Rush, *So Many Roads*

Blues Song of the Year: Luther Allison, "Cherry Red Wine"

Sixteenth Annual W.C. Handy Blues Awards (1995)

Blues Entertainer of the Year: Buddy Guy

Blues Band of the Year: Charlie Musselwhite Band

Contemporary Blues—Male Artist of the Year: Otis Rush

Contemporary Blues—Female Artist of the Year: Etta James

Soul/Blues—Male Artist of the Year: Little Milton

Soul/Blues—Female Artist of the Year: Irma Thomas

Traditional Blues—Male Artist of the Year: Pinetop Perkins

Traditional Blues—Female Artist of the Year: Katie Webster

Country/Acoustic Blues—Artist of the Year: John Hammond

Male Vocalist of the Year: Charles Brown

Female Vocalist of the Year: Koko Taylor

Blues Instrumentalist—Guitar: Buddy Guy

Blues Instrumentalist—Harmonica: Charlie Musselwhite

Blues Instrumentalist—Keyboards: Pinetop Perkins

Blues Instrumentalist—Bass: Willie Kent

Blues Instrumentalist—Other: Clarence "Gatemouth" Brown (fiddle)

Contemporary Blues Album of the Year: Buddy Guy, *Slippin' In*

Soul/Blues Album of the Year: Solomon Burke, *Live at the House of Blues*

Traditional Blues Album of the Year: Jimmy Rogers, *Blue Bird*

Country/Acoustic Blues Album of the Year: Keb' Mo', *Keb' Mo'*

Reissue Album of the Year: MCA Records, *One More Mile*, Muddy Waters

Blues Song of the Year: Otis Rush for "Ain't Enough Comin In"

Crossover Artist of the Year: Eric Clapton

Fifteenth Annual W.C. Handy Blues Awards (1994)

Blues Entertainer of the Year: Albert Collins

Blues Band of the Year: Anson Funderburgh and the Rockets with Sam Myers

Contemporary Blues—Male Artist of the Year: Albert Collins

Contemporary Blues—Female Artist of the Year: Koko Taylor

Soul/Blues—Male Artist of the Year: Bobby "Blue" Bland

Soul/Blues—Female Artist of the Year: Etta James

Traditional Blues—Male Artist of the Year: Robert Jr. Lockwood

Traditional Blues—Female Artist of the Year: Jessie Mae Hemphill

Acoustic Blues—Artist of the Year: John Hammond

Male Vocalist of the Year: Otis Rush

Female Vocalist of the Year: Etta James

Blues Instrumentalist—Guitar: Albert Collins

Blues Instrumentalist—Harmonica: Charlie Musselwhite

Blues Instrumentalist—Keyboards: Pinetop Perkins

Blues Instrumentalist—Other: Clarence "Gatemouth" Brown

Contemporary Blues Album of the Year: B.B. King, *Blues Summit*

Soul/Blues Album of the Year: Bobby "Blue" Bland, *Years of Tears*

Traditional Blues Album of the Year: Taj Mahal, *Dancin' the Blues*

Acoustic Blues Album of the Year: Pinetop Perkins, *Portrait of a Delta Bluesman*

Reissue Album of the Year: Muddy Waters, *The Complete Plantation Recordings*

Blues Song of the Year: "My Next Ex-Wife," written by Rick Estrin, recorded by Little Charlie and the Nightcats

Fourteenth Annual W.C. Handy Blues Awards (1993)

Blues Entertainer of the Year: Buddy Guy

Blues Band of the Year: Albert Collins and the Icebreakers

Contemporary Blues—Male Artist of the Year: Buddy Guy

Contemporary Blues—Female Artist of the Year: Katie Webster

Soul/Blues—Male Artist of the Year: Bobby "Blue" Bland

Soul/Blues—Female Artist of the Year: Etta James

Traditional Blues—Male Artist of the Year: John Lee Hooker

Traditional Blues—Female Artist of the Year: Koko Taylor

Acoustic Blues—Artist of the Year: Snooky Pryor

Male Vocalist of the Year: Charles Brown

Female Vocalist of the Year: Etta James

Blues Instrumentalist—Guitar: Buddy Guy

Blues Instrumentalist—Harmonica: Charlie Musselwhite

Blues Instrumentalist—Keyboards: Pinetop Perkins

Blues Instrumentalist—Other: Papa John Creach (violin)

Contemporary Blues Album of the Year: Buddy Guy, *Feels Like Rain*

Soul/Blues Album of the Year: Etta James, *The Right Time*

Traditional Blues Album of the Year: Lowell Fulson, *Hold On*

Acoustic Blues Album of the Year: John Hammond, *Got Love If You Want It*

Reissue Album of the Year: Elmore James, *King of the Slide Guitar*

Blues Song of the Year: "Working Man," Lowell Fulson

Thirteenth Annual W.C. Handy Blues Awards (1992)

Blues Entertainer of the Year: Buddy Guy

Blues Band of the Year: Anson Funderburgh and the Rockets with Sam Myers

Contemporary Blues—Male Artist of the Year: Albert Collins

Contemporary Blues—Female Artist of the Year: Etta James

Traditional Blues—Male Artist of the Year: Willie Dixon

Traditional Blues—Female Artist of the Year: Koko Taylor

Acoustic Blues—Artist of the Year: Johnny Shines

Blues Vocalist of the Year: Buddy Guy

Blues Instrumentalist—Guitar: Buddy Guy

Blues Instrumentalist—Harmonica: Charlie Musselwhite

Blues Instrumentalist—Keyboards: Pinetop Perkins

Blues Instrumentalist—Other: Clarence "Gatemouth" Brown (fiddle)

Contemporary Blues Album of the Year (U.S.): Buddy Guy, *Damn Right I've Got the Blues* (Silvertone)

Contemporary Blues Album of the Year (Foreign): Guitar Shorty and Otis Grand Blues Band, *My Way or the Highway* (JSP)

Vintage/Reissue Album of the Year (U.S./Foreign): Howlin' Wolf, *The Chess Box* (MCA/Chess)

Traditional Blues Album (U.S./Foreign): Champion Jack Dupree, *Forever and Ever* (Bullseye Blues)

Blues Song of the Year: "Damn Right I've Got the Blues," Buddy Guy

Twelfth Annual W.C. Handy Blues Awards (1991)

Blues Entertainer of the Year: Buddy Guy

Blues Band of the Year: The B.B. King Orchestra

Contemporary Blues—Male Artist of the Year: Joe Louis Walker

Contemporary Blues—Female Artist of the Year: Koko Taylor

Traditional Blues—Male Artist of the Year: Champion Jack Dupree

Traditional Blues—Female Artist of the Year: Katie Webster

Acoustic Blues—Artist of the Year: Taj Mahal

Blues Vocalist of the Year: Charles Brown

Blues Instrumentalist—Guitar: Buddy Guy
Blues Instrumentalist—Harmonica: James Cotton
Blues Instrumentalist—Keyboards: Charles Brown
Blues Instrumentalist—Other: Clarence "Gatemouth" Brown (fiddle)
Contemporary Blues Album of the Year (U.S.): *Harp Attack,* various artists (Alligator)
Contemporary Blues Album of the Year (Foreign): Magic Slim, *Live on Stage—Magic Slim*
Traditional Album: Jimmy Rogers, *Ludella* (Antone's)
Country Blues Album: Jessie Mae Hemphill, *Feelin' Good* (Highwater)
Vintage/Reissue Album of the Year: Robert Johnson, *The Complete Recordings of Robert Johnson* (Columbia)
Blues Song of the Year: "Must Be Jelly," William Clarke (Alligator)

Eleventh Annual W.C. Handy Blues Awards (1990)

Blues Entertainer of the Year: Buddy Guy
Traditional Blues—Male Artist of the Year: Sunnyland Slim
Traditional Blues—Female Artist of the Year: Queen Ida
Traditional Blues Album: John Cephas and Phil Wiggins, *Guitar Man* (Flying Fish)
Vintage/Reissue Album (Foreign): *Memphis Days,* Howlin' Wolf (Bear Family)
Vintage/Reissue Album (U.S.): *The Chess Box,* Muddy Waters (MCA/Chess)
Blues Vocalist of the Year: John Lee Hooker
Contemporary Male Blues Artist: John Lee Hooker
Contemporary Female Blues Artist: Koko Taylor
Contemporary Blues Album (U.S.): *The Healer,* John Lee Hooker (Chameleon)
Contemporary Blues Album (Foreign): *Chicago Blues Session—Vol. 10,* Magic Slim (Wolf Records)
Blues Instrumentalist—Guitar: Buddy Guy
Blues Instrumentalist—Harmonica: Charlie Musselwhite
Blues Song of the Year: "The Middle Aged Blues Boogie," Saffire-Gaye Adegbalola (Alligator)
Blues Single of the Year: "Big Leg Women/Cadillac Baby," Sonny Rogers and the Cat Scratchers (Blue Moon)
Blues Band of the Year: Buddy Guy and His Chicago Blues Band

Tenth Annual W.C. Handy Blues Awards (1989)

Blues Song of the Year: "Don't Be Afraid of the Dark," written by Dennis Walker, recorded by Robert Cray
Contemporary Blues Album (U.S.): *Blues at Sunrise,* Albert King (Stax)
Traditional Blues Album (U.S./Foreign): *Gateway to the Delta,* James Son Thomas (Rustron)

Vintage/Reissue (U.S.): *The Chess Box,* Willie Dixon (Chess)
Blues Single of the Year (U.S./Foreign): "Don't Be Afraid of the Dark," written by Dennis Walker, recorded by Robert Cray (High Tone)
Contemporary Album (Foreign): *Blues at the Top,* Buster Benton (Blue-Phoenix)
Vintage/Reissue Album (Foreign): *Mouth Harp Maestro,* Big Walter Horton (Ace/England)
Contemporary Female Blues Artist: Etta James
Contemporary Male Blues Artist: Albert Collins
Traditional Male Blues Artist: John Lee Hooker
Traditional Female Blues Artist: Queen Ida
Blues Vocalist of the Year: Sam Myers
Blues Instrumentalist (Guitar): Albert Collins
Blues Instrumentalist (Miscellaneous): James Cotton, Katie Webster
Blues Band of the Year: Albert Collins and the Icebreakers

Ninth Annual W.C. Handy Blues Awards (1988)

Blues Song of the Year: "Changing Neighborhoods," written by Sam Myers and Anson Funderburgh, recorded by Anson Funderburgh and the Rockets with Sam Myers
Contemporary Blues Album (U.S.): *Sins,* recorded by Anson Funderburgh and the Rockets (Blacktop)
Contemporary Blues Album (Foreign): *Rides Again,* recorded by Lazy Lester (Blue Horizon/England)
Traditional Blues Album (U.S./Foreign): *Giants of Country Blues Guitar 1967–81,* recorded by various artists (Wolf/Austria)
Vintage/Reissue Album (U.S.): *Down and Out Blues,* recorded by Sonny Boy Williamson (Chess)
Vintage/Reissue Album (foreign): *Killing Floor: Masterworks Vol. 5,* recorded by Howlin' Wolf (P-Vine Special-Chess/Japan)
Blues Single of the Year (U.S./Foreign): "Women Look at What You're Doing to Me/Nine Below Zero," recorded by Luther Johnson (Pulsar)
Contemporary Female Blues Artist: Koko Taylor
Contemporary Male Blues Artist: Joe Louis Walker
Traditional Female Blues Artist: Jessie Mae Hemphill
Traditional Male Blues Artist: John Lee Hooker
Blues Vocalist of the Year: Johnny Adams
Blues Instrumentalist (Guitar): Albert Collins
Blues Instrumentalist (Miscellaneous): Sam Myers
Blues Band of the Year: Anson Funderburgh and the Rockets with Sam Myers

Eighth Annual W.C. Handy Blues Awards (1987)

Blues Song of the Year: "Right Next Door (Because of Me)," written by Dennis Walker, recorded by Robert Cray
Contemporary Blues Album (U.S.): *Strong Persuader,* recorded by Robert Cray (Mercury/High Tone)

Contemporary Blues Album (Foreign): *Chicago Blues Sessions Vol. 3*, recorded by Magic Slim (Wolf/Austria)

Traditional Blues Album (U.S./Foreign): *Dog Days of August*, recorded by Bowling Green John Cephas and Harmonica Phil Wiggins (Flying Fish)

Vintage/Reissue Album (U.S.): *Moanin' in the Moonlight*, recorded by Howlin' Wolf (Chess)

Vintage/Reissue Album (Foreign): *Let's Cut It*, recorded by Elmore James (Ace/England)

Blues Single of the Year (U.S./Foreign): "Smoking Gun/Fantasized," recorded by Robert Cray (Mercury/High Tone)

Contemporary Female Blues Artist: Koko Taylor

Contemporary Male Blues Artist: Robert Cray

Traditional Female Blues Artist: Jessie Mae Hemphill

Traditional Male Blues Artist: John Lee Hooker

Blues Vocalist of the Year: Robert Cray

Blues Instrumentalist (Guitar): Albert Collins

Blues Instrumentalist (Harmonica): James Cotton

Blues Band of the Year: Robert Cray Band

Seventh Annual W.C. Handy Blues Awards (1986)

Blues Song of the Year: "False Accusations," written by Deannie Walker, Robert Cray, Richard Cousins; recorded by Robert Cray

Contemporary Blues Album (U.S.): *Showdown*, recorded by Albert Collins, Robert Cray, Johnny Copeland (Alligator Records)

Traditional Blues Album (U.S./Foreign): *Jealous*, recorded by John Lee Hooker (Pausa)

Vintage/Reissue Album (U.S.): *King of the Slide Guitar*, recorded by Elmore James (Kent)

Blues Single of the Year (U.S./Foreign): "Change of Heart/I Got Loaded/Phone Booth/Bad Influence," recorded by Robert Cray (Demon/England)

Contemporary Blues Album of the Year (Foreign): *Live in Europe*, Otis Rush (Isabel/France)

Vintage/Reissue Album of the Year (Foreign): *The Chess Years*, Sonny Boy Williamson (Charly-Chess Box/England)

Contemporary Female Blues Artist: Koko Taylor

Contemporary Male Blues Artist: Robert Cray

Traditional Female Blues Artist: Sippie Wallace

Traditional Male Blues Artist: John Lee Hooker

Blues Vocalist of the Year: Robert Cray

Blues Band of the Year: Fabulous Thunderbirds

Blues Band of the Year (Foreign): Powder Blues

Sixth Annual W.C. Handy Blues Awards (1985)

Blues Entertainer of the Year: Koko Taylor

Blues Vocalist of the Year: Koko Taylor

Contemporary Blues Female Artist of the Year: Koko Taylor

Contemporary Blues Male Artist of the Year: Robert Cray

Traditional Blues Female Artist of the Year: Alberta Hunter

Traditional Blues Male Artist of the Year: John Lee Hooker

Blues Instrumentalist of the Year: Stevie Ray Vaughan

Blues Band of the Year: Albert Collin and the Icebreakers

Blues Song of the Year: "My Toot Toot," written by Sidney Simien

Blues Single of the Year (U.S./Foreign): "My Toot Toot/My Zydeco Shoes," Rockin Sidney (Maison De Soul)

Contemporary Blues Album of the Year (U.S.): *Bad Axe*, Son Seals (Alligator)

Contemporary Blues Album of the Year (Foreign): *I Didn't Give a Damn If Whites Bought It!* Jimmy Johnson/Eddy Clearwater (Red Lighting/England)

Traditional Blues Album of the Year (U.S./Foreign): *Nothin' But the Blues*, Joe Williams (Delos)

Vintage/Reissue Blues Album (U.S.): *Rare and Unissued*, Muddy Waters (Chess)

Vintage/Reissue Blues Album (Foreign): *The Chess Box*, Muddy Waters (Pine Special – Chess/Japan)

Fifth Annual W.C. Handy Blues Awards (1984)

Blues Single of the Year (U.S./Foreign): "Phone Booth," Robert Cray

Contemporary Blues Male Artist of the Year: Robert Cray

Traditional Blues Male Artist of the Year: John Lee Hooker

Contemporary Blues Female Artist of the Year: Koko Taylor

Traditional Blues Female Artist of the Year: Alberta Hunter

Blues Instrumentalist of the Year: Stevie Ray Vaughan

Blues Vocalist of the Year: Z.Z. Hill

Contemporary Blues Album of the Year (U.S.): *Bad Influence*, Robert Cray

Traditional Blues Album of the Year (U.S./Foreign): *New Orleans Piano Professor*, Tuts Washington (Rounder)

Vintage/Reissue Blues Album (U.S.): *The Original Peacock Recordings*, Clarence "Gatemouth" Brown (Rounder)

Vintage/Reissue Blues Album (Foreign): *Nobody Knows Chicago Like I Do*, Otis Spann (Charly/England)

Contemporary Blues Album of the Year (Foreign): *Rockin' the Blues*, Freddie King (Crosscut/Germany)

Fourth Annual W.C. Handy Blues Awards (1983)

Blues Vocalist of the Year: Z.Z. Hill

Contemporary Blues Female Artist of the Year: Koko Taylor

Contemporary Blues Male Artist of the Year: Johnny Copeland

Traditional Blues Female Artist of the Year: Alberta Hunter

Traditional Blues Male Artist of the Year: Louisiana Red

Blues Instrumentalist of the Year: Albert Collins

Blues Song of the Year: "Country Preacher," written and recorded by Jimmy Johnson Band

Blues Single of the Year (U.S. or Foreign): "Got My Mojo Working/Rocket 88," Muddy Waters/Jackie Brentson (Chess)

Contemporary Blues Album of the Year (U.S.): *Don't Lose Your Cool*, Albert Collins (Alligator)

Contemporary Blues Album of the Year (Foreign): *Grand Slam*, Magic Slim and the Teardrops (Rooster Blues/England)

Traditional Blues Album of the Year (U.S./Foreign): *Sippie*, Sippie Wallace (Atlantic)

Vintage/Reissue Blues Album (U.S.): *The OKeh Sessions*, Big Maybelle (Epic)

Vintage/Reissue Blues Album (Foreign): *King of the Slide Guitar*, Elmore James (Ace/England)

Third Annual W.C. Handy Blues Awards (1982)

Male Blues Artist of the Year: Johnny Copeland

Female Blues Artist of the Year: Koko Taylor

Blues Vocalist of the Year: Bobby "Blue" Bland

Blues Instrumentalist of the Year: Clarence "Gatemouth" Brown

Blues Album of the Year (U.S.): *Funny Stuff*, Larry Davis (Rooster Blues)

Blues Album of the Year (Foreign): *Big Brown's Chicago Blues*, Andrew Brown (Black Magic/Holland)

Blues Album of the Year (U.S. or Foreign-Traditional): *Woke Up Screaming*, Buddy Guy and Junior Wells (Isabel/France)

Vintage/Reissue Blues Album (U.S.): *Live*, Magic Sam (Delmark)

Vintage/Reissue Blues Album (Foreign): *Woke Up Screaming*, Bobby "Blue" Bland (Ace/England)

Blues Single of the Year: "Since I Been Loving You/Walk Out Like a Lady," Larry Davis (Rooster Blues)

Blues Song of the Year: "Down Home Blues," written by Memphian, George Jackson; recorded by Z.Z. Hill

Traditional Blues Male Artist of the Year: Robert Jr. Lockwood

Traditional Blues Female Artist of the Year: Sippie Wallace

Classics of Blues: Literature—*Blues and Gospel Records 1902–1942,* by J. Godrich and R.M.W. Dixon; Magazines—*Blues Unlimited* and *Living Blues*

Classics of Blues Recording: *King of the Blues,* Robert Johnson (Columbia)

Blues Promoter of the Year: Purvis Spann

Entertainer of the Year: Bobby "Blue" Bland

Second Annual W.C. Handy Blues Awards (1981)

Entertainer of the Year: B.B. King

Blues Vocalist of the Year: Bobby "Blue" Bland

Blues Instrumentalist of the Year: Albert Collins

Males Blues Artist of the Year: Albert Collins

Female Blues Artist of the Year: Koko Taylor

Blues Album of the Year (Foreign): *London Concert,* Professor Longhair

Blues Album of the Year (U.S.): *Copeland Special,* Johnny Copeland (Rounder Records)

Vintage/Reissue Blues Album (U.S.): *Mardi Gras in New Orleans,* Professor Longhair (Nighthawk Records)

Vintage/Reissue Blues Album (Foreign): *Blues from the Gut,* Champion Jack Dupree (Atlantic Records - Japan)

Blues Single of the Year: "Teardrop," Magic Slim and the Teardrops (Rooster Records)

Special Recognition Awards:

Book: Sheldon Harris, *Bible of the Blues,* D.A. Capo Press International, New York

Book: Dr. David Evans, *Big Road Blues*

Harry Godwin: U.S. Senate naming Memphis the Official Home of the Blues

WLOK-AM Radio: Contribution to the Community

Rufus Thomas: Promotion of the blues in the entertainment field throughout the world

Nancy Ferguson and George Caldwell: Orff and Blues in the Schools programs

George Lindstrom: Developed Blues Brass Band

Abe Schwab: Blues Museum

First Annual W.C. Handy Blues Awards (1980)

Traditional Female Blues Artist: Alberta Hunter

Traditional Male Blues Artist: Lightnin' Hopkins

Contemporary Female Blues Artist: Koko Taylor

Contemporary Male Blues Artist: Albert Collins

Blues Single of the Year: "I Need Some Easy Money," Jimmy Johnson

Traditional Blues Album: *Crawfish Fiesta,* Professor Longhair

Contemporary Blues Album: *Hanging On,* Robert Jr. Lockwood and Johnny Shines

Vintage/Reissue Album: *Live on Maxwell Street— 1964*

Special Recognition Awards for creating and preserving the blues:

Sam Phillips, Little Laura Dukes, Rufus Thomas, Jim Stewart, Evelyn Young, Dave Clark, Paul Savarin, Nat D. Williams, Furry Lewis, Otto Lee, Sunbeam Mitchell, A.C. Williams, Harry Godwin,

Memphis Slim, Ma Rainey II, Grandma Dixie
Davis, Ironing Board Sam, Hammie Nixon, Mrs.
Van Zula Hunt, Mose Vinson.
Special Presentations:
WMC-FM/WMC-TV: Supporting Memphis Music
through station advertising

PBS: (series) *From Jumpstreet,* programs on the
blues
Jim and Amy O'Neal: Founders of *Living Blues*
magazine

BLUES HALL OF FAME

Since its inception in 1980, the Blues Foundation, a Memphis-based nonprofit organization dedicated to preserving and promoting the blues, has inducted new members into the Blues Hall of Fame in five categories: performers, nonperformers, classics of blues literature, classics of blues recordings (single), and classics of blues recordings (album). The following are the Hall of Fame inductees from 1980 to 1999.

Performers

Luther Allison
Chuck Berry
Blind Blake
Bobby "Blue" Bland
Big Bill Broonzy
Charles Brown
Clarence "Gatemouth" Brown
Roy Brown
Leroy Carr
Ray Charles
Clifton Chenier
Albert Collins
Arthur "Big Boy" Crudup
Willie Dixon
Champion Jack Dupree
David "Honeyboy" Edwards
Sleepy John Estes
Lowell Fulson
Buddy Guy
Slim Harpo
Wynonie Harris
John Lee Hooker
Lightnin' Hopkins
Big Walter Horton
Son House
Howlin' Wolf
J.B. Hutto
Elmore James
Skip James
Blind Lemon Jefferson
Lonnie Johnson
Robert Johnson
Tommy Johnson
Louis Jordan
Albert King
B.B. King
Freddie King
Leadbelly
Robert Jr. Lockwood

Little Walter
Magic Sam
Percy Mayfield
Fred McDowell
Brownie McGhee
Jay McShann
Blind Willie McTell
Memphis Minnie
Memphis Slim
Little Milton
Mississippi John Hurt
Muddy Waters
Robert Nighthawk
Johnny Otis
Charley Patton
Professor Longhair
Ma Rainey
Jimmy Reed
Otis Rush
Johnny Shines
Bessie Smith
Otis Spann
Roosevelt Sykes
Tampa Red
Jimmy Rogers
Eddie Taylor
Hound Dog Taylor
Koko Taylor
Sonny Terry
Big Momma Thornton
Big Joe Turner
Stevie Ray Vaughn
T-Bone Walker
Junior Wells
Bukka White
Big Joe Williams
Sonny Boy Williamson #1 (John Lee Williamson)
Sonny Boy Williamson #2 (Rice Miller)
Johnny Winter

Nonperformers

Bill "Hoss" Allen
Leonard Chess
Phil Chess
Bruce Iglauer
Bob Koester
Alan Lomax
John Lomax
Lillian Shedd McMurry
Lester Melrose
Gene Nobles
Sam Phillips
John "R" Richbourg
Chris Strachwitz
Dick Waterman
Pete Welding

Classics of Blues Literature

Big Bill Blues, by Bill Broonzy and Yannick
   Bruynoghe
Big Road Blues, by Dr. David Evans
Blues and Gospel Records 1902–1942, by J. Godrich
   and R.M.W. Dixon
Blues from the Delta, by William Ferris
Blues Records 1943–1966, by Mike Leadbetter and
   Neil Slaven
Blues Who's Who, by Sheldon Harris
Chicago Breakdown (Chicago Blues), by Mike Rowe
Conversation with the Blues, by Paul Oliver
Country Blues, by Sam Charters
Deep Blues, by Robert Palmer
Feel Like Going Home, by Peter Guralnick
*Honkers and Shouters: The Golden Years of Rhythm
   and Blues,* by Arnold Shaw
I Am the Blues, by Willie Dixon and Don Snowden
The Land Where the Blues Began, by Alan Lomax
Nothing But the Blues, by Lawrence Cohn
Searching for Robert Johnson, by Peter Guralnick
Sweet Soul Music, by Peter Guralnick
The Story of the Blues, by Paul Oliver
The World Don't Owe Me Nothing, by David
   "Honeyboy" Edwards
Urban Blues, by Charles Keil

Classics of Blues Recordings (Singles)
(1920 to present)

"Baby Please Don't Go" (Bluebird), Big Joe Williams
"Baby Scratch My Back" (Excello), Slim Harpo
"Big Boss Man" (VeeJay), Jimmy Reed
"Big Road Blues" (Victor), Tommy Johnson
"Boogie Chillen" (Modem), John Lee Hooker
"Call It Stormy Monday" (Black & White), T-Bone
   Walker
"Come On in My Kitchen" (ARC), Robert Johnson
"Cross Road Blues" (ARC), Robert Johnson

"Dark Was the Night" (Vocalion), Blind Willie
   Johnson
"Don't Start Me Talkin'" (Chess), Sonny Boy
   Williamson #2
"Down Home Blues" (Malaco), Z.Z. Hill
"Driftin' Blues" (Exclusive), Charles Brown
"Dust My Broom" (Trumpet), Elmore James
"Good Morning Little School Girl" (Bluebird), John
   Lee, Sonny Boy Williamson, and Big Joe Williams
"Got My Mojo Working" (Chess), Muddy Waters
"Hell Hound on My Trail" (ARC), Robert Johnson
"Help Me" (Chess), Sonny Boy Williamson #2
"I Can't Quit You Baby" (Cobra), Otis Rush
"I'm a King Bee" (Excello), Slim Harpo
"I'm Your Hoochie Coochie Man" (Chess), Muddy
   Waters
"I'm Ready" (Chess), Muddy Waters
"Juke" (Checker), Little Walter
"The Killing Floor" (Chess), Howlin' Wolf
"Long Distance Call" (Chess), Muddy Waters
"Manish Boy" (Chess), Muddy Waters
"Messin' with the Kid" (Vanguard), Junior Wells
"Nine Below Zero" (Trumpet), Sonny Boy
   Williamson #2
"Please Send Me Someone to Love" (Specialty), Percy
   Mayfield
"Reconsider Baby" (Checker), Lowell Fulson
"Rocket 88" (Chess), Jackie Brentson
"The Sky Is Crying" (Fire), Elmore James
"Smokestack Lightning" (Chess), Howlin' Wolf
"Statesboro Blues" (Victor), Blind Willie McTell
"Sweet Home Chicago" (Vocalion), Robert Johnson
"Terraplane Blues" (ARC), Robert Johnson
"The Things That I Used To Do" (Specialty), Guitar
   Slim
"The Thrill Is Gone" (ABC Bluesway), B.B. King
"Wang Dang Doodle" (MCA/Chess), Koko Taylor
"Worried Life Blues" (Bluebird), Big Maceo

Classics of Blues Recordings (Albums)

A.K.A. Howlin' Wolf (Chess), Howlin' Wolf
The Best of Bobby "Blue" Bland (Duke), Bobby
   "Blue" Bland
Black Magic (Delmark), Magic Slim
Blues Before Sunrise (Columbia), Leroy Carr
Blues from the Gutter (Atlantic), Champion Jack Dupree
Blues Hit Big Town (United), Junior Wells
Born Under a Bad Sign/Livewire Blues Power (Stax),
   Albert King
Boss Blues Harmonica (Chess), Little Walter
Boss of the Blues (Atlantic), Big Joe Turner
Paul Butterfield Blues Band (Elektra), Paul Butterfield
   Blues Band
The Chess Box Set (MCA), Willie Dixon
Chicago Bound (Chess), Jimmy Rogers
Chicago, the Blues Today (Vanguard), various artists

Father of Folk Blues (Columbia), Son House
Founder of the Delta Blues (Yazoo), Charley Patton
Hideaway (King), Freddie King
Hoodoo Man Blues (Delmark), Junior Wells
Hound Dog Taylor and the Houserockers (Alligator),
  Hound Dog Taylor and the Houserockers
I Am the Blues (Columbia), Willie Dixon
Ice Pickin' (Alligator), Albert Collins
I'll Play the Blues for You (Stax), Albert King
King of the Delta Blues Singers Vols. I and II
  (Columbia), Robert Johnson
The Best of Little Walter (MCA/Chess), Little Walter
Live on Maxwell Street—1964 (Rounder), Robert
  Nighthawk
Live at the Regal (ABC), B.B. King
Mississippi Delta Blues (Arhoolie), "Mississippi,"
  Fred McDowell
The Muddy Waters Box Set (MCA/Chess), Muddy Waters

The Best of Muddy Waters and McKinley Morgan-
  field/a.k.a. Muddy Waters (Chess), Muddy Waters
Otis Span Is the Blues (Candid), Otis Span
Parchman Farm (Columbia), Bukka White
Right Place, Wrong Time (High Tone), Otis Rush
Robert Johnson, the Complete Recordings (Columbia),
  Robert Johnson
Showdown (Alligator), Albert Collins/Robert
  Cray/Johnny Copeland
Skip James—the Complete 1931 Session (Yazoo), Skip
  James
The Complete T-Bone Walker, 1940–1954 (Cobra),
  T-Bone Walker
West Side Soul (Delmark), Magic Sam
The World's Greatest Blues Singer (Columbia), Bessie
  Smith
Two Steps from the Blues (Duke), Bobby "Blue" Bland

LIFETIME ACHIEVEMENT AWARDS

*S*ince 1995 the Blues Foundation has awarded Lifetime Achievement Awards to the following individuals:
  B.B. King, John Lee Hooker, Jerry Wexler, Bobby "Blue" Bland, Ahmet Ertegun, Ray Charles, Etta
James, Koko Taylor, and Ruth Brown. (List current to 2000.)

FOLK ALLIANCE LIFETIME ACHIEVEMENT AWARDS

*T*he North American Folk Music and Dance Alliance began in January 1989, when Elaine and Clark Weissman of the California Traditional Music Society invited 125 people to a retreat in Malibu to discuss the
formation of a coalition of folk organizers. The assemblage included members of the Philadelphia Folksong Society, *Sing Out!*, the Vancouver Folk Festival, Chicago's Old Town School of Folk Music, the California Traditional
Music Society, Charlotte's Fiddle and Bow Society, the International Bluegrass Music Association, the Augusta
Heritage Center, and Woods Music and Dance Camp, among others. The group set forth some bylaws in Philadelphia and thus created the North American Folk Music and Dance Alliance in January 1990.

Since then, the Folk Alliance has held conferences in Chicago (January 1991), Calgary (January 1992), Tucson
(February 1993), Boston (February 1994), Portland, Oregon (February 1995), Washington, D.C. (February 1996),
Toronto (February 1997), Memphis (February 1998), and Albuquerque (February 1999). Conferences are sched-
uled for Cleveland in 2000, Vancouver in 2001, and Pittsburgh in 2002.

Each year the Folk Alliance selects up to three honorees for its Lifetime Achievement Award. The awards are
presented to individuals or organizations who have had a significant impact on the field of folk music and dance,
and whose work has inspired a continuation of the voice of folk music and dance in society.

Award Recipients:

	Performers	Business/Organization
1995:	Pete Seeger	Alan Lomax
1996:	Woody Guthrie	Moe Asch, founder Folkways Records
1997:	Bruce "Utah" Phillips	Chris Strachwitz, founder Arhoolie Records
1998:	Jean Ritchie Huddie Ledbetter	American Folklife Center, Library of Congress
1999:	Bernice Johnson Reagon, the Carter Family	Anne and Frank Warner
2000:	Doc Watson Dewey Balfa	Edith Fowke
2001:	Paul Robeson Lydia Mendoza	Ralph Rinzler

FOLK ALLIANCE SHOWCASES

*W*hat follows is a list of folk music and dance performers who have been featured at the Folk Alliance Conferences:

First Formational Conference—Malibu, California, 1989

Mark Graham and Sandy Silva (U.S.)
Keith and Rusty MacNeil (U.S.)
Madelaine MacNeil (U.S.)
Sukay (U.S./Latin America)

Second Annual Conference—Philadelphia, Pennsylvania, 1990 (partial list)

Fiddlepuppets (U.S.)
Jane Gilman (U.S.)
Ginny Hawker (U.S.)
Hesperus (U.S.)
James Keelaghan (Canada)
Anne Lederman (Canada)

Third Annual Conference—Chicago, Illinois, 1991

Kwasi Aduonum (U.S./Ghana)
Anderson and Brown (Canada)
Howard Armstrong (U.S.)
Ralph Blizzard (U.S.)
Guy Carawan (U.S.)
Iris Dement (U.S.)
Kitty Donohoe (U.S.)
Marie-Lynn Hammond (Canada)
Robert Earl Keen Jr. (U.S.)
Eileen McGann (Canada)
Lynn Morris Band (U.S.)
Bill Morrissey (U.S.)
Joel Mabus (U.S.)
David MacIsaac (Canada)
Cathy Miller (Canada)
Lee Murdock (U.S.)
The Polish Highlanders (U.S.)
Raices del Ande (U.S./Bolivia)
Tanushree Sarkar and Ustad Tari Kahn (U.S./India)
Carla Sciaky (U.S.)
Sotavento (U.S./Latin America)
Jody Stecher and Kate Brislin (U.S.)
Sugar Blue (U.S.)
Tamarack (Canada)

Fourth Annual Conference—Calgary, Alberta, 1992

Ad Vielle Que Pourra (Canada)
Sarah Bauhan (U.S.)
Tony Bird (South Africa)
Bourne and MacLeod (Canada)
Howie Burnsen (U.S.)

Cooper and Nelson (U.S.)
Darcie Deaville (U.S.)
Theresa Doyle (Canada)
Great Western Orchestra (Canada)
Hoag and Sagan (U.S.)
Juba (Canada)
Laurie Lewis and Grant Street (U.S.)
Oscar Lopez (Canada/Chile)
Mad Love (Canada)
Masterson and Blackburn (U.S.)
Dave Moore (U.S.)
Pete Morton (U.K.)
Ann Reed (U.S.)
Lesley Schatz (Canada)
Laura Smith (Canada)
Chris Smither (U.S.)
Aileen Vance (U.S.)
Bobby Watt (Canada/Scotland)
David Wilcox (U.S.)

Fifth Annual Conference—Tucson, Arizona, 1993

Antonia Apodaca (U.S.)
Austin Lounge Lizards (U.S.)
Ira Bernstein (U.S.)
Anita Best and Pamela Morgan (Canada)
Sophia Bilides (U.S.)
Don Charles and Deb Gessner (U.S.)
Margaret Christi (U.S./Scotland)
Freyda and the Atta Boys (U.S.)
Flying Bulgar Klezmer Band (Canada)
Bob Franke (U.S.)
Steve Gillette and Cindy Mangsen (U.S.)
Good Ol' Persons (U.S.)
Tish Hinojosa (U.S.)
David Holt (U.S.)
Alain LaMontagne (Canada)
Lewis, Pint, and Dale (Canada)
Nosotros (U.S./Mexico)
Queztalcoatl (Latin America)
Nat Reese (U.S.)
Mike Seeger (U.S.)
Uzume Taiko (Canada)

Sixth Annual Conference—Boston, Massachusetts, 1994

Bird Sisters (Canada)
Wild Child Butler (Canada)
The Dorkestra (U.S.)
Flor de Caña (U.S./Latin America)

Fourin A Feire (U.S.)
Stanley Greenthal (U.S.)
Peter Keane (U.S.)
Loose Ties (U.S.)
The Mendes Brother (Cape Verde)
Lynn Miles (Canada)
Karen Mueller (U.S.)
The New St. George (U.S.)
Ouzo Power (Canada)
Tom Paxton (U.S.)
John Roberts and Tony Barrand (U.S./U.K.)
Garnet Rogers (Canada)
Tommy Sands (Ireland)
Fred Small (U.S.)
Tip Splinter (Canada)
Tolino (Puerto Rico)
The Vanaver Caravan (U.S.)
Zhentian Zhang (U.S./China)
Zlatne Uste Balkan Brass Band (U.S.)

Seventh Annual Conference—Portland, Oregon, 1995

The Billys (U.S.)
Kevin Burke's Open House (U.S.)
Cornerstone (U.S.)
Catie Curtis (U.S.)
Pat Donohue (U.S.)
Irene Farrerra (U.S.)
Ferron (Canada)
The Five Chinese Brothers (U.S.)
Cate Friesen (Canada)
Laura Love Band (U.S.)
Marley's Ghost (U.S.)
Dannielle Martineau et Rockabayou (Canada)
Rory McLeod (U.K.)
Carrie Newcomer (U.S.)
Willy Porter (U.S.)
Janet Russell and Christine Kydd (Scotland)
The Oliver Schroer Band (Canada)
Silk Road (Canada/China)
Ernie Sites (U.S.)
Lora and Sukutai Marimaba Ensemble (U.S.)
Trout Fishing in America (U.S.)
Dar Williams (U.S.)
Word of Mouth (U.S.)

Eighth Annual Conference—Washington, D.C., 1996

Alter Ego (Canada)
Charlotte Blake Alston (U.S.)
Roy Book Binder (U.S.)
Cordelia's Dad (U.S.)
Dan Crary (U.S.)
Footworks (U.S.)
The Foremen (U.S.)
The Gospel Pearls (U.S.)
Hapa (U.S.)

Helicon (U.S.)
Ginny Hawker and Kay Justice (U.S.)
Connie Kaldor (Canada)
Mary Jane Lamond (Canada)
Katy Moffatt (U.S.)
The Lynn Morris Band (U.S.)
La Musgaña (Spain)
Mystic Warriors (U.S./South America)
The Nile Ethiopian Ensemble (U.S./Ethiopia)
Bonnie Rideout (U.S.)
Steve Riley and the Mamou Playboys (U.S.)
Satan and Adam (U.S.)
Athena Tergis and Laura Risk (U.S.)
Three Sheets to the Wind (Canada)
Brooks Williams (U.S.)

Ninth Annual Conference—Toronto, Ontario, 1997

Les Barker (U.K.)
Bourque and Bernard (Canada)
Kate Campbell (U.S.)
Famous Steve Denyes (U.S.)
Alpha Yaya Diallo (Canada/Guinea)
Dinastia Hedalguense (Mexico)
Fred J. Eaglesmith (Canada)
Stephen Fearing (Canada)
Flying Bulgar Klezmer Band (Canada)
La Galvaude (Canada)
Edward Gerhard (U.S.)
Vance Gilbert (U.S.)
Molly Johnson (Canada)
Barbara Kessler (U.S.)
Malaika (Canada)
Nazka (Canada)
The Paperboys (Canada)
Murray Porter (Canada)
Quartette (Canada)
Salamander Crossing (U.S.)
Martin Sexton (U.S.)
Sin E (U.K.)
Christina Smith and Jean Hewson (Canada)
Sons of the Never Wrong (U.S.)
Hans Theessink and Blue Groove (U.S.)
Trilogy (Canada)
UHF (Canada)
Jackie Washington (Canada)
David Wilkie and Cowboy Celtic (Canada)

Tenth Anniversary Conference—Memphis, Tennessee, 1998

Anam (Ireland)
Artisan (England)
Asza (Canada)
Balfa Toujours (U.S.)
Ira Bernstein (U.S.)
Keith Brown (U.S.)

J.P. Cormier (Canada)
Mike Dowling (U.S.)
Tony Ellis (U.S.)
Corey Harris (U.S.)
Bruce Molksy (U.S.)
Blind Mississippi Morris (U.S.)
Nickel Creek with Chris Thile (U.S.)
Ellis Paul (U.S.)
Eddie Pennington (U.S.)
Seanachie (Canada)
Sid Selvidge (U.S.)
Jo Serrapere (U.S.)
Cosy Sheridan (U.S.)
Sones de Mexico Ensemble (Mexico via Chicago)
Louise Taylor (U.S.)
Don Walser and the Pure Texas Band (U.S.)

Eleventh Annual Conference—Albuquerque, New Mexico, 1999

Terri Allard (U.S.)
Barachois (Canada)
Robin Bullock (U.S.)
Dave Carter with Tracy Grammer (U.S.)
Carlos del Junco Band (Canada)
Todd Denman (U.S.)
Frifot (Sweden)
Annie Gallup (U.S.)
Sid Hausman (U.S.)
Hedzoleh Soundz (Ghana)
Hot Club of Cowtown (U.S.)
Ray Wylie Hubbard (U.S.)
JPP (Finland)
Joel Mabus (U.S.)
Los Matachines de Bernalillo (U.S.)
Peter Mulvey (U.S.)
Mollie O'Brien (U.S.)
Pierce Pettis (U.S.)
Dana Robinson (U.S.)
Sourdough Slim (U.S.)
Cipriano Vigil and Family (U.S.)

Susan Werner (U.S.)
The Westerleys (U.S.)
Johnny Whelan (U.S.)
Whirligig (U.S.)
Wylie and the Wild West (U.S.)
The Wyrd Sisters (Canada)

Twelfth Annual Conference—Cleveland, Ohio, 2000

Alex Bevan (U.S.)
Catfish Keith (U.S.)
Cleveland Junior Tamburitzana (U.S.)
Maria Dunn (Canada)
Judith Edelman Band (U.S.)
Adie Grey (U.S.)
HillBilly Idol (U.S.)
David Holt (U.S.)
Inca Son (U.S./Andes)
Kathy Kallick (U.S.)
Jimmy LaFave (U.S.)
Dean Magraw (U.S.)
David Mallett (U.S.)
Bill Miller (U.S.)
The Mollys (U.S.)
Dave Moore (U.S.)
Nerissa & Katryna Nields (U.S.)
Tom Russell (U.S.)
Takadja (Canada/West Africa)
The Joey Tomsick Orchestra (U.S.)
Volo Bogtrotters (U.S.)
Yiddishe Cup Klezmer Band (U.S.)
The Zeke and Charlie Band (U.S.)

For more information about the Folk Alliance, contact:
Folk Alliance
1001 Connecticut Avenue, NW
Suite 501
Washington, D.C. 20036-5504
Phone: 202-835-3655; Fax: 202-835-3656
Executive Director: Phyllis Barney
E-mail: fa@folk.org

THE INTERNATIONAL BLUEGRASS MUSIC AWARDS

*T*he International Bluegrass Music Association, founded in 1985, is a nonprofit professional trade organization created to advance the recognition of bluegrass music. IBMA's worldwide membership is composed of artists, songwriters, record companies, event producers, print and broadcast media reps, associations, agents, educators, and bluegrass fans from all fifty United States and twenty-nine additional countries.

Hall of Honor Inductees

Bill Monroe—1991
Earl Scruggs—1991
Lester Flatt—1991
The Stanley Brothers, Carter and Ralph—1992

Don Reno and Arthur Lee "Red" Smiley—1992
Mac Wiseman—1993
Jim and Jesse McReynolds—1993
The Osborne Brothers—1994
Jimmy Martin—1995

"The Classic" Country Gentlemen—1996
Peter V. Kuykendall—1996
Josh Graves—1997
Carlton Haney and Chubby Wise—1998
Kenny Baker—1999

Entertainer of the Year

Hot Rize—1990
Alison Krauss and Union Station—1991, 1995
The Nashville Bluegrass Band—1992, 1993
Del McCoury—1996
The Del McCoury Band—1994, 1997, 1998, 1999

Vocal Group of the Year

The Nashville Bluegrass Band—1990, 1991, 1992, 1993
IIIrd Tyme Out—1994, 1995, 1996, 1997, 1998

Instrumental Group of the Year

The Bluegrass Album Band—1990
California—1992, 1993, 1994
The Tony Rice Unit—1991, 1995
The Del McCoury Band—1996, 1997
Ricky Skaggs and Kentucky Thunder—1998, 1999

Female Vocalist of the Year

Laurie Lewis—1992, 1994
Alison Krauss—1990, 1991, 1993, 1995
Lynn Morris—1996, 1998, 1999
Claire Lynch—1997

Male Vocalist of the Year

Del McCoury—1990, 1991, 1992, 1996
Tim O'Brien—1993
Russell Moore—1994, 1997
Ronnie Bowman—1995, 1998, 1999

Song of the Year

"Little Mountain Church," Doyle Lawson and Quicksilver (artists), Jim Rushing and Carl Jackson (songwriters)—1990
"Colleen Malone," Hot Rize (artists), Pete Goble and Leroy Drumm (songwriters)—1991
"Blue Train," Nashville Bluegrass Band (artists), Dave Allen (songwriter)—1992
"Lonesome Standard Time," Lonesome Standard Time (artists), Larry Cordle and Jim Rushing (songwriters)—1993
"Who Will Watch the Home Place," Laurie Lewis (artist), Kate Long (songwriter)—1994
"Cold Virginia Night," Ronnie Bowman (artist), Timmy Massey (songwriter)—1995
"Mama's Hand," Lynn Morris (artist), Hazel Dickens (songwriter)—1996

"High Lonesome Sound," Vince Gill with Alison Krauss and Union Station (artists), Vince Gill (songwriter)—1997
"Lonesome Old Home," Longview (artist), Ed Hamilton (songwriter)—1998

Album of the Year

At the Old Schoolhouse, The Johnson Mountain Boys, Rounder—1990
I've Got that Old Feeling, Alison Kraus and Union Station, Rounder—1991
Carrying the Tradition, the Lonesome River Band, Rebel—1992
Every Time You Say Goodbye, Alison Krauss and Union Station, Rounder—1993
A Deeper Shade of Blue, Del McCoury, Rounder—1994
Cold Virginia Night, Ronnie Bowman, Rebel—1995
It's a Long, Long Road, Blue Highway, Rebel—1996
True Life Blues—the Songs of Bill Monroe, Sam Bush, Vassar Clements, Mike Compton, Jerry Douglas, Stuart Duncan, Pat Enright, Greg Garing, Richard Greene, David Grier, David Grisman, John Hartford, Bobby Hicks, Kathy Kallick, Laurie Lewis, Mike Marshall, Del McCoury, Ronnie McCoury, Jim Nunally, Scott Nygaard, Mollie O'Brien, Tim O'Brien, Alan O'Bryant, Herb Pedersen, Todd Phillips, John Reischman, Peter Rowan, Craig Smith, Chris Thile, Tony Trischka, Roland White; Sugar Hill Records—1997
Bluegrass Rules!, Ricky Skaggs and Kentucky Thunder; produced by Ricky Skaggs, Skaggs Family/Rounder Records—1998
Clinch Mountain Country, Ralph Stanley & Friends, produced by Bil Vorn Dick, Rebel Records–1999

Instrumental Album of the Year

The Masters, Adcock, Baker, Graves, and McReynolds, CMH—1990
Norman Blake & Tony Rice—2, Norman Blake and Tony Rice, Rounder—1991
Slide Rule, Jerry Douglas, Sugar Hill—1992
Stuart Duncan, Stuart Duncan, Rounder—1993
Skip, Hop and Wobble, Douglas, Barenberg, and Meyer, Sugar Hill—1994
The Great Dobro Sessions, Various Artists, Sugar Hill—1995
Ronnie and Rob McCoury, Ronnie and Rob McCoury, Rounder—1996
Bluegrass Instrumentals, Volume 6, the Bluegrass Album Band, Rounder—1997
Fiddle Patch, Bobby Hicks; produced by Bobby Hicks and Traci Todd—1998
Bound to Ride, Jim Mills, produced by Jim Mills, Sugar Hill—1999

Recorded Event of the Year

Classic Country Gents Reunion, Duffey, Waller, Adcock, and Gray, Sugar Hill—1990
Families of Tradition, Parmley and McCoury, BGC—1991
Slide Rule, Jerry Douglas, Sugar Hill—1992
Saturday Night and Sunday Morning, Ralph Stanley and Special Guests, Freeland Recordings—1993
A Touch of the Past, Larry Perkins and Friends, Pinecastle Records—1994
The Great Dobro Sessions, Various Artists, Sugar Hill—1995
Bluegrass '95, Vestal, Haynie, Steffey, Benson, Bales, and Jones; Pinecastle Records—1996
True Life Blues—the Songs of Bill Monroe, Sugar Hill Records—1997
Longview, Longview; produced by Ken Irwin and Longview, Rounder Records—1998
Clinch Mountain Country, Ralph Stanley & Friends, produced by Bil Vorn Dick, Rebel Records–1999

Gospel Recorded Performance of the Year

One Beautiful Day, Front Range, Sugar Hill—1995
There's a Light Guiding Me, Doyle Lawson and Quicksilver, Sugar Hill—1996
"God Moves in a Windstorm," from the album *Wind to the West,* Blue Highway, Rebel—1997
Stanley Gospel Tradition: Songs about Our Savior, featuring Tim Austin, Barry Bales, Ronnie Bowman, Aubrey Haynie, James King, Dwight McCall, Dale Perry, Don Rigsby, James Shelton, Junior Sisk, Charlie Sizemore, Craig Smith, Steve Sparks, Adam Steffey, Ernie Thacker, and Dan Tyminski; produced by Tim Austin and Dan Tyminski, Doobie Shea Records—1998
"Three Rusty Nails, from *The Man I'm Tryin' to Be,* Ronnie Boroman, Sugar Hill—1999

Emerging Artist of the Year

Lou Reid, Terry Baucom, and Carolina—1994
David Parmley, Scott Vestal, and Continental Divide—1995
Blue Highway—1996
The James King Band—1997
The Gibson Brothers—1998
Mountain Heart—1999

Instrumental Performers of the Year

Banjo

Béla Fleck—1990
Alison Brown—1991
Tom Adams—1992, 1993
J.D. Crowe—1994
Scott Vestal—1996 (tie)

Sammy Shelor—1995, 1996 (tie), 1997, 1998
Jim Mills—1999

Guitar

David Grier—1992, 1993, 1995
Tony Rice—1990, 1991, 1994, 1996, 1997
Kenny Smith—1998, 1999

Fiddle

Stuart Duncan—1990, 1991, 1992, 1993, 1994, 1995, 1996
Jason Carter—1997, 1998
Randy Howard—1999

Bass

Roy Huskey Jr.—1990, 1991, 1992, 1993
Mark Schatz—1994, 1995
Mike Bub—1996, 1997
Missy Raines—1998, 1999

Dobro

Jerry Douglas—1990, 1991, 1992, 1993, 1994, 1995
Rob Ickes—1996, 1997, 1998, 1999

Mandolin

Sam Bush—1990, 1991, 1992
Ronnie McCoury—1993, 1994, 1995, 1996, 1997, 1998, 1999

Print Media Personality

Art Menius, *International Bluegrass*—1990
Peter V. Kuykendall, *Bluegrass Unlimited*—1991
Hub Nitchie, *Banjo Newsletter*—1992
Edward Morris, *Billboard*—1993
John Wright, author—1994
Frank Godbey, Bgrass-L, writer—1995
Wayne Bledsoe, *Bluegrass Now*—1996
Murphy Henry, *Women in Bluegrass Newsletter, Banjo Newsletter, Bluegrass Unlimited*—1997
Saburo Watanabe Inoue, *Moonshiner Magazine*—1998
Walt Saunders, *Bluegrass Unlimited*—1999

Broadcast Personality

Orin Friesen, KFDI—1990
Lee Michael Demsey, WAMU—1991
Dell Davis, KVOO—1992
Col. Tom Riggs, ABN Group—1993
Frank Javorsek, KCSN—1994
Wayne Rice, KSON—1995
Eddie Stubbs, WSM—1996
Bill Knowlton, WNCY—1997
Terry Herd, Bluegrass Radio Network—1998
Gary Henderson, WAMU—1999

Graphic Design—Recorded Project

I Got a Bullfrog: Folksongs for the Fun of It, David Holt, High Windy Audio—1994

Old Time, New Times, Benton Flippen, Rounder—1995

Lonesome and Then Some, James King, Rounder—1996

Hogs on the Highway, the Bad Livers, Sugar Hill—1997

Midnight Storm, Blue Highway, Craig Henson (designer) Rebel Records—1998

Restless on the Farm, Jerry Douglas (artist), Sue Meyer (designer) Sugar Hill—1999

Liner Notes—Recorded Project

Don Reno and Red Smiley: 1951–1959, King Records/IMG—1994

Hazel and Alice, Hazel Dickens and Alice Gerrard, Rounder—1995

Lonesome and Then Some, James King, Rounder—1996

Watson Country, Doc and Merle Watson, Flying Fish—1997

Country Gentlemen: The Early Recordings 1962–1971, Gary B. Reid (writer), Rebel Records—1999

Award of Merit Recipients/Distinquished Achievement Award

1986

Albert E. Brumley
Ray Davis
Bill Monroe
Ruby Baker Moody
Cuzin' Isaac Page
Dr. Neil V. Rosenberg

1987

Dewitt "Snuffy" Jenkins
Bill Jones
Don Owens
Ralph Rinzler
Charlie Waller

1988

John Duffey
Tom Henderson
Peter V. Kuykendall
Ola Belle Reed
Earl Scruggs
Bill Vernon

1989

Lester Flatt
David Freeman

Kathy Kaplan
Robert Larkin
Dr. Bill C. Malone

1990

Carlton Haney
Wade Mainer
Joe Stuart
Dr. Charles Wolfe

1991

Ralph Epperson
Don Stover
The Blue Sky Boys (Bill and Earl Bolick)

1992

The Louvin Brothers (Charlie and Ira)
Bill Clifton
Lloyd Loar
Burkett "Uncle Josh" Graves

1993

Curly Ray Cline
Hazel Dickens
Jim Eanes
Charles Richard Freeland

1994

Wilma Lee Cooper
Lance LeRoy
Ken Irwin
Johnnie Wright and Jack Anglin

1995

Rose Maddox
Mike Seeger
Joe Val
Toshio and Saburo Watanabe

1996

Curly Seckler
George Shuffler
The Martha White Flour Company
G.B. Grayson

1997

Mary Tyler Doub
Vern Williams and Ray Park
Kenny Baker
Benny Martin

1998

Ed Ferris, bass player
Barry Poss, Sugar Hill Records
Gary Ferguson, radio broadcaster
Bob and Jean Cornett, festival promoters

1999

The Martin Guitar Company
Lee Moore, radio broadcaster
Carl Pagter, event producer
Gloria Belle, vocalist & multi-instrumentalist

For more information about the IBMA, contact:
IBMA
207 E. Second Street
Owensboro, KY 42303
Phone: 270-684-9025, 888-GET-IBMA
Fax: 270-686-7863
E-mail: ibmal@occ-uky.campus.mci.net

Dan Hays, Executive Director
Nancy Cardwell, Special Projects Coordinator
Susan Cooke, Member Services/Convention Services

ASSOCIATION FOR INDEPENDENT MUSIC

*A*FIM (formerly known as the National Association of Independent Record Distributors) was founded in 1972 by a handful of labels and distributors. Initially the primary goal of the group was to establish channels for effective communication regarding the issue of independent distribution. Today, this is still a top priority. In addition, AFIM is dedicated to stimulating growth and promoting the independent recording industry. Other goals include addressing issues of importance to and improving communication among all segments of the independent music industry, identifying and promoting cooperative activities for the independent music industry, publicizing the achievements and activities of the independent music industry, and educating the members on how to succeed in the music industry.

HALL OF FAME

*T*he Independent Music Hall of Fame was established in 1987 by the NAIRD board as a way of recognizing persons who have made significant and lasting contributions to independent music. Each year, the board has selected a person or persons involved primarily with the business aspects of the industry and one recording artist or group.

1987: Moses Asch, Folkways Records; Kate Wolf, Kaleidoscope Records (posthumously)
1988: Sam Phillips, Sun Records; Clifton Chenier, King of Zydeco (posthumously)
1989: Ahmet Ertegun, Atlantic Records; Pete Seeger, activist/singer-songwriter
1990: George Hocutt, California Record Distributors Inc.; Creedence Clearwater Revival, Fantasy Records
1991: Gene Norman, GNP Crescendo Records; Little Richard, Specialty Records
1992: Huey P. Meaux, producer/Crazy Cajun Music; George Thorogood, Rounder Records

1993: Bruce Kaplan, Flying Fish (posthumously); Arthel "Doc" Watson, guitarist, singer
1994: Lillian S. McMurry, Trumpet Records; Albert Collins, Alligator Records (posthumously)
1995: Chris Strachwitz, Arhoolie Records; Jerry Garcia, Grateful Dead Records
1996: Hy Weiss, Old Town Records; Sylvia Robinson, Sugar Hill Records
1997: Jerry and Sunny Richman, Richard Brothers Records; Professor Longhair, pianist (posthumously)
1998: Leonard, Phil, and Marshall Chess, Chess Records; Junior Wells, bluesman

THE INDIE AWARDS

*E*ach year the AFIM presents "Indies" to outstanding performers in various categories. After 1997, when NAIRD changed its name to AFIM, they became known as the AFIM Indie Awards. (*Note:* there are no winners listed for 1996. That was the year AFIM changed the designation from the release year to the presentation year. So the 1997 Indies were actually released during the 1996 calendar year.)

Acoustic Instrumental

1994—*Broken Silence,* by Dean Magraw on Red House Records

1995—*Heart of the Heartland,* by Peter Ostroushko on Red House Records

1997—*DGQ-20,* by the David Grisman Quintet on Red House Records

1998—*Cool and Unusual,* by Martin Simpson on Red House Records

1999—*All the Rage,* by the Nashville Mandolin Ensemble on New World Records

2000—*The Gateway,* by Hayes & Blazer on Ben Lauren Productions

Adult Contemporary

1988—*Good Thing He Can't Read My Mind,* by Christine Lavin on Philo Records

1989—*One Big Town,* by Greg Brown on Red House Records

1990—*Rhythm, Blues, Soul and Grooves,* by Bobby King and Terry Evans on Rounder Records

1991—*Havin' a Party with Jonathan Richman,* by Jonathan Richman on Rounder Records

1992—*Louisiana Love Call,* by Maria Muldaur on Black Top Records

1993—*Danko/Fjeld/Andersen,* by Rick Danko/Jonas Fjeld/Eric Andersen on Rykodisc

1994—*Angel of Mercy,* by Rory Block on Rounder Records

1995—*River of Fallen Stars,* by Pete and Maura Kennedy on Green Linnet/Redbird Records

1997—*Tornado,* by Rory Block on Rounder Records

Americana

1997—*Rig Rock Deluxe,* by various artists on Upstart/Diesel Only

1998—*It Had to Happen,* by James McMurtry on Sugar Hill

1999—*The Harry Smith Collection,* by various artists on Smithsonian/Folkways

2000—*In Spite of Ourselves,* by John Prine on Oh Boy Records

Bluegrass

1984—*Down South,* by Doc and Merle Watson on Sugar Hill Records

1985—*Blue Ridge,* by Jonathan Edwards and the Seldom Scene on Sugar Hill

1986—*Riding the Midnight Train,* by Doc Watson on Sugar Hill Records

1987—*Untold Stories,* by Hot Rize on Sugar Hill

1988—*Home Is Where the Heart Is,* by David Grisman on Rounder Records

1989—*Live,* by New Grass Revival on Sugar Hill

1990—*I've Got that Old Feeling,* by Alison Krauss on Rounder Records

1991—*All on a Rising Day,* by Peter Rowan on Sugar Hill Records

1992—*Everytime You Say Goodbye,* by Alison Krauss on Rounder Records

1993—*Waitin' for the Hard Times to Go,* by the Nashville Bluegrass Band on Sugar Hill Records

1994—*A Deeper Shade of Blue,* by Del McCoury on Rounder

1995—*Unleashed,* by Nashville Bluegrass Band on Sugar Hill Records

1997—*Cold Hard Facts,* by the Del McCoury Band on Rounder Records

1998—*Longview,* by Longview on Rounder Records

1999—*Mac, Doc & Del,* by Del McCoury, Doc Watson & Mac Wiseman on Sugar Hill Records

2000—*The Grass Is Blue* by Dolly Parton on Sugar Hill Records

Blues

1980—*Crawfish Fiesta,* by Professor Longhair on Alligator Records

1981—*Magic Sam Live,* by Magic Sam on Delmark Records

1982—*Don't Lose Your Cool,* by Albert Collins on Alligator Records

1983—*Sunnyland Train,* by Sunnyland Slim on Red Beans

1984—*Guitar Slinger,* by Johnny Winter on Alligator Records

1985—*False Accusations,* by Robert Cray on High-Tone Records

1986—*Cold Snap,* by Albert Collins on Alligator Records

1987—*Take Me Back,* by James Cotton on Blind Pig Records

1988—*The Swamp Boogie Queen,* by Katie Webster on Alligator Records

1989—*Juke Box Music,* by Doug Sahm on Antone's

1990—*Dreams Come True,* by Angela Strehli, Lou Ann Barton, and Marcia Ball on Antone's Records

1991—*Mighty Long Time,* by James Cotton on Antone's Records

1992—*No Looking Back,* by Clarence "Gatemouth" Brown on Alligator Records

1993—*Force of Nature,* by Koko Taylor on Alligator Records

1994—*Live at B.B. King's,* by Rod Piazza and the Mighty Flyers on Big Mo

1995—*Blue Streak,* by Luther Allison on Alligator Records

1995—*Eldorado Cadillac,* by Billy Boy Arnold on Alligator Records

1997—*Leaving Here Walking,* by Jimmy Burns on Delmark

Electric Blues

1998—*Reckless,* by Luther Allison on Alligator

1999—*Black Tornado,* by Magic Slim and the Teardrops on Blind Pig Records

2000—*Live in Chicago,* by Luther Allison on Alligator Records

Acoustic Blues

1998—*Fish Ain't Bitin',* by Corey Harris on Alligator

1999—*You Don't Know My Mind,* by Guy Davis on Red House Records

2000—*Living Country Blues,* by Various Artists on Evidence Music

Cajun/Zydeco

1987—*Hot Chili Mama,* by BeauSoleil on Arhoolie Records

1988—*Cajun Brew,* by Michael Doucet on Rounder Records

1989—*Cookin' with Queen Ida,* by Queen Ida on GNP

1990—*Zydeco Trail Ride,* by Boozoo Chavis on Maison de Soul

1991—*Quand J'ai Parti,* by David Doucet on Rounder Records

1992—*Home Music with Spirits,* by the Savoy-Doucet Cajun Band on Arhoolie Records

1993—*Boozoo, That Is Who,* by Boozoo Chavis on Rounder Records

1994—*Live! At the Dance,* by the Savoy-Doucet Cajun Band on Arhoolie

1995—*La Toussaint,* by Steve Riley and the Mamou Playboys on Rounder Records

1995—*Nonc Adam Two-Step,* by the California Cajun Orchestra on Arhoolie Record

1997—*The Big Squeeze,* by C.J. Chenier and the Red Hot Louisiana Band on Alligator Records

1998—*Friday at Last,* by Steve Riley and the Mamou Playboys on Flat Town Music

Celtic/British Isles

1981—*Star Spangled Molly,* by De Dannan on Shanachie Records

1982—*The New Land,* by Touchstone on Green Linnet Records

1983—*Song for Ireland,* by De Dannan on Sugar Hill Records

1984—*Airs and Graces,* by Phil Cunningham on Green Linnet Records

1985—*Relativity,* by Relativity on Green Linnet Records

1986—*A Glint of Silver,* by Silly Wizard on Green Linnet Records

1987—*Ballroom,* by De Dannan on Green Linnet Records

1988—*The Light of Other Days,* by Celtic Thunder on Green Linnet Records

1989—*Sidewaulk,* by Capercaillie on Green Linnet Records

1990—*The Red Crow,* by Altan on Green Linnet Records

1991—*Think of Tomorrow,* by Pentangle on Green Linnet Records

1992—*Harvest Storm,* by Altan on Green Linnet Records

1993—*Island Angel,* by Altan on Green Linnet Records

1994—*Capernaum,* by the Tannahill Weavers on Green Linnet Records

1995—*Dawn Dance,* by Alasdair Fraser on Culburnie Records

1995—*Many Happy Returns,* by Arcady on Shanachie

1997—*Solas,* by Solas, featuring Seamus Egan on Shanachie Records

1998—*Sunny Spells and Scattered Showers,* by Solas on Shanachie Records

1999—*The Words that Remain,* by Solas on Shanachie Records

2000—*Broken Ground,* by Waterson: Carthy on Topic Records

Children's Music

1983—*Wha'd Ya Wanna Do?,* by Peter Alsop on Flying Fish Records

1984—*Howjadoo,* by John McCutcheon on Rounder Records

1985—*Saddlepals,* by Riders in the Sky on Rounder Records

1986—*The Marvelous Toy,* by Tom Paxton on Flying Fish Records

1987—*Stayin' Over,* by Peter Alsop on Moose School Records

1988—*Shake Sugaree,* by Taj Mahal on Music for Little People

1989—*All for Freedom,* by Sweet Honey in the Rock on Music for Little People

1990—*Songs for Little Pickers*, by Doc Watson on Alcazam!/Sugar Hill

1991—*Pluggin' Away*, by Peter Alsop on Moose School Productions

1992—*What Can One Little Person Do?*, by Sally Rogers on Round River Records

1993—*At Quiet O'Clock*, by Sally Rogers on Round River Records

1994—*Mine!*, by Trout Fishing in America on Trout Records

1995—*Wintersongs*, by John McCutcheon on Rounder Records

1996—*Nora's Room*, by Jessica Harper on Alcazam!

1997—*My World*, by Trout Fishing in America on Trout Records

1999—*Doctor Looney's Remedy*, by Parachute Express on Trio Lane Records

2000—*Goin' Wild*, by Banana Slug String Band on Slug music

Children's Storytelling

1993—*River of Stars*, by Marcia Lane on A Gentle Wind

1994—*Why the Dog Chases the Cat: Great Animal Stories*, by David Holt and Bill Mooney on High Windy Audio

1995—*Kipling: Jungle Books*, by Madhav Sharma on Naxos Audio Books

1997—*Stellaluna*, by David Holt on High Windy Audio

1998—*The Hidden Grail: Sir Percival and the Fisher King*, by Odds Bodkin on Rivertree

1999—*Weezie and the Moon Pies*, by Bill Harley on Round River Records

2000—*Little Proto's T-Rex Adventure* by Odds Bodkin on Rivertree Productions

Children's Video

1992—*On Top of Spaghetti*, by Little Richard on Walt Disney Records

1993—*Wake Up!*, by Peter Alsop on Moose School Productions

1994—*Sing, Stretch and Play with Mom and Dad*, by various artists on Brentwood Kids Co.

Comedy

1988—*Old Feathers/New Bird*, by Wavy Gravy on Relix Records

1989—*Stand by Your Dan*, by Capitol Steps on Capitol Steps

1990—*Backsliders Tractor Pull*, by the Rev. Billy C. Wirtz on HighTone Records

1993—*Shut Up and Sing*, by the Bobs on Rounder Records

Country

1981—*Cowboy Jubilee*, by Riders in the Sky on Rounder Records

1982—*Electricity*, by Sleepy LaBeef on Rounder Records

1983—*Swing Boogie*, by Cowboy Jazz on Rounder Records

1984—*Desert Rose*, by Chris Hillman on Sugar Hill Records

1985—*She Sings, They Play*, by Skeeter Davis and NRBQ on Rounder Records

1986—*Last of the True Believers*, by Nanci Griffith on Philo Records

1987—*Together at Last*, by Vassar Clements and Stephane Grappelli on Flying Fish

1988—*Sleazy Roadside Stories*, by Commander Cody on Relix Records

1989—*Love Chooses You*, by Laurie Lewis on Flying Fish Records

1990—*Aces High*, by Commander Cody and His Lost Planet Airmen on Relix Records

1991—*Odd Man In*, by Tim O'Brien on Sugar Hill Records

1992—*Infamous Angel*, by Iris DeMent on Philo Records

1993—*Rodeo Waltz*, by Sweethearts of the Rodeo on Sugar Hill Records

1994—*Straw Into Gold*, by Barry and Holly Tashian on Rounder Records

1995—*Beyond the City*, by Cox Family on Rounder Records

1995—*Just One Love*, by Willie Nelson on Justice Records

1997—*Texas Top Hand*, by Don Walser on Watermelon Records

1998—*Way Out West*, by Wylie and the Wild West on Rounder Records

1999—*Spyboy*, by Emmylou Harris on Eminent Records

2000—*What I Deserve*, by Kelly Willis on Rykodisc

Folk

1980—*Longtime Gone*, by John Starling on Sugar Hill Records

1981—*Red Rocking Chair*, by Doc and Merle Watson on Flying Fish Records

1982—*In the Circle of the Sun*, by Sally Rogers on Thrushwood Records

1983—*Give Yourself to Love*, by Kate Wolf on Kaleidoscope Records

1984—*Elizabeth Cotten: Live!*, on Arhoolie

1985—*HARP*, by Holly Near, Arlo Guthrie, Ronnie Gilbert, and Pete Seeger on Redwood Records

1986—*Poet's Heart*, by Kate Wolf on Kaleidoscope Records

1987—*Gold in California,* by Kate Wolf on Kaleidoscope Records

1988—*Dust Bowl Ballads,* by Woody Guthrie on Rounder Records

1989—*An Evening in Austin,* by Kate Wolf on Kaleidoscope Records

1990—*Dust Bowl Children,* by Peter Rowan on Sugar Hill Records

1991—*The Missing Years,* by John Prine on Oh Boy Records

1992—*Culture Swing,* by Tish Hinojosa on Rounder Records

1993—*Happier Blue,* by Chris Smither on Flying Fish Records

1994—*Memorial Anthology,* by Mississippi John Hurt on Adelphi/Genes Blues Vault Series

1995—*Stories,* by Maura O'Connell on Hannibal Records

Traditional Folk

1997—*The Long Memory,* by U. Utah Phillips and Rosalie Sorrels on Red House Records

1998—*Saddle Songs,* by Don Edwards on Shanachie Records

1999—*Chattanooga Sugar Babe,* by Norman Blake on Shanachie Records

2000—*Oh the Wind and Rain,* by Jody Strecher on Appleseed Records

Contemporary Folk

1997—*Matapedia,* by Kate and Anna McGarrigle on Hannibal Records

1998—*Reunion Hill,* by Richard Shindell on Shanachie

1999—*Where Have all the Flowers Gone: The Songs of Pete Seeger,* by Various Artists on Appleseed Records

2000—*The Crossing,* by Tim O'Brien on Alula Records

Singer-Songwriter

1994—*The Poet Game,* by Greg Brown on Red House Records

1995—*Train A Comin',* by Steve Earle on Winter Harvest Entertainment

Gospel

1983—*We All . . . Every One of Us,* by Sweet Honey in the Rock on Flying Fish Records

1984—*Take a Look at My People,* by Jane Sapp on Flying Fish Records

1985—*Feel Something Drawing Me On,* by Sweet Honey in the Rock on Flying Fish Records

1986—*Beyond the Shadows,* by Doyle Lawson on Sugar Hill Records

1987—*River of Love,* by Bernice Johnson Reagon on Flying Fish Records

1988—*The Live Album by the Florida Mass Choir,* by the Florida Mass Choir on Malaco Records

1989—*Mom and Pop Winans,* by Mom and Pop Winans on Sparrow Records

1990—*On Praying Ground,* by Doc Watson on Sugar Hill Records

1991—*Strong Again,* by Marion Williams on Spirit Feel Records

1997—*Count on God,* by Dottie Peoples on Atlanta International Records

1998—*Hattie B's Daughter,* by Dorothy Norwood on Malaco

1999—*Let the Church Say Amen . . . Again!,* by Rev. Gerald Thompson on Atlanta International Records

2000—*Emmanuel (God with Us),* by Mississippi Mass Choir On Malaco

Gospel/Religious

1992—*Steppin' Out,* by Gospel Hummingbirds on Blind Pig Records

1993—*It Remains to Be Seen,* by Mississippi Mass Choir on Malaco Records

1994—*I Know Who Holds Tomorrow,* by Alison Krauss and the Cox Family on Rounder Records

1995—*Georgia Live,* by the Kingsmen on Horizon Records

Southern and Bluegrass Gospel

1997—*Renaissance,* by the Freemans on Daywind Records

1998—*Kept and Protected,* by Doyle Lawson and Quicksilver on Sugar Hill

1999—*A Vision,* by Don Rigsby on Sugar Hill Records

2000—*Winding Thorugh Life,* by Dolye Lawson & Quicksilver on Sugar Hill Records

Historical

1981—*Mardi Gras in New Orleans,* by Professor Longhair on Nighthawk Records

1982—*The Great Twenty Eight,* by Chuck Berry on Chess Records

1983—*The Original Peacock Recordings,* by Clarence "Gatemouth" Brown on Rounder Records

1984—*Best of the Tiffanies,* by Bob Wills and His Texas Playboys on Kaleidoscope Records

1985—*Steamboat Whistle Blues,* by Roy Acuff on Rounder Records

1986—*The First Recordings,* by Hank Williams on Country Music Foundation

1987—*Columbia River Collection,* by Woodie Guthrie on Rounder Records

1988—*The Library of Congress Recordings*, by Woodie Guthrie on Rounder Records

1989—*The Legendary Dial Sessions*, by Charlie Parker on Stash Records

1990—*Blues in the Mississippi Night*, by Big Bill Broonzy, Memphis Slim, and Sonny Boy Williamson on Rykodisc

1991—*The Complete Early Transcriptions*, by Nat King Cole on VJC Records

1992—*Duke Ellington and His World Famous Orchestra: The Collection '46–'47*, by Duke Ellington on Hindsight Records

1993—*Tougher than Tough: The Story of Jamaican Music*, by various artists on Mango Records

1994—*Joe Henderson: The Milestone Years*, by Joe Henderson on Milestone

1995—*Complete Prestige Recordings*, by Eric Dolphy on Prestige Records

1997—*The Singles*, by Sun Ra on Evidence Music

1998—*Anthology of American Folk Music*, edited by Harry Smith, by various artists on Smithsonian/Folkways

1999—*Time is Tight*, by Booker T. & the MGs on Stax Records

2000—*From Spirituals to Swing*, by Various Artists on Vanguard

String Band Jazz

1981—*At the Winery*, by Stephane Grappelli on Concord Jazz Records

1982—*Tea for One*, by Jethro Burns on Kaleidoscope Records

1983—*David Grisman's Acoustic Christmas*, by David Grisman on Rounder Records

1984—*First Dibs*, by Robin Flower on Flying Fish Records

Latin

1986—*Sensacion*, by Tito Puente on Picante Records

1987—*Un Poco Loco*, by Tito Puente on Concord Picante

1988—*Flaco's Amigos*, by Flaco Jimenez on Arhoolie Records

1990—*Goza Mi Timbal*, by Tito Puento on Concorde Picante

1991—*Out of this World*, by Tito Puento on Concorde Picante

1992—*Mambo of the Times*, by Tito Puento on Concorde Picante

1993—*Una Sola Casa*, by Conjunto Cespedes on Green Linnet Records

1994—*944 Columbus,*by Mario Bauza on Messidor Musik

1995—*Vivito y Coleando*, by Conjunto Cespedes on Xenophile Records

1997—*Celebremos Navidad*, by Yomo Toro on Ashe/Rounder

1998—*Malembe*, by Cubanismo, starring Jesus Alemany, on Hannibal Records

1999—*Reencarnacion*, by Cubanismo on Hannibal Records

2000—*Maferefun*, by Tony Martinez on Blue Jackel

New Age

1985—*Imagination*, by Inti-Illimani on Redwood Records

1986—*Harpes Du Nouvel*, by Alan Stivell on Rounder Records

1987—*The Great Road*, by Metamora on Sugar Hill Records

1988—*Here Goes Nothing*, by Zero on Relix Records

1989—*Freedom Chants from the Roof of the World*, by the Gyuto Monks on Rykodisc

1990—*At the Edge*, by Mickey Hart on Rykodisc

1991—*Borrasca*, by Ottmar Liebert on Higher Octave Music

1992—*Migration*, by Peter Kater/R. Carlos Nakai on Silver Wave Records

1993—*Change of Face*, by Wind Machine on Blue Meteor

1994—*Earth Island*, by Suspended Memories on Hearts of Space

1995—*Trust*, by Patrick O'Hearn on Deep Cave Records

1997—*Metaphor*, by Patrick O'Hearn on Deep Cave Records

1998—*Bridge*, by Oystein Sevag on Hearts of Space

1999—*Prophecies*, by Dik Darnell & Steven Halpern on Etherean Music

2000—*Afterglow*, by Hoppé/Tilman/Wheater on Hearts of Space

North American Native Music

1995—*Touch the Sweet Earth*, by Sharon Burch on Canyon Records

1997—*Matriarch (Iroquois Women's Songs)*, by Joanne Shenandoah on Silver Wave Records

1998—*Circle Dance Songs of the Paiute and Shoshone*, by Judy Trejo with Delgadina Gonzalez and Christina Gonzalez on Canyon Records

1999—*Mythic Dreamer*, by R. Carlos Nakai on Canyon Records Productions

2000—*Heart of the World*, by Mary Youngblood on Silver Wave Records

Pop

1992—*Over the Limit*, by Trout Fishing in America on Trout Records

1993—*Swim Away*, by Toni Price on Antone's Records

1994—*The Impossible Bird*, by Nick Lowe on Upstart

1995—*Love Story,* by Lloyd Cole on Rykodisc
1997—*The Laughing Man,* by Yazbek on W.A.R.?
What Are Records?
1998—*Mirmama,* by Eddi Reader on Compass Records
1999—*Words and Music,* by Paul Kelly on Vanguard
Records
2000—*Ten Year Night,* by Lucy Kaplansky on Red
House Records

R&B

1989—*Walking on a Tightrope,* by Johnny Adams on
Rounder Records
1990—*Between a Rock and a Hard Place,* by
Clarence Carter on Ichiban Records
1991—*Sons of the P,* by Digital Underground on
Tommy Boy Music
1992—*I'll Treat You Right,* by Otis Clay on Bullseye
Blues
1993—*People Get Ready—a Tribute to Curtis Mayfield,* by various artists on Shanachie Records
1994—*Blasters of the Universe,* by Bootsy's New
Rubber Band on Rykodisc
1995—*Right on Time!,* by Little Buster on Bullseye
Blues
1997—*Good Love,* by Johnnie Taylor on Malaco
Records
1998—*Soul of a Woman,* by Shirley Brown on Malaco
1999—*For Real,* by Little Milton on Malaco Records
2000—*Gonna Get the Groove Back,* by Johnnie Taylor
on Malaco

Rap

1989—*Loc-ed After Dark,* by Tone-Loc on Delicious
Vinyl
1990—*Sex Packets,* by Digital Underground on
Tommy Boy Music
1991—*Nature of a Sista!,* by Queen Latifah on
Tommy Boy Music
1992—*House of Pain,* by House of Pain on Tommy
Boy Music
1993—*19 Naughty III,* by Naughty by Nature on
Tommy Boy Music
1994—*The Sun Rises in the East,* by Jeru the Damaja
on Payday/FFRR
1995—*Jealous One's Envy,* by Fat Joe on Relativity
1997—*Stakes Is High,* by De La Soul on Tommy Boy
1998—*One Day This Will All Make Sense,* by Common on Relativity
1999—*N.O.R.E.,* by Noreaga on Tommy Boy Music
2000—*Prince Among Thieves,* by Prince Paul on
Tommy Boy

Reggae

1982—*Who Feels It Knows It,* by Rita Marley on
Shanachie Records

1983—*Roots, Radics, Rockers, Reggae,* by Bunny
Wailer on Shanachie Records
1984—*Scattered Lights,* by the Scatelites on Alligator
Records
1985—*Alive in Jamaica,* by the Blue Riddim Band on
Flying Fish Records
1986—*City Down,* by Casselberry-Dupree on
Icegergg Records
1987—*Groovin',* by Killer Bees on Jungle Records
1988—*Positive Dub,* by Black Uhuru on ROIR
1989—*Live in Berlin,* by Killer Bees on ROIR
1990—*Dancing Floor,* by Gregory Isaacs on
Heartbeat Records
1991—*Jah Kingdom,* by Burning Spear on Mango
Records
1992—*House of Exile,* by Lucky Dube on Koch
International
1993—*The World Should Know,* by Burning Spear on
Heartbeat Records
1994—*Hi-Bop Ska,* by Skatalites on Shanachie
Records
1995—*Rasta Business,* by Burning Spear on Heartbeat
Records
1997—*Free to Move,* by Israel Vibration on Ras
Records
1998—*Trust Me,* by Culture on Ras Records
1999—*One Calling,* by Morgan Heritage on VP
Records
2000—*The Sound of Channel One: King Tubby
Collection,* by Various Artists on Triple X

Rock

1980—*Disconnected,* by Stiv Bators on Bomp
Records
1981—*Everybody Needs It,* by Ellen McIlwaine on
Blind Pig Records
1982—*Shoot Out the Lights,* by Richard and Linda
Thompson on Hannibal Records
1983—*Hand of Kindness,* by Richard Thompson on
Hannibal Records
1984—*Nevillization,* by the Neville Brothers on Black
Top Records
1985—*The Pitts Bear Down,* by the Zasu Pitts
Memorial Orchestra on Kaleidoscope Records
1986—*Passion,* by Robin Trower on Crescendo
Records
1987—*Lord of the Highway,* by Joe Ely on HighTone
Records
1988—*You Can't Do That on Stage Anymore,* by
Frank Zappa on Rykodisc
1989—*Live From Austin,* by Delbert McClinton on
Alligator Records
1990—*Passion and Warfare,* by Steve Vai on
Relativity Records
1991—*Blue Blvd.,* by Dave Alvin on HighTone
Records

1992—*The Extremist,* by Joe Satriani on Relativity Records

1993—*Burning Daylight,* by Loose Diamonds on Dos Records

1994—*Autopilot,* by the Samples on W.A.R.?

1995—*Lost Dogs and Mixed Blessings,* by John Prine on Oh Boy Records

1997—*Acid Bubblegum,* by Graham Parker on Razor and Tie

1998—*The Last Rock 'n' Roll Tour,* by Graham Parker and the Figgs on Razor and Tie

1999—*Rockin' in the Weary Land* by Donna the Buffalo on Sugar Hill Records

2000—*Somewhere Between Heaven and Earth* by Cindy Bullens on Artemis

Seasonal

1986—*Oh Chanukah,* by the Klezmer Conservatory Band on Rounder Records

1987—*Merry Cajun Christmas, Vol. 2,* by various artists on Swallow Records

1988—*Christmas Spirituals,* by Odetta on Alcazar

1989—*American Folk Songs for Christmas,* by Mike, Peggy, and Penny Seeger on Rounder Records

1990—*The Christmas Rose,* by Patrick Ball on Fortuna Records

1991—*Sugar Plums—Holiday Treats from Sugar Hill,* by various artists on Sugar Hill Records

1992—*Christmas in Maine,* by Paul Sullivan on River Music

1993—*A John Prine Christmas,* by John Prine on Oh Boy Records

1994—*A Concord Jazz Christmas,* by various artists on Concord Jazz

1995—*I Want a Smile for Christmas,* by Freddy Cole on Fantasy Records

1997—*Christmas Songs,* by Carolling Carollers on Satellites Records

1998—*Holiday Guitar,* by Dan Crary on Sugar Hill

1999—*Noëls Celtique,* by the Ensemble Choral du Bout du Monde on Green Linnet

2000—*A Winter Solstice with Helicon,* by Helicon on Dorian Recordings

Sound Track/Cast Recording

1985—*Star Trek—the Original TV Sound Track,* on GNP Crescendo Records

1986—*Children of a Lesser God—Cast Recordings,* on GNP Crescendo Records

1987—*Country Characters,* by Jackie Torrence on Earwig Music Company

1988—*The Unforgettable Lightness of Being,* cast recording on Fantasy Records

1989—*Black and Blue (Orig. Broadway Cast),* by Ruth Brown and Linda Hopkins on DRG Records

1990—*Star Trek—the Next Generation: The Best of Both Worlds I and II,* Star Trek—the Next Generation on GNP Crescendo Records

1992—*Aladdin,* by Ashman, Menken, and Rice on Walt Disney Records

1993—*Tim Burton's the Nightmare Before Christmas,* by Danny Elfman and original cast voices on Walt Disney Records

1994—*Elmer Bernstein: The Magnificent Seven,* by Phoenix Symphony/Jim Sedares on Koch International Classics

1995—*Crumb: Original Sound Track,* by various artists on Rykodisc

1997—*The English Patient,* by Gabriel Yared, composer, on Fantasy

1998—*The Boys from Syracuse,* by New York 1997 cast on DRG

1999—*The Ladykillers,* by The Royal Ballet Sinfonia on Silva America

2000—*Do Re Mi,* by New York 1999 cast on DRG

Storytelling/Spoken Word

1987—*Matewan,* by various artists on Daring Records

1988—*Stories and Songs for Little Children,* by Pete Seeger on High Windy Audio

1989—*Classic Children's Tales,* by Jackie Torrence on Rounder Records

1990—*Dreams and Ilusions: Tales of the Pacific Rim,* by Brenda Wong Aoki on Rounder Records

1991—*Report from Grimes Creek,* by Rosalie Sorrels on Green Linnet Records

1992—*Storyteller in a Groove,* by Bobby Norfolk on Earwig Music Company

Spoken Word

1986—*A Child's Look at What It Means to Be Jewish,* by various artists on Kids' Records

1993—*Spare Ass Annie and Other Tales,* by William Burroughs on Island Red Label

1994—*The Ice Opinion,* by Ice T on the Publishing Mills

1995—*Storyteller,* by Patrick Ball on Celestial Harmonies

1997—*White on White,* by Joel White and Paul Sullivan on River Music

1998—*Jacob Marley's Christmas Carol,* by Tom Mula on Woodside Avenue

1999—*The Queen's Garden,* by Brenda Wong Aoki/Mark Izu on Asian Improv. Arts

2000—*Richard Fawkes: The History of Opera,* by Robert Powell on Naxos Audiobooks

String Band Music

1981—*After Midnight,* by the Seldom Scene on Sugar Hill Records

1982—*Eight String Swing*, by Mike Auldridge on Sugar Hill Records

1983—*Doc and Merle's Guitar Album*, by Doc and Merle Watson on Flying Fish Records

1985—*Pickin' the Blues*, by Doc and Merle Watson on Flying Fish Records

1986—*Step by Step*, by John McCutcheon on Rounder Records

1987—*Rude Awakening*, by Rude Girls on Flying Fish Records

1988—*Take 5*, by No Strings Attached on Turquoise Records

1989—*Heart's Ease*, by Madeline MacNeil on Turquoise Records

1990—*Treasures Untold*, by Mike Auldridge on Sugar Hill Records

1991—*Thunderation*, by Dan Crary on Sugar Hill/Pamlico Sound

1992—*Rambler*, by the Red Clay Ramblers on Sugar Hill Records

1993—*Skip, Hop and Wobble*, by Douglas, Barenberg, and Meyer on Sugar Hill Records

1994—*The Art of Taksim*, by Goksel Kartal on Traditional Crossroads

Women's Music

1985—*The Other Side*, by Sweet Honey in the Rock on Flying Fish Records

1986—*The Pfister Sisters*, by the Pfister Sisters on Great Southern Records

1987—*Babies with Glasses*, by Robin Flower and the Bleachers on Flying Fish Records

1988—*Live at Carnegie Hall*, by Sweet Honey in the Rock on Flying Fish Records

1989—*Skydances*, by Holly Near on Redwood Records

1990—*In the Square*, by Patty Larkin on Philo Records

World Music

1981—*The Klezmorim Metropolis*, by Klezmorim on Flying Fish Records

1982—*Revolutionary Songs of El Salvador*, by Yolocombo Ita on Flying Fish Records

1983—*In San Francisco*, by Queen Ida and the Zydeco Band on GNP/Crescendo Records

1984—*Palimpsesto*, by Inti-Illimani on Redwood Records

1985—*Caught in the Act*, by Queen Ida on GNP/Crescendo Records

1986—*Inala*, by Ladysmith Black Mambazo on Shanachie Records

1987—*Back in Town*, by Boyoyo Boys on Rounder Records

1988—*Drums of Passion: The Invocation*, by Babatunde Olatunji on Rykodisc

1989—*Huayarasan*, by Sukay on Flying Fish Records

1990—*Soup of the Century*, by 3 Mustaphas 3 on Rykodisc

Traditional World

1991—*Mexico*, by Los Folkloristas on Flying Fish Records

1992—*Tzigane, the Gypsy Music of Turkey*, by Erkose Brothers on CMP Records

1993—*Maramaros*, by Muzsikas on Hannibal Records

1994—*Tibetan Buddhist Rites from the Monasteries of Bhutan*, by Tibetan Monks on Lyrichord Discs

1995—*Bayaka*, by BaBenzelle Pygmies on Ellipsis Arts

1997—*The Music of Armenia Volume 3*, by George Dagbagian on Celestial Harmonies

1998—*The Music of Islam Sampler*, by various artists on Celestial Harmonies

1999—*String Glamour*, by Hong-Mei Yu on Wind Records

2000—*The Raga Guide*, by Various Artists on Nimbus Records

Contemporary World

1991—*Friends, Fiends, and Fronds*, by 3 Mustaphas 3 on Omnium Records

1992—*A World out of Time*, by Henry Kaiser and David Lindley on Koch International

1993—*A Meeting by the River*, by Ry Cooder and V.M. Bhatt on Water Lily Acoustics

1994—*Songhai2*, by Songhai on Hannibal Records

1995—*Aitara*, by Varttina on Xenophile Records

1997—*IHU Todos Os Sons*, by Marlui Miranda on Blue Jackel

1998—*Son Egal*, by Tarika on Xenophile

1999—*In Search of the Lost Riddim*, by Ernest Ranglin on Palm Pictures

2000—*Bilbao OO:OOh*, by Kepa Junkera on Alula

Video

1992—*Picture Show*, by John Prine on Oh Boy Records

1993—*We're the Boyz*, by Robby Bee and the Boyz from the Rez on Warrior Records

1994—*High Lonesome—the Story of Bluegrass Music*, by various artists on Shanachie Entertainment

Longform Video

1995—*Djabote*, by Doudou N'Daye Rose Senegal Drumming Group on Multicultural Media

1997—*At Home in Renfro Valley*, by New Coon Creek Girls on Pinecastle Records

1998—*The Live Experience*, by Phil Coulter on Shanachie Records

Artist	Title	Company	Date

1966

Simon and Garfunkel	Sounds of Silence (S)	Columbia	Feb. 14
Smothers Brothers	*Think Ethnic*	Mercury	Aug. 16

1967

Harry Belafonte	*An Evening with Belafonte*	RCA Victor	Apr. 10
Donovan	*Mellow Yellow*	Epic	Jan. 19
Bob Dylan	*Blonde on Blonde*	Columbia	Aug. 25
Bob Dylan	*Highway 61 Revisited*	Columbia	Aug. 25
Bob Dylan	*Bringing It All Back Home*	Columbia	Aug. 25
Simon and Garfunkel	*Parsley, Sage, Rosemary and Thyme*	Columbia	July 6
Simon and Garfunkel	*Sounds of Silence*	Columbia	Aug. 25
Smothers Brothers	*The Two Sides of the Smothers Brothers*	Mercury	Feb. 22

1968

Byrds	*The Byrds Greatest Hits*	Columbia	Mar. 13
Chambers Brothers	*The Time Has Come*	Columbia	Dec. 4
Bob Dylan	*Bob Dylan's Greatest Hits*	Columbia	Jan. 5
Bob Dylan	*John Wesley Harding*	Columbia	Mar. 19
Jose Feliciano	*Feliciano*	RCA Victor	Oct. 4
Simon and Garfunkel	*Bookends*	Columbia	Apr. 18
Simon and Garfunkel	Mrs. Robinson (S)	Columbia	June 10
Smothers Brothers	*At the Purple Onion*	Mercury	Nov. 13
Sound Track	*The Graduate*	Columbia	Mar. 27

1969

Band	*The Band*	Capitol	Nov. 26
Judy Collins	*Wildflowers*	Elektra	Jan. 20
Judy Collins	*Who Knows Where the Time Goes*	Elektra	Nov. 8
Crosby, Stills and Nash	*Crosby, Stills and Nash*	Atlantic	Sept. 30
Jackie DeShannon	Put a Little Love in Your Heart (S)	Imperial	Sept. 29
Donovan	*Donovan's Greatest Hits*	Epic	Apr. 22
Bob Dylan	*Nashville Skyline*	Columbia	May 7
Arlo Guthrie	*Alice's Restaurant*	Reprise	Sept. 29
Peter, Paul and Mary	*Album 1700*	Warner Brothers	Jan. 27
Peter, Paul and Mary	Leaving on a Jet Plane (S)	Warner Brothers	Dec. 30
Simon and Garfunkel	*Wednesday Morning 3 A.M.*	Columbia	Mar. 4
Youngbloods	Get Together (S)	RCA Victor	Oct. 7

1970

Judy Collins	*In My Life*	Elektra	Dec. 21
Crosby, Stills, Nash and Young	*Déjà Vu*	Atlantic	Mar. 25
Donovan	*A Gift from a Flower to a Garden*	Epic	Apr. 1
Bob Dylan	*Self Portrait*	Columbia	June 22
Bob Dylan	*New Morning*	Columbia	Dec. 11
Bob Dylan	*The Freewheelin' Bob Dylan*	Columbia	Dec. 18
Jose Feliciano	*Alive Alive-O!*	RCA	Feb. 9
Jose Feliciano	*Feliciano/10 to 23*	RCA	Mar. 20
Joni Mitchell	*Ladies of the Canyon*	Reprise	Dec. 23
Peter, Paul and Mary	*See What Tomorrow Brings*	Warner Brothers	Jan. 29
Peter, Paul and Mary	*A Song Will Rise*	Warner Brothers	Apr. 30

Artist	Title	Company	Date
1970 (cont.)			
Peter, Paul and Mary	*The Best of Peter, Paul and Mary's (Ten) Years Together*	Warner Brothers	Oct. 16
Simon and Garfunkel	*Bridge over Troubled Water*	Columbia	Feb. 9
Simon and Garfunkel	Bridge over Troubled Water (S)	Columbia	Feb. 27
Simon and Garfunkel	Cecilia (S)	Columbia	June 12
Stephen Stills	*Stephen Stills*	Atlantic	Nov. 24
Stephen Stills, Mike Bloomfield, and Al Kooper	*Super Session*	Columbia	Dec. 4
Neil Young	*After the Gold Rush*	Reprise	Nov. 2
Neil Young with Crazy Horse	*Everybody Knows This Is Nowhere*	Reprise	Oct. 16
1971			
Allman Brothers Band	*The Allman Brothers Band at Fillmore East*	Capricorn	Oct. 25
Joan Baez	The Night They Drove Old Dixie Down (S)	Vanguard	Oct. 22
Band	*Rock of Ages*	Capitol	Nov. 2
Judy Collins	*Whales and Nightingales*	Reprise	Apr. 6
David Crosby	*If I Could Only Remember My Name*	Atlantic	Apr. 8
Crosby, Stills, Nash and Young	*Four-Way Street*	Atlantic	Apr. 12
John Denver	Take Me Home, Country Roads (S)	RCA	Aug. 18
John Denver	*Poems, Prayers and Promises*	RCA	Sept. 15
Carole King	*Tapestry*	Ode	June 7
Carole King	It's Too Late (S)	Ode	July 21
Carole King	*Carole King Music*	Ode	Dec. 9
Melanie	Brand New Key (S)	Neighborhood	Dec. 16
Joni Mitchell	*Blue*	Reprise	Nov. 15
Graham Nash	*Songs for Beginners*	Atlantic	Aug. 26
Stephen Stills	*Stephen Stills 2*	Atlantic	Aug. 26
James Taylor	*Mud Slide Slim and the Blue Horizon*	Warner Brothers	Apr. 30
James Taylor	You've Got a Friend (S)	Warner Brothers	Sept. 13
Various Artists	*Woodstock II*	Cotillion	Apr. 1
1972			
Joan Baez	*Blessed Are*	Vanguard	Jan. 31
Joan Baez	*Any Day Now*	Vanguard	Jan. 31
John Denver	*Aerie*	RCA	Jan. 5
John Denver	*Rocky Mountain High*	RCA	Dec. 30
Roberta Flack	The First Time Ever I Saw Your Face (S - Ewan MacColl, songwriter)	Atlantic	Apr. 19
Carole King	*Rhymes and Reasons*	Ode	Nov. 1
Don McLean	American Pie (S)	United Artists	Jan. 3
Don McLean	*American Pie*	United Artists	Jan. 3
Melanie	*Gather Me*	Neighborhood	June 13
Joni Mitchell	*For the Roses*	Asylum	Dec. 22
Graham Nash and David Crosby	*Graham Nash and David Crosby*	Atlantic	May 30
Harry Nilsson	*Nilsson Schmilsson*	RCA	Mar. 3
Harry Nilsson	Without You (S)	RCA	Mar. 3
Harry Nilsson	*Son of Schmilsson*	RCA	Dec. 30
Seals and Crofts	*Summer Breeze*	Warner Brothers	Dec. 14

Artist	Title	Company	Date

1972 (cont.)

Artist	Title	Company	Date
New Seekers	I'd Like to Teach the World to Sing (S)	Elektra	Jan. 27
Paul Simon	*Paul Simon*	Columbia	Mar. 3
Simon and Garfunkel	*Simon and Garfunkel's Greatest Hits*	Columbia	July 6
Stephen Stills	*Manassas*	Atlantic	May 30
Neil Young	*Harvest*	Warner/Reprise	Feb. 18
Neil Young	Heart of Gold (S)	Warner/Reprise	Apr. 21

1973

Artist	Title	Company	Date
Jim Croce	Bad, Bad Leroy Brown (S)	ABC/Dunhill	July 24
Jim Croce	*Life and Times*	ABC/Dunhill	Nov. 2
Jim Croce	*You Don't Mess Around with Jim*	ABC/Dunhill	Nov. 26
Jim Croce	*I Got a Name*	ABC/Dunhill	Dec. 6
John Denver	*Farewell Andromeda*	RCA	Aug. 27
John Denver	*John Denver's Greatest Hits*	RCA	Dec. 11
Bob Dylan	*Dylan*	Columbia	Dec. 21
Art Garfunkel	*Angel Clare*	Columbia	Oct. 24
Carole King	*Fantasy*	Ode	June 26
Loggins and Messina	*Loggins and Messina*	Columbia	Feb. 2
Loggins and Messina	Your Mama Don't Dance (S)	Columbia	Mar. 7
Loggins and Messina	*Sittin' In*	Columbia	May 11
Loggins and Messina	*Full Sail*	Columbia	Dec. 7
Seals and Crofts	*Diamond Girl*	Warner Brothers	June 25
Paul Simon	*There Goes Rhymin' Simon*	Columbia	June 15
Paul Simon	Loves Me Like a Rock (S)	Columbia	Oct. 9
Neil Young	*Time Fades Away*	Warner/Reprise	Dec. 7

1974

Artist	Title	Company	Date
Jackson Browne	*Late for the Sky*	Asylum	Dec. 24
Harry Chapin	*Verities and Balderdash*	Elektra	Dec. 17
Harry Chapin	Cat's in the Cradle (S)	Elektra	Dec. 31
Judy Collins	*Colors of the Day*	Elektra	Jan. 22
Jim Croce	Time in a Bottle (S)	ABC	Jan. 3
Jim Croce	*Photographs and Memories, His Greatest Hits*	ABC	Oct. 22
Crosby, Stills, Nash and Young	*So Far*	Atlantic	Sept. 19
John Denver	Sunshine on My Shoulder (S)	RCA	Mar. 28
John Denver	Annie's Song (S)	RCA	July 26
Bob Dylan	*Planet Waves*	Asylum	Jan. 22
Bob Dylan and the Band	*Before the Flood*	Asylum	July 8
Carole King	*Wrap Around Joy*	Ode	Oct. 16
Gordon Lightfoot	*Sundown*	Reprise	May 31
Gordon Lightfoot	Sundown (S)	Reprise	June 18
Loggins and Messina	*On Stage*	Columbia	June 18
Loggins and Messina	*Mother Lode*	Columbia	Nov. 25
Joni Mitchell	*Court and Spark*	Asylum	Feb. 27
Joni Mitchell	*Miles of Aisles*	Asylum	Nov. 27
Maria Muldaur	*Maria Muldaur*	Reprise	May 13
Seals and Crofts	*Unborn Child*	Warner Brothers	Mar. 12
Paul Simon	*Live Rhymin'*	Columbia	June 11
James Taylor and Carly Simon	Mockingbird (S)	Elektra	May 14
Neil Young	*On the Beach*	Reprise	Sept. 23

Artist	Title	Company	Date

1975

Artist	Title	Company	Date
Joan Baez	*Diamonds and Rust*	A&M	Nov. 11
Bobby Bland and B.B. King	*Together for the First Time*	ABC/Dunhill	Feb. 28
Jackson Browne	*For Everyman*	Asylum	Oct. 8
Judy Collins	*Judith*	Elektra	Nov. 19
Rita Coolidge and Kris Kristofferson	*Full Moon*	A&M	Oct. 20
David Crosby and Graham Nash	*Wind on the Water*	ABC Records/ Atlantic Tape	Nov. 7
John Denver	Back Home Again (S)	RCA	Jan. 3
John Denver	*An Evening with John Denver*	RCA	Feb. 19
John Denver	Thank God I'm a Country Boy (S)	RCA	June 26
John Denver	*Windsong*	RCA	Sept. 19
John Denver	*Rocky Mountain Christmas*	RCA	Oct. 24
John Denver	I'm Sorry (S)	RCA	Nov. 18
Bob Dylan	*Blood on the Tracks*	Columbia	Feb. 12
Art Garfunkel	*Breakaway*	Columbia	Dec. 5
Janis Ian	*Between the Lines*	Columbia	Sept. 11
Joni Mitchell	*The Hissing of Summer Lawns*	Asylum	Dec. 4
Michael Martin Murphy	Wildfire (S)	Epic	July 21
Michael Martin Murphy	*Blue Sky—Night Thunder*	Epic	Nov. 17
Linda Ronstadt	*Heart Like a Wheel*	Capitol	Jan. 31
Linda Ronstadt	*Don't Cry Now*	Asylum	Aug. 25
Linda Ronstadt	*Prisoner in Disguise*	Asylum	Oct. 8
Seals and Crofts	*I'll Play for You*	Warner Brothers	Sept. 29
Seals and Crofts	*Seals and Crofts' Greatest Hits*	Warner Brothers	Dec. 5
Paul Simon	*Still Crazy After All These Years*	Columbia	Nov. 17
Bruce Springsteen	*Born to Run*	Columbia	Oct. 8
James Taylor	*Gorilla*	Warner Brothers	Sept. 12

1976 (gold)

Artist	Title	Company	Date
Jackson Browne	*The Pretender*	Asylum	Nov. 15
Jackson Browne	*Jackson Browne*	Asylum	Nov. 16
David Crosby and Graham Nash	*Whistling down the Wire*	Atlantic	Oct. 19
John Denver	*Spirit*	RCA	Aug. 17
Bob Dylan	*Desire*	Columbia	Jan. 14
Bob Dylan	*Hard Rain*	Columbia	Sept. 22
Dan Fogelberg	*Souvenirs*	Epic	May 21
Carole King	*Thoroughbred*	Ode	Mar. 25
Gordon Lightfoot	*Summertime Dream*	Reprise	Oct. 26
Loggins and Messina	*Native Sons*	Columbia	Aug. 19
Joni Mitchell	*Hejira*	Asylum	Dec. 23
Linda Ronstadt	*Hasten down the Wind*	Asylum	Aug. 30
Linda Ronstadt	*Greatest Hits*	Asylum	Dec. 8
Seals and Crofts	*Get Closer*	Warner Brothers	Aug. 25
Paul Simon	50 Ways to Leave Your Lover (S)	Columbia	Mar. 11
Starland Vocal Band	Afternoon Delight (S)	Windsong	July 15
James Taylor	*In the Pocket*	Warner Brothers	Oct. 19
James Taylor	*James Taylor's Greatest Hits*	Warner Brothers	Dec. 22

Artist	Title	Company	Date

1976 (platinum)

John Denver	*Spirit*	RCA	Oct. 6
Bob Dylan	*Desire*	Columbia	Mar. 4
Linda Ronstadt	*Hasten down the Wind*	Asylum	Oct. 28

1977 (gold)

Jackson Browne	*Running on Empty*	Elektra/Asylum	Dec. 28
Rita Coolidge	*Anytime . . . Anywhere*	A&M	Aug. 18
Rita Coolidge	(Your Love Has Lifted Me) Higher and Higher (S)	A&M	Aug. 30
Crosby, Stills and Nash	*CSN*	Atlantic	June 28
John Denver	*John Denver's Greatest Hits, Volume II*	RCA	Mar. 30
Dan Fogelberg	*Nether Lands*	Full Moon/Epic	Aug. 9
Dan Fogelberg	*Captured Angel*	Full Moon/Epic	Nov. 1
Carole King	*Simple Things*	Capitol	Sept. 23
Gordon Lightfoot	*Gord's Gold*	Warner/Reprise	Apr. 19
Kenny Loggins	*Celebrate Me Home*	Columbia	Sept. 20
Loggins and Messina	*The Best of Friends*	Columbia	May 10
Linda Ronstadt	*Simple Dreams*	Elektra/Asylum	Sept. 19
Bruce Springsteen	*The Wild, the Innocent, and the E Street Shuffle*	Columbia	May 2
James Taylor	*J.T.*	Columbia	July 5
Stills and Young Band	*Long May You Run*	Warner/Reprise	Jan. 12
Neil Young	*American Stars 'n' Bars*	Warner Brothers	Oct. 11

1977 (platinum)

Jackson Browne	*The Pretender*	Elektra/Asylum	Apr. 12
Crosby, Stills and Nash	*CSN*	Atlantic	Aug. 18
Linda Ronstadt	*Greatest Hits*	Elektra/Asylum	Jan. 19
James Taylor	*J.T.*	Columbia	Aug. 1

1978 (gold)

Blues Brothers	*Briefcase Full of Blues*	Atlantic	Dec. 22
Harry Chapin	*Greatest Stories—Live*	Elektra	June 7
Rita Coolidge	We're All Alone (S)	A&M	Feb. 2
Rita Coolidge	*Love Me Again*	A&M	June 21
Bob Dylan	*Street Legal*	Columbia	June 27
Dan Fogelberg and Tim Weisberg	*Twin Sons of Different Mothers*	Full Moon/Epic/CBS	Sept. 29
Art Garfunkel	*Watermark*	Columbia	Mar. 2
Carole King	*Carole King . . . Her Greatest Hits*	Ode/CBS	Apr. 4
Gordon Lightfoot	*Endless Wire*	Warner Brothers	Apr. 25
Kenny Loggins	*Nightwatch*	Columbia	Sept. 14
Joni Mitchell	*Don Juan's Reckless Daughter*	Asylum	Feb. 13
Linda Ronstadt	Blue Bayou (S)	Asylum	Jan. 23
Linda Ronstadt	*Living in the USA*	Asylum	Sept. 22
Linda Ronstadt	*A Retrospective*	Capitol	Nov. 13
Bruce Springsteen	*Darkness on the Edge of Town*	Columbia	June 16
Bruce Springsteen	*Greetings From Asbury Park, New Jersey*	Columbia	Nov. 21
Neil Young	*Comes a Time*	Warner/Reprise	Nov. 21
Warren Zevon	*Excitable Boy*	Asylum	Apr. 17

Artist	Title	Company	Date
	1978 (platinum)		
Jackson Browne	*Running on Empty*	Asylum	Aug. 25
John Denver	*I Want to Live*	RCA	May 12
Don Fogelberg and Tim Weisberg	*Twin Sons of Different Mothers*	Full Moon/Epic/CBS	Dec. 12
Kenny Loggins	*Nightwatch*	Columbia	Oct. 13
Linda Ronstadt	*Living in the USA*	Asylum	Sept. 22
Paul Simon	*Greatest Hits, Etc.*	Columbia	Feb. 1
Bruce Springstein	*Darkness on the Edge of Town*	Columbia	June 27
	1979 (gold)		
John Denver	*John Denver*	RCA	Jan. 19
Bob Dylan	*Slow Train Coming*	CBS	Dec. 26
Dan Fogelberg	*Home Free*	CBS	Dec. 26
Rickie Lee Jones	*Rickie Lee Jones*	Warner Brothers	May 22
Nicolette Larson	*Nicolette Larson*	Warner Brothers	Feb. 27
James Taylor	*Flag*	Columbia	May 15
Neil Young	*Decade*	Reprise	Aug. 9
Neil Young	*Rust Never Sleeps*	Reprise	Aug. 28
	1979 (platinum)		
Blues Brothers	*Briefcase Full of Blues*	Atlantic	Jan. 5
Dan Fogelberg	*Nether Lands*	Full Moon/Epic	Dec. 26
Rickie Lee Jones	*Rickie Lee Jones*	Warner Brothers	Aug. 7
	1980 (gold)		
Blues Brothers	*The Blues Brothers* (sound track)	Atlantic	Sept. 10
John Denver and the Muppets	*A Christmas Together*	RCA	Feb. 1
Dan Fogelberg	*Phoenix*	Full Moon/Epic	Mar. 13
Kenny Loggins	*Keep the Fire*	Columbia	Feb. 6
Kenny Loggins	*Alive*	Columbia	Nov. 14
Bonnie Raitt	*Sweet Forgiveness*	Warner Brothers	Oct. 24
Linda Ronstadt	*Mad Love*	Asylum	May 12
Linda Ronstadt	*Linda Ronstadt's Greatest Hits, Vol. II*	Asylum	Dec. 5
Paul Simon	*One Trick Pony*	Warner Brothers	Oct. 14
Bruce Springsteen	*The River*	Columbia	Dec. 12
Neil Young and Crazy Horse	*Live Rust*	Warner Brothers	Mar. 11
	1980 (platinum)		
Jackson Browne	*Hold Out*	Elektra	Sept. 15
John Denver and the Muppets	*A Christmas Together*	RCA	Feb. 1
Bob Dylan	*Slow Train Coming*	Columbia	May 9
Dan Fogelberg	*Phoenix*	Full Moon/Epic	Mar. 13
Gordon Lightfoot	*Summertime Dream*	Reprise	Feb. 7
Kenny Loggins	*Celebrate Me Home*	Columbia	Dec. 22
Linda Ronstadt	*Mad Love*	Asylum	May 12
Bruce Springsteen	*The River*	Columbia	Dec. 12
Neil Young	*Rust Never Sleeps*	Warner Brothers	Feb. 7

Artist	Title	Company	Date
1981 (gold)			
Kim Carnes	Bette Davis Eyes (S, co-written by Jackie DeShannon and Donna Weiss)	EMI/America	June 10
John Denver	*Some Days Are Diamonds*	RCA	Dec. 30
Dan Fogelberg	*The Innocent Age*	Full Moon	Nov. 3
Rickie Lee Jones	*Pirates*	Warner Brothers	Sept. 30
James Taylor	*Dad Loves His Work*	Columbia	May 5
1981 (platinum)			
John Denver	*John Denver's Greatest Hits, Vol. II*	RCA	June 5
Dan Fogelberg	*The Innocent Age*	Full Moon	Nov. 10
Loggins and Messina	*The Best of Friends*	Columbia	Dec. 30
1982 (gold)			
John Cougar (Mellencamp)	*American Fool*	Riva	July 6
John Cougar (Mellencamp)	Hurts So Good (S)	Riva	Oct. 8
John Cougar (Mellencamp)	Jack and Diane (S)	Riva	Oct. 29
Crosby, Stills and Nash	*Daylight Again*	Atlantic	Aug. 27
John Denver and Placido Domingo	*Perhaps Love*	Command	Mar. 8
Dan Fogelberg	*Greatest Hits*	Full Moon/Epic	Dec. 27
Kenny Loggins	*High Adventure*	Columbia	Nov. 22
Linda Ronstadt	*Get Closer*	Asylum	Nov. 23
Simon and Garfunkel	*The Concert in Central Park*	Warner Brothers	May 12
Bruce Springsteen	*Nebraska*	Columbia	Dec. 19
1982 (platinum)			
John Cougar (Mellencamp)	*American Fool*	Riva	Aug. 26
1983 (gold)			
Jackson Browne	*Lawyers in Love*	Asylum	Nov. 8
John Denver	*Seasons of the Heart*	RCA	Dec. 7
John Cougar Mellencamp	*Uh-Huh*	Riva	Dec. 16
Linda Ronstadt	*What's New*	Asylum	Nov. 17
1983 (platinum)			
Crosby, Stills and Nash	*Daylight Again*	Atlantic	Jan. 7
Dan Fogelberg	*Greatest Hits*	Full Moon/Epic	July 18
John Cougar Mellencamp	*Uh-Huh*	Riva	Dec. 16
Linda Ronstadt	*What's New*	Asylum	Dec. 14
1984 (gold)			
Bob Dylan	*Infidels*	Columbia	Jan. 23
Dan Fogelberg	*Windows and Walls*	Full Moon/Epic	Apr. 2
Bruce Springsteen	*Born in the U.S.A.*	Columbia	Aug. 7

Artist	Title	Company	Date
1984 (platinum)			
Bruce Springsteen	*Born in the U.S.A.*	Columbia	Aug. 7
1985 (gold)			
John Cougar Mellencamp	*Scarecrow*	Riva	Oct. 24
Bonnie Raitt	*Give It Up*	Warner Brothers	Dec. 3
Linda Ronstadt	*Lush Life*	Elektra	Jan. 17
Stevie Ray Vaughan and Double Trouble	*Couldn't Stand the Weather*	Epic	Dec. 23
1985 (platinum)			
John Cougar Mellencamp	*Scarecrow*	Riva	Oct. 24
Linda Ronstadt	*Lush Life*	Elektra	Jan. 17
1986 (gold)			
Jackson Browne	*Lives in the Balance*	Asylum	July 8
Fabulous Thunderbirds	*Tuff Enuff*	CBS Assoc.	July 25
Peter Gabriel	*So*	Geffen	July 22
Loggins and Messina	*Full Sail*	Columbia	Nov. 21
Linda Ronstadt	*For Sentimental Reasons*	Elektra	Dec. 8
Paul Simon	*Graceland*	Warner Brothers	Oct. 29
1986 (platinum)			
Byrds	*The Byrds Greatest Hits*	Columbia	Nov. 21
Bob Dylan	*Bob Dylan's Greatest Hits*	Columbia	Nov. 21
Bob Dylan	*Bob Dylan's Greatest Hits, Vol. II*	Columbia	Nov. 21
Bob Dylan	*Nashville Skyline*	Columbia	Nov. 21
Dan Fogelberg	*Souvenirs*	Epic	Nov. 21
Peter Gabriel	*So*	Geffen	Aug. 13
Art Garfunkel	*Breakaway*	Columbia	Nov. 21
Arlo Guthrie	*Alice's Restaurant*	Reprise	Oct. 13
Janis Ian	*Between the Lines*	Columbia	Nov. 21
Gordon Lightfoot	*Gord's Gold*	Reprise	Oct. 13
Gordon Lightfoot	*Sundown*	Reprise	Oct. 13
Loggins and Messina	*Loggins and Messina*	Columbia	Nov. 21
Joni Mitchell	*Blue*	Reprise	Oct. 13
Joni Mitchell	*Ladies of the Canyon*	Reprise	Oct. 13
Peter, Paul and Mary	*Peter, Paul and Mary*	Warner Brothers	Oct. 13
Peter, Paul and Mary	*The Best of Peter, Paul and Mary's (Ten) Years Together*	Warner Brothers	Oct. 13
Seals and Crofts	*Seals and Crofts' Greatest Hits*	Warner Brothers	Oct. 13
Paul Simon	*Paul Simon*	Columbia	Nov. 21
Paul Simon	*There Goes Rhymin' Simon*	Columbia	Nov. 21
Paul Simon	*Graceland*	Warner Brothers	Dec. 22
Simon and Garfunkel	*The Concert in Central Park*	Warner Brothers	May 13
Simon and Garfunkel	*Parsley, Sage, Rosemary and Thyme*	Columbia	Nov. 21
Simon and Garfunkel	*Bookends*	Columbia	Nov. 21
Simon and Garfunkel	*Bridge over Troubled Water*	Columbia	Nov. 21
Simon and Garfunkel	*Simon and Garfunkel's Greatest Hits*	Columbia	Nov. 21
Bruce Springsteen	*Born to Run*	Columbia	Nov. 21

Artist	Title	Company	Date
	1986 (platinum) (cont.)		
James Taylor	*Mud Slide Slim and the Blue Horizon*	Warner Brothers	Oct. 13
James Taylor	*Sweet Baby James*	Warner Brothers	Oct. 13
Neil Young	*After the Gold Rush*	Reprise	Oct. 13
Neil Young	*Everybody Knows This Is Nowhere*	Reprise	Oct. 13
Neil Young	*Harvest*	Reprise	Oct. 13
Neil Young	*Decade*	Reprise	Dec. 22
	1986 (multiplatinum)		
John Cougar Mellencamp	*American Fool* (3 M)	Riva	Apr. 7
John Cougar Mellencamp	*Scarecrow* (3 M)	Riva	Apr. 7
Bob Dylan	*Bob Dylan's Greatest Hits* (2 M)	Columbia	Nov. 21
Dan Fogelberg	*Souvenirs* (2 M)	Epic	Nov. 21
Peter, Paul and Mary	*Peter, Paul and Mary* (2 M)	Warner Brothers	Oct. 13
Seals and Crofts	*Seals and Crofts' Greatest Hits* (2 M)	Warner Brothers	Oct. 13
Simon and Garfunkel	*Bookends* (2 M)	Columbia	Nov. 21
Simon and Garfunkel	*Bridge over Troubled Water* (5 M)	Columbia	Nov. 21
Simon and Garfunkel	*Parsley, Sage, Rosemary and Thyme* (3 M)	Columbia	Nov. 21
Simon and Garfunkel	*Simon and Garfunkel's Greatest Hits* (5 M)	Columbia	Nov. 21
Bruce Springsteen	*Born to Run* (3 M)	Columbia	Nov. 21
James Taylor	*Sweet Baby James* (3 M)	Warner Brothers	Oct. 13
Neil Young	*After the Gold Rush* (2 M)	Reprise	Oct. 13
Neil Young	*Harvest* (3 M)	Reprise	Oct. 13
	1987 (gold)		
Robert Cray	*Strong Persuader*	Mercury	Mar. 10
Peter Gabriel	*Security*	Geffen	May 14
John Cougar Mellencamp	*The Lonesome Jubilee*	Mercury	Oct. 22
R.E.M.	*Life's Rich Pageant*	I.R.S.	Jan. 23
R.E.M.	*Document*	I.R.S.	Nov. 2
Linda Ronstadt, Dolly Parton, Emmylou Harris	*Trio*	Warner Brothers	July 14
Bruce Springsteen	*Bruce Springsteen and the E Street Band Live*	Columbia	Feb. 2
Bruce Springsteen	*Tunnel of Love*	Columbia	Dec. 31
Stevie Ray Vaughan	*Soul to Soul*	Epic	Aug. 11
Suzanne Vega	*Solitude Standing*	A&M	July 15
	1987 (platinum)		
John Cougar Mellencamp	*The Lonesome Jubilee*	Mercury	Oct. 22
Linda Ronstadt, Dolly Parton, Emmylou Harris	*Trio*	Warner Brothers	July 17
Bruce Springsteen	*Bruce Springsteen and the E Street Band Live*	Columbia	Feb. 2
Bruce Springsteen	*Tunnel of Love*	Columbia	Dec. 31

Artist	Title	Company	Date

1987 (multiplatinum)

Artist	Title	Company	Date
Peter Gabriel	*So* (2 M)	Geffen	July 21
Paul Simon	*Graceland* (2 M)	Warner Brothers	May 6
Bruce Springsteen	*Bruce Springsteen and the E Street Band Live 1975–1985* (3 M)	Columbia	Feb. 2
Bruce Springsteen	*Tunnel of Love* (2 M)	Columbia	Dec. 31

1988 (gold)

Artist	Title	Company	Date
Tracy Chapman	*Tracy Chapman*	Elektra	June 22
Robert Cray Band	*Don't Be Afraid of the Dark*	Mercury	Oct. 26
Bob Marley and the Wailers	*Legend*	Legend	June 22
Ziggy Marley and the Melody Makers	*Conscious Party*	Virgin	June 30
Linda Ronstadt	*Canciones de Mi Padre*	Elektra	Feb. 17
Robbie Robertson	*Robbie Robertson*	Geffen	Oct. 21
James Taylor	*Never Die Young*	Columbia	Apr. 11

1988 (platinum)

Artist	Title	Company	Date
Tracy Chapman	*Tracy Chapman*	Elektra	July 27
Robert Cray	*Strong Persuader*	Mercury	Feb. 10
Fabulous Thunderbirds	*Tuff Enuff*	CBS Assoc.	June 1
Bob Marley and the Wailers	*Legend*	Island	June 22
R.E.M.	*Document*	I.R.S.	Jan. 25
Neil Young	*Live Rust*	Reprise	Feb. 17

1988 (multiplatinum)

Artist	Title	Company	Date
Tracy Chapman	*Tracy Chapman* (2 M)	Elektra	Sept. 27
John Cougar Mellencamp	*The Lonesome Jubilee* (2 M)	Mercury	Jan. 14
Paul Simon	*Graceland* (3 M)	Warner Brothers	Jan. 14

1989 (gold)

Artist	Title	Company	Date
Tracy Chapman	*Crossroads*	Elektra	Nov. 21
Crosby, Still, Nash and Young	*American Dream*	Atlantic	Jan. 10
Bob Dylan	*Biograph*	Columbia	Mar. 29
Bob Dylan	*Dylan and the Dead*	Columbia	Aug. 3
Enya	*Waterman*	Geffen	Apr. 6
Indigo Girls	*Indigo Girls*	Epic	Aug. 11
Kenny Loggins	*Vox Humana*	Columbia	July 24
John Cougar Mellencamp	*Big Daddy*	Mercury	July 10
Bonnie Raitt	*Nick of Time*	Capitol	July 26
R.E.M.	*Green*	Warner Brothers	Jan. 10
Linda Ronstadt	*Cry Like a Rainstorm Howl Like the Wind*	Elektra	Nov. 21
Linda Ronstadt	*Don't Know Much*	Elektra	Dec. 6
Traveling Wilburys	*Traveling Wilburys*	Warner Brothers	Jan. 4

Artist	Title	Company	Date
	1989 (platinum)		
Jackson Browne	*For Everyman*	Elektra	May 16
Jackson Browne	*Late for the Sky*	Elektra	May 16
Tracy Chapman	*Crossroads*	Elektra	Nov. 21
Crosby, Stills, Nash and Young	*American Dream*	Atlantic	Jan. 27
Bob Dylan	*Blood on the Tracks*	Columbia	Aug. 9
John Cougar Mellencamp	*Big Daddy*	Mercury	July 10
R.E.M.	*Green*	Warner Brothers	Feb. 14
Linda Ronstadt	*Greatest Hits, Vol. II*	Asylum	Sept. 13
Linda Ronstadt	*Prisoner in Disguise*	Asylum	Sept. 13
Linda Ronstadt	*Cry Like a Rainstorm Howl Like the Wind*	Elektra	Dec. 6
Bruce Springsteen	*Nebraska*	Columbia	July 6
Traveling Wilburys	*Traveling Wilburys*	Warner Brothers	Jan. 4
	1989 (multiplatinum)		
Tracy Chapman	*Tracy Chapman* (3 M)	Elektra	Mar. 29
Linda Ronstadt	*Greatest Hits, Vol. I* (4 M)	Asylum	Aug. 13
Bruce Springsteen	*Darkness on the Edge of Town* (2 M)	Columbia	July 6
Bruce Springsteen	*Born in the U.S.A.* (11 M)	Columbia	Aug. 9
James Taylor	*James Taylor's Greatest Hits* (3 M)	Warner Brothers	June 1
James Taylor	*J.T.* (2 M)	Columbia	July 6
Traveling Wilburys	*Traveling Wilburys* (2 M)	Warner Brothers	Mar. 1
	1989 (videos - gold)		
Bruce Springsteen	*Video Anthology/1978–1988*	CBS Music Video Enterprises	Mar. 29
	1989 (videos - platinum)		
Bruce Springsteen	*Video Anthology/1978–1988*	CBS Music Video Enterprises	Mar. 29
	1989 (videos - multiplatinum)		
Bruce Springsteen	*Video Anthology/1978–1988* (350,000)	CBS Music Video Enterprises	Mar. 29
	1990 (gold)		
Vaughan Brothers	*Family Style*	Epic	Nov. 19
Stevie Ray Vaughan and Double Trouble	*Live Alive*	Epic	May 24
Stevie Ray Vaughan and Double Trouble	*Texas Flood*	Epic	Aug. 13
Stevie Ray Vaughan and Double Trouble	*In Step*	Epic	Feb. 13
Neil Young	*Freedom*	Reprise	Feb. 21
	1990 (platinum)		
Kenny Loggins	Footloose (S)	Columbia	Jan. 17
Bonnie Raitt	*Nick of Time*	Capitol	Mar. 1
Linda Ronstadt	Blue Bayou (S)	Elektra	Nov. 27

Artist	Title	Company	Date

1990 (platinum) (cont.)

Artist	Title	Company	Date
Bruce Springsteen	*The Wild, the Innocent, and the E Street Shuffle*	Columbia	July 10
Vaughan Brothers	*Family Style*	Epic	Nov. 19
Stevie Ray Vaughan and Double Trouble	*Couldn't Stand the Weather*	Epic	Sept. 26

1990 (multiplatinum)

Artist	Title	Company	Date
Bob Marley and the Wailers	*Legend* (2 M)	Island	July 20
Bonnie Raitt	*Nick of Time* (3 M)	Capitol	May 7
Linda Ronstadt	*Cry Like a Rainstorm Howl Like the Wind* (2 M)	Elektra	Nov. 27
Linda Ronstadt	*Simple Dreams* (3 M)	Elektra	Nov. 27
Bruce Springsteen	*Born in the U.S.A.* (12 M)	Columbia	Mar. 12
Bruce Springsteen	*The River* (2 M)	Columbia	Aug. 21

1990 (videos - gold)

Artist	Title	Company	Date
Bob Marley and the Wailers	*The Bob Marley Story*	Island Visual Arts	Nov. 27
R.E.M.	*Pop Screen*	Warner Music Video	May 22
R.E.M.	*R.E.M. Tour Film*	Warner Music Video	Nov. 30

1991 (gold)

Artist	Title	Company	Date
Robert Johnson	*The Complete Recordings* (box set)	Columbia	Jan. 22
R.E.M.	*Fables of the Reconstruction*	I.R.S.	June 24
R.E.M.	Losing My Religion (S)	Warner Brothers	Sept. 12
R.E.M.	*Murmur*	I.R.S.	Oct. 10
R.E.M.	Out of Time	Warner Brothers	May 24
R.E.M.	*Reckoning*	I.R.S.	June 24
Bonnie Raitt	*Luck of the Draw*	Capitol	Aug. 26
Paul Simon	*Negotiations and Love Songs 1971–1986*	Warner Brothers	Mar. 19
Paul Simon	*The Rhythm of the Saints*	Warner Brothers	Jan. 8
James Taylor	*New Moon Shine*	Columbia	Dec. 16
Traveling Wilburys	*Volume 3*	Warner Brothers	Jan. 8

1991 (platinum)

Artist	Title	Company	Date
The Band	*The Band*	Capitol	Dec. 2
Loggins and Messina	*On Stage*	Columbia	July 22
Loggins and Messina	*Sittin' In*	Columbia	July 22
Ziggy Marley and the Melody Makers	*Conscious Party*	Virgin	Aug. 27
R.E.M.	*Out of Time*	Warner Brothers	May 24
Bonnie Raitt	*Luck of the Draw*	Capitol	Aug. 26
Linda Ronstadt	*Canciones De Mi Padre*	Elektra	Aug. 27
Linda Ronstadt	*Heart Like a Wheel*	Capitol	Nov. 27
Simon and Garfunkel	*Sounds of Silence*	Columbia	July 22
Paul Simon	*The Rhythm of the Saints*	Warner Brothers	Jan. 8
Bruce Springsteen	*Greetings from Asbury Park, New Jersey*	Columbia	Aug. 9
Traveling Wilburys	*Volume 3*	Warner Brothers	Jan. 8
Stevie Ray Vaughan and Double Trouble	*In Step*	Epic	Jan. 29

Artist	Title	Company	Date

1991 (multiplatinum)

Artist	Title	Company	Date
Peter Gabriel	*So* (3 M)	Geffen	Dec. 4
R.E.M.	*Out of Time* (2 M)	Warner Brothers	June 19
R.E.M.	*Out of Time* (3 M)	Warner Brothers	Oct. 11
Bonnie Raitt	*Luck of the Draw* (2 M)	Capitol	Dec. 13
Bonnie Raitt	*Nick of Time* (3 M)	Capitol	Oct. 10
Linda Ronstadt	*Heart Like a Wheel* (2 M)	Capitol	Nov. 27
Simon and Garfunkel	*Sounds of Silence* (2 M)	Columbia	July 22
Paul Simon	*The Rhythm of the Saints* (2 M)	Warner Brothers	Sept. 12
James Taylor	*James Taylor's Greatest Hits* (4 M)	Warner Brothers	Oct. 23

1991 (videos - gold)

Artist	Title	Company	Date
R.E.M.	*This Film Is On*	Warner/Reprise Music Video	Nov. 26
Stevie Ray Vaughan and Double Trouble	*Pride and Joy*	Sony Music Video	Feb. 15

1991 (videos - platinum)

Artist	Title	Company	Date
Stevie Ray Vaughan and Double Trouble	*Pride and Joy*	Sony Music Video	Feb. 15

1992 (gold)

Artist	Title	Company	Date
Crosby, Stills and Nash	*Crosby, Stills and Nash* (box set)	Atlantic	Aug. 20
Peter Gabriel	*Peter Gabriel*	Geffen	Aug. 3
Peter Gabriel	*Shaking the Tree—16 Golden Greats*	Geffen	Aug. 3
Peter Gabriel	*Us*	Geffen	Dec. 2
Bob Marley	*Songs of Freedom* (box set)	Island	Dec. 7
Simon and Garfunkel	*Collected Works* (box set)	Columbia	July 8
Bruce Springsteen	Dancin' in the Dark (S)	Columbia	May 5
Bruce Springsteen	*Human Touch*	Columbia	May 28
Bruce Springsteen	*Lucky Town*	Columbia	May 28
Bruce Springsteen	Santa Claus Is Coming to Town (S)	Columbia	May 5
Stevie Ray Vaughan and Double Trouble	*The Sky Is Crying*	Epic	Jan. 24

1992 (platinum)

Artist	Title	Company	Date
Crosby, Stills, Nash and Young	*Déjà Vu*	Atlantic	Nov. 4
Crosby, Stills, Nash and Young	*Four Way Street*	Atlantic	Dec. 18
Crosby, Stills, Nash and Young	*So Far*	Atlantic	Dec. 18
Donovan	*Donovan's Greatest Hits*	Epic	Aug. 11
Peter Gabriel	*Us*	Geffen	Dec. 14
Bob Marley	*Songs of Freedom* (box set)	Island	Dec. 7
Bruce Springsteen	Dancin' in the Dark (S)	Columbia	May 5
Bruce Springsteen	*Human Touch*	Columbia	May 28
Bruce Springsteen	*Lucky Town*	Columbia	May 28
Stevie Ray Vaughan and Double Trouble	*Texas Flood*	Epic	Jan. 22
Stevie Ray Vaughan and Double Trouble	*The Sky Is Crying*	Epic	Jan. 24
Stevie Ray Vaughan	*Soul to Soul*	Epic	Aug. 11

Artist	Title	Company	Date
1992 (multiplatinum)			
Crosby, Stills and Nash	*CSN* (4 M)	Atlantic	Nov. 4
Crosby, Stills, Nash and Young	*Déjà Vu* (7 M)	Atlantic	Nov. 4
Crosby, Stills, Nash and Young	*Four Way Street* (4 M)	Atlantic	Dec. 18
Crosby, Stills, Nash and Young	*So Far* (6 M)	Atlantic	Dec. 18
Bob Marley and the Wailers	*Legend* (3 M)	Island	Mar. 31
Bonnie Raitt	*Luck of the Draw* (4 M)	Capitol	July 20
Paul Simon	*Graceland* (4 M)	Warner Brothers	Feb. 5
Bruce Springsteen	*Bruce Springsteen and the E Street Band Live, 1975–1985* (12 M)	Columbia	July 8
Bruce Springsteen	*Greetings from Asbury Park, New Jersey* (2 M)	Columbia	Apr. 9
1992 (videos - gold)			
Stevie Ray Vaughan and Double Trouble	*Live at the El Mocambo—1983*	Sony Music Video	Apr. 9
1993 (gold)			
John Mellencamp	*Human Wheels*	Mercury	Nov. 10
Peter, Paul and Mary	*Peter, Paul and Mommy*	Warner Brothers	Apr. 2
John Princ	*The Best of John Prine*	Atlantic	Jan. 26
Bonnie Raitt	*Bonnie Raitt Collection*	Warner Brothers	June 29
Paul Simon	*Paul Simon 1964–1993* (box set)	Warner Brothers	Dec. 17
James Taylor	*James Taylor Live* (box set)	Columbia	Oct. 25
Neil Young	*Harvest Moon*	Reprise	Jan. 15
Neil Young	*Unplugged*	Reprise	Nov. 16
1993 (platinum)			
Jim Croce	*Photographs and Memories, His Greatest Hits*	SAJ	June 30
Enya	*Enya*	Atlantic	Aug. 10
Carole King	*Tapestry*	Epic	Mar. 1
John Mellencamp	*Human Wheels*	Mercury	Nov. 10
James Taylor	*James Taylor Live* (box set)	Columbia	Nov. 16
Neil Young	*Harvest Moon*	Reprise	Feb. 3
1993 (multiplatinum)			
Enya	*Shepherd Moons* (2 M)	Reprise	Jan. 15
Enya	*Watermark* (2 M)	Reprise	Jan. 15
Carole King	*Tapestry* (2 M)	Epic	Mar. 1
Bob Marley and the Wailers	*Legend* (4 M)	Island	June 24
R.E.M.	*Automatic for the People* (3 M)	Warner Brothers	Nov. 16
Linda Ronstadt	*What's New* (3 M)	Elektra	May 28
1993 (videos - gold)			
Bruce Springsteen	*MTV Unplugged*	Columbia	Feb. 18

Artist	Title	Company	Date

1994 (gold)

Artist	Title	Company	Date
Beck	*Loser*	DGC	Apr. 11
Beck	*Mellow Gold*	DGC	May 3
Bob Dylan	*The Times They Are a-Changin'*	Columbia	Nov. 14
Dan Fogelberg	*High Country*	Epic	Nov. 9
Hootie and the Blowfish	*Cracked Rear View*	Atlantic	Nov. 10
Indigo Girls	*Swamp Ophelia*	Epic	July 5
Kenny Loggins	*Return to Pooh Corner*	Columbia	Dec. 5
Sarah McLachlan	*Fumbling Towards Ecstasy*	Arista	Aug. 8
John Mellencamp	*Dance Naked*	Mercury	Nov. 14
R.E.M.	*Monster*	Warner Brothers	Dec. 6
Bonnie Raitt	*Longing in Their Hearts*	Capitol	May 23
Sound Track	*Philadelphia*	Epic	Mar. 22
Bruce Springsteen	Streets of Philadelphia (S)	Columbia	Apr. 26
Various Artists	*Bob Dylan—30th Anniversary Concert Celebration* (box set)	Columbia	Jan. 14
Neil Young and Crazy Horse	*Sleeps with Angels*	Reprise	Oct. 18

1994 (platinum)

Artist	Title	Company	Date
Indigo Girls	*Rites of Passage*	Epic	Nov. 18
Robert Johnson	*Robert Johnson—the Complete Recordings* (box set)	Columbia	Apr. 26
John Mellencamp	*Dance Naked*	Mercury	Nov. 14
R.E.M.	*Monster*	Warner Brothers	Dec. 6
Bonnie Raitt	*Longing in Their Hearts*	Capitol	May 23
Paul Simon	*Negotiations and Love Songs 1971–1986*	Warner Brothers	Aug. 17
Sound Track	*Philadelphia*	Epic	Apr. 8
James Taylor	*Flag*	Columbia	Oct. 28
James Taylor	*Never Die Young*	Columbia	Oct. 3
James Taylor	*New Moon Shine*	Columbia	Dec. 13
James Taylor	*That's Why I'm Here*	Columbia	Oct. 6
Stevie Ray Vaughan and Double Trouble	*Live Alive*	Epic	Dec. 5
The Wailers	*Burnin'*	Island	May 23

1994 (multiplatinum)

Artist	Title	Company	Date
Bob Dylan	*Blood on the Tracks* (2 M)	Columbia	Nov. 14
Bob Dylan	*Bob Dylan's Greatest Hits, Volume II* (2 M)	Columbia	Nov. 14
Enya	*Shepherd Moons* (3 M)	Reprise	Mar. 25
Peter Gabriel	*So* (4 M)	Geffen	Nov. 9
Gordon Lightfoot	*Gord's Gold* (2 M)	Reprise	Aug. 4
Loggins and Messina	*Best of Friends* (2 M)	Columbia	Nov. 21
Bob Marley and the Wailers	*Legend* (5 M)	Island	May 23
Bob Marley and the Wailers	*Songs of Freedom* (box set, 4 CDs) (2 M)	Island	Sept. 28
Peter, Paul and Mary	*The Best of Peter, Paul and Mary's (Ten) Years Together* (2 M)	Warner Brothers	Aug. 4
R.E.M.	*Green* (2 M)	Warner Brothers	Aug. 17
R.E.M.	*Monster* (2 M)	Warner Brothers	Dec. 6
Bonnie Raitt	*Longing in Their Hearts* (2 M)	Capitol	May 23
Bonnie Raitt	*Luck of the Draw* (5 M)	Capitol	Jan. 26
Bonnie Raitt	*Nick of Time* (4 M)	Capitol	Dec. 13

Artist	Title	Company	Date
	1994 (multiplatinum) (cont.)		
Linda Ronstadt	*Greatest Hits, Volume I* (5 M)	Asylum	June 28
Simon and Garfunkel	*Simon and Garfunkel's Greatest Hits* (6 M)	Columbia	Nov. 14
Bruce Springsteen	*Born in the U.S.A.* (14 M)	Columbia	Oct. 17
Bruce Springsteen	*Born to Run* (4 M)	Columbia	Nov. 17
Bruce Springsteen	*The River* (3 M)	Columbia	Oct. 17
James Taylor	*James Taylor's Greatest Hits* (7 M)	Warner Brothers	Aug. 4
James Taylor	*Mud Slide Slim and the Blue Horizon* (2 M)	Warner Brothers	Aug. 5
Traveling Wilburys	*Traveling Wilburys* (3 M)	Warner Brothers	Aug. 4
Neil Young	*Harvest* (4 M)	Reprise	June 27
	1995 (gold)		
Jackson Browne	*I'm Alive*	Elektra	Dec. 6
Robert Cray	*Midnight Stroll*	Mercury	May 15
Ziggy Marley	*One Bright Day*	Island	Nov. 16
John Mellencamp	*John Cougar*	Mercury	Feb. 17
John Mellencamp	*Nothin' Matters and What If It Did*	Mercury	Feb. 15
Bruce Springsteen	*Greatest Hits*	Columbia	Apr. 24
Neil Young	*Mirror Ball*	Reprise	Sept. 12
	1995 (platinum)		
Beck	*Mellow Gold*	DGC	Aug. 8
Hootie and the Blowfish	*Cracked Rear View*	Atlantic	Jan. 25
Carole King	*Carole King Music*	Ode	July 17
Sarah McLachlan	*Fumbling Towards Ecstasy*	Arista	Jan. 19
John Mellencamp	*Nothin' Matters and What If It Did*	Mercury	July 13
Bruce Springsteen	*Greatest Hits*	Columbia	Apr. 24
	1995 (multiplatinum)		
Enya	*Shepherd Moons* (4 M)	Reprise	Feb. 9
Enya	*Watermark* (3 M)	Reprise	Mar. 8
Dan Fogelberg	*Nether Lands* (2 M)	Epic	Feb. 10
Dan Fogelberg	*Phoenix* (2 M)	Epic	Aug. 8
Hootie and the Blowfish	*Cracked Rear View* (2 M)	Atlantic	Mar. 14
Hootie and the Blowfish	*Cracked Rear View* (3 M)	Atlantic	May 9
Hootie and the Blowfish	*Cracked Rear View* (4 M)	Atlantic	May 24
Hootie and the Blowfish	*Cracked Rear View* (6 M)	Atlantic	Aug. 8
Hootie and the Blowfish	*Cracked Rear View* (10 M)	Atlantic	Oct. 19
Hootie and the Blowfish	*Cracked Rear View* (11 M)	Atlantic	Nov. 13
Carole King	*Tapestry* (10 M)	Ode	July 17
John Mellencamp	*American Fool* (4 M)	Polygram	Jan. 27
John Mellencamp	*Scarecrow* (4 M)	Mercury	Jan. 27
John Mellencamp	*The Lonesome Jubilee* (3 M)	Mercury	Jan. 27
John Mellencamp	*Uh-Huh* (3 M)	Mercury	Jan. 27
R.E.M.	*Automatic for the People* (4 M)	Warner Brothers	Feb. 9
R.E.M.	*Monster* (3 M)	Warner Brothers	Mar. 22
R.E.M.	*Monster* (4 M)	Warner Brothers	Aug. 10
Paul Simon	*Graceland* (5 M)	Warner Brothers	Jan. 31
Bruce Springsteen	*Born in the U.S.A.* (15 M)	Columbia	Apr. 19
Bruce Springsteen	*Greatest Hits* (2 M)	Columbia	Apr. 24
Stevie Ray Vaughan and Double Trouble	*In Step* (2 M)	Epic	June 6
Stevie Ray Vaughan and Double Trouble	*The Sky Is Falling* (2 M)	Epic	June 6

Artist	Title	Company	Date

1995 (videos - platinum)

| Stevie Ray Vaughan and Double Trouble | *Live at the Mocambo—1983* | Sony Music Video | Oct. 13 |

1996 (gold)

Artist	Title	Company	Date
Tracy Chapman	*New Beginning*	Elektra	Mar. 22
Tracy Chapman	Give Me One Reason (S)	Elektra	June 11
Enya	*The Memory of Trees*	Reprise	Feb. 27
Enya	*The Celts*	Reprise	June 27
Hootie and the Blowfish	*Fairweather Johnson*	Atlantic	June 11
Indigo Girls	*1200 Curfews*	Epic	Aug. 14
Indigo Girls	*Strange Fire*	Epic	Nov. 15
Jewel	*Pieces of You*	Atlantic	May 13
Bob Marley and the Wailers	*Uprising*	Island	Mar. 14
Bob Marley and the Wailers	*Rastaman Vibration*	Island	Mar. 14
Bob Marley and the Wailers	*Live!*	Island	Mar. 14
Bob Marley and the Wailers	*Kaya*	Island	Mar. 14
Bob Marley and the Wailers	*Exodus*	Island	Mar. 14
Bob Marley and the Wailers	*Confrontation*	Island	Mar. 14
John Mellencamp	*Mr. Happy Go Lucky*	Mercury	Dec. 3
R.E.M.	*New Adventures in Hi-Fi*	Warner Brothers	Nov. 18
Bonnie Raitt	*Road Tested*	Capitol	Feb. 2
Bruce Springsteen	*Ghost of Tom Joad*	Columbia	Aug. 1
Various Artists	*Tapestry Revisited—a Tribute to Carole King*	Lava	June 12
Stevie Ray Vaughan and Double Trouble	*Greatest Hits*	Epic	Apr. 11

1996 (platinum)

Artist	Title	Company	Date
Tracy Chapman	*New Beginning*	Elektra	May 3
Tracy Chapman	Give Me One Reason (S)	Elektra	Aug. 27
Judy Collins	*Judith*	Elektra	Mar. 20
Enya	*The Memory of Trees*	Reprise	Feb. 27
Peter Gabriel	*Shaking the Tree—16 Golden Greats*	Geffen	June 24
Hootie and the Blowfish	*Fairweather Johnson*	Atlantic	June 11
Indigo Girls	*Swamp Ophelia*	Epic	Aug. 14
Jewel	*Pieces of You*	Atlantic	Aug. 6
R.E.M.	*New Adventures in Hi-Fi*	Warner Brothers	Nov. 18

1996 (multiplatinum)

Artist	Title	Company	Date
Tracy Chapman	*Tracy Chapman* (4 M)	Electra	Aug. 19
Tracy Chapman	*New Beginning* (2 M)	Elektra	July 9
Tracy Chapman	*New Beginning* (3 M)	Electra	Aug. 27
Robert Cray	*Strong Persuader* (2 M)	Mercury	June 13
Enya	*Shepherd Moons* (5 M)	Reprise	Mar. 15
Enya	*Watermark* (4 M)	Reprise	Mar. 15
Enya	*The Memory of Trees* (2 M)	Reprise	Aug. 7
Peter Gabriel	*Shaking the Tree—16 Golden Greats* (2 M)	Geffen	June 24

Artist	Title	Company	Date
1996 (multiplatinum) (cont.)			
Peter Gabriel	*So* (5 M)	Geffen	Oct. 25
Hootie and the Blowfish	*Cracked Rear View* (12 M)	Atlantic	Jan. 24
Hootie and the Blowfish	*Cracked Rear View* (13 M)	Atlantic	Mar. 12
Hootie and the Blowfish	*Cracked Rear View* (14 M)	Atlantic	June 13
Hootie and the Blowfish	*Fairweather Johnson* (2 M)	Atlantic	June 11
Bob Marley and the Wailers	*Legend* (7 M)	Island	Mar. 20
Bob Marley and the Wailers	*Legend* (8 M)	Island	Mar. 22
Bob Marley and the Wailers	*Legend* (9 M)	Island	Nov. 1
Sarah McLachlan	*Fumbling Towards Ecstasy* (2 M)	Arista	Aug. 1
John Mellencamp	*American Fool* (5 M)	Polygram	May 23
Simon and Garfunkel	*The Concert in Central Park* (2 M)	Warner Brothers	May 1
James Taylor	*James Taylor's Greatest Hits* (8 M)	Warner Brothers	May 16
James Taylor	*James Taylor's Greatest Hits* (11 M)	Warner Brothers	Aug. 7
1996 (videos - gold)			
Hootie and the Blowfish	*Summer Camp with Trucks* (video longform)	Atlantic	Apr. 11
Bob Marley and the Wailers	*Legend* (video longform)	Island Video	Mar. 20
Stevie Ray Vaughan and Double Trouble	*Live from Texas* (video longform)	Sony Music Video	Feb. 14
1996 (videos - platinum)			
Bob Marley and the Wailers	*The Bob Marley Story* (video longform)	Island Video	Feb. 14
1997 (gold)			
Allman Brothers	*Where It All Begins*	Epic	Nov. 26
B.B. King	*Best of B.B. King*	MCA	Nov. 18
Paula Cole	*This Fire*	Warner Brothers	May 8
Shawn Colvin	*A Few Small Repairs*	Columbia	May 30
John Denver	*Wildlife Concert*	Legacy/Columbia	Nov. 12
Bob Dylan	*Bootleg Series Vols. 1–3, Rare and Unreleased*	Columbia	Aug. 19
Bob Dylan	*Pat Garrett and Billy the Kid*	Columbia	Aug. 19
Bob Dylan	*Time out of Mind*	Columbia	Oct. 27
Peter Gabriel	*Secret World Live*	Geffen	Nov. 18
Indigo Girls	*Shaming of the Sun*	Epic	July 7
Jewel	You Were Meant for Me (S)	Atlantic	Feb. 28
Rickie Lee Jones	*Flying Cowboys*	Geffen	Sept. 18
Bob Marley and the Wailers	*Natural Mystic*	Island	Sept. 19
Sarah McLachlan	*Solace*	Arista	Apr. 2
Sarah McLachlan	*Surfacing*	Arista	Sept. 3
John Mellencamp	*The Best That I Could*	Mercury	Dec. 15
James Taylor	*Hourglass*	Columbia	July 16
Suzanne Vega	*99.9°F*	A&M	Oct. 22
Neil Young	*Zuma*	Reprise	Feb. 7

Artist	Title	Company	Date
1997 (platinum)			
Beck	*Odelay*	DGC	Jan. 28
Jackson Browne	*Jackson Browne*	Elektra	Dec. 17
B.B. King	*Best of B.B. King*	MCA	Nov. 18
Harry Chapin	*Greatest Stories—Live*	Asylum	Feb. 12
Paula Cole	*This Fire*	Warner Brothers	Oct. 22
Judy Collins	*Colors of the Day*	Elektra	Dec. 12
Bob Dylan	*Highway 61 Revisited*	Columbia	Aug. 19
Bob Dylan and the Band	*Before the Flood*	Columbia	Sept. 8
Jewel	You Were Meant for Me (S)	Atlantic	June 20
Sarah McLachlan	*Surfacing*	Arista	Sept. 3
John Mellencamp	*Mr. Happy Go Lucky*	Mercury	May 7
Joni Mitchell	*Court and Spark*	Elektra	Dec. 12
Simon and Garfunkel	*The Graduate (sound track)*	Columbia	Jan. 31
Simon and Garfunkel	*Wednesday Morning, 3 A.M.*	Columbia	Nov. 5
Stevie Ray Vaughan and Double Trouble	*Greatest Hits*	Epic	Jan. 8
Suzanne Vega	*Solitude Standing*	A&M	Oct. 22
Warren Zevon	*Excitable Boy*	Elektra	Nov. 7
1997 (multiplatinum)			
Alllman Brothers	*A Decade of Hits* (2 M)	Polydor	Apr. 23
Jackson Browne	*The Pretender* (2 M)	Elektra	Dec. 12
Jackson Browne	*Runing on Empty* (5 M)	Elektra	Dec. 12
Bob Dylan	*Bob Dylan's Greatest Hits, Vol. II* (5 M)	Columbia	Aug. 8
Dan Fogelberg	*The Innocent Age* (2 M)	Epic	Jan. 29
Dan Fogelberg	*Dan Fogelberg—Greatest Hits* (3 M)	Epic	Jan. 10
Hootie and the Blowfish	*Cracked Rear View* (15 M)	Atlantic	Jan. 24
Indigo Girls	*Indigo Girls* (2 M)	Epic	June 3
Jewel	*Pieces of You* (2 M)	Atlantic	Jan. 10
Jewel	*Pieces of You* (3 M)	Atlantic	Feb. 28
Jewel	*Pieces of You* (4 M)	Atlantic	May 28
Jewel	*Pieces of You* (5 M)	Atlantic	July 9
Jewel	*Pieces of You* (6 M)	Atlantic	Sept. 24
Jewel	*Pieces of You* (7 M)	Atlantic	Nov. 5
Joni Mitchell	*Court and Spark* (2 M)	Elektra	Dec. 12
Linda Ronstadt	*Living in the U.S.A.* (2 M)	Elektra	Dec. 12
Simon and Garfunkel	*Bridge over Troubled Water* (6 M)	Columbia	Jan. 31
Simon and Garfunkel	*The Graduate* (sound track) (2 M)	Columbia	Apr. 28
Bruce Springsteen	*Greatest Hits* (3 M)	Columbia	Apr. 28
James Taylor	*Live* (2 M)	Columbia	Jan. 31
James Taylor	*J.T.* (3 M)	Columbia	Jan. 31
Stevie Ray Vaughan and Double Trouble	*Texas Flood* (2 M)	Epic	Mar. 6
Stevie Ray Vaughan and Double Trouble	*Couldn't Stand the Weather* (2 M)	Epic	June 20
Neil Young	*Harvest Moon* (2 M)	Reprise	July 16
1997 (videos - gold)			
Bruce Springsteen	*Blood Brothers* (longform)	Columbia Music	July 23

Artist	Title	Company	Date
	1998 (gold)		
Beck	*Mutations*	DGC	Dec. 7
Enya	*Paint the Sky with Stars—The Best of Enya*	Reprise	June 6
Peter Gabriel	*Passion: Music for the Last Temptation of Christ*	Geffen	July 23
Hootie and the Blowfish	*Musical Chairs*	Atlantic	Oct. 13
Jewel	*Spirit*	Atlantic	Nov. 24
B.B. King	*Deuces Wild*	MCA	Mar. 18
Loreena McKennitt	*Book of Secrets*	Quinlan Road	Mar. 2
Sarah McLachlan	*Adia* (S)	Arista	July 8
John Mellencamp	*John Mellencamp*	Columbia	Nov. 4
Bonnie Raitt	*Fundamental*	Capitol	May 8
Bruce Springsteen	*Tracks*	Columbia	Dec. 9
Warren Zevon	*A Quiet Normal Life—the Best of Warren Zevon*	Asylum	Dec. 4
	1998 (platinum)		
Shawn Colvin	*A Few Small Repairs*	Columbia	Mar. 31
Bob Dylan	*Time out of Mind*	Columbia	June 2
Enya	*Paint the Sky with Stars—the Best of Enya*	Reprise	June 6
Enya	*The Celts*	Reprise	May 21
Hootie and the Blowfish	*Musical Chairs*	Atlantic	Oct. 13
Jewel	*Spirit*	Atlantic	Nov. 24
Loreena McKennitt	*Book of Secrets*	Warner Brothers	Mar. 2
John Mellencamp	*The Best That I Could*	Mercury	July 20
Bruce Springsteen	*Tracks*	Columbia	Dec. 9
James Taylor	*Hourglass*	Columbia	June 30
	1998 (multiplatinum)		
Beck	*Odelay* (2 M)	DGC	July 15
Paula Cole	*This Fire* (2 M)	Warner Brothers	June 30
Hootie and the Blowfish	*Fairweather Johnson* (3 M)	Atlantic	Sept. 21
Jewel	*Pieces of You* (8 M)	Atlantic	Jan. 26
Jewel	*Spirit* (2 M)	Atlantic	Dec. 2
Sarah McLachlan	*Fumbling Towards Ecstasy* (3 M)	Arista	June 25
Sarah McLachlan	*Surfacing* (2 M)	Arista	Jan. 12
Sarah McLachlan	*Surfacing* (3 M)	Arista	June 2
Sarah McLachlan	*Surfacing* (4 M)	Arista	Nov. 6
Bonnie Raitt	*Nick of Time* (5 M)	Capitol	Apr. 3
Bonnie Raitt	*Luck of the Draw* (7 M)	Capitol	Apr. 3
	1998 (videos - gold)		
Peter Gabriel	*Secret World Live* (video longform)	Geffen	Mar. 16
Bob Marley and the Wailers	*Time Will Tell* (video longform)	Polygram	July 28
Stevie Ray Vaughan and Double Trouble	*Live from Austin, Texas* (video longform)	Sony Music Video	July 8

BIBLIOGRAPHY

Aaron, John, "Gordon Lightfoot," *Guitar Player,* December 1973, p. 20.

Ainsworth, Bill, "Anarchy in Songs—Utah Phillips Keeps the Wobbly Flame Alive," *Sacramento News & Review,* July 25, 1991.

Alarik, Scott, Interview with Si Kahn, *Performing Songwriter,* September–October 1995.

———, Interview with Patty Larkin, *Performing Songwriter,* September–October 1993.

———, Interview with Ellis Paul, *Performing Songwriter,* January–February 1994.

Anonymous, "Champion Country Picker" (Doc Watson), *Time,* August 25, 1967, pp. 40–41.

———, "James Taylor, One Man's Family of Rock," *Time,* March 1, 1971, pp. 45–53.

———, "Latin Soul," (Jose Feliciano) *Time,* September 27, 1968.

———, "A Loose Federation" (Crosby, Stills, Nash and Young), *Time,* March 30, p. 70, 1962.

———, "Montage of Loss" (Don McLean), *Time,* February 1972, p. 55.

Ansorge, Rick, "Goodman Leads His Flock from the Wilderness" (Steve Goodman), *Chicago Lakes Countryside,* March 16, 1978.

Arnold, Christine, "Three Ex-Birds Fly a New Course" (McGuinn, Clark, and Hillman), *Miami Herald,* October 20, 1978.

Arsenault, Charlene J., "Ellis Paul Catches a Buzz," *Worcester Magazine,* July 17, 1966.

Asch, Moses, and Silber, Irwin, *The Ballads, Blues, and Folksongs of Cisco Houston,* Oak Publications, New York, 1965.

Atkinson, Terry, "Life Isn't Quite So Blue for Van Zandt," (Townes Van Zandt), *Los Angeles Times,* July 26, 1985.

Avery, Kevin, "The Bioponic Songman" (Vince Bell), *Gallery,* April 1995.

Axton, Mae Boren, "Hoyt Axton," *Picking Up the Tempo,* February–March 1976.

Azerrad, Michael, "Luka Bloom Doesn't Want to Be Just Another Boring Folkie," *Rolling Stone,* March 19, 1992.

Bedeaux, Ed, "Please Don't Tell What Train I'm On" (Elizabeth Cotten), *Sing Out!,* September 1964.

Baez, Joan, *And A Voice to Sing With* (autobiography), Summit, 1987.

Baggelar, Kristin, and Milton, Donald, *Folk Music: More Than a Song,* Thomas Y Crowell Co., New York, 1976.

Bartlett, Ellen J., Interview with Arlo Guthrie, *Boston Globe,* December 7, 1988.

Becker, Terry, "Politics Proved Final Note to Weavers' Brief Reign" (Lee Hayes obit),

Berkowitz, Kenny, Interview with David Doucet (BeauSoleil), *Ithaca Times,* March 23, 1995.

Bessman, Jim, Interview with Mary Black, *Billboard,* August 28, 1993.

———, "Siberry's Sheeba Takes Indie Route," (Jane Siberry), *Billboard,* June 1, 1996.

———, Interview with Chris Smither, *Billboard,* December 21, 1996.

Biederman, Patricia Ward, "At Home on the Range" (Ian Tyson), *Los Angeles Times,* Valley Edition Calendar, April 3, 1987.

Billboard [weekly], New York, New York, BPI Communications, various issues.

Blackstock, Peter, "Son Volt—Jay Farrar Traces a Path Away from Uncle Tupelo," *No Depression,* Fall 1995.

Blume, Mary, "The Rise of Leonard Cohen," *Los Angeles Times,* Part IV, August 28, 1970, P. 16.

Boehm, Mike, "Back on Home 'Turf'" (Luka Bloom), *Los Angeles Times,* Calendar Section, June 14, 1994.

———, "Flatpicking Professor Enjoys a Double Life" (Dan Crary), *Los Angeles Times,* Calendar Section, June 4, 1989.

———, Interview with John Hammond, *Los Angeles Times,* September 24, 1992.

———, Interview with Maggie Roche, *Los Angeles Times,* July 11, 1991.

———, Interview with Jose Feliciano, *Los Angeles Times,* July 18, 1998.

Bond, Lahri, "Brewer & Shipley—More Tokes for Old Folks," *Dirty Linen,* February–March 1996.

———, Interview with Maire Brennan of Clannad, *Dirty Linen,* August–September 1993.

———, "The Voice of Ireland Dolores Keane," *Dirty Linen,* June–July 1993.

———, Interview with Dougie MacLean, *Dirty Linen,* October–November 1995.

———, "Roger McGuinn—Throw a Dime to the Tambourine Man," *Dirty Linen,* August–September 1995, pp. 54–58.

————, Interview with Maggie Roche, *Dirty Linen,* October–November 1995.

Boxer, Sarah, "Slogans and Images, with Talking Heads Bending Your Ears" (David Byrne), *New York Times,* Arts and Leisure Section, August 18, 1996.

Boyd, Joe, Liner notes to *Way to Blue* album (Nick Drake), 1994.

Bradley, Jeff, "'My Best Shot,' Folksinger Tom Paxton Says of New Album," *Denver Post,* January 2, 1995.

Bragg, Billy, Liner notes to *Mermaid Avenue* album, Elektra Records, 1998.

Brand, Oscar, *The Ballad Mongers,* Funk & Wagnalls, New York, 1962.

Brennan, Maureen, Frankie Kennedy Obituary, *Sing Out!,* December '94–January '95

Brooks, Michael, "David Bromberg," *Guitar Player,* March 1973, pp. 24–25, 36.

————, "John Fahey," *Guitar Player,* April 1972, p. 20.

Broonzy, Big Bill, *Big Bill Blues* (as told to Yannick Bruynoghe), England, 1955; revised, with additional material, Oak Publications, New York, 1964.

Broughton, Simon; Ellingham, Mark; Muddyman, David; Trillo, Richard; and Burton, Kim, *World Music: The Rough Guide,* Rough Guides Ltd., London, 1994.

Brown, Alison, Interview with Béla Fleck, *Banjo Newsletter,* May 1995.

Brown, Joe, "Songs Support Near and Dear" (Holly Near), *Washington Post,* October 20, 1989.

Brown, Peter, Reminiscences of talks with Professor Longhair, *Welcomat,* December 8, 1993.

Browne, David, "Beck in the High Life," *Entertainment Weekly,* February 14, 1997.

————, "Tim Hardin Defied Convention," *New York Times,* February 20, 1994.

Burr, Ramiro, "Rooted in Two Cultures—Tish Hinojosa," *Sing Out!,* May–July 1995.

Cairn, North, Interview with Jean Redpath, *Cape Cod Times,* May 2, 1988.

Cash Box [weekly], New York, New York, Cash Box Publishing Co., various issues.

Catalano, Jim, Interview with Rory Block, *Ithaca Journal,* January 27, 1994.

Charters, Samuel, *The Country Blues,* Rinehart, Winston & Co., New York, 1959.

————, *The Bluesmen,* Oak Publications, New York, 1968.

————, *The Blues Makers* (comprising *The Bluesmen* and *Sweet As the Rain: The Bluesmen Volume II*), Da Capo Press, New York, 1991.

Chlipala, Bonnie, "Cheryl Wheeler a Not-to-be-missed Experience," *Crested Butte Chronicle & Pilot,* November 3, 1995.

Christgau, Robert, "What If Woody Guthrie Had Led a Rock Band?" (Billy Bragg and Wilco), *New York Times,* Arts & Leisure Section, June 28, 1998, pp. 26, 36.

Coats, Art, and Coats, Leota, "Bryan Bowers," *Frets,* May 1979.

Cohen, Belissa, "In the Driver's Seat" (Ferron), *Out,* October 1995.

Cohen, John, "Joan Baez," *Sing Out!,* Summer 1963, pp. 5–7.

————, "Roscoe Holcomb: First Person," *Sing Out!,* April–May 1966, pp. 3–7.

Cohen, John, and Seeger, Mike, eds., *The New Lost City Ramblers Song Book,* Oak Publications, New York, 1964.

Cohn, Lawrence, "Mississippi John Hurt," *Sing Out!,* November 1964, pp. 16–21.

Collier, Pat, "Clarence 'Gatemouth' Brown—American Music, Texas Style," *Sing Out!,* vol. 40, no. 4, 1995.

Collins, Lisa, Interview with Clarence Fountain, *Billboard,* September 16, 1995.

Condran, Ed, "The Wheel Deal in Newtown" (Cheryl Wheeler), *Bucks County Courier Times,* October 5, 1995.

Conover, Kristen A., Interview with Christine Lavin, *Christian Science Monitor,* March 2, 1992.

Cook, Bruce, *Listen to the Blues,* Charles Scribner's Sons, New York, 1973.

Coupe, Stuart, Interview with Rickie Lee Jones, *Sydney Melbourne & Brisbane Rhythms Magazine,* June 27, 1994.

Crawford, Wayne, "There's Much More Now for Dion DiMucci," *Chicago Daily News,* February 28, 1970.

Cromelin, Richard, "'Blackjack' Deals a Dark View of Love" (Dave Alvin), *Los Angeles Times,* July 4, 1998, p. F12.

————, Interview with Nanci Griffith, *Los Angeles Times,* March 28, 1993.

————, "For Joady Guthrie, an Unhappy, Fearful Legacy" (Woody Guthrie), *Los Angeles Times,* January 25, 1980.

————, "The Same Old Dan Hicks Returns to L.A.—Sort Of," *Los Angeles Times,* Part VI, January 23, 1987.

————, "Rollin' with Etta" (Etta James), *Los Angeles Times,* Calendar Section, November 1, 1992.

————, "Laura Nyro Returns for a Soulful Connection," *Los Angeles Times,* August 11, 1988.

————, "Folk Singer Enjoys Being Phranc at Last," *Los Angeles Times,* July 22, 1989.

————, "DeShannon's Back on the Charts," *Los Angeles Times,* Calendar Section, December 4, 1977, p. 80.

————, "Old School Folk from Eric Andersen," *Los Angeles Times,* June 1975.

Cromonic, Richard, "The Spider's Web" (Spider John Koerner), *Boston Phoenix,* July 20, 1990.

D'Agostino, Interview with Pete Seeger, *Los Angeles Times,* January 31, 1992.

Damsker, Matt, "Richie Havens Sells His Soulfulness," *Los Angeles Times,* Calendar Section, September 16, 1984.

Dane, Barbara, "Lone Cat Jesse Fuller," *Sing Out!,* December 1963–January 1964, pp. 5–11

Daughtry, Sheila, Interview with John Hammond, *Players,* January 23, 1992.

———, Interview with Catie Curtis, *Dirty Linen,* June–July 1996.

Davies, Barbara, "Freedy Johnston's 'Perfect World,'" *Billboard,* May 21, 1994.

Davis, Frances, *The History of the Blues: The Roots, the Music, the People from Charley Patton to Robert Cray,* Hyperion Press, New York, 1995.

Davis, John T., "Sinking No Deeper—Van Zandt Hangs in the Real Balance Between Melancholy and Redemption" (Townes Van Zandt), *Austin American-Statesman,* January 19, 1995.

DeCurtis, Tony, "An Apostle of Love Returns as a Pop Mystic" (Donovan), *New York Times,* Art & Leisure Section, October 13, 1996.

De Lisle, Tim, Interview with Leonard Cohen, *Sunday Independent,* October 12, 1997.

DesRosiers, Mary, "Jean Ritchie: An Unbroken Circle," *Sing Out!,* December 1996–January 1997.

Dexter, Kerry, Interview with Chris Smither, *Acoustic Musician,* November 1995.

Diehl, Digby, "Lightnin' Hopkins: Bolt from the Blue," *Los Angeles Times,* Part IV, July 12, 1968, p. 12.

Dietz, Roger, "Female Folk Artists Fight Pigeonholing" (Ferron), *Billboard,* November 11, 1995.

———, "Sorrels Remains True to Her Green Linnet 'Heart,'" *Billboard,* November 11, 1995.

DiMartino, Dave, *Singer-Songwriters,* Billboard Books, an Imprint of Watson-Guptil Publications, New York, 1994.

Dixon, Willie, *I Am the Blues,* 1989.

Dr. John (Mac Rebennack), *Under a Hoodoo Moon,* St. Martin's Press, New York, 1994.

Dold, R. Bruce, "Roads Less Traveled" (David Bromberg), *Chicago Tribune,* October 12, 1989.

Dollar, Steve, Interview with Vic Chesnutt, *Atlanta Journal & Constitution,* May 8, 1994.

Drust, Greg, Liner notes for *John Lee Hooker: The Ultimate Collection, 1948–1990* (Rhino), 1991.

———, Liner notes for *Lightnin' Hopkins Anthology: Mojo Hand* (Rhino), 1993.

Dudick, J. Mark, Interview with Cliff Eberhardt, *Anchorage Daily News,* October 3, 1997.

Dunphy, Martin, "Sainte-Marie Seeks Heaven Here," *Georgia Straight,* April 25–May 2, 1996.

Dylan, Bob, *The Freewheelin' Bob Dylan,* M. Widmark & Sons, New York, 1964.

Eichenberger, Bill, "Rice Has His Own, Perfect Style of Bluegrass" (Tony Rice), *Ohio Columbus Dispatch,* July 28, 1994.

Ellison, Todd, Interview with Kristina Olsen, *Acoustic Guitar,* April 1996.

Epand, Len, "Country Joe" (McDonald), *City,* December 26, 1974, pp. 24–25.

Everett, Todd, Interview with Mike Nesmith, *Phonograph Record,* December 1970.

Eyre, Banning, Interview with Mickey Hart, *Boston Phoenix,* November 22–28, 1991.

Fahey, Jym, Interview with Rory Block, *Relix,* June 1983.

Farley, Christopher John, "Southern Exposure" (Hootie and the Blowfish), *Time,* February 27, 1995.

———, "The Power of Two" (Indigo Girls), *Time,* May 23, 1994.

Farrell, Tim, Interview with Tony Trischka, *Bluegrass Canada,* September–October 1993.

Feather, Leonard, "Woody Guthrie, Noted Folk Singer, Dies at 55" (Obit), *Los Angeles Times,* October 4, 1967, p. 24.

Feniak, Peter, "Irish Soul" (Loreena McKennitt), *Saturday Night,* February 1994.

Flisher, Chris, "Street Wise—For Britain's Ralph McTell One Hit Wasn't Enough," *Worcester Phoenix,* November 24, 1995.

———, Interview with Kristina Olsen, *Performing Songwriter,* March–April 1994.

Flynn, Bob, Dick Gaughan concert review, *The Guardian,* December 17. 1995.

Freeman, Mark, Interview with Rosalie Sorrels, *San Francisco Weekly,* February 21, 1990.

Freeman, Paul, Interviw with Rory Block, *West County Times,* Richmond, California, April 8, 1994.

Fricke, David, Liner notes for *Great Days: The John Prine Anthology* (Rhino), 1993.

Furnish, David, "Music View Woman" (Jane Siberry), *Interview,* May 30, 1986.

Geisel, Ellen, "Timeless Treasures: The Music of Paul Seibel," *Dirty Linen,* June–July 1996.

———, "Taj Mahal—The Root of the Matter," *Dirty Linen,* February–March 1996.

———, Interview with John Hartford, *Dirty Linen,* February–March 1997.

Gettleman, Parry, Interview with Jean Redpath, *Middlesex* (Massachusetts) *News,* January 22, 1988.

Gewertz, Daniel, Interview with Catie Curtis, *Boston Globe,* January 29, 1996.

Gill, Doug, "Songwriter for the Stars Sees Himself as Just a Guy with His Guitar" (Dave Mallett), *Baltimore Sun,* February 17, 1995.

Givens, Steve, "Bill Staines—Passing It on with Clarity," *Performing Songwriter,* September–October 1994.

Glatt, John, *The Chieftains: The Authorized Biography,* St. Martin's Press, New York, 1997.

Glennon, Sean, Interview with Tracy Chapman, *Springfield Advocate,* December 30, 1995.

Goering, Laurie, "Folk Music Dean Win Stracke," *Chicago Tribune,* June 30, 1991.

Goldstein, Patrick, Interview with Michelle Shocked, *Los Angeles Times,* July 7, 1991.

Goodman, Fred, Ani DiFranco article, *Rolling Stone,* August 24, 1995.

Goreau, Lorraine, *Just Mahalia Baby,* Texas Word Books, Waco, 1995.

Graustark, Barbara, and Abramson, Pamela, "Paganini of the Mandolin" (David Grisman), *Newsweek,* November 10, 1980, p. 81.

Greenberg, Mark, "The State of Old-Time Music from New Lost City to Siberia" (Mike Seeger), *Sing Out!,* 1993.

Gritten, David, "Enya Dreams," *Los Angeles Times,* Calendar Section, January 7, 1996.

Gunderson, Edna, "*Odelay* is Perfect Mix of Imperfections," *USA Today,* July 11, 1996.

———, "Rock Band a Foursome on Fairways, Too" (Hootie and the Blowfish), *USA Today,* April 18, 1995.

Guralnick, Peter, *Last Train to Memphis: The Rise of Elvis Presley,* Back Bay Books, Little Brown & Co., Boston, 1994.

Guthrie, Woody, *American Folksong/Woody Guthrie* (Edited by Moses Asch), Disc. Co. of America, New York, 1947; Oak Publications, New York, 1961.

———, *Born to Win,* Macmillan, New York, 1965.

Guy, George "Buddy," and Wilcox, Donald, *Damn Right I've Got the Blues,* Woodford Press, San Francisco, 1996.

Hamner, Anne, Interview with Nanci Griffith, *Record Exchange Music Monitor,* December 1991.

Hampel, Paul, "Don't Call Him Prodigal" (Jay Farrar, Son Volt), *St. Louis Post-Dispatch,* August 7, 1997.

Handelman, David, Review of John Hiatt *Little Head* album, *People,* July 7, 1997.

Harper, Colin, Interview with Bert Jansch, *Folk Roots,* March 1994.

Harris, Craig, *The New Folk Music,* White Cliffs Media Co., 1991.

———, Interview with Pete Seeger, *Dirty Linen,* December 1994–January 1995.

Harris, Sheldon, *Blues Who's Who: A Biographical Dictionary of Blues Singers,* Da Capo Press, New York, 1979, paperback, January 1994.

Hart, Mickey, with Stevens, Jay, *Drumming at the Edge of Magic,* 1990.

———, Lieerman, Fredric; and Sonneborn, D.A., *Planet Drum,* Harper, San Francisco, 1991.

Heckman, Don, "Spirit of Colonus Still Moves this Group," (Blind Boys of Alabama), *Los Angeles Times,* March 3, 1997, pp. F1; F4.

Heffley, Lynne, Interview with Joseph Shabalala, leader of Ladysmith Black Mambazo, *Los Angeles Times,* March 8, 1994.

Helm, Levon, and Davis, Stephen, *This Wheel's on Fire,* William Morrow, 1993.

Hentoff, Nat, "Profile: Bob Dylan," *New Yorker,* October 24, 1964, pp. 61–62.

Herbst, Peter, Interview with Clannad, *Rolling Stone,* November 29, 1979.

Herzhaft, Gerhard, *Encyclopedia of the Blues,* University of Arkansas Press, Fayetteville, Arkansas, 1992.

Hilburn, Robert, "Reflections on the Age of a Real Rock Band" (Robbie Robertson interview), *Los Angeles Times,* January 19, 1994.

———, "Wading Beyond the Gene Pool" (Jeff Buckley), *Los Angeles Times,* Calendar Section, February 19, 1995.

———, "'Sketches' for Her Son" (Jeff Buckley), *Los Angeles Times,* May 25, 1998.

———, Interview with Tracy Chapman, *Los Angeles Times,* April 17, 1988.

———, Interview with Leonard Cohen, *Los Angeles Times,* September 24, 1995.

———, "For All It's Worth" (Steve Stills), *Los Angeles Times,* May 6, 1997.

———, Interview with Ani DeFranco, *Los Angeles Times,* May 5, 1996.

———, "Reborn Again" (Bob Dylan), *Los Angeles Times,* Calendar Section, December 14, 1997, pp. 3, 72.

———, "Icons of the '60s Paired on Tour" (Dylan, Grateful Dead), *Los Angeles Times,* July 13, 1987.

———, "Oh Yeah, Life Goes On . . . and Thrill of Living Is Back" (John Mellencamp), *Los Angeles Times,* September 10, 1996.

———, "Nyro Returns to Public Eye with Artistry Intact" (Laura Nyro), *Los Angeles Times,* August 15, 1988.

———, "Bob Dylan: Still Playing Guitar and Singing His Songs," *Los Angeles Times,* May 28, 1978, p. 66.

———, "Bruised Orange: Prine Gets His Second Wind," *Los Angeles Times,* May 21, 1978, pp. 64, 86.

———, "I Larned That Jesus Is Real and I Wanted That" (Bob Dylan), *Los Angeles Times,* November 23, 1980, p. 1.

———, "Simon Without Garfunkel Makin' It As a Single," *Los Angeles Times,* May 27, 1973.

———, "A Texan Tries It As a Lone Star" (Doug Sahm), *Los Angeles Times,* June 16, 1974, p. 58.

———, "Not Fade Away" (Bonnie Raitt) *Los Angeles Times,* Calendar Section, March 20, 1994.

Hinton, Brian, *Joni Mitchell: Both Sides Now,* Sanctuary Publishing, London, 1996.

Hinton, Sam, "Bess Hawes," *Sing Out!,* September 1965, pp. 26–30.

Hitchner, Earle, "Never Tire of the Road—Trade Legend Andy Irvine Keeps on Truckin'," *Irish Echo,* April 28–May 4, 1993.

Hochman, Steve, Interview with Michael Doucet (BeauSoleil), *Los Angeles Times,* May 31, 1994.

———, "Don't Get Bitter on Us, Beck," *Los Angeles Times,* Calendar Section, February 20, 1994, pp. 4, 60–61.

———, "The Meaning of 'Earth'? Duo Isn't Sure" (John Cale and Bob Neuwirth), *Los Angeles Times,* April 29, 1994.

———, C.J. Chenier, *Los Angeles Times,* March 14, 1988.

———, "Crosby, Stills, & Nash Display Special Chemistry," *Los Angeles Times,* September 30, 1997, p. F2.

———, Interview with Si Kahn, *Los Angeles Times,* February 19, 1987.

———, "Country Joe Singing a Pro-Veteran Tune Now" (Country Joe McDonald), *Los Angeles Times,* February 24, 1986.

———, "A Homecoming for Odetta," *Los Angeles Times,* November 24, 1992.

———, "The Oyster Band: In One Era and Out Another," *Los Angeles Times,* April 4, 1989.

———, Interview with Ziggy Marley, *Los Angeles Times,* February 10, 1987.

———, Interview with Mickey Hart, *Escape,* Spring 1994.

Hodari, Cleo, "Singer Bland Turns It On at Long Beach Blues Fest," *Los Angeles Times,* Sept. 2, 1996.

Hoffman, Jan, "Hazel Dickens—Union Blues," *Village Voice,* September 1, 1987.

Holden, Stephen, "Jackson Browne vs. Madison Avenue," *New York Times,* February 18, 1996.

———, Review of Tracy Chapman album *Crossroads, New York Times,* October 1, 1989.

———, "A Self-Effacing Ascetic in Folk-Rocker's Clothing" (Bruce Cockburn), *New York Times,* October 1, 1994.

———, "Folk Tunes That Address Real Folks" (Hazel Dickens), *New York Times,* May 29, 1992.

———, "Jane Siberry," *New York Times,* May 30, 1986.

Hoskyns, Barney, *Across the Great Divide: The Band and America,* Hyperion, New York, 1993.

House, Son, "I Can Make My Own Songs," *Sing Out!,* July 1965, pp. 38–45.

Houston, Cisco, "Autobiographical Notes," Smithsonian Institution Center for Folklife Programs and Cultural Studies Archive.

Hoyt, Larry, Interview with Tony Trischka, *Syracuse New Times,* May 18–25, 1994.

Humphrey, Mark, "Bert Jansch," *Frets,* March 1980, pp. 18–23.

Hunt, Dennis, "Joan Baez Raising Her Voice Again," *Los Angeles Times,* June 14, 1987.

———, Interview with Shawn Colvin, *Los Angeles Times,* December 8, 1992.

———, "Judy Collins Near 40," *Los Angeles Times,* Part IV, February 16, 1979, p. 28.

———, "Faces: In Charge of Her Career" (Bonnie Raitt), *Los Angeles Times,* Calendar Section, December 9, 1979.

Hunt, Ken, Interview with Pete Seeger, *Folk Roots,* March 1994.

Hunter, Mark, "Tony Rice," *Frets,* April 1980, pp. 26–30.

Hurley, F. Jack, and Evans, David, *Tom Shley, Sam McGee, Bukka White: Tennessee Traditional Singers,* University of Tennessee Press, Knoxville, 1981.

Hurst, Jack, "The Rankins Bring Canadian Stardom Across the Border," *Chicago Tribune,* April 10, 1995.

Hutchinson, Lydia, Interview with Dougie MacLean, *Performing Songwriter,* May–June 1995.

———, "Tom Paxton—A Songwriter for All Seasons," *Performing Songwriter,* January–February 1994.

Irwin, Colin, Bothy Band concert review, *Melody Maker,* 1975.

———, Interview with Terre Roche, *Folk Roots,* January–February 1996.

Ives, Burl, *Wayfaring Stranger,* Whittlesey House, New York, 1948.

Jenings, Dana Andrews, "Doc Watson, Down-Home Virtuoso," *New York Times,* Arts & Leisure Section, November 12, 1995.

Johnson, David W., "Move Over Woody, Make Room for My Manager" (Bill Staines), *Boston Globe,* May 7, 1996.

Johnson, Tom, "Josh White Jr.," *Performance,* March 30, 1979, pp. 4–5.

Katz, Larry, "The Gospel According to Clarence Fountain" (Blind Boys of Alabama), *Boston Herald,* July 28, 1995.

Keil, Charles, *Urban Blues,* University of Chicago Press, 1966.

Kelp, Larry, "Q and A with Tish Hinojosa," *San Francisco Examiner-Chronicle,* October 29, 1995.

Kerstetter, Rich, "Chesapeake," *Sing Out!,* vol. 41, no. 2.

Kessler, Lee, Interview with Tony Trischka, *Banjo Newsletter,* October 1986.

King, B.B., with Ritz, David, *Blues All Around Me,* Avon Books, New York, 1996.

Kingsley, Michelle Pelick, "Wanted: Byron Berline," *Frets,* June 1979, pp. 34–36.

Kirchner, Cynthia, "Aiming at the Audience" (John McCutcheon), *Lambertville* (New Jersey) *Beacon,* October 11, 1995.

Klein, Joe, *Woody Guthrie: A Life,* Ballantine Books, New York, 1980.

Klomar, William, "Laura Nyro: She's the Hippest—and Maybe the Hottest," *New York Times,* October 6, 1968.

Kohlhaase, Jim, Interview with John Hammond, *Los Angeles Times,* June 3, 1994.

LaVere, Stephen C., Liner notes for *Robert Johnson: The Complete Recordings,* August 1990.

Lawless, Ray McKinley, *Folksingers and Folksongs in America,* Duell, Sloan & Pearce, New York, 1960; rev. ed., 1965.

Lee, Jim, Interview with Bryndle, *Dirty Linen,* June–July 1996, pp. 34, 35.

Levenson, Laura, Commentary on the Chieftains, *San Francisco Chronicle,* March 5, 1995.

Libowitz, Steven, "Capturing Details of Life's Poignant Moments" (Cheryl Wheeler), *Santa Barbara News-Press,* September 22, 1995.

Lieb, Sandra, *Mother of the Blues: A Study of Ma Rainey,* University of Massachusetts Press, 1981.

Locey, Bill, Interview with John Hammond, *Los Angeles Times,* April 14, 1994.

Loggins, Kenny, and Loggins, Julia, *Unimaginable Life,* Avon Books, New York, 1997.

Lomax, Alan, *The Land Where the Blues Began,* Pantheon, New York, 1993.

———, *The Folk Songs of North America,* Doubleday, Garden City, N.Y., 1960.

———, ed., *The Penguin Book of American Folk Songs,* Penguin Books, Baltimore, Maryland, 1965.

Lomax, Alan; Guthrie, Woody; and Seeger, Pete, *Hard Hitting Songs for Hard Hit People,* Oak Publications, New York, 1967.

Lomax, John Avery, *Adventures of a Ballad Hunter,* Macmillan, New York, 1947.

Lomax, John A., and Lomax, Alan, *Folksong U.S.A.,* Duell, Sloan & Parce, New York, 1947.

———, *Out Singing Country,* Macmillan, New York, 1941.

Longino, Miriam, "Late Success Surprises Blueswoman" (Tracy Nelson), *Atlanta Journal & Constitution,* April 17, 1998.

———, "*Up* Unbuttons Three-Piece R.E.M. from Its Past," *Atlanta Journal & Constitution,* September 3, 1998.

MacColl, Ewan, *The Essential Ewan MacColl Songbook,* Music Sales, 1999.

MacMillan, Kyle, Interview with Jean Redpath, *Omaha World-Herald,* October 9, 1988.

Mahalia and Wylie, Evan McLeod, *Moving On Up,* Hawthorn Books, New York, 1966.

Marsh, David, and Swenson, John, *The Rolling Stone Record Guide,* Random House/Rolling Stone Press, New York, 1979.

Masello, Robert, Interview with Leonard Cohen, *People,* March 25, 1996.

Maslin, Janet, Interview with Leonard Cohen, *New York Times,* November 6, 1997.

———, "There's Nothing I Like About It—But It May Be a Classic" (Leonard Cohen), *New York Times,* November 6, 1977.

Mason, Bobbie Ann, "Breaking New Ground, But the Roots Hold Fast" (R.E.M.), *New York Times,* September 8, 1996.

McCall, Michael, Interview with John Prine, *Nashville Scene,* June 29, 1995.

McCarty, David, "The Living Tradition" (Dan Crary), *Acoustic Guitar,* January–February 1991.

McCray, Michael, "Patty Griffin's Songs Are Outlet for Angst," *The Tab,* May 28–June 3, 1996.

McGhee, Brownie, "Brownie McGhee on Playing the Blues," as told to Michael Brooks, *Guitar Player.*

McGrail, Steve, "Holding Up the Bar" (Dougie MacLean), *Folk Roots,* December 1998.

McGrath, T.J., Interview with Dougie MacLean, *Dirty Linen,* October–November 1990.

McKeough, "Woody Guthrie Cuts a New Album" (Jeff Tweedy, Wilco), *St. Louis Post-Dispatch,* June 28, 1998.

McNeil, Liz, "Talking with . . . B.B. King," *People Weekly,* December 2, 1996.

McMahon, Regan, "Holly Near: Power in the Darkness," *BAM Magazine,* November 2, 1979.

Meade, Don, "Super Show from a Young Legend" (Sharon Shannon), *Irish Voice,* June 15, 1993.

Medwick, Joe, "Love, Canadian Style" (Bruce Cockburn), *Hits,* June 6, 1994, p. 60.

Mellencamp, John, *Mellencamp: Painting and Reflections,* HarperCollins, New York, 1998.

Melrose, Julie, Interview with Catie Curtis, *Daily Hampshire Gazette,* February 5, 1996.

Mervis, Scott, "Perfectly Good Musician" (John Hiatt), *Pittsburgh Post Gazette,* November 3, 1995.

Millar, Jeff, "Leadbelly—Music Man with a Mean Streak," *Los Angeles Times,* Calendar Section, December 22, 1974, p. 44.

Miller, Michael, "Texas' Influence Is Apparent in Eric Taylor's New Album," Columbia, South Carolina, *The State,* October 6, 1995.

Miller, Michele, "Look What Melanie's Done to the House, Ma," *St. Petersburg Times,* April 20, 1998.

Mitchell, Joe, "Back from the Obit" (Vince Bell), *Austin Chronicle,* March 31, 1995.

———, "Deliveries Abound for Sara Hickman," *Austin Chronicle,* May 1996.

Mitchell, Sean, Interview with Nanci Griffith, *Los Angeles Times Magazine,* May 7, 1995.

Moon, Tom, "Echoes from the Highway in Son Volt's Debut Album," *Philadelphia Enquirer,* September 24, 1995.

Morris, Chris, "John Hiatt Struts His Stuff on Capitol Set," *Billboard,* September 16, 1995.

Morse, Steve, Interview with Tracy Chapman, *Boston Globe,* November 10, 1995.

———, Interview with Micky Hart, *Boston Globe,* June 14, 1996.

Morton, Cole, "A Rebel with a Cause" (Billy Bragg), *UK Sunday Independent,* May 26, 1996, pp. 18–20.

Mosey, Chris, Interview with Eric Bogle, *Folk Roots,* January–February 1998.

Mothner, I., "Big Folk-Singers on Campus: Peter, Paul & Mary," *Look,* July 2, 1963, pp. 59–62.

Nash, Alanna, Eric Andersen record review, *Stereo Review,* August 1991.

———, Album review, Greg Brown's *The Poet Game, Stereo Review,* February 1995.

Near, Holly, *Fire in the Rain . . . Singer in the Storm,* William Morrow & Co., New York, 1990.

Nelligan, Tom, "Ralph McTell Still Weathering the Storm," *Dirty Linen,* April–May 1996.

Nelson, Peter, Interview with Cliff Eberhardt, *Performing Songwriter,* November–December 1995.

Nichols, Natalie, "British Brand of Blues Is Celebrated at Long Beach Fest," *Los Angeles Times,* September 8, 1998.

Nicks, Stevie, Interview with Sarah McLachlan, *Interview,* March 1995.

Niles, John Jacob, *The Ballad Book,* Houghton Mifflin, Boston, 1961.

Nuccio, Tom, Interview with Darden Smith, *Illinois Entertainer,* November 1993.

Obrecht, Jas, Interview with Bert Jansch, *Guitar Player,* May 1994.

O'Brien, Karen, *Hymn to Her: Women Musicians Talk,* Virago, United Kingdom, 1995.

O'Neal, Chip, Interview with Karla Bonoff, *Fullerton Hornet,* December 3, 1976.

O'Neal, Jim, and O'Neal, Amy, "John Lee Hooker," *Living Blues,* Autumn 1979, pp. 14–22.

Orr, Jay, Interview with J.D. Crowe, *Nashville Banner,* July 17, 1995.

Palmer, Robert, "Tom Waits, All-Purpose Troubadour," *New York Times,* Arts & Leisure Section, November 14, 1993.

Pancake, Jon, "Mike Seeger: The Style of Tradition," *Sing Out!,* July 1964, pp. 6–11.

Pareles, Jon, "A Pop Post-Modernist Gives Up on Irony" (Beck) *New York Times,* Arts & Leisure Section, November 8, 1998, pp. 33, 40.

———, "Elizabeth Cotten at 90, Bigger than the Tradition," *New York Times,* section 3, January 7, 1983.

———, Interview with Joseph Shabalala of Ladysmith Black Mambazo, *New York Times,* March 21, 1993.

Parrish, Michael, Interview with Mickey Hart, *Sing Out!,* February–March–April 1995.

———, "Musical Ambassadors to Norway" (David Lindley and Henry Kaiser), *Dirty Linen,* April–May 1995.

Paxton, Tom, "Courting the Music," *Sing Out!,* August–September–October 1996.

Peabody, Dave, "1 Guy Named Mo'" (Keb' Mo'), *Folk Roots,* December 1995.

Phillips, Chuck, Interview with John Lee Hooker, *Los Angeles Times,* April 23, 1989.

Piazza, Tom "Night Tripping with the Good Doctor," *New York Times,* Arts & Leisure Section, May 22, 1994.

Pierce, Michael, "Brewer & Shipley," *Guitar Player,* July–August 1973, p. 13.

Podolinsky, Gil, Interview with Leo Kottke, *Guitar Player,* August 1977.

Pond, Steve, "Almost 20 Years of Reunion Music," (Hamilton Camp and Bob Gibson), *Los Angeles Times,* May 22, 1987.

Powell, Betsy, "Every Song Tells a Story for Tune-smith" (Freedy Johnston), *Toronto Star,* October 15, 1998.

Powell, Bryan, Interview with Chris Smither, *Acoustic Guitar,* May–June 1995.

Proffitt, Frank, "Good Memories for Me," *Sing Out!,* November 1965, pp. 34–37.

Purdy, Jack, "Forty-three Going on Fourteen" (Bob Gibson), *City Paper,* March 22, 1991.

Rabey, Frank, "You Ain't Heard Nothin' till Hearing Marty Sexton Sing," *Mountain Xpress,* March 6, 1996.

Ramsey, Frederic Jr., "Leadbelly: A Great Long Time," *Sing Out!,* March 1965, pp. 7–24.

Rauzi, Robin, "Up-and-Coming Singer Knows the Score" (Paula Cole), *Los Angeles Times,* Valley Edition, Calendar Section, August 1, 1996, p. 18.

Rayburn, Heather, Interview with Michelle Shocked, *Asheville Citizen-Times,* May 10, 1996.

Rea, Steven, "Melancholy Genius" (Eric Andersen), *Music World,* November 1973, p. 70.

Record World [weekly], Record World Publishing Co., New York, various issues.

Regenstreif, Mike, "Kate & Anna McGarriglc: On Their Own Terms," *Sing Out!,* February–March 1997.

Reiss, Al, Interview with Ani DiFranco, *Dirty Linen,* October–November 1994.

Reynolds, Malvina, *Little Boxes and Other Handmade Songs by Malvina Reynolds,* Oak Publications, 1963.

Richardson, Derk, "All-Americana" (Jay Farrar, Son Volt), *San Francisco Bay Guardian,* November 29, 1995.

Ritchie, Jean, *Singing Family of the Cumberlands,* Oxford University Press, 1955; issued in paperback by Oak Publications, New York, 1963; reprinted by University Press of Kentucky, 1988.

———, *Apple Seeds and Soda Straws: Love Charms and Legends Written Down for Young and Old,* Henry Walck, 1963.

———, *The Dulcimer People,* Oak Publications, New York, 1974.

Robicheau, Paul, Interview with Mary Black, *Boston Globe,* October 21, 1993.

———, Interview with Catie Curtis, *Boston Globe,* January 26, 1996.

———, Interview with Ani DiFranco, *Boston Globe,* May 12, 1994.

———, "Irish Voices . . . Sharon Shannon's Road to Success Follows the Traditional Route," *Boston Globe,* Calendar Section, March 17, 1994.

Rockwell, John, "Folk Music Is Back with a Twang," *New York Times,* section 2, April 30, 1978, pp. 1, 22.

————, "Steve Forbert, New Folk Singer," *New York Times,* December 1977.

Rogovoy, Seth, "Ferron Rising," *Boston Globe,* October 27, 1995.

————, Interview with Bill Morrissey, *Berkshire Eagle,* April 19, 1996.

Roos, John, "Future Celtic Shock" (Battlefield Band), *Los Angeles Times,* March 4, 1995.

————, Interview with John Lee Hooker, *Los Angeles Times,* May 15, 1998.

Ross, John, "The Travelin' Lady Alights" (Rosalie Sorrels), *San Francisco Bay Guardian,* April 2, 1986.

Rotenstein, David S., Interview with C.J. Chenier, *Pittsburgh Tribune-Review,* August 24, 1995.

Rule, Sheila, "Solitude as Therapy for Writing" (Sarah McLachlan), *New York Times,* March 24, 1994.

Russell, Tom, and Tyson, Sylvia, *And Then I Wrote: The Songwriter Speaks,* Arsenal-Pulp Press, Canada, 1995.

Sandberg, Larry, and Weissman, Dick, *The Folk Music Sourcebook,* Alfred A. Knopf, New York, 1976.

Sander, Ellen, "Paul Siebel: Homegrown Weed," *Saturday Review,* January 30, 1971.

————, "Crosby, Stills & Nash: Renaissance Fare," *Saturday Review,* May 31, 1969.

Santelli, Robert, *The Big Book of Blues,* Penguin Books USA, New York, 1993.

Sawyer, Charles, *The Arrival of B.B. King,* Doubleday, Garden City, N.Y., 1980.

Scaduto, Anthony, *Bob Dylan,* W.H. Allen & Co., 1972.

Scherman, Tony, "Danceable, Eclectic Folk-Pop" (Geoff Muldaur), *New York Times,* December 13, 1998.

Schoemer, Karen, "Tom Waits Finds a Purity in Debris," *New York Times,* September 30, 1992.

Schumacher, Michael, *There But for Fortune* (Phil Ochs), Hyperion Books, New York, 1996.

Schwartz, Harriet, Interview with Catie Curtis, *Philadelphia Gay News,* February 16–22, 1996.

Scribner, Sara, "Jewel's Folk Gem Is the Real Thing," *Los Angeles Times,* May 4, 1996.

Scruggs, Louise, "A History of America's Favorite Folk Instrument," *Sing Out!,* December 1963–January 1964, pp. 26–29.

Scully, Alan, Interview with Jeff Tweedy, *St. Louis Post-Dispatch,* April 1995.

Seder, Jennifer, "Buffy" (Buffy Sainte-Marie), *Los Angeles Times,* March 31, 1978.

Seeger, Mike, and Cohen, John, *New Lost City Ramblers Songbook,* Oak Publications, 1964.

Seeger, Peggy, *The Peggy Seeger Songbook, Warts and All,* Music Sales, 2000.

Seeger, Pete, *Where Have All the Flowers Gone,* Sing Out! Publications, Bethlehem, Pa., 1993.

Segel, Joel, "At Acoustic Disc, the Boss Works Like a Dawg" (David Grisman), *Rhythmmusic,* vol. V, no. 3, 1996, pp. 26–29.

Segell, Michael, Interview with Robert Cray, *Cosmopolitan,* February 1987.

Selvin, Joel, Mary Black concert review, *San Francisco Chronicle,* April 5, 1991.

————, Interview with Mickey Hart, *San Francisco Sunday Examiner & Chronicle,* May 26, 1996.

Shapiro, Stephanie, "Mike Seeger: Preserver of Mountain Music," *Baltimore Evening Sun,* May 24, 1990.

Shulgold, Marc, "The Clancys: Hello Again and Goodbye," *Los Angeles Times,* November 15, 1985.

Signorelli, Cathy, "Yesterday Is Today & Today Is Tomorrow" (Brownie McGhee), *Sing Out!,* December 1995–January 1996.

Silverman, Edward M., "Working Heroine Folksinger Hazel Dickens," *Option Magazine,* September–October 1990.

Skelly, Richard, "David Bromberg," *Relix,* February 1990.

————, "Richie Havens—Mixed Bag," *Goldmine,* June 10, 1994.

Smith, Andy, "John Hiatt Takes an Acoustic Turn," *Providence Journal Bulletin,* October 30, 1995.

Snider, Eric, "Singer Rosalie Sorrels Has Laughed All Her Life," *Sarasota Herald Tribune,* February 1, 1994.

Snowden, Don, Interview with Joseph Shabalala of Ladysmith Black Mambazo, *Los Angeles Times,* June 10, 1987.

Sofranko, Denise, Interview with Mary Black, *Sing Out!,* February–March 1991.

————, "Folk Trailblazer Carolyn Hester Sings to a New Generation," *Sing Out!,* December 1993–January 1994, pp. 26–28.

Solondz, Simone, "Suzanne Vega—Breaking the Singer-Songwriter Mold," *Acoustic Musician,* August 1995.

Sowd, David, Interview with Michael Doucet, *Scene,* August 16, 1994.

Stambler, Irwin, *Encyclopedia of Pop, Rock & Soul,* St. Martin's Press, New York, 1974, 1977, 1989.

Stambler, Irwin, and Landon, Grelun, *Encyclopedia of Folk, Country & Western Music,* 1st ed., St. Martin's Press, New York, 1969; 2nd ed., St. Martin's Press, New York, 1983.

Stewart, Zan, Interview with Béla Fleck, *Los Angeles Times,* August 26, 1992.

————, "Waits Does a Guest Turn with Saxophonist Edwards" (Tom Waits), *Los Angeles Times,* November 22, 1991.

Sullivan, Jerry, "Magic Fingers" (Doc Watson), *Chicago Sun Times,* October 3, 1977.

Sullivan, Kevin, Interview with Arlo Guthrie, *Providence Journal,* July 15, 1990.

Swenson, John, BeauSoleil concert review, *Rolling Stone,* December 21, 1991.

Symkus, Ed, Interview with Rory Block, *The Tab,* April 9–16, 1996.

Tayler, Letta, "Ronstadt Reveling in a Lullaby Style and Motherhood," *Newsday,* July 19, 1996.

Taylor, Jonathan, Interview with Jane Siberry, *Daily News* (Los Angeles), August 29, 1985.

Thompson, Toby, *Positively Main Street: An Unorthodox View of Bob Dylan,* Coward, McCann, New York, 1971.

Thorpe, Helen, Interview with Shawn Colvin, *Texas Monthly,* ca. 1985.

Tick, Judith, *Ruth Crawford Seeger: A Composer's Search for American Music,* Oxford University Press, 1997.

Tillotson, Kristin, "Suzzy Roche, Singular Sister, *Minneapolis Star Tribune,* September 19, 1997.

Tobler, John, "The Man Who Made Folk Rock" (Roger McGuinn), *Folk Roots,* October 1997.

Trubo, Richard, "Tim Can Almost Smell the Roses Now" (Tim Rose), *Los Angeles Times,* Calendar Section, July 16, 1972, p. 78.

Tucker, Ken, "Bonnie Raitt Takes a Journey into the Heart of Darkness," *New York Times,* March 20, 1994.

Underwood, Lee, "Tim Buckley Remembered," *Downbeat,* June 16, 1977, pp. 25–27, 56.

Van Matre, Lynn, "Liberation/She's too Busy Being Free" (Rosalie Sorrels), *Chicago Tribune,* September 7, 1973.

Victor, Allen F., "All in the Rankin Family," *Performance,* March 24, 1995.

Wakefield, Dan, "Joan Baez," *Redbook,* January 1967, p. 114.

Wald, Elijah, Interview with Rory Block, *Acoustic Guitar,* December 1995.

———, "Dick Gaughan's New Traditions," *Boston Globe,* July 1995.

———, "Folk Music's Mayor of Greenwich Village" (Dave Van Ronk), *Sing Out!,* vol. 41, no. 1.

Walters, Neal, and Mansfield, Brian, *MusicHound Folk: The Essential Album Guide,* Visible Ink, Division of Gale Research, Detroit, Michigan, 1998.

Warner, Anne; Warner, Jeff; and Epstein, Jerome S., *Traditional American Folk Songs from the Anne & Frank Warner Collection,* Syracuse University Press, 1984.

Warner, Frank, "Traditional Singers #3: Frank Proffitt," *Sing Out!,* October–November 1963, pp. 6–11.

Washburn, Jim, Interview with J.J. Cale, *Los Angeles Times,* May 11, 1990.

———, Interview with Paddy Moloney of the Chieftains, *Los Angeles Times,* December 13, 1991.

———, Interview with John Hammond, *Los Angeles Times,* May 25, 1995.

———, Interview with John Renbourn, *Los Angeles Times,* April 29, 1995.

———, Interview with Michelle Shocked, *Los Angeles Times,* May 29, 1990.

———, Interview with Richard Thompson, *Los Angeles Times,* September 5, 1990.

Watson, Doc, "Folksinging Is a Way of Life," *Sing Out!,* February–March 1964, pp. 8–12.

Watts, Michael, "A Breath of Early Beatles from Lindisfarne," *Melody Maker,* December 19, 1970.

Weir, Rob, "Battlefield Band's Colorful Past & Future," *Sing Out!,* vol. 41, no. 3, pp. 37–41.

Welding, Pete, "B.B. King, the Mississippi Giant," *Downbeat,* October 5, 1978, pp. 20–22, 64; October 19, 1978, pp. 17, 39–40.

Wheeler, Steven P., "Hootie & the Blowfish," *Music Connection,* March 20–April 2, 1996.

Whitburn, Joel, Best-selling records based on *Billboard* charts, Record Research, Menominee Falls, Wisconsin, various editions.

White, Alana J., Interview with Béla Fleck, *Banjo Newsletter,* September 1986.

White, Timothy, "Enya 'Memory,' Myth & Melody," *Billboard,* November 25, 1995.

———, "Sarah McLachlan Irony & 'Ecstasy'," *Billboard,* January 8, 1994.

———, Death of Professor Longhair, *Rolling Stone,* March 20, 1980.

Wihlborg, Ulrica, and Day, Carol, "Getting Settled: A Husband and a Hit Help Sarah McLachlan Shed Her Longtime Angst," *People,* October 20, 1997.

Willging, Dan, Interview with Geno Delafose, *ZydE-Zine* (on-line), December 27, 1997.

Williams, Roger Neville, "Jesse Winchester: The Return of the Native," *San Francisco Bay Guardian,* June 9, 1977.

Willman, Chris, "Browne Getting on with Life after Daryl" (Jackson Browne), *Los Angeles Times,* November 27, 1993.

———, "Holly Near Edges Closer to a Mainstream Sound," *Los Angeles Times,* November 4, 1987.

Wilonsky, Robert, Interview with Michelle Shocked, *Dallas Observer,* April 25, 1996.

Wilson, John S., "Newport Is His Just for a Song" (Arlo Guthrie), *New York Times,* July 18, 1967.

Wittenberg, Rich, "Eric Taylor Not a Secret Anymore," *Houston Chronicle,* September 21, 1995.

Wolfe, Charles K., "The White Man's Blues, 1922–40" (Dock Boggs), *Journal of Country Music,* vol. 15, no. 3, 1993.

Wolmuth, Roger, "After Years of Hard Traveling, Mountain Maestro Doc Watson Looks to Find Some Easy Pickin' at Last," *People Weekly,* August 10, 1987.

———, Interview with Willie Dixon, *People Weekly,* September 11, 1989.

Wright, Frankie, Interview with Mickey Hart, *Los Angeles Times,* November 16, 1991.

Yao, Link, "Bloom: Irish Sensibility, American Style" (Luka Bloom), *Ann Arbor News,* July 12, 1994.

Yaryan, Bill, "Ramblin' Jack Elliott," *Sing Out!,* November 1965, pp. 25–28.

Young, Jon, Eric Andersen interview, *Musician,* August 1991.

Younger, Joseph D., "Richie Havens, American Troubadour," *Amtrak Express,* March–April 1993.

Zwicker, Brant, "The Rankin Family," *Acoustic Musician,* December 1995.

INDEX